UNIVERSITY CASEBOOK SERIES

CASES AND MATERIALS

THE INTERNATIONAL LEGAL SYSTEM

FIFTH EDITION

by

CHRISTOPHER L. BLAKESLEY
J.Y. Sanders Professor of Law
Louisiana State University Law Center
William S. Boyd School of Law
The University of Nevada at Las Vegas (Beginning Fall, 2002)

EDWIN B. FIRMAGE
Samuel D. Thurman Professor of Law
University of Utah College of Law

RICHARD F. SCOTT
Distinguished Professor of International Law
Thomas Jefferson School of Law
Professor of International Law Emeritus
The American University of Paris

SHARON A. WILLIAMS
Professor of International Law
Osgoode Hall Law School, York University
Judge ad litem, International Criminal Tribunal for the Former Yugoslavia

NEW YORK, NEW YORK
FOUNDATION PRESS
2001

Foundation Press, a division of West Group, has created this publication to provide you with accurate and authoritative information concerning the subject matter covered. However, this publication was not necessarily prepared by persons licensed to practice law in a particular jurisdiction. Foundation Press is not engaged in rendering legal or other professional advice, and this publication is not a substitute for the advice of an attorney. If you require legal or other expert advice, you should seek the services of a competent attorney or other professional.

 *TEXT IS PRINTED ON 10% POST CONSUMER RECYCLED PAPER*

Dedicated to our spouses:
Suzy Eliason Blakesley, Annie Firmage, Lorraine L. Scott, and
to Robert W. Cosman

*

PREFACE TO THE FIFTH EDITION

Although public international law is still principally the study of the law concerning the relations among sovereign states, its scope has expanded to include vital impacts on international organizations and on the individual directly. It creates and governs international organizations, and in turn these organizations contribute to the creation of new law in this field. The individual may now constitute a full-blown subject of international law in relation to human rights and offenses in international criminal law. In the subject areas of international law and in the creation of new institutions, critical issues include: how international law arises, the sources of its authority, how it applies, how it works, and how lawyers use it.

International law is no longer the reserved province of government lawyers and the large "major" law firms, but engages in one fashion or another practically all lawyers at times. As the world shrinks, businesses extend their markets; as individuals and society become more mobile, the general practitioner must be more "internationally literate." The lawyer practicing "business law," encounters questions of jurisdiction, trade and finance, business and banking record keeping requirements, which put every lawyer and his or her client, the corporate officer or banker, at risk for prosecution or extradition, to mention only a few relevant areas of potential involvement with international law.

All of the chapters of the book make this exceedingly clear. *See Chapters 1, 3, 6, 13, and 16, for example).* Even the practice of family law does not escape international legal problems, nor does the serious mistreatment of citizens by local governmental authority acting on national territory. Virtually all of law practice has been internationalized. The practitioner, thus, the student must know what issues will arise in any international litigation or even domestic litigation in which the governing rules may arise from international law, and know how to resolve these issues, or how to avoid their arising. The compleat attorney must also be able to draft agreements well enough to put his or her client in the best tactical position in case of dispute (or best strategic position to avoid dispute).

Public international law is still the comprehensive course where the world's current affairs and changing relationships are analyzed from a broad legal perspective. The Fourth Edition of THE INTERNATIONAL LEGAL SYSTEM went to press in August, 1994. The changes in international law that occurred between the time of the Fourth and the Fifth Editions, namely between 1994 and 2001 are indeed molar changes that have altered the planetary societal environment that had developed after World War II. During the period covered by the first three editions of this work

[1972-1988], major conditioning factors bearing on the status, effectiveness and growth of world legal order included Doomsday-like dangers of mass destruction, seemingly unbridgeable ideological conflicts between groups of nation-states, particularly the superpowers. In 1994, when we published the Fourth Edition, the "Cold War" had ended and new and intractable problems became more evident, such as the division of the world between "Rich Nations — Poor Nations." The "new" problems of globalization, ethnic division, the potential for environmental devastation, plagues and other medical and health problems have become more acute between 1994 and 2001 when we publish this Fifth Edition.

Perhaps the most significant, positive, legal development in this period has been the increased importance of human rights as a law-involving development, although this realm of law is still uncertain and developing. International criminal law is related to human rights law and the impact of this body of law and practice has become tremendously important and vigorous. Unmet challenges for the earlier editions included gridlock in the United Nations, resulting from the effect of the Cold War on the use of the veto power in the Security Council and the domination of the General Assembly by underdeveloped, often defensive and perturbed, countries. Judicial resolution of legal issues between states by the World Court was sporadic and halting. At the time of the Persian Gulf War, the U.N. gridlock was overcome for a period, but has arisen again since. Peacekeeping and peacemaking have become more difficult and complex. Despite the negative factors, however, scholarly attention to and student participation in "international legal studies" grew robustly to include oceans, atmosphere and space law; international trade, investment and financial law; international legal theory, "peace-keeping" by United Nations forces; and, as already mentioned, human rights. The international system is also strengthening by fresh institution building, including the U.N's creation of the two ad hoc International Criminal Tribunals, by the now growing role of the World Court, the new U.N. Tribunal for the Law of the Sea, and the future International Criminal Court.

Today, legal norms, principles, and structures are being subjected to stresses that may alter materially some of the contours of planetary legal order. Among these stressed areas are the territorial reach of state authority, individual and group human rights, access to and sharing of planetary resources, participation in international trade and investment and the new World Trade Organization, protection of the physical environment of a small planet, evermore heavily populated; and equilibrium between ethnicity and statehood. This Edition gives attention to such areas, including the new chapter on International Criminal Law and expansion of our chapter on Environmental Law, as well as a wholly revised and updated introductory Chapter on International Economic Law. Each of these chapters, along with other supporting chapters could be used as fully separate courses. Or, of course, the material is accessible and teachable in the basic or advanced course in public international law. We continue to draw cases and materials from other legal systems than that of the United States where we deem them useful. But the majority of users will remain American and we must continue to deal with some aspects of the `foreign affairs law of the United

States and Canada, such as these nations' ways with treaties, immunity of foreign sovereignties, and separation of powers within the Federal triad. Thus, the course book is fully accommodating to undergraduate or graduate courses in International Relations or International Law. The Fifth edition remains dedicated to keeping the scope, sense and "feel" of the earlier versions, as adjusted to the environment of change and new dimensions described above.

Professors Leech and Sweeney, two of the originating editors, chose for personal reasons not to continue with the project for the Fourth Edition. Covey Oliver, the other original editor, decided the same for this Fifth edition. But their solid contributions to the earlier books continue to influence the substance, tone and style of this edition, especially as to the encouragement of student interest and involvement. Professors Blakesley, Scott and Williams ensure continuation of the linkages to European and Latin American outlooks heretofore provided by Professors Sweeney and Oliver. Professor Firmage adds the dimensions of constitutional law, dispute resolution, and religion in international law.

*

SUMMARY OF CONTENTS

*

TABLE OF CONTENTS

*

TABLE OF ABBREVIATIONS

The following are abbreviations that have been used by the editors in their citations to principal cases and major materials and in their notes.

A.B.A.J. --------------------------American Bar Association Journal

A.C.--------------------------------Law Report series [British] House of Lords

ADIZ -------------------------------Air Defense Identification Zone

A.F. L. Rev. ----------------------Air Force Law Review

All E.R.----------------------------All England Law Reports [1936-date]

A.J.I.L. ----------------------------American Journal of International Law

A.S.I.L. ----------------------------American Society of International Law

ANCOM--------------------------Andean Common Market

Ann.Dig. -------------------------Annual Digest and Reports of International Law Cases [title of Int'l Law Reports prior to 1953]

APEC ------------------------------Asia Pacific Economic Cooperation Forum

BITS --------------------------------Bilateral Investment Treaties

Brit.Y.B. Int'l L. ----------------British Yearbook of International Law

Brook. J. Int'l L.----------------Brooklyn Journal of International Law

C.A.---------------------------------Law Report series, Court of Appeal

CACM ----------------------------Central American

Cal.2d-----------------------------California Reports, Second Series

CCH Trade Cases --------------Trade Regulation Reporter [Commerce Clearing House]

C.F.R. -----------------------------Code of Federal Regulations

Ch. ---------------------------------Law Report series, Chancery [1891-date]

Chicago J. Int'l L. --------------Chicago Journal of International Law

Colum. J. Trans'l L. -----------Columbia Journal of Transnational Law

Common Mkt. L.R. ------------Common Market Law Reports

Cornell Int'l L.J. ---------------Cornell International Law Journal

C.M.A. ----------------------------Court of Military Appeals Reports

C.-M.Rep. ------------------------Court-Martial Reports

Cr.Cas.Res.----------------------Law Report Series, Crown Cases Reserved [1865-1875]

CSCE ----------------------------------- Conference on Security and Co-operation in Europe

D.----------------------------------- Recueil Dalloz, [French Reporter]

Dall ----------------------------------- Dallas, United States Supreme Court Reports

DEWIZ ----------------------------------- Distant Early Warning Identification Zone

Doc. Supp. . ----------------------- Documentary Supplement

DSB ----------------------------------- Dispute Settlement Body

DSU ----------------------------------- Dispute Settlement Understanding

E.C.----------------------------------- European Community

E.Comm.Ct.J.Rep. -------------- European Community Court of Justice Reports

ECOSOC Off.Rec. --------------- United Nations Economic and Social Council, Official Records

EEC ----------------------------------- European Economic Community

EFTA ----------------------------------- European Free Trade Association

E.U. ----------------------------------- European Union

F.2d ----------------------------------- Federal Reporter, Second Series [1924-date]

F.R.D.----------------------------------- Federal Rules Decisions

F.Supp. ----------------------------------- Federal Supplement

FCN ----------------------------------- Friendship, Commerce and Navigation Treaties

FDI ----------------------------------- Foreign Direct Investment

Fletcher For. Wld. Aff. -------- Fletcher Forum of World Affairs

FM----------------------------------- Department of the Army Field Manual

Fordham Int'l L. J. ------------- Fordham International Law Journal

For. Aff. ----------------------------- Foreign Affairs

FSIS----------------------------------- Food Safety and Inspection Service

Ga. ----------------------------------- Georgia Supreme Court Reports

Ga.J.Int'l L. ---------------------- Georgia Journal of International Law

G.A.Off.Rec. ---------------------- General Assembly Office of Records

G.A.Res.----------------------------- General Assembly Resolution

GATT----------------------------------- General Agreement on Tariffs and Trade

GSP ----------------------------------- Generalized System of Preference

Harv.Int'l L.J.-------------------- Harvard International Law Journal

Harv. L. Rev. --------------------- Harvard Law Review

IATA----------------------------------- International Air Transport Association

ICC ----------------------------------- International Criminal Court

ICI ----------------------------------- Imperial Chemical Industries, Ltd.

I.C.A.O.----------------------------- International Civil Aviation Organization

I.C.J.. ----------------------------------- International Court of Justice

I.C.J.Rep. ----------------------------- International Court of Justice Reports

ICSID ------------------------------International Center for Settlement of Investment Disputes

ICTFY ------------------------------International Criminal Tribunal for the Former Yugoslavia

ICTY -------------------------------International Criminal Tribunal for Yugoslavia

ICRC -------------------------------International Committee of the Red Cross

ICTR -------------------------------International Criminal Tribunal for Rwanda

IFOR -------------------------------Implementation Force

Ill.Rev.Stat. ----------------------Illinois Revised Statutes

I.L.O.Off.Bull---------------------International Labour Office, Official Bulletin

Ind. L. Rev. ----------------------Indiana Law Review

Int'l & Comp.L.Q.----------------International and Comparative Law Quarterly

IEL --------------------------------International Economic Law

I.L.M. -----------------------------International Legal Materials

Int'l L.Rep.------------------------International Law Reports

IMF--------------------------------International Monetary Fund

IMT--------------------------------International Military Tribunal

J.Crim.L.& Criminol. -----------Journal of Criminal Law and Criminology

J. Int'l Econ. L. ------------------Journal of Economic Law

JNA -------------------------------Yugoslav Peoples Army

K.B.--------------------------------Law Report series, Kings Bench

LAFTA ----------------------------Latin American Free Trade Association

L.Ed.2d----------------------------Lawyer's Editors, Second Series, United States Supreme Court Reporter

L.N.T.S. ---------------------------League of Nations Treaty Series

Mich.J.Int'l L.---------------------Michigan Journal of International Law

Mich. L. Rev. ---------------------Michigan Law Review

MFN ------------------------------Most favored nation

MFO ------------------------------Multinational Force & Observers

MIGA -----------------------------Multilateral Investment Guarantee Agency

M.I.T.I. ---------------------------Ministry of International Trade and Industry

N.Y.Misc.2d----------------------New York Miscellaneous, Second Series, [1955-date]

MNEs-----------------------------Multinational enterprises

NATO-----------------------------National Atlantic Treaty Organization

N.E. -------------------------------North Eastern Reporter [1885-1936]

NGO ------------------------------Non-Governmental Organization

NTR-------------------------------Normal Trade Relations

N.Y. -------------------------------New York Reports

N.Y.S.2d --------------------------New York Supplement, Second Series [1937-date]

N.Y.U.J.Int'l L. & Pol. -------- New York University Journal of International Law and Politics

OECD ---------------------------- Organization for Economic Cooperation and Development

OPIC ----------------------------- Overseas Private Investment Corporation

P. --------------------------------- Law Report series, Probate, Divorce and Admiralty

P.2d ----------------------------- Pacific Reporter, Second Series

Pas. -------------------------------- Pasicrisie [Belgian Reporter]

PCA . ------------------------------ Permanent Court of Arbitration

P.C.I.J. ---------------------------- Permanent Court of International Justice

PRC ------------------------------- Peoples Republic of China

Pub.L.No. ------------------------- Public Law Number

Q.B. -------------------------------- Law Report series, Queen's Bench

SALT I --------------------------- Strategic Arms Limitation Talks I

SFOR ----------------------------- Stabilization Force

SNC ------------------------------- Supreme National Council

SPS -------------------------------- Sanitary and Phytosanitary Measures

S.Ct. ------------------------------ Supreme Court Reporter [U.S., 1882-date]

S.C. Res -------------------------- Security Council Resolution

Sirey ------------------------------ Sirey, Recueil Général des Lois et des Arrêts [France]

S.E. -------------------------------- Southeastern Reporter

So.2d ----------------------------- Southern Reporter, Second Series [1941-date]

So.African L.Rep. --------------- South African Law Reports

Spec. Sess. ------------------------ Special Session

Stan L. Rev. ---------------------- Stanford Law Review

Stat -------------------------------- Statutes at Large, United States

Tex.Int'l L. J. -------------------- Texas International Law Journal

T.I.A.S. --------------------------- Treaties and Other International Acts Series

TPRM ---------------------------- Trade Policy Review Mechanism

TRIMS --------------------------- Trade-Related Investment Measures

TRIPS --------------------------- Trade-Related Aspects of Intellectual Property Rights

TRNC ----------------------------- Turkish Republic of Northern Cyprus

TS---------------------------------- Treaty Series

U.K. -------------------------------- United Kingdom

UDI-------------------------------- Unilateral Declaration of Independence

U.Ill L. Rev. ---------------------- University of Illinois Law Review

U.Ill Press. ----------------------- University of Illinois Press

U.Miami Inter-Am.L.Rev ----- University of Miami Inter-American Law Review

U.Pa L. Rev. ---------------------- University of Pennsylvania Law Review

UNCITRAL ---------------------- United Nations Commission on International Trade Law

U.N.Conf.Int'l Org. ------------- United Nations Conference on International Organization [San Francisco Conference]

UNCTAD ------------------------- United Nations Conference on Trade and Development

U.N.Doc -------------------------- United Nations Document

UNDOF -------------------------- United Nations Disengagement Observer Force

UNEF ----------------------------- United Nations Emergency Force

UNIFIL --------------------------- United Nations Interim Force in Lebanon

UNCOK . ------------------------- United Nations Commission on Korea

U.N.Gen.Ass.Off.Rec. ---------- United Nations General Assembly, Official Records

UNICEF ------------------------- United Nations Children's Fund

UNFICYP ----------------------- United Nations Force in Cyprus

UNMOGIP. ---------------------- United Nations Military Observer Group for India and Pakistan

UNOC --------------------------- United Nations Operation in the Congo

UNOGIL. ------------------------ United Nations Observer Mission to Lebanon

UNOSOM ----------------------- United Nations Operation in Somalia

UNPAs -------------------------- United Nations Protected Areas

UNPROFOR. ------------------- United Nations Protection Force

U.N.Rep.Int'l Arb. Awards --- United Nations Reports of International Arbitration Awards

U.N.Sec.Council Off.Rec. ----- United Nations Security Council, Official Records

U.N.S.C.O.B.. ------------------- United Nations Special Committee on the Balkins

UNTAC ------------------------- United Nations Transitional Authority in Cambodia

U.N.T.S. ------------------------- United Nations Treaty Series

U.Pa.L.Rev. ---------------------- University of Pennsylvania Law Review

U.Pitt. L.Rev. ------------------- University of Pittsburgh Law Review

U.S. ------------------------------ United States Supreme Court Reports

U.S.C. ---------------------------- United States Code

U.S.C.A. ------------------------- United States Code Annotated

U.S.Dep't State Bull. ----------- United States Department of State Bulletin

USIA --------------------------- United States Information Agency

U.S.T. ------------------------------U.S. Treaties and Other International Agreements

USTR -----------------------------United States Trade Representative

Va.J.Int'l L. ----------------------Virginal Journal of International Law

Weekly Comp.Pres.Doc.-------Weekly Compilation of Presidential Documents

WL---------------------------------WestLaw

W.L.R. ----------------------------Weekly Law Reports [England, 1953-date]

Western Weekly Rep. ----------Western Weekly Reports, New Series [Canada]

Wm. & Mary L. Rev. -----------William & Mary Law Review

Yale L. Rev. ----------------------Yale Law Review

Y.B.U.N. -------------------------Year Book of the United Nations

ACKNOWLEDGMENTS

We would like to thank our Research assistants: Dan Stigall; Elena Arcos; Angela Wangeshi Gatheru; Mark Dereig; Douglas Palomboi Rachael Wilcox and Muriel Certa. We would also like to thank the Library, research, and staff colleagues at Louisiana State University Law Center, the University of Utah College of Law, the Thomas Jefferson School of Law, and the University of San Diego School of Law, including: Gladys Dreher; Linda Duplessis; Kandi Prejean; George Jacobsen; Charlotte Melius; Cynthia Lane.

We would like to acknowledge our indebtedness to the following authors, publishers and organizations for giving us permission to reprint excerpts from the books, periodicals and other documents indicated below:

A.B.C. News, This Week With David Brinkley, October 13, 1985, Interview with Abraham D. Sofaer.

Agence France Presse, August 11, 1991, excerpts from, World's Smallest States at Risk Over Environment.

The American Institute of Aeronautics & Astronautics, excerpt from, Rosenfield, Some Thoughts on the Distinction Between Air Space and Outer Space, Proceedings of the Twenty-sixth Colloquium on the Law of Outer Space, 93-94 (1984).

The American Institute of Aeronautics & Astronautics, Gnady Danilenko, The Boundary Between

Air Space and Outer Space in Modern International Law, Proceedings of the Twenty-sixth Colloquium on the Law of Outer Space 71, 73 (1984).

The American Law Institute, the Inferred Legislative Intent not to Violate International Law, 1987 Restatement of the Foreign Relations Law of the United States, § 115.

The American Law Institute, The 1987 Restatement of the Foreign Relations Law of the United States, § 401, Categories of Jurisdiction; § 404, Universal Jurisdiction to Define and Punish Certain Offenses.

The American Law Institute, 1987 Restatement, Introductory Note to Part V, The Law of the Sea.

The American Society of International law, excerpt from, Ruling of the Secretary General of the United Nations on the Rainbow Warrior Affair Between France and New Zealand, July 6, 1986, 26 I.L.M.1346 (1987).

The American Society of International Law, excerpt from, A Report of the Joint committee Established by the American Society of International Law and the International Law Association, 85 Am.J.Int'l L. 358 (1991).

The American Society of International Law, excerpt from the Letter from the U.S. Secretary of the Treasury to the Chairman of the Senate Finance Committee, April 7, 1986, 25 I.L.M. 760 (1986), under the title "United States: Letter of the Secretary of the Treasury Concerning Opposition to Tax Reform Legislation That Overrides Bilateral Tax Treaties."

The American Society of International Law, excerpt from, Promoting the Rule of Law in U.S. Foreign Policy, Murphy, Contemporary Practice of the United States Relating to International Law, 93 American Journal of International Law 470 (1999).

The American Society of International Law Schwebel, excerpt from Fifty Years of the World Court: A Critical Appraisal, 90 American Society of International Law Proceedomgs 339 (1996).

The American Society of International Law, excerpt from, Response of the International Court of Justice to General Assembly Resolution 52/161 of 15 December 1997, 37 I.L.M. 1466 (1998).

The American Society of International Law, Case Concerning East Timor (PORTUGAL v. AUSTRALIA), International Court of Justice, (1995): [1995] ICJ Reps. 90; 34 I.L.M. 1581.

The American Society of International Law, excerpt from, Caron, The Nature of the Iran-United States Claims Tribunal and the Evolving Structure of International Dispute Resolution, 84 American Journal of International Law 104 (1990).

The American Society of International Law, excerpt from, European Community Declaration on Yugoslavia and on the Guidelines on the Recognition of New States, December 16, 1991, 31 I.L.M. 1485 (1992).

The American Society of International Law, excerpt from, Kenneth Abbott, International Relations Theory, International Law, and the Regime Governing Atrocities in International Conflicts, in Symposium on Method in International Law 93 American Journal of International Law 291, 361 (1999).

The American Society of International Law, excerpt from, Dunoff and Trachtman, The Law and Economics of Humanitarian Law Violations in Internal Conflict, in International Conflicts, in Symposium on Method in International Law 93 American Journal of International Law 291, 394 (1999).

The American Society of International Law, excerpt from, Thomas Franck, Legitimacy in the International System, 82 American Journal of International Law 705 (1988).

The American Society of International Law, The M.V. "Saiga" Case, (Saint Vincent and the Grenadines v. Guinea), The International Tribunal for the Law of the Sea, Year 1999, 1 July 1999, 38 International Legal Materials 1323 (1999).

The American Society of International Law, excerpt from, Objection of the United States to the Assertion of Sovereignty Over the Gulf of Sirte [Sidra] by Libya, 68 American Journal of International Law 510 (1974).

The American Society of International Law, excerpt from, Statement by the Legal Adviser of the U.S. Department of State Concerning a TwelveB-

Mile Limit, August 3, 1971, 66 American Journal of International Law 133 (1972).

The American Society of International Law, excerpt from, The Twelve-Mile Limit at Unclos III, Stevenson and Oxman, the Third United Nations Conference on the Law of the Sea: The 1974 Caracas Session, 69 American Journal of International Law, 1, 13B14, (1975).

The American Society of International Law, excerpt from, United States: Presidential Proclamation on the Territorial Sea of the United States [December 27, 1988]. 28 I.L.M. 284 (1989).

American Society of International Law, excerpt from, Goedhuis, Civil Aviation After the War, 36 American Journal of International Law 596, 605 (1942).

The American Society of International Law, Report of Investigation by the Secretary General of Civil Aviation Organization (December 1983), 23 International Legal Materials 867 (1984).

American Society of International Law, excerpt from, Preliminary Information on Progress of the USSR Investigation into the Accident to a South Korean Aeroplane on 1 September 1983, 23 International Legal Materials 910 (1984).

American Society of International Law, excerpt from, Review of Secretary-General's Report by the Air Navigation Commission of the ICAO, 23 International Legal Materials 924 (1984).

American Society of International Law, excerpt from, Resolution adopted by the Council of the ICAO, March 6, 1984, 23 International Legal Materials 937 (1984).

American Society of International Law, excerpt from, North Pacific Route System: Emergency Communications, 80 American Journal of International Law 152 (1986).

American Society of International Law, excerpt from, Staple, The New World Satellite Order: A Report from Geneva, 80 American Journal of International Law 699, 700 (1986).

The American Society of International Law, excerpt from, Buergenthal, The advisory Practice of the Inter-American Human Rights Court, 79 American Journal of International Law 1, 8 (1985).

The American Society of International Law, excerpt from, Letter Dated 2 April 1992, from the Permanent Representative of Venezuela to the U.N., Addressed to the President of the Security Council, 31 I.L.M. 753 (1992).

The American Society of International Law, excerpt from, Marian Nash Leach, Contemporary Practice of the U.S. Relating to International Law, 83 American Journal of International Law 905 (1989).

The American Society of International Law, excerpt from, Sean B. Murphy, Waiver of Georgian Diplomat's Immunity from Criminal Prosecution, 93 American Journal of International Law 470, 485 (1999).

The American Society of International Law, Additional Protocol to the 1949 Geneva Conventions, 16 I.L.M. 1391 (1977).

The American Society of International Law, excerpt from, Joyner, Reflections on the Lawfulness of Invasion, 78 American Journal of International Law 131 (1984).

The American Society of International Law, excerpt from, Wright, Legal Aspects of the Vietnam Situation, 60 American Journal of International Law 570, 755 (1966).

The American Society of International Law, excerpt from, Bianchi, Review of Terrorismo Internazionale e Garanzie Colletive, 87 American Journal of International Law 175, 177 (1993).

The American Society of International Law, 15 International Legal Materials 1224, McDowell, Introductory Note to Summary Account of Entebbee Incident.

American Society of International Law, excerpt from, Framework Convention on Climate Change Principles U.N. Doc. A/AC 237/18 (Pt. II) Add. 1; 31 International Legal Materials 851 (1992).

American Society of International Law, excerpt from, Rio Declaration on Environment and Development, June 13, 1992; A/CONF. 151/5/Rev. 1, 31 International Legal Materials 874 (1992).

American Society of International Law, excerpt from, KYOTO PROTOCOL to the United Nations Framework Convention on Climate Change, 37 International Legal Materials (1998).

The American Society of International Law, excerpt from, Ratner & Slaughter, Appraising the Methods of International Law: A Prospectus for Readers, 93 American Journal of International Law 291 (1999).

The American Society of International Law, excerpt from, Oscar Schachter, Philip Jessup's Life and Ideas, 80 American Journal of International Law 878, 890 (1986).

The American Society of International Law, excerpt from, Martii Koskenniemi, Letter to the Editors of the Symposium, in Symposium on Method in International Law 93 American Journal of International Law 291, 351 (1999).

American Society of International Law, excerpt from, Environmental Law Interest Group Newsletter, Vol. 3(1), 2 (1992).

American Society of International Law, excerpt from, General Agreement on Tariffs and Trade: Dispute Settlement Panel Report on United States Restrictions on Imports of Tuna (TUNA I), 30 International Legal Materials 1594 (1991).

American Society of International Law, excerpt from, General Agreement on Tariffs and Trade: Dispute Settlement Panel Report on United States Restrictions on Imports of Tuna (TUNA II), 33 International Legal Materials 842 (1994).

American Society of International Law, excerpt from, United States – Import Prohibition of Certain Shrimp and Shrimp Products, World Trade Organization: Report of the Panel, WT/DS58/R, 15 May, 1998, 37 International Legal Materials 834 (1998).

American Society of International Law, excerpt from, Legality of the Threat or Use of Nuclear Weapons, International Court of Justice, 1996, Advisory Opinion, 35 International Legal Materials 814 (1996).

American Society of International Law, excerpt from, G. Berrisch, American Society of International Law Environmental Interest Group Newsletter, Vol. 3(1), 3-4 (1992).

The American Society of International Law, excerpt from, Jordan Paust, Self-Executing Treaties, 82 American Journal of International Law 760 (1988).

The American Society of International Law, excerpt from, Stefan Reisenfeld, The Doctrine of Self-Executing Treaties & U.S. v. Postal: Win at Any Price, 74 American Journal of International Law 892, 896 (1980).

The American Society of International Law, excerpt from, Van de Velde, The Political Economy of a Bilateral Investment Treaty, 92 American Journal of International Law 621 (1998).

The American Society of International Law, excerpt from, 35 International Legal Materials 357 (1996) Cuban Liberty and Democratic Solidarity Act of 1996 (Helms-Burton Act).

The American Society of International Law, excerpt from, European Union; Demarche Protesting the Cuban Liberty and Democratic Solidarity (Libertad) Act, March 5, 1995, 35 International Legal Materials 397 (1996).

The American Society of International Law, excerpt from, Organization of American States; Inter- American Juridical Committee Opinion Examining the U.S. Helms-Burton Act, 35 I.L.M. 1332 (1996).

The American Society of International Law, excerpt from, European Union: Council Regulation (EC) No. 2271/96, Protecting Against the Effects of the Extra-Territorial Application of Legislation Adopted by a Third Country, 36 I.L.M. 125 (1996).

The American Society of International Law, excerpt from, Canada: Foreign Extraterritorial Measures Act, Oct. 9, 1996, 36 I.L.M. 111 (1996).

The American Society of International Law, excerpt from, European Union–U.S.: Memorandum of Understanding Concerning the U.S. Helms-Burton Act and the U.S. Iran and Libya Sanctions Act, April 11, 1997, 36 I.L.M. 529.

The American Society of International Law, ROME STATUTE OF THE INTERNATIONAL CRIMINAL COURT, Adopted July 17, 1998, 37 I.L.M. 999, 1017 (1998).

The American Society of International Law, excerpt from, Georges Delaume, Case Note, Société Iranienne du Gaz v. Société Pipeline Service [NIGC], French Cour de Cassation, May 2, 1990, 80 Revue Critique de Droit International Privé 140 (1991), 85 AJIL 696 (1991).

The American Society of International Law, excerpt from, The United States of America v. The Public Service Alliance of Canada, the Attorney General of Canada and the Canada Labour Relations Board, Supreme Court of Canada, 1992, 32 I.L.M. 1 (1993).

The American Society of International Law, excerpt from, Bruce Smith, Paul Hudson, et al. v. Socialist People's Libyan Arab Jamahiriya, etc., November 26, 1996, 36 I.L.M. 100 (1997).

American Society of International Law, excerpt from, Alejandre v. Republic of Cuba, International Law in Brief, Summary, March 22 - April 2, 1999.

American University Journal of International Law and Policy Edith Brown Weiss, In Fairness to Future Generations, Conference on Human Rights, Public Finance, and the Development Process, 8, 19-22 (1992).

The American Society of International Law, excerpt from, Brief of the Government of Canada as Amicus Curiae in Support of the Respondent in the Case of U.S. v. Alvarez Machain, 31 International Legal Materials 919 (1992).

The American Society of International Law, excerpt from, United Nations Convention on the Law of the Sea, December 10, 1982. 21 I.L.M. 1261 (1982).

The American Society of International Law, excerpt from, European Convention on Nationality, November 6, 1997, 37 I.L.M. 44 (1998).

The American Society of International Law, excerpt from, United Nations Compensation Commission: Report with Decisions of the Governing Council, 31 I.L.M. 1009, 1055 (1992).

The American Society of International Law, excerpt from, E.U. Treaty of Amsterdam: Consolidated Version of the Treaty, Establishing the European Community, October 7, 1997, 37 I.L.M. 56, 82 (1998).

The American Society of International Law, excerpt from, Guha Roy, Is the Law of Responsibility of States for Injuries to Aliens a Part of Universal International Law?, 55 American Journal of International Law 863, 866, 888 (1961).

The American Society of International Law, excerpt from, Jurisdiction – NATO Status of Forces Agreement-U.S. Serviceman Charged with Criminal Offenses Overseas European Convention on Human Rights, 85 AJIL 698, 701 (1991).

The American Society of International Law, excerpt from, Hilary Charlesworth, Feminist Methods in International Law 93 American Journal of International Law 379 (1999).

The American Society of International Law, International Law: Classic & Contemporary Readings (Ku & Diehl eds. 1998), excerpt from, Christopher L. Blakesley, Obstacles to the Creation of A Permanent War Crimes Tribunal.

The American Society of International Law, excerpt from, Weller, The International Response to the Dissolution of the Socialist Federal Republic of Yugoslavia, 86 American Journal of International Law 569 (1992).

The American Society of International Law, excerpt from, Case Concerning the Vienna Convention on Consular Relations (Paraguay v. U.S.) (International Court of Justice, April 9, 1998), 37 International Legal Materials 810 (1998).

The American Society of International Law, excerpt from, Evan T. Bloom, Protecting Peacekeepers: the Convention on the Safety of U.N. and Associated Personnel, 89 American Journal of International Law 621 (1995).

The American Society of International Law, excerpt from, Schwelb, Some Aspects of International Jus Cogens as Formulated by the International Law Commission, 61 American Journal of International Law 946, 949 (1967).

The American Society of International Law, excerpt from, Kearney and Dalton, The Treaty on Treaties: The Negotiating History of Jus Cogens at Vienna, 64 American Journal of International Law 495, 535 (1970).

The American Society of International Law, excerpt from, International Law Commission, Draft Articles on the Law of Treaties, 61 American Journal of International Law 255, 349 (1967).

The American Society of International Law, excerpt from, Fitzmaurice, Vae Victis or Woe to the Negotiators! Your Treaty or Our "Interpretation of It, 61.

The American Society of International Law, excerpt from, Judgment in Case Concerning the Gabcikovo-Nagymaros Project, 37 International Legal Materials 162 (1998).

The American Society of International Law, excerpt from, Franck, Editorial Comment, The "Powers of Appreciation": Who is the Ultimate Guardian of UN Legality?, 86 American Journal of International Law 519, 520-23 (1992).

Annuaire Suisse de Droit International, Swiss Federal Political Department, Opinion of the Office for Public International Law, Status of Families and "Husband-in-Fact" of Diplomat, 33 Annuaire Suisse de Droit International 224 (1977).

The Association of the Bar of the City of New York, excerpt from, Ruth Wedgwood, The Use of Armed Force in International Affairs: The Case of Panama.

Auden, W. H., Epitaph on a Tyrant.

Auden, W. H., Gare du Midi.

Austin, John, excerpt from, 1 Austin, Jurisprudence 177, 189 (1861).

BBC News, Tuesday, 3 April 2001, 83–Year-old NAZI Convicted.

Bridges Weekly Trade News Digest, excerpt from, Big-Mac Targeted by French Farmers, 3

Bridges Weekly Trade News Digest, No. 34, 30 Aug. 1999.

Belhaven Press, London; New York excerpt from G. Plant, Introduction and Elements of a "Fifth Geneva" Convention on the Protection of the Environment in Time of Armed Conflict, in G. Plant (ed.) Environmental Protection and the Law of War, 17-18, 37-42 (1992) .

Berkeley Journal of International Law, excerpt from,Weiss, The U.N.'s Prevention Pipe-Dream, 14 Berkeley Journal of International Law 423, 431-34 (1996).

Burroughs & Co., Ltd., Calgary, Alberta, Canada. Re Immigration Act and Hanna Canada, Supreme Court of British Columbia, 1957, in 21 Western Weekly Rep. 400.

Butterworths, Toronto, excerpt from, Sharon A. Williams & A.L.C. De Mestral, An Introduction to International Law, 267-269 (2d ed., 1987).

Butterworths, Toronto, excerpt from, Sharon A. Williams and A.L.C. De Mestral, an Introduction to International Law, 280-281 (2nd ed. 1987).

Calvocaressi, Nuremberg 141 (1947).

Cambridge University Press, Cambridge [England]; New York : excerpt from, Byers, Custom, Power, and the Power of Rules, p. xi, 3 (1999).

Cambridge University Press, British Law Officers Opinion in the Silesian Loan Case 1753, in 2 McNair, International Law Opinions 303-304 (Cambridge 1956).

Carnegie Endowment for International Peace, Foreign Policy – excerpt from Simmons, Learning to Live with NGOs, Foreign Policy 82, Fall 1998.

The Carnegie Endowment, excerpt from, Phillipson, Introduction to Gentili, De Jure Belli Libri Tres (2 Trans., Carnegie Endowment 1933).

The Carnegie Endowment, Foreign Policy, excerpt from, Statement on Human Rights by the Secretary General of the International Commission of Jurists, November 1978, Human Rights in the United States and United Kingdom, Foreign Policy 23-26, 72 (Stewart ed. 1979).

The Carnegie Endowment, excerpt from, 2 Wolff, Classics of International Law 11, 19 (1934).

Case Western Reserve Journal of International Law, excerpt from, Sharon A. Williams, Public International Law and Water Quantity Management in a Common Drainage Basin: The Great Lakes, 18 Case Western Reserve Journal of International Law 155, 165-168 (1986).

Case Western Reserve Journal of International Law, excerpt from, Sharon A. Williams, Public International Law and Water Quantity Management in a Common Drainage Basin: The Great Lakes Basin, 18 Case Western Reserve Journal of International Law 155, 178-179 (1986).

Columbia Journal of Transnational Law, Abraham Sofaer, The Legality of United States Action in Panama.

Columbia Journal of Transnational Law, Henkin, The Invasion of Panama Under International Law: A Gross Violation.

Detroit Mercy Law Review, excerpt from, Louis René Beres. After the Gulf War: Iraq, Genocide and International Law, Detroit Mercy L.Rev. 13 (1991).

Dickenson Journal of International Law, excerpt from, Rene Louis Beres, The United States and Nuclear Terrorism in a Changing World: A Jurisprudential View, 12 Dickenson Journal of International Law 327.

De Vattel, The Law of Nations or Principles of the Law of Nature, Applied to the Conduct and Affairs of Nations and Sovereigns (1758), Book II ch. VI, p. 162 (Chitty, ed. 1849).

The Economist, excerpt from Unban the Taliban: It is time to Recognize the Taliban as the Rulers of Afghanistan, The Economist, July 13, 1999, p. 19.

Editions Techniques, S.A., Paris, Denunciation to the Enemy Case, Netherlands Court of Cassation, 1958, 88 Journal du Droit International 893 (1961).

Editions Techniques, S.A., Paris. Public Ministry v. Mogens Glistrup Denmark, Maritime and Commercial Court, 1967. 95 Journal du Droit International 979 (1968).

Emond Montgomery [Toronto], excerpts from, Hugh M. Kindred et al, International Law Chiefly as interpreted and Applied in Canada, 969-971, (6th ed., 2000).

Etcheson, Craig, excerpt from, Terror in the East: Phases of Repression in Region 23.

Experts Group on Environmental Law of the World Commission on Environment and Development, Judge Nagendra Singh, Environmental Protection and Sustainable Development Legal Principles and Recommendations, Forward to the Report of the Experts Group on Environmental Law of the World Commission on Environment and Development, at xi (1987).

Experts Group on Environmental Law of the World Commission on Environment and Development, Environmental Protection and Sustainable Development, Legal Principles and Recommendations, Elements for a Draft Convention 42-45 (1987).

Fletcher Forum of World Affairs, excerpt from Christopher L. Blakesley, Obstacles to the Creation of a Permanent War Crimes Tribunal, 18 The Fletcher Forum of World Affairs 77 (1994).

Georgia Journal of International and Comparative Law, excerpt from, Buser, the Jaffe Case and the Use of International Kidnaping as an Alternative to Extradition.

Georgetown Law Journal, Glennon & Howard, Collective Security and the Constitution: Can the Commander in Chief Power be Delegated to the United Nations?

Hague Academy, excerpts from, Rosalyn Higgins, in her General Course on Public International Law: International Law and the Avoidance, Containment and Resolution of Disputes, [1991–V] Recueil Des Cours 100–104.

Harvard Human Rights Law Journal, excerpt from, John Quigley, Criminal Law & Human Rights: Implications of the United States Ratification of the International Covenant on Civil and Political Rights, 6 Harv.Hum.Rts.J. 59, 59B63 (1993).

Harvard International Law Journal, excerpt from, Beth Van Schaack, In Defense of Civil Redress: The Domestic Enforcement of Human Rights Norms in the Context of the Proposed Hague Judgments Convention, 42 Harvard International Law Journal 141, 161-162 (2001).

Hartunian, Vartan,excerpt from, The Armenian Genocide: A Survivor of the Armenian Genocide Remembers: An Interview with Reverend Vartan Hartunian,(2001). www.hatewatch.com

Houston Journal of International Law, excerpt from, A. Gallagher, The "New" Montreal Protocol and the Future of International Law for Protection of the Global Environment, 14 Houston Journal of International Law 267, 274-277 (1992).

Human Rights Law Journal, excerpt from, Nowak, The African Charter on Human and Peoples' Rights, 7 Human Rights Law Journal 399 (1986).

The Indian Society of International Law, excerpts from, Anand, U.N. Convention on the Law of the Sea and the United States, 24 Indian Journal of International Law 153, 154, 163B164, 184B187, 188, 190B191, 193.

Indiana Law Journal, excerpt from, Delbrück, A Fresh Look at Humanitarian Intervention Under the Authority of the United Nations, 67 Indiana Law Journal 887 (1992).

Indiana University Press, excerpt from, Matthew H. Kramer and Bloomington :, excerpts from, Legal Theory, Political Theory, and Deconstruction : Against Rhadamanthus 238-239, 254-255 (1991).

L'Institut de Droit International, Draft Convention Regime of Aerostats and Wireless Telegraphy (1906), 21 Annuaire de l'Institut de Droit International 293, 327.

Instituto Interamericano de Drechos Humanos San José, Costa Rica, excerpt from, Günter Handl, Human Rights and Protection of the Environment: A Mildly "Revisionist" View in A. Cancado Trindade (ed.), Human Rights, Sustainable Development and the Environment 117-122 (1992)

The International Bar Association, excerpt from, R. Frye, Uncle Sam and UNCED: A United States Perspective on the Earth Summit, International Newsletter of Committee F of the Section of Business Law of the International Bar Association 5 (1993).

International Business Lawyer, excerpt from Sharon A. Williams, State Responsibility and the Standard of Fault, in Public International Law Governing Transboundary Pollution, 243, 244- 245 (1984).

International Herald Tribune, excerpt from, Craig R. Whitney, Leniency Asked for Envoy Who Killed 2 in France, International Herald Tribune, 26 March 1997.

International Law Reports, for the Eichmann Case.

International Law Reports, People v. Robert J. Thomas, Eire, Supreme Court, 1954, 22 Int'l L.Rep. 295 (1958).

American Society of International Law, excerpt from, Cosmos 954 Claim (Canada v. U.S.S.R.) 18 International Legal Materials 899 (1979).

Italian Yearbook of International Law, Re Pulos and Others, Italy, Tribunal of Naples, 1976. 3 282, 286 (1977).

Journal du Droit International, excerpt from, Seidl-Hohenveldern, Notes on Austrian Judicial Decisions, Textuality or Contextuality Case on Interpretation of the Austrian State Treaty, 86 Journal du Droit International 835, 837 (1959).

Journal of Commerce, excerpts from, Spain, Finland Joining Rush to Form Flags of Convenience, November 18, 1986, p. 1.

Journal of Criminal Law and Criminology, excerpt from, Christopher L. Blakesley, Autumn of the Patriarch: The Pinochet Extradition Debacle & Beyond, 90 Journal of Criminal Law and Criminology 1 (2001).

Journal of Criminal Law & Criminology and Northwestern University School of Law, excerpts from Christopher L. Blakesley, Autumn of the Patriarch: The Pinochet Extradition Debacle and Beyond, 90 Journal of Criminal Law & Criminology 1, 63-84 (2000).

Journal of International Economic Law, excerpt from, John Jackson, Global Economics & International Economic Law, 1 Journal of International Economic Law 1, 8 (1998).

2 Kiss, Répertoire de la Pratique Française en Matière de Droit International Public 651 (1966).

Kluwer Academic Publishers, and Dordrecht; Boston : M. Nijhoff ; Hingham, MA : Distributors for the U.S. and Canada, excerpt from, Covey T. Oliver, The Future of Idealism in International Law: Structuralism, Humanism, and Survivalism, in The Structure and Process of International Law: Essays in Legal Philosophy, Doctrine and Theory 1207, 1208 (Macdonald & Johnston, eds. 1983).

Kluwer Law and Taxation Publishers, excerpt from Cristol, Space Law: Past, Present and Future (Kluwer, 1991).

Kluwer Academic Publishers, Martinus Nijhoff, Pub., excerpt from Mostafa K. Tolba, Preface, Global Environmental Interdependence.

Kluwer Academic Publishers, Martinus Nijhoff, Dordrecht; Boston,, 1986, excerpt from, Barbara Kwiatkowska & A.H.A. Soons, Transboundary Movements & Disposal of Hazardous Wastes in International Law XXII (eds.1993).

Kluwer Academic Publishers, Martinus Nijhoff, Pub., excerpt from ,Environmental Protection and Sustainable Development, Legal Principles and Recommendations Judge Nagendra Singh, Forward in Experts Group on Environmental Law of the World Commission on Environment and Development IX (1987).

Kluwer Academic Publishers, Martinus Nijhoff, experts from, Group on Environmental Law of the World Commission on Environment and Development, Environmental Protection and Sustainable Development, Legal Principles and Recommendations, Elements for a Draft Convention 38-42 (1987).

Law Quarterly Review , excerpt from, Hans Kelson, The Pure Theory of Law, 51 517 (1935).

Law and Policy in International Business, excerpt from, Note, The Haitian Crisis and the Future of Collective Enforcement of Democratic Governance, 27 Law and Policy in International Business 477.

Locke, John, excerpts from, Second Treatise of Government (1690) In Two Treatises of Government § 123, p. 368 (Critical Edition 1963).

Loyola L.A. Law Review, excerpt from, Michael Glennon, The War Powers Resolution: Sad Record, Dismal Promise.

Loyola of L.A. International and Comparative Law Journal, excerpt from Sharon A. Williams, Extradition and the death Penalty Exception in Canada: Resolving the Ng and Kindler Cases, 13 Loyola of L.A. International and Comparative Law Journal 799, 801-804.

McGill University, Institute and Centre of Air and Space Law, excerpts from, Mishra and Pavlasek, on the Lack of Physical Bases for Defining a Boundary Between Air Space and Outer Space, 7 Annals of Air and Space Law 399, 412 (1982).

Macmillan, New York [1963-68], excerpts from, Schwartz, Bernard, a Commentary on the Constitution of the United States: The Powers of Government (1963).

Martinus Nihjoff, Publisher, excerpt from, Oscar Schachter, International Law in Theory and Practice 11 (1991).

Michigan Journal of International Law, excerpt from, Joyner & Rothbaum, Libya and the Aerial Incident at Lockerbie: What Lessons for International Extradition Law, 14 Michigan Journal of International Law (1993).

Michigan Journal of International Law, excerpt from, Mutharika, The Role of the United Nations Security Council in African Peace Management: Some Proposals, 17 Michigan Journal of International Law 537 (1996).

Michigan Journal of International Law, Malvina Halberstam, The Right of Self-Defense Once the Security Council Takes Action.

Michigan Law Review , excerpt from, Comment, Punishment for War Crimes: Duty of Discretion, 69 Michigan Law Review 1312 (1971).

Michigan Law Review, David Luban, Alan Strudler, and David Wasserman, Moral Responsibility in the Age of Bureaucracy 90 Michigan Law Review 2348 (1993).

Montreal Gazette & Southam, Inc., excerpt from, Amanda Jelowicki, A first: local Armenians: Turks should admit 1915 genocide, gathering told, The Gazette (Montreal), April 26, 2000, FINAL

Morgenthau, Henry, excerpt from, Politics Among Nations 290 (4th ed. 1967).

The Nation, Johathan Schell, The New Nuclear Danger, Monday, June 25, 2001.

Netherlands Yearbook of International Law, Minister of Foreign Affairs, The Netherlands, Statement on Sanctions Against Diplomats, 2 Netherlands Yearbook of International Law 170 (1971).

New York Times Book Review, excerpt from, Judith Shapiro, Book Review of, David Chandler, Beyond the Grave An account of Pol Pot's genocide in Cambodia told through the records of its victims VOICES FROM S-21: Terror and History in Pol Pot's Secret Prison. Berkeley: University of California Press. New York Times Book Review, January 30, 2000.

New York University Journal of International and Politics, excerpt from, Ethan Nadelman, The Evolution of U.S. Involvement in the International Rendition of Fugitive Criminals, 25 N.Y.U. Journal of International and Politics 313, 324 (1993).Natural Resources Lawyer, excerpt from,

Collins, Mineral Exploitation of the Seabed: Problems, Progress, and Alternatives, 12 Natural Resources Lawyer 599, 636 (1979).

Oceana Publications, Sharon A. Williams, The International and National Protection of Cultural Property: A Comparative Study, 173-174 (1978).

Osgoode Hall Law School, Sharon A. Williams and the, The Rome Statute on the International Criminal Court: from 1947-2000 (2000).

Oxford University Press, Ian Brownlie, International Law 4 (5th ed., 1998).

Oxford University Press, excerpt from, Allyn & Bacon/Longman, 1 Jennings and Watts, Oppenheim's International Law 114 (1996).

Oxford University Press, excerpt from Allyn & Bacon/Longman, 1 Jennings and Watts, Oppenheim's International Law 127 (9th Ed.,1996) .

Oxford University Press, excerpt from, Allyn & Bacon/Longman, 1 Jennings and Watts, Oppenheim's International Law 146 (9th Ed.,1996).

Oxford University Press, excerpt from, Allyn & Bacon/Longman, 1 Jennings and Watts, Oppenheim's International Law 146, et seq., Parts 2-4, pp. 886-7, (9th Ed., 1996).

Oxford University Press, Clarendon Press, excerpt from, Roth, Governmental Illegitimacy in International Law, p.. 253ff, 1999.

Oxford University Press, Clarendon Press; New York, excerpt from, P. Birnie and A. Boyle, International Law and the Environment 3-6, 121-122 (1992).

Oxford University Press, Clarendon Press, New York, excerpt from, Ian Brownlie, Principles of Public International Law, pp. 428-432 (5th Ed.1998).

Oxford University Clarendon Press, New York, excerpt from Eileen Denza, Diplomatic Law: A Commentary on the Vienna Convention on Diplomatic Relations 373 (2nd ed. 1998).

Praeger, New York, excerpt from, Humphrey, The UN Charter and the Universal Declaration of Human Rights, in The International Protection of Human Rights 39, 51 (Luard, ed. 1967).

Princeton University Press, excerpt from Devisscher, Theory and Reality in Public International Law 404 (P.E. Corbett, transl. 1968).

Quadrangle Books, Chicago, distributed by Random House, excerpt from, Telford Taylor, Nuremberg and Vietnam: an American Tragedy (1970).

Rinehart, New York, 1954, excerpt from Julius Stone, Legal controls of international conflict; a treatise on the dynamics of disputes- and war-law.

Royal Institute of International Affairs, excerpt from John Jackson, The World Trade Organisation: Constitution and Jurisprudence (1998).

San Diego Justice Journal, excerpt from, Matthew Lippman, War Crimes: The My Lai Massacre and the Vietnam War, San Diego Justice Journal 295 (1993).

The San Francisco Chronicle, Pirates Raid Ship Leased to U.S. Navy, The San Francisco Chronicle, January 31, 1985, p. 1.

Simon & Shuster-Prentice-Hall Publishers, excerpt from, E. Østrom, Governing the Commons 1-3.

Smith, Forward to Sherr, A Legal Analysis of the "New Interpretation" of the Anti- Ballistic Missile Treaty (1986).

Solzhenitsyn, Alexander, excerpts from, The Gulag Archipelago (T. Whitney trans., 1974).

South Dakota Law Review, excerpt from, Goldberg, The Shoot–Out at the Libyan Self-Styled People's Bureau: A Case of State-Supported Terrorism, 30 So. Dakota Law Review 1 (1984).

Stanford Law Review, excerpt from, Phillip Trimble, International Law, World Order and Critical Legal Studies, 42 Stanford Law Review 811, 833-834 (1990).

Stanford Law Review, excerpt from, Kahn, Essay: Lessons for International Law from the Gulf War, 45 Stanford Law Review 425 (1993).

Stevens & Sons, Ltd., London, excerpt from, McNair, The Law of the Air 4 (Kerr & Evans, 3d ed. 1964).

Stevens & Sons, Ltd., London, excerpts from, O'Connell, International Law 38 (2nd ed. 1970).

Stevens, London; New York, Praeger, Woetzel, Robert K., The Nürnberg Trials in International Law, 1 Trial of the Major War Criminals 171 (1960).

Texas International Law Journal, excerpt from,Terry, The Criteria for Intervention: An Evaluation of U.S. Military Policy in U.N. Operations.

Transnational Publishers, Inc., excerpts from, Christopher L. Blakesley, Terrorism, Drugs, International Law and the Protection of Human Liberty, 132–134, 136–37 (1992).

Transnational Publishers Inc., excerpt from, J. Brunée, Acid Rain and Ozone Layer Depletion: International Law and Regulation 47 (1988).

Transnational Publishers Inc., excerpt from, E. Brown Weiss, In Fairness to Future Generations, Core Features, 38, 157-159 (1989).

Transnational Publishers, Inc., excerpt from, A. Kiss and D. Shelton, International Environmental Law, 9-18, 21-22, 28-31, 48-50, 54, 249, 257-258, (1991).

Triffterer, Otto, editor, Commentary on the Rome Statute of the International Criminal Court (1999), W. J. Fenrick, Responsibility of Commanders and Other Superiors.

United Nations University Press, excerpt from, Edith Brown Weiss, Global Environmental Change and International Law: the Introductory Framework, Environmental Change and International Law, 3-7 (1992).

United Nations University Press, excerpt from, Ploman, Global Learning: Concept and Applications Edith Brown Weiss (ed.), Environmental Change and International Law 459, 476- 478 (1992).

University of Glascow School of Law, John P. Grant, The Lockerbie Case, Background, www.law.gla.ac.uk/lockerbie/backgroundsummary.cfm

University of Illinois Press, excerpt from, Warmuth and Firmage, To Chain the Dog of War (2d ed. 1989).

University of Pennsylvania Press, excerpt from, Abdullah Ahmed An'Naim, Human Rights in Cross-Cultural Perspectives, pp. 1-6 (1992).

University of Pittsburgh Law Review, excerpt from, Parker, Cultural Autonomy: A Prime Directive for the Blue Helmets, 55 University of Pittsburgh Law Review 207, 208 (1993).

University of Tasmania, Environmental Law and Policy Workshop papers and proceedings Environmental Law and Policy Workshop (1990), excerpt from, "Towards Common Action: Proposals for Institutional and Legal Change," Our Common Future, World Commission on Environment and Development 308-311, 312-314, 323-324, 330-333, 334-337 (1987).

U.S. Department of State, excerpt from, II Hackworth, Digest of International Law, Asylum on a Vessel 641 (1941).

U.S. Department of State, excerpt from, Whiteman, Digest of International Law (1967).

The Vancouver Sun, excerpt from, Mugabo, Lama, Confronting the face of genocide: On the sixth anniversary of the Rwandan massacres that left one million dead, scholars, politicians & survivors are gathering in Vancouver to examine the fateful circumstances and mistakes that engendered the tragedy April 8, 2000).

Vicuña, F. Orrego, State Responsibility, Liability, and Remedial Measures Under International Law: New Criteria for Environmental Protection, in E. Brown Weiss (ed.), Environmental Change and International Law, 124, 144-147 (1992).

Virginia Journal of International Law, Fernando R. Tesón, Feminism and International Law: A Reply, 33 Virginia Journal of International Law 647 (1993).

Virginia Journal of Internal Law, excerpt from, McDougal, Lasswell, Reisman, Theories About International Law: Prologue to a Configurative Jurisprudence, 8 Virginia Journal of Internal Law 188, 195 (1968).

Virginia Journal of International Law, excerpt from, Moore, Toward a New Paradigm: Enhanced Effectiveness in United Nations Peacekeeping, Collective Security, and War Avoidance, 37 Virginia Journal of International Law 811 (1997).

Virginia Journal of International Law, Rebecca J. Cook, Reservations to the Convention on the Elimination of all Forms of Discrimination Against Women,, 30 Va.J.Int'l L. 643, 693–696 (1990).

West Publishing Inc., Symeon C. Symeonides, Wendy Collins Perdue, Arthur T. von Mehren, Conflict of Laws: American, Comparative, International 58-563 (1998).

World Affairs, International Air Transport and Foreign Policy, Campbell, United States in 1947–1948, 276, at 280 (1948).

John Wylie and Sons and Dr. Morton A. Kaplan, excerpts from, Kaplan and Katzenback, The Political Foundations of International Law 5 (1961).

Yale University Press, 1978, excerpt from, Lee Buchheit, Succession: The Legitimacy of Self- Determination (1978).

Yale University Press, excerpt from, Harold Hongju Koh, The National Security Constitution (1990).

TABLE OF CASES

Principal cases are in bold type. Non-principal cases are in roman type. References are to Pages.

*

THE INTERNATIONAL LEGAL SYSTEM

*

CHAPTER 1

APPLICATION OF THE LAW OF THE INTERNATIONAL SYSTEM

Our view of the "international legal system" includes not only the traditional and evolving body of international law in the public sector but also extends to the surrounding areas of the national law that bear on a state's conduct of foreign relations: the domestic constitutional systems treatment of international law and particularly of treaties, and the domestic legislative and regulatory measures employed to implement international law. A major example of the the domestic law feature of the system is found in Chapter 12 on treaties in United States law. The legal status of international organizations is taken up in Chapter 2, Section C. The work of international organizations appears in relation to most topics developed in the Casebook.

Chapter 1 introduces the wide variety of foreign affairs situations in which international law questions arise in practice, sometimes in unsuspected places and in exciting ways. These materials are intended to stimulate judgements about the uses and implementation of international law, and to show that as in domestic legal systems serious violations occur and receive perhaps excessive attention. In most areas of international law, states regularly respect and apply the rules and insist on being seen to do so, as they must for the successful transaction of even the simplest forms of intergovernmental business.

International system studies are intended to demonstrate some of the most important or useful rules, to show how the system works overall, to distinguish between effective and reliable rules in context versus the few others that are less respected and reliable, and to anticipate the kinds of problems that arise in the application of rules in international work. Whether or not one chooses to see these rules as fully qualified "law" in the positivist—Austinian sense–like domestic legal rules, the practitioner must be familiar with the international system and know how to use it within its own terms, the way lawyers operate in the various sectors of domestic law. Otherwise he or she may prove to be unable to act effectively in the international system where adversaries may come better equipped professionally to deal with the problems at hand. It is not a matter of international relations alone but a matter of *law* as well.

Study of this system inevitably brings early confrontation with such theoretical systemic questions as the nature, the validity, the reality and the utility of international law, without need at this stage to search in depth for the answers to these recurrent and vexing questions (more on that appears in Chapter 17 on Theories About International Law). While this Chapter also looks briefly at the sources of international law, the authors have not sought to cover these sources in systematic form, for much is left to the more concrete materials throughout the *Cases* to present typical problems of the sources of law and the hierarchy of international norms. The *Cases* identify and make convincing use of the sources in addressing substantive issues in context.

An appreciation of the key sources in this field of the law is of course critical at the outset, as is a sense of a workable definition of international law, which might be taken as "a body of legally binding rules principally governing relations among states, rules applicable to international organizations, and rules evolving to provide increasing rights to individuals particularly in the fields of human rights and crimes against humanity."

Focusing on a brief summary of the generally accepted functions of international law (with some reference to national law counterparts) should also prove to be instructive at this point. Broadly sketched, some functions and domestic parallels are:

1. To establish and support the international system (constitutional law)

2. To provide substantive legal rules for resolving disputes

    Treaties—(contracts, legislation)

    International organizations—(governments, corporations)

    International civil responsibility—(torts)

    Criminal responsibility (criminal law)

    Jurisdiction of states, territory, law of sea, air and space—(jurisdiction, property)

    Judicial settlement—(civil jurisdiction, civil procedure)

    Arbitration—(arbitration)

    Human Rights (civil liberties)

    Environment (environment)

Economic law (trade, investment)

3. To do justice in relations between states and other actors on the international scene, in place of anarchy or the imposition of the unregulated interest of the stronger

4. To keep the peace: rules about pacific settlement of disputes, the use of force, and the enforcement of international law

5. To provide practical aids to the smooth conduct of foreign relations: establishment of systems and rules which do not require reinvention and renegotiation each time a problem arises.

Chapter 1 is also analytically descriptive of the main features of the system. It introduces a number of its major operational challenges, viz: (a) universality, (b) effectiveness, (c) state dissent from binding effect, (d) some of the uses and limitations of the arbitral-adjudicatory process as a means of resolving conflicts, and (e) the law making and application role of the United Nations.

1. The traditional sources of international law.

Article 38 of the Statute of the International Court of Justice:

1. The Court, whose function is to decide in accordance with international law such disputes as are submitted to it, shall apply:

   a. international conventions, whether general or particular, establishing rules expressly recognized by the contesting states;

   b. international custom, as evidence of a general practice accepted as law;

   c. the general principles of law recognized by civilized nations;

   d. subject to the provisions of Article 59, judicial decisions and the teachings of the most highly qualified publicists of the various nations, as subsidiary means for the determination of rules of law.

   * * *

This hierarchy of legal authority is *"civilian"* or derived largely from Roman law influence as established on the European continent and other areas that have been influenced by that model. International conventions (like legislation or the code in *civilian* jurisdictions), international custom, and general principles of law, are all binding or primary authority. Judicial decisions and teachings of the most highly qualified publicists, or doctrine, are persuasive authority. The latter, principally are to be used to prove the existence of custom. This is the same as in *civilian* domestic systems. Take, for example, the Civil Code of Louisiana, which originally was adopted from the French *Projet* or Digest for their *Code Napoléon*:

Art. 1: The sources of law are legislation and custom.

Art. 2: Legislation is the solemn expression of legislative will.

Art. 3: Custom results from practice repeated for a long time and generally accepted as having acquired the force of law. Custom may not abrogate legislation.

Art. 4: When no rule for a particular situation can be derived from legislation or custom, the court is bound to proceed according to equity. To decide equitably, resort is made to justice.

Or note the Iraqi Code, which follows essentially the same hierarchy of authority, adding general principles of Islam:

§ 1: The Code governs all questions of law which come within the letter or spirit of any of its provisions.

§ 2: If the Code does not furnish an applicable provision, the court shall decide in accordance with customary law, and failing that, in accordance with those *principles of Muslim law* (Shari'a) which are most in keeping with the provisions of this Code, without being bound by any particular school of jurisprudence, and, failing that, in accordance with the principles of equity.

§ 3: In all of this, the Court shall be guided by judicial decisions and by the principles of jurisprudence in Iraq and in foreign countries whose laws are similar to those of Iraq.

Thus, to understand international law properly, to be able to negotiate, litigate, or even to communicate effectively in the arena of international law, it is necessary to understand that its origin and discipline, its philosophical context, and the mindset of many of its practitioners is "civilian" or a variation on that theme, rather than common law in inspiration. To practice international law well, one should also be a comparativist.

———

Questions

How does this hierarchy of sources compare to that in "common law" systems? What is binding authority? Will the nature of the sources of international law make a difference in how you will research, negotiate, or litigate an international legal problem? Where will you look to find evidence of authoritative sources such as Custom and General Principles? Keep these issues in mind as you proceed.

2.   *International Custom.*

Byers, Custom, Power and the Power of Rules

p. xi, 3, (1999).

At the beginning of his or her career, every international lawyer has to grapple with the concept of customary international law, with the idea that there are informal, unwritten rules which are binding upon States. This is because there remain important areas of international law, such as the laws of State responsibility and State immunity, where generally applicable treaties do not exist. And despite the lack of an explicit, general consent to rules in these areas, no international lawyer doubts that there is a body of law that applies to them.

        * * *

    The International Court of Justice has observed that international law is not a static set of rules, that it undergoes "continuous evolution' " The evolution of international law is a subject that has absorbed international lawyers for centuries, for, among other things, the way in which law develops and changes clearly determines the rules that are applicable today. * * * [O]ne particular characteristic of the evolution of international law, is * * * that it does not occur in a legal vacuum, but is instead circumscribed and regulated by fundamental rules, principles and processes of international law. One such process is the process of customary international law, which is also referred to here as the "customary process". This process governs how one particular kind of rules—rules of customary international law—is developed, maintained and changed.

    Unlike treaty rules, which result from formal negotiation and explicit acceptance, rules of customary international law arise out of frequently ambiguous combinations of behavioural regularity and expressed or inferred acknowledgments of legality. Despite (or perhaps because of) their informal origins, rules of customary international law provide substantive content to many areas of international law, as well as the procedural framework within which most rules of international law, including treaty rules, develop, exist and change. Customary rules are particularly important in areas of international law, such as State immunity and State responsibility, where multilateral treaties of a general scope have yet to be negotiated. They are also important in areas, such as human rights, where many States are not party to existing treaties nor subject to the relevant treaty enforcement mechanisms. Finally, customary rules would seem to exist alongside many treaty provisions, influencing the interpretation and application of those provisions, and in some cases modifying their content.

Brownlie, International Law 4 (5TH Ed., 1998)*

Definition. Article 38 refers to "international custom, as evidence of a general practice accepted as law", and Brierly remarks that "what is sought for is a general recognition among States of a certain practice as obligatory". Although occasionally the terms are used interchangeably, "custom" and "usage" are terms of art and have different meanings. A usage is a general practice which does not reflect a legal obligation, and examples are ceremonial salutes at sea and the practice of exempting diplomatic vehicles from parking prohibitions.

Evidence. The material sources which establish custom are very numerous and include the following: diplomatic correspondence, policy statements, press releases, the opinions of official legal advisers, official manuals on legal questions, e.g. manuals of military law, executive decisions and practices, orders to naval forces etc., comments by governments on drafts produced by the International Law Commission, state legislation, international and national judicial decisions, recitals in treaties and other international instruments, a pattern of treaties in the same form, the practice of international organs, and resolutions relating to legal questions in the United Nations General Assembly. Obviously the value of these sources varies and much depends on the circumstances.

The elements of custom

* * *

(c) Generality of the Practice. This is an aspect which complements that of consistency, Certainly universality is not required, but the real problem is to determine the value of abstention from protest by a substantial number of states in face of a practice followed by some others. Silence may denote either tacit agreement or a simple lack of interest. * * *

(d) Opinio juris et necessitatis. The Statute of the International Court refers to "a general practice *accepted as law*". Brierly speaks of recognition by states of a certain practice "as obligatory", and Hudson requires a "conception that the practice is required by, or consistent with, prevailing international law". Some writers do not consider this psychological element to be a requirement for the formation of custom, but it is in fact a necessary ingredient. The sense of legal obligation, as opposed to motives of courtesy, fairness, or morality, is real enough, and the practice of states recognizes a distinction between obligation and usage. The essential problem is surely one of proof, and especially the incidence of the burden of proof.

In terms of the practice of the International Court of Justice—which provides a general guide to the nature of the problem—there are two methods of approach. In many cases the Court is willing to assume the existence of an *opinio juris* on the basis of evidence of a general practice, or a consensus in the literature, or the previous determinations of the Court or other international tribunals. However, in a significant minority of cases the Court has adopted a more rigorous approach and has called for more positive evidence of the recognition of the validity of the rules in question in the practice of states. The choice of approach appears to depend upon the nature of the issues (that is, the state of the law may be a primary point in contention), and the discretion of the Court.

* * *

Proof of custom. In principle a court is presumed to know the law and may apply a custom even if it has not been expressly pleaded. In practice the proponent of a custom has a burden of proof, the nature of which will vary according to the subject-matter and the form of the pleadings. Thus in the *Lotus* case [*infra*, ch. 3] the Court spoke of the plaintiff's burden in respect of a general custom. Where a local or regional custom is alleged, the proponent "must prove that this custom is established in such a manner that it has become binding on the other Party".

Schachter, International Law in Theory and Practice 11 (1991)*

Does it follow * * * that a particular State may reject the system and opt out of it? In a speculative way, one may conceive of a régime in control of a territory resting its claim to authority solely on its naked power (or perhaps on assertion of religious authority) without a claim of rights under international law as such. Whether the exercise of authority in such cases would be acquiesced in by other States is an empirical matter. In practice, no State in the contemporary period has attempted to reject the system as a whole. However, on occasion, representatives of newly independent States asserted in the 1960s that they could not be bound by a system of law in whose creation they had no opportunity to participate. However, this sweeping assertion did not in fact preclude their explicit or implicit claim of rights of territorial integrity and political independence (and other basic rights) under international law. The acceptance of international law was a necessary implication of their assertion of sovereign equality and their claim to be treated as a State. In actuality, the claim that they could not be bound by the rules to which they had not assented was aimed at specific customary law rules (such as those in State responsibility), and not at the whole body of customary law.

* * *

[Another] * * * proposition constitutes the "strongest" use of voluntarist theory. It would allow a State to reject the application of a customary rule to it simply on the ground that it was contrary to the State's present will. No State, to my knowledge, has openly espoused that position. It would amount to a denial of customary law and it is most unlikely that any State would be prepared to take that position. However, a State may seek to avoid submitting to a rule by adopting a more moderate form of consensualism and asserting that it had manifested its objection in the past or that its lack of explicit consent taken together with similar lack of acceptances by other States has been enough to defeat the application of the rule as universally binding. * * *

Voluntarism in a somewhat different guise can also be found when a State objects to a rule on the ground that it is incompatible with a vital interest of the State. In such case, the recalcitrant State rests not simply on its will per se but on a superior norm of self-interest that is said to prevail over law. An example well known in the United States was the statement of the former Secretary of State, Dean Acheson, at the time of the Cuban missile case that the "quarantine" imposed by the United States could not be dealt with as a legal issue since international law "does not deal with questions of ultimate power" and "the survival of States is not a matter of law". The statement has been taken to mean that a State may decide for itself whether its "ultimate power" or survival are at stake and, if so, to disregard the law. This view, it should be noted, is not the same as reliance on the legal right of self-defence. It is a claim that the State's will, if based on a vital State interest, must prevail over law. The position in effect

* Reprinted with the permission of Martinus Nihoff.

denies the applicability of the law to critical issues particularly involving the right to use force.

SECTION A.   APPLICATION WITHIN NATIONAL LEGAL SYSTEMS

1.   RULES OF CUSTOMARY INTERNATIONAL LAW NOT IN CONFLICT WITH DOMESTIC LAW

The Paquete Habana
The Lola

United States Supreme Court, 1900.
175 U.S. 677, 20 S.Ct. 290, 44 L.Ed. 320.

MR. JUSTICE GRAY delivered the opinion of the court.

These are two appeals from decrees of the District Court of the United States for the Southern District of Florida, condemning two fishing vessels and their cargoes as prize of war.

Each vessel was a fishing smack, running in and out of Havana, and regularly engaged in fishing on the coast of Cuba; sailed under the Spanish flag; was owned by a Spanish subject of Cuban birth, living in the city of Havana; was commanded by a subject of Spain also residing in Havana * * *. Her cargo consisted of fresh fish, caught by her crew from the sea, put on board as they were caught, and kept and sold alive. Until stopped by the blockading squadron, she had no knowledge of the existence of the war, or of any blockade. She had no arms or ammunition on board, and made no attempt to run the blockade after she knew of its existence, nor any resistance at the time of the capture.

* * *

Both the fishing vessels were brought by their captors into Key West. A libel for the condemnation of each vessel and her cargo as prize of war was there filed * * * a claim was interposed by her master, on behalf of himself and the other members of the crew, and of her owner; evidence was taken, showing the facts above stated; and on May 30, 1898, a final decree of condemnation and sale was entered, "the court not being satisfied that as a matter of law, without any ordinance, treaty or proclamation, fishing vessels of this class are exempt from seizure."

Each vessel was thereupon sold by auction; the Paquete Habana for the sum of $490; and the Lola for the sum of $800. * * *

* * *

We are then brought to the consideration of the question whether, upon the facts appearing in these records, the fishing smacks were subject to capture by the armed vessels of the United States during the recent war with Spain.

By an ancient usage among civilized nations, beginning centuries ago, and gradually ripening into a rule of international law, coast fishing vessels, pursuing their vocation of catching and bringing in fresh fish, have been recognized as exempt, with their cargoes and crews, from capture as prize of war.

This doctrine, however, has been earnestly contested at the bar; and no complete collection of the instances illustrating it is to be found, so far as we are aware, in a single published work, although many are referred to and discussed by the writers on international law, notably in 2 Ortolan, Règles Internationales et Diplomatie de la Mer, (4th ed.); in 4 Calvo, Droit International, (5th ed.); in De Boeck, Propriété Privée Ennemie sous Pavillon Ennemi; and in Hall, International Law, (4th ed.). It is therefore worth the while to trace the history of the rule, from the earliest accessible sources, through the increasing recognition of it, with occasional setbacks, to what we may now justly consider as its final establishment in our own country and generally throughout the civilized world.

[The court then proceeds to trace the history of the rule through an extensive examination of inconsistent state practice, beginning with the issuance of orders by Henry IV to his admirals in 1403 and 1406.]

Since the English orders in council of 1806 and 1810 * * * in favor of fishing vessels employed in catching and bringing to market fresh fish, no instance has been found in which the exemption from capture of private coast fishing vessels, honestly pursuing their peaceful industry, has been denied by England, or by any other nation. And the Empire of Japan, (the last State admitted into the rank of civilized nations,) by an ordinance promulgated at the beginning of its war with China in August, 1894, established prize courts, and ordained that "the following enemy's vessels are exempt from detention"—including in the exemption "boats engaged in coast fisheries," as well as "ships engaged exclusively on a voyage of scientific discovery, philanthropy or religious mission."

International law is part of our law, and must be ascertained and administered by the courts of justice of appropriate jurisdiction, as often as questions of right depending upon it are duly presented for their determination. For this purpose, where there is no treaty, and no controlling executive or legislative act or judicial decision, resort must be had to the customs and usages of civilized nations; and, as evidence of these, to the works of jurists and commentators, who by years of labor, research and experience, have made themselves peculiarly well acquainted with the subjects of which they treat. Such works are resorted to by judicial tribunals, not for the speculations of their authors concerning what the law ought to be, but for trustworthy evidence of what the law really is. Hilton v. Guyot, 159 U.S. 113, 163, 164, 214, 215.

       * * *

This review of the precedents and authorities on the subject appears to us abundantly to demonstrate that at the present day, by the general consent of the civilized nations of the world, and independently of any express treaty or other public act, it is an established rule of international law, founded on considerations of humanity to a poor and industrious order of men, and of the mutual convenience of belligerent States, that coast fishing vessels, with their implements and supplies, cargoes and crews, unarmed, and honestly pursuing their peaceful calling of catching and bringing in fresh fish, are exempt from capture as prize of war.

The exemption, of course, does not apply to coast fishermen or their vessels, if employed for a warlike purpose, or in such a way as to give aid or information to the enemy; nor when military or naval operations create a necessity to which all private interests must give way.

Nor has the exemption been extended to ships or vessels employed on the high sea in taking whales or seals, or cod or other fish which are not brought fresh to market, but are salted or otherwise cured and made a regular article of commerce.

This rule of international law is one which prize courts, administering the law of nations, are bound to take judicial notice of, and to give effect to, in the absence of any treaty or other public act of their own government in relation to the matter.

* * *

The United States [position] during the recent war with Spain was quite in accord with the rule of international law, now generally recognized by civilized nations, in regard to coast fishing vessels.

On April 21, 1898, the Secretary of the Navy gave instructions to Admiral Sampson commanding the North Atlantic Squadron, to "immediately institute a blockade of the north coast of Cuba, extending from Cardenas on the east to Bahia Honda on the west." The blockade was immediately instituted accordingly. On April 22, the President issued a proclamation, declaring that the United States had instituted and would maintain that blockade, "in pursuance of the laws of the United States, and the law of nations applicable to such cases." And by the act of Congress of April 25, 1898, c. 189, it was declared that the war between the United States and Spain existed on that day, and had existed since and including April 21.

On April 26, 1898, the President issued another proclamation, which, after reciting the existence of the war, as declared by Congress, contained this further recital: "It being desirable that such war should be conducted upon principles in harmony with the present views of nations and sanctioned by their recent practice." This recital was followed by specific declarations of certain rules for the conduct of the war by sea, making no mention of fishing vessels. But the proclamation clearly manifests the general policy of the Government to conduct the war in accordance with the principles of international law * * *.

* * *

Upon the facts proved in either case, it is the duty of this court, sitting as the highest prize court of the United States, and administering the law of nations, to declare and adjudge that the capture was unlawful, and without probable cause; and it is therefore, in each case,

Ordered, that the decree of the District Court be reversed, and the proceeds of the sale of the vessel, together with the proceeds of any sale of her cargo, be restored to the claimant, with damages and costs.

Trendtex Trading Corporation v. Central Bank of Nigeria

England, Queen's Bench, 1977.
[1977] Q.B. 529, 553–554.*

[The issue was whether the bank was entitled to sovereign immunity i.e., whether it was immune from suit in the courts of England.

At the time the suit was brought, the applicable rule of customary international law did not require the court to grant the immunity. Lord Denning discussed the manner in which this rule of international law became part of the law of England. A portion of his opinion follows.]

* * *

A fundamental question arises. * * * What is the place of international law in our English law? One school of thought holds to the doctrine of *incorporation*. It says that the rules of international law are incorporated into English law automatically and considered to be part of English law unless they are in conflict with an Act of Parliament. The other school of thought holds to the doctrine of *transformation*. It says that the rules of international law are not to be considered as part of English law except in so far as they have been already adopted and made part of our law by the decisions of the judges, or by Act of Parliament, or long established custom. The difference is vital when you are faced with a change in the rules of international law. Under the doctrine of incorporation, when the rules of international law change, our English law changes with them. But, under the doctrine of transformation, the English law does not change. It is bound by precedent. It is bound down to those rules of international law which have been accepted and adopted in the past. It cannot develop as international law develops.

(i) The doctrine of incorporation. The doctrine of incorporation goes back to 1737 in Buvot v. Barbut [sic] (1736) 3 Burr. 1481 in which Lord Talbot L.C. (who was highly esteemed) made a declaration which was taken down by young William Murray (who was of counsel in the case) and adopted by him in 1764 when he was Lord Mansfield C.J. in Triquet v. Bath (1764) 3 Burr. 1478:

> Lord Talbot declared a clear opinion—"That the law of nations in its full extent was part of the law of England." * * *

That doctrine was accepted, not only by Lord Mansfield himself, but also by Sir William Blackstone, and [numerous] other great names.

* * *

---

* Reprinted by permission of the Incorporated Council of Law Reporting for England and Wales, London.

(iii) Which is correct? * * * I now believe that the doctrine of incorporation is correct. Otherwise I do not see that our courts could ever recognise a change in the rules of international law. It is certain that international law does change. I would use of international law the words which Galileo used of the earth: "But it does move." International law does change: and the courts have applied the changes without the aid of any Act of Parliament. * * *

(iv) Conclusion on this point. Seeing that the rules of international law have changed—and do change—and that the courts have given effect to the changes without any Act of Parliament, it follows to my mind inexorably that the rules of international law, as existing from time to time, do form part of our English law. It follows, too, that a decision of this court—as to what was the ruling of international law 50 or 60 years ago—is not binding on this court today. International law knows no rule of stare decisis. * * *

    * * *

Note: In the first Pinochet appeal in the House of Lords on 25 November 1998, (*Regina v. Battle et al*, 37 I.L.M. 1302, 1311 (1998), later set aside for reasons unrelated to the following point, Lord Slynn of Hadley wrote:

Rules of customary international law change, however, and as Lord Denning, M.R. said in *Trendtex Trading Corporation v. Central Bank of Nigeria* [1977] Q.B. 529, "we should give effect to those changes and not be bound by any idea of stare decisis in international law". Thus, for example, the concept of absolute immunity for a Sovereign has changed to adopt a theory of restrictive immunity in so far as it concerns the activities of a State engaging in trade (I Congresso del Partido [1983] A.C. 244). One must therefore ask is there "sufficient evidence to show that the rule of international law has changed?" (p. 556).

Notes and Questions

1. It may be impossible to find a national legal system which arbitrarily refuses to apply rules of customary international law not in conflict with domestic law. The main issue in this section is not whether courts in national legal systems give effect to such rules, but how they go about it. The two preceding cases are illustrative.

2. ***Where there is no constitutional provision directing courts to apply rules of customary international law.*** In common law states courts usually justify their application of customary international law by stating that international law is part of the law of the land. The simplicity of the proposition is deceptive, for if it were accepted as literally true, courts would need only to determine whether there was an applicable rule of customary international law and apply it so long as they found an applicable rule not in conflict with domestic law. Yet this is not quite the

way the courts proceeded in the cases set forth above. Did the court apply international law? Domestic law? Both?

In *The Paquete Habana*, what was the applicable rule of customary international law ? How was it proved? Did the Court hold that custom was the law of the land under all circumstances? The Court determined the applicable rule of customary international law only after ascertaining that there was no applicable rule of domestic law already established by previous executive or legislative act or judicial decision. Why was the court concerned with the possibility that a rule of domestic law might be available? And why would a nation be determined to apply a rule of customary international law even before it had been explicitly transformed into a rule of domestic law?

Did the Court hold that Congress could abrogate custom? How about the President? Can the courts abrogate custom, or must they follow it? In the *Paquete Habana* case, specifically who breached customary international law? Did that individual breach international law, domestic law or both? Did the Court indicate some sort of hierarchy of "law" in this context? In many "civil law" jurisdictions, if there is no constitutional provision commanding the application of customary international law, the courts show the same proclivity as common law courts to search for an applicable rule of domestic law. Illustrative of this propensity is the decision in *the Immunity Case,* Yugoslavia, Supreme Court of the People's Republic of Croatia, 86 Journal de Droit International 525 (1959). As in the *Trendtex* case, the issue was sovereign immunity, i.e., whether a foreign state could claim immunity from suit. The court found the foreign state was entitled to immunity by a rule of customary international law. But it also found there was a rule of domestic law which provided immunity for the foreign state and gave judgment accordingly.

Suppose that in the Yugoslav case, the court had found there was no applicable rule of domestic law. Would it have applied the rule of customary international law as the rule of decision? Did the Supreme Court of the United States apply a rule of customary international law as the rule of decision in *The Paquete Habana*? In these two cases, did the Yugoslav and the American courts follow identical theories concerning the relationship of customary international law to domestic law? Do these theories differ from the theory implicit in the opinion of Lord Denning in the *Trendtex* case?

3. ***Provisions in constitutions.*** National constitutions may provide a specific legal basis for the application of rules of customary international law. Among those a number of modest formulations provide (or contain language to the effect) that "The State shall endeavour to * * * foster respect for international law and treaty obligations in the dealings of organized peoples with one another" Article 51(c) of the Constitution of India, 1950.* Comparable provisions are found in the constitutions of a

* The source of constitutional material in this chapter is Constitution Finder on the Internet:www.richmond.edu/?jpjones/confinder, See also Blaustein and Flanz, Constitutions of the Countries of the World, (1990), a multi-volume work.

number of countries, including Bulgaria Article 24(1), 1991, Nepal Article 26(15), 1990, Namibia Article 96(d), 1990, The Netherlands Article 90, 1990, and Romania, Article 10, 1991.

Stronger terms of acceptance of international law are found in other national constitutions, including Article 143, of the Paraguay Constitution of 1992. Article 29(3) of the Constitution of Ireland (text of 1990), provides that : "Ireland accepts the generally recognized principles of international law as its rule of conduct in its relations with other States." Article 98(2) of the Japanese Constitution of 1946 provides that "The * * * established laws of nations shall be faithfully observed".

Whether a broadly worded constitutional provision justifies application of customary international law depends on past practice. French courts have traditionally given effect to such rules and for this reason some argue that the preamble to the French Constitution of 1946 merely acknowledged the fact: "The French Republic, faithful to its tradition, abides by the rules of international law." 2 Peaslee, *Constitutions of Nations* 7 (2d ed. 1956). The provision was incorporated by reference in the 1958 Constitution of the Fifth French Republic. It has been contended by a French author that the provision is not only unnecessary but also dangerous, because it might put into question the inherent power of French courts to apply rules of international law. Rousseau, *Droit International Public* 14 (Précis Dalloz, 5th ed. 1970). Compare Article 55 of the French Constitution of 1958 which provides specifically for the binding force of qualified treaties and agreements—but not for customary international law. Treaties have a status *superior* to that of legislation. The lesser status for customary law is regretted by at least one French author. Dupuy, *Droit International Public* 304 (Précis Dalloz, 1992); but see Carreau, *Droit International Public* 57 (3rd ed. 1991) The Hungarian Constitution of 1949 as amended in 1997, is exceptional in providing in Chapter 1, sec. 7 that: "The legal system of the Republic of Hungary accepts the generally recognized principles of international law, and shall harmonize the country's domestic law with the obligations assumed under international law."

Some constitutions may provide a basis for courts to apply rules of customary international law by declaring specifically that international law is part of the law of the land. Thus the Austrian Constitution of 1928 states in Article 9(1): "[t]he generally recognized principles of International Law are integral parts of the Federal Law". Article 2(2) of the 1987 Constitution of the Philippines states: "The Philippines * * * adopts the generally accepted principles of international law as part of the law of the land. Article 15 of the Russian Constitution of 1993 states that: 'the commonly recognized principles and norms of international law and the international treaties of the Russian Federation shall be a component part of its legal system.' " Do these provisions mean that custom is automatically integrated or must something further be done to integrate it?

2. RULES OF DOMESTIC LAW IN CONFLICT WITH CUSTOMARY INTERNATIONAL LAW

Attorney–General of Israel v. Eichmann

Israel, District Court of Jerusalem, 1961.
36 Int'l L.Rep. 5, 24 (1968).*

[After Israeli agents kidnaped Adolf Eichmann in Argentina and brought him to Israel for trial without consent of the Argentine authorities, Eichman was tried in Israel under a law punishing Nazis and their collaborators for crimes against the Jewish people committed in Germany during World War II. His counsel argued that, under applicable rules of customary international law, the court had no jurisdiction to try him for crimes committed outside Israel when neither the law, nor Israel, yet existed. He also argued that Israel law was in conflict with international law.]

The argument that Israel law is in conflict with international law and that it cannot vest jurisdiction in this Court, raises the preliminary question of the validity of international law in Israel and whether, in the event of conflict, it is to be preferred to the law of the land. The law in force in Israel resembles that in force in England in this regard. * * *

As to the question of the incorporation of the principles of international law in the national law [of Israel] we rely on Blackstone, Commentaries on the Laws of England (Book IV, Chap. 5):

In England * * * the law of nations * * * is * * * adopted in its full extent by the common law, and it is held to be a part of the law of the land * * * without which it must cease to be a part of the civilized world.

The same applies to other countries, such as the United States of America, France, Belgium and Switzerland, where the usages of international law have been recognized as part of the national law.

* * *

With respect to statutory law, Justice Agranat said in High Court:

B. It is a well-known maxim that a municipal statute should—except where its contents require a different interpretation—be interpreted in accordance with the rules of public international law.

And in Criminal Appeal No. 5/51 Mr. Justice Sussman said (p. 1065):

It is a well-known rule that in interpreting a statute the Court will as far as possible try to avoid a conflict between the municipal law and the obligations incumbent on the State by virtue of international law. But this is only one of the canons of interpretation. That is to say, where we are dealing not with the Common Law but with a written statute which expresses the will of the legislator, then the Court must carry out the will of the legislator without considering if there exists a

* Reprinted with the permission of the
Editor of the International Law Reports.

contradiction between the statute and international law * * *. Furthermore, the Courts here derive their jurisdiction from municipal law and not from international law.

Our jurisdiction to try this case is based on the Nazi and Nazi Collaborators (Punishment) Law, an enacted Law the provisions of which are unequivocal. The Court has to give effect to a law of the Knesset, and we cannot entertain the contention that this Law conflicts with the principles of international law. For this reason alone counsel's first submission must be rejected.

We have, however, also considered the sources of international law, including the numerous authorities cited by learned defence counsel in his basic written brief upon which he based his oral pleadings, and by the learned Attorney–General in his comprehensive oral pleadings, and have failed to find any foundation for the contention that Israel law is in conflict with the principles of international law. On the contrary, we have reached the conclusion that the Law in question conforms to the best traditions of the law of nations.

* * *

———

Notes and Questions

1. The basis for jurisdiction of Israel is taken up by the Israeli Supreme Court in the *Eichmann* case; excerpts from this opinion are found, infra, in Chapter 16. For consideration of apparently conflicting provisions of domestic law with international law, see excerpts from *United States v. Palestine Liberation Organization*, infra Chapter 10 in which Judge Palmieri quotes the maxim of statutory interpretation that "an act of Congress ought never to be construed to violate the law of nations, if any other possible construction remains", from *Weinberger v. Rossi*, 456 U.S. 25, 32 (1982) and other authorities cited. See also the 1987 Restatement § 115.

2. How might Argentina have responded to Israel having its agents kidnap Eichmann on Argentine territory? Argentina protested the violation of its sovereignty and lodged a formal complaint with the Security Council which in turn condemned the kidnaping and requested the Government of Israel to make reparation in accordance with the rules of the Charter and international law. U. N. Doc. S/4349. June 23, 1960. Compare the *Alvarez-Machain* case, infra, Chapters 3 and 16.

3. If the statute is applied contrary to the rule of international law, what are the consequences for the forum state? Is that the end of the affair?

4. Absent a constitutional provision commanding precedence, the courts of national legal systems frequently assert that they must give effect to their domestic law if it is in clear conflict with customary international law. Should a court resolve the conflict in this manner, the state to which it belongs would be in violation of international law. Thus, in the United States an act of Congress supersedes an inconsistent rule of customary international law, but that "does not relieve the United States of its international obligation or of the consequences of a violation of that

obligation." Section 115(1)(b) of Restatement of the Law Third, The Foreign Relations Law of the United States (1987).[b] English courts make a point of stating that they would give effect to the will of parliament if its legislation were in clear conflict with customary international law.

Actually courts in national legal systems are rarely confronted with the necessity of resolving the conflict by giving precedence to their domestic law. A Norwegian scholar characterizes the conflicts between domestic law and international law, including customary international law, as relating to "pathological cases" and that, "clear conflict situations are rare. * * * [s]carcely one has been brought before the Norwegian Supreme Court * * *." Smith, International Law in Norwegian Courts, 12 Scandinavian Studies in Law 1968, at 153, 160 (1968). The main reason for the rarity of the conflict is that courts can avoid it by construction of the rule of domestic law involved, as in the reference above to *United States v. Palestine Liberation Organization*.

5. ***Provisions in constitutions.*** Article 25 of the 1949 German Constitution, as amended, provides: "The general rules of public international law constitute an integral part of federal law. They take precedence over statutes and directly create rights and duties for the inhabitants of the federal territory."Article 10 of the Italian Constitution states: "Italy's legal system conforms with the generally recognized principles of international law." Conformity between the two means that rules of municipal law which are contrary to customary international law "must be eliminated." *Re Martinez*, Italy, Court of Cassation, 1959, 28 Int'l L.Rep. 170 (1963).

Article 28(1) of the Greek Constitution of 1975 declares that "the generally recognized rules of international law * * * shall be an integral part of domestic Greek law and shall prevail over any contrary provision of law" Id., VII at 26 (1988). The Constitution of Slovenia in 1997 provided in Article 8, that "Statutes and other legislative measures shall comply with generally accepted principles of international law * * * ".

3. RULES OF DOMESTIC LAW IN CONFLICT WITH INTERNATIONAL AGREEMENTS

A conflict between domestic law and an international agreement may arise in either of two ways. First, the agreement may be in conflict with a rule of domestic law already in effect at the time the international agreement becomes binding. Second, a conflicting rule of domestic law may come into effect after the agreement has become binding. In either case, a state would be in violation of international law if it gave effect to the conflicting domestic law, for it cannot invoke its contrary domestic law as justification for its failure to abide by international agreement or customary international law.

1. ***International agreement in conflict with constitutional provision.*** If an international agreement is in conflict with a nation's constitution, domestic law prevails, unless the constitution provides otherwise. In

---

b. Hereafter cited as the 1987 Restatement, while Restatement of the Law Second, The Foreign Relations Law of the United States (1965) is cited as the 1965 Restatement.

United States law, the last in time prevails only with regard to legislation; a treaty not in compliance with the United States Constitution will not be given effect by United States courts, *Reid v. Covert*, 354 U.S. 1 (1957) See Chapter 12 infra. The international rule would not apply in Chile under these circumstances (see *Skrabs v. Kriegler*, 89 Int'l L. Rep. 59 (1992). Neither would it be internally operative in Mexico. *In re Vera,* Supreme Court, 1948, [1948] Ann.Dig. 328 (No. 114). The Court of Appeal for East Africa at Nairobi took the same position in *Criminal Appeal No. 156 of 1969*, 9 ILM 561 (1970). Article 182 of the 1987 Constitution of Nicaragua provides that any treaties that "oppose it or alter its dispositions shall have no value." Blaustein and Flanz, Vol. XIII at 33 (1987)). For Paraguay, the Constitution of 1992, Article 137 refers to the Constitution, international treaties, conventions and agreements among others "in descending order of preeminence, as listed".

The constitutions of some national systems provide for resolving conflicts between the constitution and an international agreement. Thus the 1983 Netherlands Constitution provides in Article 91.3 that, "[a]ny provisions of a treaty that conflict with the Constitution or which lead to conflicts with it may be approved by the Chambers of the States General only if at least two-thirds of the votes cast are in favor." The 1978 Spanish Constitution provides in Article 95.1 that "The conclusion of an international treaty which contains stipulations contrary to the Constitution shall require a prior constitutional revision," and in Article 95.2: "The Government or either of the Chambers may request the Constitutional Court to declare whether or not such a contradiction exists." In *Re: Treaty on European Union*, the Spanish Constitutional Court determined that certain European citizenship provisions of the Maastricht Treaty conflicted with Spain's constitutional rules on voting in local elections. In consequence the Spanish Constitution was amended to comply with Maastricht, and the treaty was then ratified (98 Int'l L.Rep. 251 (1994)).

Under similar constitutional provisions, the French Conseil Constitutional determined in 1992 that the Maastricht Treaty on European Union contained provisions contrary to the French Constitution, which resulted in the requirement that the Constitution be amended as provided in Article 54 before Maastricht could be ratified or approved. (See Kokott, *French Case Note*, 86 A.J.I.L. 824 (1992)). The same procedure was invoked and followed before France could ratify the Treaty of Amsterdam in 1999 (Decision No. 97–394, December 31,1997) and for the Statute of the International Criminal Court, noted in ASIL, *International Law in Brief*, May 3, 1999.

2. *International agreement in conflict with legislation.* Where the conflict is between an international agreement and anterior legislation, courts usually resolve a conflict in favor of the international agreement, but usually do not take the position that the agreement is intrinsically superior to existing legislation. Instead, they treat it as equal in rank with the legislation and apply the rule of construction that, as between anterior and posterior laws in conflict, the one later in time prevails.

In the United States, the equality in rank of treaties and acts of Congress is provided by Article VI, Clause 2, of the Constitution. Since neither is superior, the one later in time prevails. Hence, a self-executing treaty, i.e. one whose provisions are directly applicable as rules of domestic law without the need of implementation by an act of Congress, supersedes the provisions of prior and inconsistent federal legislation. Should the treaty not be self-executing, its provisions, once enacted into rules of domestic law by act of Congress, also supersede the provisions of prior and inconsistent federal legislation. On these and other aspects of the internal effect of international agreements of the United States, see Chapter 12.

The *United States Supreme Court's position is illustrative:* "[we have] repeatedly taken the position that an Act of Congress * * * is on a full parity with a treaty, and that when a statute which is subsequent in time is inconsistent with a treaty, the statute to the extent of conflict renders the treaty null." *Reid v. Covert,* 354 U.S. 1, 18 (1957). In recent years, the courts of some other national legal systems have shown a willingness to give more weight to international agreements in conflict with subsequent domestic law than might be expected under the doctrine of precedence for the one later in time. The matter is discussed in the following decision.

3. *Decision of the French Cour de Cassation*

Administration des Douanes v. Societe Cafes Jacques Vabre

France, Cour de Cassation Chambres Reunies), 1975.
2 Common Market Law Reports 336 (1975)

[The facts. The plaintiffs imported from Holland soluble coffee and mixtures of soluble coffee and chicory for resale on the French market. The French Customs Administration imposed a consumption tax on imports at a rate higher than the one used for soluble coffees manufactured and sold in France. The rate applicable to the imports was established by ministerial orders which were issued in 1967 on the basis of legislative authority incorporated in the Customs Code in 1966.

In their suit against the Customs Administration, the plaintiffs argued that the discriminatory tax on their imports was in violation of Article 95 of the Rome Treaty of 1957, establishing the European Economic Community, now Article 90 under the Consolidated Version adopted by the Treaty of Amsterdam of 1999. Article 95 provided in part:

> No Member State shall impose, directly or indirectly, on the products of other Member States any internal taxation of any kind in excess of that imposed directly or indirectly on similar domestic products.

The Customs Administration defended that the legislation of 1966, being later in time, prevailed. Both the Tribunal d'Instance and the Cour d'Appel de Paris held that the treaty prevailed by virtue of Article 55 of the French Constitution according to which treaties "have an authority superior to that of laws." The Customs Administration appealed to the supreme court of France, the Cour de Casssation, contending that the term "laws" did not include legislation enacted subsequent to the treaty.

The Cour de Cassation gives very great weight to the views of the procureur général, although it does not always agree with him. But, in accordance with tradition, it gives its judgments in terms so terse they are nearly delphic. As a result, the only sensible way to evaluate the judgment is to read it together with the text of the "submissions", i.e. the oral pleading delivered by the procureur général at the hearing before the court. Indeed, it is for this reason that his pleading—often a long one—is published by the French reporters together with the judgment of the court.]

Submissions of the Procureur Général
(M. Adolphe Touffait)

[The procureur général first argued that the term "laws" in Article 55 of the French Constitution covered legislation enacted subsequent to the treaty. A portion of his argument on this point follows.]

* * *

The relations between international law and internal law have been constructed, thought out and set out in the framework of systems classified under the headings of dualism and monism, each of these being the expression of a measure of historical truth, according to the dominant ideas on the national level and the evolution of international society.

* * *

The idea emerges irresistibly that there can be no international relations if the diplomatic agreements can be put in balk by unilateral decisions of the contracting powers, and the duty of the State to respect its international obligations becomes a fundamental principle, and on the morrow of the liberation politicians who were often lawyers realised that their ideas—which might fall under the weight of legal and judicial tradition—would have to be incorporated solemnly in the Constitution if they were to triumph. That is how for the first time in France the Constitution of 27 October 1946, in its Articles 26 and 28, expressly and in general form incorporated the principle of the primacy of international treaties over internal laws.

Article 26 relates to laws prior to the Treaty. *Article 28 relates to laws subsequent to the Treaty.*

The fact that the equivalent of these two Articles of the 1946 Constitution is a single Article 55 in that of 1958 does not represent a change in will in the constitution-makers.

* * *

Besides, how is one to understand Article 55 otherwise? The concept of superiority only has sense with regard to subsequent laws.

If Article 55 had been intended to refer only to laws prior to the treaty it would have been sufficient for it to provide that "a treaty has statutory force", since it is an absolute principle that subsequent statute prevails over a prior statute.

An analysis of the texts, in accord with the international ethic intended by the makers of the Constitutions of 1946 and 1958, thus ineluctably leads to the consideration that the concept of superiority of treaties over statutes only has sense with regard to statutes subsequent to the treaty, as it is clear that the international legal order can only be realised and developed if the States loyally apply the treaties they have signed, ratified and published. (at 360–362)

> [The procureur général went on to suggest the court should not rely on Article 55 in the French Constitution in holding that the treaty prevailed over the subsequent statute. He argued as follows.]

> It would be possible for you to give precedence to the application of Article 95 of the Rome Treaty over the subsequent statute by relying on Article 55 of our Constitution, but personally I would ask you not to mention it and instead base your reasoning on the very nature of the legal order instituted by the Rome treaty.

> Indeed, in so far as you restricted yourselves to deriving from Article 55 of our Constitution the primacy in the French internal system of Community law over national law you would be explaining and justifying that action as regards our country, but such reasoning would let it be accepted that it is on our Constitution and on it alone that depends the ranking of Community law in our internal legal system.

> In doing so you would impliedly be supplying a far from negligible argument to the courts of the Member States which, lacking any affirmation in their constitutions of the primacy of the Treaty, would be tempted to deduce therefrom the opposite solution, as the Italian Constitutional court did in 1962 when it claimed that it was for internal constitutional law to fix the ranking of Community law in the internal order of each Member State.

> Those are the reasons, Gentlemen, why I ask you not to base your reasoning on Article 55 of our Constitution; you will thus recognise that the transfer made by the States from their internal legal order to the Community legal order, within the limits of the rights and obligations corresponding to the provisions of the Treaty, involves a definitive limitation of their sovereign rights against which a subsequent unilateral act which is incompatible with the notion of Community cannot prevail.

>   * * *

> In this great but difficult and delicate task of building Europe, *difficult* because it often comes up against national economic differences which have to be eliminated, *delicate* because all the institutions of the country are involved, Parliament, Government, Conseil Constitutionnel, Conseil d'Etat, Cour de Cassation, it is indispensable that all the decisions of these various organs should be compatible with the objectives of the Community, as it is necessary that the finalities of the Rome Treaty should inspire the interpretative law of all the Member States. [The Court then examines the history of these questions in the other Member States.]

>   * * *

This panoramic survey of the case law of the Member States of the European Economic Community suffices to demonstrate that after some years of groping and hesitation there has been created under the guidance of the Court of Justice of the European Communities, that attentive guardian of the will of the authors of the Treaty, by demonstrating, but avoiding the reefs of government by the judiciary-a European legal con-

sciousness within all the national courts concerned to recognise the primacy of Community law without which there could not be created that unity
of the market which is desired by the signatory governments and approved
by their national sovereignty, reaffirmed at the conferences in The Hague
on 2 December 1969 and Paris on 20–21 October 1972; and it is for all
these reasons that I conclude very firmly that the second ground of appeal
should be dismissed. (at 363–367)

Judgment (of the Cour de Cassation)

[The court summarized the opposite contentions very briefly, including
the position of the Customs Administration that the relevant section of the
Customs Code had "the absolute authority which belongs to legislative
provisions and which are binding on all French courts." It then went on to
say:]

But the treaty of 25 March 1957, which by virtue of the above
mentioned Article of, the Constitution has an authority greater than that of
statutes, institutes a separate legal order integrated with that of the
Member States. Because of that separateness, the legal order which it has
created is directly applicable to the nationals of those States and is binding
on their courts. Therefore, the Cour d'Appel was correct and did not exceed
its powers in deciding that Article 95 of the Treaty was to be applied in the
instant case, and not section 265 of the Customs Code, even though the
latter was later in date. Whence it follows that the ground [of appeal] must
be dismissed. (at 369)

Questions regarding the French decision. Why did the French
Supreme Court fail to adopt the suggestion of the procureur général—an
unusual occurrence—and rely on Article 55 of the French Constitution? If
Article 55 had not been in the French Constitution, would the court have
held that the treaty prevailed over the latter statute? If it had, could it have
based its conclusion on the particular character of the legal order created
by the EEC treaty, or would it have held broadly for prevalence of any
treaty over later inconsistent legislation? Does the pleading of the procureur général suggest the answer?

4. *Parliamentary sovereignty in the United Kingdom.* When the
United Kingdom became a member of the European Economic Community,
it enacted legislation which Lord Denning construed as conferring priority
to the treaty over subsequent inconsistent acts of Parliament.

* * *

That priority is given by our own law. It is given by the European
Communities Act 1972 itself. Community law is now part of our law:
and whenever there is any inconsistency, Community law has priority.
It is not supplanting English law. It is part of our law which overrides
any other part which is inconsistent with it. Macarthys Ltd. v. Smith,
England, Court of Appeal, 1981, [1981] Q.B. 180, 200.

At an earlier stage of the same litigation, Lord Denning also said:

I pause here, however, to make one observation on a constitutional point. Thus far I have assumed that our Parliament, whenever it passes legislation, intends to fulfil its obligations under the Treaty. If the time should come when our Parliament deliberately passes an Act with the intention of repudiating the Treaty or any provision in it or intentionally of acting inconsistently with it and says so in express terms then I should have thought that it would be the duty of our courts to follow the statute of our Parliament. I do not however envisage any such situation. As I said in Blackburn v. Attorney–General: "But if Parliament should do so, then I say we will consider that event when it happens." Unless there is such an intentional and express repudiation of the Treaty, it is our duty to give priority to the Treaty. * * * *Id.*

In a quite different context involving the insolvency of the International Tin Council, Lord Templeman spoke not specifically about the European Union but more generally:

The Government may negotiate, conclude, construe, observe, breach, repudiate or terminate a treaty. Parliament may alter the laws of the United Kingdom. The courts must enforce those laws; judges have no power to grant specific performance of a treaty or to award damages against a sovereign state for breach of a treaty or to invent laws or misconstrue legislation in order to enforce a treaty.

A treaty is a contract between the governments of two or more sovereign states. International law regulates the relations between sovereign states and determines the validity, the interpretation and the enforcement of treaties. A treaty to which Her Majesty's Government is a party does not alter the laws of the United Kingdom. A treaty may be incorporated into and alter the laws of the United Kingdom by means of legislation. Except to the extent that a treaty becomes incorporated into the laws of the United Kingdom by statute, the courts of the United Kingdom have no power to enforce treaty rights and obligations at the behest of a sovereign government or at the behest of a private individual. * * * *Australia and New Zealand Banking Group Ltd., et al. v. Commonwealth of Australia and 23 Others, etc.*, House of Lords [1989] 3 W.L.R. 969; 29 I.L.M. 670 (1990).

———

*5. **Constitutional Provisions**.* Some constitutional provisions which apparently give primacy to treaties over domestic legislation are not altogether clear about whether subsequent as well as prior legislation is trumped by the treaty. Article 5(4) of the Bulgarian Constitution of 1991, for example, provides that qualified international treaties "shall be considered part of the domestic legislation of the country. They shall supersede any domestic legislation stipulating otherwise". See for Paraguay Article 137 (1992)) and for the Netherlands Article 94 of the Constitution of 1983. The Rumanian Constitution of 1991 states in Article 11.2 that "The treaties ratified by Parliament, according to the law, are part of national law." For Russia, "If an international treaty of the Russian Federation stipulates other rules than those stipulated by the law, the rules of the international treaty shall apply" (1993, Article 15).

A number of constitutions have directly addressed the problem of treaty conflict with subsequent legislation. Article 10 of the 1993 Constitution of the Czech Republic provides "Ratified and promulgated international accords on human rights and fundamental freedoms, to which the Czech Republic has committed itself, are immediately binding and are superior to law".

According to Article 28(1) of the Greek Constitution of 1975, "international conventions * * * shall be an integral part of domestic Greek law and shall prevail over any contrary provision of the law". See Roucounas, *Le Droit International dans la Constitution de la Grèce du 9 Juin 1975*, 29 Revue Hellénique du Droit International 63, 65 (1976), where the author asserts that the article gives primacy to the treaty over both anterior and posterior domestic laws. Article 96.1 of the Spanish Constitution of 1978 states that "Validly concluded international treaties once officially published in Spain shall constitute part of the internal legal order. Their provisions may only be abolished, modified or suspended in the manner provided for in the treaties themselves or in accord with general norms of international law." Similarly, see Article 134 of the Croatian Constitution of 1990. The 1991 Constitution of Slovenia provides in Article 8 that "Statutes and other legislative measures shall comply with generally accepted principles of international law and shall accord with international agreements which bind Slovenia from time to time". Also, see in Chapter 10, the Portuguese Constitution and the Statute of 1999 on extradition.

Questions: What if a treaty is inconsistent with national law? How do you reconcile the U.S. "last in time" doctrine, which favors subsequent Congressional legislation, with Article 27 of the Vienna Convention on the Law of Treaties (in the Documentary Supplement) which provides in part that "[a] party may not invoke the provisions of its internal law as justification for its failure to perform a treaty"? See also the ICJ's views to the same effect expressed in paragraph 57 of its Advisory Opinion in the UN Headquarters Agreement case, *infra* this Chapter, Section C. How would this problem of inconsistency be handled in the United States? See Chapter 12.

How do you think courts in the United Kingdom would resolve the problem of legislation in conflict with a subsequent treaty?

What are the domestic and international consequences of the rule? What do the foregoing materials teach us about the overall relationship between domestic law and international law? Are they two different systems? Or only one, of which each is an integral part? These questions foreshadow the theoretical question of *dualism* v. *monism*, taken up *infra*, in Chapter 17, Section B.

Are the approaches to international law of Mr. Justice Gray in *The Paquette Habana* and of Chief Justice Rehnquist in *Alvarez–Machain* (in Chapter 16) compatible? Read the brief excerpts from Mr. Justice Story in *The Schooner La Jeune Eugenie* and from Chief Justice Marshall in *The Antelope,* presented in the introduction to Chapter 18; consider how each

Justice would likely approach the two cases; consider also the question of whether customary international law is law in the United States at all until it has been explicitly incorporated by legislation. See different views expressed in Bradley & Goldsmith, *Customary International Law as Federal Common Law: A Critique of the Modern Position*, 110 Harv. L. Rev. 815 (1997); Koh, *Is International Law Really State Law?*, 111 Harv. L. Rev .. 1824 (1998).

4.   DOMESTIC ACTION TO APPLY AND TO CONFORM WITH INTERNATIONAL LAW

Trimble, International Law, World Order and Critical Legal Studies
42 Stanford Law Review 811, 833–834 (1990).*

A quick look at the "rules" of international law shows why governments love international law. Contrary to the realist/idealist view of law as a restraint on unruly governments, international law confirms much more authority and power than it denies. For example, the basic rule of international law is that a state generally has the exclusive authority to regulate conduct within its territory. International law thus confers authority to control entry and exit, to establish police control, to determine economic structure, to tax, to regulate, and to reinforce in many other ways the power and legitimacy of government. Public international law also grants governments sovereignty over air space and control over the continental shelf and economic resources 200 miles into the sea.

Of course, each rule conferring authority on a government denies it to all others. The United States government may be restrained in attempts to enforce its law in Canada, and Japanese fisherman may be barred from fishing near California's coast. Nevertheless, governments have little interest in extending their authority to that extent, at least when compared with their interest in controlling matters at home. For the most part, governments do not want to invade other countries or apply their law or send their fishermen to other territories. To be sure, there are exceptions, and these exceptions can be of vital importance to the actors involved. In the aggregate, however, they are less important than the effect of the general rules.

Even the rules of public international law that expressly restrain government authority may at the same time give a government an excuse to impose its authority throughout its own society so that it can effectively discharge its obligations under international law. International human rights law. for example, promotes national judicial review, general criminal law procedures, and a host of objectives that can best be met by assertions of national government power, especially against village or other traditional structures. For example, a government's international responsibility for injuries to aliens gives that government a mandate to control local officials and practices.

* Reprinted with the permission of Stanford Law Review.

Even when the rules do prevent a government from doing something that it otherwise wants to do, such as denying overflight rights to a hostile state's aircraft (contrary to the Chicago Convention), it may decide to forgo the short-term advantages derived from violating those rules because it has an overriding interest in maintaining the overall system. The rules comprising the system as a whole enable each government to achieve welfare goals for important parts of its population, and hence solidify its standing and legitimacy. Thus, the United States government may decide not to block transit of Cuban aircraft over United States territory because it derives support from the airline industry and the traveling public, both of which in turn benefit from transit over Cuba or from the system of which such transit rights are an integral part. The rules of international law accordingly are very congenial to governments. They mostly justify or legitimate the practical exercise of state power.

Legal Advisers to Government Departments
The Role of the Legal Adviser of the Department of State

A Report of the Joint Committee Established by the American Society of International Law and the American Branch of the International Law Association
85 Am.J.Int'l L. 358 (1991).*

* * *

* * * The position of Legal Adviser is established by statute. The Legal Adviser is appointed by the President, by and with the advice and consent of the Senate, and heads an office at present comprising some 100 government attorney-advisers. The Legal Adviser is responsible for furnishing legal advice on all problems, domestic and international, which arise in the course of the work of the Department of State. Thus, the Legal Adviser's responsibilities generally correspond to those of General Counsel of other Executive Branch agencies. In this capacity, the Legal Adviser and attorneys of that office are involved in many aspects of formulating and implementing the foreign policy of the United States. More particularly, they have special responsibilities regarding the handling of international legal issues arising in the conduct of U.S. foreign relations, as well as for promoting respect for and the development of international law and institutions as a fundamental element of U.S. foreign policy.

* * *

II.   Compliance With International Law

The U.S., like most countries, generally complies with its international treaty and customary law obligations. But, as is the case with almost every

---

* Reprinted by permission, American Society of International Law.

other country, problems of compliance occasionally arise, particularly in situations where international norms appear to conflict with what are perceived as national security or other vital national interests. It is in regard to these situations that the role of the Legal Adviser is of particular interest.

Whether the United States has complied with international law in any given case is * * * a matter for individual scrutiny and study. Lawyers often divide in their views as do governments. It is pertinent to recall that in recent years the United States has taken a number of actions that have been widely questioned on legal grounds both within the United States and by foreign governments in international bodies. Examples of such actions include the U.S. military operation in Grenada, mining of Nicaraguan harbors and armed support for the "contras," bombing of Libya, forcing down of the Egyptian airliner carrying the *Achille Lauro* terrorists, failure to pay UN contributions, reinterpretation of the ABM Treaty, rejection of the World Court's judgment in the *Nicaragua* case, assertion of the right to seize fugitives from a foreign state's territory without the foreign government's consent, and the invasion of Panama. In addition to these publicized actions, many other situations have arisen of a specialized character in regard to which the legality of U.S. actions under international law has been questioned. [See also] international trade, tax treaties, and the law of the sea. * * *

* * *

III. The Legal Adviser's Special Role Regarding U.S. Participation in the International Legal System

As counsel to the Secretary of State and Department of State, the Legal Adviser's responsibilities involve not only the usual business of a general counsel to a major Executive Branch department, but also responsibility for matters relating to U.S. participation in the international legal system.

First, unlike most other lawyers, the Legal Adviser operates within the framework of two separate legal systems. Thus, the Legal Adviser must consider the consequences of legal advice, and of U.S. government decisions and actions based on that advice, not only on the national legal system but also on the international legal system.

Second, the Legal Adviser's "client"—the U.S. government—is one of some 160 or so nations that constitute the international society and through their actions and interactions make international law. This means that, in contrast to most other lawyers, the Legal Adviser's advice may significantly affect the content and integrity of international rules and institutions. If legal advisers did no more than provide legal rationalizations of their government's political actions, the international legal system would be the elaborate charade that some detractors of international law consider it to be.

* * *

IV. The Conflict Between the Legal Adviser's Different Responsibilities

As the U.S. government official primarily responsible for ensuring that the U.S. complies with its international obligations, the Legal Adviser must be in a position to present an objective analysis of any questions of international law arising in the formulation and conduct of U.S. foreign policy, and to tell the Secretary of State and other policy-making officials if their proposed actions or policies may violate international law. On the other hand, the Legal Adviser is usually a political appointee, and is also expected to act as adviser to the Secretary of State, and sometimes as advocate for Administration policies.

It seems clear that these two roles contain the seeds of conflict.

Thus, the Legal Adviser's first responsibility is to tell the Secretary of State and Administration candidly and objectively what existing law is or requires in a given situation. Every lawyer owes this duty to his or her client. As indicated, unless the Secretary and other policy officials are given competent, objective and honest advice as to the legal consequences of proposed actions and decisions, they cannot make informed and intelligent foreign policy judgments or properly balance the national interests involved; indeed, the success of a decision or policy may depend on its compliance with international law. [T]he Legal Adviser can, and often should, accompany an objective legal analysis with concrete suggestions as to how particular policy objectives can be achieved in a manner consistent with international law and U.S. obligations. It is also desirable that, in dealing with particular cases, the Legal Adviser seek to further the long-range international law objectives of the United States.

However, once the Secretary or other responsible officials decide upon a particular policy, the nature of the Legal Adviser's role changes. Some Committee members believe that, even if the decision reached is contrary to what the Legal Adviser believes is the better view, the Legal Adviser, like other attorneys with respect to their clients, can properly serve as the Secretary's advocate and make the best case possible in support of the Administration's position—at least so long as the arguments presented are in good faith and legally responsible. Of course, if the Legal Adviser believes that a situation involves an important issue of conscience or professional or personal ethics, the Legal Adviser may be unwilling to participate further in the matter and, in an extreme case, may wish to resign.

* * *

Note: *See also,* Cassese, *The Role of Legal Advisors in Ensuring that Foreign Policy Conforms to International Legal Standards,* 14 Mich.J.Int'l L. 139 (1992); *Symposium: The Impact of International Law on Foreign Policy–Making,* 2 EJIL 131 (1991).

———

United States: Department of Defense Report to Congress on the Conduct of the Persian Gulf War—Appendix on the Role of the Law of War

31 I.L.M. 612 (1992)

THE ROLE OF THE LAW OF WAR

> *"Decisions were impacted by legal considerations at every level, [the law of war] proved invaluable in the decision-making*

process." General Colin Powell, Chairman, Joint Chiefs of Staff

* * *

ROLE OF LEGAL ADVISERS

The Office of General Counsel of the Department of Defense (DOD), as the chief DOD legal office, provided advice to the Secretary of Defense, the Deputy Secretary of Defense, the Under Secretary of Defense for Policy, other senior advisers to the Secretary and to the various components of the Defense legal community on all matters relating to Operations Desert Shield and Desert Storm, including the law of war. For example, the Secretary of Defense tasked the General Counsel to review and opine on such diverse issues as the means of collecting and obligating for defense purposes contributions from third countries; the Wars Powers Resolution; DOD targeting policies; the rules of engagement; the rules pertinent to maritime interception operations; issues relating to the treatment of prisoners of war; sensitive intelligence and special access matters; and similar matters of the highest priority to the Secretary and DOD. In addition, military judge advocates and civilian attorneys with international law expertise provided advice on the law of war and other legal issues at every level of command in all phases of Operations Desert Shield and Desert Storm. Particular attention was given to the review of target lists to ensure the consistency of targets selected for attack with United States law of war obligations.

COUNT VON MOLTKE IN NAZI GERMANY

Count von Moltke was a German international lawyer, a descendent of the family of Bismarck's renowned field marshal. A member of the Foreign Division of the German Military Intelligence Service (*Abwehr*) under Admiral Canaris and a legal advisor to the Supreme Command of the Armed Forces (Öberkommando der Wehrmacht OKW) during World War II, he had written numerous illuminating letters about his official legal work to his wife Freya. Published under the title "Letters to Freya" (1990), von Moltke's letters portray some of the problems faced by a conscientious government legal adviser under extreme conditions of adversity.

On April 29, 1941, from Berlin, Count von Moltke wrote "Suddenly there is a big row here on matters of principle concerning Schmitz in Belgrade". Having played his way into the foreground on this case, von Moltke expected to be told to report to Admiral Canaris about it, when he would be able to induce Canaris to face the serious issues of policy that the case represented., and to make a difficult decision, rather than avoiding it altogether. Von Moltke stated in a letter bearing the above date:

> "I certainly shall treat [the issues] exclusively as matters of principle and shall see what happens. I'll be alone with Canaris, so that his only possible reason for dissimulation would be one that lies in me. I can only hope that I'll have a good day. My basic theme is this: what is right and lawful is good for the people, what is international law is

good for the conduct of the war. And that is how I will formulate it. Perhaps I'll be thrown out. If not, my position will be firmer."

On April 30, Count von Moltke wrote that his discussion with Canaris had lasted an hour. He felt that it had been "thoroughly satisfactory." He said that he had left no doubt about his views and "[Canaris] completely agreed with me," although nothing was decided in the meeting. Von Moltke at least was happy to have "learned" where Canaris stood and hoped that the process would move forward properly.

On November 3, 1942, Von Moltke wrote that he had just had a "decisive exchange" with Admiral Bürkner. Bürkner had been refusing to sign a paper that "mattered a great deal" to Von Moltke. The two had argued about the "justification for an undiluted murder Order by the Führer".[2] During the argument, Von Moltke stated to Bürkner:

> You see, Herr Admiral, the difference between us is that I can't argue about such questions. As long as I recognize imperatives that cannot be repealed by any Führer Order and that must be followed against a Führer Order, I cannot let such things pass, because for me the difference between good and evil, justice and injustice exists *a priori*. It is not subject to considerations of expediency or argument.

After that vigorous and courageous statement, Bürkner "signed without demur." Von Moltke found it interesting to see how "such people can be swayed to the right side by a resolute stand." It is also interesting to note that, Von Moltke was later convicted of attempting to change the Reich's Constitution by force and was executed in January, 1945. See also, and more broadly on this subject, Detlev Vagts, *International Law in the Third Reich*, 84 Am.J.Int'l L. 661 (1990).

———

Executive Opposition to Proposed Legislation Violative of International Law

Letter From the U.S. Secretary of the Treasury to the Chairman of the Senate Finance Committee April 7, 1986

25 I.L.M. 760 (1986).*

* * *

2. The "Order" referred to was undoubtedly the infamous *"Commando Order* of October 18, 1942, which had recently come to the notice of the Abwehr. Hitler's order was made in light of the Allied commando and sabotage operations becoming more frequent in Africa and in the Western theater. He ordered that all participants were to be killed and not to be taken prisoner. Even those one or two who were taken to be inter-

rogated first, they, too, were to be shot immediately afterwards."

* Reprinted with the permission of the American Society of International Law from material published at 25 I.L.M. 760 under the title "United States: Letter of the Secretary of the Treasury Concerning Opposition to Tax Reform Legislation That Overrides Bilateral Tax Treaties."

Certain provisions of the tax reform legislation recently passed by the House of Representatives and now under consideration by the Senate conflict with U.S. obligations under existing tax treaties. In some instances, the intention to override treaties is made explicit, either in the Bill or in the committee report. As you are aware, under our Constitutional system a later enacted statute takes precedence over a pre-existing treaty where that is the manifest intent of the Congress. * * * This administration strongly opposes treaty overrides in tax reform legislation.

* * *

I urge that you not enact treaty override provisions as part of tax reform legislation and that you reaffirm in the accompanying committee reports the U.S. commitment to honor its outstanding treaty obligations. Bilateral negotiation, not unilateral override, is the appropriate way to deal with treaty abuses. In the long run, such an approach will best serve the interests of the United States in the international marketplace.

* * *

———

Relative success. On July 31, 1986, the Secretary of the Treasury also wrote to the Chairman of the House Ways and Means Committee concerning the tax reform provisions in conflict with tax treaties of the United States, and emphasized again the opposition of the executive to them. An official of the Treasury Department later claimed success in obtaining deletion in the final bill of many, but not all, of the treaty overrides. The remaining discrepancies between the legislation and the treaties would thus become a matter of diplomatic negotiations.

Legislative override. In 1989 the OECD Committee on Fiscal Affaires made a report on this subject as respects tax treaty override by national legislation. It made its Report to the Council of OECD, where 24 member states from the traditional market economy countries of North America, Western Europe and the Far East are represented. In acting on the Committee's Report, the OECD Council acting by consensus on October 2, 1989, 717th Session, recommended Member Countries:

1. To undertake promptly bilateral or multilateral consultations to address problems connected with tax treaty provisions, whether arising in their own country or raised by countries with which they have tax treaties:

2. To avoid enacting legislation which is intended to have effects in clear contradiction to international treaty obligations.

* * *

———

Inferred Legislative Intent Not to Violate International Law

1987 Restatement, Section 115*

Comment *a*.

* * * It is assumed that Congress does not intend to repudiate an international obligation * * * by nullifying a rule of international law or an international agreement * * * or by making it impossible for the United States to carry out its obligations. * * * Therefore, when an act of Congress and an international agreement or a rule of customary law relate to the same subject, the courts, regulatory agencies, and the Executive Branch will endeavor to construe them so as to give effect to both. The courts do not favor a repudiation of an international obligation by implication and require clear indication that Congress, in enacting legislation, intended to supersede the earlier agreement or other international obligation. The fact that an act of Congress does not expressly exclude matters inconsistent with international law or a United States agreement does not necessarily imply a Congressional purpose to supersede [those obligations].

―――――――

Standing Instructions for Administration and Implementation of International Law

In the services of the Government of the United States such as the Armed Forces, the Coast Guard, the Foreign Service and the Immigration and Naturalization Service, standing instructions are issued to officers who, because of their position or mission, may have to handle situations susceptible of creating serious international repercussions. The instructions may anticipate some specific situations and spell out procedures for meeting them in conformity with international law. With respect to situations which cannot be specifically anticipated, the instructions usually call for referral to higher authority and eventually the Department of State. The issuance of standing instructions to services for insuring national action in conformity with international law is a practice followed in many national systems.

―――――――

Department of Defense Directive No. 5100.77 December 9, 1998

SUBJECT: DoD Law of War Program

* * *

2. APPLICABILITY AND SCOPE

2.1. This Directive applies to the Office of the Secretary of Defense, the Military Departments, the Chairman of the Joint Chiefs of Staff, the

* Copyright 1987 by the American Law
Institute. Reprinted with permission.

Combatant Commands, the Defense Agencies, and the DoD Field Activities (hereafter referred to collectively as "the DoD Components").

* * *

3. DEFINITIONS

3.1. Law of War. That part of international law that regulates the conduct of armed hostilities. It is often called the law of armed conflict. The law of war encompasses all international law for the conduct of hostilities binding on the United States or its individual citizens, including treaties and international agreements to with the United States is a party, and applicable customary international law.

* * *

4. POLICY

It is DoD policy to ensure that:

4.1.1. The law of war obligations of the United States are observed and enforced by the DoD Components.

4.2. An effective program to prevent violations of the law of war, is implemented by the DoD Components.

4.3. All reportable incidents by or against U.S. or enemy persons are promptly reported, thoroughly investigated, and, where appropriate, remedied by corrective action.

* * *

5. RESPONSIBILITIES

5.3 The Heads of DoD Components shall:

5.3.1. Ensure that the members of their Components comply with the law of war during all armed conflicts, however such conflicts are characterized, and with the principles and spirit of the law of war during all other operations,

5.3.2. Institute and implement effective programs to prevent violations of the law of war, including law of war training and dissemination are required, * * *

5.3.3. Ensure that qualified legal advisors are immediately available at all levels of command to provide advice about the law of war compliance during planning and execution of exercises and operations; and institute and implement programs to comply with the reporting requirements

* * *

United States Navy Regulations Subpart F
Commanders in Chief and Other Commanders
Code of Federal Regulations, 32 C.F.R. 700.605 (1999).

§ 700.605 Observance of international law.

At all times a commander shall observe, and require his command to observe, the principles of international law. Where necessary to fulfillment of this responsibility, a departure from other provisions of Navy Regulations is authorized.

———

UCMJ, art. 92 provides that a violation of a lawful general regulation, such as the foregoing Section of 32 C.F.R., is punishable by court-martial. See Naval War College, *Annotated Supplement to the Commander's Handbook on the Law of Naval Operations*, 4 (Newport, R.I., 1997). See also, Reisman and Leitzau, *Moving International Law from Theory to Practice: The Role of Military Manuals in Effectuating the Law of Armed Conflict*, in 64 International Law Studies, The Law of Naval Operations 1 (1991).

———

National Apology for Violation of International Law

Ruling of the Secretary–General of the United Nations on the Rainbow Warrior Affair Between France and New Zealand, July 6, 1986

26 I.L.M.1346 (1987).*

[On July 10, 1985, the Rainbow Warrior was sunk in Auckland harbor, New Zealand, as a result of extensive damage caused by explosives. A Dutch crewman drowned. The ship was owned by the Greenpeace organization and used by it in its campaign against French nuclear tests in the Pacific. Two agents of the French secret service, Major Alain Mafart and Captain Dominique Prieur, were arrested in New Zealand, prosecuted and sentenced to prison for the crimes. In a communique issued September 22, 1985, the Prime Minister of France acknowledged that the Rainbow Warrior had been sunk by the two agents acting on instructions from higher authority.

On the same date, the French Minister for External Affairs indicated that France was prepared to undertake reparations for the consequences of its action and enter into negotiations for this purpose with New Zealand. Having failed to reach an agreement, the parties referred the affair to the Secretary–General of the United Nations and agreed to abide by his ruling. He invited them to submit written statements of their positions. The parties' positions and the ruling of the Secretary–General, follow].

* * *

Memorandum of the Government of New Zealand

Reparations Sought by New Zealand

New Zealand seeks redress as follows:

* Reprinted with permission of the American Society of International law.

(A) Apology

The Government of New Zealand is entitled, in accordance with international law, to a formal and unqualified apology for the violation of its sovereignty and its rights under international law.

* * *

Memorandum of the Government of France

Reparations Sought by New Zealand

A.   Apologies

The violation of New Zealand territory by France did not in itself cause any material damage to New Zealand. It may, [however], be admitted that it has caused it moral damage which, according to international law, may be compensated by the offer of regrets and apologies.

The Government of New Zealand requests the French Government to offer it such apologies. The French Government is prepared to make compensation * * * for the moral damage suffered by New Zealand and the French Prime Minister is ready, therefore, to address to the New Zealand Prime Minister a formal and unconditional letter of apology for the attack carried out on 10 July 1985.

* * *

Ruling of the Secretary General

1.   Apology

New Zealand seeks an apology. France is prepared to give one. My ruling is that the Prime Minister of France should convey to the Prime Minister of New Zealand a formal and unqualified apology for the attack, contrary to international law, on the "Rainbow Warrior" by French service agents which took place on 10 July 1985.

* * *

———

Other reparations. Among other reparations, New Zealand sought compensation for the violation of its sovereignty and all the costs, including the costs of investigation, incurred as a direct result of the incident. The Secretary–General ruled that the French Government should pay $7 million to the Government of New Zealand "as compensation for all the damage it has suffered." As to the death of the crewman, New Zealand did not have standing to claim compensation on behalf of his family, because he was not one of its nationals, but wanted to make sure the French Government made appropriate arrangements. The French Government did so. As to the sinking of the Rainbow Warrior, the French Government agreed with the Greenpeace organization to submit the issue of damages suffered to an arbitral tribunal. On October 2, 1987, the tribunal awarded Greenpeace the sum of $8,159,000. *Le Monde,* 5 October 1987, at 16. (Editors' translation).

———

The Second National Apology in the Rainbow Warrior Affair

[The *Rainbow Warrior Affair* did not end there. A second arbitration took place and an apology was made.] The two French officers (known in France as the "false couple Turinge") * * * had been sentenced to ten years in prison by a New Zealand court. This term was reduced to a minimum period of three years following an agreement between the Secretary–General of the United Nations and the two governments, on the condition that the term be served at the French military base at Hao in the Pacific to which they were transferred for that purpose. They were forbidden to leave their place of forced residence for any reason except by agreement between the two governments.

In contravention of that condition, France, in which the political majority in Parliament had changed in the meantime, decided to repatriate Major Mafart, invoking his state of health, and then Captain Prieur in May, 1988, because she was pregnant and her father was ill. These successive decisions displeased the New Zealand Government, which appealed to international law in complaining of France's non-respect of its engagements.

The Tribunal rendered a condemnation of pure form against France, noting that in evacuating Major Mafart from Hao, the French Republic did not violate its obligations to New Zealand, because his health condition required it.

On the other hand, the Tribunal held that France had violated those obligations in not ordering the return of the officer to the atoll after his treatment. Regarding Captain Prieur, France violated its obligations on three successive occasions: [1] in not seeking in good-faith to obtain the agreement of New Zealand for her departure from the island; [2] in evacuating her in May 1988; [3] and finally in not returning her to the atoll. The Tribunal found, however, that the obligations to maintain the two officers on the island were extinguished on 22 July, 1989 (end of the minimal period of three years). Therefore, the Tribunal could not accept New Zealand's application requesting it to order the two officers returned to the island. All considered, the judgement against France for violations of its obligations to New Zealand "constitutes, in view of the circumstances, adequate reparation for the juridical and moral prejudice suffered by New Zealand."[a] Rousseau, *Chroniques des Faits Internationaux*, 94 Rev.Gen. de Droit Int'l 1069 (1990). Editors's translation.

[Later Major Mafart was promoted to the rank of Colonel and decorated for distinguished service before leaving the French Army. In 1995 Captain Prieur published her memoires of the affair under the title "*Agente Secrète*" (Fayard, Paris) See Le Monde, May 12, 1995, p. 14, Col. 1. Ultimately France and New Zealand reconciled].

---

a. Translations by the editors.

SECTION B.   APPLICATION IN DIPLOMATIC PRACTICE

Charter of the United Nations

Article 33.

1. The parties to any dispute, the continuance of which is likely to endanger the maintenance of international peace and security, shall, first of all, seek a solution by negotiation, enquiry, mediation, conciliation, arbitration, judicial settlement, resort to regional agencies or arrangements, or other peaceful means of their own choice.

———

Promoting the Rule of Law in U.S. Foreign Policy

Murphy, Contemporary Practice of the United States Relating to International Law.
93 AJIL 470 (1999).

In a speech at the University of Washington School of Law on October 28, 1998, U.S. Secretary of State Madeleine K. Albright discussed the relevance of the rule of law to U.S. foreign policy:

> Law is a theme that ties together the broad goals of our foreign policy. It is at the heart of virtually everything we do at the Department of State—from the negotiation of arms control treaties to seeking a fair deal for our salmon fishermen to guaranteeing that the intellectual property rights of our software companies are protected. And one of the great lessons we have learned is that the rule of law and global prosperity go hand in hand.

> * * *

> * * * [T]he global financial crisis requires that we focus not only on the rules governing international trade but also on the rules governing the regulation and management of economies within nations. For it is clear that an insufficient commitment to the rule of law in key countries was a major contributor to the current crisis.

> * * *

> The United States relies on the rule of law to help build a world that is safer and more secure. But we are also prepared, through our armed forces, to protect our citizens and our vital interests should the rule of law break down. A case in point is the battle against international terror.

> * * *

> Almost exactly 50 years ago, representatives from nations around the world came together to draft and sign the Universal Declaration of Human Rights. Since its unveiling, the Declaration has been incorporated or referred to in dozens of national constitutions, and its princi-

ples have been reaffirmed many times. It is a centerpiece of the argument we make today that respect for human rights is the obligation not just of some but of every government.

* * *

A centerpiece of our efforts has been our strong backing for the international war crimes tribunals for Rwanda and the Balkans * * *

We must not forget. The killings in Bosnia and Rwanda were not the inevitable result of ethnic grievances. They were not the products of drunken excess or battlefield passions. On the contrary, they were carefully planned and ruthlessly orchestrated by ambitious men seeking expanded power.

We all have a stake in seeing that these individuals are brought to justice. We all have a stake in establishing a precedent that will deter future atrocities. And we all have an interest in seeing that those who consider rape just another tactic of war are held accountable for their crimes.

* * *

Among the most basic rights spelled out in the Universal Declaration is the right to take part in government either directly or through freely chosen representatives. Article 21 provides that "the will of the people shall be the basis of the authority of government."

The promotion of this right is a top priority of our foreign policy. We know that democracy is not an import; it must find its roots internally. But outsiders can help nourish those roots by backing efforts to build democratic institutions.

* * *

——————

Diplomatic Representations

Diplomatic practice. The primary means of resolving claims asserted under international law by one state against another is diplomatic correspondence. It is the everyday working method of the international system for settling legal disputes. Centuries of practice attest to its effectiveness. Hence correspondence recording the diplomatic negotiations of states in settling their legal claims is a vast and valuable repository of information on the application of international law. See the ICJ's discussion of the international claims process in the *Reparations Case*, infra, Chapter 2, Section C. Official representations contained in diplomatic correspondence and other communications are often employed to prove the existence of rules of customary international law. Excellent examples are found in the diplomatic correspondence between Canada and the USSR in 1978 on the subject of the Cosmos 954 Claim of Canada, 18 I.L.M. 899 (1979). Parts of the Canadian claim are reproduced , infra, in Chapter 6.

A note of caution is in order. Remember that the assertion of a claim under international law by one state against another is a contentious statement. The diplomatic presentation of its claim is the state's partisan position, a one-sided view of the facts and the law applicable to them. In some cases, the claim may be exactly stated and incontrovertible on both facts and law. In many more cases, however, the defending state questions either or both. Not until the parties have achieved mutual agreement as to both can it be said they have recognized a particular rule of international law as applicable to the particular case, although a claim based upon a stated legal proposition, even if not agreed by the other party, should constitute a recognition of the proposition by the claimant state. Some agreements may be fully based on compromise, *not law*.

Thus the totality of the relevant diplomatic exchanges has to be considered before any conclusion can be reached regarding the rule of international law applied to the resolution of a claim. Moreover, it must be kept in mind that the resolution of a claim by diplomatic negotiation may turn in the end, not on considerations of international law, but partly or entirely on political, economic and other empirical factors. Diplomatic representations often are made not only by formal correspondence but also by other direct communications of representatives meeting in Foreign Offices or Embassies and increasingly by press, television and radio announcements or even "leaks." All of this process may offer valuable evidence of the evolution and acceptance of rules of customary international law.

Digests of International Law published in the United States contain, inter alia, a great deal of diplomatic correspondence on issues of international law. They are valuable tools for the international lawyer. The Moore Digest of 1906 was followed by that of Hackworth in 1940. Between 1963 and 1972 fifteen volumes of Whiteman's Digest of International Law were published. Supplemental volumes have been published as The Digest of United States Practice in International Law and as Cumulative Digests. The American Journal of International Law has also published updating material regularly under the title "Contemporary Practice of the United States Relating to International Law". Other Digests published from 20 to 25 years after the events, frequently throw light on legal issues involved in originally highly classified documents.

Foreign Digests: Information on diplomatic practice relating to international law is also becoming increasingly available in other states. It may be provided by specialized publications such as the British Digest of International Law, the Réportoire de la Pratique Française en Matière de Droit International Public and the *Prassi Italiana di Diritto Internazionale*. More often a national journal of international law will reserve a section for periodic reports on national diplomatic practice. Journals so doing include not only the American Journal of International Law but also the *Annuaire Francais de Droit International*; the *Annuaire Suisse de Droit International*; the Australian Yearbook of International Law; the Canadian Yearbook of International Law; the Indian Journal of International Law; the Italian Yearbook of International Law; the Japanese Annual of International Law;

the Netherlands Yearbook of International Law; the *Revue Belge de Droit International*; the Malaya Law Review.

———

Commissions of inquiry. For a description of arrangements for commissions of inquiry, their structure and function, see Chapter 14, *infra* and the United Nations Handbook on the Pacific Settlement of Disputes Between States 24–33 (N.Y., 1992). * * *

Commissions for conciliation. A feature of some international conventions is the provision of commissions for conciliation to which parties can resort for an amicable solution of their disputes, either in place of or prior to submission of the dispute to arbitration or to adjudication. Among the conventions in the Documentary Supplement see, e.g., the following: Article 42 of the International Covenant on Civil and Political Rights, Article 12 of the *International Convention on the Elimination of all Forms of Racial Discrimination*, Article 66 of the Vienna Convention on the Law of Treaties, Article III of the Optional Protocol to the Vienna Convention on Diplomatic Relations, and Article 284 and Annex V of the United Nations Convention on the Law of the Sea. Historically, few disputes have been brought before conciliation commissions.

———

SECTION C.   APPLICATION IN INTERNATIONAL TRIBUNALS

The International Court of Justice is the judicial centerpiece of the international system. The principle judicial organ of the United Nations and integrated with the Organization by Charter provision and by attachment of the Court's founding Statute to the Charter, the ICJ enjoys a unique international status meriting the name "World Court" often applied to it. Membership in the ICJ coincides with that of the United Nations (and is enlarged by arrangement with non-Member States), ICJ subject matter jurisdiction spreads over the entire field of public international law, its jurisdiction to adjudicate (though limited by the requirements of consent of the parties in contentious cases) has no regional or other geographical boundaries. Information about the Court, its basic documents, names and background and elections of the judges, the pending and decided cases and opinions as well as other useful information are readily found at its Internet site, http://www.icj-cij.org/.

Although this Section focuses on the ICJ, one should not lose sight of the many other international courts. The European Court of Justice appears in Chapter 2, infra. The European and other Courts of Human Rights are seen in Chapter 9 infra, the United Nations Tribunal on the Law of the Sea is taken up in Chapter 4, and the Rome Statute of the International Criminal Court and the Ad Hoc War Crimes Tribunals in Chapter 16. These and the many other international courts acting in their specific geographical or substantive areas have also made enormous contributions to the realization of the objectives of international adjudication.

1.   THE INTERNATIONAL COURT OF JUSTICE

Schwebel,[a] Fifty Years of the World Court: A Critical Appraisal

90 ASIL Proc. 339 (1996).[*]

Now what of the record of the Court the last fifty years? That record may indeed be said to stretch back to 1922, to the initiation of the Permanent Court of International Justice (PCIJ). That Court proved to be an outstandingly successful innovation in the affairs of mankind. Between 1922 and 1940, it dealt with sixty-six cases. Thirty-eight were contentious and twenty-eight advisory; twelve were settled out of court. The PCIJ demonstrated that an international court of justice could work. Its judgments were generally well received and virtually uniformly implemented; its advisory opinions were given great weight by the League Council and the states and organizations on whose behalf the Council flexibly transmitted questions. The only opinion that attracted widespread criticism was the *Customs Union* opinion, in which the Court narrowly held that the proposed customs union between Germany and Austria was incompatible with the Peace Treaties regime of 1919.

In the 1920s, in a period of international detente, the Court flourished. In the 1930s, with the rise of international tensions engendered by what came to be known as the Axis Powers, the Court declined. Significant an institution as the Court was, and concerned as it was with a number of cases arising out of the Peace Treaties, and with tensions between Germany and Poland, it could hardly prevent the Second World War. The history of the interwar period suggests that, rather than international adjudication producing peace, peace is conducive to international adjudication. It demonstrated as well that an international court could and did make great contributions to the development of international law.

Reconsideration in 1945

It is a striking fact that the founders of the United Nations from the outset agreed that the League of Nations would be dissolved and displaced by the United Nations but that the Permanent Court of International Justice would be maintained by the International Court of Justice. Statesmen and lawyers never for a moment doubted that the Court should be preserved.

They were not prepared to agree on much more. The International Court of Justice is the immediate offspring of the Permanent Court. The United Nations Charter provides that its Statute is based upon the Statute of the Permanent Court. The ICJ Statute is in large measure unchanged, down to the very numbering of its articles. Its jurisdiction is similarly consensual and hence sharply limited. The two great states that had never become parties to the Statute of the Permanent Court, the United States

a. Vice–President of the International Court of Justice, later President of the Court.

* Reprinted with the permission of the American Society of International Law.

and the Soviet Union, were no more willing in 1945 to accept statutory provision for compulsory jurisdiction than had been the United Kingdom, Italy and Japan in 1920. Recalling the unsuccessful battles in the Senate over adherence to the Statute of the Permanent Court, the State Department was unwilling to risk ratification of the Charter of which the Statute was part. The USSR had an ideological antipathy toward submitting to international adjudication, which began to soften only with the advent of Gorbachev.

But in 1945 there were a few significant innovations. The International Court of Justice is an organ of the United Nations, whereas the Permanent Court was not an organ of the League; an important result is that all members of the United Nations ipso facto are parties to the Statute. Provision was introduced authorizing the Court to form a chamber for dealing with a particular case. And Article 94 of the Charter provides that each member of the United Nations must undertake to comply with the Court's decision in any case to which it is a party and that the Security Council may make recommendations or decide upon measures to give effect to the judgment.

The International Court of Justice has fifteen judges, as did the PCIJ. They too sit in the Peace Palace in The Hague. The International Court of Justice inherited not only the quarters, the archives, the registry, the rules, and the jurisdiction of the Permanent Court; it inherited its jurisprudence as well. Counsel in argument before the Court, judges in their deliberations, and the Court in its judgments and advisory opinions, invoke the jurisprudence of the Permanent Court as they invoke the jurisprudence of this Court.

An Appraisal of the International Court of Justice

Jurisdiction. The hope at San Francisco was that, by preserving adherences to the compulsory jurisdiction of the Permanent Court under the optional clause and treaties specifying recourse to the Court for settlement of disputes arising thereunder, and by fresh adherences by United Nations members under these titles, the jurisdiction of the Court would grow.

In fact, for some years jurisdiction under the optional clause contracted, in numbers and content. Not only did fewer states—relative to the large expansion in the number of independent states—adhere to the optional clause. Many of the states that did adhere, did so with far-reaching reservations unknown in the League era. Sir Humphrey Waldock was moved to write his well-known article on "The Decline of the Optional Clause,'" a decline whose angle widened when France and the United States withdrew their adherences altogether.

But more recently, that trend has turned upward. Currently fifty-nine states adhere to the Court's compulsory jurisdiction under the optional clause, out of 187 parties to the Statute. The geographical spread is wide, and it now includes states from Eastern Europe as well as Africa and Asia. Yet in percentage terms far fewer states adhere than in 1939, when thirty-six out of forty-eight parties to the Statute of the Permanent Court adhered to the optional clause. In all, then, the record on this count is mixed. While the number of adherences appears to be slowly increasing, the majority of states remains outside the system and that majority today includes four of the five permanent members of the Security Council.

All this said, it is clear that the optional clause as a meaningful source of the Court's jurisdiction has not disappeared. On the contrary, significant cases have been brought on the basis of it in recent years.

Some 264 treaties provide that disputes arising thereunder may at the instance of a party be submitted to the Court for determination. Some 106 of these treaties are multilateral.With the passing of the ideological opposition to the Court's jurisdiction of the former Soviet Union and its former allies, and with much greater recourse to the Court by states of the developing world, it is to be expected that more and more treaties, multilateral and bilateral, will invest the Court with jurisdiction. It is equally to be expected that there will continue to be special agreements between states to take disputes to the Court.

As it is, despite the limitations on its jurisdiction, the Court today is busy and as busy as it has been since 1922. The Court has evolved a jurisdictional jurisprudence which is unique in its complexity and subtlety. In the construction of its jurisdiction, it has been criticized at times for undue conservatism; at other times, for excessive liberalism. Having not infrequently dissented in matters of jurisdiction and admissibility, I cannot say that I think that such diverse criticism shows that the Court has achieved the golden mean. But in this sphere as in others, I believe that its record is, with relatively few exceptions, rather good.

Recourse to the Court. Recourse to the International Court of Justice has been uneven; it has had its ups and downs. There were a considerable number of contentious cases and advisory proceedings in the period 1946–1966. Then, for more than a dozen years, the Court experienced a sharp diminution in cases. With the bringing of the *Hostages* case, in 1979, pace in and publicity about the Court quickened. In the 1980s, recourse to the Court burgeoned. In recent years, the Court has had as many as thirteen cases on its docket.

Why this is so is not clear. Some speculate that increased recourse to the Court by developing states flows from an increase in confidence in the Court engendered by its judgments in *Military and Paramilitary Activities in and against Nicaragua.* If so, that would be paradoxical, since those judgments gave rise to unprecedented criticism of the Court, above all in the United States, but also in some other states and among many international legal scholars.

Whatever the cause, the fact is that the Court is no longer underemployed. Indeed, so busy is it that, if its workload continues to increase, it may have to enlarge significantly its Registry and the services it renders—as by the addition of clerks to judges—and reform the Court's ponderous procedures. Those procedures are designed to accord considerable latitude to sovereign litigants, while affording each of the fifteen judges the fullest opportunity for shaping the Court's judgments and opinions. But they evolved in times of less recourse to the Court. The Court is falling behind in its expeditious disposition of cases, and there are understandable proposals for accelerating the pace of its work. Yet the financial pressures on the Court of which I have spoken cut the other way.

* * *

The Prospects of the Court

If the Statute remains unchanged. The Statute of the Court cannot be easily amended, governed as it is in this respect by the amendment provisions of the United Nations Charter: that is, adoption and ratification by two-thirds of the membership of the United Nations, including all the permanent members of the Security Council.

Taking the Statute as it is, the Court today is accomplishing much. Tomorrow it may accomplish more still, if its flow of cases is maintained and expanded. That is true, whether the cases are large or small in import. For the Court to play a significant role in the settlement of international disputes and the development of international law, it is not necessary for international disputes of great moment to be submitted to it. What is important is that states increasingly acquire the habit of submitting legal disputes not otherwise settled—and most disputes are and should be otherwise settled—to the Court. It is likely that the more they do, the more they will do.

Not only are most international disputes rightly settled without judicial recourse. Numbers of disputes that have been submitted to the Court have been settled in the course of litigation, occasionally with the Court's encouragement. That may be no less desirable on an international plane than it is on national and local planes.

If the Statute were to be amended. If the Statute were to be amended, the scope for change—progressive, but also regressive—would be wide. Any amendments would require the most careful consideration, which these remarks do not purport to offer. A few tentative thoughts:

* The amendment that may at once be the most desirable and the most portentous and problematic is that of amending Article 34's provision that only states may be parties in contentious cases before the Court. But if the gates are to be opened, how wide? Presumably, to include intergovernmental international organizations. Even that relatively modest innovation would entail multiple difficulties. But nongovernmental international organizations? Corporations incorporated under national law? Private associations? Individuals? The prospects are daunting.

* Extending the capacity to request advisory opinions from UN organs and the UN specialized agencies so as to include other intergovernmental international organizations should be sympathetically canvassed. The UN Secretary–General should be authorized to request advisory opinions on legal questions arising within the scope of his responsibilities (the latter step requires no Charter amendment).

* Affording other international courts the facility of appeal to the International Court of Justice merits consideration. As specialized international courts multiply, the importance of preserving the posi-

tion of the International Court of Justice grows, lest various international courts develop conflicting interpretations of international law.

* Enabling the highest national courts to refer questions of international law in cases arising before them to the International Court of Justice for its opinion on those questions, the case being remitted to the national court for disposition thereafter, is another proposed innovation that may deserve examination.

* Lengthening the current judicial term of office of nine years to fifteen years, but specifying that it shall not be subject to renewal, might enhance the independence of the members of the Court.

* * *

Response of the International Court of Justice to General Assembly Resolution 52/161 of 15 December 1997

37 I.L.M. 1466 (1998).*

The International Court of Justice was invited to submit to the General Assembly by 30 June 1998 its "comments and observations on the consequences that the increase in the volume of cases before the Court has on its operation, on the understanding that whatever action may be taken as a result of this invitation will have no implications for any changes in the Charter of the United Nations or the Statute of the International Court of Justice" (General Assembly resolution 52/161, paragraph 4).

The Assembly will find below the observations it invited. After explaining the current workload of the Court, this Report examines the effects of the increase in the volume of its work and the budgetary difficulties that it faces. It then analyses the responses of the Court to this double challenge and its needs that have yet to be met.

THE COURT AND ITS WORKLOAD

The International Court of Justice is one of the six principal organs of the United Nations and its principal judicial organ, a body whose independence and autonomy are recognized by the Charter of the United Nations and the Statute of the Court, which itself is an integral part of the Charter. The Court must at all times be able to exercise the functions entrusted to it if the terms and intent of the Charter are to be implemented.

The entire raison d'etre of the Court is to deal with the cases submitted to it by States Members of the United Nations and parties to the Statute and with the requests for advisory opinions made by United Nations organs or specialized agencies. These statutory duties of the Court mean that it does not have programmes which may be cut or expanded at will, although such possibilities may exist for certain other United Nations organs.

* Reprinted with the permission of the American Society of International Law.

Since its establishment in 1946, the Court has had to deal with 76 disputes between States and 22 requests for an advisory opinion. Of those, 28 of the contentious cases were brought before the Court since the 1980s. Whereas in the seventies the Court characteristically had one or two cases at a time on its docket, from the early eighties there has been a marked increase in recourse to the Court. Throughout the 1990s the figures have been large, standing at 9 in 1990, 12 in 1991, 13 in the years 1992–1995, 12 in 1996, 9 in 1997. Ten cases are currently pending.

In reality, there is a still larger number of matters awaiting the Court's decision. This is because the jurisdiction of the Court being based on consent, there are often "cases within cases" to determine questions of jurisdiction and admissibility when this is contested by one of the parties. * * * Just as in proceedings on the merits, these preliminary questions have to be dealt with by multiple rounds of written pleadings, oral arguments, deliberations and judgments, thus considerably multiplying further the "real" number of cases on the Court's docket at any given time. In certain recent cases the respondent State has not only replied on the merits but has also brought counter-claims (*Oil Platforms; Genocide*). The admissibility of the counter-claims and the subsequent exchanges of pleadings that they engender have given rise to yet further "cases within cases" upon the Court's listed docket.

Furthermore, it is not uncommon for the Court suddenly to receive a request for provisional measures. Such a request takes priority over everything else and entails written pleadings, hearings, deliberations and an Order issued by the Court. During the last 2 1/2 years there have been three such cases on provisional measures.

It must be appreciated that the Court deals with cases involving sovereign States, bearing on issues of great importance and complexity, in which the States have mobilized their full resources to submit heavy written pleadings and present detailed oral argument. In order to cope with such cases, the practice has been that after reviewing the written and oral pleadings each judge of the Court prepares a written Note—in fact a detailed analysis of the legal issues and the judicial conclusions that follow. Each Judge then studies the Notes of his or her colleagues before engaging in deliberations on the various complex issues. At the end of these deliberations—which may last over several days—a drafting committee is selected to prepare the Court's Judgment or Opinion. All judges then prepare comments and amendments to the draft Judgment or Opinion, which is further refined by the drafting committee and put again before the Court, before being adopted in its final form. The fashioning of the Court's decisions accordingly brings to bear the contributions of every Member of the Court, as befits a court of universal composition and mission.

The evidence is clear, both from the history of the Permanent Court of International Justice and of this Court, that judicial recourse is resorted to more frequently in times of detente rather than of tension. The increasing tendency to bring cases to the Court by Special Agreement is testimony to this. Further, more and more multilateral conventions include reference clauses to the International Court for the settlement of disputes. Moreover, 13 more States today accept the "Optional Clause" under Article 36, paragraph 2, of the Statute, allowing cases to be brought against them by States accepting the same obligation, than was the case in the early eighties. There is thus every reason to suppose that the rise since this period in the number of cases coming to the Court represents a fundamental change, which is likely to endure and perhaps expand.

Speech by the President of France, Jacques Chirac to the International Court of Justice, 29 February 2000

http://www.icj-cij.org/

[President Chirac was welcomed to the Court by Judge Gilbert Guillaume, of France, President of the Court. Selections from President Chirac's speech follow.]

Mr. President,

Judges of the International Court of Justice

Thank you for your hospitality and for your words of welcome. They are witness to the long and dense relationship between my country and the institution over which you preside. They reflect the harmony that exists between your mission and France's conception of a civilized international society—an international society ordered and regulated by law.

From the moment the principle of my State visit to the Netherlands was agreed upon, I expressed the wish to attend an official session of the Court. I wanted to pay tribute to the eminent position it occupies in the service of peace and the peaceful settlement of international disputes.

I wanted to pay homage to The Hague as home of international public law and international justice. Three centuries ago already, the Abbé de Saint–Pierre proposed to establish in the Netherlands the Senate and Tribunal charged with the control of security in Europe. "Here," he said, "is the most peaceable of all peoples, and those most interested in preserving the peace."

This visit is also an opportunity for me to pay homage to you, Mr. President. You belong to an illustrious line of French jurists, from René Cassin, whose irreplaceable contribution to the emergence of a universal conscience is known to us all, to Jules Basedevant, one of the founding fathers of the Court, and to your predecessor Guy Lacharrière, too soon taken from us.

Your election by your peers bears witness to the authority you wield and to the confidence you enjoy. It is an honour for France, and you may rest assured that our country remains an ally and support of the Court in the service of our vision of international relations. More and more, the world is in need of a supreme judicial body in order to ensure the primacy of the rule of law.

The nuclear threat has receded with the end of the Cold War. But at the same time, new circumstances have prompted a resurgence of regional and internal confrontation, of conflicts between ethnic and national groups, of wars based on territorial claims. These developments, with their attendant atrocities, are taking place before our very eyes.

The closing years of the century have been marked by crimes against humanity, by genocides. The accompanying trial of horrors has deeply shocked the conscience of mankind. Our citizens are increasingly well-informed, and they demand an end to these massacres and destruction. They demand that the international community react. That justice be done. They place their hopes in the deterrent force of effective sanction.

This demand has led to the creation of the International Criminal Tribunals. Such progress would have been unthinkable just ten years ago.The same spirit presides over the Tribunal for the Former Yugoslavia, whose members I shall be meeting shortly, the Tribunal set up to judge those responsible for the genocide in Rwanda, and the coming International Criminal Court. World public opinion no longer tolerates a situation in which the worst criminals can shelter behind reasons of State or national sovereignty to commit their crimes within impunity. It demands investigations and sanctions.

But isn't the very fact of resorting to these tribunals proof that the irreparable has already been committed, that the international community has failed in its mission?

Similarly, when war breaks out, isn't this a sign of the international community's failure in its mission to preserve peace? More than ever, we need to develop mechanisms for conflict prevention and for the peaceful settlement of disputes.

We all know what the role of the Security Council is in this task. But we also know that the United Nations Charter confers an essential mission on the International Court of Justice as the main judicial organ of the United Nations, a key forum for the resolution of international disputes, and we should promote it with determination.

The jurisdictional approach marks a step forward for civilization, being rooted in the will of the States that resort to it. This is as true for States as it is for individuals. Recourse to the courts offers the benefits of neutrality, impartiality, independence, and of submission to a law recognized by all.

When everyone shows good will, the search for a negotiated settlement is that much easier. Sometimes, even, the case is dropped and, properly encouraged, the parties reach a settlement before the judges reach a decision.

Recourse to the courts can help to "save face", which is so important in international life: no one yields to force; everyone bows before the law and reason.

That is why, since its creation in 1946, the International Court of Justice has gained such widespread recognition, as evidenced by the growing number of cases brought before it, especially since the end of the East–West confrontation.

The credit for the confidence States have shown in the Court is due to its judges above all. Decade after decade, they have overcome their national, political and cultural differences to develop procedures for examination and judgment that have won unanimous recognition and acceptance. Above all, they have succeeded in adopting a common understanding of international rules.

The authority of their decisions, their speed when circumstances demand, their wise, deliberate pace when the facts of the case remain too uncertain, have made the Court an organ towards which States turn increasingly naturally. France has always come before the Court with confidence whenever it has felt the need to make its voice heard.

In future, it will doubtless be necessary to institute more systematic recourse to your jurisdiction for the settlement of disputes between States. France would like to see the Court assume the responsibilities incumbent upon it to their fullest extent, just as, at the dawn of the 21st century, France is determined to see the United Nations play its roles to the full.

States encumbered by longstanding disputes unable to be resolved by negotiation should be firmly encouraged to refer their cases to the Court. The settlement of the painful dispute between Libya and Chad has been exemplary in this regard. And I want to welcome, here, the wisdom of many other States, particularly African ones, that have recently referred sensitive territorial disputes to the Court.

The extraordinary acceleration of growth in exchanges among people has given birth to a new international society. The number of actors is multiplying, and dialogue is taking place on a global scale. Alongside States and their increasingly dense relations, we are witnessing the rising influence of international and regional organizations, corporations and NGOs.

We all want to control and humanize this process of globalization. But who is to set the rules? That is the task of States first and foremost. It is for them to formulate the necessary mechanisms to permit the emergence of a rule-based society on the scale of our planet, ensuring justice and stability among its members.

On the world scene, the State is increasingly swapping its long-time role of diplomat and warrior for that of lawmaker. As long ago as 1923, the Permanent Court of International Justice noted that, when it concludes a treaty, a State does not abandon its sovereignty, it exercises it.

The proliferation of institutions and treaties that has accompanied globalization, embracing and ever-broader diversity of fields, raises one essential question: are we still capable of ensuring their overall coherence in the service of a common goal? How can we ensure the convergence of law when faced with a juxtaposition of specialized jurisdiction responsible for enforcing the profusion of international agreements?

I would like to see the Court invested with a specific role in that regard—a regulatory role, advising the international organizations, as is indeed provided for in the Charter.

When international law on the environment, trade, and labor standards conflict, we need a place where they can be reconciled. Why not request consultative opinions from your Court in such cases? We should reflect on ways to facilitate referrals for such purposes.

In the same spirit, perhaps we should see to it that treaties containing dispute-settlement mechanisms ought to establish an explicit linkage with the Court. When these treaties or conventions set up a new jurisdiction, would it not be desirable for that jurisdiction to be able to refer questions to the Court for preliminary ruling, for guidance on points of law of general interest?

I have talked about greater recourse to your jurisdiction for the settlement of disputes between States, to ensure coherence between the activities of the international organizations and between conventions. This additional workload will inevitably entail increased resources. And, while your institution has consistently and scrupulously measured its requests for funds, it must nevertheless have the material had human means to perform all of its tasks, while fully respecting the principle of bilingualism. France will help you in this.

In a sense, the Court has turned a page in its history with the passing of the century. And a brilliant page it has been, having witnessed the birth of your jurisdiction and its rise to become one of the great institutions working for peace and dialogue among Nations.

Today, in a world where international law is increasingly taking hold, in a world that is fortunately increasingly unwilling to tolerate the use of unilateral force, the task before the International Court of Justice is an immense one. A new era is opening up for it.

I feel sure that the influence of the Court will continue to grow under your leadership, thanks to the wisdom, the justice and the equity of its decisions. More and more, States will put their trust in it, France foremost among them.

Jurisdiction By Consent

United Nations, Handbook on the Pacific Settlement of Disputes Between States 70 (1992)

* * *

(a) *Jurisdiction, competence and initiation of the process*

202.   Settlement of international disputes by international courts is subject to State acceptance of jurisdiction over such disputes. This recognition may be expressed by way of a special agreement between the States parties (*compromis*) conferring jurisdiction upon a court in a particular dispute, or by a compromissory clause providing for an agreed or unilateral reference of a dispute to a court, or by other means. In the event of a dispute as to whether a court has jurisdiction, the matter is settled by the decision of the court. For example, the court may rule on questions of competence or other substantive preliminary objections that can be raised by a respondent State. Issues relating to procedural preliminary objections under the rule of exhaustion of local remedies are also heard.

(i) *Special agreement*

203.   Article 36, paragraph 1, of the Statute of the International Court of Justice provides that the "jurisdiction of the Court comprises all cases which the parties refer to it", which is done normally by way of notification

to the Registry of a special agreement (*compromis*) concluded by the parties for that purpose. The Special Agreement of 23 May 1976 concerning the Delimitation of the Continental Shelf (Libya/Malta), for example, provides:

"The Government of the Republic of Malta and the Government of the Libyan Arab Republic agree to recourse to the International Court of Justice as follows:

"*Article I,*

"The Court is requested to decide the following questions:

"What principles and rules of international law are applicable to the delimitation of the area of the continental shelf which appertains to the Republic of Malta and the area of continental shelf which appertains to the Libyan Arab Republic and how in practice such principles and rules can be applied by the two parties in this particular case in order that they may without difficulty delimit such areas by an agreement * * *.''

205. Article 36, paragraph 1, of the Statute * * * provides also that the jurisdiction * * * comprises "all matters specially provided for * * * in treaties and conventions in force". There are numerous treaties containing such a compromissory clause, some of which provide for unilateral reference of all or certain categories of disputes to the International Court of Justice. At the global level, for example, under the General Act for the Pacific Settlement of International Disputes of 26 September 1928 and 28 April 1949 all legal disputes are subject to compulsory adjudication by the Court, unless the parties agree to submit them to arbitration or conciliation. * * *

206. At the regional level, * * * the European Convention for the Peaceful Settlement of Disputes of 29 April 1957, * * * provides for the submission of all international legal disputes to the International Court of Justice.

(iii) *Other means of conferring jurisdiction*

207. * * * States parties to the Statute of the [International Court of Justice] have the option of making a declaration under Article 36, paragraph 2, of the Statute by which they accept in advance the jurisdiction of the Court "in all legal disputes concerning (*a*) the interpretation of a treaty; (*b*) any question of international law; (*c*) the existence of any fact which, if established, would constitute a breach of an international obligation; (*d*) the nature or extent of the reparation to be made for the breach of an international obligation". States are bound by this declaration only with respect to States which have also made such a declaration. The declaration may be made unconditionally or on condition of reciprocity on the part of several or certain States, or for a certain time. Optional clauses of compulsory jurisdiction also exist with respect to the European Court of Human Rights and the Inter–American Court of Human Rights.

208. By contrast, other treaties establishing an international court automatically confer jurisdiction to that court with respect to its scope of activities. The States parties do not need and do not have the option to make a declaration of acceptance of the compulsory jurisdiction of that

court. Thus, by becoming a party to the Treaties establishing the European Communities, member States automatically subject themselves to the jurisdiction of the Court of Justice of the European Communities for disputes connected with the application and interpretation of the Treaties. States parties to the 1982 United Nations Convention on the Law of the Sea *ipso facto* accept the compulsory jurisdiction of various forums for the settlement of law of the sea disputes. However, under the Convention, States parties have to make a declaration on the choice of the forum for judicial settlement established thereunder.

(iv) *Initiation of process*

209.   Contentious proceedings before international courts are instituted either unilaterally by one of the parties to a dispute or jointly by the parties, depending upon the terms of the relevant agreement in force between them.[202] Thus, if under the agreement the parties have accepted the compulsory jurisdiction of the International Court of Justice in respect of the dispute, then proceedings may be instituted unilaterally by the applicant State. In the absence of such a prior acceptance, however, proceedings can only be brought before international courts on the basis of the mutual consent of the parties.

210.   The procedure for instituting contentious proceedings is defined in the basic statute of the respective international courts. The Statute of the International Court of Justice provides under Article 40 as follows:

"1. Cases are brought before the Court, as the case may be, either by the notification of the special agreement or by a written application addressed to the Registrar. In either case the subject of the dispute and the parties shall be indicated.

"2. The Registrar shall forthwith communicate the application to all concerned.

"3. He shall also notify the Members of the United Nations through the Secretary–General, and also any other States entitled to appear before the Court."

* * *

(v) *Advisory opinions*

212.   International courts may be empowered to give an advisory opinion on a legal question relating to an existing international dispute between States referred to them by an international entity. The opinion does not bind the requesting entity, or any other body, or any State. Nevertheless, procedure in advisory cases, as in contentious cases, involves elaborate written and oral proceedings in accordance with the predetermined rules of the court in question, and as such advisory opinions could

---

202.   In some regional courts, cases may be brought to them by entities other than States (e.g., the European Commission of Human Rights with respect to the European Court of Human Rights; the Council or the Commission with respect to the Court of Justice of the European Communities; the Inter–American Commission on Human Rights with respect to the Inter–American Court of Human Rights) or even by individuals (e.g., the Court of Justice of the European Communities). * * *

assume the character of judicial pronouncements which, while not binding, might entail practical consequences * * *.

———

Acceptance of the Jurisdiction of the Court. By the year 2000 the jurisdiction of the court had been accepted in some 280 international agreements, but only 62 states had made declarations accepting the Court's jurisdiction under the optional clause. Still, this was up substantially from a few years earlier. Jurisdiction for advisory opinions, provided in Article 96 of the U.N. Charter, is conferred case by case by request of the competent organ of the United Nations or of the Agency entitled to make the request, as will be seen below. The Internet site of the Court contains a current list of cases filed since 1946, as well as the texts of opinions and decisions. See www.icj-cij.org. Texts of jurisdiction documents, including special agreements conferring jurisdiction and Declarations under the Optional clause, appear in the ICJ's Yearbooks, published by the Court.

Examples of Declarations Under Article 36(2) of the Statute of the International Court of Justice

NICARAGUA

International Court of Justice, Yearbook 1990–1991 at 93 (1992) [Translation from French]

On behalf of the Republic of Nicaragua I recognize as compulsory unconditionally the jurisdiction of the Permanent Court of International Justice. Geneva, 24 September 1929. (Signed) T.F. MEDINA.

UNITED STATES OF AMERICA

International Court of Justice, Yearbook 1984–1985, at 99 (1985)

I, Harry S. Truman, President of the United States of America, declare on behalf of the United States of America, under Article 36, paragraph 2, of the Statute of the International Court of Justice, and in accordance with the Resolution of 2 August 1946 of the Senate of the United States of America (two-thirds of the Senators present concurring therein), that the United States of America recognizes as compulsory ipso facto and without special agreement, in relation to any other State accepting the same obligation, the jurisdiction of the International Court of Justice in all legal disputes hereafter arising concerning

(a) the interpretation of a treaty;

(b) any question of international law;

(c) the existence of any fact which, if established, would constitute a breach of an international obligation;

(d) the nature or extent of the reparation to be made for the breach of an international obligation;

Provided, that this declaration shall not apply to

(a) disputes the solution of which the parties shall entrust to other tribunals by virtue of agreements already in existence or which may be concluded in the future; or

(b) disputes with regard to matters which are essentially within the domestic jurisdiction of the United States of America as determined by the United States of America; or

(c) disputes arising under a multilateral treaty, unless (1) all parties to the treaty affected by the decision are also parties to the case before the Court, or (2) the United States of America specially agrees to jurisdiction; and

Provided further, that this declaration shall remain in force for a period of five years and thereafter until the expiration of six months after notice may be given to terminate this declaration.

Done at Washington this fourteenth day of August 1946.

(Signed) HARRY S. TRUMAN.

[The declaration was terminated on October 7, 1985. See *infra* pp. 59 et seq.]

Case Concerning Military and Paramilitary Activities In and Against Nicaragua (Nicaragua v. United States of America)

International Court of Justice, 1984.
[1984] I.C.J.Rep. 392.

[On April 9, 1984, the Government of Nicaragua filed an application instituting proceedings against the United States with respect to its military and paramilitary activities in Nicaragua.

On April 6, 1984, i.e. three days before the filing, the Secretary of State of the United States sent to the Secretary–General of the United Nations the letter which follows.]

* * *

I have the honor on behalf of the Government of the United States of America to refer to the Declaration of my Government of August 26, 1946, concerning the acceptance by the United States of America of the compulsory jurisdiction of the International Court of Justice, and to state that the aforesaid Declaration shall not apply to disputes with any Central American state or arising out of or related to events in Central America, any of which disputes shall be settled in such manner as the parties to them may agree.

Notwithstanding the terms of the aforesaid Declaration, this *proviso* shall take effect immediately and shall remain in force for two years, so as to foster the continuing regional dispute settlement process which seeks a negotiated solution to the interrelated political, economic and security problems of Central America.

* * * 23 International Legal Materials 670 (1984).

[The United States appeared and pleaded that the court lacked jurisdiction relying, inter alia, on its letter of April 6, 1984, and on proviso (c) of its reservations to its acceptance of the compulsory jurisdiction of the court. See the text of the declaration supra p. 53.

By eleven votes to five, the court held that it had jurisdiction to entertain the application of Nicaragua on the basis of Article 36, paragraphs 2 and 5 of the I.C.J. Statute. It rejected the United States' arguments based on the letter of April 6, 1984, as will be seen in the language which follows.]

57. The terms of the 1984 notification, introducing substantial changes in the United States Declaration of Acceptance of 1946, have been quoted above; they constitute an important element for the development of the Court's reasoning. The 1984 notification has two salient aspects: on the one hand it states that the 1946 Declaration of acceptance shall not apply to disputes with any Central American State or arising out of or related to events in Central America; on the other hand it states that it is to take effect immediately, notwithstanding the terms of the 1946 Declaration, and is to remain in force for two years.

* * *

59. Declarations of acceptance of the compulsory jurisdiction of the Court are facultative, unilateral engagements, that States are absolutely free to make or not to make. In making the declaration a State is equally free either to do so unconditionally and without limit of time for its duration, or to qualify it with conditions or reservations. In particular, it may limit its effect to disputes arising after a certain date; or it may specify how long the declaration itself shall remain in force, or what notice (if any) will be required to terminate it. However, the unilateral nature of declarations does not signify that the State making the declaration is free to amend the scope and the contents of its solemn commitments as it pleases.
* * *

60. In fact, the declarations, even though they are unilateral acts, establish a series of bilateral engagements with other States accepting the same obligation of compulsory jurisdiction, in which the conditions, reservations and time-limit clauses are taken into consideration. In the establishment of this network of engagements, which constitutes the Optional–Clause system, the principle of good faith plays an important role: the Court has emphasized the need in international relations for respect for good faith and confidence in particularly unambiguous terms. * * *

61. The most important question relating to the effect of the 1984 notification is whether the United States was free to disregard the clause of six months' notice which, freely and by its own choice, it had appended to its 1946 Declaration. In so doing the United States entered into an obligation which is binding upon it vis-à-vis other States parties to the Optional–Clause system. Although the United States retained the right to modify the contents of the 1946 Declaration or to terminate it, a power which is inherent in any unilateral act of a State, it has, nevertheless assumed an inescapable obligation towards other States accepting the Optional Clause, by stating formally and solemnly that any such change

should take effect only after six months have elapsed as from the date of notice.

62.   The United States has argued that the Nicaraguan 1929 Declaration, being of undefined duration, is liable to immediate termination, without previous notice, and that therefore Nicaragua has not accepted "the same obligation" as itself for the purposes of Article 36, paragraph 2, and consequently may not rely on the six months' notice proviso against the United States. The Court does not however consider that this argument entitles the United States validly to act in non-application of the time-limit proviso included in the 1946 Declaration. The notion of reciprocity is concerned with the scope and substance of the commitments entered into, including reservations, and not with the formal conditions of their creation, duration or extinction. It appears clearly that reciprocity cannot be invoked in order to excuse departure from the terms of a State's own declaration, whatever its scope, limitations or conditions. As the Court observed in the Interhandel case:

> "Reciprocity enables the State which has made the wider acceptance of the jurisdiction of the Court to rely upon the reservations to the acceptance laid down by the other party. There the effect of reciprocity ends. It cannot justify a State, in this instance, the United States, in relying upon a restriction which the other party, Switzerland, has not included in its own Declaration." * * *

The maintenance in force of the United States Declaration for six months after notice of termination is a positive undertaking, flowing from the time-limit clause, but the Nicaraguan Declaration contains no express restriction at all. It is therefore clear that the United States is not in a position to invoke reciprocity as a basis for its action in making the 1984 notification which purported to modify the content of the 1946 Declaration. On the contrary it is Nicaragua that can invoke the six months' notice against the United States—not of course on the basis of reciprocity, but because it is an undertaking which is an integral part of the instrument that contains it.

   * * *

65.   In sum, the six months' notice clause forms an important integral part of the United States Declaration and it is a condition that must be complied with in case of either termination or modification. Consequently, the 1984 notification, in the present case, cannot override the obligation of the United States to submit to the compulsory jurisdiction * * * vis-à-vis Nicaragua, a State accepting the same obligation.

   * * *

[The court then rejected United States' arguments based on proviso (c) of its reservations, i.e. the so-called multilateral treaty (Vandenberg) reservation, in the language which follows.]

   * * *

72.   The multilateral treaty reservation in the United States Declaration has some obscure aspects, which have been the subject of comment since its making in 1946. There are two interpretations of the need for the presence of the parties to the multilateral treaties concerned in the pro-

ceedings before the Court as a condition for the validity of the acceptance of the compulsory jurisdiction by the United States. It is not clear whether what are "affected", according to the terms of the proviso, are the treaties themselves or the parties to them. Similar reservations to be found in certain other declarations of acceptance, such as those of India, El Salvador and the Philippines, refer clearly to "all parties" to the treaties. The phrase "all parties to the treaty affected by the decision" is at the centre of the present doubts. The United States interprets the reservation in the present case as referring to the States parties affected by the decision of the Court, merely mentioning the alternative interpretation, whereby it is the treaty which is "affected", so that all parties to the treaty would have to be before the Court, as "an *a fortiori* case". This latter interpretation need not therefore be considered. The argument of the United States relates specifically to El Salvador, Honduras and Costa Rica, the neighbour States of Nicaragua, which allegedly would be affected by the decision of the Court.

73. It may * * * be noted that the multilateral treaty reservation could not bar adjudication by the Court of all Nicaragua's claims, because Nicaragua * * * does not confine those claims only to violations of the four multilateral conventions referred to above (paragraph 68). On the contrary, Nicaragua invokes a number of principles of customary and general international law that, according to the Application, have been violated by the United States. The Court cannot dismiss the claims of Nicaragua under principles of customary and general international law, simply because such principles have been enshrined in the texts of the conventions relied upon by Nicaragua. The fact that the above-mentioned principles, recognized as such, have been codified or embodied in multilateral conventions does not mean that they cease to exist and to apply as principles of customary law, even as regards countries that are parties to such conventions. Principles such as those of the non-use of force, non-intervention, respect for the independence and territorial integrity of States, and the freedom of navigation, continue to be binding as part of customary international law, despite the operation of provisions of conventional law in which they have been incorporated. Therefore, since the claim before the Court in this case is not confined to violation of the multilateral conventional provisions invoked, it would not in any event be barred by the multilateral treaty reservation in the United States 1946 Declaration.

* * *

75. The United States Declaration uses the word "affected", without making it clear who is to determine whether the States referred to are, or are not, affected. The States themselves would have the choice of either instituting proceedings or intervening for the protection of their interests, in so far as these are not already protected by Article 59 of the Statute. As for the Court, it is only when the general lines of the judgment to be given become clear that the States "affected" could be identified. By way of example we may take the hypothesis that if the Court were to decide to reject the Application of Nicaragua on the facts, there would be no third State's claim to be affected. Certainly the determination of the States "affected" could not be left to the parties but must be made by the Court.

76.   At any rate, this is a question concerning matters of substance relating to the merits of the case: obviously the question of what States may be "affected" by the decision on the merits is not in itself a jurisdictional problem. The present phase of examination of jurisdictional questions was opened by the Court itself by its Order of 10 May 1984, not by a formal preliminary objection submitted by the United States; but it is appropriate to consider the grounds put forward by the United States for alleged lack of jurisdiction in the light of the procedural provisions for such objections. That being so, and since the procedural technique formerly available of joinder of preliminary objections to the merits has been done away with since the 1972 revision of the Rules of Court, the Court has no choice but to avail itself of Article 79, paragraph 7, of the present Rules of Court, and declare that the objection based on the multilateral treaty reservation of the United States Declaration of Acceptance does not possess, in the circumstances of the case, an exclusively preliminary character, and that consequently it does not constitute an obstacle for the Court to entertain the proceedings instituted by Nicaragua under the Application of 9 April 1984.

* * *

U.S. Withdrawal From the Proceedings Initiated by Nicaragua in the ICJ

United States Department of State Bulletin, March 1985, p. 64. Statement, Jan. 18, 1985.

The United States has consistently taken the position that the proceedings initiated by Nicaragua in the International Court of Justice (ICJ) are a misuse of the Court for political purposes and that the Court lacks jurisdiction and competence over such a case. The Court's decision of November 26, 1984, finding that it has jurisdiction, is contrary to law and fact. With great reluctance, the United States has decided not to participate in further proceedings in this case.

* * *

The conflict in Central America, * * * is an inherently political problem that is not appropriate for judicial resolution. The conflict will be solved only by political and diplomatic means—not through a judicial tribunal. The ICJ was never intended to resolve issues of collective security and self-defense and is patently unsuited for such a role. Unlike domestic courts, the World Court has jurisdiction only to the extent that nation-states have consented to it. When the United States accepted the Court's compulsory jurisdiction in 1946, it certainly never conceived of such a role for the Court in such controversies. Nicaragua's suit against the United States—which includes an absurd demand for hundreds of millions of dollars in reparations—is a blatant misuse of the Court for political and propaganda purposes.

* * *

This decision is erroneous as a matter of law and is based on a misreading and distortion of the evidence and precedent.

* * *

[After stating some reasons for this assertion, the Department continued]: For these reasons, we are forced to conclude that our continued participation in this case could not be justified.

* * *

Questions. Does it really show respect for the rule of law to argue that the Court lacks jurisdiction and, having lost on that issue, to refuse to proceed on the merits? Does it show respect for the court to label its decision "erroneous as a matter of law" and "based on a misreading and distortion of the evidence"? It should be noted in this connection that by combining the votes on the various grounds of decision, the court eventually held it had jurisdiction by fifteen votes in favor and one vote against, the dissenting voice being that of the judge from the United States.

U.S. Terminates Acceptance of ICJ Compulsory Jurisdiction

United States Department of State Bulletin, January 1986, p. 67. Secretary's Letter to UN Secretary General, Oct. 7, 1985.

* * *

I have the honor on behalf of the Government of the United States of America to refer to the declaration of my Government of 26 August 1946, as modified by my note of 6 April 1984, concerning the acceptance by the United States of America of the compulsory jurisdiction of the International Court of Justice, and to state that the aforesaid declaration is hereby terminated, with effect six months from the date hereof.

* * *

Legal Advisor Soafer's statement defending this action also appears in the State Department Bulletin, January 1986. For a statement supporting compulsory jurisdiction, see U.S. Decision to Withdraw from the International Court of Justice, Hearing before the Subcommittee on Human Rights and International Organizations of the House Committee on Foreign Affairs, 99th Cong., 1st Sess. 92–109 (1986) (statement of Burns H. Weston and Bessie D. Murray for the Independent Commission on Respect for International Law).

End of the Nicaragua Case. In 1991 the Agent for Nicaragua informed the Court that Nicaragua did not wish to go on with these proceedings, and the Legal Advisor of the Department of State advised the Court that the United States welcomed the Nicaraguan request for discontinuance of the proceedings in this case. See 31 I.L.M. 103 (1992). The

Order removing the case from the Court's list was made on 26 September, 1991. I.C.J. Reports 1991, 47; 31 I.L.M. 103 (1992).

Case Concerning East Timor (Portugal v. Australia)

International Court of Justice, (1995):
[1995] ICJ Reps. 90; 34 I.L.M. 1581

11. The Territory of East Timor corresponds to the eastern part of the island of Timor; it includes the island of Atauro, 25 kilometres to the north, the islet of Jaco to the east, and the enclave of Oe–Cusse in the western part of the island of Timor. Its capital is Dili, situated on its north coast. The south coast of East Timor lies opposite the north coast of Australia, the distance between them being approximately 430 kilometres.

In the sixteenth century, East Timor became a colony of Portugal; Portugal remained there until 1975. The western part of the island came under Dutch rule and later became part of independent Indonesia.

12. In resolution 1542 (XV) of 15 December 1960 the United Nations General Assembly recalled "differences of views ... concerning the status of certain territories under the administrations of Portugal and Spain and described by these two States as 'overseas provinces' of the metropolitan State concerned"; and it also stated that it considered that the territories under the administration of Portugal, which were listed therein (including "Timor and dependencies") were non-self-governing territories within the meaning of Chapter XI of the Charter. Portugal, in the wake of its "Carnation Revolution", accepted this position in 1974.

13. Following internal disturbances in East Timor, on 27 August 1975 the Portuguese civil and military authorities withdrew from the mainland of East Timor to the island of Atauro. On 7 December 1975 the armed forces of Indonesia intervened in East Timor. On 8 December 1975 the Portuguese authorities departed from the island of Atauro, and thus left East Timor altogether. Since their departure, Indonesia has occupied the Territory, and the Parties acknowledge that the Territory has remained under the effective control of that State. Asserting that on 31 May 1976 the people of East Timor had requested Indonesia "to accept East Timor as an integral part of the Republic of Indonesia", on 17 July 1976 Indonesia enacted a law incorporating the Territory as part of its national territory.

18. * * *Australia and Indonesia then turned to the possibility of establishing a provisional arrangement for the joint exploration and exploitation of the resources of an area of the continental shelf. A Treaty to this effect was eventually concluded between them on 11 December 1989, whereby a "Zone of Cooperation" was created "in an area between the Indonesian Province of East Timor and Northern Australia". Australia enacted legislation in 1990 with a view to implementing the Treaty; this law came into force in 1991. * * *

* * *

19. In these proceedings Portugal maintains that Australia, in negotiating and concluding the 1989 Treaty, in initiating performance of the Treaty, in taking internal legislative measures for its application, and in

continuing to negotiate with Indonesia, has acted unlawfully, in that it has infringed the rights of the people of East Timor to self-determination and to permanent sovereignty over its natural resources, infringed the rights of Portugal as the administering Power, and contravened Security Council resolutions 384 and 389. * * *

* * *

23.   The Court will now consider Australia's principal objection, to the effect that Portugal's Application would require the Court to determine the rights and obligations of Indonesia. The declarations made by the Parties under Article 36, paragraph 2, of the Statute do not include any limitation which would exclude Portugal's claims from the jurisdiction thereby conferred upon the Court. Australia, however, contends that the jurisdiction so conferred would not enable the Court to act if, in order to do so, the Court were required to rule on the lawfulness of Indonesia's entry into and continuing presence in East Timor, on the validity of the 1989 Treaty between Australia and Indonesia, or on the rights and obligations of Indonesia under that Treaty, even if the Court did not have to determine its validity. Portugal agrees that if its Application required the Court to decide any of these questions, the Court could not entertain it. The Parties disagree, however, as to whether the Court is required to decide any of these questions in order to resolve the dispute referred to it.

24.   Australia argues that the decision sought from the Court by Portugal would inevitably require the Court to rule on the lawfulness of the conduct of a third State, namely Indonesia, in the absence of that State's consent. In support of its argument, it cites the Judgment in the case concerning *Monetary Gold Removed from Rome in 1943*, in which the Court ruled that, in the absence of Albania's consent, it could not take any decision on the international responsibility of that State since "Albania's legal interests would not only be affected by a decision, but would form the very subject-matter of the decision" (I.C.J. Reports 1954, p. 32).

Port. contends

25.   In reply, Portugal contends, first, that its Application is concerned exclusively with the objective conduct of Australia, which consists in having negotiated, concluded and initiated performance of the 1989 Treaty with Indonesia, and that this question is perfectly separable from any question relating to the lawfulness of the conduct of Indonesia. According to Portugal, such conduct of Australia in itself constitutes a breach of its obligation to treat East Timor as a non-self-governing territory and Portugal as its administering Power; and that breach could be passed upon by the Court by itself and without passing upon the rights of Indonesia. The objective conduct of Australia, considered as such, constitutes the only violation of international law of which Portugal complains.

26.   The Court recalls in this respect that one of the fundamental principles of its Statute is that it cannot decide a dispute between States without the consent of those States to its jurisdiction. This principle was reaffirmed in the Judgment given by the Court in the case concerning Monetary Gold Removed from Rome in 1943 and confirmed in several of its subsequent decisions [citations omitted]

27.   The Court notes that Portugal's claim that, in entering into the 1989 Treaty with Indonesia, Australia violated the obligation to respect Portugal's status as administering Power and that of East Timor as a non-self-governing territory, is based on the assertion that Portugal alone, in its capacity as administering Power, had the power to enter into the Treaty on behalf of East Timor; that Australia disregarded this exclusive power, and, in so doing, violated its obligations to respect the status of Portugal and that of East Timor.

The Court also observes that Australia, for its part, rejects Portugal's claim to the exclusive power to conclude treaties on behalf of East Timor, and the very fact that it entered into the 1989 Treaty with Indonesia shows that it considered that Indonesia had that power. Australia in substance argues that even if Portugal had retained that power, on whatever basis, after withdrawing from East Timor, the possibility existed that the power could later pass to another State under general international law, and that it did so pass to Indonesia; Australia affirms moreover that, if the power in question did pass to Indonesia, it was acting in conformity with international law in entering into the 1989 Treaty with that State, and could not have violated any of the obligations Portugal attributes to it. Thus, for Australia, the fundamental question in the present case is ultimately whether, in 1989, the power to conclude a treaty on behalf of East Timor in relation to its continental shelf lay with Portugal or with Indonesia.

28.   The Court has carefully considered the argument advanced by Portugal which seeks to separate Australia's behaviour from that of Indonesia. However, in the view of the Court, Australia's behaviour cannot be assessed without first entering into the question why it is that Indonesia could not lawfully have concluded the 1989 Treaty, while Portugal allegedly could have done so; the very subject-matter of the Court's decision would necessarily be a determination whether, having regard to the circumstances in which Indonesia entered and remained in East Timor, it could or could not have acquired the power to enter into treaties on behalf of East Timor relating to the resources of its continental shelf. The Court could not make such a determination in the absence of the consent of Indonesia.

                         * * *

In the Court's view, Portugal's assertion that the right of peoples to self-determination, as it evolved from the Charter and from United Nations practice, has an *erga omnes* character, is irreproachable. The principle of self-determination of peoples has been recognized by the United Nations Charter and in the jurisprudence of the Court *(see Legal Consequences for States of the Continued Presence of South Africa in Namibia (South West Africa) notwithstanding Security Council Resolution 276 (1970), Advisory Opinion, I.C.J. Reports 1971*, pp. 31–32, paras. 52–53; *Western Sahara, Advisory Opinion, I.C.J. Reports 1975*, pp. 31–33, paras. 54–59); it is one of the essential principles of contemporary international law. However, the Court considers that the *erga omnes* character of a norm and the rule of consent to jurisdiction are two different things. Whatever the nature of the obligations invoked, the Court could not rule on the lawfulness of the conduct of a State when its judgment would imply an evaluation of the lawfulness of the conduct of another State which is not a party to the case.

Where this is so, the Court cannot act, even if the right in question is a right erga omnes.

* * *

35.   The Court concludes that it cannot, in this case, exercise the jurisdiction it has by virtue of the declarations made by the Parties under Article 36, paragraph 2, of its Statute because, in order to decide the claims of Portugal, it would have to rule, as a prerequisite, on the lawfulness of Indonesia's conduct in the absence of that State's consent. This conclusion applies to all the claims of Portugal, for all of them raise a common question: whether the power to make treaties concerning the continental shelf resources of East Timor belongs to Portugal or Indonesia, and, therefore, whether Indonesia's entry into and continued presence in the Territory are lawful. * * *

* * *

———

Role of the United Nations. Article 94 of the United Nations Charter provides:

> 1.   Each Member of the United Nations undertakes to comply with the decision of the International Court of Justice in any case to which it is a party.
>
> 2.   If any party to a case fails to perform the obligations incumbent upon it under a judgment rendered by the Court, the other party may have recourse to the Security Council, which may, if it deems necessary, make recommendations or decide upon measures to be taken to give effect to the judgment.

The Security Council * * * has never decided upon measures to be taken "to give effect to the judgment." Questions as yet undecided include the following: Does the Security Council have power under the Charter to order a state to comply with a judgment? Can the Security Council direct or authorize the use of force to enforce such an order? Is the council limited, in its use of force to enforce a judgment of the court, to those situations in which non-performance of an order of the court can be considered a threat to the peace, breach of the peace, or act of aggression under Article 39 of the Charter of the United Nations?

Advisory Opinions

Advisory Opinion on the Legality of the Threat or Use of Nuclear Weapons

International Court of Justice: [1996] ICJ Reports. p. 226; 35 I.L.M. 809 (1996)

[Other excerpts from this Opinion may be found in Chapters 3 and 16]

10.   The Court must first consider whether it has the jurisdiction to give a reply to the request of the General Assembly for an Advisory Opinion

and whether, should the answer be in the affirmative, there is any reason it should decline to exercise any such jurisdiction.

The Court draws its competence in respect of advisory opinions from Article 65, paragraph 1, of its Statute. Under this Article, the Court

"may give an advisory opinion on any legal question at the request of whatever body may be authorized by or in accordance with the Charter of the United Nations to make such a request".

11. For the Court to be competent to give an advisory opinion, it is thus necessary at the outset for the body requesting the opinion to be "authorized by or in accordance with the Charter of the United Nations to make such a request". The Charter provides in Article 96, paragraph 1, that:

"The General Assembly or the Security Council may request the International Court of Justice to give an advisory opinion on any legal question."

Some States which oppose the giving of an opinion by the Court argued that the General Assembly and Security Council are not entitled to ask for opinions on matters totally unrelated to their work. They suggested that, as in the case of organs and agencies acting under Article 96, paragraph 2, of the Charter, and notwithstanding the difference in wording between that provision and paragraph 1 of the same Article, the General Assembly and Security Council may ask for an advisory opinion on a legal question only within the scope of their activities.

In the view of the Court, it matters little whether this interpretation of Article 96, paragraph 1, is or is not correct; in the present case, the General Assembly has competence in any event to seise the Court. Indeed, Article 10 of the Charter has conferred upon the General Assembly a competence relating to "any questions or any matters" within the scope of the Charter. Article 11 has specifically provided it with a competence to "consider the general principles ... in the maintenance of international peace and security, including the principles governing disarmament and the regulation of armaments". Lastly, according to Article 13, the General Assembly "shall initiate studies and make recommendations for the purpose of ... encouraging the progressive development of international law and its codification".

13. The Court must furthermore satisfy itself that the advisory opinion requested does indeed relate to a "legal question" within the meaning of its Statute and the United Nations Charter.

The Court has already had occasion to indicate that questions

"framed in terms of law and rais[ing] problems of international law ... are by their very nature susceptible of a reply based on law ... [and] appear ... to be questions of a legal character" (*Western Sahara, Advisory Opinion, I.C.J. Reports 1975*, p. 18, para. 15).

The question put to the Court by the General Assembly is indeed a legal one, since the Court is asked to rule on the compatibility of the threat or use of nuclear weapons with the relevant principles and rules of international law. To do this, the Court must identify the existing principles and rules, interpret them and apply them to the threat or use of nuclear weapons, thus offering a reply to the question posed based on law.

The fact that this question also has political aspects, as, in the nature of things, is the case with so many questions which arise in international life, does not suffice to deprive it of its character as a "legal question" and to "deprive the Court of a competence expressly conferred on it by its Statute" (*Application for Review of Judgement No. 158 of the United Nations Administrative Tribunal, Advisory Opinion, I.C.J. Reports 1973*, p. 172, para. 14). Whatever its political aspects, the Court cannot refuse to admit the legal character of a question which invites it to discharge an essentially judicial task, namely, an assessment of the legality of the possible conduct of States with regard to the obligations imposed upon them by international law [Citations omitted].

Furthermore, as the Court said in the Opinion it gave in 1980 concerning the *Interpretation of the Agreement of 25 March 1951 between the WHO and Egypt:*

"Indeed, in situations in which political considerations are prominent it may be particularly necessary for an international organization to obtain an advisory opinion from the Court as to the legal principles applicable with respect to the matter under debate ... " (*Interpretation of the Agreement of 25 March 1951 between the WHO and Egypt, Advisory Opinion, I.C.J. Reports 1980*, p. 87, para. 33.)

The Court moreover considers that the political nature of the motives which may be said to have inspired the request and the political implications that the opinion given might have are of no relevance in the establishment of its jurisdiction to give such an opinion.

14.   Article 65, paragraph 1, of the Statute provides: "The Court *may* give an advisory opinion ... " (Emphasis added.) This is more than an enabling provision. As the Court has repeatedly emphasized, the Statute leaves a discretion as to whether or not it will give an advisory opinion that has been requested of it, once it has established its competence to do so. In this context, the Court has previously noted as follows:

"The Court's Opinion is given not to the States, but to the organ which is entitled to request it; the reply of the Court, itself an 'organ of the United Nations', represents its participation in the activities of the Organization, and, in principle, should not be refused." [Citations omitted]

The Court has constantly been mindful of its responsibilities as "the principal judicial organ of the United Nations" (Charter, Art. 92). When considering each request, it is mindful that it should not, in principle, refuse to give an advisory opinion. In accordance with the consistent jurisprudence of the Court, only "compelling reasons" could lead it to such a refusal [Citations omitted]. There has been no refusal, based on the discretionary power of the Court, to act upon a request for advisory opinion in the history of the present Court; in the case concerning the *Legality of the Use by a State of Nuclear Weapons in Armed Conflict*, the refusal to give the World Health Organization the advisory opinion requested by it was justified by the Court's lack of jurisdiction in that case. The Permanent Court of International Justice took the view on only one occasion that it could not reply to a question put to it, having regard to the very particular circumstances of the case, among which were that the question directly concerned an already existing dispute, one of the States parties to which was neither a party to the Statute of the Permanent Court nor a Member of the League of Nations, objected to the proceedings, and refused to take part in any way (*Status of Eastern Carelia, P.C.I.J., Series B, No. 5*).

15. Most of the reasons adduced in these proceedings in order to persuade the Court that in the exercise of its discretionary power it should decline to render the opinion requested by General Assembly resolution 49/75K were summarized in the following statement made by one State in the written proceedings:

"The question presented is vague and abstract, addressing complex issues which are the subject of consideration among interested States and within other bodies of the United Nations which have an express mandate to address these matters. An opinion by the Court in regard to the question presented would provide no practical assistance to the General Assembly in carrying out its functions under the Charter. Such an opinion has the potential of undermining progress already made or being made on this sensitive subject and, therefore, is contrary to the interest of the United Nations Organization." (United States of America, Written Statement, pp. 1–2; * * *

In contending that the question put to the Court is vague and abstract, some States appeared to mean by this that there exists no specific dispute on the subject-matter of the question. In order to respond to this argument, it is necessary to distinguish between requirements governing contentious procedure and those applicable to advisory opinions. The purpose of the advisory function is not to settle—at least directly—disputes between States, but to offer legal advice to the organs and institutions requesting the opinion (cf. *Interpretation of Peace Treaties I.C.J. Reports 1950*, p. 71). The fact that the question put to the Court does not relate to a specific dispute should consequently not lead the Court to decline to give the opinion requested.

Moreover, it is the clear position of the Court that to contend that it should not deal with a question couched in abstract terms is "a mere affirmation devoid of any justification", and that "the Court may give an advisory opinion on any legal question, abstract or otherwise" * * *
* * *

16. Certain States have observed that the General Assembly has not explained to the Court for what precise purposes it seeks the advisory opinion. Nevertheless, it is not for the Court itself to purport to decide whether or not an advisory opinion is needed by the Assembly for the performance of its functions. The General Assembly has the right to decide for itself on the usefulness of an opinion in the light of its own needs.
* * *

18. Finally, it has been contended by some States that in answering the question posed, the Court would be going beyond its judicial role and would be taking upon itself a law-making capacity. It is clear that the Court cannot legislate, and, in the circumstances of the present case, it is not

called upon to do so. Rather its task is to engage in its normal judicial function of ascertaining the existence or otherwise of legal principles and rules applicable to the threat or use of nuclear weapons. The contention that the giving of an answer to the question posed would require the Court to legislate is based on a supposition that the present corpus juris is devoid of relevant rules in this matter. The Court could not accede to this argument; it states the existing law and does not legislate. This is so even if, in stating and applying the law, the Court necessarily has to specify its scope and sometimes note its general trend.

19. In view of what is stated above, the Court concludes that it has the authority to deliver an opinion on the question posed by the General Assembly, and that there exist no "compelling reasons" which would lead the Court to exercise its discretion not to do so.

An entirely different question is whether the Court, under the constraints placed upon it as a judicial organ, will be able to give a complete answer to the question asked of it. However, that is a different matter from a refusal to answer at all.

Applicability of the Obligation to Arbitrate Under Section 21 of the United Nations Headquarters Agreement of 26 June 1947

Advisory Opinion of 26 April 1988

International Court of Justice, 1988
I.C.J. Reports 1988, p. 12

* * *

7. The question upon which the opinion of the Court has been requested is whether the United States of America (hereafter referred to as "the United States"), as a party to the United Nations Headquarters Agreement, is under an obligation to enter into arbitration. The Headquarters Agreement of 26 June 1947 came into force in accordance with its terms on 21 November 1947 by exchange of letters between the Secretary–General and the United States Permanent Representative. The Agreement was registered the same day with the United Nations Secretariat, in accordance with Article 102 of the Charter. In section 21, paragraph (a), it provides as follows:

> "Any dispute between the United Nations and the United States concerning the interpretation or application of this agreement or of any supplemental agreement, which is not settled by negotiation or other agreed mode of settlement, shall be referred for final decision to a tribunal of three arbitrators, one to be named by the Secretary–General, one to be named by the Secretary of State of the United States, and the third to be chosen by the two, or, if they should fail to agree upon a third, then by the President of the International Court of Justice."

There is no question but that the Headquarters Agreement is a treaty in force binding the parties thereto. What the Court has therefore to determine, in order to answer the question put to it, is whether there exists a dispute between the United Nations and the United States of the kind contemplated by section 21 of the Agreement. * * *

* * *

8. The events in question centred round the Permanent Observer Mission of the Palestine Liberation Organization (referred to hereafter as "the PLO") to the United Nations in New York. The PLO has enjoyed in relation to the United Nations the status of an observer since 1974, the Organization was invited to "participate in the sessions and the work of the General Assembly in the capacity of observer". Following this invitation, the PLO established an Observer Mission in 1974, and maintains an office, entitled office of the PLO Observer Mission at 115 East 65th Street, in New York City, outside the United Nations Headquarters District. Recognized observers are listed as such in official United Nations publications: the PLO appears in such publications in a category of "organizations which have received a standing invitation from the General Assembly to participate in the sessions and the work of the General Assembly as observers".

* * *

* * * Section 11 of the Headquarters Agreement provides that

> "The federal, state or local authorities of the United States shall not impose any impediments to transit to or from the headquarters district of: (1) representatives of Members * * * or the families of such representatives * * *; * * * (5) other persons invited to the headquarters district by the United Nations * * * on official business * * *."

Section 12 provides that, "[T]he provisions of section 11 shall be applicable irrespective of the relations existing between the Governments of the persons referred to in that section and the Government of the United States."

Section 13 provides (*inter alia*) that, "[L]aws and regulations in force in the United States regarding the entry of aliens shall not be applied in such manner as to interfere with the privileges referred to in section 11."

* * *

24. On 11 March 1988 the Acting Permanent Representative of the United States to the United Nations wrote to the Secretary–General, referring to General Assembly resolutions 42/229A and 42/229B and stating as follows:

> "I wish to inform you that the Attorney General of the United States has determined that he is required by the Anti–Terrorism Act of 1987 to close the office of the Palestine Liberation Organization Observer Mission to the United Nations in New York, irrespective of any obligations the United States may have under the Agreement between the United Nations and the United States regarding the

Headquarters of the United Nations. If the PLO does not comply with the Act, the Attorney General will initiate legal action to close the PLO Observer Mission on or about March 21, 1988, the effective date of the Act. This course of action will allow the orderly enforcement of the Act.
* * *

This letter was delivered by hand to the Secretary–General by the Acting Permanent Representative of the United States. * * * On receiving the letter, the Secretary–General protested to the Acting Permanent Representative and stated that the decision taken by the United States Government as outlined in the letter was a clear violation of the Headquarters Agreement between the United Nations and the United States.

* * *

[The Court examined the requirements of Section 21 and found that they were satisfied.]

57. The Court must therefore conclude that the United States is bound to respect the obligation to have recourse to arbitration under section 21 of the Headquarters Agreement. The fact remains however that, as the Court has already observed, the United States has declared (letter from the Permanent Representative, 11 March 1988) that its measures against the PLO Observer Mission were taken "irrespective of any obligations the United States may have under the [Headquarters] Agreement". If it were necessary to interpret that statement as intended to refer not only to the substantive obligations laid down in, for example, sections 11, 12 and 13, but also to the obligation to arbitrate provided for in section 21, this conclusion would remain intact. It would be sufficient to recall the fundamental principle of international law that international law prevails over domestic law. This principle was endorsed by judicial decision as long ago as the arbitral award of 14 September 1872 in the *Alabama* case between Great Britain and the United States, and has frequently been recalled since, for example in the case concerning the *Greco–Bulgarian "Communities"* in which the Permanent Court of International Justice laid it down that

> "it is a generally accepted principle of international law that in the relations between Powers who are contracting Parties to a treaty, the provisions of municipal law cannot prevail over those of the treaty" (*P.C.I.J., Series B, No. 17*, p. 32).

* * *

58. For these reasons,

THE COURT,

Unanimously,

Is of the opinion that the United States of America, as a party to the Agreement between the United Nations and the United States of America regarding the Headquarters of the United Nations of 26 June 1947, is under an obligation, in accordance with section 21 of that Agreement, to enter into arbitration for the settlement of the dispute between itself and the United Nations.

————

Notes & Questions

1. For further developments in the United States concerning the effort to close the PLO Observer Mission, *see United States v. Palestine Liberation Organization*, 695 F.Supp. 1456 (S.D.N.Y.1988) in which the U.S. government's motion for an injunction closing the P.L.O. office was denied and the PLO's motion to dismiss was granted. Excepts are found in Chapter 10.

2. How would you characterize the status of I.C.J. advisory opinions? Are these opinions obligatory, and if so, in what sense and on whom? Or as advice to the requesting organ, are they merely hortatory but to be taken into account? Are they any more or less binding than other decisions of the I.C.J.? *See* U.N. Charter Article 96 and I.C.J. Statute Articles 65–68. Compare Charter Article 94 which makes I.C.J. decisions in contentious cases binding on the parties. Does Statute Article 38 affect your analysis?

3. What procedures might be employed to make advisory opinions formally binding in the sense of Charter Article 94 as applied to contentious cases? What would be the effect of an agreement providing that "[t]he opinion of the Court shall be accepted as decisive by the parties"? *See* in the Documentary Supplement, Section 30 of the Convention on the Privileges and Immunities of the United Nations.

4. Organs and agencies authorized to request advisory opinions under Charter Article 94 are limited to 5 U.N. organs (General Assembly, Security Council, Economic and Social Council, Trusteeship Council and the Interim Committee of the General Assembly) and U.N. Specialized Agencies (see listing in Chapter 2, Section C 1 below). Should access to the Court's advisory jurisdiction be expanded to include the Secretary–General and even other public international organizations not directly affiliated with the United Nations, such as the Council of Europe, OECD, NATO, the OAS? Or to states? Or to non-state parties such as NGOs, companies and individuals? How might that be done in formal terms?

5. For use of the advisory opinion procedure in a case of actual dispute without the consent of the state concerned, see *Applicability of Article VI, Section 22 on the Convention on the Privileges and Immunities of the United Nations, Advisory Opinion, I.C.J. Reports 1989*, p. 177; 29 I.L.M. 100 (1990). Does that suggest a possible means for expanding the role and impact of the I.C.J.?

6. Should the decisions of the ICJ in contentious cases and advisory opinions have a stare decisis quality? Do they have precedential value in any case? Is there a distinction to be made on these issues between contentious cases and advisory opinions? Have you noticed how the ICJ actually treats its decisions and opinions on parallel issues presented in later cases? How would you compare the ICJ practice to the notion of stare decisis in the common law world?

2.   INTERNATIONAL ARBITRATION

United Nations Handbook on the Pacific Settlement of Disputes Between States 55 (1992)[1]

168.   The 1899 and 1907 Hague Conventions for the Pacific Settlement of International Disputes described the object of international arbitration as the settlement of disputes between States by judges chosen by the parties themselves and on the basis of respect for law. They further provided that recourse to the procedure implied submission in good faith to the award of the tribunal. Accordingly, one of the basic characteristics of arbitration is that it is a procedure which results in binding decisions upon the parties to the dispute.

169.   The power to render binding decisions is, therefore, a characteristic which arbitration shares with the method of judicial settlement by international courts whose judgements are not only binding but also, as in the case of the International Court of Justice, final and without appeal, as indicated in article 60 of the I.C.J. Statute. For this reason, arbitration and judicial settlement are both usually referred to as compulsory means of settlement of disputes.

170.   However, while both arbitration and judicial settlement are similar in that respect, the two methods of settlement are nevertheless structurally different from each other. Arbitration, in general, is constituted by mutual consent of the States parties to a specific dispute where such parties retain considerable control over the process through the power of appointing arbitrators of their own choice. By contrast, judicial settlement relies upon pre-constituted international courts or tribunals, the composition of which is not to the same extent subject to control by the parties to the dispute.

* * *

(a) *Types of arbitration agreements*

174.   Consent of the parties to arbitration may be expressed prior to or after the occurrence of a dispute. Parties may agree to submit all or special categories of future disputes to arbitration. Such commitment may be made in multilateral or bilateral treaties entirely devoted to the peaceful settlement of disputes.[116] A more common method is by inclusion of a

---

1.   Reprinted with the permission of the United Nations.

116.   One of the well-known multilateral general dispute settlement agreements is the Hague Convention for the Pacific Settlement of International Disputes of 18 October 1907. It was one of the more successful first attempts to design a multilateral convention aimed specifically at proposing a variety of means and procedures for the peaceful settlement of disputes. The Convention establishes a system of arbitration for which new agencies were created. The most important part of

the Convention was devoted to the organization and the operation of the Permanent Court of Arbitration. The Permanent Court was created with the object of facilitating an immediate recourse to arbitration of international disputes which could not be settled by diplomacy.

The Revised General Act for the Pacific Settlement of International Disputes of 1949 is another important multilateral general dispute settlement agreement. Chapter III is devoted to arbitration. The chapter provides a system for the establishment of the tribu-

compromissory clause in a treaty, by which parties agree to submit all or part of their future disputes regarding that treaty to arbitration. Parties may also agree to go to arbitration by a special agreement or a *compromis* after the occurrence of a dispute.

* * *

Caron, The Nature of the Iran–United States Claims Tribunal and the Evolving Structure of International Dispute Resolution

84 Am.J.Int'l L. 104 (1990).*

The Iran–United States Claims Tribunal[1] has been called "the most significant arbitral body in history"; its awards, "a gold mine of information for perceptive lawyers." In a recent international commercial arbitration, however, an arbitrator reportedly stated that decisions of the Tribunal, although on point, were not persuasive because the Tribunal, after all, involves a special type of arbitration. This arbitrator is not alone. A lecturer at the Hague Academy of International Law, speaking on international commercial arbitration, reportedly did not refer to the Tribunal's jurisprudence because he did not find it relevant to his work for the same reason. Viewed as a gigantic experiment in international dispute resolution rather than merely a claims settlement device for this particular group of disputes, the Tribunal thus appears (at least to some) to yield decisions of unclear precedential value. Millions of dollars have been spent on its operation and hundreds of awards rendered, yet an apparently not uncommon perception is that the work of this, in some respects unique, institution is not applicable elsewhere.

nal, including the mode of appointment and number of arbitrators, the cases of vacancies and so forth. Under article 21 of the Revised General Act the parties may agree to a different mode of establishing the tribunal. See United Nations, *Treaty Series,* vol. 71, p. 101.

An example of a bilateral treaty wholly devoted to the peaceful settlement of disputes is the Treaty for Conciliation, Judicial Settlement and Arbitration (with annexes) between the United Kingdom of Great Britain and Northern Ireland and Switzerland, signed at London on 7 July 1965. Chapter IV of the Treaty is devoted to arbitration. It sets out the number of arbitrators, their nationality and their appointment. It also deals with the question of vacancy and the scope of the competence of the arbitration tribunal. The annex to this Treaty contains recommended rules of procedure for the arbitration tribunal that the parties may wish to choose. Under

article 15 of the Treaty the parties may agree to a different mode of establishment of the arbitral tribunal. * * *

* Reprinted with the permission of the American Society of International Law.

1. The Iran–United States Claims Tribunal was established in 1981 pursuant to the Declaration of the Government of the Democratic and Popular Republic of Algeria (hereinafter General Declaration) and the Declaration of the Government of the Democratic and Popular Republic of Algeria concerning the Settlement of Claims by the Government of the United States of America and the Government of the Islamic Republic of Iran (hereinafter Claims Settlement Declaration), collectively referred to as the Algiers Accords. For the text of the Accords, see 1 Iran–United States Claims Tribunal Reports [hereinafter Iran–U.S. C.T.R.] 3 (1981–2), 75 AJIL 418 (1981).

In one sense, the doubt about the relevance of the Tribunal's work reflects a more fundamental uncertainty about the proper place of the Tribunal and its work within traditional categories of international dispute resolution. Like any truly nagging question, that fundamental uncertainty comes to be phrased in various ways. A phrasing frequently used by scholars inquires into the "nature" of the Tribunal. The assumption apparently underlying this question is that there are basically two distinct types of international arbitration: interstate arbitration such as the *Beagle Channel* arbitration between Chile and Argentina (sometimes referred to here as public international arbitration); and international commercial arbitration such as proceedings between private companies before the International Chamber of Commerce (ICC) (sometimes more broadly referred to here as private international arbitration). Practitioners often regard the inquiry into the nature of the process as irrelevant to lawyering until it is pointed out that many practical questions, such as the enforceability of an award and the ability to challenge an award, turn upon the answer.

* * *

Interstate Arbitration

The internal world of interstate arbitration typically is created and defined by treaty. The agreement to arbitrate and (where applicable) the treaty establishing the responsible institution are the most relevant treaties. The external world may be of little significance for two reasons. So far as the relationship of the customary international legal system to the arbitration is concerned, the international lawmaking capability of the parties may lead to a merging of the internal/external models. The models can collapse into one because states by their agreements both define the internal world of the arbitration *and* modify the applicable international law. In this sense, international law leaves the structuring and conduct of the arbitration entirely in the control of the parties. Consequently, the prime question is whether by their agreement to arbitrate the state parties intend to adopt, supplement or, instead, replace entirely the customary international law that governs such processes. Many agreements to ad hoc arbitration are quite brief and are intended to rest upon the pertinent customary international practice. Even a brief agreement, however, may raise the question whether aspects of customary practice have been displaced.

II.   The Legal System Supervising the Iran–U.S. Claims Tribunal

One of the most innovative and intellectually satisfying aspects of the Algiers Accords is that they establish for the Iran–United States Claims Tribunal a rather complete internal world. There is little need for the parties to request assistance from powers external to the Tribunal. The UNCITRAL Arbitration Rules provide for an appointing authority to resolve disputes between the parties over the composition of the Tribunal. More importantly, the Algiers Accords established a fund, the Security Account, with a portion of the Iranian assets that the United States had frozen. With the Algerian Government acting as escrow agent for the Security Account pursuant to the Tribunal's instructions, the Security

Account assures the availability of funds to satisfy most awards of the Tribunal.

* * *

Another factor in analyzing the Tribunal's relationship to the external legal world is the Tribunal's three primary jurisdictional grants. It must be asked whether the legal system supervising the arbitral process before the Tribunal is a function of the particular basis of jurisdiction. First, the Tribunal may hear "claims of nationals of the United States against Iran and claims of nationals of Iran against the United States" (claims of nationals). Second, the Tribunal has jurisdiction over "official claims of the United States and Iran against each other arising out of [certain] contractual arrangements between them" (official claims). Third, the Tribunal may hear disputes between Iran and the United States concerning the interpretation or performance of any provision of the General Declaration or the interpretation or application of the Claims Settlement Declaration (interpretive disputes). * * *

* * *

Treaty Between the United States and the Russian Federation Concerning the Encouragement and Reciprocal Protection of Investment, April 3, 1992, 31 I.L.M. 794 (1992)*

Article VII[a]

1. Any dispute between the Parties concerning the interpretation or application of the Treaty which is not resolved through consultations or other diplomatic channels, shall be submitted, upon the request of either Party, to an arbitral tribunal for binding decision in accordance with the applicable rules of international law. In the absence of an agreement by the Parties to the contrary, the UNCITRAL Rules, except to the extent modified by the Parties, shall govern.

2. Within two months of receipt of a request, each Party shall appoint an arbitrator. The two arbitrators shall select a third arbitrator as Chairman, who is a national of a third State. The UNCITRAL Rules for appointing members of three member panels shall apply to the appointment of the arbitral panel, except that the appointing authority referenced in those rules shall be the Secretary–General of the Permanent Court of Arbitration.

3. Unless otherwise agreed, all submissions shall be made and all hearings shall be completed within six months of the date of selection of the third arbitrator, and the Tribunal shall render its decisions within two months of the date of the final submissions or the date of the closing of the hearings, whichever is later.

* Reprinted with the permission of the American Society of International Law.

a. Arbitration between a state party and a national or company of the other party is provided in Article VI. Arbitration of cer-tain international law questions is provided in Article 5 of the Investment Incentive Agreement between the United States and the Russian Federation, April 3, 1992, 31 I.L.M. 777 (1992).

4.   Expenses of the Chairman, the other arbitrators, and other costs of the proceedings shall be paid for equally by the Parties. The Tribunal may, however, at its discretion, direct that a higher proportion of the costs be paid by one of the Parties.

SECTION D.   LAW MAKING AND APPLICATION IN THE UNITED NATIONS

Brownlie, Principles of Public International Law
694 (5th Ed., 1998)[b]

The varied roles played by organizations may be distinguished as follows:

(a) Forums for state practice. Statements on legal questions by governments through their representatives in organs and committees of organs provide evidence of customary law. So it is also with the voting on resolutions concerned with legal matters, for example the resolution of the General Assembly affirming the principles of the Nuremberg Charter.

(b) Prescriptive resolutions. A resolution not in itself binding may prescribe principles of international law and be, or purport to be, merely declaratory. However, the mere formulation of principles may elucidate and develop the customary law. When a resolution of the General Assembly touches on subjects dealt with in the United Nations Charter, it may be regarded as an authoritative interpretation of the Charter: obvious examples are the Universal Declaration of Human Rights and the Declaration on the Granting of Independence to Colonial Countries and Peoples contained in resolutions of the General Assembly. Resolutions on new legal problems provide a means of corralling and defining the quickly growing practice of states, while remaining hortatory in form.

(c) Channels for expert opinion. Organizations often establish bodies of legal experts in connection with projects for the codification or progressive development of the law, the most important being the International Law Commission of the United Nations General Assembly, and, like governments, organizations have a staff of legal advisers from whom proceed expert and highly influential opinions.

(d) Decisions of organs with judicial functions. Clearly decisions of judicial organs, such as the Court of Justice of the European Communities, may contribute to the development of the law of treaties, principles of interpretation, and general international law The specialized function of such bodies may of course limit their contribution to the latter.

(e) The practice of political organs. Political organs, and particularly the General Assembly and Security Council of the United Nations, make numerous recommendations and decisions relating to specific issues, which involve the application of general international law, or, where there is no identity of the two, the provisions of the Charter or some other constituent instrument. Such practice provides evidence of the state of the law and also

of the meaning of texts, and has considerable legal significance. However, as with the practice of states, the nature of the particular decision and the extent to which legal matters were considered must be examined before much legal weight is given to the decision. Furthermore, to give legal significance to an omission of an organ to condemn is problematical, since this omission turns often on the political attitude of the majority in the organ concerned. Moreover, many jurists regard the decisions of political organs in terms of the arithmetic of voting, the decisions being taken to represent the views of n states in the majority and their cogency being roughly on a scale n majority divided by n minority states. Obviously states cannot by their control of numbers of international organizations raise in some sense the value of their state practice by reference to the 'practice of organizations'.

In certain instances a consistent and uniform interpretation by members of an organ placed upon a persistent practice, for example, in matters of voting, adopted by *that organ* will be opposable to *all* members provided that there is substantial evidence of general acceptance by members of the organization. On this basis in its Advisory Opinion in the *Namibia* case the International Court rejected the South African argument that the key Security Council resolution was invalid since two permanent members had abstained. The consistent practice of the members of the Security Council had been to interpret such abstention as not constituting a bar to the adoption of resolutions in spite of the provisions of Article 27, paragraph 3, of the Charter which refer to the 'concurring votes' of the permanent members.

(f) External practice of organizations. Organizations may make agreements with member and non-member states and with other organizations, and may present international claims and make official pronouncements on issues affecting them. Subject to what has been said above the need for care in evaluating acts of political organs, the practice of organizations provides evidence of the law.

(g) Internal law-making. Organizations have considerable autonomy in making rules on internal matters such as procedure and the relations of the organization and its staff. Resolutions of organs of the United Nations on questions of procedure create internal law for the members. However, questions of internal powers, for example concerning budgetary control, have a delicate relation to issues as to external ultra vires, if budgetary approval were given to sums allocated for operations under resolutions alleged to be ultra vires the Charter as a whole. The United Nations has developed a code of staff regulations and rules governing the conditions of service of its officials, and the General Assembly has established a United Nations Administrative Tribunal to adjudicate upon applications alleging non-observance of employment contracts of staff members of the Secretariat.

* * *

1 Jennings and Watts, Oppenheim's International Law 114 (1996)*

§ 32 The revision of international law The primary objective of codifications and development of international law as envisaged in Article

* Reprinted with the permission of Oxford University press.

13 of the Charter is to give clear expression to those branches of international law with regard to which there is already either a common measure of agreement or a sufficient amount of practice to warrant attempts at improvement. From the codification and development of international law thus conceived there must be distinguished the deliberate revision and change of existing law with a view to adapting it to changed conditions. The distinction, however, is no longer clear-cut: not only is the process of codification in practice inseparable from a measure of progressive development of the law, but it may involve—as negotiations within the framework of the Third United Nations Law of the Sea Conference demonstrated—conscious attempts to make radical changes to existing law. Nevertheless, there is no machinery of international legislation for effecting changes of this nature against the dissent of a minority of interested states. The establishment of such machinery would amount, to a substantial degree, to setting up an international legislature. That development is not one which governments are at present prepared to accept. Its realization requires further abandonment of the principle of unanimity and far-reaching changes in the matter of equality of voting and representation.

* * *

United Nations Security Council Resolutions on the Persian Gulf Crisis

(Iraq–Kuwait) (1990–1991).

In the course of the 1990–1991 Persian Gulf Crisis, the Security Council adopted a number of measures applying international law to Iraq or creating legal obligations on states in relation to Iraq. In each case the Council acted under Chapter VII of the United Nations Charter in which Article 39 broadly empowers the Council to "decide" on measures to be taken in accordance with Articles 41 and 42. Charter Article 25 provides that "Members of the United Nations agree to accept and carry out the decisions of the Security Council in accordance with the present Charter". Iraq was a member of the United Nations at all relevant times. Portions of a number of those measures are presented in the Documentary Supplement and analyzed in Chapter 15.

CHAPTER 2

THE STRUCTURE OF THE INTERNATIONAL LEGAL SYSTEM: STATES, INTERNATIONAL ORGANIZATIONS AND OTHER ENTITIES

SECTION A. STATES AND STATEHOOD: THE AURA OF SOVEREIGNTY

1. *Nomenclature, Standing, and Role of States.* In the international legal system the terms "nations," "peoples," "states," and "nation-states" are used interchangeably and somewhat imprecisely, from a socio-anthropological standpoint, to refer to the legally-organized political power-structures that are the highest authority in a country, i.e., states. These entities have long been, and still are, the major structural units of the

legal-political order of the planet. Historically, the imprecision noted above goes back to ancient usages, to the times when emperors and kings really ruled their peoples, or nations. States inherited the aura of sovereignty from them. Sovereignty has been the sine qua non of statehood: traditionally there has been no higher earthly authority. States are not often composed of one people, but are still seen as normally exercising the supreme authority over the inhabitants of their territories. They are legally endowed with independence, equality, and the capacity to deal with other states, whether in war or peace. For centuries, states have been the recognized actors in the international legal system, where living persons as such theoretically have had no standing, except through their states. In classical theory, states are the "subjects" of "inter-state" law that they make for themselves, either by accepted custom or by specific agreements. We still call it "inter*national* law," a term coined by Bentham quite casually, and it is too late to change that; but most states rule over more than one race or nationality.

States traditionally, therefore, have had the virtually exclusive role in the evolution of the modern international legal system. Some scholars recently have seen international law as almost entirely the product of the Western World, having entered its "modern" stage at the end of the Thirty Years War, via the treaties made at Westphalia, in 1648, when sovereign equality moved from a few key monarchies, the Holy Roman Empire, and the Holy See, to a number of newly-independent states. See Gross, *The Peace of Westphalia*, 1648–1948, 42 Am.J.Intl.Law 20 (1948); Falk, *The Interplay of Westphalia and Charter Conceptions of International Legal Order*, essay in International Law: A Contemporary Perspective 116 (1985), *"The End of Sovereignty?"*, Roundtable, ASIL Proceedings of the 88th Annual Meeting 71, April 6–9, 1994, and *"A Conversation with Oscar Schachter"* at the end of this Chapter.

However, international organizations now play increasingly important roles as subjects of international law and as major contributors to it. You will see that regional economic integration organizations (REIOs) as supranational organizations have new roles in acting directly and significantly on the legal rights and duties of individuals, companies and other entities in the Members States as well as directly upon the Member States as such. Traditional international organizations which normally function as centers of cooperation among their Member States are also increasingly moving in such fields of human rights law to act directly on the rights and duties of individuals and other non-state entities. Non–Governmental organizations as well are active participants in the development and administration of international law, as seen in the valuable work of the International Committee of the Red Cross. In such major fields as international environment, human rights, world trade and investment law, and in the development of the International Criminal Court, non-governmental organizations have made signal contributions.

It seems that civilization is moving now into an era in which states are not the only subjects of international law and are no longer entirely sovereign. These notions will be studied throughout. Nonetheless, statehood is still highly relevant, perhaps the most relevant, subject-matter in the study of the international legal system. We focus on that in this Section looking at the minimum factual criteria for statehood, the territory of states, and the recognition of states and governments.

————

2. ***The Elements of Statehood.*** The definition of state in Section 201 of the 1987 Restatement may be useful: " * * * an entity which has a defined territory and permanent population, under the control of its own government, and which engages in, or has the capacity to engage in, formal relations with other such entities." This definition does not make reference to any central legal process by which those facts are to be determined. The lack of a central legal process for this purpose stands in contrast to domestic legal systems in which legal entities such as corporations are created by explicitly required legal processes. A corporation can be defined as an entity that has been created by compliance with that prescribed process. No such legal process exists in the case of the formation of entities called states.

The nearest international law analogues are (a) the process by which new members are admitted to the United Nations and (b) the phenomenon known as recognition of the international system. These analogues are imperfect. Admission to the United Nations is not automatically accorded to every entity that meets the factual criteria for statehood, since Article 4 of the Charter lays down additional criteria. Moreover, under exceptional circumstances, public entities that do not fully meet all of the criteria have been admitted into the U.N. As for the process of recognition, (i) there is no central recognizing authority, for each state in the international community makes its own unilateral determination to recognize a new state (or a new government of an existing state) and (ii) there is some disagreement among legal theorists on the question whether the fact of recognition by other states is one of the minimum facts necessary for a new state to come into existence, is merely a neutral acknowledgment of an historical fact, i.e., that a new state has come into existence, or is purely political. The question of recognition will be explored in Section B, *infra*.

If the relevant "factual prerequisites" to statehood are: territory, population, government and engagement or capacity to engage, in foreign relations, what normal legal consequences follow from establishment of these facts? Some of these consequences can be gleaned from an examination of the charters of international organizations. Extracts from the United Nations Charter, the Charter of the Organization of American States, the Statute of the International Court of Justice, the Vienna Conventions on the Law of Treaties and on Diplomatic Relations, and related materials are set out below (and more fully in the Documentary Supplement). In the Documentary Supplement, see also the Declaration on Principles of International Law Concerning Friendly Relations and Cooperation among States, adopted by the General Assembly in 1970. Note the emphasis on independence, territorial inviolability and equality.

————

UNITED NATIONS CHARTER
Article 3

The original Members of the United Nations shall be the states which, having participated in the United Nations Conference on International Organization at San Francisco, or having previously signed the Declaration by United Nations of 1 January 1942, sign the present Charter and ratify it in accordance with Article 110.

Article 4

1. Membership in the United Nations is open to all other peace-loving states which accept the obligations contained in the present Charter and, in the judgment of the Organization, are able and willing to carry out these obligations.

2. The admission of any such state to membership in the United Nations will be effected by a decision of the General Assembly upon the recommendation of the Security Council.

CHARTER OF THE ORGANIZATION OF AMERICAN STATES
Article 9

States are juridically equal, enjoy equal rights and equal capacity to exercise these rights, and have equal duties. The rights of each State depend not upon its power to ensure the exercise thereof, but upon the mere fact of its existence as a person under international law.

Statute of the International Court of Justice

Article 34–1. Only states may be parties in cases before the Court.

Vienna Convention on the Law of Treaties
Article 1

Scope of the present Convention

The present Convention applies to treaties between States.[1]

Vienna Convention on Diplomatic Relations of April 18, 1961

Article 48

The present Convention shall be open for signature by all States Members of the United Nations or of any of the specialized agencies or

1. Compare Article 3 of this Convention on the subject of other international agreements.

Parties to the Statute of the International Court of Justice, and by any other State invited by the General Assembly of the United Nations to become a Party to the Convention * * *.

Minimum facts for statehood not clearly present. It is easy enough to identify entities of long standing as states and to concede that whatever one normally believes to be the rights and duties of states inheres in those entities. France is a state, without doubt, and has the normal rights and duties of a state. The same can be said for most of the members of the United Nations.

But cases may arise when evidence of the factual criteria to support a finding of statehood are either not clearly discernible, or when parties to a controversy take differing views on the existence or non-existence of the facts, or when essential facts clearly do not exist. What, then, are the rights and duties of such an entity? For example, as a result of political compromise it was agreed at the founding of the United Nations that two of the federal states of the Union of Soviet Socialist Republics would be admitted to the United Nations as members: Byelorussian Soviet Socialist Republic and Ukranian Soviet Socialist Republic. The founders of the United Nations agreed to this compromise, even though these units of the USSR did not freely engage in international relations with the rest of the world. This did not prevent these Members from exercising the rights flowing from U.N. membership (subject of course to the influence of the USSR over them) during the long period before they achieved independence from the USSR.

Thus political entities which did not satisfy the minimum factual criteria for statehood were treated, at least for purposes of membership in the United Nations, as though they were states. *Did they thereby become states*? This is not just an abstract question. Rather, the lawyer is presented with the concrete issue: whether such an entity, not fully meeting the factual criteria for statehood, will or will not have a given legal right and obligation normally accorded to states, this attribute to be identified as problems arise. How should his cluster of questions be treated in any future cases in which an entity does not fulfill completely the criteria for statehood?

Acceleration of changes in the roster of states: Over the years, a number of entities accepted as states exhibited somewhat unusual characteristics, such as the Holy See, Namibia, the two Koreas, and the two Germanies. The United States continued recognition of Estonia, Latvia, and Lithuania, although they were administered by the Soviet Union as internal sub-entities for many years. The "mini-state" phenomenon has also appeared. Yet solutions to problems of this kind have been emerging from changed factual situations and from policy changes. The three Baltic states are free again; in 1991 they became members of the U.N. The two Germanies are one. Czechoslovakia split peaceably into two states. The Soviet Union has become the Russian Federation, with some unusual characteristics for some of its internal units. Ukraine is an independent state, as is former Byelorussia, the two one-time second and third UN votes of the USSR; and a number of new states now exist in former territories of the USSR. The former Yugoslavia has sanguinously fractured into a number of states, with perhaps more to come. Somalia and Haiti suffer all but complete disappearance of effective internal order. Palestine edges toward becoming an independent state (see *Klinghoffer v. S.N.C. Achille Lauro*, 937 F.2d 44 (2d Cir.1991), perhaps East Timor as well. Tension persists over the question of one China (unified with Taiwan) or two Chinas (Taiwan as a separate state). Meanwhile, more former colonial territories have become states or may be expected to achieve that status, some of them "micro"-ministates.

Might it be anticipated that the current "inflation" of statehood will alter, in some particulars, the status of statehood itself? What would you foresee as possible consequences and problems?

In re Citizenship of X[a]

Federal Republic of Germany, Administrative Court of Cologne, 1978.

Report by Stefan Riesenfeld, 77 A.J.I.L. 160 (1983).

Plaintiff, a German citizen by birth, obtained a document, issued on August 26, 1975, conferring upon him citizenship of the "Duchy of Sealand." The so-called Duchy consists of a former anti-aircraft platform, erected by the United Kingdom approximately 8 nautical miles off its southern coast, outside its [then] territorial waters. The platform rests on strong pillars connecting it with the seabed, and it has an area of approximately 1,300 square meters. The British forces abandoned the installation after the end of World War II, and in 1967 a British army officer, Major R.B., took possession and proclaimed it the Duchy of Sealand. Major R.B. issued a constitution for his territory, assuming the title of Roy of Sealand. At present, 106 persons are citizens of the Duchy of Sealand, and 40 persons reside on it. Plaintiff occupies the office of Minister of Foreign Affairs and President of the State Council.

Plaintiff instituted proceedings for a declaratory judgment establishing loss of his German nationality by virtue of his having acquired the citizenship of a foreign nation. The court dismissed the action for the reason that the Duchy of Sealand did not qualify as a foreign state under international law and therefore could not confer foreign nationality so as to warrant loss of German citizenship in accordance with the German Law on Nationality of 1913.

The court held that to constitute a state under international law three essential attributes had to be present,. territory, population, and government. The Duchy of Sealand lacked at least two of these. First, territory must consist of a naturally created portion of the earth's surface and not of a man-made island. Second, population denotes a group of persons leading a common life and forming a living-community, a bond that did not exist

a. Reprinted by permission of the American Society of International Law among the citizens of the Duchy of Sealand, not even among the 40 persons staying on the platform.

This case is another unsuccessful attempt to establish a new state on an artificial island in order to escape the laws of the coastal state. Similar efforts in Italy and the United States have also failed.

———

Questions. Was the ruling on the character of territory requisite to statehood based on law? What other characteristics might have been considered? Distance from a mainland or natural island? Permanence of the installation? What of a permanent undersea colony on the ocean floor? Or a space station? Should that question await technological developments and population growth by the year 2500? The Sealand saga did not end with the German case discussed above.

For more about Sealand, visit http://www.sealandgov.com/ and see "L'homme qui voulait être prince" *Le Monde*, 14 June 2000, p. 14. Consider possible roles (with corresponding problems for states) that Sealand and like locations might play in the world of Internet transactions.

———

Statehood in United Nations practice. Denial of United Nations membership to a political entity is at best ambiguous on the question of statehood. Under Article 4 of the Charter, admission of new members is not automatic but requires affirmative action by two political bodies, the Security Council and the General Assembly. The reasons for non-admission can be numerous, unspecified, and in fact based upon political criteria having no relation to the legal indicia of statehood.

When an entity is admitted to membership in the United Nations before meeting the standard minimum criteria for statehood as defined by international law, is one to assume that the members have acted illegally or, at least, outside the law? Or are the members saying that the purposes of the Charter may be fulfilled when an entity is well on the way to meeting those criteria and that it is thus a state as that term is used in Article 4 of the Charter?

Qualitative factors as elements of statehood? The generally accepted definition of statehood does not include qualitative factors, except as they may be subsumed under the rubric of capacity to engage in formal relations with other states (which probably also denotes the ability to carry out their obligations under international law) Should the size of an entity's territory be a factor? The size of its population? Its gross national product? Its ability to survive without foreign aid? Such factors have not been considered relevant in international law. Statehood is a question of fact; a question of power. If an aggregation of people claim that they are independent and *can get away with it,* international law recognizes that fact. There are many reasons why a people may wish to separate from a particular state. *See,* inter alia, the Declaration of Independence of the United States. The means of secession are various: force of arms; force of public opinion (a major factor in the rise to statehood of former colonial peoples); agreement due to their own lack of economic or militarily strategic value to any other state.

Newly independent states want the dignity, prestige and overt recognition of their independence that flow from United Nations membership. Not surprisingly, the major powers sometimes chafe at the notion that a vote in the organization by a member with a population of less than 100,000 is as significant as that of China with its population of well over one billion. However, the so-called "mini-state" problem is less significant than a decade ago, as one has become habituated to the phenomenon.

----

3.   *The Territorial Element in Statehood.*

Acquisition of land territory. The existence of a state is conditioned upon its occupation of a defined area. Territory often correlates with the other organic requirements for statehood: the requirement of a defined population and the requirement of a government in control of it.

Historically, competition for the acquisition of land territory has been a main feature of the rise of the nation state and the source of bitter and violent conflicts as well. Conquest was a common and legally recognized form of acquisition of title to territory, and this mode of establishing a right to permanent occupation of a defined area is not extinct, though it occurs much less frequently than it used to. Peaceful means of title acquisition, such as purchase, prescription, and, as to water boundaries, accretion (but not avulsion) also developed. Usually any state-to-state land transfer is eventually formalized by international agreement providing for cession. Discovery, once a major means of land acquisition, is no longer possible for lack of land to discover. All known land is owned by one state or another, except for the Antarctic continent. The Arctic is not land, but, as it is said in Russian, "the Northern Frozen Ocean". "Territory" in "Outer Space" is another issue considered in Chapter 5.

Antarctica, once subject to various claims, including discovery and sectorial longitudinal projections, is immunized from national territorial claims by an "internationalizing" agreement, the *Antarctic Treaty* of December 1, 1959, 12 U.S.T. 794, 402 U.N.T.S. 71. It entered into force on June 23, 1961, upon the deposit of ratifications by all the signatory states: Argentina, Australia, Belgium, Chile, France, Japan, New Zealand, Norway, Union of South Africa, Union of Soviet Socialist Republics, United Kingdom and the United States.

The intent of the treaty is to ensure that Antarctica shall be used exclusively for peaceful purposes and not become the object of international discord. It is to promote freedom of and international cooperation in scientific investigation in the area. Article 4 provides that nothing in the treaty shall be interpreted as a renunciation of asserted rights of sovereignty or bases for claims of sovereignty by the parties, or prejudice their recognition or non-recognition of claims by other states. It further states that the acts or activities of the parties taking place within Antarctica shall not constitute a basis for asserting, supporting or denying claims of sovereignty there or for creating rights of sovereignty therein.

As to the maritime territory of states, see Chapter 4, and as to their airspace above their land and maritime territory, see Chapter 5.

Territorial boundaries. Over the centuries, many contests between states concerning territorial questions have been over the location of land boundaries delimiting their respective areas of sovereignty. Even when allocations of territory have been agreed upon by two or more states, the actual boundary demarcation problem remains.

In parts of the earth where allocations of territory have been stable for a long time, and descriptions and demarcations of boundaries made long ago, there is still controversy over portions of boundaries involving small areas. The issue may be resolved by litigation before the International Court of Justice, as in the *Case Concerning Sovereignty Over Certain Frontier Land,* (Belgium v. Netherlands), [1959] I.C.J.Rep. 209. Or it may be resolved by some other settlement, as in the Italian Peace Treaty of February 10, 1948, where provisions were made for changes in the Franco–Italian boundary. A border issue was also involved in the case before the International Court of Justice concerning the *Temple of Preah Vihear* (Cambodia v. Thailand), [1962] I.C.J.Rep. 6. Hostilities over a border question broke out between India and Pakistan in 1965 and the issue was submitted to arbitration. *Rann of Kutch Arbitration,* 1968, 7 I. L.M.633 (1968). In 2000, the bitter dispute between India and Pakistan risked war, possibly even the use of nuclear weapons. The People's Republic of China and India have been embroiled over the years in border disputes which flare up occasionally into limited hostilities. Old boundary disputes contributed to the causes of the armed conflict between Iraq and Iran beginning in 1980, and between Iraq and Kuwait resulting in the Persian Gulf War. See Chapter 14. Indeed in 1993, the Security Council settled the demarcation of the boundary between Iraq and Kuwait (Res 833 of 27 May 1993, 32 I.L.M. 1463 (1993)), demanded that the two states respect the inviolability of the boundary, and underlined and affirmed its decision to guarantee its inviolability.

It would be all but pointless to try to derive specific international law principles from boundary cases because the issues nearly always have a long particularized history and often come down to a matter of interpretation of agreements. There is an exception to this, however, when the boundary between two states is a navigable river, where the location of the boundary is the *thalweg,* i.e. the middle of the channel of navigation. See the *1965 Restatement,* Section 12, which also states that when the boundary between two states is a non-navigable river or lake, its location is in the middle of the river or lake. For the settlement of the *Chamizal Boundary Dispute* between the United States and Mexico, which involved the Rio Grande, see 49 U. S. State Dept. Bull. 199 (1963).

Newly independent states. Since World War II, the breaking-up of colonial empires has brought about the creation or re-emergence of a substantial number of independent states which previously were dependent territories of a colonial power or were subjected in various degrees to administrative control by another state, e.g., mandates or trusteeships. The break-up of the USSR and the Socialist Federal Republic of Yugoslavia led to the creation of additional new states. These events and the merger of East Germany with the Federal Republic have created difficult problems of succession, including those concerning succession to territorial boundary treaties.

At its 1972 Session, the International Law Commission adopted *Draft Articles* on the Succession of States in Respect of Treaties, II Yearbook of the International Law Commission 1972, at 223. Part V of the draft is entitled: Boundary Regimes or Other Territorial Regimes Established by a Treaty.

Rights over territory short of title. A state may cede to another a portion of its territory, just as a person may pass title to his property in private law. Also, just as rights in property short of title may be created in private law, so it is in international law with respect to the territory of a state. A state may lease to another a portion of its territory for a term of years. The convention between the United States and Panama of November 18, 1903, granted to the United States in perpetuity the use, occupation and control of a ten-mile strip of Panamanian territory for the purpose of constructing and operating a ship canal, and in this zone the United States exercised all the rights it "would possess and exercise if it were the sovereign of the territory" to the entire exclusion of the exercise by Panama of any such sovereign rights. For discussion of the termination of this convention, see Chapters 11 and 12.

Supreme Court of Canada: Reference Re: Secession of Quebec

August 2, 1998, 37 I.L.M. 1340 (1998).

[The Governor in Council of Canada referred to the Supreme Court questions concerning the right of Quebec to secede from Canada. After giving a negative response to the first question (Can Quebec secede unilaterally under Canada's constitution?), the Court turned to the second question: (Can Quebec unilaterally secede under international law?]

B. *Question 2*

Does international law give the National Assembly, legislature or government of Quebec the right to effect the secession of Quebec from Canada unilaterally? In this regard, is there a right to self-determination under international law that would give the National Assembly, legislature or government of Quebec the right to effect the secession of Quebec from Canada unilaterally?

109 For reasons already discussed, the Court does not accept the contention that Question 2 raises a question of "pure" international law which this Court has no jurisdiction to address. Question 2 is posed in the context of a Reference to address the existence or non-existence of a right of unilateral secession by a province of Canada. The amicus curiae argues that this question ultimately falls to be determined under international law. In addressing this issue, the Court does not purport to act as an arbiter between sovereign states or more generally within the international community. The Court is engaged in rendering an advisory opinion on certain legal aspects of the continued existence of the Canadian federation. International law has been invoked as a consideration and it must therefore be addressed.

110 The argument before the Court on Question 2 has focused largely on determining whether, under international law, a positive legal right to unilateral secession exists in the factual circumstances assumed for the purpose of our response to Question 1. Arguments were also advanced to the effect that, regardless of the existence or non-existence of a positive right to unilateral secession, international law will in the end recognize effective political realities—including the emergence of a new state—as facts. While our response to Question 2 will address considerations raised by this alternative argument of "effectivity", it should first be noted that the existence of a positive legal entitlement is quite different from a prediction that the law will respond after the fact to a then existing political reality. These two concepts examine different points in time. The questions posed to the Court address legal rights in advance of a unilateral act of purported secession. While we touch below on the practice governing the international recognition of emerging states, the Court is as wary of entertaining speculation about the possible future conduct of sovereign states on the international level as it was under Question 1 to speculate about the possible future course of political negotiations among the participants in the Canadian federation. In both cases, the Reference questions are directed only to the legal framework within which the political actors discharge their various mandates.

(1) *Secession at International Law*

[The Supreme Court's Summary of conclusions are set forth below. In reaching these conclusions, the Court's citations of authority included the following: R. Y. Jennings, *The Acquisition of Territory in International Law* (1963) at pp. 8–9; A. Cassese, *Self–Determination of Peoples: A legal reappraisal* (1995) at pp. 171–72; K, Doehring, "*Self–Determination*" in B. Simma, ed., *The Charter of the United Nations: A Commentary* (1994) at pp. 60, 70; United Nations Charter, Articles 1 and 55; Article 1 of the International Covenant on Civil and Political Rights, 999 U.N.T.S. 171 and the International Covenant on Economic, Social and Cultural Rights,993 U.N.T.S. 3; the Declaration on Principles of International law Concerning Friendly Relations and Co-operation Among States in Accordance with the Charter of the United Nations, GA Res. 2625 (XXV), 24 October 1970; the Vienna Declaration and Programme of Action, adopted by the U,N, World Conference on Human Rights, A/Conf. 157/24, 25 June 1993; the Declaration on the Occasion of the Fiftieth Anniversary of the United Nations, GA RES 50/6, 9 November 1995; the Final Act of the Conference on Security and Co-operation in Europe, 14 I.L.M. 1292 (1972) (Part VIII); H.W.R. Wade, *The Basis of Legal Sovereignty* [1955] Camb. L.J. 172, 196; the *European Community Declaration on the Guidelines on the Recognition of New States in Eastern Europe and in the Soviet Union*, 31 I.L.M. 1485 (1992) p. 1487 (set *forth below in Section B*); S.A. de Smith, *Constitutional Lawyers in Revolutionary Situations* [1968] 7 West. Ont.L. Rev. 93, 96, and Reference re Manitoba Language Rights [1985] 1 S.C.R. 721, 753.]

          * * *

IV.   *Summary of Conclusions*
          * * *

154 We have also considered whether a positive legal entitlement to secession exists under international law in the factual circumstances con-

templated by Question 1, i.e., a clear democratic expression of support on a clear question for Quebec secession. Some of those who supported an affirmative answer to this question did so on the basis of the recognized right to self-determination that belongs to all "peoples". Although much of the Quebec population certainly shares many of the characteristics of a people, it is not necessary to decide the "people" issue because, whatever may be the correct determination of this issue in the context of Quebec, a right to secession only arises under the principle of self-determination of peoples at international law where "a people" is governed as part of a colonial empire; where "a people" is subject to alien subjugation, domination or exploitation; and possibly where "a people" is denied any meaningful exercise of its right to self-determination within the state of which it forms a part. In other circumstances, peoples are expected to achieve self-determination within the framework of their existing state. A state whose government represents the whole of the people or peoples resident within its territory, on a basis of equality and without discrimination, and respects the principles of self-determination in its internal arrangements, is entitled to maintain its territorial integrity under international law and to have that territorial integrity recognized by other states. Quebec does not meet the threshold of a colonial people or an oppressed people, nor can it be suggested that Quebecers have been denied meaningful access to government to pursue their political, economic, cultural and social development. In the circumstances, the National Assembly, the legislature or the government of Quebec do not enjoy a right at international law to effect the secession of Quebec from Canada unilaterally.

155 Although there is no right, under the Constitution or at international law, to unilateral secession, that is secession without negotiation on the basis just discussed, this does not rule out the possibility of an unconstitutional declaration of secession leading to a de facto secession. The ultimate success of such a secession would be dependent on recognition by the international community, which is likely to consider the legality and legitimacy of secession having regard to, amongst other facts, the conduct of Quebec and Canada, in determining whether to grant or withhold recognition. Such recognition, even if granted, would not, however, provide any retroactive justification for the act of secession, either under the Constitution of Canada or at international law.

156 The reference questions are answered accordingly.

Judgment accordingly.

SECTION B. RECOGNITION OF STATES AND THEIR GOVERNMENTS

1. RECOGNITION POLICY AND LAW

1 Jennings and Watts, Oppenheim's International Law 127 (9th Ed.,1996)*

§ 38 **Recognition in general** In a broad sense recognition involves the acceptance by a state of any fact or situation occurring in its relations with

---

* Reprinted with the permission of Oxford University press.

other states. In the context of recognition of states and governments, however, recognition is of particular significance. It is of great importance both as a device of international law and as a political act of the state granting recognition. Because of its important legal and political consequences, recognition in this particular sense must be distinguished from a looser use of the term conveying mere acknowledgement or cognisance of an existing situation.

Recognition is accorded to a particular body in a particular capacity. Thus usually a community is recognised as a sovereign state, or an administration is recognised as the government of such a state. But circumstances may call for recognition only in some special capacity: for example, a régime may be recognised only as the government of that part of the territory of the state which it controls, or a community may be recognised as something else than a sovereign state.

The grant of recognition is an act on the international plane, affecting the mutual rights and obligations of states, and their status or legal capacity in general. Recognition also has consequences at the national level, as where the application of rules of municipal law is affected by a decision to recognise a new state or government. Furthermore, the rules of international law relating to recognition are rules of customary international law, and their application in particular circumstances may be modified by treaty obligations.

§ 39   Recognition and membership of the international community The international community is composed primarily of states. Any changes in the composition of the international community are of immediate concern to existing states, whether those changes involve members of that community (usually states) or the authorities (usually governments) through which they act. The matter is of legal importance because it is when an entity becomes a member of the international community that it thereupon becomes bound by the obligations, and a beneficiary of the rights, prescribed by international law for states and their governments.

There is, however, no settled view whether recognition is the only means through which a new state becomes part of the international community. On the one view if a new state comes into existence as a matter of fact, it thereupon enters into the international community and becomes of right an international person regardless of whether it has been recognised.

Although in practice recognition is necessary to enable every new state to enter into official intercourse with other states, theoretically every new state becomes, according to this view, a member of the international community *ipso facto* by its rising into existence: recognition is thus viewed as purely declaratory or confirmatory in nature, supplying only the necessary evidence of the fact of a state's existence.

The opposed view is that it is a rule of international law that no new state has a right as against other states to be recognised by them; that no state has a duty to recognise a new state; that a new state before its recognition cannot claim any right which a member of the international community has as against other members; and that it is recognition which constitutes the new state as a member the international community.

The problem is largely theoretical because state practice is inconclusive and may be rationalised either way. The international community is still largely decentralised. The extent to which a new state is able to participate in the international community is in practice largely determined by the extent of its bilateral relationships with other states, which in turn depends primarily on its recognition by them. Only by being granted recognition is a new state fully admitted by an existing state into its circle of bilateral relationships within the framework of international law; this is precisely what the existing state intends when granting recognition, and what it knows it is preventing when withholding recognition. The grant of recognition by a state is a unilateral act affecting essentially bilateral relations, and neither constitutes nor declares the recognised state to be a member of the international community as a whole. Recognition of a new state by only one state will make it an international person to the limited extent of its relations with that state, but such limited personality cannot realistically be regarded as membership of the international community in general. That is the result of recognition by a significant number of existing states, for example by a sufficient majority to secure admission to the major multilateral organisations. Such a degree of recognition is usually present when, but is unlikely to be present unless, the new state is in effective existence in fact.

The overwhelming practice of states does not accept that the mere claim of a community to be an independent state automatically gives it a right to be so regarded, or that an existing state is justified in recognising or refusing to recognise a new community as a state in disregard of whether it fulfils the factual requirements of statehood. While the grant of recognition is within the discretion of states, it is not a matter of arbitrary will or political concession, but is given or refused in accordance with legal principle. That principle, which applies alike to recognition of states, governments, belligerents, or insurgents, is that, when certain conditions of fact (not in themselves contrary to international law) are shown to exist, recognition is permissible and is consistent with international law in that it cannot (as may recognition accorded before those facts are clearly established) be considered to constitute intervention; and that, while recognition is accordingly declaratory of those facts, it is also constitutive of the rights and duties of the recognised community in its relations with the recognising state.

     * * *

Although not always consistent, the bulk of state practice probably supports the view that governments do not deem themselves free to grant or refuse recognition to new states in an arbitrary manner, by exclusive reference to their own political interests, and regardless of legal principle. Undoubtedly, quite apart from the element of discretion left to states in assessing the facts concerning the existence of a new state and in determining the timing of an act of recognition, it is unavoidable that political considerations from time to time influence the grant or refusal of recognition; some states, indeed, go further and assert that recognition is essentially a matter within their political discretion. It may be, however, that it is largely a matter of degree, since there probably are no states which do not allow some role to considerations of policy, while those states which treat recognition as a matter of policy do not usually in practice disregard the imperatives to which a new state's effective existence gives rise. These variations do not affect the essential legal nature of the process of recognition. Recognition, while declaratory of an existing fact, is constitutive in its nature, at least so far as concerns relations with the recognising state. It marks the beginning of the effective enjoyment of the international rights and duties of the recognized community.

Query: What should be the policy of the international community on the question of recognition of territory taken in violation of the U. N. Charter Article 2.4 rule against the threat or use of force? In the 1990–1991 Gulf Crisis, after Iraq invaded and occupied Kuwait, the territory of Kuwait was incorporated into Iraq as the 19th province of that country. The Security Council adopted a policy of non-recognition of this action in S.C. Res. 662 of 9 August, 1990. The Security Council implemented that policy by deciding that "the annexation has no legal validity, and is considered null and void", and called upon all States and international organizations not to recognize the annexation either directly or indirectly, and by demanding that " * * *Iraq rescind its actions purporting to annex Kuwait" (see text in the Documentary Supplement). See also 1987 *Restatement*, The Foreign Relations Law of the United States § 203.

European Community: Declaration on Yugoslavia and on the Guidelines on the Recognition of New States

December 16, 1991, 31 I.L.M. 1485 (1992).*

DECLARATION ON YUGOSLAVIA

(Extraordinary EPC Ministerial Meeting, Brussels, 16 December 1991)

The European Community and its member States discussed the situation in Yugoslavia in the light of their guidelines on the recognition of new states in Eastern Europe and in the Soviet Union. They adopted a common position with regard to the recognition of Yugoslav Republics. In this connection they concluded the following:

The Community and its member States agree to recognise the independence of all the Yugoslav Republics fulfilling all the conditions set out below. The implementation of this decision will take place on January 15, 1992.

They are therefore inviting all Yugoslav Republics to state by 23 December whether:

— they wish to be recognised as independent States;

— they accept the commitments contained in the above-mentioned guidelines;

* Reprinted with the permission of the American Society of International Law.

— they accept the provisions laid down in the draft Convention— especially those in Chapter II on human rights and rights of national or ethnic groups—under consideration by the Conference on Yugoslavia;

— they continue to support

— the efforts of the Secretary General and the Security Council of the United Nations, and

— the continuation of the Conference on Yugoslavia.

The applications of those Republics which reply positively will be submitted through the Chair of the Conference to the Arbitration Commission for advice before the implementation date.

In the meantime, the Community and its member States request the UN Secretary General and the UN Security Council to continue their efforts to establish an effective cease-fire and promote a peaceful and negotiated outcome to the conflict. They continue to attach the greatest importance to the early deployment of a UN peace-keeping force referred to in UN Security Council Resolution 724.

The Community and its member States also require a Yugoslav Republic to commit itself, prior to recognition, to adopt constitutional and political guarantees ensuring that it has no territorial claims towards a neighbouring Community State and that it will conduct no hostile propaganda activities versus a neighbouring Community State, including the use of a denomination which implies territorial claims.

DECLARATION ON THE "GUIDELINES ON THE RECOGNITION OF NEW STATES IN EASTERN EUROPE AND IN THE SOVIET UNION"

* * *

In compliance with the European Council's request, Ministers have assessed developments in Eastern Europe and in the Soviet Union with a view to elaborating an approach regarding relations with new states.

In this connection they have adopted the following guidelines on the formal recognition of new states in Eastern Europe and in the Soviet Union:

"The community and its Member States confirm their attachment to the principles of the Helsinki Final Act and the Charter of Paris, in particular the principle of self-determination. They affirm their readiness to recognise, subject to the normal standards of international practice and the political realities in each case, those new states which, following the historic changes in the region, have constituted themselves on a democratic basis, have accepted the appropriate international obligations and have committed themselves in good faith to a peaceful process and to negotiations."

Therefore, they adopt a common position on the process of recognition of these new states, which requires:

— respect for the provisions of the Charter of the United Nations and the commitments subscribed to in the Final Act of Helsinki and in the Charter of Paris, especially with regard to the rule of law, democracy and human rights;

— guarantees for the rights of ethnic and national groups and minorities in accordance with the commitments subscribed to in the framework of the CSCE;

— respect for the inviolability of all frontiers which can only be changed by peaceful means and by common agreement;

— acceptance of all relevant commitments with regard to disarmament and nuclear non-proliferation as well as to security and regional stability;

— commitment to settle by agreement, including where appropriate by recourse to arbitration, all questions concerning state succession and regional disputes.

The Community and its Member States will not recognise entities which are the result of aggression. They would take account of the effects of recognition on neighbouring states.

The commitments to these principles opens the way to recognition by the Community and its Member States and to the establishment of diplomatic relations. It could be laid down in agreements.

Brussels, The Hague, 16 December 1991

———

Recognition of Governments

1 JENNINGS AND WATTS, OPPENHEIM'S INTERNATIONAL LAW 146 (9th Ed.,1996)*

§ 42 Recognition of new heads and governments of old states
Recognition of a change in the headship of a state, or in its government, or in the title of an old state, are matters of importance. But such recognition must not be confused with recognition of the state itself. If a foreign state refuses to recognise a new Head of State or a change in the government of an old state, the latter does not thereby lose its recognition as an international person, although no formal official intercourse is possible between the two states as long as recognition is not given either expressly or tacitly. Recognition of a government as the government of a state presupposes, and will normally imply, recognition of a state. If no state is recognised, the 'government' cannot be recognised as the government of a state, although it may be recognised in some other capacity.

* * *

§ 43 When coming into power normally and constitutionally On the accession of a new Head of State, other states are as a rule notified and usually recognise the new head of State by some formal act such as a

* Reprinted by permission of Allyn & Bacon/Longman.

message of congratulations; in the case of a normal constitutional change of government there is usually no such formal notification or recognition. In practice, when a new Head of State has come into his position in a normal and constitutional manner, such as succession to the throne on the death of the reigning monarch or at a presidential election, recognition is a matter of course; as it also is where a state changes its constitutional form from, for instance, a monarchy to a republic, in a constitutional manner and without anything in the nature of a revolution. Nor would there be any question of withholding recognition of the new government after a change in the government following elections. In such cases recognition causes no difficulties and often takes place informally and by implication from a continuation of normal bilateral diplomatic dealings in such a way as to leave no doubt as to the intention to continue recognition.

§ 44 When coming into power abnormally and in a revolutionary manner When, however, the new Head of State or government comes into power not in a constitutional manner but after a *coup d'etat,* a revolution (which need not involve bloodshed), or any other event involving a break in legal continuity, the determination by other states of the attitude to be adopted towards the new Head of State or government is often difficult. They are called upon to decide whether the new authority can be properly regarded as representing the state in question.

Such a decision is unavoidable, since states act through their governments and most if not all aspects of international relations depend upon acceptance of a government's right to act and speak for the state. The decision that a new government may properly represent the state concerned is not, however, one which needs to be formally or publicly announced, and a number of states, including since 1980 the United Kingdom, now follow the policy of not doing so. Instead, the nature of their relations with an authority claiming to be the government of a state is determined by and deduced from the circumstances of each case: recognition will be more a matter of implication than of express declaration. In deciding whether formally to recognise a new government, or whether the circumstances are such that relations with it should be those which are normal between governments, the recognising state exercises a discretion which, although necessarily wide, is not arbitrary.

* * *

§ 45 Criteria for recognition of governments As with recognition of new states, so also with recognition of governments the decision is not one determined solely by political considerations on the part of the recognising state. A government which is in fact in control of the country and which enjoys the habitual obedience of the bulk of the population with a reasonable expectancy of permanence, can be said to represent the state in question and as such to be deserving of recognition. The preponderant practice of states, in articular that of the United Kingdom, in the recognition of governments has been based on the principle of effectiveness thus conceived.

* * *

46 *De facto* Recognition States granting recognition often distinguish between *de jure* and *de facto* recognition. These terms are convenient but elliptical: the terms *de jure* or *de facto* qualify the state or government recognised rather than the act of recognition itself. Those terms are in this context probably not capable of literal analysis, particularly in terms of the *ius* to which recognition *de jure* refers. The distinction between *de jure* and *de facto* recognition is in essence that the former is the fullest kind of recognition while the latter is a lesser degree of recognition, taking account on a provisional basis of present realities. Thus *de facto* recognition takes place when, in the view of the recognising state, the new authority, although actually independent and wielding effective power in the territory under its control, has not acquired sufficient stability or does not as yet offer prospects of complying with other requirements of recognition.

Thus after the First World War, the governments of various new states, such as Finland, Latvia and Estonia, which formerly constituted part of the Russian Empire, were recognised in the first instance as *de facto* governments pending the final territorial settlement in that part of the world. The Government of the Soviet Union, although, to all appearances, firmly and effectively established, was recognised for a number of years after its establishment by many states *de facto* only on the ground that, in their view, it was unwilling to fulfil its international obligations in such matters as compensation for the confiscated property of foreign subjects and acknowledgement of liability for financial obligations incurred by its predecessors. Recognition of a government de facto may be limited to such areas as are actually under its control. Such recognition will often in time be replaced by the grant of *de jure* recognition. While *de facto* recognition usually falls to be considered in the context of new states or governments, it may also be relevant in other circumstances such as the extension of a state's territory or its absorption of another previously independent state.

* * *

Roth, Governmental Illegitimacy in International Law*

p. 253ff, 1999.

* * *

Apart from the special circumstances of "colonial, alien, or racist domination", the international community has made every effort to avoid judgments regarding the legitimacy of member state governments. Officially, it has no process for conferring collective recognition on governments. Recognition and non-recognition continue to be spoken of as political acts within the sovereign discretion of individual states, and a regime's legal capacity to assert rights, incur obligations and authorize acts on behalf of state is subject to no systematic process of authoritative determination. Yet international bodies cannot evade the responsibility of collective legal recognition; where rival ruling apparatuses purport to act in the name of the

* Reprinted with the permission of the
Oxford University Press.

political community, the question of a putative government's legal capacities thrusts itself upon the international community.

* * *

Collective bodies must, inevitably, assess the legitimacy of rival ruling apparatuses in determining (1) whether to accept state delegation credentials issued by a putative government; and (2) whether to condemn foreign military assistance rendered to a putative government. The two questions, both occasioned by conditions of internal armed conflict, are frequently very closely connected: the putative government that gains the seat is poised to establish which foreign military assistance is duly "invited", and which constitutes unlawful intervention. Notwithstanding the disclaimers rendered by its participants, the credentials process serves as a process of collective legal recognition.

In its first 45 Years, the U.N. General Assembly was the site of eight major credentials contests. One case, South Africa, has been elaborated above under the heading of self-determination, and another controversy, concerning Israel, turned on matters of external behavior (and, implicitly, the legitimacy of the political community itself) rather than on the capacity of the ruling apparatus to represent the political community. The other cases were: China (Nationalists v. Communists, 1949–71); Hungary (Soviet-installed Kadar Government, 1956–63); Congo–Leopoldville (President Kasavubu v. ousted Prime Minister Lumumba, 1960); Yemen (Egyptian-backed Republic v. ousted monarchy, 1962); Cambodia I (Lon Nol Government v. Royalist-backed Khmer Rouge insurgency, 1973–74); and Cambodia II (Vietnamese-installed "People's Republic" v. "Democratic Kampuchea" resistance, 1979–90).

Regional bodies have faced analogous contests with implications for the admissibility of foreign involvement in internal armed conflict. In January 1976, the Organization of African Unity faced the choice of admitting the People's Republic of Angola, thereby recognizing the MPLA government at the expense of the rival "Democratic People's Republic of Angola", both of which were backed by foreign troops. In June 1979, the Organization of American States faced the choice of "prematurely" withdrawing recognition of Nicaragua's Somoza government in favor of the Sandinista-led Provisional government, which was being assisted by neighboring states.

* * *

A. U.N. Credentials and Collective Legal Recognition

1. The U.N. Credentials Process

> ... From the standpoint of legal theory, the linkage of representation in an international organization and recognition of a government is a confusion of two institutions which have superficial similarities but are essentially different.
>
> The recognition of a new State, or of a new government of an existing State, is a unilateral act which the recognizing government can grant or withhold....

... On the other hand, membership of a State in the United
Nations and representation of a State in organs is clearly determined by a collective act of the appropriate organ.

So noted a U.N. Legal Memorandum in 1950, as it sought to grapple with
problem of Chinese representation, the first of the U.N. credentials controversies. It is the General Assembly's practice to accept delegation credentials where they have been properly issued by the head of state, head of
government or foreign minister of a member state; where delegations
present credentials issued by officials of rival ruling apparatuses, the
General Assembly is forced to choose which ruling apparatus shall represent the state in that body. In emphasizing that the credentials process is
not a form of collective recognition, the quoted Legal Memorandum sought
to reassure the wary that U.N. representation is without prejudice to
member states' political disapproval—expressed by a denial of recognition—of the government that the seated delegation represents.

The Memorandum sidestepped the larger issue: the need to establish
with clarity for the international community which of two contestants is
the bearer of the state's rights, powers and responsibilities at international
law. If the credentials decision is a collective process, whereas the recognition decision is a matter of individual state prerogative, the need for
coherence in the international legal system clearly argues for the former to
be preferred as the arbiter of legal capacity.

* * *

The United Nations Charter nowhere expressly grants the General
Assembly the capacity to make so weighty a determination, whether
declaratory or constitutive, regarding the legal legitimacy of governments.
The Charter's drafters apparently understood that [i]n the course of the
operations from day to day of the various organs of the Organization, it is
inevitable that each organ will interpret such parts of the Charter as are
applicable to its function. Since, as one expert has put it, "the General
Assembly's exercise of authority in [this area] is based not on a grant of
authority in the Charter but on necessity, the scope of such authority is
defined by and is coextensive with the necessity that gave rise to it". * * *

More generally, a General Assembly vote on credentials gauges the
balance of legal opinion in the international community on the question of
which contestant apparatus is entitled to represent the state in deliberations on international problems. Where the vote goes overwhelmingly in
favor of one of the contestants, the collective *opinio juris* has far-reaching
implications: it is either constitutive of a putative government's *de jure*
status or persuasively declaratory of the presence of underlying facts
sufficient to establish that status.

Thus, a General Assembly vote on credentials cannot be dissociated
from the matter of legal recognition, notwithstanding that a simple majority decision on a delegation's credentials may be insufficient to resolve the
issue of the putative government's legal capacity to assert rights, incur
obligations and authorize acts on behalf of the state. (By contrast, a joint
decision of the General Assembly and Security Council to admit a putative
state to the United Nations establishes clearly the entity's legal entitlement

to the protections of the international system, as the discourse on Bosnia–Herzegovina reflects). There is thus ample basis to take credentials decisions seriously.

* * *

Unban the Taliban?

It is Time to Recognize the Taliban as the Rulers of Afghanistan*

The Economist, July 13, 1999, p. 19.

Diplomats can recognise a duck when they see one: if it looks, acts and quacks like a duck, it's a duck. So why can't they recognise the Taliban? Over the past three years, the Taliban have been looking, acting and quacking like the government of Afghanistan, yet only three countries—all Muslim—recognise them as such.

Afghanistan badly needs a recognisable government. Like many another country, it is an artificial affair, a cartographical concept matched on the ground not by a harmonious nation but by peoples who have fought each other for generations, and been fought over by outsiders for just as long. Sometimes seen as a buffer state, it has proved better at providing shocks than at absorbing them. It has certainly not provided stability of government.

Yet, under the Taliban, something like a stable government seems to have emerged * * *. Though they are still challenged by opposition groups, their grip on the 90% of the country that they now control is hardly in doubt. After the setback to peace talks in Ubekistan this week, the opposition is left with the choice of resuming, in due course, the search for a power-sharing agreement or of seeking contentment in an extended sulk. It has little prospect of gaining power through victory on the battlefield. So why does the West not give diplomatic recognition to Afghanistan's rulers?

The answer is that the Taliban are a bunch of Islamic Zealots who treat their own people, especially their women, with scant regard for modern liberal norms, and would dearly love to see others treated in the same way. Several countries in their neighbourhood, notably Russia, India and Iran, regard them with the utmost suspicion. The United States regards them with horror. They give sanctuary to militants—some would say terrorists—including Osama bin Laden, who is accused by America of masterminding the blowing-up of its embassies in Kenya and Tanzania last year. If the Taliban are ducks, they are undeniably ugly ducks.

Moreover, some would argue that, whatever the old rules of diplomacy, times have moved on. Nowadays, ex-dictators like Augusto Pinochet find themselves arrested on medical trips to London, NATO goes to war to stop ethnic cleansing in Kosovo, and the world is trying to set up an international criminal court. Morality is now the name of the game. The Taliban may be no more wicked than the Soviet Union was; they may be no more

* Reprinted with the permission of the Economist.

destabilising than China; they may treat women no worse than the Saudis do; but sooner or later new rules must be brought in. Now is the time.

Yet diplomatic recognition need not be the enemy of morality. Countries recognise each other not because they like or approve of their counterparts' politics, but because they must deal with them. Western countries have plenty to discuss with Afghanistan: drugs, human rights and terrorism, for a start. By all means seek to win concessions in return for diplomatic recognition, but do not imagine that all the benefits of having the Taliban accepted in world counsels lie with them; it is very much in the interests of all sorts of outsiders to see the rulers of Afghanistan crack down on the export of both drugs and terror. And those who preach morality should want to see the better treatment of Afghan citizens too. The motto for the West should be recognise and pressurise. Isolation, after all, does not necessarily breed moderation. Conversation, by contrast, may.

----

2.   SOME PROBLEMS OF NONRECOGNITION IN DOMESTIC JUDICIAL PROCEEDINGS AND IN EXECUTIVE DEPARTMENTS

By far the majority of legal issues concerning recognition and nonrecognition have arisen in domestic courts. The classic issue has been: in the absence of diplomatic recognition of a state or of a regime by the pertinent department or branch of the forum state government, may such entity or regime be treated by domestic courts as having juridical existence? The courts of a forum state may be incapable of acting at all. Or, the courts might feel that the characterizations of parties as state entities or as governments should be made by the diplomatic branch. The courts, however, might make such decisions for themselves. If so, what law would they apply? International? Principles of law common to the world's major legal systems? Judicial notice? Analogies to the private law of entities such as corporations?

Access to courts. Access to courts was denied to the non-recognized Soviet government in a number of states. See, *R.S.F.S.R. v. Cibrario*, 235 N.Y. 255, 139 N.E. 259 (1923). The non-recognized Soviet government was refused the right to sue in *Soviet Government v. Ericsson*, Sweden, Supreme Court, 1921, [1919–1922] Ann.Dig. 54 (No. 30). The outcome was the same in *Societé Despa v. USSR*, Belgium, Court of Appeal of Liège, 1931, Pasicrisie II, 108 (1931). In *USSR v. Luxembourg and Saar Company*, Luxembourg, Tribunal of Commerce of Luxembourg, 1935, Sirey, IV, 26 (1936), the USSR was allowed to sue but on the ground it had been impliedly recognized by Luxembourg and hence the bar against bringing the suit had been removed. In some states, however, the unrecognized regime has been allowed to sue. *Commercial Representation of the USSR v. Levant Red Sea Coal Co.*, Egypt, Tribunal of Alexandria, 1933, 62 J.Dr. Int'l 199 (1935); *Republic of the South Moluccas v. Netherlands New Guinea*, Netherlands, District Court of the Hague, 1954, 21 Int'l L.Rep. 48

(1957). The policy to deny an unrecognized government access to courts does not extend to corporations or its assignee owned by the unrecognized government. *See* 1987 *Restatement*, Comment *a* to Section 205 and Reporters' Note 1 to that section setting forth United States cases in point.

Non–Recognition Distinguished From Severance of Diplomatic Relations

Banco Nacional de Cuba v. Sabbatino
United States Supreme Court, 1964.
376 U.S. 398, 84 S.Ct. 923, 11 L.Ed.2d 804.

[Banco Nacional, an instrumentality of the Cuban government, brought an action in the Federal District Court for the Southern District of New York alleging conversion of bills of lading representing sugar previously expropriated by the Cuban government; the action seeks recovery of proceeds from the sale of the sugar. At the outset several procedural questions were presented to the court, one of which was dealt with when Mr. Justice HARLAN delivered the opinion of the court, as follows.]

* * *

It is first contended that this petitioner, an instrumentality of the Cuban Government, should be denied access to American courts because Cuba is an unfriendly power and does not permit nationals of this country to obtain relief in its courts. * * * If the courts of this country should be closed to the government of a foreign state, the underlying reason is one of national policy transcending the interests of the parties to the action, and this Court should give effect to that policy sua sponte even at this stage of the litigation.

Under principles of comity governing this country's relations with other nations, sovereign states are allowed to sue in the courts of the United States * * *. [P]rior to some recent lower court cases which have questioned the right of instrumentalities of the Cuban Government to sue in our courts, the privilege of suit has been denied only to governments at war with the United States * * *.

Respondents, pointing to the severance of diplomatic relations, commercial embargo, and freezing of Cuban assets in this country, contend that relations between the United States and Cuba manifest such animosity that unfriendliness is clear, and that the courts should be closed to the Cuban Government. We do not agree. This Court would hardly be competent to undertake assessments of varying degrees of friendliness or its absence, and, lacking some definite touchstone for determination, we are constrained to consider any relationship, short of war, with a recognized sovereign power as embracing the privilege of resorting to United States courts. Although the severance of diplomatic relations is an overt act with objective significance in the dealings of sovereign states, we are unwilling to say that it should inevitably result in the withdrawal of the privilege of bringing suit. Severance may take place for any number of political reasons, its duration is unpredictable, and whatever expression of animosity it may imply does not approach that implicit in a declaration of war.

It is perhaps true that non-recognition of a government in certain circumstances may reflect no greater unfriendliness than the severance of diplomatic relations with a recognized government, but the refusal to recognize has a unique legal aspect. It signifies this country's unwillingness to acknowledge that the government in question speaks as the sovereign authority for the territory it purports to control * * *. Political recognition is exclusively a function of the Executive. The possible incongruity of judicial "recognition," by permitting suit, of a government not recognized by the Executive is completely absent when merely diplomatic relations are broken.

* * *

The Lawmaking Authority of Unrecognized Governments

A.M. Luther Co. v. James Sagor & Co.

England, Court of Appeal, 1921.
[1921] 3 K.B. 532, 539.*

BANKES, L.J. The action was brought to establish the plaintiff company's right to a quantity of veneer or plywood which had been imported by the defendants from Russia. The plaintiffs' case was that they are a Russian company having a factory or mill at Staraja in Russia for the manufacture of veneer or plywood, and that in the year 1919 the so-called Republican Government of Russia without any right or title to do so seized all the stock at their mill and subsequently purported to sell the quantity in dispute in this action to the defendants. The plaintiffs contended that the so-called Republican Government had no existence as a government, that it had never been recognized by His Majesty's Government, and that the seizure of their goods was pure robbery. As an alternative they contended that the decree of the so-called government nationalizing all factories, as a result of which their goods were seized, is not a decree which the Courts of this country would recognize.

The answer of the defendants was two-fold. In the first place they contended that the Republican Government which had passed the decree nationalizing all factories was the de facto Government of Russia at the time, and had been recognized by His Majesty's Government as such, and that the decree was one to which the Courts of this country could not refuse recognition. Secondly they contended that the plaintiff company was an Estonian and not a Russian company * * *. Roche, J. decided the two main points in the plaintiffs' favour. Upon the evidence which was before the * * * judge I think that his decision was quite right. As the case was presented in the Court below the appellants relied on certain letters from the Foreign Office as establishing that His Majesty's Government had

* Reprinted with the permission of The Incorporated Council of Law Reporting for England and Wales, London.

recognized the Soviet Government as the de facto Government of Russia. The principal letters are referred to by the learned judge in his judgment. He took the view that the letters relied on did not establish the appellants' contention. * * * I entirely agree.

In this Court the appellants asked leave to adduce further evidence, and as the respondents raised no objection, the evidence was given. It consisted of two letters from the Foreign Office dated respectively April 20 and 22, 1921. The first is in reply to a letter dated April 12, which the appellants' solicitors wrote to the Under Secretary of State for Foreign Affairs, asking for a "Certificate for production to the Court of Appeal that the Government of the Russian Socialist Federal Soviet Republic is recognized by His Majesty's Government as the de facto Government of Russia." To this request a reply was received dated April 20, 1921, in these terms: "I am directed by Earl Curzon of Kedleston to refer to your letter of April 12, asking for information as to the relations between His Majesty's Government and the Soviet Government of Russia. (2.) I am to inform you that His Majesty's Government recognize the Soviet Government as the de facto Government of Russia." The letter of April 22 is in reply to a request for information whether His Majesty's Government recognized the Provisional Government of Russia, and as to the period of its duration, and the extent of its jurisdiction. The answer contains (inter alia) the statement that the Provisional Government came into power on March 14, 1917, that it was recognized by His Majesty's Government as the then existing Government of Russia, and that the Constituent Assembly remained in session until December 13, 1917, when it was dispersed by the Soviet authorities. The statement contained in the letter of April 20 is accepted by the respondents' counsel as the proper and sufficient proof of the recognition of the Soviet Government as the de facto Government of Russia.

 * * *

* * * [U]pon the construction which I place upon the communication of the Foreign Office to which I have referred, this Court must treat the Soviet Government, which the Government of this country has now recognized as the de facto Government of Russia, as having commenced its existence at a date anterior to any date material to the dispute between the parties to this appeal.

An attempt was made by the respondents' counsel to draw a distinction between the effect of a recognition of a government as a de facto government and the effect of a recognition of a government as a government de jure, and to say that the latter form of recognition might relate back to acts of state of a date earlier than the date of recognition, whereas the former could not. Wheaton quoting from Mountague Bernard states the distinction between a de jure and a de facto government thus (1): "A de jure government is one which, in the opinion of the person using the phrase, ought to possess the powers of sovereignty, though at the time it may be deprived of them. A de facto government is one which is really in possession of them, although the possession may be wrongful or precarious." For some purposes no doubt a distinction can be drawn between the effect of the recognition by a sovereign state of the one form of government or of the other, but for the present purpose in my opinion no distinction can be drawn. The Government of this country having, to use the language just quoted, recognized the Soviet Government as the Government really in possession of the powers of sovereignty in Russia, the acts of that Government must be treated by the Courts of this country with all the respect due to the acts of a duly recognized foreign sovereign state.

* * *

Since writing this judgment a further communication from the Foreign Office dated May 4, 1921, has been supplied by the respondents' solicitors to the members of the Court, and to the appellants' solicitors. The communication was made to a firm of solicitors interested in some other litigation. In the communication the writer states that he is instructed to state that His Majesty's Government recognize the Soviet Government of Russia as the de facto Government of that country as from March 16, 1921. I have ascertained that the words "as from" should be read "as on." So read the communication adds nothing to the information already before the Court and I need not refer to it further.

[Other opinions omitted.]

———

The Problem of one China or two. In 1949, at the close of the civil war in China between the Nationalist authority of Chiang kai-shek and the communists led by Mao Zedong, the defeated Nationalists repaired to Taiwan and the communists established on the mainland the Peoples Republic of China (PRC). Until 1979 the United States continued to recognize only the Taiwan regime as "China". At the United Nations the Taiwan authorities continued to represent "China" as a member of that organization. This could not, of course, continue forever, and eventually consideration was given to the recognition of the PRC and its communist government. Part of that problem was: what to do about Taiwan as "China".

Some states, including the United States, have viewpoints on record that do not exclude the possibility that the recognition of a regime as a government can be withdrawn; see the 1987 Restatement Section 203(f) and Reporter's Note 3. When it recognized the People's Republic of China as the government of all the territory of the state of China, the United States "derecognized" the regime on Taiwan as the government of even a part of the territory (Taiwan) of the state of China and invoked the termination clause in the Mutual Defense Treaty with Taiwan. *See* Unger (the last American ambassador to Taiwan), *Derecognition Worked*, Foreign Policy No. 36,105 (Fall 1979). What is United States cognition of the regime on Taiwan following the resumption of relations with a government on the mainland? The Joint Communiqué states that "the people of the United States will maintain cultural, commercial, and other unofficial relations with the people of Taiwan." A Presidential memorandum, *Relations with the People on Taiwan*, December 30, 1978 provides that all programs with the people of Taiwan will be carried out through "an unofficial instrumentality in corporate form, to be identified shortly." The 1979 Taiwan Relations Act, 22 USC § 3301 et seq., identifies this instrumentality as The American Institute of Taiwan, 22 USC § 3305. Section 4 of the Public Law, 22 USC § 3303, provides very interestingly for the continuation in legal effect so far as the United States is concerned "of laws of the United States with respect to Taiwan." Congressional oversight of the act is provided, 22 USC § 3313. For detail as to the institute, consult 22 USC §§ 3306 through 3312, and 3315. In October, 1980, an arrangement as to immunities for the United States personnel of the American Institute was concluded with the regime on Taiwan.

Richard M. Nixon established political relations with the People's Republic of China, having begun to indicate a shift in the United States position early in his first administration. Diplomatic relations between the United States and Beijing were formally established by the *Joint Communiqué on the Establishment of Diplomatic Relations between the United States of America and the People's Republic of China*, January 1, 1979, U.S. Dept. of State Bull., January 1979, pp. 25–26, in which each of the parties agreed to recognize the other, a formula that the People's Republic had insisted upon with other well-recognized states, such as the United Kingdom and France, when these, some years earlier, shifted relations from Taiwan to Beijing. Agreements were concluded—and became effective at signature on January 31, 1979,—concerning: Consular Relations, 30 U.S.T. 17; Cultural Relations, 30 U.S.T. 26; and Scientific Cooperation, 30 U.S.T. 35.

On May 11, 1979 an Agreement on the Settlement of Claims was signed (effective at signature) 30 U.S.T. 19. The United States waived the nationalization claims of itself and its nationals for takings on or after October 1, 1949, for a lump sum payment of $80.5 million, the United States to be solely responsible for its distribution among claimants. The People's Republic waived claims arising from the blocking of Chinese assets after December 17, 1950; and the United States agreed to unblock these assets and further agreed [Art. II(b)] " * * * that prior to unblocking * * * it will notify the holders of blocked assets which the records of the Government of the United States indicate are held in the name of residents of the PRC that the Government of the PRC requests * * * not be transferred or withdrawn without its consent." An Agreement on Trade Relations came into force on February 1, 1980, 31 U.S.T. 4651.

———————

Notes & Questions. In view of the unofficial relations maintained with Taiwan by so many states, should it be considered to be a state, although perhaps a state a bit different from the usual? Why should that not be possible? In fact, it appears that the American Institute of Taiwan functions like an embassy and actually all U.S. relations with Taiwan are much like those with any state or government. Are there not entities, such as the Holy See, which do not meet the requirements expected of a state in the traditional sense? According to Reporters' Note 8 to Section 201 of the 1987 *Restatement*, the authorities on Taiwan do not even claim that it is a state. See *International Agreements and U.S.–Taiwan Relations*, 22 Harv. I.L.J. 451 (1981). On July 9, 1999, Taiwan President Lee Teng-hui made a suggestion that Taiwan–Chinese relations should be reclassified as "special state-to-state" ties, but Beijing responded with hostile rhetoric and threats of the use of force to prevent the "independence" of Taiwan, notwithstanding that Taiwan continues to function in most respects as a fully independent state. (*see* New York Times, 13 July 1999, p. A1, Col, 1).

SECTION C. OTHER STRUCTURES AND ELEMENTS OF THE INTERNATIONAL SYSTEM

1. International Organizations and the United Nations System: A Collective But "Softer" Sovereignty?

Although the keystone of the international system in operation remains the "sovereign" state, seen close-up in the preceding Section, possible competitors over the past hundred years or so have been visible on or over the horizon. Has the development and recent integration of the United Nations system and other intergovernmental organizations caused the disintegration of sovereignty? Have competitors to state sovereignty arrived? If not, do they have a reasonable prospect of arriving in the foreseeable future? To consider those questions, you need to look at some of the defining legal characteristics of international organizations, especially those which have a generally worldwide or "universal" membership of states and which exercise a number of specified powers and functions more or less in parallel to those of states. We focus primarily on the United Nations system in which are found some seventeen organizations in addition to the U.N. itself, qualified under Article 57 of the Charter as Specialized Agencies. These include:

International Labor Organization (ILO)

Food and Agriculture Organization (FAO)

United Nations Educational, Scientific and Cultural Organization (UNESCO)

World Health Organization (WHO)

World Bank Group:

   International Bank for Reconstruction and Development (IBRD)

   International Development Association (IDA)

   International Finance Corporation (IFC)

   Multilateral Investment Guarantee Agency (MIGA)

International Monetary Fund (IMF)

International Civil Aviation Organization (ICAO)

Universal Postal Union (UPU)

International Telecommunication Union (ITU)

World Meteorological Organization (WMO)

International Maritime Organization (IMO)

World Intellectual Property Organization (WIPO)

International Fund for Agricultural Development (IFAD)

United Nations Industrial Development Organization (UNIDO).

Although the United Nations and each of its specialized agencies is legally independent in accordance with its respective constituent treaty, those organizations have many parallel structural and operational elements and coordinate their activities on a regular and systematic basis.

A much larger group of other organizations operates outside of the United Nations system. Some are universal, others regional or functional or technical. These include the World Trade Organization (WTO), International Atomic Energy Agency (AIEA), North Atlantic Treaty Organization (NATO), Organization for Economic Co-operation and Development (OECD), Council of Europe, International Energy Agency (IEA), Organization of Petroleum Exporting Countries (OPEC), Organization of American States (OAS), Organization of African Unity (OAU) and Western European Union (WEU), to mention only a few of the several hundred existing international organizations (I.O.s) in this category. The European Union, fully worthy of separate discussion in Subsection 2 below, is a "regional economic integration organization" exercising quite extensive powers, making it perhaps *sui generis*.

International organizations are sometimes referred to as "public international organizations" or "intergovernmental organizations" to distinguish them from *Nongovernmental Organizations (NGOs)* which are also important actors in the international system as you will see in Subsection 3 below. NGOs are normally established under and are governed by a *national legal system* rather than international law. However, the international organizations considered in this Subsection *are* established under and pursuant to *international law,* in each case by a treaty, to which the Vienna Convention on the Law of Treaties applies (see Article 5; the text is found in the Documentary Supplement).

International organizations are not yet properly characterized as "states", of course. I.O.s have no territory as such but hold private titles of ownership or rights under leases to the real property they occupy at their headquarters or other locations. Organizations also lack populations in the sense that states are populated with individual human beings and various forms of domestic entities made subject to the states' clearly sovereign powers. Organizations, however, do have constituent states as members and do exercise certain powers with respect to them. They have Secretariats which correspond broadly to national civil services and are subject to institutional command. Organizations do enjoy international legal personality as required for the full and effective exercise of their functions. The comparison becomes more blurred, however, when we look at the criterion of a "government" exercising independent (or "sovereign") control over the "population" and having effective power to engage in foreign relations. Some institutional elements analogous to government are present in international organizations, and they do carry out "foreign relations" in the regular use of diplomatic forms and in entering into legally binding treaty relations. In the U.N. system (as well as in other organizations) there are internal bodies fulfilling some legislative-like functions, notably the U.N. Security Council and the General Assembly, but they are subject to the extensive limitations set forth in the United Nations Charter. There is an "executive" type function exercised by the Secretary–General and the

Secretariat, again with limited although potentially far reaching powers. There is also a judicial "branch", in the form of the International Court of Justice, the Law of the Sea Tribunal, and the forthcoming International Criminal Court, but with limitations on jurisdiction provided in the constituent instrument of each. Are the elements of statehood present here in more than merely a formal or theoretical legal sense?

a. ***Legal Personality.*** Perhaps a threshold question is whether the U.N. enjoys the capacity to act as an institution in its own name through the device of international legal personality, as states do. Functional legal personality is provided clearly in Article 104 of the Charter: "in the territory of each of its Members," but the Charter is silent about the territory of non-Members and sheds little direct light on the question of the U.N.'s capacity to pursue international claims as states may do on behalf of themselves and their nationals. These questions were presented in one of the earliest advisory cases brought to the International Court of Justice. In reaching its conclusions favorable to United Nations powers, the Court considered some of the broader issues of the function and nature of the United Nations. See the *Reparations Case*, below in this Section.

If the United Nations enjoys sufficient international legal personality to pursue an international claim, the Organization also enjoys under the applicable texts the capacity to enter into contracts, to acquire and dispose of immovable property and movable property as well as to institute legal proceedings (see Section 1 of the Convention on the Privileges and Immunities of the United Nations, in the Documentary Supplement). On the international level, these are powers analogous to those of states which in fact enjoy more legal status than legal personality and capacity. Under the international law doctrine of sovereign immunity taken up in Chapter 7, states also enjoy effective immunity from the jurisdiction of other states. The United Nations and other organizations enjoy immunities similar in most respects to those applicable to states, perhaps even more protective immunities. *See,* Ch. 7, § B. Moreover, a House of Lords ruling emphasized that an international organization is not regarded as merely an unincorporated association of states in which the member states would be exposed to liability for debts of the organization in case of its insolvency; in *Australia and New Zealand Banking Group Ltd. et al. v. Commonwealth of Australia and 23 others*, [1989]; 29 I.L.M. 670 (1990), the House of Lords rejected claims that the member states of the International Tin Council should be liable for the unsatisfied debts of the Council. Does this suggest an analogy with states?

Another question is whether, as legal entities separate from their member states, organizations are empowered to enter into international treaties. They do so regularly under powers specifically provided in their respective constituent treaties or inferred from Article 104 of the U.N. Charter and similar provisions for other organizations. The treaty power is now clearly recognized in the Vienna Convention on the Law of Treaties Between States and International Organizations or Between International Organizations (25 I.L.M. 543 (1986), in early 2001 with 38 signatories and 33 parties but not in force)); see Report of the International Law Commission on the Work of its Thirty-fourth Session, ORGA 34th Sess.Supp. No. 10, A/37/10). Is the treaty power another line of analogy?

b. ***Legislative power.*** The United Nations' legislative power may also be compared to that of states, but here the differences are perhaps more striking. Chapter 14, below considers the several legislative measures adopted by the Security Council during the Persian Gulf Crisis. When framed in obligatory terms, those decisions are binding on the states to which they are addressed (Charter Articles 2.2 and 25), and may be acted upon as applicable to non-Members as well (Article 2.6). Are those institutional arrangements indicia of "government?"

But what about the effect of United Nations decisions on individuals? Are Security Council embargo decisions, for example, binding upon individuals and companies in the member states? How does that compare with national legislative powers? Where does sovereignty lie with respect to embargo decisions? How may they be enforced? Viewing them from Saddam Hussein's perspective at the close of Desert Storm, would you expect him to have a different response from yours? From that of Presidents Bush or Clinton? The "Statute" of the newly created I.C.C. functions as a "penal code" for specified international crimes. Individuals will be prosecuted, convicted and punished for committing those offenses.

Does the U.N. system include a "Super–Legislature"? Would you consider it wise to characterize the U.N. as including a Super–Legislature? Or to establish one?

One other way of looking at legislative powers in the U.N. is that decisions are often made *by* the members and *for* the members themselves. These decisions are often made quite independently of the U.N. in the treaty process or by international custom. In acting through the U.N., rather than by direct diplomacy, have nations not merely changed place and procedure? At times that might be true, but would it be true when one third of the Members is outvoted in the General Assembly? Nine members of the Security Council, including the five permanent members, can legally bind the entire membership in the neighborhood of 188 states. Some non-members can be compelled to comply. Do these situations affect your assessment of the possible "sovereignty" of the United Nations? When a member or non-member refuses to comply and the U.N. does nothing, does that mean that the decision was non-binding?

c. ***Executive power.*** In the United Nations, the executive power is divided between the Secretary–General and the member states themselves. The powers of the Secretary–General as provided in Chapter XV of the Charter are largely dependant upon actions of the Security Council and the General Assembly. Enforcement actions are adopted by the Security Council under Chapter VII on Action with Respect to Threats to the Peace, Breaches of the Peace and Acts of Aggression, (or possibly by the General Assembly under the Uniting for Peace Resolution), and are carried out by the Member States with quite far-reaching and powerful consequences, as will be seen in Chapter 14 below. In enforcement actions, the most consequential of all organization activities, there has always been a *political* decision to be taken as part of the *operational* one. That carries the obvious advantage in a decentralized sanction system of ensuring that the political will exists for the decision to be implemented but also the clear disadvantage of risking failure to take the decision and the loss of enforcement and deterrence when the political will is weak or entirely absent. How does this element of "government" compare to its national counterpart?

d. ***Judicial Institutions.*** International judicial institutions have been described in some detail in Chapter 1. Jurisdiction over responding parties and access by international organizations present some of the major difficulties. How would you compare the ICJ with a national sovereign's judicial jurisdiction over disputing citizens or institutions on the domestic scene? Organizations themselves suffer a serious infirmity with respect to contentious cases, by virtue of their access to the Court being denied under Article 36 of the Court's Statute, which admits only States. While the U.N. and Specialized Agencies are generally afforded access in *advisory* cases (only), even that avenue is shut off for other organizations, such as the WTO, Council of Europe, NATO, OECD and all others outside of the U.N. system. Action under Charter Article 94.2 to enforce an ICJ judgment requires a prior political decision in the Security Council, subject to the veto. How does that compare to the enforcement of domestic court judgments under national sovereignties? Can the U.N. create *ad hoc* War Crimes Tribunals? A permanent International Criminal Court? If so, by what authority? It has already created Ad Hoc Tribunals for the Former Yugoslavia and Rwanda by decisions of the Security Council. The I.C.C. is in the process of creation by separate treaty. See discussion in Chapter 16.

e. ***Compulsory Funding.*** The organizations in the United Nations system are largely dependent upon the member states for financing of their operations; however, the decisions on budget levels and funding are made by the competent organ in each case. For the U.N. itself, the rules are contained in Article 17 of the Charter along lines which established the pattern for most other organizations both within and without the U.N. system. Article 17 provides that the General Assembly shall consider and approve the budget of the Organization. The expenses of the Organization shall be borne by the Members as apportioned by the General Assembly. The General Assembly shall consider and approve any financial and budgetary arrangements with specialized agencies referred to in Article 57 and shall examine the administrative budgets of such specialized agencies with a view to making recommendations to the agencies concerned.

United Nations funding consists of assessed contributions of the members, voluntary contributions and income from sales and services. In adopting the budgets and fixing the assessed contributions of members, the General Assembly acts by a two-thirds majority of the members present and voting (Article 18.2), with each member having one vote irrespective of its share in the financing. The Assembly's powers are stated in terms which make it clear that these decisions are legally binding on *all* of the members, including those in opposition. (See the International Court of Justice opinion in *Certain Expenses of the United Nations* (Advisory Opinion), in Chapter 14, in which the Court answered in the affirmative the question: "Do the expenditures authorized in General Assembly resolutions * * * relating to the United Nations operations in the Congo * * * and the expenditures authorized in General Assembly resolutions * * * relating to the operations of the United Nations Emergency Force * * * constitute 'expenses of the Organizations' within the meaning of Article 17, paragraph 2, of the Charter of the United Nations?'')

————

What does the foregoing tell us about whether the U.N.'s sovereignty is "hard", "soft" or non-existent?

————

Reparation for Injuries Suffered in the Service of the United Nations

International Court of Justice, Advisory Opinion, April 11, 1949.
1949 I.C.J. 174.

[The General Assembly submitted the following legal question to the Court for an advisory opinion:

Question I: In the event of an agent of the United Nations in the performance of his duties suffering injury in circumstances involving the responsibility of a State, has the United Nations, as an Organization, the capacity to bring an international claim against the responsible de jure or de facto government with a view to obtaining the reparation due in respect of the damage caused (a) to the United Nations, (b) to the victim or to persons entitled through him? (Question II is omitted)].

THE COURT:

* * *

Competence to bring an international claim is, for those possessing it, the capacity to resort to the customary methods recognized by international law for the establishment, the presentation and the settlement of claims. Among these methods may be mentioned protest, request for an enquiry, negotiation, and request for submission to an arbitral tribunal or to the Court in so far as this may be authorized by the Statute.

This capacity certainly belongs to the State; a State can bring an international claim against another State. Such a claim takes the form of a claim between two political entities, equal in law, similar in form, and both the direct subjects of international law. It is dealt with by means of negotiation, and cannot, in the present state of the law as to international jurisdiction, be submitted to a tribunal, except with the consent of the States concerned.

When the Organization brings a claim against one of its Members, this claim will be presented in the same manner, and regulated by the same procedure. It may, when necessary, be supported by the political means at the disposal of the Organization. In these ways the Organization would find a method for securing the observance of its rights by the Member against which it has a claim.

But, in the international sphere, has the Organization such a nature as involves the capacity to bring an international claim? In order to answer this question, the Court must first enquire whether the Charter has given the Organization such a position that it possesses, in regard to its Members, rights which it is entitled to ask them to respect. In other words, does the Organization possess international personality? This is no doubt a doctrinal expression, which has sometimes given rise to controversy. But it will be used here to mean that if the Organization is recognized as having that personality, it is an entity capable of availing itself of obligations incumbent upon its Members.

To answer this question, which is not settled by the actual terms of the Charter, we must consider what characteristics it was intended thereby to give to the Organization.

* * *

The Charter has not been content to make the Organization created by it merely a centre 'for harmonizing the actions of nations in the attainment of these common ends' (Article I, para. 4). It has equipped that centre with organs, and has given it special tasks. It has defined the position of the Members in relation to the Organization by requiring them to give it every assistance in any action undertaken by it (Article 2, para. 5), and to accept and carry out the decisions of the Security Council; by authorizing the General Assembly to make recommendations to the Members; by giving the Organization legal capacity and privileges and immunities in the territory of each of its Members; and by providing for the conclusion of agreements between the Organization and its Members. Practice—in particular the conclusion of conventions to which the Organization is a party—has confirmed this character of the Organization, which occupies a position in certain respects in detachment from its Members * * *

In the opinion of the Court, the Organization was intended to exercise and enjoy, and is in fact exercising and enjoying, functions and rights which can only be explained on the basis of the possession of a large measure of international personality and the capacity to operate upon an international plane. It is at present the supreme type of international organization, and it could not carry out the intentions of its founders if it was devoid of international personality. It must be acknowledged that its Members, by entrusting certain functions to it, with the attendant duties and responsibilities, have clothed it with the competence required to enable those functions to be effectively discharged.

Accordingly, the Court has come to the conclusion that the Organization is an international person. That is not the same thing as saying that it is a State, which it certainly is not, or that its legal personality and rights and duties are the same as those of a State. Still less is it the same thing as saying that it is 'a super-State', whatever that expression may mean. It does not even imply that all its rights and duties must be upon the international plane, any more than all the rights and duties of a State must be upon that plane. What it does mean is that it is a subject of international law and capable of possessing international rights and duties, and that it has capacity to maintain its rights by bringing international claims.

The next question is whether the sum of the international rights of the Organization comprises the right to bring the kind of international claim described in the Request for this Opinion. That is a claim against a State to obtain reparation in respect of the damage caused by the injury of an agent of the Organization in the course of the performance of his duties. Whereas a State possesses the totality of international rights and duties recognized by international law, the rights and duties of an entity such as the Organization must depend upon its purposes and functions as specified or implied in its constituent documents and developed in practice. The functions of the Organization are of such a character that they could not be effectively discharged if they involved the concurrent action, on the international plane, of fifty-eight or more Foreign Offices, and the Court concludes that the Members have endowed the Organization with capacity to bring international claims when necessitated by the discharge of its functions.

* * *

The Charter does not expressly confer upon the Organization the capacity to include, in its claim for reparation, damage caused to the victim or to persons entitled through him. The Court must therefore begin by enquiring whether the provisions of the Charter concerning the functions of the Organization, and the part played by its agents in the performance of those functions, imply for the Organization power to afford its agents the limited protection that would consist in the bringing of a claim on their behalf for reparation for damage suffered in such circumstances. Under international law, the Organization must be deemed to have those powers which, though not expressly provided in the Charter, are conferred upon it by necessary implication as being essential to the performance of its duties. This principle of law was applied by the Permanent Court of International Justice to the International Labour Organization in its Advisory Opinion No. 13 of July 23rd, 1926 (Series B., No. 13, p. 18), and must be applied to the United Nations.

Having regard to its purposes and functions already referred to, the Organization may find it necessary, and has in fact found it necessary, to entrust its agents with important missions to be performed in disturbed parts of the world. Many missions, from their very nature, involve the agents in unusual dangers to which ordinary persons are not exposed. For the same reason, the injuries suffered by its agents in these circumstances will sometimes have occurred in such a manner that their national State would not be justified in bringing a claim for reparation on the ground of diplomatic protection, or, at any rate, would not feel disposed to do so. Both to ensure the efficient and independent performance of these missions and to afford effective support to its agents, the Organization must provide them with adequate protection.

* * *

The obligations entered into by States to enable the agents of the Organization to perform their duties are undertaken not in the interest of the agents, but in that of the Organization. When it claims redress for a breach of these obligations, the Organization is invoking its own right, the right that the obligations due to it should be respected. On this ground, it asks for reparation of the injury suffered, for 'it is a principle of international law that the breach of an engagement involves an obligation to make reparation in an adequate form'; as was stated by the Permanent Court in its Judgment No. 8 of July 26th, 1927 (Series A., No. 9, p. 21). In claiming reparation based on the injury suffered by its agent, the Organization does not represent the agent, but is asserting its own right, the right to secure respect for undertakings entered into towards the Organization.

   * * *

[The Court Answered Question I (a) and I (b) in the affirmative.]

———

2.   Regional Economic Integration Organization (REIOs). Now broaden the focus of your analysis beyond states and the U.N. System to include the European Union (EU) as well. The EU provides an additional comparison point. More importantly, the EU qualifies as a major and innovative international organization in itself. The EU is so advanced in many respects over conventional international organizations in structure, powers and operations that it is sometimes seen as establishing an entirely new category of international institution designated as a "regional economic integration organization," with the emphasis clearly on "integration".

The Maastricht Treaty of European Union establishes what appears to be a single international entity, although for many legal purposes the three underlying European Communities will continue to exist, and it is not clear whether the European Union as such is endowed with international legal personality separate from the three underlying European Communities. The three Communities are the familiar European Coal and Steel Community (ECSC), the European Atomic Energy Community (EURATOM) and the European Economic Community (EEC), each created under its own treaty. The institutional components of the three Communities have been integrated into the single set of operational institutions analyzed in the following materials.

You will note that the European Union's functions extend far beyond those normally conferred upon traditional international organizations like the United Nations and its specialized agencies which are essentially intergovernmental *cooperative* organizations. In cooperative organizations, governments are normally not bound legally without their consent, given either by formal agreement or by consent to be bound as a party to international agreements developed under the auspices of the organizations (but compare the powers of the Security Council under Chapter VII of the United Nations Charter).

More dramatically, the EU's institutions have received extensive powers to establish and enforce legislation binding legally not only upon the Member States but also upon individuals and other entities, and not always with each Member State's specific consent. When the EU legislates in that fashion, it is clearly more than a "cooperative international institution." The EU then acts as an *integrated supranational* body much like the central government of a federation. For further background on these points, see Hartley, *The Foundations of European Community Law* 3–7 (4th Ed., 1998).

As you study the EU materials below, consider the differences between the competences of United Nations type organizations and those of the EU. In your view, would some of the operational problems of the United Nations become more manageable if EU-like powers were conferred upon it? Where does sovereignty lie now under the EU system? Do EU powers suggest future directions for more traditional international organizations? Do you see serious political problems in moving in that direction?

The European Union: A Guide for Americans

www.eurunion.org/infores/euguide, September 11, 1999.

What is the European Union?

The European Union is a unique, treaty-based, institutional framework that defines and manages economic and political cooperation among its fifteen European member countries. The Union is the latest stage in a process of integration begun in the 1950s by six countries—France, Germany, Italy, the Netherlands, Belgium and Luxembourg—whose leaders signed the original treaties establishing various forms of European integration. These treaties gave life and substance to the novel concept that, by creating communities of shared sovereignty in matters of coal and steel production, trade and nuclear energy, another war in Europe would be unthinkable. While the EU has evolved common policies in a number of other sectors since then, the fundamental goal of the Union remains the same: to create an ever closer union among the peoples of Europe.

Due largely to the success of Europe's economic integration, there are now 15 EU member states (Austria, Belgium, Denmark, Finland, France, Germany, Greece, Ireland, Italy, Luxembourg, the Netherlands, Portugal, Spain, Sweden, and the United Kingdom), and membership will likely increase to more than twenty soon after 2000.

The European Union used to be called the European Community until 1993 when the Maastricht Treaty took effect and made a number of important revisions to the founding treaties. 'Maastricht' made it constitutionally possible to achieve Economic and Monetary Union (EMU), and to develop the Union's inherent political dimension through the new Common Foreign and Security Policy (CFSP).

The new Treaty of Amsterdam, agreed by the 15 EU member states on June 17, 1997, [brings] the Union into the 21st century. The treaty's main objectives are: to make the EU's institutions more efficient in preparation for the next enlargement, to strengthen the Union's foreign policy, to develop a more coherent EU strategy to boost employment, and to remove remaining barriers to free movement of people across internal borders.
* * *

A United States of Europe?

The Union is often compared to the United States, and there are some similarities. Member countries have agreed to pool some of their sovereign powers for the sake of unity, just as American states did to create a federal republic. In the fields where such pooling of national sovereignty has occurred—for example, in trade and agriculture—the Union negotiates directly with the United States and other countries. Member states retain their sovereign powers in such fields as security and defense, although since Maastricht, they can take joint action in certain agreed-upon foreign and security policy areas. Although the US federal model continues to inspire the search for political unity, Europe is constructing its own model for unification, ensuring respect for its richest asset the historical, cultural and linguistic diversity of the European nations.

* * *

The Maastricht Treaty on European Union, which took effect in November 1993, was a major overhaul of the founding treaties. It created the 'three pillar' European Union as it exists today.

Pillar One incorporates the three founding treaties [single market, democratization of the institutions, European Citizenship, and economic and monetary union] and sets out the institutional requirements for EMU. It also provides for supplementary powers in certain areas, e.g. environment, research, education and training.

Pillar Two established the Common Foreign and Security Policy which makes it possible for the Union to take joint action in foreign and security affairs.

Pillar Three created the Justice and Home Affairs policy, dealing with asylum, immigration, judicial cooperation in civil and criminal matters, and customs and police cooperation against terrorism, drug trafficking and fraud.

The CFSP and JHA operate by intergovernmental cooperation, rather than by Community institutions which operate Pillar One. Maastricht also created European citizenship and strengthened the European Parliament's legislative role in certain areas.

* * *

Governing Institutions

The European Union is governed by five institutions—Parliament, Council of Ministers, Commission, Court of Justice, and Court of Auditors. In addition, the Heads of State and Government and the Commission President meet at least twice a year in European Council summits to provide overall strategy and political direction. The European Central Bank is responsible for monetary policy and managing the euro in the Economic and Monetary Union, which comprises eleven states at the outset. [Twelve states by early 2001]

The governing system differs from all previous national and international models. Unlike the United States, the EU is founded on international treaties among sovereign nations rather than a Constitution. The power to enact laws that are directly binding on all EU citizens throughout the EU territory also distinguishes the Union from international organizations.

The Union has been described as a supranational entity. The member states have relinquished part of their national sovereignty to the EU institutions. The member states work together, in their collective interest, through the joint administration of their sovereign powers. The Union also operates according to the principle of "subsidiarity", which characterizes most federal systems. Under this principle, the Union is granted jurisdiction only for those policies that cannot be handled effectively at lower levels of government, i.e., national, regional, or local.

The EU system is inherently evolutionary. It was designed to allow for the gradual development of European unification and has not yet achieved its final form.

* * *

Legislation

Legislation takes different forms, depending on the objectives to be achieved.

Regulations are binding in their entirety, are self-executing and directly applicable and obligatory throughout the EU territory. They can be compared to federal laws.

Directives are binding in terms of the results to be achieved, and are addressed to the member states, which are free to choose the best forms and methods of implementation.

Decisions are binding in their entirety upon those to whom they are addressed—member states, natural and/or legal persons.

Recommendations and **Opinions** are not binding.

* * *

Court of Justice

The Court of Justice, sitting in Luxembourg, is the Community's "Supreme Court." It ensures that the treaties are interpreted and applied correctly by other EU institutions and by the member states. The Court comprises 15 judges, one from each member state, appointed for renewable terms of six years. Judgements of the Court in the field of EC law are binding on EU institutions, member states, national courts, companies and private citizens, and overrule those of national courts.

Since 1988 a Court of First Instance, consisting of 15 members, has assisted the Court of Justice. This court has power to hear actions brought by EU officials, competition and coal and steel cases, and actions for damages. Its decisions are subject to appeal to the Court of Justice on points of law only.

Louis, The Community Legal Order 50–54

(3rd ed., by J.D. Louis, 1995)*

* * *

* Reproduced from THE COMMUNITY LEGAL ORDER (3nd ed. 1995, by J.V. Louis) by permission of the publisher, The Office for Official Publications, European Communities, L–2895 Luxembourg.

22.   Itself a creature of the law and dependent on the law for its effectiveness, the legal order of the European Community is also, as we have seen, a major source of law. It has highly developed machinery for producing legislation and also for enforcing the law it creates through a judicial authority.

Unlike international courts of the traditional kind such as the International Court of Justice, the Court of Justice of the European Communities automatically has jurisdiction in the cases where the Treaties so provide; it is not necessary for the Member State concerned first to submit to that jurisdiction. Its jurisdiction is mandatory simply by virtue of the entry into force of the Treaties. It should also be noted that the Court of Justice is accessible not only to the Member States and the EC institutions but also (to varying extents in the different Treaties)[1] to companies and individuals. Finally, judgments of the Court imposing fines or daily default penalties on firms are enforceable without an enforcement order from a national court; the national authority responsible for enforcement merely has the right to check the authenticity of the judgment.

A central judicial authority is essential in any integration process. The transfers of control which integration involves require some guarantee for the member countries that both the supranational institutions and their partner countries are playing by the rules. If the central institutions could overstep the limits of their authority, a transfer of sovereignty would be unacceptable. Similarly, it would be difficult for a member country to comply with the rules laid down by the central institutions unless it were sure that the rules were being applied uniformly by all the other members.

The Court of Justice thus performs a vital function, that of assuring observance of the law in the interpretation and application of the European Treaties (Article 164 of the EC Treaty, Article 136 of the Euratom Treaty and Article 31 of the Coal and Steel Treaty)[1]. The description of the office of Advocate–General, who is required, 'acting with complete impartiality and independence, to make, in open court, reasoned submissions on cases brought before the Court of Justice' (second paragraph of Article 166, EC Treaty), is a good illustration of the task of the whole Court.

* * *

27.   Besides the features described above, the Court of Justice differs from an international court of the traditional kind in the aims it serves, its role and its relations with national courts. While the Court of Justice is not a federal court that is hierarchically superior to the individual state courts,

---

1. For example, coal and steel firms can ask the Court to annul decisions of the High Authority (Commission) in a larger number of cases than can private firms or individuals under the EEC or Euratom Treaties: see the second paragraph of Article 33 of the ECSC Treaty and the second paragraph of Article 173 of the EEC Treaty. Under the EEC and Euratom Treaties, firms and individuals cannot challenge regulations.

1. Editor's. Note: The Treaty of Amsterdam provides a complete renumbering of the articles, titles, and sections of the existing Treaty on European Union and of the Treaty establishing the European Community. The Consolidated version showing the new and the former article numbers is found in 37 I.L.M. 56 (1998).

the importance of its role in determining the legality, its direct relations with national courts, and the access to it enjoyed by private individuals do make the Court the central judicial authority of a community of nations engaged in a process of integration.

* * *

* * * Charged with interpreting the law and determining the validity of Community legislation, the Court has no power to overturn decisions of national courts that are contrary to Community law or to say how Community law applies to the facts of a particular case. It is not a court of appeal. Nor, as already noted, does it have all the powers of a typical federal court. In this respect its status is not free of ambiguity, because in its relations with the Member States and the EC institutions it is necessarily looking more and more like a court of the federal type. Understandably in these circumstances, the draft Treaty establishing the European Union provided, in article 43, for the Court to be given jurisdiction to hear appeals against decisions by national courts from which there is no right of appeal in which they have refused to refer a question for a preliminary ruling or have ignored such ruling.

———

Question: What now can be said about sovereignty and the European Union? Professor Louis' views on this subject follow.

Louis, The Community Legal Order

11 (3rd ed., 1995).*

* * *

4. The law of the European Community is, in the truest sense of the term, a legal order, that is to say, an "organized and structured system of legal rules, with its own sources, and its own institutions and procedures for making, interpreting and enforcing those rules".[1]

Section 1. The transfer of sovereignty

5. The basis of the Community legal order is a transfer of decision-making to common institutions and a corresponding limitation of the areas of decision-making remaining with the individual Member States. This fundamental fact, the transfer of national sovereignty to the Community, has been stated in many judgments both of the European Court of Justice and of national courts. It is worth quoting from some.

One of the most forceful statements is found in the judgment of the Court of Justice of 15 July 1964 in Costa v ENEL,[3] whose influence on national supreme courts has been considerable. There the Court said:

---

* Reproduced from THE COMMUNITY LEGAL ORDER (3rd ed. 1995) by permission of the Office for Official Publications, European Communities, L–2895 Luxembourg.

1. G. Isaac, Droit communautaire général, Paris (Masson), 1983, p. 111.

3. Case 6/64 [1964] ECR 585, at p. 593.

"By contrast with ordinary international treaties, the EEC Treaty has created its own legal system which, on the entry into force of the Treaty, became an integral part of the legal systems of the Member States and which their courts are bound to apply.

By creating a Community of unlimited duration, having its own institutions, its own personality, its own legal capacity and capacity of representation on the international plane and, more particularly, real powers stemming from a limitation of sovereignty or a transfer of powers from the States to the Community, the Member States have limited their sovereign rights, albeit within limited fields, and have thus created a body of law which binds both their nationals and themselves."

In this judgment the Court harked back to the very origins of the European unification movement after the Second World War. The Hague Congress held on 7 to 10 May 1948 had declared in a political resolution that "the time has come for the nations of Europe to transfer certain of their sovereign rights in order henceforward to exercise those rights jointly, and so to coordinate and develop their resources".

No significance may be attached to the fact that the Court referred to sovereignty only being "limited", not "transferred" as advocated by the Hague Congress.

The artificiality of such a distinction is clear from the following passage in a later judgment:

"The States have thus conferred on the Community institutions power to take measures fixing the levy such as those which form the subject-matter of Regulation No 22, thus submitting their sovereign rights to a corresponding limitation. More particularly, to the extent to which this concerns fiscal sovereignty, such a result is perfectly in accordance with the system of the Treaty."

The granting to the Community of power to tax imports of agricultural products had taken this power away from the Member States, thereby limiting the total extent of their sovereignty.

* * *

The surrender of sovereignty is final as long as the Community continues in existence, barring a duly enacted amendment of the Community's constitution, the Treaties. * * *

6. The notion of sovereignty to which the Court is referring is clearly not the traditional abstract, indeed semi-metaphysical, view of sovereignty developed by philosophers from Bodin, through Hobbes and others, to Hegel, which lies behind the nineteenth century view of the State. On that view, sovereignty is indivisible and inalienable.

A new concept of sovereignty, consistent with sovereignty being divisible, is apparent in the Hague declaration. However, transfers of sovereignty are not to be seen in a quantitative sense like surrendering pieces of territory. Rather, certain powers are vested in the Community and from that vesting of powers and the Community's exercise of them it must be determined which of the two, Member State or Community, has jurisdiction over a particular matter. In appropriate cases jurisdiction may be shared or the Member States may be delegated certain subordinate tasks.

The view of sovereignty as something divisible is fundamental to the idea of any process of integration in which sovereignty is said to be altered, pooled or exercised collectively.

* * *

8. The corollary of the "division of sovereignty" is the direct effect and primacy of Community law. As the German Federal Constitutional Court pointed out in an order made on 9 June 1971, the lawful delegation of powers necessarily entails the recognition that the acts adopted by the new holder of the powers have direct effect in domestic law and prevail over contrary national law. These principles have repeatedly been emphasized by the Court of Justice. * * *

* * *

The EEC Treaty—and especially its provisions on specific policies, such as agriculture, transport and overseas trade—sets a framework of tasks that the central institutions are to perform in pursuance of the Treaty's general goals and the particular objectives of individual chapters of it, and in accordance with a prescribed procedure. It is the performance of these duties that ousts the jurisdiction of the Member States.

* * *

————

Questions: Do you agree with Professor Louis' reasoning and conclusions about European Union sovereignty? Applying his reasoning to the United Nations would you give the same response? Why? Why not? For discussions from the German, Italian, Swiss, European Union, and U.S. reaction, *see* BLAKESLEY, ESER, and LAGODNEY, THE INDIVIDUAL IN FACE OF INTERNATIONAL COOPERATION (MAX-PLANK-INSTITUTE, FREIBURG 2001).

Europe in the World

www.eurunion.org/euguide. September 11, 1999

* * *

From the outset, the Community had wide powers for shaping its trade relations with the outside world. It also undertook development aid and technical assistance programs, initially in the former colonies and dependencies of member states, and subsequently throughout the developing world.

Over the last two decades, the EU has created a dense network of international agreements and relationships whose purpose extends well beyond the development of commercial ties and development cooperation. These remain central to the many bilateral and multilateral agreements that have been signed, but they have also launched regular high-level political contacts with many countries, cooperation between companies and industries, as well as investment promotion and cultural exchanges.

* * *

Asserting the EU's New Role in the World–CFSP

The Common Foreign and Security Policy (CFSP) is a framework for member states to coordinate policy by formulating "common positions" and conducting "joint actions" under the Union. The aim is to use these new instruments to create consistent policies which are preventive rather than reactive and which assert the EU's political identity. This is a recent and relatively untried ambition compared with the European Union's long-established constitutional responsibility to act on behalf of its member states in the fields of external economic relations and development policies. It is generally recognized that the speed of development of a common foreign and security policy cannot be forced.

Decision-making procedures are intergovernmental and, therefore, different from those which apply to external economic relations. Heads of State and Government in the European Council agree in broad terms to joint actions. Foreign ministers of the member states decide the specifics. The European Commission participates in all discussions, can make proposals, and has a right of initiative, but not the sole right of initiative it has in community policies. The European Parliament is regularly consulted but has no direct powers.

The Amsterdam Treaty contains provisions designed to improve the functioning of CFSP. It creates a CFSP planning and analysis secretariat staffed by officials from the Council, the Commission, member states, and the Western European Union (WEU). The WEU is the vehicle for military cooperation and for the coordination of European Union positions within NATO. A High Representative, popularly known as Mr. or Ms. CFSP, will personify the EU's foreign and security policy for the first time. Security roles such as peace keeping, monitoring, and conflict prevention, known as Petersberg tasks (originally agreed at a conference in Petersberg, Germany) are spelled out for the WEU acting on behalf of the EU.

* * *

Denzer, Two Legal Orders: Divergent or Convergent?

48 Int'l & Comp. L. Q. 257 (1999)*

The conclusion of the Treaty of Amsterdam and its progress through the ratification procedures of the 15 member States of the European Union provides an occasion to re-examine a familiar question. What is meant by the claim by the European Court of Justice, that the European Community Treaties have created "a new legal order of international law" or, more radically, "a new legal order"? Is EC law to be regarded as a particularly effective system of regional international law, or has it been created as, or mutated into, an entirely new species of law? If there are, indeed, two legal

* Reprinted with the permission of Oxford University Press.

orders, to what extent are they still capable of cross-fertilisation? What about,"European Union law"? Have the Treaty on European Union and now the Treaty of Amsterdam eroded the dichotomy between the two legal orders of public international law and EU law? Is public international law itself taking on some of the characteristics which have made EC law an attractive as well as an effective system for regulating relations between sovereign States? Are the two streams converging?

* * *

Both public international law and EC law are essentially law between sovereign states. Setting aside for the moment the question of their effect on the rights and duties of individuals, and the way in which they may change national constitutions or national legal orders, the States which form and are governed by both legal orders remain separate sovereign States. In contrast to any national legal system, international law and EC law are essentially horizontal rather than vertical in nature. Although the European Community may claim to be "supranational" and some at least of its peoples and its governments had or have clear political aspirations to drive "ever closer Union among the peoples of Europe" towards a single federal State, such a change has not happened. The member States continue to satisfy the established criteria for recognition as independent sovereign States and to be recognised as such by the rest of the world. EC law is based on the Community Treaties concluded between these independent States, not superimposed by any higher authority, and although these Treaties do not provide explicitly for withdrawal or termination of membership of the Union, it is accepted politically that in the unlikely event of a State wishing to leave, it could not ultimately be compelled to remain a member. It should be noted that the UN Charter likewise makes no provision for deliberate withdrawal from membership (as opposed to expulsion) and it has never been suggested that the members of the United Nations have thereby forfeited their character as independent sovereign states.

* * *

In practice the European Community and later the European Union by its example, through the conduct of its external relations and its participation in international conferences and organisations has had an important influence in the development of many aspects of international law-making and diplomacy. The governments of the member States to an increasing extent have seen that in certain areas there are still advantages in the public international law method of working together. Certain Ideals—transparency in law-making, effective judicial supervision, full integration into national legal systems within a predictable time-scale and effective remedies for individuals—have been perceived to be not the monopoly of one or other legal order but, rather, ideals of general application. The nation States of the European Union have survived intact, and the agony of the process of ratification of Maastricht showed that there was little appetite for self-destruction or fusion among the national parliaments or the citizens of Europe. There is a whole range of ways for States to work and make laws together, and no one method has a monopoly of rightness for all contexts.

It is to the credit of the Treaty of Amsterdam that it carries forward this flexibility of approach. It is indeed a muddle—but it is a glorious muddle.

3. NONGOVERNMENTAL ORGANIZATIONS (NGOs)

Simmons, Learning to Live With NGOs
Foreign Policy 82, Fall 1998.*

* * *

The question facing national governments, multilateral institutions, and national and multinational corporations is not whether to include NGOS in their deliberations and activities. Although many traditional centers of power are fighting a rear-guard action against these new players, there is no real way to keep them out. Instead, the real challenge is figuring out how to incorporate NGOs into the international system in a way that takes account of their diversity and scope, their various strengths and weaknesses, and their capacity to disrupt as well as to create.

WHY NGOs MATTER

Defining NGOS is not an exercise for the intellectually squeamish. A 1994 United Nations document, for example, describes an NGO as a

> nonprofit entity whose members are citizens or associations of citizens of one or more countries and whose activities are determined by the collective will of its members in response to the needs of the members of one or more Communities with which the NGO Cooperates.

This formulation embraces just about every kind of group except for private businesses, revolutionary or terrorist groups, and political parties. Other popular substitutes for the term NGO (private voluntary organizations, civil society organizations, and the independent sector) are likewise almost terminally vague. A better approach to understanding NGOs and what they are would focus on. their respective goals, membership, funding, sources, and other such factors . . .

Yet although there may be no universal agreement on what NGOs are exactly, there is widespread agreement that their numbers, influence, and reach are at unprecedented levels. . . . In 1948, for example, the UN listed 41 consultative groups that were formally accredited to cooperate and consult with the UN Economic and Social Council (ECOSOC); in 1998, there were more than 1,500 with varying degrees of participation and access. Until recently, NGO)s clustered in developed and democratic nations; now groups sprout up from Lima to Beijing. They are changing societal norms, challenging national governments, and linking up with counterparts in powerful transnational alliances. And they are muscling their way into areas of high politics, such as arms control, banking, and trade, that were previously dominated by the state.

In general terms, NGOs affect national governments, multilateral institutions, and national and multinational corporations in four ways: setting agendas, negotiating outcomes, conferring legitimacy, and implementing solutions.

Setting Agendas

NGOs have long played a key role in forcing leaders and policymakers to pay attention. * * *. In 1945, NGOs Were largely responsible for inserting human-rights language in the UN Charter and have since put almost every major human-rights issue on the international agenda. Likewise, NGO activism since the 1960s and 1970s successfully raised the profile of global environmental and population issues.

Instead of holding marches or hanging banners off buildings, NGO members now use computers and cell phones to launch global public-relations blitzes that can force issues to the top of policymakers' "to do" lists. Consider the 1997 Nobel Prize-winning campaign by NGOs to conclude a treaty banning landmines over the objections of the United States. The self-described "full working partnership" between the Canadian government and a loose coalition of more than 350 humanitarian and arms-control NGOs from 23 countries was key to the negotiations' success. But what seized the attention of the public and policymakers was the coalition's innovative media campaign using the World Wide Web, faxes, e-mail, newsletters, and even *Superman* and *Batman* comic books. Treaty supporters won the signatures of 122 nations in 14 months. When several coalition members announced plans for a follow-on campaign against small aims, the U.S. government sprang into action, meeting with 20 other countries in July 1998 to launch official talks on a possible treaty.

Negotiating Outcomes

NGOs can be essential in designing multilateral treaties that work. Chemical manufacturing associations from around the world helped set up an effective verification regime for the 1997 Chemical Weapons Convention that could be supported by industries and militaries. Throughout the various sessions of negotiations on climate change, groups such as the Environmental Defense Fund and the World Business Council for Sustainable Development have helped craft compromise proposals that attempt to reconcile environmental and commercial interests; meanwhile, NGOs have been instrumental in helping government negotiators understand the science behind the issues that they seek to address.

NGOs can also build trust and break deadlocks when negotiations have reached an impasse. In 1990, a sole Italian NGO, the Comunitá di Sant'Egidio, started the informal meetings between the warring parties in Mozambique that eventually led to a peace settlement. During talks in 1995 to extend the Treaty on the Non–Proliferation of Nuclear Weapons, NGOs from several countries working with the South African government delegation helped forge a compromise that led to the treaty's permanent extension.

* * *

Making Solutions Work

NGOs on the ground often make the impossible possible by doing what governments cannot or will not. Some humanitarian and development

NGOs have a natural advantage because of their perceived neutrality and experience. The International Committee of the Red Cross, for example, is able to deliver health care to political prisoners in exchange for silence about any human-rights violations that its members witness. Other groups such as Oxfam International provide rapid relief during and after complex humanitarian disasters—with and without UN partners. Moreover, as governments downsize and new challenges crowd the international agenda, NGOs increasingly fill the breach. Willy nilly, the UN and nation-states are depending more on NGOs to get things done. Total assistance by and through international NGOs to the developing world amounted to about $8 billion in 1992—accounting for 13 percent of all development assistance and more than the entire amount transferred by the UN system.

International NGOs also play critical roles in translating international agreements and norms into domestic realities. Where governments have turned a blind eye, groups such as Amnesty International and the Committee to Protect journalists call attention to violations of the UN Declaration on Human Rights. Environmental NGOs police agreements such as the Convention on International Trade in Endangered Species, uncovering more accurate data on compliance than that provided by member nations. Perhaps one of the most vital but overlooked NGO roles is to promote the societal changes needed to make international agreements work. Signatories of the Organization for Economic Cooperation and Development's 1997 Bribery Convention, for example, are counting on the more than 80 chapters of Transparency International to help change the way their societies view bribery and corruption.

Increasingly, however, NGOs operate outside existing formal frameworks, moving independently to meet their goals and establishing new standards that governments, institutions, and corporations are themselves compelled to follow through force of public opinion.

* * *

* * * NGOs, governments, and multilateral institutions need to devise systems of public participation that draw on the expertise and resources of NGOs, their grassroots connections, sense of purpose and commitment, and freedom from bureaucratic constraints. Those NGOs that have seen the most rapid growth in their power will have to contend with inevitable limits on their influence and access. Those governments and institutions that have resisted the advance of these new players will have to permit an unprecedented level of public scrutiny and participation. Over time, this process of give-and-take promises to transform the way that international affairs are conducted. Yet as it plays out, both sides may realize that the new system that they have sought to create or resist is in many respects no different from the clash of competing interests that has characterized democracies since their inception.

* * *

1999 Annual Report of the International Committee of the Red Cross

www.icrc.org (March 5, 2001).

The ICRC and the International Red Cross and Red Crescent Movement

The International Red Cross and Red Crescent Movement is made up of the National Societies, the ICRC and the International Federation of Red Cross and Red Crescent Societies. Although each of the Movement's components engages in different activities, they are all united by the same Fundamental Principles: humanity, impartiality, neutrality, independence, voluntary service, unity and universality.

As its founding institution, the ICRC has certain statutory responsibilities towards the Movement. In particular, it is responsible for ensuring respect for and promoting knowledge of the Fundamental Principles, recognizing new National Red Cross or Red Crescent Societies which meet the current conditions for recognition, and discharging the mandates entrusted to it by the International Conference of the Red Cross and Red Crescent. The ICRC takes an active part in the Movement's statutory meetings, which it often organizes jointly with the Federation.

In accomplishing these tasks the ICRC maintains close relations with the National Societies, cooperating with them in areas of mutual interest such as preparedness for situations of armed conflict, development and ratification of and respect for the Geneva Conventions, and dissemination of humanitarian law and the Fundamental Principles. It also acts as lead agency for international relief operations conducted by the Red Cross and Red Crescent in situations of inter-national and non-international armed conflict, internal strife and their direct results, as well as in situations of armed conflict concomitant with natural or technological disasters.

Finally, while fully respecting the Federation's competence in the matter, the ICRC cooperates actively in the development of National Red Cross and Red Crescent Societies, in particular through technical and legal assistance, by supporting the National Societies' dissemination programmes and by contributing to the training of their staff in areas that fall within its mandate.

Legal Bases

The work of the ICRC is based upon the Geneva Conventions and their Additional Protocols, the Statutes of the International Red Cross and Red Crescent Movement, and the resolutions of International Conferences of the Red Cross and Red Crescent. The ICRC's mission is to provide protection and assistance to victims of armed conflicts. It takes direct and immediate action in response to emergency situations, at the same time promoting preventive measures by developing and spreading knowledge of international humanitarian law.

It was at the prompting of the ICRC that governments adopted the initial Geneva Convention in 1864. In the years since, the ICRC, with the support of the entire Movement, has put constant pressure on governments to adapt international humanitarian law to changing circumstances, especially developments in methods and means of warfare, in order to provide more effective protection and assistance for the victims of armed conflicts.

Today almost all States are bound by the four Geneva Conventions of 12 August 1949, which, in times of armed conflict, protect wounded, sick and shipwrecked members of the armed forces, prisoners of war and civilians.

Moreover, two Protocols additional to these Conventions were adopted in June 1977. Protocol I protects the victims of international armed conflicts, while Protocol II protects the victims of non-international armed conflicts; in particular, these Additional Protocols have codified the rules which protect the civilian population against the effects of hostilities.

More than three-quarters of all States are now bound by the Protocols.

The legal bases of any action undertaken by the ICRC may be summed up as follows:

* In the four Geneva Conventions of 1949 and Additional Protocol I, the international community gave the ICRC a mandate in the event of international armed conflict. In particular, the ICRC has the right to visit prisoners of war and civilian internees. The Conventions also confer on the ICRC a broad right of initiative.

* In situations of armed conflict which are not international in character, the ICRC also has a right of initiative recognized by the States and enshrined in the four Geneva Conventions.

* In the event of internal disturbances and tension, and in any other situation which warrants humanitarian action, the ICRC has a right of humanitarian initiative which is recognized in the Statutes of the International Red Cross and Red Crescent Movement and allows it to offer its services to a government without that offer constituting interference in the internal affairs of the State concerned.

A Conversation With Oscar Schachter*

ASIL, Proceedings of the 91st Annual Meeting 343, April 9–10, 1997 (1998).**

BRIGITTE STERN:[a] Oscar Schachter, in his own words, has shared the passions of our time. I invite you tonight to share them with him. * * * if we look at the structure of international law today, we are conscious that the state plays less and less of a role, although still quite a role. You have written, Oscar, that international law is moving away from a state-centered orientation .. My question is multifold. First, I must say that I agree with you on the existence of this trend. But do you welcome such an evolution? In other words, do you think the state is no longer a suitable framework for the development of a social and legal order?

* Ed. Note: Hamilton Fish Professor Emeritus of Law and Diplomacy, Columbia University, School of Law

** Reprinted with the permission of the American Society of International Law.

a. Ed. Note: Professor, University of Paris I, Panthèon-Sorbonne.

PROFESSOR SCHACHTER: The decline of state authority has become a popular subject with political scientists, economists and businessmen. They relate it to the globalization of the economy, the spread of free market economies and the weakness of governments in controlling the flow of capital. One of the legal consequences, apart from the erosion of governmental controls, is a growth of nonstate functional rules applied in transnational enterprises and relationships, with only a minimal linkage to state legislation and judicial authority. They may be regarded as stateless law which, like the *lex mercatoria*, is based on agreements and practices developed outside of governments.

Another subject that has also become fashionable is civil society—that is, voluntary associations and their influence in political life. At least in the American tradition such associations are seen often as authentic expressions of what people want, more so than government. Civil society has its transnational side influencing international action and law. Many see this as a counterforce to "statism," especially when nongovernmental organizations (NGOs) support causes they favor—such as women's rights, environmental rules, arms control and human rights. Not all, of course, are devoted to the public good—many serve special interests. Clearly, NGOs have a greater role in influencing international law and its application today than formerly. Democratization and technology (especially in communication) are important factors. We might also bear in mind that not all voluntary associations are "civil." Transnational criminal networks flourish today, revealing the weakness of states to control drug trade, money laundering, and illegal arms sales.

Another aspect I would call "the resurgence of particularisms," that is, the movements that seek to cut down the power of the national state and to favor regional or ethnic or other nonstate identities. This seems to be a worldwide trend. It may be a psychological reaction to globalization, a response to the feeling that anonymous and remote forces control much of our lives. In any case, it is a threat to the centralized power of nation states.

The weakness of states is also evidenced by the inability of governments to maintain public order. Even powerful states cannot prevent serious international crimes—money laundering, drugs, arms traffic—not to mention the so-called "failed states" where internal anarchy seems to prevail.

To answer Brigitte's question, I am not tempted by a stateless world or by philosophical anarchism (which was somewhat fashionable in the nineteenth century). Nor do I buy the "minimal state" based upon libertarian ideals. It seems to me that juridical authority exercised on a territorial basis is still the realistic foundation for governing people of different classes, origins, and values. The vulnerable and the poor are almost sure to lose out if state authority were replaced by private or localized authority. At one time (when I was about 18) I thought the state would and should wither away. I do not hold that view today–not even as a Utopian idea.
* * *

* * * I regard group identity pride as positive elements in human life, and some place should be given to that in national societies. Whether

minorities ought to have voices in the international world depends on cases and situational judgments. I still feel that, from the point of view of justice and the notion of a common good, the territorial nexus of existing authority of the state remains better than breaking up state authority into parochial entities or unmitigated free markets.

————

INDIVIDUALS

Systematic and comprehensive treatment of individuals in relation to other actors in the international system is found below in Chapters 9 (Human Rights) and 16 (Individual Responsibility International Criminal Law).

CHAPTER 3

JURISDICTION

———

Introduction

Allocation of Jurisdiction in the International System
Introduction.

Meaning of Jurisdiction: General. Jurisdiction is the authority to
effect and affect legal interests—to prescribe rules of law, to adjudicate

131

legal questions, and to compel or induce compliance. Jurisdiction, therefore, makes law functional.

Jurisdiction in national legal systems. Does the term, jurisdiction, play the same role in domestic and international realms? In the United States, for example, we speak of federal versus state jurisdiction. The nature or scope of jurisdiction varies, depending on the context in which it is asserted. Most nations have sets of courts with jurisdiction over civil matters, others over commercial, and still others over criminal matters. Civil courts are often specialized, some having jurisdiction over certain civil matters but not others. Jurisdiction of criminal courts is determined by the level of gravity of the offense. There are states where jurisdiction over litigation between individuals and the government is vested in a system of administrative courts, separate and distinct from other civil courts (e.g., the *Conseil d'Etat* in France).

Jurisdiction in the international legal system. In the international legal system, jurisdiction refers to the authority of the state as a whole, not of its constituent units or political subdivisions. Whether an alien is tried by a court of New York State or by a federal court, or whether in France he is tried by a court in Paris or Marseilles, does not create an international issue. When we speak of a state's jurisdiction in the international system, we mean that the state is entitled under international law to subject certain categories of persons, events or places to its rules of law. The rules of international law determining whether a state has jurisdiction over a particular person, event or place, are often different from those used in a national legal system. Accordingly it is advisable to discuss the jurisdiction of states under international law in terms that are neutral as to the organs of government exercising the jurisdiction.

Recently, issues of separation of powers among international organs have arisen. For example, Security Council actions in relation to the Gulf War, Somalia, Bosnia, Cambodia, and other hot spots, or its creation of the ad hoc criminal trubunals, may suggest that the Council is exercising some executive, legislative, and judicial power.

Jurisdiction to prescribe, to adjudicate, and enforce. The term jurisdiction is often used imprecisely. Effective analysis requires a sharp distinction between rule-making and rule-enforcing jurisdiction. A state first prescribes a rule, which is to say that either by act of the legislature, decree of the executive, administrative regulation, or decision of a court, it declares a principle or legal norm. Second, the state enforces the rule. That is, it arrests, subpoenas witnesses and documents, extradites, tries, or punishes a person for violation of the rule. A court enters a judgment vindicating the rule. Jurisdiction to adjudicate, where the judiciary decides questions of law and fact and metes out the punishment or remedy, is sometimes carved out of enforcement jurisdiction as a separate category. Jurisdiction to enforce or to adjudicate is dependant on jurisdiction to prescribe.

———

The 1987 Restatement.*

§ 401, Categories of Jurisdiction

Under international law, a state is subject to limitations on

(1) jurisdiction to prescribe, i.e., to make its law applicable to the activities, relations, or status of persons, or the interests of persons in things, whether by legislation, by executive act or order, by administrative rule or regulation, or by determination of a court;

(2) jurisdiction to adjudicate, i.e., to subject persons or things to the process of its courts or administrative tribunals, whether in civil or in criminal proceedings, whether or not the state is a party to the proceedings;

(3) jurisdiction to enforce, i.e., to induce or compel compliance or punish noncompliance with its laws or regulations, whether through the courts or by use of executive, administrative, police, or other non-judicial action.

This chapter examines the accepted jurisdictional bases in the international legal system. As you read, you should consider questions, such as whether these bases are adequate foundations for a state's prescriptive, adjudicative, or enforcement needs? Are they too broad or too narrow? Are they antiquated? Some jurisdictional issues are considered in more depth in other chapters, where relevant. *E.g.,* Ch. 4 (the High Seas), Ch. 5 (Airspace).

5.   *Jurisdiction, vel non, not always dispositive.* Do not read too much into the term jurisdiction. To say that a state has acted outside its jurisdiction implies an immediate legal consequence. But to say that it has acted within its jurisdiction may be only the first step in analysis. A state is considered to owe special obligations of fair treatment to aliens who are within its territory. Failure to provide the alien with a fair trial gives the state of his nationality a claim against the failing country, even though that nation, in trying the alien at all, acted within its rights under international rules of jurisdiction. Consequences of not having jurisdiction are frequently different in domestic systems from those in the international legal system. Domestically, for example, to convict a person for conduct beyond the scope of the law results in his or her release. Yet should a court violate an international jurisdictional rule, it is possible that no domestic legal consequence may follow. On the other hand, the individual or his state may have a remedy under international law may have a claim against the offending state.

6.   For more detail, see Blakesley, Terrorism, Drugs, International Law, and the Protection of Human Liberty Chs. 2 and 3 (1992); Blakesley, Extraterritorial Jurisdiction, Ch 3, in II International Criminal Law (2nd ed. Bassiouni 1998).

SECTION A.   JURISDICTION TO PRESCRIBE RULES OF LAW GOVERNING CONDUCT—THEORIES OF JURISDICTION

International law recognizes four basic theories of jurisdiction: (1) territorial (subjective and objective); (2) nationality (active & passive personality); (3) the protective principle; and (5) universality. The pages that follow allow you to consider each.

A hypothetical used in European course books illustrates all of the bases, except for universality. A German national, standing in France, next to the French border with both Switzerland and Italy, shoots an Austrian who is standing across the border in Switzerland. The victim is hit and mortally wounded in Switzerland, but manages to stumble across the border into Italy, where he succumbs to his wounds. Would each country named have jurisdiction over the homicide? On what theory? Would any of the bases have priority? Study the following material to decide.

1.   TERRITORIAL JURISDICTION

Territorial jurisdiction has traditionally been predominant. A state has jurisdiction to prescribe rules of law governing conduct taking place within its territory. No state has jurisdiction to prescribe rules of domestic law governing all conduct of everyone everywhere in the world. Sovereignty requires that no state's authority obtain on the territory of another. *See*, Chief Justice Marshall's holding on the territorial nature of enforcement jurisdiction in *The Schooner Exchange v. McFaddon*, 11 U.S. (7 Cranch) 116, 136 (1812). The jurisdiction of the nation within its own territory is necessarily exclusive and absolute. It is susceptible of no limitation not imposed by itself. Any restriction upon it, deriving validity from an external source, would imply a diminution of its sovereignty to the extent of the restriction, and an investment of that sovereignty to the same extent in that power which could impose such restriction. His point in *The Antelope*, 23 U.S. (10 Wheat.) 66, 123 (1825) is also apt: "[t]he courts of no country execute the penal laws of another. . . ." Permission is required for one state to gather evidence, arrest, or to take other enforcement action on the territory of another. Subjective and objective territoriality are the two types of territorial jurisdiction. They may overlap, so concurrent jurisdiction is not uncommon.

Computer technology and the era of cyberspace presents new jurisdictional complexity. The speed and facility with which a criminal can hide in cyberspace for illegal gambling, pornography, bank and securities fraud, money laundering, theft of information and funds, and even terrorism, sex tourism, and slave trade have outstripped the law's capacity to react. Serious jurisdictional issues arise, like what constitutes a constituent element of cyber conduct, where does it occur, where do its effects occur? These problems, along with many governments' attempts to gain a monopoly on "data-encription" raise issues of domestic constitutional interests and international human rights. *See, gen.*, Doris Estelle Long & Anthony D'Amato, A COURSEBOOK IN INTERNATIONAL INTELLECTUAL PROPERTY (2000).

a. SUBJECTIVE TERRITORIALITY: Subjective Territoriality obtains when an essential part of the conduct covered by legislation occurs within the state. This may be when a constituent element of a crime, or when employment, marriage, acquisition of property, disposition of wealth, conclusion of contracts, commission of torts occurs within the territory. *See, e.g.* French *Code de Procédure Pénale* art. 693, which provides that an offense is considered to have been committed in France when "an act characterizing one of its elements is accomplished in France." Jurisdiction obtains even if all of the other elements of an offense and its effect occur abroad. *See, e.g. R. v. Nel, South Africa Supreme Court,* App.Div. 1953, 20 Int'l L.Rptr. 192 (1957) (receipt of stolen property). The state in which the effect occurs also has jurisdiction on the basis of objective territoriality.

The Case of the Artsy Austrian Pornographers, Austria S.Ct, 101 J.Dr.Int'l 632 (1974). Sometimes a state will prosecute conduct that it considers illegal, even though the conduct is not criminal in the state where it culminates. In this case, two Austrians assembled, arranged, and published an illustrated book in Germany, through a German publisher. They were prosecuted in Austria for publishing pornography. The pornography charge against them in Germany had been dismissed as being non-criminal; their illustrations accepted there as modern art. Thus, they argued that they could not be prosecuted in Austria. The Austrian court rejected their argument and they were convicted. They were held to have committed some elements of the crime of pornography in Austria.

Denunciation to the Enemy Case, **Netherlands Court of Cassation, 1958, 88 J. du Dr. Int'l 893 (1961):**[b] Conduct may consist of a series of acts, some taking place inside and some outside a state's territory.

> Benders, an employee of the Twentsche Bank, revealed to German authorities in 1936 that the Spier brothers, Jews of German nationality, had, contrary to the legislation then in force in Germany, placed a considerable fortune in safety in the Twentsche Bank in the Netherlands. By * * * imprisoning one of the Spier brothers and the wife of the other the German authorities were able to constrain them to return the fortune to Germany, after which, naturally under a cloak of legitimacy, it was almost entirely confiscated. The heirs sued Benders and the Bank.
>
> What is the law governing Benders' unlawful act? In order to carry out his * * * design, he went just beyond the Netherlands frontier, to make contact in Germany with Oberzollrat Kinzel of Düsseldorf. The interview consummating this betrayal, which netted 10,000 deniers for Benders, therefore took place in Germany. Was Germany therefore the locus delicti and German law for that reason applicable? The Court of Appeal of Amsterdam rightly thought that this was a little too easy. The execution of the design, the Court said, began by the compilation

---

b. English text in the Journal. Reprinted with the permission of Editions Techniques, S.A., Paris.

of documents in the offices of the Bank in the Netherlands; the infamous act was directed against a fortune in the Netherlands, while it was at the same time calculated to injure the Bank in the Netherlands. "In the light of all these facts", notes the Court, "Benders" act took place to such an extent in the Netherlands that the Tribunal was fully justified in subjecting it to Netherlands law.

b. Objective Territoriality Jurisdiction: The Effects Theory.

In Strassheim v. Daily, **221 U.S. 280 (1911),** Justice Holmes stated the correct rule in the most commonly cited decision in on the objective territoriality theory: "[a]cts done outside a jurisdiction, but *intended to produce and producing* detrimental effects within it, justify a state in punishing a cause of the harm as if he had been present at the effect, if the state should succeed in getting him within its power." Justice Holmes' opinion and historical precedent make it clear that the objective territorial theory does not apply when parties merely intend to cause an effect within a state. A significant effect or the result of the offense must actually occur within the state's territory. Lately, however, many U.S. federal courts (and the 1987 Restatement, §§ 402 and 403) have applied it upon the mere intent to cause an effect Section 402 reads: "[s]ubject to § 403, a state has jurisdiction to prescribe law with respect to (c) conduct outside its territory that has or is intended to have substantial effect within its territory ..." It has been applied to *thwarted* extraterritorial conspiracies, where some other theory may be more appropriate. Courts have confused the substantive elements of federal narcotics conspiracy with the jurisdictional prerequisite (an effect occurring on the territory). Federal conspiracy law requires an agreement to import, but no overt act. From this, the courts have "reasoned" that, since no overt act is required for the offense, objective territorial jurisdiction obtains, as long as an intent to import is proved. Do you agree? Has an effect occurred upon the territory? Think about this as you consider the other theories of jurisdiction.

Perhaps the most famous international decision on extraterritorial jurisdiction is the *S.S. Lotus Case.*

The S.S. "Lotus" (France v. Turkey)

Permanent Court of International Justice, 1927.
P.C.I.J., Ser. A, No. 10.

* * * By a special agreement signed at Geneva on October 12th, 1926, between the Governments of * * * [France and Turkey], [who] have submitted to the Permanent Court of International Justice the question of jurisdiction which has arisen between them following upon the collision which occurred on August 2nd, 1926, between the steamships Boz–Kourt and Lotus.

According to the special agreement, the Court has to decide the following questions:

(1) Has Turkey, contrary to Article 15 of the Convention of Lausanne of July 24th, 1923, respecting conditions of residence and business and jurisdiction, acted in conflict with the principles of international law—and if so, what principles—by instituting, following the collision which occurred on August 2nd, 1926, on the high seas between the French steamer Lotus and the Turkish steamer Boz–Kourt and upon the arrival of the French steamer at Constantinople— as well as against the captain of the Turkish steamship—joint criminal proceedings in pursuance of Turkish law against M. Demons, officer of the watch on board the Lotus at the time of the collision, in consequence of the loss of the Boz–Kourt having involved the death of eight Turkish sailors and passengers?

* * *

On August 2nd, 1926, just before midnight, a collision occurred between the French mail steamer Lotus, proceeding to Constantinople, and the Turkish collier Boz–Kourt, between five and six nautical miles to the north of Cape Sigri (Mitylene). The Boz–Kourt, which was cut in two, sank, and eight Turkish nationals who were on board perished. After having done everything possible to succour the shipwrecked persons, of whom ten were able to be saved, the Lotus continued on its course to Constantinople, where it arrived on August 3rd.

At the time of the collision, the officer of the watch on board the Lotus was M. Demons, a French citizen, lieutenant in the merchant service and first officer of the ship, whilst the movements of the Boz–Kourt were directed by its captain, Hassan Bey, who was one of those saved * * *

* * *

On August 5th, Lieutenant Demons was requested by the Turkish authorities to go ashore to give evidence. The examination * * * led to the * * * [arrest] of Lieutenant Demons—without previous notice being given to the French Consul–General—and Hassan Bey, amongst others. This arrest, which has been characterized by the Turkish Agent as arrest pending trial (arrestation préventive), was effected in order to ensure that the criminal prosecution instituted against the two officers, on a charge of manslaughter, by the Public Prosecutor of Stamboul, on the complaint of the families of the victims of the collision, should follow its normal course.

The case was first heard by the Criminal Court of Stamboul on August 28th. * * * Lieutenant Demons submitted that the Turkish Courts had no jurisdiction; the Court, however, overruled his objection. * * *

* * * [T]he Criminal Court delivered its judgment, the terms of which have not been communicated to the Court by the Parties. It is, however, common ground, that it sentenced Lieutenant Demons to eighty days' imprisonment and a fine of twenty-two pounds, Hassan Bey being sentenced to a slightly more severe penalty.

* * *

The action of the Turkish judicial authorities with regard to Lieutenant Demons at once gave rise to many diplomatic representations and other steps on the part of the French Government or its representatives in Turkey, either protesting against the arrest of Lieutenant Demons or demanding his release, or with a view to obtaining the transfer of the case from the Turkish Courts to the French Courts.

As a result of these representations, [both the Turkish and the French Governments] * * * appointed their plenipotentiaries with a view to the drawing up of the special agreement to be submitted to the Court; this special agreement was signed at Geneva on October 12th, 1926 * * *.
      * * *

I

Before approaching the consideration of the principles of international law contrary to which Turkey is alleged to have acted—thereby infringing the terms of Article 15 of the Convention of Lausanne of July 24th, 1923, respecting conditions of residence and business and jurisdiction—, it is necessary to define, in the light of the written and oral proceedings, the position resulting from the special agreement. * * *

1.   The collision which occurred * * *, between the S.S. Lotus, flying the French flag, and the S.S. Boz–Kourt, flying the Turkish flag, took place on the high seas: the territorial jurisdiction of any State other than France and Turkey therefore does not enter into account.

2.   The violation, if any, of the principles of international law would have consisted in the taking of criminal proceedings against Lieutenant Demons. It is not therefore a question relating to any particular step in these proceedings—such as his being put to trial, his arrest, his detention pending trial or the judgment given by the Criminal Court of Stamboul—but of the very fact of the Turkish Courts exercising criminal jurisdiction. That is why the arguments put forward by the Parties in both phases of the proceedings relate exclusively to the question whether Turkey has or has not, according to the principles of international law, jurisdiction to prosecute in this case.

The discussions have borne exclusively upon the question whether criminal jurisdiction does or does not exist in this case.

3.   The prosecution was instituted because the loss of the Boz–Kourt involved the death of eight Turkish sailors and passengers. * * * It is * * * a case of prosecution for involuntary manslaughter. * * * There is no doubt that [the death of the victims] may be regarded as the direct outcome of the collision, and the French Government has not contended that this relation of cause and effect cannot exist.
      * * *

5.   The prosecution was instituted in pursuance of Turkish legislation.
* * *

Article 6 of the Turkish Penal Code, * * * runs as follows:

[Translation]   Any foreigner who, apart from the cases contemplated by Article 4, commits an offence abroad to the prejudice of

Turkey or of a Turkish subject, for which offence Turkish law pre-scribes a penalty involving loss of freedom for a minimum period of not less than one year, shall be punished in accordance with the Turkish Penal Code provided that he is arrested in Turkey. * * *

* * *

Even if the Court must hold that the Turkish authorities had seen fit to base the prosecution of Lieutenant Demons upon the above-mentioned Article 6, the question submitted to the Court is not whether that article is compatible with the principles of international law; it is more general. The Court is asked to state whether or not the principles of international law prevent Turkey from instituting criminal proceedings against Lieutenant Demons under Turkish law. Neither the conformity of Article 6 in itself with the principles of international law nor the application of that article by the Turkish authorities constitutes the point at issue; it is the very fact of the institution of proceedings which is held by France to be contrary to those principles. * * *

II

Having determined the position resulting from the terms of the special agreement, the Court must now ascertain which were the principles of international law that the prosecution of Lieutenant Demons could conceiv-ably be said to contravene.

It is Article 15 of the Convention of Lausanne of July 24th, 1923, respecting conditions of residence and business and jurisdiction, which refers the contracting Parties to the principles of international law as regards the delimitation of their respective jurisdiction. [The clause reads]:

> Subject to the provisions of Article 16, all questions of jurisdiction shall, as between Turkey and the other contracting Powers, be decided in accordance with the principles of international law.

* * * In these circumstances it is impossible—except in pursuance of a definite stipulation—to construe the expression "principles of international law" otherwise than as meaning the principles which are in force between all independent nations and which therefore apply equally to all the contracting Parties.

* * *

III

* * * The French Government contends that the Turkish Courts, * * * to have jurisdiction, should be able to point to some title to jurisdic-tion recognized by international law in favour of Turkey. * * * The Turkish Government takes the view that Article 15 allows Turkey jurisdic-tion whenever such jurisdiction does not * * * conflict with a principle of international law.

* * *

International law governs relations between independent States. The rules of law binding upon States therefore emanate from their own free will as expressed in conventions or by usages generally accepted as expressing principles of law and established in order to regulate the relations between these co-existing independent communities or with a view to the achievement of common aims. Restrictions upon the independence of States cannot therefore be presumed.

Now the first and foremost restriction imposed by international law upon a State is that—failing the existence of a permissive rule to the contrary—it may not exercise its power in any form in the territory of another State. In this sense jurisdiction is certainly territorial; it cannot be exercised by a State outside its territory except by virtue of a permissive rule derived from international custom or from a convention.

It does not, however, follow that international law prohibits a State from exercising jurisdiction in its own territory, in respect of any case which relates to acts which have taken place abroad, and in which it cannot rely on some permissive rule of international law. Such a view would only be tenable if international law contained a general prohibition to States to extend the application of their laws and the jurisdiction of their courts to persons, property and acts outside their territory, and if, as an exception to this general prohibition, it allowed States to do so in certain specific cases. But this is certainly not the case under [current] international law. Far from laying down a general prohibition . . . that States may not extend the application of their laws and the jurisdiction of their courts to persons, property and acts outside their territory, it leaves them in this respect a wide measure of discretion which is only limited . . . by prohibitive rules; as regards other cases, every State remains free to adopt the principles which it regards as . . . most suitable.

This discretion left to States by international law explains the great variety of rules which they have been able to adopt without objections or complaints on the part of other States; it is * * * to remedy the difficulties resulting from such variety that efforts have been made for many years past, both in Europe and America, to prepare conventions the effect of which would be precisely to limit the discretion at present left to States in this respect by international law, thus making good the existing lacunae in respect of jurisdiction or removing the conflicting jurisdictions arising from the diversity of the principles * * * [in] various States.

In these circumstances, all that can be required of a State is that it should not overstep the limits which international law places upon its jurisdiction; within these limits, its title to exercise jurisdiction rests in its sovereignty. It follows from the foregoing that the contention of the French Government to the effect that Turkey must in each case be able to cite a rule of international law authorizing her to exercise jurisdiction, is opposed to the generally accepted international law to which Article 15 of the Convention of Lausanne refers. * * *

* * *

[We] therefore must * * * ascertain whether * * * there exists a rule of international law limiting the freedom of States to extend the criminal jurisdiction [under the] circumstances of the present case.

IV

The Court will now proceed to ascertain whether general international law, to which Article 15 of the Convention of Lausanne refers, contains a rule prohibiting Turkey from prosecuting Lieutenant Demons.

For this purpose, it will in the first place examine the value of the arguments advanced by the French Government, without however omitting to take into account other possible aspects of the problem, which might show the existence of a restrictive rule applicable in this case.

The arguments advanced by the French Government [include]:

(1) International law does not allow a State to take proceedings with regard to offences committed by foreigners abroad, simply by reason of the nationality of the victim; and such is the situation in the present case because the offence must be regarded as having been committed on board the French vessel.

* * *

As regards the first argument, the Court * * * [recalls] that its examination is strictly confined to the specific situation in the present case, [based on the *compromis* submitting to jurisdiction].

* * * The characteristic features of the situation of fact are as follows: there has been a collision on the high seas between two vessels flying different flags, on one of which was one of the persons alleged to be guilty of the offence, whilst the victims were on board the other.

This being so, the Court does not think it necessary to consider the contention that a State cannot punish offences committed abroad by a foreigner simply by reason of the nationality of the victim. For this contention only relates to the case where the nationality of the victim is the only criterion on which the criminal jurisdiction of the State is based. Even if that argument were correct generally speaking—and in regard to this the Court reserves its opinion—it could only be used in the present case if international law forbade Turkey to take into consideration the fact that the offence produced its effects on the Turkish vessel and consequently in a place assimilated to Turkish territory in which the application of Turkish criminal law cannot be challenged, even in regard to offences committed there by foreigners. But no such rule of international law exists. No argument has come to the knowledge of the Court from which it could be deduced that States recognize themselves to be under an obligation towards each other only to have regard to the place where the author of the offence happens to be at the time of the offence. On the contrary, it is certain that the courts of many countries, even of countries which have given their criminal legislation a strictly territorial character, interpret criminal law in the sense that offences, the authors of which at the moment of commission are in the territory of another State, are nevertheless to be regarded as having been committed in the national territory, if one of the constituent elements of the offence, and more especially its effects, have taken place there. French courts have, in regard to a variety of situations, given decisions sanctioning this way of interpreting the territorial principle. Again, the Court does not know of any cases in which governments have protested against the fact that the criminal law of some country contained a rule to this effect or that the courts of a country construed their criminal law in this sense. Consequently, once it is admitted that the effects of the offence were produced on the Turkish vessel, it becomes impossible to hold that there is a rule of international law which prohibits Turkey from prosecuting Lieutenant Demons because of the fact that the author of the offence was on board the French ship. Since, as has already been observed, the special agreement does not deal with the provision of Turkish law under which the prosecution was instituted, but only with the question whether the prosecution should be regarded as contrary to the principles of international law, there is no reason preventing the Court from confining itself to observing that, in this case, a prosecution may also be justified from the point of view of the so-called territorial principle.

* * * The fact that the judicial authorities may have committed an error in their choice of the legal provision applicable to the particular case and compatible with international law only concerns municipal law and can only affect international law in so far as a treaty provision enters into account, or the possibility of a denial of justice arises.

* * *

The offence for which Lieutenant Demons appears to have been prosecuted was an act—of negligence or imprudence—having its origin on board the Lotus, whilst its effects made themselves felt on board the Boz–Kourt. These two elements are, legally, entirely inseparable, so much so that their separation renders the offence nonexistent. Neither the exclusive jurisdiction of either State, nor the limitations of the jurisdiction of either State, nor the limitations of the jurisdiction of each to the occurrences which took place on the respective ships would appear calculated to satisfy the requirements of justice and effectively to protect the interests of the two States. It is only natural that each should be able to exercise jurisdiction and to do so in respect of the incident as a whole. It is therefore a case of concurrent jurisdiction.

* * *

For These Reasons, the COURT, having heard both Parties, gives, by the President's casting vote—the votes being equally divided—, judgment to the effect

. . . that, following the collision which occurred on August 2nd, 1926, on the high seas between the French steamship Lotus and the Turkish steamship Boz–Kourt, and upon the arrival of the French ship at Stamboul, and in consequence of the loss of the Boz–Kourt having involved the death of eight Turkish nationals, Turkey, by instituting criminal proceedings in pursuance of Turkish law against Lieutenant Demons, officer of the watch on board the Lotus at the time of the collision, has not acted in conflict with the principles of international law, contrary to Article 15 of the Convention of Lausanne of July 24th, 1923, * * *;

* * * [Separate and dissenting opinions omitted.]

———

Questions & Notes

1. Does the *Lotus* decision state (a) a rule of jurisdiction in international law or (b) the legal consequences of not having one? Is it concerned with the lack of a rule of international law, generally, or just of jurisdiction?

2. Is the following comment by the PCIJ still true today? "[T]he rules of law binding upon States therefore emanate from their own free will as expressed in conventions or by usages generally accepted as expressing principles of law and established in order to regulate the relations between these co-existing independent communities or with a view to the achievement of common aims. Restrictions upon the independence of States cannot therefore be presumed . . ."

3. The Court's discussion of what is required to prove custom is interesting and informative. What must be established? Would France win today?

> "The Court explained that the dearth of criminal cases being brought merely showed that states had 'often, in practice, abstained from instituting criminal proceedings, *and not that they recognized themselves as constrained by law to do so.* Only if such abstention were based on their being conscious of having a duty to abstain would it be possible to speak of international custom. If no states official had ever articulated this consciousness of duty, no custom!' "

4. What bases of jurisdiction would the Court find acceptable? What is its attitude toward "passive personality?"

5. *Current rule as to prosecution for high seas collision.* Article 11 of the 1958 Convention on the High Seas and Article 97 of the U.N. Convention on the Law of the Sea, both provide:

> In the event of a collision * * * concerning a ship on the high seas, involving the penal or disciplinary responsibility of the master or of any person in the service of the ship, no penal or disciplinary proceedings may be instituted against such persons except before the judicial or administrative authorities either of the flag state or of the state of which such person is a national.

———

In the 1996 Nuclear Weapons Case, the International Court of Justice took the opportunity to consider the scope of the Lotus decision.

Legality of the Threat or Use of Nuclear Weapons 1996 I.C.J. 226.

* * *

[at p. 237] ". . . The use of the word 'permitted' in the question put by the General Assembly was criticized before the Court by certain States on the ground that this [the use of the term 'permitted'] implied that the threat or the use of nuclear weapons would only be permissible if authorization could be found in a treaty provision or in customary international law."

Such a starting point, those states submitted, was incompatible with the very basis of international law, which rests upon the principles of sovereignty and consent; accordingly, and contrary to what was implied by use of the word "permitted", states are free to threaten or use nuclear weapons unless it can be shown that they are bound not to do so by reference to a prohibition in either treaty law or custom . . .

Support for this contention was found in dicta of the [PCIJ] in the case what "restrictions upon the independence of States cannot . . . be presumed" & that I/L leaves to states "a wide measure of discretion which is only limited in certain cases by prohibitive rules."

Later, the International Court of Justice stated:

[at p. 270] "[T]he case . . . should be understood to be of very limited application in the particular context of the question which is the subject of this Advisory Opinion. It would be to exaggerate the importance of that decision of the [PCIJ] and to distort its scope were it to be divorced from the particular context, both judicial and temporal, in which it was taken. No doubt this decision expressed the spirit of the times, the spirit of an international society which as yet had few institutions and was governed by an international law of strict co-existence, itself a reflection of the vigour of the principle of state sovereignty. . . ."

Some Questions:

What was the Question presented to the PICJ for an Advisory Opinion, in *The Lotus Case* ? Did it have something to do with whether Turkey had jurisdiction to prosecute for the wreck on the High Seas?

What does the term "temporal" mean in the above-quoted language from the *Nuclear Use or Threat Case* (ICJ, 1996)? Could it mean that times have changed and that issues of nuclear dangers are different from matters of jurisdiction? Is there a hint that the ICJ may have changed its mind on jurisdiction since it rendered the *Lotus* decision? Could it now be leaning toward limiting jurisdiction? Keep this in mind for when you read the *Alvarez-Machain* decision.

Ethereal Effects

The grand old *Alcoa case* elaborated the classic effects doctrine. Consider *Alcoa* and, whether a European counterpart has developed since *Wood Pulp Cartel*, [1988] E.C.R 5214.

United States v. Aluminum Co. of America

United States Court of Appeals, Second Circuit, 1945.
148 F.2d 416, 442.

[This was a prosecution for violation of the Sherman Act. One of the defendants was Aluminum Limited, a Canadian corporation formed to take over properties of the Aluminum Company of America outside the United States. Not quite half of each company's shares were owned by the same group of individuals. The court was concerned about the participation of each company in a foreign cartel, called the Alliance. The court concluded that the American company, Alcoa, was not a party to the Alliance and "did not join in any violation of § 1 of the Act, so far as concerned foreign commerce." Judge Learned Hand, for the Court:]

Whether "Limited" itself violated that section depends upon the character of the "Alliance." It was a Swiss corporation, created in pursuance of an agreement entered into on July 3, 1931, the signatories to which were a French corporation, two German, one Swiss, a British, and "Limited." The original agreement, or "cartel," provided for the formation of a corporation in Switzerland which should issue shares, to be taken up by the signatories. This corporation was from time to time to fix a quota of production for each share, and each shareholder was to be limited to the quantity measured by the number of shares it held, but was free to sell at any price it chose. The corporation fixed a price every year at which it would take off any shareholder's hands any part of its quota which it did not sell. No shareholder was to "buy, borrow, fabricate or sell" aluminum produced by anyone not a shareholder except with the consent of the board of governors, but that must not be "unreasonably withheld." * * *

The agreement of 1936 abandoned the system of unconditional quotas, and substituted a system of royalties. Each shareholder was to have a fixed free quota for every share it held, but as its production exceeded the sum of its quotas, it was to pay a royalty, graduated progressively in proportion to the excess; and these royalties the "Alliance" divided among the shareholders in proportion to their shares. This agreement—unlike the first—did not contain an express promise that the "Alliance" would buy any undisposed of stocks at a fixed price, although perhaps [part of the agreement] may have impliedly recognized such an obligation. Probably during the two years in which the shareholders operated under this agreement, that question did not arise for the demand for aluminum was very active. Nevertheless, we understand from "Limited's" answer to an interrogatory that the last price fixed under the agreement of 1931 was understood to remain in force. Although this agreement, like its predecessor, was silent as to imports into the United States, when that question arose during its preparation, as it did, all the shareholders agreed that such imports should be included in the quotas. The German companies were exempted from royalties—for obvious reasons—and that, it would seem, for practical purposes put them out of the "cartel" for the future, for it was scarcely possible that a German producer would be unable to dispose of all its production, at least within any future period that would be provided for. The shareholders continued this agreement unchanged until the end of March, 1938, by which time it had become plain that, at least for the time being, it was no longer of service to anyone. Nothing was, however, done to end it, although the German shareholders . . . became enemies of the French, British and Canadian shareholders in 1939. The "Alliance" . . . has apparently never been dissolved; and indeed it appeared on the "Proclaimed List of Blocked Nationals" of September 13, 1944.

Did either the agreement of 1931 or that of 1936 violate § 1 of the Act? The answer does not depend upon whether we shall recognize as a source of liability a liability imposed by another state. * * * We are concerned only with whether Congress chose to attach liability to the conduct outside the United States of persons not in allegiance to it. That being so, the only question open is whether Congress intended to impose the liability, and whether our own Constitution permitted it to do so: as a court of the United States, we cannot look beyond our own law. Nevertheless, it is quite true that we are not to read general words, such as those in this Act, without regard to the limitations customarily observed by nations upon the exercise of their powers; limitations which generally correspond to those fixed by the "Conflict of Laws." We should not impute to Congress an intent to punish all whom its courts can catch, for conduct which has no consequences within the U.S. *American Banana Co. v. United Fruit Co.*; *United States v. Bowman*; *Blackmer v. U.S.*; on the other hand, *it is settled law*—as *"Limited"* itself agrees—*that any state may impose liabilities, even upon persons not within its allegiance, for conduct outside its borders that has consequences within its borders which the state reprehends;*[a] and these liabilities other states will ordinarily recognize. *Strassheim v. Daily.* * * * It may be argued that this Act extends further. Two situations are possible. There may be agreements made beyond our borders not intended to affect imports, which do affect them, or which affect exports. Almost any limitation of the supply of goods in Europe, for example, or in South America, may have repercussions in the United States if there is trade between the two. Yet when one considers the international complications likely to arise from an effort in this country to treat such agreements as unlawful, it is safe to assume that Congress certainly did not intend the Act to cover them. Such agreements may on the other hand intend to include imports into the United States, and yet it may appear that they have had no effect upon them. That situation might be thought to fall within the doctrine that intent may be a substitute for performance in the case of a contract made within the United States; or it might be thought to fall within the doctrine that a statute should not be interpreted to cover acts abroad which have no consequence here. We shall not choose between these alternatives; but for argument we shall assume that the Act does not cover agreements, even though intended to affect imports or exports, unless its performance is shown actually to have had some effect upon them. Where both conditions are satisfied, the situation certainly falls within such decisions as *United States v. Pacific & Arctic R. & Navigation Co.*; *Thomsen v. Cayser*; and. *U.S. v. Sisal Sales Corporation* (*United States v. Nord Deutcher Lloyd*, illustrates the same conception in another field.) * * *

Both agreements would clearly have been unlawful, had they been made within the United States; and it follows from what we have just said that both were unlawful, though made abroad, if they were intended to affect imports and did affect them. Since the shareholders almost at once agreed that the agreement of 1931 should not cover imports, we may ignore it and confine our discussion to that of 1936: indeed that we should have to do anyway, since it superseded the earlier agreement. The judge found that it was not the purpose of the agreement to "suppress or restrain the exportation of aluminum to the United States for sale in competition with Alcoa." By that we understand that he meant that the agreement was not

---

a. Emphasis supplied by the editors.

specifically directed to "Alcoa," because it only applied generally to the production of the shareholders. If he meant that it was not expected that the general restriction upon production would have an effect upon imports, we cannot agree, for the change made in 1936 was deliberate and was expressly made to accomplish just that. It would have been an idle gesture, unless the shareholders had supposed that it would, or at least might, have that effect. The first of the conditions which we mentioned was therefore satisfied; the intent was to set up a quota system for imports.

The judge also found that the 1936 agreement did not "materially affect the * * * foreign trade or commerce of the United States"; apparently because the imported ingot was greater in 1936 and 1937 than in earlier years. We cannot accept this finding, based as it was upon the fact that, in 1936, 1937 and the first quarter of 1938, the gross imports of ingot increased. It by no means follows from such an increase that the agreement did not restrict imports; and incidentally it so happens that in those years such inference as is possible at all, leads to the opposite conclusion. It is true that the average imports—including "Alcoa's"—for the years 1932–1935 inclusive were about 15 million pounds, and that for 1936, 1937 and one-fourth of 1938 they were about 33 million pounds; but the average domestic ingot manufacture in the first period was about 96 million and in the second about 262 million; so that the proportion of imports to domestic ingot was about 15.6 per cent for the first period and about 12.6 per cent for the second. We do not mean to infer from this that the quota system of 1936 did in fact restrain imports, as these figures might suggest; but we do mean that nothing is to be inferred from the gross increase of imports. We shall dispose of the matter therefore upon the assumption that, although the shareholders intended to restrict imports, it does not appear whether in fact they did so. Upon our hypothesis the plaintiff would therefore fail, if it carried the burden of proof upon this issue as upon others. We think, however, that, after the intent to affect imports was proved, the burden of proof shifted to "Limited." In the first place a depressant upon production which applies generally may be assumed, ceteris paribus, to distribute its effect evenly upon all markets. Again, when the parties took the trouble specifically to make the depressant apply to a given market, there is reason to suppose that they expected that it would have some effect, which it could have only by lessening what would otherwise have been imported. If the motive they introduced was over-balanced in all instances by motives which induced the shareholders to import, if the United States market became so attractive that the royalties did not count at all and their expectations were in fact defeated, they to whom the facts were more accessible than to the plaintiff ought to prove it, for a prima facie case had been made. Moreover, there is an especial propriety in demanding this of "Limited," because it was "Limited" which procured the inclusion in the agreement of 1936 of imports in the quotas.

There remains only the question whether this assumed restriction had any influence upon prices * * *. To that Socony–Vacuum Oil Co. v. U.S., *supra*, is an entire answer. * * * The underlying doctrine was that all factors which contribute to determine prices, must be kept free to operate unhampered by agreements. For these reasons we think that the agreement of 1936 violated § 1 of the Act.

* * *

American Banana Co. v. United Fruit Co.

United States Supreme Court, 1909.
213 U.S. 347, 29 S.Ct. 511, 53 L.Ed. 826.

* * * The plaintiff is an Alabama corporation, organized in 1904. The defendant is a New Jersey corporation, organized in 1899. Long before the plaintiff was formed, the defendant, with intent to prevent competition and to control and monopolize the banana trade, bought the property and business of several of its previous competitors, with provision against their resuming the trade, made contracts with others, including a majority of the most important, regulating the quantity to be purchased and the price to be paid, and acquired a controlling amount of stock in still others. For the same purpose it organized a selling company, of which it held the stock, that by agreement sold at fixed prices all the bananas of the combining parties. By this and other means it did monopolize and restrain the trade and maintained unreasonable prices. The defendant being in this ominous attitude, one McConnell in 1903 started a banana plantation in Panama, then part of the United States of Colombia, and began to build a railway (which would afford his only means of export), both in accordance with the laws of the United States of Colombia. He was notified by the defendant that he must either combine or stop. Two months later, it is believed at the defendant's instigation, the governor of Panama recommended to his national government that Costa Rica be allowed to administer the territory through which the railroad was to run, and this although that territory had been awarded to Colombia under an arbitration agreed to by treaty. The defendant, and afterwards, in September, the government of Costa Rica, it is believed by the inducement of the defendant, interfered with McConnell. In November, 1903, Panama revolted and became an independent republic, declaring its boundary to be that settled by the award. In June, 1904, the plaintiff bought out McConnell and went on with the work, as it had a right to do under the laws of Panama. But in July, Costa Rican soldiers and officials, instigated by the defendant, seized a part of the plantation and a cargo of supplies and have held them ever since, and stopped the construction and operation of the plantation and railway. In August one Astua, by ex parte proceedings, got a judgment from a Costa Rican court, declaring the plantation to be his, although, it is alleged, the proceedings were not within the jurisdiction of Costa Rica, and were contrary to its laws and void. Agents of the defendant then bought the lands from Astua. The plaintiff has tried to induce the government of Costa Rica to withdraw its soldiers and also has tried to persuade the United States to interfere, but has been thwarted in both by the defendant and has failed. The government of Costa Rica remained in possession down to the bringing of the suit.

As a result of the defendant's acts the plaintiff has been deprived of the use of the plantation, and the railway, the plantation and supplies have been injured. The defendant also, by outbidding, has driven purchasers out of the market and has compelled producers to come to its terms, and it has prevented the plaintiff from buying for export and sale. This is the substantial damage alleged. * * * It is contended, however, that, even if the main argument fails and the defendant is held not to be answerable for acts depending on the cooperation of the government of Costa Rica for their effect, a wrongful conspiracy resulting in driving the plaintiff out of business is to be gathered from the complaint and that it was entitled to go to trial upon that.

[The court affirmed the dismissal of the complaint as not setting forth a cause of action. Justice Holmes wrote for the Court:]

* * * It is obvious that, however stated, the plaintiff's case depends on several rather startling propositions. In the first place the acts causing the damage were done, so far as appears, outside the jurisdiction of the United States and within that of other states. It is surprising to hear it argued that they were governed by the act of Congress.

* * *

* * * The general and almost universal rule is that the character of an act as lawful or unlawful must be determined wholly by the law of the country where the act is done. * * *

* * *

For another jurisdiction, if it should happen to lay hold of the actor, to treat him according to its own notions rather than those of the place where he did the acts, not only would be unjust, but would be an interference with the authority of another sovereign, contrary to the comity of nations, which the other state concerned justly might resent. * * *

* * *

The foregoing considerations would lead in case of doubt to a construction of any statute as intended to be confined in its operation and effect to the territorial limits over which the lawmaker has general and legitimate power. "All legislation is prima facie territorial." * * * Words having universal scope, such as "Every contract in restraint of trade," "Every person who shall monopolize," etc., will be taken as a matter of course to mean only every one subject to such legislation, not all that the legislator subsequently may be able to catch. In the case of the present statute the improbability of the United States attempting to make acts done in Panama or Costa Rica criminal is obvious, yet the law begins by making criminal the acts for which it gives a right to sue. We think it entirely plain that what the defendant did in Panama or Costa Rica is not within the scope of the statute so far as the present suit is concerned. * * *

Notes & Questions

1.   *Why was a circuit court decision in Alcoa this important?* This case has the theoretical standing of a Supreme Court decision, because it was decided on certification and transfer from the Supreme Court for lack of a quorum of qualified justices. The Supreme Court has decided other antitrust cases along similar lines: *U.S. v. Sisal Sales Corp.*, 274 U.S. 268

(1927); *Holophane Co. v. U.S.*, 352 U.S. 903 (1956) (per curium affirmance of lower court order under the Sherman Act requiring the defendants to compete actively in foreign markets); *Continental Ore Co. v. Union Carbide & Carbon Corp.*, 370 U.S. 690 (1962). In the 1911 dissolution of the American *Tobacco Trust in U.S. v. American Tobacco Co.*, 221 U.S. 106 (1910).

2.   *ALCOA* makes it clear that where express statutory language calls for it, U.S. courts will apply federal statutes extraterritorially. Is *ALCOA* consistent with the *Paquete Habana Case, supra*, Ch. 1, or with *U.S. v. Alvarez–Machain, infra*? Is the rule different when the statute is silent on whether it is to be applied extraterritorially, as statutes usually are? *See* the *Hartford Fire Case, infra*.

3.   Certain groups have sought to direct attention to the harmful effects on U.S. economic activity abroad that extending the reach of U.S. antitrust laws may cause. To what extent does the statement of the Department of Justice suggest that moderation may be jurisdictional? Suppose the United States should abandon or modify the use of the effects doctrine in antitrust cases, either outright or by casting the balance against application. Would concern over the negative impact be alleviated by this balancing or have other nations or unions of nations taken a cue from the aggressive U.S. approach, which has now overtaken any desire for balancing and moderation?

Hartford Fire Ins. Co. v. California

509 U.S. 764 (1993).

Justice Souter[.] * * * The Sherman Act makes every contract, combination, or conspiracy in unreasonable restraint of interstate or foreign commerce illegal,15 U.S.C. § 1. These consolidated cases present questions about the application of that Act to the insurance industry, both here and abroad. The plaintiffs (respondents here) allege that both domestic and foreign defendants (petitioners here) violated the Sherman Act by engaging in various conspiracies to affect the American insurance market.* * * [A] group of domestic defendants argues that the McCarran–Ferguson Act, 15 U.S.C. § 1011 et seq., precludes application of the Sherman Act to the conduct alleged; a group of foreign defendants argues that the principle of international comity requires the District Court to refrain from exercising jurisdiction over certain claims against it. We hold that most of the domestic defendants' alleged conduct is not immunized from antitrust liability by the McCarran–Ferguson Act, and that, even assuming it applies, the principle of international comity does not preclude District Court jurisdiction over the foreign conduct alleged.

I.   The two petitions before us stem from consolidated litigation comprising the complaints of 19 States and many private plaintiffs alleging that the defendants, members of the insurance industry, conspired in violation of § 1 of the Sherman Act to restrict the terms of coverage of commercial general liability (CGL) insurance available in the United States. Because the cases come to us on motions to dismiss, we take the allegations of the complaints as true.

A.   According to the complaints, the object of the conspiracies was to force certain primary insurers (insurers who sell insurance directly to consumers) to change the terms of their standard CGL insurance policies to conform with the policies the defendant insurers wanted to sell.* * * [The complaints alleged a violation of § 1 of the Sherman Act by certain London reinsurers who conspired to: (a) coerce primary insurers in the United States to offer CGL coverage on a claims-made basis, thereby making "occurrence CGL coverage ... unavailable in the State of California for many risks;" (b) limit coverage of pollution risks in North America, thereby rendering "pollution liability coverage ... almost entirely unavailable for the vast majority of casualty insurance purchasers in the State of California;" and (c) limit coverage of seepage, pollution, and property contamination risks in North America, "thereby eliminating such coverage in the State of California."]

C.   * * * After the actions had been consolidated for litigation in the Northern District of California * * * [t]he District Court * * * dismissed the three claims that named only certain London-based defendants, invoking international comity and applying the Ninth Circuit's decision in Timberlane Lumber Co. v. Bank of America....

The Court of Appeals reversed. * * * [A]s to the three claims brought solely against foreign defendants, the court applied its Timberlane analysis, but concluded that the principle of international comity was no bar to exercising Sherman Act jurisdiction.

We granted certiorari * * * to address the application of the Sherman Act to the foreign conduct at issue. [cit.] We now affirm [.] * * *

III.   * * * At the outset, we note that the District Court undoubtedly had jurisdiction of these Sherman Act claims, as the London reinsurers apparently concede. ("Our position is not that the Sherman Act does not apply in the sense that a minimal basis for the exercise of jurisdiction doesn't exist here. Our position is that there are certain circumstances, and that this is one of them, in which the interests of another State are sufficient that the exercise of that jurisdiction should be restrained").[u] Although the proposition was perhaps not always free from doubt, see American Banana Co. v. United Fruit Co., 213 U.S. 347, (1909), it is well established by now that the Sherman Act applies to foreign conduct that was meant to produce and did in fact produce some substantial effect in the United States.[cit.][v] Such is the conduct alleged here: that the London reinsurers engaged in unlawful conspiracies to affect the market for insur-

---

u. One of the London reinsurers * * * argues that the Sherman Act does not apply to its conduct in attending a single meeting at which it allegedly agreed to exclude all pollution coverage from its reinsurance contracts. * * * [Nevertheless] the allegations, which we are bound to credit, remain that it participated in conduct that was intended to and did in fact produce a substantial effect on the American insurance market.

v. Justice SCALIA believes that what is at issue in this litigation is prescriptive, as opposed to subject-matter, jurisdiction. The parties do not question prescriptive jurisdiction, however, and for good reason: it is well established that Congress has exercised such jurisdiction under the Sherman Act. See G. Born & D. Westin, International Civil Litigation in United States Courts 542, n. 5 (2d ed. 1992) (Sherman Act is a "prime exampl[e] of the simultaneous exercise of prescriptive jurisdiction and grant of subject matter jurisdiction").

ance in the United States and that their conduct in fact produced substantial effect.[w]

According to the London reinsurers, the District Court should have declined to exercise such jurisdiction under the principle of international comity.[x] The Court of Appeals agreed that courts should look to that principle in deciding whether to exercise jurisdiction under the Sherman Act. This availed the London reinsurers nothing, however. To be sure, the Court of Appeals believed that "application of [American] antitrust laws to the London reinsurance market 'would lead to significant conflict with English law and policy,' " and that "[s]uch a conflict, unless outweighed by other factors, would by itself be reason to decline exercise of jurisdiction." (citation omitted). But other factors, in the court's view, including the London reinsurers' express purpose to affect U.S. commerce and the substantial nature of the effect produced, outweighed the supposed conflict and required the exercise of jurisdiction in this litigation.

When it enacted the [Foreign Trade Antitrust Improvements Act] FTAIA, 15 U.S.C. § 6a, Congress expressed no view on the question whether a court with Sherman Act jurisdiction should ever decline to exercise such jurisdiction on grounds of international comity. See H.R.Rep. No. 97–686, p. 13 (1982) ("If a court determines that the requirements for subject matter jurisdiction are met, [the FTAIA] would have no effect on the court['s] ability to employ notions of comity ... or otherwise to take account of the international character of the transaction") (citing Timberlane). We need not decide that question here, however, for even assuming that in a proper case a court may decline to exercise Sherman Act jurisdiction over foreign conduct (or, as JUSTICE SCALIA would put it, may conclude by the employment of comity analysis in the first instance that there is no jurisdiction), international comity would not counsel against exercising jurisdiction in the circumstances alleged here.

The only substantial question in this litigation is whether "there is in fact a true conflict between domestic and foreign law." Societe Nationale Industrielle Aerospatiale v. U.S. Dist. Court for Southern Dist. of Iowa, 482 U.S. 522, 555, (1987) (BLACKMUN, J., concurring in part and dissenting in

---

w. Under § 402 of the Foreign Trade Antitrust Improvements Act of 1982 (FTAIA), 96 Stat. 1246, 15 U.S.C. § 6a, the Sherman Act does not apply to conduct involving foreign trade or commerce, other than import trade or import commerce, unless "such conduct has a direct, substantial, and reasonably foreseeable effect" on domestic or import commerce. § 6a(1)(A). The FTAIA was intended to exempt from the Sherman Act export transactions that did not injure the United States economy, [cit.], and it is unclear how it might apply to the conduct alleged here. Also unclear is whether the Act's "direct, substantial, and reasonably foreseeable effect" standard amends existing law or merely codifies it. [cit.]. We need not address these questions here. Assuming that the FTAIA's standard affects this litigation, and assuming further that this standard differs from the prior law, the conduct alleged plainly meets its requirements.

x. JUSTICE SCALIA contends that comity concerns figure into the prior analysis whether jurisdiction exists under the Sherman Act. [cit]. This contention is inconsistent with the general understanding that the Sherman Act covers foreign conduct producing a substantial intended effect in the United States, and that concerns of comity come into play, if at all, only after a court has determined that the acts complained of are subject to Sherman Act jurisdiction. * * * In any event, the parties conceded jurisdiction at oral argument, and we see no need to address this contention here.

part). The London reinsurers contend that applying the Act to their conduct would conflict significantly with British law, and the British Government, appearing before us as amicus curiae, concurs.[cit.] They assert that Parliament has established a comprehensive regulatory regime over the London reinsurance market and that the conduct alleged here was perfectly consistent with British law and policy. But this is not to state a conflict. "[T]he fact that conduct is lawful in the state in which it took place will not, of itself, bar application of the United States antitrust laws," even where the foreign state has a strong policy to permit or encourage such conduct. Restatement (Third) Foreign Relations Law § 415, Comment j; [cit.] No conflict exists, for these purposes, "where a person subject to regulation by two states can comply with the laws of both." Restatement (Third) Foreign Relations Law § 403, Comment e. Since the London reinsurers do not argue that British law requires them to act in some fashion prohibited by the law of the United States, [cit.], or claim that their compliance with the laws of both countries is otherwise impossible, we see no conflict with British law. See Restatement (Third) Foreign Relations Law § 403, Comment e, § 415, Comment j. We have no need in this litigation to address other considerations that might inform a decision to refrain from the exercise of jurisdiction on grounds of international comity.

IV.   The judgment of the Court of Appeals is affirmed * * * and the cases are remanded for further proceedings consistent with this opinion. It is so ordered.

JUSTICE SCALIA[.] * * * I dissent from the Court's ruling concerning the extraterritorial application of the Sherman Act. * * *

The Petitioners * * *, various British corporations and other British subjects, argue that certain of the claims against them constitute an inappropriate extraterritorial application of the Sherman Act. It is important to distinguish two distinct questions raised by this petition: whether the District Court had jurisdiction, and whether the Sherman Act reaches the extraterritorial conduct alleged here. On the first question, I believe that the District Court had subject-matter jurisdiction over the Sherman Act claims against all the defendants (personal jurisdiction is not contested). Respondents asserted nonfrivolous claims under the Sherman Act, and 28 U.S.C. § 1331 vests district courts with subject-matter jurisdiction over cases "arising under" federal statutes. As precedents such as *Lauritzen v. Larsen*, [*supra*], make clear, that is sufficient to establish the District Court's jurisdiction over these claims. * * *

The second question—the extraterritorial reach of the Sherman Act—has nothing to do with the jurisdiction of the courts. It is a question of substantive law turning on whether, in enacting the Sherman Act, Congress asserted regulatory power over the challenged conduct. See EEOC v. Arabian American Oil Co., 499 U.S. 244 (1991) (Aramco)("It is our task to determine whether Congress intended the protections of Title VII to apply to United States citizens employed by American employers outside of the United States"). If a plaintiff fails to prevail on this issue, the court does not dismiss the claim for want of subject-matter jurisdiction—want of power to adjudicate; rather, it decides the claim, ruling on the merits that

the plaintiff has failed to state a cause of action under the relevant statute.
* * *

There is, however, a type of "jurisdiction" relevant to determining the extraterritorial reach of a statute; it is known as "legislative jurisdiction," Aramco, supra, 499 U.S., at 253, Restatement (First) Conflict of Laws § 60 (1934), or "jurisdiction to prescribe," 1 Restatement (Third) of Foreign Relations Law of the United States 235 (1987) (hereinafter Restatement (Third)). This refers to "the authority of a state to make its law applicable to persons or activities," and is quite a separate matter from "jurisdiction to adjudicate," There is no doubt, of course, that Congress possesses legislative jurisdiction over the acts alleged in this complaint: Congress has broad power under Article I, § 8, cl. 3, "[t]o regulate Commerce with foreign Nations," and this Court has repeatedly upheld its power to make laws applicable to persons or activities beyond our territorial boundaries where United States interests are affected. [cit.] But the question in this litigation is whether, and to what extent, Congress has exercised that undoubted legislative jurisdiction in enacting the Sherman Act.

Two canons of statutory construction are relevant in this inquiry. The first is the "longstanding principle of American law 'that legislation of Congress, unless a contrary intent appears, is meant to apply only within the territorial jurisdiction of the United States.' " Aramco, supra. Applying that canon in Aramco, we held that the version of Title VII of the Civil Rights Act of 1964 then in force, [cit.], did not extend outside the territory of the United States even though the statute contained broad provisions extending its prohibitions to, for example, " 'any activity, business, or industry in commerce.' " [Aramco], 499 U.S., at 249. We held such "boiler-plate language" to be an insufficient indication to override the presumption against extraterritoriality. The Sherman Act contains similar "boilerplate language," and if the question were not governed by precedent, it would be worth considering whether that presumption controls the outcome here. We have, however, found the presumption to be overcome with respect to our antitrust laws; it is now well established that the Sherman Act applies extraterritorially. [cit.]

But if the presumption against extraterritoriality has been overcome or is otherwise inapplicable, a second canon of statutory construction becomes relevant: "[A]n act of congress ought never to be construed to violate the law of nations if any other possible construction remains." Murray v. Schooner Charming Betsy, 2 Cranch 64, 118, (1804) (Marshall, C.J.). This canon is "wholly independent" of the presumption against extraterritoriality. It is relevant to determining the substantive reach of a statute because "the law of nations," or customary international law, includes limitations on a nation's exercise of its jurisdiction to prescribe. See Restatement (Third) §§ 401–416. Though it clearly has constitutional authority to do so, Congress is generally presumed not to have exceeded those customary international-law limits on jurisdiction to prescribe.

Consistent with that presumption, this and other courts have frequently recognized that, even where the presumption against extraterritoriality does not apply, statutes should not be interpreted to regulate foreign persons or conduct if that regulation would conflict with principles of international law. * * * [T]he principle was expressed in [*ALCOA, supra*], the decision that established the extraterritorial reach of the Sherman Act. In his opinion for the court, Judge Learned Hand cautioned "we are not to read general words, such as those in [the Sherman] Act, without regard to the limitations customarily observed by nations upon the exercise of their powers; limitations which generally correspond to those fixed by the 'Conflict of Laws.' "Id., at 443.

More recent lower court precedent has also tempered the extraterritorial application of the Sherman Act with considerations of "international comity." [cit] The "comity" they refer to is not the comity of courts, whereby judges decline to exercise jurisdiction over matters more appropriately adjudged elsewhere, but rather what might be termed "prescriptive comity": the respect sovereign nations afford each other by limiting the reach of their laws. That comity is exercised by legislatures when they enact laws, and courts assume it has been exercised when they come to interpreting the scope of laws their legislatures have enacted. It is a traditional component of choice-of-law theory. See J. Story, Commentaries on the Conflict of Laws § 38 (1834) (distinguishing between the "comity of the courts" and the "comity of nations," and defining the latter as "the true foundation and extent of the obligation of the laws of one nation within the territories of another"). Comity in this sense includes the choice-of-law principles that, "in the absence of contrary congressional direction," are assumed to be incorporated into our substantive laws having extraterritorial reach. Romero, supra,; see also Lauritzen, supra, Hilton v. Guyot, 159 U.S. 113, 162–166, (1895). Considering comity in this way is just part of determining whether the Sherman Act prohibits the conduct at issue.

In sum, the practice of using international law to limit the extraterritorial reach of statutes is firmly established in our jurisprudence. In proceeding to apply that practice to the present cases, I shall rely on the Restatement (Third) for the relevant principles of international law. Its standards appear fairly supported in the decisions of this Court construing international choice-of-law principles (Lauritzen, Romero, and McCulloch) and in the decisions of other federal courts, especially Timberlane. Whether the Restatement precisely reflects international law in every detail matters little here, as I believe this litigation would be resolved the same way under virtually any conceivable test that takes account of foreign regulatory interests.

Under the Restatement, a nation having some "basis" for jurisdiction to prescribe law should nonetheless refrain from exercising that jurisdiction "with respect to a person or activity having connections with another state when the exercise of such jurisdiction is unreasonable." Restatement (Third) § 403(1). The "reasonableness" inquiry turns on a number of factors including, but not limited to: "the extent to which the activity takes place within the territory [of the regulating state]," id., § 403(2)(a); "the connections, such as nationality, residence, or economic activity, between the regulating state and the person principally responsible for the activity to be regulated," id., § 403(2)(b); "the character of the activity to be regulated, the importance of regulation to the regulating state, the extent to which other states regulate such activities, and the degree to which the desirability of such regulation is generally accepted," id., § 403(2)(c); "the extent to which another state may have an interest in regulating the activity," id., § 403(2)(g); and "the likelihood of conflict with regulation by another state," id., § 403(2)(h). Rarely would these factors point more clearly against application of United States law. The activity relevant to the counts at issue here took place primarily in the United Kingdom, and the defendants in these counts are British corporations and British subjects having their principal place of business or residence outside the United States. Great Britain has established a comprehensive regulatory scheme governing the London reinsurance markets, and clearly has a heavy "interest in regulating the activity," id., § 403(2)(g). [cit.] Finally, § 2(b) of the McCarran–Ferguson Act allows state regulatory statutes to override the Sherman Act in the insurance field, subject only to the narrow "boycott" exception set forth in § 3(b)—suggesting that "the importance of regulation to the [United States]," Restatement (Third) § 403(2)(c), is slight. Considering these factors, I think it unimaginable that an assertion of legislative jurisdiction by the United States would be considered reasonable, and therefore it is inappropriate to assume, in the absence of statutory indication to the contrary, that Congress has made such an assertion.

It is evident from what I have said that the Court's comity analysis, which proceeds as though the issue is whether the courts should "decline to exercise ... jurisdiction," [cit.], rather than whether the Sherman Act covers this conduct, is simply misdirected. I do not at all agree, moreover, with the Court's conclusion that the issue of the substantive scope of the Sherman Act is not in the cases. [cit.] To be sure, the parties did not make a clear distinction between adjudicative jurisdiction and the scope of the statute. Parties often do not, as we have observed (and have declined to punish with procedural default) before. [cit.] It is not realistic, and also not helpful, to pretend that the only really relevant issue in this litigation is not before us. In any event, if one erroneously chooses, as the Court does, to make adjudicative jurisdiction (or, more precisely, abstention) the vehicle for taking account of the needs of prescriptive comity, the Court still gets it wrong. It concludes that no "true conflict" counseling nonapplication of United States law (or rather, as it thinks, United States judicial jurisdiction) exists unless compliance with United States law would constitute a *violation* of another country's law. [cit.] That breathtakingly broad proposition, which contradicts the many cases discussed earlier, will bring the Sherman Act and other laws into sharp and unnecessary conflict with the legitimate interests of other countries—particularly our closest trading partners.

In the sense in which the term "conflic[t]" was used in Lauritzen, and is generally understood in the field of conflicts of laws, there is clearly a conflict in this litigation. The petitioners here, like the defendant in Lauritzen, were not compelled by any foreign law to take their allegedly wrongful actions, but that no more precludes a conflict-of-laws analysis here than it did there. [cit.] Where applicable foreign and domestic law provide different substantive rules of decision to govern the parties' dispute, a conflict-of-laws analysis is necessary ...

Literally the only support that the Court adduces for its position is § 403 of the Restatement (Third)—or more precisely Comment e to that provision, which states:

"Subsection (3) [which says that a State should defer to another state if that State's interest is clearly greater] applies only when one state requires what another prohibits, or where compliance with the regulations of two states exercising jurisdiction consistently with this section is otherwise impossible. It does not apply where a person subject to regulation by two states can comply with the laws of both...."

The Court has completely misinterpreted this provision. Subsection (3) of § 403 (requiring one State to defer to another in the limited circumstances just described) comes into play only after subsection (1) of § 403 has been complied with—i.e., after it has been determined that the exercise of jurisdiction by both of the two States is not "unreasonable." That prior question is answered by applying the factors (inter alia) set forth in subsection (2) of § 403, that is, precisely the factors that I have discussed in text and that the Court rejects.

* * *

I would reverse the judgment of the Court of Appeals on this issue, and remand to the District Court with instructions to dismiss for failure to state a claim on the three counts at issue * * *.

———

Notes & Questions

1. On this subject, see, generally, Symeon C. Symeonides, Wendy Collins Perdue, Arthur von Mehren, CONFLICT OF LAWS: AMERICAN, COMPARATIVE, INTERNATIONAL 58–563 (1998). *Professor Symeonides explains* that both the Majority and Dissenting opinions agree that the U.S. Congress has constitutional authority to promulgate laws (prescriptive jurisdiction, as opposed to adjudicative or enforcement jurisdiction) occurring outside U.S. territory. Their disagreement is whether Congress intended to have this law reach the conduct at issue. It is clear that Congress has authority to legislate, even criminalize, fully extraterritorial conduct. See, e.g., U.S. Const. Art. 1 § 8. On the issue of the "effects doctrine," Justice Souter reiterates the holding of *Strassheim v. Daily, supra*, which requires the concurrence of two elements for jurisdiction to obtain: (1) the foreign conduct must be intended to produce effects in the U.S.; and (2) it must have actually produced such effects. What are the benefits and the disadvantages of this rule?

2. Professor Symeonides also notes the reality that most statutes are silent on whether they are to apply extraterritorially or have "boilerplate language" that is so catholic that, if taken literally, would always apply everywhere at all times. The courts must determine whether Congress really intended this to occur. In reality, there is a "presumption against extraterritoriality." Symeonides, et al., at 557–558, citing *The Apollon*, 22 U.S. (9 Wheat.) 362 (1824), decided by Justice Joseph Story, who wrote that, "[t]he laws of no nation can justly extend beyond its own territory,

except so far as regards its own citizens. . . ." *The Apollon*, at 370. Justice Story continued, relying on "the law of nations": "[H]owever general and comprehensive the phrases used in our municipal laws may be, they must always be restricted in construction, to places and persons, upon whom the legislature have authority and jurisdiction." *Id.* American Banana shows how rigidly this anti-extraterritoriality presumption was applied during the 19th Century and the first two decades of the 20th. Symeonides, et al., *supra*, at 558, also noting Justice Holmes holding that, "[for a nation] to lay hold of the actor, to treat him according to its own notions rather than those of the place where he did the acts, not only would be unjust, but would be an interference with the authority of another sovereign, contrary to the comity of nations." *Milliken v. Pratt*, 125 Mass. 374 (1878); *Id.* This presumption was a bit weak until resurrected in 1991, when the Supreme Court decided *EEOC v. Arabian American Oil Co.*, 499 U.S. 244 (1991) and followed by *Smith v. U.S.*, 507 U.S. 197 (1993); and *Sale v. Haitian Centers Council, Inc.*, 509 U.S. 155 (1993). *Id.* These latter cases dealt with applying citizens rights and interests extraterritorially, rather than limiting them. *Hartford Insurance* turns this trend around again, without mentioning its decisions noted immediately above. Does this mean that the presumption against extraterritoriality has been abandoned? *Id.* What, if anything, does the *Alvarez-Machain* decision suggest in this regard?

3. ***The Principle of Reasonableness***. U.S. jurisprudence has also expanded the application of the traditional bases of jurisdiction. Jurisdiction has been expanded to apply to thwarted extraterritorial narcotics conspiracies, even when no element of the offense (or any effect) has occurred in U.S. territory. The Restatement (3rd) endorses this expansion. Even when a narcotics conspiracy has occurred abroad and was thwarted before any effect or element occurs in the territory, the Restatement and the courts provide that *"territorial"* jurisdiction applies, as long as the intent was to violate U.S. law or territory. Jurisdiction, however, is not to be asserted if it will violate a significant interest of another state or is otherwise exorbitant. The rule of reasonableness limits the impact somewhat by providing that even where a basis for jurisdiction applies, it should not be asserted if such assertion is unreasonable or exorbitant. U.S. courts have utilized this rule in conjunction to expanding the territoriality theories of jurisdiction. In his dissenting opinion in *Hartford Fire*, *supra*, Justice Scalia, joined by 3 other Justices, accepted the "rule of reasonableness."

4. ***More on the economic effects doctrine, antitrust and jurisdictional conflicts.*** The U.S. and other nations have traditionally tried to exclude domestic economic impacts resulting from external conduct. The rationale is that such effects, although not palpable like those resulting from bullets and poisoned chocolates, are harmful and may be considered to be *"territorial"* nonetheless. Harm has become a proxy for territory. Foreign economic activity is argued to be within a state's prescriptive jurisdiction if it produces discernible and serious economic damage. Both the 1965 and 1987 Restatements of Foreign Relations Law claim that this idea is a matter of customary international law. German legislation explicitly recognizes the effects doctrine for such matters. This also seems implicit in the economic regulatory laws of some other states. This may also be true for the European Union.

5. *Professor Symeonides discusses Justice Scalia's dissent in Hartford, which noted* the claim of no true conflict between American and British law to be a "breathtakingly broad proposition, which . . . will bring the Sherman Act and other laws into sharp and unnecessary conflict with the legitimate interests of other countries—particularly our closest trading partners." He said that, in the sense in which the term "conflict" is generally understood in the field of conflicts of laws, there is clearly a conflict whenever applicable foreign and domestic law provide different substantive rules of decision to govern the parties' dispute, and that in such a case a conflict-of-laws analysis is necessary. Justice Scalia distinguished between adjudicatory jurisdiction and legislative or prescriptive jurisdiction. He agreed with the majority that the district court unquestionably did have adjudicatory jurisdiction, and that Congress did possess legislative jurisdiction to regulate the defendants' London activity. However, the question was whether Congress had actually done so, which in turn depended on how one delineates the extraterritorial reach of the Sherman Act. In such delineation, Scalia said that one should keep in mind that, even when the presumption against extraterritoriality is overcome, an act of Congress ought not to be construed in a way that violates the principles of international law, including "international comity," which is a traditional component of choice-of-law theory. Relying on section 403 of the Restatement (3rd) of Foreign Relations Law, Scalia concluded that an interpretation of the Sherman Act that would make it applicable to defendant's London activities would be "unreasonable." He pointed out that the defendants' activity took place primarily in the United Kingdom, and that the defendants are British corporations having their principal place of business or residence outside the United States. Great Britain has established a comprehensive regulatory scheme governing the London reinsurance markets, and clearly has a heavy "interest in regulating the activity."

6. The European approach was "updated" in the *"Wood Pulp"* decision, *In re Wood Pulp Cartel,* 1985 O.J. (L § 85) 1, (1985), 3 C.M.L.R. 474 (1985, *aff'd sub nom, Case 89/85, A Ahlstoöm Osakeyhito v. Comm'n,* 1988 E.C.R. 5193, 1988) 4 C.M.L.R. 901 (1988); Joseph P. Griffin, *Foreign Governmental Reactions to U.S. Assertions of Extraterritorial Jurisdiction,* 6 Geo.Mason L.Rev. 505 (1998). The European Court of Justice established an *"implementation"* basis for jurisdiction, holding, in *Wood Pulp,* that pursuant to article 85 of the Treaty of Rome, jurisdiction obtains over non-European companies functioning outside the European Union, if they *"implement"* an anticompetitive agreement, even when this agreement is entered outside EU territory, if they sell their product to purchasers inside the Union. Griffin, *Foreign Reactions, supra.* The *Avocat–Général* of the Court of Justice recommended, not long after this decision, in *Dyestuffs Cartel,* that cartels located outside the Community be reached under the effects doctrine, but the Court chose to apply Community antitrust law on the ground that such external parent companies had wholly-owned subsidiaries within the Community. *Imperial Chemical Industries Ltd. v. E.C. Commission,* 11 Comm.Mkt.L.R. 557 (1972). Thus, the EU Commission has claimed jurisdiction based on the *"effects"* theory, but the European Court of Justice has refused to adopt "U.S. version" of the effects theory, distinguishing it from its own *"implementation"* doctrine. Griffin, *Foreign*

Reactions, supra. **Query:** *are these theories functional equivalents?* They certainly have produced similar results, except in certain narrow circumstances, such as when a U.S. firm refuses to sell to firms in the EU This may cause an effect, but would not fit the "implementation" theory. *Id.*

c. Jurisdiction to Prescribe Choice of Law Rules

It has been noted that "choice of law is a mess ... It is a 'dismal swamp,' a morass of confusion, a body of doctrine 'killed by a realism intended to save it,' and now universally said to be a 'disaster.' ... One way to demonstrate its tribulations would be to look at the academic dissensus and the hopelessly underdeterminative Restatement (Second)." Kermit Roosevelt III, *The Myth of Choice of Law: Rethinking Conflicts*, 97 Mich.L.Rev. 2448 (1999). We will do that, but will leave further study of this to scholarly authority on Conflicts of Law.

SECTION 19

1965 Restatement

JURISDICTION TO PRESCRIBE RULES FOR ADJUDICATION
OR OTHER DETERMINATION OF CLAIMS

(1) Subject to the limitation of Subsection (2), a state has jurisdiction to prescribe a rule as to choice of the law governing the substantive adjudication or other determination of a claim asserted in its territory against a person, or with respect to a thing, located there, or another interest localized there, even though the state does not otherwise have a basis of jurisdiction under § 10 to prescribe a rule of law with respect to the conduct giving rise to the claim.

(2) In prescribing a rule of choice of law as indicated in Subsection (1), a state is acting within its jurisdiction if it gives effect either

(a) to a rule of law applicable to the conduct giving rise to the claim, prescribed by a state having jurisdiction to prescribe with respect to that conduct, or

(b) to a rule of its own law that would have been applicable to the conduct giving rise to the claim if the state had had jurisdiction to prescribe with respect to that conduct. However, the rule of choice of law prescribed under Subsection (1) must be a conflict of laws rule designed primarily for the adjudication or other determination of claims of a private nature rather than a rule designed to control conduct not within the state's jurisdiction to prescribe.

1987 RESTATEMENT SECTION 401: CATEGORIES OF JURISDICTION

Under international law, a state is subject to limitations on

(1) jurisdiction to prescribe, *i.e.,* to make its law applicable to the activities, relations, or status of persons, or the interests of persons in things, whether by legislation, by executive act or order, by administrative rule or regulation, or by determination of a court;

(2) jurisdiction to adjudicate, *i.e.,* to subject persons or things to the process of its courts or administrative tribunals, whether in civil or in

criminal proceedings, whether or not the state is a party to the proceedings;

(3) jurisdiction to enforce, *i.e.*, to induce or compel compliance or punish noncompliance with its laws or regulations, whether through the courts or by use of executive, administrative, police, or other non-judicial action.

(4.) *Comparison.* Section 401(2) of the 1987 Restatement appears to cover what is in Section 19 of the 1965 Restatement.

Recent Scholarship. Although the American Law Institute was formulating a new Restatement of Conflict of Laws in the same decade, this work did not follow the interest analysis approach in either its original or its modified versions. See, however, Restatement, Second, Conflict of Laws, § 6. *See also,* Symeon Symeonides, Wendy C. Perdue, & Arthur T. von Mehren, CONFLICT OF LAWS: AMERICAN, COMPARATIVE, INTERNATIONAL (1998).

2.   NATIONALITY THEORY: ACTIVE, ASCRIBED AND PASSIVE PERSONALITY[a]

The active and passive personality theories have applied since the days of Roman Law. The active personality principle provides jurisdiction over a state's nationals. The passive personality principle provides jurisdiction over those who injure a state's nationals. Ascribed nationality is where a state's nationality is ascribed to a legal person like a ship or a corporation. They were adapted and expanded, becoming widespread during the Middle Ages. German criminalists of the 19th century promoted their *Realsystem,* which combined *passive personality with active personality* (nationality) jurisdiction and the *protective principle. Realsystem* emphasized the role of the state's duty to protect its sovereignty, dignity and security, which were infringed when a national committed a crime or was the victim of a crime. Sovereignty is considered to a degree to be based on a state's ability to control and protect its nationals.

----

a.   Active Personality (*personalité active*)

The nationality principle stems from the Roman Law that a citizen carried his law on his back. For many *"Civil Law"* nations this is a very important, almost sacrosanct (often constitutional), basis of jurisdiction which permits a state to prescribe rules of conduct for nationals even when they are outside its territory. The rationale is that national sovereign pride and honor are tainted when a national commits an offense abroad. It is considered necessary that the state have authority to control its nationals to ensure that its laws, reputation, and sovereignty are respected. Another aspect of this principle is that it assumes that the national's own system of justice is the more appropriate and fair one to apply to nationals. Thus, they refuse to extradite them. *See gen.*, Michael Plachta, *(Non)-Extradition of Nationals: A Neverending Story?*, 13 Emory I.L.Rev. 77 (1999). Although the application and use of nationality jurisdiction is not as pronounced in Anglo–American systems as it is on the Continent or in Latin America, it is not uncommon. Unlike most European and Latin American counterparts, however, the U.S. does not refuse to extradite its nationals. Colombia and the Dominican Republic have recently passed non-retroactive legislation allowing discretion to extradite nationals. *See, e.g., Acto Legislativo No. 10 de 1997, art. 1 ("[a]demas, la extradicion de los colombianos por nacimiento se concedera por delitos cometidos en el exterior.").*

Samuel Sheinbein Case–A rather stark example of both aspects of the nationality principle arose in the *Sheinbein case* that arose in the U.S. and Israel. Israel refused to extradite a national, but prosecuted him. Samuel Sheinbein was a dual-national (U.S. and Israel), because his father was born in Israel. The father had left Israel as a child and Samuel had never been to Israel, until he arrived to try to escape prosecution in Maryland for a gruesome murder that he committed there. The U.S. sought Sheinbein's extradition, but Israel's law forbade extradition of Israeli nationals, so the request, although approved by the District Court, was denied by the Israeli Supreme Court. Quite interestingly, in this case, the U.S.–Israel Extradition Treaty at the time explicitly prohibited refusal of extradition on the basis of nationality, but also provided that extradition would be governed by the law of the requested state. The Supreme Court, in a 3–2 decision held that he was a national, that he could not be extradited, but stated that the law on extradition on this point should be changed. Sheinbein ultimately pled guilty in Israel and was sentenced to 24 years in prison, a sentence that many considered to be light for his very gruesome murder. Israel, embarrassed by the case and amended its law to allow extradition of nationals, on condition that they would be allowed to serve their sentences in Israel. For background, see, Abraham Abramovsky & Jonathan Edelstein, *The Sheinbein Case and the Israeli–American Extradition Experience: A Need for Compromise*, 32 Vand.J.Transnat'l L. 305 (1999); Yaffa Zilbershats, *Extraditing Israeli Citizens to the U.S.–Extradition & Citizenship Dilemmas*, 21 Mich.J.Int'l L. 297 (2000).

――――――

b. *Ascribed Nationality*

1. *General principle.* A state may ascribe its nationality to "legal persons," like corporations, vessels, aircraft, or even military services or bases. The nationality of these entities provides a basis for jurisdiction. The scope of the jurisdiction, however, is not exactly the same as that for nationality of a natural person.

2. *Vessels, aircraft and military services.* Prescriptive jurisdiction based on the nationality of vessels, aircraft and military services generally obtains either in the state in which the entity is registered, licensed, or has its legal and managerial control. Jurisdiction to enforce the rules prescribed accompanies the vessels, aircraft or military services wherever they go. Enforcement jurisdiction is limited even more rigorously by sovereignty

and other rules of international law. Thus, it is illegal, for example, to board a foreign flag vessel without the permission of the flag state. Jurisdiction extends, moreover, to persons aboard the vessels or aircraft, as well as to members of the military services, regardless of the nationality of the individuals. In *The Queen v. Anderson,* [1868] L.R. 1 Cr.Cas.Res. 161, a U.S. seaman was convicted of manslaughter for a killing on a British vessel navigating some 45 miles upstream on the Garonne River in France. France chose not to exercise its concurrent jurisdiction, deciding that British law applied. The British convict the perpetrator. Jurisdiction over military services is more complex, controlled by Status of Forces Agreements or their equivalent, discussed *infra.*

3. *Corporations.* Corporations and other legal persons are generally considered to have the nationality of the place of their incorporation. *See, The Barcelona Traction, Light & Power Co., Ltd. (Belgium v. Spain),* 1970 I.C.J. 3. Do you think that there may be a better way to determine this? Should courts consider the place of management, the nationality of the directors or such like? Suppose a corporation formed in a foreign state and doing all its business there is a subsidiary of a U.S. corporation. Does the United States government have jurisdiction to order the U.S. parent corporation to order its subsidiary to take action in that wholly owned subsidiary's home country even if to take such action would violate the law of its home state? In *Dresser Industries and the Siberian Pipeline,* 549 F.Supp. 108 (D.D.C.1982), a U.S. federal court approved, in 1982, a Commerce Department plan to penalize *Dresser Industries,* a U.S. Company, for supplying equipment to the Siberian pipeline in defiance of Reagan Administration sanctions (*Export Administration Act of 1979*). *Dresser France,* a wholly owned French subsidiary operating in France, was required by French law to supply the equipment. *Dresser France* argued that complying with the U.S. order would subject it to penalties in France. Dresser US had refused to order its French subsidiary to defy a French Government order to deliver. The press reported that both companies could face criminal sanctions in the US and that *Dresser France* would be placed on a "denial list," which would prevent it from having any commercial dealings with the U.S. Does the U.S. or the French government have the right to control the conduct of Dresser France? Was it appropriate for the U.S. Government to sanction a wholly owned foreign subsidiary of a U.S. company for complying with its own government's orders? The U.S. Department of Justice refused to concede that the French order was "valid under French law." European Governments registered protests against such expansive extraterritorial jurisdiction. Do you agree with the Justice Department official, who argued that France could not validly exercise jurisdiction over Dresser France? Does the U.S. have authority under U.S. law to order Dresser France not to ship the equipment or to punish them for doing so? What about under international law? If the answer differs in each, which is the better rule?

----

c. Passive Personality
The Cutting Case Letter, Secretary of State to United States Ambassador to Mexico

[1887]   Foreign Relations of the United States 751 (1888).

Department of State, Washington, November 1, 1887.

SIR: On the 19th of July 1886, the minister of the United States at the City of Mexico was instructed to demand ... the Mexican Government [to] release ... A.K. Cutting, a [U.S.] citizen ... , then imprisoned at Paso del Norte since, on a charge of libel alleged to have been published by him in Texas.

The case was first brought to the notice of the Department by Mr. Brigham, consul of the United States at Paso del Norte, who ... reported that Mr. Cutting had been arrested and imprisoned ... for the publication in Texas ... of an alleged libel against a citizen of Mexico * * *

* * * It is sufficient here to state, ... that the ground upon which Mr. Cutting's release was demanded was that the judicial tribunals of Mexico were not competent under the rules of international law to try a [U.S.] citizen ... for an offense committed and consummated in his own country, merely because the person offended happened to be a Mexican. * * *

* * * Not only was this claim, which is defined in Article 186 of the Mexican penal code, defended and enforced by [Trial] Judge Zubia, ... whose decision was affirmed by the supreme court of Chihuahua * * *, but the claim was defended and justified by the Mexican Government. * * *

The statement of the consul at Paso del Norte that Mr. Cutting was arrested on the charge of the publication in Texas of an alleged libel against a Mexican is fully sustained by the opinion of Judge Zubia. It is stated that on the 22nd of June, 1886, "the plaintiff enlarged the accusation, stating that although the newspaper, the El Paso Sunday Herald, is published in Texas, Mr. Cutting had circulated a great number in this town (Paso del Norte) and in the interior of the Republic, it having been read by more than three persons, for which reason an order had been issued to seize the copies which were still in the office of the said Cutting." The conclusive inference from this statement is that the charge upon which the warrant of arrest was issued was the publication of the alleged libel in Texas. * * * It appears, however, that the claim made in Article 186 of the Mexican penal code was actually enforced in the case in question as a distinct and original ground of prosecution. [Judge Zubia's decision] was framed in the alternative, and it was held that, even supposing the defamation arose solely from the publication of the alleged libel in the El Paso (Texas) Sunday Herald, Article 186 of the Mexican penal code provided for punishment in that case; Judge Zubia saying that it did not belong to the judge to examine the principle laid down in that article but to apply it fully, it being the law in force in the State of Chihuahua. It nowhere appears that the Texas publication was ever circulated in Mexico so as to constitute the crime of defamation under the Mexican law. As has been seen, this was not a part of the original charge on which the warrant for Mr. Cutting's arrest was issued; and while it is stated in Judge Zubia's decision that an order was issued for the seizure of copies of the Texas paper which might be found in the office of Mr. Cutting in Paso del Norte, it nowhere appears from that decision that any copies were actually found in that place or elsewhere in Mexico.

But, however this may be, this Government is still compelled to deny what it denied on the 19th of July, 1886, and what the Mexican Government has since executively and judicially maintained, that a citizen of the United States can be held under the rules of international law to answer in Mexico for an offense committed in the United States, simply because the object of that offense happens to be a citizen of Mexico. * * *

* * *

As to the question of international law, I am unable to discover any principle upon which the assumption of jurisdiction made in Article 186 of the Mexican penal code can be justified. There is no principle better settled than that the penal laws of a country have no extraterritorial force. Each state may, it is true, provide for the punishment of its own citizens for acts committed by them outside of its territory; but this makes the penal law a personal statute, and while it may give rise to inconvenience and injustice in many cases, it is a matter in which no other Government has the right to interfere. To say, however, that the penal laws of a country can bind foreigners and regulate their conduct, either in their own or any other foreign country, is to assert a jurisdiction over such countries and to impair their independence. Such is the consensus of opinion of the leading authorities on international law at the present day * * *. There being then no principle of international law which justifies such a pretension, any assertion of it must rest, as an exception to the rule, either upon the general concurrence of nations or upon express conventions. Such a concurrence in respect to the claim made in Article 186 of the Mexican penal code can not be found in the legislation of the present day. Though formerly asserted by a number of minor states, it has now been generally abandoned, and may be regarded as almost obsolete.

* * *

It has constantly been laid down in the United States as a rule of action, that citizens of the United States can not be held answerable in foreign countries for offenses which were wholly committed and consummated either in their own country or in other countries not subject to the jurisdiction of the punishing state. When a citizen of the United States commits in his own country a violation of its laws, it is his right to be tried under and in accordance with those laws, and in accordance with the fundamental guaranties of the Federal Constitution in respect to criminal trials in every part of the United States.

To say that he may be tried in another country for his offense, simply because its object happens to be a citizen of that country, would be to assert that foreigners coming to the United States bring hither the penal laws of the country from which they come, and thus subject citizens of the United States in their own country to an indefinite criminal responsibility. Such a pretension can never be admitted. * * *

* * *

You are therefore instructed to say to the Mexican Government, not only that an indemnity should be paid to Mr. Cutting for his arrest and detention in Mexico on the charge of publishing a libel in the United States against a Mexican, but also, in the interests of good neighborhood and future amity, that the statute proposing to confer such extraterritorial jurisdiction should, as containing a claim invasive of the independent sovereignty of a neighboring and friendly state, be repealed. * * *

     * * *

T.F. BAYARD.

Questions & Discussion

1.   Consider the spirit of Secretary of State Bayard's language again after you read the *Alvarez–Machain Case, infra.* Secretary of State Bayard objected to Mexico's prosecution of a U.S. national "merely because the person offended [was] a Mexican."

2.   The passive personality theory has traditionally been anathema to U.S. law and practice. It began in ancient Rome and was revitalized in medieval Europe, when it was widespread especially in Italy. Its rationale is that, because criminal law has as its essential object to protect public and private interests (the private ones implicating the public), the victim's national system has the better appreciation of what protection should be afforded. It fell into desuetude during the heyday of positivism in the 19th and early 20th centuries, but rebounded and is gaining popularity, especially in relation to terrorism.

3.   In the *Lotus case, supra,* France argued before the Permanent Court of International Justice that "international law does not allow a State to [proceed against] offences committed by foreigners abroad, simply by reason of the nationality of the victim," but the court did not decide whether France was correct. Since then, France has enacted legislation based on passive nationality—*Code de Procédure Pénale,* Article 689 (1).

4.   Article 5 of the 1979 International Convention Against the Taking of Hostages and the Omnibus Diplomatic Security and Anti–Terrorism Act of 1986, Ch. 113A, added to 18 U.S.C. § 2331, provide for jurisdiction when a U.S. national is taken hostage, injured or killed in certain circumstances. The Anti–Terrorism Act provides jurisdiction, without the benefit of an international convention, over terrorist acts of violence abroad against U.S. nationals. The basis of jurisdiction is actually a combination of the passive personality and protective principles. An implication of *national* interests is required, in addition to the violence against a national. Thus, they are actually more like the protective principle than passive personality. Terrorism virtually by definition threatens national security or important governmental interests. See full discussion in Blakesley, TERRORISM, DRUGS * * * *supra* at 132–134, 136–37.

3.   THE PROTECTIVE PRINCIPLE: EXTRATERRITORIAL CONDUCT AFFECTING IMPORTANT STATE INTERESTS

United States v. Pizzarusso

United States Court of Appeals, Second Circuit, 1968.
388 F.2d 8.

MEDINA, CIRCUIT JUDGE. This case ... brings before this Court for the first time the question of the jurisdiction of the District Court to indict and convict a foreign citizen of the crime of knowingly making a false statement under oath in a visa application to an American consular official located in a foreign country, in violation of 18 U.S.C. Section 1546.[a] Supreme Court cases give some guidance but none of them passes on this question directly.

The indictment charges that Pizzarusso wilfully made under oath a number of false statements in her "Application for Immigrant Visa And Alien Registration" at the American Consulate, Montreal, Canada. * * * Although at all times pertinent to this case she was a citizen of Canada, she was taken into custody in the Southern District of New York. * * *

Upon the issuance of the visa and by its use Mrs. Pizzarusso immediately entered [U.S. territory], but this fact is not [relevant or] . . . material, as we find the crime was complete when the false statements were made to an American consular official in Montreal. * * *

The evidence to sustain the charge is so overwhelming that we shall not pause to discuss it. Indeed, the only contention made on this appeal is that the District Court lacked jurisdiction to indict appellant and convict her of the crime alleged. As we find no lack of jurisdiction, we affirm the judgment. Our reasons follow.

　　　* * *

International law has recognized, in varying degrees, five bases of jurisdiction with respect to the enforcement of the criminal law. * * * Thus both the territoriality and nationality principles, under which jurisdiction is determined by either the situs of the crime or the nationality of the accused, are universally accepted. The third basis, the protective principle, covers the instant case. By virtue of this theory a state "has jurisdiction to prescribe a rule of law attaching legal consequences to conduct outside its territory that threatens its security as a state or the operation of its governmental functions, provided the conduct is generally recognized as a crime under the law of states that have reasonably developed legal systems." * * *

Traditionally, the United States has relied primarily upon the territoriality and nationality principles, * * * and judges have often been reluctant to ascribe extraterritorial effect to statutes. * * * Our courts have developed what has come to be termed the objective territorial principle as a means of expanding the power to control activities detrimental to the state. This principle has been aptly defined by Mr. Justice Holmes in Strassheim v. Daily. "Acts done outside a jurisdiction, but intended to produce and producing detrimental effects within it, justify a state in punishing the cause of the harm as if he had been present at the effect * * *." * * * Underlying this principle is the theory that the "detrimental effects" constitute an element of the offense and since they occur within the country, jurisdiction is properly invoked under the territorial principle. * * *

However, the objective territorial principle is quite distinct from the protective theory. Under the latter, all the elements of the crime occur in the foreign country and jurisdiction exists because these actions have a

_____

a. Fraud and misuse of visas, permits and other entry documents. * * *

"potentially adverse effect" upon security or governmental functions, and there need not be any actual effect in the country as would be required under the objective territorial principle. Courts have often failed to perceive this distinction. Thus, the Ninth Circuit, in upholding a conviction under a factual situation similar to the one in the instant case, relied on the protective theory, but still felt constrained to say that jurisdiction rested partially on the adverse effect produced as a result of the alien's entry into the United States. The Ninth Circuit also cited Strassheim and Aluminum Company of America as support for its decision. With all due deference to our brothers of the Ninth Circuit, however, we think this reliance is unwarranted. A violation of 18 U.S.C.A. Section 1546 is complete at the time the alien perjures himself in the foreign country. It may be possible that the particular criminal sanctions of Section 1546 will never be enforced unless the defendant enters the country, but entry is not an element of the statutory offense. Were the statute re-drafted and entry made a part of the crime we would then be presented with a clear case of jurisdiction under the objective territorial principle.

Statutes imposing criminal liability on aliens for committing perjury in United States Consulates in foreign countries have been in existence for over one hundred years * * *. Only one court has ever held that the United States did not have jurisdiction to proceed against an alien under the legislation governing this case. U.S. v. Baker ... In Baker it was conceded that there was authority for deporting an alien for making perjurious statements to a United States Consul, U.S. ex rel. Majka v. Palmer, ... but the court thought the imposition of criminal sanctions was "far different" from deportation and dismissed the indictment. We would have sustained jurisdiction in Baker had the case been before us, and in this view we are apparently joined by the judge who decided Baker, since he presided over the instant case in the court below.

Affirmed.

✦ a. *Distinction Between the Territorial, the Protective Principle, and Passive Personality.*

The protective principle requires no territorial nexus. Its focus is the nature of the interest that is or may be injured, rather than the territory upon which the conduct or its effects occur. It provides jurisdiction over offenses committed *outside* the forum state's territory, but *only when* the conduct injures or threatens to injure that state's security, sovereignty, or an important governmental function. Conduct, such as terrorism or hostage taking, designed to intimidate a government or to extort a concession would meet this test. The protective principle is the only accepted theory that allows jurisdiction over conduct that poses only a *potential* threat to the interests of the asserting state.

Early drafts of the *Omnibus Anti–Terrorism Act of 1986* used language considered too broad because it covered all serious extraterritorial criminal violence against U.S. nationals, rather than terrorism. Ultimately, Congress attempted to make the Act apply strictly to terrorist violence, providing:

"No prosecution for any offense described in this section shall be undertaken by the United States except on written certification of the Attorney General or the highest ranking subordinate * * * with responsibility for criminal prosecutions that, in the judgment of the certifying official, such *offense was intended to coerce, intimidate, or retaliate against a government or a civilian population.*" What do you think of the language calling for the Attorney General to determine what conduct is terroristic? For analysis of the British approach, *see*, Clive Walker, *Constitutional Governance & Special Powers Against Terrorism: Lessons from the United Kingdom's Prevention of Terrorism Acts*, 35 Colum.J.Trans'l L. 1 (1997); Clive Walker, *The Bombs in Omagh & their Aftermath: The Criminal Justice (Terrorism & Conspiracy) Act 1998*, 62 The Mod.L.Rev. 879 (1999).

Rosalyn Higgins, in her *General Course on Public International Law: International Law and the Avoidance, Containment and Resolution of Disputes*, [1991–V] Recueil Des Cours 100–104, states:

* * * we must also admit that in recent years there has been a revived interest in invoking the passive personality principle. This has occurred against the background of the explosion of international terrorism. * * * Accordingly, other States with a direct legal interest in the events and a strong political belief in the need to combat terrorism have sought to identify a possible basis for asserting jurisdiction themselves. The United States and France provide interesting examples.* * * [The U.S. Terrorist Prosecution Act of 1985, and the Omnibus Diplomatic Security and Anti-terrorism Act of 1986 appear][196] * * * to establish a passive personality basis of jurisdiction. However, it would seem that the assertion of jurisdiction is still intended to be limited to offences that would commonly be described as "terrorist" offences. There appears to be no intention to assert jurisdiction (notwithstanding the broad wording of the Act), where, for example, Americans abroad are the victims of bar room violence or robberies. * * *

Thus the passive personality principle is invoked by the United States, but only in relation to terrorist-type offences. The confinement of a passive personality claim to terrorist-type cases points to a constellation of facts which touches on a State's sovereignty and the security of its citizens in relation thereto. It has been pointed out that this "triggers the protective principle. Thus, there is no need to call upon the more controversial and less accepted passive personality theory."

In France too[199] traditional hostility to the passive personality principle has been overtaken by more recent legislation based on this principle. Once again, it has been explained by those responsible for such legislation that its invocation is intended to be restricted to cases involving national security.

---

196. 18 USC § 2331 (1986). For commentary, see C. Blakesley, "Jurisdictional Issues and Conflicts of Jurisdiction" in Legal Responses to International Terrorism, US Procedural Aspects (ed. Bassiouni) 1988, 131–181. Blakesley criticizes generally the attempts to extend the reach of US jurisdiction; and specifically the US Restatement as contrary to international legal principles. Ibid., fn. 26.

199. This aspect is very well explained in Blakesley, *supra*, at 172–177. * * *

b. *Expansion of the Protective Principle.* The court in Pizzarusso held that the principle was be applicable because the conduct of aliens abroad had a *"potentially* adverse effect" upon an important governmental function. The alternative would have been to hold that an effect in the territory had taken place when the aliens entered the United States. Traditionally the U.S. has applied the protective principle sparingly. The expanding use of the protective principle is consistent with an international practice. The 1987 Restatement provides in § 403 that a state has jurisdiction to prescribe with respect to "conduct outside its territory by persons not its nationals that is directed against the security of the state or against a limited class of other state interests."

Do you detect any dangers inherent in the protective principle?

c. Constitutional Limitations on Extraterritorial Jurisdiction: The "Nexus Requirement".

U.S. courts have taken to combining jurisdictional bases as factors to determine whether a sufficient nexus exists between a defendant and the U.S. sufficient to satisfy Due Process. The courts have considered some bases insufficient by themselves, but sufficient when combined with others. *See, e.g., U.S. v. Juda,* 46 F.3d 961 (9th Cir.1995), *cert. denied sub nom. Paris v. U.S.,* 514 U.S. 1090, & *cert. denied,* 515 U.S. 1169 (1995);*U.S. v. Davis,* 905 F.2d 245, 248–49 (9th Cir.1990), *cert. denied* 498 U.S. 1047 (1991) (noting that a federal criminal statute will apply extraterritorially only if there is a sufficient nexus); *U.S. v. Greer,* 956 F.Supp. 531, 535 (D.Vt.1997).

Notes & Questions: Traditionally, U.S. courts applied a fairly relaxed due process scrutiny in relation to jurisdiction over defendants on stateless vessels on the high seas. Is the traditional distinction between registered and stateless vessels constitutionally meaningful? What sorts of *nexes* ought to be sufficient to allow jurisdiction? The 9th Circuit in *Juda, cited supra* excluded a non-U.S. national from jurisdiction, notwithstanding the fact that members of the conspiracy committed material elements of the crime within U.S. territory Subjective territoriality clearly provided a sufficient nexus. The 9th Circuit in *Juda* also considered the protective principle insufficient by itself to be a nexus that would satisfy due process. Do you agree?

The traditional rule for registered vessels is that permission is required from the government for registry before boarding and seizure are legal. What is the rule for stateless vessels? Courts have held, however, that this nexus requirement does not apply to stateless vessels. *U.S. v. Caicedo,* 47 F.3d 370 (9th Cir.1995) ("... A nexus requirement, imposed as a matter of due process, makes sense when the 'rough guide' of international law also requires a nexus ... But where a defendant attempts to avoid the law of all nations by travelling [sic] on a stateless vessel, he has forfeited these protections ..."); *see, also, U.S. v. Wright–Barker,* 784 F.2d 161, 167–70, 175–76 (3d Cir.1986); *U.S. v. Rasheed,* 802 F.Supp. 312 (D.Hawai'i 1992). On some recent extension of constitutional protections to extradition, *see,* Lis Wiehl, *Extradition Law and the Crossroads: The Trend Toward Extend-*

ing Greater Constitutional Procedural Protections to Fugitives Fighting Extradition from the U.S., 19 Mich.J.Int'l L. 729 (1998).

4.   UNIVERSAL JURISDICTION

1987 Restatement, Section 404*

Universal Jurisdiction To Define And Punish Certain Offenses

"A state has jurisdiction to define and prescribe punishment for certain offenses recognized by the community of nations as of universal concern, such as piracy, slave trade, attacks on or hijacking of aircraft, genocide, war crimes, and *perhaps certain acts of terrorism,* even where none of the bases of jurisdiction indicated in § 402 is present."

1.   This theory provides that some conduct, wherever it occurs, creates jurisdiction and an obligation to prosecute or extradite in any nation that obtains custody of the perpetrator. *See, e.g., Demjanjuk v. Petrovsky,* 776 F.2d 571, 581–82 (6th Cir.1985), *infra,* Ch. 11 (explicitly recognizing the universality principle). *What conduct fits the universality theory? Who decides?* Piracy and slave trade have been widely considered to be the most ancient universal crimes. It is argued that piracy became a universal crime under customary international law because it was in the common interest of maritime states to preserve freedom of navigation. Is it clear that universal crimes are universal crimes or are they just crimes that all or most nations proscribe? Is there a difference? Some dispute the claim that piracy is an international crime, at least insofar as adjudicative and enforcement jurisdiction are concerned. *See,* Alfred P. Rubin, PIRACY (1997). Other crimes may also have become recognized as universal, perhaps arising from a non-derogable general principle recognized by all nations (*jus cogens*), or from customary international law. Many offenses are made "universal" by treaties to which virtually all or most nations are parties. If this is so, are the crimes in the treaties universal because they have been become custom? If not, what would make them universal crimes? Refer to Ch. 1 to see what is required for custom to develop. Some crimes covered by treaty include: Acts of violence against diplomats, see Chapter 12; Genocide (Chs. 9 & 15), Hijacking (Ch. 5), Sabotage of Civil Aircraft (Ch.5), Slave trade (*see,* Doc. Supp. for Articles 13 and 22 of the 1958 Convention on the High Seas and Articles 99 and 110 of the Convention on the Law of the Sea; Apartheid Convention), War crimes (Chs. 15, 16). These treaties must be consulted to determine the requirements for a state, which otherwise would have no jurisdiction, may participate in the repression of the particular crime.

2.   *Is terrorism a universal crime?* Despite the increase in the number of acts of terrorism in recent years, it is still a matter of controversy over whether it is a universal crime, especially given the difficulty arriving at an

acceptable definition sufficient for prosecution. For discussion of terrorism, see Ch. 11.

5. Extraterritorial Acts of Terrorism: What is the Basis of Jurisdiction?

a. What is Terrorism?

Defining terrorism is controversial. Some argue that the core of terrorism is "the use or threat of violence, a method of combat or a strategy to achieve certain goals, that its aim is to induce a state of fear in the victim, that it is ruthless and does not conform to humanitarian norms, and that publicity is an essential factor in terrorist strategy." Laqueur, *Reflections on Terrorism*, 65 For.Aff. at 86, 88 (1986). This may be true, but is the definition sufficient to allow prosecution? Is it too vague or broad? British law defines terrorism in the Criminal Justice (Terrorism & Conspiracy) Act 1998, as "the threat and use of violence for political ends". Would this definition satisfy Due Process in the U.S? *See* analysis in, Clive Walker, *The Bombs in Omagh & their Aftermath: The Criminal Justice (Terrorism & Conspiracy) Act 1998*, 62 The Mod.L.Rev. 879 (1999). If terrorism is a crime, what are its elements? What is the difference between Professor Laqueur's definition of terrorism and most conduct in war? Do all war crimes violate humanitarian norms? Is analogous conduct without belligerency terrorism? Does universal jurisdiction appropriately cover the conduct indicated in Laqueur's definition both during belligerency and non-belligerency? Is his definition clear enough to meet standards of *légalité* or the U.S. constitutional "vagueness" doctrine? Does Laqueur's element of "violating humanitarian norms" resolve the difficulty? Definitions have meaning and value only incident to and in the context of the purpose for which they are used. An anthropologist sees it one way, a political scientist another, a politician another, an international lawyer another, as would a prosecutor or defense attorney. Also any definition is complicated by propagandists who appropriate it to demonize their enemies and to promote their own ends. Do you think it is possible to arrive at a good legal definition of terrorism sufficient to justify the use of force or to prosecute its perpetrators?

U.S. v. Yunis

United States District Court, District of Columbia, 1988.
681 F.Supp. 896.

* * * In the original multi-count indictment, * * * the United States charged Fawaz Yunis, a resident and citizen of Lebanon, for his alleged involvement in the hijacking of a Jordanian civilian aircraft in the Middle East.

Defendant's counsel has moved to dismiss the indictment on grounds that this Court lacks subject matter jurisdiction under general principles of international law * * * [and] provisions of the United States Code. The motion is predicated on grounds that the Jordanian aircraft never flew over United States airspace and had no contact whatsoever with United States territory. Without such connection, Yunis' * * * counsel argues that this Court has no basis for asserting either subject matter or personal jurisdiction. In analyzing whether physical contact with the United States is necessary to proceed with the indictment, the Court first reviews the events surrounding the hijacking. The Court also examines various principles of international law to determine whether they afford grounds for exercising jurisdiction over defendant. Lastly, two relevant statutes, the Hostage Taking Act, 18 U.S.C. § 1203, and the several discrete provisions invoked under the Destruction of Aircraft Act, 18 U.S.C. §§ 82(a) and (b) [also referred to as The Aircraft Piracy Act] are examined to determine whether they apply to offenses committed overseas.[1]

* * *

[T]he Court concludes that consistent with reputable and generally accepted treatises and international law principles, there are sufficient grounds for asserting both subject matter and personal jurisdiction. Further, the Hostage Taking Act and Section 32(b) of the Aircraft Piracy Act impose liability for offenses allegedly committed by defendant. However, for the reasons explained more fully below, the Court concludes that Section 32(a) of the Aircraft Piracy Act does not apply. The alleged offenses thereunder have no connection whatsoever to United States territory.

I.

BACKGROUND

This criminal proceeding and indictment arise from the hijacking of a Jordanian civil aircraft. There is no dispute that the only nexus to the United States was the presence of several American nationals on board the flight. The airplane was registered in Jordan, flew the Jordanian flag and never landed on American soil or flew over American airspace.

* * *

* * * Its flightpath was limited to an area within and around the Mediterranean Sea. Based on the absence of any nexus to United States territory, Yunis has moved to dismiss the entire indictment, arguing that no United States federal court has jurisdiction to prosecute a foreign national for crimes committed in foreign airspace and on foreign soil. *He further claims that the presence of the American nationals on board the aircraft is an insufficient basis for exercising jurisdiction under principles of international law.* [emphasis added]

* * * [T]hreshold inquiries: whether * * * there is a basis for jurisdiction under international law, and if so, whether Congress intended to and had authority to extend jurisdiction of our federal courts over criminal offenses and events * * * committed and occurred overseas and out of the territorial jurisdiction of such courts.

---

1. Section 32(a) covers offenses committed on aircraft having some physical nexus to the United States, either operating in "the special aircraft jurisdiction" or in "overseas or foreign air commerce." Section 32(b) authorizes jurisdiction over offenses committed entirely in foreign airspace if the "offender is later found" in the United States.

II.

ANALYSIS

A.   JURISDICTION UNDER INTERNATIONAL LAW

The parties agree that there are five traditional bases of jurisdiction over extra-territorial crimes under international law: *Territorial; National; Protective; Universal; Passive personal.*

These general principles were developed in 1935 by a Harvard Research Project in an effort to codify principles of jurisdiction under international law. Most courts, including our Court of Appeals, have adopted the Harvard Research designations on jurisdiction.

* * *

The Universal and the Passive Personal principle appear to offer potential bases for asserting jurisdiction over the hostage-taking and aircraft piracy charges against Yunis. However, his counsel argues that the Universal principle is not applicable because neither hostage-taking nor aircraft piracy are heinous crimes encompassed by the doctrine. He urges further, that the United States does not recognize Passive Personal as a legitimate source of jurisdiction. The government flatly disagrees and maintains that jurisdiction is appropriate under both.

1. *Universal Principle*

The Universal principle recognizes that certain offenses are so heinous and so widely condemned that "any state if it captures the offender may prosecute and punish that person on behalf of the world community regardless of the nationality of the offender or victim or where the crime was committed." M. Bassiouni, II International Criminal Law, Ch. 6 at 298 (ed. 1986). The crucial question for purposes of defendant's motion is how crimes are classified as "heinous" and whether aircraft piracy and hostage taking fit into this category.

Those crimes that are condemned by the world community and subject to prosecution under the Universal principal [sic] are often a matter of international conventions or treaties. See Demjanjuk v. Petrovsky (treaty against genocide signed by a significant number of states made that crime heinous; therefore, Israel had proper [universal] jurisdiction over a Nazi war criminal. * * *

Both offenses are the subject of international agreements. A majority of states in the world community including Lebanon, have signed three treaties condemning aircraft piracy: The Tokyo Convention, The Hague Convention, and The Montreal Convention. The Hague and Montreal Conventions explicitly rely on the principle of Universal jurisdiction in mandating that all states "take such measures as may be necessary to establish its jurisdiction over the offences * * * where the alleged offender is present in its territory." Hague Convention Art. 4 § 2; Montreal Convention Art. 5 § 2. Further, those treaties direct that all "contracting states * * * of which the alleged offender is found, * * * shall, be obliged, *without exception whatsoever and whether or not the offense was committed in its territory,* to submit the case to its competent authorities for the purpose of prosecution." These two provisions together demonstrate the international community's strong commitment to punish aircraft hijackers irrespective of where the hijacking occurred.

The global community has adopted the International Convention for the Taking of Hostages, an agreement which condemns and criminalizes the offense of hostage taking. Like the conventions denouncing aircraft piracy, this treaty requires signatory states to prosecute any alleged offenders "present in its territory."

In light of the global efforts to punish aircraft piracy and hostage taking, international legal scholars unanimously agree that these crimes fit within the category of heinous crimes for purposes of asserting universal jurisdiction. See * * * Blakesley, United States Jurisdiction over Extraterritorial Crime, 73 J. Crim. L. & Criminology (1982).

Our Circuit has cited the Restatement with approval and determined that the Universal principle, standing alone, provides sufficient basis for asserting jurisdiction over an alleged offender. "The premise of universal jurisdiction is that a state 'may exercise jurisdiction to define and punish certain offenses recognized by the community of nations as of universal concern,' * * * even where no other recognized basis of jurisdiction is present." Therefore, under recognized principles of international law, and the law of this Circuit, there is clear authority to assert jurisdiction over Yunis for the offenses of aircraft piracy and hostage taking.

2. *Passive Personal Principle*

This principle authorizes states to assert jurisdiction over offenses committed against their citizens abroad. It recognizes that each state has a legitimate interest in protecting the safety of its citizens when they journey outside national boundaries. Because American nationals were on board the Jordanian aircraft, the government contends that the Court may exercise jurisdiction over Yunis under this principle. Defendant argues that this theory of jurisdiction is neither recognized by the international community nor the United States and is an insufficient basis for sustaining jurisdiction over Yunis.

Although many international legal scholars agree that the principle is the most controversial of the five sources of jurisdiction, they also agree that the international community recognizes its legitimacy. Most accept that "the extraterritorial reach of a law premised upon the * * * principle would not be in doubt as a matter of international law." * * * More importantly, the international community explicitly approved of the principle as a basis for asserting jurisdiction over hostage takers. The Hostage Taking Convention set forth certain mandatory sources of jurisdiction. But it also gave each signatory country discretion to exercise extraterritorial jurisdiction when the offense was committed "with respect to a hostage who is a national of that state if that state considers it appropriate." Art. 5(a)(d). Therefore, even if there are doubts regarding the international community's acceptance, there can be no doubt concerning the application of this principle to the offense of hostage taking, an offense for which Yunis is charged. * * *

Defendant's counsel correctly notes that the Passive Personal principle traditionally has been an anathema to United States lawmakers.[8] But his reliance on the Restatement (Revised) of Foreign Relations Laws for the claim that the United States can never invoke the principle is misplaced. In the past, the United States has protested any assertion of such jurisdiction for fear that it could lead to indefinite criminal liability for its own citizens. This objection was based on the belief that foreigners visiting the United States should comply with our laws and should not be permitted to carry their laws with them. Otherwise Americans would face criminal prosecutions for actions unknown to them as illegal. However, in the most recent draft of the Restatement, the authors noted that the theory "has been increasingly accepted when applied to terrorist and other organized attacks on a state's nationals by reason of their nationality, or to assassinations of a state's ambassadors, or government officials." Restatement (Revised) § 402, comment g * * * The authors retreated from their wholesale rejection of the principle, recognizing that perpetrators of crimes unanimously condemned by members of the international community, should be aware of the illegality of their actions. Therefore, qualified application of the doctrine to serious and universally condemned crimes will not raise the specter of unlimited and unexpected criminal liability.

This case does not present the first time that the United States has invoked the principle to assert jurisdiction over a hijacker who seized an American hostage on foreign soil. The government relied on this very principle when it sought extradition of Mohamed Abbas Zaiden, the leader of the terrorists who hijacked the Achille Lauro vessel in Egyptian waters and subsequently killed Leon Klinghoffer, an American citizen. As here, the only connection to the United States was Klinghoffer's American citizenship. Based on that link, an arrest warrant was issued charging Abbas with hostage taking, conspiracy and piracy.

Thus the Universal and Passive Personality principles, together, provide ample grounds for this Court to assert jurisdiction over Yunis. In fact, reliance on both strengthens the basis for asserting jurisdiction. Not only is the United States acting on behalf of the world community to punish alleged offenders of crimes that threaten the very foundations of world order, but the United States has its own interest in protecting its nationals.

B. JURISDICTION UNDER DOMESTIC LAW

Even if there is authority to assert jurisdiction over Yunis under International law, defendant's counsel argues that the Court has no jurisdiction under domestic law. He contends that Congress neither had the power nor the intention to authorize jurisdiction over the offenses of hostage taking and aircraft piracy committed "half way around the world".

But defendant's argument fails to recognize the power of the Congress to legislate overseas and to define and punish offenses committed on foreign soil. Article I, section 8, Clause 11 of the Constitution gives Congress the power to "define and punish Piracies and Felonies committed

---

8. However, defendant improperly relies on United States v. Layton, 509 F.Supp. 212, 215 (N.D.Cal.1981) for the proposition that the United States categorically rejects this principle.

on the High Seas and Offenses against the Law of Nations." As explained, * * * both hostage taking and aircraft piracy have been defined as offenses against the law of nations.

The reliance that Yunis' counsel places on _United States v. Bowman_, to argue that Congress has no power to extend jurisdiction outside its territorial boundaries, is misplaced. _Bowman_ stands for the contrary proposition. Indeed, it is routinely quoted for the holding that "there is no constitutional bar to the extraterritorial application of penal laws." * * *

A more accurate interpretation of _Bowman_ and its progeny is that Congress has the power to punish crimes committed overseas but it must evince such an intent with clarity. "If punishment * * * is extended to include those [acts] committed outside of the strict territorial jurisdiction, it is natural for Congress to say so in the statute and failure to do so will negate the purpose of Congress in this regard."

The two statutes under which the defendant was indicted, the Hostage Taking Act and the Aircraft Piracy Act, were part of a three bill package enacted by Congress in 1984 aimed at combating the rise of terrorism. Both were promulgated to extend jurisdiction over extraterritorial crimes and satisfy the country's obligations as a party to various international conventions. Because of the newness of the statutes, no court has been called upon to analyze the scope of the jurisdictional provisions. Therefore, the Court must rely on the recognized tools of statutory interpretation, the language of the statute along with the statutory history, to evaluate whether these provisions apply to the particular offenses charged in this indictment.

1. _Hostage Taking Act, 18 U.S.C. 1203_

This statute imposes liability on any individual who takes an American national hostage irrespective of where the seizure occurs. Congress wrote the jurisdictional reach of the statute in clear and unambiguous language. Subsection (b)(1) provides that a defendant is properly chargeable for offenses occurring outside the United States if _any one_ of the following circumstances exists:

(A) the offender or the person seized or detained is a national of the United States;

(B) the offender is found in the United States; or

(C) the governmental organization sought to be compelled is the Government of the United States.

Congress enacted the Hostage Taking Act to meet its obligations as a signatory state to the Hostage Taking Convention, _supra_. Article 5 of that treaty required signatory states to extend jurisdiction over hijacking committed outside the United States when the offender was a citizen of the states, or "present" in the state. It also provided states with the discretion to assert jurisdiction when their nationals were taken hostage. Congress' voluntary decision to adopt this permissive basis of jurisdiction underscores its intent to exercise broad jurisdiction over any offender who threatens American nationals. Therefore, the plain language of the statute coupled with its legislative history and purpose clearly support a finding that

Congress intended to assert extraterritorial jurisdiction over offenders such as Yunis who allegedly seized Americans hostage in foreign territory.

   2.   *Destruction of Aircraft Act, 18 U.S.C. 32*

   (a.) *Application of 32(b):* jurisdiction over offenders later "found" in the United States.

   This provision expressly extends jurisdiction over an alleged saboteur who commits offenses against an aircraft located in foreign airspace and has no other nexus to the United States other than that he or she "is later found in the United States." 18 U.S.C. 32(b)(4). Defendant was charged with violating these provisions, in the superceding indictment of October 1, 1987 that was filed after Yunis was arrested and flown to this country aboard a naval plane.

   Defendant's counsel argues that his client was not "found" in the United States within the meaning of the statute. He purports that the word "found" only pertains to individuals who voluntarily entered the United States and were later discovered by the government; the term was never envisioned to apply to defendants forcibly abducted and brought to the United States. Yunis did not voluntarily enter the country. To the contrary, he was lured through efforts and stratagem of FBI agents to international waters off the coast of Cyprus, where he was arrested and forcibly brought to the United States. Therefore, counsel argues that the government's forcible kidnaping of Yunis obviates any jurisdiction under this statute. In response, the government states that the term "found" is neither defined in the statute nor explained in the legislative history. Indeed, the statute neither precludes nor approves the extension of jurisdiction over offenders who have been brought to this country by force. However, the government urges that the legislative history and purpose behind the statute support asserting jurisdiction over the defendant.

   Defendant's attempt to limit the Court's jurisdiction is unavailing. Once a defendant is brought within the jurisdiction of the Court he is subject to prosecution for all federal offenses. Yunis was seized for alleged violation of the hostage taking statute. Physical presence in United States territory is not a necessary element for exercising subject matter jurisdiction over that offense. Only after he stepped onto American soil was the defendant charged with aircraft piracy. Indeed, once he was within the boundaries of the United States, the government was obligated by statute and the Montreal Convention to prosecute him for destroying the aircraft. As discussed earlier, both the Hague Convention and the Montreal Convention require all contracting states to exercise jurisdiction over individuals charged with seizing control of an aircraft. Any state that secures custody of the alleged hijackers is obligated to prosecute or extradite them.[20]

   (b.) *Application of 32(a):* jurisdiction over aircraft in "overseas or foreign air commerce".

   This provision imposes liability on individuals who damage and destroy an aircraft and/or perform acts of violence against passengers on board a

---

20. See, Blakesley, Jurisdiction as Legal Protection against Terrorism, 19 Conn.   L.Rev. 895, 918 (1987).

civil aircraft that operates in "overseas or foreign air commerce." Yunis has been charged specifically in Count I with conspiracy to hijack and destroy an aircraft; Count III with destroying a civil aircraft; Count IV with placing a destructive device on a civil aircraft; and in Count V with performing acts of violence against passengers of a civil aircraft. * * *

The 32(a) provision does not become operative unless the aircraft flies in "overseas or foreign air commerce." Defendant contends that the terms "overseas air commerce" and "foreign air commerce" require some nexus to the United States. Because the ALIA flight never landed on or even flew over American air space, he urges the Court to dismiss these counts. In turn, the government argues that Congress intended to regulate air commerce broadly and impose liability against alleged perpetrators of aircraft piracy irregardless [sic] of where the offense took place or which country operated the aircraft.

The Court agrees that Counts III, IV, and V must be dismissed. Section (a) of this provision is applicable only to aircraft operating in "interstate, overseas or foreign air commerce." The definitional provision of the Act, 18 U.S.C. § 31, relies on the "meaning ascribed to those terms in the Federal Aviation Act of 1958, as amended." That statute provides:

> "interstate air commerce, overseas air commerce, and foreign air commerce respectively, mean the carriage by aircraft of persons * * * or the operation or navigation of aircraft in the conduct or furtherance of a business or vocation, in commerce between, respectively,—
>
> (a) a place in any State of the United States * * * through the airspace over any place outside thereof; or between places in the same Territory or possession of the United States,
>
> (b) a place in any State of the United States and any place in a Territory or possession of the United States; and
>
> (c) a place in the United States and any place outside thereof whether such commerce moves wholly by aircraft or partly by aircraft and partly by other forms of transportation."

49 U.S.C. § 1301(23).

By focusing solely on the passengers and their connection to United States soil no matter how remote, the government's definition makes almost every aircraft subject to regulation by the United States. Airline companies operating exclusively overseas which wanted to avoid such regulation would be forced to research the travel history of every potential passenger and then exclude any person who had ever traveled to the United States.

When exposed to its core, the government's extreme interpretation is rejected. Neither the courts nor the United States Department of Transportation ("DOT"), the agency in charge of administering the Act, have ever adopted the government's broad, open-ended definition. Indeed, the agency has expressly rejected the mirror image of the interpretation urged by the government here.

Based on the above, Counts III, IV and V of the indictment must be dismissed. Dismissal of those Counts also requires dismissal of the corresponding sections of Count I; ¶ 4b, c, & d, charging the defendant with violations under 18 U.S.C. § 32(a). However, the remaining section of the conspiracy count, ¶ 4a, charging defendant with violations under 18 U.S.C. §§ 1203 and 2 shall stand. * * **

Notes & Questions

1. Does it seem appropriate that U.S. jurisdiction obtain over conduct perpetrated by a Lebanese national against Jordanian aircraft in the Middle East, and aimed at coercing a foreign entity? What nexus did Yunis's crime really have with the U.S? What theories of jurisdiction did the court apply? With regard to enforcement jurisdiction, does it give you any pause that FBI agents arrested Yunis aboard a foreign flag vessel in foreign or international waters? Should the flag-state have exclusive enforcement jurisdiction on board? Was permission obtained? If no permission were obtained, was the FBI conduct legal under international law? Under the law of the flag-ship? Under U.S. law? Would the U.S. government consider it legal for a foreign government to board a U.S. flag-vessel without permission to make an arrest?

2. President Reagan's Attorney General "authorized FBI agents to arrest defendants anywhere, including foreign territory." This policy seems to have continued. *US OKs Kidnapping Terrorists*, Chicago Tribune Feb. 5, 1997 Section 1. Does such expansive application put U.S. nationals traveling abroad in danger? Terrorists and drug traffickers ought to be apprehended and prosecuted, but do you see a danger in allowing abduction and harsh treatment to obtain incriminating evidence for prosecution? Immediately after the Attorney General's order, the Iranian Government issued an order providing for the arrest of U.S. nationals anywhere for violations of Iranian law. Do you think that U.S. protestations will ring true if a U.S. national were abducted? Were not at least some of the hostages in the Middle–East held under a pretext sounding similar to the one made in the Yunis case?

3. The Attorney General insisted that law enforcement officials had legal authority to seize Yunis and transport him to the U.S. under a hostage-taking law enacted in 1984. The statute provided jurisdiction over extraterritorial offenses when U.S. nationals are among those taken hostage. A senior Justice Department official said Yunis is a "full-time employee of the Amal militia and works for Nabih Berri." Berri had been Lebanon's justice minister and the leader of Amal, Lebanon's largest Shiite organization. Berri offered to help mediate the release of U.S. hostages and served as an intermediary in the resolution of another hijacking—that of T.W.A. Flight 847 in 1985, in which Navy Seal Robert Stethem, a passenger, was murdered by a hijacker and dumped to the tarmac in Beirut. Mohammed Ali Hamadei, was arrested in Germany and convicted of murder and kidnaping for his role in this hijacking. Germany rejected American appeals to extradite Hamadei to the United States.

4. ***Problems concerning jurisdiction to prescribe with respect to hostage taking abroad.*** 18 U.S.C. § 1203 is based on Article 5 of the *International Convention Against the Taking of Hostages*, to which the U.S. became a party in 1985. The preamble specifies that "all acts of taking of hostages" are "international terrorism." The Yunis prosecution was based on § 1203(b)(1)(A) which makes hostage taking an offense against the United States if the "person seized or detained is a national of or found in the United States." This provision is based in turn on Article 5(d) of the Convention, which provides that a state may exercise jurisdiction with respect to the offender when the hostage is one of its nationals "if that state considers it appropriate." Lebanon was not a party to the Convention at the time of Yunis's capture or prosecution. Is this relevant? Would your answer be different under international, as opposed to domestic law? Would customary international law provide jurisdiction? Another basis of jurisdiction is provided in Article 5, 1(c) of the Convention and 18 U.S.C. § 1203(b)(1)(C). According to these provisions, the U.S. would have jurisdiction over the terrorist if he had taken the passengers hostage to compel the United States "to do or abstain from doing any act." The hostage taking in *Yunis,* however, was an attempt to compel members of the Arab League to cancel one of its resolutions. Should this fact be considered in deciding whether the U.S. was vested with jurisdiction? Does the fact that only four Americans were among the passengers taken hostage weigh against U.S. jurisdiction?

5. ***When a U.S. national is killed.*** U.S. nationals were killed in hijackings in the TWA 837 and the *Achillea Lauro* incidents. Robert Stethem was murdered while the hijacked plane was on the tarmac in Beirut. Leon Klinghoffer was murdered on board the "hijacked" Italian cruise ship on the High Seas. The following materials are pertinent to these incidents.

b.   "Omnibus Anti–Terrorism Act"—Terrorist Acts of Violence Abroad Against United States Nationals: Law of the United States

18 U.S.C. 2331.

(a) HOMICIDE.—Whoever kills a [U.S.] national, while such national is outside the United States, shall—

(1) if the killing is a murder as defined in section 1111(a) of this title, be fined under this title or imprisoned for any term of years or for life, or both so fined and so imprisoned;

(2) if the killing is a voluntary manslaughter as defined in section 1112(a) of this title, be fined under this title or imprisoned not more than ten years, or both; and

(3) if the killing is an involuntary manslaughter as defined in section 1112(a) of this title, be fined under this title or imprisoned not more than three years, or both.

(b) Attempt or Conspiracy With Respect to Homicide.—Whoever outside the [U.S.] attempts to kill, or engages in a conspiracy to kill, a [U.S.] national shall [be subject to listed penalties.]

(c) Other Conduct.—Whoever outside the U.S. engages in physical violence—

(1) with intent to cause serious bodily injury to a national of the United States; or

(2) with the result that serious bodily injury is caused to a [U.S.] national;

shall be fined under this title or imprisoned not more than five years, or both.

* * *

(e) Limitation on Prosecution.—No prosecution for any offense described in this section shall be undertaken by the United States except on written certification of the Attorney General or the highest ranking subordinate of the Attorney General with responsibility for criminal prosecutions that, in the judgment of the certifying official, such offense was intended to coerce, intimidate, or retaliate against a government or a civilian population.

* * *

———

Notes & Questions

1. *Problem concerning jurisdiction to prescribe terrorist acts of violence abroad against U.S. nationals.* The Anti–Terrorism Act is not based on a treaty. Would customary international law allow this jurisdiction? The Legal Adviser of the Department of State appeared before the Senate Judiciary Committee asserting that the "proposed extension of jurisdiction is both warranted by reality and logic, and consistent with international law ... [T]here is no compelling reason why the seizure of a private U.S. citizen abroad as a hostage should be a U.S. federal crime but the terrorist murder of that same U.S. citizen should not." He endorsed the view that the *protective principle* could be extended to cover the proscribed conduct.

2. What is the purpose of ¶ (e) of the Act? Is it a substantive rule of law and an element of an offense? What special type of violence against U.S. citizens allows this jurisdiction? Would attacking a U.S. military unit engaged in military action constitute terroristic violence under the Act? What if the unit was asleep in its barracks? Any military battle is violent and is intended to intimidate the U.S. into quitting the fight. Does that make it terrorism; would the Act apply?

3. *The Antiterrorism and Effective Death Penalty Act of 1996 (AEDPA), 28 U.S.C. ___, 110 Stat. 1214,* amending various parts of the U.S. Code, including titles 8, 18, 22, 28, 40, and 42, was promulgated after the Oklahoma City bombing. Did the Act improve or diminish its potential for combating terrorism by attaching it to the popular expansion of the

death penalty. *See,* e.g., 18 U.S.C. 2332(b) and 18 U.S.C. 2332b(c)(1)(a). The trend in Europe Canada, Mexico, and other Latin American States is in opposition to the death penalty, resulting less extradition or other cooperation. The AEDPA prohibits persons within the U.S. or subject to U.S. jurisdiction to provide any support or resources to any "terrorist activity" or to any group designated by the Department of State as a "foreign terrorist organization." 18 U.S.C. 2339A and 2339B. It also provides that all U.S. territorial sea, as defined by Presidential Proclamation 5928 of December 27, 1998, is part of U.S. territory for purposes of Federal criminal jurisdiction. [110 Stat. 1214 (1996).

4.   ***U.N. Resolution on international terrorism***. On December 9, 1985, the General Assembly adopted Resolution 40/61 concerning measures to prevent international terrorism. *See,* 25 ILM 239 (1986). It "unequivocally condemns, as criminal, all acts, methods and practices of terrorism wherever and by whomever committed." Did this create a normative rule making any act of terrorism a crime under international law, thus justifying the enactment of 18 U.S.C. § 2331? If such was the intent, why does the preamble to the resolution state that the General Assembly reaffirms "the inalienable right to self-determination and independence of all peoples under colonial and racist regimes" and upholds "the legitimacy of their struggle, in particular the struggle of national liberation movements"?

5.   ***Regional Treaties***. The member states of the Council of Europe elected to deal with acts of terrorism by eliminating the application of the "political exception to extradition" for hostage taking and acts of violence against the life or physical integrity of a person. *See,* 15 I.L.M. 1272 (1976). The U.S. and several Latin American states entered *The Convention to Prevent and Punish the Acts of Terrorism Taking the Form of Crimes Against Persons and Related Extortion That Are of International Significance.* 27 U.S.T. 3949 (1976).

SECTION B.   JURISDICTION TO ENFORCE RULES OF LAW

1.   SOVEREIGNTY AND THE EXCLUSIVE CHARACTER OF JURISDICTION TO ENFORCE WITHIN THE TERRITORY

The Schooner Exchange v. McFaddon

United States Supreme Court, 1812.
11 U.S. (7 Cranch) 116, 136, 3 L.Ed. 287.

MARSHALL, C.J. * * *

   * * *

   The jurisdiction of the nation within its own territory is necessarily exclusive and absolute. It is susceptible of no limitation not imposed by itself. Any restriction upon it, deriving validity from an external source, would imply a diminution of its sovereignty to the extent of the restriction, and an investment of that sovereignty to the same extent in that power which could impose such restriction. * * *

2.   JURISDICTION TO ENFORCE DEPENDS ON JURISDICTION TO PRESCRIBE

Arret Fornage

France, *Cour de Cassation*, 1873.
84 Journal du Palais 299 (1873).[a]

[The accused was prosecuted in France for grand larceny that he committed in Switzerland. French procedure allowed the indictment to be presented to a court whose function was to decide whether the evidence was sufficient to support a French prosecution. This court found sufficient evidence for prosecution before the *Cour d'Assizes*. The accused could have appealed this jurisdictional decision to the *Cour de Cassation* but failed to do so. At trial, defendant claimed that French courts had no authority to prosecute him for a crime committed in a foreign country. Defendant was convicted. His appeal was heard by the Criminal Section of the *Cour de Cassation*. Arguments presented by a *conseiller rapporteur,* a member of the court appointed to make recommendations, and those made by the *avocat général* were accepted by the Criminal Chamber. The *conseiller rapporteur* conceded the ruling of the *Court d'Assizes* was in accord with precedents established by the *Cour de Cassation,* but followed this with the argument presented below.]

. . . Is it not possible also to say that, in the case presented to you, there are considerations of a superior nature justifying an exception to the general rule? The only basis for the right to punish is sovereignty, which dies at the border. If French law allows the prosecution of French nationals for crimes or offenses committed in a foreign country, it is because criminal law applies both on a territorial and personal basis. A French national, even abroad, still remains a citizen of his country and as such remains subject to French law, which has power over him as soon as he comes back to France. But [without an exceptional basis,] the law itself cannot give French courts the power to try foreign nationals for crimes or offenses committed outside French territory; such exorbitant jurisdiction, whose basis could neither be territorial nor personal, would constitute a violation of international law, a breach of the sovereignty of other states. There [are a limited number of] exceptions to this rule of international law. When, [for example,] a foreign national has committed, even abroad, a crime against the security of the state, he can be prosecuted, tried and punished in France. [This exception] is based on the right of self-defense [others may be based on universality or passive personality. Apart from these, which are very limited], foreign nationals can only be prosecuted by the courts of their own country for acts committed outside the territory. * * * The *Cour d'Assizes*, by punishing this act, would commit an abuse of power; it would usurp a right of sovereignty belonging to a foreign power. Would it not be contrary to all principles of justice to force the judges into knowingly

a. Translation by the editors. A *cour d'Assizes* is the trial level court for the equiv-alent of felonies.

becoming guilty of an arbitrary act, a violation of international law? * * * [The *Cour d'Assizes*] must examine the evidence presented by the accused in support of his claims and declare itself without jurisdiction if it finds that he is an alien and the act of which he is accused has been committed outside French territory.

Indeed, French justice has jurisdiction only to try French nationals for crimes committed by them outside the territory * * *; it has no jurisdiction over aliens; so the question of nationality must be decided beforehand; for the right of jurisdiction depends upon the resolution of the question. The ruling which is challenged appears to me to have overlooked those fundamental principles.

* * * [I]t is a general principle that * * * jurisdiction, however broad it may be, cannot extend to crimes committed outside the territory by aliens who, in respect to those acts, are not punishable in French courts. * * * [T]his lack of jurisdiction in this regard is absolute, permanent; it can be cured neither by the silence nor by the consent of the accused; it continues to exist at all levels * * * [and the indicting court] cannot give the *Cour d'Assizes* a right it does not itself possess, to try acts which do not come under the jurisdiction of French law. * * * [Fornage] was sent to the *Cour d'Assizes* of Haute–Savoie and accused of having committed grand larceny in the *Canton de Valais* (Switzerland); before the trial began, he presented arguments to the effect that the court was without jurisdiction * * * the *Cour d'Assizes* wrongly applied * * * [the law]; and by ordering the trial to proceed without deciding the motion based on nationality * * * disregarded the rights of the defendant.

––––––

Comment & Query: *Treatment of subject in 1987 Restatement & Relevance of the Lotus Decision.* Comment *a* to § 431 states: "[U]nder international law, a state may not exercise authority to enforce law that it has no jurisdiction to prescribe." The Reporters' Note to this section refers to the *Lotus Case*, *supra*. Why is Lotus relevant?

SECTION C.   REDUCTION AND RESOLUTION OF JURISDICTIONAL CONFLICTS

1.   CONFLICTS OF JURISDICTION–CAUSES

Concurrent and conflicting jurisdiction are not uncommon. The parties may agree as to which among them ought to assert jurisdiction. Successful challenges to enforcement jurisdiction is more common than successful challenge to prescriptive jurisdiction.

*a.   **General Problems.*** Broad expansion of prescriptive jurisdiction has caused problems. Some ad hoc arrangements have developed to allocate primary jurisdiction. These ad hoc arrangements are not numerous and have had limited impact. For example, anti-double taxation treaties are used, not when State A asserts jurisdiction and denies it entirely to State B, but where both states have a basis of jurisdiction which the other acknowledges. This resolution of a jurisdictional conflict is essentially a re-allocation of exclusive authority by mutual agreement. The agreements themselves usually designate one of the states as having *"primary"* jurisdiction.

b. **Conflicts of Law, Enforcement, and Adjudicative Jurisdiction.** Conflicts of law focuses on the rights of private parties before a state forum. Courts by their actions in such cases usually do not raise questions involving conflict of public law. *See, Laker Airways v. Sabena, Belgian World Airlines,* 731 F.2d 909 (D.C.Cir.1984). The international legal community is accustomed to domestic courts trying conflicts of law cases that include significant foreign elements, but do not involve governmental or public interests that have been cast by a state into legal rules, such as tax law , business regulation, or criminal law.

c. **Boarding foreign ships on the High Seas.** Most nations, including the United States, have entered into arrangements for high seas boarding of ships suspected of transporting narcotics. These arrangements require specific, explicit prior clearance with the flag state for each case. The states agree to "waive" their right to exclusive enforcement jurisdiction on their vessels.

d. **International Finance: Money Laundering, Stock Fraud, Insider Trading, and Such Like.** States heavily involved in international finance, banking, and securities regulation are opening the way to jurisdictional cooperation to combat stock fraud, "insider trading," and other criminal manipulations. Even Switzerland, that mountain fortress of bank secrecy, recently has come to moderate its once rigidly territorial exclusivity in deference to the interests of other states on behalf of investors entitled to their help or protection. This cooperation and reduction of jurisdictional conflicts has been state driven, with only limited and indirect assistance from international organizations. *See, discussion of German and other European law in* Blakesley & Lagodny, *Finding Harmony Amidst Disagreement Over Extradition, Jurisdiction, the Role of Human Rights, and Issues of Extraterritoriality Under International Criminal Law,* 24 Vand.J.Trans'l L. 1 (1991); Blakesley & Lagodny, *Competing National Criminal Laws: Network or Jungle, in Principles and Procedures for a New Transnational Criminal Law, (Max–Planck Institute für Ausländisches und Internationales Strafrecht,* Freiburg, Germany, 1992).

2. INTERNATIONAL ARRANGEMENTS AND AGREEMENTS AS TO JURISDICTION IN REGARD TO VISITING FOREIGN MILITARY FORCES

Persons in the armed services may fail in the performance of their military duties on or off-post, or they may misbehave when off duty and amidst the civilian community, with resultant injury to a local resident. These types of situations are the most common causes of jurisdictional conflict between a host state and a visiting military unit. As experience with friendly foreign forces present in a state at the invitation of that state has accumulated, principles have been worked out for the allocation of primary jurisdiction to one or the other of the states concerned. Some types of conduct, are easy to resolve. At one end of the spectrum, all agree that the military person should be responsible only to the law of his military unit. At the opposite extreme, all agree that he or she should be treated like anyone else within the civilian population in which he has acted. The following cases show that application of the rules of jurisdictional allocation pose problems inherently more difficult than the drafting of the rules themselves. In addition to the immediate issue of allocation, important incidental issues arise, such as those involving human rights, or double jeopardy, or denial of certain defenses.

Whitley v. Aitchison

France, Court of Cassation, 1958.
26 Int'l L.Rep. 196 (1963).[a]

Facts: Article VII(3)(b) of the N.A.T.O. Status of Forces Agreement [S.O.F.A.], provides that in the case of offences not arising out of acts done in the performance of the official duty of a member of a visiting force, "the authorities of the receiving State shall have the primary right to exercise jurisdiction". Subparagraph (c) of the same paragraph provides that "if the State having the primary right decides not to exercise jurisdiction, it shall notify the authorities of the other State as soon as practicable * * *." Article VII(8) * * * provides:

> Where an accused has been tried by the authorities of one Contracting Party and has been acquitted, or has been convicted and is serving, or has served, his sentence or has been pardoned, he may not be tried again for the same offence within the same territory by the authorities of another Contracting Party.

On November 25, 1953, the appellant, a major of the United States Air Force stationed in France under the provisions of the North Atlantic Treaty, was driving his car at high speed along a road within the judicial district of the French town of Corbeil. He was carrying as a passenger one Aitchison, an officer in the Royal Canadian Air Force. As subsequently found, the applicant drove negligently and as a result of his driving the car crashed and Aitchison was killed. It was also found that when driving the car the appellant was not acting in the performance of his official duty; and in accordance with Article VII(3)(b) of the Agreement of June 19, 1951, the primary right of jurisdiction was vested in the French courts. The United States military authorities requested the French authorities to waive their primary right of jurisdiction, and this request was approved by the French Ministry of Justice and the Prosecutor of the Court of Corbeil. The French authorities duly notified the United States military authorities in accordance with Article VII(3)(c) of the Agreement that they had decided not to exercise jurisdiction.

Notwithstanding the waiver of their primary right of jurisdiction by the French authorities * * * the widow of Aitchison (the respondent herein) instituted proceedings against the appellant for damages as *partie civile*, as is customary under French law in connection with criminal proceedings. At that time the United States military authorities had not yet

a. Reprinted with the permission of the Editor of the International Law Reports.

made any decision as to the manner in which they intended to proceed against the appellant in the exercise of the right of jurisdiction granted to them by the French authorities, but subsequently they decided not to take any action against the appellant.

The appellant objected to the jurisdiction of the French court on the ground that the waiver by the French authorities of their primary right of jurisdiction was irrevocable, and that the right once waived could not be revived by the decision of the United States authorities not to prosecute. The Court of Corbeil overruled the objection and held itself competent to adjudicate the respondent's claim for damages. The Paris Court of Appeal dismissed the appellant's appeal against that decision.[1]

On further appeal to the Court de Cassation,

Held: (i) that the appeal must be allowed. Once the French authorities had waived their right to primary jurisdiction and notified United States military authorities of the waiver, their right to exercise jurisdiction was incapable of being revived, notwithstanding that the United States military authorities decided not to prosecute.

(ii) Even though under French municipal law a prosecutor cannot definitively waive the right to prosecute, the Agreement, in accordance with Article 26 of the French Constitution of October 27, 1946, must take precedence and as, according to the Agreement, a right of primary jurisdiction once waived cannot be revived, the French courts were no longer competent. [A portion of the opinion of the court appears below.]

* * * The notice of appeal alleges a violation of Articles VII(3)(c) and XX(3) of the N.A.T.O., S.O.F.A., promulgated by Decree dated October 13, 1952; a violation of Articles 26 et seq. of the Constitution of October 27, 1946; of Articles 3 and 182 of the Code of Criminal Procedure; and of Article 7 of the Law of April 20, 1810. It is contended that the judgment under appeal, notwithstanding the waiver of the right of primary jurisdiction by the Minister of Justice as well as by the Prosecutor of the Court of Corbeil, in favour of the United States authorities, wrongly considered the Magistrates' Court of Corbeil entitled to deal with the civil action and the criminal prosecution. The Court of Corbeil, it is said, took this view on the ground that a waiver by the authorities of the country entitled to the right of primary jurisdiction is neither irrevocable nor unconditional, and that in order to be final and irrevocable and generally binding, a waiver must be subject to the requirement of the existence of a judgment against the accused. As long as such a judgment has not come into existence the victim, according to the view expressed by the lower courts, cannot be deprived of his right to bring proceedings in the criminal courts with a view to obtaining damages for the injury sustained. Neither the Minister of Justice nor the Public Prosecutor, according to this view, is in full control of the criminal proceedings, and they cannot waive these because such waiver would have no legal effect and could not, in any event, deprive the claimant (*partie civile*) of his own rights which the law confers on him.

---

1.   The judgment of the Court of Appeal of Paris is reported in International Law Reports, 1956, p. 255.

If the host State which has the right of primary jurisdiction decides to waive this right, there arises a genuine lack of competence for the benefit of the other State which is not entitled to the right of primary jurisdiction. The State which has waived its right can no longer exercise jurisdiction unless the State which benefits from the waiver decides not to exercise jurisdiction and notifies the State which has waived its right. *International conventions have the force of law even if they conflict with municipal law*, and they must be applied instead of the latter where occasion demands. The provisions of the North Atlantic Treaty necessarily imply that it is the Public Prosecutor's department which is entitled to waive the right of primary jurisdiction, and that when the right has been waived the French courts are no longer competent, notwithstanding that according to French municipal law the Public Prosecutor cannot waive the right to institute criminal proceedings. The victim of the criminal offence, who can always bring his claim before the civil courts, cannot question a renunciation of competence which has been made for reasons of international courtesy.

Article VII(3)(c) of the Agreement of June 19, 1951, between the Parties to N.A.T.O., as published in the Decree dated October 11, 1952, provides:

> If the State having the primary right decides not to exercise jurisdiction, it shall notify the authorities of the other State as soon as practicable. Authorities of the State having primary right shall give sympathetic consideration to a request from the authorities of the other State for a waiver of its right in cases where that other State considers such waiver to be of particular importance.

Where, in accordance with this provision, the authorities of the State which has the right of primary jurisdiction have, at the request of the other State, waived that right, their decision is final, and the criminal courts of the State concerned can no longer exercise jurisdiction over facts in respect of which there has been a waiver. There is no need to enquire whether the State in whose favour the right has been waived has exercised jurisdiction through its own courts. The only exception to this would be the case where the State which has been granted the right to exercise jurisdiction by the State in which the primary right was vested, expressly informs the latter that it does not wish to exercise jurisdiction and leaves the matter to the judicial authorities of the other Contracting Party.

Article 26 of the Constitution of October 27, 1946, provides that international treaties duly ratified and published have the force of law even if they conflict with French municipal law. After the death of Aitchison, the latter's widow instituted proceedings against Whitley before the criminal court of Corbeil–Essonnes, alleging involuntary homicide committed against her husband while Whitley was not acting in the performance of his official duties. That Court, in arriving at a finding that the subsidiary civil action (*action de la partie civile*) was subject to the jurisdiction, held that if before the institution of these proceedings the Minister of Justice and the Public Prosecutor of Corbeil–Essonnes agreed, at the request of the United States authorities and in accordance with the [N.A.T.O., S.O.F.A.], to waive the right of primary jurisdiction, this did not imply a waiver of the right subsequently to exercise jurisdiction if, as in this case, the alleged offender has not been tried by the judicial authorities of his home State, because the Agreement itself contemplates the case of an accused who has not been tried in the home State and of an accused who, though convicted, has not served his sentence—unless there has been an amnesty.

The appealed judgment has misinterpreted the Agreement of June 19, 1951, and violated the provisions referred to in the notice of appeal, because it arrived at its finding notwithstanding the absence of any express declaration by the home State that it waived its right to exercise jurisdiction, which jurisdiction had been recognized by France when that country agreed not to exercise its primary right of jurisdiction. The judgment of the Court of Appeal of Paris is therefore reversed, and there is no need for remand.

* * *

Wilson, Secretary of Defense v. Girard

United States Supreme Court, 1957.
354 U.S. 524, 77 S.Ct. 1409, 1 L.Ed.2d 1544.

PER CURIUM. [the U.S. and Japan became involved in a controversy whether the respondent Girard should be tried by a Japanese court for causing the death of a Japanese woman. * * *

Girard, a Specialist Third Class in the United States Army, was engaged on January 30, 1957, with members of his cavalry regiment in a small unit exercise at Camp Weir range area, Japan. Japanese civilians were present in the area, retrieving expended cartridge cases. Girard and another Specialist Third Class were ordered to guard a machine gun and some items of clothing that had been left nearby. Girard had a grenade launcher on his rifle. He placed an expended 30–caliber cartridge case in the grenade launcher and projected it by firing a blank. The expended cartridge case penetrated the back of a Japanese woman gathering expended cartridge cases and caused her death.

The United States ultimately notified Japan that Girard would be delivered to the Japanese authorities for trial. Thereafter, Japan indicted him for causing death by wounding. Girard sought a writ of habeas corpus in the United States District Court for the District of Columbia. The writ was denied, but Girard was granted declaratory relief and an injunction against his delivery to the Japanese authorities. The petitioners appealed to the Court of Appeals for the District of Columbia, and, without awaiting action by that court on the appeal, invoked the jurisdiction of this Court under 28 U.S.C.A. § 1254(1). Girard filed a cross-petition for certiorari to review the denial of the writ of habeas corpus.

———

Note on the Girard case. What is the proper result in a case like this? The U.S. military decision to turn Girard over to Japanese justice, once the authorities admitted in an official statement that: " * * * This was upheld by the U.S. Supreme Court, after it reversed District Court injunction against his delivery to Japan. Girard's action in firing empty shell cases from a rifle grenade launcher was not authorized * * * ", was sharply criticized in some quarters in the United States; and there was great public interest in the action brought in the United States on Girard's behalf. A professor of international law on temporary duty in the Department of Justice, was speeding into Washington on a Sunday to work on the government's side of the case before the Supreme Court. The traffic police officer was skeptical both as to Sunday work and haste, until told that the professor was working on the Girard case. Then, tearing up the ticket, the policeman exclaimed: "Get on in there and get that boy out, ya hear?" Girard was convicted in Japan of bodily injury resulting in death. He served a comparatively light sentence without further attention from the public.

Do the same sorts of issues arise with regard to U.N. peacekeeping forces?

3. INTERNATIONAL ARRANGEMENTS AND AGREEMENTS AS TO CONFLICTING STATE DEMANDS BASED ON NATIONALITY OR ALLEGIANCE

States may make demands for service of various kinds on the basis of jurisdiction over nationals or the existence of obligations arising from allegiance. See Ch. 9. Such demands conflict when more than one state considers itself entitled to demand service of the person on nationality or related grounds, as in cases of demands for military service. When the United States had compulsory military service (the draft) it sought by international agreements to eliminate or lower the risk that a person might have to serve in more than one military system.

CHAPTER 4

A VIEW FROM THE BRIDGE: SEA LAW IN HISTORICAL AND CURRENT PERSPECTIVE

The term "Law of the Sea" is used here as international lawyers usually use it, to refer to the rules of law, increasingly from positive law sources, that govern the rights and duties of states as to the exercise of jurisdiction and the pursuit of benefits in, on, under, and even over, this planet's waters. Reference should be made to R.R. Churchill and A.V. Lowe, The Law of the Sea (3rd ed., 1999); J.B. Morrell, The Law of the Sea, An

Historical Analysis of the 1982 Treaty and Its rejection by the United states (1992); D.P. O'Connell, The Law of the Sea, 2 Vols (1982–84) and D. Vidas and W. Østreng (eds) Order for the Oceans at the Turn of the Century (1999). In a broader, historical sense the term also covers the private law of vessel ownership and management, carriage of goods by sea, rules of the maritime road, maritime torts such as collisions at sea, maritime liens, salvage, and processes in special courts that apply the general law maritime, called courts of Admiralty. Maritime law has a very long history, beginning as customary law over 5,000 years ago, passing through various partial codification in different lands, and existing in the United States today as a mixture of customary law and national statutes applied exclusively by federal judges without juries. The Admiralty or private law side of the law of the sea remains essentially national, rather than international (as by codification in treaties) but nonetheless, remarkably uniform as between various national legal systems.

SECTION A. CODIFICATION OF THE LAW OF THE SEA

1. THE UNITED NATIONS CONVENTION ON THE LAW OF THE SEA

Historical background. Navigation, fishing and extraction of minerals take place on or under the sea. For centuries, there has been an ongoing struggle over whether these activities can be engaged in freely by all states and their nationals almost anywhere in the sea or whether states can carve out maritime areas for their exclusive use and control. The law of the sea is one of the most dramatic examples of the dynamic evolution of international law. Even though codification has taken place as will be detailed in this Chapter customary international law has and will continue to be a focal point in its future development.

Attempts at resolving the issue by codification of the law of the sea began as early as 1930 at a conference of some 40 states held at The Hague under the auspices of the League of Nations, but it was not successful.

Following work undertaken by the International Law Commission more than 80 states participated in the 1958 Geneva conference on the law of the sea and produced four conventions, which have all entered into force, codifying portions of the customary law and creating new law in some cases. Three of these are still carried in the Documentary Supplement, because, as we shall explain later, they may still contain some law of the United States. They are:

1. Convention on the Territorial Sea and the Contiguous Zone, which entered into force on September 10, 1964; as of June 30, 2000, 51 states were parties to this Convention;

2. Convention on the High Seas, which entered into force on September 30, 1962; as of June 30, 2000, 62 states were parties to this Convention; and

3. Convention on the Continental Shelf, which entered into force on June 10, 1964; as of June 30, 2000, 57 states were parties to this Convention.

The fourth, the Convention on Fishing and Conservation of the Living Resources of the High Seas, in force on June 10, 1963 is not included; as of June 30, 2000, 37 states were parties to this Convention. The text of this Convention can be found in 17 U.S.T. 138, 559 U.N.T.S. 285. Only the Convention on the High Seas states in the preamble that it is "generally declaratory of established principles of international law". In practice the Conventions on the Territorial Sea and the Contiguous Zone and the Continental Shelf were also viewed as codifying certain aspects of customary international law as well. Reference should be made to the decision of the International Court of Justice in the *North Sea Continental Shelf* Cases, [1969] I.C.J. Rep. 3, concerning whether certain of the norms contained in the Convention on the Continental Shelf were paralleled in or had crystallized into customary international law.

After the second conference on the law of the sea failed in 1960 to agree on the fundamental question of the breadth of the territorial sea, the General Assembly of the United Nations convened a third conference in 1973. Apart from the territorial sea and consequential questions concerning international straits and archipelagic states, other issues had also appeared outdating the Geneva Conventions, notably fishing rights beyond the territorial sea, pollution control and exploration and exploitation of oil, gas and minerals beyond national jurisdiction. After eleven sessions, from 1973 to 1982 UNCLOS III adopted the United Nations Convention on the Law of the Sea of December 10, 1982. An edited version of the text is in the Documentary Supplement. The actual text contains 320 Articles and 9 Annexes. The1982 Convention as a multilateral treaty is a product of compromise. The aim was to arrive at a package-deal basically acceptable to all states and to adopt it by consensus. However, at the end of the Conference the then new Reagan administration in the United States requested a vote after changes it had wished in the deep seabed mining Articles were not realized. The 1982 Convention was then adopted in Montego Bay, Jamaica, by 130 states in favour to 4 against (Israel, Turkey, United States and Venezuela) with 17 abstentions (Belgium, Bulgaria, Byelorussia, Czechoslovakia, GRD, FRG, Hungary, Italy, Luxembourg, Netherlands, Mongolia, Poland, Spain, Thailand, United Kingdom, Ukraine and the former USSR).

The sixtieth state having acceded pursuant to Article 308 (1), the Convention came into force on November 16, 1994. No member of the Group of Seven (the major developed countries) had become a party at that time due to concerns with respect to the International Seabed Area and dissatisfaction with some of the terms of Part XI, dealing with seabed mining beyond national jurisdiction. However, as of November 30, 2000, 135 states were parties to this Convention. The seabed mining regime is considered in Section E of this Chapter. In July 1990 informal consultations were initiated and culminated in the adoption on July 28, 1994 by U.N. General Assembly Resolution 48/263 of the Agreement Relating to the Implementation of Part XI of the United Nations Convention on the Law of the Sea of 10 December, 1982. The Agreement was prompted by the desire to achieve universal participation in the 1982 Convention on the Law of the Sea and recognized that political and economic changes had necessitated the re-evaluation of some parts of Part XI. The Agreement entered into force July 28, 1996 and as of November 30, 2000 there were 100 states parties. The United States signed on November 16, 1994 but has not ratified. In his report to the President of the United States (upon which the President based a Message to the Senate, proposing Senate approval of the entire Convention) the Secretary of State wrote:

"... The legally binding changes set forth in the Agreement meet the objections of the United States to Part XI of the Convention. The United States and all other major industrialized states have signed the Agreement."

Would its provisions prevail over corresponding and inconsistent provisions of the Geneva Conventions of 1958, to which the United States is a party?

1987 Restatement, Introductory Note to Part V, the Law of the Sea[a]

* * * [M]any * * * provisions of the Convention follow closely provisions in the 1958 conventions * * * which largely restated customary law as of that time. Other provisions in the LOS Convention set forth rules that, if not law in 1958, became customary law since that time, as they were accepted at the Conference by consensus and have influenced, and came to reflect, the practice of states. * * * In particular, in March 1983 President Reagan proclaimed a 200–nautical-mile exclusive economic zone for the United States and issued a policy statement in which the United States in effect agreed to accept the substantive provisions of the Convention, other than those dealing with deep sea-bed mining, in relation to all states that do so with respect to the United States. Thus, by express or tacit agreement accompanied by consistent practice, the United States, and states generally, have accepted the substantive provisions of the Convention, other than those addressing deep sea-bed mining, as statements of customary law binding upon them apart from the Convention. * * * In a few instances, however, there is disagreement whether a provision of the Convention reflects customary law. * * * Some provisions of the Convention, notably those accepting particular arrangements for settling disputes, clearly are not customary law and have not been accepted by express or tacit agreement.

The 1994 Agreement should be referred to in the Documentary Supplement. The Agreement is comprised of 10 Articles and an Annex. The Annex deals with various matters including consent to be bound, costs and decision-making mechanisms for the International Seabed Authority. As of November 30, 2000 the 1982 Convention of the Law of the Sea has 135 states parties including France, Germany, Italy, Japan, the Russian Federation and the United Kingdom. The European Community as a regional entity has also ratified. Canada signed on December 10, 1982 but has not yet ratified.

The Agreement and Part XI of the Convention are to be applied as a single instrument. In the event of inconsistency the provisions of the Agreement will apply. Of extreme importance is the fact that ratifications or accessions to the Convention following the adoption by the General Assembly of the Agreement represent consent to be bound by the Agreement and consent to be bound by the Agreement is not permitted unless consent to be bound by the Convention is established. See B.H. Oxman, The 1994 Agreement and the Convention, 88 AJIL 687 (1994); L.B. Sohn, International Law Implications of the 1994 Agreement, *id.*, at 696; J. Charney, U.S. Provisional Application of the 1994 Deep Seabed Agreement, *id.*, 705 and A. de Marffy–Mantuano, The Procedural Framework of the Agreement Implementing the 1982 United Nations Convention on the Law of the Sea, 89 AJIL 814 (1995).

The question arises: Why did so few states ratify or accede to the 1982 Convention until after the 1994 Agreement was adopted? Was it because Article 309 forbids all reservations or exceptions to the Convention unless expressly permitted in particular articles. But see Article 310, on declarations and statements made at ratification, and Articles 312 and 313, on amendments proposed by parties to the Convention. Why were reservations prohibited? Consider this question again when studying Reservations to Treaties in Chapter 11. Note that Article 2 (2) of the Agreement likewise applies Articles 309–319 of the Convention. The Reagan Administration, while rejecting the Convention as a whole, declared it to be the best exposition of international law of a customary nature relating to the delineations of national and international areas of the oceans, a matter of obvious concern to a naval power. The President's Statement is in, 18 Weekly Compilation of Presidential Documents 887 (July 12, 1982). In its view, the provisions to which the U.S. agrees do not state new rules of law but, instead, only restate rules of customary international law. James L. Malone, former Assistant Secretary of State for Oceans and International Environmental and Scientific Affairs, defended the claim in a speech. Excerpts follow.

————

Malone, Freedom and Opportunities: Foundation for a Dynamic Oceans Policy

United States Department of State Bulletin, December 1984, p. 76.

* * *

Recognizing that the peaceful uses of the world's oceans and the management and conservation of marine resources remain a matter of fundamental concern—as well as a potential source of boundless opportunity—to all maritime states, President Reagan set forth on March 10, 1983,

the principles upon which the U.S. would base its future oceans policy
* * *.

In order to fully grasp and appreciate that policy, however, a key
principle underlying it—namely, that the nonseabed sections of the treaty
reflect customary law in distinction to those prescribing the mining regime—must be understood.

Of paramount importance in assigning the proper meaning to the
various sections of the LOS Convention is the need to recognize that unlike
all former oceans-related conventions, UNCLOS III does two things: it
codifies existing law and prescribes new law. The attempt was made to both
set out present and developing law in familiar areas in light of circumstances since 1958 as well as to provide new regimes for unregulated
activities. Navigation rights, as seen in the very wording of the LOS
Convention articles on navigation, were frequently drawn from the 1958
Geneva Conventions on the Territorial Sea and Contiguous Zone and that
on the High Seas, which embodied customary law as it had developed to
that time. As such, it is void of merit to argue that only parties to the LOS
Convention enjoy customary international legal rights of longstanding
status.

Similarly, it is without legal foundation to maintain, on the basis of the
so-called contractual theory, that the convention is a package and that for a
non-party all rights are lost if a state does not become a party to it. Absent
a peremptory norm to the contrary, customary rights of sovereign states
remain inviolate and cannot otherwise be denied. I do not subscribe to the
views of critics of the U.S. position who accuse nonsignatories of "picking
and choosing" among sections of the convention. The "package deal"
concept was, it must be remembered, nothing more than a procedural
device, based on a December 1973 "gentleman's agreement" and designed
to further the achievement of consensus. As such, the concept died upon
the conclusion of the LOS negotiations. It has no continuing merit whatever.

States certainly are free to continue to apply customary international
law and ignore *de novo* prescriptive provisions which have neither been
tried nor admitted by wide practice to be a source of recognized international law.

It is the position of the United States then that, despite its shortcomings, the Law of the Sea Convention does reflect a successful effort to
articulate and codify existing rules of maritime law and actual state
practice with respect to the traditional uses of the oceans, such as navigation and overflight. Indeed, the United States believes that most of the
provisions of the treaty, apart from the seabed mining text in part XI, fairly
balance the interests of all states and are fully consistent with norms of
customary international law. Hence, it is prepared to accept and act in
accordance with these provisions on a reciprocal basis.

But, since the seabed mining portions of the convention establish
wholly new law and new obligations, which are contractual in nature and
not part of customary international law, the provisions will be binding only
on parties to the convention and, then, only when and if it enters into

force. The provisions in part XI of the convention are predicated on the establishment of a new international organization, the International Seabed Resource Authority, and on the acceptance by parties of that organization's jurisdiction and of their own obligation to act in accordance with its mandates. Such obligations must be willingly assumed by states and cannot be thrust upon them. The United States does not and will not accept them and is not bound by them.

In nonseabed areas, however, as I have said, the United States does recognize the existence of an international law of the sea entirely independent of—though reflected in—the Law of the Sea Convention and based upon accepted principles of customary international law. The United States will continue to honor those principles and will assert its rights consistent with those principles on a global basis.

     * * *

Customary international law and treaty law. The position of the United States raises fundamental questions about the nature of customary international law and its relationship to treaty law. Can it be argued, for example, that the whole of the United Nations Convention on the Law of the Sea, including provisions on deep seabed mining, is declaratory of customary international law or not, especially in the light of the need to adopt the 1994 Agreement, *supra*? Note that the following decisions of the International Court of Justice considered the 1982 convention and customary international law: the *Gulf of Maine* case (Canada v. The United States), before a Chamber of the Court, [1985] I.C.J. Rep. 246, 294; the Continental Shelf (Tunisia v. Libya) Case, [1982] I.C.J. Rep. 18, 74 and the *Continental Shelf (Libya v. Malta) case*, [1985] I.C.J. Rep. 13, 30. Consider the following but note that it was written two years after the adoption of the Convention and consequently before it came into force.

Anand, U.N. Convention on the Law of the Sea and the United States

24 Indian Journal of International Law 153, 154, 163–164, 184–187, 188, 190–191, 193 (1984).*

     * * *

On April 30, 1982, after nine years of intense, arduous, sometimes bitter and protracted negotiations, the Third United Nations Conference on the Law of the Sea adopted what has been called "a comprehensive constitution for the Oceans", a Convention which was said to be "the most significant international agreement since the Charter of the United Nations," providing a legal regime for nearly 70 per cent of the earth's surface. Largely put together through compromises and consensus in a conference which was in session for 93 weeks from the time it opened in December 1973 until it concluded its substantive work in September 1982,

     * Reprinted by permission of the Indian Society of International Law.

it was the largest conference in history in which 157 countries participated and 11 delegations attended as observers.

Following the consensus procedure all through its deliberations requiring all delegations to make efforts, in good faith, to accommodate the interests of others, resisting the temptation of putting substantive proposals to the vote, the Conference in the end was forced to adopt the Convention, on the insistence of the United States, by a vote of 130 in favour to 4 against (Israel, Turkey, United States and Venezuela), with 17 abstentions which included the Soviet Union and its allies and a few West European industrialized countries like Germany, Italy, Luxembourg, Netherlands, Spain and the United Kingdom. Based on numerous "mini-packages"—balanced compromises on at least 25 different contested subjects and issues ranging from seabed production to marine scientific research in offshore waters negotiated in different negotiating fora—the Convention was accepted in the end as "a package" and "an integral whole." It was for this reason that, as President of the Conference, Dr. Tommy Koh explained,

> * * * the Convention does not provide for reservations. It is therefore not possible for States to pick what they like and disregard what they do not like. In International law, as in domestic law, rights and duties go hand in hand. It is, therefore, legally impermissible to claim rights under the Convention without being willing to assume the correlative duties.

> He added: "Let no nation put asunder this landmark achievement of the international community."

> * * *

Seabed Beyond the Limits of National Jurisdiction

While the international society, almost for the first time in history, came to agree on a large part of international law of the sea, and UNCLOS–III, despite its cumbersome and time-consuming rules of procedure, settled most of the issues which in the beginning seemed unsolvable, one issue which threatened the disintegration of the entire conference was the mining of the deep seabed manganese nodules. It is important to note that although there were sharp disagreements amongst states about the structure and powers of an international seabed authority that must be established to control and manage the deep seabed and its resources, the acceptance of the area as "common heritage of mankind" which could not be appropriated by any state and must be explored and exploited for the benefit of mankind as a whole, was unquestioned. This principle, iterated and reiterated by the General Assembly in numerous resolutions, not only symbolized the interests and aspirations of the developing countries, but had been endorsed by all the developed countries, including the United States. As early as 1966, President Johnson wanted to "ensure that the deep seas and the ocean bottoms are, and remain, the legacy of all human beings." In 1970, President Nixon, renouncing all sovereign rights to the seabed and its resources and announcing the American policy to help establish an international machinery to administer the licensing of exploration and exploitation of the resources of the seabed, declared:

The International Seabed Area would be *the common heritage of mankind* and no state could exercise sovereignty or sovereign rights over this area or its resources.

Presidents Ford and Carter recognized these principles without any question and enthusiastically participated at the UNCLOS–III to develop an international regime to govern seabed mining activities. Even after the United States got frustrated with the slow progress in the UNCLOS–III and decided to enact an interim legislation for the exploration and exploitation of deep seabed resources to prod the conference to expedite its work, it acknowledged the commitment of the United States to the 1970 UN Declaration. Sections 7 and 8 of the U.S. Deep Seabed Hard Minerals Resources Act of 1980 stated:

> (7) On December 17, 1970, the United States supported (by affirmative vote) General Assembly Resolution 2749 (XXV) declaring inter alia the principle that the mineral resources of the deep seabed are the common heritage of mankind, with the expectation that this principle would be legally defined under the terms of a comprehensive international Law of the Sea Treaty yet to be agreed upon.

> (8) It is in the national interest of the United States and other nations to encourage a widely acceptable Law of the Sea Treaty, which will provide a new legal order for the oceans covering a broad range of ocean interests, including exploration for and commercial recovery of hard mineral resources of the deep seabed.

> * * *

[Having asserted that the United States originally subscribed to the "common heritage principle," the author later argues that emerging principles of customary international law are binding on states which fail to object to them from the outset. He begins with an analysis of the growth of customary international law in state practice, which includes most of the analysis of custom and is presented in chapter 1.]

> * * *

Treaty Custom Dichotomy

Another significant * * * custom-creating process is through "generalizable provisions in bilateral and multilateral treaties (which) generate customary rules of law binding upon all states". * * *

Although a codifying treaty normally presupposes a fair amount of established customary law which it seeks to codify, a treaty which breaks entirely new ground may stimulate the crystalization of customary rules binding even on non-parties to the treaty. * * *

The 1969 Vienna Convention on the Law of Treaties * * * clearly recognized this phenomenon. After dealing with the pacta tertiis problem in Articles 34 to 37, Article 38 states that:

> Nothing in Articles 34 to 37 precludes a rule set forth in a treaty from becoming binding upon a third state as a customary rule of international law, recognized as such.

> * * *

* * * [S]trong dissent to a treaty by a small number of states, or even a single powerful and influential state, whose interests are directly affected, especially if they have consistently and openly maintained their dissent, would distract from the authority of the treaty and adversely affect the emergence of customary law on the subject. However, the dissent of certain states may be ineffective if there is general acceptance of a practice "as law", or the dissentient states have not made their views heard until the rule has in practice crystallized and become firmly established, or the dissent relates to some fundamental principle. * * * [W]hile a state may acquire an exceptional position with regard to some general rule of customary law, there is no such right for the state to isolate itself from the impact of a fundamental principle. In other words, it is submitted that no state can evade a treaty or the operation of a principle which has emerged as jus cogens, or avoid the operation of a rule or rules which are so bound up with the essential nature of a concept of international law, which has become universally binding, that they cannot be excluded without denying the existence of the concept. * * * For this situation, when a treaty seeks to codify a general fundamental norm and effects the sudden acceleration of usage the position of dissenting states which are in a small minority may be made more difficult. *In the normal course of inter-state relations, the state which declines to accept an emerging rule of general law has to object to its application to itself, consistently and openly, from the time when the rule begins to crystallize.* [Italics supplied] But if the dissenting state itself has been a party to the emergence and acceptance of a general norm of international law sought to be codified, it cannot decline its acceptance by refusing to sign and ratify the treaty and may find it difficult to resist the application of the general rule to its own interests at a subsequent stage.

* * *

* * * [T]he basic tenets of the "common heritage" principle have come to be universally accepted, and have become jus cogens. The traditional law can never be interpreted to permit the exclusive exploitation of hundreds of miles of a seabed mining site for extended periods of time by any nation or its nationals. Acceptance of the Convention by a vast majority of states with abstentation [sic] by a few industrialized Western Powers which did not oppose it, can be said to have created a strong presumption in favour of an emergent custom which even the strongest Power on earth cannot violate except at a considerable cost and without being challenged.

* * *

2.   THE CONVENTION AND THE PRACTICE OF STATES

Extent of Maritime Zones Under the United Nations Convention

III. OTHER INFORMATION

Worldwide claims to maritime zones[a]

1. Summary of national claims to maritime zones

	African States	Asian and Pacific States	European and North American States	Latin American and Caribbean States	Total
Outer limits					
Territorial Sea					
12 mm or less	30	46	30	27	135
More than 12 mm	6	3	–	4	13
Contiguous zone					
24 mm or less	18	24	9	16	67
	–	1	–	–	1
Exclusive economic zone					
200 mm or less (up to delimitation line, median line, determination by coordinates, etc.)	27	36	19	27	109
Fishery zone					
200 mm or less	3	2	10	–	15
200 mm and/or outer edge of continental margin	10	16	5	13	44
Depth 200 meters and/or exploitability	4	7	10	3	25
Others (natural prolongation, no definition provided, etc.)	1	6	8	7	22

[a] From R.R. Churchill and A.V. Lowe, THE LAW OF THE SEA, at p. 39 (3rd ed. 1999). Reprinted with the permission of Juris Publishing, Manchester University Press.

Extent of Maritime Zones Established by National Legislation

U.N. Office of the Special Representative of the Secretary–General for the Law of the Sea, Law of the Sea Bulletin No. 2, March 1985, p. 1

One of the most important consequences of the Third United Nations Conference on the Law of the Sea was the acceleration of the process of revision of national laws undertaken by Governments, in particular those laws regulating the nature and breadth of maritime areas subject to sovereignty or national jurisdiction. Since the beginning of deliberations, several States have amended their maritime legislation in order to reflect the new trends and concepts that were emerging in the Conference; this is evidenced, inter alia, by the fact that 54 States have since 1974 adopted laws establishing an exclusive economic zone * * *. This important development was recognized by the Secretary–General of the United Nations at the closing session of the Conference in these terms: "In order to affirm that international law is now irrevocably transformed so far as the seas are concerned, we need not wait for the process of ratification to begin."

The Office of the Special Representative for the Law of the Sea considered that it might be useful for governments and bodies of the United Nations system to have quick and convenient access to updated information on the status of national legislation concerning maritime zones around the world. This information may be of assistance to States in their process of ratification of the Convention on the Law of the Sea and for the adjustment of their legislation to it. For this purpose, this Office has prepared the present issue of the Law of the Sea Bulletin Series containing a tabulation of national legislation establishing the breadth and régimes governing maritime zones over which coastal States exercise their sovereignty or jurisdiction (territorial sea, contiguous zone, exclusive economic zone, fishery zone, continental shelf and others). * * *

SECTION B.   CONTROL OF NATIONAL VESSELS

Source Note: the material in Section B. blends some older customary and treaty law with influences from the 1982 Law of the Sea Convention.

1.   NATIONALITY OF VESSELS

Public Ministry v. Mogens Glistrup

Denmark, Maritime and Commercial Court, 1967.
95 Journal du Droit International 979 (1968).[a]

A vessel belonging to a Danish corporation and registered in Denmark and flying the Danish flag, was bareboat chartered[b] to an American

---

a. Translation by the editors. Reprinted by permission of Editions Techniques, S.A., Paris.

b. Leased without provision of officers or crew by the owner.

company which used it in Nigerian waters. While the vessel was under charter, it had a crew which did not meet the conditions of the Danish Act on the Manning of Ships of 1965. According to paragraph 1, the act applies to all Danish vessels. The director of the American corporation had interpreted this provision as applying only to vessels under actual Danish control.

The court held however that the act applied to all Danish vessels even when bareboat chartered. The law of the flag controls. Otherwise, said the court, a vessel flying the Danish flag could escape all legislation or public control [of Denmark].

Even though Denmark has not ratified the Geneva Convention on the High Seas, the rule in Article 5 of the convention which makes the nationality of vessels depend upon the existence of a genuine link between the state and vessel flying its flag, must be considered without any question to be a part of public international law. The decision [therefore] seems to be perfectly in accord with the principle expressed in that article: genuine link means that the state effectively exercises its jurisdiction and its control
* * *.

1. *Genuine Link in Article 5 of the 1958 Convention on the High Seas.* The article provides, in Paragraph 1:

> Each state shall fix the conditions for the grant of its nationality to ships, for the registration of ships in its territory, and for the right to fly its flag. Ships have the nationality of the state whose flag they are entitled to fly. There must exist a genuine link between the state and the ship; in particular, the state must effectively exercise its jurisdiction and control in administrative, technical and social matters over ships flying its flag.

What is the function of the genuine link? Consider in connection with this question the statement made before the United States Senate Committee on Foreign Relations by Mr. Arthur H. Dean, the head of the delegation of the United States at the 1958 Geneva Conference. He said:

> The International Law Commission did not decide upon a definition of the term "genuine link." This article as originally drafted by the Commission would have authorized other states to determine whether there was a "genuine link" between a ship and the flag state for purposes of recognition of the nationality of the ship.

> It was felt by some states attending the Conference on the Law of the Sea that the term "genuine link" could, depending upon how it were defined, limit the discretion of a state to decide which ships it would permit to fly its flag. Some states, which felt their flag vessels

were at a competitive disadvantage with vessels sailing under the flags of other states, such as Panama and Liberia, were anxious to adopt a definition which states like [the latter] could not meet.

By a vote of 30 states, including the United States, against 15 states for, and 17 states abstaining, a provision was eliminated which would have enabled states other than the flag state to withhold recognition of the national character of a ship if they considered that there was no "genuine link" between the state and the ship.

Thus, under the Convention on the High Seas, it is for each state to determine how it shall exercise jurisdiction and control in administrative, technical and social matters over ships flying its flag. The "genuine link" requirement need not have any effect upon the practice of registering American built or owned vessels in such countries as Panama or Liberia. The existence of a "genuine link" between the state and the ship is not a condition of recognition of the nationality of a ship; that is, no state can claim the right to determine unilaterally that no genuine link exists between a ship and the flag state. * * * Excerpt from Executive Report No. 5—Law of the Sea Conventions, 106 Cong.Rec. 11189, 11190 (1960). This topic is covered in Chapter 8, as to persons, and Chapter 3 as to jurisdiction.

Note the importance of the *Nötteböhm* case (Liechtenstein v. Guatemala), [1955] I.C.J. Rep. 4 Although that case concerned the "genuine link" between a person and the state claiming him as his or her own national, it was because of this case that the requirement was inserted into the International Law Commission's Draft Articles which were the vehicle for negotiation in Geneva in 1958. See Article 5 of the 1958 Convention on the High Seas and Article 91(1) of the 1982 Convention, both in the Documentary Supplement.

   2. Nationality and Genuine Link in Article 91 of the United Nations Convention. The International Tribunal for the Law of the Sea, considered *infra*, had occasion to deal with this issue in its second case which concerned the Saiga, an oil tanker which was attacked and seized by a Guinean patrol boat while beyond the EEZ of Guinea. The extract below deals with the factual background and one of the challenges to admissibility based on nationality of claims, that is that St. Vincent and the Grenadines had no legal standing to bring the claim, *inter alia*, in respect of the ship, because the *Saiga* did not have the nationality of Saint Vincent and the Grenadines at the time of its arrest.

The M/V "Saiga" (No. 2) Case

(Saint Vincent and the Grenadines v. Guinea)

INTERNATIONAL TRIBUNAL FOR THE LAW OF THE SEA
YEAR 1999

1 July 1999

List of Cases
No. 2

38 International Legal Materials 1323 (1999)*

31. The *Saiga* is an oil tanker. At the time of its arrest on 28 October 1997, it was owned by Tabona Shipping Company Ltd. of Nicosia, Cyprus, and managed by Seascot Shipmanagement Ltd. of Glasgow, Scotland. The ship was chartered to Lemania Shipping Group Ltd. of Geneva, Switzerland. The *Saiga* was provisionally registered in Saint Vincent and the Grenadines on 12 March 1997. The Master and crew of the ship were all of Ukrainian nationality. There were also three Senegalese nationals who were employed as painters. The *Saiga* was engaged in selling gas oil as bunker and occasionally water to fishing and other vessels off the coast of West Africa. The owner of the cargo of gas oil on board was Addax BV of Geneva, Switzerland.

32.   Under the command of Captain Orlov, the *Saiga* left Dakar, Senegal, on 24 October 1997 fully laden with approximately 5,400 metric tons of gas oil. On 27 October 1997, between 0400 and 1400 hours and at a point 10°25′03′N and 15°42′06′W, the Saiga supplied gas oil to three fishing vessels, the *Giuseppe Primo* and the *Kriti*, both flying the flag of Senegal, and the *Eleni S*, flying the flag of Greece. This point was approximately 22 nautical miles from Guinea's island of Alcatraz. All three fishing vessels were licensed by Guinea to fish in its exclusive economic zone. The *Saiga* then sailed in a southerly direction to supply gas oil to other fishing vessels at a pre-arranged place. Upon instructions from the owner of the cargo in Geneva, it later changed course and sailed towards another location beyond the southern border of the exclusive economic zone of Guinea.

33.   At 0800 hours on 28 October 1997, the *Saiga*, according to its log book, was at a point 09°00′01N and 14°58′58′W. It had been drifting since 0420 hours while awaiting the arrival of fishing vessels to which it was to supply gas oil. This point was south of the southern limit of the exclusive economic zone of Guinea. At about 0900 hours the *Saiga* was attacked by a Guinean patrol boat (P35). Officers from that boat and another Guinean patrol boat (P328) subsequently boarded the ship and arrested it. On the same day, the ship and its crew were brought to Conakry, Guinea, where its Master was detained. The travel documents of the members of the crew were taken from them by the authorities of Guinea and armed guards were placed on board the ship. On 1 November 1997, two injured persons from the *Saiga*, Mr. Sergey Klyuyev and Mr. Djibril Niasse, were permitted to leave Conakry for Dakar for medical treatment. Between 10 and 12 November 1997, the cargo of gas oil on board the ship, amounting to 4,941.322 metric tons, was discharged on the orders of the Guinean authorities. Seven members of the crew and two painters left Conakry on 17 November 1997, one crew member left on 14 December 1997 and six on 12 January 1998. The Master and six crew members remained in Conakry until the ship was released on 28 February 1998.

* * *

---

* Reprinted with the permission of the
American Society of International Law.

Challenges to admissibility

Registration of the *Saiga*

55.   The first objection raised by Guinea to the admissibility of the claims set out in the application is that Saint Vincent and the Grenadines does not have legal standing to bring claims in connection with the measures taken by Guinea against the *Saiga*. The reason given by Guinea for its contention is that on the day of its arrest the ship was "not validly registered under the flag of Saint Vincent and the Grenadines" and that, consequently, Saint Vincent and the Grenadines is not legally competent to present claims either on its behalf or in respect to the ship, its Master and the other members of the crew, its owners or its operators.

56.   This contention of Guinea is challenged by Saint Vincent and the Grenadines on several grounds.

57.   The facts relating to the registration of the *Saiga*, as they emerge from the evidence adduced before the Tribunal are as follows:

(1) The *Saiga* was registered provisionally on 12 March 1997 as a Saint Vincent and the Grenadines ship under section 36 of the Merchant Shipping Act of 1982 of Saint Vincent and the Grenadines (hereinafter "the Merchant Shipping Act"). The Provisional Certificate of Registration issued to the ship on 14 April 1997 stated that it was issued by the Commissioner for Maritime Affairs of Saint Vincent and the Grenadines on behalf of the Government of Saint Vincent and the Grenadines under the terms of the Merchant Shipping Act. The Certificate stated: "This Certificate expires on 12 September 1997".

(2) The registration of the ship was recorded in the Registry Book of Saint Vincent and the Grenadines on 26 March 1997. The entry stated: "Valid thru: 12/09/1997".

(3) A Permanent Certificate of Registration was issued on 28 November 1997 by the Commissioner for Maritime Affairs of Saint Vincent and the Grenadines on behalf of the State. The Certificate stated: "This Certificate is permanent".

58.   Guinea contends that the ship was unregistered between 12 September 1997 and 28 November 1997 because the Provisional Certificate of Registration expired on 12 September 1997 and the Permanent Certificate of Registration was issued on 28 November 1997. From this Guinea concludes: "It is thus very clear that the MV 'SAIGA was not validly registered' in the time period between 12 September 1997 and 28 November 1997. For this reason, the MV 'SAIGA' may [be] qualified to be *a ship without nationality* at the time of its attach." Guinea also questioned whether the ship had been deleted from the Maltese Register where it was previously registered.

59.   Saint Vincent and the Grenadines controverts Guinea's assertion that the expiry of the Provisional Certificate of Registration implies that the ship was not registered or that it lost the nationality of Saint Vincent and the Grenadines. It argues that when a vessel is registered under its flag "it remains so registered until deleted from the registry." It notes that the

conditions and procedures for deletion of ships from its Registry are set out in Part I, sections 9 to 42 and 59 to 61, of the Merchant Shipping Act, and emphasizes that none of these procedures was at any time applied to the *Saiga*. In support of its claim, Saint Vincent and the Grenadines refers to the declaration dated 27 October 1998 by the Commissioner for Maritime Affairs of Saint Vincent and the Grenadines which states that the ship was registered under the Saint Vincent and the Grenadines flag on 12 March 1997 "and is still today validly registered."

60.   Saint Vincent and the Grenadines further contends that, under the Merchant Shipping Act, a ship does not lose Vincentian nationality because of the expiry of its provisional certificate of registration. In support of its contentions, Saint Vincent and the Grenadines refers to section 36(2) of the Merchant Shipping Act which states that a provisional certificate "shall have the same effect as the ordinary certificate of registration until the expiry of one year from the date of its issue." Saint Vincent and the Grenadines argues that, pursuant to this provision, a provisional certificate of registration remains in force until the expiry of one year from the date of its issue. In further support for this contention, Saint Vincent and the Grenadines points out that, under section 36(3) of the Merchant Shipping Act, payment of "the annual fee for one year" is required when an application is made for provisional registration. It further maintains that, just as a person would not lose nationality when his or her passport expires, a vessel would not cease to be registered merely because of the expiry of a provisional certificate. According to Saint Vincent and the Grenadines, the provisional certificate, like a passport, is evidence, but not the source, of national status. For these reasons, Saint Vincent and the Grenadines contends that the Provisional Certificate in this case remained in force after 12 September 1997 and at all times material to the present dispute. With regard to the question raised by Guinea concerning the previous registration of the ship, Saint Vincent and the Grenadines states that its authorities had received from the owner of the ship "satisfactory evidence that the ship's registration in the country of last registration had been closed" as required by section 37 of the Merchant Shipping Act.

61.   Guinea argues that automatic extension of a provisional certificate of registration is neither provided for nor envisaged under the Merchant Shipping Act. In this connection, it argues that the declarations by the Commissioner for Maritime Affairs of 27 October 1998 and the Deputy Commissioner for Maritime Affairs of 1 March 1999, to the effect that the *Saiga* Aremained validly registered in the Register of Ships of Saint Vincent and the Grenadines as at 27th October 1997 do not suffice to fill the gap in registration between 12 September 1997 and 28 November 1997, when the Permanent Certificate of Registration of the *Saiga* was issued. It further argues that these declarations on the registration status cannot be accepted as independent documentary evidence in the context of the present proceedings. According to Guinea, the *Saiga's* registration could only have continued after the expiry of its Provisional Certificate if the Provisional Certificate had been replaced with another provisional certificate or its expiry date had been extended. Guinea points out that there is no evidence that any such action was taken after the Provisional Certificate expired. It states that a comparison of a provisional certificate of registra-

tion of a ship with a person's passport is misplaced, since a ship acquires nationality by registration and is required to have a certificate, while a person's nationality does not depend on the acquisition or retention of a passport. For these reasons, Guinea maintains that the *Saiga* did not have the nationality of Saint Vincent and the Grenadines during the period between the expiry of the Provisional Certificate on 12 September 1997 and the issue of the Permanent Certificate on 28 November 1997.

62.   The question for consideration is whether the *Saiga* had the nationality of Saint Vincent and the Grenadines at the time of its arrest. The relevant provision of the Convention is article 91, which reads as follows:

Article 91
Nationality of ships

1.   Every State shall fix the conditions for the grant of its nationality to ships, for the registration of ships in its territory, and for the right to fly its flag. Ships have the nationality of the State whose flag they are entitled to fly. There must exist a genuine link between the State and the ship.

2.   Every State shall issue to ships to which it has granted the right to fly its flag documents to that effect.

63.   Article 91 leaves to each State exclusive jurisdiction over the granting of its nationality to ships. In this respect, article 91 codifies a well-established rule of general international law. Under this article, it is for Saint Vincent and the Grenadines to fix the conditions for the grant of its nationality to ships, for the registration of ships in its territory and for the right to fly its flag. These matters are regulated by a State in its domestic law. Pursuant to article 91, paragraph 2, Saint Vincent and the Grenadines is under an obligation to issue to ships to which it has granted the right to fly its flag documents to that effect. The issue of such documents is regulated by domestic law.

64.   International law recognizes several modalities for the grant of nationality to different types of ships. In the case of merchant ships, the normal procedure used by States to grant nationality is registration in accordance with domestic legislation adopted for that purpose. This procedure is adopted by Saint Vincent and the Grenadines in the Merchant Shipping Act.

65.   Determination of the criteria and establishment of the procedures for granting and withdrawing nationality to ships are matters within the exclusive jurisdiction of the flag State. Nevertheless, disputes concerning such matters may be subject to the procedures under Part XV of the Convention, especially in cases where issues of interpretation or application of provisions of the Convention are involved.

66.   The Tribunal considers that the nationality of a ship is a question of fact to be determined, like other facts in dispute before it, on the basis of evidence adduced by the parties.

67.   Saint Vincent and the Grenadines has produced evidence before the Tribunal to support its assertion that the *Saiga* was a ship entitled to fly

its flag at the time of the incident giving rise to the dispute. In addition to making references to the relevant provisions of the Merchant Shipping Act, Saint Vincent and the Grenadines has drawn attention to several indications of Vincentian nationality on the ship or carried on board. These include the inscription of "Kingstown" as the port of registry on the stern of the vessel, the documents on board and the ship's seal which contained the words SAIGA "Kingstown" and the then current charter-party which recorded the flag of the vessel as "Saint Vincent and the Grenadines."

68.   The evidence adduced by Saint Vincent and the Grenadines has been reinforced by its conduct. Saint Vincent and the Grenadines has at all times material to the dispute operated on the basis that the *Saiga* was a ship of its nationality. It has acted as the flag State of the ship during all phases of the proceedings. It was in that capacity that it invoked the jurisdiction of the Tribunal in its Application for the prompt release of the *Saiga* and its crew under article 292 of the Convention and in its Request for the prescription of provisional measures under article 290 of the Convention.

69.   As far as Guinea is concerned, the Tribunal cannot fail to note that it did not challenge or raise any doubts about the registration or nationality of the ship at any time until the submission of its Counter–Memorial in October 1998. Prior to this, it was open to Guinea to make inquiries regarding the registration of the *Saiga* or documentation relating to it. For example, Guinea could have inspected the Register of Ships of Saint Vincent and the Grenadines. Opportunities for raising doubts about the registration or nationality of the ship were available during the proceedings for prompt release in November 1997 and for the prescription of provisional measures in February 1998. It is also pertinent to note that the authorities of Guinea named Saint Vincent and the Grenadines as civilly responsible to be summoned in the schedule of summons by which the Master was charged before the Tribunal of First Instance in Conakry. In the ruling of the Court of Appeal, Saint Vincent and the Grenadines was stated to be the flag State of the *Saiga*.

70.   With regard to the previous registration of the *Saiga*, the Tribunal notes the statement made by Saint Vincent and the Grenadines in paragraph 60. It considers this statement to be sufficient.

71.   The Tribunal recalls that, in its Judgment of 4 December 1997 and in its Order of 11 March 1998, the *Saiga* is described as a ship flying the flag of Saint Vincent and the Grenadines.

72.   On the basis of the evidence before it, the Tribunal finds that Saint Vincent and the Grenadines has discharged the initial burden of establishing that the *Saiga* had Vincentian nationality at the time it was arrested by Guinea. Guinea had therefore to prove its contention that the ship was not registered in or did not have the nationality of Saint Vincent and the Grenadines at that time. The Tribunal considers that the burden has not been discharged and that it has not been established that the *Saiga* was not registered in or did not have the nationality of Saint Vincent and the Grenadines at the time of the arrest.

73.   The Tribunal concludes:

(a) it has not been established that the Vincentian registration or nationality of the *Saiga* was extinguished in the period between the date on which the Provisional Certificate was stated to expire and the date of issue of the Permanent Certificate of Registration;

(b) in the particular circumstances of this case, the consistent conduct of Saint Vincent and the Grenadines provides sufficient support for the conclusion that the *Saiga* retained the registration and nationality of Saint Vincent and the Grenadines at all times material to the dispute;

(c) in view of Guinea's failure to question the assertion of Saint Vincent and the Grenadines that it is the flag State of the *Saiga* when it had every reasonable opportunity to do so and its other conduct in the case, Guinea cannot successfully challenge the registration and nationality of the *Saiga* at this stage;

(d) in the particular circumstances of this case, it would not be consistent with justice if the Tribunal were to decline to deal with the merits of the dispute.

74. For the above reasons, the Tribunal rejects Guinea's objection to the admissibility of the claims of Saint Vincent and the Grenadines based on the ground that the *Saiga* was not registered in Saint Vincent and the Grenadines at the time of its arrest and that, consequently, the *Saiga* did not have Vincentian nationality at that time.

Genuine Link

75. The next objection to admissibility raised by Guinea is that there was no genuine link between the *Saiga* and Saint Vincent and the Grenadines. Guinea contends that "without a genuine link between Saint Vincent and the Grenadines and the M/V '*Saiga*' Saint Vincent and the Grenadines' claim concerning a violation of its right of navigation and the status of the ship is not admissible before the Tribunal *vis-a-vis* Guinea, because Guinea is not bound to recognize the Vincentian nationality of the M/V '*Saiga*', which forms a prerequisite for the mentioned claim in international law."

76. Guinea further argues that a State cannot fulfil its obligations as a flag State under the Convention with regard to a ship unless it exercises prescriptive and enforcement jurisdiction over the owner or, as the case may be, the operation of the ship. Guinea contends that, in the absence of such jurisdiction, there is no genuine link between the ship and Saint Vincent and the Grenadines and that, accordingly, it is not obliged to recognize the claims of Saint Vincent and the Grenadines in relation to the ship.

77. Saint Vincent and the Grenadines maintains that there is nothing in the Convention to support the contention that the existence of a genuine link between a ship and a State is a necessary precondition for the grant of nationality to the ship, or that the absence of such a genuine link deprives a flag State of the right to bring an international claim against another State in respect of illegal measures taken against the ship.

78. Saint Vincent and the Grenadines also challenges the assertion of Guinea that there was no genuine link between the *Saiga* and Saint

Vincent and the Grenadines. It claims that the requisite genuine link existed between it and the ship. Saint Vincent and the Grenadines calls attention to various facts which, according to it, provide evidence of this link. These include the fact that the owner of the *Saiga* is represented in Saint Vincent and the Grenadines by a company formed and established in that State and the fact that the *Saiga* is subject to the supervision of the Vincentian authorities to secure compliance with the International Convention for the Safety of Life at Sea (SOLAS), 1960 and 1974, the International Convention for the Prevention of Pollution from Ships, 1973, as modified by the Protocol of 1978 relating thereto (MARPOL 73/78), and other conventions of the International Maritime Organization to which Saint Vincent and the Grenadines is a party. In addition, Saint Vincent and the Grenadines maintains that arrangements have been made to secure regular supervision of the vessel's seaworthiness through surveys, on at least an annual basis, conducted by reputable classification societies authorized for that purpose by Saint Vincent and the Grenadines. Saint Vincent and the Grenadines also points out that, under its laws, preference is given to Vincentian nationals in the manning of ships flying its flag. It further draws attention to the vigorous efforts made by its authorities to secure the protection of the *Saiga* on the international plane before and throughout the present dispute.

79.   Article 91, paragraph 1, of the Convention provides: "There must exist a genuine link between the State and the ship." Two questions need to be addressed in this connection. The first is whether the absence of a genuine link between a flag State and a ship entitles another State to refuse to recognize the nationality of the ship. The second question is whether or not a genuine link existed between the *Saiga* and Saint Vincent and the Grenadines at the time of the incident.

80.   With regard to the first question, the Tribunal notes that the provision in article 91, paragraph 1, of the Convention, requiring a genuine link between the State and the ship, does not provide the answer. Nor do articles 92 and 94 of the Convention, which together with article 91 constitute the context of the provision, provide the answer. The Tribunal, however, recalls that the International Law Commission, in article 29 of the Draft Articles on the Law of the Sea adopted by it in 1956, proposed the concept of a "genuine link" as a criterion not only for the attribution of nationality to a ship but also for the recognition by other States of such nationality. After providing that "ships have the nationality of the State whose flag they are entitled to fly", the draft article continued: "Nevertheless, for purposes of recognition of the national character of the ship by other States, there must exist a genuine link between the State and the ship." This sentence was not included in article 5, paragraph 1, of the Convention on the High Seas of 29 April 1958 (hereinafter "the 1958 Convention"), which reads, in part, as follows:

> There must exist a genuine link between the State and the ship; in particular, the State must effectively exercise its jurisdiction and control in administrative, technical and social matters over ships flying its flag.

Thus, while the obligation regarding a genuine link was maintained in the 1958 Convention, the proposal that the existence of a genuine link should be a basis for the recognition of nationality was not adopted.

81.   The Convention follows the approach of the 1958 Convention. Article 91 retains the part of the third sentence of article 5, paragraph 2, of the 1958 Convention which provides that there must be a genuine link between the State and the ship. The other part of that sentence, stating that the flag State shall effectively exercise its jurisdiction and control in administrative, technical and social matters over ships flying its flag, is reflected in article 94 of the Convention, dealing with the duties of the flag State.

82.   Paragraphs 2 to 5 of article 94 of the Convention outline the measures that a flag State is required to take to exercise effective jurisdiction as envisaged in paragraph 1. Paragraph 6 sets out the procedure to be followed where another State has "clear grounds to believe that proper jurisdiction and control with respect to a ship have not been exercised." That State is entitled to report the facts to the flag State which is then obliged to "investigate the matter and, if appropriate, take any action necessary to remedy the situation." There is nothing in article 94 to permit a State which discovers evidence indicating the absence of proper jurisdiction and control by a flag State over a ship to refuse to recognize the right of the ship to fly the flag of the flag State.

83.   The conclusion of the Tribunal is that the purpose of the provisions of the Convention on the need for a genuine link between a ship and its flag State is to secure more effective implementation of the duties of the flag State, and not to establish criteria by reference to which the validity of the registration of ships in a flag State may be challenged by other States.

84.   This conclusion is not put into question by the United Nations Convention on Conditions for Registration of Ships of 7 February 1986 invoked by Guinea. This Convention (which is not in force) sets out as one of its principal objectives the strengthening of "the genuine link between a State and ships flying its flag." The Tribunal observes that Guinea has not cited any provision in that Convention which lends support to its contention that "a basic condition for the registration of a ship is that also the owner or operator of the ship is under the jurisdiction of the flag State."

85.   The conclusion is further strengthened by the Agreement for the Implementation of the Provisions of the United Nations Convention on the Law of the Sea of 10 December 1982 Relating to the Conservation and Management of Straddling Fish Stocks and Highly Migratory Fish Stocks opened for signature on 4 December 1995 and the Agreement to Promote Compliance with International Conservation and Management Measures by Fishing Vessels on the High Seas of 24 November 1993. These Agreements, neither of which is in force, set out, *inter alia*, detailed obligations to be discharged by the flag States of fishing vessels but do not deal with the conditions to be satisfied for the registration of fishing vessels.

86.   In the light of the above consideration, the Tribunal concludes that there is no legal basis for the claim of Guinea that it can refuse to recognize the right of the *Saiga* to fly the flag of Saint Vincent and the Grenadines

on the ground that there was no genuine link between the ship and Saint Vincent and the Grenadines.

87. With regard to the second question, the Tribunal finds that, in any case, the evidence adduced by Guinea is not sufficient to justify its contention that there was no genuine link between the ship and Saint Vincent and the Grenadines at the material time.

88. For the above reasons, the Tribunal rejects the objection to admissibility based on the absence of a genuine link between the *Saiga* and Saint Vincent and the Grenadines.

3. *Flags of Convenience and the United Nations Convention on the Law of the Sea.* The attempt made at the 1958 Geneva Conference to frame an effective genuine link requirement was intended to curb the use of flags of convenience. The term refers, broadly speaking, to vessels operating under the flags of states that do not require the owners to be nationals or long term residents. The practice, also called open registry, means that such states are seldom directly concerned with the management of the vessels and, in some cases, show little interest in regulating their operation. The opportunity is thereby created for less scrupulous owners to run substandard vessels with inadequate equipment or incompetent crews.

It is well known that substandard vessels and incompetent crews can also be found in fleets from certain states with closed registries. Nevertheless, much of the pressure for the adoption of regulations was generated in recent years by spectacular oil spills from wrecked or sinking tankers flying flags of convenience and the publicity given thereafter to the lack of competence of the crew, the inadequacy of the equipment aboard and the faulty design of the vessel.

The United Nations Convention on the Law of the Sea does not deal directly with the definition of genuine link. Instead, its provisions specify in detail the duties incumbent upon a state in order effectively to exercise jurisdiction and control over its flag vessels. These provisions require the state to take measures regarding: the construction, equipment and seaworthiness of vessels; the manning of vessels, labour conditions and the training of crews; and the use of signals, the maintenance of communications and the prevention of collisions. See Article 94 of the convention in the Documentary Supplement.

The convention does not go so far as to strip from a vessel the nationality of the flag state in the event the flag state fails to take such measures. Section 6 of Article 94 provides only the following recourse:

> A State which has clear grounds to believe that proper jurisdiction and control with respect to a ship have not been exercised may report the facts to the flag State. Upon receiving such a report, the flag State shall investigate the matter and, if appropriate, take any action necessary to remedy the situation.

The problem of defining the genuine link which should exist between a vessel and the state whose flag it flies was considered in a conference called especially to deal with it pursuant to a resolution of the General Assembly of the United Nations. The conference adopted on February 7, 1986 the convention set forth in part below.

The United Nations Convention on Conditions for Registration of Ships

U.N. Office of the Special Representative of the Secretary–General for the Law of the Sea, Law of the Sea Bulletin No. 7, April 1986, pp. 87, 93. The Convention is in the Documentary Supplement. Please analyze articles 7, 8, and 9.

Entry into force of the convention. It was open for signature from May 1, 1986 to April 30, 1987 and will go into effect when ratified by 40 states whose combined tonnage amounts to at least 25 per cent of the world registered tonnage. [As of June 2000 there are 11 states parties.] Statistics on world registered tonnage are available in the Law of the Sea Bulletin, No. 7, April 1986, p. 103, published by the U.N. Office of the Special Representative of the Secretary–General for the Law of the Sea. They reflect the importance of flags of convenience in world shipping.

Rounded off to the millionth ton, the world registered tonnage—vessels of 500 gross tons and above—is 384,000,000 tons. The two states best known as suppliers of flags of convenience, Liberia and Panama account for more than 25 per cent of the world tonnage between them. The tonnage given for the Bahamas, for Cyprus, and for Singapore, also reflect the fact that they are important suppliers of flags of convenience.

The United States is reputed to be the largest beneficiary of flags of convenience. The statistics bear this out. The economic pressure generated by the use of flags of convenience has led to the curious practice described in the following material.

Spain, Finland Joining Rush to Form Flags of Convenience

The Journal of Commerce, November 18, 1986, p. 1.*

Spain and Finland have joined the growing list of European nations seeking to establish domestic flags of convenience to try to halt or even reverse the exodus of shipowners from their national flags.

Luxembourg also is keen to include a shipping register in its drive to expand its financial services sector.

The Spanish government is mulling a proposal to turn the Canary Islands into an offshore registry for the country's hard-pressed shipowners. Authorities on the Aland Islands, midway between Finland and Sweden, are seeking special status to attract Finnish ships sailing under foreign flags.

The proposed Canary Islands registry is part of a package designed to help Spanish shipowners, who have accumulated debts of about $1.5 billion. Eighty companies are likely to move their operations to the Canaries,

* Reprinted by permission of the Journal of Commerce.

bringing about 360 of the country's 580 ships, according to the Spanish Maritime Institute.

The semi-autonomous administration of the Aland Islands is seeking changes in Finland's constitution that would allow a more favorable fiscal and labor regime to attract the 40% of the national fleet registered overseas.

Fifteen Finnish ships have switched flags this year to Panama, Cyprus and the Cayman Islands.

Several European countries have already set up offshore registries to compete with Liberia and Panama. * * *

Norway, whose shipowners are deserting in droves to flags of convenience, pioneered the concept of an offshore flag earlier this year with a plan to establish a registry on the Svalbard Islands in the Spitzbergen archipelago. Shipowners would enjoy the same benefits there as they would in Panama or Liberia.

Other maritime nations quickly followed suit. British owners are transferring the registry of their ships to the Isle of Man, the small self-governing island in the Irish Sea, while French owners are hoisting their flag on the Kerguelen Islands in the Antarctic.

The new registries are "flags with a flag," allowing shipowners to reap the financial benefits of offshore operation while remaining under the sovereignty of their national registries.

Time is running out for European nations to halt shrinkage of their fleets. Last year Norway's flag fleet dwindled by 10 million deadweight tons to a record low of 16.9 million dwt. The exodus is accelerating, with the flag losing 67 ships of almost 5 million deadweight tons in the first nine months of the year.

Norwegian-owned tonnage under foreign flags is now equal to the size of the domestic fleet.

At the end of this year the size of the British-flag fleet will be smaller than that of the flagged-out fleet controlled by U.K.-registered companies, according to the General Council of British Shipping.

More than 50 vessels have left the West German fleet this year, with Cyprus the favored location. About 45% of the German-owned fleet is operating under foreign flags and the figure is rising fast.

Several national fleets could disappear within the next few years as shipowners seek cover from falling freight rates, rising labor costs and intensified low-cost competition from the Far East.

West European shipowners, especially bulk operators, cannot afford to compete with Asian lines employing cheaper crews. The annual wage bill for a 10,000–ton U.K.-crewed ship is about $1 million, twice that of a Hong Kong-registered vessel crewed by Asians.

* * *

1. Reflagging of Kuwaiti tankers as United States vessels. A foreign vessel may qualify for registry in the United States, and fly the American flag, if its ownership is transferred to a person or entity of American nationality, as for example, a Delaware corporation, and it meets a number of technical requirements as to design, construction and other such matters. See Section 2101 and following of Title 46 of the United States Code. Should the vessel not meet these requirements, it may still qualify for registry in the United States if the President directs they be waived because the needs of foreign commerce so require. See Section 3101 of the same title.

In the case of the Kuwaiti tankers, however, the authority to waive the requirements was provided by Article 27 of the Act of December 27, 1950, Ch. 1155, '1, 64 Stat. 1120. It empowers the Secretary of Defence to direct the waiver in the interests of national defence.

2. Use of flags of convenience by the former USSR and the Peoples Republic of China. In February of 1977, the People's Republic of China was reported as having placed some 80 of its merchant vessels under the Panamanian flag, thereby following the example of the former USSR which long before that had placed about one hundred of its merchant vessels under the same flag. 81 Revue Générale de Droit International Public 1120 (1977). What benefits do you suppose were derived by these nations from the use of flags of convenience? This was ironic, given their earlier vigorous attacks upon the employment of flags of convenience as economic colonialism.

2. JURISDICTION OVER VESSELS

Discussion and analysis of jurisdiction in general, including issues of jurisdiction over vessels and on the High Seas is found in Chapter 3.

The People v. Robert J. Thomas

Eire, Supreme Court, 1954.
22 Int'l L.Rep. 295 (1958).*

The Facts. The accused was convicted of the manslaughter of one Humphries. The accused and Humphries were travelling together on the Irish ship Munster, from Liverpool to Dublin. They had both been drinking, when, some 15 miles out from the Welsh coast, about midnight, there was a fight in which Humphries went overboard and was lost. Thomas was not an Irish citizen.

There was an appeal on the ground, first, of alleged lack of evidence, and secondly on the ground that the Court had no jurisdiction to try an offence of manslaughter on an Irish ship where the death did not occur on board the ship, or within the jurisdiction.

Held (affirming the Court of Criminal Appeal): that the appeal failed on both grounds.

* Reprinted with the permission of the
Editor of the International Law Reports.

* * * The next ground of appeal is that there was no jurisdiction in the Central Criminal Court to try the appellant for manslaughter as the death did not occur on board the ship and so was not within the jurisdiction of the Court. It is clear that the Central Criminal Court has all the jurisdiction formerly exercised by the Admiral and later exercised by the Commissioners of Oyer and Terminer appointed to exercise the Admiralty jurisdiction in criminal cases. This was not contested. Mr. Bell [counsel for the accused] contended that the jurisdiction was confined to the trial of persons committing offences on board an Irish ship on the high seas where such offences were committed and completed on the ship. Manslaughter, Mr. Bell says, is a complex crime consisting of two essential ingredients. The first is some unlawful act or culpable neglect, which causes the death, and the second is the fact of death itself. The death admittedly did not take place on the ship. The crime, therefore, according to the argument, not being completed on board the ship was not committed within the jurisdiction. Mr. Bell referred at length to the case of The Queen v. Keyn. Keyn, a foreigner, was in command of a foreign ship which ran into a British ship within three miles of the English shore and sank her. A passenger on board the English ship was drowned. The facts were such as would in English law amount to manslaughter. On his being indicted for that offence in the Central Criminal Court the jury found Keyn guilty. Counsel for the prisoner objected that the Court had no jurisdiction. Pollock B., the trial Judge, stated a case on the point for the opinion of the Court for Crown Cases Reserved. The majority * * * held that as the offence was not committed on a British ship there was no jurisdiction to try the prisoner, even though the ship at the time of the occurrence was within what has become known as the "three-mile limit."

* * *

Applying these observations, the contention on behalf of the appellant is that since the death took place, if at all, in the water, the crime was not complete upon the Irish ship and therefore no crime in fact or in law took place on the ship, and it follows that the jurisdiction of the Central Criminal Court which is confined in its admiralty jurisdiction to trying cases of crimes committed in Irish ships is not brought into operation. If the argument is correct it would appear that there is no jurisdiction in any Court of this country to try either a citizen or foreigner on an Irish ship who by culpable negligence or design throws another overboard with the result that death occurs in the water.

* * *

It will be convenient in discussing the matter of the Admiral's jurisdiction to consider it from two aspects. First, what jurisdiction the Admiral had as regards the place where the crime was committed, and, secondly, in respect of what persons that jurisdiction operated.

* * *

* * * It is sufficient to say that it is clear law that the jurisdiction extends to a foreigner on an Irish ship.

It being undoubted that crimes committed by foreigners on board British or Irish ships are cognizable by British or Irish Courts, as the case may be, without any statute, is there anything in the origins or the legal theory giving rise to this rule of law to indicate that whatever jurisdiction attaches is limited to the punishment of a crime begun and completed on board the ship, as distinct from a crime completed by the death taking place in the water surrounding the ship?

[J]urisdiction is the right of the country to which the ships belong to control the conduct of those on board from the point of good order and the prevention of crime by virtue of the protection afforded to such persons while sailing in such ship. In The Queen v. Anderson, Blackburn, J., says: "There are a vast number of cases which decide that when a ship is sailing on the high seas and bearing the flag of a particular nation, the ship forms a part of that nation's country, and all persons on board of her may be considered as within the jurisdiction of that nation whose flag is flying on the ship, in the same manner as if they were within the territory of that nation." Coke says: "Protectio trahit subjectionem et subjectio protectionem." Lord Coleridge in The Queen v. Carr, says: "The true principle is, that a person who comes on board a British ship where English law is reigning, places himself under the protection of the British flag, and as a correlative, if he thus becomes entitled to our law's protection, he becomes amenable to its jurisdiction, and liable to the punishment it inflicts upon those who there infringe its requirements." He adds that there is no distinction to be drawn between a member of the crew and a passenger.

* * *

The verdict of manslaughter in this case involved a finding of fact that Humphries is dead. The evidence points only to a death by drowning on the high seas. The other ingredient of the crime, the act or omission causing the death, occurred on board the M.V. "Munster", an Irish ship. Thus the event leading to the death also took place upon the high seas. The two elements necessary to give jurisdiction were thus both present. The crime was committed on the high seas and the appellant was at the time of its commission on an Irish ship. The appellant was, therefore, properly triable in the Central Criminal Court.

The appeal in so far as it was based on want of jurisdiction also fails.

Question. Consider the discussion by the court of *The Queen* v. *Keyn* in which it was held that "as the offense was not committed on a British ship there was no jurisdiction to try the prisoner, even though the ship at the time of the occurrence was within what has become known as the three-mile limit." Was this a statement of a rule of international law? See discussion of territorial jurisdiction in Chapter 3, supra.

Re Bianchi

Argentina, Cámara Nacional Especial, 1957.
24 Int'l L.Rep. 173 (1961).*

The Facts. The appellant, Gerónimo C. Bianchi, a member of the crew of the R.T., a ship of Argentine registry, was charged with the commission of a theft on board the ship while it was anchored in the harbour of Río de Janeiro, Brazil. In the absence of any action in the matter by Brazilian authorities, charges were brought against Bianchi in Argentina. It was unsuccessfully argued for the defendant that the Argentine court lacked jurisdiction over an offence which had been committed in foreign territorial waters. On appeal,

Held: that the judgment appealed from must be affirmed. Where local authorities did not take jurisdiction over an offence committed on board a ship anchored in foreign territorial waters, jurisdiction reverted to the courts of the State of registry of the ship.

* * * [I]n the trial Court, an inquiry was made into a theft which was allegedly committed on board the R.T., a ship of Argentine registry, while it was at anchor in the port of Río de Janeiro. Article 1, para. 1, of the Penal Code provides that [it] is applicable to offences committed in places subject to the national jurisdiction. According to the rules of public international law, which have not been reproduced for obvious reasons in the said Article but which are none the less binding upon Argentine courts, offences committed on board a private ship fall within the jurisdiction of the courts of the flag State if the ship is on the high seas, and fall within the jurisdiction of a foreign State only in the event that such offences have been committed while the ship is in the territorial waters of that other State.

This latter principle is not an absolute rule, however, for if the foreign State does not choose to exercise its right to institute proceedings because it considers that the act has not affected the community at large or the peace of the port (as maintained in French and Italian doctrine)[a], the flag State may then assert full authority over the ship for the purpose of restoring order and discipline on board or protecting the rights of the passengers. We may reasonably conclude with regard to the case before us, given the fact that the preliminary hearing was apparently held "en route", that the Brazilian authorities had relinquished jurisdiction over the alleged offence, so that this offence then became subject to the jurisdiction of the Argentine courts. As this reasoning accords with the judgment of the trial Court * * * regarding the case, the judgment under appeal is affirmed.

---

* Reprinted with the permission of the Editor of the International Law Reports.

a. But see infra the *Wildenhus's* case and the peace of the port doctrine, according to which the exercise of jurisdiction by the flag state is not contingent upon the decision of the territorial state not to exercise jurisdiction.

Special Maritime and Territorial Jurisdiction of the United States

18 U.S.C. § 7.

The term "special maritime and territorial jurisdiction of the United States", as used in this title, includes:

(1) The high seas, any other waters within the admiralty and maritime jurisdiction of the United States and out of the jurisdiction of any particular State [of the United States], and any vessel belonging in whole or in part to the United States, or any citizen thereof, or to any corporation created by or under the laws of the United States, or of any State, Territory, District, or possession thereof, when such vessel is within the admiralty and maritime jurisdiction of the United States and out of the jurisdiction of any particular State.

(2) Any vessel registered, licensed, or enrolled under the laws of the United States, and being on a voyage upon the waters of any of the Great Lakes, or any of the waters connecting them, or upon the Saint Lawrence River where the same constitutes the International Boundary Line.

* * *

---

1. *Crimes included in special maritime jurisdiction of the United States.* Title 18 of the United States Code defines as criminal a number of acts that are performed within the special maritime jurisdiction of the United States: Sections 113, assaults; 114, maiming; 661, theft; 662, receiving stolen goods; 1111, murder; 1112, manslaughter; 1113, attempt to commit murder or manslaughter; 2031, rape; 2032, statutory rape; 2111, robbery. (See, also Title 49, Section 1472(k), dealing with these same crimes when committed within the "special aircraft jurisdiction of the United States." This jurisdiction is discussed in Chapter 5.)

2. *Vessels included in special maritime jurisdiction of the United States.* In civil matters involving vessels on the high seas such as collision and salvage, the United States as well as other states apply the rules of maritime law to foreign flag vessels as well as to vessels sailing under their national flag. The general law maritime is not itself a part of international law. Rather, it is a body of rules reflecting the universal interest of states in achieving a substantial degree of uniformity in the handling of civil claims arising on the high seas. In the application of such rules, each state may use its own understanding or domestic version of the rules without subjecting itself thereby to a claim under international law by another state.

But would it be valid under international law for the United States to apply rules of criminal law under Section 7 of Title 18 to vessels owned by United States citizens or corporations if the vessels were registered under a foreign flag?

For more discussion of Jurisdiction on the High Seas and otherwise on vessels, see also Chapter 3, *supra*.

U.S. v. Aikins

United States Court of Appeal, Ninth Circuit, 1990.
923 F.2d 650.

* * *

Before CANBY, NOONAN and RYMER, CIRCUIT JUDGES.

NOONAN, CIRCUIT JUDGE:

George Aikins, Manuel Angulo–Castillo, Roberto Cayasso–Schellett, Lai Chai Hai, Anastacio Henry–Barnard, Roosevelt Rodney, Eusebio Samudio–Jiminez, and William Snyder were convicted of possessing with intent to distribute 21,000 pounds of marijuana on the high seas on February 19, 1988 and of distributing a separate 14,000 pounds of marijuana on the high seas on February 17, 1988, all in violation of the Maritime Drug Enforcement Act, 46 U.S.C.App. '1903(a). We reverse their convictions and remand for a new trial.

FACTS

The facts are well set out by Judge Takasugi in the district court and with minor editorial revisions are restated here:

During an ongoing undercover investigation of marijuana trafficking/importation, approximately two weeks preceding the seizure in this case, an undercover United States Customs agent was solicited by a marijuana trafficker to off-load a large quantity of marijuana from a mother ship located on the high seas southeast of the Hawaiian Islands. The undercover agent agreed to provide a vessel to off-load marijuana from the mother ship and transport the substance to the Bay Area of Northern California as directed by the trafficker.

A plan was developed among members of United States Customs, Drug Enforcement Administration and the United States Coast Guard whereby a crew of federal agents, posing as marijuana traffickers, would rendezvous with the mother ship and off-load the marijuana. The plan included the United States Coast Guard cutter *Mallow*'s following the undercover off-load vessel at a safe distance and remaining in radio contact with the off-load vessel.

On February 16 and 17, 1988, the undercover vessel rendezvoused with the mother ship approximately 600B800 miles southeast of the Hawaiian Islands. The mother ship was identified as the *Christina M*, a Panamanian coastal freighter bearing a Panamanian flag. After off-loading to a capacity of approximately 14,000 pounds of marijuana from the *Christina M*, the undercover agents were able to ascertain that the Panamanian freighter still had a large quantity of marijuana remaining aboard. All identification, registry and description of the *Christina M* were relayed by radio from the undercover crew to the *Mallow*.

Thereafter, the government contends that on February 18, 1988, U.S. Coast Guard officials on the *Mallow* sought and received permission from Panamanian officials "to the enforcement of United States law by the United States against the individuals found aboard the *M/V Christina M*." The *Christina M* was not then proceeding toward the United States.

On February 19, 1988, some 48 hours after the previous off-loading operation by the undercover vessel, the *Mallow* closed within visual distance of the *Christina M*. Lt. Commander Christian Bohner, Commanding Officer of the *Mallow,* identified the *Mallow* as a United States Coast Guard vessel and requested permission to board the *Christina M*. Defendant Augustus Rodney, Captain of *Christina M,* initially refused Bohner's request. Bohner then indicated to Rodney that the Coast Guard had permission of the Panamanian authorities to board and search the *Christina M* and that he, Bohner, had "other means" to stop the *Christina M*. Rodney relented and the *Christina M* made no effort to flee.

Shortly thereafter, without a search or arrest warrant or any efforts to secure same, the Coast Guard personnel from *Mallow* boarded the *Christina M* for the express purpose of searching the freighter for marijuana. A strong odor of marijuana was immediately apparent to all members of the boarding party, except for one who was stuffy. They found in excess of 21,000 pounds of marijuana in the aft hold. Although no other cargo was found, other than the bales of marijuana, documents and other personal effects were found and seized from the living quarters assigned to the crew. Rodney and his crew of seven men were arrested. The *Mallow* possessed radio equipment capable of communicating with a magistrate in Hawaii or the mainland. Captain Rodney and the seven crew members were arrested and subsequently indicted.

* * *

2. The Search and Seizure of the *Christina M.*

The defendants raise the protection of the Fourth Amendment in objection to the Coast Guard's search and seizure of the vessel. The Fourth Amendment was not "understood by contemporaries of the Framers to apply to activities of the United States directed against aliens in foreign territory or in international waters." United States v. Verdugo–Urquidez. The Fourth Amendment does not apply to a search of aliens conducted in foreign territory. Id. The Fourth Amendment does not apply to the search of non-resident aliens on a ship in international waters. United States v. Davis. All but one of the defendants here was an alien to whom the guarantees of the Fourth Amendment do not apply. William Snyder, who is an American citizen, has no standing to challenge the search of the *Christina M,* "it being well settled that the crew has no legitimate expectation of privacy in the cargo hold of a vessel." United States v. Peterson.

3. The Constitutionality of the Maritime Drug Law Enforcement Act.

The defendants contend that the Maritime Drug Law Enforcement Act, 46 U.S.C.App. § 1903(a), is unconstitutional as applied to them. It has been established that the Act is intended by Congress to apply to conduct on the high seas. It is clear that Congress has power "to define and punish piracies and felonies committed on the high seas." United States Constitution, Art. I, Sec. 8, cl. 10. The statute is not void for vagueness: it expressly prohibits the possession of drugs on certain vessels with intent to distribute. United States v. Mena, 863 F.2d 1522, 1527 (11th Cir., 1989). The statute is not applied to the defendants ex post facto; although Panama gave its consent after they had set to sea, they took the risk of such consent being given.

Due process is not offended by the extent of the jurisdiction created if there is a sufficient nexus between the conduct condemned and the United States. A sufficient nexus exists where the ship with drugs is bound ultimately for the United States. Id. In the present case, although the *Christina M* at the moment of seizure was not headed in the direction of the United States, the entire operation of off-loading was set up by an agreement that was designed to bring the off-loaded marijuana into the United States. A sufficient nexus existed. * * * Conviction reversed and case remanded to determine whether the consent of Panama to enforce U.S. law aboard the Panamanian vessel.

SECTION C.   WATERS WITHIN THE TERRITORY

1.   BASELINE SEPARATING INTERNAL WATERS FROM TERRITORIAL SEA

1.   *Significance of baseline*. The baseline separates internal waters from the territorial sea; the breadth of the territorial sea is measured from that line and so is the breadth of the exclusive economic zone. The manner in which the baseline is drawn is important because this can be done in such a way as to thrust it far away from the coast with two resulting consequences: first, expansion of the area of inland waters lying between the coast and the baseline; second, placing the outer limit of the territorial sea, and of the exclusive economic zone, which are measured from the baseline, at great distances from the coast.

Suppose, by way of exaggerated example, that the baseline on the eastern coast of the United States were drawn by means of a straight line running from Maine to the tip of Florida. A huge area of the sea inside the baseline would become internal waters, i.e. assimilated to land territory so far as concerns the jurisdiction of the United States. Moreover the outer limit of the territorial sea of the United States would at some points be so many miles from the coast as to make arguments about the breadth of the territorial sea entirely meaningless.

2.   *The Fisheries Case in the International Court of Justice*. Both the 1958 Convention on the Territorial Sea and the Contiguous Zone and the United Nations Convention on the Law of the Sea contain provisions on the delineation of the baseline which are consistent with international law and the earlier decision of the International Court of Justice the *Anglo-Norweigan Fisheries Case* (U.K. v. Norway), [1951] I.C.J.Rep. 116.

The case involved a portion of the coastline of Norway with a very distinctive configuration, i.e., a mountainous coast on the mainland constantly opening into indentations penetrating great distances inland (fjords) and in front of it a "skjærgaard", or rock rampart, made up of large and small islands mountainous in character, islets, rocks and reefs, all in effect an extension of the mainland. Of this coastline the court said: "The coast of the mainland does not constitute, as it does in practically all other countries, a clear dividing line between land and sea. What matters, what really constitutes the Norwegian coastline, is the outerline of the 'skjærgaard.' " (at 127) Norway delineated its baseline in this region by drawing straight lines connecting fixed points on the islands, islets, rocks, and reefs of the skjærgaard, thus claiming as inland waters the rich and extensive fishing grounds landward of the baseline. The court held that the straight baselines method used by Norway, and the straight baselines drawn by Norway in application of this method, were not contrary to international law.

3. *Baseline under 1958 Convention and U.N. Convention.* The 1958 Convention on the Territorial Sea and the Contiguous Zone deals in detail with the drawing of the baseline in Articles 3–5 and 7–13. The United Nations Convention on the Law of the Sea essentially reproduces those provisions, with a few additions, in Articles 4 through 16. For both, see the Documentary Supplement.

Article 4 of the first and 7 of the second deal specifically with the use of the straight baselines method. Consider the grounds on which a state may claim to utilize this method in accordance with these Articles.

Article 5 of the 1958 text and Article 8(2) of the U.N. Convention make provision for a right of innocent passage, under certain conditions, through inland waters created by the use of the straight baselines method. Why?

4. *Archipelagic baselines.* Totally new in the U.N. Convention is the provision made by Article 47 for the drawing of straight archipelagic baselines. The drawing of such baselines, limited in length to 100–125 miles between the islands of an archipelago, obviously is susceptible of enclosing vast areas of waters previously considered as high seas and used for international navigation. Article 49 stipulates for them a new status, archipelagic waters, over which the archipelagic state has sovereignty except for the regime of sea lanes.

The sea lanes which the archipelagic state may establish in its archipelagic waters are intended to provide continuous and expeditious passage of foreign ships (and aircraft), and all ships (and aircraft) enjoy the right of archipelagic sea lane passage in such sea lanes. See the elaborate provisions in point in Article 53. Apparently, the right of innocent passage can be restricted by the coastal state by compelling the use of sea lanes.

Within archipelagic waters, the archipelagic state may draw closing lines for the delineation of internal waters. Article 50.

What is the status of archipelagic waters in international law? Are the rules concerning them in the United Nations Convention rules of customary international law? See the discussion in Section A of this chapter, *supra*. What then of the controversy in the documents below?

Declaration of The Philippines Upon Ratification of the United Nations Convention on the Law of the Sea

U.N. Office for Oceans Affairs and the Law of the Sea, Law of the Sea Bulletin, Special Issue 1, March 1987, Annex II, p. 6.

* * *

1.   The signing of the Convention by the Government of the Republic of the Philippines shall not in any manner impair or prejudice the sovereign rights of the Republic of the Philippines under and arising from the Constitution of the Philippines;

2.   Such signing shall not in any manner affect the sovereign rights of the Republic of the Philippines as successor of the United States of America, under and arising out of the Treaty of Paris between Spain and the United States of America of December 10, 1898, and the Treaty of Washington between the United States of America and Great Britain of January 2, 1930;

3.   Such signing shall not diminish or in any manner affect the rights and obligations of the Contracting Parties under the Mutual Defence Treaty between the Philippines and the United States of America of August 30, 1951, and its related interpretative instruments; nor those under any other pertinent bilateral or multilateral treaty or agreement to which the Philippines is a party;

6.   The provisions of the Convention on archipelagic passage through sea lanes do not nullify or impair the sovereignty of the Philippines as an archipelagic State over the sea lanes and do not deprive it of authority to enact legislation to protect its sovereignty, independence, and security;

7.   The concept of archipelagic waters is similar to the concept of internal waters under the Constitution of the Philippines, and removes straits connecting these waters with the economic zone or high sea from the rights of foreign vessels to transit passage for international navigations.
* * *

Objection by the [Former] Union of Soviet Socialist Republics to the Understanding Recorded Upon Signature by the Philippines and Confirmed Upon Ratification

U.N. Office for Oceans Affairs and the Law of the Sea.
Law of the Sea Bulletin, Special Issue 1, March 1987, p. 14.

The [former] Union of Soviet Socialist Republics considers that the statement made by the Philippines upon signature, and then confirmed upon ratification, of the United Nations Convention on the Law of the Sea in essence contains reservations and exceptions to the Convention, which is prohibited under article 309 of the Convention. At the same time, the statement of the Philippines is incompatible with article 310 of the Convention, under which a State, when signing or ratifying the Convention, may make declarations or statements only "provided that such declarations or statements do not purport to exclude or to modify the legal effect of the provisions of this Convention in their application to that State''.

The discrepancy between the Philippine statement and the Convention can be seen, inter alia, from the affirmation by the Philippines that ''the concept of archipelagic waters is similar to the concept of internal waters under the Constitution of the Philippines, and removes straits connecting these waters with the economic zone or high sea from the rights of foreign vessels to transit passage for international navigation''. Moreover, the statement emphasizes more than once that, despite its ratification of the Convention, the Philippines will continue to be guided in matters relating to the sea, not by the Convention and the obligations under it, but by its domestic law and by agreements it has already concluded which are not in line with the Convention. Thus, the Philippines not only is evading the harmonization of its legislation with the Convention but also is refusing to fulfill one of its most fundamental obligations under the Convention— namely, to respect the régime of archipelagic waters, which provides that foreign ships enjoy the right of archipelagic passage through, and foreign aircraft the right of overflight over, such waters.

In view of the foregoing, the [former] USSR cannot recognize as lawful the statement of the Philippines and considers it to be without legal effect in the light of the provisions of the Convention.

* * *

Illustrations of Baselines from Churchill and Lowe

Note that whereas drawing of the baselines remains the same since 1988, the United States has adopted a 12 nautical mile territorial sea. See, infra.

Diagram of the Construction of Baselines

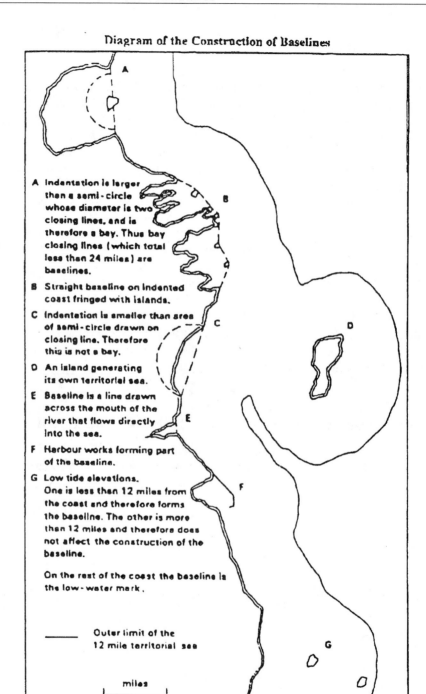

A Indentation is larger than a semi-circle whose diameter is two closing lines, and is therefore a bay. Thus bay closing lines (which total less than 24 miles) are baselines.

B Straight baseline on indented coast fringed with islands.

C Indentation is smaller than area of semi-circle drawn on closing line. Therefore this is not a bay.

D An island generating its own territorial sea.

E Baseline is a line drawn across the mouth of the river that flows directly into the sea.

F Harbour works forming part of the baseline.

G Low tide elevations. One is less than 12 miles from the coast and therefore forms the baseline. The other is more than 12 miles and therefore does not affect the construction of the baseline.

On the rest of the coast the baseline is the low-water mark.

——— Outer limit of the 12 mile territorial sea

miles
0   12

From Churchill and Lowe, supra,   at 36.

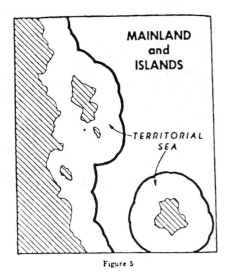

MAINLAND
and
ISLANDS

TERRITORIAL
SEA

Figure 5

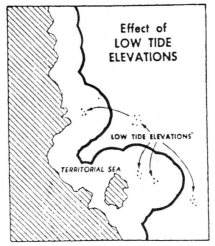

Effect of
LOW TIDE
ELEVATIONS

LOW TIDE ELEVATIONS

TERRITORIAL SEA

Figure 6

CONSTRUCTION
of the
BASE LINE
in the
MISSISSIPPI DELTA
AREA

BASE LINE

Figure 7

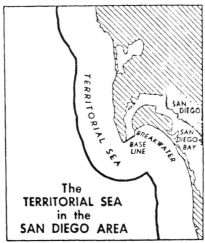

TERRITORIAL SEA

SAN
DIEGO

BREAKWATER

SAN
DIEGO
BAY

BASE
LINE

The
TERRITORIAL SEA
in the
SAN DIEGO AREA

Figure 8

[C3008]

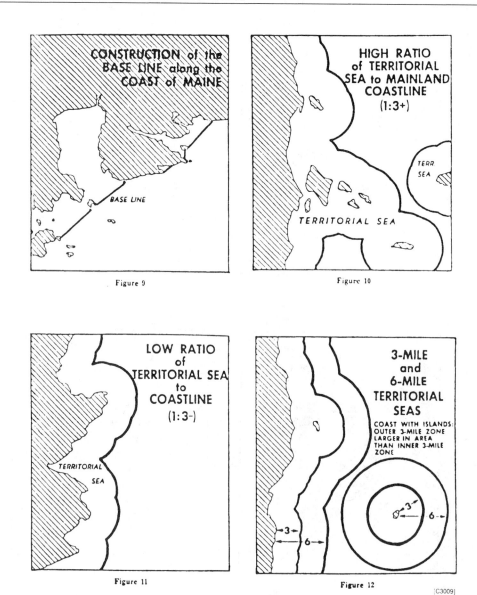

Figure 9

Figure 10

Figure 11

Figure 12

[C3009]

Historic Bays

4 Whiteman, Digest of International Law 233 (1965).

Historic bays are those which fall outside of the general delimitation rules. Some writers hold that claims to historic bays are based on prescription. Jessup states that "the legality of the claim is to be measured, not by the size of the area affected, but by the definiteness and duration of the assertion and the acquiescence of foreign powers. The evidence of international practice and usage does not indicate that a claim to a large bay is illegal." Jessup, The Law of Territorial Waters and Maritime Jurisdiction, p. 382. Hyde on the other hand disagrees with this theory and states that historic bays are illustrative of a habit of maritime States rather than a token of an exception to an accepted rule. Hyde argues that since historic bays constitute fresh and initial claims of a State to dominion over bodies of water of a wide area, such claims cannot be thought to operate by prescription because generally they are neither initially adverse vis à vis another State nor initially considered wrongful by another State. Hyde, International Law, Vol. I, 2nd. ed., pp. 469, 470. The International Law Commission specifically excepts historic bays from the article on bays in the Commission's draft code of the law of the sea. In view of the importance of a number of bodies of water considered (or claimed) to be historic bays it may be useful at this point to briefly mention a number of them.

The Gulf of Aqaba

The exact status of this body of water is still a matter open to controversy. The Department of State in a recent statement published in the New York Times on June 24, 1957, declared that:

> The United States position is that the Gulf of Aqaba comprehends international waters. That no nation has the right to prevent free and innocent passage in the gulf and through the straits giving access thereto. A denial of those waters to vessels of United States registry should be reported to the nearest United States diplomatic or consular offices. (Printed in full in XXXVII Bulletin, Department of State, No. 942, July 15, 1957, pp. 112B113.)

* * *

The Gulf of Bothnia

This gulf has a mouth more than fifty miles wide, is about five hundred miles long and has a width of between fifty to one hundred miles. This body of water formerly lay entirely within Swedish territory and was at one time considered to be Swedish. After Finland was ceded to Russia by the Treaty of Friederichsham of 1809, some argued that the Gulf of Bothnia belonged jointly to Russia and Sweden. Now that this body of water lies between Finland and Sweden and in the absence of a general historic claim, it would appear that the Gulf of Bothnia is open sea.

* * *

Bay of Chaleurs (a hot one)

This bay has a maximum depth of one hundred miles, and opens into the Gulf of St. Lawrence through a passage sixteen miles wide. This bay has been claimed as part of Canadian waters and statutes have been passed assuring jurisdiction over the whole bay. 47 Geo. 111, c. 12, s. 15; 4 Geo. iv, c. 1, s. 25. The Supreme Court of Canada in the case of Morvat v. McFee, 5 Supp.Ct.R. 66 (1880) has held that the bay is entirely within British territory.

Chesapeake Bay

This bay is twelve miles wide at its entrance between Cape Henry and Cape Charles and one hundred and seventy miles in length to the mouth of the Susquehanna River (following mid-channel). The Commissioners in the

Alabama Claims Case held that the waters of the bay constitute United States waters. Second Court of Commissioners of Alabama Claims, Stetson v. United States, No. 3993; Moore, Dig., I, 741B742.

* * *

Delaware Bay

Delaware Bay is ten marine miles wide at its entrance, and forty miles in length from that entrance to the Delaware River. In 1793 the French frigate "L'Embuscade" captured the British ship "Grange" within Delaware Bay between the shores of Delaware and New Jersey, several miles from the bay's mouth. Attorney General Randolph stated that in his opinion Delaware Bay constituted American waters and the seizure within its waters was an illegal act within neutral territory. Opinion of Mr. Randolph, Atty.Gen. May 14, 1793; Moore, Digest of International Law, Vol. I, pp. 735B739. Secretary of State Jefferson declared that the Government of the United States deemed the capture "to have been unquestionably within its jurisdiction", and consequently demanded the release of the ship and its crew. Mr. Jefferson to Mr. Morris, Aug. 16, 1793, I American State Papers Foreign Relations, 148, 167, 169.

* * *

Hudson Bay

Hudson Bay is about six hundred miles wide and one thousand miles long. Canada claims the bay as part of its territory and this is disputed by the United States. In 1670 the English Government, by grant to the Hudson's Bay Company assumed possession of, and title to, Hudson Bay. By the charter of the Hudson's Bay Company, the British Crown granted to the Company all water, land, etc., within entrance to Hudson Strait, not possessed by any foreign state or other British company or colony. From 1670 until 1713 France and England disputed possession of Hudson Bay; in 1713 by the Treaty of Utrecht, France relinquished her claim to the area to Great Britain.

By the Treaty of 1818, citizens of the United States were granted the privilege of fishing along the coasts of Labrador indefinitely northwards, but without prejudice, however, to any of the exclusive rights of the Hudson's Bay Company. In 1870 the territorial and jurisdictional rights of the Hudson's Bay Company were transferred to Canada and those rights held by the British Government were transferred in 1880. In 1906 the Government of Canada passed a statute declaring the waters of Hudson Bay to be territorial waters of Canada. R.S.C. 1927, cap. 73, sec. 9, sub-sec. 10; Statutes of Canada, 1906, cap. 45, sec. 9(12). See: V. Kenneth Johnston, 15 British Yearbook of International Law, pp. 1B20 (1934).

The Treaty of July 20, 1912, which was concluded for the purpose of carrying out the award of the Tribunal in the North Atlantic Coast Fisheries Arbitration of 1910, provides "that it is understood that the award does not cover Hudson Bay." Redmond, Treaties, etc., 1923, Vol. III, p. 2632. The United States has continued to dispute Canada's claim to include Hudson Bay in its territory. See Hackworth, Digest of International Law, Vol. I, pp. 700, 701.

* * *

Long Island Sound

Long Island Sound is surrounded entirely by American territory. It is one hundred miles in length and has a maximum width of twenty miles. The New York Court of Appeals has held that the waters of Long Island Sound are entirely within the territory of the United States. Mahler v. Transp., 35 N.Y. 352 (1866). This decision has not been disputed.

* * *

Monterey Bay

"The State of California has by its constitution declared Monterey Bay, of which the opening headlands are about nineteen miles apart, to be within its limits, and has asserted control over the fisheries within the bay. In 1927, the Supreme Court of California, declaring that there could not be said to be 'any rule of international law upon the subject', expressed the view that the whole matter rested 'in the undisputed assertion of jurisdiction by the power possessing the inclosing shore line of the bay or inlet in question'. Ocean Industries, Inc. v. Superior Court of California, in and for Santa Cruz County, 200 Cal. 235 (1927). This claim on the part of California has not been acceded to by the United States and in the same year as the above-cited decision, Mr. Grew, Under Secretary of State, wrote that: 'In the absence of any accepted standard as to their size and conformation, it is difficult to determine in any given case whether a bay, gulf or recess in a coast line can be regarded as territorial waters. Under the applicable general principles of international law, however, as evidenced by writers on the subject, it may be stated that gulfs and bays surrounded by land of one and the same littoral State whose entrance is of such a width that it cannot be commanded by coast batteries are regarded as nonterritorial.' " Hackworth, Digest of International Law, Vol. I, p. 708.

In the case of the United States v. California before the Special Master, the position of the United States was set forth at some length in the government brief. It was stated that there could be certain exceptions to the general delimitation rules but only based on historical grounds and that it was up to California to prove these exceptions. * * * Before the Special Master, United States Supreme Court, October Term, 1951, p. 95. It was further argued that California had not made such a showing of proof that it could take advantage of this historical exception to the general rule. Ibid., pp. 107B110. The Special Master in his report concurred with the contentions of the United States. United States v. California, Report of the Special Master, United States Supreme Court, October Term, 1952, p. 21.

* * *

The Zuyder Zee

This body of water once lay in two parts, one forty miles long by twenty miles wide, connected with the inner part, which was forty-five miles by thirty-five miles, by a narrow passage about nine miles wide. The Dutch have largely reclaimed this area by pumping out the water and treating the soil so that it can be used for crop production. What is left of this former "inland sea" is now called "Ysselmeer".

Juridical Regime of Historic Waters, Including Historic Bays

2 Yearbook of the International Law Commission 1 (1962).

[The Geneva Convention of 1958 on the Territorial Sea and the Contiguous Zone makes provisions in paragraph 1 through 5 of Article 7 for the drawing of the baseline in bays. Paragraph 6 then provides: The foregoing provisions shall not apply to so-called "historic bays" * * * . See the Documentary Supplement. The Geneva Conference resolved to leave the subject of historic bays for further study and eventually such a study was prepared by the Secretariat, an extract from which follows. Note that Article 10(6) of the 1982 U.N. Convention on the Law of the Sea likewise provides for historic bays as an exception to normal methods of delimiting bays. However, there is no provision for the criteria necessary to substantiate the claim.]

III.   Conclusions

182.   The above discussion of the principles and rules of international law relating to "historic waters, including historic bays" would seem to justify a number of conclusions, provided that it is understood that some of these must necessarily be highly tentative * * *.

183.   In the first place, while "historic bays" present the classic example of historic title to maritime areas, there seems to be no doubt that, in principle, a historic title may exist also to other waters than bays, such as straits or archipelagos, or in general to all those waters which can form part of the maritime domain of a State.

185.   In determining whether or not a title to "historic waters" exists, there are three factors which have to be taken into consideration, namely,

(i) The authority exercised over the area by the State claiming it as "historic waters";

(ii) The continuity of such exercise of authority;

(iii) The attitude of foreign States.

186.   First, effective exercise of sovereignty over the area by the claiming State is a necessary requirement for title to the area as "historic waters" of that State. Secondly, such exercise of sovereignty must have continued during a considerable time so as to have developed into a usage. Thirdly, the attitude of foreign States to the activities of the claiming State in the area must have been such that it can be characterized as an attitude of general toleration. * * *

188.   The burden of proof of title to "historic waters" is on the State claiming such title, in the sense that, if the State is unable to prove to the

satisfaction of whoever has to decide the matter that the requirements necessary for the title have been fulfilled, its claim to the title will be disallowed. * * *

189. The legal status of "historic waters", i.e., the question whether they are to be considered as internal waters or as part of the territorial sea, would in principle depend on whether the sovereignty exercised in the particular case over the area by the claiming State and forming a basis for the claim, was sovereignty as over internal waters or sovereignty as over the territorial sea. It seems logical that the sovereignty to be acquired should be commensurate with the sovereignty actually exercised.

190. The idea of establishing a definitive list of "historic waters" in order to diminish the uncertainty which claims to such waters might cause has serious drawbacks. An attempt to establish such a list might induce States to overstate both their claims and their opposition to the claims of other States, and so give rise to unnecessary disputes. Moreover, it would in any case be extremely difficult, not to say impossible, to arrive at a list which would be really final.

Objection of the United States to the Assertion of Sovereignty over the Gulf of Sirte [Sidra] by Libya

68 American Journal of International Law 510 (1974).*

On October 11, 1973, the Embassy of the Libyan Arab Republic in Washington sent a note to the Department of State asserting a claim to the Gulf of Sirte as internal or territorial waters. The Department of State sent a reply, dated February 11, 1974, which characterized the Libyan claim as "unacceptable as a violation of international law." The note continued:

> * * * The Libyan action purports to extend the boundary of Libyan waters in the Gulf of Sirte northward to a line approximately 300 miles long at a latitude of 32 degrees, 30 minutes, and to require prior permission for foreign vessels to enter that area. Under international law, as codified in the 1958 Convention on the Territorial Sea and Contiguous Zone, the body of water enclosed by this line cannot be regarded as the juridical internal or territorial waters of the Libyan Arab Republic. Nor does the Gulf of Sirte meet the international law standards of past open, notorious and effective exercise of authority, continuous exercise of authority, and acquiescence of foreign nations necessary to be regarded historically as Libyan internal or territorial waters. The United States Government views the Libyan action as an attempt to appropriate a large area of the high seas by unilateral action, thereby encroaching upon the long-established principle of freedom of the seas. This action is particularly unfortunate when the international community is engaged in intensive efforts to obtain broad international agreement on law of the sea issues, including the nature and extent of coastal state jurisdiction. Unilateral actions of this type can only hinder the process of achieving an accommodation of the interests of all nations at the Law of the Sea Conference.

* Reprinted with the permission of the American Society of International Law.

In accordance with the positions stated above, the United States Government reserves its rights and the rights of its nationals in the area of the Gulf of Sirte affected by the action of the Government of Libya.

––––––––

Notes

1. *Incident of August 19, 1981.* Two Libyan planes were shot down over the Gulf of Sirte by United States planes operating from an aircraft carrier. The latter claimed to have acted in self defense in international airspace over international waters. In reporting the incident and the challenge by the United States of the claim by Libya that the waters of the gulf were "historic waters," Professor Rousseau pointed out that they had never been claimed to be such by predecessors in title to the Libyan territory, such as Turkey and Italy. 86 Revue Générale de Droit International Public 145 (1982)

2. *Incident of March 24, 1986.* United States naval forces, claiming their aircraft was fired upon with surface-to-air missiles while operating in international airspace over the Gulf of Sirte, attacked the missile site on the Libyan shore and destroyed in the gulf a Libyan missile patrol boat. A statement from the White House noted: "U.S. forces were intent only upon making the legal point that, beyond the internationally recognized 12–mile limit, the Gulf of Sidra belongs to no one and that all nations are free to move through international waters and airspace." United States Department of State Bulletin, May 1986, p. 76.

3. *Customary international law.* The International Court of Justice has had occasion to deal with historic bays at customary international law in the *Land, Island and Maritime Frontier Case*, [1992] I.C.J. Rep. 351 between Nicaragua, Honduras and El Salvador and in the *Continental Shelf (Tunisia v. Libya) Case*, [1982] I.C.J. Rep. 73. Note the importance of the acquiesence by other states to such claims.

2.   FOREIGN VESSELS IN INTERNAL WATERS

Consent to entry into internal waters. States have plenary jurisdiction in these waters in the same way as over their land mass. Foreign vessels enter the internal waters of a coastal state only with its consent. As to merchant vessels, the consent is usually implied. Prohibiting the entry of foreign merchant vessels is the exception rather than the rule in practice. The entry, however, may be conditioned upon the giving of notice. In September 1980, the merchant vessels of the People's Republic of China received permission to enter 55 ports in the United States on four-day notice and other ports on a longer notice, while merchant vessels of the United States were given access to 20 Chinese ports on seven-day notice. Editorial, The Times–Picayune, September 20, 1980, Sec. 1, p. 12. Once a foreign merchant vessel enters these waters the coastal state has jurisdiction over any criminal conduct occurring on board. However, in most cases it will not be exercised and the concurrent flag state jurisdiction will be allowed to deal with the matter. The *Wildenhus'* case extracted below illustrates the important practical issue of whether the coastal state views the criminal conduct to have affected its interest significantly.

As to naval vessels, formal notification of their intended visit is customary. Unless the coastal state expressly prohibits the visit, naval vessels are deemed to have received the necessary consent. Some states, nevertheless, insist on issuing a prior authorization before allowing a foreign naval vessel to enter its internal waters. Algeria, for example, permits entry following notification alone only if the foreign naval vessel is compelled to come in by bad weather or by some other force majeure. *Bendeddouche, Note sur la Réglementation Algérienne du Passage et du Séjour des Navires de Guerre Etrangers dans les Eaux Territoriales et Intérieures de l'Algérie (Décret du 5 Octobre 1972), XI Revue Algérienne des Sciences Juridiques Economiques et Politiques 461, 469 (1974).*

Wildenhus' Case

United States Supreme Court, 1887.
120 U.S. 1, 7 S.Ct. 385, 30 L.Ed. 565.

This appeal brought up an application made to the Circuit Court of the United States for the District of New Jersey, by Charles Mali, the "Consul of His Majesty the King of the Belgians, for the States of New York and New Jersey, in the United States," for himself as such consul, "and in behalf of one Joseph Wildenhus, one Gionviennie Gobnbosich, and one John J. Ostenmeyer," for the release, upon a writ of habeas corpus, of Wildenhus, Gobnbosich, and Ostenmeyer from the custody of the keeper of the common jail of Hudson County, New Jersey, and their delivery to the consul, "to be dealt with according to the law of Belgium." The facts on which the application rested were thus stated in the petition for the writ:

> Second. That on or about the sixth day of October, 1886, on board the Belgian steamship Noordland, there occurred an affray between the said Joseph Wildenhus and one Fijens, wherein and whereby it is charged that the said Wildenhus stabbed with a knife and inflicted upon the said Fijens a mortal wound, of which he afterwards died.
>
> * * *
>
> Fifth. That at the time said affray occurred the said steamship Noordland was lying moored at the dock of the port of Jersey City, in said state of New Jersey.
>
> Sixth. That the said affray occurred and ended wholly below the deck of the said steamship, and that the tranquility of the said port of Jersey City was in nowise disturbed or endangered thereby.
>
> * * *

Article XI of a Convention between the United States and Belgium "concerning the rights, privileges, and immunities of consular officers," concluded March 9, 1880, and proclaimed by the President of the United States, March 1, 1881, 21 Stat. 776, 781, is as follows:

> The respective consuls-general, consuls, vice-consuls, and consular agents shall have exclusive charge of the internal order of the mer-

chant vessels of their nation, and shall alone take cognizance of all differences which may arise, either at sea or in port, between the captains, officers, and crews, without exception, particularly with reference to the adjustment of wages and the execution of contracts. The local authorities shall not interfere, except when the disorder that has arisen is of such a nature as to disturb tranquility and public order on shore, or in the port, or when a person of the country or not belonging to the crew, shall be concerned therein.

In all other cases, the aforesaid authorities shall confine themselves to lending aid to the consuls and vice-consuls or consular agents, if they are requested by them to do so, in causing the arrest and imprisonment of any person whose name is inscribed on the crew list, whenever, for any cause, said officers shall think proper.

The claim of the consul was, that, by the law of nations, and the provisions of this treaty, the offence with which Wildenhus was charged is "solely cognizable by the authority of the laws of the Kingdom of Belgium," and that New Jersey was without jurisdiction in the premises. The Circuit Court refused to deliver the prisoners [the other two men were being held as witnesses] to the consul and remanded them to the custody of the jailer. To reverse that decision this appeal was taken.

* * *

MR. CHIEF JUSTICE WAITE, after stating the case as above reported, delivered the opinion of the court.

* * *

It is part of the law of civilized nations that when a merchant vessel of one country enters the ports of another for the purposes of trade, it subjects itself to the law of the place to which it goes, unless by treaty or otherwise the two countries have come to some different understanding or agreement; for, as was said by Chief Justice Marshall in *The Exchange,* 7 Cranch, 116, 144, "it would be obviously inconvenient and dangerous to society, and would subject the laws to continual infraction, and the government to degradation, if such * * * merchants did not owe temporary and local allegiance, and were not amenable to the jurisdiction of the country." * * * And the English judges have uniformly recognized the rights of the courts of the country of which the port is part to punish crimes committed by one foreigner on another in a foreign merchant ship. * * * As the owner has voluntarily taken his vessel for his own private purposes to a place within the dominion of a government other than his own, and from which he seeks protection during his stay, he owes that government such allegiance for the time being as is due for the protection to which he becomes entitled.

From experience, however, it was found long ago that it would be beneficial to commerce if the local government would abstain from interfering with the internal discipline of the ship, and the general regulation of the rights and duties of the officers and crew towards the vessel or among themselves. And so by comity it came to be generally understood among civilized nations that all matters of discipline and all things done on board which affected only the vessel or those belonging to her, and did not involve the peace or dignity of the country, or the tranquillity [sic] of the port, should be left by the local government to be dealt with by the authorities of the nation to which the vessel belonged as the laws of that nation or the interests of its commerce should require. But if crimes are committed on board of a character to disturb the peace and tranquillity [sic] of the country to which the vessel has been brought, the offenders have never by comity or usage been entitled to any exemption from the operation of the local laws for their punishment, if the local tribunals see fit to assert their authority. Such being the general public law, * * * treaties and conventions have been entered into by nations having commercial intercourse, the purpose of which was to settle and define the rights and duties of the contracting parties with respect to each other in these particulars, and thus prevent the inconvenience that might arise from attempts to exercise conflicting jurisdictions.

* * *

Next came a form of convention which in terms gave the consuls authority to cause proper order to be maintained on board and to decide disputes between the officers and crew, but allowed the local authorities to interfere if the disorders taking place on board were of such a nature as to disturb the public tranquillity, [sic] and that is substantially all there is in the convention with Belgium which we have now to consider. This treaty is the law which now governs the conduct of the United States and Belgium towards each other in this particular. Each nation has granted to the other such local jurisdiction within its own dominion as may be necessary to maintain order on board a merchant vessel, but has reserved to itself the right to interfere if the disorder on board is of a nature to disturb the public tranquillity [sic].

The treaty is part of the supreme law of the United States, and has the same force and effect in New Jersey that it is entitled to elsewhere. If it gives the consul of Belgium exclusive jurisdiction over the offence which it is alleged has been committed within the territory of New Jersey, we see no reason why he may not enforce his rights under the treaty by writ of habeas corpus in any proper court of the United States. This being the case, the only important question left for our determination is whether the thing which has been done—the disorder that has arisen—on board this vessel is of a nature to disturb the public peace, or, as some writers term it, the "public repose" of the people who look to the state of New Jersey for their protection. If the thing done—"the disorder," as it is called in the treaty—is of a character to affect those on shore or in the port when it becomes known, the fact that only those on the ship saw it when it was done is a matter of no moment. Those who are not on the vessel pay no special attention to the mere disputes or quarrels of the seamen while on board, whether they occur under deck or above. Neither do they as a rule care for anything done on board which relates only to the discipline of the ship, or to the preservation of order and authority. Not so, however, with crimes which from their gravity awaken a public interest as soon as they become known, and especially those of a character which every civilized nation considers itself bound to provide a severe punishment for when committed within its own jurisdiction. In such cases inquiry is certain to be instituted at once to ascertain how or why the thing was done, and the popular excitement rises or falls as the news spreads and the facts become known. It is not alone the publicity of the act, or the noise and clamor which attends it, that fixes the nature of the crime, but the act itself. If that is of a character to awaken public interest when it becomes known, it is a "disorder" the nature of which is to affect the community at large, and consequently to invoke the power of the local government whose people have been disturbed by what was done. The very nature of such an act is to disturb the quiet of a peaceful community, and to create, in the language of the treaty, a "disorder" which will [sic] "disturb tranquillity [sic] and public order on shore or in the port." The principle which governs the whole matter is this: Disorders which disturb only the peace of the ship or those on board are to be dealt with exclusively by the sovereignty of the home of the ship, but those which disturb the public peace may be suppressed, and, if need be, the offenders punished by the proper authorities of the local jurisdiction. It may not be easy at all times to determine to which of the two jurisdictions a particular act of disorder belongs. Much will undoubtedly depend on the attending circumstances of the particular case, but all must concede that felonious homicide is a subject for the local jurisdiction, and that if the proper authorities are proceeding with the case in a regular way, the consul has no right to interfere to prevent it. That, according to the petition for the habeas corpus, is this case.

* * *

The judgment of the Circuit Court is affirmed.

————

1. *Peace of the port doctrine in customary international law.* Is a treaty necessary for the application of the doctrine enunciated by the court in *Wildenhus*, or is it a rule of international law arising from custom?

According to 22 U.S. Code of Federal Regulations '838b, an offense which does not involve the peace of the port "is usually left" by local governments to be adjusted by officers of the vessel. The jurisdiction of U.S. vessels in foreign ports in such a class of cases, the section indicates, is insured in many places by a treaty of friendship, commerce and navigation or by a consular convention. Even in the absence of a treaty, the section specifies, the local foreign government "will usually refrain" from intervening.

The *State v. Jannopulos*, Italy, Court of Naples, 1974, I Italian Yb. Int'l L. 268 (1975)*, involved a Greek sailor on a Cypriot vessel in the port of Naples. He was charged with possession of drugs when a considerable quantity of marijuana was found in his cabin. There was no applicable treaty between Italy and Cyprus. The court acquitted the defendant on the ground that the mere possession of drugs aboard a foreign vessel, without a showing of an intent to sell the drugs in Italy, was an internal matter:

> * * * Modern writers on international law and international state practice * * * recognise the existence of an international custom

———

* Reprinted by permission of Editoiale Scientifica s.r.l., Naples.

whereby a foreign ship retains its separate identity as long as it does not interfere in local life by acts which cause or are likely to cause a breach of the peace on shore. Only such an interference would create a link between the shore and the ship, so that in that case the coastal State would be entitled to intervene because of its interest in the peaceful course of life in its own community on shore.

That means that all so-called internal matters on board the ship are outside the criminal jurisdiction of the coastal State, unless they infringe the interest of that State in the peaceful course of life in its own community on shore.

* * *

In the case before us the defendant was in possession of drugs in his cabin on board a Cypriot ship, and there is no evidence at all that he intended to sell it in Italy (and in particular within the jurisdiction of the Court of Naples). We must suppose that he intended to sell it in some other port on the ship's route. There is therefore no link at all between this purely "internal" fact, on board, and the community on shore, whose safety and peaceful course of life and activity were not affected in the slightest by the simple fact of possession. Since the fact occurred in a place which cannot be considered subject to Italian sovereignty because of an exception under international law, we declare that the Italian legal authorities have no jurisdiction and that the case falls under the criminal jurisdiction of the Republic of Cyprus. (at 269B270)

Compare the language used by the Argentinian court in Re Bianchi, *supra* p. 220, which identifies peace of the port as Italian doctrine. The doctrine, so far as it applies to passage through the territorial sea, is labelled "peace of the country" in Article 19, 1(b) of the 1958 Convention on the Territorial Sea and Contiguous Zone and Article 27, 1(b) of the United Nations Convention, in the Documentary Supplement.

2. *Foreign naval vessels in port.* In the *Schooner Exchange v. McFaddon*, 11 U.S. (7 Cranch) 116 (1812), Chief Justice Marshall said: "[T]he Exchange being a public armed ship, in the service of a foreign sovereign, with whom the government of the United States is at peace, and having entered a U.S. port open for her reception, on the terms on which ships of war are generally permitted to enter the ports of a friendly power, must be considered as having come into the American territory, under an implied promise that * * * she should be exempt from the jurisdiction of the country."

In 1975, two sailors from the HMS Hermes, a British aircraft carrier, were arrested and held in jail in Quebec for breaking into the apartment of a Canadian, beating him up and causing considerable damage to the premises. Thereupon a Canadian federal court enjoined the vessel from departing. It left, without the two sailors, in defiance of the injunction. The British consulate in Quebec issued a communiqué justifying the departure on the ground that the order of a federal court in Canada could not be enforced against a vessel of the sovereign forces of Her Majesty. Rousseau, in reporting the incident in his Chronique des Faits Internationaux, approved. 80 Revue Générale de Droit International Public 233 (1976).

3. *Note.* Neither the 1958 Convention on the Territorial Sea and the Contiguous Zone nor the U.N. Convention deals with the jurisdictional issues raised by the presence in port of foreign merchant or naval vessels.

Hoff, Administratrix (United States v. United Mexican States)

General Claims Commission, 1929.
4 U.N.Rep.Int'l Arb. Awards 444.

COMMISSIONER NIELSEN, for the Commission:

Claim in the amount of $10,000.00 with interest is made in this case by the United States of America in behalf of Kate Allison Hoff, Administratrix of the estate of Samuel B. Allison. The latter was the owner of a small American schooner called the Rebecca, which together with its cargo was seized by Mexican authorities at Tampico in 1884. Allegations with respect to the occurrences on which the claim is predicated are made in the Memorial in substance as follows:

The Rebecca was built in the United States and registered at Galveston, Texas. Its approximate value was $5,000.00. In the month of January, 1884, Gilbert F. Dujay, the master of the vessel, loaded it at a small port called Patersonville, nine miles above Morgan City [try their crawfish] in the State of Louisiana, with a cargo consisting of six cases of merchandise destined for Brazos Santiago, Texas, and of a consignment of lumber for Tampico, Mexico. The vessel cleared at Brashear City, now known as Morgan City, on the 30th day of January, 1884, bound for Santiago, Texas. When it reached a point off this port the wind and the tide were so high that it was unsafe to enter. While lying off Brazos Santiago, on the 13th of February, waiting for a favorable opportunity to enter the port, an adverse wind from the north became so strong and the sea so rough, that the vessel was driven to the southward before a furious wind and sea, and when the wind abated it was found that the vessel was in a disabled and unsafe condition off the port of Tampico. The master, realizing the dangerous condition of his vessel, entered the port of Tampico as the nearest place of safety for the vessel, cargo and crew. The crew concurred in and advised such action. When the Rebecca entered the port she was leaking badly. Her standing rigging had been torn away. The cabin windows were broken. The cooking stove was so badly broken it could not be used. While at sea the vessel began to leak so that the water reached the cases of merchandise, and the crew was compelled to break open the packages and store them so that they would not be ruined by the water.

When the Rebecca entered the port the master presented to the Mexican customs official a manifest for the goods destined for Tampico and a so-called "master's manifest" for the consignment for Brazos Santiago, Texas, which met the requirements of the law of the United States. As soon as the vessel reached Tampico, which was on Sunday afternoon, February

17th, it was anchored off the custom house and a protest of distress was immediately entered with A.J. Cassard, the American Consul at that port.

On the day following the arrival at Tampico, February 18, 1884, the Mexican custom house officials demanded from the master of the Rebecca the packages of merchandise on board the vessel. The demand was refused and thereupon the packages were taken by force and no receipt or other evidence of possession by the custom house authorities was given.

On the 21st of February the master was arrested on a charge of attempt to smuggle, was placed in the barracks with armed soldiers guarding him, was not permitted to speak to anyone, and was kept in close confinement until the day following, a period of 28 hours, when he was brought before the Judge of the District Court at Tampico, and without the privilege of having counsel, was tried and was acquitted and released. On the 23rd of February the master was again arrested by the Mexican authorities and was required to give bond for his appearance before the Criminal Court at Tampico to answer a charge of bringing goods into a Mexican port without proper papers. While awaiting trial he remained under bond, but without permission to leave Mexico, until the 24th day of April, a period of over two months. On that date a decree was entered by the court which released the master from bail but assessed treble damages against the merchandise seized, and charged the master with the cost of revenue stamps used in the proceedings. Because of the refusal and inability of the master to pay the penalties thus assessed, the Rebecca and its cargo were sold by order of court, and the proceeds were applied to the Federal Treasury, a balance being distributed among certain customs employees.

* * *

It is of course well established that, when a merchant vessel belonging to one nation enters the territorial waters of another nation, it becomes amenable to the jurisdiction of the latter and is subject to its laws, except in so far as treaty stipulations may relieve the vessel from the operation of local laws. On the other hand, there appears to be general recognition among the nations of the world of what may doubtless be considered to be an exception, or perhaps it may be said two exceptions, to this general, fundamental rule of subjection to local jurisdiction over vessels in foreign ports.

Recognition has been given to the so-called right of "innocent passage" for vessels through the maritime belt in so far as it forms a part of the high seas for international traffic. Similarly, recognition has also been given— perhaps it may be said in a more concrete and emphatic manner—to the immunity of a ship whose presence in territorial waters is due to a superior force. The principles with respect to the status of a vessel in "distress" find recognition both in domestic laws and in international law. * * *

* * *

While recognizing the general principle of immunity of vessels in distress, domestic courts and international courts have frequently given consideration to the question as to the degree of necessity prompting vessels to seek refuge. It has been said that the necessity must be urgent. It seems possible to formulate certain reasonably concrete criteria applicable and controlling in the instant case. Assuredly a ship floundering in distress, resulting either from the weather or from other causes affecting management of the vessel, need not be in such a condition that it is dashed helplessly on the shore or against rocks before a claim of distress can properly be invoked in its behalf. The fact that it may be able to come into port under its own power can obviously not be cited as conclusive evidence that the plea is unjustifiable. If a captain delayed seeking refuge until his ship was wrecked, obviously he would not be using his best judgment with a view to the preservation of the ship, the cargo and the lives of people on board. An important consideration may be the * * * whether there is any evidence in a given case of a fraudulent attempt to circumvent local laws. And even in the absence of any such attempt, it can probably be correctly said that a mere matter of convenience in making repairs or in avoiding a measure of difficulty in navigation can not justify a disregard of local laws.

The Rebecca did sail into Tampico, as observed by the judge who condemned the vessel, under its own power. However, it did not enter the port until after it had for three days, in a crippled condition, been contending with a storm in an attempt to enter the port at Brazos Santiago, Texas. It is therefore certain that the vessel did not by choice abandon its attempt to make port at that place, but only because according to the best judgment of the captain and his crew absolute necessity so required. In such a case a captain's judgment would scarcely seem subject to question. It may also be concluded from the evidence in the case that a well grounded apprehension of the loss of the vessel and cargo and persons on board prompted the captain to turn south towards Tampico. It was argued in behalf of the United States that under the conditions of the weather it could be assumed that no other port of refuge was available. And even if such were not the case, there would seem to be no reason why refuge should not have been sought at Tampico. The fact that the ship had cargo for that place in addition to that consigned to Brazos Santiago, did not make the former any less available as the port of refuge. It may be concluded from the evidence that the captain had no intent to perpetrate a fraud on Mexican customs laws. Indeed his acquittal on the criminal charge preferred against him appears to be conclusive on that point, even if there were no other evidence bearing on the matter which there is. It may also be concluded that the captain had no intent merely as a matter of convenience to flout Mexican laws. This very small vessel had been driven before a strong north wind; its cabin had been damaged; its pumps had been broken and repaired; the cooking stove on the vessel had been rendered useless; there were one and a half to two feet of water in the vessel; and it had been leaking. * * * The ship entered the port of Tampico in distress, and the seizure of both the vessel and cargo was wrongful.

                    * * *

Decision

The United Mexican States shall pay to the United States of America on behalf of Kate A. Hoff the sum of $5,000.00, with interest at the rate of six per centum per annum from April 24, 1884, to the date on which the last award is rendered by the Commission.

---

1. ***Basis of decision.*** The compromise establishing the USA/Mexican General Claims Commission provided that the claims to be submitted to the commission should be decided "in accordance with the principles of international law, justice and equity." 4 U.N.Rep.Int'l Arb.Awards 11, 12.

2. ***Nuclear vessels.*** The Brussels Convention on the Liability of Operators of Nuclear Ships of May 25, 1962, provides in Article 17:

> Nothing in this Convention shall affect any right which a Contracting State may have under international law to deny access to its waters and harbours to nuclear ships licensed by another Contracting State, even when it has formally complied with the provisions of this Convention. 57 Am. J. Int'l L. 268 (1963).

Does a contracting state have a right under international law to deny access to a nuclear vessel entering in distress? What if the distress is a leaking nuclear reactor? See the Reporters' Note to Section 48 of the 1965 Restatement.

3. ***Law of the former USSR recognized a right of entry in distress for foreign naval vessels.*** Rules for Navigation and Sojourn of Foreign Warships in the Territorial and the Internal Waters and Ports of the former U.S.S.R., 24 International Legal Materials 1715, 1722 (1985).

4. ***No provision in conventions.*** Neither the 1958 Convention on the Territorial Sea and the Contiguous Zone nor the United Nations Convention on the Law of the Sea deals with the jurisdictional issues raised by a foreign vessel's entry in distress into internal waters. However, the right has been recognized in state practice and renders immunity to a ship that is in genuine distress. This exception to port state jurisdiction has over the years been used by smugglers and more latterly drug traffickers but it has been strictly construed. Distress caused by bad weather or the need to make repairs has been based on necessity. In *Cashin* v. *The King*, [1935] 4 D.L.R. 547, 551–52, the Canadian Exchequer Court held as a rule of customary international law that:

> a ship, compelled through stress of either, duress or other unavoidable cause to put into a foreign port, is * * * exempt from liability to the penalties and forfeitures which, had she entered the port voluntarily she would have incurred.

3. Breadth of the Territorial Sea

Evolution of the position of the United States. From the time of Jefferson until 1958, the United States consistently supported a three-mile limit as the appropriate breadth of the territorial sea. At the First Geneva Conference on the Law of the Sea in 1958, the United States first maintained its support of the three-mile limit, but eventually shifted to a compromise proposal providing for a six-mile limit of territorial sea and, subject to certain qualifications, a six-mile fishing zone beyond it. The proposal was not adopted. The Conference failed to achieve agreement on the extent of the territorial sea and the resulting Article 24 (2) simply stipulated that the contiguous zone could not extend beyond 12 miles from the baseline from which the territorial sea is measured, giving contracting states the flexibility to delimit the territorial sea and contiguous zone within that overall maximum. The United States supported a similar proposal at the Second Geneva Conference on the Law of the Sea in 1960 and again the proposal failed. Since then the position of the United States has continued to evolve, as shown by the materials that follow.

Statement by the Legal Adviser of the U.S. Department of State Concerning a Twelve–mile Limit, August 3, 1971

66 American Journal of International Law 133 (1972).*

[Before the third conference on the law of the sea, commonly called UNCLOS III, was convened, the United Nations had assigned the task of preparing draft articles for the conference to its Committee on the Peaceful Uses of the Seabed and the Ocean Floor Beyond the Limits of National Jurisdiction. The Committee met in Geneva from July 19 to August 27, 1971. John R. Stevenson, Legal Adviser of the Department of State and U.S. Representative to the Committee, submitted on August 3 draft articles to Subcommittee II and made a statement:

> The first article presented by my Government would establish a maximum breadth of 12 miles for the territorial sea. The prime distinguishing characteristic of the territorial sea is that the coastal state exercises jurisdiction over navigation and overflight, subject to a limited right of innocent passage for vessels. We believe agreement must be reached on a narrow territorial sea. While my Government adheres to the traditional 3–mile limit, it is prepared to take into account the views of others and to agree to a treaty fixing the maximum breadth of the territorial sea at 12 nautical miles, if there is an adequate agreement concerning international straits—to which I shall refer shortly. We use the 12–mile figure because it represents the best—probably the only—possibility for reaching agreement. It is apparent that the overwhelming majority of states are prepared to accept the 12–mile limit. In most cases where broader jurisdictional claims have been made, the reasons for those claims were resource-oriented. We believe that the real concerns of those few states that have claimed broader limits for the territorial sea can be accommodated in the course of the work of this and the other subcommittees.]

The Twelve–Mile Limit at Unclos III

Stevenson and Oxman, the Third United Nations Conference on the Law of the Sea: The 1974 Caracas Session, 69 American Journal of International Law, 1, 13B14, (1975).**

* Reprinted by permission of the American Society of International Law.

** Reprinted by permission of the American Society of International Law.

[John R. Stevenson, author of the preceding statement, had become Ambassador and Special Representative of the President of the United States for the Law of the Sea Conference, by the time he wrote the article.] "Agreement on a 12–mile territorial sea is so widespread that there were virtually no references to any other limit in the public debate, although other alternatives are presented in the working paper. Major conditions for acceptance of 12 miles as a maximum limit were agreement on unimpeded transit of straits and acceptance of a 200–mile exclusive economic zone. * * * "

United States: Presidential Proclamation on the Territorial Sea of the United States***

[December 27, 1988].
28 I.L.M. 284 (1989).

Proclamation of December 27, 1988

TERRITORIAL SEA OF THE UNITED STATES

By the President of the United States of America—A Proclamation

International law recognizes that coastal nations may exercise sovereignty and jurisdiction over their territorial seas.

The territorial sea of the United States is a maritime zone extending beyond the land territory and internal waters of the United States over which the United States exercises sovereignty and jurisdiction, a sovereignty and jurisdiction that extend to the airspace over the territorial sea, as well as to its bed and subsoil.

Extension of the territorial sea by the United States to the limits permitted by international law will advance the national security and other significant interests of the United States.

Now, Therefore, I, Ronald Reagan, by the authority vested in me as President by the Constitution of the United States of America, and in accordance with international law, do hereby proclaim the extension of the territorial sea of the United States of America, the Commonwealth of Puerto Rico, Guam, American Samoa, the United States Virgin Islands, the Commonwealth of the Northern Mariana Islands, and any other territory or possession over which the United States exercises sovereignty.

The territorial sea of the United States henceforth extends to 12 nautical miles from the baselines of the United States determined in accordance with international law.

In accordance with international law, as reflected in the applicable provisions of the 1982 United Nations Convention on the Law of the Sea, within the territorial sea of the United States, the ships of all countries enjoy the right of innocent passage and the ships and aircraft of all countries enjoy the right of transit passage through international straits.

*** [Reproduced from U.S. Weekly Compilation of Presidential Documents, Volume 24, Number 52 (January 2, 1989), p. 1661. The 1982 United Nations Convention on the Law of the Sea as in Doc.Supp.].

Nothing in this Proclamation:

(a) extends or otherwise alters existing Federal or State law or any jurisdiction, rights, legal interests, or obligations derived therefrom; or

(b) impairs the determination, in accordance with international law, of any maritime boundary of the United States with a foreign jurisdiction.

In Witness Whereof, I have hereunto set my hand this twenty-seventh day of December, in the year of our Lord nineteen hundred and eighty-eight, and of the Independence of the United States of America the two hundred and thirteenth.

/s/ Ronald Reagan

4.   FOREIGN VESSELS IN THE TERRITORIAL SEA

Corfu Channel Case (United Kingdom v. Albania)

International Court of Justice, 1949.
[1949] I.C.J. Rep. 4, 28.

[On May 5, 1946, British cruisers were fired upon by an Albanian battery while passing through the Corfu Channel, which, on that date, was clear of minefields. "The government of the United Kingdom protested on the ground that innocent passage through straits was a right recognized by international law. The government of Albania answered that neither foreign naval vessels, nor foreign merchant vessels, had a right under international law to pass through Albanian territorial waters without prior notification to, and permission of, the Albanian authorities."

On October 22, 1946, a squadron of British naval vessels proceeded through the Corfu Channel without the permission of the Albanian authorities and in the passage two destroyers were heavily damaged by mines, with loss of life.

By special agreement, the parties submitted questions to the International Court of Justice, one of which was whether the acts of the Royal Navy on October 22, 1946, violated the sovereignty of Albania.

The court dealt with the question as follows:]

The Court will now consider the Albanian contention that the United Kingdom Government violated Albanian sovereignty by sending the warships through this Strait without the previous authorization of the Albanian Government.

It is, in the opinion of the Court, generally recognized and in accordance with international custom that states in time of peace have a right to send their warships through straits used for international navigation between two parts of the high seas without the previous authorization of a coastal state, provided that the passage is innocent. Unless otherwise prescribed in an international convention, there is no right for a coastal state to prohibit such passage through straits in time of peace.

The Albanian Government does not dispute that the North Corfu Channel is a strait in the geographical sense; but it denies that this

Channel belongs to the class of international highways through which a right of passage exists, on the grounds that it is only of secondary Nations Convention on the Law of the Sea deals with it in Articles 17B32. [For both texts, see the Documentary Supplement.]

Some of the articles in the United Nations Convention deal with matters not covered in the 1958 text. Article 21, for example, is new in providing a list of the matters with respect to which a coastal state may enact laws and regulations applicable to foreign vessels in innocent passage. So is Article 22, which specifies a coastal state may establish sea lanes and traffic separation schemes in the territorial sea and lists the factors it must take into account in so doing. Article 23 is also new in dealing with foreign nuclear-powered vessels and vessels carrying nuclear or other dangerous substances.

Other articles incorporate principles already in the 1958 text, but expand them by elaborating their meaning or application in great detail. Such is the case with Article 19. It repeats paragraph 4 of Article 14 in the 1958 text: "Passage is innocent so long as it is not prejudicial to the peace, good order or security of the coastal state." Then it goes on to give a list of 12 activities which will render the passage prejudicial if engaged in by a foreign vessel in the territorial sea.

The net effect of such additions and expansions may be to give coastal states more control over foreign vessels in innocent passage than granted in the 1958 Convention.

Anand, Transit Passage and Overflight in International Straits

26 Indian Journal of International Law 72, 91–95 (1986).*

* * *

The United States representative said in Sub-committee of the Seabed Committee that "in addition to the importance of sea navigation for their international trade, many states depended upon air and sea mobility in order to exercise their inherent right of individual and collective self-defence". He pointed out that "the security of the United States and its allies depended to a very large extent on the freedom of navigation and on the overflight of the high seas. More extensive territorial seas, without the right to free transit of straits, would threaten that security". The United States maintained that the invulnerability of its nuclear missile submarines (SSBNs)Ccurrently the Polaris/Poseidon fleet—and hence their indispensable role in an adequate second strike force depended on their right to pass through straits submerged and unannounced. In the U.S. view, the right of free transit through straits was "an indispensable adjunct to the freedom of navigation and that of overflight on the high seas themselves". Moreover, the regime of innocent passage provided for in the 1958 Convention on the Territorial Sea was "inadequate when applied to international straits" because it was a subjective standard subject to abuse. Some states, he said,

* Reprinted by permission of the Indian
Society of International Law.

had in fact claimed that certain types of passage—by nuclear-powered ships and super tankers—should be considered as non-innocent per se.

The United States made it clear time and again that it would not accept any extension of the territorial sea from three miles to twelve miles unless the right of *free passage* through international straits was accepted. It demanded freedom of unobstructed passage for warships, including nuclear submarines, on the surface or submerged, without notification and irrespective of mission. Further, it wanted freedom of civilian and military flights through the superjacent airspace. All these rights were claimed not only in those straits that were wider than six miles and were supposed to have, at least theoretically, a corridor of high seas in their midst, but in *all straits irrespective of their breadth or importance.*

The United States was willing to accept and "observe reasonable traffic safety and marine pollution regulations"; regulations that were "consistent with the basic right of transit". The safety standards to be applied in straits, however, should be established by international agreement and should not be unilaterally imposed by the coastal state.

As to the free transit of aircraft, the United States stated that civil aircraft already enjoyed transit rights over national territory of other states, under the Convention on International Civil Aviation and the International Air Service Transit Agreement. But such rights were not available to state aircraft. The United States demanded a right of free transit for all aircraft over straits, but also stated that such aircraft need not be routed over the strait itself but, at the coastal state's discretion, could be directed through "suitable corridors over land areas".

The United States was supported on this issue not only by the western maritime powers, like the United Kingdom, France, West Germany and others but also by the Soviet Union and Communist bloc countries which also insisted that the limited right of "innocent passage" was not sufficient and "had never been and could never be applied to such straits as those of Gibraltar, Dover, Malacca, Singapore and Bab-el-Mandeb, where freedom of navigation had always been enjoyed." In accordance with these views on 25 July 1972, the Soviet Union proposed "Draft Articles on Straits used for International Navigation".

Although "the coastal state should be given appropriate guarantees of its security and protection against pollution of the waters of its adjacent straits", the Soviet Union, like the United States, was absolutely convinced that "the concept of innocent passage could not be accepted as applying to the principal straits used for international navigation because it was too widely interpreted as a concept giving, so to speak, the last word to the coastal state or states concerned". Refusal to recognize the principle of free passage would mean, according to the Soviet Union, "establishing the domination of only 12 to 15 states adjacent to straits over the passage of vessels of some 130 states of the world". * * *

* * *

Despite all the misgivings and apprehensions of the smaller coastal and strait states * * *, the maritime powers were not prepared to give up their demands. Both the superpowers and their allies left no one in doubt that unless unimpeded passage on, over and under straits used for international navigation was conceded to all commercial vessels and warships, including submarines, there was simply no possibility of coming to an agreement on the subject of national jurisdiction. * * *

* * * As finally adopted, the Convention provides for a guaranteed non-suspendable transit passage through straits and archipelagic waters, subject only to the power of the coastal state to make certain rules related to navigational safety, pollution, and fishing. For the first time, the Convention provides separate regimes for "innocent passage" through territorial sea, laid down in Part II, Section 3 (Articles 17 to 32), and "Transit Passage," through International Straits, laid down in Part III, Section 2 (Articles 37 to 44), and Section 3 (Article 45), the latter applicable only to special straits. The right of transit passage applies to "straits which are used for international navigation between one part of the high sea or an exclusive economic zone and another part of the high seas or an exclusive economic zone" [Article 37]. But transit passage does not apply to:

(1) Straits formed by an island of a state bordering the strait and its mainland if there exists seaward of the island a route through the high seas or through an EEZ of similar convenience with respect to navigational and hydrographical characteristics [Article 38(1)].

(2) Straits used for international navigation between one area of the high seas or an EEZ and the territorial sea of a foreign state [Article 45(1)(b)].

For these two categories the right of "innocent passage" is deemed sufficient which however cannot be suspended [Article 45(2)].

Transit passage is defined as: "the exercise in accordance with this part of the freedom of navigation and overflight solely for the purpose of continuous and expeditious transit of the strait between one part of the high seas or an EEZ and another part of the high seas or an EEZ. However, the requirement of continuous and expeditious transit does not preclude passage through the strait for the purpose of entering, leaving or returning from a state bordering the strait, subject to the conditions of entry to that state [Art. 38(2)]."

Article 39 lays down the duties of ships and aircraft while exercising the right of transit passage, such as, to (1) proceed without delay through or over the strait; (2) refrain from use of force against the sovereignty, integrity or independence of the bordering states, or in any manner in violation of the principles of international law; (3) refrain from any activities other than those incidental to their normal modes of continuous and expeditious transit unless rendered necessary by force majeure or by distress.

* * *

———

World straits. There are at least 120 straits in the world 24 miles in width, or less. Thus the universal adoption of 12 miles as the breadth of the territorial sea would place the waters in all such straits under the national jurisdiction of bordering states, subject only to a right of innocent passage. Transit through many of these straits is not important for international traffic, but transit through certain of them is essential for international maritime commerce and crucial for global deployment of naval power.

In preparation for the 1958 Geneva Conference on the Law of the Sea, the Secretariat of the United Nations made a study of straits constituting routes for international traffic which would be affected should 12 miles become the breadth of the territorial sea. The study listed 33. I United Nations Conference on the Law of the Sea 114 (1958).

The Office of the Geographer of the United States Department of State has issued a chart entitled World Straits Affected by a 12 Mile Territorial Sea on which there appears the notation: "Capitalization used to denote major straits from other and minor straits." From this notation, Pirtle infers that the straits whose names are in capitals are of strategic significance to the security of the United States. Transit Rights and U.S. Security Interests in International Straits: The "Straits Debate" Revisited, 5 Ocean Development and International Law 477, 488 (1978). These straits include some straits not listed in the United Nations study.[a]

Question: In what respect do you think that transit passage through an international strait differs from innocent passage? Consider the type of straits to which transit passage applies in Articles 37—44 of the 1982 Convention in the Documentary Supplement.

Public Prosecutor v. Kairismaa

Sweden, Court of Appeal of Svea, 1960.
Supreme Court, 1960.
32 Int'l L.Rep. 117 (1966).*

The Facts. Kairismaa, a Finnish citizen, was charged before the City Court of Stockholm with, inter alia, obtaining a loan of 1,000 Swedish crowns from another Finnish citizen, Stjernvall, superintendent on the Finnish ship the Bore II, by fraudulently alleging that he needed the money immediately for a business transaction concerning an automobile and that he would repay it later the same day. The Public Prosecutor alleged that the crime had been committed within Swedish territorial waters. The City Court having found the defendant guilty, he appealed. Referring to the fact that the ship was Finnish, that both he himself and Stjernvall were Finnish

---

a. The United Nations study lists the following straits: Bab el Mandeb, Gibraltar, Zanzibar Channel, The Serpent's Mouth, The Dragon's Mouth, St. Lucia Channel, Strait between St. Lucia and St. Vincent, Dominica Channel, Straits between Dominica and Guadeloupe, Magellan, Juan de Fuca, Chosen, Hainan, Palk, Malacca, Ombae, Soenda, San Bernardino, Surigao, Hormuz, St. George's Channel (Bismarck Archipelago), Cook, Foveaux, Kaiwi Channel, Dover, Canal de Menorca, Messina, Bonifacio, The Dardanelles, Sea of Marmara and the Bosphorus, Kithera, Carphatos, The Sound and Singapore Strait.

Pirtle lists the 16 straits of strategic importance to the United States as follows: West Korean, Malacca, Sunca, Lombok, Ombae, West Bering, Juan de Fuca, Old Bahamas Channel, Dominica Channel, Martinique Channel, St. Lucia Channel, St. Vincent Passage, Gibraltar, Bab el Mandeb, Hormuz.

* Reprinted with the permission of the Editor of the International Law Reports.

citizens, and claiming that the transaction had taken place while the Bore II was outside Swedish territorial waters, the defendant urged the Appeal Court to reject the present part of the charge.

Held (by the Court of Appeal of Svea): that the appeal must fail and the judgment of the Court below must be confirmed. [The Court said:]

> * * * It has been made clear [however], chiefly by the evidence given by Stjernvall before the City Court, that the transaction had taken place after the ship's entry into the Stockholm archipelago. As the Bore II—which plies in regular passenger traffic between Stockholm and Helsinki—thus at the time when the act was committed was in Swedish territorial waters, the Court of Appeal finds that the act shall be deemed to have taken place within the country. Under Chapter 1, Article 2, paragraph 1, of the Penal Code, a Swedish Court is consequently competent to consider the present part of the charge.

Kairismaa applied for permission to appeal to the Supreme Court and urged that Court to reject the charge. * * *

> * * *

Kairismaa also contended that it was not clear from the reasons given by the Court of Appeal for its judgment whether the present charge could be brought in Sweden on the sole ground that, at the time when the crime was committed, the ship was in Swedish territorial waters, or whether a second condition was required, namely, that the ship be plying in regular traffic between a Swedish and a foreign port. * * * It was true that the principle applied by the Court of Appeal had been expressed earlier, in cases concerning crimes by Swedish citizens. * * * It was much more natural, however, to consider a crime committed against an alien on a foreign ship within Swedish territorial waters as a matter of Swedish concern when committed by a Swede than when it was committed by an alien. * * *

Held (by the Supreme Court): that the application for permission to appeal must be rejected. The Court found no reason to alter the decision of the City Court. Accordingly, the judgment of the Court of Appeal must be affirmed.

---

1. *Amendment of Swedish law subsequent to decision.* The decision appears to have been the cause of an amendment to the Swedish code of criminal law which went into effect on January 1, 1965. Under this amendment, special permission from the executive is required before prosecution is initiated for an offense committed by an alien aboard a foreign vessel in Swedish territory and affecting another alien or alien interests. The amendment is reported in a note at the end of a comment on the case by Eek, *Chronique de Jurisprudence Suédoise Relative au Droit International Privé* 1960–1964, 93 *Journal du Droit International* 410 (1965–1966).

2. *Jurisdiction over merchant vessels in innocent passage under 1958 Convention and U.N. Convention.* As to criminal jurisdiction, see in the Documentary Supplement Article 19 of the 1958 Convention on

the Territorial Sea and the Contiguous Zone and Article 27 of the United Nations Convention on the Law of the Sea. As to civil jurisdiction, see Article 20 of the former and Article 28 of the latter.

   3. *Warships*. Concerning the right of warships to innocent passage see The Joint Statement by the United States and the former USSR on Uniform Interpretation of Rules of International Law Governing Innocent Passage, 1989, reprinted in D.J. Harris, Cases and Materials on International Law (5th ed., 1998), 405–406. The 1958 and 1982 Conventions do not expressly deal with this issue. Consider, the heading of Part II, Section 3 (A.) entitled "Rules Applicable to All Ships".

SECTION D.   WATERS BEYOND THE TERRITORIAL SEA

1.   FREEDOM OF NAVIGATION

The Principle

Negroponte,[a] Who Will Protect the Freedom of the Seas?

United States Department of State, Bureau of Public Affairs,
Current Policy No. 855.

          * * *

   The world's oceans are vital to mankind in diverse ways. We are just beginning to understand their environmental significance. We have always used their fishery resources. We have begun to learn how to exploit some of their other resources. And through the centuries the world's oceans have been essential as waterways, and now airways, necessary to preserve the peace and to move world trade and commerce.

   The freedom of use of the world's marine waters is what we mean by the freedom of the seas. It is perhaps our oldest customary international law doctrine.

   The freedom of the seas was not given to mankind. It was won through scholarly and legal debate and in naval engagements. Over the years, the freedom of the seas has undergone some changes and refinements. Its exercise has become geographically compressed; its composition has been broken into fragments, and some of those have been lost. So, today, when we speak of the freedom of the seas, we mean, primarily, the freedom of movement on the world's seas and oceans by navies and maritime commerce: the freedom to navigate and to fly from one continent to another over broad expanses; the freedom to navigate and to fly from one sea to another through even the narrowest of straits.

   a. At the time—July 21, 1986—he gave the speech, John D. Negroponte was the Assistant Secretary of State for Oceans and International Environmental and Scientific Affairs, in the U.S. Department of State.

Without the freedom of the seas, the world would be a different place. Maritime commerce as we know it would not exist. The global balance of power would be unalterably shifted.

* * *

Agreement Allowing U.S. Authorities to Seize British Flag Vessels Outside the Territorial Sea and Contiguous Zone

21 International Legal Materials 439 (1982).*

Foreign and Commonwealth Office

London SW.1A 2AH, 13 November 1981

His Excellency

The Honourable

John J. Louis Jr.

Embassy of the United States of America

Your Excellency,

I have the honour to refer to the recent discussions between representatives of our two Governments concerning the desire of the authorities of the United States to take more effective measures to suppress the unlawful importation of cannabis and other narcotic drugs into the United States.

Bearing in mind the special nature of this problem and having regard to the need for international co-operation in suppressing the illicit traffic in narcotic drugs, which is recognised in the Single Convention on Narcotic Drugs of 1961, I have the honour to propose the following:

1. The Government of the United Kingdom of Great Britain and Northern Ireland agree that they will not object to the boarding by the authorities of the United States, outside the limits of the territorial sea and contiguous zone of the United States and within the areas described in paragraph 9 below, of private vessels under the British flag in any case in which those authorities reasonably believe that the vessel has on board a cargo of drugs for importation into the United States in violation of the laws of the United States.

2. On boarding the vessel the authorities of the United States may address enquiries to those on board, examine the ship's papers and take such other measures as are necessary to establish the place of registration of the vessel. When these measures suggest that an offence against the laws of the United States relative to the importation of narcotic drugs is being committed, the Government of the United Kingdom agree that they will not object to the authorities of the United States instituting a search of the vessel.

---

* Reprinted by permission of the American Society of International Law from material published at 21 I.L.M. 439 under the title "United Kingdom: Letters to U.S. Concerning Measures to Suppress the Unlawful Importation of Narcotic Drugs into the United States."

3. If the authorities of the United States then believe that an offence against the laws referred to in paragraph 2 above is being committed, the Government of the United Kingdom agree that they will not object to the vessel being seized and taken into a United States port.

4. The Government of the United Kingdom may, within 14 days of the vessel's entry into port, object to the continued exercise of United States jurisdiction over the vessel for purposes of the laws referred to in paragraph 2 above, and the Government of the United States shall thereupon release the vessel without charge. The Government of the United States shall not institute forfeiture proceedings before the end of the period allowed for objection.

5. The Government of the United Kingdom may, within 30 days of the vessel's entry into port, object to the prosecution of any United Kingdom national found on board the vessel, and the Government of the United States shall thereupon release such person. The Government of the United Kingdom agree that they will not otherwise object to the prosecution of any person found on board the vessel.

6. Any action by the authorities of the United States shall be taken in accordance with this Agreement and United States law.

7. In any case where a vessel under the British flag is boarded the authorities of the United States shall promptly inform the authorities of the United Kingdom of the action taken and shall keep them fully informed of any subsequent developments.

8. If any loss or injury is suffered as a result of any action taken by the United States in contravention of these arrangements or any improper or unreasonable action taken by the United States pursuant thereto, representatives of the two Governments shall meet at the request of either to decide any question relating to compensation. Representatives of the two Governments shall in any case meet from time to time to review the working of these arrangements.

9. The areas referred to in paragraph 1 above comprise the Gulf of Mexico, the Caribbean Sea, that portion of the Atlantic Ocean West of longitude 55E West and South of latitude 30E North and all other areas within 150 miles of the Atlantic coast of the United States.

10. I have the honour to suggest that if the foregoing proposals are acceptable to the Government of the United States, this Note and Your Excellency's confirmatory reply shall constitute an Agreement between the Government of the United Kingdom of Great Britain and Northern Ireland and the Government of the United States which shall enter into force on the date of your reply. It may be terminated by either Government on one month's notice but will continue to remain effective in respect of any proceedings based on action taken during its validity.

Accept, Excellency, the renewed assurance of my highest consideration. (For the Secretary of State)

———

Status of vessels on the high seas under 1958 Convention and U.N. Convention. Article 6 of the 1958 Convention on the High Seas and Article 92 of the United Nations Convention on the Law of the Sea both provide that vessels on the high seas are under the exclusive jurisdiction of the state of their flag. However, concerning the right of visit by a warship of a vessel of another flag state, where there is a reasonable ground to suspect that the ship has been engaged in piracy, the slave trade, amongst other matters, see Article 22 of the 1958 Convention on the High Seas and Article 110 of the 1982 Convention, both reproduced in the Documentary Supplement. Warships and ships used only on government non-commercial service have complete immunity on the high seas from any state other than their flag state. See Articles 8—9 of the 1958 Convention on the High Seas and Articles 95—96 of the 1982 Convention.

———

Note the solution to pirate broadcasting in Article 109 of the 1982 U.N. Convention in the Documentary Supplement which allows arrest of individuals and seizure vessels engaged in pirate broadcasting.

———

The Contiguous Zone

In Re Martinez

Italy, Court of Cassation, 1959.
28 Int'l L.Rep. 170 (1963).*

The Facts. [Article 2 of the Italian Maritime Code fixed the limit of territorial waters at six miles from the coast. Article 33 of the Customs Law of September 25, 1940, on the other hand, provide[d] that Italy shall be entitled to exercise jurisdiction over a further six-mile zone for the purpose of preventing and punishing smuggling along the Italian coast. This latter zone is referred to as the "zone of vigilance" (contiguous zone).] The appellants, who were foreign nationals, were convicted of smuggling in the following circumstances: while their vessel was at a distance of nine miles from the coast, warning shots were fired, and upon these shots being ignored the vessel was pursued and ultimately captured at a distance of 54 miles from the coast. The appellants appealed their conviction and contended that Article 24 of the Geneva Convention of 1958 on the Territorial Sea and the Contiguous Zone was declaratory of existing customary international law and accordingly a coastal State, while entitled to prevent customs offences from being committed in the contiguous zone, was not entitled to exercise jurisdiction and inflict punishment in respect of such offences; that jurisdiction could only be exercised if an offence had actually been committed within the territorial sea, and therefore Article 33 of the

* Reprinted with the permission of the
Editor of the International Law Reports.

Customs Law was contrary to Article 10 of the Italian Constitution, which provided that Italian law must be consistent with international law. * * *

[Article 24 provides in part:

1. In a zone of the high seas contiguous to its territorial sea, the coastal state may exercise the control necessary to:

(a) Prevent infringement of its customs, fiscal, immigration or sanitary regulations within its territory or territorial sea;

(b) Punish infringement of the above regulations committed within its territory or territorial sea.]

Held: that the appeal must be dismissed: * * *

The contention that Article 33 of the Customs Law is contrary to the Constitution is misconceived and has been rejected by the judgment under appeal. It is undoubtedly true that the rule laid down in Article 10 of the Constitution, according to which Italian law must comply with generally recognized rules of international law, ensures the compatibility of Italian municipal law with international law, viz., with the duties imposed upon the State by international law, so that rules of municipal law which are contrary to international law must be eliminated. However, in order for this to be so, it is necessary for the rules of international law to be generally recognized, and it is admitted on behalf of the defendants that the Geneva Convention, which has been signed by Italy, is not yet in force.

It is not true that Article 24 of the Convention constitutes a customary rule of international law governing the delimitation of the territorial sea in the sense that the sovereignty of the coastal State is limited to the territorial sea itself, without being capable of being extended over the contiguous zone when smuggling has occurred in the latter and not in the territorial sea. No such rule can be said to have been generally accepted in international law. In substance custom is a manifestation of social life which hardens by means of constant and uniform repetition of certain acts on the part of States or individuals, extending over a period of time, to which municipal law attributes legal relevance. In the international field this presupposes the existence of a substantive element, namely, the constant repetition of certain rules of conduct between States, and a psychological element, namely, the conviction that such conduct is obligatory for everybody, so that others can insist upon it, and which does not depend on purely subjective judgment. Only then can custom be a source of law equal to municipal law.

* * *

It is contended on behalf of the defendants that the [International Law] Commission was set up for the progressive development and codification of international law, and that when preparing the report on which the Convention is based it investigated substantially the rules of customary international law. This, it is argued, shows that these rules existed prior to codification, which was merely intended to lay down in codified form what was already custom. Hence the wording of the rule contained in Article 24 of the Convention, which is said to be a faithful reproduction of a pre-existing customary rule which as such is generally recognized and must be considered, by virtue of Article 10 of the Constitution, as having been automatically incorporated in Italian law, and which must not be contrary to the rule laid down in that article.

* * * [T]his rule cannot be said to be a generally recognized rule of customary international law because the rule relating to the width of the territorial sea is still under discussion between States. States apply different rules according to their respective municipal laws, which fact in itself precludes recognition of any pre-existing custom in the matter. In fact, although the Conference on the Law of the Sea was successful in defining a number of rules governing the matter under discussion, it left unsolved the problem of the width of the territorial sea, as can be seen from the preparatory work of the Conference. The disagreement was due to different contrasting views put forward by participating States, one group being in favour of the three-mile limit for territorial waters, as in the past, another holding the opposite view and applying various criteria to the actual width of the territorial sea, without affirming a right to twelve miles. Although various proposals were put forward to reconcile the opposing wishes of States, no positive solution was found. Accordingly, * * * the rule contained in Article 24 of the Convention existed previously as a generally recognized customary rule when the conditions surrounding the delimitation of the territorial sea and the contiguous zone were very different from those contained in that article and when agreement could not be reached. * * *

In fact, not all States have accepted the three-mile limit, which in the past represented a compromise between States: Norway and Sweden have fixed the limit of their territorial sea at four miles; Spain, Portugal, Yugoslavia, Italy and other countries at six, while Bulgaria, the Soviet Union, Communist China, Egypt, Ethiopia, Rumania and Guatemala have fixed it at twelve miles, and Chile and other countries at two hundred. Italy, on the other hand, has not accepted the limit of the contiguous zone in the form in which it is expressed in Article 24. The rules of municipal law of coastal States have therefore remained in force. In Italy it is the rule laid down in Article 33 of the Customs Law, which cannot be said to be contrary to Article 10 of the Constitution. It follows that the offence of smuggling committed in the zone of vigilance, the so-called contiguous zone, is punishable in Italy, and that the arrest of a foreign national is lawful by Article 137 of the Customs Law. Equally lawful is the pursuit of a foreign vessel. * * *

The appellants contend that as Article 2 of the Maritime Code fixes the limit of the territorial sea at six miles from the coast and provides that this is without prejudice to various legal provisions which are to apply in specific cases, the only purpose of the Code was to lay down a six-mile limit for the territorial sea, reserving the right to extend the limit for specific purposes other than sovereignty, and less extensive than the latter. Accordingly, the zone of vigilance provided for by Article 33 of the Customs Law as being between six and twelve miles is not the territorial sea but merely an area of the sea which is subject to control for the purpose of prevention only and not punishment. Although in theory it may seem as if in the contiguous zone only police and preventive measures may be taken, because this zone forms part of the open sea rather than the territorial sea, a different view must be taken when one considers that the draft code of the Institute of International Law on the contiguous zone clearly recognizes the right to exercise jurisdiction. The International Law Commission, in its 1953 report was decidedly in favour of acknowledging the right to exercise jurisdiction, while in its 1951 draft it merely referred to preventive measures.

* * *

———

1. *Contraband outside the customs zone.* A British vessel transferred contraband goods to an Italian vessel outside the Italian 12 mile customs zone. An Italian coast guard crew boarded the British vessel on the high seas and arrested its crew. The Supreme Court of Italy ordered the release of the British crew on the ground that a state cannot exercise its jurisdiction over foreign vessels on the high seas, save in the exceptional case of hot pursuit. Re McSporran et al.; SS Sito, Court of Cassation, 1957, 89 J. de Dr. Int'l. 229 (1962).

2. *Contiguous zone under 1958 Convention and U.N. Convention.* Article 33 of the United Nations Convention reproduces verbatim Article 24 of the 1958 Convention on the Territorial Sea and the Contiguous Zone, except that it extends the breadth of the contiguous zone to 24 miles from the baseline, instead of the 12 miles provided in the 1958 Convention.

———

Hot Pursuit

Re Pulos and Others

Italy, Tribunal of Naples, 1976.
3 Italian Yearbook of International Law 282, 286 (1977).*

* * * On 11 November 1976 the vessel "Olimpios Hermes", flying the Greek flag, left the port of Antwerp carrying 25,000 cartons of cigarettes. * * * The voyage was regular until the Straits of Gibraltar were navigated after which, from 16 November there is no further entry in the log-book or the radio-telephone journal: the vessel was surprised on the morning of 29 November 1976 off the coast of the island of Ischia, 27 miles at 220 degrees from Punta Imperatore (this is clear from the file), that is on the high seas, surrounded by some 20 motor-boats whilst another 12 motor-boats were further away and nearer the land which was some 15 miles distant.

* * * It must be held established that one of the said motor-boats was carrying from the "Olimpios Hermes" 80 cartons of cigarettes (it should

———

* Reprinted by permission of Editoriale
Scientifica, s.r.l., Naples.

have taken 100 cartons but evidently the arrival of the Guardia di Finanza interrupted the operation).

* * * It is also clear from the file that after the motor-boat had taken on board the said cigarettes it fled despite the orders of the servicemen to stop; however, pursued without interruption first by helicopters and then by coastguards and the patrol boat of the Guardia di Finanza, it sailed initially towards the coast, returning, however, amongst the other motor-boats which were still in the vicinity of the vessel, and endeavoured, by reckless manoeuvres entailing a risk of collision, to hinder the pursuing craft and finally turned again towards the coast; it was captured in territorial waters (10 miles at 220 degrees from Punta Imperatore, Ischia) after the discharge of 70 rounds from light machine guns, some of which damaged the driving gear of the two 350 HP engines of the motor-boat. Thereafter the naval unit notified the capture of the motor-boat in territorial waters to the coastguard vessels Guglielmi and Di Sessa which were lying near the "Olimpios Hermes"; the latter was slowly moving away in a south-south-west direction and the coastguards called upon it to stop by visual and auditory signals and ultimately by hailing; when this proved fruitless the "Olimpios Hermes" was boarded 28 miles at 220 degrees from Punta Imperatore, that is on the high seas, the remainder of the cargo of cigarettes was seized and the persons on board the vessel were arrested. It was subsequently established that the contraband cigarettes carried by the "Olimpios Hermes", part of which had already been unloaded and part of which was about to be unloaded whilst on the high seas to the motor-boats for transshipment to the coast, had been sold in advance in Naples by a person or persons unknown to the prosecution.

* * * To that extent, since it is clear from the file that the police operation against the motor-boat which was captured, concerned an Italian-registered craft, with Italian nationals on board and moreover ended in Italian territorial waters following the said commission of the crime of smuggling 800 kg of foreign cigarettes, it merely remains to consider the lawfulness of that operation since the defence for the accused contests this point because, so far as the "Olimpios Hermes" is concerned, it constitutes the seizure of a foreign vessel on the high seas.

Italian criminal legislation covers all persons, apart from exceptions concerning so-called immunity, whether nationals or foreign, who are on the territory of the state (Art. 3, para. 1, c.p.), that is the territory of the Republic of Italy and accordingly all other places subject to the sovereignty thereof, including Italian vessels or aircraft wherever they may be, apart from exceptions created by international law (Art. 4, para. 2, c.p.). The sovereign right of the State covers the territorial waters up to 12 miles from the coast * * *.

Beyond the territorial waters lies the open sea or high seas. It is precisely the absence of State sovereignty over the area of sea lying beyond the territorial waters which creates the principle of the freedom of such seas which, as it is expressed in Article 2 of the Geneva Convention of 29 April 1958 on the High Seas, are open "to all nations" * * * and are guaranteed for the use of all States (for navigation, use of the resources and any other freedom acknowledged by the general principles of international law).

Upon this is based the further principle of international law, whether customary or conventional—Art. 6 of the said Geneva Convention—, which has also been adopted in municipal legislation (in the case of Italy in Art. 4 c.p. and Art. 4 c. nav.) whereby ships sailing on high seas come under the exclusive jurisdiction of the State whose flag they fly, save in exceptional cases expressly provided for in international law. Naturally the principle of freedom of the high seas is not without its limits since it is subject to derogations and restrictions on the basis of international customary law and international agreements. * * *

[The court said one limit was the right of a state to repress smuggling and the mother ship had engaged in smuggling through the use of small boats to take the cigarettes ashore.]

The other (specific) limit to the principle in question is that concerning the right of pursuit whereby the coastal State may pursue and seize on the high seas foreign civil vessels which are guilty of infringements of its legislation on internal waters or territorial waters. It must be held that this right is established first of all on the basis of international customary law, as is clear from its usual application in international disputes (in which the disputes were chiefly settled on the basis of the conduct of the State concerned in the exercise of that right) or in the replies given in this connexion by States in the course of the travaux préparatoires for the Hague Codification Conference of 1930; these States, by providing unanimously an affirmative answer to the questions drawn up by the League of Nations and arriving easily at agreement on the wording of Art. II of Appendix No. I to the Report of the second Commission which was systematizing the right, merely noted the existence of that custom for the purpose of establishing its details, prescribing limits to prevent abuses of it.

The same conclusions were reached in substance by the Geneva Conference on the High Seas which repeated at Art. 23 the old principles whilst extending their scope (by providing in the contiguous zone for pursuit by aircraft, that the ship or aircraft need not also be in territorial waters, that the ship or aircraft undertaking the arrest need not be that which initiated the pursuit where boats are operating as a team). In sum it may be stated that with regard to the right of pursuit, Art. 23 of the Geneva Convention, whilst going beyond the scope of the Codification Conference of 1930, is nevertheless narrower than the rules of the relevant customary international law where no specific limits are laid down, which indicates that States are tending to return to a broad conception of the right in order to provide better protection for their national interests which are increasingly threatened by well-trained and highly organised groups of criminals.

The said Art. 23 in fact lays down that foreign civil vessels may be arrested on the high seas if the following conditions are met:

(1) The laws and regulations of the coastal state were infringed;

(2) The vessel itself, or one of its boats, or other craft working as a team and using the said vessel as a mother ship was within the internal waters, territorial waters or the contiguous zone;

(3) Pursuit, begun in territorial waters or the contiguous zone and continued on the high seas, was uninterrupted, although the pursuing craft may have changed;

(4) Visual or auditory signals, which can be seen or heard, conveying an order to halt were given;

(5) Pursuit was given by warships or military aircraft, or other ships or aircraft on government service especially authorized to that effect.

With regard to the first condition it has been established above that there was an infringement of the customs legislation of the coastal State, Italy. The foreign vessel stationed itself near the boundary of the Italian territorial waters, following the sale in advance in Naples of the entire cargo of foreign cigarettes with which it was laden, and supplied those cigarettes to the numerous motor-boats which came from the coast to which they transshipped the cigarettes, in breach of customs legislation, until the arrival of the Guardia di Finanza cut short the unloading.

With regard to the second condition it is established that the vessel was supplying from its cargo the said motor-boats which, drawn up in a queue and in groups alongside the vessel (as is clear from the photographs taken from the helicopters), transshipped, or intended to transship, to the shore to the purchasers. The foreign vessel accordingly acted as the mother ship to those boats by furnishing the latter with the relevant materials, that is the cigarettes, which the boats took to the destination and then returned for more until the vessel was completely unloaded. * * * It may be inferred from the foregoing that those boats operated as a team with the vessel. The whole unloading and subsequent transshipment to the coast, organised by a buyer and sellers unknown, by their agents and by the person in charge of the vessel, with the assistance of the skippers of the motor-boats shows clearly that all those persons acted in concert for the same purpose namely to convey the cigarettes to the shore in breach of Italian customs legislation. This constitutes working as a team and in pursuance of the rule in question the situation is the same as if the vessel itself had entered the territory of the State in order to unload the cigarettes. * * *

With regard to the third condition it has already been shown that after the pursuit of the motor-boat, which carried over into and terminated in the territorial waters, the other craft of the Guardia di Finanza immediately began continuous pursuit of the foreign vessel which soon terminated in the seizure of the vessel on the high seas through which it had been slowly proceeding. It is quite clear that no relevance in the present case can attach to the fact that pursuit of the motor-boat began on the high seas (it nevertheless continued in the territorial waters where it also terminated) in that, since the boat in question was Italian, pursuit and any capture which took place on the high seas was entirely lawful. Accordingly, commencement of pursuit in the territorial waters constituted the precise circumstance permitting the pursuers to hold that they had obtained fulfilment of the condition for "extending" the right of pursuit to the foreign vessel on the high seas.

With regard to the fourth and fifth conditions it has been shown that they were fully complied with since visual and auditory signals were given to halt and the pursuit was carried out by the military craft of the Guardia di Finanza. * * *

———

1. *Hot pursuit under 1958 Convention and U.N. Convention.* The provisions of Article 23 of the Geneva Convention on the High Seas are extended *mutatis mutandis* by Article 111 of the United Nations Convention to violations in the exclusive economic zone or on the continental shelf. In *M/V "Saiga"* (No. 2), *supra*, pages 1352–1356, before the International Law of the Sea Tribunal it was contended by the applicant Saint Vincent and the Grenadines that the right of hot pursuit under Article 111 had not been exercised lawfully. Saint Vincent noted that assuming but without conceding that the *Saiga* had violated the laws of New Guinea its arrest did not satisfy the conditions of Article 111 of the Convention, as the pursuit was commenced when the vessel was well outside of the Guinean contiguous zone. The Tribunal stated that:

> 140.   Saint Vincent and the Grenadines asserts that, even if the *Saiga* violated the laws and regulations of Guinea as claimed, its arrest on 28 October 1997 did not satisfy the other conditions for hot pursuit under article 111 of the Convention. It notes that the alleged pursuit was commenced while the ship was well outside the contiguous zone of Guinea. The *Saiga* was first detected (by radar) in the morning of 28 October 1997 when the ship had crossed the southern border of the exclusive economic zone of Guinea.

> 141.   Saint Vincent and the Grenadines further asserts that, wherever and whenever the pursuit was commenced, it was interrupted. It also contends that no visual and auditory signals were given to the ship prior to the commencement of the pursuit, as required by article 111 of the Convention.

> 142.   Guinea denies that the pursuit was vitiated by any irregularity and maintains that the officers engaged in the pursuit complied with all the requirements set out in article 111 of the Convention. In some of its assertions, Guinea contends that the pursuit was commenced on 27 October 1997 soon after the authorities of Guinea had information that the *Saiga* had committed or was about to commit violations of the customs and contraband laws of Guinea and that the pursuit was continued throughout the period until the ship was spotted and arrested in the morning of 28 October 1997. In other assertions, Guinea contends that the pursuit commenced in the early morning of 28 October 1997 when the *Saiga* was still in the exclusive economic zone of Guinea. In its assertions, Guinea relies on article 111, paragraph 2, of the Convention.

> 143.   Guinea states that at about 0400 hours on 28 October 1997 the large patrol boat P328 sent out radio messages to the *Saiga* ordering it to stop and that they were ignored. It also claims that the small patrol boat P35 gave auditory and visual signals to the *Saiga* when it came

within sight and hearing of the ship. The Guinean officers who arrested the ship testified that the patrol boat sounded its siren and switched on its blue revolving light signals.

144. Guinea admits that the arrest took place outside the exclusive economic zone of Guinea. However, it points out that since the place of arrest was not in the territorial sea either of the ship's flag State or of another State, there was no breach of article 111 of the Convention.

* * *

146. The Tribunal notes that the conditions for the exercise of the right of hot pursuit under article 111 of the Convention are cumulative; each of them has to be satisfied for the pursuit to be legitimate under the Convention. In this case, the Tribunal finds that several of these conditions were not fulfilled.

147. With regard to the pursuit alleged to have commenced on 27 October 1997, the evidence before the Tribunal indicates that, at the time the Order for the Joint Mission of the Customs and Navy of Guinea was issued, the authorities of Guinea, on the basis of information available to them, could have had no more than a suspicion that a tanker had violated the laws of Guinea in the exclusive economic zone. The Tribunal also notes that, in the circumstances, no visual or auditory signals to stop could have been given to the *Saiga*. Furthermore, the alleged pursuit was interrupted. According to the evidence given by Guinea, the small patrol boat P35 that was sent out on 26 October 1997 on a northward course to search for the *Saiga* was recalled when information was received that the *Saiga* had changed course. This recall constituted a clear interruption of any pursuit, whatever legal basis might have existed for its commencement in the first place.

148. As far as the pursuit alleged to have commenced on 28 October 1998 is concerned, the evidence adduced by Guinea does not support its claim that the necessary auditory or visual signals to stop were given to the *Saiga* prior to the commencement of the alleged pursuit, as required by article 111, paragraph 4, of the Convention. Although Guinea claims that the small patrol boat (P35) sounded its siren and turned on its blue revolving light signals when it came within visual and hearing range of the *Saiga*, both the Master who was on the bridge at the time and Mr. Niasse who was on the deck, categorically denied that any such signals were given. In any case, any signals given at the time claimed by Guinea cannot be said to have been given at the commencement of the alleged pursuit.

149. The Tribunal has already concluded that no laws or regulations of Guinea applicable in accordance with the Convention were violated by the *Saiga*. It follows that there was no legal basis for the exercise of the right of hot pursuit by Guinea in this case.

150. For these reasons, the Tribunal finds that Guinea stopped and arrested the *Saiga* on 28 October 1997 in circumstances which did not justify the exercise of the right of hot pursuit in accordance with the Convention.

2. *Use of force in hot pursuit.* In 1977 a local union in Nantes, France, opposed the departure of a merchant vessel flying the Panamanian flag in a dispute over the wages paid the crew. It sailed down the estuary of the Loire river and to sea without taking a pilot aboard as required by law. The pursuit was begun by a small boat of the customs service and taken up by a submarine chaser. After ordering it to stop and firing warning shots, the submarine chaser fired machine gun bursts in the hull above the water, which were ignored. Thereupon the submarine chaser "deeming the infraction not serious enough to risk sinking the vessel," gave up the pursuit and the vessel escaped to the high seas. 81 Revue Générale de Droit International Public 1161–1162 (1977). Compare the case of *The I'm Alone, infra.* Note also the following extract:

The M/V "Saiga" (No. 2) Case

(Saint Vincent and the Grenadines v. Guinea)

International Tribunal for the Law of the Sea

38 International Legal Materials 1323 (1999).*

* * *

Use of force

153.   Saint Vincent and the Grenadines claims that Guinea used excessive and unreasonable force in stopping and arresting the *Saiga*. It notes that the *Saiga* was an unarmed tanker almost fully laden with gas oil, with a maximum speed of 10 knots. It also notes that the authorities of Guinea fired at the ship with live ammunition, using solid shots from large-calibre automatic guns.

154.   Guinea denies that the force used in boarding, stopping and arresting the *Saiga* was either excessive or unreasonable. It contends that the arresting officers had no alternative but to use gunfire because the *Saiga* refused to stop after repeated radio messages to it to stop and in spite of visual and auditory signals from the patrol boat P35. Guinea maintains that gunfire was used as a last resort, and denies that large-calibre ammunition was used. Guinea places the responsibility for any damage resulting from the use of force on the Master and crew of the ship.

155.   In considering the force used by Guinea in the arrest of the *Saiga*, the Tribunal must take into account the circumstances of the arrest in the context of the applicable rules of international law. Although the Convention does not contain express provisions on the use of force in the arrest of ships, international law, which is applicable by virtue of article 293 of the Convention, requires that the use of force must be avoided as far as possible and, where force is unavoidable, it must not go beyond what is reasonable and necessary in the circumstances. Considerations of humanity must apply in the law of the sea, as they do in other areas of international law.

---

* Reprinted with the permission of the American Society of International Law.

156. These principles have been followed over the years in law enforcement operations at sea. The normal practice used to stop a ship at sea is first to give an auditory or visual signal to stop, using internationally recognized signals. Where this does not succeed, a variety of actions may be taken, including the firing of shots across the bows of the ship. It is only after the appropriate actions fail that the pursuing vessel may, as a last resort, use force. Even then, appropriate warning must be issued to the ship and all efforts should be made to ensure that life is not endangered (*S.S. "I'm Alone"* case (*Canada/United States*, 1935), *U.N.R.I.A.A., Vol. III*, p. 1609; *The Red Crusader* case (*Commission of Enquiry, Denmark— United Kingdom*, 1962), *I.L.R., Vol. 35*, p. 485). The basic principle concerning the use of force in the arrest of a ship at sea has been reaffirmed by the Agreement for the Implementation of the Provisions of the United National Convention on the Law of the Sea of 10 December 1982 Relating to the Conservation and Management of Straddling Fish Stocks and Highly Migratory Fish Stocks. Article 22, paragraph (f), of the Agreement states:

1. The inspecting State shall ensure that its duly authorized inspectors:

   . . .

   (f) avoid the use of force except when and to the degree necessary to ensure the safety of the inspectors and where the inspectors are obstructed in the execution of their duties. The degree of force used shall not exceed that reasonably required in the circumstances.

157. In the present case, the Tribunal notes that the *Saiga* was almost fully laden and was low in the water at the time it was approached by the patrol vessel. Its maximum speed was 10 knots. Therefore it could be boarded without much difficulty by the Guinean officers. At one stage in the proceedings Guinea sought to justify the use of gunfire with the claim that the *Saiga* had attempted to sink the patrol boat. During the hearing, the allegation was modified to the effect that the danger of sinking to the patrol boat was from the wake of the *Saiga* and not the result of a deliberate attempt by the ship. But whatever the circumstances, there is no excuse for the fact that the officers fired at the ship itself with live ammunition from a fast-moving patrol boat without issuing any of the signals and warnings required by international law and practice.

158. The Guinean officers also used excessive force on board the *Saiga*. Having boarded the ship without resistance, and although there is no evidence of the use or threat of force from the crew, they fired indiscriminately while on the deck and used gunfire to stop the engine of the ship. In using firearms in this way, the Guinean officers appeared to have attached little or no importance to the safety of the ship and the persons on board. In the process, considerable damage as done to the ship and to vital equipment in the engine and radio rooms. And, more seriously, the indiscriminate use of gunfire caused severe injuries to two of the persons on board.

159. For these reasons, the Tribunal finds that Guinea used excessive force and endangered human life before and after boarding the *Saiga*, and

thereby violated the rights of Saint Vincent and the Grenadines under international law.

Right of Approach and Visit

Right of Approach

4 Whiteman, Digest of International Law 667 (1965).

The right of any ship to fly a particular flag must obviously be subject to verification by proper authority, and from this it follows that warships have a general right to verify the nationality of any merchant ship which they may meet on the high seas. This "right of approach" (*vérification du pavillon* or *reconnaissance*) is the only qualification under customary law of the general principle which forbids any interference in time of peace with ships of another nationality upon the high seas. Any other act of interference (apart from the repression of piracy) must be justified under powers conferred by treaty. Provided that the merchant vessel responds by showing her flag the captain of the warship is not justified in boarding her or taking any further action, unless there is reasonable ground for suspecting that she is engaged in piracy or some other improper activity. In the absence of good cause for suspicion his government may have to accept substantial responsibility for any interference. If the vessel approached shows a foreign flag even suspicious conduct will not justify active interference except in those cases, such as slave trading, where it is authorized by treaty. Otherwise the captain should merely report the incident to superior authority so that further action, if deemed necessary, may be taken through diplomatic channels.

In the past the question of the right of approach has been the subject of some controversy and has occasionally given rise to friction. Under modern conditions the general use of wireless and other developments have made the matter one of very small importance. Smith, The Law and Custom of the Sea (1959) 64–65.

Right of visit under 1958 Convention and U.N. Convention. See in the Documentary Supplement Article 22 of the 1958 Convention on the High Seas and Article 110 of the U.N. Convention on the Law of the Sea.

Note on Naval Incidents in and Near Territorial Waters

Naval people have a natural and understandable professional interest in getting in as close as feasible under the circumstances to the shoreside and operating bases of other naval powers. In modern times this interest has been whetted by the development of electronic and other sensing gear. This professional interest is served by the development of clear and widely-accepted rules about foreign naval presence in particular offshore zones, especially that of the territorial sea. All naval powers, including the United States, welcomed the specificity of the 1982 United Nations Convention in this regard, considering the earlier uncertainties resulting from differing views as to the width of the territorial sea. But navies will be navies and, perhaps, sometimes, enter or traverse a foreign territorial sea for reasons that do not appeal to the landside state or come absolutely within the privileges of innocent passage.

The former Soviet Union in a sense responded to its ship's treatment by the U.S. Navy in the incident reported above when in 1988 two small Soviet naval units deliberately bumped two American naval vessels, a cruiser and a destroyer, which had entered Soviet territorial waters in the Black Sea. There was a bit of hull damage; but the Americans left, claiming innocent passage, while the Soviets implied illicit intelligence-gathering and asserted a closed Black Sea. Under the 1982 Convention, the Americans would have been in violation of Article 19 if they had been doing anything specified in paragraph 2 thereof, and if the Convention had then been in effect and both the USSR and the United States parties thereto. *Mutatis mutandis,* the USSR could not close the Black Sea legally.

Questions: 1.   Article 19(2)(c) of the Convention is known as the "Pueblo Clause." Why? For further analysis and useful citations, see Butler, Innocent Passage and the 1982 Convention: The Influence of Soviet Law and Policy, 81 Am.J.Intl.L. 331 (1987).

2.   Assume both Russia and the United States are parties to the Convention and it is in effect. The Executive Officer of the American cruiser in Russian territorial waters is an ardent fisherman and wets a line whilst traversing. What is the legal situation if the Russians should come along-side and order departure?

3.   What if members of the crew of the U.S. cruiser were looking at bathers on Black Sea beaches, (a) by "*naked*" eyepower; (b) with binoculars or, (e) photographing them with telescopic lenses? Are there any legal remedies? If not, should there be proposed a convention against "offshore eaves-dropping", or some type of invasion of privacy out to, say 500 to 1000 nautical miles? Why or why not?

Piracy

Pirates Raid Ship Leased to U.S. Navy

The San Francisco Chronicle, January 31, 1985, p. 1.**

By the Associated Press. A band of pirates boarded an American cargo ship leased to the Navy as it passed through the Strait of Malacca on Tuesday, tying up the ship's master and making off with $19,471 from the ship's safe, the Pentagon said yesterday.

The attack occurred at night off the coast of Indonesia as the Falcon Countess was traveling from Bahrain to Guam, according to the Military Sealift Command. No one was injured, and the ship continued on its route.

** Reprinted by permission of the Associated Press.

The assault by the six pirates, who were reported to have been armed with knives and bayonets and traveling in a speedboat, is the second in two years involving a Navy-chartered ship in the Strait of Malacca. The Sealift Arctic was boarded by pirates on Jan. 10, 1983, prompting the Navy to issue instructions calling for guards to be posted when traveling through the area.

The Military Sealift Command said guards had been posted on the Falcon Countess, but their special watch "had just ended as the ship was leaving the 'pirate zone.' "

According to the command, piracy attacks in the area have become almost routine since 1981 and most commercial oil tankers traversing the strait have begun posting guards as well.

The Falcon Countess was travelling at 13 knots at the time of the attack, according to the Pentagon. The pirates apparently used bamboo poles with hooks to climb from their boat onto the ship's stern.

The pirates then rifled the ship's safe, taking $19,471, and threatened and tied up the master, * * *

The ship is chartered to the Military Sealift Command * * *, and was transporting jet fuel and diesel oil under Navy contract.

The Achille Lauro Affair. Five Palestinian passengers boarded the *Achille Lauro*, an Italian cruise liner, while it was in Genoa. On October 7, 1985, they seized the vessel as it proceeded from Alexandria to Port Said, beyond Egyptian territorial waters, having been discovered by a steward as "dubious" passengers. It would appear that their original intent was not to hijack the vessel but to use it as a means of gaining entry as tourists to the Israeli port of Ashod to carry out terrorist acts there. Claiming to be members of the Palestine Liberation Organization, they threatened to kill some of the approximately 450 persons_ crew and passengers, aboard unless Israel released fifty Palestinians it held in prison. Israel refused to negotiate. On October 9, Egypt arranged the removal of the terrorists, whereupon it was learned the latter had killed one of the passengers, an American national, Leon Klinghoffer. All these events and their aftermath, including the interception by U.S. military aircraft of a civilian plane believed to be carrying the terrorists, were reported at length by the media. It is discussed further in Chapter 17, *infra*.

On October 16, the Attorney General of the United States announced the terrorists were being charged with a number of crimes, including piracy. See 24 International Legal Materials 1555 (1985).

Article 15 of the 1958 Convention on the High Seas and Article 101 of the United Nations Convention on the Law of the Sea, both provide:

Piracy consists of the following acts:

(1) Any illegal acts of violence, detention, or any act of depredation, committed for private ends by the crew or the passengers of a private ship * * *, and directed:

> (a) On the high seas, against another ship * * *, or against persons or property on board such ship * * *

See the full text, as well as other provisions on piracy, in the two conventions, which appear in the Documentary Supplement.

On the basis of the facts stated above and the law in the documents, was the charge of piracy justified? If so, what is the point of the convention discussed in the material which follows? On the issue of piracy see Alfred P. Rubin's comprehensive work, THE LAW OF PIRACY (Naval War College 1988) and William R. Casto, *The Origins of Federal Admiralty Jurisdiction in an Age of Privateers, Smugglers, and Pirates,* 37 Am.J.Leg.Hist. (1993).

It was the *Achille Lauro* incident, which within reason should have been predictable, that illustrated the gaps in the piece-meal approach to dealing with international terrorism that caused a flurry of rapid activity, by international standards. No multilateral convention covered maritime hijacking and thus no obligations to extradite or prosecute in that situation existed. On March 10, 1988 the International Maritime Organization (IMO), a specialized agency of the United Nations, remedied this deficit by adopting an international Convention by consensus, for the Suppression of Unlawful Acts Against the Safety of Maritime Navigation, 27 ILM 672 (1988), along with a Protocol dealing with fixed platforms on the Continental Shelf. As with the other conventions dealing with specific aspects of international terrorism the Convention adopted which is reproduced in the Documentary Supplement contains wide bases of jurisdiction over the offence and the obligation, *aut dedere, aut judicare,* that is to extradite or submit the case to a state's own authorities for the purposes of prosecution. Note article 4 concerning the application of the Convention if the ship is navigating in or scheduled to navigate beyond the territorial sea of a single state.

Why do you think that Article 2(2) states that the Convention does not affect the immunities of warships and other governmental ships used for non-commercial purposes, and further in Article 9 that nothing in this Convention shall affect the rights of visit of foreign ships? On the Convention see Sharon A. Williams, *International Law and Terrorism: Age–Old Problems, Different Targets,* XXVI CYBIL 87 (1988), C. Blakesley, *Drugs International Law, and Protection of Human Liberty* (1992) and M. Halberstam, *Terrorism on the High Seas: The Achille Lauro, Piracy and the IMO Convention on Maritime Safety,* 82 AJIL 269 (1988). On the *Achille Lauro* incident before the adoption of the Convention see J. Paust, *Extradition and United States Prosecution of the Achille Lauro Hostage Takers: Navigating the Hazards,* 20 Vand. J. Int'l l. 235 (1987).

Convention for the Suppression of Unlawful Acts Against the Safety of Maritime Navigation

Adopted, Rome, March 10, 1988; 1678 UNTS 201 Reprinted in (1988), U.N.Doc. A/CONF. 183/9, IMO Doc. SUA/CON/15/Rw.1; 1993 Can.T. Series No. 10; 27 I.L.M. 668 (1988). Reproduced in the Documentary Supplement

2. THE EXCLUSIVE ECONOMIC ZONE

Table 1. *Leading EEZ beneficiaries**

State	Area of 200-mile zone (square nautical miles)	Offshore oil production 1992 in '000 tonnes (proven reserves in million tonnes)		Offshore natural gas production 1992 in million cubic metres (proven reserves in billion cubic metres)		Fish Catches or estimated potential (EP) in 200-mile zone (million tonnes)
1. USA	2,831,400	35,308	(707)	103,471	(1,189)	5.5 (1994)
2. France	2,083,400	0		0		Not available
3. Indonesia	1,577,300	57,270	(286)	7,236	(1,447)	6.7 (EP)
4. New Zealand	1,409,500	797	(18)	2,998	(82)	0.7 (1995)
5. Australia	1,310,900	24,153	(258)	16,952	(538)	2.5 (1995)
6. Russia	1,309,500	10,558	(41)	10,337	(17)	3.0 (1994)
7. Japan	1,126,000	697	(1)	286	(0)	6.5 (1994)
8. Brazil	924,000	26,145	(631)	7,236	(2)	0.6 (1995)
9. Canada	857,000	498	(162)	0	(298)	0.8 (1995)
10. Mexico	831,500	85,656	(5,712)	11,370	(1,926)	1.2 (1995)
11. Kiribati	770,000	Not available		Not available		Not available
12. Papua New Guinea	690,000	0	(37)	0	(314)	Not available
13. Chile	667,300	847	(54)	569	(65)	7.5 (1995)
14. Norway	590,500	89,640	(2,364)	32,044	(3,088)	3.0 (1995)
15. India	587,600	35,856	(1,047)	6,202	(430)	2.0 (EP)
Total all States	37,745,000	909,398	(37,276)	355,697	(25,393)	91.9 (1995)

Note: The figures for the areas of the EEZs of the USA and France include their overseas and dependent territories. There appear to be no separate figures for their metropolitan territories. The figure given for the area of Russia's EEZ is that given for the former Soviet Union. Russia's EEZ is unlikely to be significantly smaller. Micronesia and the Marshall Islands are almost certainly in the top fifteen States in terms of the area of their EEZs, but there appear to be no figures for these areas.

Source: Cols 1 and 2: *Limits in the Seas* No. 36, 4th revision (1981), p. 12; Cols 3 and 4: World Resources Institute, *World Resources 1994-95* (Oxford, Oxford University Press), 1994, pp. 354-5; Col 5: the figures (which are very approximate) have been calculated from a variety of EC, FAO and OECD publications.

---

* From R.R. Churchill and A.V. Lowe, THE LAW OF THE SEA, at 178 (3rd ed. 1999). Reprinted with the permission of Juris Publishing, Manchester University Press.

Table 2. *Distribution of world merchant shipping tonnage as at 31 December 1997: leading twenty States ('000 gross tons)*[*]

Panama	91,128		United Kingdom[c]	14,046
Liberia	60,058		Russia	12,282
Bahamas	25,523		USA	11,789
Greece	25,288		Philippines	8,849
Cyprus	23,653		St. Vincent	8,374
Malta	22,984		South Korea	7,430
Norway[a]	22,839		Germany	6,950
China[b]	22,110		India	6,934
Singapore	18,875		Turkey	6,567
Japan	18,516		Marshall Islands	6,314
			Other States	101,688
			Total all States	522,197

[*] From R.R. Churchill and A.V. Lowe, THE LAW OF THE SEA, at 256 (3rd ed. 1999). Reprinted with the permission of Juris Publishing, Manchester University Press.

[a] Includes 19,780 million gross tons on the Norwegian International Ship Register.

[b] Includes 5.771 million gross tons registered in Hong Kong, but excludes Taiwan.

[c] Includes 4.759 million gross tons registered in the Isle of Man, 4.610 registered in bermuda and 1.191 registered in other UK dependent territories.

Source: Lloyd's Register of Shipping, *World Fleet Statistics 1997*, London, 1998, pp. 13-15.

Summary of claims[a]

1. Territorial sea

Three miles: four
Four miles: one
Six miles: two (excluding Turkey)
Twelve miles: 121 (including Turkey)
Twenty miles: one

Thirty miles: two
Thirty-five miles: one
Fifty miles: one
200 miles: ten
No precise claim/not known: five

2. EFZ or EEZ

Twenty-five mile EFZ: one
32-52 mile EFZ: one
200 mile EFZ: nine
EFZ up to boundaries with
   neighboring States: two

EFZ of unspecified area: one
200 mile EFZ: ninety-three
EEZ up to boundaries with neighboring
   States: six
Other EEZ: three

3. Continental shelf

CSC definition: twenty-three
200 metres: three
200 miles:[**] forty-four
200 miles or edge of continental margin:
   thirty-three
Up to boundary with neighboring States: five

To depth of exploitation: six
Edge of continental margin: one
350 miles: one
100 miles beyond 2,500-metre isobath:
   two (including Madagascar)
No precise claim: thirty (not including Chile)

4. Other zones

Fifteen-mile contiguous zone: one
Eighteen-mile contiguous zone plus
   security: four (including Gambia)
Twenty-four mile contiguous zone for
   LOSC purposes: thirty-three
   (including Djibouti)
Twenty-four mile contiguous zone for
   LOSC purposes plus security: eleven
   (including Egypt, Haiti and Iran)
Twenty-four mile contiguous zone for
   Unspecified/unknown purposes: seven
Forty-one mile contiguous zone for
LOSV purposes plus security: one
Four-mile customs zone: one
Ten-mile customs zone: one
Twelve-mile anti-liquor smuggling zone: one

Twenty-four mile customs zone: one
Ten-mile security zone: one
Fifty-mile security zone: one
Fifty-mile pollution control zone: one
200-mile pollution control zone: one
Twenty-four mile zone for wrecks/cultural
   remains: three (including South Africa)
Continental shelf jurisdiction over wrecks
   and archeological remains: one
100-mile anti-pollution zone in Arctic
   waters: one

---

[a] From R.R. Churchill and A.V. Lowe, THE LAW OF THE SEA, at 471-472 (3rd ed. 1999). Reprinted with the permission of Juris Publishing, Manchester University Press.

[**] This includes claims to a 200-mile continental shelf as such, and claims to a 200-mile EEZ or territorial sea where no precise claim is made to a continental shelf.

United States: Proclamation of an Exclusive Economic Zone

22 International Legal Materials 461 (1983).*

THE WHITE HOUSE

Office of the Press Secretary fact sheet, March 10, 1983

UNITED STATES OCEANS POLICY

Today the President announced new guidelines for U.S. oceans policy

---

* Reprinted by permission of the American Society of International Law.

and proclaimed an Exclusive Economic Zone (EEZ) for the United States. This follows his consideration of a senior interagency review of these matters.

The EEZ Proclamation confirms U.S. sovereign rights and control over the living and non-living natural resources of the seabed, subsoil and superjacent waters beyond the territorial sea but within 200 nautical miles of the United States coasts. This will include, in particular, new rights over all minerals (such as nodules and sulphide deposits) in the zone that are not on the continental shelf but are within 200 nautical miles. Deposits of polymetallic sulphides and cobalt/manganese crusts in these areas have only been recently discovered and are years away from being commercially recoverable. But they could be a major future source of strategic and other minerals important to the U.S. economy and security.

The EEZ applies to waters adjacent to the United States, the Commonwealth of Puerto Rico, the Commonwealth of the Northern Mariana Islands (consistent with the Covenant and UN Trusteeship Agreement), and United States overseas territories and possessions. The total area encompassed by the EEZ has been estimated to exceed two million square nautical miles.

The President's statement makes clear that the proclamation does not change existing policies with respect to the outer continental shelf and fisheries within the U.S. zone.

Since President Truman proclaimed U.S. jurisdiction and control over the adjacent continental shelf in 1945, the U.S. has asserted sovereign rights for the purpose of exploration and exploitation of the resources of the continental shelf. Fundamental supplementary legislation, the Outer Continental Shelf Lands Act, was passed by Congress in 1953. The President's proclamation today incorporates existing jurisdiction over the continental shelf.

Since 1976 the United States has exercised management and conservation authority over fisheries resources (with the exception of highly migratory species of tuna) within 200 nautical miles of the coasts, under the Magnuson Fishery Conservation and Management Act. The U.S. neither recognizes nor asserts jurisdiction over highly migratory species of tuna. Such species are best managed by international agreements with concerned countries. In addition to confirming the United States sovereign rights over mineral deposits beyond the continental shelf but within 200 nautical miles, the Proclamation bolsters U.S. authority over the living resources of the zone.

The United States has also exercised certain other types of jurisdiction beyond the territorial sea in accordance with international law. This includes, for example, jurisdiction relating to pollution control under the Clean Water Act of 1977 and other laws.

The President has decided not to assert jurisdiction over marine scientific research in the U.S. EEZ. This is consistent with the U.S. interest in promoting maximum freedom for such research. The Department of State will take steps to facilitate access by U.S. scientists to foreign EEZ's under reasonable conditions.

The concept of the EEZ is already recognized in international law and the President's Proclamation is consistent with existing international law. Over 50 countries have proclaimed some form of EEZ; some of these are consistent with international law and others are not.

The concept of an EEZ was developed further in the recently concluded Law of the Sea negotiations and is reflected in that Convention. The EEZ is a maritime area in which the coastal state may exercise certain limited powers as recognized under international law. The EEZ is not the same as the concept of the territorial sea, and is beyond the territorial jurisdiction of any coastal state.

The President's proclamation confirms that, without prejudice to the rights and jurisdiction of the United States in its EEZ, all nations will continue to enjoy non-resource related freedoms of the high seas beyond the U.S. territorial sea and within the U.S. EEZ. This means that the freedom of navigation and overflight and other internationally lawful uses of the sea will remain the same within the zone as they are beyond it.

The President has also established clear guidelines for United States oceans policy by stating that the United States is prepared to accept and act in accordance with international law as reflected in the results of the Law of the Sea Convention that relate to traditional uses of the oceans, such as navigation and overflight. The United States is willing to respect the maritime claims of others, including economic zones, that are consistent with international law as reflected in the Convention, if U.S. rights and freedoms in such areas under international law are respected by the coastal state.

The President has not changed the breadth of the United States territorial sea. It remains at 3 nautical miles. The United States will respect only those territorial sea claims of others in excess of 3 nautical miles, to a maximum of 12 nautical miles, which accord to the U.S. its full rights under international law in the territorial sea. [But note the Presidential Proclamation, supra, extending the U.S. territorial sea to twelve nautical miles].

Unimpeded commercial and military navigation and overflight are critical to the national interest of the United States. The United States will continue to act to ensure the retention of the necessary rights and freedoms.

By proclaiming today a U.S. EEZ and announcing other oceans policy guidelines, the President has demonstrated his commitment to the protection and promotion of U.S. maritime interests in a manner consistent with international law.

UNITED STATES OCEANS POLICY
STATEMENT BY THE PRESIDENT.
MARCH 10, 1983

The United States has long been a leader in developing customary and conventional law of the sea. Our objectives have consistently been to provide a legal order that will, among other things, facilitate peaceful, international uses of the oceans and provide for equitable and effective management and conservation of marine resources. The United States also recognizes that all nations have an interest in these issues.

Last July I announced that the United States will not sign the United Nations Law of the Sea Convention that was opened for signature on December 10. We have taken this step because several major problems in the Convention's deep seabed mining provisions are contrary to the interests and principles of industrialized nations and would not help attain the aspirations of developing countries.

The United States does not stand alone in those concerns. Some important allies and friends have not signed the convention. Even some signatory states have raised concerns about these problems.

However, the convention also contains provisions with respect to traditional uses of the oceans which generally confirm existing maritime law and practice and fairly balance the interests of all states.

Today I am announcing three decisions to promote and protect the oceans interests of the United States in a manner consistent with those fair and balanced results in the Convention and international law.

First, the United States is prepared to accept and act in accordance with the balance of interests relating to traditional uses of the oceans— such as navigation and overflight. In this respect, the United States will recognize the rights of other states in the waters off their coasts, as reflected in the Convention, so long as the rights and freedoms of the United States and others under international law are recognized by such coastal states.

Second, the United States will exercise and assert its navigation and overflight rights and freedoms on a worldwide basis in a manner that is consistent with the balance of interests reflected in the convention. The United States will not, however, acquiesce in unilateral acts of other states designed to restrict the rights and freedoms of the international community in navigation and overflight and other related high seas uses.

Third, I am proclaiming today an Exclusive Economic Zone in which the United States will exercise sovereign rights in living and nonliving resources within 200 nautical miles of its coast. This will provide United States jurisdiction for mineral resources out to 200 nautical miles that are not on the continental shelf. Recently discovered deposits there could be an important future source of strategic minerals.

Within this Zone all nations will continue to enjoy the high seas rights and freedoms that are not resource related, including the freedoms of navigation and overflight. My proclamation does not change existing United States policies concerning the continental shelf, marine mammals, and fisheries, including highly migratory species of tuna which are not subject to United States jurisdiction. The United States will continue efforts to achieve international agreements for the effective management of these species. The proclamation also reinforces this government's policy of promoting the United States fishing industry.

While international law provides for a right of jurisdiction over marine scientific research within such a zone, the proclamation does not assert this right. I have elected not to do so because of the United States interest in encouraging marine scientific research and avoiding any unnecessary burdens. The United States will nevertheless recognize the right of other coastal states to exercise jurisdiction over marine scientific research within 200 nautical miles of their coasts, if that jurisdiction is exercised reasonably in a manner consistent with international law.

The Exclusive Economic Zone established today will also enable the United States to take limited additional steps to protect the marine environment. In this connection, the United States will continue to work through the International Maritime Organization and other appropriate international organizations to develop uniform international measures for the protection of the marine environment while imposing no unreasonable burdens on commercial shipping.

The policy decisions I am announcing today will not affect the application of existing United States law concerning the high seas or existing authorities of any United States Government agency.

In addition to the above policy steps, the United States will continue to work with other countries to develop a regime, free of unnecessary political and economic restraints, for mining deep seabed minerals beyond national jurisdiction. Deep seabed mining remains a lawful exercise of the freedom of the high seas open to all nations. The United States will continue to allow its firms to explore for and, when the market permits, exploit these resources. The administration looks forward to working with the Congress on legislation to implement these new policies.

Question: What do you think that the main issues were in negotiating the EEZ? Why and how is the EEZ considered *sui generis*? Do states automatically have sovereign rights as defined in Article 56(1)(a) and jurisdiction in Article 56(1)(b) or must they expressly assert such? Consider the difference between sovereign rights and sovereignty. When you consider the materials in the next section on the Continental Shelf consider whether the 200 mile EEZ was a compromise struck in Montego Bay in 1982 with those states not having a continental shelf.

Notes: 1. Straddling stocks. One of the sovereign rights a coastal state exercises in the EEZ is that of exclusive fisheries jurisdiction. Even before the 1982 United Nations Convention on the Law of the Sea was adopted many states including the United States in 1976 and Canada in 1977 had extended their fisheries jurisdiction to 200 nautical miles. However, the Articles contained in the 1982 Convention, including Article 63 and 64 did not address adequately the acute problem of fish stocks that straddled the EEZ of a coastal state and the high seas and highly migratory fish stocks. Refer also to Article 116. Based on these Articles could a coastal state seek to conserve and manage such stocks beyond its EEZ or would this amount to a violation of the high seas which are not amenable to the sovereignty of any state? A Convention was adopted to this end by the United Nations on August 4, 1995. Entitled The Agreement for the Implementation of the Provisions of the United Nations Convention on the Law of the Sea of 10 December 1982 Relating to the Conservation and Management of Straddling Fish Stocks and Highly Migratory Fish Stocks, U.N. Doc. A–CONF.164–37, its objective is to ensure long term conservation and sustainable use of such stocks and it mandates states to apply the precautionary approach in order to protect living marine resources and preserve the environment. It contains important provisions on state cooperation for conservation and management. As of June 30, 2000, it is not yet in force as 30 ratifications are necessary. There are so far 59 signatories and 28 states parties. An edited version is contained in the Documentary Supplement. See M. Hayashi, *The 1995 Agreement on Straddling Fish Stocks and Highly Migratory Fish Stocks: Significance For the Law of the Sea Convention*, 12 Ocean Y.B. 5 (1995) and 29 Oceans and Coastal Management 51 (1996) and D.H. Anderson, *The Straddling Stocks Agreement of 1995—An Initial Assessment*, 45, Int'l and Comp. L.Q. 463 (1996).

2. *Canadian Seizure of the Estai*. Canadian concerns concerning the depletion of northern cod, and later turbot, in the North Atlantic and the inability of the North Atlantic Fisheries organization, NAFO to control over-fishing in the NAFO Regulatory Area beyond the Canadian EEZ resulted in Canada enacting in 1994 the *Coastal Fisheries Protection Act*. This legislation provided that Canadian fisheries protection officers may board and inspect fishing vessels in Canadian waters or beyond in the NAFO Regulatory Area and seize a fishing vessel on reasonable grounds that the legislation has been violated. At the same time Canada entered a reservation to its acceptance of the jurisdiction of the International Court of Justice with respect to conservation and management measures and their enforcement by Canada in the NAFO Regulatory Area. The Regulations to the legislation contained a list of states whose vessels could be arrested. On March 3, 1995 Canada added Spain and Portugal. On March 9, 1995 Canada arrested the Spanish fishing vessel the *Estai*, 245 miles from the Canadian coast and escorted it to a Canadian port. Eventually, Canada and the European Union reached agreement on enforcing conservation in the NAFO Regulatory Area and the vessel and catch were released. Based on the Law of the Sea Convention, what would you consider the arguments that Canada and Spain would have raised if the International Court of Justice had heard the merits of the case? Spain had initiated a claim before the Court but based on the Canadian reservation the Court decided it lacked jurisdiction. See *Case Concerning Fisheries Jurisdiction* (Spain v. Canada), decision rendered December 1998.

3. *Question*: Do you think that conservation and management of a fisheries resource on the high seas with respect to straddling stocks can be justified on the grounds of necessity, retorsion, the precautionary principle and the principle of compatibility. Concerning the latter see Article 7 of the Agreement in the Documentary Supplement. See B. Kwiatkowska, *Expansion of Protective Jurisdiction: Future Challenges*, in Lessons From the Past—Blueprints for the Future, Proceedings of the 25th Canadian Council on International Law , (1997), and P.H. Bekker, *Grabcikovo–Nagymaros Project (Hungary v. Slovskia) Judgement*, 92 AJIL 273 (1998).

Report to the White House

Turning to the Sea: America's Ocean Future

September 2, 1999.
http:/www.publicaffairs.noaa.gov/oceanreport/intro.html

To the President:

In June of last year, you and Vice president Gore presided over the National Ocean Conference in Monterey, which drew together for the first time the full array of ocean interests–from government to industry, science to conservation. Among the many initiatives you and the Vice President launched at that historic gathering were new steps to restore coastal reefs, rebuild marine fisheries, preserve freedom of the seas, provide public access to military data and technology, enhance the competitiveness of America's ports, and protect our national marine sanctuaries from oil drilling.

In your address to the Conference, you also directed your Cabinet to report back to you with additional recommendations for a coordinated, disciplined, long-term federal ocean policy. Today, on behalf of the Cabinet and independent agencies with responsibility for ocean affairs, we are pleased to submit this report with our recommendations for a comprehensive policy to guide federal efforts into the 21st century.

The national dialogue begun in Monterey reflects the diverse, sometimes competing values inherent in our oceans. The seas are not only a source of economic benefit and a major avenue of world trade, but they are also a vital component of our national defense, a natural treasure to be preserved, and a fascinating frontier with secrets yet to be discovered. Our recommendations build on the broad consensus among Conference participants on the vital importance of the oceans to our nation's future–our economy, our security, our health and well-being–and the challenges we face in ensuring that all the oceans' many resources are protected and sustained.

* * *

[W]e have come to understand that the "boundless" oceans have their limits. They cannot provide unlimited fish to feed the growing populations of the world, nor can they absorb unlimited wastes from human activities. * * * [U]nchecked coastal development risks destroying ocean habitats that sustain economic activity and the natural splendour * * * [of] the sea.

* * *

In developing the recommendations contained in this report we have been guided by the following core principles:

SUSTAINING THE ECONOMIC BENEFITS OF THE OCEANS–Future generations deserve to inherit healthy, bountiful oceans.

STRENGTHENING GLOBAL SECURITY–Freedom of the seas is integral to the strength and security of our nation.

PROTECTING MARINE RESOURCES–Strong protection of our ocean and coastal environment using a precautionary approach and sound management, is no longer a choice but a necessity.

DISCOVERING THE OCEANS–Exploring and understanding the oceans is critical to our well-being and survival.

[The recommendations offered were in twenty-five subject areas. For example:]

To sustain economic benefits, we recommend working with coastal communities on plans for sustainable development; creating new incentives to reduce overfishing and develop guidelines for environmentally sound aquaculture; and increasing support for identifying and harvesting marine resources with pharmaceutical benefits.

To strengthen global security, we recommend working with the U.S. Senate to ensure early ratification of the Law of the Sea Convention; improving our ability to detect and deter maritime threats before they reach our shores; expanding efforts to maintain and exercise traditional freedoms of navigation and overflight around the world; and extending to 24 nautical miles the "contiguous zone" for enhanced federal law enforcement purposes.

To protect marine resources, we recommend coordinating federal efforts with state and local "smart growth" initiatives in the coastal zone; taking new steps to reduce urban and agricultural runoff; strengthening efforts to protect and restore essential fish habitat; and exploring the concept of marine wilderness areas.

To better understand and use the oceans, we recommend expanding coastal, open-ocean, and seafloor observations; integrating satellite, buoy, and other observing networks; advancing basic and applied research to increase our knowledge of ocean and coastal areas; supporting exploration in underwater areas; and establishing a coordinated effort to promote ocean science education.

To ensure a coordinated, focused federal effort to implement this report, we recommend establishment of a high-level taskforce composed of undersecretaries of relevant agencies and departments to be chaired by the Deputy National Security Advisor and the Chair of the Council on Environmental Quality.

We believe this report makes an important contribution to the national dialogue begun last year in Monterey. We look forward to working with you in developing and implementing a comprehensive federal policy to explore, protect, and sustain our oceans in the new millennium.

Sincerely,

William M. Daley
Secretary of Commerce

Richard Danzig
Secretary of the Navy

SECTION E.   ALLOCATION OF THE RESOURCES OF THE SEABED

1.   THE CONTINENTAL SHELF

1. ***Evolution of the doctrine of the continental shelf.*** President Truman proclaimed on September 28, 1945, that "the natural resources of the subsoil and sea bed of the continental shelf beneath the high seas but contiguous to the coasts of the United States" were regarded by the United States as appertaining to it and "subject to its jurisdiction and control." Thereafter, claims to the resources of the continental shelf were made by a large number of other states. Only thirteen years after the presidential proclamation, the Convention on the Continental Shelf was signed. As of June 30, 2000, 57 states were parties to it. The ready acceptance of the new basis of jurisdiction illustrates the capacity of international law to adapt and change very rapidly when the international community so demands. See also Articles 76–85 of the 1982 UN Convention on the Law of the Sea in the Documentary Supplement.

2. ***Exclusivity of Continental Shelf Rights***. All coastal states possessing a continental shelf have sovereign rights. The 1982 Convention is here in accord with customary international law and the 1958 Convention. When you consider the outer delimitation of the Continental Shelf contained Article 1 of the 1958 Convention why could it be viewed as defective? How does the 1982 Convention seek to remedy this? With respect to the Shelf beyond the 200 mile mark analyze the provisions on revenue sharing.

3. ***Commission on the Limits of the Continental Shelf***. The Commission was set up in March 1997 by the states parties to the 1982 Convention. Its mandate is to guide states whose actual shelf excedes 200 nautical miles. In particular look at Article 76(6) of the 1982 Convention. A state that makes a continental shelf claim beyond 200 miles is obligated to submit data to the Commission within a ten year period following ratification. At the 1999 meeting of the Commission scientific and and technical guidelines were adopted to facilitate the preparations for states making submissions.

4. ***Division of the resources of the continental shelf between the States and the federal government.*** In the Submerged Lands Act of May 22, 1953, 67 Stat. 29, the States of the U.S. were granted rights to the lands which are part of the continental shelf of the United States up to three nautical miles from the coast on the Atlantic and Pacific Oceans, and up to nine nautical miles in the Gulf of Mexico if the states involved could establish an historical claim to such distance. Beyond those limits, the federal government controls the resources of the continental shelf. Outer Continental Shelf Lands Act, August 7, 1953, 67 Stat. 462. The division of the resources does not create an issue of international law, however. This presents a domestic law issue, as illustrated in the following case.

United States v. Florida

United States Supreme Court, 1976.
425 U.S. 791, 96 S.Ct. 1840, 48 L.Ed.2d 388.

DECREE

The joint motion for entry of a decree is granted.

For the purpose of giving effect to the decision and opinion of this Court announced in this case on March 17, 1975, 420 U.S. 531, and to the Supplemental Report of the Special Master filed January 26, 1976, it is Ordered, Adjudged, and Decreed as Follows:

As against the State of Florida, the United States is entitled to all the lands, minerals, and other natural resources underlying the Atlantic Ocean more than 3 geographic miles seaward from the coastline of that State and extending seaward to the edge of the Continental Shelf, and the State of Florida is not entitled to any interest in such lands, minerals, and resources. As used in this decree, the term "coastline" means the line of ordinary low water along that portion of the coast which is in direct contact with the open sea and the line marking the seaward limit of inland waters, as determined under the Convention on the Territorial Sea and the Contiguous Zone, 15 U.S.T. (Pt. 2) 1606.

As against the United States, the State of Florida is entitled to all the lands, minerals, and other natural resources underlying the Atlantic Ocean extending seaward from its coastline for a distance of 3 geographic miles, and the United States is not entitled, as against the State of Florida, to any interest in such lands, minerals, or resources, with the exceptions provided by Section 5 of the Submerged Lands Act, 43 U.S.C. § 1313.

As against the State of Florida, the United States is entitled to all the lands, minerals and other natural resources underlying the Gulf of Mexico more than 3 marine leagues from the coastline of that State; the State of Florida is not entitled to any interest in such lands, minerals, and resources. Where the historic coastline of the State of Florida is landward of its coastline, the United States is additionally entitled, as against the State of Florida, to all the lands, minerals, and other natural resources underlying the Gulf of Mexico more than 3 marine leagues from the State's historic coastline (but not less than 3 geographic miles from its coastline), and the State of Florida is not entitled to any interest in such lands, minerals, and resources. As used in this decree, the term "historic coastline" refers to the coastline as it existed in 1868, as to be determined by the parties.

As against the United States, the State of Florida is entitled to all the lands, minerals, and other natural resources underlying the Gulf of Mexico extending seaward for a distance of 3 marine leagues from its coastline or its historic coastline, whichever is landward, but for not less than 3 geographic miles from its coastline; the United States is not entitled, as against the State of Florida, to any interest in such lands, minerals, or resources, with the exceptions provided by Section 5 of the Submerged Lands Act, 43 U.S.C. § 1313.

For the purpose of this decree, the Gulf of Mexico lies to the north and west, and the Atlantic Ocean to the south and east, of a line that begins at a point on the northern coast of the island of Cuba in 83° west longitude, and extends thence to the northward along that meridian of longitude to 24°35' north latitude, thence eastward along that parallel of latitude through Rebecca Shoal and the Quicksands Shoal to the Marquesas Keys, and thence through the Florida Keys to the mainland at the eastern end of Florida Bay, the line so running that the narrow waters within the Dry Tortugas Islands, the Marquesas Keys, and the Florida Keys, and between the Florida Keys and the mainland, are within the Gulf of Mexico.

There is no historic bay on the coast of the State of Florida. There are no inland waters within Florida Bay, or within the Dry Tortugas Islands, the Marquesas Keys, and the lower Florida Keys (from Money Key to Key West), the closing lines of which affect the right of either the United States or the State of Florida under this decree.

Jurisdiction is reserved by this Court. . . .

ODECO (Ocean Drilling and Exploration Co.) v. Torao Oda, Superintendent of Shiba Revenue Office

Japan, District Court of Tokyo, 1982;
27 Japanese Annual of International Law 148 (1984).[a]

TEXT OF JUDGMENT

1. All of the plaintiff's claims are dismissed.

2. The cost of the action shall be borne by the plaintiff.

* * *

Summary: The plaintiff of the case is a company incorporated under the laws of Panama. From 1971 to 1973, the company undertook exploring activities of the seabed outside the territorial sea of Japan under a contract concluded with a Japanese and an American company. Taxes were levied by the Revenue Office on the income derived from the boring activities of the seabed for the years 1971, 1972 and 1973. The company did not file final income tax returns by reason that the seabed outside the territorial sea does not fall within the "enforcement area" as defined in the Japanese Corporation Tax Law. The State authorities rejected this view.

* * *

OPINION OF THE COURT

* * *

When a foreign corporation like the plaintiff has the "income accruing from domestic areas" defined in Article 138 of the Corporation Tax Law, it is under obligation to pay corporation taxes [Article 4(2) of the same Law]. The range of taxable incomes includes the kinds of income accruing from domestic areas enumerated in each paragraph of Article 141 of the same Law and is determined in accordance with the kinds of foreign corporation

a. Original in Japanese. Translation into English by the editorial staff of The Japanese Annual of International Law. Re- printed with the permission of the International Law Association of Japan.

enumerated in each paragraph of the same Article [Article 9 of the same Law]. The defendant contends that the plaintiff's incomes from the drilling activities concerned correspond to the "income derived from activities within the domestic areas" defined as one of the incomes accruing from domestic areas in Article 138(1) of the Corporation Tax Law; that the plaintiff corresponds to a "foreign corporation which engages in other activities within the domestic areas for more than one year" defined in Article 141(2) of the same Law; and that the plaintiff is under obligation to pay corporation taxes in respect to the income derived from the drilling activities concerned among its income in each business year. On the other hand, the plaintiff contends that the region where the plaintiff engaged in the drilling activities concerned is outside the territorial sea of Japan; that Japan's right to impose taxes does not extend over such a region; that the effect of the Corporation Tax Law does not extend, either; and that the region does not correspond to the "domestic areas" defined in the same Law.

And so, in the first place, the question is whether Japan's right to impose taxes extends over the region where the drilling activities were performed. The defendant contends that the region is outside the territorial sea of Japan but it is part of Japan's continental shelf, and that Japan has sovereign rights over the continental shelf by virtue of customary international law, whereby Japan can exercise a right to impose taxes in the region concerned. The Court must examine the existence and contents of customary international law in relation to the continental shelf.

According to the evidence [omitted], with regard to the existence and contents of customary international law concerning the continental shelf at the time of 1971 to 1973, the following facts can be recognized:

A. Harry S. Truman, President of the United States, proclaimed "the Policy of the United States of America with regard to the Natural Resources of the Subsoil and Seabed of the Continental Shelf" on September 28, 1945. This Proclamation read as follows:

* * *

Now therefore, I, Harry S. Truman, President of the United States of America, do hereby proclaim the following policy of the United States of America with respect to the natural resources of the subsoil and seabed of the continental shelf.

Having concern for the urgency of conserving and prudently utilizing its natural resources, the Government of the United States regards the natural resources of the subsoil and seabed of the continental shelf beneath the high seas but contiguous to the coasts of the United States as appertaining to the United States, subject to its jurisdiction and control. In cases where the continental shelf extends to the shores of another state, or is shared with an adjacent state, the boundary shall be determined by the United States and the state concerned in accordance with equitable principles. The character as high seas of the waters above the continental shelf and the right to their free and unimpeded navigation are in no way thus affected.

Although the scope of the continental shelf is not defined in this proclamation itself, it was thought, according to the statement reported in the newspapers, that it extends to where the depth of the superjacent waters is 100 fathoms (approximately 200 meters).

The Truman Proclamation awakened the states to the possibility of a right over the resources beneath the seabed of the high seas and initiated the formulation of international law with regard to the continental shelf. Following the Truman Proclamation, a great number of states made proclamations or legislation concerning the continental shelf, but their contents were not uniform.

B.   Under these circumstances the U.N. International Law Commission (I.L.C.) embarked in 1949 on the codification of rules of the high seas. Within that framework, it discussed draft articles on the continental shelf from 1950 to 1956. In 1956 it adopted draft conventions on the law of the seas and submitted them to the United Nations. Article 68 of the draft convention provides that the coastal state may exercise over the continental shelf sovereign rights for the purpose of exploring it and exploiting its natural resources. As to the meaning of natural resources, the attitude of the I.L.C. changed. According to the understanding of the I.L.C. in 1951, natural resources, no doubt, were limited to the mineral resources. In the fourth report (1953) by Francois, special rapporteur, which was the basis of the deliberation of the I.L.C., the words "natural resources" were replaced by the words "mineral resources." In the session of 1953, however, the opinion was put forward that the living resources belonging to sedentary species should be regarded as part of the resources in the continental shelf, and this opinion was supported by the majority of the I.L.C. Eventually, the I.L.C. concluded that the natural resources in the continental shelf should include the living organisms belonging to sedentary species.

C.   The United Nations, having discussed the draft on the Law of Sea that the I.L.C. had proposed, and according to the recommendation of the commission, decided by resolution on February 24, 1957 to convene the Conference on the Law of Sea and to provide for the result in a proper treaty or other documents. The conference was convened on February 24, 1958 at the European headquarters of the U.N., and the Convention on the Continental Shelf was adopted by 57 votes to three (Japan, West Germany, and Belgium) with eight abstentions. This Convention was signed by 46 states and came into effect on June 10, 1964 by the ratification or accession of 22 states. As of March 15, 1969, the number of the states that ratified or acceded to the convention was 39. Japan has neither ratified nor acceded to the convention. The provisions of the Convention on the Continental Shelf are as follows.

[The court quotes Articles 1, 2, 3 and 12 of the convention.]

Japan, West Germany, and Belgium criticized the system of the continental shelf itself in the conference, but the basic idea that the coastal state has monopolistic rights for the development of resources of the area called continental shelf was approved by most of the states; this gained a position which could no longer change. But, an agreement about the nature of the rights the coastal state has and the scope of the resources involved in the continental shelf system could never be easily reached. The argument about the nature of the rights * * * never [left] in much doubt that the coastal state could monopolize the development of the continental shelf. Getting into actual problems, the subject of warmest debate was what particular resources the coastal state should have the monopoly to develop.

The European states such as Sweden, Norway, Greece, Spain, Denmark, and Italy insisted that these should be limited to mineral resources. At the other end of the debate, Latin American states, Iceland, and Indonesia insisted, although this insistence was virtually neglected, that the resources should include deep-sea fishes and species living in the bottom of the sea. A compromise proposal of the six states, Australia, Ceylon, Malaya, India, Norway, and the United Kingdom eventually became the text of Article 2, paragraph 4 of the adopted convention * * *. France, in its accession on June 14, 1965, made an interpretative declaration: "France considers that the crustacea except for the crab called barnade are excluded for living organisms belonging to sedentary species."

[Japan objected to the inclusion in "natural resources" of living organisms belonging to sedentary species, because of its fishermen's long established practice of recovering oysters—for pearls—on the continental shelf of other states such as Australia.

France's objections were based on the interest of its fishermen in lobsters off the coast of Brazil.]

D. The International Court of Justice made the following judgment on the so-called North Sea Continental Shelf Case, February 20, 1969.

* * * [This] is the most fundamental of all the rules of law relating to the continental shelf, enshrined in the 1958 Geneva Convention,—namely that the rights of the coastal State in respect of the area of continental shelf that constitutes a natural prolongation of its land territory into and under the sea exist *ipso facto* and *ab initio*, by virtue of its sovereignty over the land, and as an extension of it in an exercise of sovereign rights for the purpose of exploring the seabed and exploiting its natural resources. In short, there is here an inherent right. In order to exercise it, no special legal process has to be gone through, nor have any special legal acts to be performed. Its existence can be declared (and many States have done this) but does not need to be constituted. To echo the language of the Geneva Convention, it is "exclusive" in the sense that if the coastal State does not choose to explore or exploit the areas of shelf appertaining to it, that is its own affair, but no one else may do so without its express consent.

More fundamental than the notion of proximity appears to be the principle of the natural prolongation or continuation of the land territory or domain, or land sovereignty of that State. There are various ways of formulating this principle, but the underlying idea, namely of an extension of something already possessed, is the same, and it is this idea of extension which is, in the Court's opinion, determinant. Submarine areas do not really appertain to the coastal State because * * * they are near it. They are near it of course; but this would not suffice to confer title, * * * What confers the ipso jure title which international law attributes to the coastal State in respect of its continental shelf, is the fact that the submarine areas concerned may be deemed to be actually part of the territory over which the coastal State already has dominion,—in the sense that, although covered with water, they are a prolongation or continuation of that territory, an extension of it under the sea.

* * * [S]peaking generally, it is a characteristic of purely conventional rules and obligations that, in regard to them, some faculty of making unilateral reservations may, within certain limits, be admitted, * * * whereas this cannot be so in the case of general or customary law rules and obligations which, by their very nature, must have equal force for all the members of the international community, and cannot therefore be the subject of any right of unilateral exclusion exercisable at will by any one of them in its own favor. Consequently, it is to be expected when, for whatever reasons, rules or obligations of this order are embodied, or are intended to be reflected in certain provisions of a convention, such provisions will figure amongst those in respect of which a right of unilateral reservation is not conferred, or is excluded. This expectation is, in principle, fulfilled by Article 12 of the Geneva Continental Shelf Convention "other than to Article 1 to 3 inclusive"— these three Articles being the ones which, it is clear, were then regarded as reflecting, or as crystallizing, received or at least emergent rules of customary international law relative to the continental shelf, amongst them the question of the seaward extent of the shelf; the kind of the natural resources to which these relate; and the preservation intact of the legal status as high seas of the waters over the shelf, and the legal status of the superjacent air-space.

E.   As was mentioned above, in spite of the claim of rights of each country to its continental shelf, which the Truman Proclamation had led, followed by discussions in the International Law Commission of the United Nations, the international law on the continental shelf has been formed gradually. The adoption of the Convention on the Continental Shelf in the Conference on the Law of Sea and the subsequent practice of states (Judge Lachs states in his dissenting opinion in the judgment of the North Sea Continental Shelf Case of the ICJ, it is noteworthy that about seventy states are now engaged in the exploration and development of the continental shelf areas) make the basic idea of the continental shelf incorporated in Articles 1 through 3 of the Convention on the Continental Shelf into rules-of-custom international law. The existence of the customary international law was affirmed by the judgment on the North Sea Continental Shelf Case of the ICJ.

But it cannot be said that all of the provisions of Articles 1 through 3 have become rules-of-custom international law. The judgment of the ICJ states: "These three provisions were at that time clearly regarded to reflect or embody the received or appearing rules on customary international law relating to the continental shelf." It does not state that all these three Articles are rules already received as customary international law. Article 2, paragraph 4 of the Convention includes "living organisms belonging to sedentary species" in the resources whose development the coastal state can monopolize, but, as is stated above, this point met a division in opinions in the U.N. International Law Committee and the Committee on the Law of Sea. * * * It was only the result of the compromise between the states in the Conference on the Law of Sea that living organisms belonging to sedentary species were incorporated into resources of the continental shelf.

In addition, * * * France made an interpretative declaration that "France thinks that the crustacea except for the crab called barnade are excluded from living organisms belonging to sedentary species," and from these facts, the very concept of "living organisms belonging to sedentary species" itself allows various interpretations and is not necessarily clear. Accordingly, it is a rule legislated by the Convention on the Continental Shelf and cannot be said to be a rule-of-custom international law that the coastal state can monopolize the capture of living organisms belonging to sedentary species. And there is no document attesting that that rule has, after the conclusion of the convention, grown into customary international law. On the other hand, the rules incorporated in Articles 1–3, except for the resources of sedentary species, are the basic system of the continental shelf and can be seen by the time of the judgment on the North Sea Continental Shelf Case of the ICJ, February 1969, at the latest to have become customary international law.

F.   Accordingly, in the years * * * [involved in this case,] Japan could exercise its sovereign rights for exploring and developing the mineral resources of the Japanese continental shelf, (the continental shelf contiguous to the Japanese coast but outside the territorial seas of Japan) as a warrant of customary international law, even if Japan has not acceded to the convention. The nature and content of the sovereign rights are as follows.

1.   The territorial sovereignty of a state is a right to exercise governmental functions toward the territorial area belonging to the state (territory, territorial sea, and territorial air) generally and exclusively, and for the purpose of realizing the aims that state fixes in its disposition. The sovereign rights to the continental shelf are extensions of the territorial sovereignty to the area of the bottom of the high seas, but the reason it is called sovereign rights and not sovereignty is based on the fact that these rights are limited by the purpose of exploring (exploring the continental shelf itself when the varied resources are not yet known) and developing (mining the already known resources); and furthermore they cannot affect any status of the superjacent waters as high seas or that of the air space above those waters or high air, except to the extent necessary to the realization of this purpose. But the sovereign rights to the continental shelf include all the sovereign rights necessary to the exploration and development of the mineral resources of the continental shelf or relate to it—that is, legislative, executive, and judicial powers. Namely, they are limited by the purpose, but have a complete nature in the scope of the purpose mentioned above, comprehensive and exclusive, and are not different from sovereignty.

2.   Accordingly, the sovereign rights to the continental shelf include, ipso facto, the right of taxation which is a side of the sovereignty. That is, the sovereign rights to the continental shelf is extension of the territorial

sovereignty as long as its subject is the exploration or development of mineral resources or related activities, and it exercises jurisdiction over these activities as a domestic withheld income. Furthermore, the services by the contract are also included in the scope of the above-mentioned purpose as long as they are related to the exploration or development of mineral resources in the continental shelf, and taxes are imposed as those within the territorial jurisdiction as long as the services are done on the continental shelf.

3.   The sovereign rights to the continental shelf are based on the idea of extension of the territorial sovereignty to the sea bottom area under high seas, which is an inherent right of a state and independent to neither an effective or ideal preoccupation nor an express declaration. Accordingly, the exercise of the sovereign rights need neither express declaration by the state in advance, nor special legal processes or acts.

* * *

———

Note: Within the Canadian confederation there has also been an issue of whether the federal government or the provinces have jurisdiction over the Continental Shelf. See *Re Newfoundland Continental Shelf*, [1984] 1 S.C.R. 86 for an interesting analysis of the evolution of international law on this topic.

2.   MINERAL RESOURCES BEYOND NATIONAL JURISDICTION

Technological advances induce quest for law as to mineral resources under the high seas. For most of the modern era, conflicts of national interest did not arise as to the extraction of substances from the waters, bed, and subsoil of what once were called the high seas but now must be more exactly characterized as areas beyond national jurisdiction. By analogy to high seas fishing, anyone could take natural materials from these waters and even the fixing of installations by mooring and other methods was considered not to be illegal *per se.*

By the 1960s, technologies for the drilling for oil and gas in very deep water and collection and lifting from the seabed of polymetallic nodules became feasible. These technological developments coincided in a general way with increasing need everywhere for liquid hydrocarbons and deficiencies in national production by some states, particularly highly industrialized states such as the United States, of highly strategic alloy metals contained in the seabed nodules, viz., manganese, cobalt, and nickle. Copper and iron (usually in highly attractive ferromanganese compounds) are also found in nodular form. Nodules vary in metallic composition and content from place to place. The quantities are immense, and the areas of concentration are vast.

It was the developed states, particularly the United States in its private sector, that brought about the improvements in technology that have made extraction of the substances referred to feasible. These states also have capabilities for mobilizing the capital such operations will require. The less well developed states, faced with disappointments as to expectations for rapid growth and in an environment of a widening gap— rather than a narrowing one—between rich countries and poor countries, viewed with apprehension the prospect that the planet's last source of natural wealth not already appropriated would be denied to them through preemption by states able to take the lead in exploitation.

In the developed states, the profit motive in the private sector (reflected, of course, in national politics) and a security interest in the public sector created pressures for action to use the new technology on an individual state basis. But in these same states, a prudent concern for national image, the verdict of history, and the broader national interest in world stability supported the search for means to achieve equitable sharing of the new resources on the basis of respective needs and national contributions.

In 1968 a private international consortium, without leave of any state, claimed exclusive rights to the extraction of seabed brine from a large area in the Red Sea, asserting that no licensing authority existed anywhere. See Nanda, Some Legal Questions on the Peaceful Uses of Ocean Space, 9 Va.J.Int'l L. 343, 384 (1969). Other plans to act unilaterally were announced and received publicity. The basic issues came rapidly to the attention of various segments of the United Nations, the Senate Committee on Foreign Relations, and legal writers.

Collins, Mineral Exploitation of the Seabed: Problems, Progress, and Alternatives, 12 Natural Resources Lawyer 599, at 636 (1979)*, describes what has come to be recognized as a key development:

> * * * August 17, 1967, was the date on which the seabed question was born. On that date Malta's United Nations ambassador, Arvid Pardo, proposed that an item entitled "Declaration and Treaty Concerning the Reservation Exclusively for Peaceful Purposes of the Seabed and of the Ocean Floor Underlying the Seas Beyond the Limits of Present National Jurisdiction and the Use of their Resources in the Interests of Mankind" be added to the agenda of the General Assembly. It was Dr. Pardo's subsequent speech to the General Assembly that set off the explosion of international interest in the formation of a regime to exploit the seabed not then under national jurisdiction. Pardo * * * mesmerized many United Nations delegations from developing countries with his assertions that the vast, readily exploitable mineral wealth of the seabed could quickly redress the inequities of economic development * * *.

The Pardo proposal contained the following essential points:

— that the ocean floor and its resources * * * are to be considered the common property of mankind;

— that they are not subject to national appropriation;

— that they must be used for peaceful purposes only;

* Reprinted by permission of the Section   Bar Association.
on Natural Resources Law of the American

— that the resources should be developed cooperatively, not competitively, and particularly for the benefit of developing nations; and

— that an international regime be created, within the framework of the United Nations or emanating from the United Nations, to guarantee these principles and plan for the development of common ocean resources.

The initiative just described set in train a long process of negotiations at UNCLOS III. However, as early as 1969 the General Assembly had adopted Resolution 2574 (XXIV) calling for a moratorium on deep seabed activities pending the establishment of an international regime. In 1970 the same body adopted the Declaration of Principles Governing the Seabed and the Ocean Floor, and Subsoil Thereof Beyond National Jurisdiction, Resolution 2749 (XXV), without a vote. Article 3 of this resolution declared that:

No State or person, natural or juridical, shall claim, exercise or acquire rights with respect to the area or its resources incompatible with the international regime to be established and the principles of this Declaration.

On the one hand the less well developed states made determined efforts to vest exclusive rights of exploitation of seabed resources beyond national jurisdiction in an international authority so organized they could dominate it by taking full advantage of their number. On the other hand the developed states, while willing to accommodate the principles expressed above, resisted the creation of an international authority not responsive to their interests even though the successful operation of the authority would depend on technology and risk capital that they alone could provide.

In some quarters in developed states, the free enterprise system as to mining was seen as imperilled by the insistence of the developing states that structured international controls be provided for all significant activities in the seabed area beyond national jurisdiction. Concern about national security in relation to supplies of scarce substances was prominent in developed states. Some states, mainly developing ones, are producers on land of vital metals found also on the ocean floor in nodules. These feared damage to markets and price structure from additional production of these metals from the new source and wished to have such production controllable in support of their interests, or alternatively, guaranteed commodity price support systems for their production of the minerals concerned.

The seabed beyond national jurisdiction is named "The Area" in the Convention on the Law of the Sea and Articles 133–191 of Part XI of the Convention are devoted to organizing the exploitation of its resources which are declared in Article 136 to be "the common heritage of mankind". The Authority set up to function in the Area consists of an Assembly, Articles 159–160, a Council which is the executive body of the seabed authority, Articles 161–165, a Secretariat, Articles 166–169, and an Enterprise, Article 170, which is to carry out the activities in the Area. In this authority, however, the conflicting state interests sketched above were not harmonized. See the 1994 agreement relating to the implementation of Part XI (in the Documentary Supplement), the aim of which is to facilitate universal participation in the convention, and deals, *inter alia*, with the treatment of registered pioneer investors.

Note of January 13, 1986, from the United States Mission to the United Nations Addressed to the Secretary–General of the United Nations

U.N. Office of the Special Representative of the Secretary–General for the Law of the Sea, Law of the Sea Bulletin No. 7, April 1986, p.74.

The Government of the United States wishes to provide the United Nations with the attached notices published in the Federal Register of the United States, which provide public notices of the issuance, by the National Oceanic and Atmospheric Administration, United States Department of Commerce, of four licences authorizing deep seabed hard mineral resource exploration in specified areas of the east-central Pacific Ocean * * *. Included in the Federal Register notices are the geographical coordinates of the deep seabed areas within which deep seabed hard mineral exploration has been authorized.

These licences were issued pursuant to the Deep Seabed Hard Mineral Resources Act. In accordance with section 102(b)(2) of that Act, these licences are exclusive as against "any other United States citizen or any citizen, national or government agency of, or any legal entity organized or existing under the laws of, any reciprocating State." Reciprocating States are those states designated as such in accordance with section 118 of the Act.

The Government of the United States also calls attention to section 3(a) of the Act, which states:

By the enactment of the Act, the United States:

(1) Exercises jurisdiction over United States citizens and vessels, and foreign persons and vessels otherwise subject to its jurisdiction, in the exercise of the high seas freedom to engage in exploration for, and commercial recovery of, hard mineral resources of the deep seabed in accordance with generally accepted principles of international law recognized by the United states, but

(2) Does not thereby assert sovereignty or sovereign or exclusive rights or jurisdiction over, or the ownership of, any areas or resources in the deep seabed.

In addition to confirming for the United Nations, and through its Member States, the existence of licences for exploration of the hard mineral resources of the deep-sea bed, the Government of the United States takes this opportunity to state that, in view of the international legal obligation of all States to avoid unreasonable interference with the interests of other States in the exercise of the freedoms of the high seas, the Government of the United States stands ready to consult on this subject with any other Government. The Government of the United States also notes that it has been informed by representatives of the recipients of United States licences that they are also prepared to discuss the subject of avoidance of interference of activities with any other entity engaged in such activities in the areas within which their deep seabed hard mineral mining has been authorized.

The Government of the United States requests that this note, and the attached Federal Register notices, be circulated by the United Nations as part of the next Law of the Sea Bulletin prepared by the Office of the Special Representative of the Secretary–General for the Law of the Sea.

————

Notes and Questions: 1. Part XI of the UN Convention. It was Part XI of the 1982 Convention that caused the United States to call for a vote on the Convention and then refuse to sign. Furthermore, the United States then proceeded to enter into a scheme of reciprocal recognition of seabed claims by other similarly interested states. As was discussed at the beginning of this Chapter, the dissatisfaction with Part XI led to the adoption in 1994 of the Agreement Relating to the Implementation of Part XI of the United Nations Convention on the Law of the Sea of 10 December, 1982, adopted by General Assembly Resolution 48/263, 28 July, 1994. This Agreement, reproduced in the Documentary Supplement, entered into force on July 28, 1996 and as of November 30, 2000, has 100 states parties. See 34 ILM 1428–1438.

2. *Common heritage of mankind*. The concept that no state can acquire an exclusive right to use certain areas, deposits, or other things of value, because they belong to all mankind has been advanced in regard to orbits in space, mineralized areas of the Moon and other celestial bodies, and the Antarctic continent. See the Agreement Governing the Activities of States on the Moon and other Celestial Bodies (the "Moon Treaty") UN Doc. A/34/664; 18 ILM 1434 (1979), Article 11(1). However, nowhere else has this doctrine been as firmly asserted as with respect to the minerals on the deep sea bed beyond national jurisdiction. Refer back to the Pardo declaration in this section and look at the following Articles in the UN Convention: 137, 140, 149, 150, 151, 156, 159, 161, 162, 163, 164, 165, 166, 170, 171, 174 and 187. The ethical concept of the common heritage fits in a general way with the long held view that the high seas are not subject to exclusive appropriations by any state. Did the common heritage principle create a common economic right? Do you think that the drive by the less developed countries, under the banner of the Group of 77 was fanned, as to Part XI, by then great expectations as to immense wealth at the bottom of the seas or was it also symbolic and even the cornerstone of the then declared New International Economic Order?

Consider the Articles in Part XI of the 1982 Convention and then the 1994 Agreement. What were the significant compromises that were struck? Further, to what extent do you think the fact that technical and economic issues have hindered commercial deep seabed mining played a part in this process?

SECTION F.   DISPUTE SETTLEMENT

The settlement of disputes since the 1982 United Nations Convention entered into force in 1994 is governed by Part XV of the Convention,

Articles 279–299. If a dispute has not been settled by peaceful means in accordance with Article 2 (3) of the United Nations Charter, by the means indicated in Article 33 of the Charter, including negotiation, mediation or conciliation, then the provisions in Articles 286 and 287 of the Convention contained in the Documentary Supplement for the compulsory settlement of disputes by any one of the following means apply:

- The International Tribunal for the Law of the Sea;
- The International Court of Justice;
- Arbitration; or
- Special arbitration.

Of particular note the Convention created the International Tribunal for The Law of the Sea. It has 21 judges and its seat is in Hamburg.

Hugh M. Kindred Et Al. International Law Chiefly as Interpreted and Applied In Canada

969–971, (6th ed., 2000, footnotes omitted)*

The International Tribunal of the Law of the Sea

The entry into force of the Law of the Sea Convention in 1994 was particularly significant in terms of the settlement of law of the sea disputes. The 1982 Convention created the International Tribunal of the Law of the Sea (the Tribunal), an international judicial institution established specifically to resolve disputes involving nation States or other entities in law of the sea matters.

Part XV of the 1982 Convention stipulates that in case of a dispute between two States, the parties are to proceed expeditiously to an exchange of views regarding its settlement by negotiation or other peaceful means. As a consequence, a state that has acceded to the 1982 Convention and that finds itself involved in a dispute under the Convention must submit the conflict to compulsory dispute settlement. The Convention provides four possible procedures for states to follow; the parties may agree to submit the dispute to (1) the Tribunal, (2) ICJ, (3) arbitration, or (4) special arbitration. In a situation where the parties have failed to make a declaration of their preferred forum of compulsory dispute settlement, arbitration in some form will be necessary.

In contrast to other international tribunals, one of the main features of the Tribunal is its broader rules with respect to access, since both private parties and international organizations may be granted standing as well as states. The varied types of disputes that may be referred to the Tribunal include fisheries, navigation, ocean pollution, and the delimitation of maritime zones. Furthermore, the Tribunal exercises compulsory jurisdiction over the release of arrested vessels and their crews under certain conditions. The Tribunal has a separate Seabed Disputes Chamber in order to ensure that a forum exists which can hear cases involving both states and

* Reprinted with the permission of Hugh
M. Kindred.

private actors regarding investment and exploration in the international seabed.

The first case heard by the Tribunal concerned the *M/V Saiga* case. The case involved the arrest by the West African country of Guinea of an oil tanker, the *Saiga* that, at the time of the arrest, was flying the flag of Saint Vincent and the Grenadines. Guinean authorities made the arrest of both the ship and its crew members on the grounds that the *Saiga* was engaged in smuggling activities in Guinean territorial waters and it justi-fied the arrest as an exercise of the right of hot pursuit. In its defence, Saint Vincent and the Grenadines accused the Guinean authorities of piracy. Since both parties to the dispute could not agree on the forum for the dispute resolution and since both states are parties to the 1982 Convention and especially given the humanitarian considerations for the crew of the *Saiga* who were under arrest, the Tribunal was under an obligation to reach a decision rapidly. Nonetheless, lawyers representing Guinea contended that the Tribunal lacked jurisdiction to hear the case. In its decision on December 4, 1997, the Tribunal ordered the release of the *Saiga* and its crew from detention in Guinea upon a security deposit from Saint Vincent and the Grenadines. Significantly, in response to the ques-tion of jurisdiction, the judgment was unanimous in favour of the tribunal having compulsory jurisdiction over the matter. On the merits of the case, the Tribunal subsequently decided on July 1, 1999 that the arrest and detention of the *Saiga* and crew was unlawful and the hot pursuit was illegally effected with excessive force. Consequently, Guinea was ordered to pay substantial damages to St. Vincent and the Grenadines.

The system of dispute settlement outlined above may seem cumber-some, but it was the only way in which it was possible to reach agreement on the principle of compulsory dispute resolution of the whole Convention without a right of reservation. The system was negotiated during the 1975 Geneva session of the Law of the Sea Conference and the so-called Montreux compromise? was reached at a meeting of an informal working group meeting in Montreux. Some states insisted on maintenance of the International Court of Justice (ICJ). Others considered that only a new tribunal would be acceptable given their reservations and past experience with the ICJ. Still others refused to submit to any standing tribunal and therefore opted for arbitration either of a general character or some form of special arbitration as found at different points in the Law of the Sea Convention. Thus, in a highly pragmatic way, the fundamental principle of compulsory dispute settlement was enshrined in this profoundly important renewal of the international law of the sea. In practice, the new Tribunal, which has only been in existence for a few years, has received little business. This may reflect simply initial uncertainty before a new institu-tion, but it does not bode well for what many governments consider a new tribunal of great importance.

The ICJ has continued to play a vital role in international maritime boundary delimitation and it would appear that this function will continue, given its relative success in this area. Arbitration has been used by many governments during and subsequent to the period leading up to the adoption of the U.N. Convention on the Law of the Sea. Arbitration will doubtless continue to be the preferred option for some countries or the preferred option in certain circumstances. Canada has had a recourse to arbitration as well as to the ICJ. Decisions in this area seem to be taken on a pragmatic basis by most governments, when and as they have recourse to compulsory dispute settlement.

Conciliation continues to be an option under the U.N. Charter and general principles of public international law. However, there is very little evidence that conciliation is a preferred option for many governments at the present time. Finally, a special procedure was established by the U.N. Convention on the Law of the Sea for delimitation of the Continental Shelf boundary beyond two hundred miles. Article 76(8) calls for a Commission on the limits of the Continental Shelf, which is set up by Annex II to the Convention. Its procedure is compulsory in the event of a dispute and any state as beneficiary of an interest in the common heritage of mankind may be a party to its proceedings.

CHAPTER 5

LAW OF AIRSPACE, OUTER SPACE AND CELESTIAL BODIES

Overview
Section A. Airspace.
        1. Aerial Transit.
        2. Offenses Aboard Aircraft.
        General Offenses.
        Hijacking.
        Sabotage.
        Extradition and Aircraft Offenses.
Section B. Outer Space.
        Round-up on Other Legal Aspects of the Use of Space.
Section C. Celestial Bodies.

Overview

The twentieth century saw the rise of the technologies of both air and space flight, and a concomitant evolution and creation of legal principles. Today, legal principles regarding airspace and its utilization have become relatively stabilized. Space law is in a holding pattern after a flurry of development incident to the orbital flight of Sputnik 1 in 1957, which produced a few, generalized international agreements, along with the creation of proto-law by the U.N. General Assembly and considerable additions to scholarly legal literature. In 2001, President Bush has prompted some murmuring among friends and enemies alike, by reviving the issue of the so-called "Star Wars" missile defense shield.

Flight operations of powered, steerable aircraft, both lighter-than-air and heavier-than-air, developed in the World War I along the military lines of aerial observation, combat, and bombing, especially of cities. Between the two world wars, commercial aviation began, grew, and came under a number of legal controls, national and international. Virtually all of this law, the subject of a recognized and active legal specialty, is positive, rather than customary, in its origins. Air law, unlike much law of the sea, is not consuetudinarian. Significantly, for instance, a freedom for aerial transit, like freedom on the "high seas," though advanced by early scholars, did not survive the Zeppelin bombing raids on London. The only free airspace today is that above the high seas. And, as we shall see, that freedom narrows as national airspace is approached.

In the course of its relatively brief and partial development, space law has had to deal with many problems, like where space begins? Or does the definition of space depend on the purpose to which it was put? How if at all, will advantages, such as orbits and substances from celestial bodies be shared. How will space debris or liability for it be handled? What should be the proper use of space for military operations. Space law as a specialty is still mainly in the hands of scholars and national and international officials. However, communications law has developed a practitioner specialty related to satellite ownership, financing, control, launching, and utilization.

SECTION A. AIRSPACE

1. AERIAL TRANSIT

Draft Convention, Regime of Aerostats and Wireless Telegraphy (1906)

21 Annuaire de l'Institut de Droit International 293, 327 (1907).[a]

Mr. Fauchille, rapporteur, * * * summarizes the main conclusions:

* * *

The fundamental difficulty * * * concerns the nature of airspace and the rights of states in the atmosphere. How can this question be solved? It must be defined. The atmosphere can be divided into three zones. Above 5000 meters [there is] a zone where breathing is impossible and where balloons cannot penetrate. Close to earth, [is] a zone [which is] subject to appropriation through building up to, at present, a height of 330 meters since the highest construction today, the Eiffel Tower, is 300 meters high and the highest telegraphic masts reach 30 meters. But even in that situation, airspace is subject to appropriation by the state. What is state property is not airspace but the constructions in the airspace. Thus, it is only in that airspace from the ground up, where there are no constructions, and up to 5000 meters, that there exists a [third] zone whose [legal] regime must be determined.

Two absolute theories have been advanced.

In one * * * airspace is completely free in all its zones, be it for aerial navigation or for radio telegraphy. In the other, the subjacent state has a right of property or sovereignty in airspace within a limit, according to one view, * * * [equivalent] to the range of a cannon, or according to another view, * * * within limits to be determined by an international agreement similar to the one proposed by the Netherlands in 1895 for territorial waters.

The first system does not take into account the dangers for states in the matter of espionage, especially, and the operation of radio telegraphy, [which would result] from the passage of aerostats at low altitude. [In the second], the range of a cannon varies widely and may attain, it is said, a range of 4800 meters, it would follow that aerial navigation would in fact become impossible. * * * [To the extent] the second system involves determining the rights of the subjacent state by international agreement,

---

a. Translation by the editors. The text in the Annuaire is a summary minute of what the rapporteur said rather than the verbatim transcript of his statement.

the determination, has no rational basis and would be arbitrary. [A single observation] applies both aspects of this second system: Airspace, by its very nature, is not susceptible of appropriation or subjection to sovereignty.

The rapporteur proposes, accordingly, a combination of two uncontested principles: (1) airspace is not susceptible of appropriation or subjection to sovereignty, and therefore is free; (2) a state has a right of self-preservation and of self-defense to guaranty the essential elements of its existence, both in a material sense and as a legal person. Hence this formula: airspace is free, subject to the right of self-preservation and self-defense of the subjacent state.

Two consequences follow from the proposal:

(1) What is the most serious danger from aerostats? Espionage. What form does this danger take? Photography. But useful photography of a country's fortifications can be made only at an altitude of less than 1500 meters. Thus, under 1500 meters, the navigation of aerostats should be forbidden.

(2) What is today the most serious problem for wireless telegraphy? It is the possibility of interference with telephone communications and ordinary telegraphy.

* * * [The following text was adopted by the Institute.]

Article 1. Airspace is free. States have in it, in time of peace or in time of war, only the rights necessary for their self-preservation.

* * *

From Theory to Treaty Law

McNair, The Law of the Air 4 (Kerr & Evans, 3d ed. 1964).*

* * * Until after the war of 1914–18 the only aspects of aerial navigation which had engaged the serious attention of English lawyers, and, indeed, of [most] lawyers, were the rules of public international law and of the Conflict of Laws which ought to govern it. * * *

It was generally admitted that the airspace was free [over the high seas]. * * *

(1) *That the airspace is free, subject only to the rights of states required in the interests of their self-preservation.* This theory, which will always be associated with the name of its champion, Fauchille, was adopted by the Institute of International Law in 1906. * * *

(2) The second theory was that *upon the analogy of the maritime belt or territorial waters there is over the land and waters of each state a lower zone of territorial airspace, and a higher, and unlimited, zone of free airspace.*

(3) The third theory was that *a state has complete sovereignty in its superincumbent airspace to an unlimited height,* thus applying the *cujus est solum* maxim in its crude form.

* Reprinted with the permission of Stevens & Sons, Ltd., London.

(4) The fourth theory was the third *with the addition of a servitude of innocent passage for foreign non-military aircraft,* akin to the right of innocent passage of merchant ships through territorial waters.

The war of 1914–18 brought about a realisation of the importance of aerial navigation and of its potential danger to the subjacent state and its inhabitants. It is therefore not surprising to find now the almost universal adoption by international treaty and by national legislation of the theory of complete sovereignty (No. (3) above), subject to a mutual, carefully safe-guarded, and easily determinable treaty right of free entry and passage for the non-military aircraft of foreign countries.

Thus the first Article of the Paris Convention of 1919 [read]: "The High Contracting Parties recognise that every Power has complete and exclusive sovereignty over the air space above its territory.

For the purpose of the present Convention the territory of a State shall be understood as including the national territory, both that of the Mother Country and of the Colonies, and the territorial waters adjacent thereto."

* * *

Goedhuis, Civil Aviation After the War

36 American Journal of International Law 596, 605 (1942).*

The * * * accelerated speed of change in the last thirty years has been such that, politically, air navigation has already passed through many of the phases which it took sea navigation centuries to span.

As to air navigation, * * * in 1910 the states were preoccupied only with guaranteeing the safety of their territory; the necessity of permitting other states to navigate freely to and over their territory was recognized to the fullest extent where this freedom did not affect the security of the state. The period 1910–1919 can thus be compared with that period in the history of shipping in which the adjacent seas were appropriated primarily to secure the land from invasion.

In 1919 the first consideration was still the security of the states, but the study of the minutes of the meetings held by the Aeronautical Commis-sion of the Peace Conference reveals the fact that some small clouds were already appearing on the horizon of the free sky. In the minds of some of the delegates the idea took shape to use the power of the state over the air to protect its own air navigation against foreign competition. As in ship-ping, the pretensions to the appropriation of the sea and the power to restrict foreign sea commerce grew in proportion to the increase of the direct profits to be expected from them, so in aviation the pretensions to unrestricted sovereignty—not in doctrine but in practice—grew in propor-tion to the development of aviation during the period from 1919 to 1929.
* * *

* * *

International Air Transport and Foreign Policy

Campbell, The United States in World Affairs, 1947–1948, 276, at 280 (1948).**

* * *

The present concern of the United States with foreign air policy questions is of comparatively recent origin. The United States participated in the drafting but later failed to ratify the Convention Relating to the Regulation of Aerial Navigation, signed at Paris in 1919 and later accepted by most European nations. It signed and ratified the Pan American Convention on Commercial Aviation concluded at Havana in 1928, but this convention had little practical effect since it was almost ignored even by the few nations which had accepted it.

* * *

Even before the outbreak of the second World War, the United States had entered into intergovernmental negotiations for the establishment of international air services. The transatlantic route discussions with Great Britain, Canada and Ireland in 1935–1937 and an exchange of notes with France in 1939 paved the way for the inauguration of Pan American Airways' service to Great Britain and to France a few months before the outbreak of war. During the war U.S. flag international air transport increased beyond any possible prior contemplation. Part of the enormous amount of flying was conducted directly by commercial air carriers, part by such air carriers acting on government account, and a large part by the Army Air Transport Command and the Naval Air Transport Services. The routes used were expanded where the war effort required by informal arrangements made between the United States and its allies. But the very informality of the wartime expansion made it more than clear that urgent and important foreign policy problems would be involved in stabilizing the general international air transport position when the war ended, particularly if the routes desired by the United States were to be put into operation.

* * *

Toward the end of the war it was clear that the great changes which had taken place called for some measure of international agreement beyond the prewar pattern. Faced with the certain reorganization of world air transport that would follow the termination of hostilities, the United States consulted with various foreign nations, particularly Great Britain, and, as a result of such negotiations, invited its allies and the neutral powers to an International Civil Aviation Conference at Chicago in November 1944.

The Chicago conference was by far the most important ever held dealing with international civil aviation. It provided a forum for foreign air policy discussions such as had never existed before. * * *

* * *

At the conclusion of the conference, three executive agreements and one formal convention were opened for signature. The United States signed all four. Through the executive branch of the government, it later formally accepted the executive agreements, and, through the formal constitutional procedure, duly ratified the convention.

* * *

Under the terms of the Chicago convention, agreement was reached on certain questions of major importance affecting world aviation. The agreed principles included the following: acceptance of airspace sovereignty as in the Paris convention of 1919 and the Havana convention of 1928; authority without further permit for aircraft of contracting states not engaged in international air service to fly non-stop across the territory of other contracting states and to make stops for non-traffic purposes, with the provision that such aircraft may take on or discharge passengers, cargo or mail "subject to the right of any state where such embarkation or discharge takes place to impose such regulations, conditions or limitations as it may consider desirable"; provisions that no scheduled international air service may be operated over or into the territory of a contracting state except by special permission; that any contracting state may refuse permission to aircraft of other contracting states to carry cabotage traffic (i.e., traffic from one point to another within the same country); that contracting states may set up prohibited areas for reasons of military necessity or public safety; that aircraft shall have the nationality of the state in which they are registered; that contracting states will adopt all practicable measures to facilitate navigation between their territories; that contracting states, so far as practicable, will install and provide air navigation facilities for international air navigation; that all aircraft shall carry certain documents and be equipped (including radio equipment) in the manner set out in the convention; that each contracting state may designate routes to be followed and airports to be used by any international air service within its territory; that the convention should supersede the Paris and Havana conventions; and that the formation of an International Civil Aviation Organization should be undertaken.

* * *

The convention made no provision, however, for the general automatic or other grant of the privilege of regular scheduled air services of one contracting state to fly over or into the territory of other contracting states, or the terms under which such services should or could be organized and operated. On this question hinged the long discussions and futile compromise efforts of the conference. Basically divergent foreign policy views were involved.

Australia and New Zealand proposed the establishment of an international air transport authority which would be responsible for the operation of air services on international trunk routes and which would own the aircraft and ancillary equipment employed on these routes. Canada proposed the organization of an international authority to fix routes, frequencies, capacity and rates applicable to international air services and to issue permits to international civil aviation operators much as the Civil Aeronautics Board does in the United States for U.S. flag operators. Great Britain also favored such an authority with power to allocate operating frequencies and capacity and to fix rates. The United States opposed these suggestions, favoring instead a wide exchange of transit privileges by which scheduled services of any contracting state could fly over or land for refueling or other technical purposes in the territory of another contracting state. The transit privileges (the right to fly over, or to land for technical purposes) are sometimes called the first and second freedoms, and the transport privileges (the right to carry traffic to another contracting state, bring back traffic from such state, or to carry traffic between another contracting state and other states) are referred to as the third, fourth and fifth freedoms.

The Australian and New Zealand position found little support. Many efforts were made to find a compromise between the British insistence on some type of economic regulation which they deemed necessary to assure "order in the air" and the American opposition to any prior allocation of frequencies or capacity, or to any other form of international economic regulation of the growing United States air transport services. Various automatic and semi-automatic formulas were suggested, but without result. In the absence of general agreement on economic regulation of scheduled services, the transit and transport agreements were drafted separately, apart from the convention. Both were supported by the United States. The Transit Agreement covered the first and second freedoms, and, in addition, authorized any nation flown over to require the international operator to land and offer reasonable commercial services. The Transport Agreement covered all five freedoms, including both transit and commercial privileges.
* * *

* * *

Thus by the close of the war, the foreign air policy of the United States, so far as it could be determined from the position of the executive branch of the government, had taken definite shape. * * *

* * *

The Chicago Convention

61 Stat. 1180, 15 U.N.T.S. 295.

The Convention resolved many of the issues that had arisen over the course of the first half of the 20th century. It applies only to civil (not military or governmental) aircraft. Read articles 1, 2, 5, 6, 17, in the Documentary Supplement.

Notes & Questions

1. *The International Air Services Transit Agreement*. The United States became a party in 1945. 84 U.N.T.S. 389. Article 1 § 1, provides the so-called *"two freedoms"* for scheduled air services:

Each contracting State grants to the other contracting States the following freedoms of the air in respect of scheduled international air services:

(1) The privilege to fly across its territory without landing;

(2) The privilege to land for non-traffic purposes.

The privileges of this section shall not be applicable with respect to airports utilized for military purposes to the exclusion of any scheduled international air services. In areas of active hostilities or of military occupation, and in time of war along the supply routes leading to such areas, the exercise of such privileges shall be subject to the approval of the competent military authorities.

2.   *The International Air Transport Agreement.* The United States became a party in 1945, but so few states joined that the U.S. withdrew in 1947. Article 1, Section 1, provides the so-called *"five freedoms"* for scheduled air service: Each contracting State grants to the other contracting States the following freedoms of the air in respect of scheduled international air services:

(1) The privilege to fly across its territory without landing;

(2) The privilege to land for non-traffic purposes;

(3) The privilege to put down passengers, mail and cargo taken on in the territory of the State whose nationality the aircraft possesses;

(4) The privilege to take on passengers, mail and cargo destined for the territory of the State whose [aircraft's] nationality;

(5) The privilege to take on passengers, mail and cargo destined for the territory of any other contracting State and the privilege to put down passengers, mail and cargo coming from any such territory.

With respect to the privileges specified under paragraphs (3), (4) and (5) of this Section, the undertaking of each contracting State relates only to through services on a route constituting a reasonably direct line out from and back to the homeland of the State [of the aircraft's] nationality.

3.   *Scheduled air services.* The package of agreements emanating from the Chicago conference thus did not include a multilateral agreement of wide acceptance sufficient to deal with the question of scheduled air service. To provide the authorizations and permissions foreshadowed in Article 6 of the Chicago Convention, states entered into a vast network (or cobweb) of bilateral agreements, covering routes, types of traffic and volume of traffic (capacity), as well as a variety of administrative and legal matters of concern to the airline industry. See Lissitzyn, Bilateral Agreements on Air Transport, 30 J. of Air L. & Commerce 248 (1964); Hill, Bermuda II: The British Revolution of 1976, 44 J. of Air L. & Commerce 111 (1978). Following the Chicago conference, rates were set for many years by conference machinery established by the International Air Transport Association (IATA), a private association of airlines, sometimes referred to as a cartel. With the onset of airline industry deregulation in the United States in the late 70s and the removal of IATA's antitrust immunity, IATA's ratemaking function ceased. Schwartz, Flynn & First, Free Enterprise and Economic Organization: Government Regulation 625 (6th ed. 1985).

The Powers Case

Union of Soviet Socialist Republics, Supreme Court Military Collegium, 1960.
30 Int'l L.Rep. 69 (1966).*

* * * On May 1, 1960, at 5 hours 36 minutes, Moscow time, a military unit of the Soviet anti-aircraft defence in the area of the city of Kirovabad, the Tajik S.S.R., at an altitude of 20,000 metres, unattainable for planes of the civil air fleet, spotted an unknown aircraft violating the State frontier of the U.S.S.R.

The military units of the Soviet anti-aircraft defence vigilantly followed the behaviour of the plane as it flew over major industrial centres and important objectives, and only when the intruder plane had penetrated 2,000 kilometres into Soviet territory and the evil purpose of the flight, fraught with disastrous consequences for world peace in an age of thermo-nuclear weapons, became absolutely obvious, a battery of ground-to-air missiles brought the aggressor plane down in the area of Sverdlovsk at 8 hours 53 minutes as ordered by the Soviet Government.

The pilot of the plane bailed out and was apprehended upon landing. On interrogation, he gave his name as Francis Gary Powers, citizen of the United States of America. Examination of the wreckage of the plane which had been brought down showed that it was of American make, specially designed for high altitude flights and fitted with various equipment for espionage reconnaissance tasks.

In view of this, the pilot Powers was arrested and committed for trial on charges of espionage against the Soviet Union.

During the court hearings, the defendant Powers testified in detail about his espionage activity and the circumstances connected with the violation of Soviet air space on May 1, 1960.

* * *

On the night of April 30, 1960, Colonel Shelton gave Powers the assignment to fly over the territory of the Soviet Union at an altitude of 20,000 metres along the following course: Peshawar, the Aral Sea, Sverd-lovsk, Kirov, Archangel, Murmansk, and to land in Norway, at Bodoe airport, with which Powers familiarized himself back in 1958.

Flying over Soviet territory, Powers, on Shelton's orders, was to switch on at definite points his special equipment for aerial photography and the registration of the operation of Soviet anti-aircraft defence radar stations. Powers was to give special attention to two spots—in one of them American intelligence suspected the presence of missile launching ramps and in the other a particularly important defence objective.

The material evidence of the case and his testimony has established that Powers fulfilled the criminal mission given him.

Having taken off from Peshawar airport in Pakistan, Powers flew over the territory of Afghanistan and for more than 2,000 kilometres over the Soviet Union in accordance with the established course. Besides Powers' testimony, this is confirmed by the American flight map discovered in the

---

* Reprinted with the permission of the
Editor of the International Law Reports.

debris of the U–2 plane and submitted to the Court, bearing the route plotted out by Major Dulak, navigator of the detachment "Ten–Ten", and also notes and signs made by Powers, who marked down on this map several important defence objectives of the Soviet Union he had spotted from the plane.

Throughout the flight, to the very moment the plane was shot down, Powers switched on his special intelligence equipment, photographed important defence objectives and recorded signals of the country's anti-aircraft radar installations. The development of the rescued aerial photography films established that defendant Powers photographed from the U–2 plane industrial and military objectives of the Soviet Union—plants, depots, oil storage facilities, communication routes, railway bridges and stations, electric transmission lines, aerodromes, the location of troops and military equipment.

The numerous photos of the Soviet Union's territory, taken by defendant Powers from an altitude of 20,000 metres, in possession of the Military Collegium of the U.S.S.R. Supreme Court, make it possible to determine the nature of industrial establishments, the design of railway bridges, the number and type of aircraft on the airfields, the nature and purpose of military material.

Powers tape-recorded impulses of certain [USSR] radar stations with a view to detecting the country's anti-aircraft defence system.

According to the conclusion of experts, the information collected by defendant Powers during his flight in Soviet air space on May 1, 1960, constitutes a State and military secret of the Soviet Union, which is specially guarded by law.

* * *

Thus, the court hearings have established definitely that the Lockheed U–2 reconnaissance aircraft belonged to the United States Air Force and that defendant Powers was a secret agent of the Central Intelligence Agency of the United States of America.

Powers was an obedient executor of the perfidious designs of the Central Intelligence Agency of the United States of America, carried out with the consent of the American Government.

Powers himself admitted that he realized when intruding into the air space of the Soviet Union that he was violating the national sovereignty of the U.S.S.R. and flying over its territory on an espionage mission, whose main purpose consisted of detecting and marking down missile launching sites.

* * *

Article 2 [of the Law on Criminal Responsibility for State Crimes]:

Espionage

The giving away, theft or collection with the intention of conveying to a foreign Power, a foreign organization, or their agents, of information constituting a State or military secret, as well as the giving away or collection on the instructions of foreign intelligence agencies of other information to be used against the interests of the U.S.S.R., if the espionage is committed by a foreigner or by a stateless person—is punishable by deprivation of liberty for a period of from seven to fifteen years with confiscation of property, or by death and confiscation of property.

* * * [T]he Military Collegium of the U.S.S.R. Supreme Court takes into account that the intrusion of the American military intelligence plane constitutes a criminal breach of a generally recognized principle of international law, which establishes the exclusive sovereignty of every State over the air space above its territory. This principle, laid down by the Paris Convention of October 13, 1919, for the regulation of aerial navigation, and several other subsequent international agreements, is proclaimed in the national legislations of different States, including the Soviet Union and the United States of America.

Violation of this sacred and immutable principle of international relations creates in the present conditions a direct menace to universal peace and international security.

At the present level of military technology, when certain States possess atomic and hydrogen weapons, as well as the means of delivering them quickly to targets, the flight of a military intelligence plane over Soviet territory could have directly preceded a military attack. This danger is the more possible in conditions when the United States of America, as stated by American generals, constantly keeps bomber patrols in the air, always ready to drop bombs on earlier marked-out targets of the Soviet Union.

Under these conditions the aggressive act of the United States of America, carried out on May 1 of this year by defendant Powers, created a threat to universal peace.

* * *

Having examined the materials of the case, material and other evidence and expert findings, and having heard the testimony of the defendant and the witnesses, the speeches of the State Prosecutor and of the Defence Counsel, and also the last plea of the defendant, the Military Collegium of the U.S.S.R. Supreme Court holds established that defendant Powers was for a long time an active secret agent of the United States Central Intelligence Agency, directly fulfilling espionage missions of this agency against the Soviet Union; and that on May 1, 1960, with the knowledge of the Government of the United States of America, in a specially equipped U–2 intelligence plane, he intruded into Soviet air space and with the help of special radio-technical and photographic equipment collected information of strategical importance, which constitutes a State and Military secret of the Soviet State, thereby committing a grave crime covered by Article 2 of the Soviet Union's Law "On Criminal Responsibility for State Crimes".

At the same time, weighing all the circumstances of the given case in the deep conviction that they are inter-related, taking into account Powers' sincere confession of his guilt and his sincere repentance, proceeding from the principles of socialist humaneness, and guided by Articles 319 and 320 of the Code of Criminal Procedure of the Russian Federation, the Military Collegium of the U.S.S.R. Supreme Court

Sentences: Francis Gary Powers, on the strength of Article 2 of the U.S.S.R. Law "On Criminal Responsibility for State Crimes", to ten years' confinement with the first three years to be served in prison.

* * *

———

Notes & Questions

1. ***Reprise on Powers, the Lockheed U–2 aircraft, and aerial surveillance***. Much still has to come out about spying-by-aircraft during the Cold War period. The U–2 operation was run by the CIA, not the Air Force or the Defense Intelligence Agency. We know that Powers was not the only U.S. pilot downed. The Lockheed U–2 was a marvel of specialty design for observation operations above 60,000 feet. The Soviet Report on the *Powers Case* stated that the claimed interception by a surface-to-air missile was at 20,000 meters * * * [an altitude] "unattainable for planes in the civilian air fleet * * *." Civil? But what about the Soviet military air fleet?. No U.S. interceptions of Soviet surveillance aircraft were ever reported. Powers ultimately was exchanged at the classic spy-exchange bridge into East Berlin for Col. Rudolf Abel, a brilliant Soviet spymaster who had operated for years from a photography shop in Brooklyn. Ironically, Powers died in Los Angeles, while engaged in an aerial journalism mission.

President Eisenhower's early evasion of this Soviet report was almost immediately blown, whereupon he reiterated his call for an "Open Skies" policy, that he had originally made in 1955, which is presented, *infra*.

Aerial surveillance during the Cuban Missile Crisis was of great importance to President Kennedy and his emergency staff.

2. ***Sanctions against aircraft entering airspace***. Does the fact that a state has prescriptive jurisdiction mean that it has freedom of choice in the methods used to exercise that jurisdiction? For example, does a state have a right to shoot down any plane that enters its airspace? In 1955, an El Al Israel Airlines Ltd. commercial airliner, with passengers aboard, entered Bulgarian airspace for some unknown reason. Bulgarian fighter aircraft shot the plane down, as it exploded in flight and crashed in Bulgarian territory. killing all 58 persons aboard, including some U.S. and British passengers. The U.S, the U.K., and Israel instituted proceedings against Bulgaria in the International Court of Justice, protesting the Bulgarian inhuman and excessive use of force, the lack of adequate warning, and their failure to recognize the right of entry in distress. The cases did not proceed to the merits, however, because of Bulgaria's refused consent to the Court's jurisdiction. *See*, 9 Whiteman, DIGEST OF INTERNATIONAL LAW 326–340 (1963).

3. In early 2001, a U.S. spy plane was running a mission over the High Seas, but near the Peoples Republic of China. These spy planes are frequently "buzzed" by Chinese Migs, one of which came too close and hit the U.S. plane. The engines and the nose of the U.S. aircraft were damaged. The Mig fell into the Sea, presumably killing it pilot. After a steep, long dive, the U.S. pilot was able to gain control. The crew radioed MAYDAY and landed on the Chinese island of Hainan. The plane was held,

as was the crew. The crew were kept for several days and were interrogated, but apparently were treated well, except for some sleep deprivation. The crew were released unharmed. Is it "legal" for the U.S. to fly spy planes over international waters, but close to other nations? Was it legal for the Captain to land the plane on Hainan Island?

4. ***Excessive use of force: analogies from the law of the sea. The I'm Alone case*** 1935, 3 U.N.Rep.Int'l Arb. Awards 1609, involved a dispute between Canada and the US, arising out of the sinking of a Canadian rumrunning vessel. The U.S. and Britain had entered into a convention permitting US authorities to engage in search and seizure of British vessels suspected of liquor smuggling, if the vessels were found close to, although outside, US territorial waters. US authorities entered into hot pursuit of the *I'm Alone* chasing her some 200 miles away from the Louisiana coast in the Gulf of Mexico. The commanding officer of the pursuing coast guard cutter ordered the *I'm Alone* to stop and informed the her commander that it would be sunk unless it stopped. The cutter shot warning shots, then put enough shots into the hull of the *I'm Alone* to sink her. Commissioners were appointed to report on this event. They held:

> * * * The question is whether, in the circumstances, the Government of the United States was legally justified in sinking the I'm Alone.

The answer given to this question is as follows:—

> On the assumptions stated in the question, the United States might, consistently with the Convention, use necessary and reasonable force for the purpose of effecting the objects of boarding, searching, seizing and bringing into port the suspected vessel; and if sinking should occur incidentally, as a result of the exercise of necessary and reasonable force for such purpose, the pursuing vessel might be entirely blameless. But the Commissioners think that, in the circumstances stated in paragraph eight of the Answer, the admittedly intentional sinking of the suspected vessel was not justified by anything in the Convention.

> * * *

The *I'm Alone* was sunk on the 22nd day of March, 1929, on the high seas, in the Gulf of Mexico, by the United States revenue cutter Dexter. By their interim report the Commissioners found that the sinking of the vessel was not justified by anything in the Convention. The Commissioners now add that it could not be justified by any principle of international law.

Are there special risks associated with aircraft that require peremptory use of destructive force?

———

A Proposed Open Skies Treaty: A Post–Cold War Initiative

There is, pending advice and consent in the United States Senate, a proposed Open Skies Treaty whose negotiation was initiated by the U.S., on the basis of a concept announced by President Eisenhower in 1955. Senate action approved this Treaty on August 6, 1993. Salient provisions of the Treaty are in the Documentary Supplement. Hearings were conducted in the Foreign Relations Committee on this Treaty in which officials from the Joint Chiefs of Staff, the Departments of State and Defense, and the Arms Control and Disarmament Agency testified in its favor.

In essence the Treaty provides for states' acceptance of unarmed, short-notice overflights of each others' territories for general observation related to confidence-and-security-building knowledge of each other's offensive and defensive installations. Signers of the Treaty, subject to ratification or accession, include the 16 NATO countries, the East European members of the former Warsaw Pact, Russia and at least four other successor states of the former Soviet Union, and the former Czechoslovakian state, now divided, with both new states intending to re-acknowledge signature and seek ratifications.

Various overflight arrangements of interest to particular states have been declared, and the data from any overflight by any participating country is to be made available by purchase to any and all treaty parties.

Question: Is it likely that this treaty will significantly reduce the dangers of air disasters such as those that immediately follow? Why or why not?

Destruction of Korean Air Lines Boeing 747 Over Sea of Japan, 31 August 1983

Report of Investigation by Secretary General of Civil Aviation Organization (December 1983)

23 International Legal Materials 867 (1984).*

SUMMARY OF FINDINGS AND CONCLUSIONS

On 31 August 1983, a Korean Air Lines Boeing 747, designated KE007, departed John F. Kennedy International Airport, New York, United States, on a one-stop scheduled flight for Kimpo International Airport, Seoul, Republic of Korea. The en-route stop occurred at Anchorage International Airport, Alaska. At Anchorage, the aircraft was refuelled, serviced for the remainder of the flight to Seoul, and, in accordance with the standing company practice, the flight and cabin crews were changed.

The flight departed at the planned estimated time of departure (ETD) which, in keeping with the standard Korean Air Lines' procedure, was separately calculated for each flight of KE007. The ETD at Anchorage was planned so that its arrival in Seoul was at its scheduled arrival time of 0600 (local time) or as close thereto as possible. The actual departure time of 1300 hours on 31 August should have resulted in an on-time arrival of

---

* Reprinted with the permission of the American Society of International Law from materials published in 23 I.L.M. 864–937 under the general title "International Civil Organization: Action with Regard to the Downing of the Korean Air Lines Aircraft."

KE007 at Seoul had the flight been completed successfully and fully in accordance with its filed flight plan.

On departing Anchorage, the flight had 269 persons on board consisting of three flight crew members, twenty cabin attendants, six crew employees of KAL being repositioned to Seoul for duty assignments and 240 passengers.

Soon after its departure from Anchorage, KE007 began deviating to the right (north) of its assigned direct route to Bethel. This deviation resulted in a progressively ever greater lateral displacement to the right of its planned route which, ultimately, resulted in its penetration of adjacent high seas airspace in flight information regions (FIRs) operated by the Union of Soviet Socialist Republics (USSR), as well as of sovereign USSR airspace overlying portions of the Kamchatka Peninsula and Sakhalin Island and their surrounding territorial waters.

No evidence was found * * * to indicate that the flight crew of KE007 was, at any time, aware of the flight's deviation from its planned route in spite of the fact that it continued along the same general off-track flight path for some five hours and twenty-six minutes.

At about 1820 hours when it was in the vicinity of Sakhalin Island, USSR, the flight was intercepted by military aircraft operated by the USSR. At 1827 hours, the aircraft was hit by at least one of two air-to-air missiles fired from one of the USSR interceptor aircraft whose pilot had been directed by his ground command and control unit to terminate the flight of KE007.

As a direct result of the missile attack, KE007 crashed and sank into the Sea of Japan southwest of Sakhalin Island. There were no survivors among the passengers, flight crew and cabin attendants. Only fragmentary pieces of the aircraft and a small number of items of personal property have been salvaged to-date. Most of this debris apparently was either dislodged as a result of impact forces at the time the aircraft struck the water or subsequently floated to the surface where they were dispersed by tidal currents.

The search and rescue and salvage efforts of the several interested ICAO Contracting States have now been suspended or terminated completely after more than two months of sustained effort.

Due to the absence or unavailability of: 1) surviving crew members with whom discussions might have taken place; 2) some of the communications which might have shed light on the reasons for KE007's major course deviation; 3) indications of flight crew awareness of their being off track; 4) indication that the crew of KE007 knew they were the subject of interception activity; 5) a record of communications emanating from ground intercept control units; 6) vital flight instrumentation, communications and avionics equipment from the wreckage of KE007 and, finally; 7) the flight data and the cockpit voice recorders from KE007, the investigative effort was compelled to proceed on the basis of limited hard evidence and facts, circumstantial evidence, assumptions and calculations and to base some of its key findings on postulated and then simulated, most-likely scenarios of what may have transpired.

Several potentialities for KE007's straying off track were ultimately discarded by this ICAO investigation as being too unlikely to warrant further consideration. They are:

a) unlawful interference;

b) crew incapacitation;

c) deliberate crew action associated with fuel savings incentives; and

d) extensive cockpit avionics-navigation systems failures or malfunctions.

In light of the information in the second paragraph above concerning the revised ETD of KE007 which should have resulted in an "on-time" arrival at Seoul, the investigation did not consider further the hypothesis considered by the USSR Accident Investigation Commission that there was a deliberate delay in KE007's departure from Anchorage and a premeditated deviation from the flight plan route for intelligence gathering purposes.

As the investigation proceeded, many postulations were heard and considered as to how and why KE007 strayed so far off track. It was possible to narrow the number of plausible explanations to three, each of which were amenable to study, analysis, testing and verification through simulation or sophisticated calculation methodologies. They are:

1) That the crew inadvertently flew virtually the entire flight on a constant magnetic heading (in the "heading mode") due to its unawareness of the fact that "heading" had been selected as the mode of navigation rather than "inertial navigation system" (INS). In such a situation, with the INS system activated although not controlling flight navigation, the crew would have been provided with regular indications of INS waypoint passages at or near the flight plan estimates for such passages and could, therefore, have been under the impression they were navigating in the INS mode.

2) That an undetected 10 degree longitudinal error was made in inserting the "present position" coordinates of the Anchorage gate position into one or more of the INS units on board the aircraft. Such an entry mistake could be made by a single "finger error" in entering more than 100 digits and letters that would be needed to fully load a single INS unit at the outset of the flight.

3) That at some point a crew member inserted the Seoul (destination) coordinates into the INS steering unit as a waypoint merely to obtain an indication of the direct distance to Seoul. In so doing, rather than using the "remote ranging" capability of the INS, he erroneously entered the present position to Seoul as a directed track change. Such an inadvertent action would produce the information desired but also cause the aircraft to take up the direct, great circle track to Seoul bypassing all other waypoints which, in the early stages of the flight would result in a change in heading, which would easily remain undetected.

After a simulation study which included four flights, three of which were of four to five and one half hours in duration, the scenarios in 1) and 2) presented possible explanations for the straying to the right of track by

KE007 virtually from the beginning of its ill-fated flight. Each of the scenarios assumes a considerable degree of lack of alertness and attentiveness on the part of the entire flight crew but not to a degree that is unknown in international civil aviation.

Concerning the interception and associated identification, signalling and communications the investigation found the following:

1) Interceptions of KE007 were attempted by USSR military interceptor aircraft, over Kamchatka Peninsula and in the vicinity of Sakhalin Island.

2) The USSR authorities assumed that KE007 was an "intelligence" aircraft and, therefore, they did not make exhaustive efforts to identify the aircraft through in-flight visual observations.

3) KE007's climb from FL 330 to FL 350 during the time of the last interception, a few minutes before its flight was terminated, was interpreted as being an evasive action thus further supporting the presumption that it was an "intelligence" aircraft.

4) ICAO was not provided any radar recordings, recorded communications or transcripts associated with the first intercept attempt or for the ground-to-interceptor portion of the second attempt, therefore, it was not possible to fully assess the comprehensiveness or otherwise of the application of intercept procedures, signalling and communications.

5) In the absence of any indication that the flight crew of KE007 was aware of the two interception attempts, it was concluded that they were not.

Preliminary Information on Progress of the U.S.S.R. Investigation Into the Accident to a South Korean Aeroplane on 1 September 1983

23 International Legal Materials 910 (1984).*

1.1 General information

On the night of 1 September 1983, at 05.30 Kamchatka time (20.30 Moscow summer time on 31 August 1983), an unknown aeroplane violated the State frontier of the Union of Soviet Socialist Republics and penetrated deep into USSR airspace. The intruder aeroplane spent about 2 hours over the Kamchatka Peninsula, the area of the Okhotsk Sea and the Island of Sakhalin.

Interception procedures were executed within USSR airspace, over the Kamchatka Peninsula, by aircraft of the USSR Air Defence Command (PVO) in accordance with the established USSR regulations, for the purpose of compelling the aeroplane to land on USSR territory. The intruder aeroplane did not comply with the demands of the interceptors but continued flying in the direction of the Sea of Okhotsk.

---

* Reprinted with the permission of the
American Society of International Law.

In the course of the intruder aircraft's onward flight in Soviet airspace over the Island of Sakhalin the regulatory USSR interception procedures were executed once more. In view of the refusal of the intruder aircraft to comply with the demands of the USSR anti-aircraft defence forces to land on USSR territory, the flight was terminated in Soviet airspace over USSR territory—above the Pravda housing project in the southwest part of Sakhalin Island—on 1 September 1983 at 06.24 Sakhalin time (22.24 Moscow time on 31 August 1983).

On 1 September—10 hours after the termination of the intruder aircraft's flight—the USSR received an official request from the United States for information concerning a South Korean aeroplane which "according to the information of American tracking stations, has lost its way in the area of Sakhalin".

It thus became known from foreign sources that the sovereignty of the USSR, the rules of Soviet and international law and the Standards of the International Civil Aviation Organization (ICAO) had been violated by an aircraft registered in South Korea. No official confirmation of this has been communicated to the Soviet side by South Korea.

* * *

CONCLUSIONS

1. The investigation of the violation of the State frontier of the USSR and deep penetration of USSR airspace by the intruder aeroplane in the areas of Kamchatka and South Sakhalin on the night of 31 August_1 September has brought to light numerous breaches of Soviet law, and specifically of the Air Code of the USSR and the Law on the State Frontier of the USSR, and violations of the terms of the 1944 Chicago Convention, Annexes 2 and 10 and the rules promulgated in AIP USSR and the requirements of ICAO air navigation documents.

2. [T]hat the intruder aeroplane belonged to a South Korean airline was received by the Soviet authorities from foreign sources only after its flight had been terminated by the Air Defence Command.

3. It has been established that the flight of the South Korean aeroplane over Soviet territory was conducted with prior intent.

This is confirmed by the following:

a) a deviation from track of more than 500 km far exceeds the permissible navigational errors for this type of aeroplane;

b) the indications of the airborne radar equipment made it possible for the crew to be aware of the fact that they were crossing the Kamchatka Peninsula and Island of Sakhalin, which was clearly inconsistent with the plan to fly on airway R20;

c) the ATS units of the United States and Japan, notwithstanding the absence of the South Korean aeroplane from its prescribed track for over 3 hours in their controlled airspace, took no steps to return the aeroplane to that track;

d) the flight crew of the intruder aeroplane did not respond to the series of actions taken by the Soviet Air Defence forces to attract the attention of the South Korean aeroplane to the fact that it was being intercepted and oblige it to land;

e) the deviation of the * * * aeroplane from the international airway was such that its flight took place over strategically important Soviet centres in the Far East and coincided with a stepped-up operation by United States intelligence forces in this area.

4. The South Korean aeroplane was engaged in a preplanned intelligence-gathering and provocative mission.

5. The actions of the Soviet anti-aircraft defence interceptors were conducted in strict conformity with current Soviet legislation and the provisions set out in AIP USSR. The intruder aeroplane ignored the actions of the intercepting fighters and altered its heading, altitude and flight speed, which proves that the crew was in full control of the flight. In view of the complete refusal of the intruder aeroplane to obey the instructions given by the Air Defence aircraft, the intruder aeroplane's flight was terminated on orders from the ground.

6. The ATC services of the United States and Japan, which were responsible for providing navigational support to the South Korean aeroplane on flight KAL 007 along the Anchorage–Tokyo airway, did not utilize the possibilities open to them of detecting and forestalling such a glaring deviation by the aeroplane.

Chairman of the Accident Investigation Commission, A.I. Okhonsky

Review of Secretary–General's Report by the Air Navigation Commission of the I.C.A.O.

23 International Legal Materials 924 (1984).*

* * *

4.4 Although the preliminary information provided by the USSR in Appendix F to C–WP_7764 is that the actions of the USSR intercepting aircraft were conducted in strict conformity with the interception procedures promulgated in the USSR AIP, which are essentially in line with the ICAO procedures, the transcript in Appendix D to C–WP_7764 of air-ground communications between the intercepting aircraft and intercept control units gives no clear indication that the intercepting aircraft had taken up a position "within view of the pilot of the intercepted aircraft" or "to enable the pilot of the latter aircraft to see the visual signals given" as recommended in Attachment A to Annex 2. This has been highlighted because the Commission realizes that many factors have to be considered in assessing the ideal position for an interceptor to be seen by the pilot of the civil aircraft. Therefore, it is of paramount importance for the interceptor aircraft to ensure that it attracts the attention of the pilot-in-command of the civil aircraft.

4.5 The Air Navigation Commission is unable to establish the exact cause for the significant deviation from tract. The magnitude of the

* Reprinted with the permission of the
American Society of International Law.

diversion cannot be explained, particularly as the aircraft was equipped with navigation equipment which should have enabled the crew to adhere to its track. It has to be understood that operators have extensive ab-initio and recurrent training programmes to train pilots in the use of self-contained navigation aids. This is the case also for Korean Air Lines.

* * *

5. Conclusions

5.1 During the technical review of the Secretary General's report as contained in C–WP_7764, the Air Navigation Commission has not attempted to offer any firm conclusions regarding the various aspects of the incident, because the information presented to the Commission in relation to the total period of flight KE007 was incomplete and some of the information received by ICAO had differences which could not be cleared up. Furthermore, the Commission found it difficult to validate and endorse the conclusions connected with the scenarios postulated in the Secretary General's report because any one of them contained some points which could not be explained satisfactorily.

5.2 The Commission noted that the evaluations and simulations conducted did not include an extensive evaluation of INS equipment malfunctions or other failures involving significant track deviations which have occurred in the past and is of the opinion that study of this subject should be pursued.

* * *

Resolution Adopted by the Council of the I.C.A.O., March 6, 1984

23 International Legal Materials 937 (1984).*

THE COUNCIL,

1) RECALLING the resolutions adopted and the decisions taken on 16 September 1983 at the Extraordinary Session of the ICAO Council and endorsed by the 24th Session of the ICAO Assembly in October 1983 as well as the Council Resolution of 13 December 1983, relating to the destruction of a Korean Air Lines civil aircraft on 1 September 1983 by Soviet military aircraft;

2) HAVING CONSIDERED the report of the investigation by the Secretary General and the subsequent technical review by the Air Navigation Commission;

3) RECOGNIZING that, although this investigation was unable, because of lack of necessary data, to determine conclusively the precise cause for the serious deviation of some 500 kilometers from its flight plan route by the Korean aircraft into the airspace above the territory under the sovereignty of the Soviet Union, no evidence was found to indicate that

* Reprinted with the permission of the American Society of International Law.

the deviation was premeditated or that the crew was at any time aware of the flight's deviation;

4) REAFFIRMING that, whatever the circumstances which, according to the Secretary General's report, may have caused the aircraft to stray off its flight plan route, such use of armed force constitutes a violation of international law, and invokes generally recognized legal consequences;

5) RECOGNIZING that such use of armed force is a grave threat to the safety of international civil aviation, and is incompatible with the norms governing international behavior and with the rules, Standards and Recommended Practices enshrined in the Chicago Convention and its Annexes and with elementary considerations of humanity;

6) EXPRESSING its continuing sympathy with the families bereaved in this tragic incident;

1) CONDEMNS the use of armed force which resulted in the destruction of the Korean airliner and the tragic loss of 269 lives;

2) DEEPLY DEPLORES the Soviet failure to cooperate in the search and rescue efforts of other involved States and the Soviet failure to cooperate with the ICAO investigation of the incident by refusing to accept the visit of the investigation team appointed by the Secretary General and by failing so far to provide the Secretary General with information relevant to the investigation;

3) URGES all Contracting States to cooperate fully in the work of examining and adopting an amendment to the Chicago Convention at the 25th Session (Extraordinary) of the ICAO Assembly and in the improvement of measures for preventing a recurrence of this type of tragedy.

——————

Notes. *Reaction to the destruction of KAL Flight 007.* The United States presented diplomatic notes to the Soviet Union demanding compensation for the attack on the airliner. The Soviet Union refused to accept the notes. Similar notes were presented by Australia, Canada, Japan, Malaysia, the Philippines, Thailand, the United Kingdom and (through the U.S.) Korea. 22 International Legal Materials 1190 (1983). Public controversy over the affair highlighted one question: did the Soviets know they were attacking a civilian airliner or did they mistakenly believe that the aircraft was a military reconnaissance plane? *See* Hersh, THE TARGET IS DESTROYED (1986).

North Pacific Route System: Emergency Communications

80 American Journal of International Law 152 (1986).*

By a trilateral exchange of notes at Tokyo on October 8, 1985 among American Ambassador Mike Mansfield, Soviet Ambassador to Japan Pyotr

* Reprinted with the permission of the
American Society of International Law.

Abrasimov and Japanese Minister of Foreign Affairs Shintaro Abe, the United States of America, the Union of Soviet Socialist Republics and Japan brought into force arrangements to enhance the safety of flights over the North Pacific Route System. These arrangements were set out in a memorandum of understanding signed by representatives of the three Governments at Tokyo on July 29, 1985. The trilateral exchange confirmed the memorandum, which provides for a new communications network among the parties' respective air control centers at Anchorage, Tokyo and Khabarovsk in order to coordinate actions to assist a civil aircraft in an emergency.

Recognizing the complete and exclusive sovereignty of each state over the airspace above its territory, the memorandum designates the area control centers (ACCS) at Anchorage, Tokyo and Khabarovsk as points of contact among the parties' respective air traffic control services, with the center at Tokyo the principal point of contact. Contact among the three air traffic control services is to be conducted on a priority basis. To achieve coordination of their actions, the area control centers at Anchorage and Tokyo will initiate communication with the Khabarovsk area control center to provide all available information regarding a civil aircraft assigned to a North Pacific route when they are aware of its possible entry into a Soviet flight information region (FIR). When necessary, the area control center at Khabarovsk will initiate communication with the Tokyo and Anchorage area control centers to exchange information about an unidentified aircraft appearing in a Soviet flight information region. To the extent available, the following will be exchanged: information provided by the appropriate area control center that the situation has occurred; data on the type of aircraft; its radio call sign, transponder code, nationality, operator, location, altitude, and speed; the time and type of the event; the pilot's intentions if known; actions taken and assistance requested; information to the responsible search and rescue agencies. The communication facilities between the Anchorage, Tokyo and Khabarovsk area control centers are to be available on a round-the-clock basis.

A new dedicated direct speech circuit, using the currently existing telephone cable, is to be established between the Tokyo and Khabarovsk area control centers. The existing high-frequency speech circuit between the Sapporo (Japan) and Khabarovsk area control centers, connected by domestic telephone channel to the Tokyo area control center, is to be used as a backup to the direct speech circuit.

KAL–007 Black Boxes Retrieved by the USSR

Russian President Yeltsin announced in October, 1992 that the Soviets had retrieved the downed aircraft's flight recorders from the depths of the Sea of Japan. The bearing of this source of possible information on what really happened is not yet clear.

———

Notes & Questions. 1. *Beyond trespass: espionage as a state offense*. Issues other than technical trespass of Soviet airspace were involved in the U–2 incident. The criminal charge against Powers in the Soviet Union was of espionage as defined in the domestic law of that state.[a] The Soviets also claimed that espionage was involved in the KAL case. In the tradition of the international spy, fictional and real, the espionage agent is alone "out in the cold." He expects to be disowned if caught. The conventional practice of states is not overtly to charge another state with espionage but to counter-attack in kind, in what Dean Acheson once called "the underworld of international relations." In the U–2 case, however, although Powers was caught and prosecuted under Soviet law at the time, the former USSR openly charged the US with responsibility, calling for the Security Council to condemn the "aggressive acts." President Eisenhower responded with the unprecedented admission that the US was responsible for Powers' flight, justifying it "to obtain information now concealed behind the iron curtain in order to lessen the danger of surprise attack on the free world * * *." Wright, *Legal Aspects of the U–2 Incident*, 54 Am.J.Int'l L. 836, 838 (1960).

Are there, therefore, issues of espionage at the international level? That is, is the law of espionage purely domestic, directed at the individual only, or is there state responsibility to the state spied upon? In view of the practices of states over centuries, it is not possible to find a consentio juris that spying per se is an offense under customary law. Has it become so under the U.N. Charter, either as to (a) conventional espionage through the penetration of the state's ground frontier, or (b) aerial espionage through the penetration of airspace? *See* Article 2(4). Also, espionage is a purely political offense, exempting alleged perpetrators from extradition.

2. ***Identification zones.*** The US has established air defense identification zones (ADIZ) and a distant early warning identification zone (DEWIZ) in areas of the airspace over the high seas adjacent to its coasts. Similar zones have been established by some other states. Aircraft operating in or penetrating such zones are subject to requirements with respect to filing flight plans; pilots of aircraft entering the US through an ADIZ or a DEWIZ are required to report positions.14 C.F.R., Part 99. Since these zones extend seaward several hundreds of miles, do they entail a violation of international law respecting the jurisdiction of the US over airspace? Can the US lawfully prescribe rules regulating activity in these zones on the ground that obedience to the rules is a condition to entry into the territory of the US? *See, Comment e* to § 21, and the 1987 Restatement, Reporters' *Note 2* to § 521.

3. ***The Air Tragedy at Lockerbie, Scotland.*** The destruction of Pan–Am 103, Dec. 21, 1988, with loss of all passengers and crew due to the explosion of an infernal machine placed aboard it at Frankfurt, apparently by Libyan nationals, two of whom were prosecuted in the Hague, by Scottish judges and upon Scottish and internationallaw. This case will be considered under *Sabotage* in the next sub-division of this Chapter, *Offensives Aboard Aircraft*. One question may be posed now: If it should be shown that the saboteurs or the baggage handlers at Frankfurt were the

---

a. Compare 18 U.S.C. § 796, with respect to photography of military installations   from aircraft.

agents of the State of Libya, does an international claim against Libya in the *Pan–Am Case* differ from a possible claim against Russia as the successor to the Soviet State for the KAL–007 loss? Are the *délits* of the two states, if both are involved, the same or different? What do you think?

Where to Draw the Line between the International Public Law of Airspace and This Private Law of Transnational Air Transport

In chapter 4, we alluded to traditional differences in the origins and natures of sea law as to what is public international law and what is not. The difference is disappearing generally, and in Air law it is much more complex, chiefly because almost all of air law is treaty based, insofar as over-borders operations are concerned. We have decided that the Chicago Convention and its progeny, bilateral civil aviation route and passenger-handling agreements, should be presented, because of the very large direct involvement of state interests, including territorial airspace. But we think the Warsaw Convention and its progeny in international agreement form, dealing with liabilities of contractual commercial carriers to passengers, baggage and cargo, mainly belong to another arena. We present only a brief summary of an intensely litigated area of private claims against carriers and insurers, that of the Warsaw Convention and its modifications. An exception to this is litigation that arose over the KAL disaster, which has given rise to two important Supreme Court decisions, which follow after a brief note.

International Aircarrier Liability to Passengers, "Offenses" in a Nutshell

Establishing tort liability (or is it contractual?) of a common carrier is difficult enough on the ground and within a single jurisdiction. It is much more difficult in the case of civil aviation operations among states, because of the ways in which aircraft losses happen and the widely different treatment of liabilities for losses in diverse legal systems, especially as between common law and civil law jurisdictions. The operative heart of the Warsaw Convention of 1925–29 should be printed on your ticket if you fly abroad, in at least 10–point type.

But if the print is smaller or you lose the ticket stub, the Convention still applies. It limits death or injury claims to $75,000, without proof of fault, or, in some American states, $58,000 exclusive of legal fees and costs. There are also baggage loss limitations. A comparative law scholar will instantly see the relationship of this scheme to the civil law limits on tort recovery for personal injury. Not unnaturally, common law lawyers and judges are not wildly enthusiastic about such a system, but then they begin to think of the difficulties of proving fault of the flight crew and the ground management of an air-carrier. Recent disasters such as KAL–007 have "pushed the envelope" in U.S. tort jurisprudence a bit, but the courts have held firm in favor of the Convention's application as against technical and constitutional-level attacks. Of perhaps only minor consolation is the provision in the Convention that removes the recovery limitation if wilful misconduct on the part of the aircarrier can be proved. The international air traveler is well advised to insure himself up to any amount he wishes or can afford, above the difficult to avoid Warsaw Convention capped recovery.

Questions for a Torts Class or a Beer Hall:

1.   Would the Warsaw Convention scheme be better for automobile passengers than mandatory no-fault auto insurance?

2.   Would the Warsaw Convention scheme be better than trying to enforce adequate auto insurance policy injury liability limits, say, in California?

Zicherman v. Korean Air Lines, Co., Ltd.

516 U.S. 217 (1996).

SCALIA, J.

This action presents the question whether, in a suit brought under Article 17 of the Warsaw Convention governing international air transportation . . . a plaintiff may recover damages for loss of society resulting from the death of a relative in a plane crash on the high seas.

On September 1, 1983, Korean Air Lines Flight KE007, en route from Anchorage, Alaska, to Seoul, South Korea, strayed into air space of the Soviet Union and was shot down over the Sea of Japan. All 269 persons on board were killed, including Muriel Kole. Petitioners Marjorie Zicherman and Muriel Mahalek, Kole's sister and mother, respectively, sued respondent Korean Air Lines Co., Ltd. (KAL), in the United States District Court for the Southern District of New York. Petitioners' final amended complaint contained three counts, entitled, respectively, "Warsaw Convention," "Death on the High Seas Act," and "Conscious Pain and Suffering." At issue here is only the Warsaw Convention count, in which petitioners sought "judgment against KAL for their pecuniary damages, for their grief and mental anguish, for the loss of the decedent's society and companionship, and for the decedent's conscious pain and suffering. "

Along with other federal-court actions arising out of the KAL crash, petitioners' case was transferred to the United States District Court for the District of Columbia for consolidated proceedings on common issues of liability. There, a jury found that the destruction of Flight KE007 was proximately caused by "willful misconduct" of the flight crew, thus lifting the Warsaw Convention's $75,000 cap on damages. See Warsaw Convention, Art. 25, 49 Stat. 3020; Order of Civil Aeronautics Board Approving Increases in Liability Limitations of Warsaw Convention and Hague Protocol, reprinted in note following 49 U.S.C.App. § 1502 (1988 ed.). The jury awarded $50 million in punitive damages against KAL. The Court of Appeals for the District of Columbia Circuit upheld the fuiding of "willful misconduct," but vacated the punitive damages award, holding that the Warsaw Convention does not permit the recovery of punitive damages. *In re Korean Air Lines Disaster of Sept. 1, 1983*, 932 F.2d 1475, 1479–1481, 1484–1490, cert. denied, 502 U.S. 994, (1991). The individual cases were then remanded by the Judicial Panel on Multidistrict Litigation to the original transferor courts for trial of compensatory damages issues.

At petitioners' damages trial in the Southern District of New York, KAL moved for determination that the Death on the High Seas Act (DOHSA), 41 Stat. 537, 46 U.S.C.App. § 761 *et seq.* (1988 ed.), prescribed the proper claimants and the recoverable damages, and that it did not permit damages for loss of society. The District Court denied the motion and held, *inter alia*, that petitioners could recover for loss of "love, affection, and companionship." *In re Korean Air Lines Disaster of Sept. 1, 1983*, 807 F.Supp. 1073, 1086–1088 (S.D.N.Y.1992). The jury awarded loss-of-society damages in the amount of $70,000 to Zicherman and $28,000 to Mahalek.

The Court of Appeals for the Second Circuit set aside this award. Applying its prior decisions in *In re Air Disaster at Lockerbie, Scotland, on Dec. 21, 1988*, 928 F.2d 1267, 1278–1279 (*Lockerbie I*), cert. denied *sub nom. Rein v. Pan American World Airways, Inc.*, 502 U.S. 920, (1991), and *In re Air Disaster at Lockerbie, Scotland, on Dec. 21, 1988*, 37 F.3d 804 (1994) (*Lockerbie II*), cert. denied *sub nom. Pan American World Airways, Inc. v. Pagnucco*, 513 U.S. 1126, (1995), it held that general maritime law supplied the substantive law of compensatory damages to be applied in an action under the Warsaw Convention. 43 F.3d 18, 21–22 (1994). Then, following its decision in *Lockerbie II*, it held that, under general maritime law, a plaintiff is entitled to recover loss-of-society damages, but only if he was a dependent of the decedent at the time of death. The court concluded that as a matter of law Mahalek had not established that status, and therefore vacated her award; it remanded to the District Court for determination of whether Zicherman was a dependent of Kole.

In their petition for certiorari, petitioners contended that under general maritime law dependency is not a requirement for recovering loss-of-society damages. In a cross-petition, KAL contended that the Warsaw Convention does not allow loss-of-society damages in this case, regardless of dependency. We granted certiorari. 514 U.S. 1062,(1995).

Article 17 of the Warsaw Convention, as set forth in the official American translation of the governing French text, provides as follows: "The carrier shall be liable for *damage sustained* in the event of the death or wounding of a passenger or any other bodily injury suffered by a passenger, if the accident which caused the damage so sustained took place on board the aircraft or in the course of any of the operations of embarking or disembarking." 49 Stat. 3018 (emphasis added). The first and principal question before us is whether loss of society of a relative is made recoverable by this provision.

It is obvious that the English word "damage" or "harm"—or in the official text of the Convention, the French word "*dommage*"—can be applied to an extremely wide range of phenomena, from the medical expenses incurred as a result of Kole's injuries (for which every legal system would provide tort compensation) to the mental distress of some stranger who reads about Kole's death in the paper (for which no legal system would provide tort compensation). It cannot seriously be maintained that Article 17 uses the term in this broadest sense, thus exploding tort liability beyond what any legal system in the world allows, to the farthest reaches of what could be denominated "harm." We therefore reject petitioners' initial proposal that we simply for Petitioners 7–9.

There are only two thinkable alternatives to that. First, what petitioners ultimately suggest: that *"dommage"* means what French law, in 1929, recognized as *legally cognizable* harm, which petitioners assert included not only *"dommage materiel"* (pecuniary harm of various sorts) but also *"dommage moral"* (nonpecuniary harm of various sorts, including loss of society). In support of that approach, petitioners point out that in a prior case involving Article 17 we were guided by French legal usage: *Air France v. Saks*, 470 U.S. 392 (1985) (interpreting the term *"accident"*). See also *Eastern Airlines, Inc. v. Floyd*, 499 U.S. 530 (1991) (interpreting the Article 17 term *"lesion corporelle"*). What is at issue here, however, is not simply whether we will be guided by French legal usage *vel non*. Because, as earlier discussed, the dictionary meaning of the term *"dommage"* embraces harms that no legal system would compensate, it must be acknowledged that the term is to be understood in its distinctively *legal* sense—that is, to mean only *legally cognizable harm*. The nicer question, and the critical one here, is whether the word *"dommage"* establishes *as the content of the concept "legally cognizable harm"* what French law accepted as such in 1929. No case of ours provides precedent for the adoption of French law in such detail. In *Floyd,* we looked to French law to determine whether *"lesion corporelle"* indeed meant (as it had been translated) "bodily injury"—not to determine the subsequent question (equivalent to the question at issue here) whether "bodily injury" encompassed psychic injury. See *id.,* at 536–540, 111 S.Ct., at 1494–1496, And in *Saks,* once we had determined that in French legal terminology the word *"accident"* referred to an unforeseen event, we did not further inquire whether French courts would consider the event at issue in the case unforeseen; we made that judgment for ourselves.

See 470 U.S., at 405–407.

It is particularly implausible that "the shared expectations of the contracting parties," *id.,* at 399, were that their mere use of the French language would effect adoption of the precise rule applied in France as to what constitutes legally cognizable harm. Those involved in the negotiation and adoption of the Convention could not have been ignorant of the fact that the law on this point varies widely from jurisdiction to jurisdiction, and even from statute to statute within a single jurisdiction. Just as we found it "unlikely" in *Floyd* that Convention signatories would have understood the general term *"lesion corporelle"* to confer a cause of action available under French law but unrecognized in many other nations, see 499 U.S., at 540. So also in the present case we find it unlikely that they would have understood Article 17's use of the general term *"domniage"* to require compensation for elements of harm recognized in France but unrecognized elsewhere, or to forbid compensation for elements of harm *unrecognized* in France but recognized elsewhere. Many signatory nations, including Czechoslovakia, Denmark, Germany, the Netherlands, the Soviet Union, and Sweden, did not, even many years after the Warsaw Convention, recognize a cause of action for nonpecuniary harm resulting from wrongful death. See 11 International Encyclopedia of Comparative Law: Torts, ch. 9, pp. 15–18 (A. Tunc ed. 1972); *Floyd, supra,* at 544–545, n. 10.

The other alternative, and the only one we think realistic, is to believe that *"dommage"* means (as it does in French legal usage) "legally cognizable harm," but that Article 17 leaves it to adjudicating courts to specify what harm is cognizable . . .

The postratification conduct of the contracting parties displays the same understanding that the damages recoverable—so long as they consist of compensation for harm incurred *(dommage survenu)*—are to be determined by domestic law. Some countries, including England, Germany and the Netherlands, have adopted domestic legislation to govern the types of damages recoverable in a Convention case. See Haanappel, The right to sue in death cases under the Warsaw Convention, 6 Air Law 66, 72, 74 (1981); E. Giemulla, R. Schmid, & P. Ehlers, Warsaw Convention 39, n. 5 (1992); German Law Concerning Air Navigation (Luft VG) of Jan. 10, 1959, Arts. 35–36, 38, reprinted in 1 Senate Committee on Commerce, Air Laws and Treaties of the World, 89th Cong., 1st Sess., 766–768 (Comm. Print 1965); R. Mankiewicz, The Liability Regime of the International Air Carrier ¶ 187, pp. 160–161 (1981). Canada has adopted legislation setting forth who may bring suit under Article 24(2), but has left the question of what types of damages are recoverable to provincial law. Haanappel, *supra,* at 70–71. The Court of Appeals of Quebec has rejected the argument that Article 17 permits damages unrecoverable under domestic Quebec law. *Dame Surprenant v. Air Canada,* [19731 C.A. 107, 117–118, 126–127 (opinion of Deschenes, J.). But see *Preston v. Hunting Air Transport Ltd.,* [19561 1 Q.B. 454, 461–462 (granting damages under Convention, but without considering Article 24). Finally, the expert commentators are virtually unanimous that the type of harm compensable is to be determined by domestic law. See, *e.g.,* H. Drion, Limitation of Liabilities in International Air Law I III, pp. 125–126 (1954); Giemulta, Schmid, & Ehlers, *supra,* at 33; D. Goedhuis, National Air Legislations and the Warsaw Convention 269 (1937); Mankiewicz, *supra,* ¶ 187, at 160–161; G. Miller, Liability in International Air Transport: The Warsaw System in Municipal Courts 125 (1977); see also Cha, The Air Carrier's Liability to Passengers in International Law, 7 Air L.Rev. 25, 56–57 (1936). . . .

We conclude that Articles 17 and 24(2) of the Warsaw Convention permit compensation only for legally cognizable harm, but leave the specification of what harm is legally cognizable to the domestic law applicable under the forum's choice-of-law rules. Where, as here, an airplane crash occurs on the high seas, DOHSA supplies the substantive United States law. Because DOHSA permits only pecuniary damages, petitioners are not entitled to recover for loss of society. We therefore need not reach the question whether, under general maritime law, dependency is a prerequisite for loss-of-society damages. . . .

El Al Israel Airlines, Ltd. v. Tseng

525 U.S. 155 (1999)

GINSBURG, J.

Plaintiff-respondent Tsui Yuan Tseng was subjected to an intrusive security search at John F. Kennedy International Airport in New York before she boarded an El Al Israel Airlines May 22, 1993 flight to Tel Aviv. Tseng seeks tort damages from El Al for this occurrence. The episode-in-suit, both parties now submit, does not qualify as an "accident" within the meaning of the treaty popularly known as the Warsaw Convention, which governs air carrier liability for "all international transportation." Tseng alleges psychic or psychosomatic injuries, but no "bodily injury," as that term is used in the Convention. Her case presents a question of the Convention's exclusivity: When the Convention allows no recovery for the episode-in-suit, does it correspondingly preclude the passenger from maintaining an action for damages under another source of law, in this case, New York tort law?

The exclusivity question before us has been settled prospectively in a Warsaw Convention protocol (Montreal Protocol No. 4) recently ratified by the Senate. In accord with the protocol, Tseng concedes, a passenger whose injury is not compensable under the Convention (because it entails no "bodily injury" or was not the result of an "accident") will have no recourse to an alternate remedy. We conclude that the protocol, to which the United States has now subscribed, clarifies, but does not change, the Convention's exclusivity domain. We therefore hold that recovery for a personal injury suffered "on board [an] aircraft or in the course of any of the operations of embarking or disembarking," Art. 17, 49 Stat. 3018, if not allowed under the Convention, is not available at all.

I

We have twice reserved decision on the Convention's exclusivity. In *Air France v. Saks*, 470 U.S. 392 (1985), we concluded that a passenger's injury was not caused by an "accident" for which the airline could be held accountable under the Convention, but expressed no view whether that passenger could maintain "a state cause of action for negligence." *Id.*, at 408. In *Eastern Airlines, Inc. v. Floyd,* 499 U.S. 530 (1991), we held that mental or psychic injuries unaccompanied by physical injuries are not compensable under Article 17 of the Convention, but declined to reach the question whether the Convention "provides the exclusive cause of action for injuries sustained during international air transportation." *Id.*, at 553. We resolve in this case the question on which we earlier reserved judgment.

At the outset, we highlight key provisions of the treaty we are interpreting. Chapter I of the Warsaw Convention, entitled "SCOPE—DEFINITIONS," declares in Article 1(1) that the "[C]onvention shall apply to all international transportation of persons, baggage, or goods performed by aircraft for hire." 49 Stat. 3014. Chapter III, entitled "LIABILITY OF THE Carrier," defines in Articles 17, 18, and 19 the three kinds of liability for which the Convention provides. Article 17 establishes the conditions of liability for personal injury to passengers. . . .

II

With the key treaty provisions as the backdrop, we next describe the episode-in-suit. On May 22, 1993, Tsui Yuan Tseng arrived at John F.

Kennedy International Airport (hereinafter JFK) to board an El Al Israel Airlines flight to Tel Aviv. In conformity with standard El Al preboarding procedures, a security guard questioned Tseng about her destination and travel plans. The guard considered Tseng's responses "illogical," and ranked her as a "high risk" passenger. Tseng was taken to a private security room where her baggage and person were searched for explosives and detonating devices. She was told to remove her shoes, jacket, and sweater, and to lower her blue jeans to midhip. A female security guard then searched Tseng's body outside her clothes by hand and with an electronic security wand.

After the search, which lasted 15 minutes, El Al personnel decided that Tseng did not pose a security threat and allowed her to board the flight. Tseng later testified that she "was really sick and very upset" during the flight, that she was "emotionally traumatized and disturbed" during her month-long trip in Israel, and that, upon her return, she underwent medical and psychiatric treatment for the lingering effects of the body search. . . .

Tseng filed suit against El Al in 1994 in a New York state court of first instance. Her complaint alleged a state law personal injury claim based on the May 22, 1993 episode at JFK. Tseng's pleading charged, *inter alia*, assault and false imprisonment, but alleged no bodily injury. El Al removed the case to federal court.

The Court of Appeals reversed in relevant part. See 122 F.3d 99 (C.A.2 1997). The Second Circuit concluded first that no "accident" within Article 17's compass had occurred; in the Court of Appeals' view, the Convention drafters did not "ai[m] to impose close to absolute liability" for an individual's "personal reaction" to "routine operating procedures," measures that, although "inconvenien[t] and embarass[ing]," are the "price passengers pay for . . . airline safety." *Id.*, at 103–104.[9] In some tension

---

9. Notes that the District Court, "[u]sing the flexible application prescribed by the Supreme Court," concluded that El Al's search of Tseng was an "accident": "[A] routine search, applied erroneously to plaintiff in the course of embarking on the aircraft, is fairly accurately characterized as an accident." 919 F.Supp. 155, 158 (S.D.N.Y.1996).

The Court of Appeals disagreed. That court described security searches as "routine" in international air travel, part of a terrorism-prevention effort that is "widely recognized and encouraged in the law," and "the price passengers pay for the degree of airline safety so far afforded them." 122 F.3d, at 103. The court observed that passengers reasonably should be aware of "routine operating procedures" of the kind El Al conducts daily. *Ibid.* The risk of mistakes, *i.e.*, that innocent persons will be erroneously searched, is "inherent in any effort to detect malefactors," the court explained. *Ibid.* Tseng thus encountered "ordffiary events

and procedures of air transportation," the court concluded, and not "an unexpected or unusual event." *Id.*, at 104. It is questionable whether the Court of Appeals "flexibly applied" the definition of "accident" we set forth in *Saks*. Both parties, however, now accept the Court of Appeals' disposition of that issue.

In any event, even if El Al's search of Tseng was an "accident," the core question of the Convention's exclusivity would remain. The Convention provides for compensation under Article 17 only when the passenger suffers "death, physical injury, or physical manifestation of injury," *Eastern Airlines, Inc. v. Floyd*, 499 U.S. 530, 552, a condition that both the District Court and the Court of Appeals determined Tseng did not meet, see 919 F.Supp., at 158, 122 F.3d, at 104. The question whether the Convention precludes an action under local law when a passenger's claim fails to satisfy Article 17's conditions for liability does not turn on *which* of those conditions the claim fails to satisfy.

with that reasoning, the Second Circuit next concluded that the Convention does not shield the very same "routine operating procedures" from assessment under the diverse laws of signatory nations (and, in the case of the United States, States within one Nation) governing assault and false imprisonment. See *id.*, at 104.

Article 24 of the Convention, the Court of Appeals said, "clearly states that resort to local law is precluded only where the incident is 'covered' by Article 17, meaning where there has been an accident, either on the plane or in the course of embarking or disembarking, which led to death, wounding or other bodily injury." *Id.*, at 104–105. The court found support in the drafting history of the Convention, which it construed to "indicate that national law was intended to provide the passenger's remedy where the Convention did not expressly apply." *Id.*, at 105. The Second Circuit also rejected the argument that allowance of state-law claims when the Convention does not permit recovery would contravene the treaty's goal of uniformity. The court read our decision in *Zichernwn v. Korean Air Lines Co.*, 516 U.S. 217 (1996), to "instruct specifically that the Convention expresses no compelling interest in uniformity that would warrant ... supplanting an otherwise applicable body of law." 122 F.3d, at 107.

III

We accept it as given that El Al's search of Tseng was not an "accident" within the meaning of Article 17, for the parties do not place that Court of Appeals conclusion at issue. We also accept, again only for purposes of this decision, that El Al's actions did not constitute "wilful misconduct"; accordingly, we confront no issue under Article 25 of the Convention ... The parties do not dispute that the episode-in-suit occurred in international transportation in the course of embarking.

Our inquiry begins with the text of Article 24, which prescribes the exclusivity of the Convention's provisions for air carrier liability. "[I]t is our responsibility to give the specific words of the treaty a meaning consistent with the shared expectations of the contracting parties." *Saks*, 470 U.S., at 399, 1338. "Because a treaty ratified by the United States is not only the law of this land, see U.S. Const., Art. II, § 2, but also an agreement among sovereign powers, we have traditionally considered as aids to its interpretation the negotiating and drafting history (*travaux preparatoires*) and the postratification understanding of the contracting parties." *Zicherman*, 516 U.S., at 226.

Article 24 provides that "cases covered by article 17"—or in the governing French text, "les cas prevus a l'article 17"]—may "only be brought subject to the conditions and limits set out in th[e] [C]onvention." 49 Stat. 3020. That prescription is not a model of the clear drafter's art. We recognize that the words lend themselves to divergent interpretation.

In Tseng's view, and in the view of the Court of Appeals, "les cas prevus a l'article 17" means those cases in which a passenger could actually maintain a claim for relief under Article 17. So read, Article 24 would permit any passenger whose personal injury suit did not satisfy the liability conditions of Article 17 to pursue the claim under local law.

In El Al's view, on the other hand, and in the view of the United States as *amicus curiae*, "les cas prevus a l'article 17" refers generically to all personal injury cases stemming from occurrences on board an aircraft or in embarking or disembarking, and simply distinguishes that class of cases (Article 17 cases) from cases involving damaged luggage or goods, or delay (which Articles 18 and 19 address). So read, Article 24 would preclude a passenger from asserting any air transit personal injury claims under local law, including claims that failed to satisfy Article 17's liability conditions, notably, because the injury did not result from an "accident," see *Saks*, 470 U.S., at 405, 105 S.Ct. 1338, or because the "accident" did not result in physical injury or physical manifestation of injury, see *Floyd*, 499 U.S., at 552.

Respect is ordinarily due the reasonable views of the Executive Branch concerning the meaning of an international treaty. See *Sumitomo Shoji America, Inc. v. Avagliano*, 457 U.S. 176, 184–185(1982) ("Although not conclusive, the meaning attributed to treaty provisions by the Government agencies charged with their negotiation and enforcement is entitled to great weight."). We conclude that the Government's construction of Article 24 is most faithful to the Convention's text, purpose, and overall structure.

A

The cardinal purpose of the Warsaw Convention, we have observed, is to "achieve uniformity of rules governing claims arising from international air transportation." *Floyd,* 499 U.S., at 552; see *Zicherman,* 516 U.S., at 230. The Convention signatories, in the treaty's preamble, specifically "recognized the advantage of regulating in a uniform manner the conditions of ... the liability of the carrier".... To provide the desired uniformity, Chapter III of the Convention sets out an array of liability rules which, the treaty declares, "apply to all international transportation of persons, baggage, or goods performed by aircraft." *Ibid.* In that Chapter, the Convention describes and defines the three areas of air carrier liability (personal injuries in Article 17, baggage or goods loss, destruction, or damage in Article 18, and damage occasioned by delay in Article 19), the conditions exempting air carriers from liability (Article 20), the monetary limits of liability (Article 22), and the circumstances in which air carriers may not limit liability (Articles 23 and 25).... Given the Convention's comprehensive scheme of liability rules and its textual emphasis on uniformity, we would be hard put to conclude that the delegates at Warsaw meant to subject air carriers to the distinct, nonuniform liability rules of the individual signatory nations.

The Court of Appeals looked to our precedent for guidance on this point, but it misperceived our meaning. It misread our decision in *Zicherman* to say that the Warsaw Convention expresses no compelling interest in uniformity that would warrant preempting an otherwise applicable body of law, here New York tort law. See 122 F.3d, at 107. *Zicherman* acknowledges that the Convention centrally endeavors "to foster uniformity in the law of international air travel." 516 U.S., at 230. It further recognizes that the Convention addresses the question whether there is airline liability *vel non*. See *id.*, at 231. The *Zicherman* case itself involved auxiliary issues: who may seek recovery in lieu of passengers, and for what harms they may be compensated. See *id.*, at 221, 227. Looking to the Convention's text, negotiating and drafting history, contracting states' postratification understanding of the Convention, and scholarly commentary, the Court in *Zicherman* determined that Warsaw drafters intended to resolve *whether there is liability,* but to leave to domestic law (the local law identified by the forum under its choice of law rules or approaches) determination of the compensatory damages available to the suitor. See *id.*, at 231.

A complementary purpose of the Convention is to accommodate or balance the interests of passengers seeking recovery for personal injuries, and the interests of air carriers seeking to limit potential liability. Before the Warsaw accord, injured passengers could file suits for damages, subject only to the limitations of the forum's laws, including the forum's choice of law regime. This exposure inhibited the growth of the then-fledgling international airline industry. See *Floyd,* 499 U.S., at 546; Lowenfeld & Mendelsohn, The United States and the Warsaw Convention, 80 Harv. L.Rev. 497, 499–500 (1967). Many international air carriers at that time endeavored to require passengers, as a condition of air travel, to relieve or reduce the carrier's liability in case of injury. See Second International Conference on Private Aeronautical Law, October 4–12, 1929, Warsaw, Minutes 47 (R. Homer & D. Legrez transls. 1975) (hereinafter Minutes). The Convention drafters designed Articles 17, 22, and 24 of the Convention as a compromise between the interests of air carriers and their customers worldwide. In Article 17 of the Convention, carriers are denied the contractual prerogative to exclude or limit their liability for personal injury. In Articles 22 and 24, passengers are limited in the amount of damages they may recover, and are restricted in the claims they may pursue by the conditions and limits set out in the Convention.

Construing the Convention, as did the Court of Appeals, to allow passengers to pursue claims under local law when the Convention does not permit recovery could produce several anomalies. Carriers might be exposed to unlimited liability under diverse legal regimes, but would be prevented, under the treaty, from contracting out of such liability. Passengers injured physically in an emergency landing might be subject to the liability caps of the Convention, while those merely traumatized in the same mishap would be free to sue outside of the Convention for potentially unlimited damages. The Court of Appeals' construction of the Convention would encourage artful pleading by plaintiffs seeking to opt out of the Convention's liability scheme when local law promised recovery in excess of that prescribed by the treaty. See *Potter v. Delta Air Lines, Inc.*, 98 F.3d 881, 886 (C.A.5 1996). Such a reading would scarcely advance the predictability that adherence to the treaty has achieved worldwide....

The drafting history of Article 17 is consistent with our understanding of the preemptive effect of the Convention. The preliminary draft of the Convention submitted to the conference at Warsaw made air carriers liable "in the case of death, wounding, or any other bodily injury suffered by a traveler." Minutes 264; see *Saks,* 470 U.S., at 401, 105 S.Ct. 1338. In the later draft that prescribed what is now Article 17, airline liability was narrowed to encompass only bodily injury caused by an "accident." See Minutes 205. It is improbable that, at the same time the drafters narrowed the conditions of air carrier liability in Article 17, they intended, in Article 24, to permit passengers to skirt those conditions by pursuing claims under local law.

Inspecting the drafting history, the Court of Appeals stressed a proposal made by the Czechoslovak delegation to state in the treaty that, in the absence of a stipulation in the Convention itself, " 'the provisions of laws and national rules relative to carriage in each [signatory] State shall apply.' " 122 F.3d, at 105 (quoting Minutes 176). That proposal was withdrawn upon amendment of the Convention's title to read: "CONVENTION FOR THE UNIFICATION OF *CERTAIN* RULES RELATING TO INTERNATIONAL TRANSPORTATION BY AIR." 49 Stat. 3014 (emphasis added); see 122 F.3d, at 105. The Second Circuit saw in this history an indication "that national law was intended to provide the passenger's remedy where the Convention did not expressly apply." 122 F. 3d, at 105.

The British House of Lords, in *Sidhu v. British Airways plc*, [1997] 1 All E.R. 193, considered the same history, but found it inconclusive. Inclusion of the word "certain" in the Convention's title, the Lords reasoned, accurately indicated that "the [C]onvention is concerned with certain rules only, not with all the rules relating to international carriage by air." Id., at 204. For example, the Convention does not say "anything ... about the carrier's obligations of insurance, and in particular about compulsory insurance against third party risks." *Ibid.* The Convention, in other words, is "a partial harmonisation, directed to the particular issues with which it deals," *ibid.*, among them, a carrier's liability to passengers for personal injury. As to those issues, the Lords concluded, "the aim of the [C]onvention is to unify." *Ibid.* Pointing to the overall understanding that the Convention's objective was to "ensure uniformity," *id.*, at 209, the Lords suggested that the Czechoslovak delegation may have meant only to underscore that national law controlled "chapters of law relating to international carriage by air with which the [C]onvention was not attempting to deal." *Ibid.* In light of the Lords' exposition, we are satisfied that the withdrawn Czechoslovak proposal will not bear the weight the Court of Appeals placed on it.

Montreal Protocol No. 4, ratified by the Senate on September 28, 1998, amends Article 24 to read, in relevant part: "In the carriage of passengers and baggage, any action for damages, however founded, can only be brought subject to the conditions and limits set out in this Convention....."[15] Both parties agree that, under the amended Article 24, the

---

15. Article 24, as amended by Montreal Protocol No. 4, provides: "I. In the carriage of passengers and baggage, any action for damages, however founded, can only be brought subject to the conditions and limits set out in this Convention, without prejudice to the question as to who are the persons who have the right to bring suit and what are their respective rights.

"2. In the carriage of cargo, any action for damages, however founded, whether under this Convention or in contract or in tort or otherwise, can only be brought subject to the conditions and limits of liability set out in this Convention without prejudice to the question as to who are the persons who have the right to bring suit and what are their

Convention's preemptive effect is clear: The treaty precludes passengers from bringing actions under local law when they cannot establish air carrier liability under the treaty. Revised Article 24, El Al urges and we agree, merely clarifies, it does not alter, the Convention's rule of exclusivity.

Supporting the position that revised Article 24 provides for preemption not earlier established, Tseng urges that federal preemption of state law is disfavored generally, and particularly when matters of health and safety are at stake. See Brief for Respondent 31–33. See also post, at 677 ("[A] treaty, like an Act of Congress, should not be construed to preempt state law unless its intent to do so is clear.") (STEVENS, J., dissenting). Tseng overlooks in this regard that the nation-state, not subdivisions within one nation, is the focus of the Convention and the perspective of our treaty partners. Our home-centered preemption analysis, therefore, should not be applied, mechanically, in construing our international obligations.

Decisions of the courts of other Convention signatories corroborate our understanding of the Convention's preemptive effect. In *Sidhu*, the British House of Lords considered and decided the very question we now face concerning the Convention's exclusivity when a passenger alleges psychological damages, but no physical injury, resulting from an occurrence that is not an "accident" under Article 17. See 1 All E. R., at 201, 207. Reviewing the text, structure, and drafting history of the Convention, the Lords concluded that the Convention was designed to "ensure that, in all questions relating to the carrier's liability, it is the provisions of the [C]onvention which apply and that the passenger does not have access to any other remedies, whether under the common law or otherwise, which may be available within the particular country where he chooses to raise his action." *Ibid.* Courts of other nations bound by the Convention have also recognized the treaty's encompassing preemptive effect. The "opinions of our sister signatories," we have observed, are "entitled to considerable weight." *Saks,* 470 U.S., at 404, (internal quotation marks omitted). The text, drafting history, and underlying purpose of the Convention, in sum, counsel us to adhere to a view of the treaty's exclusivity shared by our treaty partners.

* * *

For the reasons stated, we hold that the Warsaw Convention precludes a passenger from maintaining an action for personal injury damages under local law when her claim does not satisfy the conditions for liability under the Convention. Accordingly, we reverse the judgment of the Second Circuit. . . .

JUSTICE STEVENS, dissenting.

My disagreement with the Court's holding today has limited practical significance, not just because the issue has been conclusively determined for future cases by the recent amendment to the Warsaw Convention, but also because it affects only a narrow category of past cases. The decision is

respective rights. Such limits of liability constitute maximum limits and may not be exceeded whatever the circumstances which gave rise to the liability." S. Exec. Rep. No. 105–20, at 29.

nevertheless significant because, in the end, it rests on the novel premise that preemption analysis should be applied differently to treaties than to other kinds of federal law. . . . Because I disagree with that premise, I shall briefly explain why I believe the Court has erred.

I agree with the Court that the drafters of the Convention intended that the treaty largely supplant local law. Article 24 preempts local law in three major categories: (1) personal injury claims arising out of an accident; (2) claims for lost or damaged baggage; and (3) damage occasioned by transportation delays. Those categories surely comprise the bulk of potential disputes between international air carriers and their passengers.

The Convention, however, does not preempt local law in cases arising out of "wilful misconduct." Article 25 expressly provides that a carrier shall not be entitled to avail itself of the provisions of the Convention that "exclude or limit" its liability if its misconduct is willful. Moreover, the question whether the carrier's wrongful act "is considered to be equivalent to wilful misconduct" is determined by "the law of the court to which the case is submitted." *Ibid.* Accordingly, the vast majority of the potential claims by passengers against international air carriers are either preempted by Article 24 or unequivocally governed by local law under Article 25.

Putting these cases aside, we are left with a narrow sliver of incidents involving personal injury that arise neither from an accident nor willful misconduct. . . .

The overriding interest in achieving " 'uniformity of rules governing claims arising from international air transportation,' . . . will be accommodated in the situations explicitly covered by Article 24, regardless of how the Court decides this case. In those circumstances, the Convention's basic tradeoff between the carriers' interest in avoiding unlimited liability and the passengers' interest in obtaining compensation without proving fault will be fully achieved."

On the other hand, the interest in uniformity is disregarded in the category of cases that involve willful misconduct. Under the treaty, a reckless act or omission may constitute willful misconduct. See *Koirala v. Thai Airways Int'l, Ltd.*, 126 F.3d 1205, 1209–1210 (C.A.9 1997); Goldhirsch, *supra* n. 1 at 121 (stating that most civil law jurisdictions have found that gross negligence satisfies Article 25). This broad definition increases the number of cases not preempted by the Convention. In these circumstances, the delegates at Warsaw did decide "to subject air carriers to the distinct, nonuniform liability rules of the individual signatory nations"

Thus, the interest in uniformity would not be significantly impaired if the number of cases not preempted, Re those involving willful misconduct, was slightly enlarged to encompass those relatively rare cases in which the injury resulted from neither an accident nor a willful wrong. That the interest in uniformity is accommodated in one category of cases but not the other simply raises, without resolving, the question whether the drafters of the treaty intended to treat personal injury nonaccident cases as though they involved accidents. A plaintiff in such a case, unlike those injured by an accident, receives no benefit from the treaty, and normally should not have a claim that is valid under local law preempted, unless the treaty expressly requires that result.

Everyone agrees that the literal text of the treaty does not preempt claims of personal injury that do not arise out of an accident. It is equally clear that nothing in the drafting history requires that result. On the contrary, the amendment to the title of the Convention made in response to the proposal advanced by the Czechoslovak delegation, ... suggests that the parties assumed that local law would apply to all nonaccident cases. I agree with the Court that that inference is not strong enough, in itself, to require that the ambiguity be resolved in the plaintiff's favor. It suffices for me, however, that the history is just as ambiguous as the text. I firmly believe that a treaty, like an Act of Congress, should not be construed to preempt state law unless its intent to do so is clear.... For this reason, I respectfully dissent.

Notes & Questions

1.   Do you agree with the Supreme Court in these two decisions? What is the proper method of treaty interpretation? See our Ch. 11 and the Vienna Convention on Treaties, at art. 31 (in Doc. Supp.). What should be the meaning of "shared expectations" of the parties to a treaty? Is it what is "expected," as manifest in each party's domestic law? Is it only what all of them expect? Some? Most? Is there an "ordinary" or "plain" meaning to these treaty terms?

2.   Is the Montreal Convention self-executing? *See, T.W.A. v. Franklin Mint, Corp.*, 466 U.S. 243, 252 (1984), and discussion in Ch. 12, *infra*.

3.   How should damages be measured—by some international standard or by the domestic law of the victims? Consider article 25(*l*) of the treaty. When a treaty is self-executing, what is its impact on state or local law? *See*, U.S. Constitution, Article VI, cl. 2, and Chs. 9, and 12, *infra*.

4.   In the El Al decision, do you consider the majority or the dissenting opinion the better reasoned in terms of treaty interpretation? Does the Montreal Convention apply to cases other than accidents? Does it apply to passengers when they are not embarking or disembarking?

2.   OFFENSES ABOARD AIRCRAFT GENERAL OFFENSES

Silberwacht v. Attorney–General

Israel, District Court of Tel Aviv, 1953.
20 Int'l L.Rep. 153 (1957).*

The Facts. This was an appeal from a decision of the Magistrate's Court convicting the appellant of smuggling and of being in possession of smuggled goods. The appellant was employed at Lydda Airport where there existed a clandestine organization for purchasing tinned food from South African airmen and bringing it on to the market without customs examina-

---

* Reprinted with the permission of the
Editor of The International Law Reports.

tion and payment of customs duty. By section 2 of the Customs Ordinance smuggling is defined as:

> Any importation, exportation, carriage coastwise or over the land frontiers, or attempted importation, exportation, carriage coastwise or over the land frontiers, of goods, with intent to defraud the revenue or to evade any prohibition of, restriction on, or regulations as to, the importation, exportation, carriage coastwise or over the land frontiers of any goods; and "smuggle" and "smuggled goods" have corresponding meanings.

Held: that the appeal must be admitted and the conviction dismissed. [A portion of the opinion of the court appears below.]

* * * This ground of appeal raises several important questions of public international law The question whether the removal of the goods from the aircraft (which, it seems, was a South African aircraft, although it is not clear whether it was privately owned or a State aircraft) constitutes their importation into Israel, or whether the goods entered Israel at the moment when the aircraft entered Israel, is connected with the question whether an aircraft has to be regarded as foreign territory. Although the rule is nowhere explicitly laid down, it seems that the law of Israel presupposes that the law governing territorial sovereignty (from the point of view of jurisdiction) is similar to the concept of ownership of land, and includes authority not only over the surface of the land but also down to its depth and also in the skies above jusque ad coelum. The general opinion in public international law is similar. See Article I of the Chicago Air Agreement of 1944. * * *

  * * *

[E]ven if South Africa has jurisdiction over acts performed in her aircraft in accordance with South African laws regarding the air and regarding jurisdiction (assuming that the existence of extraterritorial laws of that character is not contrary to international law and the public policy of Israel)—nevertheless the foreign aircraft is not foreign territory. The result, therefore, is that the act of smuggling came to an end when the pilot imported the tins into Israel with the intention of defrauding the customs. The act of smuggling did not continence at the moment when the tins were removed from the aircraft since they were already within Israel. * * *

Judge Avissar, dissenting, said: "As to the smuggling, it seems to me to make no difference to the appellant whether the pilot who landed at Lydda Airport with the tinned goods on board and intending to smuggle them was guilty of an offence or not." * * * When the appellant received the goods from the aircraft and removed them from Lydda Airport without paying customs—as has been proved to have occurred—he committed the offence. The position of a person who receives goods from an aircraft at an airport cannot be any different from the position of a person who receives goods from a ship within the territorial waters of the country and imports them by smuggling. At all events, such a person is to be considered as an importer in the sense of the definition of smuggling contained in section 2 of the Customs Ordinance; and why should any discrimination be made in favour of the man who conunits the smuggling by recieving the goods from an aircraft which has landed at an airport? * * *

Problem. A South African commercial aircraft is making a nonstop transit through the airspace of Israel on a flight to Turkey at an altitude of 30,000 feet. No Israeli nationals are on board the plane. A passenger in the plane assaults a stewardess. Both are South African nationals. If the passenger subsequently travels to Tel Aviv, and is arrested and tried there for assault, does South Africa have any basis for complaint under international law?

Chumney v. Nixon

United States Court of Appeals, Sixth Circuit, 1980.
615 F.2d 389.

EDWARDS, CHIEF JUDGE.

Plaintiffs-appellants Chumney, man and wife, appeal from dismissal of their complaint. The District Judge before whom this matter was argued, after considerable deliberation, granted defendants-appellees' motions to dismiss. He reached his final conclusion on motion to reconsider or rehear his dismissal, at which point he held that "the claims could not be said to arise under this criminal statute." The statute referred to, 18 U.S.C. § 113, is a criminal statute which provides penalties for personal assaults on any aircraft within the special aircraft jurisdiction of the United States.

This is a strange case on the alleged facts. It is also a difficult one as far as legal concepts are concerned.

THE ALLEGATIONS OF FACT

[**Facts**] Chumney claims that, while he and his wife were returning from a Memphis, Tennessee, Shrine Temple charter flight to Rio de Janeiro, a physical assault on him by defendant Nixon, the mayor of Shelby County, Tennessee, and the other individual defendants, broke some of his teeth and resulted in other serious, possibly permanent injuries. At the time of the assault, the complaint alleges that the aircraft was approximately 2½ hours out of Rio de Janeiro en route to Memphis, Tennessee. At oral argument, the parties appeared to agree that at the time concerned, the aircraft was at 29,000 feet over the Brazilian jungle. Judicial notice of a world map strongly suggests that plaintiffs' pleading should be so construed.

The motivation for this assault is alleged by Chumney to have originated in the fact that Nixon had once been sheriff of Shelby County and that Chumney, as a lawyer, had represented one of Nixon's deputies who had been fired by Nixon and had succeeded in getting him ordered replaced on the job.

There are sundry other interesting facts alleged in the background of this involved case, such as that Mr. and Mrs. Chumney were using this charter flight for their honeymoon following their recent marriage, that the Chumneys were seated next to an unnamed man (who did not participate in this assault) whose "body odor" was highly offensive to the Chumneys and they were much offended by having to continue to sit near him, which complaint they had made known to the individual defendants who were officers of the Shrine Temple and that, as alleged by the complaint, Braniff Airlines served quantities of liquor to everybody concerned, including both the plaintiffs and the individual defendants, and failed to prevent the assault.

THE LEGAL ISSUES

It is plaintiffs' contention that the individual defendants named as having participated in the assault clearly violated 18 U.S.C. § 113(d) and that their actions did damage which exceeded $10,000. They assert that their complaint arose under the laws of the United States as a civil action under 28 U.S.C. § 1331(a), the federal question jurisdictional statute. * * *

Plaintiffs in their tendered amended complaint assert that the United States District Court for the Western District of Tennessee, Western Division, has federal question jurisdiction under 28 U.S.C. § 1331 (1976) because defendants violated 18 U.S.C. § 113 (1976) which statute punishes assaults within the maritime and territorial jurisdiction of the United States. They claim the cited statute is made specifically applicable to the current fact problem by 49 U.S.C. § 1472(k)(1) (1976) pertaining to the special aircraft jurisdiction of the United States.

The federal question statute 28 U.S.C. § 1331(a) which plaintiffs rely upon reads:

(a) The district courts shall have original jurisdiction of all civil actions wherein the matter in controversy exceeds the sum or value of $10,000, exclusive of interest and costs, and arises under the Constitution, laws, or treaties of the United States.

18 U.S.C. § 113 reads:

Whoever, within the special maritime and territorial jurisdiction of the United States, is guilty of an assault shall be punished as follows:

* * *

(d) Assault by striking, beating, or wounding, by fine of * * * or imprisonment for not more than six months, or both.

(e) Simple assault, by fine * * * or imprisonment for not more than three months, or both.

(f) Assault resulting in serious bodily injury, by fine * * * or imprisonment for not more than ten years, or both.

The applicability of 18 U.S.C. § 113 is established by the following statutory provisions:

18 U.S.C. § 7 reads:

The term "special maritime and territorial jurisdiction of the United States", as used in this title [18 U.S.C. § 1 et seq.] includes:

* * *

(5) Any aircraft belonging in whole or in part to the United States, or any citizen thereof, or to any corporation created by or under the laws of the United States, or any State, Territory, district, or possession thereof, while such aircraft is in flight over the high seas, or over any other waters within the admiralty and maritime jurisdiction of the United States and out of the jurisdiction of any particular State.

49 U.S.C. § 1472(k)(1) reads:

(k)(1) Whoever, while aboard an aircraft within the special aircraft jurisdiction of the United States, commits an act which, if committed within the special maritime and territorial jurisdiction of the United States, as defined in section 7 of Title 18, would be in violation of section 113, 114, 661, 662, 1111, 1112, 1113, 2031, 2032, or 2111 of such Title 18 shall be punished as provided therein.

Finally, 49 U.S.C. § 1301(34)(d)(i) reads:

(34) The term "special aircraft jurisdiction of the United States" includes—

* * *

(d) any other aircraft outside the United States—

(i) that has its next scheduled destination or last point of departure in the United States, if that aircraft next actually lands in the United States;[13]

We believe that these statutes clearly indicate that the Congress of the United States has undertaken to apply federal law to American (and other) aircraft while such aircraft are en route from an airport in the United States or are returning from a foreign country directly to an airport in the United States. The nature of 18 U.S.C. § 113 is that of a criminal statute designed to protect law abiding passengers on such an aircraft from either simple or felonious assault. The sanctions created by § 113 and made applicable to the subject circumstances by 49 U.S.C. §§ 1472(k)(1) and 1301(34)(d) are, however, purely criminal sanctions.

This leaves for our resolution the following question: Are plaintiffs entitled to a civil cause of action for damages against defendants which is derived from the federal criminal statutes described above and over which the federal courts would have jurisdiction under 28 U.S.C. § 1331(a)? The answer is anything but easy to come by. The District Judge accurately defined the question and answered it in the negative. Although it is certainly a close question, we disagree.

* * *

In our instant case, each plaintiff is clearly "one of the class for whose especial benefit" the statutes here involved were created. We find no specific language in the legislative history of the statutes previously cited which shows specific intent to create a civil remedy or which prohibits inference of such intent. It is clear to us that Congress has taken care in comprehensive legislation to protect the safety of passengers flying on United States airlines or flying on aircraft intended to land at United

---

13. The definition now appears as paragraph 38 of 49 U.S.C. § 1301.

States airports or on aircraft bound for foreign lands after departure from an airport in the United States. A clear-cut purpose has been defined in federal legislation and the federal courts have been given specific jurisdiction to impose criminal penalties against those who commit simple or felonious assaults on aircrafts under the conditions described above. A civil action for damages would certainly be consistent with the over-all congressional purpose and we believe should be inferred therefrom.

Indeed the existence or nonexistence of a civil cause of action in this case may create a legal precedent which will affect other possible fact situations (aircraft kidnapping or terrorism) some of which may well cry out for more than the criminal remedy.

Finally, the maintenance of civil peace on airlines flying to and from the United States and foreign lands is clearly a topic of federal, not state, significance. The State of Tennessee has not legislated on this subject and we believe that most state courts would be loath to reach for jurisdiction over the results of an altercation which occurred at 29,000 feet over the Brazilian jungle. This problem is certainly not one "traditionally relegated to the state courts."

It seems to this court to be an appropriate step under the legal doctrines which we have outlined above to approve a civil cause of action for damages derived from criminal statutes which plaintiffs alleged were violated in this case.

We recognize, of course, that when and if this case is finally tried, it may result in a swearing match between individuals, all of whom are now alleged to have been under some influence of liquor, and that sorting out who hit whom first may appear to be a task more appropriate for a police court than a federal district court.[1]

As to the portions of the complaint seeking damages from the individual defendants, the judgment of the District Court is reversed and the case is remanded for further proceedings consistent with this opinion.

* * *

1. *Notes and Questions.* What basis of jurisdiction under international law supports US federal prosecution in *Chumney*? Would the result in *Chumney* have been different if the airline had been Brazilian? What if the individuals involved had also been Brazilian nationals? In particular: (a) Would the assault have been covered by the statutes in those cases? (b) Would Brazil have a basis for complaint against the United States if the defendants had been convicted in those cases?

2. *Hijacking—Problem*

A passenger in a commercial airplane threatens to explode a bomb which, he says, is in his carry-on. The pilot diverts the flight to a

---

1. Indeed, the district judge was of a view that the action could be maintained appropriately in the state court since all parties involved were residents of Memphis, Tennessee.

destination demanded by the passenger. The passenger leaves the plane at that destination and the plane is flown to its original destination. Even this simple example raises a number of domestic and international law problems. The plane may be registered in the U.S. or in some other country. The passenger may hijack the plane on the ground in New York, or while it is over the Atlantic on its way to London, or while it is on the ground in London. The hijacker may be a U.S. national, or the national of another state. He may or may not eventually return to the United States and thus be subject to its enforcement jurisdiction. The U.S. may ask the government of the foreign state in which the hijacker is found to return him to the U.S. by extradition proceedings. The government of a state to which the hijacker has fled may decide to try him even though that state has had no connection with the event other than having become a place of refuge. The following material will elucidate.

3.   INTERNATIONAL CONVENTIONS.

The Tokyo Convention (Convention on Offenses and Certain Other Acts Committed on Board Aircraft, 20 U.S.T. 2941; In Documentary Supplement) was drafted under the auspices of the International Civil Aviation Organization and signed in 1963, entering into force for the United States on December 4, 1969. The Convention is concerned broadly with the question of crimes on board aircraft in flight, on the surface of the high seas or any other area outside the jurisdiction of a nation state. A special purpose of the convention is to provide that there be no lapse of jurisdiction with respect to such crimes. To that end Article 3(l) provides that at least one state shall have jurisdiction-"The State of registration of the aircraft is competent to exercise jurisdiction over offenses and acts committed on board." This jurisdiction is not exclusive, however. The convention deals in detail with the powers of the aircraft commander to "off-load" and to restrain offenders or suspected offenders.

Article 11 deals specifically with hijacking, but in a limited way. It merely requires states parties to restore control of a hijacked airplane to the lawful commander or to preserve his control. The provision for extradition is relatively weak. Article 16 specifies that, for purposes of extradition, offenses on board shall be treated as though they had been committed not only in the place in which they occurred but also in the territory of the state of registration of the aircraft. However, the article expressly provides that it does not create an obligation to grant extradition.

The Hague Convention (Convention for the Suppression of Unlawful Seizure of Aircraft, 22 U.S.T. 1641, Documentary Supplement) was also the product of the work of the ICAO. It was approved at a diplomatic conference at The Hague in 1970 and entered into force for the United States on October 14, 1971. In contrast to the Tokyo Convention, the Hague Convention is directed narrowly at hijacking. Its major provisions create universal jurisdiction for the prosecution of hijackers and impose an obligation on the parties either to prosecute or extradite a hijacker who is found. See, Arts. 4, 7 and 8. Jurisdiction is recognized in the state of the plane's registration, as well as in the state on whose territory the aircraft lands with the offender still on board. The innovative thrust of this is that it provides for universal jurisdiction. Articles 7 and 8 provides that hijacking is deemed to be included as an extraditable offense in existing extradition treaties and is to be included in future extradition treaties.

Problem. Suppose that a hijacker commandeers a British plane en route from London to South Africa. He forces it to Land in Libya, is arrested there, but escapes, ultimately being found in Italy. Suppose that the U.S. government, wishing to make a statement against terrorism, wishes to prosecute. Would the U.S. have jurisdiction to seek extradition? Look at the U.S—Italy extradition treaty in the Documentary Supplement.

2. **United States legislation.** Even before becoming a party to the Hague Convention, it proscribed "any seizure or exercise of control, by force or violence or threat of force or violence and with wrongful intent, of an aircraft within the special aircraft jurisdiction of the United States", 49 U.S.C. § 1472. After becoming a party to the convention, the U.S. enacted legislation to broaden its definition of special aircraft jurisdiction to take account particularly of article 4 (1) (b) and (c) of the Convention. 49 U.S.C. § 1301(38). In implementation of Article 4(2), 49 U.S.C. § 1472 was added, criminalizing hijacking outside the special aircraft jurisdiction of the United States if the offender is later found in the U.S.

3. *Hijacking as piracy?* Some scholars stress the traditional rule that piracy refers to an assault upon one vessel and its passengers, crew and cargo by criminal elements from another vessel. This would mean that an infiltration of a vessel not from another vessel is not piracy jure gentium. Thus, it was not piracy when infiltrators from within the vessel took control of it for purposes of making a political demonstration, killing the watch officer and wounding several of the crew. *See the Santa Maria,* 4 Whiteman, DIGEST OF INTERNATIONAL LAW 665 (1965). What would this position do for aircraft hijacking? On the other hand, the 1985 infiltration and seizure of the Italian liner the *Achille Lauro* followed by murder of passenger Leon Klinghoffer was deemed by some in the media and some writers, to be piracy jure gentium giving jurisdiction to the state of the vicatim's as well as to the state of the vessel's registration. Actually, however, to be piracy, it must be done for private ends. *See* the *Achille Lauro Case,* 24 ILM 1509 (1985); Art. 101 U.N. Convention on the Law of the Sea.

4. *Problem.* Suppose that a national of State Z hijacked an Israeli aircraft. Assume that the hijacker forced the plane to fly to Hungary, escaped and made his way to the U.S., where he was "found" and prosecuted. State Z, the state of the hijacker's nationality, is not a party to the Hague Convention. Would this prosecution violate State Z's rights or interests? Can the U.S. justify its assertion of jurisdiction by claiming that its anti-hijacking legislation is an implementation not only of the Hague Convention's grant of jurisdiction but also of jurisdiction that is recognized by the customary international law of piracy? What would be the proper theory?

Sabotage

The Montreal Convention for the Suppression of Unlawful Acts Against the Safety of Civil Aviation—was adopted by a Conference on

International Air Law in 1971, 24 U.S.T. 564. It entered into force in the U.S. on January 26, 1973. *Also see*, the 1988 Montreal protocol for the Suppression of Unlawful Acts of Violence at Airports, 27 I.L.M. 627 (1988). The convention's scope was described by the head of the U.S. delegation:

> Although this convention is similar to the Hijacking Convention in many respects, it is significantly distinct: It does not, basically, require states to define any new offenses—it covers acts which already are common crimes; it does not, for the most part, establish new crimes to fall within the extradition process—most of the acts already are extraditable crimes. These were important elements of the Hijacking Convention. It might be said that states could punish offenders or extradite them without this convention.

> What this convention does is to impose an obligation on states *requiring* them to prosecute or extradite offenders. It serves as a warning to any person who contemplates such acts that the international community has responded with unanimity to condemn such acts. In this respect it is like the Hijacking Convention.

> And in an important respect this convention does more than the Hijacking Convention. It covers acts against aircraft in a state's domestic service, even when the acts take place wholly within that same state, if the offender escapes to another state. While this element is not critical for the Hijacking Convention, it is crucial for the effectiveness of the convention we have concluded, because of the possibility that offenders may escape before they are discovered. This convention declares that no one who sabotages a civil aircraft—whether in domestic or international service—no one who places a bomb on board such an aircraft, no evildoer who commits violence aboard such an aircraft in flight, no criminal of this character shall ever find sanctuary anywhere in the world, no matter how deviously he may seek to evade retribution for his deeds. The parties to this convention have declared that this despicable criminal shall be pursued without respite. 65 U.S.Dept.State Bull. 464 (1971).

Pan Am 103

John P. Grant, the Lockerbie Case, Background

University of Glasgow School of Law,
www.law.gla.ac.uk/lockerbie/backgroundsummary.cfm*

The Charges

By the time of the trial of the two Libyan nationals accused of placing an explosive device on Pan Am Flight 103, resulting in a total of 270 deaths, over eleven years will have elapsed. While this seems a long time, it appeared, until August of 1998, that there might never be a criminal trial,

* Reprinted with the permission of Glascow University School of Law.

so entrenched had become the positions of the states involved. Libya argued that it had no legal obligation to surrender the suspects, and the United Kingdom and United States argued that nothing short of a trial in either Scotland or the United States was acceptable. This stalemate was broken only by a compromise whereby the Libyans would be tried in a neutral venue, the Netherlands, before a panel of Scottish judges (with no jury) under Scots criminal law and procedure.

In the evening of 21 December 1988, Pan Am Flight 103 was en route from London Heathrow to JFK New York when it blew up in mid-air and fell to the ground at Lockerbie in the Scottish Borders. All 259 passengers and crew on the 'plane were killed instantly, and a total of eleven local people also died in the crash.

The Investigation

A major police investigation was mounted immediately and run for a period of years, involving not only the local force from Dumfries and Galloway, but law enforcement officers from around the world, including the FBI. CAA Air Accident Investigation Branch investigated and reported in July 1990 on the circumstances of the crash. It concluded that "the detonation of an improvised explosive device led directly to the destruction of the aircraft with the loss of all 259 persons on board and eleven of the residents of the town of Lockerbie."

As is normal in circumstances of this kind, a Fatal Accident Inquiry was held. The Sheriff Principal convening the inquiry like wise had no doubt about the cause of the tragedy. In his findings in fact of February 1991, Sheriff Principal John Mowat Q.C. found that a Semtex-type plastic explosive contained in a Toshiba radio-cassette player in a Samsonite suitcase had been carried by Pan Am from Frankfurt to London Heathrow and then transferred to Flight 103; that this and other inter-line baggage had not been counted, weighed, reconciled with passengers travelling on Flight 103 or x-rayed; and that the cause of all the deaths was the detonation of this device in the left side of the forward hold of the 'plane. He concluded that "the primary cause of the deaths was the criminal act of murder."

By early 1991 it was absolutely clear that the tragedy was not the result of mechanical failure or pilot error, but was instead the direct consequence of an explosive device placed in luggage in one of the plane's holds.

The Impasse

On 27 November 1991, the Lord Advocate obtained a warrant for the arrest of two Libyans, Abdelbasset Ali Ahmed al-Megrahi and Ali Amin Khalifa Fhimah, on charges of conspiracy to murder, murder and breaches of the Aircraft Security Act of 1982. An indictment in similar terms was handed down by the U.S. District Court of the District of Columbia on the same day.

Thereupon, the British and American governments demanded that the two Libyans be surrendered so that they could stand trial in either Scotland or the United States. Libya refused to surrender the suspects, claiming that it had no extradition treaties with either the U.K. or the U.S. and that, in any case, Libyan law prohibited the extradition of its own nationals.

The two governments then went to the UN Security Council, which in Resolution 731 of 21 January 1992 requested the surrender for trial of the suspects. After that request was refused, the Security Council adopted Resolution 748 on 31 March 1992, this time in the form of a demand that Libya renounce terrorism and surrender al-Megrahi and Fhimah for trial. The resolution gave just over two weeks to comply after which a range of sanction would be—and in the event were—imposed sanctions on Libya. When the two Libyans were still not handed over after a further 18 months, the sanctions were extended and tightened by the Security Council in Resolution 883 of 11 November 1993.

In the meantime, Libya applied to the International Court of Justice against the U.K. and U.S.A., claiming that the matter was governed by an international agreement, the Montreal Convention of 1971. Libya claimed that it had fulfilled all its obligations under the Convention by detaining the suspects and investigating the matter. The UK and US countered by arguing that the Security Council resolutions over-rode the Convention.

The Compromise

The Court decided in October 1992 that the matter was not of sufficient urgency to grant Libya provisional measures of protection. In the Court ruled February 1998 the Court ruled on a number of preliminary objections made by the two governments and declared that it had jurisdiction to deal with the merits of the dispute between Libya and the U.K. and U.S. The Court is currently engaged in considering the merits of the case and its decision is expected sometime in 2001.

It was thought that a breakthrough had been made in early 1994, when Professor Robert Black of Edinburgh University and Dr. Ibrahim Legwell, the head of the Libyan defence team, agreed on a trial in a neutral venue before a panel of international judges. Britain and America refused to accept this compromise, demanding a trial in either Scotland or the United States.

It became clear at the beginning of 1998 that, despite sanctions, the two Libyans would not be surrendered for trial. On 24 August, the two governments went back to the Security Council, proposing that the trial should be held in the Netherlands before a panel of three Scottish judges and with no jury. This offer was broadly accepted by Libya, which reiterated its stance that it was for the two suspects and their legal advisers to decide whether they would appear in the Netherlands for trial.

On 5 April 1999, after some months of discussions on concerns from the accused and their lawyers, al-Megrahi and Fhimah surrendered for trial in the Netherlands at the Dutch military airbase of Valkenburg, just outside The Hague. They were swiftly extradited to Scottish jurisdiction at Camp Zeist, just outside Utrecht. Camp Zeist, a former American airbase, had been agreed between the British and Dutch governments as the most suitable site for the trial. On the second of two appearances before Sheriff

Principal Graham Cox Q.C., sitting at Camp Zeist, they were committed for trial on 14 April 1999. The normal period under Scots law within which the trial must commence, 110 days from the date of full committal, has been extended on application to the High Court, again sitting at Camp Zeist. The trial proper begins in early 2000 and is expected to last for at least a year. The trial will be the international trial of the decade—but it will be the Scottish trial of the century.

It involves allegations of the largest mass murder in Scottish legal history. It will be the first occasion that a Scottish criminal court has sat abroad. It will be the first time that charges of this seriousness have been heard without a jury. It will probably be the longest and most expensive trial in Scottish legal history.

But, in a sense, all these "firsts" do not matter. What is important is that those thought responsible for the tragic loss of 270 lives be brought to trial; the families of those who perished over Lockerbie in 1988 deserve no less. And it is equally important that the suspects have their day in court.

Extradition and Aircraft Offenses

1. ***The prosecute or extradite principle.*** While there were earlier uses of this principle in regard to terrorism, such as in a 1936 League of Nations treaty, it quickly became a standard legal and political response when modern terrorism began to exploit the vulnerability of the passenger plane. One result was the promulgation of the treaties examined in this Chapter. Terrorism and hijacking conventions, however, still suffer from a disinclination of some states to accept their obligations. Other problems as to their effectiveness include: (i) unsuccessful prosecution in the state that first gains custody of the accused, leading to acquittal or the dropping of charges; (ii) contradictions between the prosecute or extradite undertaking and pre-existing bilateral general extradition treaties, especially as to the specification of extraditable offenses, or occasional defenses; (iii) the legal competence of the requesting state under its own law (or possibly under international law) to try the accused criminally; and (iv) the factor of the nationality or allegiance of the person sought to be extradited. By far the major problem for extradition in the context of modern terrorism, including hijacking, has been the assertion of the political offense exception. At its most difficult, the problem involves good people using illegal means such as hijacking to escape from "tyranny." It also arises when underground resistance movements use terrorism as a means to political ends, themselves not necessarily reprehensible. The decision on the applicability of the political offense exception lies with the authorities in the state of which extradition has been requested, unless the states parties to an extradition agreement mutually provide otherwise, as in the U.S.–U.K. agreement. Extradition is presented in Chapter 16, and today most if not all conventions, given the terms of the Hague Hijacking Convention.

2. ***Extradition under the Hague Hijacking Convention.*** Article 8(1) of the Hague Convention provides, in effect, for the automatic amendment of extradition treaties to add hijacking to the list of extraditable crimes. What, then, of the individual who seeks to escape from a tyrannical regime by hijacking a plane in that country and requiring the pilot to fly to

a country of refuge? If the underlying extradition treaty provides for the usual exception for offenses of a political character, can the requested state consider that hijacking under those circumstances is such a crime? Do the hijacking conventions eliminate it as a political offense? If a country considers this to be a political offense and refuses to extradite, the obligation to prosecute, under Article 7 of the Hague Convention, comes into play. But what does the obligation to prosecute mean? If a U.S. prosecutor decided to drop charges based on his or her political views, would this violate or satisfy the treaty obligation?

A Case of Refusal to Extradite

McDowell, Digest of United States Practice in International Law 1975, at 168 (1976).

On April 14, 1975, the Chambre d'accusation of the Cour d'appel of Paris refused a request of the United States for extradition of Willie Roger Holder and Mary Katherine Kerkow for trial in the United States on aircraft hijacking charges. The refusal was based on the fugitives' allegations of political motive. They had been indicted in June 1972 in both New York and California in connection with the 1972 hijacking of a flight between Los Angeles and Seattle, followed by a forced landing in San Francisco, a stop for refueling in New York, and a forced flight to Algeria.

In support of its request for extradition, the United States had submitted to the French Foreign Ministry and to the Justice Ministry the following memorandum of law, dated April 3, 1975:

Memorandum of Law

* * *

The fugitives, Holder and Kerkow, have been indicted for the crimes of aircraft piracy, kidnapping and extortion, which are extraditable offenses under Article II of the Extradition Treaty between the United States and France, of January 6, 1909, as amended by the supplementary convention of February 12, 1970. Thus, France has a treaty obligation to surrender these fugitives for prosecution in the United States, unless the case comes within the terms of the exemption established in Article VI for political offenses. Article VI provides: Extradition shall not be granted in any of the following circumstances:

* * *

4.   If the offense for which the individual's extradition is requested is of a political character, or if he proves that the requisition for his surrender has, in fact, been made with a view to try or punish him for an offense of a political character. If any question arises as to whether a case comes within the provisions of this subparagraph, the authorities of the government on which the requisition is made shall decide.

* * *

Under this provision the requested state determines whether a crime is of a political character. However, the determination does not involve an exercise of discretion. It is a legal determination as to whether a treaty obligation exists on the facts of the particular case. No allegation has been made in this case, nor could it be sustained, that the United States requests the surrender of these fugitives in order to punish them for any offense other than the common crimes for which extradition is requested. Therefore, the sole question for the court is whether the crimes charged constitute offenses of a "political character" in the legal sense of Article VI.

Although the treaty does not prescribe a specific definition of offenses of a "political character" there is considerable jurisprudence and international extradition practice which establish the parameters of this concept. Offenses "of a political character" include traditional political crimes such as sedition and treason. The concept may also include common crimes which are clearly connected with offenses of a political character under special circumstances which have been defined by the tribunals of states and international practice.

There are numerous decisions holding that ordinary common crimes cannot be considered offenses of a political character unless they occur in the context of a civil war, rebellion or similar political disturbance. * * * [See chapters 3 and 16.]

Although political offenses have been found by tribunals in some other circumstances—usually involving compelling human considerations—it is well established that political motive alone does not give a common crime the character of a political offense.

* * *

In this case the fugitives were not engaged in any attempt to overthrow the Government of the United States or in any other political offense with which their crime could be connected. There is no evidence and no allegation that they belonged to any political group or had engaged in any political activities in the past. There is no allegation that the fugitives were subject to political persecution or harassment of any kind. The defense bases its claim of political offense exclusively on the alleged motive of the defendants to have the hijacked aircraft fly to Hanoi. The only evidence on this point is that the defendant Holder asked that the first plane fly to Hanoi and did not persist in that request when he was provided a second aircraft with the capacity to do so. His references to Angela Davis at the outset of the flight and to Eldridge Cleaver near the destination at Algiers evidence a confused mixture of vague and ill-defined motives. There is no precedent and no basis for construing the criminal activity of these fugitives as an offense of a political character.

Aircraft piracy is a serious, common crime which threatens the lives of innocent persons, disrupts international civil aviation, and causes tensions in international relations. It is an offense against the human rights of passengers and crew, and against the public order of all states. As such, it has been repeatedly condemned by the Security Council, the * * * General Assembly and the International Civil Aviation Organization in solemn resolutions supported by France and the United States. The General Assembly resolution of November 25, 1970, "condemns, without exception whatsoever, all acts of aircraft hijacking" and "calls upon states to take all appropriate measures to deter, prevent or suppress such acts within their jurisdiction * * *.'' The Hague Convention for the Suppression of Unlawful Seizure of Aircraft, signed December 16, 1970, to which France and the United States are party, provides for the extradition or prosecution of the perpetrators of such crimes.

While there are cases in years past in which states held a particular hijacking to be a political offense where the persons involved were fleeing from tyranny and faced severe political persecution if they were returned, the danger inherent in the increasing incidence of aircraft hijacking in more recent years has alarmed the entire international community and given grounds for a presumption that aircraft hijacking is a most serious common crime regardless of the circumstances. Moreover, there is wide recognition in the international community that cases of aircraft hijacking involving extortion or actual injury to passengers or crew represent an aggravated form of the offense which requires punishment as a common crime. * * *

In this case there is no suggestion that the fugitives were subject to any political persecution or needed the transportation to leave the country; they did threaten the lives of passengers and crew to extort $500,000 from the airline. This extortion contradicts any notion of idealism or of "political character" in this case.

It is recognized that extradition is the most effective deterrent to the crime of aircraft hijacking. Surrender of these fugitives for prosecution in the United States will contribute to such deterrence and thus protect lives and the interests of France as well as those of the United States. Refusal of extradition on the specious grounds that this crime is an offense of a political character would appear to condone hijacking and could contribute to repetition of such crimes to the danger of the entire international community.

[End of Memorandum of Law.]

On July 7, 1975, the United States Embassy at Paris delivered to the Acting Legal Adviser in the French Foreign Ministry a note with respect to the French refusal of extradition and the applicability of the U.S.–French extradition convention, as supplemented. The substantive portion of the note follows:

* * *

The Embassy notes that the decision of the Chambre d'accusation regarding the question of extradition is final and that in accordance with the Convention for the Suppression of Unlawful Seizure of Aircraft, signed at The Hague on December 16, 1970, a case has been opened against the accused at the Parquet de Paris on charges of the illegal seizure of an aircraft and restraint of hostages under threat. The Embassy trusts that these proceedings will result, in the event the accused are found guilty, in the application of the penalty which is proportionate to the seriousness of the crime and which will further the purposes of the Hague Convention to deter aircraft hijacking.

The interested officials of the United States Government have now had the opportunity to review the decision of the Chambre d'accusation on the request for extradition made by the United States, and this

Embassy has been instructed to bring to the attention of the Foreign Ministry the serious concern of the United States Government over the rejection of its extradition request.

In the view of the United States Government the decision of the French Government in this case to deny extradition on the sole grounds of an alleged political motivation for the crime is inconsistent with France's obligations under the Treaty of Extradition between the United States of America and the Republic of France of January 6, 1909, as amended by the supplementary convention signed at Paris on February 12, 1970. * * *

Although the treaty does not prescribe a specific definition of an offense of a "political character," and international practice is somewhat varied, the considerable jurisprudence and * * * cases in this field clearly establish that mere political motive is not sufficient to characterize a serious common crime as a political offense. * * *

    * * *

A strong case can be made that serious crimes such as aircraft hijacking are so dangerous to human life and so inimical to international order that they should not be regarded as "political offenses" regardless of the circumstances. Even if it is assumed that there are special circumstances in which an act of hijacking may be considered to have a political character, it is an extreme position to argue that the mere plea of political motive is sufficient to establish the political nature of the offense. * * *

The effect of the decision by the *Cour d'appel* is to construe hijacking as a "political offense" in any case in which a political motive is alleged, even where large sums of money are extorted under the threat of murder of the passengers and crew. The effect of the decision in this case, if it were followed by other states, would be virtually to eliminate extradition as a remedy in hijacking cases, and by suppressing the most effective deterrent to aircraft hijacking, would encourage the commission of more such crimes in the future.

    * * *

———

1. ***Subsequent conviction.*** On June 13, 1980, Willie Holder received a suspended five-year prison sentence in France for the hijacking. The New York Times, June 15, 1980, Sec. A, p. 8.

2. ***Questions.*** There are several cases involving hijackers from states behind the former Iron Curtain, in which the authorities of the state where they landed—Denmark, Austria, Western Germany—denied the requests for extradition and handed down light sentences when they tried the hijackers. *See, e.g., 76 Rev. Gén. de Dr. Int'l Pub.* 484, 509 (1972); Vol. 82 at 1083 (1978); and 83 *Rev. Gén. de Dr. Int'l Pub.* 480 (1979), where two persons from East Germany hijacked a Polish plane and forced it to land at Tempelhof airport, in the American zone of Berlin. Extradition was immediately refused. Was the refusal consistent with the letter of the Hague

Convention? With its spirit? Is it consistent with current definitions of a political offense? Since a strong case can be made that hijacking is so dangerous to human life it should not be regarded as a political offense regardless of the circumstances, is the political offense exception, nevertheless, sometimes appropriate? See Chapter 16.

3.   *Self help*. The rescue of hijacked airplane passengers is considered in Chapter 17 from the standpoint of territorial intervention by the rescuing state. Such rescue efforts, which are unilateral remedies for unlawful activity, must satisfy international legal requirements of necessity and proportionality, and must also conform to U.N. Charter obligations. *See* the 1987 Restatement, Section 905.

4.   *On Extradition and Hijacking* generally, and other acts of terrorism in the air, see Christopher L. Blakesley, TERRORISM, *supra* at pp. 84–100, 129, 146, 202–215.

SECTION B.   OUTER SPACE

Theories about airspace and outer space delimitation. Speakers at the Twenty-sixth Colloquium on the Law of Outer Space, sponsored by the International Institute of Space Law, October, 1983, addressed perhaps the most intractable question of the boundary between airspace and outer space. Some views follow.

Rosenfield, Some Thoughts on the Distinction Between Air Space and Outer Space

Proceedings of the Twenty-sixth Colloquium on the Law of Outer Space
93–94 (1984).*

* * *

In researching this question I went back through all of the previous twenty-five colloquia. To my surprise I found that this question was on the first colloquium, and it has appeared on almost every subsequent colloquium since that time. During the first colloquium the question was addressed by Andrew Haley of the United States who supported a scientific approach, the Von Karman line;[a] by Luig de Gonzaga Bevilacqua of Brazil, who advocated a theory that the boundary should depend on the nature of the craft involved, namely the altitude to which a specific craft remained dependent on the atmosphere; John Cobb Cooper who suggested several different possibilities without selecting between them. His list included: the

---

* Reprinted with the permission of the American Institute of Aeronautics & Astronautics.

a.   "[The Von Karman line] accepts the basic concept of aerodynamic lift but argues that such lift need not be the only 'support' and that present law could be interpreted as extending sovereignty up to the point where any aerodynamic lift is available. For an object traveling at 25,000 feet per second, that line is said to be about 275,000 feet from the earth's surface. * * * [I]t would * * * vary with atmospheric conditions and with design changes and other factors affecting the flight of objects." Lipson and Katzenbach, The Law of Outer Space 12 (1961).

height to which a craft can proceed while using aerodynamic lift; the height at which a satellite would go into orbit; the Von Karman line theory; the height at which no atmosphere exists (estimated to be about 1000 miles); a nation's sovereignty extends without limit above its territory; and, the height to which a state may exercise "effective control". Finally, Robert Jastrow of the United States advocated the lowest point at which a vehicle could orbit the earth, estimated at approximately 100 miles.

It is surprising to me to note that even the arguments have changed very little over the years. It is particularly surprising when it is recalled that this first meeting was in 1958, shortly after the first artificial earth satellite was placed in orbit, but ten years prior to the first legal space treaty. The early arguments were more technical and more theoretical emphasizing, inter alia, the Von Karman line, the point where gravity ceases, the layers of the atmosphere or the maximum altitude of flight. However the foundation for today's arguments were also being laid. Functionalism, use of an arbitrary height, a free zone between air space and outer space—these are not ideas developed in the 1970's and 1980's. They were also being suggested in the earliest meeting of the 1950's.

* * *

It may be that the real problem is that there does not seem to be a problem. A part of the solution has been the functional approach of the outer space treaties. Any problems that have come up have been solved through the functionalism of the existing treaties. The result is that there is in fact no problem to be resolved.

Danilenko, The Boundary Between Air Space and Outer Space in Modern International Law

Proceedings of the Twenty-sixth Colloquium on the Law of Outer Space.
71, 73 (1984).*

* * *

The evaluation of the current practice of states leads to the formulation of the rule of conduct which is observed by all states of the international community. In their mutual relations all states observe the rule according to which space objects in orbit, including the orbit with the technically lowest perigee achieved by any satellite so far placed in orbit, are within the sphere of application of the principle of freedom of outer space. This means that the sovereignty of underlying states does not extend at least over limits outlined by lowest perigees of earth-orbiting satellites. Thus according to established international practice the lower limit of outer space and the upper limit of national air space at present are broadly defined by the lowest altitudes at which the satellites can be maintained and used in orbit in an unpowered flight ($100(\pm10)$ km above sea-level).

The practice of states constituting the rule of international law which establishes the boundary between air space and outer space meets the

* Reprinted by permission of the American Institute of Aeronautics & Astronautics.

requirements of generality, consistency, uniformity and continues over the period of time of more than 25 years. * * *

　　　* * *

The recognition or acceptance of customary rules of conduct by which air space and outer space are demarcated as a rule of international law on the part of space powers was primarily manifested through their actual space activities connected with the launching and operation of space objects. These activities amounted to an implied legal claim to the right to carry out the exploration and use of outer space at various altitudes over the territories of subjacent states. At the same time the acting states recognized the right of other states of the international community to carry out similar activities over their territories. At least one of the space powers—the Soviet Union—has expressly recognized the existence of "an international legal custom" defining the boundary between air space and outer space on the basis of the criterion of the lowest perigee of orbiting satellite, i.e. at a height of approximately 100–110 km above sea-level. The acceptance of the established practice on the part of non-space powers was primarily manifested through their passive conduct expressing consent to the legal claims of space powers. Tacit consent of states who are not as yet capable of launching and operating space objects is evidenced by absence of protests based on the principle of state sovereignty against the space activities at the lowest altitudes over their territorial air space. * * *

　　　* * *

Definition and Delimitation of Outer Space

Summary Report of a Discussion in the Legal Sub–Committee of the United Nations Committee on the Peaceful Uses of Outer Space, March–April 1984.
21 UN Chronicle No. 4, p. 32 (1984).

Where does outer space begin? Does it have a physical boundary by which States could stake claim to areas above them? What problems would ensue from establishing legal definitions and boundaries?

The Legal Sub–Committee established a working group to deal with the problems of definition and delimitation of outer space and the character and use of the geostationary orbit. The working group, on a proposal of its Chairman, agreed on separate consideration of the two subjects. However, it felt time should also be allotted to consider the item as a whole.

Some countries maintained that a definition and delimitation of outer space was necessary and wanted a multilateral agreement, open to all States, to establish a specific altitude as the upper limit of air space. Related questions are whether outer space should be considered as beginning where air space ends; and at what altitude air space should be regarded as ending.

A number of nations favouring a "spatial definition" supported the Soviet proposal that the boundary between outer space and air space be at an altitude not exceeding 110 kms above sea level. Provision could be made for that to be changed in the future, by international agreement, should circumstances make it necessary, according to the proposal.

In the debate, the Soviet Union said delimitation and definition of outer space was needed to guarantee effectively a reliable legal basis for new spheres of space activity and to guarantee that the study and use of space would be carried out in the interests of all States. The problem of defining the boundary between the two types of space was important. That boundary was the limit of the height of the application of State sovereignty. Definition of the boundary was a means of establishing the area for applying international air and space law.

Bulgaria said the absence of a boundary between air and outer space opened the door to countless violations of State sovereignty. The absence of a clearly defined limit would compel States whose security would be threatened to enact measures to prevent such violation.

India said outer space should be defined and delimited because of the existence of different legal régimes for air and outer space. There was a need to provide a clear area for applying existing outer space law and facilitating the further development of that law to determine the upper limit of State sovereignty, to safeguard the security of national air space and prevent disputes between States.

Hungary said as there were two law régimes, of outer space and of air space, there could well be situations in the future which would raise the question as to which applied. Explicit definitions of outer space and air space were technically possible.

Nigeria said a definition was needed as a requirement for the full exercise of State sovereignty. Czechoslovakia said delimitation of space was important to preserve it for activities of a peaceful nature only.

Some States, while favouring the "spatial definition" approach, did not agree with the proposed altitude for the demarcation between air space and outer space. Kenya, for example, had some reservations regarding setting a specific distance in terms of delimiting outer space, as it seemed arbitrary. A definition of air space would be possible only after outer space had been defined.

Other delegations stated that: there was no present scientific basis for defining and delimiting outer space or for placing the boundary at any particular altitude; the development and application of the law of outer space had proceeded satisfactorily without such a definition or delimitation; and it would be unreasonable to adopt an arbitrary definition or delimitation which could give rise to difficulties and impede the development of space technology.

The United States said the establishment of a demarcation between outer space and air space in advance of a genuine and practical need for doing so would be an inherently arbitrary exercise having unforeseeable and almost certainly detrimental consequences for future outer space activities.

The United Kingdom said it was premature to define outer space, and was not convinced of the need for such a definition. The Netherlands said to draw a boundary between outer space and air space at a certain altitude was not only unnecessary but undesirable, as it could create problems that did not now exist.

Italy said a rigid and general delimitation of outer space did not meet the scientific criteria or respond to practical and functional criteria. A number of space agreements had been formulated without such a definition. A rigid definition would create major problems for certain smaller States in contradiction of the principle of free access to space activity.

Brazil said any definition could not be separated from the scientific knowledge available. The drawing of an arbitrary line to divide outer space and air space was always a possibility, but other approaches, such as spatial or functional, could be taken.

Some delegations considered that as the positions of delegations had not moved closer over many years, the Sub–Committee should, without prejudice to its future work on the question of the definition and delimitation of outer space, concern itself with such matters as the definition of "space objects" and "space activities". Others felt a consensus on the definition of a "space object" would be more difficult to achieve than on a definition and delimitation of outer space.

France said a definition of space objects or space activities would make possible a definition of the basic legal concepts for outer space law and determine all implications of a future definition of outer space.

Bulgaria said the Sub–Committee could not attribute privileges to space objects if it were to base its work on definition of space objects and activities. Violation of air space by a space object rather than an aircraft represented the same danger to States as overflight by aircraft.

———

Notes & Questions.   Launching and landing of space objects. Members of the Committee on the Peaceful Uses of Outer Space expressed views, similar to those summarized above, at its 1986 session. Among matters discussed was a Soviet proposal for a "multilateral agreement establishing the beginning of outer space at an altitude not exceeding 110 kilometres above sea level and allowing for innocent passage, at lower altitudes, through the airspace of one State of another State's space object for the purpose of reaching orbit or returning to Earth. It was noted during the discussion that the particular altitude of demarcation was open to negotiation." 23 UN Chronicle No. 4 (1986), p. 86.

The editors of an earlier edition of this book asked the General Counsel of NASA (National Aeronautics and Space Administration): "Is it the practice of NASA to procure the permission of a state through whose airspace a space vehicle may pass on launching or landing? If so, how is airspace defined for the purpose of determining whether permission is needed?"

General Counsel John E. O'Brien response, on June 18, 1986 follows:

Regarding your question, it should be noted that there is no boundary between air space and outer space that has been endorsed by the world community. For a number of years, the question of where air space ends and outer space begins has been on the agenda of the Legal Subcommittee of the U.N. Committee on the Peaceful Uses of Outer

Space. It is the position of the United States that there is a gray area between air space and outer space which does not permit us to agree that an arbitrary boundary should be set between these two areas.

While experimental airplanes have flown to about 50 miles, there is no clarity as to where air space ends. Due to this circumstance, it has not been necessary for the United States to obtain the permission of a State through whose air space a space vehicle may pass during launching or landing. We do not know of any instance where on launching or landing a space vehicle has clearly been passing through the air space of another state. If a space vehicle were clearly passing through the air space of another State, on launching or landing, we would, of course, notify that State and obtain its permission if it were determined that such permission were required.

You should be aware that a practice has evolved over the past twenty-five years which permits a space vehicle, upon launching or landing, to pass over other States. As far as I know, there has been no protest by any State in this area.

———

As of May 2001, the above summary of NASA practice and nonobjection thereto by other states seemingly still holds. Is it possible that a legal principle governing tolerated foreign airspace passage in climb-to-orbit, free movement in "outer" space, and tolerated re-entry through foreign airspace is evolving or has evolved? Does it matter, in this regard, whether the vehicle is winged, so that it flies through airspace after it drops out of "outer space"? Would you analogize launch and re-entry tolerations in airspace above national territory to innocent passage and port-entry in the Law of the Sea? On the other hand, is an American shuttle-craft an airplane when in glide path, under aero-dynamic lift? Should a flight plan be filed with an ADIZ[a] county transited whilst approaching landing in the United States?

When Russia allowed Dennis Tito to tag along into space for a handsome price, would the Warsaw Convention apply if he were injured or lost some of his belongings?, (a) on launch before orbit; (b) to air-lift glidepath after re-entry?

Mishra and Pavlasek, on the Lack of Physical Bases for Defining a Boundary Between Air Space and Outer Space

7 Annals of Air and Space Law 399, 412 (1982).[*]

* * *

a. Aircraft Defense Identification Zone regulations, which require a flight plan to be filed prior to take-off on a flight that is planned to come within certain distances from a state so requiring. * * *

* Reprinted by permission of the Institute and Centre of Air and Space Law, McGill University.

The objective of this statement has been to examine physical factors which might be considered as bases for the definition of a boundary between air space and outer space. For this purpose, pertinent physical phenomena and their practical applications were considered under the following groupings or "regimes": 1. "State of Matter". 2. "Gravitational Field", 3. "Electromagnetic", 4. "Geometrical/Geographical", 5. "Biological/Environmental" and 6. "Technological".

In the ongoing "legal debate" of the past, since "space activities" started, it appears that two basic seemingly different types of arguments have been advanced for the definition of a boundary, which may appear to be contradictory. These are characterizable as the "physical boundary" versus the "functional boundary" arguments. * * * From a physical world point of view there is *no real difference* between these two_ The "Physical Boundary" hypothesis considers the possibility of a physical *condition* whereas the "Functional Boundary" approach concerns the use of physical means towards a particular *application*. Both of these are "physical" and there is thus no fundamental difference, there is merely a change in vantage point and perspective.

It is the conclusion of this statement that there in fact exist no physical bases which might be used as a sound and absolute reason for defining a boundary between air space and outer space. In examining the first five regimes enumerated above it is clear that there exists no definite physical condition which can be described as a boundary. Furthermore, an overview of the technological applications shows equally well that there are no useful "functional" boundaries either. In fact the examination simply confirms the obvious, namely that the planet earth is only a minor component of, but forms an indivisible integral part of the universe. It does so both materially and in terms of the "physical laws" by which its existence is governed. The "indivisibility principle" is fundamental and cannot be altered regardless of human desires or imaginings to do so.

The consequences of this conclusion to the problem of defining a boundary between air space and outer space are quite clear. The notion of a "boundary" is simply a humanly conceived constraint, possibly a matter of convenience or a means of controlling conflicting human objectives. The definition must therefore be sought in human terms. In terms of human experience this means that such a definition is an act of willful desire, an arbitrary decision and the answer must be achieved through well known processes of human decision making in such cases. Such decisions may be achieved on social, cultural, economic, historical and political grounds as an act of collective will, through negotiated agreement or, regrettably even the use of force. Since such a decision will have no physical foundation it will benefit from an inherently flexible definition with a built in possibility of subsequent revision or even ultimate abolishment, as the human perspective of the problem evolves in the future.

Any attempt however to make use of physical arguments to define a boundary will be contrived, artificial, illusory and therefore intellectually unsound—even if temporarily expedient as a masking of the human urge for imagining a boundary.

———

The delimitation, or boundary, between a nation's "territorial" airspace and outer space remains perhaps the most difficult of all space law issues. We have seen various theories on making this boundary. These boil down to "spatialist" and functionalist approaches, with the "spatialists" apparently winning the argument to date. There is still no clear answer to the question of where space begins. But equally clearly, at some point above the earth, there exists an environment completely different from that in which we live. "A sort of customary law has developed ... to the effect than any object in orbit is in space, and that seems enough to satisfy everyone for the time being." *See* Robert A. Ramey, *Armed Conflict on the Final Frontier: The Law of War in Space*, 48 Air Force Law Review 1, 158, n. 556 (2000); Leo Malagar & Marlo Apalisok Magdoza–Malagar, *International Law of Outer Space & the Protection of Intellectual Property Rights*, 17 B.U. Int'l L.J. 311, 316–18 (1999).

———

* * *

International conventions. Several international conventions address the legal problems of space.

The Outer Space Treaty (Treaty on Principles Governing the Activities of States in the Exploration and Use of Outer Space, Including the Moon and Other Celestial Bodies), 18 U.S.T. 2410, 610 U.N.T.S. 205—see the Documentary Supplement—entered into force for the United States on October 10, 1967. The following articles indicate the generality of its provisions:

Article I

The exploration and use of outer space, including the moon and other celestial bodies, shall be carried out for the benefit and in the interests of all countries, irrespective of their degree of economic or scientific development, and shall be the province of all mankind.

Outer space, including the moon and other celestial bodies, shall be free for exploration and use by all States without discrimination of any kind, on a basis of equality and in accordance with international law, and there shall be free access to all areas of celestial bodies.

There shall be freedom of scientific investigation in outer space, including the moon and other celestial bodies, and States shall facilitate and encourage international co-operation in such investigation.

Article III

States Parties to the Treaty shall carry on activities in the exploration and use of outer space, including the moon and other celestial bodies, in accordance with international law, including the Charter of the United Nations, in the interest of maintaining international peace and security and promoting international cooperation and understanding.

In analyzing this treaty, which purports to set general principles, the following questions should be addressed:

i. Has the treaty made any change in the law that would be applicable without the treaty? Another way of putting this question is whether a non-party is freer than a party to do as it wishes in outer space and, if so, in what respects?

ii. Are enough facts known about space to justify a state's committing itself at this stage of technological development to the principles enunciated in the treaty? What would the U.S. status be, were it to develop the "Star Wars" missile shield? How can a state protect its interests if startling new facts are discovered about outer space in the future?

The Agreement on the Rescue of Astronauts, the Return of Astronauts, and the Return of Objects Launched Into Outer Space, 19 U.S.T. 7570, entered into force for the United States on December 3, 1968.

The Convention on International Liability for Damage Caused by Space Objects—see the Documentary Supplement—entered into force for the United States on October 9, 1973. 88 states were parties as of January 2000. The convention provides that the launching state shall be liable for damage caused by its space object absolutely in some cases, or for its fault in others. Claims procedure involves a Claims Commission, whose decision shall be binding if the parties have so agreed or whose award is recommendatory, "which the parties shall consider in good faith." (Article XIX). The legal principles to be applied in determining compensation are particularly interesting:

Article XII

The compensation which the launching State shall be liable to pay for damage under this Convention shall be determined in accordance with international law and the principles of justice and equity, in order to provide such reparation in respect of the damage as will restore the person, natural or juridical, State or international organization on whose behalf the claim is presented to the condition which would have existed if the damage had not occurred.

The Liability Convention, defines "space object" as including the "component parts of a space object as well as its launch vehicle and parts thereof." Convention on International Liability for Damage Caused by Space Objects, Mar. 29, 1972, art. 1(d), 24 U.S.T. 2389, 961 U.N.T.S. 187 (entered into force Sept. 1, 1972)[hereinafter Liability Convention]. How helpful is this definition? Can an astronaut be a "space object"? *See,* Article VI of the Outer Space Treaty, provided that States Parties "shall bear international responsibility for national activities in outer space. . . ." There remain many questions, however, as W.F. Foster notes in *The Convention on International Liability for Damage Caused by Space Objects,* 1972 CAN. Y.B. INT'L L. 137, 143 n.3:

(a) what flight instrumentalities are covered by the term "object?";

(b) what is meant by the phrase "internationally liable"?;

(c) what regime will govern the liability of States engaged in a joint venture—will they be jointly and severally liable or only severally liable?;

(d) what is encompassed by the term "damage"?;

(e) how is an international organization to be responsible under the Treaty when it cannot become a party to, or even accept the obligations contained in the Treaty?; and

(f) what mechanisms will be used to settle disputes arising when damage is caused?

Has the Liability Convention answered any of these in any meaningful way? *See discussion in Armed Conflict on the Final Frontier: The Law of War in Space,* Major Robert A. Ramey, 48 Air Force Law Review 1 (2000).

Convention on Registration of Objects Launched into Outer Space, entered into force for the United States on September 15, 1976. 28 U.S.T. 695.

2. *Work on new conventions at the United Nations.* The committee on the Peaceful Uses of Outer Space has for a number of years worked on the drafting of agreements relating to remote sensing of the environment of the earth from outer space, the definition and or delimitation of outer space (see Part 2b, below relating to the geostationary orbit). The progress of the Outer Space Committee is reported from time to time in the UN Chronicle (e.g. 23 UN Chronicle No. 4, 1986, p. 84).

a. *Remote sensing.* Satellites orbiting the earth can collect photographic information about military affairs, such as troop concentrations, military installations, naval movements and missile emplacements and today a person's features. Remote sensing of the earth also produces vast quantities of information of a non-military nature, useful in such matters as weather prediction, maritime navigation, geological exploration, estimating agricultural crops, monitoring the growth of deserts, surveying natural disasters and map-making, to mention only a few uses.

Some countries have objected to being observed from outer space without their consent, but the more recent concerns have dealt with access to the non-military information that is being gathered by the few countries that have the capacity to conduct remote sensing operations.

In December 1986, the General Assembly adopted a resolution setting forth fifteen principles on remote sensing, recommended by the Committee on Peaceful Uses of Outer Space and its Legal Sub–Committee. Principle XII deals with the right of observed states to have access to primary and processed data and to analyzed information concerning their territory. The principle provides that such access shall be made available on a non-discriminatory basis and at reasonable cost.

b. *The geostationary orbit.* Communications satellites are put into orbit directly above the equator at a distance of 22,300 miles above the earth. The speed of the satellite in orbit is synchronized to that of the earth so that a satellite appears to be located permanently in a particular, stationary spot above the earth. Certain states located at the equator have claimed special territorial rights with respect to the space occupied by the orbiting satellites, but the consensus of the remainder of states appears to be to reject that claim. It is generally considered that the geostationary orbit falls within outer space under the terms of the Outer Space Treaty and thus, under Article I, is free for use by all states. So many satellites have been placed in geostationary orbit that developing states have voiced concern that the orbit will become saturated with satellites by developed states, so as to preclude the use of the orbit by other states when their technology has developed. The matter has been a frequent subject of contention in the UN Committee on Peaceful Uses of Outer Space. At the 1985 World Administrative Radio Conference sponsored by the International Telecommunications Union, one hundred twelve nations made a beginning on meeting the concerns of all states in the use of the orbit, as described below.

———

Military uses of outer space. Article IV of the Outer Space Treaty provides that the parties "undertake not to place in orbit around the Earth any objects carrying nuclear weapons or any other kinds of weapons of mass destruction, install such weapons on celestial bodies, or station such weapons in outer space in any other manner." See the Documentary Supplement. Despite this commitment, already made, the former Soviet Union proposed a draft treaty on the prohibition of stationing of weapons of any kind in outer space. It has also proposed a treaty on the prohibition of the use of force in outer space and from outer space with regard to the earth. To what extent would a treaty on the latter subject place limits on states not already provided by the U.N. Charter or by customary international law? Although Article 2(4) of the Charter limits a state's use of force generally, Article 51 expressly preserves the right of self defense. See Chapter 15.

The most current international controversy on the military use of space involves the use of anti-satellite weaponry, in particular on the interpretation of the 1972 Anti–Ballistic Missile Treaty between the United States and the former Soviet Union. The question whether the United States is free under that treaty to deploy anti-satellite devices under its Strategic Defense Initiative (popularly called Star Wars) involves a question of treaty interpretation which is posed in Chapter 15. President Bush has given new life to the controversy in 2001, by stating that the United States is going to study the viability of the missile shield. Russia, China, and even most of our European allies have protested this, stating that studying the creation of such a "shield" violates the ABM Treaty and risks a renewal of the Cold War arms race.

———

Round–Up on Other Legal Aspects of the Use of Space

1. A very useful source book in this field is Cristol, Space Law: Past, Present and Future (1991), especially *Part I, Where We Have Been and Where We Are.*

2.   The common heritage of mankind concept, dealt with heretofore in regard to deep sea mining, Part XI of the 1982 Law of the Sea Convention, is linked (in various phrasings) to the space treaties carried in the Documentary Supplement. So far, however, the concept has not been sought to be applied to space law with the rigor, detail, and structure of that not-yet-in-force treaty. Note that the so-called "Moon Treaty" (Doc.Supp.) is in force with very few participants, not including the United States, the former USSR, or the Russian Federation, the only two states so far that have, by different means, brought anything back from the Moon. Activity on the Moon does not seem to be on the "take action" agenda of any "space power"; but, suppose, there should be a flurry of interest in the extraction of very valuable or security-important substances from the Moon, would we see a replay of Part XI of the Law of the Sea Convention?

3.   *The problem of geosynchronous (or geostationary) orbits:* Satellites orbiting in equatorial regions at altitudes essentially equal to the circumference of the Earth can be arranged so as to "accompany" the planet in its revolution on its own axis. Such positions give great advantages as to optical observation, signals projection and detection ("remote sensing"); and communications, including radio frequencies and new light-beam technologies. In the 1970's a group of equatorial states, led by Colombia, made a determined effort in the United Nations and elsewhere to assert sovereign claims of an essentially territorial nature to the areas of such orbits. They failed. Meanwhile, the International Telecommunications Union (ITU), a specialized agency under Articles 57 and 63 of the Charter, has managed to "keep the peace" as to utilizations of the limited number of orbital paths available. For the prospects of possibly greater demand for use, see Gleick, *The Telephone Transformed—Into Almost Everything,* New York Times Magazine (May 16, 1993).

4.   *Radio and Television Broadcasting from Space.* Technical problems of electronic interference (which usually are manageable) aside, what if a state feels invaded, culturally, socially, or even politically, by broadcasts from space vehicles by another state? Are such broadcasts legally distinguishable from broadcasts beamed from land, vessels, or aircraft? Is the problem different from, say, broadcasts from vessels or aircraft operating within the territorial jurisdiction of the target state? Why or why not? Is there a legal right of a state and its people "to be let alone" from foreign broadcasts intentionally and specifically directed toward it and them, regardless of source? There is virtually no "hard" (or real?) law in this area. Diplomacy, retaliation, and getting along are the main resorts of offended states. Efforts at "soft law" through General Assembly Resolutions have not fared well even when limited to obligations to inform, consult, and, inferentially, receive prior consent.

A question for a first course in international law: should the source of the objectionable broadcast be in and of itself, a key variable as to the claimed "rights" of the objecting state and the assertion liability of the "state of the broadcast"? Suppose an objecting state should criminalize all unauthorized (by it) broadcasts heard or seeable in its territory, from whatever source emanating, then sit back and wait for the broadcasters to be (a) found in or (b) hauled into its territory? Should "source" of a satellite in space or on the ground in the sending state be crucial?

Actually, so far, most of the transitional problems involving broadcasting have been the simple over-lapping of signals areas, such as in national sectors along the Canadian, United States and Mexican borders, and in Europe. Propaganda broadcasting by radio was at its height during World War II and the Cold War. Some can still be heard between Castro's Cuba and the United States. (Television seems not to have lent itself as well to direct and unadorned propaganda.)

5. Telecommunications law is a well-developed specialty practice, both nationally and transnationally.

6. *Remote Sensing.* Space satellites, mainly un-manned, have an extensive use in observing, measuring, classifying, and otherwise appraising aspects and characteristics of the planet Earth and its atmosphere, including weather. As is to be expected, states that are more observed than observing of others develop a degree of sensitivity and even concern. Tensions are reduced by the degree to which states with developed sensing capabilities share the results of their observances with other states. See, generally, Christol, Space Law, op. cit. sup., pp. 73–95. "Soft law" through a unanimous Resolution of the General Assembly in 1986 (A–41_65) has linked the sharing of remote sensing results to the "Space Activities Treaty of 1967". Sensing by the United States purports to comply with this and other re-assuring principles. The United States sensing operation was privatized in 1985, on a subsidized basis which, it is assumed by us, is not excessively costly to foreign and other users of the sensed data. One has to assume, however, that observations from space of a military intelligence nature take place and are classified, rather than shared, in view of the secrecy with which certain satellites for military use are launched.

SECTION C.   CELESTIAL BODIES

———

1. *The Outer Space Treaty.* Article II of the treaty provides: "Outer space, including the moon and other celestial bodies, is not subject to national appropriation by claim of sovereignty, by means of use or occupation, or by any other means." As of January 2000, 101 States were parties.

Suppose that a state discovers a particularly rare and valuable mineral on the moon, which it is able to mine cheaply with manned or unmanned equipment. Does the treaty prohibit that state from exploiting the moon's resources for its own exclusive benefit? Can the state set up a base over which it has exclusive control so as to prevent another state from exploiting resources within that base? See Article XII.

What law governs the state, not a party to the treaty (or one that has withdrawn pursuant to Article XVI) that wishes to claim a portion of the moon as its territory? Do the principles relating to the acquisition of territory on the surface of the earth apply? If so, what facts would support a claim that a state has lawfully acquired a portion of the moon as its territory?[a]

2. *The Moon Treaty.* In Dec. 1979, the General Assembly adopted an Agreement Governing the Activities of States on the Moon and other Celestial Bodies. Although the treaty came into force on July 11, 1984, it has very few adherents. Only 8 states were parties to the treaty on Jan. 1, 1993. Developed states parties include France, Austria and the Netherlands, but not the United States or the Soviet Union.

The text of the treaty is set forth in the Documentary Supplement. Article 3 of the Treaty prohibits any threat or use of force or any other hostile act or threat of hostile act on the moon, which France stated upon signature to be only a reaffirmation of the principle of prohibition of use of force which states are obligated to observe under the provisions of the Charter of the United Nations. In Article 11(2) the treaty reiterates the prohibition against national appropriation set forth in the Outer Space Treaty.

A striking feature of the treaty is its declaration that the moon and its natural resources are the common heritage of mankind (Article 11). (Compare the provisions of the Treaty on the Law of the Sea adopting the same concept with respect to the seabed and ocean floor and subsoil beyond the limits of national jurisdiction. Article 136.)

In addition to provisions dealing with notice of activities undertaken on the moon (and other celestial bodies), freedom of scientific investigation, and protection of the moon's environmental balance, the agreement looks ahead to an eventual partial internationalization of the moon. Article 11 provides:

> States Parties to this Agreement hereby undertake to establish an international regime, including appropriate procedures, to govern the exploitation of the natural resources of the moon as such exploitation is about to become feasible. * * *

One of the main purposes of such an international regime is:

> An equitable sharing by all States Parties in the benefits derived from those resources, whereby the interests and needs of the developing countries, as well as the efforts of those countries which have contributed either directly or indirectly to the exploration of the moon, shall be given special consideration.

To what extent does the treaty inhibit commercial exploitation of the moon's resources by a state party? Does the agreement provide for a moratorium on such exploitation prior to the establishment of the projected

a. Of some utility in the analysis of the legal problems of celestial bodies is a study of Antarctica. See the Antarctic Treaty, 12 U.S.T. 794, 402 U.N.T.S. 71, which entered into force for the United States on June 23, 1961; 42 states were parties as of January 1, 1993. The treaty is briefly discussed in Chapter 11. The text of the treaty and bibliographic references are also in Lay and Taubenfeld, The Law Relating to Activities of Man in Space 59–62 (1970).

international regime? These questions were the subject of debate in the United States.

———

3.   *What About Space Stations?* From the movies we are familiar enough with them. Remember the stop at the space station in *2001: A Space Odyssey?* The scene was not unlike coming aboard a United States Navy ship-of-the-line, except that there was no quarter-deck to salute and liquor was served. The Moon launch in 2001 was from the Space Station. Of course, the hugeness of the movie station, more like a city than a mere vessel, contrasts with the modest size of the only station now in space, Russia's *Mir*. In fact, it is difficult to distinguish *Mir* from a mere shuttle, except that *Mir* cannot fly back to Earth but is doomed to burn on re-entry and probably drop debris. The legal literature on space stations is rather iffy and vague, as is to be expected, given their virtually negative state of development and inability to maintain orbit or flight control on re-entry. But, *Mir* has stayed "up" longer than any American shuttle has ever remained in space, thus tending, perhaps, to induce considering a space station as a short-life artificial satellite with people aboard, thus giving rise to questions that would not be relevant as to an un-manned remote-sensing vehicle or a TV repeater. At least one scholar worries about whether the state of the nationality of a space station has any priority of claim as to its orbit, once it drops and has to be replaced. Stay tuned.

4.   *The Unmet Problems of Space Debris.* The problem of debris within space was highlighted at mid-summer, 1993, when an American shuttle crew had to take evasive action to avoid collision. There is a lot of trash in orbit and so far nothing has been done about it. The old 1950s treaty on liability for objects falling from space has not been made the basis for liability claims so far.

CHAPTER 6

INTERNATIONAL PROTECTION OF THE ENVIRONMENT

———

1. *The development of international environmental law and emerging principles.* The last twenty-eight years since the 1972 Stockholm Conference on the Human Environment has evidenced the increasing international and national concern for environmental protection. There has been a growing realization that the ecosystem is complex and interrelated and the approach to combat environmental harm must also be interrelated and integrated among states. Environmental problems do not respect state boundaries and are a common vital concern for all people.

This Chapter begins with an analysis of the genesis of the international legal protection of the environment as exemplified in the trilogy of cases, the Trail Smelter Arbitration, the Corfu Channel and the Lake Lanoux

365

Arbitration, which can be regarded as the jurisprudential backing for the 1972 Stockholm Declaration. It then goes on to survey the treatment given to particular areas of environmental concern such as, *inter alia,* transboundary air pollution and acid rain, the ozone layer, climate change, marine pollution and protection of endangered species. The Rio Declaration on Environment and Development and Agenda 21 will also be discussed. The second part of the Chapter addresses emerging international law principles such as sustainable development, inter-generational equity and environmental rights as human rights. The aim here is to give the reader a sense of the new imperatives that are called for to strengthen the legal framework, increase international cooperation and protect the environment for future generations.

2. *Environmental issues and the world community.* The balancing of environmental issues and development present the world community with a unique challenge, as they involve not only conflicting interests but also the interdependence of environmental, economic, political, social and security issues. A cross-sectoral integrated approach is called for.

What on Earth's the Matter?

The Rio Conference

UNESCO Sources, No. 37, May 1992, 7–8.

The degradation of the planet's environment is accelerating. It has been estimated that 10 to 20 million hectares of forest—an area five times the size of Belgium—are destroyed each year, while another six million hectares of arable land turn into desert. Whole species vanish and ecosystems are destroyed at a dizzying pace, shrinking the earth's genetic capital before when we have even explored all of its resources.

For the first time in history, human deeds have an impact that goes beyond local boundaries and encompasses the globe: witness, for example, climatic changes caused by the greenhouse effect. And such changes could well prove irreversible.

The human factors accounting for the worsening of our environment are known. Foremost among them are the world's demographic explosion—the population of the Third World will have quadrupled between 1950 and 2025, the damaging consequences of global manufacturing and consumerism, and the inability of our existing forms of government and social practices to resolve such problems. These human factors are all linked; unsustainable development and the environmental crisis are but two sides of the same coin.

The physical phenomena involved, be they local or worldwide, are increasingly understood by scientists. Today, these phenomena can be forecast with enough accuracy to set the alarm bells ringing. Changing climatic patterns, for example, could lead to rising temperatures and sea levels which, in turn would modify the agricultural potential of entire regions, submerge hundreds of thousands of square kilometers of coastal areas where three-quarters of the world's population live today and disrupt, maybe ruin, the lives of millions.

* * *

Humanity is therefore living with a paradox: it is certain that apathy or sporadic and incoherent explosions of activity, will lead us to catastrophe, yet this certainty does not rid us of our impotence and paralysis. This paradox, at the heart of the environmental crisis, is so acute that it can't be explained by circumstantial factors, such as lack of funds, but rather by structural problems.

If paralysis stems from ignorance of the accumulating risks, the environmental crisis then reveals tremendous inefficiency in research methods and/or communication of knowledge.

Environmental problems completely ignore borders, whether they be between nations or scientific disciplines; interdisciplinary approaches, involving not only natural sciences but also social sciences, and cooperation among communities of scientists throughout the world are the only way that environmental research can leap ahead.

* * *

E. Brown Weiss, Global Environmental Change and International Law: The Introductory Framework

in E. Brown Weiss (ed.) Environmental Change and International Law, 3–7 (1992).*

International law has been based on the relationship between independent states that exercise exclusive national sovereignty over their territories. Global change is altering this vision by causing states to realize that they are locked together in sharing the use of a common global environment. While human activities have always contributed to environmental change, it is only within the last half of this century that their effects have become global and serious, and in many cases irreversible. This has led to a growing awareness that the interests of humankind must constrain the interests of individual states. Moreover, actors other than states have become essential to managing global environmental change. These developments are leading to a fundamental shift in the paradigm of international law that is evolving in the international environmental field.

* * * Concern among primarily industrialized countries about the serious risk of environmental harm to countries around the world motivated states to convene the 1972 Conference on the Human Environment, the first world conference on the environment.

By 1970 the world population had more than doubled since the beginning of the century (from 1.6 to 3.4 billion), industrial processes were generating unprecedented amounts of pollutants, and in some countries popular concern for the environment had sky-rocketed. The United States, for example, had passed its first piece of national environmental legislation, the National Environmental Policy Act of 1969.

At the time of the Stockholm Conference countries were deeply divided over the issue of whether environmental protection and economic development were compatible. The conceptual breakthrough that provided the paradigm for joining these two important goals emerged from a meeting of experts held in Founex, Switzerland, just prior to the Stockholm Conference. Today countries recognize that sound economic development must be environmentally sustainable and are concerned about how to do this. They realize that we need to substantially increase the living standards of the poor in a manner that is environmentally sustainable. The issue in 1992 that divides countries is an equity one: how to finance environmentally sustainable economic development for present and future generations.

Today, 20 years after the Stockholm Conference, countries are concerned with global environmental problems that were either not yet identified or barely addressed. These include acid precipitation, ozone depletion, climate change, hazardous waste disposal, loss of biological diversity, and forest degradation and loss and land-based sources of marine pollution.

The trends in population, resource consumption, and environmental degradation that caused such concern in the early 1970s have continued, or accelerated, while our capacity to address them has increased at a slower rate, albeit arguably more rapidly than for some other problems.

Population growth, resource consumption, and technological development continue to be primary catalysts for global environmental change. By 1990, world population had reached 5.3 billion, more than triple than in 1900 and almost 2 billion more than in 1970. Current estimates are that world population will reach at least 8.5 billion by the year 2025. The bulk of population growth is projected to be in the developing world.

The link between population growth and environmental degradation is complex and not well understood, as reflected in the several competing schools of thought on the issues. However, a larger population generally translates into greater demands on the Earth's resources. As has been demonstrated, population size that exceeds local carrying capacity of the ecosystems can cause soil depletion, deforestation, and desertification. If we multiply projected population increases by the substantially higher standard of living that equity requires for impoverished communities today and for future populations, the potential demands on the environment in the decades ahead are dramatic.

Since 1968, the world's consumption of energy has grown. Overall, the total energy requirements of industrialized countries have increased almost 30 per cent from 1970 to 1988, although this masks two periods of decline after the oil-price shocks. The rate of increase in energy consumption in the developing countries has declined, but remains high. Most of the world's energy continues to come from burning fossil fuels, whose general by-products are a primary contributor to global warming. Annual emissions of carbon dioxide from fossil fuels more than doubled from 1960 to 1988.

In addition, the release of ozone-depleting chloro-fluorocarbons (e.g. CFC–11 and CFC–12), which were virtually non-existent prior to World

War II, has risen from 35 million kilograms in 1950, to 506 million kilograms in 1970, and to 707 million kilograms by 1988. Fortunately, countries have now agreed to phase out their production and consumption by the year 2000, and likely sooner. Human-caused emissions of trace metals have followed a similar growth pattern.

Agriculture demands and practices have also raised important environmental concerns. Irrigated crop land, which accounts for about 17 per cent of the world's crop land and one-third of the global harvest, is being eroded by waterlogging and made less productive by salinization (the cumulative build-up of salts left by evaporation of irrigation water). Deforestation, loss of biological diversity, and soil erosion have significantly increased.

Fresh water continues to be a critical resource. In addition to the well-documented water-quality problems of surface waters, new concern has emerged over groundwater resources. Contamination results from the disposal of wastes, both hazardous and non-hazardous, and from the seepage of chemicals such as pesticides and fertilizers into the aquifers. Pesticides, whose use has doubled in the US since 1961, have created groundwater contamination problems in 40 of the 50 US states. Pesticides are used worldwide, with an over–$18–billion market in 1987, and their use is frequently unregulated or not well monitored. The agricultural use of chemicals has also grown dramatically, leading to increased run-off and contamination of lakes, streams, and groundwater. While the open oceans remain relatively undisturbed by humankind's activities, the oceans' coastal zones, the most biologically productive areas, are under severe pressure from population growth and development activities. In addition, there is evidence that we may be reaching the limits of the seas' natural productive capacity. The average annual catch of marine fisheries (79 million metric tons for 1987) are at or near estimates of their sustainable yield (between 62 and 96 million metric tons per year).

In the past, pollution and environmental degradation have operated largely on the local level and hence their effects have been isolated in impact. Given the increasingly global scale of environmental degradation and the ever-increasing volume of pollutants entering the environment, however, their effects are now being felt on regional and global levels. In addition, the scope and irreversible nature of some global changes reach through time to affect the well-being of future generations.

Ploman, Global Learning: Concept and Applications

in E. Brown Weiss (ed.) Environmental Change and International.
Law 459, 476–478 (1992).*

Concerns about the environment are not new. Yet only in recent years have ecological crises reached such pervasive, disruptive, and potentially disastrous levels that "suddenly the world itself has become a world issue." Thus, today's environmental problems are closely interlinked, planetary in scale, and, literally, deadly serious.

However, more important than another list of issues is the interlinkage of environmental problems, particularly what they all amount to in the aggregate. The Brundtland Commission has aptly used the image of our earth seen from space as an entry point when it said, "From space we see a small and fragile ball, dominated not by human activity and edifices, but by a pattern of clouds, oceans, greenery, and soil. Humanity's inability to fit its doings into that pattern is fundamentally changing planetary systems. Many such changes are accompanied by life-threatening hazards. This new reality, from which there is no escape, must be recognized—and managed."

* * * Social unrest due to environmental degradation, resource depletion, and social injustice have already occurred in various countries. Analysts also foresee that if present trends continue unchecked, environmental problems might well become major reasons for international conflict, and even war. In the coming decades such problems will range from squabbles over mineral deposits and other natural resources to controversies over unilateral decisions in one country that will affect situations in other countries (transborder pollution, downstream effects of effluents, deforestation, over-fishing, and destruction of habitat).

In fact, analysts have pointed out that comparisons to the environmental changes now under way can only be found by going back millions of years in earth's history; the situation is thus totally outside of any human experience. As a result, learning how to cope with these changes is, and will continue to be, a new and difficult experience.

The reluctant and/or partial recognition of this new reality has already led to some action. Despite often bitter scientific and sociopolitical controversy in this area, the ecological crises have reached such a level that the scientific community has merged and agreed on a number of scientific projects on a global scale.

There have also been some surprisingly rapid intergovernmental agreements on specific problems such as the Vienna Ozone Treaty and its Montreal Protocol, as well as a series of high-level meetings. However, in addition to the difficulties in getting even limited agreements accepted and implemented, voices are already raised in concern that what has been done is not enough and often too late. In general, the agreements are attacking symptoms rather than causes.

Even though the reality of the situation is only partly perceived and accepted even less so, it has led to a new look at the causes, trends, and phenomena that make current measures appear inadequate, insufficient, and sometimes frivolous. It would be easy to find some examples of these newly perceived issues that hint at the kind of changes that are required. However, it is more important to recognize the interlinkage between development, population, and environment. Far from being antagonistic to development, environmental protection is an irreplaceable partner to development. Environment and development are now seen as opposite sides of the same coin.

* * * In summary, what is required is a change in thinking, and changes in the way things are done and organized. While little has so far

been said about the global learning that is required, it is obvious that the learning dimension will be crucial if we are to achieve:

— the necessary integration of population, environment, and development policies;

— growth beyond such immature attitudes as growth for growth's sake or hiding behind "technological fixes";

— economic stability by rethinking our economies;

— a change in attitudes towards nature and the interrelationship between man and nature.

SECTION A.   THE DEVELOPMENT OF INTERNATIONAL ENVIRONMENTAL LAW

1.   FOUNDATION IN EARLY RULES OF PUBLIC INTERNATIONAL LAW

Sharon A. Williams & A.L.C. De Mestral, An Introduction to International Law

267–269 (2d ed., 1987) (footnotes omitted).*

* * *

The term transboundary pollution encompasses environmental pollution from many sources. The connecting factor is that the phrase is used to denote "pollution" that emanates from the territory of one state and causes injury, actual or prospective in another state. It is clear that pollution does not respect international boundaries. Hazardous air pollution may be produced in one state and cause damage within the borders of another state. Environmental pollution may be caused by chemicals such as sulphur dioxide (SO_2) and oxides of nitrogen (NO_x) being put into the air in state X and along with other products being vented upwards, especially by tall stacks, undergoing complex chemical reactions high in the atmosphere and then circulating with the air masses, with the end result that after perhaps travelling hundreds or even thousands of miles, acid precipitation falls in state Y. Smoke and fumes may be blown from one state to another. Hazardous liquid and solid wastes may be discharged onto the land and into inland waters causing damage to health and property in another state. This may be of particular danger where two states share a common drainage basin. Oil pollution and effluent waste disposal may cause damage to the maritime environment offshore. Other methods of possible injury could include: thermal pollution; radiation of the atmosphere; nuclear emissions into the atmosphere; disturbance of the oxygen-carbon dioxide balance and the nitrogen cycle and by the use of pesticides, defoliants and other chemicals harmful to people and to the environment that surrounds them.

    * Published by Butterworths Canada, Ltd., reprinted with their permission.

* * * Due to the novelty of this subject, the law is still very much in the process of development. There are glaring gaps in the law and the fundamental principles underlying the law are not always easy to discern. Any analysis of international environmental law must begin with existing rules of international law. Thus, the fundamental rules of sovereignty, territorial integrity, state responsibility, and maritime jurisdiction, however inappropriate, provide the basic framework within which the law has developed, but it is also true that many of the rules of international law which are slowly emerging contain much that is different in content and purpose from traditional international law.

The process of development of international environmental law has been rapid and complex. As one might expect with a new body of law, the United Nations and other international organizations such as the United Nations Environment Program (U.N.E.P.) and the International Maritime Organization (I.M.O.) have played an important role. Nongovernmental organizations such as the International Law Association and the International Council on Environmental Law have also contributed. International conferences have played a conspicuous part: in particular the United Nations Conference on the Human Environment, held at Stockholm in 1972, marked a watershed in the development of international environmental law. Also of great importance was the Third United Nations Conference on the Law of the Sea culminating in the 1982 Convention on the Law of the Sea. Treaty law has been a most important source of law both for specific areas such as marine pollution and for the development of general principles. Bilateral and regional state practice has also begun to follow a number of significant patterns concerning such issues as transboundary water pollution or marine pollution. Unilateral state action such as the adoption of the *Arctic Waters Pollution Prevention Act* by Canada in 1970 has also been a significant, albeit controversial, source of law.

Trail Smelter Arbitration (United States v. Canada)

Arbitral Tribunal, 1941.
3 U.N.Rep.Int'l Arb. Awards 1905, 1907 (1949).

Convention for Settlement of Difficulties Arising From Operation of Smelter at Trail, B.C.

* * *

Article III

The Tribunal shall finally decide the questions, hereinafter referred to as "the Questions", set forth hereunder, namely:

(1) Whether damage caused by the Trail Smelter in the State of Washington has occurred since the first day of January, 1932, and, if so, what indemnity should be paid therefor?

(2) In the event of the answer to the first part of the preceding Question being in the affirmative, whether the Trail Smelter should be required to refrain from causing damage in the State of Washington in the future, and if so, to what extent?

(3) In the light of the answer to the preceding Question, what measures or régime, if any, should be adopted or maintained by the Trail Smelter?

(4) What indemnity or compensation, if any, should be paid on account of any decision or decisions rendered by the Tribunal pursuant to the next two preceding Questions?

Article IV

The Tribunal shall apply the law and practice followed in dealing with cognate questions in the United States as well as international law and practice, and shall give consideration to the desire of the high contracting parties to reach a solution just to all parties concerned.

* * *

DECISION

Reported on March 11, 1941, to the Government of the United States of America and to the Government of the Dominion of Canada, Under the Convention Signed April 15, 1935.

* * *

On April 16, 1938, the Tribunal reported its "final decision" on Question No. 1, as well as its temporary decisions on Questions No. 2 and No. 3, and provided for a temporary régime thereunder. The decision reported on April 16, 1938, will be referred to hereinafter as the "previous decision".

* * *

In conclusion (end of Part Two of the previous decision), the Tribunal answered Question No. 1 as follows:

> Damage caused by the Trail Smelter in the State of Washington has occurred since the first day of January, 1932, and up to October 1, 1937, and the indemnity to be paid therefor is seventy-eight thousand dollars ($78,000), and is to be complete and final indemnity and compensation for all damage which occurred between such dates. * * *

* * *

In 1896, a smelter was started under American auspices near the locality known as Trail, B.C. In 1906, the Consolidated Mining and Smelting Company of Canada, Limited, obtained a charter of incorporation from the Canadian authorities, and that company acquired the smelter plant at Trail as it then existed. Since that time, the Canadian company, without interruption, has operated the Smelter, and from time to time has greatly added to the plant until it has become one of the best and largest equipped smelting plants on the American continent. In 1925 and 1927, two stacks of the plant were erected to 409 feet in height and the Smelter greatly increased its daily smelting of zinc and lead ores. This increased production resulted in more sulphur dioxide fumes and higher concentrations being emitted into the air. In 1916, about 5,000 tons of sulphur per month were emitted; in 1924, about 4,700 tons; in 1926, about 9,000 tons—an amount which rose near to 10,000 tons per month in 1930. In other words, about

300–350 tons of sulphur were being emitted daily in 1930. (It is to be noted that one ton of sulphur is substantially the equivalent of two tons of sulphur dioxide or SO_2.)

From 1925, at least, to 1937, damage occurred in the State of Washington, resulting from the sulphur dioxide emitted from the Trail Smelter as stated in the previous decision.

* * *

The second question under Article III of the Convention is as follows:

In the event of the answer to the first part of the preceding question being in the affirmative, whether the Trail Smelter should be required to refrain from causing damage in the State of Washington in the future and, if so, to what extent?

Damage has occurred since January 1, 1932, as fully set forth in the previous decision. To that extent, the first part of the preceding question has thus been answered in the affirmative.

* * *

The first problem which arises is whether the question should be answered on the basis of the law followed in the United States or on the basis of international law. The Tribunal, however, finds that this problem need not be solved here as the law followed in the United States in dealing with the quasi-sovereign rights of the States of the Union, in the matter of air pollution, whilst more definite, is in conformity with the general rules of international law.

Particularly in reaching its conclusions as regards this question as well as the next, the Tribunal has given consideration to the desire of the high contracting parties "to reach a solution just to all parties concerned".

As Professor Eagleton puts it (Responsibility of States in International Law, 1928, p. 80): "A State owes at all times a duty to protect other States against injurious acts by individuals from within its jurisdiction." A great number of such general pronouncements by leading authorities concerning the duty of a State to respect other States and their territory have been presented to the Tribunal. These and many others have been carefully examined. International decisions, in various matters, from the Alabama case onward, and also earlier ones, are based on the same general principle, and, indeed, this principle, as such, has not been questioned by Canada. But the real difficulty often arises rather when it comes to determine what, pro subjecta materia, is deemed to constitute an injurious act.

A case concerning, as the present one does, territorial relations, decided by the Federal Court of Switzerland between the Cantons of Soleure and Argovia, may serve to illustrate the relativity of the rule. Soleure brought a suit against her sister State to enjoin use of a shooting establishment which endangered her territory. The court, in granting the injunction, said: "This right (sovereignty) excludes * * * not only the usurpation and exercise of sovereign rights (of another State) * * * but also an actual encroachment which might prejudice the natural use of the territory and the free movement of its inhabitants." As a result of the decision, Argovia made plans for the improvement of the existing installations. These, however, were considered as insufficient protection by Soleure. The Canton of Argovia then moved the Federal Court to decree that the shooting be again permitted after completion of the projected improvements. This motion was granted. "The demand of the Government of Soleure", said the court, "that all endangerment be absolutely abolished apparently goes too far." The court found that all risk whatever had not been eliminated, as the region was flat and absolutely safe shooting ranges were only found in mountain valleys; that there was a federal duty for the communes to provide facilities for military target practice and that "no more precautions may be demanded for shooting ranges near the boundaries of two Cantons than are required for shooting ranges in the interior of a Canton".

No case of air pollution dealt with by an international tribunal has been brought to the attention of the Tribunal nor does the Tribunal know of any such case. The nearest analogy is that of water pollution. But, here also, no decision of an international tribunal has been cited or has been found.

There are, however, as regards both air pollution and water pollution, certain decisions of the Supreme Court of the United States which may legitimately be taken as a guide in this field of international law, for it is reasonable to follow by analogy, in international cases, precedents established by that court in dealing with controversies between States of the Union or with other controversies concerning the quasi-sovereign rights of such States, where no contrary rule prevails in international law and no reason for rejecting such precedents can be adduced from the limitations of sovereignty inherent in the Constitution of the United States.

In the suit of Missouri v. Illinois (200 U.S. 496, 521) concerning the pollution, within the boundaries of Illinois, of the Illinois River, an affluent of the Mississippi flowing into the latter where it forms the boundary between that State and Missouri, an injunction was refused. "Before this court ought to intervene", said the court, "the case should be of serious magnitude, clearly and fully proved, and the principle to be applied should be one which the court is prepared deliberately to maintain against all considerations on the other side. (See Kansas v. Colorado, 185 U.S. 125.)" The court found that the practice complained of was general along the shores of the Mississippi River at that time, that it was followed by Missouri itself and that thus a standard was set up by the defendant which the claimant was entitled to invoke.

* * *

In the more recent suit of New York against New Jersey (256 U.S. 296, 309), concerning the pollution of New York Bay, the injunction was also refused for lack of proof * * *. What is true between States of the Union is, at least, equally true concerning the relations between the United States and the Dominion of Canada.

In another recent case concerning water pollution (283 U.S. 473), the complainant was successful. The City of New York was enjoined, at the request of the State of New Jersey, to desist, within a reasonable time limit, from the practice of disposing of sewage by dumping it into the sea, a practice which was injurious to the coastal waters of New Jersey in the vicinity of her bathing resorts.

In the matter of air pollution itself, the leading decisions are those of the Supreme Court of Georgia v. Tennessee Copper Company and Ducktown Sulphur, Copper and Iron Company, Ltd. Although dealing with a suit against private companies, the decisions were on questions cognate to those here at issue. Georgia stated that it had in vain sought relief from Tennessee, on whose territory the smelters were located, and the court defined the nature of the suit by saying: "This is a suit by a State for an injury to it in its capacity of quasi-sovereign. In that capacity, the State has an interest independent of and behind the titles of its citizens, in all the earth and air within its domain."

On the question whether an injunction should be granted, the court said (206 U.S. 230):

> It (the State) has the last word as to whether its mountains shall be stripped of their forests and its inhabitants shall breathe pure air. * * * It is not lightly to be presumed to give up quasi-sovereign rights for pay and * * * if that be its choice, it may insist that an infraction of them shall be stopped. This court has not quite the same freedom to balance the harm that will be done by an injunction against that of which the plaintiff complains, that it would have in deciding between two subjects of a single political power. Without excluding the considerations that equity always takes into account * * * it is a fair and reasonable demand on the part of a sovereign that the air over its territory should not be polluted on a great scale by sulphurous acid gas, that the forests on its mountains, be they better or worse, and whatever domestic destruction they may have suffered, should not be further destroyed or threatened by the act of persons beyond its control, that the crops and orchards on its hills should not be endangered from the same source. * * * Whether Georgia, by insisting upon this claim, is doing more harm than good to her own citizens, is for her to determine. The possible disaster to those outside the State must be accepted as a consequence of her standing upon her extreme rights.

Later on, however, when the court actually framed an injunction, in the case of the Ducktown Company (237 U.S. 474, 477) (an agreement on the basis of an annual compensation was reached with the most important of the two smelters, the Tennessee Copper Company), they did not go beyond a decree "adequate to diminish materially the present probability of damage to its (Georgia's) citizens".

* * *

The Tribunal, therefore, finds that the above decisions, taken as a whole, constitute an adequate basis for its conclusions, namely, that, under the principles of international law, as well as of the law of the United States, no State has the right to use or permit the use of its territory in such a manner as to cause injury by fumes in or to the territory of another or the properties or persons therein, when the case is of serious consequence and the injury is established by clear and convincing evidence.

The decisions of the Supreme Court of the United States which are the basis of these conclusions are decisions in equity and a solution inspired by them, together with the regime hereinafter prescribed, will, in the opinion of the Tribunal, be "just to all parties concerned", as long, at least, as the present conditions in the Columbia River Valley continue to prevail.

Considering the circumstances of the case, the Tribunal holds that the Dominion of Canada is responsible in international law for the conduct of the Trail Smelter. Apart from the undertakings in the Convention, it is, therefore, the duty of the Government of Canada to see to it that this conduct should be in conformity with the obligation of the Dominion under international law as herein determined.

The Tribunal, therefore, answers Question No. 2: (2) So long as the present conditions in the Columbia River Valley prevail, the Trail Smelter shall be required to refrain from causing any damage through fumes in the State of Washington; the damage herein referred to and its extent being such as would be recoverable under the decisions of the courts of the United States in suits between private individuals. The indemnity for such damage should be fixed in such manner as the Governments, acting under Article XI of the Convention should agree upon.

The third question under Article III of the Convention is as follows: "In the light of the answer to the preceding question, what measures or régime, if any, should be adopted and maintained by the Trail Smelter?"

Answering this question in the light of the preceding one, since the Tribunal has, in its previous decision, found that damage caused by the Trail Smelter has occurred in the State of Washington since January 1, 1932, and since the Tribunal is of opinion that damage may occur in the future unless the operations of the Smelter shall be subject to some control, in order to avoid damage occurring, the Tribunal now decides that a régime or measure of control shall be applied to the operations of the Smelter and shall remain in full force unless and until modified in accordance with the provisions hereinafter set forth. * * *

* * *

---

1. ***Jurisdiction to legislate with respect to air pollution.*** Does either the State of Washington or the United States have jurisdiction to prescribe laws regulating the pollution of Washington or United States airspace by Canadian polluters?

2. ***Applicable law.*** Heretofore in Chapter 5, the law governing events occurring in airspace has been domestic law and the inquiry has been whether or not a state has jurisdiction to prescribe the relevant rule. In what respect does the *Trail Smelter* case present a different problem? What is the source of the governing rule?

Why is Canada held responsible in this case? By what standard is its conduct measured? Does international law impose an obligation on Canada only after a showing of historical injury, or would a showing of potential injury be sufficient? For a discussion of the implications of the *Trail*

Smelter case for situations in which modern technological developments threaten the environment (e.g., weather modification), *see* Kirgis, *Technological Challenge to the Shared Environment: United States Practice,* 66 Am.J.Int'l L. 290 (1972).

Corfu Channel Case (Merits) (United Kingdom v. Albania)

International Court of Justice 1949.
[1949] I.C.J. Rep. 4.

[During transit of the Corfu Channel within the territorial sea of Albania two British warships were damaged heavily by mines. Following this two other British warships mine-swept the Corfu Channel. From the international environmental law perspective the Court's pronouncement on the question of Albanian responsibility and liability to compensate for damage and loss of life caused by the explosions occurring in its waters is of relevance.]

THE COURT:

* * * It is clear that knowledge of the minelaying cannot be imputed to the Albanian Government by reason merely of the fact that a minefield discovered in Albanian territorial waters caused the explosions of which the British ships were the victims. It is true, as international practice shows, that a State on whose territory or in whose waters an act contrary to international law has occurred, may be called upon to give an explanation. It is also true that that State cannot evade such a request by limiting itself to a reply that it is ignorant of the circumstances of the act and of its authors * * *. [I]t cannot be concluded from the mere fact of the control exercised by a State over its territory and waters that that State necessarily knew, or ought to have known, of any unlawful act perpetrated therein, nor yet that it necessarily knew, or should have known, the authors. This fact, by itself and apart from other circumstances, neither involves *prima facie* responsibility nor shifts the burden of proof.

On the other hand, the fact of this exclusive territorial control exercised by a State within its frontiers has a bearing upon the methods of proof available to establish the knowledge of that State as to such events. By reason of this exclusive control, the other State, the victim of a breach of international law, is often unable to furnish direct proof of facts giving rise to responsibility. Such a state should be allowed a more liberal recourse to inferences of fact and circumstantial evidence. This indirect evidence is admitted in all systems of law, and its use is recognized by international decisions. It must be regarded as of special weight when it is based on a series of facts linked together and leading logically to a single conclusion.

The court must examine therefore whether it has been established by means of indirect evidence that Albania has knowledge of minelaying in her territorial waters independently of any connivance on her part in this operation. The proof may be drawn from inferences of fact, provided that they leave no room for reasonable doubt * * *.

From all the facts and observations * * * the Court draws the conclusion that the laying of the minefield which caused the explosions * * * could not have been accomplished without the knowledge of the Albanian Government. * * *

[It is] every State's obligation not to allow knowingly its territory to be used for acts contrary to the rights of other States. * * *

Lake Lanoux Arbitration (France v. Spain)

12 U.N. Rep. Int'l Arb. Awards 281 (1957).

[Spain objected to a French proposal to use Lake Lanoux for hydroelectric purposes, in that it would interfere with the flow of boundary waters contrary to an 1866 bilateral treaty. The arbitral tribunal first found for France, that its development scheme would not breach the bilateral treaty. In doing so it made an important finding concerning liability for environmental harm. The Tribunal then considered what conduct was expected of France in its relations with Spain over the project and Spain's contention that prior agreement of both States was needed.]

THE TRIBUNAL: * * *

One might have attacked this conclusion [that the French plans were not in breach of the treaty] in several different ways.

It could have been argued that the works would bring about an ultimate pollution of the waters of the Carol or that the returned waters would have a chemical composition or temperature or some other characteristic which could injure Spanish interests. Spain could then have claimed that her rights had been impaired in violation of the Additional Act. Neither in the *dossier* nor in the pleadings in this case is there any trace of such an allegation.

[As to the Spanish contention that its agreement with the French scheme was necessary, the Tribunal said:]

* * * To admit that jurisdiction in a certain field can no longer be exercised except on the condition of, or by way of, an agreement between two States, is to place an essential restriction on the sovereignty of a State, and such restriction could only be admitted if there were clear and convincing evidence. Without doubt, international practice does reveal some special cases in which this hypothesis has become reality; thus, sometimes two States exercise conjointly jurisdiction over certain territories (joint ownership, *co-imperium*, or *condominium*); likewise, in certain international arrangements, the representatives of States exercise conjointly a certain jurisdiction in the name of those States or in the name of organizations. But these cases are exceptional, and international judicial decisions are slow to recognize their existence, especially when they impair the territorial sovereignty of a State, as would be the case in the present matter.

In effect, in order to appreciate in its essence the necessity for prior agreement, one must envisage the hypothesis in which the interested States cannot reach agreement. In such case, it must be admitted that the

State which is normally competent has lost its right to act alone as a result of the unconditional and arbitrary opposition of another State. This amounts to admitting a "right of assent", a "right of veto", which at the discretion of one State paralyses the exercise of the territorial jurisdiction of another.

That is why international practice prefers to resort to less extreme solutions by confining itself to obliging the States to seek, by preliminary negotiations, terms for an agreement, without subordinating the exercise of their competences to the conclusion of such an agreement. Thus, one speaks, although often inaccurately, of the "obligation of negotiating an agreement". In reality, the engagements thus undertaken by States take very diverse forms and have a scope which varies according to the manner in which they are defined and according to the procedures intended for their execution; but the reality of the obligations thus undertaken is incontestable and sanctions can be applied in the event, for example, of an unjustified breaking off of the discussions, abnormal delays, disregard of the agreed procedures, systematic refusals to take into consideration adverse proposals of interests, and, more generally, in cases of violation of the rules of good faith.

* * * States are today perfectly conscious of the importance of the conflicting interests brought into play by the industrial use of international rivers, and of the necessity to reconcile them by mutual concessions. The only way to arrive at such compromises of interests is to conclude agreements on an increasingly comprehensive basis. International practice reflects the conviction that States ought to strive to conclude such agreements: there would thus appear to be an obligation to accept in good faith all communications and contracts which could, by a broad comparison of interests and by reciprocal good will, provide States with the best conditions for concluding agreements. This point will be referred to again later on, when enquiring what obligations rest on France and Spain in connection with the contracts and the communications preceding the putting in hand of a scheme such as that relating to Lake Lanoux.

But international practice does not so far permit more than the following conclusion: the rule that States may utilize the hydraulic power of international watercourses only on condition of a *prior* agreement between the interested States cannot be established as a custom, even less as a general principle of law. * * *

The * * * question is to determine the method by which these interests can be safeguarded. If that method necessarily involves communications, it cannot be confined to purely formal requirements, such as taking note of complaints, protests or representations made by the downstream State. The Tribunal is of the opinion that, according to the rules of good faith, the upstream State is under the obligation to take into consideration the various interests involved, to seek to give them every satisfaction compatible with the pursuit of its own interests, and to show that in this regard it is genuinely concerned to reconcile the interests of the other riparian State with its own. * * *

As a matter of form, the upstream State has, procedurally, a right of initiative; it is not obliged to associate the downstream State in the elaboration of its schemes. If, in the course of discussions, the downstream State submits schemes to it, the upstream State must examine them, but it has the right to give preference to the solution contained in its own scheme provided that it takes into consideration in a reasonable manner the interests of the downstream State.

* * * In the case of Lake Lanoux, France has maintained to the end the solution which consists in diverting the waters of the Carol to the Ariege with full restitution. By making this choice France is only making use of a right; the development works of Lake Lanoux are on French territory, the financing of and the responsibility for the enterprise fall upon France, and France alone is the judge of works of public utility which are to be executed on her own territory, save for the provisions of Articles 9 and 10 of the Additional Act, which, however, the French scheme does not infringe.

On her side, Spain cannot invoke a right to insist on a development of Lake Lanoux based on the needs of Spanish agriculture. In effect, if France were to renounce all of the works envisaged on her territory, Spain could not demand that other works in conformity with her wishes should be carried out. Therefore, she can only urge her interests in order to obtain, within the framework of the scheme decided upon by France, terms which reasonably safeguard them.

It remains to be established whether this requirement has been fulfilled * * *.

When one examines the question of whether France, either in the course of the dealings or in her proposals, has taken Spanish interests into sufficient consideration, it must be stressed how closely linked together are the obligation to take into consideration, in the course of negotiations, adverse interests and the obligation to give a reasonable place to these interests in the solution finally adopted. A State which has conducted negotiations with understanding and good faith * * * is not relieved from giving a reasonable place to adverse interests in the solution it adopts simply because the conversations have been interrupted, even though owing to the intransigence of its partner. Conversely, in determining the manner in which a scheme has taken into consideration the interests involved, the way in which negotiations have developed, the total number of the interests which have been presented, the price which each Party was ready to pay to have those interests safeguarded, are all essential factors in establishing * * * the merits of that scheme.

[In conclusion, the Tribunal was of the view that France had sufficiently involved Spain in the preparations of the project.]

Declaration of the United Nations Conference on the Human Environment

U.N. Document A/CONF. 48/14 and Corr. 1.
11.International Legal Materials 1416 (1972), in the Doc. Supp.

Colloquy

Proceedings, 77th Annual Meeting, American Society of International Law

433–34 (1983).*

CHRISTIAN HERTER: * * * In terms of the Trail Smelter case and the precedent it set for the development of Principle 21, has there been any comparable case since the Trail Smelter? If not, why not?

* * *

Professor HANDL: In response to why there has not been a second Trail Smelter case, the answer perhaps is related to why there has been a decline in the amount of international adjudication. Today, there seems to be a reluctance on the part of most states to submit to international adjudication coupled with a tendency of states to negotiate and arbitrate informally. I also think that we are seeing a movement toward the adoption of soft norms, reflecting a sense of soft responsibility on the part of states for international matters. On the other hand, it can be argued that Principle 21 is widely accepted by states as customary international law and that it is no longer contested. However, Principle 21 has a different impact today, a different application from what it originally had in the Trail Smelter context.

State Responsibility and the Standard of Fault

Sharon A. Williams, Public International Law Governing Transboundary Pollution,

International Business Lawyer, 243, 244–245 (1984).*

Of particular relevance and difficulty is the question of liability and on what basis is it to be determined. Is it to be based on subjective fault criteria, objective fault criteria or strict or absolute liability? According to many writers it is the objective fault or responsibility principle that has been followed by states in their practice, by arbitral tribunals and by the International Court of Justice. It follows that if in the area of transboundary pollution fault should play a part, it should only be in the objective sense.

It has been suggested that the use of strict liability may be still *de lege ferenda*. However, there is some support for it at the present time. It can be argued that in the Corfu Channel case and in the Trail Smelter Arbitration fault of no kind was established. Likewise, in the Gut–Dam Arbitration [between Canada and the U.S.] the tribunal was not interested in fault or knowledge of prospective injuries by Canada. Canada was held liable. This decision, however, is of less value when it is added that Canada had accepted the obligation of compensation payment in advance. In the Lac Lanoux arbitration between France and Spain, fault on the part of France was not a requirement. The matter is not addressed in the Stockholm Declaration of June 16th, 1972. It has been argued that this might negate any requirement for the establishment of fault. Further, some O.E.C.D. states have argued that a system of strict liability should be introduced in

---

* Reprinted with the permission of the American Society of International Law.

* Reprinted with the permission of the International Bar Association.

all cases of transboundary pollution, regardless of any safeguard measures that have been taken.

On this basis, it can be argued that strict liability may become, in the not too distant future, the accepted norm re liability in customary international law. This argument is justified if the aforementioned arbitral decisions, declarations and statements by governments can be seen to indicate the required state practice and *opinio juris* necessary to form a rule of customary international law.

It is impossible to designate any similar status to the absolute liability theory. There is no indication through any of the forms of state practice or judicial or arbitral decisions that would allow the supposition that this theory is presently or is imminently on the verge of crystallizing into a role of customary international law. Unless states agreed to such a rule of liability in an international agreement, the notion of absolute liability does not appear to merit practical consideration.

In international law the effect of a finding of state responsibility is that the state found responsible to another must make reparation. The usual type of reparation for a wrongful act or omission is an indemnity that corresponds to the damage suffered. In the context of damage caused by transboundary pollution restitution in the majority of cases would not be a possibility. It is impossible to re-establish the situation as it existed prior to the delinquent act and hence to wipe out the consequences of the illegality. Therefore compensation in monetary terms and formal apologies, statements of consideration or intent for the future might be in order. It has been suggested by one author that international tribunals may impose injunctions to restrain pollution activities in the future. Also the International Court of Justice may grant interim measures to prevent further damage ensuing during the conduct of an action before it.

F. Orrego Vicuña, State Responsibility, Liability and Remedial Measures Under International Law: New Criteria for Environmental Protection

in E. Brown Weiss (ed.), Environmental Change and International Law 124, 134–135, 138–140 (1992).*

* * * [T]he fact that international law has been exploring more stringent forms of responsibility is, in and of itself, indicative of the sense of change that is taking place. The most significant of these changes is the introduction of the concept of absolute and strict liability. Delinking the adverse effects of a given hazardous or dangerous activity from the element of *culpa* of the state or operator incorporates the test of "objective" responsibility as opposed to the "subjective" criteria of traditional international law. Still more stringent criteria have been emerging lately, particularly as concerns the idea of holding a state responsible for damage ensuing from given activities irrespective of whether it took all necessary measures to prevent injury. The result is that responsibility will attach in spite of due

diligence having been observed. Liability for acts not prohibited by international law is another major development * * *.

* * * [T]he International Law Commission has made the point that material damage would not be an essential element in the case of responsibility for wrongful acts. The attribution of the conduct to the state and the breach of an international obligation would suffice to invoke responsibility. Under traditional international law, however, the violation of the obligation would be sufficient to engage responsibility, which means that the old rules are very helpful indeed to broaden the scope of the law at present. On the other hand, when the international liability is for acts not prohibited by international law, material damage would be the essential basis of compensation, resulting in the paradox that, on this point, the new rules are more restrictive than the old.

Although the seriousness of the damage is another issue where the practice is not entirely uniform, certain gravity is, without a doubt, required. This requirement, however, is qualified by two considerations that relate to the evolving state of international law. First, given the emphasis on preventive measures characterizing present environmental law, the adoption of all necessary preventive and remedial measures even where no injury has occurred is beginning to emerge as a new type of obligation. Second, as mentioned in the *Restatement of the Law (Third)*, when pollution is caused by substances that are highly dangerous to human life and health, there is no need to prove a significant impact or injury, thereby altering rather dramatically the traditional standards of international law. Examples of this trend are blacklisting of hazardous products and abnormally dangerous activities like the launching of space objects.

* * * International liability for acts not prohibited by international law involves a rather stringent form of responsibility-liability, which in turn has a strong impact on the nature and extent of remedial measures in the field. It follows that the debate about the present state of international law on this point has been most lively.

First, it should be noted that the much discussed decision of the International Law Commission in 1976, referred to above (which lists among international crimes those relating to the breach of an international obligation of essential importance for the safeguarding and preservation of the human environment), has to be understood more as an expression of concern in line with the Stockholm Conference than as a radical departure in terms of the consequences attached to the breach of such an obligation.

The work of the International Law Commission on "International Liability" reveals a cautious approach to the state of international law on the matter. On the one hand the separation of liability for acts not prohibited by international law from State Responsibility is indicative of the policy of attaching a legal consequence-liability-even to international lawful activities, yet on the other hand State Responsibility could well apply to extra-hazardous operations, thus also attaching a legal consequence to activities that are not, *per se,* unlawful. In this regard the remedial aspect of the law would not be different under either approach. What is of importance is that international law is accepting legal consequences for a variety of activities that may result in an adverse impact upon the environment.

The "compound 'primary' obligation" identified by the International Law Commission in its schematic outline on "international liability" refers to four basic duties: prevent, inform, negotiate, and repair. The emphasis is on preventive measures as well as the new obligation to notify and consult. However, it is surprising that the failure to comply with the first three duties mentioned is not regarded as wrongful and, consequently, no action can be brought against such failure; only the failure to make reparations is ultimately identified with a wrongful act and, hence, engages the State's responsibility.

It follows that from the perspective of the International Law Commission, there is really not much difference between international liability and state responsibility, since the ultimate test of wrongfulness in both lies in the failure to make a reparation. While it is true that under international liability the initial activity can be lawful and under state responsibility normally it will be unlawful (although neither excludes both lawful and unlawful activities), the two are equated in terms of the end result.

It has been rightly observed that one consequence of the International Law Commission approach could "allow a state to persist in an unlawful act even without the consent of the injured state, as long as the acting state pays monetary reparations to the injured state." In the field of environmental protection this result would be utterly unacceptable and self-defeating, which is why there has been an emphasis on both preventive measures and new developments that require that pollution be terminated and allow all states to bring actions to this effect.

Although there has also been debate about whether the *Trail Smelter* decision involved, in addition to its pioneering invocation of international liability, an element of international responsibility given that a wrongful act had been committed, it is quite clear that the effect of the decision never would have allowed the harmful activity to persist. As noted above it ordered the smelter to "refrain" from such activity and put in place a regime for the control of emissions. This result is in line with the emerging consensus that international law ought to provide adequate protection of the environment.

Another element of the debate prompted by the International Law Commission's work is the method of determining reparation. The schematic outline favours the method of reparation determined by a "balance-of-interests" test, which takes into account the shared expectations of the states involved, a number of principles and factors, and the extent to which the duties to prevent, inform, and negotiate have been complied with. This approach offers the advantage of introducing an element of flexibility that allows the weighing of the different circumstances of the case, but, on the other hand, it involves greater subjectivity. The alternative test of strict liability is in a sense more objective, because the harmful result will be separated from the intention of the state and even from the fact of having discharged the relevant duties. Again this last approach is more in line with the needs of environmental protection.

Cosmos 954 Claim (Canada v. U.S.S.R.)

18 International Legal Materials 899 (1979)*

[The satellite Cosmos 954 was placed in orbit in space by the former U.S.S.R. on September 18, 1977. The Secretary–General of the United Nations was officially informed. The satellite had on board a nuclear reactor that worked on uranium enriched with isotope of uranium 235. On January 24, 1978 Cosmos 954 re-entered the earth's atmosphere and intruded into Canada's air space. Debris from the satellite was found on Canadian territory, specifically in the Northwest Territories, Alberta and Saskatchewan. The Canadian Armed Forces and the Canadian Atomic Energy Control Board immediately began to locate, recover, remove and test the debris and to clean up the sites where it had landed. The total cost of these operations which were conducted in two phases in 1978 was approximately 14 million dollars. Canada claimed 6 million dollars from the U.S.S.R. The following extract is taken from Canada's Statement of Claim.] "On behalf of CANADA:" * * *

(a) International Agreements

15. Under Article II of the Convention on International Liability for Damage Caused by Space Objects, hereinafter referred to as the Convention, "A launching State shall be absolutely liable to pay compensation for damage caused by its space object on the surface of the earth * * *." The Union of Soviet Socialist Republics, as the launching State of the Cosmos 954 satellite, has an absolute liability to pay compensation to Canada for the damage caused by this satellite. The deposit of hazardous radioactive debris from the satellite throughout a large area of Canadian territory, and the presence of that debris in the environment rendering part of Canada's territory unfit for use, constituted "damage to property" within the meaning of the Convention.

16. The intrusion into Canadian air space of a satellite carrying on board a nuclear reactor and the break-up of the satellite over Canadian territory created a clear and immediate apprehension of damage, including nuclear damage, to persons and property in Canada. The Government of the Union of Soviet Socialist Republics failed to give the Government of Canada prior notification of the imminent re-entry of the nuclear powered satellite and failed to provide timely and complete answers to the Canadian questions of January 24, 1978 concerning the satellite. It thus failed to minimize the deleterious results of the intrusion of the satellite into Canadian air space.

17. Under general principles of international law, Canada had a duty to take the necessary measures to prevent and reduce the harmful consequences of the damage and thereby to mitigate damages. Thus, with respect to the debris, it was necessary for Canada to undertake without delay operations of search, recovery, removal, testing and clean-up. * * * Article VI of the Convention imposes on the claimant State a duty to observe reasonable standards of care with respect to damage caused by a space object.

* Reprinted with the permission of the American Society of International Law.

18. * * * Costs included by Canada * * * were incurred solely as a consequence of the intrusion into Canadian air space and the deposit on Canadian territory of hazardous radioactive debris from the satellite.

19. In respect of compensation for damage caused by space objects, the Convention provides for " * * * such reparation in respect of the damage as will restore * * * [the claimant State] to the condition which would have existed if the damage had not occurred" (Article XII). In accordance with its Preamble, the Convention seeks to ensure " * * * the prompt payment * * * of a full and equitable measure of compensation to victims of such damage" * * *. Canada's claim includes only those costs which were incurred in order to restore Canada to the condition which would have existed if the damage inflicted by the Cosmos 954 satellite had not occurred. The Convention also provides that "The compensation which the launching State shall be liable to pay for damage under this Convention shall be determined in accordance with international law and the principles of justice and equity * * * "(Article XII). In calculating the compensation claimed, Canada has applied the relevant criteria established by general principles of international law and has limited the costs included in its claim to those costs that are reasonable, proximately caused by the intrusion of the satellite and deposit of debris and capable of being calculated with a reasonable degree of certainty.

20. The liability of the [U.S.S.R.] * * * for damage caused by the satellite is also founded in Article VII of the Treaty on Principles Governing the Activities of States in the Exploration and Use of Outer Space, including the Moon and Other Celestial Bodies, done in 1967, and to which both Canada and the [U.S.S.R.] * * * are parties. This liability places an obligation on the [U.S.S.R.] * * * to compensate Canada in accordance with international law for the consequences of the intrusion of the satellite into Canadian air space and the deposit on Canadian territory of hazardous radioactive debris from the satellite.

(b) General Principles of International Law

21. The intrusion of the Cosmos 954 satellite into Canada's air space and the deposit on Canadian Territory of hazardous radioactive debris from the satellite constitutes a violation of Canada's sovereignty. * * * International precedents recognize that a violation of sovereignty gives rise to an obligation to pay compensation.

22. The standard of absolute liability for space activities, in particular activities involving the use of nuclear energy, is considered to have become a general principle of international law. * * * The principle of absolute liability applies to fields of activities having in common a high degree of risk. It is repeated in numerous international agreements and is one of "the general principles of law recognized by civilized nations" (Article 38 of the Statute of the International Court of Justice). Accordingly, this principle has been accepted as a "general principle of international law."

Notes and Questions

1. ***Cosmos 954 Settlement.*** In February, June and November 1980 negotiations took place between Canada and the former U.S.S.R. The result was a three million dollar settlement in the form of a Protocol signed by the Canadian Ambassador and the Soviet Deputy Minister of Foreign Affairs. It did not acknowledge liability formally.

2. ***Territorial sovereignty versus common interest.*** The crux of the international environmental debate is whether a state being sovereign, may carry out, or permit to be carried out, hazardous activities in its territory that are injurious to the environment. Can other states complain, even if they have not suffered actual injury? Is the obligation to protect the environment owed *erga omnes,* because of the common interest of humanity in its well-being? Note the recognition of this by the International Court of Justice in the *Barcelona Traction* case [1970] I.C.J.Rep. 3, when the Court stated that:

> [A]n essential distinction should be drawn between the obligations of a State towards the international community as a whole, and those arising vis-à-vis another State in the field of diplomatic protection. By their very nature the former are the concern of all states. In view of the importance of the rights involved, all states can be held to have a legal interest in their protection; they are obligations *erga omnes.*

The 1992 Report of the International Law Commission on the Work of its Forty–Fourth Session on the topic of state responsibility had this to say on the question of differently injured states, U.N. GAOR 47th Sess. Supp. No. 10 (A/47/10) 93–95:

> The violation of obligations arising, for example, under rules concerning disarmament, promotion of and respect for human rights and environmental protection, termed *"erga omnes* obligations", simultaneously injured the subjective rights of all the States bound by the norm, whether or not they were specifically affected * * *. The Special Rapporteur * * * arrived at the conclusion that the distinction between "directly" and "indirectly" injured States did not hold water and that the differing situations were distinguished by the nature or the extent of the injury. * * * It must therefore be determined to what extent each of those States was, on the one hand, entitled to claim cessation, restitution in kind, pecuniary compensation, satisfaction and/or guarantees of non-repetition, and, on the other hand, entitled to resort to sanctions or countermeasures.

These questions go to the heart of the problem, in that under the traditional customary international law rules of state responsibility discussed in Chapter 10(A), a state is only responsible for damage caused resulting from an illegal activity. Also, the jurisprudence on state responsibility has concerned for the most part injuries to aliens occurring within the territory of the respondent state. (See G. Handl, Territorial Sovereignty and the Problem of Transnational Pollution, 69 Am.J.Int'l L. 50 (1975).) Can these traditional rules be extended to and cope with transnational ecosystem damage and the threat thereof?

3. The principle of imputability is important in determining state responsibility. Would a state be able to plead a domestic law or lack of same in defence of any environmental claims made against it by other states? See the *Free Zones case*, P.C.I.J.Ser. A/B, No. 46, 167 (1932). When cross-border pollution or other environmental harm occurs does state responsibility arise when no action is taken either to prosecute the alleged perpetrators or to give access to remedies to the victims?

4. ***The standard of fault.*** There has been a great deal of discussion as to the appropriate standard to be applied in transnational environmental cases. Is it to be based on fault, or strict or absolute liability irrespective of fault? In the absence of a specific treaty obligation such as illustrated above in the Cosmos 954 claim under, *inter alia,* the 1972 Convention on International Liability for Damage Caused by Space Objects, 24 U.S.T. 2389, T.I.A.S. No. 7762, it is doubtful that customary international law has gone this far. The cases reproduced above would seem to indicate this.

5. ***Sic utere tuo, ut non alienum laedas.*** Apart from and in addition to the rules of customary international law that may be applied to environmental protection are certain general principles of law such as that expressed in this latin maxim, meaning "use your property so as not to injure that of another". This fundamental principle may be seen as equivalent to the general principle of "good neighbourliness" which is specifically recognized in Article 74 of the U.N. Charter and may be said to fall under Article 38(1)(c) of the Statute of the International Court of Justice. It may be said to have been the underlying principle in the *Trailer Smelter* case considered earlier in this section. It is also reflected in Article X of the International Law Association's Helsinki Rules on the Uses of Waters of International Rivers, referred to infra. (See S.A. Williams, Public International Law Governing Transboundary Pollution, International Business Lawyer 243, 249 (June 1984)).

6. ***Causal link.*** It is a general principle accepted by states that there must be a causal link between the conduct and the injury. On account of the nature of environmental pollution this can be problematic in that a great distance may separate the source of the pollution from the locus of the injury. A second factor is the time between the emission of the pollutants and the injury and thus the possibility of intervening causes that may be argued to have broken the chain of causation. A third factor is that emissions emanating from several states may cumulatively cause the environmental damage.

7. ***Stockholm Declaration.*** This Declaration was adopted at the 1972 U.N. Conference on the Human Environment by acclamation. There were 113 states present. Although not a treaty but a declaration, it represents a basic charter of environmental protection and its principles are reflected in, *inter alia,* Article 30 of the Charter of Economic Rights and Duties of States, U.N.G.A.Res. 3281 (XXI) December 12, 1974, 29 U.N. GAOR Supp. (No. 31) 50, U.N.Doc. A/9631 (1974), Articles 192–194 of the 1982 Law of the Sea Convention, U.N.Doc. A/CONF. 62/122 (1982), the OECD Principles Concerning Transfrontier Pollution, Council Rec. C(74) 224, 14 Int'l Leg.Mat. 242 (1975), the 1979 ECE Convention on Long Range Transboundary Pollution, Preamble, T.I.A.S. 10541, the 1985 Vienna Convention for

the Protection of the Ozone Layer, Preamble, 26 Int'l Leg.Mat. 1516
(1987), the 1991 Canada–United States Air Quality Agreement, Preamble,
30 Int'l Leg.Mat. 678 (1991), the 1992 United Nations Framework Convention on Climate Change, Preamble, 31 Int'l Leg.Mat. 851 (1992), the 1992
United Nations Convention on Biodiversity, Article 3, 31 Int'l Leg.Mat. 822
(1992), the Statement of Principles for a Global Consensus on the Management, Conservation and Sustainable Development of all Types of Forests,
31 Int'l Leg.Mat. 818 (1992), and the 1992 Rio Declaration on Environment
and Development, 31 Int'l Leg.Mat. 874 (1992). In the *Nuclear Tests Cases*,
[1974] I.C.J.Rep. 253, 457, it was argued by Australia and New Zealand
that it reflected the attitude of the international community.

The 1972 Declaration was accompanied by 109 recommendations. The
U.N. General Assembly endorsed these recommendations and in December
1972 created the United Nations Environmental Programme (UNEP),
headquartered in Nairobi, Kenya, to carry them out. See UNGA Res.
2997/27, UN GAOR, 27th Sess. Supp. (No 30) 43, UN Doc. No. A/8730
(1972) and Petsonk, The Role of the United Nations Environmental Programme (UNEP) in the Development of International Environmental Law,
5 Am.U.J.Int.L. & Pol. 351 (1990). In 1991 the U.N. Convention on
Environmental Impact Assessment in a Transboundary Context was
signed, 30 Int'l Leg.Mat. 809 (1991). This Convention provides, *inter alia*,
for an assessment procedure that must be undertaken for any activity that
is proposed that falls within Appendix I that is likely to cause significant
adverse transboundary impact. There are provisions for notification and
consultation of affected states parties and the public in those states. See
also the 1998 U.N. ECE Convention on Access to Information, Public
Participation in Decision–Making and Access to Justice in Environmental
Matters, 38 ILM 517 (1999).

8. ***The 1987 Restatement.*** See Section 601, which obligates states to
take "such measures as may be necessary, to the extent practicable under
the circumstances" with respect to the environment of other states and
imposes responsibility for significant injury resulting from violation of this
obligation. Comment *d* to this section makes an additional observation:
"However, even if it has taken the necessary and practicable measures, a
state is responsible where injury results from a discharge of highly dangerous substances (radioactive, toxic, etc.), or from abnormally dangerous
activities (e.g. launching of space satellites)."

9. ***Necessity.*** Draft Article 33 of the International Law Commission's
Draft Articles on State Responsibility, was introduced by the Special
Rapporteur in 1999. See, The Report of the International Law Commission
on the Work of its 51st Session, 3 May–23 July, 1999, UN GAOR Off. Rec.
44th Sess. Supp. No. 10 (A/54/10). Draft Article 33 deals with the invocation
of necessity by a state as a ground for precluding the wrongfulness of an
act not in conformity with international law. Such a ground may only be
successful if the act is the only means open to a state for "safeguarding an
essential interest of that state against a grave and imminent peril". The
Special Rapporteur noted that necessity of action may be so compelling that
it justifies a course of conduct, for example in relation to the urgent
conservation of a species as in the *Russian Fur Seals case, ibid.*, 183. Draft

Article 33 was expressly endorsed by the International Court of Justice in the *Case Concerning the Gabčíkovo–Nagymaros Project*, [1997] I.C.J. Rep. 7, reproduced in part below. The International Court of Justice considered, as well, many other issues concerning termination and suspension of treaties, succession of states to treaties and most importantly vigilance and prevention in environmental protection because of the often irreversible nature of damage to the environment.

Case Concerning the Gabčíkovo–Nagymaros Project (Hungary v. Slovakia)

International Court of Justice.
[1997] I.C.J. Rep. 7.

[On September 16, 1977 Hungary and Czechoslovakia entered into a Treaty concerning the construction and operation of a series of locks as a joint investment for the development of water resources, energy, transport, agriculture and other sectors of the national economies of both states. It was aimed at producing hydroelectricity, improving navigation on relevant sections of the River Danube and protection of the areas along the banks against flooding. Both states also undertook to ensure water quality of the River Danube was not impaired as a result of the Project. Work began in 1978. The Danube is the second longest river in Europe and for 142 kilometres it forms the border between the two states. Due to intense criticism of the Project in Hungary in 1989, Hungary suspended and later on abandoned the Project. The Hungarian concerns and uncertainties stemmed from apprehension of environmental damage and the effect on Budapest's water supply. Hungary justified its conduct on a "state of ecological necessity" that constituted a circumstance that relieved it from incurring international responsibility. During that period Czechoslovakia started to investigate other solutions and decided on an alternative project that entailed a unilateral diversion of the River Danube on its territory. Work on this began in 1991. Discussions broke down between the two states and in 1992 Hungary terminated the 1977 Treaty. In 1993 Slovakia became an independent state. As the successor state to Czechoslovakia, Slovakia's position was that Hungary was bound to carry out its Treaty obligations. Hungary argued that it had been by the alternative project deprived of an equitable and reasonable share of the natural resources of the River Danube. Hungary presented five arguments in support of its unilateral termination of the joint Project. These were the existence of a state of necessity, the impossibility of performance of the Treaty, the occurrence of a fundamental change of circumstances, a material breach of the Treaty by Czechoslovakia and lastly the development of new norms of international law appertaining to the environment.]

THE COURT:

    * * *

44. In the course of the proceedings Slovakia argued at length that the state of necessity upon which Hungary relied did not constitute a reason for the suspension of a treaty obligation recognized by the law of treaties.

At the same time, it cast doubt upon whether "ecological necessity" or "ecological risk" could, in relation to the law of state responsibility constitute a circumstance precluding the wrongfulness of an act.

In any event, Slovakia denied that there had been any kind of "ecological state of necessity" in this case either in 1989 or subsequently [and that] * * * Hungary had given an exaggeratedly pessimistic description of the situation.

* * *

50.   In the present case, the parties are in agreement in considering that the existence of a state of necessity must be evaluated in the light of the criteria laid down by the International Law Commission in Article 33 of the Draft Articles on the International Responsibility of States * * *

51.   The Court considers, first of all, that the state of necessity is a ground recognized by customary international law for precluding the wrongfulness of an act not in conformity with an international obligation. It observes moreover that such ground for precluding wrongfulness can only be accepted on an exceptional basis. The International Law Commission was of the same opinion * * *

Thus, according to the Commission, the state of necessity can only be invoked under strictly defined conditions which must be cumulatively satisfied; and the State concerned is not the sole judge of whether those conditions have been met.

52.   In the present case, the following basic conditions set forth in Draft Article 33 are relevant: it must have been occasioned by an "essential interest" of the State which is the author of the act * * * ; that interest must have been threatened by a "grave and imminent peril"; the act being challenged must have been the "only means" of safeguarding that interest; that act must not have "seriously impair[ed] an essential interest of the State towards which the obligation existed; and the State which is the author of that act must not have 'contributed to the occurrence of the state of necessity' ". Those conditions reflect customary international law.

* * *

53.   The Court has no difficulty in acknowledging that the concerns expressed by Hungary for its natural environment in the region affected by the Gabčíkovo–Nagymaros Project related to an "essential interest" of the State * * *

The Commission, in its Commentary * * * included among the situations that could occasion a state of necessity, "a grave danger to * * * the ecological preservation of all or some of the [territory] of the State * * * and specified with reference to state practice, that 'It is primarily in the last two decades that safeguarding the ecological balance has come to be considered an "essential interest" of all States'."* * *

54.   * * * The Court considers, however, that, serious though these uncertainties might have been they could not, alone, establish the objective existence of a "peril" in the sense of a component element of a state of necessity. The word "peril" certainly evokes the idea of "risk"; that is precisely what distinguishes "peril" from material damage. But a state of

necessity could not exist without a "peril" duly established at the relevant point in time; the mere apprehension of a possible "peril" could not suffice in that respect. It could moreover hardly be otherwise, when the "peril" constituting the state of necessity has at the same time to be "grave" and "imminent". "Imminence" is synonymous with "immediacy" or "proximity" and goes far beyond the concept of "possibility". As the International Law Commission emphasized in its Commentary, the "extremely grave and imminent" peril must "have been a threat to the interest at the actual time." That does not exclude, in the view of the Court, that a "peril" appearing in the long term might be held to be "imminent" as soon as it is established, at the relevant point in time, that the realization of that peril, however far off it might be, is not thereby any less certain and inevitable.
* * *

55. * * * Hungary maintained that, if the works at Nagymaros had been carried out as planned, the environment–and in particular the drinking water resources–in the area would have been exposed to serious dangers on account of problems linked to the upstream reservoir on the one hand and, on the other, the risks of erosion of the riverbed downstream.

The Court notes that the dangers ascribed to the upstream reservoir were mostly of a long-term nature and, above all, that they remained uncertain. * * * It follows that, even if it could have been established– which, in the Court's appreciation of the evidence before it was not the case–that the reservoir would ultimately have constituted a "grave peril" for the environment in the area, one would be bound to conclude that the peril was not "imminent" at the time at which Hungary suspended and then abandoned the works related to the dam. * * * The Court would stress that, however, that even supposing, as Hungary maintained, that the construction and operation of the dam would have created serious risks, Hungary had means available to it, other than the suspension and abandonment of the works, of responding to that situation. It could for example have proceeded regularly to discharge gravel into the river downstream of the dam. It could likewise, if necessary, have supplied Budapest with drinking water by processing the river water in an appropriate manner * * * [although] the purification of the river water, like the other measures envisaged, clearly would have been a more costly technique.

56. * * * [With respect to the Gabčíkovo sector] [t]he Court also notes that, in these proceedings, Hungary acknowledged that, as a general rule, the quality of the Danube waters had improved over the past 20 years * * *.

However "grave" it might have been, it would accordingly have been difficult * * * to see the alleged peril as sufficiently certain and therefore imminent in 1989.

The Court moreover considers that Hungary could, in this context also, have resorted to other means in order to respond to the dangers it apprehended. * * *

57. The Court concludes * * * that, with respect to both Nagymaros and Gabčíkovo, the perils invoked by Hungary, without prejudging their possible gravity, were not sufficiently established in 1989, nor were they

imminent; and that Hungary had available to it at that time means of responding to these perceived perils other than the suspension and abandonment of works with which it had been entrusted. What is more negotiations were under way which might have led to a review of the Project and the extension of some of the time limits without there being need to abandon it. * * *

What is more, the Court cannot fail to note the positions taken by Hungary after the entry into force of the 1977 Treaty. In 1983, Hungary asked that the works under the Treaty should go forward more slowly, for reasons that were essentially economic but also, subsidiarily, related to ecological concerns. In 1989, when, according to Hungary itself, the state of scientific knowledge had undergone a significant development, it asked for the works to be speeded up, and then decided, three months later to suspend them and subsequently to abandon them. The Court is not unaware that profound changes were taking place in Hungary in 1989, and that, during that transitory phase, it might have been more than difficult to co-ordinate the different points of view prevailing from time to time.

The Court infers from all these elements that, in the present case, even if it had been established that there was, in 1989, a state of necessity linked to the performance of the 1977 Treaty, Hungary would not have been permitted to rely upon that state of necessity in order to justify its failure to comply with its treaty obligations, as it had helped by act or omission to bring it about.

* * *

[The Court then considered the arguments of Hungary based on Articles 61, 62 and 60 of the Vienna Convention on the Law of the Law of Treaties, reproduced in the Documentary Supplement, dealing with supervening impossibility of performance, fundamental change of circumstances and termination or suspension of a treaty as a consequence of a material breach by one of the parties and the argument that international environmental law had evolved into an *erga omnes* obligation of prevention of damage pursuant to the "precautionary principle" and the argument of Slovakia that none of the intervening developments in environmental law had given rise to norms of *jus cogens* that would override the bilateral Treaty of 1977.]

99. * * * The Vienna Convention is not directly applicable to the 1977 Treaty inasmuch as both States ratified that Convention only after the [1977] Treaty's conclusion. Consequently only those rules which are declaratory of customary international law are applicable to the 1977 Treaty. * * * [T]his is the case in many respects, with Articles 60 to 62 of the Vienna Convention * * *.

101. The Court will now turn to the first ground advanced by Hungary, that of the state of necessity. In this respect the Court will merely observe that, even if a state of necessity is found to exist, it is not a ground for the termination of a treaty. It may only be invoked to exonerate from its responsibility a State which has failed to implement a treaty. Even if found justified, it does not terminate a Treaty; the Treaty may be ineffective as long as the condition of necessity continues to exist; it may in fact be

dormant, but–unless the parties by mutual agreement terminate the Treaty–it continues to exist. As soon as the state of necessity ceases to exist, the duty to comply with treaty obligations revives.

102.   * * * Hungary's interpretation of the wording of Article 61 [of the Vienna Convention on impossibility of performance] is, however, not in conformity with the terms of that Article, nor with the intentions of the Diplomatic Conference which adopted the Convention. Article 61, paragraph 1, requires the "permanent disappearance or destruction of an object indispensable for the execution" of the treaty to justify the termination of a treaty. * * *

103.   Hungary contended that the essential object of the Treaty–an economic joint investment which was consistent with environmental protection * * * had permanently disappeared and that the Treaty had thus become impossible to perform. * * * [I]f the joint exploitation of the investment was no longer possible, this was originally because Hungary did not carry out most of the works for which it was responsible under the 1977 Treaty. Article 61, paragraph 2, of the Vienna Convention expressly provides that impossibility of performance may not be invoked for the termination of a treaty when it results from that party's own breach of an obligation flowing from that treaty.

104.   * * * [Concerning fundamental change of circumstances Hungary had specified] profound changes of a political nature, the Project's diminishing economic viability, the progress of environmental knowledge and the development of new norms and prescriptions on international environmental law. * * *

The changed circumstances advanced * * * are, in the Court's view, not of such a nature, either individually or collectively, that their effect would radically transform the extent of the obligations still to be performed in order to accomplish the Project. A fundamental change of circumstances must have been unforeseen; the existence of the circumstances at the time of the Treaty's conclusion must have constituted an essential basis of the consent of the parties to be bound by the Treaty. * * * [T]he plea of fundamental change of circumstances [can] be applied only in exceptional cases.

* * *

106.   * * * [The Court considered Hungary's submission of material breach by Czechoslovakia of the 1977 Treaty and other conventions and rules of general international law and breach of the 1977 Treaty by the planning and construction of the alternative project and held that with respect to] * * * the other treaties and general rules of international law * * * it is only a material breach of the treaty itself, by a State party to that treaty, which entitles the other party to rely on it as a ground for terminating the treaty. The violation of other treaty rules or of rules of general international law may justify the taking of certain measures including countermeasures, by the injured State, but it does not constitute a ground for termination under the law of treaties.

108. [The Court concluded that, the termination of the 1977 Treaty by Hungary in 1992 was premature as] no breach of the Treaty by Czechoslovakia had yet taken place. * * *

    * * *

111. Finally, the Court will address Hungary's claim that it was entitled to terminate the 1977 Treaty because new requirements of international law for the protection of the environment precluded performance of the Treaty.

112. Neither of the Parties contended that new peremptory norms of environmental law had emerged sine the conclusion of the 1977 Treaty, and the Court will consequently not be required to examine the scope of Article 64 of the Vienna Convention on the Law of Treaties. On the other hand the Court wishes to point out that newly developed norms of environmental law are relevant for the implementation of the Treaty and that the Parties could, by agreement, incorporate them * * *. [The 1977 Treaty had required that] the parties, in carrying out their obligations to ensure that the quality of water in the Danube is not impaired and that nature is protected, to take new environmental norms into consideration when agreeing upon the means to be specified in the Joint Contractual Plan.

By inserting these evolving provisions in the Treaty, the parties recognized the potential necessity to adapt the Project. Consequently, the Treaty is not static and is open to adapt to emerging norms of international law. * * *

The responsibility to do this was a joint responsibility. The obligations [in the Treaty] are, by definition general and have to be transformed into specific obligations of performance through a process of consultation and negotiation. Their implementation thus requires a mutual willingness to discuss in good faith actual and potential environmental risks. * * *

The awareness of the vulnerability of the environment and the recognition that environmental risks have to be assessed on a continuous basis have become much stronger in the years since the Treaty's conclusion. * * *

113. The Court recognizes that both Parties agree on the need to take environmental concerns seriously and to take the required precautionary measures, but they fundamentally disagree on the consequences this has for the Joint Project. In such a case, third-party involvement may be helpful and instrumental in finding a solution, provided each of the Parties is flexible in its position.

114. Finally, Hungary maintained that by their conduct both parties had repudiated the Treaty and that a bilateral treaty repudiated by both parties cannot survive. The Court is of the view, however, that although it has found that both Hungary and Czechoslovakia failed to comply with their obligations under the 1977 Treaty, this reciprocal wrongful conduct did not bring the Treaty to an end nor justify its termination. The Court would set a precedent with disturbing implications for treaty relations and the integrity of the rule *pacta sunt servanda* if it were to conclude that a treaty in force between States, which the parties have implemented in considerable measure and at great cost over a period of years, might be unilaterally

set aside on grounds of reciprocal non-compliance. It would be otherwise, of course, if the parties decided to terminate the Treaty by mutual consent. But in this case, while Hungary purported to terminate the Treaty, Czechoslovakia consistently resisted this act and declared it to be without legal effect.

* * *

139.   The Court is of the opinion that the Parties are under a legal obligation, during the negotiations to be held by virtue of Article 5 of the Special Agreement, [by which they were before the Court] to consider, within the context of the 1977 Treaty, in what way the multiple objectives of the Treaty can best be served, keeping in mind that all of them should be fulfilled.

140.   It is clear that the Project's impact upon, and its implications for, the environment are of necessity a key issue. The numerous scientific reports which have been presented to the Court by the Parties–even if their conclusions are often contradictory–provide abundant evidence that this impact and these implications are considerable.

In order to evaluate the environmental risks, current standards must be taken into consideration. This is not only allowed by the wording of [the Treaty] * * *, but even prescribed, to the extent that these articles impose a continuing–and thus necessarily evolving–obligation on the parties to maintain the quality of the water and to protect nature.

The Court is mindful that, in the field of environmental protection, vigilance and prevention are required on account of the often irreversible character of damage to the environment and of the limitations inherent in the very mechanism of reparation of this type of damage.

Through the ages, mankind has, for economic and other reasons, constantly interfered with nature. In the past, this was often done without consideration of the effects upon the environment. Owing to new scientific insights and to a growing awareness of the risks for mankind–for present and future generations–of pursuit of such interventions at an unconsidered and unabated pace, new norms and standards have been developed, set forth in a number of instruments during the last two decades. Such new norms have to be taken into consideration, and such new standards given proper weight, not only when States contemplate new activities but also when continuing with activities begun in the past. This need to reconcile economic development with protection of the environment is aptly expressed in the concept of sustainable development.

* * *

141.   It is not for the Court to determine what shall be the final result of these negotiations to be conducted by the Parties. It is for the Parties themselves to find an agreed solution, that takes account of the objectives of the Treaty, which must be pursued in a joint and integrated way, as well as the norms of international environmental law and the principles of international watercourses. * * *

152.   * * * The Court has not been asked at this stage to determine the quantum of damages due, but to indicate on what basis they should be

paid. Both parties claimed to have suffered considerable financial losses and both claim pecuniary compensation for them.

It is a well-established rule of international law that an injured State is entitled to obtain compensation from the State which has committed an internationally wrongful act for the damage caused by it. In the present Judgement, the Court has concluded that both Parties committed internationally wrongful acts, and it has noted that those acts gave rise to the damage sustained by the Parties; consequently, Hungary and Slovakia are both under an obligation to obtain compensation and are both entitled to obtain compensation.

Slovakia is accordingly entitled to compensation for the damage suffered by Czechoslovakia as well as by itself as a result of Hungary's decision to suspend and subsequently abandon the work * * *.

Hungary is entitled to compensation for the damage sustained as a result of the diversion of the Danube [by the alternative project].* * *

Draft Code of Crimes Against the Peace and Security of Mankind

Report of the International Law Commission on the Work of Its 48th Session, 6 May–26 July, 1996

UN GAOR 51th Session Supp. No. 10 (A/51/10), ch. II.
See Article 20(g) in the Documentary Supplement.

Rome Statute on the International Criminal Court

Adopted by the United Nations Diplomatic Conference of Plenipotentiaries on the Establishment of an International Criminal Court.
U.N. Doc. A/CONF. 183/9, 17 July, 1998
Reissued with Corrections as Doc. PCNICC/1999/INF/3

Article 8

1. The Court shall have jurisdiction in respect of war crimes in particular when committed as part of a plan or policy or as part of a large-scale commission of such crimes.

2. For the purpose of this Statute, "war crimes" means:

    * * *

    (b) Other serious violations of the laws and customs applicable in international armed conflict, within the established framework of international law, namely, any of the following acts:

    * * *

    (iv) Intentionally launching an attack in the knowledge that such attack will cause incidental loss of life or injury to civilians or damage to civilian objects or widespread, long-term and severe damage to the natural environment which would be clearly excessive in relation to the concrete and direct overall military advantage anticipated.

1. ***Work of the International Law Commission.*** The ILC worked
on the Draft Code of Crimes (formerly called Offences) since 1949, follow-
ing its establishment by the U.N. General Assembly in 1947 by
U.N.G.A.Res. 174(II), U.N.Doc. A/519, 105–10 (1947). For a history of the
Draft Code of Crimes see Gross, Some Observations on the Draft Code of
Offences Against the Peace and Security of Mankind, 13 Is. Yearbook
Human Rights 9 (1983); Williams, The Draft Code of Offences Against the
Peace and Security of Mankind, in Bassiouni (ed.) International Criminal
Law (1985), vol. I, 109 and Bassiouni, The History of the Draft Code of
Crimes Against the Peace and Security of Mankind, 27 Is.L.Rev. 247
(1993).

In its 1991 Report on the Work of its 44th Session, UN GAOR 46th
Session Supp. No. 10 (A/46/10), the International Law Commission had a
specific crime on damage to the environment. Draft Article 26 entitled
"Wilful and severe damage to the environment" read:

> "An individual who wilfully causes or orders the causing of widespread,
> long-term and severe damage to the natural environment shall, on
> conviction thereof, be sentenced . . .".

The inclusion of this draft Article was controversial and members of the
International Law Commission were divided. In its Report on the Work of
its 47th Session, 2 May–21 July, 1995, UN GAOR Off. Rec. 50th Session,
Supp. No. 10 (A/50/10), 62, some members shared the view of the Special
Rapporteur that such a crime as defined therein, even though a criminal
act was not one that met the criteria for a crime against the peace and
security of mankind. Others wanted it to be retained. The view was
expressed that there could be certain types of environmental damage that
would threaten the peace and security of mankind. Examples given were
the "deliberate detonation of nuclear explosives or pollution of entire
rivers". Concern was also expressed about criminal attempts to dump
illicitly chemical or radioactive waste in the land or maritime territory of
developing states, as well as the possibility of environmental terrorism.
Reference was made to draft Article 19 of Part I on State Responsibility
and the need for the Commission to have "some unity of purpose in the
work" that it produces.

Following comments by states on draft Article 26, the 1996 Draft Code
does not contain a separate crime dealing with the environment, but
includes it in draft Article 20(g) under war crimes. It provides that it is a
war crime against the peace and security of mankind, when committed in a
systematic manner or on a large scale for:

> "in the case of armed conflict, using methods or means of warfare not
> justified by military necessity with the intent to cause widespread
> damage, long-term and severe damage to the natural environment and
> thereby gravely prejudice the health or survival of the population and
> such damage occurs."

Notes and Questions

Consider the terms of reference of draft Article 26. Do you think that it
was too broad in encompassing "any individual" and not just state agents,

as well as applying to peace time and armed conflicts? Also, what is your view on the meaning of the term "wilfully"? Consider under draft Article 20(g) the difficulty in waiting for proof of long term damage to emerge. How does this gel with the right of an accused person to a trial within a reasonable period of time under international human rights law, as well as the domestic legal systems of many countries?

Draft Article 19(3)(d) of the ILC's Draft Articles on State Responsibility, provides that "a serious breach of an international obligation of essential importance for the safeguarding and preservation of the human environment" is an international crime. It should be noted that the term "international crime" as it is used there according to the Commission meant international wrongs that are serious in the extreme and for which there is state responsibility. Although the designation sounded confusing, it was not thought to entail incrimination of states or individuals. (See [1976] Y.B.I.L.C. 11, 109, 119). In its 1994 Report, the ILC re-opened discussion on this issue. (See UN GAOR 49th Sess. Supp. No. 10 (A/49/10), 327.) In its 1998 Report on the Work of its 50th Session, the ILC following a long debate concluded that there was no agreement between the members on the issue of division of state conduct into "crimes" or "delicts" and that more work was necessary. Article 19(3) was viewed as defective for many reasons. Comments of states were likewise divided. Some states were vehemently opposed to the notion of crimes in a draft convention dealing with civil state responsibility and considered that it would destroy the draft as a whole. Others believed that there was a distinction to be made without necessarily using the term "crime". Still other states, while in support of the distinction felt that the current article was unsatisfactory because it did not address adequately the procedural implications or consequences of crimes. It was decided that draft Article 19 should be deferred for the time being while the ILC proceeded to concentrate on other aspects of Part One. (See UN GAOR 53rd Sess. Supp. No. 10 (A/53/50), 108, 118, 119, 147.)

For its work on state responsibility the Commission decided to separate the concepts of international responsibility and international liability. The former deals with the consequences of prohibited or wrongful activity, while the concept of liability entails the harmful consequences of lawful activity. A significant distinction between the two is that, although a state may be obligated (liable) to pay compensation for harm caused by lawful activity, the underlying activity as such (e.g., the maintenance of a nuclear power station) need not be stopped. The separation of the two concepts has created analytical problems. The work on state responsibility and liability has occupied the Commission for many years and is in the year 2001 still ongoing. (See G. Handl, Liability as an Obligation Established By a Primary Rule of International Law, 16 Netherlands Yb. Int'l L. 49 (1985).)

The work of the ILC on International Liability for Injurious Consequences Arising Out Of Acts not Prohibited by International Law (Prevention of Transboundary Damage From Hazardous Activities) has been ongoing since 1978. (See Handl, State Liability for Accidental Harm by Private Persons, 74 Am.J.Int'l.L. 525 (1980); Boyle, State Responsibility and International Liability for Injurious Consequences of Acts Not Prohibited by International Law: A Necessary Distinction, 39 Int. & Comp.L.Q. 1

(1990)). The draft Articles apply to activities that are not prohibited by international law which involve a risk of causing serious transboundary harm. The draft Articles concentrate, *inter alia*, on prevention, liability, cooperation between states and international organizations, prior authorization for activities within the scope of the draft Articles, impact assessment, notification and information, equitable balance of interests, national security and industrial secrets and settlement of disputes. (See the 1998 Report of the ILC on the Work of its 50th Session, UNGAOR 53rd Sess. Supp. No. 10 (A/53/10), 11). In August 1998 the Commission adopted on first reading a set of 17 draft Articles on prevention of transboundary pollution damage from hazardous activities. In its 1999 Report on the Work of its 51st Session the ILC decided to defer consideration of international liability, until the second reading of draft Articles 1–17 is completed. (See UNGAOR 54th Sess. Supp. No. 10 (A/54/10).

2. ***International Criminal Court***. The Statute adopted in Rome in 1998 will enter into force when 60 States have ratified. As of July 2001 there are 37 ratifications and 139 signatures. The United States has signed but not ratified. Canada ratified in June 2000. Article 8(2)(b)(iv) deals with the war crime of intentionally causing "widespread, long-term and severe damage to the natural environment". Fenrick, in Triffterer (ed.), Commentary on the Rome Statute, Article 8, 173, 197 (1999) has suggested this threshold is "quite high" and would probably exclude "the sort of damage caused by heavy shelling during World War I battles on the Western Front". Note the language that follows concerning the damage being "clearly excessive in relation to the concrete and direct overall military advantage anticipated." Fenrick suggests that "prosecutors would probably be reluctant to prosecute unless the proportionality requirement was clearly breached."

3. ***Council of Europe***. The Council of Europe adopted in 1998 a Convention on the Protection of the Environment Through Criminal Law, E.T.S. No. 172 (1998), 38 ILM 259 (1999). The Preamble to the Convention recognizes that "whilst the prevention of the impairment of the environment must be achieved primarily through other measures, criminal law has an important part to play" in its protection. The purpose of the Convention is to pursue a common criminal policy and to take effective measures to ensure that through international co-operation environmental crime perpetrators will not escape prosecution.

2. TRANSBOUNDARY AIR POLLUTION AND ACID RAIN

In 1991, the United States and Canada entered an agreement dealing with the problems of transboundary air pollution and acid rain between the two countries. This agreement delineated specific objectives for air quality; assessment, notification and mitigation of proposed activities, actions and projects; and provided for a dispute settlement mechanism and the establishment of a Bilateral Air Quality Commission. A portion of the Agreement between Canada and the United States on Air Quality, 30 Int'l Leg. Mat. 676 (1991) is in the Documentary Supplement.

1. ***Acid rain.*** A joint United States–Canada Research Consultation Group on Long–Range Transport of Air Pollutants concluded in 1979: "The

transport of air pollutants over distances of hundreds to thousands of kilometres is taking place in eastern North America. The [group] has identified acidic precipitation as the problem of greatest common concern at the present time. Acidic precipitation is primarily the result of sulphur dioxide and oxides of nitrogen emissions which are transformed as they are transported by the atmosphere. The most recent estimates of sulphur dioxide emissions are 25.7 million metric tons for the United States and 5.0 million metric tons for Canada.'' The group found that these emissions crossed the border between the two countries. While noting that the greater part of each country's pollutants was caused by its own emissions, it reported that more acid rain was being sent to Canada by the United States.

It took fifty years after the decision in the Trail Smelter arbitration for the U.S. and Canada to negotiate an air quality agreement requiring specific government controls on industries causing cross-frontier deposits of acid rain. Although the Canadian government had pushed for such controls, in particular with respect to industries in the Ohio Valley burning coal with high sulphur content, the United States government had hesitated pending more research. Such agreements as were entered into dealt with research, monitoring, notification and exchange of information. See, e.g., Memorandum of Intent Concerning Transboundary Air Pollution, August 5, 1980, 32 UST 2521, TIAS 9856. (Note Brunée, Acid Rain and Ozone Layer Depletion: International Law and Regulation (1988) and Flinterman, Kwiatkowska and Lammers (eds.) Transboundary Pollution (1986).)

2. *Specific objectives of the 1991 Air Quality Agreement.* Annex 1 requires that the United States: 1) reduce its annual sulphur dioxide emissions by approximately 10 million tons from 1980 levels by the year 2000; 2) achieve a permanent national emission cap of 8.95 million tons of sulphur dioxide per year for electric utilities by the year 2010; 3) promulgate new or revised standards or such other action under the Clean Air Act as the Administrator of the Environmental Protection Agency deems appropriate aimed at sulphur dioxide emissions from industrial sources in the event that annual sulphur dioxide emissions from industrial sources may reasonably be expected to exceed 5.6 million tons and 4) concerning nitrogen oxides with a view to reducing total annual emissions by approximately 2 million tons from 1980 emission levels, the implementation of stated nitrogen oxide programs. The requirements for Canada under Annex 1 are: 1) the reduction of sulphur dioxide emissions in the seven easternmost provinces to 2.3 million tonnes (metric) per year by 1994 and the achievement of a cap on sulphur dioxide emissions in the seven easternmost provinces at 2.3 million tonnes per year from 1995 through December 31, 1999; 2) achievement of a permanent national emissions cap of 3.2 million tonnes per year by 2000; 3) as an interim requirement the reduction by 2000 of annual national emissions of nitrogen oxides from stationary sources by 10,000 tonnes below the year 2000 forecast of 970,000 tonnes, and by January 1, 1995, the development of further annual national emission reduction requirements from stationary sources to be achieved by 2000 and/or 2005, and 4) the implementation of a more stringent mobile source nitrogen oxides control program for gasoline and diesel powered vehicles and engines.

3. *The International Joint Commission (IJC).* This body was established pursuant to Article VII of the 1909 Boundary Waters Treaty, 1909 T.S. No. 548, 12 Bevans 319, between the United States and Great Britain acting then on behalf of Canada. Its purpose is to aid in the prevention and settlement of disputes over the uses of boundary waters. Article IV provides that the boundary waters "shall not be polluted on either side to the injury of health or property on the other". It is noteworthy that pursuant to Article IX that the IJC must examine, report and make recommendations upon the request of either one of the governments, on any difference between the two states or their inhabitants along the common border. There have been many references under this Article. There are arbitral powers, where both states consent under Article X. So far, this has not been used. The 1991 Air Quality Agreement, augments the activities of the IJC in the air pollution field. An annex that deals with ground level ozone and its precursors was concluded on October 12, 2000.

4. *Reciprocal Access.* In response to Principle 22 of the Stockholm Declaration, the American and Canadian Bar Associations, the National Conference of Commissioners on Uniform State Laws and the Uniform Law Conference of Canada recommended legal procedures to compensate victims of transboundary pollution through litigation. This would enable out of jurisdiction victims to have standing to sue in the courts of the jurisdiction where the pollution is situated. Based upon reciprocity, the victim would only have such court access if both the state or province of the victim and alleged polluter have such legislation. Under U.S. federal legislation, in the form of the Clean Water Act, 33 U.S.C. § 1251–1376 and the Clean Air Act, 42 U.S.C. § 7401–7642, there can be the participation of a foreign state, on the basis of reciprocity, in hearings held for the revision of a state implementation plan, for the purposes of eliminating adverse consequences for that foreign state. Note also the 1980 Comprehensive Environmental Response, Compensation and Liability Act, 42 U.S.C. § 9601.

5. *Multilateral conventions.* The United States and Canada are parties to the United Nations Economic Commission for Europe (UNECE) Convention on Long Range Transboundary Air Pollution (LRTAP) of 1979 (in force March 16, 1983), 1302 U.N.T.S. 217, TIAS 10541, 18 Int'l Leg.Mat. 1442 (1979), to which states from both Eastern Europe, including the Russian Federation and western Europe are also parties. The 1984 Protocol on long term financing of the co-operative programme for monitoring and evaluation of air pollutants in Europe entered into force on January 28, 1988. As of June 30, 2000 there are 38 states parties including Canada and the United States. Note the 1985 and 1994 Protocols to that Convention on reduction of sulphur dioxide and the 1988 Protocol on the control of nitrogen oxide emissions respectively. See 27 Int'l Leg.Mat. 707 (1988) and 28 Int'l Leg.Mat. 214 (1989). The 1985 Protocol entered into force on September 2, 1987 and as of June 30, 2000 there are twenty two states parties including Canada. The 1994 Protocol entered into force on August 5, 1998 and as of June 30, 2000 there are twenty two states parties including Canada. The 1988 Protocol entered into force on February 14, 1991 and as of June 30, 2000 there are twenty seven states parties including Canada and the United States. The emphasis of the Convention is on research and the exchange of information, and there are few real

obligations concerning emission limitations and liability. (See Fraenkel, the Convention on Long–Range Transboundary Air Pollution: Meeting the Challenge of International Cooperation, 30 Harvard Int.L.J. 447 (1989)). A third protocol on the Control of Emissions of Volatile Organic Compounds or their Transboundary Fluxes has been signed but not ratified by Canada and the United States. It entered into force on September 29, 1997 and as of June 30, 2000 there are forty seven states parties. See Doc. ECE–EB AIR–30, 31 Int'l Leg.Mat. 573 (1992). Two other Protocols were adopted in 1998 on Persistent Organic Pollutants and Heavy Metals. See 37 ILM 505 (1998). Neither Protocol is yet in force, but as of June 30, 2000, both have thirty six signatures and six and five ratifications respectively. Canada has ratified both Protocols. The United States has signed but not ratified. Finally, the Protocol to Abate Acidification, Eutrophication and Ground-level Ozone was adopted in 1999. It is not yet in force as of June 30, 2000, but there are thirty one signatories including Canada and the U.S.

6. ***European Union (EU) action.*** The EU Commission in Brussels proposed in September 1993 far reaching measures for an integrated approach to the control of air, water and land pollution from large industrial plants. New industries would be expected to introduce the latest technology to reduce pollution, while older plants would have until 2005 to clean up and comply. The Commission proposed a licensing procedure based on admissible levels of pollutants for each individual sector. However, although existing national controls would be coordinated, the member states would still set their own emission limits within EU margins. Heavy industries would have to submit themselves for pollution inspection by national authorities before being granted a license to operate. The Directive also provides for the public to scrutinize member states' control measures.

3. TRANSBOUNDARY NUCLEAR DAMAGE

The Three Mile Island warning and the 1986 Chernobyl disaster have brought home a realization that nuclear accidents can result in pollution in a form and of an intensity beyond levels previously contemplated. What should be the international legal reaction to this newly recognized fact? A multilateral convention that does no more than restate recognized obligations under existing customary international law will not go far to address the problem. The threat of an international obligation to pay reparations for past injuries probably does not provide any greater deterrence on a state than does concern for the safety of the state's own citizens (and rulers). Conventions finely-tailored to specific aspects of the problem are more promising. On September 26, 1986, the International Atomic Energy Agency opened for signature two such conventions: a Convention on Early Notification of a Nuclear Accident and a Convention on Assistance in the Case of a Nuclear Accident or Radiological Emergency, 25 I.L.M. 1370 and 1377 (1986). (See Sands, Chernobyl: Law and Communication (1988) and Handl, Transboundary Nuclear Accidents: The Post–Chernobyl Multilateral Legislative Agenda, 15 Ecology L.Q. 203 (1988)). Note also the IAEA Convention on Nuclear Safety, of June 17, 1994, 33 ILM 1518 (1994), the IAEA Convention Joint Convention on the Safety of Spent Fuel

Management and on the Safety of Radioactive Waste Management of September 5, 1997, 36 ILM 1435 (1997).

The Treaty Banning Nuclear Weapon Tests in the Atmosphere, in Outer Space and Under Water, 14 U.S.C. 1313, 480 U.N.T.S. 43, in the Documentary Supplement, entered into force for the United States on October 10, 1963. The preamble to the treaty recites that the parties desired "to put an end to the contamination of man's environment by radioactive substances." Concerning civil liability the 1960 Paris Convention, 8 E.Y.B. 203, 55 A.J.I.L. 1082, drafted by the O.E.C.D. addresses transboundary nuclear accidents within the Western European member states. The 1963 Vienna Convention, 1063 U.N.T.S. 265, 2 I.L.M. 727 is similar but global in scope. The U.S. is not a party. (See Birnie and Boyle, International Law and the Environment, 371 (1992)). See also the 1997 Protocol to Amend the Vienna Convention and the 1997 Convention on Supplementary Compensation for Nuclear Damage, 36 ILM 1461 (1997).

Nuclear Tests (Australia v. France), Interim Protection, Order of 22 June 1973

International Court of Justice, 1973.
[1973] I.C.J. Rep. 99.[a]

The International Court of Justice,

* * *

Having regard to the Application by Australia filed in the Registry of the Court on 9 May 1973, instituting proceedings against France in respect of a dispute concerning the holding of atmospheric tests of nuclear weapons by the French Government in the Pacific Ocean, and asking the Court to adjudge and declare that the carrying out of further atmospheric nuclear weapon tests in the South Pacific Ocean is not consistent with applicable rules of international law, and to order that the French Republic shall not carry out any further such tests,

Makes the following Order:

1. Having regard to the request * * * whereby the Government of Australia * * * asks the Court to indicate, pending the final decision in the case brought before it by the Application of the same date, the following interim measures of protection: "The provisional measures should be that the French Government should desist from any further atmospheric nuclear tests pending the judgment of the Court in this case;" * * *

* * *

6. Whereas by a letter dated 16 May 1973 from the Ambassador of France to the Netherlands, handed by him to the Registrar the same day, the French Government stated that it considered that the Court was manifestly not competent in the case and that it could not accept the Court's jurisdiction, and that accordingly the French Government did not

a. Parallel proceedings were instituted
by New Zealand. [1973] I.C.J. Reports 135.

intend to appoint an agent, and requested the Court to remove the case from its list;

* * *

13.   Whereas on a request for provisional measures the Court need not, before indicating them, finally satisfy itself that it has jurisdiction on the merits of the case, and yet ought not to indicate such measures unless the provisions invoked by the Applicant appear, prima facie, to afford a basis on which the jurisdiction of the Court might be founded;

* * *

17.   Whereas the material submitted to the Court leads it to the conclusion, at the present stage of the proceedings, that the provisions invoked by the Applicant appear, prima facie, to afford a basis on which the jurisdiction of the Court might be founded; * * *.

* * *

22.   Whereas the claims formulated by the Government of Australia in its Application are as follows:

(i) The right of Australia and its people, in common with other States and their peoples, to be free from atmospheric nuclear weapon tests by any country is and will be violated;

(ii) The deposit of radio-active fall-out on the territory of Australia and its dispersion in Australia's airspace without Australia's consent:

(a) violates Australian sovereignty over its territory;

(b) impairs Australia's independent right to determine what acts shall take place within its territory and in particular whether Australia and its people shall be exposed to radiation from artificial sources;

(iii) the interference with ships and aircraft on the high seas and in the superjacent airspace, and the pollution of the high seas by radioactive fall-out, constitute infringements of the freedom of the high seas;

* * *

25.   Whereas the Government of Australia alleges, inter alia, that a series of atmospheric nuclear tests have been carried out by the French Government in the Pacific during the period from 1966 to 1972, including the explosion of several hydrogen bombs and a number of devices of high and medium power; that during recent months there has been a growing body of reports, not denied by the French Government, to the effect that the French Government is planning to carry out a further series of atmospheric nuclear tests in the Pacific in 1973; that this series of tests may extend to 1975 and even beyond that date; that in diplomatic correspondence and in discussions earlier in the present year the French Government would not agree to cease nuclear testing in the atmosphere in the Pacific and would not supply Australia with any information as to the dates of its proposed tests or the expected size and yield of its explosions; and that in a statement made in the French Parliament on 2 May 1973 the French Government indicated that, regardless of the protests made by

Australia and other countries, it did not envisage any cancellation or modification of the programme of nuclear testing as originally planned;

* * *

27. Whereas the Government of Australia also alleges that the atmospheric nuclear explosions carried out by France in the Pacific have caused wide-spread radio-active fall-out on Australian territory and elsewhere in the southern hemisphere, have given rise to measurable concentrations of radio-nuclides in foodstuffs and in man, and have resulted in additional radiation doses to persons living in that hemisphere and in Australia in particular; that any radio-active material deposited on Australian territory will be potentially dangerous to Australia and its people and any injury caused thereby would be irreparable; that the conduct of French nuclear tests in the atmosphere creates anxiety and concern among the Australian people; that any effects of the French nuclear tests upon the resources of the sea or the conditions of the environment can never be undone and would be irremediable by any payment of damages; and any infringement by France of the rights of Australia and her people to freedom of movement over the high seas and superjacent airspace cannot be undone;

28. Whereas the French Government, in a diplomatic Note dated 7 February 1973 and addressed to the Government of Australia, the text of which was annexed to the Application in the present case, called attention to Reports of the Australian National Radiation Advisory Committee from 1967 to 1972, which all concluded that the fall-out from the French tests did not constitute a danger to the health of the Australian population; whereas in the said Note the French Government further expressed its conviction that in the absence of ascertained damage attributable to its nuclear experiments, they did not violate any rule of international law, and that, if the infraction of the law was alleged to consist in a violation of a legal norm concerning the threshold of atomic pollution which should not be crossed, it was hard to see what was the precise rule on which Australia relied;

29. Whereas for the purpose of the present proceedings it suffices to observe that the information submitted to the Court, including Reports of the U.N. Scientific Committee on the Effects of Atomic Radiation between 1958 and 1972, does not exclude the possibility that damage to Australia might be shown to be caused by the deposit on Australian territory of radio-active fall-out resulting from such tests and to be irreparable;

* * *

33. Whereas the decision given in the present proceedings in no way prejudges the question of the jurisdiction of the Court to deal with the merits of the case, or any questions relating to the admissibility of the Application, or relating to the merits themselves, and leaves unaffected the right of the French Government to submit arguments in respect of those questions;

* * *

Accordingly, The COURT, Indicates, by 8 votes to 6, pending its final decision in the proceedings instituted on 9 May 1973 by Australia against France, the following provisional measures: The Governments of Australia and France should each of them ensure that no action of any kind is taken which might aggravate or extend the dispute submitted to the Court or prejudice the rights of the other Party in respect of the carrying out of whatever decision the Court may render in the case; and, in particular, the French Government should avoid nuclear tests causing the deposit of radio-active fall-out on Australian territory; * * *

———

Subsequent proceedings in the Nuclear Tests Cases. Despite the court's order for interim measures of protection, France continued to conduct tests during the summer months of 1973 and 1974. The court held hearings on the question of its jurisdiction, France not participating. Thereafter the court took note of a number of public declarations by the French government, including a communiqué issued by the President of France stating that "in view of the stage reached in carrying out the French nuclear defence programme France will be in a position to pass on to the stage of underground explosions as soon as the series of tests planned for this summer is completed." The court read these unilateral acts as creating a legally binding obligation on the part of France to cease testing in the atmosphere in the South Pacific. Since the court concluded that Australia's objective in this proceeding was to obtain termination of French atmospheric nuclear tests in the South Pacific, it found, by a vote of nine to six "that the claim of Australia no longer has any object and that the court is therefore not called upon to give a decision thereon." [1974] I.C.J. Reports 253. The same result was reached in the New Zealand proceedings. *Id.* at 457. See also the Order of the International Court of Justice in the Request for an Examination of the Situation in Accordance with Paragraph 63 of the Court's Judgment of 20 December 1974 in the Nuclear Tests (New Zealand v. France) Case, I.C.J. Rep. [1995].

Legality of the Threat or Use of Nuclear Weapons. The General Assembly asked the International Court of Justice in December 1994 for an Advisory Opinion on this question. The Court advised that the threat or use of nuclear weapons was neither authorized nor prohibited by conventional or customary international law. However, states must comply with the U.N. Charter obligations contained in Articles 2(4) and 51. The extract below addresses the position of international environmental law in this debate.

Legality of the Threat or Use of Nuclear Weapons

International Court of Justice, 1996.
Advisory Opinion, 35 International Legal Materials 814 (1996).

THE COURT:

* * *

29.   * * * [T]he environment is under daily threat and * * * the use of nuclear weapons could constitute a catastrophe for the environment. * * * The existence of the general obligation of States to ensure that activities

within their jurisdiction and control respect the environment of other States or of other areas beyond national jurisdiction is now part of the corpus of international law relating to the environment.

30.   * * * [T]he issue is not weather the treaties relating to the protection of the environment are or are not applicable during an armed conflict, but rather whether the obligations stemming from these treaties were intended to be obligations of total restraint during military conflict.

The Court does not consider that the treaties in question could have intended to deprive a State of the exercise of its right to self-defence under international law because of its obligations to protect the environment. Nonetheless, States must take environmental considerations into account when assessing what is necessary and proportionate in the pursuit of legitimate military objectives. Respect for the environment is one of the elements that go to assessing whether an action is in conformity with the principles of necessity and proportionality

[The Court then considered in support of this view, Principle 24 of the Rio Declaration, Articles 35(3) and 55 of Additional Protocol I to the Geneva Conventions and United Nations General Assembly Resolution 47/37 of November 25, 1992 on the Protection of the Environment in Times of Armed Conflict.]

33.   * * * The Court thus finds that while the existing international law relating to the protection of the environment does not specifically prohibit the use of nuclear weapons, it indicates important environmental factors that are properly to be taken into account in the context of the implementation of the principles and rules of the law applicable in armed conflict.

---

4.   PROTECTING THE OZONE LAYER

The ozone layer is a protective screen that filters ultraviolet radiation and thus protects the earth from over-exposure. It is estimated that approximately ninety per cent of all the atmospheric ozone is to be found in the stratosphere. (See Brunée, Acid Rain and Ozone Layer Depletion: International Law and Regulation, 35 (1988)). The balance of the ozone layer has been undermined by industrial and human actions, whereby deterioration is caused by chemicals, especially chlorofluorocarbons (CFCs), but also by methane, nitrogen oxides and halons. CFCs are used in many consumer goods such as refrigerators, air conditioners, aerosol cans, solvents and styro-foam. It is not known exactly how the chemicals are transported into the stratosphere. The impact of this ozone layer depletion is that more harmful rays of UVBB have increased and global scale effects will result on human health and in fact on the whole eco-system with some variations based on latitude, unless the situation is rapidly ameliorated. (See, *id.*, 43). There is also the relation between ozone layer depletion and climate change, otherwise commonly known as the "greenhouse effect", in that ozone absorbs and then emits what is termed "thermally significant terrestrial infrared radiation". (See Gallagher, The New Montreal Protocol and the Future of International Law for Protection of the Global Environment, 14 Houston J.Int.L. 267, 274B277 (1992)). The two are linked because the gases CO_2, methane, N_2O, CFC 11 and 12 are among the major greenhouse gases and are also responsible for ozone layer deterioration. In 1985 the Vienna Convention for the Protection of the Ozone Layer, 1513 U.N.T.S. 293, 26 ILM 1516 (1987), became the first multilateral convention to deal with this dangerous problem. It came into force on September 22, 1988. As of June 30, 2000, there are 176 states parties including Canada and the United States. However, as with the ECE Long Range Transboundary Air Pollution Convention considered earlier in section A.2 of this Chapter, it is only a framework for cooperation, with no real substantive obligations. The aim was, and has been since, to adopt protocols or amendments to existing protocols that deal with specific obligations. The 1987 Montreal Protocol, which entered into force on January 1, 1989, 26 ILM 1541 (1987) and the 1990 London Adjustments thereto, which entered into force on August 10, 1992, 30 ILM 537 (1991), that are reproduced in the Documentary Supplement, are part of that process. There are 175 and 140 states parties respectively, including Canada and the U.S. The Ozone secretariat is in Nairobi, Kenya. In 1992 a further meeting in Copenhagen produced other adjustments and amendments to the Montreal Protocol. See 32 ILM 874 (1993). These amendments entered into force on June 14, 1994 and there are 109 states parties including Canada and the United States. Subsequent meetings have been held in Vienna in 1995, in San José, Costa Rica in 1996, in Montreal in 1997, in Paris in 1997, in Cairo in 1998 and Beijing in 1999. The 1997 Montreal amendments entered into force on November 10, 1999 and as of June 30, 2000 there are thirty eight states parties. The 1999 Beijing amendments are not yet in force, with to date only one state party, Chile. One of the issues in the Cairo meeting was how to harmonize the Montreal Protocol policies with the Kyoto Protocol to the United Nations Framework Convention on Climate Change, 37 ILM 32 (1998), contained in the Documentary Supplement. (*See* Landers, *The Black Market Trade in Chloroflurocarbons: The Montreal Protocol Makes Banned Refrigerants a Hot Commodity*, 26 Ga J. Int'l & Comp. L. 457 (1997) and Oberthûr, *Montreal Protocol: 10 Years After*, 27 Env. Pol. & L. 432 (1997).) *See also* the 1994 Instrument Establishing the Global Environmental Facility, as a permanent financial mechanism to provide grants and funds to developing states for projects and activities that will protect the environment, 33 ILM 1273 (1994).

Global Ozone Trends

A. Gallagher, The "New" Montreal Protocol and the Future of International Law for Protection of the Global Environment

14 Houston Journal of International Law 267, 274B277 (1992).*

Despite several decades of observation and the utilization of increasingly sophisticated equipment, scientists have found it difficult to accurately

* Reprinted with the permission of the
Houston J. Int'l L.

measure past changes in global ozone. Considerable natural variations, due, *inter alia,* to cyclical changes in atmospheric motion and solar activity, have hindered efforts to assess net ozone losses. In 1986, the National Aeronautical Space Administration (NASA), in conjunction with other national and international organizations, including the World Meteorological Association (WMO) and the United Nations Environment Programme (UNEP), conducted a major review and re-analysis of all available data relating to atmospheric ozone concentrations. A final report from NASA and the Ozone Trends Panel was released in 1988, and included results from the NASA-backed Airborne Antarctic Ozone Experiment conducted the previous year. The Panel, after adjusting measurements to allow for natural geophysical variability, detected small but statistically significant changes in both total column ozone and its vertical distribution between 1979 and 1986. The Panel concluded that such changes may well be due to the increased abundance of atmospheric trace gases-primarily CFCs.

Of far greater magnitude were the levels of stratospheric ozone depletion measured over Antarctica during the 1987 Experiment. The springtime "hole" has been observed since the early eighties, each year growing progressively deeper, despite what appeared to be explicable turnarounds in 1986 and 1988. Some think the unique winter/spring Antarctic meteorology permits the creation of an isolated air-mass (polar vortex) with temperatures sufficiently cold to perturb the critical composition of the upper atmosphere. Within this vortex, the anthropogenically influenced processes by which ozone is destroyed are hastened and intensified.

In 1989, NASA launched another expedition, this time an investigation of the winter Arctic stratosphere. The expedition's final report revealed that the chemistry responsible for Antarctic ozone depletion was also present in the atmosphere above the North Pole. The Arctic ozone layer, it appears, is "primed for destruction." Parallel investigations conducted by a Canadian research team using specially filled balloons confirmed the NASA group's findings.

Rapid advances in the field of polar atmospheric photochemistry helped explain the large decreases in Antarctic ozone and confirmed the existence of Arctic conditions indicating potential for a similar level of destruction. What remains unclear is whether this phenomena forebodes ozone thinning elsewhere in the stratosphere, whether the processes responsible could be important at other latitudes, and whether a hemispheric depletion of ozone is possible through dilution of the wider layer.

The search for answers to these questions is becoming increasingly urgent. The 1990 springtime hole over Antarctica was far deeper and persisted for considerably longer than expected. In April 1991 NASA completed analysis of data collected by its total ozone mapping satellite over a period of eleven years and seven months. The Agency confirmed that ozone depletion in the northern hemisphere is occurring between two and five times faster than previously predicted by theoretical models and is extending further away from the polar regions.

5.   CLIMATE CHANGE AND THE PRECAUTIONARY PRINCIPLE

J. Brunée, Acid Rain and Ozone Layer Depletion: International Law and Regulation

47 (1988).*

* * * The Earth's temperature depends on the amounts of sunlight coming in, in relation to the amounts which are reflected back into space. This reflection is prevented by the [greenhouse] gases [CO_2, methane, N_2O, CFC 11 and 12 and tropospheric ozone] which have the effect of a screen and retain heat comparable to a greenhouse. With concentrations of these gases rising at current levels, global temperatures could rise between 1.5E C by the middle of the next century. However, noticeable changes may occur within the next decade * * *.

The consequences would, of course, be immense: climate zones could shift and impair global agriculture and food supplies, sea levels could rise between 20 and 140 meters due to thermal expansion and melting of glaciers and polar ice, human health could be directly affected, at least in an adaption period.

Because of the immense impact of CO_2 emissions and the difficulty of controlling them (they occur necessarily in every combustion process), the greenhouse effect might be an even more pressing problem than the depletion of the ozone layer. Some scientists consider global warming to be inevitable and suggest that even now we begin preparations of countries and economies for climatical, geographical, and social changes.

---

1.   ***The Problem***. The use of fossil fuels and increased industrialization have produced carbon dioxide and other greenhouse gases such as methane, nitrous oxide which in turn produce global warming. Massive deforestation is also a cause as forests assist in carbon dioxide absortion. In 1988 The Intergovernmental Panel on Climate Change was established by UNEP and the World Meteorological Organization (WMO) to provide scientific and technical research on climate change. The United Nations General Assembly endorsed this in its Resolution on protection of Global Climate for Present and Future Generations of Mankind. See U.N.G.A. Res. 43/53, of December 6, 1988, which was adopted without a vote, reprinted in 28 ILM 1326 (1988). In its second Resolution on this topic the General Assembly supported UNEP and the WMO's initiative to initiate negotiations for a framework convention on climate change. See U.N.G.A. Res. 44/207, of December 22, 1989.

2.   ***Non-binding Declarations.*** On March 11, 1989, a non-binding declaration was signed at the Hague, the Netherlands, by twenty-four state

* Reprinted with the permission of Transnational Publishers Inc.

leaders. It called for a new approach to dealing with matters pertaining to the atmosphere through new principles of international law being developed and new international institutional authority. (See 28 ILM 1308 (1989)). Note also the 1989 Malé Declaration on Global Warming and Sea Level Rise by so-called "small states" and the 1989 Noordwijk Declaration on Atmospheric Pollution and Climate Change made by the 67 state representatives, the Commission of the European Communities and ten international organizations. (See Molitor (ed.) International Environmental Law: Primary Materials (1991)). The 1990 Ministerial Declaration of the Second World Climate Conference, attended by representatives of 137 states, amongst other things urged developed states to limit non-Montreal Protocol greenhouse gases and called for a framework convention on climate change to be ready for signature at the 1992 Rio Conference on Environment and Development. (See Handl (ed.) 1 Yb. Int'l Env.L. 473 (1990)).

3. ***Convention on Climate Change.*** On June 5, 1992, the United Nations Framework Convention on Climate Change was opened for signature, at the U.N. Conference on Environment and Development. No reservations to this Convention are allowed. It entered into force on March 21, 1994. As of June 30, 2000 there were 184 states parties. Canada and the United states have ratified. See the Documentary Supplement for the Convention and related U.N. General Assembly resolutions. Two of the most important portions of these documents concerning the precautionary principle are reproduced below. (*See also* Bodansky, *Scientific Uncertainty and the Precautionary Principle*, 33(7) Environment 4 (1991) and Cameron & Abouchar, *The Precautionary Principle: A Fundamental of Law and Policy for the Protection of the Global Environment*, 14 B.C. Int'l & Comp.L.Rev. 1 (1991)).

Framework Convention on Climate Change Principles

U.N. Doc. A/AC 237/18 (Pt. II) Add. 1; 31 International Legal Materials 851 (1992).*

* * *

3. Parties should take precautionary measures to anticipate, prevent or minimize the causes of climate change and mitigate its adverse effects. Where there are threats of serious or irreversible damage, lack of full scientific certainty should not be used as a reason for postponing such measures, taking into account that policies and measures to deal with climate change should be cost-effective so as to ensure global benefits at the lowest possible cost. To achieve this, such policies and measures should take into account different socio-economic contexts, be comprehensive, cover all relevant sources, sinks and reservoirs of greenhouse gases and adaptation, and comprise all economic sectors. Efforts to address climate change may be carried out cooperatively. * * *

* Reprinted with the permission of the
American Society of International Law.

Rio Declaration on Environment and Development
June 13, 1992; A/CONF. 151/5/Rev. 1, 31 International Legal Materials 874 (1992).*

Principle 15

In order to protect the environment, the precautionary approach shall be widely applied by States according to their capabilities. Where there are threats of serious or irreversible damage, lack of full scientific certainty shall not be used as a reason for postponing cost-effective measures to prevent environmental degradation.

Note: Concerning the precautionary principle see the International Court of Justice decision in *Gabčíkovo–Nagymaros Project* (Hungary v. Slovakia), [1997] I.C.J. Rep.7 reproduced in Section A.1. The WTO has also had occasion to address this in the *Beef Hormones* case. See *EC Measures Concerning Meat and Meat Products (Hormones)*, Report of January 16, 1998, AB–1997–4,WT/DS 26/AB/R. P. Sands, "Environmental Protection in the Twenty–First Century: Sustainable Development and International Law" in R. Revesz, P. Sands & R. Stewart (eds) Environmental Law, The Economy and Sustainable Development (2000),369, 376 states that although the "precautionary principle" is "potentially the most radical and far-reaching of environmental principles, its meaning and effect are unclear and remain mired in controversy." He suggests at 384 that the International Court of Justice "appears to be concluding that a state of environmental necessity can only be invoked * * * if there is a sufficient degree of certainty and inevitability that the peril *will* occur * * *. And the Court does not indicate what degree of certainty or inevitability will be 'sufficient' ". Refer to The International Law Commission's Draft Articles on State Responsibility, Draft Article 33, Report of the International Law Commission on the Work of its 51st Session, 3 May–23 July, 1999, UN GAOR Off. Rec. 44th Sess. Supp. No. 10 (A/54/10). See Section A.1 in this Chapter. The WTO Appellate Body in the *Beef Hormones* case was faced with the issue of whether a European Community ban on importation of American beef that had been produced with artificial hormones could be justified as a threat to health and the environment. The United States submitted that there was no adequate scientific basis for such action and consequently the ban was not based on an assessment of risk and was inconsistent with the international trade treaty obligations of the European Communities. At paragraph 121 the Appellate Body noted that the basic submission of the European Communities was that the precautionary principle "is or has 'become a general customary rule of international law' " and further that it was its position that "it is not necessary for *all* scientists around the world to agree on the 'possibility and magnitude' of the risk, nor for *all* or most of the WTO Members to perceive and evaluate the risk in the same way." The United States had, to the contrary, considered that it represented an approach rather than a principle and was not representative of customary international law (para. 122).The Appellate Body considered it unnecessary "and probably imprudent * * * to take a position on this important but abstract question" concerning the status of the precautionary principle in international law. It noted in footnote 44 to

* Reprinted with the permission of the American Society of International Law.

paragraph 123 that the International Court of Justice in the *Gabčíkovo–Nagymaros* case, *supra*, in paragraph 140 of its judgment had not specifically identified the precautionary principle as one of the recently developed norms of international law. The Appellate Body found that on the basis of the trade rules that it was applying that the import ban was not warranted as "no risk assessment that reasonably support[ed] or warrant[ed]" it had been provided to the Panel (para. 208). Thus the WTO required that "the results of risk assessment must sufficiently warrant–that is to say, reasonably support the * * * measure at stake. * * * [This] is a substantive requirement that there be a rational relationship between the measure and the risk assessment" (para.193). Of particular interest is the conclusion that even where there is divergent scientific opinion this will not necessarily mean that there is an absence of such a relationship, "especially where the risk involved is life-threatening in character and is perceived to constitute a clear and imminent threat to public safety. Determination of the presence or absence of that relationship can only be done on a case-to-case basis, after account is taken of all considerations rationally bearing upon the issue of potential adverse health effects" (para. 194). As Sands, *ibid.*, 387 points out this approach "does not exclude the possibility that a risk assessment could be relied upon even if it indicated a degree of uncertainty".

Kyoto Protocol to the United Nations Framework Convention on Climate Change

37 International Legal Materials (1998).
See the Documentary Supplement.

Notes: Article 7 of the Climate Change Convention provided that the Conference of states parties would review implementation of the Convention and any future agreements. The first Conference of the state parties to the Climate Convention was held in Berlin in 1995. The result was the "Berlin Mandate" which provided that the stated objectives of the developed states parties to reduce emissions of greenhouse gases to 1990 levels by 2000 were not adequate and it also aimed at producing a protocol or other agreement which would contain new emission reductions to be adopted at the third meeting. An *Ad Hoc* Group was created in Berlin to keep check on the negotiations. The Secretariat was also to be located in Berlin. In 1996 the second meeting was held in Geneva and the third in 1997 in Kyoto, Japan. The Kyoto Protocol was adopted on December 11, 1997. Canada signed it on April 29, 1998 and the United States on November 12, 1998. As of September, 2000 it is not yet in force. There are 84 signatories and 29 states have ratified. The Protocol contains greenhouse gas emission reduction commitments that are aimed at reducing global emissions by at least 5% below the 1990 levels in a period of initial commitment of 2008–2012. (*See* Davies, *Global Warming and the Kyoto Protocol*, 47 Int. & Comp. L. Q. 466 (1998); Hanafi, *Joint Implementation: Legal and Institutional Issues for an Effective International program to Combat Climate Change*, 22 Harv. Env. L. Rev. 331 (1998) and Smeloff, *Global Warming: The Kyoto Protocol and Beyond*, 28 Env. Pol. & L. 63 (1998).The fourth meeting was held in Buenos Aires in 1998, the result being the "BA Adoption Plan". It established 2000 as the deadline for the implementation of the Kyoto Protocol mechanisms, including the transfer of technology provisions, emissions trading scheme, financial mechanism and joint implementation. Concerning compliance the Protocol provides that "effective and appropriate" compliance procedures must be approved by the first meeting of the parties to the Protocol, once in force. The binding consequences of non-compliance will require an amendment to the Protocol. These are key and as yet unresolved issues.

President George W. Bush has refused to support the Kyoto Protocol of 1998. On this refusal, read the following.

Scott Barrett, "KYOTO'S FALL" (2000)

The American Institute for Contemporary German Studies*

The announcement by the White House of President George W. Bush's opposition to the Kyoto Protocol came as a shock to Europe. It must have been especially galling for Chancellor Schröder, since the statement was issued only hours before he was to meet with the president.

The Kyoto process has been underway for almost ten years, and about 180 countries have invested a substantial amount of political energy into constructing this agreement. Europe has accommodated U.S. concerns on numerous occasions—a hard pill for the Greens in the Schröder coalition to swallow. Now the U.S. has turned its back to the entire process, without offering an alternative. Europe feels gutted.

However, George W. Bush has been consistent in showing his distaste for Kyoto, and so his announcement should not have come as a surprise. Even more importantly, Kyoto was lifeless even before the White House condemned it. The U.S. constitution requires that a treaty be sent to the Senate for its "advice and consent." Two-thirds of the Senate must approve of a treaty before it can become law. And yet even before the Kyoto Protocol was negotiated, the Senate rejected it. In the summer of 1997, the Senate voted against a Kyoto-style treaty by a 95–0 margin. President Clinton signed Kyoto, but he did not send it to the Senate because he knew he did not have the votes. Al Gore felt more passionately about climate change than did President Clinton, but his passion would not have changed the minds of 66 senators. Ratification of this agreement by the U.S. was always a poor bet.

What should the rest of the world do now? Different opinions are being voiced. Australia has hinted that it will not ratify Kyoto now. Many European leaders, by contrast, have said that they will proceed with Kyoto with or without the United States. My guess, however, is that Kyoto will not survive.

* Reprinted with the permission of American Institute for Contemporary German Studies. Scott Barrett is a professor at the School of Advanced International Studies, Johns Hopkins University. He is also a contributing author to the third assessment report of the Intergovernmental Panel on Climate Change. The views expressed in this publication are those of the author(s) alone. They do not necessarily reflect the views of the American Institute for Contemporary German Studies.

To enter into force, Kyoto would have to be ratified by at least 55 countries, making up at least 55 percent of the emissions of the industrialized countries. It is technically possible for Kyoto to enter into force without the U.S. Ratification by the European Union, Japan, Russia, and the European economies in transition would be enough. However, this seems a long shot.

So far, only one of the industrialized countries has ratified Kyoto: Romania. But Romania accounts for just 1.2% of the emissions of the so-called Annex I countries, and so there is still a long way to go. More importantly, the agreement will only require real reductions in emissions by countries like the European Union and Japan. These countries are going to have to consider very carefully if the effort is worth it. Without U.S. participation, the agreement will have next to no effect on global emissions of greenhouse gases. The U.S. accounts for about a quarter of global emissions, and the agreement does not constrain the emissions of developing countries—a sore point for Mr. Bush. Moreover, Europe will be worried that participation without the U.S. would damage its competitiveness. Europe backed off from imposing a carbon tax in 1992, largely for the same reasons.

There are even more problems. Kyoto is also a work in progress. It imposes specific obligations upon industrial countries as regards their emissions of greenhouse gases, but it leaves many important details undecided. That is why the negations in The Hague foundered last November. Even without the U.S., negotiators will find it difficult to take Kyoto forward—the U.S. has merely been a lightning rod for every disagreement to this point.

Another problem is that Kyoto does not give countries much time to resolve the remaining issues. It fixes the date at which emissions are capped. Much time has already been lost, and the longer it takes to complete the negotiations, the higher will be the cost to every country of participating in it.

Finally, in my view the negotiations to this point have utterly failed to come up with a credible compliance enforcement mechanism. Even if Kyoto did enter into force, my guess is that it would not survive for long.

All of this adds to Europe's frustration. It cannot go forward without the U.S., and yet it cannot get the U.S. to move forward. At the same time, Europe should see the silver lining in this cloud. The Bush rejection does provide the opportunity for all parties to reconsider the basic architecture of Kyoto—which, as I noted above, was flawed from the beginning.

For the U.S. to become re-engaged, two things would seem to be necessary. First, the president will have to see that his stance is a vote loser. It is worth recalling that the president got fewer votes than Kyoto's friend, Al Gore, and that he was only able to take the White House because Gore lost votes to an even greener Ralph Nader. Domestic pressure may force Bush to change tack. He will not reverse his position on Kyoto, but he may become more engaged in the renewed process.

Second, the president will have to see climate change for what it really is—a foreign policy issue, and not a domestic environmental issue. He will have to see that the interests of the United States are tied to those of all other nations; that the rest of the world is looking to the U.S. for solutions, not excuses; and that the United States has a responsibility—to its own citizens and especially to its children, but also to the rest of the world—to do something about climate change.

Do you agree with the positions taken by this article? Why? Why not? Does the U.S. have an obligation to support the Kyoto Protocol? If so, upon what authority?

6.   INTERNATIONAL RIVERS, LAKES AND DRAINAGE BASINS

Environmental protection of international rivers, lakes and drainage basins, including groundwater as well as surface water is fundamental. However, here we are not only talking about protection from pollution, but also of water quantity issues. Reference should be made to the International Law Association's Helsinki Rules on the Uses and Waters of International Rivers, the Montreal Rules on Water Pollution in an International Drainage Basin, to the U.N. ECE Convention on the Protection and Use of Transboundary Water Courses and Lakes, 31 ILM 1312 (1992), which entered into force on October 6, 1996 and the International Law Commission's work which led to the adoption by the U.N. General Assembly in 1997 of the Convention on the Law of the Non–Navigational Uses of International Watercourses, 36 ILM 703 (1997), not yet in force, contained in the Documentary Supplement. Note should also be taken of the 2000 Report of the International Law Association's Committee on Water Resources which presents the Campione Consolidation of the Helsinki and Montreal Rules. It consolidates the original texts but does not change the substance. See the International Law Association, Report of the 96th Conference, London, 2000, 443, 835–851.

Equitable Utilization or Participation

Sharon A. Williams, Public International Law and Water Quantity Management in a Common Drainage Basin: The Great Lakes

18 Case Western Reserve Journal of International Law 155, 165B168 (1986).*

This theory of equitable utilization, currently described as equitable participation is clearly accepted by States and can be designated today as a rule of customary international law.

This theory was the basis for "equitable apportionment" in the case of Kansas v. Colorado [206 U.S. 46 (1907)] and was adopted as "equitable utilization" by the Helsinki Rules on the Uses of the Waters of International Rivers adopted by the International Law Association in 1966. The phrase "equitable participation" can be found in the draft articles on the Law of the Non-Navigational Uses of International Watercourses adopted by the

* Reprinted with the permission of Case West.J.Int'l L.

International Law Commission. [Adopted by the General Assembly in 1997].

* * * Under these rules, basin states include all states whose territories contribute to the international drainage basin, whether or not they are "riparian" states. Thus, it is recognized in the Helsinki Rules (which although not a binding agreement between states, but rather a document produced by a non-governmental organization seeks to state the rules of customary international law) that underground waters may contribute to an international drainage basin. Article IV is illustrative of the key principle of the Rules, which is that every basin state in an international drainage basin has the right to reasonable use and an equitable share of the waters of the basin. The Rules reject outright the "Harmon Doctrine" of unlimited sovereignty. This rejection is based on state practice. A basin state is obligated to look to the rights and needs of other states and each is entitled to an equitable share. This latter concept is to provide the maximum benefit to each basin state from the waters in question, along with a minimum of detriment.

The determination of what is a reasonable and equitable share is to be determined "in the light of all the relevant factors in each particular case." [Article V of the Helsinki Rules] Naturally, rights which are "equal in kind and correlative with those" of co-basin states will not necessarily mean that the share in the uses of waters are identical. This will depend upon the weight given to relevant factors. The rules consider the reasonable uses of international drainage basins.

Each of * * * [the factors listed in Article V of the Helsinki Rules are] deemed relevant must "aid in the determination or satisfaction of the social and economic needs of co-basin states." Consider the following scenario: In the case of a common drainage basin where state A, the lower "co-basin" state, uses the waters for irrigation purposes but state B, the upper "co-basin" state, wants to produce hydroelectric power from the shared waters, the question arises as to whose use is preeminent. The two uses are * * * partially at odds as the storage period for the hydroelectric power may overlap with the growing season of crops in state A when the water is needed for nourishment. A number of elements [are] crucial to a resolution of this dilemma. State A has always used the inundation method of irrigation. An objective study indicates that the use of the water of the basin for hydroelectric purposes would be more valuable than irrigation methods. The dam would allow flow control of seasonal flooding and economically speaking would in the long term result in reasonable agricultural productivity. However, it would not be as high as that before the dam was built. Even though the population of state A for many centuries depended upon the agriculture in the basin area of state A, this is not now the case. Alternative sources for food are present, but not enough to completely rule out the need for the old produce area. A survey in state A indicates that there are substantial underground waters in state A. The new hydroelectric production from the basin would benefit several hundred thousand people in state B. Power obtained from other resources would cost much more.

The following factors, based on Article V would appear relevant: (1) an existing reasonable use; (2) the relative dependence on the waters; (3) the population; (4) the climatic and weather conditions; (5) alternative sources of food in state B; (6) inefficient utilization of water in state B; and (7) the financial status of the two co-basin states.

An analysis of this situation would probably show that although state A has an existing reasonable use, irrigation, the other competing factors militate for some modification of that use. State A has other sources of food and is using an antiquated method of irrigation which could be replaced with a system that wastes less of the basin's water. This replacement would be within state A's economic capacity. The potential use of the water for hydroelectric purposes is very valuable. A balancing here of all the factors would lead to a conclusion that modification of A's utilization and accommodation of state B's is desirable.

Reconciliation of the problem between states A and B would seem to lie in state A either changing its system of irrigation for a more water-efficient method, using alternate food supplies, using its underground water, or any combination of all of these options. However, state B might be required to help bear the costs involved in developing, for example, the new system of irrigation, or alternative food supplies. Compensation might be required should state A have to abandon any permanent installations or parts thereof.

If no combination of the above suggested solutions is agreeable to both states, then one of the uses, existing irrigation or new hydroelectric power will prevail with the other use being impaired or stopped. At that juncture, the state deprived of its use would undoubtedly seek compensation. Basin states therefore must share the waters equitably. * * *

Notes and Questions

1. **Common Interest.** The equitable utilization principle is an excellent example of the recognition of common interest in a shared resource. The international concern with fresh water pollution resulted in the inclusion of Articles IXBXI in the International Law Association's Helsinki Rules, reproduced in the Documentary Supplement. The definition of "water pollution" contained in Article IX is very broad and should be contrasted with Principle 6 of the 1972 Stockholm Declaration. (Lipper, Equitable Utilization, in Garretson et al., The Law of International Drainage Basins, 15 (1967), Handl, Balancing of Interests and International Liability for the Pollution of International Watercourses: Customary Principles of Law Revisited, 13 Can. Yb. Int'l L. 156 (1975), and Benvenisti, Collective Action in the Utilization of Shared Freshwater: The Challenges of International Water Resources Law, 90 AJIL 384 (1996).)

2. **Harmon Doctrine.** This is the most extreme view of plenary jurisdiction. Stemming from a dispute in 1895 over the right of the United States to divert water from the Upper Rio Grande, at a point where that river was completely within United States territory, the doctrine was named after

U.S. Attorney General Judson Harmon who in a legal opinion to the Secretary of State of the United States, 21 Op.Att'y Gen. 274, 281 (1895), stated that absolute sovereignty within its territory is a fundamental principle of international law. The International Law Association took the view in 1966 that this doctrine, as it pertained to international rivers, had never had a wide acceptance. (See Austin, Canadian–United States Practice and Theory Respecting the International Law of International Rivers: A Study of the History and Influence of the Harmon Doctrine, 37 Can. Bar Rev. 393 (1959)).

3. ***Canada–United States Great Lakes Cooperation.*** The Great Lakes system had become extremely polluted by 1970 from many sources including industrial and urban usages and maritime vessel wastes. A study and report that revealed this convincingly was produced by the International Joint Commission (IJC), a body set up in 1909 by the Boundary Waters Treaty, U.S.T.S. 548, between the United States and Great Britain, on behalf of Canada, for the purpose of helping the settlement of and preventing disputes over the use of boundary waters. Article IV of the 1909 Treaty declares that the boundary waters "shall not be polluted on either side to the injury of health or property on the other". It did not, however, give to the IJC a specific mandate with respect to pollution. Over the years, the IJC has assisted in resolving mostly navigation and water diversion matters, but it seems that its major impact was the Report on the polluted state of Lakes Erie and Ontario, as well as the international section of the St. Lawrence River. This led to the 1978 Canada-United States Great Lakes Water Quality Agreement, 30 U.S.T.S., TIAS 9257, which superceded the earlier 1972 Agreement. This does not abrogate Article IV of the 1909 Treaty, but rather supplements it. The Agreement seeks to provide for more effective cooperative actions to restore and enhance water quality in the Great Lakes basin ecosystem, by adopting common objectives and implementing cooperative programs and measures. The purpose, as laid out in Article II is to restore and maintain through a maximum effort, the chemical, physical and biological integrity of the waters of the basin. Key to this Agreement and the manner in which it supercedes the previous 1972 Agreement is that it is not only dealing with the boundary waters within the Great Lakes system itself, but also with the elimination or reduction of the discharge of pollutants into the basin ecosystem. Article I(g) defines this ecosystem as "the interacting components of air, land, water and living organisms, including man, within the drainage basin of the St. Lawrence River at or upstream from the point at which this river becomes the international boundary between Canada and the United States". The IJC under Article VII shall assist, *inter alia,* in the implementation of the Agreement through collation, analysis and dissemination of data, tendering of advice and recommendations to the parties and their component states and provinces, coordination of joint activities and such investigations as the parties may refer to it. In discharging these responsibilities the IJC may under the powers given to it in the Agreement and by domestic legislation passed pursuant thereto conduct public hearings and compel the testimony of witnesses and the production of documents. (See S.A. Williams, Public International Law and Water Quantity Management in a Common Drainage Basin: The Great Lakes, 18 Case W.Res.J.Int.L. 155 (1986); E. Brown

Weiss, New Directions for the Great Lakes Water Quality Agreement: A Commentary, 65 Chic.-Kent L. Rev. 375 (1989)).

In 1985 the Great Lakes states and the Canadian provinces of Ontario and Quebec signed the Great Lakes Charter. This provides for ongoing consultation and management of the Great Lakes ecosystem. As the component entities of both federal states do not have treaty-making capacity, what status does this "Charter" have? (See Great Lakes Governors Task Force on Water Diversion and Great Lakes Institutions, Final Report and Recommendations–A Report to the Governors and Premiers of the Great Lakes States and Provinces (1985)). Note also that in 1994 an Agreement Respecting the Great Lakes Basin Ecosystem was reached between Canada and Ontario that focuses on implementation.

4. ***The Global Environmental Monitoring System.*** Global deterioration of water quality and quantity has been pinpointed as the key to sustainable development in the twenty-first century, for more than a third of the developing countries. The Water Quality Program of the Global Environmental Monitoring System (GEMS), a U.N. program coordinated by UNEP and the central part of the U.N.'s Earthwatch program, is the first international program to address global freshwater quality issues using a worldwide network of monitoring stations of surface and ground-water. GEMS/Water has 57 participating countries. It played the pivotal role in developing the freshwater chapter of Agenda 21.

Water Quantity

In emphasizing the problems of pollution, water quantity issues cannot be overlooked. The Great Lakes basin is a case on point, being the largest single fresh water resource in the world shared by Canada and the United States. Questions are raised concerning diversion of some of the water out of the basin to help solve drought problems in the west.

Sharon A. Williams, Public International Law and Water Quantity Management in a Common Drainage Basin: The Great Lakes Basin

18 Case Western Reserve Journal of International Law 155, 178–179 (1986)*

The Boundary Waters Treaty of 1909 signed by Great Britain (on behalf of Canada) and the United States is still the most important bilateral treaty on the subject of management of the shared fresh water resource between the two states today.

The preamble to the Treaty details its purpose as being:

[t]o prevent disputes regarding the use of boundary waters and to settle all questions which are now pending between the United States and the Dominion of Canada involving the rights, obligations, or interests of either in relation to the other or to the inhabitants of the other, along their common frontier, and to make provision for the

* Reprinted with the permission of Case West.J.Int'l L.

adjustment and settlement of all such questions as may hereafter arise
* * *.

The preliminary article defines boundary waters as the waters that
stretch from main shore to main shore of the lakes, rivers and connecting
waterways through which the international boundary passes. It does not
include tributary waters which "in their natural channels would flow into
such lakes, rivers or waterways * * *" or waters flowing from such. The
Treaty provides in Article II that the purpose enunciated in the preamble
was to be achieved by granting parties injured by one state's use or
diversion of the tributary waters the same legal remedies as if the injury
took place in the country where such diversion or use occurred. Secondly,
the Treaty sets up a joint commission, known as the International Joint
Commission, with the requirement that the Commission give approval
before uses, obstructions or diversions, temporary or permanent, of boundary waters that affect the natural level or flow of the waters take place. The
International Joint Commission was given the power to examine, report
and make recommendations.

Under Articles III and IV the International Joint Commission has a
quasi-judicial role in that it may approve or disapprove of any use, obstruc-
tion or diversion of boundary waters or waters that flow from boundary
waters or in waters at a lower level than the boundary in rivers that flow
across the boundary, if such would have the effect of raising the water level
on the other side of the boundary, unless agreed to by the states' parties.

Conditions of approval may be imposed. Such a condition could be, for
example, that injured parties be compensated.

Under Article IX the Commission has an investigative and advisory
role. It may examine and report on any questions that are referred to it by
either the United States or Canada. It may then follow up with conclusions
and recommendations. Although, the two states could act alone in referring
a matter to the Commission, this has not occurred in practice. The reports
made are not considered "as decisions of the questions or matters so
submitted either on the facts or the law, and shall in no way have the
character of an arbitral award." Where both parties consent, the Commission may act as an arbitration panel with a binding power of decision.

The Commission is given the authority by Article XII to employ
technical staff, such as engineers and clerical assistants, to conduct open
hearings, take evidence on oath, compel the attendance of witnesses and
adopt rules of procedure that are in accordance with justice and equity.

Trends before the Commission indicate that although originally the
majority of its cases concerned approval under Article III and Article IV, in
recent years it has been dealing with references under Article IX.

The Commission takes note of Canadian and United States statutes
but has never considered itself bound by them. It has not applied the
doctrine of stare decisis.

The Commission has had success in the area of adjudication and
advisory opinions. However, it does have some drawbacks, notably that it is

confined by the 1909 Treaty itself and by the appointment of its Commissioners by the two governments. The United States and Canada can limit the references made to the Commission. Having said this, practice seems to show that the Commissioners have handled matters with neutrality * * *.

This being said, it must be realized that in the context of a proposed large scale water diversion into or out of the Great Lakes, the national ties of the six Commissioners might well come to the fore. Should either state propose such a project and the other strenuously object, it would remain to be seen whether the International Joint Commission is as impartial as its record appears to indicate.

7.   THE MARINE ENVIRONMENT

Marine pollution has caused great concern for several decades. Under the auspices of the International Maritime Organization (IMO), formerly called the International Maritime Consultative Organization (IMCO), the United Nations Environmental Program (UNEP) and regional organizations, many conventions have been adopted dealing with, *inter alia*, design and construction of ships, oil pollution damage, a compensation fund and the dumping of wastes at sea. See, the 1954 International Convention for the Prevention of Pollution of the Sea by Oil (OILPOL) 12 U.S.T.S. 2989; TIAS 4900; the 1973 International Convention for the Prevention of Pollution from Ships (MARPOL), 12 ILM 1319 (1973) and 17 ILM 546 (1979); the 1990 International Convention on Oil Pollution Readiness, Response and Cooperation, 30 ILM 735 (1991); the 1969 Convention on Civil Liability for Oil Pollution Damage, 9 ILM 45 (1970); 1976 Protocol, 16 ILM 617 (1977), 1984 Protocol, Misc. No. 8 (1986), Cmnd. 9927 and 1992 Protocol, IMO Doc. LEG/CONF. 9/15 (1992); the 1971 International Convention on the Establishment of a Fund for Compensation for Oil Pollution Damage, 11 ILM 284 (1972), 1976 Protocol, 16 ILM 621, 1984 Protocol, 23 ILM 195 (1984) and 1992 Protocol, IMO Doc. LEG/CONF. 9/16 (1992); the 1976 London Convention on Civil Liability for Oil Pollution Damage Resulting From Exploration for and Exploitation of Seabed Mineral Resources, 16 ILM 1450 (1977), and the 1972 Convention on the Prevention of Marine Pollution by Dumping of Wastes and Other Matter, 26 U.S.T.S. 2403, TIAS 8165, 11 ILM 1291 (1972). Intervention Against Maritime Casualties is provided for in the 1969 Convention Relating to Intervention on the High Seas in Cases of Oil Pollution Casualties, 26 U.S.T. 765, T.I.A.S. No. 8068, 9 ILM 25 (1970) and the Protocol Relating to Intervention on the High Seas in Cases of Pollution by Substances Other Than Oil, TIAS 10561, 13 ILM 605 (1974).

Regional agreements dealing with the maritime environment include the 1974 Helsinki Convention on the Protection of the Marine Environment of the Baltic Sea Area, 13 ILM 546 (1974); the 1976 Barcelona Convention for the Protection of the Mediterranean Sea Against Pollution and its Protocols of 1976 and 1980, 15 ILM 290, 300 and 306 (1976), and 19 ILM 869 (1980); the 1978 Kuwait Regional Convention for Cooperation on the Protection of the Marine Environment from Pollution and Protocol, 17

ILM 511 and 526; the 1981 Abidjan Convention for Cooperation in the Protection and Development of the Marine and Coastal Environment of the West and Central African Region and Protocol, 20 ILM 746 and 756 (1981); the 1983 Cartenega Convention for the Protection and Development of the Marine Environment of the Wider Caribbean Region and Its Protocols, TIAS 11085, 22 ILM 227 and 240 (1983) and the 1986 Noumea Convention for the Protection of the National Resources and Environment of the South Pacific Region and Protocols, 26 ILM 38 and 58 (1987). The most recent agreement, the 1992 Paris Convention for the Protection of the Marine Environment of the North–East Atlantic, 32 ILM 1072 (1993), seeks to coordinate protection of the North–East Atlantic. Until it comes into force the 1972 Oslo Convention for the Prevention of Marine Pollution by Dumping from Ships and Aircraft, 11 ILM 262 (1972) and the 1974 Paris Convention for the Prevention of Marine Pollution from Land Based Sources and Protocol, 13 ILM 352 (1974), 27 ILM 625 (1988), remain in force. The 1992 Bucharest Convention on the Protection of the Black Sea Against Pollution and Its Protocols on Protection of the Black Sea Marine Environment Against Pollution from Land Based Sources, on Cooperation in Combatting Pollution of the Black Sea Environment by Oil and Other Harmful Substances in Emergency Situations and on the Protection of the Black Sea Marine Environment Against Pollution By Dumping, is not yet in force, 32 ILM 1110, 1122, 1127 and 1129 (1993).

The efficacy of the above Conventions has been frustrated to a great extent by lack of ratification and lack of consequent necessary domestic implementation. Enforcement mechanisms are also missing. At the 1992 United Nations Conference on Environment and Development in Rio de Janeiro emphasis was laid on the crucial need for such full participation.

The 1982 United Nations Convention on the Law of the Sea

Sharon A. Williams and A.L.C. De Mestral, An Introduction to International Law

280–281 (2nd ed. 1987).*

The most ambitious attempt to protect the marine environment is to be found in the provisions of the 1982 Convention on the Law of the Sea. At the onset of negotiations, Canada, among other states, in a working paper presented to the Seabed Committee [U.N.Doc. A/AC 138/S.C. III/L. 26, August 18, 1972, 733] and Draft Articles [U.N.Doc. A/AC 138/S. III/L. 28, March 8, 1973, 762] called for treaty provisions which would provide a comprehensive framework for the conclusion of a complete network of treaties dealing with all aspects of marine pollution. This approach is reflected in the 1982 Convention, Part XII which [now that it is in force, since November 1994] will have the effect of committing all states parties

* Published by Butterworths Canada, Ltd., reprinted with their permission.

to taking measures, nationally and internationally, to prevent pollution from the principal sources of marine pollution: land, sea, continental shelf and atmospheric. States parties will be under an obligation to conclude international conventions dealing with the different manifestations of pollution of the marine environment or to take measures at least as effective as "generally accepted international standards". Failure to live up to such minimum international standards will constitute a violation of the Law of the Sea Convention and in appropriate circumstances will give rise to state responsibility.

The Convention contains general provisions committing states to protect the marine environment from pollution from all sources and prohibiting the transfer of pollution from one area to another. The text also provides for global and regional cooperation, notification of other states in the event of imminent or actual damage, the preparation of joint contingency plans, environmental monitoring and assessment of data, and technical assistance. The subsequent articles will have the effect of committing states to develop national and international rules on pollution from land-based sources, seabed activities, and ocean dumping. Complementary articles deal with enforcement of these rules. Articles 211 and 217 to 236 deal with pollution caused by ships. Traditional flag state obligations are somewhat strengthened. Most noteworthy are the new rules allowing limited jurisdiction to "coastal" and "port" states to enforce international rules and standards against foreign ships in strictly defined circumstances. Of great interest to Canada is article 234 allowing coastal states broad jurisdiction to adopt and enforce their own rules for the prevention, reduction and control of marine pollution from ships in "ice-covered areas" within the limits of the exclusive economic zone. This authority shall have due regard to navigation.

Perhaps the most significant development of the Convention is the duty set out in article 194(2) not to "cause damage by pollution to other states and their environment" which, coupled with article 235 on liability and responsibility, will make states liable for damages attributable to natural or juridical persons under their jurisdiction and responsible to ensure prompt and adequate recourse against persons under their jurisdiction who cause pollution affecting other states or their nationals. Failure to respect this obligation or other international treaty obligations will make the state responsible liable to compensate the injured party. States' parties are obligated to cooperate also in the development of criteria and procedures for payment of adequate compensation, such as compulsory insurance or compensation funds. It remains to be seen whether this approach to state responsibility and liability for pollution damage will be adopted more generally in international environmental law for other forms of pollution damage. Evidence that the 1982 Convention may afford a model for other areas can be seen in the work of U.N.E.P. on shared natural resources and the even more recent work of the U.N.E.P. Committee on International Environmental Law. It is also noteworthy that the Convention is already complemented by a number of important regional conventions dealing with pollution of the marine environment.

F. Orrego Vicuña, State Responsibility, Liability, and Remedial Measures Under International Law: New Criteria for Environmental Protection

in E. Brown Weiss (ed.), Environmental Change and International Law, 124, 144–147 (1992).*

The 1982 Convention on the Law of the Sea and related treaties have significantly developed the rules of international law applicable to the preservation of the marine environment and illustrate the evolution of state responsibility. In point of fact, states are under the obligation to ensure that activities under their jurisdiction or control "are so conducted as not to cause damage by pollution to other States and their environment" and that any pollution arising from such activities "does not spread beyond the areas where they exercise sovereign rights." The activities included in this obligation are those undertaken both by the state and by entities of a private nature under state jurisdiction and control. It is also quite apparent that this provision covers not only transboundary effects of pollution but also harm to areas beyond national jurisdiction. In other words, the global scale of environmental effects is incorporated into this particular regime.

This regime encompasses all sources of pollution, a further indication of the broadening concern and scope of international law. In addition, a broad definition of pollution of the marine environment is included in this and other treaty regimes as an expression of the very same concern. Important IMO and related conventions have developed a well-structured normative regime dealing with specific questions of marine pollution particularly in terms of oil pollution, discharge and dumping of waste, and safety at sea.

In light of this more advanced regime, it follows quite naturally that international law has accepted holding a state responsible for pollution injuries resulting from a violation of its obligations in this field. Although the primary obligation to enforce the law is bestowed upon the flag state of the ships concerned, other states are not prevented from taking the necessary preventive or remedial actions. In addition to the powers allocated to the coastal state and the port state in given instances, there is the most important right of intervention on the high seas, which is ultimately related to a measure of self-help under international law. The obligation to notify is also prominent in this field. These developments of course do not prejudice the rules dealing specifically with issues such as the environmental consequences of seabed-mining operations, cooperation in emergencies, or the protection of fragile ecosystems.

Remedial measures have also evolved significantly in the area of the law of the sea. In addition to recourse to the general remedies provided for under international law, coastal and port states can participate actively by detaining and investigating ships and by instituting proceedings.

———

Notes and Questions

1. *The 1982 Law of the Sea Convention.* This Convention which entered into force on November 14, 1994 and is reproduced in the Documentary Supplement, was the product of the Third U.N. Law of the Sea Conference (UNCLOS III). Part XII, dealing with the protection and preservation of the marine environment seeks to balance the interests of coastal states and flag states. National jurisdiction to control is moderated by the reference to "generally accepted international law rules". (See generally Timagenis, International Control of Pollution (1980), Sand, Marine Environmental Law in the U.N. Environmental Program: An Emergent Eco–Regime (1989) and The International Law Association's Committee on Coastal State Jurisdiction Relating to Maritime Pollution, The International Law Association, Report of the 69th Conference, 2000, 443, 448–512.).

2. *Ice covered areas.* Article 234 of the 1982 Law of the Sea Convention that gives coastal states extensive jurisdiction over such areas is of special importance to states such as Canada which border the extensive ecologically fragile Arctic. Do you think that this Article affirms the unilateral action taken by Canada when it enacted in 1970 the Arctic Waters Pollution Prevention Act, R.S.C. 1985, c. AB12, whereby it provided for regulation of shipping within one hundred nautical miles of land into the Arctic? The United States strongly protested against this legislation. Note that in 1988 Canada and the United States entered into an Agreement on Cooperation in the Arctic, 1988 Can.T.S. No. 29, T.I.A.S. 11565 in which they agreed to seek permission of the other before sending icebreaking ships into the Arctic areas under their respective territorial jurisdictions. (*See* Bilder, The Canadian Arctic Waters Pollution Prevention Act: New Stresses on the Law of the Sea, 69 Mich.L.Rev. 1 (1970–71) and Henkin, Anti–Pollution: Does Canada Make or Break International Laws? 65 AJIL 131 (1971)). It is interesting to observe more recent action concerning Arctic environmental protection, in the form of official meetings between the eight Arctic states, Canada, Denmark, Finland, Iceland, Norway, Sweden, the former U.S.S.R. and the United States. With the assistance of observers from other governments, as well as international governmental and non-governmental organizations, in 1991 an Arctic Environmental Protection Strategy was developed. The Arctic states are committed to international cooperation to ensure environmental protection in the region and its sustainable and equitable development, while protecting the cultures of indigenous peoples. *See* 30 ILM 1624 (1991). See 35 ILM 1386 (1996) for the establishment of the Arctic Council. (See Rothwell, International Law and the Protection of the Arctic Environment, 44 Int. & Comp. L.Q. (1995) and The Arctic Environmental Protection Strategy and International Environmental Cooperation in the Far North, 5 Yr Bk Int'l Env. L 65 (1995). Note also the Report of the International Law Association's Committee on Coastal State Jurisdiction Relating to Marine Pollution, *supra*, 468–473.)

Note the Convention on the Regulation of Antarctic Mineral Resource Activities, 27 ILM 868 (1988), especially Article 4 that provides that mineral resource activity is pre-conditioned by a judgment that it is environmentally safe and also the 1959 Antarctica Treaty, 19 ILM 860

(1980) and the 1991 Protocol on Environmental Protection to the Antarctic Treaty, 30 ILM 1455 (1991). (See Pineschi, The Antarctic Treaty System and General Rules of International Environmental law, in Francioni and Scovazzi (eds.) International Law of Antarctica, 187 (1987) and Watts, International Law and the Antarctic Treaty System (1992).)

8. THE WORLD CULTURAL AND NATURAL HERITAGE

Sharon A. Williams, The International and National Protection of Cultural Property: a Comparative Study
173–174 (1978).*

The 1972 UNESCO Convention [for the Protection of the World Cultural and Natural Heritage, 1976 Can. T. S. No. 45, 11 Int'l Leg.Mat. 1358 (1972), which entered into force on December 17, 1975, and is reproduced in the Documentary Supplement] * * * reiterates the concept that parts of the cultural heritage are of outstanding interest and therefore need to be preserved as part of the "world heritage of mankind as a whole". It is stated that in view of the magnitude and gravity of the dangers caused to the world cultural and natural heritage, by traditional decay as well as the new dangers of the changing social and economic conditions which aggravate the situation with a more formidable phenomenon of damage and destruction, it is incumbent upon the international community as a whole to participate in the protection of the cultural and natural heritage of outstanding value, by the granting of collective assistance, which will serve as a complement to the action taken by the states concerned. * * * Whilst the parties fully respect the sovereignty of the states on whose territory the cultural and natural heritage is situated, and without prejudice to property rights provided by national legislation, they recognize that such heritage constitutes a world heritage for whose protection it is the duty of the international community as a whole to co-operate. For the purpose of the Convention, the term international protection is to be understood to mean the establishment of a system of international co-operation and assistance designed to support states in their efforts to conserve and identify their heritage. The Convention establishes an Intergovernmental Committee [World Heritage Committee] to ensure proper functioning of the terms of the Convention and "World Heritage Fund" whose purpose is to support the protection of the world cultural and natural heritage of outstanding value.

Note

1. *World Heritage List.* The 1972 Convention, which Canada and the United States are parties to, 27 U.N.T.S. 37; T.I.A.S. 8226, also sets up a World Heritage List. Under Article 11(1), it is provided that every state party shall submit to the World Heritage Committee an inventory of property forming part of the natural and cultural heritage, situated in its

---

* Reprinted with the permission of Sharon A. Williams.

territory and suitable for inclusion in the list. The United States has listed, for example, the Grand Canyon. Canada has listed several sites including the Rocky mountain and Gros Morne National parks. It is further provided in Article 11(4) that the Committee shall establish and keep up to date a List of World Heritage in Danger. This list may only contain property forming the part of the cultural and natural heritage that is threatened by, *inter alia,* serious and specific dangers, such as the threat of disappearance caused by accelerated deterioration, large-scale public or private projects or rapid urban or tourist development projects; destruction caused by changes in the use or ownership of land; the outbreak of or the threat of armed conflict and other calamities, serious fires, earthquakes, landslides, floods and so on.

2. ***Obligations under the 1972 UNESCO Convention.*** In *Commonwealth of Australia* v. *State of Tasmania* (1983), 46 A.L.R. 625 (H.C.) it was held that Articles 4 and 5 of the 1972 Convention imposed legal obligations upon Australia to protect a World Heritage listed site, the listed wilderness parks in Tasmania. See also *State of Queensland* v. *Commonwealth of Australia* (1989), 86 A.L.R. 519 and *Richardson* v. *Forestry Commission* (1988), 164 C.L.R. 261.

9.   PROTECTION OF WETLANDS

A. Kiss and D. Shelton, International Environmental Law

249 (1991).*

* * * *The Convention on Wetlands of International Importance* was the first treaty based on the idea that the habitat of endangered species should be the focus of protection. One of the first major conservation treaties, it is relatively simple in its structure. It is based on recognition that wetlands are among the most productive sources of ecological support on earth, acting as habitat for myriad species and as flood control regions.

The preamble affirms that wetlands constitute a resource of great economic, cultural, scientific and recreational value, the loss of which would be irreparable. Wetlands are defined in Article 1 as being areas of marsh, fen, peatland or water, whether natural or artificial, permanent or temporary, with water that is static or flowing, fresh, brackish or salt, including areas of marine water whose depth does not exceed six meters at low tide. Waterfowl, whose protection was the purpose of this convention, are defined as birds ecologically dependent on wetlands.

The original objective of the Convention was to protect the habitat of waterfowl. However, its importance has outstripped that objective as the ecological importance of wetlands has become recognized, particularly their role in supporting marine life. Unfortunately, during recent decades drain-

* Reprinted with the permission of Transnational Publishers, Inc.

age operations and drought, as well as landfill, have considerably reduced the extent of wetlands.

————

Note: Refer to the Convention on Wetlands of International Importance (RAMSAR Convention) that entered into force on December 21, 1975, in the Documentary Supplement. A Protocol to the Convention was adopted in 1982. See Can T. S. No. 46 (1986). See Lyster, International Wildlife Law (1985), Navid, The International Law of Migratory Species: The RAMSAR Convention, 29 Nat. Res. J. 1001 (1989) and Bowman, The RAMSAR Convention Comes of Age, 42 Neth. Int'l L. Rev. (1995).

10.   PROTECTION OF FORESTS

The 1992 United Nations Conference on Environment and Development at Rio adopted a non-binding statement of principles on the protection of forests. In the lead-up time to the 1992 Rio Conference the possibility of adoption of a convention at the conference on point was rejected. See the Resulting Statement of Principles for a Global Consensus on the Management, Conservation and Sustainable Development of All Types of Forests, UN Doc. A/CONF. 151/6/Rev. 1; 31 ILM 818 (1992), reproduced in the Documentary Supplement. (See also Shally, Forests: Toward an International Legal Regime, 4 Yr Bk Int'l Env. L. 30 (1993). Note that the Convention on Biological Diversity and the World Heritage Convention contained in the Documentary Supplement also have application to forest preservation. Further, the Climate Change Convention and the 1997 Kyoto Protocol in the Documentary Supplement should be reviewed as forests act as carbon sinks. See in particular article 3(3) of the Kyoto Protocol.

Earth Summit in Focus

No. 5, February 1992, U.N. Department of Public Information, DP1/1198–92173.

Saving the Forests:

Forging a Global Compact

* * *

The divergence of views on the forestry issue is not surprising. Trees mean different things to different people.

* * *

Developing countries in particular—desperate to provide basic necessities for their people and to earn foreign exchange to pay their debts—are under great economic pressure to exploit or clear their forests. They are also under increasing pressure from environmentalists and Northern Governments to preserve tropical forests, both as wildlife habitats and to counter global warming.

But developing countries question why they should bear the economic burden for solving a problem created largely by pollution in the North:

most greenhouse gases are caused by the burning of fossil fuels in industrialized countries.

These conflicting views, especially those between the Northern industrialized nations and Southern developing countries, surfaced clearly during early preparations for the Earth Summit. The North's focus on tropical forests has been met with the South's requirement that the global forest—including that which has been cut in the North in the past—be considered.

* * *

The value of forests [is often] described in narrow economic terms, as an exploitable resource. However, in recent years a wider view has emerged of the varied functions forests serve, many of which have far-reaching economic and social implications. Increasingly, forests are seen:

- as homes for indigenous peoples.

- as "sinks" for converting carbon dioxide through photosynthesis into the oxygen needed to keep us alive.

- as protection for watersheds. Forests help prevent avalanches, floods, landslides and mud-flows, and protect hydroelectric power plants, irrigation and municipal water supplies.

- as wildlife habitats for a rich diversity of species of plant, animal and insect life. Tropical forests are believed to be home to more than half the species on earth, including medicinal plants and food crops. Fallen leaves are a primary source of humus, the topsoil which sustains plant life.

- as key players in maintaining crucial ecological balances, such as the annual cycle of sediments and flood water needed for the production of rice to feed hundreds of millions of people.

- as recreation areas.

- as fuel used daily by some two billion people in developing countries. Half the annual forest harvest is for fuel. Where forests are degraded, women must walk farther to find cooking fuel; but in some areas, there is no wood at all. By 2000, the fuel-wood deficit could reach 960 million cubic metres a year, the energy equivalent of $30 billion worth of oil annually.

* * *

Today's situation is made urgent by the rate at which forests are being lost, the increased burning of fossil fuels and the contribution of forest-burning to climate change.

* * *

While forests are diminishing at an alarming rate, the use of fossil fuels stands to increase dramatically—a combination projected to accelerate global warming and other climate change. Industrialized nations are currently the primary source of air pollution from the use of fossil fuels, but it is expected that the rate of energy consumption in some developing nations will be twice that of industrialized nations from now to the year 2000.

Every country consumes energy at a faster rate at the beginning of its industrial growth than it does in later stages. Peoples in developing countries seek to raise their standard of living and own the same appliances and automobiles enjoyed by peoples in the North. Unless they are technically and financially assisted to use fuels more efficiently and to make a transition to alternative, "environmentally cleaner" technologies, they will not be able to avoid creating the same pollution—on a far more massive scale—than has been produced by countries in the industrialized world.

The effects of forest burning also are directly linked to global warming. The Earth's forests store 450 billion metric tons of carbon, much of it gathered from carbon dioxide found in air pollution. When burned, forests release carbon dioxide. Forest burning is the second largest source of greenhouse gases, after the use of fossil fuels.

* * *

To sustain the forests while maintaining economic development, people will have to change the way they view forests. Experts point to three phases: in the first, the forest is viewed as an unlimited resource. Its destruction may be promoted by encouraging agricultural expansion. In the second phase, destruction of the forest may cause concern that leads to the institution of controls. In the third phase, attempts are made to re-create the forest.

* * *

Now, although deforestation rates are soaring, satellites and other technology make it possible to inventory and plan for reforestation projects on a regional and global scale. Regional and international organizations and businesses are playing an expanded role. * * *

Many nations are now taking steps to change destructive practices. Parts of Scandinavia, Canada and the former USSR are carrying out sustainable management practices. More than 60 countries have agreed to prepare national forestry programmes under the Tropical Forestry Action Plan, launched in 1985 by FAO. Logging in the tropics has not traditionally had sustainability as a goal. Typically, only 10 to 20 per cent of the trees are harvested, but up to half are destroyed in the logging process. The soil is so disturbed that the forest does not regenerate and becomes degraded. Simply changing logging techniques would be a significant step.

Although plantation forests can play an important role, many species will need protected native habitats if they are to survive. The setting aside of selected forests is already under way. Recently, Bolivia has launched a five-year ecological moratorium, temporarily suspending logging concessions. Guyana has set aside 360,000 hectares of tropical forest for conservation and research. India and Viet Nam have launched conservation efforts.

Public policy and trade are also being used as tools to encourage sustainable forestry practices. Brazil has modified its incentives for cattle ranching, which encouraged clearing the Amazon. Germany, the United Kingdom and the Netherlands have placed special restrictions and controls on the use and imports of tropical timber, although such regulations have been sharply criticized by some developing countries as unfair trade practices.

* * *

Governments and a variety of local and international organizations have identified sustainable forestry practices as a priority. The process of understanding the problem, establishing plans to fix it and finding the resources to apply to the task has at least begun. * * *

1. ***The International Tropical Timber Agreement***. The objectives of the ITTA are the promotion of the management of tropical forests on a sustainable basis and to provide a framework for cooperation between producing and consumer states. The International Tropical Timber Organization set up under the Agreement, with its Secretariat in Japan has as one of its prime objectives the expansion of forest estates in producer countries that are almost all developing states to produce timber for processing *in situ* rather than exporting the timber as a raw material. See UNCTAD, Doc.TO/TIMBER/II, Geneva, November 18, 1983.

2. ***The Intergovernmental Panel on Forests.*** The IPF was set up in 1995 by the Commission on Sustainable Development. The IPF's mandate was to develop initiatives on conservation and sustainable development of Forests. It produced its final report to the Commission in 1997. However, there was no agreement on a multilateral forest treaty at that time. In 1997 the International Forum on forests was established at a special session of the U.N. General Assembly. See ECOSOC res. 1997/65, 42nd Plenary Meeting, July 25, 1997. The International Forum will consider implementation of the IPF's proposals and the issue of a treaty. It will report to the Commission in 2000. (See, L. Reif, Environmental Policy: The Rio Summit Five Years later, in F. Hampson and M. Molot (eds), Canada Among Nations 1998: Leadership and Dialogue, 267 (1998).

11. DESERTIFICATION

Desertification is a matter of urgent concern in those states experiencing serious drought. The 1994 United Nations Convention to Combat Desertification in those countries experiencing serious drought and or deforestation, particularly in Africa, 33 ILM 1328 (1994), reproduced in the Documentary Supplement, has sought to deal with this acute problem. (See Burns, The International Convention to Combat Desertification: Drawing a Line in the Sand? 16 Mich. Int'l L. J. 831 (1995); Iles, The Desertification Convention: A Deeper Focus on Social Aspects of Environmental Degradation? 36 Harv. Int. L. J. 207 (1995).) The objective laid down in Article 2(1) is to combat desertification and mitigate the effects of drought, particularly in Africa, while not neglecting other developing countries in other regions that are similarly affected, through effective action at all levels and supported by international cooperation. It seeks an integrated strategy, supported by international cooperation and partnership agreements consistent with Agenda 21. The view is to achieve sustainable development in those areas affected. As Articles 2(2) and 4(1) and (2) indicate the attainment of this objective will involve long term strategies that focus at the same time on improvements in the productivity of land and the rehabilitation, conservation and sustainable management of resources leading to improved living conditions. Article 5 lays out the obligations of affected country parties. These include giving due priority to combating the problem of desertification and mitigating the effects of drought, allocating adequate resources in accordance with their circumstances and capabilities, addressing the underlying causes of desertification, paying special attention to the socio-economic factors that contribute to the desertification processes and promoting awareness and facilitating the participation of local populations, particularly women and youth with the support of NGOs.

12. ENDANGERED SPECIES

Kiss Shelton, International Environmental Law

257–258 (1991).*

* * * Unlike the prior conventions, the *Convention on International Trade in Endangered Species of Wild Fauna and Flora (CITES),* is not based on a spatial concept of protection, but on a given activity relating to wildlife: international trade. One of the most powerful motives for the exploitation of plant and animal species is income production, especially in poor countries lacking other major resources. Certain products derived from wildlife species, such as the rhinoceros horn, which is powdered for use as a medicine or stimulant, ivory, tortoise shell, and fur skins, can command high prices and attract hunters, traders and poachers. It is estimated that near the end of the 1960s, five to ten million crocodile skins were traded on the international market. In 1972, the record year, the exports of ivory from Kenya reached 150 tons. To counter trade in animals, plants and their derivatives, to eliminate this source of income, quotas or duties may be imposed. However, no measure of this type can be truly effective without international cooperation between exporting, transit, and importing states. The major framework in this regard is CITES, the most complete treaty at present on trade in endangered species, to which the majority of states in the world are parties.

———

Notes

1. *Lacunae in the Convention.* It is apparent from the 1973 Convention on International Trade in Endangered Species, 993 U.N.T.S. 243, 27 U.S.T.S. 1087; T.I.A.S. 8249, reproduced in the Documentary Supplement, that there are a number of exemptions from the imposed permit system, such as for what is called a "pre-Convention" specimen, and those that are categorized as "personal or household effects". The recent controversy over the trade in ivory is illustrative. In 1979 the African elephant was moved from Appendix II to Appendix I to stop the ivory trade that was killing great numbers of the animal. Some states parties to the Convention argued that ivory stockpiled in their states before their adherence to the Conven-

tion were "pre-Convention" specimens. The second gap that the elephant case indicates is that of the allowance of specific reservations to the Convention which both ivory-producing and consuming states used. Another problem is that the Convention only applies to species that fall within its Article I definition and thus does not go so far as to protect endangered species not being traded in, but in danger because of habitat destruction. (See Sands and Bedecarre, Convention on International Trade in Endangered Species: The Role of Public Interest Non-Governmental Organizations in Ensuring the Effective Enforcement of the Ivory Trade Ban, 17 Boston Coll.Env.Aff.L.Rev. 799 (1990) and Glenon, Has International Law Failed the Elephant, 84 Am.J.Int.L.1 (1990)). Concerning other species of concern see Crawford, Conflicts Between the Convention on International Trade in Endangered Species and the GATT in Light of Actions to Halt the Rhinoceros and Tiger Trade, 7 Georgetown Int. Env. L. Rev. 555 (1995) and Patel, The Convention on International Trade in Endangered Species: Enforcement and the Last Unicorn, 18 Houston J. Int. L. 157 (1995).

2. *Migratory species.* The Bonn Convention on the Conservation of Migratory Species of Wild Animals, 19 ILM 15 (1980) deals with the obligations of states whose territories are part of the range of such wild animals. Appendix I deals with wild animals in danger of extinction. Neither Canada nor the United States are parties to this Convention. Note also the 1931 Convention for the Regulation of Whaling, 3 Bevans 26, 155 L.N.T.S.; The 1946 International Convention for the Regulation of Whaling, 161 U.N.T.S. 72, and 1956 Protocol, 10 U.S.T.S. 952, 338 U.N.T.S. 366; The 1973 Agreement on the Conservation of Polar Bears, 27 U.S.T.S. 3918; T.I.A.S. 8409; The 1972 Convention for the Conservation of Antarctic Seals, 29 U.N.T.S. 441; T.I.A.S. 8826 and most recently in order to prevent the killing of dolphins and porpoises, The 1989 Convention for the Prohibition of Fishing with Long Driftnets in the South Pacific, which entered into force for the United States on February 28, 1992 and Protocols, 29 ILM 1453 (1990). (See Eldridge, Whale for Sale? New Developments in the Convention on International Trade in Endangered Species of Wild Fauna and Flora, 24 Ga J. Int. & Comp. L. 549 (1995) and van Heijnsbergen, International Legal Protection of Wild Fauna and Flora (1997).)

Canada and the United States have several bilateral treaties on point. They are firstly, the 1916 Convention for the Protection of Migratory Birds, 12 Bevans 375. This Convention does not protect the habitat of migratory birds, but addresses protection from killing and nest despoilation. Second, there is The 1987 Agreement on the Conservation of the Porcupine Caribou Herd with annex, T.I.A.S. 11259, which provides for conservation and habitat. It should be noted that this agreement recognizes the traditional rights of aboriginal peoples to harvest subject to the need to establish bilateral cooperative mechanisms to coordinate conservation. Third, there is an informal mechanism in the 1988 North American Waterfowl Management Plan for the protection of migratory species. (See Osterwoldt, Implementation and Enforcement Issues in the Protection of Migratory Species—Two Case Studies: Waterfowl in North America, Seals in Europe, 29 Nat.Res.J. 1017 (1989)).

3. ***Leghold Traps***. The use of leghold traps that clamp down on an animal's leg or other limb has been targeted by animal protection activist groups, particularly because of their use in Canada, the Russian Federation, and the United States. In 1991 the European Union Council adopted a regulation prohibiting this type of trap being used in its member states and further banned the importation into the EU of both fur and products made from animals caught in such leghold traps or by other means that did not meet humane standards. See EC Council Reg. No. 3254/91 of November 4, 1991 and other EC Commission Regulations in 37 ILM 532 (1998). The ban was to have taken effect on January 1, 1995 but was not activated while negotiations between the EU and involved states was taking place. An Agreement on International Humane Trapping Standards was signed by Canada and the EU on December 15, 1997 and by the Russian Federation and the EU on April 22, 1998. See 37 ILM 532, 542 (1998). These agreements commit the parties to specific obligations and provide for dispute settlement through arbitration. The United States signed an Agreed Minute and Side Letter Relating to Humane Trapping Standards with the EU on December 18, 1997. However, in contrast this is of a non-binding nature. The position of the United States is that authority to regulate traps and trapping methods resides primarily in the State and tribal authorities concerned. See 37 ILM 532, 556 (1998).

13.   BIOLOGICAL DIVERSITY

Refer to the 1992 Convention on Biological Diversity contained in the Documentary Supplement. No reservations may be made to this Convention, which was adopted in Nairobi, by the Intergovernmental Negotiating Committee in May 1992. It entered into force on December 29, 1993. The Conference of states parties has the mandate of overseeing and reviewing the implementation of the Convention. Montreal is the headquarters of the Biodiversity Secretariat. (See McConnell, The Biodiversity Convention: A Negotiating History (1996), Bowman and Redgwell (eds), International Law and the Conservation of Biological Diversity (1996) and Symposium, Biodiversity: Opportunities and Issues, 28 Vand. J. Trnnat'l L. (1995).)

American Society of International Law, Environmental Law Interest Group Newsletter

Vol. 3(1), 2 (1992).*

The Convention is directed at the conservation and sustainable use of biological diversity, the fair and equitable sharing of the benefits arising out [of] its utilization, and the regulation of biotechnology. The Convention stresses national measures to conserve biodiversity and does not require the development of international lists of threatened species and areas of biological importance, as some countries had urged. Under the Convention:

- Parties are required to develop national plans or programs for the conservation and sustainable use of biological diversity, and to integrate, as far as possible and as appropriate, the conservation and

* Reprinted with the permission of the
American Society of International Law.

sustainable use of biological diversity into their relevant sectoral and cross-sectoral plans, programs and policies.

- Access to and transfer of technology "shall be provided and/or facilitated under fair and favourable terms, including on concessional and preferential terms where mutually agreed." Patented technologies shall be transferred "on terms which recognize and are consistent with the adequate and effective protection of intellectual property rights." The Parties shall cooperate to ensure that intellectual property rights are "supportive of and do not run counter to" the Convention's objectives.

- Contracting Parties are required to take "all practicable measures to promote and advance [the source country's] priority access on a fair and equitable basis * * * to the results and benefits arising from biotechnologics based upon genetic resources provided by [it]." Access shall be on mutually agreed terms.

- Developed country Parties shall provide "new and additional financial resources to enable developing country Parties to meet the agreed full incremental costs * * * of implementing measures which fulfil the obligations" of the Convention and are agreed between a developing country Party and the Convention's financial mechanism.

- The financial mechanism shall operate under the "authority and guidance of, and be accountable to" the Conference of the Parties. Provided it has been "fully restructured," the GEF will serve as the financial mechanism on an interim basis, until the first meeting of the Conference of the Parties.

While many Western countries expressed reservations about the Convention, all but the US ended up signing. In declining to sign the Convention, the United States said that the text was "seriously flawed," and identified three areas of concern: the provision on intellectual property rights; the funding provisions, which the US said would establish a different role for the Global Environment Facility than agreed at the April GEF Participants Meeting * * * and the biotechnology provisions.

Frye, Uncle Sam and UNCED: A United States Perspective on the Earth Summit

International Newsletter of Committee F of the Section of Business Law of the International Bar Association 5 (1993).*

Biodiversity Convention

The Framework Convention on Biological Diversity is a good example of the competing interests of developed and developing nations. As *Newsweek* magazine commented: "While few delegates know a fungus from a mold, they do know the most important thing about biodiversity: the rich North needs, the poor South has it." Maintaining biodiversity, a wide range and assortment of plants, helps to provide protection against pests and disease and is vital for the breeding of improved crop varieties. Under the

---

* Reprinted with the permission of the International Bar Association.

terms of the Biodiversity Convention, its contracting parties agree to pursue "conservation of biological diversity, the sustainable use of its components and the fair and equitable sharing of the benefits arising out of the utilization of genetic resources * * *."

The U.S. refused to sign the Biodiversity Convention because of concern about its effect on intellectual property rights. Advocates of the Convention offer that, while it does call for transfer of technology to developing countries which provide genetic resources, it is only on mutually agreed terms. Critics of the Biodiversity Convention, however, suggest that the convention might have been acceptable to the United States had the staff "stuck to [the] subject of preserving species." Unsure how the Biodiversity Convention might affect their property rights, private biotechnology companies may elect to reduce investment in potentially affected businesses where they may later be required to surrender technology or pay royalties to other countries.

14. ENVIRONMENTAL PROTECTION AND INTERNATIONAL TRADE

The relationship between environmental protection and international trade is an issue of major debate. The liberalization of international trade exemplified by the General Agreement on Tariffs and Trade (GATT), 61 Stat. (5), (6), T.I.A.S. 1700, 4 Bevans 639, the 1987 Free Trade Agreement, between Canada and the United States with exchanges of letters, 27 ILM 293 (1988), and the 1992 North American Free Trade Agreement, between Canada, Mexico and the United States, 32 ILM 296 (1993) and the 1996 Canada–Chile Free Trade Agreement, 36 ILM 1079 (1997), envision this by providing that domestic measures intended to protect the environment must in turn comply with international trade law. If they fail, they may be classified as an unlawful restriction on trade. Note also the side agreement to the NAFTA on Environmental Cooperation, 32 ILM 1480 (1993) and the side agreement to the Canada–Chile Agreement on Environmental Cooperation, 36 ILM 1193 (1997). Refer also to the international implications of other conventions in this Chapter such as the Convention on the Trade in Endangered Species, the Basel Convention on the Control of Transboundary Movements of Hazards Wastes and their Disposal, The Montreal Convention on Substances that Deplete the Ozone Layer, all contained in the Documentary Supplement. On September 11, 1998 the Rotterdam Convention on the Prior Informed Consent Procedure for Certain Hazardous Chemicals and Pesticides in International Trade was adopted. (See Jackson, "World Trade Rules and Environmental Policies: Congruence or Conflict?" 49 Wash. Lee L. Rev. 1227 (1992), Thomas and Tereposky, The Evolving Relationship Between Trade and Environmental Regulation, 27 J. World Trade 23 (1993), Steinberg, Trade–Environment Negotiations in the EU, NAFTA and WTO, Schoenbaum, International Trade and Protection of the Environment: The Continuing Search for Reconciliation, 91 AJIL 268 (1997), Van Calster, International and EU Trade Law: The Environmental Challenge (2000), Reverz, Sands & Stewart, (eds) Environmental Law, The Economy and Sustainable Development (2000) and Bosselmann & Richardson, (eds) Environmental Justice and Market Mechanisms (1999)).

A key issue that has emerged has been whether international trade rules restrict states from taking measures to protect the environment. The decisions of the GATT panels and the WTO extracted below illustrate the dilemma. The question is whether a domestic measure taken as part of an environmental policy by a state is in reality for environmental protection or whether its actual purpose is protectionist and in effect a barrier to trade and in contravention of international trade law.

General Agreement on Tariffs and Trade: Dispute Settlement Panel Report on United States Restrictions on Imports of Tuna (Tuna I).

30 International Legal Materials 1594 (1991).*

[This case concerned the method of fishing for tuna in the Eastern Tropical Pacific Ocean (ETP), where purse-seine nets are used. In the ETP there has long been an association between dolphins and tuna. Schools of underwater tuna are found by chasing dolphins on the ocean surface and intentionally encircling them to catch the tuna underneath. This association between tuna and dolphins has not been observed elsewhere in the world. The United States Marine Mammal Protection Act, as amended in 1990 dealt with, *inter alia*, this situation and banned the importation of yellow fin tuna harvested with purse-seine nets in the ETP and products there from unless certain dolphin protection standards were met that would be in compliance with United States' standards imposed upon American fishing fleets. The United States Government imposed an embargo on imports of yellow fin tuna harvested with such nets in the ETP by Mexico. Mexico took this case to the GATT. The embargo also applied to "intermediary" states that had processed and canned the tuna.]

* * *

5. *FINDINGS*

A. *Introduction*

5.1.   The Panel noted that the issues before it arose essentially from the following facts: the Marine Mammal Protection Act (MMPA) regulates, *inter alia,* the harvesting of tuna by United States fishermen and others who are operating within the jurisdiction of the United States. The MMPA requires that such fishermen use certain fishing techniques to reduce the taking of dolphin incidental to the harvesting of fish. The United States authorities have licensed fishing of yellowfin tuna by United States vessels in the ETP on the condition that the domestic fleet not exceed an incidental taking of 20,500 dolphins per year in the ETP.

5.2.   The MMPA also requires that the United States Government ban the importation of commercial fish or products from fish caught with commercial fishing technology which results in the incidental killing or incidental serious injury of ocean mammals in excess of United States standards. Under United States customs law, fish caught by a vessel

* Reprinted with the permission of the
American Society of International Law.

registered in a country is deemed to originate in that country. As a condition of access to the United States market for the yellowfin tuna or yellowfin tuna products caught by its fleet, each country of registry of vessels fishing yellowfin tuna in the ETP must prove to the satisfaction of the United States authorities that its overall regulatory regime regarding the taking of marine mammals is comparable to that of the United States. To meet this requirement, the country in question must prove that the average rate of incidental taking of marine mammals by its tuna fleet operating in the ETP is not in excess of 1.25 times the average incidental taking rate of United States vessels operating in the ETP during the same period. The exact methods of calculating and comparing these average incidental taking rates have been specified by regulation.

5.3.   The MMPA also provides that ninety days after imports of yellowfin tuna and yellowfin tuna products from a country have been prohibited as above, importation of such tuna and tuna products from any "intermediary nation" shall also be prohibited, unless the intermediary nation proves that it too has acted to ban imports of such tuna and tuna products from the country subject to the direct import embargo.

5.4.   Six months after either the direct embargo or the "intermediary nations" embargo goes into effect, the United States authorities are required to take action which triggers Section 8 of the Fishermen's Protective Act (the Pelly Amendment). This provision enables the President in his discretion to prohibit imports of all fish or wildlife products from the country in question, "for such duration as the President determines appropriate and to the extent that such prohibition is sanctioned by the General Agreement on Tariffs and Trade."

5.5.   Under the MMPA, the United States currently prohibits importation into its customs territory of yellowfin tuna and yellowfin tuna products from Mexico which were caught with purse-seine nets in the ETP. A predecessor embargo was imposed on such tuna and tuna products on 28 August 1990; the embargo in its present form has been in place since 26 March 1991. Since 24 May 1991 the United States has also implemented the "intermediary nations" embargo provisions of the MMPA by prohibiting the importation of yellowfin tuna or yellowfin tuna products from any other country if the tuna was harvested with purse-seine nets in the ETP by vessels of Mexico. If either of these prohibitions is in effect six months after its inception, then as of that date the President will have the discretionary authority under the Pelly Amendment to prohibit imports of all fish products of Mexico or of any "intermediary nation" for such duration as he determines appropriate and to the extent that such action is "sanctioned by the General Agreement".

5.6.   The Dolphin Protection Consumer Information Act (DPCIA) provides that when a tuna product exported from or offered for sale in the United States bears the optional label "Dolphin Safe" or any similar label indicating it was fished in a manner not harmful to dolphins, this tuna product may not contain tuna harvested on the high seas by a vessel engaged in driftnet fishing, or harvested in the ETP by a vessel using a purse-seine net unless it is accompanied by documentary evidence showing that the purse-seine net was not intentionally deployed to encircle dolphins.

The use of the label "Dolphin Safe" is not a requirement but is voluntary. The labelling provisions of the DPCIA took effect on 28 May 1991.

5.7.   The Panel decided to examine successively:

(a) the prohibition of imports of certain yellowfin tuna and certain yellowfin tuna products from Mexico imposed by the United States and the provisions of the MMPA on which it is based;

(b) the prohibition of imports of certain yellowfin tuna and certain yellowfin tuna products from "intermediary nations" imposed by the United States and the provisions of the MMPA on which it is based;

(c) the possible extension of each of these import prohibitions to all fish products from Mexico and the "intermediary nations", under the MMPA and Section 8 of the Fishermen's Protective Act (the Pelly Amendment); and

(d) the application to tuna and tuna products from Mexico of the labelling provisions of the DPCIA, as well as these provisions as such.

In accordance with the established practice, the Panel further decided that it would examine each of the above issues first in the light of the provisions of the General Agreement which Mexico claims to have been violated by the United States and then, if it were to find an inconsistency with any of the provisions invoked by Mexico, in the light of the exceptions in the General Agreement raised by the United States.

* * *

Article XX

General

5.22.   The Panel noted that the United States had argued that its direct embargo under the MMPA could be justified under Article XX(b) or Article XX(g), and that Mexico had argued that a contracting party could not simultaneously argue that a measure is compatible with the general rules of the General Agreement and invoke Article XX for that measure. The Panel recalled that previous panels had established that Article XX is a limited and conditional exception from obligations under other provisions of the General Agreement, and not a positive rule establishing obligations in itself. Therefore, the practice of panels has been to interpret Article XX narrowly, to place the burden on the party invoking Article XX to justify its invocation, and not to examine Article XX exceptions unless invoked. Nevertheless, the Panel considered that a party to a dispute could argue in the alternative that Article XX might apply, without this argument consti-tuting *ipso facto* an admission that the measures in question would other-wise be inconsistent with the General Agreement. Indeed, the efficient operation of the dispute settlement process required that such arguments in the alternative be possible.

5.23. The Panel proceeded to examine whether Article XX(b) or Article XX(g) could justify the MMPA provisions on imports of certain yellowfin tuna and yellowfin tuna products, and the import ban imposed under these provisions. The Panel noted that Article XX provides that:

"Subject to the requirement that such measures are not applied in a manner which would constitute a means of arbitrary or unjustifiable discrimination between countries where the same conditions prevail, or a disguised restriction on international trade, nothing in this Agreement shall be construed to prevent the adoption or enforcement by any contracting party of measures * * *

(b) necessary to protect human, animal or plant life or health; * * *

(g) relating to the conservation of exhaustible natural resources if such measures are made effective in conjunction with restrictions on domestic production or consumption; * * * ".

Article XX(b)

5.24.   The Panel noted that the United States considered the prohibition of imports of certain yellowfin tuna and certain yellowfin tuna products from Mexico, and the provisions of the MMPA on which this prohibition is based, to be justified by Article XX(b) because they served solely the purpose of protecting dolphin life and health and were "necessary" within the meaning of that provision because, in respect of the protection of dolphin life and health outside its jurisdiction, there was no alternative measure reasonably available to the United States to achieve this objective. Mexico considered that Article XX(b) was not applicable to a measure imposed to protect the life or health of animals outside the jurisdiction of the contracting party taking it and that the import prohibition imposed by the United States was not necessary because alternative means consistent with the General Agreement were available to it to protect dolphin lives or health, namely international co-operation between the countries concerned.

5.25.   The Panel noted that the basic question raised by these arguments, namely whether Article XX(b) covers measures necessary to protect human, animal or plant life or health outside the jurisdiction of the contracting party taking the measure, is not clearly answered by the text of that provision. It refers to life and health protection generally without expressly limiting that protection to the jurisdiction of the contracting party concerned. The Panel therefore decided to analyze this issue in the light of the drafting history of Article XX(b), the purpose of this provision, and the consequences that the interpretations proposed by the parties would have for the operation of the General Agreement as a whole.

5.26.   The Panel noted that the proposal for Article XX(b) dated from the Draft Charter of the International Trade Organization (ITO) proposed by the United States, which stated in Article 32, "Nothing in Chapter IV [on commercial policy] of this Charter shall be construed to prevent the adoption or enforcement by any Member of measures: * * * (b) necessary to protect human, animal or plant life or health". In the New York Draft of the ITO Charter, the preamble had been revised to read as it does at present, and exception (b) read: "For the purpose of protecting human, animal or plant life or health, if corresponding domestic safeguards under similar conditions exist in the importing country". This added proviso reflected concerns regarding the abuse of sanitary regulations by importing countries. Later, Commission A of the Second Session of the Preparatory

Committee in Geneva agreed to drop this proviso as unnecessary. Thus, the record indicates that the concerns of the drafters of Article XX(b) focused on the use of sanitary measures to safeguard life or health of humans, animals or plants within the jurisdiction of the importing country.

5.27.   The Panel further noted that Article XX(b) allows each contracting party to set its human, animal or plant life or health standards. The conditions set out in Article XX(b) which limit resort to this exception, namely that the measure taken must be "necessary" and not "constitute a means of arbitrary or unjustifiable discrimination or a disguised restriction on international trade", refer to the trade measure requiring justification under Article XX(b), not however to the life or health standard chosen by the contracting party. The Panel recalled the finding of a previous panel that this paragraph of Article XX was intended to allow contracting parties to impose trade restrictive measures inconsistent with the General Agreement to pursue overriding public policy goals to the extent that such inconsistencies were unavoidable. The Panel considered that if the broad interpretation of Article XX(b) suggested by the United States were accepted, each contracting party could unilaterally determine the life or health protection policies from which other contracting parties could not deviate without jeopardizing their rights under the General Agreement. The General Agreement would then no longer constitute a multilateral framework for trade among all contracting parties but would provide legal security only in respect of trade between a limited number of contracting parties with identical internal regulations.

5.28.   The Panel considered that the United States' measures, even if Article XX(b) were interpreted to permit extrajurisdictional protection of life and health, would not meet the requirement of necessity set out in that provision. The United States had not demonstrated to the Panel—as required of the party invoking an Article XX exception—that it had exhausted all options reasonably available to it to pursue its dolphin protection objectives through measures consistent with the General Agreement, in particular through the negotiation of international cooperative arrangements, which would seem to be desirable in view of the fact that dolphins roam the waters of many states and the high seas. Moreover, even assuming that an import prohibition were the only resort reasonably available to the United States, the particular measure chosen by the United States could in the Panel's view not be considered to be necessary within the meaning of Article XX(b). The United States linked the maximum incidental dolphin taking rate which Mexico had to meet during a particular period in order to be able to export tuna to the United States to the taking rate actually recorded for United States fishermen during the same period. Consequently, the Mexican authorities could not know whether, at a given point of time, their policies conformed to the United States' dolphin protection standards. The Panel considered that a limitation on trade based on such unpredictable conditions could not be regarded as necessary to protect the health or life of dolphins.

5.29.   On the basis of the above considerations, the Panel found that the United States' direct import prohibition imposed on certain yellowfin tuna and certain yellowfin tuna products of Mexico and the provisions of the MMPA under which it is imposed could not be justified under the exception in Article XX(b).

Article XX(g)

5.30.   The Panel proceeded to examine whether the prohibition on imports of certain yellowfin tuna and certain yellowfin tuna products from Mexico and the MMPA provisions under which it was imposed could be justified under the exception in Article XX(g). The Panel noted that the United States, in invoking Article XX(g) with respect to its direct import prohibition under the MMPA, had argued that the measures taken under the MMPA are measures primarily aimed at the conservation of dolphin, and that the import restrictions on certain tuna and tuna products under the MMPA are "primarily aimed at rendering effective restrictions on domestic production or consumption" of dolphin. The Panel also noted that Mexico had argued that the United States measures were not justified under the exception in Article XX(g) because, *inter alia,* this provision could not be applied extrajurisdictionally.

5.31.   The Panel noted that Article XX(g) required that the measures relating to the conservation of exhaustible natural resources be taken "in conjunction with restrictions on domestic production or consumption". A previous panel had found that a measure could only be considered to have been taken "in conjunction with" production restrictions "if it was primarily aimed at rendering effective these restrictions". A country can effectively control the production or consumption of an exhaustible natural resource only to the extent that the production or consumption is under its jurisdiction. This suggests that Article XX(g) was intended to permit contracting parties to take trade measures primarily aimed at rendering effective restrictions on production or consumption within their jurisdiction.

5.32.   The Panel further noted that Article XX(g) allows each contracting party to adopt its own conservation policies. The conditions set out in Article XX(g) which limit resort to this exception, namely that the measures taken must be related to the conservation of exhaustible natural resources, and that they not "constitute a means of arbitrary or unjustifiable discrimination * * * or a disguised restriction on international trade" refer to the trade measure requiring justification under Article XX(g), not however to the conservation policies adopted by the contracting party. The Panel considered that if the extrajurisdictional interpretation of Article XX(g) suggested by the United States were accepted, each contracting party could unilaterally determine the conservation policies from which other contracting parties could not deviate without jeopardizing their rights under the General Agreement. The considerations that led the Panel to reject an extrajurisdictional application of Article XX(b) therefore apply also to Article XX(g).

5.33.   The Panel did not consider that the United States measures, even if Article XX(g) could be applied extrajurisdictionally, would meet the conditions set out in that provision. A previous panel found that a measure could be considered as "relating to the conservation of exhaustible natural resources" within the meaning of Article XX(g) only if it was primarily aimed at such conservation. The Panel recalled that the United States linked the maximum incidental dolphin-taking rate which Mexico had to meet during a particular period in order to be able to export tuna to the United States to the taking rate actually recorded for United States fishermen during the same period. Consequently, the Mexican authorities could not know whether, at a given point of time, their conservation policies conformed to the United States conservation standards. The Panel considered that a limitation on trade based on such unpredictable conditions could not be regarded as being primarily aimed at the conservation of dolphins.

5.34.   On the basis of the above considerations, the Panel found that the United States direct import prohibition on certain yellowfin tuna and certain yellowfin tuna products of Mexico directly imported from Mexico, and the provisions of the MMPA under which it is imposed, could not be justified under Article XX(g).

* * *

6. *Concluding Remarks*

6.1.   The Panel wished to underline that its task was limited to the examination of this matter "in the light of the relevant GATT provisions", and therefore did not call for a finding on the appropriateness of the United States' and Mexico's conservation policies as such.

6.2.   The Panel wished to note the fact, made evident during its consideration of this case, that the provisions of the General Agreement impose few constraints on a contracting party's implementation of domestic environmental policies. The Panel recalled its findings in paragraphs 5.10–5.16 above that under these provisions, a contracting party is free to tax or regulate imported products and like domestic products as long as its taxes or regulations do not discriminate against imported products or afford protection to domestic producers, and a contracting party is also free to tax or regulate domestic production for environmental purposes. As a corollary to these rights, a contracting party may not restrict imports of a product merely because it originates in a country with environmental policies different from its own.

6.3   The Panel further recalled that the import restrictions examined in this dispute, imposed to respond to differences in environmental regulation of producers, could not be justified under the exceptions in Articles XX(b) or XX(g). These exceptions did not specify criteria limiting the range of life or health protection policies, or resource conservation policies, for the sake of which they could be invoked. It seemed evident to the panel that, if the Contracting Parties were to permit import restrictions in response to differences in environmental policies under the General Agreement, they would need to impose limits on the range of policy differences justifying such responses and to develop criteria so as to prevent abuse. If the Contracting Parties were to decide to permit trade measures of this type in particular circumstances it would therefore be preferable for them to do so not by interpreting Article XX, but by amending or supplementing the provisions of the General Agreement or waiving obligations thereunder. Such an approach would enable the contracting parties to impose such limits and develop such criteria.

6.4   These considerations led the Panel to the view that the adoption of its report would affect neither the rights of individual contracting parties to pursue their internal environmental policies and to co-operate with one another in harmonizing such policies, nor the right of the Contracting Parties acting jointly to address international environmental problems which can only be resolved through measures in conflict with the present rules of the General Agreement.

7. CONCLUSIONS

7.1.   (a) The prohibition of imports of certain yellowfin tuna and certain yellowfin tuna products of Mexico and the provisions of the Marine Mammal Protection Act under which it is imposed are contrary to Article XI:I and are not justified by Article XX(b) or Article XX(g).

(b) The import prohibitions imposed by the United States with regard to certain yellowfin tuna and certain yellowfin tuna products of "intermediary nations" and the provisions of the Marine Mammal Protection Act under which they are imposed are contrary to Article XI:I and are not justified by Article XX(b), XX(d) or XX(g).

(c) The Panel recommends that the Contracting Parties request the United States to bring the above measures into conformity with its obligations under the General Agreement.

General Agreement on Tariffs and Trade: Dispute Settlement Panel Report on United States Restrictions on Imports of Tuna (Tuna II)

33 International Legal Materials 842 (1994).*

[The European Union laid its own complaint with the GATT. The fact pattern was the same as in Tuna I, the difference being that it concerned the embargo with respect to "intermediary" states.]

* * *

5.11   The Panel noted the United States argument that both the primary and intermediary embargoes, even if inconsistent with Articles III or XI, were justified by Article XX(g) as measures relating to the conservation of dolphins, an exhaustible natural resource. The united States argued that there was no requirement in Article XX(g) for the resources to be within the the territorial jurisdiction of the country taking the measure. The United States further argued that the measures were taken in conjunction with restrictions on domestic production and consumption. Finally, it argued that the measures met the requirement of the preamble to Article XX.

5.12   * * * The Panel observed that the text of Article XX(g) suggested a three step analysis:

First, it had to be determined whether the policy in respect of which these provisions were invoked fell within the range of policies to conserve exhaustible natural resources.

---

* Reprinted with the permission of the American Society of International Law.

Second, it had to be determined whether the measure for which the exception was being invoked—that is the particular trade measure inconsistent with the obligations under the General agreement—was "related to" the conservation of exhaustible natural resources, and whether it was made effective "in conjunction" with restrictions on domestic production or consumption.

Third, it had to be determined whether the measure was applied in conformity with the requirement set out in the preamble to Article XX, namely that the measure not be applied in a manner which would constitute a means of arbitrary or unjustifiable discrimination between countries where the same conditions prevail or in a manner which would constitute a disguised restriction on international trade.

* * *

5.25 The Panel then examined whether, under Article XX(g), measures primarily aimed at the conservation of exhaustible natural resources, or primarily aimed at rendering effective domestic restrictions on their production or consumption, could include measures taken so as to force other countries to change their policies with respect to persons or things within their own jurisdictions, and requiring such changes in order to be effective. The Panel noted that the text of Article XX does not provide a clear answer to this question. It therefore proceeded to examine the text of Article XX(g) in the light of the object and purpose of the General Agreement.

5.26 The Panel observed that Article XX provides for an exception to obligations under the General Agreement. The long-standing practice of panels has accordingly been to interpret the provision narrowly, in a manner that preserves the basic objectives and principles of the General Agreement. If Article XX were interpreted to permit contracting parties to deviate from the obligations of the General Agreement by taking trade measures to implement policies, including conservation policies, within their own jurisdiction, the basic objectives of the General Agreement would be maintained. If however Article XX were interpreted to permit contracting parties to take trade measures so as to force other contracting parties to change their policies within their jurisdiction, including their conservation policies, the balance of rights and obligations among contracting parties, in particular the right of access to markets, would be seriously impaired. Under such an interpretation the General Agreement could no longer serve as a multilateral framework for trade among contracting parties.

5.27 The Panel concluded that measures taken so as to force other countries to their policies, and that were effective only if such changes occurred, could not be primarily aimed either at the conservation of an exhaustible natural resource, or at rendering effective restrictions on domestic production or consumption, in the meaning of Article XX(g). Since an essential condition of Article XX(g) had not been met, the Panel did not consider it necessary to examine whether the United States measures had also met the other requirements of Article XX. The Panel accordingly found that the import prohibitions on tuna and tuna products maintained by the

United States inconsistently with Article XI:1 were not justified by Article XX(g).

* * *

5.42 The Panel noted that the objective of sustainable development, which includes the protection and preservation of the environment, has been widely recognized by the contracting parties to the General Agreement. The Panel observed that the issue in this dispute was not the validity of the environmental objectives of the United States to protect and conserve dolphins. The issue was whether, in the pursuit of its environmental objectives, the U.S. could impose trade embargoes to secure changes in the policies which other contracting parties pursued within their own jurisdiction. The Panel therefore had to resolve whether the contracting parties, by agreeing to give each other in Article XX the right to take trade measures necessary to protect the health and life of plants, animals and persons or aimed at the conservation of exhaustible natural resources, had agreed to accord each other the right to impose trade embargoes for such purposes. The Panel had examined this issue in the light of the recognized methods of interpretation and had found that none of them lent any support to the view that such an agreement was reflected in Article XX.

* * *

————

Note. Under the old GATT system there had to be consensus by the GATT Council to adopt the Panel Report. There was none in the above two extracted cases. Thus, they do not "form part of 'official' GATT jurisprudence [but] they have had an enormous influence" according to G. Van Calster, International & EU Trade Law: The Environmental Challenge, 222 (2000). Concerning Tuna I, Mexico and the United States entered into bilateral consultations to reach an agreement. The major difference with the World Trade Organization system is that Reports of the Panels and Appellate Body are considered adopted automatically unless unanimously rejected after 60 days. As to domestic case law in the United States concerning the Marine Mammal Protection Act, see *Earth Island Institute* v. *Mosbacher,* 929 F.2d 1449 (9th Cir.1991).

United States–Import Prohibition of Certain Shrimp and Shrimp Products

World Trade Organization: Report of the Panel, WT/DS58/R, 15 May, 1998
37 International Legal Materials 834 (1998).*

[As with Tuna I and II the case extracted below dealt with an embargoed product. See Section 609 of U.S. Public Law 101–162, 16 U.S.C. 1537 note amending the Endangered Species Act of 1973, 16 U.S.C. § 1531 et seq. and the "Revised Notice of Guidelines for Determining Comparability of Foreign Programs for the Protection of Turtles in Shrimp Trawl Fishing Operations", 61 Fed. Reg.17342, (19 April 1996)] (WT/DS58/1).

* Reprinted with permission of the American Society of International Law.

This time the issue was shrimp harvested in a manner not complying with United States sea turtle protection legislation. Malaysia, Thailand, Pakistan and then India, in what became consolidated requests asked the WTO Dispute Settlement Body to examine the embargo on the importation of shrimp and shrimp products, after consultations had not resulted in a satisfactory solution of the matter.]

VII. FINDINGS

7.1 We note that the dispute arose from the following facts. Most sea turtles are distributed around the world, in sub-tropical or tropical areas. Sea turtles are affected by human activity. They have been exploited for their meat, shell and eggs but they are also affected by the pollution of the oceans and the destruction of their habitats. In addition, they are subject to incidental capture in fisheries. Presently, most populations of sea turtles are considered to be endangered or threatened. In this respect, all marine turtles are included in Appendix I to the 1973 Convention on International Trade in Endangered Species (hereafter "CITES") as species threatened with extinction.

7.2 Pursuant to US Endangered Species Act of 1973 (hereafter "ESA"), all sea turtles that occur in US waters are listed as endangered or threatened species. Research programmes carried out by the United States have led to the conclusion that incidental capture and drowning of sea turtles by shrimp trawlers is a significant source of mortality for sea turtles. * * * In 1987, the United States issued regulations under the ESA whereby shrimp fishermen are required to use TEDs [turtle excluder devices] or tow time restrictions in specified areas where there is a significant mortality of sea turtles in shrimp trawls. Since December 1994, these regulations have eliminated the option for small trawl vessels to restrict tow times in lieu of using TEDs.

7.3 In 1989, the United States enacted Section 609 of Public Law 101–162 (hereafter "Section 609"). Section 609 calls upon the US Secretary of State, in consultation with the US Secretary of Commerce, *inter alia* to initiate negotiations for the development of bilateral or multilateral agreements for the protection and conservation of sea turtles, in particular with governments of countries engaged in commercial fishing operations likely to have a negative impact on sea turtles. Section 609 further provides that shrimp harvested with technology that may adversely affect certain sea turtles protected under US law may not be imported into the United States, unless the President annually certifies to the Congress that the harvesting country concerned has a regulatory programme governing the incidental taking of sea turtles in the course of such harvesting that is comparable to that of the United States, that the average rate of that incidental taking by the vessels of the harvesting country is comparable to the average rate of incidental taking of sea turtles by United States vessels in the course of such harvesting, or that the fishing environment of the harvesting country does not pose a threat of incidental taking to sea turtles in the course of such harvesting.

7.4 The United States issued guidelines in 1991 and 1993 for the implementation of Section 609. Pursuant to these guidelines, Section 609 was applied only to countries of the Caribbean/Western Atlantic. In September 1996, the United States concluded the Inter–American Convention for the Protection and Conservation of sea Turtles with a number of countries of that region. In December 1995, the US Court of International Trade (hereafter "CIT") found the 1991 and 1993 guidelines illegal insofar as they limited the geographical scope of section 609 to shrimp harvested in the wider Caribbean/Western Atlantic area. The CIT directed the US Department of State to prohibit, no later than 1 May 1996, the importation of shrimp or products of shrimp wherever harvested in the wild with commercial fishing technology which may affect adversely those species of sea turtles the conservation of which is the subject of the regulations of the Secretary of Commerce.

7.5   In April 1996, the Department of State published revised guidelines to comply with the CIT order of December 1995. The new guidelines extended the scope of section 609 to shrimp harvested in all countries. The Department of state further determined that, as of 1 May 1996, all shipments of shrimp and shrimp products must be accompanied by a declaration attesting that the shrimp or shrimp product in question has been harvested "either under conditions that do not adversely affect sea turtles * * * or in waters subject to the jurisdiction of a nation currently certified pursuant to Section 609." * * *

7.6   In October 1996, the CIT ruled that the embargo on shrimp and shrimp products enacted by Section 609 applies to "all shrimp and shrimp products harvested in the wild by citizens or vessels of nations which have not been certified". The CIT found that the 1996 guidelines are contrary to Section 609 when allowing, with a shrimp exporter declaration form, imports of shrimp from non-certified countries, if the shrimp was harvested with commercial fishing technology that did not adversely affect sea turtles. The CIT later clarified its decision in ruling that shrimp harvested by manual methods which do not harm sea turtles, by aquaculture and in cold water, could continue to be imported even from countries which have not been certified under Section 609. * * *

7.15   * * * the United States, in reply to one of our questions, "does not dispute that with respect to countries not certified under Section 609, Section 609 amounts to a restriction on the importation of shrimp within the meaning of Article XI: 1 of GATT 1994". * * * It is the usual legal practice for domestic and international tribunals, including GATT panels, to consider that, if a party admits a particular fact, the judge may be entitled to consider such a fact as accurate.

7.16   Even if the above-mentioned US declaration does not amount to an admission of a violation of Article XI: 1, we consider that the evidence made available to the Panel is sufficient to determine that the United States prohibition of imports of shrimp from non-certified Members violates Article XI: 1. * * *

7.24   The United States claims that the measures at issue * * * are justified under Article XX(b) and (g) of GATT 1994. India, Pakistan and Thailand argue that Article XX(b) and (g) cannot be invoked to justify a measure which applies to animals not within the jurisdiction of the Member enacting the measure. Malaysia contends that, since Section 609 allows the United States to take actions unilaterally to conserve a shared resource, it is therefore in breach of the sovereignty principle under international law. The United States responds that Article XX(b) and (g) contain no jurisdictional limitations, nor limitations on the location of the animals or natural resources to be protected and conserved and that, under general principles of international law relating to sovereignty, States have the right to regulate imports within their jurisdiction. * * *

[The Panel considered the object and purpose of the WTO Agreement, of which Article XX:1 of GATT is an integral part and in particular looked at the Preamble of that Agreement.]

7.42   * * * On the one hand, the first paragraph of the Preamble of the WTO Agreement acknowledges that the optimal use of the world's resources must be pursued "in accordance with the objective of sustainable development, seeking both to protect and preserve the environment and to enhance the means of doing so in a manner consistent with [Members'] respective needs and concerns at different levels of economic development." On the other hand, the second paragraph of the Preamble of GATT and the third paragraph of the WTO Preamble refer to "entering into reciprocal and mutually advantageous arrangements directed to the substantial re-duction of tariffs and other barriers to trade and to the elimination of discriminatory treatment" in international trade relations. While the WTO Preamble confirms that environmental considerations are important for the interpretation of the WTO Agreement, the central focus of that Agreement remains the promotion of economic of economic development through trade; and the provisions of GATT are essentially turned toward liberaliza-tion of access to markets on a non-discriminatory basis.

7.43   We also note, that by its very nature, the WTO Agreement favours a multilateral approach to trade issues. The Preamble to the WTO Agreement provides that Members are "resolved to develop an integrated, more viable and durable *multilateral trading system* [and] determined to preserve the basic principles and to further the objectives underlying this *multilateral trading system*" (emphasis added).* * *

7.44   Therefore, we are of the opinion that the chapeau of Article XX, interpreted within its context and in the light of the object and purpose of GATT and of the WTO Agreement, only allows Members to derogate from GATT provisions so long as, in doing so, they do not undermine the WTO multilateral trading system, thus also abusing the exceptions contained in Article XX. * * *

7.50   The United States argues that the Panel should consider the many examples of import bans under various international agreements that show that Members may take actions to protect animals, whether they are located *within or outside their jurisdiction*. We are of the view that these treaties show that environmental protection through international agree-ment—as opposed to unilateral measures—have for a long time been a recognized course of action for environmental protection. [We note in this respect that the WTO Committee on Trade and Environment endorsed and supported "multilateral solutions based on international cooperation and consensus as the best and most effective way for governments to tackle environmental problems of a transboundary or global nature. WTO Agreements and multilateral environmental agreements (MEAs) are representative of efforts of the international community to pursue shared goals, and in the development of a mutually supportive relationship between them due respect must be afforded to both". (Report (1996) of the Committee on trade and environment, WT/CTE/l, 12 November 1996, para.171).] We note that this US argument addresses the issue of a potential jurisdictional scope of Article XX. However, we consider that this argument bears no direct relation to our finding, which rather addresses the inclusion of certain unilateral measures within the scope *ratione materiae* of Article XX. In addition, in the present case, we are not dealing with measures taken by the United States in application of an agreement to which it is a party, as the United States does not claim that it is allowed or required by any international agreement (other than GATT 1994) to impose an export ban on shrimp in order to protect sea turtles. Rather, we are limiting our finding to measures—taken independently of any such international obligation—conditioning access to the US market for a given product on the adoption by the exporting member of certain conservation policies.* * *

7.51 The United States further argues that the complainants confuse the difference between extrajurisdictional application of a country's law and the application by a country of its law, within its jurisdiction, in order to protect resources located outside its jurisdiction. However, we note that we are not basing our findings on an extrajurisdictional application of US law. Many domestic governmental measures can have an effect outside the jurisdiction of the government which takes them. What we found above was that a measure cannot be considered as falling within the scope of Article XX if it operates so as to affect other governments' policies in a way that threatens the multilateral trading system * * * . * * * [R] equiring that other Members adopt policies comparable to the US policy for their domestic markets and all other markets represents a threat to the WTO multilateral trading system. * * *

7.52 The United States argues that the right of WTO Members to take measures under Article XX to conserve and protect natural resources is reaffirmed and reinforced by the Preamble to the WTO Agreement. Although we not disagree in general with this statement, we are not persuaded that this argument is a reason to change our finding.* * * [C]onservation measures should be adapted, *inter alia,* to the environmental, social and economic conditions prevailing where they are to be applied. We further note that the Rio declaration on Environment and Development recognizes the right of States to design their own environmental policies on the basis of their particular environmental situations and responsibilities. It also stresses the need for international cooperation and for avoiding unilateral measures. In this light, we consider that the Preamble does not justify interpreting Article XX to allow a Member to condition access to its market for a given product on the adoption of certain conservation policies by exporting Members in order to bring them into line with those of the importing Member. On the contrary, the diversity of the environmental and development situations underlined by the Preamble can best be taken into account through international cooperation. * *

7.53   The United States further claims that sea turtles are a shared global resource and that, therefore, it has an interest and a right to impose the measures at issue.* * * that sea turtles are a shared global resource because they are highly migratory creatures which travel through large expanses of sea, within the range of thousands of kilometres, from the jurisdiction of one Member to those of other Members. Secondly, the United States argues that, even if sea turtles were not migratory at all, they may still represent a shared global resource in terms of biological diversity in the protection of which the United States may have a legitimate interest.* * * This said, even assuming that sea turtles were a shared global resource, we consider that the notion of "shared" resource implies a common interest in the resource concerned. If such a common interest exists, it would be better addressed through the negotiation of international agreements than by measures taken by one Member * * *.

8.1   In the light of the findings above, we conclude that the import ban on shrimp and shrimp products as applied by the United States on the basis of Section 609 of Public Law 101–162 is not consistent with Article XI:1 of GATT 1994, and cannot be justified under Article XX of GATT 1994.

8.2   The panel recommends that the Dispute settlement Body request the United States to bring this measure into conformity with its obligations under the WTO Agreement.

* * *

9.1   * * *

We consider that the best way for the parties to the dispute to contribute effectively to the protection of sea turtles in a manner consistent with WTO objectives, including sustainable development, would be to reach cooperative agreements on integrated conservation strategies * * * while taking into account the specific conditions in the different geographical areas concerned.

* * *

Note

1.   The WTO Appellate Body was later seized of the matter. See 38 International Legal Materials 118 (1999). Of particular interest are paragraphs 185–186 where the Appellate Body stresses what they "have not decided" in the appeal. They did not decide "that the protection and preservation of the environment is of no significance to the Members of the WTO. Clearly it is." It did not decide that members of the WTO "cannot adopt effective measures to protect endangered species, such as sea turtles. Clearly they can and should". It did not decide that "sovereign states should not act together bilaterally, plurilaterlally or multilaterally, either within the WTO or in other international fora, to protect endangered species or to otherwise protect the environment. Clearly, they should do so". What the Appellate Body found, however, was that the United States measure while qualifying under Article XX(g) for "provisional justification

failed to meet the requirements of the chapeau of article XX, and, therefore [was] not justified under article XX of the GATT". The WTO according to G. Van Calster, International Trade & EU Trade Law: The Environmental Challenge (2000), 269, "stuck to its decision, and then added the type of 'environmentally friendly' *obiter* which would seem to be classic in this kind of Reports * * * " when it stated that the findings did not question the legitimacy of environmental policies but stressed the need to resought to international cooperation before unilateral measures are taken. Note that the International Law Association's Committee on Legal Aspects of Sustainable Development in International Law Association, Report of the 69th Conference, London (2000), 655, 668 stated that even though the Appellate Body "ultimately decided that the US measures constituted an unjustifiable discrimination, the various references to sustainable development and legitimate environmental concerns contrast this decision with earlier decisions of GATT panels", notably Tuna I and II. In the *Southern Blue Fish Tuna* cases (Australia and New Zealand v. Japan), the first arbitration under Part XV of the 1982 Convention on the Law of the Sea, reproduced in the Documentary Supplement, the arbitral tribunal found on August 4, 2000, that it lacked jurisdiction to decide on the merits of the claims by the applicant states concerning Japanese fishing on the high seas for southern blue fish tuna. See http//www.worldbank.org.iscid. Australia and New Zealand had submitted that the Japanese fishing was contrary to the 1982 Law of the Sea Convention, the 1983 Convention for the Conservation of Southern Bluefish Tuna and customary international law. Prior to this the International Tribunal for the Law of the Sea on August 27, 1999, had held that once constituted such a tribunal would have jurisdiction. See http// www.un.org/Depts/los/ITLOS/Ordertuna34.htm. (See Mensah, "The International Tribunal and the Protection and Preservation of the Marine Environment" 28 E.P.L. 216 (1998).)

2. ***Endangered species.*** As discussed, *supra,* international trade in endangered species is governed by the Convention on International Trade in Endangered Species of Wild Fauna and Flora, 993 U.S.T.S. 243. Concerning marine turtles see the 1999 Memorandum of Understanding Concerning Conservation Measures for Marine Atlantic Turtles of the Atlantic Coast of Africa, 39 ILM 1 (2000).

3. ***Hazardous Wastes.*** International trade in hazardous wastes is restricted by the Basel Convention on the Control of Transboundary Movements of Hazardous Wastes and their Disposal, 28 ILM 657 (1989). Note also the 1991 Organization of African Unity Bamako Convention on the Ban of the Import into Africa and the Control of Transboundary Movement and Management of Hazardous Wastes Within Africa, 30 ILM 775 (1991) and the Canada–United States Agreement concerning the Transboundary Movement of Hazardous Waste, T.I.A.S. 11099. *(See* G. Handl and R. Lutz, *Transferring Hazardous Technologies and Substances* (1989)). Also, the Montreal Protocol on Substances that Deplete the Ozone Layer, 26 ILM 1541 (1987), considered in Section A.4, imposes trade restrictions on non-state parties. Additional serious problems occur in relation to armed conflict and the environment. Consider the following.

15. THE PROTECTION OF THE ENVIRONMENT IN TIME OF ARMED CONFLICT

The Iraq–Kuwait armed conflict, discussed in Chapter 14 illustrates the use of the environment as a weapon of war, in that intentionally millions of barrels of oil were spilled into the Persian Gulf and hundreds of oil wells were set alight by the Iraqi forces. Not only have the waters of the Gulf been affected but the atmosphere and the wildlife in the area. The question that remains is whether existing international humanitarian law and international criminal law are sufficient to the task of criminalizing such behaviour or whether a new fifth Geneva Convention is necessary. Refer to Protocol I to the four Geneva Conventions 1949, 16 ILU 1391 (1977), and the 1977 Convention on the Prohibition of Military or Any Other Hostile Use of Environmental Modfication Techniques, 31 U.S.T.S. 333 (1977) contained in the Documentary Supplement. (See Schmitt, Green War: An Assessment of the Environmental Law of International Armed Conflict, 22 Yale J. Int'l L. 1 (1997) and Joyner and Kirkhope, The Persian Gulf War Oil Spill: Reassessing the Law of Environmental Protection and the Law of Armed Conflict, 24 Case West. Res. J. Int. L. 29 (1992). Parsons, The Fight to Save the Planet: U.S. Armed During Armed Forces, "Greenkeeping" and Enforcement of the Law Pertaining to Environmental Protection During Armed Conflict, 10 Georgetown Int'l Rev. 441 (1998).)

Plant, Introduction and Elements of a "Fifth Geneva" Convention on the Protection of the Environment in Time of Armed Conflict

in Plant (ed.) Environmental Protection and the Law of War, 17–18, 37–42 (1992).*

The common ground on the law of war may be stated as follows:

1. The law of war has been concerned with environmental protection since ancient times at least in the sense of prohibiting wanton destruction of forests, orchards, fruit trees and vines and forbidding the poisoning of wells, springs and rivers.

2. Deliberate and wanton destruction of the environment in circumstances where no legitimate military objective is served is contrary to international law.

3. The principle of proportionality between means and methods employed in an attack and the military objective sought to be attained by it, the prohibition against military operations not directed against legitimate military targets, the prohibition against the destruction of enemy property not imperatively demanded by the necessities of war and other well established principles of customary international law have the indirect effect of protecting the environment in many wartime situations.

4. The Martens Clause, as formulated in its most modern version in Protocol I, reads as follows:

* Reprinted with the permission of Bellhaven Press.

In cases not covered by this Protocol or by other international agreements, civilians and combatants remain under the protection and authority of the principles of international law derived from established custom, from the principles of humanity and from the dictates of public conscience.

Thus the customary law of war, in reflecting the modern increase in concern for the environment as one of the dictates of public conscience in the sense understood in that Clause, now includes a requirement to avoid unjustifiable damage to the environment.

5. Violations of Article 23(g) of the Regulations attached to the Hague Convention of 1907 (IV) Respecting the Laws and Customs of War on Land, or of Article 53 of the 1949 Geneva Convention (IV) Relative to the Protection of Civilian Persons in Time of War, which prohibit destruction by an Occupying Power of enemy property not required by military necessity, give rise to civil liability. Wanton destruction is considered a grave breach, for which individual criminal responsibility can be attributed by virtue of Article 147 of the latter Convention.

6. States should ensure the wide dissemination and effective implementation of their existing obligations under the law of armed conflict as they may be relevant to the protection of the environment, as well as proper instruction of the military in their application. They should be adequately incorporated into military manuals and rules of engagement, in particular, through instructions to military commanders on the planning and preparation of military activities.

* * *

The deliberate, massive environmental damage in the recent Gulf conflict calls for a distinct instrument on the laws of war and the environment.

It seems desirable to include in this clear statements on the relevant rules of customary law concerning, *inter alia,* state responsibility and international criminal law.

It seems desirable in this connection to bring the laws of war up to date to reflect major developments in international environmental law as it applies in time of peace.

It also seems desirable to improve existing Geneva and Hague law to afford greater protection to the environment. It is necessary to establish a specific threshold of protection.

This calls for a new Convention, rather than a Protocol to the existing Geneva Conventions, because it essentially marks a new departure within Geneva law.

It is appropriate at this initial juncture to await developments in disarmament fora and elsewhere before seeking to regulate in such a new instrument the use or first use of nuclear weapons and other weapons of mass destruction.

Consideration should be given to the possibility of the establishment of a rapid response body which could carry out in the environmental field functions similar to that of the Red Cross/Crescent in the humanitarian field, including acting as a Protecting Power for the Environment.

It will be difficult to define 'environment' for these purposes. The main problem is to distinguish attacks upon humans and their environment from attacks upon the environment as such, in so far as this is a meaningful distinction. Similarly it will be difficult to determine the degree of damage to the environment warranting regulation or prohibition.

* * *

The outrage felt at Iraq's actions alone arguably makes it desirable for the international community to mark in a new instrument the concern that in future the need to give protection to the *environment* as such in time of armed conflict should be *explicitly* catered for, if only in relation to deliberate environmental damage. This is so even if it is agreed that Iraq's actions were already proscribed by customary or treaty norms, since the existing relevant norms do not address themselves to the environmental impact of the destruction so much as to the indiscriminate and excessive nature of damage to enemy *property*. Most existing norms which might be construed to apply to environmental damage do not expressly mention the environment.

It is also arguably no longer sufficient to rely on the fact that the environment as such *is* expressly protected in the odd provision in one or two instruments, such as Article 35(3) of Additional Protocol I to the Geneva Conventions (Protocol I), especially when the efficacy of those provisions is seriously in doubt.

In addition, there is growing evidence that the prohibition of actions like those in question either is or is developing into a norm of international criminal law. It seems desirable to state this clearly in an international instrument.

This is not the first time that the environment has been blatantly abused in time of armed conflict, but it is perhaps the first time that the facts have been broadcast on such a wide scale. An unscrupulous leader, moreover, is more likely to have increasing destructive possibilities for causing such harm at his disposal as the world moves to more and more intensive exploitation of natural resources and energy sources.

As regards collateral damage to the environment, two matters might suggest the need, at the very least, to update existing Geneva and Hague law to improve the protection afforded to the environment, notwithstanding that many areas of this body of law were re-examined and improved upon during the decade commencing in 1970. Those improvements, after all, were made largely for humanitarian rather than environment-protection purposes. First, the 1980s and early 1990s have seen the development of new generations of weapons systems, which are available in varying degrees to military establishments worldwide; many of these pose an enhanced threat to the environment either by their very nature or in circumstances where they are used intensively or indiscriminately. Second, those years have also seen an environmentally significant diversification of military options in relation to possible targets, in two senses: that new weapons systems might be taken to make possible (and 'legitimize') precision (or other) attacks against targets which it would formerly have been impracticable, or even unlawful, to attack, in such a way as to increase the risk of damage to the environment; and that the number of targets, such as nuclear-power stations, chemical facilities and high dams, the destruction of which might result in environmental disaster, has grown greatly. The Chernobyl disaster is a sobering indication of the potential effects of a strike against the core of a nuclear reactor in time of armed conflict, when evacuation and other response measures will be even more difficult than they are in peacetime.

This document, therefore, suggests improvements mainly in the Geneva law, but also in the Hague law, which cannot be entirely separated from Geneva law, as is illustrated by Protocol I itself. It calls for a new Convention, rather than a Protocol to the existing Geneva Conventions because it essentially marks a new departure within Geneva law, rather than an improvement upon an existing corpus of law. The author is conscious of the many fora in which the laws of war are dealt with. If it is felt that this document contains too much Hague law, it is suggested that to that extent the regulation of weapons systems might be pursued with a view to environmental protection within the review processes set upon under the various relevant conventions.

It is a trite proposition, too, that both Geneva law and Hague law are in practice closely connected with the law of disarmament. It is, for example, much easier to regulate attacks upon targets or the use of certain weapons in armed conflicts, if those weapons are not being developed, tested or stockpiled or have not already been used in practice by armed forces. Improvement of the Geneva law, moreover, is frequently the first step in movements towards disarmament measures. The author is aware that disarmament negotiations are proceeding in various fora on various types of weapons and does not wish the round table conference to prejudice those negotiations.

It follows that, while nuclear and other weapons of mass destruction, for example, should properly be regulated by any new Geneva law instrument concerning the environment, being obvious examples of weapons which, if used, seriously threaten the environment, it is, in the author's view, appropriate at this initial juncture to await developments elsewhere before seeking to regulate or further regulate in such a new instrument the use or first use of such weapons. This is certainly true of nuclear weapons, which form part of the deterrent forces of a number of states and are stockpiled in vast numbers; disarmament measures are likely to be far more important than Geneva law measures in their case. However, it might be that participants will consider that a provision or provisions concerning chemical, biological and other toxin weapons, the stockpiling of which is much less acceptable among the vast majority of states, should be included in a new instrument.

In this context, too, it is recognized that over-strict attempts to regulate weaponry and targetry in an indirect attempt to induce disarmament raises the danger of bringing the law into disregard, given the capacities of modern weaponry, and to weaken its legal and moral force. It is, therefore, necessary to seek a realistic threshold of regulation. What is clear is that this threshold should be expressed in specific, * * * terms; it must have a real impact, at least sufficient to cover the excesses in the Gulf conflict, and not merely seek to prohibit or regulate weaponry or targetry which in practical terms is unlikely to be used.

A third reason for the consideration of a new instrument governing the laws of war and the environment is the desirability of updating the laws of war to reflect major developments in international environmental law as it applies in time of peace. Changes in state practice and the adoption of a large number of international environmental law instruments since the 1970s have reinforced the establishment or imminent emergence of a number of principles and norms of international law. Few of the international instruments refer expressly to their application in time of armed conflict, and the precise applicability of the norms and principles at such times is not clear. Nevertheless, a number, if not all, of them have potential applications at such time too. They include: the principle that states are responsible for ensuring that activities within their jurisdiction or control do not cause damage to the environment of other states or of areas beyond the limits of national jurisdiction; (possibly) a duty to carry out an environmental impact assessment prior to such activities; requirements of notification of such activities and (possibly) of consultation with affected states; (possibly) the application of the precautionary principle to such activities; and requirements to warn neighbouring states when an injurious transboundary escape in fact takes place. A new 'Geneva' convention could be used to clarify their application in wartime. Even taking into account the difficulties surrounding the practical application of several of these principles and norms in peacetime, their application in time of armed conflict might have useful consequences, especially upon the geographical limitation of the effects of such conflict.

A number of states, inter-governmental and non-governmental organizations have been involved in trying to put out the burning oil-wells and clean up the pollution in the Gulf region following the recent conflict. With all due respect to their valiant efforts and cooperation through existing coordinating structures, the response has been both improvised and delayed by the absence of a neutral body with access to the war zone during the conflict. The possibility of establishing a rapid response body which could also be accepted as a sort of Protecting Power for the Environment and could perhaps carry out other functions parallel to those of the ICRC and/or League of the Red Cross and Red Crescent Societies in the humanitarian field, called perhaps the 'Green Cross/Crescent', ought to be considered.

Finally, the author makes no attempt to define the term 'environment'. Many have failed in this difficult venture. A definition is not, however, a unique problem in this context; it has not always been easy to find a workable distinction between civilians and combatants. A new 'Geneva' Convention would clearly be concerned with: damage to the marine environment as a whole and marine wildlife and habitats in particular; pollution of the atmosphere, destructive climate modification, enhanced global warming and degradation of the ozone layer; and the destruction or degradation of terrestrial fauna and flora and their habitats. It should take an ecosystems approach.

Difficulties will be encountered in defining what amounts to destruction or degradation and what degrees of destruction or degradation warrant regulation or prohibition under a new Convention. Particularly strict protection would be justified, for example, of areas of special vulnerability or importance in aesthetic, evolutionary (biodiversity) or other similar terms.

Perhaps the greatest difficulty, however, is posed by the fact that man and many of his works form part of the environment. It is accordingly very difficult to determine whether or not, for example, attacks on the means of survival of human populations themselves, such as attacks upon agricultural land or harvested forest or attacks which result in the spread of malnutrition or disease among humans as well as animals or plants, should always be considered as attacks upon the environment. If all attacks which cause human suffering were treated as attacks upon the environment for these purposes, the result would be absurdity; a dividing line must be found.

Similar considerations might also be applied to attacks upon culturally important sites and monuments. No provision is included concerning these, because they are already protected by the Hague Convention for the Protection of Cultural Property in the Event of Armed Conflict 1954 and by provisions in Protocol I. If such a provision were added to a new Convention, it would only make sense if it were intended to remove the exception to the prohibition of attacks on such objects on grounds of military necessity.

Notes

1. ***Convention parties.*** At the time of the Gulf War, Iraq, the United Kingdom and the United States were not parties to Protocol I. Kuwait had acceded to it on January 17, 1985. Kuwait, the United Kingdom and the United States were parties to the Environmental Modification Convention, but Iraq was not.

2. ***Security Council action.*** The Security Council Resolution 687 of 1991, 30 ILM 846 (1991) adopted by 12 votes in favor to 1 (Cuba) against

with two abstentions (Ecuador and Yemen) reaffirmed that Iraq was " * * * liable under international law for any direct loss, damage, including environmental damage and the depletion of natural resources, or injury to foreign Governments, nationals and corporations, as a result of Iraq's unlawful invasion and occupation of Kuwait." (Plant, Environmental Protection and the Law of War (1992); Joyner and Kirkhope, the Persian Gulf War Oil Spill: Reassessing the Law of Environmental Protection and the Law of Armed Conflict, 24 Case W.Res.J.Int.L. 29 (1992)).

Draft Code of Crimes Against the Peace and Security of Mankind

Report of the International Law Commission on the Work of Its 48th Session, 6 May–26 July, 1996.

U.N. GAOR 51st Session Supp. No. 10 (A/51/10), Ch II
See the Documentary Supplement and Section A.2 of this Chapter.

Legality of the Threat or Use of Nuclear Weapons

International Court of Justice, 1996.
Advisory Opinion, 35 International Legal Materials 814 (1996).

See *supra*, Section A.3.

Rome Statute on the International Criminal Court

Adopted by the United Nations Diplomatic Conference of Plenipotentaries on the Establishment of an International Criminal Court.

U.N. Doc. A/CONF.183/9, 17 July 1998

Reissued with Corrections as Doc. PCNICC/1999/INF/3

See Article 8(2)(b)(iv) in the Documentary Supplement

Question: Do you think that the threshold of "widespread, long-term and severe" contained in the Draft Code and the Rome Statute is too high? Do you think that there is a need for a "fifth" Geneva Convention?

Note: At the 1998 Rome Conference on the Establishment of an International Criminal Court, a hotly debated issue and one of the most difficult in the context of war crimes was that of prohibited weapons. When it was evident that there was major opposition to the inclusion of nuclear weapons, some delegations opposed the inclusion of biological and chemical weapons, labelling them the "poor" states' weapons of mass destruction. Thus all three were excluded. This is clearly a significant weakness in the Statute, but was necessary to make it marketable in Rome. Article 8 (2) (xvii), (xviii) and (xix) prohibit poison or poisoned weapons, asphyxiating, poisonous or other gases and expanding bullets, respectively. The accommodation that was struck was to provide in Article 8(2) (b) (xx) that further weapons may be added by an amendment after the expiry of seven years from the entry into force of the Statute. The Statute will enter into force when 60 states have ratified.

16. TRANSBOUNDARY MOVEMENT AND DISPOSAL OF HAZARDOUS WASTES GLOBAL ENVIRONMENTAL INTERDEPENDENCE

Mostafa K. Tolba, Preface

in Kwiatkowska & Soons (eds.), Transboundary Movements and Disposal of Hazardous Wastes in International Law, XIII–XV (1993).*

* * *

The Basel Convention on the Control of Transboundary Movements of Hazardous Wastes and their Disposal represents new norms, rules and procedures in law governing the movement and disposal of hazardous wastes at [the] national and international level. The instrument represents the intention of the international community to solve a global environmental problem in a collective manner.

Institutionalized international cooperation was needed to address the growing amount of hazardous wastes generation, their transboundary movements and disposal. Precise estimates of world wide hazardous wastes volume are difficult to determine, but range from 300 to 400 million tons or more hazardous wastes generated each year. On average, a country who has a gross domestic product of 1 billion U.S. dollars is likely to have to manage about 35,000 tons of hazardous wastes per year. Approximately 2.2 million tons of hazardous wastes made 100,000 border crossings in Europe in 1983. In the OECD countries, a cargo of hazardous wastes cross a national frontier more than once every five minutes.

* * *

As most hazardous wastes come from industries that are among the most important to the growth and maintenance of a modern industrial society, such as iron and steel, nonferrous or precious metals, and the chemical industry, generation of hazardous wastes would continue to be one of the major consequences of industrial development. And when a "not in my backyard" rejection accompanies the growing industrial development transboundary movements of hazardous wastes—even illegal movements— become a boom industry.

* * *

Incentives of wastes brokers are the price and regulation difference in the disposal of hazardous wastes between developing and developed countries. The problem is particularly acute in Africa, where waste disposal rates are, at highest, $40 per ton while European disposal costs are 4–25 times greater and US costs are 12–36 times greater than those in Africa. The prospect of South-South traffic—as developing countries push towards industrialization—is also likely to develop in the near future.

---

* Reprinted with the permission of Martinus Nijhoff.

Kwiatkowska & Soons, Transboundary Movements & Disposal of Hazardous Wastes in International Law
XXII (1993).*

* * *

The problem solving part of the question is of global and regional dimensions, as the TMHW occur both between industrialized states themselves (North-North/West-East) and from these states to developing countries (North-South). Whereas in the OECD context most TMHW take place between member states (some 100,000 such movements occurring in OECD European states and 6,000 in North America annually), the most publicized are exports from the developed to the developing states and, to a lesser extent, also those from West to East European states, both these categories of importing states not possessing environmentally sound waste disposal facilities.

* * *

Instances of the North-South TMHW were provided by incidents involving the *Khian Sea* ship subsequently renamed to the *Felicia* (carrying aboard the U.S. incinerator ash from Philadelphia), the Nigerian *Koko* (port) dump site (wherefrom toxic wastes were subsequently removed aboard the Italian *Karin B* and *Deepsea Carrier* ships), the *Pro Americana* ship (which sailed to the port of Rotterdam with the toxic wastes of Belgian, Danish and Italian origin upon refusal of their acceptance by Brazil), or the presumed instances of dumping of radioactive wastes from France and the Soviet Union in Benin.

* * *

The 1989 Basel Convention/1990 IAEA Code system [the latter deals with radioactive wastes, a lacuna in the Basel Convention] plays * * * a central role in the international regulation of the TMHW.

* * *

The main rules of the Basel Convention provide for: the sovereign right of every state to ban the import of hazardous wastes; the prohibition of export of hazardous wastes if the exporting state has reason to believe that their environmentally sound management and disposal would not be guaranteed in the prospective state of import; the prohibition of the export of hazardous wastes to a group of states belonging to an economic and/or political integration organization, particularly of developing states, which have banned imports of wastes; and the prohibition of export of hazardous wastes to non-parties and imports from non-parties, unless such export/import is in accordance with a specific treaty provided it is not less environmentally sound than the Basel Convention. The exporting state is prohibited from allowing TMHW to commence until it has given written notification (with detailed information) to the importing state in which the wastes will be disposed or recycled and until it has obtained the written consent to receive the wastes from the latter state. In cases when an importing state has given its consent, but disposal cannot be completed

* Reprinted with the permission of Martinus Nijhoff.

in an environmentally sound manner, the state of export has the duty to ensure alternative arrangements, including, if necessary, the re-importation of the wastes for domestic disposal. The optimum solution—which however, appeared so far too far-reaching for the developed states—would be to allow exports only if the wastes were to be handled and disposed in the importing state in no less strict a manner than that required in the exporting state.

The Convention declares illegal the TMHW carried out in contravention of its provisions, qualifying such movements as 'criminal'. It also commits the parties to reduce the generation of hazardous wastes to a minimum and introduces the proximity principle requiring to dispose wastes as close as possible to the source of generation. All state parties are obliged to strengthening their cooperation in order to improve and achieve the environmentally sound waste management. This duty to cooperate is primarily designed to benefit the developing countries, through: information exchange; monitoring the effects of the hazardous waste management on human health and the environment; developing and implementing new, and improving the existing, low-waste technologies; as well as transferring technology and waste management systems.

Notes

1. ***Basel Convention***. The Convention, 28 ILM 657 (1989) came into force on May 5, 1992. See also the Amendment to the Basel Convention done in Geneva on September 22, 1995 which is not yet in force. See Doc. UNEP–CHW. 3–35. See also The Basel Protocol on Liability and Compensation Resulting from Tranboundary Movements of Hazardous Wastes and Their Disposal of December 10, 1999, not yet in force, Doc. UNEP–CHW.1–WG–1–9–2.

2. ***Work of some of the specialized agencies of the United Nations.*** Since the adoption of the Hazardous Wastes Decision by the Governing Council of UNEP in 1990, Decision 16/30 (No. 6.2.4) UNEP has focused its energy on the development of an International Strategy and an Action Programme for the Environmentally Sound Management of Hazardous Wastes. Note should also be taken of the work of the ECOSOC Committee of Experts on the Transport of Dangerous Goods and the International Maritime Organization (IMO), which seek to harmonize other global agreements with the Basel Convention. See B. Kwiatkowska and A.H.A. Soons, ibid., XL–XLVII. Also see Abrams, Regulating the International Hazardous Waste Trade, 28 Colum.J.Trans.L. 801; Mahalu, The OAU Council of Ministers Resolution on Dumping of Nuclear and Industrial Waste in Africa and the Basel Convention, 2 African J. Int'l & Comp.L. 61 and Handl, The 1989 Basel Convention, *supra*. The 1989 Basel Convention and its Bamaco (O.A.U.) Convention are reproduced in the Documentary Supplement. The United States is not a party to Basel Convention.

3. ***UNCED and the future.*** Subsequent to the adoption of Agenda 21 the Commission on Sustainable Development, discussed infra, has been established. Part of its mandate is to address the problem of hazardous wastes and toxic chemicals.

Rio Declaration on Environment and Development

UN Doc. A/CONF. 151/26, vol. I, 8–18 (1992).

Principle 14

States should effectively cooperate to discourage or prevent the relocation and transfer to other States of any activities and substances that cause severe environmental degradation or are found to be harmful to human health.

———

For a discussion of the controversy over the transboundary movement of hazardous wastes see the following extract:

World's Smallest States at Risk Over Environment

Agence France Presse, August 11, 1993.*

NAURU, Aug. 11 (AFP) A gathering of some of the world's smallest nations ended here Wednesday with a loud plea for global recognition that their survival is at risk through continued environmental degradation. Prime ministers and presidents from 13 small Pacific states, plus Australia and New Zealand, ended their annual South Pacific Forum here with a communique dominated by environmental issues.

* * *

The forum said that another problem, the movement of hazardous industrial waste, could have a disastrous impact on the people and natural resources of the region. "In this context the forum noted that numerous approaches had been made to certain South Pacific Island countries by unscrupulous foreign waste dealers for the importation into, and the treatment within the region of, hazardous and other wastes produced in other countries."

The offending countries were not named in the communique, but previous reports have cited Tonga and the Marshall Islands as willing to store hazardous waste. It called on countries to adopt a London Convention amendment later this year to totally outlaw the dumping of radioactive waste at sea. The forum "expressed its grave concern over the dumping of Russian nuclear wastes into the north Pacific, called for its immediate cessation and called for retrieval of those wastes if feasible and safe."

The forum also reaffirmed "its strong commitment to sustainable development". "The vulnerability of the region to natural disasters, environmental degradation and high population growth underlined the need for careful and sustainable management in order to meet the needs of future generations," the communique said.

* * *

* Reprinted with the permission of Agence France Presse.

Notes

1. ***More opposition on the South Pacific:*** It was widely reported that a
U.S. company's intended storage of large amounts of toxic waste on a
volcanic island in Tonga triggered violent opposition by New Zealand and
other nearby states. The Tongan government apparently had received an
offer of $5 million per year for storing up to 35,000 barrels of waste per
year on the actively volcanic island of Niuafo'ou. Reporters claimed that
Tonga had referred the company's offer to its environmental experts to
help them decide whether to accept the reported deal. Neighboring governments, including New Zealand protested and noted that the region's heads
of state had voiced strong concern about such dumping one month prior to
the report of the deal. The governments of Western Samoa and Niue
expressed vigorous opposition. Niue had just previously rejected an offer to
have a toxic waste incinerator built on its territory. Environmentalist
groups have frequently accused international industrial groups of seeking
to dump their waste in areas such as the South Pacific, to avoid dumping it
at home. *Reuters Business Report,* Sept. 29, 1993, *Pacific Toxic Waste
Proposal Stirs Controversy.*

2. ***Regional or global?*** It seems that the member states of the OAU
were dissatisfied with the 1989 Basel Convention, in that in their view it
controlled rather than prohibited the TMHW. As Kwiatkowska and Soons,
supra, LXXII, suggest the Bamako Convention

> "largely duplicates the definitions and principles of the Basel Conven-
> tion, but it provides for a total ban of imports into Africa of hazardous,
> including radioactive wastes from non-parties. [It] permits, thus, the
> intra-African TMHW between its parties and the exports from parties
> to non-parties (be them developed or non-African developing states).
> Import from a non-party is deemed illegal and a criminal act. In
> addition, unlike the Basel Convention, the Bamako Convention prohib-
> its ocean dumping of hazardous wastes, including their incineration at
> sea and disposal in the seabed and sub-seabed * * *."

3. ***The United States and its neighbours.*** The United States which is
the major exporter of waste in the world has agreements on TMHW with
Canada (1986), TIAS 11099 and Mexico (1987), TIAS 11269 which it has
been estimated import some 20% and between 74% and 85% of U.S.
hazardous wastes respectively. The U.S. position is that they are specific
bilateral treaties permitted by the Basel Convention, because they are
compatible with its requirements for environmentally sound management
of hazardous wastes. See Kwiatkowska and Soons, *ibid.,* LII. However, in
the context of the U.S.-Mexico agreement, which is based on prior notification from the U.S. Environmental Protection Agency to the Mexican
government of shipments of hazardous wastes to Mexico that have been
generated in the United States, the same authors suggest at LXXVI that
Mexico has a "lack of capacity to handle and dispose of most hazardous
wastes". They suggest that Canada, Mexico and the United States should
conclude a regional treaty modelled on the 1991 U.N. ECE Convention on
Environmental Impact Assessment in a Transboundary Context. See also
the 1998 U.N. ECE Convention on Access to Information, Public Partic-

ipation in Decision–Making and Access to Justice in Environmental Matters, 38 ILM 517 (1999).

4. ***Antarctica.*** The 1989 Basel Convention bans the export of hazardous wastes and any other wastes for disposal in Antarctica. The 1991 Madrid Protocol on Environmental Protection, 30 ILM 1455 (1991) which supplements the 1959 Antarctica Treaty, 12 U.S.T. 794, TIAS 4780, deals comprehensively with environmental protection including waste disposal in the fragile ecological setting of Antarctica. Annex III deals with waste disposal and management. The Protocol's emphasis is on the principle that what is brought to Antarctica is taken away. See Kwiatkowska and Soons (eds.), Transboundary Movements *supra* LXXXV (1993); Francioni and Scovazzi (eds.) International Law for Antarctica (1987) and Kimball, Antarctica, 1 Yb. Int'l Env.L. 176; and 2 Yb. Int'l L. 190.

SECTION B.   EMERGING INTERNATIONAL LAW PRINCIPLES

1.   NEW IMPERATIVES FOR CO–OPERATION AMONG NATIONS AND INTERNATIONAL LAW

Environmental Protection and Sustainable Development, Legal Principles and Recommendations

Judge Nagendra Singh, Foreward

in Experts Group on Environmental Law of the World Commission on Environment and Development IX (1987).*

* * * National boundaries are now so very permeable that traditional distinctions between local, national, and international issues have become blurred. Policies formerly considered to be exclusively matters of "national concern" now have an impact on the ecological basis of other nations' development and survival. Conversely, the way in which the policies of certain nations—including economic, trade, monetary, and most sectoral policies—are increasingly tending to reach into the "sovereign" territory of other nations, serves to limit those nations' options in devising national solutions to their "own" problems. This fast-changing context for national action has introduced new imperatives and new opportunities for international co-operation—and for international law.

The international legal framework needs to be significantly strengthened in support of sustainable development. Although international law relating to the environment has evolved rapidly since the 1972 Stockholm Conference on the Human Environment, there are still major gaps and deficiencies that must be overcome as part of the transition to sustainable development. A great deal of the evidence and conclusions presented in the report of the World Commission on Environment and Development [Our Common Future (1987)] calls into question the desirability—or even the feasibility—of maintaining an international system that cannot prevent one

---

* Reprinted with the permission of Martinus Nijhoff.

or more States from damaging the ecological basis for development and the very prospects for survival of other—or, possibly, all—States.

Both municipal and international law have all too frequently lagged behind events. Today, legal regimes are being rapidly outdistanced by the accelerating pace and expanding scale of actions affecting the environmental base of development. Human laws must be reformulated to keep human activities in harmony with the unchanging and universal laws of nature. There is at the present time an urgent need:

- to strengthen and extend the application of existing laws and international agreements in support of sustainable development;

- to recognize and respect the reciprocal rights and responsibilities of individuals and States regarding sustainable development, and to apply new norms for State and interstate behaviour to enable this to be achieved;

- to reinforce existing methods and develop new procedures for avoiding and resolving disputes on environmental and resource management issues.

2.   SUSTAINABLE DEVELOPMENT

Birnie and Boyle, International Law and the Environment

3–6 (1992).*

Environment and Development: What is "Sustainable Development"?

It was perceived at the time of the Stockholm Conference that progress on environmental protection was inextricably linked, especially for developing states, with progress in economic development. The UNCHE declaration recognized this need and provided for it in several of its principles. Problems soon emerged, however, because of the political and economic implications of restricting industrial, agricultural, fisheries, and other developmental activities in order to protect the environment from pollution or to conserve resources, and although they continue to arise for all states they do so in an increasingly acute form for developing countries whose incomes are everywhere declining. Their attempts in the 1970s to create a New International Economic Order based on a Charter of Economic Rights and Duties of states were embodied in the General Assembly resolutions * * * but made no reference to and took little account of the impacts of development on the environment.

In the 1980s, however, strategies were promulgated which, though primarily aimed at environmental protection, did take account of the need for development whilst recognizing that the environment could not in all

* Reprinted with the permission of Oxford University Press.

cases sustain unlimited development. The International Union for Conservation of Nature's World Conservation Strategy adopted in 1980 was premised on sustainable utilization of species and ecosystems. The World Charter for Nature adopted by the General Assembly in 1982 aimed, *inter alia,* at optimal sustainable productivity of all resources coupled with conservation and protection.

In 1987, the World Commission on Environment and Development (WCED) [Our Common Future, 43] synthesized these aims in pointing to the need to ensure 'sustainable development' and to provide mechanisms to increase international co-operation to this end. It defined 'sustainable development' as 'development that meets the needs of the present without compromising the ability of future generations to meet their own needs' and UNEP has since added that it requires 'the maintenance, rational use and enhancement of the natural resource base that underpins ecological resilience and economic growth' and 'implies progress towards international equity' [UNEP Governing Council Decision 15/2, May 1989, Annex II, GAOR, 44th Session Supp. No. 25 (A/44/25)].

It follows that goals of economic and social development now have to be defined in all states in terms of sustainability. The role of law in achieving sustainable development has been little discussed but is crucial in regulating use of resources and the biosphere. New concepts are emerging such as the inherent rights or interests of future generations, of equitable utilization, and the 'precautionary principle'. The problem of achieving 'sustainable development' is, however, easier to identify than to solve and is essentially one of negotiating balanced solutions taking account of both developmental and environmental factors in the particular context of the problem at issue, and of the wider environmental impacts of possible solutions. International law cannot provide the answers to this dilemma but it can, in its constitutional role, provide mechanisms for negotiating the necessary accommodations, settling disputes, and supervising implementation of treaties and customs, and in its regulatory, prescriptive role can embody the necessary protective measures and techniques in conventions, codes, and standards, and provide flexible procedures for amending and updating these as required, in the light of technological developments and advances in scientific and other information. * * * Moreover, international law can also be used to secure harmonization and development of national environmental law, facilitate compensation for environmental damage, and provide for offences, penalties and other sanctions to be employed under national law against individuals and companies whose activities are harmful to the environment.

* * * Sustainable development is a seductively simple concept, basic to human survival and [sic] though it cannot yet be said to be a norm of international law. As one leading commentator has pointed out 'it is a notion around which legally significant expectations regarding environmental conduct have begun to crystallize' and which he considers might in time become a peremptory norm of international law (*jus cogens*). [Handl, 1 Yb. Int'l Env.L. 25 (1991).] The problems of its content, however, will remain.

The Brundtland Report

"Towards Common Action: Proposals for Institutional and Legal Change," Our Common Future

World Commission on Environment and Development 308–311, 312–314, 323–324, 330–333, 334–337 (1987).*

In the middle of the 20th century, we saw our planet from space for the first time. Historians may eventually find that this vision had a greater impact on thought than did the Copernican revolution of the 16th century, which upset humans' self-image by revealing that the Earth is not the centre of the universe. From space, we see a small and fragile ball dominated not by human activity and edifice but by a pattern of clouds, oceans, greenery, and soils. Humanity's inability to fit its activities into that pattern is changing planetary systems fundamentally. Many such changes are accompanied by life-threatening hazards, from environmental degradation to nuclear destruction. These new realities, from which there is no escape, must be recognized and managed.

The issues we have raised in this report are inevitably of far-reaching importance to the quality of life on earth—indeed, to life itself. We have tried to show how human survival and well-being could depend on success in elevating sustainable development to a global ethic. In doing so, we have called for such major efforts as greater willingness and co-operation to combat international poverty, to maintain peace and enhance security world-wide, and to manage the global commons. We have called for national and international action in respect of population, food, plant and animal species, energy, industry, and urban settlements. * * *

The onus for action lies with no one group of nations. Developing countries face the challenges of desertification, deforestation, and pollution, and endure most of the poverty associated with environmental degradation. The entire human family of nations would suffer from the disappearance of rain forests in the tropics, the loss of plant and animal species, and changes in rainfall patterns. Industrial nations face the challenges of toxic chemicals, toxic wastes, and acidification. All nations may suffer from the releases by industrialized countries of carbon dioxide and of gases that react with the ozone layer, and from any future war fought with the nuclear arsenals controlled by those nations. All nations will also have a role to play in securing peace, in changing trends, and in righting an international economic system that increases rather than decreases inequality, that increases rather than decreases numbers of poor and hungry.

The time has come to break out of past patterns. Attempts to maintain social and ecological stability through old approaches to development and environmental protection will increase instability. Security must be sought through change. The Commission has noted a number of actions that must be taken to reduce risks to survival and to put future development on paths that are sustainable.

* Reprinted with the permission of Oxford University Press.

Without such reorientation of attitudes and emphasis, little can be achieved. We have no illusions about 'quick-fix' solutions. We have tried to point out some pathways to the future. But there is no substitute for the journey itself, and there is no alternative to the process by which we retain a capacity to respond to the experience it provides. We believe this to hold true in all the areas covered in this report. But the policy changes we have suggested have institutional implications, and it is to these we now turn— emphasizing that they are a complement to, not a substitute for, the wider policy changes for which we call. Nor do they represent definitive solutions, but rather first steps in what will be a continuing process.

In what follows we put forward, in the first place, what are essentially conceptual guidelines for institutions at the national level. We recognize that there are large differences among countries in respect of population size, resources, income level, management capacity, and institutional traditions; only governments themselves can formulate the changes they should make. Moreover, the tools for monitoring and evaluating sustainable development are rudimentary and require further refinement.

* * *

The next few decades are crucial for the future of humanity. Pressures on the planet are now unprecedented and are accelerating at rates and scales new to human experience: a doubling of global population in a few decades, with most of the growth in cities; a five- to tenfold increase in economic activity in less than half a century; and the resulting pressures for growth and changes in agricultural, energy, and industrial systems. Opportunities for more sustainable forms of growth and development are also growing. New technologies and potentially unlimited access to information offer great promise.

Each area of change represents a formidable challenge in its own right, but the fundamental challenge stems from their systemic character. They lock together environment and development, once thought separate; they lock together 'sectors', such as industry and agriculture; and they lock countries together as the effects of national policies and actions spill over national borders. Separate policies and institutions can no longer cope effectively with these interlocked issues. Nor can nations, acting unilaterally.

The integrated and interdependent nature of the new challenges and issues contrasts sharply with the nature of the institutions that exist today. These institutions tend to be independent, fragmented, and working to relatively narrow mandates with closed decision processes. Those responsible for managing natural resources and protecting the environment are institutionally separated from those responsible for managing the economy. The real world of interlocked economic and ecological systems will not change; the policies and institutions concerned must.

This new awareness requires major shifts in the way governments and individuals approach issues of environment, development, and international co-operation. Approaches to environment policy can be broadly characterized in two ways. One, characterized as the 'standard agenda', reflects an approach to environmental policy, laws, and institutions that focuses on environmental effects. The second reflects an approach concentrating on the policies that are the sources of those effects. These two approaches represent distinctively different ways of looking both at the issues and at the institutions to manage them.

The effects-oriented 'standard agenda' has tended to predominate as a result of growing concerns about the dramatic decline in environmental quality that the industrialized world suffered during the 1950s and 1960s. New environmental protection and resource management agencies were added on to the existing institutional structures, and given mainly scientific staffs.

* * *

National boundaries have become so porous that traditional distinctions between local, national, and international issues have become blurred. Policies formerly considered to be exclusively matters of 'national concern' now have an impact on the ecological bases of other nations' development and survival. Conversely, the growing reach of some nations' policies—economic, trade, monetary, and most sectoral policies—into the 'sovereign' territory of other nations limits the affected nations' options in devising national solutions to their 'own' problems. This fast-changing context for national action has introduced new imperatives and new opportunities for international co-operation.

* * *

The ability to choose policy paths that are sustainable requires that the ecological dimensions of policy be considered at the same time as the economic, trade, energy, agricultural, industrial, and other dimensions—on the same agendas and in the same national and international institutions.

* * *

The future—even a sustainable future—will be marked by increasing risk. The risks associated with new technologies are growing. The numbers, scale, frequency, and impact of natural and human-caused disasters are mounting. The risks of irreversible damage to natural systems regionally (for example through acidification, desertification, or deforestation) and globally (through ozone layer depletion or climate change) are becoming significant.

Fortunately, the capacity to monitor and map Earth change and to assess risk is also growing rapidly. Data from remote sensing platforms in space can now be merged with data from conventional land-based sources. Augmented by digital communications and advanced information analysis, photos, mapping, and other techniques, these data can provide up-to-date information on a wide variety of resource, climatic, pollution, and other variables. High-speed data communications technologies, including the personal computer, enable this information to be shared by individuals as well as corporate and governmental users at costs that are steadily falling. Concerted efforts should be made to ensure that all nations gain access to them and the information they provide either directly or through the UNEP Earthwatch and other special programmes.

* * *

National and international law has traditionally lagged behind events. Today, legal regimes are being rapidly outdistanced by the accelerating pace and expanding scale of impacts on the environmental base of development. Human laws must be reformulated to keep human activities in harmony with the unchanging and universal laws of nature.

* * *

Principle 1 of the 1972 Stockholm Declaration said that 'Man has the fundamental right to freedom, equality and adequate conditions of life, in an environment of a quality that permits a life of dignity and well-being'. It further proclaimed the solemn responsibility of governments to protect and improve the environment for both present and future generations. After the Stockholm Conference, several states recognized in their Constitutions or laws the right to an adequate environment and the obligation of the state to protect that environment.

Recognition by states of their responsibility to ensure an adequate environment for present as well as future generations is an important step towards sustainable development. However, progress will also be facilitated by recognition of, for example, the right of individuals to know and have access to current information on the state of the environment and natural resources, the right to be consulted and to participate in decision making on activities likely to have a significant effect on the environment, and the right to legal remedies and redress for those whose health or environment has been or may be seriously affected.

* * *

The enjoyment of any right requires respect for the similar rights of others, and recognition of reciprocal and even joint responsibilities. States have a responsibility towards their own citizens and other states:

- to maintain ecosystems and related ecological processes essential for the functioning of the biosphere;
- to maintain biological diversity by ensuring the survival and promoting the conservation in their natural habitats of all species of flora and fauna;
- to observe the principle of optimum sustainable yield in the exploitation of living natural resources and ecosystems;
- to prevent or abate significant environmental pollution or harm;
- to establish adequate environmental protection standards;
- to undertake or require prior assessments to ensure that major new policies, projects, and technologies contribute to sustainable development; and
- to make all relevant information public without delay in all cases of harmful or potentially harmful releases of pollutants, especially radioactive releases.

It is recommended that governments take appropriate steps to recognize these reciprocal rights and responsibilities. However, the wide variation in national legal systems and practices makes it impossible to propose an approach that would be valid everywhere. Some countries have amended their basic laws or constitution; others are considering the adoption of a special national law or charter setting out the rights and responsibilities of citizens and the state regarding environmental protection and sustainable development. Others may wish to consider the designation of a national council or public representative or 'ombudsman' to represent the interests and rights of present and future generations and act as an environmental watchdog, alerting governments and citizens to any emerging threats.

* * *

We have endeavoured to show that it makes long-term economic sense to pursue environmentally sound policies. But potentially very large financial outlays will be needed in the short term in such fields as renewable energy development, pollution control equipment, and integrated rural development. Developing countries will need massive assistance for this purpose, and more generally to reduce poverty. Responding to this financial need will be a collective investment in the future.

* * *

The Concept of Sustainable Development

Environmental Protection and Sustainable Development Legal Principles and Recommendations

In his Forward to the *Report of the Experts Group on Environmental Law of the World Commission on Environment and Development,* at xi (1987), Judge Nagendra Singh wrote:

The right to development does, however, have certain limitations inasmuch as it cannot be asserted at the expense of the community or even at the expense of neighbouring States whose prospects may be jeopardized. For example a State cannot, in the name of development, proceed to applications of nuclear energy in such a way as to harm the environment and imperil human life, whether in the immediate neighbourhood or in the surrounding region. In fact, environment and development go together and have to be examined simultaneously in this context. In the process of advocating sustainable development, one has to examine the rights and responsibilities of States, both bilaterally and in relation to the international community as a whole. The need for co-operation among nations has to be viewed in the light of new imperatives. The efforts of the World Commission need to be briefly mentioned here because it makes a major contribution to the concept of development in relation to sustainability. The Commission's emphasis on "Sustainable Development" is vital to the well being of humanity not only today but in the context of future generations.

Notes and Questions

1. *Bruntland as Rationalization of Northern Global Ideological Hegemony.* Graf in "Sustainable Ideologies and Interests: Beyond Brunt-

land" 13 Third World Quarterly 553 (1992) argued that the Bruntland Report was an attempt "to reassert and rationalise Northern global ideological hegemony"; that "the 'ecological interdependence among nations' which [it] advance[d] is a sham when viewed in the context of its concept of sustainable development. The environment cannot be the starting point from which to derive coherent prescriptions for global reform. * * * " What is your opinion of this perspective?

2. ***Rio Declaration.*** The initial intention had been to adopt an "Earth Charter" at Rio. However, in the end result the 1992 Declaration reproduced in the Documentary Supplement was adopted. It reflected a compromise position between developed and developing states. In June 2000, however, the Earth Charter was launched as an NGO initiative in The Hague. See http//www.earthcharter.org. for the full text. In its Preamble it states that "The emergence of a global civil society is creating new options to build a democratic and humane world. Our environmental, political, social and spiritual challenge are interconnected, and together we can forge inclusive solutions." There are four parts in this Charter: Respect and care for the community of life; Ecological integrity; Social and economic justice and democracy, non-violence and peace. The International Law Association's Committee on Legal Aspects of Sustainable Development notes in the International Law Association Report of the 69th Conference, London (2000), 667, that the Earth Charter is "meant to serve as a common standard for a sustainable way of life by which the conduct of all individuals, organizations, businesses, governments, and transnational institutions is to be guided and assessed." The Committee states that it "is still somewhat unclear to what extent States and international organs such as UNEP will support this process" but that as a "private, if not 'civil society' initiative" its principles "can certainly provide a useful contribution to discussion and dialogue and serve as another source of inspiration for the progressive development of international law in the field of sustainable development."

3. ***Agenda 21.*** A non-binding plan of action entitled Agenda 21 was drafted at the Rio Conference in 1992. It is reproduced in part in the Documentary Supplement. It has four sections covering (1) social and economic dimensions; (2) conservation and management of resources for development; (3) strengthening the role of major groups; and (4) means of implementation. The creation of a Commission on Sustainable Development as a subsidiary organ of the United Nations was supported here. See A/CONF. 151. (See N. Robinson, (ed.) Agenda 21 and the UNCED Proceedings, 2 vols. (1992).) Agenda 21 in paragraph 38.11 stated that the purpose behind the creation of the Commission was "to enhance cooperation and rationalize the inter-governmental capacity for the integration of environment and development and to examine progress in the implementation of agenda 21 at the national, regional and international levels."

4. ***The Commission on Sustainable Development (CSD).*** The CSD held its first substantive session in June 1993. This meeting had two major outcomes. First, it confirmed the structure and multi-tier thematic work plan of the CSD. Second, it was the vehicle for bringing together over forty environment ministers who together with the other participants met at the

end of the session for two days to discuss how they could provide support politically for the CSD's goals through concrete governmental and international action. It meets annually in New York. However, consider the views of P. Sands, "Environmental Protection in the Twenty–First Century: Sustainable Development and International Law" in Revesz, Sands & Stewart (eds), Environmental Law, The Economy and Sustainable Development (2000), 369, 396, where he states that the CSD "needs to be critically examined, and if found to be wanting measures should be taken to institute effective reform or abolish the body altogether". In his view the CSD has been "little more than a talking shop which has made little, if any, real contribution to the development of the environmental agenda or to the integration of environment and development." In his opinion the CSD's contribution "has been virtually non-existant," apart from "conscious-raising generally". A key point in his analysis is that there should be a rationalization of the plethora of institutions established under the various international environmental treaties and perhaps a merger which would lead to the sharing of expertise and a minimization of costs.

Rio One Year Later,

UNESCO Sources, No. 47, 7–8 (1993).

* * *

What has this unprecedented event achieved? Texts? Certainly. The *"new world partnership for sustainable development"*, called for in Agenda 21? Undoubtedly. New funding? Not really.

UNCED kicked off a preparatory process, begun in 1989 and placed under the auspices of the General Assembly of the United Nations. From the start, this process was universal. All States in all regions were included. Every organization within the UN system cooperated with the secretariat set up by Maurice Strong. From this point of view, the Rio texts reflect a worldwide consensus on the action necessary to achieve sustainable development.

The two conventions drawn up for Rio, on climate and biodiversity, were signed by 150 nations. The United States, which at the time refused to put its signature to these documents, has recently announced that it will now do so.

* * *

And yet Rio's main actors are divided in their reactions to the results of the efforts made since the conference.

* * *

Some are violently critical. For Warren Lindner from the Geneva-based NGO, the Centre for Our Common Future, *"we have not come very far at all"*. *"Non binding agreements and agendas for action and unenforceable declarations of principles are simply not enough"* he stresses. Even recognizing that Rio saw a *"herculean effort made to convince the global community of the need for change"*, he believes the determination necessary for such change is lacking. *"We clearly lack global and national political leadership in respect of most of the issues addressed in Rio. And this applies to both the North and the South".*

In fact, the challenge set by Rio requires a veritable revolution in methods of production, lifestyles, government and education. However, revolutions do not happen from one day to the next, or even over the course of one year.

Even Warren Lindner admits that *"we were expecting more from UNCED than it could give". "The state of the world demands radical change. It is not difficult to see that we cannot continue very much longer with the environment in the state it is, with a swelling population and the existing financial imbalance,"* he says. But at the same time, he acknowledges, *"we cannot change the world in 15 days".*

* * *

The real impact of the texts adopted in Rio will only be felt in the long term. In the meantime, despite the inherent constraints of international organizations, an impressive diplomatic machine has been set up in very short time. The Commission for Sustainable Development was created by the UN General Assembly towards the end of [1992]. * * * States must provide it with information on the measures undertaken to implement Agenda 21; non-governmental organizations will be able to participate, and its deliberations should result in more *"operational"* conclusions than the texts usually prepared by such institutions.

The negotiation committee for the desertification convention has also been established and will meet for the first time in May in Nairobi and should be ready by June next year. A conference on small island states will be held in Barbados, also in 1994, while another on the fishing industry is planned for July in New York.

To a certain extent, Rio has revitalized the dialogue between North–South, setting a new base for discussions, and providing a different ideological context to that of the 1970s. That the industrialized countries join forces with the developing nations to make environmentally rational development a common goal represents a major step forward.

This partnership is not limited to states. It includes NGOs, the private sector, and the scientific community to which the Rio texts constantly refer. The mobilization of the NGOs and their involvement in different conferences and follow-up committees indicates their solid commitment to the process. National commissions for sustainable development, including NGOs, have been set up in several countries such as Canada, throughout Africa and Asia.

The partnership should include a financial dimension, essentially in the form of transfers to the South. From the start of the preparatory negotiations, the subject of resources has been considered as crucially important. This question was, along with the fate of the forests, the last to be dealt with in Rio, and the resulting *"financial packet"* relies on several supports: chapter 33 in Agenda 21, which contains general commitments concerning *"new and additional"* resources, the announcements made by various States during the conference, and the verification that these commitments be met by the Commission of Sustainable Development.

It is difficult to quantify the extra resources generated so far by Rio. No calendar was set for countries to put aside the agreed 0.7 per cent of their GNP for development aid. Rough estimates, however, would indicate that the conference has raised only about one billion dollars in supplementary resources for the South—hardly more than the normal increase in public aid. Even so, external resources are not everything. To have a clearer picture, we would have to evaluate on a national level, how much countries are devoting to the implementation of Agenda 21.

On the basis of initial, admittedly vague commitments, the results are very poor. The fate of two, spectacular announcements made at Rio, serve as revealing examples. The President of the World Bank had proposed an "Earth increment" to the resources of the Bank's International Development Association (IDA). This "increment", amounting to several billion dollars, should have been negotiated by donors during the 10th replenishment of IDA's resources. In fact, the negotiations achieved little more than a renewal, in real terms, of the funds made available at IDA–9.

In the second case, Portugal, in the name of the European Community, announced a four billion dollar plan to finance Agenda 21. Since then, the EEC has been debating how this sum should be divided up between its Member States.

In the coming months, the coffers of the Global Environment Facility managed by the World Bank, UNDP and UNEP, will need topping up, providing another test of the capacity of industrialized countries to turn words into action.

The financial difficulties can, in part, be attributed to budgetary deficits and economic recession in donor countries. However they are also the result of a certain ordering of priorities in these countries, which have chosen to give precedence to other urgent problems such as national unemployment and international peacekeeping.

* * *

Disappointing as they may be, these initial results should not lead to the dismissal of UNCED as an impossible quest. As Gisbert Glaser, Coordinator of UNESCO's environmental programmes points out *"the recession will not last forever"*. *"Agenda 21 has the advantage of being ready to go once the economy turns around."*

His optimism is echoed in the comment often repeated by Maurice Strong that Rio was not just an event, but the launch of a long-term process whose results will be judged in the decades to come.

The scientific community is also thinking along these lines. While the Executive Director of the International Council of Scientific Unions, Julia Marton–Lefêvre, deplores the heavy bureaucracy of international organizations and the barriers that continue to separate them from the non-governmental sector, she is *"not disenchanted"*. *"Rio has forced everyone, even us, the scientists, to think of environment and development as a pair. And that is no small achievement."*

The NGO network is more active than ever and has upped the pressure on governments to ensure that they move in the right direction. The UN

Secretary General, and the entire UN family, have made the follow-up to Rio central part of their action.

Further encouragement has come from the new administration in Washington. The announcement that the U.S. would sign the Convention on Biodiversity, review energy taxes and increase foreign aid for environmentally sound projects, indicates a new spirit. * * *

* * *

European Community and Sustainable Development

Berrisch, American Society of International Law Environmental Interest Group Newsletter
Vol. 3(1), 3–4 (1992).*

On 18 March 1992, the Commission unveiled the 5th Environmental Programme of the Community, entitled "Towards Sustainability: A European Community Programme of Policy and Action in Relation to the Environment and Sustainable Development." The Commission considers the Programme, which was adopted by the Council on 26 May, as a turning point for the Community. If the task for the Community in the 1980s was to complete the internal market, "the reconciliation of environment and development is one of the principal challenges facing the Community and the world at large in the 1990s." The approach of the Programme differs from previous programmes: it is no longer a merely legislative approach but aims at the involvement and commitment of all sectors of society and business in the process of sustainable development. In order to achieve this objective, the Programme broadens the range of instruments from legislative/regulatory instruments, designed to set fundamental levels of protection for the environment and public health, to three new categories of instruments: (1) market-based instruments aimed at internalizing external environmental costs; (2) horizontal, supporting instruments relating to such matters as scientific research, planning, and improved consumer and producer information; and (3) financial support mechanisms such as LIFE. The Programme explicitly recognizes the responsibility of the Community to help protect the global environment. It is intended to cover the period through the year 2000, but shall be reviewed in 1995; a new feature of the Programme is the inclusion of proposed concrete measures for the main sectors, including in each case the envisaged time frame and actors.

Economic Development and the Environment

Kiss and Shelton, International Environmental Law
48–50, 54 (1991).*

Developing countries contain more than three-quarters of the world's population, with 90 percent of the estimated population increase during the

* Reprinted with the permission of the American Society of International Law.   * Reprinted with the permission of Transnational Publishers, Inc.

next quarter-century projected to occur in the urban centers of the world's poorest countries. At the same time, developing countries account for only 30 percent of the world income, with the income gap continuing to widen. Over half the developing countries experienced declines in per capita gross domestic product during the early 1980s, with an overall decline of 10 percent occurring during the decade. In its preamble the Stockholm Declaration recognized that

> [i]n the developing countries most of the environmental problems are caused by underdevelopment. Millions continue to live far below the minimum levels required for health and sanitation. Therefore, the developing countries must direct their effort to development, bearing in mind their priorities and the need to safeguard and improve the environment. For the same purpose, the industrialized countries should make efforts to reduce the gap between themselves and the developing countries * * *.

The Third World view of development as an absolute priority became a problem during preparation for the Stockholm Conference, because initially these states did not favor the idea that the cooperation of all countries was necessary to protect the environment. Environmental problems were considered predominately an ailment of rich, industrialized countries. From this perspective, deterioration of the environment was assimilated to industrial pollutants, a perspective that has not disappeared. Even in 1989, the Brasilia Declaration of the Latin American and Caribbean summit asserted that "the seriousness of the environmental problems facing the world today stem mainly from industrialization, consumer and disposal patterns in the developed countries, which are at the root of the rapid wear and tear on natural resources on the planet and the ever increasing introduction of pollutants in the biosphere." At Stockholm, the reaction of developing countries wishing to become industrialized was to ignore the environmental costs. The priorities are reflected in the comment of one Third World representative who exclaimed, "let me die polluted."

A second Third World preoccupation arose from the perception that for industrialized countries development issues were considered as less urgent than and subordinated to efforts to protect the environment. Some feared that funds previously dedicated to development would be diverted to fight environmental deterioration. These fears seemed to be borne out several days before the Stockholm meeting, when the Third United Nations Conference on Trade and Development produced particularly disappointing results on development aid.

These circumstances explain parts of the Stockholm Declaration and Action Plan which reflect the agenda of the Third World. Beginning with the condemnation of apartheid and racial discrimination in Principle 1 of the Declaration, subsequent provisions are dedicated to economic and social development as a condition of environmental protection.

＊ ＊ ＊

In principle, the problems which surfaced at Stockholm have been resolved. Third World countries now largely accept the need for world cooperation to safeguard the planet. The Brasilia Declaration which condemns the industrial origin of pollution adds that Latin American and Caribbean countries "are committed to a course of action that will be able to prevent a repetition of the mistakes of those development patterns and their consequences." In practice, Kenya, India and Indonesia have taken a leadership role in environmental matters. Zaire, ten years after Stockholm, initiated the World Charter for Nature in the United Nations General Assembly. Finally, Third World countries have adopted regional environmental treaties and largely ratified the global instruments.

* * *

In developed countries and in international organizations, pressure has been exerted to encourage adoption of measures to assess the environmental impact of development assistance. The World Bank has announced plans to assess environmental threats in the thirty most vulnerable developing countries. A February 1990 UNEP meeting stressed the need for grants, investments, and loans to alleviate the critical need for data collection and analysis in developing countries. OECD has adopted a recommendation concerning an environmental checklist for development assistance, calling on member countries to ensure that for both bilateral and multilateral development assistance, environmental aspects are taken into account in the identification, planning, implementation and evaluation of those development projects which are proposed for funding.

There is growing concern among Third World countries that environmental criteria will become a new factor of "conditionality" influencing development assistance and establishing trade barriers. Such conditions are seen as constraints on development opportunities and national sovereignty as well as attempts to protect markets rather than the environment. As a result, the Amazon Declaration specifically objects to attempts to impose conditions in the allocation of international resources for development. As an alternative, an innovative program has begun in some areas to allow developing countries to pay off part of their external debt by committing themselves to invest such funds in environmental protection. These "debt for nature swaps" have been undertaken by private foundations and commercial banks and have found support in national government policies. Proposals also have been made to the World Bank to forgive outstanding loans in exchange for the implementation of specific conservation programs.

In conclusion, developing countries today generally agree on the necessity of safeguarding the environment and integrating methods to protect it in the development process. On the international level, there remain diverse issues over implementation of environmental norms, but the split over the need for and content of these norms has substantially decreased.

3.   INTER-GENERATIONAL EQUITY

E. Brown Weiss, In Fairness to Future Generations, Conference on Human Rights, Public Finance, and the Development Process

8 American University Journal of International Law and Policy.
19–22 (1992).*

Sustainable development is inherently an *inter* generational question as well as an *intra* generational question. Sustainable development relies on a commitment to equity with future generations. I suggest that this ethical and philosophical commitment acts as a constraint on a natural inclination to take advantage of our temporary control over the earth's resources, and to use them only for our own benefit without careful regard for what we leave to our children and their descendants. This may seem a self-centered philosophy, but it is actually embodied in the logic that controls economic decisions over the use of our resources in day-to-day life.

The recent and valid concern over environmental externalities focuses mainly on the costs that we and our contemporaries must bear when we pollute the air, water and soil by industrial expansion, deforestation and other aspects of economic development. Concern over these externalities is intended to ensure that the benefits from a contemplated action exceed its costs and that those who bear its costs are adequately compensated. But in practice the costs and benefits are assessed from the perspective of the present generation.

The discount rate, or in some ways the tyranny of the discount rate, ensures that short-term benefits nearly always outweigh long-term costs. For this reason it is useful to address the issue of sustainability philosophically and legally, as well as from an economic perspective. Sustainability requires that we look at the earth and its resources not only as an investment opportunity, but as a trust passed to us by our ancestors for our benefit, but also to be passed on to our descendants for their use.

This notion conveys both rights and responsibilities. Most importantly, it implies that future generations have rights too. These rights have meaning only if we, the living, respect them, and in this regard, transcend the differences among countries, religions, and cultures.

It is also important, as we discuss the appropriate economic instruments for sustainable economic development, to ensure the effective transfer of rights and responsibilities from one generation to the next. If we safeguard this transfer, then we can develop the economic instruments to ensure the most efficient use of resources to protect these rights and responsibilities. But we may continue to have difficulties until we firmly establish the transfer of rights and responsibilities as an entitlement.

* Reprinted with the permission of the   Law and Policy.
American University Journal of International

Fortunately, the notion that each generation holds the earth as a trustee or steward for its descendants strikes a deep chord with all cultures, religions and nationalities. Nearly all human traditions recognize that we, the living, are sojourners on earth and temporary stewards of our resources. The theory of intergenerational equity states that we, the human species, hold the natural environment of our planet in common with other species, other people, and with past, present and future generations. As members of the present generation, we are both trustees, in a sense responsible for ensuring its integrity, and beneficiaries, with the right, the entitlement, to use and benefit from it for ourselves.

Two relationships must shape any theory of intergenerational equity in the environmental context. The first is our relationship with our natural system, through which we are intricately linked with other parts of the natural system. The second is our relationship with other generations.

The natural system is not always beneficent. Deserts, glaciers, volcanoes and tsunamis are hostile to humans, but we alone, among all other living creatures, have the capacity to significantly shape our relationship with this system. We can use its resources on a sustainable basis or we can degrade the system, and destroy its integrity. Because of our unique ability to control our environment, we have a special responsibility to care for it.

The second fundamental relationship is that among different generations of people. All generations are linked by the ongoing relationship with the earth. The theory of intergenerational equity states that all generations have an equal place in relation to the natural system, and that there is no basis for preferring past, present or future generations for use of the system. This notion has deep roots in international law. The preamble to the universal declaration of human rights begins:

> Whereas recognition of the inherent dignity and of the equal and inalienable rights of all members of the human family is the foundation of freedom, justice and peace in the world. * * *

The reference to all members of the human family has a temporal dimension which brings all generations within its scope. The reference to equal and inalienable rights affirms the basic equality of such generations in the human family.

Every generation should use the natural system to improve the human condition. But when one generation severely degrades the environment, it violates its intergenerational obligations to care for the natural system. In such cases, other generations may in fact have an obligation to restore the robustness of the system, though not to bear all the costs. Those costs must be distributed across generations; and we possess the tools for doing just that.

The state of the legal framework for distributing these costs is the notion of equality as the norm connecting successive generations in the care and use of the environment. A corollary to this principle is the concept of a partnership between humans and nature, as well as among generations. It is useful to refer to Edmund Burke to fully understand this concept:

As the ends of such a partnership cannot be obtained in many generations, it becomes a partnership, not only between those who are living but between those who are living, those who are dead, and those who are to be born.

The purpose of this partnership must be to realize and protect the welfare and well-being of every generation in relation to the planet. The integrity of the planet requires proper care of the life support systems of the planet, the ecological processes and the environmental conditions necessary for a healthy human environment.

* * * A future generation would want to inherit the earth and have access to its resources as did prior generations. This requires that each generation leave the planet in no worse condition than it received it, and to provide succeeding generations equitable access to its resources and benefits.

Experts Group on Environmental Law of the World Commission on Environment and Development, Environmental Protection and Sustainable Development, Legal Principles and Recommendations, Elements for a Draft Convention

42–45 (1987).*

Article 2
Conservation for present and future generations

States shall ensure that the environment and natural resources are conserved and used for the benefit of present and future generations.

Comment

The present article stipulates that the environment and natural resources are to serve the needs of both present *and future* generations. It purports to give effect to the statement in the Preamble of the 1972 UN Declaration on the Human Environment that: "To defend and improve the human environment for present *and future* generations has become an imperative goal for mankind * * * "(emphasis added). It obliges States to manage the environment and natural resources for the benefit of present generations in such a way that they are held in trust for future generations.

This implies, in the first place, a basic obligation for States to conserve options for future generations by maintaining to the maximum extent possible the diversity of the natural resource base. It requires a management of natural resources of the environment in such a manner that they may yield the greatest sustainable benefit to present generations while maintaining their potential to meet the needs and aspirations of future generations. Conservation of the diversity of the natural resource base for the benefit of future generations is warranted as the possibilities to develop

---

* Reprinted with the permission of Martinus Nijhoff.

substitute products or to improve production and/or extraction technologies are not unlimited. Or else because future generations may otherwise only be able to obtain the same benefits at considerably higher costs.

The second basic obligation for States following from the duty to hold the natural heritage of mankind in trust for future generations concerns the prevention or abatement of pollution or other forms of degradation of natural resources or the environment, which would reduce the range of uses to which the natural resources or environment could be put or which would confront future generations with enormous financial burdens to clean up the environment.

Support for the duty of States to ensure that the natural heritage of mankind is used and conserved for the benefit of both present and future generations is to be found in many international instruments.

Thus, Principle 1 of the 1972 UN Declaration on the Human Environment provides that: "Man * * * bears a solemn responsibility to protect and improve the environment for present and future generations". Principle 2 of the 1972 UN Declaration lays down that: "The natural resources of the earth including the air, water, land, flora and fauna and especially representative samples of natural ecosystems must be safeguarded for the benefit of present and future generations through careful planning or management, as appropriate." Principle 5 provides that: "The non-renewable resources of the earth must be employed in such a way as to guard against the danger of their future exhaustion * * * ", while Principle 6 states that: "The discharge of toxic substances or of other substances and the release of heat, in such quantities or concentrations as to exceed the capacity of the environment to render them harmless, must be halted in order to ensure that serious or irreversible damage is not inflicted on ecosystems * * * ".

Numerous references to the need to conserve the natural heritage of mankind for the benefit of present and future generations also are to be found (usually in the preamble) in many international agreements concluded after the adoption of the 1972 UN Declaration on the Human Environment, e.g., in:

1972   Paris Convention concerning the Protection of World Cultural and Natural Heritage;

1973   Washington Convention on International Trade in Endangered Species of Wild Fauna and Flora;

1976   Barcelona Convention for the Mediterranean Sea;

1976   Apia Convention on the Conservation of Nature in the South Pacific;

1977   Geneva Convention on the Prohibition of Military or Any Other Hostile Use of Environmental Modification Techniques;

1978   Kuwait Regional Convention;

1979   Berne Convention on the Conservation of European Wildlife and Natural Habitats;

1979   Bonn Convention on the Conservation of Migratory Species of Wild Animals;

1983   Cartagena de Indias Convention for the Wider Caribbean Region; and

1985   ASEAN Agreement on the Conservation of Nature and Natural Resources.

Reference must also be made to Article 30 of the Charter of Economic Rights and Duties of States proclaimed in UNGA Resolution No. 3281; to UNGA Resolution No. 36/7 of 27 October 1981 on the Historical Responsibility of States for the Preservation of Nature for Present and Future Generations; and to UNGA Resolution No. 37/7 of 28 October 1982 on the World Charter for Nature.

Although in the preceding observations special emphasis has been laid on the obligation to conserve natural resources and the environment for the benefit of *future* generations, one should not forget that such an obligation also exists for the benefit of *present* generations. The basic obligation for the benefit of both present and future generations is further elaborated in the following articles.

To the extent that this basic obligation concerns international or transboundary natural resources or environmental interferences, it already may in many respects be deemed to find substantial support in existing general international law.

In this connection it may finally be observed that the conservation or use of the environment and natural resources for the benefit of present and future generations also implies certain restraints for the parties to an international or non-international armed conflict in that they shall abstain from methods or means of warfare which are intended, or may be expected, to cause wide-spread, long-lasting or severe damage to the environment. Support for this idea may, inter alia, be found in the 1977 Geneva Convention on the Prohibition of Military or Any Other Hostile Use of Environmental Modification Techniques.

Core Features
Brown–Weiss, In Fairness to Future Generations
38 (1989).*

First, each generation should be required to conserve the diversity of the natural and cultural resource base, so that it does not unduly restrict the options available to future generations in solving their problems and satisfying their own values, and should also be entitled to diversity comparable to that enjoyed by previous generations. This principle may be called "conservation of options". Second, each generation should be required to maintain the quality of the planet so that it is passed on in no worse condition than the present generation received it, and should be entitled to

___

* Reprinted   with   the   permission   of   Brown Weiss.
Transnational Publishers, Inc., and Edith

a quality of the planet comparable to the one enjoyed by previous generations. This is the principle of "conservation of quality". Third, each generation should provide its members with equitable rights of access to the legacy from past generations and should conserve this access for future generations. This is the principle of "conservation of access".

Notes and Questions

1. ***Intertemporal Concerns.*** Professor Brown Weiss notes in her above-quoted book at 34–38, the intertemporal dimension in international law and the long held tradition of using principles of equity to interpret international documents and reach decisions. In this sense equity is used to mean equitable standards or principles and must be distinguished from equity in the sense of a decision *ex aequo et bono* to which the parties must consent under Article 38(2) of the Statute of the International Court of Justice.

2. ***Global Commons.*** Should only those areas beyond national jurisdiction such as the deep sea bed, high seas and outer space be considered as the "global commons"? Brown Weiss is of the view (id., 289) that "the planet is a 'global commons' shared by all generations." (See also Brown Weiss, Our Rights and Obligations to Future Generations for the Environment, 84 American Journal of International Law 198 (1990). Note also D'Amato, Do We Owe a Duty to Future Generations to Preserve the Global Environment? 84 AJIL 190 (1990)). Do you think that the environmental concerns dealt with in this Chapter fall under this heading of "global commons" or under that of "shared natural resources" that do not fall exclusively within any one state's jurisdiction, but neither are they the common property of all states? Alternatively, can the principle of the "common heritage" as seen in the 1979 Moon Treaty and in Articles 136 and 137 of the 1982 Law of the Sea Treaty be applied in the international environmental context?

Reflections on the Commons, in E. Ostrom, Governing the Commons: The Evolution of Institutions for Collective Action, at 1–3 (1990).*

Hardly a week goes by without a major news story about the threatened destruction of a valuable natural resource. In June of 1989, for example, a *New York Times* article focused on the problem of overfishing in the Georges Bank about 150 miles off the New England coast. Catches of cod, flounder, and haddock are now only a quarter of what they were during the 1960s. Everyone knows that the basic problem is overfishing; however, those concerned cannot agree how to solve the problem. Congressional representatives recommend new national legislation, even though

---

* Reprinted with the permission of Elinore Ostrom and Simon & Shuster–Prentice– Hall Publishers.

the legislation already on the books has been enforced only erratically. Representatives of the fishers argue that the fishing grounds would not be in such bad shape if the federal government had refrained from its sporadic attempts to regulate the fishery in the past. The issue in this case—and many others—is how best to limit the use of natural resources so as to ensure their long-term economic viability. Advocates of central regulation, of privitization, and of regulation by those involved have pressed their policy prescriptions in a variety of different arenas.

Similar situations occur on diverse scales ranging from small neighbor-hoods to the entire planet. The issues of how best to govern natural resources used by many individuals in common are no more settled in academia than in the world of politics. Some scholarly articles about the "tragedy of the commons" recommend that "the state" control most natural resources to prevent their destruction; others recommend that privatizing those resources will resolve the problem. What one can observe in the world, however, is that neither the state nor the market is uniformly successful in enabling individuals to sustain long-term, productive use of natural resource systems.

* * *

The tragedy of the commons

Since Garrett Hardin's challenging article in *Science* (1968), the ex-pression "the tragedy of the commons" has come to symbolize the degrada-tion of the environment to be expected whenever many individuals use a scarce resource in common. To illustrate the logical structure of his model, Hardin asks the reader to envision a pasture "open to all." He then examines the structure of this situation from the perspective of a rational herder. Each herder receives a direct benefit from his own animals and suffers delayed costs from the deterioration of the commons when his and others' cattle overgraze. Each herder is motivated to add more and more animals because he receives the direct benefit of his own animals and bears only a share of the costs resulting from overgrazing. Hardin concludes: "Therein is the tragedy. Each man is locked into a system that compels him to increase his herd without limit—in a world that is limited. Ruin is the destination toward which all men rush, each pursuing his own best interest in a society that believes in the freedom of the commons." (Hardin 1968, p. 1,244).

Hardin was not the first to notice the tragedy of the commons. Aristotle long ago observed that "what is common to the greatest number has the least care bestowed upon it. Everyone thinks chiefly of his own, hardly at all of the common interest" (*Politics,* Book II, ch. 3). Hobbes's parable of man in a state of nature is a prototype of the tragedy of the commons: Men seek their own good and end up fighting one another. In 1833, William Forster Lloyd (1977) sketched a theory of the commons that predicted improvident use for property owned in common. More than a decade before Hardin's article, H. Scott Gordon (1954) clearly expounded similar logic in another classic: "The Economic Theory of a Common-Property Research: The Fishery." Gordon described the same dynamic as Hardin:

There appears then, to be some truth in the conservative dictum that everybody's property is nobody's property. Wealth that is free for all is valued by no one because he who is foolhardy enough to wait for its proper time of use will only find that it has been taken by another * * *. The fish in the sea are valueless to the fisherman, because there is no assurance that they will be there for him tomorrow if they are left behind today. (Gordon 1954, p. 124).

* * *

* * * Standard analyses in modern resource economics conclude that where a number of users have access to a common-pool resource, the total of resource units withdrawn from the resource will be greater than the optimal economic level of withdrawal * * *.

If the only "commons" of importance were a few grazing areas or fisheries, the tragedy of the commons would be of little general interest. That is not the case. Hardin himself used the grazing commons as a metaphor for the general problem of overpopulation. The "tragedy of the commons" has been used to describe such diverse problems as the Sahelian famine of the 1970s, * * * firewood crises throughout the Third World, * * * the problem of acid rain, * * *. Much of the world is dependent on resources that are subject to the possibility of a tragedy of the commons.

4. COMMON HERITAGE

Birnie and Boyle, International Law and the Environment, 121–122 (1992).*

* * * [T]here remains the objection that common heritage is still of doubtful legal status following its well-known rejection by the United States and other countries opposed to ratification of the 1982 UNCLOS and the Moon Treaty. Significantly, it was not employed in the Ozone Convention. Some conventions do use the term or others such as the "world heritage of mankind" in their preambles in a horatory sense. But these are better viewed, like the term "common concern", as expressions of the common interest of all states in certain forms of ecological protection, and not as attempts to internationalize ownership of resources. Common heritage is important, however, in providing one of the most developed applications of trusteeship or fiduciary relationship in an environmental context, and in that sense it represents a significant precedent * * *.

Kiss and Shelton, International Environmental Law, 9–18 (1991).*

* * * According to a UNESCO program entitled "Man and the Biosphere", the term biosphere designates the totality of our environment,

* Reprinted with the permission of Oxford University Press.   * Reprinted with the permission of Transnational Publishers, Inc.

that part of the universe in which, as far as we know, all life is concentrated. In fact, it is a very narrow stratum encircling the globe. It comprises the earth and several hundred meters above and under the surface of the earth and oceans.

Lawyers may question whether it is possible to legally protect the entire biosphere, as such. One means of protection derived from familiar juridical techniques would be to confer on it a status similar to legal personality, giving the biosphere a legally recognized existence currently afforded juridical entities such as corporations, trusts and, on the international level, international organizations and trust territories. Although such a solution for the entirety of our universe is difficult to imagine, the 1982 Convention on the Law of the Sea moves in this direction by proclaiming the deep seabed and its mineral resources (the Area) to be the common heritage of mankind and investing all humanity with rights and responsibilities over the Area. An implementing international authority is established to act for all humanity. In this way, a sector of the globe is given a juridical status and its representation is simultaneously assured. A similar solution might be possible for the biosphere, although this appears highly unlikely.

In the current state of the law, protection of the environment occurs on the international plane, as it does within national legal systems, by adoption of measures targeting sectors of the biosphere such as air or water, based on their importance or benefit to humans. At the beginning of the 1970s some suggested that the legal personality of certain of these environmental sectors be recognized. However, legal systems have difficulty integrating such solutions because the systems are created by humans to serve human interests. This anthropocentric approach to resources is reflected in one of the fundamental international environmental texts, the 1972 Stockholm Declaration on the Human Environment: "The natural resources of the earth, including the air, water, and flora and fauna and especially representative samples of natural ecosystems, must be safeguarded for the benefit of present and future generations through careful planning or management, as appropriate."

More recently, international instruments increasingly have recognized an intrinsic value in components of the environment. The preamble of the 1979 Bern Convention on the Conservation of European Wildlife and Natural Habitats is particularly significant in this regard: "Recognizing that wild flora and fauna constitute a natural heritage of aesthetic, scientific, cultural, recreational, economic, and intrinsic value that needs to be preserved and handed on to future generations."

The text demonstrates an integrated approach: the common heritage of mankind presents a certain number of qualities important for humanity, but these do not lessen its inherent value. It is possible to go further. The most important text of principles since the Stockholm Declaration, the 1982 World Charter for Nature, proclaimed by the United Nations General Assembly, marks an evolution in this regard and indicates possible limits: "Every form of life is unique, warranting respect regardless of its worth to man and, to accord other organisms such recognition, man must be guided by a moral code of action[.]"

An intrinsic value is thus recognized in the basic elements of the environment, but their protection is governed by moral rather than legal rules. Given the refusal to confer legal status on sectors of the environment and to thus recognize their intrinsic, independent value, it seems that another approach is necessary to establish the purpose of environmental protection. The first phrases of the preamble of the World Charter for Nature set out such an alternative: "Mankind is a part of nature and life depends on the uninterrupted functioning of natural systems which ensure the supply of energy and nutrients[.]"

The intrinsic value of the biosphere is not rejected but is integrated with a recognition that man makes up part of the universe and cannot exist without conservation of the biosphere and the ecosystems which comprise it. In this perspective all sectors of the environment have a value not only in their short-term utility to humans, as the earlier exclusively anthropocentric approach would have it, but also as indispensable elements of an interrelated system which must be protected to ensure human survival. While this ultimate aim of human survival remains anthropocentric, humans are not viewed as apart from or above the natural universe, but as an interlinked and interdependent part of it. It follows that because all parts of the natural web are linked, they must each be protected and conserved. It is in this sense that "intrinsic value" may be understood.

* * * [T]he concept of an interrelated system leads to the conclusion that protection of the biosphere is in the common interest of humanity, a conclusion that has important consequences not only for environmental law, but for all of international law. The "common interest" of humanity is, above all, human survival, which underlies all legal and social systems and may be grounded in a genetic or biological imperative. Inevitably, this interest requires that "humanity" be seen to include not only present but also future generations. In fact, the right of future generations is implicit in all which touches environmental protection and the preservation of natural resources. It also is increasingly explicit in international texts, beginning with Principle 2 of the Stockholm Declaration and Article 4 of the UNESCO World Heritage Convention.

Conservation makes sense only in a temporal perspective; absent this consideration everything could be consumed or wasted in the present and human survival foreclosed. Moreover, the conditions of life for those to come—who will be increasingly numerous for at least the coming decades—should not be less favorable than those which the present generations have inherited from their predecessors. These include the required conditions for individuals and peoples * * * to lead materially satisfying lives in dignity and liberty.

* * * Toward the end of the 1960s, when international environmental law was born, the term "common heritage of mankind" appeared in international texts, applied by virtue of international instruments relating to the deep seabed and the moon and other celestial bodies. In fact, the common heritage of mankind, a concretization in law of the common interest of humanity, already existed in general terms in regimes such as those governing Antarctica and its seas, the radio frequency spectrum, and the orbit of geostationary satellites, all of which contain obligations of

nonappropriation, conservation, and rational use. States freely undertake to respect these obligations without obtaining any immediate advantage. The purpose is to serve more long-term objectives which are in mankind's common interest: to prevent international tensions from creating dangers to the maintenance of peace, to respect and ensure the dignity and fundamental rights and liberties of all humans, and to halt the deterioration and destruction of natural resources. It may be that the common interest of humanity is identifiable precisely where conventions are not based on reciprocity. Of course, in the environmental field the concept of "common interest" also reflects the physical reality of an indivisible environment, notwithstanding the claims of states to "permanent" sovereignty over natural resources.

* * *

Rules of international environmental law fall into the category of norms adopted in the common interest of humanity. They generally do not bring immediate advantages to contracting states when their objective is to protect species of wild plant and animal life, the oceans, the air, the soil, and the countryside. Even in regard to treaties concluded among a small number of states, reciprocity normally is not the primary purpose of the contracting parties. For example, states upstream on a river are not in the same situation as those downstream. The general direction of winds and ocean currents can substantially affect legal obligations, cut against the equality of the parties, and diminish the importance of reciprocity.

The common interest of humanity also is mentioned, usually in the preamble, among the objectives of several treaties aimed at protecting particular elements of the environment. For example, the 1972 UNESCO Convention concerning the Protection of the World Cultural and Natural Heritage proclaims that, "the deterioration or disappearance of any item of the cultural or natural heritage constitutes a harmful impoverishment of the heritage of all nations of the world."

A veritable profession of faith even more characteristically opens the preamble of the 1979 Bonn Convention on the Conservation of Migratory Species of Wild Animals:

> * * * wild animals in their innumerable forms are an irreplaceable part of the earth's natural system which must be conserved for the good of mankind;

> * * * each generation of man holds the resources of the earth for future generations and has an obligation to ensure that this legacy is conserved and, where utilized, is used wisely[.]

Finally, a regional example can be taken from the 1974 Paris Convention for the Prevention of Marine Pollution from Land–Based Sources:

> "the marine environment and the flora and fauna which it supports are of vital importance to all nations."

Thus, the purpose of international environmental law can be seen as serving the general interest of humanity, its survival and well-being, rather than exchanging reciprocal rights and duties.

Note: Kiss "International Trade and the Common Concern of Humankind" in Bosselmann & Richardson (eds) (2000),143, 150–151, notes that the protection of the human environment has been recognized as "part of the common concern of humanity". He links the common concern of humanity and the rights of future generations. He states that in "one way or another, all the activities aiming at the protection of the environment are directly or indirectly based on the implicit recognition that it constitutes one of the major components of the common concern of humanity".

5. ENVIRONMENTAL RIGHTS AS HUMAN RIGHTS

Experts Group on Environmental Law of the World Commission on Environment and Development, Environmental Protection and Sustainable Development, Legal Principles and Recommendations, Elements for a Draft Convention
38–42 (1987).*

Article 1

Fundamental human right

All human beings have the fundamental right to an environment adequate for their health and well-being.

Comment

This article stipulates the fundamental right of every individual human being to an environment adequate for his health and well-being. The formulation of this fundamental right differs in various respects from that proclaimed in Principle 1 of the 1972 UN Declaration on the Human Environment which provides: "Man has the fundamental right to freedom, equality and adequate conditions of life, in an environment of a quality that permits a life of dignity and well-being * * *." The formulated fundamental right is to be preferred to the one contained in Principle 1 of the 1972 UN Declaration. Firstly, because its *direct* and *immediate* object is the maintenance and/or restoration of an adequate environment. The principle in the 1972 UN Declaration on the contrary has as its direct and immediate object "freedom, equality and adequate conditions of life", putting the requirement of an adequate environment merely in second place. Secondly, the formulated fundamental right refers to the more concrete notion of "health" as an interest to be protected and avoids an explicit reference to the concept of "a life of dignity", which may be deemed to be comprised in the notion of "well-being".

Although the environment to which the fundamental right formulated above relates clearly comprises the environment in which human beings live, it also is intended to comprise those parts of the earth and the surrounding sphere which hold important natural resources for man (e.g. marine waters) or which, when disturbed or degraded, may eventually

* Reprinted with the permission of Martinus Nijhoff.

detrimentally affect areas normally inhabited by man (e.g. rain forests or the ozone layer).

Of course, the requirement that the environment must be "adequate for [human] health and well-being" is extremely vague. In any case both physical and mental health and well-being are to be protected and promoted. The adjective "adequate" makes clear that there are limits to the protection of the environment for the purpose of promoting the health and well-being of human beings. Indeed, those limits may to some extent even be dictated by the need to promote the health or well-being of human beings (e.g. by food production or housing). Apart from that, the determination of the adequacy of the environment for the health and well-being of human beings will depend to a considerable extent on many regional or local factors, such as the nature of the environment concerned, the kind of use made of it, the means at the disposal of the public authorities and the population, and the expectations of the human beings themselves.

The fundamental human right to an adequate environment implies at least the existence of an international obligation on the part of States vis-à-vis other States, if not also vis-à-vis individual human beings, to adequately protect the environment for the benefit of individual human beings (substantive human right) and/or to grant to such individual human beings the procedural legal means necessary to protect their interests in an adequate environment (procedural human right) against infringements by the State or by other entities or persons (e.g. private companies or individuals).

By postulating in Article 1 the fundamental human right to an adequate environment, it is made clear that the obligations of States formulated in the subsequent articles are not merely intended to protect the interests of States *inter se* in maintaining or restoring an adequate environment, but also those of individual human beings irrespective of their nationality. Moreover, Article 2 makes clear that these obligations do not merely exist in the interest of *present* human beings, but also for the benefit of *future* generations.

Article 1 only purports to establish a fundamental right of human beings to an adequate environment vis-à-vis other human beings or entities created by man such as States. In other words the emphasis laid in Article 1 on the protection of the interests of human beings may not be deemed to imply a choice for an anthropocentric approach in environmental questions.

It cannot be said that the fundamental human right to an adequate environment already constitutes a well-established right under present international law. As a matter of fact there are as yet no treaties which provide for a specific human right to an adequate environment. Efforts made within the framework of the Council of Europe during the 1970s to adopt such a human right in an additional protocol to the 1950 European Convention for the Protection of Human Rights and Fundamental Freedoms or through an amendment of the 1961 European Social Charter unfortunately failed to obtain the required support. It is true that the 1974 Nordic Environmental Protection Convention grants inhabitants of a country who are (possibly) detrimentally affected by a (planned) environmentally harmful activity in another country, a right of equal access to and of equal treatment by the administrative or judicial authorities of the latter country. However, this convention does not provide for an *independent* (substantive and/or procedural) right to an adequate environment for the inhabitants of the country of origin of the environmentally harmful activity and consequently neither for the inhabitants of countries (possibly) affected by such an activity. The argument of the absence of an independent right to an adequate environment applies, of course, likewise to all those OECD or other recommendations which recommend the granting of a right of equal access or treatment to individuals (possibly) affected by a transboundary environmental interference.

Certain treaties provide for human rights which may imply a corollary duty not to impair the environment beyond a certain degree. Reference may be made here to the inherent right to life of every human being stated in Article 6(1) of the 1966 UN Covenant on Civil and Political Rights. However, it should be kept in mind that this right can only be invoked when the environmental degradation has reached such an extent that life itself is endangered, so that it must be deemed to be of little use to safeguard a certain *quality* of life. Another limitation is to be found in the last sentence of Article 6(1) which provides that "No one shall be *arbitrarily* deprived of his life." (emphasis added).

Certain provisions in the 1966 UN Covenant on Economic, Social and Cultural Rights are more promising. The States Parties to this covenant recognize in Article 11(1) " * * * the right of everyone to an *adequate standard of living * * * and to the *continuous improvement of living conditions*" (emphasis added) and in Article 12(1) " * * * the right of everyone to the enjoyment of the *highest attainable standard of physical and mental health*", the full realization of which is to be achieved, inter alia, by "the improvement of all aspects of *environmental * * * hygiene*" (emphasis added). It is clear that the realization of the right to an adequate standard of living and to the highest attainable standard of physical and mental health may well require the taking of measures to prevent or abate impairment of the environment. However, it should also be borne in mind that, according to the 1966 UN Covenant on Economic, Social and Cultural Rights (see Article 2(1)), the realization of these rights need only be progressively achieved by States which are a party to the covenant "by all appropriate means" and "to the maximum of [their] available resources".

En dehors treaties, some indirect support for a right of human beings to an adequate environment also may be found in everyone's right to life (Article 3) or everyone's right to a standard of living adequate for the health and well-being of himself and of his family (Article 25) which are proclaimed in UNGA Resolution No. 217 of 10 December 1948 adopting the Universal Declaration of Human Rights. Noteworthy, however, also is Article 29(2) which provides that the rights proclaimed in the Universal Declaration may be limited by law "for the purpose of * * * meeting the just requirements of * * * the general welfare in a democratic society". Like the 1966 UN Covenant on Economic, Social and Cultural Rights, the

Universal Declaration sets only certain standards of achievement (see the Preamble), but, unlike the 1966 UN Covenant, does not constitute a legally binding instrument for States.

Reference to a specific international human right to an adequate environment is, in fact, only to be found in the above-quoted Principle 1 of the 1972 UN Declaration on the Human Environment. Apart from the fact that the States which adopted the 1972 UN Declaration probably regarded the principle as not legally binding but stating merely a goal to be achieved, there also remains the problem of the clear incompatibility of the proclaimed fundamental human right with the statement in Principle 21 of the 1972 UN Declaration that: "States have, in accordance with the Charter of the United Nations and the principles of international law, the sovereign right to exploit their own resources pursuant to their own environmental policies * * * ". This sovereign right is, in Principle 21, only restricted in case damage is caused to the environment of other States or of areas beyond the limits of national jurisdiction.

The source of many human rights which have eventually found recognition on the international plane is to be found in municipal law. Hence, support for an emerging specific fundamental human right to an adequate environment may possibly be found in national constitutional or other legislation. While there are a fair number of constitutional or other legal provisions which impose a basic duty on the State to protect (certain parts of) the environment, there are only very few provisions which provide for a specific right of individual human beings to an adequate environment (see, e.g., Article 45(1) of the 1978 Constitution of Spain; Article 123 of the 1979 Constitution of Peru; and perhaps Article 71 of the 1976 Polish Constitution) or provide that the State must protect the environment for the benefit of individual human beings. Hence, it is as yet not possible to maintain that there already exists a general principle of (national) law recognized by civilized nations in the sense of Article 38(1)(c) of the Statute of the International Court of Justice which embodies a fundamental human right to an adequate environment.

The fundamental human right laid down in Article 1 therefore remains an ideal which must still be realized.

Environmental Rights as Human Rights—differing opinions. From the above extract it can be seen that group of experts of the WCED did not find that there exists at the present time a "fundamental human right to an adequate environment" under international law. Consider the views of the writers extracted below on this issue. See also P. Gormley, Human Rights and Environment: The Need for International Cooperation (1976); P. Gormley, The Legal Obligation of the International Community to Guarantee a Pure and Decent Environment: The Expansion of Human Rights Norms, 3 Georgetown Int'l Env.L.Rev. 85 (1990) and A. Cancado Trindade, The Parallel Evolutions of International Human Rights Protection and of Environmental Protection and the Absence of Restrictions upon the Exercise of Recognized Human Rights, 13 Revista del Instituto Interamericano de Derochos Humanos 35 (1991).

Kiss and Shelton, International Environmental Law, 21–22, 28–31 (1991).*

The Right to Environment

Just as environmental law derives from the common interest of humanity, so does international recognition of human rights and fundamental freedoms. There is no contradiction between the two concepts. The opening paragraph of the preamble to the Universal Declaration of Human Rights, unanimously proclaimed by the General Assembly of the United Nations on December 10, 1948, underlines a common purpose, stating that, "recognition of the inherent dignity and of the equal and inalienable rights of all members of the human family is the foundation of freedom, justice and peace in the world."

The link between human rights and environmental protection is clearly established by Principle 1 of the Stockholm Declaration: "Man has the fundamental right to freedom, equality and adequate conditions of life, in an environment of a quality that permits a life of dignity and well-being. * * *."

This formulation stops short of proclaiming a direct right to a healthy environment. Rather, it reaffirms the right to freedom, equality and adequate conditions of life; the requirement of an adequate environment is viewed as a means to achieve the protection of that right. Of course, this approach is true as far as it goes; clearly an environment damaged by pollutants and robbed of all beauty and variety is contrary to adequate conditions of life, just as rupturing the ecosystems endangers physical and mental health.

However, there is value in recognizing an independent right to a safe and healthy environment. First, it reinforces and complements other rights guaranteed to each person. For example, inequalities of economic status are accentuated by environmental harm: the wealthy have available the material means necessary to escape both the air pollution and environmental damage of poor urban areas, and to create for themselves safe and healthy zones, at least until environmental damage becomes too widespread. Recognizing the right to a safe and healthy environment thus can become a means to implement other fundamental human rights.

The concept of a right to environment also is inherent in recognizing the interests of future generations. Immediately after the Stockholm Declaration proclaims that man has the right to live in an environment whose quality permits a life of dignity and well-being, it adds that man has the "solemn responsibility to protect and improve the environment for present and future generations." Economic, social and cultural rights cannot be enjoyed in a world where resources are inadequate due to the waste of irresponsible generations. Thus, the right to environment as one form of the expression of human dignity may be seen as a necessary precondition to the realization of other rights in the future.

* Reprinted with the permission of Transnational Publishers, Inc.

* * * [I]n 1989, the International Labor Organization adopted a new Convention concerning Indigenous and Tribal Peoples in Independent Countries. [28 ILM 1384 (1989).] This treaty requires that states parties take special measures to safeguard the environment of the peoples concerned. In particular governments must ensure that studies are carried out to assess the environmental impact of planned development activities and take measures, in cooperation with the peoples concerned, to protect and preserve the environment of the territories they inhabit. The Convention also recognizes the importance of traditional activities of indigenous peoples, including hunting, fishing, trapping, and gathering. As discussed below, most international instruments for the protection of wildlife contain exceptions permitting traditional hunting by indigenous populations, even with regard to endangered species. Although there is potential conflict between concerns for maintenance of traditional cultures and protection of endangered wildlife species, such conflict remains theoretical at the present time due to the limitations included in the wildlife treaties and traditional indigenous respect for nature.

* * * United Nations organs responsible for human rights issues have begun to consider the inter-relationship of the environment and human rights. The United Nations Subcommission on the Prevention of Discrimination and Protection of Minorities has adopted several resolutions in this field since 1989. One reaffirms that the movement of toxic and dangerous products endangers basic human rights such as the right to life, the right to live in a sound and healthy environment and the right to health, and calls on UNEP to find global solutions to the problem. Another resolution appointed a special rapporteur to study the environment and its relation to human rights, while affirming "the inextricable relationship between human rights and the environment". The UN Human Rights Commission also adopted a resolution in 1990 in which it stressed the importance of the preservation of life-sustaining ecosystems to the promotion of human rights.

* * * It is possible that in the foreseeable future, the right to conservation of the environment will be incorporated more frequently in obligatory international instruments. Besides its procedural aspects, it carries a temporal perspective which could become fundamental for the enjoyment of all other rights guaranteed to individuals, including the interests of future generations in the safeguarding or conservation of resources.

Handl, Human Rights and Protection of the Environment: A Mildly "Revisionist" View

in A. Cancado Trindade (ed.), Human Rights, Sustainable Development and the Environment 117–122 (1992).*

The concept of environmental rights as "new" human rights—"third generation", so-called "human needs" or "solidarity" rights—is a relatively

* Reprinted with the permission of Instituto Interamericano de Drechos Humanos   San José, Costa Rica.

old one. So is the debate over whether such entitlements presently are, are about to be, or should be guaranteed in international law. However, the upcoming 1992 United Nations Conference on Environment and Development which presents a potentially unique opportunity to write and refine basic international environmental law for the rest of the century and beyond, has again focused attention on the concept of international environmental human rights.

For example, in September 1990, the Parliamentary Assembly of the Council of Europe adopted Recommendation 1130 (1990) (1) which provides for a human right to "an environment * * * conducive to * * * good health, well-being and full development of the human personality". In October 1991, an ECE Experts Meeting in Oslo adopted a draft Charter on Environmental Rights and Obligations which proclaims among its fundamental principles everybody's "right to an environment adequate for his general health and well-being." This formulation follows closely Principle 1 of a text adopted by the Experts Group on Environmental Law of the World Commission on Environment and Development in 1986. More recently, the meeting of Associations of Environmental Law adopted a "Declaration of Limoges," which, once again, recommends recognition of a "human right to the environment" (recommendation 4). These proposals have been made against the background of an on-going study by the United Nations Human Rights Commission's Sub-commission on [the] Prevention of Discrimination and Protection of Minorities of the problem of the environment and its relation to human rights.

During the meetings of Working Group III of the UNCED Preparatory Committee itself, a number of states submitted proposals for a similar entitlement for inclusion in the Conference's final document on general rights and obligations, the "Earth Charter": the Chairman's consolidated draft-now replaced by a set of draft principles proposed by the Chairman-contained several provisions that emphasized a human right to a "healthy environment."

Support for international environmental human rights thus cuts across a wide spectrum of international public opinion. * * * Increasingly, it is also being claimed that there exists already, or there is about to emerge, a broad generic entitlement to a healthy, decent or otherwise qualified environment. Indeed, often this entitlement is referred to simply as a "human right to the environment"—unqualified.

The assumption that inspires a significant portion of the public discourse, namely that today the cause of environmental protection is furthered by the postulation of a generic human right to a decent or healthy environment, however, is a problematical one. While it should be self-evident that there is a direct functional relationship between protection of the environment and the promotion of human rights, it is much less obvious that environmental protection ought to be conceptualized in terms of a generic human right. Indeed, the emphasis on such a perspective on the interrelationship of human rights and environmental protection carries significant costs; it reflects a maximalist position that offers little prospect of becoming reality in the near term while its propagation diverts attention and efforts from other more pressing and promising environmental and human rights objectives. In short, a generic international environmental entitlement, both as an already existing and an emerging human rights concept, is a highly questionable proposition.

II.   *Environmental Rights as Human Rights*
A.   *The Right to a Healthy Environment as an Existing or Emerging Human Right*

1.   The Probative Value of International Practice (i) Some Theoretical Observations

At the outset it might be advisable to point out that the international human rights discourse continues to suffer from an unresolved "contradiction between conceptions of human rights as either inherent in human beings by virtue of their humanity or as benevolently granted by the state * * * ". This affects not just the perception of the burden of proof but the very nature of the argument regarding the existence of such rights in general international law. For example, some adherents of a natural law theory of human rights might be apt to view any "just claim" as an existing human right. Most international lawyers, however, are likely to agree that the process of international recognition of human rights evinces overlapping positive and natural law conceptions. They are also likely to insist, notwithstanding the relative dearth of traditional state practice in the sense of international claims and counterclaims involving human rights, on evidence of actual supportive state practice remain[ing] an essential element of any persuasive argument that a given human rights claim is recognized by general international law.

This evidentiary requirement applies firstly, even if we assume that by now states implicitly recognize the United Nations General Assembly's special declaratory authority to determine the human rights nature of claims; and secondly, notwithstanding the possibility that with respect to human rights claims, actual state practice may be less of an essential underpinning of international normativity than [it] would be in * * * other claims contexts. After all, from the perspective of assessing allegedly new customary international legal norms, including human rights norms, deeds speak louder than words: only actual practice endorsing a claimed entitlement may provide a realistic measure of determination to render the prescriptive standard effective. Absent a "credible communication" to that effect, the alleged human rights standard is a mere paper right.

In any event, a diminished evidentiary standard regarding actual practice might be applicable only to human rights that are fundamental or inalienable ones. What can be said with confidence, therefore, is that the more attenuated the natural law basis of an alleged human right, the more important will be support of evidence of its reflection in positive international law, i.e., the practice of states and other relevant transnational actors.

Leaving aside for the moment the problem of its intrinsic relativity, the so-called "right to environment", or the right to a "clean," even to a "healthy environment" would be difficult to conceptualize as an inalienable one, notwithstanding the important objectives it purports to serve. If "inalienability" implies the impermissibility of derogations from the human right concerned, it should be evident why any meaningful environmental entitlement would not qualify: The evolution of environmental protection measures has involved a constant re-ordering of socio-economic priorities, of accomodating, adjusting, or off-setting mutually restrictive, if not exclusive, public policy objectives. Environmental entitlements have been and will continue to be susceptible to restrictions for the sake of other, socio-economic objectives, such as ensuring continued "development" or "saving jobs". In short, since a generic environmental entitlement would not be inalienable, it would not therefore share either a characteristic that is traditionally viewed as a hallmark of "natural" rights. Conceptually, it is instead squarely rooted in positive law.

Those who attempt to make the case for an existing or emerging generic environmental human right, therefore, would have to back up their claims by solid positive legal evidence. Alas, when analyzed in light of this evidentiary standard, the claims concerned are unpersuasive: Thus far, the idea of a generic entitlement—as against "sectoral" environmental rights of individuals—has not found express affirmation in any binding or effective international legal instrument.

6.   DEBT FOR NATURE SWAPS

Brown Weiss, In Fairness to Future Generations
157–159 (1989).*

One of the most innovative international financing initiatives operating at the national level is the debt for nature swap, or debt/conservation swap, which is a method of allowing developing countries to pay off a portion of their external debt by committing themselves to protecting their own natural resources. This indirectly facilitates funds for conservation projects, which are scarce. The idea is an extension of the debt/equity conversions employed by a number of heavily indebted States, in which foreign holders of the country's commercial debt are allowed to exchange it for local currency which can then be reinvested in specified domestic commercial and industrial projects.

The debt/conservation swap can take several forms, depending upon whether the debts are owed to private banks or to multilateral and bilateral lending agencies. If the debts are owed to foreign private banks, there is typically a secondary market where the obligations are bought and sold at only a fraction of their face value, because of the high risk that they may be uncollectible. In a debt/conservation swap, a private party who has bought the obligation at the deeply discounted price, returns it to the issuing government in exchange for the latter's agreeing to undertake a specific conservation program in the indebted country. The first successful transaction involved a private charitable foundation, the Weeden Foundation, which provided money to an environmental organization, Conservation International, to buy deeply discounted Bolivian bonds at 15 cents to the

* Reprinted with the permission of Transnational Publishers, Inc.

dollar. Bolivia agreed to set aside 3.7 million acres of its tropical forest in exchange for cancellation of the debt, and also agreed to allocate money to the maintenance of the reserve. Other such arrangements are being negotiated by private environmental groups such as the World Wildlife Fund.

These swaps are devices to help countries develop on a sustainable basis rather than by destructive short-term resource exploitation in the hope of keeping up with interest payments. They are in essence a form of development assistance that is conditioned on specific programs of environmental conservation. They require for their effectiveness a source of grant funds or concessional loans, preferably one that constitutes a new source of such finance and is not subtracted from funds now being devoted to development assistance.

Bills have been introduced in the U.S. Congress to provide for favorable tax treatment of the debt cancellation or donation. This is intended to encourage commercial banks to donate the outstanding dollar denominated obligations of certain debtor countries to conservation organizations in return for taking a charitable deduction equal, according to the proposed legislation, to the donor's basis in the debt.

When the developing country has borrowed money not from private banks, but from other states through bilateral or multilateral lending agencies, there is no secondary market where the obligations are discounted to third parties. Proposals have been made to encourage the World Bank to forgive certain outstanding loans to developing countries that agree to implement specific conservation programs. These programs could take many different forms depending on the circumstances of each country.

In 1987 the U.S. Secretary of the Treasury expressed support for the principle of debt forgiveness in return for investment in environmental protection measures. Bills have been before both Houses of Congress to require the Executive Director of the World Bank from the United States to propose a pilot program by which countries with debts held by the Bank might suspend repayment by establishing "conservation easements" to protect endangered parts of tropical forests and wetlands.

At the Fourth World Wilderness Congress in September 1987, a World Conservation Bank was proposed to finance conservation projects and address debt problems in developing countries. The World Commission on Environment and Development has proposed that a special international banking facility or program be established in connection with the World Bank to provide loans or develop joint financing activities for conserving critical habitats or ecosystems. This should extend to activities for conserving the knowledge of traditional peoples about these areas.

Notes and Questions

1. *The World Wildlife Fund for Nature.* This NGO has been an active pioneer in this area of debts-for-nature swaps. In 1987–1988 the WWF entered into debts-for-nature swaps with Costa Rica, Ecuador and the Philippines. What concerns do you think might be raised here by the debtor state concerning sovereignty? (Barrans, Promoting Environmental Protec-

tion Through Foreign Debt Exchange Transactions, 24 Cornell Int.L.J. 1 (1991); Hamlin, Debt-for-Nature Swaps: A New Strategy for Protecting Environmental Interests in Developing Nations, 16 Ecol.L.Q. 1065 (1989)).

2. *The Global Environmental Facility*. In 1994 the Global Environmental Facility (GEF), which had been established as a pilot program in 1991, 30 ILM 1735 (1991), was restructured into a permanent financial institution, whose purpose is to provide grants and funds to developing states for projects that will protect the environment. See 33 ILM 1273 (1994). Agenda 21 had singled out at the 1992 Rio Conference the GEF as of vital importance. *See*, introductory note on the GEF by Prang in 33 ILM 1273, 1275, where he states that the agreement "emphasizes the importance of leveraging additional resources from other sources, including the private sector, broadening the range of partners with access to GEF funds; and making more information available about GEF and associated projects."

CHAPTER 7

THE IMMUNITIES OF STATES AND INTERNATIONAL ORGANIZATIONS, THE ACT OF STATE DOCTRINE

SECTION A. THE IMMUNITY OF STATES

1. ABSOLUTE AND RESTRICTIVE PRINCIPLES

Modern doctrines of foreign sovereign immunities are a product of evolving customary international law influenced by Twentieth Century legislation, judicial decision, and efforts to develop and codify by the treaty process. Immunity shields a sovereign from the exercise of jurisdiction, principally from the jurisdiction of other states' courts in cases where the sovereign has not given consent. Its purpose is to allow a sovereign to act in the nation's best interest without fear that its actions will become the subject of adjudication in another state. It also is to ensure that the public property of the state remain available for public purposes, free from the constraints of the forum's powers of attachment and execution. The international legal rules on sovereign immunity still are not free from dispute and uncertainty, despite several centuries of attempts to refine them in treaties, judicial decisions, and doctrine. It is now at least clear, however, that immunity can be justified only on the basis of the most compelling considerations of public policy. This trend seems to favor the reduction of sovereign immunity coverage.

In the *Schooner Exchange v. McFadden,* 11 U.S. (7 Cranch) 116, 3 L.Ed. 287 (1812): Chief Justice Marshall stated the classical formulation of the rationale for sovereign immunity:

> The world being composed of distinct sovereignties, possessing equal rights and equal independence, whose mutual benefit is promoted by intercourse with each other, and by an interchange of those good offices which humanity dictates and its wants require, all sovereigns have consented to a relaxation in practice, in cases under certain circumstances, of that absolute and complete jurisdiction within their respective territories which sovereignty confers.

> * * *

> This full and absolute territorial jurisdiction being alike the attribute of every sovereign, and being incapable of conferring extra-territorial power, would not seem to contemplate foreign sovereigns nor their sovereign rights to its objects. One sovereign being in no respect amenable to another; and being bound by obligations of the highest character not to degrade the dignity of his nation, by placing himself or its sovereign rights within the jurisdiction of another, can be supposed to enter a foreign territory only under an express license, or in confidence that the immunities belonging to his independent sovereign station, though not expressly stipulated, are reserved by implication, and will be extended to him.

> This perfect equality and absolute independence of sovereigns, and this common interest impelling them to mutual intercourse, and an interchange of good offices with each other, have given rise to a class of cases in which every sovereign is understood to waive the exercise of a part of that complete exclusive territorial jurisdiction, which has been stated to be the attribute of every nation.

The fiction of "perfect equality and absolute independence of sovereigns" arose in the 18th and 19th Centuries. Having served as one of the theoretical bases of international law, it is not altogether forgotten today. We must now consider whether Chief Justice Marshall's elegant formulations still fit comfortably with either the appearance or reality of modern international relations. The international system has evolved toward a more realistic and pragmatic policy oriented vision of the sovereign's status. Notions of sovereignty, equality and independence have become qualified, indeed severely limited. Theoretically, since the American Revolution, the "people" are generally considered sovereign, rather than the head of State. More realistically, the "sovereign" may be a public trading institution or other subordinate governmental operating entity; the sovereign's commercial activities, in acting like a trader, have led to the "restrictive theory" that relaxes sovereign immunity for commercial and certain other activities. The modern sovereign state's equality and independence are severely constrained in institutions like the U.N. or other international organizations. A sovereign can be subject to the most far-reaching and even humiliating formal condemnations, such as occurred with Iraq in the Security Council actions taken in the course of the Persian Gulf Crisis in 1990–1991. "Perfect equality" does not exist outside ideal legal abstraction. It is no wonder that sovereign immunity doctrine has receded from its most extreme form, "*absolute immunity*", in many (but by no means all) countries. With "absolute immunity" now finding only minority support, the international system is moving to accommodate immunity problems in particular sectors or situations and to find new applications and exceptions.

If the concerns about formal doctrine of equality, dignity, and avoidance of embarrassment no longer carry their former weight, there remain other considerations which explain the durability of the sovereign immunity doctrine. The judicial branch may be, or at least may feel, constrained at hearing charges or claims against a sovereign. Judicial determinations rendered against a foreign state or its leader can interfere with the conduct of foreign relations. Although this problem is sometimes exaggerated, serious problems can arise. For example, embarrassment and international conflict could occur if a court were to adopt a rule, apply a treaty interpretation or make a decision at variance with the views of the forum executive, that had been advanced in negotiations with another state. Protecting a foreign state from nuisance cases, from the abusive use of the courts as a negotiating tool or as a "public forum" for political advantage is another reason for sovereign immunity continued viability. The case for immunity is strong when judicial action may interfere with the forum state's continuing or future foreign relations. Concerns about protecting operations are particularly noteworthy in cases of attachment and execution affecting a foreign government's property situated in the forum state. The foregoing policy concerns have affected outcomes of decisions, resulting in the continuing uncertainty and at times inconsistency in the law. The materials below cover many of these situations.

In sum, the case for sovereign immunity, particularly in the traditional absolute sense, has become much less acceptable. State practice is not uniform and uncertainty as to the rules and role of sovereign immunity is widespread among and even within countries. More erosion of the traditional doctrine may be reasonably foreseen. The former socialist countries of central and eastern Europe remain among the last bastions of the absolute principle, but as they evolve more fully into market economies, they may find that they have the same incentive as traditional market economy countries to find ways of limiting sovereign immunity. They too might well adopt the "restrictive principle" which relaxes the immunity for commercial and a number of other specified activities.

Absolute Theory of Immunity

Chief Justice Marshall articulated the principle of absolute immunity in the famous *Schooner Exchange* Case, quoted above. Cf. Aldona S. v. U.K., 90 J. du Dr. Int'l 190 (1963) (S. Ct, Poland 1948). Absolute immunity was attacked in the early part of the 20th century, often in cases in which foreign state owned vessels were engaged in maritime commerce. In 1926, however, the United States Supreme Court refused to limit the scope of the immunity in an *in rem* proceeding to enforce a cargo damage claim against a merchant vessel owned and operated by Italy. The Court stated:

> We think the principles [of immunity] are applicable alike to all ships held and used by a government for a public purpose, and that when, for the purpose of advancing the trade of its people or providing revenue for its treasury, a government acquires, mans and operates ships in the carrying trade, they are public ships in the same sense that war ships are. We know of no international usage which regards the maintenance and advancement of the economic welfare of a people in time of peace as any less a public purpose than the maintenance and training of a naval force. *Berizzi Bros. Co. v. S.S. Pesaro*, 271 U.S. 562 (1926).

Some Substantive Exceptions to Sovereign Immunity. Forum state policy considerations have traditionally led to a few exceptions to the absolute immunity principle, such as those relating to rights in immovable property (real property) situated in the forum state and rights in movable property there when acquired by succession or gift. Section 1605(4) of the U.S. Foreign Sovereign Immunities Act provides for these exceptions, (See the Documentary Supplement.) Article 7 of the Charter of the International Military Tribunal established for the Nuremberg Trials after World War II provided another exception which precluded sovereign immunity for war crimes. The Security Council in S/RES/827 (1993) adopted a parallel exception incident to the creation of the International Tribunal to prosecute crimes against humanity in the former Yugoslavia (see Chapter 16). Article 7.2 of the Annex to that Resolution provides that: "The official position of any accused person, whether as Head of State or Government or as a responsible Government official, shall not relieve such person of criminal responsibility nor mitigate punishment". An identical provision was made for the Rwanda Tribunal (see Article 6.2 of that Tribunal's Statute, 33 I.L.M. 1598, 1604 (1994)) and another is provided more permanently in the Rome Statute of the International Criminal Court.

Rome Statute of the International Criminal Court

Adopted July 17, 1998, 37 I.L.M. 999, 1017 (1998).

Article 27 Irrelevance of official capacity

1.   This Statute shall apply equally to all persons without any distinction based on official capacity. In particular, official capacity as a Head of State or Government, a member of a Government or parliament, an elected representative or a government official shall in no case exempt a person from criminal responsibility under this Statute, nor shall it, in and of itself, constitute a ground for reduction of sentence.

2.   Immunities or special procedural rules which may attach to the official capacity of a person, whether under national or international law, shall not bar the Court from exercising its jurisdiction over such a person.

Restrictive Theory of Immunity

In 1952, the U.S. Department of State indicated that it would follow the *"restrictive"* theory of sovereign immunity, as stated in the famous "Tate Letter". This theory was applied in the *Foreign Sovereign Immunities Act of 1976*. A period of extensive *state* participation in commercial activity during the 19th and early 20th centuries precipitated the change.

United States: Letter From the Acting Legal Adviser of the Department of State to the Department of Justice, May 19, 1952 (The Famous "Tate Letter")

26 United States Department of State Bulletin 984 (1952).

MY DEAR MR. ATTORNEY GENERAL:

The Department of State has for some time had under consideration the question whether the practice of the Government in granting immunity from suit to foreign governments made parties defendant in the courts of the United States without their consent should not be changed. The Department has now reached the conclusion that such immunity should no longer be granted in certain types of cases. In view of the obvious interest of your Department in this matter I should like to point out briefly some of the facts which influenced the Department's decision.

A study of the law of sovereign immunity reveals the existence of two conflicting concepts of sovereign immunity, each widely held and firmly established. According to the classical or absolute theory of sovereign immunity, a sovereign cannot, without his consent, be made a respondent in the courts of another sovereign. According to the newer or restrictive theory of sovereign immunity, the immunity of the sovereign is recognized with regard to sovereign or public acts (*jure imperii*) of a state, but not with respect to private acts (*jure gestionis*). There is agreement by proponents of both theories, supported by practice, that sovereign immunity should not be claimed or granted in actions with respect to real property (diplomatic and perhaps consular property excepted) or with respect to the disposition of the property of a deceased person even though a foreign sovereign is the beneficiary.

The classical or virtually absolute theory of sovereign immunity has generally been followed by the courts of the United States, the British Commonwealth, Czechoslovakia, Estonia, and probably Poland.

The decisions of the courts of Brazil, Chile, China, Hungary, Japan, Luxembourg, Norway, and Portugal may be deemed to support the classical theory of immunity if one or at most two old decisions anterior to the development of the restrictive theory may be considered sufficient on which to base a conclusion.

The position of the Netherlands, Sweden, and Argentina is less clear since although immunity has been granted in recent cases coming before the courts of those countries, the facts were such that immunity would have been granted under either the absolute or restrictive theory. However, constant references by the courts of these three countries to the distinction between public and private acts of the state, even though the distinction was not involved in the result of the case, may indicate an intention to leave the way open for a possible application of the restrictive theory of immunity if and when the occasion presents itself.

A trend to the restrictive theory is already evident in the Netherlands where the lower courts have started to apply that theory following a Supreme Court decision to the effect that immunity would have been applicable in the case under consideration under either theory.

The German courts, after a period of hesitation at the end of the nineteenth century have held to the classical theory, but it should be noted that the refusal of the Supreme Court in 1921 to yield to pressure by the lower courts for the newer theory was based on the view that theory had not yet developed sufficiently to justify a change. In view of the growth of the restrictive theory since that time the German courts might take a different view today.

The newer or restrictive theory of sovereign immunity has always been supported by the courts of Belgium and Italy. It was adopted in turn by the courts of Egypt and of Switzerland. In addition, the courts of France, Austria, and Greece, which were traditionally supporters of the classical theory, reversed their position in the 20's to embrace the restrictive theory. Rumania, Peru, and possibly Denmark also appear to follow this theory.

Furthermore, it should be observed that in most of the countries still following the classical theory there is a school of influential writers favoring the restrictive theory and the views of writers, at least in civil law countries, are a major factor in the development of the law. Moreover, the leanings of the lower courts in civil law countries are more significant in shaping the law than they are in common law countries where the rule of precedent prevails and the trend in these lower courts is to the restrictive theory.

Of related interest to this question is the fact that ten of the thirteen countries which have been classified above as supporters of the classical theory have ratified the Brussels Convention of 1926 under which immunity for government owned merchant vessels is waived. In addition the United States, which is not a party to the Convention, some years ago announced and has since followed, a policy of not claiming immunity for its public owned or operated merchant vessels. Keeping in mind the importance played by cases involving public vessels in the field of sovereign immunity, it is thus noteworthy that these ten countries (Brazil, Chile, Estonia, Germany, Hungary, Netherlands, Norway, Poland, Portugal, Sweden) and the United States have already relinquished by treaty or in practice an important part of the immunity which they claim under the classical theory.

It is thus evident that with the possible exception of the United Kingdom little support has been found except on the part of the Soviet Union and its satellites for continued full acceptance of the absolute theory of sovereign immunity. There are evidences that British authorities are aware of its deficiencies and ready for a change. The reasons which obviously motivate state trading countries in adhering to the theory with perhaps increasing rigidity are most persuasive that the United States should change its policy. Furthermore, the granting of sovereign immunity to foreign governments in the courts of the United States is most inconsistent with the action of the Government of the United States in subjecting itself to suit in these same courts in both contract and tort and with its long established policy of not claiming immunity in foreign jurisdictions for its merchant vessels. Finally, the Department feels that the widespread and increasing practice on the part of governments of engaging in commercial activities makes necessary a practice which will enable persons doing business with them to have their rights determined in the courts. For these reasons it will hereafter be the Department's policy to follow the restrictive theory of sovereign immunity in the consideration of requests of foreign governments for a grant of sovereign immunity.

It is realized that a shift in policy by the executive cannot control the courts but it is felt that the courts are less likely to allow a plea of sovereign immunity where the executive has declined to do so. There have been indications that at least some Justices of the Supreme Court feel that in this matter courts should follow the branch of the Government charged with responsibility for the conduct of foreign relations.

In order that your Department, which is charged with representing the interests of the Government before the courts, may be adequately informed it will be the Department's practice to advise you of all requests by foreign governments for the grant of immunity from suit and of the Department's action thereon.

Sincerely yours,

For the Secretary of State:

JACK B. TATE
Acting Legal Adviser

* * *

Testimony of the Legal Adviser of the Department of State of the United States on the Foreign Sovereign Immunities Act of 1976

Hearings on H.R. 11315 before the Subcommittee on Administrative Law and Governmental Relations of the Committee on the Judiciary, House of Representatives, 94th Cong., 2d Sess. 24, 26–27 (1976).

[Monroe Leigh, the Legal Adviser, testified]: The first objective is to vest sovereign immunity decisions exclusively in the courts. The bill would accomplish this by prescribing the standards the courts are to apply in deciding questions of sovereign immunity.

* * * [A]fter a foreign-state defendant raises the defense of sovereign immunity, it has an option: either the foreign state can litigate this legal defense entirely in court, or, as is more usually the case, it can make a formal diplomatic request to have the State Department decide the issue.

If it does the latter, and if the State Department believes that immunity is appropriate, the State Department asks the Department of Justice to file a "suggestion of immunity" with the court hearing the case. Under the Supreme Court's decision in *Ex Parte Peru*, which was decided in 1943, U.S. courts automatically defer to such suggestions of immunity from the executive branch.

In response to various developments in international law, the State Department in 1952 adopted its so-called *Tate letter*. Prior to the Tate letter, the Department of State, when called on to decide questions of immunity, followed the so-called absolute rule of sovereign immunity: a state was immune from suit irrespective of whether it was engaged in a government or a commercial act.

Under the Tate letter, the Department undertook to decide future sovereign immunity questions in accordance with the international legal principle which I have mentioned and which is known as the "restrictive theory"—namely, that a foreign state's immunity is "restricted" to cases based on its public acts, and does not extend to cases based on its commercial or private acts. The Tate letter was based on a realization that the prior absolute rule of sovereign immunity was no longer consistent with modern international law.

The Tate letter, however, has not been satisfactory. * * * From a legal standpoint, it poses a devil's choice. If the Department follows the Tate letter in a given case, it is in the incongruous position of a political institution trying to apply a legal standard to litigation already before the courts.

On the other hand, if forced to disregard the Tate letter in a given case, the Department is in the self-defeating position of abandoning the very international law principle it elsewhere espouses.

From a diplomatic standpoint, the Tate letter has continued to leave the diplomatic initiative to the foreign state. The foreign state chooses which case it will bring to the State Department and in which case it will try to raise diplomatic considerations.

Leaving the diplomatic initiative in such cases to the foreign state places the United States at a disadvantage. This is particularly true since the United States cannot itself obtain similar advantages in other countries. In virtually every other country in the world, sovereign immunity is a question of international law decided exclusively by the courts and not by institutions concerned with foreign affairs.

For this reason, when we and other foreign states are sued abroad, we realize that international law principles will be applied by the courts and that diplomatic relations will not be called into play.

Moreover, from the standpoint of the private citizen, the current system generates considerable commercial uncertainty. A private party who deals with a foreign government entity cannot be certain of having his day in court to resolve an ordinary legal dispute. He cannot be entirely certain that the ordinary legal dispute will not be artificially raised to the level of a diplomatic problem through the government's intercession with the State Department.

The purpose of sovereign immunity in modern international law is not to protect the sensitivities of 19th–century monarchs or the prerogatives of the 20th–century state. Rather, it is to promote the functioning of all governments by protecting a state from the burden of defending law suits abroad which are based on its public acts.

However, when the foreign state enters the marketplace or when it acts as a private party, there is no justification in modern international law for allowing the foreign state to avoid the economic costs of the agreements which it may breach or the accidents which it may cause.

The law should not permit the foreign state to shift these everyday burdens of the marketplace onto the shoulders of private parties. * * *

———

1. *Foreign Sovereign Immunities Act of 1976.* Selections from the Act, as amended, appear in the Documentary Supplement. The act went into effect in January 1977. It incorporates the restrictive theory. As the Legal Adviser put it in * * * his testimony: "Under international law today, a foreign state is entitled to sovereign immunity only in the cases based on its 'public' acts. However, where a law suit is based on a commercial transaction or some other 'private' act of the foreign state, the foreign state is not entitled to sovereign immunity. The specific applications of this principle of international law are codified in * * * the proposed bill."

The *fundamental rule* is stated in Section 1604: "Subject to existing international agreements to which the United States is a party at the time of enactment of this Act a foreign state shall be immune from the jurisdiction of the courts of the United States and of the States except as provided in sections 1605 to 1607 of this chapter." In accordance with the terms of those sections, there are ten categories of exceptions to section 1604:

(1) waiver of immunity

(2) commercial activity

(3) rights in property taken in violation of international law

(4) rights in property in the United States acquired by succession or gift or rights in immovable property in the United States

(5) money damage tort actions for personal injuries or death or damage to or loss of property occurring in the United States

(6) enforcement of an arbitration agreement made by a foreign state with or for the benefit of a private party, in prescribed situations

(7) money damage actions for personal injuries or death that was caused by an act of torture, extrajudicial killing, or aircraft sabotage, or hostage taking

(8) maritime liens against a vessel where the lien is based upon commercial activities and in certain other situations

(9) foreclosure of a preferred mortgage under the Ship Mortgage Act of 1920

(10) counterclaims.

In *Verlinden B.V. v. Central Bank of Nigeria*, 461 U.S. 480 (1983), the U.S. Supreme Court upheld the constitutional power of Congress to enact this legislation.

––––––

2. ***United Kingdom: State Immunity Act of 1978.*** The United Kingdom became a signatory to the European Convention on State Immunity on May 16, 1972. That Convention, found in 11 I. L.M. 470 (1972) (entered into force on June 11, 1976), incorporates the restrictive theory. To give effect to the Convention, the U.K. enacted the State Immunity Act of 1978, found in 17 I. L.M. 1123 (1978). For a recent discussion of sovereign immunity in the United Kingdom, see *Holland v. Lampen-Wolf*, House of Lords, 20 July 2000, especially the opinion of Lord Millet, [2000] 3 All ER 833, 1 WLR 1573, unanimously recognizing the immunity in a defamation action against a civilian U.S. educational official serving at a U.S. Air Force base in Britain. The action was brought by a civilian professor at the base who also was a U.S. citizen. *See also*, The Canadian State Immunity Act, R.S.C. 1885, c. S–18asam.

The 1987 Restatement noted that nearly all "non-Communist" states now accept the restrictive theory. Comment *a* to Section 451. It remains to be seen whether former communist countries will adopt it. None so far are a party to the European Convention discussed below.

3. ***International Agreements.*** Movement toward the "restrictive principle" is occurring as a function of a number of treaty provisions in force or under consideration as well as national legislation and judicial decisions. These sources may well be moving customary law in that direction by accretion. The first of these treaties is the Brussels Convention of 1926, which applied the restrictive principle to government owned or operated vessels involved in trade (*See also*, the 1982 U.N. Convention on the Law of the Sea provisions on the subject of vessels *e.g.*, Articles 27–32, 95 and 96). The European Convention on State Immunity and Additional Protocol of May 16, 1972 adopted the restrictive principle on a broader basis, including the commercial exception as provided in Article 7.1, which reads:

> A Contracting state may not claim immunity from the jurisdiction of a court of another Contracting State if it has on the territory of the State of the forum an office, agency, or other establishment through which it engages, in the same manner as a private person, in an industrial, commercial or financial activity, and the proceedings relate to that activity of the office, agency or establishment.

By early 2001, there were 9 signatories to the European Convention (Austria, Belgium, Cyprus, Germany, Luxembourg, Netherlands, Portugal, Switzerland and the United Kingdom) and 7 countries which had given their consent to be bound (all but Portugal).

In 1991 the International Law Commission adopted "Draft Articles on Jurisdictional Immunities of States and their Property" (UN A/46/405, 11 September, 1991; 30 I.L.M. 1554, 1565). Article 5 contains the following broad provision: "A State enjoys immunity, in respect of itself and its property, from the jurisdiction of the courts of another State subject to the provisions of the present articles." This is qualified by a number of exceptions, including: "express consent" (Article 7); proceedings initiated by the State invoking immunity (Articles 8 & 9); commercial transactions (Article 10); contracts of employment (Article 11); personal injuries and damage to property (Article 12); ownership, possession and use of property (Article 13); intellectual and industrial property (Article 14); participation in companies or other collective bodies (Article 15); ships owned or operated by a State for other than government non-commercial purposes (Article 16); and certain proceedings related to an arbitration to which the State had agreed in writing (Article 17).

Articles 18 and 19 cover state immunity from "measures of constraint". They provide for the immunity except in described cases of consent, allocation or earmarking of property for satisfaction of a claim, and certain property in use or intended for use by the State for other than government non-commercial purposes. Moreover, specific categories of qualifying property may not be reached: immovable and some movable property (bank accounts included) "used or intended for use for the purposes of the diplomatic mission of the State" (Article 19).

That the Draft Articles do not yet enjoy a consensus is made clear by the work of the 1991 General Assembly Sixth Committee which encountered doctrinal disagreement as well as problems of detail and drafting (see U.N. A/CN.4/L. 456, February 6, 1991). The Draft Articles, nevertheless, currently represent the most advanced efforts to resolve the numerous uncertainties in the sovereign immunity arena.

U.N. Convention on the Law of the Sea

Article 95

Immunity of warships on the high seas

Warships on the high seas have complete immunity from the jurisdiction of any State other than the flag State.

Article 96

Immunity of ships used only on government non-commercial service

Ships owned or operated by a State and used only on government non-commercial service shall, on the high seas, have complete immunity from jurisdiction of any State other than the flag State.

————

4. ***French Administrative Law Concepts.*** After the French Revolution of 1789, France established two parallel systems of courts: one judicial and the other administrative. For all practical purposes, they are equal in rank. The judicial system essentially was given jurisdiction over

disputes between private parties, while the administrative system was given jurisdiction over disputes between private parties and the state. The administrative courts have developed—on a case by case basis (similar to the way "case-law" developed in the "common law" world)—a body of administrative law which has no exact counterpart in England or the United States. This "case law" development has become the basis of administrative law in much of continental Europe and has influenced the administrative law of a number of states elsewhere. It was and is in these administrative courts that the individual is protected from official abuse.

It cannot be entirely an accident that states whose courts led the development of the restrictive theory, or eventually adopted it, are also, in the main, those which adopted or were influenced by French administrative law. For in the French system, a fundamental distinction is drawn between situations where the state exercises its *public power*, and those where the state acts in its *private capacity*. In the former, litigation authority belongs to the administrative courts. In the latter, it belongs to the judiciary. The distinction is elementary to civil law lawyers, even though it is subject in its application to exceptions, qualifications and refinements as complex as those surrounding the application of the concept of due process in U.S. courts.

Because of their experience with concepts of administrative law in the French, the courts, by the turn of the century, of a number of civil law states were intellectually conditioned to engage in a critical analysis of the doctrine of sovereign immunity. They did not take it for granted that all acts of a foreign state were sovereign. Borrowing a differentiation from French administrative law and using it as the basis for determining immunity vel non, the theory worked out to delimit acts of sovereignty entitled to immunity (public acts) and to separate them from other acts not entitled to immunity (private acts).

Consider the following application of the distinction between public and private acts.

Georges Delaume, Case Note, Société Iranienne Du Gaz v. Société Pipeline Service

[NIGC]   80 Revue Critique de Droit International Privé 140 (1991).
French Court of Cassation, May 2, 1990.
85 AJIL 696 (1991).[1]

In 1978 a French company (Pipeline) and the National Iranian Gas Company (NIGC) entered into a contract (governed by Iranian law) for the supply and erection of gas pipeline installations linking certain Iranian cities. Apparently not paid for its services, Pipeline brought an action in France against NIGC. NIGC's plea of immunity was denied by the Court of Appeal of Versailles, whose decision was reversed by the Court of Cassation.

From the decision of the Court of Cassation (which, as usual, is essentially abstract and does not supply detailed information on the facts of

---

1. Reprinted by permission of the American Society of International Law.

the case and the arguments of the parties), it appears that NIGC based its plea of immunity on the consideration that it was intimately linked to the Iranian Government and that its activities relating to gas transmission throughout Iran were intended to meet the needs of a "public service" (service public). The court of appeal had considered this line of argument irrelevant because the decisive factor in determining the issue of immunity was the nature of the transaction. In its view, under the French lex fori, the transaction fell within the category of a "public work subcontract," which should be characterized as a purely commercial transaction. The Court of Cassation disagreed with that characterization, stating: "Foreign states and instrumentalities acting under the direction or on behalf of states are entitled to immunity from suit not only in regard to governmental acts but also in respect of acts performed in furtherance of a public service."[2]

This decision is surprising. It is contrary to a consistent line of cases in which the Court of Cassation has held that, for the implementation of immunity rules, the relevant factor is the nature of the transaction from which the dispute arises, rather than its purpose.[3] The nature of the transaction has been considered decisive in cases involving both immunity from suit and immunity from execution.

A return to the traditional test is apparent from another decision of the Court of Cassation rendered barely a few weeks after the NIGC case. The plaintiff, a British newspaperman, brought suit against the Kuwait News Agency following the agency's decision not to renew his contract. The agency pleaded immunity on the grounds that (1) it was an agency of Kuwait linked to the Ministry of Information; (2) its managing board was appointed by the Government; and (3) the contract of employment had a governmental character since the plaintiff's activities regarding the collection of information were carried out for the exclusive benefit of the Kuwaiti Government and, as such, should be regarded as directly related to the pursuit of a "public service." The plea was denied. Although the decision could have been based on the sole ground that the agency had an independent juridical personality and enjoyed financial autonomy, the Court went further and said that, even if the agency were in effect part of the Kuwaiti Government, the employment contract should be regarded as a commercial act with respect to which there was no immunity from suit.

Under the circumstances, the rationale of the NIGC decision is not readily apparent. It may be that the Court of Cassation was influenced by domestic administrative law concepts regarding the respective jurisdictions of the administrative and judicial courts. If that were the case, the NIGC

---

2. Judgment of May 2, 1990, Cass. civ. 80 Revue Critique De Droit International Privé [RCDIP] 140, 141.

3. France long ago adopted the restrictive theory of sovereign immunity. * * * Under the "purpose" test, an act would be considered sovereign if performed for a public purpose. That test has been criticized on the ground that, literally applied, it would eviscerate the "restrictive" theory of immunity since all acts of the sovereign might be construed as having a public purpose. Victory Transport Inc. v. Comisaria General, 336 F.2d 354 (2d Cir.1964). In the United States, the "nature of the act" test was codified in the Foreign Sovereign Immunities Act of 1976, 28 U.S.C. § 1603(d) (1988) and applied by the U.S. Supreme Court in Republic of Argentina etc v, Weltover, taken up below.

decision would be a matter of concern because these concepts are not as clear as would be desirable. To project them into the international arena would inject unwarranted uncertainties into the implementation of immunity rules. Another possibility is that the Court may have been influenced by nonlegal considerations due to the improvement in the political climate between France and Iran. In any event, in light of the Kuwait News Agency decision, it is not clear whether the Court intended to signal a change in immunity rules in the NIGC case.

———

Questions: What are the conceptual differences between the approach of the Cour de Cassation in the NIGC and the Kuwait cases as described above? Can they be reconciled? Which would lead to the preferred policy result as you see it? Why?

General Rule of Immunity

Argentine Republic v. Amerada Hess Shipping Corp.

United States Supreme Court, 1989.
488 U.S. 428, 109 S.Ct. 683, 102 L.Ed.2d 818.

■ CHIEF JUSTICE REHNQUIST delivered the opinion of the Court.

Two Liberian corporations sued the Argentine Republic in a United States District Court to recover damages for a tort allegedly committed by its armed forces on the high seas in violation of international law. We hold that the District Court correctly dismissed the action, because the Foreign Sovereign Immunities Act of 1976 (FSIA), 28 U.S.C. § 1330 et seq., does not authorize jurisdiction over a foreign state in this situation.

Respondents alleged the following facts in their complaints. Respondent United Carriers, Inc., a Liberian corporation, chartered one of its oil tankers, the Hercules, to respondent Amerada Hess Shipping Corporation, also a Liberian corporation. The contract was executed in New York City. Amerada Hess used the Hercules to transport crude oil from the southern terminus of the Trans–Alaska Pipeline in Valdez, Alaska, around Cape Horn in South America, to the Hess refinery in the United States Virgin Islands. On May 25, 1982, the Hercules began a return voyage, without cargo but fully fueled, from the Virgin Islands to Alaska. At that time, Great Britain and petitioner Argentine Republic were at war over an archipelago of some 200 islands—the Falkland Islands to the British, and the Islas Malvinas to the Argentineans—in the South Atlantic off the Argentine coast. On June 3, United States officials informed the two belligerents of the location of United States vessels and Liberian tankers owned by United States interests then traversing the South Atlantic, including the Hercules, to avoid any attacks on neutral shipping.

By June 8, 1982, after a stop in Brazil, the Hercules was in international waters about 600 nautical miles from Argentina and 500 miles from the Falklands; she was outside the "war zones" designated by Britain and Argentina. At 12:15 Greenwich mean time, the ship's master made a routine report by radio to Argentine officials, providing the ship's name, international call sign, registry, position, course, speed, and voyage description. About 45 minutes later, an Argentine military aircraft began to circle the Hercules. The ship's master repeated his earlier message by radio to Argentine officials, who acknowledged receiving it. Six minutes later, without provocation, another Argentine military plane began to bomb the Hercules; the master immediately hoisted a white flag. A second bombing soon followed, and a third attack came about two hours later, when an Argentine jet struck the ship with an air-to-surface rocket. Disabled but not destroyed, the Hercules reversed course and sailed to Rio de Janeiro, the nearest safe port. At Rio de Janeiro, respondent United Carriers determined that the ship had suffered extensive deck and hull damage, and that an undetonated bomb remained lodged in her No. 2 tank. After an investigation by the Brazilian Navy, United Carriers decided that it would be too hazardous to remove the undetonated bomb, and on July 20, 1978, the Hercules was scuttled 250 miles off the Brazilian coast. * * *

* * * In the FSIA, Congress added a new chapter 97 to Title 28 of the United States Code, 28 U.S.C. §§ 1602–1611, which is entitled "Jurisdictional Immunities of Foreign States." Section 1604 provides that "[s]ubject to existing international agreements to which the United States [was] a party at the time of the enactment of this Act[,] a foreign state shall be immune from the jurisdiction of the courts of the United States and of the States except as provided in sections 1605 to 1607 of this chapter." The FSIA also added § 1330(a) to Title 28; it provides that "[t]he district courts shall have original jurisdiction without regard to amount in controversy of any nonjury civil action against a foreign state * * * as to any claim for relief in personam with respect to which the foreign state is not entitled to immunity under sections 1605–1607 of this title or under any applicable international agreement." § 1330(a).

We think that the text and structure of the FSIA demonstrate Congress' intention that the FSIA be the sole basis for obtaining jurisdiction over a foreign state in our courts. Section 1604 and § 1330(a) work in tandem: § 1604 bars federal and state courts from exercising jurisdiction when a foreign state is entitled to immunity, and § 1330(a) confers jurisdiction on district courts to hear suits brought by United States citizens and by aliens when a foreign state is not entitled to immunity. As we said in Verlinden, the FSIA "must be applied by the district courts in every action against a foreign sovereign, since subject-matter jurisdiction in any such action depends on the existence of one of the specified exceptions to foreign sovereign immunity." *Verlinden B.V. v. Central Bank of Nigeria*, 461 U.S. 480, 493 (1983).

The Court of Appeals acknowledged that the FSIA's language and legislative history support the "general rule" that the Act governs the immunity of foreign states in federal court. The Court of Appeals, however, thought that the FSIA's "focus on commercial concerns" and Congress' failure to "repeal" the Alien Tort Statute indicated Congress' intention that federal courts continue to exercise jurisdiction over foreign states in suits alleging violations of international law outside the confines of the FSIA. The Court of Appeals also believed that to construe the FSIA to bar the instant suit would "fly in the face" of Congress' intention that the FSIA be interpreted pursuant to " 'standards recognized under international law.' " Ibid., * * *.

Taking the last of these points first, Congress had violations of international law by foreign states in mind when it enacted the FSIA. For example, the FSIA specifically denies foreign states immunity in suits "in which rights in property taken in violation of international law are in issue." 28 U.S.C. § 1605(a)(3). Congress also rested the FSIA in part on its power under Art. I, § 8, cl. 10, of the Constitution "[t]o define and punish Piracies and Felonies committed on the high Seas, and Offenses against the Law of Nations." From Congress' decision to deny immunity to foreign states in the class of cases just mentioned, we draw the plain implication that immunity is granted in those cases involving alleged violations of international law that do not come within one of the FSIA's exceptions.

As to the other point made by the Court of Appeals, Congress' failure to enact a pro tanto repealer of the Alien Tort Statute when it passed the FSIA in 1976 may be explained at least in part by the lack of certainty as to whether the Alien Tort Statute conferred jurisdiction in suits against foreign states. Enacted by the First Congress in 1789, the Alien Tort Statute provides that "[t]he district courts shall have original jurisdiction of any civil action by an alien for a tort only, committed in violation of the law of nations or a treaty of the United States." 28 U.S.C. § 1350. The Court of Appeals did not cite any decision in which a United States court exercised jurisdiction over a foreign state under the Alien Tort Statute, and only one such case has come to our attention—one which was decided after the enactment of the FSIA.

* * * [R]espondents argue that cases were brought under the Alien Tort Statute against foreign states for the unlawful taking of a prize during wartime. The Alien Tort Statute makes no mention of prize jurisdiction, and § 1333(2) now grants federal district courts exclusive jurisdiction over "all proceedings for the condemnation of property taken as a prize." In the *Santissima Trinidad*, 20 U.S. (7 Wheat.) 283, 353–354, 5 L.Ed. 454 (1822), we held that foreign states were not immune from the jurisdiction of United States courts in prize proceedings. That case, however, was not brought under the Alien Tort Statute but rather as a libel in admiralty. Thus there is a distinctly hypothetical cast to the Court of Appeals' reliance on Congress' failure to repeal the Alien Tort Statute, and respondents' arguments in this Court based on the principle of statutory construction that repeals by implication are disfavored.

We think that Congress' failure in the FSIA to enact an express pro tanto repealer of the Alien Tort Statute speaks only faintly, if at all, to the issue involved in this case. In light of the comprehensiveness of the statutory scheme in the FSIA, we doubt that even the most meticulous draftsman would have concluded that Congress also needed to amend pro tanto the Alien Tort Statute and presumably such other grants of subject-matter jurisdiction in Title 28 as § 1331 (federal question), § 1333 (admiralty), § 1335 (interpleader), § 1337 (commerce and antitrust), and § 1338 (patents, copyrights, and trademarks). Congress provided in § 1602 of the FSIA that "[c]laims of foreign states to immunity should henceforth be decided by courts of the United States in conformity with the principles set forth in this chapter," and very likely it thought that should be sufficient. § 1602 (emphasis added); see also H.R.Rep., at 12; S.Rep., at 11 * * * (FSIA "intended to preempt any other State and Federal law (excluding applicable international agreements) for according immunity to foreign sovereigns").

Having determined that the FSIA provides the sole basis for obtaining jurisdiction over a foreign state in federal court, we turn to whether any of the exceptions enumerated in the Act apply here. These exceptions include cases involving the waiver of immunity, § 1605(a)(1), commercial activities occurring in the United States or causing a direct effect in this country, § 1605(a)(2), property expropriated in violation of international law, § 1605(a)(3), real estate, inherited, or gift property located in the United States, § 1605(a)(4), non-commercial torts occurring in the United States, § 1605(a)(5), and maritime liens, § 1605(b). We agree with the District Court that none of the FSIA's exceptions applies on these facts.

Respondents assert that the FSIA exception for noncommercial torts, § 1605(a)(5), is most in point. This provision denies immunity in a case

> "in which money damages are sought against a foreign state for personal injury or death, or damage to or loss of property, occurring in the United States and caused by the tortious act or omission of that foreign state or of any official or employee of that foreign state while acting within the scope of his office or employment." 28 U.S.C. § 1605(a)(5).

Section 1605(a)(5) is limited by its terms, however, to those cases in which the damage to or loss of property occurs in the United States. Congress' primary purpose in enacting § 1605(a)(5) was to eliminate a foreign state's immunity for traffic accidents and other torts committed in the United States, for which liability is imposed under domestic tort law. See H.R.Rep., at 14, 20–21. * * *

In this case, the injury to respondents' ship occurred on the high seas some 5,000 miles off the nearest shores of the United States * * *.

    * * *

The result * * * is not altered by the fact that petitioner's alleged tort may have had effects in the United States. Respondents state, for example, that the Hercules was transporting oil intended for use in this country and that the loss of the ship disrupted contractual payments due in New York. Under the commercial activity exception to the FSIA, § 1605(a)(2), a foreign state may be liable for its commercial activities "outside the territory of the United States" having a "direct effect" inside the United States. But the noncommercial tort exception, § 1605(a)(5), upon which respondents rely, makes no mention of "territory outside the United States" or of "direct effects" in the United States. Congress' decision to use explicit language in § 1605(a)(2), and not to do so in § 1605(a)(5), indicates that the exception in § 1605(a)(5) covers only torts occurring within the territorial jurisdiction of the United States. Respondents do not claim that § 1605(a)(2) covers these facts.

We also disagree with respondents' claim that certain international agreements entered into by petitioner and by the United States create an exception to the FSIA here. As noted, the FSIA was adopted "[s]ubject to international agreements to which the United States [was] a party at the time of [its] enactment." § 1604. This exception applies when international agreements "expressly conflic[t]" with the immunity provisions of the FSIA, H.R.Rep., at 17; S.Rep., at 17, hardly the circumstances in this case. Respondents point to the Geneva Convention on the High Seas, Apr. 29, 1958, [1962] 13 U.S.T. 2312, T.I.A.S. No. 5200, and the Pan American Maritime Neutrality Convention, Feb. 20, 1928, 47 Stat. 1989, 1990–1991, T.S. No. 845. These conventions, however, only set forth substantive rules of conduct and state that compensation shall be paid for certain wrongs. They do not create private rights of action for foreign corporations to recover compensation from foreign states in United States courts. Cf. *Head Money Cases*, 112 U.S. 580, 598–599 (1884); *Foster v. Neilson*, 27 U.S. (2 Pet.) 253, 314 (1829). Nor do we see how a foreign state can waive its immunity under § 1605(a)(1) by signing an international agreement that contains no mention of a waiver of immunity to suit in United States courts or even the availability of a cause of action in the United States. We find similarly unpersuasive the argument of respondents and Amicus Curiae Republic of Liberia that the Treaty of Friendship, Commerce and Navigation, Aug. 8, 1938, United States–Liberia, 54 Stat. 1739, T.S. No. 956, carves out an exception to the FSIA. Article I of this Treaty provides, in pertinent part, that the nationals of the United States and Liberia "shall enjoy freedom of access to the courts of justice of the other on conforming to the local laws." The FSIA is clearly one of the "local laws" to which respondents must "conform" before bringing suit in United States courts.

We hold that the FSIA provides the sole basis for obtaining jurisdiction over a foreign state in the courts of this country, and that none of the enumerated exceptions to the Act applies to the facts of this case. The judgment of the Court of Appeals is therefore

REVERSED.

Questions: Were the U.S. contacts and interests in this case sufficiently strong for U.S. courts to take jurisdiction, compared, for example, to contacts and interests for the courts of the United Kingdom or Liberia? What harm might be done if U.S. courts were to take jurisdiction in such cases? Are there any benefits? Would a decision taking jurisdiction have carried the risk that U.S. courts might become a world judiciary in actions grounded on international law violations of foreign governments? What remedies remained for *Amerada Hess* after this proceeding was concluded against it?

———

Note: *Gould, Inc. v. Mitsui Min. & Smelting Co. Ltd.*, et al, 750 F.Supp. 838 (N.D.Ohio 1990), involved issues of trade secret misappropriation sufficient to amount to a "pattern of racketeering (per RICO)". The action was dismissed because the predicate acts of "mail and wire fraud" were insufficiently alleged. Gould alleged that some of its trade secrets were transferred to foreign companies and that a plant was built in France based at least partly upon the trade secrets. Defendants Pechiney/Trefimetaux argued that, at the time of the alleged predicate acts, they were owned by France and that the FSIA, therefore, applied. They contended that the RICO claim should fail because the FSIA provided the only basis of jurisdiction and that a foreign sovereign is not subject to U.S. criminal jurisdiction. Plaintiff countered that the FSIA applies only to civil actions and that RICO was irrelevant. The Court held that the language of RICO suggests that the kind of fraud which may be a "predicate act" may only be criminal fraud, and only when the defendant is subject to being prosecuted. Since sovereigns are not subject to *criminal* prosecution, there is no basis for jurisdiction over the French defendants in this case. See, 18 U.S.C. § 1961(1)(B); 18 U.S.C. §§ 1341, 1343.

2.   APPLICATIONS OF THE RESTRICTIVE PRINCIPLE TO COMMERCIAL AND OTHER ACTIVITIES

In a pre-FSIA case, *Victory Transport Inc. v. Comisaria General*, 336 F.2d 354, 360 (2d Cir..1964), the Court applied the restrictive theory as formulated by the Department of State and looked at whether the government action was public, private or commercial. The Court stated that it was disposed to deny a claim of immunity:

> * * * unless it is plain that the activity in question falls within one of the categories of strictly political or public acts about which sovereigns have traditionally been quite sensitive. Such acts are generally limited to the following categories:
>
> (1) internal administrative acts, such as expulsion of an alien.
>
> (2) legislative acts such as naturalization.
>
> (3) acts concerning the armed forces.
>
> (4) acts concerning diplomatic activity.
>
> (5) public loans.

Republic of Argentina and Banco Central De La Republica Argentina, Petitioners v. Weltover, Inc.

United States Supreme Court, 1992.
504 U.S. 607, 112 S.Ct. 2160, 119 L.Ed.2d 394.

■ JUSTICE SCALIA delivered the opinion of the Court.

This case requires us to decide whether the Republic of Argentina's default on certain bonds issued as part of a plan to stabilize its currency was an act taken "in connection with a commercial activity" that had a "direct effect in the United States" so as to subject Argentina to suit in an American court under the Foreign Sovereign Immunities Act of 1976, 28 U.S.C. §§ 1602 et seq.

I

* * * Argentina's currency is not one of the mediums of exchange accepted on the international market. Argentine businesses engaging in

foreign transactions must pay in U.S. dollars or some other internationally accepted currency. [It has been] difficult for Argentine borrowers to obtain such funds, principally because of the instability of the Argentine currency. To address these problems, petitioners, the Republic of Argentina and its central bank, Banco Central (collectively Argentina), in 1981 instituted a foreign exchange insurance contract program (FEIC), under which Argentina effectively agreed to assume the risk of currency depreciation in cross-border transactions involving Argentine borrowers. This was accomplished by Argentina's agreeing to sell to domestic borrowers, in exchange for a contractually predetermined amount of local currency, the necessary U.S. dollars to repay their foreign debts when they matured, irrespective of intervening devaluations.

* * * Argentina did not possess sufficient reserves of U.S. dollars to cover the FEIC contracts as they became due in 1982. The Argentine government thereupon adopted certain emergency measures, including refinancing of the FEIC-backed debts by issuing to the creditors government bonds. These bonds, called "Bonods," provide for payment of interest and principal in U.S. dollars; payment may be made through transfer on the London, Frankfurt, Zurich, or New York market, at the election of the creditor. [T]he foreign creditor had the option of either accepting the Bonods in satisfaction of the initial debt, thereby substituting the Argentine government for the private debtor, or maintaining the debtor/creditor relationship with the private borrower and accepting the Argentine government as guarantor.

When the Bonods began to mature in May 1986, Argentina concluded that it lacked sufficient foreign exchange to retire them. Pursuant to a Presidential Decree, Argentina unilaterally extended the time for payment, and offered bondholders substitute instruments as a means of rescheduling the debts. [Three creditors] refused to accept the rescheduling, and insisted on full payment, specifying New York as the place where payment should be made. Argentina did not pay, and respondents then brought this breach-of-contract action, * * * relying on the Foreign Sovereign Immunities Act of 1976 as the basis for jurisdiction. * * *

II

The Foreign Sovereign Immunities Act of 1976, 28 U.S.C. § 1602 et seq., establishes a comprehensive framework for determining whether a court in this country, state or federal, may exercise jurisdiction over a foreign state. Under the Act, a "foreign state *shall* be immune from the jurisdiction of the courts of the United States and of the States" unless one of several statutorily defined exceptions applies. § 1604 (emphasis added). The FSIA thus provides the "sole basis" for obtaining jurisdiction over a foreign sovereign in the United States. See Argentine Republic v. Amerada Hess [supra.] The most significant of the FSIA's exceptions—and the one at issue in this case—is the "commercial" exception of § 1605(a)(2). * * *

In the proceedings below, respondents relied only on the third clause of § 1605(a)(2) to establish jurisdiction and our analysis is therefore limited to considering whether this lawsuit is (1) "based * * * upon an act outside the territory of the United States"; (2) that was taken "in connection with a commercial activity" of Argentina outside this country; and (3) that "cause[d] a direct effect in the United States." The complaint in this case alleges only one cause of action on behalf of each of the respondents, viz., a breach-of-contract claim based on Argentina's attempt to refinance the Bonods rather than to pay them according to their terms. The fact that the cause of action is in compliance with the first of the three requirements—that it is "based upon an act outside the territory of the United States" (presumably Argentina's unilateral extension)—is uncontested. The dispute pertains to whether the unilateral refinancing of the Bonods was taken "in connection with a commercial activity" of Argentina, and whether it had a "direct effect in the United States." We address these issues in turn.

A

Respondents and their *amicus,* the United States, contend that Argentina's issuance of, and continued liability under, the Bonods constitute a "commercial activity" and that the extension of the payment schedules was taken "in connection with" that activity. The latter point is obvious enough, and Argentina does not contest it; the key question is whether the activity is "commercial" under the FSIA. The FSIA defines "commercial activity" to mean: "[E]ither a regular course of commercial conduct or a particular commercial transaction or act. The commercial character of an activity shall be determined by reference to the nature of the course of conduct or particular transaction or act, rather than by reference to its purpose." 28 U.S.C. § 1603(d).

This definition, however, leaves the critical term "commercial" largely undefined: The first sentence simply establishes that the commercial nature of an activity does *not* depend upon whether it is a single act or a regular course of conduct, and the second sentence merely specifies what element of the conduct determines commerciality (i.e., nature rather than purpose), but still without saying what "commercial" means. Fortunately, however, the FSIA was not written on a clean slate. As we have noted, see *Verlinden B.V. v. Central Bank of Nigeria,* 461 U.S. 480, 486–489 (1983), the Act (and the commercial exception in particular) largely codifies the so-called "restrictive" theory of foreign sovereign immunity first endorsed by the State Department in 1952. The meaning of "commercial" is the meaning generally attached to that term under the restrictive theory at the time the statute was enacted. See *McDermott Int'l, Inc. v. Wilander,* * * * ("[W]e assume that when a statute uses [a term of art], Congress intended it to have its established meaning").

This Court did not have occasion to discuss the scope or validity of the restrictive theory of sovereign immunity until our 1976 decision in *Alfred Dunhill v. Cuba,* 425 U.S. 682. Although the Court there was evenly divided on the question whether the "commercial" exception that applied in the foreign-sovereign-immunity context also limited the availability of an act-of-state defense, compare id., at 695–706 (plurality) with id., at 725–730 (Marshall, J., dissenting), there was little disagreement over the general scope of the exception. The plurality noted that, after the State Department endorsed the restrictive theory of foreign sovereign immunity in 1952, the lower courts consistently held that foreign sovereigns were not immune from the jurisdiction of American courts in cases "arising out of purely commercial transactions." [The plurality also noted that the "state sovereign" and "state commercial" acts were not entirely novel to U.S. law]. * * * The plurality stated that the restrictive theory of foreign sovereign immunity would not bar a suit based upon a foreign state's participation in the marketplace in the manner of a private citizen or corporation. 425 U.S., at 698–705. A foreign state engaging in "commercial" activities "do[es] not exercise powers peculiar to sovereigns"; rather, it "exercise[s] only those powers that can also be exercised by private citizens." The dissenters did not disagree with this general description. Given that the FSIA was enacted less than six months after our decision in *Alfred Dunhill* was announced, we think the plurality's contemporaneous description of the then-prevailing restrictive theory of sovereign immunity is of significant assistance in construing the scope of the Act.

In accord with that description, we conclude that when a foreign government acts, not as regulator of a market, but in the manner of a private player within it, the foreign sovereign's actions are "commercial" within the meaning of the FSIA. Moreover, because the Act provides that the commercial character of an act is to be determined by reference to its "nature" rather than its "purpose," 28 U.S.C. § 1603(d), the question is not whether the foreign government is acting with a profit motive or instead with the aim of fulfilling uniquely sovereign objectives. Rather, the issue is whether the particular actions that the foreign state performs (whatever the motive behind them) are the *type* of actions by which a private party engages in "trade and traffic or commerce," Black's Law Dictionary 270 (6th ed. 1990). See, e.g., *Rush–Presbyterian–St. Luke's Medical Center v. Hellenic Republic*, 877 F.2d 574, 578 (CA7), cert. denied. Thus, a foreign government's issuance of regulations limiting foreign currency exchange is a sovereign activity, because such authoritative control of commerce cannot be exercised by a private party; whereas a contract to buy army boots or even bullets is a "commercial" activity, because private companies can similarly use sales contracts to acquire goods, see, e.g., *Stato di Rumania v. Trutta*, [1926] Foro It. I 584, 585–586, 589 (Corte di Cass. del Regno, Italy), translated and reprinted in part in 26 Am.J.Int'l L. 626–629 (Supp.1932).

Argentina contends that, although the FSIA bars consideration of "purpose," a court must nonetheless fully consider the *context* of a transaction in order to determine whether it is "commercial." Accordingly, Argentina claims that the Court of Appeals erred by defining the relevant conduct in what Argentina considers an overly generalized, a contextual manner and by essentially adopting a *per se* rule that all "issuance of debt instruments" is "commercial."

Argentina points to the fact that the transactions in which the Bonods were issued did not have the ordinary commercial consequence of raising capital or financing acquisitions. Assuming for the sake of argument that this is not an example of judging the commerciality of a transaction by its purpose, the ready answer is that private parties regularly issue bonds, not just to raise capital or to finance purchases, but also to refinance debt. * * * Engaging in a commercial act does not require the receipt of fair value, or even compliance with the common-law requirements of consideration.

* * *

However difficult it may be in some cases to separate "purpose" (i.e., the *reason* why the foreign state engages in the activity) from "nature" (i.e., the outward form of the conduct that the foreign state performs or agrees to perform), see *De Sanchez, supra*, at 1393, the statute unmistakably commands that to be done. 28 U.S.C. § 1603(d). We agree with the Court of Appeals, see 941 F.2d, at 151, that it is irrelevant *why* Argentina participated in the bond market in the manner of a private actor; it matters only that it did so. We conclude that Argentina's issuance of the Bonods was a "commercial activity" under the FSIA.

B

The remaining question is whether Argentina's unilateral rescheduling of the Bonods had a "direct effect" in the United States, 28 U.S.C. § 1605(a)(2).

We * * * have little difficulty concluding that Argentina's unilateral rescheduling of the maturity dates on the Bonods had a "direct effect" in the United States. Respondents had designated their accounts in New York as the place of payment, and Argentina made some interest payments into those accounts before announcing that it was rescheduling the payments. Because New York was thus the place of performance for Argentina's ultimate contractual obligations, the rescheduling of those obligations necessarily had a "direct effect" in the United States: Money that was supposed to have been delivered to a New York bank for deposit was not forthcoming. We reject Argentina's suggestion that the "direct effect" requirement cannot be satisfied where the plaintiffs are all foreign corporations with no other connections to the United States. We expressly stated in *Verlinden* that the FSIA permits "a foreign plaintiff to sue a foreign sovereign in the courts of the United States, provided the substantive requirements of the Act are satisfied." * * *

* * *

We conclude that Argentina's issuance of the Bonods was a "commercial activity" under the FSIA; that its rescheduling of the maturity dates on those instruments was taken in connection with that commercial activity and had a "direct effect" in the United States; and that the District Court therefore properly asserted jurisdiction, under the FSIA, over the breach-of-contract claim based on that rescheduling. Accordingly, the judgment of the Court of Appeals is *Affirmed*.

Note: Article 2.2 of the I.L.C's Draft Articles on Jurisdictional Immunity of States and Their Property cited above provides that:

In determining whether a contract or transaction is a "commercial transaction" under paragraph 1 (c), reference should be made primarily to the nature of the contract or transaction, but its purpose should also be taken into account if, in the practice of the State which is a party to it, that purpose is relevant to determining the non-commercial character of the contract or transaction.

———————

Questions: If this provision were applicable, would Justice Scalia have reached the same result? If the "context" of the transaction indicated potentially high public importance, would this be taken into account under the FSIA? Should it? Compare the French case NIGC above at p. 516. What are the differences in conceptual approach that led to different outcomes?

The United States of America v. The Public Service Alliance of Canada, The Attorney General of Canada and the Canada Labour Relations Board

Supreme Court of Canada, 1992.
32 I.L.M. 1 (1993).

[The Canadian Supreme Court addressed sovereign immunity in a case involving Canadian civilian employees of a U.S. naval base (leased by the U.S.) in Argentia, Newfoundland. The U.S. claimed immunity from proceedings before the Canadian Labor Relations Board. The issue was whether the Board's proceedings "relate to any U.S. commercial activity." The base was used by the U.S. in its anti-submarine warfare command. The Canadian employees did most of the base's maintenance and had only minimal exposure to the military operations. A dispute arose relating to unionization and a no-strike clause in the employment contracts].

LA FOREST, J.: Before delving into the specific questions posed by this case, it is useful to consider first the common law antecedents of the *State Immunity Act,* and then to compare Canada's codification of the common law with the statutory model in the United States. As will become apparent, the law in this area reveals a consistent pattern of development that has arrived at a point where state activity can be characterized only after appreciating its entire context. Rigid dichotomies between the "nature" and "purpose" of state activity are not helpful in this analysis. * * *

In determining the nature of the activity in question, it is useful to begin by acknowledging that employment at a military base is a multi-faceted relationship. It is simply not valid to isolate one aspect of this activity and label it as either "sovereign" or "commercial" in nature. A better approach is to determine which aspects of the activity are relevant to the proceedings in issue, and then to assess the impact of the proceedings on these attributes as a whole.

The United States argues that the work performed by the Canadian civilian personnel is an integral and indispensable part of its stated defence mission and that it takes place within the context of an international agreement—the Lease—which gives the United States the right of management and control over the base. The Board, on the other hand, argues that this Court should only consider the threshold nature of the activity, namely a contract of employment, and ignore its context or purpose. PSAC is prepared to go a little further and characterizes the relevant activity as employment to provide maintenance services to a military base in return for remuneration. The Canadian personnel involved are essentially trades-men who "fix water pipes, run boilers, perform new construction, and generally maintain the physical buildings on the base". The nature of the contract of employment is similar to an employment contract in the private sector, because the employees are using the same trade skills as they would use in the employ of a private contractor.

* * *

It is impossible to ignore the sovereign purpose of this latter aspect of the employment relationship. Argentia is a military post, conceived in times of war as an air and naval base. In peacetime it has served as a highly sensitive communications and surveillance post. In another war the base could play a crucial role in American military activities in the North Atlantic. I can think of no activity of a foreign state that is more inherently sovereign than the operation of such a base. As such, the United States government must be granted the unfettered authority to manage and control employment activity at the base.

* * *

In the result, the "activity" at Argentia has a double aspect. It is at once sovereign and commercial. The question becomes, do the certification proceedings "relate" to the commercial aspect of this activity? To this issue I now turn.

* * *

I also agree with the Attorney General of Canada that the objective of the Board's proceedings is the imposition of collective bargaining by the Canadian state, and under the control of a Canadian court. The nexus between this objective and the management of the base constitutes an unacceptable interference with American sovereignty. This is more than just a theoretical concern, as becomes apparent upon consideration of the consequences of submission to the Board's jurisdiction.

Collective bargaining carries with it the right of employees to strike to enforce their contract demands. A strike at the Argentia base would, at a minimum, disrupt its military mission. It is true that the employees' services are not directly required to achieve this mission. However, the indirect effect of the loss of 60 full-time employees cannot be lightly dismissed. I am not prepared to concede that a boiler plant operator or an engineer at the base does not contribute in some important way to the successful operation of the base. Simply put, the United States is entitled to absolute control of the base and so over the availability of its labour force, particularly in times of war. At all events, it can hardly be said not to interfere seriously with the control of the base, which is expressly conferred upon the United States by the Lease.

* * *

Finally, PSAC points out that the effect of granting immunity to the United States is to deprive Canadian employees of their right to the protection of labour relations legislation, a right enjoyed by all other

Canadians. However, this regrettable result is a necessary consequence of Canada's commitment to policies of international comity and reciprocity. Any time sovereign immunity is asserted, the inevitable result is that certain domestic parties will be left without legal recourse. This is a policy choice implicit in the Act itself. A policy choice with a similar effect in the field of labour law is the exclusion from union membership of "a person who performs management functions or is employed in a confidential capacity in matters relating to industrial relations," under § 3 of the *Canada Labour Code*. That regrettable exclusion is necessitated by valid labour relations policy considerations. The exclusion in the present case is required by policy considerations of international comity and reciprocity. Indeed, more than mere comity comes into play here. As noted, it is required by Canada's obligation under the Lease—an international agreement. Article 1 of that document, we saw, accords the U.S. "all the rights, power and authority within the Leased Areas which are necessary for the establishment, use, operation and defence thereof, or appropriate for their control. * * * "I find it difficult to see how the U.S. can fully exercise these rights without having full control of its labour relations on the base.

Disposition

For these reasons I would allow the appeal, and answer the first referred question in the affirmative.

———

Notes and Questions: How do you think Justice La Forest would have approached the *Weltover* case? The Canadian case being later in time than *Weltover*, do you think that the U.S. Supreme Court might look at "context" in a more flexible way the next time the issue is presented?

Plaintiff in ***Saudi Arabia v. Nelson***, 507 U.S. 349 (1993), alleged that he was detained and tortured by Saudi Arabian authorities. He had been hired in the United States to work as a monitoring systems engineer at a Saudi Arabian (government) hospital. Nelson alleged that agents of the Saudi Government arrested him after he made complaints about safety defects in the hospital. He claimed that he was shackled, beaten, kept for days without food, tortured and confined in a rat infested overcrowded cell. In addition, he claimed that his wife was told by a government official that her husband's release could be arranged, if she provided sexual favors.

Nelson was released after 39 days of confinement. Upon his return, he brought an action in the Federal District Court for the Southern District of Florida, claiming that the Saudi conduct violated his human rights. He sought damages from the Saudi Government for, among other things, negligent failure to warn him of the dangers of working in a Saudi hospital, for various intentional torts, including "battery, unlawful detainment, wrongful arrest and imprisonment, false imprisonment, inhuman torture, disruption of normal family life, and infliction of mental anguish."

A majority of the Supreme Court held that the suit could not properly be maintained under the FSIA, because the conduct of which Nelson complained was not "based upon commercial activity," but "upon an abuse of sovereign power." It noted that the Act requires more than "mere connection with" or "relation to" commerce for conduct to be "based upon commercial activity." 28 U.S.C. § 1603(d). Justices White and Blackmun concurred, arguing that the conduct *was, indeed, based upon commercial activity,* "but went along with the decision, because they found that the activity was neither carried on in nor connected to the United States."

Note: In *Siderman de Blake v. Republic of Argentina,* 965 F.2d 699 (9th Cir.1992), the plaintiffs sued in the United States for damages from the Argentine Republic for torture and wrongful seizure of property. The opinion relating to torture and wrongful seizure of property by Argentine authorities is presented in Chapter 9. Their complaint alleged eighteen causes of action arising out of the torture of Jose Siderman and the expropriation of the Sidermans' property by Argentine military officials. The District Court dismissed the expropriation claims on the basis of the act of state doctrine, but granted a default judgment on the torture claims. The Court of Appeals ruled that Argentina had waived its sovereign immunity defense when it requested California State Courts by letter rogatory to assist it in proceedings it had undertaken in Argentina against the plaintiffs in this case and based upon the conduct in Argentina that prompted plaintiffs' action in the United States:

The Sidermans argued that their claims fall within the international takings exception to the FSIA's rule of immunity. The Ninth Circuit held that advertising and receiving profits from the Sidermans' expropriated hotel in Argentina constituted commercial activity. Id., at 708–09. It also held that the Sidermans could take advantage of the "commercial activities exception "to immunity, but could not benefit from the "expropriation exception." It held that even a claim based on a foreign government's violation of a jus cogens principle (a peremptory norm) could be heard in a U.S. court only if it falls within one of the exceptions to immunity.

Questions: What should be the test for "commercial activity" under the FSIA: the overall character of the operation or the particular actions complained of? Is there an element of subjectivity in determinations of this kind? Is the definition of "commercial activity" in 28 USC 1603(d) satisfactory? It seems to be mutually circular. How much guidance can it give the Courts? The Supreme Court has looked at the precise conduct involved. Note the differences in the United States, United Kingdom, and Canadian legislation. The U.S. legislation applies the "nature of the transaction" test, rather than its "purpose." The U.K. legislation gives a list of activities that are considered "commercial." The Canadian legislation uses the "nature of the transaction" test. However, the Supreme Court of Canada in the *PSAC Case,* extracted above, held that this did not preclude consideration of its purpose. With the uncertainty which remains, do you think that this subject is ready for codification or would codification simply continue the uncertainty? See the I.L.C.'s Draft Articles cited above.

MK v. Republic of Turkey

The Netherlands, Sub–District Court of the Hague
1 August 1985, 94 Int'l L. Rep. 350 (1994).*

[The plaintiff, a Dutch national, was employed as a secretary in the Embassy of Turkey in the Netherlands. She was dismissed from her employment and then brought this action to have the dismissal declared void. The following portion of the Court's opinion dealt with Turkey's defense of sovereign immunity.]

Defense III

The immunity which the defendant has claimed comes within the exceptions recognized in international law and referred to in Article 13(a) of the General Provisions of Legislation Act,[5] but that these exceptions are in turn subject to an exception as soon as the defendant performs acts which it performs on the same footing as a natural or legal person under private law; that this immunity only applies in respect of so-called *acta jure imperii* i.e., purely governmental acts.

The view that a sovereign State cannot be subjected to the jurisdiction of another State against its will can nowadays no longer be regarded as a rule of international law and that the rule which now obtains is more limited, namely that the State is only exempted from the jurisdiction of another State in respect of *acta jure imperii* i.e., purely governmental acts.

The conclusion of a contract of employment with a Dutch clerical worker who has no diplomatic or civil service status was an act which the defendant performed on the same footing as a natural or legal person under private law and that there was therefore no question of a purely governmental act in the present case: the defendant, represented by its Ambassador, entered into a legal transaction of this kind in the same way as a private legal person (see, *inter alia*, The Hague Court of Appeal, (NJ (1969) No 484) and HR 26 October 1973 (NJ (1974) No 361).

Note: In this case the Dutch court applied the nature of the transaction analysis later adopted by Justice Scalia in *Weltover.* (*See also Edwards v. BV Wijsmuller, etc, Amsterdam Court of Appeal*, 94 Int'l L. Rep. 362 (1994) applying the same analysis to salvage work performed on a U.S. warship. The Polish Supreme Court in a case still earlier (1948) and similar to the Turkish case applied the absolute immunity theory and found no jurisdiction. (*Aldona S. v. United Kingdom*, 90 J. du Dr. Int'l 190 (1963).

Bruce Smith, Paul S. Hudson et al. v. Socialist People's Libyan Arab Jamahiriya, etc.

November 26, 1996, 101 F.3d 239 (2d Cir., 1996), 36 I.L.M. 100 (1997).**

■ JON O. NEWMAN, CHIEF JUDGE:

In *Kadic v. Karadzic*, 70 F.3d 232 (2d Cir.1995), this Court ruled that a violation of certain fundamental norms of international law can be re-

---

* Reprinted with the permission of the Editor, International Law Reports.

5. Article 13(a) provides: "The juridical jurisdiction of the courts and the execution of court decisions and of legal instruments drawn up by legally authorized officials [authentieke akte] are subject to the exceptions acknowledged under international law".

** Reprinted with the permission of the American Society of International Law.

dressed by a civil suit brought in a U.S. district court against private citizens under the Alien Tort Act, 28 U.S.C. s 1350 (1994). The decision is presented in Chapter 9. The pending appeal presents the issue of whether such violations can be redressed by a civil suit brought in a United States district court against a foreign state. The more precise issue is whether such a suit—brought primarily on behalf of victims of an aircraft bombing—is prohibited by the Foreign Sovereign Immunities Act, 28 U.S.C. §§ 1602–1611 (1994), as it read prior to the recent amendment that explicitly permits suits against foreign states in some circumstances for acts in violation of fundamental international norms such as aircraft sabotage, see Antiterrorism and Effective Death Penalty Act of 1996 ("AEDPA"), Pub. L. No. 104–132, s 221(a), 110 Stat. 1214, 1241 (1996) (to be codified at 28 U.S.C. § 1605(a)(7)).

* * *

The complaints allege that the Libyan governmental defendants, acting principally through two Libyan agents, Abdel Basset Ali Al–Megrahi and Lamen Khalifa Fhimah, planned and carried out the bombing of Pan Am Flight 103. Al-Megrahi and Fhimah have been indicted in the District of Columbia for their roles in the bombing.

* * *

The parties are in agreement that the issue of Libya's amenability to suit in a United States court is governed by the Foreign Sovereign Immunities Act ("FSIA"). The FSIA "provides the sole basis for obtaining jurisdiction over a foreign state in the courts of this country." *Argentine Republic v. Amerada Hess Shipping Corp.*, 488 U.S. 428, 443 (1989). The FSIA recognizes the immunity of foreign states, 28 U.S.C. § 1604, subject to specified exceptions. The appellants advance four bases for asserting jurisdiction over Libya–[the first two are taken up below in connection with waiver] * * * (3) occurrence of the alleged bombing on "territory" of the United States, id. § 1605(a)(5); and (4) conflict with the United Nations Charter, id. § 1604.

* * *

3. Occurrence on "Territory" of the United States

The FSIA removes immunity "in any case ... in which money damages are sought against a foreign state for personal injury or death ... occurring in the United States and caused by the tortious act or omission of that foreign state...." 28 U.S.C. § 1605(a)(5). The Act defines the "United States" to include "all territory and waters, continental or insular, subject to the jurisdiction of the United States." Id. s 1603(c). Appellants contend that Pan Am Flight 103 should be considered to have been "territory" of the United States for purposes of the FSIA. They rely on the principle that a nautical vessel "is deemed to be a part of the territory" of "the sovereignty whose flag it flies." *United States v. Flores*, 289 U.S. 137, 155 (1933).

Even if we assume, without deciding, that for some purposes an American flag aircraft is like an American flag vessel, but see *United States v. Cordova*, 89 F. Supp. 298, 301 (E.D.N.Y.1950), the fact that a location is subject to an assertion of United States authority does not necessarily mean that it is the "territory" of the United States for purposes of the FSIA. Cases rejecting FSIA jurisdiction over foreign states for torts committed at United States embassies make this point clear. See *Persinger v. Islamic Republic of Iran*, 729 F.2d 835, 839–42 (D.C.Cir.1984). If FSIA immunity prevails with respect to torts in United States embassies, it cannot be displaced with respect to United States aircraft flying over a foreign land. Moreover, in *Amerada Hess*, the Supreme Court declined an invitation to equate "territory ... of the United States," for purposes of the FSIA, with all areas over which any United States jurisdiction might be asserted. The Court ruled that though the high seas were within the admiralty jurisdiction of United States courts, see *The Plymouth*, 70 U.S. (3 Wall.) 20, 36 (1865), they were not the "territory ... of the United States" within the meaning of the FSIA. *Amerada Hess*, 488 U.S. at 440.

4.   Conflict with the United Nations Charter

The FSIA provides that a foreign state's immunity is "[s]ubject to existing international agreements to which the United States is a party at the time of enactment of [the FSIA]." 28 U.S.C. § 1604. Appellants contend that Libya's immunity has been displaced by reason of a conflict with the UN Charter. Appellants do not assert that any provision of the UN Charter subjects Libya to suit in the United States. Instead, they reason that Article 25 of the Charter binds all member nations to abide by decisions of the Security Council taken under Chapter VII of the Charter and contend that Security Council Resolution 748, adopted on March 31, 1992, commits Libya to pay compensation to the victims of Pan Am Flight 103.

Libya resists this contention on numerous grounds, including the arguments that Resolution 748 is not self-executing, that it was not intended to create judicially enforceable private rights, and that it does not compel payment by Libya. We reject the contention for the threshold reason that the FSIA's displacement of immunity, applicable to international agreements in effect at the time the FSIA was adopted, does not contemplate a dynamic expansion whereby FSIA immunity can be removed by action of the UN taken after the FSIA was enacted. Such a contention would encounter a substantial constitutional issue as to whether Congress could delegate to an international organization the authority to regulate the jurisdiction of United States courts. It would take an explicit indication of Congressional intent before we would construe an act of Congress to have such an effect. Cf. *Industrial Union Dep't, AFL–CIO v. American Petroleum Institute*, 448 U.S. 607, 645–46 (1980) (delegation of Congressional power narrowly construed to avoid constitutional issue). There is no such indication in section 1604.

Conclusion

The bombing of Pan Am Flight 103 was an act of terrorism that has properly drawn the condemnation of the world community. Horrific as that act was, it cannot provide a basis for giving an unwarranted interpretation to an act of Congress simply to achieve a result beneficial to the families of the victims of the bombing. We hold that the FSIA, prior to the recent amendment, does not subject Libya to the jurisdiction of the District Court with respect to the bombing. Whether the recent amendment affords a remedy to some or all of the appellants remains to be determined in subsequent litigation.

The judgment of the District Court is affirmed.

Rein v. Socialist People's Libyan Arab Jamahiriya

United States Court of Appeals, 162 F.3d 748 (2d Cir.1998), 38 I.L. M. 447 (1999).

■ CALABRESI, CIRCUIT JUDGE:

Defendants-appellants, collectively "Libya," appeal from the denial of their motion to dismiss. The plaintiffs, who are the survivors and representatives of persons killed aboard Pan Am 103 above Lockerbie, Scotland, brought suit against Libya alleging wrongful death, pain and suffering, and a variety of other injuries. Libya moved to dismiss for lack of subject matter jurisdiction, contending that 28 U.S.C. § 1605(a)(7), the provision of the Foreign Sovereign Immunities Act ("FSIA") on which jurisdiction is alleged to be founded, is void as an unconstitutional delegation of the power to establish the jurisdiction of the federal courts. It also sought dismissal for lack of personal jurisdiction or, if its jurisdictional challenges failed, dismissal of certain of the plaintiffs' claims for failure to state a claim on which relief could be granted. The district court denied all aspects of the motion to dismiss, and Libya appealed. We conclude that we have no jurisdiction, on this interlocutory appeal, to review any of the issues that Libya raised in its motion to dismiss other than its challenge to subject matter jurisdiction. We therefore dismiss so much of the appeal as raises these other issues. With respect to the question of subject matter jurisdiction, we find that § 1605(a)(7) is constitutional as applied in this case. We therefore affirm the district court's ruling that it has subject matter jurisdiction over Libya.

BACKGROUND

In December 21, 1988, Pan Am Flight 103 exploded over Lockerbie, Scotland. All 259 persons on board were killed, as were eleven people on the ground below. The two men named as individual defendants in this suit, both of whom are Libyan, have been indicted in the United States and the United Kingdom in connection with the bombing. Negotiations are currently in progress among the United States, the United Kingdom, and Libya to hold a criminal trial in the Netherlands at which those two men would be tried under Scottish law for allegedly perpetrating the bombing.

In 1994, some of the present plaintiffs brought suit against some of the present defendants, claiming that Libya and its agents were responsible for destroying Pan Am 103. Libya moved to dismiss for lack of jurisdiction under the FSIA or any other applicable law. The FSIA establishes that foreign states are generally immune from suit. But it gives the federal district courts jurisdiction over actions against such states when either

§§ 1605–07 of the Act or relevant international agreements permit them to be sued. Sections 1605–07 enumerate categories of cases in which foreign states are not entitled to sovereign immunity and are, therefore, subject to district court jurisdiction. When the previous litigation was brought in 1994, no provision of the FSIA deprived Libya of sovereign immunity in suits of this sort. Accordingly, the United States District Court for the Eastern District of New York (Platt, J.) dismissed the case for lack of subject matter jurisdiction. *Smith v. Socialist People's Libyan Arab Jamahiriya*, 886 F.Supp. 306 (E.D.N.Y.1995). We affirmed. *Smith v. Socialist People's Libyan Arab Jamahiriya*, 101 F.3d 239 (2d Cir.1996), cert. denied, 117 S.Ct. 1569 (1997).

In 1996, the Antiterrorism and Effective Death Penalty Act ("AEDPA") amended the FSIA by adding what is now 28 U.S.C. § 1605(a)(7). Under this new section, foreign states that have been designated as state sponsors of terrorism are denied immunity from damage actions for personal injury or death resulting from aircraft sabotage.[3] Shortly after passage of the AEDPA, the present plaintiffs filed (against the present defendants) substantially the same claims that had been previously dismissed.

* * *

(C) Relationship between subject matter and personal jurisdiction

1. Extricability

Accordingly, we now inquire whether any of the other issues Libya has raised are inextricably intertwined with its claim of sovereign immunity (that is, with its defense to subject matter jurisdiction). We begin with the question of personal jurisdiction. It is true, as the parties urge, that the two kinds of jurisdiction—subject matter and personal—are interrelated under the FSIA. Pursuant to that statute, there is personal jurisdiction over foreign sovereigns with respect to all claims (a) over which there is subject matter jurisdiction, and (b) as to which process has been properly served. 28 U.S.C. § 1330(b). In other words, the statute makes both service of process and subject matter jurisdiction elements of personal jurisdiction over foreign sovereigns.

3. 28 U.S.C. § 1605 (Supp.1996), another provision of the FSIA, reads, in pertinent part:

"(a) A foreign state shall not be immune from the jurisdiction of courts of the United States or of the States in any case—

. . .

(7) ... in which money damages are sought against a foreign state for personal injury or death that was caused by an act of torture, extrajudicial killing, aircraft sabotage, hostage taking, or the provision of material support or resources (as defined in section 2339A of title 18) for such an act if such act or provision of material support is engaged in by an official, employee, or agent of such foreign state while acting within the scope of his or her office, employment, or agency, except that the court shall decline to hear a claim under this paragraph—

(A) if the foreign state was not designated as a state sponsor of terrorism under section 6(j) of the Export Administration Act of 1979 (50 U.S.C.A pp. 2405(j)) or section 620A of the Foreign Assistance Act of 1961 (22 U.S.C. 2371) at the time the act occurred, unless later so designated as a result of such act[.]"

It does not follow, however, that a court cannot decide issues of subject matter jurisdiction without at the same time making definitive findings as to personal jurisdiction. For instance, a court could find subject matter jurisdiction without passing on whether there had been effective service of process, thus leaving the personal jurisdiction question open. The current case presents a different example of the same point. Libya's challenge to personal jurisdiction is based on due process and the principle of minimum contacts. We can readily decide whether the district court had subject matter jurisdiction over Libya without at all considering whether it would violate due process to subject Libya to personal jurisdiction. Because review of the latter is not necessary for review of the former, we conclude that the issues of subject matter jurisdiction and personal jurisdiction are not inextricably intertwined in this case.

2. Impact of foreign sovereignty

The plaintiffs claim, however, that the special nature of suits against foreign sovereigns renders review of the subject matter jurisdiction issue less than meaningful if there is no simultaneous resolution of the personal jurisdiction question. One could understand this argument as having two strands, the first of which is addressed to Libya's foreignness and the second of which goes to its sovereignty. First, the plaintiffs argue that a foreign sovereign claiming immunity from suit in an American court may justifiably fail to see the distinction between the two kinds of jurisdiction. All that sovereign is interested in is whether the suit will proceed or not. In other words, counsel for the plaintiffs suggests that we should not insist on procedural niceties that from Libya's point of view are either too subtle to be grasped or too provincial to be easily understood.

We reject this contention. It is, in essence, a claim that we should not apply general principles of our law to Libya because Libya, as a foreign litigant, might not comprehend them. But we have no reason to think that sovereign states are less able to understand basic principles of American law than are other litigants. Instead, it seems likely that a foreign nation that maintains laws and courts of its own has considerably greater legal sophistication than do most ordinary plaintiffs and defendants. Moreover, Libya does not appear before this court pro se. It has hired distinguished professional counsel whose office it is to explain the law to its client.

The second aspect of this argument is, in essence, that if we are going to release the defendant sovereign from our jurisdiction on appeal from a final order, the comity that one government owes to another instructs that we do so now, thus sparing the sovereign the expense and embarrassment of litigation. This contention might be in point if the litigant to which it was applied were entitled to sovereign immunity. But if Libya were entitled to sovereign immunity, the case would be dismissed for lack of subject matter jurisdiction. And then the question of whether we could review personal jurisdiction interlocutorily would be moot. That question will only be before us if we decide—as we do today—that Libya is not entitled to immunity from the present suit. Once we have adjudicated the sovereign immunity question and concluded that there is no immunity, Libya cannot procure dismissal by pressing its failed claim to immune status under another heading (i.e., that of personal rather than subject matter jurisdiction).

* * *

The decision to subject Libya to jurisdiction under § 1605(a)(7) was manifestly made by Congress itself rather than by the State Department. At the time that § 1605(a)(7) was passed, Libya was already on the list of state sponsors of terrorism. No decision whatsoever of the Secretary of State was needed to create jurisdiction over Libya for its alleged role in the destruction of Pan Am 103. That jurisdiction existed the moment that the AEDPA amendment became law.

* * *

The district court's determination that subject matter jurisdiction exists over the present action is affirmed. All other aspects of this interlocutory appeal are dismissed for want of appellate jurisdiction.

Questions: Do you find that any of the theories justifying sovereign immunity would be properly applied to cases of this kind? Is there a case to be made for universal jurisdiction in cases of some or any violations of international law? The case's jurisdictional, human rights, and international criminal law implications are found in Chapters 3, 9 and 16.

Mcelhinney v. Williams and Her Majesty's Secretary of State for Northern Ireland

Ireland, Supreme Court. 15 December 1995, 104 Int'l L. Rep. 691 (1997).*

SUMMARY: *The facts:*—The first respondent was a British soldier stationed in Northern Ireland. It was alleged that while he was guarding a checkpoint on the border between Northern Ireland and the Republic of Ireland he had involuntarily entered the Republic of Ireland and had attempted to fire a gun at the appellant. The appellant claimed damages for the alleged assault. The appellant brought proceedings against the second respondent, the United Kingdom Secretary of State for Northern Ireland, on the ground that he was responsible for the affairs of Northern Ireland, including the soldier's actions. The Secretary of State applied to set aside service on him on the ground of sovereign immunity. The High Court held that sovereign immunity applied because the relevant activities were of a governmental, not a private law character, and granted the Secretary of State's application.

The appellant appealed to the Supreme Court, arguing that sovereign immunity did not apply in respect of claims for damages arising from torts committed by foreign States or their agents within the jurisdiction. He argued that this constituted an exception to sovereign immunity and was recognized as such under international law as was evidenced by the practice of other States.

* * *

The following is the text of the judgment of the Court, delivered by Hamilton, CJ:

* * *

---

* Reprinted with the permission of the
Editor, International Law Reports.

The appellant alleges that these acts were tortious and that he has suffered personal injuries as a result thereof.

There can be no doubt but that the first named defendant in carrying out his duties at the said checkpoint was acting within the sphere of governmental or sovereign activity and the acts complained of must be regarded as jure imperii even though alleged to have been committed within this jurisdiction.

It is submitted on behalf of the appellant that as the acts complained of were tortious and caused personal injuries to him that the principle of foreign sovereign immunity should not apply to such acts and that it was a near-universally recognized principle of international law that claims for personal injuries allegedly inflicted in the forum state by or on behalf of a foreign government constitute an exception to the sovereign immunity principle.

In support of such submission, counsel for the appellant referred in particular to the United Kingdom State Immunities Act of 1978; the USA Foreign Sovereign Immunities Act of 1976; the Canadian State Immunity Act 1982; the Australian Foreign Sovereign Immunities Act 1985 and the European Convention on State Immunity, 1972.

Section 5 of the UK Act provides that:

A State is not immune as respects proceedings in respect of—

(a) death or personal injury; or

(b) damage to or loss of tangible property, caused by an act or omission in the United Kingdom.

The relevant section of the. USA Act provides that:

(a) A foreign State shall not be immune from the jurisdiction of courts of the United States or of the states in any case–

in which money damages are sought against a foreign State for personal injury or death, or damage to or loss of property occurring in the United States and caused by the tortious act or omission of that foreign State or of any official or employee of that foreign State while acting within the scope of his office or employment.

Similar provisions are contained in the Canadian and Australian legislation on this point. The appellant relies on these statutes as indicative of a recognized principle of public international law.

* * *

Distinction must be drawn between the provisions of legislation in a number of States and the provisions of public international law and the principles set forth in individual State legislation cannot be regarded as establishing principles of public international law.

The provisions of statutes cannot be used as evidence of what international law is: statutes are evidence of the domestic law in the individual States and not evidence of international law generally.

Article 11 of the European Convention on State Immunity provides that:

A Contracting State cannot claim immunity from the jurisdiction of a court of another Contracting State in proceedings which relate to redress for injury to the person or damage to tangible property, if the facts which occasioned the injury or damage occurred in the territory of the State of the forum, and if the author of the injury or damage was present in that territory at the time when those facts occurred.

I do not have to decide, in the circumstances of this case, whether the terms of the Convention are part of the domestic law of this State because even if they were, the appellant's claim herein would fail by virtue of the terms of Article 31 of the said Convention which provides that:

Nothing in this Convention shall affect any immunities or privileges enjoyed by a Contracting Party in respect of anything done or omitted to be done by, or in relation to armed forces when on the territory of another Contracting State.

The terms of Article 31 recognize that as a matter of international law immunities and privileges in respect of anything done or omitted to be done by, or in relation to armed forces when on the territory of another Contracting State, exist.

* * *

Despite the Herculean efforts of the appellant's legal advisers in making available to this Court, copies of all relevant decisions, articles, and draft conventions and the cogent arguments of counsel, I am not satisfied that it is a principle of public international law that the immunity granted to sovereign States should be restricted by making them liable in respect of tortious acts committed on their behalf by their servant or agent causing personal injuries to the person affected by such act or omission when such act or omission is committed jure imperii and I would dismiss the appeal on this point.

———

Arbitration. Section 1605(a)(6) of the U.S. Foreign Sovereign Immunities Act of 1976 as amended (see text in the Documentary Supplement) establishes the rules governing an exception for actions brought to enforce an agreement made by the foreign state with or for the benefit of a private party to submit to arbitration or an action to confirm an award made pursuant to the agreement. Section 1610(a)(6) states the rules for a parallel exception from attachment or execution. See *In the Matter of the Arbitration of Certain Controversies between Chromalloy and the Arab Republic of Egypt,* (D. D.C. 1996) 35 I.L.M. 1359 in which the Court found jurisdiction under Section 1605(a)(6), citing also the U.S. Arbitration Act, 9 U.S.C. Section 203. In *Cargill International S.A. v. M/T Pavel Dybenko,* 991 F.2d 1012 (2d Cir.1993), the Court of Appeals affirmed jurisdiction to determine whether the plaintiff was a third party beneficiary of an arbitration agreement entered into by an instrumentality of the former Soviet Union and whether the arbitration exception was applicable in that case.

3. MEASURES OF CONSTRAINT

United States, Foreign Sovereign Immunities Act of 1976

§ 1609: Immunity from attachment and execution of property of a foreign state

Subject to existing international agreements to which the United States is a party at the time of enactment of this Act the property in the United States of a foreign state shall be immune from attachment arrest and execution except as provided in sections 1610 and 1611 of this chapter.

———

Note: Details of the United States exceptions in sections 1610 and 1611 as well as the exceptions to the exceptions are set forth in the Documentary Supplement with other provisions of the FSIA.

Liberian Eastern Timber Corp. v. Government of the Republic of Liberia

United States District Court, S.D.N.Y., 1986.
650 F.Supp. 73 (1986), aff'd without opinion, 854 F.2d 1314 (2d Cir.1987).

■ EDWARD WEINFELD, DISTRICT JUDGE.

The Government of the Republic of Liberia ("Liberia" or "Republic") moves to vacate a judgment entered ex parte by Judge John F. Keenan enforcing an arbitration award issued under the rules of the International Centre for the Settlement of Investment Disputes ("ICSID"). The Republic also moves for a preliminary injunction enjoining the enforcement of, and execution upon, the aforesaid judgment pending determination of Liberia's motion: (1) to vacate the judgment, or, in the alternative, (2) to vacate the execution of that judgment on its property located in the United States. Liberia's contention is that the ex parte judgment violated its sovereign immunity which it did not waive.

* * *

What Liberia seeks to vacate is the judgment entered in this court based upon the arbitration award and to enjoin the issuance of executions to seize its property or assets in order to satisfy the judgment. It contends that this court was without jurisdiction to enter the judgment or to enforce the award by the issuance of executions against its property in the United States under the Foreign Sovereign Immunities Act ("FSIA"), and that it did not surrender or waive its sovereign immunity by entering into the Concession Agreement, by agreeing to arbitration, or by reducing the forestry area and then finally cancelling the contract.

* * *

In support of its position plaintiff emphasizes Article 54 of the [ICSID] Convention, which provides:

Each Contracting State shall recognize an award rendered pursuant to this Convention as binding and enforce the pecuniary obligations imposed by that award within its territories as if it were a final judgment of a court in that State.

* * *

Liberia, as a signatory to the Convention, waived its sovereign immunity in the United States with respect to the enforcement of any arbitration award entered pursuant to the Convention. When it entered into the concession contract with LETCO, with its specific provision that any dispute thereunder be settled by arbitration under the rules of ICSID and its enforcement provision thereunder, it invoked the provision contained in Article 54 of the Convention which requires enforcement of such an award by Contracting States. That action, and reading the treaty as a whole, leaves little doubt that the signatories to the Convention intended that awards made pursuant to its provisions be given full faith and credit in their respective jurisdictions subject to such rights as are reserved by signatories thereunder. Therefore, Liberia clearly contemplated the involvement of the courts of any of the Contracting States, including the United States as a signatory to the Convention, in enforcing the pecuniary obligations of the award.

The fact that LETCO is a French entity and Liberia a foreign sovereign does not deprive the district court of subject matter jurisdiction. Thus, this Court had jurisdiction to direct the entry of judgment against Liberia to enforce the pecuniary obligations of the arbitration award in favor of LETCO. The motion to vacate the judgment is denied.

We next consider the separate issue of Liberia's motion to vacate the executions issued against Liberia's property or assets to enforce and collect the judgment. Article 55 of the Convention provides that "Nothing in Article 54 shall be construed as derogating from the law in force in any Contracting State relating to immunity of that State or of any foreign state from *execution*." (emphasis supplied). 28 U.S.C. § 1610(a) provides exceptions to the immunity of a foreign state from execution upon a judgment entered by a Court of the United States if the property is or was "used for a commercial activity in the United States."

The essence of Liberia's argument concerning its immunity from execution of the judgment, however variously stated, is that the executions upon the judgment entered in this court have been served on, among other entities, shipowners located in the United States and agents of Liberia appointed to collect from such shipowners tonnage fees, registration fees and other taxes due the government—that these fees are collected as taxes designed to raise revenues for the Republic of Liberia and, as such, are sovereign not commercial assets under the Liberian maritime law and regulations, and thus immune from execution since they are not "property * * * used for a commercial activity."

LETCO, with respect to the registry fees and tonnage taxes that have been levied upon within this district, does not dispute that they are tax revenues ultimately payable to Liberia, but asserts that of the gross amounts due and collected from companies under Liberian registry, 27% is retained for operating and administrative expenses and profits by United States corporations or citizens who render services in collecting the funds. In consequence, LETCO argues that those payments reflect commercial activities within the purview of section 1610(a). Upon the argument of this motion, LETCO conceded that if, instead of employing United States corporations or citizens to collect the registry fees and tonnage taxes, Liberia had engaged personnel of the Liberian Consulate stationed in the United States, that taxes so collected would be beyond the reach of execution. This rather fine distinction is without substance. It does not make sense to say that because Liberia engaged and gave employment to United States citizens, instead of utilizing the services of its consulate employees stationed in the United States, it thereby forfeited its sovereign immunity with respect to its right to the taxes so collected. The nature of the amounts due from ships flying the Liberian flag, the registration fees or taxes, is constant. They are tax revenues for the benefit of the Government of Liberia, and the method employed to effect their collection does not destroy the basic nature of that collection. The levy and collection of taxes intended to serve as revenues for the support and maintenance of governmental functions are an exercise of powers particular to a sovereign. Accordingly, Liberia's motion to vacate the executions upon such funds is granted and the United States Marshal is directed to release the funds so attached (less his lawful fees). Further, LETCO is enjoined from issuing executions against such registry fees and taxes; however, LETCO is not enjoined from issuing executions with respect to any properties which are used for commercial activities and that may fall within one of the exceptions delineated in section 1610.

So ordered.

Note: LETCO later recorded the judgement in the U.S. District Court in the District of Columbia and writs of attachment were thereafter served on Riggs National Bank and First American Bank where Liberia held accounts. On Liberia's emergency motion for relief from orders attaching the accounts, treated as a motion to quash the writs of attachment, the Court stated:

> In conclusion, the bank accounts of the Liberian Embassy are immune from attachment both because they enjoy diplomatic immunity under the Vienna Convention and because no exception of the FSIA applies to deprive the bank accounts of their grant of sovereign immunity. Also, as noted above, the bank account used for the central bank of Liberia is immune under 28 U.S.C. § 1611(b)(1).

MK v. State Secretary for Justice

The Netherlands, Council of State. 24 November 1986, 94 Int'l L. Rep. 357 (1994).*

[The earlier phase of this case seen above, in which the petitioner received an award of damages for wrongful dismissal from her employment with the Embassy of Turkey at the Hague, did not bring MK satisfaction. She then sought to attach a bank account belonging to the Turkish Embassy, but the Dutch Secretary of State for Justice instructed the bailiffs not to attach the bank account because that would be in violation of

* Reprinted with the permission of the
editor, International Law Reports.

international law. MK appeals to the Council of State against the State Secretary's actions.]

It has been established that there are no treaty rules applicable between the State of the Netherlands and Turkey regarding immunity from the compulsory execution of judgments by means of the attachment of recoverable debts or goods belonging to the Turkish State. Although there is no rule of international law that prohibits executions levied on the assets of a foreign State which are in the territory of another State * * * it is equally beyond doubt that rules of customary law prescribe immunity from execution in respect of the enforcement of a judgment, even if the court which gave the judgment was competent to do so under these rules (as in the present case) if this execution relates to assets intended for public purposes.

* * *

On request the respondent lodged with us a note verbale dated 25 November 1986 from the Turkish Embassy in The Hague in which it is stated that all the money in the attached account had been transferred, by the Turkish Government in order to defray the costs of the Turkish Embassy in The Hague in the performance of its functions. We consider that a declaration of this kind must be deemed to be a sufficient basis for assuming that these moneys were indeed intended for the public purposes of the Turkish State, since the petitioner has not been able to prove the contrary and we see no other reason for doubting this.

We have taken into account in this connection that great importance has traditionally been attached to the efficient performance of the functions of embassies and consulates; confirmation of this is provided in the Vienna Conventions on Diplomatic Relations (1961) and Consular Relations (1963). The respondent is not therefore in a position to require the Turkish mission in the Netherlands to provide a further and more detailed account of the uses to which the account will be put. This would, after all, amount under international law to an unjustified interference in the internal affairs of this mission. [On the application of the Vienna Conventions, see Chapter 10 above.]

* * *

4. SOME HORIZONTAL QUESTIONS

1. *States*

Since sovereign immunity applies to "states", questions regarding the scope of "statehood" necessarily arise. (*See* Chapter 2 above.) The international law rule for sovereign immunity reaches statehood in all of its manifestations. See e.g., *Krajina v. The Tass Agency*, [1949] 2 All E.R. 274 where Cohen, L.J. stated in the Court of Appeal that the evidence "falls far short of that which would be necessary to establish that Tass is a legal entity and that the USSR, by procuring its incorporation, has deprived that particular department of the immunity which normally attaches to a department of a sovereign State in accordance with the principles of comity established by international law and recognized by this country. * * * I ought to say just a few words on what the position would be had we come to the opposite conclusion and been of opinion that the evidence did establish that Tass was given the status of a separate juridical entity. It does not seem necessary to follow that it would thereby have been deprived of its immunity." [Lord Justice Cohen then analyzed the parallel situation in the U.K. and concluded that "One must look at every case at the facts to reach a conclusion whether the Crown had intended to give up its immunity generally or only for limited and defined purposes."]

Courts should no longer find it troublesome, as did the Court in Krajina, to deal with the separate legal entity problem, for the statutory and treaty provisions now clearly recognize the state owned or controlled entity. For example Article 2.1(b) of the I.L.C. Draft Articles define "State" for the purpose of those draft articles to mean:

(i) the State and its various organs of government;

(ii) constituent units of a federal state;

(iii) political subdivisions of the State which are entitled to perform acts in the exercise of the sovereign authority of the State;

(iv) agencies or instrumentalities of the State and other entities, to the extent that they are entitled to perform acts in the exercise of the sovereign authority of the State;

(v) representatives of the State acting in that capacity.

The U.S. Foreign Sovereign Immunities Act of 1976 (in the Documentary Supplement) contains a definition of "foreign state" which is more specific than the definition contained in the Draft Articles above. Section 1603 includes in the definition, "an agency or instrumentality of a foreign state as defined in subsection (b) which refers to any entity

(1) which is a separate legal person, corporate or otherwise, and

(2) which is an organ of a foreign state or political subdivision thereof or a majority of whose shares or other ownership interest is owned by a foreign state or political subdivision thereof, and

(3) which is neither a citizen of a State of the United States as defined in section 1332(c) of this title, nor created under the laws of any third country."

For applications of the foregoing rules see *Vermeulen v. Renault, U.S.A., Inc.*, 985 F.2d 1534 (11th Cir.1993) and *Gould, Inc. v. Mitsui Mining and Smelting Co., Ltd.*, cited above, where the courts acted favorably upon claims that two French industrial corporations (Regie National des Usines Renault and Pechiney/Trefimetaux) were state entities for purposes of sovereign immunity. Compare *Alejandre v. Telefonica Larga Distancia de Puerto Rico, Inc.*, 183 F.3d 1277 (11th Cir.1999) in which the Court, in a garnishment proceeding, applied to a government instrumentality a presumption of separate juridical status vis-a-vis a foreign government to which the instrumentality is related. Payments to that instrumentality were held not be subject to garnishment to satisfy a judgment against the Cuban government in a case involving the claims of family members of Americans whose plane was shot down over international waters by the Cuban Air Force in 1996.

Any tendency to recognize claims for FSIA status for a state has not been extended to an association which seeks that status but has failed to satisfy fully the established criteria for statehood. In *Klinghoffer v. S.N.C. Achille Lauro*, 937 F.2d 44 (2d Cir.1991), an action was brought against the Palestine Liberation Organization in connection with the 1985 seizure of the passenger liner "Achille Lauro". The PLO claimed the status of state entitled to immunity under the FSIA, but the court, finding the absence of a defined territory, permanent population and a government in control, held that the PLO does not qualify as a FSIA "state." This, despite the fact that the PLO had been recognized by other countries (but not the United States). What would be the status of the PLO today?

Notes and Questions

Can an individual qualify as a foreign sovereign under the U.S. Act? Although the language does not suggest natural persons, States act through individuals who should be protected where a corporate entity would be protected under the same circumstances. See *Chuidian v. Philippine National Bank*, 912 F.2d 1095 (9th Cir.1990) (upholding an individual's FSIA claim). In the United Kingdom, the House of Lords considered this issue in the dramatic *Pinochet case*.

Regina v. Bartle and the Commissioner of Police for the Metropolis and Others Ex Parte Pinochet

United Kingdom, House of Lords, 24 March 1999, Pinochet III, [1999] 2 All ER 97, 170, 2 WLR. 827, 38 I.L.M.581, 644 (1999).

[The facts of this singular case are shown with selections of the opinions in Chapters 9 and 16 in the discussion of individual responsibility and in Chapter 10 on diplomatic immunities. For the moment, we may note that the case was before the British Courts pursuant to a Spanish request for Pinochet's extradition incident to allegations of his role in the disappearances, torture and murder occurring while he was the Chilean head of state. The Pinochet case can be considered as falling within the scope of immunity of states or of diplomatic immunities. Consider the following views of Lord Millet on this question.]

Two overlapping immunities are recognised by international law; immunity ratione personae and immunity ratione materiae. They are quite different and have different rationales.

Immunity ratione personae is a status immunity. An individual who enjoys its protection does so because of his official status. It enures for his benefit only so long as he holds office. While he does so he enjoys absolute immunity from the civil and criminal jurisdiction of the national courts of foreign states. But it is only narrowly available. It is confined to serving heads of state and heads of diplomatic missions, their families and servants. It is not available to serving heads of government who are not also heads of state, military commanders and those in charge of the security forces, or their subordinates. It would have been available to Hitler but not to Mussolini or Tojo. It is reflected in English law by section 20(l) of the State Immunity Act 1978, enacting customary international law and the Vienna Convention on Diplomatic Relations (1961).

The immunity of a serving head of state is enjoyed by reason of his special status as the holder of his state's highest office. He is regarded as the personal embodiment of the state itself. It would be an affront to the dignity and sovereignty of the state which he personifies and a denial of the equality of sovereign states to subject him to the jurisdiction of the municipal courts of another state, whether in respect of his public acts or private affairs. His person is inviolable; he is not liable to be arrested or detained on any ground whatever. The head of a diplomatic mission represents his head of state and thus embodies the sending state in the territory of the receiving state. While he remains in office he is entitled to the same absolute immunity as his head of state in relation both to his public and private acts.

This immunity is not in issue in the present case. Senator Pinochet is not a serving head of state. If he were, he could not be extradited. It would be an intolerable affront to the Republic of Chile to arrest him or detain him.

Immunity ratione materiae is very different. This is a subject-matter immunity. It operates to prevent the official and governmental acts of one state from being called into question in Proceedings before the courts of another, and only incidentally confers immunity on the individual. It is therefore a narrower immunity but it is more widely available. It is available to former heads of state and heads of diplomatic missions, and any one whose conduct in the exercise of the authority of the state is afterwards called into question, whether he acted as head of government, government minister, military commander or chief of police, or subordinate public official. The immunity is the same whatever the rank of the office-holder. This too is common ground. It is an immunity from the civil and criminal jurisdiction of foreign national courts but only in respect of governmental or official acts. The exercise of authority by the military and security forces of the state is the paradigm example of such conduct. The immunity finds its rationale in the equality of sovereign states and the doctrine of non-interference in the internal affairs of other states: see *Duke of Brunswick v. King of Hanover* (I 848) 2 H.L.Cas, 1; *Hatch v. Baez* (1876) 7 Hun. 596 U.S.; *Underhill v. Hernandez* (1897) 168 U.S. 456. These hold that the courts of one state cannot sit in judgment on the sovereign acts of another. The immunity is sometimes also justified by the need to prevent the serving head of state or diplomat from being inhibited in the performance of his official duties by fear of the consequences after he has ceased to hold office. This last basis can hardly be prayed in aid to support the availability of the immunity in respect of criminal activities prohibited by international law.

Given its scope and rationale, it is closely similar to and may be indistinguishable from aspects of the Anglo–American Act of State doctrine. As I understand the difference between them, state immunity is a creature of international law and operates as a plea in bar to the jurisdiction of the national court, whereas the Act of State doctrine is a rule of domestic law which holds the national court incompetent to adjudicate upon the lawfulness of the sovereign acts of a foreign state.

* * *

2. *Waiver*

Bruce Smith, Paul S. Hudson et al. v. Socialist People's Libyan Arab Jamahiriya, etc.

101 F.3d 239, 241 (2d Cir.1996), 36 I.L.M. 100, 104 (1997)

■ Jon O. Newman, Chief Judge:

[Other parts of this opinion are presented, *supra*. The excerpts below relate to the Court's holdings on waiver.]

The parties are in agreement that the issue of Libya's amenability to suit in a United States court is governed by the Foreign Sovereign Immunities Act ("FSIA"). The FSIA "provides the sole basis for obtaining jurisdiction over a foreign state in the courts of this country." *Argentine Republic v. Amerada Hess Shipping Corp.*, [supra] at 443. The FSIA recognizes the immunity of foreign states, 28 U.S.C. § 1604, subject to specified exceptions. The appellants advance four bases for asserting jurisdiction over Libya—(1) implied waiver, id. § 1605(a)(1), arising from Libya's alleged participation in actions that violate fundamental norms of international law; (2) implied waiver, id. § 1605(a)(1), arising from Libya's alleged guaranty of any damage judgment against the individual defendants

* * *

1. Implied Waiver for *Jus Cogens* Violations

The FSIA removes the immunity of a foreign state in any case "in which the foreign state has waived its immunity either explicitly or by implication." id. § 1605(a)(1). The appellants contend that an implied waiver has occurred by virtue of Libya's violation of fundamental international norms ("*jus cogens*"). Libya concedes, for purposes of this appeal, that its alleged participation in the bombing of Pan Am Flight 103 would be a violation of *jus cogens*, but it contests the premise of appellants' argument that such a violation demonstrates an implied waiver of sovereign immunity within the meaning of the FSIA.

* * *

The contention that a foreign state should be deemed to have forfeited its sovereign immunity whenever it engages in conduct that violates fundamental humanitarian standards is an appealing one. The argument was persuasively developed a few years ago in the *California Law Review*. See Adam C. Belsky et al., *Implied Waiver Under the FSIA: A Proposed Exception to Immunity for Violations of Peremptory Norms of International Law*, 77 Cal. L. Rev. 365 (1989). The argument is premised on the idea that because observance of jus cogens is so universally recognized as vital to the functioning of a community of nations, every nation impliedly waives its traditional sovereign immunity for violations of such fundamental standards by the very act of holding itself out as state:

> *Jus cogens* norms ... do not depend on the consent of individual states, but are universally binding by their very nature. Therefore, no explicit consent is required for a state to accept them; *the very fact that it is a state implies acceptance.* Also implied is that when a state violates such a norm, it is not entitled to immunity. Id. at 399 (emphasis added).

The issue we face, however, is not whether an implied waiver derived from a nation's existence is a good idea, but whether an implied waiver of that sort is what Congress contemplated by its use of the phrase "waive[r] ... by implication" in section 1605(a)(1) of the FSIA. We have no doubt that Congress has the authority either to maintain sovereign immunity of foreign states as a defense to all violations of jus cogens if it prefers to do so or to remove such immunity if that is its preference, and we have no doubt that Congress may choose to remove the defense of sovereign immunity selectively for particular violations of jus cogens, as it has recently done in the 1996 amendment of the FSIA. To determine which course Congress chose when it enacted the FSIA in 1976, we examine first the terms of the statute and then the legislative history.

The text of section 1605(a)(1) is not conclusive as to the meaning of an implied waiver. It simply says that a foreign state shall not be immune in any case in which the foreign state has waived its immunity "either explicitly or by implication." We and other courts have observed that "the implied waiver provision of Section 1605(a)(1) must be construed narrowly." [Citations omitted].

The concept of an "implied" waiver can have at least three meanings. First, such a waiver can mean that an actor intended to waive a protection, even though it did not say so expressly. Second, an implied waiver might arise whenever an act has been taken under circumstances that would lead a reasonable observer to conclude that the act generally manifests an intent to waive, whether or not the actor had such intent in the particular case. Both of these meanings involve a requirement of intentionality, the first being subjective and the second objective. A third meaning is that the law deems an actor to have surrendered a protection, regardless of the actor's subjective or objectively reasonable intent. "Waiver" in this third sense is more properly termed "forfeiture." The text of the FSIA gives no indication as to the sense in which waiver "by implication" is used.

The legislative history of the FSIA provides important clues as to Congress's meaning. The Report of the House Judiciary Committee includes the following:

> With respect to implicit waivers, the courts have found such waivers in cases where a foreign state has agreed to arbitration in another country or where a foreign state has agreed that the law of a particular country should govern a contract. An implicit waiver would also include a situation where a foreign state has filed a responsive pleading in an action without raising the defense of sovereign immunity. * * * [Citations omitted]

* * *

Whether or not an implied waiver might, in some circumstances, arise from a foreign state's actions not intimately related to litigation, we conclude that Congress's concept of an implied waiver, as used in the FSIA, cannot be extended so far as to include a state's existence in the community of nations—a status that arguably should carry with it an expectation of amenability to suit in a foreign court for violations of fundamental norms of international law.

The appellants vigorously argue that Congress would not have wanted to condone, by insulating from legal redress, such outrageous violations of *jus cogens* as the bombing of a passenger aircraft. The emotional power of that argument is not persuasive for at least two reasons. First, Congress's use of the concept of implied waiver in a sense less expansive than permitting suit for all violations of jus cogens is not equivalent to condonation of such lawless conduct. Congress might well have expected the response to such violations to come from the political branches of the Government, which are not powerless to penalize a foreign state for international terrorism. Second, when Congress recently amended the FSIA to remove the sovereign immunity of foreign states as a defense to acts of international terrorism, it enacted a carefully crafted provision that abolishes the defense only in precisely defined circumstances. * * *

Our reluctance to construe the concept of implied waiver to include all violations of *jus cogens* is not grounded, however, on an inference from the action of the 104th Congress; it is based on our understanding of what the 94th Congress meant when it illustrated the inexact phrase "waive[r] ... by implication" with examples drawn entirely from the context of conduct related to the litigation process. We recognize that the examples given in the House Report are not necessarily the only circumstances in which an implied waiver might be found. *See Siderman de Blake v. Republic of Argentina*, 965 F.2d 699, 721 (9th Cir.1992). Nevertheless, they indicate the principal context that Congress had in mind, *see id.* at 720 (remanding for consideration of implied waiver based on initiation of malicious criminal proceedings against FSIA plaintiff and request to United States court for judicial assistance), and, at a minimum, they preclude a sweeping implied waiver for all violations of *jus cogens*.

Two circuits have considered whether a violation of a jus cogens standard constitutes an implied waiver within the meaning of the FSIA, and both have rejected the claim. *See Princz v. Federal Republic of Germany*, 26 F.3d 1166, 1174 (D.C.Cir.1994); *Siderman de Blake*, 965 F.2d at 714–19. *Princz* rejected the claim on the D.C. Circuit's view that an implied waiver under the FSIA will be found only where a foreign state intended to permit suit. *See Princz, supra* at 1174 ("[T]he *amici's jus cogens* theory of implied waiver is incompatible with the intentionality requirement implicit in § 1605(a)(1)."). *Siderman* reasoned that the Supreme Court's decision in *Amerada Hess* precludes viewing jus cogens violations as an implied waiver. 965 F.2d at 718–19. That contention is questionable since no claim of waiver arising from a *jus cogens* violation was made in *Amerada Hess*. Though the Court there ruled that "immunity is granted in those cases involving alleged violations of international law that do not come within one of the FSIA's exceptions," *Amerada Hess*, 488

U.S. at 436, the Court was not asked to determine whether a jus cogens violation could constitute an implied waiver within the meaning of section 1605(a)(1). Our rejection of the claim that a jus cogens violation constitutes an implied waiver within the meaning of the FSIA rests neither on reading a subjective "intentionality" requirement into section 1605(a)(1), nor on the precedent of *Amerada Hess*. It rests on our understanding that Congress did not intend the implied waiver exception of section 1605(a)(1) to extend so far, however desirable such a result might be.

2.   Implied Waiver from Alleged Guaranty of Damages Judgment

The appellants contend that Libya impliedly waived its immunity from suit in United States courts by reason of the following paragraph contained in a February 27, 1992, letter from Ibrahim M. Bishari, Secretary of the Libyan government's "People's Committee for Foreign Liaison and International Cooperation" to the Secretary General of the United Nations:

> Despite the fact that discussion of the question of compensation is premature, since it would only follow from a civil judgement based on a criminal judgement, Libya guarantees the payment of any compensation that might be incurred by the responsibility of the two suspects who are its nationals in the event that they were unable to pay.

This paragraph concerning guaranty of payment of a judgment against Al–Megrahi and Fhimah was contained in a three-page document that included proposals concerning handing the suspects over to a "third party," and various steps relating to "the issue of terrorism."

Libya rejects the claim of an implied waiver arising from the guaranty provision for several reasons. First, Libya contends that the letter is an integrated document, subject to conditions, and was not accepted by the United Nations. Second, Libya asserts that even if the guaranty paragraph can be considered as an independent proposal, it is not binding for lack of consideration. Third, Libya contends that even if a binding guarantee obligation arose, there was no waiver of immunity from suit in the courts of the United States to enforce such an obligation.

We agree with the third contention and do not consider the other lines of defense. The paragraph in Mr. Bishari's letter concerning a guaranty of payment contains no express or indirect reference to a waiver of sovereign immunity. *See Amerada Hess*, 448 U.S. at 442–43 ("[W]e [do not] see how a foreign state can waive its immunity under s 1605(a)(1) by signing an international agreement that contains no mention of a waiver of immunity to suit in the United States courts or even the availability of a cause of action in the United States."). Though a guaranty is somewhat related to the litigation context illustrated by the three examples of implied waiver in the House Report, the paragraph in Mr. Bishari's letter does not bear such a close relationship to litigation as to support an implied waiver. If a foreign state undertook to guarantee payment of a judgment entered against its nationals in a United States court, the argument for an implied waiver would be much stronger. A generalized undertaking to pay the debt of a national, however, does not imply that the guaranteeing state agrees to be sued on such an undertaking in a United States court.

* * *

Creighton Limited v. Government of the State of Qatar.

181 F.3d 118 (D.C.Cir.1999).

■ GINSBURG, CIRCUIT JUDGE:

Creighton Limited, a Cayman Islands corporation with offices in Tennessee, contracted with the Government of the State of Qatar to build a hospital in Doha, the Qatari capital. Following a dispute over its performance, Creighton obtained an arbitral award against Qatar from the International Chamber of Commerce in Paris. Creighton now seeks to enforce the award in the United States District Court for the District of Columbia. Qatar claims the court lacks subject matter jurisdiction over the action pursuant to the Foreign Sovereign Immunities Act of 1976, 28 U.S.C. §§ 1330, 1602–1611

* * *

Creighton claims that Qatar, by agreeing to arbitrate in France, implicitly waived its sovereign immunity in the United States for, by virtue of the New York Convention, Qatar was "on notice" that an arbitral award rendered in France would be enforceable in this country. Qatar responds that "the FSIA and decisions applying it make clear that a sovereign's agreement to arbitrate in a New York Convention state is not a waiver of immunity to suit in the U.S. unless the foreign sovereign is also party to the New York Convention."

The FSIA does not define an implied waiver. We have, however, followed the "virtually unanimous" precedents construing the implied waiver provision narrowly.

We follow the Second Circuit in rejecting such a broad reading of the "implicit waiver" exception.

> [I]f the language of the legislative history [were] applied literally, a foreign government would be subject to the United States's jurisdiction simply because it agreed to have the contract governed by another country's laws, or agreed to arbitrate in a country other than itself, even though the agreement made no reference to the United States. Such an interpretation of § 605(a)(1)'s "implicit waiver" exception would vastly increase the jurisdiction of the federal courts over matters involving sensitive foreign relations. *Seetransport Viking Trader v. Navimpex Centrals*, 989 F.2d 572, 577 (2d Cir.1993) * * *

* * *

b.   Arbitration

The Congress added the following exception to the FSIA in 1988:

A foreign state shall not be immune from the jurisdiction of courts of the United States or of the States in any case . . . in which the action is brought ... to confirm an award made pursuant to ... an agreement to arbitrate, if ... the agreement or award is or may be governed by a treaty or other international agreement in force for the United States calling for the recognition and enforcement of arbitral awards. 28 U.S.C. § 1605(a)(6).

Qatar does not contest Creighton's assertion that because the New York Convention calls for enforcement of any arbitral award rendered within the jurisdiction of a signatory country, the quoted exception applies by its terms to this action. Indeed, it has been said with authority that the New York Convention "is exactly the sort of treaty Congress intended to include in the arbitration exception." * * *

Qatar's sole defense is that application of the arbitral exception here would be impermissibly retroactive because it was added to the statute after the contract was signed, indeed after the Paris arbitration was commenced. In reply, Creighton suggests that because the FSIA is a jurisdictional statute, its application to events that occurred before it was enacted would not be retroactive, for the FSIA speaks not to the primary conduct of the parties but rather to the question of which tribunal may enforce the arbitral award.

[Discussion of personal jurisdiction over Qatar omitted]

III. Conclusion

For the foregoing reasons, we hold that the district court had subject matter jurisdiction over this suit but lacked personal jurisdiction over Qatar. The judgment of the district court is therefore

Affirmed.

***Note*s:** Under the New York Convention on the Recognition and Enforcement of Arbitration Awards, there is considerable potential for waiver in arbitration cases, since there were by October 2000, 121 states parties to that convention. See www.uncitral.org/.

Waiver of execution measures has also arisen in the World Bank's arbitration system. *See,* the International Centre for Settlement of Investment Disputes (ICSID). ICSID Model Clauses, Doc. ICSID/5/Rev. 2, at 15, February 1, 1993 states:

> Under Article 54 of the [ICSID] Convention, all Contracting States, whether or not parties to the dispute, must recognize awards rendered pursuant to the Convention as binding and enforce the pecuniary obligations imposed thereby. Article 55 of the Convention nevertheless makes it clear that a State does not by becoming a party to the Convention waive such immunity from execution of an award as the State might enjoy under national laws. Such a waiver may, however, be effected by an express stipulation of which the following is an example.

Clause 15

The Host State hereby waives any right of sovereign immunity as to it and its property in respect of the enforcement and execution of any award rendered by an Arbitral Tribunal constituted pursuant to this agreement.

3.   *International Law and National Law in this Sector.*

How does the international legal system deal with a conflict between the international system itself and a national one? Part of the problem is the persistence of divergent policy views, certainly influenced by some of the "hard cases" such as *Smith* and *Rein* in the United States as seen above. Another part of the problem is the uncertainty and ambiguity in the law of sovereign immunity. Each doubtless contributes to the other.

Codification efforts and treaty provisions, including the European Convention, are improving the coherency of the international law on sovereign immunity (see above Section A.2). As a comprehensive and integrated statement of the modern law, the I.L.C. Draft Articles must also be included in this assessment. Those texts can now be seen as providing a certain measure of codification of the existing customary law in this sector.

Although some constitutions call for the application of international law in the event of conflict between national and international law, others do not. National courts will normally apply their national law when they are required by their constitutions to do so. (see Chs. 1, 12 and 17). Whether a true conflict exists depends on whether the international rule is mandatory or permissive. If the rule in question is a mandatory rule of immunity, for example the rule affording immunity to warships, the application of an inconsistent national rule by national courts would necessarily constitute a violation of international law and give rise to the international responsibility of the state denying immunity. If, on the other hand, a state extends immunity on the basis of national law to a state owned merchant ship, when international law permits, but seems no longer to require, there is no apparent violation of international law.

Notes and Questions

The means of protecting claimants who are damaged when immunity is applied are matters of concern and attention. *Are the alternative means of redress adequate?* The problem of doing justice is clear in the Turkish and British personal employment cases noted in Section A.2 above. The Polish Court in *Aldona*, referred to the possibilities of Aldona's seeking justice before English courts or making in effect an international claim through her Foreign Ministry to its British counterpart. Are these alternatives realistic? Can you envisage other means? Would requiring or encouraging the immune government to waive immunity except in cases of demonstrable risk of disruption of government operations resolve the difficulty? Should the immune government be required to accept arbitration? Should the immunity be relaxed except in cases where the court might make a specific finding of the disruption risk? What other alternatives would you suggest?

SECTION B.   THE IMMUNITY OF INTERNATIONAL ORGANIZATIONS

1987 Restatement: Immunities of International Organizations*

p. 492 (Third, 1987).

Introductory Note:

International organizations have achieved independent legal personality under international law largely since the Second World War. * * * Earlier, they were seen largely as "unincorporated" associations of individual states and sometimes claimed the immunities of one or all of their member states. When international organizations acquired legal personality by international agreement, they also acquired privileges and immunities in their own right.

The privileges and immunities of an international organization and its officials, and of member representatives, are generally established by the constitution of the organization, e.g., Article 105 of the United Nations Charter, and are often supplemented by special agreement. See, e.g., the Convention on Privileges and Immunities of the United Nations, 21 U.S.T., to which (as of 1986) 120 states (including the United States) [120 states in early 2001] were party, and the Convention on Privileges and Immunities of the Specialized Agencies, 33 U.N.T.S. 261, to which (as of 1986) 88 states [106 states in early 2001] were party (but not the United States). An international organization sometimes enjoys additional privileges and immunities by agreement with a particular state, for example, an agreement between the organization and the state that is the seat of its headquarters, such as the Headquarters Agreement between the United States and the United Nations. * * * Strictly, those agreements are binding only on states parties to them, but an organization may also enjoy basic privileges and immunities vis-à-vis non-member states under customary law. * * *

The privileges and immunities of international organizations are "functional," and, though modeled after those of states, differ from them in some measure, both in conception and content. Unlike states, international organizations are not "sovereign" and draw on no history of sovereignty and no tradition of sovereign immunity. State and diplomatic immunities apply equally and reciprocally between one state and another; the immunities of an international organization are claimed, without reciprocity, by an organization vis-à-vis a state, generally a member state. Most such claims, in fact, arise in the few particular states in whose territories the organizations have their headquarters or conduct their principal activities. Officials of an international organization represent no sending state but may be "sent" to all states; unlike diplomatic personnel they are not nationals of a sending state but bear various nationalities, in some instances the nationality of the state from whose laws they seek immunity. The absence of reciprocity is reflected also in the privileges and immunities enjoyed by representatives of member states to international organizations, as compared with the privileges and immunities of diplomatic agents. * * *

Broadbent v. Organization of American States

United States Court of Appeals, 628 F.2d 27 (D.C.Cir.1980).

■ LEVENTHAL, CIRCUIT JUDGE: This is an appeal from a District Court judgment dismissing an action by the appellants claiming they had been improperly discharged by the Organization of American States (OAS). The district court held the OAS was absolutely immune from suit. We affirm on the ground that, even assuming for discussion the applicability of the lesser, "restrictive" immunity doctrine, which permits a lawsuit based on "commercial" activity to be maintained against a sovereign without its consent, this case does not present such "commercial" activity.

I. Background

The plaintiffs-appellants are seven former staff members of the General Secretariat of OAS. Before their termination, they had been employed at the permanent headquarters of the organization in Washington, D.C., for periods ranging from six to twenty-four years. They are all United States citizens or foreign nationals admitted to permanent residency in the United States.

The appellants were dismissed from the Secretariat on August 31, 1976, due to a reduction in force mandated by the OAS General Assembly. At various times between October 31 and November 8, 1976, they filed complaints with the Administrative Tribunal of the OAS, the internal court created to resolve personnel disputes. On June 1, 1977, the Tribunal held that the discharges had been improper and that the appellants should be reinstated at the grades they held when they were separated from service. In accordance with its governing statute, the Tribunal also fixed an indemnity to be paid to each appellant should the Secretary General choose to exercise the option of refusing to reinstate them. Subsequently, the Secretary General denied reinstatement, and each appellant received the indicated indemnity.[3]

* * * [A]ppellants brought this action in the district court, alleging breach of contract and seeking damages totaling three million dollars. The OAS moved to quash service and dismiss the complaint, asserting that the district court lacked subject matter jurisdiction and that the OAS is immune from service of process * * *

---

3. The amounts of the indemnities ranged from $9,000 to $12,000 plus attorney's fees.

II. Analysis

A. Jurisdiction

In its final order, the district court concluded that it lacked subject matter jurisdiction, and the OAS advances that position on appeal. Appellants—and the district court in its January 25 order—rely upon a conjunctive reading of the International Organizations Immunity Act (IOIA) of 1945, 22 U.S.C. § 288a(b) (1979), and the Foreign Sovereign Immunities Act (FSIA) of 1976, 28 U.S.C. § 1330 (1979), to establish jurisdiction. The OAS counters that § 288a(b) confers immunity, not jurisdiction, and that § 1330 establishes jurisdiction over suits against foreign *states,* not international organizations.

* * *

The International Organizations Immunities Act of 1945, 22 U.S.C. § 288a(b) (1979), grants to international organizations which are designated by the President[10] "the same immunity from suit and every form of judicial process as is enjoyed by foreign governments, except to the extent that such organizations may expressly waive their immunity for the purpose of any proceedings or by the terms of any contract." As of 1945, the statute granted absolute immunity to international organizations, for that was the immunity then enjoyed by foreign governments.

. The Foreign Sovereign Immunities Act of 1976, 28 U.S.C. § 1602 et seq. (1979), codified what, in the period between 1946 and 1976, had come to be the immunity enjoyed by sovereign states—restrictive immunity. The central feature of restrictive immunity is the distinction between the governmental or sovereign activities of a state (acts jure imperii) and its commercial activities (acts jure gestionis). Foreign states may not be found liable for their governmental activities by American courts; but they enjoy no immunity from liability for their commercial activities.

Contention for restrictive immunity

Appellants—and the United States as amicus curiae—submit the following syllogism: the IOIA conferred on international organizations the same immunity enjoyed by foreign governments; the FSIA indicates that foreign governments now enjoy only restrictive immunity; therefore, international organizations enjoy only restrictive immunity. They are supported by the general doctrine that ordinarily, "[a] statute which refers to the law of a subject generally adopts the law on the subject as of the time the law was invoked * * * includ[ing] all the amendments and modifications of the law subsequent to the time the reference statute was enacted."

Contention for absolute immunity

The OAS and several other international organizations as amici curiae counter that Congress granted international organizations absolute immunity in the IOIA, and it has never modified that grant. They rely on three

---

10. By Executive Order 10533 (June 3, 1954), 19 Fed.Reg. 3289 (1954), President Eisenhower designated the OAS an international organization entitled to the privileges and immunities conferred by the IOIA.

implications of a legislative intent *not* to apply to international organizations the post World War II evolutions in the doctrine of sovereign immunity.

[T]he FSIA is generally silent about international organizations. No reference to such organizations is made in the elaborate definition of "state" in § 1603, and only § 1611 even alludes to their existence. True, § 1611, dealing as it does with the attachment of property belonging to international organizations, presupposes a successful action against an international organization. However, that could follow a waiver of immunity. Alternatively, § 1611 would have application in case of an attempt to execute a judgment against a foreign state by attaching funds of that foreign state held by an international organization.[16]

[B]y its own terms the IOIA provides for the modification, where appropriate, of the immunity enjoyed by one or more international organizations.

Under the statute, the President can withdraw or restrict the immunity and privileges thereby conferred. Specifically, it provides:

The president (is) authorized, in the light of the functions performed by any such international organization, by appropriate executive order to withhold or withdraw from any such organization or its officers or employees any of the privileges, exemptions, and immunities provided for in this title * * * or to condition or limit the enjoyment by any such organization or its officers or employees of any such privilege, exemption, or immunity.[17]

The Senate Report on the IOIA stated: "This provision will permit the adjustment or limitation of the privileges in the event that any international organization should engage for example, in activities of a commercial nature." And, in floor debate on the legislation, its supporters pointed again to this provision as a limitation on commercial abuses by an international organization.[19] Hence this provision may reveal that Congress intended to grant absolute immunity to international organizations giving to the President the authority to relax that immunity, including removal or restriction of immunity in cases involving the commercial activities of international organizations.

Finally, Congress may have concluded that the policies and considerations that led to the development of the restrictive immunity concept for foreign nations do not apply to international organizations like the OAS.[20]

---

16. According to the House Report: The purpose of this section is to permit international organizations designated by the President pursuant to the International Organization Immunities Act, 22 U.S.C. 288 et seq., to carry out their functions from their offices located in the United States without hindrance by private claimants seeking to attach the payment of funds to a foreign state; such attachments would also violate the immunities accorded to such international institutions. H.R.Rep. No. 94–1487, 94th Cong., 2d Sess. 30 (1976). The Report continues, even more pointedly

This reference to "international organizations" in this subsection is not intended to restrict any immunity accorded to such international organizations under any law or international agreement.

17. 22 U.S.C. § 288a(a) (1979).

19. See 91 Cong.Rec. 12,432 (daily ed. Dec. 20, 1945) and 12,530 (daily ed. Dec. 21, 1945).

20. Prior to its modification, the absolute immunity of states was justified by "the desirability of avoiding adjudication which might affront a foreign nation and thus em-

We need not decide this difficult question of statutory construction. On *either* theory of immunity—absolute or restrictive—an immunity exists sufficient to shield the organization from lawsuit on the basis of acts involved here.

C.   The "Commercial" Activity Concept in the Restrictive Immunity Doctrine

Even under the restrictive immunity doctrine, there is immunity from lawsuits based on governmental or sovereign activities—the jure imperii—as distinct from commercial activities. We discuss the narrower standard of restrictive immunity not because it is necessarily the governing principle, but because we discern that an organization conducting the activities at issue in this case is shielded even under the restrictive immunity formula, and a fortiori on the absolute immunity theory.

Section 1605 of the FSIA provides that foreign states shall not be immune from the jurisdiction of American courts in any case based upon their commercial activity in the United States, with the commercial character of an activity determined by reference to its "nature" rather than to its "purpose." The conceptual difficulties involved in differentiating jure gestionis from jure imperii have led some commentators to declare the distinction unworkable. The restrictive immunity doctrine is designed to accommodate the legal interests of citizens doing business with foreign governments on the one hand, with the interests of foreign states in avoiding the embarrassment of defending the propriety of political acts before a foreign court.

In our view, the employment by a foreign state or international organization of internal administrative personnel—civil servants—is not properly characterized as "doing business." That view is supported by the legislative history of the FSIA, and the definition of "commercial activity" in § 1603. The House Report commented:

> (d) Commercial activity.—Paragraph (c) of section 1603 defines the term "commercial activity" as including a broad spectrum of endeavor, from an individual commercial transaction or act to a regular course of commercial conduct. A "regular course of commercial conduct" includes the carrying on of a commercial enterprise such as a

barrass the executive branch in its conduct of foreign relations." See Hearings on H.R. 11315 before the Subcommittee on Administrative Law and Governmental Relations, House Committee on the Judiciary, 94th Cong., 2d Sess. 29 (1976). As sovereign nations become more and more involved in the market place, as merchants rather than sovereigns, claims arising out of commercial transactions do not affront the sovereignty of the nations involved. Id. Recognition of this growing involvement in commercial activity was the basis of the movement to a restrictive concept. Moreover, most other commercial nations embrace restrictive immunity with regard to sovereigns. Thus, when our

government and its instrumentalities are sued abroad in commercial litigation, the sovereign immunity defense is rarely available. H.R.Rep. [supra]. Congressional proponents of the restrictive immunity could thus indicate that use of the restrictive immunity concept would bring the United States into step with foreign nations. But neither rationale for adopting the restrictive notion of immunity would seem to apply to international organizations. Such organizations do not regularly engage in commercial activities, nor do other nations apply the concept of restrictive immunity to them. Cf. *Alfred Dunhill of London, Inc. v. Cuba*, 425 U.S. 682, 699–702 (1975).

mineral extraction company, an airline or a state trading corporation. Certainly, if an activity is customarily carried on for profit, its commercial nature could readily be assumed. At the other end of the spectrum, a single contract, if of the same character as a contract which might be made by a private person, could constitute a "particular transaction or act."

As the definition indicates, the fact that goods or services to be procured through a contract are to be used for a public purpose is irrelevant; it is the essentially commercial nature of an activity or transaction that is critical. Thus, a contract by a foreign government to buy provisions or equipment for its armed forces or to construct a government building constitutes a commercial activity. The same would be true of a contract to make repairs on an embassy building. Such contracts should be considered to be commercial contracts, even if their ultimate object is to further a public function.

By contrast, a foreign state's mere participation in a foreign assistance program administered by the Agency for International Development (AID) is an activity whose essential nature is public or governmental, and it would not itself constitute a commercial activity. By the same token, a foreign state's activities in and "contacts" with the United States resulting from or necessitated by participation in such a program would not in themselves constitute a sufficient commercial nexus with the United States so as to give rise to jurisdiction (see sec. 1330) or to assets which could be subjected to attachment or execution with respect to unrelated commercial transactions (see sec. 1610(b)). However, a transaction to obtain goods or services from private parties would not lose its otherwise commercial character because it was entered into in connection with an AID program. Also public or governmental and not commercial in nature, would be the employment of diplomatic, civil service, or military personnel, but not the employment of American citizens or third country nationals by the foreign state in the United States.[23]

This report clearly marks employment of civil servants as noncommercial for purposes of restrictive immunity. The Committee Reports establish an exception from the general rule in the case of employment of American citizens or third country nationals by foreign states. The exception leaves foreign states free to conduct "governmental" matters through their own citizens. A comparable exception is not applicable to international organizations, because their civil servants are inevitably drawn from either American citizens or "third" country nations. In the case of international organizations, such an exception would swallow up the rule of immunity for civil service employment disputes.

The United States has accepted without qualification the principles that international organizations must be free to perform their functions and that no member state may take action to hinder the organization.[24]

23. H.Rep. No. 94–1487, 94th Cong., 2d Sess. 16 (1976) (emphasis added).

24. See e.g., XIII Documents of the United Nations Conference on International Organizations 704–05 (1945), reprinted in 13 Whiteman, Digest of International Law 36 (1968).

The unique nature of the international civil service is relevant. International officials should be as free as possible, within the mandate granted by the member states, to perform their duties free from the peculiarities of national politics. The OAS charter, for example, imposes constraints on the organization's employment practices.[25] Such constraints may not coincide with the employment policies pursued by its various member states.[26] It would seem singularly inappropriate for the international organization to bind itself to the employment law of any particular member, and we have no reason to think that either the President or Congress intended this result. An attempt by the courts of one nation to adjudicate the personnel claims of international civil servants would entangle those courts in the internal administration of those organizations. Denial of immunity opens the door to divided decisions of the courts of different member states passing judgment on the rules, regulations, and decisions of the international bodies. Undercutting uniformity in the application of staff rules or regulations would undermine the ability of the organization to function effectively.

We hold that the relationship of an international organization with its internal administrative staff is noncommercial, and, absent waiver, activities defining or arising out of that relationship may not be the basis of an action against the organization—regardless of whether international organizations enjoy absolute or restrictive immunity.

D. The Activities at Issue Here

The appellants were staff members of the General Secretariat of the OAS. Their appointments, terms of employment, salaries and allowances, and the termination of employment were governed by detailed "Staff Rules of the General Secretariat" promulgated by the OAS. The Staff Rules further establish an elaborate grievance procedure within the OAS, with ultimate appeal to the Administrative Tribunal of the OAS.

The Tribunal is competent to determine the lawfulness of an employee's termination of employment. If an employee has been wrongfully discharged, the Tribunal may order reinstatement. If reinstatement is ordered, the Tribunal may also establish an indemnity to be paid to the

---

25. See e.g., OAS Charter, Article 143 (forbidding discrimination on the basis of "race, creed or sex"), Article 126 (requiring staff recruitment on as wide a geographic basis as possible).

26. For example, the Age Discrimination in Employment Act of 1978, (ADEA) 29 U.S.C. § 621 et seq., forbids in most circumstances a requirement that a person retire at a particular age. Yet other countries consider early retirement an important social goal, the achievement of which facilitates advancement by younger people. Since there is no inconsistent provision in the OAS Charter (and since, even if there were, the ADEA was enacted after the latest amendment to the OAS Char-

ter), the ADEA presumably would govern, and unless its provisions were construed not to cover international employment, see 29 U.S.C. §§ 630 and 633a, the OAS and other international organizations who are thought not immune from suit would be required to abide by the terms of the Act in their employment here.

Or for another example, the rigid quotas employed as an integral part of recruiting a "balanced" international civil service, see, e.g., General Assembly Resolution 33/143, December 18, 1978, might run afoul of the emerging law of "affirmative action" in the United States.

employee in the event the Secretary General exercises his authority to indemnify the employee rather than effect the reinstatement.

The employment disputes between the appellants and OAS were disputes concerning the internal administrative staff of the Organization. The internal administration of the OAS is a non-commercial activity shielded by the doctrine of immunity. There was no waiver, and accordingly the appellant's action had to be dismissed.

Affirmed.

———

Note: in 1998 the District of Columbia Circuit Court of Appeals confirmed much of the reasoning of the *Broadbent* case, above. In *Atkinson v. Inter–American Development Bank* 156 F.3d 1335 (D.C.Cir.1998), appellant sought a declaratory judgment that her husband's employer, the appellee Bank, an international organization, was not immune from garnishment proceedings under the International Organizations Immunities Act of 1945 which was applicable to the Bank. The Court declined, as it did in *Broadbent*, to find that the IOIA incorporated subsequent changes in the law governing immunity of foreign sovereigns. Hence the IOIA did not incorporate the 1952 restrictive theory of immunity but retained the absolute theory of immunity as it existed in 1945. On the question of the "commercial activities exception" under the restrictive theory, the Court said at pp. 98–99:

Even if we concluded that the IOIA's reference to the law of immunity of foreign sovereigns is an evolving one that incorporates the commercial activities exception to immunity, we think appellant's garnishment proceeding would not come within that exception. As relevant here, the FSIA's formulation finds the commercial activities exception satisfied where "the action is based upon a commercial activity carried on in the United States by the foreign state." 28 U.S.C. § 1605(a)(2). To determine whether an action is "based upon a commercial activity," we look to "those elements of a claim that, if proven, would entitle a plaintiff to relief under his theory of the case." *Saudi Arabia v. Nelson* [*supra*],

A garnishment proceeding would require appellant to demonstrate two principal elements. To obtain a writ of garnishment, appellant would need to show the amount of the debt owed by [former husband] Kestell to her and the judgment giving rise to that debt. D.C. Code § 16–501(c)(1)-(2). To levy the writ on the Bank as garnishee, appellant would have to demonstrate that the Bank owed wages to Kestell. Id. § 16–544. Neither of these elements relates to a commercial activity of the Bank. * * * Nor is the Bank's payment of wages to Kestell a commercial activity. *See Broadbent v. Organization of Am. States*, 628 F.2d 27, 34 (D.C.Cir.1980) (holding that an international organization's employment of civil servants, regardless of their nationality, is not a commercial activity).

Because neither of these principal elements of a garnishment proceeding rests on a commercial activity of the Bank, the commercial activities exception would not apply and the Bank would remain immune from jurisdiction under the general rule of 28 U.S.C. § 1604. The judgment of the district court is

Affirmed.

Questions: What is the argument for maintaining absolute immunity for international organizations? Purely textual? *See Food & Agriculture Org. v. INPDAI*, 87 Int'l L.Rep.1 (Italy, Court of Cassation, 1992) in which the Court reached a restrictive and functional result, finding jurisdiction in a rent increase dispute between the FAO and a lessor of office space in Rome.

Consider the questions posed at the close of Section A above, now from the standpoint of international organizations as well as states. Note that Articles 20 and 31 of the Convention on the Privileges and Immunities of the United Nations (1 U.N.T.S. 15) and Articles 22 and 31 of the Convention on the Privileges and Immunities of the Specialized Agencies (33 U.N.T.S. 261) *require* waiver of immunity and appropriate provision for the settlement of disputes in certain situations. Should formal and systematic arrangements be made for the implementation of these provisions? Should such arrangements be made also with respect to the immunities of states? What might be the scope and reach of such provisions?

SECTION C.   THE ACT OF STATE DOCTRINE

The act of state doctrine is a judicially-created limitation on the exercise of federal adjudicatory jurisdiction. It is not a jurisdictional bar, but is a mechanism of judicial abstention to allow the judiciary prudentially to avoid litigating a foreign sovereign's public conduct committed within its own territory. The judiciary avoids being enmeshed in matters of foreign affairs which could risk embarrassment to the executive. Most of the Supreme Court decisions have related to expropriation of private property, or political crises in foreign countries. Questions of civil damages for loss of consortium or for *"Foreign Corrupt Practices "*relating to alleged bribery of foreign officials by a U.S. contractor have also been at issue, as have been questions of human rights abuses by foreign officials and responsibility of a U.S. company cooperating with a foreign government in a project in which such abuses allegedly take place.

The act of state doctrine arises in a litigation context. It involves the question whether an otherwise dispositive governing foreign legal principle is to be invalidated by a "municipal" court. It does not arise in a purely foreign relations context, as where the foreign office of State A should reject official conduct of State B in a diplomatic protection case (refer to Chapters 8 and 13B). A foreign ministry might assert that the foreign state's conduct violates international law, and it might even try to proceed in an international tribunal, where official conduct and major policy are concerned. But no state uses its courts to sue another to invalidate the latter state's official conduct, especially that taken in the latter state's territory. True, in the leading U.S. case, *Banco National de Cuba v. Sabbatino, infra*, the plaintiff was an agency of Cuba, but you will understand shortly how it came to be the plaintiff. In all other act of state cases in U.S. courts, the plaintiffs are private parties who have taken the initiative to bring cases. The dispositive issue, however, whether the act of a foreign state is legitimate, is usually raised by the defendant.

The act of state doctrine is not part of the Foreign Sovereign Immunities Act and is governed by different variables as to application, *vel non,* although it will cause a plaintiff to lose in a similar fashion. These cases could be dealt with as an ordinary, strictly judicial, conflicts of law case. The choice of law would be to apply that of the foreign state, unless the plaintiff could convince the court that the foreign law should be rejected as fundamentally and inherently contrary to the law and policy of the forum. But major act of state cases have not taken this approach. Why? Simply put: it is because non-judicial issues arise, including policy issues of concern to the executive and the legislative branches.

1.   THE BASIC COURT-MADE DOCTRINE

The U.S. act of state doctrine and political crises in foreign relations. The U.S. act of state doctrine is closely linked to foreign political crises in the course of which officials of a foreign government take actions harmful or outrageous to a person who, later, seeks redress by bringing a suit in the United States.

Legislation could be enacted or executive action could be taken to require that the act of state doctrine not apply unless the Department of State calls for its application. The justification for side-tracking the doctrine is that the courts should be allowed to do justice for less sensitive cases, for plaintiffs who are victims of foreign governmental acts committed in their own territories. What happens to justice when the Executive or the Congress intervene in support of one outcome or the other as to the rejection or acceptance of the foreign act of state? The potential separation-of-powers problem is obvious. Should the Supreme Court be the final arbiter? Should the trial court solicit the foreign policy view of the Department of State on the matter? Should the court be required to follow the Department of State position? Should Congress resolve these and related issues by comprehensive legislation on act of state?

In the matter of U.S. business investment abroad, the customary tensions escalated into crisis when Castro nationalized American private property in Cuba belonging to U.S. nationals in retaliation for actions such as Congressional suspension of the Cuban sugar quota. Later, Allende, the former president of Chile, nationalized what had already been reduced to minority U.S. interests in Chilean copper mining companies. He evaded paying compensation by inducing the enactment of a retroactive excess profits tax that exceeded the compensation claim. In Peru, elements of the military overthrew an elected president who had tried to settle a long-smouldering controversy about sub-surface oil and gas rights and had trumped up a bad faith extraction claim that washed out compensation. Libya's Colonel Qadhafi cancelled without compensation some (but not all) oil concessions that had been made by the deposed king of Libya, See in Chapter 13 below Section B 2 on expropriation of foreign property.

Banco Nacional de Cuba v. Sabbatino, Receiver

United States Supreme Court, 1964.
376 U.S. 398, 84 S.Ct. 923, 11 L.Ed.2d 804.

■ MR. JUSTICE HARLAN delivered the opinion of the Court.

The question which brought this case here, and is now found to be the dispositive issue, is whether the so-called act of state doctrine serves to sustain petitioner's claims in this litigation. Such claims are ultimately founded on a decree of the Government of Cuba expropriating certain property, the right to the proceeds of which is here in controversy. The act of state doctrine in its traditional formulation precludes the courts of this country from inquiring into the validity of the public acts a recognized foreign sovereign power committed within its own territory.

[In 1960, the U.S. Congress reduced the import quota for Cuban sugar. The Cuban government characterized the reduction as "aggression" and retaliated by nationalizing the sugar industry, expropriating many U.S. owned companies or companies in which Americans held significant interests. Farr Whitlock, an American commodities broker had entered into a contract to buy a shipload of C.A.V. (*Compañia Azucarera Vertientes,* one of the U.S. companies) sugar. Farr Whitlock entered into a new agreement to buy the shipload of sugar from the Cuban government, and turned the proceeds over to *C.A.V.,* instead of Cuba. Farr Whitlock's defense in this action was that title to the sugar never actually passed to Cuba, because the expropriation violated international law.]

* * *

The classic American statement of the act of state doctrine, which appears to have taken root in England as early as 1674, and began to emerge in the jurisprudence of this country in the late eighteenth and early nineteenth centuries, see e.g., *Ware v. Hylton,* 3 Dall. 199, 230; *The Santissima Trinidad,* 7 Wheat. 283, 336, is found in *Underhill v. Hernandez,* where Chief Justice Fuller said for a unanimous Court: "Every sovereign State is bound to respect the independence of every other sovereign State, and the courts of one country will not sit in judgment on the acts of the government of another done within its own territory. Redress of grievances by reason of such acts must be obtained through the means open to be availed of by sovereign powers as between themselves." Following this precept the Court in that case refused to inquire into acts of Hernandez, a revolutionary Venezuelan military commander whose government had been later recognized by the United States, which were made the basis of a damage action in this country by Underhill, an American citizen, who claimed that he had been unlawfully assaulted, coerced, and detained in Venezuela by Hernandez.

None of this Court's subsequent cases in which the act of state doctrine was directly or peripherally involved manifest any retreat from *Underhill.* * * * On the contrary in *Oetjen* and *Ricaud,* the doctrine as announced in Underhill was reaffirmed in unequivocal terms.

* * *

The Court of Appeals relied in part upon an exception to the unqualified teachings of *Underhill, Oetjen,* and *Ricaud* which that court had earlier indicated. In *Bernstein v. Van Heyghen Freres Société Anonyme,* suit was brought to recover from an assignee property allegedly taken, in effect, by the Nazi Government because plaintiff was Jewish. Recognizing the odious nature of this act of state, the court, through Judge Learned Hand, nonetheless refused to consider it invalid on that ground. Rather, it looked to see if the Executive had acted in any manner that would indicate that United States Courts should refuse to give effect to such a foreign decree. Finding no such evidence, the court sustained dismissal of the complaint. In a later case involving similar facts the same court again assumed examination of the German acts improper, *Bernstein v. N.V. Neder-landsche–Amerikaansche Stoomvaart–Maatschappij,* but, quite evidently following the implications of Judge Hand's opinion in the earlier case, amended its mandate to permit evidence of alleged invalidity, subsequent to receipt by plaintiff's attorney of a letter from the Acting Legal Adviser to the State Department written for the purpose of relieving the court from any constraint upon the exercise of its jurisdiction to pass on that question.

This Court has never had occasion to pass upon the so-called *Bernstein* exception, nor need it do so now. For whatever ambiguity may be thought to exist in the two letters from State Department officials on which the Court of Appeals relied, is now removed by the position which the Executive has taken in this Court on the act of state claim; respondents do not indeed contest the view that these letters were intended to reflect no more than the Department's then wish not to make any statement bearing on this litigation.

The outcome of this case, therefore, turns upon whether any of the contentions urged by respondents against the application of the act of state doctrine in the premises is acceptable: (1) that the doctrine does not apply to acts of state which violate international law, as is claimed to be the case here; (2) that the doctrine is inapplicable unless the Executive specifically interposes it in a particular case; and (3) that, in any event, the doctrine may not be invoked by a foreign government plaintiff in our courts.

Preliminarily, we discuss the foundations on which we deem the act of state doctrine to rest, and more particularly the question of whether state or federal law governs its application in a federal diversity case.

We do not believe that this doctrine is compelled either by the inherent nature of sovereign authority, as some of the earlier decisions seem to imply, see *Underhill, American Banana,* and *Oetjen, supra,* or by some principle of international law. If a transaction takes place in one jurisdiction and the forum is in another, the forum does not by dismissing an action or by applying its own law purport to divest the first jurisdiction of its territorial sovereignty; it merely declines to adjudicate or makes applicable its own law to parties or property before it. The refusal of one country to enforce the penal laws of another * * * is a typical example of an instance when a court will not entertain a cause of action arising in another jurisdiction. While historic notions of sovereign authority do bear upon the wisdom of employing the act of state doctrine, they do not dictate its existence.

That international law does not require application of the doctrine is evidenced by the practice of nations. Most of the countries rendering decisions on the subject fail to follow the rule rigidly. No international arbitral or judicial decision discovered suggests that international law prescribes recognition of sovereign acts of foreign governments and apparently no claim has ever been raised before an international tribunal that failure to apply the act of state doctrine constitutes a breach of international obligation. If international law does not prescribe use of the doctrine, neither does it forbid application of the rule even if it is claimed that the act of state in question violated international law. The traditional view of international law is that it establishes substantive principles for determining whether one country has wronged another. Because of its peculiar nation-to-nation character the usual method for an individual to seek relief is to exhaust local remedies and then repair to the executive authorities of his own state to persuade them to champion his claim in diplomacy or before an international tribunal. Although it is, of course, true that United States courts apply international law as a part of our own in appropriate circumstances * * * the public law of nations can hardly dictate to a country which is in theory wronged how to treat that wrong within its domestic borders.

Despite the broad statement in *Oetjen* that "The conduct of the foreign relations of our Government is committed by the Constitution to the Executive and Legislative * * * Departments," it cannot of course be thought that "every case or controversy which touches foreign relations lies beyond judicial cognizance." The text of the Constitution does not require the act of state doctrine; it does not irrevocably remove from the judiciary the capacity to review the validity of foreign acts of state.

The act of state doctrine does, however, have "constitutional" underpinnings. It arises out of the basic relationships between branches of government in a system of separation of powers. It concerns the competency of dissimilar institutions to make and implement particular kinds of decisions in the area of international relations. The doctrine as formulated in past decisions expresses the strong sense of the Judicial Branch that its engagement in the task of passing on the validity of foreign acts of state may hinder rather than further this country's pursuit of goals both for itself and for the community of nations as a whole in the international sphere. Many commentators disagree; they have striven by means of distinguishing and limiting past decisions and by advancing various considerations of policy to stimulate a narrowing of the apparent scope of the rule. Whatever considerations are thought to predominate, it is plain that the problems involved are uniquely federal in nature. If federal authority, in this instance this Courtorders the field of judicial competence in this area for the federal courts, and the state courts are left free to formulate their own rules, the purposes behind the doctrine could be as effectively undermined as if there had been no federal pronouncement on the subject.

* * *

If the act of state doctrine is a principle of decision binding on federal and state courts alike but compelled by neither international law nor the Constitution, its continuing vitality depends on its capacity to reflect the proper distribution of functions between the judicial and political branches of the Government on matters bearing upon foreign affairs. It should be apparent that the greater the degree of codification or consensus concerning a particular area of international law, the more appropriate it is for the judiciary to render decisions regarding it, since the courts can then focus on the application of an agreed principle to circumstances of fact rather than on the sensitive task of establishing a principle not inconsistent with the national interest or with international justice. It is also evident that some aspects of international law touch much more sharply on national nerves than do others; the less important the implications of an issue are for our foreign relations, the weaker the justification for exclusivity in the political branches. The balance of relevant considerations may also be shifted if the government which perpetrated the challenged act of state is no longer in existence, as in the *Bernstein* case, for the political interest of this country may, as a result, be measurably altered. Therefore, rather than laying down or reaffirming an inflexible and all-encompassing rule in this case, we decide only that the Judicial Branch will not examine the validity of a taking of property within its own territory by a foreign sovereign government, extant and recognized by this country at the time of suit, in the absence of a treaty or other unambiguous agreement regarding controlling legal principles, even if the complaint alleges that the taking violates customary international law.

There are few if any issues in international law today on which opinion seems to be so divided as the limitations on a state's power to expropriate the property of aliens. There is, of course, authority, in international judicial and arbitral decisions, in the expressions of national governments, and among commentators for the view that a taking is improper under international law if it is not for a public purpose, is discriminatory, or is without provision for prompt, adequate, and effective compensation. However, Communist countries, although they have in fact provided a degree of compensation after diplomatic efforts, commonly recognize no obligation on the part of the taking country. Certain representatives of the newly independent and underdeveloped countries have questioned whether rules of state responsibility toward aliens can bind nations that have not consented to them and it is argued that the traditionally articulated standards governing expropriation of property reflect "imperialist" interests and are inappropriate to the circumstances of emergent states.

* * *

The possible adverse consequences of a conclusion to the contrary of that implicit in these cases is highlighted by contrasting the practices of the political branch with the limitations of the judicial process in matters of this kind. Following an expropriation of any significance, the Executive engages in diplomacy aimed to assure that United States citizens who are harmed are compensated fairly. Representing all claimants of this country, it will often be able, either by bilateral or multilateral talks, by submission to the United Nations, or by the employment of economic and political sanctions, to achieve some degree of general redress. Judicial determinations of invalidity of title can, on the other hand, have only an occasional impact, since they depend on the fortuitous circumstance of the property in question being brought into this country. Such decisions would, if the acts involved were declared invalid, often be likely to give offense to the expropriating country; since the concept of territorial sovereignty is so deep seated, any state may resent the refusal of the courts of another sovereign to accord validity to acts within its territorial borders. * * *

The dangers of such adjudication are present regardless of whether the State Department has, as it did in this case, asserted that the relevant act violated international law. If the Executive Branch has undertaken negotiations with an expropriating country, but has refrained from claims of violation of the law of nations, a determination to that effect by a court might be regarded as a serious insult, while a finding of compliance with international law, would greatly strengthen the bargaining hand of the other state with consequent detriment to American interests.

Even if the State Department has proclaimed the impropriety of the expropriation, the stamp of approval of its view by a judicial tribunal, however impartial, might increase any affront and the judicial decision might occur at a time, almost always well after the taking, when such an impact would be contrary to our national interest. Considerably more serious and far-reaching consequences would flow from a judicial finding that international law standards had been met if that determination flew in the face of a State Department proclamation to the contrary. When articulating principles of international law in its relations with other states, the Executive Branch speaks not only as an interpreter of generally accepted and traditional rules, as would the courts, but also as an advocate of standards it believes desirable for the community of nations and protective of national concerns. In short, whatever way the matter is cut, the possibility of conflict between the Judicial and Executive Branches could hardly be avoided.

* * *

Another serious consequence of the exception pressed by respondents would be to render uncertain titles in foreign commerce, with the possible consequence of altering the flow of international trade. If the attitude of the United States courts were unclear, one buying expropriated goods would not know if he could safely import them into this country. Even were takings known to be invalid, one would have difficulty determining after goods had changed hands several times whether the particular articles in question were the product of an ineffective state act.

Against the force of such considerations, we find respondents' countervailing arguments quite unpersuasive. Their basic contention is that United States courts could make a significant contribution to the growth of international law, a contribution whose importance, it is said, would be magnified by the relative paucity of decisional law by international bodies. But given the fluidity of present world conditions, the effectiveness of such a patchwork approach toward the formulation of an acceptable body of law concerning state responsibility for expropriations, is, to say the least, highly conjectural. Moreover, it rests upon the sanguine presupposition that the decisions of the courts of the world's major capital exporting country and principal exponent of the free enterprise system would be accepted as disinterested expressions of sound legal principle by those adhering to widely different ideologies.

* * *

Respondents claim that the economic pressure resulting from the proposed exception to the act of state doctrine will materially add to the protection of United States investors. We are not convinced, even assuming the relevance of this contention. * * *

It is suggested that if the act of state doctrine is applicable to violations of international law, it should only be so when the Executive Branch expressly stipulates that it does not wish the courts to pass on the question of validity. We should be slow to reject the representations of the Government that such a reversal of the *Bernstein* principle would work serious inroads on the maximum effectiveness of United States diplomacy. Often the State Department will wish to refrain from taking an official position particularly at a moment that would be dictated by the developing of private litigation but might be inopportune diplomatically. Adverse domestic consequences might flow from an official stand which could be assuaged, if at all, only by revealing matters best kept secret. Of course, a relevant consideration for the State Department would be the position contemplated in the court to hear the case. It is highly questionable whether the examination of validity by the judiciary should depend on an educated guess by the Executive as to probable result and, at any rate, should a prediction be wrong, the Executive might be embarrassed in its dealings with other countries. We do not now pass on the *Bernstein* exception, but even if it were deemed valid, its suggested extension is unwarranted.

However offensive to the public policy of this country and its constituent States an expropriation of this kind may be, we conclude that both the national interest and progress toward the goal of establishing the rule of law among nations are best served by maintaining intact the act of state doctrine in this realm of its application.

* * *

The judgment of the Court of Appeals is reversed and the case is remanded to the District Court for proceedings consistent with this opinion.

It is so ordered.

■ MR. JUSTICE WHITE dissenting.

I am dismayed that the Court has, with one broad stroke, declared the ascertainment and application of international law beyond the competence of the courts of the United States in a large and important category of cases. I am also disappointed in the Court's declaration that the acts of a sovereign state with regard to the property of aliens within its borders are beyond the reach of international law in the courts of this country. However clearly established that law may be, a sovereign may violate it with impunity, except insofar as the political branches of the government may provide a remedy. This backward-looking doctrine, never before declared in this Court, is carried a disconcerting step further: not only are the courts powerless to question acts of state proscribed by international law but they are likewise powerless to refuse to adjudicate the claim founded upon a foreign law; they must render judgment and thereby validate the lawless act. Since the Court expressly extends its ruling to all acts of state expropriating property, however clearly inconsistent with the international community, all discriminatory expropriations of the property of aliens, as for example the taking of properties of persons belonging to certain races, religions or nationalities, are entitled to automatic validation in the courts of the United States. No other civilized country has found such a rigid rule necessary for the survival of the executive branch of its government; the executive of no other government seems to require such insulation from international law adjudications in its courts; and no other judiciary is apparently so incompetent to ascertain and apply international law.

I do not believe that the act of state doctrine as judicially fashioned in this Court, and the reasons underlying it, require American courts to decide cases in disregard of international law and of the rights of litigants to a full determination on the merits.

* * *

2. SOME POST-SABBATINO APPLICATIONS OF THE ACT OF STATE DOCTRINE

In *Alfred Dunhill of London, Inc. v. Republic of Cuba*, 425 U.S. 682, 695, 96 S.Ct. 1854, 1861 (1976), Mr. Justice White stated that the Court was: * * * persuaded by the arguments of petitioner and by those of the United States that the concept of an act of state should not be extended to include the repudiation of a purely commercial obligation owed by a foreign sovereign or by one of its commercial instrumentalities * * * and noted that it is the position of the United States, stated in an amicus brief * * * that * * * a line should be drawn in defining the outer limits of the act of state concept and that repudiations by a foreign sovereign of its commercial debts should not be considered to be acts of state beyond legal question in our courts. * * *

W.S. Kirkpatrick & Co., Inc. v. Environmental Tectonics Corporation, International

United States Supreme Court, 1990.
493 U.S. 400, 110 S.Ct. 701, 107 L.Ed.2d 816.

■ JUSTICE SCALIA delivered the opinion of the Court.

In this case we must decide whether the act of state doctrine bars a court in the United States from entertaining a cause of action that does not rest upon the asserted invalidity of an official act of a foreign sovereign, but that does require imputing to foreign officials an unlawful motivation (the obtaining of bribes) in the performance of such an official act.

I

[Facts]: * * * In 1981, Harry Carpenter, who was then Chairman of the Board and Chief Executive Officer of petitioner W.S. Kirkpatrick & Co.,

Inc. (Kirkpatrick) learned that the Republic of Nigeria was interested in contracting for the construction and equipment of an aeromedical center at Kaduna Air Force Base in Nigeria. He made arrangements with Benson "Tunde" Akindele, a Nigerian citizen, whereby Akindele would endeavor to secure the contract for Kirkpatrick. It was agreed that, in the event the contract was awarded to Kirkpatrick, Kirkpatrick would pay to two Panamanian entities controlled by Akindele a "commission" equal to 20% of the contract price, which would in turn be given as a bribe to officials of the Nigerian Government. In accordance with this plan, the contract was awarded to petitioner W.S. Kirkpatrick & Co., International (Kirkpatrick International), a wholly owned subsidiary of Kirkpatrick; Kirkpatrick paid the promised "commission" to the appointed Panamanian entities; and those funds were disbursed as bribes. All parties agree that Nigerian law prohibits both the payment and the receipt of bribes in connection with the award of a government contract.

Respondent Environmental Tectonics, * * * an unsuccessful bidder for the Kaduna contract, learned of the 20% "commission" and brought the matter to the attention of the Nigerian Air Force and the United States Embassy in Lagos. Following an investigation by the Federal Bureau of Investigation, the United States Attorney for the District of New Jersey brought charges against both Kirkpatrick and Carpenter for violations of the Foreign Corrupt Practices Act of 1977, 15 U.S.C. § 78dd–1 et seq., and both pleaded guilty.

Respondent then brought this civil action against Carpenter, Akindele, petitioners, and others, seeking damages under the Racketeer Influenced and Corrupt Organizations Act [RICO], 18 U.S.C. § 1961 et seq., the Robinson–Patman Act, 15 U.S.C. § 13 et seq., and the New Jersey Anti–Racketeering Act. The defendants moved to dismiss the complaint under Rule 12(b)(6) of the Federal Rules of Civil Procedure on the ground that the action was barred by the act of state doctrine.

The District Court, having requested and received a letter expressing the views of the legal advisor to the United States Department of State as to the applicability of the act of state doctrine, treated the motion as one for summary judgment under Rule 56 of the Federal Rules of Civil Procedure, and granted the motion. *Environmental Tectonics v. Kirkpatrick*, 659 F.Supp. 1381 (1987). The District Court concluded that the act of state doctrine applies "if the inquiry presented for judicial determination includes the motivation of a sovereign act which would result in embarrassment to the sovereign or constitute interference in the conduct of foreign policy of the United States." Applying that principle to the facts at hand, the court held that respondent's suit had to be dismissed * * *

The Court of Appeals for the Third Circuit reversed. Although agreeing with the District Court that "the award of a military procurement contract can be, in certain circumstances, a sufficiently formal expression of a government's public interests to trigger application" of the act of state doctrine, it found application of the doctrine unwarranted on the facts of this case. The Court of Appeals found particularly persuasive the letter to the District Court from the legal advisor to the Department of State, which had stated that in the opinion of the Department judicial inquiry into the purpose behind the act of a foreign sovereign would not produce the "unique embarrassment, and the particular interference with the conduct of foreign affairs, that may result from the judicial determination that a foreign sovereign's acts are invalid." The Court * * * acknowledged that "the Department's legal conclusions as to the reach of the act of state doctrine are not controlling on the courts," but concluded that "the Department's factual assessment of whether fulfillment of its responsibilities will be prejudiced by the course of civil litigation is entitled to substantial respect." In light of the Department's view that the interests of the Executive Branch would not be harmed by prosecution of the action, the Court of Appeals held that Kirkpatrick had not met its burden of showing that the case should not go forward; accordingly, it reversed the judgment of the District Court and remanded the case for trial. We granted certiorari.

II

This Court's description of the jurisprudential foundation for the act of state doctrine has undergone some evolution over the years. We once viewed the doctrine as an expression of international law, resting upon "the highest considerations of international comity and expediency," *Oetjen v. Central Leather Co.* We have more recently described it, however, as a consequence of domestic separation of powers, reflecting "the strong sense of the Judicial Branch that its engagement in the task of passing on the validity of foreign acts of state may hinder" the conduct of foreign affairs, *Banco Nacional de Cuba v. Sabbatino.* Some Justices have suggested possible exceptions to application of the doctrine, where one or both of the foregoing policies would seemingly not be served: an exception, for example, for acts of state that consist of commercial transactions, since neither modern international comity nor the current position of our Executive Branch accorded sovereign immunity to such acts, see *Alfred Dunhill of London,* (opinion of WHITE, J.), or an exception for cases in which the Executive Branch has represented that it has no objection to denying validity to the foreign sovereign act, since then the courts would be impeding no foreign policy goals, see *First National City Bank v. Banco Nacional de Cuba,* (opinion of REHNQUIST, J.).

The parties have argued at length about the applicability of these possible exceptions, and, more generally, about whether the purpose of the act of state doctrine would be furthered by its application in this case. We find it unnecessary, however, to pursue those inquiries, since the factual predicate for application of the act of state doctrine does not exist. Nothing in the present suit requires the court to declare invalid, and thus ineffective as "a rule of decision for the courts of this country," the official act of a foreign sovereign.

In every case in which we have held the act of state doctrine applicable, the relief sought or the defense interposed would have required a court in the United States to declare invalid the official act of a foreign sovereign performed within its own territory. * * * In the present case, by contrast, neither the claim nor any asserted defense requires a determination that Nigeria's contract with Kirkpatrick International was, or was not, effective.

Petitioners point out, however, that the facts necessary to establish respondent's claim will also establish that the contract was unlawful. Specifically, they note that in order to prevail respondent must prove that petitioner Kirkpatrick made, and Nigerian officials received, payments that violate Nigerian law, which would, they assert, support a finding that the contract is invalid under Nigerian law. Assuming that to be true, it still does not suffice. The act of state doctrine is not some vague doctrine of abstention but a "principle of decision binding on federal and state courts alike." *Sabbatino, supra,* (emphasis added). As we said in *Ricaud,* "the act within its own boundaries of one sovereign State * * * becomes * * * a rule of decision for the courts of this country." Act of state issues only arise when a court *must decide*—that is, when the outcome of the case turns upon—the effect of official action by a foreign sovereign. When that question is not in the case, neither is the act of state doctrine. That is the situation here. Regardless of what the court's factual findings may suggest as to the legality of the Nigerian contract, its legality is simply not a question to be decided in the present suit, and there is thus no occasion to apply the rule of decision that the act of state doctrine requires. Cf. *Sharon v. Time, Inc.,* ("The issue in this litigation is not whether [the alleged] acts are valid, but whether they occurred").

* * *

Petitioners insist, however, that the policies underlying our act of state cases—international comity, respect for the sovereignty of foreign nations on their own territory, and the avoidance of embarrassment to the Executive Branch in its conduct of foreign relations—are implicated in the present case because, as the District Court found, a determination that Nigerian officials demanded and accepted a bribe "would impugn or question the nobility of a foreign nation's motivations," and would "result in embarrassment to the sovereign or constitute interference in the conduct of foreign policy of the United States." The United States, as *amicus curiae,* favors the same approach to the act of state doctrine, though disagreeing with petitioners as to the outcome it produces in the present case. We should not, the United States urges, "attach dispositive significance to the fact that this suit involves only the 'motivation' for, rather than the 'validity' of, a foreign sovereign act," and should eschew "any rigid formula for the resolution of act of state cases generally." In some future case, perhaps, "litigation * * * based on alleged corruption in the award of contracts or other commercially oriented activities of foreign governments could sufficiently touch on 'national nerves' that the act of state doctrine or related principles of abstention would appropriately be found to bar the suit," (quoting *Sabbatino*) and we should therefore resolve this case on the narrowest possible ground, viz., that the letter from the legal advisor to the District Court gives sufficient indication that, "in the setting of this case," the act of state doctrine poses no bar to adjudication, ibid.[a]

---

a. Even if we agreed with the Government's fundamental approach, we would question its characterization of the legal advisor's letter as reflecting the absence of any policy objection to the adjudication. The letter, which is reprinted as an appendix to the opinion of the Court of Appeals, see 847 F.2d 1052, 1067–1069 (C.A.3 1988), did not purport to say whether the State Department would like the suit to proceed, but rather

These urgings are deceptively similar to what we said in *Sabbatino,* where we observed that sometimes, even though the validity of the act of a foreign sovereign within its own territory is called into question, the policies underlying the act of state doctrine may not justify its application. We suggested that a sort of balancing approach could be applied—the balance shifting against application of the doctrine, for example, if the government that committed the "challenged act of state" is no longer in existence. But what is appropriate in order to avoid unquestioning judicial acceptance of the acts of foreign sovereigns is not similarly appropriate for the quite opposite purpose of expanding judicial incapacities where such acts are not directly (or even indirectly) involved. It is one thing to suggest, as we have, that the policies underlying the act of state doctrine should be considered in deciding whether, despite the doctrine's technical availability, it should nonetheless not be invoked; it is something quite different to suggest that those underlying policies are a doctrine unto themselves, justifying expansion of the act of state doctrine (or, as the United States puts it, unspecified "related principles of abstention") into new and uncharted fields.

The short of the matter is this: Courts in the United States have the power, and ordinarily the obligation, to decide cases and controversies properly presented to them. The act of state doctrine does not establish an exception for cases and controversies that may embarrass foreign governments, but merely requires that, in the process of deciding, the acts of foreign sovereigns taken within their own jurisdictions shall be deemed valid. That doctrine has no application to the present case because the validity of no foreign sovereign act is at issue.

The judgment of the Court of Appeals * * * is affirmed. *It is so ordered.*

Note and Questions: Some say that the act of state doctrine is in desuetude. It has long confounded international lawyers and the *Kirkpatrick case* has done nothing to provide guidance. Indeed, it has been argued that, since *Kirkpatrick,* the act of state doctrine cannot be understood in any coherent fashion. As you saw in Justice Scalia's terse opinion, the Court held that the act of state doctrine functions as a special "rule of decision" or special choice of law rule, which requires courts faced with challenges to apparently official acts of sovereign foreign governments, to apply the law of the latter state. *See,* Fox, *Reexamining the Act of State Doctrine: An Integrated Conflicts Analysis,* 33 Harv.Int'l L.J. 521 (1992). Did Justice Scalia oversimplify? If so, does that invite further use by counsel for foreign states and agencies, who would otherwise not be immune to suit under the restrictive theories of the FSIA? Sovereign immunity is an important shield where applicable. When it is removed, however, defense of the foreign state falls back to the *act of state* doctrine. Does Justice Scalia's opinion create enough incoherence on these issues to breed additional such use? Ambiguity may be the medium of good lawyers.

responded (correctly, as we hold today) to the question whether the act of state doctrine was applicable.

A Limited v. B Bank and Bank of X

England, Court of Appeal, 31 July 1996, 111 Int'l L. Rep. 590.*

The following is the text of the judgments delivered in the Court of Appeal:

* * *

The appellants are registered proprietors of a United Kingdom patent relating to the invention of a type of security paper suitable for use in the manufacture of bank notes and other security documents. The interveners are the central bank of a foreign country which I shall call X. They had security paper manufactured for them in Italy, which the appellants say is within the claims of their United Kingdom patent. Bank notes printed on that paper were then issued as currency of the State of X. The respondents as a commercial Bank have kept for disposal and have disposed of such bank notes in England. This action against the respondents is for infringement of the United Kingdom patent in so doing, contrary to Patents Act 1977 * * *

Judge Ford upheld the application to set aside the proceedings on the grounds that the issues in the action were non-justiciable, and that the grant or relief would be contrary to international comity. He dealt with both matters succinctly in his judgment, saying of non-justiciability:

It must be inherent in the recognition by an English court of the prerogative right of a State to issue paper money that English courts will not interfere with the free circulation of the lawful paper money of another State in this country without express authority from the Crown or Parliament.

Of comity he said: " ... if ... notes are printed on the [allegedly infringing] paper and put into circulation, it would seem to be a breach of the rules comity for English Courts to seek to interfere with that circulation".

For the interveners Mr Richard Plender QC argues that the issue of bank notes is relevant because it forms the kernel of the dispute. He submits that there are objections to the English courts adjudicating upon the alleged infringement of patent by the use of bank notes of the State of X here. Those objections are practical, legal and under patent law. Although for the future the interveners could alter any paper on which their bank notes are printed, it would be impossible to separate currency already circulating abroad, if that proved to infringe the patent, from currency circulating at home. According to Mr Plender's submission the appellants seek to challenge the disposal within the United Kingdom of "bank notes, being the currency of the State of X put into circulation in the United Kingdom and elsewhere by" the Interveners. But here the bank notes are not currency, they are commodities. There is nothing to show that the interveners put the bank notes into circulation here, and if they had, it would not have been a sovereign act. No sovereign has the right to insist on the circulation of his bank notes in a foreign country. To seek to do so would itself constitute an invasion of sovereignty, palpably contrary to comity.

* * *

---

* Reprinted with the permission of the Editor, International Law Reports.

The notion that the keeping and disposal of foreign bank notes for commercial purposes in this country should be treated as sovereign acts outside the purview of the English courts is not only unattractive but is contrary to principle. If the interveners have had any bank notes printed on infringing paper, they have only themselves to blame for any adverse monetary or commercial consequences that may have ensued.

* * *

Even if the disposal of banknotes of the State of X were held to have infringed the appellants' patent, the fact that they could not have been disposed of unless they had been issued by or on behalf of the government of the State of X will not avail the respondents or the interveners because the court is not asked to adjudicate upon, or even to consider the lawfulness of the issue of currency, nor is any claim made that might interfere with sovereign functions of the State of X: cf. the *Playa Larga* [1983] 2 Lloyd's Rep. 171. Scalia J conclusively summarized the matter in *W. S. Kirkpatrick & Co. Inc. v. Environmental Tectonics supra* when he said, delivering the opinion of the Supreme Court of the United States:

Courts in the United States have the power, and ordinarily the obligation, to decide cases and controversies properly presented to them. The act of state doctrine does not establish an exception for cases and controversies that may embarrass foreign governments, but merely requires that, in the process of deciding, the acts of foreign sovereigns taken within their own jurisdictions shall be deemed valid. That doctrine has no application to the present case because the validity of no foreign sovereign act is at issue.

* * *

The judge's assertion that it follows from the right to issue bank notes that English courts will not interfere with their circulation in this country is a *non sequitur*. A sovereign has the right to issue bank notes in his own country and to treat them as currency there. He has no right to impose that obligation on others. Since foreign bank notes are not legal tender here, they circulate only in the sense and to the extent that they may be bought and sold in this country. In principle it is English law that determines what may be done with foreign bank notes here. Were it otherwise, a foreign sovereign's right to circulate his bank notes here would considerably impair the right of English courts to regulate their use here, and might interfere with the sovereign prerogative of issuing currency in this country. If the State of X is put to the inconvenience of having to meet the allegation that some of its bank notes are printed on paper that infringes copyright or alternatively of having to print them on other paper, that cannot render the question of infringement of copyright unsuitable for determination by English courts and so non-justiciable. It cannot be regarded as a breach of comity to restrain the use in this country of foreign bank notes that infringe a United Kingdom patent. The judge therefore erred both as to non-justiciability and as to comity.

* * *

3. HUMAN RIGHTS ABUSES

National Coalition Government of the Union of Burma v. Unocal, Inc.

United States District Court, C.D. California, November 5, 1997, 176 F.R.D. 329

ORDER GRANTING IN PART AND DENYING IN PART UNOCAL'S
   MOTION TO DISMISS * * *

■ PAEZ, DISTRICT JUDGE.

Introduction

Plaintiffs, John Doe I, * * * bring this action for compensatory and equitable relief against defendants Unocal Corporation ("Unocal") and the Yadana Natural Gas Project (the "Project"). In essence, plaintiffs allege that they, and, with respect to the NCGUB and the FTUB, their members, have been injured as a result of violations of international human rights allegedly committed by the controlling government in Burma, the State Law and Order Restoration Council's ("SLORC"). According to plaintiffs, SLORC has engaged in numerous human rights abuses, including torture, forced labor and confiscation of property, in the furtherance of a joint venture to extract natural gas from the Andaman Sea and transport it across Burma to Thailand.

[At the invitation of the Court to the State Department to express its views on the potential foreign policy ramifications of this litigation, the Department's Acting Legal Advisor stated that "at this time adjudication of the claims based on allegations of torture and slavery would not prejudice or impede the conduct of U.S. foreign relations with the current government of Burma."]

* * *

Plaintiffs allege that in early 1993, Unocal joined the Yadana Natural Gas Project (the "Project") as a joint venturer and implied partner. Plaintiffs contend that the Project is a joint venture and implied partnership to exploit natural gas resources in the Yadana gas field off the coast of Burma by developing platforms there and constructing a pipeline to transport gas from the Yadana field to the Thai border. Plaintiffs allege that the Project members include: Unocal Corporation; Total S.A., a French oil company; the reigning government of Burma, better known as the State Law and Order Restoration Council ("SLORC"); the Myanma Oil and Gas Enterprise ("MOGE"), a company wholly owned and operated by SLORC; and the Petroleum Authority of Thailand Exploration & Production Public Co. Ltd. ("PTTEP").

* * *

B. Subject–Matter Jurisdiction

This Court has subject-matter jurisdiction over plaintiffs' action against defendants Unocal and the Project because the Doe plaintiffs' claim under the Alien Tort Claims Act ("ATCA") presents a federal question.

The ATCA provides that [t]he district courts shall have original jurisdiction of any civil action by an alien for a tort only, committed in violation of the law of nations or a treaty of the United States. 28 U.S.C. § 1350. * * *

1. Violation of International Law

    * * *

Jurisdiction under the ATCA may be premised on alleged violations of a jus cogens, or peremptory, norm. Id. at 500; see also *Estate II*, 25 F.3d at 1475. The Ninth Circuit recently reiterated that torture, murder, genocide and slavery all constitute violations of jus cogens norms. *United States v. Matta–Ballesteros*, 71 F.3d 754, 763–65 (9th Cir.1996), as amended, 98 F.3d 1100 (1996) (citing *Siderman de Blake*, 965 F.2d at 717), cert. denied, 117 S.Ct. 965, (1997). In *Siderman de Blake*, the Ninth Circuit explicitly concluded that the prohibition against official torture rises to the level of a jus cogens norm. *Siderman de Blake, supra* at 717. Thus, John Doe I's claims of torture in violation of international law easily satisfy the ATCA's requirement that the individual plaintiffs allege a violation of international law.

    * * *

C. Act of State Doctrine

The act of state doctrine precludes a court of the United States from considering a plaintiff's claims where either the claims or the defenses asserted would require the court to determine that a foreign sovereign's official acts performed in its own territory were invalid. *W.S. Kirkpatrick & Co., Inc. v. Environmental Tectonics Corp. International, supra* at 405. Unocal argues, in asserting the applicability of the doctrine, that by adjudicating plaintiffs' claims, this Court will necessarily pass judgment on the validity of SLORC's official acts, thereby interfering with the foreign policy efforts of the United States Congress and the President.

    * * *

Here, plaintiffs seek review of alleged violations of international law, including forced labor, torture and expropriation of property. Based on the foregoing authority, the Court must determine whether SLORC is a foreign sovereign, whether the case turns on SLORC's official actions and whether the Sabbatino factors support or undermine application of the act of state doctrine to bar plaintiffs' claims.

    * * *

In addition, the Court notes that plaintiffs contend Burma is a signatory to International Labor Organization Convention No. 29, which purportedly bans the use of forced labor. Plaintiffs' Opposition Memorandum at 3. Consequently, the so-called "treaty exception," may apply here, even if plaintiffs' allegations do not constitute slavery or slave trading per se.

Finally, because nations do not, and cannot under international law, claim a right to torture or enslave their own citizens, inquiry into whether a government has committed such acts should have no detrimental effect on the policies underlying the act of state doctrine, particularly where, as here, that inquiry is in keeping with the prior conclusions of the coordinate branches of government and has been specifically authorized by the Department of State.

b. Sensitivity of National Nerves

Sabbatino also cautions courts to consider that where the impact on foreign relations of the international issues presented is small, the justification for application of the act of state doctrine is commensurately weak. *Sabbatino*, 376 U.S. at 428, 84 S.Ct. at 940. Here, the coordinate branches of government have already denounced the foreign state's human rights abuses and imposed sanctions. More importantly, in his response to the Court's inquiry concerning the Department's views on the potential ramifications of this litigation on the foreign policy of the United States, the Acting Legal Advisor of the United States Department of State, Michael J. Matheson, stated that "at this time adjudication of the claims based on allegations of torture and slavery would not prejudice or impede the conduct of U.S. foreign relations with the current government of Burma." Statement of Interest of the United States at 2, filed July 9, 1997. In light of that statement, the Court concludes that the issues presented here have only limited implications for our foreign relations, tipping the balance against invocation of the act of state doctrine to bar plaintiffs' claims.

* * *

d. Public Interest

Although *Sabbatino* did not list additional considerations in its balancing test, the Ninth Circuit has included an inquiry into "whether the foreign state was acting in the public interest." Liu, 892 F.2d at 1432. Here, it would be difficult to contend that SLORC officials' alleged jus cogens violations of international human rights were "in the public interest," despite the fact that they are allegedly directly connected to decisions regarding allocation and profit from Burma's natural resources.

Taking all of the factors together, the balance weighs against invocation of the act of state doctrine to bar plaintiffs' claims of torture and slavery, even if the doctrine were technically applicable.

4. *Bernstein* Exception

* * *

In short, the viability of the exception is highly questionable. For the sake of completeness, however, the Court notes that the Statement of Interest submitted by the United States would qualify as a *Bernstein* letter authorizing the Court to proceed with plaintiffs' claims based on torture and slavery because separation of powers concerns, which underlie the act of state doctrine and allocate foreign policy to the coordinate branches of government, would not be served by invocation of the doctrine.

5. Expropriation of Property

The foregoing discussion aside, Unocal is correct that under *Sabbatino*, the Court may not examine the validity of a taking of property within its own territory by a foreign sovereign government, extant and recognized by this country at the time of suit, in the absence of a treaty or other unambiguous agreement regarding controlling legal principles, even if the complaint alleges that the taking violates customary international law.

* * *

In response to the Supreme Court's decision in *Sabbatino*, Congress enacted the Second Hickenlooper Amendment, which states, in pertinent part:

> Notwithstanding any other provision of law, no court in the United States shall decline on the ground of the federal act of state doctrine to make a determination on the merits giving effect to the principles of international law in a case in which a claim of title or other right to property is asserted by any party ... based upon ... a confiscation or other taking ... by an act of that state in violation of international law[.] 22 U.S.C. § 2370(e)(2). The primary purposes of the Hickenlooper Amendment was to promote and protect U.S. investments in foreign countries. *West v. Multibanco Comermex.*

More significantly, the Hickenlooper Amendment, by its own terms, is only properly invoked as an exception to the act of state doctrine where the expropriation at issue would constitute a violation of international law. The Ninth Circuit has explicitly concluded that "[e]xpropriation by a sovereign state of the property of its own nationals does not implicate settled principles of international law." *Chuidian*, 912 F.2d at 1105 (considering applicability of FSIA where Philippine bank official instructed California branch of bank not to honor letter of credit issued to Philippine national); see also *Bank Tejarat v. Varsho–Saz*, 723 F.Supp. 516, 520 (C.D.Cal.1989) (confiscation by Iranian government of property of its national located in Iran was not a violation of international law and Hickenlooper exception did not apply). Here, each of the individual plaintiffs asserts claims for expropriation of property, including claims for conversion and trespass under California law. Plaintiffs have not alleged a violation of international law, however, because they are Burmese nationals seeking relief for alleged expropriation by SLORC of property located in Burma. Consequently, the act of state doctrine requires the Court to refrain from reviewing plaintiffs' expropriation claims.

* * *

In sum, although the act of state doctrine does not preclude review of plaintiffs' claims based on allegations of torture and forced labor, the doctrine does apply in the context of plaintiffs' claims for expropriation of property.

* * *

4.   CONGRESS AND THE ACT OF STATE DOCTRINE

A few paragraphs of history. Various interests concerned about nationalizations of direct foreign investment, and others hoping to reduce or prevent even legal nationalizations combined immediately after the Supreme Court's decision in *Sabbatino* to add a second anti-nationalization provision to the Foreign Assistance [AID] Act. A key congressional figure in the drive was the late Senator whose name is given to the Hickenlooper amendments.

The first Hickenlooper Amendment mandated that the President cut off development assistance to any country that did not (within a time frame for reassessment) conform as to Americans' investments to the international minimum standard for nationalizations asserted by the U. S.

Shortly after the remand of the *Sabbatino case* for disposition in conformity with the Supreme Court decision, Congress enacted the second Hickenlooper Amendment.

Foreign Assistance Act

22 U.S.C. § 2370.

* * *

(e)(2) Notwithstanding any other provision of law, no court in the United States shall decline on the ground of the federal act of state doctrine to make a determination on the merits giving effect to the principles of international law in a case in which a claim of title or other right to property is asserted by any party including a foreign state (or a party claiming through such state) based upon (or traced through) a confiscation or other taking after January 1, 1959, by an act of that state in violation of the principles of international law [according to the standards set by Congress]: Provided, That this subparagraph shall not be applicable (1) in any case in which an act of a foreign state is not contrary to international law or with respect to a claim of title or other right to property acquired pursuant to an irrevocable letter of credit of not more than 180 days duration issued in good faith prior to the time of the confiscation or other taking, or (2) in any case with respect to which the President determines that application of the act of state doctrine is required in that particular case by the foreign policy interests of the United States and a suggestion to this effect is filed on his behalf in that case with the court.

Cuban Liberty and Democratic Solidarity Act of 1998 (Helms–Burton Act)

Public Law 104–114, 110 Stat.785, Mar 12, 1996, 35 I.L.M. 357 (1996).

In a continuing chapter of relations between the United States and Castro's Cuba, on March 12, 1996 the Helms–Burton Act became law. Title III creates a federal cause of action enabling U.S. citizens whose property was confiscated without compensation by Cuba to recover money damages against persons who "traffic" in that property (see Section 302(1)). Section 4(13) provides that "... a person 'traffics' in confiscated property if that person knowingly and intentionally–

(i) sells, transfers, distributes, dispenses, brokers, manages or otherwise disposes of confiscated property, or purchases, leases, receives, possesses, obtains control of, manages, uses, or otherwise acquires or holds an interest in confiscated property. ...." (among other actions provided in Section 12).

Title III thus potentially set the stage for act of state defenses, but Congress anticipated this problem with the following provision of Section 302(6):

(6) INAPPLICABILITY OF ACT OF STATE DOCTRINE–No court of the United States shall decline, based upon the act of state doctrine, to make a determination on the merits in an action brought under paragraph (1).

———

Questions: Compare sovereign immunity cases, in which the foreign sovereign is usually directly involved in the proceedings, with act of state cases. Do the act of state cases, where the sovereign is not directly involved, present an *a fortiori* situation for courts *not* to refrain from acting? As to clearly commercial transactions, should the test for act of state be the same as it is for foreign state immunity under the Foreign Sovereign Immunities Act? Should the test of commercial versus sovereign conduct be the same in both situations? Are there any of the exceptions to sovereign immunity contained in FSIA § 1605 that you would consider not appropriate, *mutatus mutandus*, as exceptions to the act of state doctrine? How do you think United States courts would now handle a claim that jus cogens norms should override the act of state doctrine?

Is there a case to be made for abandoning the act of state doctrine altogether? How would you balance the various elements of the problem?

———

CHAPTER 8

NATIONALITY, PROTECTION AND ALLEGIANCE

One of the indispensable requirements of statehood is a "permanent population," the presence of "a group of persons leading a common life and forming a living-community", as seen in *In Re Citizenship of X* above in Chapter 2. These persons ordinarily have a durable legal relationship to the state, either residence, domicile or nationality or most often a combination of these relationships. This is usually, but not always, accompanied by physical presence in the state. The norm is for the individuals to hold the nationality of the state. This supports a requirement of statehood and defines the relationship of the individuals to the state and to the international system.

A basic feature of these relationships is the individual's relative dependency on the state. A person becomes a member of a state in the international system. The state essentially affords protection from violence. Domestically, the state's police and courts may offer protection. Its military may offer protection from harm caused by external aggression. Yet protection offered by the individual's home state may not always be sufficient.

A state has no authority, without permission, to take affirmative action to protect its nationals, when they are in other states. As a practical matter, a person's security, therefore, may diminish outside the state. If injured by an individual in another state, the injured party, generally, may only seek redress, if any, in *that* state, or in an international tribunal of some sort. On state responsibility to protect aliens within its borders, *see* Chapter 9, Section A, *infra*. Doctrines of sovereign immunity may bar redress for injuries caused by that state itself. On the other hand, a state has an affirmative duty to protect aliens within its borders. International law provides that an individual, as a last resort, may appeal to his own government for assistance. International law authorizes one's government to provide this assistance, in the form of "diplomatic protection." If the home state chooses, it may come to the individual's aid by espousing a claim against the wrongdoing state through diplomatic channels, or possibly through arbitration or judicial means, such as the International Court of Justice. In some cases the individual may also seek redress in the United Nations or regional regimes governing human rights.

The home state demands obligations of its nationals in return for the protection it offers at home and abroad. For example, a national is required:

1.   To obey his country's laws, even when they confer jurisdiction over nationals for offenses committed abroad; this is known as the "active personality," or nationality, basis of jurisdiction, taken up in Chapter 3;

2.   To pay its taxes, including taxes on income derived from world wide sources. The state may choose to tax this income in whole, in part, or not at all; in practice the hard edges of this jurisdiction are softened by double taxation treaties which usually prevent full taxation by more than one state party on the same income (see the *Restatement* on the Foreign Relations Law of the United States §§ 411 and 412 (1987); and

3.   To provide allegiance to the country and service in the military and civilian sectors as the state may require. United States nationals have thus been subject to prosecution for treason (*see D'Aquino v. United States* 192 F.2d 338 (9th Cir.1951), and have been required to perform compulsory military service.

The fact of an individual's presence within a state has been the major basis from which the state exerts its power to protect the individual and to demand allegiance. But the processes of history have developed legal relationships between the state and the individual that do not depend solely upon physical presence in the territory of the state. The state has a special relationship to those it designates as its nationals. Unless otherwise provided by treaty or customary international law, the state's nationals are entitled—in broad and inexact terms—to greater rights than non-nationals in some sectors (e.g., in states with voting systems, the national is permitted to vote, the non-national usually is not, and this practice is giving way in the European Union; see Section D below).

The practices of states in creating the classes of people upon whom they confer nationality vary widely. Some states accord nationality to individuals born within the territory; this right of nationality is referred to as *jus soli*. Some states accord nationality at birth only to individuals born of parents who are already nationals: this right of nationality is referred to as *jus sanguinis*. An increasing number of states recognize both bases. In addition to according nationality based upon facts associated with birth, states afford naturalization processes by which individuals may apply for and be granted nationality. With such a variety of bases for nationality existing in the international system it is possible for an individual to be designated a national by more than one state and thus to have dual nationality or even multiple nationality. Also, there are circumstances under which a person may have no nationality at all and thus be "stateless". See generally, R. Donner, The Regulation of Nationality in International Law (1994).

From the perspective of the international legal system, several general questions immediately arise:

1. How should the international system resolve the problems of statelessness?

2. Is a state free to set its own standards for conferring nationality upon an individual? Or does international law set some minimum standards and requirements? See the *Notteböhm* case below. So far we have been considering the nationality of individuals. What is the nationality of a corporation? Or a ship or aircraft? Or a manned space vehicle?

3. May states arrange to modify the customary rules of international law by adopting treaty regimes which create new principles and systems governing the nationality relationships?

4. May an international organization such as the United Nations confer nationality or exercise with respect to its officials some of the prerogatives that the traditional home state exercises with respect to its nationals?

5. What does European Union "citizenship" suggest about future directions that the international legal system might take in this sector?

This chapter explores these questions. In succeeding chapters the question will be asked whether the developments in the law of human rights and individual responsibility significantly modify the legal situation of the individual as sketched above. For now, note that the Universal Declaration on Human Rights (found in the Documentary Supplement) provides comprehensively that:

Article 15:

1. Everyone has the right to a nationality.

2. No one shall be arbitrarily deprived of his nationality nor denied the right to change his nationality.

SECTION A.   NATIONALITY: LOSS OF ITS BENEFITS

Re Immigration Act and Hanna

Canada, Supreme Court of British Columbia, 1957.
21 Western Weekly Rep. 400.*

■ SULLIVAN, J. This is a "hard case" of the kind of which it is said that bad law is made. The applicant George Christian Hanna, whom I shall refer to

* Reprinted by permission of Burroughs & Co., Ltd., Calgary, Alberta, Canada.

as "Hanna" in these reasons for judgment, is a young man without a country—one of those unfortunate "stateless" persons of the world whose status is a matter of concern to humanitarians and has prompted men and women of good will of all countries to seek relief for such persons through the agency of the Economic and Social Council of the United Nations. A convention was adopted by that council in September 1954, to which, however, Canada is not a signatory.

The matter comes before me by way of habeas corpus with certiorari in aid. Hanna seeks a judicial declaration that his detention under a deportation order made by F. Wragg, an immigration officer (acting as a special inquiry officer) dated January 18, 1957, and confirmed on appeal to an immigration appeal board duly constituted under the provisions of the Immigration Act, RSC, 1952, ch. 325, is illegal: (1) Because the deportation order is defective, incomplete, impossible of interpretation or enforcement and beyond the statutory authority of Mr. Wragg to make; and (2) Because the immigration appeal board improperly denied Hanna the right to be heard, either in person or by counsel, at the appeal proceedings before such board.

The issues thus presented for my determination are strictly legal in nature and narrow in their scope. I have no right to reflect upon and must guard against the danger that the strictly legal opinion which I am required to express should be influenced in any degree by considerations of human sympathy for this unfortunate (23–year–old) young applicant in the frustrating dilemma with which fate seems to have confronted him throughout his lifetime prior to his last arrival in Canada as ship-bound prisoner aboard a tramp motor-ship in her ceaseless meanderings from port to port throughout the world. The deportation order in question is in the words and figures following:

Department of Citizenship and Immigration Deportation Order Against Christian George Hanna of Djibouti, French Somaliland

under section 28 of the Immigration Act. On the basis of the evidence adduced at an inquiry held at the Immigration Building, Vancouver, B.C., on January 18, 1957 I have reached the decision that you may not come into or remain in Canada as of right and that you are a member of the prohibited class described in paragraph (t) of Section 5 of the Immigration Act, in that you do not fulfil or comply with the conditions or requirements of Subsection (1), Subsection (3) and Subsection (8) of Section 18 of the Immigration Regulations.

I hereby order you to be detained and to be deported to the place whence you came to Canada, or to the country of which you are a national or citizen, or to the country of your birth, or to such country as may be approved by the minister.

Date 18 January 1957, [Sgd.] F. WRAGG, Special Inquiry Officer [Sgd.] C.G. HANNA.

Subsecs. (1), (3) and (8) of sec. 18 of the regulations to which said deportation order refers require that an immigrant possess a passport and visa; and that his passport or other travel document bear a medical certificate in approved form.

It should be stated at the outset that no Canadian court has power to assist Hanna in his plea that he be given right of residence in Canada. That is a decision for immigration officials, and for them alone, to make. Similarly all right of exercise of discretionary power to exempt from strict compliance with the requirements of the Immigration Act or regulations made thereunder is vested in and is the prerogative of only the minister, deputy minister, director, or such other persons as may be authorized to act for the director. * * *

        * * *

It may be helpful to outline Hanna's history and background as it is disclosed by the scanty material before me. Most of such material consists of Hanna's sworn testimony, given in the English language, when he was before Mr. Wragg on January 18, 1957, at which time his knowledge and proficiency in the use of our language was not as great as it may be now. He says that he was born at sea and that no known record of his birth is extant. The name of the vessel aboard which he was born, and particulars of her nationality or port of registry are unknown. His father was named George Hanna and supposedly travelled to French Somaliland from Liberia, a small republic situate on the west coast of Africa. His mother's maiden name was Marian Marika and she was a native of Ethiopia (or Abyssinia)— a country whose status either as empire or vassal of Italy at any given time can be determined only by reference to historical data bearing upon Emperor Haile Selassie's struggles in warfare with the late Benito Mussolini. Hanna understands that his parents met and were married at Djibouti, the capital city of French Somaliland. The accuracy of his information in this respect should be easy to check. French Somaliland is a very small country. It has been a French colony for about 80 years. * * * Hanna was the only child born of his parents' marriage and both of his parents are dead. Continuing the narrative according to Hanna's understanding of events, his father left his mother to seek employment in Liberia. Subsequently his mother, being pregnant at the time, and seeking to rejoin her husband, took passage on a ship sailing out of Djibouti. She became ill and gave birth to Hanna when the ship was one day at sea, and because of her illness the ship was put about and returned to Djibouti where she and her newborn child were placed in a hospital or home for women. Thereafter Hanna was cared for by his mother who worked at various times at Addis Ababa and Dire Wawa (both in Ethiopia) and at Djibouti in French Somaliland, until Hanna was six years of age. She then died and thereafter Hanna more or less "raised himself" as he puts it, with some assistance from a kindly old Turkish gentleman at Djibouti and others, including a Japanese gentleman at Dire Wawa in Ethiopia.

During his years of infancy and adolescence Hanna seems to have crossed and recrossed the international boundaries of Ethiopia, French Somaliland, British Somaliland and Eritrea (formerly an Italian colony but now a province of Ethiopia by virtue of the recommendation of a United Nations' committee adopted by the General Assembly in 1952) without encountering difficulty with the immigration officials of those countries. I suppose that youth was in his favour at the outset, and I suppose, too, that the international boundaries referred to were not too well defined at that time. That still seems to be the case. I understand that the accurate fixation of the international borders convergent upon the small area of French Somaliland is a problem which presently engages the attention of the United Nations' General Assembly.

In this way Hanna lived and worked from time to time (inter alia) in the ports of Zeila and Berbera in British Somaliland where he picked up a smattering of English. He says that his mother spoke English and, although he never saw his father, it is his understanding that his parents conversed in English. This would be consistent with Hanna's theory that his father was a native of Liberia—a republic which most people look upon as a virtual protectorate of the United States of America, and where English is spoken.

As he grew older Hanna seems to have encountered and had difficulty with the immigration officers of these adjacent countries, in none of which he could claim right of residence. He thereby learned that possession of a birth certificate is an indispensable requirement of modern society. He learned "the hard way" that some of the fundamental human rights with which all men are endowed by their Creator at birth were not his to enjoy without the intervention and benevolent assistance of some temporal power—a power to be exercised in many cases according to the whim or opinion of immigration officers whose numbers are legion in most sovereign states. That is not to say, of course, that he or anyone else possesses an inherent right to enter or remain in Canada unless born here. The late Right Honorable W.L. Mackenzie King, Prime Minister of Canada, said in the House of Commons on May 1, 1947, that "It is not a 'fundamental human right' of an alien to enter Canada. It is a privilege. It is a matter of domestic policy."

* * *

Almost three years ago, when he was in the port of Massaua, Eritrea, Hanna stowed away in an Italian tramp steamer in the hope of being carried in her to some country which would grant him asylum and right of residence. His plan met with frustration because upon arrival of such ship at any port he was immediately locked up and denied permission to land. After a year or more of such aimless wandering and imprisonment, Hanna escaped from the Italian vessel when she called at Beirut in the republic of Lebanon, and concealed himself in the hold of the Norwegian motor-ship "Gudveig." As a stowaway in such latter vessel he fared no better than before. He was held prisoner aboard "The Gudveig" for more than 16 months and made three or more trips to Canada in her until his release under writ of habeas corpus in these proceedings. He first came before Clyne, J., upon return of a show cause summons on January 18, 1957, wherein he challenged the legality of his detention by the master of The "Gudveig." My learned brother there held (correctly, in my respectful opinion) that the master's detention of Hanna was not illegal since the master was subject to and bound by the regulations applicable to "stowaways" as passed pursuant to the provisions of the Immigration Act. Thereafter Hanna made application to enter Canada and his status was thereby changed from that of "stowaway" to that of "immigrant." An immigrant is defined by sec. 2(i) of the Immigration Act as follows: (i) "immigrant" means a person who seeks admission to Canada for permanent residence.

* * * And so, at a time when it had become a widely publicized matter of general public knowledge or repute that Hanna possessed no proof of birth nor documents of any kind, he was granted the privilege of appearing before three separate departmental tribunals for the purpose of proving—if he could—that he did in fact possess such documents. Of course, he was unable to discharge that onus, and the deportation order followed which is now under attack in these proceedings.

[Now to] that deportation order. Was it an order which the special inquiry officer had legal authority to make in all of the circumstances existing at the time of its making? It contains four separate directives which are stated in the alternative and, presumably, in the order of their importance.

The most important directive is, No. 1, that Hanna be deported to the place whence he came to Canada. The next directive is, No. 2, that he be deported to the country of which he is a national or citizen. The next is, No. 3, that he be deported to the country of his birth. The final alternative is, No. 4, that he be deported to such country as may be approved by the minister.

The No. 4 directive is meaningless in the absence of anything to show a possibility of the minister ever finding a country which would be willing to admit this young man in the face of Canada's refusal to admit him. It cannot be assumed that travel documents are of less significance in other countries than here. The thing goes further than that, however, because sec. 40(2) of our Act makes the minister's power of designation and approval of "such country" conditional upon the owners of the M.S. "Gudveig" first making request for such ministerial approval. Even then, as I interpret the statute, the approval of the minister could have no effect unless after finding "a country that is willing to receive him," Hanna were to indicate that such country is "acceptable" to him.

Directives No. 2 and No. 3 referring, respectively, to country of nationality or citizenship and country of birth, may be discussed together. Neither of these directives could possibly be complied with. In the absence of satisfactory evidence of nationality of a legitimate father and lack of any evidence as to the nationality or registry of the ship aboard which Hanna was born, these directives of the deportation order are meaningless.

The inescapable fact is that Hanna is a "stateless person," and the efforts of the department to prove otherwise have not been impressive. I was presented with evidence (consisting of affidavits by lawyers in Oslo, Norway, and a Canadian immigration officer) in support of the submission that Hanna is not "stateless" and that the words of the directive "country of your birth," therefore, are not meaningless. The trouble is that whilst the affidavit of the immigration officer fixes Hanna's birthplace as Djibouti in French Somaliland, the Norwegian lawyers suggest that he is an Egyptian who was born at Alexandria. None of this conflicting evidence is credible. It is all based on hearsay and, perhaps, the least said about it, the better.

[Now for] consideration of directive No. 1—that Hanna be deported to the place whence he came to Canada. What does it mean?

The department's position, as I understand it, is that it could mean a number of things which it leaves to other people to determine for themselves. The place whence Hanna came to Canada might be the port of Beirut in the republic of Lebanon since that is the place where he first stowed away in the M.S. "Gudveig." Perhaps that interpretation is favoured by the department since it has presented certain material tending to show that if Lebanese authorities can be satisfied that Hanna stowed away at Beirut, they might permit him to land in their country—a country, incidentally, which is quite as foreign to Hanna as it is to me. Then again the department seems to suggest that the place whence Hanna came to Canada could be the United Kingdom and an affidavit is presented for the purpose of showing that "The Gudveig" sailed non-stop from the United Kingdom to Vancouver on her last voyage with Hanna aboard. Perhaps the place whence Hanna came to Canada could be the port of Massaua in Eritrea, since that was the starting point of his aimless wanderings as a stowaway in search of a country which would give him right of residence. Other interpretations are possible, but it seems to me that the matter of correct interpretation is of comparative unimportance here. The thing of importance, is that the special inquiry officer delegated to the master or owners of "The Gudveig" the responsibility for saying what his deportation order means; and, apart from the circumstances that he himself does not seem to know what it means, I am of opinion that he has not that power of delegation under the Act. I have had reference to the authorities cited by counsel wherein it was held that deportation orders made (as this one was) in form approved by the minister were valid and enforceable notwithstanding their multiplicity of alternative directives, but in none of such cases were the facts comparable to the extraordinary facts of this amazing case. In each of such cases the meaning of the deportation order in the form used was clearly apparent to everyone concerned or affected by it. In no case did the deportation order require subsequent inquiry or investigation by anyone for determination of its meaning. In none was there a necessarily incidental delegation of his authority by the special inquiry officer who made the order for deportation. These are some of the things which distinguish Hanna's case from all others.

From whatever angle one views it, so far as Hanna is concerned, this deportation order amounted to a sentence of imprisonment aboard "The Gudveig" for an indefinite term, and in my opinion and finding, no immigration officer has the legal right to exercise such drastic power.

* * *

For the reasons previously expressed, there will be judgment for Hanna in these proceedings, with costs. That does not mean that he has established any legal right to enter or remain in Canada. As previously stated, it is for immigration officials and for them alone to grant or withhold that privilege. This judgment does not mean that Hanna may not be deported legally from Canada by further proceedings properly instituted and conducted in accordance with the provisions and intent of the Immigration Act. It means only that the present deportation order is illegal and that Hanna is entitled to be released from detention thereunder; and I so order.

* * *

Consequences of Statelessness

1. **What happens to Hanna now?** In *Staniszewski v. Watkins,* 80 F.Supp. 132 (S.D.N.Y.1948), a stateless seaman was released after being detained at Ellis Island for about seven months. The court observed that the government was "willing that he go back to the ship, but if he were sent back aboard ship and sailed to the port * * * from which he last sailed to the United States, he would probably be denied permission to land." The court said, "There is no other country that would take him, without proper documents." The court sustained the seaman's writ of habeas corpus and ordered his release: "He will be required to inform the immigration officials at Ellis Island by mail on the 15th of each month, stating where he is employed and where he can be reached. If the government does succeed in arranging for petitioner's deportation to a country that will be ready to receive him as a resident, it may then advise the petitioner to that effect and arrange for his deportation in the manner provided by law."

Similarly, in *Public Prosecutor v. Zinger*, France, Tribunal of the Seine, 1936, [1935–37] Ann.Dig. 307 (No. 138), the court ordered the release of a stateless person who had been imprisoned for failure to obey expulsion orders. The court weighed the alternatives of releasing the man or imprisoning him "at the cost of the French taxpayer" for an offence which he could not help committing, since he was unable to leave French territory. The court concluded: "release is the best solution."

Three more recent cases led to favorable results for the detained aliens. In *Zadvydas v. Davis* and *Ashcroft v. Kim Ho Ma,* 28 June, 2001, the U.S. Supreme Court applied an implicit reasonableness limitation of detention and presumptive reasonableness duration of six months in cases where the were detained by U.S. immigration authorities beyond the 90 day removal period under U.S. law (69 USLW 4581 and 4626). The third case had a belated but happy ending under administrative action. In September 1999, at the Charles de Gaulle Airport near Paris, French authorities finally allowed Marham Karimi Nasseri to leave the airport where he had been living in the passenger area for 11 years because, on account of unlawful entry, authorities would not permit him to enter France, and because other countries would not accept him. New York Times, 27 September 1999, p. A4, Col. 1.

Jennings and Watts (Eds), Oppenheim's International Law

VOL. 1, Parts 2–4, pp. 886–7 (ed. 1996).*

§ 396 **How statelessness occurs** An individual may be without nationality knowingly or unknowingly, intentionally or through no fault of his

* Reprinted with the permission of *Longman Publishers.*

own. Even by birth a person may be stateless, as where an illegitimate child is born in a state which does not apply *jus soli* to an alien mother under whose national law the child does not acquire her nationality, or where a legitimate child is born in such a state to parents who have no nationality themselves. Statelessness may occur after birth, for instance as the result of deprivation or loss of nationality by way of penalty or otherwise. All individuals who have lost their original nationality without having acquired another are, in fact, stateless.

§ 397 **Position of stateless individuals** Since stateless individuals do not possess a nationality, the principal link by which they could derive benefits from international law is missing. They may, therefore, lack the possibility of diplomatic protection or of international claims being presented in respect of harm suffered by them at the hands of a state. In practice, stateless individuals are in most states treated more or less as though they were nationals of foreign states. If they are maltreated, they in general fall outside the protection afforded by international law, with the important exception of provisions of the Charter of the United Nations, the Covenants on human rights and other treaties concerning human rights and fundamental freedoms, and such other treaties as expressly regulate their position. In such cases every contracting party may, depending on the treaty in question, acquire the right to seek to secure the application of the treaty in respect of them notwithstanding the rule as to nationality of claims.

§ 398 *Regulation of statelessness by treaty*. There has for some time been an effort to reduce by international conventions the possibilities of statelessness or, where that is impossible, to render less difficult the position of stateless persons.

The attempts made to reduce the occasions for statelessness are not only an expression of the desire to do away with a source of inconvenience to governments and of grave hardship to individuals. They also constitute recognition of the fact that so long as nationality is the link between the individual and the protection of rights accruing to him by virtue of international law, it is illogical that international law should permit a condition of statelessness, and the admissibility of statelessness must be regarded as a serious defect in this branch of international law. There are no vital interests of states which stand in the way of introducing such a measure of uniformity in the law relating to acquisition of nationality by birth, marriage, naturalization or otherwise as may be sufficient to prevent statelessness arising on that account. The same applies to the abandonment of the practice, which is of comparatively recent origin, of adding the penalty of deprivation of nationality for disloyalty or other reasons to the manifold and severe punishments available to states under their municipal law.[a]

a. The numerous treaties on this subject are outlined in Oppenheim § 398, including the 1961 Convention on the Reduction of Statelessness which provides for a Contracting State to grant its nationality to persons born on its territory who would otherwise remain stateless (Article 1). Foundlings found in the territory of a Contracting State are considered, in the absence of proof to the contrary, to be born of parents within that territory of parents possessing the nationality of that State (Article 2), 989 U.N.T.S. 195. See also the 1954 Convention on the Status of Stateless Persons, 360 U.N.T.S. 117. These

SECTION B.   INTERNATIONAL CRITERIA

1.   THE GENUINE LINK DOCTRINE

Notteböhm Case (Liechtenstein v. Guatemala)

International Court of Justice, 1955.
[1955] I.C.J.Rep. 4.

* * *

By the Application filed, the Government of Liechtenstein instituted proceedings before the Court in which it claimed restitution and compensation on the ground that the Government of Guatemala had "acted towards the person and property of Mr. Friedric Notteböhm, a citizen of Liechtenstein, in a manner contrary to international law". In its Counter–Memorial, the Government of Guatemala contended that this claim was inadmissible on a number of grounds, and one of its objections to the admissibility of the claim related to the nationality of the person for whose protection Liechtenstein had seised the Court.

It appears to the Court that this plea in bar is of fundamental importance and that it is therefore desirable to consider it at the outset.

Guatemala has referred to a well-established principle of international law, which it expressed in Counter–Memorial, where it is stated that "it is the bond of nationality between the State and the individual which alone confers upon the State the right of diplomatic protection". * * *

Liechtenstein considers itself to be acting in conformity with this principle and contends that Notteböhm is its national by virtue of the naturalization conferred upon him. Notteböhm was born at Hamburg [in] 1881. He was German by birth, and still possessed German nationality when, in October 1939, he applied for naturalization in Liechtenstein.

In 1905 he went to Guatemala. He took up residence there and made that country the headquarters of his business activities, which increased and prospered; these activities developed in the field of commerce, banking and plantations. Having been an employee in the firm of Notteböhm Hermanos, which had been founded by his brothers Juan and Arturo, he became their partner in 1912 and later, in 1937, he was made head of the firm. After 1905 he sometimes went to Germany on business and to other countries for holidays. He continued to have business connections in Germany. He paid a few visits to a brother who had lived in Liechtenstein since 1931. Some of his other brothers, relatives and friends were in Germany, others in Guatemala. He himself continued to have his fixed abode in Guatemala until 1943, until the occurrence of the events which constitute the basis of the present dispute.

and other treaty rules mark a certain progress, but much remains to be done, including a coherent solution to the Hanna problem.

In 1939, after having provided for the safeguarding of his interests in Guatemala by a power of attorney given to the firm of Notteböhm Hermanos on March 22nd, he left that country at a date fixed by Counsel for Liechtenstein as at approximately the end of March or the beginning of April, when he seems to have gone to Hamburg, and later to have paid a few brief visits to Vaduz where he was at the beginning of October 1939. It was then, on October 9th, a little more than a month after the opening of the second World War marked by Germany's attack on Poland, that his attorney, Dr. Marxer, submitted an application for naturalization on behalf of Notteböhm.

The Liechtenstein Law of January 4th, 1934, lays down the conditions for the naturalization of foreigners, specifies the supporting documents to be submitted and the undertakings to be given and defines the competent organs for giving a decision and the procedure to be followed. The Law specifies certain mandatory requirements, namely, that the applicant for naturalization should prove: (1) "that the acceptance into the Home Corporation (Heimatverband) of a Liechtenstein commune has been promised to him in case of acquisition of the nationality of the State"; (2) that he will lose his former nationality as a result of naturalization, although this requirement may be waived under stated conditions. It further makes naturalization conditional upon compliance with the requirement of residence for at least three years in the territory of the Principality, although it is provided that "this requirement can be dispensed with in circumstances deserving special consideration and by way of exception". In addition, the applicant for naturalization is required to submit a number of documents, such as evidence of his residence in the territory of the Principality, a certificate of good conduct issued by the competent authority of the place of residence, documents relating to his property and income and, if he is not a resident in the Principality, proof that he has concluded an agreement with the Revenue authorities, "subsequent to the revenue commission of the presumptive home commune having been heard". The Law further provides for the payment by the applicant of a naturalization fee, which is fixed by the Princely Government and amounts to at least one half of the sum payable by the applicant for reception into the Home Corporation of a Liechtenstein commune, the promise of such reception constituting a condition under the Law for the grant of naturalization.

* * *

As to the consideration of the application by the competent organs and the procedure to be followed by them, the Law provides that the Government, after having examined the application and the documents pertaining thereto, and after having obtained satisfactory information concerning the applicant, shall submit the application to the Diet. If the latter approves the application, the Government shall submit the requisite request to the Prince, who alone is entitled to confer nationality of the Principality.

* * *

This was the legal position with regard to applications for naturalization at the time when Notteböhm's application was submitted.

On October 9th, 1939, Notteböhm, "resident in Guatemala since 1905 (at present residing as a visitor with his brother, Hermann Notteböhm, in Vaduz)", applied for admission as a national of Liechtenstein and, at the same time, for the previous conferment of citizenship in the Commune of Mauren. He sought dispensation from the condition of three years' residence as prescribed by law, without indicating the special circumstances warranting such waiver. He submitted a statement of the Crédit Suisse in Zurich concerning his assets, and undertook to pay 25,000 Swiss francs to the Commune of Mauren, 12,500 Swiss francs to the State, to which was to be added the payment of dues in connection with the proceedings. He further stated that he had made "arrangements with the Revenue Authorities of the Government of Liechtenstein for the conclusion of a formal agreement to the effect that he will pay an annual tax of naturalization amounting to Swiss francs 1,000, of which Swiss francs 600 are payable to the Commune of Mauren and Swiss francs 400 are payable to the Principality of Liechtenstein, subject to the proviso that the payments of these taxes will be set off against ordinary taxes which will fall due if the applicant takes up residence in one of the Communes of the Principality". He further undertook to deposit as security a sum of 30,000 Swiss francs. He also gave certain general information as to his financial position and indicated that he would never become a burden to the Commune whose citizenship he was seeking.

* * *

A document dated October 15th, 1939, certifies that on that date the Commune of Mauren conferred the privilege of its citizenship upon Mr. Notteböhm and requested the Government to transmit it to the Diet for approval. A certificate of October 17th, 1939, evidences the payment of the taxes required to be paid by Mr. Notteböhm. On October 20th, 1939, Mr. Notteböhm took the oath of allegiance and a final arrangement concerning liability to taxation was concluded on October 23rd. This was the procedure followed in the case of the naturalization of Notteböhm. A certificate of nationality has also been produced, signed on behalf of the Government of the Principality and dated October 20th, 1939, to the effect that Notteböhm was naturalized by Supreme Resolution of the Reigning Prince dated October 13th, 1939.

Having obtained a Liechtenstein passport, Notteböhm had it visaed by the Consul General of Guatemala in Zurich on December 1st, 1939, and returned to Guatemala at the beginning of 1940, where he resumed his former business activities and in particular the management of the firm of Notteböhm Hermanos.

* * * Liechtenstein requests the Court to find and declare, first, "that the naturalization of Mr. Notteböhm in Liechtenstein on October 13th, 1939, was not contrary to international law", and, secondly, "that Liechtenstein's claim on behalf of Mr. Notteböhm as a national of Liechtenstein is admissible before the Court".

The Final Conclusions of Guatemala, on the other hand, request the Court "to declare that the claim of the Principality of Liechtenstein is inadmissible", and set forth a number of grounds relating to the nationality of Liechtenstein granted to Notteböhm by naturalization.

Thus, the real issue before the Court is the admissibility of the claim of Liechtenstein in respect of Notteböhm. Liechtenstein's first submission referred to above is a reason advanced for a decision by the Court in favour of Liechtenstein, while the several grounds given by Guatemala on the question of nationality are intended as reasons for the inadmissibility of Liechtenstein's claim. The present task of the Court is limited to adjudicating upon the admissibility of the claim of Liechtenstein in respect of Notteböhm on the basis of such reasons as it may itself consider relevant and proper.

To decide upon the admissibility of the Application, the Court must ascertain whether the nationality conferred on Notteböhm by Liechtenstein by means of a naturalization which took place in the circumstances which have been described, can be validly invoked as against Guatemala, whether it bestows upon Liechtenstein a sufficient title to the exercise of protection in respect of Notteböhm as against Guatemala and therefore entitles it to seise the Court of a claim relating to him. In this connection, Counsel for Liechtenstein said: "the essential question is whether Mr. Notteböhm, having acquired the nationality of Liechtenstein, that acquisition of nationality is one which must be recognized by other States". This formulation is accurate, subject to the twofold reservation that, in the first place, what is involved is not recognition for all purposes but merely for the purposes of the admissibility of the Application, and, secondly, that what is involved is not recognition by all States but only by Guatemala.

The Court does not propose to go beyond the limited scope of the question which it has to decide, namely whether the nationality conferred on Notteböhm can be relied upon as against Guatemala in justification of the proceedings instituted before the Court. It must decide this question on the basis of international law; to do so is consistent with the nature of the question and with the nature of the Court's own function.

* * *

Since no proof has been adduced that Guatemala has recognized the title to the exercise of protection relied upon by Liechtenstein as being derived from the naturalization which it granted to Notteböhm, the Court must consider whether such an act of granting nationality by Liechtenstein directly entails an obligation on the part of Guatemala to recognize its effect, namely, Liechtenstein's right to exercise its protection. In other words, it must be determined whether that unilateral act by Liechtenstein is one which can be relied upon against Guatemala in regard to the exercise of protection. The Court will deal with this question without considering that of the validity of Notteböhm's naturalization according to the law of Liechtenstein.

It is for Liechtenstein, as it is for every sovereign State, to settle by its own legislation the rules relating to the acquisition of its nationality, and to confer that nationality by naturalization granted by its own organs in accordance with that legislation. It is not necessary to determine whether international law imposes any limitations on its freedom of decision in this domain. Furthermore, nationality has its most immediate, its most far-reaching and, for most people, its only effects within the legal system of the State conferring it. Nationality serves above all to determine that the person upon whom it is conferred enjoys the rights and is bound by the obligations which the law of the State in question grants to or imposes on its nationals. This is implied in the wider concept that nationality is within the domestic jurisdiction of the State.

But the issue which the Court must decide is not one which pertains to the legal system of Liechtenstein. It does not depend on the law or on the decision of Liechtenstein whether that State is entitled to exercise its protection, in the case under consideration. To exercise protection, to apply to the Court, is to place oneself on the plane of international law. It is international law which determines whether a State is entitled to exercise protection and to seise the Court. The naturalization of Notteböhm was an act performed by Liechtenstein in the exercise of its domestic jurisdiction. The question to be decided is whether that act has the international effect here under consideration.

    * * *

* * * International arbitrators, having before them allegations of nationality by the applicant State which were contested by the respondent State, have sought to ascertain whether nationality had been conferred by the applicant State in circumstances such as to give rise to an obligation on the part of the respondent State to recognize the effect of that nationality. To decide this question arbitrators have evolved certain principles for determining whether full international effect was to be attributed to the nationality invoked. The same issue is now before the Court: it must be resolved by applying the same principles.

The courts of third States, when confronted by a similar situation, have dealt with it in the same way. * * *

International arbitrators have decided in the same way numerous cases of dual nationality, where the question arose with regard to the exercise of protection. They have given their preference to the real and effective nationality, that which accorded with the facts, that based on stronger factual ties between the person concerned and one of the States whose nationality is involved. Different factors are taken into consideration, and their importance will vary from one case to the next: the habitual residence of the individual concerned is an important factor, but there are other factors such as the centre of his interests, his family ties, his participation in public life, attachment shown by him for a given country and inculcated in his children, etc.

Similarly, the courts of third States, when they have before them an individual whom two other States hold to be their national, seek to resolve the conflict by having recourse to international criteria and their prevailing tendency is to prefer the real and effective nationality.

The same tendency prevails in the writings of publicists and in practice. This notion is inherent in the provisions of Article 3, ¶ 2, of the court's Statute. National laws reflect this tendency.

    * * *

The practice of certain States which refrain from exercising protection in favour of a naturalized person when the latter has in fact, by his prolonged absence, severed his links with what is no longer for him anything but his nominal country, manifests the view of these States that, in order to be capable of being invoked against another State, nationality must correspond with the factual situation. * * *

The character thus recognized on the international level as pertaining to nationality is in no way inconsistent with the fact that international law leaves it to each State to lay down the rules governing the grant of its own nationality. The reason for this is that the diversity of demographic conditions has thus far made it impossible for any general agreement to be reached on the rules relating to nationality, although the latter by its very nature affects international relations. It has been considered that the best way of making such rules accord with the varying demographic conditions in different countries is to leave the fixing of such rules to the competence of each State. On the other hand, a State cannot claim that the rules it has thus laid down are entitled to recognition by another State unless it has acted in conformity with this general aim of making the legal bond of nationality accord with the individual's genuine connection with the State which assumes the defence of its citizens by means of protection as against other States.

* * *

According to the practice of States, to arbitral and judicial decisions and to the opinions of writers, nationality is a legal bond having as its basis a social fact of attachment, a genuine connection of existence, interests and sentiments, together with the existence of reciprocal rights and duties. It may be said to constitute the juridical expression of the fact that the individual upon whom it is conferred, either directly by the law or as the result of an act of the authorities, is in fact more closely connected with the population of the State conferring nationality than with that of any other State. Conferred by a State, it only entitles that State to exercise protection vis-à-vis another State, if it constitutes a translation into juridical terms of the individual's connection with the State which has made him its national.

Diplomatic protection and protection by means of international judicial proceedings constitute measures for the defence of the rights of the State. * * *

Since this is the character which nationality must present when it is invoked to furnish the State which has granted it with a title to the exercise of protection and to the institution of international judicial proceedings, the Court must ascertain whether the nationality granted to Notteböhm by means of naturalization is of this character or, in other words, whether the factual connection between Notteböhm and Liechtenstein in the period preceding, contemporaneous with and following his naturalization appears to be sufficiently close, so preponderant in relation to any connection which may have existed between him and any other State, that it is possible to regard the nationality conferred upon him as real and effective, as the exact juridical expression of a social fact of a connection which existed previously or came into existence thereafter.

Naturalization is not a matter to be taken lightly. * * *

To appraise its international effect, it is impossible to disregard the circumstances in which it was conferred, the serious character which attaches to it, the real and effective, and not merely the verbal preference of the individual seeking it for the country which grants it to him.

At the time of his naturalization does Nottebőhm appear to have been more closely attached by his tradition, his establishment, his interests, his activities, his family ties, his intentions for the near future to Liechtenstein than to any other State? * * *

* * *

The essential facts are as follows: At the date when he applied for naturalization Nottebőhm had been a German national from the time of his birth. He had always retained his connections with members of his family who had remained in Germany and he had always had business connections with that country. His country had been at war for more than a month, and there is nothing to indicate that the application for naturalization then made by Nottebőhm was motivated by any desire to dissociate himself from the Government of his country.

He had been settled in Guatemala for 34 years. He had carried on his activities there. It was the main seat of his interests. He returned there shortly after his naturalization, and it remained the centre of his interests and of his business activities. He stayed there until his removal as a result of war measures in 1943. He subsequently attempted to return there, and he now complains of Guatemala's refusal to admit him. There, too, were several members of his family who sought to safeguard his interests.

In contrast, his actual connections with Liechtenstein were extremely tenuous. No settled abode, no prolonged residence in that country at the time of his application for naturalization: the application indicates that he was paying a visit there and confirms the transient character of this visit by its request that the naturalization proceedings should be initiated and concluded without delay. No intention of settling there was shown at that time or realized in the ensuing weeks, months or years—on the contrary, he returned to Guatemala very shortly after his naturalization and showed every intention of remaining there. If Nottebőhm went to Liechtenstein in 1946, this was because of the refusal of Guatemala to admit him. No indication is given of the grounds warranting the waiver of the condition of residence, required by the 1934 Nationality Law, which waiver was implicitly granted to him. There is no allegation of any economic interests or of any activities exercised or to be exercised in Liechtenstein, and no manifestation of any intention whatsoever to transfer all or some of his interests and his business activities to Liechtenstein. It is unnecessary in this connection to attribute much importance to the promise to pay the taxes levied at the time of his naturalization. The only links to be discovered between the Principality and Nottebőhm are the short sojourns already referred to and the presence in Vaduz of one of his brothers: but his brother's presence is referred to in his application for naturalization only as a reference to his good conduct. Furthermore, other members of his family have asserted Nottebőhm's desire to spend his old age in Guatemala.

These facts establish, on the one hand, the absence of any bond of attachment between Notteböhm and Liechtenstein and, on the other hand, the existence of a long-standing and close connection between him and Guatemala, a link which his naturalization in no way weakened. That naturalization was not based on any real prior connection with Liechtenstein, nor did it in any way alter the manner of life of the person upon whom it was conferred in exceptional circumstances of speed and accommodation. In both respects, it was lacking in the genuineness requisite to an act of such importance, if it is to be entitled to be respected by a State in the position of Guatemala. It was granted without regard to the concept of nationality. * * *

Naturalization was asked for not so much for the purpose of obtaining a legal recognition of Notteböhm's membership in fact in the population of Liechtenstein, as it was to enable him to substitute for his status as a national of a belligerent State that of a national of a neutral State, with the sole aim of thus coming within the protection of Liechtenstein but not of becoming wedded to its traditions, its interests, its way of life or of assuming the obligations—other than fiscal obligations—and exercising the rights pertaining to the status thus acquired.

Guatemala is under no obligation to recognize a nationality granted in such circumstances. Liechtenstein consequently is not entitled to extend its protection to Notteböhm vis-à-vis Guatemala and its claim must, for this reason, be held to be inadmissible.

The Court is not therefore called upon to deal with the other pleas in bar put forward by Guatemala or the Conclusions of the Parties other than those on which it is adjudicating in accordance with the reasons indicated above. For these reasons, The COURT, by eleven votes to three, Holds that the claim submitted by the Government of the Principality of Liechtenstein is inadmissible. * * * [Dissenting opinions omitted.]

Notes and Questions:

1. **Earlier adjudication in the Permanent Court of International Justice: The classical View.** In its *Advisory Opinion on Nationality Decrees in Tunis and Morocco* (France and Great Britain), 1923, P.C.I.J., Ser. B, No. 4, the court was asked whether a dispute between France and Great Britain as to nationality decrees in Tunis and Morocco was or was not, by international law, solely a matter of domestic jurisdiction under Article 15, paragraph 8, of the Covenant of the League of Nations (compare U.N. Charter Article 2.7 which now governs the question of domestic jurisdiction). Apparently on the ground that the relations between France and Great Britain and their protectorates were determined by international agreements and that "it will be necessary to resort to international law in order to decide what the value of an agreement of this kind may be as regards third States," the court expressed the opinion that the dispute was not, by international law, solely a matter of domestic jurisdiction. But for the existence of the agreements, however, the court presumably would not have taken jurisdiction: "The question whether a certain matter is or is not

solely within the jurisdiction of a State is an essentially relative question; it depends upon the development of international relations. Thus, in the present state of international law, questions of nationality are, in the opinion of the Court, in principle within this reserved domain." However, the evolution of customary and treaty law, particularly in the field of human rights, raises the question whether the International Court of Justice should be expected to reach the same conclusion today.

2. ***How far does Notteböhm reach?*** Liechtenstein's claim was asserted against another state, Guatemala, with which Notteböhm had, in the language of the court, "a long-standing and close connection," a "link" which his naturalization in no way weakened. Notteböhm had been sent by Guatemala to the United States for internment during World War II. Suppose that the United States had injured Notteböhm by seizing and retaining, without compensation, property that he had removed to a bank in the United States. Suppose that Liechtenstein brought an action against the United States in the International Court of Justice on behalf of Notteböhm. Suppose also that the United States asked the Court to declare the claim inadmissible on the ground that Liechtenstein has no standing. *How should the court rule?* See *Flegenheimer Case*, 14 Rep. of Int'l Arb. Awards 327 (Italian–United States Conciliation Commission, 1958). The International Law Commission (I.L.C.), in its *Report on Diplomatic Protection*, the most, in its 52nd Session, May 1–June 9th and 10th–August, 2000, UNGAOR Fifty-fifth Session, Supp. No.10 (A/55/10), 141, 158–164 (2000), of its Fifty-second session, May 1–June 9 & July 10–August 2000, UNGAOR Fifty-fifth session Supp. No. 10 (A/55/10), 141, 158–164, discussed this issue and the view of the special rapporteur was that based on doubts about the legality of Liechtenstein's conferral of nationality on *Notteböhm* and his closer ties to Guatemala than with Liechtenstein that the International Court of Justice "had not purported to pronounce on the status of Notteböhm's nationality vis-a-vis all States. Note that in the *Barcelona Traction case* 1 I.C.J. Rep. 3 [1970], that the International Court of Justice held that in the case of severe human rights abuses, which are viewed as being severe enough that all states have an obligation erga omnes not to participate in them, *any state may intervene.* See more discussion on this in the notes immediately below.

3. ***Problem:*** Refer to the *Hanna case*, above. Suppose that Hanna had resided in Canada for a period of twenty years, was married there, raised a family and conducted a business there, and as a result of the international operation of his business, he had accumulated large sums of money in a bank in State X. Now suppose that State X expropriated his bank account without compensation. Although Hanna has not been declared a national by Canada, assume that Canada espoused his claim against State X and eventually brought an action against State X in the International Court of Justice. If State X asked the Court to declare the claim inadmissible on the ground that Hanna is not a Canadian national, how should the court rule?

If Canada in fact had accorded Hanna its protection domestically over the years, and if in fact Hanna had with Canada's acquiesence established a close link or tie with Canada, is a formal grant of nationality by Canada necessary? See Leigh, *Nationality and Diplomatic Protection*, 20 Int'l. &

Comp.L.Q. 453 (1971). What interest would State X have in Canada's formally according Hanna Canadian nationality?

4. **Query:** If a stateless person were able to persuade *any* state to espouse his claim against a state that wrongfully harmed him, but with which he previously had no link, why should the requested state not be permitted to make a claim on his behalf before the Court?

5. **Query.** The International Law Commission, *ibid*, 170–173 considered whether the diplomatic protection for refugees and stateless persons was an issue for the progressive development of international law based on residence, provided that the injury occurred after that person became a resident of that state. An overwhelming majority of members of the Commission were in favor of it.

6. **Dual or Multiple Nationality.** The traditional rule codified in the 1930 Hague Convention on Conflict of Nationality Laws, 179 L.N.T.S. 89, article 4 provides that a state "may not afford diplomatic protection to one of its nationals against a state whose nationality such a person also possesses." *See the Canevaro Case (Italy v. Peru)* 11 R.I.A.A. 397 1912). However, in *Iran–U.S. Case No. A/18 (Iran–U.S. Claims Tribunal),* 5 Iran–U.S.C.T. 251 (1984), it was held that this rule did not apply where the dual national brought an individual claim. Furthermore, the Tribunal cast doubt on the present day validity of the 1930 Hague Convention and held that the rule should be that of dominant or effective nationality. The International Law Commission since 1996 has taken up the issue of diplomatic protection and although there is a division of opinion with the Commission itself some members have taken the position similar to the Iran–United States Claims Tribunal that dominant or effective nationality is the key even in cases of state espousal of claims and that dual nationals should not be subject to disadvantages because of their status. The special rapporteur John Dugard noted that many states do not permit persons to relinquish their nationality and even though a person may have severed all ties with that state and acquired another nationality he or she would still be tied by nationality to the state of origin, under that state's law. *See, Report of the International Law Commission, ibid,* 141, 165–168.

2. DISCRIMINATION AGAINST WOMEN

Reservations to the Convention on the Elimination of All Forms of Discrimination Against Women

REBECCA J. COOK, 30 Va.J.Int'l L. 643, 693–696 (1990).*

* * *

"C. *Nationality: Article 9*

Women's capacity to possess citizenship and nationality separate from their husbands' affects both their capacity to be represented by state subjects of international law and their ability legally to transmit such

* Reprinted by permission of Virginia Jnl. of Int'l Law.

capacity to their children. The ability to invoke the protection of a country with which they retain a genuine and effective link while they reside in another may be an important source of security for women who go to live in a country where they are disadvantaged as aliens.

Article 9 of the Women's Convention requires that:

1. States Parties shall grant women equal rights with men to acquire, change or retain their nationality. They shall ensure in particular that neither marriage to an alien nor change of nationality by the husband during marriage shall automatically change the nationality of the wife, render her stateless or force upon her the nationality of the husband.

2. States Parties shall grant women equal rights with men with respect to the nationality of their children.

Explanations on reservations to this article vary.[a] A traditional explanation is that family solidarity and cohesiveness is served by the family having the same nationality, which should be that of its leader, who traditionally has been an adult man. Another explanation is the prevention of statelessness that would arise when a woman's original national law attributes to her on marriage her husband's nationality, but her husband's national law recognizes her separate nationality and does not extend its nationality to her. The Republic of Korea, Iraq and Tunisia consider themselves not to be bound by this article.

Egypt's reservation to article 9(2) was made to afford a child born within marriage its father's nationality 'in order to prevent a child's acquisition of two nationalities, since this may be prejudicial to his future.' This goal would be served, of course, if the child had only its mother's nationality, but another explanation is offered: [I]t is clear that the child's acquisition of his father's nationality is the procedure most suitable for the child and that this does not infringe upon the principle of equality between men and women, since it is the custom for a woman to agree, on marrying an alien, that her children shall be of the father's nationality. Since Egypt claims that its existing law does not infringe upon equality of men and women, it is questionable why it reserved with respect to this article.

The proposition that the man's nationality should govern his wife and his child was rejected by the Inter–American Court on Human Rights and the Human Rights Committee. The Inter–American Court referred to article 9 in an Advisory Opinion sought by Costa Rica on a number of amendments proposed to the naturalization provisions of its Constitution. One of the proposed amendments would have distinguished the naturalization provisions governing foreign women and foreign men who marry Costa Ricans. The Court noted that the proposed amendment follows the formula

---

a. Countries which have not reserved this article are not necessarily in compliance. For example in Gabon, which ratified the Women's Convention without reservations, a Gabonese woman must renounce her nationality in order to marry a foreigner, and if she divorces she cannot have her nationality rein- stated. Moreover, a foreign woman who marries a Gabonese man cannot retain her nationality. Implementation in Africa of the Convention on the Elimination of All Forms of Discrimination Against Women, Doc. E/ECA/CM.13/27 at para. 33 (1987).

adopted in the current Constitution, which gives women but not men who marry Costa Ricans a special status for * * * naturalization. This approach or system was based on the so-called principle of family unity and is traceable to two assumptions * * * [that] all members of a family should have the same nationality. The other derives from notions about paternal authority and the fact that authority over minor children was as a rule vested in the father and that it was the husband on whom the law conferred a privileged status of power, giving him authority, for example to fix the marital domicile and to administer the marital property. Viewed in this light, the right accorded to women to acquire the nationality of their husbands was an outgrowth of conjugal inequality.

The Court unanimously expressed the opinion that this proposed naturalization amendment 'which favors only one of the spouses, does constitute discrimination incompatible with article 17(4) [on equality of rights and responsibilities within marriage] and article 24 [on equal protection of the law] of the [American] Convention'. The Human Rights Committee in the *Aumeeruddy–Cziffra* decision considered that a Mauritian woman's inability (in contrast to a Mauritian man's ability) to transmit her nationality to her children constituted sex discrimination in the field of family life and cannot be justified on grounds of national security.

Discriminatory nationality laws between the sexes might have a marginal impact among static, perhaps isolated, populations but will be of major significance in countries where sizeable numbers of immigrants, such as workers, refugees and students, have intermarried. A reservation to the Women's Convention that upholds the imposition of a husband's alien nationality on a married woman, and the related withdrawal of the nationality of the country in which she and her family have lived and in which she intends to rear her children, will cause a comprehensive withdrawal of legal rights and capacities that the Women's Convention is designed to prevent. Such reservations, if permitted, would undermine the object and purpose of the Convention. The reservations themselves, founded on a stereotype of women's domestic roles, indicate an attitude or perception that states parties to the Women's Convention undertake to strive to change. It is inconsistent with adherence to the Women's Convention and its principle of progressive development for a country to anchor women's enduring incapacity in such a stereotypical attitude.

3. NATIONALITY OF CORPORATIONS.

The leading judicial decision on the nationality of corporations is the *Barcelona Traction Case* (1970) excerpted below. Its basic holding is that a corporation may be protected diplomatically only by the state in which it is incorporated. Belgium lost its case, brought before the ICJ against Spain on behalf of the Belgian shareholders, because the corporation was chartered in Canada, and thus had the nationality of that country. This is the prevailing rule; *see* 1987 Restatement § 213, especially Reporters' Notes 1–9. "Civil law" countries have been said to ascribe nationality on the basis of the locus of corporate activity (*siège social*), but the Restatement takes the position that this is an additional, not a different, requirement; *see* Reporters' Note 6. What does this mean? What if a corporation organized in

Canada has its *siège social* in France? American corporation law tends to permit "piercing the veil" between a corporation and its shareholders when the court finds police-power public interest. Would this make a difference? Transnational and international decisions do not seem to have accepted this U.S. practice, although European Community law has adopted it for antitrust actions. At a time when the United Kingdom was not a Community member, *Imperial Chemicals Industries, Ltd.,* a British parent corporation, was held subject to (then) EEC (now EU) prosecution as a member of the dye-stuffs cartel, because it was "present" within the EEC through subsidiaries. See, *Imperial Chemical Industries Ltd. v. Commission,* Case, 11 Com.Mkt.L.R. 557 (1972). Would the then EEC countries have accepted a British claim to assert diplomatic protection as to ICI on the "present-through-subsidiary" principle, if the subsidiary, but not ICI, had a *siège social* in an EEC country? What if the subsidiary, organized in an EU country were entirely managed by a non-EU parent corporation operating in that country, say Norway? Consider, *Elettronica Sicula* S.P.A. (ELST Case) (U.S. v. Italy) 1989 I.C.J.Rep. 15 (1989).

Barcelona Traction, Light and Power Co., Ltd (Belgium v. Spain)

International Court of Justice, 1970.
[1970] I.C.J.Rep. 3.

[The essence of the Belgian claim on the merits in the case that follows would have been that Belgian nationals as stockholders in Barcelona Traction were the victims of foreign exchange, bankruptcy and related official actions that squeezed out the Belgian equity investment in the Barcelona Traction corporate complex. The important facts include the following: the parent company, in the corporate complex involved in this action, was incorporated in 1911 in Canada; after the First World War, however, approximately 85% of its shares came to be held by Belgian nationals, largely through complicated arrangements involving some very large Belgian holding companies. Belgium wished to be allowed to show that its national shareholders had been seriously harmed by actions of Spain after the Spanish Civil War. These included, according to Belgian memorials in an earlier ICJ case dropped in 1961 in expectation of a diplomatic settlement: denial since 1940 of foreign exchange licenses to the Traction Company and some of its Spanish subsidiaries to permit service on bonds payable in pounds sterling; a 1948 bankruptcy proceeding in Spain brought by Spanish purchasers of "defaulted" sterling bonds of which the Traction Company itself had not received fair notice; and an unfair time limit on appeal in the bankruptcy case. A portion of the opinion appears below]

* * *

31. The Court has to deal with a series of problems arising out of a triangular relationship involving the State whose nationals are shareholders in a company incorporated under the laws of another State, in whose territory it has its registered office; the State whose organs are alleged to have committed against the company unlawful acts prejudicial to both it

and its shareholders; and the State under whose laws the company is incorporated, and in whose territory it has its registered office.

32. In these circumstances it is logical that the Court should first address itself to what was originally presented as the subject-matter of the third preliminary objection: namely the question of the right of Belgium to exercise diplomatic protection of Belgian shareholders in a company which is a juristic entity incorporated in Canada, the measures complained of having been taken in relation not to any Belgian national but to the company itself.

36. * * * [I]t is the existence or absence of a right, belonging to Belgium and recognized as such by international law, which is decisive for the problem of Belgium's capacity.

> This right is necessarily limited to intervention [by a State] on behalf of its own nationals because, in the absence of a special agreement, it is the bond of nationality between the State and the individual which alone confers upon the State the right of diplomatic protection, and it is as a part of the function of diplomatic protection that the right to take up a claim and to ensure respect for the rules of international law must be envisaged. Note Panevezys–Saldutiskis Railway Judgment, 1939, P.C.I.J., Series A/B, No. 26, p. 16.

It follows that the same question is determinant in respect of Spain's responsibility towards Belgium. Responsibility is the necessary corollary of a right. In the absence of any treaty on the subject between the Parties, this essential issue has to be decided in the light of the general rules of diplomatic protection.

* * *

46. It has also been contended that the measures complained of, although taken with respect to Barcelona Traction and causing it direct damage, constituted an unlawful act vis-à-vis Belgium, because they also, though indirectly, caused damage to the Belgian shareholders in Barcelona Traction. This again is merely a different way of presenting the distinction between injury in respect of a right and injury to a simple interest. But, as the Court has indicated, evidence that damage was suffered does not ipso facto justify a diplomatic claim. Persons suffer damage or harm in most varied circumstances. This in itself does not involve the obligation to make reparation. Not a mere interest affected, but solely a right infringed involves responsibility, so that an act directed against and infringing only the company's rights does not involve responsibility towards the shareholders, even if their interests are affected.

50. Turning to the international legal aspects of the case, the Court must, as already indicated, start from the fact that the present case essentially involves factors derived from municipal law—the distinction and the community between the company and the shareholder—which the Parties, however widely their interpretations may differ, each take as the point of departure of their reasoning. If the Court were to decide the case in disregard of the relevant institutions of municipal law it would, without justification, invite serious legal difficulties. It would lose touch with reality, for there are no corresponding institutions of international law to

which the Court could resort. Thus the Court has not only to take cognizance of municipal law but also to refer to it. It is to rules generally accepted by municipal legal systems which recognize the limited company whose capital is represented by shares, and not to the municipal law of a particular State, that international law refers. In referring to such rules, the Court cannot modify, still less deform them.

51.   On the international plane, the Belgian Government has advanced the proposition that it is inadmissible to deny the shareholders' national State a right of diplomatic protection merely on the ground that another State possesses a corresponding right in respect of the company itself. In strict logic and law this formulation of the Belgian claim to jus standi assumes the existence of the very right that requires demonstration. In fact the Belgian Government has repeatedly stressed that there exists no rule of international law which would deny the national State of the shareholders the right of diplomatic protection for the purpose of seeking redress pursuant to unlawful acts committed by another State against the company in which they hold shares. This, by emphasizing the absence of any express denial of the right, conversely implies the admission that there is no rule of international law which expressly confers such a right on the shareholders' national State.

58.   * * * [T]he process of lifting the veil, being an exceptional one admitted by municipal law in respect of an institution of its own making, is equally admissible to play a similar role in international law. It follows that on the international plane also there may in principle be special circumstances which justify the lifting of the veil in the interest of shareholders.

85.   The Court will now examine the Belgian claim from a different point of view, disregarding municipal law and relying on the rule that in inter-State relations, whether claims are made on behalf of a State's national or on behalf of the State itself, they are always the claims of the State. As the Permanent Court said, "The question whether the * * * dispute originates in an injury to a private interest, which in point of fact is the case in many international disputes, is irrelevant from this standpoint." (Mavrommatis Palestine Concessions, Judgment; Notteböhm, Second Phase).

* * *

89.   Considering the important developments of the last half-century, the growth of foreign investments and the expansion of the international activities of corporations, in particular of holding companies, which are often multinational, and considering the way in which the economic interests of States have proliferated, it may at first sight appear surprising that the evolution of law has not gone further and that no generally accepted rules in the matter have crystallized on the international plane. Nevertheless, a more thorough examination of the facts shows that the law on the subject has been formed in a period characterized by an intense conflict of systems and interests. It is essentially bilateral relations which have been concerned, relations in which the rights of both the State exercising diplomatic protection and the State in respect of which protection is sought have had to be safeguarded. Here as elsewhere, a body of rules could only

have developed with the consent of those concerned. The difficulties encountered have been reflected in the evolution of the law on the subject.

90.   Thus, in the present state of the law, the protection of shareholders requires that recourse be had to treaty stipulations or special agreements directly concluded between the private investor and the State in which the investment is placed. States ever more frequently provide for such protection, in both bilateral and multilateral relations, either by means of special instruments or within the framework of wider economic arrangements. Indeed, whether in the form of multilateral or bilateral treaties between States, or in that of agreements between States and companies, there has since the Second World War been considerable development in the protection of foreign investments. The instruments in question contain provisions as to jurisdiction and procedure in case of disputes concerning the treatment of investing companies by the States in which they invest capital. Sometimes companies are themselves vested with a direct right to defend their interests against States through prescribed procedures. No such instrument is in force between the Parties to the present case.

92.   Since the general rule on the subject does not entitle the Belgian Government to put forward a claim in this case, the question remains to be considered whether nonetheless, as the Belgian Government has contended during the proceedings, considerations of equity do not require that it be held to possess a right of protection. It is quite true that it has been maintained that, for reasons of equity, a State should be able, in certain cases, to take up the protection of its nationals, shareholders in a company which has been the victim of a violation of international law. Thus a theory has been developed to the effect that the State of the shareholders has a right of diplomatic protection when the State whose responsibility is invoked is the national State of the company. Whatever the validity of this theory may be, it is certainly not applicable to the present case, since Spain is not the national State of Barcelona Traction.

93.   On the other hand, the Court considers that, in the field of diplomatic protection as in all other fields of international law, it is necessary that the law be applied reasonably. It has been suggested that if in a given case it is not possible to apply the general rule that the right of diplomatic protection of a company belongs to its national State, considerations of equity might call for the possibility of protection of the shareholders in question by their own national State. This hypothesis does not correspond to the circumstances of the present case.

94.   In view, however, of the discretionary nature of diplomatic protection, considerations of equity cannot require more than the possibility for some protector State to intervene, whether it be the national State of the company, by virtue of the general rule mentioned above, or, in a secondary capacity, the national State of the shareholders who claim protection. Account should also be taken of the practical effects of deducing from considerations of equity any broader right of protection for the national State of the shareholders. It must be observed that it would be difficult on an equitable basis to make distinctions according to any quantitative test: it would seem that the owner of 1 per cent. and the owner of 90 per cent. of

the share-capital should have the same possibility of enjoying the benefit of diplomatic protection. The protector State may, of course, be disinclined to take up the case of the single small shareholder, but it could scarcely be denied the right to do so in the name of equitable considerations. In that field, protection by the national State of the shareholders can hardly be graduated according to the absolute or relative size of the shareholding involved.

95.   The Belgian Government, it is true, has also contended that as high a proportion as 88 per cent. of the shares in Barcelona Traction belonged to natural or juristic persons of Belgian nationality, and it has used this as an argument for the purpose not only of determining the amount of the damages which it claims, but also of establishing its right of action on behalf of the Belgian shareholders. Nevertheless, this does not alter the Belgian Government's position, as expounded in the course of the proceedings, which implies, in the last analysis, that it might be sufficient for one single share to belong to a national of a given State for the latter to be entitled to exercise its diplomatic protection.

96.   The Court considers that the adoption of the theory of diplomatic protection of shareholders as such, by opening the door to competing diplomatic claims, could create an atmosphere of confusion and insecurity in international economic relations. The danger would be all the greater inasmuch as the shares of companies whose activity is international are widely scattered and frequently change hands. It might be claimed that, if the right of protection belonging to the national States of the shareholders were considered as only secondary to that of the national State of the company, there would be less danger of difficulties of the kind contemplated. However, the Court must state that the essence of a secondary right is that it only comes into existence at the time when the original right ceases to exist. As the right of protection vested in the national State of the company cannot be regarded as extinguished because it is not exercised, it is not possible to accept the proposition that in case of its non-exercise the national States of the shareholders have a right of protection secondary to that of the national State of the company. Study of factual situations in which this theory might possibly be applied gives rise to the following observations.

* * *

100.   It is clear from what has been said above that Barcelona Traction was never reduced to a position of impotence such that it could not have approached its national State, Canada, to ask for its diplomatic protection, and that there was nothing to prevent Canada from continuing to grant its diplomatic protection to Barcelona Traction if it had considered that it should do so.

101.   For the above reasons, the Court is not of the opinion that, in the particular circumstances of the present case, jus standi is conferred on the Belgian Government by considerations of equity.

* * *

103. Accordingly, The Court rejects the Belgian Government's claim by fifteen votes to one, twelve votes of the majority being based on the reasons set out in the present Judgment.

———

[Judge Jessup discusses the general requirement of effective nationality in the *Barcelona Traction Case*, [1970] I.C.J.Rep. 3, at 182. A portion of his opinion follows.]

38. There is no question that, under international law, a State has in general a right to extend its diplomatic protection to a corporation which has its nationality, or national character as it is more properly called. The proposition raises two questions:

(1) What are the tests to determine the national character of a corporation?

(2) Assuming the appropriate tests are met, must that national character be "real and effective" as shown by the "link" between the corporation and the State, just as, in the Notteböhm case, this Court decided that a certain claim to nationality is not enough in all situations to justify a State in extending its diplomatic protection to a natural person?

39. There are two standard tests of the "nationality" of a corporation. The place of incorporation is the test generally favoured in the legal systems of the common law, while the siège social is more generally accepted in the civil law systems. There is respectable authority for requiring that both tests be met.

It is not possible to speak of a single rule for all purposes. The tests used in private international law have their own character.

Commercial treaties and claims conventions often contain their own definitions of which companies shall be considered to have the nationality of a State for purposes of the treaty. The tests used for such purposes may be quite different—even in the practice of the same State—from the tests used for other purposes. For example, the "control" test was widely used to determine the enemy character of property during war, but it is not established in international law as a general test of the nationality of a corporation. On the other hand, control may constitute the essential link which, when joined to nationality, gives the State the right to extend diplomatic protection to the corporation. It is a familiar fact that the laws of certain States provide favourable conditions for companies incorporating therein, especially in relation to taxation. Canada is one such State, Liechtenstein is another. In the United States, many companies find it advantageous, for various reasons, to incorporate in Delaware or New Jersey. Charters secured for such reasons may be called "charters of convenience".

40. The Judgment of the Court of Notteböhm, Second Phase, in 1955, has been widely discussed in the subsequent literature of international law particularly with reference to the so-called "link theory" by which the effectiveness of nationality may be tested. It has been

argued that the doctrine is equally applicable in the case of ships flying "flags of convenience" and in relation to the diplomatic protection of corporations. I have maintained the view that it should apply in both those situations.

43. It has also been argued that the Court should not pass judgment on the question whether there existed the necessary link between Canada and Barcelona Traction without hearing argument on behalf of Canada. Canada might have sought to intervene in the instant case under Article 62 of the Statute, but it did not do so. It is said that after judgment is pronounced in this case of Belgium v. Spain, Canada might find some jurisdictional ground to found an application to institute a case of Canada v. Spain. It is known that no such jurisdictional ground now exists. It seems quite unreal to suppose that Spain would now agree with Canada upon a compromise submitting to the Court a Canadian claim on behalf of Barcelona Traction, thus exposing Spain to the new hazard of being required to pay some two hundred millions of dollars of damages. But if the Court were properly seised of an application by Canada, it would have to take cognizance of the fact that following Article 59 of the Statute, "The decision of the Court has no binding force except between the parties and in respect of that particular case". Had the Court endorsed the application of the link principle to juristic persons, in its present decision in Belgium v. Spain, Canada could have argued against that conclusion in the hypothetical case of Canada v. Spain, or might have relied on Spanish admissions that Canada was entitled to protect the company.

44. It seems to be widely thought that the "link" concept in connection with the nationality of claims, originated in the International Court of Justice's Judgment in Notteböhm. I do not agree that in that instance the Court created a new rule of law. Indeed the underlying principle was already well established in connection with diplomatic claims on behalf of corporations. To look for the link between a corporation and a State is merely another example of what is now the familiar practice of "lifting the veil". The practice of such States as the United States and Switzerland had already given weight to the proposition that a corporation would not be protected solely because it was incorporated in the State, i.e., had the State's nationality; some other link was required and that link usually was related to the ownership of shares. Such abstention, being as it were "against interest", has special probative value.

Three years after the decision in Notteböhm, the Italian–United States Conciliation Commission, under the presidency of the late Professor Sauser Hall, in the Flegenheimer case stated:

> The right of challenge of the international court, authorizing it to determine whether, behind the nationality certificate or the acts of naturalization produced, the right to citizenship was regularly acquired, is in *conformity with the very broad rule* of *effectivity* which dominates the law of nationals entirely and allows the

court to fulfill its legal function and remove the inconveniences specified. (Emphasis supplied.)

* * *

Notes and Questions

In what circumstances would the state of nationality of shareholders have standing to bring an international claim? For the U.S. position, *see* Steiner and Vagts, TRANSNATIONAL LEGAL PROBLEMS (4th ed. 1999) at 222.

4. NATIONALITY OF SHIPS, AIRCRAFT AND SPACE VEHICLES[a]

United Nations Convention on the Law of the Sea

December 10, 1982. 21 I.L.M. 1261 (1982).

Article 91

Nationality of ships

1.   Every State shall fix the conditions for the grant of its nationality to ships, for the registration of ships in its territory, and for the right to fly its flag. Ships have the nationality of the State whose flag they are entitled to fly. There must exist a genuine link between the State and the ship.

2.   Every State shall issue to ships to which it has granted the right to fly its flag documents to that effect.

Article 92

Status of ships

1.   Ships shall sail under the flag of one State only and, save in exceptional cases expressly provided for in international treaties or in this Convention, shall be subject to its exclusive jurisdiction on the high seas. A ship may not change its flag during a voyage or while in a port of call, save in the case of a real transfer of ownership or change of registry.

2.   A ship which sails under the flags of two or more States, using them according to convenience, may not claim any of the nationalities in question with respect to any other State, and may be assimilated to a ship without nationality.

Article 93

Ships flying the flag of the United Nations, its specialized agencies and the International Atomic Energy Agency

The preceding articles do not prejudice the question of ships employed on the official service of the United Nations, its specialized agencies or the International Atomic Energy Agency, flying the flag of the organization.

a. See Chapters **4** and **5** infra for additional material on nationality aspects of these topics.

Article 94

Duties of the flag State

1.   Every State shall effectively exercise its jurisdiction and control in administrative, technical and social matters over ships flying its flag.

2.   In particular every State shall:

(a) maintain a register of ships containing the names and particulars of ships flying its flag, except those which are excluded from generally accepted international regulations on account of their small size; and

(b) assume jurisdiction under its internal law over each ship flying its flag and its master, officers and crew in respect of administrative, technical and social matters concerning the ship.

3.   Every State shall take such measures for ships flying its flag as are necessary to ensure safety at sea with regard, inter alia, to:

(a) the construction, equipment and seaworthiness of ships;

(b) the manning of ships, labour conditions and the training of crews, taking into account the applicable international instruments;

(c) the use of signals, the maintenance of communications and the prevention of collisions.

* * *

The M/V "Saiga" (No. 2) Case (Saint Vincent and the Grenadines v. Guinea)

International Tribunal for the Law of the Sea,
1 July 1999, 38 I.L.M. 1323 (1999).*

[Saint Vincent and Grenadines commenced this proceeding seeking damages for losses arising out of the actions of Guinea described below. The Tribunal took jurisdiction by agreement of the parties. Guinea interposed a number of preliminary objections, including the three Challenges to admissibility concerning Registration of the Saiga, Genuine Link, and Nationality of Claims, discussed in the following excerpts from the Judgment of the Tribunal.]

31.   The Saiga is an oil tanker. At the time of its arrest on 28 October 1997, it was owned by Tabona Shipping Company Ltd. of Nicosia, Cyprus, and managed by Seascot Shipmanagement Ltd. of Glasgow, Scotland. The ship was chartered to Lemania Shipping Group Ltd. of Geneva, Switzerland. The Saiga was provisionally registered in Saint Vincent and the Grenadines on 12 March 1997. The Master and crew of the ship were all of Ukrainian nationality. There were also three Senegalese nationals who were employed as painters. The Saiga was engaged in selling gas oil as bunker and occasionally water to fishing and other vessels off the coast of West Africa. The owner of the cargo of gas oil on board was Addax BV of Geneva, Switzerland.

32.   Under the command of Captain Orlov, the Saiga left Dakar, Senegal, on 24 October 1997 fully laden with approximately 5,400 metric

* Reprinted with the permission of the
American Society of International Law.

tons of gas oil. On 27 October 1997, between 0400 and 1400 hours [at an identified point], the Saiga supplied gas oil to three fishing vessels, the Giuseppe Primo and the Kriti, both flying the flag of Senegal, and the Eleni S, flying the flag of Greece. The point was approximately 22 nautical miles from Guinea's island of Alcatraz. All three fishing vessels were licensed by Guinea to fish in its exclusive economic zone. The Saiga then sailed in a southerly direction to supply gas oil to other fishing vessels at a pre-arranged place. Upon instructions from the owner of the cargo in Geneva, it later changed course and sailed towards another location beyond the southern border of the exclusive economic zone of Guinea.

33.   At 0800 hours on 28 October 1997, the Saiga, according to its log book, was at [another identified point] * * *. It had been drifting since 0420 hours while awaiting the arrival of fishing vessels to which it was to supply gas oil. This point was south of the southern limit of the exclusive economic zone of Guinea. At about 0900 hours the Saiga was attacked by a Guinean patrol boat (P35). Officers from that boat and another Guinean patrol boat (P328) subsequently boarded the ship and arrested it. On the same day, the ship and its crew were brought to Conakry, Guinea, where its Master was detained. * * * The travel documents of the members of the crew were taken from them by the authorities of Guinea and armed guards were placed on board the ship. On 1 November 1997, two injured persons from the Saiga, Mr. Sergey Klyuyev and Mr. Djibril Niasse, were permitted to leave Conakry for Dakar for medical treatment. Between 10 and 12 November 1997, the cargo of gas oil on board the ship, amounting to 4,941.322 metric tons, was discharged on the orders of the Guinean authorities. Seven members of the crew and two painters left Conakry on 17 November 1997, one crew member left on 14 December 1997 and six on 12 January 1998. The Master and six crew members remained in Conakry until the ship was released on 28 February 1998.

* * *

Challenges to admissibility

Registration of the Saiga

55.   The first objection raised by Guinea to the admissibility of the claims set out in the application is that Saint Vincent and the Grenadines does not have legal standing to bring claims in connection with the measures taken by Guinea against the Saiga. The reason given by Guinea for its contention is that on the day of its arrest the ship was "not validly registered under the flag of Saint Vincent and the Grenadines" and that, consequently, Saint Vincent and the Grenadines is not legally competent to present claims either on its behalf or in respect of the ship, its Master and the other members of the crew, its owners or its operators.

* * *

57.   The facts relating to the registration of the Saiga, as they emerge from the evidence adduced before the Tribunal, are as follows:

(a) The Saiga was registered provisionally on 12 March 1997 as a Saint Vincent and the Grenadines ship under section 36 of the Merchant Shipping Act of 1982 of Saint Vincent and the Grenadines (hereinafter "the

Merchant Shipping Act''). The Provisional Certificate of Registration issued to the ship on 14 April 1997 stated that it was issued by the Commissioner for Maritime Affairs of Saint Vincent and the Grenadines on behalf of the Government of Saint Vincent and the Grenadines under the terms of the Merchant Shipping Act. The Certificate stated: ''This Certificate expires on 12 September 1997.''

(b) The registration of the ship was recorded in the Registry Book of Saint Vincent and the Grenadines on 26 March 1997. The entry stated: ''Valid thru: 12/09/1997''.

(c) A Permanent Certificate of Registration was issued on 28 November 1997 by the Commissioner for Maritime Affairs of Saint Vincent and the Grenadines on behalf of that State. The Certificate stated: ''This Certificate is permanent.''

58. Guinea contends that the ship was unregistered between 12 September 1997 and 28 November 1997 because the Provisional Certificate of Registration expired on 12 September 1997 and the Permanent Certificate of Registration was issued on 28 November 1997. From this Guinea concludes: ''It is thus very clear that the MV 'SAIGA was not validly registered' in the time period between 12 September 1997 and 28 November 1997. For this reason, the MV 'SAIGA' may [be] qualified to be a ship without nationality at the time of its attack.'' Guinea also questioned whether the ship had been deleted from the Maltese Register where it was previously registered.

60. * * * With regard to the question raised by Guinea concerning the previous registration of the ship, Saint Vincent and the Grenadines stated that its authorities had received from the owner of the ship ''satisfactory evidence that the ship's registration in the country of last registration had been closed'' as required by section 37 of the Merchant Shipping Act.

62. The question for consideration is whether the Saiga had the nationality of Saint Vincent and the Grenadines at the time of its arrest. The relevant provision of the Convention is article 91, * * * * [see text above].

63. Article 91 leaves to each State exclusive jurisdiction over the granting of its nationality to ships. In this respect, article 91 codifies a well-established rule of general international law. Under this article, it is for Saint Vincent and the Grenadines to fix the conditions for the grant of its nationality to ships, for the registration of ships in its territory and for the right to fly its flag. These matters are regulated by a State in its domestic law. Pursuant to article 91, paragraph 2, Saint Vincent and the Grenadines is under an obligation to issue to ships to which it has granted the right to fly its flag documents to that effect. The issue of such documents is regulated by domestic law.

64. International law recognizes several modalities for the grant of nationality to different types of ships. In the case of merchant ships, the normal procedure used by States to grant nationality is registration in accordance with domestic legislation adopted for that purpose. This proce-

dure is adopted by Saint Vincent and the Grenadines in the Merchant Shipping Act.

65.   Determination of the criteria and establishment of the procedures for granting and withdrawing nationality to ships are matters within the exclusive jurisdiction of the flag State. Nevertheless, disputes concerning such matters may be subject to the procedures under Part XV of the Convention, especially in cases where issues of interpretation or application of provisions of the Convention are involved.

66.   The Tribunal considers that the nationality of a ship is a question of fact to be determined, like other facts in dispute before it, on the basis of evidence adduced by the parties.

67.   Saint Vincent and the Grenadines has produced evidence before the Tribunal to support its assertion that the Saiga was a ship entitled to fly its flag at the time of the incident giving rise to the dispute. In addition to making references to the relevant provisions of the Merchant Shipping Act, Saint Vincent and the Grenadines has drawn attention to several indications of Vincentian nationality on the ship or carried on board. These include the inscription of "Kingstown" as the port of registry on the stern of the vessel, the documents on board and the ship's seal which contained the words "SAIGA Kingstown" and the then current charter-party which recorded the flag of the vessel as "Saint Vincent and the Grenadines".

68.   The evidence adduced by Saint Vincent and the Grenadines has been reinforced by its conduct. Saint Vincent and the Grenadines has at all times material to the dispute operated on the basis that the Saiga was a ship of its nationality. It has acted as the flag State of the ship during all phases of the proceedings. It was in that capacity that it invoked the jurisdiction of the Tribunal in its Application for the prompt release of the Saiga and its crew under article 292 of the Convention and in its Request for the prescription of provisional measures under article 290 of the Convention.

69.   As far as Guinea is concerned, the Tribunal cannot fail to note that it did not challenge or raise any doubts about the registration or nationality of the ship at any time until the submission of its Counter–Memorial in October 1998. Prior to this, it was open to Guinea to make inquiries regarding the registration of the Saiga or documentation relating to it. * * *

70.   With regard to the previous registration of the Saiga, the Tribunal notes the statement made by Saint Vincent and the Grenadines in paragraph 60. It considers this statement to be sufficient.

71.   The Tribunal recalls that, in its Judgment of 4 December 1997 and in its Order of 11 March 1998, the Saiga is described as a ship flying the flag of Saint Vincent and the Grenadines.

72.   On the basis of the evidence before it, the Tribunal finds that Saint Vincent and the Grenadines has discharged the initial burden of establishing that the Saiga had Vincentian nationality at the time it was arrested by Guinea. Guinea had therefore to prove its contention that the ship was not registered in or did not have the nationality of Saint Vincent and the Grenadines at that time. The Tribunal considers that the burden

has not been discharged and that it has not been established that the Saiga was not registered in or did not have the nationality of Saint Vincent and the Grenadines at the time of the arrest.

73.   The Tribunal concludes:

(a) it has not been established that the Vincentian registration or nationality of the Saiga was extinguished in the period between the date on which the Provisional Certificate of Registration was stated to expire and the date of issue of the Permanent Certificate of Registration;

(b) in the particular circumstances of this case, the consistent conduct of Saint Vincent and the Grenadines provides sufficient support for the conclusion that the Saiga retained the registration and nationality of Saint Vincent and the Grenadines at all times material to the dispute;

(c) in view of Guinea's failure to question the assertion of Saint Vincent and the Grenadines that it is the flag State of the Saiga when it had every reasonable opportunity to do so and its other conduct in the case, Guinea cannot successfully challenge the registration and nationality of the Saiga at this stage;

(d) in the particular circumstances of this case, it would not be consistent with justice if the Tribunal were to decline to deal with the merits of the dispute.

74.   For the above reasons, the Tribunal rejects Guinea's objection to the admissibility of the claims of Saint Vincent and the Grenadines based on the ground that the Saiga was not registered in Saint Vincent and the Grenadines at the time of its arrest and that, consequently, the Saiga did not have Vincentian nationality at that time.

Genuine link

75.   The next objection to admissibility raised by Guinea is that there was no genuine link between the Saiga and Saint Vincent and the Grenadines. Guinea contends that "without a genuine link between Saint Vincent and the Grenadines and the M/V 'Saiga', Saint Vincent and the Grenadines' claim concerning a violation of its right of navigation and the status of the ship is not admissible before the Tribunal vis-a-vis Guinea, because Guinea is not bound to recognise the Vincentian nationality of the M/V 'Saiga', which forms a prerequisite for the mentioned claim in international law".

79.   Article 91, paragraph 1, of the Convention provides: "There must exist a genuine link between the State and the ship." Two questions need to be addressed in this connection. The first is whether the absence of a genuine link between a flag State and a ship entitles another State to refuse to recognize the nationality of the ship. The second question is whether or not a genuine link existed between the Saiga and Saint Vincent and the Grenadines at the time of the incident.

80. With regard to the first question, the Tribunal notes that the provision in article 91, paragraph 1, of the Convention, requiring a genuine link between the State and the ship, does not provide the answer. Nor do articles 92 and 94 of the Convention, which together with article 91 constitute the context of the provision, provide the answer. The Tribunal, however, recalls that the International Law Commission, in article 29 of the Draft Articles on the Law of the Sea adopted by it in 1956, proposed the concept of a "genuine link" as a criterion not only for the attribution of nationality to a ship but also for the recognition by other States of such nationality. After providing that "ships have the nationality of the State whose flag they are entitled to fly", the draft article continued: "Nevertheless, for purposes of recognition of the national character of the ship by other States, there must exist a genuine link between the State and the ship". This sentence was not included in article 5, paragraph 1, of the Convention on the High Seas of 29 April 1958 (hereinafter "the 1958 Convention"), which reads, in part, as follows:

> There must exist a genuine link between the State and the ship; in particular, the State must effectively exercise its jurisdiction and control in administrative, technical and social matters over ships flying its flag.

Thus, while the obligation regarding a genuine link was maintained in the 1958 Convention, the proposal that the existence of a genuine link should be a basis for the recognition of nationality was not adopted.

81. The Convention follows the approach of the 1958 Convention. Article 91 retains the part of the third sentence of article 5, paragraph 1, of the 1958 Convention which provides that there must be a genuine link between the State and the ship. The other part of that sentence, stating that the flag State shall effectively exercise its jurisdiction and control in administrative, technical and social matters over ships flying its flag, is reflected in article 94 of the Convention, dealing with the duties of the flag State.

82. Paragraphs 2 to 5 of article 94 of the Convention outline the measures that a flag State is required to take to exercise effective jurisdiction as envisaged in paragraph 1. Paragraph 6 sets out the procedure to be followed where another State has "clear grounds to believe that proper jurisdiction and control with respect to a ship have not been exercised". That State is entitled to report the facts to the flag State which is then obliged to "investigate the matter and, if appropriate, take any action necessary to remedy the situation". There is nothing in article 94 to permit a State which discovers evidence indicating the absence of proper jurisdiction and control by a flag State over a ship to refuse to recognize the right of the ship to fly the flag of the flag State.

83. The conclusion of the Tribunal is that the purpose of the provisions of the Convention on the need for a genuine link between a ship and its flag State is to secure more effective implementation of the duties of the flag State, and not to establish criteria by reference to which the validity of the registration of ships in a flag State may be challenged by other States.

84. This conclusion is not put into question by the United Nations Convention on Conditions for Registration of Ships of 7 February 1986 invoked by Guinea. This Convention (which is not in force) sets out as one of its principal objectives the strengthening of "the genuine link between a State and ships flying its flag". In any case, the Tribunal observes that Guinea has not cited any provision in that Convention which lends support to its contention that "a basic condition for the registration of a ship is that also the owner or operator of the ship is under the jurisdiction of the flag State".

85. The conclusion is further strengthened by the Agreement for the Implementation of the Provisions of the United Nations Convention on the Law of the Sea of 10 December 1982 Relating to the Conservation and Management of Straddling Fish Stocks and Highly Migratory Fish Stocks opened for signature on 4 December 1995 and the Agreement to Promote Compliance with International Conservation and Management Measures by Fishing Vessels on the High Seas of 24 November 1993. These Agreements, neither of which is in force, set out, inter alia, detailed obligations to be discharged by the flag States of fishing vessels but do not deal with the conditions to be satisfied for the registration of fishing vessels.

86. In the light of the above considerations, the Tribunal concludes that there is no legal basis for the claim of Guinea that it can refuse to recognize the right of the Saiga to fly the flag of Saint Vincent and the Grenadines on the ground that there was no genuine link between the ship and Saint Vincent and the Grenadines.

Nationality of claims

103. In its last objection to admissibility, Guinea argues that certain claims of Saint Vincent and the Grenadines cannot be entertained by the Tribunal because they relate to violations of the rights of persons who are not nationals of Saint Vincent and the Grenadines. According to Guinea, the claims of Saint Vincent and the Grenadines in respect of loss or damage sustained by the ship, its owners, the Master and other members of the crew and other persons, including the owners of the cargo, are clearly claims of diplomatic protection. In its view, Saint Vincent and the Grenadines is not competent to institute these claims on behalf of the persons concerned since none of them is a national of Saint Vincent and the Grenadines. During the oral proceedings, Guinea withdrew its objection as far as it relates to the shipowners, but maintained it in respect of the other persons.

104. In opposing this objection, Saint Vincent and the Grenadines maintains that the rule of international law that a State is entitled to claim protection only for its nationals does not apply to claims in respect of persons and things on board a ship flying its flag. In such cases, the flag State has the right to bring claims in respect of violations against the ship and all persons on board or interested in its operation. Saint Vincent and the Grenadines, therefore, asserts that it has the right to protect the ship flying its flag and those who serve on board, irrespective of their nationality.

105. In dealing with this question, the Tribunal finds sufficient guidance in the Convention. The Convention contains detailed provisions concerning the duties of flag States regarding ships flying their flag. Articles 94 and 217, in particular, set out the obligations of the flag State which can be discharged only through the exercise of appropriate jurisdiction and control over natural and juridical persons such as the Master and other members of the crew, the owners or operators and other persons involved in the activities of the ship. No distinction is made in these provisions between nationals and non-nationals of a flag State. Additionally, articles 106, 110, paragraph 3, and 111, paragraph 8, of the Convention contain provisions applicable to cases in which measures have been taken by a State against a foreign ship. These measures are, respectively, seizure of a ship on suspicion of piracy, exercise of the right of visit on board the ship, and arrest of a ship in exercise of the right of hot pursuit. In these cases, the Convention provides that, if the measures are found not to be justified, the State taking the measures shall be obliged to pay compensation "for any loss or damage" sustained. In these cases, the Convention does not relate the right to compensation to the nationality of persons suffering loss or damage. Furthermore, in relation to proceedings for prompt release under article 292 of the Convention, no significance is attached to the nationalities of persons involved in the operations of an arrested ship.

106. The provisions referred to in the preceding paragraph indicate that the Convention considers a ship as a unit, as regards the obligations of the flag State with respect to the ship and the right of a flag State to seek reparation for loss or damage caused to the ship by acts of other States and to institute proceedings under article 292 of the Convention. Thus the ship, every thing on it, and every person involved or interested in its operations are treated as an entity linked to the flag State. The nationalities of these persons are not relevant.

107. The Tribunal must also call attention to an aspect of the matter which is not without significance in this case. This relates to two basic characteristics of modern maritime transport: the transient and multinational composition of ships' crews and the multiplicity of interests that may be involved in the cargo on board a single ship. A container vessel carries a large number of containers, and the persons with interests in them may be of many different nationalities. This may also be true in relation to cargo on board a break-bulk carrier. Any of these ships could have a crew comprising persons of several nationalities. If each person sustaining damage were obliged to look for protection from the State of which such person is a national, undue hardship would ensue.

108. The Tribunal is, therefore, unable to accept Guinea's contention that Saint Vincent and the Grenadines is not entitled to present claims for damages in respect of natural and juridical persons who are not nationals of Saint Vincent and the Grenadines.

109. In the light of the above considerations, the Tribunal rejects the objection to admissibility based on nationality of claims.

Brownlie, Principles of Public International Law

pp. 428–432 (5th Ed.1998).*

In the maintenance of a viable regime for common use of the high seas the law of the flag and the necessity for a ship to have a flag are paramount. The opinion commonly expressed by jurists was strongly in favour of the unqualified freedom of each state to determine for itself the conditions under which national status could be conferred on vessel. * * * The act of conferment of nationality (registration) is within the competence of states, but registration is in principle only evidence of nationality, and valid registration under the law of the flag state does not preclude issues of validity under international law. The *Notteböhm* principle applies equally here * * *

* * *

The Convention for the Regulation of Aerial Navigation of 1919, and later the Chicago Convention of 1944, provided that the nationality of aircraft is governed by the state of registration. The former stipulated that registration could only take place in the state of which the owners were nationals, while the latter merely forbids dual registration. Neither Convention applied in time of war, and the latter Convention does not apply to state aircraft, i.e. aircraft used in military, customs and police services'. The Tokyo Convention on Offenses Committed on Board Aircraft provides that the state of registration has jurisdiction over offenses and acts committed on board. * * * Obviously the *Notteböhm* principle ought to apply to aircraft as it does to ships. It must surely apply at the least to discover to which state non-civil aircraft belong, but it is probable that even where the Chicago Convention applies, issues of diplomatic protection are not precluded by registration. In bilateral treaties the United States has reserved the right to refuse a carrier permit to an airline designated by the other contracting party 'in the event substantial ownership and effective control of such airlines are not vested in nationals of the other contracting party'.

* * *

The Space Treaty of 1967 does not employ the concept of nationality in relation to objects launched into outer space. Article VIII of the Treaty provides in part that the state of registration shall retain jurisdiction and control over such object, and over any personnel thereof, while in outer space or on a celestial body'. In the [1975] Convention on Registration of Objects Launched into Outer Space it is provided that the launching state shall maintain a register of space objects. Each state of registry has a duty to furnish certain information to the Secretary–General of the United Nations.

Note

All member states of the International Civil Aviation Organization are required to have their civilian registered aircraft display their nationality

* Reprinted with the permission of Oxford University Press.

and registration marks. *See*, Annex to the Chicago Convention 15 U.N.T.S. 295.

5. COUNCIL OF EUROPE CONVENTION ON NATIONALITY

European Convention on Nationality[a]

November 6, 1997, 37 I.L.M. 44 (1998).*

[The European Convention on Nationality is the first international agreement to deal coherently and comprehensively with this subject. The full text is found in the Documentary Supplement. Chapter II on general principles is reproduced below. Other topics treated in the Convention include: rules on the acquisition and loss of nationality (Chapter III), multiple nationality (Chapters V and VI), state succession (Chapter VI and military service (Chapter VII)].

Chapter II—General principles relating to nationality

Article 3—Competence of the State

1 Each State shall determine under its own law who are its nationals.

2 This law shall be accepted by other States in so far as it is consistent with applicable international conventions, customary international law and the principles of law generally recognised with regard to nationality.

Article 4—Principles

The rules on nationality of each State Party shall be based on the following principles:

a everyone has the right to a nationality;

b statelessness shall be avoided;

c no one shall be arbitrarily deprived of his or her nationality;

d neither marriage nor the dissolution of a marriage between a national of a State Party and an alien, nor the change of nationality by one of the spouses during marriage, shall automatically affect the nationality of the other spouse.

Article 5—Non-discrimination

1 The rules of a State Party on nationality shall not contain distinctions or include any practice which amount to discrimination on the grounds of sex, religion, race, colour or national or ethnic origin.

2 Each State Party shall be guided by the principle of non-discrimination between its nationals, whether they are nationals by birth or have acquired its nationality subsequently.

a. By early 2001, the number of signatories of this Convention was 17 and the number of ratifying states was 4. The Convention entered into force on 1 March 2000.

* Reprinted with the permission of the American Society of International Law.

SECTION C.   THE UNITED NATIONS: THE ORGANIZATION AND ITS OFFICIALS

Note: The United Nations's public responsibilities for operational activities on a global basis raise nationality questions. As the ICJ has clearly stated (see Chapter 2 above), the U.N. is not a state, nor is it anything like a "super-state". Although the U.N. does exercise a number of functions which over-lap or sometimes parallel those of states, there is no provision in the Charter for the U.N. to confer nationality, either on its officials, or on stateless persons, refugees or others. In the *Reparations Case*, the ICJ confirmed the limited nature of the U.N.'s powers. If it does not have the power to confer nationality, is the U.N. empowered to provide diplomatic protection for its officials and agents? These officials normally hold the nationality of their own home state, a Member State of the U.N. That State presumably would itself enjoy the traditional power to provide diplomatic protection over its own nationals even when they serve the U.N. What then, is the result of this possibly competing or parallel authority? Beyond the question of individual officials, what about a U.N. official's surviving family when the official is killed or otherwise incapacitated in the performance of his U.N. duties? Does the U.N. have the authority to act in the interest of the official's survivors? These questions are considered in the portions of the ICJ's Advisory Opinion presented below. *See also* in Chapter 2 other parts of this Opinion.

1.   THE UNITED NATIONS

Reparations for Injuries Suffered in the Service of the United Nations

International Court of Justice, 1949.
[1949]   I.C.J. Rep. 174, 183.

* * *

Question I (b) is as follows:

> * * * 'has the United Nations, as an Organization, the capacity to bring an international claim * * * in respect of the damage caused * * * (b) to the victim or to persons entitled through him?'

* * *

It is not possible, by a strained use of the concept of allegiance, to assimilate the legal bond which exists, under Article 100 of the Charter,[a] between the Organization on the one hand, and the Secretary–General and

---

a. Ed. Note: Article 100 is set forth below with other material on international   officials.

the staff on the other, to the bond of nationality existing between a State and its nationals.

* * *

Having regard to its purposes and functions already referred to, the Organization may find it necessary, and has in fact found it necessary, to entrust its agents with important missions to be performed in disturbed parts of the world. Many missions, from their very nature, involve the agents in unusual dangers to which ordinary persons are not exposed. For the same reason, the injuries suffered by its agents in these circumstances will sometimes have occurred in such a manner that their national State would not be justified in bringing a claim for reparation on the ground of diplomatic protection, or, at any rate, would not feel disposed to do so. Both to ensure the efficient and independent performance of these missions and to afford effective support to its agents, the Organization must provide them with adequate protection.

This need of protection for the agents of the Organization, as a condition of the performance of its functions, has already been realized, and the Preamble to the Resolution of December 3rd, 1948 (supra, p. 175), shows that this was the unanimous view of the General Assembly.

For this purpose, the Members of the Organization have entered into certain undertakings, some of which are in the Charter and others in complementary agreements. The content of these undertakings need not be described here; but the Court must stress the importance of the duty to render to the Organization 'every assistance' which is accepted by the Members in Article 2, paragraph 5, of the Charter. It must be noted that the effective working of the Organization-the accomplishment of its task, and the independence and effectiveness of the work of its agents-require that these undertakings should be strictly observed. For that purpose, it is necessary that, when an infringement occurs, the Organization should be able to call upon the responsible State to remedy its default, and, in particular, to obtain from the State reparation for the damage that the default may have caused to its agent.

In order that the agent may perform his duties satisfactorily, he must feel that this protection is assured to him by the Organization, and that he may count on it. To ensure the independence of the agent, and, consequently, the independent action of the Organization itself, it is essential that in performing his duties he need not have to rely on any other protection than that of the Organization (save of course for the more direct and immediate protection due from the State in whose territory he may be). In particular, he should not have to rely on the protection of his own State. If he had to rely on that State, his independence might well be compromised, contrary to the principle applied by Article 100 of the Charter. And lastly, it is essential that whether the agent belongs to a powerful or to a weak State; to one more affected or less affected by the complications of international life; to one in sympathy or not in sympathy with the mission of the agent-he should know that in the performance of his duties he is under the protection of the Organization. This assurance is even more necessary when the agent is stateless.

Upon examination of the character of the functions entrusted to the Organization and of the nature of the missions of its agents, it becomes clear that the capacity of the Organization to exercise a measure of functional protection of its agents arises by necessary intendment out of the Charter.

* * *

Having regard to the foregoing considerations, and to the undeniable right of the Organization to demand that its Members shall fulfil the obligations entered into by them in the interest of the good working of the Organization, the Court is of the opinion that, in the case of a breach of these obligations, the Organization has the capacity to claim adequate reparation, and that in assessing this reparation it is authorized to include the damage suffered by the victim or by persons entitled through him.

* * *

The affirmative reply given by the Court on point I (b) obliges it now to examine Question II. When the victim has a nationality, cases can clearly occur in which the injury suffered by him may engage the interest both of his national State and of the Organization. In such an event, competition between the State's right of diplomatic protection and the Organization's right of functional protection might arise, and this is the only case with which the Court is invited to deal. In such a case, there is no rule of law which assigns priority to the one or to the other, or which compels either the State or the Organization to refrain from bringing an international claim. The Court sees no reason why the parties concerned should not find solutions inspired by goodwill and common sense, and as between the Organization and its Members it draws attention to their duty to render 'every assistance' provided by Article 2, paragraph 5, of the Charter.

Although the bases of the two claims are different, that does not mean that the defendant State can be compelled to pay the reparation due in respect of the damage twice over. International tribunals are already familiar with the problem of a claim in which two or more national States are interested, and they know how to protect the defendant State in such a case.

The risk of competition between the Organization and the national State can be reduced or eliminated either by a general convention or by agreements entered into in each particular case. There is no doubt that in due course a practice will be developed, and it is worthy of note that already certain States whose nationals have been injured in the performance of missions undertaken for the Organization have shown a reasonable and co-operative disposition to find a practical solution.

* * *

The question of reconciling action by the Organization with the rights of a national State may arise in another way; that is to say, when the agent bears the nationality of the defendant State.

The ordinary practice whereby a State does not exercise protection on behalf of one of its nationals against a State which regards him as its own national, does not constitute a precedent which is relevant here. The action of the Organization is in fact based not upon the nationality of the victim but upon his status as agent of the Organization. Therefore it does not matter whether or not the State to which the claim is addressed regards him as its own national, because the question of nationality is not pertinent to the admissibility of the claim.

In law, therefore, it does not seem that the fact of the possession of the nationality of the defendant State by the agent constitutes any obstacle to a claim brought by the Organization for a breach of obligations towards it occurring in relation to the performance of his mission by that agent.

———

Note: The United Nations Claims Commission was set up in 1992 to resolve claims brought against Iraq in consequence of the 1990 invasion of Kuwait by Iraq. There has been a vast number of these claims, requiring an extraordinary claims process. The claims raise a number of nationality questions, as reflected in the Commission's Rules which provide forthcoming solutions. Query whether these Rules are fully consistent with the principles and rules developed in the readings above in this Chapter?

United Nations Compensation Commission: Report With Decisions of the Governing Council

31 I.L.M. 1009, 1055 (1992).*

Provisional Rules for Claims Procedure

Article 5. Who may submit claims

1. Governments and international organizations are entitled to submit claims to the Commission.

(a) A Government may submit claims on behalf of its nationals and, at its discretion, of other persons resident in its territory. In the case of Governments existing in the territory of a former federal state, one such Government may submit claims on behalf of nationals, corporations or other entities of another such Government, if both Governments agree.

(b) A Government may submit claims on behalf of corporations or other entities that, on the date on which the claim arose, were incorporated or organized under the law of that State. If the Governments concerned agree, one Government may submit claims in respect of joint ventures on behalf of the nationals, corporations or other entities of other Governments.

(c) Claims may be submitted on behalf of an individual, corporation or other entity by only one Government.

(d) International organizations may submit claims only on their own behalf.

* Reprinted with the permission of the American Society of International Law.

2.   An appropriate person, authority, or body appointed by the Governing Council may submit claims on behalf of persons who are not in a position to have their claims submitted by a Government.

3.   A corporation or other private legal entity is required to request the State of its corporation or organization to submit its claim to the Commission. In the case of a corporation or other private legal entity whose State of incorporation or organization fails to submit, within the time-limit established by the Governing Council, such claims falling within the applicable criteria, the corporation or other private legal entity may itself make a claim to the Commission within three months thereafter. It must provide at the same time an explanation as to why its claim is not being submitted by a Government.

———

2.   INTERNATIONAL OFFICIALS

Numbering now in the thousands, "international officials" are persons appointed to positions of responsibility in international organizations, such as the United Nations, in the U.N.'s specialized agencies (listed above in Chapter 2, Section C), in the European Union and in many other universal, regional and functional intergovernmental organizations. The officials are usually nationals of member countries. They do not relinquish their personal nationality as a consequence of accepting the status of international officials. Nor do they acquire anything like an internationally created special nationality. They do, however, enjoy certain privileges and immunities. (see Chapter 10). They also undertake certain obligations of loyalty to their organization. Those obligations may at times conflict with the policies of their own governments.

Typically international organizations adopt rigorous rules requiring the utmost loyalty of their officials. The officials are subject to the authority of the executive heads of their respective organizations and are solely responsible to them in the discharge of their duties. Officials may neither seek nor accept instructions from any member state, or government or other external authority. They must carry out their duties and conduct themselves solely with the interests of the organization in mind. They may not engage in any political activities or carry out, state or publish anything incompatible with their duties as international public servants. Their loyalty to the organization must take precedence over any other interests, and they must act as necessary to ensure their independence of any person or authority outside of the organization. This is essential to the objective and effective operation of the organizations which are created to serve the entire community of their member states.

If international officials owe such a far-reaching duty of loyalty to the organization, do their governments have any proper interest in their continuing national loyalty? Are international officials in a sense also representatives of their own governments, or at least subject to their respective law in the same way as other nationals? If so, is that legally compatible with the rules described above? How should executive heads of international organizations handle such questions when they arise in the form of a demand by a government that in considering its nationals for appointment to staff positions, the organization should appoint only those holding a national loyalty clearance? In the event that a United Nations official carries out instructions of the Secretary–General for certain actions which are considered by the official's national government to violate his duty of loyalty to the official's *own* state, does international law permit that state to prosecute? What if the official acted beyond instructions or authority and violated international law or the law of his or her own country? Could that official be prosecuted before an international tribunal (e.g. a war crimes tribunal) or before a national tribunal? If the Secretary— General waived the official's immunity, would that affect your views?

Charter of the United Nations

Article 100

1. In the performance of their duties the Secretary–General and the staff shall not seek or receive instructions from any government or from any other authority external to the Organization. They shall refrain from any action which might reflect on their position as international officials responsible only to the Organization.

2. Each Member of the United Nations undertakes to respect the exclusively international character of the responsibilities of the Secretary– General and the staff and not to seek to influence them in the discharge of their responsibilities.

Statute of the International Court of Justice

Article 20

Every member of the Court shall, before taking up his duties, make a solemn declaration in open court that he will exercise his powers impartially and conscientiously.

Hinton v. Devine

United States District Court, Eastern District of Pennsylvania, 1986.
633 F.Supp. 1023.

MEMORANDUM AND ORDER

■ TROUTMAN, SENIOR DISTRICT JUDGE.

In 1953 the President of the United States issued Executive Order No. 10422, providing for an investigation of United States citizens employed or being considered for employment by the United Nations or other international organizations. The Order establishes an International Organizations Employees Loyalty Board, the function of which is to evaluate all such citizens and render an advisory opinion as to their loyalty to the United States. That opinion is transmitted to the Secretary of State for ultimate transmittal to the executive head of the involved international organization. The opinion is developed in accordance with procedures described in the Order, and rules and regulations promulgated by the Board.* The plaintiff, William Hinton, a resident of Fleetwood, Pennsylvania, and a graduate of the Cornell College of Agriculture and the author of several books on China, challenges the constitutionality of Executive Order No. 10422.

In 1980 Hinton was hired by the Food and Agriculture Organization (FAO), an agency of the United Nations, to serve for six months as a consultant to the Grasslands Development Project in the Inner Mongolia Region of the Peoples Republic of China (PRC). Pursuant to Executive Order No. 10422, he requested and received a loyalty clearance. In 1981 and 1982 he received similar FAO offers of employment and again sought and received loyalty clearances. In 1983, having once again been advised that he was being considered for an FAO consultancy, Hinton, for his fourth consecutive year, requested a loyalty clearance. This time his clearance was unaccountably delayed. Having failed to receive a clearance for 1983, Hinton was not offered FAO employment, but did return to the project, on which he had served for the preceding three years, as an employee of the PRC.

Early in 1984, with another FAO offer allegedly on the horizon, Hinton filed the instant suit, contending that because his 1983 loyalty clearance request had not been processed for over a year, he lost an employment opportunity in 1983. More importantly, he feared that the lack of a clearance would adversely affect his expected 1984 FAO appointment. Accordingly, plaintiff filed a motion for a preliminary injunction, requesting that the Court direct immediate action on his pending application for a loyalty clearance. On April 5, 1984, after a March 28 conference before the Court, Hinton received a loyalty clearance, obviating the need for an immediate ruling on his request for a preliminary injunction. Thereafter, on June 26, 1984, plaintiff filed a motion for summary judgment seeking a declaratory judgment that Executive Order No. 10422 is unconstitutional and a permanent injunction against its further and continued enforcement. * * *

* * *

IV.   *Nature of the Government's Interest*

We begin this phase of the analysis by examining the government's stated interest as set forth in § [6] of the Preamble to Executive Order No. 10422: " * * * it is in the interest of the United States that United States citizens who are employees of the Secretariat of the United Nations be of the highest integrity and not persons who have been, are, or are likely to be, engaged in espionage or subversive activities against the United States". Conceding that this is an important interest, it would be ludicrous to conclude that the Order as it is written approaches the "precision of regulation" contemplated by the Supreme Court in situations where government regulation impinges upon First Amendment freedoms. Our exhaustive analysis of the means used to fulfill the government's stated purpose reveals that the procedures for obtaining a loyalty clearance are

---

* Executive Order No. 10422, as amended, is found at 22 U.S.C. § 287.

not narrowly drawn to reach only subversion, espionage or even lack of integrity. Instead, a wide range of activities and associations may be examined, and the resulting advisory opinion purports to pass upon the individual's "loyalty", a vague and sometimes illusory concept. Another inherent problem is the fact that the need for an advisory opinion as to loyalty extends to all employees or prospective employees of international organizations regardless of their duty stations or the nature of their duties.

* * *

The government made no effort to identify specific positions that might implicate significant foreign policy concerns of the United States. Instead, it seeks to justify the loyalty clearance program on the insubstantial and conclusory basis that all employees of international organizations are *"de facto "*representatives of the United States and have "affirmatively chosen to enmesh themselves in the delicate foreign affairs concerns of the United States". Just as the Supreme Court declined to allow "war powers" to "be invoked as a talismanic incantation" to support overbroad Congressional action because even that power "does not remove constitutional limitations safeguarding essential liberties", so this Court, for the same reason, may not allow the President's power over foreign affairs to be invoked in that manner.

A closer scrutiny of the government's rationale for the loyalty clearance program, particularly as it concerns the plaintiff in this case, reveals the true nature of what the government seeks to accomplish and clearly illustrates why it is legally and constitutionally impermissible. The *Ozonoff* court concluded, and we agree, that the government's interest in regulating the employment of United States citizens by international organizations is more attenuated than if the individuals subject to investigation were employees of this government. In doing so, the court observed that: "The appellee is a medical doctor. He does not want to represent the United States abroad, engage in diplomacy, or practice politics. His object— prolonging human life—is technical and scientific, not political. His employer is an international organization, not the American government."

Although we believe that only the last sentence of the foregoing observation is truly relevant to the issue, the government argues vigorously and at length that the issue of expertise was essential to the result reached in the *Ozonoff* case. Upon that premise, the government argues that Hinton does not fit the criteria set forth by the First Circuit and, hence, that it has a stronger interest in investigating his loyalty. To support that contention, defendant characterized the plaintiff as an "author of political propaganda who resides on a one-man farm" and who "has interacted with international political figures and practices politics". * * * Thus, it appears that the government is contending, at the least, that politically active citizens who seek to work for international organizations in whatever capacity ought to be subject to investigations into their loyalty to the United States.

* * *

From the government's more general defense of the loyalty clearance program, it appears that it seeks to use the Executive Order, if necessary, to discriminate against United States citizens on the basis of their political beliefs and activities. Defendant's most basic rationale for the Order can best be summarized by the following: In addition, * * * the international organization will not be misled into assuming that, for example, if it assigns such an individual to a 'balanced' team (one representing the conflicting interests of the constituent members of the international organization), that the organization is thereby fairly representing the interests of the United States on that team. * * * " As previously stated, an appropriate order will issue invalidating and enjoining the Order in question.

Section D.   European Union Citizenship

The Amsterdam Treaty: A Comprehensive Guide

European Union, www.europa.eu.int (19 May 1999).

CITIZENSHIP of the EUROPEAN UNION

* * *

Union citizenship and the rights accompanying it must be seen in perspective in order to understand the dynamics of the process launched by the Treaty setting up the European Economic Community (signed in Rome in 1957). This Treaty gave people the right to move freely within the European Community. Free movement of people was closely linked to economic status as employee, self-employed or service provider. The right of residence throughout the Community was first given to employees and the self-employed and members of their families in conjunction with the right to work there.

The Single European Act (1986) wrote provisions into the Treaty of Rome to establish an area without frontiers and to abolish checks on persons at internal frontiers, irrespective of nationality. Unfortunately, this area was not established before the scheduled date of 31December1992. But in 1990 the Council, acting under the Single Act, extended the right of residence to persons who are not engaged in an occupation, provided they have sufficient resources and social insurance cover. The final stage in attaining the general right to movement and residence was its incorporation in the concept of Union citizenship in the Treaty on European Union (1992). In 1997 the Amsterdam Treaty produced a political solution for further progress on free movement, incorporating the Schengen Agreement into the Union Treaty (although some member states wanted to have special status and will retain controls at their border with other Member States).

As early as the Paris Summit in 1974, attempts had been made to define the "special rights" to be conferred on nationals of the European Economic Community as it then was. In 1992 the EU Treaty wrote Union citizenship into the Treaty establishing the European Community (Article 17, ex Article 8). After the signing of the Treaty, the Declaration by the Birmingham European Council in October 1992 made clear that "... citizenship of the Union brings our citizens additional rights and protection without in any way taking the place of their national citizenship". A

Declaration attached to the Treaty setting up the European Community notes that "the question whether an individual possesses the nationality of a Member State shall be settled solely by reference to the national law of the Member State concerned".

The Treaty on European Union, by establishing Union citizenship, confers on every Union citizen a fundamental and personal right to move and reside freely without reference to an economic activity. The right to vote and to stand as a candidate in elections to the European Parliament and in municipal elections in the Member State in which he resides and the right to protection by the diplomatic or consular authorities of any Member State in a non-member country are a concrete expression of the feeling of common citizenship. Directives adopted in 1993 and 1994 laid down the rules for giving effect to these rights. The same Treaty makes it possible to strengthen and amplify these rights.

However, European citizens still encounter real obstacles, both practical and legal, when they wish to exercise their rights to free movement and residence in the Union.

ADDITIONS by the AMSTERDAM TREATY

Amendments have been made to Articles 17 and 21 (ex Articles 8 and 8(d)) of the EC Treaty, which define European citizenship.

Firstly, the Amsterdam [treaty] clarifies the link between European and national citizenship. It states unequivocally that "citizenship of the Union shall complement and not replace national citizenship". Two practical conclusions follow from this:

- it is first necessary to be a national of a Member State in order to enjoy citizenship of the Union;

- European citizenship will supplement and complement the rights conferred by national citizenship.

E.U. Treaty of Amsterdam: Consolidated Version of the Treaty Establishing The European Community

October 7, 1997, 37 I.L.M. 56, 82 (1998).*

CITIZENSHIP OF THE UNION

Article 17 (ex Article 8)

1. Citizenship of the Union is hereby established. Every person holding the nationality of a Member State shall be a citizen of the Union. Citizenship of the Union shall complement and not replace national citizenship.

2. Citizens of the Union shall enjoy the rights conferred by this Treaty and shall be subject to the duties imposed thereby.

* Reprinted with the permission of the American Society of International Law.

Article 18 (ex Article 8a)

1.   Every citizen of the Union shall have the right to move and reside freely within the territory of the Member States, subject to the limitations and conditions laid down in this Treaty and by the measures adopted to give it effect.

2.   The Council may adopt provisions with a view to facilitating the exercise of the rights referred to in paragraph 1; save as otherwise provided in this Treaty, the Council shall act in accordance with the procedure referred to in Article 251. The Council shall act unanimously throughout this procedure.

Article 19 (ex Article 8b)

1.   Every citizen of the Union residing in a Member State of which he is not a national shall have the right to vote and to stand as a candidate at municipal elections in the Member State in which he resides, under the same conditions as nationals of that State. This right shall be exercised subject to detailed arrangements adopted by the Council, acting unanimously on a proposal from the Commission and after consulting the European Parliament; these arrangements may provide for derogations where warranted by problems specific to a Member State.

2.   Without prejudice to Article 190(4) and to the provisions adopted for its implementation, every citizen of the Union residing in a Member State of which he is not a national shall have the right to vote and to stand as a candidate in elections to the European Parliament in the Member State in which he resides, under the same conditions as nationals of that State. This right shall be exercised subject to detailed arrangements adopted by the Council, acting unanimously on a proposal from the Commission and after consulting the European Parliament; these arrangements may provide for derogations where warranted by problems specific to a Member State.

Article 20 (ex Article 8c)

Every citizen of the Union shall, in the territory of a third country in which the Member State of which he is a national is not represented, be entitled to protection by the diplomatic or consular authorities of any Member State, on the same conditions as the nationals of that State. Member States shall establish the necessary rules among themselves and start the international negotiations required to secure this protection.

Article 21 (ex Article 8d)

Every citizen of the Union shall have the right to petition the European Parliament in accordance with Article 194.

Every citizen of the Union may apply to the Ombudsman established in accordance with Article 195.

Every citizen of the Union may write to any of the institutions or bodies referred to in this Article or in Article 7 in one of the languages mentioned in Article 314 and have an answer in the same language.

Article 22 (ex Article 8e)

The Commission shall report to the European Parliament, to the Council and to the Economic and Social Committee every three years on the application of the provisions of this Part. This report shall take account of the development of the Union.

On this basis, and without prejudice to the other provisions of this Treaty, the Council, acting unanimously on a proposal from the Commission and after consulting the European Parliament, may adopt provisions to strengthen or to add to the rights laid down in this Part, which it shall recommend to the Member States for adoption in accordance with their respective constitutional requirements.

Re: Treaty on European Union

Spain, Constitutional Court (Plenary Session) 1992.
98 Int'l L. Rep. 251 (1994).*

* * * In a Resolution of the Council of Ministers of 24 April 1992, it was resolved to commence the consultation procedure provided for in Article 95(2) of the Constitution,[a] for the purpose of obtaining the opinion of this Court on a possible contradiction between the Constitution and Article 8B(1) of the EEC Treaty, in the wording given to it by Article G B10 of the EUT * * *

2. For the purpose of clearly establishing the terms of the present Application, the government first of all sets out the history of the matter, stating that the EUT, far from confining itself to the creation of an organic and procedural framework rendering possible the establishment of a common foreign relations policy and providing for security and defence at a European level, whilst at the same time reinforcing the process of economic and social integration, also involves a process of political integration on the basis of a true European Community and introduces a "citizenship of the Union" as a civil status, different from the citizenship of the Member states, based on but not co-extensive with that citizenship and of a higher order. The nucleus of this "European citizenship" consists of acknowledging the right of Community residents to vote in and to stand as candidates at municipal elections on the same terms as the nationals of the member state in which those elections take place (Article 8(B)(1) of the EEC treaty, introduced by Article G B 10 of the EUT). The same applies as regards elections to the European Parliament (Article 8B(2) of the EEC Treaty).

* * *

To sum up, under Article 93, the Spanish Parliament can grant or transfer the exercise of "powers derived from the Constitution", but cannot dispense with the Constitution itself, by contradicting or permitting the contradiction of its provisions. The possibility of amending the Constitution is not a "power" whose exercise can be granted. Moreover, the Constitution

---

* Reprinted with the permission of the Editor, International Law Reports.

a. Ed. Note: Under the Spanish Constitution only Spanish nationals had the right to stand as a candidate in municipal elections under Article 13(2), as explained in this opinion, p. 252–253.

cannot be amended save by the means provided for in Chapter X through the procedures and guarantees laid down there and by means of an express amendment of the text of the Constitution. This is the conclusion that the wording of Article 95(1) requires . . .

It must therefore be concluded that the a contradiction which exists between Article 13(2) of the Constitution and Article 8B(1) of the Treaty establishing the European Economic Community, as amended, cannot be circumvented through the mere expedient of authorizing the conclusion of the Treaty on the European Union under the provisions of Article 93. It is clear that Article 8B(*l*), in so far as it directly grants a right to stand as a candidate at elections, does not grant powers of any kind but rather personal rights, and that for this purpose, in view of the wording of Article 13(2) of the Constitution, it will in any event first be necessary to amend the Constitution.

5.   The conflict between the provision whose constitutional compatibility is at issue and Article 13(2) of the Constitution cannot therefore be avoided by means of the provisions of Article 93 of the Constitution. But it is also necessary to comment on a suggestion contained in the Application, made for the purpose of overcoming or circumventing the restrictions laid down in the Constitution and hence avoiding the need for amendment of the Constitution. That suggestion consists of possible legislation treating citizens of the European Union, for the purposes of the right to stand as a candidate at municipal elections, as if they were Spanish nationals.

It is indeed the case that the Constitution does not define Spaniards (this task is left to the legislature under Article 1l(1)). It is also indisputable that there is no uniform set of legal provisions governing all nationals and that the rules applicable to them may differ from those applicable to certain aliens. Nevertheless it is clear that Article 13 of the Constitution does lay down binding and unavoidable provisions appertaining to all Spanish public authorities (Article 9(*l*) of the Constitution) concerning the recognition of constitutional rights in favour of non-Spaniards. Those provisions include, as stated above, the reservation to Spaniards of the possession and exercise of certain specific fundamental rights. These rights, including the right to stand for election which is at issue here, cannot be granted, either by law or by treaty, to persons who are not Spaniards. This means that these rights can only be conferred on foreigners by means of an amendment to the Constitution. This constitutional restriction would disappear, and with it the binding force of the Constitution, if the interpretation put forward by the Government were to take legal-form and be accepted. That interpretation would amount to enabling the legislature to "mint" nationalities on an ad hoc basis for the sole and exclusive purpose of avoiding the applicability of the limitation contained in Article 13(2) of the Constitution. The Spanish legislature clearly must define which persons are Spaniards, that is to say those persons who potentially have the capacity to hold posts provided for by law in the legal order, and on this subject the Constitution does not lay down any relevant guidelines. However, the legislature cannot, without acting contrary to the Constitution, divide up or manipulate Spanish nationality, acknowledging it only in certain respects, for the sole purpose of granting to persons who are not nationals a fundamental right which, as in the case of the right to stand as a candidate at elections, is expressly withheld from them by Article 13(2) of the Constitution.

It is clearly not possible to escape the consequences of what has been said above by the allusion, made in the Application, to the expedient of legal fictions. A legal fiction is merely a legal construction whose purpose, contrary to reality, is to introduce into the scope of the applicability of an existing legal provision a matter which would otherwise be excluded from that provision. One of the essential characteristics of such a fiction is that it must not consist of a convenient device for achieving the legally impossible, as is the case with amending the Constitution otherwise than by the procedures expressly laid down for such purpose in Articles 167 and 168 of the Constitution. The legislature, since it is subject to the principle of the supremacy of the Constitution, cannot evade those procedures either directly or by means of the indirect, exceptional and supplementary technique consisting of a legal fiction.

6. It follows that the inevitable conclusion is that there exists contradiction, which no amount of interpretation can overcome between Article 8B(l) of the Treaty establishing the European Community, in the version contained in the Treaty on European Union, on the one hand, and Article 13(2) of the Constitution, on the other hand. This contradiction appertains to that part of Article 8B(1) which gives the right to stand as a candidate at municipal elections to a generic group of persons (nationals of other Member States of the Community) who are not Spaniards. The only means available at law to overcome this contradiction, so as to sign or ratify the Treaty, is therefore the means provided for in Article 95(l) of the Constitution, namely the prior amendment of the Constitution. The amendment to the Constitution will have to remove the obstacle contained in Article 13(2), which prohibits the right to stand as a candidate at municipal elections from being extended to non-Spaniards.

* * *

Note.—To comply with the ruling of the Constitutional Court, the Government immediately proposed a constitutional amendment, which was approved by the Spanish Parliament and became law on 27 August 1992. The amended version of Article 13(2) provides:

Only Spanish nationals shall have the rights recognized in Article 23, except for the right to vote and stand as a candidate in municipal elections which, consistently with the criteria of reciprocity, may be established [for other persons] by treaty or by law.

Subsequently a draft law ratifying the Maastricht Treaty was approved by almost unanimous votes of both Chambers of the Spanish Parliament and the Law of Ratification was promulgated on 28 December 1992 (for further details see European Law Review, 1993, p. 247, Report on Ratification of the Treaty in Spain by Marta Arpio Santacruz).

Notes and Questions: While the foregoing authorities already show a significant measure of flexibility and a pragmatic approach to nationality issues in order to do justice in particular situations, recent years have witnessed a comprehensive reconsideration of the role of nationality in the international system. This should not be at all surprising in a period of reducing roles of state sovereignty, of growth of NGOs and other competing actors in bringing heavy influences to bear on governments, and of the increasing mobility and functions of individuals on the international scene. The sociological and legal background of these developments is examined in Linda Bosniak, *Citizenship Denationalized*, 7 Indiana Journal of Global Law Studies 447 (2000) and in Daniel Adler and Kim Rubenstein, *International Citizenship: The Future of Nationality in a Globalized World*, 7 Indiana Journal of Global Legal Studies 519 (2000).

Two recent cases also reflect the pragmatic approach. See *Karpa v. Mexico* (Interim Decision on Preliminary Jurisdictional Issues) Case No. ARB(AF)/99/1 (December 6, 2000), noted in ASIL, *International Law in Brief* (February 3–9 (2001) (A U.S. citizen's permanent residence in Mexico held not to bar his claim against Mexico under NAFTA). In *Prosecutor v. Delalic*, the International Criminal Tribunal for the Former Yugoslavia applied "ethnic" rather than "national characteristics" for purposes of Geneva Convention IV Relative to the Protection of Civilian Persons in Time of War. See: http://www.un.org/icty/celebici/appeal/judgement/cel-aj010220e–1.htm.

Now reconsider questions 1–5 set forth in the introduction to this Chapter. How would you characterize today the role of nationality as applied in the international system to individuals. companies and other entities?

CHAPTER 9

HUMAN RIGHTS: THE GROWTH OF STATE RESPONSIBILITY TO INDIVIDUALS

INTRODUCTION

The catalog of abuses to which human beings have subjected each other is one of unrelieved horror. Abuses range from murder and physical torture and rape of the individual to the slaughter and rape of religious, racial and ethnic masses. They also include slavery, sex-slavery and traffic in women and children, forced labor mass dislocations and deprivations of liberty. Freedom to speak, to practice one's religion, to select one's own occupation, and to marry whom one pleases are repressed. Arbitrary arrest, imprisonment without trial, unfair trials and degrading punishments are not uncommon. In his stunning book, A MIRACLE, A UNIVERSE: SETTLING ACCOUNTS WITH TORTURERS (1990), Lawrence Weschler chronicles the story of torture and its impact on Brazil and Uruguay during the 1960's and 1970's: "[T]hey [the political prisoners] have been tortured, kept in secret places of detention, questioned—all of them, without exception * * *. In some units, prisoners are tortured with electrodes, in others they are suspended by their arms, which have been previously tied behind their backs, or kept with their heads under water until suffocation, not to mention similar refinements * * *." Weschler provides details on how the U.S. provided Uruguayan officers with up-to-date "anti-subversion techniques," and "more scientifically effective methods of interrogation." We must be ever vigilant in minding ourselves. *See also*, Feitlowitz, A LEXICON OF TERROR: ARGENTINA AND THE LEGACIES OF TORTURE (1998).

Many of these are abuses to the human personality, recently called human dignity, committed by people upon people. Some are also common crimes, such as murder, matters of domestic criminal law. Others are perpetrated by individuals acting in some official capacity for the state. Still others are committed by violent opponents of the state. Protections against these abuses are frequently afforded by the internal laws of the state. Domestic laws are designed not only to deter private individuals from harming their fellows but also, as in the case of the U.S. Constitution, to protect the individual from abuses by the state. But what protects people when the machinery of domestic law fails or even violates them? Does the international legal system offer protection? The traditional rule, until a generation ago, was chilling: a state could treat its own citizens "according to discretion." I Oppenheim, INTERNATIONAL LAW 682 (Lauterpacht 8th ed. 1955). Is this still true today? What substantive legal norms have been developed in the international system for the protection of the individual? Are they effective? Are citizens and aliens equally protected? By what processes are those norms applied and protections afforded both internationally and domestically?

As the nation-state became the organizing unit of the European peoples an early, if halting, recognition developed that, in some circumstances, a state might be circumscribed in the way it treated its nationals. Doctrines of natural law furnished a major impetus. DeVisscher noted: "[T]he treaties by which States bound themselves to treat their own nationals in a certain way appear only as isolated phenomena inspired first by political interest and later by considerations of humanity. The series of particular agreements inaugurated in 1660 by the Treaty of Oliva after a century and a half of religious commotions bore this aspect. In these, states receiving cessions of territory guaranteed to the ceding states the continuance and protection of the religion existing in the ceded territories. This protection, granted first to individuals, was gradually extended to minority groups, to religious minorities first and afterwards ethnic or national minorities." DeVisscher, THEORY AND REALITY IN PUBLIC INTERNATIONAL LAW 126 (Corbett trans., 1968).

SECTION A.   RESPONSIBILITY OF STATES FOR INJURIES TO ALIENS

1.   THE PRINCIPLE OF DIPLOMATIC PROTECTION

The Traditional Rule.

Administrative Decision No. V

Mixed Claims Commission (United States—Germany), 1924
7 U.N.Rep.Int'l Arb. Awards 119, 152.

* * * Ordinarily a nation will not espouse a claim on behalf of its national against another nation unless requested so to do by such national. When on such request a claim is espoused, the nation's absolute right to control it is necessarily exclusive. In exercising such control it is governed not only by the interest of the particular claimant but by the larger interests of the whole people of the nation and must exercise an untrammeled discretion in determining when and how the claim will be presented and pressed, or withdrawn or compromised, and the private owner will be bound by the action taken. Even if payment is made to the espousing nation in pursuance of an award, it has complete control over the fund so paid to and held by it and may, to prevent fraud, correct a mistake, or protect the national honor, at its election return the fund to the nation paying it or otherwise dispose of it. * * *

———

Note: Diplomatic protection in the 18th and 19th centuries was the means by which a state sought protection for its own nationals when they had left its territory. If a foreign state did not protect another's nationals, diplomatic protests were made, asserting that the foreign state had violated its treaty obligations or other obligations imposed by general international law. Diplomatic protest remains a major vehicle for this. In theory, it was the rights of the protecting state that had been violated, not those of the injured individual. An injured individual had no standing to assert his or her own rights or interests. In the absence of an international judiciary in which the rights of the offended state could be litigated, states occasionally resorted to arbitration and authorized ad hoc tribunals to decide claims based upon alleged injuries to individuals. A substantial body of precedent, establishing a primitive law of human rights, was developed but the practice of arbitrating violations of personal rights began to slacken after World War II. As you read these materials, ask yourselves whether the artificial derivative theory of rights and protection continues its dominance.

2.   IS THERE AN INTERNATIONAL MINIMUM STANDARD?

———

Notes and Questions

1. *Equality vs. International Minimum Standard for prosecution and trial*. When European nationals began to travel to trade and colonize, their governments became concerned for their personal safety and property. European states asserted diplomatic protests on behalf of their nationals, claiming that there existed a *minimum standard of justice* to which all states must adhere in their treatment of aliens. Dawson and Head, International Law, National Tribunals and the Rights of Aliens, Chapter I (1971). The General Claims Commission in *Roberts v. Mexico,* 4 U.N.Rpt. Int'l Arb. Awards 17 (1976) adopted this standard, holding that aliens are to be treated in accordance with *ordinary standards of civilization.* Does international law actually recognize a minimum standard? If a minimum standard exists, what is it? Is it violated, when an Islamic state punishes an alien for violating its prohibition of the consumption of alcohol? Would the answer be different or the same for punishing a woman for being in public without a veil? Is the "minimum standard" only an imposition of Western values or something more? Is it possible that there is a minimum standard in some and not other subjects? The alternative provides that a state must merely assure that aliens are not treated any worse than its own nationals? These are the two competing positions, the latter having been urged by scholars representing developing nations.

2. *Standard for determining that there has been a denial of justice*. By what standard will a court decide that there has been a denial of justice? Must the complaining party show that there has been a failure to meet the standards of local law? Or may the standards of local law be so high that a failure to meet those high standards is not, of itself, a denial of justice, or so low that even meeting them violate the standard? Traditionally, some jurists have denied that there is an international standard. Some argue that the alien is entitled only to equality of treatment with nationals. In analyzing this proposition note that the broad question of state responsibility for injury to aliens has been discussed somewhat indiscriminately in connection with two types of problems: injury to an alien individual in his personal rights (*e.g.,* rights to physical security and personal freedom, rights to fair trial in cases involving personal liberty) on one hand and the alien individual's (or corporation's) rights to property, on the other. During much of the 20th Century, the latter rights have been the subject of considerable controversy, particularly with respect to the expropriation of property by states socializing and collectivizing the means of production. Would you expect a system of international law to be more protective of personal rights than of property rights?

3. *Influence of the emergence of new states on the question of the international minimum standard*. The Western World prior to World War II debated whether the standard for justice was national treatment or an international minimum standard. This debate may be viewed as one within a single established legal system in which the members of that system sought to delineate the contours of a body of customary law acceptable to them. With the influx of new states into the community of nations, mostly former colonies, the debate took on a different tone.

Guha Roy, Is the Law of Responsibility of States for Injuries to Aliens a Part of Universal International Law?

55 AJIL 863, 866, 888 (1961).[1]

The international community in its inception was confined to only some Christian states of Europe. It expanded within very narrow limits to embrace, first, the other Christian states of Europe and next their own offshoots in other continents. It thus retained until recently its racial exclusiveness in full and its geographical and other limitations in part. The international law which the worldwide community of states today inherits is the law which owes its genesis and growth, first, to the attempts of these states to regulate their mutual intercourse in their own interests and, secondly, to the use made of it during the period of colonialism.

The contacts of the members of the restricted international community of the past with other states and peoples of the much larger world outside its own charmed circle were not governed by any law or scruples beyond what expediency dictated. The history of the establishment and consolidation of empires overseas by some of the members of the old international community and of the acquisition therein of vast economic interests by their nationals teems with instances of a total disregard of all ethical considerations. A strange irony of fate now compels those very members of the community of nations on the ebb tide of their imperial power to hold up principles of morality as shields against the liquidation of interests acquired and held by an abuse of international intercourse. Rights and interests acquired and consolidated during periods of such abuse cannot for obvious reasons carry with them in the mind of the victims of that abuse anything like the sanctity the holders of those rights and interests may and do attach to them. To the extent to which the law of responsibility of states for injuries to aliens favors such rights and interests, it protects an unjustified status quo or, to put it more bluntly, makes itself a handmaid of power in the preservation of its spoils. * * *

The law of responsibility then, is not founded on any universal principles of law or morality. Its sole foundation is custom, which is binding only among states where it either grew up or came to be adopted. It is thus hardly possible to maintain that it is still part of universal international law. Whatever the basis of obligation in international law in the past, when the international community was restricted to only a few states, including those, fewer still, admitted into it from time to time, the birth of a new world community has brought about a radical change which makes the traditional basis of obligation outmoded.

Once it is found that the right of diplomatic protection of their nationals abroad, claimed by states as a customary right, is not universally binding, the structure of this law as part of universal international law crumbles, for this right is assumed to be the sole basis of a state's claim to stretch out its protecting hand to its nationals in the territory of another state independently of its consent. Its elimination from universal interna-

---

1. Reprinted with the permission of the American Society of International Law.

tional law necessarily means that, even outside the limited zone of the applicability of this law, the responsibility of a state for injuries to aliens remains in every case in which it may be held to be responsible exactly in the same way as in the case of its own nationals, but it remains its responsibility not to the home state of the injured alien but to the injured alien himself. It ceases to be an international responsibility and becomes a responsibility only under the municipal law of the state concerned.

Notes and Questions

1. *What variations in legal systems are comprehended by the international minimum standard?* National legal systems differ considerably as to how they deal with an accused in a criminal proceeding pending trial on the merits. In some countries, the accusation of a criminal offense results in the accused being put into detention pending investigation by a magistrate on the question of probable cause. In most Civil Law countries, bail is not allowed for the period pending trial (they consider it scandalous that one with money can buy this liberty). Individuals who do not pose a threat of danger or pose a risk of disappearing are not detained. Often, the physical conditions of detention centers are rather grim. In many Civil Law countries, exclusionary and other rigorous rules of evidence traditionally have been sparse and the defendant was often not allowed directly to confront witnesses against him. In view of these differences, can it be said that the international minimum standard of criminal procedural justice takes its contents from Anglo–American Systems? This is changing, however. Moreover, it is not uncommon as stated by the dissent in the *Chattin Case*, below, General Claims Commission, 1927, 4 U.N.Rpt. Int'l Awards 282, in ¶¶ 17–23, the majority did not understand the Mexican Legal System:

> "All the criticism which has been made of these proceedings, I regret to say, appears to arise from lack of knowledge of the judicial system and practice of Mexico, and, what is more dangerous, from the application thereto of tests belonging to foreign systems of law. For example, in some of the latter the investigation of a crime is made only by the police magistrates and the trial proper is conducted by the Judge. Hence the reluctance in accepting that one same judge may have the two functions and that, therefore, he may have to receive in the preliminary investigation (*instrucción*) of the case all kinds of data, with the obligation, of course, of not taking them into account at the time of judgment, if they have no probative weight."

2. It is certain that the secret report, so much discussed in this case, would have been received by the police of the countries which place the investigation exclusively in the hands of such branch. This same police would have been free to follow all the clues or to abandon them at its discretion; but the Judge is criticized here because he did not follow up completely the clue given by Ramirez with respect to *Chattin*. The same domestic test–to call it such–is used to understand what is a trial or open trial imagining at the same time that it must have the sacred forms of

common-law and without remembering that the same goal is reached by many roads. And the same can be said when speaking of the manner of taking testimony of witnesses, of cross-examination, of holding confrontations, etc. Trials in Mexico, like in other "Civil Law" systems are generally short and formal "confirmations of the written documents * * *".

3. The protections for the accused traditionally are supposed to be built into the investigative stage, where a judge, trained to protect the "liberty interests" of the accused, often oversees the process. Hence, the majority's misconception about the process in Mexico is often held by common law jurists as to any "Civil Law" system. Do differences such as this mean that there is no international minimum standard?

3. U.S. Ratification of the International Covenant on Civil and Political Rights

In June 1992, the Senate gave its Advice and Consent to the *International Covenant on Civil and Political Rights*. Reservations and understandings similar to those issued when the Genocide convention was ratified were attached to the ratification.

John Quigley, Criminal Law & Human Rights: Implications of the United States Ratification of the International Covenant on Civil and Political Rights

6 Harv.Hum.Rts.J. 59, 59–63 (1993).*

The 1992 ratification by the United States of the International Covenant on Civil and Political Rights ("Covenant") opens U.S. practice on human rights issues to scrutiny under international standards. To be sure, human rights standards found in the customary law of nations already bound the United States, apart from this country's adherence to any human rights treaty. With every decision, domestic courts around the globe contribute to the customary law of nations; in a similar way, the opinions and practices of intergovernmental human rights committees and courts claim authority in the domestic courts of the United States. Customary law notwithstanding, accession to the Covenant may significantly enlarge our obligations under human rights standards. Ideally, the Covenant provides the human rights advocate with what customary law is wanting: an authoritative, textual exposition of protected rights and routinized mechanisms for their enforcement.

The Covenant requires governments to observe a broad spectrum of standards in their treatment of individuals and provide remedies for violations. It is no less than an international bill of rights, part of an effort to codify the Universal Declaration of Human Rights, the United Nations' post-war proclamation of the rights of man ...

The General Assembly approved the text and opened the Covenant for ratification in 1966; at the prospect of accession, the United States demurred. It was not until 1977 that President Carter made the United

* Reprinted with the permission of the Harvard Human Rights Journal.

States a treaty signatory and asked the Senate to give its advice and consent to ratification ...

In 1991, President Bush requested the Senate's consent to ratification, but, seeking to limit U.S. obligations under the Covenant, submitted a package of formal reservations and qualifying statements. The Senate Foreign Relations Committee unanimously recommended the Covenant to the Senate, and the Senate voted in favor of ratification, subject to the Administration's proposed emendations. On June 8, 1992, the President deposited the signed instrument of ratification with the U.N. Secretary–General; three months later, on September 8, 1992, the treaty entered into force in the United States.

Criminal law is a principal area of concern in the Covenant. Rights guarantees in such areas as speech, assembly, and privacy limit the criminalization of conduct. The Covenant provides certain procedural protections to criminal suspects, the accused, and convicted prisoners,[3] and several provisions pertain to the conduct of criminal trials.[4] * * *

II.   Limitations on U.S. Obligations under the Covenant

The U.S. government took steps, in ratifying the Covenant, to minimize international scrutiny into its domestic policies. The Bush Administration hedged U.S. acceptance of the Covenant with reservations, understandings, and declarations ... To the qualifications proposed by President Bush, the Senate added the so-called "Helms proviso": the Covenant should not be read to require or authorize legislation or other action by the United States that the U.S. Constitution would prohibit.

On the international level, the United States has protected itself from effective legal oversight on its compliance with Covenant provisions, particularly in refusing to sign the treaty's Optional Protocol. Pursuant to the Optional Protocol, individuals whose protected rights have "been violated by State action" have filed complaints with the Human Rights Committee, the body established by the treaty to monitor compliance with its provisions ...

The enforcement mechanisms to which the United States is subject have little bite ...

3. The Covenant treats the following procedural topics: capital punishment, Covenant, art. 6; torture and lesser forms of brutality, art. 7; arbitrary arrest, art. 9(1); the right upon arrest to be informed of the charges, art. 9(2); prompt arraignment, art. 9(3); habeas corpus, art. 9(4); compensation for unlawful detention, art. 9(5); and prison conditions, art. 10; prosecution only for an act that was an offense at the time committed, art. 15(1).

4. A partial list: the right to a fair hearing, Covenant, art. 14(1); openness of court proceedings; the presumption of innocence, art. 14(2); the right to be informed in detail of the charges, art. 14(3)(a); an opportunity to prepare a defense, art. 14(3)(b); speedy trial, art. 14(3)(c); the right to defend oneself in person or through counsel of choice, including free counsel where required, art. 14(3)(d); the right to cross-examine prosecution witnesses and to compel the attendance of defense witnesses, art. 14(3)(e); assistance without charge of an interpreter, art. 14(3)(f); protection against self-incrimination, art. 14(3)(g); special proceedings for juveniles, art. 14(4); the right to appeal a conviction, art. 14(5); compensation for punishment under a false conviction, art. 14(6).

Article 2 mandates that states provide enforcement mechanisms through their domestic law. The United States government, however, entered a declaration in apparent opposition to this mandate. The declaration asserts that the prescriptive provisions of the Covenant (Articles 1 to 27) are not "self-executing": absent further action by the Congress to incorporate provisions into the domestic law, the courts may not enforce them. "The intent," explained the Foreign Relations Committee, was "to clarify that the Covenant will not create a private cause of action in U.S. courts * * *. [E]xisting U.S. law generally complies with the covenant; hence implementing legislation is not contemplated."

The Senate declaration has uncertain legal status. It is neither an Act of Congress, having the force of federal law, nor a reservation to the Covenant, having all the authority of treaty law under the Supremacy Clause....

––––––––––

Notes and Questions

1.   For more on U.S. "implementation" of the Covenant, see Henkin, *U.S. Ratification of Human Rights Conventions: The Ghost of Senator Bricker*, 89 AJIL 341 (1995); Henkin, Neuman, Orentlicher & Leebron, HUMAN RIGHTS 783, et seq. (1999). Treaties in U.S. law are either self-executing or non-self-executing. To determine whether treaty provisions are "self-executing," the Supreme Court examines the intent of the parties to the treaty: did the states parties to the covenant intend to confer legal rights upon individuals? If it is true that the U.S. already provides, by Constitution or statute, most of the rights granted by these covenants, what is to be gained or lost by binding the U.S. *by treaty*? To the extent that some of the rights granted by the Covenant are not already provided in U.S. law, should they be? Presumably the main purpose of the Covenant is to require states who become parties to raise their human rights standards to the level required. Is that purpose served when a nation makes reservations to provisions in the convention because they "go beyond its domestic law?"

The State Department's position with respect to the four human rights conventions submitted in 1978 can fairly be described as cautious. Why so hesitant? In December 1998, President Clinton issued an executive order to "implement the human rights treaties." Exec.Order No. 13107, 63 Fed.Reg. 68,991 (1998), declared that it is the policy and practice of the U.S. Government to respect and honor its obligations under the human rights treaties to the fullest extent. This includes the ICCPR, the Convention Against Torture, and against Genocide, among others. It orders the executive agencies to perform their functions so as to respect all relevant human rights obligations. What is the actual effect of this executive order?

––––––––––

4.   What is the influence of the International Criminal Courts on the International Minimum Standard? The question of whether there is an international minimum standard for justice, and if there is one, what is it, is a matter of serious debate today. Since the Nuremberg Trials, and with some momentum during the decade of the 1990's, and now moving into the 21st century, international tribunals have been created to prosecute crimes against humanity and war crimes. The Ad Hoc Tribunals for the former Yugoslavia and Rwanda and the Rome Statute for the International Criminal Court have had an impact on the evolution of an international minimum standard. These tribunals will be discussed more fully in Chapter 16, but a discussion of their impact on issues relating to an international minimum standard of a fair investigation, prosecution and trial follows immediately below.

Christopher L. Blakesley, Obstacles to the Creation of a Permanent War Crimes Tribunal

18, The Fletcher Forum of World Affairs 77 (1994).[5]

Basic notions of fairness and human rights in relation to investigation, prosecution, and trial are paramount, and are part of the minimum standard. *But what are these basic notions of fairness?* If we are not scrupulous in protecting individuals accused from abuses and deprivation of civil liberties, we will ultimately condemn the viability of an international criminal tribunal. Justice Jackson summed up the importance of this point in his opening statement during the Nuremberg Trial:"Before I discuss the particulars of evidence, some general considerations which may affect the credit of this trial in the eyes of the world should be candidly faced. There is a dramatic disparity between the circumstances of the accusers and the accused that might discredit our work if we should falter, in even minor matters, in being fair and temperate. Unfortunately, the nature of these crimes is such that both prosecution and judgment must be by victor nations over vanquished foes [*a problem (or blessing?) not faced by the Ad Hoc Tribunals for Rwanda or the former Yugoslavia or for the International Criminal Court*] * * * We must never forget that the record on which we judge these defendants is the record on which history will judge us tomorrow. To pass these defendants a poisoned chalice is to put it to our lips as well. We must summon such detachment and intellectual integrity to our task that this Trial will commend itself to posterity as fulfilling humanity's aspirations to do justice." Justice Robert H. Jackson, Chief Counsel for the Prosecution in the Nuremberg Trials, *Opening Statement,* delivered, November 20, 1945, *quoted in* Telford Taylor, The Anatomy of the Nuremberg Trials: A Personal Memoir 167–169 (1992).

Notes and Questions

1. *Is there an International Minimum Standard for Conviction of a Crime?* International human rights law provides the minimum standard of protection for an accused person. Increasingly, United States requests for extradition and renditions under status of forces agreements have been

---

5. (Reprinted with the permission of the Fletcher Forum of World Affairs), *also* *reprinted in* A.S.I.L. Classic & Contemp. Readings 281 (Ku & Diehl, eds., 1998).

overridden by international and foreign courts which have ruled that international human rights provisions take precedence. In two cases, concerns over capital punishment in the U.S. have resulted in litigation in which courts outside the United States have held that turning persons over to states with the death penalty (and the concomitant death row syndrome) would in certain circumstances violate provisions of international human rights conventions. *See, e.g., Soering v. U.S.* International human rights conventions contain analogues to many of the protections guaranteed by the U.S. Constitution, including the right to a fair trial, to "equality of arms" and access to court, to the presumption of innocence, to the right of confrontation, and to the right to counsel of choice. Though some of the international human rights protections meet, and even exceed, U.S. constitutional standards, some do not. Article 20(1) of the *Statute for the ICTY* provides that the "[t]rial chambers shall ensure that a trial is fair and expeditious and that proceedings are rendered in accordance with the rules of procedure and evidence, with full respect for the rights of the accused and due regard for the protection of victims and witnesses." The accused's Geneva Law and human right to consult a lawyer and to have adequate time to prepare a defense must be ensured. To be acceptable, this protection must be applicable to the entire process. *See also*, Lawyers Committee for Human Rights, *What Is a Fair Trial?: A Basic Guide to Legal Standards and Practice* (Oct. 1995) (focusing mainly on the International Covenant on Civil and Political Rights (ICCPR). *See*, especially, Covenant articles 6 and 14; and The American Convention on Human Rights (OAS Convention), art. 8 in the Documentary Supplement.

2. Do these sources meet the minimum standard? Do they help create one? Is there a right under customary international law to a fair trial? Is there customary international law providing what constitutes a fair trial? If so, is it equal to or less than U.S. constitutional standards? Are their standards more or less vague than those in the covenant for civil and political rights? Suppose that a U.S.–Serbian or U.S.–Rwandan dual national had been charged with violations of humanitarian law. Suppose that he was sought for prosecution before the relevant ad hoc tribunal. If he were present in the U.S., could the U.S. Government constitutionally send him to be prosecuted? If you were assigned as defense counsel, what would you argue? As prosecutor? If "minimum international standards" do not meet minimum U.S. constitutional standards, can our courts accept the U.S. participation in the creation of a court that does not apply the protections afforded U.S. citizens and send one there for prosecution? If so, upon what rationale? If not, why not? Do we do just that in extradition? Is there a difference? Is this extradition? *See, Surrender of Elizaphan Ntakirutimana*, 988 F.Supp. 1038 (S.D.Tex.1997), *reprinted in* 37 ILM 398 (1998); *Ntakirutimana v. Reno*, 184 F.3d 419, 430 (5th Cir.1999), *cert denied*, 120 S.Ct. 977 (2000). Does the U.S. extradite fugitives to countries without questioning the quality of their justice? For more on this see Chapter 16 on extradition.

3. Is evidence sufficient for probable cause required to bring an individual to trial under the statute of either *Ad Hoc Tribunal* or the Rome Statute for the ICC? The statutes are in the Documentary Supplement. Is proof beyond a reasonable doubt necessary for conviction? This standard has controlled in "Common Law countries" for over two hundred years. John

Locke and even the famous German Lutheran jurist, Samuel Pufendorf, linked the concept of *"conscience "*(similar to the French idea of *intime conviction*) to a sense of moral certainty and of proof beyond a reasonable doubt. The Israeli Supreme Court applied the reasonable doubt standard in the *Demjanjuk Case* studied in chapter 16. Is the "reasonable doubt" standard part of the international minimum standard? If so, what does it require? Must the evidence be sufficient to establish that there is no reasonable hypothesis or explanation of the evidence other than that of the defendant's guilt? If this standard is not part of the international minimum, what is the test?

4. *Has the Right of Confrontation become part of the International Minimum Standard?* If so, is cross-examination the only thing that constitutes confrontation? Should ex-parte affidavits or video-taped depositions, etc., be admissible at trial, or is their use inconsistent with the right to confrontation. Trial rights for defendants were taken verbatim from article 14(3)(e) of the International Covenant on Civil and Political Rights. Article 21(4) of the ICTY Statute provides the right of "accused person to examine or have examined the witnesses against him." The same is provided in the ICTR and the Rome Statute provides in Article 67(1)(a-g) that an accused has the right to be present at trial, to be represented by counsel, and to "examine or have examined" the witnesses against him. What does the term "have examined" mean in this context? Is it closer to eye to eye cross-examination required by the 6th Amendment to the U.S. Constitution or to the civil law systems' approach which allows a judge to do the questioning? Article 56 of the Rome Statute, which allows the Pre–Trial Chambers to take a deposition of a victim or witness, when the situation presents a unique opportunity, which may not present itself subsequently. This will be admissible at trial, based on the judge's view of its "probative value," its admissibility, and "any prejudice that such evidence may cause to a fair trial or to a fair evaluation of the testimony...." Rome Statute, art. 69(4). Does this rule protect victims and witnesses? If so, is the trade-off with the right to confrontation worth the benefit obtained? Does the Statute mix procedural and substantive issues (on the merits of the case) in a way that a jury trial would not do? Does the fact that the case is tried before a judge make a difference on this point? Does the reality that the Judge has authority in Article 69(3) to admit evidence on its own initiative, in the long-standing inquisitorial fashion. He or she may request the submission of evidence that he or she believes is, "necessary for the determination of the truth"? Finally, is it clear in Statute Article 67 (d) right to counsel is the same as that guaranteed by the U.S. 5th and 6th Amendments? Does it appear that this right obtains at the point of custodial interrogation as required by the 5th Amendment? What about at the pre-trial "critical stages," as the U.S. Supreme Court has required incident to the 6th Amendment? Finally, does it appear that the right to counsel obtains at all times after indictment? What do you think, especially given your reading of article 67 in light of Articles 21(4), 69(4), and Article 56, of the Rome Statute and the discussion in this paragraph? See further discussion below and in Chapter 16.

5. *Tension between the primary responsibility of a tribunal to ensure a fair trial and the obligation to protect victims and wit-*

nesses. To provide protections for the accused without adequate safeguards for victims of war crimes, rape, and torture risks not only severe psychological harm to those victims, but even jeopardizes their very lives and those of their family members. Supporters of perpetrators of such crimes often use militia or paramilitary forces to intimidate or harm the witnesses and victims. In the case of the former Yugoslavia, the ABA Task Force suggested that any derogation from the principle *against the use* of *ex-parte* affidavits should be limited to permitting their use as corroborative evidence in cases involving sexual assault against women, and that an *ex-parte* affidavit might be used at the investigatory stage, but not at trial.

Some have strong reservations about the use of the adversarial model of confrontation and cross-examination, unless adequate safeguards for rape and torture victims are incorporated. It is argued that, first, these procedural safeguards may be easily abused and cause distortion of the truth-seeking process. Second, the U.S. model disregards the legitimate rights and interests of the victim-witness. Third, the model assumes that other mechanisms in society will protect the victim-witness, which is unlikely in an international tribunal. Finally, the model lends itself to the further victimization of witnesses, including assassination and other forms of reprisals and harassment. Hence, while it is clear that human rights norms require some sort of confrontation-type examination (or the right to have examined), there is disagreement over what that means and should mean in the international tribunal context. Whatever approach one takes presents serious problems.

In a meeting held under the auspices of the International Scientific and Professional Advisory Council (ISPAC) in Spain on 3 May 1993, several recommendations were made with a view to protecting victims and witnesses while still providing for the accused's right to confrontation. Suggested protections included adding the following passage to Article 21 (*Rights of the Accused*) paragraph 4(e) of the Statute for the Ad Hoc Tribunal: "With regard to child witnesses this examination will be restricted to questions through the Tribunal only. In other cases where the International Tribunal considers it appropriate for the protection of the witness, it may similarly restrict the questioning." Article 18 (*Investigation and Preparation of Indictment*) paragraph 3 was to be amended to include: "The views and concerns of victims shall be presented and considered at appropriate stages of the proceedings where their personal interests are affected, without prejudice to the accused and consistent with the other rules of the International Tribunal." Further, it was recommended that the Tribunal "[take] into account the victims' needs for privacy and their special sensitivities. For example, screens or facilities for giving evidence from a separate room and separate waiting areas for defence and prosecution witnesses can be provided for protection. In this context, child victims should be offered special protection and interview procedures." These recommendations were taken into account for the Rules of Evidence and Procedure in both the Rwanda and the Yugoslavia Ad Hoc Tribunals. The principle behind the adoption was based on the U.N. Declaration on Victims, which was carried forward to be adopted in the Rome Statute for the International Criminal Court. The ICC Statute provides in article 68, that "special measures" must be taken to protect victims and witnesses, because their fear of retribution, public humiliation or other harm to them or their families may be a stumbling block for them to take part in any proceedings. "Special measures" include excluding the public from the hearing, use of electronic or special means to transmit testimony, increased security, counseling where appropriate, or any other measure that the judge deems proper. *See*, The Rome Statute of the International Criminal Court (ICC) [Statute], U.N. Doc. A/CONF.183/9, *reissued for technical reasons,* July 17, 1998, at art. 68. Protection for victims and witnesses has proved quite valuable for the ICTR and the ICTY, although the quality of protection has sometimes gone wanting. The Statute also provides, in article 75(2), for the deciding court to make appropriate compensation to the victims of the person convicted.

This is somewhat related to the rules in the Rome Statute that are designed to protect victims and witnesses.

Even if done well, would these safeguards be sufficient for the victims, the witnesses, and the accused? Providing some of the traditional Anglo–American, *"adversarial,"* safeguards for the accused without establishing serious protective measures for victims will simply ensure that no victims will come forth, or if they do, that the risk of harm will be significant. Not including them will render the tribunal suspect. The international community would run the risk of facing another fiasco such as that at the Leipzig Trials. The result may be no serious or important convictions, but plenty of trauma for the victims and witnesses. *Does this discussion suggest that there is or is not an international minimum standard for a fair trial?*

———

g.   Other situations raising questions about "a minimum international standard." The *"Michael Fay "*incident in Singapore again raised issues of whether there was a "minimum standard." Michael Fay had been charged with vandalism, among other offenses. Fay claimed that he was coerced into confessing,. The result of his confession was sentencing to four months in prison and *caning (six "lashes"* with a ratan "cane"). The caning part of his sentence was eventually "commuted" to four lashes. The reader may also recall the incident in which Malaysia executed (hanged) a young Australian who had smuggled drugs into that country, apparently naively believing that if he traveled first class, he would not be searched at customs. These were punishments meted out to locals and to foreign nationals within the country. What do these cases indicate about an international minimum standard?

———

h.   Do Prisoner Transfer or Mutual Cooperation in Criminal Matters Treaties promote a minimum standard? Many nations warn their nationals when they travel that methods of justice may be different abroad. They have attempted to ameliorate their situation through *prisoner transfer treaties.* The U.S. is party to 12 bilateral Prisoner transfer treaties and is a party to the Council of Europe (COE) Convention on the Transfer of Sentenced Persons, referred to as the "Strasbourg Convention" by European nations. For a graphic account of brutal treatment of U.S. nationals arrested by Mexican authorities and convicted there for illegal importation of cocaine *see Rosado v. Civiletti*, 621 F.2d 1179 (2d Cir.1980). Sentenced to eight years and nine months imprisonment, they were subsequently transferred to complete their sentences in the U.S., under the terms of the U.S.–Mexico treaty. They subsequently sought release from confinement in the U.S., claiming that they had been coerced into consenting to their transfer and that their continued detention was a deprivation of due process. The court denied their motion for release, holding that they had consented voluntarily and intelligently.

On prisoner transfer treaties generally, *see* Michael Abbell and Bruno Ristau, 6 INTERNATIONAL JUDICIAL ASSISTANCE (*Vol. 6, Prisoner Transfers*) (Looseleaf, 1990); Theodore Simon & Richard D. Atkins, *Prisoner Transfer Treaties: Crucial Times Ahead*, in THE ALLEGED TRANSNATIONAL OFFENDER 69 (Atkins ed. 1995); Michael Plachta, *Human Rights Aspects of the Prisoner Transfer in a Comparative Perspective*, 53 La.L.Rev. 1043 (1993).

---

i. *Mutual Assistance Treaties*. An ever-growing web of bilateral and multilateral treaties, executive agreements, and memoranda of understanding enable governments to obtain information on various offenses. *See*, Christopher Blakesley, Albin Eser, Otto Lagodny, THE INDIVIDUAL IN THE FACE OF INTERNATIONAL COOPERATION IN CRIMINAL MATTERS (Max–Planck Inst. 2001). Bruce Zagaris, *A Brave New World: Recent Developments in anti-Money Laundering and Related Litigation Traps for the Unwary in International Trust Matters*, 32 Vand.J.Transnat'l L. 1023 (1999).

j. *Do Status of Forces Agreement [S.O.F.A.] help create a minimum standard?* The United States has concluded agreements with states on whose territory U.S. military forces are stationed. Among other matters, these agreements allocate jurisdiction over criminal offenses committed by members of the forces. In general, duty-related offenses are triable by U.S. authorities. Other offenses by the receiving state. The NATO SOFA, June 19, 1951, [1953] 4 U.S.T. 1792, 199 U.N.T.S. 67, provides the principles governing criminal trials conducted by the receiving state when it exercises its jurisdiction. Paragraph 9 of Article VII states: [w]henever a member of a force or civilian component or a dependent is prosecuted under the jurisdiction of a receiving State he shall be entitled

(a) to a prompt and speedy trial;

(b) to be informed, in advance of trial, of the specific charge or charges made against him;

(c) to be confronted with the witnesses against him;

(d) to have compulsory process for obtaining witnesses in his favor, if they are within the jurisdiction of the receiving State;

(e) to have legal representation of his own choice for his defence or to have free or assisted legal representation under the conditions prevailing for the time being in the receiving State;

(f) if he considers it necessary, to have the services of a competent interpreter; and

(g) to communicate with a representative of the Government of the sending State and, when the rules of the court permit, to have such a representative present at his trial.

Are these guarantees different from those which would be provided under an international minimum standard in accordance with ordinary standards of civilization? Would all the members of NATO provide these guarantees without reference to the agreement? Does paragraph 9 incorporate into status of forces jurisprudence the guarantees of the United States Constitution?

k.   *Raising the Minimum Standard?* In some situations, European nations may afford more protection than the U.S.: *Short v. Kingdom of the Netherlands,* 92 ILM 1388 (1990). See the following discussion.

Jurisdiction—NATO Status of Forces Agreement–U.S. Serviceman Charged With Criminal Offenses Overseas European Convention on Human Rights

85 AJIL 698, 701 (1991) (footnotes omitted).*

* * *

The *Short* case represents perhaps the most serious example of this dilemma. On March 30, 1988, Staff Sergeant Charles D. Short, a member of theU.S. Air Force stationed at Soesterberg Air Base in the Netherlands, was arrested by the Dutch Royal Marechaussee (military police) as a suspect in the murder of his wife, a Turkish national. At some point during his interrogation, SSgt Short admitted killing his wife, dismembering her, and placing her remains in plastic bags by a dike somewhere near Amsterdam. Depending on such additional factors as his state of mind at the time of the murder, SSgt Short clearly might have been charged with capital murder under the Uniform Code of Military Justice. Knowing this, the Dutch authorities refused to turn him over to his superiors at the *Soesterberg base.* Although the NATO SOFA vested jurisdiction over this offense in the United States, the Dutch rationale for refusing to comply with that treaty was that to do so would subject SSgt Short to the risk of capital punishment.

The path this case traveled through the Dutch courts was just as interesting to the U.S. military as the High Court's ultimate refusal to surrender SSgt Short. Requests for the surrender of visiting force members to the state with primary jurisdiction are generally made and approved (or disapproved) at the lowest levels possible. Rarely will the host nation's courts get involved; the local police chief or prosecutor is usually the decisional authority. SSgt Short's case was destined to be different when his appointed Dutch attorney's first act was to secure a local court

* Reprinted with the permission of the American Society of Int'l Law.

injunction preventing his surrender. After a full hearing, the civil trial court at The Hague acknowledged that the NATO SOFA gave the United States primary jurisdiction over the alleged offense. Nevertheless, it refused to allow the Dutch Government to surrender SSgt Short because the Netherlands was bound by the Sixth Protocol to the European Convention not to subject anyone to the risk of capital punishment. The court added that it would order his surrender to U.S. authorities only if they could guarantee that the death penalty either would not be imposed or would not be carried out. For policy and legal reasons, the Commander in Chief, United States Air Forces in Europe (CinCUSAFE), refused to give such assurances.

While the Dutch Ministry of Justice appealed the civil trial court's decision, a Dutch criminal trial court convicted SSgt Short of manslaughter and sentenced him to six years' imprisonment. Very shortly thereafter, the civil appeals court in The Hague reversed the initial civil court decision on the ground that the NATO SOFA allocates primary jurisdiction to the United States. Instead of interpreting the Convention and Dutch law as superseding the SOFA, it construed them as consistent with it: since the SOFA exempted Short from Dutch criminal jurisdiction, it also removed him from its civil and convention-based jurisdiction. Thus, the latter laws and treaty did not apply. The appeals court accordingly ordered his surrender but agreed to stay execution of its judgment until the High Court had an opportunity to review it.

At this point, the decisions of the criminal trial court and the civil appeals court conflicted. Both were appealed. The criminal appeals court reversed the criminal trial court, holding that since the United States had jurisdiction, Dutch courts lacked authority to hear the criminal case. The Dutch High Court (Hoge Raad), however, reversed the civil appeals court, ruling that the state's obligations under the Convention must prevail over the conflicting SOFA allocation of jurisdiction. This double reversal led to an even more frightening paradox: unless either decision was somehow reversed, the ultimate result would be that SSgt Short—by his own admission, a brutal murderer—would be a free man in the Netherlands. Both judgments stood.

———

3. HUMAN RIGHTS AND THE EXHAUSTION OF LOCAL REMEDIES. THE INTERHANDEL CASE (*Switzerland v. U.S.*), [1959] I.C.J.Rep. 6, 27, held that "[t]he rule that local remedies must be exhausted before international proceedings may be instituted is a well-established rule of customary international law. It has been generally observed in cases in which a state has adopted the cause of its national where rights are claimed to have been disregarded in another State in violation of international law. Before resort may be had to an international court in such a situation, it has been considered necessary that the State where the violation occurred should have an opportunity to redress it by its own means, within the framework of its own domestic legal system." *See, e.g.*, the American Convention on Human Rights, art. 46 (1)(a), Nov. 22, 1969, OEA/Ser. K/XVI/1.1, doc 65 rev. 1 corr. (1970); European Convention for the Protection of Human Rights and Fundamental Freedoms, art. 26, Nov. 4, 1950, 213 UNTS 222; and the *Optional Protocol to the U.N. Covenant on Civil & Political Rights*, 999 UNTS 171, arts. 1–2 (1967). The rule is applicable to claims based upon violations of personal human rights as well as to claims arising from violations of property rights. In view of the exhaustion of local remedies rule, how can a claimant state assert that the acting state has violated its own law? If, for example, an individual has been imprisoned for a long time before trial and complains of this through appropriate court proceedings until a court of final appeal has ruled that the local law does not prohibit such imprisonment, can an international tribunal properly hold that there has been a violation of local law? In the *Roberts Case*, the commission asserted that Roberts' imprisonment was a violation of the Mexican Constitution. Does Article V of the General Claims Convention governing the Roberts arbitration provide the answer?

> The High Contracting Parties, being desirous of effecting an equitable settlement of the claims of their respective citizens thereby affording them just and adequate compensation for their losses or damages, agree that no claim shall be disallowed or rejected by the Commission by the application of the general principle of international law that the legal remedies must be exhausted as a condition precedent to the validity or allowance of any claim.

C.F. Amerasinghe, in his book LOCAL REMEDIES IN INTERNATIONAL LAW (1990) argues that the exhaustion of remedies rule applies to human rights cases. A.A. Cançado Trindate, reviewing Amerasinghe's book, counters:

> * * * to claim that the local remedies rule should be applied in human rights protection exactly as diplomatic protection, to claim that the content or scope of the rule is not affected by contextual differences, and, in particular, by considerations of superior common values or *ordre public* in respect of the protection of the rights of the human person and not of the state, is to close one's eyes to reality. Generally recognized rules of international law, besides undergoing an evolution of their own within the contexts in which they are applied, necessarily undergo, when enshrined in human rights treaties, some adjustment, dictated by the special character of the object and purpose of those treaties and by the generally recognized specificity of the international protection of human rights.

> This is the lesson drawn from the experience accumulated in this domain; progress in the international protection of human rights has been made possible in the last decades, as well as in relation to the operation of the local remedies rule, by an awareness of the specificity of this *droit de protection* (which calls for an interpretation of its own), by a proper understanding of the basic premises underlying the mechanisms of protection and by faithful pursuit of their object and purpose. It is fortunate that international supervisory organs in the domain of

human rights protection have espoused an understanding of the local remedies rule and have proceeded on a basis wholly at variance with [its application in matters of diplomatic protection]. 86 AJIL 626, 631 (1992) (reprinted by permission).

Still, the exhaustion of remedies rule is the most commonly asserted preliminary objection before human rights tribunals and commissions, but it is subject to exceptions. Domestic remedies must be adequate and effective. If it is clear that exhaustion of local remedies would be futile, incapable of producing a meaningful result, or if the remedy is not applied impartially by the government, or if it is a senseless formality, the claimant will be exempted from pursuing them. For example, the Inter–American Court of Human Rights granted jurisdiction on the ground that there were no meaningful local remedies to exhaust in Honduras, in *Valásquez Rodriguez Case,* Inter.Am.Ct.H.Rts., OAS_ser. L._V._III.19, doc. 13 (1988), 28 I.L.M. 291, 305–06 (1989); *see also,* the *Fairen Garbi & Solis Corrales Case,* Merits, Inter–Am.Ct.H.R., Jdt. of March 15, 1989, Ser. C, No. 6; *see also,* Claudio Grossman, *Moving Toward Improved Human Rights Enforcement in the Americas,* 27–Sum Hum.Rts. 16, 17–18 (2000); Pasqualucci, *Preliminary Objections Before the Inter–American Court of Human Rights: Legitimate Issues & Legitimate Tactics,* 40 Va.J.Int'l L. 1 (1999).

SECTION B.   THE ARTICULATION OF HUMAN RIGHTS STANDARDS

INTRODUCTION

The Optional Protocol to the International Covenant on Civil and Political Rights, [U.N.Doc. A_6316 (1966), 999 UNTS 302] provides in article 5, that the Human Rights Committee may hear submissions by individuals without exhaustion of local remedies, "where the application of the [local] remedies is unreasonably prolonged." This has created a body of law through the Human Rights Committee, providing that gross violations of human rights will have a remedy, including the obligation to pay adequate compensation to victims or their families. Gross violations of human rights have been deemed to include violations of fundamental freedoms, the crime of genocide, torture or other cruel, inhuman or degrading treatment or punishment, systematic racial discrimination, and a consistent pattern of gross violations of internationally recognized human rights. *See,* van Boven, *Special Rapporteur,* for the *Study Concerning Right to Restitution, Compensation and Rehabilitation for Victims of Gross Violations of Human Rights and Fundamental Freedoms,* U.N.Doc. E_CN.4_Sub.2_10, at 8 (1990); *reported in* Lee, *The Preventive Approach to the Refugee Problem,* 28 Willamette L.Rev. 821 (1992); Shelton, *Individual Complaint Machinery Under the U.N. 1503 Procedure & the Optional Protocol to the International Covenant on Civil and Political Rights,* in GUIDE TO INTERNATIONAL HUMAN RIGHTS PRACTICE 59, 62 (1984). Consider the following:

Beth Van Schaack, In Defense of Civil Redress: The Domestic Enforcement of Human Rights Norms in the Context of the Proposed Hague Judgments Convention

42 Harvard International Law Journal 141, 161–162 (2001)*

Institutions based on the U.N. Charter, international multilateral treaties, or regional agreements typically address state responsibility and norm compliance but do not assign liability to individual defendants, generate enforceable remedies, or provide victims with a judicial forum in which to bear witness and confront their abusers. For example, the Human Rights Committee ("the Committee") of the International Covenant on Civil and Political Rights (ICCPR) is one of the few international treaty-based bodies empowered to receive human rights complaints from individuals. The Committee can entertain communications from victims of violations of the ICCPR at the hands of a State Party, but the Committee cannot consider violations by private entities rather than states themselves. Not all Parties to the ICCPR have ratified the Optional Protocol, and the Committee may not receive complaints against States Parties that have not done so.

Further, the Committee is not an adjudicatory body. Instead, it employs a policy of constructive dialogue that limits the Committee to "forward[ing] its views" to the individual and government concerned and to seeking "explanations or statements clarifying the matter." There is no judicial process, confrontation between the parties, investigation, oral hearings or formal judgment, and no perpetrator is identified or held individually liable. The Committee can recommend specific remedies for victims, but it has little leverage to ensure that states implement these recommendations. As such, the case is effectively closed once the Committee forwards its views.

Individuals may convey communications to the U.N. Sub–Commission on the Promotion and Protection of Human Rights ("the Sub–Commission") alleging human rights abuses within both member and non-member states. This is the only U.N. procedure capable of accepting individual petitions. In order for such petitions to be admissible, they must be submitted within a reasonable time after the exhaustion of local remedies, provided such remedies are "effective and not unreasonably prolonged." This procedure was designed for the consideration of systematic violations of human rights by states, as opposed to individual or isolated violations. Allegations of singular incidents involving human rights violations will be considered as evidence of such patterns if they are of sufficient quantity. However, these individual cases do not give rise to judgments or remedies in and of themselves. In fact, the Sub-Commission may refuse to consider a situation that is not sufficiently serious or systematic, notwithstanding that a violation has clearly occurred.

Further, the authors of such communications are denied direct involvement in the process of review; once a communication is filed the dispute

---

* Reprinted with the permission of the   notes omitted.
Harvard Journal of International Law. Foot-

becomes a confidential matter between the Sub–Commission (or the entire Commission) and that state. The outcome may be a decision by the entire Human Rights Commission to conduct a thorough study of, or investigation within, the state complained against, with or without the consent of the state. Despite the potential of such bodies, international adjudicatory mechanisms in the U.N. system remain inherently ineffective.

———

A new view of the older precedents. The flow of third party decisions on questions of human rights violations practically ceased with World War II. It has been observed that the desire of states for freedom to act unilaterally has been strong during the whole life of the United Nations and that states have been reluctant to take disputes to the International Court of Justice. Leo Gross said: "[i]t may be noted in this context that, whereas the number of arbitral decisions since 1945 was not spectacular, it was not insignificant, although it is probably true that, as the Secretary General of the United Nations pointed out, 'most of them concerned minor questions, many of them of a commercial nature, which were not in the least likely to disturb peace and security.' " Leo Gross, *The International Court of Justice: Consideration of Requirements for Enhancing its Role in the International Legal Order,* 65 AJIL 253, 268 (1971). Is this more or less true today? The U.N. has made the development of new legal norms protecting human rights a matter of major concern. Today is it possible for arbitral commissions, domestic, or international courts to ignore the Universal Declaration of Human Rights or the relevant human rights conventions or customary law promulgated in recent decades?

1. THEORIES OF HUMAN RIGHTS

Natural Law

De Vattel, The Law of Nations or Principles of the Law of Nature, Applied to the Conduct and Affairs of Nations and Sovereigns (1758)

Book II ch. VI, p. 162 (Chitty, ed. 1849).

§ 71. * * * [I]t remains for us to examine what share a state may have in the actions of her citizens, and what are the rights and obligations of sovereigns in this respect.

Whoever offends the state, injures its rights, disturbs its tranquility, or does it a prejudice in any manner whatsoever, declares himself its enemy, and exposes himself to be justly punished for it. Whoever uses a citizen ill, indirectly offends the state, which is bound to protect this citizen; and the sovereign of the latter should avenge his wrongs, punish the aggressor, and, if possible, oblige him to make full reparation; since otherwise the citizen would not obtain the great end of the civil association, which is, safety.

§ 72. But, on the other hand, the nation or the sovereign, ought not to suffer the citizens to do an injury to the subjects of another state, much less to offend that state itself: and this, not only because no sovereign ought to permit those who are under his command to violate the precepts of the law of nature, which forbids all injuries,—but also because nations ought mutually to respect each other, to abstain from all offence from all injury, from all wrong,—in a word, from every thing that may be of prejudice to others. If a sovereign, who might keep his subject within the rules of justice and peace, suffers them to injure a foreign nation either in its body or its members, he does not less injury to that nation than if he injured it himself. In short, the safety of the state, and that of human society, requires this attention from every sovereign. If you let loose the reigns to your subjects against foreign nations, these will behave in the same manner to you; and, instead of that friendly intercourse which nature has established between all men, we shall see nothing but one vast and dreadful scene of plunder between nation and nation.

During the reign of *"Natural Law,"* it was a matter of principle that the law protected individuals from certain abuses. *John Locke provided the following thoughts:*

John Locke, Second Treatise of Government (1690) in Two Treatises of Government

§ 123, p. 368 (critical edition 1963).

Of the Ends of Political Society and Government.

If Man in the State of Nature be so free, as has been said; If he be absolute Lord of his own Person and Possessions, equal to the greatest, and subject to no Body, why will he part with his Freedom? Why will he give up this Empire, and subject himself to the Dominion and Controul of any other Power? To which 'tis obvious to Answer, that though in the state of Nature he hath such a right, yet the Enjoyment of it is very uncertain, and constantly exposed to the Invasion of others. For all being Kings as much as he, every Man his Equal, and the greater part no strict Observers of Equity and Justice, the enjoyment of the property he has in this state is very unsafe, very unsecure. This makes him willing to quit a Condition, which however free, is full of fears and continual dangers: And 'tis not without reason, that he seeks out, and is willing to joyn in Society with others who are already united, or have a mind to unite for the mutual *Preservation* of their Lives, Liberties and Estates, which I call by the general Name, *Property*.

Positivism

British Law Officers Opinion in the Silesian Loan Case

1753, in 2 McNair, International Law Opinions, (Cambridge 1956) 303–304.

In the famous Report of the Law Officers of 18 January 1753 upon what is known as the Silesian Loan, the matter is touched upon incidentally. It was signed by Lee, Paul, Ryder and Murray (then Solicitor–General, later Lord Chief Justice Mansfield). * * * If the Matter of Complaint be a Capture at Sea during War, and the Question relative to Prize, he ought to apply to the Judicatures established to try these Questions.

The Law of Nations, founded upon Justice, Equity, Convenience and the Reason of the Thing, and confirmed by long Usage, don't allow of Reprizals, except in Case of violent Injuries, directed or supported by the State, and Justice, absolutely denied, *in Re minime dubiâ,* by all the Tribunals, and afterwards by the Prince.

When the Judges are left free, and give Sentence according to their Conscience, though it should be erroneous, that would be no Ground for Reprizals. Upon doubtful Questions, different Men think and judge differently; and all a Friend can desire, is, that Justice should be as impartially administered to him, as it is to the Subjects of that Prince, in whose Courts the Matter is try'd.

On 6 November 1819, Robinson, in reporting upon certain depredations upon British trade by armed vessels acting under the orders of the captain-general of Valencia, which amounted "to an absolute denial of justice or failure of justice on appeal by reason of the acts of a principal officer of the Spanish Government", remarked:

The ancient remedy in such cases was by granting Special Letters of Reprizal to the injured party. But that practice has been disused, not on account of any intrinsic injustice in the principle, but on account of the inconveniences attending it. The remedy of Force however must always remain the last resort of the injured Government. But it is a question of extreme delicacy when and in what manner it may be expedient to use it.

———

Notes & Questions: Do philosophical positivists recognize the validity of Human Rights law? Can they, given their position on the status of the individual in international law? If they can, how do they rationalize this acceptance? For more detail and writings of Austin and others, see Ch. 17 *infra.*

"Cross–Cultural Perspectives"

Abdullahi Ahmed An'na'im

Human Rights in Cross–Cultural Perspectives, pp. 1–6 (1992).*

* * * [A] cross-cultural approach may be helpful in deepening our understanding of the underlying causes of the continuing discrepancy between the theory and practice of human rights, and in addressing those causes more effectively. Clearly, the credibility and practical efficacy of national and international human rights standards would be enhanced by increasing their legitimacy in the widest possible range of cultural traditions. Current and foreseeable new human rights cannot be seen as truly

* Reprinted with the permission of University of Pennsylvania Press.

universal unless they are conceived and articulated within the widest possible range of cultural traditions.

The term *culture* is used here in its broadest sense as the "totality of values, institutions and forms of behavior transmitted within a society * * * this wide conception of culture covers *Weltanschauung* [world view], ideologies and cognitive behavior." In this sense, liberalism and Marxism, for example, are part of, or ideological manifestations of, the culture of some societies. As normative propositions, human rights are much more credible and thereby stand a better chance of implementation if they are perceived to be legitimate within the various cultural traditions of the world.

Some scholars and political leaders have argued that the current international standards of human rights, together with the machinery for promoting and implementing them, may not be sufficiently universal because they lack legitimacy in major cultural traditions. Others argue that these standards and machinery are universal because the vast majority of governments have either participated in the formulation process or subsequently ratified the relevant international instruments. They also warn against the dangers of claiming cultural relativity as a pretext for justifying human rights violations. While appreciating that the first position might be adopted cynically to justify human rights violations, and that the second position might reflect undue formalism or naive idealism, I suggest that a constructive approach can draw on the element of truth in each position in order to enhance the credibility and efficacy of international human rights standards.

* * * [It] is not realistic to deny the real or apparent insufficiency of cultural legitimacy of some human rights standards. Because there are obvious areas of conflict and tension between the current international standards of human rights and major cultural traditions, relativist arguments often seem plausible. Nevertheless, the dangers of extreme relativism should not be underestimated. My view, therefore, is that scholars and activists should neither underestimate the challenge of cultural relativism to the universality of human rights nor concede too much to its claims. Rather, it is preferable to adopt a constructive approach that recognizes the problems and addresses them in the context of each cultural tradition, as well as across cultural boundaries.

The proposed approach seeks to explore the possibilities of cultural reinterpretation and reconstruction through *internal cultural discourse and cross-cultural dialogue,* as a means to enhancing the universal legitimacy of human rights. * * *

Since cultural norms and attitudes influence individual and collective or institutional human behavior, one may reasonably expect cultural antagonism toward some human rights standards to diminish the efficacy of these standards in a particular society. Although such antagonism may reflect the prevailing or dominant view of the cultural position, it may not necessarily be the only available view. There may therefore be room for changing a cultural position from within, through *internal discourse* about the fundamental values of the culture and the rationale for these values. * * *

Feminist Approaches.

Are women's human rights different from those of men? If so, how and why? Does feminist legal scholarship provide different perspective from which to consider human rights law? *See generally*, WOMEN AND INTERNATIONAL HUMAN RIGHTS LAW (3 vols., Askin & Koenig, eds. 1999–2000); White & Blakesley, *Women or Rights: How Should Women's Rights be Conceived & Implemented*, Ch 3, in II WOMEN AND INTERNATIONAL HUMAN RIGHTS LAW, *supra*, at 50 (2000).

Hilary Charlesworth, Feminist Methods in International Law

93 AJIL 379 (1999) (footnotes omitted).

. . . I am conscious of the limits of my analysis and its unrepresentativeness—the particularity of my nationality, race, class, sexuality, education and profession shapes my outlook and ideas on international law. I clearly cannot speak for all women participants in and observers of the international legal system . . . My reservations are also more general because presenting feminism as one of seven rival methodological traditions may give a false sense of its nature . . . I do not see feminist methods as ready alternatives to any of the other methods represented in this symposium. Feminist methods emphasize conversations and dialogue rather than the production of a single, triumphant truth. They will not lead to neat "legal" answers because they are challenging the very categories of "law" and "nonlaw." Feminist methods seek to expose and question the limited bases of international law's claim to objectivity and impartiality and insist on the importance of gender relations as a category of analysis. The term "gender" here refers to the social construction of differences between women and men and ideas of "femininity" and "masculinity"—the excess cultural baggage associated with biological sex. * * *

Editor's Question: *If feminist approaches challenge the very categories of law vs. non-law, as Professor Charlesworth states, does that not belie her claim that they do not attempt to establish one triumphant truth?*

[Professor Charlesworth continues]:

In writing about feminist perspectives on the law concerning human rights abuses in armed conflict, I am conscious that I am able to do so precisely because I am not at daily risk of these harms . . .

. . .

I think that this impurity is inevitable in the analysis of complex situations. Feminist investigations of international law require "situated judgment" rather than an overarching theory to work out the most appropriate technique at any time.

. . .

How might a feminist international lawyer approach the specific question of individual accountability for human rights abuses in armed conflict? There is considerable empirical evidence that women are affected by armed conflict in ways that men are not. The savagery of warfare seems closely linked to a wild form of male sexuality, a type of "toxic testosterone" in Michael Ignatieff's words, and women and girls are the most obvious objects of this violence. Rape has been understood as one of the spoils of the victor, serving also to humiliate the vanquished. Globally, women form only 2 percent of regular army personnel, but as civilians they suffer disproportionately from armed conflict. For example, women and children constitute the majority of the victims in African conflict zones. In northern Uganda, young girls have been abducted to become the "wives" of commanders in the Lord's Resistance Army, which is fighting President Musuveni's government forces. In refugee camps, women tend to be responsible for the collection of food, fuel and water, requiring them to venture from the relative safety of the camps and thus to risk rape, torture and death from rebels, government soldiers and land mines. Women's lower social status also disadvantages them in the "relief" operations conducted during and after armed conflict. For example, in Somalia relief agencies often consult "household heads" when making decisions about the distribution of food and medicines, and these are usually regarded as the men. In Uganda women survivors of decades of conflict claim that reproductive health has not been adequately attended to in relief work. Violence against women has been described more generally as "among the most serious and pervasive human rights abuses that the international community [now] confront[s]." Nongovernmental organizations have chronicled, in particular, massive violence against women during armed conflict in Bosnia and Rwanda and the failure of their governments, international donors, humanitarian organizations, and reconstruction and development agencies to respond to women's needs in the "postwar" period.

Whether and how individuals should be held criminally accountable for human rights abuses in internal conflicts has increasingly exercised international lawyers. These questions have been prompted by the fact that the major overt manifestation of tension in the international community has shifted from wars between states to armed conflicts within states. What directions do feminist methodologies suggest for analyzing international law in this area? On one level, the acknowledgment of women's lives and the use of the vocabulary of gender in the statutes of the ad hoc Tribunals for the former Yugoslavia and for Rwanda and the international criminal court (ICC) might suggest that feminist activism has had a progressive effect on the law. On another level, it appears that even the "new" international criminal law remains primarily a system based on men's lives.

International law has traditionally drawn a distinction between the principles of individual conduct that apply in times of armed conflict (international humanitarian law, IHL) and those that operate in peacetime (human rights law). This dichotomy has led to many anomalies and inconsistencies. From a feminist perspective, the distinction has allowed IHL, with its basis in codes of warriors' honor, to factor out issues that do not relate to the warrior caste. For example, the guardian of IHL, the International Committee of the Red Cross (ICRC), was able to consider the

Taliban's exclusion of women from any workplace in Afghanistan as completely outside its mandate. Ignatieff has described the self-imposed constraints of the ICRC in this situation: "Its legitimacy depends on its working with warriors and warlords: if they insist that women be kept out of sight, it has no choice but to go along." The honor of warriors has nothing to say about the oppression of women. Human rights law, while more expansive in its coverage than IHL, has, as indicated above, provided a more limited response to the harms that women generally face compared with those confronting men. International criminal law, the topic of this symposium, is an amalgam of IHL and human rights law. In many ways, it has combined the gendered blind spots of both traditions.

... What is the nature of international legal knowledge in this context? What knowledge is privileged and what knowledge is silenced and devalued? ....

Notes & Questions. Is it really true that to consider mass rape and rape as a military and political strategy part of public international law renders all other rapes of lesser importance? If so, why? If not, why not? Is it helpful or harmful to the protection of women and men to suggest that rape of women, punishable as a common crime, is a violation of human rights, but that the common crime of murder of men (or women) is not? Is this what Professor Charlesworth is suggesting? Is she suggesting that the "hate crime model" is the one to apply? Is that model helpful or not? On this issue, *see*, John V. White & Christopher Blakesley, *Women or Rights: How Should Women's Rights Be Conceived?*, in II WOMEN & INTERNATIONAL HUMAN RIGHTS LAW 51–75 (2000).

Critical Race Theory.

See, gen., Wing, *Critical Race Feminism and International Human Rights of Women in Bosnia, Palestine, and south Africa: Issues for Lat Crit Theory*, 28 U. Miami Inter–Am. L. Rev. 337 (1997); White & Blakesley, *Women or Rights: How Should Women's Rights be Conceived & Implemented*, Ch 3, in II WOMEN AND INTERNATIONAL HUMAN RIGHTS LAW, *supra*, at 51 (2000).

2. HUMAN RIGHTS PROVISIONS OF THE U.N. CHARTER

Articles 1, 2, 55, and 56 are the most commonly cited articles in the UN Charter for their human rights content. Read each carefully.

Highlights of the drafting history of Chapter IX & Article 56 of the Charter. Some say that article 56 imposes an international legal obligation on states to take immediate national action to correct internal human rights deficiencies. Others claim that it serves merely as a statement of political principle that human rights are important. What do you think? The U.S. government was particularly concerned that nothing in Chapter IX, "be construed as giving authority to the 'Organization' to intervene in the domestic affairs of member states." *See*, 10 *U.N.Conf.Int'l Org.* 83 (1945). At one point, the U.S. position was that the Charter Article 2(7) reservation for domestic jurisdiction would not be sufficient by itself to keep human rights from becoming matters of international concern, as long as Article 56 were worded to include a pledge by members "to take such independent action as they deem appropriate to achieve these purposes within their own territories.'' The U.S. ultimately supported the language of Article 56, however, without insisting upon a special reservation to retain domestic jurisdiction over human rights matters. *Id.*, at 161. As to the nature of the commitment, the following submission from a drafting sub-committee was rejected: ''[a]ll members undertake to cooperate jointly and severally with the Organization for the achievement of these purposes.'' The proposal for a pledge to take ''independent action,'' was also rejected. The ultimate language as found in the charter includes toe term, ''*separate action* in cooperation with the Organization.'' *Id.*, at 139, *emphasis supplied*. Do you think that this is the best solution?

The Meaning of Article 56

In the formative stages of the United Nations the members sought to give content to the commitments made in Article 56. An obvious place to begin was South Africa's practice of apartheid. The South African Government responded that the U.N. was, by the law of the Charter, forbidden to intervene in its domestic jurisdiction, including its ''racial policy.'' This presented very sharply the issue of whether the U.N. had broken decisively with the past. The traditional claim that how a nation treated its own citizens was its own business was powerful. The ''apartheid'' debate in a General Assembly is interesting historically and illustrates the legal argumentation that was advanced at this early stage in the development of the relation between Article 56 and Article 2(7)'s prohibition against intervention in domestic jurisdiction. It is still enlightening given the history-making events of 1994, including the end of apartheid and the election of Nelson Mandela, which, at least, resolved South Africa's terrible period of apartheid. *See, The Question of Race Conflict in South Africa Resulting from the Policies of Apartheid*, U.N. Res. 721 (VIII), adopted by the Gen. Ass., Dec. 8, 1953, UNGA Off.Rec., 8th Sess. 1953 Supp. No. 17 (A_2630).

Article 56 and Self–Execution of Human Rights Treaties under United States Law

As will be developed further in Chapters 11 and 12, some treaties become domestic law in the United States immediately upon ratification, without need for implementing legislation. These so-called self-executing treaties may also afford individual rights that are immediately enforceable in the courts. Is Article 56 self-executing? Does it afford enforceable rights? It was held not to be such a treaty in *Sei Fujii v. State*, 38 Cal.2d 718, 242 P.2d 617 (1952). Although holding that California's law that prohibited ownership of land by a Japanese citizen ineligible for American citizenship was unconstitutional under the Fourteenth Amendment, the court said, with respect to the Charter: ''[T]he provisions in the charter pledging cooperation in promoting observance of fundamental freedoms lack the mandatory quality and definitiveness which would indicate an intent to create justiciable rights in private persons immediately upon ratification.'' Is the California court correct in its appraisal of the provisions of Article 56? Would the result be different if some ''mandatory quality'' were found? Can a self-executing theory lead to the conclusion, in a particular case, that the state is obligated internationally at some time after ratification not to discriminate on the basis of alien status but that, without promulgation of additional law, the alien, even after ratification, is not protected by national law? If this occurs, what is the status of the United States in relation to the treaty and international law? Was it inevitable in 1952 that a court would find the alien land law unconstitutional? Jordan Paust writes that human rights are inalienable and, therefore, human rights treaties are the supreme law of the land. As such, he argues, that claims that they are not self-executing or that latter promulgated legislation overrides them is incorrect.

Christopher L. Blakesley, Autumn of the Patriarch: The Pinochet Extradition Debacle & Beyond

90 Journal of Criminal Law & Criminology 1 (2001).*

* * *

SELF-EXECUTING TREATIES AND THEIR IMPACT ON HUMAN RIGHTS IN EXTRADITION PRACTICE–GENERAL

A "self-executing treaty" is one that needs no implementing domestic legislation; it takes effect upon ratification. It is aimed at the judiciary, not the legislature. In the U.S., if a treaty is not self-executing, or if Congress has not passed enabling legislation, it does not create a cause of action or provide a remedy. Non-self-executing treaties do not create adjudicative or enforcement jurisdiction in United States courts. Thus, if a treaty is non-self-executing, it provides no specific legal effect, although it may influence policy or legislation. Human rights conventions generally are not considered self-executing in the United States. In fact, to try to ensure this result, the United States often includes non-self-executing declarations in its ratification instruments. The principle of non self-executing treaties in the United States, therefore, hampers human rights protection generally and in relation to extradition.

It can be argued that the entire idea of considering treaties, duly entered and ratified, not to be self-executing is "unavoidably unconstitutional,"at least for purposes of supremacy. The idea seems to be, "inconsistent with the language, history, and purpose" of Article VI, paragraph 2, of the Constitution.

The principle of non self-executing treaties in the United States hampers human rights protection in relation to extradition. Article VI, paragraph 2, of the Constitution, of course, makes treaties that have received the "Advice and Consent" of the Senate, the Supreme Law of the Land. On the other hand, most courts and commentators allow that treaties do not have the force of law in the United States, unless they are self-executing, or have been implemented by legislation.

Self-executing treaties have been held to confer rights enforceable by private persons; they are fully operative without implementing legislation. It is held that to provide a private right of action, a treaty must be self-

* Reprinted with the permission of the
Journal of Criminal Law & Criminology.

executing, "that is, 'it must prescribe [ ] rules by which private rights may be determined.' "The 9th Circuit Court of Appeals noted that, "[o]n a general level, the Supreme Court has recognized that treaties can in some circumstances create individually enforceable rights . . . " The proposition that self-executing treaties confer rights on private parties is not undisputed.

Some courts and commentators argue that they give standing to individuals and create private causes of action and remedies. Non-self-executing treaties, on the other hand, are not enforced until legislation is passed incorporating or enabling them.

A vigorous debate has arisen over whether the idea of non-self-executing treaties is inconsistent with the Supremacy Clause. Professor John Yoo argues that the British and colonial approaches to treaty making and treaty enforcement, as well as the experience under the Articles of the Confederation, the debates at the Constitutional Convention and the debates in some of the state ratifying conventions do not provide conclusive or definitive support for the proposition that treaties automatically become the law of the land upon ratification. In fact, claims Professor Yoo, some of this historical evidence supports the position that all, or at least most, treaties do not have the force of law and, therefore, may be ignored by the courts, the citizens, and other state or federal officials who enforce domestic law. Professor Carlos Manuel Vazquez counters, arguing that the Supremacy Clause is more correctly read to call for a "default rule," whereby a treaty automatically will be considered the law of the land, unless the treaty itself is entered with an explicit reservation that clearly provides that the treaty is considered non-self-executing.

Given the current viability in the United States of the notion of non-self-executing treaties, it may be wise, in order to protect individuals being extradited, to establish, either a specific human rights clause barring extradition that would have to be incorporated into each extradition treaty for each particular human right considered appropriate or to expand the traditional exemptions to extradition to include more human rights protections. The reality in United States extradition practice is that no human rights clauses are being incorporated and the traditional exemptions to extradition are being significantly constricted, rather than expanded.

DETERMINING WHICH TREATIES ARE SELF–EXECUTING– MORE ON THE STATUS OF HUMAN RIGHTS CONVENTIONS.

To establish whether a given treaty is self-executing, courts look to the "intent of the signatory parties, as manifested by the language of the instrument, and, if the instrument is uncertain, recourse must be had to the circumstances surrounding its execution."

Treaties that condemn conduct as criminal are non-self-executing. It is accepted that the President and the Senate will not make criminal law by treaty. I have noted that most human rights treaties are also considered non-self executing. This is generally because the Senate, upon giving its Advice & Consent so indicates. This was the case for The Convention Against Torture and Other Cruel, Inhuman or Degrading Treatment or Punishment, and [t]he *International Covenant* on Civil and Political Rights.

The Torture Convention, in article III, § 1, provides: "[N]o State Party shall expel, return (*'refouler'*) or extradite a person to another State where there are substantial grounds for believing that he would be in danger of being subjected to torture ... " The Torture Convention, as noted, has been held to be non-self-executing. At the time the Convention was sent to the Senate for Advice and Consent, Secretary of State, George Schultz, included a "Declaration Regarding the Non–Self–Executing Nature of the Convention," which provided, in part: "[t]he United States that articles 1 through 16 of the Convention are not self-executing." Articles 1–16, are the Convention's protective provisions, designed to protect individuals from the proscribed acts and, as indicated in Article 1, quoted above, to ensure that no State Party will send a fugitive, by way of extradition or other means, to a place where these depredations may well occur. Finally, to close the embarrassing circle of U.S. action, Congress has not promulgated legislation granting jurisdiction to federal courts to hear claims involving the Torture Convention's protective provisions. On the other hand, the principle of non-self-executing treaties was judicially created, so the issue of whether a given treaty is or is not self-executing should be decided by the judiciary. Moreover, some argue persuasively, at least in terms of supremacy in contexts other than that of creating criminal sanctions, that the notion of non-self-executing treaties is anathema and unavoidably unconstitutional.

Nevertheless, the Second Circuit Court of Appeals, in *Gallina v. Fraser,* recognized in dicta a potential exception. The Court noted that there could be some "procedures or punishment so antipathetic to a federal court's sense of decency as to require reexamination of the exception to the principle [of non-inquiry]". The 9th Circuit Court of Appeals took up the gauntlet in 1999, noting that some jurisdictions. "have discussed the possibility of a humanitarian exception to extradition, tracing the idea from *Gallina v. Fraser.*"

Congress recently promulgated legislation implementing Article 3 of the Torture Convention. This was part of the Foreign Affairs Reform and Restructuring Act [FARR Act]. Thus, although the Torture Convention is not considered self-executing, Article 3 has been enabled. The FARR Act provides that it is "the policy of the United States not to expel, extradite, or otherwise effect the involuntary return of any person to a country in which there are substantial grounds for believing the person would be in danger of being subjected to torture.... " Following the promulgation of the FARR Act, the Department of State prescribed regulations to implement Article 3 of the Torture Convention. These Regulations state: "[p]ursuant to [18 U.S.C. §§ 3184 and 3186], the Secretary [of State] is the U.S. official responsible for determining whether to surrender a fugitive to a foreign country by means of extradition ... [Incident to the U.S. obligations under Article 3 of the Convention], the Department [of State] considers the question of whether a person facing extradition from the U.S. is more likely than not to be tortured in [the requesting state]...."

The principle of non-self-executing treaties prevents any impact that human rights might have on extradition or deportation, except insofar as these treaties allow courts to broaden the traditional exemptions from extradition as a disguised method of applying human rights protections, or otherwise to so interpret extradition treaties. Therefore, to protect individuals being extradited, either a specific human rights clause barring extradition would have to be incorporated into each extradition treaty or the traditional exemptions to extradition would have to be expanded by interpretation to include more human rights protections. U.S. practice has been, albeit meagerly and reluctantly, to use the traditional, statist exemptions to extradition as repositories for human rights protections. The quality of this protection, has never been great and has been diminishing, along with other protections for those accused of crime, over the past several years. No human rights clauses have been incorporated and the traditional exemptions to extradition are being significantly constricted.

Notes, Decisions, & Readings

Sloss, *The Domestication of International Human Rights: Non–Self–Executing Declarations and Human Rights Treaties*, 24 Yale J.Int'l l. 129 (1999). *See,* US Constitution art. VI, § 2; 18 USC. § 3181; *Head Money Cases*, 112 U.S. 580 (1884); *Chew Heong v. U.S.*, 112 U.S. 536, 540, 556 (1884). On the judicial provenance of self executing treaties, *see*, Vazquez, *The Four Doctrines of Self-Executing Treaties*, 89 AJIL 695 (1995); Riesenfeld & Abbott, *The Scope of U.S. Senate Control Over the Conclusion and Operation of Treaties*, 77 Chi.–Kent L.Rev. 571 (1991); de la Vega & Brown, *Can a U.S. Treaty Reservation Provide a Sanctuary for the Juvenile Death Penalty*, 32 U.S.F.L. Rev. 735, 762 (1998). *See also*, Yoo, *Globalism and the Constitution: Treaties, Non–Self–Execution and the Original Understanding*, 99 Colum.L.Rev. 1955, 1978–1979 (1999); Yoo, *Treaties and Public Lawmaking: A Textual and Structural Defense of Non–Self–Execution*, 99 Colum.L.Rev. 2218 (1999). Professor Yoo is challenged by Flaherty, *History Right?: Historical Scholarship, Original Understanding, and Treaties as "Supreme Law of the Land,"* 99 Colum.L.Rev. 2095 (1999) (finding that history and the material available from the founding contradicts Professor Yoo's position; confirms the opposite); Vasquez, *Response, Laughing at Treaties,* 99 Colum. L. Rev. 2154, 2156, 2157, and authority and discussion in n. 10 (1999) (finding Professor Yoo's position implausible from the textual and doctrinal standpoints). *Also see,* Halberstam, *United States Ratification of the Convention on the Elimination of all Forms of Discrimination Against Women*, 31 G.W.J.Intl L. & Econ. 49, 64, 67–69 (1997); Quigley, *The International Covenant on Civil and Political Rights and the Supremacy Clause*, 42 DePaul L.Rev. 1287 (1993); Schabas, *Invalid Reservations to the International Covenant on Civil and Political Rights: Is the U.S. Still a Party?*, 21 Brooklyn J.Int'l L. 277 (1995); Henkin, FOREIGN AFFAIRS AND THE UNITED STATES CONSTITUTION 198–204 (2nd ed. 1996); Paust, *Self-Executing Treaties*, 82 A.J.I.L. 760 (1988); Vazquez, *The Self–Executing Character of the Refugee Protocol's Nonrefoulement Obligation*, 7 Geo. Immigr. L.J. 39, 44–49 (1993); Vazquez, *Treaty-Based Rights and Remedies of Individuals*, 92 Colum. L.Rev. 1082, 1101–1010 (1992). *See also and compare*, authority in *U.S. v. Nai Fook Li*, 206 F.3d 56 (1st Cir.2000); "treaties do not generally create rights that are privately enforceable in the federal courts [as they are] primarily compacts between independent nations ..., *citing Head Money Cases*, 598; *Charltòn v. Kelly*, 229 U.S. 447, 474 (1913; *Foster v. Neilson*, 27 U.S. (2 Pet.) 253, 306 (1829) ("The judiciary is not that department of the government to which the assertion of its interest against foreign powers is confided.") ... [E]ven where a treaty provides ... benefits to a national of a given state, [that] individual's rights are derivative through the states." *But see*, *U.S. v. Alvarez–Machain*, 504 U.S. 655, 667 (1992) (suggesting in dictum that the issues of a treaty's self-executing nature and its being *"the Law of the Land"* are separate). *Sandhu v. U.S.*, 2000 WL 191707 (S.D.N.Y.2000), as well as the discussion and authority in notes 126–143, *infra*, and accompanying text.

3.   THE TORTURE CONVENTION

The Senate finally has given its Advice & Consent to the Torture Convention, which codifies an internationally recognized human right. Article 1, defines torture as "any act by which severe pain or suffering, whether physical or mental, is intentionally inflicted ... for such purposes as obtaining ... information or a confession, [punishment] ... , intimidating or coercing him or a third person, or for any reason based on discrimination of any kind, when such pain or suffering is inflicted by or at the instigation of or with the consent or acquiescence of a public official or other person acting in an official capacity." It excludes pain and suffering inherent in or incidental to lawful sanctions. The Convention also incorporates the principle of *non-refoulement*, whereby no state party shall expel, return *(refouler)* or extradite an individual where there exists substantial grounds to believe that he or she would be in danger of being tortured. The U.S. Refugee Act of 1980 provides that grounds for *non-refoulement* obtain when it *"is more likely than not"* that the person will suffer or be threatened with persecution, etc. upon return? *See, INS v. Stevic*, 467 U.S. 407 (1984); *Sale v. Haitian Refugee Center, infra*. Is the U.S. standard the same as that called for in the Torture Convention? See Convention in the Documentary Supplement.

The *Torture Victim Protection Act* of 1991. Article 14 of the Torture Convention calls for each Party to accord the victim of torture both a legal right to redress and an enforceable right to fair and adequate compensation. Congress promulgated the *Torture Victim Protection Act*, which provides: "[a]n Act to carry out obligations of the United States under the United Nations Charter and other international agreements pertaining to the protection of human rights by establishing a civil action for recovery of damages from an individual who engages in torture or extrajudicial killing * * *." It continues:

§ 2.   Establishment of Civil Action

(a) Liability.–An individual who, under actual or apparent authority, or color of law, of any foreign nation–

    (1) subjects an individual to torture shall, in a civil action, be liable for damages to that individual; or

(2) subjects an individual to extrajudicial killing shall, in a civil action, be liable for damages to the individual's legal representative, or to any person who may be a claimant in an action for wrongful death.

(b) Exhaustion of Remedies–A court shall decline to hear a claim under this section if the claimant has not exhausted adequate and available remedies in the place in which the conduct giving rise to the claim occurred.

(c) Statute of Limitations.–No action shall be maintained under this section unless it is commenced within 10 years after the cause of action arose.

§ 3.   Definitions

(a) Extrajudicial Killing.—For the purposes of this Act, the term "extrajudicial killing" means a deliberated killing not authorized by a previous judgment pronounced by a regularly constituted court affording all the judicial guarantees which are recognized as indispensable by civilized peoples. Such term, however, does not include any such killing that, under international law, is lawfully carried out under the authority of a foreign nation.

(b) Torture.—For the purposes of this Act—

(1) * * * means any act, directed against an individual in the offender's custody or physical control, by which severe pain or suffering (other than pain or suffering arising only from or inherent in, or incidental to, lawful sanctions), whether physical or mental, is intentionally inflicted on that individual for such purposes as obtaining from that individual or a third person information or a confession, punishing that individual for an act that individual or a third person has committed or is suspected of having committed, intimidating or coercing that individual or a third person, or for any reason based on discrimination of any kind; and

(2) mental pain or suffering refers to prolonged mental harm caused by or resulting from

(A) the intentional infliction or threatened infliction of severe physical pain or suffering;

(B) the administration or application, or threatened administration or application, of mind altering substances or other procedures calculated to disrupt profoundly the senses or the personality;

(C) the threat of imminent death; or

(D) the threat that another individual will imminently be subjected to death, severe physical pain or suffering, or the administration or application of mind altering substances or other procedures calculated to disrupt profoundly the senses or personality. *Approved March 12, 1992.*

Notes

The Senate adhered to the *Torture Convention*, but adopted significant reservations as it did in the Genocide Convention and in the Covenant on

Civil and Political Rights our reservation was to make all of these treaties specifically *"non-self-executing."* For discussion, *see above* and Chapters 1, 11, and 12. The U.S. also limited its obligation to prevent "cruel, inhuman or degrading treatment or punishment," to what is meant by those terms in the judicial gloss on the 5th, 8th, and 14th Amendments to the Constitution, being especially concerned about the death penalty. Ratification of the *Torture Convention* included an *"understanding"* that the U.S. considered itself obligated only to provide judicially-imposed punishments and other enforcement measures authorized by U.S. law. Thus, the death penalty as practiced in the U.S. was "held" not to violate the U.S. obligation under the Convention. The Senate also included a "federal-state understanding," that the federal government will implement the Convention,"to the extent that it exercises legislative and judicial jurisdiction over the matters covered by the Convention and otherwise by the state and local governments * * *," where we put someone to death, are we in violation of international law? For more on capital punishment and human rights, *see infra*, this chapter.

4. THE GENOCIDE CONVENTION

One day before the General Assembly adopted the Universal Declaration of Human Rights, On December 9, 1948, as it addressed the holocaust of World War II. By a unanimous vote, it adopted the *Genocide Convention*, which proscribes genocide as a crime under international law which the contracting states undertook to prevent and punish. The Convention is in the Documentary Supplement. Article II of the convention defines Genocide: "In the present Convention, *genocide means* any of the following acts committed with intent to destroy, in whole or in part, a national, ethnical, racial or religious group, as such:

(a) Killing members of the group;

(b) Causing serious bodily or mental harm to members of the group;

(c) Deliberately inflicting on the group conditions of life calculated to bring about its physical destruction in whole or in part;

(d) Imposing measures intended to prevent births within the group;

(e) Forcibly transferring children of the group to another group.

Notes and Questions

1. Is Genocide a type of "hate crime?" Would laws that you would expect to find in a country's municipal penal code cover the acts specified in Article II? In the U.S., would current state and federal murder, assault and kidnaping statutes satisfy the Convention's obligation to prevent and punish genocide? Is that enough or is more needed?

2. Is every instance of mass slaughter genocide? What of a government's mass execution of its political opponents? Or of a government's administration of a population resettlement policy for economic and political reasons. Would it be required that the policy be brutally or recklessly carried out so that many people are killed? Was the bombing of Hiroshima or Nagasaki genocide? How about the fire-bombing of Dresden, Tokyo, or London? What

about the blanket bombing of North Vietnam? If the answer is yes, why? If not, why not?

3.   Does the convention impose any obligation upon states aside from the obligation to enact proscribing legislation under Article V? Does a state, as distinct from the individuals under a state's jurisdiction, have any treaty obligation not to commit genocide? If a state has not become a party to the Convention, does it violate international law if it commits genocide? In other words, apart from the treaty, is there an obligation not to commit genocide? If so, on what is it based? What if a country condones genocide by individuals under its jurisdiction as a matter of state policy? What if a state fails to take action to prevent or punish genocide by groups within? By groups outside the country?

Consider the policy position on Human Rights as articulated by the Department of State under President Bush and Secretary of State Colin Powell. Available at httl2://www.state.gov, along with other Senior State Department Official's statements and testimonies.

Under Secretary of State Paula Dobriansky
U.S. Human Rights Policy

Senate Foreign Relations Committee
May 24, 2001

Mr. Chairman, Members of the Foreign Relations Committee,

It is an honor to be here to discuss the Bush Administration's democracy promotion and human rights policy and the importance of maintaining our leadership in this field. This is my first chance to address this committee since I became the Under Secretary of State for Global Affairs. I look forward to future discussions with you on these important issues. My purpose today is to highlight the Bush Administration's commitment to democracy and human rights promotion and the policies we intend to pursue in support of them.

U.S. commitment to human rights dates from the Declaration of Independence and our nation's founding. This reflects our nation's values and our deeply rooted belief in the importance of developing and maintaining democratic governments, subject to the rule of law, that respect and protect individual liberty. At the same time, the defense of human rights clearly serves our national interest.

As the history of the past century has shown, the strongest, most stable, tolerant, and prosperous countries are precisely those which respect universal human rights. For that reason, we have long made the promotion of human rights a focus of our foreign policy and our foreign assistance programs.

Since the end of the Second World War, the United States has been without equal in articulating a vision of international human rights and having the grit to carry it out. Whether crafting the United Nations

Charter and the Universal Declaration of Human Rights, championing freedom and democracy throughout the Cold War, insisting on human rights in the Helsinki Final Act, compiling the Country Reports on Human Rights Practices for the past 25 years, or helping establish the Community of Democracies in Warsaw last year, the United States has been the country that has set the agenda and has done the heavy lifting. Throughout these years, our message has not wavered. Promoting democracy and protecting the individual against the excesses of the state is the policy of the United States.

Fortunately, that effort has been successful. The U.S. vision has come to be shared by many other states, and is now a fundamental component of NATO, the Organization for Security and Cooperation in Europe, and the Organization of American States and the Summit of the Americas, and in the basic laws of many states that have emerged since the end of World War H.

It is increasingly an important factor in decisions of countries in other regions, for example in Africa.

Let me turn now to a subject that has been much in the news recently: the United Nations Commission on Human Rights. I am sure you are all aware of the UN Economic and Social Council vote in New York on May 3, which resulted in the United States losing its seat for the first time since the Commission was created in 1947 under the chairmanship of Eleanor Roosevelt.

As President Bush said on Cuban Independence Day last week at the White House: "Last month, the UN Human Rights Commission called on Castro's regime to respect the basic human rights of all its people. The United States' leadership was responsible for passage of that resolution. Some say we paid a heavy price for it, but let me be clear: I'm very proud of what we did. And repressed people around the world must know this about the United States: We might not sit on some commission, but we will always be the world's leader in support of human rights."

The President was right: we did pay a price for taking forthright, principled positions at the Commission this year. Secretary of State Colin Powell spoke about this when he addressed the Senate Appropriations Subcommittee on Foreign Operations May 15, and he stressed that the future policy of the United States toward the Commission would be the result of a review and ultimately a decision by the President. This review is now under way within the Administration.

As the President said, the United States will remain committed to human rights. It will be a crucial part of our approach to China, Cuba, Indonesia, the Balkans, Iran, Sudan and all the other places where fundamental freedoms are at stake. We are working ever closer with our friends and allies at the UN, the OSCE, OAS, NATO, and other multilateral organizations, and the State Department remains strongly committed to its round-the-clock, round the year, round-the-world human rights monitoring portfolio.

We shall continue to be the world's leading advocate for democracy and human rights. We shall continue to meet foreign government officials, and insist that our views on human rights be known. We shall speak up for the dissidents, the victims of persecution, the tortured and the dispossessed. We shall continue to tell the truth when we submit our Country Reports on Human Rights Practices to Congress and to the millions who now access them via the Internet. We shall continue our reports on International Religious Freedom, now in its third cycle, and a new report on Trafficking in Persons to be released on June 1.

Is this easy? No. Is it always appreciated by our friends and allies? Unfortunately, not. But it is necessary. It is worthwhile. To quote the President again:

"History tells us that forcing change upon oppressive regimes requires patience. But history also proves, from Poland to South Africa, that patience and courage and resolve can eventually cause oppressive regimes to fear and then to fall." The vote at by the member states of ECOSOC has limited our role in one highly visible forum, but it has hardly crippled us. Those states which voted against us in the hope that they would prevent us from being forceful advocates for human rights were sadly mistaken. Indeed, in the policy review, to which I earlier referred, we are taking a close look at new approaches and new opportunities to pursue our human rights objectives worldwide. We may be forced, for a time, to shift our tactics, but we will never abandon our goal.

I would like to say a brief word about the proposal by some to link the payment of our arrears to the outcome of the Commission election. The Administration believes strongly that any attempt to link U.S. payments to the UN—now or in the future—to U.S. membership in or support for the Commission is counterproductive. Not only will withholding money or adding additional conditions on arrears payments provide ammunition to our adversaries, but it will also frustrate our efforts to further U.S. political interests and push for reform of the institution and its agencies. In the words of the President, "a deal's a deal."

While the Commission on Human Rights is far from a perfect institution, it has done much good over the years. It established Special Rapporteurs on country situations like the Former Yugoslavia or Iraq, and on crucial thematic issues such as Torture or the Independence of Judges and Lawyers. These special mechanisms of the CHR are among the activities of the Office of the UN High Commissioner for Human Rights, former Irish President Mary Robinson, which also maintains field offices in trouble spots like Congo and Colombia.

We would caution against penalizing the UN, the UN human rights program, or the Office of the High Commissioner, for the vote by a small number of UN Member States in the Economic and Social Council over membership in the CHR. I strongly urge the Committee to proceed very cautiously in this regard.

Thank you.

Louis René Beres, After the Gulf War: Iraq, Genocide and International Law

Det.Mercy L.Rev. 13 (1991) (footnotes omitted).*

"Truly, I live in dark times. The guileless word is folly. A smooth forehead suggests insensitivity. The man who laughs has simply not yet had the terrible news." (Bertolt Brecht)

The poet Brecht's "terrible news" has now been heard by all, but there is still considerable laughter. Tragically embedded in a world system that seemingly draws comfort from the outermost extremes of human torment, we residents of this defiled planet have not yet learned that politics is unheroic and that innocence counts for nothing. Aware, as legal scholars, that reason of state always preempts human rights, we know that Realpolitik has produced our Age of Atrocity, yet we steadfastly refuse to place enforceable limits around Realpolitik. As a result, the shadow of crimes against humanity darkens not only our discredited recent past but also our most probable immediate future. * * * Genocide, of course, is a crime under international law. * * *

[W]hat is genocide? Based upon a combination of the Greek genos (meaning race or tribe) with the Latin cide (meaning killing), it means the commission of certain specific acts with intent to destroy, wholly or in part, a national, ethnic, racial or religious group as such. Coined in 1944 by Raphael Lemkin, a Polish–Jewish lawyer who escaped the German occupation of his homeland, it describes what Winston Churchill once called "a crime without a name." In this connection, it describes a crime that is juristically distinct from other sorts of wartime killing (killing long since prohibited by the laws of war of international law) and from other sorts of non-wartime political repression * * *.

Although legal scholars may understand that genocide has always been prohibited by international law, the post World War II criminalization of genocide has been especially explicit and far-reaching. Building upon the norms established by international custom, the general principles of law recognized by civilized nations, the writings of highly qualified publicists, various treaties and conventions, and the overriding principles of natural law, this criminalization has flowed almost entirely from universal reaction to the Holocaust. * * *

Today, there exists a well-established regime for the protection of all human rights. This regime is comprised of peremptory norms, rules that endow all human beings with a basic measure of dignity and that permit no derogation by States. These internationally protected human rights can be grouped into three broad categories:

— First, the right to be free from governmental violations of the integrity of the person—violations such as torture, cruel, inhuman

* Reprinted with the permission of Detroit–Mercy Law Rev. and Louis René Beres.

or degrading treatment or punishment; arbitrary arrest or imprisonment; denial of fair public trial; and invasion of the home.

— Second, the right to the fulfillment of vital needs such as food, shelter, health care and education;

— Third, the right to enjoy civil and political liberties, including freedom of speech, press, religion and assembly; the right to participate in government; the right to travel freely within and outside one's own country; the right to be free from discrimination based on race or sex.

Taken together with other important covenants, treaties and declarations which comprise the human rights regime, the Genocide Convention represents the end of the idea of absolute sovereignty concerning non-intervention when human rights are in grievous jeopardy. The Charter * * * stipulates in its Preamble and several articles that human rights are protected by international law. In the Preamble, the peoples of the United Nations reaffirm their faith "in fundamental human rights, in the dignity and worth of the human person, in the equal rights of men and women and of nations large and small" and their determination "to promote social progress and better standards of life in larger freedom."

In light of these codified expressions of the international law of human rights, it is abundantly clear that individual states can no longer claim sovereign immunity from responsibility for gross mistreatment of their own citizens. Notwithstanding Article 2(7) of the U.N. Charter, which reaffirms certain areas of "domestic jurisdiction," each state is now clearly obligated to uphold basic human rights. Even the failure to ratify specific treaties or conventions does not confer immunity from responsibility, since all states are bound by the law of the Charter and by the customs and general principles of law from which such agreements derive * * *.

Looking over the current landscape of international relations, we recognize immediately that politics has become the primary ground of total misfortune. The myth of progress has run its course and calculated visions of a more perfect global society are no longer the reasonable product of creative imaginations. Against genocide and genocide-like crimes, collective legal sanctions and deterrents are indispensable, yet we are sobered by the timeless remark of the poet Yeats: "There is no longer a virtuous nation, and the best of us live by candle light." * * *

U.N. Sub–Commission on Discrimination and Minorities

35 Review of the International Commission of Jurists 12 (1985).*

The Sub–Commission met in Geneva in August 1985.

* Reprinted with the permission of the International Commission of Jurists, Geneva, Switzerland.

Genocide. Under the Item Review of further developments in fields with which the Sub–Commission has been concerned, it discussed the revised and updated report on the question of the prevention and punishment of the crime of genocide, prepared by the Special Rapporteur.

Besides referring to the Nazi holocaust in Europe, he also cited as cases of genocide the German massacre of Hereros in 1904, the Ottoman massacre of Armenians in 1915–1916, the Ukranian pogrom of Jews in 1919, the Tutsi massacre of Hutu in Burundi in 1965 and 1972, the Paraguayan massacre of Ache Indians prior to 1974, the Khmer Rouge massacre in Kampuchea between 1975–78 and the contemporary killings of Bahai'is in Iran. This passage in the report was criticized by many members of the Sub–Commission. After analyzing the Convention on Genocide, he has made the following recommendations:

- the definition should be extended to include a sexual group, such as women, men or homosexuals;

- the inclusion of cultural genocide or ethnocide, meaning the physical destruction of indigenous communities, and also ecocide in terms of irreparable damage to the environment;

- an additional protocol to include the killings of political and other groups;

- addition to Article II of the Convention of words such as ''in any of the above conduct, a conscious act or acts of advertent omission may be as culpable as an act of commission'';

- to include specific wording in the Convention to the effect that in judging culpability a plea of obeying superior orders shall not be a defence;

- to include State responsibility for genocide, together with reparations;

- to make genocide a matter of universal jurisdiction and include in the Convention a provision similar to that of Article 8 of the Convention against torture;

- renewed efforts by the UN to persuade the remaining Member States to ratify the Convention;

- conducting interdisciplinary research into the psychological character and motivation of individuals and groups who commit genocide or acts of racism;

- developing an effective early warning system to monitor impending genocidal conflict and taking timely action on receiving such a warning; and

- establishment of a new impartial and respected international body to deal with genocide.

Notes

Speaking under this item, the Secretary–General of the International Commission of Jurists suggested that rather than seek to amend the Convention to include the "acts of omission", the International Law Commission might be asked to express an opinion on whether the words in Article II include acts of conscious and deliberate omission with that intent. He also suggested that the Commission on Human Rights could establish a working group to deal with alleged cases of genocide, as well as to consider the proposals for universal jurisdiction or for an international penal tribunal and other additions and amendments to the Convention recommended by the Special *Rapporteur*. The Sub–Commission, in a resolution, took note of the revised and updated study and recommended that the UN renew its efforts to make ratification of the Convention * * * universal as soon as possible. *See General Assembly Resolution and Declaration on the Rights of Persons Belonging to National or Ethnic, Religious and Linguistic Minorities*, December 18, 1992, 32 I.L.M. 911 (1993).

THE UNITED STATES AND THE GENOCIDE CONVENTION.

The United States signed the Convention two days after it was adopted by the General Assembly in 1948. President Truman submitted it to the Senate in 1949. The Senate did not give its advice and consent, however, until February 1986, although each president from Kennedy to Reagan urged Senate's approval. The Senate conditioned its action upon two reservations, five understandings and one declaration:

RESERVATIONS:

1. [Regarding] Article IX of the Convention, before any dispute to which the United States is a party may be submitted to the jurisdiction of the International Court of Justice under this article, the specific consent of the United States is required in each case.

2. That nothing in the Convention requires or authorizes legislation or other action by the United States prohibited by the Constitution of the United States as interpreted by the United States.

UNDERSTANDINGS:

1. That the term "intent to destroy, in whole or in part, a national, ethnical, racial, or religious group, as such" appearing in Article II means the specific intent to destroy, in whole or in substantial part, a national, ethnical, racial, or religious group as such by the acts specified in Article II.

2. That the term "mental harm" in Article II(b) means permanent impairment of mental faculties through drugs, torture or similar techniques.

3. That the pledge to grant extradition in accordance with a state's laws and treaties in force found in Article VII extends only to acts which are criminal under the laws of both the requesting and the

requested state and nothing in Article VI affects the right of any state to bring to trial before its own tribunals any of its nationals for acts committed outside a state.

4. That acts in the course of armed conflicts committed without the specific intent required by Article II are not sufficient to constitute genocide as defined by this Convention.

5. That with regard to the reference to an international penal tribunal in Article VI of the Convention, the United States declares that it reserves the right to effect its participation in any such tribunal only by a treaty entered into specifically for that purpose with the advice and consent of the Senate.

DECLARATION:

That the President will not deposit the instrument of ratification until after the implementing legislation referred to in Article V has been enacted. 132 Congressional Record SB1377B8 (daily ed., Feb. 19, 1986).

––––––––

Question

What do you think of these reservations, understandings, and declaration? For example, see the so-called sovereignty reservation, which reads: "[t]hat nothing in the [Genocide] Convention requires or authorizes legislation or other action by the United States of America prohibited by the Constitution of the United States as interpreted by the United States." Was this necessary? *See* Chapter 12. What does such a reservation, included with the U.S. instruments of ratification, do to the perception of the U.S. commitment to the treaty and to oppose genocide? What is the Constitutions's relationship to treaties? Do the other reservations, understandings and the declaration have more of an impact on this than the Constitution? Due to the problems prompted by the *sovereignty reservation,* the U.S. Senate did not include one when it adopted the Torture Convention *supra,* but did include a "statement" in its Resolution of Advice and Consent, that "[t]he President of the United States shall not deposit the instrument of ratification until such time as he has notified all present and prospective ratifying party [sic] to this Convention that nothing in this Convention requires or authorizes legislation, or other action, by the United States prohibited by the Constitution of the United States as interpreted by the United States." This was not considered to be a "reservation" or an "understanding."

Genocide & Human Rights in Cambodia

Cambodia is in the process of negotiating with the U.N. and among its own people over whether to establish another Ad Hoc Tribunal, this time for the depredations of the Khmer Rouge in the killing fields. The following material is most pertinent to this issue.

Beyond the Grave an Account of Pol Pot's Genocide in Cambodia Told Through the Records of its Victims Voices from S–21: Terror and History in Pol Pot's Secret Prison.

By David Chandler.
Berkeley: University of California Press.
Reviewed by JUDITH SHAPIRO
New York Times Book Review, January 30, 2000.*

From 1975 to 1979, in a former high school called Tuol Sleng on the outskirts of Phnom Penh, the Khmer Rouge interrogated and tortured 14,000 political prisoners and extracted lengthy written confessions from them. No one was released. A satisfactory confession brought a trip to the killing field at Cheong Euk, where a lethal blow was administered with an iron oxcart axle.

In an effort to explain what happened inside Tuol Sleng (then known by the code name S–21), David Chandler, the preeminent historian of Cambodia, spent years examining the voluminous archives discovered in the compound when the Vietnamese seized power in Cambodia in 1979. He plumbed comparative materials on state-sponsored terror and sought insight in psychological studies of the human capacity to inflict pain. "Voices From S–21" is the wrenching and dispassionate result.

Most of the archives, Chandler tells us, consist of typed or handwritten confessions, some of them hundreds of pages long. Six thousand photographs were found, including many of the haunting mug shots that the Khmer Rouge took of every prisoner. But information about what went on in the former school remains sparse. Only 12 prisoners are known to have survived, seven of whom have given valuable interviews. Surviving prison workers have been circumspect. However, the confessions of 79 former interrogators, document workers and guards who themselves became victims provided insight into interrogation techniques, the use of torture and the prison workers' mostly rural backgrounds.

Why were such extensive records of such horrific behavior maintained? Chandler offers several explanations, including preparations for a future party history and the regime's need for reassurance that it was keeping external and internal enemies at bay. S–21's mission, Chandler writes, "had always been to validate the Party Center's worst suspicions. ... The killing machine at S–21 had no brakes because the paranoia of the Party Center had no limits."

Interrogation was surrealistic in that neither prisoner nor interrogator knew what crimes the prisoner was supposed to have committed. "Prisoners struggled to 'remember' the kinds of crimes that the relentless and similarly terrified interrogators wanted them to confess." Formulaic as they are, the confessions reveal the prisoners' humanity–one planted fruit trees without permission, another forgot to water plants. Almost all wrote of joining the C.I.A.; many clearly had no idea what it was.

* Reprinted with the permission of the New York Times Book Review. Judith Shapiro is co-author with Liang Heng of "Son of the Revolution."

The Party Center eventually destroyed itself with its conspiracy theories and inquisitions. Most of Cambodia's rulers disappeared into Tuol Sleng. Whole sectors of Cambodia's administration, and the leadership of entire districts, were exterminated. If not for the Vietnamese invasion, Chandler suggests, Son Sen, the deputy prime minister under whose jurisdiction S–21 operated, would soon have been a victim.

Chandler describes his immersion in the S–21 archives as at times "akin to drowning." His fascinating comparisons of Tuol Sleng with the Nazi camps, the Moscow show trials, the Chinese Cultural Revolution, events in Bosnia and Rwanda and other atrocities distance us from the horror. Despite the title, we are left wanting to hear even more from the victims than Chandler seems able to provide.

Foreign, Communist or Cambodian influence are inadequate to explain the amalgam that was Tuol Sleng; in Chandler's view, the roots lie even deeper. By defining their victims as subhuman, interrogators became capable of shutting down empathy, and torture became routinized. "Turning the victims into 'others,' in a racist fashion—and using words associated with animals to describe them—made them easier to mistreat and easier to kill." The source of the evil enacted in Tuol Sleng, Chandler argues, lies within all of us.

Terror in the East Terror in the East: Phases of Repression in Region 23 of Democratic Kampuchea*

Craig Etcheson, Crimes of the Khmer Rouge: The Search for Peace and Justice in Cambodia, Chapter 11(Mellen, forthcoming 2001).
From September 1, 2001–August 30, 2002. Visiting Scholar, John Hopkins-University's School of Advanced International Studies.

Introduction. This ... is a case study of state terror in Democratic Kampuchea (DK), Pol Pot's Khmer Rouge state. I examine the relationship between political authority and the intensity of human rights violations in one region of the Khmer Rouge state. Some scholars argue that levels of political violence were relatively constant across all political factions of the Khmer Rouge. Others argue that extreme violence was a characteristic only of those regions controlled by factions loyal to the "Party Center," and that levels of repression tended to be less extreme in regions outside the control of the central political authorities. Thus the question is: Was there any change in overall levels of violence when a given region came under the authority of the Party Center? [This] study examines primary documents and other evidence newly uncovered by the Cambodian Genocide Program in an attempt to shed light on this question.

* Reprinted with the permission of Craig Etcheson, who is an independent genocide researcher working out of Washington DC. He is also Advisor to the Documentation Center of Cambodia and has published extensively on the Cambodian Genocide. This chapter is an updated and revised version of, Craig Etcheson, *Terror in the East: Phases of Repression in Region 23 of Democratic Kampuchea,* paper presented to the Annual Meeting of the Society for Historians of American Foreign Relations, Washington, DC, June 19–22, 1997.

Overview. There is a common view of the Khmer Rouge revolution in Cambodia which holds that when the insurgent communist forces took control of Phnom Penh on April 17, 1975, a unified, tightly knit organization came into control of Cambodia nationwide. The reality was much more complex. What is called the "Khmer Rouge" was actually a loose coalition of revolutionary groupings who had been united largely by the common goal of overthrowing the US-backed Lon Nol regime. Even before that common goal was achieved, however, another struggle—in many ways a much more desperate struggle—began with a deadly serious aim: control of the revolution. Within the revolutionary movement, there were many tendencies. Some Cambodian revolutionaries traced their lineage to the revolution in Vietnam; others tended toward allies in the People's Republic of China; still others were motivated by a nationalistic ideology, or were more interested in returning Prince Norodom Sihanouk to the position of power snatched from his grasp by Lon Nol. Imposing unity and central control over this fractious collection of tendencies was the task set by Pol Pot, the Chairman of the Central Committee of the Communist Party of Kampuchea (CPK), the man at the heart of the "Party Center."

Cambodia had been divided into "zones" of control during the war of 1970–1975, defined in large part by whose troops controlled which areas of the country. Over the course of the war, Pol Pot formed a close alliance with the infamous Ta Mok, whose ferocious forces controlled the southwestern areas of Cambodia. In the eastern areas of Cambodia, troops under the command of So Phim pursued a policy of cooperation and friendship with Vietnamese communist forces, who had done so much to help the Cambodian revolutionaries in the early stages of their war against Lon Nol. This fact alone made So Phim and his Eastern Zone forces suspect in the eyes of Pol Pot and his allies, who viewed Vietnam as the historic enemy. Through a complex series of maneuvers, forces loyal to the Party Center—i.e., Pol Pot—staged a creeping coup against the forces loyal to So Phim, gradually purging region cadre and replacing them with cadre loyal to the Party Center. This series of maneuvers culminated in So Phim's death in May 1978, and the military rout of his remaining Eastern Zone forces.

The particular region I will examine was known as *Damban* 23, or Region 23, which is almost exactly contiguous with Cambodia's Svay Rieng Province. There are two general views of difference in the intensity of human rights violations in areas controlled by Pol Pot versus areas controlled by other Cambodian revolutionary forces. I will employ arguments advanced by two prominent analysts of the Khmer Rouge regime to elaborate these general perspectives.

I will attempt to shed light on [some] interpretations [of evidence of the degree of Genocide] by examining evidence newly uncovered by the Cambodian Genocide Program.

Political Authority in Region 23. Given the extreme secrecy which was characteristic of the Communist Party of Kampuchea, it is difficult to establish the facts of leadership within the organization ... , [but] it is now becoming easier to identify lines of command and control within Khmer Rouge organizations, and to track changes in leadership across time ... Within Khmer Rouge organizations, leadership was structured according to the classic communist cell structure, with a three-person committee in charge of affairs at each level of the organization . . .

I have been able to identify three different individuals who occupied the post of Region Chair or Region Secretary over the Democratic Kampuchea regime. Beginning in 1975, presumably soon after or even prior to the April 17th fall of Phnom Penh, a cadre named Chan Sovan was named Secretary of Region 23. Sometime in late 1975 or early 1976, Sovan was replaced by a cadre named Sin So. He was to have a brief tenure. According to Kiernan, Sin So was purged by Southwest Zone forces loyal to the Party Center in March 1977, presumably indicating that he did not have Pol Pot's confidence. Evidently at this same time, a man named Seng Hong took the position of Secretary for both Regions 23 and 24. Thus we can date the takeover of Region 23 by the Party Center to approximately March of 1977.

This was not the end of the purges of Region 23, as there is evidence that the Deputy Secretary of the Region Committee, Maung Vuth, and the Member of the Region Committee, Neth Yun, were sent to the infamous Tuol Sleng prison in Phnom Penh for interrogation and execution in April of 1978. Still, this information gives us a benchmark to identify the transition of political authority from Eastern Zone to Party Center cadre in Region 23. Thus, we will examine the intensity of human rights violations in Region 23, both before and after March 1977.

These leaders ruled over a highly simplified, ideologically constructed class structure. There were only three classes of citizens in the Khmer Rouge state. The foundation of Democratic Kampuchea society was a class of citizen known as a *"full rights" person, also called "old people" or "base people."* The base people were those of impeccable socio-economic status, meaning that they were from the poorest strata of the peasantry, and that they had lived in areas controlled by the revolutionary forces prior to the final victory on April 17, 1975. *A second class of citizen was the "candidate,"* i.e., a person who was theoretically qualified to rise to the status of a full-rights person through service to the revolution, military or otherwise, but whose biography was marred by dint of a questionable socio-economic background, such as having come from a less-than-impoverished peasant family. *Finally, there was the "new people."* The new people were those who lived in the cities, and who did not "join" the revolution until the cities fell to revolutionary forces on April 17, 1975. For this reason, the new people were often called the "April 17" people. The official term for this lowest class was "depositee," an apt term insofar as immediately after the April 17 victory, all city dwellers were evacuated from the cities and "deposited" in rural areas. These new people—including many poor peasants who had fled to the cities to escape the violence of the war—were all suspected as traitors and enemies, because they had remained in the enclaves of Lon Nol's Khmer Republic and had failed to rally to the revolution until it was forced upon them through the victory of the revolution. There is substantial evidence that the central authorities of Democratic Kampuchea regime planned to simply kill all of the new people, bit by bit, over time, through starvation, overwork, and outright execution.

Prisons and Killing Fields in Region 23. According to a report prepared by the People's Republic of Kampuchea (PRK) Information, Culture and Press Center in Svay Rieng province in 1981, there were 74 "genocide sites" in Svay Rieng province dating from the Democratic Kampuchea regime. The term, "genocide sites," generally refers to detention, interrogation and torture facilities, as well as mass grave sites (known in the vernacular as "killing fields"). The 1981 PRK report does not give an exhaustive listing of these alleged sites, so one is left to reconstruct the particulars from other sources. In the documentation work completed to date by the Cambodian Genocide Program, our information remains fragmentary and incomplete. Nonetheless, we have assembled a good deal of data, enough to reconstruct a partial inventory of these sites.

Based on these various sources, I can identify a total of 42 "genocide sites" in Region 23 (Svay Rieng province). Of these, 26 were the locations of Khmer Rouge detention, interrogation and torture facilities, hereafter referred to as prisons. . . . [there were other] mass grave pits dating to the Khmer Rouge regime. The 26 prison sites are distributed across every district in Region 23, but not in every commune. . . . From the substantial amount of witness commentary discussing killing rates during 1975 at other prisons in Region 23, it is safe to assume that the majority of the facilities were in operation from early 1975 or before. Thus it seems clear that there was an elaborate network of prisons and interrogation centers in operation in Region 23 long before the forces of the Party Center assumed control of the region in March 1977.

A quick inventory of the seven districts of Region 23 illustrates the ubiquitous nature of the Khmer Rouge security services and their works, even at the outset of the revolution in April 1975. In Romeas Hek district of Region 23, we believe that we can identify eleven prisons and four sites containing mass grave pits. According to one witness, a 48–year old man who was a base person in the area during the Khmer Rouge regime, people were imprisoned in Romeas Hek district on charges of "immorality," of stealing food, or of "talking arbitrarily." "Victims taken to be confined here had to work one or two days, and then somehow disappeared." Where they "disappeared" to was the "killing fields." . . .

At the Wat Kdey Rumduol prison in Sang Kur commune, an individual who was classified as base person during the Khmer Rouge regime recalls seeing victims marched in a line from the prison to the killing fields near the temple. They did not return. According to this witness, many of these victims, particularly early in the Khmer Rouge regime, were provincial officials from the Lon Nol regime.

According to a local farmer, in areas adjacent to the remaining obvious sites [in Chantrea], it is common to find human remains while plowing the fields there.

In Kompong Ro district there "were six pagodas transformed into detention centers and another 12 detention centers, one in each commune." . . . At the prison site Wat Russei Sang, one witness of the killing field associated with this particular prison that "when he was about 14 years old, he saw 15 prisoners buried up to their necks in the fields nearby, and others tied to a bamboo tree to die. Two other boys who were walking past and saw this were shot by KR soldiers."

The other known KR prison site in Svay Chrum district is at Tlork, and was known as the "Tuol Sleng" of Svay Rieng province. Tuol Sleng, ... is the Phnom Penh headquarters of the Khmer Rouge secret police....

Finally, the Svey Rieng city prisons—the facility at Tuol Prich—was known as the "hot prison," and a "main killing center." This suggests that this place was part of the headquarters for state security in Region 23. Besides Tuol Prich's location at the district seat, and its reputation as a "main killing center," another factor suggests its importance. The designation of Tuol Prich as a "hot prison" recalls the name of an elite group of interrogators—the "hot group"—at Khmer Rouge security services headquarters.

Witnesses to Terror. What were the patterns of operation for these prisons before and after March 1977? This is a difficult question, but we can gain some insight into the matter based on interviews carried out by the CGP with witnesses who observed the operation of prisons and killing fields ... Several witnesses have testified about Khmer Rouge state-organized killing ... One man, now graduated from Phnom Penh University, described his family's ordeal ... On April 17, 1975, his entire family was evacuated from Phnom Penh and settled in Tnoat village, ... quite close to the Vietnam border.[8]

> My mother was told my grandmother was taken to be shot dead along with many other people in a pit, and the slaughters left the bodies on the ground like those of animals. It was afterwards in 1977 that a new chief of the Phum came in charge and at the time there were lots of youth escaping from the place to live in Vietnam as the place was close to Vietnam just a passage as far as a canal, and one other kilometer walk from the canal—then there was safety. As many tried to escape, some were caught and taken to be killed but not all members of the family were killed, as in the former chief's time ... Then the previous chief including all members of his family were taken to be killed, and a new chief was put in place. This was in fact the second renewed suffering burden ...

This witness testifies to varying degrees of brutality by successive leaders of his village, beginning with a high level of killing in 1975 and 1976, changing to a lower lethality under a less brutal village chief in 1977, and then, after another purge and a new chief, a return to very high levels of brutality and killing in 1978. The first village chief in 1975–76 followed the *Khmer Rouge policy of "root and branch,"* whereby when one member of a family was accused of wrongdoing, the entire family was executed....

... [A] 56–year old man from Romeas Hek district told of a different killing field....[9] "Every day, around 40 to 50 victims were ordered by the killers to walk in lines. They were people from Svay Rieng and many others from Phnom Penh during 1975–76." Another witness says he saw victims being taken to be killed. "Most of the victims were male members of the 17 April people evacuated from Svay Rieng and the city. Other victims were people chosen through their biographies, and those taken from the security

8. Ros Visal, "My Family During the 3–Year 8–Month and 20–Day Period," Documentation Center of Cambodia Document #604.

9. Testimony taken on March 24, 1997, in Romeas Hek district, from 56 year old male. 1997 CGP Mapping Report, Svay Rieng Province.

office in Prey Romdeng village, Chrey commune, and from the security office at Veal Svay. . . . In 1977, victims were brought to dig pits in Prey Akrian. In 1978, lines of 40 to 50 victims were taken to be killed there during the nighttime." The "biographies" mentioned were the autobiographies which all citizens were periodically required to produce, and through which the Khmer Rouge identified "enemies" who should be eliminated. . . .

Another Romeas Hek witness, a 67–year old male, told us what he witnessed at Svay Tateum village in Trapaeng Sdao commune. He said he saw "victims being walked in lines, taken from everywhere. . . . Approximately 50 to 60 persons walked the victims to where the killers waited, received and temporarily put the victims in prison. During the following days, victims were interrogated and taken to be killed gradually during the night . . ." This witness testified that by "late 1977 and 1978, all the victims were killed; there were no survivors." Another witness to events at this same facility, a 60–year old male, said, "Victims taken to be killed in the prison . . . included military police, soldiers, policemen, civil servants, teachers, and students during 1976 and 1977. Until 1978, it was a mass and cruel killing."

Speaking of a killing site at Khpoap Ampil, through the gateway of Wat Kampong Ampil, one witness told us that "victims taken to be killed here included soldiers, civil servants, teachers, students and intellectuals. They were people of both sexes and all ages. In 1975, during a period of 2 to 3 months, victims evacuated from Phnom Penh were taken to be killed here. It was the first phase of killing." . . .

Elsewhere in Rumduol district, at Tuol Popok Vil, a 58–year old witness described ruses used by the Khmer Rouge to select who would be executed first.

All the victims were taken both from the security office and the prison at Tuol Popok Vil, as well as from Trapaeng Veng in Phum Tuol Chres, Khum Chork. Among the victims were civil servants evacuated from the city and from all the collectives throughout Romduol district. In 1976, people were moved from one commune to another throughout the district. At that time, people were selected to be killed in accordance with the rule that anyone who was a soldier, second lieutenant, or first lieutenant was the first to be killed; subordinates, policemen, military police and spies were preferably the first to be killed. Although civil servants, teachers and students were deceived into thinking that they were assigned to plant potatoes and bananas, and would be allowed to have enough to eat, they instead were taken to be killed one by one gradually.

Yet another Rumduol district witness, a 65–year old male, described the killing fields where the Tuol Popok Vil victims were taken for disposal: "There are 9 big pits and some 400 to 500 small pits. Each victim family of 4 to 6 members were put in the small pits, while 40 to 50 victims were buried in the big pits. . . .

Beyond this witness testimony on the high levels of killing in Region 23 before March 1977, there is also evidence that the Region 23 prisons were functioning as elements of an integrated national security system. People from Region 23, both "new people" (i.e., those evacuated from the cities after April 17, 1975) and "old people" (those living in areas controlled by revolutionary forces before April 17) were arrested and transported to Tuol Sleng Prison in Phnom Penh for processing. Among the forced confessions of prisoners . . . is one from Sa Son, a 31–year old Khmer man, born in Tanor village. . . . Working in engineering for the Lon Nol regimes Ministry of Information before April 17, he was sent out from Svay Rieng city to a farm in Region 22. On May 28, 1975, barely six weeks after the revolutionary victory, Sa Son was arrested and sent for interrogation and execution at Tuol Sleng. Not only were personnel of the defeated regime persecuted, but also revolutionaries were already falling under suspicion of the new regime. An example is the forced confession Kul Thai, a 44 year old Khmer male. . . . Both before and after April 17, 1975, he served in a Khmer Rouge military logistics force. He was arrested at South Boeng Trabek on November 14, 1975, transferred to Tuol Sleng, interrogated and executed.

Finally, it seems clear that in 1978, very large mass executions of Eastern Zone citizens became common. The indiscriminate 1978 slaughter of Eastern Zone people has been well documented in previous scholarship, but one example will illustrate this development. During the 1979 People's Revolutionary Tribunal in Phnom Penh, a witness described his own culpability in carrying out some of these massacres. Siv Samon recounted that ". . . on 12 Aug 78, the Mean Cheay Security issued a circular of the Communist Party of Kampuchea to purge away lives of the people. We had 8 people altogether. We were assigned to kill 250 people of Krosaom Ark . . . they were clubbed on the back side of the head with bamboo pipes and kicked into pits. I myself killed 20 of those people . . ." The prosecutor of the tribunal pressed this line of questioning: "What type of people were killed? What were the accusations? How were they killed?" The witness answered, "We used iron bar to kill them, so the victims did not scream and we didn't cut their limbs. They were people from Svay Rieng and they were under the accusations of being associated with Vietnam. The order was that those who had connection with Vietnam had to be exterminated." It appears that a "connection with Vietnam" became defined as anyone who lived in East Zone districts along the border with Vietnam.* * *

Conclusions. This study has examined only one region of one zone of Democratic Kampuchea.

. . . [B]ased on the evidence examined, we can gain insight into the differing interpretations of the relative levels of violence in various regions. It seems clear that the authorities in So Phim's Eastern Zone were cooperating fully in the Party Center's plan to liquidate the "depositee" class. Virtually all of the witnesses cited here say that those imprisoned and killed before March 1977 were primarily the "new people." As the forces of the Party Center seized control of the east, a new class of victims arose:

Eastern Zone Khmer Rouge cadre and military personnel. With time, it appears, this class of victims was expanded to include all residents of the east; they were seen as complicit in the "rebelliousness" of Eastern Zone authorities, and as fatally compromised by their physical proximity to Vietnam. Thus, Kiernan seems to be correct insofar as it is clear that levels of repression and extrajudicial execution escalated dramatically after the seizure of power by forces of the Party Center in Region 23. The policy of the Party Center appears to have evolved toward the utter annihilation of all living persons in Region 23, the ultimate indicia of state terror.... Although it evolved through distinct phases, and grew worse over time as political authorities changed, we can conclude that the Khmer Rouge terror in the East was continuous and ubiquitous.

The Armenian Genocide

A Survivor of the Armenian Genocide Remembers: An Interview with Reverend Vartan Hartunian, www.hatewatch.org. (March 3, 2001).*

My name is Vartan Hartunian and I am the pastor of the First Armenian Church in Belmont, Massachusetts. I am one of a diminishing number of survivors of the Armenian genocide. I was born on February 11, 1915 and the genocide broke out on April 24, 1915. Prior to the genocide, in the 11th and 12th centuries, the Armenian people were subjugated by the Ottoman Turks. Since that time, they have been tolerated, but have had few civil rights, not comparable to the civil rights of the Turks. The Armenian people lived under tension, because of their situation, vis a vis the Turkish government. They lived in fear and massacres would break out here and there for various reasons. The greatest one was in 1895, when Abdul Hamid, "the bloody Sultan", ordered the massacres; some 300,000 Armenians were slaughtered throughout Turkey. The massacre began at a given hour and ended at a given hour 3 or 4 days later. This put the entire Armenian community in great jeopardy. When the Young Turks came to power and overthrew the Sultan Hamid, the Armenian political parties joined the Young Turks and the Young Turks welcomed them. When the new government was established, both the Armenians and the Turks rejoiced, but obviously the Armenians were unaware of the ultimate plan of the Young Turks.

In 1909 there was a massacre in Adana, and 30,000 Armenians were slaughtered. For a few years after that there was reasonable calm, and the thought was that perhaps Armenians and Turks could get along together. When World War I broke out, this gave the Young Turks the opportunity to fulfill a Turkish desire that had continued for centuries: to rid Turkey of all Armenians, perhaps to rid Turkey of all Christians, because in addition to the Armenians there were Greeks and other Armenian minorities in Turkey. ... I was born on February 11, 1915, and the genocide broke out on April 24, 1915. Even before I was born, the Turkish mayor of Marash, the city where I was born, called my father to his office and showed him the

* Reprinted with the permission of Hate-watch.org.

orders from Constantinople for the extermination of all the Armenian people. And this good mayor, this good Turk, pleaded with my father and said "What shall I do?" and my father told him to stay in office and to help him, his family and his people as much as he could. This good Turk did that, and we know he was later removed from office due to his lack of cooperation. . . .

When I was born, my father knew that the decree had been given for my death, and for the death of his other children, his wife and for himself. But fortunately, under the mayor's guidance, my mother and I were hidden in a hospital room. My three sisters were kept safe in the German orphanage and my father was finally deported. My father was in a death march of 12,000 Armenian men, women, and children, and by the time he had played dead and managed to escape to the American College in Aintab, there were less then 1,000 of those 12,000 remaining.

During the genocide, [which had been] deliberated in the Turkish parliament, where all objections were silenced, 1.5 million Armenian men, women and children were slaughtered in various ways. Some 500,000 died after the armistice and not only from disease, heartbreak and starvation, but because even after the armistice, the troops of Mustafa Kemal, armed by the French and the English, went through Turkey and destroyed towns, cities and the survivors of the genocide. During 1920, 1921, as a child of 5 to 6, I witnessed an Armenian church in which there were 2,000 Armenian men, women and children taking refuge. The Turks surrounded the church and poured kerosene all around and set the church on fire, ready to shoot anyone who came out of the building. . . .

"The suffering of the Armenian people is a gathering of all the suffering of peoples throughout the history of the world," were the words of Ambassador Henry Morgenthau. He realized how tragic it was. The Turks went to the extent of cutting off the hands of children and letting them bleed and yell themselves to death. They buried children alive in ditches in the desert, and they drove thousands of Armenians in death marches until they dropped dead or were shot dead. They were robbed on the way and they were forbidden to drink. At the end of the war, when an American official went into the area called Der-el-Zor, which was really the last stopping place of the deportees, he found piles and piles of dead bodies. He asked the Turkish official there how did these people die. The Turkish official said they died of thirst. The official asked if the Euphrates River had dried up. The Turkish official replied that they were forbidden to give the Armenians any water. Therefore, it was a deliberate plan of the Turkish nation to eliminate the Armenian Christian population. They succeeded to such a degree that for about 50 years after, the Armenians were unable to properly speak about, document and reveal to the world the occurrence of this horrendous experience.

As a matter of fact, there were several reasons why the Armenian genocide was called, and is still called, the unremembered genocide. First of all, the world thought the first world war was a war to end all wars. If one had that belief, one would try to minimize all the tragedies of World War I.

As a result, both the western powers and America and the American Congregation of Missionaries, in the delusion that the first world war was a war to end all wars, felt that all the tragedy should be minimized and not talked about. Turkey should be forgiven, and allowed to reestablish themselves in that area for stability purposes. The second reason was the Armenians were so disseminated, and so deeply hurt in their minds, hearts and souls that they were unable to speak as to what happened. It was only in 1965 that they finally began to proclaim to the world that this horrendous act had taken place.

Thirdly, the Turks found it very convenient to deny that a genocide ever took place; they said it was a civil war and both sides suffered. Ever since and to 1998, they have denied that the genocide ever took place, because they feel, that if this is established, they would be responsible to return lands, to return property, and to apologize. In denying the Armenian genocide, the Turks are denying themselves of their proper place in present civilization, because in accepting that genocide, and in doing whatever is necessary as a consequence, they would say to the world that they have not only participated in this evil, but that they are ready to do something for its good in the future. . . . [The archives of] Washington, . . . England, France, Germany and Austria, even the Turkish archives if by this time they have not been corrupted, which will clearly reveal that the Armenian genocide was deliberately planned and executed by the Young Turks, and that it was very, very successful. It was so successful that it inspired Hitler when he decided to exterminate the Jews, to say to his troops who were ready to go into battle to kill, "Go kill men, women and children without mercy . . . who now remembers the Armenians? When we are successful, the world will worship us."

Notes and Questions

Vartan Hartunian is editor-translator of Abraham Hartunian, neither to laugh or to weep: A memoir of the Armenian Genocide (1968). Does the conduct of the Khmer Rouge and that of the Turks done within their own territory constitute a violation of human rights sufficient to allow intervention.

In 2001, there appears to be ramblings from Turkish scholars and intellectuals that are prompting Turkey to accept accountability for the Armenian Genocide. The following article from The Montreal Gazette recounts one Turkish intellectual's attempts to speak out about the genocide of the Armenians. Dr. Ragip Zarakolu, who is a member and founder of Turkey's Association for Human Rights, spoke to about 200 members of Montreal's Armenian community. He "admitted that his country committed a great wrong 85 years ago. . . . In what the Montreal Armenian community is calling a first, a Turkish intellectual said yesterday that his government should admit that the massacre of countless Armenians in 1915 by the Ottoman Turks was genocide." Zarakolu, however, has been attacked in Turkey for similar comments. He and his wife run a book-publishing business in Turkey, which has been bombed, and he and his wife have been persecuted, threatened, and imprisoned for printing books and essays about the poor human-rights record in Turkey.

A First: Local Armenians: Turks Should Admit 1915 Genocide, Gathering Told

by Amanda Jelowicki the Gazette (Montreal), April 26, 2000, Final.*

In what the Montreal Armenian community is calling a first, a Turkish intellectual said yesterday that his government should admit that the massacre of countless Armenians in 1915 by the Ottoman Turks was genocide. Dr. Ragip Zarakolu, a member and founder of Turkey's Association for Human Rights, spoke to about 200 members of Montreal's Armenian community last night, and admitted that his country committed a great wrong 85 years ago. Zarakolu was invited to Montreal by the Armenian National Committees of Canada and Montreal. Zarakolu, who has been arrested and attacked in his native country for his radical views on Turkish atrocities committed against Armenians, said his country can only become a democratic nation once it admits its past assassination and expulsion of Armenians from Turkey. He said the only way to prevent similar genocides from being committed again is for Turkey to recognize and admit to its violent past.

The Armenian National Committee of Canada maintains that the 1915 massacre and displacement of 1.5 million Armenians was the 20th century's first genocide. The Turkish government has refused to recognize the events of 1915 as genocide, and places the death toll at a much lower level. He said his business has been bombed, and he and his wife have been imprisoned for printing books and essays on Turkey's poor human-rights record. Zarakolu said Turkey's candidacy for membership of the European Union will force the country into a radical overhaul of its political and social policies and ideologies. "Turkey must change and accept the universal rules of rights and standards. Turkey is very late to catch on." Zarakolu declined to comment on the Canadian government's refusal to acknowledge the events of 1915 as genocide, while Ontario and Quebec have both acknowledge that Turkish actions during World War I amounted to genocide. Zakarian said the ANCM will continue to pressure the federal government to change its policy.

Notes

Excellent works on the Armenian Genocide include: Boass, Stay the Hand of Vengeance at ch. 4 (Princeton 2000); Akcapu Tanner, Armenian und der Völkermord: Die Istarzbuler Progesse und der Turkische National bewegung (1996); V.N. Dadrian, Genocide as a problem of National and International Law: The World War I Armenian case and its Contemporary Ramificatious, 14 Yale J.Int'l L. 221 (1989).

* Reprinted with the permission of the
Montreal Gazette & Southam, Inc.

Rwanda the Genocide in Rwanda Could Have Been Prevented

Hrvoje Hranjski, *"We could have done more, and we could have done better": Belgian PM apologizes for failings in Rwanda,* The Ottawa Citizen, April 8, 2000.

In 90 days of slaughter in 1994, Hutu extremists killed as many as a million people, most of their Tutsies and many were hacked to death with machetes. The beginning of the attacks was on April 7, 1994. On April 6th, the plane carrying Hutu President Juvenal Habyarimana and Burundian president Cyprien Ntaryamira (also a Hutu) was shot down (apparently by a missile) by suspects, as yet not convicted, but who were likely militia or soldiers. The plane was downed as it neared the Kigali airport. French Examining Magistrate, Jean–Louis Bruguiere, acting on behalf of the families of four French crew-members has been investigating the downing. It has been reported that suspects include Hassan Ngeze, former editor of Kangura, the extremist Hutu newspaper. Ngeze has stated that the downing of the plane was masterminded by Paul Kagame, President of Rwanda, then a Hutu rebel leader. This information was in a leaked U.N. document The incident enraged a murderous mass of soldiers and militiamen. They hunted down hundreds of thousands of Tutsi and moderate Hutu children, women, and men, hacking many of them to death on the spot with machetes. The number of slaughtered Hutus is estimated at between 500,000 and 800,000.

Belgium had been Rwanda's colonial ruler until 1962, and had supplied most (1,500 troops) of the U.N. force that had been deployed in 1993, to buffer between the Tutsi-led rebels and the Hutus, who ruled at that time. This force evacuated Rwanda, after 10 Belgian troops were shot and hacked to death. The genocide of the Tutsies followed. Belgian Prime Minister, Guy Verhoftadt, has apologized stated that the ten troops fought for three hours against superior numbers, before being overcome and killed. He stated that, "for reasons beyond our understanding, nothing was done to help them [by the] hesitant command, the final, irresponsible bastion of a badly planned, badly equipped system that exhibited to an absurd degree a culpable lack of concern...." *See also, French Investigator Probes 1994 Rwandan Plane Downing, Agence France–Presse,* May 16, 2000]. President Clinton also made a weak and trifling apology. Thus, more than six years too late, apologies, finger-pointing, the excuses, along with the quest for understanding of what might have happened and how it might have been prevented, continue.

Rape as a Crime Against Humanity and a War Crime— Rwanda & Yugoslavia.

This issue will be discussed in more detail in Chapter 16, but for now, it is important to note that the Ad Hoc Tribunal for Rwanda held in *Prosecutor v. Jean–Paul Akayesu,* Case No. ICTR–96–4–T, Trial Chamber 1, Judgment, paragraph 598 (Sept. 2, 1998), that rape is a crime against humanity, defined as: "a physical invasion of a sexual nature, committed on a person under circumstances which are coercive. Sexual violence, which includes rape, is considered to be any act of a sexual nature which is committed on a person under circumstances which are coercive." This definition of rape was adopted by the Ad Hoc Tribunal for the Former Yugoslavia, in the context of torture and is a War Crime. *See,* Prosecutor v. Zejnil Delaić, et al., Case No. IT–96–21–T, in paragraph 493 (ICTY, Nov. 16, 1998). *See, gen.,* Kelly Dawn Askin, *Sexual Violence in Decisions and Indictments of the Yugoslav and Rwandan Tribunals: Current Status,* 93 Am.J.Int'l L. 97 (1999).

Summary of the Judgement in Jean–Paul Akayesu Case

ICTR–96–4–T
Delivered on 2 September 1998.

[The actual judgment is nearly 300 pages long. The Trial Chamber, therefore, delivered a summary which is extracted below. The accused was elected *bourgmestre* of Taba commune in 1993 and held that position until June 1994. The *bourgmestre* in Rwanda traditionally has had extensive powers, as the Tribunal noted. He was indicted with 15 counts relating to genocide, crimes against humanity and violations of article 3 common to the Geneva Conventions 1949 and Additional Protocol 11 of 1977. These Documents are in the Documentary Supplement. Acayesu's specific offenses included murder, torture, rape in addition to the genocide, crimes against humanity, and public incitement to commit genocide.]

19. Based on the evidence submitted to the Chamber, it is clear that the massacres which occurred in Rwanda in 1994 had a specific objective, namely the extermination of the Tutsi, who were targeted especially because of their Tutsi origin and not because they were RPF fighters. In any case, the Tutsi children and pregnant women would, naturally, not have been among the fighters. The Chamber concludes that, alongside the conflict between the RAF and RPF, genocide was committed in Rwanda in 1994 against the Tutsi as a group. The execution of this genocide was probably facilitated by the conflict in the sense that the conflict with the RPF forces served as a pretext for the propaganda inciting genocide against the Tutsi by branding RPF fighters and Tutsi civilians together through the notion widely disseminated, particularly by *Radio Television Libre des Mille Collines (RTLM)*, to the effect that every Tutsi was allegedly an accomplice of the RPF soldiers or "Inkotanyi". However, the fact that the genocide occurred while the RAF were in conflict with the RPF, obviously, cannot serve as a mitigating circumstance for the genocide.

20. Consequently, the Chamber concludes from all the foregoing that it was, indeed, genocide that was committed in Rwanda in 1994, against the Tutsi as a group. The Chamber is of the opinion that the genocide appears to have been meticulously organized. . . .

21. The Chamber holds that the genocide was organized and planned not only by members of the RAF, but also by the political forces who were behind the "Hutu-power", that it was executed essentially by civilians including the armed militia and even ordinary citizens, and above all that

the majority of the Tutsi victims were non-combatants, including thousands of women and children.

22.   Having said that, the Chamber then recalled that the fact that genocide was, indeed, committed in Rwanda in 1994, and more particularly in Taba, cannot influence it in its findings in the present matter. It is the Chamber's responsibility alone to assess the individual criminal responsibility of the Accused, Jean–Paul Akayesu, for the crimes alleged against him, including genocide, for which the Prosecution has to show proof. Despite the indisputable atrociousness of the crimes and the emotions evoked in the international community, the judges have examined the facts adduced in a most dispassionate manner, bearing in mind that the accused is presumed innocent. . . .

Note. The remainder of the Akayesu decision is in Chapter 16.

In 1999, Elizaphan Ntakirutimana was extradited to the Arusha Tribunal from the United States, despite the lack of an extradition treaty. Until 1996, no extradition from the U.S. was allowed without a treaty. In 1996, however, the extradition law was amended to allow surrender of fugitives to the Ad Hoc Tribunals for the former Yugoslavia and Rwanda.[1] Today, the law reads: "[t]he provisions of this chapter relating to the surrender of persons who have committed crimes in foreign countries shall continue in force only during the existence of any treaty of extradition with such governments."[2] This extradition decision is found below, *supra.* It may be worthwhile reviewing at this point. *See, Re Ntakirutimana v. Reno,* 184 F.3d 419 (5th Cir. 1999) (reversing District Court that had refused extradition of Rwandan génocidaire).

When genocide was ignited in the spring of 1994, the international community and the western media that had ignored the brewing crisis in Africa's Great Lakes region were caught off-guard. Unable to devote necessary resources to provide an adequate analysis of the complexities that involved African, as well as Western actors, they went to the reductive and simplistic filter of making sense of African conflicts through the narrow lens of tribal hatred.

The UN General Assembly dragged its feet for weeks before acknowledging that genocide was taking place in Rwanda. Meanwhile, hundreds of thousands of Tutsi along with Hutu moderates were slaughtered in a systematically planned campaign to wipe out anyone resembling a Tutsi,

---

1.   Id. Recently, the U.S. Congress promulgated the Judicial assistance to the International Tribunal for Yugoslavia and to the International Tribunal for Rwanda, Pub.L. 104–106, Div.A., Title XIII, § 1342, Feb. 10, 1996, 110 Stat. 486, provided that: ". . . 118 U.S.C. § 3181, et seq.], relating to the extradition of persons to a foreign country pursuant to a treaty or convention for extradition . . ., shall apply in the same manner and extent to the surrender of persons, including United States citizens, to—(A) [the ICTY]; and (B) [the ICTR]. . . . *See, Surrender of Ntakirutimana,* 988 F.Supp. 1038 (S.D.Tex. 1998) (holding this to be unconstitutional); *reversed in, In re Surrender of Ntakirutimana,* 184 F.3d 419 (5th Cir. 1999). Also, 18 U.S.C. 3181(b), allows the Attorney General of the U.S. to surrender non-U.S. nationals without a treaty (by way of comity), persons who have committed crimes of violence against U.S. nationals in foreign countries.

2.   18 U.S.C. § 3181, et seq. *See, US v. Herbage,* 850 F.2d 1463, 1465 (11th Cir. 1989); *see discussion, infra;* Blakesley, Terrorism, Drugs, *supra* at 224–250.

and any Hutus who got in the way. One explanation why the UN was slow to act is that the U.S. was worried that if the term genocide was used, it would be required to send in its marines. President Bill Clinton did not want to risk the repeat of the Mogadishu fiasco, where Somalis retaliated by killing an American marine and dragging his naked body through the streets of their capital. But the U.S. didn't have to intervene. At issue was whether the UN could alter its mandate from peacekeeping to peacemaking, and authorize the Canadian UN Commander Gen. Romeo Dallaire, to protect Rwandan civilians. Clearly, the UN forces in Rwanda would have had no resistance from the ill-equipped Rwandan army and its Interahamwe militia, which was engaged in the extermination of the Tutsi. But the international community turned a blind eye. Although the UN did not assist Rwandans, it did evacuate the expatriate population out of Rwanda. With the foreigners gone, the media left and turned off the lights, thus giving carte blanche to the génocidaires to carry out their objectives. The slaughter was carried out very efficiently. It took only three months to kill the same number of people that were killed in the three-year "ethnic cleansing" in Bosnia. This year marks the sixth memorial of this tragedy, and the Rwandan community in Vancouver hopes that this symposium can serve as a forum to reflect on the causes, as well as on the effects of the genocide. It will be an annual event where we can begin to map strategies to help prevent a repeat of such heinous crimes against humanity.

5. THE UNIVERSAL DECLARATION OF HUMAN RIGHTS[a]

The declaration was adopted by the United Nations General Assembly, Resolution 217A(III), on December 10, 1948, by a vote of 48 to 0, *Gen.Ass.*

a. Other Human Rights Declarations. In addition to the Universal Declaration, a number of other declarations dealing with particular aspects of human rights have been adopted by the General Assembly. Among them are:

Declaration of the Rights of the Child, November 20, 1959, G.A.Res. 1386 (XIV), U.N.Gen.Ass.Off.Rec., 14th Sess., Supp. 16(A/4354), p. 19.

Declaration on the Granting of Independence to Colonial Countries and Peoples, December 14, 1960, G.A.Res. 1514(XV), U.N.Gen.Ass. Off.Rec., 15th Sess., Supp. 16(A/4684), p. 66.

United Nations Declaration on the Elimination of All Forms of Racial Discrimination, November 20, 1963, G.A.Res. 1904 (XVIII), U.N.Gen.Ass.Off.Rec., 18th Sess., Supp. 15(A/5515), p. 35.

Declaration on the Elimination of Discrimination Against Women, November 7, 1967, G.A.Res. 2263(XXII), U.N.Gen.Ass.Off.Rec., 22nd Sess., Supp. 16(A/6716), p. 35.

Declaration on Territorial Asylum, December 14, 1967, G.A.Res. 2312(XXII), U.N.Gen.Ass. Off.Rec., 22nd Sess., Supp. 16(A/6716), p. 81.

Declaration on the Protection of all Persons from Being Subjected to Torture and Other Cruel, Inhuman or Degrading Treatment or Punishment, December 9, 1975, G.A.Res. 3452(XXX), U.N.Gen.Ass.Off.Rec., 30th Sess., Supp. 34(A/10034), p. 91.

Declaration on the Rights of Mentally Retarded Persons, December 20, 1971, G.A.Res. 2856(26), U.N.Gen.Ass.Off.Rec., 26th Sess., Supp. 29(A/8429), p. 93.

Declaration on the Protection of Women and Children in Emergency and Armed Conflict, December 14, 1974, G.A.Res. 3318(29), U.N.Gen.Ass.Off.Rec., 29th Sess., Supp. 31(A/9631), p. 146.

Declaration on the Rights of Disabled Persons, December 9, 1975, G.A.Res. 3447(30), U.N.Gen.Ass.Off.Rec., 30th Sess., Supp. 34(A/10034), p. 88.

Declaration on the Elimination of All Forms of Intolerance and of Discrimination Based on Religion or Belief, November 25, 1981, G.A.Res. 36/55, U.N.Gen.Ass.Off.Rec., 36th Sess., Supp. 51(A/36/51), p. 171.

Off.Rec., 3rd Sess., Part 1, Resolutions, p. 71. Although there were no dissenting votes, the following states abstained: Byelorussia SSR, Czechoslovakia, Poland, Saudi Arabia, Ukranian SSR, USSR, Union of South Africa and Yugoslavia.

————

CONTENTS OF THE DECLARATION

The General Assembly proclaims the listed rights as a "common standard of achievement." These rights are applicable to "all human beings," to "everyone." The rights include such personal rights as equal protection of the law, right to a fair hearing, to be presumed innocent, to freedom of movement and asylum, to marry and found a family. Also included are economic and social rights such as to social security, to work, to form and join trade unions, to a standard of living adequate for health and well-being, to education. For example:

Article 5

No one shall be subjected to torture or to cruel, inhuman or degrading treatment or punishment.

Article 9

No one shall be subjected to arbitrary arrest, detention or exile.

Article 10

Everyone is entitled in full equality to a fair and public hearing by an independent and impartial tribunal, in the determination of his rights and obligations and of any criminal charge against him.

Is the Declaration Law? A Drafter's View

5 Whiteman, Digest of International Law 243 (1965).

As the General Assembly neared its final vote on the Declaration, Mrs. Franklin D. Roosevelt, as the Chairman of the Commission on Human Rights and a representative of the United States in the Assembly, stated: In giving our approval to the declaration today, it is of primary importance that we keep clearly in mind the basic character of the document. It is not a treaty; it is not an international agreement. It is not and does not purport to be a statement of law or of legal obligation. It is a declaration of basic principles of human rights and freedoms, to be stamped with the approval of the General Assembly by formal vote of its members, and to serve as a common standard of achievement for all peoples of all nations.

A Diplomatic View

2 Kiss, *Répertoire de la Pratique Française en Matière de Droit International Public* 651 (1966).*

Declaration of the French Government of August 1, 1951. The French Government has followed with the greatest attention the measures of deportation taken in Hungary against numerous components of the population [which have been] suddenly declared "undesirable." According to the information received [by the French Government] these measures appear to have been extraordinarily far reaching and harsh and to strike pitilessly a great diversity of persons within the population. Such acts constitute a flagrant violation of the principle of respect for human beings and the rights of man [which is] recognized by the international community and embodied in the Declaration of the United Nations of December 10, 1948.

The French Government notes with the greatest concern that the information has now been confirmed by official statements of the Hungarian authorities. Faithful to its traditions, the French Government regards it as its duty solemnly to denounce practices which openly violate the human rights that the Government of the People's Republic of Hungary has formally committed itself to observe in the Peace Treaty of February 10, 1947.

A Publicist's View

Humphrey, *The UN Charter and the Universal Declaration of Human Rights*, The International Protection of Human Rights 39, 51 (Luard, ed. 1967).

Even more remarkable than the performance of the United Nations in adopting the Declaration has been its impact and the role which it almost immediately began to play both within and outside the United Nations-an impact and a role which probably exceed the most sanguine hopes of its authors. No other act of the United Nations has had anything like the same impact on the thinking of our time, the best aspirations of which it incorporates and proclaims. It may well be that it will live in history chiefly as a statement of great moral principles. As such its influence is deeper and more lasting than any political document or legal instrument. [Some] are more apt to be impressed by the political and legal authority which it has established for itself. Its political authority is now second only to that of the charter itself. Indeed its reception at all levels has been such that, contrary to the expressed intention of its authors, it may have now become part of international law.

A Jurist's View

Separate Opinion of Vice–President Ammoun in Advisory Opinion on the Continued Presence of South Africa in Namibia (South West Africa) [1971] I.C.J. Reports 16, 76.

The Advisory Opinion takes judicial notice of the Universal Declaration of Human Rights. In the case of certain of the Declaration's provisions,

* Translation by the editors. Reprinted   *de la Recherche Scientifique*, Paris. by permission, *Editions du Centre National*

attracted by the conduct of South Africa, it would have been an improvement to have dealt in terms with their comminatory nature, which is implied in paragraphs 130 and 131 of the Opinion by the references to their violation.

In its written statement the French Government, alluding to the obligations which South Africa accepted under the Mandate and assumed on becoming a Member of the United Nations, and to the norms laid down in the Universal Declaration of Human Rights, stated that there was no doubt that the Government of South Africa had, in a very real sense, systematically infringed those rules and those obligations. Nevertheless, referring to the mention by resolution 2145(XXI) of the Universal Declaration of Human Rights, it objected that it was plainly impossible for non-compliance with the norms it enshrined to be sanctioned with the revocation of the Mandate, inasmuch as that Declaration was not in the nature of a treaty binding upon States.

Although the affirmations of the Declaration are not binding qua international convention within the meaning of Article 38, paragraph 1(a), of the Statute of the Court, they can bind States on the basis of custom within the meaning of paragraph 1(b) of the same Article, whether because they constituted a codification of customary law as was said in respect of Article 6 of the Vienna Convention on the Law of Treaties, or because they have acquired the force of custom through a general practice accepted as law, in the words of Article 38, paragraph 1(b), of the Statute. One right which must certainly be considered a preexisting binding customary norm which the Universal Declaration of Human Rights codified is the right to equality, which by common consent has ever since the remotest times been deemed inherent in human nature.

The equality demanded by the Namibians and by other peoples of every colour, the right to which is the outcome of prolonged struggles to make it a reality, is something of vital interest to us here, on the one hand because it is the foundation of other human rights which are no more than its corollaries and, on the other, because it naturally rules out racial discrimination and apartheid, which are the gravest of the facts with which South Africa, as also other States, stands charged. The attention I am devoting to it in these observations can therefore by no means be regarded as exaggerated or out of proportion.

It is not by mere chance that in Article 1 of the Universal Declaration of the Rights * * * there stands * * * this primordial principle or axiom: "All human beings are born free and equal in dignity and rights." From this first principle flow most rights and freedoms.

* * * The ground was thus prepared for the legislative and constitutional process which began with the first declarations or bills of rights in America and Europe, continued with the constitutions of the nineteenth century, and culminated in positive international law in the San Francisco, Bogota and Addis Ababa charters, and in the Universal Declaration of Human Rights which has been confirmed by numerous resolutions of the United Nations, in particular the above-mentioned declarations adopted by the General Assembly in resolutions 1514(15), 2625(25) and 2627(25). The

Court in its turn has now confirmed it. *See,* the *Filartiga* and *Siderman* cases, *infra.* * * *

6.   THE HUMAN RIGHTS COVENANTS

Under the aegis of the League of Nations and the United Nations, a number of conventions on particular human rights have been prepared by a variety of conferences, committees and commissions. Drafts of these conventions have progressed through many stages. They are typically given final approval by some plenary international body before being submitted to states for ratification. In some cases that approval has been issued by resolution of the General Assembly. In others, the final text is prepared and approved by an ad hoc U.N. conference. In still other cases, the final text has come from a specialized agency, such as the International Labor Organization.

The two conventions that are the most general in scope of all of the human rights conventions are the *International Covenant on Economic, Social and Cultural Rights* and the *International Covenant on Civil and Political Rights.*[a] These two covenants comprehensively carry into detailed treaty form most of the provisions of the *Universal Declaration of Human Rights.* You should compare the declaration with covenants.

What disparities exist within these covenants and between them and the Declaration? Is the fact of these disparities significant? Does the fact that certain rights were included in the Declaration but not in the more detailed covenants weaken the general legal significance that has been accorded the Declaration? Does the fact that certain rights appear in the covenants but not in the Declaration (such as the right to self-determination) suggest that some are less than universal or that they do not reflect general principles of international law? Does the worldwide recognition of a particular right as international law depend upon factors more complex than whether the verbal recognition of that right was made in the declaration or in one or the other of the covenants? If so, what are the factors and do they have a legal impact?

The covenants were the product of many years' work, first in the Commission on Human Rights (from 1949 until 1954) and thereafter in the Third Committee of the General Assembly (from 1954 until 1966). The Commission's original conception had been to prepare a single draft covenant. Insistence by some states that the covenant include provisions for economic, social and cultural rights resulted in a decision by the General Assembly that two covenants be drafted. One dealing with economic, social and cultural rights; the other with civil and political rights. Contrast the wide difference between the two covenants with respect to methods of implementation with the sense of assurance by which the various rights are asserted in each. Compare each of these instruments with the *Convention on the Elimination of All Forms of Discrimination Against Women.* What impact do you think the Statutes for the Ad Hoc Tribunals for Rwanda and

a. In 1978, the U.N. Office of Public Information published the texts of the Universal Declaration, these two covenants, and an official protocol relating to implementation of the latter covenant under the title: The International Bill of Human Rights.

the former Yugoslavia, and the International Criminal Court have on the human rights indicated in all these instruments? How do the rights provided in the *Covenant on Civil and Political Rights* compare with those recognized decisions of commissions for the protection of women, refugees, minorities, or ethnic groups, or with the statutes for the *Ad Hoc Tribunals for Rwanda, the former Yugoslavia*, or the Statute for the *International Criminal Court?* Who is entitled to these rights? Are the substantive standards different? *See* Chapter 10, *infra*, and the Documentary Supplement.

———

The Helsinki Final Act. The Helsinki Conference on Security and Cooperation in Europe, held from September 1973 to August 1975, concluded with a *Final Act*, signed by representatives of 35 states, including the countries of "Western Europe," the "Soviet-bloc," the U.S. and Canada. The legal status of this document was described by President Ford before he attended the closing days of the conference: "I would emphasize that the document I will sign is neither a treaty nor is it legally binding on any participating state. The Helsinki documents involve political and moral commitments aimed at lessening tensions and opening further the lines of communication between the peoples of East and West." 73 U.S. Dept. State Bull. 204, 205 (1975). The Final Act was deposited by the Finnish delegate with the following statement: "I have also been asked * * * to draw your attention to the fact that this Final Act is not eligible, in whole or in part, for registration with the Secretariat under Article 102 of the Charter, * * * as would be the case were it a matter of a treaty or international agreement. * * * "

The Final Act is a comprehensive document covering the following matters: Questions Relating to Security in Europe (so-called Basket I); Cooperation in the Field of Economics, of Science and Technology, and of the Environment (Basket II); Questions Relating to Security and Cooperation in the Mediterranean, and Cooperation in Humanitarian and Other Fields (Basket III). A major outcome of the conference was an assurance that existing European territorial arrangements (e.g. borders) would not be disturbed by force. Human rights matters were also included in the Final Act, as Principle VII in a Declaration of Principles Guiding Relations between Participating States. The complete text of the Final Act may be found at 73 U.S. Dept. State Bull. 323 (1975). At a follow-up conference in Madrid in 1983, a Concluding Document amplified the Helsinki agreements with respect to cooperation in the humanitarian field. Department of State Bulletin, October 1983, p. 53. Although the Helsinki Final Act does not constitute a legally binding international agreement, Principle VII of the Declaration of Principles seeks to tie the signatory states to international law with the following statement: "In the field of human rights and fundamental freedoms, the participating States will act in conformity with the purposes and principles of the [U.N.] Charter and with the Universal Declaration of Human Rights. They will also fulfill their obligations as set forth in the international declarations and agreements in this field, including inter alia the International Covenants on Human Rights, by which they may be bound.''

––––––––

7. U.S. RATIFICATION OF THE INTERNATIONAL COVENANT ON CIVIL AND POLITICAL RIGHTS

This material is presented *supra* at pages 654–756, in relation to the section on Self–Executing Treaties, in Blakesley, *Autumn of the Patriarch, supra.*

Human Rights and the Environment. Do you think human rights law should encompass environmental concerns? *See* Chapter 6.

SECTION C. HUMAN RIGHTS AS CUSTOMARY INTERNATIONAL LAW

The Universal Declaration of Human Rights and the human rights conventions spell out in considerable detail a great number of rights. The conventions are legally binding documents detailing the correlative duties of state parties to give effect to human rights. Is the Universal Declaration a codification of international law? Do the human rights conventions reflect international law that exists outside treaty regimes? Do they create or reflect law that is binding on parties and non-parties alike? The American Law Institute has taken the position that there are certain core human rights that have entered into the body of international law, rights that must be recognized by each state whether or not the state has become otherwise bound to do so by international agreement.

1987 Restatement, Section 702

Customary International Law of Human Rights

A state violates international law if, as a matter of state policy, it practices, encourages or condones

    (a) genocide,

    (b) slavery or slave trade,

    (c) the murder or causing the disappearance of individuals,

    (d) torture or other cruel, inhuman or degrading treatment or punishment,

    (e) prolonged arbitrary detention,

    (f) systematic racial discrimination, or

    (g) a consistent pattern of gross violations of internationally recognized human rights.

Comment: k. Consistent pattern of gross violations of human rights. The acts enumerated in clauses (a) to (f) are violations of customary law even if the practice is not consistent, or not part of a "pattern," and those acts are inherently "gross" violations of human rights. Clause (g) includes other infringements of recognized human rights which, when committed singly or sporadically, are not violations of customary law (although they may be forbidden to states parties to the International Covenants or other particular agreements); they become violations of customary law if the state is guilty of a "consistent pattern of gross violations" as state policy. A violation is gross if it is particularly shocking because of the importance of the right or the gravity of the violation. While all the rights proclaimed in the Universal Declaration and protected by the principal International Covenants * * * are internationally recognized human rights, some rights are fundamental and intrinsic to human dignity, and a consistent pattern of violation of such rights as state policy may be deemed "gross" ipso facto. It includes, for example, systematic harassment, invasions of the privacy of the home, arbitrary arrest and detention (even if not prolonged); denial of fair trial in criminal cases; grossly disproportionate punishment; denial of freedom to leave a country when a country of haven is available; denial of the right to return to one's own country; mass uprooting of a country's population; denial of freedom of conscience and religion; denial of personality before the law; denial of basic privacy such as the right to marry and raise a family; invidious racial or religious discrimination. A party to the Covenant on Civil and Political Rights is responsible even for a single, isolated violation of one of these rights; any state is liable under customary law for a consistent pattern of violations of any such right as state policy. *See also,* the *Karadzic, Filartiga* and *Siderman* cases, *infra, this chapter.*

SECTION D.   IMPLEMENTATION OF THE INTERNATIONAL LAW OF HUMAN RIGHTS

1.   IMPLEMENTATION AT THE UNITED NATIONS

Statement on Human Rights by the Secretary General of the International Commission of Jurists, Nov. 1978

Human Rights in United States and United Kingdom Foreign Policy 23–26, 72 (Stewart ed. 1979).*

The UN bodies concerned with human rights are chiefly the Commission on Human Rights; its Sub–Commission on the Prevention of Discrimination and Protection of Minorities; and the Human Rights Committee set up under the International Covenant on Civil and Political Rights. Many other UN bodies also cope with human rights issues.

There is a frequent complaint about too much politics in the Human Rights Commission; but human rights are a very political subject. One must accept that. Paradoxically, it is very rare for politicians to attend the

* Reprinted with the permission of the American Association of the International Commission of Jurists.

Human Rights Commission. [But, recall that the U.S. was voted off the commission in the spring of 2001.]

There is a need for people with continuing experience in human rights to head delegations.

The Human Rights Commission and the Sub–Commission's work is threefold: standard setting, studies, and implementation.

Standard Setting is the formulation of principles in Conventions or Declarations of Principles such as the two International Covenants prepared by the Commission, and the Draft Convention on Torture. The Draft Body of Principles for the Protection of Persons in All Forms of Detention or Imprisonment was delegated to the Sub–Commission. . . .

Implementation takes two forms:

Reports from States and Parties on legislative and administrative action to implement the various conventions and declarations. A number of them, such as on Freedom of Information and of the Press, go to the Commission. They do not form a large part of the Commission's activities and are not very effective. More impressive are the reporting procedures under the Convention on the Elimination of Racial Discrimination and under the Convention on Civil and Political Rights.

Alleged Violations Procedures can be public or private. They are public when a government raises an issue. . . . An ad hoc committee is set up to study the subject and receive evidence, usually from NGOs and individuals. They tend to be one-sided in their views, often because the government under investigation has failed to cooperate. Governments do not regard them as fair tribunals.

The other system is the confidential so-called communications procedure directed to situations of a consistent pattern of gross violations of human rights, rather than to individual complaints. The UN receives [more than] 30,000–40,000 complaints yearly, mostly from individuals and most of which do not begin to provide evidence of a consistent pattern. * * * The Commission acts on complaints from NGOs. The Human Rights Commission can set up a Commission of Enquiry with the consent of the concerned government; or it can order a thorough study. . . . Occasionally a complaint has been referred to a government for its comment. That is another delaying tactic. . . .

―――――

Investigation of human rights violations. United Nations implementation of human rights policies generally consists of resolutions condemning violations of human rights standards. Ad hoc groups of experts or working groups are occasionally created by the General Assembly or the Human Rights Commission, to investigate and publicize human rights violations. From time to time, a special rapporteur may be asked to address a specific problem. The General Assembly may request the Secretary–General to investigate and publicize violations. The Human Rights Commission has discussed for many years the creation of a High Commissioner for Human Rights to serve as an ombudsman, dealing with specific situations as the need might arise. How much do you think these processes help to create customary international law?

2.   INTERNATIONAL ADJUDICATION

There is no universal court in which an individual can maintain an action to enforce the rights that international law has begun to recognize. True, we have recently seen the creation of two ad hoc tribunals and a permanent international criminal court (ICC), but these courts have the purpose of prosecuting individuals for criminal conduct thus only incidentally protecting the victim's rights. These courts do not provide an outlet for individual victims to sue or to receive direct vindication for their rights having been abused. In mid–2001, he only universal court is the International Court of Justice where only states may be parties in cases before the court.[a] Are there nevertheless means by which an individual's rights can be vindicated in this court?

Problem. A is a national of State D, a party to the International Convention on the Elimination of All Forms of Racial Discrimination. A claims that because of his race he has been denied equal opportunity by State D with respect to housing and employment, in violation of Article 5 of the convention. A persuades the foreign office of State P to become interested in his case by reason of the opportunity it affords State P to publicly embarrass State D over its racial policies. State P is unsuccessful in procuring any change in State D's policies or its treatment of A. All of the procedures provided for in the convention are exhausted without effect see Articles 11, 12 and 13 *in the Documentary Supplement.* Pursuant to Article 22, State P refers its dispute with State D, over D's treatment of A, to the International Court of Justice. Article 22 provides:"Any dispute between two or more States Parties with respect to the interpretation or application of this Convention, which is not settled by negotiation or by the procedures expressly provided for in this Convention, shall, at the request of any of the parties to the dispute, be referred to the International Court of Justice for decision, unless the disputants agree to another mode of settlement." Will the court take jurisdiction of such a claim? Will it recognize the standing or interest of the complainant state?

Notteböhm Case (Liechtenstein v. Guatemala)

International Court of Justice, 1955.
[1955] I.C.J.Rep. 4.

Re-read the opinion of *Notteböhm*, found in Chapter 8, *supra.* In the problem case the individual, A, whose rights were allegedly violated, is not a national of State by any definition of nationality. Does the reasoning of *Notteböhm* suggest that P cannot maintain this proceeding?

a. Of course, when the International Criminal Court (ICC) receives its 60 ratifications necessary for its beginning to function, we will have another "universal court." Still, this court will be for prosecutors to bring cases against individual indictees. Indictments will be triggered either by states, international organizations or sometimes individuals through their representatives. For discussion of the ICC, see Chapter 16, *infra.*

Inter–American Court of Human Rights: Judgment in Velásquez Rodríguez Case*

(Forced Disappearance and Death of Individual in Honduras) [July 29, 1988], 28 I.L.M. 291 (1989).

Introductory Note by Thomas Buergenthal

In 1986 the Inter–American Commission on Human Rights referred three cases to the Inter–American Court of Human Rights for adjudication in accordance with the provisions of the American Convention of Human Rights. [See 9 I.L.M. 673 (1970)]. In all three cases-*Velásquez Rodríguez, Godínez Cruz,* and *Fairen Garbi and Sollis Corrales*-the Republic of Honduras was charged with a series of violations of human rights that were allegedly committed in that country between 1981–1984 and resulted in the forced disappearance and death of four individuals.

The Government of Honduras, which had accepted the Court's jurisdiction in accordance with the provisions of Article 62 of the Convention, challenged the admissibility of the cases and the tribunal's jurisdiction to hear them on various grounds relating to the Commission's handling of the cases and for failure to exhaust domestic remedies. The Court dealt with these contentions in separate but almost identical judgments which were rendered on June 26, 1987. * * * In them, it rejected all but one of the preliminary objections of the Government. As to that objection, which alleged the failure to exhaust domestic remedies, the Court ordered it joined to the merits of the proceedings. This decision, the Court concluded, was compelled by the fact that it could not dispose of the objection without examining the question whether there existed in Honduras, between 1981 and 1984, a practice of disappearances, carried out or tolerated by the Government, which was the very issue the Court would have to address in dealing with the merits.

Although the Court was able to dispose of the preliminary objections in three separate judgments rendered on the same day, it has thus far adjudicated the merits of only two of the cases, *viz., Velásquez Rodríguez,* the instant case, and the *Godínez Cruz* case. The Court's reasoning in the latter case, which was decided on January 20, 1989, is for all practical purposes identical to that of *Velásquez.* * * * In all three cases the Commission invited Messrs. Claudio Grossman, Juan Méndez and José Miguel Vivanco, the lawyers who represented the private parties in the proceedings before the Commission, to serve as advisers to its delegation in the proceedings. * * *

――――

Notes and Questions

1. *The case concerning the Barcelona Traction, Light and Power Company, Limited (Belgium v. Spain)* **[1970]** I.C.J.Rep. 3. A portion of

――――

* Reproduced from the English text provided to *International Legal Materials* by the Inter–American Court of Human Rights. Reprinted with the permission of the American Society of Int'l Law. The Introductory Note was prepared for *International Legal Materials* by Thomas Buergenthal, Professor of Law, George Washington University School of Law; nominated to be Judge, International Court of Justice.

the decision is in Chapter 13. The case concerned claimed injury to a corporation's property. In the course of an opinion dealing with the question of the proper state to maintain an action to redress this injury, the court stated:

33. When a State admits into its territory foreign investments or foreign nationals, * * * it is bound to extend to them the protection of the law and assumes obligations concerning the treatment to be afforded them. These obligations, however, are neither absolute nor unqualified. In particular, an essential distinction should be drawn between the obligations of a State towards the international community as a whole, and those arising vis-à-vis another State in the field of diplomatic protection. By their very nature the former are the concern of all States. In view of the importance of the rights involved, all States can be held to have a legal interest in their protection; they are obligations erga omnes.

34. Such obligations derive, for example, in contemporary international law, from the outlawing of acts of aggression, and of genocide, as also from the principles and rules concerning the basic rights of the human person, including protection from slavery and racial discrimination. Some of the corresponding rights of protection have entered into the body of general international law (*Reservations to the Convention on the Prevention and Punishment of the Crime of Genocide, Advisory Opinion*, I.C.J. Reports 1951, p. 23); others are conferred by international instruments of a universal or quasi-universal character.

35. Obligations the performance of which is the subject of diplomatic protection are not of the same category. It cannot be held, when one such obligation in particular is in question, in a specific case, that all States have a legal interest in its observance. In order to bring a claim in respect of the breach of such an obligation, a State must first establish its right to do so, for the rules on the subject rest on two suppositions:

The first is that the defendant State has broken an obligation towards the national State in respect of its nationals. The second is that only the party to whom an international obligation is due can bring a claim in respect of its breach. (Reparation for Injuries Suffered in the Service of the United Nations, Advisory Opinion, I.C.J. Reports 1949, pp. 181–182.)

* * *

Despite the expansiveness of its language in ¶ ¶ 33 and 34, the court made the following puzzling observation later in its opinion:

91. With regard more particularly to human rights, to which reference has already been made in paragraph 34 of this Judgment, it should be noted that these also include protection against denial of justice. However, on the universal level, the instruments which embody human rights do not confer on States the capacity to protect the victims of infringements of such rights irrespective of their nationality. It is therefore still on the regional level that a solution to this problem

has had to be sought; thus, within the Council of Europe, of which Spain is not a member, the problem of admissibility encountered by the claim in the present case has been resolved by the European Convention on Human Rights, which entitles each State which is a party to the Convention to lodge a complaint against any other contracting State for violation of the Convention, irrespective of the nationality of the victim.

The Reporters of the 1987 Restatement addressed the Court's statement: " * * * Apparently, the Court meant that, as a matter of interpretation, general human rights agreements ordinarily do not contemplate diplomatic protection by one state party on behalf of an individual victim of a violation by another state party, at least where the victim was not a national of the protecting state. However, unless otherwise provided or clearly implied, there appears to be no reason why a party may not make an inter-state claim for a violation of such an agreement as for any other multilateral agreement. * * * " Section 703, Reporters' Note 2.

2. *Remedies and Advisory Opinions.* The International Court of Justice has two forms of jurisdiction: contentious and advisory. If a state refers a dispute about one state's treatment of the latter state's own nationals, what relief may be granted? Would monetary relief be administrable? Would a declaratory judgment be more workable? Would it be effective? See Judge Jessup's dissenting opinion in *the South West Africa cases*, [1966] I.C.J.Rep. at 329. Article 65(1) of the I.C.J. Statute provides authority for the Court to render advisory opinions, when requested is there any way that human rights can be vindicated in an advisory opinion? An individual needs the support of some other state to enlist the aid of the General Assembly or the Security Council (or some other body authorized under Articles 65 and 96 to request the opinion. The political difficulties that would be encountered by a single individual in pursuit of an advisory opinion through these channels would be virtually insurmountable. On the other hand, a group of individuals alleging a gross violation of a convention or general international legal obligation might possibly have more success. Beyond the political problems involved in procuring the request for an advisory opinion, there is the problem of inducing the Court to render the opinion. *As an example, see, the Western Sahara Case* [1975] ICJ Rep. 12, 22.

———

Contentious Cases

Case Concerning Application of the Convention on the Prevention and Punishment of the Crime of Genocide (Bosnia and Herzegovina v. Yugoslavia (Serbia and Montenegro), Request for the Indication of Provisional Measures, [1993] I.C.J.Reports 3, 32 I.L.M. 890 (1993).

International Court of Justice, 1993, 1993 I.C.J. 3 (Apr.8).
(Order on Request for the Indication of Provisional Measures).

[Bosnia and Herzegovina brought an action against Serbia and Montenegro "for violating the Genocide Convention" and other illegal conduct in violation of customary international law. Although atrocities were committed by all sides, this suit was based on Bosnia's allegations that Yugoslavia through its agents "has killed, murdered, wounded, raped, robbed, tortured, kidnapped, illegally detained, and exterminated the citizens of Bosnia. . . ." On April 8, 1993, the International Court of Justice in response to the suit filed by Bosnia and Herzegovina, called upon Serbia and Montenegro to "immediately * * * take all measures within its power to prevent commission of the crime of genocide * * * whether directed against the Muslim population of Bosnia and Herzegovina or against any other national, ethnical, racial, or religious group." This was an interim decision. The Court noted that facts were still in dispute. It also noted that it was unable to render a decision in relation to disputed rights falling outside the ambit of the Genocide Convention.]

1.   Whereas . . . Bosnia–Herzegovina, basing the jurisdiction of the Court on Article IX of the Genocide Convention, recounts a series of events in Bosnia–Herzegovina from April 1992 up to the present day which, in its contention, amount to acts of genocide within the definition given in the Genocide Convention . . . ; and whereas Bosnia–Herzegovina claims that the acts complained of have been committed by former members of the Yugoslav People's Army (YPA) and by Serb military and paramilitary forces under the direction of, at the behest of, and with assistance from Yugoslavia; and whereas Bosnia–Herzegovina claims that Yugoslavia is therefore fully responsible under international law for their activities;

2.   Whereas on the basis of the facts alleged in the Application Bosnia–Herzegovina requests the Court to adjudge and declare as follows:

"(a) that Yugoslavia . . . has breached, and is continuing to breach, its legal obligations toward the people and State of Bosnia and Herzegovina under Articles I, II(a), II(b), II(c), II(d), III(a), III(b), III(c), III(d), III(e), IV, and V of the Genocide Convention;"

3.Whereas by a request filed . . . on 20 March 1993 . . . Bosnia–Herzegovina, invoking Article 41 of the Statute of the Court . . ., urgently requested that the Court indicate [enumerated] provisional measures to be in effect while the Court is seised of this case . . .;* * *

9.   Whereas in written observations, submitted to the Court on 1 April 1993, on the request for the indication of provisional measures, the Government of Yugoslavia [requested provisional measures instructing Bosnian authorities to take various measures to cease alleged mistreatment of and atrocities against Serbs in Bosnia];

. . .

14.   Whereas on a request for provisional measures the Court need not, before deciding whether or not to indicate them, finally satisfied itself that it has jurisdiction on the merits of the case, yet it ought not to indicate such measures unless the provisions invoked by the Applicant or found in the Statute appear, prima facie, to afford a basis on which the jurisdiction of the Court might be established; . . .

* * *

19. Whereas ... if Bosnia–Herzegovina and Yugoslavia are both parties to the Genocide Convention, disputes to which Article IX [of that Convention] applies are ... prima facie within the jurisdiction *ratione personae* of the court [pursuant to Article 35(2) of its Statute];

[Despite some question about whether Bosnia had become a party to the Genocide Convention at the time necessary to support the Court's jurisdiction, the Court concluded that a prima facie case had been established that it had jurisdiction *ratione materiae* under Article IX of the Genocide Convention. It reached a preliminary conclusion rejecting Bosnia's claim that a letter dated June 8, 1992, which had been signed by the Presidents of Yugoslavia's two constituent republics, constituted a basis for jurisdiction over "all outstanding legal disputes" between Yugoslavia and Bosnia. Accordingly, it confined its examination of the request for provisional measures and the grounds asserted in support thereof "to those which fall within the scope of the Genocide Convention."]

* * *

40. Whereas the Applicant has brought before the Court ... accounts of military and paramilitary activities, including the bombing and shelling of towns and villages, the destruction of houses and forced migration of civilians, and of acts of violence, including execution, murder, torture, and rape which, in the circumstances in which they have occurred, show, in the view of the Applicant, that acts of genocide have been committed, and will continue to be committed against, in particular, the Muslim inhabitants of Bosnia–Herzegovina;

41. Whereas Bosnia–Herzegovina claims in the Application that the acts there complained of have been committed by former members of the Yugoslav People's Army (YPS) and by Serb military and paramilitary forces under the direction of, at the behest of, and with assistance from Yugoslavia, and that Yugoslavia is therefore fully responsible under international law for their activities; and whereas in its request for the indication of provisional measures Bosnia–Herzegovina similarly contends that the facts stated in the Application show that Yugoslavia is committing acts of genocide, both directly and by means of its agents and surrogates, and that there is no reason to believe that Yugoslavia will voluntarily desist from this course of conduct while the case is pending before the Court;

42. Whereas Yugoslavia observes that the situation is not one of aggression by one State against another, but a civil war, and asserts that it has no soldiers in the territory of Bosnia–Herzegovina, that it does not militarily support any side in the conflict, and that it does not support or abet in any way the commission of crimes cited in the Application; that Yugoslavia and its subordinate bodies, including the military, have not committed and are not committing any of the acts to which Article III of the Genocide Convention refers. . . . ;

43. Whereas Yugoslavia in its written observations on the request for the indication of provisional measures "requests the Court to establish the responsibility of the authorities" of Bosnia–Herzegovina for acts of genocide against the Serb people in Bosnia–Herzegovina, and indicates its

intention to submit evidence to that effect; and whereas Yugoslavia claimed at the hearings that genocide and genocidal acts are being carried out against Serbs living in Bosnia–Herzegovina; whereas Bosnia–Herzegovina for its part contends however that there is on basis in fact or in law for the indication of provisional measures against it, there being no credible evidence that its Government has committed acts of genocide against anyone;

44.   Whereas the Court, in the context of the present proceedings on a request for provisional measures, has in accordance with Article 41 of the Statute to consider the circumstances drawn to its attention as requiring the indication of provisional measures, but cannot make definitive findings of fact or of imputability, and the right of each Party to dispute the facts alleged against it, to challenge the attribution to it of responsibility for those facts, and to submit arguments in respect of the merits, must remain unaffected by the Court's decision;

45.   Whereas Article I of the Genocide Convention provides that

> "The Contracting Parties confirm that genocide, whether committed in time of peace or in time of war, is a crime under international law which they undertake to prevent and to punish"

Whereas all parties to the Convention have thus undertaken"to prevent and to punish" the crime of genocide; whereas in the view of the Court, in the circumstances brought to its attention and outlined above in which there is a grave risk of acts of genocide being committed, Yugoslavia and Bosnia–Herzegovina, whether or not any such acts in the past may be legally imputable to them, are under a clear obligation to do all in their power to prevent the commission of any such acts in the future;

46.   Whereas the Court is not called upon, for the purpose of its decision on the present request for the indication of provisional measures, now to establish the existence of breaches of the Genocide Convention by either Party, but to determine whether the circumstances require the indication of provisional measures to be taken by the Parties for the protection of rights under the Genocide Convention; and whereas the Court is satisfied, taking into account the obligation imposed by Article I of the Genocide Convention, that the indication of measures is required for the protection of such rights; and whereas Article 75, paragraph 2, of the Rules of Court recognizes the power of the Court, when a request for provisional measures has been made, to indicate measures that are in whole or in part other than those requested, or that ought to be taken or compiled with by the party which has itself made the request;

* * *

48.   Whereas in its request for the indication of provisional measures Bosnia–Herzegovina has also maintained that the Court should exercise its power to indicate provisional measures with a view to preventing the aggravation or extension of the dispute whenever it considers that circumstances so require; whereas from the information available to the Court it is satisfied that there is a grave risk of action being taken which may

aggravate or extend the existing dispute over the prevention or punishment of the crime of genocide, or render it more difficult of solution;

49.   Whereas the crime of genocide "shocks the conscience of mankind, results in great losses to humanity ... and is contrary to moral law and to the spirit and aims of the United Nations", in the words of General Assembly resolution 96 (I) of 11 December 1946 on "the Crime of Genocide" ...;

50.   Whereas in the light of the several considerations set out above, the Court finds that the circumstances require it to indicate provisional measures, as provided by Article 41 of the Statute of the Court;

51.   Whereas the decision given in the present proceedings in no way prejudges the question of the jurisdiction of the Court to deal with the merits of the case, or any questions relating to the admissibility of the Application, or relating to the merits themselves, and leave unaffected the right of the Governments of Bosnia–Herzegovina and Yugoslavia to submit arguments in respect of those questions;

52.   For these reasons,

The Court,

Indicates, pending its final decision in the proceedings instituted on 20 March 1993 by the Republic of Bosnia and Herzegovina against the Federal Republic of Yugoslavia (Serbia and Montenegro) the following provisional measures

A.   (1) Unanimously,

The Government of the Federal Republic of Yugoslavia (Serbia and Montenegro) should immediately, in pursuance of its undertaking in the Convention on the Prevention and Punishment of the Crime of Genocide of 9 December 1948, take all measures within its power to prevent commission of the crime of genocide;

(2) By 13 votes to 1,

The Government of the Federal Republic of Yugoslavia (Serbia and Montenegro) should in particular ensure that any military, paramilitary or irregular armed unites which may be directed or supported by it, as well as any organizations and persons which may be subject to its control, direction or influence, do not commit any acts of genocide, of conspiracy to commit genocide, of direct and public incitement to commit genocide, or of complicity in genocide, whether directed against the Muslim population of Bosnia and Herzegovina or against any other national, ethnical, racial or religious groups;

In Favour: *President* Sir Robert Jennings; Vice–President Oda; Judges Ago, Schweble, Bedjaoui, Ni, Evensen, Guillaume, Shahabuddeen, Aguilar Mawdsley, Weeramantry, Ranjeva, Ajibola;

Against: *Judge* Tarassov;

B.   Unanimously,

The Government of the Federal Republic of Yugoslavia (Serbia and Montenegro) and the Government of the Republic of Bosnia and Herzegovina should not take any action and should ensure that no action is taken which may aggravate or extend the existing dispute over the prevention or punishment of the crime of genocide, or render it more difficult of solution.

* * *

Declaration of JUDGE TARASSOV

The appalling atrocities which have taken place in the territory of the former State of Yugoslavia move me no less than they move my colleagues. Nevertheless I have not been able to join with them in voting for all of the operative paragraphs of the Order, and I wish to say why.

I am generally in agreement with the consideranda and conclusions of the Order.... I support the provisional measures indicated by the Court in paragraph 52A(1) and paragraph 52B. I agree that the Government of the Federal Republic of Yugoslavia "should immediately ... take all measures within its power to prevent commission of the crime of genocide"–meaning, of course, measures within its real power. In my opinion, the same measures should be taken under the same understanding in respect of the Government of the Republic of Bosnia and Herzegovina, which has responsibility over acts committed on its territory. Unfortunately, the Court did not find it necessary to so provide....

... I regret that I have not been able to vote for the provision of paragraph 52A(2) that the Government of the Federal Republic of Yugoslavia should in particular "ensure" that any military, paramilitary or irregular armed units which "may" be directed or supported by it, and organizations or persons which "may be subject to its control, direction or influence" do not commit any acts of genocide, "of conspiracy to commit genocide", of incitement to genocide or of "complicity in genocide". In my view, these passages of the Order are open to the interpretation that the Court believes that the Government of the Federal Republic of Yugoslavia is indeed involved in such genocidal acts, or at least that it may very well be so involved. Thus, on my view, these provisions are very close to a prejudgment of the merits, despite the Court's recognition that, in an Order indicating provisional measures, it is not entitled to reach determination of fact or law. Moreover, these passages impose practically unlimited, ill-defined and vague requirements for the exercise of responsibility by the Respondent in fulfilment of the Order of the Court, and lay the Respondent open to unjustifiable blame for failing to comply with this interim measure....

Moreover, these objectionable provisions lack not only balance but practicality. Is it really within the realm of the practical for the Yugoslav Government to "ensure" that all persons who may claim to be subject to its influence do not conspire to commit genocide or incite genocide? Particularly when the persons who are accused of such acts are not its citizens and not within its territorial jurisdiction? Someone may affirm that he is under the influence of the Yugoslav Government without that being the fact. I am convinced that he Court should not imply that the Yugoslav Government may have responsibility for the commission of acts which in fact may be beyond its control.

———

Case Concerning Application of the Convention on the Prevention and Punishment of the Crime of Genocide (Bosnia–Herzegovina v. Yugoslavia)

International Court of Justice, 1996, 1996 I.C.J. 595 (July 11).
Preliminary Objections
Judgment, July 11, 1996

* * *

27.   In order to determine whether it has jurisdiction to entertain the case on the basis of Article IX of the Genocide Convention, it remains for the Court to verify whether there is a dispute between the Parties that falls within the scope of that provision. . . .

30.   . . . Yugoslavia disputes this. It contests the existence in this case of an "international dispute" within the meaning of the Convention, basing itself on two propositions: first, that the conflict occurring in certain parts of the Applicant's territory was of a domestic nature, Yugoslavia was not party to it and did not exercise jurisdiction over that territory at the time in question; and second, that State responsibility, as referred to in the requests of Bosnia–Herzegovina, was excluded from the scope of application of Article IX.

3.   The Court will begin with a consideration of Yugoslavia's first proposition. In doing so, it will start by recalling the terms of Article I of the Genocide Convention, worded as follows:

> "The Contracting Parties confirm that genocide, whether committed in time of peace or in time of war, is a crime under international law which they undertake to prevent and to punish."

The Court sees nothing in this provision which would make the applicability of the Convention subject to the condition that the acts contemplated by it should have been committed within the framework of a particular type of conflict. The contracting parties expressly state therein their willingness to consider genocide as "a crime under international law", which they must prevent and punish independently of the context "of peace" or "of war" in which it takes place. In the view of the Court, this means that the Convention is applicable, without reference to the circumstances linked to the domestic or international nature of the conflict, provided the acts to which it refers in Article II and III have been perpetrated. In other words, irrespective of the nature of the conflict forming the background to such acts, the obligations of prevention and punishment which are incumbent upon the States parties to the Convention remain identical.

As regards the question whether Yugoslavia took part–directly or indirectly–in the conflict at issue, the Court would merely note that the Parties have radically differing viewpoints in this respect and that it cannot, at this stage in the proceedings, settle this question, which clearly belongs to the merits.

Lastly, as to the territorial problems linked to the application of the Convention, the Court would point out that the only provision relevant to this, Article VI, merely provides for persons accused of one of the acts prohibited by the Convention to "be tried by a competent tribunal of the

State in the territory of which the act was committed … ". It would also recall its understanding of the object and purpose of the Convention, as set out in its Opinion of 28 May 1951, cited above:

> "The origins of the Convention show that it was the intention of the United Nations to condemn and punish genocide as 'a crime under international law' involving a denial of the right of existence of entire human groups, a denial which shocks the conscience of mankind and results in great losses to humanity, and which is contrary to moral law and to the spirit and aims of the united Nations (Resolution 96 (I) of the General Assembly, December 11th 1946). The first consequence arising from this conception is that the principles underlying the Convention are principles which are recognized by civilized nations as binding on States, even without any conventional obligation. A second consequence is the universal character both of th4e condemnation of genocide and of the co-operation required 'in order to liberate mankind from such an odious scourge' (Preamble to the Convention)." (I.C.J. Reports 1951, p. 23.)

It follows that the rights and obligations enshrined by the Convention are rights and obligations *erga omnes*. The Court notes that the obligation each State thus has to prevent and to punish the crime of genocide is not territorially limited by the Convention.

32.   The Court now comes to the second proposition advanced by Yugoslavia, regarding the type of State responsibility envisaged in Article IX of the Convention. According to Yugoslavia, that Article would only cover the responsibility flowing from the failure of a State to fulfil its obligations of prevention and punishment as contemplated by Articles V, VI, and VII; on the other hand, the responsibility of a State for an act of genocide perpetrated by the State itself would be excluded from the scope of the Convention. The Court would observe that the reference to Article IX to "the responsibility of a State for genocide or for any of the other acts enumerated in Article III", does not exclude any form of State responsibility. Nor is the responsibility of a State for acts of its organs excluded by Article IV of the Convention, which contemplates the commission of an act of genocide by "rulers" or "public officials".

33.   In the light of the foregoing, the Court considers that it must reject the fifth preliminary objection of Yugoslavia. It would moreover observe that it is sufficiently apparent from the very terms of that objection that the Parties not only differ with respect to the facts of the case, their imputability and the applicability to them of the provisions of the Genocide Convention, but are moreover in disagreement with respect to the meaning and legal scope of several of those provisions, including Article IX. For the Court, there is accordingly no doubt that there exists a dispute between them relating to "the interpretation, application or fulfilment of the … Convention, including … the responsibility of a State for genocide …", according to the form of words employed by that latter provision….

* * *

[Case Concerning Legality of Use of Force (Yugoslavia v. Belgium), Request for the Indication of Provisional Measures, (Order, June 2, 1999).

In April 1999, the Federal Republic of Yugoslavia (FRY) filed its applications against the NATO countries that were participating in the bombardment of its territory. The ICJ was requested to indicate provisional measures, ordering NATO to "cease immediately [it's] ... use of force ... [and to] refrain from any act of threat or use of force against the FRY." The FRY claimed Article IX of the Genocide Convention as the basis for jurisdiction, but On June 2, 1999, the ICJ held that it lacked jurisdiction to indicate provisional measures, as it "is ... not in a position to find, at this stage of the proceedings, that the acts imputed by [FRY] ... are capable of coming within the provisions of the Genocide Convention;...." *See also, Press Communiqué*, International Court of Justice, 99/23, June 2, 1999.]

Individual Petitions

Is there a right under national law. If so, where and how? If not, why not? To bring individual petitions for human rights violations? In 1947, the Human Rights Commission and the Economic and Social Council decided that the Commission "has no power to take any action in regard to any complaints concerning human rights." ECOSOC Off.Rec., 4th Sess., Supp. 3, *Report of the Commission on Human Rights, First Sess.*, p. 6. Although attempts were made for two decades to reverse this position, the many communications from individuals that came to the UN informally each year were not acted upon, although a state named in a complaint was sent an anonymous copy. This position was changed by ECOSOC *Resolution 1503* (XLVIII) of May 27, 1970. It provided that the Sub–Commission on Prevention of Discrimination and Protection of Minorities may appoint a working group to consider communications from individuals and to bring to the sub-commission's attention those communications "which appear to reveal a consistent pattern of gross and reliably attested violations of human rights and fundamental freedoms within the terms of reference of the sub-commission." The resolution provided for consideration of the communications by the sub-commission, with reference thereafter to the Human Rights Commission and possibly a study and report by the commission or an investigation by an ad hoc committee appointed by the commission and recommendation to ECOSOC. Limitations of significance are that the ad hoc investigation can be made only with the consent of the state concerned and that the matter must remain confidential until the commission decides to make a recommendation to ECOSOC.

Procedures to carry out ECOSOC Resolution 1503 were adopted by the sub-commission in August 1971. Paragraph 2 of the procedures discloses that a broad range of persons and groups is empowered to originate communications. Paragraph 1 indicates that the procedures are useful for a single individual only if he is a victim of a "consistent pattern of gross and reliably attested violations of human rights and fundamental freedoms." It is significant, however, that the injured person can communicate directly with the UN without the necessity of enlisting the aid of a foreign state. Although the 1503 procedure was hailed at the time of its creation as a major advance in human rights law, its accomplishments have largely been shrouded by the requirement of confidentiality.

———

Racial discrimination. A procedure for hearing individual communications is contained in the International Convention on the Elimination of All Forms of Racial Discrimination and a Committee on the Elimination of Racial Discrimination exists under Article 8 of that Convention. Under Article 14, no communication from individuals is to be received by the committee if it concerns a state party that has not made a declaration recognizing the competence of the committee. *See, gen.,* Slye, *Apartheid as a Crime Against Humanity: A Submission to the South African Truth & Reconciliation Commission,* 20 Mich.J.Int'l L.267 (1999).

———

Optional Protocol to the International Covenant on Civil and Political Rights. The right to make individual communications is also provided by the *Optional Protocol.* The Human Rights Committee, established by Part IV of the Covenant, is the mechanism for dealing with such communications.[32] Under Article 1 of the Protocol, a state party "recognizes the competence of the Committee to receive and consider communications from individuals subject to its jurisdiction who claim to be victims of a violation by that State Party of any of the rights set forth in the Covenant." This provision allows an individual to claim a single violation (i.e. it is not necessary to identify a pattern of violations as under the 1503 procedure). In addition, although Article 5(3) of the protocol calls for closed meetings, the committee is not held to the level of confidentiality that surrounds the 1503 procedure. It has issued a number of reports with respect to communications that it has received.

4. Public Denunciation

It is the practice of the Department of State to issue periodic reports on the implementation of these provisions. In 1960's, '70's and 80's, the focus of these reports was often on the countries of Eastern Europe. Recently, they have focused on other hot-spots like: the territory of the former Yugoslavia, Rwanda, East Timor, and the Peoples Republic of China, among others.

5. Pursuit of Human Rights Under Customary International Law in National Courts

Filartiga v. Pena–Irala

United States Court of Appeals, Second Circuit, 1980.
630 F.2d 876.

Kaufman, Circuit Judge:

Upon ratification of the Constitution, the thirteen former colonies were fused into a single nation, one which, in its relations with foreign states, is

---

32. The Human Rights Committee under the Optional Protocol is a different institution from the United Nations Commission on Human Rights and is not to be confused therewith.

bound both to observe and construe the accepted norms of international law, formerly known as the law of nations. Under the Articles of Confederation, the several states had interpreted and applied this body of doctrine as a part of their common law, but with the founding of the "more perfect Union" of 1789, the law of nations became preeminently a federal concern.

Implementing the constitutional mandate for national control over foreign relations, the First Congress established original district court jurisdiction over "all causes where an alien sues for a tort only [committed] in violation of the law of nations." Judiciary Act of 1789, ch. 20, § 9(b), (1789), *codified at* 28 U.S.C. § 1350. Construing this rarely-invoked provision, we hold that deliberate torture perpetrated under color of official authority violates universally accepted norms of the international law of human rights, regardless of the nationality of the parties. Thus, whenever an alleged torturer is found and served with process by an alien within our borders, § 1350 provides federal jurisdiction. Accordingly, we reverse the judgment of the district court dismissing the complaint for want of federal jurisdiction.

I

The appellants, plaintiffs below, are citizens of * * * Paraguay. Dr. Joel Filartiga, a physician, describes himself as a longstanding opponent of the government of President Alfredo Stroessner, which held power in Paraguay since 1954. His daughter, Dolly Filartiga, arrived in the U.S. in 1978 under a visitor's visa, and has since applied for permanent political asylum. The Filartigas brought this action in the Eastern District of New York against Pena–Irala (Pena), also a citizen of Paraguay, for wrongfully causing the death of Dr. Filartiga's seventeen-year old son, Joelito. Because the district court dismissed the action for want of subject matter jurisdiction, we must accept as true the allegations contained in the Filartigas' complaint and affidavits.

The appellants contend that on March 29, 1976, Joelito Filartiga was kidnapped and tortured to death by Pena, who was then Inspector General of Police in Asuncion, Paraguay. Later that day, the police brought Dolly Filartiga to Pena's home where she was confronted with the body of her brother, which evidenced marks of severe torture. As she fled, horrified, from the house, Pena followed after her shouting, "Here you have what you have been looking for for so long and what you deserve. Now shut up." The Filartigas claim that Joelito was tortured and killed in retaliation for his father's political activities and beliefs. * * *

In July of 1978, Pena sold his house in Paraguay and entered the United States under a visitor's visa. He was accompanied by Juana Bautista Fernandez Villalba, who had lived with him in Paraguay. The couple remained in the United States beyond the term of their visas, and were living in Brooklyn, New York, when Dolly Filartiga, who was then living in Washington, D.C., learned of their presence. . . .

. . . Dolly [had Pena served] with a summons and civil complaint at the Brooklyn Navy Yard, where he was being held pending deportation. The complaint alleged that Pena had wrongfully caused Joelito's death by torture and sought compensatory and punitive damages of $10,000,000. The Filartigas also sought to enjoin Pena's deportation to ensure his availability for testimony at trial. The cause of action is stated as arising under "wrongful death statutes; the U.N. Charter; the Universal Declaration on Human Rights; the U.N. Declaration Against Torture; the American Declaration of the Rights and Duties of Man; and other pertinent declarations, documents and practices constituting the customary international law of human rights and the law of nations," as well as 28 U.S.C. § 1350, Article II, sec. 2 and the Supremacy Clause of the U.S. Constitution. Jurisdiction is claimed under the general federal question provision, 28 U.S.C. § 1331 and, principally on this appeal, under the Alien Tort Statute, 28 U.S.C. § 1350. * * *

II

Appellants rest their principal argument in support of federal jurisdiction upon the Alien Tort Statute, 28 U.S.C. § 1350, which provides: "The district courts shall have original jurisdiction of any civil action by an alien for a tort only, committed in violation of the law of nations or a treaty of the United States." Since appellants do not contend that their action arises directly under a treaty of the United States, a threshold question on the jurisdictional issue is whether the conduct alleged violates the law of nations. In light of the universal condemnation of torture in numerous international agreements, and the renunciation of torture as an instrument of official policy by virtually all of the nations of the world (in principle if not in practice), we find that an act of torture committed by a state official against one held in detention violates established norms of the international law of human rights, and hence the law of nations.

The Supreme Court has enumerated the appropriate sources of international law. The law of nations "may be ascertained by consulting the works of jurists, writing professedly on public law; or by the general usage and practice of nations; or by judicial decisions recognizing and enforcing that law." * * *

"[*The Paquete Habana*], ... is particularly instructive for present purposes, for it held that [a] traditional prohibition ... , [which] began as one of comity only, had ripened over the preceding century into 'a settled rule of international law' by 'general assent of civilized nationa.' Thus, it is clear that courts must interpret international law not as it was in 1789, but as it has evolved and exists among the nations of the world today."

The requirement that a rule command the "general assent of civilized nations" to become binding upon them all is a stringent one. Were this not so, the courts of one nation might feel free to impose idosyncratic legal rules upon others, in the name of applying international law. Thus, in Sabbatino, 376 U.S. 398 (1964), the Court declined to pass on the validity of the Cuban government's expropriation of a foreign-owned corporation's assets, noting the sharply conflicting views on the issue propounded by the capital-exporting, capital-importing, socialist and capitalist nations.

The case at bar presents * * * situation diametrically opposed to the conflicted state of law that confronted the Sabbatino Court. Indeed, to paraphrase that Court's statement, there are few, if any, issues in international law today on which opinion seems to be so united as the limitations on a state's power to torture persons held in its custody.

The United Nations Charter (a treaty of the United States, (1945)) makes it clear that in this modern age a state's treatment of its own citizens is a matter of international concern. * * *

* * * [This broad mandate has been held not fully self-executing, but this does not end the inquiry]. [A]lthough there is no universal agreement as to the precise extent of the "human rights and fundamental freedoms" guaranteed to all by the Charter, there is at present no dissent from the view that the guaranties include, at a bare minimum, the right to be free from torture. This prohibition has become part of customary international law, as evidenced and defined by the Universal Declaration of Human Rights, General Assembly Resolution 217(III)(A) (Dec. 10, 1948) which states, in the plainest of terms, "no one shall be subjected to torture." The General Assembly has declared that the Charter precepts embodied in this Universal Declaration "constitute basic principles of international law." G.A.Res. 2625(25) (Oct. 24, 1970).

Particularly relevant is the Declaration on the Protection of All Persons from Being Subjected to Torture, General Assembly Resolution 3452, 30 U.N. GAOR Supp., (n. 34) 91, U.S.Doc. A_1034 (1975) * * *. The Declaration expressly prohibits any state from permitting the dastardly and totally inhuman act of torture. Torture, in turn, is defined as "any act by which severe pain and suffering, whether physical or mental, is intentionally inflicted by or at the instigation of a public official on a person for such purposes as * * * intimidating him or other persons." The Declaration goes on to provide that "[w]here it is proved that an act of torture or other cruel, inhuman or degrading treatment or punishment has been committed by or at the instigation of a public official, the victim shall be afforded redress and compensation, in accordance with national law." This Declaration, like the Declaration of Human Rights before it, was adopted without dissent by the General Assembly. * * *

These U.N. declarations are significant because they specify with great precision the obligations of member nations under the Charter. Since their adoption, "[m]embers can no longer contend that they do not know what human rights they promised in the Charter to promote." * * * Moreover, a U.N. Declaration is, according to one authoritative definition, "a formal and solemn instrument, suitable for rare occasions when principles of great and lasting importance are being enunciated." * * * Accordingly, it has been observed that the Universal Declaration of Human Rights "no longer fits into the dichotomy of 'binding treaty' against 'non-binding pronouncement,' but is rather an authoritative statement of the international community." * * * Thus, a Declaration creates an expectation of adherence, and "insofar as the expectation is gradually justified by State practice, a declaration may by custom become recognized as laying down rules binding upon the States." Indeed, several commentators have concluded that the Universal Declaration has become, in toto, a part of binding, customary international law. * * *

Turning to the act of torture, we have little difficulty discerning its universal renunciation in the modern usage and practice of nations. The international consensus surrounding torture has found expression in numerous international treaties and accords. * * * The substance of these international agreements is reflected in modern municipal–i.e. national–law as well. Although torture was once a routine concomitant of criminal interrogations in many nations, during the modern and hopefully more enlightened era it has been universally renounced. According to one survey, torture is prohibited, expressly or implicitly, by the constitutions of over fifty-five nations, including both the United States and Paraguay. * * *

Having examined the sources from which customary international law is derived–the usage of nations, judicial opinions and the works of jurists– we conclude that official torture is now prohibited by the law of nations. The prohibition is clear and unambiguous, and admits of no distinction between treatment of aliens and citizens. Accordingly, we must conclude that the dictum in Dreyfus v. von Finck, supra, to the effect that "violations of international law do not occur when the aggrieved parties are nationals of the acting state," is clearly out of tune with the current usage and practice of international law. The treaties and accords cited above, as well as the express foreign policy of our own government, all make it clear that international law confers fundamental rights upon all people vis-a-vis their own governments. While the ultimate scope of those rights will be a subject for continuing refinement and elaboration, we hold that the right to be free from torture is now among them. We therefore turn to the question whether the other requirements for jurisdiction are met.

III

Appellee submits that even if the tort alleged is a violation of modern international law, federal jurisdiction may not be exercised consistent with the dictates of Article III of the Constitution. The claim is without merit. Common law courts of general jurisdiction regularly adjudicate transitory tort claims between individuals over whom they exercise personal jurisdiction, wherever the tort occurred. Moreover, as part of an articulated scheme of federal control over external affairs, Congress provided, in the First Judiciary Act, Sec. 9(b), 1 Stat. 73, 77 (1789), for federal jurisdiction over suits by aliens where principles of international law are in issue. The constitutional basis for the Alien Tort Statute is the Law of Nations, which has always been part of the federal common law. * * *

Although the Alien Tort Statute has rarely been the basis for jurisdiction during its long history [28 USC 1350] in light of the foregoing discussion, there can be little doubt that this action is properly brought in federal court. This is undeniably an action by an alien, for a tort only, committed in violation of the law of nations. * * *

* * *

Since federal jurisdiction may properly be exercised over the Filartigas' claim, the action must be remanded for further proceedings. Appellee Pena, however, advances several additional points that lie beyond the scope of our holding on jurisdiction. Both to emphasize the boundaries of our holding, and to clarify some of the issues reserved for the district court on remand, we will address these contentions briefly.

IV

Pena argues that the customary law of nations, as reflected in treaties and declarations that are not self-executing, should not be applied as rules of decision in this case. In doing so, he confuses the question of federal jurisdiction under the Alien Tort Statute, which requires consideration of the law of nations, with the issue of the choice of law to be applied, which will be addressed at a later stage in the proceedings. The two issues are distinct. Our holding on subject matter jurisdiction decides only whether Congress intended to confer judicial power, and whether it is authorized to do so by Article III. The choice of law inquiry is a much broader one, primarily concerned with fairness. Should the district court decide that the Lauritzen analysis requires it to apply Paraguayan law, our courts will not have occasion to consider what law would govern a suit under the Alien Tort Statute where the challenged conduct is actionable under the law of the forum and the law of nations, but not the law of the jurisdiction in which the tort occurred.

Pena also argues that "[i]f the conduct complained of is alleged to be the act of the Paraguayan government, the suit is barred by the Act of State doctrine." This argument was not advanced below, and is therefore not before us on this appeal. We note in passing, however, that we doubt whether action by a state official in violation of the Constitution and laws of the Republic of Paraguay, and wholly unratified by that nation's government, could properly be characterized as an act of state. See *Sabbatino, supra*; Underhill v. Hernandez. Paraguay's renunciation of torture as a legitimate instrument of state policy, however, does not strip the tort of its character as an international law violation, if it in fact occurred under color of government authority. See Declaration on the Protection of All Persons from Being Subjected to Torture, supra; cf. Ex parte Young (state official subject to suit for constitutional violations despite immunity of state).
* * *

In the twentieth century the international community has come to recognize the common danger posed by the flagrant disregard of basic human rights and particularly the right to be free of torture. Spurred first by the Great War, and then the Second, civilized nations have banded together to prescribe acceptable norms of international behavior. From the ashes of the Second World War arose the United Nations Organization, amid hopes that an era of peace and cooperation had at last begun. Though many of these aspirations have remained elusive goals, that circumstance cannot diminish the true progress that has been made. In the modern age, humanitarian and practical considerations have combined to lead the nations of the world to recognize that respect for fundamental human rights is in their individual and collective interest. Among the rights universally proclaimed by all nations, as we have noted, is the right to be free of physical torture. Indeed, for purposes of civil liability, the torturer has become–like the pirate and slave trader before him–ostis humani generis, an enemy of all mankind. Our holding today, giving effect to a jurisdictional provision enacted by our First Congress, is a small but important step in the fulfillment of the ageless dream to free all people from brutal violence.

––––––

Notes

1. ***Further proceedings in Filartiga.*** On remand, the District Court granted a default judgment to plaintiffs. In addition to actual damages, it awarded punitive damages of $5,000,000 to each plaintiff. In looking for the applicable law, the court concluded that Section 1350 did not merely provide jurisdiction but also set the substantive principles to be applied. International law and not just the national law of the state where the tort was committed. The remedy of punitive damages was devised pursuant to the following syllogism: "The international law prohibiting torture established the standard and referred to the national states the task of enforcing it. By enacting Section 1350 Congress entrusted that task to the federal courts and gave them power to choose and develop federal remedies to effectuate the purposes of the international law incorporated into United States common law." *Filartiga v. Pena–Irala*, 577 F.Supp. 860, 863 (E.D.N.Y.1984).

2. **In *Rodriguez Fernandez v. Wilkinson***, 505 F.Supp. 787 (D.Kan. 1980), aff'd, 654 F.2d 1382 (10th Cir.1981), the court found legal principles similar to those employed by the court in *Filartiga,* and held that customary international law required release of an excludable alien from indefinite detention, even though his country (Cuba) would not take him back. The court of appeals, affirmed specifically on U.S. domestic law grounds, but noted that its construction of the relevant statute was "consistent with accepted international law principles that individuals are entitled to be free of arbitrary imprisonment."

3. ***Tel-Oren v. Libyan Arab Republic,*** 726 F.2d 774 (D.C.Cir.1984), *cert. denied* 470 U.S. 1003 (1985) addressed the Alien Tort Statute and came up with the opposite result. Survivors and representatives of victims of an armed attack on two Israeli buses, a taxi, and a passing car in Israel, sued the P.L.O. in a U.S. court for compensatory and punitive damages. Their claim was that this was a tort arising from a violation of international law. The case was dismissed for want of subject matter jurisdiction. A three-judge panel of the Washington D.C. Court of Appeal affirmed. Each judge wrote a separate opinion.

Judge Edwards "endorsed the legal principles [in] *Filartiga,* but found that the Alien Tort Statute) was inapplicable because the 'law of nations [fails to impose] the same responsibility or liability on non-state actors, such as the PLO, as it does in states and persons acting under color of state law.' "*Judge Bork,* on the other hand, argued that *Filartiga* was fundamentally wrong on the merits. Section 1350 simply did not apply. No jurisdiction obtained and no cause of action could arise, unless it were granted explicitly either by international law (general principles, custom, or treaty) or other domestic law. *Judge Robb* simply found that the case came within the political question doctrine, so was non-justiciable.

4. See also, Forti v. Suarez–Mason, 672 F.Supp. 1531 (N.D.Cal.1987), *modified* in 694 F.Supp. 707 (N.D.Cal.1988); *Republic of Philippines v. Marcos,* 818 F.2d 1473 (9th Cir.1987). The Supreme Court has held that the Foreign Sovereign Immunity Act applies to actions under the Alien Tort Statute. *See, Argentine Republic v. Amerada Hess Shipping Corp., 488 U.S. 428 (1989); Saudi Arabia v. Nelson, 507 U.S. 349 (1993)* (where a U.S. national was tortured by Saudi police when he "blew the whistle" on what he considered improper conduct in a Saudi hospital).

Kadic, Et Al. v. Karadzic

70 F.3d 232 (2d Cir. 1995)

■ JON O. NEWMAN, CHIEF JUDGE:

Most Americans would probably be surprised to learn that victims of atrocities committed in Bosnia are suing the leader of the insurgent Bosnian-Serb forces in a United States District Court in Manhattan. Their claims seek to build upon the foundation of this Court's decision in *Filartiga v. Pena–Irala,* which recognized the important principle that the venerable *Alien Tort Act,* 28 U.S.C. § 1350 (1988), enacted in 1789 but rarely invoked since then, validly creates federal court jurisdiction for suits alleging torts committed anywhere in the world against aliens in violation of the law of nations. The pending appeals pose additional significant issues as to the scope of the Alien Tort Act: whether some violations of the law of nations may be remedied when committed by those not acting under the authority of a state; if so, whether genocide, war crimes, and crimes against humanity are among the violations that do not require state action; and whether a person, otherwise liable for a violation of the law of nations, is immune from service of process because he is present in the United States as an invitee of the United Nations.

[The 2nd Circuit reversed and remanded the decision noted above].

The plaintiffs-appellants are Croat and Muslim citizens of the internationally recognized nation of Bosnia–Herzegovina, formerly a republic of Yugoslavia. Their complaints, which we accept as true for purposes of this appeal, allege that they are victims, and representatives of victims, of various atrocities, including brutal acts of rape, forced prostitution, forced impregnation, torture, and summary execution, carried out by Bosnian-Serb military forces as part of a genocidal campaign conducted in the course of the Bosnian civil war. Karadzic, formerly a citizen of Yugoslavia and now a citizen of Bosnia–Herzegovina, is the President of a three-man presidency of the self-proclaimed Bosnian–Serb republic within Bosnia–Herzegovina, sometimes referred to as "Srpska," which claims to exercise lawful authority, and does in fact exercise actual control, over large parts of the territory of Bosnia-Herzegovina. In his capacity as President, Karadzic possesses ultimate command authority over the Bosnian–Serb military forces, and the injuries perpetrated upon plaintiffs were committed as part of a pattern of systematic human rights violations that was directed by Karadzic and carried out by the military forces under his command. The complaints allege that Karadzic acted in an official capacity either as the titular head of Srpska or in collaboration with the government of the recognized nation of the former Yugoslavia and its dominant constituent republic, Serbia.

* * *

The ... plaintiffs asserted causes of action for genocide, rape, forced prostitution and impregnation, torture and other cruel, inhuman, and degrading treatment, assault and battery, sex and ethnic inequality, summary execution, and wrongful death. They sought compensatory and punitive damages, attorney's fees, and, in one of the cases, injunctive relief ...

In early 1993, Karadzic was admitted to the United States on three separate occasions as an invitee of the United Nations. According to affidavits submitted by the plaintiffs, Karadzic was personally served with the summons and complaint in each action during two of these visits while he was physically present in Manhattan ...

... Karadzic moved for dismissal of both actions on the grounds of insufficient service of process, lack of personal jurisdiction, lack of subject-matter jurisdiction, and nonjusticiability of plaintiffs' claims.

Though the District Court dismissed for lack of subject-matter jurisdiction, the parties have briefed not only that issue but also the threshold issues of personal jurisdiction and justiciability under the political question doctrine. Karadzic urges us to affirm on any one of these three grounds. We consider each in turn.

    I.   Subject–Matter Jurisdiction

* * *

A.   The Alien Tort Act

1.   General Application to Appellants' Claims

... Our decision in *Filartiga* established that this statute confers federal subject-matter jurisdiction when the following three conditions are satisfied: (1) an alien sues (2) for a tort (3) committed in violation of the law of nations (i.e., international law) ... The first two requirements are plainly satisfied here, and the only disputed issue is whether plaintiffs have pleaded violations of international law. * * *

[The District Judge] accepted Karadzic's contention that "acts committed by non-state actors do not violate the law of nations," Doe, 866 F.Supp. at 739, and considered him to be a non-state actor. The Judge appears to have deemed state action required primarily on the basis of cases determining the need for state action as to claims of official torture, without consideration of the substantial body of law, discussed below, that renders private individuals liable for some international law violations.

We do not agree that the law of nations, as understood in the modern era, confines its reach to state action. Instead, we hold that certain forms of conduct violate the law of nations whether undertaken by those acting under the auspices of a state or only as private individuals. An early example of the application of the law of nations to the acts of private individuals is the prohibition against piracy. *See United States v. Smith*, 18 U.S. (5 Wheat.) 153, 161 (1820). In *The Brig Malek Adhel*, 43 U.S. (2 How.) 210, 232 (1844), the Supreme Court observed that pirates were "hostis humani generis" (an enemy of all mankind) in part because they acted "without . . . any pretense of public authority." Later examples are prohibitions against the slave trade and certain war crimes.

. . . The Executive Branch has emphatically restated in this litigation its position that private persons may be found liable under the Alien Tort Act for acts of genocide, war crimes, and other violations of international humanitarian law. *See Statement of Interest of the United States* at 5–13.

The Restatement (Third) of the Foreign Relations Law of the United States (1986) ("Restatement (Third)") proclaims: "Individuals may be held liable for offenses against international law, such as piracy, war crimes, and genocide." Restatement (Third) pt. II, introductory note. The Restatement is careful to identify those violations that are actionable when committed by a state, Restatement (Third) § 702, and a more limited category of violations of "universal concern," id. § 404. A state has jurisdiction to define and prescribe punishment for certain offenses recognized by the community of nations as of universal concern, such as piracy, slave trade, attacks on or hijacking of aircraft, genocide, war crimes, and perhaps certain acts of terrorism, even where [no other basis of jurisdiction] is present. partially overlapping with those listed in section 702. Though the immediate focus of section 404 is to identify those offenses for which a state has jurisdiction to punish without regard to territoriality or the nationality of the offenders, cf. id. § 402(1)(a), (2), the inclusion of piracy and slave trade from an earlier era and aircraft hijacking from the modern era demonstrates that the offenses of "universal concern" include those capable of being committed by non-state actors. Although the jurisdiction authorized by section 404 is usually exercised by application of criminal law, international law also permits states to establish appropriate civil remedies . . . * * *

Karadzic also contends that Congress intended the state-action requirement of the Torture Victim Act to apply to actions under the Alien Tort Act. We disagree. Congress enacted the *Torture Victim Act* to codify the cause of action recognized by this Circuit in *Filartiga,* and to further extend that cause of action to plaintiffs who are U.S. citizens. *See* H.R.Rep. No. 367, 102d Cong., 2d Sess., at 4 (1991), *reprinted in* 1992 U.S.C.C.A.N. 84, 86 (explaining that codification of *Filartiga* was necessary in light of skepticism expressed by Judge Bork's concurring opinion in *Tel-Oren*). At the same time, Congress indicated that the Alien Tort Act "has other important uses and should not be replaced," because

> Claims based on torture and summary executions do not exhaust the list of actions that may appropriately be covered [by the Alien Tort Act]. That statute should remain intact to permit suits based on other norms that already exist or may ripen in the future into rules of customary international law. *Id.*

The scope of the Alien Tort Act remains undiminished by enactment of the Torture Victim Act.

2. Specific Application of Alien Tort Act to Appellants' Claims

In order to determine whether the offenses alleged by the appellants in this litigation are violations of the law of nations that may be the subject of

Alien Tort Act claims against a private individual, we must make a particularized examination of these offenses, mindful of the important precept that "evolving standards of international law govern who is within the [*Alien Tort Act's*] jurisdictional grant." *Amerada Hess, supra* In making that inquiry, it will be helpful to group the appellants' claims into three categories: (a) genocide, (b) war crimes, and (c) other instances of inflicting death, torture, and degrading treatment.

(a) Genocide. In the aftermath of the atrocities committed during the Second World War, the condemnation of genocide as contrary to international law quickly achieved broad acceptance by the community of nations. In 1946, the General Assembly ... declared that genocide is a crime under international law that is condemned by the civilized world, whether the perpetrators are "private individuals, public officials or statesmen." G.A.Res. 96(I), 1 U.N.GAOR, U.N. Doc. A/64/Add.1, at 188–89 (1946) ...

The Convention on the Prevention and Punishment of the Crime of Genocide entered into force Jan. 12, 1951 [for the US Feb. 23, 1989 (hereinafter "Convention on Genocide"), provides a more specific articulation of the prohibition of genocide in international law ... Especially pertinent to the pending appeal, the Convention makes clear that "[p]ersons committing genocide ... shall be punished, whether they are constitutionally responsible rulers, public officials or private individuals." *Id.* art. IV (emphasis added) ...

The applicability of this norm to private individuals is also confirmed by the Genocide Convention Implementation Act of 1987, 18 U.S.C. § 1091 (1988), which criminalizes acts of genocide without regard to whether the offender is acting under color of law, see id. § 1091(a) ("[w]hoever" commits genocide shall be punished), if the crime is committed within the United States or by a U.S. national, id. § 1091(d). Though Congress provided that the Genocide Convention Implementation Act shall not "be construed as creating any substantive or procedural right enforceable by law by any party in any proceeding," id. § 1092, the legislative decision not to create a new private remedy does not imply that a private remedy is not already available under the Alien Tort Act. Nothing in the Genocide Convention Implementation Act or its legislative history reveals an intent by Congress to repeal the Alien Tort Act insofar as it applies to genocide, and the two statutes are surely not repugnant to each other. Under these circumstances, it would be improper to construe the Genocide Convention Implementation Act as repealing the Alien Tort Act by implication. *See Rodriguez v.U.S.,* 480 U.S. 522, 524 (1987) ("[R]epeals by implication are not favored and will not be found unless an intent to repeal is clear and manifest.") ...

Appellants' allegations that Karadzic personally planned and ordered a campaign of murder, rape, forced impregnation, and other forms of torture designed to destroy the religious and ethnic groups of Bosnian Muslims and Bosnian Croats clearly state a violation of the international law norm proscribing genocide, regardless of whether Karadzic acted under color of law or as a private individual. The District Court has subject-matter jurisdiction over these claims pursuant to the Alien Tort Act.

(b) War crimes. Plaintiffs also contend that the acts of murder, rape, torture, and arbitrary detention of civilians, committed in the course of hostilities, violate the law of war. Atrocities of the types alleged here have long been recognized in international law as violations of the law of war. *See In re Yamashita*, 327 U.S. 1, 14 (1946). Moreover, international law imposes an affirmative duty on military commanders to take appropriate measures within their power to control troops under their command for the prevention of such atrocities. Id. at 15–16.

After the Second World War, the law of war was codified in the four Geneva Conventions, which have been ratified by more than 180 nations, including the United States, see Treaties in Force, supra, at 398–99. Common article 3, which is substantially identical in each of the four Conventions, applies to "armed conflict[s] not of an international character" and binds "each Party to the conflict . . . to apply, as a minimum, the following provisions" . . .

* * *

Under the law of war as codified in the Geneva Conventions, all "parties" to a conflict—which includes insurgent military groups—are obliged to adhere to these most fundamental requirements of the law of war.

The offenses alleged by the appellants, if proved, would violate the most fundamental norms of the law of war embodied in common article 3, which binds parties to internal conflicts regardless of whether they are recognized nations or roving hordes of insurgents. The liability of private individuals for committing war crimes has been recognized since World War I and was confirmed at Nuremberg after World War II . . . The District Court has jurisdiction pursuant to the *Alien Tort Act* over appellants' claims of war crimes and other violations of international humanitarian law.

(c) Torture and summary execution. In *Filartiga,* we held that official torture is prohibited by universally accepted norms of international law, see 630 F.2d at 885, and the Torture Victim Act confirms this holding and extends it to cover summary execution. Torture Victim Act §§ 2(a), 3(a). However, torture and summary execution—when not perpetrated in the course of genocide or war crimes—are proscribed by international law only when committed by state officials or under color of law . . .

In the present case, appellants allege that acts of rape, torture, and summary execution were committed during hostilities by troops under Karadzic's command and with the specific intent of destroying appellants' ethnic-religious groups. Thus, many of the alleged atrocities are already encompassed within the appellants' claims of genocide and war crimes. Of course, at this threshold stage in the proceedings it cannot be known whether appellants will be able to prove the specific intent that is an element of genocide, or prove that each of the alleged torts were committed in the course of an armed conflict, as required to establish war crimes. It suffices to hold at this stage that the alleged atrocities are actionable under the Alien Tort Act, without regard to state action, to the extent that they were committed in pursuit of genocide or war crimes, and otherwise may be

pursued against Karadzic to the extent that he is shown to be a state actor
. . .

3.   The State Action Requirement for International Law Violations

In dismissing plaintiffs' complaints for lack of subject-matter jurisdiction, the District Court concluded that the alleged violations required state action and that the "Bosnian–Serb entity" headed by Karadzic does not meet the definition of a state . . . Appellants contend that they are entitled to prove that Srpska satisfies the definition of a state for purposes of international law violations and, alternatively, that Karadzic acted in concert with the recognized state of the former Yugoslavia and its constituent republic, Serbia.

* * *

Although the Restatement's definition of statehood requires the capacity to engage in formal relations with other states, it does not require recognition by other states . . . Recognized states enjoy certain privileges and immunities relevant to judicial proceedings, *see, e.g., Pfizer Inc. v. India*, 434 U.S. 308, 318–20 (1978) (diversity jurisdiction); *Banco Nacional de Cuba v. Sabbatino*, 376 U.S. 398, 408–12 (1964) (access to U.S. courts); *Lafontant*, 844 F.Supp. at 131 (head-of-state immunity), but an unrecognized state is not a juridical nullity. Our courts have regularly given effect to the "state" action of unrecognized states . . .

The customary international law of human rights, such as the proscription of official torture, applies to states without distinction between recognized and unrecognized states . . .

* * *

(b) Acting in concert with a foreign state. Appellants also sufficiently alleged that Karadzic acted under color of law insofar as they claimed that he acted in concert with the former Yugoslavia, the statehood of which is not disputed. The "color of law" jurisprudence of 42 U.S.C. § 1983 is a relevant guide to whether a defendant has engaged in official action for purposes of jurisdiction under the Alien Tort Act. *See Forti v. Suarez-Mason*, 672 F.Supp. 1531, 1546 (N.D.Cal.1987)

B.   The Torture Victim Protection Act

The Torture Victim Act [1992, in § 2(a)]provides a cause of action for official torture and extrajudicial killing: An individual who, under actual or apparent authority, or color of law, of any foreign nation—

(1) subjects an individual to torture shall, in a civil action, be liable for damages to that individual; or

(2) subjects an individual to extrajudicial killing shall, in a civil action, be liable for damages to the individual's legal representative, or to any person who may be a claimant in an action for wrongful death.

* * *

By its plain language, the Torture Victim Act renders liable only those individuals who have committed torture or extrajudicial killing "under actual or apparent authority, or color of law, of any foreign nation."

Legislative history confirms that this language was intended to "make[ ] clear that the plaintiff must establish some governmental involvement in the torture or killing to prove a claim," and that the statute "does not attempt to deal with torture or killing by purely private groups." H.R.Rep. No. 367, 102d Cong., 2d Sess., at 5 (1991), reprinted in 1992 U.S.C.C.A.N. 84, 87. In construing the terms "actual or apparent authority" and "color of law," courts are instructed to look to principles of agency law and to jurisprudence under 42 U.S.C. § 1983, respectively. Id.

Though the Torture Victim Act creates a cause of action for official torture, this statute, unlike the Alien Tort Act, is not itself a jurisdictional statute. The Torture Victim Act permits the appellants to pursue their claims of official torture under the jurisdiction conferred by the Alien Tort Act and also under the general federal question jurisdiction of section 1331, *see Xuncax v. Gramajo*, 886 F.Supp. 162, 178 (D.Mass.1995) . . .

* * *

II.   Service of Process and Personal Jurisdiction

The Court held that service of process upon Karadzic was proper and that he was not immune from being served pursuant to the UN Headquarters Agreement, because he was outside the "headquarters district" when served. In addition, he was not a designated representative of any member of the U.N. In addition, the Court declined to infer that there was any immunity for U.N. invitees beyond the terms of the Headquarters Agreement, either as a matter of federal common law or interpretation of the Agreement.]

III.   Justiciability

We recognize that cases of this nature might pose special questions concerning the judiciary's proper role when adjudication might have implications in the conduct of this nation's foreign relations. We do not read Filartiga to mean that the federal judiciary must always act in ways that risk significant interference with United States foreign relations. To the contrary, we recognize that suits of this nature can present difficulties that implicate sensitive matters of diplomacy historically reserved to the jurisdiction of the political branches. *See First National Bank v. Banco Nacional de Cuba*, 406 U.S. 759, 767 (1972). We therefore proceed to consider whether, even though the jurisdictional threshold is satisfied in the pending cases, other considerations relevant to justiciability weigh against permitting the suits to proceed.

Two nonjurisdictional, prudential doctrines reflect the judiciary's concerns regarding separation of powers: the political question doctrine and the act of state doctrine. It is the " 'constitutional' underpinnings" of these doctrines that influenced the concurring opinions of Judge Robb and Judge Bork in *Tel-Oren*. Although we too recognize the potentially detrimental effects of judicial action in cases of this nature, we do not embrace the rather categorical views as to the inappropriateness of judicial action urged by Judges Robb and Bork. Not every case "touching foreign relations" is nonjusticiable, *see Baker v. Carr*, 369 U.S. 186, 211 (1962) . . . and judges should not reflexively invoke these doctrines to avoid difficult and somewhat sensitive decisions in the context of human rights. We believe a preferable approach is to weigh carefully the relevant considerations on a case-by-case basis. This will permit the judiciary to act where appropriate in light of the express legislative mandate of the Congress in section 1350, without compromising the primacy of the political branches in foreign affairs.

Karadzic maintains that these suits were properly dismissed because they present nonjusticiable political questions. We disagree. Although these cases present issues that arise in a politically charged context, that does not transform them into cases involving nonjusticiable political questions. "[T]he doctrine 'is one of "political questions," not one of "political cases." ' " Klinghoffer, 937 F.2d at 49

* * *

... Although the present actions are not based on the common law of torts, as was Klinghoffer [in the *Achille Lauro*], our decision in Filartiga established that universally recognized norms of international law provide judicially discoverable and manageable standards for adjudicating suits brought under the Alien Tort Act, which obviates any need to make initial policy decisions of the kind normally reserved for nonjudicial discretion. Moreover, the existence of judicially discoverable and manageable standards further undermines the claim that such suits relate to matters that are constitutionally committed to another branch ...

* * *

In the pending appeal, we need have no concern that interference with important governmental interests warrants rejection of appellants' claims. After commencing their action against Karadzic, attorneys for the plaintiffs in Doe wrote to the Secretary of State to oppose reported attempts by Karadzic to be granted immunity from suit in the United States; a copy of plaintiffs' complaint was attached to the letter. Far from intervening in the case to urge rejection of the suit on the ground that it presented political questions, the Department responded with a letter indicating that Karadzic was not immune from suit as an invitee of the United Nations ... After oral argument in the pending appeals, this Court wrote to the Attorney General to inquire whether the United States wished to offer any further views concerning any of the issues raised. In a "Statement of Interest," signed by the Solicitor General and the State Department's Legal Adviser, the United States has expressly disclaimed any concern that the political question doctrine should be invoked to prevent the litigation of these lawsuits: "Although there might be instances in which federal courts are asked to issue rulings under the Alien Tort Statute or the Torture Victim Protection Act that might raise a political question, this is not one of them." Statement of Interest of the United States at 3. Though even an assertion of the political question doctrine by the Executive Branch, entitled to respectful consideration, would not necessarily preclude adjudication, the Government's reply to our inquiry reinforces our view that adjudication may properly proceed.

As to the act of state doctrine, the doctrine was not asserted in the District Court and is not before us on this appeal ... Moreover, the appellee has not had the temerity to assert in this Court that the acts he allegedly committed are the officially approved policy of a state. Finally, as noted, we think it would be a rare case in which the act of state doctrine precluded suit under section 1350. [*Banco Nacional de Cuba v. Sabbitino*] was careful to recognize the doctrine "in the absence of . . . unambiguous agreement regarding controlling legal principles," 376 U.S. at 428, 84 S.Ct. at 940, such as exist in the pending litigation, and applied the doctrine only in a context—expropriation of an alien's property—in which world opinion was sharply divided . . .

Finally, we note that at this stage of the litigation no party has identified a more suitable forum, and we are aware of none. Though the Statement of the United States suggests the general importance of considering the doctrine of forum non conveniens, it seems evident that the courts of the former Yugoslavia, either in Serbia or war-torn Bosnia, are not now available to entertain plaintiffs' claims, even if circumstances concerning the location of witnesses and documents were presented that were sufficient to overcome the plaintiffs' preference for a United States forum.

The judgment of the District Court dismissing appellants' complaints for lack of subject-matter jurisdiction is reversed, and the cases are remanded for further proceedings in accordance with this opinion.

In the Bow Street Magistrates' Court the Kingdom of Spain v. Augusto Pinochet Ugarte

Mr Ronald David Bartle Metropolitan Magistrate 8th October 1999.

Before I commence my judgment there are certain preliminary matters which I feel I should mention. I do so because of the enormous public attention which this case has received both in this country and abroad, and because of the emotions, indeed passions, to which it has given rise.

Extradition is a branch of law relatively unknown to the general public, and therefore I think it is very important that I should say a few words at the outset to explain proceedings and my role as the Presiding Magistrate. I shall, by way of explanation deal with the following: the proper approach of the court to the case before it; the nature of the hearing; the function of the court; and my own duties including the delivery of my judgment.

With regard to the first point I cannot do better than quote the words of Lord Browne–Wilkinson in the early part of his judgment delivered on 24th March of this year when this case was before the House of Lords Appellate Committee. What the learned law lord said was this:

"In 1998 Senator Pinochet came to the United Kingdom for medical treatment. The judicial authorities in Spain sought to extradite him in order to stand trial in Spain on a large number of charges. Some of those charges had links with Spain. But most of the charges had no connection Spain. The background to the case", said the learned law lord, "is to those of left-wing political convictions Senator Pinochet is seen as an arch-devil: to those of right-wing persuasions he is seen as the saviour Chile. It may well be thought", he continued, "that the trial of Senator Pinochet in Spain for offences all of which related to the State of Chile and of which occurred in Chile is not calculated to achieve the best justice. But I cannot emphasise too strongly that that is no concern of your Lordships. Although others perceive our task as being to choose between two sides on the grounds of personal preference or political inclination, that is an entire misconception".

I respectfully adopt those words so far as this court is concerned, It is unfortunate that this point has to be made at all, but having regard to the appearance in the press of one two foolish articles hinting at the possibility of bias, and taking into account the great of public debate, including statements of opinion by prominent public figures, I feel incumbent upon me to emphasise that my decision in this case will be based upon the law and the law alone, in accordance with the judicial oath "to do right to all manner of persons, after the laws and ordinances of the realm, without fear or favour, affection or ill-will". If my understanding of the law is at fault a higher court will put that right.

Next I turn to the nature of these proceedings. The Spanish request is made under the terms of the European Convention on Extradition, entered into by a number of states, mostly though not entirely, European, for the purpose of simplifying and expediting the process of the return of fugitive offenders. Both Spain and the United Kingdom are signatories to the Convention and both have embodied its terms, with few reservations, into their own domestic law. In the case of this country the relevant law is contained in the Extradition Act 1989 and in The European Convention on Extradition Order 1990. The purpose of the Convention would appear to be to expedite and streamline the extradition process and so avoid the previous situation under which fugitives from justice, by taking every conceivable technicality, were able to delay, in some instances for years, their return to the requesting state.

The purpose of such Conventions is to assist the forces of law and order to counter the increasing sophistication with which international criminals, be they terrorists, drug traffickers, perpetrators of fraud on an international scale and such like, exploit advanced technology and communications to commit their crimes and avoid detection and subsequent apprehension. In recent years a number of such agreements between states have been entered into, including one which has been an important factor in this case, namely the United Nations Convention against Torture and Other Cruel, Inhuman or Degrading Treatment or Punishment, adopted by the United Nations General Assembly on 10th December 1984, referred to for convenience as "The Torture".

These Conventions represent the growing trend of the international community to combine together to outlaw crimes which are abhorrent to civilized society whether they be offences of the kind to which I have referred or crimes of cruelty and violence which may be committed by individuals, by terrorist groups seeking to influence or overthrow democratic governments or by undemocratic governments against their own citizens.

This development may be said to presage the day when, for the purposes of extradition, there will be one law for one world.

Against that background let me now turn to the function of this court. In this respect I cannot do better than quote the words of Lord Justice Kennedy in the case of *In Re Anthony*: "The whole purpose of the Convention and those parts of the statute, to which I have referred, is to provide a simplified form of procedure which does not become bogged down in detailed consideration of evidence. The person whose extradition is sought needs to know, in general terms, what he is supposed to have done, and both the Secretary of State and the Magistrate need to be satisfied that the conduct alleged would amount to a serious crime in either country". But as Lord Templeman said in Evans: "The magistrate is not concerned with proof of the facts, the possibilities of other relevant facts, or the emergence of any defence; these are matters for trial".

It cannot be too strongly emphasized that these proceedings are not conducted for the purpose of deciding the guilt or innocence of Senator Pinochet in respect of the allegations made against him, nor would a finding on my part that the request of Spain should be complied with be any indication whatever that I have formed a view as to his guilt or innocence.

The purpose of this hearing is to enable me as the presiding magistrate, to decide whether or not the conditions are in place which would oblige me to order the committal of Senator Pinochet to await the decision of the Secretary of State.

This is an accusation case under the Convention. No evidence is called, except on very restricted issues, and there is no requirement for the Government of Spain to establish a prima facie case. This is because the whole purpose of this procedure is to ensure that, so far as possible, contentious matters should be thrashed out in the courts of the requesting state. Hence, it would be in the Spanish court, should the case go that far, that evidence would be called and tested. It is there that Senator Pinochet would be able to establish any defence.

I refer to my own position as magistrate. My decision is not final. Firstly, both the government and the defence have the right to appeal my ruling, depending on which way it goes, to the Divisional Court of the High Court, and thereafter, with leave, to the House of Lords. Secondly, if Senator Pinochet is not discharged, the final decision regarding his extradition to Spain rests with the Secretary of State and not with the courts.

One further matter. The Divisional Court of the High Court, which hears appeals from this court in extradition cases, has indicated, very understandably, that when such appeals are heard it is helpful to the judges if they are provided with a statement of the magistrate's reasons for his decision. It is not my proper task to give a long judgment tracing through in detail all the submissions and dwelling in depth on the authorities. I therefore now return to what I understand to be the main issues, my ruling on each of these, and my reasons for so ruling.

The first question for my consideration is whether I can properly entertain material produced by the requesting state which was not before and had not been requested by the Secretary of State when he issued his authority to proceed on the 14th April 1999.

I can find nothing in Articles 12 or 13 of the Convention or Section 7 of the Extradition Act which states this. I am also satisfied that the case of Cuoghi is clear authority against it.

Article 12 sets out the necessary form and contents of the Request. Article 13, under the heading "Supplementary Information" states: "If the information communicated by the requesting party is found to be insufficient to allow the requested party to make a decision in pursuance of this Convention, the latter party shall request the necessary supplementary information and may fix a time-limit for the receipt thereof".

The power of the Secretary of State under Article 13 to request further information is for the purpose of enabling him the better to formulate the correct offences to be contained in the authority to proceed. I draw no inference from this that further material which was not before him when he issued his authority is not receivable by the court. The purpose of Article 13 is to assist the Secretary of State perform his task, not to deprive the court of necessary information to enable it perform its function.

I have been referred by the defence to a letter dated 15th April 1999 from a Home Office official to solicitors for the defence. I am not at all sure that in reaching my decision on this point it is appropriate for me to have regard to the contents of such a letter. But in any event I do not accede to the interpretation that the defence place upon the passages marked. The most significant appears to be paragraph 22. That paragraph that the Secretary of State has declined the invitation of The Crown Prosecution Service to consider fresh material dated 10th December 1998, 24th December 1998, 26th March 1998(9) and 5th April 1999 subsequent to the formal request received in the Home Office on 11th November 1998.

The following words are important however. "He does not regard the material to be 'supplementary material' Article 13 of the ECE since, as the requested party in that Article, he has considered it necessary to request such material from Spain in order to make his decision".

The authority to proceed is, as the Government of Spain submits, the document which starts the proceedings moving. I can find no basis for the proposition that material therefore be unavailable to the court. Section 7(2)(b) of the Extradition Act which refers to "particulars of the offence of which he is accused . . ." which "shall be furnished with any such request" does not in my view confine the court to those particulars which were furnished with the original request or which were before the Secretary of State when he issued his authority to proceed.

The further material, objected to by the defence is in my view supplementary to and in amplification of the conduct alleged against Senator Pinochet, namely his involvement in acts of torture and conspiracy to commit such acts. If such material described totally different offences the position would be different.

The relevant authority in point is that of Re Cuoghi. The Government and the defence each place a different construction on this case. I have to say I find the Government view more persuasive. The crucial words of Lord

Justice Kennedy are these: "If the magistrate is satisfied that the authority to proceed has been issued in respect of the person arrested and that the offence to which the authority to proceed relates is an extradition crime he is required to commit. Nothing in the statute requires him to reach that state of mind on the basis of information as it was before the Secretary of State".

My ruling is therefore that I am entitled to receive and consider the further information which was not before the Secretary of State at the time he issued his authority to proceed on 14th April.

The next matter for my consideration is whether the conduct of which Senator Pinochet stands accused is conduct which if it occurred in this country and also in Spain would, under the law of each country constitute extraditable offences. This is called the "double criminality rule" which must be satisfied before I can properly commit Mr Pinochet to await the Secretary of State's further direction.

Section 2(1)(a) of the Extradition Act 1989 defines an extradition crime as "conduct in the territory of a foreign state ... which, if it occurred in the United Kingdom, would constitute an offence punishable with imprisonment for a term of 12 months, or any punishment, and which, however described in the law of the foreign state ... so punishable under that law".

May I say straight away that I feel sure that the House of Lords at the March hearing had under review the question of extradition crimes and immunity as two separate issues. Lord Browne–Wilkinson made that clear when he said at the commencement of his judgment:

> "Our job is to decide two questions of law: are there any extradition crimes and, if so, is Senator Pinochet immune from trial for committing crimes. If, as a matter of law, there are no extradition crimes or he is entitled to immunity in relation to whichever crimes there are, then there is legal right to extradite Senator Pinochet to Spain, or indeed to stand in way of his return to Chile. If, on the other hand, there are extradition in relation to which Senator Pinochet is not entitled to state then it will be open to the Home Secretary to extradite him.

> "The task of this House is only to decide those points of law".

I have carefully and respectfully read and re-read the judgments of their Lordships and I am satisfied that the majority of the House regarded the Torture Convention to be of universal application. Chile, Spain and the United Kingdom are all signatories to Convention. The Criminal Justice Act 1988 Section 134 applies the Convention to the law of this country. Section 134(3) provides that the offence can be committed by act omission, and the torture may be mental or physical. It has been submitted to me that the Government of Spain have to provide information that the alleged torture must be widespread and systematic. A majority of the House held that one act of torture was sufficient to establish the necessary conduct, Lord Goff dissenting. However, having admitted the further information, I respectfully adopt the view of their Lordships that the conduct alleged against Senator Pinochet would be extraditable offences under English law if the accusations were substantiated. But even without the guidance of the highest court in the land I would have come to the same conclusion.

What is the position regarding the law of Spain? The defence submit that I cannot be satisfied that by the law of Spain the conduct as alleged against Senator Pinochet is an extraditable offence in that country. Am I bound by the insistence of Spain that the conduct would be punishable in Spain with a sentence of twelve months' imprisonment or more or should I examine the situation more closely?

Here I receive great assistance from the leading House of Lords case of In Re Evans. I ask the indulgence of counsel who I know are all too familiar with it, but I feel that it has such a powerful bearing on my judgment that I propose to cite those passages in the landmark judgment of Lord Templeman which I consider most important.

Mr Nicholls has, I think, conceded that on the authority of Evans he is not entitled to call evidence of foreign law. He is entitled to make submissions, and I have to ask myself what is my position as a presiding magistrate having heard those submissions.

After reviewing the law generally as attaching to accusation cases under the Convention, Lord Templeman said "If the magistrate in committal proceedings were not limited to consideration of the conduct of the accused as alleged in the request for extradition, in the light of the law of the foreign state as presented with the request, then no one would ever be extradited until he had been tried and found guilty in the United Kingdom of an offence against the law of a foreign country committed in the foreign country". He then states later: "For the purposes of the court of committal, the conduct facts are those set forth in the request for extradition; the relevant law of the state is that set forth in the request for extradition".

Then again he states: "The magistrate will then consider whether the conduct set out in the particulars of conduct furnished by the requested state constituted an offence under the law set out in the particulars of law supplied by the requesting state. The magistrate will be aware that the authorities which issued the foreign warrant for arrest and the government which requested extradition must have been satisfied that the conduct constituted an offence".

I read that passage as saying that having heard submissions the relevant foreign law to which I must direct my attention is that contained in the request. Can I go behind the claim in the request that the foreign law has been infringed by the alleged conduct.

To do so would surely involve me in an investigation of the foreign law of a kind which the full House in Evans declared impermissible. Foreign experts would surely have to assist the court. But that would be a reversion to the old system which has been ruled in Evans in Convention accusation cases. Moreover the High Court of Spain has twice ruled that the conduct complained of would amount to Extradition offences under the law of Spain. Could I, a magistrate with no particular knowledge, or quite frankly no knowledge of Spanish law challenge the rulings of Spanish High Court judges regarding the law of their own country? I think not.

Two further significant passages in Lord Templeman's judgment are worthy of note in this context: "If the presentation of the law of the foreign state set forth in the request for were inaccurate or incomplete in a relevant and material respect and the correct law could not be presented by agreement, then the accused would have his remedy in habeas corpus proceedings".

The learned Law Lord is not there speaking in a derogatory manner of the committing magistrate, but emphasising the very limited nature of the role he or she has to play.

One final passage I would cite: "In my opinion where requests for extradition allege acts violence, theft, fraud or the like courts should be slow to pay heed to any representations that such acts do not constitute offences under foreign law".

I conclude therefore that I am bound by the Spanish representations as to their own law and I accordingly find that the double criminality rule is satisfied.

The remaining issues I propose to deal with quite briefly.

The matter of immunity has been ruled upon by the House of Lords with one dissentient voice. That ruling is binding upon this court. Accordingly I find that the information before me relating to allegations after 8th 1988 constitute a course of conduct amounting to torture and conspiracy to torture for which Senator Pinochet enjoys no immunity. The attack on the charges relate in my view to matters of evidence appropriately dealt at the court of trial. Again I pray in aid a passage from Lord Templeman's judgment in Evans: "The magistrate is not concerned with proof of the facts, the possibilities of other relevant facts, or the emergence of any defence; these are matters for trial". The issues raised on the charges essentially go to Senator Pinochet's defence for which the appropriate court is the court of trial, which this is not.

I take the view that information relating to the allegation of conspiracy prior to 8th 1988 can be considered by the court, as conspiracy is a continuing offence. However, this would not be my ruling relating to the substantive offences. Whether the disappearances amount to torture; the effect on the families of those who can amount to mental torture. Whether or not this was intended by the regime of Senator Pinochet is in my view a matter of fact for the trial court. On the basis of my findings I am therefore satisfied that all the conditions are in place which oblige me under the terms of Section 9(8) of the Extradition Act 1989 to commit Senator Pinochet to await the decision of the Secretary of State.

Autumn of the Patriarch:* The Pinochet Extradition Debacle & Beyond–Human Rights Clauses Compared to Traditional Derivative Protections

90 J. Criminal Law & Criminology 1 (2001)**

This article will analyze human rights law to see whether it plays any role in the protection of the individual in the face of extradition or other

* In honor of Gabriel Garcia Marquez, THE AUTUMN OF THE PATRIARCH (1976).

** Reprinted with the permission of the Journal of Criminal Law & Criminology.

cooperation in criminal matters. Two approaches to extradition and human rights that seem to be vying for position in the world arena and the tension between them. The first is to apply the traditional statist exemptions to extradition, which sometimes have enabled human rights protections. This approach, of course, is based on the concept that states are the only subjects of international law. Thus, it is state's interests, rights, and obligations that are to be vindicated. If a fugitive is to be protected, it is because the state wills it so. The second approach considers the individual, at least to a degree, to be a subject of international law. It is the fugitive's interests and rights that are at issue and that human rights law protects. Thus, extradition law (treaties, custom, and domestic law) should include certain specific, basic human rights clauses or rules, through which the fugitive, if they obtain, will be exempt from extradition. These may include specific, wholesale human rights clauses in extradition treaties and domestic extradition laws. It can be argued that, even without a specific clause, established international human rights rules are incorporated by reference.

The two approaches and the battle to have each accepted, illustrate the tension between the value of protecting individual human rights in the criminal justice arena and the need to provide effective international law enforcement. This tension and both theories or approaches were presented dramatically by the process leading to and the English decision not to extradite Augusto Pinochet to Spain. I will begin with issues related to the attempted Pinochet extradition. I will move quickly beyond Pinochet to consider the above-noted tensions in some detail.

. . . I will argue that if we are seriously going to try to end impunity for crimes against humanity and war crimes, it must be done in a way that is consistent with the highest protection of human rights interests for those being prosecuted. Otherwise, the system will ultimately fall of its own weight or become a tool of repression itself. If we are not scrupulous in protecting accused persons from abuses and deprivation of civil liberties and related human rights protections during extradition, investigation, and trial. we will ultimately condemn the viability of the human rights and criminal justice. As Justice Jackson stated in his opening statement as Chief Prosecutor in the Nuremberg Trials:

> "[b]efore I discuss the particulars of evidence, some general considerations which may affect the credit of this trial in the eyes of the world should be candidly faced. There is a dramatic disparity between the circumstances of the accusers and the accused that might discredit our work if we should falter, in even minor matters, in being fair and temperate. Unfortunately, the nature of these crimes is such that both prosecution and judgment must be by victor nations over vanquished foes. . . . We must never forget that the record on which we judge these defendants is the record on which history will judge us tomorrow. To pass these defendants a poisoned chalice is to put it to our lips as well.

We must summon such detachment and intellectual integrity to our task that this Trial will commend itself to posterity as fulfilling humanity's aspirations to do justice.''[1]

The very same principles obtain in any criminal justice system, whether domestic or international. We will look at these issues through the prism of international extradition. Extradition is the traditional and the legal method for one state to return a fugitive to face prosecution or to serve his or her sentence. The traditional positivist approach to extradition is still predominant on most issues. It prescribes that the state is *the* subject of international law and that the individual is an object to be extradited. It is the state, not the individual that has rights and obligations.[2] Barriers to extradition, therefore, obtain for the protection of the state and as the means for the state to insist on protection for its nationals, or to insist on the limits it to which the requesting state must abide.... This is a matter of sovereignty. Thus, limitations on and exemptions from extradition, like the double criminality principle, the principle of speciality, ne bis in idem, or the political offense exception apply at the prerogative and benefit of the state. They are not exclusively or even primarily, aimed at protecting the fugitive, who, under this view, generally does not even have standing to raise their violation. Rather, the fugitive's right or protection is derivative. For example, the political offense exception is applied to allow a state to protect its nationals, to avoid participation in the prosecution of the losers in a political conflict or to protect a person from being extradited to a place where he or she will be persecuted for reasons of race, gender, ethnicity, religion, or politics. The rule of non-inquiry ... is applied by courts to avoid considering the propriety of extradition, when questions about the fairness of the requesting state's justice system are raised. The requested state sees its interest in not embarrassing the requesting state.... Human rights protections in extradition practice are only incremental and casuistic at best.

A. Emergence of Pro-active Human Rights Clauses

The view that human rights for individuals are merely derivative is also part of the vision of the Ad Hoc tribunals for Rwanda and the former Yugoslavia and for the Permanent International Criminal Court. The

---

1. Justice Robert H. Jackson, Chief Counsel for the Prosecution in the Nuremberg Trials, *Opening Statement,* delivered, November 20, 1945, *quoted in* Telford Taylor, THE ANATOMY OF THE NUREMBERG TRIALS: A PERSONAL MEMOIR 167–169 (1992); *see elaboration in* Christopher L. Blakesley, *Obstacles to the Creation of an Permanent War Crimes Tribunal,* 18 The Fletcher Forum of World Affr's 77 (1994); and in Christopher L. Blakesley, *Atrocity & its Prosecution: The Ad Hoc Tribunals for the Former Yugoslavia and Rwanda,* Ch. 8, in, THE LAW OF WAR CRIMES: NATIONAL AND INTERNATIONAL APPROACHES 189 (Timothy L.H. McCormack & Gerry J. Simpson, eds. 1997).

2. *See, e.g., R.v. Bow Street Metropolitan Stipendiary Magistrate, ex parte Pinochet Ugarte* (Amnesty International and others intervening (No. III), 2 All E.R. 97, 170 (H.L. 1999), [1999] 2 W.L.R. 827 (Lord Millett, stating: "[The classical theory of international law] taught that states were the only actors on the international plane; the rights of individuals were not the subject of international law ..."); William J. Aceves, *Liberalism and International Legal Scholarship; The Pinochet Case and the Move Toward a Universal System of Transnational Law Litigaiton,* 41 Harv.Int'l L.J. 131 (2000).

Appeals Chamber of the International Tribunal for the former Yugoslavia stated in the *Tadic Case* that the derivative nature of human rights interests has more impact on domestic courts than in the international arena. I will show that the same vision is beginning to develop in domestic systems. Human rights are protected directly and in increasing measure through enforcement in domestic litigation and through other domestic institutions or mechanisms. Thus, I will focus on extradition as one of the mechanisms for the potential development of human rights in general, especially for the rights related to criminal prosecution. ... Extradition is at the intersection of international and domestic law.

... Some nations, especially in Europe, are adopting the more proactive human rights approach in their extradition law and practice. Some are including new bars or limits to extradition based on international and domestic human rights protections. This includes rights that arise not only from treaty, customary international law, but also from domestic legislation, and constitutional principles. Indeed, for some international norms protecting human rights are seen as having a constitutional character. Some nations are considering the adoption of explicit human rights clauses into their extradition treaties and laws.... German extradition treaties, in the future, for example, will likely contain a clause which with something like: "extradition will not be granted, if it is contrary to international and Constitutional Basic Rights ..." Basic Rights in Germany include international human rights.

Traditionally, at least since the Peace of Westphalia, sovereignty has been sacrosanct, an unassailable attribute, indeed, the essence of, statehood. Sovereignty, however, has suffered some erosion through progressive forces at work in democratic societies, often prompted by the human rights movement. In the international system and in many domestic legal systems, it is arguable that an extradition treaty must be read to promote basic human rights.[4] Human rights norms inform and infuse the treaty. Ambiguous terms must be interpreted to be consistent with relevant human right principles and gaps must be filled so as to promote human rights.[5] Traditionally, however, the opposite has been true; ambiguity was to be read in favor of extradition. The House of Lords found a way to apply a fairly rigid, dualistic, traditional rule of double criminality in the Pinochet case [the decision did recognize] case torture committed abroad as a crime in England. The decision, while important, was clearly in the rank of traditional, statist international law.

B.   Is there a Need for an Humanitarian Exception to Extradition?–Or Worrisome Tendencies.

Whatever slight human rights protections obtain for individuals charged with crime in either the domestic or the international systems, may be eroded even further by an ironic partnership of anti-crime zealots

---

4. *But see, U.S. v. Alvarez–Machain,* 112 S.Ct. 2188 (1992) (official abduction of accused, for purposes of prosecution in US, although admittedly illegal under international law does not provide remedy of release, even upon protest of nation from which defendant was abducted); *US v. Verdugo–Urquidez,* 494 US 259 (1990).

5. This is similar to how public policy principles function in the US judicial system.

and some human rights activists. Of course, it is most important to find a way to disestablish impunity for perpetrators of all crime, especially crimes against humanity. A major theme of this article, however, is to warn against a tendency into which we all sometimes stumble. We allow ourselves to believe that short-cuts to the processes of "finding the truth" and eliminating impunity are appropriate, in the face of the more horrendous crimes committed. ... It is sadly interesting to me that many of vigorous proponents of human rights, who, by instinct are also vigorous promoters of protections against police and prosecutorial abuses, are tempted to seek shortcuts when it comes to fighting serious international evil. This phenomenon reminds me of the tendencies of true-believers in the "war on drugs,...."

If we are not careful, we may fall into the trap laid for all those who are too certain about the righteousness of their indignation. They become willing to "do what is necessary" to fulfill their righteousness. Recently, for example, in discussion of the eminently proper extradition of Elizaphan Ntakirutimana, it was argued that the procedural hurdles that had to be overcome before rendering Ntakirutimana to the International Criminal Court for Rwanda (ICTR) were, "... unnecessary procedural complexities of American Extradition law...." "There is no doubt that criminals, including international criminals, will and do "take advantage of" (in every sense of the term) any procedural or substantive devices they have available to them. Abuse occurs, but abuse occurs just as often by governments who prosecute or extradite. The answer is not to panic and eliminate the protections available, but to insist on efficiency in policing, extradition, and prosecution."

Voltaire's *"everyman"* in *Candide* cynically assessed international law and the laws of war, as consisting of righteous brutality on a grand scale and simple suffering on a human scale. Voltaire's assessment of international law, terror, and our own tendency to become barbaric, makes one pause. Exploitation of human weakness by the few with power may be the actual culprit. Primo Levi drove himself to despair (perhaps to suicide) over the issue of why common, every-day, "civilized" people may fall into a miasma of evil. Sadly, many of us tend to distrust, denigrate, and discriminate against those whom we perceive as being different from us. This tendency is often manipulated by "leaders," who appropriate it for their own nefarious purposes. We are made to believe that those "who are different" are dangerous. Sometimes we may even succumb to this and to discriminate invidiously. Worse, we may adopt a mob mentality in prosecutions. Even worse, we may participate in ethnic, racial, or other mindless violence.

Herman Melville also beautifully makes us feel what happens to us, when we let hatred of our so-called "enemies" fester and well-up in us:

> *"[a]ll that most maddens and torments; all that stirs up the lees of things; all truth with malice in it; all that cracks the sinews and cakes the brain; all the subtle demonisms of life and thought; all evil to crazy Ahab, were visibly personified, and made practically assailable in Moby Dick. He piled upon the whale's white hump the sum of all the general rage and hate felt by his whole race from Adam down; and then, as if*

his chest had been a mortar, he burst his hot heart's shell upon it."
Herman Melville, MOBY DICK (1851).

Herman Melville brilliantly prompts us to address our own tendencies through Captain Ahab. We sense the risk of our own potential for destructive rage, hatred and violence.

Terroristic outrage is sickeningly common; few, if any of us escape its taint. Chemical warfare has recently been reinstituted against combatants and non-combatants alike. It is now well known that on or about March 23, 1988, the Iraqi Air Force bombed villages in Kurdistan, spreading mustard and possibly nerve gas over villagers, dropping them in their panicked tracks, many holding their babies to their breasts. Iraq accused Iran of using similar weapons. It has been proposed often that the United States Government increase its capacity in research into biological agents to be used as weapons or defenses. The Salvadoran Army participated in a program of mass execution of civilians to intimidate "its enemies." In September 1982, innocent men, women and children were slaughtered in the refugee camps at Sabra and Shatila, Lebanon by Lebanese–Christian forces dependent on Israel. The Achille Lauro Affair is well known. The former Soviets, among other things, used booby-trapped dolls for Afghan Moujahadeen children. Later, the Russians continued committing atrocities in Georgia and in Chechnya. The outrage of the desaparacidos is now well known. At least some of the culprits may now be preparing to meet a proper legal fate. The United States Government has supported, both directly and indirectly, the Nicaraguan "Contras" who, themselves, killed innocent Nicaraguans in conjunction with their guerilla warfare. Sandinistas in Nicaragua and their enemies, too, apparently killed many innocents in maintaining their power. The depredations in Cambodia are renown. In 1975, the Khmer Rouge destroyed the Cambodian legal system and culture, slaughtering by starvation, torture, and mass murder at the very least 800,000 to one million Cambodians, in their "auto-genocide." The former South African Government terrorized and oppressed its non-white population. There are so many other tragic episodes. Our *Mal du siècle*, our nauseating modern equivalent of the ancient blood-feud, this ugly saga of crimes against humanity and terrorism continues to accelerate. Makes one wonder.

Are these horrors and the responses to them all of one cloth or at least risk becoming so? I will try to argue one way in which they are indeed. I believe that Simone Weill and Thomas Merton were not far off in their belief that the monster, "the great beast," is the urge to collective power, "the grimmest of all the social realities of our time."[8] his lust for power is masked by the symbols of "nationalism, 'fundamentalism,' of capitalism, fascism, racism."

We have hoped and still hope that something can be done about the Khmer Rouge killers. At least we are trying, belatedly, to do something

---

8. Thomas Merton, *The Answer of Minerva: Pacifism and Resistance in Simone Weil*, in Merton, THE LITERARARY ESSAYS OF THOMAS MERTON 134 (1968) (Brother Patrick Hart, ed. (New Direction, 1981) (first published in Faith and Violence (Notre Dame, Press, 1968).

about the *genocidaires* of Rwanda and the former Yugoslavia. We will see whether something can be done in relation to Kosovo. . . .

This century has been terrible. The Armenians in Turkey, so many in Stalinist USSR, the Jewish people, the Gypsies, and others in Nazi Germany, the Kurds, Blacks in South Africa, and on and on. There are so many others. Every day it seems, some institution, government or group uses innocent children, women and men as fodder in their "war" against enemies; in their attempt at promoting a perverted vision of lex talionis. Some claim that the pusillanimous carnage was in retaliation for the slaughter of innocent children, women and men aboard the Iranian Air Bus, blown out of the sky by American forces. Others suggest that it was committed by those interested in thwarting prospects of peace in the Middle East. The melodrama of terrorism, war crimes, and crimes against humanity has penetrated each of our lives.

. . . Innocent children, women and men aboard Pan Am Flight 103 were used as fodder in some "cause" or "war". Two Libyans are now being prosecuted in the Hague, under Scottish law and before Scottish judges. But, consider all the innocents slaughtered aboard the Iranian Air Bus, blown out of the sky by American forces. Perhaps the pusillanimous carnage wrought on Pan Am 103, was in retaliation for the slaughter of other innocent children, women and men aboard the Airbus.

. . . These dangers apply, not only in the tendency to become caught up in perpetrating crimes against humanity, but we risk the same phenomenon in our reaction to such crimes. This article argues that a similar risk obtains in the criminal justice arena; in the way we proscribe and prosecute these offenses. . . .

We need to work toward developing a society in which the rule of law may begin to compete more efficiently with violence and terror. Do international law and its intersection with domestic law provide a means to stop these sorts of atrocities and to prosecute the accused, consistently with international norms of justice? The crimes against humanity and violations of human rights in the former Yugoslavia and Rwanda prompted the Security Council [to create the Ad Hoc Tribunals]. . . .[10]

II Humanitarian Exception to Extradition?—Pinochet not Competent to Stand Trial or to be Extradited?

> *Perfection, of a kind, was what he was after,*
> *And the poetry he invented was easy to understand;*
> *He knew human folly like the back of his hand,*
> *And was greatly interested in armies and fleets;*
> *When he laughed, respectable senators burst with laughter,*
> *And when he cried the little children died in the streets.*
> *W.H. Auden, Epitaph on a Tyrant,*

This section will consider some so-called "humanitarian" exemptions from extradition, such as refusing to extradite on the basis of the fugitive's

---

10. *See, Rome Statute of the International Criminal Court*, art. 5(1), U.N. Diplomatic Conference of Plenipotentiaries on the Establishment of an International Criminal Court, U.N.Doc. A/CONF.183/8 (July 17, 1998); presented in chapter 16.

physical infirmity or mental incompetency. These were the grounds that informed the English government's decision not to extradite Augusto Pinochet to Spain. The Spanish extradition request for Pinochet is quite well known by now, as is the House of Lords decision that he did not enjoy former head of state immunity for acts of torture that he or his government committed during his reign.[11]

Extradition is an admixture of national and international law. . . . [Since extradition sends a person to trial in the requesting state]. Perhaps, it is not inappropriate that extradition be refused upon evidence of an individual's incompetence to stand trial, as British Home Secretary, Jack Straw did in the Pinochet extradition case. On March 2, 2000, he . . . decided to free Pinochet [on humanitarian grounds], who immediately returned to Chile. Mr. Straw stated that either extradition or a trial in Britain, however desirable, was simply no longer possible on medical grounds. Pinochet was "unfit to stand trial and that no significant improvement in his condition could be expected." The evidence of Pinochet's incapacity and the decision not to let a court make the judgment are hotly disputed.

. . . The primary questions I will address are: what, if any, human rights or humanitarian protections ought to obtain at the extradition stage; and, if any obtain, how will the balance be struck between enforcement interests and human rights? Apparently, in England, like in the United States, it is the prerogative of the executive branch to apply humanitarian grounds to refuse extradition. In the United States, it is the prerogative of the Secretary of State. Pinochet should have been extradited, unless the defense actually proved that he is incompetent to stand trial. The test for this is whether the accused is capable of understanding the charges against him and to participate meaningfully in his defense. Secretary Straw's decision not to extradite was based mainly on his belief in Pinochet's mental incapacity, although he also mentioned his physical deterioration. Mr. Straw must have realized that Pinochet's physical deterioration is not relevant unless it impacts his capacity to enter a plea and to work with counsel. Certainly, an elderly person's physical capacity to withstand travel or a trial are pertinent to humanitarian concerns, and may impact on sentencing, but they are not sufficient to allow a court to deny extradition or prosecution altogether. It seems to me that it would have been better for a court to have decided this issue, although I understand that it was fully within the prerogative of the Home Secretary. Even so, one is still torn over whether he should have been extradited, so that Spanish courts could make the competency decision. Still, it would have been better for a British court to have made this decision than for the Home Secretary's decision to have been the final word.

Pinochet's Medical Report, which was the basis for Mr. Straw's decision to allow Pinochet to return to Chile, was leaked to the Spanish press. The Medical Report was written by esteemed British doctors and was reviewed by British chief medical officer Dr. Liam Donaldson, who confirmed its quality and thoroughness. It is important to determine whether Pinochet feigned the symptoms that allowed his apparent escape from

---

11. *See, Regina v. Bow Street Metropolitan Stipendiary Magistrate ex parte Pinochet*   *Ugarte* (III)[1999] (U.K.), 2 All E.R. 97, 170 (H.L. 1999), [1999] 2 W.L.R. 827.

earthly justice. The doctors who examined Pinochet concluded that his condition could not be feigned. . . .

It seemed that Pinochet was frail, but quite alert immediately after a very long plane trip and he was obviously happy to be home. . . . There has been enough fury over the evidence and the decision to justify the question being raised before the Chilean courts . . . One important human rights value, which is also a basic criminal law principle, is that a person who does note have the mental capacity or competence to grasp the purpose of his punishment, to understand the proceedings against him, or to assist his counsel should not be prosecuted. All legal systems that honor human rights must have a mechanism for protecting those who are not competent to stand trial. No doubt, sometimes even people who have done the most evil things become incompetent. Deciding not to extradite Pinochet may or may not accommodate this important value of not abusing people who are beyond earthly sanction due to incompetence. . . . It is ironic, that a person charged with having violated the most basic human rights of so many may be the beneficiary of those human rights protections he mocked in a most heinous way. Nevertheless, we must remain worthy of our human rights principles. . . .

C. The House of Lord's Decisions on Torture and Impunity

The decision not to extradite Pinochet or to prosecute him in Britain was a terrible blow to the survivors of his torture and to the relatives of his victims, but some hope can be found in the decision on whether Pinochet was immune from extradition or prosecution. Reed Brody, Advocacy Director for Human Rights Watch, tried to put a nice face on the situation, stating that, notwithstanding the non-extradition, the Pinochet case itself is a milestone. Brody stated that, . . . "the very fact that [Pinochet] was arrested, and that his claim of immunity was rejected, has already changed the calculus of dictators around the world. The Pinochet case signified the beginning of the end of their impunity." On February 3rd, for example, a Senegalese judge indicted the former Chadian dictator, Hissein Habré, on charges of torture, and apparently former President of Indonesia, Suharto, decided not to seek medical care abroad, because of the risk of prosecution. No doubt, then, some impunity was dissipated. Brody stated that, "a sea change is underway in how the world deals with the worst abuses." In its attempt to make the best of the bad situation in Pinochet's release, however, Human Rights Watch did overstate the legal value of the House of Lords decision on impunity.

It is true that Pinochet's arrest, detention, and the House of Lords decision that he was not immune as a former head of state from prosecution for torture, is very important—a milestone. Nevertheless, there is a "down-side" to the House of Lords decision. The Lords clearly applied a straight forward, traditional dualist position on torture, let alone on all the other horrible crimes with which Pinochet was charged. The House of Lords majority actually insisted on applying classic, rigid, traditional extradition law, applying a pedantic position on the "special use" of dual criminality. . . . The House of Lords held: (1) that for extradition to be allowed, not only must the fugitive's conduct be criminal in both states

(Spain and England); also, (2) a common theory of jurisdiction over the conduct must obtain in both states. This is the special use of double criminality. The majority's view is, first, that torture was NOT a crime of universal jurisdiction prior to the promulgation of the Torture Convention and that, even if it were, it was not extraditable in England, until promulgation of the Criminal Justice Act of 1988. It insisted that jurisdiction be based on an explicit English "incorporation" of torture. Thus, although it held that Pinochet was not immune from extradition or prosecution for torture, this was *only* on the basis of the Torture Convention and the Criminal Justice Act of 1988, which incorporated it.[14] This position is clearly antagonistic to the idea of torture being a universal crime or a crime that allows universal jurisdiction on the basis of customary international law.

Torture: Actus Reus and Mens Rea: The position taken by the English and the House of Lords regarding the offense of torture is interesting. Home Secretary Straw agreed with the House of Lords that the Torture Convention, as incorporated into British Law in the Criminal Justice Act of 1988, § 134, requires intent to "[inflict] severe pain or suffering on another in the performance or purported performance of . . . official duties . . ." whether the suffering is caused by act or omission, and whether it is committed directly by the defendant or by aiding, abetting, consent, instigation, by an official person or one acting on his behalf. The House of Lords held that only those acts of torture attributable to Pinochet that occurred after the promulgation of this Act were extraditable or justiciable, if there were to be any prosecution in England. It seems to me that the disappearances and continued pain and suffering caused in the families and loved ones of those who were made to "disappear," constitutes a continuing offense of torture to those families. This should give a basis for any nation to prosecute Pinochet (if he is competent) or his cronies. So, the Spanish request for Pinochet's extradition was refused by the British Government (along with requests from the Belgians, the French, and the Swiss). Amnesty International reported that all four of these nations that had sought Pinochet, are unconvinced that the medical report proves that Pinochet lacks the capacity to stand trial.

Notes and Questions

We have seen how the British have recently reacted to a human rights issue; now consider the U.S. approach.

1. Mental Incapacity and Human Rights. Do you agree with Lord Jack Straw and Professor Blakesley that, if even a former tyrant and human rights abuser of the first order is suffering from such mental degradation that he cannot assist in his defense, that he cannot be extradited or prosecuted consistently with human rights norms?

---

14. *See, Ex Parte Pinochet* (II), [1999] 2 W.L.R. 827 (H.L.); *Criminal Justice Act of 1988* § 134(1), (2) and (3).

2. *Torture as a Universal Violation of Human Rights.* Do you believe that torture on the scale that Pinochet is charged with constitutes a crime against humanity, such that it implicates universal jurisdiction? Is it this the law of England? If it is, at what point did the House of Lords find that torture as a universal crime obtained in English law? Do you believe that universality jurisdiction is part of customary international law? On the international law side of these issues, see Ch.3 (Jurisdiction) and Ch. 16, International Criminal Law.

3. *Head of State and Former Head of State Immunity*. For issues of head of state and former head of state immunity, see Ch. 7.

4. *Do you believe that any human rights protections should apply at the extradition phase.*

5. *U.S. Courts and Human Rights Law.* *Is it your impression that U.S. courts have been receptive to international human law? If not, why not?* effect On April 2, 1992, the Senate gave its advice and consent to the *International Covenant on Civil and Political Rights.* It had been open for signature since 1966. Why did it take the Senate so long? The US often includes severely limiting reservations on its ratifying instruments to human rights treaties, such as one providing that the convention is non-self-executing. What does this mean? If it is non-self-executing, what international effect does our "ratification" have? What is domestic effect?

6. *Would the Torture Victim Protection Act of 1991, supra and the Victims of Crime Act of 1984* (42 U.S.C. § 10601), which includes penalties for "international terrorism" change the outcome in cases like *Tel-Oren*?

Siderman v. Republic of Argentina

United States Court of Appeals, Ninth Circuit, 1992.

■ FLETCHER, CIRCUIT JUDGE:

* * *

FACTS

The factual record, which consists only of the Sidermans' complaint and numerous declarations they submitted in support of their claims, tells a horrifying tale of the violent and brutal excesses of an anti-Semitic military junta that ruled Argentina. On March 24, 1976, the Argentine military overthrew the government of President Maria Estela Peron and seized the reins of power for itself, installing military leaders of the central government and the provincial governments of Argentina. That night, ten masked men carrying machine guns forcibly entered the home of Jose and Lea Siderman, husband and wife, in Tucuman Province, Argentina. The men, who were acting under the direction of the military governor of Tucuman, ransacked the home and locked Lea in the bathroom. They then blindfolded and shackled 65–year old Jose, dragged him out of his home, tossed him into a waiting car, and drove off to an unknown building. For seven days the men beat and tortured Jose. Among their tools of torture was an electric cattle prod, which they used to shock Jose until he fainted.

As they tortured him, the men repeatedly shouted anti-Semitic epithets, calling him a "Jew Bastard" and a "Shitty Jew." They inflicted all of these cruelties upon Jose Siderman because of his Jewish faith.

At the end of this nightmarish week, his body badly bruised and his ribs broken, Jose was taken out of the building and driven to an isolated area, where the masked men tossed him out of the car. The men told Jose that if he and his family did not leave Tucuman and Argentina immediately, they would be killed. On the day of Jose's release, he and Lea fled to Buenos Aires in fear for their lives. Their son Carlos followed shortly thereafter, and the night Carlos left Tucuman, military authorities ransacked his home. In June 1976, Jose, Lea, and Carlos left Argentina for the United States, where they joined Susana Siderman de Blake. She is the daughter of Jose and Lea and is a United States citizen.

Before the hasty flight from Tucuman to Buenos Aires, Jose was forced to raise cash by selling at a steep discount part of his interest in 127,000 acres of land. Prior to their departure for the United States, the Sidermans also made arrangements for someone to oversee their family business, Inmobiliaria del No–Oeste, S.A. ("INOSA"), an Argentine corporation. Susana Siderman de Blake, Carlos Siderman and Lea Siderman each owned 33% of INOSA and Jose owned the remaining one percent. Its assets comprised numerous real estate holdings including a large hotel in Tucuman, the Hotel Gran Corona. The Sidermans granted management powers over INOSA to a certified public accountant in Argentina.

After the Sidermans left Argentina for the United States, Argentine military officers renewed their persecution of Jose. They altered real property records in Tucuman to show that he had owned not 127,000, but 127, acres of land in the province. They then initiated a criminal action against him in Argentina, claiming that since he owned only 127 acres he had sold land that did not belong to him. Argentina sought the assistance of our courts in obtaining jurisdiction over his person, requesting via a letter rogatory that the Los Angeles Superior Court serve him with documents relating to the action. The court, unaware of Argentina's motives, complied with the request.

Soon thereafter, while he was travelling in Italy, Jose was arrested pursuant to an extradition request from Argentina to the Italian government. Argentina charged that Jose had fraudulently obtained the travel documents enabling him to leave Argentina in 1976. Jose was not permitted to leave Cremora, Italy, for seven months, and actually was imprisoned for 27 days, before an Italian Appeals Court finally held that Argentina's extradition request would not be honored, as it was politically motivated and founded on pretextual charges.

The Argentine military also pursued INOSA with vigor. In April 1977, INOSA was seized through a sham "judicial intervention," a proceeding in which property is put into receivership. The purported reasons for the intervention were that INOSA lacked a representative in Argentina and that INOSA had obtained excessive funds from a Tucuman provincial bank. Though these reasons were pretexts for persecuting the Sidermans because of their religion and profiting from their economic success, the Sidermans were unable to oppose the intervention because Argentine officials had imprisoned and killed the accountant to whom they had granted management powers over INOSA. In 1978, the Sidermans retained an attorney in Argentina and brought a derivative action in a Tucuman court in an effort to end the intervention. The court ordered that the intervention cease, and the order was upheld by the Supreme Court of Tucuman, but the order remains unenforced and the intervention has continued. Argentine military officials and INOSA's appointed receivers have extracted funds from INOSA, purchased various assets owned by INOSA at sharply discounted prices, and diverted INOSA's profits and revenues to themselves.

In 1982, Jose, Lea, and Carlos, who by then had become permanent residents of the United States, and Susana, a United States citizen since 1967, turned to federal court for relief. They filed a complaint asserting eighteen causes of action based on the torture and harassment of Jose by Argentine officials and the expropriation of their property in Argentina. Named defendants included the Republic of Argentina, the Province of Tucuman, INOSA, and numerous individual defendants who participated in the wrongdoing. In December 1982, the Sidermans properly served Argentina and Tucuman with the Summons and Complaint. The Argentine Embassy subsequently sought assistance from the U.S. State Department, which informed Argentina that it would have to appear and present any defenses it wished to assert to the district court, including the defense of sovereign immunity, or risk a default judgment. The State Department also provided a directory of lawyer referral services. Despite receiving this information, Argentina did not enter an appearance, and the Sidermans filed a motion for default judgment.

On March 12, 1984, the district court dismissed the Sidermans' expropriation claims sua sponte on the basis of the act of state doctrine and ordered a hearing for the Sidermans to prove up their damages on the torture claims. The Sidermans moved for reconsideration of the court's dismissal of the expropriation claims. On September 28, 1984, the court denied the motion for reconsideration and entered a default judgment on the torture claims, awarding Jose damages and expenses totalling $2.6 million for his torture claims and awarding Lea $100,000 for her loss of consortium claim.

The damages award finally elicited a response from Argentina, which filed a motion for relief from judgment on the ground that it was immune from suit under the FSIA and that the district court therefore lacked both subject matter and personal jurisdiction. The United States filed a suggestion of interest, asking the court to consider the issue of foreign sovereign immunity but indicating no view of the merits. On March 7, 1985, the district court vacated the default judgment and dismissed the Sidermans' action on the ground of Argentina's immunity under the FSIA. The Sidermans filed a timely notice of appeal. We have jurisdiction over the appeal pursuant to 28 U.S.C. § 1291. * * *

II. Torture Claims

The question of Argentina's immunity from the Sidermans' torture claims is squarely presented, without the procedural complications surrounding the district court's treatment of the expropriation claims. The district court dismissed the torture claims on the ground that they fell within no exception to immunity under the FSIA. In defending the district court's decision on appeal, Argentina argues that the Sidermans' claims are foreclosed by the Supreme Court's opinion in Argentine Republic v. Amerada Hess. Since Amerada Hess represents the Court's most extensive treatment of the FSIA and its exceptions to immunity, we begin with a discussion of the case before turning to the Sidermans' arguments about why the case does not preclude their torture claims.

* * *

A.   Jus Cogens

The Sidermans contend that Argentina does not enjoy sovereign immunity with respect to its violation of the jus cogens norm of international law condemning official torture. While we agree with the Sidermans that official acts of torture of the sort they allege Argentina to have committed constitute a jus cogens violation, we conclude that Amerada Hess forecloses their attempt to posit a basis for jurisdiction not expressly countenanced by the FSIA.

As defined in the Vienna Convention on the Law of Treaties, a jus cogens norm, also known as a "peremptory norm" of international law, "is a norm accepted and recognized by the international community of states as a whole as a norm from which no derogation is permitted and which can be modified only by a subsequent norm of general international law having the same character." Vienna Convention on the Law of Treaties, art. 53, May 23, 1969, [*hereinafter "Vienna Convention"*]; *see also* Restatement § 102 Reporter's Note 6. Jus cogens is related to customary international law (the direct descendant of the law of nations), which the Restatement defines as the "general and consistent practice of states followed by them from a sense of legal obligation." Restatement § 102(2). Courts ascertain customary international law "by consulting the works of jurists, writing professedly on public law; or by the general usage and practice of nations; or by judicial decisions recognizing and enforcing that law." *U.S. v. Smith*, * * * (Story, J.); *see also The Paquete Habana* * * * (in ascertaining and administering customary international law, courts should resort "to the customs and usages of civilized nations, and, as evidence of these, to the works of jurists and commentators"); *Filartiga v. Pena–Irala* * * * Courts seeking to determine whether a norm of customary international law has attained the status of jus cogens look to the same sources, but must also determine whether the international community recognizes the norm as one "from which no derogation is permitted." Committee of U.S. Citizens Living in *Nicaragua v. Reagan* * * * [hereinafter "CUSCLIN"] (quoting Vienna Convention, art. 53). In CUSCLIN, the only reported federal decision to give extended treatment to jus cogens, the court described jus cogens as an elite subset of the norms recognized as customary international law.

While jus cogens and customary international law are related, they differ in one important respect. Customary international law, like international law defined by treaties and other international agreements, rests on the consent of states. A state that persistently objects to a norm of customary international law that other states accept is not bound by that norm, see Restatement § 102 Comment d, just as a state that is not party to an international agreement is not bound by the terms of that agreement. International agreements and customary international law create norms known as jus dispositivum, the category of international law that "consists of norms derived from the consent of states" and that is founded "on the self-interest of the participating states * * *." Jus dispositivum binds only "those states consenting to be governed by it."

In contrast, jus cogens "embraces customary laws considered binding on all nations," * * * and "is derived from values taken to be fundamental by the international community, rather than from the fortuitous or self-interested choices of nations * * *." Whereas customary international law derives solely from the consent of states, the fundamental and universal norms constituting jus cogens transcend such consent, as exemplified by the theories underlying the judgments of the Nuremberg tribunals following World War II * * *. The legitimacy of the Nuremberg prosecutions rested not on the consent of the Axis Powers and individual defendants, but on the nature of the acts they committed: acts that the laws of all civilized nations define as criminal * * *. The universal and fundamental rights of human beings identified by Nuremberg-rights against genocide, enslavement, and other inhumane acts * * * are the direct ancestors of the universal and fundamental norms recognized as jus cogens. In the words of the International Court of Justice, these norms, which include "principles and rules concerning the basic rights of the human person," are the concern of all states; "they are obligations erga omnes." *The Barcelona Traction* (Belgium v. Spain), 1970 I.C.J. 3, 32.

Because jus cogens norms do not depend solely on the consent of states for their binding force, they "enjoy the highest status within international law." CUSCLIN. For example, a treaty that contravenes jus cogens is considered under international law to be void ab initio. See Vienna Convention, art. 53; Restatement § 102 Comment k. Indeed, the supremacy of jus cogens extends over all rules of international law; norms that have attained the status of jus cogens "prevail over and invalidate international agreements and other rules of international law in conflict with them." Restatement § 102 Comment k. A jus cogens norm is subject to modification or derogation only by a subsequent jus cogens norm. *Id.*

The Sidermans claim that the prohibition against official torture has attained the status of a jus cogens norm. There is no doubt that the prohibition against official torture is a norm of customary international law, as the Second Circuit recognized more than ten years ago in the landmark case of Filartiga v. Pena–Irala * * *. Dr. Filartiga and his daughter, citizens of Paraguay, [sued] Paraguayan officials who had tortured Dr. Filartiga's son to death. They alleged jurisdiction under the Alien Tort Statute, which grants the district courts "original jurisdiction of any civil action by an alien for a tort only, committed in violation of the law of nations or a treaty of the United States." 28 U.S.C. § 1350. Dr. Filartiga claimed that the defendants' torture of his son, perpetrated under color of official authority, violated a norm of customary international law prohibiting official torture, and the court agreed. Judge Kaufman, writing for the court, explained that "there are few, if any, issues in international law today on which opinion seems to be so united as the limitations on a state's power to torture persons held in its custody." * * * Judge Kaufman catalogued the evidence in support of this view, citing several declarations of the General Assembly and human rights conventions prohibiting torture modern municipal law to the same effect, and the works of jurists, and finally concluded "that official torture is now prohibited by the law of nations."

Other authorities have also recognized that official torture is prohibited by customary international law. In *Forti v. Suarez–Mason [supra]*, a suit predicated on atrocities committed by the same Argentine military government alleged to be responsible for the torture of Jose Siderman, the district court held that "official torture constitutes a cognizable violation of the law of nations," and described the prohibition against official torture as "universal, obligatory, and definable." Similarly, in *Tel-Oren v. Libyan Arab Republic*, *[supra]* (opinion of Edwards, J.) which involved an action against the Palestine Liberation Organization for its acts of terrorism, Judge Edwards identified torture as a violation of customary international law. Judge Bork, although raising considerable opposition to the application of customary international law in U.S. courts, see id. (opinion of Bork, J.), at the same time conceded that the international law prohibition against torture is not disputed. *Id.* The Restatement of Foreign Relations also holds to the view that customary international law prohibits official torture. Restatement § 702(d). Finally, the world now has an international agreement focused specifically on the prohibition against torture: The Convention Against Torture and Other Cruel, Inhuman or Degrading Treatment or Punishment, 39 U.N.GAOR Supp. (No. 51), 23 I.L.M. 1027 (1984) [hereinafter "Torture Convention"], which entered into force on June 26, 1987. The United States signed the Torture Convention in April 1988, the United States Senate gave its advice and consent in October 1988, see 136 Cong.Rec. S17486–92 (daily ed. October 27, 1990), and it now awaits the President's filing of the instrument of ratification with the Secretary–General of the United Nations.

In light of the unanimous view of these authoritative voices, it would be unthinkable to conclude other than that acts of official torture violate customary international law. And while not all customary international law carries with it the force of a jus cogens norm, the prohibition against official torture has attained that status. In CUSCLIN, the D.C. Circuit announced that torture is one of a handful of acts that constitute violations of jus cogens. In Filartiga, though the court was not explicitly considering jus cogens, Judge Kaufman's survey of the universal condemnation of torture provides much support for the view that torture violates jus cogens. In Judge Kaufman's words, "[a]mong the rights universally proclaimed by all nations, as we have noted, is the right to be free of physical torture." Supporting this case law is the Restatement, which recognizes the prohibition against official torture as one of only a few jus cogens norms. Restatement § 702 Comment n (also identifying jus cogens norms prohibiting genocide, slavery, murder or causing disappearance of individuals, prolonged arbitrary detention, and systematic racial discrimination). Finally, there is widespread agreement among scholars that the prohibition against official torture has achieved the status of a jus cogens norm * * *.

Given this extraordinary consensus, we conclude that the right to be free from official torture is fundamental and universal, a right deserving of the highest status under international law, a norm of jus cogens. The crack of the whip, the clamp of the thumb screw, the crush of the iron maiden, and, in these more efficient modern times, the shock of the electric cattle prod are forms of torture that the international order will not tolerate. To subject a person to such horrors is to commit one of the most egregious violations of the personal security and dignity * * *. That states engage in official torture cannot be doubted, but all states believe it is wrong, all that engage in torture deny it, and no state claims a sovereign right to torture its own citizens. See Filartiga, * * * (noting that no contemporary state asserts "a right to torture its own or another nation's citizens"); at n. 15 ("The fact that the prohibition against torture is often honored in the breach does not diminish its binding effect as a norm of international law."). Under international law, any state that engages in official torture violates jus cogens.

The question in the present case is what flows from the allegation that Argentina tortured Jose Siderman and thereby violated a jus cogens norm. The Sidermans contend that when a foreign state's act violates jus cogens, the state is not entitled to sovereign immunity with respect to that act. This argument begins from the principle that jus cogens norms "enjoy the highest status within international law," CUSCLIN, [supra] and thus "prevail over and invalidate * * * other rules of international law in conflict with them," Restatement § 102 Comment k. The Sidermans argue that since sovereign immunity itself is a principle of international law, it is trumped by jus cogens. In short, they argue that when a state violates jus cogens, the cloak of immunity provided by international law falls away, leaving the state amenable to suit. [For the sovereign immunity discussion in Siderman, see Chapter 7, supra].

* * *

* * * [W]e conclude that if violations of jus cogens committed outside the United States are to be exceptions to immunity, Congress must make them so. The fact that there has been a violation of jus cogens does not confer jurisdiction under the FSIA.

* * *

The district court erred in dismissing the Sidermans' torture claims.

CONCLUSION

The Sidermans' complaint and the evidence they have presented in support of their allegations paint a horrifying portrait of anti-Semitic, government-sponsored tyranny. The record that so far has been developed in this case reveals no ground for shielding Argentina from the Sidermans' claims that their family business was stolen from them by the military junta that took over the Argentine government in 1976. It further suggests that Argentina has implicitly waived its sovereign immunity with respect to the Sidermans' claims for torture.

We REVERSE and REMAND.

———

Notes and Questions

This case was settled generously in Siderman's favor just before trial. *See* N.Y.T., 14 Sept. 1996 and N.Y.T., 2 Sept. 1996. Are jus cogens normal pacts of customary international law or general principles? See chapters 1 and 17.

SECTION E. HUMAN RIGHTS AND REGIONAL ORGANIZATIONS

These include the European Union, the Council of Europe, the Organization of American States, the Organization of African Unity, among others. Several of these have enforcement mechanisms including Human Rights Commissions and Courts. *See, gen.*, Henkin, Neuman, Orentlicher, & Leebron, HUMAN RIGHTS (1999).

1. THE COUNCIL OF EUROPE

The Council of Europe was created in 1949 by European states with the aim, in the language of the statute, "to achieve a greater unity [among] its Members for the purpose of safeguarding and realizing the ideals and principles which are their common heritage," this aim to be pursued "by discussion of questions of common concern * * * and in the maintenance and further realization of human rights and fundamental freedoms." 87 UNTS 103. Pursuant to that aim, and in the light of the *Universal Declaration of Human Rights*, the *European Convention for the Protection of Human Rights and Fundamental Freedoms* was brought into force in 1953, 213 UNTS 221.

European Commission and European Court of Human Rights. The Convention is notable because it provides a working system for the international protection of human rights. The international organs of enforcement are the European Commission on Human Rights and the European Court of Human Rights. These organs have established a substantial body of precedent under the Convention. The Commission's function is to ascertain the facts as to alleged breaches of the convention and to secure a friendly settlement. There are two ways in which the Commission can be activated. One, any state party may refer an alleged breach by another party. Second, individual victim of a violation by a state party can petition the Commission, but this right of petition can be exercised against a state only if that state has declared that it recognizes the competence of the Commission to receive petitions. In the event a friendly settlement is not reached through conciliation, the Commission renders a report providing, "its opinion as to whether the facts found disclose a breach by the State concerned of its obligations under the Convention." The Convention provides for further decision and for measures by the Committee of Ministers, also an organ of the Council.

The Court on the other hand, has a jurisdiction which is more remote to the individual. Its jurisdiction comprises cases referred to it by the Commission or by a state party to the Convention. A state may refer the case to the Court if its national is alleged to be a victim. An individual's case can come before the Court, if a state, or if it had referred the case to the Commission. A case cannot be brought to the Court until after the Commission's efforts for a friendly settlement have failed. An individual, therefore, is protected only derivatively in a case before the Court. Nevertheless, a state other than that of the claimant's nationality can "represent" him. Also, if remedies are exhausted and the Commission deems it appropriate, it can trigger action in the Court. *Why are states, even in a regional organization of states with a common heritage, reluctant to permit individuals to have direct access to a court of human rights?*

Case of Ireland v. The United Kingdom

European Court of Human Rights.
Judgment of January 18, 1978, Series A, No. 25.

"[The judgment of the European Court of Human Rights begins with a long presentation of the history of the *'troubles'* in Northern Ireland. The case was 'referred to the Court' by the Government of Ireland against the United Kingdom (U.K.). This historical presentation ends with the U.K.'s introduction in 1971 of internment without trial of persons suspected of being *'suspected terrorists'* and *'key members of the I.R.A. (the Special Powers Act).'* It also includes the U.K.'s 1972 imposition of its own *direct rule* over Northern Ireland. The Court then focuses in some detail on two principal claims: (1) that suspects taken pursuant to the *Special Powers Act* after August 9, 1971 had been subjected to treatment which constituted torture and inhuman and degrading treatment contrary to Article 3 of the European Convention on Human Rights; and (2) that whether or not (1) was established, internment without trial as implemented after August 9, 1971, constituted a violation of Article 5 of the European Convention, which guarantees security of the person and liberty.]" * * *

[The "methods" applied] sometimes termed "disorientation" or "sensory deprivation" techniques, were not used in any cases other than the fourteen so indicated above. It emerges from the Commission's establishment of the facts that the techniques consisted of:

(a) *wall-standing:* forcing the detainees to remain for periods of some hours in a "stress position", described by those who underwent it as being "spreadeagled against the wall, with their fingers put high above the head against the wall, the legs spread apart and the feet back, causing them to stand on their toes with the weight of the body mainly on the fingers";

(b) *hooding:* putting a black or navy coloured bag over the detainees' heads and, at least initially, keeping it there all the time except during interrogation;

(c) *subjection to noise:* pending their interrogations, holding the detainees in a room where there was a continuous loud and hissing noise;

(d) *deprivation of sleep:* pending their interrogations, depriving the detainees of sleep;

(e) *deprivation of food and drink:* subjecting detainees to a reduced diet pending interrogations.

* * *

97.   From the start, it has been conceded by the respondent Government that the use of the five techniques was authorised at "high level". Although never committed to writing or authorised in any official document, the techniques had been orally taught to members of the RUC by the English Intelligence Centre at a [1971] seminar.

* * *

152.   The U.K. Government contest neither the breaches of Article 3 as found by the Commission * * *, nor–a point moreover that is beyond doubt–the Court's jurisdiction to examine such breaches. However, relying inter alia on the case-law of the International Court of Justice (*Northern Cameroons case*, judgment of 2 December 1963, and Nuclear Tests cases, judgments of 20 December 1974), they argue that the European Court has power to decline to exercise its jurisdiction where the objective of an application has been accomplished or where adjudication on the merits would be devoid of purpose. Such, they claim, is the situation here. They maintain that the findings in question not only are not contested but also have been widely publicised and that they do not give rise to problems of interpretation or application of the Convention sufficiently important to require a decision by the Court. Furthermore, for them the subject-matter of those findings now belongs to past history in view of the abandonment of the five techniques (1972), the solemn and unqualified undertaking not to reintroduce these techniques (8 February 1977) and the other measures taken by the United Kingdom to remedy, impose punishment for, and prevent the recurrence of, the various violations found by the Commission.

This argument is disputed by the applicant Government. Neither is it accepted in a general way by the delegates of the Commission; they stated, however, that they would express no conclusion as to whether or not the above-mentioned undertaking had deprived the claim concerning the five techniques of its object.

153.   The Court takes formal note of the undertaking given before it, at the hearing on 8 February 1977, by the United Kingdom Attorney–General on behalf of the respondent Government. The terms of this undertaking were as follows:

> "The Government of the United Kingdom have considered the question of the use of the 'five techniques' with very great care and with particular regard to Article 3 of the Convention. They now give this unqualified undertaking, that the 'five techniques' will not in any circumstances be reintroduced as an aid to interrogation."

The Court also notes that the United Kingdom has taken various measures designed to prevent the recurrence of the events complained of and to afford reparation for their consequences. For example, it has issued to the police and the army instructions and directives on the arrest, interrogation and treatment of persons in custody, reinforced the procedures for investigating complaints, appointed commissions of enquiry and paid or offered compensation in many cases * * *.

154. Nevertheless, the Court considers that the responsibilities assigned to it within the framework of the system under the Convention extend to pronouncing on the non-contested allegations of violation of Article 3. The Court's judgments in fact serve not only to decide those cases brought before the Court but, more generally, to elucidate, safeguard and develop the rules instituted by the Convention, thereby contributing to the observance by the States of the engagements undertaken by them as Contracting Parties (Article 19). * * *

155. Accordingly, that part of the present case which concerns the said allegations cannot be said to have become without object; the Court considers that it should rule thereon, notwithstanding the initiatives taken by the respondent State.

162. As was emphasized by the Commission, ill-treatment must attain a minimum level of severity if it is to fall within the scope of Article 3. The assessment of this minimum is, in the nature of things, relative; it depends on all the circumstances of the case, such as the duration of the treatment, its physical or mental effects and, in some cases, the sex, age and state of health of the victim, etc.

163. The Convention prohibits in absolute terms torture and inhuman or degrading treatment or punishment, irrespective of the victim's conduct. Unlike most of the substantive clauses of the Convention and of Protocols Nos. 1 and 4, Article 3 makes no provision for exceptions and, under Article 15 § 2, there can be no derogation therefrom even in the event of a public emergency threatening the life of the nation.

164. In the instant case, the only relevant concepts are "torture" and "inhuman or degrading treatment", to the exclusion of "inhuman or degrading punishment".

165. The facts concerning the five techniques are summarised * * * above. In the Commission's estimation, those facts constituted a practice not only of inhuman and degrading treatment but also of torture. The applicant Government ask for confirmation of this opinion which is not contested before the Court by the respondent Government.

166. The police used the five techniques on fourteen persons in 1971, that is on twelve, including T 6 and T 13, in August before the Compton Committee was set up, and on two in October whilst that Committee was carrying out its enquiry. Although never authorised in writing in any official document, the five techniques were taught orally by the English Intelligence Centre to members of the RUC at a seminar held in April 1971. There was accordingly a practice.

167. The five techniques were applied in combination, with premeditation and for hours at a stretch; they caused, if not actual bodily injury, at least intense physical and mental suffering to the persons subjected thereto and also led to acute psychiatric disturbances during interrogation. They accordingly fell into the category of inhuman treatment within the meaning of Article 3. The techniques were also degrading since they were such as to

arouse in their victims feelings of fear, anguish and inferiority capable of humiliating and debasing them and possibly breaking their physical or moral resistance.

On these two points, the Court [agrees with] the Commission.

In order to determine whether the five techniques should also be qualified as torture, the Court must have regard to the distinction, embodied in Article 3, between this notion and that of inhuman or degrading treatment. In the Court's view, this distinction derives principally from a difference in the intensity of the suffering inflicted.

The Court considers in fact that, whilst there exists on the one hand violence which is to be condemned both on moral grounds and also in most cases under the domestic law of the Contracting States but which does not fall within Article 3 of the Convention, it appears on the other hand that it was the intention that the Convention, with its distinction between "torture" and "inhuman or degrading treatment", should by the first of these terms attach a special stigma to deliberate inhuman treatment causing very serious and cruel suffering. Moreover, this seems to be the thinking lying behind Article 1 *in fine* of Resolution 3452(30) adopted by the General Assembly ... on 9 December 1975, which declares: "Torture constitutes an *aggravated* and deliberate form of cruel, inhuman or degrading treatment or punishment".

Although the five techniques, as applied in combination, undoubtedly amounted to inhuman and degrading treatment, although their object was the extraction of confessions, the naming of others and_or information and although they were used systematically, they did not occasion suffering of the particular intensity and cruelty implied by the word torture as so understood.

168. The Court concludes that recourse to the five techniques amounted to a practice of inhuman and degrading treatment, which practice was in breach of Article 3.

186. In a letter dated 5 January 1977, the applicant Government requested the Court to order that the respondent Government refrain from reintroducing the five techniques, as a method of interrogation or otherwise; proceed as appropriate, under the criminal law of the United Kingdom and the relevant disciplinary code, against those members of the security forces who have committed acts in breach of Article 3 referred to in the Commission's findings and conclusions, and against those who condoned or tolerated them.

At the hearings, the applicant Government withdrew the first request following the solemn undertaking given on behalf of the United Kingdom Government on 8 February 1977 (see paragraph 153 above); on the other hand, the second request was maintained.

187. The Court does not have to consider in these proceedings whether its functions extend, in certain circumstances, to addressing consequential orders to Contracting States. In the present case, the Court finds that the sanctions available to it do not include the power to direct one of those

States to institute criminal or disciplinary proceedings in accordance with its domestic law.

* * *

FOR THESE REASONS, THE COURT

I. *ON ARTICLE* 3, 1. holds unanimously that, although certain violations of Article 3 were not contested, a ruling should nevertheless be given thereon; 2. holds unanimously that it has jurisdiction to take cognisance of the cases of alleged violation of Article 3 to the extent that the applicant Government put them forward as establishing the existence of a practice; 3. holds by sixteen votes to one that the use of the five techniques in August and October 1971 constituted a practice of inhuman and degrading treatment, which practice was in breach of Article 3; 4. holds by thirteen votes to four that the said use of the five techniques did not constitute a practice of torture within the meaning of Article 3;

* * * 10. holds unanimously that it cannot direct the respondent State to institute criminal or disciplinary proceedings against those members of the security forces who have committed the breaches of Article 3 found by the Court and against those who condoned or tolerated such breaches;

* * *

[Separate opinions omitted.]

2.   THE ORGANIZATION OF AMERICAN STATES

In the Charter of the Organization of American States, which entered into force on December 13, 1951, "proclaim(s) the fundamental rights of the individual without distinction as to race, nationality, creed or sex." 119 UNTS 3. The 1948 Conference of the American States, which gave birth to the Charter, also adopted the American Declaration of the Rights and Duties of Man. In 1959, the Inter–American Commission on Human Rights was created. In addition to its powers of study and advice, the commission was given authority to receive and examine individual communications charging the violation of fundamental human rights set forth in the American Declaration and to make recommendations to governments with respect thereto. A conference in 1969 approved the American Convention on Human Rights, which contains provisions widening the American Declaration, re-establishing the Inter–American Commission and establishing the Inter–American Court of Human Rights. Individuals do not have standing. Only states parties and the commission have the right to submit a case to the Court; as usual, the court's jurisdiction depends upon the state's consenting thereto. For the statute of the court, *see* 19 ILM 634 (1980). President Carter submitted this Convention to the Senate for its advice and consent in 1978. Ratification of the convention does not, of itself, constitute a state's consent to the court's jurisdiction. As in the case of the International Court of Justice, a further declaration of submission to the court's jurisdiction (or a special agreement) is necessary. *See* Article 62 of the Convention. The President did not call upon the Senate to make such a declaration.

Buergenthal, The Advisory Practice of the Inter-American Human Rights Court

79 American Journal of International Law 1, 8 (1985).*

* * *

Disguised Contentious Cases. International tribunals exercising advisory and contentious jurisdiction have at times had to confront a problem that arises when they are asked to render an advisory opinion on an issue that is, at one and the same time, the subject of a dispute between two or more states or between a state and an international organization. Here the argument frequently made is that the request for an advisory opinion is a disguised contentious case and that it should be heard only if all the parties have accepted the tribunal's contentious jurisdiction. The International Court of Justice, for example, has consistently rejected such arguments and complied with the requests. The inter-American human rights system adds a new dimension to this problem that is unique to the advisory functions of the Court. Under Article 64(1) of the Convention, the Court's advisory jurisdiction may be invoked not only by organs or organizations, as is the case in the UN system, for example, but also by states. The Court might therefore confront a petition by a state asking it to render an advisory opinion relating to a dispute between the petitioner and another state, which dispute could not be referred to the Court as a case because one of the states had not accepted its contentious jurisdiction. Moreover, the Inter–American Commission on Human Rights, which has the right to request advisory opinions, exercises powers under the Convention comparable to that of a tribunal of first instance in dealing with charges alleging violations of human rights by a state party and may also refer contentious cases to the Court. Since the Commission may only bring such cases to the Court if the states concerned have accepted the Court's jurisdiction, the question arises whether the Commission has the power, in the absence of a state's consent, to seek an advisory opinion under Article 64(1) regarding a legal issue in dispute in a case being considered by the Commission.

The Court has dealt with only one case bearing on these issues. The Inter–American Commission had embarked on a country study of the human rights situation in Guatemala, which was charged with numerous human rights violations. The authority of the Commission to prepare country reports derives from its status as an OAS Charter organ and is governed by different provisions of the Convention and its Statute from those which deal with the disposition of petitions filed by individuals and communications presented by states parties charging another state party with violations of the human rights guaranteed in the Convention. When the Commission prepares country studies and reports, it acts first and foremost as an OAS Charter organ; whereas, when it deals with petitions and communications filed under the Convention, it discharges the functions of a tribunal of first instance or Convention institution which, together with the Court, comprises the judicial and enforcement machinery provided for by the Convention.

* Reprinted with the permission of the American Society of International Law.

These different functions need to be kept in mind when analyzing the Court's advisory opinion involving Guatemala. The Court was asked by the Commission to render an advisory opinion on a legal issue only. The issue was one of a number of disputed matters, both legal and factual, to arise between the Commission and the Government of Guatemala while the former was examining the human rights situation in that country. In rejecting Guatemala's claim that there was a dispute between it and the Commission and that, as a result, the Court lacked the power to hear the dispute because Guatemala had not accepted its jurisdiction, the Court emphasized that the Commission's request was designed to assist it in performing its functions under Article 112 of the OAS Charter:

> The powers conferred on the Commission require it to apply the Convention or other human rights treaties. In order to discharge fully its obligations, the Commission may find it necessary or appropriate to consult the Court regarding the meaning of certain provisions whether or not at the given moment in time there exists a difference between a government and the Commission concerning an interpretation, which might justify the request for an advisory opinion. If the Commission were to be barred from seeking an advisory opinion merely because one or more governments are involved in a controversy with the Commission over the interpretation of a disputed provision, the Commission would seldom, if ever, be able to avail itself of the Court's advisory jurisdiction. Not only would this be true of the Commission, but the OAS General Assembly, for example, would be in a similar position were it to seek an advisory opinion from the Court in the course of the Assembly's consideration of a draft resolution calling on a Member State to comply with its international human rights obligations.

This language suggests that the Court treated the request for an advisory opinion * * * as it would have treated a similar request from any other OAS organ acting in the discharge of its OAS Charter functions. If the holding is limited to matters under consideration by the Commission in its role as OAS Charter organ, it permits the argument that the advisory route may not be used to circumvent the restrictions applicable to the contentious process, which is initiated by individual petition or interstate communication. There is a great deal of language in the Court's opinion, however, that suggests that the holding is much broader. Thus, for example, the Court noted that "[t]he mere fact that this provision [Article 4] may also have been invoked before the Commission in petitions and communications filed under Articles 44 and 45 of the Convention" did not affect the Court's conclusion about the legitimacy of the Commission's request. The Court indicated, moreover, that "the Convention, by permitting Member States and OAS organs to seek advisory opinions, creates a parallel system to that provided for under Article 62 [on the Court's contentious jurisdiction] and offers an alternate judicial method of a consultative nature, which is designed to assist states and organs to comply with and to apply human rights treaties without subjecting them to the formalism and the sanctions associated with the contentious judicial process." If the advisory route is in fact seen as in all respects a "parallel system" and "alternate judicial method" to the Court's contentious jurisdiction, the Commission or any interested state would be able to resort to it in the midst of a pending contentious proceeding. Here one might hypothe-size a situation in which an individual has lodged a petition with the Commission against state *X*, a party to the Convention, alleging that *X* has violated various rights guaranteed in the Convention. Let us assume further that in the course of the proceedings state *X* and the individual litigant disagree as to the meaning of one of the disputed provisions of the Convention. May the Commission at that stage request an advisory opinion from the Court on the meaning of the disputed provision? May state *X* do so? Does it matter at all whether state *X* has accepted the jurisdiction of the Court? Is the consent of state *X* necessary before the Commission may request the advisory opinion?

The Court's advisory opinion relating to Guatemala does not provide any ready answers to these questions. However, one consideration men-tioned in the opinion deserves to be noted. In dealing with the question whether to comply with the Commission's request, the Court made the following observation:

> The Court has already indicated that situations might arise when it would deem itself compelled to decline to comply with a request for an advisory opinion. In *Other Treaties* * * * the Court acknowledged that resort to the advisory opinion route might in certain situations inter-fere with the proper functioning of the system of protection spelled out in the Convention or that it might adversely affect the interests of the victim of human rights violations. . . .

* * * The instant request of the Commission does not fall within the category of advisory opinion requests that need to be rejected on those grounds because nothing in it can be deemed to interfere with the proper functioning of the system or might be deemed to have an adverse effect on the interests of a victim.

It may well be, therefore, that the crucial question for the Court will not be whether the advisory opinion is or is not tied to proceedings pending in the Commission. Instead, the Court might seek to ascertain what impact in a particular case its decision to grant the request for an advisory opinion would have on the victim or on the Convention system.

> * * *

3.   THE ORGANIZATION OF AFRICAN UNITY

Nowak, The African Charter on Human and Peoples' Rights

7 Human Rights Law Journal 399 (1986).*

On 21 October 1986 the African Charter on Human and Peoples' Rights, adopted by the 18th Ordinary Session of the Assembly of Heads of State and Government of the Organization of African Unity (OAU) held in

* Reprinted with the permission of N.P. Engel, and Kehlam Rhein/Strasbourg/Arling-ton, Va.

June 1981, entered into force. This date marks an important day in the history of international promotion and protection of human rights. After the European and American Conventions on Human Rights the African Charter is the third regional human rights instrument of great political and legal significance. It provides for the establishment of an African Commission on Human and Peoples' Rights consisting of eleven African experts in the field of human rights. The members of the Commission will be elected at the 23rd Ordinary Session of the Assembly of Heads of State and Government which [was] in 1987

The idea of establishing both an African Human Rights Convention and Commission dates back to 1961 when the first congress of African jurists was organized by the International Commission of Jurists at Lagos. It was further discussed at several regional human rights seminars organized by the United Nations. The decisive step forward was taken however only after the bitter experiences of serious human rights violations which had occurred in Africa during the seventies, above all in Uganda, the Central African Empire and Equatorial Guinea. In July 1979 the Assembly of Heads of State * * * at its 16th Ordinary Session held in Monrovia called on the Secretary–General of the OAU to "organize as soon as possible in an African capital a restricted meeting of highly qualified experts to prepare a preliminary draft of an African Charter on Human Rights providing, inter alia, for the establishment of bodies to promote and protect human rights". After less than two years of drafting negotiations the African Charter was adopted in Nairobi in June 1981.

The African Charter on Human and Peoples' Rights contains some major *conceptual innovations* in the field of international human rights law. By incorporating a number of collective rights of peoples it marks a major step forward in the development of a third generation of human rights. For the first time an international treaty undertakes to ensure to peoples not only the right to self-determination, but as well the rights of existence, equality, development, peace, security and a general satisfactory environment. Secondly, the African Charter provides for a number of fundamental duties of the individual towards his family and society, the State, other legally recognized communities and the international community. One of these duties is to preserve and strengthen positive African cultural values in the relation with other members of the society. The emphasis on the protection of morals and traditional values recognized by the community and on the family as the natural unit and basis of society underlines the specific *community-oriented approach* that distinguishes the African Charter from other international human rights instruments.

* * *

SECTION F.   SELF-HELP: ASYLUM AND REFUGEE LAW

So long as the level of human rights protections varies among the states of the world, the individual will continue the age-old human practice of leaving a state where he is oppressed to live in another state where, he believes, his rights will be protected. But it is said: "The reception of aliens is a matter of discretion, and every state is by reason of its territorial supremacy competent to exclude aliens from the whole, or any part, of its territory." I. Oppenheim, International Law 675 (Lauterpacht, 8th ed. 1955). The writer further asserts that the Universal Declaration of Human Rights does not give an alien a right to demand asylum. The declaration provides:

Article 13.

1. Everyone has the right to freedom of movement and residence within the borders of each State. * * *

Article 14

1. Everyone has the right to seek and to enjoy in other countries asylum from persecution.

2. This right may not be invoked in the case of prosecutions genuinely arising from non-political crimes or from acts contrary to the purposes and principles of the United Nations.

If an alien cannot lawfully demand that a state grant him asylum, what is the content of the right to seek asylum?

The United Nations adopted a Declaration on Territorial Asylum, Resolution 2312(22) of December 14, 1967, U.N.Gen.Ass.Off.Rec., 22nd Sess., Supp. 16(A_6716), p. 81. It stated:

Article 1

1. Asylum granted by a State, in the exercise of its sovereignty, to persons entitled to invoke article 14 of the Universal Declaration of Human Rights, including persons struggling against colonialism, shall be respected by all other States.

Article 3

1. No person referred to in article 1, paragraph 1, shall be subjected to measures such as rejection at the frontier or, if he has already entered the territory in which he seeks asylum, expulsion or compulsory return to any State where he may be subjected to persecution.

It is doubtful that the international community is prepared to accept an absolute obligation on the part of each state to grant asylum. In the preparation of a draft convention designed to give real effect to the apparent rights proclaimed in Article 14, what interests should be taken into account? Would a convention binding a state to "use its best endeavors to grant asylum in its territory" promote the humanitarian objectives of the Universal Declaration of Human Rights?

Note: See, gen., LAW AND MIGRATION (Selina Goulbourne, ed. 1998) (essays and articles on immigration, refugee law and human rights); Helene Lambert, *Protection Against Refoulement from Europe,* 48 Int'l & Comp. L.!. 515 (1999). The International Red Cross movement has left its mark in the history of humanitarian law, beginning with the initiative taken in 1863 by its founder, Henri Dunant, for the relief of the wounded on the battlefield, and culminating in four successive Geneva Conventions governing the treatment of wounded soldiers in armed conflicts, whether international or not, prisoners of war and civilians in internal disturbances. These provisions, in the impersonal and cold language of legal drafters, prohibit taking any measure of such a character as to cause the physical suffering or extermination of protected persons in their hands * * * [and applies] * * * to murder, torture, corporal punishment, mutilation and medical or scientific experiments not necessitated by the medical treatment of a protected person, * * * [and] * * * any other measures of brutality whether applied by civilian or military agents.

Refugees—The Trauma of Exile puts a human face on the suffering of these victims. The book is a collection of papers presented at a workshop sponsored by the League of the Red Cross and Red Crescent Societies in 1987, dealing with the psychological and medical problems of persons uprooted by war, revolution, counter-revolution and naked terror. As narrated by the editor:

We heard about some of the worst forms of evil man can perpetrate against man: physical and psychological torture, incarceration in inhuman conditions, forced separation of families, sudden deportation, violence on the high seas * * * [death or murder] * * * in prison * * *. Many of the victims of gross human rights abuses are children, some of whom have been forced to witness unspeakable horrors * * *. (Miseres, p. 6)

The persons who have been treated by the International Red Cross societies have come from diverse cultural, linguistic and religious backgrounds and from every continent, including the millions who fled Laos, Cambodia and Vietnam; the Tamils from Sri Lanka; the tens of thousands from Chile, El Salvador, Nicaragua and Cuba; the thousands who left Iran, Iraq and Afghanistan; countless people who have fled from the various African countries-Ethiopia, Sudan, Zaire and Ghana, among others-and refugees from Eastern European countries, including Jewish Holocaust survivors. [*See* further discussion in Chapter 2B, *supra.*]

Sale v. Haitian Centers Council, Inc.

United States Supreme Court,509 U.S. 155, 113 S.Ct. 2549, 125 L.Ed.2d 128 (1993).

[After the coup that ousted elected President Jean–Bertrand Aristide, unprecedented numbers of Haitians began to flee Haiti for the U.S.]

■ STEVENS, J., delivered the opinion of the Court, in which REHNQUIST, C.J., and WHITE, O'CONNOR, SCALIA, KENNEDY, SOUTER, and THOMAS, JJ., joined. BLACKMUN, J., filed a dissenting opinion.

■ JUSTICE STEVENS delivered the opinion of the Court.

The President has directed the Coast Guard to intercept vessels illegally transporting passengers from Haiti to the United States and to return those passengers to Haiti without first determining whether they may qualify as refugees. The question presented in this case is whether such forced repatriation, "authorized to be undertaken only beyond the territorial sea of the United States,[1] violates § 243(h)(1) of the Immigration and Nationality Act of 1952 (INA or Act). We hold that neither § 243(h) nor Article 33 of the United Nations Protocol Relating to the Status of Refugees applies to action taken by the Coast Guard on the high seas. [Jan. 31, 1967, 19 U.S.T. 6223, T.I.A.S. No. 6577.] * * *

III

Both parties argue that the plain language of § 243(h)(1) is dispositive. It reads as follows: "The Attorney General shall not deport or return any alien (other than an alien described in section 1251(a)(4)(D) of this title) to a country if the Attorney General determines that such alien's life or freedom would be threatened in such country on account of race, religion, nationality, membership in a particular social group, or political opinion." 8 U.S.C. § 1253(h)(1).

Respondents emphasize the words "any alien" and "return"; neither term is limited to aliens within the United States. Respondents also contend that the 1980 amendment deleting the words "within the United States" from the prior text of § 243(h), see n. 2, supra, obviously gave the statute an extraterritorial effect. This change, they further argue, was required in order to conform the statute to the text of Article 33.1 of the Convention, which they find as unambiguous as the present statutory text.

Petitioners' response is that a fair reading of the INA as a whole demonstrates that § 243(h) does not apply to actions taken by the President or Coast Guard outside the United States; that the legislative history of the 1980 amendment supports their reading; and that both the text and the negotiating history of Article 33 of the Convention indicate that it was not intended to have any extraterritorial effect.

We shall first review the text and structure of the statute and its 1980 amendment, and then consider the text and negotiating history of the Convention. * * *

B.   THE HISTORY OF THE REFUGEE ACT OF 1980

As enacted in 1952, § 243(h) authorized the Attorney General to withhold deportation of aliens "within the United States." Six years later we considered the question whether it applied to an alien who had been paroled into the country while her admissibility was being determined. We held that even though she was physically present within our borders, she was not "within the United States" as those words were used in § 243(h). *Leng May Ma v. Barber*, 357 U.S. 185, 186 (1958). We explained the

---

1. This language appears in both Executive Order No. 12324, 3 CFR 181 (1981B1983 Comp.), issued by President Rea-gan, and Executive Order No. 12807, 57 Fed. Reg. 23133 (1992), issued by President Bush.

important distinction between "deportation" or "expulsion," on the one hand, and "exclusion," on the other:

"It is important to note at the outset that our immigration laws have long made a distinction between those aliens who have come to our shores seeking admission, such as petitioner, and those who are within the United States after an entry, irrespective of its legality. In the latter instance the Court has recognized additional rights and privileges not extended to those in the former category who are merely 'on the threshold of initial entry.' * * * The distinction was carefully preserved in Title II of the Immigration and Nationality Act * * *.

"Under the INA, both then and now, those seeking "admission" and trying to avoid "exclusion" were already within our territory (or at its border), but the law treated them as though they had never entered the United States at all; they were within United States territory but not "within the United States." Those who had been admitted (or found their way in) but sought to avoid "expulsion" had the added benefit of "deportation proceedings"; they were both within United States territory and "within the United States." Although the phrase "within the United States" presumed the alien's actual presence in the United States, it had more to do with an alien's legal status than with his location.

The 1980 amendment erased the long-maintained distinction between deportable and excludable aliens for purposes of § 243(h). By adding the word "return" and removing the words "within the United States" from § 243(h), Congress extended the statute's protection to both types of aliens, but it did nothing to change the presumption that both types of aliens would continue to be found only within United States territory. The removal of the phrase "within the United States" cured the most obvious drawback of § 243(h): as interpreted in Leng May Ma, its protection was available only to aliens subject to deportation proceedings.

Of course, in addition to this most obvious purpose, it is possible that the 1980 amendment *also* removed any territorial limitation of the statute, and Congress might have intended a double-barreled result. That possibility, however, is not a substitute for the affirmative evidence of intended extraterritorial application that our cases require. Moreover, in our review of the history of the amendment, we have found no support whatsoever for that latter, alternative, purpose.

The addition of the phrase "or return" and the deletion of the phrase "within the United States" are the only relevant changes made by the 1980 amendment to § 243(h)(1), and they are fully explained by the intent to apply § 243(h) to exclusion as well as to deportation proceedings. That intent is plainly identified in the legislative history of the amendment. There is no change in the 1980 amendment, however, that could only be explained by an assumption that Congress also intended to provide for the statute's extraterritorial application. It would have been extraordinary for Congress to make such an important change in the law without any mention of that possible effect. Not a scintilla of evidence of such an intent can be found in the legislative history.

In sum, all available evidence about the meaning of § 243(h)—the government official at whom it is directed, its location in the Act, its failure to suggest any extraterritorial application, the 1980 amendment that gave it a dual reference to "deport or return," and the relevance of that dual structure to immigration law in general—leads unerringly to the conclusion that it applies in only one context: the domestic procedures by which the Attorney General determines whether deportable and excludable aliens may remain in the United States.

IV

Although the protection afforded by § 243(h) did not apply in exclusion proceedings before 1980, other provisions of the Act did authorize relief for aliens at the border seeking protection as refugees in the United States. *See INS v. Stevic, [supra].* When the United States acceded to the Protocol in 1968, therefore, the INA already offered *some* protection to both classes of refugees. It offered no such protection to any alien who was beyond the territorial waters of the United States, though, and we would not expect the Government to assume a burden as to those aliens without some acknowledgment of its dramatically broadened scope. Both Congress and the Executive Branch gave extensive consideration to the Protocol before ratifying it in 1968; in all of their published consideration of it there appears no mention of the possibility that the United States was assuming any extraterritorial obligations.[8] Nevertheless, because the history of the 1980 Act does disclose a general intent to conform our law to Article 33 of the Convention, it might be argued that the extraterritorial obligations imposed by Article 33 were so clear that Congress, in acceding to the Protocol, and then in amending the statute to harmonize the two, meant to give the latter a correspondingly extraterritorial effect. Or, just as the statute might have imposed an extraterritorial obligation that the Convention does not (the argument we have just rejected), the Convention might have established an extraterritorial obligation which the statute does not; under the Supremacy Clause, that broader treaty obligation might then provide the controlling rule of law.[9] With those possibilities in mind we shall consider both the text and negotiating history of the Convention itself.

Like the text and the history of § 243(h), the text and negotiating history of Article 33 of the United Nations Convention are both completely silent with respect to the Article's possible application to actions taken by a country outside its own borders. Respondents argue that the Protocol's

8. "The President and the Senate believed that the Protocol was largely consistent with existing law. There are many statements to that effect in the legislative history of the accession to the Protocol. *E.g.,* S.Exec. Rep. No. 14, 90th Cong., 2d Sess., 4 (1968) ('refugees in the United States have long enjoyed the protection and the rights which the Protocol calls for'); id., at 6, 7 ('the United States already meets the standards of the Protocol')."

9. U.S. Const., Art. VI, cl. 2 provides: "This Constitution, and the Laws of the United States; and all Treaties made, or which shall be made, under the Authority of the United States, shall be the supreme Law of the Land; * * *" In *Murray v. The Charming Betsy,* 2 Cranch 64, 117B118 (1804), Chief Justice Marshall wrote that "an act of congress ought never to be construed to violate the law of nations if any other possible construction remains * * *."

broad remedial goals require that a nation be prevented from repatriating refugees to their potential oppressors whether or not the refugees are within that nation's borders. In spite of the moral weight of that argument, both the text and negotiating history of Article 33 affirmatively indicate that it was not intended to have extraterritorial effect.

A. The Text of the Convention

Two aspects of Article 33's text are persuasive. The first is the explicit reference in Article 33.2 to the country in which the alien is located; the second is the parallel use of the terms "expel or return," the latter term explained by the French word *"refouler."*

The full text of Article 33 reads as follows: *"Article 33.2–Prohibition of expulsion or return ('refoulement')*

> "1. No Contracting State shall expel or return ('refouler') a refugee in any manner whatsoever to the frontiers of territories where his life or freedom would be threatened on account of his race, religion, nationality, membership in a particular social group or political opinion.

> "2. The benefit of the present provision may not, however, be claimed by a refugee whom there are reasonable grounds for regarding as a danger to the security *of the country in which he is,* or who, having been convicted by a final judgment of a particularly serious crime, constitutes a danger to the community of that country." Convention Relating to the Status of Refugees, 1951, 19 U.S.T. 6259, 6276.

Under the second paragraph of Article 33 an alien may not claim the benefit of the first paragraph if he poses a danger to the country in which he is located. If the first paragraph did apply on the high seas, no nation could invoke the second paragraph's exception with respect to an alien there: an alien intercepted on the high seas is in no country at all. If Article 33.1 applied extraterritorially, therefore, Article 33.2 would create an absurd anomaly: dangerous aliens on the high seas would be entitled to the benefits of 33.1 while those residing in the country that sought to expel them would not. It is more reasonable to assume that the coverage of 33.2 was limited to those already in the country because it was understood that 33.1 obligated the signatory state only with respect to aliens within its territory.

Article 33.1 uses the words "expel or return ('refouler')" as an obvious parallel to the words "deport or return" in § 243(h)(1). There is no dispute that "expel" has the same meaning as "deport"; it refers to the deportation or expulsion of an alien who is already present in the host country. The dual reference identified and explained in our opinion in *Leng May Ma v. Barber,* suggests that the term "return ('refouler')" refers to the exclusion of aliens who are merely " 'on the threshold of initial entry.' "

This suggestion–that "return" has a legal meaning narrower than its common meaning–is reinforced by the parenthetical reference to *"refouler ",* a French word that is not an exact synonym for the English word "return." Neither of two respected English–French Dictionaries mentions *"refouler"* as one of many possible French translations of "return." Conversely, the English translations of *"refouler "*do not include the word "return." They do, however, include words like "repulse," "repel," "drive back," and even "expel." To the extent that they are relevant, these translations imply that "return" means a defensive act of resistance or exclusion at a border rather than an act of transporting someone to a particular destination. In the context of the Convention, to "return" means to "repulse" rather than to "reinstate."

The text of Article 33 thus fits with Judge Edwards' understanding "that 'expulsion' would refer to a 'refugee already admitted into a country' and that 'return' would refer to a 'refugee already within the territory but not yet resident there.' Thus, the Protocol was not intended to govern parties' conduct outside of their national borders." Haitian Refugee Center v. Gracey. From the time of the Convention, commentators have consistently agreed with this view.

The drafters of the Convention and the parties to the Protocol–like the drafters of § 243(h)–may not have contemplated that any nation would gather fleeing refugees and return them to the one country they had desperately sought to escape; such actions may even violate the spirit of Article 33; but a treaty cannot impose uncontemplated extraterritorial obligations on those who ratify it through no more than its general humanitarian intent. Because the text of Article 33 cannot reasonably be read to say anything at all about a nation's actions toward aliens outside its own territory, it does not prohibit such actions.[15]

* * *

V

Respondents contend that the dangers faced by Haitians who are unwillingly repatriated demonstrate that the judgment of the Court of Appeals fulfilled the central purpose of the Convention and the Refugee Act of 1980. While we must, of course, be guided by the high purpose of both the treaty and the statute, we are not persuaded that either one places any limit on the President's authority to repatriate aliens interdicted beyond the territorial seas of the United States.

It is perfectly clear that 8 U.S.C. § 1182(f), grants the President ample power to establish a naval blockade that would simply deny illegal Haitian migrants the ability to disembark on our shores. Whether the President's chosen method of preventing the "attempted mass migration" of thousands of Haitians—to use the Dutch delegate's phrase—poses a greater risk of harm to Haitians who might otherwise face a long and dangerous return voyage, is irrelevant to the scope of his authority to take action that neither the Convention nor the statute clearly prohibits. As we have already noted, Acts of Congress normally do not have extraterritorial application unless such an intent is clearly manifested. That presumption has special force when we are construing treaty and statutory provisions that may involve foreign and military affairs for which the President has unique responsibility. Cf. United States v. Curtiss–Wright Export Corp., 299 U.S. 304 (1936). We therefore find ourselves in agreement with the conclusion expressed in Judge Edwards' concurring opinion in Gracey: "This case presents a

15. The Convention's failure to prevent the extraterritorial reconduction of aliens has been generally acknowledged (and regretted). * * *

painfully common situation in which desperate people, convinced that they can no longer remain in their homeland, take desperate measures to escape. Although the human crisis is compelling, there is no solution to be found in a judicial remedy."

The judgment of the Court of Appeals is reversed. *It is so ordered.*

■ JUSTICE BLACKMUN, dissenting.

When, in 1968, the United States acceded to the UN Protocol Relating to the Status of Refugees, Jan. 31, 1967, [1968] 19 U.S.T. 6223, T.I.A.S. 6577, it pledged not to "return (*'refouler'*) a refugee in any manner whatsoever" to a place where he would face political persecution. In 1980, Congress amended our immigration law to reflect the Protocol's directives. Refugee Act of 1980. *See INS v. Cardoza–Fonseca,* [*supra*] *INS v. Stevic,* [*supra*]. Today's majority nevertheless decides that the forced repatriation of the Haitian refugees is perfectly legal, because the word "return" does not mean return, because the opposite of "within the United States" is not outside the United States, and because the official charged with controlling immigration has no role in enforcing an order to control immigration.

I believe that the duty of nonreturn expressed in both the Protocol and the statute is clear. The majority finds it "extraordinary," that Congress would have intended the ban on returning "any alien" to apply to aliens at sea. That Congress would have meant what it said is not remarkable. What is extraordinary in this case is that the Executive, in disregard of the law, would take to the seas to intercept fleeing refuges and force them back to their persecutors–and that the Court would strain to sanction that conduct.

I

I begin with the Convention, for it is undisputed that the Refugee Act of 1980 was passed to conform our law to Article 33, and that "the nondiscretionary duty imposed by § 243(h) parallels the United States' mandatory *nonrefoulement* obligations under Article 33.1 * * *." *INS v. Doherty,* (SCALIA, J., concurring in the judgment in part and dissenting in part). The Convention thus constitutes the backdrop against which the statute must be understood.

A

Article 33.1 of the Convention states categorically and without geographical limitation:

"No Contracting State shall expel or return (*'refouler'*) a refugee in any manner whatsoever to the frontiers of territories where his life or freedom would be threatened on account of his race, religion, nationality, membership in a particular social group or political opinion."

The terms are unambiguous. Vulnerable refugees shall not be returned. The language is clear, and the command is straightforward; that should be the end of the inquiry. Indeed, until litigation ensued, see Haitian Refugee Center v. Gracey, the Government consistently acknowledged that the Convention applied on the high seas.

The majority * * * has difficulty with the Treaty's use of the term "return (*'refouler'*)." "Return," it claims, does not mean return, but instead has a distinctive legal meaning. For this proposition the Court relies almost entirely on the fact that *American* law makes a general distinction between *deportation* and *exclusion*. Without explanation, the majority asserts that in light of this distinction the word "return" as used in the Treaty somehow must refer only to "the exclusion of aliens who are * * * 'on the threshold of initial entry' " * * * The text of the Convention does not ban the "exclusion" of aliens who have reached some indeterminate "threshold"; it bans their "return." It is well settled that a treaty must first be construed according to its "ordinary meaning." Article 31.1 of the Vienna Convention on the Law of Treaties, 1155 U.N.T.S. 331 (1980). The ordinary meaning of "return" is "to bring, send, or put (a person or thing) back to or in a former position." Webster's Third New International Dictionary 1941 (1986). That describes precisely what petitioners are doing to the Haitians. By dispensing with ordinary meaning at the outset, and by taking instead as its starting point the assumption that "return," as used in the Treaty, "has a legal meaning narrower than its common meaning," the majority leads itself astray.

The straightforward interpretation of the duty of nonreturn is strongly reinforced by the Convention's use of the French term *"refouler."* The ordinary meaning of *"refouler,"* as the majority concedes, is "[t]o repulse, * * *; to drive back, to repel." *Dictionnaire Larousse* 631. Thus construed, Article 33.1 of the Convention reads: "No contracting state shall expel or [repulse, drive back, or repel] a refugee in any manner whatsoever to the frontiers of territories where his life or freedom would be threatened * * *." That, of course, is exactly what the Government is doing. It thus is no surprise that when the French press has described the very policy challenged here, the term it has used is *"refouler." See, e.g., Le bourbier haitian*, Le Monde, May 31–June 1, 1992 ("*[L]es Etats–Unis ont decide de* refouler *directement les refugies recueillis par la garde cotire."* (The U.S. has decided [de refouler] directly the refugees picked up by the Coast Guard)).

And yet the majority insists that what has occurred is not, in fact, *"refoulement."* It reaches this conclusion in a peculiar fashion. After acknowledging that the ordinary meaning of *"refouler "*is "repulse," "repel," and "drive back," the majority without elaboration declares: "To the extent that they are relevant, these translations imply that 'return' means a defensive act of resistance or exclusion at a border * * *." I am at a loss to find the narrow notion of "exclusion at a border" in broad terms like "repulse," "repel," and "drive back." * * *

Article 33.1 is clear not only in what it says, but also in what it does not say: it does not include any geographical limitation. It limits only where a refugee may be sent "to", not where he may be sent from. This is not surprising, given that the aim of the provision is to protect refugees against persecution.

Article 33.2, by contrast, *does* contain a geographical reference, and the majority seizes upon this as evidence that the section as a whole applies only within a signatory's borders. That inference is flawed. Article 33.2 states that the benefit of Article 33.1

"may not * * * be claimed by a refugee whom there are reasonable grounds for regarding as a danger to the security of the country in which he is, or who, having been convicted by a final judgment of a particularly serious crime, constitutes a danger to the community of that country."

The signatories' understandable decision to allow nations to deport criminal aliens who have entered their territory hardly suggests an intent to permit the apprehension and return of noncriminal aliens who have not entered their territory, and who may have no desire ever to enter it. One wonders what the majority would make of an exception that removed from the Article's protection all refugees who "constitute a danger to their families." By the majority's logic, the inclusion of such an exception presumably would render Article 33.1 applicable only to refugees with families.

Far from constituting "an absurd anomaly," the fact that a state is permitted to "expel or return" a small class of refugees found within its territory but may not seize and return refugees who remain outside its frontiers expresses precisely the objectives and concerns of the Convention. Non-return is the rule; the sole exception (neither applicable nor invoked here) is that a nation endangered by a refugee's very presence may "expel or return" him to an unsafe country if it chooses. The tautological observation that only a refugee already in a country can pose a danger to the country "in which he is" proves nothing.

* * *

II

* * *

C

That the clarity of the text and the implausibility of its theories do not give the majority more pause is due, I think, to the majority's heavy reliance on the presumption against extraterritoriality. The presumption runs throughout the majority's opinion, and it stacks the deck by requiring the Haitians to produce "affirmative evidence" that when Congress prohibited the return of "any" alien, it indeed meant to prohibit the interception and return of aliens at sea.

The judicially created canon of statutory construction against extraterritorial application of United States law has no role here, however. It applies only where congressional intent is "unexpressed." Here there is no room for doubt: a territorial restriction has been deliberately deleted from the statute. Even where congressional intent is unexpressed, however, a statute must be assessed according to its intended scope. The primary basis for the application of the presumption (besides the desire—not relevant here—to avoid conflict with the laws of other nations) is "the common-sense notion that Congress generally legislates with domestic concerns in mind." Where that notion seems unjustified or unenlightening, however, generally-worded laws covering varying subject matters are routinely applied extraterritorially * * *.

In this case we deal with a statute that regulates a distinctively international subject matter: immigration, nationalities, and refugees. Whatever force the presumption may have with regard to a primarily domestic statute evaporates in this context. There is no danger that the Congress that enacted the Refugee Act was blind to the fact that the laws it was crafting had implications beyond this Nation's borders. The "common-sense notion" that Congress was looking inwards—perfectly valid in a case involving the Federal Tort Claims Act, such as Smith,–cannot be reasonably applied to the Refugee Act of 1980.

In this regard, the majority's dictum that the presumption has "special force" when we construe "statutory provisions that may involve foreign and military affairs for which the President has unique responsibility," is completely wrong. The presumption that Congress did not intend to legislate extraterritorially has less force—perhaps, indeed, no force at all—when a statute on its face relates to foreign affairs. What the majority appears to be getting at, as its citation to *U. S. v. Curtiss–Wright Export Corp.*, suggests, is that in some areas, the President, and not Congress, has sole constitutional authority. Immigration is decidedly not one of those areas. " '[O]ver no conceivable subject is the legislative power of Congress more complete * * *.' " And the suggestion that the President somehow is acting in his capacity as Commander-in-Chief is thwarted by the fact that nowhere among Executive Order No. 12,807's numerous references to the immigration laws is that authority even once invoked.

If any canon of construction should be applied in this case, it is the well-settled rule that "an act of congress ought never to be construed to violate the law of nations if any other possible construction remains." Murray v. The Charming Betsy. The majority's improbable construction of § 243(h), which flies in the face of the international obligations imposed by Article 33 of the Convention, violates that established principle.

III

The Convention that the Refugee Act embodies was enacted largely in response to the experience of Jewish refugees in Europe during the period of World War II. The tragic consequences of the world's indifference at that time are well known. The resulting ban on *refoulement,* as broad as the humanitarian purpose that inspired it, is easily applicable here, the Court's protestations of impotence and regret notwithstanding.

The refugees attempting to escape from Haiti do not claim a right of admission to this country. They do not even argue that the Government has no right to intercept their boats. They demand only that the United States, land of refugees and guardian of freedom, cease forcibly driving them back to detention, abuse, and death. That is a modest plea, vindicated by the Treaty and the statute. We should not close our ears to it.

———

Note: *See Haitian Centers Council v. Sale,* 823 F.Supp. 1028, 1042 (E.D.N.Y.1993); Koh, *Reflections on Refoulement and Haitian Centers Council,* 34 Harv.Int'l L.J. 1 (1994).

Additional problems and questions. Several additional problems concerning asylum and the reception of refugees require consideration. (1) Is a state that grants asylum to the national of another state violating the rights of that state? See the language of Article 1 of the Declaration on Territorial Asylum. (2) If a state admits individuals seeking asylum or refuge, how must they be treated? On a basis of equality with other aliens; with nationals of the asylum state? See the Convention Relating to the Status of Refugees, 1951, 189 U.N.T.S. 137. At what locations may a state receive persons seeking asylum so as not to violate the rights of the state of his nationality or from which he is fleeing? Compare the following cases.

Defection from the "Ukraina"

8 Whiteman, Digest of International Law 669 (1967).

In connection with the circumstances in which a refugee escaping from a Soviet fishing fleet off Shetland was pursued by Soviets across British soil in June 1958, the Secretary of State for the Home Department and Lord Privy Seal, R.A. Butler, furnished the House of Commons with the following information:

> A man named Erich Teayn, stated to be an Estonian, came ashore in the Shetland Islands early this morning from the Russian fishing vessel "Ukraina", one of three Russian trawlers anchored in a bay at Walls. He made his way to a crofter's house and indicated that he did not want to go back to the Russian vessel. He was followed by a party of Russians, said to number about 30, who landed from two small boats in pursuit of him. He was taken into custody for interrogation under the Aliens Order. Three Russians subsequently called at Lerwick police station and sought access to him. This was refused.

In response to a question whether immediate protest would be made to the Russians if the facts as stated were confirmed, and the person involved were a genuine political refugee, Mr. Butler replied: "First, we have to examine the case. If this man asks for political asylum, it will certainly be considered." * * *

Asylum on a Vessel

II Hackworth, Digest of International Law 641 (1941).

The American Minister in Guatemala reported to the Department of State, in October 1922, that in reply to an inquiry of the Mexican Minister as to whether a certain Guatemalan to whom the Mexican Legation had given asylum would be safe from arrest if placed aboard an American vessel in a Guatemalan harbor, he had informed the Minister that the Guatemalan authorities would have the right to effect the arrest of a person in such circumstances so long as the vessel was within Guatemalan waters. In an instruction of November 3, 1922 the Department approved the attitude assumed by the Minister.

Would the result be different if the Guatemalan were placed aboard a United States naval vessel in Guatemalan waters? That is, could Guatemala lawfully arrest the man; would Guatemala have a basis for diplomatic protest in such a case? For the United States Department of State statement of general policy for dealing with requests for asylum by foreign nationals, *see* 66 U.S.Dept. of State Bull. 124 (1972).

The Immigration and Naturalization Act, and related Acts, have nearly eviscerated the opportunity for asylum in cases of human rights abuse.

G.   HUMAN RIGHTS AND THE NEW WORLD ORDER

Most of the materials in this chapter relate to the so-called "new world order." After the fall of the former Soviet Union and the re-emergence of most of its "Republics" and former "satellites" as independent nation-states, problems of human rights abuse increased. Under the totalitarian regimes, much of the ethnic hatreds were kept in check through the power of the police state. After that fell apart, many traditionally antagonistic groups have become embroiled in extremely violent confrontations. Thus, we have had wars in Chechnya, Bosnia, Kosovo, along with tensions elsewhere. For example there is potential for trouble in Romania and the Czech Republic in relation to their Hungarian minority.

Moreover, virtually the entire continent of Africa has fallen into protracted warfare, which is exacerbated by rampant epidemics, poverty, drought, famine, and hatred. The civil wars and other wars there have been truly horrible, with massive egregious human rights violations.

There is no doubt that the 21st century had better be a century of promoting and protecting human rights, or it will be disastrous, not only for those places mentioned above, but for every nation, kindred, tongue, and people.

CHAPTER 10

DIPLOMATIC AND CONSULAR IMMUNITIES AND IMMUNITIES OF PERSONS CONNECTED WITH INTERNATIONAL ORGANIZATIONS

Diplomatic protection in most of its manifestations developed as customary international law over the centuries to become one of the most venerable, vital, and well respected parts of the international legal system. The principal source of diplomatic law in recent times has been the Vienna Convention on the Law of Diplomatic Relations of 1961, set forth in full in the Documentary Supplement, in force in 2001 in 179 countries. It clearly merits careful study, not only for the articles cited or reproduced in this Chapter, but the Convention in its entirety. This body of international law is so well codified in the Convention, that most of the rules are now readily available in understandable and mostly in relatively unambiguous form from a working standpoint. The rules reflect years of application and experience. Their all but universal acceptance testifies to their reliability, despite the many violations which appear in the readings to follow. The rules of diplomatic protection are supported by internal legislation in most countries, and by the practical notion of reciprocity which carries the substantial risk that violation by one country is quite likely to lead to consideration of reciprocal counter-violations by others. The Vienna Convention also carries the promise of further adaptability and evolution through customary international law, as suggested in the last paragraph of the Preamble.

The Preamble serves as an excellent introduction to this subject. The Preamble correctly recognizes the status of diplomatic agents going back to "ancient times", and refers to such basic concepts as the doctrine of "sovereign equality of states", the "maintenance of international peace and security", and the "development of friendly relations among nations, irrespective of their differing constitutional and social systems", all reflecting United Nations formulations which have particular application in the diplomatic field. Privileges and immunities are conferred for the purpose "not to benefit the individuals but to ensure the efficient performance of the *functions* of diplomatic missions as representing states", a concept employed repeatedly by the authorities represented in this Chapter. Finally, the Preamble foresees a continuing role for customary international law as a source for further development of diplomatic law.

———

The Vienna Convention on Diplomatic Relations (1961) provides in Article 3:

1. The functions of a diplomatic mission consist inter alia in:

(a) representing the sending State in the receiving State;

(b) protecting in the receiving State the interests of the sending State and of its nationals, within the limits permitted by international law;

(c) negotiating with the Government of the receiving State;

(d) ascertaining by all lawful means conditions and developments in the receiving State, and reporting thereon to the Government of the sending State;

(e) promoting friendly relations between the sending State and the receiving State, and developing their economic, cultural and scientific relations.

———

SECTION A.   CRIMES AGAINST DIPLOMATIC

Agents and Other Persons Entitled to Immunities

1. *Risks of diplomatic life.* Diplomatic representation is essential to the operation of the international legal system. For diplomatic representation to function effectively, diplomatic representatives must be protected from receiving state interference with the discharge of diplomatic duties. Lord Mansfield in Triquet v. Bath noted the verity of this in the incident which led to the enactment in England of the Diplomatic Privileges Act of 1708:

This privilege of foreign ministers and their domestic servants depends upon the law of nations. The Act of Parliament of 7 Ann. c. 12, is declaratory of it. All that is new in this Act, is the clause which gives a summary jurisdiction for the punishment of the infractors of this law.

The Act of Parliament was made upon occasion of the Czar's Ambassador being arrested. If proper application had been immediately made for his discharge from the arrest, the matter might and doubtless would have been set right. Instead of that, bail was put in, before any complaint was made. An information was filed by the then Attorney General against the persons who were thus concerned, as infractors of the law of nations: and they were found guilty; but never brought up to judgment.

The Czar took the matter up, highly. No punishment would have been thought, by him, an adequate reparation. Such a sentence as the Court could have given, he might have thought a fresh insult.

Another expedient was fallen upon and agreed to: this Act of Parliament passed, as an apology and humiliation from the whole nation. It was sent to the Czar, finely illuminated by an ambassador extraordinary, who made excuses in a solemn oration. 3 Burr. 1478, 1480 (K.B.1764).

Protection from authorities in the receiving state has not always been sufficient, however, to insure the inviolability of diplomatic representatives. Private individuals have at times felt compelled physically to vent frustrations of one kind or another upon the persons of foreign ambassadors. On the whole, though, interference with the function of diplomatic representation, either by authorities or by individuals resorting to violence, seems, until recently, to have been minimal.

----

2. *United States Experience.* In recent years United States diplomatic missions have been targeted by private individuals under circumstances which do not entirely exclude the possibility of terrorists receiving state participation, encouragement or acquiescence. One of the more egregious cases was the assault on the U.S. Embassy in Tehran in 1979, described in part in the following paragraphs. In 1998 the bombing attacks on the U.S. Embassies in Nairobi and Dar es Salam were reported to have killed a number of American and local inhabitants, wounded many more, and caused extensive damage to mission premises. Given the high visibility of the United States as the sole super-power with its active and energetic foreign policy world wide, the United States has to face the risk of continued exposure to aggressive and destructive actions against its diplomatic personnel and missions.

Some flavor of the more extreme violations of diplomatic rules can be seen in the following extracts from the opinion of the International Court of Justice in the Case Concerning United States Diplomatic and Consular

Staff in Tehran [1980] I.C.J. Rep. 3 [other excerpts are found in Section B–2 below]:

17. At approximately 10.30 a.m. on 4 November 1979, during the course of a demonstration of approximately 3,000 persons, the United States Embassy compound in Tehran was overrun by a strong armed group of several hundred people. The Iranian security personnel are reported to have simply disappeared from the scene; at all events it is established that they made no apparent effort to deter or prevent the demonstrators from seizing the Embassy's premises. The invading group (who subsequently described themselves as "Muslim Student Followers of the Imam's Policy", and who will hereafter be referred to as "the militants") gained access by force to the compound and to the ground floor of the Chancery building. Over two hours after the beginning of the attack, and after the militants had attempted to set fire to the Chancery building and to cut through the upstairs steel doors with a torch, they gained entry to the upper floor; one hour later they gained control of the main vault. The militants also seized the other buildings, including the various residences, on the Embassy compound. In the course of the attack, all the diplomatic and consular personnel and other persons present in the premises were seized as hostages, and detained in the Embassy compound; subsequently other United States personnel and one United States private citizen seized elsewhere in Tehran were brought to the compound and added to the number of hostages.

18. During the three hours or more of the assault, repeated calls for help were made from the Embassy to the Iranian Foreign Ministry, and repeated efforts to secure help from the Iranian authorities were also made through direct discussions by the United States Chargé d'affaires, who was at the Foreign Ministry at the time, together with two other members of the mission. From there he made contact with the Prime Minister's Office and with Foreign Ministry officials. A request was also made to the Iranian Chargé d'affaires in Washington for assistance in putting an end to the seizure of the Embassy. Despite these repeated requests, no Iranian security forces were sent in time to provide relief and protection to the Embassy. In fact when Revolutionary Guards ultimately arrived on the scene, despatched by the Government "to prevent clashes", they considered that their task was merely to "protect the safety of both the hostages and the students", according to statements subsequently made by the Iranian Government's spokesman, and by the operations commander of the Guards. No attempt was made by the Iranian Government to clear the Embassy premises, to rescue the persons held hostage, or to persuade the militants to terminate their action against the Embassy.

19. During the morning of 5 November, only hours after the seizure of the Embassy, the United States Consulates in Tabriz and Shiraz were also seized; again the Iranian Government took no protective action. The operation of these Consulates had been suspended since the attack in February 1979 (paragraph 14 above), and therefore no United States personnel were seized on these premises.

20. The United States diplomatic mission and consular posts in Iran were not the only ones whose premises were subjected to demonstrations

during the revolutionary period in Iran. On 5 November 1979, a group invaded the British Embassy in Tehran but was ejected after a brief occupation. On 6 November 1979 a brief occupation of the Consulate of Iraq at Kermanshah occurred but was brought to an end on instructions of the Ayatollah Khomeini; no damage was done to the Consulate or its contents. On 1 January 1980 an attack was made on the Embassy in Tehran of the USSR by a large mob, but as a result of the protection given by the Iranian authorities to the Embassy, no serious damage was done.

21. The premises of the United States Embassy in Tehran have remained in the hands of militants; and the same appears to be the case with the Consulates at Tabriz and Shiraz. Of the total number of United States citizens seized and held as hostages, 13 were released on 18–20 November 1979, but the remainder have continued to be held up to the present time. The release of the 13 hostages was effected pursuant to a decree by the Ayatollah Khomeini addressed to the militants, dated 17 November 1979, in which he called upon the militants to "hand over the blacks and the women, if it is proven they did not spy, to the Ministry of Foreign Affairs so that they may be immediately expelled from Iran".

22. The persons still held hostage in Iran include, according to the information furnished to the Court by the United States, at least 28 persons having the status, duly recognized by the Government of Iran, of "member of the diplomatic staff" within the meaning of the Vienna Convention on Diplomatic Relations of 1961; at least 20 persons having the status, similarly recognized, of "member of the administrative and technical staff" within the meaning of that Convention; and two other persons of United States nationality not possessing either diplomatic or consular status. Of the persons with the status of member of the diplomatic staff, four are members of the Consular Section of the Mission.

23. Allegations have been made by the Government of the United States of inhumane treatment of hostages; the militants and Iranian authorities have asserted that the hostages have been well treated, and have allowed special visits to the hostages by religious personalities and by representatives of the International Committee of the Red Cross. The specific allegations of ill-treatment have not however been refuted. Examples of such allegations, which are mentioned in some of the sworn declarations of hostages released in November 1979, are as follows: at the outset of the occupation of the Embassy some were paraded bound and blindfolded before hostile and chanting crowds; at least during the initial period of their captivity, hostages were kept bound, and frequently blindfolded, denied mail or any communication with their government or with each other, subjected to interrogation, threatened with weapons.

24. Those archives and documents of the United States Embassy which were not destroyed by the staff during the attack on 4 November have been ransacked by the militants. Documents purporting to come from this source have been disseminated by the militants and by the Government-controlled media.

3. ***Panama, Kuwait, and Iraq.*** At the time of the events in
Panama and in Kuwait and Iraq related below, Professor Charles Rousseau
of the University of Paris Law School published regularly in the *Revue
Générale de Droit International Public, Chronique des Faits Internationaux.*
This chronicle of diplomatic and legal happenings was based upon official
and unofficial sources, including newspaper reports. It discloses in recent
years a rather constant stream of violence concerning diplomatic personnel,
premises and property in violation of international law. His reports on two
recent cases, Panama and Kuwait, are particularly noteworthy:

Rousseau, *Chronique des Faits Internationaux,* 95 Rev. Gén. de Droit
Int'l Pub. 495 and 1096 (1991):[a]

On Panama: Infringements of Diplomatic Privileges. General
Noriega surrendered voluntarily on January 3, 1990 to American armed
forces without any bargaining or negotiation and was immediately transferred by a C–130 aircraft from Howard military base to Holmstead in
Florida. The fact that he had taken refuge at the Papal Nunciature in
Panama as early as December 24 (a building enjoying diplomatic immunity)
posed "unsolvable" problems for the American "occupation forces." The
position of the United States consisted in not recognizing in this instance
diplomatic asylum which in its opinion could benefit only political refugees
and not common criminals such as General Noriega. President Endara
terminated Noriega's command, thereby ending his special status and
personnel immunity.

The encirclement of the Cuban and Peruvian Embassies in Panama,
the search of the Nicaraguan Embassy,[1] the searches of the Nuncio's car on
each of his departures from the Nunciature were [serious] infringements of
immunities traditionally recognized to diplomatic personnel and buildings.
This resulted in the expulsion by the government of Nicaragua of 20 out of
the 28 American diplomats accredited to Managua and the reduction from
120 to 100 non-diplomatic members of the American Embassy.

On Iraq: Measures against Diplomatic Missions and Agents.
From the moment the annexation of Kuwait was proclaimed, the government of Iraq announced the expulsion of the foreign diplomatic missions
established in Kuwait. Iraq indicated that it would no longer recognize the
diplomatic status of agents accredited to a State "which no longer existed."
But 28 out of 60 embassies, as of September 1, 1990—refused to bow to the
orders of Iraq and continued to function, declaring that they would give
way only in the face of force.

The Iraqi government responded by blocking the embassies. They were
encircled by the army and police and deprived of any communication with
the outside. The Iraqi authorities cut off water, electricity and telephone
services.

a. Translation by the editors.

1. [The search was on Jan. 3] On January 8 the OAS protested this measure which
was characterized by President Bush as a
"screw-up". It nevertheless permitted the
discovery of machine guns, rifles, bayonets
and a rocket launcher, materials not habitually seen in the private residence of a foreign
ambassador.

Two incidents constituting a particularly serious infringement of the inviolability of embassies and their members occurred: (1) The arrest by the Iraqi army—announced on August 27 but carried out several days earlier—of the Ambassador of Lebanon and twelve members of his staff, followed by their transfer to the Lebanese Embassy in Baghdad which they were forbidden to leave; (2) the invasion by the Iraqi army on September 14 of several foreign embassies in Kuwait (France, Belgium, Netherlands and Canada) and the arrest of the French military attaché, the consuls of the United States, Canada, Ireland and Austria, as well as three French refugees. All were taken to an unknown destination, but the French military attaché and the consuls were released in the evening. The residence of the French Ambassador was pillaged and ransacked.

This conduct infringed international law; it was a scandalous violation of the principle of the inviolability of embassies and diplomatic agents. Articles 22.1, 9 and 30 of the Vienna Convention of April 18, 1961 on Diplomatic Relations condemn it. * * * Iraq would also expel on September 20 and October 4 the military attachés of several Member States of the E.U. (France, Great Britain, FRG, Spain and Italy), the military attaché of the United States, seven French diplomats (but not the Chargé d'affaires), and Egyptian diplomats.[b]

4. ***Convention on the Prevention and Punishment of Crimes against Internationally Protected Persons, including Diplomatic Agents.*** The Convention, signed December 14, 1973, entered into force for the United States on October 26,1976. 28 U.S.T. 1975, 1035 U.N.T.S. 167, 13 I.L.M. 41 (1974). By 2001, 102 states were parties. Article 1 of the convention provides that "internationally protected person" means:

> * * * (a) a Head of State, including any member of a collegial body performing the functions of a Head of State under the constitution of the State concerned, a Head of Government or a Minister for Foreign Affairs, whenever any such person is in a foreign State, as well as members of his family who accompany him;

> (b) any representative of a State or any agent of an international organization of an intergovernmental character who, at the time when and in the place where a crime against him, his official premises, his private accommodation or his means of transport is committed, is entitled pursuant to international law to special protection from any attack on his person, freedom or dignity, as well as members of his family forming part of his household;

> * * *

The Convention is designed to deny safe haven to those who attack, kidnap or inflict grievous bodily harm upon diplomatic agents or other internationally protected persons. A main feature of the Convention is the requirement that a party in whose territory the offender is found must either

---

b.   Translation by the editors.

prosecute or extradite offender, and the inclusion of wide cases of criminal jurisdiction over the offense, considered in Chapters 3, 5, and 16.

5. ***United States legislation to protect foreign representatives.*** Threats of violence and violent acts against foreign representatives have also been on the rise in the United States. The situation in New York, with repeated hostile demonstrations and attacks on diplomatic representatives to the United Nations, led the General Assembly to pass a resolution urging the United States to take measures for ensuring the protection and security of the United Nations Headquarters, the missions accredited to it and their personnel. See the statements of the Deputy Under Secretary of State for Management and of the United States Representative to the United Nations, 67 U.S. Dept. St.Bull. 609 (1972). At the request of the Department of State, legislation was enacted on October 24, 1972 making it a federal offense to commit certain crimes, e.g., murder, kidnapping, assault, harassment, property damage, against internationally protected persons: foreign embassy personnel, and representatives to and of international organizations, and their families. See 18 U.S. Code §§ 112, 970, 1116, 1117 and 1201, as amended.

Section B.   Diplomatic Immunity

1.   Inviolability of Diplomatic Premises

767 Third Avenue Associates et al, Plaintiffs–Appellees v. Permanent Mission of the Republic of Zaire, Defendant–Appellant

988 F.2d 295 (2d Cir.1993).

■ Cardamone, Circuit Judge:

This appeal emerges out of a landlord-tenant dispute. When the Zaire mission to the United Nations occupying leased space on the east side of midtown Manhattan repeatedly fell into arrears on its rent, it was sued by its landlord. The tenant's defense against being evicted was diplomatic immunity. A district court refused to credit this defense and instead granted summary judgment to the landlord for back rent and also awarded it possession of the premises, ordering United States Marshals to remove the Mission physically if it failed to vacate in a timely manner.

Enforcement of an owner's common law right to obtain possession of its premises upon the tenant's non-payment of rent may not override an established rule of international law. Nor under the guise of local concepts of fairness may a court upset international treaty provisions to which the United States is a party. The reason for this is not a blind adherence to a rule of law in an international treaty, uncaring of justice at home, but that by upsetting existing treaty relationships American diplomats abroad may well be denied lawful protection of their lives and property to which they would otherwise be entitled. That possibility weighs so heavily on the scales of justice that it militates against enforcement of the landlord's right to obtain possession of its property for rental arrears.

* * *

DISCUSSION

I Inapplicability of Foreign Sovereign Immunities Act

The inviolability of a United Nations mission under international and U.S. law precludes the forcible eviction of the Mission. Applicable treaties, binding upon federal courts to the same extent as domestic statutes, *see Trans World Airlines, Inc. v. Franklin Mint Corp.*, 466 U.S. 243, 260–61, 104 S.Ct. 1776, 1786–87, 80 L.Ed.2d 273 (1984); *United States v. Palestine Liberation Org.*, 695 F.Supp. 1456, 1464 (S.D.N.Y.1988), establish that Zaire's Permanent Mission is inviolable. The district court erred in misinterpreting the applicable treaties and in carving out a judicial exception to the broad principle of mission inviolability incorporated in those agreements.

Although the United States' support for appellant is based solely on a number of relevant treaties, the district court rested its decision in part on an interpretation of the Foreign Sovereign Immunities Act, 28 U.S.C. §§ 1602–1611 (1988). That Act deserves brief discussion since the landlord continues to raise its provisions. While Sage Realty correctly asserts that Congress aimed to permit courts to make sovereign immunity determinations, see id. § 1602, plaintiffs give short shrift to the Act's explicit provision that it operates "[s]ubject to existing international agreements to which the United States is a party." *Id.* § 1609. Because of this provision the diplomatic and consular immunities of foreign states recognized under various treaties remain unaltered by the Act. *See Mashayekhi v. Iran*, 515 F.Supp. 41, 42 (D.D.C.1981) ("Under the FSIA ..., what were then 'existing international agreements' remain[ ] valid and superior to the FSIA wherever terms concerning immunity contained in the previous agreement conflict with the FSIA."); * * *

II International Agreements

A. Generally

The international agreements presented us and relied upon by the United States all pre-date the Foreign Sovereign Immunities Act. They include the United Nations Charter, 59 Stat. 1031 (1945), the Agreement Between the United Nations and the United States of America Regarding the Headquarters of the United Nations, June 26–Nov. 21 1947, 61 Stat. 754, 756 [hereafter the U.N. Headquarters Agreement], the Convention on the Privileges and Immunities of the United Nations, adopted Feb. 13, 1946, 21 U.S.T. 1418 [hereafter the U.N. Convention on Privileges and Immunities], and the Vienna Convention on Diplomatic Relations, done Apr. 18, 1961, 23 U.S.T. 3227 [hereafter the Vienna Convention].

The first three of those treaties provide for various diplomatic protections and immunities without specific reference to mission premises. The U.N. Charter, for example, provides "[r]epresentatives of the Members of the United Nations and officials of the Organization shall similarly enjoy such privileges and immunities as are necessary for the independent exercise of their functions in connection with the Organization." U.N. Charter, supra, Art. 105(2). The U.N. Headquarters Agreement states that representatives of member states "shall, whether residing inside or outside the headquarters district, be entitled in the territory of the United States to the same privileges and immunities . . . as it accords to diplomatic envoys accredited to it." U.N. Headquarters Agreement, supra, Art. V(4). The Convention on Privileges and Immunities of the United Nations recites in somewhat more detail that representatives of member states shall "enjoy the following privileges and immunities: (a) immunity from personal arrest or detention . . .; (b) inviolability for all papers and documents; . . . (g) such other privileges, immunities and facilities not inconsistent [with] the fore-going as diplomatic envoys enjoy. . . ." U.N. Convention on Privileges and Immunities, supra, Art. IV, § 11.

B.   Vienna Convention

While these Treaty provisions standing alone shed little light on the immunities granted a permanent mission, the 1961 Vienna Convention speaks directly to the issue of mission premises. Article 22 of that Convention declares:

> 1.   The premises of the mission shall be inviolable. The agents of the receiving State may not enter them, except with the consent of the head of the mission. Article 22, section 2 of the Vienna Convention goes on to note a host state's "special duty" to protect "the premises of the mission" from "any intrusion or damage" and "prevent any disturbance of the peace of the mission or impairment of its dignity"; Article 22, section 3 further states that the premises of a mission shall be immune from "search, requisition, attachment or execution." Mission premises covered by the Convention include both owned and leased property. *See Report of the International Law Commission,* Diplomatic Intercourse and Immunities, U.N. GAOR, 13th Sess., Supp. 9, U.N. Doc. a/3859 (1958), reprinted in [1958] II Y.B. Int'l L. Comm'n 89, 95, U.N. Doc. a/CN.4/SER.A/1958/Add.1
>
> * * *

As the United States correctly points out, the drafters of the Vienna Convention considered and rejected exceptions, opting instead for broad mission inviolability. For instance, one proposal in an early Convention draft offered an exception to the prohibition on any non-consensual entry by the receiving state. The exception posed was one to be strictly limited to emergencies presenting "grave and imminent risks" to life, property or national security. See *Diplomatic Intercourse and Immunities,* Projet de codification du droit relatif aux relations et immunités diplomatiques, U.N. Doc. a/CN.4/91, *reprinted in* [1955] II Y.B. Int'l L. Comm'n 9, 11, U.N. Doc. a/CN.4/SER.a./ 1955/Add.1. This proposed exception that would have altered the rule of mission inviolability then existing under customary international law, *id.* at 16, was not adopted. The 1957 draft of the article covering the subject of mission inviolability rejected the proposed exception, and this exception never resurfaced in later drafts. *See Report of the International Law Commission,* Diplomatic Intercourse and Immunities,

U.N. GAOR, 12th Sess., Supp. 9, U.N. Doc. A/3223 (1957), *reprinted in* [1957] II Y.B. Int'l L. Comm'n 131, 136, U.N. Doc. a/CN.4/SER.a/1957/Add.1 [hereafter 1957 Report of Int'l Law Comm'n]. The commentary to the draft article that was ultimately adopted explicitly emphasized the lack of exceptions to inviolability, stating "the receiving State is obliged to prevent its agents from entering the premises for any official act whatsoever." *Id.* at 137. Nothing could be stated more plainly.

* * *

III Inviolability Recognized Without Exception
A.   Under International Law

The fact that the Vienna Convention codified longstanding principles of customary international law with respect to diplomatic relations further supports the view that the Convention recognized no exceptions to mission inviolability. *See* Higgins, *Abuse of Diplomatic Privileges, supra*, at 642 (The Vienna Convention "is agreed to be largely confirmatory of existing customary law."); Secretariat Memorandum, *supra*, at 134. The Convention codified a wide range of diplomatic protections accorded foreign missions over the centuries, *see* Higgins, *Abuse of Diplomatic Privileges, supra*, at 641–42, and recognized the independence and sovereignty of mission premises that existed under customary international law.

Under such law the inviolability of mission premises had become by the 18th century an established international practice, *see Satow's Guide to Diplomatic Practice, supra*, at 106–09, and represented an integral part of the diplomatic privileges accorded envoys abroad. See Francis Deak, *Immunity of a Foreign Mission's Premises From Local Jurisdiction*, 23 Am.J.Int'l L. 582, 587 (1929); 1 L. Oppenheim, *International Law* 793–95 (H. Lauterpacht ed., 8th ed. 1955). The United States and other nations had abided by the inviolability of mission premises long before the Vienna Convention entered into force. *See* IV Green H. Hackworth, *Digest of International Law* 562 (1942) (noting that Foreign Service regulations recognized mission inviolability years before the convention was concluded).

Although diplomatic privilege and mission inviolability arose under various now-outdated theories, including Grotius' notion of the "sacredness of Ambassadors" and the conception of the diplomat as personifying the foreign state's sovereign, *see* Lori J. Shapiro, *Foreign Relations Law: Modern Developments in Diplomatic Immunity*, 1989 Ann.Surv.Am.L. 281, 282 [hereafter Shapiro, Developments], modern international law has adopted diplomatic immunity under a theory of functional necessity. *See id.* at 283. Under that doctrine, the United States recognizes the privileges of foreign diplomats in the U.S. with the understanding that American diplomats abroad will be afforded the same protections from intrusions by the host state. The most secure way to guarantee this protection, the United States tells us, is through blanket immunities and privileges without exception.

The risk in creating an exception to mission inviolability in this country is of course that American missions abroad would be exposed to incursions that are legal under a foreign state's law. Foreign law might be vastly different from our own, and might provide few, if any, substantive or procedural protections for American diplomatic personnel. Were the United States to adopt exceptions to the inviolability of foreign missions here, it would be stripped of its most powerful defense, that is, that international law precludes the non-consensual entry of its missions abroad. Another related consideration is the frequent existence of a small band of American nationals residing in foreign countries, often business personnel. Recent history is unfortunately replete with examples demonstrating how fragile is the security for American diplomats and personnel in foreign countries; their safety is a matter of real and continuing concern. Potential exposure of American diplomats to harm while serving abroad and to American nationals living abroad is not "pure conjecture," as plaintiffs blithely assert.

* * *

Perhaps most telling, no support may be found for an interpretation of limited inviolability in either the commentary to the Vienna Convention or the scholarly literature concerning the convention and the customary international law principles it codified.

Plaintiffs' position is also refuted by what has occurred in practice. The United States has consistently respected the complete inviolability of missions and consulates. Even in extreme cases U.S. authorities will not enter protected premises without permission following, for example, bomb threats. Nor have local authorities been permitted to enter to conduct health and building safety inspections without the consent of the mission involved. *See, e.g.*, Eleanor C. McDowell, Digest of United States Practice in International Law 1976 198–99 (1977). An affidavit from the counselor for Host Country Affairs for the United States Mission to the United Nations attests that after the Soviet mission to the U.N. was bombed in 1979, the FBI and local police officers were all refused entry to the mission until the Soviets consented to allow certain law enforcement officers to enter. Absent such consent, the United States tells us, government officials would not have attempted to enter the Soviet mission's premises.

Additional support for the position we take here is found in decisional law. The Supreme Court has made clear: "When the parties to a treaty both agree to the meaning of a treaty provision, and that interpretation follows from the clear treaty language, [the court] must, absent extraordinarily strong contradictory evidence, defer to that interpretation." *Sumitomo Shoji America, Inc. v. Avagliano*, 457 U.S. 176, 184–85 (1982); *accord In re Air Disaster at Lockerbie, Scotland* on December 21, 1988, 928 F.2d 1267, 1280 (2d Cir.), *cert. denied*, 502 U.S. 920 (1991). This case presents such a situation. Treaty language uses the term "inviolability" and the Convention contains no exceptions relevant to this case. Because the United States agrees to an accepted interpretation of the Vienna Convention, and because no evidence appears of a contrary interpretation advanced by any of the United Nation members, all of whom are parties to the Convention, see G.A. Res. 41/78, U.N. GAOR, 41st Sess., Supp. No. 53, at 260, U.N. Doc. A/41.53 (1986) (General Assembly resolution emphasizing inviolability of missions as prerequisite to carrying on diplomatic functions and stressing States' duties to protect mission premises as required by international law), federal courts must defer to the language of Article 22.

Cf. Concerned Jewish Youth v. McGuire, 621 F.2d 471, 474 (2d Cir.1980) (recognizing U.S. obligations under Article 22 of the Vienna Convention), *cert. denied,* 450 U.S. 913 (1981).

Hence, that portion of the district court's order awarding Sage Realty immediate possession of the premises and directing U.S. Marshals to remove the mission, its effects, and its personnel physically from the premises must be reversed.

* * *

Congress is of course the branch of government best suited to address the full array of concerns involved in altering the Vienna Convention. Already, the legislature has enacted the Diplomatic Relations Act of 1978, 22 U.S.C. §§ 254a-e (1988), to counter some of the more flagrant abuses of diplomatic privilege observed in this country. That Act gives the President the power "on the basis of reciprocity" to establish privileges and immunities for missions and their members "which result in more favorable or less favorable treatment than is provided under the Vienna Convention." *Id.* § 254c. Although the act requires liability insurance coverage for diplomatic missions and their representatives and families to insure against negligence arising from the operation of motor vehicles, vessels or aircraft, *id.* § 254e, it contains no restrictions on mission inviolability. While Congress and the President—via the Diplomatic Relations Act—possess the power to limit mission inviolability, neither has chosen to exercise that power. Our sister branches of government may more appropriately initiate whatever revision, if any, of the Vienna Convention is deemed necessary. *Cf. Palestine Liberation Org.,* 695 F.Supp. at 1465 ("Congress has the power to enact statutes abrogating prior treaties or international obligations entered into by the United States").

* * *

CONCLUSION

Accordingly, the portion of the district court's order granting the landlord possession of the premises and ordering the U.S. Marshals forcibly to seize the premises, if necessary, is reversed. That portion of the district court's order awarding plaintiffs monetary damages is affirmed.

Affirmed, in part, reversed, in part.

The Canadian Foreign Missions and International Organizations Act, S.C 1991, c. 41, provides in similar terms.

Republic of Zaire v. Duclaux

The Netherlands, Court of Appeal of the Hague, 18 February 1988.
94 Int'l L. Rep. 368 (1994).

The following is the text of the relevant part of the judgment of the Court: Under Dutch law a declaration of bankruptcy is a very far-reaching measure. It constitutes judicial seizure of the entire assets of the debtor concerned with a view to their forced sale to enable the assets thus realized to be distributed among all the creditors. By virtue of being declared bankrupt the debtor also automatically, by law, forfeits control over and the use of the assets which form part of the bankrupt estate.

It cannot be denied that if a Dutch court were to declare a sovereign State (which has an embassy or diplomatic mission in the Netherlands) bankrupt, as the Court of first instance did to the Republic of Zaire, this would in no small measure impede the efficient performance of the functions of that State's official diplomatic representation in the Netherlands in view of the nature, effects and consequences of a bankruptcy under the Dutch Bankruptcy Act, which have been considered above. This would be particularly true if, as in the present case, the trustee in bankruptcy were also to be declared competent to open letters and telegrams addressed to the sovereign sending State.

Since such a bankruptcy would therefore entail a by no means insubstantial infringement of the independence of the sending State vis-á-vis the receiving State, given that, at the. very minimum, the diplomatic mission would not be able to function properly, the sending State can, under the generally recognized rules of international law, invoke its immunity from execution in proceedings before a court in the receiving State asked to give judgment on a petition for the sending State to be declared bankrupt.

It follows from the above that the Court of first instance was wrong to reject the Republic of Zaire's reliance on its right of immunity in relation to the aforementioned bankruptcy petition and was wrong to declare the Republic of Zaire bankrupt. The judgment appealed against must be quashed and the Court of Appeal, giving judgment again, must declare that the Court does not have jurisdiction on the grounds of exceptions recognized under international law. [Report: 20 NYIL (1989), p. 296 (English translation)]

Radwan v. Radwan

England, Family Division, 1972.
[1972] 3 W.L.R. 735.*

CUMMING–BRUCE J. Mrs. Mary Isobel Radwan filed a petition for dissolution of marriage on November 27, 1970, seeking dissolution on the ground of her husband's cruelty. * * *

   * * *

The facts are as follows. The husband was born in Cairo. He is and at all material times was a Mohammedan. He was and remains a subject of the United Arab Republic. By the date of the institution of these proceedings, and by the date of the pronouncement of divorce by talaq in April 1970, he had acquired a domicile of choice in England. On April 1, 1970, he entered the Egyptian Consulate in London; the procedure stated in the affidavit of the deputy consul of the Consulate General was followed. The husband three times declared the prescribed form of divorce in the presence of two witnesses. All the steps were carried out in accordance with

---

Egyptian law. After the prescribed 90 days the divorce was finalised in accordance with Egyptian law, and in accordance with that law it was no impediment to the efficacy of the proceedings that the wife knew nothing about it at all. The deputy consul states * * * that the Egyptian Consulate in London is regarded as being Egyptian territory on Egyptian soil. I take it that he means so regarded by the sending sovereign state * * *.

The question for my decision is whether by English law the Egyptian Consulate General is part of a country outside the British Isles within the meaning of section 2(a) of the Divorce Act. By that Act the relevant sections providing for recognition will have effect in respect of overseas divorces if they have been obtained by means of judicial or other proceedings in any country outside the British Isles, and it is necessary for the efficacy of the talaq divorce that it should have been obtained outside the British Isles by reason of the fact that at the material time the husband had acquired English domicile. Curiously, the question has not arisen for decision in England before—the question whether the premises of an embassy or consulate are part of the territory of the sending state as compared to the territory of the receiving state. * * *

* * *

The term "extraterritorial" has been used to describe in a compendious phrase that bundle of immunities and privileges which are accorded by receiving civilized states to the envoys sent by foreign states. One such immunity included in the term is the inviolable character of the premises of a mission, which the agents of the receiving state may not enter without the consent of the head of the mission. The phrase was used by Grotius * * *. The word "extra-territorialitas" was used by Wolff in 1749 and has been in use in English, French and German for some 250 years. Three theories have been invoked to explain the admitted principles that diplomatic premises and property are inviolable by the agents of the receiving state:

    (a) The strict extraterritorial fiction. The premises are regarded by a legal fiction as outside the territory of the receiving state and as part of the territory of the sending state. (b) The representative theory. The premises are immune from entry without consent of the head of the mission, as the mission represents or personifies the sovereignty of the sending state. (c) The theory of functional necessity. The immunity is granted by the receiving state because it is necessary to enable the mission to carry out its functions.

Mr. Ewbank submits, and I agree, that (a) should be discarded as obsolete in the sense that international lawyers have long regarded it as unsound, and it is inconsistent with modern foreign decisions and international convention. He asks me to prefer (c) to (b), though both avoid the practical dangers which (a) is liable to produce.

This view is rested on the foundation of the consensus of authors learned in international law, the approach of courts of law abroad in such cases in modern times as have involved consideration of the immunity of diplomatic land and buildings, and inferences from the international conventions by which civilized states in modern times have sought to define the immunities which they will accord to diplomatic missions.

* * *

I quote and adopt the observations of Mr. J.E.S. Fawcett.

> But there are two popular myths about diplomats and their immunities which we must clear away; one is that an embassy is foreign territory * * * The premises of a mission are inviolable, and the local authorities may enter them only with the consent of the head of the mission. But this does not make the premises foreign territory or take them out of the reach of the local law for many purposes: for example, a commercial transaction in an embassy may be governed by the local law, particularly tax law; marriages may be celebrated there only if conditions laid down by the local law are met; and a child born in it will, unless his father has diplomatic status, acquire the local nationality.
>
> * * *

3.   International conventions.

Though international conventions do not have the force of law unless embodied in municipal legislation, they may in the field of international law be valuable as a guide to the rules of international law which this country as a signatory respects. The Vienna Convention on Consular Relations in 1963, by article 31 sets out the agreed immunities adherent to consular premises under the heading: "Inviolability of the consular premises": "1. Consular premises shall be inviolable to the extent provided in this article," and the article then sets out that extent in its several different ways. There is no suggestion that it was in the mind of any of the signatories that the premises themselves were part of the territory of the sending state. So, too, the Vienna Convention on Diplomatic Relations 1961, by article 22 * * *

What is significant about those articles is not so much what they say as what they do not say. If it was the view of the high contracting parties that the premises of missions were part of the territory of the sending state, that would undoubtedly be formulated and it would have been quite unnecessary to set out the immunities in the way in which it has been done.

* * *

For those reasons the husband, being at the material time a gentlemen of English domicile, did not go through a proceeding for divorce in a country outside the British Isles when he pronounced the talaq three times in the Consulate General in 1970.

* * *

Notes and Questions

1.   *Jurisdiction of sending state over crimes committed within diplomatic premises. In United States v. Erdos*, 474 F.2d 157 (4th Cir.1973),

the chargé d'affairs at the American Embassy in Equitorial Guinea was convicted of killing another Embassy employee within the Embassy compound. The Court construed 18 U.S.C. § 7(3), which deals with the special maritime and territorial jurisdiction of the United States, as embracing an Embassy in a foreign country.

In 1978, the former Ambassador of Austria to Yugoslavia was sentenced by an Austrian court to a heavy fine for accidentally killing the French Ambassador to Yugoslavia upon their return from a hunting trip. The court relied on Article 31(4) of the Vienna Convention which specifies that immunity from the jurisdiction of the receiving state does not exempt the diplomat from the jurisdiction of the sending state. 82 Revue Générale de Droit International Public 1086 (1978).

2. **Diplomatic asylum.** Latin American states assert that a right to grant asylum in the diplomatic premises exists by virtue of a regional custom peculiar to them. The existence of such a right was tested and denied in the *Asylum Case* (Colombia v. Peru) [1950] I.C.J.Rep. 266. The holding of the court that the Colombian government had failed to prove the existence of a regional custom of asylum may have induced the adoption of a new convention on asylum by the Tenth Inter–American Conference at Caracas in 1954. 6 Whiteman Digest *supra* at 436.

The United States Department of State has consistently maintained that a state does not have a right to grant asylum under international law. The granting of asylum to Cardinal Mindszenty by the American Embassy in Budapest in 1956 was explained as "exceptional." 6 Whiteman Digest supra at 463–464. It lasted for 15 years. Still, the U.S. loses granted asylum to dissidents from the former USSR and from China in its Embassies.

Goldberg,[a] The Shoot–Out at the Libyan Self–Styled People's Bureau: A Case of State–Supported Terrorism

30 South Dakota Law Review 1 (1984).*

* * *

The facts of the shoot-out at the Libyan People's Bureau in London have been extensively reported. Two gunmen in the Libyan self-styled "People's Bureau" in London opened fire on a crowd of peaceful anti-Qaddafi demonstrators. These demonstrators were conducting their peaceful protest on a sidewalk adjacent to the Libyan People's Bureau, yet the gunmen inside chose to shoot at them, killing Constable Fletcher and wounding eleven demonstrators and bystanders. Ten days after this barbaric incident, the British Government provided the killers and their murder weapons with safe passage out of the country.

On the same day that British police escorted the murderers to Heathrow Airport, Constable Fletcher was buried. At the time of her funeral, the

---

a. The author, Arthur G. Goldberg, was formerly Associate Justice of the Supreme Court of the United States and Ambassador to the United Nations.

* Reprinted with the permission of the South Dakota Law Review.

Home Secretary, Mr. Leon Brittan, stated that the British police were prevented under the terms of the Vienna Convention on Diplomatic Relations from storming the so-called People's Bureau to apprehend the killers and bring them to justice. Mr. Brittan asserted Her Majesty's government could not act because the murderers, the premises of the People's Bureau, and the bags within which the lethal weapons were concealed were all immune according to the Convention. Prime Minister Thatcher and the Foreign Secretary Howe, supported the Home Secretary's view in the debate in the House of Commons. With all respect, I disagree. The Vienna Convention, like all treaties, must be sensibly interpreted. In this unruly age of state-sponsored terrorism, the Vienna Convention must not be construed so as to be a suicide pact for civilized countries. Treaties must be read in their entirety, with some provisions necessarily modified by others. Nothing could be more foolish than to accept a simple-minded, literal reading of each of the Convention's articles. The privileges and immunities granted by the Convention are rights declared in words, but rights declared in words are not to be lost in reality.

* * *

[T]he Home Secretary * * * claimed the British police under the Vienna Convention could not storm the so-called Libyan People's Bureau to capture the killers and confiscate their weapons as material evidence. * * * I disagree. Colonel Qaddafi's People's Bureau in London scarcely qualifies as a *bona fide* embassy whose premises are inviolable under the Vienna Convention. * * * [T]he London People's Bureau, according to reliable evidence, has harbored assassination teams directed by Qaddafi against Libyan dissidents. Murder factories are not embassies, and therefore do not come within the scope of the Vienna Convention. That treaty is designed to grant immunity to a proper embassy devoted to diplomatic relations. Article 41, section 3 of the Convention states that the "premises of the mission must not be used in any manner incompatible with the functions of the mission as laid down in the * * * Convention or by other rules of general international law * * *." Harboring hit squads clearly does not come within the protection of that provision.

The People's Bureau in London therefore is not a *bona fide* embassy. It was, in my opinion, subject under established rules of international law to search and seizure by the British police after the brutal murder of Constable Fletcher and the wounding of others.

* * *

Britain Agrees to Restore Ties to Libya

Warren Hoge, International Herald-Tribune, 8 July 1999, p. 1.*

LONDON—Britain said Wednesday it was resuming diplomatic relations with Libya after 15 years because Tripoli had agreed to assist British police in the investigation of the fatal shooting of a London police officer outside the Libyan Embassy in London in 1984.

Foreign Secretary Robin Cook told the House of Commons that Libya had also agreed to pay compensation to the family of the slain constable

* Reprinted with the permission of the International Herald Tribune.

and accepted "general responsibility," for the killing, which caused the severing of relations. The policewoman, Yvonne Fletcher, 25, died from a single wound in the back, and witnesses have said the shot came from a window of the embassy.

* * *

Though the killing of Constable Fletcher occurred 15 years ago, it is an especially unforgettable event for the British because they witnessed it unfold on live television. For days after her body was removed, her police helmet remained in the middle of the no-man's land that St. James's Square had become, a particularly forlorn sight for the millions of people who saw it. There was added poignancy in the fact that among the policemen who frantically dragged her away so she could be taken to a hospital was her fiancé, Constable Michael Liddle. She died 15 minutes after arriving at Westminster Hospital.

Anti–Gadhafi protesters had gathered outside the building when a burst of automatic gunfire was heard and 11 demonstrators fell wounded. The fatal shot that hit Constable Fletcher in the back was thought to have come from the first floor. The murder weapon was later identified as a British-made Sterling submachine gun, which was standard issue to the Libyan Army. No one was ever charged in the shooting, and 22 Libyan Embassy officials were allowed to leave the building 10 days later under police escort to Heathrow Airport.

Britain cut off diplomatic relations with Tripoli immediately, and public outrage in Britain grew when the Libyan diplomats were given a heroes welcome on their return home. Mr. Cook said Wednesday's break-through would lead to the British Interests Section in Tripoli being upgraded to full embassy status and the appointment of an ambassador "as quickly as practical." He said a joint British–Libyan statement "accepts general responsibility for the actions of those in the Libyan People's Bureau at the time of the shooting." The Libyans "express deep regret to the family for what occurred and offer to pay compensation now to the family. Libya agrees to participate and cooperate with the continuing police investigation and to accept its outcome," he said.

The Fletcher family issued a statement welcoming Libya's new willing-ness to assist the investigation and said, "We hope that there can now be progress on identifying precisely who was responsible for Yvonne's death. The path to full justice is now open." In a statement, Scotland Yard called the move "a positive step."

Letter Dated 2 April 1992 From the Permanent Representative of Venezuela to the United Nations Addressed to the President of the Security Council

31 I.L.M. 753 (1992) (reprinted by permission of the American Society of Int'l Law).

I have the honour to transmit to Your Excellency the text in Spanish of the Declaration of the Government of Venezuela, in regard to the violation to the diplomatic mission of Venezuela in Tripoli, on 2 April 1992. I would greatly appreciate if Your Excellency distributed the text of the present letter and its annex as a document of the Security Council.

(Signed) Diego ARRIA Ambassador of Venezuela
Permanent Representative to the United Nations
Annex [Original: Spanish]

The Ministry of Foreign Affairs hereby informs public opinion that today, at 10:30 a.m. Libyan time, the administrative headquarters of the Venezuelan Embassy in Tripoli was attacked. A mob consisting of students who had arrived in two buses and people from the street broke into the Embassy shouting slogans against Venezuela because of the latter's vote in the Security Council in favour of the anti-terrorist resolution on 31 March 1992. The mob then began to ransack and destroy the premises of our diplomatic representation. Neither the four Libyan guards assigned to protect the Embassy nor anyone from the police force of the city of Tripoli intervened to stop the looting and arson of the diplomatic premises, which were carried out with total impunity. The members of the Venezuelan diplomatic staff, with whom this Ministry remains in contact through various channels, suffered no physical injury to speak of.

On the same date, the Ministry of Foreign Affairs delivered an official note to the representative of the Libyan Government in Venezuela to protest about the violation of the standards of protection for diplomatic premises which are laid down in the relevant international agreements, and to demand assurances guaranteeing the physical integrity of the Venezuelan diplomats accredited to Libya and the inviolability of the Venezuelan Embassy residence, together with an adequate official explanation of the incident in question within 48 hours.

Caracas, 2 April 1992

Letter Dated 8 April 1992 From the Permanent Representative of Venezuela to the United Nations Addressed to the President of the Security Council

31 I.L.M. 754 (1992) (reprinted by permission of the American Society of Int'l Law).

With regard to the letter dated 2 April 1992 from the Permanent Representative of Venezuela to the United Nations addressed to the President of the Security Council, concerning the attack on the Venezuelan diplomatic mission at Tripoli, Libya, I have the honour to transmit herewith the communiqué issued on 5 April 1992 by the Ministry of Foreign Affairs of Venezuela concerning the official reply by the People's Bureau for Foreign Liaison and International Cooperation of the Libyan Arab Jamahiriya to the Venezuelan protest note. I should be grateful if you would have this text issued as a document of the Security Council.

(Signed) Diego Arria Permanent Representative
of Venezuela to the United Nations

Annex

The Ministry of Foreign Affairs reports that on 5 April Venezuela received from the People's Bureau for Foreign Liaison and International

Cooperation of Libya (Ministry of Foreign Affairs) the official reply to the Venezuelan protest note concerning the attack on the Venezuelan Embassy in Tripoli conveying " * * * the deepest regret and apologies of the Socialist People's Libyan Arab Jamahiriya for the damage sustained by the Venezuelan Embassy at Tripoli". The note of apology adds:

"The Jamahiriya, in condemning this act, feels that it was directed in the first place against the Jamahiriya, rather than against Venezuela, a friendly country. The Jamahiriya takes responsibility for the consequences of this incident and will provide compensation in the fairest manner so as to satisfy the Government of Venezuela since this is a legitimate right of the Government of Venezuela. The Jamahiriya reiterates that what occurred will not be repeated in respect of the Venezuelan Embassy or of the other Embassies accredited to the Jamahiriya. The Jamahiriya hopes that this passing incident will not have any adverse effect on the good relations between our two countries."

The Ministry of Foreign Affairs accepts the apologies of the Government of Libya on the understanding that there will be no repetition of such acts of violence, that there will be full compensation for the material damage and that the diplomatic relations between the two countries will be conducted, both in matters on which they agree and in matters on which they disagree, in accordance with the norms of international law and of civilized coexistence among nations. At all events, national public opinion will be informed that Venezuela's diplomatic representatives in Libya have been called back to Caracas for consultations with the Ministry.

Yener and Erez Deceased

France, Conseil d'Etat (1987).
89 Int'l L.Rptr. 1 (1992).

The following is the text of the judgment of the *Conseil d'Etat*:

1. The application of the dependants of Mr. Yener seeks:

    a) the annulment of the judgment of 7 July 1982 of the *Tribunal administratif* of Paris which rejected their claim against the State for the award of damages as compensation for the loss suffered by them as a result of the assassination of Mr. Yener, the chauffeur of the Turkish Ambassador in France, which occurred on 24 October 1975 in Paris; and

    b) the award of various sums as compensation for this loss.

2. The application of the dependants of Mr. Erez seeks:

    a) the annulment of the judgment of 7 July 1982 of the *Tribunal administratif* of Paris which rejected their claim for damages against the State as compensation for the loss suffered by them as a result of the assassination of Mr. Erez, Turkish Ambassador in France, which occurred on 24 October 1975 in Paris; and

    b) the award of various sums as compensation for this loss.

The *Conseil d'Etat* has considered the Decree of 29 March 1971 whereby the Vienna Convention on Diplomatic Relations was published * * *.

[The *Conseil d'Etat* decided to join the two applications and continued:] Mr. Erez, Turkish Ambassador in France, and Mr. Yener, his chauffeur, were the victims of a terrorist attack in Paris on 24 October 1975 at approximately 1.30 p.m., when they were travelling in a car on the bridge of Bir–Hakeim in the direction of the embassy premises, which were a few hundred meters away. In the circumstances of the case, proceedings to establish State responsibility for the alleged inadequacy of measures taken to ensure the protection of the victims of the attack in question, having regard to their membership of a diplomatic mission, do not bring into question the conduct of international relations by France. Their outcome merely depends upon an assessment which can be separated from questions of international relations.

It does not appear from the available information that the police ought to have provided tighter security surveillance than they actually gave. In particular it is not established from the documents in the file that the Turkish Ambassador made any request for special protection (*protection rapprochée*) in the days leading up to the attack. In failing to take additional measures the French police did not therefore commit any serious fault capable of engaging the responsibility of the State.

In the absence of any express legislative provision, the responsibility of the State cannot be engaged merely on the basis of the actual risk of acts of terrorism on French territory. It follows * * * that the dependents of Erez and Yener are not entitled to claim that, in the judgments being challenged, the *Tribunal administratif* of Paris wrongly rejected their claims that the State should be declared responsible for the consequences of the attack in question and ordered to pay damages. * * * [The applications were rejected.]

2.   IMMUNITY AND INVIOLABILITY OF DIPLOMATIC AGENTS

The Vienna Convention on Diplomatic Relations was signed by 81 states on April 18, 1961. It entered into force on April 24, 1964; by 2001, there were 179 states parties to the Convention. It entered into force for the U.S. on December 13, 1972. The legislation prior to ratification dated from the eighteenth century (Act of 30 April 1790, ch. 9, § 25, 22 U.S.C. § 252). It conferred broad immunity from both criminal and civil jurisdiction upon ambassadors, their domestic servants, and upon other diplomatic personnel. The Convention on the other hand granted a narrower measure of immunity to all diplomatic personnel. The Department of Justice took the position that the Convention did not repeal or supersede the greater measure of immunity provided by existing legislation. Rovine, Digest of United States Practice in International Law 1973, at 143 (1974). The Diplomatic Relations Act, repealing the previous legislation and giving effect to the Convention as controlling domestic law, was enacted on

September 30, 1978. 22 U.S.C. §§ 254a–254e, 28 U.S.C. § 1364. The text of the Convention and the Act are in the Documentary Supplement.

———

Notes.

1. ***Protection Afforded.*** Articles 29–44 of the Vienna Convention afford broad protection to diplomatic agents: including personal inviolability for himself and his personal residence, immunity from arrest or detention, immunity from the jurisdiction of local courts, from criminal, and (subject to certain exceptions) civil and administrative jurisdiction, immunity from certain local laws, from execution, from local dues and taxes (subject to exceptions such as indirect taxes included in the price of goods), immunity from customs duties, personal service (military and jury service) and social security requirements as well as immunity from the obligation to give evidence as a witness. The specific terms of these immunities and their exceptions are provided in the Convention articles cited above.

2. ***Rationale: immunity of diplomatic agents.*** Diplomatic immunity rests on two grounds: (1) it ensures the effective performance by the diplomatic agent; and (2) it protects the diplomatic agent's person and dignity. Before the Vienna Convention, however, a number of states rejected the representational considerations, i.e., those pertaining to the personal dignity of diplomatic agents. They took the position that functional necessity was the sole basis of diplomatic immunity.

In the states adopting the rationale of functional necessity, the courts distinguished between the official acts and the private acts of a diplomatic representative, immunity being granted for the former, but not for the latter. The distinction had an obvious parallel in the distinction made by many courts in civil law states between the public acts of a foreign state (for which immunity is granted) and its private acts (for which no immunity is given). See Chapter 7 on Immunity of states.

Marian Nash Leach, Contemporary Practice of the United States Relating to International Law

83 A.J.I.L. 905, 910 (1989).*

DIPLOMATIC MISSIONS AND EMBASSY PROPERTY (U.S. DIGEST, CH. 4, § 1)

Appointment, Accreditation and Notification: The Department of State has observed that it is necessary and useful periodically to reiterate and clarify the standards for the accreditation of foreign diplomatic personnel assigned to the United States. By a circular note to the Chiefs of Mission at Washington, dated May 23, 1989, Secretary of State James A. Baker III reiterated the Department's requirement that, to be recognized as a diplomatic agent, a person must possess a recognized diplomatic title and must, as well, perform duties of a diplomatic nature. Secretary Baker reminded the Chiefs of Mission that the accreditation of diplomats was solely within

* Reprinted with the permission of the American Society of Int'l Law.

the discretion of the Department of State and that requests for accreditation in diplomatic status of personnel performing duties of an administrative and technical nature were incompatible with both Department policy and the Vienna Convention on Diplomatic Relations (1961). The Secretary informed them, further, that any promotion from the administrative and technical staff to diplomatic agent status must be accompanied by a formal position description for each person * * *.

Enclosed with the note of May 23, 1989, was an earlier circular note in greater detail on the same subject, dated May 1, 1985, and reading, in part, as follows:

> Requests for exceptions to the general guidelines will be considered infrequently and only in extenuating circumstances. Such requests must be forwarded in the form of a diplomatic note to the Department and must set forth in detail the exact nature of the exception requested, justification for such exception, the duration thereof, and possible alternative courses of action.

So that the accreditation policy of the United States Government may be uniformly a matter of record for all missions, the criteria governing accreditation are set forth as follows:

"DIPLOMATIC AGENTS"

> To be recognized as a "diplomatic agent", and in order to retain such status, a person must: (1) possess a valid diplomatic passport if diplomatic passports are issued by his government or, if diplomatic passports are not issued, present a diplomatic note from the mission formally representing the intention of the sending government to assign to him diplomatic duties; (2) possess a recognized diplomatic title; (3) be a holder of an A–1 nonimmigrant visa; (4) be over 21 years of age; (5) with the exception of certain designated senior financial, economic, and commercial positions in New York City or certain other positions expressly agreed to by the Department, reside in the Washington, D.C. area * * *; and (6) devote official activities to diplomatic functions on an essentially full-time basis. * * *

Notes and Questions

1. **Private acts of diplomatic agent not covered by immunity.** The Division of Juridical Affairs of the Swiss Federal Political Department issued an opinion as to whether a lien could be secured on a building owned by a high official of an international organization. Workers who provide services and materials for the construction of a building are protected for their payment under the Swiss Code by a lien against the property, even if the owner is not the one owing the debt. The lien must be recorded and this can be done only if the debtor acknowledges the debt or if a court orders the recordation following a summary proceeding. Where a cantonal court ordered provisional recordation of a lien upon the property of a high official of the United Nations, the lien is effective. Under Article 31(1) of

the Vienna Convention, a diplomatic agent shall enjoy immunity from civil and administrative jurisdiction of the receiving state, but not with respect to private immovable property in the territory of the receiving state. Since the property was private in this case, the opinion concluded there was no need to seek a waiver of diplomatic immunity. 32 Ann. Suisse de Dr. Int'l 143 (1976).

For the rule concerning two types of private acts not covered by diplomatic immunity, (certain succession matters and private professional or commercial activity) see Article 31(1) in the Documentary Supplement.

2. *Abuse of Immunities.* In the aftermath of the "shoot-out" at the Libyan Peoples' Bureau in London and other developments, there were a number of reviews and second thoughts about the scope of diplomatic immunity, particularly in relation to criminal prosecution where the immunity could be abused. The U.S. Congress ordered a State Department study and report. Hearings were held in the spring of 1988. The State Department reported that there were in the U.S. 26,282 persons with criminal immunity, 29,689 with official acts immunity, for a total of 55,971, but that the number of crimes committed by those persons is "very small" and there was not a "diplomatic crime wave." Draft legislation before the Congress to tighten procedures was not adopted. *See The Diplomatic Privileges and Immunities Act, Hearing before the Subcommittee on International Operations of the Committee on Foreign Affairs,* 100th Cong. 2nd Sess. 7, March 30 and April 13, 1988; and Miscellaneous International Affairs Authorizations Act of 1988, Report to accompany S. 2757, submitted by Mr. Pell, from the Committee on Foreign Relations 100th Cong. 2nd Sess. Report 100–500, September 7, 1988. In the United Kingdom, the review process and report are described in Higgins, U.K. Foreign Affairs Committee Report on the Abuse of Diplomatic Immunities and Privileges: Government Response and Report, 80 A.J.I.L. 135 (1986).

3. *Questions*: Had there been evidence of more rampant and serious abuse—or should there be rampant and serious abuse in the future—what remedies might be employed by the receiving state without impairing the diplomatic immunity? What might be the risk to the receiving state in limiting the scope of the immunity?

Waiver of Diplomatic Immunity

Waiver may provide a solution in some but perhaps not all cases. Some governments are reluctant to permit a waiver of immunity even in cases where the sending state's interest might be minimal, as in the automobile accident cases, especially if the sending state senses a risk of higher pressure being exerted upon it to waive immunity in future cases where the sending state might have superior interests it wished to protect. Nevertheless, waiver by the sending state (but not by the diplomatic agent) is clearly available under Article 32 of the Vienna Convention, subject to the rules that it "must always be express". The Makharadze case in Washington provides a dramatic example. For analysis of Article 32, see Eileen Denza, Diplomatic.Law 271 (2nd Ed., 1998) An equally dramatic French case which theoretically might have been resolved by waiver was not, since an equally effective alternative was employed under the end of mission rules as will be seen below.

Waiver of Georgian Diplomat's Immunity From Criminal Prosecution

Sean B. Murphy, Ed., Contemporary Practice of the United States Relating to International Law, 93 AJIL 470, 485 (1999).*

On January 3, 1997, a diplomat posted at the Embassy of Georgia in Washington, D.C., Gueorgui Makharadze, was speeding in his car when it crashed, causing a multicar collision that killed sixteen-year-old-Joviane Waltrick and injured four other persons. At the time of her death, Waltrick was a citizen of Brazil on a tourist visa in the United States.

The U.S. Attorney's office for the District of Columbia informed the Department of State that its initial review of the evidence indicated that Makharadze could be charged with negligent homicide, involuntary manslaughter, or second-degree murder. Consequently, on January 9, the Department of State requested that the Georgian Embassy waive Makharadze's immunity from criminal prosecution. On January 10, President Eduard A. Shevardnadze of the Republic of Georgia announced that Georgia was prepared to waive the diplomat's immunity.

After further discussions between the two governments regarding the charges that would be brought against Makharadze, the Department of State, on February II, 1997, transmitted to the Embassy of Georgia an affidavit setting forth the U.S. Attorney's evidence in the case and providing information on the maximum sentence that could be imposed if Makharadze were charged and convicted of involuntary manslaughter and aggravated assault. By diplomatic note dated February 14, the Embassy responded as follows:

The Government of Georgia has considered the request of the United States Department of State and according to Article 32 of the Vienna Convention on Diplomatic Relations has waived the diplomatic immunity for Mr. George Makharadze, so he can be prosecuted in the United States, for the accident that took place on January 3, 1997, in Washington, DC.

After welcoming this decision, State Department spokesman Nicholas Burns noted that it was "highly unusual in modem diplomacy for a head of state to take a step like this. But given the emotions in the United States, given the feelings of the family and the local community here in Washington, D.C., we think it's the appropriate step for the Government of Georgia to take."

On February 20, 1997, Makharadze was charged with one count of involuntary manslaughter and four counts of aggravated assault for the death of Waltrick and injuries to four others. In October, Makharadze pleaded guilty. As part of a plea bargain, prosecutors agreed not to object to the diplomat's request to serve his sentence in a federal prison instead of in the District's Lorton Correctional Complex. He was sentenced to seven to twenty years in prison on December 19.

* Reprinted with the permission of the American Society of International Law.

On December 31, 1997, the estate of Joviane Waltrick filed a civil suit in federal court against various parties: Makharadze, the Republic of Georgia (for letting Makharadze drive despite a history of traffic violations), Yanni's Greek Tavern (where Makharadze drank wine immediately prior to the accident), the Ford Motor Co. and Jerry's Ford Sales (based on Makharadze's claims that the brakes had failed), and certain insurance and credit companies. In order to establish the responsibility of the Republic of Georgia, the complaint alleged that Makharadze had been acting within the scope of his employment since the accident occurred after he had consumed alcohol at an official dinner function and while he was using a vehicle leased by the Embassy.

On January 9, 1998, plaintiffs counsel in the case requested that the Department of State seek a waiver from the Republic of Georgia of Makharadze's immunity from civil suit. The Department of State responded, in part:

Mr. Makharadze was a diplomatic agent accredited to the Embassy of Georgia. However, when he was incarcerated after having entered guilty pleas to criminal charges arising from the accident in which Miss Waltrick was killed, he ceased to perform diplomatic functions. Therefore, pursuant to Article 39(2) of the Vienna Convention on Diplomatic Relations, Mr. Makharadze has residual immunity from civil jurisdiction of U. S—courts only "with respect to acts performed ... in the exercise of his functions as a member of the mission."

It is not the Department's practice to seek the waiver of immunity in civil cases in instances where the defendant's immunity is limited to acts done within the scope of his diplomatic functions. We note that Mr. Makharadze would be amenable to suit if the court were to determine that his actions were nondiplomatic in nature. If the court finds otherwise, your clients would continue to have recourse against the insurance company and other named defendants.

On April 22, 1998, counsel for Makharadze sought his dismissal from the civil case on grounds of diplomatic immunity. On May 29, U.S. District judge Thomas F. Hogan granted the motion, concluding:

Plaintiff has not established a waiver of defendant Makharadze's immunity from civil jurisdiction. Neither the Republic of Georgia's explicit waiver of criminal immunity nor the circumstances surrounding that waiver support such a conclusion. Furthermore, although defendant Makharadze no longer enjoys the blanket immunity granted to acting diplomatic officers, he enjoys residual immunity for actions taken in performance of his former duties. Because plaintiff explicitly pleads that the accident occurred in the course of defendant Makharadze's official duties, the Court must conclude that residual immunity attaches. Therefore, because defendant Makharadze enjoys immunity from the civil jurisdiction of this Court, the Court must dismiss him from the case.[10]

10. Knab v. Republic of Georgia, No.97–CV–03118 (TFH), 1998 U.S.Dist LEXIS 8820 (D.D.C. May 29, 1998) (mem.).

On October 14, 1998, all remaining defendants except Yanni's Greek Tavern agreed to settle the lawsuit for an undisclosed amount in excess of $250,000.

Leniency Asked for Envoy Who Killed 2 in France

Craig R. Whitney, International Herald Tribune, 26 March 1997.*

PARIS—The former ambassador of Zaire to France appeared voluntarily Tuesday in a court in Nice for trial on involuntary homicide charges in the deaths of two schoolboys he hit while driving his car at high speed in November.

The former envoy, Ramazani Baya, had diplomatic immunity at the time of the accident, on Nov. 23 near the Mediterranean resort of Menton, where a week later 5,000 people protested, demanding that he be tried anyway. Mr. Baya and President Mobutu Sese Seko of Zaire agreed to lift the envoy's immunity, and Mr. Baya, recalled as ambassador in December, returned to France in January as an ordinary Zairian citizen.

In court Tuesday, the French state prosecutor asked for a three-year suspended sentence for manslaughter by negligence, plus a fine of 20,000 francs ($3,500), with 4,000 francs in damages and a three-year ban on driving in France. The court will rule April 29.

"We need to be reasonable, although we feel inclined to pass judgment with our heart," said the prosecutor, Didier Durand, as the parents of the two boys who were killed, Raphael Lenoir, 13, and Ronald Lehartel, 12, were sitting in the courtroom. "Justice cannot return your children to you."

Mr. Baya told the police that he had not seen the boys at a crosswalk while he was rushing to a meeting with Marshal Mobutu, who was recuperating from cancer treatment in a nearby Mediterranean villa. The envoy stayed at the scene and submitted to a blood alcohol test that showed he had not been drinking.

Mr. Durand cited these factors as reasons for not requesting a harsher sentence, although Mr. Baya had been driving at more than twice the legal speed limit of 50 kilometers (32 miles) an hour. Mr. Baya could be sent to jail for three years and fined 300,000 francs.

French diplomats said that Mr. Baya was stricken with remorse and had volunteered to waive diplomatic immunity shortly after the accident, but that only the Zairian authorities could waive it for him. Foreign Minister Herve de Charette formally asked Zaire to lift his immunity, but only after the ambassador had left the country, and the French authorities seemed surprised when the request was granted. "I will not be at ease until after the verdict," Mr. Baya said upon returning to France in January.

* * *

---

* Reprinted with the permission of the International Herald Tribune.

Notes. The Finale.

1.   In the end, Mr. Mobutu did not waive Ambassador Baya's immunity. The Ambassador was permitted to leave France in accordance with his diplomatic rights. After he returned to Zaire, he resigned from the Zaire diplomatic service. At that point he continued to enjoy diplomatic immunity in France only "with respect to acts performed by such a person in the *exercise of is functions* as a member of the mission" (Vienna Convention, Article 39(2) emphasis added), but not for his *private acts* committed during his period of service. In this case the French court could properly take jurisdiction because there was no claim that the Ambassador's acts causing the accident were carried out in the "exercise of his functions" as ambassador, although that would have been an arguable position had the claim been made. (See various news sources: Le Monde, 23 January and March 27 1997, Le Figaro, 23 and 27 January 1997, and International Herald Tribune, January 27 and April 30 1997.)

2.   ***Death of a Canadian killed by Russian Diplomat.***

Duties of the Mission Towards the Receiving State

Vienna Convention, Article 41.

EILEEN DENZA, DIPLOMATIC LAW 373 (2nd Ed. 1998)*

The Duty to Respect Laws and Regulations of the Receiving State

This is much the most important of the four general obligations of a diplomatic agent. " * * * In the older writers this duty was seen as a corollary of the duty on the part of the receiving State to accord privileges and immunities. Many of these writers saw the diplomat as being exempt as a matter of substance from the legal duties and liabilities prescribed by the laws of the receiving State, but having instead a moral duty, or a duty of courtesy to respect them. The duty to 'respect' the laws of the receiving State was something less than a legal duty to obey them. The modern theory, however, is that certainly in regard to his private acts and now even in regard to his official acts a diplomat is subject as a matter of legal substance to the laws of the receiving State except where these laws make a specific exception in his favour. Such exceptions may be made in order to give effect to an inter-national rule (as in matters of tax and social security) or they may be made as a matter of domestic policy, perhaps for reasons of comity or of reciprocity. To regard a diplomat as not merely protected by immunity from enforcement of the laws of the receiving State but also exempt from liability under them would produce absurd results. It would mean that a diplomat could pay a debt and sue for recovery of the money on the basis that it had been paid in the absence of any obligation. It would lead to an absurd position where immunity was waived or came to an end on termination of functions or operation of law in that the defendant could again plead his status in order to dispute liability. In the cases already discussed in the context of Article 31.1 regarding the legal effect of the establishment or lifting of immunity, national courts have emphasized that

* Reprinted with the permission of the
Oxford University Press.

immunity is procedural in character and does not affect any underlying substantive liability, and this is now a well-established rule.''

* * *

Duty not to Interfere in Internal Affairs

The International Law Commission discussed at length in 1957 the nature of this duty. It became apparent that there was some confusion between the duty of the sending State not to intervene in the domestic affairs of the receiving State—an important rule of international relations, but one which it was ultimately agreed was not suitable for inclusion in a codification of diplomatic law—and the much more limited question of the duty of the diplomat in his personal activities not to meddle in the domestic affairs of the receiving State. It may sometimes be difficult to determine whether it is the duty of the State or the duty of the diplomat which is in issue—this will normally be determined by whether the diplomat was acting on instructions of his sending State. It was the second of the two duties which was reflected in Article 12 of the Havana Convention regarding Diplomatic Officers which stated: ''Foreign diplomatic officers may not participate in the domestic or foreign policies of the State in which they exercise their functions.'' Where a diplomat on instructions made some statement or took some step which was regarded by the receiving State as interference in its internal affairs, the question was whether the sending State had locus standi in the matter—as it would if the treatment of its own nationals or relations between the two States were involved. The longstanding rule now reflected in Article 41.1, however, related to personal comments or activities by diplomats not made on instructions. There were many cases where disregard or alleged disregard of the rule led to the offending diplomat being declared persona non grata. The most famous was the incident where Lord Sackville, British Minister in Washington, in 1888 wrote a letter advising the recipient, who had pretended to be a naturalized citizen of British birth, how he should vote in the forthcoming Presidential election. This letter was made public and led to the dismissal of Lord Sackville by the Government of the United States.

* * *

Duty to Communicate through the Ministry of Foreign Affairs

Just as a diplomatic mission is entitled to insist that communications to it from organs of the receiving State, and in particular from its courts should be channeled through the Ministry of Foreign Affairs, that Ministry is in return entitled to regard itself as prima facie the sole channel of communication to receive communications from the diplomatic mission to the government. The rule is a long-established and universal one, based on common sense. In France it was prescribed by Decrees of 1799 and of 1810 issuing from the Emperor Napoleon. The task of the Ministry of Foreign Affairs is made smoother and relations are conducted more efficiently if all communications are normally channeled through the Ministry which is in the light of its overall knowledge of the bilateral relations between the two countries best qualified to help with requests, information, and negotiations. Article 13 of the 1928 Havana Convention on Diplomatic Officers set out the rule without any qualification. Under modern practice, however, which is reflected in Article 41.2, it is becoming more usual for direct contact with other government departments to be permitted by agreement in particular cases or by practice. It has long been the understanding that specialist attachés, whether·military, cultural or economic, are authorized to do business directly with the corresponding specialist ministry in the receiving State. The extension of this practice to wider categories of diplomatic staff reflects the degree to which the substance of international relations has become highly technical as well as a greater tendency in the conduct of relations between States to use the most informal and effective channels for communication. The Ministry of Foreign Affairs will, however, always expect to be kept informed of the substance of exchanges of any importance or potential political sensitivity between an embassy and another ministry. This was in effect what was meant by the reply given in 1979 by the United Kingdom Prime Minister to a Parliamentary Question: "All foreign countries which maintain missions accredited to the Court of St. James's conduct their business with Ministers and officials of Her Majesty's Government under the auspices of the Foreign and Commonwealth Office." The German Ministry of Foreign Affairs by circular Note to diplomatic missions has made clear that they are not permitted to correspond directly with provincial or local authorities on general questions.

* * *

Duty regarding Use of Mission Premises

The duty not to use mission premises in any manner incompatible with the functions of the mission is to some extent an aspect of the duty in Article 41.1 to respect the laws and regulations of the receiving State. To take the most extreme case, the members of the diplomatic mission may not use the premises to plot the removal or the destabilization of the government or the political system of the receiving State. On a more mundane level, if for example the receiving State bans the manufacture of alcohol or the operation of gaming houses, then mission premises may not be used for those purposes. Just as personal immunity from jurisdiction does not confer or imply exemption from local laws and regulations, so inviolability of mission premises does not confer or imply exemption from local laws for acts or events taking place on these premises. The meaning of inviolability and of the now discredited theory of exterritoriality [sic] is discussed more fully above under Article 22. Even although the local law can not be supervised by inspection from local fire or building safety officers·or enforced through legal proceedings, States do in general accept without question that they are subject to local law on such matters as obtaining planning permission before carrying out structural alterations to their premises.

The duty in regard to use of mission premises is, however, wider than the duty to respect local laws. It would for example cover such activities as running a commercial restaurant or a trade promotion shop on mission premises—activities which are not in themselves illegal but which are not within the scope of the proper functions of a diplomatic mission as described in Article 3 and which if carried on in mission premises are likely to offend the receiving State or to constitute an abuse of the special status of the premises. Premises which are used solely for such purposes may of course not be accepted by the receiving State as constituting "premises of the mission" at all within the definition given in Article 1 of the Convention. Thus, for example, the United Kingdom Government in their Review of the Vienna Convention said:

> we will take appropriate administrative action in the event of abuse or suspected abuse, including withdrawal of diplomatic status from existing premises where they are not being used for purposes compatible with the legitimate functions of a mission. As a general rule we regard the following types of activity as being incompatible with the functions of a mission: trading or other activities conducted for financial gain (e.g. selling tickets for airlines or holidays, or charging fees for language classes or public lectures) and educational activities (e.g. schools or students' hostels).

The United States Secretary of State, in a circular Note to Chiefs of Mission at Washington in 1987, emphasized the Government's position that the use of premises or other property of diplomatic missions to engage in commercial activity (other than that incidental to the maintenance and operation of the post or performance of diplomatic functions) was incompatible with the status of these establishments. Particular attention was drawn to the use of mission bank accounts for commercial transactions other than those identified above.

Sanctions Against Diplomats

Statement of the Minister for Foreign Affairs of the Netherlands.
2 Netherlands Yearbook of International Law 170 (1971).*

During a * * * debate in the Parliamentary Standing Committee for Foreign Affairs, the Minister for Foreign Affairs made, inter alia, the following remarks: * * * a foreign diplomat cannot be prosecuted, unless his Government or he himself waives his right to immunity * * *

> Yet, there are some sanctions. First, expulsion from the host country, which goes further than recall. * * * Secondly, the person in question can be called to account through his ambassador * * * and one can ensure that civil liability, at least, be assumed. Thirdly, the foreign government does sometimes take this liability on itself. There have been cases of ordinary offences such as nonpayment of large amounts for the purchase of cars, food, etc. being committed; in these cases the nomination of a new ambassador was made conditional on previous settlement of those questions. * * * [I]t is a principle of public international law that the host country should put nothing in the way of a diplomat which would hinder him from complete freedom to exercise his functions and should remove any existing hindrances. [But there] are of course limits; for instance, when a diplomat obviously abuses his position. I am thinking of cases in which espionage activities lead to expulsion. Then there are local customs: one should

---

* Reprinted by permission of T.M.C. Asser Instituut, The Hague.

behave according to local standards. One also oversteps the limit, therefore, by violating unwritten morals of a host country, by behaving in a provocative manner, by being drunk in a public place or, in countries where ladies go veiled, by insisting on seeing what is going on behind the veil. I just give a few examples that do not require the exercise of much imagination on the part of this illustrious assembly. In these cases of what I would call overstepping the limit, the diplomat concerned may be declared persona non grata * * *

Case Concerning United States Diplomatic And Consular Staff In Tehran (United States v. Iran)

International Court of Justice, 1980 [1980] I.C.J.Rep. 3.

[On November 27, 1979, the United States instituted proceedings in the International Court of Justice against Iran with respect to the seizure and holding as hostages in Tehran on November 4, 1979, of American diplomatic and consular personnel. Iran did not file any pleading and did not appoint an agent to appear on its behalf. It sent to the court, however, two letters in which it defined its position and contended that the taking of the hostages might be justified by the existence of special circumstances. The court examined that contention]:

* * *

81.   In his letters of 9 December 1979 and 16 March 1980, as previously recalled, Iran's Minister for Foreign Affairs referred to the present case as only "a marginal and secondary aspect of an overall problem". This problem, he maintained, "involves, inter alia, more than 25 years of continual interference by the United States in the internal affairs of Iran, the shameless exploitation of our country, and numerous crimes perpetrated against the Iranian people, contrary to and in conflict with all international and humanitarian norms". In the first of the two letters he indeed singled out amongst the "crimes" which he attributed to the United States an alleged complicity on the part of the [CIA] in the coup d'état of 1953 and in the restoration of the Shah to the throne of Iran. Invoking these alleged crimes, the Iranian Foreign Minister took the position that the United States' Application could not be examined by the Court divorced from its proper context, which he insisted was "the whole political dossier of the relations between Iran and the United States over the last 25 years".

82.   [Other information before the court suggested that the criminal activities asserted in the letter consisted of espionage and U.S. interference in Iran centered upon its embassy in Tehran.]

* * *

85.   * * * It is for the very purpose of providing a remedy for such possible abuses of diplomatic functions that Article 9 of the 1961 Convention on Diplomatic Relations stipulates:

1.   The receiving State may at any time and without having to explain its decision, notify the sending State that the head of the mission or any member of the diplomatic staff of the mission is persona

non grata or that any other member of the staff of the mission is not acceptable. In any such case, the sending State shall, as appropriate, either recall the person concerned or terminate his functions with the mission. A person may be declared non grata or not acceptable before arriving in the territory of the receiving State.

2.   If the sending State refuses or fails within a reasonable period to carry out its obligations under paragraph 1 of this Article, the receiving State may refuse to recognize the person concerned as a member of the mission.

The 1963 Convention contains, in Article 23, paragraphs 1 and 4, analogous provisions in respect of consular officers and consular staff. Paragraph 1 of Article 9 of the 1961 Convention, and paragraph 4 of Article 23 of the 1963 Convention, take account of the difficulty that may be experienced in practice of proving such abuses in every case or, indeed, of determining exactly when exercise of the diplomatic function, expressly recognized in Article 3(1)(d) of the 1961 Convention, of "ascertaining by all lawful means conditions and developments in the receiving State" may be considered as involving such acts as "espionage" or "interference in internal affairs". The way in which Article 9, paragraph 1, takes account of any such difficulty is by providing expressly in its opening sentence that the receiving State may "at any time and without having to explain its decision" notify the sending State that any particular member of its diplomatic mission is "persona non grata" or "not acceptable" (and similarly Article 23, paragraph 4, of the 1963 Convention provides that "the receiving State is not obliged to give to the sending State reasons for its decision"). Beyond that remedy for dealing with abuses of the diplomatic function by individual members of a mission, a receiving State has in its hands a more radical remedy if abuses of their functions by members of a mission reach serious proportions. This is the power which every receiving State has, at its own discretion, to break off diplomatic relations with a sending State and to call for the immediate closure of the offending mission.

86.   The rules of diplomatic law, in short, constitute a self-contained regime which, on the one hand, lays down the receiving State's obligations regarding the facilities, privileges and immunities to be accorded to diplomatic missions and, on the other, foresees their possible abuse by members of the mission and specifies the means at the disposal of the receiving State to counter any such abuse. These means are, by their nature, entirely efficacious, for unless the sending State recalls the member of the mission objected to forthwith, the prospect of the almost immediate loss of his privileges and immunities, because of the withdrawal by the receiving State of his recognition as a member of the mission, will in practice compel that person, in his own interest, to depart at once. But the principle of the inviolability of the persons of diplomatic agents and the premises of diplomatic missions is one of the very foundations of this long-established regime, to the evolution of which the traditions of Islam made a substantial contribution. The fundamental character of the principle of inviolability is, moreover, strongly underlined by the provisions of Articles 44 and 45 of the Convention of 1961 (cf. also Articles 26 and 27 of the Convention of 1963). Even in the case of armed conflict or in the case of a breach in diplomatic

relations those provisions require that both the inviolability of the members of a diplomatic mission and of the premises, property and archives of the mission must be respected by the receiving State. Naturally, the observance of this principle does not mean—and this the Applicant Government expressly acknowledges—that a diplomatic agent caught in the act of committing an assault or other offence may not, on occasion, be briefly arrested by the police of the receiving State in order to prevent the commission of the particular crime. But such eventualities bear no relation at all to what occurred in the present case.

* * *

[By 13 votes to 2, the court decided, inter alia, that the conduct of Iran was in violation of the rules of international law on diplomatic immunity and by 12 votes to 3 decided that Iran was under an obligation to make reparation to the United States for the injury.]

Notes and Questions

1. **Deterrence.** The sanctions discussed above should have sufficient adverse effects upon the diplomatic agent's career to provide a stronger deterrent than even the waiver of immunity. However, those sanctions do not respond to the need to do justice to third parties who are prevented by immunity from pursing just claims. Nor do they point to criminal penalties which might reflect strongly established policies of both the sending the receiving state. Does the international system provide solutions to these problems?

2. **Prosecution in the sending state.** Vienna Convention Article 31 takes an important step in that direction in providing in para 4 that "The immunity of a diplomatic agent from the jurisdiction of the receiving state does not exempt him from the jurisdiction of the sending state." The active nationality principle could also help with jurisdiction of the sending state. What else might be required for this procedure to be effective?

3. **Civil actions.** Another possibility in civil actions is legal action by the claimant in the civil courts of the diplomat's home country. Even assuming the service of process could be effected, do you see any problems in this procedure? Another is for the claimant to enlist the assistance of its own government, not only to apply pressures as suggested in the readings, but ultimately also to lodge a formal diplomatic claim against the sending state, or even to take the case to the International Court of Justice. In what situations would that help?

4. **Reform.** In all of these possibilities, the international system is still decentralized and fragmented. If you were devising a comprehensive reform of the system what elements would you consider? How would you take into account the known sensitivities of governments about dignity, embarrassment and sovereignty?

Other Persons Entitled to Diplomatic Immunity

Organization of a diplomatic mission. The Vienna Convention divides the personnel of a diplomatic mission into four categories and assigns different privileges and immunities to each. In assessing the difference in treatment of each of these categories, it is useful to know who are the persons in each and what they do. The information below is a simplified organization of a diplomatic mission.

The first category is the diplomatic staff. Its members have diplomatic rank. They are the ones who are engaged in the performance of the diplomatic function in the strict sense of the term. These diplomatic agents, as they are called in the Vienna Convention, include the chief of mission (ambassador, or minister or chargé d'affaires), counsellor or deputy chief of mission, the first, second and third secretaries (of embassy), the military attachés (air, army, navy) and such other attachés (for commerce, labor, treasury and other matters) as the receiving state may agree to recognize as diplomatic agents.

Variant state interests as to the reach of immunity. Many diplomatic missions, including those of the United States, make heavy use of nationals of the host state. It is in the general interest of states housing missions to have a fairly wide reach of immunity for all members of the embassy community, including the local employees. On the other hand, objections are often publicly raised if diplomatic immunity were widely accorded to fellow nationals and resident aliens because of their employment by a foreign mission.

Status of Families and "Husband–In–Fact" of Diplomat

Opinion of the Office for Public International Law of the Swiss Federal Political Department. 33 Annuaire Suisse De Droit International 224 (1977).[a]

[In a note dated July 13, 1976, the Office for Public International Law of the Federal Political Department handed down a ruling on the question whether the de facto husband of a woman diplomat accredited to Switzerland could avail himself of the privileges and immunities accorded by Article 37, paragraph 1, of the Vienna Convention on Diplomatic Relations of April 18, 1961, " * * * to members of the family of a diplomatic agent who are part of his household and not nationals of the accrediting state."]

Doctrine is silent on this question. Jurisprudence [case law] appears to be nonexistent. Albeit, we can cite a decision of the Tribunal Civil of the Seine in 1907 holding that the wife of a diplomat, who had been authorized to establish a separate domicile as a result of a suit for separation, continued to enjoy diplomatic privileges and immunities.

The working papers of the International Law Commission (ILC) do not address themselves to the precise question of a spouse-in-fact. But they do furnish useful guidelines as to the circle of members of the family entitled to diplomatic privileges. The ILC has noted in particular that the chief, or member, of a mission may be elderly or a bachelor and be assisted by a sister, an adult daughter or even a sister-in-law, who acts as lady of the house * * *. In its comments on Article 36 (practically identical to the

a. Translation by the editors. Reprinted by permission of Schulthess Polygraphischer Verlag AG, Zurich.

future Article 37 of the Convention) of the draft articles (concerning diplomatic relations and immunities), the ILC comments:

> So far as concerns diplomatic agents * * * who enjoy the full range of privileges and immunities, the Commission, in conformity with existing practice, proposed that these prerogatives be equally accorded to members of their families, on the condition they be members of their households and they not be nationals of the accrediting state. The Commission did not want to go so far as precisely to define the meaning of the term "members of the family" or to set a maximum age for children. The spouse and the minor children, at least, are universally acknowledged to be members of the family, but there can be cases where other relatives also qualify if they are part of the household. In stipulating that in order to claim privileges and immunities, a member of the family must be part of the household, the Commission means to indicate that close relationships or special circumstances must be involved. These special circumstances may exist when a relative keeps house for the ambassador though they may not be closely related or when a distant relative has lived in the bosom of the family for so long he ends up being a part of it.

Strictly speaking the term family means a group of persons linked to each other by marriage (relationship by affinity), by descent (relationship by consanguinity) or by adoption. But the commentary clearly leads one to think that the ILC preferred to put the emphasis on the common household rather than on the links of marriage. Therefore it seems to be in conformity with the spirit of the Convention to include a spouse-in-fact among the members of the family. The Convention never made it its goal to regulate the private lives of diplomatic agents, but [rather made it its goal] to regulate the granting of diplomatic privileges.

In conformity with the preamble to the Vienna Convention, the purpose of the Convention's privileges is not to create advantages for individuals but to insure the effective performance of the functions of diplomatic missions insofar as they represent states. They are extended to the family that is part of the household of the diplomatic agent because the family is supposed to represent that which is dearest to him and because, by threats to it, one would be able to compromise the free exercise of the mission of the agent. Besides, the family in the sense of the Convention includes a limited number of persons. Giving a privileged status to its members would not in itself involve major risks of abuse. The family does not vary every day in its composition. It is relatively stable. It exists within the orbit of the diplomatic agent who can exert upon it a certain control.

All of these elements are present in the case at bar. The theoretical foundation of the law of diplomatic privileges and immunities rests on the idea that certain persons—first of all the members of his family—may be considered as an extension of the personality of the diplomatic agent * * *. As it were, there are sometimes circumstances under which one must hold them to be special and assimilate a person, even though a stranger to the agent (diplomat) by blood or by marriage, to a member of the family within the meaning of Article 37, paragraph 1, of the Convention. Such is the case with a long-time liaison, officially recognized as such by the accrediting state, between two spouses-in-fact who travel together, each with an official passport. The closeness of the bond seems to us further strengthened when the husband-in-fact, far from wanting to create his own center of interests and ·exercise a gainful activity in the accrediting state, manifests an intention to live under the same roof and in the financial orbit of the diplomatic agent. * * *

3. SPECIAL MISSIONS AND HEADS OF STATE OR PERSONS OF HIGH RANK

Notes

1. *Special missions.* On December 8, 1969, the General Assembly of the United Nations adopted and opened for signature on December 16, 1969, a Convention on Special Missions. For its text, see U.N. Document A/Res/2530(24) of December 8, 1969 and A/Res/2530(24)_Corr. 1 of January 2, 1970. The Convention entered into force on June 21, 1985. As of 2001, 31 states were parties to the Convention; the United States was not. In Article I, a special mission is defined as a "temporary mission, representing the State, which is sent by one State to another State with the consent of the latter for the purpose of dealing with it on specific questions or of performing in relation to it a specific task."

Like the Vienna Convention on Diplomatic Relations, the Convention on Special Missions breaks down their personnel into four categories— diplomatic staff, administrative and technical staff, service staff and private staff—and grants to the members in each the same immunities, subject to one qualification, as are granted to personnel in the corresponding categories by the Vienna Convention on Diplomatic Relations. The qualification is that in addition to the three types of private acts for which a diplomatic agent is not entitled to immunity from civil and administrative jurisdiction under the Vienna Convention on Diplomatic Relations, a member of the diplomatic staff of a special mission has no immunity from civil and administrative jurisdiction in the case of "an action for damages arising out of an accident caused by a vehicle used outside the official functions of the person concerned." Article 32 (2)(d). By Article 25, the premises of a special mission are made inviolable, and the members of its diplomatic staff enjoy personal inviolability under Article 29.

2. Heads of state and persons of high rank. Article 21 of the Convention on Special Missions provides:

> 1. The Head of the sending State, when he leads a special mission, shall enjoy in the receiving State or in a third State the facilities, privileges and immunities accorded by international law to Heads of State on an official visit.

> 2. The Head of the Government, the Minister for Foreign Affairs and other persons of high rank, when they take part in a special mission of the sending State, shall enjoy in the receiving State or in a

third State, in addition to what is granted by the present Convention, the facilities, privileges and immunities accorded by international law.

The federal department of foreign affairs in Switzerland sent to an embassy in Berne in 1983 a note setting forth its views on the immunities, under customary international law, of foreign chiefs of state and their families. The note stated that a head of state is entitled in a foreign state to absolute immunity from criminal jurisdiction, as are the members of his close family. As to immunity from jurisdiction in civil matters, the practice of states varies. Some states distinguish between the official acts of the head of state and his private acts, the immunity extending only to the official ones. If the department were asked to take a position regarding the private acts of a foreign head of state in Switzerland, it would recognize the immunity, except for litigation involving an interest in immovable property, an interest in an estate locally administered, or an illegal act committed in his private capacity. 40 Ann. Suisse Dr. Int'l 182 (1984).

United States v. Noriega

746 F.Supp. 1506 (S.D.Fla.1990).

OMNIBUS ORDER

■ HOEVELER, DISTRICT JUDGE. [The facts and non-immunity aspects of the case are presented in Ch. 15].

* * *

Subsequent to the indictment, the Court granted General Noriega's motion to allow special appearance of counsel, despite the fact that Noriega was a fugitive and not before the Court at that time. Noriega's counsel then moved to dismiss the indictment on the ground that United States laws could not be applied to a foreign leader whose alleged illegal activities all occurred outside the territorial bounds of the United States. Counsel further argued that Noriega was immune from prosecution as a head of state and diplomat, and that his alleged narcotics offenses constituted acts of state not properly reviewable by this Court.

* * *

As is evident from the unusual factual background underlying this case, the Court is presented with several issues of first impression. This is the first time that a leader or de facto leader of a sovereign nation has been forcibly brought to the United States to face criminal charges. The fact that General Noriega's apprehension occurred in the course of a military action only further underscores the complexity of the issues involved. * * *

* * *

A. Head of State Immunity

Grounded in customary international law, the doctrine of head of state immunity provides that a head of state is not subject to the jurisdiction of foreign courts, at least as to official acts taken during the ruler's term of ◁— office. The rationale behind the doctrine is to promote international comity and respect among sovereign nations by ensuring that leaders are free to perform their governmental duties without being subject to detention, arrest, or embarrassment in a foreign country's legal system[11] * * *

In order to assert head of state immunity, a government official must be recognized as a head of state. Noriega has never been recognized as Panama's Head of State either under the Panamanian Constitution or by the United States. Title VI, Article 170 of the Panamanian Constitution provides for an executive branch composed of the President and Ministers of State, neither of which applies to Noriega. Officially, Noriega is the Commandante of the Panamanian Defense Forces, but he was never elected to head Panama's government and in fact abrogated the Panamanian presidential elections of May 7, 1989. More importantly, the United States government has never accorded Noriega head of state status, but rather continued to recognize President Delvalle as the legitimate leader of Panama while Noriega was in power. As this Court held in a previous case involving the Republic of Panama, the Executive's decision to recognize President Delvalle and not the Defendant as Panama's head of state is binding on the Court. The ruling in that case—which I find no reason to depart from here—was based on a line of case law holding that recognition of foreign governments and their leaders is a discretionary foreign policy decision committed to the Executive branch and thus conclusive upon the courts.

* * *

Aside from the fact that neither Panama nor the United States recognizes Noriega as a head of state, the defendant concedes that he does not fit within traditional notions of a head of state as defined by customary international law.[13] He nonetheless argues that he is entitled to head of state immunity as the de facto ruler of Panama, "regardless of the source of his power or the nature of his rule." The defendant cites numerous newspaper reports and excerpts of congressional testimony to the effect that Noriega effectively controlled Panama. In fact, this Court has previously acknowledged that, despite the official recognition of Delvalle, Noriega was the de facto head of Panama's government. United States v. Noriega, 683 F.Supp. at 1374, n. 3. But simply because Noriega may have in fact run the country of Panama does not mean he is entitled to head of state immunity, since the grant of immunity is a privilege which the United

11. Given this rationale, there is ample doubt whether head of state immunity extends to private or criminal acts in violation of U.S. law. See In re Doe, 860 F.2d at 45; In re Grand Jury Proceedings, Doe #700, 817 F.2d at 1111; Philippines v. Marcos (Marcos I), 806 F.2d 344, 360 (2d Cir. 1986). Criminal activities such as narcotics trafficking with which Defendant is charged can hardly be considered official acts or governmental duties which promote a sovereign state's interests, especially where, as here, the activity was allegedly undertaken for the sole benefit of the foreign leader. * * *

13. The provision of customary international law cited by Defendant as an accept-able definition of a head of state would not include Noriega. The Convention on the Prevention and Punishment of Crimes Against Internationally Protected Persons, Including Diplomatic Agents (T.I.A.S. No. 8532; 28 U.S.T.1975) defines "internationally protected person" as "(a) a Head of State," including any member of a collegial body performing the functions of a Head of State under the constitution of the State concerned, a Head of Government or a Minister of Foreign Affairs? * * * Noriega has not shown that he was either the ceremonial or official head of government, and he does not otherwise fulfill the definition.

States may withhold from any claimant. The Schooner Exchange v. M'Faddon * * * Indeed, deference to the Executive branch in matters concerning relations with foreign nations is the primary rationale supporting immunity for heads of state. Since the only reason Noriega would be entitled to immunity as a head of state is because of such judicial deference to the Executive, his claim to a "right" of immunity against the express wishes of the Government is wholly without merit.

The "head of state" argument comes to the Court unencumbered by evidence; the arguments were made largely on the basis of general information made available by the media. However, accepting as true statements of counsel regarding Defendant's position of power, to hold that immunity from prosecution must be granted "regardless of his source of power or nature of rule" would allow illegitimate dictators the benefit of their unscrupulous and possibly brutal seizures of power. No authority exists for such a novel extension of head of state immunity, and the Court declines to create one here. Since the United States has never recognized General Noriega as Panama's head of state, he has no claim to head of state immunity.

* * *

Regina v. Bartle and the Commissioner of Police for the Metropolis and Others (Appellants) v. Ex Parte Pinochet (Respondent)

United Kingdom, House of Lords March 24,1999,38 I.L.M. 581 (1999).

[A chronology of the numerous opinions and actions in this case up to April 15, 1999 is set forth in a note from the Editors of the I.L.M. at 38 I.L.M. 581. On March 24, 1999 individual opinions were delivered by each of the seven members of the Law Lords panel that decided this phase of the Pinochet case, including the opinion of Lord Browne–Wilkinson from which the excerpts below are taken. Briefly stated, the Spanish authorities sought to extradite Mr. Pinochet from the United Kingdom to Spain to stand trial on a number of charges, including conspiracy to torture, conspiracy to take hostages, conspiracy to torture in which murder was committed, torture, conspiracy to murder, and attempted murder.

The Queen's Bench Divisional Court quashed warrants of arrest on the ground, among others, that Mr. Pinochet was entitled as a former head of state to immunity from these charges. Acting on behalf of the Spanish government, the U.K Crown Prosecution Service appealed to the House of Lords, with leave of the Divisional Court which certified the point of law of general importance as being: "The proper interpretation and scope of the immunity enjoyed by a former head of state from arrest and extradition proceedings in the United Kingdom in respect of acts committed while he was head of state." The excerpts below from Lord Browne–Wilkinson's opinion consider that question with respect to a limited period found to be consistent with U.K. law, when torture committed abroad was criminal in the U.K and qualified as an extradition crime. By a majority of six to one, the House of Lords denied immunity on the torture charges. Excerpts on other issues appear in Chapters 3 on Jurisdiction, 16 on the International Criminal Law, and 9 on Human Rights.]

LORD BROWNE–WILKINSON

My Lords,

As is well known, this case concerns an attempt by the Government of Spain to extradite Senator Pinochet from this country to stand trial in Spain for crimes committed (primarily in Chile) during the period when Senator Pinochet was head of state in Chile. The interaction between the various legal issues which arise is complex. I will therefore seek, first, to give a short account of the legal principles which are in play in order that my exposition of the facts will be more intelligible.

State immunity

This is the point around which most of the argument turned. It is of considerable general importance internationally since, if Senator Pinochet is not entitled to immunity in relation to the acts of torture alleged to have occurred after 29 September 1988, it will be the first time so far as counsel have discovered when a local domestic court has refused to afford immunity to a head of state or former head of state on the grounds that there can be no immunity against prosecution for certain international crimes.

Given the importance of the point, it is surprising how narrow is the area of dispute. There is general agreement between the parties as to the rules of statutory immunity and the rationale which underlies them. The issue is whether international law grants state immunity in relation to the international crime of torture and, if so, whether the Republic of Chile is entitled to claim such immunity even though Chile, Spain and the United Kingdom are all parties to the Torture Convention and therefore "contractually" bound to give effect to its provisions from 8 December 1988 at the latest.

It is a basic principle of international law that one sovereign state (the forum state) does not adjudicate on the conduct of a foreign state. The foreign state is entitled to procedural immunity from the processes of the forum state. This immunity extends to both criminal and civil liability. State immunity probably grew from the historical immunity of the person of the monarch. In any event, such personal immunity of the head of state persists to the present day: the head of state is entitled to the same immunity as the state itself The diplomatic representative of the foreign state in the forum state is also afforded the same immunity in recognition of the dignity of the state which he represents. This immunity enjoyed by a head of state in power and an ambassador in post is a complete immunity attaching to the person of the head of state or ambassador and rendering him immune from all actions or prosecutions whether or not they relate to matters done for the benefit of the state. Such immunity is said to be granted ratione personae.

What then when the ambassador leaves his post or the head of state is deposed? The position of the ambassador is covered by the Vienna Convention on Diplomatic Relations, 1961. After providing for immunity from arrest (Article 29) and from criminal and civil jurisdiction (Article 31),

Article 39(1) provides that the ambassador's privileges shall be enjoyed from the moment he takes up post, and subsection (2) provides:

"(2) When the functions of a person enjoying privileges and immunities have come to an end, such privileges and immunities shall normally cease at the moment when he leaves the country, or on expiry of a reasonable period in which to do so, but shall subsist until that time, even in case of armed conflict. However, with respect to acts performed by such a person in the exercise of his functions as a member of the mission, immunity shall continue to subsist."

The continuing partial immunity of the ambassador after leaving post is of a different kind from that enjoyed ratione personae while he was in post. Since he is no longer the representative of the foreign state he merits no particular privileges or immunities as a person. However in order to preserve the integrity of the activities of the foreign state during the period when he was ambassador, it is necessary to provide that immunity is afforded to his official acts during his tenure in post. If this were not done the sovereign immunity of the state could be evaded by calling in question acts done during the previous ambassador's time. Accordingly under Article 39(2) the ambassador, like any other official of the state, enjoys immunity in relation to his official acts done while he was an official. This limited immunity, ratione materiae, is to be contrasted with the former immunity ratione personae which gave complete immunity to all activities whether public or private.

In my judgment at common law a former head of state enjoys similar immunities, ratione materiae, once he ceases to be head of state. He too loses immunity ratione personae on ceasing to be head of state: see Watts The Legal Position in International Law of Heads of States, Heads of Government and Foreign Ministers p. 88 and the cases there cited. He can be sued on his private obligations: Ex–King Farouk of Egypt v. Christian Dior (I 957) 24 I.L.R. 228, Jimenez v. Aristeguieta (I 962) 31 1 F. 2d 547. As ex head of state he cannot be sued in respect of acts performed whilst head of state in his public capacity: Hatch v. Baez [1876] 7 Hun. 596. Thus, at common law, the position of the former ambassador and the former head of state appears to be much the same: both enjoy immunity for acts done in performance of their respective functions whilst in office.

* * *

The question then which has to be answered is whether the alleged Organisation of state torture by Senator Pinochet (if proved) would constitute an act committed by Senator Pinochet as part of his official functions as head of state. It is not enough to say that it cannot be part of the functions of the head of state to commit a crime. Actions which are criminal under the local law can still have been done officially and therefore give rise to immunity ratione materiae. The case needs to be analyzed more closely.

Can it be said that the commission of a crime which is an international crime against humanity and jus cogens is an act done in an official capacity on behalf of the state? I believe there to be strong ground for saying that the implementation of torture as defined by the Torture Convention cannot be a state function. This is the view taken by Sir Arthur Watts (supra) who said (at p. 82):

> "While generally international law ... does not directly involve obligations on individuals personally, that is not always appropriate, particularly for acts of such seriousness that they constitute not merely international wrongs (in the broad sense of a civil wrong) but rather international crimes which offend against the public order of the international community. States are artificial legal persons: they can only act through the institutions and agencies of the state, which means, ultimately through its officials and other individuals acting on behalf of the state. For international conduct which is so serious as to be tainted with criminality to be regarded as attributable only to the impersonal state and not to the individuals who ordered or perpetrated it is both unrealistic and offensive to common notions of justice.

> "The idea that individuals who commit international crimes are internationally accountable for them has now become an accepted part of international law. Problems in this area—such as the non-existence of any standing international tribunal to have jurisdiction over such crimes, and the lack of agreement as to what acts are internationally criminal for this purpose—have not affected the general acceptance of the principle of individual responsibility for international criminal conduct."

Later, at p. 84, he said:

> "It can no longer be doubted that as a matter of general customary international law a head of state will personally be liable to be called to account if there is sufficient evidence that he authorised or perpetrated such serious international crimes."

It can be objected that Sir Arthur was looking at those cases where the international community has established an international tribunal in relation to which the regulating document expressly makes the head of state subject to the tribunal's jurisdiction: see, for example, the Nuremberg Charter Article 7, the Statute of the International Tribunal for former Yugoslavia, the Statute of the International Tribunal for Rwanda and the Statute of the International Criminal Court. It is true that in these cases it is expressly said that the head of state or former head of state is subject to the court's jurisdiction. But those are cases in which a new court with no existing jurisdiction is being established. The jurisdiction being established by the Torture Convention and the Hostages Convention is one where existing domestic courts of all the countries are being authorised and required to take jurisdiction internationally. The question is whether, in this new type of jurisdiction, the only possible view is that those made subject to the jurisdiction of each of the state courts of the world in relation to torture are not entitled to claim immunity.

I have doubts whether, before the coming into force of the Torture Convention, the existence of the international crime of torture as jus cogens was enough to justify the conclusion that the organization of state torture could not rank for immunity purposes as performance of an official function. At that stage there was no international tribunal to punish torture and no general jurisdiction to permit or require its punishment in domestic courts. Not until there was some form of universal jurisdiction for the punishment of the crime of torture could it really be talked about as a fully constituted international crime. But in my judgment the Torture Convention did provide what was missing: a worldwide universal jurisdiction. Further, it required all member states to ban and outlaw torture: Article 2. How can it be for international law purposes an official function to do something which international law itself prohibits and criminalises? Thirdly, an essential feature of the international crime of torture is that it must be committed "by or with the acquiescence of a public official or other person acting in an official capacity." As a result all defendants in torture cases will be state officials. Yet, if the former head of state has immunity, the man most responsible will escape liability while his inferiors (the chiefs of police, junior army officers) who carried out his orders will be liable. I find it impossible to accept that this was the intention.

Finally, and to my mind decisively, if the implementation of a torture regime is a public function giving rise to immunity ratione materiae, this produces bizarre results. Immunity ratione materiae applies not only to ex-heads of state and ex-ambassadors but to all state officials who have been involved in carrying out the functions of the state. Such immunity is necessary in order to prevent state immunity being circumvented by prosecuting or suing the official who, for example, actually carried out the torture when a claim against the head of state would be precluded by the doctrine of immunity. If that applied to the present case, and if the implementation of the torture regime is to be treated as official business sufficient to found an immunity for the former head of state, it must also be official business sufficient to justify immunity for his inferiors who actually did the torturing. Under the Convention the international crime of torture can only be committed by an official or someone in an official capacity. They would all be entitled to immunity. It would follow that there can be no case outside Chile in which a successful prosecution for torture can be brought unless the State of Chile is prepared to waive its right to its officials' immunity. Therefore the whole elaborate structure of universal jurisdiction over torture committed by officials is rendered abortive and one of the main objectives of the Torture Convention—to provide a system under which there is no safe haven for torturers—will have been frustrated. In my judgment all these factors together demonstrate that the notion of continued immunity for ex-heads of state is inconsistent with the provisions of the Torture Convention.

For these reasons in my judgment if, as alleged, Senator Pinochet organised and authorised torture after 8 December 1988, he was not acting in any capacity which gives rise to immunity ratione materiae because such actions were contrary to international law, Chile had agreed to outlaw such conduct and Chile had agreed with the other parties to the Torture Convention that all signatory states should have jurisdiction to try official torture (as defined in the Convention) even if such torture were committed in Chile.

As to the charges of murder and conspiracy to murder, no one has advanced any reason why the ordinary rules of immunity should not apply and Senator Pinochet is entitled to such immunity.

For these reasons, I would allow the appeal so as to permit the extradition proceedings to proceed on the allegation that torture in pursuance of a conspiracy to commit torture, including the single act of torture which is alleged in charge 30, was being committed by Senator Pinochet after 8 December 1988 when he lost his immunity.

Notes and Questions.

1. *Sovereign immunity or diplomatic immunity?* The Pinochet opinion, like others in the readings above, raises at times the question whether the issue being decided is one of sovereign immunity or of diplomatic immunity. Or are both part and parcel of the same thing? Does it help to speak of the ratione materiae or ratione personae? Does Article 39(2) apply to persons who are not diplomatic agents? Lord Browne–Wilkinson spoke of the common law as the bridge. Is that an appropriate solution?

2. *The impact of Pinochet.* Pinochet is theoretically quite far reaching if it applies broadly to violations of humanitarian law and serious war crimes, including international aggression committed by government officers, or to all subjects of universal jurisdiction under international law? Would this be a desirable outcome when the law of aggression, for example, may not yet be fully developed and free from ambiguity? Would cases like Mr. Pinochet's be better heard by a multinational forum, like the International Criminal Court, rather than national courts? Why? What would be a reasonable interim solution during the possibly long period before the I.C.C. becomes operational?

3. *Query.* How would you advise former heads of state to conduct themselves in the light of the Pinochet case?

SECTION C.   CONSULAR IMMUNITY
Consular Function

The Vienna Convention on Consular Relations was signed on April 24, 1963. The Convention entered into force on March 19, 1967; in 2001, there were 165 parties, up from 38 parties in 1992. This Convention entered into force for the United States in 1969. 21 U.S.T. 77, 596 U.N.T.S. 261. Selected text is reproduced in the Documentary Supplement.

————————

Re Rissmann
Italy, Court of Genoa, 1970.
1 Italian Yearbook of International Law 254 (1975).*

Facts.—By complaint lodged with the Prosecutor of Genoa dated 13 July 1966, Mrs. Mancuso Santa in Cucco declared: * * * by decision dated 21 July 1964 the Genoa Minors Court had given her custody of her minor daughter Maria Luisa, born in Genoa [in] 1947 from her first marriage with the German citizen Muller Werner; which marriage was dissolved by

* Reprinted with the permission of Editoriale Scientifica, s.r.l., Naples.

the Hannover Court with a sentence of divorce on 2 October 1956, recognized and made effective in Italy by the Court of Appeal of Genoa by judgment dated 31 March 1961; that following such judgment the minor had acquired Italian citizenship, in accordance with a note dated 5 July 1965 from the Prefettura of Genoa; that by letter dated 8 March 1966 addressed to the Consul General for Germany in Genoa and, with a copy to the Head of the Police, she, as legitimate guardian of the said minor child, had given notice of her disapproval to the issuing of a passport or of any other equivalent document to the said minor, even if requested by a third party; * * * that in March 1966, she, following a serious act of indiscipline by the minor * * * had agreed for her to stay in the boarding house Istituto Madri Pie, Genoa * * *; that, however, on the morning of 11 July 1966 a nun of the Institute had informed her that her daughter had gone out * * * and had not come back * * *.

* * *

Therefore the complainant formally called for punishment of whoever was responsible for the disappearance of her daughter, a minor, of the removal of her from her mother's guardianship and of any other criminal action arising from the facts reported by her or subsequently arising therefrom * * *. Following the summons the Prosecutor proceeded to verify the facts reported therein and the further circumstances arising therefrom * * *. On the basis of such results and after acquiring copies of the statements made during the guardianship proceedings by the minor to the President of the Genoa Court for Minors, * * * the Prosecutor made the charge referred to in the heading against Dr. Rissmann, sending a copy thereof to the Consulate of the German Federal Republic in Genoa under cover of a note dated 8 August 1966.

However, the German Embassy in Rome, by memorandum dated 25 August 1966 addressed to the Ministry of Foreign Affairs and through it transmitted to the Ministry of Justice who also sent a copy to the Prosecutor in Genoa, stated that Dr. Rissmann had "in the exercise of his functions and following written request by the father of the German national Maria Luisa Muller, born 7 June 1947, whom he had the right to legally represent, issued her with a German passport", and invoked for the Consul Rissmann the consular immunity provided for in the first paragraph of art. 43 of the Vienna Convention on Consular Relations ratified by both Italy and Germany, stating that in view of this the Consul Rissmann had been ordered not to appear in Court.

* * *

Law.—The question as to whether or not consular immunity exists is clearly a preliminary question to be decided since it is relevant to whether or not Dr. Rissmann is exempt from the jurisdiction of this criminal Court. First and foremost, it calls for consideration as to the nationality of the minor Maria Luisa Muller. There is no doubt that she, German iure sanguinis having been born of parents who were both German at that time, never lost German nationality according to the German law on citizenship.

* * *

It is * * * established that in the same way as Italy, maintaining that Muller had acquired Italian nationality iure communicationis, could legitimately consider her purely as an Italian citizen ignoring her dual nationality, so also could the German Federal Republic, and consequently also the Consul, Rissmann, who was one of the representatives operating abroad, legitimately consider her a German citizen.

Clearly, in view of the fact that, inter alia, the minor had been legally entrusted by the Italian judge to her mother, the Consul in issuing her with a passport as a German citizen and facilitating her return to Germany was certainly acting in conflict with the Italian legal system and behaving in a manner liable to give rise to the criminal charge contained in the indictment in this case.

But it is necessary to clarify the question as to whether there exists in the present case the necessary conditions and circumstances for the application of consular immunity. According to agreed doctrine (developed from jurisprudence of the principal States) and to general international law, even prior to the last Convention on Consular Relations concluded in Vienna [in] 1963 in conformity with the principles of the Charter of the United Nations, there existed functional immunity for Consuls: namely, exemption from local jurisdiction in civil and criminal matters in respect of acts performed in the exercise of their office. Following the same doctrine, a demonstration of the common feeling of states on this matter was afforded by Article II of the Convention of Montreux dated 8 May 1937. This provided that "foreign consuls are subject to the jurisdiction of mixed Courts subject always to the exceptions recognised by international law. In particular, they are not subject to indictment in respect of actions carried out in the exercise of their office".

It should be added that functional immunity, already then generally recognised even in the absence of specific provisions in consular conventions, finds its justification in the general principle according to which the Consul's acts, even though they may be valid within the legal system of territorial State and thus produce legal consequences therein, constitute an activity of the State to which the Consul belongs, and not of the Consul personally, since, in the exercise of his office, he must answer to his government. Such an immunity is not, therefore, confined to judicial proceedings. It is based on a principle of substantive law, and continues even after his tour of office as Consul has terminated.

      * * *

We now come to the Convention on Consular Relations signed in Vienna [in] 1963 by 92 States members of the United Nations, including Italy and the German Federal Republic, and implemented by law. The Court observes that the functional immunity of consuls is explicitly covered by Art. 43 of the Convention, under the title "Immunity from Jurisdiction", the first paragraph of which provides as follows: "Consular officers and consular employees shall not be amenable to the jurisdiction of the judicial or administrative authorities of the receiving State in respect of acts performed in the exercise of consular functions". * * *

We must now examine whether or not the action of the Consul Rissmann which gives rise to this case fell within the scope of his consular functions. As far as concerns the present judgment, suffice to observe that Art. 5 of the Convention includes among consular functions at letters d) and e) respectively, the issuing of passports and travel documents to citizens of the State concerned and the giving of assistance to the same: textually "Consular functions consist in: * * * d) issuing passports and travel documents to nationals of the sending State, * * * e) helping and assisting nationals of the sending State." It is certain that Muller was a German citizen, [so] there can be no doubt that Rissmann, in issuing her with a German passport, was carrying out a true and proper official act as Consul, and this is because, in view of the fact that a minor was in question, he had not only the consent but even the express request on the part of the father, a German citizen, entitled to guardianship of her which entitlement had never lapsed * * *.

It should not be forgotten that Consuls, being State agents operating abroad, do not exceed the scope of their functions when they act in accordance with the laws of their country which they must comply with in so far as these laws are to be applied abroad.

As far as concerns the cooperation of Rissmann in furthering the return of the minor to Germany by means of booking and acquiring the air ticket and the assistance given to her for this purpose, it must be stressed that this undoubtedly pertains to the consular office. First and foremost, such an assistance was given to a minor German citizen, upon the request of the father, a German national, exercising guardianship rights over her. From the knowledge that the Consul had of the history of Muller, as it had been referred to him by her and her father, he had valid reason—even independently from actual truth of the case that, as proved by evidence before the Court, had been explained to him only by the afore-mentioned as a situation of dramatic tension and intolerability—to respond to the appeal for assistance directed to him by a fellow country woman who, among other things, was by then 19 years of age.

* * * [W]e must * * * hold that proceedings cannot be brought against Rissmann in respect of the charges made against him, since, as a person who enjoys consular immunity, he is exempted from criminal action * * *.

Case Concerning the Vienna Convention on Consular Relations (Paraguay v. United States)

International Court of Justice, April 9,1998, 37 I.L.M. 810 (1998).*

The International Court of Justice,

* * *

After deliberation,

Having regard to Articles 41 and 48 of the Statute of the Court and to Articles 73, 74 and 75 of the Rules of Court,

* Reprinted with the permission of the American Society of International Law.

Having regard to the Application filed in the Registry of the Court on 3 April 1998, whereby the Republic of Paraguay (hereinafter "Paraguay") instituted proceedings against the United States of America (hereinafter "the United States") for "violations of the Vienna Convention on Consular Relations [of 24 April 1963]" (hereinafter the "Vienna Convention") allegedly committed by the United States,

Makes the following Order:

1.   Whereas, in its aforementioned Application, Paraguay bases the jurisdiction of the Court on Article 36, paragraph 1, of the Statute of the Court and on Article I of the Optional Protocol concerning the Compulsory Settlement of Disputes, which accompanies the Vienna Convention on Consular Relations ("the Optional Protocol");

2.   Whereas, in the Application, it is stated that in 1992 the authorities of the Commonwealth of Virginia arrested a Paraguayan national, Mr. Angel Francisco Breard; whereas it is maintained that he was charged, tried, convicted of culpable homicide and sentenced to death by a Virginia court (the Circuit Court of Arlington County) in 1993, without having been informed, as is required under Article 36, subparagraph I*(b)*, of the Vienna Convention, of his rights under that provision; whereas it is specified that among these rights are the right to request that the relevant consular office of the State of which he is national be advised of his arrest and detention, and the right to communicate with that office; and whereas it is also alleged that the authorities of the Commonwealth of Virginia also did not ad-vise the Paraguayan consular officers of Mr. Breard's detention, and that those officers were only able to render assistance to him from 1996, when the Paraguayan Government learnt by its own means that Mr. Breard was imprisoned in the United States',

* * *

6.   Whereas, on 3 April 1998, after having filed its Application, Paraguay also submitted an urgent request for the indication of provisional measures in order to protect its rights, pursuant to Article 41 of the Statute of the Court and to Articles 73, 74 and 75 of the Rules of Court;

* * *

8.   Whereas, in its request for the indication of provisional measures of protection, Paraguay states that, on 25 February 1998, the Circuit Court of Arlington County, Virginia, ordered that Mr. Breard be executed on 14 April 1998; whereas it emphasizes that "[t]he importance and sanctity of an individual human life are well established in international law" and "[a]s recognized by Article 6 of the International Covenant on Civil and Political Rights, every human being has the inherent right to life and this right shall be protected by law"; and whereas Paraguay states in the following terms the grounds for its request and the possible consequences of its dismissal:

> "Under the grave and exceptional circumstances of this case, and given the paramount interest of Paraguay in the life and liberty of its nationals, provisional measures are urgently needed to protect the life of Paraguay's national and the ability of this Court to order the relief

to which Paraguay is entitled: restitution in kind. Without the provisional measures requested, the United States will execute Mr. Breard before this Court can consider the merits of Paraguay's claims, and Paraguay will be forever deprived of the opportunity to have the status quo ante restored in the event of a judgment in its favour";

* * *

18. Whereas at the hearing, the United States argued that Mr. Breard's guilt was well established, and pointed out that the accused had admitted his guilt, which Paraguay did not dispute; whereas it recognized that Mr. Breard had not been informed, at the time of his arrest and trial, of his rights under Article 36, subparagraph 1(b), of the Vienna Convention, and indicated to the Court that this omission was not deliberate; whereas it nonetheless maintained that the person concerned had all necessary legal assistance, that he understood English well and that the assistance of consular officers would not have changed the outcome of the proceedings brought against him in any way; whereas, referring to State practice in these matters, it stated that the notification provided for by Article 36, subparagraph 1(b), of the Vienna Convention is unevenly made, and that when a claim is made for failure to notify, the only consequence is that apologies are presented by the government responsible; and whereas it submitted that the automatic invalidation of the proceedings initiated and the return to the *status quo ante* as penalties for the failure to notify not only find no support in State practice, but would be unworkable;

19. Whereas the United States also indicated that the State Department had done everything in its power to help the Government of Paraguay as soon as it was informed of the situation in 1996; and whereas it stated that when, on 30 March 1998, Paraguay advised the Government of the United States of its intention to bring proceedings before the Court if the United States Government did not take steps to initiate consultation and to obtain a stay of execution for Mr. Breard, the Government of the United States had emphasized *inter alia* that a stay of execution depended exclusively on the United States Supreme Court and the Governor of Virginia;

24. Whereas Article I of the Optional Protocol, which Paraguay invokes as the basis of jurisdiction of the Court in this case, is worded as follows:

"Disputes arising out of the interpretation or application of the Convention shall lie within the compulsory jurisdiction of the International Court of Justice and may accordingly be brought before the Court by an application made by any party to the dispute being a Party to the present Protocol";

25. Whereas, according to the information communicated by the Secretary–General of the United Nations as depositary, Paraguay and the United States are parties to the Vienna Convention and to the Optional Protocol, in each case without reservation;

35. Whereas the power of the Court to indicate provisional measures under Article 41 of its Statute is intended to preserve the respective rights of the parties pending its decision, and presupposes that irreparable prejudice shall not be caused to rights which are the subject of a dispute in

judicial proceedings; whereas it follows that the Court must be concerned to preserve by such measures the rights which may subsequently be adjudged by the Court to belong either to the Applicant, or to the Respondent; and whereas such measures are only justified if there is urgency;

37.   Whereas the execution of Mr. Breard is ordered for 14 April 1998; and whereas such an execution would render it impossible for the Court to order the relief that Paraguay seeks and thus cause irreparable harm to the rights it claims;

41.   For these reasons,

THE COURT

Unanimously,

Indicates the following provisional measures:

The United States should take all measures at its disposal to ensure that Angel Francisco Breard is not executed pending the final decision in these proceedings, and should inform the Court of all the measures which it has taken in implementation of this Order;

Decides, that, until the Court has given its final decision, it shall remain seised of the matters which form the subject-matter of this Order.

Breard v. Fred W. Greene, Warden, etc.

United States Supreme Court 1998. 523 U.S. 371, 118 S.Ct. 1352, 140 L.Ed.2d 529, 37 I.L.M. 824 (1998).

■ PER CURIAM.

Angel Francisco Breard is scheduled to be executed by the Commonwealth of Virginia this evening at 9:00 p.m. Breard, a citizen of Paraguay, came to the United States in 1986, at the age of 20. In 1992, Breard was charged with the attempted rape and capital murder of Ruth Dickie. At his trial in 1993, the State presented overwhelming evidence of guilt, including semen found on Dickie's body matching Breard's DNA profile and hairs on Dickie's body identical in all microscopic characteristics to hair samples taken from Breard. Breard chose to take the witness stand in his defense. During his testimony, Breard confessed to killing Dickie, but explained that he had only done so because of a Satanic curse placed on him by his father-in-law. Following a jury trial in the Circuit Court of Arlington County, Virginia, Breard was convicted of both charges and sentenced to death. On appeal, the Virginia Supreme Court affirmed Breard's convictions and sentences, Breard v. Commonwealth, 445 S.E.2d 670 (1994), and we denied certiorari, 513 U.S. 971 (1994). State collateral relief was subsequently denied as well.

Breard then filed a motion for habeas relief under 28 U.S.C. § 2254 in Federal District Court on August 20, 1996. In that motion, Breard argued for the first time that his conviction and sentence should be overturned because of alleged violations of the Vienna Convention on Consular Relations (Vienna Convention), April 24, 1963, [1970] 21 U.S.T. 77, T.I.A.S. No. 6820, at the time of his arrest. Specifically, Breard alleged that the Vienna Convention was violated when the arresting authorities failed to inform him that, as a foreign national, he had the right to contact the Paraguayan Consulate. The District Court rejected this claim, concluding that Breard procedurally defaulted the claim when he failed to raise it in state court and that Breard could not demonstrate cause and prejudice for this default. Breard v. Netherland, 949 F.Supp. 1255, 1266 (E.D.Va.1996). The Fourth Circuit affirmed. Breard v. Pruett, 134 F.3d 615, 620 (1998). Breard has petitioned this Court for a writ of certiorari.

In September 1996, the Republic of Paraguay, the Ambassador of Paraguay to the United States, and the Consul General of Paraguay to the United States (collectively Paraguay) brought suit in Federal District Court against certain Virginia officials, alleging that their separate rights under the Vienna Convention had been violated by the Commonwealth's failure to inform Breard of his rights under the treaty and to inform the Paraguayan consulate of Breard's arrest, conviction, and sentence. In addition, the Consul General asserted a parallel claim under 42 U.S.C. § 1983, alleging a denial of his rights under the Vienna Convention. The District Court concluded that it lacked subject-matter jurisdiction over these suits because Paraguay was not alleging a "continuing violation of federal law" and therefore could not bring its claims within the exception to Eleventh Amendment immunity established in Ex parte Young, 209 U.S. 123 (1908). *Republic of Paraguay v. Allen,* 949 F.Supp. 1269, 1272–1273 (E.D.Va.1996). The Fourth Circuit affirmed on Eleventh Amendment grounds. *Republic of Paraguay v. Allen,* 134 F.3d 622 (1998). Paraguay has also petitioned this Court for a writ of certiorari.

On April 3, 1998, nearly five years after Breard's conviction became final, the Republic of Paraguay instituted proceedings against the United States in the International Court of Justice (ICJ), alleging that the United States violated the Vienna Convention at the time of Breard's arrest. On April 9, the ICJ noted jurisdiction and issued an order requesting that the United States "take all measures at its disposal to ensure that Angel Francisco Breard is not executed pending the final decision in these proceedings.... The ICJ set a briefing schedule for this matter, with oral argument likely to be held this November. Breard then filed a petition for an original writ of habeas corpus and a stay application in this Court in order to 'enforce' the ICJ's order. Paraguay filed a motion for leave to file a bill of complaint in this Court, citing this Court's original jurisdiction over cases 'affecting Ambassadors ... and Consuls.'" U.S. Const., Art. III, § 2.

It is clear that Breard procedurally defaulted his claim, if any, under the Vienna Convention by failing to raise that claim in the state courts. Nevertheless, in their petitions for certiorari, both Breard and Paraguay contend that Breard's Vienna Convention claim may be heard in federal court because the Convention is the "supreme law of the land" and thus trumps the procedural default doctrine. Pet. for Cert. in No. 97–8214, pp. 15–18–5 Pet. for Cert. in No. 97–1390, p. 14, n.

8.   This argument is plainly incorrect for two reasons.

First, while we should give respectful consideration to the interpretation of an international treaty rendered by an international court with jurisdiction to interpret such, it has been recognized in international law that, absent a clear and express statement to the contrary, the procedural rules of the forum State govern the implementation of the treaty in that State. *See Sun Oil Co. v. Wortman*, 486 U.S. 717, 723 (1988); *Volkswagenwerk, Aktiengesellschaft v. Schlunk,* 486 U.S. 694 (1988); *Societe Nationale Industrielle, Aerospatiale v. United States Dist. Court for Southern Dist. of Iowa*, 482 U.S. 522, 539 (1987). This proposition is embodied in the Vienna Convention itself, which provides that the rights expressed in the Convention "shall be exercised in conformity with the laws and regulations of the receiving State," provided that "said laws and regulations must enable full effect to be given to the purposes for which the rights accorded under this Article are intended." Article 36(2), [1970] 21 U.S. T., at 101. It is the rule in this country that assertions of error in criminal proceedings must first be raised in state court in order to form the basis for relief in habeas. *Wainwright v. Sykes*, 433 U.S. 72 (1977). Claims not so raised are considered defaulted. *Ibid.* By not asserting his Vienna Convention claim in state court, Breard failed to exercise his rights under the Vienna Convention in conformity with the laws of the United States and the Commonwealth of Virginia. Having failed to do so, he cannot raise a claim of violation of those rights now on federal habeas review.

* * *

[The Court's discussion of the relations between the U.S. Constitution and Federal legislation is taken up below in Chapters 9 and 12]

As for Paraguay's suits (both the original action and the case coming to us on petition for certiorari), neither the text nor the history of the Vienna Convention clearly provides a foreign nation a private right of action in United States' courts to set aside a criminal conviction and sentence for violation of consular notification provisions. The Eleventh Amendment provides a separate reason why Paraguay's suit might not succeed. That Amendment's "fundamental principle" that "the States, in the absence of consent, are immune from suits brought against them ... by a foreign State" was enunciated in *Principality of Monaco v. Mississippi*, 292 U.S. 313, 329–330 (1934). Though Paraguay claims that its suit is within an exemption dealing with continuing consequences of past violations of federal rights, see *Milliken v. Bradley*, 433 U.S. 267 (1977), we do not agree. The failure to notify the Paraguayan Consul occurred long ago and has no continuing effect. The causal link present in *Milliken* is absent in this case.

Insofar as the Consul General seeks to base his claims on § 1983, his suit is not cognizable. Section 1983 provides a cause of action to any "person within the jurisdiction" of the United States for the deprivation "of any rights, privileges, or immunities secured by the Constitution and laws." As an initial matter, it is clear that Paraguay is not authorized to bring suit under § 1983. Paraguay is not a "person" as that term is used in § 1983. [Citations omitted] Nor is Paraguay "within the jurisdiction" of the United States. And since the Consul General is acting only in his official capacity, he has no greater ability to proceed under § 1983 than does the country he represents. Any rights that the Consul General might have by virtue of the Vienna Convention exist for the benefit of Paraguay, not for him as an individual.

It is unfortunate that this matter comes before us while proceedings are pending before the ICJ that might have been brought to that court earlier. Nonetheless, this Court must decide questions presented to it on the basis of law. The Executive Branch, on the other hand, in exercising its authority over foreign relations may, and in this case did, utilize diplomatic discussion with Paraguay. Last night the Secretary of State sent a letter to the Governor of Virginia requesting that he stay Breard's execution. If the Governor wishes to wait for the decision of the ICJ, that is his prerogative. But nothing in our existing case law allows us to make that choice for him.

For the foregoing reasons, we deny the petition for an original writ of habeas corpus, the motion for leave to file a bill of complaint, the petitions for certiorari, and the accompanying stay applications filed by Breard and Paraguay.

Notes and Questions

1. What are the differences between the scope of immunities of a diplomatic agent and a consular officer? What is the immunity of a diplomatic agent who performs consular functions?

2. *The ICJ judgment and U.S. law.* Note that neither the ICJ order nor the U.S. Supreme Court opinion states views on the status of the ICJ's interim protection order. Is it legally binding on the U.S? Should it be? *See, LeGrand Case* (Germany v. U.S.), 27 June 2001, ICJ Aress Rel. 2001/16.

3. In your opinion, should the ICJ Order have convinced the Supreme Court that it should find the means of ordering a stay while considering the issues further and until the ICJ issues its decision on the merits? Why?

4. What do these cases teach us about the problems of enforcing international law in the U.S. federal system?

5. Is world law a single unity encompassing both national law and international law (monism theory)? Or do the national and international systems exist separately (dualism theory)? See Chapters 9 and 17.

SECTION D.   IMMUNITY OF PERSONS CONNECTED WITH INTERNATIONAL ORGANIZATIONS

1.   OFFICIALS AND EXPERTS OF INTERNATIONAL ORGANIZATIONS

In addition to diplomatic agents and consular agents, a third group of protected individuals is composed of persons appointed by international organizations, commonly referred to as officials or experts. U.N. officials are afforded functional immunity under Charter Article 105(2) and Article V of the General Convention on the Privileges and Immunities of the United Nations, set forth in the Documentary Supplement. A separate but similar Convention covers the U.N. Specialized Agencies, and other organizations usually have comparable protection under independent arrangements. There is provision for immunity of "experts on mission for the United Nations" in Article VI of the General Convention, as will be seen in the I.C.J. Advisory Opinion that follows.

Difference Relating to Immunity From Legal Process of a Special Rapporteur of the Commission on Human Rights

International Court of Justice, Advisory Opinion, 29 April 1999, 38 I.L.M. 873 (1999).

[In 1994 The U.N. Economic and Social Council endorsed the decision of the Commission on Human Rights to appoint Mr. Dato' Param Cumaraswamy, a Malasian jurist, as Rapporteur to conduct an inquiry into the independence of judges, lawyers and court officials, and to identify and record attacks on them. The following year the Rapporteur gave an interview on this subject to International Commercial Litigation, a U.K. publication circulated in Malaysia, which resulted in the filing in Malaysia of defamation actions against the Rapporteur. Thereafter, U.N. Legal Counsel and the Secretary General informed the Malaysian authorities that the Rapporteur was entitled to immunity from legal process. The authorities were also requested to inform the Malaysian courts accordingly, but this was not done, even after repeated requests and efforts on the part of the United Nations. Indeed, the Malaysian authorities disputed this application of immunity. The Rapporteur's motion to quash the writ was denied by the Malaysian court which assessed him with costs in a significant amount. On August 5, 1998, ECOSOC requested the ICJ to give an advisory opinion on the immunity question. Selections from the ICJ's opinion on that request follow].

38.   The Court will initially examine the first part of the question laid before the Court by the Council, which is:

> "the legal question of the applicability of Article VI, Section 22, of the Convention on the Privileges and Immunities of the United Nations in the case of Cumaraswamy as Special Rapporteur of the Commission on Human Rights on the independence of judges and lawyers, taking into account the circumstances set out in paragraphs 1 to 15 of the note by the Secretary–General . . . ."

* * *

40.   Pursuant to Article 105 of the Charter of the United Nations:

> "1. The Organization shall enjoy in the territory of each of its Members such privileges and immunities as are necessary for the fulfilment of its purposes.
>
> 2.   Representatives of the Members of the United Nations and officials of the Organization shall similarly enjoy such privileges and immunities as are necessary for the independent exercise of their functions in connexion with the Organization.
>
> 3.   The General Assembly may make recommendations with a view to determining the details of the application of paragraphs 1 and 2 of this Article or may propose conventions to the Members of the United Nations for this purpose."

Acting in accordance with Article 105 of the Charter, the General Assembly approved the General Convention on 13 February 1946 and proposed it for accession by each Member of the United Nations. Malaysia became a party to the General Convention, without reservation, on 28 October 1957.

41.   The General Convention contains an Article VI entitled "Experts on Missions for the United Nations." It is comprised of two Sections (22 and 23). Section 22 provides:

"Experts (other than officials coming within the scope of Article V) performing missions for the United Nations shall be accorded such privileges and immunities as are necessary for the independent exercise of their functions during the period of their missions, including time spent on journeys in connection with their missions. In particular they shall be accorded:

. . .

(b) in respect of words spoken or written and acts done by them in the course of the performance of their mission, immunity from legal process of every kind. This immunity from legal process shall continue to be accorded notwithstanding that the persons concerned are no longer employed on missions for the United Nations.

. . . . ."

42.   In its Advisory Opinion of 14 December 1989 on the *Applicability of Article VI, Section 22, of the Convention on the Privileges and Immunities of the United Nations*, the Court examined the applicability of Section 22 *ratione personae, ratione temporis* and *ratione loci*.

In this context the Court stated:

"The purpose of Section 22 is ... evident, namely, to enable the United Nations to entrust missions to persons who do not have the status of an official of the Organization, and to guarantee them 'such privileges and immunities as are necessary for the independent exercise of their functions'.... The essence of the matter lies not in their administrative position but in the nature of their mission." *(I.C.J. Reports 1989, p. 194, para. 47.)*

In that same Advisory Opinion, the Court concluded that a Special Rapporteur who is appointed by the Sub–Commission on Prevention of Discrimination and Protection of Minorities and is entrusted with a research mission must be regarded as an expert on mission within the meaning of Article VI, Section 22, of the General Convention (*ibid.*, p. 197, para. 55).

43.   The same conclusion must be drawn with regard to Special Rapporteurs appointed by the Human Rights Commission, of which the Sub–Commission is a subsidiary organ. It may be observed that Special Rapporteurs of the Commission usually are entrusted not only with a research mission but also with the task of monitoring human rights violations and reporting on them. But what is decisive is that they have been entrusted with a mission by the United Nations and are therefore entitled to the privileges and immunities provided for in Article VI, Section 22, that safeguard the independent exercise of their functions.

45. The Commission extended by resolution 1997/23 of 11 April 1997 the Special Rapporteur's mandate for a further period of three years.

In the light of these circumstances, the Court finds that Mr. Cumaraswamy must be regarded as an expert on mission within the meaning of Article VI, Section 22, as from 21 April 1994, that by virtue of this capacity the provisions of this Section were applicable to him at the time of his statements at issue, and that they continue to be applicable.

46. The Court observes that Malaysia has acknowledged that Mr. Cumaraswamy, as Special Rapporteur of the Commission, is an expert on mission and that such experts enjoy the privileges and immunities provided for under the General Convention in their relations with States parties, including those of which they are nationals or on the territory of which they reside. Malaysia and the United Nations are in full agreement on these points, as are the other States participating in the proceedings.

* * *

47. The Court will now consider whether the immunity provided for in Section 22 (b) applies to Mr. Cumaraswamy in the specific circumstances of the case; namely, whether the words used by him in the interview, as published in the article in International Commercial Litigation (November issue 1995), were spoken in the course of the performance of his mission, and whether he was therefore immune from legal process with respect to these words.

48. During the oral proceedings, the Solicitor General of Malaysia contended that the issue put by the Council before the Court does not include this question. She stated that the correct interpretation of the words used by the Council in its request

"does not extend to inviting the Court to decide whether, assuming the Secretary-General to have had the authority to determine the character of the Special Rapporteur's action, he had properly exercised that authority"

and added:

"Malaysia observes that the word used was 'applicability' not 'application'. 'Applicability' means 'whether the provision is applicable to someone' not 'how it is to be applied'."

49. The Court does not share this interpretation. It follows from the terms of the request that the Council wishes to be informed of the Court's opinion as to whether Section 22 (b) is applicable to the Special Rapporteur, in the circumstances set out in paragraphs 1 to 15 of the note of the Secretary–General and whether, therefore, the Secretary–General's finding that the Special Rapporteur acted in the course of the performance of his mission is correct.

50. In the process of determining whether a particular expert on mission is entitled, in the prevailing circumstances, to the immunity provided for in Section 22 (b), the Secretary–General of the United Nations has a pivotal role to play. The Secretary–General, as the chief administrative officer of the Organization, has the authority and the responsibility to

exercise the necessary protection where required. This authority has been recognized by the Court when it stated:

> "Upon examination of the character of the functions entrusted to the Organization and of the nature of the missions of its agents, it becomes clear that the capacity of the Organization to exercise a measure of functional protection of its agents arises by necessary intendment out of the Charter." (*Reparation for Injuries Suffered in the Service of the United Nations, Advisory Opinion, I.C.J. Reports* 1949, p. 184.)

51. Article VI, Section 23, of the General Convention provides that "[p]rivileges and immunities are granted to experts in the interests of the United Nations and not for the personal benefit of the individuals themselves." In exercising protection of United Nations experts, the Secretary–General is therefore protecting the mission with which the expert is entrusted. In that respect, the Secretary–General has the primary responsibility and authority to protect the interests of the Organization and its agents, including experts on mission. As the Court held:

> "In order that the agent may perform his duties satisfactorily, he must feel that this protection is assured to him by the Organization, and that he may count on it. To ensure the independence of the agent, and, consequently, the independent action of the Organization itself, it is essential that in performing his duties he need not have to rely on any other protection than that of the Organization ..." (*Ibid.*, p. 183.)

53. As is clear from the written and oral pleadings of the United Nations, the Secretary–General was reinforced in this view by the fact that it has become standard practice of Special Rapporteurs of the Commission to have contact with the media. This practice was confirmed by the High Commissioner for Human Rights who, in a letter dated 2 October 1998, included in the dossier, wrote that: "it is more common than not for Special Rapporteurs to speak to the press about matters pertaining to their investigations, thereby keeping the general public informed of their work".

57. The Court will now deal with the second part of the Council's question, namely, "the legal obligations of Malaysia in this case".

58. Malaysia maintains that it is premature to deal with the question of its obligations. It is of the view that the obligation to ensure that the requirements of Section 22 of the Convention are met is an obligation of result and not of means to be employed in achieving that result. It further states that Malaysia has complied with its obligation under Section 34 of the General Convention, which provides that a party to the Convention must be "in a position under its own law to give effect to [its] terms", by enacting the necessary legislation; finally it contends that the Malaysian courts have not yet reached a final decision as to Mr. Cumaraswamy's entitlement to immunity from legal process.

59. The Court wishes to point out that the request for an advisory opinion refers to "the legal obligations of Malaysia in this case". The difference which has arisen between the United Nations and Malaysia originated in the Government of Malaysia not having informed the competent Malaysian judicial authorities of the Secretary–General's finding that Mr. Cumaraswamy had spoken the words at issue in the course of the

performance of his mission and was, therefore, entitled to immunity from legal process (see paragraph 17 above). It is as from the time of this omission that the question before the Court must be answered.

60.   As the Court has observed, the Secretary–General, as the chief administrative officer of the Organization, has the primary responsibility to safeguard the interests of the Organization; to that end, it is up to him to assess whether its agents acted within the scope of their functions and, where he so concludes, to protect these agents, including experts on mission, by asserting their immunity. This means that the Secretary–General has the authority and responsibility to inform the government of a member State of his finding and, where appropriate, to request it to act accordingly and, in particular, to request it to bring his finding to the knowledge of the local courts if acts of an agent have given or may give rise to court proceedings.

61.   When national courts are seised of a case in which the immunity of a United Nations agent is in issue, they should immediately be notified of any finding by the Secretary–General concerning that immunity. That finding, and its documentary expression, creates a presumption which can only be set aside for the most compelling reasons and is thus to be given the greatest weight by national courts.

* * *

63.   Section 22 (b) of the General Convention explicitly states that experts on mission shall be accorded immunity from legal process of every kind in respect of words spoken or written and acts done by them in the course of the performance of their mission. By necessary implication, questions of immunity are therefore preliminary issues which must be expeditiously decided *in limine litis*. This is a generally-recognized principle of procedural law, and Malaysia was under an obligation to respect it. The Malaysian courts did not rule *in limine litis* on the immunity of the Special Rapporteur (see paragraph 17 above), thereby nullifying the essence of the immunity rule contained in Section 22 (b). Moreover, costs were taxed to Mr. Cumaraswamy while the question of immunity was still unresolved. As indicated above, the conduct of an organ of a State—even an organ independent of the executive power—must be regarded as an act of that State. Consequently, Malaysia did not act in accordance with its obligations under international law.

64.   In addition, the immunity from legal process to which the Court finds Mr. Cumaraswamy entitled entails holding Mr. Cumaraswamy financially harmless for any costs imposed upon him by the Malaysian courts, in particular taxed costs.

65.   According to Article VIII, Section 30, of the General Convention, the opinion given by the Court shall be accepted as decisive by the parties to the dispute. Malaysia has acknowledged its obligations under Section 30.

Since the Court holds that Mr. Cumaraswamy is an expert on mission who under Section 22 (b) is entitled to immunity from legal process, the Government of Malaysia is obligated to communicate this advisory opinion to the competent Malaysian courts, in order that Malaysia's international obligations be given effect and Mr. Cumaraswamy's immunity be respected.

67.   For these reasons,

The Court

Is of the opinion:

(1) (a) By fourteen votes to one,

That Article VI, Section 22, of the Convention on the Privileges and Immunities of the United Nations is applicable in the case of Dato' Param Cumaraswamy as Special Rapporteur of the Commission on Human Rights on the Independence of Judges and Lawyers;

* * *

(b) By fourteen votes to one,

That Dato' Param Cumaraswamy is entitled to immunity from legal process of every kind for the words spoken by him during an interview as published in an article in the November 1995 issue of International Commercial Litigation;

* * *

[The Court also advised that Malaysia had the obligation to inform the Malaysian courts of the finding of the Secretary–General that Mr Cumaraswamy was entitled to immunity from legal process, that the Malaysian courts had the obligation to deal with the question of immunity from legal process as a preliminary issue to be expeditiously decided *in limine litis*; that Mr. Cumaraswamy shall be held financially harmless for any costs imposed upon him by the Malaysian courts, in particular taxed costs; and that the Government of Malaysia has the obligation to communicate this advisory opinion to the Malaysian courts, in order that Malaysia's international obligations be given effect and Cumaraswamy's immunity be respected.]

People v. Leo

United States, Criminal Court of the City of New York, 1978.
95 Misc.2d 408, 407 N.Y.S.2d 941.

Defendant moves for dismissal of the complaint charging him with assault in the third degree (Penal Law § 120.00) and resisting arrest (Penal Law § 205.30) on the ground that he "is a person who has international diplomatic immunity and as such the court lacks jurisdiction". The relevant facts underlying the charges arose on July 29, 1977, when defendant, who was then working at his office in the United Nations Building at about 10 P.M., received a telephone call from his wife advising him of the uninvited presence of complainant in their apartment and her refusal to leave despite requests that she do so. Defendant then left his office and returned home, where a scuffle with complainant ensued resulting in the arrival of the police to place defendant under arrest for assault and his resistance to such arrest.

Defendant contends that a dismissal is mandated in this case because he is insulated from prosecution by the cloak of diplomatic immunity and, further, because this court lacks jurisdiction over the subject matter which, according to defendant, constitutes the commission of a federal crime by the complainant. It may be noted that defendant has pressed a cross-complaint against complainant in this court and has also made a formal complaint to the U.S. Attorney's office against her apparently under 18 U.S.C. § 112.

It is essential to establish the precise status occupied by defendant in this country. It is uncontradicted that he is a Tanzanian national who is employed by the United Nations at its headquarters in New York in the capacity of Economic Affairs Officer, Economic Affairs Section, Centre for Natural Resources, Energy, and Transportation. While defendant is concededly sponsored for this position by the government of Tanzania, he holds no other diplomatic position on behalf of the government of Tanzania, has never been issued a diplomatic passport and he resides in the United States under a G4 visa which is issued to international civil servants. Thus, it is clear that defendant's status is solely that of an employee of the United Nations with whatever rights and immunities may inure to him by virtue of that position.

The controlling authorities are in Article 105 of the United Nations Charter, of which the United States is a signatory, and in the International Organizations Immunities Act (22 U.S.C. § 288d[b]) which was enacted in 1945 to implement the immunities provisions embodied in the United Nations Charter and was made applicable to that organization by Executive Order No. 9698 of February 19, 1946.

Article 105 of the United Nations Charter, provides that:

1. The Organization shall enjoy in the territory of each of its Members such privileges and immunities as are necessary for the fulfillment of its purposes.

2. Representatives of Members of the United Nations and officials of the Organization shall similarly enjoy such privileges and immunities as are necessary for the independent exercise of their functions in connection with the Organization.

Section 288d, sub-paragraph (b) of Title 22 of the U.S. Code states that:

Representatives of foreign governments in or to international organizations and officers and employees of such organization shall be immune from suit and legal process relating to acts performed by them in their official capacity and falling within their function as such representatives, officers, or employees except insofar as such immunity may be waived by the foreign government or international organization concerned. (underscoring added.)

The underscored language clearly delineates the perimeters of the immunity applicable to defendant, as an employee of the United Nations. It is limited in scope and purpose to protection for acts committed by United Nations officials in the course of accomplishing their functions as United Nations' employees in distinction to the unlimited form of immunity traditionally accorded to diplomats.

While defendant asserts that the statutory immunity under Section 288d(b) applies in this instance because complainant did in fact obstruct him "in the performance of his duties", an analysis of the facts in this case, in the most liberal perspective possible, fails to demonstrate any basis whatsoever upon which to conclude that defendant was acting in his official capacity or that there was some reasonable relationship between the alleged altercation and defendant's United Nations employment. On the contrary, the acts underlying the charges took place away from defendant's office when he returned home in response to his wife's call concerning an unwanted visitor whose presence at defendant's residence has not been shown to have been in any way connected with defendant's employment. The defendant's acts took place wholly within the context of a personal, domestic matter and as such are outside the scope of the limited immunity to which he is entitled as a United Nations' employee. The tenuous circumstance that he was at his office when he received his wife's call affords no rational basis for holding that his subsequent acts of violence in ejecting complainant and in resisting arrest were in some way related to the purposes of the United Nations or to the performance or fulfillment of defendant's duties and functions as an Economic Affairs Officer of that organization.

Nor is there merit to defendant's argument that this court lacks jurisdiction over the subject matter herein because such jurisdiction is vested solely in the Federal Courts. In support of this contention defendant points to the fact that, under his version of the incident, complainant is chargeable with a violation of the federal law (i.e. 18 U.S.C. § 112[a] and [b]) which provides for the imposition of criminal penalties for injury to the person or property of a foreign official, including trespass upon the residence of such official. It is apparently defendant's position that if he initiates charges against complainant under such statute, he is thereby rendered immune from criminal prosecution for any acts committed against complainant, however egregious. Aside from the fact that defendant does not fall within the category of "foreign official" covered by the statute, he seriously misapprehends its scope and purpose. The statute is designed to provide foreign officials with a protective shield against harm by imposing severe criminal penalties upon those who would interfere with such foreign officials in the performance of their functions and duties. There is no language whatsoever in Section 112(a) and (b) of Title 18 which deals with the granting of immunity or which can give rise to a construction of the statute permitting it to be converted into a sword authorizing the perpetration of criminal acts with impunity by those whom the statute seeks to protect. The purpose of this legislation is simply to deal with the protection of diplomatic officials by preventing and discouraging crimes against such persons. Any immunities from prosecution which they or other persons may enjoy derive from other statutory provisions. Insofar as defendant is concerned the controlling statute is 22 U.S.C. § 288d(b) which, as has already been discussed, affords him only the limited diplomatic immunity applicable to a United Nations employee, an immunity which in no way proscribes the instant prosecution. It is undoubtedly in recognition of the limited scope of 22 U.S.C. § 288 that defendant seeks to create a more expansive immunity by a strained and distorted interpretation of 18 U.S.C.

§ 112. Significantly, defendant has submitted no authority whatsoever in support of such untenable construction of that statute.

* * *

Accordingly, defendant's motion to dismiss on the ground of diplomatic immunity is in all respects denied.

Evan T. Bloom, Protecting Peacekeepers: The Convention on the Safety of United Nations and Associated Personnel

89 AJIL 621 (1995).

On December 9, 1994, the United Nations General Assembly adopted a new multilateral convention of particular importance to United Nations peacekeeping, the Convention on the Safety of United Nations and Associated Personnel [The text is found in 34 I.L.M. 482 (1995); by 2001, the Convention had 51 parties, not including the United States. It entered into force on January 15, 1999.] The treaty addresses a critical gap in international law. While the conduct of combatants in international armed conflicts is regulated by the Geneva Conventions of 1949 and related norms and principles, no instrument prohibited or provided legal remedies for attacks against forces performing traditional noncombat peacekeeping functions as such. Thus, as the Security Council in the post-Cold War period deployed larger and larger numbers of peacekeepers to areas of extreme risk, and casualties to UN forces rose, UN member states realized that there was an urgent need for an international agreement that would deter and ensure punishment of such attacks. The new Convention addresses this problem by creating a regime for prosecution or extradition of persons accused of attacking UN peacekeepers and other persons associated with operations under UN mandates. It also contains provisions concerning the relationship of peacekeepers and others with host and transit states.

2.   REPRESENTATIVES OF MEMBER STATES AND OFFICIAL INVITEES

United States Ex rel. Casanova v. Fitzpatrick

United States District Court, S.D. New York, 1963.
214 F.Supp. 425.

■ WEINFELD, DISTRICT JUDGE. The petitioner, Roberto Santiesteban Casanova, seeks his release from custody on a writ of habeas corpus on the ground of lack of the Court's jurisdiction over his person. He is under arrest and detention by virtue of a two-count indictment wherein he, two codefendants and two others not named as defendants are charged with conspiracy to commit sabotage and to violate the Foreign Agents Registration Act. He was originally arrested on a warrant issued by the United States Commissioner, based upon a complaint, and held on $250,000 bail fixed by the Commissioner. Thereafter, following his indictment by a grand jury, this Court set bail in the sum of $75,000, which it later reduced to $50,000. Petitioner has been confined since his arrest in default of bail.

Petitioner contends he is entitled to diplomatic immunity and is not subject to Federal arrest, detention or prosecution. The basic facts upon which his claim to immunity rests are not in dispute. He is a Cuban national, appointed by his government as an attaché and Resident Member of the Staff of the Permanent Mission of Cuba to the United Nations (hereafter "Cuban Mission".) He entered the United States on October 3, 1962 with a diplomatic passport issued by his own government, a nonimmigrant visa issued by our Department of State, and a landing card issued by the Immigration and Naturalization Service. From the time of his admission to the United States to the date of his arrest he was employed as a Resident Member of the staff of the Cuban Mission.

Petitioner contends that he enjoys diplomatic immunity from arrest and prosecution under (1) Article 105 of the United Nations Charter, (2) Section 15(2) of the Headquarters Agreement, and (3) the Law of Nations. He further contends that even if his claim to immunity is overruled, nonetheless the writ must be sustained, since the Supreme Court of the United States has exclusive and original jurisdiction to try him under Article III of the Constitution of the United States and 28 U.S.C. § 1251. Before considering his contentions, it is desirable to localize the issue with which we deal. The petitioner is not a member of a diplomatic staff accredited to, and recognized by, the United States Government. He is not a representative to, or an employee of, the United Nations. His claim to diplomatic immunity derives solely from his status as a Resident Member of the Cuban Permanent Mission to the United Nations. Whatever right to immunity exists must be considered within the context of that status.

A.   The Claim of Diplomatic Immunity Under the United Nations Charter

　　＊ ＊ ＊

The thrust of the relator's contention is that the declaration in section 2 is self-executing and requires absolute diplomatic immunity be accorded to representatives of members and their staffs. The argument rests upon the postulate, universally recognized in international law, that diplomatic agents are accorded immunity from judicial process so that their governments may not be hampered in their foreign relations by the arrest or harassment of, or interference with, their diplomatic representatives. Petitioner urges that this rationale applies with equal force to the members of a mission to the United Nations and its staff; that unless they enjoy diplomatic immunity they can be prevented from fulfilling their diplomatic functions vis-a-vis the United Nations, if the host country, in this instance the United States, were able to arrest and detain them—in short, that diplomatic immunity is required to assure the independence of the Organization and its members in the discharge of their duties and functions. Accordingly, he contends that Article 105 intended, and in fact confers, full diplomatic immunity. The language of Article 105, its history, as well as subsequent acts by the United States and the United Nations, require rejection of petitioner's claim that by its own force full diplomatic immunity was either intended or granted.

　　＊ ＊ ＊

The Court concludes that Article 105 of the Charter does not purport to nor does it confer diplomatic immunity. The broadest claim that can be made is that it is self-operative with respect to functional activities. And even if it were so construed, it avails not the petitioner, since by its very language the immunity is confined to acts necessary for the independent exercise of functions in connection with the United Nations. Conspiracy to commit sabotage against the Government of the United States is not a function of any mission or member of a mission to the United Nations. Accordingly, the Court holds that the petitioner does not enjoy diplomatic immunity against prosecution on the indictment by virtue of Article 105 of the United Nations Charter.

B.   The Claim of Diplomatic Immunity Under the Headquarters Agreement

(1) Is the Court concluded by the certificate of the State Department?

The development and growth of international organizations over the past two decades, particularly the United Nations as a world force, have brought into being new problems and concepts relating to the immunities and privileges to be accorded the organization, its officials and representatives of member states and their staffs. From the start it was evident that unless adequate immunity was provided to protect them in the exercise of their respective functions, the independence of the organization would be undermined and its effectiveness greatly hampered, if not destroyed. The location of the headquarters presents special problems to the host country and the organization. Access to the headquarters to all persons having legitimate business with the organization is required and, on the other hand, the host country is entitled to protection against the admission of persons likely to engage in activities subversive of its national interests and internal security. These matters are usually provided for by the basic charter or constitution, special agreements or national legislation. With the United States as the site of the United Nations headquarters, our Government was particularly sensitive to the problem of assuring the independence and proper functioning of the United Nations, and also to the protection of its own security. The Headquarters Agreement was one of the means adopted to protect the respective interests.

* * *

Under the above provisions, those who come within its embrace are entitled to the broad diplomatic privileges and immunities enjoyed by diplomatic envoys accredited to the United States. And there would appear to be no question that if the petitioner is entitled to the benefits of Article 15, he is immune from prosecution upon the charges contained in the indictment. Petitioner relies upon section 15(2) as conferring diplomatic immunity upon him by reason of his position as an attaché and a Resident Member of the Cuban Mission. The Government challenges his claim, pointing out that the subsection expressly provides that immunity thereunder is accorded only to "such resident members * * * as may be agreed upon between the Secretary–General, the Government of the United States and the Government of the Member concerned." It denies that any such agreement was ever manifested, although it admits that an application therefor was made by the Secretary–General of the United Nations pursuant to the request of the Cuban Mission.

The prosecution has filed an authenticated affidavit of the Chief Protocol Officer of the Department of State certifying that the Government of the United States has not agreed to grant diplomatic immunity to petitioner under section 15(2) of the Headquarters Agreement, "and that he does not enjoy any diplomatic privileges and immunities under the aforesaid Article 15 of the Agreement." Accordingly, it presses that the Court is concluded by this certification. Thus, a threshold question is presented. The precise issue before the Court is whether, in the light of section 15(2) of the Headquarters Agreement, certification by the Department of State that an individual acknowledged to be a resident attache of the Permanent Cuban Mission to the United Nations has not been "agreed upon" by the Government as entitled to diplomatic privileges and immunities thereunder, concludes the question. A number of leading authorities do hold that the State Department certification is conclusive where the issue pertains to a diplomatic envoy accredited to the United States. This Court is of the view that such authorities do not control the question here presented. There is a sharp distinction between a diplomatic envoy accredited to the Government of the United States and a representative of a member state to the United Nations, an international organization. The status of each is different and immunity rests upon and is derived from entirely different desiderata.

Acceptance of a diplomatic envoy from a foreign government to the United States rests upon the exercise by our Executive of its power to conduct foreign affairs. It either accepts or rejects the diplomat in its sole and absolute discretion and, if he is received, he thereby is entitled, without more, under the Law of Nations, to full diplomatic immunity. These are political judgments by the Executive Branch of the Government and the Court is concluded thereby. In contrast, a representative of a member state to an international organization, such as the United Nations, is designated by his Government entirely independent of the views of other member states and indeed of the Organization. The United States has no say or veto power with respect to such representative of any member state. These representatives acquire immunity only to the extent that it is granted by legislation, or by agreement, whether under the basic charter, a general convention, or a separate agreement, as in the instant case by the Headquarters Agreement. Accordingly, whether or not a particular individual is entitled to immunity is to be decided within the framework of the applicable document. The Headquarters Agreement simply provides that the three designated parties are to agree upon those entitled to immunity. * * *

Whether, upon the facts presented by both the Government and the individual involved or his government, immunity exists by reason of the agreement, is not a political question, but a justiciable controversy involving the interpretation of the agreement and its application to the particular facts. In this instance the decision is for the Court and it is not concluded by the unilateral statement of the Government, a party to that agreement and to this controversy, that the individual is not entitled to immunity thereunder. * * *

The scope of the inquiry is narrowly confined. Did the United States of America, as one of the parties to the Headquarters Agreement, make its decision under section 15(2) either that it agreed or did not agree that petitioner was entitled to diplomatic immunity? The Government's statement that it did not so agree is evidential but not conclusive. Petitioner asserts that by various acts the necessary agreement was manifested; the Government denies it. * * * Thus we proceed to consider the petitioner's contention upon the merits.

(2) The claim that section 15(2) of the Headquarters Agreement contemplates agreement only as to categories and not as to individuals.

The petitioner's contention is that the clause "such resident members as may be agreed upon" contemplates an agreement with respect to categories of persons and does not require agreement upon persons within the category. The petitioner's main props in support of his contention are comments and reports of committees of the United Nations with respect to immunity proposals. While the unilateral views of any United Nations committee or member cannot serve to defeat the express language of the final agreement (the Headquarters Agreement), nonetheless, analysis of such comments and reports negates rather than supports the plaintiff's position.

* * *

The argument that unless petitioner's construction of class agreement is adopted the United States would obtain "a discriminatory, unilateral and effective control of and sanctions against nations of equal sovereignty in the United Nations" is unpersuasive. As already demonstrated, full diplomatic immunity is accorded under subdivision 1 of section 15 to top echelon representatives of member nations identical to that accorded to accredited diplomats to the United States. As to their staff members, pending agreement by the United States under section 15(2), which would entitle them to diplomatic immunity, there is available under the International Organizations Immunities Act the immunity necessary for the independent exercise of their functions, apart from Article 105 of the Charter, if in fact it is self-executing. No member state is prevented from appointing whomever it will to serve on the resident staff of its mission to the United Nations, but the United States, under section 15(2), is not required, simply by reason of one's employment in a particular category, to grant diplomatic immunity. It retains the rights thereunder to agree or not to agree that diplomatic immunity shall extend to individuals who qualify under the broad category "Resident Members of their Staffs." While it has exercised this right sparingly, it has refused, in the instance of at least five individuals, to agree to the request for immunity, without objection by either the Secretary–General or the member state who submitted the request.

The construction advanced would mean that a member state of the United Nations which may be hostile to our interests is free to send to the United States individuals designated as resident members of their staffs, to engage in conduct destructive of our national interest and security and yet have them protected from criminal prosecution on the theory that their designated status cloaked them with diplomatic immunity. It would open the flood gates for the entry of saboteurs, agents provocateur and others under a built-in guarantee that no matter what the criminal conduct, the Government could not prosecute them.

The language of the section controls. There is nothing in its history or in the practice under it to support petitioner's claim. To accept his contention would in effect amend section 15(2) by inserting therein the words "classes of" to read "such classes of resident members * * *."

The Court holds that the status of petitioner as an attache and resident member of the Cuban Mission does not by itself entitle him to diplomatic immunity under section 15(2) and that unless there was the agreement of the United States, as provided therein, the prosecution is not barred. The petitioner claims there was such agreement.

(3) The claim that the United States did agree that petitioner was entitled to diplomatic immunity.

The essence of petitioner's claim is that the issuance of the visa and the landing permit constituted, under the facts and law, the agreement of the Government of the United States that he was entitled to diplomatic privileges and immunities under section 15(2) of the Headquarters Agreement. * * *

    * * *

I am of the view that petitioner's contention cannot be upheld. To do so is to transmute the G–1 visa issued by the State Department into the agreement of the United States required under section 15(2) before diplomatic immunity extends to staff members of missions to the United Nations. The fact that the G–1 visa recognized that petitioner had the status encompassed within section 15(2) does not mean that by reason thereof the United States gave the required agreement thereunder. The visa was issued at the request of the Cuban Mission upon presentation of a diplomatic passport issued by the Cuban government and its representation of petitioner's appointment as "diplomatic attaché". Since the designation rested with the Cuban government, the United States was obligated under sections 11 and 13 of the Headquarters Agreement not to impose any impediment in his transit to and from the Headquarters District and to provide him with the necessary visa. The visa was the basic document of entry into the United States enroute to his post with his mission.

Petitioner argues that the State Department did not have to issue a G–1 visa in order to fulfill its obligations under the Headquarters Agreement; that so long as petitioner was accorded free access to the Headquarters District, the obligations of the United States Government were met. But as the prosecution contends, once the State Department determined that petitioner, upon the documents and representations contained therein, qualified for a G–1 visa, its issuance to the petitioner was pursuant to rules promulgated under the Immigration and Naturalization Act. The question of the agreement of the United States Government to diplomatic immunity was entirely separate from facilitating petitioner's entry to assume his duties with his mission.

I conclude that the Government of the United States did not, by the issuance of the visa and the landing permit, give its agreement that petitioner, on his entry into the United States to assume his duties as a member of the Cuban Mission, was thereby entitled to diplomatic immunity under section 15(2) of the Headquarters Agreement.

C. THE CLAIM OF DIPLOMATIC IMMUNITY UNDER THE LAW OF NATIONS

Here the petitioner's position is that under the Law of Nations he had diplomatic immunity from the time of his entry until the Government of the United States took definitive action upon the request of the Cuban Mission that he be "agreed upon" for diplomatic immunity under the Headquarters Agreement. Again, the claim centers in part about the G–1 visa and landing permit. He urges in substance that by this issuance the United States acknowledged his status for the purpose of entry into the United States to assume his duties with his mission, aware that he was eligible for diplomatic immunity. Accordingly, he contends that he was entitled to diplomatic immunity from the time of his entry on the same principle as that applicable under the Law of Nations to diplomats awaiting acknowledgment by governments to which they are accredited and which attaches even before they have been received by it—in fine, that until he was either agreed upon or rejected in response to his government's request, he was protected. * * *

> * * *

Petitioner's path is blocked by the same reasoning upon which the Court rejected the Government's position that its unilateral determination that he was not entitled to diplomatic immunity under the Headquarters Agreement was conclusive. As the Government's suggestion of an analogy to diplomats accredited to the United States was refused above, so is petitioner's in this instance. It is the Headquarters Agreement, the Charter and the applicable statutes of the United States that govern the determination of his rights, not the Law of Nations. The Law of Nations comes into play and has applicability in defining the nature and scope of diplomatic immunity only once it is found a person is entitled thereto under an applicable agreement or statute.

The Court concludes that petitioner is not entitled to diplomatic immunity by virtue of the Law of Nations.

> * * *

The petition for a writ of habeas corpus is dismissed upon the merits.

Note

The Vienna Convention on the Representation of States in Their Relations with International Organizations of a Universal Character. This Convention was adopted by a United Nations conference in March 1975 and by 2001 had 30 parties but had not yet entered into force. The United States became a signatory but has not given its consent to be bound by the convention. The head of the United States delegation to the conference Considered the Convention as needlessly expanding the obligations of host states. "Article 66, for example, is an expansion of current privileges and immunities for which no justification has been given. Administrative and technical staff, who have no representational functions, are accorded virtually the same privileges and immunities as would be accorded the ambassador to the host state." McDowell, Digest of United States Practice in International Law 1975, at 40 (1976).

United States v. Palestine Liberation Organization

United States District Court, S.D.N.Y.1988.
695 F.Supp. 1456, 27 I.L.M. 1055.

■ PALMIERI, J.:

The Anti-terrorism Act of 1987 (the "ATA"), is the focal point of this lawsuit. At the center of controversy is the right of the Palestine Liberation Organization (the "PLO") to maintain its office in conjunction with its work as a Permanent Observer to the United Nations. The case comes before the court on the government's motion for an injunction closing this office and on the defendants' motions to dismiss.

I

Background

The United Nations' Headquarters in New York were established as an international enclave by the Agreement Between the United States and the United Nations Regarding the Headquarters of the United Nations[2] (the "Headquarters Agreement"). This agreement followed an invitation extended to the United Nations by the United States, one of its principal founders, to establish its seat within the United States.

As a meeting place and forum for all nations, the United Nations, according to its charter, was formed to:

> maintain international peace and security * * *; to develop friendly relations among nations, based on the principle of equal rights and self-determination of peoples * * *; to achieve international cooperation in solving international problems of an economic, social, cultural or humanitarian character * * *; and be a centre for harmonizing the actions of nations in the attainment of these common ends.

U.N. Charter art. 1. Today, 159 of the United Nations' members maintain missions to the U.N. in New York. U.N. Protocol and Liaison Service, Permanent Missions to the United Nations No. 262 3–4 (1988) (hereinafter "Permanent Missions No. 262 "). In addition, the United Nations has, from its incipiency, welcomed various non-member observers to participate in its proceedings. See Permanent Missions to the United Nations: Report of the Secretary–General, (hereinafter Permanent Missions: Report of the Secretary–General). Of these, several non-member nations, intergovernmental

---

2. G.A.Res. 169(II), 11 U.N.T.S. 11, No. 147 (1947). T.I.A.S. No. 1676, *authorized by* S.J.Res. 144, 80th Cong., 1st Sess., *set out in* 22 U.S.C. § 287 note (1982). We refer to the Headquarters Agreement as a treaty, since we are not concerned here with making a distinction among different forms of international agreement. The applicable law implicates all forms, including the Headquarters Agreement. *Weinberger v. Rossi*, 456 U.S. 25, 29–30 (1982).

organizations, and other organizations currently maintain "Permanent Observer Missions" in New York.

The PLO falls into the last of these categories and is present at the United Nations as its invitee. See Headquarters Agreement, § 11 (22 U.S.C. § 287 note). The PLO has none of the usual attributes of sovereignty. It is not accredited to the United States and does not have the benefits of diplomatic immunity. There is no recognized state it claims to govern. It purports to serve as the sole political representative of the Palestinian people. The PLO nevertheless considers itself to be the representative of a state, entitled to recognition in its relations with other governments, and is said to have diplomatic relations with approximately one hundred countries throughout the world.

In 1974, the United Nations invited the PLO to become an observer at the U.N., to "participate in the sessions and the work of the General Assembly in the capacity of observer." The right of its representatives to admission to the United States as well as access to the U.N. was immediately challenged under American law. Judge Costantino rejected that challenge in Anti–Defamation League of B'nai B'rith v. Kissinger. The court upheld the presence of a PLO representative in New York with access to the United Nations, albeit under certain entrance visa restrictions which limited PLO personnel movements to a radius of 25 miles from Columbus Circle in Manhattan. It stated from the bench:

This problem must be viewed in the context of the special responsibility which the United States has to provide access to the United Nations under the Headquarters Agreement. It is important to note that a primary goal of the United Nations is to provide a forum where peaceful discussions may displace violence as a means of resolving disputed issues. At times our responsibility to the United Nations may require us to issue visas to persons who are objectionable to certain segments of our society.

* * *

Since 1974, the PLO has continued to function without interruption as a permanent observer and has maintained its Mission to the United Nations without trammel, largely because of the Headquarters Agreement, which we discuss below.

II

The Anti–Terrorism Act

In October 1986, members of Congress requested the United States Department of State to close the PLO offices located in the United States. That request proved unsuccessful, and proponents of the request introduced legislation with the explicit purpose of doing so. The result was the ATA, 22 U.S.C. §§ 5201–5203. It is of a unique nature. We have been unable to find any comparable statute in the long history of Congressional enactments. The PLO is stated to be "a terrorist organization and a threat to the interests of the United States, its allies, and to international law and should not benefit from operating in the United States." 22 U.S.C. § 5201(b). The ATA was added, without committee hearings, as a rider to the Foreign Relations Authorization Act for Fiscal Years 1988–89, which provided funds for the operation of the State Department, including the operation of the United States Mission to the United Nations. The bill also authorized payments to the United Nations for maintenance and operation. Id., § 102(a)(1); see also id. § 143.

The ATA, which became effective on March 21, 1988, forbids the establishment or maintenance of "an office, headquarters, premises, or other facilities or establishments within the jurisdiction of the United States at the behest or direction of, or with funds provided by" the PLO, if the purpose is to further the PLO's interests. 22 U.S.C. § 5202(3). The ATA also forbids spending the PLO's funds or receiving anything of value except informational material from the PLO, with the same mens rea requirement.

* * *

The United States commenced this lawsuit the day the ATA took effect, seeking injunctive relief to accomplish the closure of the Mission. The United States Attorney for this District has personally represented that no action would be taken to enforce the ATA pending resolution of the litigation in this court.

* * *

V

The Anti–Terrorism Act and the Headquarters Agreement

If the ATA were construed as the government suggests, it would be tantamount to a direction to the PLO Observer Mission at the United Nations that it close its doors and cease its operations instanter. Such an interpretation would fly in the face of the Headquarters Agreement, a prior treaty between the United Nations and the United States, and would abruptly terminate the functions the Mission has performed for many years. This conflict requires the court to seek out a reconciliation between the two.

* * *

We believe the ATA and the Headquarters Agreement cannot be reconciled except by finding the ATA inapplicable to the PLO Observer Mission.

A. The Obligations of the United States under the Headquarters Agreement.

The obligation of the United States to allow transit, entry and access stems not only from the language of the Headquarters Agreement but also from forty years of practice under it. Section 11 of the Headquarters Agreement reads, in part: "The federal, state or local authorities of the United States shall not impose any impediments to transit to or from the headquarters district of: (1) representatives of Members * * *, (5) other persons invited to the headquarters district by the United Nations * * * on official business." (22 U.S.C. § 287 note).[23] These rights could not be

23. Section 12 requires that the provisions of Section 11 be applicable "irrespective of the relations existing between the Governments of the persons referred to in that Sec-

effectively exercised without the use of offices. The ability to effectively organize and carry out one's work, especially as a liaison to an international organization, would not be possible otherwise. It is particularly significant that Section 13 limits the application of United States law not only with respect to the entry of aliens, but also their residence. The Headquarters Agreement thus contemplates a continuity limited to official United Nations functions and is entirely consistent with the maintenance of missions to the United Nations. The exemptions of Section 13 are not limited to members, but extend to invitees as well.

There can be no dispute that over the forty years since the United States entered into the Headquarters Agreement it has taken a number of actions consistent with its recognition of a duty to refrain from impeding the functions of observer missions to the U.N. It has, since the early days of the U.N.'s presence in New York, acquiesced in the presence of observer missions to the U.N. in New York. *See Permanent Missions: Report of the Secretary–General.*

After the United Nations invited the PLO to participate as a permanent observer, the Department of State took the position that it was required to provide access to the U.N. for the PLO. The State Department at no time disputed the notion that the rights of entry, access and residence guaranteed to invitees include the right to maintain offices.

* * *

In sum, the language of the Headquarters Agreement, the longstanding practice under it, and the interpretation given it by the parties to it leave no doubt that it places an obligation upon the United States to refrain from impairing the function of the PLO Observer Mission to the United Nations. The ATA and its legislative history do not manifest Congress' intent to abrogate this obligation. We are therefore constrained to interpret the ATA as failing to supersede the Headquarters Agreement and inapplicable to the Mission.

* * *

VI

Conclusions

The Anti–Terrorism Act does not require the closure of the PLO Permanent Observer Mission to the United Nations nor do the act's provisions impair the continued exercise of its appropriate functions as a Permanent Observer at the United Nations. The PLO Mission to the United Nations is an invitee of the United Nations under the Headquarters Agreement and its status is protected by that agreement. The Headquarters Agreement remains a valid and outstanding treaty obligation of the

tion and the Government of the United States." (22 U.S.C. § 287 note).

Section 13 limits the applicability of the United States laws and regulations regarding the entry and residence of aliens, when applied to those affiliated with the United Nations by virtue of Section 11. (22 U.S.C. § 287 note).

United States. It has not been superceded by the Anti–Terrorism Act, which is a valid enactment of general application.

* * *

The motion of the United States for summary judgment is denied, and summary judgment is entered for the defendants, dismissing this action with prejudice.

———

Note: On August 29, 1988, the U.S. Dept. of Justice announced that the Administration would not appeal this decision in the P.L.O. case. "The Administration based its decision on foreign policy considerations. Specifically, the State Department expressed concern that the closure of the mission would violate the U.S. obligations as the host country under the United Nations Headquarters Agreement." 27 I.L.M. 1704 (1988).

SECTION E.   UNITED STATES ADMINISTRATIVE PRACTICE

Notes and Questions

1. Study the United States Department of State Guidance for Law Enforcement Officers With Regard to Personal Rights and Immunities of Foreign Diplomatic and Consular Personnel (1988). 27 I.L.M. 1617 (1988), found in the Documentary Supplement, and the following chart on Diplomatic and Consular Privileges and Immunities.

2. **Query.** How would you characterize succinctly the immunities of the consular officers and officials of international organizations on the one hand, and the immunities of the diplomats and representatives to international organizations, on the other hand?

3. **Query.** What are your views on the standards that should be applied by host governments of international organizations with respect to the admission of diplomatic personnel for residence for the purpose of joining the mission of their countries to the organization? Did Judge Weinfeld reach the correct conclusion in the Casanova case? On the applicable law? On the preferable policy?

Diplomatic and Consular Privileges and Immunities
Summary of Law Enforcement Aspects

	Category	May be Arrested or Detained	Residence May be Entered Subject to Ordinary Procedures	May be Issued Traffic Citation	May be Subpoenaed as Witness	May be Prosecuted	Recognized Family Member
Diplomatic	Diplomatic Agent	No[2]	No	Yes	No	No	Same as sponsor (full immunity & inviolability).
Diplomatic	Member of Admin. and Tech. Staff	No[2]	No	Yes	No	No	Same as sponsor (full immunity & inviolability).
Diplomatic	Service Staff	Yes[1]	Yes	Yes	Yes	No—for official acts. Otherwise, Yes[1]	No immunity or inviolability.[1]
Consular	Career Consular Officers	Yes, if for a felony & pursuant to a warrant[1]	Yes[4]	Yes	No—for official acts. Testimony may not be compelled in any case.	No—for official acts. Otherwise, Yes[1]	No immunity or inviolability.[1]
Consular	Honorable Consular Officers	Yes	Yes	Yes	No—for official acts. Yes, in all other cases.	No—for official acts. Otherwise, Yes	No immunity or inviolability.
Consular	Consular Employees	Yes[1]	Yes	Yes	No—for official acts. Yes, in all other cases.	No—for official acts. Otherwise, Yes[1]	No immunity or inviolability.[1]
International Organizations	International Organization Staff[3]	Yes[3]	Yes[3]	Yes	Yes[3]	No—for official acts. Otherwise, Yes[3]	No immunity or inviolability.
International Organizations	Diplomatic-Level Staff of Missions to Int'l Orgs.	No[2]	No	Yes	No	No	Same as sponsor (full immunity & inviolability).
International Organizations	Support Staff of Missions to International Organizations	Yes	Yes	Yes	Yes	No—for official acts. Otherwise, Yes	No immunity or inviolability.

[1] This table presents general rules. Particularly in the cases indicated, the employees of certain foreign countries may enjoy higher levels of privileges and immunities on the basis of special bilateral agreements.

[2] Reasonable constraints, however, may be applied in emergency circumstances involving self-defense, public safety, or the prevention of serious criminal acts.

[3] A small number of senior officers are entitled to be treated identically to "diplomatic agents."

[4] Note that consular residences are sometimes located within the official consular premises. In such cases, only the official office space is protected from police entry.

CHAPTER 11

THE INTERNATIONAL LAW ABOUT INTERNATIONAL AGREEMENTS

SECTION A. INTRODUCTION

Notes and Questions

1. *Article 38 of the Statute of the International Court of Justice* sets out the *sources* of international law. First in the hierarchy is "[i]nternational conventions, whether general or particular, establishing rules expressly recognized by the contesting states * * *" Not only are treaties a basic source of international law, they are *the* key vehicle by which the international system changes most rapidly. They are the modii vivendi of states; they provide the mechanism for the various subjects of international law to arrange their relations, indeed, to make their own law. This aspect of treaties is really not much different from citizens of states in their contractual relationships. What one calls a treaty is not important; they are called conventions, *modii vivendi, concordats*, charters, articles of agreement, pacts, protocols, and accords, agreements, memoranda of understanding, among other designations. On the other hand, differences are important between multilateral and bilateral treaties and other agreements in which reservations or other special rules govern are allowed.

855

2. ***The Law of Treaties*** is a segment of international law governing treaties. It is comprised of customary international law, general principles, including *jus cogens*, and the 1969 Vienna Convention on the Law of Treaties. The Vienna Convention on Treaties, purports to codify customary international law on treaties. Article 2.1(a) defines treaty for purposes of the Convention as "an international agreement concluded between States in written form and governed by international law, whether embodied in a single instrument or in two or more related instruments and whatever its particular designation."

Keep the following questions in mind as you study this chapter. Does the Vienna Convention actually codify international law on treaties? Is general international law on treaties different from that in the Vienna Convention? Is the Convention's definition of treaties broader or narrower than that in general international law? May a state and an international organization or a state and a corporation enter into a treaty? Are the *agreements* between Israel and the Palestinian Liberation Organization treaties? Is a treaty in U.S. constitutional law more restrictive than one in international law? The Constitution, Article II Section 2[2], defines a treaty as an international agreement that is entered into by the President and receives the Advice and Consent of ⅔ of the Senators present. U.S. law on treaties is explored in the next chapter.

Studying the law on treaties helps one understand law in general. *What makes treaties binding?* By the same token, why are contracts in a domestic system binding? The *Code Civil* in France provides that the conventional obligation (i.e., the contract) is the means by which the parties make their own law as between themselves (as long as what they do does not violate important public policy). Is there a parallel in international treaty law? What makes a Code binding? The social contract? Public policy? General principles? Does the Constitution make treaties binding? In antiquity, religious solemnity provided the obligatory force for both contracts and treaties. The *jus cogens* principle, *pacta sunt servanda,* is often said to be *The Law* of international relations and apparently makes treaties binding. *Why? How?*

3. ***The Treaty on Treaties: present status and significance as evidence of customary law.*** The Convention entered into force January 27, 1980. President Nixon referred the Vienna Convention to the Senate on November 21, 1971, but it has never received that body's Advice and Consent. The Convention was developed from draft articles prepared by the International Law Commission (ILC). The work of the last *rapporteur* (Sir Humphrey Waldock, later a judge of the International Court of Justice) was overwhelmingly the most influential on the final draft that went to the Convention at Vienna. The ILC's Draft Articles, with commentary, can be found in 61 AJIL 263 (1967). Authoritatively comments by two major American negotiators, Kearney and Dalton may be read in their article: *The Treaty on Treaties*, 64 A.J.I.L. 495 (1970):

> The Convention on the Law of Treaties sets forth the code of rules that will govern the indispensable element in the conduct of foreign affairs, the mechanism without which international intercourse could not exist, much less function. It is possible to imagine a future in which the

treaty will no longer be the standard device for dealing with any and all international problems—a future in which for example, the use of regulations promulgated by international organizations in special fields of activity, such as the World Health Organization's sanitary regulations, will become the accepted substitute for the lawmaking activity now effected through international agreement. But, in the present state of international development, this is crystal-gazing. For the foreseeable future, the treaty will remain the cement that holds the world community together.

The State Department has stated, since 1973, the Convention to be a codification or at least good evidence of customary international law on treaties. It is worth considering to what extent this is so. Common-law lawyers may agree that it is a "code," but a "civilian" would not. Is the Vienna Convention comprehensive, complete and exclusive? Is it coherent and systematic? If not, it is not a true code. A true Code preempts the field.

There are also questions about whether the Treaty may fully or accurately reflect customary international law. The Convention's preamble, states: "rules of customary international law will continue to govern questions not regulated by the * * * Convention." Does this mean that if an issue is "regulated by the Convention," no new custom may develop? Will custom modify the Convention? Is Custom a source of law relating to agreements along with the Convention? Does pre-existing custom control interpretation? Can inconsistent custom, still be followed even by member states, overrule the Convention? Consider whether agreements really must be written to be binding? If not, are such agreements treaties? What body of law controls? If some other body of law controls, is the Convention a code? There are many other questions that we will raise in the Chapter, but it may be supposed that the Convention is neither a code nor a full or true reflection of customary international law. It may be a compilation of rules or a digest of some sort.

The executive branch and the judiciary have considered the Vienna Convention to be authoritative with respect to the executive's treatment of issues related to international agreements arising after May 22, 1969. See, Rovine, *Digest of U.S. Practice in International Law* 1973, at 307, 482–83 (1974). Study of the law about treaties during the usable life of this edition ought to be undertaken with knowledge of the Convention's treatment of the various international legal issues that follow. Ask yourselves when you finish this chapter: Is the Vienna Convention either silent or a poor guide on any of the issues raised in this chapter? What issues does it clarify well or seem to settle? Where does it fall? Where, if anywhere, does the Convention expand doctrine?

4. ***The wide application of international agreements.*** Undertakings among states are major tools of operations in the international legal system. Other mechanisms, such as rules of customary law, derived from the usual modes of conduct of international relations, right reason, judicial decisions, general principles of law common to the world's major legal systems and the like. They also lag behind developing needs within the international community and lack specificity due to the technologically complicated and politically sophisticated situations they address. Interna-

tional agreements, on the other hand, are often made because the parties have realized a need to reach specific accord upon some common concern. Like contracts or trusts in private law, international agreements are cut to the cloth of the parties' interests.

International agreements cover a wide range of interests. The spectrum extends from those that are in effect conveyances of real estate (treaties of lease, cession and measurement of boundaries), through mutual promises to pursue common lines of action (military alliances, mutual defense, safety at sea), to organic arrangements that function much as constitutions (the U.N. Charter). Some international agreements are regarded as executed internationally as between the parties when made (boundary treaties). Others are executory, such as the mutual promises of the members of the NATO to consider an attack on one an attack on all and to respond effectively. Still others may require implementing legislation.

International agreements have given the international legal system almost all the rules that exist on international economic law. In the more traditional political areas, international agreements may alter, expand, or restate customary international law. Treaties may have a "common-law" like customary law-creating, characteristic. A series of treaties, or even one overwhelmingly adopted, may create customary international law. Treaties also may "codify" rules of customary international law. Finally, given the lack so far of an effective international parallel to national legislatures or judiciaries, multilateral agreements are used to make new law, such as those relating to pollution of the high seas, uses of the moon, Antarctica, aerial hijacking, protection of human rights, or the creation of an international criminal court. Treaties that have legislative characteristics are sometimes called *traité-lois,* or law-making treaties. They establish a series of legislation-like rules among nations. The Hague and the Geneva Conventions, UNCLOS, and the U.N. Treaty on Drug Trafficking are examples. These *traités-lois* raise the analytical issue of whether the rules therein stated are themselves international law.

Some treaties have constitutional characteristics. They create international institutions and organizations. The U.N. Charter and the Treaty of Rome are examples. All treaties have contract like elements. Some agreements actually are simple contracts. Are these treaties? They are called *traités contrats.* A simple agreement by one country to buy grain from another is an example. The Louisiana Purchase was a *traités contrat.* Is it the same genre as an agreement to purchase grain? Some treaties are "merely" aspirational, such as the Helsinki Final Act. Aspirational agreements tend often to impact both domestic and international law. We saw such an impact from the Helsinki Accords in Eastern Europe. Many from the Czechoslovak and other underground movements stated that the Accords helped them and eventually were incorporated into law . See, Chapters 9 (Human Rights), 16 (Individual Responsibility), 14 (International Resolution of Disputes), and 15 (States and the Use of Force).

5. ***Treaties & the European Union.*** One of the more significant modern uses of treaties is to create international structures such as those that underlie the European Union (EU). Treaties established new institu-

tions and bound the member states to uniform courses of action. The treaties made EU law (and that deriving therefrom as declared by EU agencies) superior to member states' national laws in enumerated situations, and provided for centralized budgeting and financing of important activities. Examples include the Community Agricultural Policy (CAP) and the community treaty on economic matters (the European Economic Community treaty).

The EU system is neither a conventional international organization nor (so far) a federation that eliminates the international statehood of its members. If community authority to make superior law that is directly applicable in some, but not all, situations of governance should expand appreciably into general governmental affairs, the EU might one day become a new federated state. If the authority of the EU should decline to the extent of becoming non-binding directly within member states, it would become indistinguishable from ordinary international organizations.

The modern international practitioner must of necessity have a lot to do with international agreements and the International Court of Justice has subject-matter jurisdiction as to issues concerning international agreements. Treaties are a most vital part of international law; they promote trade and commerce, allow cooperation in other economic and even criminal law matters, provide for common defense, they promote friendship, cooperation in all areas of international intercourse, such as providing for the post, protect the environment and protect the rights and interests of individuals.

———

Section B. International Agreements as Bases of Legal Rights and Duties

———

1. *Pacta Sunt Servanda, the Standard of Performance.* The rule that a treaty undertaking should be performed in good faith, certainly preceded the Vienna Convention, but some authorities contended that the proper standard, at least for some types of treaties, was utmost fidelity (*uberrima fides*). The concept is similar to that of fiduciary obligation in Anglo–American law. Article 26 of the Vienna Convention adopts the first (pacta sunt servanda) standard, although some delegates at the Vienna Treaty conference wanted it stated that only valid treaties in force should be so entitled. Some others wished to confine the performance standard to treaties in force which conformed to the Convention, which would have raised a serious retroactivity problem. What is the difference between the two standards? Judge Lauterpacht's separate opinion in the *Norwegian Loans Case* (1957) (in Ch. 1), noted that "[u]nquestionably, the obligation to act in accordance with good faith, being a general principle of law, is also part of international law." Did Judge Lauterpacht see *pacta sunt servanda*

as a rule of customary international law? As a general principle of international law? As both?

————

Yalta Conference, Agreement Regarding Entry of the Soviet Union Into the War Against Japan, Feb. 11, 1945

59 Stat. 1823.

The leaders of the three Great Powers—the Soviet Union, the United States of America and Great Britain—have agreed that in two or three months after Germany has surrendered and the war in Europe has terminated the Soviet Union shall enter into the war against Japan on the side of the Allies on condition that:

1. The status quo in Outer–Mongolia (The Mongolian People's Republic) shall be preserved;

2. The former rights of Russia violated by the treacherous attack of Japan in 1904 shall be restored, viz:

> (a) the southern part of Sakhalin as well as all the islands adjacent to it shall be returned to the Soviet Union,

> (b) the commercial port of Dairen shall be internationalized, the preeminent interests of the Soviet Union in this port being safeguarded and the lease of Port Arthur as a naval base of the USSR restored,

> (c) the Chinese–Eastern Railroad and the South–Manchurian Railroad which provides an outlet to Dairen shall be jointly operated by the establishment of a joint Soviet–Chinese Company it being understood that the preeminent interests of the Soviet Union shall be safeguarded and that China shall retain full sovereignty in Manchuria;

3. The Kuril islands shall be handed over to the Soviet Union.

It is understood, that the agreement concerning Outer–Mongolia and the ports and railroads referred to above will require concurrence of Generalissimo Chiang Kai–Shek. The President will take measures in order to obtain this concurrence on advice from Marshal Stalin. The Heads of the three Great Powers have agreed that these claims of the Soviet Union shall be unquestionably fulfilled after Japan has been defeated. For its part the Soviet Union expresses its readiness to conclude with the National Government of China a pact of friendship and alliance between the USSR and China in order to render assistance to China with its armed forces for the purpose of liberating China from the Japanese yoke.

II.   CTAJINH (J. STALIN)
FRANKLIN D. ROOSEVELT
WINSTON S. CHURCHILL

————

United States Position on Soviet–Japanese Peace Treaty Negotiations

35 United States Department of State Bulletin 484 (1956).

Following is the text of an *aide memoire* which was given to the Japanese Ambassador at Washington on September 7 and to the Japanese Foreign Minister at Tokyo on September 8. Pursuant to the request made by the Japanese Foreign Minister, Mr. Shigemitsu, in the course of recent conversations in London with the Secretary of State, Mr. Dulles, the Department of State has reviewed the problems presented in the course of the current negotiations for a treaty of peace between the Union of Soviet Socialist Republics and Japan, with particular reference to the interest of the United States as a signatory of the San Francisco Peace Treaty, and on the basis of such review makes the following observations.

The Government of the United States believes that the state of war between Japan and the Soviet Union should be formally terminated. Such action has been overdue since 1951, when the Soviet Union declined to sign the San Francisco Peace Treaty. Japan should also long since have been admitted to the United Nations, for which it is fully qualified; and Japanese prisoners of war in Soviet hands should long since have been returned in accordance with the surrender terms.

With respect to the territorial question, as the Japanese Government has been previously informed, the United States regards the so-called Yalta agreement as simply a statement of common purposes by the then heads of the participating powers, and not as a final determination by those powers or of any legal effect in transferring territories. The San Francisco Peace Treaty (which conferred no rights upon the Soviet Union because it refused to sign) did not determine the sovereignty of the territories renounced by Japan, leaving that question, as was stated by the Delegate of the United States at San Francisco, to "international solvents other than this treaty".
* * *

Department of State, Washington, September 7, 1956.

Legal Status of Eastern Greenland (Denmark v. Norway)

Permanent Court of International Justice, 1933.
P.C.I.J., Ser. A_B, No. 53.

* * *

By an Application instituting proceedings, filed with the Registry of the Court on July 12th, 1931, in accordance with Article 40 of the Statute and Article 35 of the Rules of Court, the Danish Government, relying on the optional clause of Article 36, paragraph 2, of the Statute, brought before the Permanent Court of International Justice a suit against the Norwegian Government on the ground that the latter had, on July 10th, 1931, published a proclamation declaring that it had proceeded to occupy certain territories in Eastern Greenland, which, in the contention of the Danish Government, were subject to the sovereignty of the Crown of Denmark.

The Application, after thus indicating the subject of the dispute, proceeds to formulate the claim by asking the Court for judgment to the effect that "the promulgation of the above-mentioned declaration of occupation and any steps taken in this respect by the Norwegian Government constitute a violation of the existing legal situation and are accordingly unlawful and invalid."

* * *

The Danish submission in the written pleading, that the Norwegian occupation of July 10th, 1931, is invalid, is founded upon the contention that the area occupied was at the time of the occupation subject to Danish sovereignty; that the area is part of Greenland, and at the time of the occupation Danish sovereignty existed over all Greenland; consequently it could not be occupied by another Power. In support of this contention, the Danish Government advances two propositions. First, that the sovereignty which Denmark now enjoys over Greenland has existed for a long time, has been continuously and peacefully exercised and, until the present dispute, has not been contested by any Power. This proposition Denmark sets out to establish as a fact. Second, that Norway has by treaty or otherwise herself recognized Danish sovereignty over Greenland as a whole and therefore cannot now dispute it.

* * *

The Court will now consider the second Danish proposition that Norway had given certain undertakings which recognized Danish sovereignty over all Greenland. These undertakings have been fully discussed by the two Parties, and in three cases the Court considers that undertakings were given.

* * *

In addition to the [above] engagements, the Ihlen declaration, viz. the reply given by M. Ihlen, the Norwegian Minister for Foreign Affairs, to the Danish Minister on July 22nd, 1919, must also be considered.

* * *

* * * [T]he point is whether the Ihlen declaration—even if not constituting a definitive recognition of Danish sovereignty—did not constitute an engagement obliging Norway to refrain from occupying any part of Greenland. The Danish request and M. Ihlen's reply were recorded by him in a minute . . .

* * *

II.   Today I informed the Danish Minister that the Norwegian Government would not make any difficulties in the settlement of this question. 22/7—19Ih.

The incident has reference, first to the attitude to be observed by Denmark before the Committee of the Peace Conference at Paris in regard to Spitzbergen, this attitude being that Denmark would not "oppose the wishes of Norway in regard to the settlement of this question"; as is known, these wishes related to the sovereignty over Spitzbergen. Secondly, the request showed that "the Danish Government was confident that the Norwegian Government would not make any difficulty" in the settlement of the Greenland question; the aims that Denmark had in view in regard to the last-named island were to secure the "recognition by all the Powers concerned of Danish sovereignty over the whole of Greenland," and that there should be no opposition "to the Danish Government extending their political and economic interests to the whole of Greenland." It is clear from the relevant Danish documents which preceded the Danish Minister's démarche at Christiania on July 14th, 1919, that the Danish attitude in the Spitzbergen question and the Norwegian attitude in the Greenland question were regarded in Denmark as interdependent, and this interdependence appears to be reflected also in M. Ihlen's minutes of the interview. Even if this interdependence—which, in view of the affirmative reply of the Norwegian Government, in whose name the Minister for Foreign Affairs was speaking, would have created a bilateral engagement—is not held to have been established, it can hardly be denied that what Denmark was asking of Norway ("not to make any difficulties in the settlement of the [Greenland] question") was equivalent to * * * indicating her readiness to concede in the Spitzbergen question (to refrain from opposing "the wishes of Norway in regard to the settlement of this question"). What Denmark desired to obtain from Norway was that the latter should do nothing to obstruct the Danish plans [for] Greenland. The declaration which the Minister * * * gave on July 22nd, 1919, on behalf of the Norwegian Government, was definitely affirmative: "I told the Danish Minister to-day that the Norwegian Government would not make any difficulty in the settlement of this question."

The Court considers it beyond all dispute that a reply of this nature given by the Minister for Foreign Affairs on behalf of his Government in response to a request by the diplomatic representative of a foreign Power, in regard to a question falling within his province, *is binding upon the country to which the Minister belongs.* (emphasis added).

* * *

It follows that, as a result of the undertaking involved in the Ihlen declaration of July 22nd, 1919, Norway is under an obligation to refrain from contesting Danish sovereignty over Greenland as a whole, and a fortiori to refrain from occupying a part of Greenland.

* * *

For these reasons, the court, by twelve votes to two, (1) decides that the declaration of occupation promulgated by the Norwegian Government on July 10th, 1931, and any steps taken in this respect by that Government, constitute a violation of the existing legal situation and are accordingly unlawful and invalid;

* * *

Dissenting Opinion of Mr. ANZILOTTI:

* * *

The question whether the so-called Ihlen declaration was merely a provisional indication (Norwegian contention) or a definitive undertaking (Danish contention) has been debated at length.

* * *

The outcome of all this is therefore an agreement, concluded between the Danish Minister, on behalf of the Danish Government, and the Norwegian Minister for Foreign Affairs, on behalf of the Norwegian Government, by means of purely verbal declarations. The validity of this agreement has been questioned, having regard, in the first place, to its verbal form, and to the competence of the Minister for Foreign Affairs. As regards the form, it should be noted that as both Parties are agreed as to the existence and tenor of these declarations, the question of proof does not arise. Moreover, there does not seem to be any rule of international law requiring that agreements of this kind must necessarily be in writing, in order to be valid. The question of the competence of the Minister for Foreign Affairs is closely connected with the contents of the agreement in question; and these have already been determined.

No arbitral or judicial decision relating to the international competence of a Minister for Foreign Affairs has been brought to the knowledge of the Court; nor has this question been exhaustively treated by legal authorities. In my opinion, it must be recognized that the constant and general practice of States has been to invest the Minister for Foreign Affairs—the direct agent of the chief of the State—with authority to make statements on current affairs to foreign diplomatic representatives, and in particular to inform them as to the attitude which the government, in whose name he speaks, will adopt in a given question. Declarations of this kind are binding upon the State.

As regards the question whether Norwegian constitutional law authorized the Minister for Foreign Affairs to make the declaration, that is a point which, in my opinion, does not concern the Danish Government: it was M. Ihlen's duty to refrain from giving his reply until he had obtained any assent that might be requisite under the Norwegian laws. * * *

[Observations and another dissenting opinion omitted.]

———

Comment on the Anzilotti dissent. This luminary of the Permanent Court of International Justice agreed with the majority on the issues of oral treaties and the binding effect internationally of a foreign minister's commitment in excess of his constitutional authority. (Cf. Articles 27, 46, and 47 of the Vienna Convention.). How and why was the Ihlen declaration sufficient to bind Norway? Did the majority opinion, and especially the dissent, accept agency principles as part of international law? If so, by what authority? What are the boundaries of this "agency" that the Court and international law recognize? *See,* Vienna Convention article 7(1)(b): "[if it] appears from the practice of the states concerned or from other circumstances that their intention was to consider that person as representing the state for such purposes and to dispense with full powers * * *." See also article 47. Was this an application of international, contract, and agency law? Was there any sort of *quid pro quo?* Was any sort of agreement made? Did Denmark give anything to Norway? Denmark conceded that Norway had sovereignty over Spitzbergen. Is that sufficient for a contract? Would the result be the same in a simple contract case before common law nation's domestic court? Would it be the same in a court of a civil law country? Anzilotti's dissent was on a broader ground: he was not prepared to rule that the Norwegian occupation was invalid, even though unlawful. For further explanation, *see* Hudson, *The Twelfth Year of the Permanent Court of International Justice*, 28 AJIL 1, 8 (1934).

2. RIGHTS AND OBLIGATIONS OF STATES NOT PARTIES TO AN INTERNATIONAL AGREEMENT

Read articles 34 through 37 of the Vienna Convention in the Documentary Supplement.

Free Zones of Upper Savoy and the District of Gex (France v. Switzerland)

Permanent Court of International Justice, 1932.
P.C.I.J., Ser. A–B, No. 46.

[France contended that the Treaty of Versailles (1919) abrogated certain tariff-free areas within France, on the border with Switzerland in the region of Geneva. Switzerland claimed that her rights in these areas had been provided in the post-Napoleonic settlement of Europe, by various treaties stemming from the Congress of Vienna, in the years 1814–15. The court found that Switzerland had sufficiently participated in the earlier arrangements as to have acquired rights as to the free zones. It also decided that the Treaty of Versailles was not intended to abrogate these rights. Nevertheless, the court expressed a viewpoint on the question whether rights that Switzerland might have acquired as a non-party to the 1814–15 treaties could have been taken away by France and other parties to the Versailles treaty, to which Switzerland was not a party. On third party rights the court made a statement which a common law lawyer would call obiter dictum. It appears below.]

It cannot be lightly presumed that stipulations favourable to a third State have been adopted with the object of creating an actual right in its favour. There is however nothing to prevent the will of sovereign States from having this object and this effect. The question of the existence of a right acquired under an instrument drawn between other States is therefore one to be decided in each particular case: it must be ascertained whether the States which have stipulated in favour of a third State meant to create for that State an actual right *which the latter has accepted as such.* [Emphasis supplied.]

Question. Before the Vienna Convention, the statement above was the main authority on the point. Does the Convention follow the dictum squarely? See Article 36.

Jus Cogens

Notes and Questions. Are there overriding restrictions on what states may do by international agreement? The Latin term jus cogens (compelling law) may supply an answer. Read article 53 of the Vienna Convention on Treaties in the Documentary Supplement. What is a peremptory norm? Is it a "super custom" or some sort of peremptory public policy principle. Could it function like a constitutional principle?

Schwelb, Some Aspects of International Jus Cogens as Formulated by the International Law Commission

61 American Journal of International Law 946, 949 (1967).*
Jurisprudence on International Jus Cogens.

* * * [There have been very few instances involving authoritative invocation of jus cogens. Many of its invocations have been in dissenting opinions or in domestic judicial decisions.]

* * *

In the case of the S.S. Wimbledon the question was whether Germany, as a neutral in the Polish–Russian war, was in 1921 under the obligation to permit contraband destined for Poland to pass through the Kiel Canal. The Court decided that Article 380 of the Peace Treaty of Versailles applied, under which the Canal was to be maintained open to the vessels of all nations at peace with Germany. Mr. Schücking, the German national judge, dissented. One of his arguments was the consideration that, by permitting the passage of the ship carrying contraband, Germany would have violated the duties of a neutral. It cannot have been the intention of the victorious states, he said, to bind Germany to commit offenses against third states. It would have been impossible to give effect to such an intention because it is impossible to undertake by treaty a valid obligation to perform acts which would violate the rights of third parties. Judges Anzilotti and Huber, who also dissented from the decision of the Court, did not adduce an argument based on the partial invalidity of the Peace Treaty article. * * *

The Negotiating History of Jus Cogens at Vienna Kearney and Dalton, The Treaty on Treaties.

64 American Journal of International Law 495, 535 (1970).*

* * * The committee of the whole moved immediately to one of the most controversial articles produced by the Commission—Article 53 on treaties conflicting with a peremptory norm of international law or, as it is customarily described, the Jus Cogens Doctrine. The Commission [proposed]: "A treaty is void if it conflicts with a peremptory norm of general international law from which no derogation is permitted and which can be modified only by a subsequent norm of general international law having the same character." Although the principle that there are fundamental requirements of international behavior that cannot be set aside by treaty is considered a fairly recent development, it has been incorporated into Section 116 of the Restatement in the following terms: "An international agreement may be made with respect to any matter except to the extent that the agreement conflicts with, a) the rules of international law incorpo-

* Reprinted with the permission of the American Society of International Law.

rating basic standards of international conduct. * * * '' Both the Commission's article and the Restatement, however, present the same difficulty: they leave open the question what is a peremptory norm or what is a basic standard of international conduct.

* * *

In his second report Waldock had proposed three categories of jus cogens: (a) the use or threat of force in contravention of the principles of the United Nations Charter; (b) international crimes so characterized by international law; (c) acts or omissions whose suppression is required by international law. The discussion in the Commission indicated such varying viewpoints on what constituted jus cogens that the categories were dropped. A comment regarding the resulting draft is pertinent: "Mr. Bartoš explained that the drafting committee had been compelled to refrain from giving any definition of jus cogens whatever, because two-thirds of the Commission had been opposed to each formula proposed." The position in the conference reflected the position in the Commission. There was no substantial attack made upon the concept of jus cogens. Indeed, it would be very difficult to make a sustainable case that two states are free to make a treaty in which they agree to attack and carve up a third state or to sell some of their residents to each other as slaves. But as Minagawa points out, "examples such as the treaty permitting piracy or re-establishing slavery appear to concern merely *'une pure hypothèse d'école'*." The real problem was how to define the test for recognizing a rule of jus cogens.

* * *

The Austrian jurist, Hanspeter Neuhold, gives in his analysis of the 1968 session a lively account of the conclusion of debate:

> After five meetings had been devoted to discussing the various problems of jus cogens, the scene was set for the final showdown at a night meeting which lasted almost till midnight. It was fought with all the weapons which the arsenal of the rules of procedure offered the delegates. Thus, the representative of the USA introduced a motion to defer the vote on article [53] and to refer all amendments to the Drafting Committee with a view to working out a more acceptable text. This proposal was endorsed by the United Kingdom and France. Conversely, the Ghanaian delegate, who was supported by the representatives of India and the USSR, moved to take a vote immediately, since the various delegations had made their positions sufficiently clear. Motions to adjourn the debate and to close the discussion were defeated. Other motions requesting a division of the original United States proposal caused considerable confusion. At last, a roll call was taken on the motion submitted by the USA to defer voting on article [53] and the amendments thereto, which failed to obtain the necessary majority by the narrowest margin possible: 42 votes were cast in favour, the same number against, with 7 abstentions_ Ironically enough, if a request by Ghana for priority of her motion to vote at once had been adopted and the votes cast in the same way, the United States motion would have prevailed indirectly * * *. [r]eference to recognition of jus cogens by the national and regional legal systems of the world was rejected. * * *

A dispute then arose as to the meaning of that vote and whether the principle of jus cogens had been adopted. The chairman settled the matter by ruling that the jus cogens principle had been adopted and that the drafting committee was to see if the text could be made clearer. A peremptory norm was defined as "a norm accepted and recognized by the international community of States as a whole * * *."

Notes and Questions

1. ***Ruminations on jus cogens?*** Is jus cogens a general principle or a custom in the ICJ Statute article hierarchy of sources? What is the difference? How does the Vienna Convention on Treaties see it: custom or super custom? Does it function like a fundamental principle of public policy or constitutional law? The basic idea seems to be that certain norms are so compelling as to be peremptory. What does this mean? Who or what decides which norms are peremptory? How do they become peremptory? Can *jus cogens* principles be modified? If so, how? Can custom overcome them or does it take a subsequent formulation of a new peremptory norm—a new "super-custom?" Is there some analogy between the notion of *jus cogens* and principles of public policy in both civilian jurisdictions and common law states? Both systems have certain rules for which no derogation by contract will be countenanced. Can a treaty derogate from a regular (*non-jus cogens*) norm of customary international law?

2. ***Vienna Convention Article 53 defines a peremptory norm as one "accepted and recognized by the international community of states as a whole * * *" What is the "international community of states?"*** What norms reach the level of being peremptory? Who decides? Does this mean every nation? A majority? A two-thirds majority? The most influential? If there is a community, does it ever accept anything "as a whole?" One hopes that it can be shown that the "community" had accepted the prohibition of the slave trade and genocide, but has it? Could it be argued that it has also accepted a principle prohibiting environmental pollution? See Chapter 6. Is there any relationship between obligations *erga omnes* and *jus cogens*?

Does *jus cogens* supersede domestic law? From the point of view of international law? From the point of view of domestic law? *See, Committee of U.S. Citizens Living in Nicaragua v. Reagan*, 859 F.2d 929, 940 (D.C.Cir. 1988) ("*Jus cogens* describes peremptory norms of law, which are nonderogable and form the highest level of international law"): *Siderman v. Argentina, supra* (the prohibition against official torture "carries with it the force of *jus cogens.*") ("[*Jus cogens*] is an elite subset of norms recognized as customary international law."). We present the pertinent part of Siderman in chapter 9. Please read the *jus cogens* portion now.

3. ***How may the substantive content of jus cogens be established?*** What state conduct beyond Waldock's three categories may come to be included in *jus cogens*? What institutions, by what modalities, may add to the basic list of peremptory norms? Category (a) in Waldock's enumeration is generally assumed to be established by *opinio juris* and the

U.N. Charter, although in Chapter 14 the argument is raised that the anti-force provisions of the Charter are not as firm as the language and negotiating history of the Charter might otherwise indicate. Some suggest that, analytically, *jus cogens* is a rule about valid and invalid treaties, classified as to purpose. Indeed, it is argued that it is not a rule about legal and illegal use of force by states that would be raised even if no agreement were involved. However, see ¶ 190 of the *Nicaragua Case, supra*— where the International Court states that the principle against the use of force, is "a conspicuous example of a rule of international law having the character of *jus cogens*." Also, look at article 103 of the Charter. Does this suggest that articles in the Charter are or have become general *jus cogens* principles invalidating any treaty inconsistent with them? Consider also the treatment of *jus cogens* in the 1987 Restatement, Section 331(2).

SECTION C.   RESERVATIONS TO INTERNATIONAL AGREEMENTS

———

Notes.

1.   ***What are reservations and why are they made?*** A nation may wish to have the advantages of being a party to a treaty, but is unwilling or unable to accept certain aspects. Thus, a state may try to become a party to the convention, while excepting itself out of or modifying "unacceptable" provisions. Vienna Convention, article 1(d) provides that a *reservation* is "a unilateral statement, however phrased or named, made by a State, when signing, ratifying, accepting, approving or acceding to a treaty, whereby it purports to exclude or to modify the legal effect of certain provisions of the treaty in their application to that state." Does this article consider a unilateral interpretation of an ambiguous treaty clause in a treaty be a reservation? Can there be a reservation to a bilateral treaty? Would that not simply be a rejection of the treaty? Or would a reservation in a bilateral negotiation be a counter-offer, which, if not accepted, means no treaty. Even when negotiations are among a few states, reservations have little utility.

A state interested in entering into a treaty relationship will attempt during the negotiations to shape the agreement to its wishes. If it succeeds, there is no further problem. If it cannot convince its negotiating partners, but wishes to protect itself against becoming obligated in a manner or to a degree that it unsuccessfully tried to avoid in the negotiations, it may attempt to enter into the treaty relationship under the safeguard of a reservation.

Sometimes state-parties accept other parties' reservations to increase world-wide participation. The price to be paid for this, however, may be to compromise the value or integrity of the convention. Some recent treaties have not allowed reservations. For example, *see* "fast track" (up or down vote—no amendments) procedures in the Law of the Sea, the Rome Statute on the International Criminal Court, and NAFTA treaties.

2. ***When are reservations put?*** In the case of some multilateral agreements, particular issues are intensely disputed in the negotiating conference. Sometimes, a reservation will be put forward by a state that has decided to try to be seen as the treaty community, while maintaining its contrarian position. In times past, when most chiefs of state were autocrats, reservations were at the time the agent signed for the sovereign. Today, the signature of the final act of the negotiating conference is almost always *ad referendum* to an internal authorization process, leading to ratification. Signature indicates that the negotiators have agreed to the text language. Even so, reservations are sometimes made at signature, so as to give clear notice to the other states involved or to protect the negotiators from criticism at home.

An international agreement may provide that it is open for acceptance or accession by states that did not participate in the negotiation. In such cases, obviously, an acceding state wishing to make a reservation would do so at the time of attempted accession.

In many states the internal authorization to become bound involves the consent of the legislative branch. In the United States, the Senate provides its advice and consent by a two-thirds majority of the senators present. Legislative authorization may itself be conditioned upon a reservation. Under most constitutional systems when this happens the executive has no alternative, if it wishes to participate in the treaty association. Such a second stage reservation often reflects imperfect foresight on the part of the executive at the time of the negotiations. The classic and tragic example is that of President Woodrow Wilson and a minority (more than one-third) of the Senate as to the Covenant of the League of Nations. In negotiating the Covenant at Paris in 1919, the President did not take into account that a group of dissident senators would insist on reservations or block approval. President Wilson realized this too late. You recall that the Covenant was an annex to the Versailles peace treaty with Germany. A re-convention of the peace conference was politically impossible because Germany was in internal turmoil; the Weimar Republic was weak, hyperinflation was raging, and revanchist elements that Hitler later mobilized already were active against the treaty. Thus, we see that relationships between the President and the Senate with respect to the conclusion of treaties causes both domestic and international complications. See Chap. 14.

3. ***Effect of reservation on other states.*** A reservation presents other states with the following problem: shall State X be allowed to enter the treaty community on its altered version of the treaty or shall it be excluded? Substantive and procedural issues are presented. The pre-WWII rule bluntly prohibited State X to participate, unless its reservation were unanimously accepted. There has since been a shift in direction, as reflected in the Vienna Convention, resulting in greater flexibility. See Restatement § 313(2)(c). A growing trend is developing to prohibit reservations, especially in complicated, multisubject, multiparty conventions, such as the U.N. Convention on the Law of the Sea. Such prohibitions, obviously hinder universality in acceptance but preserve uniformity of treatment. The materials that follow deal with this shift.

Vienna Convention on the Law of Treaties

[The text of the convention is in the Documentary Supplement. Read articles 20 through 23 in conjunction with article 19, quoted below.]

Article 19

Formulation of reservations

A State may, when signing, ratifying, accepting, approving or acceding to a treaty, formulate a reservation unless:

(a) the reservation is prohibited by the treaty;

(b) the treaty provides that only specified reservations, which do not include the reservation in question, may be made; or

(c) in cases not falling under sub-paragraphs (a) and (b), the reservation is incompatible with the object and purpose of the treaty.

Note.

Vienna Convention provisions on reservations: types of treaties providing for the codification and progressive development of international law. Articles 19–23 of the Convention are the product of the General Assembly's request to the International Law Commission. Law-making international agreements may be an orderly formulation in concise text of widely accepted norms of customary international law [*codification*]. Or, they may be a formulation of proposed new rules [*progressive development*]. Sometimes both of these exist in the same treaty. The Treaty on Treaties, itself, is, on the whole, more digest than code or progressive development, but some aspects of the articles on reservations may go beyond what is clearly accepted as customary international law.

Reservations to the Convention on Genocide (Advisory Opinion)

International Court of Justice, 1951.
[1951] I.C.J.Rep. 15.

[On November 16th, 1950, the General Assembly requested the Court to respond to the following questions concerning the Genocide Convention:] I. Can the reserving State be regarded as being a party to the Convention while still maintaining its reservation if the reservation is objected to by one or more of the parties to the Convention but not by others? II. If the answer to Question I is in the affirmative, what is the effect of the reservation as between the reserving State and: (a) The parties which object to the reservation? (b) Those which accept it? III. What would be the legal effect as regards the answer to Question I if an objection to a reservation is made: (a) By a signatory which has not yet ratified? (b) By a State entitled to sign or accede but which has not yet done so?

* * *

The Court observes that the three questions referred to it for an Opinion have certain common characteristics. All three questions are expressly limited by the terms of the Resolution of the General Assembly to

the Convention on the Prevention and Punishment of the Crime of Genocide, * * * [t]he replies which the Court is called upon to give to them are
necessarily and strictly limited to that Convention. The Court will seek
these replies in the rules of law relating to the effect to be given to the
intention of the parties to multilateral conventions. The * * * questions
are purely abstract in character. They refer neither to the reservations
which have, in fact, been made to the Convention by certain States, nor to
the objections which have been made to such reservations by other States.
They do not even refer to the reservations which may in future be made in
respect of any particular article; nor do they refer to the objections to which
these reservations might give rise. * * *

The Court observes that this question [I] refers, not to the possibility
of making reservations to the Genocide Convention, but solely to the
question whether a contracting State which has made a reservation can,
while still maintaining it, be regarded as being a party to the Convention,
when there is a divergence of views between the contracting parties
concerning this reservation, some accepting the reservation, others refusing
to accept it.

* * *

The Court recognizes that an understanding was reached within the
General Assembly on the faculty to make reservations to the Genocide
Convention and that it is permitted to conclude therefrom that States
becoming parties to the Convention gave their assent thereto. It must now
determine what kind of reservations may be made and what kind of
objections may be taken to them.

The solution of these problems must be found in the special characteristics of the Genocide Convention. * * * The origins of the Convention
show that it was the intention of the United Nations to condemn and
punish genocide as "a crime under international law" involving a denial of
the right of existence of entire human groups, a denial which shocks the
conscience of mankind and results in great losses to humanity, and which is
contrary to moral law and to the spirit and aims of the United Nations
(Resolution 96(I) of the General Assembly, December 11th 1946). The first
consequence arising from this conception is that the principles underlying
the Convention are principles which are recognized by civilized nations as
binding on States, even without any conventional obligation. A second
consequence is the universal character both of the condemnation of genocide and of the co-operation required "in order to liberate mankind from
such an odious scourge" (Preamble to the Convention). The Genocide
Convention was therefore intended by the General Assembly and by the
contracting parties to be definitely universal in scope. It was in fact
approved on December 9th, 1948, by a resolution which was unanimously
adopted by fifty-six States.

The objects of such a convention must also be considered. The Convention was manifestly adopted for a purely humanitarian and civilizing
purpose. It is indeed difficult to imagine a convention that might have this
dual character to a greater degree, since its object on the one hand is to
safeguard the very existence of certain human groups and on the other to
confirm and endorse the most elementary principles of morality. In such a

convention the contracting States do not have any interests of their own; they merely have, one and all, a common interest, namely, the accomplishment of those high purposes which are the raison d'être of the convention. Consequently, in a convention of this type one cannot speak of individual advantages or disadvantages to States, or of the maintenance of a perfect contractual balance between rights and duties. The high ideals which inspired the Convention provide, by virtue of the common will of the parties, the foundation and measure of all its provisions.

* * *

The object and purpose of the Genocide Convention imply that it was the intention of the General Assembly and of the States which adopted it that as many States as possible should participate. The complete exclusion from the Convention of one or more States would not only restrict the scope of its application, but would detract from the authority of the moral and humanitarian principles which are its basis. It is inconceivable that the contracting parties readily contemplated that an objection to a minor reservation should produce such a result. But even less could the contracting parties have intended to sacrifice the very object of the Convention in favour of a vain desire to secure as many participants as possible. The object and purpose of the Convention thus limit both the freedom of making reservations and that of objecting to them. It follows that it is the compatibility of a reservation with the object and purpose of the Convention that must furnish the criterion for the attitude of a State in making the reservation on accession as well as for the appraisal by a State in objecting to the reservation. Such is the rule of conduct which must guide every State in the appraisal which it must make, individually and from its own standpoint, of the admissibility of any reservation.

Any other view would lead either to the acceptance of reservations which frustrate the purposes which the General Assembly and the contracting parties had in mind, or to recognition that the parties to the Convention have the power of excluding from it the author of a reservation, even a minor one, which may be quite compatible with those purposes. It has nevertheless been argued that any State entitled to become a party to the Genocide Convention may do so while making any reservation it chooses by virtue of its sovereignty. The Court cannot share this view. It is obvious that so extreme an application of the idea of State sovereignty could lead to a complete disregard of the object and purpose of the Convention.

On the other hand, it has been argued that there exists a rule of international law subjecting the effect of a reservation to the express or tacit assent of all the contracting parties. This theory rests essentially on a contractual conception of the absolute integrity of the convention as adopted. This view, however, cannot prevail if, having regard to the character of the convention, its purpose and its mode of adoption, it can be established that the parties intended to derogate from that rule by admitting the faculty to make reservations thereto.

It does not appear, moreover, that the conception of the absolute integrity of a convention has been transformed into a rule of international law. The considerable part which tacit assent has always played in estimating the effect which is to be given to reservations scarcely permits one to state that such a rule exists, determining with sufficient precision the effect of objections made to reservations. In fact, the examples of objections made to reservations appear to be too rare in international practice to have given rise to such a rule. It cannot be recognized that the report which was adopted on the subject by the Council of the League of Nations on June 17th, 1927, has had this effect. At best, the recommendation made on that date by the council constitutes the point of departure of an administrative practice which, after being observed by the Secretariat of the League of Nations, imposed itself, so to speak, in the ordinary course of things on the Secretary–General of the United Nations in his capacity of depositary of conventions concluded under the auspices of the League. But it cannot be concluded that the legal problem of the effect of objections to reservations has in this way been solved. * * *

It may, however, be asked whether the General Assembly of the United Nations, in approving the Genocide Convention, had in mind the practice according to which the Secretary–General, in exercising his functions as a depositary, did not regard a reservation as definitively accepted until it had been established that none of the other contracting States objected to it. If this were the case, it might be argued that the implied intention of the contracting parties was to make the effectiveness of any reservation to the Genocide Convention conditional on the assent of all the parties. The Court does not consider that this view corresponds to reality. It must be pointed out, first of all, that the existence of an administrative practice does not in itself constitute a decisive factor in ascertaining what views the contracting States to the Genocide Convention may have had concerning the rights and duties resulting therefrom. It must also be pointed out that there existed among the American States members both of the United Nations and of the Organization of American States, a different practice which goes so far as to permit a reserving State to become a party irrespective of the nature of the reservations or of the objections raised by other contracting States. The preparatory work of the Convention contains nothing to justify the statement that the contracting States implicitly had any definite practice in mind. Nor is there any such indication in the subsequent attitude of the contracting States: neither the reservations made by certain States nor the position adopted by other States towards those reservations permit the conclusion that assent to one or the other of these practices had been given. Finally, * * * the debate on reservations to multilateral treaties which took place in the Sixth Committee at the fifth session of the General Assembly reveals a profound divergence of views, some delegations being attached to the idea of the absolute integrity of the Convention, others favouring a more flexible practice which would bring about the participation of as many States as possible. It results from the foregoing considerations that Question I, on account of its abstract character, cannot be given an absolute answer. The appraisal of a reservation and the effect of objections that might be made to it depend upon the particular circumstances of each individual case.

[Portions of the opinion setting forth the Court's reasoning as to Questions II and III omitted.]

The COURT is of the opinion,

In so far as concerns the Convention on the Prevention and Punishment of the Crime of Genocide, in the event of a State ratifying or acceding to the Convention subject to a reservation made either on ratification or on accession, or on signature followed by ratification,

On Question I: by seven votes to five, that a State which has made and maintained a reservation which has been objected to by one or more of the parties to the Convention but not by others, can be regarded as being a party to the Convention if the reservation is compatible with the object and purpose of the Convention; otherwise, that State cannot be regarded as being a party to the Convention.

On Question II: by seven votes to five, (a) that if a party to the Convention objects to a reservation which it considers to be incompatible with the object and purpose of the Convention, it can in fact consider that the reserving State is not a party to the Convention; (b) that if, on the other hand, a party accepts the reservation as being compatible with the object and purpose of the Convention, it can in fact consider that the reserving State is a party to the Convention. * * * That an objection to a reservation made by a State which is entitled to sign or accede but which has not yet done so, is without legal effect. * * * [Dissenting opinions omitted.]

———

Notes & Questions. Finally, on November 4, 1988, President Reagan signed the *Genocide Convention Implementation Act.* The Senate gave its Advice and Consent, enabling the U.S. to become the 88th party to the Genocide Convention, however, subject to major reservations, five understandings, and a declaration. These were intended to modify the legal effects of certain provisions of the Convention. For example, the Senate stipulated that the U.S. must consent specifically before submitting to the jurisdiction of the International Court called for by the Convention. In addition, the Senate provided that the Convention was "non-self-executing." This means that the Convention is not effective under U.S. law, until enabling legislation is promulgated. *See, e.g., Asakura, Sei Fijii cases*, and others in Chapter 12, *infra.*

The Senate further provided the so called "sovereignty reservation," "[t]hat nothing in the [Genocide] Convention requires or authorizes legislation or other action by the United States of America prohibited by the Constitution of the United States as interpreted by the United States." Was this reservation necessary? Does it make the Genocide Convention meaningless in and for the United States? Does it give other nations an argument that the U.S. may claim the right of non-compliance with any obligation under the Convention? Is this reservation "compatible with the object and purpose of the Convention," as required by the Vienna Convention on Treaties, arts. 18 and 19? For more on the U.S. Constitution and Treaties, see Chapter 14.

The Senate also stipulated five *"understandings"* designed to "clarify" interpretation of the Convention and its obligations. First, the mens rea element, "the intent [to destroy a group in whole or in part]" provided in article II is held to require "specific intent." Also, "mental harm" element was defined, the obligation to extradite was limited. Another "understanding" is aimed at protecting members of the U.S. armed forces from prosecution for genocide in combat situations. Another, limits U.S. submission to the jurisdiction of any future international criminal court created under terms of the Convention. Is an understanding any different from a reservation? Can you find the term *"understanding"* or *"declaration"* in the Vienna Convention on Treaties?

Due to the problems caused by its "sovereignty" reservation in the Genocide Convention, the U.S. Senate did not include one for the Torture Convention. The Senate, however, did include a *"declaration"* in its Resolution of Advice and Consent: "[t]he President ... shall not deposit the instrument of ratification until such time as he has notified all present and prospective ratifying party [sic] to this Convention that nothing in this Convention requires or authorizes legislation, or other action, by the United States prohibited by the Constitution ... as interpreted by the United States." This "declaration" was *not* considered to be a *"reservation"* or an *"understanding."* See, gen., Stewart, *The Torture Convention and the Reception of International Criminal Law Within the United States,* 15 Nova L.Rev. 449 (1991).

In the International Covenant on Civil and Political Rights, the Senate gave its advice and consent, but did include the so-called *"states rights understanding,"* which provides that the U.S. Government will only "take appropriate measures to the end" of meeting the requirement of Covenant article 50. Article 50 provides that "the Covenant shall extend to all parts of federal states without any limitations or exceptions" and to fulfill "this Covenant." What do you think the effect of this *understanding* will be? See Ch. 9, *supra.*

Hypothetical Problems on Reservations.

a.   State X, with nuclear capability, has not yet acceded to the Nuclear Test Ban Treaty. What would be the legal consequences (a) under the Genocide case and (b) under the Vienna Convention if State X were to deposit the following instrument with the three depositary governments? "State X accedes to the Treaty Banning Nuclear Weapons Tests in the Atmosphere, in Outer Space and under Water done at Moscow, August 5, 1963, subject to the reservation that the treaty shall not be deemed to inhibit the use of nuclear weapons in armed conflict."

b.   State Y, a new state that has just come into existence, proposes to accede to a number of multipartite international agreements open for accession including the Geneva Convention Relative to the Treatment of Prisoners of War, 75 U.N.T.S. 135. It offers for deposit this reservation: "Provided, however, that persons guilty of war crimes shall not be entitled in State Y to treatment as prisoners of war under this Convention." At the time this proposal is made, military personnel of State A, which is engaged in armed conflict with State Y, have been captured in large numbers by State Y. State A is a party to the Geneva Convention. Assume the Vienna

Convention is in force. What position would you as an official of State A take as to this reservation under the Vienna Convention?

c. The U.S. and Canada negotiated a Treaty Concerning the Uses of the Waters of the Niagara River, 1 U.S.T. 694 (1950). The major purpose of the treaty was to allocate as between the two countries the amount of hydro-static potential each could use for the generation of electrical power. The Senate resolution of advice and consent included a reservation that the United States for its part reserves the right to provide by legislation for the use of the United States' share of the waters of the Niagara and that no project for the use of the United States' share should be undertaken until specifically authorized by Congress. This reservation was officially called to the attention of the government of Canada. What, if any, response do you think Canada should make? *See* Reporters' Note 7 to Section 133 of the 1965 Restatement. Internal legal aspects of this situation, in relationship to the Federal Power Act of 1920 and the jurisdiction of the Federal Power Commission in the absence of any new legislation, were involved in *Power Authority of New York v. Federal Power Commission*, 247 F.2d 538 (D.C.Cir.1957).

_____

Section D.   Interpretation of International Agreements

1.   General

Are there formalized guidelines for interpretation of international agreements? Older systemic scholarship sometimes presented canons for interpretation. These have fallen into desuetude. The influences of relatively modern developments of thought about semiotics, semantics, social psychology, linguistics, and mental processes are manifest in current scholarly discussions. A restraining influence on the movement away from lexicographical emphasis is the continued validity of an international relations assumption that states, being free to make agreements, always intend to make the least detrimental of several otherwise plausible interpretative alternatives.

The basic principles for interpreting treaties are: ordinary meaning in context, good faith, object and purpose. *See* arts. 31 and 32 of the Vienna Convention. The determination of the meaning of language in relationship to the rights and duties of parties to an international agreement is a process that parallels interpretation of contracts, wills, trusts and other consensual arrangements in private law. Do words and phrases in international agreements (in domestic contracts) always, sometimes, or never have clear, mutually understood, and constant meanings? Although the parallel is clear, are the rules the same as those a U.S. judge would apply in the domestic contractual setting? Some problems are particular to operations in the international legal system. For example, would interpretation be the same or different, if the jurisdiction International Court of Justice is invoked, as compared to a domestic court, where the issue is one of asserted private party rights under an international agreement? Here we assume the parallels and focus on the special problems.

To what extent is the type or nature of a given international agreement involved to be taken into account, as say, between a land boundary agreement, an international agreement codifying private carriage of goods at sea, and the Charter of the United Nations? How is the authority of the authorized interpreter to interpret the agreement to be determined? Is an arbitral panel chosen by the states involved more or less free to interpret than the legal adviser of one of the foreign offices? How and when, if at all, is the negotiating history of the agreement legally acceptable as relevant to the interpretative process? Would acceptable negotiating history include actions taken and statements made during the internal ratification of the agreement by a party?

International Law Commission, Draft Articles on the Law of Treaties

61 American Journal of International Law 255, 349 (1967).*

Commentary on Rules of Interpretation**

(1) The utility and even the existence of rules of international law governing the interpretation of treaties are sometimes questioned. The first two of the Commission's Special Rapporteurs on the law of treaties in their private writings also expressed doubts as to the existence in international law of any general rules for the interpretation of treaties. Other jurists, although they express reservations as to the obligatory character of certain of the so-called canons of interpretation, show less hesitation in recognizing the existence of some general rules for the interpretation of treaties. * * *

(2) Jurists also differ to some extent in their basic approach to the interpretation of treaties according to the relative weight which they give to: (a) The text of the treaty as the authentic expression of the intentions of the parties; (b) The intentions of the parties as a subjective element distinct from the text; and (c) The declared or apparent objects and purposes of the treaty.

* * *

(3) Most cases submitted to international adjudication involve the interpretation of treaties, and the jurisprudence of international tribunals is rich in reference to principles and maxims of interpretation. In fact, statements can be found in the decisions of international tribunals to support the use of almost every principle or maxim of which use is made in national systems of law in the interpretation of statutes and contracts.

* Reprinted with the permission of the American Society of International Law.

** Draft Articles 27 and 28, which correspond to Articles 31 (as supplemented) and 32 in the Convention.

Treaty interpretation is, of course, equally part of the everyday work of Foreign Ministries.

* * *

(11) The article as already indicated is based on the view that the text must be presumed to be the authentic expression of the intentions of the parties; and, that, in consequence, the starting point of interpretation is the elucidation of the meaning of the text, not an investigation ab initio into the intentions of the parties. The Institute of International Law adopted this—the textual—approach to treaty interpretation. The objections to giving too large a place to the intentions of the parties as an independent basis of interpretation find expression in the proceedings of the Institute. The textual approach on the other hand, commends itself by the fact that, as one authority has put it, "le texte signé est, sauf de rares exceptions, la seule et la plus récente expression de la volonté commune des parties." Moreover, the jurisprudence of the International Court contains many pronouncements from which it is permissible to conclude that the textual approach to treaty interpretation is regarded by it as established law. In particular, the Court has more than once stressed that it is not the function of interpretation to revise treaties or to read into them what they do not, expressly or by implication, contain.

Kearney and Dalton, The Treaty on Treaties

64 American Journal of International Law 495, 518 (1970).*

* * *

The articles on interpretation demonstrate that a quite conservative (even old-fashioned) series of rules would be accepted by the conference if endorsed by the Commission. Articles 31 and 32 deal, respectively, with the general rule and supplementary means of interpretation. The Commission's formulation established a hierarchy of sources in which primacy was accorded to the text.

Paragraph 1 of Article 31 requires that a treaty be "interpreted in good faith in accordance with the ordinary meaning to be given to the terms of the treaty in their context and the light of its object and purpose." Context is narrowly defined as comprising, "in addition to the text, including its preamble and annexes," related agreements made by all the parties and instruments made by less than all the parties but accepted by all as related to the treaty. Paragraph 3 of Article 31, listing elements "extrinsic to the text" which shall be "taken into account" in interpretation, is limited to subsequent agreements between the parties, subsequent practice establishing agreement and relevant rules of international law.

Article 32 allows "supplementary means of interpretation" to be resorted to, "including preparatory work on the treaty and the circumstances of its conclusion, in order to confirm the meaning resulting from the application of article 31, or to determine the meaning when the interpretation according to article 31: (a) leaves the meaning ambiguous or

* Reprinted with the permission of the American Society of International Law.

obscure; or (b) leads to a result which is manifestly absurd or unreasonable.''

A member of the Commission has observed that the method of presentation in both Articles 31 and 32 "is designed to stress the dominant position of the text itself in the interpretative process."

In the Commission Messrs. Briggs, El Erian, Rosenne and Tsuruoka supported a proposal to combine the substance of Articles 31 and 32 into a single article. In addition, Mr. Barto stated that he was inclined to favor the proposal, and Mr. Amado that he had no strong feelings either way. Among the governments which in their comments on the Commission's articles criticized treating the travaux préparatoires as a secondary means of interpretation were Hungary and the United States.

In light of the division in the Commission on the subject, the expressions of concern in governmental comments, and the traditional United States position in favor of according equal weight to travaux, the United States formally proposed an amendment, the principal objective of which was to eliminate the hierarchy between the sources of evidence for interpretation of treaties by combining the articles containing the general rule and the supplementary means of interpretation: "A treaty shall be interpreted in good faith in order to determine the meaning to be given to its terms in the light of all relevant factors, including in particular:

(a) the context of the treaty;

(b) its objects and purposes;

(c) any agreement between the parties regarding the interpretation of the treaty;

(d) any instrument made by one or more parties in connexion with the conclusion of the treaty and accepted by the other parties as an instrument related to the treaty;

(e) any subsequent practice in the application of the treaty which establishes the common understanding of the meaning of the terms as between the parties generally;

(f) the preparatory work of the treaty;

(g) the circumstances of its conclusion;

(h) any relevant rules of international law applicable in the relations between the parties;

(i) the special meaning to be given to a term if the parties intended such term to have a special meaning.

In introducing the amendment Professor McDougal adverted to the practice of Ministries of Foreign Affairs in looking at the travaux when considering a problem of treaty interpretation and to the practice of international tribunals, as illustrated by the Lotus case, of looking at the preparatory work before reaching a decision on the interpretation of a treaty described as "sufficiently clear in itself."

In the ensuing debate in the committee of the whole, the U.S. amendment received scant support. A principal source of arguments against it was the 1950 debates in the Institute of International Law which had adopted the textual approach. Fear was expressed that "too ready admission of the preparatory work" would afford an opportunity to a state which had "found a clear provision of a treaty inconvenient" to allege a different interpretation "because there was generally something in the preparatory work that could be found to support almost any intention." Other arguments advanced included the assertion that recourse to travaux would favor wealthy states with large and well-indexed archives, fear that non-negotiating states would hesitate to accede to multilateral conventions, since they could hardly be aware of or wish to have their rights based on recourse to the travaux, and the characterization of the International Law Commission text as a "neutral and fair formulation of the generally recognized canons of treaty interpretation." Given the tenor of the debate, the rejection of the amendment was a foregone conclusion.

The adoption by the conference of two articles which the United States viewed as somewhat archaic and unduly rigid does not seriously weaken the value of the convention. It seems unlikely that Foreign Offices will cease to take into consideration the preparatory work and the circumstances of the conclusion of treaties when faced with problems of treaty interpretation, or that international tribunals will be less disposed to consult Article 32 sources in determining questions of treaty interpretation.

The reaction of the conference to a United States amendment to Article 33, which deals with interpretation of plurilingual treaties, was more favorable. The amendment was referred to the drafting committee, which incorporated it in paragraph 4. The new rule provides that when a treaty has been authenticated in two or more languages, neither of which has been accorded priority, and a difference in meaning persists after recourse to the other articles on interpretation, "the meaning which best reconciles the texts, having regard to the object and purpose of the treaty, shall be adopted."

———

Notes. *See* McDougal, Lasswell, & Miller, *The Interpretation of Agreements and World Public Order: Principles of Content and Procedure* (1967), where these authors of the "Yale School" argue that the rules of interpretation ought to permit consideration of *any* relevant evidence to achieve the goal of determining the *"shared expectations of the parties."* They argue that this should be done even when to do so would require contravention of the clear meaning of the text. *What approach does the Vienna Convention on Treaties take? See,* articles 31 and 32; *see also,* Francowska, *The Vienna Convention on the Law of Treaties Before United States Courts,* 28 Va.J.Int'l L. 281 (1988); Günter Handl, *Regional Arrangements and Third State Vessels: Is the Pacta Tertiis Principle Being Modified?,* in COMPETING NORMS IN THE LAW OF MARINE ENVIRONMENTAL PROTECTION—FOCUS ON SHIP SAFETY & POLLUTION PREVENTION 217, 240 (Ringbom, ed. 1997).

Fitzmaurice, Vae Victis or Woe to the Negotiators! Your Treaty or Our "Interpretation" of It?

65 American Journal of International Law 358, 370 (1971).*

[Taken from an article-length book review of McDougal, Lasswell and Miller, The Interpretation of Agreements, *supra.*] The most striking feature of the authors' system is, however, that it subordinates the interpretation of a treaty—or rather (for the matter has little to do with interpretation stricto sensu) its application—to the attainment of certain objectives,—a process which is summed up * * * under the head of the "policing * * * goal." This is defined in general terms * * * as "requiring the rejection of the parties' explicit expectations which [sc. if and insofar as they] contradict community policies." In other words the intentions of the parties, even if clear and ascertained and—what is even more important—common to them both, or all (in short the intentions of the *treaty*—* * *), are not to be given effect to if, in the opinion of the "decision-maker," such intentions are inconsistent with * * * "the goals of public order." Since it is thus left to the adjudicator to decide not only whether there is such inconsistency but also what *are* the goals of public order (and of which public order) to be taken into account, it is evident that on this wideranging, indeed almost illimitable basis, the parties could never be sure how their treaty would be applied or whether it would be applied at all. The process would, in fact, confer on the "decision-maker" a discretion of a kind altogether exceeding the normal limits of the judicial function, amounting rather to the exercise of an administrative rôle. This is well illustrated by the character of the only "community goal" which, so far as this reviewer can see, the authors themselves actually specify, namely, that of the preservation of "human dignity" * * *.

* * *

The *second* goal contemplates the case where the search for * * * the "genuine shared expectations" of the parties "must falter or fail because of gaps, contradictions or ambiguities" in their "communication"—(an unclear term which might mean in the course of the negotiations leading up to the agreement, or in the agreement itself). In such event (ibid.) "a decision-maker should supplement or *augment* (our italics) the relatively more explicit expressions of the parties [sc. what they actually wrote into the agreement] by making reference to the basic constitutive policies of the larger community * * *." Here again, therefore, community policies come in as a criterion, and also, once more, human dignity,—for (ibid.) "no conceivable alternative goal" could be "in accord with the aspiration to defend and expand a social system compatible with the overriding objectives of human dignity."

This, however excellent, is not law but sociology; and although the aim is said to be "in support of search for the genuine shared expectations of the parties," it would in many cases have—and is perhaps subconsciously designed to have—quite a different effect, namely, in the guise of interpretation, to substitute the will of the adjudicator for that of the parties, since

* Reprinted with the permission of the
American Society of International Law.

the intentions of the latter are, by definition (in the given circumstances) unascertainable because not sufficiently clearly or fully expressed,—and therefore presumed intentions, based on what the adjudicator thinks would be good for the community, or in accordance with "overriding objectives of human dignity" etc., must be attributed to them.

* * *

2.   TEXTUALITY OR CONTEXTUALITY?

Textuality or Contextuality Case on Interpretation of the Austrian State Treaty

Seidl–Hohenveldern, Notes on Austrian Judicial Decisions.
86 J. du Droit International 835, 837 (1959).*

The German text of Article 16, Austrian State Treaty (BGBl., Nr. 152–1955; J.O. 2nd Sept. 1955; 49 AJIL, 1955, Off.Doc., p. 162), is worded as follows: "Prohibition relating to Civil Aircraft of German and Japanese Design". "Austria shall not acquire or manufacture civil aircraft which are of German or Japanese design or which embody major assemblies of German or Japanese manufacture or design". Pursuant to this regulation, the Federal Ministry of communications and electric power—Air Navigation Division—denied the request filed by an Austrian glider club for licensing a glider of German construction type; and the glider club, in protest, brought an action before the Verwaltungsgerichtshof. It pointed out, to start with, that in the German language version of the Treaty there was an inherent contradiction, since the Title of Article 16 read "Zivilflugzeuge" (airplanes), whereas in the Article proper one referred to "Luftfahrtzeugen" (aircraft). In Austrian terminology, the plaintiff asserted, "Zivilflugzeuge" indicates in principle that the plane is engine-driven, while "Luftfahrtzeuge" covers gliders as well. Pursuant to Article 38, State Treaty, the Russian, English, French and German texts are authentic. The French version makes use, for both title and text of Article 16, of the word "Avion", which corresponds to the "Zivilflugzeug" concept, instead of using "aéronef", which would render "Luftfahrtzeug"; and so does the Russian text. The English version, on the contrary, reads—for both title and text of Article 16—"aircraft", which corresponds to "Luftfahrtzeug", whereas "Zivilflugzeug", in English, would be "airplane".

The glider club considered that, account being taken of the aforementioned discrepancies between texts, one was faced here, essentially, with an error in the translation into German. Article 16 * * * brings about a limitation of Austrian sovereignty, but even according to the basic principles of international law the existence of diverging authentic texts of a State Treaty results in considering that version which infringes least on sovereignty, as the only one which may be regarded as consonant with the will of the contracting parties and the principles of International Law.

---

* English text in the Journal. Reprinted by permission of Editions Techniques, S.A., Paris.

Moreover, it claimed, the French text is most authoritative, because in the Convention on International Civil Aviation French terminology is clearly defined—French being the official language of ICAO. * * * French wording does not provide any reason for further limiting Austria's sovereignty.

The Verwaltungsgerichtshof decided that, for the purpose of implementing the State Treaty—which in the domestic sphere is to be regarded as directly applicable law—one must infer from its Article 39, paragraph 1, that its German version became domestic law. Pursuant to Austrian practice, headings are to be called upon for construing a legal text only in the event that the text proper is not clear or does not make sense—which is not the case here. In the light of the purpose which, among others, underlies Part II of the State Treaty—namely, to prevent coordination of the Austrian Air Force and civilian aviation with those of Germany and Japan—, the importance of civil aviation as a whole in war time, together with the widespread use of all types of aircraft, including gliders and balloons, for war aims, make a prohibition against any aircraft (even one which is not engine-propelled) appear perfectly logical, however harsh such a rule may seem to glider pilots.

Nor is anything to be gained in favour of thus construing this legal text by underlining the existing contradictions between the German version and those in other languages, since the latter turn out to be just as diverging. Therefore, as long as the differences are not settled by an authentic interpretation of Article 16, made in accordance with the procedure provided for in Article 35 of the Treaty—a procedure which can only be initiated at the international public law level—, the Austrian authorities must continue to abide by the German text, application of which as positive law is mandatory for them and in which the wording does not admit—as already pointed out—of the kind of interpretation proposed by the plaintiff. A legal text may be interpreted in the manner most favourable to the sovereignty of the country concerned only when there exists a doubt as to how that regulation ought to be interpreted; since the provisions of Article 16, in its German version, are unambiguous, this does not apply here.

* * *

Textuality or Contextuality In the Light of Special Circumstances

In the *Anglo–Iranian Oil Co. Case, United Kingdom v. Iran*, [1952] I.C.J.Rep. 4, the optional clause jurisdiction of the World Court turned on the interpretation of the Iranian declaration under Article 36(2) of the Statute of the Court. The issue was whether the limitation of acceptance of jurisdiction was as to (i) treaties or (ii) events coming after the ratification of the Iranian declaration. On linguistic grounds, stressing the French text of the declaration, the court held for Iran, but in doing so it went into the background of why, at the time of making its declaration, Iran sought to be as restrictive as possible as to old treaties. Iran wished to exclude "capitulations treaties," and other impositions on middle eastern countries, made in the Age of Imperialism.

In dissent, Judge Alvarez strongly rejected any notion that a declaration under Article 36(2) should be interpreted on linguistic grounds and then listed and rejected a set of old-fashioned canons of interpretation: The traditional methods of interpretation may be summarized by the following points:

(1) It is considered that the texts have an everlasting and fixed character as long as they have not been expressly abrogated.

(2) Strict respect for the letter of the legal or conventional texts.

(3) Examination of these texts, considered by themselves without regard to their relations with the institution or convention as a whole.

(4) Recourse to travaux préparatoires in case of doubt as to the scope of these texts.

(5) Use, in reasoning, of out-and-out logic, almost as in the case of problems of mathematics or philosophy.

(6) Application of legal concepts or doctrines of the law of nations as traditionally conceived.

(7) Application of the decisions of the present International Court, or of the earlier Court, in similar cases which arise, without regard to the question whether the law so laid down must be modified by reason of the new conditions of international life.

(8) Disregard for the social or international consequences which may result from the construction applied.

Some form of reaction is necessary against these postulates because they have had their day. In the first place the legal or conventional texts must be modified and even regarded as abrogated if the new conditions of international life or of States which participated in the establishment of those texts, have undergone profound change. Then it is necessary to avoid slavish adherence to the literal meaning of legal or conventional texts; those who drafted them did not do so with a grammar and a dictionary in front of them; very often, they used vague or inadequate expressions. The important point is to have regard above all to the spirit of such documents, to the intention of the parties in the case of a treaty, as they emerge from the institution or convention as a whole, and indeed from the new requirements of international life.

Recourse should only be had to travaux préparatoires when it is necessary to discover the will of the parties with regard to matters which affect their interests alone. A legal institution, a convention, once established, acquires a life of its own and evolves not in accordance with the ideas or the will of those who drafted its provisions, but in accordance with the changing conditions of the life of peoples.

A single example will suffice to show the correctness of this assertion. Let us assume that in a commercial convention there is a stipulation that all questions relating to maritime trade are to be governed by the principles of international law in force. These principles may have been followed by the parties for a century, perhaps, without any disputes arising between them; but one of the parties may, at the present time, by reason of the changes which have recently taken place in such matters, come to Court to claim that the century-old practice hitherto followed should be changed on the ground that it must be held that the will of the parties is no longer the same as it was at the time when the convention was signed. This is in many ways similar to the rebus sic stantibus clause which is so well known in the law of nations.

It is to be observed that out-and-out reliance upon the rules of logic is not the best method of interpretation of legal or conventional texts, for international life is not based on logic; States follow, above all, their own interests and feelings in their relations with one another. Reason, pushed to extremes, may easily result in absurdity. It is also necessary to bear in mind the fact that certain fundamental legal conceptions have changed and that certain institutions and certain problems are not everywhere understood in the same way. * * *

SECTION E.   PERFORMANCE OF INTERNATIONAL AGREEMENTS

1.   NOVATION, AMENDMENT AND MODIFICATION OF INTERNATIONAL AGREEMENTS

As in the private law of contracts, the parties to an international agreement may, if third party rights protected by international law are not involved, agree to end the agreement, substitute another agreement for it, or otherwise change particulars in it. Consult articles 37, 39, 40, and 41 of the Vienna Convention. *Cf.* The 1987 Restatement, §§ 334 and 339 (semble, as to modification).

2.   INVALIDATION

As in the private law of contracts, an international agreement may be or become unenforcible for strong public policy reasons. *Jus cogens*, to the extent it has developed or will develop, is one such reason. The niceties of common law distinctions between void and voidable contracts do not carry over into customary international law, but under certain circumstances an obligated party under a treaty may prevail against performance by succeed to establish a legal basis for invalidation. Such bases have been expanded by the Vienna Convention beyond what they were in pre-convention customary international law, thus providing an instance in which the Vienna Convention progressively develops, rather than merely digests, customary international law. Another example involves force and duress. In pre-Charter times, force and duress (military, political, or economic) were two of the legitimate means by which a state was required to become legally obligated to another state or states, contrary to the obligated states' wishes. Many territory grabs were thus established over many centuries. Likewise, error, even fraud in the inducement, were not defenses. Study now articles 46 through 53 of the Vienna Convention. Only article 51 (coercion of the representative of a state) was an assuredly recognized legal basis for later invalidation prior to the Vienna Convention. Does the Vienna Convention go too far the other way, say as to fraud (article 49)? In diplomacy, as in war, ruses and deceptions have a long history of usage, and it cannot assuredly be affirmed that their actual use has ended in post-Charter, post-Vienna Convention days. Treaty capitulations imposed upon a state by use or threat of force impermissible under the U.N. Charter, however, seem clear targets for subsequent successful invalidation. On what ground, other than article 52 of the Vienna Convention? See also the 1987 Restatement, § 331, especially Comment *d* and Reporters' Note 3.

3.   DURATION, SUCCESSION, SUSPENSION, TERMINATION

Notes and Questions

1. ***Duration, (general).*** International agreements may be for fixed time periods, ending automatically at the expiration of the time set. Others provide for automatic renewal if nothing is done at the end of the period. If no time period is fixed, an international agreement continues until legally terminated. Treaties may declare that they continue in perpetuity, but some, such as the 1903 canal treaty between the United States and Panama have not so continued. *See*, Vienna Convention article 4, which allows for termination * * * when and in the manner indicated in the agreement. It also allows termination of an agreement when all of the parties agree. What would be the result if a sufficient number of parties withdrew from a multilateral agreement to put the number of parties remaining below that required for "entry into force?" Do articles 54 or 55 help?

A few international agreements that fix no time period are considered to be of perpetual duration, such as those creating the European Union. Many treaties that create international organizations (often called constitutive treaties) provide procedures for amendment (e.g., the U.N. Charter, articles 108 and 109.) Typically such treaties do not provide for withdrawal but withdrawals have taken place nevertheless.

2. ***Relative durability of various types of international agreements.*** International agreements are all equally durable in strict legal sense, but actual practices indicates that some are more durable than others. In international relations practice treaties, bipartite and multipartite, that create territorial rights (said to be executed treaties) are usually stable. So are treaties that deal with a common problem or need shared by the parties. Bilateral treaties that are or become out of balance as to mutuality of interests are susceptible to unilateral termination. Where, in the past, war has either terminated or suspended international agreements, peace treaties may clarify the situation by stipulating the pre-war bilateral treaties that the parties deem still to be in force and by stating for the negotiating history of the peace treaty that multipartite treaties remain in force, unless specific counter-stipulation is made. The peace treaties negotiated with Italy, Finland, Hungary, Rumania and Bulgaria at Paris in 1946 followed the method just described. When the issue is whether an international agreement has an internal legal effect, a national court looks to the element of the national government that has charge of international relations for guidance as to whether the agreement is still in effect. In some

nations subsequent inconsistent national law may affect the internal legal standing of the international agreement, although internationally it has not been legally ended. Various cases in Chapter 12 illustrate this problem in United States law.

3. *Two significant instances of treaty instability. The Treaty of Versailles, 1919* was negotiated to end World War I with Germany, having the Covenant of the League of Nations as an annex. President Wilson suffered the stroke that led to his death while trying to convince the American people to support the treaty. Far less than half the Senate refused to ratify it without reservations that were politically impossible to re-negotiate with Germany or the Allies. A young John Maynard Keynes became famous (*see*, his Economic Consequences of the Peace (1919), for his attack on its reparations provisions and his study of the disintegration of Wilson's principles under the pounding of vengeful European leaders, especially Georges Clémenceau, Premier of France. In addition to reparations that Germany claimed it could not pay without an expansion of its export trade unacceptable to the Allies, Germany from the beginning evaded the arms limitations provisions of the treaty. Hitler, after he was elected chancellor in 1933, denounced the treaty, armed openly, and stated as an objective of his 1,000 year Reich the elimination of the injustices done to Germany under Versailles, including the imposition on Germany of onerous terms that would not have been acceptable but for disintegration of the German economy following the Armistice of November 11, 1918. As World War II approached, during, and since that war, many have wondered whether a more benign Versailles Treaty would have avoided a second terrible war in Europe, or whether a more severe and effectively policed 1919 treaty would have prevented World War II. Following World War II, unconditional surrender and Allied military occupation were imposed upon Germany. No peace treaty has yet been signed with Germany. The western Allies successfully resisted Soviet demands for heavy reparations charges (20 billion dollars in current production), so far as the occupation zones administered by France, the United Kingdom and the United States were concerned. The division of Germany was directly linked to this resistance.

The Panama Canal Treaty of 1903 granted to the U.S. a zone eleven miles wide through the fledgling state of Panama, along with the authority to act "as if sovereign" in perpetuity. In 1964 internal objection in Panama erupted into riot at a high school within the zone when the Panamanian flag was hauled down by U.S. students. To avoid further unrest negotiations to replace the treaty of 1903 began in 1965 but did not result in mutually agreed terms until after a military coup in Panama in 1968 and the subsequent mobilization by Panama of world opinion in its favor, including a special session of the Security Council held in Panama. Under two treaties entered, Panama and the U.S. are jointly responsible for the security of the Panama Canal, U.S. law has been replaced in the zone by Panamanian law and courts, various public installations in the zone are in the process of being transferred to Panama, and by the year 2000 the canal itself is to pass to Panamanian ownership and control. *See, generally* and as to other instances, Malawer, *Imposed Treaties and International Law*, 7 Cal.W.I.L.J. 1 (1977); Stone, *De Victoribus Victis: The International Law Commission and Imposed Treaties of Peace*, 8 Va.J. of Int'l L. 356

(1968); David Bederman, *Deference or Deception: Treaty Rights as Political Questions,* 70 Colo.L.Rev. 1439 (1999); David, *The Strategy of Treaty Termination—Lawful Breaches and Retaliations* (1975); Halberstam, *A Treaty is a Treaty is a Treaty,* 33 Va.J.Int'l L. 51 (1992); Johnstone, *Treaty Interpretation: The Authority of Interpretive Communities,* 12 Mich.J.Int'l L. 371 (1991). *Cf.,* the meta-legal literature of conflict resolution and negotiating science, such as Deutsch, *Cooperation and Trust, Some Theoretical Notes, Nebraska Symposium on Motivation* (1962); Bilder, *Managing the Risks in International Agreements* (1981).

4. ***Duration and the territorial applicability of international agreements as affected by the life of states, growth and division of states.*** States have always had a high survival rate, although they do occasionally disappear. International agreements not otherwise terminated, to which the former German Reich was a party, were carried on through the former two divided Germanies to continue in today's unified Germany. This, despite the unconditional surrender of the Reich and the exercise of supreme authority in the territory of the former Reich by the occupying powers for from seven to ten years and technically much longer for Berlin. However, it was decided that the statehood of Austria should be re-established by treaty after the 1938 incorporation of Austria into the Reich by Hitler. Technically, and insofar as treaty law is concerned, the Republic of Italy is the former Kingdom of Savoy territorially expanded and governmentally altered.

Although propagandistically the Marxist–Leninist structure was depicted as a new arrangement for a new species of humanity, the USSR was the Tsarist Russian Empire with a different ideology. Shortly after the 1917 Revolution, Lenin canceled unilaterally some treaties giving Russia imperialistic territorial and other rights in Iran. This was quickly reversed has been cast upon the ash heap of history by Lenin's successors, clung tenaciously to all Russian rights under Tsarist treaties.

The post World War I Treaty of St. Germain split up the Austrio–Hungarian Empire into a vestigial Austria and a somewhat altered Hungary. It restored Serbia as a part of a new Yugoslav state and made Bohemia, after centuries of non-treatment as a state, into a new Czechoslovak state, which has now divided itself in two. Many of the "nations" created in that era are now becoming independent. All of them have retained the treaties of their predecessors.

In the decades since World War II, many former colonies have seceded to become new states. In the arrangements for their independence the issue of which treaties of the metropole shall continue in force for the new entity. If third states are concerned, the "mother country" has often negotiated for the continuation or cessation of such treaties as to the people or territory of the new state. Usually newly-created states opt for the continuation of boundary and other territorial interests, including servitudes, transit rights, and similar arrangement. Sometimes the retiring sovereignty is able to negotiate for the new state the continuation for it of advantages it formerly enjoyed as a colony under multilateral treaties. The new state usually elects to decide for itself what multipartite treaties open for accession. The new state must apply to be admitted to the United Nations as a member under Article 4(2) of the Charter.

Historically, the appearance of entirely new states out of revolution is comparatively rare, except for the states of the Western Hemisphere, beginning with the United States. The former French Indochina, Israel, Bangladesh, and, possibly the Republic of Indonesia, are the major post World War II instances. And the fall of the former USSR caused the rebirth of many nations that had been absorbed into that "Union." That fall also prompted the dissolution of other states such as the former Yugoslavia.

———

5. ***Treaty provisions on termination and related matters.*** Treaties contained in the Documentary Supplement display a variety of approaches to the question of termination, including:

a. No express provision appears in the following:

(i) International Covenant on Economic, Social and Cultural Rights.

(ii) International Covenant on Civil and Political Rights.

(iii) Vienna Convention on the Law of Treaties.

(iv) Vienna Convention on Diplomatic Relations.

(v) 1958 Conventions on the Law of the Sea.

b. Denunciation [Termination] at any time by notice to Secretary–General of United Nations (to take effect one year after receipt of notice): International Convention on the Elimination of all forms of Racial Discrimination, article 21.

c. After ten years the convention remains in force for successive periods of five years, for parties that have not denounced (by notice to Secretary–General) six months before end of current period: Convention on the Prevention and Punishment of the Crime of Genocide, article XIV.

d. Notice of withdrawal may be given to Depository Governments after one year after treaty in force (to take effect one year after receipt of notice): Space Treaty, article XVI.

Some conventions provide an amendment process (e.g., Nuclear Test Ban, Space Treaty, United Nations Charter, and the 1982 Law of the Sea Convention). Some provide that parties may request revision by notifying the Secretary–General of the United Nations, in which event the General Assembly shall decide what steps to take (e.g., conventions on Racial Discrimination, the Territorial Sea, the High Seas, the Continental Shelf). The 1958 Law of the Sea Conventions provide that such requests can be made only after five years from the date of entry into force.

Article 56 of the Vienna Convention on Treaties provides that if there is no provision for termination, denunciation or withdrawal, a treaty is not subject to denunciation unless "it is established that the parties intended to admit the possibility of denunciation or withdrawal" or "a right of denunciation or withdrawal may be implied by the *nature* of the treaty." [Emphasis supplied.]

Treaties and War. Article 73 of the Vienna Convention on Treaties provides: "The provisions of the present Convention shall not prejudge any question that may arise in regard to a treaty * * * from the outbreak of hostilities between States." In *Clark v. Allen,* 331 U.S. 503, 508 (1947), the court said: "[W]e start from the premise that the outbreak of war does not necessarily suspend or abrogate treaty provisions ... There may be such an incompatibility between a particular treaty provision and the maintenance of a state of war as to make clear that it should not be enforced ... Or the Chief Executive or the Congress may have formulated a national policy quite inconsistent with the enforcement of a treaty in whole or in part. This [is the correct view]. That case concerned the right of a resident alien enemy to inherit real property in New York. Under New York law, as it then stood, an alien enemy had no such right. The question was whether the right was granted by a reciprocal inheritance provision in a treaty with Austria which was couched in terms practically identical with those we have here. The court found nothing incompatible with national policy in permitting the resident alien enemy to have the right of inheritance granted by the treaty. * * *

Suspension and revival of treaties. The Supreme Court view in *Clark v. Allen, supra,* that if hostilities do not necessarily suspend or abrogate treaty provisions is elaborated by some text-writers, who say that hostilities abrogate political treaties, such as those for mutual security or alliance, but only suspend less sensitive ones, such as consular, navigation, and commercial arrangements. Suspension is sometimes used as an alternative to cancellation for failure of performance by the other party either in the same treaty or under general international law. Suspension of treaty concessions is common in international trade law under the General Agreement on Tariffs and Trade (GATT). Suspension is also used in some instances to manifest political disapproval of another treaty party's policies. See, Resolution, The Effects of Armed Conflicts on Treaties, 61 Ann.Inst. Dr.Int'l (I 986); *Sedeo Inc. v. National Iranian Oil Co.* and the Islamic Republic of Iran, 84 ILR 521 (Iran–US Claims Trib. 1986).

4. CHANGE OF CIRCUMSTANCES (REBUS SIC STANTIBUS)

The clause rebus sic stantibus. The Vienna Convention on Treaties provides in Article 62 for terminating, withdrawing from or suspending a treaty upon a fundamental change of circumstances. Read this article carefully and in conjunction with the procedures established in Articles 65–68, which also refer to invalidity, termination, withdrawal from or suspension of a treaty. Why is article 62 couched in negative terms? Does article 62 appear to limit the application of *rebus sic stantibus*? When is a change of a "fundamental character" an "essential basis" of the consent? What is meant by the term to "radically transform" the party's obligation? Is a change in government sufficient? What if the change occurs as a result of the acts of the party raising the issue of *rebus sic stantibus*? Can a private party raise *rebus sic stantibus*—say, for example, that a person's extradition has been requested and the regime of the requesting state is now much more hostile to him than the prior one? *See, T W.A. v. Franklin Mint Corp.*, 466 U.S. 243, 253 (1984) (not allowed). Scholars have raised doubts about the viability and wisdom of *rebus sic stantibus*. See, e.g., Schwarzenberger, *Clausula Rebus Sic Stantibus*, 7 Ency.Pub.Int'l L. 22 (1984). Others have argued that the rule is valuable as being a mechanism for enhancing stability and peace, through providing an outlet for intolerably burdensome treaties or for those in which the community no longer has a strong interest. Lissitzyn, *Stability and Change: Unilateral Denunciation or Suspension of Treaties by Reason of Changed Circumstances*, 61 ASIL Proceedings 186 (1967); Bederman, *The 1871 London Declaration, Rebus Sic Stantibus and a Primitivist View of the Law of Nations*, 82 A.J.I.L. 1 (1998).

Can *rebus sic stantibus* be invoked-unilaterally by a state as a defense for a breach? Does the Vienna Convention allow an unlimited right to terminate a treaty unilaterally on the basis of *rebus sic stantibus*? Do you think that unilateral denunciation of a treaty based on *rebus sic stantibus* is often tested in the courts or in arbitration?

To avoid the doctrinal implication of the term *rebus sic stantibus*, the International Law Commission decided not to use it either in the text or the title of the Vienna Convention article on fundamental change in circumstances. See the Commentary of the International Law Commission on Draft Article 59 (now Treaty Article 62) 61 AJIL 428 (1967). It is clear, however, that the Commission was carefully and narrowly stating its preferred version of *rebus sic stantibus*. The International Court of Justice had avoided taking a position on the existence of the rule by finding in *Free Zones of Savoy and Gex,* P.C.I.J., 1932, Series A–B, No. 46. Although municipal courts "have not infrequently recognized the relevance of the principle in international law, [they have] always ended by rejecting the application of it in the particular circumstances of the case before them." However, the Commission found in state practice "a wide acceptance of the view that a fundamental change of circumstances may justify * * * termination or revision of a treaty."

The doctrine of *rebus sic stantibus*, either in those terms or in other words, is to be found in the domestic law of states in cases not involving treaties but in commercial contracts. If *rebus sic stantibus* is common to municipal systems of law, why, then, should there be such hesitancy to recognize that the rule is a rule of international law? Are there any peculiar risks to its application in international law that do not exist, or exist to a lesser extent, in municipal law.? Is the weakness of international adjudication one such risk?

Impossibility of performance article 61 of the Vienna Convention sharply differentiates supervening impossibility of performance from fundamental change of circumstances (article 62). But, like the latter, Article 61 is tightly drafted against excuse from performance. Is impossibility related to *rebus sic stantibus*? Does it have a legal foundation at least as solid as that of *rebus sic stantibus*? It would seem so. It has been utilized less than has *rebus sic stantibus*, however.

5. TERMINATION: PRIOR BREACH BY THE OTHER PARTY

Similarities to the private law of contracts. Neither parties to private contracts nor states parties to treaties are disposed to carry out their obligations if the other side has not lived up to its undertaking or has made it clear that it does not intend to perform. There are public international public law parallels to failure of consideration in the common law world, or failure of cause in the civilian world. There are parallels to prior breach of condition precedent, material breach, anticipatory breach, frustration of expectations, and the like. The international law rules, however are not sharply etched in the conduct of states as legal principles. For more on this in U.S. law, *see* Ch. 13, *infra.*

Remedies. Most jurists agree that a violation of a treaty by one party allows the other party to abrogate the treaty or to suspend its own performance. Jurists are split on the scope of the right to abrogate or to take reprisals, otherwise unlawful. Some jurists see abrogation as the only viable sanction, but others see it as being too risky for wide use. Generally the right is limited to breaches of *material, fundamental,* or other *primary* aspects of a treaty. These "limitations" cause uncertainty and potential dispute. *See gen., International Law Commission Draft Articles on the Law of Treaties, Commentary on "Breach."* 61 AJIL 263, 422 (1967).

The Vienna Convention on Breach—see Article 60 in the Documentary Supplement. What constitutes a *material breach*? For example, did France breach its extradition treaty with the U.S. in the case of the attempted extradition of hijacker Willie Holder discussed below. In Holder, the *Avocat Général,* the official designated to "represent" the U.S. before the French courts presented the documentary evidence and proceeded to argue against the extradition. The Secretary of State wrote a diplomatic note protesting and claiming breach. See whether you think a breach occurred or whether the dispute arose over a failure to understand a foreign criminal justice system or the desire to ensure adoption of a treaty by avoiding a negotiation snag. For more, see, Setear, *Responses to Breach of a Treaty & Rationalist International Relations Theory: The Rules of Release & Remediation in the Law of Treaties and th Law of State Responsibility,* 83 Va.J.Int'l L. 1 (1997); Setear, *An Iterative Perspective on Treaties: A Synthesis of International Relations Theory and International Law,* 37 Harv.Int'l L.J. 139 (1996).

International Court of Justice: Judgment In Case Concerning the Gabcikovo-Nagymaros Project

September 25, 1997, 37 I.L.M. 162 (1998).

* * *

89. By the terms of Article 2, paragraph 1 (c), of the Special Agreement, the Court is asked, thirdly, to determine "what are the legal effects of the notification, on 19 May 1992, of the termination of the Treaty by the

Republic of Hungary". The Court notes that it has been asked to determine what are the legal effects of the notification given on 19 May 1992 of the termination of the Treaty. It will consequently confine itself to replying to this question.

90. The Court will recall that, by early 1992, the respective parties to the 1977 Treaty had made clear their positions with regard to the recourse by Czechoslovakia to Variant C. Hungary in a Note Verbale of 14 February 1992 had made clear its view that Variant C was a contravention of the 1977 Treaty (see paragraph 64 above); Czechoslovakia insisted on the implementation of Variant C as a condition for further negotiation. On 26 February 1992, in a letter to his Czechoslovak counterpart, the Prime Minister of Hungary described the impending diversion of the Danube as "a serious breach of international law" and stated that, unless work was suspended while further enquiries took place, "the Hungarian Government [would] have no choice but to respond to this situation of necessity by terminating the 1977 inter-State Treaty". In a Note Verbale dated 18 March 1992, Czechoslovakia reaffirmed that, while it was prepared to continue negotiations "on every level", it could not agree "to stop all work on the provisional solution".

On 24 March 1992, the Hungarian Parliament passed a resolution authorizing the Government to terminate the 1977 Treaty if Czechoslovakia did not stop the works by 30 April 1992. On 13 April 1992, the Vice–President of the Commission of the European Communities wrote to both parties confirming the willingness of the Commission to chair a committee of independent experts including representatives of the two countries, in order to assist the two Governments in identifying a mutually acceptable solution. Commission involvement would depend on each Government not taking "any steps . . . which would prejudice possible actions to be undertaken on the basis of the report's findings". The Czechoslovak Prime Minister stated in a letter to the Hungarian Prime Minister dated 23 April 1992, that his Government continued to be interested in the establishment of the proposed committee "without any preliminary conditions"; criticizing Hungary's approach, he refused to suspend work on the provisional solution, but added, "in my opinion, there is still time, until the damming of the Danube (i.e., until October 31, 1992), for resolving disputed questions on the basis of agreement of both States".

On 7 May 1992, Hungary, in the very resolution in which it decided on the termination of the Treaty, made a proposal, this time to the Slovak Prime Minister, for a six-month suspension of work on Variant C. The Slovak Prime Minister replied that the Slovak Government remained ready to negotiate, but considered preconditions "inappropriate".

91. On 19 May 1992, the Hungarian Government transmitted to the Czechoslovak Government a Declaration notifying it of the termination by Hungary of the 1977 Treaty as of 25 May 1992. In a letter of the same date from the Hungarian Prime Minister to the Czechoslovak Prime Minister, the immediate cause for termination was specified to be Czechoslovakia's refusal, expressed in its letter of 23 April 1992, to suspend the work on Variant C during mediation efforts of the Commission of the European Communities. In its Declaration, Hungary stated that it could not accept

the deleterious effects for the environment and the conservation of nature of the implementation of Variant C which would be practically equivalent to the dangers caused by the realization of the original Project. It added that Variant C infringed numerous international agreements and violated the territorial integrity of the Hungarian State by diverting the natural course of the Danube.

* * *

92. During the proceedings, Hungary presented five arguments in support of the lawfulness, and thus the effectiveness, of its notification of termination. These were the existence of a state of necessity; the impossibility of performance of the Treaty; the occurrence of a fundamental change of circumstances; the material breach of the Treaty by Czechoslovakia; and, finally, the development of new norms of international environmental law. Slovakia contested each of these grounds.

93. On the first point, Hungary stated that, as Czechoslovakia had "remained inflexible" and continued with its implementation of Variant C, "a temporary state of necessity eventually became permanent, justifying termination of the 1977 Treaty".

Slovakia, for its part, denied that a state of necessity existed on the basis of what it saw as the scientific facts; and argued that even if such a state of necessity had existed, this would not give rise to a right to terminate the Treaty under the Vienna Convention of 1969 on the Law of Treaties.

94. Hungary's second argument relied on the terms of Article 61 of the Vienna Convention, which is worded as follows:

"Article 61
Supervening impossibility of performance

1. A party may invoke the impossibility of performing a treaty as a ground for terminating or withdrawing from it if the impossibility results from the permanent disappearance or destruction of an object indispensable for the execution of the treaty. If the impossibility is temporary, it may be invoked only as a ground for suspending the operation of the treaty.

2. Impossibility of performance may not be invoked by a party as a ground for terminating, withdrawing from or suspending the operation of a treaty if the impossibility is the result of a breach by that party either of an obligation under the treaty or of any other international obligation owed to any other party to the treaty. Hungary declared that it could not be "obliged to fulfil a practically impossible task, namely to construct a barrage system on its own territory that would cause irreparable environmental damage". It concluded that "By May 1992 the essential object of the Treaty—an economic joint investment which was consistent with environmental protection and which was operated by the two parties jointly—had permanently disappeared, and the Treaty had thus become impossible to perform." In Hungary's view, the "object indispensable for the execution of the treaty", whose disappearance or destruction was required by Article 61 of the Vienna Convention, did not have to be a physical object, but could also include, in the words of the International

Law Commission, "a legal situation which was the raison d'etre of the rights and obligations".

Slovakia claimed that Article 61 was the only basis for invoking impossibility of performance as a ground for termination, that paragraph 1 of that Article clearly contemplated physical "disappearance or destruction" of the object in question, and that, in any event, paragraph 2 precluded the invocation of impossibility "if the impossibility is the result of a breach by that party . . . of an obligation under the treaty".

95. As to "fundamental change of circumstances", Hungary relied on Article 62 of the Vienna Convention on the Law of Treaties which states as follows:

"Article 62

Fundamental change of circumstances

1. A fundamental change of circumstances which has occurred with regard to those existing at the time of the conclusion of a treaty, and which was not foreseen by the parties, may not be invoked as a ground for terminating or withdrawing from the treaty unless:

(a) the existence of those circumstances constituted an essential basis of the consent of the parties to be bound by the treaty; and

(b) the effect of the change is radically to transform the extent of obligations still to be performed under the treaty.

2. A fundamental change of circumstances may not be invoked as a ground for terminating or withdrawing from a treaty:

(a) if the treaty establishes a boundary; or

(b) if the fundamental change is the result of a breach by the party invoking it either of an obligation under the treaty or of any other international obligation owed to any other party to the treaty.

3. If, under the foregoing paragraphs, a party may invoke a fundamental change of circumstances as a ground for terminating or withdrawing from a treaty it may also invoke the change as a ground for suspending the operation of the treaty. Hungary identified a number of "substantive elements" present at the conclusion of the 1977 Treaty which it said had changed fundamentally by the date of notification of termination. These included the notion of "socialist integration", for which the Treaty had originally been a "vehicle", but which subsequently disappeared; the "single and indivisible operational system", which was to be replaced by a unilateral scheme; the fact that the basis of the planned joint investment had been overturned by the sudden emergence of both States into a market economy; the attitude of Czechoslovakia which had turned the "framework treaty" into an "immutable norm"; and, finally, the transformation of a treaty consistent with environmental protection into "a prescription for environmental disaster". Slovakia, for its part, contended that the changes identified by Hungary had not altered the nature of the obligations under the Treaty from those originally undertaken, so that no entitlement to terminate it arose from them.

96. Hungary further argued that termination of the Treaty was justified by Czechoslovakia's material breaches of the Treaty, and in this regard it invoked Article 60 of the Vienna Convention on the Law of Treaties, which provides:

"Article 60

Termination or suspension of the operation of
a treaty as a consequence of its breach

1. A material breach of a bilateral treaty by one of the parties entitles the other to invoke the breach as a ground for terminating the treaty or suspending its operation in whole or in part.

2. A material breach of a multilateral treaty by one of the parties entitles:

(a) the other parties by unanimous agreement to suspend the operation of the treaty in whole or in part or to terminate it either:

(i) in the relations between themselves and the defaulting State, or

(ii) as between all the parties;

(b) a party specially affected by the breach to invoke it as a ground for suspending the operation of the treaty in whole or in part in the relations between itself and the defaulting State;

(c) any party other than the defaulting State to invoke the breach as a ground for suspending the operation of the treaty in whole or in part with respect to itself if the treaty is of such a character that a material breach of its provisions by one party radically changes the position of every party with respect to the further performance of its obligations under the treaty.

3. A material breach of a treaty, for the purposes of this article, consists in:

(a) a repudiation of the treaty not sanctioned by the present Convention; or

(b) the violation of a provision essential to the accomplishment of the object or purpose of the treaty.

4. The foregoing paragraphs are without prejudice to any provision in the treaty applicable in the event of a breach.

5. Paragraphs 1 to 3 do not apply to provisions relating to the protection of the human person contained in treaties of a humanitarian character, in particular to provisions prohibiting any form of reprisals against persons protected by such treaties. Hungary claimed in particular that Czechoslovakia violated the 1977 Treaty by proceeding to the construction and putting into operation of Variant C, as well as failing to comply with its obligations under Articles 15 and 19 of the Treaty. Hungary further maintained that Czechoslovakia had breached other international conventions (among them the Convention of 31 May 1976 on the Regulation of Water Management Issues of Boundary Waters) and general international law.

Slovakia denied that there had been, on the part of Czechoslovakia or on its part, any material breach of the obligations to protect water quality and nature, and claimed that Variant C, far from being a breach, was devised as "the best possible approximate application" of the Treaty. It furthermore denied that Czechoslovakia had acted in breach of other international conventions or general international law.

97.   Finally, Hungary argued that subsequently imposed requirements of international law in relation to the protection of the environment precluded performance of the Treaty. The previously existing obligation not to cause substantive damage to the territory of another State had, Hungary claimed, evolved into an erga omnes obligation of prevention of damage pursuant to the "precautionary principle". On this basis, Hungary argued, its termination was "forced by the other party's refusal to suspend work on Variant C".

Slovakia argued, in reply, that none of the intervening developments in environmental law gave rise to norms of jus cogens that would override the Treaty. Further, it contended that the claim by Hungary to be entitled to take action could not in any event serve as legal justification for termination of the Treaty under the law of treaties, but belonged rather "to the language of self-help or reprisals".

* * *

98.   The question, as formulated in Article 2, paragraph 1 (c), of the Special Agreement, deals with treaty law since the Court is asked to determine what the legal effects are of the notification of termination of the Treaty. The question is whether Hungary's notification of 19 May 1992 brought the 1977 Treaty to an end, or whether it did not meet the requirements of international law, with the consequence that it did not terminate the Treaty.

99.   The Court has referred earlier to the question of the applicability to the present case of the Vienna Convention of 1969 on the Law of Treaties. The Vienna Convention is not directly applicable to the 1977 Treaty inasmuch as both States ratified that Convention only after the Treaty's conclusion. Consequently only those rules which are declaratory of customary law are applicable to the 1977 Treaty. As the Court has already stated above (see paragraph 46), this is the case, in many respects, with Articles 60 to 62 of the Vienna Convention, relating to termination or suspension of the operation of a treaty. On this, the Parties, too, were broadly in agreement.

100.   The 1977 Treaty does not contain any provision regarding its termination. Nor is there any indication that the parties intended to admit the possibility of denunciation or withdrawal. On the contrary, the Treaty establishes a long-standing and durable regime of joint investment and joint operation. Consequently, the parties not having agreed otherwise, the Treaty could be terminated only on the limited grounds enumerated in the Vienna Convention.

* * *

101.   The Court will now turn to the first ground advanced by Hungary, that of the state of necessity. In this respect, the Court will

merely observe that, even if a state of necessity is found to exist, it is not a ground for the termination of a treaty. It may only be invoked to exonerate from its responsibility a State which has failed to implement a treaty. Even if found justified, it does not terminate a Treaty; the Treaty may be ineffective as long as the condition of necessity continues to exist; it may in fact be dormant, but—unless the parties by mutual agreement terminate the Treaty—it continues to exist. As soon as the state of necessity ceases to exist, the duty to comply with treaty obligations revives.

* * *

102.   Hungary also relied on the principle of the impossibility of performance as reflected in Article 61 of the Vienna Convention on the Law of Treaties. Hungary's interpretation of the wording of Article 61 is, however, not in conformity with the terms of that Article, nor with the intentions of the Diplomatic Conference which adopted the Convention. Article 61, paragraph 1, requires the "permanent disappearance or destruction of an object indispensable for the execution" of the treaty to justify the termination of a treaty on grounds of impossibility of performance. During the conference, a proposal was made to extend the scope of the article by including in it cases such as the impossibility to make certain payments because of serious financial difficulties (Official Records of the United Nations Conference on the Law of Treaties, First Session, Vienna, 26 March–24 May 1968, Doc. A/CONF.39/11, Summary records of the plenary meetings and of the meetings of the Committee of the Whole, 62nd Meeting of the Committee of the Whole, pp. 361–365). Although it was recognized that such situations could lead to a preclusion of the wrongfulness of non-performance by a party of its treaty obligations, the participating States were not prepared to consider such situations to be a ground for terminating or suspending a treaty, and preferred to limit themselves to a narrower concept.

103.   Hungary contended that the essential object of the Treaty—an economic joint investment which was consistent with environmental protection and which was operated by the two contracting parties jointly—had permanently disappeared and that the Treaty had thus become impossible to perform. It is not necessary for the Court to determine whether the term "object" in Article 61 can also be understood to embrace a legal regime as in any event, even if that were the case, it would have to conclude that in this instance that regime had not definitively ceased to exist. The 1977 Treaty—and in particular its Articles 15, 19 and 20—actually made available to the parties the necessary means to proceed at any time, by negotiation, to the required readjustments between economic imperatives and ecological imperatives. The Court would add that, if the joint exploitation of the investment was no longer possible, this was originally because Hungary did not carry out most of the works for which it was responsible under the 1977 Treaty; Article 61, paragraph 2, of the Vienna Convention expressly provides that impossibility of performance may not be invoked for the termination of a treaty by a party to that treaty when it results from that party's own breach of an obligation flowing from that treaty.

* * *

104.   Hungary further argued that it was entitled to invoke a number of events which, cumulatively, would have constituted a fundamental change of circumstances. In this respect it specified profound changes of a political nature, the Project's diminishing economic viability, the progress of environmental knowledge and the development of new norms and prescriptions of international environmental law (see paragraph 95 above).

The Court recalls that, in the Fisheries Jurisdiction case (I.C.J. Reports 1973, p. 63, para. 36), it stated that. "Article 62 of the Vienna Convention on the Law of Treaties, . . . may in many respects be considered as a codification of existing customary law on the subject of the termination of a treaty relationship on account of change of circumstances".

The prevailing political situation was certainly relevant for the conclusion of the 1977 Treaty. But the Court will recall that the Treaty provided for a joint investment programme for the production of energy, the control of floods and the improvement of navigation on the Danube. In the Court's view, the prevalent political conditions were thus not so closely linked to the object and purpose of the Treaty that they constituted an essential basis of the consent of the parties and, in changing, radically altered the extent of the obligations still to be performed. The same holds good for the economic system in force at the time of the conclusion of the 1977 Treaty. Besides, even though the estimated profitability of the Project might have appeared less in 1992 than in 1977, it does not appear from the record before the Court that it was bound to diminish to such an extent that the treaty obligations of the parties would have been radically transformed as a result.

The Court does not consider that new developments in the state of environmental knowledge and of environmental law can be said to have been completely unforeseen. What is more, the formulation of Articles 15, 19 and 20, designed to accommodate change, made it possible for the parties to take account of such developments and to apply them when implementing those treaty provisions.

The changed circumstances advanced by Hungary are, in the Court's view, not of such a nature, either individually or collectively, that their effect would radically transform the extent of the obligations still to be performed in order to accomplish the Project. A fundamental change of circumstances must have been unforeseen; the existence of the circumstances at the time of the Treaty's conclusion must have constituted an essential basis of the consent of the parties to be bound by the Treaty. The negative and conditional wording of Article 62 of the Vienna Convention on the Law of Treaties is a clear indication moreover that the stability of treaty relations requires that the plea of fundamental change of circumstances be applied only in exceptional cases.

* * *

105.   The Court will now examine Hungary's argument that it was entitled to terminate the 1977 Treaty on the ground that Czechoslovakia had violated its Articles 15, 19 and 20 (as well as a number of other conventions and rules of general international law); and that the planning,

construction and putting into operation of Variant C also amounted to a material breach of the 1977 Treaty.

106. As to that part of Hungary's argument which was based on other treaties and general rules of international law, the Court is of the view that it is only a material breach of the treaty itself, by a State party to that treaty, which entitles the other party to rely on it as a ground for terminating the treaty. The violation of other treaty rules or of rules of general international law may justify the taking of certain measures, including countermeasures, by the injured State, but it does not constitute a ground for termination under the law of treaties.

107. Hungary contended that Czechoslovakia had violated Articles 15, 19 and 20 of the Treaty by refusing to enter into negotiations with Hungary in order to adapt the Joint Contractual Plan to new scientific and legal developments regarding the environment. Articles 15, 19 and 20 oblige the parties jointly to take, on a continuous basis, appropriate measures necessary for the protection of water quality, of nature and of fishing interests.

Articles 15 and 19 expressly provide that the obligations they contain shall be implemented by the means specified in the Joint Contractual Plan. The failure of the parties to agree on those means cannot, on the basis of the record before the Court, be attributed solely to one party. The Court has not found sufficient evidence to conclude that Czechoslovakia had consistently refused to consult with Hungary about the desirability or necessity of measures for the preservation of the environment. The record rather shows that, while both parties indicated, in principle, a willingness to undertake further studies, in practice Czechoslovakia refused to countenance a suspension of the works at Dunakiliti and, later, on Variant C, while Hungary required suspension as a prior condition of environmental investigation because it claimed continuation of the work would prejudice the outcome of negotiations. In this regard it cannot be left out of consideration that Hungary itself, by suspending the works at Nagymaros and Dunakiliti, contributed to the creation of a situation which was not conducive to the conduct of fruitful negotiations.

108. Hungary's main argument for invoking a material breach of the Treaty was the construction and putting into operation of Variant C. As the Court has found in paragraph 79 above, Czechoslovakia violated the Treaty only when it diverted the waters of the Danube into the bypass canal in October 1992. In constructing the works which would lead to the putting into operation of Variant C, Czechoslovakia did not act unlawfully.

In the Court's view, therefore, the notification of termination by Hungary on 19 May 1992 was premature. No breach of the Treaty by Czechoslovakia had yet taken place and consequently Hungary was not entitled to invoke any such breach of the Treaty as a ground for terminating it when it did.

109. In this regard, it should be noted that, according to Hungary's Declaration of 19 May 1992, the termination of the 1977 Treaty was to take effect as from 25 May 1992, that is only six days later. Both Parties agree that Articles 65 to 67 of the Vienna Convention on the Law of Treaties, if

not codifying customary law, at least generally reflect customary international law and contain certain procedural principles which are based on an obligation to act in good faith. As the Court stated in its Advisory Opinion on the Interpretation of the Agreement of 25 March 1951 between the WHO and Egypt (in which case the Vienna Convention did not apply): "Precisely what periods of time may be involved in the observance of the duties to consult and negotiate, and what period of notice of termination should be given, are matters which necessarily vary according to the requirements of the particular case. In principle, therefore, it is for the parties in each case to determine the length of those periods by consultation and negotiation in good faith." (I.C.J. Reports 1980, p. 96, para. 49.)

The termination of the Treaty by Hungary was to take effect six days after its notification. On neither of these dates had Hungary suffered injury resulting from acts of Czechoslovakia. The Court must therefore confirm its conclusion that Hungary's termination of the Treaty was premature.

110. Nor can the Court overlook that Czechoslovakia committed the internationally wrongful act of putting into operation Variant C as a result of Hungary's own prior wrongful conduct. As was stated by the Permanent Court of International Justice: "It is, moreover, a principle generally accepted in the jurisprudence of international arbitration, as well as by municipal courts, that one Party cannot avail himself of the fact that the other has not fulfilled some obligation or has not had recourse to some means of redress, if the former Party has, by some illegal act, prevented the latter from fulfilling the obligation in question, or from having recourse to the tribunal which would have been open, to him." (Factory at Chorzow, Jurisdiction, Judgment No. 8, 1927, P.C.I.J., Series A, No. 9, p. 31.) Hungary, by its own conduct, had prejudiced its right to terminate the Treaty; this would still have been the case even if Czechoslovakia, by the time of the purported termination, had violated a provision essential to the accomplishment of the object or purpose of the Treaty.

* * *

111. Finally, the Court will address Hungary's claim that it was entitled to terminate the 1977 Treaty because new requirements of international law for the protection of the environment precluded performance of the Treaty.

112. Neither of the Parties contended that new peremptory norms of environmental law had emerged since the conclusion of the 1977 Treaty, and the Court will consequently not be required to examine the scope of Article 64 of the Vienna Convention on the Law of Treaties. On the other hand, the Court wishes to point out that newly developed norms of environmental law are relevant for the implementation of the Treaty and that the parties could, by agreement, incorporate them through the application of Articles 15, 19 and 20 of the Treaty. These articles do not contain specific obligations of performance but require the parties, in carrying out their obligations to ensure that the quality of water in the Danube is not impaired and that nature is protected, to take new environmental norms into consideration when agreeing upon the means to be specified in the Joint Contractual Plan.

By inserting these evolving provisions in the Treaty, the parties recognized the potential necessity to adapt the Project. Consequently, the Treaty is not static, and is open to adapt to emerging norms of international law. By means of Articles 15 and 19, new environmental norms can be incorporated in the Joint Contractual Plan.

The responsibility to do this was a joint responsibility. The obligations contained in Articles 15, 19 and 20 are, by definition, general and have to be transformed into specific obligations of performance through a process of consultation and negotiation. Their implementation thus requires a mutual willingness to discuss in good faith actual and potential environmental risks.

It is all the more important to do this because as the Court recalled in its Advisory Opinion on the Legality of the Threat or Use of Nuclear Weapons, "the environment is not an abstraction but represents the living space, the quality of life and the very health of human beings, including generations unborn" (I.C.J. Reports 1996, para. 29; see also paragraph 53 above).

The awareness of the vulnerability of the environment and the recognition that environmental risks have to be assessed on a continuous basis have become much stronger in the years since the Treaty's conclusion. These new concerns have enhanced the relevance of Articles 15, 19 and 20.

113. The Court recognizes that both Parties agree on the need to take environmental concerns seriously and to take the required precautionary measures, but they fundamentally disagree on the consequences this has for the joint Project. In such a case, third-party involvement may be helpful and instrumental in finding a solution, provided each of the Parties is flexible in its position.

114. Finally, Hungary maintained that by their conduct both parties had repudiated the Treaty and that a bilateral treaty repudiated by both parties cannot survive. The Court is of the view, however, that although it has found that both Hungary and Czechoslovakia failed to comply with their obligations under the 1977 Treaty, this reciprocal wrongful conduct did not bring the Treaty to an end nor justify its termination. The Court would set a precedent with disturbing implications for treaty relations and the integrity of the rule pacta sunt servanda if it were to conclude that a treaty in force between States, which the parties have implemented in considerable measure and at great cost over a period of years, might be unilaterally set aside on grounds of reciprocal non-compliance. It would be otherwise, of course, if the parties decided to terminate the Treaty by mutual consent. But in this case, while Hungary purported to terminate the Treaty, Czechoslovakia consistently resisted this act and declared it to be without legal effect.

* * *

115. In the light of the conclusions it has reached above, the Court, in reply to the question put to it in Article 2, paragraph 1 (c), of the Special Agreement (see paragraph 89), finds that the notification of termination by Hungary of 19 May 1992 did not have the legal effect of terminating the 1977 Treaty and related instruments.

* * *

TREATIES AND OTHER INTERNATIONAL AGREEMENTS IN THE CONSTITUTIONAL AND STATUTORY LAW OF THE UNITED STATES

The Vienna Convention on the Law of Treaties has contributed significantly to the modernization of the law about treaties; but when the result is compared with any modern, developed legal system's treatment of the law of conventional obligations (contract), it is apparent that the international legal system lags behind. On review, ask yourselves where does it fail to meet the standard of a domestic system? Absent compulsory judicial process against an alleged treaty non-performer, how much improvement is reasonably foreseeable?

Confining inquiry to the policing and enforcement of treaties as contracts between states, the contrast between the array of remedies in the

Anglo–American national legal systems and their scarcity in the international legal system is marked. As at common law, before the rise of equity, "damages" are still the basic remedy in the international system. Justice Holmes and other jurists have played contrapuntally with the notion that the common law of contract gives a "bad man" an option to breach his undertaking and pay damages. But equity will put him in jail until he does carry out his undertaking in a number of situations that matter. The civil law system, however, never developed injunction and specific performance, although it resorts to criminal law in promise-enforcement more widely than the Anglo–American systems do. We have seen, though, that a promisee state can use the pressure of withholding its performance pending compliance with undertaking on the other side. This toleration is functionally a kind of invalidation. As such it is a sanction beyond damages. Some added inducement to performance also comes from the law *in* treaties, when it is also internal law to be applied by national courts. Can you think of situations where a state wishing to rid itself of a treaty obligation might provoke or induce non-performance on the other side, or charge that side with a bad record of treaty performance?

———

Study the Constitution of the United States: Article I, Section 10; Article II, § 2; Article II, § 3; Article VI; and Amendment X, in the Doc. Supp. This chapter presents the American way of dealing with international agreements. It is unique, in the unmodifiable, true sense of the word. Largely this is caused by the federalistic, separation-of-powers constitutional structure of the United States. Problems beyond those dealt with in Chapter 11 result. We consider them in this book for this reason and because they are not usually analyzed in any depth in courses on constitutional law. Moreover, as a U.S. practitioner of international law, you cannot function without it. Also, non–U.S. lawyers must understand this to work with matters that have a U.S. component. Against the background of Chapter 11, we begin with the Constitution of 1789, as amended. Problems involving the difficulty of the federal government under the first U.S. Constitution in requiring the states to respect the obligations of the nation under international agreements were major among the reasons for convening at Philadelphia in 1787 the convention that framed the Constitution. Federal-state issues as to foreign affairs operations under treaties and other international agreements still exist, but by far the more difficult and numerous problems are those involving the federal legislative chambers, between themselves and between each of them and the President. Also, the role and authority of the Supreme Court to decide contentions as to the respective foreign affairs authorities of the Congress and the President are contentious.

A point as to word usage: in Chapter 11 we saw that what one called an international agreement was not very important. But in United States foreign affairs law, *"treaty"* has a very specific and significant meaning; and all other international agreements are usually called "executive agreements," even though not always made by the President's branch alone.

SECTION A.   THE CONSTITUTION, THE FOREIGN AFFAIRS POWER, AND TREATIES AS FEDERAL LAW

It is usually said that the United States has contributed two inventions to political science: federalism and judicial review. And this is more or less true. But two other ideas which have played a great part in our constitutional history were not American in origin: checks and balances and the separation of powers.*

* * *

During the colonial period [in the U.S.] the virtues of the mixed state and of checks and balances were learned from the mother country. In 1784 John Adams published his *Defense of the Constitutions of the United States.* Adams lauded the partition of power established by all the state constitutions of the revolutionary period, Luther Martin, in his report to the Maryland legislature on the Constitutional Convention, said that the reviewers had justly observed that Adams "appears to be as fond of *checks* and *balances* as Lord Chesterfield of the Graces." * * * But Martin himself thought checks and balances appropriate to a state government; he merely protested that bicameralism was unnecessary to a simple confederation of states, which the United States had been under the Articles of Confederation and which he hoped they would continue to be.

In England, checks and balances reflected social divisions: monarchy, the aristocracy, and the commonalty. But in the United States there was neither a monarchy nor an aristocracy. In No. 14 of the *Federalist* James Madison asserted that America had shown that representation might be made the basis of "unmixed and extensive republics." He might have added that America had also shown that checks and balances might exist in an unmixed republic, balancing institutions rather than social classes against each other. The institutions that the framers of the Constitution counterpoised were determined by the theory of the separation of powers.

Frank J. Goodnow observed in 1914 that there were only two functions of government—the formulation of policy and the execution of policy. This analysis had first been stated during the English Civil Wars: the formulation of policy was assigned to the legislative power, and the execution of policy was attributed to what was called either the executive or the judicial power. At its first appearance the separation of powers was therefore a twofold separation. . . .

Thereafter the propriety of separating the legislative power from the executive or judicial function became universally accepted. * * * The distinction of "the legislative from the ministerial authority" was "the most vital part of freedom."

John Locke, in his *Two Treatises of Government,* offers us a view of the Stuart constitution as modified by the radical political theory that had

---

* Wormuth & Firmage, To Chain the Dog of War. Excerpts from 1–15, 192–93 (2d ed. 1989). Reprinted with the permission of the University of Illinois press.

developed during the Civil Wars: the doctrines of social contract, of individualism and equality, and of the separation of powers. The principal omission is the theory of the mixed state. Locke wrote the major part of the book between 1679 and 1683 to express the philosophy of the Whig party in its contest with Charles II * * *. That publication was extremely influential; it not only justified the Glorious Revolution but also helped shape constitutional discussion in England and America in the eighteenth century. Locke wrote:

> In all Cases, whilst the Government subsists, *the Legislative is the Supreme Power.* For what can give Laws to another, must needs be superior to him: and since the Legislative is no otherwise Legislative of the Society, but by the right it has to make Laws for all the parts and for every Member of the Society, prescribing Rules to their actions, and giving power of Execution, where they are transgressed, the *Legislative* must needs be the *Supreme,* and all other Powers in any Members or parts of the Society, derived from and subordinate to it. [Locke, Two Treatises of Government 385–86 (Lasswell ed. 1907)]

There are two other powers of government. "But because the Laws, that are at once, and in a short time made, have a constant and lasting force, and need a *perpetual Execution,* or an attendance thereunto: Therefore 'tis necessary there should be a *Power always in being,*' which should see to the *Execution* of the Laws that are made, and remain in force. And thus the *Legislative* and *Executive* Power come often to be separated." * * *

> This therefore contains the Power of War and Peace, Leagues and Alliances, and all the Transactions, with all Persons and Communities without the Commonwealth, and may be called *Federative,* if any one pleases.

> The executive power may be placed in the hands of several persons or of one, who may also have a share in the legislative power. But he is merely the *"Supreme Executor* of the Law," and if he violates law "and acts by his own private Will, he degrades himself, and is but a single private person without power, and without Will, that has any right to *Obedience;* the Members owing no Obedience but to the publick Will of the Society."

Locke, although he, like Lilburne, believed that "the Ruling Power ought to govern by *declared* and *received Laws,* and not by extemporary Dictates and undetermined Resolutions", trusted the legislative supremacy to accomplish this result. There was one feature of the Stuart constitution that Locke felt unable to disavow. The King had long claimed a "prerogative" to act outside—that is, contrary to—the law in cases of necessity. Locke wrote that: "there is a latitude left to the Executive power," to do many things of choice, which the Laws do not prescribe * * *.

It may strike the reader that Locke made a bad choice in granting a prerogative to violate the law for the public good and leaving no remedy for abuse of this power other than revolution. The inconveniences of the absence of prerogative are surely outweighed by the inconveniences of revolution. But the alternatives were those suggested by seventeenth-century English history. American law has made a better choice than either.

Lilburne's primary motive for the separation of powers was to insure impartiality: the legislature should be confined to the making of general rules, and the executive to the enforcement of these rules. Locke shared this view, but his principal purpose in separating the executive from the legislature was to make the King subject to the representative body, the Parliament.

In his Commentaries on the Laws of England, Sir William Blackstone used the idea of checks and balances and the seventeenth-century twofold separation of powers, joined with the rule that counseled the independence of the judiciary. In his famous argument in the *Case of Writs of Assistance* in 1761, James Otis employed the same analysis and said that the "executive courts" must pass into disuse acts of Parliament that violated the British constitution. * * * The first New Hampshire constitution, of 1776, spoke of the "executive courts." As late as 1827 Chief Justice John Marshall spoke of "the judicial power as part of the executive."

Montesquieu's was the dominant analysis in America. The first constitutions of Virginia, Maryland, North Carolina, Georgia, and Massachusetts, and the second constitution of New Hampshire, decreed that the legislative, executive, and judicial powers were and should remain distinct. This was more easily decreed than accomplished. In his *Notes on the State of Virginia,* first published in 1785, Thomas Jefferson, a former governor of the state, complained of "very capital defects" in the constitution. The principal defect was the fact that the constitution had been adopted by the legislature, and its provisions might be altered by any subsequent act of the legislature.

.   .   .

Jefferson proposed that "the powers of government should be so divided and balanced among several bodies of magistracy, so that no one could transcend their legal limits, without being effectually checked and restrained by the others." So Jefferson called in checks and balances—not, as previously, of social classes, but of governmental institutions—to safeguard the separation of powers. Madison adopted the same argument in No. 48 of the *Federalist,* describing the arrangements he thought would perhaps accomplish the desired result. * * * The executive, legislative, and judicial officers should draw their authority from the people through channels having no communication with one another; the method of choosing the judiciary, however, offered difficulties. ... To these internal checks of the national government he added the states as further checks, and he revived the argument of No. 10 of the *Federalist:* in an extensive republic, interests would be so numerous that a tyrannical majority would not come into existence.

In No. 78 of the *Federalist* Alexander Hamilton completed the argument on checks and balances. In a discussion of the judiciary he quoted Montesquieu, "There is no liberty, if the power of judging be not separated from the legislative and executive powers." In a constitution that limits legislative power, the judiciary must pronounce legislative acts contrary to the constitution as void, for the constitution is a fundamental law, and the courts must prefer it to a statute inconsistent with it. Jefferson had expressed the same opinion two years earlier in his answer to the inquiries of Jean Nicolas Démeunier, who was compiling an article on the United States for the *Encyclopédi Methodique*. Repeating his complaint that people considered the constitution of Virginia an ordinary statute because it had been created by the legislature, and therefore many laws inconsistent with the constitution had been passed, Jefferson said, "I have not heard that in the other states they have ever infringed their constitutions; and I suppose they have not done it; as the judges would consider any law void, which was contrary to the constitution." [Thomas Jefferson, The Papers of Thomas Jefferson at X, & XIV (Boyd ed. 1954).]

Like Madison, Jefferson believed that "the tyranny of the legislature is the most formidable dread at present." (Id.) * * * But at the Constitutional Convention of 1787 the liveliest apprehension centered on the executive.

* * *

Notes and Questions

1. ***The treaty-making power*** is allocated between the executive and legislative branches, reflecting the intent of the framers for a partnership in the conduct of foreign relations. But while the Constitution provides that the President "shall have Power, by and with the Advice and Consent of the Senate, to make treaties, provided two-thirds of the senators present concur," the Constitution does not indicate how the President is to "make" treaties or how the Senate is to give its advice and consent to presidential action. This lack of specificity on how the treaty power was to be exercised is probably the result of the fact that the framers simply assumed that the international customs and practices of their time would be the model for treaty making under the Constitution. This assumption is supported by the fact that the treaty-making process received but little consideration in the Constitutional Convention.

2. ***Authority to Negotiate Treaties.*** As a consequence of the lack of constitutional guidelines on how the treaty power is to be exercised, the treaty-making process has evolved as a matter of custom. For the most part, "the President exclusively has exercised the power to negotiate treaties," and it is now commonly accepted that neither the Senate nor the Congress as a whole has the authority to enter into the negotiating process. In addition to the President's power to "make treaties," the President's constitutional power to "receive Ambassadors and other public Ministers" is customarily cited as a basis for this exclusive executive power of negotiation.

3. ***The Senate's Advice & Consent.*** Once a treaty has been negotiated, it is submitted by the President to the Senate. The Senate does not formally advise the President on the treaty but rather exercises its "advice and consent" power by either accepting or rejecting the treaty as submitted or by amending it in some form. Once the Senate has approved a treaty, the President may then "make" the treaty by formally concluding it with the nation(s) with which it was negotiated. The President, however, is free not

to conclude a treaty that the Senate has approved, as when the Senate approves a treaty in amended form.

4.   There is no *definition of a treaty* in the Constitution, apparently because the framers saw no need to define what was well known to them in international law. The status of treaties in national law, however, was specified in the supremacy clause: "All Treaties made, or which shall be made, under the authority of the United States, shall be the supreme Law of the Land * * *." Thus the Supreme Court has regarded treaties as being legally equivalent to the laws of Congress. The traditional rule is that an act of Congress will therefore supersede a prior treaty obligation, while a treaty will likewise supersede a previously enacted statute.

5.   *Some Preliminary notes and questions based on the Constitution.* Does Congress have a role in the conduct of foreign affairs? What is it? May Congress negotiate with other states? Directly? Indirectly? May Congress impose limitations or prior restraints on the President's power to negotiate? How, if at all? Are any such limitations on restraints unconstitutional? Will/should the federal court system attempt to decide such an issue?

   In the first constitution, the Articles of Confederation, Congress and judiciary were the entire federal government. Working through its committees, Congress appointed and received envoys, negotiated international agreements, made and carried out foreign policy. Thus Congress was once master as to all the foreign affairs of the United States. What has Congress lost in this sector from the decision of the convention to separate the executive and legislative powers of government and assign the former to a President? How clean-cut is the separation as to foreign affairs (a) policy, (b) operations? Did the framers of the present Constitution answer the question: "Who is master as to foreign affairs"? If not, why not? If so, how? If not, how are the two branches to work together in the foreign affairs field?

   The Constitution gives Congress the power to declare war and raise and support armed forces. It makes the President the commander-in-chief of such forces. If the President wants to deploy American forces in State X but Congress does not want to, what happens?

6.   *In Britain*, Parliament tamed the monarchy through the money power. The Constitution gives the Congress the money power (taxing and appropriating federal funds). Is it legitimate for Congress to use the money power to control American foreign policy?

———

Ware v. Hylton

Supreme Court of the United States, 1796.
3 U.S. (3 Dall.) 199, 220, 1 L.Ed. 568.

■ CHASE, JUSTICE.—The Defendants in error, on the 7th day of July, 1774, passed their penal bond to Farrell and Jones, for the payment of £.2,976 11 6, of good British money; but the condition of the bond, or the time of payment, does not appear on the record.

On the 20th of October, 1777, the legislature of the commonwealth of Virginia, passed a law to sequester British property. In the 3d section of the law, it was enacted, "that it should be lawful for any citizen of Virginia, owing money to a subject of Great Britain, to pay the same, or any part thereof, from time to time, as he should think fit, into the loan office, taking thereout a certificate for the same, in the name of the creditor, with an indorsement, under the hand of the commissioner of the said office, expressing the name of the payer; and shall deliver such certificate to the governor and the council, whose receipt shall discharge him from so much of the debt. And the governor and the council shall, in like manner, lay before the General Assembly, once in every year, an account of these certificates, specifying the names of the persons by, and for whom they were paid; and shall see to the safe keeping of the same; subject to the future directions of the legislature: provided, that the governor and the council may make such allowance, as they shall think reasonable, out of the interest of the money so paid into the loan office, to the wives and children, residing in the state, of such creditor."

On the 26th of April, 1780, the Defendants in error, paid into the loan office of Virginia, part of their debt, to wit, 3,111 1–9 dollars, equal to £.933 14 0 Virginia currency; and obtained a certificate from the commissioners of the loan office, and a receipt from the governor and the council of Virginia, agreeably to the above, in part recited law.

The Defendants in error being sued, on the above bond, in the Circuit Court of Virginia, pleaded the above law, and the payment above stated, in bar of so much of the Plaintiff's debt. The plaintiff, to avoid this bar, replied the fourth article of the Definitive Treaty of Peace, between Great Britain and the United States, of the 3d of September, 1783. To this replication there was a general demurrer and joinder. The Circuit Court allowed the demurrer, and the plaintiff brought the present writ of error.

The case is of great importance, not only from the property that depends on the decision, but because the effect and operation of the treaty are necessarily involved. * * *

The first point raised by the council for the Plaintiff in error was, that the legislature of Virginia had no right to make the law, of the 20th October, 1777 * * *. If this objection is established, the judgment of the Circuit Court must be reversed; because it destroys the Defendant's plea in bar, and leaves him without defence to the Plaintiff's action.

This objection was maintained on different grounds by the Plaintiff's council. One of them contended, that the legislature of Virginia had no right to confiscate any British property, because Virginia was part of the dismembered empire of Great Britain, and the Plaintiff and Defendants were, all of them, members of the British nation, when the debt was contracted, and therefore, that the laws of independent nations do not apply to the case; and, if applicable, that the legislature of Virginia was not justified by the modern law and practice of European nations, in confiscating private debts. In support of this opinion, he cited Vattel who expresses himself thus: "The sovereign has naturally the same right over what his subjects may be indebted to enemies. Therefore, he may confiscate debts of this nature, if the term of payment happen in the time of war. But at present, in regard to the advantage and safety of Commerce, all the sovereigns of Europe have departed from this rigour * * * "

* * *

I am of opinion that the exclusive right of confiscating, during the war, all and every species of British property, within the territorial limits of Virginia, resided only in the Legislature of that commonwealth. * * *

* * *

The 4th article of the treaty is in these words: "It is agreed that creditor, on either side, shall meet with no lawful impediment to the recovery of the full value, in sterling money, of all bona fide debts, heretofore contracted."

* * * I will adopt the following remarks, which I think applicable, and which may be found in Dr. Rutherforth and Vattel. * * * The intention of the framers of the treaty, must be collected from a view of the whole instrument, and from the words made use of by them to express their intention, or from probable or rational conjectures. If the words express the meaning of the parties plainly, distinctly, and perfectly, there ought to be no other means of interpretation; but if the words are obscure, or ambiguous, or imperfect, recourse must be had to other means of interpretation, and in these three cases, we must collect the meaning from the words, or from probable or rational conjectures, or from both. When we collect the intention from the words only, as they lie in the writing before us, it is a literal interpretation; and indeed if the words, and, the construction of a writing, are clear and precise, we can scarce call it interpretation to collect the intention of the writer from thence. The principal rule to be observed in literal interpretation, is to follow that sense, in respect both of the words, and the construction, which is agreeable to common use.

* * *

■ WILSON, JUSTICE.

* * *

* * * Even if Virginia had the power to confiscate, the treaty annuls the confiscation. The fourth article is well expressed to meet the very case: it is not confined to debts existing at the time of making the treaty; but is extended to debts heretofore contracted. It is impossible by any glossary, or argument, to make the words more perspicuous, more conclusive, than by a bare recital. Independent, therefore, of the Constitution of the United States, (which authoritatively inculcates the obligation of contracts) the treaty is sufficient to remove every impediment founded on the law of Virginia. The State made the law; the State was a party to the making of the treaty: a law does nothing more than express the will of a nation; and a treaty does the same. Under this general view of the subject, I think the judgment of the Circuit Court ought to be reversed.

[The court agreed, although some justices found the plight of the debtor who had paid his debt under the law of Virginia, very troublesome. The opinion of Justice Tredell is particularly anguished.]

Missouri v. Holland

United States Supreme Court, 1920.
252 U.S. 416, 40 S.Ct. 382, 64 L.Ed. 641.

■ MR. JUSTICE HOLMES delivered the opinion of the court.

This is a bill in equity brought by the State of Missouri to prevent a game warden of the United States from attempting to enforce the Migratory Bird Treaty Act of July 3, 1918, and the regulations made by the Secretary of Agriculture in pursuance of the same. The ground of the bill is that the statute is an unconstitutional interference with the rights reserved to the States by the Tenth Amendment, and that the acts of the defendant done and threatened under that authority invade the sovereign right of the State and contravene its will manifested in statutes. The State also alleges a pecuniary interest, as owner of the wild birds within its borders and otherwise, admitted by the Government to be sufficient, but it is enough that the bill is a reasonable and proper means to assert the alleged quasi sovereign rights of a State. A motion to dismiss was sustained by the District Court on the ground that the act of Congress is constitutional. The State appeals.

On December 8, 1916, a treaty between the United States and Great Britain was proclaimed by the President. It recited that many species of birds in their annual migrations traversed certain parts of the United States and of Canada, that they were of great value as a source of food and in destroying insects injurious to vegetation, but were in danger of extermination through lack of adequate protection. It therefore provided for specified close[d] seasons and protection in other forms, and agreed that the two powers would take or propose to their law-making bodies the necessary measures for carrying the treaty out. The above mentioned Act of July 3, 1918, entitled an act to give effect to the convention, prohibited the killing, capturing or selling any of the migratory birds included in the terms of the treaty except as permitted by regulations compatible with those terms, to be made by the Secretary of Agriculture. Regulations were proclaimed [in] 1918. It is unnecessary to go into any details, because, the question raised is the general one whether the treaty and statute are void as an interference with the rights reserved to the States.

To answer this question it is not enough to refer to the Tenth Amendment, reserving the powers not delegated to the United States, because by Article II, § 2, the power to make treaties is delegated expressly, and by Article VI treaties made under the authority of the United States, along with the Constitution and laws of the United States made in pursuance thereof, are declared the supreme law of the land. If the treaty is valid there can be no dispute about the validity of the statute under Article I, § 8, as a necessary and proper means to execute the powers of the Government. The language of the Constitution as to the supremacy of treaties being general, the question before us is narrowed to an inquiry into the ground upon which the present supposed exception is placed.

It is said that a treaty cannot be valid if it infringes the Constitution, that there are limits, therefore, to the treatymaking power, and that one such limit is that what an act of Congress could not do unaided, in derogation of the powers reserved to the States, a treaty cannot do. An earlier act of Congress that attempted by itself and not in pursuance of a treaty to regulate the killing of migratory birds within the States had been held bad in the District Court. Those decisions were supported by arguments that migratory birds were owned by the States in their sovereign capacity for the benefit of their people, and that under cases like Geer v. Connecticut, this control was one that Congress had no power to displace. The same argument is supposed to apply now with equal force.

Whether the two cases cited were decided rightly or not they cannot be accepted as a test of the treaty power. Acts of Congress are the supreme law of the land only when made in pursuance of the Constitution, while treaties are declared to be so when made under the authority of the United States. It is open to question whether the authority of the United States means more than the formal acts prescribed to make the convention. We do not mean to imply that there are no qualifications to the treaty-making power; but they must be ascertained in a different way. It is obvious that there may be matters of the sharpest exigency for the national well being that an act of Congress could not deal with but that a treaty followed by such an act could, and it is not lightly to be assumed that, in matters requiring national action, "a power which must belong to and somewhere reside in every civilized government" is not to be found. What was said in that case with regard to the powers of the States applies with equal force to the powers of the nation in cases where the States individually are incompetent to act. We are not yet discussing the particular case before us but only are considering the validity of the test proposed. With regard to that we may add that when we are dealing with words that also are a constituent act, like the Constitution of the United States, we must realize that they have called into life a being the development of which could not have been foreseen completely by the most gifted of its begetters. It was enough for them to realize or to hope that they had created an organism; it has taken a century and has cost their successors much sweat and blood to prove that they created a nation. The case before us must be considered in the light of our whole experience and not merely in that of what was said a hundred years ago. The treaty in question does not contravene any prohibitory words to be found in the Constitution. The only question is whether it is forbidden by some invisible radiation from the general terms of the Tenth Amendment. We must consider what this country has become in deciding what that Amendment has reserved.

The State as we have intimated founds its claim of exclusive authority upon an assertion of title to migratory birds, an assertion that is embodied in statute. No doubt it is true that as between a State and its inhabitants the State may regulate the killing and sale of such birds, but it does not follow that its authority is exclusive of paramount powers. To put the claim of the State upon title is to lean upon a slender reed. Wild birds are not in the possession of anyone; and possession is the beginning of ownership. The whole foundation of the State's rights is the presence within their jurisdiction of birds that yesterday had not arrived, tomorrow may be in another State and in a week a thousand miles away. If we are to be accurate we cannot put the case of the State upon higher ground than that the treaty deals with creatures that for the moment are within the state borders, that it must be carried out by officers of the United States within the same territory, and that but for the treaty the State would be free to regulate this subject itself.

As most of the laws of the United States are carried out within the States and as many of them deal with matters which in the silence of such laws the State might regulate, such general grounds are not enough to support Missouri's claim. Valid treaties of course "are as binding within the territorial limits of the States as they are elsewhere throughout the dominion of the United States." No doubt the great body of private relations usually fall within the control of the State, but a treaty may override its power. We do not have to invoke the later developments of constitutional law for this proposition; it was recognized early with regard to statutes of limitation, and even earlier, as to confiscation, in Ware v. Hylton. It was assumed by Chief Justice Marshall with regard to the escheat of land to the State in Chirac v. Chirac. So as to a limited jurisdiction of foreign consuls within a State. Wildenhus's Case. It only remains to consider the application of established rules to the present case.

Here a national interest of very nearly the first magnitude is involved. It can be protected only by national action in concert with that of another power. The subject-matter is only transitorily within the State and has no permanent habitat therein. But for the treaty and the statute there soon might be no birds for any powers to deal with. We see nothing in the Constitution that compels the Government to sit by while a food supply is cut off and the protectors of our forests and our crops are destroyed. It is not sufficient to rely upon the States. The reliance is vain, and were it otherwise, the question is whether the United States is forbidden to act. We are of opinion that the treaty and statute must be upheld.

■ [A]ffirmed. MR. JUSTICE VAN DEVANTER and MR. JUSTICE PITNEY dissent.

Reid v. Covert

United States Supreme Court, 1957.
354 U.S. 1, 77 S.Ct. 1222, 1 L.Ed.2d 1148.

■ MR. JUSTICE BLACK announced the judgment of the Court and delivered an opinion, in which THE CHIEF JUSTICE, MR. JUSTICE DOUGLAS, and MR. JUSTICE BRENNAN join.

These cases raise basic constitutional issues of the utmost concern. They call into question the role of the military under our system of government. They involve the power of Congress to expose civilians to trial by military tribunals, under military regulations and procedures, for offenses against the United States thereby depriving them of trial in civilian courts, under civilian laws and procedures and with all the safeguards of the Bill of Rights. These cases are particularly significant because for the first time since the adoption of the Constitution wives of soldiers have been denied trial by jury in a court of law and forced to trial before courts-martial.

* * * Mrs. Clarice Covert killed her husband, a sergeant in the United States Air Force, at an airbase in England. Mrs. Covert, who was not a

member of the armed services, was residing on the base with her husband at the time. She was tried by a court-martial for murder under Article 118 of the Uniform Code of Military Justice (UCMJ). The trial was on charges preferred by Air Force personnel and the court-martial was composed of Air Force officers. The court-martial asserted jurisdiction over Mrs. Covert under Article 2(11) of the UCMJ, which provides: "The following persons are subject to this code: * * * (11) Subject to the provisions of any treaty or agreement to which the United States is or may be a party or to any accepted rule of international law, all persons serving with, employed by, or accompanying the armed forces without the continental limits of the United States * * *."

Counsel for Mrs. Covert contended that she was insane at the time she killed her husband, but the military tribunal found her guilty of murder and sentenced her to life imprisonment. The judgment was affirmed by the Air Force Board of Review, but was reversed by the Court of Military Appeals, because of prejudicial errors concerning the defense of insanity. While Mrs. Covert was being held in this country pending a proposed retrial by court-martial in the District of Columbia, her counsel petitioned the District Court for a writ of habeas corpus to set her free on the ground that the Constitution forbade her trial by military authorities. Construing this Court's decision in *U.S. ex rel. Toth v. Quarles,* as holding that "a civilian is entitled to a civilian trial" the District Court held that Mrs. Covert could not be tried by court-martial and ordered her released from custody. The Government appealed directly to this Court under 28 U.S.C.A. § 1252.

* * * Mrs. Dorothy Smith killed her husband, an Army officer, at a post in Japan where she was living with him. She was tried for murder by a court-martial and despite considerable evidence that she was insane was found guilty and sentenced to life imprisonment. The judgment was approved by the Army Board of Review, and the Court of Military Appeals. Mrs. Smith was then confined in a federal penitentiary in West Virginia. Her father, respondent here, filed a petition for habeas corpus in a District Court for West Virginia. The petition charged that the court-martial was without jurisdiction because Article 2(11) of the UCMJ was unconstitutional insofar as it authorized the trial of civilian dependents accompanying servicemen overseas. The District Court refused to issue the writ, and while an appeal was pending in the Court of Appeals for the Fourth Circuit we granted certiorari at the request of the Government.

The cases were consolidated and argued last Term and a majority of the Court, with three Justices dissenting and one reserving opinion, held that military trial of Mrs. Smith and Mrs. Covert for their alleged offenses was constitutional. The majority held that Article III and the Fifth and Sixth Amendments which require that crimes be tried by a jury after indictment by a grand jury did not protect an American citizen when he was tried by the American Government in foreign lands for offenses committed there and that Congress could provide for the trial of such offenses in any manner it saw fit so long as the procedures established were reasonable and consonant with due process. The opinion then [expressed] the view that military trials, as now practiced, were not unreasonable or arbitrary when applied to dependents accompanying members of the armed forces overseas. In reaching their conclusion the majority found it unnecessary to consider the power of Congress "To make Rules for the Government and Regulation of the land and navel Forces" under Article I of the Constitution.

* * * The Court granted a petition for rehearing. Now, after further argument and consideration, we conclude that the previous decisions cannot be permitted to stand. We hold that Mrs. Smith and Mrs. Covert could not constitutionally be tried by military authorities.

* * *

At the time of Mrs. Covert's alleged offense, an executive agreement was in effect between the United States and Great Britain which permitted United States' military courts to exercise exclusive jurisdiction over offenses committed in Great Britain by American servicemen or their dependents.[29] For its part, the United States agreed that these military courts would be willing and able to try and to punish all offenses against the laws of Great Britain by such persons. In all material respects, the same situation existed in Japan when Mrs. Smith killed her husband. Even though a court-martial does not give an accused trial by jury and other Bill of Rights protections, the Government contends that Art. 2(11) of the UCMJ, insofar as it provides for the military trial of dependents accompanying the armed forces in Great Britain and Japan, can be sustained as legislation which is necessary and proper to carry out the United States' obligations under the international agreements made with those countries. The obvious and decisive answer to this, of course, is that no agreement with a foreign nation can confer power on the Congress, or on any other branch of Government, which is free from the restraints of the Constitution. Article VI, the Supremacy Clause of the Constitution, declares: "This Constitution, and the Laws of the United States which shall be made in Pursuance thereof; and all Treaties made, or which shall be made, under the Authority of the United States, shall be the supreme Law of the Land * * *."

There is nothing in this language which intimates the treaties and laws enacted pursuant to them do not have to comply with the provisions of the Constitution. Nor is there anything in the debates which accompanied the drafting and ratification of the Constitution which even suggests such a result. These debates as well as the history that surrounds the adoption of

---

29. Executive Agreement of July 27, 1942. The arrangement now in effect in Great Britain and the other NATO nations, as well as in Japan, is the NATO Status of Forces Agreement, T.I.A.S. 2846, which by its terms gives the foreign nation primary jurisdiction to try dependents accompanying American servicemen for offenses which are violations of the law of both the foreign nation and the United States. Art. VII, §§ 1(b), 3(a). The foreign nation has exclusive criminal jurisdiction over dependents for offenses which only violate its laws. Art. VII, § 2(b).

However, the Agreement contains provisions which require that the foreign nations provide procedural safeguards for our nationals tried under the terms of the Agreement in their courts. Art. VII, § 9.

Apart from those persons subject to the Status of Forces and comparable agreements and certain other restricted classes of Americans, a foreign nation has plenary criminal jurisdiction, of course, over all Americans—tourists, residents, businessmen, government employees and so forth—who commit offenses against its law within its territory.

the treaty provision in Article VI make it clear that the reason treaties were not limited to those made in "pursuance" of the Constitution was so that agreements made by the United States under the Articles of Confederation, including the important peace treaties which concluded the Revolutionary War, would remain in effect. It would be manifestly contrary to the objectives of those who created the Constitution, as well as those who were responsible for the Bill of Rights—let alone alien to our entire constitutional history and tradition—to construe Article VI as permitting the United States to exercise power under an international agreement without observing constitutional prohibitions. In effect, such construction would permit amendment of that document in a manner not sanctioned by Article V. The prohibitions of the Constitution were designed to apply to all branches of the National Government and they cannot be nullified by the Executive or by the Executive and the Senate combined.

There is nothing new or unique about what we say here. This Court has regularly and uniformly recognized the supremacy of the Constitution over a treaty. For example, in Geofroy v. Riggs * * * it declared:

The treaty power, as expressed in the Constitution, is in terms unlimited except by those restraints which are found in that instrument against the action of the government or of its departments, and those arising from the nature of the government itself and of that of the States. [It cannot extend] so far as to authorize what the Constitution forbids, or a change in the character of the government or in that of one of the States, or a cession of any portion of the territory of the latter, without its consent.

This Court has also repeatedly taken the position that an Act of Congress, which must comply with the Constitution, is on a full parity with a treaty, and that when a statute which is subsequent in time is inconsistent with a treaty, the statute to the extent of conflict renders the treaty null.[34] It would be completely anomalous to say that a treaty need not comply with the Constitution when such an agreement can be overridden by a statute that must conform to that instrument.

There is nothing in Missouri v. Holland, [supra], which is contrary to the position taken here. There the Court carefully noted that the treaty involved was not inconsistent with any specific provision of the Constitution. The Court was concerned with the Tenth Amendment which reserves to the States or the people all power not delegated to the National Government. To the extent that the United States can validly make treaties, the people and the States have delegated their power to the National Government and the Tenth Amendment is no barrier.

In summary, we conclude that the Constitution in its entirety applied to the trials of Mrs. Smith and Mrs. Covert. Since their court-martial did not meet the requirements of Art. III, § 2 or the Fifth and Sixth Amend-

34. In *Whitney v. Robertson*, the Court stated: "By the Constitution a treaty is placed on the same footing, and made of like obligation, with an act of legislation. Both are declared by that instrument to be the supreme law of the land, and no superior efficacy is given to either over the other * * *. [I]f the two are inconsistent, the one last in date will control the other * * *." [*See also*], Head Money Cases.

ments we are compelled to determine if there is anything within the Constitution which authorizes the military trial of dependents accompanying the armed forces overseas.

* * *

* * * The judgment of the District Court directing that Mrs. Covert be released from custody is affirmed. The judgment of the District Court is reversed and the case is remanded with instructions to order Mrs. Smith released from custody. Reversed and remanded. MR. JUSTICE WHITTAKER took no part in the consideration or decision of these cases.

* * *

■ [Opinion of MR. JUSTICE HARLAN and MR. JUSTICE FRANKFURTER, concurring in the result, omitted.] MR. JUSTICE CLARK, with whom MR. JUSTICE BURTON joins, dissenting.

* * *

Before discussing the power of the Congress under Art. I, § 8, cl. 14, of the Constitution it is well to take our bearings. * * * [No question of] U.S. jurisdiction of a military court-martial sitting within U.S. territorial limits [is involved]. * * * The power of the Government to make treaties or the legal relationship between treaties and the Constitution [is not at issue]. Nor are they concerned with the power of Congress to provide for the trial of Americans sojourning, touring, or temporarily residing in foreign nations. * * * We are to determine only whether the civilian dependents of American servicemen may constitutionally be tried by an American military court-martial in a foreign country for an offense committed in that country.

* * *

The only alternative remaining—probably the alternative that the Congress will now be forced to choose—is that Americans committing offenses on foreign soil be tried by the courts of the country in which the offense is committed. Foreign courts have exclusive jurisdiction under the principles of international law and many nations enjoy concurrent jurisdiction with the American military authorities pursuant to Article VII of the [SOFA] of Parties to NATO. Where the American military authorities do have jurisdiction, it is only by mutual agreement with the foreign sovereign concerned and pursuant to carefully drawn agreements conditioned on trial by the American military authorities. Typical of these agreements was the one concluded between the United States and Japan [in] 1952, and in force at the time one of these cases arose. Under this and like agreements, the jurisdiction so ceded to the United States military courts will surely be withdrawn if the services are impotent to exercise it. It is clear that trial before an American court-martial in which the fundamentals of due process are observed is preferable to leaving American servicemen and their dependents to the widely varying standards of justice in foreign courts throughout the world. Under these circumstances it is untenable to say that Congress could have exercised a lesser power adequate to the end proposed.

* * *

Notes and Questions

1. *"In Reid v. Covert, Justice Black held:* 'The United States is entirely a creature of the Constitution. Its power and authority have no other source. It can only act in accordance with all the limitations imposed by the Constitution.' Although Justice Black wrote for only four justices, the opinions of the two concurring justices and the two dissenting justices implied agreement with this general proposition. Three years later, in *Kinsella v. U.S.*, Justice Whittaker and Justice Stewart announced their adhesion to the proposition stated by Black in *Reid v. Covert."* See Koh, *Why the President (Almost) Always Wins in Foreign Affairs: Lessons of the Iran–Contra Affair,* 97 Yale L.J. 1255, 1261–63 (1988); Randall, *The Treaty Power,* 51 Ohio St.L.J. 1089 (1990); *See* Stevens, *Federalism and Foreign Affairs: Congress's Power to "Define & Punish"* ... *Offenses Against the Law of Nations,* 42 Wm. & Mary L.Rev. 447 (2000).

2. Do you think that Justice Black overruled *Missouri v. Holland, supra,* or any part of it? Or, did Justice Black distinguish Holland sufficiently? What was the major concern of *Reid v. Covert*? How different was that from *Holland*? Compare, *U.S. v. Toscanino,* 500 F.2d 267 (2nd Cir. 1974); with *U.S. v. Alvarez–Machain, infra this Chapter,* and in Chapter 16, *infra,* in light of *Reid v. Covert.* What, if anything, has happened to the impact of *Reid v. Covert*?

3. *On the constitutionality of the human rights conventions.*

   a. *Are there constitutional impediments to the United States becoming a party to the human rights conventions sponsored by the United Nations, at least without reservations?* Refer in particular to the following conventions in the Doc. Supp. Economic, Social and Cultural Rights; Civil and Political Rights; Elimination of All Forms of Racial Discrimination. Consider for example, Article 4 of the Convention on Racial Discrimination and Article 19 of the Convention on Civil and Political Rights. Is Article 5 of the Convention on Civil and Political Rights relevant to the question of the constitutionality of that convention as a whole? In the last decade, the U.S. Senate has given its Advice & Consent to the Genocide Convention, the International Covenant on Civil & Political Rights, the Convention against Torture, and the International Convention on the Elimination of All Forms of Racial Discrimination, but with expansive reservations, relating to the Senate's impression of their unconstitutionality. See Chapter 9, on Human Rights, and Chapter 11, on Treaties.

   b. *Do the human rights treaties embody a bargain with foreign states? Must they, to be within the treaty power?* If a treaty does not involve a bargaining of concessions between the negotiating states, some have argued that it cannot involve a matter of international concern. If a putative treaty does not involve such a matter, the argument continues, the arrangement is not really a treaty within the meaning of the Constitution. Hence the overriding power given to the federal government in Article VI, clause 2, is not activated. This argument assumes that a decision maker, presumably a court, would pass on the question, whether the supposedly necessary international concern, exists in the particular case. Is this evaluation a proper function for courts in the United States? How would the Supreme Court go about making a determination as to whether a treaty was or was not a matter of international concern? The concern about international content as a constitutional requirement has greatly diminished. It is rejected in the 1987 Restatement, Section 302, Comment c.

Even if the courts will not review a treaty at the constitutional level on the basis of whether there is an international concern, senators in giving their advice and consent to the treaty are also obligated, by their oath of office, to consider the question. Even if the senators should find that the treaty is satisfactory in this respect, it lies within their responsibility and prerogative, to determine whether the treaty is, nonetheless, undesirable from a policy point of view.

c. *Between roughly 1948 and 1953, a determined effort was made by a group of senators, elements of the American Bar Association, and others to amend the Constitution to limit the internal legal effect of treaties on the federal legislative power.* The political history of the period shows that the proponents of the *Bricker Amendment* (named for the Ohio senator who led the fight) were neo-isolationists in general alignment. Many also had a serious concern lest the conventions on human rights then being negotiated in the United Nations be given internal effect within the United States in such matters as segregated education and travel facilities. The amendment effort failed, not too long before the Supreme Court, in 1954, interpreted the due process and equal protection clauses of the 5th and 14th Amendments to prohibit different treatment based on race in public education, thus setting the stage for the general dismantling of all forms of racial discrimination involving state action. In other areas of socio-political discrimination, such as to gender, disability, disease, and age, the potential of the treaty power as an alternative path to legalizing anti-discrimination at the federal level (thus imposing the legal change on the states) still exists. Should the treaty power be used in this way, if neither formal amendment nor judicial interpretation occurs? Objection might possibly go beyond the political to a revival of constitutional arguments against such use to change the allocation of federal-state powers. Is there a residual or ultimate inherent limitation on the use of the treaty power to achieve internal socio-political change? What might it be?

Edwards v. Carter

United States Court of Appeals, District of Columbia Circuit, 1978.
580 F.2d 1055, cert. denied, 436 U.S. 907.

■ PER CURIAM: This is an appeal from the District Court's dismissal of a challenge to appellee's use of the treaty power to convey to the Republic of Panama United States properties, including the Panama Canal, located in the Panama Canal Zone. Appellants, sixty members of the House of Representatives, sought a declaratory judgment that the exclusive means provided in the Constitution for disposal of United States property requires approval of both Houses of Congress, see Art. IV, § 3, cl. 2, and that therefore the Panama Canal Zone may not be returned to Panama through the Treaty process, which invests the treaty-making power in the President by and with the advice and consent of two-thirds of the Senators present, see Art. II, § 2, cl. 2. Appellee contends that the Constitution permits United States territory to be disposed of either through congressional legislation or through the treaty process, and that therefore the President's decision to proceed under the treaty power is constitutionally permissible. * * *

* * * For the reasons appearing below, we affirm the dismissal of the complaint, not on the jurisdictional ground relied on by the District Court but for failure to state a claim on which relief may be granted.

I

* * *

* * * [T]he precise question we address is whether the constitutional delegation found in Art. IV, § 3, cl. 2 is exclusive so as to prohibit the disposition of United States property by self-executing treaty—i.e., a treaty enacted in accordance with Art. II, § 2, cl. 2, which becomes effective without implementing legislation.

II

Article IV, § 3, cl. 2, in its entirety: "The Congress shall have Power to dispose of and make all needful Rules and Regulations respecting the Territory or other Property belonging to the United States; and nothing in this Constitution shall be so construed as to Prejudice any Claims of the United States, or of any particular State."

Appellants contend that this clause gives Congress exclusive power to convey to foreign nations any property, such as the Panama Canal, owned by the United States. We find such a construction to be at odds with the wording of this and similar grants of power to the Congress, and, most significantly, with the history of the constitutional debates.[4]

The grant of authority to Congress under the property clause states that "The Congress shall have Power * * *," not that only the Congress shall have power, or that the Congress shall have exclusive power. In this respect the property clause is parallel to Article I, § 8, which also states that "The Congress shall have Power * * *." Many of the powers thereafter enumerated in § 8 involve matters that were at the time the Constitution was adopted, and that are at the present time, also commonly the subject of treaties. The most prominent example of this is the regulation of commerce with foreign nations, Art. I, § 8, cl. 3, and appellants do not go so far as to contend that the treaty process is not a constitutionally allowable means for regulating foreign commerce. It thus seems to us that, on its face, the property clause is intended not to restrict the scope of the

---

4. The Senate Foreign Relations Committee has thoroughly considered and rejected appellants' argument. That Committee reported the treaties with Panama to the full Senate by a 14 to 1 vote, and the one dissenting Senator did not dispute the power of the President, by and with the advice and consent of two-thirds of the Senate present, to transfer United States property. In addition to the American Law Institute's Restatement of Foreign Relations Law, see infra, other authorities in agreement with this conclusion include ... [and] Professor Covey Oliver, Hearings Before the Committee on Foreign Relations, Part IV, at 95, 103, 112–13 (Jan. 19, 1978).

treaty clause, but, rather, is intended to permit Congress to accomplish through legislation what may concurrently be accomplished through other means provided in the Constitution.

* * *

There are certain grants of authority to Congress which are, by their very terms, exclusive. In these areas, the treaty-making power and the power of Congress are not concurrent; rather, the only department of the federal government authorized to take action is the Congress. For instance, the Constitution expressly provides only one method—congressional enactment—for the appropriation of money: "No Money shall be drawn from the Treasury, but in Consequence of Appropriations made by Law." Art. I, § 9, cl. 7. Thus, the expenditure of funds by the United States cannot be accomplished by self-executing treaty; implementing legislation appropriating such funds is indispensable. Similarly, the constitutional mandate that "all Bills for raising Revenue shall originate in the House of Representatives," Art. I, § 7, cl. 1, appears, by reason of the restrictive language used, to prohibit the use of the treaty power to impose taxes.

These particular grants of power to Congress operate to limit the treaty power because the language of these provisions clearly precludes any method of appropriating money or raising taxes other than through the enactment of laws by the full Congress. This is to be contrasted with the power-granting language in Art. I, § 8, and in Art. IV, § 3, cl. 2. Rather than stating the particular matter of concern and providing that the enactment of a law is the only way for the federal government to take action regarding that matter, these provisions state simply that Congress shall have power to take action on the matters enumerated.

Thus it appears from the very language used in the property clause that this provision was not intended to preclude the availability of self-executing treaties as a means for disposing of United States property. The history of the drafting and ratification of that clause confirms this conclusion. The other clause in Art. IV, § 3 concerns the procedures for admission of new states into the Union, and the debates at the Constitutional Convention clearly demonstrate that the property clause was intended to delineate the role to be played by the central government in the disposition of Western lands which were potential new states. Several individual states had made territorial claims to portions of these lands; and as finally enacted the property clause, introduced in the midst of the Convention's consideration of the admission of new states, sought to preserve both federal claims and conflicting state claims to certain portions of the Western lands.

The proceedings of the Virginia state ratifying convention provide further evidence of the limited scope of the property clause. During a debate in which the meaning of the clause was questioned, Mr. Grayson noted that the sole purpose for including this provision was to preserve the property rights of the states and the federal government to the Western territory as these rights existed during the Confederation.

This history demonstrates the limited concerns giving rise to the inclusion of Article IV, § 3, cl. 2 in the Constitution. Whether or not this historical perspective might serve as a basis for restricting the scope of congressional power under the property clause, we view it as persuasive evidence for rejecting the claim that Article IV is an express limitation on the treaty power, foreclosing the availability of that process as a constitutionally permissible means of disposing of American interests in the Panama Canal Zone.

* * *

IV

In view of the lack of ambiguity as to the intended effects of the treaty and property clauses, it may be surprising that judicial pronouncements over the past two centuries relating to these constitutional provisions are somewhat vague and conflicting. However, none of the actual holdings in these cases addressed the precise issue before us—whether the property clause prohibits the transfer of United States property to foreign nations through self-executing treaties. While, therefore, neither the holdings nor the dicta of these previous cases are dispositive of the case before us, we believe that in the main they support the conclusions we have stated heretofore.

* * *

As is true of most of the cases in which the Supreme Court has addressed the scope of the treaty power * * * involved the federal government's interaction with Indian tribes. Because of the sui generis nature of the relationship between the Indian tribes and the federal government, it might be argued that these decisions are not dispositive. We think, however, that they are persuasively supportive of the authority of the President and the Senate under the treaty clause.

V

While certain earlier judicial interpretations of the interplay between the property clause and the treaty clause may be somewhat confused and less than dispositive of the precise issue before us, past treaty practice is thoroughly consistent with the revealed intention of the Framers of these clauses. In addition to the treaties with Indian tribes upheld in the cases discussed above, there are many other instances of self-executing treaties with foreign nations, including Panama, which cede land or other property assertedly owned by the United States. That some transfers have been effected through a congressional enactment instead of, or in addition to, a treaty signed by the President and ratified by two-thirds of the Senate present lends no support to appellants' position in this case, because, self-executing treaties and congressional enactments are alternative, concurrent means provided in the Constitution for disposal of United States property.

For instance, the Treaty with Panama of 1955, transferred certain property (a strip of water and other sites within the Canal Zone) to Panama without concurring legislation by the Congress, while transfer of other property (owned by the United States but within the jurisdiction of Panama) was, under the terms of the treaty itself, dependent upon concurring legislation by the Congress. The decision to cast some but not all of the articles of conveyance in non-self-executing form was a policy choice; it was not required by the Constitution.

The transfer of property contemplated in the current instance is part of a broader effort in the conduct of our foreign affairs to strengthen relations with another country, and indeed with the whole of Latin America. The Framers in their wisdom have made the treaty power available to the President, the chief executant of foreign relations under our constitutional scheme, by and with the advice and consent of two-thirds of the members of the Senate present, as a means of accomplishing these public purposes. We do not think it is relevant that many previous treaties couched in self-executing terms have been different in scope, dealing with boundary issues or otherwise ceding land which was claimed both by the United States and by a foreign nation. * * *

* * * [Thus], the judgment of the District Court dismissing the complaint is Affirmed. [Dissenting opinion of MacKINNON, CIRCUIT JUDGE, omitted.]

Notes and Questions

1. *Exclusive or concurrent?* Does the *Edwards decision* add much to the issues surrounding the debate over whether Article I, § 8, cl. 10, presents an concurrent or exclusive congressional power? *See Henfield's Case, supra.*

2. *Supreme Court Deference to Political Branches in Treaty Interpretation*. Review *United States v. Alvarez–Machain, supra*, Chapters 1, 3, 9 and 16, paying close attention to the court's treatment of customary international law and how it relates to treaty interpretation. Consider also the dissent's discussion of *Rauscher* and whether the Court adhered to the precedent set by *Rauscher*. What differences exist between the cases to justify the different treatment of the treaties?

Alvarez-Machain met with significant criticism and was immediately followed by an amendment to the U.S.-Mexico Extradition Treaty, specifically to prohibit forcible abductions. *Alvarez-Machain* also met with some support, which attempted to explain the decision in the context of the court's historical treatment of customary international law, and the doctrine of separation of powers under the United States Constitution. The commentary fairly unanimously agreed that kidnapping is a violation of international law, as was conceded by the Supreme Court, but has disagreed over whether that violation required the kidnapping state to forego jurisdiction over the foreign citizen wrongfully acquired. See further analysis and authority in chapters 1, 9, and 16.

3. *Customary International Law.* As discussed *supra* Chapter 1, the Supreme Court has typically applied customary international law only after first determining that there is no conflicting executive or legislative action. See *The Paquete Habana, supra*. This can be seen as deference to the political branches in the foreign affairs area, which the Court has long considered to be an area committed by the Constitution to the President and Congress. *See* discussion, *infra*, regarding foreign affairs power under the Constitution. Thus, the Court will, as it did in *Alvarez-Machain*, attempt to interpret the treaty so that it conforms with the executive or congressional action. *See also Sale v. Haitian Centers, supra*, in chapter 9 (interpreting refugee treaty to allow executive branch to intercept Haitian refugee boats outside of United States territory and repatriate passengers); *Barclays Bank PLC v. Franchise Tax Board of California*, 512 U.S. 298 (1994) (allowing state to impose controversial tax on foreign corporations because Congress did not act to prevent the tax). Does this type of judicial deference give sufficient consideration to customary international law? Is the Court correct to defer to the executive's interpretation of a treaty, even if it conflicts with customary international law and the spirit of the treaty, so long as it does not conflict with the express language of the treaty? Should the court intervene to prevent the executive from violating customary international law, and does it have the constitutional power to do so? Does the Constitution's mandate that the executive "take Care that the Laws be faithfully executed," *see* Art. II, § 3, include customary international law? If so, how can we justify giving the executive authority to terminate a treaty, which is "the supreme Law of the Land" under Art.VI, cl. 2 (the executive essentially has this power under *Goldwater v. Carter, infra*), but not the authority to violate customary international law, which is not mentioned in the Constitution as binding law?

SECTION B.   EXECUTIVE AGREEMENTS AND THE CONSTITUTION

Department of State Circular 175 provides that, " . . . [t]here are three bases for international agreements other than treaties . . . An international agreement may be concluded pursuant to one or more of these constitutional bases. . . . " The Circular goes on to present the following bases: (1) Agreements pursuant to treaty; (2) Agreements pursuant to Legislation; (3) Agreements pursuant to the constitutional authority of the President.

1.   PRESIDENTIAL POWER

Notes and Questions

1. *The President, the Senate and the House of Representatives.* What institutions of the federal government should participate in the formulation of foreign policy and in the making of internal law by international agreement? Despite the experience of President Washington, detailed below, Senate leaders in recent years have contended that the power as to advice and consent to treaties gives the Senate a special role of collaboration with the executive in the formulation of United States foreign policy, even where no specific international agreement is involved. Leaders of the House of Representatives have not shown enthusiasm for this concept of senatorial special responsibility.

Sometimes, as in the case of tax treaties, the special responsibility of the House as to revenue measures is respected by the practice of making such treaties subject to the enactment of tax legislation by Congress.

Further, in a revenue measure, Congress delegates to the executive, before the fact, the power to make certain types of international agreements, such as those for the reduction of tariffs or the elimination of non-tariff trade barriers. These delegations fix time limits, state maximum cuts and require periodic reports to Congress and procedural steps.

Concern as to the possibility that executive agreements not authorized bicamerally by Congress might force it to go along with the President, both as to foreign policy choices and as to internal legal effects, has from time to time been voiced in both chambers. The Senate has been more active institutionally in this regard than the House. In 1971, the Senate Committee on Foreign Relations held hearings[a] that are still significant because they covered many aspects of a basic problem of legislative participation in foreign affairs, from taxing and appropriating, through oversight of past executive actions, to the use of international agreements and the formulation of congressional foreign policy preferences. Other legislation, requiring seasonable reports from the President, is now in place, and in 1986–87 lay at the heart of the Reagan Administration's "Iran–Contragate" crisis.

2 Schwartz, A Commentary on the Constitution of the United States: The Powers of Government 101, 150 (1963)*

The conception of the Senate as a Presidential council in the diplomatic field broke down as soon as it was tried in practice. In August, 1789, Washington came personally to the Senate to seek its advice on a proposed treaty. As might have been expected, an independent legislative chamber (even one composed of only twenty-six members) was scarcely suited to perform the role of Council of State. Instead of giving the President the speedy advice he sought, the Senators made lengthy speeches on the procedure to be followed. "This defeats every purpose of my coming here!" Washington exclaimed. As he left the Senate Chamber, he is reported to have declared "That he would be damned if he ever went there again." The account is probably apocryphal, but the fact remains that, after Washington's experience in this respect, neither he nor any other President ever again sought the formal advice of the Senate on a proposed negotiation. The concept of the Senate as an executive council in the field of foreign affairs was thus all but still-born at the outset of the Republic.

* * *

That an executive agreement can, in fact, be employed to accomplish the identical purpose as a treaty covering the same subject-matter is dramatically demonstrated by Theodore Roosevelt's action in connection with a proposed treaty with the Dominican Republic. Plenipotentiaries of the two countries had signed an agreement in 1905 in treaty form provid-

a. Hearings Before the Senate Committee on Foreign Relations on S. 596, 92nd Cong., First Sess., Oct. 20–21, 1971.

* © Bernard Schwartz 1962; reprinted by permission of the publisher, The Macmillan Company, New York.

ing for the collection and disbursement of Dominican customs revenues. The treaty was submitted to the Senate, but that body failed to give its constitutional consent. President Roosevelt then proceeded to put the proposed treaty provisions into effect as an executive agreement. As T.R. put it in his Autobiography: "Somebody had to do that duty, and accordingly I did it. I went ahead and administered the proposed treaty anyhow, considering it as a simple agreement on the part of the Executive." Does the fact that he "did it" make it Constitutional?

2. *Consider President Roosevelt's actions in the context of the Bricker amendment and current practice.* A few presidential exercises of the executive agreement alternative in earlier times fed a viewpoint much emphasized by the proponents of the Bricker amendment, that important international matters are dealt with by executive agreements, not Article II treaties, and that, in any event, the two modalities are interchangeable at the option of the President. It is doubtful that the first belief was ever true, and as to the second, consider the classification of executive agreements that follows, as well as the legislation that has been enacted since the first Roosevelt president acted so independently.

Examine the connection between the rise of legislation requiring the President to keep the Congress informed on foreign affairs operations, including executive agreements, and the carrot-stick inducement used by Congress in the Trade Act of 1974, i.e., the fast-track procedure of Section 151 of that Act.

Wormuth & Firmage, To Chain the Dog of War

at 181–191, 198–200 (footnotes omitted).*

Articles I and II of the Constitution reveal the intent of the framers to give Congress the dominant hand in the establishment of basic policy regarding foreign relations. It has been observed that a stranger reading the Constitution would obtain little idea of the vast authority actually exercised by the President today. The constitutional text and the accounts of the Philadelphia Convention also make it clear that the framers envisioned a foreign affairs partnership between the two political branches. The treaty power, viewed (inaccurately as it turned out) as the major means by which our foreign relations were to be conducted * * * rests with the Senate and the President. Moreover, the ambiguities and potential overlaps of authority in the constitutional grants of power * * * as well as the theory of mixed powers articulated by some of the framers * * * provide additional evidence of the framers' anticipation: a foreign policy system emerging out of cooperation and conflict would be slow to take major steps, would lack consensus between the political branches. Finally, the constitutional text does not address all the issues that can be raised about authority in foreign affairs, indicating—or perhaps simply dictating—that custom would also play a role in the development of the allocation of power in foreign relations.

* Reprinted with the permission of the University of Illinois press.

Thus, while some powers to act in foreign affairs are expressly granted, some may be implied from textual grants of power, and still others, seemingly without any basis in the Constitution, have been "created" as a result of decades of custom and practice in the political branches. The outcome of this process is that the President almost certainly exercises greater authority over the conduct of foreign affairs than was contemplated by the framers of the Constitution. This acquisition of power by the executive proceeded at a rapid pace from the earliest days of the Republic and was aided and abetted by a Congress that recognized the natural advantages held by the executive branch. Nevertheless, in those areas where Congress has been granted clear authority, it has been given the final and authoritative word. Moreover, to recognize that presidents have on occasion ... overstepped constitutional bounds in the process of check, balance, and accommodation previously described, is not to say that the precedents necessarily legitimate such acts. The secrecy with which some executive acts have been accomplished indicates that even the actors recognized the disparity between their acts and their legal authority.

* * *

Some authors have attempted to bolster the claim for presidential war power by relying on the contention that the President is the "sole organ" of American foreign policy. According to this argument, the President's broad responsibility for America's foreign policy justified acting in the nation's interest by intervening in Vietnam. * * * A brief review of the history of the sole organ doctrine is therefore warranted.

John Marshall, speaking in the House of Representatives in defense of controversial action taken by President Adams, first described the President as "the *sole organ* of the nation in its external relations, and its sole representative with foreign nations." President Adams had given written instructions to a federal judge that a British deserter held in custody by a United States circuit court should be turned over to British authorities in accordance with extradition provisions of the Jay Treaty. In response to inaccurate charges that the President had actually delivered up an American citizen who had been impressed into British service, Marshall gave a speech outlining the facts of the case and the various legal arguments in support of the President's acts. At no time during Marshall's speech did he assert that the President's exclusive power to communicate with other nations on behalf of the United States involved power to make foreign policy.

It was Justice Sutherland who first attempted to read substantive power into the phrase. In *Curtiss–Wright*, Sutherland used Marshall's "sole organ" language to bolster his argument that the traditional prohibition against the delegation of legislative power to the President does not apply in the area of foreign affairs. In a relatively brief discussion, Sutherland moved from the accepted proposition that "the President alone has the power to speak or listen as a representative of the nation" to finding justification for the challenged delegation of authority in part in "the very delicate, plenary and exclusive power of the President as the sole organ of the federal government in the field of international relations." * * *

Just as Sutherland's theory of extra-constitutional power has been repudiated by the Supreme Court, his statements concerning the delegation doctrine and the President's authority as sole organ have been severely qualified. Two judicial statements bear repetition here. First, Justice Jackson, concurring in the *Steel Seizure Case*, reduced *Curtiss–Wright* to the holding that it would be unwise to require Congress "to lay down narrowly definite standards by which the President is to be governed." Chief Justice Warren later observed that *Curtiss–Wright* does not mean that Congress "can grant the Executive totally unrestricted freedom of choice." It is clear then that the sole organ language has been limited in its effect to a statement that the nature of the conduct of foreign relations, and the President's power over communications with foreign nations, ought to be taken into account in determining whether Congress, in granting the President contingent power, has provided sufficient statutory guidelines for presidential action. In short, *Curtiss–Wright* has been read as dealing with constitutional limits on the power of Congress, and its dictum on "sole organ" has been abandoned.

Viewed in this light, the sole organ doctrine is not novel constitutional theory. Other early officers of state had agreed with Marshall that the President held exclusive power to communicate officially with other nations * * * and this power has been continually recognized. It is also true that the President's control of the foreign affairs bureaucracy, recognized power to negotiate treaties and otherwise communicate officially with other nations, and authority to grant or withhold diplomatic recognition of other states, necessarily undermine the traditional claim that the President merely conducts foreign relations while Congress alone formulates foreign policy. Indeed, it has been correctly observed that "a President could not conduct foreign relations without thereby making foreign policy." More important, presidents do in fact formulate American foreign policy. * * *

But to acknowledge that the President makes foreign policy is a far cry from the assertion that he or she is the sole foreign policymaker. Set against the "sole organ" doctrine is what has been described as the "foreign affairs power" of Congress. It has been observed that "[n]o one knows the reaches" of this power—a power that, when combined with the generous grants of power to Congress specified in Article I, has enabled Congress to enact legislation covering a wide variety of subjects relating to the nation's foreign affairs.

Beginning with the debate between "Helvidius" (Madison) and "Pacificus" (Hamilton), recurring discussions have disputed whether Congress or the President should be dominant in determining "the condition of the nation" or in formulating American foreign policy. As part of this dialogue, Congress has frequently asserted its right to declare national policy in foreign affairs—whether by proclaiming American neutrality in times of war, repudiating treaties or directing Presidents to terminate treaties, recognizing the independence of nations formerly dominated by external powers, or directing Presidents to send delegates to international conferences and outlining the objectives to be sought and the limits of the delegates' authority. In 1864, the House of Representatives resolved:

Congress has a constitutional right to an authoritative voice in declaring and prescribing [U.S.] foreign policy, as well in the recognition of new Powers as in other matters; and it is the constitutional duty of the executive department to respect that policy, not less in diplomatic negotiations than in the use of national forces when authorized by law; and the propriety of any declaration of foreign policy by Congress is sufficiently proved by the vote which pronounces it. * * *

The "Helvidius" position has received other strong endorsements historically. In a famous 1906 debate with Senator John Spooner, Senator Augustus Bacon contended that "Congress and not the President is supreme under the Constitution in the control of foreign affairs." More recently, Senator Fulbright has maintained that, while we must acknowledge the inevitable overlap between shaping foreign policy and conducting foreign relations, Congress must no longer default on its duty "to participate actively in determining policy objectives and in the making of significant decisions."

Most significant, the Supreme Court has lent strength to the contention that Congress is the sovereign voice in determining the law and policy of the nation in its external relations. In 1889, in the *Chinese Exclusion Case*, the Supreme Court upheld the power of Congress to exclude aliens, despite the lack of any express constitutional grant of such power, on the ground that Congress could employ the "powers which belong to independent nations." Since then, the Court has frequently referred to these inherent powers of sovereignty sustaining congressional enactments and has suggested that these powers are held by the legislative branch. In *Perez v. Brownell*, the Court upheld a statute imposing loss of nationality to an American citizen for voting in a political election of a foreign state, using this reasoning: "Although there is in the Constitution no specific grant to Congress of power to enact legislation for the effective regulation of foreign affairs, there can be no doubt of the existence of this power in the lawmaking order of the Nation." Other judicial statements lend strength to the concept of sovereign power over foreign relations and provide additional support for the view that such sovereignty resides in Congress. On the other hand, the President has no power to change the law or even the applicability of comity in foreign affairs. [*See Sabbatino*].

Notes and Questions

Do you agree with Wormuth and Firmage on the relative powers of the Senate and the President in foreign affairs, including treaty practice?

1 O'Connell, International Law

206 (2d ed. 1970).*

* * * If, in [U.S.] constitutional law, a mere agreement is not a treaty, and thereby does not require Senate endorsement, the President may, by resort to informal methods of contracting, oblige the nation without the

---

* Reprinted with the permission of Stevens & Sons, Ltd., London.

democratic control that the legislative process aims at. Actually the President is rarely so isolated in the matter of executive agreements from Congressional action of some sort as to be independent of legislative control or approval. The term "executive agreement" is a wide one, designed to mark off the boundary between treaties which require the advice and consent of the Senate and those documents, widely but loosely described in international practices as "treaties," which do not. Three main categories of instruments are comprehended: (a) agreements or understandings entered into pursuant to or in accordance with specific directives or authorisation of Congress given antecedently; (b) those not given effect to without such direction or authorisation given subsequently; and (c) those made by the Executive solely in virtue of its constitutional power. Actually, those in the third category are relatively few. The critics of the executive agreements, therefore, must be taken to be attacking, not principally the dangers of Presidential commitment without legislative check, so much as the constitutional rule concerning the effect internally on the States of informal international agreements; implied in the argument is that State sovereignty is insufficiently protected by Joint Resolution of both Houses, and that the more obstructive process of a two-thirds Senate majority is necessary. The principal example of an executive agreement in the third category was the Litvinov Agreement between President Roosevelt and the Soviet Ambassador which affected suits between private claimants and the Soviet. * * *

* * *

The question is whether an international commitment of the United States is required by the Constitution to be in treaty as distinct from agreement form. The question is usually resolved on an ad hoc basis by consultation between the Executive and Congress, taking into account the extent to which the agreement can be carried out by the former without encroaching on the domain of the latter. * * *

Notes and Questions

1. Comments upon O'Connell's classification. Recognition that not all American executive agreements are based upon presidential claims to inherent power did not begin with Professor O'Connell. Their tripartite classification had been noted by writers and courts prior to its use in 1965 Restatement. Even so, the O'Connell analysis was influential in two respects: (i) it differentiated clearly the issue of interchangeability of executive agreements with Senate-approved treaties and the issue of executive agreements as sources, or not, of internal law; (ii) it analyzed the uses made of executive agreements of the various classes in foreign affairs operations. O'Connell's research showed that presidents have not widely interchanged treaties and wholly-presidential executive agreements (à la Theodore Roosevelt). It disproved Bricker amendment-era assertions that treaties were used by presidents for relatively secondary matters and executive agreements for highly significant ones. It also supports the view that even presidents know when they cannot act internally on the basis of international agreement. Finally, it shows how often, in important matters, the President and the whole Congress, through presidential negotiation and congressional delegation or ratification, have combined forces in categories 1 and 2.

2. The validity of O'Connell's analysis can be checked as to particular instances by examination of a very useful research tool for U.S. Treaty law, the Department of State yearly publication, Treaties in Force—A List of Treaties and Other International Agreements of the United States in Force. At the time of his last writing on the subject, Professor O'Connell expressed the belief that Congress and the President had worked out a protocol of general applicability as to their roles in the making of various types of executive agreements. Has time proved him right in this? Does the fast track procedure for international trade agreements support his hypothesis? Is it perhaps true that the choice between modalities of cooperation (or co-existence) between the legislative and executive branches in the United States has narrowed to either a bicameral, simple majorities legislative approval of an executively negotiated international agreement of the non-treaty type, or to presidential-senate cooperation on a non-self-executing treaty followed by bicameral implementation by bill or joint resolution?

3. ***The "sole organ" and the "twilight zone".*** Is the "sole organ" rationale properly disregarded as a justification for the practice of entering into international agreements without Senate approval? Scholars have sought to justify the practice on other grounds. One theory posits that the authority to enter into such agreements falls within a "zone of twilight" between presidential and congressional powers. This "zone of twilight," according to the theory, "may be occupied by Congress at will." The failure of Congress to fill this gray area, however, leaves a void which the President may fill. See, e.g.:

4. ***Presidential authority to enter into executive agreements*** has also been justified as a concomitant of the powers as commander in chief and chief executive. A recurring issue in this area is whether a given international agreement should be embodied in treaty form or in the form of an executive agreement. United States v. Belmont, 301 U.S. 324 (1937), has been interpreted by some as intimating that the permissible scope of executive agreements is virtually coextensive with that of treaties. So much attention has centered on the case that it requires discussion.*

It has long been the task of the chief executive of a nation, under the rules of international law, to seek the satisfaction of the claims of its nationals against a foreign state by diplomatic negotiation. In 1918 the Soviet Union confiscated the property of Russian corporations abroad and also nationalized without compensation the property of American nationals within the USSR. A Russian corporation had a sum of money on deposit in the Belmont Bank in New York in 1918. In 1933 President Roosevelt made an agreement by which he recognized the Soviet government. The Soviet government transferred its claims of property in the United States, including the deposit in the Belmont Bank, to the United States, and the Soviet

* Portions adapted from Wormuth & Firmage. To Chain the Dog of War; 196–200 (2d ed. 1989). Reprinted with the permission of University of Illinois, press.

government recognized the claims of American citizens affected by the confiscation. It was agreed that after the rival claims had been computed, whichever government had gained an advantage would pay the surplus to the other. Thus the U.S. creditors would at last gain satisfaction. The Belmont Bank refused to pay the deposit to the United States, alleging that it was founded on confiscation and that the public policy of New York did not recognize claims resulting from confiscation. In *U.S. v. Belmont* (1937), the Supreme Court, in an opinion by Justice Sutherland, held that the recognition validated the Soviet confiscation under the act of state doctrine, and the executive agreement transferred the Soviet claim to the United States. Sutherland said: "But an international compact, as this was, is not always a treaty which requires the consent of the Senate. There are many such compacts, of which a protocol, a modus vivendi, a postal convention, and agreements like that are illustrations."

Moore uses the term protocol to signify the adjustment of inconsiderable claims of citizens and also to describe agreements as to the purpose and scope of future negotiations. A modus vivendi is a provisional agreement pending formal legal action. Moore speaks of postal conventions as agreements made by the postmaster general with the advice and consent of the President under the authority of an act of Congress of 1872. By "agreements like that now under consideration" Sutherland must have referred to numerous agreements detailed by Moore to obtain the satisfaction of the claims or guarantee of the rights of U.S. citizens. In short, the *Belmont case* introduced no new principle. Since the recognition and the assignment of the Soviet claim were valid at national law, the public policy of no state could stand against them.

Notes and Questions

Do you agree with Firmage and Wormuth in this interpretation of *Belmont*? *See also, U.S. v. Pink*, 315 U.S. 203 (1942), *infra*. In Curtis Wright, is Sutherland's historical analysis accurate? *See* Lofgren, *U.S. v. Curtis–Wright: An Historical Assessment*, 83 Yale L.J. 1 (1973).

United States Department of State Circular Number 175

50 American Journal of International Law 784 (1956).*

1. Purpose of Circular: 1.1   The purpose of this circular is to insure (a) that the function of making treaties and other international agreements is carried out within traditional and constitutional limits; (b) that the objectives to be sought in the negotiation of particular treaties and other international agreements are approved by the Secretary or Under Secretary; (c) that firm positions resulting from negotiations are not undertaken without the approval of the interested Assistant Secretaries or their Deputies; (d) that the final texts developed are approved by the interested Assistant Secretaries or their Deputies and brought to the attention of the Secretary or Under Secretary a reasonable time before signature; and (e)

that authorization to sign the final text is secured and appropriate arrangements for signature are made.

* * *

2. Scope of the Treaty–Making Power: Treaties should be designed to promote United States interests by securing action by foreign governments in a way deemed advantageous to the United States. Treaties are not to be used as a device for the purpose of effecting internal social changes or to try to circumvent the constitutional procedures established in relation to what are essentially matters of domestic concern.

3. Scope of the Executive Agreement–Making Power: Executive agreements shall not be used when the subject matter should be covered by a treaty. The executive agreement form shall be used only for agreements which fall into one or more of the following categories:

    a. Agreements which are made pursuant to or in accordance with existing legislation or a treaty;

    b. Agreements which are made subject to Congressional approval or implementation; or

    c. Agreements which are made under and in accordance with the President's Constitutional power.

* * *

Notes and Questions

1. *Supreme Court Sanction.* In 1892, the U.S. Supreme Court held that these agreements were constitutional. *Field v. Clark*, 143 U.S. 649 (1892); see also, *Von Cotzhausen v. Nazro*, 107 U.S. 215 (1882); *B. Altman, Co. v. U.S.*, 224 U.S. 583 (1912).

2. *How helpful is Circular 175?* Do you think that the factors listed in Circular 175 will really be helpful in situations that require real decisions to be made as to what sorts of international agreement to be made?

3. *When may a Congressional–Executive Agreement be useful?* When do you think a President would find a Congressional–Executive Agreement to be congenial? On these sorts of agreements, see, Henkin, FOREIGN AFFAIRS AND THE CONSTITUTION 492 (2d ed. 1996).

4. *What authority do they carry?* Do you think that these agreements ought to be considered to have the same authority as Article II treaties? Why or Why not? See, Ackerman & Golov, Is NAFTA Constitutional?, 108 Harv. L. Rev. 801 (1995); John F. Murphy, *Treaties & International Agreements Other than Treaties: Constitutional Allocation of Power and Responsibility Among the President, the House of Representatives, & the Senate*, 23 Kan.L.Rev. 221 (1975).

Transmittal of United States International Agreements To Congress
1 U.S.C. 112b.

§ 112b. United States international agreements; transmission to Congress: (a) The Secretary of State shall transmit to the Congress the text of any international agreement (including the text of any oral international agreement, which agreement shall be reduced to writing), other than a treaty, to which the United States is a party, as soon as practicable after such agreement has entered into force with respect to the United States but in no event later than sixty days thereafter. However, any such agreement the immediate public disclosure of which would, in the opinion of the President, be prejudicial to the national security of the United States shall not be so transmitted to the Congress but shall be transmitted to the Committee on Foreign Relations of the Senate and the Committee on International Relations of the House of Representatives under an appropriate injunction of secrecy to be removed only upon due notice from the President. Any department or agency of the United States Government which enters into any international agreement on behalf of the United States shall transmit to the Department of State the text of such agreement not later than twenty days after such agreement has been signed.

(b) Not later than March 1, 1979, and at yearly intervals thereafter, the President shall, under his own signature, transmit to the Speaker of the House of Representatives and the chairman of the Committee on Foreign Relations of the Senate a report with respect to each international agreement which, during the preceding year, was transmitted to the Congress after the expiration of the 60–day period referred to in the first sentence of subsection (a), describing fully and completely the reasons for the late transmittal.

(c) Notwithstanding any other provision of law, an international agreement may not be signed or otherwise concluded on behalf of the United States without prior consultation with the Secretary of State. Such consultation may encompass a class of agreements rather than a particular agreement.

(d) The Secretary of State shall determine for and within the executive branch whether an arrangement constitutes an international agreement within the meaning of this section.

(e) The President shall, through the Secretary of State, promulgate such rules and regulations as may be necessary to carry out this section.

Notes and Questions

1. *The evolution of Circular 175 (1955).* Circular 175 superseded an earlier Circular 25 of 1953. Both were mollifying executive responses to the Bricker amendment controversy, as the text of paragraphs 2 and 3 of Circular 175 show. To this end also, it established a procedure for keeping track of international commitments made in the Department of State. Circular 175 was, however, insufficient to head off the congressional requirement supra, that all executive agreements be reported to the House and Senate; and after the legislation was in effect, the Circular 175 procedure reinforced the reporting requirement. The Foreign Affairs Manual (excerpted below) goes into more procedural detail than Circular 175, pulling together various internal operational instructions and procedures not within the original Circular 175. The manual's opening paragraph (720.1) refers to it as "a codification of the substance" of Circular 175. The admonition against use of any type of international agreements power "as a device for the purpose of effecting internal social changes or to try to circumvent the constitutional procedures" is no longer explicit. However, the linkage to Circular 175 at the outset, and the general tone of the manual, probably make the admonition implicit, should need for reassurance arise. For specifics, see Coordination and Reporting of International Agreements, 22 CFR § 181.2–181.7 (4/1/93), in the Documentary Supplement.

2. *A broadening of executive power?* The actions of two presidents in recent years suggests a loosening of the boundaries between Article II treaties and executive agreements. In 1987, President Ronald Reagan entered into a long-term nuclear pact with Japan, although the Senate had rejected the pact when it was presented as a Treaty. Recently, President Bill Clinton made a similar move, when he used money from the Exchange Stabilization Fund to provide loans to Mexico, following indications from Congress that they would not approve the bailout. Both actions, dealing with the powers of war and the purse explicitly granted to the legislative bodies, seem inappropriate for executive action. One problem, of course, with the executive agreement is the difficulty of drawing lines between appropriate and inappropriate use. Are these agreements constitutional uses of the executive power? Do they comply with the guidelines established by Circular 175.

3. Study the excerpt from Treaties and Other International Agreements, 11 Foreign Affairs Manual 720, United States Department of State, Publication, 1985, in the documentary supplement.

––––––

2. AGREEMENTS UNDER PRESIDENTIAL POWER: INTERNAL LAW OR PREEMPTION ON FOREIGN POLICY GROUNDS?

United States v. Pink

United States Supreme Court, 1942.
315 U.S. 203, 62 S.Ct. 552, 86 L.Ed. 796.

[The Litvinov Agreement referred to in the quotation from O'Connell above was the subject of litigation in United States v. Belmont, 301 U.S. 324, and United States v. Pink. In the *Pink* case, the relevant document is referred to as the Litvinov Assignment. As an incident to the United States recognition of the USSR on November 16, 1933, the Soviet foreign minister, Litvinov, delivered a letter to the President of the United States by which the Soviet Union assigned to the United States amounts due to the Soviet Union from United States nationals. This assignment was stated to be preparatory to a final settlement mainly of United States claims for nationalization of property of citizens of the United States situated in the USSR. In Pink the United States, assignee of the Soviet Union, sued the

New York Superintendent of Insurance, who had succeeded by a court order to the assets of the New York branch of a Russian insurance company (previously nationalized by Soviet law). One defense was that the Russian nationalization decrees were extraterritorial, confiscatory and contrary to the public policy of New York. The New York courts had dismissed the United States complaint, but the Supreme Court reversed. For the Court Mr. Justice DOUGLAS stated, in part:]

* * * The powers of the President in the conduct of foreign relations included the power, without consent of the Senate, to determine the public policy of the United States with respect to the Russian nationalization decrees. "What government is to be regarded here as representative of a foreign sovereign state is a political rather than a judicial question, and is to be determined by the political department of the government." That authority is not limited to a determination of the government to be recognized. It includes the power to determine the policy which is to govern the question of recognition. Objections to the underlying policy as well as objections to recognition are to be addressed to the political department and not to the courts. As we have noted, this Court in the Belmont case recognized that the Litvinov Assignment was an international compact which did not require the participation of the Senate. It stated: "There are many such compacts, of which a protocol, a modus vivendi, a postal convention, and agreements like that now under consideration are illustrations." Recognition is not always absolute; it is sometimes conditional. Power to remove such obstacles to full recognition as settlement of claims of our nationals certainly is a modest implied power of the President who is the "sole organ of the federal government in the field of international relations." Effectiveness in handling the delicate problems of foreign relations requires no less. Unless such a power exists, the power of recognition might be thwarted or seriously diluted. No such obstacle can be placed in the way of rehabilitation of relations between this country and another nation, unless the historic conception of the powers and responsibilities of the President in the conduct of foreign affairs * * * is to be drastically revised. It was the judgment of the political department that full recognition of the Soviet Government required the settlement of all outstanding problems including the claims of our nationals. Recognition and the Litvinov Assignment were interdependent. We would usurp the executive function if we held that that decision was not final and conclusive in the courts.

"All constitutional acts of power, whether in the executive or in the judicial department, have as much legal validity and obligation as if they proceeded from the legislature, * * *." The Federalist, No. 64. A treaty is a "Law of the Land" under the supremacy clause (Art. VI, Cl. 2) of the Constitution. Such international compacts and agreements as the Litvinov Assignment have a similar dignity. * * *

It is, of course, true that even treaties with foreign nations will be carefully construed so as not to derogate from the authority and jurisdiction of the States of this nation unless clearly necessary to effectuate the national policy. For example, in Todok v. Union State Bank, this Court took pains in its construction of a treaty, relating to the power of an alien to dispose of property in this country, not to invalidate the provisions of state law governing such dispositions. Frequently the obligation of a treaty will be dependent on state law. But state law must yield when it is inconsistent with, or impairs the policy or provisions of, a treaty or of an international compact or agreement. Then, the power of a State to refuse enforcement of rights based on foreign law which runs counter to the public policy of the forum must give way before the superior Federal policy evidenced by a treaty or international compact or agreement.

Enforcement of New York's policy as formulated by the Moscow case would collide with and subtract from the Federal policy, whether it was premised on the absence of extraterritorial effect of the Russian decrees, the conception of the New York branch as a distinct juristic personality, or disapproval by New York of the Russian program of nationalization. * * *

Notes and Questions

1. *Problem. The Nuclear Test Ban Treaty* entered into force on October 10, 1963, following its ratification by the United States, the United Kingdom and the Soviet Union. For the text, see the Doc. Supp. In its operative Article I, the treaty provides "[e]ach of the Parties to this Treaty undertakes to prohibit, to prevent, and not to carry out any nuclear weapon test explosion, or any other nuclear explosion, at any place under its jurisdiction or control: (a) in the atmosphere; beyond its limits, including outer space; or underwater, including territorial waters or high seas; or (b) in any other environment if such explosion causes radioactive debris to be present outside the territorial limits of the State under whose jurisdiction or control such explosion is conducted. * * * *"

Article II of the treaty provides for amendment as follows: "1. Any Party may propose amendments to this Treaty. The text of any proposed amendment shall be submitted to the Depositary Governments which shall circulate it to all Parties to this Treaty. Thereafter, if requested to do so by one-third or more of the Parties, the Depositary Governments shall convene a conference, to which they shall invite all the Parties, to consider such amendment. 2. Any amendment to this Treaty must be approved by a majority of the votes of all the Parties to this Treaty, including the votes of all of the Original Parties. The amendment shall enter into force for all Parties upon the deposit of instruments of ratification by a majority of all the Parties, including the instruments of ratification of all of the Original Parties."

The resolution of the Senate giving its advice and consent to the ratification of the treaty provides as follows: "Whereas the President has submitted a limited nuclear test ban treaty, providing a method of amendment, to the Senate for its advice and consent in accordance with article II, section 2 of the Constitution; and Whereas the Constitution in article II, section 2, provides 'He shall have Power, by and with the Advice and Consent of the Senate, to make Treaties, provided two-thirds of the Senators present concur'; and Whereas amendments to treaties are subject to this constitutional provision: Now, therefore, be it Resolved (two-thirds of the Senators present concurring therein), That the Senate advise and consent to the ratification of the treaty banning nuclear weapon tests in the atmosphere, in outer space, and underwater, signed at Moscow on August 5, 1963, on behalf of the United States of America, the United Kingdom of Great Britain and Northern Ireland, and the Union of Soviet Socialist Republics.''

Suppose that in conjunction with the negotiation of an arms limitation treaty the U.S. and the Russia had agreed to ban underground testing and that the President, because of expected delays in the Senate as to the approval of the entire treaty, undertook to enforce the underground testing prohibition as an executive agreement pending Senate consent to the entire treaty: (i) Is the U.S. bound internationally not to test nuclear weapons underground? (ii) Does this executive agreement legally justify no further underground testing in the U.S. as against prior legislation directing a certain number of such tests and appropriating money for them? Will it breach the ABM treaty if the U.S. begins testing of the so-called missle shield initiative? What would be the likely response of the Russian Federation?

2. ***Pink and separation of powers.*** After *Pink* was decided, the Supreme Court held in *Youngstown Sheet & Tube supra*, that the President has neither explicit nor inherent power to set aside an act of Congress for the benefit of U.S. foreign affairs interests as seen by the President. The decision was based upon the separation of powers, a principle underlying the structure of the Constitution, though not stated explicitly therein. And under its self-asserted power to say what the law is that governs the outcome of litigation, the Supreme Court has invalidated presidential and congressional acts that, if justiciable, violate the judicial version of the separation of powers principle. The basic rationale of *Youngstown* is that a president has no inherent power to repeal or suspend an act of Congress. *Buckley v. Valeo,* 424 U.S. 1 (1976), holds invalid an act of Congress providing for congressional appointment of two representative members of the Federal Elections Commission, because such a commission exercises the executive power of management, denied to Congress under separation of powers. What, then, of the President's exercise of power in the next case?

Dames & Moore v. Regan

United States Supreme Court, 1981.
453 U.S. 654, 101 S.Ct. 2972, 69 L.Ed.2d 918.

■ JUSTICE REHNQUIST * * *.

The questions presented by this case touch fundamentally upon the manner in which our Republic is to be governed. Throughout the nearly two centuries of our Nation's existence under the Constitution, this subject has generated considerable debate. We have had the benefit of commentators such as John Jay, Alexander Hamilton, and James Madison writing in The Federalist Papers at the Nation's very inception, the benefit of astute foreign observers of our system such as Alexis de Tocqueville and James Bryce writing during the first century of the Nation's existence, and the benefit of many other treatises as well as more than 400 volumes of reports of decisions of this Court. * * *

The tensions present in any exercise of executive power under the tripartite system of Federal Government established by the Constitution have been reflected in opinions by Members of this Court more than once. The Court stated in United States v. Curtiss–Wright Export Corp., [supra].

> "[W]e are here dealing not alone with an authority vested in the President by an exertion of legislative power, but with such an authority plus the very delicate, plenary and exclusive power of the President as the sole organ of the federal government in the field of international relations—a power which does not require as a basis for its exercise an act of Congress, but which, of course, like every other governmental power, must be exercised in subordination to the applicable provisions of the Constitution."

And yet 16 years later, Justice Jackson in his concurring opinion in *Youngstown, supra,* which both parties agree brings together as much combination of analysis and common sense as there is in this area, focused not on the "plenary and exclusive power of the President" but rather responded to a claim of virtually unlimited powers for the Executive by noting: "The example of such unlimited executive power that must have most impressed the forefathers was the prerogative exercised by George III, and the description of its evils in the Declaration of Independence leads me to doubt that they were creating their new Executive in his image."

As we now turn to the factual and legal issues in this case, we freely confess that we are obviously deciding only one more episode in the never-ending tension between the President exercising the executive authority in a world that presents each day some new challenge with which he must deal and the Constitution under which we all live and which no one disputes embodies some sort of system of checks and balances.

I

On November 4, 1979, the American Embassy in Tehran was seized and our diplomatic personnel were captured and held hostage. In response to that crisis, President Carter, acting pursuant to the International Emergency Economic Powers Act, 50 U.S.C. §§ 1701–1706 (hereinafter IEEPA), declared a national emergency on November 14, 1979, and blocked the removal or transfer of "all property and interests in property of the Government of Iran, its instrumentalities and controlled entities and the Central Bank of Iran which are or become subject to the jurisdiction of the United States * * *." President Carter authorized the Secretary of the Treasury to promulgate regulations carrying out the blocking order. On November 15, 1979, the Treasury Department's Office of Foreign Assets Control issued a regulation providing that "[u]nless licensed or authorized * * * any attachment, judgment, decree, lien, execution, garnishment, or other judicial process is null and void with respect to any property in which on or since [November 14, 1979,] there existed an interest of Iran." The regulations also made clear that any licenses or authorizations granted could be "amended, modified, or revoked at any time."

On November 26, 1979, the President granted a general license authorizing certain judicial proceedings against Iran but which did not allow the "entry of any judgment or of any decree or order of similar or analogous effect * * *." On December 19, 1979, a clarifying regulation was issued stating that "the general authorization for judicial proceedings contained in § 535.504(a) includes pre-judgment attachment."

On December 19, 1979, * * * Dames & Moore filed suit in the United States District Court for the Central District of California against the Government of Iran, the Atomic Energy Organization of Iran, and a number of Iranian banks. In its complaint, petitioner alleged that its wholly owned subsidiary, Dames & Moore International, S.R.L., was a party to a written contract with the Atomic Energy Organization, and that the subsidiary's entire interest in the contract had been assigned to petitioner. Under the contract, the subsidiary was to conduct site studies for a proposed nuclear power plant in Iran. As provided in the terms of the contract, the Atomic Energy Organization terminated the agreement for its own convenience on June 30, 1979. Petitioner contended, however, that it was owed $3,436,694.30 plus interest for services performed under the contract prior to the date of termination.[4] The District Court issued orders of attachment directed against property of the defendants, and the property of certain Iranian banks was then attached to secure any judgment that might be entered against them.

On January 20, 1981, the Americans held hostage were released by Iran pursuant to an Agreement entered into the day before and embodied in two Declarations of the Democratic and Popular Republic of Algeria * * *. The Agreement stated that "[i]t is the purpose of [the United States and Iran] * * * to terminate all litigation as between the Government of each party and the nationals of the other, and to bring about the settlement and termination of all such claims through binding arbitration." In furtherance of this goal, the Agreement called for the establishment of an Iran–United States Claims Tribunal which would arbitrate any claims not settled within six months. Awards of the Claims Tribunal are to be "final and binding" and "enforceable * * * in the courts of any nation in accordance with its laws." Under the Agreement, the United States is obligated: "to terminate all legal proceedings in United States courts involving claims of United States persons and institutions against Iran and its state enterprises, to nullify all attachments and judgments obtained therein, to prohibit all further litigation based on such claims, and to bring about the termination of such claims through binding arbitration." In addition, the United States must "act to bring about the transfer" by July 19, 1981, of all Iranian assets held in this country by American banks. One billion dollars of these assets will be deposited in a security account in the Bank of England, to the account of the Algerian Central Bank, and used to satisfy awards rendered against Iran by the Claims Tribunal. * * *

On January 19, 1981, President Carter issued a series of Executive Orders implementing the terms of the agreement. These Orders revoked all licenses permitting the exercise of "any right, power, or privilege" with

---

4. The contract stated that any dispute incapable of resolution by agreement of the parties would be submitted to conciliation and that, if either party was unwilling to accept the results of conciliation, "the matter shall be decided finally by resort to the courts of Iran." * * *

regard to Iranian funds, securities, or deposits; "nullified" all non-Iranian interests in such assets acquired subsequent to the blocking order of November 14, 1979; and required those banks holding Iranian assets to transfer them "to the Federal Reserve Bank of New York, to be held or transferred as directed by the Secretary of the Treasury."

On February 24, 1981, President Reagan issued an Executive Order in which he "ratified" the January 19th Executive Orders. Moreover, he "suspended" all "claims which may be presented to the * * * Tribunal" and provided that such claims "shall have no legal effect in any action now pending in any court of the United States." The suspension of any particular claim terminates if the Claims Tribunal determines that it has no jurisdiction over that claim; claims are discharged for all purposes when the Claims Tribunal either awards some recovery and that amount is paid, or determines that no recovery is due.

Meanwhile, on January 27, 1981, petitioner moved for summary judgment in the District Court against the Government of Iran and the Atomic Energy Organization, but not against the Iranian banks. The District Court granted petitioner's motion and awarded petitioner the amount claimed under the contract plus interest. Thereafter, petitioner attempted to execute the judgment by obtaining writs of garnishment and execution in state court in the State of Washington, and a sheriff's sale of Iranian property in Washington was noticed to satisfy the judgment. However, by order of May 28, 1981, as amended by order of June 8, the District Court stayed execution of its judgment pending appeal by the Government of Iran and the Atomic Energy Organization. The District Court also ordered that all prejudgment attachments obtained against the Iranian defendants be vacated and that further proceedings against the bank defendants be stayed in light of the Executive Orders discussed above. * * *

On April 28, 1981, petitioner filed this action in the District Court for declaratory and injunctive relief against the United States and the Secretary of the Treasury, seeking to prevent enforcement of the Executive Orders and Treasury Department regulations implementing the Agreement with Iran. In its complaint, petitioner alleged that the actions of the President and the Secretary of the Treasury implementing the Agreement with Iran were beyond their statutory and constitutional powers and, in any event, were unconstitutional to the extent they adversely affect petitioner's final judgment against the Government of Iran and the Atomic Energy Organization, its execution of that judgment in the State of Washington, its prejudgment attachments, and its ability to continue to litigate against the Iranian banks. * * *

　　* * *

II

The parties and the lower courts, confronted with the instant questions, have all agreed that much relevant analysis is contained in *Youngstown* [*supra*]. Justice Black's opinion for the Court in that case, involving the validity of President Truman's effort to seize the country's steel mills in the wake of a nationwide strike, recognized that "[t]he President's power, if any, to issue the order must stem either from an act of Congress or from the Constitution itself.'' Justice Jackson's concurring opinion elaborated in a general way the consequences of different types of interaction between the two democratic branches in assessing Presidential authority to act in any given case. When the President acts pursuant to an express or implied authorization from Congress, he exercises not only his powers but also those delegated by Congress. In such a case the executive action ''would be supported by the strongest of presumptions and the widest latitude of judicial interpretation, and the burden of persuasion would rest heavily upon any who might attack it.'' When the President acts in the absence of congressional authorization he may enter ''*a zone of twilight* in which he and Congress may have concurrent authority, or in which its distribution is uncertain.'' In such a case the analysis becomes more complicated, and the validity of the President's action, at least so far as separation-of-powers principles are concerned, hinges on a consideration of all the circumstances which might shed light on the views of the Legislative Branch toward such action, including ''congressional inertia, indifference or quiescence.'' Finally, when the President acts in contravention of the will of Congress, ''his power is at its lowest ebb,'' and the Court can sustain his actions ''only by disabling the Congress from acting upon the subject.''

Although we have in the past found and do today find Justice Jackson's classification of executive actions into three general categories analytically useful, we should be mindful of Justice Holmes' admonition, quoted by Justice Frankfurter in *Youngstown,* supra, at 597 (concurring opinion), that ''[t]he great ordinances of the Constitution do not establish and divide fields of black and white.'' Justice Jackson himself recognized that his three categories represented ''a somewhat over-simplified grouping,'' 343 U.S., at 635, and it is doubtless the case that executive action in any particular instance falls, not neatly in one of three pigeonholes, but rather at some point along a spectrum running from explicit congressional authorization to explicit congressional prohibition. This is particularly true as respects cases such as the one before us, involving responses to international crises the nature of which Congress can hardly have been expected to anticipate in any detail.

III

In nullifying post-November 14, 1979, attachments and directing those persons holding blocked Iranian funds and securities to transfer them to the Federal Reserve Bank of New York for ultimate transfer to Iran, President Carter cited five sources of express or inherent power. The Government, however, has principally relied on § 203 of the IEEPA, 50 U.S.C. § 1702(a)(1), as authorization for these actions. Section 1702(a)(1) provides in part:

> ''At the times and to the extent specified in section 1701 of this title, the President may, under such regulations as he may prescribe, by means of instructions, licenses, or otherwise—

> ''(A) investigate, regulate, or prohibit—

> ''(i) any transactions in foreign exchange,

"(ii) transfers of credit or payments between, by, through, or to any banking institution, to the extent that such transfers or payments involve any interest of any foreign country or a national thereof,

"(iii) the importing or exporting of currency or securities, and

"(B) investigate, regulate, direct and compel, nullify, void, prevent or prohibit, any acquisition, holding, withholding, use, transfer, withdrawal, transportation, importation or exportation of, or dealing in, or exercising any right, power, or privilege with respect to, or transactions involving, any property in which any foreign country or a national thereof has any interest;

"by any person, or with respect to any property, subject to the jurisdiction of the United States."

The Government contends that the acts of "nullifying" the attachments and ordering the "transfer" of the frozen assets are specifically authorized by the plain language of the above statute. The two Courts of Appeals that have considered the issue agreed with this contention. * * *

* * *

IV

Although we have concluded that the IEEPA constitutes specific congressional authorization to the President to nullify the attachments and order the transfer of Iranian assets, there remains the question of the President's authority to suspend claims pending in American courts. Such claims have, of course, an existence apart from the attachments which accompanied them. * * *

We conclude that although the IEEPA authorized the nullification of the attachments, it cannot be read to authorize the suspension of the claims. The claims of American citizens against Iran are not in themselves transactions involving Iranian property or efforts to exercise any rights with respect to such property. An *in personam* lawsuit, although it might eventually be reduced to judgment and that judgment might be executed upon, is an effort to establish liability and fix damages and does not focus on any particular property within the jurisdiction. The terms of the IEEPA therefore do not authorize the President to suspend claims in American courts. * * *

Concluding that neither the IEEPA nor the Hostage Act constitutes specific authorization of the President's action suspending claims, however, is not to say that these statutory provisions are entirely irrelevant to the question of the validity of the President's action. We think both statutes highly relevant in the looser sense of indicating congressional acceptance of a broad scope for executive action in circumstances such as those presented in this case. * * *

Not infrequently in affairs between nations, outstanding claims by nationals of one country against the government of another country are "sources of friction" between the two sovereigns. *United States v. Pink* [*supra*]. To resolve these difficulties, nations have often entered into agreements settling the claims of their respective nationals. As one treatise writer puts it, international agreements settling claims by nationals of one state against the government of another "are established international practice reflecting traditional international theory." Henkin, Foreign Affairs and the Constitution 262 (1972). Consistent with that principle, the United States has repeatedly exercised its sovereign authority to settle the claims of its nationals against foreign countries. Though those settlements have sometimes been made by treaty, there has also been a longstanding practice of settling such claims by executive agreement without the advice and consent of the Senate. Under such agreements, the President has agreed to renounce or extinguish claims of United States nationals against foreign governments in return for lump-sum payments or the establishment of arbitration procedures. To be sure, many of these settlements were encouraged by the United States claimants themselves, since a claimant's only hope of obtaining any payment at all might lie in having his Government negotiate a diplomatic settlement on his behalf. But it is also undisputed that the "United States has sometimes disposed of the claims of its citizens without their consent, or even without consultation with them, usually without exclusive regard for their interests, as distinguished from those of the nation as a whole." It is clear that the practice of settling claims continues today. Since 1952, the President has entered into at least 10 binding settlements with foreign nations, including an $80 million settlement with the People's Republic of China.

Crucial to our decision today is the conclusion that Congress has implicitly approved the practice of claim settlement by executive agreement. This is best demonstrated by Congress' enactment of the International Claims Settlement Act of 1949, as amended, 22 U.S.C. § 1621 et seq. The Act had two purposes: (1) to allocate to United States nationals funds received in the course of an executive claims settlement with Yugoslavia, and (2) to provide a procedure whereby funds resulting from future settlements could be distributed. To achieve these ends Congress created the International Claims Commission, now the Foreign Claims Settlement Commission, and gave jurisdiction to make final and binding decisions with respect to claims by United States nationals against settlement funds. 22 U.S.C. § 1623(a). By creating a procedure to implement future settlement agreements, Congress placed its stamp of approval on such agreements. * * *

Over the years Congress has frequently amended the International Claims Settlement Act to provide for particular problems arising out of settlement agreements, thus demonstrating Congress' continuing acceptance of the President's claim settlement authority. With respect to the Executive Agreement with the People's Republic of China, for example, Congress established an allocation formula for distribution of the funds received pursuant to the Agreement. 22 U.S.C. § 1627(f). As with legislation involving other executive agreements, Congress did not question the fact of the settlement or the power of the President to have concluded it. * * * Finally, the legislative history of the IEEPA further reveals that Congress has accepted the authority of the Executive to enter into settlement agreements. Though the IEEPA was enacted to provide for some limitation on the President's emergency powers, Congress stressed that "[n]othing in this act is intended * * * to interfere with the authority of the President to [block assets], or to impede the settlement of claims of U.S. citizens against foreign countries." 50 U.S.C. § 1706(a)(1).

* * *

The judgment of the District Court is accordingly affirmed. * * *

* * *

■ [JUSTICES STEVEN's and POWELL concurred except re U.S. duty to compensate for "taking."]

———

Notes and Questions

1. *Pink, Youngstown, Dames & Moore, and federalism.* Is the basis of the Pink decision presidential action as law under the supremacy clause [Constitution Article VI(2)] or federal preemption of a foreign affairs matter (recognition)? The Douglas opinion straddles this. The Youngstown decision cuts against presidential power to make law contrary to legislative enactment in the federal sphere. But does separation of powers in the federal system always prevent presidential law-making in the federal-state sphere? *Dames & Moore* put Youngstown into softer focus as to presidential power regarding foreign claims settlement matters, clearly a federal, not state, function. Does that focus extend to other matters, including the overriding of state law?

2. *In Zschernig v. Miller,* 389 U.S. 429 (1968), the Supreme Court, in the absence of any federal legislation or claim of preemption, held that a state could not validly require reciprocity in the treatment of legatees as between the state and iron-curtain countries. (An iron curtain legatee could not inherit in the state if an iron curtain bequest to a resident of the state would not be permitted.) In retrospect, is Pink a similar situation? Would the Supreme Court under Zschernig have ruled against the New York banking superintendent (Pink) even if President Roosevelt and Ambassador Litvinov had not made the agreement as to Russian bank assets a part of the act of recognition?

3. EXECUTIVE-CONGRESSIONAL INTERNATIONAL AGREEMENTS

Notes and Questions

1. *Current extent of use.* Most agreements to enter into international organizations are submitted to the Senate, as treaties, pursuant to Article II of the Constitution. Not all such agreements are entered in this way, however. When an agreement is passed by a simple majority of both the Senate and the House of Representatives, then signed by the President, a congressional-executive-agreement becomes law. This approach to entering international agreements gained impetus indirectly from the Senate's failure to give its Advice and Consent to the 1919 Versailles Treaty. It functions as a circumvention of the treaty clause of the Constitution. Yet, it has become more prominent in the last several years, to the point of nearly eclipsing treaties as the major instrument of international agreement.

CHAPTER 12 LAW OF THE UNITED STATES

As Professor O'Connell's classification of executive agreements shows international agreements resulting from congressional authorizations by way of delegation or ratification and presidential conclusion internationally are not unusual, but the executive-legislative agreement has not, as a modality, yet become the paramount way of committing the United States to other entities and simultaneously correlating such commitment with internal law. The use of the Executive–Congressional alternative is controlled by the President's choice; and political and other variables, such as tradition that certain types of international agreements be sent to the Senate (*see* ¶ 721.4 of the *Foreign Affairs Manual*), are often determinative. So far there is little indication that the convenience and practicality of the executive-congressional agreement for foreign affairs operations is the key factor in this choice. What are the advantages of choosing the executive-congressional agreement alternative? Its disadvantages? Do you think that this is wise? Are such agreements inherently self-executing?

2. *The fast track provision in the Trade Act of 1974.* This interesting development is considered more extensively in Chapter 16–A, but its essence is an offer along the following line. Congress, in effect, says: "Mr. President, only the executive can negotiate trade agreements, but only Congress can make trade law for the United States. When you go your way without consulting Congress in detail at every step, Congress always delays and sometimes frustrates your negotiation. But we in Congress know that Congress cannot, despite its power, actually make a national tariff schedule or set quotas or deal with non-tariff barriers on its own, because there are too many conflicting constituency issues.

"So, Mr. President, let us work together, but not in any way that would violate separation of powers. Separation of powers will not preclude this arrangement: (i) Congress sets the broad parameters of national trade law and authorizes you to negotiate trade agreements within them; (ii) if you, in such negotiations, beginning with the consultations and hearings in the United States with industry, labor, and other interest groups and continuing through the negotiations with other countries, keep the relevant committee and other elements in the Congress fully informed and show good faith in taking congressional viewpoints into account, Congress for its part will enact *now,* general legislation with respect to the procedural rules of both houses that will guarantee speedy enactment of the legislation necessary to put your international negotiation into effect."

In January, 1975, President Ford signed into law the Trade Reform Act of 1974. Section 151 of the act—19 M.S.C. § 2191—provides the above fast track. There was urgent need for the legislation, as the United States had had no trade legislation in place since the automatic demise of the Kennedy-era Trade Expansion Act of 1962. The 1974 act also contained several legislative veto provisions but President Ford could not risk using his veto. Presidents had fast-track authority until 1995, when it expired and President Clinton chose not to seek its extension, in response to opposition to fast-track because of the North American Free Trade Agreement ("NAFTA"). Although President Clinton tried to secure fast-track authority in 1997, in part so that he could extend NAFTA to include South American countries, his efforts so far have failed.

Is the result under the fast track properly classifiable as an executive-congressional agreement, or does it belong in a new, fourth classification?

3. *Are executive-congressional international agreements at the initiative of the President: always constitutionally effective?* In a pioneering article, McDougal and Lans, *Treaties and Congressional–Executive or Presidential Agreements: Interchangeable Instruments of National Policy*, 54 Yale L.J. 181, 534 (1945), the viewpoint was that such types of executive agreements are absolutely (or almost always) interchangeable, with referral to the Senate for advice and consent and to both houses for implementation, if required. *Cf.*, Oliver, *Getting the Senators to Accept the Reference of Treaties to Both Houses for Approval by Simple Majorities; Does the Sense Resolution in the 1979 Foreign Relations Authorization Act Point a Way?*, 74 AJIL 142 (1980), which focuses more on the political practicability of wide replacement of the orthodox system than on assured constitutionality in all or most situations. It is now generally assumed that the alternative of the executive-congressional international agreement has wider potential than presidents have chosen to utilize.

The executive-congressional agreement has recently received significant attention, due to President Clinton's decision to submit NAFTA to both houses of Congress, as a congressional-executive agreement, rather than to the Senate, as a treaty. NAFTA passed the Senate by a vote of sixty-one to thirty-eight, not enough to adopt it as a treaty but enough, along with a majority of the House, to adopt it as a congressional-executive agreement. This sparked a debate among three constitutional scholars, with Professor Laurence Tribe arguing that the text and structure of the Constitution preclude use of the executive-congressional agreement as an alternative to the treaty, and Ackerman and Golove arguing that Congress' powers under the Necessary and Proper Clause support the alternative. See Ackerman & Golove, *Is NAFTA Constitutional?*, 108 Harv. L. Rev. 799 (1995); Tribe, *Taking Text and Structure Seriously: Reflections on Free-Form Method in Constitutional Interpretation*, 108 Harv. L. Rev. 1221 (1995). If, as Ackerman and Golove argue, the treaty and the congressional-executive agreement are always interchangeable, what is the purpose of the Treaty Clause? Executive-congressional agreements have not been specifically tested for constitutionality by the courts. Would members of the Senate, not the Senate as a body, have standing to contend that executive-congressional agreements cannot be used to deprive them of their individual rights as senators to use the two-thirds requirement for advice and consent to prevent treaties from coming into effect? Might a worker displaced by NAFTA have standing to claim that she lost her job because her employer moved to Mexico to take advantage of the inexpensive. On executive agreements, generally, *see*, 1 Tribe, American Constitutional Law § 4–4 (3rd ed. 2000); Henkin, Foreign Affairs and the U.S. Constitution 175–230 (2nd ed. 1996).

A more difficult issue might be whether an executive-congressional international agreement can have status as a "treaty" under the supremacy clause, Article VI of the Constitution. Suppose such agreements, rather than Senate-consented treaties, had been the basis of federal supremacy in *Ware v. Hylton* and *Missouri v. Holland*, *supra*. Would the marked expansion of the federal legislative power afforded by the Supreme Court suggest that de facto interchangeability exists under Article VI? Might the court decline to decide the controversy under the political question doctrine?

It is readily apparent that the American executive-congressional international agreement comes close to the simultaneous ratification and internal implementation-by-law models in continental constitutions. Would a direct replacement of the Article II arrangement in the Constitution by a bicameral, simple majority, legislative act of approval be acceptable constitutionally, as Professors Ackerman and Golove argue? Would the political branches be violating their own oaths to "preserve, protect, and defend the Constitution" by effecting this constitutional change? Do you agree with Professors Ackerman and Golove that the congressional-executive agreement is merely another case of the evolution of the Constitution? How far would you be willing to go? Why?

4. WHERE LIES THE POWER TO END TREATIES?

The U.S. Constitution does not reveal explicitly which entity has the power to suspend or terminate treaties. *See,* Restatement (3rd), at § 339. In 1979, the Supreme Court dismissed an action brought by Senator Goldwater and others, which complained that President Carter had failed to consult Congress properly in terminating the *Mutual Defense Treaty of 1954 (with Taiwan). Goldwater v. Carter*, 444 U.S. 996, 998, et seq. (1979). This was a Treaty in the constitutional sense, having received the two-thirds vote of the Senators present. Thus, it was argued below that "proper consultation" with Congress was required before termination. The suit was dismissed, four justices arguing that the issue was a "political question," beyond the Court's competence. Another concurring justice argued that the case was not ripe.

Wormuth and Firmage, To Chain the Dog of War
at 193–94.*

The Constitution makes no mention of treaty termination. This omission leaves open questions as to the circumstances under which treaties may be terminated and, more important, whether the power to terminate treaty obligations is vested in the Senate or in the executive. Constitutional silence on the matter notwithstanding, there are several means whereby the United States may terminate its treaty obligations. Under international law, a nation has the right to terminate a treaty in response to another nation's breach of an important term of the treaty or in response to a fundamental change in the circumstances. Also, a treaty's own terms [may] provide for termination [if] notice is given to the other nation(s) affected. Finally, as a sovereign state the U.S. has the *power*—but not the right—to abrogate a treaty "and abide the international consequences" of that act.

Assuming that the United States has the right to terminate or abrogate treaties, the Constitution does not specify whether the President may act alone or must obtain the consent of the Senate in making the decision.

* Reprinted with the permission of the University of Illinois press.

There is logic in the argument that if the President must obtain the Senate's consent to conclude a treaty, the President should also obtain its consent to terminate the treaty. But it has also been argued that perhaps "the framers were concerned only to check the President in 'entangling' the United States" and that since " 'disentangling' is less risky and may have to be done quickly, and is often done piecemeal, or ad hoc, by various means or acts," senatorial approval of the President's decision to terminate a treaty should not be required. Apart from these theoretical arguments, the President has demonstrated an effective power to terminate treaties, and the Senate has not successfully challenged that right to do so. The first historical example of unilateral abrogation by a President came in 1864 under President Lincoln. Lincoln's notice to Great Britain of withdrawal from the Rush–Bagot Agreement of 1817 was subsequently ratified by Congress. It has been in the twentieth century, however, that the President has consistently and effectively asserted the right to terminate treaties. Presidents Taft, Wilson, Roosevelt, Truman, and Eisenhower invoked the power unilaterally to terminate or abrogate American treaties; more recent Presidents have followed their precedents. The larger number of modern scholars agree that the President has the effective power unilaterally to terminate treaties and that Congress is unlikely to be successful in any attempt to reassert its claim to a share in that power.

SECTION C. SELF-EXECUTING TREATIES IN THE UNITED STATES

Christopher L. Blakesley, Autumn of the Patriarch: The Pinochet Extradition Debacle & Beyond

91 Journal of Criminal Law & Criminology 1 (2001).*

* * *

SELF-EXECUTING TREATIES AND THEIR IMPACT.

A "self-executing treaty" is one that needs no implementing domestic legislation; it takes effect upon ratification. It is aimed at the judiciary, not the legislature. In the U.S., if a treaty is not self-executing, or if Congress has not passed enabling legislation, it does not create a cause of action or provide a remedy. Non-self-executing treaties do not create adjudicative or enforcement jurisdiction in United States courts. Thus, if a treaty is non-self-executing, it provides no specific legal effect, although it may influence policy or legislation. Human rights conventions generally are not considered self-executing in the United States. In fact, to try to ensure this result, the United States often includes non-self-executing declarations in its ratification instruments. The principle of non self-executing treaties in the

---

* Reprinted with the permission of the
Journal of Criminal Law & Criminology.

United States, therefore, hampers human rights protection generally and in relation to extradition.

It can be argued that the entire idea of considering treaties, duly entered and ratified, not to be self-executing is "unavoidably unconstitutional,"at least for purposes of supremacy. The idea seems to be, "inconsistent with the language, history, and purpose" of Article VI, paragraph 2, of the Constitution.

The principle of non self-executing treaties in the United States hampers human rights protection in relation to extradition. Article VI, paragraph 2, of the Constitution, of course, makes treaties that have received the "Advice and Consent" of the Senate, the Supreme Law of the Land. On the other hand, most courts and commentators allow that treaties do not have the force of law in the United States, unless they are self-executing, or have been implemented by legislation.

Self-executing treaties have been held to confer rights enforceable by private persons; they are fully operative without implementing legislation. It is held that to provide a private right of action, a treaty must be self-executing, "that is, 'it must prescribe [ ] rules by which private rights may be determined.' "The 9th Circuit Court of Appeals noted that, "[o]n a general level, the Supreme Court has recognized that treaties can in some circumstances create individually enforceable rights ... " But the proposition that self-executing treaties confer rights on private parties is not undisputed. Some courts and commentators argue that they give standing to individuals and create private causes of action and remedies. Non-self-executing treaties, on the other hand, are not enforced until legislation is passed incorporating or enabling them.

A vigorous debate has arisen over whether the idea of non-self-executing treaties is inconsistent with the Supremacy Clause. Professor John Yoo argues that the British and colonial approaches to treaty making and treaty enforcement, as well as the experience under the Articles of the Confederation, the debates at the Constitutional Convention and the debates in some of the state ratifying conventions do not provide conclusive or definitive support for the proposition that treaties automatically become the law of the land upon ratification. In fact, claims Professor Yoo, some of this historical evidence supports the position that all, or at least most, treaties do not have the force of law and, therefore, may be ignored by the courts, the citizens, and other state or federal officials who enforce domestic law. Professor Carlos Manuel Vazquez counters, arguing that the Supremacy Clause is more correctly read to call for a "default rule," whereby a treaty automatically will be considered the law of the land, unless the treaty itself is entered with an explicit reservation that clearly provides that the treaty is considered non-self-executing.

Given the current viability in the United States of the notion of non-self-executing treaties, it may be wise, in order to protect individuals being extradited, to establish, either a specific human rights clause barring extradition that would have to be incorporated into each extradition treaty for each particular human right considered appropriate or to expand the traditional exemptions to extradition to include more human rights protections. The reality in United States extradition practice is that no human rights clauses are being incorporated and the traditional exemptions to extradition are being significantly constricted, rather than expanded.

DETERMINING WHICH TREATIES ARE SELF–EXECUTING.

To establish whether a given treaty is self-executing, courts look to the "intent of the signatory parties, as manifested by the language of the instrument, and, if the instrument is uncertain, recourse must be had to the circumstances surrounding its execution."

Treaties that condemn conduct as criminal are non-self-executing. It is accepted that the President and the Senate will not make criminal law by treaty. I have noted that most human rights treaties are also considered non-self executing. This is generally because the Senate, upon giving its Advice & Consent so indicates. This was the case for The Convention Against Torture and Other Cruel, Inhuman or Degrading Treatment or Punishment, and [t]he International Covenant on Civil and Political Rights. The Torture Convention, in article III, § 1, provides: "[N]o State Party shall expel, return (*'refouler'*) or extradite a person to another State where there are substantial grounds for believing that he would be in danger of being subjected to torture ... " The Torture Convention, as noted, has been held to be non-self-executing. At the time the Convention was sent to the Senate for Advice and Consent, Secretary of State, George Schultz, included a "Declaration Regarding the Non–Self–Executing Nature of the Convention," which provided, in part: "[t]he United States that articles 1 through 16 of the Convention are not self-executing."Articles 1–16, are the Convention's protective provisions, designed to protect individuals from the proscribed acts and, as indicated in Article 1, quoted above, to ensure that no State Party will send a fugitive, by way of extradition or other means, to a place where these depredations may well occur. Finally, to close the embarrassing circle of U.S. action, Congress has not promulgated legislation granting jurisdiction to federal courts to hear claims involving the Torture Convention's protective provisions. On the other hand, the principle of non-self-executing treaties was judicially created, so the issue of whether a given treaty is or is not self-executing should be decided by the judiciary. Moreover, some argue persuasively, at least in terms of supremacy in contexts other than that of creating criminal sanctions, that the notion of non-self-executing treaties is anathema and unavoidably unconstitutional.

Nevertheless, the Second Circuit Court of Appeals, in *Gallina v. Fraser*, recognized in dicta a potential exception. The Court noted that there could be some "procedures or punishment so antipathetic to a federal court's sense of decency as to require reexamination of the exception to the principle [of non-inquiry]". The 9th Circuit Court of Appeals took up the gauntlet in 1999, noting that some jurisdictions: "have discussed the possibility of a humanitarian exception to extradition, tracing the idea from *Gallina v. Fraser*."

Congress recently promulgated legislation implementing Article 3 of the Torture Convention. This was part of the Foreign Affairs Reform and Restructuring Act [FARR Act]. Thus, although the Torture Convention is not considered self-executing, Article 3 has been enabled. The FARR Act provides that it is "the policy of the United States not to expel, extradite, or otherwise effect the involuntary return of any person to a country in which there are substantial grounds for believing the person would be in danger of being subjected to torture...." Following the promulgation of the FARR Act, the Department of State prescribed regulations to implement Article 3 of the Torture Convention. These Regulations state: "[p]ursuant to [18 U.S.C. §§ 3184 and 3186], the Secretary [of State] is the U.S. official responsible for determining whether to surrender a fugitive to a foreign country by means of extradition ... [Incident to the U.S. obligations under Article 3 of the Convention], the Department [of State] considers the question of whether a person facing extradition from the U.S. is more likely than not to be tortured in [the requesting state]...."

The principle of non-self-executing treaties prevents any impact that human rights might have on extradition or deportation, except insofar as these treaties allow courts to broaden the traditional exemptions from extradition as a disguised method of applying human rights protections, or otherwise to so interpret extradition treaties. Therefore, to protect individuals being extradited, either a specific human rights clause barring extradition would have to be incorporated into each extradition treaty or the traditional exemptions to extradition would have to be expanded by interpretation to include more human rights protections. U.S. practice has been, albeit meagerly and reluctantly, to use the traditional, statist exemptions to extradition as repositories for human rights protections. The quality of this protection, has never been great and has been diminishing, along with other protections for those accused of crime, over the past several years. No human rights clauses have been incorporated and the traditional exemptions to extradition are being significantly constricted.

Notes and Questions

1. *See,* US Constitution art. VI, § 2; Sloss, *The Domestication of International Human Rights: Non–Self–Executing Declarations and Human Rights Treaties,* 24 Yale J.Int'l l. 129 (1999). 18 USC. § 3181; Whiteman, 6 DIGEST OF INTERNATIONAL LAW 734 (1968); *Head Money Cases,* 112 U.S. 580 (1884); *Chew Heong v. U.S.,* 112 U.S. 536, 540, 556 (1884).

2. On the judicial provenance of self executing treaties, *see,* Vazquez, *The Four Doctrines of Self–Executing Treaties,* 89 AJIL 695 (1995); Riesenfeld & Abbott, *The Scope of U.S. Senate Control Over the Conclusion and Operation of Treaties,* 77 Chi.–Kent L.Rev. 571 (1991); De la Vega & Brown, *Can a U.S. Treaty Reservation Provide a Sanctuary for the Juvenile Death Penalty,* 32 U.S.F.L. Rev. 735, 762 (1998). *See also:*

3. ***The debate.*** Yoo, *Globalism and the Constitution: Treaties, Non–Self–Execution and the Original Understanding,* 99 Colum.L.Rev. 1955, 1978–1979 (1999); Yoo, *Treaties and Public Lawmaking: A Textual and Structural Defense of Non–Self–Execution,* 99 Colum.L.Rev. 2218 (1999). Yoo is challenged by Flaherty, *History Right?: Historical Scholarship, Original Understanding, and Treaties as "Supreme Law of the Land,"* 99 Colum.L.Rev. 2095 (1999) (finding that history and the material available

from the founding contradicts Professor Yoo's position; confirms the opposite); by Vasquez, *Response, Laughing at Treaties*, 99 Colum. L. Rev. 2154, 2156, 2157, and authority and discussion in n. 10 (1999) (finding Professor Yoo's position implausible from the textual and doctrinal standpoints). *Also see*, Halberstam, *United States Ratification of the Convention on the Elimination of all Forms of Discrimination Against Women*, 31 G.W.J.Intl L. & Econ. 49, 64, 67–69 (1997); Quigley, *The International Covenant on Civil and Political Rights and the Supremacy Clause*, 42 DePaul L.Rev. 1287 (1993); Schabas, *Invalid Reservations to the International Covenant on Civil and Political Rights: Is the U.S. Still a Party?*, 21 Brooklyn J.Int'l L. 277 (1995); Henkin, FOREIGN AFFAIRS AND THE UNITED STATES CONSTITUTION 198–204 (2nd ed. 1996); Paust, *Self-Executing Treaties*, 82 A.J.I.L. 760 (1988); Vazquez, *The Four Doctrines of Self-Executing Treaties*, 89 A.J.I.L. 695, 697–700 (1995); Vazquez, *The Self-Executing Character of the Refugee Protocol's Nonrefoulement Obligation*, 7 Geo. Immigr. L.J. 39, 44–49 (1993); Vazquez, *Treaty-Based Rights and Remedies of Individuals*, 92 Colum. L.Rev. 1082, 1101–1010 (1992).

4. Compare, *authority in U.S. v. Nai Fook Li*, 206 F.3d 56 (1st Cir.2000); *Sandhu v. U.S.*, 2000 WL 191707 (S.D.N.Y.2000), holding that, "treaties do not generally create rights that are privately enforceable in the federal courts [as they are] primarily compacts between independent nations ..., *citing Head Money Cases*, 112 U.S. 580, 598 (1884); *Charlton v. Kelly*, 229 U.S. 447, 474 (1913); *Foster v. Neilson*, 27 U.S. (2 Pet.) 253, 306 (1829) ("[T]he judiciary is not that department of the government to which the assertion of its interest against foreign powers is confided.") ... [E]ven where a treaty provides ... benefits to a national of a given state, [that] individual's rights are derivative through the states." *Matta-Ballesteros v. Henman*, 896 F.2d 255, 259 (7th Cir.1990).

5. *A comparative perspective.* In absolute monarchies, dictatorships *de jure* and *de facto*, and in some continental democracies, there is normally no discontinuity as to the time that an international agreement comes into effect as an international obligation and when it becomes, should that be necessary to the international undertaking, the internal law of the land. Absolute monarchs and dictators could, if they wished, provide such discontinuities but normally they do not. Under some constitutions in democracies, in Germany for instance, the legislative act that ratifies the treaty as an international obligation simultaneously makes it law within the country.

In the United Kingdom and members of the Commonwealth that still recognize the Crown, making international agreements binding internationally is a part of the prerogative of the Crown, while, as a result of historical evolution, making internal law can only be done by Parliament. Thus, theoretically, discontinuity between international obligation and internal legal effect is possible. Yet there is no possibility of discontinuity in practice, because the government (the cabinet) controls both the will of the Crown to make a treaty internationally and the will of Parliament to make a treaty-conforming law. And it is also the practice in British-type democracies to lay the treaty on the table at Parliament as a template for any necessary legislation that might be required by the international obligation.

Such laying on the table is not ratification, however; the ministers of the Crown have already committed the country internationally.

In the United States, and in the few countries with U.S.-type governmental structures, discontinuities do occur. This is rare outside the United States, but in the U.S. the choice of either a self-executing or a non-self-executing international agreement is very often difficult; all too frequently the model selected by the treaty-makers is not pre-determined.

6. *Guidelines for the U.S. system.* Some international agreements, usually treaties, require no changes or effects in internal law whatsoever. Sometimes Congress and the President work together and by their joint efforts bring into effect international agreements that in the same creative act make internal federal law. The President and two-thirds of the Senate have the power both to bind the United States internationally by treaty and to make necessary internal implementing law; i.e., the President and the Senate may make many types of self-executing treaties that require internal conformation to the international agreement. In important instances the President and the Senate either lack the power to legislate by treaty or wisely choose not to do so, e.g., where the House of Representatives must participate, as in revenue-raising, appropriations, and trade law (linked to revenue-raising). It is accepted also that the President and the Senate will not attempt to make federal criminal law by treaty. Why not? Does the Constitution speak to this? A serious operational problem arises because the President and the Senate almost never specify whether they consider a treaty self-executing. This means that when the treaty is brought into litigation as the asserted governing law, the courts must decide whether the treaty is or is not self-executing.

1. THE ROLE OF THE JUDICIARY

United States v. Percheman

United States Supreme Court, 1833.
32 U.S. (7 Pet.) 51, 8 L.Ed. 604.

[Percheman claimed title to land in Florida under a grant to his predecessor in title made by the Spanish governor of Florida in 1815, when Spain still was sovereign there, even though American military penetration had commenced. In 1819, Spain ceded Florida to the United States by a peace treaty which contained standard provisions about ceded territory, including one that private rights previously granted would be respected. As noted in detail in omitted portions of the opinion that follows, the federal government made various arrangements by acts of Congress to deal with issues of title and ownership involving some 30 million acres of newly acquired territory, pursuant to Article IV, Section 3, Paragraph 2 of the Constitution. Under an 1828 federal act, a commission was created to pass on title claims. Apparently it fell considerably short of the due process and related provision of our modern Administrative Procedures Act, and the commission ruled against Percheman's claim. Congress, despite all its other activity as to land in Florida, had never got around to implementing the provision in the 1819 treaty safeguarding prior grants. Claiming directly under the treaty, Percheman sued the United States on some waiver of sovereign immunity not disclosed in the opinion and not common to the era. Perhaps it was taken for granted that the Fifth Amendment "takings" clause overrode immunity.]

■ MARSHALL, CHIEF JUSTICE.

* * *

This state of things [the status of private property in cases of cession of territory according to the modern usage of nations] ought to be kept in view when we construe the eighth article of the treaty, and the acts which have been passed by congress for the ascertainment and adjustment of titles acquired under the Spanish government. That article in the English part of it is in these words. "All the grants of land made before the 24th of January 1818 by his catholic majesty, or by his lawful authorities, in the said territories ceded by his majesty to the United States, shall be ratified and confirmed to the persons in possession of the lands, to the same extent that the same grants would be valid if the territories had remained under the dominion of his catholic majesty."

This article is apparently introduced on the part of Spain, and must be intended to stipulate expressly for that security to private property which the laws and usages of nations would, without express stipulation, have conferred. No construction which would impair that security further than its positive words require, would seem to be admissible. Without it, the titles of individuals would remain as valid under the new government as they were under the old; and those titles, so far at least as they were consummate, might be asserted in the courts of the United States, independently of this article.

The treaty was drawn up in the Spanish as well as in the English language. Both are originals, and were unquestionably intended by the parties to be identical. The Spanish has been translated, and we now understand that the article, as expressed in that language, is, that the grants "shall remain ratified and confirmed to the persons in possession of them, to the same extent, * * * "—thus conforming exactly to the universally received doctrine of the law of nations. If the English and the Spanish parts can, without violence, be made to agree, that construction which establishes this conformity ought to prevail. If, as we think must be admitted, the security of private property was intended by the parties; if this security would have been complete without the article, the United States could have no motive for insisting on the interposition of government in order to give validity to titles which, according to the usages of the civilized world, were already valid. No violence is done to the language of the treaty by a construction which conforms the English and Spanish to each other. Although the words "shall be ratified and confirmed," are properly the words of contract, stipulating for some future legislative act; they are not necessarily so. They may import that they "shall be ratified and confirmed" by force of the instrument itself. When we observe that in the counterpart of the same treaty, executed at the same time by the same parties, they are used in this sense, we think the construction proper, if not unavoidable.

In the case of Foster v. Elam, 2 Peters, 253, this court considered these words as importing contract. The Spanish part of the treaty was not then brought to our view, and we then supposed that there was no variance between them. We did not suppose that there was even a formal difference of expression in the same instrument, drawn up in the language of each party. Had this circumstance been known, we believe it would have produced the construction which we now give to the article.

* * *

Asakura v. City of Seattle

United States Supreme Court, 1924.
265 U.S. 332, 44 S.Ct. 515, 68 L.Ed. 1041.

■ Mr. Justice Butler delivered the opinion of the Court.

Plaintiff in error is a subject of the Emperor of Japan, and, since 1904, has resided in Seattle, Washington. Since July, 1915, he has been engaged in business there as a pawnbroker. The city passed an ordinance, which took effect July 2, 1921, regulating the business of pawnbroker and repealing former ordinances on the same subject. It makes it unlawful for any person to engage in the business unless he shall have a license, and the ordinance provides "that no such license shall be granted unless the applicant be a citizen of the United States." Violations of the ordinance are punishable by fine or imprisonment or both. Plaintiff in error brought this suit in the Superior Court of King County, Washington, against the city, its Comptroller and its Chief of Police to restrain them from enforcing the ordinance against him. He attacked the ordinance on the ground that it violates the treaty between the United States and the Empire of Japan, proclaimed April 5, 1911 * * *. He had about $5,000 invested in his business, which would be broken up and destroyed by the enforcement of the ordinance. The Superior Court granted the relief. On appeal, the [State] Supreme Court held the ordinance valid and reversed the decree. * * *

Does the ordinance violate the treaty? Plaintiff in error invokes and relies upon the following provisions: "The citizens or subjects of each of the High Contracting Parties shall have liberty to enter, travel and reside in the territories of the other to carry on trade, wholesale and retail, to own or lease and occupy houses, manufactories, warehouses and shops, to employ agents of their choice, to lease land for residential and commercial purposes, and generally to do anything incident to or necessary for trade upon the same terms as native citizens or subjects, submitting themselves to the laws and regulations there established. * * * The citizens or subjects of each * * * shall receive, in the territories of the other, the most constant protection, and security for their persons and property * * *."

A treaty made under the authority of the United States "shall be the supreme law of the land; and the judges in every State shall be bound thereby, any thing in the constitution or laws of any State to the contrary notwithstanding." Constitution, Art. VI, § 2.

* * * The treaty was made to strengthen friendly relations between the two nations. The provision quoted establishes the rule of equality between Japanese subjects while in this country and native citizens. Treaties for the protection of citizens of one country residing in the territory of another are numerous, and make for good understanding between nations. The treaty is binding within the State of Washington. * * * The rule of equality established by it cannot be rendered nugatory in any part of the United States by municipal ordinances or state laws. It stands on the same footing of supremacy as do the provisions of the Constitution and laws of the United States. It operates of itself without the aid of any legislation, state or national; and it will be applied and given authoritative effect by the courts. * * *

The purpose of the ordinance complained of is to regulate, not to prohibit, the business of pawnbroker. But it makes it impossible for aliens to carry on the business. It need not be considered whether the State, if it sees fit, may forbid and destroy the business generally. Such a law would apply equally to aliens and citizens, and no question of conflict with the treaty would arise. The grievance here alleged is that plaintiff in error, in violation of the treaty, is denied equal opportunity.

* * * Decree reversed.

——————

Notes and Questions

1. *Judicial characterization of treaties as self-executing.* Are the characterizations made by American courts in the foregoing cases assuredly based upon the principles of interpretation of treaties? If so, are the interpretations textual or contextual in the terminology? Are some of the characterizations as self-executing linked to the court's response to plaintiff's claim of right based on the treaty alone? Can you formulate any reasonably reliable way of predicting outcomes on the issue, self-executing or not? If so, what is it?

When the Carter administration submitted three United Nations (and one Inter–American) human rights conventions to the Senate, the executive branch reported that the treaties had been examined for any conflicts with the Constitution and existing legislation and that any potential conflicts had been dealt with by reservations prepared by the executive and recommended to the Senate as conditions to its advice and consent. This, the President's messages claimed, would reduce the necessity for the Senate to have to weigh consent to the treaties in terms of what legislative changes might be required to put the treaties into effect as law. Why should the Senate be concerned about possible legislative changes? Would it be apt to be more concerned about possible legislative changes in the Federal Criminal Code than in some other titles of the United States Code? As to an executive branch preference for non-self executing treaties on human rights, see Chapter 10. We have already noted the reservations made to the U.S. adherence to the Genocide Convention and the International Covenant on Civil and Political Rights. One of these is a declaration that they are not self-executing. Is this a wise thing to do? Would you think that there are more advantages to having a treaty self-executing or non-self-executing? *See* Ch. 9, *supra.*

2.   *In Cannon v. U.S. Dep't of Justice (Parole Commission)*, 973 F.2d 1190, 1197 (5th Cir.1992), relating to the U.S.—Mexico Treaty on Execution of Penal Sentences, the Fifth Circuit Court of Appeals held that the Parole Commission may not authorize a "release date which results in the total period of incarceration * * * [which is] less than or greater than the total foreign-court-imposed sentence * * * " The Court noted: "Aside from the ministerial task of appointing an 'Authority' to receive transferred prisoners, the Treaty *required* [emphasis the courts] no legislative action other than ratification. Procedural legislation which makes operation of a Treaty more convenient cannot amend or abrogate a self-executing Treaty [*citing Cook v. U.S., Chew Heong v. U.S.*]. Accordingly, a foreign-court-imposed sentence is in fact one imposed by the equivalent of an Act of Congress." See also, discussion on self-executing treaties in *Alvarez–Machain, supra* and Chapters 1, 3, and 9.

Paust, Self–Executing Treaties

82 AJIL 760 (1988).*

" * * * it seems clear that the text of the Constitution, the predominant views of the Founders, and early and more modern trends in judicial decision all demand that certain notions of several text writers with respect to the inherently non-self-executing nature of certain types of treaties be abandoned. The constitutionally preferable view is that no treaty is inherently non-self-executing except those which would seek to declare war on behalf of the United States. * * * With the exception of the sui generis power of Congress to declare war, the mere existence of a congressional power does not mean that it is exclusive and would obviate any potentially self-executing effect of a treaty.

It also seems clear that all treaties are self-executing except those (or the portions of them) which, by their terms considered in context, require domestic implementing legislation or seek to declare war on behalf of the United States. All treaties are supreme federal law, but some treaties, by their terms, arc not directly operative. Finally, even non-self-executing treaties can produce and have produced domestic legal effects through indirect incorporation, by which a treaty norm is utilized as an aid in interpreting the Constitution, a statute, common law or some other legal provision."

Notes and Questions. The word "self-executing" may or may not be felicitous, but awareness of the actual text of the Constitution, the predominant views of the Founders, early and more modern judicial opinions, and a proper separation of powers should prove a useful counter to ambiguity and the contrary assumptions. It is appropriate to reaffirm the text of the

* Reprinted with the permission of the American Society of International Law.

Constitution and expectations of the Founders that all treaties will be the supreme law of the land. Do you agree? Why or why not?

2.   OTHER PROBLEMS ABOUT INTERNATIONAL AGREEMENTS AS INTERNAL LAW

Notes and Questions

What are the operational limitations on the power of the President and the Senate to legislate by treaty? We previously noted operating limitations on the President–Senate power of making self-executing treaties regarding revenue measures, appropriations, and federal criminal law. How much farther does practice carry the treaty-as-legislation power of the President and the Senate so far as concerns other enumerated powers of Congress in Article I, Section 8 of the Constitution? Is the *Asakura case* the final answer as to all aspects of the foreign commerce power under Section 8(3)? An even more difficult question is whether the President and the Senate could make a self-executing treaty fixing the exchange rate for the dollar. Look also at Section 8(4), (11), (12), and (13). We have no answers based on what has been decided, and research has not been able to draw conclusions from the non-use of the power to make law by self-executing treaties.

The problem is not entirely or even principally a legal one. Institutional attitudes in the House and Senate—attitudes beyond political alignments—are also important. Among enduring House institutional attitudes are: (i) resentment of the Senate's constitution–given role in foreign relations (a role superseded by the history of American federalism and the amendment providing for the popular election of senators); (ii) suspicion of cozy fraternization between the foreign affairs executive branches and the Senate Committee on Foreign Relations; (iii) belief that the more popular branch of the Congress is closer to grass roots than the Senate and that senators are more susceptible to foreigners' blandishments, because they are fewer, more elitist, and often more prominent; (iv) fear and dislike as to appropriations, revenue, and national security matters, of finding themselves boxed-in by national interest needs to carry out international commitments which they had no part in making; (v) concern about the erosion of House rights to participate, as in the case of the disposition of United States property in the Panama Canal Zone.

2.   *Treaties, Congress, and Judicial Interpretation.* Can Congress pass a law that violates an extant treaty? How does the judiciary interpret legislation that appears to do this? If legislation is found to violate a treaty, what is the result domestically? What is the result internationally? Read the excerpts from the following case relating to possible legislative violation of GATT.

Mississippi Poultry Ass'n, Inc. v. Madigan

United States Court of Appeals, Fifth Circuit, 1993.
992 F.2d 1359, 1369–67 *aff'd* 9 F.3d 1113; *aff'd en banc* 31 F.3d 1227.

* * *

In another variation on the absurdity theme, the Agency insists that the interpretation urged by the Associations is absurd because it would place the PPIA in violation of the 1) General Agreement on Tariffs and Trade (GATT), 2) the ongoing trade negotiations under the auspices of GATT (the Uruguay Round) and 3) the United States–Canada Free–Trade Agreement (FTA). The Agency adamantly insists that Congress cannot violate an international obligation without making a clear statement that it intends to do so. The Agency maintains further that a clear statement is especially appropriate in the instant case because the Executive Branch has exclusive responsibility for conducting international affairs. We discern fatal flaws in the Agency's position.

* * * The Agency has obfuscatorily intertwined its arguments, but when they are untangled there appear three separate but related maxims governing the construction of statutes which implicate international obligations. First, Congress may abrogate a treaty or international obligation entered into by the United States only by a clear statement of its intent to do so. Second, the extraterritorial application of domestic laws requires a clear statement of congressional intent so as "to protect against unintended clashes between our laws and those of other nations which could result in international discord." And finally, "[i]t has been a maxim of statutory construction since the decision in *Murray v. The Charming Betsy,* [*supra*] that 'an act of Congress ought never to be construed to violate the law of nations, if any other possible construction remains.'"Even when we grant arguendo that these truisms of statutory construction exist, we find them inapplicable and therefore not controlling in the instant case.

Despite the Agency's claim that Congress must clearly express its intention to violate the GATT, it fails to cite us to any authority for that specific proposition and we are aware of none. In fact, we are aware of strongly instructive authority to the contrary. The Federal Circuit recently rejected out of hand the argument that a statutory provision should be read consistently with the obligations of the United States as a signatory of GATT—the very position argued here by the Agency. The court reasoned that

> even if * * * [the] Commerce[ ] [Department's] interpretation conflicts with the GATT, * * * the GATT is not controlling. While we acknowledge Congress's interest in complying with U.S. responsibilities under the GATT, we are bound not by what we think Congress should or perhaps wanted to do, but by what Congress in fact did. The GATT does not trump domestic legislation; if the statutory provisions at issue here are inconsistent with GATT, it is a matter for Congress and not this court to decide and remedy.

We conclude that this same, flawless reasoning applies to the instant case and mandates that we give effect to Congress' intent, even if implementation of that intent is virtually certain to create a violation of the GATT.

Our adoption of this reasoning is unaffected by the maxims of statutory construction cited above. The first maxim—that a clear statement of Congress is required to abrogate a treaty—does not require a different result here because Congress is not abrogating a treaty or an international obligation. Abrogation or repeal involves nullifying an obligation. In the instant case, Congress has at most evinced an intent to place the PPIA *in violation of the GATT.* Certainly, United States has passed laws that, in a subsequent proceeding before a GATT panel, have been declared in violation of the GATT. Yet these violations have not signified the end of American involvement in the GATT.

Second, there is no need here for an Arabian American Oil Co. "clear statement" as required when Congress intends for its legislation to violate the GATT. The instant case is distinguishable from the situation in Arabian American Oil Co., which only requires such a clear statement when the intent of Congress is to apply domestic legislation extraterritorially, so as "to protect against unintended clashes between our laws and those of other nations which would result in international discord."

The factual circumstances in both of these cases are distinguishable from those in the instant case. In *Arabian American Oil Co.,* the question was whether Title VII applied to American corporations located in Saudi Arabia. Courts must be hesitant to apply American law when it would displace the law of the foreign forum. Similarly, in *Aerospatiale,* the defendants were corporations owned by France, so for all practical purposes a foreign sovereign was a party in the lawsuit. In both cases the key issue is clear: application of American law would directly *affect the sovereignty of a foreign nation.* That cannot be said of the case now before us. There is absolutely no issue of sovereignty in the instant case; in the absence of such an issue the concerns voiced in *Arabian American Oil Co.* and *Aerospatiale* are not implicated.

Like the first two maxims, the third—that an act of Congress should not be construed to violate the law of nations if there is an alternative construction available—cannot apply here. The Agency directs our attention to no supporting authority for its contention that the GATT—or for that matter any multi-lateral trade agreement—falls under the rubric of "the law of nations"; and again we have been unable to find any. Neither have we found a single case in which this canon was applied to international commercial law. Rather, all cases relying on the law-of-nations canon of construction either involve traditional rules of public international law or implicate the sovereignty of a foreign nation. We are loath, therefore, to extend this maxim to multi-lateral trade agreements. To do so in the absence of controlling authority would be to exercise raw judicial fiat.

The additional Agency argument—that a clear congressional statement is especially appropriate in this instance because the Executive Branch has exclusive authority over foreign affairs—borders on frivolity. The Agency overlooks or conveniently ignores the well recognized distinction between foreign *affairs* and *foreign commerce.* Even though the Executive Branch does have exclusive jurisdiction over foreign affairs, the Constitution grants Congress power to regulate commerce with foreign nations. To the extent that a dispute exists over possible foreign policy implications to the GATT, we decline to enter the fray. * * *

Riesenfeld, The Doctrine of Self–Executing Treaties and U.S. v. Postal: Win at Any Price?

Editorial Comment, 74 American Journal of International Law 892, 896 (1980).*

From a survey of the copious literature it emerges that the concept of self-executing treaties is in need of clarification. It has separate international and domestic constitutional aspects. The international aspect focuses on the issue of whether the treaty aims at the immediate creation of rights and duties of private individuals which are enforceable and to be enforced by domestic tribunals. The domestic constitutional aspect deals with the question whether and under what circumstances such enforceability and enforcement needs separate legislative action to accomplish this aim. The international aspect deals with the content or nature of the treaty obligation: what is to be accomplished and what is the time frame for such accomplishment. The domestic means for such accomplishment will usually not be of international concern. * * *

* * *

A survey of the constitutions, cases, and scholarly writings in other countries leads to the conclusion that even in countries in which legislative approval is needed for the conclusion of international treaties, the creation of rights, privileges, duties, and immunities cognizable in domestic courts is primarily a function of the particular treaty provision. The power of parties to invoke it in domestic courts depends upon its import, as determined from its language, context, purpose, negotiating history, and general background. The internal applicability is created *by virtue of* and—save where publication requirements dictate otherwise—*upon* the international entry into effect of the treaty provision with respect to the nation involved. The legislative approval is a condition for the valid conclusion of the treaty. Normally it does not determine the domestic applicability of the treaty provisions. Of course, this does not exclude the possibility that the legislature, in giving approval to the international engagement of the nation, may prescribe its domestic cognizability irrespective of the treaty's mandate. Conversely, where the treaty expressly or by implication provides for domestic protection of the rights and privileges created thereby, the parliamentary approval of its conclusion may not deny such cognizability, unless the legislature is empowered to prescribe internationally valid reservations or is constitutionally authorized to postpone domestic applicability until the passage of further legislation.

This analysis compels a further semantic consequence: Strictly speaking, the term "self-executing" is not a notion whose meaning is determined by international law. The self-executing nature of a treaty provision is a product of international and domestic constitutional rules. Internationally relevant is merely the determination whether the treaty provision in question mandates the cognizability in and protection by domestic tribunals of the rights, duties, privileges, and immunities created thereby.

* Reprinted with the permission of American Society of International Law.

Reservations or interpretative declarations, to the extent that they are internationally permissible and effective, may only relate to that aspect.

* * *

From what is said * * *, it follows that the panel of the United States Court of Appeals for the Fifth Circuit erred egregiously in the choice of the criteria for the determination of whether or not Article 6 of the High Seas Convention is self-executing. A treaty provision which by its terms and purpose is *meant* to stipulate the immediate and not merely progressive creation of rights, privileges, duties, and immunities cognizable in domestic courts and is *capable* of being applied by the courts without further concretization *is* self-executing by virtue of the constitutional mandate of Article VI of the U.S. Constitution. The intent or understanding of the Executive is at best an element in the interpretative task of the court. * * *

Notes and Questions. Does Professor Riesenfeld's test provide a workable basis for differentiating the questions, (a) whether a treaty is self-executing and (b) whether it creates private rights, duties, privileges or immunities? The 1965 Restatement asserts in Comment *h* to Section 131: "Whether a treaty is self-executing is not to be confused with whether the treaty creates rights and remedies." Is this merely a delphic utterance or a concurrence with Riesenfeld? Suppose that the President and two-thirds of the Senate specifically provide that the treaty they bring into effect internationally is to be deemed self-executing, but the right claimed by a private litigant is that he is entitled by the treaty to a tax break not sanctioned under the Internal Revenue Code. Would the Riesenfeld and Restatement statements lead to the same conclusion or to opposite ones? How would the Restatement utterance solve, as an original issue, Mr. Asakura's claim of right to engage in pawnbrokerage in Seattle? How does Riesenfeld know when a treaty, by its terms and purpose, is meant to be self-executing? He covers himself, does he not, if the treaty is meant to be self-executing (by whatever means of determination) but is incapable of being applied by the courts without further concretization?

United States v. Postal, 589 F.2d 862 (5th Cir.1979) involved a criminal case against persons arrested on the high seas, offshore the United States, for attempted narcotics smuggling from an unmarked, no-flag craft. The issue was whether the defendants had assertible private rights under the 1958 High Seas Convention not to be arrested by American authorities. The Court of Appeals for the Fifth Circuit held against the defense on the ground that the treaty was not executed as an international agreement, relying on the view of the executive branch that it was not such a treaty. How fundamental is Riesenfeld's critique under these circumstances? How useful the Restatement's cautionary statement? *But see, United States v. Juda,* [*supra* ch. 3] where the 9th Circuit required a nexus sufficient to meet due process, even for stateless vessels.

SECTION D.   UNITED STATES LAW AND PRACTICE AS TO RESERVATIONS, AMENDMENTS AND UNDERSTANDINGS: THE PRESIDENT AND THE SENATE

Notes and Questions

1. *The Senate of the United States.* As a part of the solution to the large-small states issue at the Constitutional Convention (1787), the executive power article (II) conditions the President's treaty-making authority by requiring that treaties be made "by and with the Advice and Consent of the Senate * * * provided two-thirds of the Senators present concur." This enforced sharing of foreign affairs power and the two-thirds vote requirement for bringing a treaty into effect are at the root of many of the aspects of uniqueness that characterize the international agreements law of the United States. In broad effect, the Senate expects (and the executive acquiesces) that any condition it attaches to its consent be respected. If the Senate does not have its way, there is no treaty, so far as United States law is concerned. The clearest form of Senate condition to consent is a reservation, i.e. a Senate imposed alteration of the legal undertaking. One notes that this type of condition is parallel to the concept of reservation in customary international law, as codified in this respect by the Vienna Convention. Sometimes, but not often, the Senate purports to amend a treaty, and this is regarded as tantamount to a reservation.

All too often (some say) the Senate approves a treaty with Senate interpretation, i.e., understandings of what it means. The rub is that while understandings are easier to get support for in the Senate (because deemed not alterations), executive practice is to communicate them to the other treaty party or parties for acceptance or rejection, exactly on the same basis as reservations. To complicate matters further, in recent times the senators have developed even less conditional caveats, such as declarations. If made by a senator or two, but not two-thirds of them, declarations would be no more than legislative history. But declarations by the approving two-thirds would seem to fall within the executive practice of transmitting all caveats by the Senate to other treaty parties. Finally, the executive may have made reservations at signature and more recently has formulated reservations recommended to the Senate. All executive reservations will be in the President's message to the Senate, and everything in that message will be sent to the other party or parties; and, eventually, if the Senate approves the treaty and the President ratifies it, the whole history of the treaty, including recitation of communication of reservations to the other side, is repeated in the presidential promulgation of the treaty. See discussion in ch. 10 of the U.S. Reservations and understandings relating to the Genocide Convention and the Covenant on Civil & Political Rights.

2. *Caveats made subsequent to a treaty entering into effect.* There are several open or only partially resolved questions here. Reservations made by other states: If these were made prior to approval by the Senate,

they would be put before the Senate by the President. But if made and acquiesced in by the executive after the treaty has come into effect for the U.S., we have no rule as yet. The other state's reservations to a bilateral treaty would virtually ensure it would not be sent to the Senate. Why?

Senate action after the treaty is in effect for the United States. In the only known case, *The Diamond Rings,* 183 U.S. 176, 180 (1901), the Supreme Court refused to take into account a Senate resolution seeking what in effect was a post-approval understanding, saying "the meaning of the treaty cannot be controlled by subsequent explanations of some of those who may have voted to ratify it". Experts on federal legislation could fashion a tighter case: the Senate is a continuing body and that body now votes by two-thirds to attach a post-promulgation reservation. Would the court ignore it?

Executive branch actions after the treaty is in effect for the United States. The treaty is in effect, and another party to it (by diplomatic note) asks whether the United States agrees with this or that interpretation of an article in the treaty. The Secretary of State says that the United States does agree. It is beyond dispute that the executive branch is the authorized interpreter of treaties vis-à-vis other states and that executive interpretations are entitled to great weight in courts in the United States. See Section 326 of the 1987 Restatement. However, the Senate, by two-thirds vote interposes a reservation to the above interpretation. What result?

This once largely hypothetical question became an acute issue of uncertain future dimensions in the spring of 1987. Responding to the President's activism in espousing a re-interpretation of the Anti–Ballistic Missile Treaty to accommodate the administration's wish to develop and (eventually) deploy the Strategic Defense Initiative, Senator Sam Nunn, a recognized Senate leader on national security and related issues, declared, for himself and some other senators, that such reinterpretation was contrary to the Senate's understanding of the ABM treaty when it was approved, and if not referred to the Senate again, would create a grave constitutional issue. Because of the unknowable possible significance of the ABM issue on United States law about treaties, we provide the following material. What issues remain the same and what new issues arise since the disintegration of the former Soviet Union? More importantly in 2001 is the fact that President George W. Bush has set in motion a plan to breach and break the ABM Treaty.

––––––

Study the Treaty Between the United States of America and the Union of Soviet Socialist Republics on the Limitation of Anti–Ballistic Missiles Systems of May 26, 1972, 23 U.S.T. 3435, T.I.A.S. 7503, in Doc. Supp.

––––––

The Reagan Re–Interpretation, 1985–1987

Prepared statement of Abraham D. Sofaer, Legal Adviser, U.S. Department of State, ABM Treaty Interpretation Dispute, Hearing Before the Sub–Committee on Arms Control, International Security and Science of the Committee on Foreign Affairs, House of Representatives, 99th Cong., 1st Sess., 9 (1986).

* * *

The ABM Treaty is an important element of our strategic arms control structure. When the President first announced the SDI program in March 1983, he made clear that it would be conducted "consistent with our obligations [under] the ABM treaty." This commitment has been maintained. The United States has scrupulously complied with the Treaty, notwithstanding such clear Soviet violations of it as the Krasnoyarsk radar station.

Soviet violations of the ABM Treaty, the implementation of our SDI program, and the ongoing arms negotiations at Geneva recently caused various agencies to consider more thoroughly than ever before the appropriate interpretation of the ABM Treaty as it relates to future or "exotic" systems. By that, I mean defensive systems that serve the same functions as ABM systems and components, but that use devices based on technology not understood in 1972 when the Treaty was negotiated and that are capable of substituting for ABM interceptor missiles, launchers, and radars. This examination has led to the conclusion that a reading of the ABM Treaty that would allow the development and testing of such systems based on physical principles other than those understood in 1972 is wholly justified.

* * *

I was well aware when I began my work on this issue that several officials associated with the SALT I negotiations, and others still in the Government, had advanced the view that the ABM Treaty is unambiguous in its treatment of such future systems. They argued that Article V of the Treaty forbids development, testing, or deployment of any future ABM systems and components other than those that are fixed land-based. They read Agreed Statement D as relevant only to fixed land-based systems and components, arguing that it permits "creation" of such systems and components when they are based on "other physical principles," but conditions their deployment on agreement between the parties on specific limitations. Other persons were contending, however, that this "restrictive" view of the ABM Treaty is based on unilateral assertions by U.S. negotiators; that the Treaty is ambiguous; and that the negotiating record supports a broader view of our freedom to develop, test, and deploy future systems.

My study of the Treaty led me to conclude that its language is ambiguous and can more reasonably be read to support a broader interpretation. An examination of the three provisions primarily at issue will demonstrate why this is so. * * *

The restrictive interpretation rests on the premise that Article V(1) is clear on its face: it says no development, testing, or deployment of "ABM systems or components" other than those that are fixed land-based. But this language does not settle the issue of the article's applicability to future systems or components. That issue depends on the meaning of the term "ABM systems or components": is that phrase limited to systems and components based on then-current technology, or does it also include those based on future technology?

In attempting to answer this question, one must turn to the definition of "ABM system" in Article II(1). Proponents of the restrictive view contend that this definition is functional: anything ever conceived that could serve the function of countering strategic missiles in flight falls within the definition. These persons argue that the three components identified in that paragraph—missiles, launchers, and radars—are merely listed as the elements of what an ABM system is "currently consisting of," and that all future components of a system that satisfies the functional definition are also covered by Article II(1). Only when armed with these meanings can proponents rely on Article V(1) as a ban on development, testing, and deployment of all non-fixed land-based systems or components, whether current or future.

* * *

Under international law, as under U.S. domestic law, once an agreement has been found ambiguous, one must seek guidance in the circumstances surrounding the drafting of the agreement. Thus, in the present situation, once we concluded that the Treaty is ambiguous, we turned to the negotiating record to see which of the possible constructions most accurately reflects the parties' intentions.

* * * I reached the firm conclusion that, although the U.S. delegates initially sought to ban development and testing of non-land based systems or components based on future technology, the Soviets refused to go along, and no such agreement was reached. The Soviets stubbornly resisted U.S. attempts to adopt in the body of the Treaty any limits on such systems or components based on future technology; their arguments rested on a professed unwillingness to deal with unknown devices or technology. The farthest the Soviets were willing to go with respect to such future systems or components was to adopt a side agreement prohibiting only the deployment of such systems and components, once created, until the parties agreed on specific limitations. The parties did not agree to ban development and testing of such systems or components, whether on land or in space.

The negotiating record also contains strong support for a reading of Article II(1) that restricts the definitions of "ABM system" and "components" to those based on current physical principles. The Soviets specifically sought to prevent broad definitions of these terms, and our negotiators acceded to their wishes. Moreover, our negotiators ultimately convinced the Soviets to adopt Agreed Statement D by arguing that, without it, the Treaty would leave the parties free to deploy systems or components based on other physical principles, such as lasers.

* * *

Smith,[a] Foreword To Sherr, A Legal Analysis of the "New Interpretation" of the Anti–Ballistic Missile Treaty (1986)*

The Anti–Ballistic Missile Treaty of 1972 is the only U.S.–Soviet strategic nuclear arms control agreement that has been ratified and remains in force today. It has effectively prevented the parties from expanding their strategic defensive arsenals as they have done so vigorously on the offensive side. It has permitted both governments to pursue—albeit with insufficient results to date—limits and reductions on strategic missiles, submarines, and bombers.

In October, 1985, the Reagan Administration suddenly revealed a new interpretation of the Treaty that would permit the development and testing of lasers and other exotic weapons that are space-, air-, sea-, or mobile land-based. This unilateral reinterpretation reversed the established understanding of the Treaty. It is inconsistent with the historic understanding accepted by the Treaty's negotiators, including myself; the U.S. Senate, which ratified it; and every Administration since President Nixon's, including the Reagan Administration itself before October, 1985.

When the supreme law of our land as set forth in this Treaty of unlimited duration is thus radically revised by an overreaching policy, it is the responsibility of the legal profession to examine the issue and support adherence to the law. In this instance, the pertinent provisions of the Treaty are clear, their meaning is readily apparent, and the public historical record is unambiguous. One does not have to be a technical expert or international lawyer to read the Treaty and the Administration's recent arguments and then draw an informed conclusion about the merits of the established and the "new" interpretations of the Treaty.

———

Perhaps in response to the problems discussed above, the United States government has begun insisting on significant detail in its weapons treaties. *See, e.g.,* USSR–U.S. 1987 Treaty on the Elimination of Their Intermediate–Range and Shorter–Range Missiles. In addition, this treaty provides that any subsequent modifications to the treaty will not be considered amendments, thus giving the executive the right to modify the treaty in the form of a note of understanding or executive agreement. Is this a permissible delegation of power to the President? Is it necessary, in order to address the many issues that might arise under a treaty of this size and significance?

a. Ambassador Gerard C. Smith was Chief U.S. Delegate to SALT I and Director of the U.S. Arms Control and Disarmament Agency from 1969 to 1973.

* Reprinted with the permission of Lawyers Alliance for Nuclear Arms Control.

Jonathan Schell, The New Nuclear Danger (demonstration against US' National Missile Defense)

The Nation, Monday, June 25, 2001, ISSN: 0027-8378; Volume 272; Issue 25*

On June 12, 1982, 1 million people assembled in Central Park in New York City to protest the reckless nuclear policies of the Reagan Administration and to call for a nuclear freeze. They never assembled in such numbers again—in part because Reagan reversed course and opened nuclear arms talks with the Soviet Union, and in part because, after (Publication page references are not available for this document.)

Mikhail Gorbachev came to power, the cold war began to wind down. The day remains in memory as a reminder of how quickly public concern over nuclear annihilation can arise and how quickly it can evaporate. When the cold war finally did end, nuclear weapons pretty much dropped out of the conscious thoughts of most Americans. The weapons themselves, however, remain in existence—some 32,000 strong at last count. Now the policies of a new administration and the rise of fresh nuclear dangers have brought the issue back to awareness. On June 10 a coalition of groups that calls itself Project Abolition will hold an antinuclear demonstration in Lafayette Park across from the White House. It will be the first major effort of its kind in the capital since the end of the cold war. The precipitating event is the new arms race that is threatened by the Bush Administration's embrace of National Missile Defense (NMD) and the weaponization of space. A million people are not expected. But the protesters hope to make up in staying power what they lack in numbers. Their underlying cause is the abolition of all nuclear arms, and their vow is to stick with it for the duration.

It is no simple matter to take stock of the nuclear predicament in the year 2001. Under the Bush Administration, the nuclear policies of the United States—and of the world—are in a state of greater confusion than at any time since the weapons were invented. Chaos would not be too strong a word to use. In fact, the greatest current danger may lie not in one policy or another but precisely in this confusion, which leaves the world's nuclear actors without any reliable road map for the future. It is nevertheless essential to try to understand at least the broad outlines of the new shape of the predicament. This exercise is complex and riddled with paradox and contradiction, not to mention wishful thinking and sheer fantasy, yet it is unavoidable if either policy or protest is to make sense.

Nuclear danger today has two main sources. The first is the mountain of nuclear arms left over from the cold war. The second is the proliferation of nuclear weapons to new countries. The leftover cold war arsenals are still governed by the policy that prevailed during the cold war, the doctrine of nuclear deterrence, which holds (in its most enlightened version) that the rival great powers are safest when each has the unchallengeable power to annihilate its rival. This way, no one is supposed to try anything, because if anyone does, all will die. Today the United States has about

* Reprinted with the permission of the
Gale Group Inc., The Nation Company L.P.

7,200 weapons poised to fire at Russia, and Russia has about 6,000 poised to fire at us, and the continued existence of each nation depends on the reliability of the other's forces, which is doubtful in the extreme in the case of Russia. Deterrence's provocative other name, of course, is mutual assured destruction, or MAD, a reference to the menace of complete annihilation on which the stability of the arrangement rests. MAD's confusing adjunct is arms control, whose aim has been to draw down the preposterous excess of offensive weapons through the Strategic Arms Reduction Talks (START) while suppressing defenses by observance of the Anti–Ballistic Missile (ABM) treaty of 1972, until this year called the "cornerstone of strategic stability" in NATO planning papers. Defenses had to be suppressed because if they ran free they would upset the laboriously negotiated offensive reductions.

MAD, however, is not a creature of the ABM treaty; it is an inescapable condition in a world of large nuclear arsenals, against which no defenses are available. The ABM treaty merely ratifies and codifies this underlying situation, the better to negotiate the reduction—though not the elimination—of offensive forces. Other things being equal, a world without an ABM treaty would not be a world without MAD; it would be a world with MAD but without arms control.

MAD was of course a product of the cold war. It was a desperate makeshift in a desperate situation. Today, however, the cold war has long been over. The extreme peculiarity—or downright absurdity—of continuing to rely on MAD is that the political antagonism that underlay and justified it ended ten years ago, when the Soviet Union disappeared. During the cold war, the two powers threatened each other with annihilation for a reason; now they do so without a reason. Russia and the United States have no quarrel that would justify the firing of a single conventional round, not to speak of mutual annihilation. The human beings resolved their quarrels, but the weapons, displaying their characteristic astonishing immunity to political influence, evidently did not get the news. Here is a state of affairs that seems ripe for radical surgery.

The second source of nuclear danger, proliferation, is most dramatically evident in South Asia, where India and Pakistan are engaged in the first nuclear face-off entirely unrelated to the cold war. It's difficult to predict where proliferation will occur next, but some of the main candidates are obvious: the Middle East, where Israel already possesses nuclear weapons and where Iraq and Iran are both known to be interested in acquiring them; and East Asia, where North Korea has well-developed nuclear and missile programs, and where Japan has just elected a prime minister who wishes to alter his nation's Constitution, which now forbids the development of offensive military forces, including nuclear weapons. If unchecked, proliferation has no logical or necessary stopping point. It points to a fully nuclearized world, in which any nation seriously threatened by another will feel itself fully entitled to build nuclear arms.

Unfortunately, the two basic elements of nuclear danger do not exist in separate worlds; they fatally interact in our one world. Most important, MAD is a standing invitation to proliferation, as the nuclearization of South Asia has already demonstrated. The simple, unavoidable truth is that possession fuels proliferation. If a country that feels threatened by the nuclear arms of another accepts MAD, as the nuclear powers teach them to do, they not only are likely to develop arms, they must do so. For a government to do otherwise would be to criminally abdicate its responsibility to defend its people. (Imagine the reactions in the United States, for example, if this country somehow did not possess nuclear arms but was suddenly threatened by a country that did possess them, and some third country lectured it on the virtues of remaining nuclear-weapon-free in the name of nonproliferation.)

Enter George W. Bush. His Administration has addressed the two major elements of nuclear danger in our world. In regard to the leftover cold war arsenals, he has proposed what on the face of it appears to be the most radical shift in policy since the inauguration of the MAD system. "The cold war logic that led to the creation of massive stockpiles on both sides," he has announced, in a refreshing acknowledgment of the new geopolitical reality, "is now outdated. Our mutual security need no longer depend on a nuclear balance of terror." The clear promise is of a fundamentally new policy, of a "new framework," in his words. In regard to proliferation, he has proposed to defend the United States with NMD (which was in fact embraced by President Clinton and both parties in the Senate before Bush took office). In sum, "it is time to leave the cold war behind, and defend against the new threats of the twenty-first century." The Bush policies have the merit of acknowledging, in a way that the seemingly insensate continuation of MAD into the post-cold war world did not, the basic new realities—on the one hand, the collapse of MAD's political underpinnings and, on the other hand, the increasing dangers of proliferation. MAD acknowledges neither. It anachronistically deals with Russia exactly as we did during the cold war (though with somewhat reduced overkill), and it fatally undercuts nonproliferation by teaching that nuclear arsenals are the key to a nation's security. It is, indeed, the impossibility, in a MAD world, of framing effective nonproliferation policies that set the stage for NMD. If diplomacy wedded to MAD cannot stop proliferation, isn't it time to try something else, namely defenses? In that respect, NMD is the product of MAD.

The Bush prescription, however, does not work merely because the policies it purported to replace have failed. The most notable problem with the Bush approach is that it has not provided—even in theory—policies that can make its promises a reality. Bush seeks to offer an exit from the balance of terror, but he provides no actual escape route. MAD, notwithstanding its deficiencies, is a tough old bird, and cannot be waved away with a phrase in a speech. The closest Bush has come to a concrete policy in this field has been to announce a unilateral reduction in offensive nuclear arsenals to "the lowest possible number"—a number, however, that he has not specified. But a low number of offensive warheads, however welcome in itself (press reports have suggested that the range might be between 1,500 and 2,500 warheads), gives no release from the balance of terror. It preserves it at lower levels of overkill. In other passages of his speeches, Bush has seemed to acknowledge that MAD will stay in effect. In a speech on May 1, he stated in a less noted passage, "Deterrence can no longer be based solely on the threat of nuclear retaliation." The word "solely" is decisive. It means that MAD will be continued. At best, it will be supplemented by something, not replaced by it. What will that something be? Bush immediately continued, "Defenses can strengthen deterrence by reducing the incentive for proliferation." But to add defenses to MAD is a far different proposition from substituting one for the other.

That brings us to the second problem with the Bush plan. It is the one that has led almost the entire world to reject national missile defenses. Russia fears that a resurgent United States, feeling protected by its shield, will bully it in the future, and China fears that its small nuclear arsenal will be negated. The initial goal of NMD is to protect against proliferators. But at the same time, it would upset arms control. Defenses do not enhance the existing MAD system; they undermine it. That is why the world is upset that the Bush Administration wants to jettison the ABM treaty. Russian Foreign Minister Igor Ivanov, for example, has recently written, "With the ABM treaty as its root, a system of international accords on arms control and disarmament sprang up in the past decades. Inseparable from this process is the creation of global and regional regimes of nuclear nonproliferation. These agreements, comprising the modern architecture of international security, rest on the ABM treaty. If the foundation is destroyed, this interconnected system will collapse, nullifying thirty years of efforts by the world community." The United States' NATO allies have just made it clear that they agree.

In the nuclear sphere, defenses and offenses are oil and water. The addition of defenses destabilizes an offensive system and vice versa. MAD is an offensive framework, depending on mutual vulnerability to make everyone cautious. A defensive framework—a so-called defense-dominated world—is imaginable. Under it, offenses would be hugely reduced or eliminated by mutual agreement, and protection from residual danger would be provided by defenses. Only when defenses could clearly overwhelm any offense would a defensive system have been achieved. At that point, and only at that point, would MAD truly be a thing of the past. This was the vision put forward, at least rhetorically, by Ronald Reagan as his ultimate goal when he first proposed strategic defenses. Like MAD, defense domination qualifies as a true framework for nuclear danger. It is one that is in fact supported by many retired civilian and military officials, including the commander of the allied air forces in the Gulf War, Charles Horner, and Reagan's chief arms negotiator, Paul Nitze, both of whom have called for the elimination of nuclear weapons together with the creation of defenses. The only way, indeed, to make sense of antimissile defenses such as NMD is to wed them to a commitment by the nuclear powers to abolish nuclear weapons.

A further problem with NMD—certainly, the strangest one—is that so far it is a technical flop, having failed most of its tests. Aristotle said that the most important attribute of a thing is existence. NMD lacks this attribute. Or, to put it differently, it has the attribute of nonexistence. It's been interesting to watch how this attribute has manifested itself politically. The Bush Administration announced that it means to "deploy" NMD. Deploy what, though? The Administration backed away from the Clinton plan—a limited deployment of ground-based missiles that would shoot down incoming missiles—and began to suggest even less-tested alternatives, including airborne, sea-based and space-based systems. When Bush recently sent his envoys to governments around the world to "persuade" them of the virtues of his plan, the governments learned to their surprise that nothing of a concrete character was on the table. It was one thing for Ivanov to say that "in order to hold a discussion, you have to have some subject for it, a plan, a concrete understanding of what the other side wants. For now, there are no such plans." It was another when the American envoy Paul Wolfowitz had to confess the truth of the charge, saying, "It is much too early, I think, even for us to ask people to agree with us, because we have not come to firm conclusions yet ourselves." The lesson may be that when you're promising pie in the sky, you should at least have some pie.

Is it possible that the nonexistence of NMD will spare us its harmful consequences? Unfortunately, not necessarily—unless the United States either abandons the scheme or weds it to a commitment to abolish nuclear weapons. Governments make their decisions according to future expectations. The looming possibility of NMD can therefore bring many of the disadvantages of actual deployment—disruption of arms control, pressure to proliferate—without any of the advantages. NMD thus creates a political problem that it cannot technically solve. When one reflects that the more ambitious NMD programs cannot be fully deployed (if they can work at all) until 2020, it becomes obvious that this is no minor consideration.

There is, we must note, one other "framework" that is possible: the framework of American military dominance, nuclear and otherwise, of the world. As the conservative commentators William Kristol and Robert Kagan have stated, Republicans "will ask Americans to face this increasingly dangerous world without illusions. They will argue that American dominance can be sustained for many decades to come, not by arms control agreements, but by augmenting America's power, and, therefore, its ability to lead." If the United States does abandon all nuclear arms control (perhaps, breaking out downward, in a manner of speaking, with unilateral cuts, the better to go upward again at will) in a bid for global dominance, and if it seeks to develop not only ballistic missile defense but—what may be more serious and technically feasible—offensive, space-based weapons, then our future framework will be neither MAD nor any version of defense dominance. It will be a hellbent military competition with the other powers of the earth—not just one but many arms races, and not, in all likelihood, in the nuclear sphere alone. Some countries will likely resort to the ugly little sisters of the family of mass destruction, chemical and biological weapons.

The great nuclear powers now rely on a system—MAD—that has lost political relevance to the world we live in. The Bush Administration has promised a new framework, in keeping with the needs of the time, but this collides both with itself and reality, political as well as technical. Absent a coherent global policy that actually does address the new shape of the nuclear predicament, events are likely to be driven in the vicious circle whose operations have already landed us in a world bristling with new nuclear dangers. Continued possession will fuel proliferation; proliferation will fuel hope for missile defense; missile defense (whether it can work or not) will disrupt arms control; and the disruption of arms control will, completing the circle, fuel proliferation. A second nuclear age has dawned, and it is running out of control. No new policies now on the horizon, in Washington or elsewhere, seem likely to turn things around anytime soon.

SECTION E.   DOES UNITED STATES PUBLIC LAW ABOUT INTERNATIONAL AGREEMENTS NEED CHANGING AND IF SO WHAT IS FEASIBLE?

Focus for the questions posed in the title. Those using this book as students will, in their professional lifetimes, probably have occasions to discharge public affairs responsibilities involving the issue whether the system of public law about treaties and other international agreements currently in place should or should not be altered. The material you have studied shows that there is an American way as to international agreements (treaties and executive agreements) that is unique in the world community. The present public law of international agreements is, of course, an important part of the foreign affairs apparatus and the operations of a super-power, and there is need for the foreign affairs ways of the United States to be better understood worldwide. On the whole they are not well understood now by the world community and remain as enigmatic as the inner mysteries of the former Soviet Union, although for different reasons.

The present public law and practice of the United States as to international agreements, internally viewed, fits reasonably well, if not perfectly, into the foreign affairs system of the country. Some argue: why bother to consider changing the former, unless the foreign affairs system can be changed, which is not likely. Others, taking into account the unlikelihood of a third United States constitution, such as a shift to a cabinet form of government would require, and the political risks of a general constitutional convention to reconsider the present Constitution across the board, support only changes in the American way with international agreements which would not alter the version of separation of powers combined with checks and balances that is the bedrock of the Constitution of 1789.

Consider, individually, whether you would change anything, support major structural change, or consider adjustments within the present system that would reduce whatever operational deficiencies exist in current American public law and practice about international agreements. If you opt for the third, the modest goal, consider the feasibility of means for change in a range from the development of non-legislated practices between the political branches, through legislation, to constitutional amendment.

CHAPTER 13

INTERNATIONAL ECONOMIC LAW

———

————

INTRODUCTION: LAW AND POLICY
Why this Chapter

We believe every person who is interested in or concerned about legal order in the world community needs to understand the basics covered in this Chapter, e.g. the rapidly expanding shifting and changing economic law sector of the international legal system. The materials chosen are broadly representative but are only a minimal introduction to specializations that are covered in advanced or graduate courses such as International Economic Law, International Business Transactions, Foreign Trade Law, and the like. This field engages more private practitioners and big law firms than any other sector. The monied levels of legal activity are so vast because the steadily increasing globalization of economic activity and the dramatic increases in world trade and direct foreign investment occurred in recent years while the legal regimes were being liberalized.

Economic equality does not prevail in our world of both "legally equal states" and various types of other international entities linked to legally equal states. There are rich states, modestly endowed states, poor states and seemingly hopeless states. The economic condition of a state is a tremendous factor in its "real-world" state of development, including politics, potential for aggression, and human rights sensitivity.

While an equilibrium of assured economic equality cannot be fashioned, it is obvious that as much as possible should be done to provide a global maximization of asset-uses. The main means are free and fair exchange of goods and services among states (Trade) and permitted and reasonably-assured movements of investment capital from state to state (Direct Foreign Investment). Some of the legal situations as to each of

977

these headings will be taken up in this Chapter. But, first, consider illustrative problems sketched below as an introduction to the subject matter in this Chapter.

———

Notes and Questions

Problem 1. Denial of entry of foreign goods. State A enjoys a large surplus of beef production, a surplus expected to continue and grow. Standards of health are quite high in State A, which fears imports from State B of meat and meat products derived from cattle produced with growth hormones. Following a "no risk" policy, State A forbids imports of such meat and products, despite the absence of scientific evidence showing health related problems with the hormones. State A refuses to carry out an assessment of the possible risks.

Problem 2. Denial of entry of foreign business capital. A high technology computer hardware manufacturer in State X decides to set up production in State Y for the State Y and near-by markets, using Y labor and materials. State Y refuses to permit the State X manufacturer to invest the requisite business capital in State Y and to commence operations.

Problem 3. Deprivation of rights flowing from ownership. A corporation organized in State Z owns 100% of two corporations chartered in State Y, one for the manufacture of industrial machinery (Sub–A) and the other for the manufacture of heavy farm equipment (Sub–B). After a long period of economic downturn, State Y expropriates both subsidiaries, without affecting other foreign manufacturers operating on its territory. No compensation is offered or paid. State Y then transfers Sub–A's assets without cost to the brother of the Finance Minister and offers for sale in international markets the assets of Sub–B.

Notwithstanding the major activities and needs reflected in the above problems, customary international law imposes no duties and creates no correlative rights governing them, except Problem 3, where the major capital-exporting states (or most of them) would argue that there is a rule of customary law requiring full compensation and some capital-receiving (usually also poor and developing) nations might disagree. Otherwise, the rules of the economic activity of international legal systems are almost entirely found in international agreements. These rules are in constant evolution toward improvement but remain ambiguous, incomplete and manipulated in their application, and many are still generally regarded as wholly unsatisfactory.

The lawyer's role in the international economic field is currently a fully active and highly important one. International lawyering in this field takes one often into national centers of law and policy and to the law in treaties. Yet the impact of international organizations like the WTO, decisions of international tribunals and the doctrines of international law publicists are steadily growing in importance to trade and investment practitioners. The market for good international lawyers in the economic sector is burgeoning, and there is every indication of still more to come in the years ahead.

* * *

Jackson, Global Economics and International Economic Law

1 J. Int'l Econ L. 1, 8 (1998).*

3.   Understanding International Economic Law

It is appropriate to ask what we mean by "international economic law". This phrase can cover a very broad inventory of subjects: embracing the law of economic transactions; government regulation of economic matters; and related legal relations including litigation and international institutions for economic relations. Indeed, it is plausible to suggest that 90 per cent of international law work is in reality international economic law in some form or another. Much of this, of course, does not have the glamour or visibility of nation-state relations (use of force, human rights, intervention etc.), but does indeed involve many questions of international law and particularly treaty law. Increasingly, today's international economic law (IEL) issues are found on the front pages of the daily newspapers.

To some extent IEL can be divided into two broad approaches which cut across most of the subjects embraced by IEL. These approaches can roughly be termed "transactional" or "regulatory". Both have their place, but activities of research and policy formulation can be substantially different, and should be understood.

Transactional IEL refers to transactions carried out in the context of international trade or other economic activities, and focuses on the way mostly private entrepreneurs or other parties carry out their activity. Much of the literature, for example, is descriptive. It can be valuable as instruction for potential players, to show "how to do it." and warn against pitfalls. It can also go further and make suggestions for change.

Regulatory IEL, however, emphasizes the role of government institutions (national, local or international). Although it can be argued that the international trade transaction is the most government regulated of all private economic transactions (usually requiring at least a report for each transaction, e.g., a customs declaration), nevertheless, most traditional attention to IEL has been focused, perhaps for practical and pragmatic reasons, on transactions. Yet arguably in today's world the real challenges for understanding IEL and its impact on governments and private citizens' lives, suggest a focus on IEL as "regulatory law", similar to domestic subjects such as tax, labour, anti-trust, and other regulatory topics.

But apart from its breadth, what are some of the characteristics of IEL which, for example, might affect the approach to it of scholars or policy makers? The following are some tentative ventures to explore these characteristics, but they are obviously by no means complete.

* Reprinted with the permission of the International Journal of Economic Law.

(1) International economic law can not be separated or compartmentalized from general or "public" international law. The activities and cases relating to IEL contain much practice which is relevant to general principles of international law, especially concerning treaty law and practice. Conversely, general international law has considerable relevance to economic relations and transactions. It is interesting, for example, to compare the number of cases handled by the GATT dispute settlement system (approximately 250) to those handled by the World Court (approaching 100). Numbers do not tell the whole tale, but there certainly are some GATT cases that have had as profound consequences on national governments and world affairs as have International Court of Justice (ICJ) cases. The GATT cases are rich with practice relating to the general question of international dispute resolution, and some of this practice has broader implications than simply for the GATT (and now WTO) system itself.

(2) The relationship of international economic law to national or "municipal" law is particularly important. It is an important part of understanding international law generally, but this "link", and the interconnections between IEL and municipal law are particularly significant to the operation and effectiveness of IEL rules. For example, an important question is the relationship of treaty norms to municipal law, expressed by such phrases as "self executing" or "direct application".

Open Markets Matter: The Benefits of Trade and Investment Liberalisation

OECD Policy Briefs, No. 6, p. 1 (1998).

Never before have so many countries at such different levels of development been involved in so much activity aimed at progressively rolling back obstacles to freer trade and investment. Yet, paradoxically, at no time during the post-war period has the prospect of further liberalisation generated so much public anxiety, not least within those countries that built much of their prosperity on a liberal trade and investment order.

* * *

The debate over open markets has changed markedly in tone and substance. Support for liberalisation has eroded in some segments of civil society in recent years because of concerns about jobs, wages, the environment and national sovereignty. Waning support points to a deficit in communications and in policy. The communications deficit can be remedied if the proponents of open markets explain clearly what trade and investment can and cannot do and what liberalisation is and is not responsible for. But it is not sufficient to point to incontrovertible evidence that liberalisation creates wealth or to the social and economic costs of failure to adjust to changing conditions. It is also necessary to confront the worries of citizens who are adversely affected by change. The challenge for policymakers is thus to design policies to help citizens and communities take advantage of the on-going, unprecedented, technology-driven structural transformation of national economies, a transformation in which trade and investment play a part, but only a part.

* * *

What are the benefits of open markets?

Trade and foreign direct investment are major engines of growth in developed and developing countries alike. Trade has consistently outperformed domestic output. The volume of world merchandise trade is 16 times greater today than it was in 1950, as compared to a six-fold increase in the volume of world production. That reflects the dismantling of import and export barriers. Outflows of foreign direct investment (FDI) have grown even faster, rising twenty-five fold during the last quarter century, from $14 billion to $350 billion a year. Trade- and investment-induced market integration has led to deeper forms of economic interdependence among nations, as a growing number of developing and former centrally-planned economies have become more closely linked to the global economy.

The case for open markets rests on solid foundations. One of these is the fact that when individuals and companies engage in specialisation and exchange, a country will exploit its comparative advantage. It will devote its natural, human, industrial and financial resources to their highest and best uses. This will provide gains to firms and consumers alike. Another is the strong preference of people the world over for more, rather than less, freedom of choice.

A more open domestic market is not a handicap; it is a source of competitive strength. Exposure to international trade is a powerful stimulus to efficiency. Efficiency, in turn, contributes to economic growth and rising incomes.

Results speak for themselves. In the last decade, countries that have been more open have achieved double the annual average growth of others. Liberalisation from the Uruguay Round alone has delivered a global tax cut estimated to be worth more than $200 billion per annum: the equivalent of adding a new Korea or Switzerland to the world economy over the next ten years. Liberalisation benefits citizens in tangible ways: in the case of Australia, for example, its recent unilateral trade liberalisation has, in effect, put A$1,000 in the hands of the average Australian family.

* * *

What is the cost of protection?

One approach has been—and remains—to protect industry and workers against imports by raising trade barriers. Societies typically pay a high price when they resort to protection. Protection raises the price of both imports and domestic products, and restricts consumer choice. It defers change and raises its cost, inflicts damage on exporting firms by making them less competitive and almost invariably translates into greater long-term hardship.

The cost to consumers of protection in OECD countries has been estimated to be as much as US$300 billion. In the United States it has been estimated that if liberalisation were stopped right now, the wages of skilled workers would decline 2—5 per cent and unskilled wages would remain flat. Imposing a 30 per cent tariff on developing country exports would inflict even greater damage; it would cut the wages of unskilled workers by 1 per cent and those of skilled workers by 5 per cent.

Protection does not deliver what it promises. The average cost to consumers of a job protected exceeds the wages of employees whose jobs are saved. In one extreme case the consumer cost of saving a single job in one OECD country was estimated to be US$600,000 per annum. Even when the cost is lower, the fact remains that protection consumes resources that could more fruitfully be used to retrain or provide transitional income support to displaced workers, or to help firms develop new products or new businesses.

How should adjustment be approached?

The fact that resort to protection is not the answer is a vital message in its own right. But it is not the whole story. Policies are still needed to ease the plight of those in the front line of adjustment. It is just as important to stress, therefore, that there is, in fact, a better way.

Properly designed labour market and social policies that provide adequate income security while facilitating the redeployment of displaced workers into expanding firms and sectors, produce important equity and efficiency gains. The effectiveness of these policies will, of course, depend on the degree of flexibility in product and labour markets, and they cannot play this role in isolation from a range of other policies. In fact, a much broader strategy is called for, one capable of increasing the flexibility of markets, upgrading the skills of workers and raising workforce mobility. Areas such as regulatory reform, education, training, taxation, pension reform and the portability of health benefits (where that is an issue) need to be dealt with in a comprehensive way. This will ensure that citizens and communities are able to take advantage of and adjust to the foremost challenge they face, technology-driven structural change.

In sum, a balanced mix of policies is needed to reinforce adaptive capacity in the face of all structural changes, including those stemming from trade and investment liberalisation. Social protection policies also need to be reoriented to ensure that those who lose their jobs—including as a result of trade or investment liberalisation—are insured against excessive income loss during the period of search for a new job. There is no inevitable connection between increased openness and less social protection. In fact, increased international trade and investment is an additional reason to improve the efficiency of public systems of social protection, rather than a rationale for reducing them.

* * *

How does market openness affect national sovereignty?

There are concerns about the way in which market openness many affect national sovereignty. More particularly, there are concerns that increasing trade and investment flows, and multilateral rules for trade and investment, may erode the capacity of governments to exercise national "regulatory" sovereignty. That is, to decide the appropriate policies and regulatory approaches for their own country or region, on issues such as environmental protection or consumer health and safety, as well as on trade and investment matters. There is also a perception that multilateral agreements encourage or even require such regulatory standards to be reduced, eliminated or harmonised.

Trade and investment liberalisation in fact forms part of a country's overall strategy to maintain and even strengthen its capacity to determine its own future (and thus its sovereignty), by improving its competitiveness and raising incomes, and making it less vulnerable to external shocks. Thus liberalisation and regulatory reform are undertaken by national governments (whether unilaterally or in the context of international negotiations between sovereign governments) to enhance national interests. Such decisions are made precisely in order to gain the added security, stability and enhanced prospects for national welfare, that internationally agreed rules provide. An agreement such as the WTO is essentially an exercise of national sovereignty rather than a surrender of it.

Multilateral trade and investment agreements do not regard all national regulatory measures simply as unnecessary. Nor do they require the removal of all barriers to foreign trade and investment or that all of these be lowered. Indeed, governments retain the sovereign right to set their own objectives on such matters. The rules do require countries to prepare, implement and administer national regulations that affect foreign goods, services and investment in a transparent, non-arbitrary and non-discriminatory way. But that is because governments have taken a sovereign decision to abide by such rules. And they have done so because they recognise that such principles help to promote fairness and stability in an international economy in which all countries have a stake and from which they benefit themselves. Such agreements explicitly provide that high-quality effective national regulation be permitted to work properly in a number of areas. Where the rules place limits on recourse to certain trade or investment restrictions, for environmental or other purposes, this arises from the agreement of sovereign member countries that it is in their mutual interest to have each other do so. Moreover, the WTO rules and dispute settlement processes recognise that there can be legitimate grounds for exceptions from these rules in certain circumstances, or to achieve other policy objectives.

* * *

SECTION A. INTERNATIONAL TRADE LAW

The shipment arrives at the frontier, usually pre-cleared, or delivered directly to a customs broker. The bill of lading describes the contents, using, if possible, the customs nomenclature of the receiving state. The goods are inspected for the accuracy and the veracity of the importer's classification. The customs inspector may change the classification and hence also the rate of duty, classifications being numerous, narrow, and sometimes surprisingly (or shockingly) variant as between items that seem not to be very different. (These differences may reflect hidden protectionism, sometimes ancient, with reasons forgotten.) If the importer does not accept a re-classification, a lawyer specializing in trade law has to be engaged to take the dispute through administrative review, and eventually, if necessary, judicial review. There is a whole body of specialist law about customs classification (and levy) issues. Note that the foregoing refers to trade in goods and things, not services. Services do not ordinarily receive customs classification for the levy of duties. Entry or denial is a matter of host state control not unlike those on direct foreign investments, treated in Section B.

There are import controls other than custom duties: quotas, sanitary and safety regulations, and importing state sanctions or other inducements to the exporting state to conform to some value or standard of interest to the import state. Quotas as to quantity or value have been often of more concern to foreign suppliers than customs duties, particularly when rates of duty have been reduced to low percentages of value, as they are now. You will see later that trade liberation arrangements, such as the WTO, approach the rate of duty and quota problems along somewhat different lines. As to health, sanitary and safety regulations, contemporary news reports of American exporters' complaints about import country "assessment" delays and alleged overreaching standards have probably come to your attention. As you will see, some of most forthcoming rule systems in world trade, like health, safety and environment, can be used as subtle or not so subtle non-tariff barriers to otherwise desirable trade.

Prohibition of imports from a particular source for foreign policy reasons or national moral values (such as human rights) involves the legal pros and cons of "economic sanctions" at times in the form of boycotts. So do controls (including absolute prohibitions) on the export of materials and devices deemed of national security concern. Exports of most goods from the U.S. require notification to the government but no longer an export licence. For security or foreign policy reasons, there are numerous restrictions appearing in an elaborate administrative regime that restricts such sensitive exports by product and destination country. Lawyers play important roles in this sector in advising clients in the face of heavy penalties for violation (including possible ban on all exporting), and in the administrative and judicial review process governing U.S. exports.

Finally, as to the customs process: beyond what happens at the customs frontier, there are in the United States and elsewhere, rather vast and complicated administrative law procedures, and in the United States, federal judicial review. To these must now be added the growing international dimension, seen dramatically in the regulatory and dispute settlement systems of the World Trade Organization.

1.   THE WORLD TRADE ORGANIZATION

What is the World Trade Organization?
www.wto.org/wto 1999, visited on 10 June, 1999.

The World Trade Organization (WTO) is the only international body dealing with the rules of trade between nations. At its heart are the WTO agreements, negotiated and signed by the bulk of the world's trading nations. These documents provide the legal ground-rules for international commerce. They are essentially contracts, binding governments to keep their trade policies within agreed limits. Although negotiated and signed by governments, the goal is to help producers of goods and services, exporters, and importers conduct their business.

Three main purposes

The system's overriding purpose is to help trade flow as freely as possible—so long as there are no undesirable side-effects. That partly means removing obstacles. It also means ensuring that individuals, companies and governments know what the trade rules are around the world, and giving them the confidence that there will be no sudden changes of policy. In other words, the rules have to be "transparent" and predictable.

Because the agreements are drafted and signed by the community of trading nations, often after considerable debate and controversy, one of the WTO's most important functions is to serve as a forum for trade negotiations.

A third important side to the WTO's work is dispute settlement. Trade relations often involve conflicting interests. Contracts and agreements, including those painstakingly negotiated in the WTO system, often need interpreting. The most harmonious way to settle these differences is through some neutral procedure based on an agreed legal foundation. That is the purpose behind the dispute settlement process written into the WTO agreements.

* * * The WTO began life on I January 1995, but its trading system is half a century older. Since 1948, the General Agreement on Tariffs and Trade (GATT) had provided the rules for the system. Before long it gave birth to an unofficial, *de facto* international organization, also known informally as GATT, and over the years GATT evolved through several rounds of negotiations.

The latest and largest round, was the Uruguay Round which lasted from 1986 to 1994 and led to the WTO's creation. Whereas GATT had mainly dealt with trade in goods, the WTO and its agreements now cover trade in services and in traded inventions, creations and designs (intellectual property).

* * *

Principles of the Trading System

The WTO agreements are lengthy and complex because they are legal texts covering a wide range of activities. They deal with: agriculture, textiles and clothing, banking, telecommunications, government purchases, industrial standards, food sanitation regulations, intellectual property, and much more. But a number of simple, fundamental principles run throughout all of these documents. These principles are the foundation of the multilateral trading system.

The principles

The trading system should be

— without discrimination—a country should not discriminate between its trading partners (they are all, equally, granted "most-favoured-nation" or MFN status); and it should not discriminate between its own and foreign products, services or nationals (they are given "national treatment").

— freer—with barriers coming down through negotiation.

— predictable—foreign companies, investors and governments should be confident that trade barriers (including tariffs, non-tariff barriers and other measures) should not be raised arbitrarily; more and more tariff rates and market-opening commitments are "bound" in the WTO.

— more competitive—by discouraging "unfair" practices such as export subsidies and dumping products at below cost to gain market share.

— more beneficial for less developed countries—by giving them more time to adjust, greater flexibility, and special privileges.

A closer look at these principles:

Trade without discrimination

1. Most-favoured-nation (MFN): treating other people equally

Under the WTO Agreements, countries cannot normally discriminate between their trading partners. Grant someone a special favour (such as a lower customs duty rate for one of their products) and you have to do the same for all other WTO members. This principle is known as most-favoured-nation (MFN) treatment * * *

It is so important that it is the first article of the General Agreement on Tariffs and Trade (GATT), which governs trade in goods. MFN is also a priority in the General Agreement on Trade in Services (GATS) (Article 2) and the Agreement on Trade–Related Aspects of Intellectual Property Rights (TRIPS) (Article 4), although in each agreement the principle is handled slightly differently. Together, those three agreements cover all three main areas of trade handled by the WTO.

Why is it called "most-favoured"?

The name sounds like a contradiction. It suggests some kind of special treatment for one particular country, but in the WTO it actually means non-discrimination—treating virtually everyone equally.

What happens under the WTO is this. Each member treats all the other members equally as "most-favoured" trading partners. If a country improves the benefits that it gives to one trading partner, it has to give the same "best" treatment to all the other WTO members so that they all remain "most-favoured".

Most-favoured nation (MFN) status did not always mean equal treatment. In the 19th Century, when a number of early bilateral MFN treaties were signed, being included among a country's "most-favoured" trading partners was like being in an exclusive club because only a few countries enjoyed the privilege. Now, when most countries are in the WTO, the MFN club is no longer exclusive. The MFN principle ensures that each country treats its over–100 fellow-members equally. But there are some exceptions . . .

Some exceptions are allowed. For example, countries within a region can set up a free trade agreement that does not apply to goods from outside the group. Or a country can raise barriers against products from specific countries that are considered to be traded unfairly. And in services, countries are allowed, in limited circumstances, to discriminate. But the agreements only permit these exceptions under strict conditions. In general, MFN means that every time a country lowers a trade barrier or opens up a market, it has to do so for the same goods or services from all its trading partners—whether rich or poor, weak or strong.

2. National treatment: treating foreigners and locals equally

Imported and locally-produced goods should be treated equally—at least after the foreign goods have entered the market. The same should apply to foreign and domestic services, and to foreign and local trademarks, copyrights and patents. This principle of "national treatment" (giving others the same treatment as one's own nationals) is also found in all the three main WTO agreements (Article 3 of GATT, Article 17 of GATS and Article 3 of TRIPS), although once again the principle is handled slightly differently in each of these.

National treatment only applies once a product, service or item of intellectual property has entered the market. Therefore, charging customs duty on an import is not a violation of national treatment even if locally-produced products are not charged an equivalent tax.

Freer trade: gradually, through negotiation

Lowering trade barriers is one of the most obvious means of encouraging trade. The barriers concerned include customs duties (or tariffs) and measures such as import bans or quotas that restrict quantities selectively. From time to time other issues such as red tape and exchange rate policies have also been discussed.

Since GATT's creation in 1947–48 there have been eight rounds of trade negotiations. At first these focused on lowering tariffs (customs duties) on imported goods. As a result of the negotiations, by the late 1980s industrial countries' tariff rates on industrial goods had fallen steadily to about 6.3% [by 2001 closer to 4%]. But by the 1980s, the negotiations had expanded to cover non-tariff barriers on goods, and to the new areas such as services and intellectual property. Opening markets can be beneficial, but it also requires adjustment. The WTO agreements allow countries to introduce changes gradually, through "progressive liberalization". Developing countries are usually given longer to fulfil their obligations.

Predictability: through binding

Sometimes, promising not to raise a trade barrier can be as important as lowering one, because the promise gives businesses a clearer view of their future opportunities. With stability and predictability, investment is encouraged, jobs are created and consumers can fully enjoy the benefits of competition—choice and lower prices. The multilateral trading system is an attempt by governments to make the business environment stable and predictable.

In the WTO, when countries agree to open their markets for goods or services, they "bind" their commitments. For goods, these bindings amount to ceilings on customs tariff rates. Sometimes countries tax imports at rates that are lower than the bound rates. Frequently this is the case in developing countries. In developed countries the rates actually charged and the bound rates tend to be the same.

A country can change its bindings, but only after negotiating with its trading partners, which could mean compensating them for loss of trade. One of the achievements of the Uruguay Round of multilateral trade talks was to increase the amount of trade under binding commitments * * *. In agriculture, 100% of products now have bound tariffs. The result of all this: a substantially higher degree of market security for traders and investors.

The system tries to improve predictability and stability in other ways as well. One way is to discourage the use of quotas and other measures used to set limits on quantities of imports—administering quotas can lead to more red-tape and accusations of unfair play. Another is to make countries' trade rules as clear and public ("transparent") as possible. Many WTO agreements require governments to disclose their policies and practices publicly within the country or by notifying the WTO. The regular surveillance of national trade policies through the Trade Policy Review Mechanism provides a further means of encouraging transparency both domestically and at the multilateral level.

Promoting fair competition

The WTO is sometimes described as a "free trade institution", but that is not entirely accurate. The system does allow tariffs and, in limited circumstances, other forms of protection. More accurately open, it is a system of rules dedicated to open, fair and undistorted competition.

The rules on non-discrimination—MFN and national treatment—are designed to secure fair conditions of trade. So too are those on dumping (exporting at below cost to gain market share) and subsidies. The issues are complex, and the rules try to establish what is fair or unfair, and how governments can respond, in particular by charging additional import duties calculated to compensate for damage caused by unfair trade.

Many of the other WTO agreements aim to support fair competition: in agriculture, intellectual property, services, for example. The agreement on government procurement (a "plurilateral" agreement because it is signed by only a few WTO members) extends competition rules to purchases by thousands of "government" entities in many countries. * * *

Encouraging development and economic reform

It is widely recognized by economists and trade experts that the WTO system contributes to development. It is also recognized that the least-developed countries need flexibility in the time they take to implement the agreements. And the agreements themselves inherit the earlier provisions of GATT that allow for special assistance and trade concessions for developing countries. Over three-quarters of WTO members are developing countries and countries in transition to market economies. During the seven and a half years of the Uruguay Round, over 60 of these countries implemented trade liberalization programmes autonomously. At the same time, developing countries and transition economies were much more active and influential in the Uruguay Round negotiations than in any previous round.

This trend effectively killed the notion that the trading system existed only for industrialized countries. It also changed the previous emphasis on exempting developing countries from certain GATT provisions and agreements.

At the end of the Uruguay Round, developing countries were prepared to take on most of the obligations that are required of developed countries. But the agreements did give them transition periods to adjust to the more unfamiliar and, perhaps, difficult WTO provisions—particularly so for the poorest, "least-developed" countries. A ministerial decision adopted at the end of the round gives least developed countries extra flexibility in implementing WTO agreements. It says better-off countries should accelerate implementing market access commitments on goods exported by the least-developed countries, and it seeks increased technical assistance for them.

Agreement Establishing the World Trade Organization[a]
www.wto.org/ 1999.

Article II

Scope of the WTO

1. The WTO shall provide the common institutional framework for the conduct of trade relations among its Members in matters related to the agreements and associated legal instruments included in the Annexes to this Agreement.

2. The agreements and associated legal instruments included in Annexes 1, 2 and 3 (hereinafter referred to as "Multilateral Trade Agreements") are integral parts of this Agreement, binding on all Members.

3. The agreements and associated legal instruments included in Annex 4 (hereinafter referred to as "Plurilateral Trade Agreements") are also part of this Agreement for those Members that have accepted them, and are binding on those Members. The Plurilateral Trade Agreements do not create either obligations or rights for Members that have not accepted them.

4. The General Agreement on Tariffs and Trade 1994 as specified in Annex 1A (hereinafter referred to as "GATT 1994") is legally distinct from the General Agreement on Tariffs and Trade, dated 30 October 1947,

---

a. On 30 November 2000, the membership of the WTO consisted of 140 states and the European Communities.

annexed to the Final Act Adopted at the Conclusion of the Second Session of the Preparatory Committee of the United Nations Conference on Trade and Employment, as subsequently rectified, amended or modified (hereinafter referred to as "GATT 1947").

Article III
Functions of the WTO

1. The WTO shall facilitate the implementation, administration and operation, and further the objectives, of this Agreement and of the Multilateral Trade Agreements, and shall also provide the framework for the implementation, administration and operation of the Plurilateral Trade Agreements.

2. The WTO shall provide the forum for negotiations among its Members concerning their multilateral trade relations in matters dealt with under the agreements in the Annexes to this Agreement. The WTO may also provide a forum for further negotiations among its Members concerning their multilateral trade relations, and a framework for the implementation of the results of such negotiations, as may be decided by the Ministerial Conference.

3. The WTO shall administer the Understanding on Rules and Procedures Governing the Settlement of Disputes (hereinafter referred to as the "Dispute Settlement Understanding" or "DSU") in Annex 2 to this Agreement.

4. The WTO shall administer the Trade Policy Review Mechanism (hereinafter referred to as the "TPRM") provided for in Annex 3 to this Agreement.

5. With a view to achieving greater coherence in global economic policy-making, the WTO shall cooperate, as appropriate, with the International Monetary Fund and with the International Bank for Reconstruction and Development and its affiliated agencies.

LIST OF **ANNEXES**
ANNEX 1

ANNEX 1A: Multilateral Agreements on Trade in Goods

General Agreement on Tariffs and Trade 1994

Agreement on Agriculture

Agreement on the Application of Sanitary and Phytosanitary Measures

Agreement on Textiles and Clothing

Agreement on Technical Barriers to Trade

Agreement on Trade–Related Investment Measures

Agreement on Implementation of Article VI of the General Agreement on Tariffs and Trade 1994

Agreement on Implementation of Article VII of the General Agreement on Tariffs and Trade 1994

Agreement on Preshipment Inspection

Agreement on Rules of Origin

Agreement on Import Licensing Procedures

Agreement on Subsidies and Countervailing Measures

Agreement on Safeguards

ANNEX 1B: General Agreement on Trade in Services and Annexes

ANNEX 1C: Agreement on Trade–Related Aspects of Intellectual Property Rights

ANNEX 2

Understanding on Rules and Procedures Governing the Settlement of Disputes

ANNEX 3

Trade Policy Review Mechanism

ANNEX 4

Plurilateral Trade Agreements

Agreement on Trade in Civil Aircraft

Agreement on Government Procurement

International Dairy Agreement

International Bovine Meat Agreement

2. WTO's MANAGEMENT OF TRADE DISPUTES

Jackson, The World Trade Organization: Constitution & Jurisprudence

pp. 59–88, (1998).*

4.1 The policies of dispute settlement procedures

For a variety of reasons, dispute settlement procedures have been growing in importance as an essential part of international economic relations and the diplomacy for those relations. The last decade of GATT, 1985–94, saw greatly increased attention to the dispute settlement procedures, and that attention continued to increase after the Uruguay Round treaty introduced numerous reforms in those procedures. Both WTO and important national leaders have lauded the dispute settlement procedures in the WTO, making them almost the centrepiece of the new Organization. For example, WTO Director–General Renato Ruggiero said in a Special Report of 30 September 1996 concerning preparations for the first Ministerial Conference in December 1996 in Singapore:

One success that stands out above all the rest is the strengthening of the dispute settlement mechanism. This is the heart of the WTO system. Not only has it proved credible and effective in dealing with disputes, it has

* Reprinted with the permission of the
Royal Institute of International Affairs.

helped resolve a significant number at the consultation stage. Furthermore, developing countries have become major users of the system, a sign of their confidence in it which was not so apparent under the old system.

* * *

Officials of the United States have several times expressed satisfaction with the procedures and noted their importance in the diplomacy of the United States.

However, throughout the history of the GATT, and now in the WTO, there has been some ambivalence about the appropriate role of dispute settlement procedures. To over-generalize a bit, there were roughly two viewpoints: one favours a "negotiation" or "diplomacy"-oriented approach whereby dispute settlement procedures should not be juridical or "legalistic", but should simply assist negotiators to resolve differences through negotiation and compromise. Another approach views the dispute settlement procedure as a relatively disciplined juridical process by which an impartial panel could make objective rulings about whether or not certain activities were consistent with GATT obligations.

I suggest that the rule-oriented approach, particularly concerning international economic affairs, has considerable advantage. It is this approach that focuses the disputing parties' attention on the rule, and on predicting what an impartial tribunal is likely to conclude about the application of a rule. This in turn will lead parties to pay closer attention to the rules of the treaty system, and hence can lead to greater certainty and predictability—essential in international affairs, particularly *economic* affairs driven by market-oriented principles of decentralized decision-making, with participation by millions of entrepreneurs. Such entrepreneurs need a certain amount of predictability and guidance so that they can make the appropriate efficient investment and market development decisions.

With a rule-oriented approach, then, there often could be some reduction in risk for the various decisions and for longer-term planning. Thus, the need for a higher rate of return to accommodate the "risk premium" of a venture would be reduced, and the risk premium lowered. This should result in a general increase in the efficiency of various economic activities, contributing to greater welfare for everyone.

The phrase "rule orientation" is used here to contrast with phrases such as "rule of law", and "rule-based system". Rule orientation implies a less rigid adherence to 'rule' and connotes some fluidity in rule approaches which seems to accord with reality (especially since it accommodates some bargaining or negotiation). Phrases that emphasize too strongly the strict application of rules sometimes scare policy-makers, although in reality the different phrases may amount to the same thing. Any legal system must accommodate the inherent ambiguities of rules and the constant changes of practical needs of human society. The key point is that the procedures of rule application, which often centre on a dispute settlement procedure, should be designed so as to promote as much as possible the stability and predictability of the rule system. For this purpose the procedure must be creditable, "legitimate", and reasonably efficient—not easy criteria.

* * *

4.3 The DSU and outline of procedure

The new text solves many, although not all, of the issues that have plagued the GATT dispute settlement system. It accomplishes the following:

(1) It establishes a unified dispute settlement system for all parts of the GATT/WTO system, including the new subjects of services and intellectual property. Thus, controversies over which procedure to use will not occur.

(2) It clarifies that all parts of the Uruguay Round legal text relevant to the matter in issue and argued by the parties can be considered in a particular dispute case.

(3) It reaffirms and clarifies the right of a complaining government to have a panel process initiated, preventing blocking at that stage.

(4) It establishes a unique new appellate procedure which will substitute for some of the former procedures of Council approval of a panel report. Thus, a panel report will effectively be deemed adopted by the new Dispute Settlement Body (DSB), unless it is appealed by one of the parties to the dispute. If appealed, the dispute will go to an appellate division. After the Appellate Body has ruled, its report will go to the DSB, but in this case it will be deemed adopted unless there is a consensus against adoption, and presumably that negative consensus can be defeated by any major objector. Thus, the presumption is the reverse of previous procedures, with the ultimate result that the appellate report will come into force as a matter of international law in virtually every case. The opportunity for a losing party to block the adoption of a panel report will no longer be available.

The DSU is designed to provide a single unified dispute settlement procedure for almost all the Uruguay Round texts. However, there remain some potential disparities. Many of the separate documents entitled "agreements", including the GATT in Annex IA and certain other texts such as the subsidies "code" or the textiles text, have clauses in them relating to dispute settlement. But the DSU Article I provides that the DSU rules and procedures shall apply to all disputes concerning "covered agreements" listed in a DSU Appendix, so presumably this trumps most of the specific dispute settlement procedures.

However, even the DSU provisions allow for some disparity. For example, parties to each of the plurilateral agreements (Annex 4) may make a decision regarding dispute settlement procedures and how the DSU shall apply (or not apply). In addition, another DSU appendix specifies exceptions for certain listed texts. Thus, the goal of uniformity of dispute settlement procedures may not be 100% achieved. Actual practice will determine to what degree this may be a problem.

    * * *

Now in turning to the new WTO procedures, we can see that these problems are part of the broader question of the legal effect of a final ruling of the dispute settlement process (that is, a report of a dispute settlement panel, or the appellate division which judges an appeal from the first-level dispute settlement report). There is some controversy about the legal status of such a report when adopted (as it will almost automatically be, under the new WTO procedures). The specific question here is whether the international law obligation deriving from such a report gives the option either to compensate with trade or other measures, or alternatively to fulfil the recommendation of the report which mandates that the member bring its practices or law into consistency with the international law treaty texts of the annexes to the WTO. In other words, does it give the choice to "compensate" or obey? There has been some confusion about this, and some important leaders, of major trading entities of the WTO have made statements that indicate this confusion, that are misleading, and that in some cases are flatly wrong. The alternative interpretation to those mentioned above is that an adopted dispute settlement report establishes an international law obligation upon the member to which the findings are directed to change its practice so as to make it consistent with the treaty text obligations of the WTO and annexed agreements. In this view, the "compensation" (or retaliation) approach is only a fall-back in the event of non-compliance. This latter approach to the question seems correct.

* * *

* * * the DSU clearly establishes a preference for an *obligation to perform* the recommendation, notes that the matter be kept under surveillance until performance has occurred, indicates compensation shall be resorted to only if the *immediate* withdrawal of the measure is impracticable, and provides that in non-violation cases, there is no obligation to withdraw an offending measure, which strongly implies that for *violation* cases, there *is* an obligation to conform.

It is true that, once the "binding" international law obligation to follow a dispute report recommendation has been established, international law has a variety of ways of dealing with a breach of such obligation, and that, understandably, those methods available to the international law system are not always very effective. However, that is a different issue from the question of whether the "WTO rules are . . . binding in the traditional sense". Certainly they are binding in the traditional *international law* sense. In fact, for many national legal systems, they are also binding in the "traditional sense" domestically, although not always in a "statute-like" sense. In the U.S. it can be argued that the WTO rules, and certainly therefore the results of a dispute settlement report, do not *ipso facto* become part of the domestic jurisprudence that courts are bound to follow as a matter of judicial notice, etc. However, the international law "bindingness" of a report certainly can and should have an important effect in domestic US jurisprudence, as in the jurisprudence of many other nation-states.

EC Measures Concerning Meat and Meat Products (Hormones)

WTO Appellate Body Report, European Communities, Approved 16 January, 1998. WT/DS26/AB/R. WT/DS48/AB/R

[These are appeals by the European Communities (EC) , the U.S. and Canada from Panel Reports on complaints of the U. S. and Canada against the EC. The appeals relate to an EC ban on imports into the EC of meat and meat products of farm animals treated with certain growth hormones. A 1997 EC Directive prohibited the use of the hormones, and the sale and importation into the EC of the affected meat and products. A US effort to counter an earlier, parallel EC Directive was successfully blocked by the EC in 1987 under the then applicable GATT 1947 Standards Code procedures requiring consensus to move forward. This early history is recounted in Dick, Note, 10 Mich. J. Int. L. 872 (1989).

Under the new WTO rules, the U.S. and Canada commenced the present proceeding challenging the 1997 Directive. They charged the EC with failing to comply with the WTO's Agreement on the Application of Sanitary and Phytosanitary Measures (SPS) which confirms the right of Members to take trade measures necessary to protect "human, animal or plant life or health" but only when the measures are consistent with this Agreement (Article 2.1). Reflecting concerns about Members using such measures as non-tariff trade barriers, ¶ 3 of Article 2 provides that:

> 3. Members shall ensure that their sanitary or phytosanitary measures do not arbitrarily or unjustifiably discriminate between Members where identical or similar conditions prevail, including between their own territory and that of other Members. Sanitary and phytosanitary measures shall not be applied in a manner which would constitute a disguised restriction on international trade.

Provisions governing the assessment of risk include the following article 5:

> 1. Members shall ensure that their sanitary and phytosanitary measures are based on an assessment, as appropriate to the circumstances, of the risks to human, animal or plant life, taking into account risk assessment techniques developed by the relevant international organizations.

> 2. In the assessment of risks, members shall take into account available scientific evidence; relevant processes and production methods; relevant inspection, sampling and testing methods; prevalence of specific diseases or pests; existence of pest-or disease-free areas; relevant ecological and environmental conditions; quarantine or other treatment.

A portion of the Appellate Body's Report follows.]

VI. The Relevance of the Precautionary Principle in the Interpretation of the *SPS Agreement*

120. We are asked by the European Communities to reverse the finding of the Panel relating to the precautionary principle. The Panel's finding and its supporting statements are set out in the Panel Reports in the following terms:

> The European Communities also invokes the precautionary principle in support of its claim that its measures in dispute are based on a risk assessment. To the extent that this principle could be considered as part of customary international law *and* be used to interpret Articles 5.1 and 5.2 on the assessment of risks as a customary rule of interpretation of public international law (as that phrase is used in

Article 3.2 of the DSU), we consider that *this principle would not override the explicit wording of Articles 5.1 and 5.2 outlined above*, in particular since the precautionary principle has been incorporated and given a specific meaning in Article 5.7 of the SPS Agreement. We note, however, that the European Communities has explicitly stated in this case that it is not invoking Article 5.7.

We thus find that *the precautionary principle cannot override our findings made above*, namely that the EC import ban of meat and meat products from animals treated with any of the five hormones at issue for growth promotion purposes, in so far as it also applies to meat and meat products from animals treated with any of these hormones *in accordance with good practice*, is, from a substantive point of view, not *based on a risk assessment*. (emphasis added) [by the Appellate Body]

121.   The basic submission of the European Communities is that the precautionary principle is, or has become, "a general customary rule of international law" or at least "a general principle of law". Referring more specifically to Articles 5.1 and 5.2 of the *SPS Agreement*, applying the precautionary principle means, in the view of the European Communities, that it is not necessary for *all* scientists around the world to agree on the "possibility and magnitude" of the risk, nor for *all* or most of the WTO Members to perceive and evaluate the risk in the same way. It is also stressed that Articles 5.1 and 5.2 do not prescribe a particular type of risk assessment and do not prevent Members from being cautious in their risk assessment exercise. The European Communities goes on to state that its measures here at stake were precautionary in nature and satisfied the requirements of Articles 2.2 and 2.3, as well as of Articles 5.1, 5.2, 5.4, 5.5 and 5.6 of the *SPS Agreement*.

122.   The United States does not consider that the "precautionary principle" represents customary international law and suggests it is more an "approach" than a "principle". Canada, too, takes the view that the precautionary principle has not yet been incorporated into the corpus of public international law; however, it concedes that the "precautionary approach" or "concept" is "an *emerging* principle of law" which may in the future crystallize into one of the "general principles of law recognized by civilized nations" within the meaning of Article 38(1)(c) of the *Statute of the International Court of Justice*.

123.   The status of the precautionary principle in international law continues to be the subject of debate among academics, law practitioners, regulators and judges. The precautionary principle is regarded by some as having crystallized into a general principle of customary international *environmental* law. Whether it has been widely accepted by Members as a principle of *general* or *customary international law* appears less than clear.[92] We consider, however, that it is unnecessary, and probably impru-

---

92.   Editor's note. Authors like P. Sands, J. Cameron and J. Abouchar, while recognizing that the principle is still evolving, submit nevertheless that there is currently sufficient state practice to support the view that the precautionary principle is a principle of customary international law. See, for example, Sands, *Principles of International Environmental Law*, Vol. I (1995) p. 212; Cameron, "The Status of the Precautionary Principle in International Law", in Cameron and O'Riordan (eds.), *Interpreting the Precautionary Principle* (Cameron May, 1994) 262, p. 283; Cameron and Abouchar, "The

dent, for the Appellate Body in this appeal to take a position on this important, but abstract, question. We note that the Panel itself did not make any definitive finding with regard to the status of the precautionary principle in international law and that the precautionary principle, at least outside the field of international environmental law, still awaits authoritative formulation.[93]

124.   It appears to us important, nevertheless, to note some aspects of the relationship of the precautionary principle to the *SPS Agreement*. First, the principle has not been written into the *SPS_Agreement* as a ground for justifying SPS measures that are otherwise inconsistent with the obligations of Members set out in particular provisions of that Agreement. Secondly, the precautionary principle indeed finds reflection in Article 5.7 of the *SPS Agreement*. We agree, at the same time, with the European Communities, that there is no need to assume that Article 5.7 exhausts the relevance of a precautionary principle. It is reflected also in the sixth paragraph of the preamble and in Article 3.3. These explicitly recognize the right of Members to establish their own appropriate level of sanitary protection, which level may be higher (i.e., more cautious) than that implied in existing international standards, guidelines and recommendations. Thirdly, a panel charged with determining, for instance, whether "sufficient scientific evidence" exists to warrant the maintenance by a Member of a particular SPS measure may, of course, and should, bear in mind that responsible, representative governments commonly act from perspectives of prudence and precaution where risks of irreversible, e.g. life-terminating, damage to human health are concerned. Lastly, however, the precautionary principle does not, by itself, and without a clear textual directive to that effect, relieve a panel from the duty of applying the normal

Status of the Precautionary Principle in International Law", in Freestone and Hey (eds.), *The Precautionary Principle in International Law* (1996) 29, p. 52. Other authors argue that the precautionary principle has not yet reached the status of a principle of international law, or at least, consider such status doubtful, among other reasons, due to the fact that the principle is still subject to a great variety of interpretations. See, for example, Birnie and Boyle, *International Law and the Environment* (1992), p. 98; Gündling, "The Status in International Law of the Precautionary Principle" (1990), 5:1,2,3 *International Journal of Estuarine and Coastal Law* 25, p. 30; de Mestral (et. al), *International Law Chiefly as Interpreted and Applied in Canada*, 5th ed. (Emond Montgomery, 1993), p. 765; Bodansky, in *Proceedings of the 85th Annual Meeting of the American Society of International Law* (ASIL, 1991), p. 415.

93. In *Case Concerning the Gabcíkovo-Nagymaros Project (Hungary/Slovakia)*, the International Court of Justice recognized_that in the field of environmental protection "... new norms and standards have been developed, set forth in a great number of instruments during the last two decades. Such new norms have to be taken into consideration, and such new standards given proper weight ...". However, we note that the Court did not identify the precautionary principle as one of those recently developed norms. It also declined to declare that such principle could override the obligations of the Treaty between Czechoslovakia and Hungary of 16 September 1977 concerning the construction and operation of the Gabcíkovo/Nagymaros System of Locks. See, *Case Concerning the Gabcíkovo-Nagymaros Project (Hungary/Slovakia)*, I.C.J. Judgement, 25 September 1997, paras. 140, 111–114. Not yet reported in the I.C.J. Reports but available on internet at http://www.icj-cij.org/idecis.htm.

(i.e. customary international law) principles of treaty interpretation in reading the provisions of the *SPS Agreement*.

125. We accordingly agree with the finding of the Panel that the precautionary principle does not override the provisions of Articles 5.1 and 5.2 of the *SPS Agreement*.

XIV. Findings and Conclusions

* * *

255. The Appellate Body *recommends* that the Dispute Settlement Body request the European Communities to bring the SPS measures found in this Report and in the Panel Reports, as modified by this Report, to be inconsistent with the *SPS Agreement* into conformity with the obligations of the European Communities under that Agreement.

Note

After the Dispute Settlement Body acted favorably (by reverse consensus) on the above Appellate Body Report, the EC announced that it intended to fulfill its obligations and that it was examining the options for compliance. However, when the parties were unable to agree on the required "reasonable time for implementation", the EC requested that it be determined by binding arbitration under DSB rules. Unable to agree on an arbitrator, the parties requested the WTO Director–General to make the appointment in accord with the applicable rules. The EC requested 4 years (later reduced to 39 months), and the U.S. and Canada requested 10 months. The arbitrator adopted 15 months, expiring on 13 May 1999. The EC not having taken measures of compliance with the decision of the Dispute Settlement body, the United States and Canada faced the questions of (1) what additional procedures might be useful or required within the WTO, and (2) whether enforcement sanctions should be sought. These questions brought into play the WTO and United States trade sanction rules addressed in the following pages.

3. MULTILATERAL VERSUS UNILATERAL ENFORCEMENT SANCTIONS

WTO Agreement, Annex 2: Understanding on Rules and Procedures Governing the Settlement of Disputes

Members hereby agree as follows:

Article 1: Coverage and Application

1. The rules and procedures of this Understanding shall apply to disputes brought pursuant to the consultation and dispute settlement provisions of the agreements listed in Appendix 1 to this Understanding (referred to in this Understanding as the "covered agreements"). The rules and procedures of this Understanding shall also apply to consultations and the settlement of disputes between Members concerning their rights and

obligations under the provisions of the Agreement Establishing the World Trade Organization (referred to in this Understanding as the "WTO Agreement") and of this Understanding taken in isolation or in combination with any other covered agreement.

Article 22: Compensation and the Suspension of Concessions

1. Compensation and the suspension of concessions or other obligations are temporary measures available in the event that the recommendations and rulings are not implemented within a reasonable period of time. However, neither compensation nor the suspension of concessions or other obligations is preferred to full implementation of a recommendation to bring a measure into conformity with the covered agreements. Compensation is voluntary and, if granted, shall be consistent with the covered agreements.

2. If the Member concerned fails to bring the measure found to be inconsistent with a covered agreement into compliance therewith or otherwise comply with the recommendations and rulings within the reasonable period of time determined pursuant to paragraph 3 of Article 21, such Member shall, if so requested, and no later than the expiry of the reasonable period of time, enter into negotiations with any party having invoked the dispute settlement procedures, with a view to developing mutually acceptable compensation. If no satisfactory compensation has been agreed within 20 days after the date of expiry of the reasonable period of time, any party having invoked the dispute settlement procedures may request authorization from the DSB to suspend the application to the Member concerned of concessions or other obligations under the covered agreements.

4. The level of the suspension of concessions or other obligations authorized by the DSB shall be equivalent to the level of the nullification or impairment.

6. When the situation described in ¶ 2 occurs, the DSB, upon request, shall grant authorization to suspend concessions or other obligations within 30 days of the expiry of the reasonable period of time unless the DSB decides by consensus to reject the request. However, if the Member concerned objects to the level of suspension proposed, or claims that the principles and procedures set forth in ¶ 3 have not been followed where a complaining party has requested authorization to suspend concessions or other obligations pursuant to ¶ 3(b) or (c), the matter shall be referred to arbitration. Such arbitration shall be carried out by the original panel, if members are available, or by an arbitrator appointed by the Director-General and shall be completed within 60 days after the date of expiry of the reasonable period of time. Concessions or other obligations shall not be suspended during the course of the arbitration.

Enforcement of United States Rights Under Trade Agreements

19 USCA Sec 2411 (Sec. 301 of U.S. Trade Act of 1974).

§ 2411. Actions by United States Trade Representative (Sec. 301)

(a) Mandatory action

(1) If the United States Trade Representative determines under section 2414(a)(1) of this title that—

(A) the rights of the United States under any trade agreement are being denied; or

(B) an act, policy, or practice of a foreign country—

(I) violates, or is inconsistent with, the provisions of, or otherwise denies benefits to the United States under, any trade agreement, or

(ii) is unjustifiable and burdens or restricts United States commerce;

the Trade Representative shall take action authorized in subsection (c) of this section subject to the specific direction, if any, of the President regarding any such action, and shall take all other appropriate and feasible action within the power of the President that the President may direct the Trade Representative to take under this subsection, to enforce such rights or to obtain the elimination of such act, policy, or practice. Actions may be taken that are within the power of the President with respect to trade in any goods or services, or with respect to any other area of pertinent relations with the foreign country.

(2) The Trade Representative is not required to take action under paragraph (1) in any case in which—

(A) The Dispute Settlement Body (as defined in section 3531(5) of this title) has adopted a report, or a ruling issued under the formal dispute settlement proceeding provided under any other trade agreement finds, that—

(i) the rights of the United States under a trade agreement are not being denied, or

(ii) the act, policy, or practice—

(I) is not a violation of, or inconsistent with, the rights of the United States * * *

(c) Scope of authority

(1) For purposes of carrying out the provisions of subsection (a) or (b) of this section, the Trade Representative is authorized to—

(A) suspend, withdraw, or prevent the application of, benefits of trade agreement concessions to carry out a trade agreement with the foreign country referred to in such subsection;

(B) impose duties or other import restrictions on the goods of, and, notwithstanding any other provision of law, fees or restrictions on the services of, such foreign country for such time as the Trade Representative determines appropriate.

Notes

1. **U.S. Procedure**. In 2000 Congress enlarged the Trade representative's sanction authority by the addition of the "carousel" procedure to be

employed in certain cases of non-compliance. with a WTO dispute settlement recommendation after a retaliation list has been established or other action has been taken under § 2411. New § 2416 provides that the Trade Representative shall "periodically revise the list or action to affect *other* goods of the country or countries", in accordance with rules stated in that Section (emphasis added). The resulting uncertainty of affected goods is expected to strengthen the impact of the sanctions.

2. **EU Procedures for Actions Under Trade Rules.** The EU has also established procedures for protection against injurious illicit practices committed in the trade field by third countries. Current EU law on this subject is contained in the Council's 1994 Regulation 3286/94 on " * * * Community procedures in field of common commercial policy in order to ensure the exercise of the Communities' rights under international trade rules, in particular, those established under the auspices of the World Trade Organization". This Regulation broadens and strengthens the EU's procedures and potential for action in appropriate cases, while conforming to the WTO associated rules.

Article 1 of Regulation 3286 provides that the procedures adopted in the Regulation are to ensure protection of the Community's rights aimed at:

> (a) responding to obstacles to trade that have an effect on the market of the Community, with a view to removing the injury resulting therefrom;

> (b) responding to obstacles to trade that have an effect on the market of a third country, with a view to removing the adverse trade effects resulting therefrom.

Under Article 12.2 Where the Community's international obligations require the prior discharge of an international procedure for consultation or for the settlement of disputes, the measures referred to in paragraph 3 shall only be decided on after that procedure has been terminated * * *. Paragraph 3 of Article 12 states that:

> 3. Any commercial policy measures may be taken which are compatible with existing international obligations and procedures, notably:

> (a) suspension or withdrawal of any concession resulting from commercial policy negotiations;

> (b) the raising of existing customs duties or the introduction of any other charge on imports;

> (c) the introduction of quantitative restrictions or any other measures modifying import or export conditions or otherwise affecting trade with the third country concerned.

WTO Authorizes Trade Retaliation Against EU in Beef Case

USIS Wahington File. Wendy Lubetkin, USIA European Correspondent.
www.usia.gov/ Visited on 28 July 1999.

Geneva–The World Trade Organization (WTO) has formally authorized the United States and Canada to impose punitive duties on a selection of

European Union (EU) imports in reaction to the EU's failure to comply with WTO rules in the transatlantic trade dispute over growth hormone-treated beef.

A July 26 meeting of the WTO Dispute Settlement Body authorized the United States to suspend tariff concessions on a range of imports from the EU worth $116.8 million a year, an amount previously determined by a group of WTO arbitrators.

Canada, also a party to the dispute, was authorized to impose sanctions in the amount of $Canadian 11.3 million.

"The requests by the U.S. and Canada were authorized today in accordance with the DSU [Dispute Settlement Understanding],"Ambassador Rita D. Hayes, deputy U.S. trade representative and U.S. permanent representative to the WTO, told a press briefing following the meeting.

"The United States intends to implement the suspension of tariff concessions and related obligations with respect to goods entered or withdrawn from the warehouse on or after July 29," she said.

Hayes emphasized, however, that the US, would prefer not to have to impose sanctions because "it does nothing to help our exports and is not to the benefit of our importers."

"The United States would prefer to settle this dispute," she said, "and we will continue to try to work with the EC [European Community] to find an acceptable solution."

The list of products subject to 100–percent ad valorem duties was made public by the Office of the U.S. Trade Representative (USTR) July 19. It includes a wide range of pork products, Roquefort cheese, foie gras, prepared mustard and truffles.

Asked whether the United States would take a "carousel" approach and change the products targeted for retaliation, Hayes said the USTR has the legal authority to change the list, but has no plans to do so at the current time.

Hayes said the United States was willing to consider compensation from the EU if the EU also offered some assurances that it would lift its barriers to U.S. beef.

"But, quite frankly, the EC's offer involving increased U.S. beef access was not adequate," she said. "The EC could not even provide assurances that this offer would in fact allow any U.S beef into the EC".

"We were also concerned that the EC would view compensation as a resolution of the dispute and the U.S. beef producers would never gain access," Hayes said. Under the WTO agreement, compensation is considered only a temporary measure for dealing with a situation like this.

Big–Mac Targeted by French Farmers

3 Bridges Weekly Trade News Digest No. 34, 30 August 1999*.

French farmers have taken up arms (and apples) against U.S. agricultural trade policy in a series of demonstrations underway since early August. Protesting punitive tariffs imposed on EU products by the U.S. in the context of the dispute over EU banning imports of U.S. hormone-treated beef, farmers in southwest France dumped 10 tonnes of nectarines in front of a McDonalds on 20 August, followed the next day by farmers in Arles and Martigues dumping tonnes of fruit, vegetables and manure in front of a McDonald's there. These protests follow similar incidents by French farmers throughout the month.

* * *

McDonalds has become the target of choice for French farmers angered by the trade situation. The French Farmers' union Confédération Paysanne said in a statement that "Globalization is creating absurd economic conflicts ," and that the protests aim to "allow farmers and others to feed themselves as they think best." French farmers have also called for a boycott of U.S. imports. Observers say these incidents show the unfairness of the Dispute Settlement System set up by the WTO: the authorized trade retaliation measures can hit small producers who had nothing to do with the initial conflict—rather than the Government—introducing a variation on the beggar-my-neighbor policies that the GATT was set up to prevent.

As tensions mounted last week, the US Embassy in Paris said it would like to hold negotiations with EU officials to find a quick solution to the trade matter. The U.S. embassy said that the retaliatory tariffs were imposed "only as a last resort." The U. S. has so far argued that it would settle for nothing less than a lifting of the EU ban on hormone treated beef, while the EU has continually said it would not lift the ban until scientific risk assessments are completed.

Meanwhile the U.S. Agriculture Department said it would resume shipments of hormone-free beef exports under a plan requiring third party verification that beef is hormone free throughout the production process. Shipments of hormone-free beef exports were halted in July after the U.S. Food Safety and Inspection Service (FSIS) said it could not certify that the U.S. beef exports were hormone free.

United States: 2001 National Trade Estimate Report on Foreign Trade Barriers

March 30, 2001.
www.ustr.gov/html/2001_Contents. Html Visited on 21 April 2001.

* * *

EUROPEAN UNION

TRADE SUMMARY

The European Union (EU) and the United States share the largest two-way trade and investment relationship in the world. In 2000, the U.S.

* Reprinted with the permission of Bridges Weekly Trade News Digest.

trade deficit with the EU was $55.5 billion, an increase of $11.8 billion from the U.S. trade deficit of $43.7 billion in 1999. U.S. merchandise exports to the 15 Member States of the EU were more than $164.8 billion, an increase of 8.7 percent from the level of U.S. exports to the EU in 1999. U.S. imports from the EU were just under $220.4 billion, an increase of 12.8 percent from the level of imports in 1999.

U.S. exports of private commercial services (i.e., excluding military and government) to the EU were $84.7 billion in 1999, and U.S. imports were $62.5 billion. Sales of services in the European Union by majority U.S.-owned affiliates were $177.3 billion in 1998, while sales of services in the U.S. by majority EU-owned firms were $135.7 billion. The stock of U.S. foreign direct investment in the EU amounted to almost USD $512.1 billion in 1999, a greater than 8.8 percent rise from 1998.

* * *

Note: This U.S. Report identified in some detail a large number of U.S. problems with EU trade policies and practices in the following sectors: (1) import policies, (2) standards, testing and labeling, (3) government procurement, (4) export subsidies, (5) intellectual property rights protection, (6) service barriers, investment barriers, internet and electronic commerce. The EU also has its problems with the U.S., as seen in its most recent report on U.S. barriers to trade.

European Union: Report on United States Barriers to Trade and Investment

European Commission, Brussels, July 2000.
http://europa.eu.int/comm/trade/pdf/usrbt2000.pdf
Visited 21 April 2001.

* * *

SUMMARY

Extraterritoriality The EU strongly opposes the extraterritorial provisions of certain US legislation, which hamper international trade and investment by seeking to regulate EU trade with third countries conducted by companies outside the US. Of particular concern at the present time are the Helms–Burton Act and the Iran Libya Sanctions Act. Important headway towards a lasting solution to this dispute was made at the 18 May 1998 EU/US Summit in London. However, implementation of the Understanding reached at that occasion continues to depend on US Congress legislative action.

Unilateralism Unilateralism in US trade legislation also remains a matter of concern. Whilst the US has in practice made extensive use of the WTO dispute settlement system, it retains the opportunity to take unilateral trade measures. Recently the EU has won two dispute settlement cases before the WTO, one against the suspension of customs liquidation in the banana dispute, and one against Sections 301 to 310 of the US 1974 Trade Act. The EU has also initiated dispute settlement proceedings against the "carousel" legislation signed into law on 18 May 2000 (section 407 of the Trade and Development Act of 2000).

* * *

Note: This Report also identified in some detail a large number of EU problems with U.S. trade policies and practices, including those in the following sectors: tariff barriers, other customs barriers, trade defense instruments (anti-dumping and others), technical barriers to trade, government procurement, national security restrictions, conditional national treatment, tax subsidies, intellectual property, and services (communications, air transport, professional and maritime).

Notes and Questions

1. *How do you distinguish between "most favored nation" and "national" treatment* in trade relations under GATT 1947 as amended Articles I and III.2 and .4? (excerpts from the GATT are reproduced in the Documentary Supplement). What elements must be present in order to establish a claim based on these concepts? In U.S. practice the "most favored nation "formulation is giving way to "normal trade relations (NTR)". What do you suppose this new formulation means? Why is it gaining currency?

2. *An earlier hormones case.* At the time the United States brought an earlier hormones case in the late 1980s under the then prevailing GATT rules, the disputes procedure required consensus to move forward. Progress in this case was stalled when the EU blocked a procedural decision. Had this case reached the enforcement stage, consensus would again have been required and doubtless again would not have been forthcoming for the same reason. As Professor Jackson indicates above in the discussion of the DSU, the 1994 WTO DSU is said to "reverse the consensus rule". How would you expect the reversed consensus rule now in effect to bear on the outcome of the 1998 hormones case reported above in this Chapter?

3. *In the 1998 hormones case,* do you agree with the Appellate Body's view that a "risk assessment" is indeed required under Article 5.1 and 5.2 of the Sanitary and Phytosanitary Agreement (SPS), even though the importing authorities seek a "no risk" position for important reasons of public health? What is the potential non-tariff barrier problem in such cases?

4. *Would you support the "precautionary principle"* as the EU sought to apply in the hormones case? The principle has been applied in multilateral instruments in developing environmental policy, particularly in the case of global warming, in the face of a weak scientific case, and in the field of living modified organisms. Would you consider that use to offer convincing precedent for applying the principle to justify an import ban in the face of clear treaty commitments? Why?

5. *How would you describe the differences* between the U.S. Trade representative's retaliation power under § 301 and the EU powers under its protective Regulation 3286/94? Do you find the U.S. law to be compatible with the WTO's DSU rules? Why? Does the EU Regulation better

conform to the DSU? Does § 301 authorize unilateral action by the U.S. without reference to the WTO? See the WTO case: *Panel on United States–§§ 301–310 of the Trade Act of 1974*, WT/DS152/R, December 22, 1999, available at www.wto.org/index.htm.

6. ***In early 2001, after many years of controversy, the hormone-beef dispute had still not been resolved.*** Does this influence your views on trade sanctions? The adoption of legislative authority for "carousel" sanctions indicated support for more severe sanctions. Do think that would be the best policy?

SECTION B. FOREIGN DIRECT INVESTMENT (FDI)

Successful trade operations frequently lead manufacturers to engage in more extended foreign operations themselves, to license their key intellectual property rights to a foreign manufacturer to produce the traded goods, or more significantly for our purposes, to establish their own manufacturing facilities in foreign countries,[a] in the form of direct foreign investment.

The manufacturer with international trade experience is often well placed to seize upon opportunities of increasing its overall economic rewards through direct investment abroad, notwithstanding new and perhaps larger risks which may be encountered. FDI benefits may take many attractive forms. They may include capture of manufacturing profits which would not return to it in licensing of intellectual property. If the investment is made in a free trade-zone country, the new goods would have duty free access to other countries in the zone, as an investment in England provides duty-free access to the other 14 Member States of the European Union. There might well be reduced transport costs, advantageous wage rates and access to resources, lower social costs in local employment markets, less-costly environmental requirements, and so forth.

Foreign direct investment carries the investor and its assets directly into the foreign country, with a number of far-reaching consequences. A manufacturer-investor typically transfers into the foreign country its production machinery, operating tools, and other tangible assets, as well as such intangible property as technology, operating procedures and trade secrets, in short all that is useful, available and economic for the new operations.

The investor also establishes a legal presence in the foreign country, usually a wholly owned subsidiary corporation formed under the law of that country. Direction and support are provided on-site by management and

a. Editor's note. This Section deals with *direct* foreign investment, although portfolio investment is always another possible means of access to foreign business. Portfolio investment abroad can give the investor a stake in a manufacturing enterprise by purchase of shares of a foreign company, without control or operating responsibility and without a legal or physical presence in the country of operations. The risks of such investments normally fall on the investor who cannot expect significant assistance of its government if the investment goes wrong. For the portfolio investor there are normally none of the operational or foreign presence risks associated with direct investment abroad.

staff, some or all of whom may be employees of the investor, and with the investor they would be regarded as "aliens" by the host state, perhaps a new and uncertain status.

The new subsidiary soon finds itself under new legal controls, not only those of the investor's home state, but also those of the host state. Both of these legal regimes function under the umbrella of a third regime, the rules of international law reflected in customary rules, bilateral investment treaties (BITS) and other agreements, and in North America under NAFTA and globally under the WTO Agreements. This international legal dimension adds the potential of another unfamiliar element to contend with.

The foreign direct investor soon confronts the fact that the economic advantages it seeks abroad come with significant attachments in the form of fresh legal risks arising in unfamiliar locations. The new legal questions include:

The right of entry and terms of entry of the investor into the host country

The management and integrity of the investment once established

The terms of departure when this time comes.

Hence it is no surprise that foreign investment lawyers in both the investor's home state and in the FDI host state have their tasks set out for themselves at all stages of the investment process.

For the successful resolution of the questions of right of entry, management and departure noted above, investors must look to their governments which have established under international law an elaborate system of facilitative and protective rules. As in the trade field, there is little customary international law of investment, except for rules about the ultimate disaster for the investor: the host country's expropriation of foreign property, which is taken up below. The bulk of the law in this sector is found in the treaties mentioned above. The treaties govern much of the detail of investment rights, and more broadly reflect the national policies of the Contracting Parties. The major policy objective in this sector in recent years has been the movement to fuller freedom of investment.

Open Markets Matter: The Benefits of Trade and Investment

OECD Policy Briefs, No. 6, p. 4, 1998*

Why Is Foreign Investment Beneficial?

The case for opening markets to foreign direct investment is as compelling as it is for trade. More open economies enjoy higher rates of private investment, which is a major determinant of economic growth and job creation. FDI is actively courted by countries, not least because it generates spillovers such as improved management and better technology.

The benefits are tangible. As is true with firms that trade, firms and sectors where FDI is intense have higher average labour productivity and

* Reprinted with the permission of OECD Policy Briefs.

pay higher wages. Outward investment enables firms to remain competitive and thus supports employment at home. Investment abroad stimulates exports of machinery and other capital goods, and increases demand for intermediary products, know-how and specialised services. A study of OECD countries found that each $1.00 of outward foreign direct investment was associated with $2.00 of additional exports, and a trade surplus of $1.70. Without FDI those exports would be smaller, sustaining fewer of the more productive, better paying jobs that go with them.

Liberalisation can benefit developed and developing countries alike. As is the case for OECD countries, foreign investment brings higher wages, and is a major source of technology transfer and managerial skills in host developing countries. This contributes to rising prosperity in the developing countries concerned, as well as enhancing demand for higher value-added exports from OECD economies. In this way, developing countries are becoming major stake-holders in the trading system today, as is evidenced by estimates that close to one half of Uruguay Round welfare gains may accrue to them.

* * *

Van De Velde, The Political Economy of a Bilateral Investment Treaty

92 AJIL 621, 624 (1998).*

* * * Liberalism seeks to insulate the markets from politics and favors an autonomous legal system to protect private property against state interference and to enforce bargained-for exchanges in the market.

* * *

Liberalism also has advocated the free movement of capital across borders. Free movement of capital complements free trade in three different ways. First, to the extent that barriers to trade exist, they can be circumvented by capital movements. Second, a state's ability to produce goods for trade depends on its endowment of the factors of production—capital, labor and technology. Foreign investment augments the supply of the factors of production of goods for export. Third, foreign subsidiaries can trade with their parent companies at lower transaction costs than with unaffiliated companies, facilitating international trade.

* * * The liberal doctrine in essence is that the state should permit the market to determine the direction of international investment flows.

1.   INTERNATIONAL INVESTMENT AGREEMENTS

Treaty law in this sector is found in bilateral and, to a lesser extent, in multilateral treaties. The U.S. has made provision for investment protection in a number of treaties of friendship, commerce and navigation (FCN Agreements). Review for example, excerpts from *Asakura vs. City of Seattle*, contained in Chapter 12 in which the Supreme Court in 1924 applied the

* Reprinted with the permission of the
American Society of International Law.

U.S. FCN with Japan. More recently the U.S. and a number of other countries have developed a network of bilateral, specialized investment treaties (BITS) which provide comprehensive protection, as will be seen below. On the multilateral side, the Uruguay Round in 1995 produced the WTO Agreement on Trade-Related Investment Measures (TRIMS) set forth in the Documentary Supplement. In addition a large number of countries joined together in the Energy Charter Treaty to deal with trade and investment among themselves in the energy sector. Excerpts of that Treaty are found below. An effort by the OECD to negotiate a comprehensive Multilateral Investment Agreement turned out in 1998 to be not fully successful, but might be continued in the WTO or elsewhere.

U.S. Bilateral Investment Treaties (BITS)

U.S.Dept.of State, Bureau of Economic and Business Affairs, November 1, 2000
www.state.gov/www/issues/economic/7treaty.html
Visited on 21 April 2001

The U.S. Bilateral Investment Treaty (BIT) program supports several key U.S. Government economic policy objectives, from protection of U.S. interests overseas to promotion of market-oriented policies in other countries to promotion of U.S. exports.

The BIT program's basic aims are to:

— protect U.S. investment abroad in those countries where U.S. investors' rights are not protected through existing agreements such as our treaties of Friendship, Commerce and Navigation;

— encourage adoption in foreign countries of market-oriented domestic policies that treat private investment fairly; and

— support the development of international law standards consistent with these objectives.

The U.S. Government also believes that adequate and effective protection for intellectual property rights is an essential element of an attractive investment climate. Consequently, prospective BIT partners are generally expected, at the time the BIT is signed, to make a commitment to implement all World Trade Organization (WTO) Trade–Related Aspects of Intellectual Property Rights (TRIPS) agreement obligations within a reasonable period of time.

The U.S. Government has placed a priority on negotiating BITs with countries undergoing economic reform and where we believe we can have a significant impact on the adoption of liberal policies on the treatment of foreign direct investment. BITs also complement and support our regional initiatives on investment liberalization in the Asia Pacific Economic Cooperation Forum (APEC) and the Free Trade Area of the Americas. In addition, BITs lay the policy groundwork for broader multilateral initiatives in the Organization for Economic Cooperation and Development (OECD) and eventually, the WTO.

U.S. Bilateral Investment Treaties provide U.S. investors with six basic benefits: First, our BITs ensure that U.S. companies are entitled to be treated as favorably as their competitors.

First, BITs assure the companies are entitled to the better of national treatment or most favored nation (MFN) treatment when they seek to initiate investment and throughout the life of that investment, subject to certain limited and specifically described exceptions listed in annexes or protocols to the treaties.

Second, BITs establish clear limits on the expropriation of investments and entitle U.S. investors to be fairly compensated.

— Expropriation can occur only in accordance with international law standards, that is, for a public purpose, in a nondiscriminatory manner, under due process of law, and accompanied by payment of prompt, adequate, and effective compensation.

Third, BITs provide U.S. investors the right to transfer funds into and out of the host country without delay using a market rate of exchange. This covers all transfers related to an investment, including interest, proceeds from liquidation, repatriated profits and infusions of additional financial resources after the initial investment has been made. Ensuring the right to transfer funds creates a predictable environment guided by market forces.

Fourth, BITs limit the ability of host governments to require U.S. investors to adopt inefficient and trade distorting practices. For example, performance requirements, such as local content or export quotas, are prohibited.

— This provision may also open up new markets for U.S. producers and increase U.S. exports. U.S. investors protected by BITs can purchase competitive U. S.-produced components without undue restriction on inputs in their production of various products.

— U.S. investors protected by BITs can also import other U.S.-produced products for distribution and sale in the local market. They cannot be forced, as a condition of establishment or operation, to export locally produced goods back to the U.S. market or to third-country markets.

Fifth, BITs give U.S. investors the right to submit an investment dispute with the treaty partner's government to international arbitration. There is no requirement to use that country's domestic courts.

Sixth, BITs give U.S. investors the right to engage the top managerial personnel of their choice, regardless of nationality.

————

The full text of U.S. and Bolivia BIT dated 17 April 1998, containing current and typical provisions, is set forth in the Documentary Supplement.

Van De Velde, The Political Economy of a Bilateral Investment Treaty

92 AJIL 621, 640 (1998).*

Beyond the BITs

Provisions comparable to those found in the BITs already have been included in a number of regional and sectoral agreements. In May 1995, the Organisation for Economic Co-operation and Development (OECD) decided to commence negotiation of a multilateral agreement on investment that would include many of the same provisions that have become typical of the BITS. Negotiations originally were to have been completed by the date of the OECD ministerial meeting scheduled for mid–1997, but as of April 1998 a number of issues remained unresolved. The negotiating group was scheduled to reconvene in October 1998. Some have proposed that similar negotiations be initiated under the auspices of the World Trade Organization (WTO). The discussions within the OECD and potentially the WTO hold out the prospect that the network of thirteen hundred bilateral treaties, with supplementing regional and sectoral instruments, will someday be largely supplanted by a single multilateral instrument.

A multilateral agreement on investment has much to commend it as an instrument of liberalism. Multilateral agreements that command widespread adherence tend to universalize norms and thus give broad scope to the core liberal principles of investment security and investment neutrality. Multilateral agreements are usually of indefinite duration and thereby create the kind of long-term commitment that is essential to the success of a liberal policy. Because they will seem to represent a global consensus, norms adopted in a multilateral negotiation will have greater and more enduring legitimacy than those adopted in a bilateral setting and for that reason will be more productive of long-term investment security and neutrality. In short, all else being equal, a multilateral agreement is likely to be more genuinely liberal than a network of bilateral treaties.

As the OECD negotiations have demonstrated, however, negotiation of a multilateral agreement is a complex undertaking because of the difficulty of balancing the desire for investment neutrality and security against the necessity of accommodating compromises. The more genuine liberalism of a multilateral agreement may be effectively undermined by the extensive qualifications that could be the price of gaining widespread adherence.

2.   EXPROPRIATION OF FOREIGN PROPERTY

3 Hackworth, Digest of International Law

p. 661, U.S. Dept of State, 1942.*

On March 18, 1938 the Mexican Government by decree undertook to expropriate the properties in Mexico of certain foreign-owned oil companies

---

operating there, including a number of American-owned companies. In a statement to the press on March 30, 1938 the Secretary of State (Hull) said that this expropriation was "but one incident in a long series of incidents of this character" and accordingly raised "no new question". He said that the subject under consideration between the two Governments was "the matter of compensation for various properties of American citizens expropriated in the past few years" and that it was his earnest hope that a fair and equitable solution of the problem might soon be found. In a note of March 31 addressed to the American Ambassador in Mexico, the President of Mexico declared that his Government would "know how to honor its obligations of today and its obligations of yesterday".

On April 2, 1938 the Department of State instructed the Embassy in Mexico City to inquire when payment might be expected and what specific guaranty would be given that payment would be made.

In a statement released to the press on August 14, 1939 the Acting Secretary of State (Welles) said with reference to the position of the Government of the United States:

> In the decree of expropriation itself, and on numerous occasions subsequently, the Mexican Government recognized its liability to make compensation and stated its willingness to discuss terms with the petroleum companies concerned. Since that time there have been discussions between representatives of the Mexican Government and of the petroleum companies in an endeavor to come to some fair and equitable agreement. This Government has continuously and consistently sought to facilitate and to further these negotiations by conferring with both sides, first with one and then with the other.

> * * *

> It is of course evident that a solution of this controversy must be found in accordance with the basic principles of international law.

The position taken by the Government of the United States was further set forth in a note of April 3, 1940 from Secretary Hull to the Mexican Ambassador in Washington:

> The Government of the United States readily recognizes the right of a sovereign state to expropriate property for public purposes. This view has been stated in a number of communications addressed to your Government during the past two years and in conversations had with you during that same period regarding the expropriation by your Government of property belonging to American nationals. On each occasion, however, it has been stated with equal emphasis that the right to expropriate property is coupled with and conditioned on the obligation to make adequate, effective and prompt compensation. The legality of an expropriation is in fact dependent upon the observance of this requirement.

> * * *

> On March 16, 1940 you were good enough to hand to me an informal memorandum pursuant to our earlier discussions of the difficulties arising

out of the expropriation by your Government of the oil properties belonging to American nationals. Without undertaking to pass in any way upon the memorandum as a whole, it is important to have a clarification of two or three of the points raised therein.

It is stated (a) that "the Mexican Government judges that the right of expropriation is beyond discussion", and (b) that "there exists no divergence of opinion between the Government of the United States and that of Mexico regarding the right of the Mexican State to expropriate any private property by payment of a just compensation, as Mexico is agreeable to paying such indemnity to the expropriated companies."

I am compelled to take exception to the statements that the "right of expropriation is beyond discussion" and that "there exists no divergence of opinion between the Government of the United States and that of Mexico" in this respect.

As above stated, in the opinion of the Government of the United States the legality of an expropriation is contingent upon adequate, effective and prompt compensation.

OECD, Protection of Foreign Property

pp. 3, 23, (1967).

OECD Resolution of the Council on the Draft Convention On the Protection of Foreign Property

(12 October, 1967).

The Council

HAVING REGARD to the provisions of the Convention on the Organisation for Economic Co-operation and Development concerning economic expansion and assistance to developing countries;

HAVING REGARD to the Reports by the Committee for Invisible Transactions and the Comments by the Payments Committee on the Draft Convention on the Protection of Foreign Property;

HAVING REGARD to the text of the Draft Convention on the Protection of Foreign Property and to the Notes and Comments constituting its interpretation (hereinafter called the "Draft Convention");

OBSERVING that the Draft Convention embodies recognised principles relating to the protection of foreign property, combined with rules to render more effective the application of these principles;

CONSIDERING that a clear statement of these principles will be a valuable contribution towards the strengthening of International economic co-operation on the basis of International law and mutual confidence;

CONSIDERING that a wider application of these principles in domestic legislation and in International agreements would encourage foreign investments;

BELIEVING that the Draft Convention will be a useful document in the preparation of agreements on the protection of foreign property;

NOTING the conclusion of a Convention on the Settlement of Investment Disputes between States and Nationals of Other States;

I. REAFFIRMS the adherence of member States to the principles of international law embodied in the Draft Convention;

II. COMMENDS the Draft Convention as a basis for further extending and rendering more effective the application of these principles;

III. APPROVES the publication of the Draft Convention as well as this Resolution.

* * *

DRAFT CONVENTION ON THE PROTECTION OF FOREIGN PROPERTY

Article I

TREATMENT OF FOREIGN PROPERTY

(a) Each Party shall at all times ensure fair and equitable treatment to the property of the nationals of the other Parties. It shall accord within its territory the most constant protection and security to such property and shall not in any way impair the management, maintenance, use, enjoyment or disposal thereof by unreasonable or discriminatory measures. The fact that certain nationals of any State are accorded treatment more favourable than that provided for in this Convention shall not be regarded as discriminatory against nationals of a Party by reason only of the fact that such treatment is not accorded to the latter.

(b) The provisions of this Convention shall not affect the right of any Party to allow or prohibit the acquisition of property or the investment of capital within its territory by nationals of another Party.

Article 3

TAKING OF PROPERTY

No Party shall take any measures depriving, directly or indirectly, of his property a national of another Party unless the following conditions are complied with:

(i) The measures are taken in the public interest and under due process of law;

(ii) The measures are not discriminatory; and

(iii) The measures are accompanied by provision for the payment of just compensation. Such compensation shall represent the genuine value of the property affected, shall be paid without undue delay, and shall be transferable to the extent necessary to make it effective for the national entitled thereto.

Note: There is an apparent conflict between the General Assembly resolution which follows and the next following Charter of Economic Rights and Duties of States. One provides for international standards and the other for national standards of compensation. In the *Texaco case, below*, the arbitrator had to make a determination as to which of the two instruments makes the proper statement of the customary international law on this subject.

Permanent Sovereignty over Natural Resources
General Assembly Resolution 1803 (XVII)

Dec. 14, 1962.
U.N. Gen .Ass. Off. Rec. 17th Sess., Supp. No. 17 (A/5217), p. 15.

The General Assembly,

Recalling its resolutions 523(VI) of 12 January 1952 and 626(VII) of 21 December 1952,

* * *

Declares that:

1.   The right of peoples and nations to permanent sovereignty over their natural wealth and resources must be exercised in the interest of their national development and of the well-being of the people of the State concerned.

4.   Nationalization, expropriation or requisitioning shall be based on grounds or reasons of public utility, security or the national interest which are recognized as overriding purely individual or private interests, both domestic and foreign. In such cases the owner shall be paid appropriate compensation, in accordance with the rules in force in the State taking such measures in the exercise of its sovereignty and in accordance with international law. In any case where the question of compensation gives rise to a controversy, the national jurisdiction of the State taking such measures shall be exhausted. However, upon agreement by sovereign States and other parties concerned, settlement of the dispute should be made through arbitration or international adjudication.

5.   The free and beneficial exercise of the sovereignty of peoples and nations over their natural resources must be furthered by the mutual respect of States based on their sovereign equality.

8.   Foreign investment agreements freely entered into by or between sovereign States shall be observed in good faith; States and international organizations shall strictly and conscientiously respect the sovereignty of peoples and nations over their natural wealth and resources in accordance with the Charter and the principles set forth in the present resolution.

Charter of Economic Rights and Duties of States
General Assembly Resolution 3281 (XXIX)

12 Dec. 1974.
14 I.L.M. 251 (1975).*

Article 2

1. Every State has and shall freely exercise full Permanent sovereignty, including possession, use and disposal, over all its wealth, natural resources and economic activities.

2. Each State has the right:

(a) To regulate and exercise authority over foreign investment within its national jurisdiction in accordance with its laws and regulations and in conformity with its national objectives and priorities. No State shall be compelled to grant preferential treatment to foreign investment;

(b) To regulate and supervise the activities of transnational corporations within its national jurisdiction and take measures to ensure that such activities comply with its laws, rules and regulations and conform with its economic and social policies. Transnational corporations shall not intervene in the internal affairs of a host State. Every State should, with full regard for its sovereign rights, co-operate with other States in the exercise of the right set forth in this subparagraph;

(c) To nationalize, expropriate or transfer ownership of foreign property, in which case appropriate compensation should be paid by the State adopting such measures, taking into account its relevant laws and regulations and all circumstances that the State considers pertinent. In any case where the question of compensation gives rise to a controversy, it shall be settled under the domestic law of the nationalizing State and by its tribunals, unless it is freely and mutually agreed by all States concerned that other peaceful means be sought on the basis of the sovereign equality of States and in accordance with the principle of free choice of means.

Texaco Overseas Petroleum Co. and California Asiatic Oil Co. v. The Government of the Libyan Arab Republic

Dupuy, Sole Arbitrator Award on the Merits, 1977. 63 Intl L.Rep. 389, 486 (1979).*

[In this arbitration the plaintiffs sought relief from the Libyan government's nationalization of the plaintiffs' property. The Sole Arbitrator's award examines the effect of the General Assembly resolutions set forth immediately above. The arbitrator decided that the arbitration clause in the concession agreements referred to international law as the rule of decision, rather than the national law of the host state. Then the Sole Arbitrator directed himself to the content of the "international law" that was to govern. One aspect of that problem is dealt with here.]

* Reprinted with the permission of the American Society of International Law.   * Reprinted with the permission of the International Law Report.

83. The general question of the legal validity of the Resolutions of the United Nations has been widely discussed by the *writers*. [Emphasis supplied; citations omitted]

85. * * *

The conditions under which Resolution 3281 (XXIX) proclaiming the Charter of Economic Rights and Duties of States, was adopted also show unambiguously that there was no general consensus of the States with respect to the most important provisions and in particular those concerning nationalization. Having been the subject matter of a roll-call vote, the Charter was adopted by 118 votes to 6, with 10 abstentions. The analysis of votes on specific sections of the Charter is most significant insofar as the present case is concerned. From this point of view, paragraph 2(c) of Article 2 of the Charter, which limits consideration of the characteristics of compensation to the State and does not refer to international law, was voted by 104 to 16, with 6 abstentions, all of the industrialized countries with market economies having abstained or having voted against it.

86. * * *

As this Tribunal has already indicated, the legal value of the resolutions which are relevant to the present case can be determined on the basis of circumstances under which they were adopted and by analysis of the principles which they state: With respect to the first point, the absence of any binding force of the resolutions of the General Assembly of the United Nations implies that such resolutions must be accepted by the members of the United Nations in order to be legally binding. In this respect, the Tribunal notes that only Resolution 1803 (XVII) of 14 December 1962 was supported by a majority of Member States representing all of the various groups. By contrast, the other Resolutions mentioned above, and in particular those referred to in the Libyan Memorandum, were supported by a majority of States but not by any of the developed countries with market economies which carry on the largest part of international trade.

87. With respect to * * * the appraisal of the legal value on the basis of the principles stated, it appears essential to this Tribunal to distinguish between those provisions stating the existence of a right on which the generality of the States has expressed agreement and those provisions introducing new principles which were rejected by certain representative groups of States and having nothing more than a de lege ferenda value only in the eyes of the States which have adopted them; as far as the others are concerned, the rejection of these same principles implies that they consider them as being contra lege. With respect to the former, which proclaim rules recognized by the community of nations, they do not create a custom but confirm one by formulating it and specifying its scope, thereby making it possible to determine whether or not one is confronted with a legal rule. As has been noted by Ambassador Castañeda, "[such resolutions] do not create the law; they have a declaratory nature of noting what does exist" (129 R.C.A.D.I. 204 (1970), at 315).

On the basis of the circumstances of adoption mentioned above and by expressing an opinio juris communes, Resolution 1803 (XVII) seems to this Tribunal to reflect the state of customary law existing in this field. Indeed, on the occasion of the vote on a resolution finding the existence of a customary rule, the States concerned clearly express their views. The consensus by a majority of States belonging to the various representative groups indicates without the slightest doubt universal recognition of the rules therein incorporated, i.e., with respect to nationalization and compensation the use of the rules in force in the nationalizing State, but all this in conformity with international law.

89. Such an attitude is further reinforced by an examination of the general practice of relations between States with respect to investments. This practice is in conformity, not with the provisions of Article 2(c) of the above-mentioned Charter conferring exclusive jurisdiction on domestic legislation and courts, but with the exception stated at the end of this paragraph. Thus a great many investment agreements entered into between industrial States or their nationals, on the one hand, and developing countries, on the other, state, in an objective way, the standards of compensation and further provide, in case of dispute regarding the level of such compensation, the possibility of resorting to an international tribunal. In this respect, it is particularly significant in the eyes of this Tribunal that no fewer than 65 States, as of 31 October 1974, had ratified the Convention on the Settlement of Investment Disputes between States and Nationals of other States, dated March 18, 1965.

* * *

Notes. Thus the Tribunal declined to accept the majority vote in the General Assembly for texts stating international legal principles on expropriation of resources in the absence of a general consensus reflecting the views not only of the majority but also the minority on that issue. The International Court of Justice employed similar reasoning in its opinion on the *Legality of the Threat or Use of Nuclear Weapons* (35 I.L.M. 809, paras 68–71 (1996)).

The Convention on the Settlement of Investment Disputes, relied upon above by the sole arbitrator, results from a World Bank initiative directed toward pragmatic, development-related, ad hoc, settlements. It does not formulate or require acceptance of legal rules as international law. Had it done so a considerable portion of the Bank's membership would not have accepted it. (See also the Bank's Guidelines on the Treatment of Foreign Direct Investment (1992) 31 I.L.M. 1363 (1992).

The Energy Charter Treaty

Done at Lisbon, December 17, 1995.
34 I.L.M. 360 (1995).[a]

ARTICLE 13

EXPROPRIATION

a. Editor's note. Entered into force on January 16, 1998. For current status see www.encharter.org. This Treaty represents one of the most recent and significant formulations of international law on expropriation. Signatories include the Russian Federation and many former members of the USSR, Eastern European and Asian countries as well as the EU and its Member States. For other reasons, the U.S. has not yet signed this treaty. Reprinted with the permission of the American Society of International Law.

(1) Investments Of Investors of a Contracting Party in the Area of any other Contracting Party shall not be nationalized, expropriated or subjected to a measure or measures having effect equivalent to nationalization or expropriation (hereinafter referred to as 'Expropriation') except where such Expropriation is:

(a) for a purpose which is in the public interest

(b) not discriminatory;

(c) carried out under due process of law, and

(d) accompanied by the payment of prompt, adequate and effective compensation.

Such compensation shall amount to the fair market value of the Investment expropriated at the time immediately before the Expropriation, or impending Expropriation became known in such a way as to affect the value of the Investment (hereinafter referred to as the "Valuation Date"). Such fair market value shall at the request of the Investor be expressed in a Freely Convertible Currency on the basis of the market rate of exchange existing for that currency on the Valuation Date. Compensation shall also include interest at a commercial rate established on a market basis from the date of Expropriation until the date of payment.

(2) The Investor shall have the right to prompt review under the law of the Contracting Party making the Expropriation by a judicial or other competent and independent authority of that Contracting Party, of its case, of the valuation of its Investment, and of the payment of compensation, in accordance with the principles set out in paragraph (1).

(3) For the avoidance of doubt, Expropriations shall include situations where a Contracting Party expropriates the assets of a company or enterprise in its Area in which an Investor of any other Contracting Party has an Investment, including through the ownership of shares.

3. THE GENERAL PROBLEM OF ENFORCEMENT

With the law of expropriation favorably developed to protect the investor, the way is now clearer for the investor to consider the various choices of procedures for pursuing its claim. The investor may look with renewed confidence at procedures for direct action as a private party; and if doctrinal support from his government provides encouragement, the possibility of enlisting the support of his government at the international level might also be considered. The international system envisages both lines of action in appropriate cases. Consider the following sketch of a number of possibilities.

A. Investor's private action against host state in host state courts. This is the traditional resort to local remedies if available. If there is no sovereign immunity or other blocking mechanism, this alternative might be possible. Indeed, the customary law requires that local remedies be exhausted before action might be taken at the international level. So there might be no effective choice at the outset. However, local action might be risky, and it is not known always to be the most objective procedure, to say the least.

B. Investor's action against host state brought in courts of other countries. While this might present the advantage of a neutral forum, there could be a defense of sovereign immunity of the host state to contend with in actions brought in the investors's home state or in any third state. Certainly in the U.S. under FSIA, 28 U.S.C. Section 1604 with exceptions provided in Section 1605, a sovereign immunity issue could be expected to arise in these circumstances. See discussion of Sovereign immunity above in Chapter 7.

C. Private arbitration against the host state. This was the solution of Texaco in its dispute with Libya. Obviously arbitration is available only with the consent of the host state, either by an arbitration clause in the contractual arrangements for the investment, or a separate *compromis*.

D. Investor's action against a private holder of the property in another state. The act of state problem could arise in the U.S. and in a number of other countries, where the courts might hold that they will not judge the legality of the act of a foreign sovereign, in such political (non-commercial) matters, because it might interfere with the executive's conduct of foreign relations and for other reasons. This subject is also taken up in Chapter 7.

E. Diplomatic Claim by home state against the host state for reparation compensation. While the diplomatic claim process might in time help in negotiations and eventually produce a solution, there is no assurance that the home state would agree to espouse the claim at all; and if it is accepted, the investor loses control of the claim which passes to his government. This might not be a desirable procedure or it might be politically counter-productive for the investor. An outgrowth of this process could be state-to-state arbitration, if the two states are willing.

F. Proceeding for reparations by home state vs. host state in the International Court of Justice. Assuming the ICJ has jurisdiction, this process is an extension of the state-to-state claim referred to in E. above and presents some of the same questions. To apply or not to the ICJ is entirely in the discretion of the home state, again assuming jurisdiction over the host state. See Chapter 1 on the possible role of the ICJ. If a judgment is obtained, there remains the question of enforcement by the home state. *See also*, chapters 7 and 9 on this subject.

G. See the inventory of other procedures provided in Article 33 of the United Nations Charter. These include negotiation, mediation, conciliation, arbitration, judicial settlement, and resort to regional agencies or arrangements.

H. Home state policy responses. Governments are often equipped with means of adding elements of persuasion or inducement to their diplomatic demands that justice be done abroad to their nationals. Adverse policy positions may be taken against the host state on a wide variety of unrelated as well as related issues. For example, donor states can withhold bilateral development assistance, oppose advantageous loan and other financial assistance or political support in multilateral financial organizations. The U.S. is relatively well situated with powers necessary to take such measures and has shown itself quite willing at times to exercise these powers.

I. Countermeasures. Subject to certain conditions, the injured state may be justified in not complying with one or more of its obligations towards a state which has committed an intentionally wrongful act, in order to induce the latter state to comply with its obligations. See the International Law Commission's Draft Articles on State Responsibility, 37 I.L.M. 440, Articles 47–50 (1998) and later ILC Reports and Chapter 9 above on Responsibility of States.

J. Home state economic embargo on the offending host state. This represents a move into high damage measures that states do not undertake lightly. Only in the severest circumstances involving quite substantial state interests would a responsible government seriously consider action of this kind. Going beyond embargoes, if an aggressive investor considers the possibility of his government employing the use of force, even light-handed measures, this is reminiscent of forcible measures in the nineteenth Century, but in the modern world forcible measures to obtain satisfaction on claims would clearly violate international law.

Investors might not find that the procedures referred to in the foregoing sketch are sufficient, either to ensure a reasonable possibility of relief, or to promise a sound basis for incurring the risks of new or increased foreign direct investment. For future FDI, the investor might examine other measures of protection which could be taken *before* the investment is made, namely insurance against expropriation risks. The World Bank's Multilateral Investment Guarantee Agency (MIGA) was created in 1988 to cover a number of non-commercial risks, including currency transfer, expropriation and similar measures, breach of contract by the host state, and war and civil disturbances. This Agency insures against partial or total loss from acts that reduce ownership or control but not against non-discriminatory acts of hosts in exercising regulatory authority. The World Bank's insurance offers some multilateral advantages and the high standing of the Bank, without being closely identified with the U.S., unlike another investment insurance issuer, the American OPIC. OPIC is the U.S. government's Overseas Private Investment Corporation. OPIC's program of investment insurance can cover inconvertibility of currency, expropriation or confiscation of property, and property loss caused by war, revolution, insurrection or civil strife, plus business interruption due to any of the foregoing.

Another approach would be (or might not be) for governments to establish new procedures and remedies for the investor. One of these might be a proceeding by the investor in courts of the home state or other states against transferees or holders (traffickers) of the expropriated property, as provided in the Helms–Burton Act to which we now turn.

4. U.S. HELMS–BURTON ACT

Cuban Liberty and Democratic Solidarity Act of 1996 (Helms–Burton Act)

35 I.L.M. 357 (1996).*

[Selected provisions of the Act governing a judicial remedy, liability, non-application of the act of state doctrine, waiver by the President, and exclusion of certain aliens are set forth in the Documentary Supplement. *See also* chapter 15, Section H.2 on this subject.]

Clagget, Title III of the Helms–Burton Act is Consistent With International Law

90 AJIL 434 (1996).**

The Cuban Liberty and Democratic Solidarity (LIBTERTAD) Act of 1996, otherwise known as the Helms–Burton Act, became law on March 12, 1996. Title III of the legislation creates a federal cause of action, on behalf of U.S. citizens whose property was confiscated without compensation by Cuba, against those who "traffic" in that property.[2] Several governments—notably Canada, Mexico and those of the European Union, whose corporate citizens are the principal "traffickers"—have denounced the legislation as an exercise of extraterritorial jurisdiction that violates customary international law. These governments apparently, see nothing wrong with permitting–even encouraging—their nationals to use and profit from property that rightfully belongs to others. The United States not only commands the moral high ground on this issue; it also has the better of the legal argument.

The genesis of Title III is found in two episodes separated by a generation: the massive confiscations of property by the Castro regime in the early 1960s, for which no reparation has been made; and, more recently, the collapse of the Soviet Union and the resulting termination of Soviet aid to Cuba, which has created severe economic and financial problems for the regime. One of its principal responses has become the solicitation of foreign investment in commercial enterprises. Such investment frequently involves property that was confiscated from U.S. or third-country nationals or from Cubans, many of whom have since become U.S. citizens.

A post-Castro government will have to deal with claims by both categories of U.S. nationals, as well as claims by confiscation victims who

---

* Reprinted with the permission of the American Society of International Law.

** Reprinted with the permission of the American Society of International Law.

2. "Traffics" is broadly defined in § 4(13), 110 Stat. at 790–91, and includes any dealing in, use of or benefitting from confiscated property or causing, directing or profiting from trafficking by others. One purpose of the definition was to reach direct traffickers' affiliates that may be subject to U.S. jurisdiction. To be actionable, trafficking must be knowing and intentional, and it must begin or continue three months after August 1, 1996. * * *

remain in Cuba or have become naturalized in other countries. The principal techniques available for making reparation will be restitution in kind and monetary compensation, which have been adopted in varying degrees and combinations in countries emerging from totalitarian rule. Another possible method is what might be called substitution—conveyance to the claimant of property similar in nature and value to the confiscated property, or the issuance of "vouchers" that he can use to acquire property of his choice.

A post-Castro government will face staggering problems in attempting to do justice to the regime's victims while reviving the economy from the wreckage in which Castro will have left it. (The claims of preconfiscation U.S. nationals alone as certified by the Foreign Claims Settlement Commission, including interest, now total more than $6 billion.) Any just solution will necessarily involve a large measure of restitution or substitution, since the payment of full monetary compensation to claimants will be far beyond Cuba's resources.

Castro's strategy of involving foreign companies in confiscated properties threatens to place significant roadblocks in the path of claims resolution. If a property remains exclusively in the hands of the Cuban state, it will be readily available for restitution or substitution. If clouds on title have been created by purported transfers to traffickers of other nationalities who claim to be holders in due course, the problem becomes, in Secretary of State Warren Christopher's words, "far more difficult."

The need to resolve such issues would, at the least, delay and complicate the task of healing Castro's legacy. The victims' rights and interests would accordingly be prejudiced. To the extent they are U.S. citizens, the prejudice to them has a substantial effect on the United States. That is one reason why the United States has a legitimate interest in trafficking by third-country nationals. In addition, the United States has a strong interest in facilitating the rapid economic development of post-Castro Cuba without the rancor, litigation and clouds on title that Castro's foreign-investment strategy will inevitably cause when he is gone.

* * *

A further reason for title III is the notorious weakness and ineffectiveness of international enforcement mechanisms. Because the jurisdiction of international tribunals is consensual, it is only rarely that a confiscation case can be brought in such a forum. Espousal of claims by the victims' government can take generations to bear any fruit at all and, even when it does, typically results in recovery by the victims of only a pathetically inadequate fraction of the just compensation to which international law entitles them. In these conditions, there is every reason for an aggrieved state to supply effective remedies on its own if it can. Cuba has given the United States that opportunity by peddling confiscated property to traffickers who may be subject to U.S. jurisdiction. Creation of such a remedy, far from violating international law, works toward rescuing that law from relative impotence.

Enactment of title III does no injustice to the "traffickers" who may become defendants. That Castro's confiscations were made without compensation, and also typically involved discrimination against U.S. nationals or political persecution of Cubans, is not one of the world's best-kept secrets. Traffickers are fully aware that they are dealing in tainted property. It can be presumed that the culpability of dealing in stolen goods is a familiar concept to them from their own legal systems. Traffickers are knowingly taking the risk that the dispossessed owners or aggrieved states might take action against them.

A wealth of authority supports the view that confiscations that violate international law are not effective in passing title to property, and a state is under no obligation to recognize a title acquired by such a confiscation. Indeed, "[i]n respect to Cuban sugar and other United States assets seized in Cuba, a good case can certainly be made for an international legal *duty* of non-recognition of Castro's titles." British, French, Swiss, Austrian, Dutch and German courts are among those that have denied effect to foreign confiscations. Certainly, at a minimum, no consensus exists that an internationally unlawful confiscation *does* pass good title that a "purchaser" can rely on and that the United States is required to recognize or respect.

Thus, it seems difficult to make a serious argument that title III infringes international law to the extent that it permits suits by confiscation victims who were U.S. nationals at the time. To the contrary, title III applies and vindicates international law. As to these lawsuits, except for some of the details of the legislation, the United States is not even exercising its jurisdiction to prescribe, but only its jurisdiction to adjudicate. It is applying international law, not just its own law.

* * *

Title III of Helms–Burton does not violate international law. To the contrary, it furthers both the development and the implementation of international law in an area where the rudimentary state of enforcement mechanisms allows rogue states to ignore that law and to violate the most elementary human rights of their own citizens and of foreigners with impunity. Title III is a powerful dissuasive to the immoral trafficking in stolen property that today plays a major role in keeping Castro in funds and therefore in power, and that directly affects the rights and interests of the United States and its nationals. It is a legitimate exercise of U.S. jurisdiction, and the international rule of law should be a principal beneficiary of its enactment. If title III is challenged by Cuba or by states that tolerate or encourage trafficking in confiscated property by their nationals, the United States will have a strong basis for vigorously defending the statute's conformity with international law. The challengers may have a more difficult task in justifying their own conduct.

European Union: Demarche Protesting the Cuban Liberty and Democratic Solidarity (Libertad) Act

March 5, 1995, 35 I.L.M. 397 (1996).*

EUROPEAN UNION

DELEGATION OF THE EUROPEAN COMMISSION

The Presidency of the Council of the European Union and the European Commission present their compliments to the Department of State and wish to refer to the Cuban Liberty and Democratic Solidarity (LIBERTAD) Act of 1996.

The European Union (EU) has consistently expressed its opposition, as a matter of law and policy, to extraterritorial applications of US jurisdiction which would also restrict EU trade in goods and services with Cuba, as already stated in various diplomatic demarches made in Washington last year, including a letter from Sir Leon Brittan to Secretary of State Warren Christopher. Although the EU is fully supportive of a peaceful transition in Cuba, it cannot accept that the US unilaterally determine and restrict EU economic and commercial relations with third countries.

The EU is consequently extremely concerned by the latest developments in the House–Senate Conference in relation to this legislation, including the position now apparently taken by the US Administration. The legislation contains several objectionable elements. In addition, provisions relating to trafficking in confiscated property and those concerning denial of visas to executives or shareholders of companies involved in transactions concerning confiscated properties in Cuba, which had been removed during the adoption procedure by the Senate last 19 October 1995, have now been reintroduced by the House–Senate Conference. These provisions, if enacted and implemented, risk leading to legal chaos.

The EU cannot accept the prohibition for US-owned or controlled firms from financing other firms that might be involved in certain economic transactions with Cuba. The EU has stated on many occasions that such an extraterritorial extension of US jurisdiction is unacceptable as a matter of law and policy. Therefore, the EU takes the position that the United States has no basis in international law to claim the right to regulate in any way transactions taking place outside the United States with Cuba undertaken by subsidiaries of US companies incorporated outside the US.

Nor can the EU accept the immediate impact of the legislation on the trade interests of the EU by prohibiting the entry of its sugars, syrups and molasses into the US, unless the former certifies that it will not import such products from Cuba. The EU considers such requests, designed to enforce a US policy which is not applied by the EU, as illegitimate. Such measures would appear unjustifiable under GATT 1994 and would appear to violate the general principles of international law and sovereignty on independent states.

In these circumstances, the EU would appreciate it if you would inform Congress that the EU is currently examining the compatibility of this

* Reprinted with the permission of the
American Society of International Law.

legislation with WTO rules and that the EU will react to protect all its legitimate rights.

The EU is also worried by the provisions that would lead the US to unilaterally reduce payments to international institutions, such as the IMF. This measure would run counter to collectively agreed upon obligations vis-a-vis those institutions and would represent an attempt to influence improperly their internal decision-making processes.

The EU also finds most worrying the reduction of US assistance to the Russian Federation as a possible consequence of this legislation. Such a measure would not only weaken Western leverage in favour of reforms, but comes at a critical junction in time.

Finally the EU objects, as a matter of principle, to those provisions that seek to assert extraterritorial jurisdiction of US Federal courts over disputes between the US and foreign companies regarding expropriated property located overseas. This measure would risk complicating not only third country economic relations with Cuba, but also any transitional process in Cuba itself. Furthermore, these provisions offer the possibility to US firms for legal harassment against foreign competitors that choose to do business in Cuba. The threat of denial of a US visa for corporate officers and shareholders accentuates this concern.

The EU considers that the collective effects of these provisions have the potential to cause grave damage to bilateral EU–US relations. For these reasons, the EU urges the US Administration to use its influence to seek appropriate modifications to the proposed legislation, or if this should not be feasible, to prevent it from being enacted.

Should the legislation be adopted, the European Union intends to defend its legitimate interests in the appropriate international fora.

The Presidency of the Council of the European Union and the European Commission avail themselves of this opportunity to renew to the Department of State the assurances of their highest consideration.

Washington, DC
5 March 1996

Morse, A Breather on Title III, but no Changes for Helms–Burton

USIA Release 96071612, 16 July 1996.
www.usinfo.state/gov/products/washfile/htm

WASHINGTON—President Bill Clinton's decision July 16 to wait another six months before allowing lawsuits to be filed under Title III of the Helms–Burton law against foreign companies invested in confiscated U.S. properties in Cuba gives these companies a "breather." But it doesn't necessarily mean there will be changes in the law, according to an administrative official.

During a background briefing at the State Department, the official predicted that U.S. allies will not execute their threats of retaliation. "My presumption would be that the allies would not rush to judgment, because there is a six-month suspension in effect. There will be no lawsuits for six months against foreign companies....".

"I would not expect them to execute the threat of sanctions that you heard about yesterday from the EU (European Union). I think that they're going to think (that) they fired a shot across our bow yesterday. They're going to think that that shot had some effect. We didn't let the law go fully into effect. They and we have a six month 'breather.'"

The official acknowledged that "this is a very difficult decision; it's got competing interests." But he added that "I don't think it's necessarily automatic that somehow we will do things differently six months from now."

The Cuban Liberty and Democratic Solidarity Act was passed by Congress and signed into law by President Bill Clinton in March after Cuba shot down two small aircraft over international waters, killing four Cuban–Americans. The law is better known as "Helms–Burton" for its Republican authors: Senate Foreign Relations Committee Chairman Jesse Helms of North Carolina, and Representative Dan Burton of Indiana.

Title III of the law allows lawsuits to be filed in U.S. courts against foreign firms that own or operate the properties of U.S. citizens seized by the Cuban government after the 1959 Communist revolution. But U.S. allies around the world—most especially Europe, Canada, Mexico—have complained that the provision could deluge their companies in lawsuits. Some have threatened to retaliate.

U.S. administration officials have maintained that the United States will faithfully carry out the law, but in a way to minimize the effect on U.S. allies while maximizing the effect on the repressive Castro regime.

Clinton announced on July 16 that he would allow Title III to go into effect August 1 as provided for under the law, but he also said he would suspend the right to file lawsuits under Title III for six months. According to the administrative official, any claims are valid, "and the claims have legal standing; it's just that you cannot pursue them in the courts for six months." After that time, Clinton may once again consider his option for another waiver.

One of the primary justifications for the six-month waiver the administration announced July 15 is, according to the administrative official, "that this, we hope, gives some of these foreign companies further time to reflect on whether or not they really want to have these investments in Cuba, or whether they want to pull out."

Clinton said in his July 15 statement that the six-month period would be used to build international support for promoting democracy in Cuba. "At the end of that period, I will determine whether to end the suspension, in whole or in part, based upon whether others have joined us in promoting democracy in Cuba," Clinton said.

———

Note. This period of suspension was followed by successive six month suspensions. At the time of this writing, the latest suspension decision was announced on January 17, 2001 for a further six months. www.usin-fo.state.gov—visited on 20 January 2001.

Organization of American States: Inter–American Juridical Committee Opinion Examining the U.S. Helms–Burton Act

August 27, 1996
35 I.L.M. 1322 (1996).*

INTRODUCTION

1. This Opinion is adopted pursuant to the provisions of Resolution AG/doc.3375/96 approved by the General Assembly on 4 June 1996 during its XXVI regular period of sessions and entitled "Freedom of Trade and Investment in the Hemisphere" (Annex A), by which it instructed the Inter–American Juridical Committee, during this period of sessions, "to examine and decide upon the validity under international law of the Helms–Burton Act [known as the "Cuban Liberty and Democratic Solidarity Act—Libertad Act"] ... as a matter of priority, and to present its findings to the Permanent Council."

2. The Committee understands that this Opinion, issued in accordance with the jurisdiction assigned to it by Article 98 of the Charter of the Organization, [FN1] has no binding effect on Member States or the organs of the Organization.

3. The Committee issues this Opinion on the basis of the following premises:

a) In the performance of its assignment the Committee did not intend to interpret or pronounce on the internal legislation of any Member State.

b) The expression "the legislation" used in this document refers to a law whose content is similar to that of the Helms–Burton Act.

c) The Committee understands that Resolution AG/doc.3375/96 adopted by the General Assembly is intended to safeguard the international public order of the hemispheric system. It is thus necessary to stress the prevalence of certain rules of international law in the inter-American system that should be respected by the juridical systems of Member States.

d) The Committee interpreted its mandate set forth in paragraph 1 of this Introduction as relating to the conformity of the legislation under examination with public international law. This has been identified with the rules of international law as alluded to in Article 38, paragraph 1 of the Statute of the International Court of Justice. However its application excludes those rules contained in instruments

---

* Reprinted with the permission of the
American Society of International Law.

of a sub-regional or universal character to which not all States of the O.A.S. are party.

e) The Committee considered that the mandate received from the General Assembly did not require an opinion on bilateral issues between Member States, which is why it makes no statement on the specific measures adopted by the Government of the United States of America in relation to Cuba such as the embargo imposed for over three decades, while nevertheless noting that such measures raise legal questions in the light of the norms established in Articles 18 and 19 of the Charter of the OAS.

* * *

A. PROTECTION OF THE PROPERTY RIGHTS OF NATIONALS

4. The Committee considered that the enactment of the legislation in some cases and its possible application in others could have the juridical effect of:

a) Transforming the espousal of a State-to-State claim under international law into a domestic legal claim asserted under internal law by a national against nationals of third States.

b) Conferring the right to make such claims on persons who were not nationals at the time of the alleged loss.

c) Attributing responsibility for acts of a foreign State to private persons who might be nationals of third States.

d) Authorizing the determination of the quantum of compensation in a manner that could increase it to three times the loss caused by the act of expropriation.

e) Creating liability for a private defendant for the total value of an asset expropriated without taking into account the value of the "benefit" derived by him from its use or the claimed "loss" caused to the alleged original owner by such use.

f) Allowing claims that should be filed against a foreign State to be enforced by means of proceedings brought against the nationals of third States without endowing them with effective means to refute or contest the allegations against them or the third State in respect of the existence or the valuation of such claims, including on the basis of conclusive certifications issued by an internal administrative commission.

g) Confusing a claim for damages or restitution, based on nationalization, with an action in rem to claim wrongfully "confiscated property" and in addition with an action in personam for unjust enrichment from the use of such wrongfully "confiscated property" by any person subsequently involved in such use in a broad-ranging and indeterminate manner.

h) Creating liability for nationals of third States for the lawful use of expropriated property in the territory of the expropriating State or for the lawful use of property which does not itself constitute expropriated property.

5. The Committee considered the rules of international law applicable to diplomatic protection, State responsibility, and the minimum rights of aliens regarding the protection of property rights of nationals. In the Committee's view the following principles and rules are generally accepted by the Member States in this regard:

a) Any State that expropriates, nationalizes or takes measures tantamount to expropriation or nationalization of property owned by foreign nationals must respect the following rules: such action must be for a public purpose, nondiscriminatory, and accompanied by prompt, adequate and effective compensation, granting to the expropriated party effective administrative or judicial review of the measure and quantum of compensation. Failure to comply with these rules will entail State responsibility.

b) The obligation of a State in respect of its liability for acts of expropriation consists of the restitution of the asset expropriated or adequate compensation for the damage caused, including interest up to the time of payment.

c) When a national of a foreign State is unable to obtain effective redress in accordance with international law, the State of which it is a national may espouse the claim through an official State-to-State claim. It is a condition for such espousal that from the time of the occurrence of the injury until the settlement of the claim the holder thereof must without interruption have been a national of the claimant State and not have the nationality of the expropriating State.

d) Claims against a State for expropriation of the property of foreign nationals cannot be enforced against the property of private persons except where such property is itself the expropriated asset and within the jurisdiction of the claimant State. Products grown or produced on such property do not under customary international law constitute expropriated property.

e) Any use by nationals of a third State of expropriated property located in the expropriating State where such use conforms to the laws of that State, as well as the use anywhere of products or intangible property not constituting the expropriated asset itself, does not contravene any norm of international law.

f) The nationals of foreign States have the right to due process of law in all judicial or administrative procedures that may affect their property. Due process includes the possibility of effectively contesting both the basis and quantum of the claim in a legal or administrative proceeding.

6. In the light of the principles and norms set out in paragraph 5 above the Committee considers that the legislation under analysis does not conform to international law in each of the following respects:

a) The domestic courts of a claimant State are not the appropriate forum for the resolution of State-to-State claims.

b) The claimant State does not have the right to espouse claims by persons who were not its nationals at the time of injury.

c) The claimant State does not have the right to attribute liability to nationals of third States for a claim against a foreign State.

d) The claimant State does not have the right to attribute liability to nationals of third States for the use of expropriated property located in the territory of the expropriating State where such use conforms to the laws of this latter State, nor for the use in the territory of third States of intangible property or products that do not constitute the actual asset expropriated.

e) The claimant State does not have the right to impose liability on third parties not involved in a nationalization through the creation of liability not linked to the nationalization or unrecognized by the international law on this subject, thus modifying the juridical bases for liability.

f) The claimant State does not have the right to impose compensation in any amount greater than the effective damage, including interest, that results from the alleged wrongful act of the expropriating State.

g) The claimant State may not deprive a foreign national of the right in accordance with due process of law to effectively contest the bases and the quantum of claims that may affect his property.

h) Successful enforcement of such a claim against the property of nationals of a third State in a manner contrary to the norms of international law could itself constitute a measure tantamount to expropriation and result in responsibility of the claimant State.

B. EXTRATERRITORIALITY AND THE LIMITS IMPOSED BY INTERNATIONAL LAW ON THE EXERCISE OF JURISDICTION

7. The Committee understands that the legislation would result in the exercise of legislative or judicial jurisdiction over acts performed abroad by aliens on the basis of a concept termed "trafficking in confiscated properties."

8. The Committee has also examined the applicable norms of international law in respect of the exercise of jurisdiction by States and its limits on such exercise. In the opinion of the Committee, these norms include the following:

a) All States are subject to international law in their relations. No State may take measures that are not in conformity with international law without incurring responsibility.

b) All States have the freedom to exercise jurisdiction but such exercise must respect the limits imposed by international law. To the extent that such exercise does not comply with these limits, the exercising State will incur responsibility.

c) Except where a norm of international law permits, the State may not exercise its power in any form in the territory of another State. The basic premise under international law for establishing legislative and judicial jurisdiction is rooted in the principle of territoriality.

d) In the exercise of its territorial jurisdiction a State may regulate an act whose constituent elements may have occurred only in part in its territory: for example an act initiated abroad but consummated within its territory ("objective territoriality") or conversely an act initiated within its territory and consummated abroad ("subjective territoriality").

e) A State may justify the application of the laws of its territory only insofar as an act occurring outside its territory has a direct, substantial and foreseeable effect within its territory and the exercise of such jurisdiction is reasonable.

f) A State may exceptionally exercise jurisdiction on a basis other than territoriality only where there exists a substantial or otherwise significant connection between the matter in question and the State's sovereign authority, such as in the case of the exercise of jurisdiction over acts performed abroad by its nationals and in certain specific cases of the protection objectively necessary to safeguard its essential sovereign interests.

9. The Committee examined the provisions of the legislation that establish the exercise of jurisdiction on bases other than those of territoriality, and concluded that the exercise of such jurisdiction over acts of "trafficking in confiscated property" does not conform with the norms established by international law for the exercise of jurisdiction in each of the following respects:

a) A prescribing State does not have the right to exercise jurisdiction over acts of "trafficking" abroad by aliens unless specific conditions are fulfilled which do not appear to be satisfied in this situation.

b) A prescribing State does not have the right to exercise jurisdiction over acts of "trafficking" abroad by aliens under circumstances where neither the alien nor the conduct in question has any connection with its territory and where no apparent connection exists between such acts and the protection of its essential sovereign interests.

Therefore, the exercise of jurisdiction by a State over acts of "trafficking" by aliens abroad, under circumstances whereby neither the alien nor the conduct in question has any connection with its territory and there is no apparent connection between such acts and the protection of its essential sovereign interests, does not conform with international law.

CONCLUSION

10. For the above reasons the Committee concludes that in the significant areas described above the bases and potential application of the legislation which is the subject of this Opinion are not in conformity with international law.

In a regular session held on 23 August 1996, this Resolution was approved unanimously in the presence of the following members: . . .

European Union: Council Regulation (EC) No. 2271/96, Protecting Against the Effects of the Extra–Territorial Application of Legislation Adopted by a Third Country

November 22, 1996.
36 I.L.M. 125 (1996).*

THE COUNCIL OF THE EUROPEAN UNION,

* * *

HAS ADOPTED THIS REGULATION:

Article 1

This Regulation provides protection against and counteracts the effects of the extra-territorial application of the laws specified in the Annex[a] of this Regulation, including regulations and other legislative instruments, and of actions based thereon or resulting therefrom, where such application affects the interests of persons, referred to in Article 11, engaging in international trade and/or the movement of capital and related commercial activities between the Community and third countries.

Acting in accordance with the relevant provisions of the Treaty and notwithstanding the provisions of Article 7 (c), the Council may add or delete laws to or from the Annex to this Regulation.

Article 2

Where the economic and/or financial interests of any person referred to in Article 11 are affected, directly or indirectly, by the laws specified in the Annex or by actions based thereon or resulting therefrom, that person shall inform the Commission accordingly within 30 days from the date on which it obtained such information; insofar as the interests of a legal person are affected, this obligation applies to the directors, managers and other persons with management responsibilities.

Article 4

No judgment of a court or tribunal and no decision of an administrative authority located outside the Community giving effect, directly or indirectly, to the laws specified in the Annex or to actions based thereon or resulting therefrom, shall be recognized or be enforceable in any manner.

Article 5

No person referred to in Article 11 shall comply, whether directly or through a subsidiary or other intermediary person, actively or by deliberate omission, with any requirement or prohibition, including requests of foreign courts, based on or resulting, directly or indirectly, from the laws

---

* Reprinted with the permission of the American Society of International Law.

a. Editor's note. The Annex refers to the Cuban Liberty and Democratic Solidarity (Libertad) Act of 1996 and specifically to Titles I, III and IV as well as to other U.S. laws and regulations.

specified in the Annex or from actions based thereon or resulting therefrom.

Persons may be authorized, in accordance with the procedures provided in Articles 7 and 8, to comply fully or partially to the extent that non-compliance would seriously damage their interests or those of the Community. The criteria for the application of this provision shall be established in accordance with the procedure set out in Article 8. When there is sufficient evidence that non-compliance would cause serious damage to a natural or legal person, the Commission shall expeditiously submit to the committee referred to in Article 8 a draft of the appropriate measures to be taken under the terms of the Regulation.

Article 6

Any person referred to in Article 11, who is engaging in an activity referred to in Article 1 shall be entitled to recover any damages, including legal costs, caused to that person by the application of the laws specified in the Annex or by actions based thereon or resulting therefrom.

Such recovery may be obtained from the natural or legal person or any other entity causing the damages or from any person acting on its behalf or intermediary.

The Brussels Convention of 27 September 1968 on jurisdiction and the enforcement of judgments in civil and commercial matters shall apply to proceedings brought and judgments given under this Article. Recovery may be obtained on the basis of the provisions of Sections 2 to 6 of Title II of that Convention, as well as, in accordance with Article 57 (3) of that Convention, through judicial proceedings instituted in the Courts of any Member State where that person, entity, person acting on its behalf or intermediary holds assets.

Without prejudice to other means available and in accordance with applicable law, the recovery could take the form of seizure and sale of assets held by those persons, entities, persons acting on their behalf or intermediaries within the Community, including shares held in a legal person incorporated within the Community.

Article 9

Each Member State shall determine the sanctions to be imposed in the event of breach of any relevant provisions of this Regulation. Such sanctions must be effective, proportional and dissuasive.

Article 10

The Commission and the Member States shall inform each other of the measures taken under this Regulation and of all other relevant information pertaining to this Regulation.

Article 11

This Regulation shall apply to:

1. any natural person being a resident in the Community and a national of a Member State,

2. any legal person incorporated within the Community,

4. any other natural person being a resident in the Community, unless that person is in the country of which he is a national,

5. any other natural person within the Community, including its territorial waters and air space and in any aircraft or on any vessel under the jurisdiction or control of a Member State, acting in a professional capacity.

Article 12

This Regulation shall enter into force on the day of its publication in the Official Journal of the European Communities.

This Regulation shall be binding in its entirety and directly applicable in all Member States. Done at Brussels, 22 November 1996.

Canada: Foreign Extraterritorial Measures Act

October 9, 1996, 36 I.L.M. 111(1996).*

RECOGNITION AND ENFORCEMENT OF FOREIGN JUDGMENTS

7.1   Any judgment given under the law of the United States entitled Cuban Liberty and Democratic Solidarity (LIBERTAD) Act of 1996 shall not be recognized or enforceable in any manner in Canada.

8.1   Where an order may not be made under section 8 in respect of a judgment because the judgment has been satisfied outside Canada, or where a judgment has been given under the law of the United States entitled Cuban Liberty and Democratic Solidarity (LIBERTAD) Act of 1996, the Attorney General of Canada may, on application by a party against whom the judgment was given who is a Canadian citizen, a resident of Canada, a corporation incorporated by or under a law of Canada or a province or a person carrying on business in Canada, by order, declare that party may recover, under the provisions of section 9 that the Attorney General identifies, any or all amounts obtained from that party under the judgment, expenses incurred by that party, or loss or damage suffered by that party.

Mexico: Act To Protect Trade and Investment From Foreign Norms That Contravene International Law

October 23, 1996, 36 I.L.M. 133.**

Article 1 It is prohibited to any [Mexican and foreign] persons, whether natural and moral, public or private, who are located in [Mexico's] national territory; those [Mexican and foreign persons] whose acts take place or produce effects in said territory, totally or partially; as well as those [Mexican and foreign persons] who are subject to Mexican laws, to engage in acts that affect trade or investment when said acts are the consequence of the extraterritorial effects of foreign statutes.

A foreign statute is understood to have extraterritorial effects affecting Mexico's trade or investment when [said statute] has or may have any of the following objectives:

I.   To attempt to impose an economic blockade or restrict the flow of investment directed to a [given] country to provoke a change in its form of government;

II.   To allow claiming payments from individuals (particulares) derived from expropriations made in the country to which the blockade is applied; [or]

III.   To restrict the entry into the country which enacted the statute [to Mexican persons] as a means to accomplish the above-mentioned objectives.

Article 2 It is prohibited to [Mexican and foreign] persons mentioned in Article 1 of this Act to provide any [kind of] information, through any means, when requested by foreign courts or authorities, pursuant to the foreign statutes referred to in Article 1.

Article 3 Those affected [Mexican and foreign] persons must notify [both] the Secretariat of Foreign Affairs (Secretaria de Relaciones Exteriores or SRE) and the Secretariat of Commerce and Industrial Development (Secretaria de Comercio y Fomento Industrial or SECOFI) of the cases in which:

I.   Their activities or investment may be injured by the effects of the foreign statutes referred to in Article 1; and

II.   They receive requests or summons (requerimientos o notificaciones) issued pursuant to the foreign statutes referred to in Article 1.

Article 4 [Mexico's] National tribunals shall deny recognition to, and enforcement of any judgments, judicial resolutions (requerimientos judiciales) or arbitral awards rendered pursuant to the foreign statutes referred to in Article 1.

Article 5 Those [Mexican and foreign persons] who have been sentenced to pay an indemnification based upon a judgment or award rendered pursuant to the foreign statutes to which Article 1 refers, shall have the right to sue, before a federal court, the Plaintiff who filed the suit in a foreign country, for the payment of:

I.   Damages (en concepto de dano), and as the principal claim, the [monetary] amount established by the foreign judgment or award (suerte principal); and

II.   Injuries caused (perjuicios ocasionados), as well as the respective expenses and judicial costs (gastos y costas judiciales).

European Union–United States: Memorandum of Understanding Concerning the U.S. Helms–Burton Act and the U.S. Iran and Libya Sanctions Act

April 11, 1997, 36 I.L.M. 529.*

Understanding Between the United States and the European Union

Libertad Act

Both sides confirm their commitment to continue their efforts to promote democracy in Cuba. On the EU side, these efforts are set out in the Common Position adopted by the Council on 2 December 1996.

The U.S. reiterates its presumption of continued suspension of Title III during the remainder of the President's term so long as the EU and other allies continue their stepped up efforts to promote democracy in Cuba. Each side will encourage other countries to promote democracy and human rights in Cuba.

The EU and the U.S. agree to step up their efforts to develop agreed disciplines and principles for the strengthening of investment protection, bilaterally and in the context of the multilateral Agreement on Investment (MAI) or other appropriate international fora. Recognizing that the standard of protection governing expropriation and nationalization embodied in international law and envisioned in the MAI should be respected by all States, these disciplines should inhibit and deter the future acquisition of investments from any State which has expropriated or nationalized such investments in contravention of international law, and subsequent dealings in covered investments. Similarly, and in parallel, the EU and U.S. will work together to address and resolve through agreed principles the issue of conflicting jurisdictions, including issues affecting investors of another party because of their investments in third countries.

The EU and US agree to make best efforts to develop the above disciplines and principles in bilateral consultations before 15 October 1997, and to subsequently introduce jointly corresponding proposals in the MAI negotiations.

The U.S. Administration, at the same time as the above bilateral consultations commence, will begin to consult with Congress with a view to obtaining an amendment providing the President with the authority to waive Title IV of the Act once the bilateral consultations are completed and the EU has adhered to the agreed disciplines and principles. In the circumstances of such adherence it is expected that such a waiver would be granted.

In the meantime, the U.S. notes the President's continuing obligation to enforce Title IV. Consistent with the guidelines for implementation, the U.S. will apply rigorous standards to all evidence submitted to the Department of State for use in enforcing Title IV. The U.S. is committed to a thorough, deliberate process in order to ensure careful implementation of

* Reprinted with the permission of the
American Society of International Law.

Title IV. This will involve discussions with all affected parties in order to consider all relevant information prior to Title IV actions.

* * *

WTO Case

In the light of all of the above, the EU agrees to the suspension of the proceedings of the WTO panel. The EU reserves all rights to resume the panel procedure, or begin new proceedings, if action is taken against EU companies or individuals under Title III or Title IV of the Libertad Act or if the waivers under ILSA referred to above are not granted or are withdrawn. The EU shall notify the United States at least seven days in advance of making a written submission to the panel, and upon delivery of such submission this Understanding shall cease to have effect. This understanding reflects the fact that the U.S. Administration is obligated to implement the Libertad Act and ILSA. * * *

––––––

Notes and Questions

1. *What possible problems might a host state foresee* in granting uncontrolled or unrestricted rights of entry for investments originating from a BIT partner country? How would the home state and the investor view the same question? Would there be an overall international policy view of this question, in terms of the generally accepted investment liberalization policy?

2. *What happens to the protected status of an investment* if the states parties to the applicable BIT terminate that treaty? See the U.S.-Bolivia BIT in the Documentary Supplement.

3. *On balance do you see more advantage or disadvantage* in a multilateral investment agreement (like the OECD draft MAI) compared to the BITs with similar provisions?

4. *Review Asakura v. City of Seattle*, above in Chapter 11 ex 12. What was the treaty basis of Mr. Asakura's claim? What if there had been a MFN type clause? What if there had been no treaty?

5. Can you *identify the effect as precedent* under international law of the State Department's action of April 2, 1938 and Secretary Hull's note of April 3, 1940 concerning the Mexican oil nationalizations?

6. *Do you see significant differences in the Hull Rule formulation* as reported in Hackworth and the OECD formulation some 30 years later? How would you analyze the legal effect of the OECD Council Resolution on the draft convention on protection of foreign property?

7. *Do you agree with the process by which Arbitrator Dupuy in the Texaco case* resolved the apparent conflict between GA RES 1803 (XVII) on Permanent Sovereignty and GA RES 3281(XXI) on the Economic Rights and Duties of States? Why?

8. *In connection with the previous question, compare the approach of the ICJ in paragraphs 68–72 of the Nuclear Weapons Opinion*

(See Chapter 13 above), particularly para 71 which refers to GA resolutions stating that use of these weapons would be a direct violation of the U.N. Charter. The Court goes on to say that " * * * several of the resolutions under consideration in the present case have been adopted with substantial numbers of negative votes and abstentions; thus, although those resolutions are a clear sign of deep concern regarding the problems of nuclear weapons, they still fall short of establishing the existence of an *opinio juris* on the illegality of the use of such weapons". How do you think the ICJ might deal with conflicting GA resolutions parallel to Arbitrator Dupuy's problem?

9. Would you consider that the Hull Rule of "adequate, effective, and prompt" compensation is now established as a rule of customary international law applicable in cases in the absence of a treaty rule?

10. In cases of uncompensated expropriations, under what circumstances would you consider it advisable to invoke one or more of the claimants' procedures discussed in this Chapter?

11. One of the main objections to the Helms–Burton Act is the claim that it has extraterritorial reach, into the territories of other states. On this subject review the material in Chapter 3. Note also that Mr. Clagget argues that the extraterritorial effect is justified in this case:

> "A state has jurisdiction to prescribe rules of law with respect to 'conduct outside its territory that has or is intended to have substantial effect within its territory,' at least when the exercise of that jurisdiction is reasonable in all the circumstances. * * *
>
> Under the *Restatement* scheme, international law is said to require that a state, even if it has jurisdiction to prescribe based on 'substantial effects,' must balance its interests against those of other states, and refrain from applying its laws when the legitimate and reasonable interests of another state are greater. The appropriate question thus becomes: what other state is entitled to complain? What state can accuse the United States of an international delinquency against it?
>
> If the 'other state' is Cuba, Cuba has no legitimate interest, which other states need or should respect, in confiscating property without compensation and profiting from foreign investment in that property. Cuba's comprehensive violations of international law fully justify U.S. countermeasures such as title III, even if those measures would otherwise be unlawful.
>
> If the 'other state' is the state of which the trafficker is a national, that state's interest in protecting its national's ability to traffic in confiscated property in a third country is, at the most, no greater (let alone more legitimate) than the United States' interest in protecting the ability of *its* national—the rightful owner—to prevent further interference with his property and perhaps ultimately to recover it. The interests of both states are equally 'extraterritorial,' since the activity with which both are concerned is taking place in a third country, Cuba. Thus, title III does not fail a balancing test, even if such a test is deemed part of international law. Title III is well within the right of the United States to prescribe rules for application by its own

courts, against defendants subject to its jurisdiction, in a matter with a demonstrable impact on the United States and its residents." (90 AJIL 434,436 (1996))

Compare paragraphs 7–8 of the OAS Juridical Committee Opinion above. What conclusion would you draw on the issue of extraterritoriality as applied to Helms–Burton?

12. *Do the blocking measures of the EU, Canada and Mexico help resolve the legal issue?* Or do they represent defensive measures which may simply lead to a stalemate? Under these circumstances, what procedures are open to the U.S and the others to resolve this kind of impasse? One possibility suggested in the readings is to negotiate a multilateral agreement authorizing and regulating a solution. This was attempted in the OECD MIA negotiations, but secondary economic boycotts and illegal expropriations figured among the issues that brought these negotiations to a standstill (See Report by the Chairman of the Negotiating Group, 28 April 1998, www.oecd.org/daf/cmis/mai/repor98.htm) and then to an unsuccessful termination.

CHAPTER 14

PEACEFUL RESOLUTION OF DISPUTES AND THE USE OF FORCE IN THE INTERNATIONAL SYSTEM

SECTION A.   THE PEACEFUL RESOLUTION OF DISPUTES IN THE INTERNATIONAL SYSTEM

At its 44th Session, in 1989, the General Assembly declared 1990–1999 to be the U.N. Decade of International Law. Objectives were to further the acceptance of the principles of international law and to promote methods for the peaceful settlement of international disputes. In the modern era of nation-states since the treaties of Utrecht and Westphalia, international law has attempted to resolve disputes by means short of war in several ways. Inspired in part by legal and theological precepts of *"Just War,"* aggressive war was proscribed, means of peaceful resolution of disputes were developed, and rules mitigating the violent effects of war were promulgated.

Modalities and techniques for the peaceful resolution of disputes were instituted through the Hague Peace Conferences of 1899 and 1907, the Bryan Treaties, the Kellogg–Briand Pact, and the League of Nations. This early history is examined in this section, culminating in a review of attempts peacefully to resolve disputes under the provisions of Chapter VI of the U.N. Charter, including fact-finding and conciliation, good offices, mediation and arbitration. Finally, this chapter describes the international community's attempts to maintain conditions of peace and justice through the use of force short of war: economic boycott and United Nations "peace-keeping" under Chapter VII of the Charter. Chapter 15, infra, completes the circle, exploring the traditional and residual rights of states to go to war.

For the most part, international disputes are resolved by negotiation between the disputants. In this way, on a day-to-day basis, international law works. If negotiation fails, the parties may seek to resolve their differences by mediation or conciliation.

Negotiation: Nations, like individuals, will attempt to resolve their problems in a non-violent way if it may give them an advantage. National leaders have negotiated with their foreign counterparts as the means to enter into relations, to prevent problems before they arise, and to resolve problems when they do arise. Thus, nations have expert negotiators in the

Legal Adviser's Office of their Department of Foreign Affairs, who conduct "negotiations", and "consultations" (e.g., the various offices in the Department of State maintain ongoing consultation on the subject of their oversight or expertise). This is the ongoing, daily business of foreign affairs, which takes place through "diplomatic channels." These negotiators negotiate treaties, but also continue ongoing "consultation" and "negotiation" on issues in their expertise.

Mediation: When consultation fails to prevent a problem and negotiation fails to resolve it, a third party may be able to intervene to resolve the impasse, helping the parties create a solution acceptable to each of them. This is offering "good offices." The third party has no power or authority to force a settlement, such as in binding arbitration. He attempts to help the parties see solutions which will be mutually advantageous or at least an acceptable alternative to continuing the dispute. The mediator may also be charged with investigation and development of proposals for consideration. This is called "conciliation."

Conciliation: A commission is set-up by disputing parties. The commission may be permanent, to resolve ongoing disputes on a given subject, or it may be ad hoc. The commission is charged to investigate the dispute or incident and to establish the facts as a neutral observer. We will examine the minimally successful attempt to utilize conciliation in disputes in the early part of the 20th century. More recently, the General Assembly has adopted a plan, *U.N. Draft Rules for the Conciliation of Disputes Between States,* Nov. 28, 1990, 30 ILM 229 (1991), which we have included in the Doc. Supp.

Adjudication: If the above methods fail, nations may resort to international adjudication either in the International Court of Justice, discussed in Chapters 1, 9, and 10, or in domestic courts, examined in Chapters 1, 9, 11, 12 and 16. Other aspects of peaceful resolution are related to fact-finding and the success of the peaceful means attempted often depends on them. These include: jurisdiction, applicable law, effect or nature of outcomes (e.g., binding or non-binding), acceptability of the various procedures (waxing or waning, for example), and workability.

1. FACT FINDING AND DISPUTE RESOLUTION UNDER THE HAGUE CONVENTIONS AND LEAGUE OF NATIONS[1]

The history of peaceful resolution of disputes through the Hague Conventions and the League of Nations is often seen as being negative, because the League and its member states failed to prevent the Second World War. While the League and its members failed adequately to confront aggressor states in the 1930's, the League was successful to some degree in resolving some disputes in Europe following the disintegration of imperial systems of government after the First World War. Then as now,

---

1. For detailed historical analysis, see Firmage, Fact–Finding in the Resolution of International Disputes—From the Hague Peace Conference to the United Nations, [1971] Utah L.Rev. 421; and, Firmage, The 1993 Kellogg Lectures, War, Peace & Faith, delivered at the Episcopal Divinity School in Cambridge, Mass. (1993) from which the following material was drawn.

contending ethnic and national groups threatened the peace. The League and its member states had somehow to redraw the map of Europe. Techniques and instruments of peaceful resolution were developed which may once again be useful in allowing contending parties in disputes to have available the means for peaceful resolution.

The enduring quest of the peacemaker has been to substitute peaceful means of dispute resolution for violent self help. The horizontal and uncentralized nature of the international system has lessened the capacity of international law to punish illegal violence and provide adequate means of peaceful resolution of disputes. There are few hierarchical, vertical, or centralizing factors in the international system to enforce its norms upon aberrant states.

Within this context of relative immaturity and weakness, the international system, nevertheless, has developed some institutional procedures to accomplish the peaceful resolution of disputes. For the most part, these procedures—good offices, conciliation, inquiry or fact-finding, negotiation, mediation, arbitration and judicial settlement—have counterparts within municipal systems. While this listing of techniques ranges from political or diplomatic to judicial, one process—inquiry or fact-finding—is instrumental to both.

Fact-finding has a common relationship to resultant conclusions of law, policy, or accommodation in dispute settlement whether the process of resolution is of a juridical or a diplomatic nature. Modern techniques of fact-finding in the process of the peaceful resolution of international disputes have an evolutionary history dating from the latter part of the last century. International commissions of inquiry have existed from before the Hague Conventions through the period of the Bryan treaties and the League of Nations to the less formal fact-finding bodies frequently created by the United Nations.

The Hague Conventions Through the League of Nations. The Hague Conventions of 1899 and 1907: Significant institutional development of international commissions of inquiry as a technique in the peaceful resolution of disputes began with the Hague Conventions of 1899 and 1907, although informal international commissions of inquiry had been employed before. Seven commissions of inquiry were established under the two Hague Conventions. The commissions all possessed the following characteristics: (1) resort to the commissions was voluntary; (2) only minor disputes were referred to the commissions; (3) each commission was *ad hoc;* (4) each commission was constituted so as to insure neutral dominance; (5) the report was recommendatory only; (6) commissions could investigate only factual differences.

One of the commissions created by the Hague, the Permanent Court of Arbitration (the "PCA"), has been revised during the last decade, in an effort to increase its utility to states. In 1991, the PCA published "New Directions," the recommendations of a group convened to review and evaluate the PCA. The suggestions of this group, most of which have since been adopted, include (1) revision of procedural rules; (2) better use of the "Members of the Court," the group of international jurists selected by states to comprise the pool of potential arbitrators; (3) organized efforts to encourage new states to become parties to the Hague; (4) cooperation with the U.N.; and, (5) creation of a steering committee to consider revisions to the 1907 Convention, to be proposed at a 1999 conference in Hague.

The Bryan Treaties: Between 1913 and 1915 the U.S. signed over 30 bilateral treaties, all entitled "Treaty for the Advancement of Peace," with other American states and with several European states. The force behind the negotiation of the treaties was William Jennings Bryan, who made his acceptance of the office of Secretary of State dependent upon the integration of his concept of commissions of inquiry into the foreign policy of the Wilson administration. While there are obvious similarities between the Hague and Bryan Commissions, the differences are more significant. Where the Hague Conventions provided for ad hoc commissions to be established by agreement between the parties, the Bryan treaties established permanent commissions within guidelines provided by the Conventions. Under the Hague Conventions, the jurisdiction of the commissions was severely limited to disputes of an incidental nature, involving neither national honor "nor vital interests." In addition, the commissions' terms of reference under the Conventions were usually limited to findings of fact rather than conclusions of law.

The League of Nations: Thirty disputes were handled by the League of Nations from 1920 to 1940. Most of these were border and territorial disputes stemming from the disintegration of the Austro–Hungarian, Turkish, and Russian empires. Franco–British solidarity accounted for the League's success in resolving most of the disputes which arose in the 1920's. This solidarity, however, proved insufficient to deal with the aggressive acts of other great powers in the 1930's.

Conclusions: Fact-finding worked best when simple, non-strategic issues were involved between parties who, in good faith, were disputing relatively simple questions of fact. All disputes handled under the Hague Conventions involved maritime incidents that did not affect the vital interests of the parties. The majority of the cases considered by the League of Nations concerned border disputes stemming from the disintegration of colonial empires.

The experience of the Hague Conventions and the League of Nations suggests that there are two essential elements of successful fact-finding efforts to aid in the peaceful settlement of international disputes: first, the parties must, to a certain degree, accept peaceful settlement as a customary means of dispute resolution; and second, the parties must believe that there is a credible threat of community sanction to enforce those means. There is a direct correlation between these two factors. As the first increases in the depth of its tradition, the necessity of the second decreases proportionally. The prerequisites are discernible in international relations, but since they are still weak, it is predictable and understandable that states will resolve the most complex and important disputes by more traditional means of diplomacy and by threatened or actual military action.

The functioning and composition of fact-finding through the League period reflects the tentative steps which the international community was willing to take along the road to increased community resolution of disputes through means of pacific settlement. The composition of most commissions was based upon individual expertise rather than national representation. Almost all commission members operated individually, without instructions from their governments. This, of course, was an operational reflection of the simplicity and relative unimportance of the disputes entrusted to their resolution. The terms of reference of the commissions became broader as the international community gained gradual confidence in this technique of dispute resolution.

The lines drawn and the nation building of the period resonate today. The disintegration of the USSR and Yugoslavia and the end of Soviet hegemony throughout Eastern Europe again confront the world with ethnic, religious and nationalist civil strife. Older imperial or multi-ethnic and multi-national forms of government have crumbled and ethnic disputes have risen to the level of civil wars, for example, in Rwanda, Burundi, Sierra Leone, The Ivory Coast, The Congo, and much of the rest of Africa, in the former Yugoslavia, in Georgia, in Chechnya, and between Azerbaijan and Armenia within the former USSR. The similarities to the disintegration of imperial systems and consequent ethnic strife following World War I are apparent. Sadly, much of the strife and issues from the earlier disputes have risen once again. In the following discussion, notice how many of the players are the same. Ask yourselves whether the legal issues are the same.

2. THE UNITED NATIONS CHARTER

At this point, consider Chapter VI of the U.N. Charter, especially Articles 33, 34, 35, 36, 37 and 38, available in the Doc. Supp. As you study, keep in mind the following: What are the means of peacemaking, peacekeeping and preventive diplomacy?

3. EARLY ATTEMPTS PEACEFULLY TO RESOLVE DISPUTES UNDER THE CHARTER

Notes and Questions, General

1. *The Greek Crisis.* The Greek crisis was the first dispute to confront the UN. Following World War II, Greece suffered internal dissent and insurrection. The Acting Chair of the Greek delegation sent a letter to the Secretary–General, asking him to bring the problem to the attention of the U.N. pursuant to articles 34 and 35 of the Charter. The Greek Government claimed that a condition of insurgency existed only in its northern provinces and that the insurgents were being trained and supplied by its northern neighbors, Yugoslavia, Albania, and Bulgaria.

The Security Council invited the representatives of the states involved to present their cases before the Council on December 10, 1946. After hearing the arguments the Security Council voted unanimously to establish a Fact–Finding Commission to investigate the alleged border violations and to report its conclusions to the Council.

Despite being denied access to three of the four states for most of its tenure, the Commission's investigation was thorough and relatively successful. The Commission concluded that Yugoslavia and, to a lesser degree,

Albania and Bulgaria, supported the guerrilla warfare in Greece. The Commission found that most of the violence had taken place in the three most northern Greek provinces, but that the level of violence did not constitute a civil war. The majority of the members of the Security Council approved the Commission's Report, but the former USSR and Poland did not. The USSR vetoed the execution of the measures called for in the Commission's Report, concluding that the evidence in the report demonstrated that a state of civil war did exist throughout Greece and was the result of internal causes. See, 1946–47 Y.B.U.N. 369.

Following the Security Council's refusal to execute the Report, the General Assembly created the United Nations Special Committee on the Balkans (UNSCOB). The Assembly ordered UNSCOB to observe compliance with its collateral call for the four involved states to "establish good neighborly relations, establish frontier agreements, settle the refugee problems and study the possibility of transferring minority groups along the border." UNSCOB had authority to investigate within each of the four states, although only Greece ultimately allowed the observer force into their country. Nevertheless, UNSCOB was successful in collecting information and ultimately provided unambiguous evidence that the three northern, neighbor states were essential accomplices in the Greek insurgency. Armed with these reports, the General Assembly condemned the actions of Yugoslavia, Albania, and Bulgaria.

2. *The India–Pakistan Conflict*. Following independence, India and Pakistan went to war over Kashmir. The combatants reached a cease-fire agreement in July, 1949. United Nations Military Observer Group (UNMOGIP), was established to investigate complaints of violations of the agreement, to observe troop build-up and deployment, and to control civilian movement in and around the cease-fire line. Although initially UNMOGIP was successful, the violence began to increase after 1955. By 1965 it had reached crisis proportions. Based on UNMOGIP reports, the Secretary General reported the escalation of violence to the Security Council in a letter. *See, gen.,* Report by the Secretary–General On the Current Situation in Kashmir with Particular Reference to the Cease–Fire Agreement, the Cease–Fire Line and the Functioning of UNMOGIP. U.N. Doc. S/6650. Consider also U.N. S.C. Resolution 211 in Doc. Supp.

Despite Resolution 211 and others which followed, the combatants in Kashmir continued to violate the cease-fire agreement. The Secretary–General and UNMOGIP continued to report violations and to attempt to mediate the dispute. Finally, on February 17, 1966, the leaders of Pakistan and India agreed to withdraw their forces and to restore the cease-fire. Sadly, in 2001, this hotspot has become inflamed once again.

Notes and Questions on Dispute Resolution Conducted by the General Assembly

1. *The Korean Conflict*. Following World War II, Korea remained divided into two nations and was occupied by the major powers. The harmony that the drafters of the U.N. Charter believed would develop and continue after World War II evaporated long before the North Korean invasion of the South in 1950. The major powers after the War found themselves involved on either side in the Korea Conflict. The Security Council already reflected institutionally the bi-polarity of the Cold War in the veto power of the permanent members and consequent paralysis of the Council. The General Assembly, however, did not find itself so constrained. Article 18(2) of the Charter, which does not include a veto, allowed the Assembly to pass Resolution 112 (II) to establish a temporary commission to inquire into whether a lawful government had been established in the Republic of Korea. Pertinent resolutions include: G.A. Res. 112; G.A. Res. 195 (III), 12 Dec. 1948; G.A. Res. 293 (IV), 21 Oct. 1949. War came to Korea, despite the efforts of the United Nations Commission on Korea (UNCOK). After delays in placing reporters in country, observers were immediately dispatched to the 38th Parallel. The observers were not allowed into North Korea and were called back to Seoul just one day before the North attacked. The Commission's report was instrumental, however, in disproving the North Korean claims of self-defense to justify their attack. Moreover, the Commission's report established that an observer group could monitor developments in a tense situation and could provide useful information, even when confined to only one side of a border.

Notes and Questions on Dispute Resolution Conducted by the Secretary–General

The Secretary–General has initiated dispute resolution without General Assembly or Security Council authority. This action has usually been met with one of two responses: (1) one or both issued a resolution providing post hoc authorization; or (2) a member of the Security Council attempted to thwart the action as an abuse of authority.

1. *The Cambodia—Thailand Border Dispute.* Cambodia and Thailand have engaged in a border dispute for centuries. External pressures from Cold War conflicts in Southeast Asia led to "good offices" missions in 1959, 1963–64, and 1966. In 1966, the Secretary–General initiated the good-offices mission on his own authority. Thus, on August 16, 1966, the Secretary–General advised the Security Council that on the invitation of the parties he had appointed a representative to attempt to mediate the border dispute. The following letters were sent in response.

a. Letter from N. Fedorenko, Permanent Representative to the President of the Security Council. 27 Aug. 1966:

> With reference to the Secretary–General's letter dated 26 August 1966 addressed to the President of the Security Council (S/7402), stating his intention to appoint a Special Representative to help to eliminate tension between Cambodia and Thailand, I consider it necessary to emphasize that under the United Nations Charter decisions on matters connected with action by the United Nations relating to the maintenance of international peace and security are taken by the Security Council. When the Security Council takes a decision on the particular candidate put forward for the post after consultation with the parties concerned, the Soviet Union will have no objection to make.

I should be grateful if you would arrange for this letter to be circulated as an official Security Council document. Accept, Sir, etc.

(*Signed*) N. FEDORENKO
Representative of the USSR
in the Security Council

b. *Letter from Raul Quijano, Deputy Permanent Representative of the Argentine Republic Addressed to the President of the Security Council. 30 Sept. 1966*

I have the honour to refer to the letter dated 27 August 1966 from the Permanent Representative of the Union of Soviet Socialist Republics to the United Nations addressed to the President of the Security Council (S/7478). The Argentine Government wishes to state that it cannot share the views expressed by the Permanent Representative of the USSR concerning the decision taken by the Secretary–General, in consultation with the Governments of Cambodia and Thailand, to appoint Ambassador Herbert de Ribbing as his Special Representative in these two countries. My Government considers that the action taken by the Secretary–General is fully justified and falls within the competence conferred upon him by the Charter of the United Nations.

In the light of the provisions of Article 99 of the Charter and the directives addressed by the General Assembly to the Secretary–General concerning his functions and responsibilities, my Government has no doubt whatever that the Secretary–General has the authority, and even the duty, to keep himself informed on all matters which may threaten the maintenance of international peace and security and to exert the utmost effort to relieve situations which may become threats to international peace and security. Most particularly, when a dispute arises between two or more countries, it lies within the authority of the Secretary–General to offer his good offices to the parties concerned, either directly or through a representative, to reduce tension and resolve the disagreement between them. The Secretary–General's appointment of a representative for this purpose is, in my Government's view, subject to only two requirements: that he should consult the parties concerned and obtain their consent to his appointment of a representative and that he should inform the Security Council of his decision.

(*Signed*) Raul QUIJANO
Deputy Permanent Representative
of the Argentine
Republic to the United Nations
Chargé d'affaires a.1.

Query, Who do you think is correct? *See also* Section B of this Chapter.

2. *The Crisis in Lebanon (1958).* On May 22, 1958, Lebanon's Representative to the United Nations sent a letter to the President of the Security Council complaining that the United Arab Republic was violating Lebanon's borders, aiding insurgents within Lebanon, and waging a media campaign calling for the overthrow of the government. This letter prompted the Security Council to invite Representatives of Lebanon and the United Arab Republic to present their case before it. Thereafter, the Security Council authorized the formation of an observer mission to Lebanon (UNOGIL).

Upon instructions from my Government, I have the honour to request you, in your capacity as President of the Security Council, to call an urgent meeting of the Council to consider the following question: "Complaint by Lebanon in respect of a situation arising from the intervention of the United Arab Republic in the internal affairs of Lebanon, the continuance of which is likely to endanger the maintenance of international peace and security."

The said intervention consists *inter alia* of the following acts: the infiltration of armed bands from Syria into Lebanon, the destruction of Lebanese life and property by such bands, the participation of United Arab Republic nationals in acts of terrorism and rebellion against the established authorities in Lebanon, the supply of arms from Syria to individuals and bands in Lebanon rebelling against the established authorities, and the waging of a violent radio and press campaign in the United Arab Republic calling for strikes, demonstrations and the overthrow of the established authorities in Lebanon, and through other provocative acts. * * *

3. *Security Council Resolution 128 (S/4023)*

The Security Council, having heard the charges of the representative of Lebanon concerning interference by the United Arab Republic in the internal affairs of Lebanon and the reply of the representative of the United Arab Republic,

1. *Decides* to dispatch urgently an observation group to proceed to Lebanon so as to ensure that there is no illegal infiltration of personnel or supply of arms or other *material* across the Lebanese borders;

2. *Authorizes* the Secretary–General to take the necessary steps to that end;

3. *Requests* the observation group to keep the Security Council currently informed through the Secretary–General.

Adopted at the 825th meeting by 10 votes to none, with 1 abstention (Former USSR).

The broad language of *Resolution 128* could have been interpreted to authorize interdiction of border violations, but the Secretary–General chose to interpret it narrowly, to include only fact-finding. On November 25, 1958, the Security Council, manifesting structural paralysis, took the approach that became its hallmark during this period. It decided "to delete the Lebanese complaint from the list of matters of which it was seized," thus leaving the parties to resolve (or to continue) their own dispute. *See* Firmage, *Fact–Finding, supra* at 435.

Assassinations in Iraq of the King, the Crown Prince, and other government leaders in a coup precipitated the landings of U.S. troops in Lebanon and U.K. forces in Jordan, at the request of those governments.

The Secretary–General rejected U.S. and Lebanese requests that UNOGIL be transformed into a peace-keeping force, on the ground that such an action had to be based on Security Council directives pursuant to Chapter VII of the Charter.

4. U.N., REGIONAL ORGANIZATION, & THIRD PARTIES COORDINATION IN REGIONAL DISPUTE RESOLUTION.

Review Articles 33, 51, 52 and 53 of the U.N. Charter. The Charter calls upon states to look to their regional organizations for dispute resolution before turning to the U.N. It also authorizes the Security Council to refer disputes to regional organizations for resolution, or to include such organizations in enforcement actions undertaken by the Council.

Notes and Questions

1. ***The Contadora Group.*** On July 19, 1979, the Sandinistas seized power in Nicaragua, overthrowing the U.S.—backed former Nicaraguan dictator, General Anastazio Somoza. The Reagan Administration, feeling that another "Marxist-led" nation in the Western Hemisphere was intolerable and presented a threat to the security of the entire region, began a campaign to undermine and contain the Sandinista Government in Nicaragua. The assistance was actually initiated by a "request" from El Salvador and, eventually from other countries. Massive financial assistance and military training programs were begun by the United States to maintain what it considered "friendly" regimes in Honduras, El Salvador, and Costa Rica. The U.S. Government created, financed, and trained the *Contra* (anti-Sandinista) rebels fighting in Nicaragua. The *Contras,* were composed largely of former members of the deposed dictator Somoza's National Guard and *Sandanistas,* who had helped overthrow Somoza, but who had become disaffected. The CIA also took direct military action against Nicaragua by reconnaissance overflights of Nicaraguan airspace by military aircraft, and mining Nicaraguan harbors.

Colombia, Mexico, Panama and Venezuela organized the Contadora Group that sought peaceful resolution by promoting dialogue among Nicaragua, Honduras, El Salvador, Costa Rica and, the two principal third-party sponsors of the violence in Nicaragua, Cuba and the United States. The methodology was mediation with good-offices aimed at ending the long-standing warfare and violence. The Contadora movement sought to prevent military intervention and conflict through a broad range of political and economic cooperative measures and in limiting the introduction of arms and military bases. *See, The Contadora Act on Peace and Co-operation in Central America,* June 7, 1986, reprinted in 25 ILM 1302 (1986), and in Contadora and the Central American Peace Process: Selected Documents, 8 SAIS Papers in International Affairs 194–217 (Bagley, et al. eds. 1985). Unfortunately, the Draft Contadora Act was never ratified. *See also,* Caminos & Lavalle, *New Departures in the Exercise of Inherent Powers by the UN and OAS Secretaries–General: The Central American Situation,* 83 A.J.I.L. 395 (1989).

2. *Haiti.* In December 1990, in an election monitored by the United Nations, more than two-thirds of the voters of Haiti elected Jean–Bertrand Aristide President. Less than a year later, on September 29, 1991, a military coup led by General Raoul Cédras ousted President Aristide, who fled to the U.S. for sanctuary. The Organization of American States (OAS) acted quickly to condemn the coup and declare Aristide the true President of Haiti. The OAS attempted to negotiate with the military and purported to impose sanctions on the country, but the sanctions put little actual pressure on Haiti because the states failed to enforce the embargo. For the next eighteen months, the OAS position regarding Aristide was ambivalent, with the Bush Administration and the CIA publicly criticizing Aristide and implicitly supporting the military. The Clinton Administration assumed a different posture toward Aristide and urged the U.N. to intervene on his behalf, although it also demonstrated some ambivalence. The U.N. did intervene on June 26, 1993, by imposing a temporary embargo on oil and military supplies. The result was the Governor's Island Agreement, which would have allowed for Aristide's eventual return in exchange for amnesty for the coup leaders and compromises regarding Aristide's cabinet.

The military, however, refused to adhere to the Governor's Island Agreement. In response, in November 1993, the U.S., Canada, France, and Venezuela (the "Friends of Haiti") organized in an attempt to force a settlement on the parties. Their negotiations failed and on July 31, 1994, following U.S. requests in light of the Haitian refugee crisis, the Security Counsil passed *Resolution 940*, urging Member States to take all necessary steps to restore Aristide to command in Haiti. In response, in September 1994, the U.S. sent a delegation, headed by former President Jimmy Carter, to attempt to negotiate a settlement. In the meantime, President Clinton deployed troops to Haiti. Perhaps realizing that the U.S. would use force to remove it, the military finally surrendered control of Haiti. General Cedras left for Panama in October 1994 and Aristide regained the presidency of Haiti within a few days. Little over a year later, Aristide relinquished the presidency to his protégé Rene Preval, who won with 87.9% of the votes. Ultimately, states from around the world contributed to the restoration of democracy in Haiti. For a thorough discussion of this and other OAS actions, *see* Schnably, *The Santiago Commitment as a Call to Democracy in the United States: Evaluating the OAS Role in Haiti, Peru, and Guatemala,* 25 U. Miami Inter–Am. L. Rev. 393 (1994).

3. *Future of Regional Enforcement Actions*. The United Nations has been strained by the many peacekeeping actions it has undertaken during the last decade, particularly in light of the failure of the United States and other countries to remain current on their financial obligations to the U.N. As a result, the U.N. has looked to regional organizations for dispute resolution. Consider the role of regional organizations, and their capabilities and limitations regarding the protection of neighboring states. Can a regional organization be an impartial intervenor so close to home? Will an increasing reliance on regional organizations improve intervention actions, many of which have been uncertain and ineffectual in the hands of the U.N.? For an interesting discussion of the role of regional organizations in dispute resolution, *see* Borgen, Note, *The Theory and Practice of Regional Organization Intervention in Civil Wars,* 26 N.Y.U. J. Int'l L. & Pol. 797

(1994). *See also* Enforcing Restraint: Collective Intervention in Internal Conflicts, Lori Fisler Damrosch, ed. (1993).

5.   ADJUSTING THE PEACE SYSTEM: RECENT ATTEMPTS TO MODERNIZE THE PROCESS—NEGOTIATION, MEDIATION & CONCILIATION

The United Nations Handbook on the Peaceful Settlement of Disputes Between States.

Introduction

By its resolutions 39/79 and 39/88 of 13 December 1984, the General Assembly requested the Secretary–General to prepare * * * in the light of the views expressed in the course of the discussions in the Sixth Committee and in the Special Committee, a draft handbook on the peaceful settlement of disputes between States.

* * *

The purpose of the handbook is to contribute to the peaceful settlement of disputes between States and to help to increase compliance with international law by providing States parties to a dispute, particularly those States which do not have the benefit of long-established and experienced legal departments, with the information they might need to select and apply procedures best suited to the settlement of particular disputes.

* * *

In conformity with the above-mentioned resolutions, the scope of the handbook was to be limited to disputes between States, excluding those disputes which although involving States fell under municipal law or were within the competence of domestic courts. However, at the request of the Consultative Group to the Secretary–General, the draft handbook now includes disputes to which subjects of law other than States may be parties. *United Nations Handbook on the Peaceful Settlement of Disputes Between States. (Handbook is in Doc. Supp.)*

* * *

Notes

1.   Guatamala Draft Resolution Calling for U.N. Rules for the Conciliation of Disputes Between States. (See, The Doc. Supp.)

2.   The General Assembly Plan: U.N. Draft Rules for the Conciliation of Disputes Between States, Nov. 28, 1990, 30 Ilm 229 (1991). (See, The Doc. Supp.)

3.   *The Secretary–General's Plan*. Boutros Boutros–Ghali, Report on an Agenda for Peace—Preventive Diplomacy, Peacemaking and Peacekeeping (June 17, 1992, 31 Ilm 953 (1992).

Introduction

1.   In its statement of 31 January 1992, adopted at the conclusion of the first meeting held by the Security Council at the level of Heads of State and Government, I was invited to prepare, for circulation to the * * * United Nations * * *, an "analysis and recommendations on ways of strengthening and making more efficient within the framework and provisions of the Charter the capacity of the United Nations for preventive diplomacy, for peacemaking and for peace-keeping."

2.   The United Nations is a gathering of sovereign States and what it can do depends on the common ground that they create between them. The adversarial decades of the cold war made the original promise of the Organization impossible to fulfil. The January 1992 Summit therefore represented an unprecedented recommitment, at the highest political level, to the Purposes and Principles of the Charter.

3.   In these past months a conviction has grown, among nations large and small, that an opportunity has been regained to achieve the great objectives of the Charter—a United Nations capable of maintaining international peace and security, of securing justice and human rights and of promoting, in the words of the Charter, "social progress and better standards of life in larger freedom". This opportunity must not be squandered. The Organization must never again be crippled as it was in the era that has now passed.

4.   I welcome the invitation of the Security Council, early in my tenure as Secretary–General, to prepare this report. It draws upon ideas and proposals transmitted to me by Governments, regional agencies, non-governmental organizations, and institutions and individuals from many countries. I am grateful for these, even as I emphasize that the responsibility for this report is my own.

5.   The sources of conflict and war are pervasive and deep. To reach them will require our utmost effort to enhance respect for human rights and fundamental freedoms, to promote sustainable economic and social development for wider prosperity, to alleviate distress and to curtail the existence and use of massively destructive weapons. The U.N. Conference on Environment and Development, the largest summit ever held, has just met at Rio de Janeiro. The second World Conference on Human Rights [follows.] In 1994 Population and Development will be addressed. In 1995 the World Conference on Women will take place, and a World Summit for Social Development has been proposed. * * * I shall be addressing all these great issues. I bear them all in mind as, in the present report, I turn to the problems that the Council has specifically requested I consider: preventive diplomacy, peacemaking and peace-keeping—to which I have added a closely related concept, post-conflict peace-building.

6.   The manifest desire of the membership to work together is a new source of strength in our common endeavour. Success is far from certain, however. While my report deals with ways to improve the Organization's capacity to pursue and preserve peace, it is crucial for all Member States to bear in mind that the search for improved mechanisms and techniques will

be of little significance unless this new spirit of commonality is propelled by the will to make the hard decisions demanded by this time of opportunity.

* * *

14. Since the creation of the United Nations in 1945, over 100 major conflicts around the world have left some 20 million dead. The United Nations was rendered powerless to deal with many of these crises because of the vetoes—279 of them—cast in the Security Council, which were a vivid expression of the divisions of that period.

15. With the end of the cold war there have been no such vetoes since 31 May 1990, and demands on the United Nations have surged. Its security arm, once disabled by circumstances it was not created or equipped to control, has emerged as a central instrument for the prevention and resolution of conflicts and for the preservation of peace. Our aims must be:

- To seek to identify at the earliest possible stage situations that could produce conflict, and to try through diplomacy to remove the sources of danger before violence results;

- Where conflict erupts, to engage in peacemaking aimed at resolving the issues that have led to conflict;

- Through peace-keeping, to work to preserve peace, however fragile, where fighting has been halted and to assist in implementing agreements achieved by the peacemakers;

- To stand ready to assist in peace-building in its differing contexts: rebuilding the institutions and infrastructures of nations torn by civil war and strife; and building bonds of peaceful mutual benefit among nations formerly at war;

- And in the largest sense, to address the deepest causes of conflict: economic despair, social injustice and political oppression. It is possible to discern an increasingly common moral perception that spans the world's nations and peoples, and which is finding expression in international laws, many owing their genesis to the work of this Organization.

U.N.Doc. A/47/227 and S/2411 (17 June 1992), reprinted in, 31 I.L.M. 953 (1992).

Query. Do the recent plans improve on the old? Why? Why not?

————

The Efficacy of Preventive Diplomacy.

Weiss, The UN's Prevention Pipe–Dream

14 Berkeley J. Int'l L. 423, 431–34 (1996) (footnotes omitted).[2]

* * *

————

2. Reprinted by permission of the Berkeley Journal of International Law.

There are substantial costs associated with reacting to threats to international peace and security, particularly for outsiders sending troops or emergency relief. But these costs pale in comparison to those borne by local populations whose social fabric is destroyed, along with its economic base for future development. With tension, violence, and war spreading, and with their consequences so dire, would it not make more sense to act earlier so as to head them off?

Although many specialists in international security are ready to answer in the affirmative, calculations by state decisionmakers about the pluses and minuses of prevention are held hostage to myopic calculations of raisons d'etat. Preventive diplomacy is merely the latest conceptual fad— one passionate but realistic advocate called it "an idea in search of a strategy." The need for prevention was originally behind Chapter VI of the UN Charter ("Pacific Settlement of Disputes"), and many efforts were part of the UN's routine by 1945, and throughout the Cold War. These early activities, as well as appropriate adaptations of such European confidence-building measures as mutual downsizing, joint exercises, and public announcements of troop movements, are plausible components of UN peacetime preventive diplomacy. Other actions, such as the expanded use of fact-finding missions, human rights monitors, and early-warning systems are being discussed and implemented. Even these measures, though, seem unlikely to deter the types of wars that are a plague on the international house at this time.

* * *

However useful such preventive peacetime measures, defusing tensions (for example, avoiding the outbreak of war in a Macedonia) and forestalling massive displacement and suffering (for example, halting even worse atrocities in a Rwanda torn by genocide) require more deliberate military action. But this sort of endeavor, given the "high politics" affecting the military forces and national security of its member states, is acutely difficult for the United Nations.

The most indispensable and cost-effective preventive measure, the deployment of troops, is considerably more problematic than such peacetime preventive measures as better early warning and fact-finding. Moreover, imposing a UN peacekeeping force to forestall the outbreak of violence and war may not be possible—or even desirable. Hence, some observers argued that an outside force in Burundi could unleash a full-scale ethnic conflict rather than prevent one. In a similar vein, the inadvisability of stopping the Rwandan Patriotic Front's (RPF) liberation of the country comes to mind as an argument for not preventing the "just" part of the 1994 Rwandan violence.

Furthermore, even when it is possible and advisable to act, the nature of the UN decision-making process often impedes the deployment of preventive forces. To be a deterrent, such UN preventive soldiers should be backed by contingency plans and empowered to retaliate against aggressors. This would advance authorization for mandatory coercive action under Chapter VII ("Action with Respect to Threats to the Peace, Breaches of the Peace, and Acts of Aggression") in the event that local forces challenge a preventive UN operation. The only example to date has been the symbolic deployment of a detachment of some one thousand blue helmets to Macedonia. Widely heralded (incorrectly in my view) as an important precedent for effective prevention, it is only effective so long as the Serbs do not call the international bluff.

Symbols are of limited utility, in the Balkans or anywhere else. Unlike states whose symbolic actions can deter aggression because they are backed by automatic military responses, the United Nations must rely upon Chapter VII to authorize one. Thomas Schelling long ago noted the need for escalation, and the effective threat of further use of force in order to deter a would-be aggressor by fear of "pain beyond endurance." Such coercive backup is not easy for the United Nations either politically or operationally. This is why it is absent in Macedonia. Beneath the rhetoric and posturing, no real line has been drawn in the sand for the Serbs. Without the ability or willingness to use force, if and when the bluff is called, the currency of UN action will be devalued to such an extent that the preventive action should not have been attempted in the first place.

The rub is obvious: Prevention is cost-effective in the long run, but cost-intensive in the short run. This is because the logic behind preventive action as an economic calculation is fundamentally flawed. As pundits and professors are fond of pointing out, democratically-elected governments rarely entertain policies whose time horizon extends beyond the next public opinion poll, and certainly not beyond the next electoral campaign. The highest elected representatives of major powers are obliged to exaggerate immediate expenditures (for their own administration) and discount future ones (for someone else's administration). Even if savings could be definitively calculated to be economically compelling (which they cannot), prevention is very risky in domestic political terms. Just a few body bags, let alone getting mired down in a protracted military operation, could mean political disaster. Devoting huge resources to humanitarian relief may not make much economic sense, but it is politically risk-free for elected officials. The proverbial bottom-line is that prevention is far more unattractive in practice than in theory.

* * *

Questions. Is Weiss overly pessimistic about the possibility of UN implementation of a long-term preventive diplomacy plan? Are politicians truly controlled by incentives in the way Weiss suggests? Consider his arguments in the context of recent interventions by the UN and its member states. Are Weiss's arguments supported by these experiences?

SECTION B. THE USE OF FORCE BY THE UNITED NATIONS

1. EVOLUTION OF LAW AGAINST USE OF FORCE BY STATES:

Conceptual and Philosophical Introduction.*

Section A, on Peaceful Resolution of Disputes, precedes this section on the use of force by the United Nations, because we see it as being primary.

---

* Portions of this introduction were adapted from Firmage, Summary and Inter-   pretation, concluding Chapter in International Law of Civil War 405–428 (Richard Falk,

Chapter VI of the U.N. Charter provides for a system of non-violent dispute resolution through fact-finding, good offices, negotiations, and mediation. There is a provision for binding third-party decisions through arbitration and judicial resolution through the International Court of Justice. The United Nations also has powers that go beyond techniques of peaceful resolution of disputes. Where the League of Nations was limited merely to recommending action, Chapter VII of the U.N. Charter allows the latter, with Security Council approval, to use force ranging from economic boycott and sanction to initiating war against an aggressive state. This section focuses on Chapter VII and provides opportunity to analyze the use of force and its limitations under the United Nations Charter.

At the end of the Cold War we face a fractionalized world of rival ethnic groups, racial, tribal, religious and national factions in conflict similar to conditions before and after the First World War. In the aftermath of that epochal confrontation, we saw the disintegration of major imperial and multi-national ethnic and linguistic systems leading to ethnic and national conflict. The aftershocks also gave birth to the Bolshevik Revolution, with profound consequences for Asia and Europe. In post-war Germany, hyper-inflation and political reaction to defeat in war brought the rise of Adolph Hitler and National Socialism. After World War II, the United Nations was created with the hope that peaceful resolution of disputes would be more feasible. The U.N. was to provide a mechanism to control violence. Soon, however, the world became divided into two, perhaps three, blocks. The Cold War dominated international law, including that relating to the use of force. The violence unleashed in World War II was only transmuted at its end as Cold War followed—overt, covert, and by proxy.

The disintegration of the former Soviet Union and the end of the Cold War provides an opportunity for the international system to function more efficiently. We now have an opportunity for peaceful resolution of disputes and an amelioration of violence to a degree not enjoyed by the leaders of nations at least since World War I. Now, however, with the disintegration of multi-ethnic states in Yugoslavia and the Soviet Union, the forms of violence which preceded and followed World War I confront us again. We now face violence among Hindu and Muslim in India and Pakistan; Serbs, Croats and Muslims in Bosnia; Armenians and Azeris in the Caucuses; Tamils and Sinhalese in Sri Lanka; Israelis and Palestinians in the West Bank; and the Hutus and the Tutsis in Rwanda, to mention but a few.

A paradox of the nuclear era is that the existence of nuclear weapons has suppressed in some circumstances massive violence with conventional weaponry of the magnitude, at least, of World War II. The nature of war in our time has tended to be internecine: wars of national liberation, civil wars, ethnic and religious conflict. Now, with the breakdown of the last imperial system to survive both world wars, and the disintegration of multi-ethnic states associated with the former Soviet Union and Communism, ethnic or tribal war, internal war and civil strife are increasingly the sorts of conflict which will challenge the peace.

ed. 1971); Firmage, Kellogg Lectures, 1993
supra at 7–8.

Solutions are not readily available. International law, when faced with the issue of third-party involvement in civil strife, has two competing lines of authority. One line of precedent allows third-party intervention in civil strife upon the invitation and in aid of the incumbent government, at least until a status of belligerency is achieved by the insurgent forces. When belligerency is reached, international law requires neutrality by third party states. The other line of cases simply requires neutrality on the part of third parties throughout the course of civil strife. There is a bias favoring incumbent governments in the former line of authority. One of the reasons for this bias is that incumbent governments perform certain invaluable services for the international community. Such an approach places value in a modicum of order provided by the incumbent government that allows for the provision of services and minimal amenities for citizens and non citizens. For a decentralized and horizontal system of law such as international law, the municipal government provides an essential role. Unlike a mature municipal system of law, with a vertical hierarchy of lawmakers, judges and police, the international system depends upon sovereign, independent incumbent governments to assure even minimal order.

But in periods of radical transformation and disintegration of old systems, this conceptually clean analysis becomes messy. When incumbent governments collapse, choosing an "incumbent" from among the various contenders may be impossible. And even if an incumbent can be identified, conditions can become so chaotic that the services normally performed by the incumbent government to earn the bias in its favor by the international community cannot be accomplished. In this situation, there is little reason to favor an incumbent.

Exceptions to the non-intervention principle exist, although colonial abuses have tarnished, if not destroyed the integrity of such exceptions. It is contended that third parties may intervene for humanitarian reasons, for example, when an incumbent government abuses its own citizens or the citizens of other states. The legality of humanitarian intervention is hotly debated and we will present the various arguments for your consideration. Protocols I and II to the 1949 Geneva Convention provide means to control internal warfare and international warfare in circumstances not covered by the Geneva Convention proper.

The neutrality principle also embodies the recognition that violence, including violent intervention in civil strife in another state, is rarely as successful, as determinative or as easily contained and terminated as it may have seemed initially. The world community has struggled with this issue in modern history for nearly a century—from the Hague Peace Conferences of 1899 and 1907, through the League of Nations, to the activities of the United Nations today. The United Nations has taken action in Suez, the Congo, Korea, Cyprus, the Greek Civil War, the war between India and Pakistan, the creation of the State of Israel, and, most recently Cambodia, the Persian Gulf War, Somalia, Rwanda, the territory of the former Yugoslavia, Haiti, and Liberia.

The ending of the Cold War offers the first chance since the inception of the United Nations for a system of international dispute resolution truly to work. If the international system is to move beyond the present level of almost total reliance upon nation states either to keep the peace or to break it, as they wish, then international institutions of law must be strengthened. The accomplishments of this century provide a foundation for peace. The machinery of the Hague Conventions of 1899 and 1906 was used in the successful resolution of maritime disputes. The League of Nations and later United Nations fact-finding groups and other institutions for peaceful resolution of disputes enjoyed considerable success in resolving conflicts, including border disputes, disputes among racial, ethnic, and national groups recently freed from imperial governmental joinder and disputes involving the protection of human rights of ethnic and religious minorities in newly created states following the disintegration of imperial and colonial systems after World War I. These newly created states following through 1930 successfully redrew the map of Europe and quite possibly arrested war among rival ethnic and religious groups, particularly in the Balkans. These successes, presented in Section A of this chapter, unfortunately and unfairly, have been eclipsed in our minds by the spectacular failure of the League and the major states of the world, in or out of the League, to deal with the aggressor states of the 1930s: Japan in Manchuria; Germany; Italy and Portugal in the Spanish Civil War; and later in those directs acts of aggression in Poland and Czechoslovakia that led to World War II. This section moves from Chapter VI actions to Chapter VII actions, presenting the law relating to the use of force by the United Nations.

2.   *EARLY HISTORICAL DEVELOPMENT AND LEGAL AUTHORITY INTERNATIONAL ORGANIZATIONS.*

The League of Nations. The Covenant of the League did not outlaw war as such. Instead, it sought to obligate states to resort to methods of peaceful settlement; in turn, members of the League agreed under certain circumstances not to resort to war. See in particular the following articles of the Covenant: *Article 12* ("* * * they agree in no case to resort to war until three months after the award by the arbitrators or the report by the Council."); *Article 13* ("The Members of the League agree that they will carry out in full good faith any award that may be rendered, and that they will not resort to war against a Member of the League which complies therewith."); *Article 15* ("If a report by the Council is unanimously agreed to by the Members thereof other than the representatives of one or more of the parties to the dispute, the Members of the League agree that they will not go to war with any party to the dispute which complies * * * "). Article 16, the primary operative section, required that economic sanctions be imposed on any state violating its covenants and that other member states support those adversely affected by the sanctions.

These qualified commitments against waging war should be contrasted to the language of the Peace Pact of Paris and *Article 2(4)* of the United Nations Charter. Also to be contrasted with *Article 2(4)* of the Charter is *Article 10* of the Covenant, in which members of the League undertook to "respect and preserve as against external aggression the territorial integrity and existing political independence of all members of the League." The mechanisms for enforcing the ambiguous and qualified obligations not to wage war were contained in *Article 10* of the Covenant ("* * * the Council shall advise upon the means by which this obligation shall be fulfilled") and in *Article 16* (the provisions for collective measures by the members of the League in the event a member of the League should "resort to war in disregard of its Covenants under Article 12, 13 or 15").

The United States did not become a member of the League of Nations. The Covenant of the League was an integral part of the Treaty of Versailles. When it was submitted to the Senate for its advice and consent, Senator Henry Cabot Lodge led the Senate to the adoption of a number of reservations, notably one to Article 10, to the effect that the United States would not assume an obligation to preserve the territorial integrity or political independence of any country unless "in any particular case the Congress, which, under the Constitution, has the sole power to declare war or authorize the employment of the military or naval forces of the United States, shall by act or joint resolution so provide." President Wilson refused to accept the Lodge reservations. As a result, the treaty (with the Covenant) was rejected by the Senate. As for the effect of the Covenant on the unilateral use of force by states and the efforts of the League to restrain that force, it can only be stated that the results were dismal.

Morgenthau, Politics Among Nations 290

(4th ed., 1967).*

* * * Collective measures of enforcement under Article 16 were applied in only one of the five cases in which undoubtedly a member of the League resorted to war in violation of the Covenant. With regard to the Sino–Japanese conflict that started in 1931, the Assembly of the League found unanimously that "without any declaration of war, part of the Chinese territory has been forcibly seized and occupied by the Japanese troops," and that far-flung hostilities, initiated by Japan, had taken place between troops of the Chinese and Japanese governments. Yet the Assembly found also that Japan had not resorted to war in violation of the Covenant and that, therefore, Article 16 did not apply.

During the Chaco War of 1932–35, when Paraguay continued hostilities against Bolivia in violation of the Covenant, many members of the League limited the arms embargo, originally imposed upon both belligerents, to Paraguay. This was a discriminatory measure falling far short of the spirit and the letter of the first paragraph of Article 16. When Japan, which by then had resigned from the League, invaded China in 1937, the Assembly found that Japan had violated the Nine Power Treaty of 1922 and the Briand–Kellogg Pact, that Article 16 was applicable, and that the members of the League had the right to take enforcement measures individually under that provision. No such measures were ever taken. When the USSR went to war with Finland in 1939, it was expelled from the League by virtue of Article 16, paragraph 4, but no collective action of enforcement was taken against it.

In contrast to these cases, the Assembly found in 1935 that the invasion of Ethiopia by Italy constituted resort to war within the meaning

* © Reprinted with the permission of Alfred A. Knopf, Inc., New York.

and in violation of the Covenant and that, therefore, Article 16, paragraph 1, was to apply. In consequence, collective economic sanctions against Italy were decided upon and applied. Yet the two measures, provided for by Article 16, paragraph 1, that offered the best chance of making international law prevail under the circumstances and that in all probability would have compelled Italy to desist from its attack upon Ethiopia—namely, an embargo on oil shipments to Italy and the closure of the Suez Canal—were not taken. "However," as Sir Lauterpacht puts it, "although the sanctions of Article 16, paragraph 1, were formally put into operation and although an elaborate machinery was set up with a view to their successive and gradual enforcement, the nature of the action taken was such as to suggest that the repressive measures were being adopted as a manifestation of moral reprobation rather than as an effective means of coercion."

[To sum up]: the attempts at establishing a centralized system of law enforcement under Article 16 of the Covenant by saying that in most cases that would have justified the application of sanctions, sanctions were not applied at all. In the sole case in which they were applied, they were applied in such an ineffective fashion as virtually to assure both their failure and the success of the recalcitrant state.

————

It should also be noted that the League system had a measure of success in the 1925 crisis between Greece and Bulgaria, noted supra, and failures in Japanese invasion of Manchuria, the Spanish Civil War, and the German Reich's invasions of the Rhineland (1936), Austria (1938), Czechoslovakia (1939), and Poland (1939).

Covenant of the League of Nations, June 28, 1919

1 Hudson International Legislation 1 (1931).

* * *

Article XVI

Should any Member of the League resort to war in disregard of its covenants under Article 12, 13 or 15, it shall ipso facto be deemed to have committed an act of war against all other Members of the League, which hereby undertake immediately to subject it to the severance of all trade or financial relations, the prohibition of all intercourse between their nationals and the nationals of the covenant-breaking State, and the prevention of all financial, commercial or personal intercourse between the nationals of the covenant-breaking State and the nationals of any other State, whether a Member of the League or not.

It shall be the duty of the Council in such case to recommend to the several Governments concerned what effective military, naval or air force the Members of the League shall severally contribute to the armed forces to be used to protect the covenants of the League. The Members of the League agree, further, that they will mutually support one another in the financial and economic measures which are taken under this Article, to minimize the loss and inconvenience resulting from the above measures, and that they will mutually support one another in resisting any special measures aimed at one of their number by the covenant-breaking State, and that they will take the necessary steps to afford passage through their territory to the forces of any of the Members which are co-operating to protect the covenants of the League.

    * * *

Notes and Questions. you read the material in this section (focusing on a series of crises, which eventuated in the use of force), ask yourself whether the result in each situation would have been different under the League Covenant or the U.N. Charter. Is "balance of power" the immutable "iron law of politics," which still [if it ever actually did] fits our "anarchic world of incorrigible power seekers," as the realists maintain? Are there viable alternative views?

Travaux—Preparatoires for the Peace Pact of Paris (The Kellogg–Briand Pact)

[1928] 1 Foreign Relations of the United States 32 (1942).

French Draft of Treaty for the Condemnation and Renunciation of War as an Instrument of National Policy

The President of the German Empire, the President of the United States of America, the President of the French Republic, His Majesty the King of England, Ireland and the British Dominions, Emperor of India, His Majesty the King of Italy, His Majesty the Emperor of Japan:

Equally desirous not only of perpetuating the happy relations of peace and friendship now existing among their peoples, but also of avoiding the danger of war between all other nations in the world.

Having agreed to consecrate in a solemn act their most formal and most definite resolution to condemn war as an instrument of national policy and to renounce it in favor of a peaceful settlement of international conflicts, expressing, finally, the hope that all the other nations of the world will be willing to join in this humane effort to bring about the association of the civilized peoples in a common renunciation of war as an instrument of national policy, have decided to conclude a treaty and to that end have designated as their respective plenipotentiaries [the above parties] who, after exchanging their full powers found to be in good and due form have agreed on the following provisions:

Article One

The High Contracting Parties without any intention to infringe upon the exercise of their rights of legitimate self-defense within the framework of existing treaties, particularly when the violation of certain of the provisions of such treaties constitutes a hostile act, solemnly declare that they condemn recourse to war and renounce it as an instrument of national policy; that is to say, as an instrument of individual, spontaneous and independent political action taken on their own initiative and not action in respect of which they might become involved through the obligation of a treaty such as the covenant of the League of Nations or any other treaty registered with the League of Nations. They undertake on these conditions not to attack or invade one another.

Article Two

The settlement or solution of all disputes or conflicts of whatever nature or origin which might arise among the High Contracting Parties or between any two of them shall never be sought on either side except by pacific methods.

Article Three

In case one of the High Contracting Parties should contravene this treaty, the other Contracting Powers would ipso facto be released with respect to that Party from their obligations under this treaty.

* * *

———

[Reply by Kellogg], Washington, April 23, 1928.

* * * In its present form the French draft treaty is wholly unacceptable to the United States since it cannot in any respect be regarded as an effective instrument for the promotion of world peace. It emphasizes war, not peace, and seems in effect to be a justification rather than a renunciation of the use of armed force. The United States will sign no treaty of the nature now under discussion which cannot reasonably be expected to lessen the danger of an outbreak of war and thus promote the cause of world peace.

* * *

There seem to be six major considerations which the French Government has emphasized in its correspondence and in its draft treaty, namely, that the treaty must not (1) impair the right of legitimate self-defense; (2) violate the Covenant of the League of Nations; (3) violate the treaties of Locarno; (4) violate certain unspecified treaties guaranteeing neutrality; (5) bind the parties in respect of a state breaking the treaty; (6) come into effect until accepted by all or substantially all of the Powers of the world. The views of the United States on these points are as follows: (1) Self-defense. There is nothing in the American draft of an anti-war treaty which restricts or impairs in any way the right of self-defense. That right is inherent in every sovereign state and is implicit in every treaty. Every nation is free at all times and regardless of treaty provisions to defend its territory from attack or invasion and it alone is competent to decide whether circumstances require recourse to war in self-defense. If it has a good case, the world will applaud and not condemn its action. Express recognition by treaty of this inalienable right, however, gives rise to the same difficulty encountered in any effort to define aggression. It is the identical question approached from the other side. Inasmuch as no treaty provision can add to the natural right of self-defense, it is not in the interest of peace that a treaty should stipulate a juristic conception of self-defense since it is far too easy for the unscrupulous to mold events to accord with an agreed definition.

* * *

General Treaty for Renunciation of War As An Instrument of National Policy of August 27, 1928

46 Stat. 2343, 94 L.N.T.S. 59 (1929).

Article I

The High Contracting Parties solemnly declare in the names of their respective peoples that they condemn recourse to war for the solution of international controversies, and renounce it as an instrument of national policy in their relations with one another.

Article II

The High Contracting Parties agree that the settlement or solution of all disputes or conflicts of whatever nature or of whatever origin they may be, which may arise among them, shall never be sought except by pacific means.

Notes and Questions

1. *Parties during World War II and Current Status.* The Pact of Paris, TS 796; 2 Bevans 732; 94 LNTS 57, signed at Paris, August 27, 1928, entered into force for the United States on July 24, 1929. It is still in effect and, in 1993, has 66 adherents. Treaties in Force lists the parties and includes a disclaimer that the Department has not passed upon the effect of war on any of the treaties in the compilation.

2. *Why was the Pact of Paris a futile bar to war?* Even before the outbreak of World War II, armed conflict had been carried on by Japan in China, by Germany, Italy and the former USSR in Spain, and by Italy in Ethiopia. Was it ever vindicated?

3. *Was the Pact of Paris vindicated in any way in World War II?* How was it to be enforced? Did it have an "enforcement clause"? Would it have been appropriate to include one? Was it vindicated at Nuremberg? For war crimes trials and related material, *see* Chapter 16.

Brown, Undeclared Wars

33 A.J.I.L. 538, 540 (1939).*

* * *

* Reprinted with the permission of the American Society of International Law.

We see, therefore, in the light of theory and practice, that the problem of the undeclared war remains largely an academic one which involves considerations more ethical than legal. And this is true also of the self-denying declaration embodied in the General Treaty of 1928 for the Renunciation of War, generally entitled the Kellogg Pact. This agreement, while purporting to renounce the use of war, really consecrated the vague and dangerous right of self-defence. The various signatories explicitly reserved the right to resort to war and to judge for themselves "whether circumstances require recourse to war in self-defence." Within four years of the signing of this Pact occurred three breaches of the Pact, namely, the aggression by Russia against China in 1929, the occupation of Manchuria by Japan in 1931, and the invasion of Colombia by Peru in 1932. The more recent instances of warlike acts by Japan, Germany, and Italy are too vividly in mind to require comment. It is necessary, however, to stress the lamentable and unforeseen consequence of the Kellogg Pact in encouraging aggressor nations hypocritically to avoid any formal declaration of war in order to elude the constraints of this pious declaration.

Still another most unexpected inducement to avoid a formal declaration of war, as revealed in the case of the conflict now going on between Japan and China, has been the natural desire to escape the disabilities of recent neutrality legislation of the United States, whereby the shipment of arms and munitions of war to belligerents is automatically forbidden. The question presents itself whether, in the absence of a formal declaration of war by either side, it should not be incumbent on neutral nations to brush all legal niceties aside and openly acknowledge a state of war where the laws of war and neutrality should apply. Nations intent on peace and determined to uphold the reign of law have a solemn duty to avoid any implied connivance in the evasion of international obligations. Neutrality is not merely to conserve national interests, but also to preserve an impartial rôle which may enable a nation to affirm with vigor the responsibilities and rights of peoples under international law.

The situation is certainly a most unhappy one. It is stultifying to discover that an idealistic agreement such as the Kellogg Pact, and neutrality legislation conceived for a generous purpose, should actually conduce to the fiction of the undeclared war. * * *

Notes and Questions. What are the reasons behind a requirement that war be declared? Did it serve as a caution to a nation of the awesome act contemplated? Did the Nuremberg Charter, Trials and Judgments have any effect on the Law relating to the Use of Force among states or the role of international alliances or organizations in relation to illegal use of force by states? Were these occurrences more important than the old rule requiring declaration of war? Less? The same? The Nuremberg Trials are discussed in Chapter 16, *on Individual Responsibility, supra,* and the role of the above-mentioned items are considered in Chapter 15, Use of Force by States, *infra*.

Charter of the United Nations

Turn to your Documentary Supplement and analyze articles 2(1) & (4), 7, 25, 39, 41, 42, 43, and 51.

Letter From Edward R. Stettinius, Secretary of State of the United States, To President Harry Truman

13 United States Department of State Bulletin 77, 80 (1945).

Summary of Report on Results of San Francisco Conference

* * *

It will be the duty of the Security Council, supported by the pledged participation, and backed by military contingents to be made available by the member states, to use its great prestige to bring about by peaceful means the adjustment or the settlement of international disputes. Should these means fail, it is its duty, as it has the power, to take whatever measures are necessary, including measures of force, to suppress acts of aggression or other breaches of the peace. It will be the duty of the Security Council, in other words, to make good the commitment of the United Nations to maintain international peace and security, turning that lofty purpose into practice. To that end the Council will be given the use and the support of diplomatic, economic and military tools and weapons in the control of the United Nations.

* * *

———

Notes and Questions

1. ***The Grand Design.*** The U.N. Charter forbade the use of force by states (article 2(4)), save in the limited area of self-defense (article 51). A near monopoly of force was reposed in the Security Council, under Chapter VII, which was empowered to respond to the dramatic conditions of article 39 ("any threat to the peace, breach of the peace, or act of aggression") by resort to the powerful measures of articles 41 and 42, including armed forces at its disposal under the terms of article 43, especially "immediately available national air-force contingents" (article 45). It was a vision of many in 1945 that the military forces of the Security Council would restrain any nation that disturbed the peace following World War II.

The language of Charter article 2(4) comprehensively prohibits the use of force, replacing and surpassing the Kellogg–Briand Pact, which prohibited the use of war as a political tool. The language, however, has traditionally been read more narrowly, to prohibit the use or threat to use force only in the international arena. Thus, in article 39, read in pari materia, the terms "breach of the peace," "aggression," and "threat to the peace" were interpreted to have only international application and implication. As you read the following material, ask whether the situations created by apartheid in South Africa and the racism in Southern Rhodesia were treated by the Security Council consistently with this traditional view? *See,* Schachter, International Law in Theory & Practice 110 (1991). Are these terms of articles 2(4) and 39 still used the same way today? Has there been a change since the end of the Cold War? Also, consider this issue when reading the material in this chapters on the Gulf War, Somalia, Cambodia and the former Yugoslavia. Can the U.N. intervene militarily without a finding that there is a threat to international peace and security? Does the Secretary–General have authority to call for military action of any kind? Can the Ad Hoc Tribunal for the former Yugoslavia call for the Security Council to sanction a nation that does not deliver a fugitive for Prosecution? Its rules call for this. See ch. 16, *infra.*

The international legal system is decentralized; the primary international law enforcement vehicle remains the state. The notion of statehood includes the characteristic of autonomy, which includes integrity of territory and freedom from intervention or coercion. It also includes notions of reciprocity, legal equality, and general adherence to international law by sister states. Failure to respect these values and interests may allow retorsion, reprisal, and self-defense. Traditionally, the state had a right under international law to use force, even to go to war, for purposes of law enforcement (liberum ius ad bellum). Does this right still exist, or has international law eliminated it and replaced it with the Security Council's authority in Chapter VII of the Charter and the residual right of individual and collective self-defense under article 51? This state-based use of force is considered in Chapter 15, *infra,* but it is important to remember that states are the engine even for U.N. efforts to "keep the peace" or to "make peace" by use of force. Keep these issues in mind as you read the following material and note the interrelationship of the "system" envisaged under the U.N. Charter and the role of individual states or other international organizations such as NATO.

2. *What went wrong?* The Charter was grounded in a belief and a hope: the belief that only with the cooperation of the great powers could the United Nations succeed, and the hope that because they had cooperated in war they would continue to do so during the peace (hence, the veto). That cooperation was not forthcoming. An immediate effect of the fragmentation of great power policy was the failure of the powers to make the agreements called for in article 43; the council thus did not have at its disposal the forces projected at the United Nation's founding. See Sohn, Basic Documents of the United Nations 89 (2nd ed. rev'd, 1968), especially Note at 98, detailing U.S.–former USSR disagreements over size and the relationships of the various force contributions to be made by the permanent members of the force.

A further factor of significance in the appraisal of the Charter provisions for dealing with threats to the peace is the fact that world tensions have taken new shapes since the days of World War II. The disintegration of old empires and the rise of the self-consciousness of formerly subject peoples have brought new demands on U.N. organs.

3. *Scope of § B of this chapter.* Section B is concerned with two principal themes that have become significant because of the foregoing political factors: first, the ways in which the United Nations has accommodated to the fact that the Security Council's monopoly of force has not worked as it was designed; and second, the development of the power of the

United Nations to use its authority to assist the drive of subject peoples toward self-determination. After the Gulf–War, the events in Somalia, Rwanda, Sierra Leone, the Ivory Coast, the Congo, the former Yugoslavia, and so many like places, do you think that the Secretary–General's vision of having U.N. military forces ready to prevent or stop breaches of the peace is realistic? What are the alternatives? Has the Security Council begun to exercise its power? Is a more broadly constituted NATO an alternative, after the Cold War? What about the E.U. so-called "Rapid Reaction Forces"? How do the Ad Hoc Tribunals for Rwanda and the former Yugoslavia or the International Criminal Court (I.C.C.) fit into this discussion?

2.   COLLECTIVE MEASURES IN THE USE OF FORCE

Korea

Background. Korea was one of the pre-World War II states that found itself divided at the end of the war. As recounted above, the United Nations was unsuccessful in its effort to unite the country and its divisions hardened into a Republic of Korea in the south (whose government was established by elections supervised by the United Nations) and a People's Republic in the north claiming jurisdiction over all of Korea. The North Korean invasion of the south precipitated a United Nations response. For discussion of attempts at peaceful resolution, *see* Section A of this Chapter. The resolutions adopted by the Council immediately following the North Korean attack on June 25, 1950, provided the authority for collective military action. They would doubtless have been vetoed by the former USSR, but the Soviets were absent from the Council, having voluntarily left their seat vacant in protest over the Council's refusal to seat the Chinese communists instead of the Chinese nationalists. First, in an emergency meeting of the Council, S.C. Resolution 82 was adopted on June 25th, which expressed grave concern over the "armed attack on the Republic of Korea by forces from North Korea" and "determin[ed] that this action constitutes a breach of the peace * * *." It also called for "the immediate cessation of hostilities * * * "and for the "authorities in North Korea to withdraw forthwith their armed forces to the 38th parallel." Resolution 82 also requested the previously created Commission on Korea: "to communicate its fully considered recommendations on the situation with the least possible delay," "to observe the withdrawal of North Korean forces to the 38th parallel," and "to keep the Security Council informed on the execution of this resolution." Finally, it called upon member states to "render every assistance to the U.N. in the execution of the Resolution and to refrain from giving assistance to the North Korean Authorities."

On June 27th, the Security Council met again, issuing Resolution 83, which reiterated that it had determined that the "armed attack upon the Republic of Korea by the forces from North Korea constitutes a breach of the peace" and called "for an immediate cessation of hostilities" and for "North Korea to withdraw forthwith" to the 38th Parallel. It noted that the North Korean forces had not withdrawn and that "urgent military measures are required to restore international peace and security" and recommended "that the Members of the United Nations furnish such assistance to the Republic of Korea as may be necessary to repel the armed attack and to restore international peace and security in the area."

On July 7th, 1950, the Security Council welcomed the prompt and vigorous support it had received. It recommended that all members providing military forces and other assistance, "make such forces and other assistance available to a unified command under the United States of America," requested that the U.S. "designate the commander of such forces," authorized the use of the U.N. flag along with the various flags of the participating states, and requested the U.S. to provide the Security Council with periodic reports. Pertinent S.C. Resolutions, are in the Documentary Supplement.

Notes and Questions

1. *How was this similar or different from the situation in Bosnia–Herzegovina? What was the legal basis for the Security Council's action?* Resolution 82 (1950) determined that the armed attack by North Korea constituted a "breach of the peace," using the language of article 39 of the Charter, although neither article 39 nor Chapter VII were actually cited. The Security Council's findings of *"threats to the [international] peace," "breaches of the [international] peace,"* or *"acts of aggression"* have accelerated over the past fifteen years. The first was in relation to Korea in 1950, when the North invaded the South. Similar findings under article 39 were made in the Rhodesian and South African cases, but the Council did not authorize the use of military force. On the other hand, in Suez (1956) and the Congo (1960), armed force was authorized by the United Nations, without any article 39 findings having been made. article 39 findings were made concerning the 1980 attack by Argentina on the Falkland Islands. A burst of activity began with Iraq's attack on Iran in 1987, followed by Iraq's invasion of Kuwait in 1990, and later the warfare in the territory of the former Yugoslavia, beginning in 1991 and the 1992 clan warfare in Somalia. By the middle of 1998, the Security Council has applied Chapter VII to authorize the collective use of force in Korea, and the Gulf War, and has authorized actions very close to that in Somalia, Haiti, the former Yugoslavia, Liberia, Rwanda and Sierra Leone.

Can the Security Council authorize the collective use of force without first finding a *"threat to international peace and security "*under article 39? Does the Security Council have authority to take actions to preserve or maintain international peace and security in a general way or is it limited to the specific measures called for in Chapter VII? Yoram Dinstein discusses this in War, Aggression and Self Defence 102–121 (1956); *see also Certain Expenses Case, infra.* One argument about the legality of the U.N. action in Korea was whether the conflict was a civil war. A portion of the debate on that question appears in chapter 2 with the concept of statehood. What is the relevance of that argument? Does article 2(7) exclude U.N. action in a civil war? Note that article 2(7) expressly preserves United Nations application of enforcement measures under Chapter VII. (article 39 is in Chapter VII.) Does the term "peace" in article 39 mean only international peace? What is "international peace?" Would that interpretation exclude U.N. involvement in a civil war? Would it have excluded U.N. involvement in the Korean case?

2.   *Nature of the forces.* Article 43 of the Charter was an agreement to agree on the composition of forces to be made available to the Security Council. As noted above, the effort to create a standing force failed for lack of agreement among the major powers. Despite that, the Council authorized member states to provide military forces to repel the North Koreans (specifically, it *recommended* that member states furnish assistance to the Republic of Korea and, in fact, sixteen member states fought in Korea under the United Nations' auspices). Was the Council acting within its powers in creating a United Nations force in this manner? Does the Charter confine the Security Council to using only a standing force?

3.   *Nature of the command.* The Security Council authorized a unified command under the United States and requested the United States to designate the commander (who was, initially, General Douglas MacArthur). Was the Council acting within its powers by delegating command, and the selection of the commander? Compare, with this mode of dealing with the command question, the assumption of command responsibility directly by the U.N. in the Suez, Congo, Persian Gulf, Somalia, and former Yugoslavia cases, considered below.

––––––––

Uniting for Peace

The Security Council's resolutions authorizing the creation of the United Nations forces in Korea were adopted in June and July of 1950. The representative of the former USSR returned to the meetings of the Security Council in August, but it was too late for the Soviets to cast a veto to undo the prior action of the Council. The forces under the aegis of the U.N. continued to fight despite the vocal opposition of the former USSR. However, it was plain that no further Security Council action would be possible in the Korean case in view of the Soviet's undoubted use of the veto. Indeed, the potential of the Security Council to act in future cases involving clashes of East–West interests was recognized as weak if not non-existent. The General Assembly was urged by a group of states acting under the leadership of the United States to assert its own authority in cases in which the Security Council failed to act because of the use of the veto. That assertion of authority was cast in the form of the Uniting for Peace Resolution, which is in the Documentary Supplement.

––––––––

Authority under the United Nations Charter. Article 11(2) of the Charter provides the basis for an argument that the General Assembly does not have the authority under the Charter to exercise the power it has asserted in operative ¶ 1 of the Uniting for Peace Resolution: "Any such question on which *action* is necessary shall be referred to the Security Council by the General Assembly either before or after discussion." [Emphasis supplied.] How do you appraise this argument? Would you make it today?

The Persian Gulf War: Post–Cold War Enforcement of the Charter Scheme

Background: On August 2, 1990, Iraq invaded Kuwait; the Emir sought refuge in Saudi Arabia. By that time, the Cold War had eroded and on the very day of the invasion, the Security Council unanimously condemned the invasion and *demanded* that the Iraqi troops "withdraw immediately and unconditionally all its armed forces * * *" deeming the invasion a *"breach of international peace and security."* [*S.C. Res. 660 (1990)*]. The S.C. Resolutions are in the Documentary Supplement.

On August 3rd, the United States dispatched naval forces to the Persian Gulf. On August 6th, the Security Council imposed a trade embargo on Iraq, except for medicine and food for humanitarian purposes. On August 7th, the U.S. deployed combat troops and planes to Saudi Arabia. On August 8th, Iraq formally annexed Kuwait. Twelve Arab leaders agreed on August 10th to send military forces to protect Saudi Arabia and on the 11th, Egyptian and British forces began to arrive in Saudi Arabia. On August 12th, Iraq ordered 4,000 Britains and 2,500 Americans in Kuwait to report to certain hotels or be rounded-up. On August 28th, Iraq declared Kuwait to be its 19th province and freed all western women and children who had been held hostage. For the ensuing three months, the United Nations attempted without success to resolve the crisis peacefully. During this period, the U.S. imposed significant and comprehensive economic sanctions on Iraq; the former USSR, Japan, the European Union, and others followed suit.

On November 29th, the Security Council issued an ultimatum to Iraq, approving *Resolution 665* and authorizing the creation of a multinational force that would be allowed to apply military force to oust Iraqi troops from Kuwait, if they did not withdraw by January 15, 1991. On January 10, 1991, the U.S. Congress debated whether to give President Bush the authority to use force in Iraq and Kuwait. The January 15th deadline passed and on January 16th Operation *Desert Shield* was transformed into *Desert Storm*. The Senate and the House of Representatives passed a resolution supporting the engagement. For the next several weeks, the U.S. population was transfixed by the events of the War shown virtually non-stop on cable television. Ultimately several Security Council Resolutions (660–678) were issued (in Doc. Supp.). It has been reported that between 100,000 and 200,000 Iraqi troops and civilians were killed and 300,000 were injured, while fewer than 400 allied deaths occurred, most by "friendly fire." *See,* Prochaska, *Disappearing Iraqis,* 4 Public Culture 91 (1992); Krishna, *Review Essay: The Importance of Being Ironic: A Postcolonial View on Critical International Relations Theory,* 18 Alternatives 385, 397 (1993). On February 13th, U.S. bombs hit an underground facility in Baghdad. The U.S. claimed that the bunker was a military command center, but 500 civilians holed up in it died. By February 25th, Saddam

Hussein ordered his troops to leave Kuwait; by the 26th Iraqi troops appeared to be in full retreat. On February 27th President Bush ordered suspension of all offensive operations. On March 3rd, Iraqi military leaders accepted the U.N. Security Council's terms for formal cease-fire. On March 12th the Iraqis crushed a Shiite Muslim rebellion in Southern Iraq. Iraq later did the same to the Kurdish rebellion in Northern Iraq, touching off a mass exodus of Kurds into Turkey. On April 5th, President Bush (1st) ordered emergency aid to be flown to the 450,000 Kurdish refugees along the Turkish/Iraqi border. On April 6th, Iraq accepted the U.N. conditions for a formal termination of the war, and on April 11th, the Security Council announced the formal end to the War and accepted Iraq's pledge to pay war damages and to destroy its weapons of mass destruction. The operation succeeded in restoring the independence of Kuwait, with far-reaching political and economic consequences.

Since the end of the war, Iraq has continued intermittently to defy U.N. resolutions. It appears that the Shiite Muslim Marsh Arabs of Southern Iraq are still being decimated by starvation, poisoning and draining of their water. The sanctions have mainly caused extreme hardship, illness and death to innocent Iraqi children and civilians. Iraq's children have not been blessed. International aid agencies estimate that about 500,000 of them have died from assorted horrors during a decade of economic sanctions: starvation, ruined schools, lack of medicine, undrinkable water, ruined sewers, land mine explosions, birth defects. The toll runs around 5,000 children a month. At 22 million, the nation's population is just ahead that of Texas. Davis, *Another voice calling for an end to sanctions in Iraq*, Austin Am.-Statesman A19, August 31, 2000), 2000 WL 7340498. See gen., Cleveland, Norm Internationalization & U.S. Economic Sanctions, 26 Yale J.I.L. 1 (2001). *See also, Opinion, End the Iraq War*, The Seattle Times, B4, May 14, 2001; The Economist, World Reporter, *Special: Iraq and the West: When sanctions don't work: Almost ten years of them have left Iraqis desperate and Saddam Hussein as defiant as ever*, The Economist, April 8, 2000, 2000 WL 8141434, noted that:

> "[s]anctions impinge on the lives of all Iraqis every moment of the day. In Basra, Iraq's second city, ... [t]ap water causes diarrhea, but few can afford the bottled sort. Because the sewers have broken down, pools of stinking muck have leached through to the surface all over town. That effluent, combined with pollution upstream, has killed most of the fish in the Shatt al-Arab river and has left the remainder unsafe to eat. The government can no longer spray for sand-flies or mosquitoes, so insects have proliferated, along with the diseases they carry ... [C]autious studies by foreign researchers show horrific rises in infant mortality, malnutrition and disease. An analysis of NGO health surveys conducted by Richard Garfield, a public-health expert at Columbia University, found that at least 100,000 (and probably as many as 227, 000) children under five had died between 1991 and 1998, as a result of the Gulf War sanctions. That works out at between 26 and 60 deaths every day among infants along. A recent UNICEF report estimated that, over the same period, some 500,000 under-fives had died.

See also, The Economist, World Reporter, *Special,* McCarthy, *Can Sanctions be smarter?: America's policy on Iraq and Iran*, The Economist, World Reporter, May 26, 2001; and Arnove, *Iraq under siege: Ten years on*, 12/1/2000 Monthly Rev. 1425, 200 WL 10947230.

In the Christian Science Monitor, Monday, April 3, 2000, WORLD, at p. 1, 2000 WL 4427149, we read the following article by Scott Peterson, *"Is the West too quick to sanction? A UN official quit last week over the human cost in Iraq of sanctions. US curbs cover half of the world population.**

> *Sanction fatigue is setting in.* This diplomatic stick, employed more times by President Clinton than any other leader in US history, is losing its effectiveness and appeal on the global stage. High-profile failings of economic sanctions—especially in Iraq—are casting doubt on the future of sanctions as a means of punishment. The paradox is that in the decades since Cuba was first embargoed in 1960, the intended target of sanctions—whether it be Cuban President Fidel Castro, Iraqi leader Saddam Hussein, or Serbia's President Slobodan Milosevic—has been able to turn sanctions to political advantage, while neatly handing off the burden to local populations. The tangle of US sanctions today affect more than half the world's population. But the severity of Iraq's case has for the first time built up a diplomatic head of steam against sanctions for what the US sees as global wrongdoing.
>
> The growing chorus of protest was capped by last Thursday's departure from Baghdad of Hans Von Sponeck, UN humanitarian chief, for Iraq. He resigned rather than preside over the further destruction of Iraq's social fabric. "Let's face it: Iraq is one of the few countries on our globe which is regressing," said the 32–year UN veteran, in his first interview since leaving Iraq. "I have no doubt that history will say that Iraq was forced to become the guinea pig for the experimentation of a sanction methodology that ultimately failed. We have to find a new approach."
>
> Sanctions may be the modern equivalent of the military siege, in which armies throughout history—from the Romans surrounding the Masada (an ancient Jewish fortress in Israel), to the Germans and Finnish blockading Leningrad in World War II—sought to compel capitulation by destroying the will to resist. Roots of the American policy reach back to President Woodrow Wilson, who said in 1919 that "a nation boycotted is a nation that is in sight of surrender." That maxim seems to have been taken to heart by President Clinton, for whom sanctions have all but replaced diplomacy. He has called the US "sanctions happy," and long with Congress, he has been responsible for imposing more than half of the 125 or so cases of sanctions ever imposed by the US.
>
> But such overuse "devalues the tool" and the "moral, disapproval value tends to be lost," says Gary Hufbauer, a sanctions expert and senior fellow at the Institute for International Economics in Washington.... The lessons of nearly 10 years of sanctions on Iraq are causing analysts to reexamine their assumptions about what few sanctions—

---

* Reprinted with the permission of the
Christian Science Monitor.

out of the 176 recorded cases this century—have caused their targets to change course, and why so many have failed. "We've done a lot of re-evaluating," Mr. Hufbauer says. "The unfortunate truth is that when you have a truly retrograde regime, and you are seeking a major goal like its overthrow, the record is close to zero." Sanctions have been applied from North Korea to Canada, and both India and Pakistan were slapped with sanctions—mandatory under US law—when they tested nuclear devices in 1998. Those sanctions hurt US farm exports badly, renewing interest in Congress for reform that would require assessing domestic impact before imposing any sanction. Despite those cases, Iraq stands out. "Iraq in our times, is like the Italian–Abyssinia case was to the League of Nations. That was the defining sanction, and it did as much as anything to destroy the League," says Hufbauer. "The Iraq case is not going to destroy the UN, but it is certainly causing a lot of rethinking. The lasting impact is that it will be much harder to put these kind of sanctions on any country."

A similar analysis has been put forward by a British parliamentary committee, that found that the Iraq example showed it would be "difficult" to justify imposing similar sanctions on any nation in the future, because they cause "impoverishment" and "only further concentrate power in the hands of the ruling elite." Comprehensive UN sanctions were slapped on Iraq in August 1990, just days after Iraqi forces invaded Kuwait—and remain the pillar of US policy toward Iraq. Since 1996, Iraq has been permitted to sell oil to buy humanitarian goods, but US officials have blocked scores of contracts, anxious that "dual use" items might be used to reinvigorate Iraq's nuclear-, chemical-, and biological-weapons programs.

The US has come under intense pressure from friend and foe alike the past two weeks in the UN Security Council. In a rare moment of criticism, UN head Kofi Annan noted that sanctions had created a "serious moral dilemma" for the UN, and that the US and Britain had blocked more than $1.5 billion worth of humanitarian contracts for Iraq—for items from breeding bulls to ambulances. "The UN has been on the side of the vulnerable and the weak, and has always sought to relieve suffering. Yet, here we are accused of causing suffering," Mr. Annan said. Senior US officials have said repeatedly that the Iraqi people are not the targets of sanctions, and have agreed to release at least 70 of the applications for humanitarian goods that it had put on hold. "There is no question that sanctions fatigue is becoming a major problem," says Anthony Cordesman, a leading Mideast security expert at the Center for Strategic and International Studies in Washington. "There is immense hardship in Iraq.... You certainly have a nation that is falling apart in every way—except in sustaining a dictatorship."

"The idea that we are engaged in a constant battle for perceptions, and that the key perception is the welfare of the Iraqi people, seems to be absolutely beyond the comprehension of the State Department," Mr. Cordesman says. "If you look back on [Secretary of State] Madeleine Albright's tenure, this will probably be recognized as one of the greatest single failures for which she has to be held responsible." Oil-rich Iraq was once one of the wealthiest nations in the Mideast. But a decade of war in the 1980s, the 1991 Gulf War, and then sanctions have all resulted in a spike in extreme malnutrition rates. Child deaths now number in the hundreds of thousands, and there has been an almost total breakdown of health and other basic services, according to UN statistics.

Mr. Von Sponeck points out that the Iraqi leadership has spent the $400 million a year from illicit smuggling of oil on everything from new palaces to whiskey, and he is disappointed at how little it spends from legal UN oil money on education. "I don't say that everything that impinges on Iraq is due to sanctions. Rubbish," he says. "But the accusation that the regime is purposefully trying to make the Iraqi people suffer doesn't hold."

"Governments are changing their attitudes to the Iraq file," says Von Sponeck. "The big question is: Can that pressure translate into swaying the very inflexible positions of the Americans and British? This has become a moral issue." Iraq should be proof that sanctions just don't work, he adds. Apartheid-era sanctions on South Africa are often a case that is raised by supporters of sanctions as a case that worked, but Von Sponeck was head of the UN in neighboring Botswana at the time, and disagrees. "People forget that the sanctions period was short, and the first victims were the blacks in South Africa," he says.

Pope John Paul II helped set the tone during his 1998 visit to Cuba—where four decades of sanctions have failed to unseat Mr. Castro—saying that sanctions are "always deplorable, because they hurt the most needy." The transformation in Von Sponeck's thinking is an apt mirror of that taking place elsewhere. When he first arrived in Iraq, "the word 'sanctions' was like a cow in India—it was very holy: don't talk about it," he says. But his "mental adjustment" was prompted by the situation in Iraqi schools, where children were learning in such isolation—printed materials have been forbidden under sanctions—that they can never be "responsible citizens."

"The biggest lesson of the last 10 years," Hufbauer says, is that "sometimes sanctions are successful when you have modest goals and an open regime. But sanctions are a fair-weather tool of diplomacy. You can't expect them to do the heavy lifting, just as you wouldn't send in a crew with shovels to dig out a major road through rock."

Notes and Questions. Do you think that economic sanctions should apply as actions under U.N. Charter Title VI (Peaceful Settlement), therefore, in this Chapter, or under Chapter VII, (on Force), therefore, under Chapter 15? For discussion of sanctions and human rights violations, see Chapter 9, *supra*, and for discussion of individual responsibility and international crime, see Chapter 16, *infra*.

See generally, Persian Gulf Chronology, Gannett News Service, June 26, 1993; 7 Saudi Arabia 16–23, 6–11 (No. 4, Winter 1991); *Entre Les Lignes: La Guerre Du Golfe et Le Droit International* (Brussels 1991); Law & Force in the New International Order (Damrosh & Scheffer eds. 1991); Moore, Crisis in the Gulf: Enforcing the Rule of Law (1992).

Notes & Questions

1. *Should President Bush have reported to Congress prior to sending troops? Does the War Power of Congress require congressional authorization?* For discussion of the legality *and* constitutionality of the Gulf War and the process leading to it, *see*, chapters 12 and 15 of this coursebook. See also, On the War Powers generally, *see*, Corn, Clinton, *Kosovo, and the Final Destruction of the War Powers Resolution*, 42 Wm. & Mary L. Rev. 1149 (2001) Stromseth, *Understanding Constitutional War Powers Today: Why Methodology Matters*, 106 Yale L.J. 845 (1996); Firmage, TO CHAIN THE DOG OF WAR 273 (1989). *See also, Authorization for Use of Military Force Against Iraq*, Pub. L. No. 102–1, 105 Stat. 3 (1991) (stating, as the first reason for the resolution, that "the Government of Iraq without provocation invaded and occupied the territory of Kuwait on August 2, 1990"); Statement on Signing the Resolution Authorizing the Use of Military Force Against Iraq, 27 Weekly Comp. Press. Doc. 48 (Jan. 14, 1991); Quigley, *The United Nations Security Council: Promethean Protector or Helpless Hostage?*, 25 Tex.Int'l L. J. 129, 141–164 (2000). The Security Council Resolutions relating to the Gulf War are in the Doc. Supp. Study them and consider the following questions.

2. *Is Resolution 661* binding? What articles of the U.N. Charter make it so? Did this Resolution provide a basis for U.S. domestic action? See, 22 U.S.C. § 287c (1982) (U.N. Participation Act). Did **Resolution 661** provide the U.S. or other member nations with authority to use military force to stop Iraqi ships from going to third nations? *See Resolutions* in Doc. Supp.

3. *Is Resolution 662* (1990) essentially security council *legislation declaring* the annexation of Kuwait null and void? Is it more like legislation, a judicial decision, or an executive ordinance?

4. *Resolution 665* was an adoption of the U.S. position on *Resolution 661*, that military force was authorized to enforce sanctions. What authority was to be in control of military forces? *In Resolution 666,* note the coordination with and use of the International Committee of the Red Cross (ICRC) discussed in Chapter 1.

5. *Note that Resolution 667* is a Security Council decision *enforcing* the Vienna Convention on Treaties, considered in Chapters 1 and 11.

In Resolution 670, the Security Council essentially sets aside the bilateral civil aviation treaties. This has not been done before. Is it an example of U.N. Charter article 103 action?

6. *In Resolution 670,* were nations authorized to order planes on their way to Iraq to land for inspection? If such a plane refused to land, was the "ordering" nation authorized to shoot it down? See, reference to the

Chicago Convention (in Doc. Supp.). *Did* Resolution 670 issue any warning to third countries? If so, what was it and how would it enforce that warning?

8.   *Does Resolution 674 explicitly mention the use of force to expel Iraq from Kuwait?* Virtually at the same time, leaders of nations which became allies during the Gulf War were sending threatening signals and were engaged in a significant military buildup in the region. The United States dispatched naval ships, combat aircraft, and troops to the Persian Gulf and to Saudi Arabia. France, Italy, Spain, Britain, Canada, and Argentina did similarly.

9.   *Did Resolution 686* allow the Security Council to play a judicial role in demanding that Iraq "accept in principle its liability under international law for any loss, damage, or injury arising in regard to Kuwait and third states * * *" or was this executive in nature?

10.   *S.C. Resolution 687* is probably the most important resolution from the standpoint of continuing enforcement. Moreover, it may be the most far-reaching "legislative" act ever adopted by the Security Council. Is this an example of international government?

Iraq's Acceptance Of The United Nations "Cease–Fire" Resolution **687 (1991)**

Identical letters dated 6 April 1991 from the permanent representative of Iraq to the United Nations addressed respectively to the Secretary–General and the President of the Security Council

On instructions from my Government, I have the honour to enclose the text of a letter dated 6 April 1991 addressed to you by the Minister for Foreign Affairs of the Republic of Iraq. I should be grateful if you would have the text of this letter and its annex circulated as a document of the Security Council. (*Signed*) Abdul Amir A. AL–ANBARI, Ambassador, Permanent Representative

Annex

Identical letters dated 6 April 1991 from the Minister for Foreign Affairs of the Republic of Iraq addressed respectively to the Secretary–General and the President of the Security Council

I have the honour to inform you that the Iraqi Government has taken note of the text of Security Council resolution 687 (1991), the authors of which are the first to recognize that it is unprecedented in the annals of the Organization, and wishes, before stating its official position, to make a number of fundamental comments regarding certain concepts and provisions contained therein:

I.   While in its preamble the resolution reaffirms that Iraq is an independent sovereign State, the fact remains that a good number of its iniquitous provisions impair that sovereignty. In fact, the resolution constitutes an unprecedented assault on the sovereignty, and the rights that stem therefrom, embodied in the Charter and in international law and practice. For example, where the question of boundaries is concerned, the Security Council has determined in advance the boundary between Iraq and Kuwait.

And yet it is well known, from the juridical and practical standpoint, that in international relations boundary issues must be the subject of an agreement between States, since this is the only basis capable of guaranteeing the stability of frontiers.

The resolution fails to take into account Iraq's view, which is well known to the Council, that the provisions relating to the boundary between Iraq and Kuwait contained in the "Agreed Minutes Between the State of Kuwait and the Republic of Iraq Regarding the Restoration of Friendly Relations, Recognition and Related Matters" dated 4 October 1963 have not yet been subjected to the constitutional procedures required for ratification of the Agreed Minutes by the legislative branch and the President of Iraq, thus leaving the question of the boundary pending and unresolved. The Council has nevertheless imposed on Iraq the line of its boundary with Kuwait. By acting in this strange manner, the Council itself has also violated one of the provisions of resolution 660, which served as the basis for its subsequent resolutions. In its paragraph 3, resolution 660 calls upon Iraq and Kuwait to resolve their differences through negotiation, and the question of the boundary is well known to be one of the main differences. Iraq officially informed the Council that it accepted resolution 660 and was prepared to apply it, but the Council has gone beyond this legal position, contradicting its previous resolution, and adopted an iniquitous resolution which imposes on Iraq, an independent and sovereign State and a Member of the United Nations, new conditions and a boundary line which deprive it of its right to establish its territorial rights in accordance with the principles of international law. Thus the Council is also depriving Iraq of its right to exercise its free choice and to affirm that it accepts that boundary without reservation. [Regarding the boundary], the Council resolution is an iniquitous resolution which constitutes a dangerous precedent, a first in the annals of the international Organization and—as some impartial members of the Council indicated in their statements when the resolution was voted on—an assault on the sovereignty of States.

It is also to be noted that the United States of America, the author of the draft resolution on which resolution 687, which imposes a solution to the boundary-related and other differences between Iraq and Kuwait, was based, refuses to impose any solution whatsoever on its ally, Israel, in accordance with conventions, United Nations resolutions and international law. Furthermore, the United States of America is preventing the Security Council from assuming the responsibilities incumbent upon it with respect to the Arab–Zionist conflict, the Israeli policy of annexation of the occupied Arab territories, the establishment of settlements, the displacement of populations and the disregard for the rights of the Palestinian people and the neighboring Arab countries, by vetoing any draft resolution approved by the remaining members of the Council, for the simple reason that Israel does not want a resolution which favours a just settlement of the conflict.

II. Iraq's position with regard to the prohibition of chemical and bacteriological weapons is clear. It is indeed a party to the Protocol for the Prohibition of the Use in War of Asphyxiating, Poisonous or Other Gases, and of Bacteriological Methods of Warfare, signed at Geneva in 1925. In a statement issued in September 1988, Iraq reiterated its attachment and adherence to the provisions of that Protocol. It also participated in the Conference of States Parties to the 1925 Geneva Protocol and Other Interested States, held at Paris from 7 to 11 January 1989, and signed the Declaration issued by the participating States. On that occasion, Iraq took a position which was unanimously shared by all the Arab countries, namely that all weapons of mass destruction, including nuclear weapons, must be eliminated from the Middle East region.

Iraq is also a party to the Treaty on the Non–Proliferation of Nuclear Weapons, of 1 July 1968. As the many reports of the International Atomic Energy Agency confirm, it is applying all the provisions of the Treaty. The Security Council resolution obliges only Iraq, and it alone, to undertake the destruction of the non-conventional weapons left to it after the heavy destruction inflicted both on these weapons and on the related installations by the military operations launched against Iraq by the 30 countries of the coalition. It does not deprive the other countries of the region, particularly Israel, of the right to possess weapons of this type, including nuclear weapons. Moreover, the Council has ignored its resolution 487 (1981), which calls on Israel to place all its nuclear facilities under international safeguards, and has not sought to ensure the implementation of that resolution in the same way as it is now seeking to impose the position it has taken against Iraq. It is thus clear that a double standard is being applied with respect to the elimination of weapons of mass destruction in the region, and an attempt being made to disrupt the military balance there. This is all the more apparent in that Iraq has not had recourse to weapons of this type. The application of this provision of the resolution cannot but seriously endanger the regional balance, as indeed was confirmed by certain impartial members of the Security Council in their statements when the resolution was voted upon. There can be no doubt that Israel, an expansionist aggressor country which is occupying the territory of neighbouring countries, usurping the right of the Palestinian Arab people against which it daily commits the most horrible atrocities, and refusing to comply with the resolutions of the Security Council, which it holds in contempt, as well as all the resolutions of the international Organization, will be the first to benefit from this imbalance.

Whereas, the resolution emphasizes the importance of all States adhering to the Convention on the Prohibition of the Development, Production and Stockpiling of Bacteriological (Biological) and Toxin Weapons, of a Convention on the Universal Prohibition of Chemical Weapons being drafted and of universal adherence thereto, it makes no mention whatsoever of the importance of universal adherence to the convention banning nuclear weapons or of the drafting of a convention on the universal prohibition of such weapons in the region. Instead, it emphasizes the importance of instituting a dialogue among the States of the region with a view to achieving a so-called balanced and comprehensive control of armaments in the region.

* * *

III.   Furthermore, Iraq's internal and external security has been and remains seriously threatened, in that continuing efforts are being made to interfere, by force of arms, in the country's internal affairs. Thus the measures taken by the Council against Iraq to deprive it of its lawful right to acquire weapons and military matériel for defence directly contribute to the intensification of these threats and to the destabilization of Iraq, thus endangering the country's internal and external security and hence peace, security and stability throughout the region.

IV.   * * * [T]he Council resolution provides mechanisms for obtaining redress from Iraq, [but] makes no reference to Iraq's rights to claim redress for the considerable losses it sustained and the massive destruction inflicted on civilian installations and infrastructures as a result of the abusive implementation of resolution 678 (1990), which were testified to by the delegation sent by the Secretary–General which visited Iraq recently, and have been referred to by the President of a permanent member of the Security Council (Soviet President Mikhail Gorbachev) and by all impartial observers who have seen with their own eyes the consequences of the military operations launched against Iraq. The Council has not explained to world public opinion and the conscience of mankind what the relationship is between its resolution 678 and the deliberate destruction of Iraq's infrastructure—generating stations, water distribution networks, irrigation dams, civilian bridges, telephone exchanges, factories producing powdered milk for infants and medicines, shelters, mosques, churches, commercial centres, residential neighbourhoods, etc. Moreover, the resolution authorizes third parties to claim compensation from Iraq for damage that may have been caused to them, even when such damage resulted from unfulfilment of their commitments to Iraq immediately following the adoption of resolution 661.

Further evidence of the resolution's biased and iniquitous nature is that it holds Iraq liable for environmental damage and the depletion of natural resources, although this liability has not been established; on the other hand, it makes no mention of Iraq's own right to obtain compensation for the established facts of damage to its environment and depletion of its natural resources as a result of more than 88,000 tons of explosives, or for the destruction of water distribution networks, generating stations and the road network, which has spread disease and epidemics and caused serious harm to the environment. These provisions partake of a desire to exact vengeance and cause harm, not to give effect to the relevant provisions of international law. The direct concrete consequences of their implementation will affect the potential and resources of millions of Iraqis, and deprive them of the right to live in dignity.

* * *

VII.   Numerous mechanisms are envisaged which will necessitate consultation in the context of the implementation of the resolution's provisions, but the resolution is not at all clear about Iraq's participation in these consultations. The fact that Iraq is concerned to the highest degree in the application of the resolution makes its effective participation in all consultations bearing on the implementation of these provisions essential. However, the Council has once again opted for an arbitrary and inequitable method.

The questions raised in the resolution and discussed in the foregoing preliminary comments constitute, in substance, an injustice, a severe assault on the Iraqi people's right to life and a flagrant denial of its inalienable rights to sovereignty and independence and its right to exercise its free choice. * * * [T]he provisions of the resolution embodying the criteria of duality in international relations and the application of a double standard to questions of the same kind hold Iraq and its population hostage to the designs harboured by certain Powers to take control of their resources, set quotas for their food and clothing needs, and deprive them of their right to live in dignity in the modern society to which they aspire.

Such injustices and such assaults on the rights of a member country of the United Nations and its people cannot under any circumstances be in conformity with the purposes and objectives of the Charter. The Council had a duty to discuss the issues before it with objectivity and in accordance with the provisions of international law and the principles of justice and equity. By adopting this unjust resolution and by this selective treatment of the Iraqi people, the Council has merely confirmed the fact that we have never ceased to emphasize, namely that the Council has become a puppet which the United States of America is manipulating in order to achieve its political designs in the region, the prime objective being to perpetuate Israel's policy of aggression and expansion, despite the empty words about peace and justice in the Middle East uttered by one or another of the Council members which voted for this resolution.

It could not be more clear to all men of honour and justice that these iniquitous and vengeful measures against Iraq are not a consequence of the events of 2 August 1990 and the subsequent period, for the essential motive underlying these measures stems from Iraq's rejection of the unjust situation imposed on the Arab nation and the countries of the region for decades, a situation which has enabled Israel, a belligerent Power heavily armed with the most modern and fearsome conventional weapons and with weapons of mass destruction, including nuclear weapons, to exercise hegemony in the region. This reality confirms what Iraq had stated before the events of 2 August 1990, namely that it was the target of a plot aimed at destroying the potential it had deployed with a view to arriving at a just balance in the region which would pave the way for the institution of justice and of a lasting peace.

It is unfortunate that States whose intention was not in any way to help the United States of America and Israel attain their objectives should involuntarily have contributed to their attainment by voting for this iniquitous resolution. As Iraq makes its preliminary comments on the juridical and legal aspects of this resolution, so as to encourage men of conscience in the countries members of the international community and world public opinion to make an effort to understand the truth as it is and the need to ensure the triumph of justice, it has no choice but to accept this resolution.

I should be grateful if you would have this letter circulated as a document of the Security Council.

(*Signed*) Ahmed HUSSEIN, Minister for Foreign Affairs of Iraq

———

S/PV.2963, 29 November 1990

The Council had before it document S/21969 containing the text of a draft resolution tabled by Canada, the former USSR, the United Kingdom and Northern Ireland and the United States [statements of Secretary Baker and Minister Shevardnadze]:

The President: [Mr. BAKER, United States of America]:

* * *

Colleagues, your very presence here, for only the fourth time in the Security Council's history that Foreign Ministers have assembled, symbolizes, I think, the seriousness of the present situation. I would like to begin today's discussion with a quotation that I believe aptly sets the context for our discussions today. The quotation is as follows:

> There is no precedent for a people being the victim of such injustice and of being at present threatened by abandonment to an aggressor. Also, there has never before been an example of any government proceeding with the systematic extermination of a nation by barbarous means in violation of the most solemn promises made to all the nations of the Earth that there should be no resort to a war of conquest and that there should not be used against innocent human beings terrible poison and harmful gases.

Those words, I think, could well have come from the Emir of Kuwait, but they do not. They were spoken in 1936, not in 1990. They come from Haile Selassie, the leader of Ethiopia, a man who saw his country conquered and occupied, much like Kuwait has been brutalized since 2 August. Sadly, that appeal to the League of Nations fell ultimately upon deaf ears. The League's efforts to redress aggression failed and international disorder and war ensued.

History has now given us another chance. With the cold war behind us, we now have the chance to build the world which was envisioned by the founders of this Organization—by the founders of the United Nations. We have the chance to make this Security Council and this United Nations true instruments for peace and for justice across the globe. We must not let the United Nations go the way of the League * * *. We must fulfil our common vision of a peaceful and just post-cold-war world.

But if we are to do so, we must meet the threat to international peace created by Saddam Hussein's aggression. And that is why the debate that we are about to begin will, I think, rank as one of the most important in the history of the United Nations. It will surely do much to determine the future of this body.

Our aim today must be to convince Saddam Hussein that the just and humane demands of this Council and of the international community cannot be ignored. If Iraq does not reverse its course peacefully, then other necessary measures, including the use of force, should be authorized. We must put the choice to Saddam Hussein in unmistakable terms. * * *

[88] Mr. Shevardnadze (U.S.S.R.) (interpretation from Russian): * * *

There is logic in the actions of our Council, which, from the outset of the crisis, has acted with cohesion and consistency and, at the same time, in a responsible, calm and prudent manner, in strict conformity with the letter and spirit of the U.N. Charter in its modern interpretation, which restores its original rights and authority. We have been faced with the first extremely grave test of the post-cold-war period, and we are coping with it, placing mankind's common interests at the centre of our policy and being guided by the principles of the new thinking in international affairs.

There is justice and a large measure of generosity in the resolution we have just adopted. As the end of the fourth month of the crisis approaches, the international community is showing genuine magnanimity and giving the side that has breached the peace time to think again. At the same time we are giving the victim in this crisis a firm pledge that it will not have to wait much longer, that help is on the way and that its rights will be fully restored.

Today we have started the count-down of the "pause of goodwill". We are confident that before the time is up events will take a turn towards peace and that the pause will usher in a transition to a political settlement. Had we thought otherwise, this resolution would have been unnecessary. It is one last sincere attempt to give common sense a chance to prevail; or, let us say, to give the instinct of self-preservation a chance to work; to give Iraq time to think about the consequences of any other than peaceful outcome of the crisis.

So we want to begin the pause of goodwill by calling upon Iraq and * * * Saddam Hussein to rise above considerations of prestige, to display wisdom and foresight and to place above all else the interests of the country and the fate of its people and of peace and stability on our planet. No member of the Council wants or seeks a tragic outcome; but nor should there be any mistake about the collective will of the international community as expressed here, or about its resolve and its readiness to act. The Council's action is based on the clear awareness and belief that shirking its duty now by failing to reverse the aggression would mean even greater hardship and suffering for the world and for all nations. Those who have breached the peace should know that "all necessary means" will indeed inexorably be used against them. All of us would be happy if only there were no need to resort to such means.

* * *

I say quite bluntly that what has happened in the Persian Gulf region strikes a blow at the emerging world of civilized behaviour. That is why it is so important to parry that blow and make sure that it does not do irreparable damage to the institutions of peace and democracy, thereby plunging the world into chaos. The world will not enter a more lucid, calm and stable phase unless it can meet the residual challenges of the past and rise to the new challenges of the present and the future.

It is of overriding importance that today we are no longer responding to these challenges in the same way as we did yesterday. We are giving preference to the law, to action under the authority of the Charter and of the Security Council, and to collective efforts. We have acted * * * collectively and in concert, throughout the long and difficult weeks of the Persian Gulf crisis, and we continue to do so. We are right to act in this way. I see it as a sign that we are truly entering a time of political maturity and have recognized that freedom and democracy are inseparable from an awareness by each one of us of our responsibility for order, for the state of our common home and for saving world civilization.

I have to say that, while it in no way minimizes our sympathy for Kuwait or our pain at its suffering, there is more at stake than the fate of that one State. Our common future is threatened. Hence the certainty that Kuwait will be reborn as an independent and sovereign State, as demanded by the resolutions adopted by the Security Council.

* * *

The purpose of the resolution we have just adopted is to put an end to the aggression and make it clear * * * that aggression cannot be rewarded. We hope the Iraqi leaders will find the strength to recognize the responsibility they bear to their own people and to history and comply with the will of the international community. We are serving them with a special warning about their personal responsibility for the fate of foreign nationals in Iraq. Endangering their lives will be regarded as a crime against humanity, with all the consequences that entails.

* * *

In conclusion, I express the confidence that we will be able to overcome this crisis peacefully—I repeat, peacefully, and in a political way—and to end it on a note of hope for a better future for all of us. * * *

* * *

The President [Mr. Baker, United States of America]: I thank the Minister for Foreign Affairs of Romania for the kind words he addressed to me. I should now like to make a statement in my capacity as Secretary of State of the United States of America. I think that today's vote marks a watershed in the history of the United Nations.

Earlier this week * * * the Security Council heard testimony of crimes committed against the citizens of Kuwait. There can be no doubt that these are crimes incompatible with any civilized order. They are part of the same pattern that includes—and many speakers have referred to this today—the taking of innocent hostages from many nations.

The entire international community has been affronted by a series of brutal acts. Iraqi forces have invaded and seized a small Arab neighbour. A once-prosperous country has been pillaged and looted. A once-peaceful country has been turned into an armed camp. A once-secure country has been terrorized. The nations of the world have not stood idly by. We have taken political, economic and military measures to quarantine Iraq and contain its aggression. We have worked out a co-ordinated international effort involving over 50 States to provide assistance to those nations most in need as a consequence of the economic embargo of Iraq. And military forces from over 27 nations have been deployed to defend Iraq's neighbours from further aggression and to implement the resolutions of this Council. The 12 resolutions adopted by the Council have clearly established that there is a peaceful way out of this conflict—and that is the complete, immediate and unconditional Iraqi withdrawal from Kuwait, the restoration of Kuwait's legitimate Government and the release of all hostages.

I do not think all this could have taken place unless most nations shared our vision of what is at stake. A dangerous man committed a blatant act of aggression in a vital region at a very critical moment in history. Saddam Hussein's actions, the vast arms he possesses and the weapons of mass destruction he seeks indicate clearly that Kuwait was not only not the first but probably not the last target on his list. If he should win this struggle, there will be no peace in the Middle East; only the prospect of more conflict and a far wider war. If he should come to dominate the resources of the Gulf, his ambitions will threaten all of us here and the economic well-being of all nations. Finally, if Iraq should emerge from this conflict with territory or with treasure or with political advantage, then the lesson will be very, very clear: aggression pays.

As I said earlier today, we must remember the lesson of the 1930s and aggression must not be rewarded. Since 2 August many nations have worked together to prove just that. Many unprecedented actions have been taken. The result is a new fact: a newly effective United Nations Security Council, free of the constraints of the cold war. Yet the sad truth is that the new fact has not yet erased the old fact of Iraqi aggression, and that—and that alone—is the ultimate test of success.

We must ask ourselves why Saddam has not recoiled from his aggression. We must wonder why he does not understand how great the forces are against him and how profound is the revulsion against his behaviour. The answer must be that he does not believe we really mean what we say. He does not believe we will stand united until he withdraws. He thinks that his fact of aggression is going to outlast our fact: that is, an international community opposed to aggression.

We are meeting here today, therefore, first and foremost—as many speakers here have already pointed out—to dispel Saddam Hussein's illusions. He must know from us that a refusal to comply peacefully with the Security Council resolutions risks disaster for him.

Fellow members of the Security Council, we are at a crossroads. Today we show Saddam Hussein that the sign marked "peace" is the direction he should take.

Today's resolution is very clear. The words authorize the use of force. But the purpose, I believe—and, again, many here have already said this— is to bring about a peaceful resolution of this problem. No one here has sought this conflict. Many nations here have had very good relations with the people of Iraq. But the Security Council of the United Nations cannot tolerate this aggression and still be faithful to the principles of the Charter of the United Nations.

With the adoption of today's resolution we concur with other Council members that this should lead to a pause in the Council's efforts— assuming, of course, no adverse change in circumstances. We do so while retaining our rights, as other nations have, to protect our foreign nationals in Iraq, and very mindful of the terms of the Fourth Geneva Convention and the Geneva Protocol of 1925, should Saddam Hussein use chemical or biological weapons.

By adopting today's resolution, which we think is a pause for peace, we say to Saddam Hussein: "We continue to seek a diplomatic solution. Peace is your only sensible option. You can choose peace by respecting the will of the international community. But if you fail to do so, you will risk all. The choice is yours."

If we fail to redress this aggression, more will be lost than just peace in the Persian Gulf. Only recently, in Europe, the nations party to the cold war assembled to bury that conflict. All the peoples of Europe and North America who had nothing to look forward to except an unending twilight struggle now have a fresh start, indeed a new opportunity. Conflict and war are no longer the watchwords of European politics.

We meet at the hinge of history. We can use the end of the cold war to get beyond the whole pattern of settling conflicts by force, or we can slip back into ever more savage regional conflicts in which might alone makes right. We can take the high road towards peace and the rule of law, or we can take Saddam Hussein's path of brutal aggression and the law of the jungle. Simply put, it is a choice between right and wrong. I think we have the courage and the fortitude to choose what is right * * *.

The Secretary–General:

The Security Council has taken a decision of immense portent. I should like to stress that, even on the most stringent reading, the resolution just adopted envisages at least 45 days of earnest effort to achieve a peaceful solution of the crisis. Mindful of the responsibility inherent in my office, I must express the hope that this time will be used to the most constructive purpose.

In my statement at the Council's ministerial meeting on 25 September I sought to point out the position of principle deriving from the Charter that is involved in this question. In requiring compliance with the resolutions of the Security Council, the United Nations seeks not surrender but the most honourable way of resolving a crisis in a manner that respects all legitimate interests and is conducive to the wider peace and the rule of law.

This * * * is not a matter simply of rhetoric. It is not a question of clothing a bellicose intent in persuasive language. To my mind, the situation requires that diplomatic efforts be made with renewed determination to put the present crisis on the road to a peaceful outcome.

A collective engagement, as I have observed before, requires a discipline all its own. Moreover, the actions of the United Nations to correct this international wrong must be perceived as part of the larger endeavour to establish peace through justice, wherever the one is imperilled and the other denied.

———

Notes and Questions

1. *Compare the role played by the Security Council in the Gulf War with that in the Korean Conflict.* The Security Council in the Korean Conflict *"recommended"* that the member states defend South Korea. What did the Security Council do in relation to Iraq and Kuwait? Do the terms: *"recommend," "authorize,"* and *"determine"* have legal significance? While the use of the veto by the Soviet Union did not occur at the beginning of the Korean War, because the Soviet Representative was absent, later the allies had to resort to the General Assembly through the *Uniting for Peace Resolution.* Was the situation during the Gulf War significantly better? If so why? What were the legal differences? The institutional differences? The allies in the Gulf War faced the possibility of a veto, both from China and Russia at various points. Difficult negotiations ultimately settled the differences, but do you think it was likely that some of the primary U.S. objectives were ultimately not taken as a consequence of the give and take of negotiation? Is it possible that the decision ultimately not to press on to Baghdad or to overthrow Saddam Hussein was one of these? Was it wise? What were the positive impacts that the Gulf War had on international law in practice and theory? Can you think of any dangers to the way the Security Council was able to function during that War? Was it a fact, as some have supported, that the Council determined the aggressor without much discussion or dissent?

Note that the Security Council never did determine that *"aggression"* had occurred or that there was an *"aggressor,"* in exactly those words. The Security Council's acts were all based on *"breach of the peace,"* until S.C. Resolution 688, which was based on *"threat to the peace."* Is the action taken in the Gulf War best characterized as collective self-defense authorized by the Security Council or as article 42 action? If the action is considered to be taken in self-defense authorized by the Security Council, do the usual requirements of proportionality and necessity obtain?

2. *Questions of domestic constitutional authority and the Gulf War precedent:* Did S.C. Resolution 678 provide the President of the United States with authority to deploy U.S. troops and armament into the Persian Gulf War? See discussion in Chapter 15, *infra.*

3. *The Gulf War and notions of sovereignty.* Did the Gulf War have an impact on the Austinian positivist notion that international law is not really law, because there is no "sovereign" to enforce it? If it could have been claimed before, can it be claimed any longer that there is no "enforcement mechanism" in international law? Could one say there *was* a sovereign? If so, what was it? The basic philosophies of international law are discussed in chapter 9 *supra*, and Chapter 17, *infra*. Was the Gulf War an example of international government at work? Was the Security Council the "sovereign"? Did the Gulf War develop the idea of "collective sovereignty," not unlike that of popular sovereignty that developed in relation to the citizens of nation-states in the eighteenth and nineteenth centuries? Did the conflicts in Bosnia, Kosovo, Rwanda, the Congo, and Macedonia, among others dash any possibility of UN or other international sovereignty?

4. *The Gulf War and the Laws of War.* Do the laws of war obtain for actions taken by the Security Council? What would be the appropriate and legal action to be taken if forces under the U.N. Command committed violations of the laws of war? Chapter 16 considers individual responsibility, addressing questions such as whether the Ad Hoc Tribunal for the former Yugoslavia should hear cases of violations committed by U.N. or NATO forces? See, Chapter 16, and Blakesley, *Obstacles to the Creation of a Permanent War Crimes Tribunal,* 18 The Fletcher Forum 77 (1994).

Kahn, Essay: Lessons for International Law From the Gulf War

45 Stan.L.Rev. 425 (1993).*

Politically and militarily, the War in the Gulf remains an unsettled event. Although nearly two years have passed since the War, its political consequences are still evolving. Militarily, the recent reintroduction of allied forces into Iraqi air space suggests that the War continues, though at a much reduced level. In the long run, the War will probably be seen as a footnote to the larger political upheavels that marked the start of this decade—noteworthy because it made visible the realignment of the international order that had already occurred.

[The war] is a major event from the perspective of international law. It marked one of the few occasions on which there was a deliberate invocation of international law to justify military force. An examination of the War can teach us much about the reality of, and possibilities for, international law. Given the continuing tumultuous politics of Eastern Europe and the former Soviet Union, this legal reconsideration is important. Already, the international-legal machinery deployed in the War has served as a precedent for Security Council action authorizing military intervention in Bosnia and Herzegovina.

We are moving rapidly toward a new world order of some sort. While it may be too early to predict the political shape of that order, it is not too early to consider the role that international law may play in it. Before we raise our hopes for a vital future for international law, we need to fully understand the character and power of existing international law. To that end, it is useful to examine international law as it operated, and failed to operate, in the Gulf War.

The international law at work during the Gulf War is the captive of an ideal of state sovereignty that assumes a harmonious relationship between a people and its government. All too often, however, the reality is not harmony but opposition. In its present form, international law cannot deal with this reality. Its focus on the ideal of state sovereignty leads international law to pursue morally unsupportable goals and to choose irrational means. When the international legal system acts to protect state sovereignty, too often the only real beneficiary is the political leadership, not the people. In those rare cases when modern international law responds to legal violations, it ends up punishing the people for the acts of their leaders, when the people too are victims.

* Reprinted by permission of the Stanford Law Review.

While at some deep level international law has grasped that it will remain a tool of powerful interests of the status quo until it rests on a foundation of human rights, justice, and equality, these ideals are not yet operative aspects of the legal system. Until the international legal system embraces those ideals, the new world order must seek a foundation somewhere outside of international law.

These may seem overly pessimistic conclusions to draw from the defeat of Saddam Hussein's effort at international aggrandisement. Admittedly, the enterprise of drawing general lessons for international law from a single event is inherently controversial. Moreover, analysis of the Gulf War is particularly difficult because the events have a complicated sequential character. The lessons drawn depend not only upon the particular events one emphasizes, but equally upon where one ends the story. For example, although the immediate aftermath of the war was a human rights disaster for Iraqi Kurds and Shiites, that disaster elicited an international response that is itself an ongoing story.

Despite such problems, international legal analysis must look to single events. This is true because particular incidents of state behavior are an important source of innovation in international law. More important, only by looking to the operation of law in particular events are we able to discuss realistically the force and effect of the formal system of international law.

     *   *   *

From the perspective of creating an effective international legal regime, the United States' action with respect to Iraq is particularly praiseworthy because a strong argument could have been made in support of unilateral action under Article 31 of the Charter. That Article recognizes a right of self-defense and, more importantly, of collective self-defense "until the Security Council has taken measures necessary to maintain international peace and security." Arguably, the United States could have defended Kuwait and Saudi Arabia merely upon a request from their governments. This exception for a unilateral recourse to force in "self-defense" has provided a large loophole through which much of the hope for the prohibition on the use of force in Article 2(4) has fallen over the last few decades. Yet another unilateral use of force, justified by reference to Article 31, would have done little to advance international law from a self-serving rhetorical system to an actual restraint on the behavior of states.

     *   *   *

———

Questions Was Iraq's invasion of Kuwait a "failure" of international law, or a violation of it? Is a robbery or murder a "failure" of domestic law?

3. PEACEKEEPING FORCES [U.N. USE OF FORCE TO KEEP THE PEACE]

In 1992, President Clinton presented new criteria for U.S. forces to become involved in "peacekeeping" efforts. In the beginning of the experiment with peacekeeping forces, the U.S. took the position that her forces would not be allowed to participate unless they were able "to make a unique military contribution." President Clinton revised this to allow U.S. forces to participate in planning, training, and engagement in peacekeeping efforts, if and when U.S. national interests justified the participation, in addition to being able to make the "unique military contribution." Factors to be considered in making the decision to participate included: public support or the lack thereof, the risk of open-ended engagement, and the relative weight of U.S. national interests. In addition, at the same time that the number and complexity of missions seemed to be multiplying, members of the U.N., including the U.S. continue to withhold funds. Several African states are collapsing and large areas of that Continent are not governed by any state: this decade alone, grave problems have developed in [Rwanda & Burundi] Zaire, Gabon, Mozambique, Angola, Cameroon, Togo, Liberia, Ethiopia, Sudan, the Congo, and Sierra Leone. Some world leaders have suggested that the triple crises of Somalia, Bosnia, Kosovo, and Cambodia indicate that the concept of absolute territorial sovereignty can no longer be considered the sole factor in maintaining order and ensuring the protection of humanity. *See,* Boutros–Ghali, *Agenda for Peace, supra,* stating: "[t]he time for absolute and exclusive sovereignty * * * has passed * * *. Its theory was never matched by reality." It appears that in the early stages of the George W. Bush administration, it appears that it will back away from participation. We will briefly discuss the development of "peacekeeping" (or peace-making?) forces and suggest that you consider the past, present and future role of U.S. involvement in these operations.

Suez

The First Peacekeeping Force: A British–French Challenge to the prohibition of the Use of Force. In Suez, after President Nasser of Egypt nationalized the Suez Canal Company, the English and French met secretly to plan and proceed with an Anglo–French "police action following an Israeli attack upon Egypt." *See,* Higgins, United Nations Peacekeeping, 1946–1967, I., The Middle East 225 (1969). Thus, the French and British challenged the prohibition of the use of force, claiming, through Sir Pierson Dixon: that their armed military action was necessary to safeguard "the Suez Canal and the restoration of peaceful conditions in the Middle East * * *. [N]either we [the British] nor the French Government have any desire whatever that the military action which we have taken should be more than temporary in its duration. It will be terminated as soon as the emergency is over. It is our intention that our action to protect the Canal, to terminate hostilities and to separate the combatants should be as short as possible * * *. The action taken by my Government and by the Government of France has been called an act of aggression against Egypt. This is a charge which we emphatically deny * * *. The action of France and the United Kingdom is not aggression. We do not seek the domination of Egypt or of any part of Egyptian territory. Our purpose is peaceful, not warlike. Our aim is to re-establish the rule of law, not to violate it; to protect and not to destroy. What we have undertaken is a temporary police action necessitated by the turn of events in the Middle East and occasioned by the imperative need not only to protect the vital interests of my own and many other countries, but also to take immediate measures for the restoration of order * * *. Our action is in no way aimed at the sovereignty of Egypt, and still less at its territorial integrity." (G.A.Off.Rec., 1st Emergency Special Sess., 1956 Plenary, p. 5).

France and the U.K. thwarted any Security Council action with their negative votes. A special emergency session of the General Assembly was called pursuant to the Uniting for Peace Resolution. The Assembly adopted Resolution 997 (ES–I), on November 2, 1956, urging a cease-fire and withdrawal of troops and that steps be taken to re-open the Canal. The next day, France and the United Kingdom declared that they were willing to cease their military action, if the Egyptian and Israeli Governments would agree to accept a U.N. Force to keep the peace. The General Assembly then established an emergency international U.N. Force ("United Nations Command for an emergency international Force to secure and supervise the cessation of hostilities," G.A. Res. 1000, later called the United Nations Emergency Force, UNEF, *see*, U.N.Doc.A/3317). *See generally*, Seyersted, U.N. Forces in the Law of Peace and War 46 (1966); G.A. Resolutions (997, 998, 1000, and 1002) establishing the Emergency Force (UNEF).

1. ***Legal basis for the United Nations Emergency Force.*** In establishing the Emergency Force, did the General Assembly avail itself of all of the power it had asserted in the Uniting for Peace Resolution? The force was not physically located on Israeli territory. Could it have lawfully entered Israeli territory to perform its function without the consent of the government of Israel?

2. ***Withdrawal of the Emergency Force.*** At the request of the government of the United Arab Republic (Egypt), the Secretary–General of the United Nations (U Thant) withdrew the Emergency Force from the territory of the Republic in May and June 1967. The action of the Secretary–General in acceding to this request at that particular time was highly controversial. He explained his action in detail in a report to the United Nations. G.A.Off.Rec., 5th Emergency Spec.Sess. (1967), Annexes (A/6730/Add. 3), p. 9.

The Congo: Preventing Dismemberment of a State. The former Belgian Congo became independent in June 1960. Shortly after independence, the Katanga Province attempted to secede, with concomitant civilian riots, including attacks on Belgians and other Europeans, and mutiny by the Congolese military. Moise Tshombe, the leader in the Katanga Province, requested the intervention of Belgian troops to restore order. Belgian troops did intervene on July 10, 1960, causing panic and bitterness in the Katangan population. Tshombe sought recognition but never received it. The Security Council, at the request of President Kasavubu and Prime Minister Lumumba of the Congo, adopted a resolution on July 14, 1960, which called for the immediate withdrawal of Belgian troops and authorized the Secretary–General to provide the Congolese Government with sufficient military assistance to bring about order. Thus, the U.N. Peacekeeping Force for the Congo was created (ONUC) (S.C.Res. 143; U.N.Doc.S/4387 1960), which did intervene, engaging in heavy fighting in Katanga Province. During 1960, several S.C. resolutions were vetoed by the USSR and a rift developed between Prime Minister Lumumba and President Kasavubu. In the beginning of the crisis, the U.N. appeared to take a neutral position on the Katangan secession, but by July 22, 1960, it requested "all states to refrain from any action which might impede the restoration of law and order and the exercise by the Government of the Congo of its authority and also to refrain from any action which might undermine the territorial integrity and the political independence of the Republic of the Congo." (S.C.Res. 145 (1960). In 1961, this was reiterated as the purpose of the U.N. involvement. [S.C.Res.U.N.SCOR, 16th Sess., U.N.Doc.S/5002 (1961)]. *See,* Franck & Carey, Working Paper, The Role of the United Nations in the Congo—A Retrospective Perspective, in The Role of the U.N. in the Congo 1, 11–12 (Tondel ed. 1963); Hoskyns, The Congo: A Chronology of Events, January 1960–December 1961 (1962); Seyersted, United Nations Forces in the Law of Peace and War 60 (1966).

The Congo problems continue. For more on the Congo, see chapter 16, *infra,* and the following Philip Gourevitch, *Forsaken,* New Yorker, Sept. 25, 2000, at 53, 59 (Democratic Republic of Congo); *In Africa, Diamonds as Gods' Tears,* Jan. 19, 2001, at http://www.msnbc.com/news/518809.asp (claiming that diamonds are exchanged for arms in Sierra Leone, Angola, and Democratic Republic of Congo); Crossette, *Rwandan Leader, in U.S., Urges Push for Peace in Congo,* N.Y. Times, Feb. 5, 2001, at A4 (expressing concern that insurgents in Congo are fighting for control of diamond mining regions).

Notes and Questions

1. *Legal basis for the United Nations operations in the Congo.* The Congolese action was authorized by the Security Council. Was its legality more firmly based on the Charter than the Emergency Force in the Middle East (which, as seen above, was authorized by the General Assembly)? Did the Council act pursuant to article 39? If so, what was the requisite threat to the peace, breach of the peace, or act of aggression? Was it the sending of troops by Belgium to maintain and restore order? The Council never made a finding to that effect. Can the Council's action be grounded on the request of the Congolese government for aid? What is the Charter basis for the Council's response to such a request?

2. *Analysis of the legal basis for peacekeeping forces by the International Court of Justice.* The legal basis for both the Emergency Force and the Congolese operations was the subject of analysis by the International Court in the *Certain Expenses Case,* which follows. The Court was asked for an advisory opinion because certain members of the U.N. refused to pay amounts assessed against them as "expenses of the Organization" (article 17). The members refusing claimed that the Middle East and Congolese operations did not qualify as such expenses. The case was significant because of its financial implications, since article 19 of the Charter prescribes a loss of the right to vote in the General Assembly in the case of certain financial delinquencies on the part of a member. But the advisory opinion of the court is also significant because of its analysis of the constitutional powers of the United Nations and its organs to employ or authorize military force.

Certain Expenses of the United Nations (Advisory Opinion)

International Court of Justice, 1962.
[1962] I.C.J.Rep. 151, 156, 162.

[The General Assembly requested an advisory opinion by Resolution 1731 (XVI), adopted on December 20, 1961. The request has been edited by omitting designations, by number and date, of specific resolutions adopted by the Security Council and the General Assembly.]

* * *

The question on which the Court is asked to give its opinion is whether certain expenditures which were authorized by the General Assembly to cover the costs of the United Nations operations in the Congo (hereinafter referred to as ONUC) and of the operations of the United Nations Emergency Force in the Middle East (hereinafter referred to as UNEF), "constitute 'expenses of the Organization' within the meaning of Article 17, paragraph 2, of the Charter * * * ".

* * *

Article 17 is the only article in the Charter which refers to budgetary authority or to the power to apportion expenses, or otherwise to raise revenue, except for Articles 33 and 35, paragraph 3, of the Statute of the Court which have no bearing on the point here under discussion. Nevertheless, it has been argued before the Court that one type of expenses, namely those resulting from operations for the maintenance of international peace and security, are not "expenses of the Organization" within the meaning of Article 17, paragraph 2, of the Charter, inasmuch as they fall to be dealt with exclusively by the Security Council, and more especially through agreements negotiated in accordance with Article 43 of the Charter.

The argument rests in part upon the view that when the maintenance of international peace and security is involved, it is only the Security Council which is authorized to decide on any action relative thereto. It is argued further that since the General Assembly's power is limited to discussing, considering, studying and recommending, it cannot impose an obligation to pay the expenses which result from the implementation of its recommendations. This argument leads to an examination of the respective functions of the General Assembly and of the Security Council under the Charter, particularly with respect to the maintenance of international peace and security.

Article 24 of the Charter provides: "In order to ensure prompt and effective action by the United Nations, its Members confer on the Security Council primary responsibility for the maintenance of international peace and security. * * * "

The responsibility conferred is "primary", not exclusive. This primary responsibility is conferred upon the Security Council, as stated in Article 24, "in order to ensure prompt and effective action". To this end, it is the Security Council which is given a power to impose an explicit obligation of compliance if for example it issues an order or command to an aggressor under Chapter VII. It is only the Security Council which can require enforcement by coercive action against an aggressor.

The Charter makes it abundantly clear, however, that the General Assembly is also to be concerned with international peace and security. Article 14 authorizes the General Assembly to "recommend measures for the peaceful adjustment of any situation, regardless of origin, which it deems likely to impair the general welfare or friendly relations among nations, including situations resulting from a violation of the provisions of the present Charter setting forth the purposes and principles of the United Nations". The word "measures" implies some kind of action, and the only limitation which Article 14 imposes on the General Assembly is the restriction found in Article 12, namely, that the Assembly should not recommend measures while the Security Council is dealing with the same matter unless the Council requests it to do so. Thus, while it is the Security Council which, exclusively, may order coercive action, the functions and powers conferred by the Charter on the General Assembly are not confined to discussion, consideration, the initiation of studies and the making of recommendations; they are not merely hortatory. * * *

       * * *

The Court has considered the general problem of the interpretation of Article 17, paragraph 2 * * *. In determining whether the actual expenditures authorized constitute "expenses of the Organization within the meaning of Article 17, paragraph 2, of the Charter", the Court agrees that such expenditures must be tested by their relationship to the purposes of the United Nations in the sense that if an expenditure were made for a purpose which is not one of the purposes of the United Nations, it could not be considered an "expense of the Organization."

The purposes of the United Nations are set forth in Article 1 of the Charter. The first two purposes as stated in paragraphs 1 and 2, may be summarily described as pointing to the goal of international peace and security and friendly relations. The third purpose is the achievement of economic, social, cultural and humanitarian goals and respect for human rights. The fourth and last purpose is: "To be a center for harmonizing the actions of nations in the attainment of these common ends".

The primary place ascribed to international peace and security is natural, since the fulfilment of the other purposes will be dependent upon the attainment of that basic condition. These purposes are broad indeed, but neither they nor the powers conferred to effectuate them are unlimited. Save as they have entrusted the Organization with the attainment of these common ends, the Member States retain their freedom of action. But when the Organization takes action which warrants the assertion that it was appropriate for the fulfilment of one of the stated purposes of the United Nations, the presumption is that such action is not ultra vires the Organization.

       * * *

In considering the operations in the Middle East, the Court must analyze the functions of UNEF as set forth in resolutions of the General Assembly. Resolution 998 (ES–I) of 4 November 1956 requested the Secretary–General to submit a plan "for the setting up, with the consent of the nations concerned, of an emergency international United Nations Force to secure and supervise the cessation of hostilities in accordance with all the terms of" the General Assembly's previous resolution 997 (ES–I) of 2 November 1956. The verb "secure" as applied to such matters as halting the movement of military forces and arms into the area and the conclusion of a cease-fire, might suggest measures of enforcement, were it not that the Force was to be set up "with the consent of the nations concerned."

In his first report on the plan for an emergency international Force the Secretary–General used the language of resolution 998 (ES–I) in submitting his proposals. The same terms are used in [G.A.] resolution 1000 (ES–I) of 5 November in which operative paragraph 1 reads: "Establishes a United Nations Command for an emergency international Force to secure and supervise the cessation of hostilities in accordance with all the terms of General Assembly resolution 997 (ES–I) of 2 November 1956." This resolution was adopted without a dissenting vote. In his second and final report on the plan for an emergency international Force of 6 November, the Secretary–General, in paragraphs 9 and 10 stated:

While the General Assembly is enabled to establish the Force with the consent of those parties which contribute units to the Force, it could not request the Force to be stationed or operate on the territory of a given country without the consent of the Government of that country. This does not exclude the possibility that the Security Council could use such a Force within the wider margins provided under Chapter VII of the Charter. I would not for the present consider it necessary to elaborate this point further, since no use of the Force under Chapter VII, with the rights in relation to Member States that this would entail, has been envisaged.

10. The point just made permits the conclusion that the setting up of the Force should not be guided by the needs which would have existed had the measure been considered as part of an enforcement action directed against a Member country. There is an obvious difference between establishing the Force in order to secure the cessation of hostilities, with a withdrawal of forces, and establishing such a Force with a view to enforcing a withdrawal of forces.

Paragraph 12 of the Report is particularly important because in resolution 1001 (ES–I) the General Assembly, again without a dissenting vote, "Concurs in the definition of the functions of the Force as stated in paragraph 12 of the Secretary–General's report". Paragraph 12 reads:

the functions of the United Nations Force would be, when a cease-fire is being established, to enter Egyptian territory with the consent of the Egyptian Government, in order to help maintain quiet during and after the withdrawal of non-Egyptian troops, and to secure compliance with the other terms established in the resolution of 2 November 1956. The Force obviously should have no rights other than those necessary for the execution of its functions, in co-operation with local authorities. It would be more than an observers' corps, but in no way a military force temporarily controlling the territory in which it is stationed; nor, moreover, should the Force have military functions exceeding those necessary to secure peaceful conditions on the assumption that the parties to the conflict take all necessary steps for compliance with the recommendations of the General Assembly.

It is not possible to find in this description of the functions of UNEF, as outlined by the Secretary–General and concurred in by the General Assembly without a dissenting vote, any evidence that the Force was to be used for purposes of enforcement. Nor can such evidence be found in the subsequent operations of the Force, operations which did not exceed the scope of the functions ascribed to it.

It could not therefore have been patent on the face of the resolution that the establishment of UNEF was in effect "enforcement action" under Chapter VII which, in accordance with the Charter, could be authorized only by the Security Council.

On the other hand, it is apparent that the operations were undertaken to fulfil a prime purpose of the United Nations, that is, to promote and to maintain a peaceful settlement of the situation. This being true, the Secretary–General properly exercised the authority given him to incur financial obligations of the Organization and expenses resulting from such obligations must be considered "expenses of the Organization within the meaning of Article 17, paragraph 2."

* * *

The operations in the Congo were initially authorized by the Security Council in the resolution of 14 July 1960 which was adopted without a dissenting vote. The resolution, in the light of the appeal from the Government of the Congo, the report of the Secretary–General and the debate in the Security Council, was clearly adopted with a view to maintaining international peace and security. However, it is argued that that resolution has been implemented, in violation of provisions of the Charter inasmuch as under the Charter it is the Security Council that determines which States are to participate in carrying out decisions involving the maintenance of international peace and security, whereas in the case of the Congo the Secretary–General himself determined which States were to participate with their armed forces or otherwise.

* * *

In the light of [the] record of reiterated consideration, confirmation, approval and ratification by the Security Council and by the General Assembly of the actions of the Secretary–General in implementing the resolution of 14 July 1960, it is impossible to reach the conclusion that the operations in question usurped or impinged upon the prerogatives conferred by the Charter on the Security Council. The Charter does not forbid the Security Council to act through instruments of its own choice: under article 29 it "may establish such subsidiary organs as it deems necessary for the performance of its functions"; under article 98 it may entrust "other functions" to the Secretary–General.

It is not necessary for the Court to express an opinion as to which article or articles of the Charter were the basis for the resolutions of the Security Council, but it can be said that the operations of ONUC did not include a use of armed force against a State which the Security Council, under article 39, determined to have committed an act of aggression or to have breached the peace. The armed forces which were utilized in the Congo were not authorized to take military action against any State. The operation did not involve "preventive or enforcement measures" against any State under Chapter VII and therefore did not constitute "action" as that term is used in article 11.

[Thus,] financial obligations which, in accordance with the clear and reiterated authority of both the Security Council and the General Assembly, the Secretary–General incurred on behalf of the United Nations, constitute obligations of the Organization for which the General Assembly was entitled to make provision under the authority of article 17.

* * * [A declaration, separate opinions and dissenting opinions omitted.]

Note. Aftermath of the Certain Expenses Case. Although the General Assembly subsequently adopted a resolution in which it accepted the advisory opinion of the International Court of Justice, members that had refused to recognize peacekeeping expenses as expenses of the organization (principally France and the former USSR) continued to refuse to accept the Court's interpretation of the Charter and became in arrears in their payments. The United States at first intended to force the application of article 19, entailing the loss of vote by non-paying members. The Nineteenth Session of the General Assembly did business without formal voting to avoid the question. The issue was subsequently dropped. The members reserved their positions and a constitutional crisis was avoided.

The Middle East: The Role of Peacekeeping Forces.

Notes and Questions

1. *United Nations Disengagement Observer Force (UNDOF)*

Genesis of the force. UNDOF was created in 1974. It had its roots in the continuous flow of hostilities in the Middle East. You have considered material on the Suez Crisis, which was the impetus for the creation of the first U.N. peace-keeping force (UNEF). Tension decreased after the UNEF force withdrew and was replaced by UAR (Egyptian) forces. Immediately after the withdrawal, at the request of Egypt of the U.N. Emergency Force in 1967, Israel launched a broad-scale offensive against Egypt and Syria which resulted in territorial gains. Following the termination of hostilities, the Security Council adopted Resolution 242 (1967) detailing the principles deemed requisite to peace in that area. But hostilities were begun again in 1973, this time on the initiative of Egypt and Syria. The Security Council adopted Resolution 338 (1973), calling for a cease fire and for the implementation of the principles in Resolution 242 (1967). After Israel and Syria entered into an agreement of disengagement, pursuant to Security Council Resolution 338 (1973), the Council authorized the establishment of the

U.N. Disengagement Observer Force. As has been its custom in the establishment of such forces, the Council put a short time limit on its authorization, subject to renewal. Three relevant resolutions were issued by the Security Council. The meaning of the resolution on principles has been the subject of debate: Resolution 242 affirms the principle of Israeli withdrawal from "territories occupied in the recent conflict"; it does not call for withdrawal from "all territories" or "the territories." *See* Rostow, *The Illegality of the Arab Attack on Israel of October 6, 1973,* 69 A.J.I.L. 272 (1975).

After the 1967 War, the Security Council's Resolution 242 enunciated two "principles": that the Israeli forces withdraw "from the territories occupied in the recent conflict" (*French version: "[r]etrait des forces armées israéliennes des territoires occupés lor du récent conflit"*); and "[t]ermination of all claims or states of belligerency and respect for and acknowledgment of the sovereignty, territorial integrity and political independence of every State in the area and their right to live in peace within secure and recognized boundaries free from threats or acts of force." Resolution 242 failed to produce peaceful settlement and Israel retained the territories occupied in the '67 War. This caused Egypt, Syria and Iraq to launch, in 1973, an attack on Israel, which was repelled after some initial success. The Security Council issued Resolution 338 (1973), which called upon the parties to "cease all firing and terminate all military activity immediately, no later than 12 hours after the moment of the adoption of this decision * * *; [T]o start immediately after the cease-fire the implementation of res. 242 (1967)," *supra;* and "that negotiations shall start between the parties * * * aimed at establishing a just and durable peace in the Middle East." Security Council Resolution 340 (1973), established the U.N. Emergency Force (UNEF). Security Council Resolution 350 (1974) established the U.N. Disengagement Observer Force (UNDOF), with the strength of 1,250 individuals. UNDOF was charged with monitoring the disengagement that Israel had finally accepted in agreements with Egypt and Syria and to occupy the buffer zone between Israel and Syria (the Golan Heights).

The provisions of the agreements, which were stated not to be "peace agreements," included the cease-fire, the separation of the forces and an agreement not to have military forces in this buffer zone. Monitoring and inspection were to be done by UNDOF. UNDOF was to have freedom of movement and communication required for its mission, was to be supplied with defensive weapons, but was required to comply with pertinent Syrian law and regulations and was not to hamper local civil administration. UNDOF was under the command of the United Nations, executed by the Secretary–General under the authority of the Security Council. The initial authorization was for six-months, renewable by the Security Council. See, *Establishment of the U.N. Disengagement Observer Force* (UNDOF), 1974 Yb.U.N. 198, 199. The mandate of UNDOF has been extended so that it continues to monitor the Golan Heights.

2. *United Nations Interim Force in Lebanon (UNIFIL)* In March of 1978, another U.N. peacekeeping force was established in the Middle East. The United Nations Interim Force in Lebanon (UNIFIL), was created to oversee and confirm the withdrawal of Israeli "forces from all Lebanese territory, to restore international peace and security," and to assist "the Government of Lebanon in ensuring the return of its effective authority in the area * * *." [S.C.Res. 425 (1978)]. UNIFIL remains today, having had its mandate extended. Some background follows.

The Situation in the Israel—Lebanon Sector

32 Yearbook of the United Nations 295, 296 (1978).

In a letter * * * to the Secretary–General, the representative of Israel charged that * * * a terrorist murder squad dispatched by the Palestine Liberation Organization (PLO) had infiltrated the Israeli coastline and carried out an indiscriminate attack against Israeli civilians along the Haifa–Tel Aviv highway, resulting in 37 dead and 76 wounded. The letter also contained excerpts from a statement by the Prime Minister of Israel in his press conference. * * * The Chief of Staff of UNTSO reported heavy Israeli ground, naval and air activity * * *. There were bombing attacks by Israeli forces to Beirut and against a Palestinian refugee camp south of Beirut, shelling in the vicinity of Tyre from Israeli naval vessels, and air attacks; mortar, artillery and tank fire were impacting in and around several other targets along the Lebanese frontier. All UNTSO personnel were reported to be safe.

In letters * * * to the President of the Security Council and the Secretary–General, the representative of Lebanon charged that * * *, Israel had committed an aggression against Lebanese territory, during which massive numbers of Israeli troops crossed into Lebanon from several axes, patrol vessels penetrated Lebanese territorial waters along the coast-line from Tyre to Sidon, and Israeli warplanes bombarded several areas in Lebanese territory. An undetermined number of citizens were killed, nota-bly in Tyre, and enormous damage was caused to property. He also stressed that Lebanon had no connection with the commando operation on the Haifa–Tel Aviv highway, that it was not responsible for the presence of Palestinian bases in southern Lebanon, and that the only solution to the problem lay in putting an end to Israeli aggression and in Israel's with-drawing its forces from Lebanon.

* * *

In a statement to the Council, the representative of Lebanon accused Israel of having committed a savage act of aggression against his country and urged the Council to demand the immediate cessation of hostilities and the withdrawal of the invaders. The United Nations should be enabled to uphold its Charter, he added, and prevent Israel from taking international law into its own hands and acting as judge, jury and executioner while the community of nations idly watched Lebanon's agony. He stressed the need for restoring the peace, restoring Lebanese sovereignty over its territory and re-establishing an acceptable international order in the Middle East.

The representative of Israel said he was convinced that the debate was unnecessary, since both parties involved in the issue wanted the same thing—the complete restoration of Lebanese sovereignty in the area in question. He charged the United Nations with blatant partiality vis-a-vis his country and regretted that neither the General Assembly nor the Security Council had issued a statement encouraging the peace talks between Israel and Egypt or urging their extension to Israel's other neighbours. Israel Defence Forces had crossed into Lebanon as a measure to deal with terror and terrorists, he continued, in carrying out Israel's inherent duty to exercise its right to self-defence in the protection of the inviolability of its territory and its people. He deplored the aid given by some Arab States and the USSR to PLO and maintained that the aim of the Israeli operation was not retaliation or to seize territory but to clear PLO from the area of southern Lebanon, bordering on Israel, where an absence of law and order reigned and over which the Lebanon Government had lost control, and to create conditions in which the Government of Lebanon could restore control and re-establish its sovereign right in the area.

* * *

Report of the Secretary–General

36 Yearbook of the United Nations 6 (1982).

* * *

Peace-keeping operations have generally been considered to be one of the most successful innovations of the United Nations, and certainly their record over the years is one of which to be proud. They have proved to be a most useful instrument of de-escalation and conflict control and have extended the influence of the Security Council into the field in a unique way. I may add that U.N. peace-keeping operations have traditionally shown an admirable degree of courage, objectivity and impartiality. This record, which is a great credit to the Organization, is sometimes overlooked in the heat of partisanship. The limitations of peace-keeping operations are less well understood. Thus when a peace-keeping operation is overrun or brushed aside, the credibility both of the United Nations and of peace-keeping operations as such is severely shaken.

It is not always realized that peace-keeping operations are the visible part of a complex framework of political and diplomatic efforts and of countervailing pressures designed to keep the peace-keeping efforts and related peace-making efforts effective. It is assumed that the Security Council itself and those Member States in a position to bring influence to bear will be able to act decisively to ensure respect for decisions of the Council. If this framework breaks down, as it did for example in Lebanon last June, there is little that a United Nations peace-keeping force can by itself do to rectify the situation. Indeed, in such circumstances it tends to become the scapegoat.

Peace-keeping operations can function properly only with the co-operation of the parties and on a clearly defined mandate from the Security Council. They are based on the assumption that the parties, in accepting a United Nations peace-keeping operation, commit themselves to co-operating with it. This commitment is also required by the Charter, under which all concerned have a clear obligation to abide by the decisions of the

Council. United Nations peace-keeping operations are not equipped, authorized, or indeed made available, to take part in military activities other than peace-keeping. Their main strength is the will of the international community which they symbolize. Their weakness comes to light when the political assumptions on which they are based are ignored or overridden.

I recommend that Member States, especially the members of the Security Council, should again study urgently the means by which our peace-keeping operations could be strengthened. An increase in their military capacity or authority is only one possibility—a possibility which may well give rise in some circumstances to serious political and other objections. Another possibility is to underpin the authority of peace-keeping operations by guarantees, including explicit guarantees for collective or individual supportive action. In recent months, two multinational forces were set up outside the framework of the United Nations to perform peace-keeping tasks, because of opposition to United Nations involvement either within or outside the Security Council. While understanding the circumstances which led to the establishment of these forces, I find such a trend disturbing because it demonstrates the difficulties the Security Council encounters in fulfilling its responsibilities as the primary organ for the maintenance of international peace and security in the prevailing political conditions.

* * *

3. *Multinational forces outside the framework of the United Nations.*

1. ***The Sinai Multinational Force and Observers.*** This force was established to implement provisions of the 1979 Treaty of Peace between Egypt and Israel. The United States contributed personnel to the force. As explained to Congress by President Reagan:

> As you know, the 1979 Treaty of Peace between Egypt and Israel terminated the existing state of war between those countries, provided for the complete withdrawal from the Sinai of Israeli armed forces and civilians within three years after the date of the Treaty's entry into force (that is, by April 25, 1982), and provided for the establishment of normal friendly relations. To assist in assuring compliance with the terms of Annex I to the Treaty, so as to enhance the mutual confidence of the parties in the security of the Sinai border area, the Treaty calls for the establishment of a peacekeeping force and observers to be deployed prior to the final Israeli withdrawal. Although the Treaty called on the parties to request the United Nations to provide the peacekeeping force and observers, it was also recognized during the negotiations that it might not be possible to reach agreement in the United Nations for this purpose. For this reason, President Carter assured Israel and Egypt in separate letters that "if the Security Council fails to establish and maintain the arrangements called for in the Treaty, the President will be prepared to take those steps necessary to ensure the establishment and maintenance of an acceptable alternative multinational force."

In fact, it proved impossible to secure U.N. action. As a result, Egypt and Israel, with the participation of the United States, entered into negotiations for the creation of an alternative multinational force and observers. These negotiations resulted in the signing on August 3, 1981 by Egypt and Israel of a Protocol for that purpose. The Protocol established the MFO and provided in effect that the MFO would have the same functions and responsibilities as those provided in the 1979 Treaty for the planned U.N. force.* * * By means of an exchange of letters with Egypt and Israel, the United States agreed, subject to Congressional authorization and appropriations, to contribute an infantry battalion, a logistics support unit and civilian observers to the MFO, as well as a specified portion of the annual costs of the MFO. The U.S. military personnel to be contributed comprise less than half of the anticipated total MFO military complement of approximately 2,500 personnel. 76 A.J.I.L. 613 (1982).

4. *The Multinational Force in Lebanon.* The United States entered into agreements in 1982 with the government of Lebanon for the establishment of this force and contributed contingents along with France, Italy and the United Kingdom. 78 AJIL 209 (1984).

Cyprus

Notes. The United Kingdom granted Cyprus its independence in 1960. The circumstances of independence were difficult, because of vitriolic conflict between Turkish and Greek Cypriot communities. *See,* Treaty Concerning the Establishment of the Republic of Cyprus, August 16, 1960, 382 U.N.T.S. 8. Fighting erupted between the Greek and Turkish Cypriot forces in December 1963. Greece supported the Greek Cypriot forces, which comprised approximately eighty percent of the population, while Turkey supported those of the Turkish Cypriot community. This situation was extremely volatile. The Security Council, after monitoring the situation for several weeks in early 1964, approved Resolution 186, establishing a peacekeeping force (UNFICYP), which was mandated "to prevent the recurrence of fighting, help maintain law and order, and promote a return to normal conditions * * * "[U.N.S.C.Res. 186, March 4, 1964]. Serious fighting, including air strikes by Turkish air forces and ground attacks by the Greek Cypriots continued, although intermittent at times, until 1967.

There was relative peace in Cyprus until 1974, when the Greek military undertook a coup d'etat and replaced Cyprus' president with one favoring union with Greece. Turkey responded within days by invading Cyprus and taking control of approximately one-third of the island. Although Turkey's actions were internationally condemned, they went unchallenged. Seven years later the Turkish Republic of Northern Cyprus ("TRNC") declared itself to be an independent state. Turkey immediately recognized its independence, but it is alone in this recognition, and the European Court of Human Rights recently held that the TRNC is not an independent state [*See Loizidou v. Turkey*, European Court of Human Rights (Dec. 19, 1996)]. The international community continues to oppose secession, insisting that the rights of the Turkish minority can be protected in a single state. Then Secretary–General Perez de Cuellar attempted to mediate a resolution and in 1992 drafted a framework for settlement, but the parties refused to adopt it. The situation remains unresolved and UNFICYP remains in Turkey, now relegated to guarding the border between the territories.

———

Cambodia

The Cambodians have suffered more than twenty years of civil war among at least four factions, preceded by saturation bombing by the U.S. during the Vietnam War. Cambodians have suffered interventions, genocide, and a series of gross violations of their human rights. Norodom Sihanouk, Cambodia's hereditary king, was overthrown. Later, the Kampuchean Communist Party (the Khmer Rouge) gained control of Cambodia in 1975 and renamed it Democratic Kampuchea, ruling from April 1975 until January 1979, when it was ousted by Vietnamese troops. During this four year period, the regime attempted total restructuring of the Khmer society, rejected all foreign influences, tried to create an agrarian economy, committed atrocities of a nature to constitute one of the worst examples of state-sponsored slaughter and other violations of human rights known to have occurred in this century. This ultimately resulted in the execution, starvation or death by disease or exhaustion of a significant portion of the Cambodian people. The 1979 Vietnamese invasion established the People's Republic of Kampuchea. The ousted Khmer Rouge occupied small rural enclaves principally close to the Thai–Cambodian border, while hundreds of thousands of Cambodians fled to Thailand and the West. The Vietnamese forces retained control throughout the 1980's, despite protestations and a call by the U.N. General Assembly to withdraw all "foreign forces." GA Res. 34/22, UN GAOR, 34th Sess., Supp. No. 46, at 16, UN Doc. A/34/46 (1979).

In 1980, the General Assembly convened an international conference to find "a comprehensive political settlement of the Kampuchean problem," [G.A.Res. 35/6, UN GAOR, 35th Sess., Supp. No. 48, at 13, 14, UN Doc. A/35/48 (1980)]. The Conference met in New York during July of 1981. It was attended by 79 states, including Democratic Kampuchea, but was boycotted by Vietnam and states aligned with the former USSR. The General Assembly subsequently passed annual resolutions and Indonesia convened the Jakarta Informal Meeting (JIM I and II), initiating a process of reconciliation.

Vietnam announced troop withdrawal in April 1989 to be completed by the end of September. The French and Indonesian Governments agreed in 1989 to convene another international conference aimed at reaching a comprehensive settlement. This Paris Conference on Cambodia included the four Cambodian factions and the ASEAN States, the five permanent members of the UN Security Council, Vietnam, Laos, Japan, Australia, India and Canada. Zimbabwe was invited to represent the non-aligned States. This Conference finally led to several agreements. [See, Paris Peace

Conference on Cambodian Agreements Elaborating the Framework for a Comprehensive Political Settlement of the Cambodian Conflict, UN Doc. A/46/608 and S/233177, reprinted in 31 I.L.M. 174 (1992)].

One of these agreements was to establish a Supreme National Council (SNC) made-up of the four formerly warring factions, to be the "unique * * * source of authority" in Cambodia, embodying Cambodian sovereignty. The SNC agreed to allow the U.N. to establish UNTAC, the U.N. Transitional Authority in Cambodia (ultimately composed of 15,000 individuals) to oversee the disarmament of the factions, to supervise free elections, and to provide some civil administrative services, including the functioning of at least five ministries. It has access to all governmental documents, to issue binding directives, and has control of all personnel. SNC and UNTAC are intertwined and present an unprecedented feature for international law. SNC virtually ran Cambodia. For discussion of the Khmer Rouge acts of Genocide, see chapter 9, and for discussion of the possibility of an Ad Hoc or mixed war crime tribunal for Cambodia, see chapter 16.

Notes and Questions

Did Cambodia become a trusteeship? If so, was that legal? See U.N. Charter Articles 77 and 78. The Security Council did not authorize any Chapter VII action to "restore international peace" in the region. Did the "nation" of Cambodia delegate power to the U.N.? Was there a single government in Cambodia accepted by all factions and able to delegate power? Was such an "entity" ingeniously created by the Comprehensive Settlement Agreement in the Supreme National Council (SNC)? The latter was defined by the agreement as the "unique legitimate body and source of authority in which, throughout the transitional period, the sovereignty, independence and unity of Cambodia are enshrined * * *" and provides that the SNC would represent Cambodia externally during this transitional period. [Comprehensive Settlement Agreement, arts. 3 and 5]. What institution would have jurisdiction if [when] SNC forces committed crimes (including crimes against humanity?) There is evidence that such conduct has occurred without appropriate resolution.

SNC is sui generis in international law. To pose the questions raised earlier, some world leaders have suggested that the triple crises of Somalia, Bosnia, and Cambodia indicate that sovereignty and national self-determination are insufficient by themselves as guiding principles for international conduct. See, Boutros–Ghali, *Agenda for Peace,* stating: "[t]he time for absolute and exclusive sovereignty * * * has passed * * *. Its theory was never matched by reality." Does the Cambodian situation give credence to this proposition?

On November 14, 1993, the last official U.N. peacekeeping troops left Cambodia, pursuant to Security Council Resolution of August 1993, which called for a November 15th deadline for a safe and orderly withdrawal from Cambodia. King Norodom Sihanouk, once and future King of Cambodia, returned on September 23rd, 1993, to sign his nation's Constitution, which will make him monarch once again. This completed the prerequisites for the withdrawal of the U.N. Peacekeeping force. Thus ended the most expensive United Nations peace-keeping effort. *See,* Ratner, *The Cambodia Settlement Agreements,* 87 A.J.I.L. 1, 3–14 (1993) (from which most of this summary was developed); Quinn, The Pattern and Scope of Violence, in Cambodia 1975–1978 Rendezvous With Death (Karl D. Jackson ed. 1989); Chanda, Brother Enemy: The War After the War (1986); Kampuchea: Decade of the Genocide (R. Kiljunen ed. 1984). Consider the following in relation to peace-keeping forces in Cambodia and other places.

Parker, Cultural Autonomy: A Prime Directive for the Blue Helmets

55 U. Pitt. L. Rev. 207, 208 (1993).*

United Nations forces increasingly are being used and promoted as tools for humanitarian intervention. The demise of the Cold War provided the catalyst for this development, resulting concurrently in a shift in international attention to the political and humanitarian concerns of individual nations, and the development of a cooperative ability within the U.N. Security Council to address those concerns using United Nations forces. As this method of intervention gains favor, important questions regarding the human rights of a subject nation's citizens, both individual and collective, must be answered.

Certain stories emerging from nations currently occupied by U.N. forces raise a subset of these questions—those relating to cultural rights. The effect of the 22,000 person United Nations Transitional Authority in Cambodia ("UNTAC") goes far beyond its official mission of preparing for elections and securing the peace. Newspaper reports describe upheavals in the economic, social, and legal life of Cambodians incidentally caused by UNTAC's authorized actions. UNTAC employees have created an unsustainable, artificial economy, luring farmers and others to Phnom Penh from their traditional vocations. Prostitution, previously almost unknown, is rampant in the larger cities. UNTAC's presence also is forcing changes in Cambodian educational practices, particularly in the language of instruction. The media, a key conduit of culture, is controlled by UNTAC monitors.

Notes and Questions

1. Are these concerns justified? Do similar concerns arise in other areas, such as Somalia, the Congo, Kosovo, or Macedonia? The Security Council Resolutions for Somalia are presented in the Doc. Supp. Analyze them. Regarding the material on international peacekeeping forces and U.S. law, would the timing provisions of the War Powers Resolution be triggered if U.S. forces were participating in such an operation and hostilities commenced between belligerents? *See,* Chapter 16, *infra.* On Peacekeeping generally, *see* Durch & Blechman, Keeping the Peace: The United

---

* Reprinted with the permission of the
U.Pitt.L.Rev.

Nations in the Emerging World Order (1992). On peacekeeping, see Reimers, *Perspective: Practicing Law on a Different Battlefield,* Chicago J.Int'l L. 275, 279–281 (2001).* ... IV. Peace Support Operations. As I describe above, modern conflicts are not the type of all-out conflicts that the world prepared for during the Cold War or had experienced in the two World Wars. Leaving aside the 1991 Gulf War, today's conflicts are most often internal struggles or local wars. The conflict in the former Yugoslavia is a good example of this type of mixed conflict with some of the military's new roles. The evolution of the various peacekeeping mandates clearly showed that the world was not prepared for a "Yugoslavian" style of conflict. The first peacekeepers in Yugoslavia—the United Nations Protection Force ('UNPROFOR')—had an extremely limited set of rules of engagement. This meant that they had little power to enforce their mandate, a role which was well in line with the United Nation's traditional approach to peacekeeping. Previous peacekeeping operations were almost always based on Chapter VI of the UN Charter, which states that a peacekeeping force must respect the limits dictated by the parties to the conflict. UN tactics did not begin to change until the failures of the mission in the former Yugoslavia became obvious. The United Nation's existing Stabilization Force ('SFOR') mission has a different set of rules of engagement that are decidedly more robust than the UNPROFOR rules. They are based on Chapter VII of the UN Charter, which empowers SFOR to impose its will on the conflicting parties.

From a legal point of view, it was evident that the basis for handling the conflicts in the Balkans was not found in the standard laws of armed conflict. Even though the situation was by Geneva Conventions all definitions to be regarded as an armed conflict, it was instead classified as a "local" conflict. Pursuant to UN resolutions and agreements, the surrounding states sent peacekeeping troops. Because the contributing states were formally at peace with the countries that they were policing, a number of agreements had to be concluded with the "hosting" countries, such as Bosnia and Croatia. Needless to say, those agreements could not be adequately disseminated down through the system in the countries of the former Yugoslavia. That made it necessary for the peacekeepers, bound by UN resolutions, to engage the local warlords, not so bound, in an uphill battle. UN forces had to maintain a precarious balance between respecting the sovereignty of the host countries and enforcing the peace treaties.

The problems that the United Nations faced were not simplified by the fact that so many countries sent peacekeeping troops. To avoid complete organizational chaos, various countries worked together in multinational units. Denmark's contribution to SFOR, for instance, was part of a battle group which included Sweden, Finland, Poland and the Baltic States. That alone could make the mouth water for any professor of international private law. It is further complicated, however, by the facts that our battle group is subordinate to the American division, and that because SFOR is operating in Bosnian territory, it had to respect Bosnian law, which is itself unclear in many relevant areas. Rules of engagement are drafted to set forth the legal limits on the use of force. These limits take into account the

* Reprinted with the permission of the
Chicago Journal of International Law.

constraints of humanitarian law, relevant international law (such as human rights laws), the mandate of the specific mission at hand, and the domestic legislation of the host nation. Even after this laundry list of variables, the Rules must take into account the variations in the domestic legislation of the contributing countries. For example, the concept of self-defense is construed differently in various countries. Some states do not allow the use of deadly force to protect objects, while some do not allow the use of deadly force to help other people; but other countries take a very expansive view of self-defense. The Danish interpretation, for example, allows for the use of deadly force to save mission personnel or equipment (regardless of the value!). The legal adviser is therefore very important for the commander who wants to ensure that he exploits the full potential of his troops, especially in multinational units.

Notes. *See also,* Bialke, *U.N. Peace Operations: Applicable Norms & the Application of the Law of Armed Conflict,* 50 A.F.L.Rev. 1 (2001); Allen, PEACEKEEPING: OUTSPOKEN OBSERVATIONS BY A FIELD OFFICER (1996); Cartledge, *Legal Constraints on Military Personnel Deployed on Peacekeeping Operations,* in THE CHANGING FACE OF CONFLICT & THE EFFICACY OF INTERNATIONAL HUMANITARIAN LAW 121 (Durham & McCormack eds. 1999); Segal, et al., *Paratroopers as Peacekeepers,* 10 Armed Forces & Society 487 (Summer 1984); Segal and Tiggle, *Attitudes of Citizen–Soldiers Toward Military Missions in the Post–Cold War World,* 23 Armed Forces & Society 373 (Spring 1997); Miller, *Do Soldiers Hate Peacekeeping? The Case of Preventive Diplomacy Operations in Macedonia,* 23 Armed Forces & Society 415 (Spring 1997); and Segal, et al., *Constabulary Attitudes of National Guard and Regular Soldiers in the U.S. Army,* 24 Armed Forces & Society 535. (Summer 1998).

4. USE OF UNITED NATIONS AUTHORITY NOT INVOLVING MILITARY FORCE

Southern Rhodesia

Although Southern Rhodesia (now Zimbabwe) was largely a self-governing territory rather than strictly a colony in the British system, it was not fully independent until the 1960s. Because it was governed by a white majority, the United Kingdom was unwilling to grant it independence until satisfactory constitutional arrangements were arrived at in Rhodesia to provide improvements in the political powers of the black minority. Negotiations between the British and the governing regime in Southern Rhodesia having failed, Southern Rhodesia declared its independence on November 11, 1965 (an act referred to as Unilateral Declaration of Independence or UDI). The General Assembly immediately requested the Security Council to take-up the Rhodesian question as a "matter of urgency." (G.A.Res. 2024, 1965).

A series of resolutions in the Security Council condemned UDI, called on the United Kingdom to quell the rebellion, and specifically called on the United Kingdom to prevent, by force if necessary, the delivery of oil by tankers destined for Rhodesia. *See* Security Council Resolutions 216 and 217 (1965) of November 12, 1965 and 221 (1966) of April 9, 1966. Selective sanctions were voted by the Council in Resolution 232, December 16, 1966. Stating that it was acting in accordance with articles 39 and 41 of the Charter, the Council determined "that the present situation in Southern Rhodesia constitutes *a threat to international peace and security.*" [Emphasis supplied.] The Council thereupon decided that all States Members of the United Nations shall prevent:

(a) the import into their territories of asbestos, iron ore, chrome, pig-iron, sugar, tobacco, copper, meat and meat products and hides, skins and leather originating in Southern Rhodesia and exported therefrom after the date of this resolution;

(b) any activities by their nationals or in their territories which promote or are calculated to promote the export of their commodities from Southern Rhodesia and any dealings by their nationals or in their territories in any of these commodities originating in Southern Rhodesia and exported therefrom after the date of this resolution, including in particular any transfer of funds to Southern Rhodesia for the purposes of such activities or dealings.

* * *

These measures having failed, the Council adopted more comprehensive sanctions two years later. Thus, in Resolution 253, the Security Council noted the failure of these sanctions to bring the "rebellion in Southern Rhodesia to an end," and called for the following sanctions, pursuant to article 25 of the Charter: a total economic blockade (inter alia, no importation of Rhodesian goods and no exportation to Rhodesia or even any activity tending to promote economic or commercial exchange or trade); and cultural and political isolation, including preventing airline registration or operation to or from Rhodesia. The dispute finally ended with an agreement reached at the Lancaster House Conference in London. As a result, on December 21, 1979, the Security Council called upon Member States of the U.N. "to terminate the measures taken against Southern Rhodesia under Chapter VII of the Charter pursuant to Resolutions 232 (1966), 253 (1968) and subsequent related resolutions * * *."

South Africa: Apartheid

The racial situation in South Africa long concerned the United Nations. For years numerous resolutions directed toward the abolition of the system of racial separation (apartheid) in that country produced no discernible effect. In 1963, the members of the Security Council apparently decided that persuasion and exhortation were insufficient to correct at least one aspect of that country's policies. Resolution 181 (1963), the text of which is in the Documentary Supplement was adopted calling upon states to impose an arms embargo. The United States claimed concern over the question of the legal basis under the Charter for the Council's action. The Council imposed a mandatory embargo by its 1977 resolution, the text of which is also in the Documentary Supplement. Read the resolutions carefully and answer the following questions. What was the legal basis for the embargo? Had the United States changed its position on the law, or on the facts? What legal position did by South Africa with respect to the council's action. Did the action eventually help in the collapse of that system? Do you think that the desired embargo of South Africa was used on the same principles as the economic sanctions against IRAO? Keep these questions in mind as you read on through the next several pages.

The Security Council reiterated its condemnation of Apartheid in Resolution 282 (1970), as "evil and abhorrent policies * * * [including] the measures being taken by the Government of South Africa to enforce and extend those policies beyond its borders * * *." It noted that "the situation resulting from the continued application of the policies of apartheid and the constant build-up of the South African military and police forces * * * constitut[ed] a potential threat to international peace and security; and recogniz[ed] that the extensive arms build-up of the military force of South Africa poses a real threat to the security and sovereignty of independent African States opposed to the racial policies of the Government of South Africa * * *." Finally, the Security Council reiterated its call for the 1963 voluntary arms embargo. The Security Council adopted Resolution 418, in 1977, portions of which are in the Doc. Supp.

Strict Implementation of 1977 Arms Embargo Against South Africa Asked By Council

24 UN Chronicle No. 1 (1987), p. 46.

The Security Council on 28 November asked States to implement strictly its 1977 mandatory arms embargo against South Africa and urged them to ensure that components of items included in that embargo did not reach the South African military establishment and police through third countries. States were also asked to refrain from any co-operation in the nuclear field with South Africa which would contribute to the manufacture and development by that country of nuclear weapons or nuclear explosive devices. The Council acted by adopting by consensus resolution 591 (1986), the text of which had been recommended by its Committee on sanctions against South Africa, formally known as the "Security Council Committee established by resolution 421 (1977) concerning the question of South Africa".

* * *

In resolution 591, States were called on to prohibit the export of spare parts for embargoed aircraft and other military equipment belonging to South Africa and any official involvement in the maintenance and service of such equipment. States were urged to ban export to South Africa of items which they had reason to believe were destined for its military and/or police forces, which had a military capacity and which were intended for military purposes—aircraft, aircraft engines, aircraft parts, electronic and telecommunication equipment, computers and four-wheel drive vehicles. The Council asked States to ensure that their national legislation or comparable policy directives guaranteed that specific provisions to implement resolution 418 included penalties to deter violations. States were also asked to adopt measures to investigate violations, prevent future circumventions and strengthen their machinery for the implementation of resolution 418 with a view to the effective monitoring and verification of transfers of arms and other equipment in violation of the arms embargo.

The embargo should, the Council stated, include—in addition to all nuclear, strategic and conventional weapons—all military, paramilitary police vehicles and equipment, "as well as weapons and ammunitions, spare parts and supplies for the aforementioned and the sale or transfer thereof". It renewed its request to States to refrain from importing arms, ammunition of all types and military vehicles produced in South Africa. States were called upon to prohibit the import or entry of all South African armaments for display in international fairs and exhibitions under their jurisdiction; to end exchanges as well as visits and exchanges of visits by government personnel, when such visits and exchanges maintained or increased South Africa's military or police capabilities; and to refrain from participating in any activities in South Africa which they had reason to believe might contribute to Pretoria's military capability. States, including those not United Nations members, were asked to act in accordance with the provisions of the resolution. * * *

* * *

Mr. Alleyne (Trinidad and Tobago) said that, while some countries had observed the letter and the spirit of Council resolutions providing for the prevention of arms shipments to South Africa, the embargo had itself been "something of a leaky barrier through which arms and military technology for bolstering a domestic arms industry in South Africa have flowed freely". The resolution sought to secure full implementation of the embargo by recommending measures to close loopholes in it, to reinforce it and to make it more effective.

* * *

Notes and Questions

1. *Resistance to mandatory sanctions.* In Resolution 569 of 1985, the Security Council voted for a series of voluntary sanctions against South Africa. Among other things, the resolution: * * *

6. Urges States Members of the Organization to adopt measures against South Africa, such as the following:

(a) Suspension of all new investment in South Africa;

(b) Prohibition of the sale of krugerrands and all other coins minted in South Africa;

(c) Restrictions in the field of sports and cultural relations;

(d) Suspension of guaranteed export loans;

(e) Prohibition of all new contracts in the nuclear field;

(f) Prohibition of all sales of computer equipment that may be used by the South African army and police;

* * *

The resolution was adopted by a vote of thirteen to none, but with the United Kingdom and the United States abstaining.

In May 1986, a resolution was proposed, declaring that South Africa's acts and policies were "a threat to international peace and security." Under this resolution, the sanctions listed in Resolution 569 would now become mandatory. The resolution failed by reason of the votes against it by the U.K. and the U.S. (with France abstaining). These three states explained their positions as follows (23 UN Chronicle, No. 4 (1986), p. 29): "The U.S. said it could not support a call for imposition of mandatory sanctions. All States should be able to decide for themselves what measures were most appropriate "as we pursue our common goal of destroying apartheid."

The destruction of the South African economy served no one's interests, least of all those who suffered under apartheid. A severance of economic ties would lead ineluctably to severance of political ones, depriving the United States of any leverage over Pretoria, and depriving the international community of any ability to work for the timely and complete dismantling of apartheid. The United States would not turn its back on the millions of blacks in South Africa and on a growing number of whites there who looked to the West to lead the South African Government out of its "crude and inhuman" political system into one where the voice of the majority participated directly in the formulation of national and international policy.

The United Kingdom said the draft contained "unacceptable" passages. It would have voted for all its provisions except that calling for sanctions. It regretted that the draft's sponsors would not accept a paragraph-by-paragraph vote. Nothing must be done to undermine the chances of a successful outcome, however hard to achieve, to the Commonwealth initiative to peacefully abolish apartheid. The United Kingdom would not take short-term steps which might endanger that long-term and fundamental goal. France said there were no grounds for replacing national measures with mandatory sanctions.

* * *

2. *The sanctions apparently helped cause* at least a temporary financial crisis in South Africa in 1985 and brought pressure to bear upon the Government. The legislation establishing and promoting apartheid was slowly repealed throughout the latter part of the 1980's; sanctions were concomitantly eliminated. In April 1993, Nelson Mandela was elected President of South Africa, in the first elections in which all were able to participate. At his request, the Security Council lifted the economic sanctions against South Africa.

Libya

Joyner & Rothbaum, Libya and the Aerial Incident at Lockerbie: What Lessons for International Extradition Law

14 Mich.J.Int'l L. 222 (1993).*

On December 21, 1988, Pan American Flight 103 took off from London's Heathrow Airport on its transatlantic flight to John F. Kennedy Airport in New York. At 6:56 P.M. EST, at an altitude of 31,000 feet, the Maid of the Seas made its last contact with ground control. Seven minutes later, the green cross-hair at air traffic control split into five bright blips as Pan Am Flight 103 exploded in midair. Her fiery skeleton, laden with the bodies of passengers and crew, rained down on the people of Lockerbie, Scotland. Within the hour, 243 passengers, 16 crew members, and 11 townspeople were dead.

Nearly three years later, following extensive international investigations, the United States indicted two Libyan intelligence officers in November 1991 for the bombing of Pan Am Flight 103. The Libyan response to informal extradition claims was not unexpected: the government refused to surrender the officers on the grounds that such an act constituted direct interference in Libya's internal affairs.

In January 1992, and again in March 1992, the United Nations Security Council responded to the Libyan position with two resolutions: the first urged the government of Colonel Muammar el-Qadhafi to cooperate with the international investigation of the bombing; the second imposed sanctions on Libya for its failure to comply with the Security Council's requests. Taken together as legal prescriptions, the Security Council's actions marked the first time that the United Nations had ever demanded extradition of nationals of one State to face trial in a second State, despite the existence of international legal principles supporting Libya's position to refuse extradition of its nationals.

The U.N. Security Council resolutions in the Lockerbie case represent a salient, albeit as yet unconsummated, step toward strengthening the international extradition process for dealing with alleged terrorist acts. In the past, international fugitives who committed unlawful acts abroad often found sanctuary behind the political veils of customary and codified law, evading extradition with the shield of State sovereignty. The lack of a universally accepted rule of law has left extradition to bilateral treaties and acts of reciprocity and comity, which provide only malleable standards that States can interpret and reinterpret to suit their needs. The subjective nature of "relative" political acts, coupled with differing State penal laws and judicial systems, has further hampered the process of transnational extradition.

The Security Council's concerted action to compel legal cooperation from Libya provokes inquiry into whether supreme authority over extradi-

* Reprinted by Permission, Michigan J. Int'l Law.

tion in the international community may be shifting slowly away from State sovereignty and toward the collective will of the United Nations. Although the full impact of the council resolutions is not yet known, such collective action is appropriate for particularly notorious cases, such as the Lockerbie bombing, fraught with myriad political complications.

The Lockerbie incident provides a means both for highlighting customary norms within the international extradition process and analyzing the legal implications of Security Council resolutions—for Libya in particular, but also for international law in general. Does concerted action taken by the U.N. Security Council against Libya bolster the international extradition process? Or do these resolutions represent little more than a new coat of legal paint on the same old political problems?

* * *

Note. Libya, the Security Council & the World Court: *Does the International Court of Justice have the power of judicial review to challenge the validity of Security Council actions?* In 1992, Libya filed actions against the U.S. and the U.K. "to enjoin the United States from pressing its claim for the extradition of the two Libyan nationals accused in the 1988 bombing of Pan Am flight 103 over Lockerbie, Scotland [Libya v. [U.S.] & U.K., 1992 I.C.J. 3 (Provisional Measures Order of April 14, 1992)]. Libya contended that the Security Council resolutions ordering extradition were ultra vires (and therefore invalid) because they disregarded a fundamental principle of international law—that a state cannot be forced to extradite its own nationals. Although the Court rejected Libya's request for provisional relief, a number of concurring and dissenting judges expressed a willingness to examine the validity of Security Council actions. For discussion of the prosecution of two Libyan functions for the downing of Part Art. 103, see chapter 16, *infra*.

Franck, Editorial Comment, The "Powers of Appreciation": Who is the Ultimate Guardian of UN Legality?

86 A.J.I.L. 519, 520–23 (1992).*

The Libyan case was based on the asserted illegality of U.S. (and UK) actions in demanding the extradition of Libyan citizens to stand trial in the United States or the United Kingdom. The Council had first decided that the Libyan Government must surrender its two nationals accused of the Lockerbie bombing; then, after the Court's oral argument but before its decision, it imposed universal mandatory commercial and diplomatic sanctions to secure compliance. In effect, Libya's request for interim relief invited the Court to decide that these Security Council resolutions might be

* Reprinted with the permission of the American Society of Int'l Law.

ultra vires and thus sanctions would impose irreparable injuries. In particular, Libya argued that, by its resolutions, "the Security Council infringes, or threatens to infringe, the enjoyment and the exercise of the rights conferred on Libya by the Montreal Convention and its economic, commercial and diplomatic rights."

Article 5(2) of the Montreal Convention for the Suppression of Unlawful Acts against the Safety of Civil Aviation of 1971, to which over 140 nations including Libya and the United States are parties, requires each state party either to take jurisdiction over persons present in its territory who are alleged to have committed acts of terrorism against a civil aircraft, or to extradite them to a state which has, and is willing to exercise, such jurisdiction. Libya asserted that it had already taken the steps necessary for "complying in full with that Convention," having "submitted the case to its competent authorities for the purpose of prosecution." Relying on those assertions, Libya asked the Court to conclude that the Security Council's resolutions are "contrary to international law" and that "the Council has employed its power to characterize the situation for purposes of Chapter VII simply as a pretext to avoid applying the Montreal Convention."

The Libyan Application essentially left the Court with three jurisprudential choices. It could have held that the sanctions ordered by Resolution 748 should be suspended until such time as the Court ascertained, at the merits stage, that Libya's claim was groundless. Or it could have decided that, since no sufficient case of *mala fides* or *ultra vires* had been established by Libya at this preliminary stage, there were no grounds upon which the Court could order such interim relief. Or, third, the Court could have held that no relief would be forthcoming at any stage of the proceedings if granting that relief would require the Court to make a finding that a chapter VII decision of the Security Council exceeded its lawful authority. It will be evident that the first two of these three options assume an implicit right of judicial review, albeit leading to opposite results, while the third assumes judicial restraint or abdication.

What did the Court's majority choose to do? It appears to have elected, if rather softly, the *second* option. The very brief majority opinion appears to turn on a finding that "both Libya and the United States, as Members of the United Nations, are obliged to accept and carry out the decisions of the Security Council in accordance with Article 25 of the Charter," including the obligations imposed by Security Council Resolution 748. It concludes, further, that "the obligations of the Parties in that respect prevail over their obligations under any other international agreement, including the Montreal Convention." This conclusion the majority reaches by an interpretation of the effect of Charter Article 103.

Most significant, however, as also in Marbury v. Madison, is what the Court left unsaid. As in *Marbury,* the Court superficially appears to accede to the broad discretionary power of the system's political "branch." But, as in Marbury, it accedes not by refusing to decide, but by exercising its power of decision. The Security Council's action in imposing sanctions is adjudged *intra vires* precisely because the majority of judges seems to agree that, for purposes of interim measures, Article 103 of the Charter "trumps" any rights Libya might have under the Montreal Convention, and thus frees the Security Council to apply sanctions as a suitable remedy in exercise of its powers under chapter VII. On the other hand, had Libya been able to allege a more general ground of *ultra vires*—that a coercive demand for extradition of a state's own national "could be deemed contrary * * * to protection of sovereign rights under general international law"—then, in the words of Acting President Oda, that "would have instituted a totally different litigation, and whether or not the Court has jurisdiction to deal with that issue is certainly a different matter." It is interesting to speculate what might have happened had Libya been a party to the Court's mandatory jurisdiction under Article 36(2) of its Statute and had it brought its action "under general international law" against Britain, as another party to 36(2), rather than under the Montreal Convention.

As it is, the interim measures decision represents a delicate balancing. As Judge Lachs noted in his separate opinion confirming the majority's result: "While the Court has the vocation of applying international law as a universal law, operating both within and outside the United Nations, it is bound to respect, as part of that law, the binding decisions of the Security Council." The operative verb is "respect"—not "defer to." The Court's decision, Lachs emphasized, "should not * * * be seen as an abdication of the Court's powers."

This carefully crafted nonabdication is succinctly put by the separate opinion, concurring in the majority's result, by Judge Shahabuddeen:

> The question now raised by Libya's challenge to the validity of resolution 748 (1992) is whether a decision of the Security Council may override the legal rights of States, and, if so, whether there are any limitations on the power of the Council to characterize a situation as one justifying the making of a decision entailing such consequences. Are there any limits to the Council's *powers of appreciation?* In the equilibrium of forces underpinning the structure of the United Nations within the evolving international order, is there any conceivable point beyond which a legal issue may properly arise as to the competence of the Security Council to produce such overriding results? If there are any limits, what are those limits and what body, if other than the Security Council, is competent to say what those limits are?

That is the nub of the matter, although the case exhibits many other interesting aspects. For example, one of those joining in the decision, as well as one dissenting judge, expressed the view that the United States was obliged by its recourse to the Security Council to renounce any right to take unilateral measures against Libya. Central, however, is the issue highlighted in the dissent of Judge Weeramantry: "does * * * the Security Council discharge[ ] its variegated functions free of all limitations, or is there a circumscribing boundary of norms or principles within which its responsibilities are to be discharged?" The majority and dissenting opinions seem to be in agreement that there are such limits and that they cannot be left exclusively to the Security Council to interpret. The legality of actions by any UN organ must be judged by reference to the Charter as a "constitution" of *delegated* powers. In extreme cases, the Court may have to be the last-resort defender of the system's legitimacy if the United Nations is to continue to enjoy the adherence of its members. This seems to be tacitly acknowledged judicial common ground. * * *

Notes and Questions

In February 1998, the I.C.J. ruled that it had jurisdiction to address the merits of Libya's challenge [Case Concerning Questions of Interpretation and Application of the 1971 Montreal Convention Arising from the Aerial Incident at Lockerbie (Order of February 27, 1998)]. The Court gave three reasons for its decision. First, it based its jurisdiction on the Montreal Convention, which gives it the authority to hear disputes that cannot be resolved through arbitration. Second, the Court held that Libya could be heard because it sought relief from the I.C.J. before the Security Council acted. Finally, the court noted that the Security Council never actually ordered Libya to surrender the bombing suspects. The Court may thus have side-stepped the constitutional confrontation that may be possible in the future. *See* Watson, *Constitutionalism, Judicial Review, The World Court*, 34 Harv. Int'l L.J. 1, 3 (1993).

5.   HUMANITARIAN INTERVENTION

Does The U.N. Charter Authorize Humanitarian Intervention?

Delbrück, A Fresh Look at Humanitarian Intervention Under the Authority of the United Nations

67 Ind.L.J. 887, 889–91 (1992) (footnotes omitted)*

* * *

The principle of nonintervention is deeply enshrined in general international law. It has its legal basis and legal policy foundations in the principles of the sovereignty and equality of states, the constitutive elements of the international legal order. Recognition of sovereignty—the independence and freedom of states from any external dominance in the determination of their domestic and foreign policies and the equality of states under law—excludes, in principle, the permissibility of interventions by third parties.

The scope, however, of the prohibition against intervention in the internal or domestic affairs of states is still controversial. On the one hand, there are those who support a broad construction of the concept of nonintervention that is based on a corresponding expansive interpretation of the concept of sovereignty. If sovereignty not only is to denote the legal independence and self-determination of states, but also is supposed to have

* Reprinted by permission of the University of Indiana Law Journal and Fred Rothman & Co.

a substantive meaning in the real world of international relations, it is argued, it must be protected from violations as a matter of law. Hence, a principle of nonintervention commensurate in scope to that of the principle of sovereignty must be recognized under international law. * * * [Some] advocate a restrictive interpretation of the principle of nonintervention. They argue that a broadly construed concept of sovereignty and a corresponding broad interpretation of the principle of nonintervention no longer meet the demands of the growing internationalization of states' responsibilities for the maintenance of international peace and security as well as for the protection of human rights. If such growing international responsibilities are recognized as a matter of law, sovereignty must be viewed as legally more limited than in the past. This, in turn, must result in a restrictive interpretation of the scope of the principle of nonintervention, leaving room for international interventions in the domestic affairs of states—if not generally, then at least under certain well-defined circumstances.

Qualifying the permissibility of international interventions in this way, however, indicates that within this second school of thought there is * * * no consensus as to the criteria or the circumstances allowing for interventions. Nor is there general agreement as to what kind of actions taken in the course of interventions could be considered legal; that is, whether such interventions could be carried out by the use of (military) force or whether they must be restricted to measures short of the use of force. According to widespread opinion, the general prohibition against the use of force under international law does not allow for unilateral forcible interventions by individual states even for the purpose of rescuing citizens of third states, or their own, from threats to their lives and physical safety. That is to say, so-called humanitarian interventions, once accepted as legal, are widely viewed as illegal today. Countermeasures even against grave and massive human rights violations are, for good reason, considered to be restricted to economic and diplomatic sanctions below the threshold of the use of force: Allowing military enforcement measures based on the "isolated" decisions of individual states would lead to an erosion of the general prohibition against the use of force and against "dictatorial interference[s]." Since the assessment of the factual situation, the determination of the appropriate means to be applied, and the execution of the intervention would all be administered by the intervening state, the door to purely arbitrary intervention, that is, acts of aggression in disguise, would be wide open.

In a world community heeding diverse values and pursuing different, often antagonistic, interests, it is easy to conceive of states invoking all kinds of justae causae as a justification for intervention. This objection to a more liberal regime governing the law of intervention need not necessarily hold true if interventions in the internal affairs of a state that commits grave human rights violations are decided on the basis of an orderly and lawful procedure and are executed by an international organization such as the UN as the representative of the international community of states. The question is, therefore, what the authority of the UN is in this regard. * * *

Notes and Questions

1. *What do you think of Delbrück's proposition?*

Collective Use of Military Force—A Hybrid? Iraq, The Former Yugoslavia & Somalia

Is the U.N. action in the territory of the former Yugoslavia the use of military force in the nature of that applied in the Korean Conflict? Is it the use of force short of military force? Have the Security Council and the Secretary–General created a hybrid in Iraq, the former Yugoslavia and in Somalia? If so, is it legal or, if you will, constitutional under the U.N. scheme? Are there differences among these cases? The General Assembly created, in 1991, a new position of *Undersecretary–General for Humanitarian Affairs.*

———

2. *Iraq* Security Council Resolution 688 (1991) (found in the Documentary Supplement), was issued in the wake of Iraq's suppression of its civilian population, particularly the Kurds and the Shiites. The Kurds had taken refuge in Turkey and Iran. Resolution 688 requested the Secretary–General to pursue humanitarian efforts and to use all resources at his disposal, including those of the relevant U.N. agencies, to address urgently the critical needs of the refugees and displaced Iraqi population. Resolution 688 could be read broadly to support writers such as Professors Lillich, McDougal, Reisman, and Téson to support humanitarian intervention.Others, such as Brownlie, Henkin, and Schachter oppose the legality of humanitarian intervention. Does U.N. Charter article 2(4) allow it? If so, on what theory?

3. *Somalia.* The Security Council specifically authorized military intervention in Somalia to establish "a secure environment for humanitarian relief efforts." This was also a hybrid situation, as the nature or status of Somalia as a state had dissipated or ceased to exist due to the non-existence of a viable government.

Read the pertinent Security Council Resolutions in the Doc. Supp. Somalia was created from an ad hoc grouping of six major clans into one state created from the 1960 merger of two former European colonies. Siad Barré seized power in a 1969 coup d'état and ruled brutally for twenty-one years, until he was overthrown in 1991 by coalition forces made up of the various clans and sub-clans. Civil war ensued wherein no one clan or coalition was able to seize control. Various clans and sub-clans maintained power over various areas by controlling resources, such as food, medicine, ammunition and weapons. The general population suffered terribly from the "civil war" and by October 1992, some 4.5 million people were near starvation.

In August 1992, the Security Council called for 3,500 troops to be sent to Somalia to protect food and other relief supplies from the warring factions. [S.C.Res. 775, Aug. 1992]. The U.N. Operation in Somalia [UNOSOM] was created to implement S.C. Resolution 733 (January 1992), which had called for the "general and complete embargo on all deliveries of weapons and military equipment to Somalia." At least 300,000 individuals had already died by that time. UNOSOM was largely prevented from performing and conditions deteriorated. The Secretary–General expressed his concern in letters to the President of the Security Council in November 1992. [See, UN Docs. S/24859 and S/24868 and S/24868, which recalled earlier S.C. Resolutions 733, 746, 571, 676 and 755 (1992)]. The Secretary–General called for military action pursuant to Article 39 of the U.N. Charter. He stated that military force was required to disarm the warring factions and to ensure the success of UNOSOM. The United States offered to commit a force of 20,000 troops to safeguard relief supplies, maintaining that its role was to be limited to opening supply lines and then turning the operation over to other U.N. peacekeeping forces. Finally, on December 3, 1992, the Security Council unanimously authorized the U.S.-led military, humanitarian intervention, to ensure the success of UNOSOM. [U.N. Security Council Resolution 794, S/Res/794, Dec. 3, 1992)]. The Resolution noted the hybrid and "unique character" of the circumstances in Somalia (essentially that there was no viable government, hence, no state) and emphasized the "magnitude of the human tragedy * * * "which constituted "*a threat to international peace and security.*" Id.

Unfortunately, UNOSOM was unable to achieve its goals, one of which was to restore civil society in Somalia. As a result, on recommendation of the Secretary–General the Security Council adopted Resolution 814, establishing UNOSOM II and giving it enforcement powers to attempt to secure Somalia. Its goal was "to complete, through disarmament and reconciliation, the task begun by UNITAF for the restoration of peace, stability, law and order" to Somalia. It was given broad powers, ranging from disarmament and control of violence through education of the Somalis and creation of governmental and administrative systems. It achieved some success and certainly ameliorated the suffering of many Somalis; however, it was unable to achieve many of its goals. Specifically, UNOSOM II's mandate expired before it was able to secure peace in Somalia, and the Security Council failed to renew it.

4. *The Former Yugoslavia.* The Security Council, in Resolution 770, August 13, 1992, authorized forcible humanitarian intervention in Bosnia–Herzegovina. Resolution 770 stated: "humanitarian assistance in Bosnia–Herzegovina is an important element in the Council's effort to restore international peace and security in the area * * *." It also called for states to facilitate relief by "all necessary measures," a euphemistic term of art, understood to include military action. While peace-keeping forces have been present and frequently have operated under great difficulty and with courage, U.N. presence has been ineffectual due to defiance by the various parties. Actual military intervention in the traditional sense has not occurred. *See* Arnison, *International Law and Non–Intervention: When Do Humanitarian Concerns Supersede Sovereignty*, 17 Fletcher For. Wld. Aff. 199, 204–05 (1993). The United States has refused to extend recognition to the recently self-proclaimed nation-state, the Federal Republic of Yugoslavia, formed out of Serbia and Montenegro on April 27, 1992, following the dissolution of the former Yugoslavia. The "Yugoslav People's Army" (JNA) attacked the Slovenian capital of Ljubljana, but the Secretary–General did not call for U.N. involvement, because this was "an internal affair." On the other hand, Bosnia–Herzegovina, Croatia, and Slovenia became members of the U.N. on May 22, 1992. Odom, *Macedonia Crisis Shows Need for NATO Expansion*, June 20, 2001, Wall St. J. A18, 2001

WL–WSJ 2867108. "For more than a decade now, the U.S. has been trailing behind the spread of war in the Balkans. First in Bosnia, then in Kosovo, and now in Macedonia, the North Atlantic Treaty Organization has been 'a day late and a dollar short,' as the old saying goes. It is time to get ahead, to make events instead of being led by them, and a larger Balkans security framework is essential to that end."

Grosberg, *Clinical Essay*: *Clinical Education in Russia: "Da and Nyet"* Spring 2001 Clinical L. Rev. 469, notes that [t]he recent deep-seated Russian opposition to U.S. policies in Kosovo also is a reminder of the independence and the enormous pride of the Russian people. George Kennan stated that he was "not surprised" at the role of Russia in opposing NATO policy in Kosovo; "it is for them largely a matter of pride." Ullman, *The US and the World: An Interview with George Kennan*, The New York Review, August 12, 1999, at 4. A Russian historian wrote: "Although Russia is weakened, it is still strong both as a nation and as a state. Its army may not have enough food to feed its soldiers, but it has great traditions and is armed with modern weapons." Roy A. Medvedev, The Talk of Moscow, *Why They Say Nyet*, Washington Post, May 2, 1999, at 1. The West is well advised not to come into Russia and contemptuously throw in their face the cold war defeat of communism.

Weller, The International Response To the Dissolution of the Socialist Federal Republic of Yugoslavia

86 A.J.I.L. 569 (1992).*

Current Developments

The [former] Yugoslavia consisted of six republics (Slovenia, Croatia, Serbia, Bosnia–Hercegovina, Montenegro and Macedonia) and two autonomous regions (Kosovo and Vojvodina).[1] Its overall population was recently estimated as 23.69 million. There were 8.14 million Serbs, 4.43 million Croats, 1.75 million Slovenes, 1.73 million Albanians, 1.34 million Macedonians and 1.22 million "Yugoslavs," as well as a variety of other minorities.

Slovenia has a population of 1.94 million, 90 percent of whom are ethnic Slovenes. There are small minorities of ethnic Serbs, Croats and Hungarians.

Croatia, with a population of 4.68 million, 85 percent of whom are ethnic Croats, contains a minority of 11.5 percent ethnic Serbs who, in 14 of 102 internal administrative districts, constitute a local majority. Among the areas predominantly inhabited by ethnic Serbs are Krajina and Petrinja.

Serbia's population totals 9.8 million, two-thirds of whom are ethnic Serbs. It includes Vojvodina and Kosovo, two formerly autonomous territories that were incorporated into Serbia in September 1990. Vojvodina

* Reprinted with the permission of the American Society of Int'l Law.

1. The following account is based on Whitacker's Almanac 1992, at 877–78 (1991);

Fischer Almanac 1992, at 90–92 (1991); and 1990–92 Keesing's Contemporary Archive.

contains a Hungarian minority of some 21 percent and Kosovo is home to a local Albanian majority of 91 percent.

Montenegro has a population of 650,000; two-thirds are ethnic Montenegrins. There are minority Muslims and Albanians.

Bosnia–Hercegovina has a population of 4.1 million, of whom some 40 percent are Muslims, 32 percent Serbs and 18 percent Croats. The various elements of the population are intermingled and pocketed throughout the territory.

Macedonia's population of 2.1 million is composed of 67 percent Macedonians, 20 percent Albanians and various other minorities.

The Federal Government was directed by a Presidential Council, or collective presidency, whose chairmanship rotated among the heads of the republics and autonomous territories. On September 27, 1990, the Slovenian parliament declared that legislation promulgated by the federal institutions would no longer be applied within the republic. In a referendum, held on December 23 of that year, 88.5 percent of the Slovenian voters opted for independence. The day before, the Croatian parliament had proclaimed the supremacy of its legislation over federal law.

* * *

———

Negotiations among the republics to achieve a loose federation of fully or semisovereign states, carried on in the spring of 1991, failed, apparently owing to the intransigence of the Serbian leadership, which had hitherto dominated the political structure of the federation. According to the London *Times,* "The Croats and Slovenes wanted a loose federation that would dilute Serbian influence. The Serbians wanted a tighter federation to preserve its centralized control of the economy and its dominant role in Yugoslav life." When agreement "on the basic functions of the future Yugoslavia" was reached among the other republics, the Serbian member of the Presidential Council walked out.

The support for maintaining the territorial integrity of the federation voiced by representatives of influential states and organizations, including the United States, the European Community (EC) and its members, and the Conference on Security and Co-operation in Europe (CSCE), undoubtedly strengthened Slobodan Milosevic, the Serbian leader, in his perception that flexibility was not required in negotiations, since independence for Slovenia and Croatia was not supported internationally. Instead of offering to accept a looser confederation, the Serbian leadership had the central army declare martial law, a move that had been explicitly ruled out by the federal presidency, which acted, or should have acted, as commander in chief.

In May, the federal council failed to elect Stipe Mesic, a Croat who, under the constitutional arrangements of the federation, was supposed to have assumed the federal presidency. Serbia, Montenegro and the representatives of the two autonomous republics effectively blocked the vote, despite Croatia's threat to secede if Mesic was not elected. On May 19, 93.24

percent of the voters in Croatia opted for independence. That month, the United States suspended all economic assistance to Yugoslavia, including support in international financial institutions for loans and credits, yet still voiced staunch support for the maintenance of national unity. On June 21, U.S. Secretary of State James A. Baker III, while visiting Belgrade, strongly endorsed a declaration adopted two days earlier at the Berlin meeting of the CSCE, which expressed support for "democratic development and [the] territorial integrity of Yugoslavia."

By June 24, 1991, after further abortive attempts at negotiations regarding secession or a loose federation of sovereign states, the Yugoslav Prime Minister warned the authorities in Zagreb and Ljubljana that "the Federal Government will use all means available to stop the republics' unilateral steps towards independence." Nevertheless, Slovenia and Croatia declared independence a day later.

On June 27, the armed forces of the central authorities (JNA) left their barracks in Slovenia and, supported by a column of heavy armor brought in through Croatia, attacked the provisional Slovenian militia. The authorities in Slovenia proclaimed that a "state of war" existed and appealed for international assistance, including action by the EC, the CSCE and the United Nations.

As the EC and the CSCE were preparing for what they hoped would be the final phase of the *Maastricht Summit* negotiations, neither was expecting, let alone prepared for, the crisis about to arise in the territory of the former Yugoslavia. Within 72 hours of the outbreak of war, the foreign ministers of Italy, Luxembourg and the Netherlands went to the former Yugoslavia in an attempt to obtain a cease-fire. Serbia soon (in July 1991) attacked Croatia, claiming that the ethnic serbian minority in Croatia had a right to self-determination and to secede. The fighting intensified and spread in 1992–93 to Bosnia–Herzegovina, where reports of Serbian atrocities, including "ethnic cleansing" and rape as a military and political strategy, starvation, and attacks on non-combatants were widely reported.

Despite the atrocities, the Security Council remained inactive for three months. When it finally met, the Council did not invoke article 2(4), and registered no conclusion that an "act of aggression" had occurred. The Security Council first adopted Resolution 713 (September 25, 1991), which called upon the EC and the CSCE to work collectively for peace in the territory of the former Yugoslavia, pursuant to Chapter VII of the United Nations Charter. Resolution 713 provided that no territorial gains or advantages within the former Yugoslavia brought about by violence were acceptable and proclaimed that "the continuation of this situation constitutes a threat to international peace and security * * *." Further, it called for a general and complete embargo on all deliveries of weapons and military equipment to Yugoslavia until the Security Council decides otherwise * * *."

Former U.S. Secretary of State Cyrus Vance undertook to obtain an agreement for a "peace-keeping" operation in the territory of the former Yugoslavia. He called for the deployment of troops and police monitors in certain areas of Croatia, designated and deemed to be demilitarized "United Nations Protected Areas" (UNPAs). [See, Report of the Secretary-

General Pursuant to S.C. Res. *721 (1991)*]. In *Resolution 724* (Dec. 15, 1991), an advance team of 12 military personnel, some police, plus supporting staff, was sent to Belgrade. *S.C. Resolution 727* (Jan. 8, 1992) provided for the dispatch of 50 military liaison officers to promote the continuation of cease-fires, but still determined that sending a larger force was not opportune.

Resolution 743 (Feb. 21, 1992) endorsed a proposal for a peacekeeping force of 13,870 personnel, and, pursuant to Charter Article 25, the Council established a U.N. Protection Force (UNPROFOR) for immediate deployment. *Resolution 757* (May 30, 1992) ordered that air links with Serbia and Montenegro be eliminated and that export and import of goods to or from these "nations" be largely prohibited.

On October 6, 1992, *Resolution 779* authorized the Peacekeeping Force, UNPROFOR, to monitor the withdrawal of the Serbian Army from Croatia. On the same date, *Resolution 780* called for international relief institutions to investigate and to compile statistics on the widely reported "ethnic cleansing." Also in October 1992, military flights were prohibited over Bosnia & Herzegovina (*S.C. Res. 781 (1992))* [this was later extended in *S.C. Resolution 816* (March 31, 1993)] and in November 1992, a naval blockade of the Danube River and the Adriatic Sea was imposed [*S.C.Res. 787* (1992)]. In December 1992, the Security Council called for 700 peacekeeping troops (including U.S. forces) to be deployed to Macedonia as a preventive measure. *See* Bell–Fialkoff, *A Brief History of Ethnic Cleansing,* 72 For. Aff. 110 (1993); William Pfaff, *Invitation to War,* 72 For.Aff. 97 (1993); Meron, *The Case for War Crimes Trials in Yugoslavia,* 72 For. Aff. 122 (1993).

In 1993 the Security Council attempted to establish six cities as "safe areas" in Bosnia and Herzegovina. It did this at the urging of France and Britain, which began to fear for their forces when the United States threatened to start bombing the Serb forces in an effort to protect the Bosnians. The warring factions refused to adhere to the Security Council mandate, so the Council adopted *Resolution 836*, authorizing UNPROFOR to use force to protect these towns. However, when UNPROFOR commanders requested the additional forces they believed necessary to implement this directive, member States reacted negatively, asserting that UNPROFOR's use of force was to remain minimal. Ultimately, the "safe areas" came under attack by Serb forces and UNPROFOR, with its minimal contingency, could not repel the attack.

The United Nations was ultimately unable to secure peace in the area. As a result, in August and September 1995, the United States led NATO in a bombing campaign against the Bosnian Serbs. Partly in response to this action against the Serbs, in late 1995 the Serbs and the Bosnians were finally able to negotiate a comprehensive peace agreement, the Dayton/Paris Peace Agreement. This signaled an end to UNPROFOR's role in the area. In its place, NATO established an Implementation Force (IFOR). Although the area remains unstable, the "ethnic cleansing" has stopped and a peaceful co-existence now seems possible. Unfortunately, peace remains elusive in many other parts of the former Yugoslavia.

As a result of this and other arguably failed United Nations missions, many observers have questioned the present ability of the United Nations to engage in "peacekeeping," particularly when it takes the form of attempted "peacebuilding" or nation-building. *See, e.g.,* Gassama, *World Order in the Post–Cold War Era: The Relevance and Role of the United Nations after Fifty Years*, 20 Brook. J. Int'l L. 255 (1994).

6. INTERVENTION FOR "DEMOCRACY"

The United Nations' "peacekeeping" policy during the past decade has reflected an increasing acceptance of intervention in governmental systems. The United Nations has been called upon to monitor elections in countries adopting new systems of government, including Albania, Angola, Cambodia, Haiti, Lesotho, Malawi, Mozambique, Nicaragua, Romania, and South Africa. Its actions in Cambodia and Haiti, in particular, reflect a belief that nation-building is a significant and appropriate role for the United Nations. However, the question arises how far this can or should go. One author has argued that the United Nations' actions in Namibia, Cambodia, El Salvador, Mozambique, Rwanda, and Somalia reflect a United Nations preference for a particular form of society. *See* Note, *Building a Peace that Lasts: The United Nations and Post–Civil War Peace Building*, 26 N.Y.U. J. Int'l L. & Pol. 837, 876, 887–888 (1994). According to this author, this "civil society" is a democracy with free and universal participation in elections, guarantees of basic civil rights, protection from and control of military and police forces, and fully functioning governmental systems—the system found in most true democracies. Other authors have expressly advocated a United Nations preference for democratic governance, some asserting in support that no democratic government has ever attacked another. *See* Donoho, *Evolution or Expediency: The United Nations Response to the Disruption of Democracy*, 29 Cornell Int'l L.J. 329 (1996); Gassama, *Safeguarding supra*; Reisman, *Humanitarian Intervention and Fledgling Democracies*, 18 Fordham Int'l L.J. 794 (1995). Opponents have pointed out that democracy is a western notion, and that it may be inappropriate for the United Nations to impose this ideal on an unwilling nation or one for which democracy would be inappropriate. Consider the following argument.

Moore, Toward a New Paradigm: Enhanced Effectiveness In United Nations Peacekeeping, Collective Security, and War Avoidance

37 Va. J. Int'l L. 811, 859–61 (1997).*

* * *

The correlation between democracy and war, democide, famine, economic malaise, and environmental protection suggests that the most effective long-run strategy to promote these goals is to promote democracy. Just as U.N. fora have been important in promoting human rights, the United

* Reprinted by permission of the University of Virginia Journal of International Law.

Nations can also play an important role in promoting democracy. And just as the struggle for human rights within the United Nations has not always pleased all the members, so too the struggle for democracy is likely to be controversial and turbulent. At the height of the cold war it would have seemed fanciful that the United Nations might play a role in promoting the growth of genuine democracy, as opposed to invocation of the term for any form of government. Today, six years after agreement on the Copenhagen Document, in which all members of NATO, the neutral and non-aligned, and all members of the CIS and former Soviet satellite states in Eastern Europe, agreed to the specifics of real democracy, it no longer seems so fanciful. Will an effort within the United Nations be greeted with universal enthusiasm? Of course not. China (the PRC), North Korea, Cuba, Iraq, Iran, Libya, and many other nations can be expected to vigorously oppose. Even Singapore has become a champion of cultural relativism. The same opposition, however, was present with respect to the struggle for human rights.

Democracy building is not a crusade to be promoted by the use of force. Such an approach would be counter to the Charter and counter-productive as well. Rather, it is a goal to be assisted through norm creation, education, electoral observation, and other modes of peaceful engagement. Nor is it a charter for an intolerant one-size-fits-all dogma. Room must always be left for the many paths to the same bottom line which honor local conditions and wishes.

The democracies should seek consistently and through time to press for opportunities in the peaceful promotion of democracy on a worldwide basis. This effort should not be one directed at any nation but rather it should be one of assisting peoples to understand the benefits of democracy and of providing assistance in implementation of its fundaments. This goal should be pursued both within and without the United Nations.

The United Nations already plays some role in democracy building, for example, its electoral observation missions and its assistance with constitution building in Namibia. As a starting point, it might be useful to seek to promote a democracy charter, similar to the Copenhagen Document, aimed at creation of a democracy norm, just as work within the United Nations aimed at creation of a human rights norm. * * *

———

Questions. Does international law permit intervention to promote democracy? *See also* Schachter, *The Legality of Pro–Democratic Invasion*, 78 A.J.I.L. 645 (1984); Reisman, *Coercion and Self–Determination: Construing Charter article 2(4)*, 78 A.J.I.L. 642 (1984); Halberstam, *The Copenhagen Document: Intervention in Support of Democracy*, 34 Harv. Int'l L.J. 163 (1993). Should the U.N. adopt democracy as its preferred form of government? Has it already done so? Does the Charter authorize such a position? If so, to what extent should the U.N. advocate democracy? How would this affect existing states with different systems of government?

7.   THE FUTURE ROLE OF THE UNITED NATIONS IN PEACE MANAGEMENT

Mutharika, The Role of the United Nations Security Council in African Peace Management: Some Proposals

17 Mich. J. Int'l L. 537, 537–39 (1996).*

The United Nations global peace management scheme is based on certain fundamental assumptions that require serious reexamination as we enter the twenty-first century. Fundamental to the 1945 vision of global peace management was the prevention of a third world war through collective action by the great powers. Structurally, this was to be achieved by a system of great power governance through the mechanism of the Security Council. While the Charter confers on the Security Council "primary responsibility" for the maintenance of international peace and security, executive decisionmaking is reserved for the great powers through permanent membership and the veto power. The present economic and military decline of Britain and France, the inability of Russia to play an effective role in world affairs, and uncertainties with respect to the succession in China have contributed to calls for a reexamination of the concept of great power governance through the mechanism of the Security Council. There was considerable agreement among the participants during the recent fiftieth anniversary celebrations that the Security Council will need to be restructured if it is to play an effective role in future global peace management. * * *

Beyond proposals for structural reform, there is need for a clear articulation of the rule of the United Nations as we enter the next century. Speeches read at the United Nations during last year's celebrations clearly demonstrate near unanimous agreement in favor of a continuing role for the United Nations in global peace management. What was lacking from these speeches was a clear vision of what that role should be. To the extent that future threats to peace are unlikely to involve cross-border conflicts, the role of the Security Council will have to be redefined as many countries increasingly face threats from internal cultural, ethnic, linguistic, and religious conflicts. Some of these internal conflicts will have an external dimension through the displacement of persons across national boundaries. Rwandan refugees in Burundi, Tanzania, Uganda, and Zaire, for example, are posing a security threat in these four countries. The Security Council needs to be reenvisioned in a manner that enables it to deal with such issues effectively.

* * *

Effective responses to these emerging threats will be achieved only if the United Nations is restructured in a manner that enables it to work in coordination with other organizations. According to the International Fed-

* Reprinted by permission of the University of Michigan Journal of International Law.

eration of Red Cross and Red Crescent Societies, there are at present 31 ongoing wars, 26 million internally displaced persons and 23 million refugees. It is predicted that man-made disasters alone will strike 350 million people by the year 2000. These developments will create a level of global insecurity of daunting proportions. To manage security threats of this magnitude, the international community will need to structure an integrated global peace management strategy. In this context, the Bosnia peace settlement provides a model for future peace management. Under the Dayton Peace Agreement, U.S.-led NATO peacekeeping forces will act as a buffer by ensuring that Bosnian Serbs and Bosnian Muslims stay in their own "zone of separation." They will also try to establish a balance of military power between the opposing forces. Of greater interest in terms of future approaches to peace management is the part of the agreement on peacebuilding. Under the peacebuilding formula, a multidimensional structure will be established to deal with the new constitution, human rights, resettlement of refugees, civilian policing, renegotiation of property claims, preservation of national monuments, and reconstruction of infrastructure. While the Implementation Force (IFOR) will operate under NATO, a diverse group of governmental and private organizations will implement different aspects of the accord.

* * *

Notes and Questions. Do you agree that the U.N. must be restructured if it is to meet the challenges currently facing it? Is it the role of the U.N. to intervene for humanitarian purposes or to impose democracy on a state, as it arguably did in Haiti, or has it in the 1990s temporarily overstepped its boundaries, as O'Connell recently argued? *See* O'Connell, *Regulating the Use of Force in the 21st Century: The Continuing Importance of State Autonomy*, 36 Colum. J. Transnat'l L. 473 (1997) (arguing that U.N. actions in Iraq, Yugoslavia, Somalia, and Haiti were aberrations, as demonstrated by the U.N.'s subsequent refusal to provide aid in Chechnya, Rwanda, and the Congo/Zaire). *See also* Kirgis, *The Security Council's First Fifty Years*, 89 A.J.I.L. 506 (1995) (arguing that peacekeeping is outside of the U.N.'s authority). If you believe that the U.N. can or should intervene absent an international breach of peace, do you also believe that its member states agree? Does the U.S. agree? If the U.N. does not intervene, who will? Is any other entity legally competent to intervene when it is necessary to end grave human suffering? In answering these questions, keep in mind that the U.N. was created in the wake of the atrocities committed by Nazi Germany before and during World War II. That situation, of course, involved an international breach of peace, but the international community ultimately intervened on behalf of Jewish people in Germany as well as those in other states. If Germany had limited its atrocities to the Jewish community within its borders, would intervention on their behalf have been forbidden by international law? If so, is this the type of system the international community *should* perpetuate?

CHAPTER 15

THE USE OF FORCE BY STATES

INTRODUCTION

1. *What is the law today governing the use of force by states?*
This question will be explored in the context of a number of instances in
which states have used force unilaterally or, even though collectively,
outside the aegis of the United Nations. This raises another question: to
what extent did the creation of the United Nations and promulgation of the
U.N. Charter change the law relating to the use of force?

Notes

1. ***Law Designed to Discourage or Control the Use of Force Prior to the United Nations:*** Since the emergence of the nation-state and the international law that developed around the system of states, notions of autonomy, territorial integrity, sovereignty, and equality have been paramount. The use of force to violate those state interests has violated international law as well.

2. ***Practical and humane rules.*** When we speak of actual armed conflict, we need to distinguish two aspects: the law governing resort to armed conflict, *jus ad bellum,* and that governing the conduct of armed conflict, *jus in bello.* Also, since Hugo Grotius wrote his classic, *De Jure Belli Ac Pacis* in 1646, international law has been divided into the law relating to peace and that relating to war. Keep these distinctions in mind as you read the material in this chapter. Antiquity saw its own control of the use of force, generally ordained by holy law and powerful leaders who often were brilliant in their practical common sense approach. Force and war were "legal" when and if consistent with the will of deity. The Code of Manu (Law of the ancient Hindus), Law 91, provided that a king who fights his foes in battle should not "strike one who has climbed on an eminence, or a eunuch, nor one who joins the palms of his hands (in supplication), nor one who (flees) with flying hair, nor one who sits down, nor one who says 'I am thine;'" 92: "Nor one who sleeps, nor one who has lost his coat of mail, nor one who is naked, nor one who is disarmed, nor one who looks on without taking part in the fight, nor one who is fighting with another (foe);" 93: "Nor one whose weapons are broken, nor one afflicted (with sorrow), nor one who has been grievously wounded, nor one who is in fear, nor one who has turned to flight; (but in all these cases let him) remember the duty (of honorable warriors) * * *." Sun Tzu said: "[T]reat your captives well, and care for them." *Chang Yü:* "all the soldiers taken must be cared for with magnanimity and sincerity so that they may be used by us * * *. Generally in war the best policy is to take a state intact; to ruin it is inferior to this * * *." In 634 A.D., Calif Abu Bakr charged the Moslem Arab Army invading Christian Syria: "Do not commit treachery, nor depart from the right path. You must not mutilate, neither kill a child or aged man or woman * * *."

3. ***Just War.*** Pascal taught: "unable to strengthen justice they have justified might; so that the just and the strong should unite, and there should be peace, which is the sovereign good * * *." St. Augustine (354–430), who contributed to the creation of the Christian doctrine of "just war," argued that "just war" could be fought to avenge the injuries caused by an enemy who has refused to make amends, to punish those wrongs, and to restore the status quo. Thomas Acquinas argued that just war was appropriate when entered for a *just cause,* such as when the wrongdoer (enemy) was subjectively guilty; no objective manifestation of that guilt was necessary. When the nation-state arose, it was jealous of the religious authority making such decisions, so *just war* was linked to the divine right of kings and sovereignty. Wars between Christian nations were difficult to justify. The attempt at justification became the impetus for the development of the gradation of causes for using military force. Just war doctrine

was *jus ad bellum* at its bottom, but it contained (and still contains) threads of *jus in bello*. For example, innocents were not to be subject to the violence of even a *just war*. In addition, proportionality formed a primary component of both *jus ad bellum* and *jus in bello*.

4. ***In the seventeenth and eighteenth centuries, Hugo Grotius and Emerich de Vattel*** attempted to secularize just war notions and to apply evidence of state practice. They actually merged religious and secular notions, distinguishing moral and legal principles (the first based on religion and the latter on nature). Grotius argued for a balancing approach by which the legality of the use of military force depended on self-defense, the defense of property and the protection of citizens. He argued against a rash use of war even for a just cause.

5. ***Shaw argued that the Peace of Westphalia killed the just war in international law.*** *See*, Shaw, International Law 539–541 (1986). Is Shaw's claim too strong? At most, does it apply to *jus ad bellum*? Just war includes, among other things, the distinction between combatant and non-combatant, care of wounded and sick prisoners, proportionality, necessity, and the requirement to attempt peaceful resolution.

6. ***Consider whether current law on the use of force is significantly more restrictive than that of the "classical period of international law,"*** which lasted from antiquity through Vitoria, Suarez, Grotius, de Vattel, Jean Bodin and others up to World War I and the Kellogg–Briand Pact. War was the prerogative of the sovereign, then the right of the state. It was a legal means to promote the state's vital interests. The late nineteenth and early twentieth centuries saw an attempt to define war, first to control its conduct, later to outlaw it. Chapter 16 (on individual responsibility) presents the Hague Convention and associated regulations, which attempted to provide the (*jus in bello*) rules of warfare. One of the very difficult issues for the International Criminal Court (I.C.C.) is that of trying to define aggression.

7. ***An early modern timorous step toward trying to outlaw war*** was taken in the Hague Convention II (1907), which provided in article I that, "[t]he contracting Powers agree not to have recourse to armed force for the recovery of contract debts claimed from the Government of one country by the Government of another country as being due to its nationals. This undertaking, however, was not applicable when the debtor State refused or neglected to reply to an offer of arbitration, or, after accepting the offer, prevented any *compromis* from being agreed on, or, after the arbitration, failed to submit to the award * * *." The League of Nations gave impetus to the attempt to outlaw war. The League was aimed at "promot[ing] international co-operation and [] achiev[ing] international peace and security." Indeed, the League Covenant provided that the "resort to war in disregard of [a Member's] covenants * * * [shall cause it] *ipso facto* [to] be deemed to have committed an act of war against all other Members of the League, which hereby undertake immediately to subject it to the severance of all trade or financial relations * * *." Bowett noted that the League's approach to achieving this was based on disarmament (art. 8), a collective guarantee of each member's independence (art. 10), pacific settlement of disputes and the outlawry of war (arts. 11–15), and sanctions for violation

of these principles (arts. 16 & 17). *See* Bowett, The Law of International Institutions 17–18 (4th ed. 1982). *See also,* Chapter 14, *supra,* on *Peaceful Resolution of Disputes and the Use of Force in the International System.* Finally, the Pact of Paris (Kellogg–Briand Pact) (July 24, 1929), in articles I and II, renounced war, "as an instrument of national policy in [the Parties] relations with one another * * * [and provided that] the settlement or solution of all disputes or conflicts of whatever nature or whatever origin they may be, which may arise among them, shall never be sought except by pacific means."

8.   ***The Law Today.*** Today, the law of the U.N. Charter along with earlier treaties such as the *Kellogg–Briand Pact* and customary rules live on. Since the end of World War II and the advent of the United Nations, reprisals have been rigorously limited to non-military countermeasures, and the former right of a sovereign state to use military force as a law enforcement measure has been abrogated. Most authorities consider the use of force now to be legal only pursuant to self-defense under article 51, or as a measure of collective security under Chapter VII of the Charter. Two issues are central to the search for an answer to the question of what the law is today: (1) Did the failure of the Security Council of the United Nations to use its theoretical near monopoly of force (during the Cold War after the Korean Conflict) affect not merely the practice of states but also the substance of the law governing the use of force by states? (2) Has the resurgence of the Security Council had an impact on the lawful use of force by states? Chapter 14 presents the law and history of the use of force by the United Nations and provides background for the development of these questions in this chapter.

9.   ***Limited Bibliography:*** Bass, Stay the Hand of Vengeance (2000); Taylor, Nuremberg and Vietnam: An American Tragedy (1970); Shaw, International Law 777 (1997); Blakesley, Terrorism, Drugs, International Law and the Protection of Human Liberty (1992); Wormuth & Firmage, To Chain the Dog of War (2d ed. 1989); Henkin, How Nations Behave (2d ed. 1979); Schachter, International Law in Theory and Practice (1991); Dinstein, War, Aggression and Self–Defense (1988); Green, Essays on the Modern Law of War (1985); Gardam, *Proportionality and Force in International Law*, 87 A.J.I.L. 391 (1993); Grew, *History of the Law of Nations: World War I to World War II*, in 7 Encyclopedia of Public International Law 252 (Bernhardt ed. 1984); Henkin, et al. Right v. Might: International Law and the Use of Force (1991); Khadduri, War and Peace in the Law of Islam (1955); Sun Tzu, The Art of War 75–77 (Griffith trans. 1963); The Laws of Manu (*Translated* by Butler, with extracts from seven commentaries, Sacred Books of the East Series, Delhi 1962). Wilson, International Law and the Use of Force by National Liberation Movements (1988); Law and Force in the New International Order (Damrosch & Scheffer, eds. 1991); Cassese, Violence and Law in the Modern Age (Greenleaves trans. 1988).

10.   ***Debate.*** Proceedings of the 77th Annual Meeting, 77 A.J.I.L. 223 (1983). *Reisman:* "There is no need to recite yet again the desuetude of the collective security arrangements envisioned in the Charter. Intractable conflicts between contending public order systems with planetary aspira-

tions paralyzed the Security Council. The UN Charter's mechanisms often proved ineffective. * * *

A sine qua non for any action—coercive or otherwise—I submit, is the maintenance of minimum order in a precarious international system. Will a particular use of force enhance or undermine world order? When this requirement is met, attention may be directed to the fundamental principle of political legitimacy in contemporary international politics: the enhancement of the ongoing right of peoples to determine their own political destinies. That obvious point bears renewed emphasis for it is the main purpose of contemporary international law: Article 2(4) is the means. The basic policy of contemporary international law has been to maintain the political independence of territorial communities so that they can continue to express their desire for political community in a form appropriate to them. Article 2(4), like so much in the Charter and in contemporary international politics, rests on and must be interpreted in terms of this key postulate of political legitimacy in the 20th century. * * * " *Coercion and Self–Determination: Construing Charter Article 2(4),* 78 A.J.I.L. 642, 643 (1984).

Schacter: "The difficulty with Reisman's argument is not merely that it lacks support in the text of the Charter or in the interpretations that states have given article 2(4) in the past decades. It would introduce a new normative basis for recourse to war that would give powerful states an almost unlimited right to overthrow governments alleged to be unresponsive to the popular will or to the goal of self-determination. The implications of this for interstate violence in a period of superpower confrontation and obscurantist rhetoric are ominous. That invasions may at times serve democratic values must be weighed against the dangerous consequences of legitimizing armed attacks against peaceful governments. * * * It is no answer to say that invasions should be allowed where there is no abuse and only for the higher good of self-determination. In the absence of an effective international mechanism to restrain force, individual governments would have wide latitude to decide on the 'reality' of democracy and self-determination in various countries. The test one side would favor would not be acceptable to others. Ideological confrontations would sooner or later become clashes of power. These considerations are so evident that we can be quite sure that governments will not adopt the suggested reinterpretation of article 2(4) as law. Not even its espousal by a powerful state would make it law. In short, it is not, will not and should not be law. * * * " *The Legality of Pro–Democratic Invasion,* 78 AJIL 645, 649 (1984).

11. ***Sources of the law governing the use of force by states.*** Discourse about the law governing the use of force has, until recently, almost exclusively referred to the U.N. Charter, in particular to articles 2(4) and 51. In the case of *Nicaragua v. United States,*[a] the International Court of Justice decided that, in spite of the United States' reservation to the compulsory jurisdiction of the Court excluding in certain circumstances

---

a. Editors note. The full name of the case is Case Concerning Military and Paramilitary Activities in and Against Nicaragua (Nicaragua v. United States of America),

[1986] I.C.J. Rep. 14. The case is more fully set forth at 1323. As to the case before the International Court of Justice on jurisdiction, see Chapter 1, p. 53.

disputes arising under a multilateral treaty (i.e., the Charter), the Court could decide the claim of Nicaragua under customary international law governing the use of force:

176. As regards the suggestion that the areas covered by the two sources of law are identical, the Court observes that the United Nations Charter, the convention to which most of the United States argument is directed, by no means covers the whole area of the regulation of the use of force in international relations. On one essential point, this treaty itself refers to pre-existing customary international law; this reference to customary law is contained in the actual text of Article 51, which mentions the "inherent right" (in the French text the "droit naturel") of individual or collective self-defence, which "nothing in the present Charter shall impair" and which applies in the event of an armed attack. The Court therefore finds that Article 51 of the Charter is only meaningful on the basis that there is a "natural" or "inherent" right of self-defence, and it is hard to see how this can be other than of a customary nature, even if its present content has been confirmed and influenced by the Charter. Moreover the Charter, having itself recognized the existence of this right, does not go on to regulate directly all aspects of its content. For example, it does not contain any specific rule whereby self-defence would warrant only measures which are proportional to the armed attack and necessary to respond to it, a rule well established in customary international law. Moreover, a definition of the "armed attack" which, if found to exist, authorizes the exercise of the "inherent right" of self-defence, is not provided in the Charter, and is not part of treaty law. It cannot therefore be held that Article 51 is a provision which "subsumes and supervenes" customary international law. It rather demonstrates that in the field in question, the importance of which for the present dispute need hardly be stressed, customary international law continues to exist alongside treaty law. The areas governed by the two sources of law thus do not overlap exactly, and the rules do not have the same content. This could also be demonstrated for other subjects, in particular for the principle of non-intervention.

177. * * * [E]ven if the customary norm and the treaty norm were to have exactly the same content, this would not be a reason for the Court to hold that the incorporation of the customary norm into treaty law must deprive the customary norm of its applicability as distinct from that of the treaty norm. The existence of identical rules in international treaty law and customary law has been clearly recognized by the Court in the North Sea Continental Shelf cases. To a large extent, those cases turned on the question whether a rule enshrined in a treaty also existed as a customary rule, either because the treaty had merely codified the custom, or caused it to "crystallize", or because it had influenced its subsequent adoption. The Court found that this identity of content in treaty law and in customary international law did not exist in the case of the rule invoked, which appeared in one article of the treaty, but did not suggest that such identity was debarred as a matter of principle: on the contrary, it considered it to be clear that certain other articles of the treaty in question "were * * * regarded as

reflecting, or as crystallizing, received or at least emergent rules of customary international law" (I.C.J. Reports 1969, p. 39, para. 63). More generally, there are no grounds for holding that when customary international law is comprised of rules identical to those of treaty law, the latter "supervenes" the former, so that the customary international law has no further existence of its own.

179. It will therefore be clear that customary international law continues to exist and to apply, separately from international treaty law, even where the two categories of law have an identical content.
* * *

12. ***The principle of non-intervention as customary international law.*** The term "intervention" has factual, political and legal connotations. Common to all three meanings, in the context of international affairs, is the series of overriding or dominant influences of one state upon the will or capabilities of another state, particularly as to events and conditions in the latter. In the history of Latin American relations prior to the coming into being of the United Nations and the Organization of American States, the opposition by Latin America to the penchant of the United States to land the Marines to protect American lives and property, and for other purposes viewed as good by the United States, coalesced into a principle of non-intervention. While some writers of that period contended that this principle was one of general international law, others viewed it as a political principle without legal content that ought eventually to be stated as a rule of international law. Since the creation of the United Nations, legal discourse has, with increased frequency, engaged the term. Does it now have legal meaning; if so, what is its scope?

The United Nations Charter does not apply the term in describing the rights and duties of states with respect to the employment of physical force. Article 2(4) forbids the use of force directed "against the territorial integrity or political independence of any state, or in any manner inconsistent with the Purposes of the United Nations." The existence of an act of aggression (not intervention), if found by the Security Council, triggers certain permissible responses, but even aggression is not in terms forbidden to states. It is from article 2(7) of the U.N. Charter that emanations have emerged forbidding intervention by states although, in its terms, that provision is directed toward the organization rather than its members: "Nothing contained in the present Charter shall authorize the United Nations to intervene in matters which are essentially within the domestic jurisdiction of any state * * *." This provision is buttressed in the Charter by broadly stated principles: self-determination of peoples, article 1(2); sovereign equality of states, article 2(1).

In elucidation of this principle, the Assembly declared: "No State or group of States has the right to intervene directly or indirectly, for any reason whatever in the internal or external affairs of any other State." And further: "Every State has an inalienable right to choose its political, economic, social and cultural systems, without interference in any form by another State." In the Nicaragua case, the Court stated its recognition of this principle as a matter of international law and defined its content to some extent:

202.   The principle of non-intervention involves the right of every sovereign State to conduct its affairs without outside interference; though examples of trespass against this principle are not infrequent, the Court considers that it is part and parcel of customary international law. As the Court has observed: "Between independent States, respect for territorial sovereignty is an essential foundation of international relations" (I.C.J. Reports 1949, p. 35), and international law requires political integrity also to be respected. Expressions of an opinio juris regarding the existence of the principle of non-intervention in customary international law are numerous and not difficult to find. Of course, statements whereby States avow their recognition of the principles of international law set forth in the United Nations Charter cannot strictly be interpreted as applying to the principle of non-intervention by States in the internal and external affairs of other States, since this principle is not, as such, spelt out in the Charter. But it was never intended that the Charter should embody written confirmation of every essential principle of international law in force. The existence in the opinio juris of States of the principle of non-intervention is backed by established and substantial practice. It has moreover been presented as a corollary of the principle of the sovereign equality of States. A particular instance of this is General Assembly resolution 2625 (XXV), the Declaration on the Principles of International Law concerning Friendly Relations and Co-operation among States. In the Corfu Channel case, when a State claimed a right of intervention in order to secure evidence in the territory of another State for submission to an international tribunal (I.C.J. Reports 1949, p. 34), the Court observed that:

> "the alleged right of intervention as the manifestation of a policy of force, such as has, in the past, given rise to most serious abuses and such as cannot, whatever be the present defects in international organization, find a place in international law. Intervention is perhaps still less admissible in the particular form it would take here; for, from the nature of things, it would be reserved for the most powerful States, and might easily lead to perverting the administration of international justice itself." (I.C.J. Reports 1949, p. 35.)

203.   The principle has since been reflected in numerous declarations adopted by international organizations and conferences in which the United States and Nicaragua have participated, e.g., General Assembly resolution 2131 (XX), the Declaration on the Inadmissibility of Intervention in the Domestic Affairs of States and the Protection of their Independence and Sovereignty. It is true that the United States, while it voted in favour of General Assembly resolution 2131 (XX), also declared at the time of its adoption in the First Committee that it considered the declaration in that resolution to be "only a statement of political intention and not a formulation of law." However, the essentials of resolution 2131 (XX) are repeated in the Declaration approved by resolution 2625 (XXV), which set out principles which the General Assembly declared to be "basic principles" of international law, and on the adoption of which no analogous statement was made by the United States representative.

205.   Notwithstanding the multiplicity of declarations by States accepting the principle of non-intervention, there remain two questions: first, what is the exact content of the principle so accepted, and secondly, is the practice sufficiently in conformity with it for this to be a rule of customary international law? As regards the first problem—that of the content of the principle of non-intervention—the Court will define only those aspects of the principle which appear to be relevant to the resolution of the dispute. In this respect it notes that, in view of the generally accepted formulations, the principle forbids all States or groups of States to intervene directly or indirectly in internal or external affairs of other States. A prohibited intervention must accordingly be one bearing on matters in which each State is permitted, by the principle of State sovereignty, to decide freely. One of these is the choice of a political, economic, social and cultural system, and the formulation of foreign policy. Intervention is wrongful when it uses methods of coercion in regard to such choices, which must remain free ones. The element of coercion, which defines, and indeed forms the very essence of, prohibited intervention, is particularly obvious in the case of an intervention which uses force, either in the direct form of military action, or in the indirect form of support for subversive or terrorist armed activities within another State. As noted above (paragraph 191), General Assembly resolution 2625 (XXV) equates assistance of this kind with the use of force by the assisting State when the acts committed in another State "involve a threat or use of force". These forms of action are therefore wrongful in the light of both the principle of non-use of force, and that of non-intervention. In view of the nature of Nicaragua's complaints against the United States, and those expressed by the United States in regard to Nicaragua's conduct towards El Salvador, it is primarily acts of intervention of this kind with which the Court is concerned in the present case.

[The Tribunal ultimately decided that the conduct of the United States constituted intervention and violated international law, including the customary rule against the use of force. The Tribunal found that the United States' conduct was not justified by any conduct by Nicaragua, and it held that the United States "should immediately cease and refrain from any action restricting, blocking, or endangering access to or from Nicaraguan ports, and, in particular, the laying of mines." Article 51 was held not to justify U.S. conduct. Did the Tribunal hold that the United States violated article 2(4)?

———

SECTION A.   THE USE OF FORCE UNDER THE UNITED STATES CONSTITUTION AND OTHER LAWS

A state operates within the strictures of both international law and its own domestic law, as we saw in Chapters 11 and 12 (the law of international agreements and the Constitution). A *monist* argues that these are one and the same and that international law controls. On the other hand, a *dualist* argues that they are two separate systems, each of which functions within its own domain, albeit with mutual impact. The drafters of the U.S. Constitution, not without vitriolic debate, developed a sophisticated system of powers both shared and separate. The brilliant mix was aimed at protecting against any one branch of government developing too much power. A major focus of this admixture was that of foreign affairs and especially the use of force. The U.S. Constitution went beyond Montesquieu's view or that of any other European Separation of Powers luminary. It provided an intricate balancing, refined by the clear understanding that if any one branch gained a monopoly on the use of force (even that applied abroad), that branch could endanger the Republic. The framers understood that what is allowed to be done abroad by government agents, eventually affects the national community, as well. The Constitution grants to Congress the decision for war or peace although the President, as Commander in Chief, may respond in self-defense to sudden attack. Scrutinize the following Constitutional provisions and the writings to see whether you agree. Read the Constitution article I, sections 8 & 9; article II, sections 1 & 2; Article III, sections 1, 2, & 3; Article IV, section 4; and Article VI, found in Documentary Supplement.

1.   THE WAR POWERS.

The Constitution does not provide under what conditions a virtuous state might resort to force and war to preserve or extend itself.* No doctrine of just war appears, though it is possible to argue that the Constitution's references to the law of nations incorporated an element of this. Rather, the framers realized that the reasons for deciding to go to war must be left for every generation to work through within the political branches of government. Is the issue of whether we should go to war and under what conditions a political question? What about the way we go to war? The procedural means were carefully stipulated. If these procedural means were wisely chosen in the first place, and if modern technology does not render them anachronistic, then do we ignore this, under the ideologically fueled heat of the moment, at our peril? At various times in our history the U.S. has ignored these procedures in favor of a total commitment to perceived ends.

Precisely because of their fear of one person's fallibility, the framers separated the power to decide for war from the power to conduct it. Firmage argues that the power to initiate war, except for sudden attack upon our country, was lodged exclusively in Congress. The President was confined to conducting war once Congress had decided upon such a course. As you study this chapter, see whether you agree.

Firmage continues, arguing that the assumptions behind this separation of war power are as vital to us two hundred years later as they were

---

* Some of the following is adapted from Wormuth & Firmage, To Chain The Dog of War, 298–300 (2d ed. 1989).

when these ideas were penned in Philadelphia. The executive or monarchical inclination to make war impulsively, without deliberate debate among a
sizeable and varied body of people, was thought by many to have contributed to decades of war that ravaged Europe. War came almost to be the
natural condition, interrupted rarely by periods of peace.

The framers thought that by denying to the President the monarchical
power of raising armies and deciding for war, and placing such powers in
the Congress, the sensitivities of the people who had to fight such wars and
pay for them would be reflected through their representatives. In other
words, the condition of peace, not war, would be considered to be normal.
The biases and presumptions of law and government, the inertia factor,
were placed on the side of peace. Those who advocate war have a burden of
persuasion not easily borne. Only after open debate in a deliberative body,
a process intentionally meant to prevent precipitous, cavalier action, will
the state move from peace to war. A number of factors have eroded these
constitutional checks against war. Two world wars and a depression in this
century have moved much power in government from the deliberative
body—Congress—to the executive. Certain advantages of administration
and dispatch are obvious. But the costs of executive abuse—Watergate, Iran
and Nicaragua, and executive war in Korea and Vietnam—have been
devastating. Apparently, government based upon an assumption of perpetual crisis fulfills its own presumption.

* * *

The war power of Congress is an institutional means of controlling the
inclination to make war [precipitately,] presumptuously. For us today, this
provision is a structural, horizontal check on war—while arms control
measures and the laws of war hit at vertical, singular issues. Even in 1789,
Thomas Jefferson noted insightfully: "We have already given * * * some
effectual check to the dog of war by transferring the power of letting him
loose, from the executive to the legislative body, from those who are to
spend to those who are to pay." Congress exclusively possesses the constitutional power to initiate war, whether declared or undeclared, public or
private, perfect or imperfect, de jure or de facto. The only exception is the
power in the President to respond self-defensively to sudden attack upon
the United States. Three points also follow from constitutional text, our
history, and pragmatic necessity. First, power over foreign relations was
meant by the Framers to be jointly held by the Congress and the President.
Today much congressional direction and control have been allowed to
wither by congressional default and presidential usurpation.

Second, the existence of nuclear weapons and missile delivery systems
reinforces this original understanding, not the reverse. The argument by
presidents and presidential counselors that the President must have the
power to wage nuclear war instantaneously because of nuclear missile
delivery time of a few minutes simply does not hold when weighed against
the cosmic implications of nuclear war. These implications favor more
rather than less institutional restraint, collegial decision rather than the
potential frailty and impetuosity of one human being who decides for or
against the continuation of human society and, possibly, the human species.

Third, Congress possesses the power, through control over expenditure, appointment, the direction of foreign policy, the government of the armed forces, censure of the President and, if necessary, impeachment, to reassert its substantial power in foreign relations and its singular power to decide for peace or war. This position—that Congress possesses the sole power to decide for war or peace—is supported with absolute clarity of intent of the founding fathers. And our history, while checkered with congressional ratification of presidential acts and by presidential abuse and congressional malfeasance on occasion, clearly reveals the norm of congressional control and presidential dependence in the decision for war and peace. This was so through the Indian wars, the Whiskey Rebellion, the Barbary pirates, and the Civil War, and from our endemic preoccupation with intervention in the Caribbean to our border crossings into Mexico and Canada. Our pattern continued through two world wars until Korea and Vietnam.

James Madison noted that "the executive is the department of power most distinguished by its propensity to war: hence it is the practice of all states, in proportion as they are free, to disarm this propensity of its influence." Even Alexander Hamilton, the advocate of presidential power in the Philadelphia Convention, nevertheless recognized that the President's power "would amount to nothing more than the supreme command and direction of the military forces," since the President lacked the British Crown's authority to declare war and raise armies. The power given Congress rests upon the constitutional text that Congress be empowered to "declare war and grant letters of marque and reprisal." This entails the power to decide for war declared or undeclared, whether fought with regular public forces or by privateers under governmental mandate. While letters of marque and reprisal originally covered specific acts, by the eighteenth century letters of marque and reprisal referred to sovereign use of private and sometimes public forces to injure another state. It was within this context that the constitutional framers vested Congress with the power to issue letters of marque and reprisal. Clearly, only Congress has the constitutional power to wage overt or covert war by private parties as well as by the armed forces * * *.

Notes and Questions

1. Were/are there any limits on *how* the president conducts war? If so, what are they?

2. *The War Clause of the Constitution reads,* "[T]he Congress shall have power * * *. To declare war, grant letters of marque and reprisal, and make rules concerning captures on land and water * * *." The corresponding provision of the Articles of Confederation, under which the United States was governed from March 2, 1781, to 1789, read: "The United States in Congress assembled shall have the sole and exclusive power of determining on peace and war, except in the cases mentioned in the sixth article * * *." The sixth article authorized the states to engage in war only if invaded or menaced with invasion by an Indian tribe. * * *

* * *

The declaration of war in 1812 said, "That war be and the same is declared to exist between the United Kingdom of Great Britain and Ireland and the dependencies thereof, and the United States of America and their territories * * *." The same form was followed in all subsequent declarations of general war.

Emerich de Vattel, the most influential writer on the law of nations * * * at the time of the adoption of the Constitution, called such a declaration a "declaration of war pure and simple." It was desirable because it gave notice to the adversary, to neutral nations, and to the subjects of the sovereign initiating the war. It ought properly to be preceded by a "conditional declaration of war"—an ultimatum demanding the satisfaction of grievances—which would first offer an alternative to war. But it was possible to enter into the state of war without making either a conditional declaration or a declaration pure and simple. The state under attack was automatically at war. And by omitting the declaration, the attacking state gained the advantage of surprise.

The Dutch jurist Bynkershoek, writing in 1737, said: "Writers on the law of nations have laid down various elements that are essential in a lawful war, and among these is the requirement that a war should be openly declared either by a special proclamation or by sending a herald; and this opinion accords with the practices of the modern nations of Europe." But compliance with this practice, he said, was "not demanded by any exigency of reason." "War may begin by a declaration, but it may also begin by mutual hostilities." In 1779, in the case of the *Maria Magdalena,* the British High Court of Admiralty held that the fact of hostilities made war.

> Where is the difference, whether a war is proclaimed by a Herald at the Royal Exchange, with his trumpets, and on the Pont Neuf at Paris, and by reading and affixing a printed paper on public buildings; or whether war is announced by royal ships, and whole fleets, at the mouths of cannon? * * * If learned authorities are to be quoted, Bynkershoek has a whole chapter to prove, from the history of Europe, that a lawful and perfect state of war may exist without proclamation.

It has always been possible at British and American law to enter into war without a formal proclamation or the services of a herald. In the [U.S.], however, war cannot lawfully be initiated by the military or its commander but only by Congress. Consequently, although a formal declaration is unnecessary, there must be some legislative act directing the cannons to speak. One of the most respected jurists of the early days of the nation, Chancellor James Kent of New York, said:

> But, though a solemn declaration, or previous notice to the enemy, be now laid aside, it is essential that some formal public act, proceeding directly from the competent source, should announce to the people at home their new relations and duties growing out of a state of war, and which should equally apprise neutral nations of the fact * * *. As war cannot lawfully be commenced on the part of the United States without an act of Congress, such an act is, of course, a formal official notice to all the world, and equivalent to the most solemn declaration.

Chancellor Kent was following established usage when he interpreted *declare* to mean *commence*. The verb *declare* had much earlier acquired this secondary meaning. It did not cease to describe a formal public proclamation of hostilities, but it was used also to mean simply the initiation of hostilities, whether or not a formal proclamation was made. In 1552 Huloet's dictionary gave the definition: "Declare warres. *Arma canere, Bellum indicere.*" There are two meanings here: to summon to arms; to announce war.

In almost every monarchical state, the power to initiate war resided in the sovereign. In discussions of constitutional arrangements at municipal law, the terms *to declare war* and *to make war* came to be used interchangeably. And while a formal declaration should be made—on the basis of obligation, according to Vattel's interpretation of the law of nations, or on the premise of generosity and justice, according to Bynkershoek's—whether or not such a formal proclamation was made had no significance for the question of the residence of power to make war at municipal law.

Comyns' Digest, an authoritative work on English law first published in 1744, said, "To the king alone it belongs to make peace and war," and also, "the king has the sole authority to declare war and peace." In 1799 in the High Court of Admiralty, Sir William Scott said, "By the law and constitution of this country, the sovereign alone has the power of declaring war and peace." It will be recalled that in the debate in the Constitutional Convention quoted above, Gerry rephrased Butler's proposal that the President be given the power to "make war" as a motion "to empower the Executive alone to declare war." Hamilton spoke of Congress as "that department which is to declare *or make war.*" Henry Clay said that "the power of declaring war" did not reside with the executive but with the legislature, which was therefore "the war-making branch."

The question of the presidential power to initiate war can be approached in another way. Retorsion is the practice of peaceful retaliation on a foreign state. Congress has often passed acts of retorsion; in 1817, 1818, and 1820, Congress closed our ports to British shipping because the British navigation acts had restricted trade, allowing only British vessels to carry to British colonies in the Western Hemisphere. During this same historical period, decisions by Justice Story on circuit and by the Supreme Court both held that the executive has no inherent power to interrupt foreign commerce; this power belongs to Congress. If the President's authority over foreign affairs does not include the peaceful practice of retorsion, it can hardly justify the initiation of war.

It remains true that the President has dominated even the decision to initiate war in recent decades. But this course of events represents a departure from the balance actually struck by the framers; it is not a simple maneuver within the gray areas or spheres of apparently overlapping authority. For these reasons, congressional action during the last decade takes on particular significance. Congress not only repented of the blank check it handed the executive in the Tonkin Gulf Resolution by repealing the Resolution in 1971, but also took a series of steps to end the Vietnam War as well as to reassert congressional authority over war. Beginning in 1970, Congress enacted the Fulbright proviso, prohibiting the use of funds for military support of Cambodia, attached a similar prohibition to every subsequent military appropriation act, prohibited the construing of any American assistance to Cambodia as an American commitment to Cambodian defense, and prohibited the use of any appropriated funds for military operations in Cambodia. Finally, and most important, Congress passed through joint resolution (over presidential veto) the *War Powers Resolution of 1973.*

The Constitution also fails to address directly the question of whether Congress or the President has the power to end war, or "to make peace." While it is undisputed that a formal treaty of peace may only be concluded by the President after approval by the Senate, it is not clear from the Constitution whether either the President or Congress may unilaterally terminate hostilities. While the President, as commander in chief, has the effective power to end the deployment of troops engaged in conflict, it is also arguable that the power of Congress to declare war "is the power to decide for *war or peace,* and should imply the power to *unmake war* as well as to make it." * * * This potential conflict between the President and Congress is addressed to a limited extent by the War Powers Resolution. Under its terms, the President must remove American forces from hostilities, in the absence of statutory authorization or a declaration of war, if "Congress so directs by concurrent resolution." This provision reflects congressional commitment to its own power over war and its belief that the President has no independent war power that would allow legal retention of forces in conflict against the will of Congress. The provision leaves unanswered, however, the more difficult question on the scope of the President's power as commander in chief once war has been authorized by Congress. In theory, it seems that Congress should have the final decision as to whether American forces should be withdrawn from conflict, but it also seems likely that the decision will in practice be a cooperative one, requiring good faith and respect for coordinate branches by both sides.

———

Franck and Weisband note that especially after World War II, up until the Vietnam War and Watergate, the President gained predominance in the foreign policy arena, especially where there was a risk of or actual war. This had been achieved, "by a zealous patriotic rallying behind the Presidential colors * * *" Franck & Weisband, Foreign Policy by Congress 3 (1979). See also, both more specifically and more generally, Mayer, With the Stroke of a Pen: Executive Orders and Presidential Power (2001); Kagan, Presidential Administration, 114 Harv.L.Rev. 1145 (2001).

Koh, The National Security Constitution

117–18 (1990).*

[The reasons may] be grouped under three headings, which not coincidentally mirror general institutional characteristics of the executive, legis-

* Reprinted with the permission of the
Yale University Press.

lative, and judicial branches. First, and most obviously, the president has won because the executive branch has taken the initiative in foreign affairs and has often done so by construing laws designed to constrain his actions as authorizations. Second, the president has won because, for all of its institutional activity, Congress has usually complied with or acquiesced in what the president has done, through legislative myopia, inadequate drafting, ineffective legislative tools, or sheer lack of political will. Third, the president has won because the federal courts have usually tolerated his acts, either by refusing to hear challenges to those acts or by hearing the challenges and then affirming presidential authority on the merits.

This simple, three-part combination of executive initiative, congressional acquiescence, and judicial tolerance explains why the president almost invariably wins in foreign affairs. Indeed, this three-part reasoning enters directly into the calculus of an executive branch lawyer asked to draft a legal opinion justifying a proposed foreign affairs initiative. If asked, for example, whether the president can impose economic sanctions on Libya or can bomb Colonel Qaddafi's headquarters, the president's lawyer must answer three questions: (1) Do we have the legal authority to act? (2) Can Congress stop us? and (3) Can anyone challenge our action in court? Or, to use the framework outlined above: (1) Do the Constitution and laws of the United States authorize the president to take this executive initiative? (2) If the executive branch takes the initiative, will Congress acquiesce? and (3) If Congress does not acquiesce and challenges the president's action (or if a private citizen sues), will the courts nevertheless tolerate the act, either by refusing to hear the challenge or by hearing it and ruling in the president's favor?

* * *

Notes and Questions

Negative reaction to the Vietnam War and to the Watergate crimes caused Congress ultimately to react, by way of the Joint War Powers Resolution. Does the Resolution practically further its stated objective of reasserting congressional power to decide for war or peace? Consider the following written by Wormuth and Firmage, in To Chain The Dog of War*: "The President has become more than the executor of the laws; she or he is now the leader of a party and of the nation. There have been similar developments in other countries—de Riencourt has written of an evolution toward executive aggrandisement of power in *The Coming Caesars*." The system of checks and balances has thus far proved to be an insuperable obstacle to the permanence of American Caesarism. Attempts have been made to revive the Stuart conception of an emergency power of the King, which John Locke recognized under the name of prerogative. In his dissenting opinion in the *Steel Seizure Case*, Chief Justice Vinson spoke vaguely of "the leadership contemplated by the Framers" and claimed a limited emergency power for the President. "With or without statutory authorization, Presidents have at such times dealt with national emergen-

---

* The following is adapted from Wormuth and Firmage, To Chain the Dog of War, 12–16 (1989). Reprinted with the permission of the University of Illinois Press.

cies by acting promptly and resolutely to enforce legislative programs, at least to save those programs until Congress could act." In 1971 Secretary of State Rogers asserted that "in emergency situations, the President has the power and responsibility to use the armed forces to protect the nation's security." The only evidence he cites is the framers' agreement that under the Constitution the President might use the armed forces to repel a sudden attack on the United States, since such an attack would initiate a state of war without a congressional joint resolution.

Does the existence of an emergency redistribute the powers of government allocated by the Constitution? In 1869, Justice Miller held that the action of the secretary of war (imputed to the President)—accepting without statutory authority bills of exchange in order to buy necessary supplies for the army—was illegal. Miller remarked, "We have no officers in this government from the President down to the most subordinate agent, who does not hold office under the law, with prescribed duties and limited authority." Miller also wrote the unanimous opinion in United States v. Lee, decided in 1882, an ejection action against two army officers in possession of the Lee estate in Virginia. Miller said:

> Shall it be said, in the face of all this, * * * that the courts cannot give remedy when the citizen has been deprived of his property by force, his estate seized and converted to the use of the government without any lawful authority, because the president has ordered it and his officers are in possession? If such be the law, it sanctions a tyranny which has no existence in the monarchies of Europe, nor in any other government which has a just claim to well-regulated liberty and the protection of personal rights. . . .

But, does a government of limited and divided powers grant an instant decision for every question that anyone, or even a large number of people, may believe requires instant decision. The price we pay for renouncing autocracy is the absence of autocracy.

The Prize Cases, decided in 1863, upheld the blockade of southern ports proclaimed by President Lincoln in 1861. Having held that the "sudden attack" of the seceding states instituted a state of war in which the President's action was constitutionally justified, Justice Grier said:

> If it were necessary to the technical existence of a war, that it should have a legislative sanction, we find it in almost every Act passed at the extraordinary session of the Legislature of 1861 * * *. And finally, in 1861 we find Congress *"ex majore cautela,"* and in anticipation of such astute objections, passing an Act "approving, legalizing and making valid all the acts, proclamations, and orders of the President, & c., as if they had been done under the previous express authority and direction of the Congress * * *."

> Without admitting that such an Act was necessary under the circumstances, it is plain that if the President had in any manner assumed powers which it was necessary should have the authority or sanction of Congress, that on the well known principle of law, *"omnis ratihabitio et mandata equiparatur,"* this ratification has operated to perfectly cure the defect.

Limited retroactive acts of immunity were passed for the protection of Union soldiers during and after the Civil War and were upheld. In 1913 the Supreme Court upheld the governor general of the Philippines in a damage suit by an alien whom he had unlawfully ordered deported because the territorial legislature had subsequently passed an act saying that his action was "approved and ratified and confirmed, and in all respects declared legal, and not subject to question or review." Justice Oliver Wendell Holmes said for a unanimous Court that "it generally is recognized that in cases like the present, where the act originally purports to be done in the name and by the authority of the state, a defect in that authority may be cured by the subsequent adoption of the act."

There is, then, a solution to the problem of emergency. If the President believes that the necessity is sufficiently great, he or she should act illegally and look to Congress for ratification of his actions. The President should not claim an emergency power to act against the law for the good of the nation, nor claim the exclusive right to determine what is good for the nation. In 1973 Congress administered a tardy rebuke for the actions of two Presidents in the War Powers Resolution, which reads in part:

> The constitutional powers of the President as Commander-in-Chief to introduce United States Armed Forces into hostilities, or into situations where imminent involvement in hostilities is clearly indicated by the circumstances, are exercised only pursuant to (1) a declaration of war, (2) specific statutory authorization, or (3) a national emergency created by attack upon the United States, its territory or possessions, or its armed forces.

*The War Powers Resolution, 50 U.S.C. §§ 1541–1548.**

THE WAR POWERS RESOLUTION interprets presidential power to introduce American forces into hostilities as being limited to the power to respond to attack or to act pursuant to authorization by congressional statute or declaration of war. Presidential consultation with Congress is required "in every possible instance" before the introduction of American forces into hostilities or situations in which imminent involvement in hostilities is likely. The Senate report on its version of the War Powers Resolution makes clear the type of involvement that would be considered imminent.

> The purpose of this provision is to prevent secret, unauthorized military activities and to prevent a repetition of many of the most controversial and regrettable activities in Indochina. The ever deepening ground combat involvement of the United States in South Vietnam began with the assignment of U.S. "advisors" to accompany South Vietnamese units on combat patrols; and in Laos, secretly and without congressional authorization, U.S. "advisors" were deeply engaged in the war * * *.

* Some parts adapted from Wormuth & Firmage, To Chain the Dog of War at 190–192; 194–95; 219–223 (1989). Reprinted with the permission of the University of Illinois Press.

The President must report to Congress the "circumstances necessitating the introduction" and the "constitutional and legislative authority" for the introduction. Within sixty days of the submission of such a report, the President must terminate the use of American armed forces, unless Congress "has declared war or has enacted a specific authorization for such use," has extended the sixty-day period, or has been unable to meet [it] because of armed attack upon the country. The requirement that congressional authorization be specific was recently upheld in the case of Crockett v. Reagan, an action brought by twenty-nine members of Congress to curb presidential action in El Salvador. Notwithstanding the sixty-day provision, the President must remove American forces from hostilities outside the "United States, its possessions and territories" if there has been no declaration of war or statutory authorization for the use of the armed forces in hostilities and if "Congress so directs by concurrent resolution."

Of significance for judicial interpretation of the exercise of the war power, the Resolution stipulates that congressional authorization for the introduction of American armed forces into "hostilities or into situations where the involvement in hostilities" may not be "inferred from any provision of law," including "any appropriation Act, unless such provision specifically authorizes" such introduction. Nor shall such an inference be drawn from "any treaty" unless it is "implemented by legislation specifically authorizing the introduction" of military forces into hostilities or into situations likely to result in hostilities. These provisions were drafted to prevent a recurrence of judicial rulings like those near the end of the Vietnam conflict, which sustained the constitutionality of the war on the ground that Congress had ratified executive war making by means of military appropriations, extensions of the draft, and other supportive legislative acts.

Notes and Questions

1. ***The invasion of Grenada.*** According to testimony by a senior State Department official, the President signed the directive ordering the invasion of Grenada at 6:00 P.M. on October 24. At 8:00 P.M. the President met with the bipartisan congressional leadership to inform them of his decision. The invasion began at 5:30 A.M. the next day. Although the administration contended that the evening meeting satisfied the consultation requirement, one ranking member of the Senate Foreign Relations committee who was not even invited to the meeting commented, "There is a world of difference between being consulted and being asked do we think this is wise or not, or being informed, saying we are doing this at 5 A.M. tomorrow."

2. ***One justification for the failure to consult may be*** lack of time. In justifying the secrecy surrounding the invasion of Grenada, President Reagan stated, "We knew that we had little time and that complete secrecy was vital to insure both the safety of the young men who would undertake this mission and the Americans they were about to rescue." While it may be that sometimes circumstances will require an expediency that provides little opportunity for discussion, even then the President could consult secretly with members of Congress, as is done with the staff and executive

branch officers, so that the decision-making process can more closely follow constitutional procedure.

3. ***Related constitutional issues*** are raised by the reporting requirements of the War Powers Resolution. Section 4(a)(1) allows the President to use military force without congressional authorization so long as she or he "reports" to Congress within forty-eight hours of deployment. This reporting requirement in turn triggers the running of a limited sixty-day time period. Under Section 5(b) the unauthorized deployment may continue for a period of sixty days unless Congress acts to either extend the time period for an additional thirty days or terminate the deployment altogether.

4. ***In practice, presidential reporting*** under Section 4(a)(1) has been less than ideal. For example, following the invasion of Grenada and the deployment of the marines in Lebanon, President Reagan reported to Congress: * * * "In accordance with my desire that the Congress be informed on this matter, and consistent with the War Powers Resolution, I am providing this report on the deployment of the United States Armed Forces * * *. This deployment * * * is being undertaken pursuant to my constitutional authority with respect to the conduct of foreign relations and as Commander-in-Chief * * *."

In neither situation did the President refer to Section 4(a)(1). By failing to mention Section 4(a)(1) in either report to Congress, the President indicated that he did not recognize any duty to withdraw the troops within the sixty day period if Congress had not acted. In the case of Lebanon, the marines were stationed in Beirut for over a year without congressional authorization. According to the Reagan administration, the resolution's "clock" did not start ticking when the marines were deployed because they were merely defensive and were not engaged in hostilities or imminent hostilities.

5. ***Foreign Policy Power.*** In refusing to acknowledge the constitutionality of the War Powers Resolution, presidents have often relied upon their power to conduct foreign policy and their position as commander-in-chief of the armed forces. However, the President's authority with respect to the conduct of foreign relations is a collegial authority to be exercised in concert with, not contrary to, congressional foreign policy authority. Moreover, the President's constitutional authority as commander-in-chief is limited to direction and conduct of hostilities following a congressional declaration of war or other congressional authorization. In fact, at the time the War Powers Resolution became law, opponents of the resolution argued that Sections 4(a)(1) and 5(b) granted "a legal basis for the President's broad claims of inherent power to initiate war" that was not present previously under the Constitution. These opponents preferred a Senate proposal that sought to reaffirm the proper role of Congress, limiting the circumstances under which the President could deploy the armed forces to those recognized by constitutional law. Instead, these limitations appear in the precatory "Purpose and Policy" section of the resolution and have no legal effect on the President's power to commence war.

Perhaps not surprisingly, the most strident critics of the War Powers Resolution do not attack it as an unconstitutional delegation of the war power of Congress, but as an unconstitutional infringement on the President's war power—a reflection of how heavily the "constitutional 'balance' of authority over warmaking has swung * * * to the President in modern times." [See Harold Koh's work]. Since the passage of the resolution, almost all of the presidents have argued that it is an unconstitutional restriction upon the inherent presidential powers. President Nixon vetoed the resolution with indignation; President Ford challenged its constitutionality; and President Reagan refused to concede that congressional authorization was required for his various military excursions, though he purported to comply with the resolution.

On October 12, 1983, when President Reagan signed into law the Multinational Force in Lebanon Resolution, which authorized the continued participation of the marines in the Multinational Force for a period of eighteen months, he expressed grave doubts as to the constitutionality of certain of its provisions. His statement, highly representative of the general Executive sentiment towards the War Powers Resolution, is worth quoting: "I would note that the initiation of isolated or infrequent acts of violence against United States Armed Forces does not necessarily constitute actual or imminent involvement in hostilities, even if casualties to those forces result. I think it reasonable to recognize the inherent risk and imprudence of setting any precise formula for making such determinations. Nor should my signing be viewed as any acknowledgement that the President's constitutional authority can be impermissibly infringed by statute, that congressional authorization would be required if and when the period specified in Section 5(b) of the War Powers Resolution might be deemed to have been triggered and the period had expired or that Section 6 of the Multinational Force in Lebanon Resolution may be interpreted to revise the President's constitutional authority to deploy United States armed forces."

Thus, President Reagan refused to concede that congressional authorization is required before the President constitutionally can deploy the United States Armed Forces in situations like those in Central America, Grenada, Lebanon, and the Persian Gulf. Do you agree?

6. *The most debated provision.* The most debated provision has been Section 5(c), which allows Congress, by concurrent resolution, to require the President to remove troops engaged in hostilities abroad. A concurrent resolution does not require the President's signature, nor is it subject to veto. The power of Congress to have the last word—the so-called legislative veto—has often been challenged and finally was held unconstitutional in *I.N.S. v. Chadha*, the reasoning of which apparently invalidates Section 5(c) of the War Powers Resolution. The Senate subsequently sought to bring that section within constitutional limits by providing that any congressional action requiring the President to withdraw United States forces engaged in hostilities abroad must follow certain priority procedures that do not constitute a legislative veto.

7. Do you think that Congress has asserted its proper constitutional role in deciding when to use the war powers remains to be seen? Do you think that the Resolution has worked? Do you think that the Resolution is a proper delegation of the war power of Congress? Or is it overbroad, essentially writing the President a blank check? Both supporters and opponents of the War Powers Resolution agree that its constitutionality is

not likely to be adjudicated. The Supreme Court has never held that
Congress may delegate the power to initiate war to the President. Even the
dictum in the *Curtiss–Wright case* said nothing of the sort. And the dictum
in Curtiss–Wright has neither [progenitors] nor progeny.

8. ***Michael Glennon's article***, immediately below, addresses the following questions: What is the record of the War Powers Resolution? What are
its prospects for resolving the problems relating to balancing the need for
quick and efficient presidential action in time of emergency and the danger
of an "Imperial Presidency?"

Michael Glennon, The War Powers Resolution: Sad Record, Dismal Promise

17 Loy.L.A.L.Rev. 656, 658–59, 661, 664–65, 670 (1984).*

* * *

[Rep. Zablocki's] first principal conclusion—that "predictions that the
Resolution would weaken the nation's ability to react to foreign policy
crises have proven unwarranted"—is difficult to quarrel with. Arguments
to the contrary are for the most part unsupported and unsupportable
assertions resting upon the major premise that anything and everything
done by a President to halt the international communist conspiracy must
perforce be constitutional.

These reflexive proponents of unfettered Presidential discretion fundamentally misapprehend the separation of powers concept. In place of the
"divisiveness" engendered by the War Powers Resolution they would
substitute an "iron demand" of "cooperation" between Congress and the
President—a cooperation that is, upon analysis, the cooperation of a valet
with his master. Brandeis, Corwin, and other boat-rockers presumably are
among those who would, if given the chance, have played into the hands of
Hanoi and Moscow. "[C]ooperation should always be the goal." Whether
one branch should play war-powers manservant to the other is perhaps an
issue that could be argued either way, but it should suffice at this point to
note that the question seems to have been ventilated and resolved in 1789.
* * *

Representative Zablocki is correct in his first conclusion only because
he is quite wrong in his second—the Resolution has not hampered the
President's ability to react to foreign policy crises precisely because it has
not served to "restore the balance in the rights and responsibilities of the
Congress and the President in the decision to commit troops." To the
contrary, it has proven virtually ineffectual in achieving that statutorily-
stated objective. Zablocki observes that "there has been more non-compliance than compliance" by the executive branch. Although I am not certain
that compliance or noncompliance can be neatly quantified, I quite agree
that the record of executive branch adherence to the requirements of the
Resolution has been dismal, and I am thus somewhat nonplussed by
Zablocki's effusive assessment—set forth after a well-documented recount-

ing of "halfhearted" consultation, inadequate reporting, and overall foot-dragging—that the product is "excellent," "workable" and that its "credibility * * * has never been higher." If credibility means the likelihood of compliance by future Presidents who, all things considered, would prefer to forget it, it seems to me that those chief executives will be on firmer ground than ever.

* * *

[The] failure of the Resolution's sponsors to articulate lucidly the reasons for its validity is disappointing because there exists a persuasive case for its validity. The argument is, in the sheerest outline, that the "fixed" powers approach to presidential power taken by the Supreme Court in *Curtiss–Wright, Pink,* and *Belmont* has given way to the very different "fluctuating" powers approach set forth initially by Chief Justice Marshall in *Little v. Barreme,* reiterated by Justice Jackson in *Steel Seizure Case,* and formally adopted by Justice Rehnquist in *Dames & Moore v. Regan.* Under the latter approach, the scope of the President's power is a function of the concurrence or non-concurrence of the Congress; once Congress acts, its negative provides "the rule of the case." That analytical framework, it seems to me, provides a general foundation for the congressional mandate of consultation and reporting as well as the imposition of a time limit upon the use of the armed forces in hostilities—all of which, in the absence of a statement by the Congress, might fall within a "zone of twilight."

* * *

* * * [A] reason for half-hearted compliance by the Executive is that fuller compliance has not been demanded—either legally by the Resolution, or politically by members of Congress. It vastly understates the problem to describe it * * * simply as a matter of "tepid congressional oversight." To cast the issue as one of oversight is to suggest that the need is merely for more hearings that generate more information. The problem has not been a lack of information, but Congress' failure to *act* on information—to act, specifically, by removing ambiguities in the Resolution and, more importantly, by living up to its responsibilities under the role it carved out for itself under the Resolution. At least three ambiguities have undermined [its] proper operation.

The Resolution should be amended to set forth a definition of "hostilities." In the absence of such a definition, officials of the executive branch and members of Congress engaged in a running argument whether United States military activities in Lebanon constituted "hostilities." When ten marines died in a twenty-day period after having been fired upon regularly by hostile forces, it seemed utterly disingenuous to claim, as the Reagan administration did, that the hostilities test was not met. Nonetheless, the term is not self-defining, and because the Resolution provides no guidance as to its meaning, a gradual escalation of hostilities can generate serious confusion as to the date on which the time limit is triggered. Similarly, there is no clear indication in the Resolution whether a variety of different activities are intended to fall within the "hostilities" test, such as exposure to minefields, missile attack, chemical or biological agents, or neutron rays. If Congress is serious about removing uncertainty and closing the door to semantic circumvention by the executive branch, it must define the term "hostilities."

Second, * * * consultation, time after time, has been perfunctory at best. This is true largely because the Executive has been allowed, time after time, to get away with perfunctory consultation. Aside from raising a political stink when such failure occurs—which congressional leaders have been loathe to do for fear of being mistakenly seen by the public as somehow critical of a military initiative—a Congress truly serious about consultation would amend the Resolution to specify precisely who is to be consulted, to make clear that "in every possible instance" does not include instances that present alleged security problems, and perhaps, to prohibit certain uses of the armed forces in the absence of genuine consultation.

Third, and most important, is the vagueness of the reporting requirement, which has led to the Resolution's virtual unraveling. Although the Executive's record here is clearly at odds with the Resolution's spirit, there is an argument to be made that presidential reports have complied with its letter. The reason is that there is in fact not one reporting requirement set forth in the Resolution, but three. Only one—that required by section 4(a)(1)—triggers the sixty-day time limit; those required by sections 4(a)(2) and 4(a)(3) are merely informational (although in the original House version of the Resolution they too triggered the time limitations). The problem arises in that the three situations overlap: facts that would require a report under section 4(a)(1) might also require a report under one of the two succeeding paragraphs, and the Resolution contains no requirement that the President specify which of the three reports he is submitting. Only the *Mayaguez* report (submitted after the military operations had terminated because they lasted less than forty-eight hours) referred expressly to section 4(a)(1). Consequently, the other reports effectively left unanswered the critical question: had the sixty-day time limit been triggered?

* * *

But these and other modifications of the Resolution will not, in themselves, "insure that the collective judgment of both the Congress and the President will apply to the introduction of United States Armed Forces into hostilities" * * * [I]t has become clear that the Resolution's sponsors were naive to believe that any law could achieve that objective. The most that a statute can do, however artfully drawn, is to facilitate the efforts of individual members of Congress to carry out their responsibilities under the Constitution. To do that requires understanding, and it also requires courage: it demands an insight into the delicacy with which our separated powers are balanced, and the fortitude to stand up to those who would equate criticism with lack of patriotism. For a Congress comprised of such members, no War Powers Resolution would be necessary; for a Congress without them, no War Powers Resolution will be sufficient.

Notes and Questions

1. Reading the following would be well worth your while: Corn, Clinton, Kosovo, and the Final Destruction of the War Powers Resolution, 42 Wm.

& Mary L.Rev. 1149 (2001); Paul, Global Governance Safe for Democracy?, 1 Chi.J.I.L. 263 (2000); Stromseth, Understanding Constitutional War Powers Today: Why Methodology Matters, 106 Yale L.J. 845, 872 (1996); Fisher, Point–Counter–Point: Unchecked Presidential Wars, 148 U.Pa. L.Rev. 1637 (2000); Yoo, Point–Counter–Point: Kosavo, War Powers and the Multilateral Future, 148 U.Pa.L.Rev. 1673 (2000).

2. *Any judicial role? What articles of the Constitution are relevant?* Consider the following review by Laudauer of Franck's Book, Political Questions/Judicial Answers, 87 A.J.I.L. 465 (1993): "Thomas Franck's new book provides an elegant and at times emotional argument against the use of the political question doctrine by U.S. courts to abstain from deciding cases that touch upon foreign policy. Troubled by the resulting lacuna in the rule of law, Franck writes: 'Judicial deference ignores the evident truth that in our system a law that is not enforceable by adjudicatory process is no law at all.' Accordingly, a 'foreign policy exempt from judicial review is tantamount to governance by men and women emancipated from the bonds of law'." [D]espite the narrowing numbers of judges directly applying the political question doctrine, Franck points out that those who find foreign policy cases justiciable remain respectful enough to the doctrine to contrive some way to appear not to be directly violating it. Nevertheless, the list of cases in which the political question doctrine was not adopted is, for Franck, a source of encouragement. But Franck is encouraged, more than by this rather uneven record, by the German judiciary, which provides for him a usable model of a judiciary that, while giving German foreign-policy makers a good deal of latitude, refuses to allow foreign policy to be made outside the rule of law. And, after suggesting several strategies for judges in the United States similarly to provide room for the foreign-policy makers within the rule of law, Franck concludes with the moral force of his opening: "To make the law's writ inoperable at the water's edge is nothing less than an exercise in unilateral moral disarmament. It is a strategy urgently in need of judicial review"....

3. *"Why the recent drift away from collegial determination of foreign policy direction by the President and Congress?* One cause may be the modern technology of war. It has been suggested that nuclear weapons capable of continental destruction borne by missiles minutes from our shores make it essential that we be able to decide for war instantaneously, by one person, without debate or restraint." However, it is [wrong] to equate collegiality with lack of effective, immediate response. Congress in the past has proven that it can quickly deliberate when required. One day after President Eisenhower asked Congress for authority to use American armed forces to protect Taiwan from attack by mainland China, the chairman of the House Rules Committee called up the resolution under a closed rule permitting only two hours of debate and no amendment. The House passed the resolution that same day.

4. *Is the belief that speed is essential in the event of a nuclear attack* open to challenge? Does precipitous action in response to an attack prevent or even mitigate the destruction a nation suffers from a nuclear strike. Unless we plan to strike first, is there any situation beyond self-

defense, which exists in any event in the President if we are under sudden attack, under which must we respond with alacrity?

5. ***The spectacular success of the American military in the war against Iraq*** not only obliterated the forces of President Saddam Hussein, but now threatens the same fate for those institutions and inclinations favoring peace and against war.* The thoroughness of Iraq's defeat and the dispatch of its accomplishment, coupled with the unpredictably low number of Allied casualties, combined to produce unparalleled euphoria and nationalistic ardor. This spirit, exploited by politicians attempting to accomplish their own purposes in such a climate, seems to be leading toward a rash of nonsequiturs in the guise of conclusions regarding the efficacy of the military option to be drawn from this short but savage conflict.

The event in this portion of history that deserves our sympathetic attention is the ending of the Cold War. The collapse of the Berlin Wall in November 1989 saw the end of nearly a century of war, physical and mental. World War I initiated a form of war both global and total. Civilian populations became the primary victims of a war affecting the entire world. A system of world governance and society ended forever. The resulting forces of inflation, depression, war guilt, reparations, and dislocation inevitably produced World War II, an aftershock predictable in its consequence if not in its particularity and severity.

But the hatreds engendered by war that normally abate with its end instead were continued into a Cold War between the two nations that emerged as superpower rivals. Almost every conflict—decolonization, civil war, or local dispute—was perceived as involving this bipolar struggle between the former USSR and the U.S. Paradoxically, even while threatening to create violence and destruction on a scale never before known, the existence of nuclear weaponry helped in deterring overt and massive violence between the superpowers. This corrosive rivalry, however, resulted in proxy wars and superpower intervention on opposing sides of civil wars throughout Asia, Africa, and Latin America. In addition, covert actions—too often covert from congressional approval and oversight, if not from the former USSR—were a characteristic of this time. Such violence, unacknowledged and often illegitimate, remains a corrosive element incongruous with principles of open debate and the rule of law within a democratic state.

Finally, may we have the opportunity to address impelling problems: the prevention of war, particularly nuclear war; the end of the arms race, nuclear and conventional; severely decreasing military spending, not only in the U.S., but also in scores of nations throughout the world forced by peculiar logic to devote enormous sums for building large military forces whose main function more realistically seems to be the preservation of the incumbent regime from internal opposition rather than as a protection against external aggression. The war against Iraq could not be considered of the same historic importance if its geopolitical consequence—the replacement of a brutal Iraqi aggressor dictator in Kuwait in favor of the more

* Some from Firmage, Book Review—Essay, 59 G.W.L.Rev. 1684, at 1685–1688 (1991). Reprinted with the permission of the George Washington University.

benign, if medieval, Arabian oligarchy that had ruled this emirate—were the criterion. The national elation that has followed what seemed like a painless and decisive victory.

Impelling reasons exist to question supposed lessons learned from the apparent success of U.S. arms. Our inclination both to objectify and personalize evil makes no more sense now than it did before the Allied victory. Even elimination of Saddam Hussein, standing alone, would produce no assurance that Iraqi alternatives for leadership will be less threatening to American interests than before. Iraq is in chaos and threatens to become fragmented beyond repair—another Lebanon. Shiite fundamentalist leadership, with Iranian influence, is not obviously in our best interest. Hussein's disappearance [would stop as] far short of insuring stability in the Middle East as General Noriega's capture was from resolving drug traffic. We have moved through a dreary procession of devil figures in American mythology; from the Ayatollah Khomeini in Iran, General Noriega in Panama, Libya's Muammar Qadhafi to Hussein, without significantly affecting the real challenges that still must be met in this hemisphere or in the Middle East: preserving interests abroad while respecting local sovereignty; guaranteeing Israeli borders and security; establishing and maintaining normal relations among the Arab states and between them and Israel; and doing justice for Palestinian interests in the Middle East, including their possession of a homeland.

6. ***The real costs of the Gulf War*** are becoming more visible to the American people: Iraqi casualties approaching mass slaughter, including several hundreds of thousands of infants, the country itself bombed into a preindustrial age, facing mass starvation and pandemic disease; Arab and Islamic hatred that will affect our relations for decades to come; an environmental disaster on a world scale never before known; and a potentially disastrous weakening of our own internal restraints against war, restraints presuming that peace is the norm and war the aberration, which has traditionally required those proposing war to bear an enormous burden of persuasion with the American people in national debate and consideration. Iraq's children have not been blessed. International aid agencies estimate that about 500,000 of them have died from assorted horrors during a decade of economic sanctions: starvation, ruined schools, lack of medicine, undrinkable water, ruined sewers, land mine explosions, birth defects. The toll runs around 5,000 children a month. At 22 million, the nation's population is just ahead that of Texas. Davis, *Another voice calling for an end to sanctions in Iraq*, Austin Am.-Statesman A19, August 31, 2000), 2000 WL 7340498. See gen., Cleveland, Norm Internationalization & U.S. Economic Sanctions, 26 Yale J.I.L. 1 (2001). *See also, Opinion, End the Iraq War*, The Seattle Times, B4, May 14, 2001; The Economist, World Reporter, *Special: Iraq and the West: When sanctions don't work: Almost ten years of them have left Iraqis desperate and Saddam Hussein as defiant as ever*, The Economist, April 8, 2000, 2000 WL 8141434, noted that:

> "[s]anctions impinge on the lives of all Iraqis every moment of the day. In Basra, Iraq's second city, . . . [t]ap water causes diarrhea, but few can afford the bottled sort. Because the sewers have broken down, pools of stinking muck have leached through to the surface all over

town. That effluent, combined with pollution upstream, has killed most of the fish in the Shatt al-Arab river and has left the remainder unsafe to eat. The government can no longer spray for sand-flies or mosquitoes, so insects have proliferated, along with the diseases they carry ... [C]autious studies by foreign researchers show horrific rises in infant mortality, malnutrition and disease. An analysis of NGO health surveys conducted by Richard Garfield, a public-health expert at Columbia University, found that at least 100,000 (and probably as many as 227, 000) children under five had died between 1991 and 1998, as a result of the Gulf War sanctions. That works out at between 26 and 60 deaths every day among infants along. A recent UNICEF report estimated that, over the same period, some 500,000 under-fives had died."

See also, The Economist, World Reporter, *Special*, McCarthy, *Can Sanctions be smarter?: America's policy on Iraq and Iran*, The Economist, World Reporter, May 26, 2001; and Arnove, *Iraq under siege: Ten years on*, 12/1/2000 Monthly Rev. 1425, 200 WL 10947230.

In the Christian Science Monitor, Monday, April 3, 2000, WORLD, at p. 1, 2000 WL 4427149, we read the following article by Scott Peterson, "*Is the West too quick to sanction? A UN official quit last week over the human cost in Iraq of sanctions. US curbs cover half of the world population.*"*

Sanction fatigue is setting in. This diplomatic stick, employed more times by President Clinton than any other leader in US history, is losing its effectiveness and appeal on the global stage. High-profile failings of economic sanctions—especially in Iraq—are casting doubt on the future of sanctions as a means of punishment. The paradox is that in the decades since Cuba was first embargoed in 1960, the intended target of sanctions—whether it be Cuban President Fidel Castro, Iraqi leader Saddam Hussein, or Serbia's President Slobodan Milosevic—has been able to turn sanctions to political advantage, while neatly handing off the burden to local populations. The tangle of US sanctions today affect more than half the world's population. But the severity of Iraq's case has for the first time built up a diplomatic head of steam against sanctions for what the US sees as global wrongdoing.

The growing chorus of protest was capped by last Thursday's departure from Baghdad of Hans Von Sponeck, UN humanitarian chief, for Iraq. He resigned rather than preside over the further destruction of Iraq's social fabric. "Let's face it: Iraq is one of the few countries on our globe which is regressing," said the 32–year UN veteran, in his first interview since leaving Iraq. "I have no doubt that history will say that Iraq was forced to become the guinea pig for the experimentation of a sanction methodology that ultimately failed. We have to find a new approach."

Sanctions may be the modern equivalent of the military siege, in which armies throughout history—from the Romans surrounding the Masada (an ancient Jewish fortress in Israel), to the Germans and Finnish

* Reprinted with the permission of the Christian Science Monitor.

blockading Leningrad in World War II—sought to compel capitulation by destroying the will to resist. Roots of the American policy reach back to President Woodrow Wilson, who said in 1919 that "a nation boycotted is a nation that is in sight of surrender." That maxim seems to have been taken to heart by President Clinton, for whom sanctions have all but replaced diplomacy. He has called the US "sanctions happy," and long with Congress, he has been responsible for imposing more than half of the 125 or so cases of sanctions ever imposed by the US.

But such overuse "devalues the tool" and the "moral, disapproval value tends to be lost," says Gary Hufbauer, a sanctions expert and senior fellow at the Institute for International Economics in Washington.... The lessons of nearly 10 years of sanctions on Iraq are causing analysts to reexamine their assumptions about what few sanctions—out of the 176 recorded cases this century—have caused their targets to change course, and why so many have failed. "We've done a lot of re-evaluating," Mr. Hufbauer says. "The unfortunate truth is that when you have a truly retrograde regime, and you are seeking a major goal like its overthrow, the record is close to zero." Sanctions have been applied from North Korea to Canada, and both India and Pakistan were slapped with sanctions—mandatory under US law—when they tested nuclear devices in 1998. Those sanctions hurt US farm exports badly, renewing interest in Congress for reform that would require assessing domestic impact before imposing any sanction. Despite those cases, Iraq stands out. "Iraq in our times, is like the Italian–Abyssinia case was to the League of Nations. That was the defining sanction, and it did as much as anything to destroy the League," says Hufbauer. "The Iraq case is not going to destroy the UN, but it is certainly causing a lot of rethinking. The lasting impact is that it will be much harder to put these kind of sanctions on any country."

A similar analysis has been put forward by a British parliamentary committee, that found that the Iraq example showed it would be "difficult" to justify imposing similar sanctions on any nation in the future, because they cause "impoverishment" and "only further concentrate power in the hands of the ruling elite." Comprehensive UN sanctions were slapped on Iraq in August 1990, just days after Iraqi forces invaded Kuwait—and remain the pillar of US policy toward Iraq. Since 1996, Iraq has been permitted to sell oil to buy humanitarian goods, but US officials have blocked scores of contracts, anxious that "dual use" items might be used to reinvigorate Iraq's nuclear-, chemical-, and biological-weapons programs.

The US has come under intense pressure from friend and foe alike the past two weeks in the UN Security Council. In a rare moment of criticism, UN head Kofi Annan noted that sanctions had created a "serious moral dilemma" for the UN, and that the US and Britain had blocked more than $1.5 billion worth of humanitarian contracts for

Iraq—for items from breeding bulls to ambulances. "The UN has been on the side of the vulnerable and the weak, and has always sought to relieve suffering. Yet, here we are accused of causing suffering," Mr. Annan said. Senior US officials have said repeatedly that the Iraqi people are not the targets of sanctions, and have agreed to release at least 70 of the applications for humanitarian goods that it had put on hold. "There is no question that sanctions fatigue is becoming a major problem," says Anthony Cordesman, a leading Mideast security expert at the Center for Strategic and International Studies in Washington. "There is immense hardship in Iraq.... You certainly have a nation that is falling apart in every way—except in sustaining a dictatorship."

"The idea that we are engaged in a constant battle for perceptions, and that the key perception is the welfare of the Iraqi people, seems to be absolutely beyond the comprehension of the State Department," Mr. Cordesman says. "If you look back on [Secretary of State] Madeleine Albright's tenure, this will probably be recognized as one of the greatest single failures for which she has to be held responsible." Oil-rich Iraq was once one of the wealthiest nations in the Mideast. But a decade of war in the 1980s, the 1991 Gulf War, and then sanctions have all resulted in a spike in extreme malnutrition rates. Child deaths now number in the hundreds of thousands, and there has been an almost total breakdown of health and other basic services, according to UN statistics.

Mr. Von Sponeck points out that the Iraqi leadership has spent the $400 million a year from illicit smuggling of oil on everything from new palaces to whiskey, and he is disappointed at how little it spends from legal UN oil money on education. "I don't say that everything that impinges on Iraq is due to sanctions. Rubbish," he says. "But the accusation that the regime is purposefully trying to make the Iraqi people suffer doesn't hold."

"Governments are changing their attitudes to the Iraq file," says Von Sponeck. "The big question is: Can that pressure translate into swaying the very inflexible positions of the Americans and British? This has become a moral issue." Iraq should be proof that sanctions just don't work, he adds. Apartheid-era sanctions on South Africa are often a case that is raised by supporters of sanctions as a case that worked, but Von Sponeck was head of the UN in neighboring Botswana at the time, and disagrees. "People forget that the sanctions period was short, and the first victims were the blacks in South Africa," he says.

Pope John Paul II helped set the tone during his 1998 visit toCuba— where four decades of sanctions have failed to unseat Mr. Castro— saying that sanctions are "always deplorable, because they hurt the most needy." The transformation in Von Sponeck's thinking is an apt mirror of that taking place elsewhere. When he first arrived in Iraq, "the word 'sanctions' was like a cow in India—it was very holy: don't talk about it," he says. But his "mental adjustment" was prompted by the situation in Iraqi schools, where children were learning in such isolation—printed materials have been forbidden under sanctions—that they can never be "responsible citizens."

"The biggest lesson of the last 10 years," Hufbauer says, is that "sometimes sanctions are successful when you have modest goals and an open regime. But sanctions are a fair-weather tool of diplomacy. You can't expect them to do the heavy lifting, just as you wouldn't send in a crew with shovels to dig out a major road through rock."

Additional Notes and Questions. Do you think that economic sanctions should apply as actions under U.N. Charter Title VI (Peaceful Settlement) or under Chapter VII, (on Force), therefore? For discussion of sanctions and human rights violations, see Chapter 9, *supra*, and for discussion of individual responsibility and international crime, see Chapter 16, *infra*.

In place of proper popular debate, we seem poised to bestow the war power on an American Caesar rather than to preserve and strengthen the constitutional decision to secure the peace by lodging the decision for war or peace within Congress—the democratic branch that must pay for the war and answer to the people for breaking the peace? Nationalistic euphoria can lead to a form of national hubris, corporate ego inflation, followed by mistakes in judgment in the form of foreign adventurism, then meeting our own nemesis in whatever form—unless we abide by our own structural checks designed to avoid this very phenomenon.

The war with Iraq was preceded by a healthy national debate culminating in the most impressive example of responsible congressional debate on the decision for war since the Second World War. But the seeming conclusiveness, the quick success, and the modest number of Allied casualties in the Gulf War have combined to give this decision for war an aura of wisdom and popularity with the people that undermines the perceived vision of those who opposed offensive action at that time before economic sanctions reasonably could be expected to work against Iraq.

Yet all the reasons for an institutional bias in favor of peace and against war remain. Does not war represent the failure of diplomatic and peaceful means of dispute resolution in favor of savagery, distinguished only by a gossamer thin cloak of respectability because the violence is done by nation-state actors?

Firmage argues that the conclusion that war, with all its violence, is a decisive and final resolver of the problems leading to war is almost always an illusion. Despite U.S. success on the battlefield, the Iraqi war inevitably was *no* exception to this rule. Most of the political and economic factors that led to the dispute still remain unresolved. Since the end of the war, Kurdish and Shiite minorities in Iraq have suffered enormous hardship, Saddam Hussein remains in power and continues his ruthless regime, and Kuwait is no closer to democracy than it was prior to August 1990. Ultimately, war only creates enormous suffering as well as economic and environmental dislocation. Do you think that the assumptions and points of the paragraphs of this, not question 4, were and are correct? Why? Why not?

2.   DELEGATION OF MILITARY COMMAND UNDER THE CONSTITUTION

Glennon & Hayward, Collective Security and the Constitution: Can the Commander In Chief Power be Delegated to the United Nations?

82 Geo. L.J. 1573, 1573–75 (1994).*

Imagine, after protracted negotiations with an intractable aggressor, that the United Nations Security Council decides to use force. Members of the Security Council agree to provide forces in the event U.N. operatives' lives are jeopardized by enemy fire. Whether that condition is met is to be decided by U.N. officials. U.N. military forces then come under attack. The designated U.N. officials decide upon air strikes, and bombs—dropped by the United States Air Force—fall upon the attackers. Security Council members, including the United States, note proudly that their agreement anticipated just this situation.

Until recently, this type of anticipatory delegation of U.S. war-making power to a multinational force would have been viewed as wildly hypothetical. Yet, this very procedure was followed in the initial bombings of Serbian forces surrounding the Bosnian town of Gorazde on April 11, 1994.

Can such anticipatory delegation of war-making power be reconciled with America's Constitution? Throughout American history, the United States has often welcomed allegiances with other nations to thwart particular threats, but with few exceptions has retained command and control over U.S. fighting forces.

Although these ad hoc agreements designed for specific situations may serve the cause of flexibility, this flexibility comes with a price. Because U.S. interests are global, American forces fight in such far-flung places as the U.S. sees its interests threatened, often without proportional assistance from other nations. Also, much of the Third World views this propensity for unilateral military action as imperialistic or neocolonial, and the United States has become to some a convenient symbol for a repressive status quo.

* * *

The superpower deadlock on the Security Council during the Cold War prevented it from developing collective security forces and procedures under Article 43 [authorizing member states to place military forces at the Security Council's command]. Given the apparent advantages of an Article 43 agreement, now possible given post-Cold War Security Council politics, it is not surprising that the idea has attracted American support. During his campaign, President Clinton expressed support for U.N. collective security schemes that would allow the U.N. to call upon U.S. troops for military operations. After protracted consideration he recently signed a directive that permits members of the U.S. Armed Forces to serve under

---

* Reprinted by permission of the Georgetown Law Journal.

foreign commanders, but opposes a standing U.N. army and declines to make standby forces available to the U.N.

Before committing to open-ended collective arrangements, the United States will have to address the numerous constitutional and statutory provisions that seem to proscribe such action. As Professor Jane Stromseth argued in Rethinking War Powers, domestic legal concerns require attention even when the Security Council has approved the use of collective force. Under the separation of powers doctrine, our legal order must observe constitutional requirements that dictate a serious role for both Congress and the President in war power decisions.

The constitutional issue most often addressed by scholars in this ares is the proper allocation of war powers between Congress and the President. This issue, however, also has an important but as yet largely unexplored second side: whether Congress or the President may delegate war powers to another body. Two constitutional questions arise here. The first is whether the Constitution permits the President to delegate his power as Commander in Chief to a foreign body. The second is whether the Constitution permits Congress to delegate its power to declare war to the President or to a foreign body. * * *

———

Notes and Questions

1. *Assignment of U.S. forces to the U.N.* On August 21, 1995, Spc. Michael New, an Army medic, was assigned to Macedonia to become part of the United Nations Peacekeeping Force. He was told that as part of the U.N. force he would be required to wear U.N. insignia and answer to U.N. commanders. He refused and ultimately was given a dishonorable discharge. Spc. New thus joined the growing debate surrounding the constitutionality of U.S. assignment of forces to the U.N. *See, e.g.,* Kaye, *Are There Limits to Military Alliance? Presidential Power to Place American Troops under Non–American Commanders,* 5 Transnat'l L. & Contemp. Probs. 399 (1995); Paust, *Peace-Making and Security Council Powers: Bosnia–Herzegovina Raises International and Constitutional Questions,* 19 S. Ill. U. L.J. 131 (1994).

2. *Congress also entered the debate* by offering a number of resolutions in an attempt to curb President Clinton's commitment of U.S. forces to U.N. peacekeeping operations. *See, e.g.,* House Bill 2606, 104th Cong., 1st Sess (1995), which sought to withdraw funds from peacekeeping operations in Bosnia and Herzegovina; National Security Revitalization Act, H.R. 7, 104th Cong., 1st Sess. (1995), which would have limited funds available for U.N. peacekeeping activities and imposed other restrictions on U.S. and U.N. cooperation; Peace Powers Act, Senate Bill 1803, 104th Cong., 1st Sess. (1995), which would have established more stringent guidelines for U.S. commitment of personnel to the U.N.; Amendment No. 1051 to the excepted committee amendment to H.R. 3116, 103d Cong., 1st Sess. (1993), which would have prohibited funding of U.S. forces in U.N. operations. In response, President Clinton issued Presidential Decision Directive 25.

Terry, The Criteria for Intervention: An Evaluation of U.S. Military Policy in U.N. Operations

31 Tex. Int'l L.J. 101, 104–05 (1996).*

Because of Congress' increased attempts to interfere legislatively with U.N. operations, the U.S. Executive branch has modified the criteria for U.S. involvement by issuing PDD–25. Under PDD–25, the United States uses a two-step analysis to determine the position it will take on a proposed intervention. In the first phase of analysis, the United States, in its position on the Security Council, must determine whether it is appropriate for the United Nations, as an organization, to intervene. This phase of analysis requires that the United States answer the following six questions: (1) is the situation a threat to international peace and security; (2) does the proposed operation have a defined scope with clear objectives; (3) is multilateral participation likely; (4) are financial and human resources available; (5) does the operation have an identifiable endpoint; and (6) if the operation is one conducted under Chapter VI of the U.N. Charter, does a working cease-fire exist?

If this first phase of inquiry results in a vote approving U.N. involvement, the United States must then apply a second set of criteria to determine whether the United States should commit U.S. forces to the U.N. operation. Six central questions comprise this second phase of analysis: (1) whether the peace operation advances U.S. interests; (2) whether personnel, funds, and resources are available; (3) whether U.S. participation is necessary for a successful operation; (4) whether an identifiable endpoint for U.S. involvement exists; (5) whether Congressional and domestic support exists; and (6) whether the command and control arrangements are acceptable. If involvement in the U.N. operation will require that the United States commit significant numbers of U.S. military personnel, PDD–25 also requires the resolution of three additional criteria. The United States must determine: (1) whether it has the ability to commit sufficient forces to achieve the defined military objectives; (2) whether the leaders of the operation possess a clear intention to achieve the stated objectives decisively; and (3) whether there is a sufficient commitment on the part of the United Nations or any other sponsoring body to reasses and adjust continually the objectives and composition of the force in order to meet changing security and operational requirements. This two-step inquiry offers prudent guidance for all U.S. commitment of forces, whether or not U.S. interests are implicated. Since national interests are no longer the primary concern, PDD–25 ensures that when the United States does intervene, clear safeguards are present.

* * *

* Reprinted with the permission of the   tions.
University of Texas School of Law Publica-

Notes and Questions. What do you think of the Clinton administration's position regarding commitment of U.S. forces to U.N. activities? This was admittedly President Clinton's attempt to retain control over the decision to commit U.S. forces. Does it resolve all of the issues it was intended to address? Do any questions remain unanswered? Do you think that the President *may* relinquish authority over U.S. forces, or must the U.S. maintain ultimate control? Are the security provisions envisioned by the U.N. charter possible if states insist on maintaining control over their own forces? What position do you think the Bush administration will take?

3.   "OPERATION JUST CAUSE"—THE PANAMA INVASION

One could place the discussion of the invasion of Panama under the rubric of unilateral self defense, humanitarian intervention, or even under extraterritorial arrest of fugitives and the expansion of jurisdiction for the purpose of curtailing drug trafficking. These were all justifications made by the U.S. Government. Consider the following questions as you read: Was the invasion justified by the claim of unilateral self-defense? What about the duty to protect U.S. nationals and interests? Also, what about the need to ensure the proper implementation of the Panama Canal treaties? Was it justified on the basis of regional self-defense and the promotion of regional security? Could it be justified as a "police action" in the basic sense of the term, to "capture a criminal?" What arguments were put by U.S. authorities? How valid were they? Ultimately with some 26,000 U.S. military, the U.S. forces met early resistance and later sniper fire, but within just 3–4 days, all resistance ended. There were at least 400 Panamanian deaths (mainly civilian) and only 23 U.S. fatalities.

The United States has long had an interest in Panama, since it participated in its creation as it seceded from Colombia in 1903. The U.S. Navy held a presence off-shore, to be sure that Colombia would submit to dismemberment. The U.S. and Panama signed a treaty within a few weeks granting the U.S. expansive rights to the area which is now the Canal Zone. The later Panama Canal Treaties (effective 1979) allow the gradual return of the Zone and the Canal to the control of Panama, to culminate in 1999.

Notes and Questions

1.   *The Invasion of Panama.* As East Berliners and the rest of eastern Europe celebrated their new freedom, the U.S. executive branch was planning an invasion of tiny Panama. Once the invasion was underway, the executive branch tried to justify the surprise attack on various grounds noted above.

2.   *For years Noriega had been coddled by U.S. officials.* The United States long had been aware of Noriega's illicit dealings, but chose to ignore them as long as Noriega remained a "stabilizing" source in the region. According to Panamanian Vice–President Arias, the U.S. government redefined Noriega as an adversary only after his regime became a "source of instability rather than stability." The executive branch suddenly reversed itself and began to treat Noriega as an enemy. Initially, economic isolation was employed. President Reagan declared a national emergency under the

National Emergencies Act and the International Emergency Economic Powers Act [EEPA] on April 8, 1988. Then in May 1989, recently-elected President Bush deployed an additional two thousand combat troops to the canal zone, ostensibly to protect American lives. Predictably, tension and hostilities escalated and President Bush ordered Operation Just Cause, the code name for the Panamanian invasion, on December 20.

3. ***Does the invasion fall under the category of acts that are denied to the Executive under the War Clause,*** so congressional approval is required *before* any military action can occur? Former President Bush (the father) made the decision to invade unilaterally and only notified Congress after initiation of action. At no point prior to or during "Operation Just Cause" was congressional approval sought by the President.

The War Clause was drafted to demand congressional authorization for acts of war taken by the U.S. Government except in response to sudden attack on the United States. Therefore, the War Clause must apply to full scale invasions such as Operation Just Cause. First, was the United States realistically ever threatened at any time? The Panamanian Assembly's "state of war" proclamation on December 15, 1989, was never more than a mouse that roared. In fact, it was only a domestic statement aimed at triggering domestic authority to Noriega. Second, was there any "sudden" turn of events that required the President to act immediately without time to consult Congress? Both an attack on the United States and a degree of surprise are necessary prerequisites to an executive military response and neither were present at the beginning of Operation Just Cause. On the contrary, Operation Just Cause was a carefully planned and executed offensive, without congressional approval, against the forces of General Noriega.

4. ***Did "Operation Just Cause" also meet the "fluctuating powers" test governing the delegation of power in foreign relations.*** Under this test, when Congress has made its intention clear, the will of Congress controls. Congress had expressed its will regarding unauthorized executive military action on numerous occasions. The War Powers Resolution of 1973, the Hughes–Ryan Amendment to the Foreign Assistance Act of 1974, the Intelligence Authorization Act for Fiscal Year 1981, and the Boland Amendments establish a record of congressional intent; namely, no offensive military activity shall be planned and staged without the knowledge and authorization of the Congress.

5. ***Should the initial deployment of two thousand troops in May 1989 also have triggered the sixty-day provision under section 5(b) of the War Powers Resolution?*** Under the Resolution, any introduction of U.S. troops into "imminent hostilities" *automatically* engages the sixty-day provision. As the House Report on the Resolution stated, the term "hostilities" "encompasses a state of confrontation in which no shots have been fired but where there is clear and present danger of armed conflict." The House Report further defined imminent hostilities as situations "in which there is a clear potential * * * for actual armed conflict."

Did the act of introducing combat troops into a nation that is being intimidated politically, economically, and militarily create a potential for armed conflict? Can the troop reinforcement of May 1989 be seen as a planned prologue to invasion? Was the "clear and present danger of armed conflict" recognized by the executive branch? Is that precisely what was intended? Did combat troop reinforcement in May 1989 constitute introduction of United States forces into "imminent hostilities," according to both the language and intent of the War Powers Resolution?

6. ***Do you think that Congress should have pressed the War Powers Resolution upon the President in May 1989?*** Some considerations include: First, the situation in Panama had deteriorated to the point where the probability of armed confrontation was clear. Second, by triggering the clock of the War Powers Resolution, Congress would have forced the President to explain his intentions concerning military activity in Panama. This would have allowed Congress to participate in the decision on whether to initiate Operation Just Cause, thus satisfying not only the War Powers Resolution, but also the constitutional war power and foreign relations power. Third, it would have provided valuably needed precedent to increase the functional credibility of the War Powers Resolution. The last reason is vital. Every time Congress allows unauthorized executive action to go unchallenged by the War Powers Resolution—even in situations where Congress agrees with the action taken—the lack of action further weakens this already troubled Resolution.

7. ***Report to Congress, former President George Bush (December 21, 1989).*** The White House, Washington, DC, December 21, 1989, to Hon. Thomas S. Foley, *Speaker of the House of Representatives, Washington, DC.*

Dear Mr. Speaker: On December 15, 1989, at the instigation of Manuel Noriega, the illegitimate Panamanian National Assembly declared that a state of war existed between the Republic of Panama and the United States. At the same time, Noriega gave a highly inflammatory anti-American speech. A series of vicious and brutal acts directed at U.S. personnel and dependents followed these events.

On December 16, 1989, a U.S. Marine officer was killed without justification by Panama Defense Forces (PDF) personnel. Other elements of the PDF beat a U.S. Naval officer and unlawfully detained, physically abused, and threatened the officer's wife. These acts of violence are directly attributable to Noriega's dictatorship, which created a climate of aggression that places American lives and interests in peril.

These and other events over the past two years have made it clear that the lives and welfare of American citizens in Panama were increasingly at risk, and that the continued safe operation of the Panama Canal and the integrity of the Canal Treaties would be in serious jeopardy if such lawlessness were allowed to continue.

Under these circumstances, I ordered the deployment of approximately 11,000 additional U.S. forces to Panama. In conjunction with the 13,000 U.S. Forces already present, military operations were initiated on December 20, 1989, to protect American lives, to defend democracy in Panama, to apprehend Noriega and bring him to trial on the drug-related charges for which he was indicted in 1988, and to ensure the integrity of the Panama Canal Treaties.

In the early morning of December 20, 1989, the democratically elected Panamanian leadership announced formation of a government, assumed power in a formal swearing-in ceremony, and welcomed the assistance of U.S. Armed Forces in removing the illegitimate Noriega regime. The deployment of U.S. Forces is an exercise of the right of self-defense recognized in Article 51 of the United Nations charter and was necessary to protect American lives in imminent danger and to fulfill our responsibilities under the Panama Canal Treaties. It was welcomed by the democratically elected government of Panama. The military operations were ordered pursuant to my constitutional authority with respect to the conduct of foreign relations and as Commander in Chief.

In accordance with my desire that Congress be fully informed on this matter, and consistent with the War Powers Resolution, I am providing this report on the deployment of U.S. Armed Forces to Panama. Although most organized opposition has ceased, it is not possible at this time to predict the precise scope and duration of the military operations or how long the temporary increase of U.S. Forces in Panama will be required. Nevertheless, our objectives are clear and largely have been accomplished. Our additional Forces will remain in Panama only so long as their presence is required.

Sincerely,
George Bush.

––––––––

8. ***Did the invasion fit within any of the exceptions to Article 51 of the U.N. Charter?*** Was safeguarding U.S. nationals a valid justification either as a form of self-defense or humanitarian intervention? Was apprehending General Noriega a valid justification in international law? Insuring the integrity of the Panama Canal Treaties? The restoration of democracy or protecting human rights in Panama?

––––––––

Sofaer, The Legality of the United States Action In Panama
29 Colum.J.Trans.L. 281 (1991).*

* * *

V.   The United States Action was Necessary and Proportionate

President Bush reasonably concluded that Operation Just Cause was both necessary and proportionate under international law. By December 20, 1989, Noriega had declared as his objective "only one territory and only one flag," and had repudiated the right of the United States to protect the Canal. He regarded Panama as being in a state of war with the United

––––

* Reprinted with the permission of the Columbia Journal of Transnational Law.   Abraham Sofaer was Legal Adviser, U.S. Dept. of State at the time.

States, having crossed the line from harassment to homicide in the escalation of hostilities. The United States had attempted to negotiate Noriega's voluntary surrender of power, had protested both Noriega's violations of the Canal Treaties and his violence against U.S. forces, and had invoked all available forms of diplomatic and economic sanctions. All these efforts failed. Under these circumstances, ousting Noriega was a legitimate and necessary foreign policy objective, only that result could end the attacks on U.S. nationals, preserve U.S. (and Panamanian) rights under the Canal Treaties, restore the legitimate, democratic government selected by the people of Panama and end Noriega's alleged involvement in international drug violations.

Because the objective of removing Noriega from authority in Panama is justifiable under international law, the substantial military action designed to achieve that result was fully warranted. The Joint Chiefs of Staff recommended, and the President adopted, a plan designed to employ a swift, overpowering force, on the belief that far fewer casualties would result than if any less intensive effort were implemented. United States diplomats and military officials on the scene emphatically concurred in this strategy, as did the democratically elected Panamanian leadership. Without total victory, the PDF or Noriega, or both, would have utilized their massive store of weapons to make democratic government impossible. A protracted operation could have been a tactical disaster, and would have exposed U.S. civilians to continuing danger.

International law, and international lawyers, should avoid utilizing the doctrine of proportionality as a vehicle for second-guessing tactical judgments as to what form a military action should take to achieve a legitimate objective. The military judgment President Bush accepted was reasonable in light of the continuing danger that otherwise would have existed for U.S. forces, for U.S. Canal rights and for President Endara's capacity to govern. U.S. forces were ordered to act in accordance with the laws of armed conflict, and the United States chose to provide all captured PDF members with prisoner-of-war protections under the Geneva Convention.

* * *

Henkin, The Invasion of Panama Under International Law: A Gross Violation

29 Colum.J.Trans.L. (1991).*

* * *

III. The Legal Adviser's Justifications

The Legal Adviser's address offers no new legal justification for the invasion of Panama but places different emphasis on those originally published, making some more explicit and less ambiguous and, in my view, more radical, more clearly erroneous in law, and more damaging to the cause of maintaining international order through international law.

* Reprinted with the permission of the Columbia Journal of Transnational Law.

To begin, the Legal Adviser strikes at the explicit language and clear meaning of Article 2(4) of the Charter which prohibits "the use of force against the territorial integrity or political independence of any state." Rather than offering a narrow interpretation of key terms, his argument concludes that the action in Panama "cannot *be viewed* as having been *intended* to *compromise* the territorial integrity or political independence of Panama." If military invasion and toppling an incumbent government is not a use of force against the territorial integrity and political independence of another state, what is? What the United States did, and intended to do, was to violate—not merely "compromise"—the territorial integrity of Panama and its political independence as asserted by its incumbent government. The Legal Adviser invokes "the cooperation and support" of Endara as lending "substantial weight" to the legitimacy of the U.S. action. That Endara controlled no Panamanian territory and exercised no governmental powers, we are told, did not deprive his consent "of legal significance." In my view, that consent has no legal significance for justifying the U.S. invasion.

The Legal Adviser would extend and expand a small exception for "humanitarian intervention" to justify not merely using minimal force to protect or extricate hostages, but a full-scale invasion to overthrow a government. The right of "humanitarian intervention" is claimed as a justification for such an invasion even though few U.S. citizens were in fact threatened and they could have been extricated or protected without armed invasion. The Legal Advisor would extend "humanitarian intervention," not only to justify the use of force to save lives, but also to overthrow undemocratic governments. There is no basis in law for such radical exceptions to Article 2(4).

The Legal Adviser's principal blow at the law of the Charter lies in his interpretation of Article 51. The United States has long rejected claims by other states of a right to act in self-defense in the absence of an armed attack. During the Suez Canal Crisis in 1957 the United States rejected such a justification by its closest NATO allies. Before the Reagan Administration, the United States was careful not to justify its own resorts to force as acts in self-defense when there had been no armed attack. Even the Reagan Administration did not claim the right of self-defense in the absence of an armed attack, though it sought to stretch the concept of armed attack to justify its uses of force against Nicaragua and its bombing of Libya in response to terrorist activities attributed to Libya's government. Now the Legal Adviser explicitly declares that it is *not* the U.S. position that the right of self-defense applies only in response to armed attack. His claim contradicts a longstanding U.S. position and the established view of international law.

Recognizing that even when force is permissible in self-defense it is limited by requirements of necessity and proportionality, the Legal Adviser declares that the U.S. action was "necessary and proportionate." In my view, international law would conclude that the invasion was not "necessary" for any lawful purpose, and that invasion by 24,000 troops—inflicting several hundred casualties and much property damage, and overthrowing an incumbent government—was out of any proportion to the attacks on

U.S. personnel cited, to the desire to bring Noriega to trial, or to anything else in the circumstances that might remotely contribute to a right to use force in self-defense. We are told, however, that "international law * * * should avoid utilizing the doctrine of proportionality as a vehicle for second-guessing tactical judgments as to what form a military action should take to achieve a legitimate objective." What, then, is left of the doctrine of proportionality?

The Legal Adviser also invokes the Panama Canal Treaties as authorizing the U.S. invasion. To support that conclusion he cites the Senate Report declaring that the Treaties would authorize U.S. action, "not only in connection with external threats to the Canal, but also with respect to internal threats." Indeed, under the Treaties, both the United States and the Government of Panama have the right to defend the Canal against internal threats, for example by terrorists. But there was no hint that the United States could defend the Canal against the Government of Panama, and surely there was no suggestion that the United States could replace one government of Panama with another in order to defend the Canal.

No government, in Panama or anywhere else, would conclude a treaty that would authorize what the United States did in Panama. Even if Panama and the United States had concluded such a treaty, it would be void: such a treaty would violate the U.N. Charter, which by its terms is to prevail over any inconsistent treaties. It would violate the principles of Article 2(4) of the Charter which are *jus cogens.*

In summary, to justify the U.S. action the Legal Adviser would:

— eviscerate Article 2(4) prohibiting "the use of force against the territorial independence or political integrity" of another state;

— expand "humanitarian intervention" to permit any state to invade another to impose the invading state's view and version of democracy;

— excise the requirement of an armed attack to justify the use of force in self-defense, and in effect accept the view that the use of force is permitted whenever a state concludes that it is the victim of various forms of "aggression" against its "vital interests" as it defines them, or that it has "just cause";

— render virtually meaningless the requirement of proportionality by insisting that the U.S. action in this case was proportionate and that international law cannot "second guess" the state using force as to what is proportional; and

— distort the clear meaning of an important treaty to render it one that no government of Panama would have concluded and giving it a meaning that will doubtless be disavowed by future governments of Panama.

In the end, the Legal Adviser has felt compelled to assert that "the threat or use of force is not inherently wrong." I disagree profoundly. His view is surely not international law. It was not the U.S. view of the law, and was not U.S. policy for at least 35 years after World War II. I deeply regret hearing that it is U.S. policy now. I profoundly hope it will not be U.S. policy tomorrow.

* * *

Notes and Questions

1. What do you think about the importance that former President Bush and Legal Adviser Sofaer seemed to put on Noriega's "Declaration of War?" Was Noriega talking to us or to his own "Legislature and people?" Alfred P. Rubin answered in the New York Times that Noriega's statement was aimed at the Panamanian Parliament to function as a means to trigger a "state of emergency" or to declare martial law.

2. ***The heavy fire-power and sheer size of the U.S. military force*** led to substantial loss of life and property. Claims for compensation were rejected by the U.S. and law suits followed. *See*, Semmelman, In re Noriega, *Non-Self–Executing Treaty Aspects of Two CCA*, cert. denied *Cases v. U.G. as to the Panama Invasion*, 87 A.J.I.L. 288 (1993).

Wedgwood Report, The Use of Armed Force In International Affairs: The Case of Panama

In the Record of the Association of the Bar of the City of New York 604; 607–609; 692–93 (1992).*

[The Report is original, as Professor Wedgwood was able to persuade the Department of Defense to release contemporaneous documents and was able to conduct interviews in Panama. She argues that there was a significant problem of violence against American troops in Panama (the harassment of American ground personnel and the repeated attacks on the Araijan Tank Farm) that had to be addressed. Nevertheless, the Report severely criticizes the rationale used to justify the use of force. These included the Noriega declaration of a state of war on the 20th anniversary of the restoration of Torrijos to power, and the incident in front of the Commandancia on December 16, 1989. In addition, the Report clearly raises serious questions about the invasion—the availability of alternative remedies and proportionality. Brief portions of the Report follow].

Following the invasion of Panama, this Association began a study of the American decision to use force in Panama. * * * In the summer of 1990, three members travelled to Panama to interview officials of the United States Department of Defense Southern Command and of the new Endara government, Panamanian businessmen, civic groups and journalists, and, in several cases where access was possible, members of the prior Noriega regime. Interviews have also been conducted in the United States with officials of the United States Department of State, Department of Defense, and Central Intelligence Agency. * * *

---

* Reprinted with the permission of Ruth Wedgwood and the Association of the Bar of the City of New York.

V.   The Place of International Law in American Politics

We conclude that the United States invasion of Panama lacks clear support under international law, on the facts developed in our study. The problem of harassment faced by American military personnel and their dependents in Panama was significant. But the United States has not addressed in any public forum why the problem could not have been met by other prudent measures, including housing troops on U.S. defense sites, early withdrawal of military dependents and other American civilians from the area of confrontation, and providing escorts outside defense sites.

The events of December 15 and 16, 1989, offered as the immediate reason for a decision to invade, are far less clear than some supposed at the time. An adequate system of national security decision-making would allow an assessment of the circumstances of events before force is committed, rather than learning of the reasons to doubt after the eggs are broken. In our dislike for Noriega, we as Americans also have not adequately assessed how our own actions may have been in tension with treaty commitments under the Panama Canal Treaties, contributing to the escalation of events in Panama. And perhaps most important, national security decision-making has not provided any process for the weighing of civilian casualties in assessing proportionality.

We do not find the claim of proportionate and necessary self-defense as a justification for the Panama invasion to be established on the facts available to us. The supplementary rationales of democracy, fighting drugs, and the integrity of the Panama Canal Treaties face the additional problems noted above. The purpose served by closely parsing the factual background and legal rationale of the United States invasion of Panama is not to criticize any Administration or decision-maker. Rather, it is to contribute to the public debate concerning the use of force in international affairs. A President may be constrained by his reading of current public attitudes; if a President expects personal or political criticism for restraint in using force, this will influence the course of events. Military force will be used soberly only where the public, the press, the Congress, and the Executive are each fluent with the standards of international law. Legal rules help form the political morality of decision-makers and the political landscape in which they act.

U.S. v. Noriega

United States District Court, S.D.Fla.1990.
746 F.Supp. 1506, *aff'd* 117 F.3d 1206 (11th Cir.1997).[a]

HOEVELER, DISTRICT JUDGE.

This cause comes before the Court on the several motions of Defendants Noriega and Del Cid to dismiss for lack of jurisdiction the indictment which charges them with various narcotics-related offenses. * * *

On February 14, 1988, a federal grand jury sitting in Miami, Florida returned a twelve-count indictment charging General Manuel Antonio

---

a. Editors note. For the immunity aspects of the case, see ch. 10.

Noriega with participating in an international conspiracy to import cocaine and materials used in producing cocaine into and out of the United States. Noriega is alleged to have exploited his official position as head of the intelligence branch of the Panamanian National Guard, and then as Commander-in-Chief of the Panamanian Defense Forces, to receive payoffs in return for assisting and protecting international drug traffickers, including various members of the Medellin Cartel, in conducting narcotics and money laundering operations in Panama.

* * * The Court is presented with several issues of first impression. This is the first time that a leader or de facto leader of a sovereign nation has been forcibly brought to the United States to face criminal charges. The fact that General Noriega's apprehension occurred in the course of a military action only further underscores the complexity of the issues involved. In addition to Defendant Noriega's motion to dismiss based on lack of jurisdiction over the offense and sovereign immunity, Defendants Noriega and Del Cid argue that they are prisoners of war pursuant to the Geneva Convention. This status, Defendants maintain, deprives the Court of jurisdiction to proceed with the case. Noriega contends that the military action which brought about his arrest is "shocking to the conscience", and that due process considerations require the Court to divest itself of jurisdiction over his person. Noriega also asserts that the invasion occurred in violation of international law. Finally, Noriega argues that, even in the absence of constitutional or treaty violations, the Court should dismiss the indictment pursuant to its supervisory powers so as to prevent the judicial system from being party to and tainted by the government's alleged misconduct in arresting Noriega.

* * *

VI.   Illegal Arrest
   * * *

B.   Violations of International Law

In addition to his due process claim, Noriega asserts that the invasion of Panama violated international treaties and principles of customary international law—specifically, Article 2(4) of the United Nations Charter, Article 20[17] of the O.A.S. Charter, Articles 23(b) and 25 of the Hague Convention, Article 3 of Geneva Convention I, and Article 6 of the Nuremberg Charter. * * *

No [private] rights are created in the sections of the U.N. Charter, O.A.S. Charter, and Hague Convention cited by Noriega. Rather, those provisions set forth broad general principles governing the conduct of nations toward each other and do not by their terms speak to individual or private rights. *See* Frolova v. USSR (articles phrased in "broad generalities" constitute "declarations of principles, not a code of legal rights"); Tel–Oren (Bork, J., concurring) (Articles 1 and 2 of the United Nations Charter "contain general 'purposes and principles,' some of which state mere aspirations and none of which can be sensibly thought to have been intended to be judicially enforceable at the behest of individuals." * * * Lujan v. Gengler (individual may not invoke Article 2(4) of the U.N. Charter or Article 20[17] of the O.A.S. Charter if the sovereign state involved does not protest). * * * Thus, under the applicable international law, Noriega lacks standing to challenge violations of these treaties in the absence of a protest by the Panamanian government that the invasion of Panama and subsequent arrest of Noriega violated that country's territorial sovereignty.

It can perhaps be argued that reliance on the above body of law, under the unusual circumstances of this case, is a form of legal bootstrapping. Noriega, it can be asserted, is the government of Panama or at least its de facto head of state, and as such he is the appropriate person to protest alleged treaty violations; to permit removal of him and his associates from power and reject his complaint because a new and friendly government is installed, he can further urge, turns the doctrine of sovereign standing on its head. This argument is not without force, yet there are more persuasive answers in response. First * * * the United States has consistently refused to recognize the Noriega regime as Panama's legitimate government, a fact which considerably undermines Noriega's position. Second, Noriega nullified the results of the Panamanian presidential election held shortly before the alleged treaty violations occurred. The suggestion that his removal from power somehow robs the true government of the opportunity to object under the applicable treaties is therefore weak indeed. Finally, there is no provision or suggestion in the treaties cited which would permit the Court to ignore the absence of complaint or demand from the present duly constituted government of Panama. The current government of the Republic of Panama led by Guillermo Endara is therefore the appropriate entity to object to treaty violations. In light of Noriega's lack of standing to object, this Court therefore does not reach the question of whether these treaties were violated by the military action in Panama. * * *

* * *

Finally, Defendant cites Article 6 of the Nuremberg Charter, which proscribes war crimes, crimes against peace, and crimes against humanity. The Nuremberg Charter sets forth the procedures by which the Nuremberg Tribunal, established by the Allied powers after the Second World War, conducted the trials and punishment of major war criminals of the European Axis. The Government maintains that the principles laid down at Nuremberg were developed solely for the prosecution of World War II war criminals, and have no application to the conduct of U.S. military forces in Panama. The Court cannot agree. As Justice Robert H. Jackson, the United States Chief of Counsel at Nuremberg, stated: "If certain acts in violation of treaties are crimes, they are crimes whether the United States does them or whether Germany does them, and we are not prepared to lay down a rule of criminal conduct against others which we would not be willing to have invoked against us." Nonetheless, Defendant fails to establish how the Nuremberg Charter or its possible violation, assuming any, has any application to the instant prosecution. As stated above, the Ker–Frisbie doctrine makes clear that violations of treaties or customary international law alone do not deprive the court of jurisdiction over the defendant in the absence of limiting language to that effect. * * * Defendant has not cited any language in the Nuremberg Charter, nor in any of the above treaties, which limits the authority of the United States to arrest foreign nationals or to assume jurisdiction over their crimes. The reason is apparent; the Nuremberg Charter, as is the case with the other treaties, is addressed to the conduct of war and international aggression. It has no effect on the ability of sovereign states to enforce their laws, and thus has no application to the prosecution of Defendant for alleged narcotics violations. "The violation of international law, if any, may be redressed by other remedies, and does not depend upon the granting of what amounts to an effective immunity from criminal prosecution to safeguard individuals against police or armed forces misconduct." United States v. Cadena * * * The Court therefore refrains from reaching the merits of Defendant's claim under the Nuremberg Charter.

C. Supervisory Authority

Having determined that Defendant Noriega fails to state a valid defense based on due process and international law principles, this Court's inquiry is nonetheless unfinished, as Defendant Noriega alternatively bases his motion on the inherent supervisory power of the Court. Noriega alleges that, by asserting jurisdiction over him, this Court would thereby sanction and become party to the Government's alleged misconduct in invading Panama and bringing Noriega to trial. * * *

* * *

* * * Noriega argues that his arrest and presence before the Court was secured as a result of deliberate and indiscriminate atrocities committed by the United States in the course of its invasion of Panama, and that such conduct "shocking to the conscience" calls for an exercise of the Court's inherent supervisory authority resulting in dismissal of the indictment. In response, the Government argues that, even pursuant to the Court's inherent supervisory authority, Noriega may not seek dismissal of the indictment based on alleged violations of the rights of third parties—in this case, the rights of individual Panamanians or of the Panamanian state. The Government's position thus seems to be that a defendant's own constitutional or statutory rights must be violated in order to trigger the exercise of a court's supervisory power. This stance blurs the critical distinction between the use of supervisory authority on the one hand and the courts' rulings based on violations of constitutional and statutory law on the other. Since use of supervisory authority presents an independent body of law and does not depend on the existence of a constitutional or statutory violation, the fact that a defendant's own such rights have not been violated is not decisive. * * *

* * * In a government of laws, existence of the government will be imperilled if its fails to observe the law scrupulously. Our government is the potent, the omnipresent teacher. For good or for ill, it teaches the whole people by its example. Crime is contagious. If the government becomes a lawbreaker, it breeds contempt for law; it invites every man to become a law unto himself; it invites anarchy. * * * This Court may someday have occasion to apply Justice Brandeis' wise words, but this is not that day, for we are confronted not with the above hypothetical but rather a military war in which innocent lives were unfortunately lost in the pursuit of foreign policy objectives. Although the motives behind the military action are open to speculation, the stated goals of the invasion were to protect American lives, support democracy, preserve the Panama Canal Treaties, and bring Noriega to stand trial for narcotics offenses. Because the President ordered Noriega arrested "in the course of carrying

out the military operations in Panama," the capture of Noriega was incident to the broader conduct of foreign policy. While the Government's asserted rationales for the invasion are not beyond challenge and need not be blindly accepted by this Court, counsel for Noriega have offered no evidence to the contrary and the evidence they have offered in fact bolsters the conclusion that the invasion was primarily an exercise in foreign policy. * * *

That foreign policy objectives rather than just law enforcement goals are implicated radically changes the Court's consideration of the government conduct complained of and, consequently, its willingness to exercise supervisory power. For the question then posed is whether a court may, under the guise of its supervisory authority, condemn armed conflict as "shocking to the conscience." Any such declaration not only runs squarely into the political question doctrine, which precludes courts from resolving issues more properly committed to the political branches, but would indeed constitute unprecedented judicial interference in the conduct of foreign policy. * * *

　　　 * * *

Noriega does not, and legally cannot, allege that President Bush exceeded his powers as Commander-in-Chief in ordering the invasion of Panama. Rather, he asks this Court to find that the deaths of innocent civilians and destruction of private property is "shocking to the conscience and in violation of the laws and norms of humanity." At bottom, then, Noriega's complaint is a challenge to the very morality of war itself. This is a political question in its most paradigmatic and pristine form. It raises the specter of judicial management and control of foreign policy and challenges in a most sweeping fashion the wisdom, propriety, and morality of sending armed forces into combat—a decision which is constitutionally committed to the executive and legislative branches and hence beyond judicial review. Questions such as under what circumstances armed conflict is immoral, or whether it is always so, are not ones for the courts, but must be resolved by the political branches entrusted by the Constitution with the awesome responsibility of committing this country to battle. * * *

In view of the above findings and observations, it is the Order of this Court that the several motions presented by Defendants relating to this Court's jurisdiction as well as that suggesting dismissal under supervisory authority be and each is DENIED.

SECTION B.   COLLECTIVE MEASURES BY REGIONAL ORGANIZATIONS

1.   SOVIET MISSILES IN CUBA

The Soviet Threat To the Americas, Address By President Kennedy

47 United States Department of State Bulletin 715 (1962).

　　　 * * *

Neither the United States nor the world community of nations can tolerate deliberate deception and offensive threats on the part of any nation, large or small. We no longer live in a world where only the actual firing of weapons represents a sufficient challenge to a nation's security to constitute maximum peril. Nuclear weapons are so destructive and ballistic missiles are so swift that any substantially increased possibility of their use or any sudden change in their deployment may well be regarded as a definite threat to peace.

For many years both the Soviet Union and the United States, recognizing this fact, have deployed strategic nuclear weapons with great care, never upsetting the precarious status quo which insured that these weapons would not be used in the absence of some vital challenge. Our own strategic missiles have never been transferred to the territory of any other nation under a cloak of secrecy and deception; and our history, unlike that of the Soviets since the end of World War II, demonstrates that we have no desire to dominate or conquer any other nation or impose our system upon its people. Nevertheless, American citizens have become adjusted to living daily on the bull's eye of Soviet missiles located inside the U.S.S.R. or in submarines.

In that sense missiles in Cuba add to an already clear and present danger—although it should be noted the nations of Latin America have never previously been subjected to a potential nuclear threat.

* * *

Acting, therefore, in the defense of our own security and of the entire Western Hemisphere, and under the authority entrusted to me by the Constitution as endorsed by the resolution of the Congress, I have directed that the following initial steps be taken immediately:

First: To halt this offensive buildup, a strict quarantine on all offensive military equipment under shipment to Cuba is being initiated. All ships of any kind bound for Cuba from whatever nation or port will, if found to contain cargoes of offensive weapons, be turned back. This quarantine will be extended, if needed, to other types of cargo and carriers. We are not at this time, however, denying the necessities of life as the Soviets attempted to do in their Berlin blockade of 1948.

Second: I have directed the continued and increased close surveillance of Cuba and its military buildup. The Foreign Ministers of the OAS [Organization of American States] in their communiqué of October 3 rejected secrecy on such matters in this hemisphere. Should these offensive military preparations continue, thus increasing the threat to the hemisphere, further action will be justified. I have directed the Armed Forces to prepare for any eventualities; and I trust that, in the interest of both the Cuban people and the Soviet technicians at the sites, the hazards to all concerned of continuing this threat will be recognized.

Third: It shall be the policy of this nation to regard any nuclear missile launched from Cuba against any nation in the Western Hemisphere as an attack by the Soviet Union on the United States, requiring a full retaliatory response upon the Soviet Union.

Fourth: As a necessary military precaution I have reinforced our base at Guantanamo, evacuated today the dependents of our personnel there, and ordered additional military units to be on a standby alert.

Fifth: We are calling tonight for an immediate meeting of the Organ of Consultation, under the Organization of American States, to consider this threat to hemispheric security and to invoke articles 6 and 8 of the Rio Treaty in support of all necessary action. The United Nations Charter allows for regional security arrangements—and the nations of this hemisphere decided long ago against the military presence of outside powers. Our other allies around the world have also been alerted.

Sixth: Under the Charter of the United Nations, we are asking tonight that an emergency meeting of the Security Council be convoked without delay to take action against this latest Soviet threat to world peace. Our resolution will call for the prompt dismantling and withdrawal of all offensive weapons in Cuba, under the supervision of U.N. observers, before the quarantine can be lifted.

Seventh and finally: I call upon Chairman Khrushchev to halt and eliminate this clandestine, reckless, and provocative threat to world peace and to stable relations between our two nations. * * *

This nation is prepared to present its case against the Soviet threat to peace, and our own proposals for a peaceful world, at any time and in any forum—in the OAS, in the United Nations, or in any other meeting that could be useful—without limiting our freedom of action.

* * *

Notes. Study the Inter–American Treaty of Reciprocal Assistance of September 2, 1947, 62 Stat. 1681, 21 U.N.T.S. 77. Also Read the Charter of the Organization of American States. Both are in the Documentary Supplement.

Resolution of Council of the Organization of American States, Meeting As the Provisional Organ of Consultation, October 23, 1962

47 United States Department of State Bulletin 722 (1962).

Whereas, The Inter–American Treaty of Reciprocal Assistance of 1947 (Rio Treaty) recognizes the obligation of the American Republics to "provide for effective reciprocal assistance to meet armed attacks against any American state and in order to deal with threats of aggression against any of them,"

* * *

The Council of the Organization of American States, Meeting as the Provisional Organ of Consultation, Resolves:

1. To call for the immediate dismantling and withdrawal from Cuba of all missiles and other weapons with any offensive capability;

2. To recommend that the member states, in accordance with Articles 6 and 8 of the Inter–American Treaty of Reciprocal Assistance, take all measures, individually and collectively, including the use of armed force, which they may deem necessary to ensure that the Government of Cuba cannot continue to receive from the Sino–Soviet powers military material and related supplies which may threaten the peace and security of the Continent and to prevent the missiles in Cuba with offensive capability from ever becoming an active threat to the peace and security of the Continent;

3. To inform the Security Council of the United Nations of this resolution in accordance with Article 54 of the Charter of the United Nations and to express the hope that the Security Council will, in accordance with the draft resolution introduced by the United States, dispatch United Nations observers to Cuba at the earliest moment;

4. To continue to serve provisionally as Organ of Consultation and to request the Member States to keep the Organ of Consultation duly informed of measures taken by them in accordance with paragraph two of this resolution.

United States Proclamation Interdiction of the Delivery of Offensive Weapons To Cuba

47 United States Department of State Bulletin 717 (1962).

Whereas the peace of the world and the security of the United States and of all American States are endangered by reason of the establishment by the Sino–Soviet powers of an offensive military capability in Cuba, including bases for ballistic missiles with a potential range covering most of North and South America;

Whereas by a Joint Resolution passed by the Congress of the United States and approved on October 3, 1962, it was declared that the United States is determined to prevent by whatever means may be necessary, including the use of arms, the Marxist–Leninist regime in Cuba from extending, by force or the threat of force, its aggressive or subversive activities to any part of this hemisphere, and to prevent in Cuba the creation or use of an externally supported military capability endangering the security of the United States; and

Whereas the Organ of Consultation of the American Republics meeting in Washington on October 23, 1962, recommended that the Member States, in accordance with Articles 6 and 8 of the Inter–American Treaty of Reciprocal Assistance, take all measures, individually and collectively, including the use of armed force, which they may deem necessary to ensure that the Government of Cuba cannot continue to receive from the Sino–Soviet powers military material and related supplies which may threaten the peace and security of the Continent and to prevent the missiles in Cuba with offensive capability from ever becoming an active threat to the peace and security of the Continent.

Now, Therefore, I, John F. Kennedy, President of the United States of America, acting under and by virtue of the authority conferred upon me by the Constitution and statutes of the United States, in accordance with the aforementioned resolutions of the United States Congress and of the Organ of Consultation of the American Republics, and to defend the security of the United States, do hereby proclaim that the forces under my command are ordered, beginning at 2:00 p.m. Greenwich time October 24, 1962, to interdict, subject to the instructions herein contained, the delivery of offensive weapons and associated materiel to Cuba. For the purposes of this Proclamation, the following are declared to be prohibited materiel: Surface-to-surface missiles; bomber aircraft; bombs, air-to-surface rockets and guided missiles; warheads for any of the above weapons; mechanical or electronic equipment to support or operate the above items; and any other classes of materiel hereafter designated by the Secretary of Defense for the purpose of effectuating this Proclamation.

To enforce this order, the Secretary of Defense shall take appropriate measures to prevent the delivery of prohibited materiel to Cuba, employing the land, sea and air forces of the United States in cooperation with any forces that may be made available by other American States. The Secretary of Defense may make such regulations and issue such directives as he deems necessary to ensure the effectiveness of this order, including the designation, within a reasonable distance of Cuba, of prohibited or restricted zones and of prescribed routes.

In carrying out this order, force shall not be used except in case of failure or refusal to comply with directions, or with regulations or directives of the Secretary of Defense issued hereunder, after reasonable efforts have been made to communicate them to the vessel or craft, or in case of self-defense. In any case, force shall be used only to the extent necessary. [The Proclamation was signed by President Kennedy at 7:06 P.M., October 23, 1962.]

Meeker, Defensive Quarantine and the Law

57 A.J.I.L. 515, 523 (1963).*

Charter Limitation on the "Threat or Use of Force"

* * *

In considering the obligations imposed on Members by [] article [2, paragraph 4], it should be noted that not all threats or uses of force are prohibited; only those which are inconsistent with the purposes of the United Nations are covered by Article 2, paragraph 4. The presence of the word "other" in the concluding clause of the paragraph makes this clear. Even assuming that the measures taken could be considered to impinge upon the territorial integrity or political independence of some state or states, they would not be contrary to Article 2, paragraph 4, as long as they were not inconsistent with the purposes of the United Nations. The

* Reprinted with the permission of the American Society of International Law.

defensive quarantine, as indicated earlier, was considered to be in accordance with Chapter VIII of the Charter.

It is clear that collective action for peace and security which the Security Council may take under Chapter VII does not contravene Article 2, paragraph 4. It is also clear that individual or collective self-defense against armed attack, in accordance with Article 51, does not violate the Charter. Here it may be noted that the United States, in adopting the defensive quarantine of Cuba, did not seek to justify it as a measure required to meet an "armed attack" within the meaning of Article 51. Nor did the United States seek to sustain its action on the ground that Article 51 is not an all-inclusive statement of the right of self-defense and that the quarantine was a measure of self-defense open to any country to take individually for its own defense in a case other than "armed attack." Indeed, as shown by President Kennedy's television address of October 22 and by other statements of the Government, reliance was not placed on either contention, and the United States took no position on either of these issues.

The quarantine was based on a collective judgment and recommendation of the American Republics made under the Rio Treaty. It was considered not to contravene Article 2, paragraph 4, because it was a measure adopted by a regional organization in conformity with the provisions of Chapter 8 of the Charter. The purposes of the Organization and its activities were considered to be consistent with the purposes and principles of the United Nations as provided in Article 52. This being the case, the quarantine would no more violate Article 2, paragraph 4, than measures voted by the Council under Chapter 7, by the General Assembly under Articles 10 and 11, or taken by United Nations Members in conformity with Article 51.

Finally, in relation to the Charter limitation on threat or use of force, it should be noted that the quarantine itself was a carefully limited measure proportionate to the threat and designed solely to prevent any further build-up of strategic missile bases in Cuba.

* * *

Notes and Questions. Was the Cuban quarantine authorized by the Security Council? The author, Deputy Legal Adviser, Department of State, addressed the question of the conformity of the Cuban quarantine to Article 53(1) of the charter: "But no enforcement action shall be taken under regional arrangements or by regional agencies without the authorization of the Security Council * * *." The first two of his three arguments were: (1) Authorization need not be prior authorization and (2) it need not be express. "The Council did not see fit to take any action in derogation of the quarantine. Although a resolution condemning the quarantine was laid before the Council by the Soviet Union, the Council subsequently, by general consent, refrained from acting upon it and instead chose to promote the cause of a negotiated settlement, with the assistance of the Secretary General." 57 A.J.I.L. at 522. Argument (3) was that, in any event, the action was not enforcement action: "As understood by the United States, 'enforcement action' means obligatory action involving the use of armed force. Thus 'enforcement action,' as the phrase appears in Article 53(1), should not be taken to comprehend action of a regional organization which is only recommendatory to the members of the organization." Is this sound? Or did the coercion exerted by the quarantine on the Soviets and Cuba render it enforcement action? The deputy legal adviser found support for the United States' definition of enforcement action in the advisory opinion of the International Court of Justice in *Certain Expenses, supra.*

Chayes,[a] The Legal Case For U.S. Action on Cuba

47 United States Department of State Bulletin 763, 765 (1962).

Some have asked whether we should not first have gone to the Security Council before taking other action to meet the Soviet threat in Cuba. And I suppose that in the original conception of the United Nations, it was thought that the Security Council would be the agency for dealing with situations of this kind. However, the drafters of the charter demonstrated their wisdom by making Security Council responsibility for dealing with threats to the peace "primary" and not "exclusive." For events since 1945 have demonstrated that the Security Council, like our own electoral college, was not a viable institution. The veto has made it substantially useless in keeping the peace.

The withering away of the Security Council has led to a search for alternative peacekeeping institutions. In the United Nations itself the General Assembly and the Secretary–General have filled the void. Regional organizations are another obvious candidate.

* * *

2. REVOLT IN THE DOMINICAN REPUBLIC

The United States Government invaded the Dominican Republic after its April 24, 1965 revolt, and defended its invasion on the basis of self-defense, defense of an international organization, and humanitarian intervention. "We landed troops in the Dominican Republic in order to preserve the lives of foreign nationals—nationals of the United States and many other countries. We continued our military presence in the Dominican Republic for the additional purpose of preserving the capacity of the OAS to function in the manner intended by the OAS Charter—to achieve peace and justice through securing a cease-fire and through reestablishing orderly political processes within which Dominicans could choose their own government, free from outside interference.* * *" Meeker, *The Dominican Situation in the Perspective of International Law,* 53 Dept.St.Bull. 60 (1965).

Notes and Questions. Threat of a communist takeover? There is more than a slight suggestion in the statement of the basis for U.S. military action in the Dominican Republic that even unilateral use of force is lawful

a. Legal Adviser, Department of State, during the Cuban missile crisis.

in aid of the preservation of democratic values. Compare the statement of the International Court of Justice in the case of *Nicaragua v. U.S.* [1986] I.C.J.Rep. 14, 109:

> 207. * * * The United States authorities have on some occasions clearly stated their grounds for intervening in the affairs of a foreign State for reasons connected with, for example, the domestic policies of that country, its ideology, the level of its armaments, or the direction of its foreign policy. But these were statements of international policy, and not an assertion of rules of existing international law.
>
> * * *
>
> 209. The Court therefore finds that no such general right of intervention, in support of an opposition within another State, exists in contemporary international law. The Court concludes that acts constituting a breach of the customary principle of non-intervention will also, if they directly or indirectly involve the use of force, constitute a breach of the principle of non-use of force in international relations.

3.   DISINTEGRATION OF POLITICAL AUTHORITY IN GRENADA

Military forces from the United States, Barbados, and Jamaica landed in Grenada in October 1983. Kenneth W. Dam, Deputy Secretary of State Dam, explained that the invasion was necessary because of the civil strife and the collapse of government in Grenada, which included the murder of Maurice Bishop and the members of his cabinet in a violent struggle for power and attempted coup. "The disintegration of political authority * * * had created a dynamic that made further violence likely and that spread uncertainty and fear * * * " Secretary Dam explained that the invasion occurred as a response to a request for assistance by the Governor–General and by the OECS (the Organization of Eastern Caribbean States). The purpose of the invasion was to restore order and human rights and to secure and evacuate endangered U.S. nationals on the island. Secretary Dam explained that the legal authority for the invasion included the request for assistance by the Governor–General, articles 3, 4, and 8, of the OECS Charter (which concern local and external threats to peace and security), articles 22 and 28 of the OAS Charter and article 52 of the U.N. Charter, which "recognize[s] the competence of regional security bodies in insuring regional peace and stability." Dam, *Statement on Grenada,* 78 A.J.I.L. 200 (1984).

Notes and Questions. Test the regional arrangement justification against the United Nations Charter; and against the Cuban missile crisis precedent. Was the United States action in Grenada on firm legal ground as a regional arrangement? What about the other justifications?

Joyner, Reflection On the Lawfulness of Invasion

78 A.J.I.L. 131 (1984).*

* * *

* Reprinted with the permission of the American Society of Int'l Law.

An especially intriguing facet of the entire diplomatic episode—and a second espoused legal justification as well—is that the United States was invited by at least five members of the Organization of Eastern Caribbean States (OECS) to intervene militarily into Grenada. Created in 1981, the OECS contains within its charter a quasi-collective security provision. Article 8 provides in relevant part:

> The Defence and Security Committee shall have responsibility for coordinating the efforts of Member States for collective defence and the preservation of peace and security against external aggression and for the development of close ties among the Member States of the Organisation in matters of external defence and security, including measures to combat the activities of mercenaries, operating with or without the support of internal or national elements, in the exercise of the inherent right of individual or collective self-defence recognised by Article 51 of the Charter.

While "collective defence" as such is called for in the Treaty, nowhere is there stipulated the option to invite outside assistance against a member state. Further, it is difficult to fathom how a treaty among seven small states could legally promote an invasion by the United States against one of its own members at the behest of the others. To be sure, considerable doubt also exists about whether the invasion of Grenada is consistent with the original intent of the signers, or for that matter, those specified treaty provisions relating to "external defence" and "arrangements for collective security against external aggression."

Several reasons rebut the use of this Treaty to legitimize U.S. intervention in Grenada. First, the United States is not a party to the Treaty and therefore legally lies outside the ambit of its concerns. (Interestingly enough, neither are Barbados and Jamaica, which also participated in the invasion.) Second, Article 8 specifically deals with "collective defence and the preservation of peace and security against external aggression." No external aggressor existed: Grenada, the state in question, was a Treaty member. In addition, the OECS Treaty makes no mention of any collective security or defensive measures to be taken against a member of the organization, should such an occasion arise. There is, in short, no provision for military action in instances other than those involving "external aggression, including mercenary aggression," and such a case was absent in the October 1983 Grenada episode.

A third contention concerns the procedure used for decision making under the OECS provisions. Paragraph 5 stipulates that decisions and directives pertaining to defense and security must be consented to unanimously by the member states. This requirement obviously was not observed for the Grenada invasion. Reportedly, three of the OECS Treaty members—Grenada, St. Kitts–Nevis and Montserrat—did not vote. In any event, even if the other two had voted affirmatively, it remains difficult to imagine that Grenada would have voted in support of foreign military intervention into its domestic affairs.

Yet this very contention—that Grenada's own Government might have advocated or even sanctioned external intervention into its domestic affairs—was advanced by the United States Government as the basis for a third prominent legal justification of the Grenadan action. In testimony before the House Foreign Affairs Committee on November 2, 1983, Deputy Secretary of State Kenneth Dam revealed that the Governor–General of Grenada, Sir Paul Scoon, had confidentially transmitted "an appeal for action by the OECS and other regional states to restore order on the island." * * *

There is no question about the legality of an external intervention occasioned by an explicit invitation that has been genuinely proffered by the legitimate government of a state; that legality is well grounded in international law. However, one may question the precise legal character of the office of Governor–General and the concomitant legal authority that the Governor–General may appropriately exercise under Grenada's operative constitutional law. Put succinctly, was the Governor–General alone constitutionally empowered to invite in foreign military forces? The political, legal and constitutional realities of Grenada in October 1983 strongly suggest that he was not.

> * * *

4.   ECOWAS INTERVENTION IN LIBERIA

On December 24, 1989, Charles Taylor undertook a coup d'etat against Samuel Doe, the president of Liberia who had himself taken Liberia by force less than a decade earlier. Taylor quickly took control of all of Liberia except the capital city, Monrovia. The U.S. and the U.N. initially refused to intervene, characterizing the dispute as entirely internal and therefore not appropriate for external aid. The Economic Community of West African States (ECOWAS) sponsored negotiations early in the conflict but failed to achieve resolution through these negotiations. As a result, in August 1990 it formed a Cease–Fire Monitoring Group (ECOMOG) to intervene in the hostilities. This group was not initially sanctioned by the U.N., and thus arguably violated Article 53 of the U.N. Charter, but it ultimately won U.N. approval. ECOMOG entered Liberia in late 1990 and was immediately attacked by Taylor's forces. It responded by ordering its troops to use force to remove Taylor. Within weeks ECOMOG forcefully secured control of Monrovia. Shortly later, Samuel Doe was killed and ECOMOG established an interim government in Monrovia.

For the next six years, Taylor's forces fought for control of Liberia. During this time, other groups developed to vie for control, making even more difficult the attainment of a binding peace accord. Twelve different peace agreements were signed, one of which resulted in the cessation of hostilities for nearly two years, but none of which were effective. ECOMOG remained in Liberia and actively participated in the hostilities, and other countries, including the United States, committed forces to encourage resolution of the dispute. Finally, in August 1996, the warring factions signed a binding peace agreement that provided for disarmament by January, 1997 and joint control of Liberia pending elections within a year. When the elections were held the following July, Taylor obtained what ECOMOG had denied him for six years—control over Liberia. Taylor won the presidency with three-fourths of the popular vote, amidst assertions by voters such as, "He killed my ma, he killed my pa, I still vote for Taylor." Although there were suggestions that he bought or coerced the vote, many observers declared it to be a fair election. ECOMOG's intervention has been both criticized and applauded in legal commentaries, with some asserting that ECOWAS had improper motives and ultimately did nothing except prolong the fighting and bloodshed, and others arguing that regional organizations are the appropriate bodies for actions such as that undertaken in Liberia, and that the U.N. Charter should be amended to codify the right of regional intervention. *Compare* Development, *The Legality of ECOWAS Intervention in Liberia*, 32 Colum. J. Transnat'l L. 381 (1994) *with* Note, *The Theory and Practice of Regional Organization Intervention in Civil Wars*, 26 N.Y.U. J. Int'l L. & Pol. 797 (1994). *See also* Wippman, *Military Intervention, Regional Organizations, and Host–State Consent*, 7 Duke J. Comp. & Int'l L. 209 (1996).

5. WAR & PEACE—SIERRA LEONE

The war in Sierra Leone has been another horrific scene. Saunders, *Rich and Rare are the Gems they War: Holding de Beers Accountable for Trading Conflict Diamonds*, 24 Fordham Int'l L.J. 1402 (2001), *citing*, Coll, *The Other War: The Gratuitous Cruelties Against Civilians in Sierra Leone Last Year Rivaled Those Committed in Kosovo at the Same Time*, Wash. Post Mag., Jan. 9, 2000, at W8, W9 (explaining that RUF is insurgent army in Sierra Leone). The civil war in Sierra Leone began when the Revolutionary United Front ("RUF") rebelled against the government in 1991. *See* Hirsch, supra, at 31 (commenting that civil war has ensued for most of decade following rebellion in 1991); Conteh–Morgan & Dixon-Fyle, *Sierra Leone at the End of the Twentieth Century: History, Politics, and Society* 126–27 (1999) (noting that RUF attacked territory in Sierra Leone in 1991); Orr, *A Nation Sinks into Savagery: Racked by a Five–Year Civil War, Sierra Leone is Now the Scene of New, Barely Imaginable Outrages*, Independent (London), May 5, 1999, at 14 (asserting that RUF attacks began in 1991); Human Rights Watch, Sierra Leone: Getting Away with Murder, Mutilation, Rape: Background, July 1999, available at http://www.hrw.org/reports/1999/sierra/SIERLE99–02.htm#P142_28430 [hereinafter HRW-Sierra Leone: Background] (maintaining that RUF rebelled in 1991, attempting to overthrow Sierra Leone government).

SECTION C. COLLECTIVE SELF-DEFENSE

1. CZECHOSLOVAKIA: DEFENSE OF THE FORMER SOCIALIST COMMUNITY

Notes and Questions

1. ***The Reagan and Breznev Doctrines.*** The disintegration of the Soviet Union also saw the repudiation of the *Brezhnev Doctrine*. The first pronouncement of the *Brezhnev Doctrine,* the Soviet analogue to the *Reagan Doctrine,* was precipitated during the Soviet intervention in Czech-

oslovakia. President Reagan had said in 1985, "freedom movements arise and assert themselves. They're doing so on almost every continent populated by man—in the hills of Afghanistan, in Angola, in Kampuchea, now Cambodia, in Central America * * * They're our brothers, these freedom fighters, and we owe them our help." *See* Reisman, *Allocating Competences to Use Coercion in the Post–Cold War World: Practices, Conditions, and Prospects, in Law and Force in the New International Order* 26, 24, n. 13 (Damrosch & Scheffer, eds. 1991). Jean Kirkpatrick and Allan Gerson have noted that "[t]he Reagan Doctrine, as we understand it, is above all concerned with the moral legitimacy of U.S. support—including military support—for insurgencies under certain circumstances: where there are indigenous opponents to a government that is maintained by force, rather than popular consent; where such a government depends on arms supplied by the Soviet Union, the Soviet bloc, or other foreign sources; and where the people are denied a choice regarding their affiliations and future." Kirkpatrick & Gerson, *The Reagan Doctrine, Human Rights, and International Law,* in Right v. Might, *supra,* at 19, 20 (1991). *See also,* Halberstam, *The Copenhagen Document: Intervention in Support of Democracy,* 34 Harv.I.L.J. 163 (1993); Franck, *The Emerging Right of Democratic Governance,* 86 A.J.I.L. 46 (1992); Reisman, *Coercion and Self–Determination: Construing Charter Article 2(4),* 78 A.J.I.L. 642, 644–45 (1984); and Schachter, *The Legality of Pro–Democratic Invasion,* 78 A.J.I.L. 645 (1984).

The Brezhnev Doctrine, on the other hand, claimed the right to use force to protect any socialist regime. The legality of the Soviet invasion of Czechoslovakia is measured against the provisions of the Charter. Article 2(1) states as a principle: "The Organization is based on the principle of the sovereign equality of all its Members." Was that "Bourgeois Law?" Were Poland, Hungary, Czechoslovakia, Bulgaria, Rumania and the three former Soviet republic members of the U.N. a single unit, with one sovereignty? Did the former USSR purport to guarantee to every segment of that unit a socialist form of government? By what right? And, if so, how is that guarantee (if enforced by arms) consistent with the Charter? Alternatively, [d]oes the United States have the right to guarantee to each state in North America (Central America) (the Western Hemisphere) (the World) a non-communist form of government?

2.   THE CLAIM OF COLLECTIVE SELF-DEFENSE IN SOUTH VIETNAM

The Legality of United States Participation in the Defense of Vietnam, Memorandum Prepared by the Legal Adviser of the Department of State
54 United States Department of State Bulletin 474 (1966).

The United States and South Vietnam Have the Right Under International Law to Participate in the Collective Defense of South Vietnam Against Armed Attack.

In response to requests from the Government of South Vietnam, the United States has been assisting that country in defending itself against armed attack from the Communist North. This attack has taken the forms of externally supported subversion, clandestine supply of arms, infiltration of armed personnel, and most recently the sending of regular units of the North Vietnamese army into the South.

International law has long recognized the right of individual and collective self-defense against armed attack. South Vietnam and the United States are engaging in such collective defense consistently with international law and with United States obligations under the United Nations Charter.

A. South Vietnam Is Being Subjected to Armed Attack by Communist
     North Vietnam

The Geneva accords of 1954 established a demarcation line between North Vietnam and South Vietnam. They provided for withdrawals of military forces into the respective zones north and south of this line. The accords prohibited the use of either zone for the resumption of hostilities or to "further an aggressive policy." During the 5 years following the Geneva conference of 1954, the Hanoi regime developed a covert political-military organization in South Vietnam based on Communist cadres it had ordered to stay in the South, contrary to the provisions of the Geneva accords. The activities of this covert organization were directed toward the kidnapping and assassination of civilian officials—acts of terrorism that were perpetrated in increasing numbers. In the 3–year period from 1959 to 1961, the North Vietnam regime infiltrated an estimated 10,000 men into the South. It is estimated that 13,000 additional personnel were infiltrated in 1962, and, by the end of 1964, North Vietnam may well have moved over 40,000 armed and unarmed guerrillas into South Vietnam.

The International Control Commission reported in 1962 the findings of its Legal Committee:

> * * * [T]here is evidence to show that arms, armed and unarmed personnel, munitions and other supplies have been sent from the Zone in the North to the Zone in the South with the objective of supporting, organizing and carrying out hostile activities, including armed attacks, directed against the Armed Forces and Administration of the Zone in the South.

> * * * [T]here is evidence that the PAVN [People's Army of Viet Nam] has allowed the Zone in the North to be used for inciting, encouraging and supporting hostile activities in the Zone in the South, aimed at the overthrow of the Administration in the South.

Beginning in 1964, the Communists apparently exhausted their reservoir of Southerners who had gone North. Since then the greater number of men infiltrated into the South have been native-born North Vietnamese. Most recently, Hanoi has begun to infiltrate elements of the North Vietnamese army in increasingly larger numbers. Today, there is evidence that nine regiments of regular North Vietnamese forces are fighting in organized units in the South.

In the guerrilla war in Vietnam, the external aggression from the North is the critical military element of the insurgency, although it is unacknowledged by North Vietnam. In these circumstances, an "armed attack'' is not as easily fixed by date and hour as in the case of traditional warfare. However, the infiltration of thousands of armed men clearly constitutes an "armed attack" under any reasonable definition. There may be some question as to the exact date at which North Vietnam's aggression grew into an "armed attack," but there can be no doubt that it had occurred before February 1965.

B.   International Law Recognizes the Right of Individual and Collective Self–Defense Against Armed Attack

International law has traditionally recognized the right of self-defense against armed attack. This proposition has been asserted by writers on international law through the several centuries in which the modern law of nations has developed. The proposition has been acted on numerous times by governments throughout modern history. Today the principle of self-defense against armed attack is universally recognized and accepted.

The Charter of the United Nations, concluded at the end of World War II, imposed an important limitation on the use of force by United Nations members. Article 2, paragraph 4, provides: All Members shall refrain in their international relations from the threat or use of force against the territorial integrity or political independence of any state, or in any other manner inconsistent with the Purposes of the United Nations. In addition, the charter embodied a system of international peacekeeping through the organs of the United Nations. Article 24 summarizes these structural arrangements in stating that the United Nations members: * * * confer on the Security Council primary responsibility for the maintenance of international peace and security, and agree that in carrying out its duties under this responsibility the Security Council acts on their behalf.

However, the charter expressly states in article 51 that the remaining provisions of the charter—including the limitation of article 2, paragraph 4 and the creation of United Nations machinery to keep the peace—in no way diminish the inherent right of self-defense against armed attack. Article 51 provides:

> Nothing in the present Charter shall impair the inherent right of individual or collective self-defense if an armed attack occurs against a Member of the United Nations, until the Security Council has taken the measures necessary to maintain international peace and security. Measures taken by Members in the exercise of this right of self-defense shall be immediately reported to the Security Council and shall not in any way affect the authority and responsibility of the Security Council under the present Charter to take at any time such action as it deems necessary in order to maintain or restore international peace and security.

Thus, article 51 restates and preserves, for member states in the situations covered by the article, a long-recognized principle of international law. The article is a "saving clause" designed to make clear that no other provision in the charter shall be interpreted to impair the inherent right of self-defense referred to in article 51.

Three principal objections have been raised against the availability of the right of individual and collective self-defense in the case of Vietnam: (1) that this right applies only in the case of an armed attack on a United Nations member; (2) that it does not apply in the case of South Vietnam because the latter is not an independent sovereign state; and (3) that collective self-defense may be undertaken only by a regional organization operating under chapter 8 of the United Nations Charter.

* * *

H. Summary

The analysis set forth above shows that South Vietnam has the right in present circumstances to defend itself against armed attack from the North and to organize a collective self-defense with the participation of others. In response to requests from South Vietnam, the United States has been participating in that defense, both through military action within South Vietnam and actions taken directly against the aggressor in North Vietnam. This participation by the United States is in conformity with international law and is consistent with our obligations under the Charter of the United Nations.

* * *

Wright, Legal Aspects of the Vietnam Situation

60 A.J.I.L. 750, 755 (1966).*

The legal issues, clarification of which might contribute to a judgment of the validity of the diverse images of the Vietnam situation, may be stated as follows:

1. Are the hostilities between North and South Vietnam international hostilities or civil strife, i.e., is Vietnam two states or one?

2. Was the requirement for an election in 1956 dependent on the development of conditions assuring that the election would be free and fair?

3. Was the requirement concerning elections in the resolutions of the Geneva Conference such an integral part of the Cease–Fire Agreement between France and the Democratic Republic of Vietnam (Ho Chi Minh) as to permit suspension of the cease-fire when the elections were frustrated?

4. If it is assumed that the cease-fire line continued in operation, was North Vietnam guilty of "armed attacks" upon South Vietnam justifying the United States bombing attacks north of the cease-fire line, which began in February, 1965, as measures of "collective self-defense"?

* * *

1. The evidence suggests that Vietnam is one state and that the hostilities of Ho Chi Minh's government against the Saigon Government would be civil strife within its domestic jurisdiction unless forbidden by the cease-fire Agreement. During the hostilities between the "Democratic Republic of Vietnam" under Ho Chi Minh and France, supporting the "Re-

* Reprinted with the permission of the American Society of International Law.

public of Vietnam'' under Bao Dai from 1946 to 1954 and during the Geneva Conference, both sides regarded Vietnam as one state, the legal issue being whether it was an independent state or a "Free State" within the French Community. When the hostilities ended with French defeat, large areas of the south were occupied by Ho Chi Minh's forces, the Viet–Minh, and areas in the north by forces of France and Bao Dai. The Cease–Fire Agreement of 1954 signed by representatives of France and the Democratic Republic of Vietnam provided for the withdrawal of these forces across the cease-fire line, substantially the 17th parallel, and very explicitly declared that this line was not an international boundary but a "provisional military demarcation line" and that the territories at each side were not states but "zones." The final resolutions of the Conference declared that "the independence, unity and territorial integrity" of Vietnam should be respected, and provided that elections "shall" be held in July, 1956, to determine the government of Vietnam. These resolutions did not constitute a formal treaty and were not signed by any of the delegates. They were, however, accepted by all of the delegates except those of the United States and Bao Dai's Republic of Vietnam, both of whom made statements "noted" by the Conference. In regard to the reservation by Bao Dai's representative, the Chairman at the final session of the Conference, Anthony Eden, said: We can not now amend our final act, which is the statement of the Conference as a whole, but the Declaration of the Representative of the State of Vietnam will be taken note of. It seems clear that the Conference recognized Vietnam as one state and provided that it should be united by one government in 1956.

* * *

Notes and Questions. Article 51 of the U.N. Charter contemplates that a state can use force in individual or collective self-defense only until action is taken by the Security Council. The design of the charter apparently envisioned only temporary self-defense measures. But fighting in Vietnam continued for many years. Why did the Security Council not take action in this case?

3. THE CLAIM OF COLLECTIVE SELF-DEFENSE IN NICARAGUA

Case Concerning Military and Paramilitary Activities In and Against Nicaragua (Nicaragua v. United States of America)[a]

International Court of Justice, 1986.
[1986] I.C.J. Reports 14.

18. The dispute before the Court between Nicaragua and the United States concerns events in Nicaragua subsequent to the fall of the Govern-

---

a. The editors have made a substantial number of omissions in this very long opin-ion. The reader can keep track of the omis-sions by referring to the paragraph numbers.

ment of President Anastasio Somoza Debayle in Nicaragua in July 1979, and activities of the Government of the United States in relation to Nicaragua since that time. Following the departure of President Somoza, a Junta of National Reconstruction and government installed by the body which had led the armed opposition to President Somoza, the Frente Sandinista de Liberación Nacional (FSLN). That body had initially an extensive share in the new government, described as a "democratic coalition", and as a result of later resignations and reshuffles, became almost its sole component. Certain opponents of the new Government, primarily supporters of the former Somoza Government and in particular ex-members of the National Guard, formed themselves into irregular military forces, and commenced a policy of armed opposition, though initially on a limited scale.

19. The attitude of the United States Government to the "democratic coalition government" was at first favourable; and a programme of economic aid to Nicaragua was adopted. However by 1981 this attitude had changed. United States aid to Nicaragua was suspended in January 1981 and terminated in April 1981. According to the United States, the reason for this change of attitude was reports of involvement of the Government of Nicaragua in logistical support, including provision of arms, for guerrillas in El Salvador. There was however no interruption in diplomatic relations, which have continued to be maintained up to the present time. In September 1981, according to testimony called by Nicaragua, it was decided to plan and undertake activities directed against Nicaragua.

20. The armed opposition to the new Government in Nicaragua, which originally comprised various movements, subsequently became organized into two main groups: the Fuerza Democrática Nicaragüense (FDN) and the Alianza Revolucionaria Democrática (ARDE). The first of these grew from 1981 onwards into a trained fighting force, operating along the borders with Honduras; the second, formed in 1982, operated along the borders with Costa Rica. * * * [A]fter an initial period in which the "covert" operations of United States personnel and persons in their pay were kept from becoming public knowledge, it was made clear, not only in the United States press, but also in Congress and in official statements by the President and high United States officials, that the United States Government had been giving support to the contras, a term employed to describe those fighting against the present Nicaraguan Government. In 1983 budgetary legislation enacted by the United States Congress made specific provision for funds to be used by United States intelligence agencies for supporting "directly or indirectly, military or paramilitary operations in Nicaragua". According to Nicaragua, the contras have caused it considerable material damage and widespread loss of life, and have also committed such acts as killing of prisoners, indiscriminate killing of civilians, torture, rape and kidnapping. It is contended by Nicaragua that the United States Government is effectively in control of the contras, that it devised their strategy and directed their tactics, and that the purpose of that Government was, from the beginning, to overthrow the Government of Nicaragua.

21.   Nicaragua claims furthermore that certain military or paramilitary operations against it were carried out, not by the contras, who at the time claimed responsibility, but by persons in the pay of the United States Government, and under the direct command of United States personnel, who also participated to some extent in the operations. These operations will also be more closely examined below in order to determine their legal significance and the responsibility for them; they include the mining of certain Nicaraguan ports in early 1984, and attacks on ports, oil installations, a naval base, etc. Nicaragua has also complained of overflights of its territory by United States aircraft, not only for purposes of intelligence-gathering and supply to the contras in the field, but also in order to intimidate the population.

23.   As a matter of law, Nicaragua claims, inter alia, that the United States has acted in violation of Article 2, paragraph 4, of the United Nations Charter, and of a customary international law obligation to refrain from the threat or use of force; that its actions amount to intervention in the internal affairs of Nicaragua, in breach of the Charter of the Organization of American States and of rules of customary international law forbidding intervention; and that the United States has acted in violation of the sovereignty of Nicaragua, and in violation of a number of other obligations established in general customary international law and in the inter-American system. The actions of the United States are also claimed by Nicaragua to be such as to defeat the object and purpose of a Treaty of Friendship, Commerce and Navigation concluded between the Parties in 1956, and to be in breach of provisions of that Treaty.

24.   The United States has not filed any pleading on the merits of the case, and was not represented at the hearings devoted thereto. It did however make clear in its Counter–Memorial on the questions of jurisdiction and admissibility that "by providing, upon request, proportionate and appropriate assistance to third States not before the Court" it claims to be acting in reliance on the inherent right of self-defence "guaranteed" * * * by Article 51, that is to say the right of collective self-defence.

81.   The operations which Nicaragua attributes to the direct action of United States personnel or "UCLAs", in addition to the mining of ports, are apparently the following:

(i) 8 September 1983: an attack was made on Sandino international airport in Managua by a Cessna aircraft, which was shot down;

(ii) 13 September 1983: an underwater oil pipeline and part of the oil terminal at Puerto Sandino were blown up;

(iii) 2 October 1983: an attack was made on oil storage facilities at Benjamin Zeledon on the Atlantic coast, causing the loss of a large quantity of fuel;

(iv) 10 October 1983: an attack was made by air and sea on the port of Corinto, involving the destruction of five oil storage tanks, the loss of millions of gallons of fuel, and the evacuation of large numbers of the local population;

(v) 14 October 1983: the underwater oil pipeline at Puerto Sandino was again blown up;

(vi) 4/5 January 1984: an attack was made by speedboats and helicopters using rockets against the Potosi Naval Base;

(vii) 24/25 February 1984: an incident at El Bluff listed under this date appears to be the mine explosion already mentioned in paragraph 76;

(viii) 7 March 1984: an attack was made on oil and storage facility at San Juan del Sur by speedboats and helicopters;

(ix) 28/30 March 1984: clashes occurred at Puerto Sandino between speedboats, in the course of minelaying operations, and Nicaraguan patrol boats; intervention by a helicopter in support of the speedboats;

(x) 9 April 1984: a helicopter allegedly launched from a mother ship in international waters provided fire support for an ARDE attack on San Juan del Norte.

85.   The Court considers that it should eliminate from further consideration under this heading the following items:

— the attack of 8 September 1983 on Managua airport (item (i)): this was claimed by the ARDE; a press report is to the effect that the ARDE purchased the aircraft from the CIA, but there is no evidence of CIA planning, or the involvement of any United States personnel or UCLAs;

— the attack on Benjamin Zeledon on 2 October 1983 (item (iii)): there is no evidence of the involvement of United States personnel or UCLAs;

— the incident of 24–25 February 1984 (item (vii)), already dealt with under the heading of the mining of ports.

86.   On the other hand the Court finds the remaining incidents listed in paragraph 81 to be established. The general pattern followed by these attacks appears to the Court, on the basis of that evidence and of press reports quoting United States administration sources, to have been as follows. A "mother ship" was supplied (apparently leased) by the CIA; whether it was of United States registry does not appear. Speedboats, guns and ammunition were supplied by the United States administration, and the actual attacks were carried out by "UCLAs". Helicopters piloted by Nicaraguans and others piloted by United States nationals were also involved on some occasions. According to one report the pilots were United States civilians under contract to the CIA. Although it is not proved that any United States military personnel took a direct part in the operations, agents of the United States participated in the planning, direction, support and execution of the operations. The execution was the task rather of the "UCLAs", while United States nationals participated in the planning, direction and support. The imputability to the United States of these attacks appears therefore to the Court to be established.

* * *

107.   To sum up, despite the secrecy which surrounded it, at least initially, the financial support given by the Government of the United States to the military and paramilitary activities of the contras in Nicaragua is a fully established fact. The legislative and executive bodies of the respondent State have moreover, subsequent to the controversy which has

been sparked off in the United States, openly admitted the nature, volume and frequency of this support. Indeed, they clearly take responsibility for it, this government aid having now become the major element of United States foreign policy in the region. As to the ways in which such financial support has been translated into practical assistance, the Court has been able to reach a general finding.

109.   What the Court has to determine at this point is whether or not the relationship of the contras to the United States Government was so much one of dependence on the one side and control on the other that it would be right to equate the contras, for legal purposes, with an organ of the United States Government, or as acting on behalf of that Government. Here it is relevant to note that in May 1983 the assessment of the Intelligence Committee, in the Report referred to in paragraph 95 above, was that the contras "constitute[d] an independent force" and that the "only element of control that could be exercised by the United States" was "cessation of aid". Paradoxically this assessment serves to underline, a contrario, the potential for control inherent in the degree of the contras' dependence on aid. Yet despite the heavy subsidies and other support provided to them by the United States, there is no clear evidence of the United States having actually exercised such a degree of control in all fields as to justify treating the contras as acting on its behalf.

114.   In this respect, the Court notes that according to Nicaragua, the contras are no more than bands of mercenaries which have been recruited, organized, paid and commanded by the Government of the United States. This would mean that they have no real autonomy in relation to that Government. Consequently, any offences which they have committed would be imputable to the Government of the United States, like those of any other forces placed under the latter's command. In the view of Nicaragua, "stricto sensu, the military and paramilitary attacks launched by the United States against Nicaragua do not constitute a case of civil strife. They are essentially the acts of the United States." If such a finding of the imputability of the acts of the contras to the United States were to be made, no question would arise of mere complicity in those acts, or of incitement of the contras to commit them.

115.   The Court has taken the view * * * that United States participation, even if preponderant or decisive, in the financing, organizing, training, supplying and equipping of the contras, the selection of its military or paramilitary targets, and the planning of the whole of its operation, is still insufficient in itself, on the basis of the evidence in the possession of the Court, for the purpose of attributing to the United States the acts committed by the contras in the course of their military or paramilitary operations in Nicaragua. All the forms of United States participation mentioned above, and even the general control by the respondent State over a force with a high degree of dependency on it, would not in themselves mean, without further evidence, that the United States directed or enforced the perpetration of the acts contrary to human rights and humanitarian law alleged by the applicant State. Such acts could well be committed by members of the contras without the control of the United States. For this conduct to give rise to legal responsibility of the United

States, it would in principle have to be proved that that State had effective control of the military or paramilitary operations in the course of which the alleged violations were committed.

116. The Court does not consider that the assistance given by the United States to the contras warrants the conclusion that these forces are subject to the United States to such an extent that any acts they have committed are imputable to that State. It takes the view that the contras remain responsible for their acts, and that the United States is not responsible for the acts of the contras, but for its own conduct vis-à-vis Nicaragua, including conduct related to the acts of the contras. What the Court has to investigate is not the complaints relating to alleged violations of humanitarian law by the contras, regarded by Nicaragua as imputable to the United States, but rather unlawful acts for which the United States may be responsible directly in connection with the activities of the contras. The lawfulness or otherwise of such acts of the United States is a question different from the violations of humanitarian law of which the contras may or may not have been guilty. It is for this reason that the Court does not have to determine whether the violations of humanitarian law attributed to the contras were in fact committed by them. At the same time, the question whether the United States Government was, or must have been, aware at the relevant time that allegations of breaches of humanitarian law were being made against the contras is relevant to an assessment of the lawfulness of the action of the United States. In this respect, the material facts are primarily those connected with the issue in 1983 of a manual of psychological operations.

122. The Court concludes that in 1983 an agency of the United States Government supplied to the FDN a manual on psychological guerrilla warfare which, while expressly discouraging indiscriminate violence against civilians, considered the possible necessity of shooting civilians who were attempting to leave a town; and advised the "neutralization" for propaganda purposes of local judges, officials or notables after the semblance of trial in the presence of the population. The text supplied to the contras also advised the use of professional criminals to perform unspecified "jobs", and the use of provocation at mass demonstrations to produce violence on the part of the authorities so as to make "martyrs".

126. The Court has before it, in the Counter–Memorial on jurisdiction and admissibility filed by the United States, the assertion that the United States, pursuant to the inherent right of individual and collective self-defence, and in accordance with the Inter–American Treaty of Reciprocal Assistance, has responded to requests from El Salvador, Honduras and Costa Rica, for assistance in their self-defence against aggression by Nicaragua. The Court has therefore to ascertain, so far as possible, the facts on which this claim is or may be based, in order to determine whether collective self-defence constitutes a justification of the activities of the United States here complained of. * * *

127. Nicaragua claims that the references made by the United States to the justification of collective self-defence are merely "pretexts" for the activities of the United States. It has alleged that the true motive for the conduct of the United States is unrelated to the support which it accuses

Nicaragua of giving to the armed opposition in El Salvador, and that the real objectives of United States policy are to impose its will upon Nicaragua and force it to comply with United States demands. In the Court's view, however, if Nicaragua has been giving support to the armed opposition in El Salvador, and if this constitutes an armed attack on El Salvador and the other appropriate conditions are met, collective self-defence could be legally invoked by the United States, even though there may be the possibility of an additional motive, one perhaps even more decisive for the United States, drawn from the political orientation of the present Nicaraguan Government. The existence of an additional motive, other than that officially proclaimed by the United States, could not deprive the latter of its right to resort to collective self-defence. The conclusion to be drawn is that special caution is called for in considering the allegations of the United States concerning conduct by Nicaragua which may provide a sufficient basis for self-defence.

152.   The Court finds, in short, that support for the armed opposition in El Salvador from Nicaraguan territory was a fact up to the early months of 1981. While the Court does not possess full proof that there was aid, or as to its exact nature, its scale and its continuance until the early months of 1981, it cannot overlook a number of concordant indications, many of which were provided moreover by Nicaragua itself, from which it can reasonably infer the provision of a certain amount of aid from Nicaraguan territory. * * *

153.   After the early months of 1981, evidence of military aid from or through Nicaragua remains very weak. This is so despite the deployment by the United States in the region of extensive technical resources for tracking, monitoring and intercepting air, sea and land traffic, described in evidence by Mr. MacMichael and its use of a range of intelligence and information sources in a political context where, the Government had declared and recognized surveillance of Nicaragua as a "high priority". The Court cannot conclude from this that no transborder traffic in arms existed, although it does not seem particularly unreasonable to believe that traffic of this kind, had it been persistent and on a significant scale, must inevitably have been discovered, in view of the magnitude of the resources used for that purpose. The Court merely takes note that the allegations of arms-trafficking are not solidly established; it has not been able to satisfy itself that any continuing flow on a significant scale took place after the early months of 1981.

160.   On the basis of the foregoing, the Court is satisfied that, between July 1979, the date of the fall of the Somoza régime in Nicaragua, and the early months of 1981, an intermittent flow of arms was routed via the territory of Nicaragua to the armed opposition in El Salvador. On the other hand, the evidence is insufficient to satisfy the Court that, since the early months of 1981, assistance has continued to reach the Salvadorian armed opposition from the territory of Nicaragua on any significant scale, or that the Government of Nicaragua was responsible for any flow of arms at either period.

164.   The Court, while not as fully informed on the question as it would wish to be, therefore considers as established the fact that certain

transborder military incursions into the territory of Honduras and Costa Rica are imputable to the Government of Nicaragua. The Court is also aware that the FDN operates along the Nicaraguan border with Honduras, and the ARDE operates along the border with Costa Rica.

172. The Court has now to turn its attention to the question of the law applicable to the present dispute. In formulating its view on the significance of the United States multilateral treaty reservation, the Court has reached the conclusion that it must refrain from applying the multilateral treaties invoked by Nicaragua in support of its claims, without prejudice either to other treaties or to the other sources of law enumerated in Article 38 of the Statute. The first stage in its determination of the law actually to be applied to this dispute is to ascertain the consequences of the exclusion of the applicability of the multilateral treaties for the definition of the content of the customary international law which remains applicable.

[The U.S. had pleaded that its reservation to the compulsory jurisdiction of the court precluded application of multilateral treaties, such as the U.N. Charter, unless all parties to the treaties affected by the decision were parties to the case. Accepting that defense, the court nevertheless held that the United States' actions could be judged under customary international law.]

179. It will therefore be clear that customary international law continues to exist and to apply, separately from international treaty law, even where the two categories of law have an identical content. Consequently, in ascertaining the content of the customary international law applicable to the present dispute, the Court must satisfy itself that the Parties are bound by the customary rules in question; but the Court is in no way bound to uphold these rules only in so far as they differ from the treaty rules which it is prevented by the United States reservation from applying in the present dispute.

180. The United States however presented a further argument, during the proceedings devoted to the question of jurisdiction and admissibility, in support of its contention that the multilateral treaty reservation debars the Court from considering the Nicaraguan claims based on customary international law. The United States observed that the multilateral treaties in question contain legal standards specifically agreed between the Parties to govern their mutual rights and obligations, and that the conduct of the Parties will continue to be governed by these treaties, irrespective of what the Court may decide on the customary law issue, because of the principle of pacta sunt servanda. Accordingly, in the contention of the United States, the Court cannot properly adjudicate the mutual rights and obligations of the two States when reference to their treaty rights and obligations is barred; the Court would be adjudicating those rights and obligations by standards other than those to which the Parties have agreed to conduct themselves in their actual international relations.

181. The question raised by this argument is whether the provisions of the multilateral treaties in question, particularly the United Nations Charter, diverge from the relevant rules of customary international law to such an extent that a judgment of the Court as to the rights and obligations of the parties under customary law, disregarding the content of the

multilateral treaties binding on the parties, would be a wholly academic exercise, and not "susceptible of any compliance or execution whatever." The Court does not consider that this is the case. On the question of the use of force, the United States itself argues for a complete identity of the relevant rules of customary international law with the provisions of the Charter. The Court has not accepted this extreme contention, having found that on a number of points the areas governed by the two sources of law do not exactly overlap, and the substantive rules in which they are framed are not identical in content * * *. However, so far from having constituted a marked departure from a customary international law which still exists unmodified, the Charter gave expression in this field to principles already present in customary international law, and that law has in the subsequent four decades developed under the influence of the Charter, to such an extent that a number of rules contained in the Charter have acquired a status independent of it. The essential consideration is that both the Charter and the customary international law flow from a common fundamental principle outlawing the use of force in international relations. * * *

193.   The general rule prohibiting force allows for certain exceptions. In view of the arguments advanced by the United States to justify the acts of which it is accused by Nicaragua, the Court must express a view on the content of the right of self-defence, and more particularly the right of collective self-defence. First, with regard to the existence of this right, it notes that in the language of Article 51 of the United Nations Charter, the inherent right (or "droit naturel") which any State possesses in the event of an armed attack, covers both collective and individual self-defence. Thus, the Charter itself testifies to the existence of the right of collective self-defence in customary international law. Moreover, just as the wording of certain General Assembly declarations adopted by States demonstrates their recognition of the principle of the prohibition of force as definitely a matter of customary international law, some of the wording in those declarations operates similarly in respect of the right of self-defence (both collective and individual). Thus, in the declaration * * * on the Principles of International Law concerning Friendly Relations and Cooperation among States in accordance with the Charter of the United Nations, the reference to the prohibition of force is followed by a paragraph stating that: "nothing in the foregoing paragraphs shall be construed as enlarging or diminishing in any way the scope of the provisions of the Charter concerning cases in which the use of force is lawful". This resolution demonstrates that the States represented in the General Assembly regard the exception to the prohibition of force constituted by the right of individual or collective self-defence as already a matter of customary international law.

194.   With regard to the characteristics governing the right of self-defence, since the Parties consider the existence of this right to be established as a matter of customary international law, they have concentrated on the conditions governing its use. In view of the circumstances in which the dispute has arisen, reliance is placed by the Parties only on the right of self-defence in the case of an armed attack which has already occurred, and the issue of the lawfulness of a response to the imminent threat of armed attack has not been raised. Accordingly the Court expresses no view on that issue. The Parties also agree in holding that whether the response to the

attack is lawful depends on observance of the criteria of the necessity and the proportionality of the measures taken in self-defence. Since the existence of the right of collective self-defence is established in customary international law, the Court must define the specific conditions which may have to be met for its exercise, in addition to the conditions of necessity and proportionality to which the Parties have referred.

195. In the case of individual self-defence, the exercise of this right is subject to the State concerned having been the victim of an armed attack. Reliance on collective self-defence of course does not remove the need for this. There appears now to be general agreement on the nature of the acts which can be treated as constituting armed attacks. In particular, it may be considered to be agreed that an armed attack must be understood as including not merely action by regular armed forces across an international border, but also "the sending by or on behalf of a State of armed bands, groups, irregulars or mercenaries, which carry out acts of armed force against another State of such gravity as to amount to" (inter alia) an actual armed attack conducted by regular forces, "or its substantial involvement therein". This description, contained in Article 3, paragraph (g), of the Definition of Aggression annexed to G.A. resolution 3314(29), may be taken to reflect customary international law. The Court sees no reason to deny that, in customary law, the prohibition of armed attacks may apply to the sending by a State of armed bands to the territory of another State, if such an operation, because of its scale and effects, would have been classified as an armed attack rather than as a mere frontier incident had it been carried out by regular armed forces. But the Court does not believe that the concept of "armed attack" includes not only acts by armed bands where such acts occur on a significant scale but also assistance to rebels in the form of the provision of weapons or logistical or other support. Such assistance may be regarded as a threat or use of force, or amount to intervention in the internal or external affairs of other States. It is also clear that it is the State which is the victim of an armed attack which must form and declare the view that it has been so attacked. There is no rule in customary international law permitting another State to exercise the right of collective self-defence on the basis of its own assessment of the situation. Where collective self-defence is invoked, it is to be expected that the State for whose benefit this right is used will have declared itself to be the victim of an armed attack.

199. At all events, the Court finds that in customary international law, whether of a general kind or that particular to the inter-American legal system, there is no rule permitting the exercise of collective self-defence in the absence of a request by the State which regards itself as the victim of an armed attack. The Court concludes that the requirement of a request by the State which is the victim of the alleged attack is additional to the requirement that such a State should have declared itself to have been attacked.

200. At this point, the Court may consider whether in customary international law there is any requirement corresponding to that found in the treaty law of the United Nations Charter, by which the State claiming to use the right of individual or collective self-defence must report to an

international body, empowered to determine the conformity with international law of the measures which the State is seeking to justify on that basis. Thus Article 51 of the United Nations Charter requires that measures taken by States in exercise of this right of self-defence must be "immediately reported" to the Security Council. * * * [A] principle enshrined in a treaty, if reflected in customary international law, may well be so unencumbered with the conditions and modalities surrounding it in the treaty. Whatever influence the Charter may have had on customary international law in these matters, it is clear that in customary international law it is not a condition of the lawfulness of the use of force in self-defence that a procedure so closely dependent on the content of a treaty commitment and of the institutions established by it, should have been followed. On the other hand, if self-defence is advanced as a justification for measures which would otherwise be in breach both of the principle of customary international law and of that contained in the Charter, it is to be expected that the conditions of the Charter should be respected. Thus for the purpose of enquiry into the customary law position, the absence of a report may be one of the factors indicating whether the State in question was itself convinced that it was acting in self-defence.

201. To justify certain activities involving the use of force, the United States has relied solely on the exercise of its right of collective self-defence. However the Court, having regard particularly to the non-participation of the United States in the merits phase, considers that it should enquire whether customary international law, applicable to the present dispute, may contain other rules which may exclude the unlawfulness of such activities. It does not, however, see any need to reopen the question of the conditions governing the exercise of the right of individual self-defence, which have already been examined in connection with collective self-defence. On the other hand, the Court must enquire whether there is any justification for the activities in question, to be found not in the right of collective self-defence against an armed attack, but in the right to take counter-measures in response to conduct of Nicaragua which is not alleged to constitute an armed attack. It will examine this point in connection with an analysis of the principle of non-intervention in customary international law.

210. When dealing with the rule of the prohibition of the use of force, the Court considered the exception to it constituted by the exercise of the right of collective self-defence in the event of armed attack. Similarly, it must now consider the following question: if one State acts towards another State in breach of the principle of non-intervention, may a third State lawfully take such action by way of counter-measures against the first State as would otherwise constitute an intervention in its internal affairs? A right to act in this way in the case of intervention would be analogous to the right of collective self-defence in the case of an armed attack, but both the act which gives rise to the reaction, and that reaction itself, would in principle be less grave. Since the Court is here dealing with a dispute in which a wrongful use of force is alleged, it has primarily to consider whether a State has a right to respond to intervention with intervention going so far as to justify a use of force in reaction to measures which do not constitute an armed attack but may nevertheless involve a use of force. The

question is itself undeniably relevant from the theoretical viewpoint. However, since the Court is bound to confine its decision to those points of law which are essential to the settlement of the dispute before it, it is not for the Court here to determine what direct reactions are lawfully open to a State which considers itself the victim of another State's acts of intervention, possibly involving the use of force. Hence it has not to determine whether, in the event of Nicaragua's having committed any such acts against El Salvador, the latter was lawfully entitled to take any particular counter-measure. It might however be suggested that, in such a situation, the United States might have been permitted to intervene in Nicaragua in the exercise of some right analogous to the right of collective self-defence, one which might be resorted to in a case of intervention short of armed attack.

211.   The Court has recalled above that for one State to use force against another, on the ground that that State has committed a wrongful act of force against a third State, is regarded as lawful, by way of exception, only when the wrongful act provoking the response was an armed attack. Thus the lawfulness of the use of force by a State in response to a wrongful act of which it has not itself been the victim is not admitted when this wrongful act is not an armed attack. In the view of the Court, under international law in force today—whether customary international law or that of the United Nations system—States do not have a right of "collective" armed response to acts which do not constitute an "armed attack". Furthermore, the Court has to recall that the United States itself is relying on the "inherent right of self-defence," but apparently does not claim that any such right exists as would, in respect of intervention, operate in the same way as the right of collective self-defence in respect of an armed attack. In the discharge of its duty under Article 53 of the Statute, the Court has nevertheless had to consider whether such a right might exist; but in doing so it may take note of the absence of any such claim by the United States as an indication of opinio juris.

213.   The duty of every State to respect the territorial sovereignty of others is to be considered for the appraisal to be made of the facts relating to the mining which occurred along Nicaragua's coasts. The legal rules in the light of which these acts of mining should be judged depend upon where they took place. The laying of mines within the ports of another State is governed by the law relating to internal waters, which are subject to the sovereignty of the coastal State. The position is similar as regards mines placed in the territorial sea. It is the sovereignty of the coastal State which is affected in such cases. It is also by virtue of its sovereignty that the coastal State may regulate access to its ports.

[The court found (paragraphs 227 and 228) that the United States had violated the prohibition against the use of force by mining Nicaraguan waters, attacking Nicaraguan ports, air installations and naval base, and arming and training the contras. It found further that those acts were not justified as collective self-defense (paragraphs 229–238). Nicaragua's arms supplies to El Salvador did not amount to armed attack; the court found it "difficult to decide" whether Nicaraguan border incursions into Honduras and Costa Rica amounted to armed attack. And, at no relevant time had El

Salvador, Honduras or Costa Rica requested U.S. aid in collective self-defense.]

292.   For these reasons, THE COURT,* * *

(2) By twelve votes to three, Rejects the justification of collective self-defence maintained by the United States in connection with the military and paramilitary activities in and against Nicaragua the subject of this case;

(3) By twelve votes to three, Decides that the United States, by training, arming, equipping, financing and supplying the contra forces or otherwise encouraging, supporting and aiding military and paramilitary activities in and against Nicaragua, has acted, against the Republic of Nicaragua, in breach of its obligation under customary international law not to intervene in the affairs of another State;

(4) By twelve votes to three, Decides that the United States, by certain attacks on Nicaraguan territory in 1983–1984, * * * has acted, against the Republic of Nicaragua, in breach of its obligation under customary international law not to use force against another State;

(5) By twelve votes to three, Decides that the United States, by directing or authorizing overflights of Nicaraguan territory, and by the acts imputable to the United States referred to in subparagraph (4) hereof, has acted, against the Republic of Nicaragua, in breach of its obligation under customary international law not to violate the sovereignty of another State;

(6) By twelve votes to three, Decides that, by laying mines in the internal or territorial waters of the Republic of Nicaragua during the first months of 1984, the United States has acted, against the Republic of Nicaragua, in breach of its obligations under customary international law not to use force against another State, not to intervene in its affairs, not to violate its sovereignty and not to interrupt peaceful maritime commerce;

(7) By fourteen votes to one, Decides that, by the acts referred to in subparagraph (6) hereof, the United States has acted, against the Republic of Nicaragua, in breach of its obligations under Article XIX of the Treaty of Friendship, Commerce and Navigation between the United States of America and the Republic of Nicaragua signed at Managua on 21 January 1956;

(8) By fourteen votes to one, Decides that the United States, by failing to make known the existence and location of the mines laid by it, referred to in subparagraph (6) hereof, has acted in breach of its obligations under customary international law in this respect;

(9) By fourteen votes to one, Finds that the United States, by producing in 1983 a manual entitled Operaciones sicologicas en guerra de guerrillas, and disseminating it to contra forces, has encouraged the commission by them of acts contrary to general principles of humanitarian law; but does not find a basis for concluding that any such acts which may have been committed are imputable to the United States of America as acts of the United States of America;

(10) By twelve votes to three, Decides that the United States, by the attacks on Nicaraguan territory referred to in subparagraph (4) hereof, and by declaring a general embargo on trade with Nicaragua on 1 May 1985,

has committed acts calculated to deprive of its object and purpose the Treaty of Friendship, Commerce and Navigation between the Parties signed at Managua on 21 January 1956;

(11) By twelve votes to three, Decides that the United States, by the attacks on Nicaraguan territory referred to in subparagraph (4) hereof, and by declaring a general embargo on trade with Nicaragua on 1 May 1985, has acted in breach of its obligations under Article XIX of the Treaty of Friendship, Commerce and Navigation between the Parties signed at Managua on 21 January 1956;

(12) By twelve votes to three, Decides that the United States is under a duty immediately to cease and to refrain from all such acts as may constitute breaches of the foregoing legal obligations;

(13) By twelve votes to three, Decides that the United States is under an obligation to make reparation to the Republic of Nicaragua for all injury caused to Nicaragua by the breaches of obligations under customary international law enumerated above;

(14) By fourteen votes to one, Decides that the United States is under an obligation to make reparation to the Republic of Nicaragua for all injury caused to Nicaragua by the breaches of the Treaty of Friendship, Commerce and Navigation between the Parties signed at Managua on 21 January 1956;

(15) By fourteen votes to one, Decides that the form and amount of such reparation, failing agreement between the Parties, will be settled by the Court, and reserves for this purpose the subsequent procedure in the case;

(16) Unanimously, Recalls to both Parties their obligation to seek a solution to their disputes by peaceful means in accordance with international law.

DISSENTING OPINION OF JUDGE SCHWEBEL

1.   To say that I dissent from the Court's Judgment is to understate the depth of my differences with it. I agree with the Court's finding that the United States, by failing to make known the existence and location of the mines laid by it, acted in violation of customary international law (in relation to the shipping of third States); I agree that the CIA's causing publication of a manual advocating acts in violation of the law of war is indefensible; and I agree with some other elements of the Judgment as well. Nevertheless, in my view the Judgment misperceives and misconstrues essential facts—not so much the facts concerning the actions of the United States of which Nicaragua complains as the facts concerning the actions of Nicaragua of which the United States complains. It misconceives and misapplies the law—not in all respects, on some of which the whole Court is agreed, but in paramount respects: particularly in its interpretation of what is an "armed attack" within the meaning of the United Nations Charter and customary international law; in its appearing to justify foreign intervention in furtherance of "the process of decolonization"; and in nearly all of its holdings as to which Party to this case has acted in violation of its international responsibilities and which, because it

has acted defensively, has not. For reasons which, because of its further examination of questions of jurisdiction, are even clearer today than when it rendered its Judgment of 26 November 1984, this Judgment asserts a jurisdiction which in my view the Court properly lacks, and it adjudges a vital question which, I believe, is not justiciable. And, I am profoundly pained to say, I dissent from this Judgment because I believe that, in effect, it adopts the false testimony of representatives of the Government of the Republic of Nicaragua on a matter which, in my view, is essential to the disposition of this case and which, on any view, is material to its disposition. The effect of the Court's treatment of that false testimony upon the validity of the Judgment is a question which only others can decide.

160.   In today's Judgment, the Court acknowledges that the views of the parties to a case as to the law applicable to their dispute are very material, particularly when their views are concordant. The Court also does not deny that the Parties to this case agree on the definition of the acts which may constitute an armed attack. Nevertheless, on the critical question of whether a State's assistance to foreign armed irregulars who seek to overthrow the government of another State may be tantamount to an armed attack by the former State upon the latter, the Court arrives at a conclusion which is discordant with the agreed views of both Parties.

161.   The Court's conclusion is inconsonant with generally accepted doctrine, law and practice as well. The Court's conclusion is inconsistent with the views of Professor Brownlie which Nicaragua's Memorial quotes that a "use of force" may comprise not merely an organized armed attack by a State's regular forces but the giving of "aid to groups of insurgents on the territory of another State". It is inconsistent with his conclusion that a general campaign by irregulars with the complicity of the government of the State from which they operate may constitute an "armed attack". It is inconsistent with what Nicaragua's Memorial describes as "a substantially unanimous modern view concerning indirect use of force * * * ". It is inconsistent with the position which the United States has maintained since 1947 that one State's support of guerrillas operating against another is tantamount to an armed attack against the latter's territorial integrity and political independence. It is inconsistent with what Nicaragua rightly observes is a consistent practice of the United Nations holding that "substantial involvement" in the activities of armed insurgent groups is a violation of "the prohibition on the use of force in Article 2(4)". It is inconsistent with repeated declarations of the UN expressive of the international legal duty of States to refrain from fomenting civil strife—a form of aggression which the General Assembly has denominated as among "the gravest of all crimes against peace and security * * * ". It is inconsistent with the terms of the "Friendly Relations" Declaration, which the Court treats as an authoritative expression of customary international law—a declaration which, in its interpretation of Article 2, paragraph 4, of the Charter, holds that, "Every State has the duty to refrain from organizing, instigating, assisting or participating in acts of civil strife or terrorist acts in another State * * * when the acts * * * involve a threat or use of force". It is inconsistent with the conclusion of Judge Lachs that "indirect means of attacking States were barred" by this Declaration. It is inconsistent with the conclusion of Judge Jiménez de Aréchaga that this Declara-

tion, "an important interstitial development of some of the implications of Article 2(4)", deals with indirect aggression, including the support given by a government to acts of civil strife in another State. Such acts, he points out, "may involve the use of force and States should not be permitted to do indirectly what they are precluded by the Charter from doing directly * * * ". The Court's conclusion is inconsistent with the terms and intent of the UN Definition of Aggression on which both Nicaragua and the Court rely.

* * *

[Judge Schwebel's 136 page opinion is accompanied by a factual appendix of 133 pages. Other opinions by members of the court are omitted.]

———

Notes and Questions. Do you agree with the Court or with Judge Schwebel? Did the Court rely too heavily on testimony from Nicaraguan officials in reaching its decision, as Judge Schwebel asserts? Even if it did, is the United States in any position to complain, given its refusal to participate in the proceedings? Were the U.S. actions justified? Is it any country's proper place to attempt to impose a system of government on another country? The United States apparently believes it is, as is evidenced by its ongoing pro-democratic actions in the Americas. Has the U.S. been acting improperly? If it has, have the U.S. and other countries nevertheless begun to form a new norm of customary international law? See Chapter 14, supra.

5.   DOES THE RIGHT TO COLLECTIVE SELF-DEFENSE SURVIVE SECURITY COUNCIL ACTION?

Halberstam, The Right To Self-Defense Once the Security Council Takes Action
17 Mich. J. Int'l L. 229 (1996).*

Article 51 of the U.N. Charter provides:

Nothing in the present Charter shall impair the inherent right of individual or collective self-defense if an armed attack occurs against a Member of the United Nations, until the Security Council has taken measures necessary to maintain international peace and security.

One of the legal issues that emerged in the context of the Gulf crisis is the interpretation of the "until" clause in Article 51 of the U.N. Charter. Specifically, does a state retain the right of self-defense once the Security Council has taken measures to deal with the problem? * * *

Five prominent international law scholars—Professors Chayes, Franck, Reisman, Rosto, and Schachter—have given differing answers as to wheth-

* Reprinted with the permission of the University of Michigan Law School.

er and to what extent self-defense is permissible once the Security Council
has acted. Three, however, appear to agree that a state that has been
attacked may lose its right to use force in self-defense if the Security
Council has taken action, even if that action has not succeeded in removing
the aggressor or stopping the attack. One believes that while such an
interpretation of Article 51 is contrary to the legislative history of Article
51, it would be permissible if that would best achieve the objectives of the
Charter, but concludes that at the present such an interpretation would
undermine rather than further those objectives. Only one takes the position that Article 51 affirms a state's right to individual and collective self-
defense until the Council has successfully dealt with the matter.

* * *

The Charter should not be interpreted as barring states from using
force in self-defense, possibly, as in the case of Kuwait, in defense of their
very existence—absent a provision that clearly so states, or, at the very
minimum, a showing that this was the intent of the drafters and that states
ratifying the Charter understood this to be its effect.

It is difficult to believe that some 180 states would have agreed to give
up the most fundamental attribute of sovereignty, the right to use force in
self-defense, to an international body, and particularly one like the Security
Council. The Security Council decides on the basis of the political interests
of the states voting—the state attacked may not even have a vote. It is
inconceivable that they would have done so in language that affirms the
"inherent right of individual or collective self-defence."

A more plausible interpretation of Article 51 is that a state retains the
right of self-defense until the Security Council has taken measures that
have succeeded in restoring international peace and security. This interpretation is overwhelmingly confirmed by the legislative history of Article 51.

* * *

Notes and Questions. Do you agree with Professor Halberstam? To
which conclusion does the language of Article 51 lead you? If the right of
self-defense remains, even after the Security Council has acted, may the
Security Council remove that right by an appropriate resolution? Is it
reasonable to expect a state to forego self-defense in the hope that the
Security Council will solve the problem? As discussed above, *see* Chapter
14, *supra*, the Security Council has been criticized extensively for its
"failures" during the past few years, including the former Yugoslavia and
Somalia. If the Security Council is not able to take effective measures to
protect a state, is there any question about that state's right of self-
defense?

SECTION D. UNILATERAL SELF-DEFENSE

Notes and Questions. 1. The easy cases, and some questions.
State A sends infantry, tanks and airplanes across the border of its

neighbor, State B, with the purpose of removing its government and substituting one of its own choosing, or to occupy State B and thereafter incorporate it into State A, or to take control of a portion of State B containing oil or some other natural resource it covets. State B responds with military force to defeat State A's forces and to send them back across the border. On these simple facts alone, so familiar to the founders of the United Nations in 1945, State B's action is an exercise in self defense against an armed attack and clearly falls within the rubric of the inherent right of self-defense recognized and preserved as among United Nations members by Article 51 of the United Nations Charter. What provocations less than the use of force such as that attributed to State A in the example just given justify a responsive unilateral use of armed force by a state today? How far does the right of self-defense encompass a state's going beyond its own border to use force against an adversary?

2.   We will see in Chapter 16 (involving individual responsibility and the permissible uses of force in the conduct of war) that retaliatory acts (sometimes called reprisals) are permitted in the give and take of warfare, acts of violence that might otherwise be unlawful but are not so considered if committed to force an adversary to comply with the laws of war. But how far, if at all, are retaliatory uses of force (reprisals) outside the context of an ongoing war permitted by the Charter, or by customary international law? The Declaration on Principles of International Law Concerning Friendly Relations and Co-operation Among States in Accordance with the Charter of the United Nations (see the Doc. Supp.) provides: "States have a duty to refrain from acts of reprisal involving the use of force." This statement appears as an elucidation of article 2(4) of the Charter, but the Declaration, in its General Part, also states that nothing therein "shall be construed as prejudicing in any manner the provisions of the Charter or the rights and duties of Member States under the Charter." Does that invite states nevertheless to resort to reprisals, but now under the rubric of article 51 and the inherent right of self defense? Indeed, what is meant by the term: self defense?

1.   ISRAELI RAID ON TUNISIA

Security Council Condemnation

22 UN Chronicle Nos. 10/11 (1985), p. 3.

The Security Council has vigorously condemned Israel's "act of armed aggression" against Tunisian territory in flagrant violation of the United Nations Charter, international law and norms of conduct, and demanded that Israel "refrain from perpetrating such acts of aggression or from the threat to do so". The Council also urgently requested United Nations Member States to take measures to dissuade Israel from resorting to such acts against the sovereignty and territorial integrity of all States. In adopting resolution 573 (1985) on 4 October, the Council considered that Tunisia had "the right to appropriate reparations as a result of the loss of human life and material damage which it has suffered and for which Israel has claimed responsibility". The vote on the text was 14 in favour to none against, with 1 abstention (United States).

The Council met following a Tunisian complaint against Israel which stated that on 1 October, six Israeli military aircraft had bombed the civilian locality at Borj–Cedria, called Hammam–Plage, situated in the southern suburbs of Tunis. The action resulted in 68 civilian dead and nearly 100 wounded, as well as wide-scale material damage and destruction, Tunisia reported.

The attack was directed against "an exclusively residential urban area which traditionally has been home to Tunisian families and a small number of Palestinian civilians who had to flee from Lebanon following the invasion of that country by the Israeli army", Tunisia stated.

Forty-six speakers participated in four Council meetings held on the complaint on 3, 4 and 7 October. Beji Caid Essebsi, Minister for Foreign Affairs of Tunisia, said any attempt to justify Israel's "act of terrorism", any "indulgence shown to its perpetrators, no matter what the pretext, can only encourage aggression and set the seal of approval on the aggressor". The "crime" was particularly "reprehensible" because it aimed at jeopardizing efforts to bring about a peaceful, just and lasting settlement of the Palestinian problem on the basis of Charter principles and relevant United Nations resolutions.

The hospitality extended by Tunisia to the Palestinian leadership fell within that framework. The headquarters of the "so-called Force 17"— which had been blamed for the attack on three Israeli civilians at Larnaca, Cyprus—were not in Tunisia. It was only the political Palestinian leadership that had been extended Tunisian hospitality. In any case, no act of terrorism had been committed from Tunisia, and no Tunisian had ever been involved in any such act.

* * *

Benjamin Netanyahu (Israel) said that for the past year, the PLO headquarters in Tunisia had initiated, planned, organized and launched hundreds of "terrorist" attacks against Israel, against Israeli targets outside Israel, and against Jews everywhere. More than 600 such attacks had killed or severely wounded more than 75 Israelis, the PLO's "designated targets". The "butchery" of three Israelis at Larnaca, Cyprus, had been perpetrated by "Force 17", Yasser Arafat's personal bodyguard unit, which occupied the PLO headquarters in Tunisia. The target of Israel's strike were those headquarters and its action was "a legitimate act of self-defence" in response to "terrorism". Any civilian casualties, were the result of the "deliberate PLO tactic * * * of planting its bases among civilians". Tunisia was strong enough to stop the "terrorists" but it "knowingly harboured the PLO and allowed it complete freedom of action in planning, training, organizing and launching murderous attacks from its soil". The Israeli action was directed against the "terrorist killers" and not against their host country. Nevertheless, the host country did bear considerable responsibility.

* * *

Claude de Kemoularia (France) condemned the Israeli attack, which was an "inadmissible" violation of international law. France was concerned at the "disastrous consequences" the attack would have on the efforts to bring about a resumption of the peace process. All parties to the conflict should replace the "language of violence and reprisals" with a spirit of dialogue which alone could make possible an overall settlement. Ole Bierring (Denmark) also condemned the Israeli action, which had violated Tunisia's sovereignty and territorial integrity and represented a further stage in the continuing violence and counter-violence in the Middle East. While Denmark condemned acts of terrorism against Israelis, it did not believe that they justified "such action".

* * *

Carlos Alzamora (Peru) rejected Israel's act of aggression against Tunisia's sovereignty and territorial integrity. "By virtue of its timing, the characteristics of the attack and its inevitable political consequences", the air raid took on "special and ominous gravity". It was "a new and disproportionate application of the principle of an eye for an eye, carried out with arrogant disregard of others".

* * *

Sir John Thomson (United Kingdom) said the Israeli raid was an "outrage". Although his country condemned any "terrorist" act anywhere by whomsoever committed, it could not accept as valid Israel's reasons for its action of "arbitrary and disproportionate" violence. Even if there had been "demonstrable responsibility" by the PLO for the Larnaca killings, that would not have justified the Israeli retaliation.

* * *

Vernon Walters (United States) said the resolution "disproportionately" placed all blame for the latest spiral of violence in the Middle East "onto only one set of shoulders", while it did not hold at fault those responsible for the "terrorist" acts which had provoked it. A State subjected to continuing "terrorist" attacks should be able to respond with appropriate use of force to defend itself against further attacks. Each State should take appropriate steps to prevent persons or groups within its territory from perpetrating "terrorist" acts. The "incident" was not an obstacle to peace, but an impetus for the peace process and "renewed efforts towards its successful completion".

* * *

2. UNITED STATES RAID ON LIBYA

On April 14, 1986, the United States bombed Tripoli, Libya, hitting a residential suburb and killing both military personnel and civilians. One of the targets bombed was the complex where Colonel Qadafi was supposed to be residing. Qadafi was not killed, but his infant daughter and at least 300 civilians were killed. The U.S. argued self-defense. *Do any of the legal standards of self-defense fit?*

Veto of Resolution of Condemnation
23 UN Chronicle No. 4 (1986), p. 46.*

Three permanent members of the Security Council—the United States, the United Kingdom and France—on 21 April cast vetoes against a draft resolution by which the Council would have condemned "the armed attack" by the United States against the Libyan cities of Tripoli and Benghazi "in violation of the Charter and the norms of international conduct". The Council would have also called on the United States to "refrain forthwith from any attacks or threats thereof".

The text also called on the Council to condemn "all terrorist activities, whether perpetrated by individuals, groups or States", and called on all parties to "refrain from resorting to force, to exercise restraint in this critical situation, and to resolve their differences by peaceful means in keeping with the Charter". The Secretary–General would have been asked to take all appropriate steps to restore and ensure peace in the Central Mediterranean and to keep the Council regularly informed of the implementation of the resolution.

* * *

Vetoes: The United States rejected the draft as "totally unacceptable". Its assumption that the essential problem before the Council stemmed from actions of the United States armed forces against Libya was false, contradicted by irrefutable evidence and by the "long and tragic list of countries which have suffered brutality after brutality at the hands of Libyan terrorism". The real issue before the Council, the United States said, was not dealt with by the draft: Libya's "blatant, unrepentant and continuing use of force" in violation of the Charter.

For the Council to endorse such an "erroneous and deficient" text would be to mock the commitment of the United Nations to oppose terrorism in all its forms as "criminal conduct that must be resisted and punished". The United States was "outraged" that the draft had not mentioned Libya's brutal, growing and increasingly violent "campaign of terror". The text would have equated the use of terrorism with an act of justified self-defence against terrorism. It would have condemned acts of the United States against Libya but ignored Libya's "undeniable use of terrorism". It would have created an "appearance of even-handedness, but not the reality". Nowhere in it had Libya been asked to refrain from its "murderous activities".

* * *

On 14 April, the United States, in a letter (S/17990) to the Secretary–General, said that it had exercised its right of self-defence by responding to "an ongoing pattern of attacks by the Government of Libya". It said it had also "exercised great care in restricting its military response to terrorist-related targets". Every possible precaution had been taken to avoid civilian casualties and to limit collateral damage, the United States said. Its objective had been to destroy facilities used to carry out Libya's "hostile

* Reprinted with the permission of U.N. Chronicle.

policy of international terrorism and to discourage Libyan terrorist attacks in the future."

* * *

Mr. Azzarouk (Libyan Arab Jamahiriya) on 15 April said the United States, using 33 aircraft, had perpetrated a "barbaric, savage" air raid against Libyan civilian targets in Benghazi and Tripoli. The act was "completely unjustified and unprovoked". The raid had taken place with the "blessing and support of certain States, first and foremost the United Kingdom, which had provided the logistics". A "number of European countries" had helped co-ordinate the carefully conceived and executed raid. Civilian airports and aircraft, schools, houses, foreign missions and a centre for the handicapped had been damaged. Fragmentation bombs had been used.

Ali Treiki (Libyan Arab Jamahiriya) on 18 April said that in Tripoli and Benghazi dozens of children, women and the elderly had fallen victim to "America's so-called civilization" and had been buried. The American Administration should permit a Security Council delegation to see for itself that all targets had been civilian. The United States had "fallen prey to the arrogance and madness of power" and wanted to become "the world's policeman". Any party that did not agree to become its "vassal and agent" was considered "an outlaw, a terrorist, a communist and a devil". The United States record was one of "colonialism, treachery and aggression".

The fault of Colonel Qaddafi and the Libyan revolution was that they had expelled Americans and their bases from Libya, had ended the American oil monopoly in Libya, and had helped the persecuted elsewhere. The United States had rejected all dialogue with Libya and wished to impose conditions. Libyans would fight to the finish in defence of their land, their dignity, their independence and their waters. Libyans condemned terrorism. They supported Palestinians and Namibians. The presence of foreign fleets and foreign bases in the Mediterranean area must be eliminated.

On 21 April, Mr. Treiki said that while Libya was proud of the international community's support, it denounced the United States' "dangerous policies" and its desire to paralyse the United Nations.

Vernon Walters (United States) on 15 April referred to a "series of carefully planned air strikes" by the United States against "terrorist-related targets in Libya". That "self-defence" had become necessary after the failure of repeated and protracted efforts to deter Libya from ongoing attacks against the United States in violation of the Charter. There was "direct, precise and irrefutable" evidence that Libya was responsible for the bombing in West Berlin on 5 April that had resulted in the deaths of a United States Army sergeant and a young Turkish woman and injury to 230 other people, among them 50 American military personnel. In the light of that "reprehensible act of violence", the latest in an ongoing pattern of attacks by Libya, and of "clear evidence that Libya was planning a multitude of future attacks", the United States was compelled to exercise its right of self-defence, he stated. The "scourge of Libyan terrorism" was not a problem for the United States alone; it threatened all members of the civilized world community. Colonel Qaddafi had made terrorism an integral part of his foreign policy. Libyan attacks were "concerted violence directed against the values, the interests and the democratic institutions of all freedom-loving States".

On 21 April, Mr. Walters said that Colonel Qaddafi had launched murderous attacks against American citizens, had fired at American ships, and was plotting "yet more deadly atrocities". How many Americans and innocents must be killed before the United States' right to respond was recognized? he asked.[a]

* * *

Andres Aguilar (Venezuela) rejected the use of violence to resolve differences between nations; that included both armed action and violence carried out by individuals or groups of individuals. Venezuela also rejected any breach of the foundations of the system to which all States owed respect. The use of military force was not the most appropriate way to fight terrorism. Violence bred violence, and sometimes the spiral of violence went far beyond what had been foreseen initially. Both parties should cooperate with the Security Council and the United Nations in general in seeking appropriate ways to end their dispute. The adoption of the draft would not have encouraged a solution by peaceful means nor alleviated tension in the region. It did not take duly into account the background of the problem in all its aspects, nor did it establish the necessary link between the crucial issues that had led to that conflict.

Sir John Thomson (United Kingdom) said it appeared that state-directed terrorism was the main policy of the Qaddafi Government. No one was safe from "Colonel Qaddafi's murderers". The United States had the inherent right of self-defence. The United Kingdom and many of its friends in Europe and the Arab world had had direct experience of Libyan terrorism. It was in their interest that effective measures be taken to end that menace so that no State would feel obliged to have recourse to armed force as a last resort in defence of its citizens or of its territory. Colonel Qaddafi had sought "to drape his nefarious activities in the colours of Arab and Palestinian nationalism"; in fact those activities did nothing but harm to the Arab and Palestinian causes. The central issue before the Council was terrorism. All should shun Colonel Qaddafi; none should act as if they were his accomplices. The Council should deal resolutely with countries which were the home of state-sponsored terrorism.

Pascal Gayama (Congo) said that the United States had reacted in "a brutal and surprisingly emotional manner" in what it had said was the only way to deal with what it called the "only source of terrorism in the world"—Colonel Qaddafi and Libya. The United States' "dangerous conduct" had unforeseeable consequences. By violating Libya's territorial integrity and sovereignty in "a flagrant and premeditated manner" with the additional "avowed intention" of removing its Head of State—"as in the worst of terrorist acts"—the United States had displayed a political

a. Mr. Walters' address to the Council, giving in detail the U.S. indictment against Libya, is reported in 80 A.J.I.L. 633 (1986).

irresponsibility that was difficult to understand from a great Power and permanent Council member.

* * *

Claude de Kemoularia (France) categorically condemned the intolerable escalation of terrorism, and shared the "legitimate indignation" of the United States and the United Kingdom concerning "the odious attacks" perpetrated against their nationals. France affirmed its solidarity with all countries' victims of "barbaric acts, which spread blind terror and in no way serve the political causes that their perpetrators claim to defend". States victims of such acts should join together in the fight against a threat affecting all of them. Determined, tenacious and patient efforts were needed, combining national measures with greater international cooperation. He appealed for reason, adding that there were serious risks of escalation in the present situation, and everything must be done to ensure that the chain of violence was broken.

* * *

Notes and Questions

1. ***Condemnation in the General Assembly.*** On November 20, 1986, the General Assembly, in Resolution 41/38, condemned the United States attack on Libya as "a violation of the U.N. Charter and international law," by a vote of 79 in favor to 28 against, with 33 abstentions. 24 UN Chronicle 1 (1987), p. 73.

2. ***Two other incidents are related to the Libyan bombing:*** (1) the U.S. commandeered an Egyptian Airliner, forced it down in Sicily, and captured those whom it felt were responsible for the Achille Lauro incident; and (2) The U.S. request for the extradition of the Libyans allegedly involved in the downing of Pan Am flight 103, over Lockerbie, Scotland has resulted in protracted conflict with Libya. For discussion of this, see, Ch. 16, on individual responsibility and international criminal law, and the latter part of this chapter on Terrorism. On the Egyptian Airliner incident and its legality, consider the material in this Chapter's section, Action Against Terrorism. *See also*, Schachter *In Defense of International Rules on the Use of Force*, 53 U.Chi.L.Rev. 113, 139–40 (1986).

3.   UNITED STATES RAIDS ON IRAQ

On June 27, 1993, the United States bombed the Iraqi intelligence headquarters building in Baghdad. The bombs were dropped in the middle of the night to avoid casualties, but three of the missiles landed on the surrounding residential area, reportedly killing eight citizens and wounding others. At a Security Council meeting convened by the United States later that day, Ambassador Albright asserted that the raid was in response to an Iraqi intelligence plot to assassinate former President George Bush. According to Ambassador Albright, the Kuwaitis discovered a car bomb on April 13, 1993, the day before President Bush was scheduled to visit Kuwait City. Kuwaiti officials advised the U.S. that their interrogation of the suspects revealed the assassination attempt, and the U.S. subsequently investigated and allegedly confirmed the reports. Ambassador Albright claimed that the United States bombed in self defense, in accordance with article 51 of the Charter. Iraq demanded that the U.S. be condemned for its actions, but many Council members voiced their support for the U.S. and none offered a resolution critical of the U.S. Ultimately, neither the Security Council nor the General Assembly criticized the U.S. for its actions.

Notes and Questions

1. ***Criticism did arise elsewhere.*** Some questioned the United States claim of self defense, considering the attack instead a reprisal, and therefore forbidden by the U.N. Charter. *See, e.g.,* Quigley, *Missiles with a Message: The Legality of the United States Raid on Iraq's Intelligence Headquarters,* 17 Hastings Int'l & Comp. L. Rev. 241 (1994). As Professor Quigley pointed out, the "evidence" offered by the United States was inadequate to definitively tie Iraq to the bomb, or even to establish that the bomb was intended to assassinate President Bush. Indeed, considering that the assassins intended to make the attempt against President Bush's motorcade, and that President Bush would be riding in an armorplated vehicle, it was unlikely that the bomb would have harmed him, much less killed him. In addition, President Clinton's comments regarding the bombing indicated that the United States' goal was retaliation and deterrence of future attacks, not self defense. Some commentators noted the similarity between the Libya raid, which was strongly condemned by the international community, and the Iraqi raid, which received little or no condemnation, and opined that this reflected a change in the law defining the limits of self defense. *See* Note, *Comparing the 1993 U.S. Airstrike on Iraq to the 1986 Bombing of Libya: The New Interpretation of Article 51,* 24 Ga. J. Int'l & Comp. L. 99 (1994). Others opined that this evolution of "self-defense," and a resulting interpretation that includes acts such as the bombing of Baghdad, is appropriate given the need to combat terrorism. *See* Note, *Terror and the Law: The Unilateral Use of Force and the June 1993 Bombing of Baghdad,* 5 Duke J. Comp. & Int'l L. 457 (1995).

2. ***Self-Defense?*** Do you agree that the U.S. action was permissible self defense? Does it conform to the parameters of self defense as understood by the drafters of the U.N. Charter? What limits remain in the Charter's prohibition against aggression if the bombing raid can be characterized as self defense? Why did the Security Council acquiesce in the U.S. characterization of the raid? Is this evidence of U.S. dominance in the Security Council, or a true belief that the attack was acceptable under the Charter?

SECTION E. ANTICIPATORY SELF-DEFENSE

1. A BIT OF HISTORY

Hugo Grotius, in 1625, noted that force could be used to forestall an attack, although it required a "present danger" which is "imminent in a point of time." He provided that the attack "may be anticipated." "It [is] lawful to kill him who is preparing to kill * * * " *See* Grotius, Di Jure Belli ac Pacis Ch. 1 (1625). Similarly, Emerich de Vattel wrote: "The safest plan is to prevent evil, where that is possible. A Nation has the right to resist the injury against the aggressor. It may even anticipate the other's design, being careful, however, not to act upon vague and doubtful suspicious, lest it should run the risk of becoming itself the aggressor." E. de Vattel, The Law of Nations IV (1758). Both warned of the danger of abusing this "right." *See*, Beres, *Perspective: After the Gulf War: Israel, Preemption, and Anticipatory Self–Defense*, 13 Hous. J. Int'l L. 259, 263–64 (1991).

2.   THE SIX DAY WAR

Situation in the Middle East

4 UN Monthly Chronicle, July 1967, p. 3, at 8.

Meeting of June 5; Following the outbreak of hostilities in the Middle East, the Security Council met in emergency session.

The Council had a letter from the representative of the United Arab Republic which stated that Israel had "committed a treacherous premeditated aggression" against his country that morning, launching attacks in the Gaza Strip, Sinai, and several airports in Cairo, the Suez Canal area, and other localities. Preliminary reports, it was stated, indicated that 23 Israeli planes had been shot down and several pilots captured. The letter went on to say that the United Arab Republic, "in repelling this aggression * * * had decided to defend itself by all means in accordance with Article 51 of the Charter of the United Nations".

The Secretary–General, U THANT, in his statement, said the United Nations had no means of ascertaining how the hostilities began. Reports coming in from the parties were conflicting, but all agreed that there was serious military action on land and in the air at a number of points which was spreading.

* * * [At a subsequent meeting of the Security Council, the spokesman for Israel delivered the following explanation of Israel's military action. Security Council, Off.Rec. 1358th Meeting].

198.   * * * On 18 May, the Government of the United Arab Republic demanded the eviction of the United Nations Emergency Force which was deployed along the Gaza Strip and the Sinai desert and at Sharm el Sheikh at the entrance to the Gulf of Aqaba, and on that day UNEF ceased to exist. Was this an act which promoted peace? Was this an act which demonstrated peaceful intent? It was not; it was preparation for aggression. The Emergency Force had to be gotten out of the way so that the aggression on Israel could be prepared and mounted.

199.   On 23 May, the United Arab Republic declared that the Strait of Tiran would be closed to Israel shipping and to ships of other nations carrying what were described as strategic goods, that is to say, anything which the United Arab Republic chose to define as strategic goods, to Israel's southernmost port of Eilat. Was this act of blockade a peaceful act? Did this re-imposition of the blockade demonstrate peaceful intent? It did

not. This was a clear act of hostility and the exercise of an internationally rejected claim to belligerency. A blockade is a classical act of war.

200. During this time, that is, the last week of May, Egypt started a massive build-up of forces in the Sinai desert. Some 80,000 men were assembled, with hundreds of assault aircraft, a thousand tanks. These huge forces were deployed in an offensive position along the Sinai frontier with Israel, along the Gaza Strip and at the approaches to Eilat. The deployment of these forces was accompanied by a mounting crescendo of warlike propaganda from Cairo. A holy war was proclaimed by the religious authorities in the Egyptian capital, and the Egyptian people were urged to march forward in a jehad to destroy Israel. The Egyptian President naturally was foremost in inciting his people for the coming war. This is what he said before the Central Council of Arab Trade Unions on 26 May 1967:

> The Arab people want to fight. We have been waiting for the suitable day when we shall be completely ready, since if we enter a battle with Israel we should be confident of victory and should take strong measures. We do not speak idly. We have lately felt that our strength is sufficient and that if we enter into battle with Israel we shall, with God's help, be victorious. Therefore, we have now decided to take real steps. The battle will be a full-scale one, and our basic aim will be to destroy Israel.

201. What were we in Israel and what was the Security Council expected to make of these words? A call for peace, or a call for war?

202. On 30 May, President Nasser signed a military agreement with King Hussein of Jordan, and Jordan began to mobilize. On 4 June, a similar agreement was signed with Iraq, and Iraqi detachments began arriving in Jordan and in Egypt. Was this evidence of peaceful intent? Were these agreements in keeping with the Charter of the United Nations? Were these aggressive movements of troops in accordance with solemn agreements which Egypt and Jordan had entered into with Israel in 1949 with the object of preventing all hostile acts and serving as a transition to permanent peace? They were clear evidence of a preparation for aggression.

203. While these military moves were going on in Egypt, Jordan and Iraq, Syria had also mobilized its forces to the last man, and 50,000 troops were poised aggressively on the heights which overlook Israel. We were surrounded. The armed ring was closed. All that the Arab forces were waiting for was the signal to start.

204. That signal was given on 5 June, when Egyptian planes in accordance with the plans contained in battle order 6/67 of Air Force and Air Defence Headquarters of the Eastern Area in Sinai, dated 26 May 1967, took off for their assigned targets in Israel, while at the same time an artillery barrage on Israel farming villages was opened from the Gaza Strip. Shortly afterwards, Jordan guns sited amid the holy places of the Holy City of Jerusalem started shelling the Israel capital, causing heavy casualties, and the Syrian artillery joined the devil's chorus in the north. The aggression had begun.

205. This is the record; this is what happened.

* * *

———

Notes and Questions

1. **Territorial control.** Israel's success in the Six Day War resulted in her military occupation of substantial territory: Sinai, the Gaza Strip, parts of Jerusalem, portions of Jordan on the West Bank of the Jordan River and the Syrian Golan Heights. However, in 1993 Israel and the P.L.O. entered into a preliminary settlement of the P.L.O.'s claims to the Gaza Strip and the West Bank of the Jordan River, and they soon thereafter began implementation of the agreement. Although full implementation has been difficult, violence and violations of international law continue to occur. Indeed in June 2001 an extremely uneasy cease-fire is in place, but not functioning very well.

2. **Was Israel's military action in the 6-Day War lawful under the Charter?** Article 51 preserves "the inherent right of individual * * * self-defense if an armed attack occurs * * *." Was Israel's response to an attack that occurred or to a threatened attack? Was Israel acting in anticipatory self-defense? Is such action lawful under the Charter? Does the U.N. Charter allow anticipatory self-defense? If so, when and under what circumstances? Must an armed attack be imminent? What is "imminent," especially in the nuclear age?

3. **What about the Israeli settlements in Palestine, the Intifada and terrorism in reaction, and the Israeli application of massive force to challenge the terrorism and the intifada?** Are any of these self-defense? See, Howlett, Palestinian Private Property Rights in Israel and the Occupied Territories, 34 Vand.J.Transnat'l L. 117 (2001).

4. **Views of certain writers.**

Stone: Writing before there had been major tests of the meaning of the Charter, Stone observed in discussing article 51: "Major troop concentrations on the border would presumably warrant anticipatory use of force * * *." Stone, Legal Controls of International Conflict 244, n. 8 (1954). Following the Cuban missile crisis and prior to the events in the Middle East in 1967, the publicists in the United States were deeply divided on anticipatory self-defense, at least as an abstract concept.

Wright: It has also been argued that the quarantine and the O.A.S. resolution were justified as measures of "individual or collective self-defense" permitted by article 51 of the Charter. It is suggested that the term "armed attack," which alone justified such defense without prior United Nations authority, must be interpreted to include a serious threat of armed attack.[a] Reference has been made to the statement by Secretary of State Webster in the Caroline case, generally accepted prior to the Charter, that military defensive action was permissible in case of "an instant and overwhelming necessity," thus creating a limited right of preventive action;

---

a. The United States has not used this argument officially * * *.

that such a construction is necessary in the nuclear age because to delay defensive action until an actual nuclear attack would be suicidal, and that the Charter supports this construction by forbidding "threat" as well as "use" of force in article 2, paragraph 4.

These arguments are not convincing. It appears that the Charter intended to limit the traditional right of defense by states to actual armed attack, even though it forbade "threat of force" and authorized the Security Council to intervene to stop "threats to the peace." Professor, later judge, Jessup wrote in 1948:

This restriction in Article 51 very definitely narrows the freedom of action which states had under international law. A case could be made out for self-defense in the traditional law where the injury was threatened but no attack had yet taken place. Under the Charter, alarming military preparations by a neighboring state would justify a resort to the Security Council, but would not justify resort to anticipatory force by the state which believed itself threatened.[b]

The obligation of states to refrain from threats to the peace under article 2, paragraph 4, and the competence of the United Nations to take action in case of a threat to the peace under article 39, were not intended to give a unilateral right of military self-defense in case of such threats. For that reason, self-defense against threats was excluded in article 51, and states were explicitly obliged to submit disputes or situations which they think threaten peace, to the United Nations and to refrain from unilateral use of force. * * * Wright, *The Cuban Quarantine*, 57 A.J.I.L. 546, 559 (1963).*

McDougal: The more important limitations imposed by the general community upon this customary right of self-defense have been, in conformity with the overriding policy it serves of minimizing coercion and violence across state lines, those of necessity and proportionality. The conditions of necessity required to be shown by the target state have never, however, been restricted to "actual armed attack"; imminence of attack of such high degree as to preclude effective resort by the intended victim to non-violent modalities of response has always been regarded as sufficient justification, and it is now generally recognized that a determination of imminence requires an appraisal of the total impact of an initiating state's coercive activities upon the target state's expectations about the costs of preserving its territorial integrity and political independence. Even the highly restrictive language of Secretary of State Webster in the Caroline case, specifying a "necessity of self defense, instant, overwhelming, leaving no choice of means and no moment for deliberation," did not require "actual armed attack,"[4] and the understanding is now widespread that a

---

b. Philip Jessup, A Modern Law of Nations 166 (New York, Macmillan, 1948). After an exhaustive discussion of "The Use of Force in Self–Defence," Ian Brownlie concludes that "the beginning of an armed attack is a condition precedent for resort to force in self-defence."37 Brit.Yr.Bk. of Int. Law 266 (1962). * * *

* Reprinted with the permission of the American Society of International Law.

4. Mr. Webster to Mr. Fox, April 24, 1841, in 29 British and Foreign State Papers 1129, 1138 (1840–41). *See also* Jennings, *The Caroline and McLeod Cases*, 32 A.J.I.L. 82 (1938).

test formulated in the previous century for a controversy between two friendly states is hardly relevant to contemporary controversies, involving high expectations of violence, between nuclear-armed protagonists. The requirement of proportionality, in further expression of the policy of minimizing coercion, stipulates that the responding use of the military instrument by the target state be limited in intensity and magnitude to what is reasonably necessary promptly to secure the permissible objectives of self-defense under the established conditions of necessity.

* * *

* * * The apparent purpose of the inept language of Article 51, commonly ascribed to the late Senator Vandenburg, was only that of accommodating regional organizations, as specifically envisioned for the inter-American system by the Act of Chapultepec, with the more comprehensive centralized system of collective security projected by the Charter. Similarly, nothing in the "plain and natural meaning" of the words of the Charter requires an interpretation that Article 51 restricts the customary right of self-defense. The proponents of such an interpretation substitute for the words "if an armed attack occurs" the very different words "if, and only if, an armed attack occurs." McDougal, *The Soviet–Cuban Quarantine and Self–Defense*, 57 A.J.I.L. 597, 598 (1963).*

Henkin: * * * While there have been few challenges to Article 2, recurring crises, we have noted, have evoked suggestions for broader readings of the exception of Article 51. One that has been strongly urged is that in the day of nuclear weapons and the ever-present possibility of sudden devastation, nations cannot wait for an armed attack to occur. At least, it is urged, the Charter must now be read to permit "anticipatory self-defense"—the right to act in self-defense in anticipation of attack.

The argument has specious appeal, but is fundamentally unpersuasive. If the Charter originally permitted force in self-defense only if an armed attack occurs, today's weapons hardly argue for extending the exception. The original reasons for barring "anticipatory self-defense" in regard to "old-fashioned war" apply even more to the new war. The logic of the deterrent and the balance of terror does not suggest that nations should be encouraged to preventive or even pre-emptive attack. The exception of Article 51 was limited to the situation "if an armed attack occurs," which is comparatively clear, objective, easy to prove, difficult to misinterpret or fabricate. To permit anticipation may virtually destroy the rule against the use of force, leaving it to every nation to claim anticipation and unleash the fury. Nations will not be prevented or deterred by the fear that later—if there is anyone left to judge—someone may determine that there had in fact been no threat of armed attack legitimately anticipated.

Proponents of anticipatory self-defense raise the specter of the all-out nuclear attack and of the obvious need to anticipate it. In fact, of course, for determining what the Charter means or should mean, the major nuclear attack and the pre-emptive strike are not the relevant concerns. A nation planning all-out attack will not be deterred by the Charter, though it may

* Reprinted with the permission of the American Society of International Law.

well talk "anticipatory self-defense" in its justification. Nor does one prescribe rules for the nation threatened with such an attack. If a nation is satisfied that another is about to obliterate it, it will not wait. But it has to make that decision on its own awesome responsibility. Anticipation in that case may have to be practiced; it need not be preached. The Charter need not make a principle of it; the law need not authorize or encourage it. But surely that extreme hypothetical case, beyond the realm of law, should not be used to justify new rules for situations that do not involve the impending mortal thrust. "Anticipatory self-defense" as a rule of law has meaning only in less extreme cases. There, anticipatory self-defense, it should be clear, becomes easily a euphemism for "preventive war." The United Nations Charter in the beginning did not authorize it. Attempts later, in relation to Suez and Sinai, to read the Charter as permitting anticipatory self-defense, were rejected. Nothing since, least of all the new weapons, suggests that international society would be better if the Charter were changed or read to authorize it. Henkin, *Force, Intervention and Neutrality in Contemporary International Law, Proceedings,* 57 A.J.I.L. 147, 150 (1963).*

5. ***Is article 51 an example of flawed draftsmanship?*** Some have argued that Article 51 was not intended to be a comprehensive statement (or restatement) of the law of self-defense, that it was hastily drafted (without full consideration) at the San Francisco conference as part of the compromise that brought the Latin American states into the organization by preserving, in part, their preference for regional arrangements. An example of draftsmanship at another constitutional convention that clarifies the question of anticipatory self-defense is contained in Article I, Section 10 of the U.S. Constitution: "No State shall, without the Consent of Congress * * * engage in War, unless actually invaded, or in such imminent Danger as will not admit of delay."

6. ***Israeli disaffection with the United Nations.*** Since 1948, the year of Israel's accession to statehood, many Arab states, including Lebanon, have regarded themselves as being in a state of war with her. This state of war has never been officially terminated; the Arab states have on numerous occasions asserted the continuing existence of war in seeking to justify various anti-Israel measures taken by them (such as the blocking of the Suez Canal and the Tiran Strait to Israeli navigation). *See* Blum, *The Beirut Raid and the International Double Standard,* 64 A.J.I.L. 73, 77 (1970). The author further states:*

> * * * One of the most disturbing aspects of the Middle East conflict—disturbing as much to the cause of "world order" as to the cause of Israel—is the fact that on no single occasion over the past fifteen years has Israel been able to get satisfaction from the political organs of the United Nations on her complaints against neighboring Arab states. The Soviet veto that has been made available to the Arabs, to block any decision by the Security Council which the latter regarded as unfavorable to them, ensured that such a decision, even if it received the requisite number of votes in the Council, would not be

---

* Reprinted with the permission of the
American Society of International Law.

adopted. This fact was naturally taken into account by other members of the Security Council more favorably disposed to Israel, and largely conditioned the very tone and formulation of many a watered-down draft resolution concerning Israeli complaints, since it was realized that the submission of a draft resolution giving satisfaction to Israel was bound to become an exercise in futility. This pattern, in turn, led to a growing conviction in Israel, which United Nations practice never effectively disproved, that it was difficult, if not impossible, for her rights to be recognized by the United Nations. * * *

---

3. DESTRUCTION OF IRAQ'S NUCLEAR REACTOR

Read the United Nations, Security Council Resolution 487 (1981) of June 19, 1981, In the Doc. Supp. The Security Council "Strongly Condemned" the Israeli Attack On Iraq's Nuclear Reactor. Resolutions and Decisions of the Security Council 1981.

U.N.Sec. Council Off.Rec., 36th year, p. 10.

Council Condemns Israel's Air Attack on Iraqi Nuclear Reactor

18 UN Chronicle No. 8 (1981), p. 5.

* * *

The Council met to consider the complaint by Iraq, contained in its letter of 8 June (S/14509), asking for an immediate meeting of the Council "to deal with a grave act of aggression committed by Israel against Iraq with far-reaching consequences for international peace and security".

The letter stated that on Sunday, 7 June, Israeli warplanes raided Baghdad. Their objective was to destroy the Iraq nuclear reactor installations. The letter also stated that Israel had admitted "this premeditated act of aggression".

In a further letter of 10 June (S/14514) Iraq emphasized that the 7 June act of aggression by Israel was not the first of its kind against Iraq. On 27 September 1980, two raids had been carried out on Baghdad which were also aimed at the nuclear installations. Due to military, political and moral considerations, the two raids were referred to in a Government communique without mentioning that Israel had perpetrated them. The Council also had before it a letter of 8 June from Israel (S/14510) stating that "on Sunday, 7 June 1981, the Israel Air Force launched a raid on the atomic reactor 'Ossirac', near Baghdad. Our pilots carried out their mission fully; the reactor was destroyed; all our aircraft returned safely to base".

The letter stated that Israel had taken that decision because for a long time it had been watching with growing concern the construction of that atomic reactor and that from sources whose reliability was beyond doubt,

Israel had learned that the reactor was designed to produce atomic bombs and that the target would be Israel, as was announced by the ruler of Iraq.

* * * Saadoon Hammadi (Iraq), Minister for Foreign Affairs, said the motives behind the zionist campaign and aggression against Iraq were the desire to cover up Israel's possession of nuclear weapons and more importantly, the determination not to allow the Arab Nation to acquire the scientific or technical knowledge necessary for their development and progress. The more the Arabs advanced their scientific knowledge, the weaker were Israel's chances of maintaining their occupation of Arab territories and their denial of the inalienable rights of the Palestinian people.

It was evident that Israel's nuclear programme had been geared to military purposes from its very inception and that all sorts of illegal means had been employed for its enhancement, in total violation of internationally accepted standards.

Despite the repeated calls upon Israel to accede to the Non–Proliferation Treaty, it had bluntly refused to do so. Iraq, in contrast, by accepting the terms of the Treaty, had fully subscribed to those standards in its nuclear programme. As noted by the Director–General of IAEA, Iraq had accepted IAEA safeguards on all its nuclear activities. The last safeguard inspection at the Iraqi nuclear centre had taken place in January of this year and all nuclear material there was satisfactorily accounted for.

* * *

The attack carried out by Israel against Iraq was clearly an act of aggression in accordance with the provisions of the Charter, as expounded in the definition of aggression in Assembly resolution 3314 (29), adopted on 14 December 1974. The Israeli allegation that it had acted in legitimate self-defence was totally unfounded, in fact and in law.

The zionist act of aggression against Iraq constituted a qualitative change in the aggressor's policy in the area. It was a clear indication of the determination of the Zionists, after the failure of Camp David, to escalate their provocations with acts of armed aggression prior to launching a full-scale war in order to subjugate the Arab countries and to impose full zionist domination over the whole Middle East.

The Israeli attack was a clear-cut case of premeditated aggression. The elaborate preparations that had preceded the commission of that act were fully described by the Prime Minister of Israel and other Israeli leaders in their press conference held in Tel Aviv on 10 June. What was worse was that Mr. Begin had stated categorically at that press conference that, if Iraq tried to rebuild the reactor, Israel would do all it could to destroy it again.

Faced with this grave situation, the Security Council should reaffirm the right of all States to develop nuclear programmes for peaceful purposes. Mandatory sanctions in accordance with the provisions of Chapter VII of the Charter should be imposed upon Israel to remove the grave menace to international peace and security posed by its actions. Israeli lawlessness should be brought to an end.

* * *

Yehuda Z. Blum (Israel) said that in destroying the Iraqi nuclear reactor Israel had performed an elementary act of self-preservation, both morally and legally. In so doing, Israel was exercising its inherent right of self-defence as understood in general international law and as preserved in Article 51 of the United Nations Charter.

A threat of nuclear obliteration was being developed against Israel by one of its most implacable enemies. Israel had tried to have that threat halted by diplomatic means, but its efforts had borne no fruit. Ultimately left with no choice, Israel was obliged to remove that mortal danger. Ever since the establishment of the State of Israel over 33 years ago, Iraq had been conspiring to destroy it. Iraq had joined several other Arab States which attacked Israel the day after it became independent in 1948. But while other Arab States—Egypt, Lebanon, Jordan and Syria—had signed armistice agreements with Israel in 1949, Iraq had adamantly refused to do so. Instead, it fomented and supported the unrelenting Arab belligerency and terrorism against Israel. It also had taken part in the Arab wars against Israel in 1967 and 1973. And it had doggedly rejected any international measure or instrument which might imply even the most indirect recognition of Israel and its right to exist.

Since 1948, Iraq had declared itself to be in a state of war with Israel. Iraq had missed no opportunity to make it clear that it would not abide by international law in respect to Israel and that it reserved its freedom of action with regard to Israel. That perverse doctrine had found expression in the so-called National Charter of Iraq, proclaimed by its President, Saddam Hussein, in 1980, which committed Iraq in no uncertain terms to all-out warfare against Israel and enjoined other Arab States to participate in that war, using "all means and techniques".

Over and beyond the development of its conventional forces, Iraq had in recent years entered the nuclear armaments field, while at the same time piously appending its signature to international instruments specifically prohibiting it from doing so. A senior member of Iraq's Revolutionary Command Council had stated at a meeting of the Arab league in 1977 that "the Arabs must get an atom bomb".

* * *

Israel had learned from unimpeachable sources that following the expected delivery of two additional shipments of weapons-grade uranium, about 24 kilograms, the nuclear reactor would have been completed, and put into operation soon—and not later than the beginning of September 1981. Thirty-six kilograms of weapons-grade uranium in Iraq's possession would enable it to make a nuclear bomb.

Iraq already possessed aircraft capable of delivering nuclear warheads. In addition, it was involved in the development of a new surface-to-surface missile with an effective range of up to 3,000 kilometres, also capable of delivering a nuclear warhead.

Unlike Israel, Iraq had not embarked on its large-scale nuclear programme for reasons of pure research, despite its protestations to the contrary. And again unlike Israel, Iraq had not embarked upon its nuclear programme because it faced an energy crisis; it was blessed with abundant supplies of natural oil and was normally one of the largest oil suppliers in the Organization of Petroleum Exporting Countries.

Israel's decision, taken in *the exercise of its right of self-defence,* was one of the most agonizing it had ever had to make. The operation was launched on a Sunday, timed for late in the day on the assumption that persons working on the site would have left. Israel regretted the loss of life, which was minimal. (emphasis added).

* * *

Natarajan Krishnan (India) said that to invoke the right to self-defence to justify a long-premeditated act of aggression was a cynical attempt to confuse the issue. To cite Article 51 of the Charter in support of an indefensible action was a travesty of the very provisions of the Charter. That Israel should have sought to present such arguments was an affront to the United Nations and the international community. It was Israel which had been making systematic efforts in the pursuit of nuclear-weapons capability. There was growing evidence to show that Israel might already have acquired such capability and a stockpile of nuclear weapons. Against that background, the development of nuclear energy for peaceful purposes by Iraq could not be deemed to be a threat to Israel. The sovereign right of a developing country to acquire and develop nuclear technology for peaceful purposes could not be denied or thwarted through discriminatory policies and practices and much less by naked aggression as committed by Israel.

The Security Council had the obligation to signal clearly to Israel that the international community would not tolerate its transgressions any more.

Sergio Correa Da Costa (Brazil) said his country joined other Member States in a clear condemnation of the aggression suffered by Iraq. The notion of "preventive aggression" was unacceptable under the legal system which bound all nations. Toleration of that notion would lead to the destruction of the United Nations and to the foundering of any hope of coexistence among States.

* * *

Jeane J. Kirkpatrick (United States) said that it was precisely because of the United States' deep involvement in efforts to promote peace in the Middle East that it was shocked by the Israeli air strike on the Iraqi nuclear facility and had promptly condemned that action, which reflected and exacerbated deeper antagonisms in the region.

However, although the United States had condemned Israel's act, it was necessary to take into account its context as well as its consequences. As President Reagan had stated in his press conference, one had to recognize that Israel had reason for concern in view of the past history of Iraq, which had never signed a cease-fire or recognized Israel as a nation, and had never joined in any peace effort. President Reagan had further stated that Israel might have sincerely believed it was a defensive move.

The strength of United States ties and commitment to Israel were well known and the Reagan administration was proud to call Israel a friend and ally. None the less, the United States believed the means Israel had chosen to quiet its fears about the purposes of Iraq's nuclear programme had hurt the peace and security of the area. Diplomatic means available to Israel had not been exhausted and the Israeli action had damaged the regional confidence that was essential for the peace process to go forward.

* * *

Mr. Blum (Israel) said that Iraq's nuclear activities had troubled many Governments and experts around the world. Israel had indicated some of the questions arising in that regard. If Iraq could not address itself to the questions raised, others had done so. They included three eminent French nuclear scientists, who had made a serious examination of those and other disturbing questions related to Iraq's nuclear development programme. The analysis and conclusions of the three scientists were to be found in a comprehensive memorandum entitled Osirak et la proliferation des armes atomiques, which they had presented to the French Government and public in May of this year. [Israel then enunciated a number of findings of the French scientists which Israel alleged undermined the reliability of the IAEA inspections, including the inspected country's right to choose the inspectors and the advance notice of inspection consistently given by the IAEA.]

* * *

[In] the debate, Sigvard Eklund, Director–General of IAEA, said:
* * *

The attack on the Iraqi nuclear centre was a serious development with far-reaching implications. Not since its establishment had IAEA been faced with a more serious matter than the implications of that development. The Agency's safeguards system was conceived as a basic element of the Non–Proliferation Treaty. The same system of safeguards was applied to facilities covered by the Tlatelolco Treaty and facilities under bilateral safeguards agreements with the Agency.

The Agency's safeguards system was the product of extensive international cooperation. Its basic principles and modus operandi had been devised and were constantly being upgraded by the foremost international experts in that field. The results of the application of the system were periodically reviewed by the Board of Governors and the General Conference and the system had not been found wanting. Its application was extremely wide. By the end of 1980 approximately 98 per cent of the nuclear facilities of which the Agency was aware outside the nuclear-weapon States were under Agency safeguards.

In fulfilling its responsibilities, the Agency had inspected the Iraqi reactors and had not found evidence of any activity not in accordance with the Non–Proliferation Treaty. Nevertheless, a country which was not a party to the Treaty had evidently not felt assured by the Agency's findings and by its ability to continue to discharge its safeguarding responsibilities effectively.

In the interest of its national security, as was stated by its leaders, it had felt motivated to take military action. From a point of principle, one could only conclude that it was the Agency's safeguards system that had also been attacked. That was a matter of grave concern to the Agency and had to be well pondered.

––––––

Notes and Questions. As you now look back, do you think that Israel was justified? Does Self–Defense work as a justification? Does the nuclear era cause a new approach to be required in relation to the issue of *"imminence"* of an armed attack? In the subsequent struggles, occupation and violence, has one side or the other been justified in any of its conduct?

––––––

SECTION F.   FURTHER STRAINS ON THE LIMITS OF CONVENTIONAL JUSTIFICATIONS

1.   NATIONAL LIBERATION MOVEMENTS

Declaration on the Granting of Independence to Colonial Countries and Peoples[a]

General Assembly Resolution 1514 (15) of Dec. 14, 1960.
U.N.Gen.Ass.Off.Rec., 15th Sess., Supp. No. 16 (A/4684), p. 66.

* * *

1.   The subjection of peoples to alien subjugation, domination and exploitation constitutes a denial of fundamental human rights, is contrary to the Charter of the United Nations and is an impediment to the promotion of world peace and co-operation.

2.   All peoples have the right to self-determination; by virtue of that right they freely determine their political status and freely pursue their economic, social and cultural development.

4.   All armed action or repressive measures of all kinds directed against dependent peoples shall cease in order to enable them to exercise peacefully and freely their right to complete independence, and the integrity of their national territory shall be respected.

5.   Immediate steps shall be taken, in Trust and Non–Self–Governing Territories or all other territories which have not yet attained independence, to transfer all powers to the peoples of those territories, without any conditions or reservations, in accordance with their freely expressed will

a.   The complete text of the declaration is in the Documentary Supplement.

and desire, without any distinction as to race, creed or colour, to enable them to enjoy complete independence and freedom.

* * *

United Nations, General Assembly Resolution 3382 (30) Of November 10, 1975

U.N.Gen.Ass.Off.Rec., 30th Sess., Sup. No. 34 (A/10034), p. 84.

The General Assembly,

Recalling its [earlier] resolutions. Reaffirming the importance of the universal realization of the right of peoples to self-determination, to national sovereignty and territorial integrity and of the speedy granting of independence to colonial countries and peoples as imperatives for the enjoyment of human rights,

* * *

1. Reaffirms the legitimacy of the peoples' struggle for independence, territorial integrity and liberation from colonial and foreign domination and alien subjugation by all available means including armed struggle;

2. Welcomes the efforts by the Fact–Finding Commission of Inquiry and Conciliation of the Organization of African Unity to resolve amicably the current conflict in Angola;

3. Rejects any foreign interference in the internal affairs of Angola and of the Comoros;

4. Condemns the policies of those members of the North Atlantic Treaty Organization and those countries whose military, economic, sporting or political relations with the racist régimes of southern Africa and elsewhere encourage these régimes to persist in their suppression of the aspirations of peoples for self-determination and independence;

5. Strongly condemns all Governments which do not recognize the right to self-determination and independence of peoples under colonial and foreign domination and alien subjugation, notably the peoples of Africa and the Palestinian people;

6. Demands full respect for the basic human rights of all individuals detained or imprisoned as a result of their struggle for self-determination and independence, and strict respect for article 5 of the Universal Declaration of Human Rights under which no one shall be subjected to torture or to cruel, inhuman or degrading treatment, and their immediate release;

8. Notes with appreciation the material and other forms of assistance that peoples under colonial and alien régimes continue to receive from Governments, United Nations agencies and intergovernmental and non-governmental organizations and calls for a maximization of this assistance.
* * *

2400th plenary meeting
10 November 1975

Notes and Questions

1. ***Assistance to liberation movements.*** Is lawful assistance to liberation movements limited to humanitarian aid? Is it lawful for states to provide military assistance (money and arms) to them? Is provision of such military assistance consistent with article 2(4) of the charter? Or is there an exception from article 2(4)'s prohibition in the case of wars of liberation waged against a colonial state by people in the colony? Does article 1(2) of the charter, referring to self-determination of peoples, supply the answer to these questions?

2. ***United Nations declaration.*** Note the following provisions of the General Assembly's Declaration on Principles of International Law Concerning Friendly Relations and Cooperation Among States in Accordance with the Charter of the United Nations, adopted in 1970:

* * *

By virtue of the principle of equal rights and self-determination of peoples enshrined in the Charter of the United Nations, all peoples have the right freely to determine, without external interference, their political status and to pursue their economic, social and cultural development, and every State has the duty to respect this right in accordance with the provisions of the Charter.

* * *

Every State has the duty to refrain from any forcible action which deprives peoples referred to above in the elaboration of the present principle of their right to self-determination and freedom and independence. In their actions against, and resistance to, such forcible action in pursuit of the exercise of their right to self-determination, such peoples are entitled to seek and to receive support in accordance with the purposes and principles of the Charter.

* * *

Nothing in the foregoing paragraphs shall be construed as authorizing or encouraging any action which would dismember or impair, totally or in part, the territorial integrity or political unity of sovereign and independent States conducting themselves in compliance with the principle of equal rights and self-determination of peoples as described above and thus possessed of a government representing the whole people belonging to the territory without distinction as to race, creed or colour.

Every State shall refrain from any action aimed at the partial or total disruption of the national unity and territorial integrity of any other State or country.

3. ***The limits of self-determination.*** National liberation movements and the notion of self-determination, of course, are related. Heather Wilson writes: "One of the most controversial issues in international law since the end of World War II has been whether self-determination is a

right in international law or simply a principle of political thought which has assumed great prominence in international affairs at various periods since the late eighteenth century." Wilson, *International Law and the Use of Force by National Liberation Movements* 55 (1988). The U.N., in specially constituted committees and the General Assembly has condemned terrorism and the illegal use of force, yet these bodies have exempted the use of force in exercise of "the inalienable right to self-determination and independence of all peoples under colonial and racist regimes and other forms of alien domination and the legitimacy of their struggle, in particular the struggle of national liberation movements, in accordance with the purposes and principles of the Charter and the relevant resolutions of the organs of the United Nations." Report of the Ad Hoc Committee on International Terrorism, U.N. GAOR, 28th Sess.Supp. No. 28, at 1, U.N.Doc. A/9028 (1973); Resolution on the Definition of Aggression, art. 7, G.A.Res. 3314, U.N. GAOR, 29th Sess., Supp. No. 31, at 144, U.N.Doc. A/9631 (1975), reprinted in 13 I.L.M. 710, 714 (1974) (in Doc.Supp.). *See also,* Beres, *Prosecuting Iraqi War Crimes: Allied and Israeli Rights Under International Law,* 16 Hast. Int'l & Comp. L. Rev. 41 (1992). *See,* Firmage, The "War of National Liberation" and the Third World, Ch. 13, in Law and Civil War in the Modern World p. 304 (Moore ed. 1974).

The notion that national liberation movements have authority to use force for purposes of self-determination challenges the traditional rule that states alone may legitimately use force. *See* Wilson, Use of Force, *supra,* at 91. Is this "special status" accorded to "national liberation movements" and the sanctioning of their use of force in contravention of the principles of the U.N. Charter? *See* Halberstam, Book Review, *A Mandate for Terror: The United Nations and the PLO,* 86 A.J.I.L. 424 (1992). Or is it promoting those principles? Judith Gardam notes that, "article 1(4) of [Protocol I of the Geneva Convention] * * * treats some wars of self-determination as international for the purposes of applying the law of armed conflict. During the negotiation of Protocol I, the majority of states took the legal position that article 1(4) was merely a recognition of the existing situation in international law. A minority of states, however, chose to couch their arguments for the extension of Protocol I in very controversial and emotive concepts, particularly that of the just war * * *. The adverse implication for civilians is that acknowledging these wars as just implicitly legitimizes lesser standards in the armed pursuit of self-determination * * * [T]he ends will justify the means * * * [Victims categorized as being] in opposition to persons exercising their right of self-determination will not be entitled to the protection of the humanitarian law of armed conflict." On the other hand, if the notion that article 1(4) represents existing international law, "[f]rom the point of view of armed conflict, * * * wars waged by such peoples to achieve the right of self-determination are wars between international entities and have the status of international wars. Thus, they should attract the application of the rules of armed conflict relative to international conflict." Gardam, *Noncombatant Immunity and the Gulf Conflict,* 32 Va.J.Int'l L. 813, 824–25, & n. 47 (1992).

Buchheit, Secession: The Legitimacy of Self–Determination

216–218 (1978).*

[W]e can draw several conclusions. First, secessionist activity is an irrepressible feature of the contemporary world scene, and the future, from all indications, will not see an abatement in the frequency of these claims. Second, many of these movements seek legal justification in the international doctrine of self-determination. Third, at the present time there is neither an international consensus regarding the status of secession within this doctrine nor (should it be conceded such a status) is there an accepted teaching regarding the nature of a legitimate secessionist movement. Fourth, by its present inability to distinguish legitimate from illegitimate claims to secessionist self-determination, the international community is seriously handicapped in its attempt to minimize instances of unwarranted third-party intervention in secessionist conflicts under the aegis of the "peremptory norm" of self-determination. Finally, aside from the immense cost of secessionist wars to the immediate parties, the danger of unrestrained intervention inevitably brings in its wake a possibility of escalation and the confrontation of major power blocs. One is left, therefore, with the disturbing result that situations involving a potentially serious threat to international world order, situations which are by their nature arguably unregulated by the general legal restrictions upon the international use of force, remain equally unfettered by any specific doctrines of international law.

There are several apparent solutions to this problem. It is possible for the world community to make an ex cathedra pronouncement that secession has no place within the doctrine of self-determination, thus embracing a limitation of this principle to cases of overseas colonization, interracial domination, or some other arbitrary category. This approach is, I believe, both dangerous and highly unrealistic. Such a transparently artificial restriction of the principle to the relatively "safe" context of European-style colonialism, when articulated by the very entities (independent States) liable to be inconvenienced by its further extension, is not likely to convince minority groups within established States that their claims have been adjudged illegitimate by an impartial collective verdict. They will therefore tend to disregard all opinions coming from that body, whether concerning the outbreak, conduct, or settlement of separatist conflicts, as hopelessly self-protective. The international community would thus effectively cast itself in a role similar to that occupied by the Holy Alliance during the last century in its goal of guarding monarchic supremacy against "anarchic" nationalism; that is, the role of an entrenched power bloc flailing against threats to its dominance arising from the dissatisfactions of its own constituents. At the very least, the community will have to abandon its fondness for decrying the evils perpetrated by colonial Powers unless it can discover a convincing method of distinguishing, in principle,

* Reprinted with the permission of Buchheit and Yale University Press.

these evil policies from the equivalent deportment of "alien" governors occupying a contiguous land mass.

* * *

[Another] solution, and the one that will be pursued here, seeks to maintain the underlying force of the self-determination principle and yet minimize the dangers to international peace and security by concentrating upon a method of ascertaining legitimate claims of this kind. Acknowledging that self-determination (insofar as it derives its strength from an innate urge to self-government coupled with a sense of the moral objections to alien domination resulting in exploitation, humiliation, and deprivation of human rights) is prima facie applicable to some but not all groups within independent States, the focus of attention ought to be on determining which groups are entitled to invoke the principle. Inevitably, this will involve an inquiry into the nature of the group, its situation within its governing State, its prospects for an independent existence, and the effect of its separation on the remaining population and the world community in general. Taken as a whole, these considerations would evolve standards by which the international community could ascertain instances of legitimate claims to separatist self-determination.

The probable benefits of this approach are significant. Most importantly, the international community would be given the chance to adjust its posture with regard to a particular separatist demand by virtue of its ability to distinguish the legal merits of the claim. This might permit a collective judgment, as was reached in the cases of Rhodesia and South Africa, concerning the proper scope of outside States' behavior toward the situation. In addition, the norms of nonintervention and proscription of force would again enjoy some protection under this scheme. Unless specifically prohibited by an authoritative international decision, of course, intervention on behalf of the "legitimate" party would still be possible and perhaps invited as enforcement of a community standard; but then, even in the halcyon days before the emergence of self-determination as a peremptory norm only a minority of jurists opposed *all* intervention. * * *

The clear trend, however, seems to be an international acceptance of minority rights, human rights, and self determination. These are no longer considered to be solely domestic issues, off-limits to any outside intervention or interference. *See, e.g.,* Smith, *NATO, the Kosovo Liberation Army, and the War for an Independent Kosovo: Unlawful Aggression or Legitimate Exercise of Self–Determination?,* 27–FEB Army Law 1, 19 (2001); Van Dyke, et al, *Self-Determination for Non–Self-Governing Peoples and for Indigenous Peoples: The Cases of Guam & Hawai'i,* 18 U.Haw.L.Rev. 623, 640–642 (1996); Ting-lun Huang, The Evolution of the Concept of Self–Determination and the Right of the People of Taiwan to Self–Determination, 14 NY Int'l L. Rev. 167 (2001).

Reimers, *Perspective: Practicing Law on a Different Battlefield,* Chicago J.Int'l L. 275, 279 (2001), wrote:**

** Reprinted with the permission of the Chicago International Law Journal.

"III. War and Peace. As I mentioned earlier, the classical conception of war is not very relevant to the modern international scene. Today, wars are mostly fought on a local scale, with the surrounding countries formally at peace. This causes some confusion about which rules apply, and all too often, military commanders get it wrong. This problem has been observed with great frequency in the Balkans (I dare say anywhere where peacekeepers are present). Even the lawyers often lack a full grasp of the countless conventions, regulations, and resolutions that apply to a conflict. Because of this confusion, as well as the military commander's frustration and desire to 'get the job done,' situations are often handled 'as we always do it' without regard to the legal requirements.

For example, the North Atlantic Treaty Organization ('NATO') bombing campaign in Kosovo in 1999 was not declared to be a 'war' within the formal meaning of that term. Nevertheless, certain human rights were suspended during the hostilities out of necessity, and now NATO has been charged with violating the human rights of some Serbians. This is paradoxical, as the campaign's primary purpose was to protect human rights. Nevertheless, because of a formality, NATO has been accused of being the violator of human rights. Thus, a formalistic view of this case ignores the fact that an actual state of war existed—even if one was not declared—which allowed for certain specific deviations from human rights conventions."

Karin von Hippel, Democracy by Force: US Military Intervention in the Post–Cold War World 172–73 (Cambridge 2000);

4. *A veiled dictum by the International Court of Justice?* In the Nicaragua case, the court made the following reference to wars of national liberation:

206. However, before reaching a conclusion on the nature of prohibited intervention, the Court must be satisfied that State practice justifies it. There have been in recent years a number of instances of foreign intervention for the benefit of forces opposed to the government of another State. The Court is not here concerned with the process of decolonization; this question is not in issue in the present case. It has to consider whether there might be indications of a practice illustrative of belief in a kind of general right for States to intervene, directly or indirectly, with or without armed force, in support of an internal opposition in another State, whose cause appeared particularly worthy by reason of the political and moral values with which it was identified. For such a general right to come into existence would involve a fundamental modification of the customary law principle of non-intervention. (Nicaragua v. United States of America, [1986] I.C.J. Reports 14, 98.)

In his dissenting opinion, Judge Schwebel commented on this statement by the court:

179. [T]he implication, or surely a possible implication, of the juxtaposition of the Court's statements is that the Court is of the view that there is or may be not a general but a particular right of intervention provided that it is in furtherance of "the process of

decolonization". That is to say, by these statements, the Court may be understood as inferentially endorsing an exception to the prohibition against intervention, in favour of the legality of intervention in the promotion of so-called "wars of liberation", or, at any rate, some such wars, while condemning intervention of another political character.

180.   In contemporary international law, the right of self-determination, freedom and independence of peoples is universally recognized; the right of peoples to struggle to achieve these ends is universally accepted; but what is *not* universally recognized and what is *not* universally accepted is any right of such peoples to foreign assistance or support which constitutes intervention. That is to say, it is lawful for a foreign State or movement to give to a people struggling for self-determination moral, political and humanitarian assistance; but it is not lawful for a foreign State or movement to intervene in that struggle with force or to provide arms, supplies and other logistical support in the prosecution of armed rebellion. This is true whether the struggle is or is proclaimed to be in pursuance of the process of decolonization or against colonial domination. Moreover, what entities are susceptible of decolonization is a matter of dispute in many cases. What is a colony, and who is the colonizer, are the subjects of sharply differing views. Examples of what may be contentiously characterized—though not necessarily unreasonably characterized—as colonies may be readily assembled. But for present purposes, it is enough to point out that the lack of beauty is in the eye of the beholder.

181.   For reasons both of principle and practicality, leading States for years have gone on record in support of the considerations recalled in the previous paragraph. It is not to be expected that their view of the law, or the content of the law, will be influenced by an acknowledged and ambiguous *dictum* of the Court on a topic of which no trace can be found in the pleadings of the Parties. Perhaps the best that can be said of this unnecessary statement of the Court is that it can be read as taking no position on the legality of intervention in support of the process of decolonization, but as merely referring to a phenomenon as to which positions in the international community differ. Even so, it is difficult to find justification for the Court raising so contentious a question, the more so when it acknowledges that that question is not in issue in the present case. (Nicaragua v.U.S. [*supra*]).

———

National Liberation, Self–Determination, and Terrorism

Bianchi, Review of Terrorismo Internazionale E Garanzie Colletive

87 A.J.I.L. 175, 177 (1993).*

* * *

Evaluating current trends in state practice can be a difficult exercise. One should not overlook the fact that, to trace general rules of international law, a consistent and general pattern of state practice is needed. In fact, one confronts a sense of uneasiness when considering the obligation to abstain from financing or directing acts of terrorism as an obligation erga omnes in terms of positive law.[1] In fact, establishing the link between a state and terrorist activities allegedly sponsored by it is often difficult. What amounts to state sponsorship remains murky. For example, can one maintain that financing a national liberation movement suspected of being involved in terrorist attacks or training its members would trigger the international responsibility of a state? It is worth noting that not even in the 1988 Rome Convention on Maritime Terrorism, a fairly sophisticated legal instrument, is mention made of state-sponsored terrorism. The absence of any such provision is not a cause for optimism about the existence or emergence of states' opinio juris. For a long time, political strains and ideological confrontation have prevented the achievement of consensus on a clear-cut distinction between terrorist acts and belligerent acts of national liberation movements. This difficulty has also overshadowed the prospects for achieving a generally accepted definition of terrorism.

Different considerations apply with respect to the punishment of individual terrorists. In this area, state practice shows a much higher degree of acceptance of the legal obligation to apprehend and prosecute those guilty of terrorist acts. Not only do extradition treaties often provide for exceptions to the political offense exemption in case of terrorist acts, but also the trend in recent practice is to invoke the universality principle in jurisdictional claims related to individual terrorist activities. One can hope that in the near future the overwhelming political condemnation of terrorism will be converted into peremptory legal terms so as to dissipate Judge Edwards's and Judge Bork's doubts about the status of terrorism in international law.

* * *

———

See also, the excellent article by Berman, *"But the Alternative is Despair": European Nationalism and the Modernist Renewal of International Law*, 106 Harv. L. Rev. 1792 (1993).

2.   ACTION AGAINST TERRORISM

Rescue of Hostages

Summary Account of Entebbe Incident
McDowell, Introductory Note.[a]

1. In 1990, however, the International Law Commission adopted, in the framework of a Draft Code of Crimes against the Peace and Security of Mankind, an article (Art. 16, International Terrorism) that expressly condemns such conduct.

a. Editor's note. The note serves as an introduction to materials concerning the incident.

15 I.L.M. 1224 (1976).*

An Air France airplane that left Israel for France with over 250 passengers and a crew of 12 aboard was hijacked by terrorists on June 28, 1976, after a stopover in Athens. The hijackers forced the plane to land first at Benghazi in Libya, and then at Entebbe Airport in Uganda. Acting for the Popular Front for the Liberation of Palestine, the hijackers demanded the release of some 153 terrorists jailed in Israel, West Germany, France, Switzerland, and Kenya. On June 30 the hijackers released 47 non-Israeli passengers, and the following day released an additional 100. The remaining 104 passengers and crew were held hostage in Uganda until rescued by an Israeli military commando unit on July 3 and taken to Israel. Reports indicated that in the rescue operation three of the hostages, one Israeli soldier, seven of the terrorists, and a number of Ugandan soldiers were killed. There were conflicting opinions on whether the Government of Uganda acted to protect the hostages and negotiate for their release, or was directly implicated in collaborating with the terrorists.

On July 9, the Security Council of the United Nations began consideration of a complaint by the Prime Minister of Mauritius, current chairman of the Organization of African Unity, which referred to the "act of aggression" by Israel against the Republic of Uganda. See U.N. Doc. S/12126. On July 12, two draft resolutions were introduced—one by the United Kingdom and the United States, the other by Tanzania, Libya, and Benin.

The U.K.–U.S. resolution, inter alia, condemned hijacking and called on states to prevent and punish all such terrorist acts, while reaffirming the need to respect the sovereignty and territorial integrity of all states.

The Tanzania–Libya–Benin draft condemned Israel's violation of Uganda's sovereignty and territorial integrity and demanded that Israel meet Uganda's claims for full compensation for damage and destruction. [Neither draft received sufficient votes for adoption.]

Excerpts From United Nations Security Council Debate on the Entebbe Incident

13 UN Monthly Chronicle, Aug.–Sept. 1976, p. 15.

* * *

* * * Kurt WALDHEIM, Secretary–General of the U.N., said he had issued a statement on 8 July immediately after his return from Africa in which he had given a detailed account of the role he had played in efforts to secure the release of the hostages at Entebbe.

The case before the Council raised a number of complex issues because, in this instance, the response of one State to the results of an act of hijacking involved an action affecting another sovereign State. In reply to a

* Reprinted with the permission of the American Society of International Law from materials published at 15 I.L.M. 1224 under the general title "United Nations: Security Council Debate and Draft Resolution Concerning the Operation to Rescue Hijacked Hostages at the Entebbe Airport."

specific question, he had said: "I have not got all the details, but it seems to be clear that Israeli aircraft have landed in Entebbe and this constitutes a serious violation of the sovereignty of a State Member of the United Nations." The Secretary–General said he felt it was his obligation to uphold the principle of the territorial integrity and sovereignty of every State.

However, that was not the only element involved in considering cases of the kind which the Council was discussing. That was particularly true when the world community was required to deal with unprecedented problems arising from acts of international terrorism, which Mr. Waldheim said he had consistently condemned and which raised many issues of a humanitarian, moral, legal and political character for which, at the present time, no commonly agreed rules or solutions existed.

It was hoped that the Council would find a way to point the world community in a constructive direction so that it might be spared a repetition of the human tragedies of the past and the type of conflict between States which the Council would now be considering.

* * *

Percy HAYNES (Guyana) said the action taken by Israel against Uganda was nothing but naked and brutal aggression. Guyana strongly condemned Israel for its aggression against the black African country of Uganda.

It was being argued that the principle of sovereignty was subordinate to the principle of human freedom and that Israel had the right, whenever it chose, to violate the sovereignty of other States in order to secure the freedom of its own citizens. That was nothing but a modern-day version of gun-boat diplomacy.

Those who, like Israel, sought to give legitimacy to the violation of the sovereignty of other States were making many small States, whose faith in and commitment to international law were unshakable, hostage to the dictates of naked power.

* * *

Kaj SUNDBERG (Sweden) said the drama was started by an abhorrent act of terrorism perpetrated by a group of extremist Palestinian Arabs and Europeans. There was no excuse for that criminal act.

The world must react vigorously against terrorist acts and take all possible protective measures. New efforts must be undertaken to achieve broad international agreement to combat terrorism, in the form of generally recognized standards of international conduct. The international community must work towards general recognition of the clear obligation resting on every State to do everything in its power, where necessary in collaboration with other States, to prevent acts of terrorism and, even more, to refrain from any action which might facilitate the perpetration of such acts.

Any State where hijackers landed with hostages must be prepared to shoulder the heavy responsibility of protecting all victims under circumstances which were bound to be difficult and delicate.

The Israeli action being considered involved an infringement of the national sovereignty and territorial integrity of Uganda. At the same time,

Sweden was aware of the terrible pressures to which the Israeli Government and people were subjected, faced with this unprecedented act of international piracy and viewing the increasing threat to the lives of so many of their compatriots.

Sweden, although unable to reconcile the Israeli action with the strict rules of the Charter, did not find it possible to join in a condemnation in such a case.

* * *

Mr. SCRANTON (United States) said the United States reaffirmed the principle of territorial sovereignty in Africa. In addition to that principle, the United States was deeply concerned over the problem of air piracy and the callous and pernicious use of innocent people as hostages to promote political ends. The Council could not forget that the Israeli operation in Uganda would never have come about had the hijacking of the Air France flight from Athens not taken place.

Israel's action in rescuing the hostages necessarily involved a temporary breach of the territorial integrity of Uganda. Normally, such a breach would be impermissible under the Charter. However, there was a well established right to use limited force for the protection of one's own nationals from an imminent threat of injury or death in a situation where the State in whose territory they were located was either unwilling or unable to protect them. The right, flowing from the right of self-defence, was limited to such use of force as was necessary and appropriate to protect threatened nationals from injury.

The requirements of that right to protect nationals were clearly met in the Entebbe case. Israel had good reason to believe that at the time it acted Israeli nationals were in imminent danger of execution by the hijackers. In addition, there was substantial evidence that the Government of Uganda cooperated with and aided the hijackers. The ease and success of the Israeli effort to free the hostages suggested that the Ugandan authorities could have overpowered the hijackers and released the hostages if they had really had the desire to do so.

* * *

Under such circumstances, the Government of Israel invoked one of the most remarkable rescue missions in history, a combination of guts and brains that had seldom, if ever, been surpassed. It was justified because innocent decent people had a right to live and be rescued from terrorists who recognized no law and who were ready to kill if their demands were not met.

* * *

Mikhail KHARLAMOV (USSR) said that the flight carried out, the material destruction wrought, the substantial number of Ugandans killed were all regarded by Israel as a measure which was just or at least justified. But there existed no laws in the world, no moral or international laws, which could justify such action.

However much the representative of Israel might have tried to refute the irrefutable, the armed action against Uganda was an act of direct, flagrant aggression and an outright violation of the Charter, especially of Article 2, ¶ 4, which stated: "All Members shall refrain in their international relations from the threat or use of force against the territorial integrity or political independence of any State, or in any other manner inconsistent with the purposes of the United Nations."

The Soviet Union consistently opposed acts of terrorism, and was prepared to do its part in order to end that phenomenon. But one could not replace one matter with another. The Council was considering not the matter of international terrorism but an attack on Uganda, the killing of Ugandans, the destruction of Entebbe Airport, and other material destruction inflicted by the Israeli action against that State.

There was a gap between individual acts of terrorism and an attack by one State—in this case Israel—against another. Therefore a policy approved by a State could not be exceptional, even in the case in question.

The Council must condemn in the most vigorous manner the Israeli aggression against the sovereignty and territorial integrity of Uganda and compel Israel to recompense Uganda for the material damage done in connection with the attack. In addition, the Council must extend a serious warning to Israel that such acts of aggression would not go unpunished in future.

* * *

Notes and Questions

1. Does the raid on Entebbe provide a precedent to justify rescue attempts.

2. ***Iranian Hostage Rescue Attempt.*** In 1980, President Carter sent a small, specially-trained unit to rescue the hostages who were still in the former Embassy compound in Tehran. Three of the helicopters, however, developed problems and the mission was aborted. The President gave the Chairman of the Joint Chiefs of Staff authority, once the mission had begun, to do what was "necessary" to accomplish the mission, while keeping civilian casualties to a minimum. What do you think would have happened if the troops had made it into Tehran, but had become trapped or engaged in a protracted conflict and then were threatened with capture or death? Did the mission comply with international law? If so, what was its justification? If not, why not? Did the mission comply with U.S. constitutional law? President Carter did "Report" to Congress on April 26, 1980, after the mission was terminated. *See* Henkin, *Use of Force: Law and U.S. Policy*, in Right v. Might, *supra*, at 31, 41–42 (recognizing a limited right to intervene, if and when the territorial state cannot or will not do so).

3. ***Rescuing nationals—Liberia.*** Day, *Legal Considerations in Noncombatant Evacuation Operations*, 40 Naval L. Rev. 45 (1992) writes: "On August 5, 1990, a reinforced rifle company of Marines arrive at the U.S. Embassy in Monrovia. Their mission was to provide additional security for the U.S. Embassy and to evacuate U.S. nationals, in response to threats made by * * * a leader of one of the rebel factions in the insurrection * * *

there." The U.S. claimed self-defense as the justification for the intervention to save U.S. nationals, citing the Israeli raid on Entebbe. The rationale was based on concepts of humanitarian intervention, which had developed despite the U.N. charter's severe limitation on a state's unilateral prerogatives to use force. The Security Council was unable to act. Is the proper basis for justifying this type of action self-defense or humanitarian intervention? *See*, Schachter, International Law in Theory and Practice (1991).

Arrest of Terrorists

Terrorists Seize Cruise Ship In Mediterranean

United States Department of State Bulletin, December 1985, p. 74.

WHITE HOUSE STATEMENT, OCT. 10, 1985

At the President's direction, U.S. military forces intercepted an aircraft over international airspace that was transporting the Achille Lauro terrorists. The aircraft was diverted to the airbase at Sigonella, Italy. In cooperation with the Government of Italy, the terrorists were then taken into Italian custody for appropriate legal proceedings.

Earlier today, upon learning that the terrorists would be flown from Egypt to their freedom, the President directed that U.S. forces intercept the aircraft and escort it to a location where the terrorists could be apprehended by those with appropriate jurisdiction. U.S. F–14 aircraft, flying from the carrier Saratoga, detected the aircraft in international airspace and intercepted it. They instructed it to follow them and escorted it to the military airbase at Sigonella, Italy. This operation was conducted without firing a shot. The aircraft landed with Italian consent and was surrounded by American and Italian troops. The terrorists aboard were taken into custody by Italian authorities. The Egyptian aircraft, with its crew and other personnel on board, is returning to Egypt.

We have been assured by the Government of Italy that the terrorists will be subject to full due process of law. For our part, we intend to pursue prompt extradition to the United States of those involved in the crime. This action affirms our determination to see that terrorists are apprehended, prosecuted, and punished.

* * *

From the onset, the U.S. Government made clear to all the governments involved our firm opposition to negotiations with the terrorists or concessions to them. We also made clear our expectation that the terrorists would be brought to justice.

We were, therefore, deeply distressed to learn that those responsible for the death of Leon Klinghoffer might be permitted to go free. We said yesterday that we were determined to see justice done and that we would use every appropriate means to that end.

The decision on ending the hijacking was an independent one by the Government of Egypt. When we were consulted, we advised strongly against any arrangements which would permit the terrorists to escape justice. Since the time the terrorists were taken off the ship, we have continued intensive contacts with the Government of Egypt to pursue that point.

* * *

In closing, the President wants to emphasize once again that the international scourge of terrorism can only be stamped out if each member of the community of civilized nations meets its responsibility squarely—passing up no opportunity to apprehend, prosecute, and punish terrorists wherever they may be found. We cannot tolerate terrorism in any form. We will continue to take every appropriate measure available to us to deal with these dastardly deeds. There can be no asylum for terrorism or terrorists.

* * *

"This Week With David Brinkley," Oct. 13, 1985

Abraham D. Sofaer,
Department of State Legal Adviser

* * *

"Q. What about the Egyptians' charge that this was piracy, that what our F–14s were doing was, in effect, no different * * * from what the terrorists have done?"

"A. That's completely inaccurate because, first of all, this was not an intercept of an Egyptian target. It's like a murderer hailing a taxi, and then the taxi company pretending that they were the target of the police arrest. The fact is, the pirates in the airplane were the target of the intercept, and they happened to be in a civilian Egyptian airliner. We have had the most excellent relations with the Egyptian military, and we did not view this as directed against them at all."

———

Notes & Questions. Did Legal Adviser Sofaer's explanation of the interception make any sense legally? Is Egypt a taxi? Was the interception of the Egyptian Airliner a precursor to the executive participation in the abduction of Alvarez–Machain, supra? Was it a violation of Egyptian sovereignty? Was it a simple arrest? If it was not a violation of Egyptian sovereignty, as the Reagan Administration claimed, what was it? What was its justification? Did Egypt invite the interception? If not, does international law provide justification for a nation to commandeer another nation's airliners? Was it an "official hijacking" prompted by a "just cause?" What "just cause" can justify hijacking? Which do we accept? How about others? Do the treaties on hijacking (Montreal, Chicago, Tokyo), to which we are a party, provide a justification? Can you meaningfully distinguish the U.S. action against the Egyptian airliner and an abduction of U.S. officials or agents who are considered to have violated the criminal laws of other regimes? *See* discussion of *U.S. v. Alvarez–Machain*, in Chapters 1 supra and 16, infra; and discussion of *U.S. v. Fawaz Yuniz*, in Chapter 3, supra.

Joyner & Rothbaum, Libya And The Aerial Incident At Lockerbie: What Lessons For International Extradition Law?

14 Mich.J.Int'l L. 222, 222–224 (1993).*

* * * At 6:56 P.M. EST, at the altitude of 31,000 feet, the Maid of the Seas made its last contact with ground control. Seven minutes later, the green cross-hair at air traffic control split into five bright blips as Pan Am Flight 103 exploded in midair. Her fiery skeleton, laden with the bodies of passengers and crew, rained down on the people of Lockerbie, Scotland. Within the hour, 243 passengers, 16 crew members, and 11 townspeople were dead.

Nearly three years later, following extensive international investigations, the United States indicted two Libyan intelligence officers in November 1991 for the bombing of Pan Am Flight 103. The Libyan response to informal extradition claims was not unexpected: the government refused to surrender the officers on the grounds that such an act constituted direct interference in Libya's internal affairs.

In January 1992, and again in March 1992, the United Nations Security Council responded to the Libyan position with two resolutions: the first urged the government of Colonel Muammar el-Qadhafi to cooperate with the international investigation of the bombing; the second imposed sanctions on Libya for its failure to comply with the Security Council's requests. Taken together as legal prescriptions, the Security Council's actions marked the first time that the United Nations had ever demanded extradition of nationals of one State to face trial in a second State, despite the existence of international legal principles supporting Libya's position to refuse extradition of its nationals.

The U.N. Security Council resolutions in the Lockerbie case represent a salient, albeit as yet unconsummated, step toward strengthening the international extradition process for dealing with alleged terrorist acts. In the past, international fugitives who committed unlawful acts abroad often found sanctuary behind the political veils of customary and codified law, evading extradition with the shield of State sovereignty. The lack of a universally accepted rule of law has left extradition to bilateral treaties and acts of reciprocity and comity, which provide only malleable standards that States can interpret and reinterpret to serve their needs. * * *

Notes and Questions

1. *Libya, for its part, has denied any involvement in the incident* and has claimed that Libya is the actual victim of terrorism, recalling the downing of a Libyan civil airplane over Sinai in 1973 and the 1986 U.S. bombing of Tripoli. Libya did offer to enter into talks with the U.S., France, and the U.K. and to submit the dispute to Libyan judges who were also investigating the bombing. See, League of Arab States—Libya: Resolu-

* Reprinted with the permission of the Michigan Journal of International Law.

tion and Statements Regarding Investigations of Aerial Incidents, 31 I.L.M. 724 (1992). In addition, there have been reports that the Libyans have attempted to compromise, offering to accept trial in Switzerland or some other "neutral" country, or even to accept responsibility in exchange for termination of sanctions and other remedies being sought. * * *

2. **Kidnapping Terrorists:** Does a notion akin to anticipatory self-defense apply to allow an exception against state-sponsored kidnapping? Some commentators have argued that self-protection, the protective principle of jurisdiction, and the defensive use of force combine to create this exception. See, discussion of this issue in relation to the *Alvarez–Machain Case, supra,* in Chapters 1, 9, 12, and 16, *supra,* and in Glennon, *Agora: State–Sponsored Abduction: A Comment on United States v. Alvarez–Machain,* 86 A.J.I.L. 746, 748–49 (1992).

* * *

Making Treaties With Terrorists.

In a series of articles, Louis Rene Beres condemned Israel for the settlement agreements with the Palestinian people (the "Oslo Accords") and for many of the actions taken under those agreements. *See, e.g.,* Beres, *Israel's Freeing of Terrorists is Contrary to International Law,* 73 U. Det. Mercy L. Rev. 1 (1995); Beres, *Why the Oslo Accords Should Be Abrogated by Israel,* 12 Am. U.J. Int'l L. & Pol'y 267 (1997). Professor Beres has even gone so far as to suggest that nuclear war is the likely result of the settlement agreements, and that Israel could rationally launch a nuclear preemptive strike if it believes its enemies in the Middle East possess nuclear weapons. *See* Beres, *After the "Peace Process:" Israel, Palestine, and Regional Nuclear War,* 15 Dick. J. Int'l L. 301 (1997). Professor Beres' argument is essentially that the P.L.O. has engaged in terrorist activities for a number of years and that as such, any agreement with the P.L.O. that serves to absolve the organization of its crimes violates international law. Professor John Quigley has responded that the Palestinian people are legally entitled to more than they received in the settlement, because they have for centuries comprised a significant majority of the population in the disputed areas. *See* Quigley, *The Oslo Accords: More than Israel Deserves,* 12 Am. U. J. Int'l L. & Pol'y 285 (1997). Professor Quigley further argues that Israel wrongfully took the Palestinian territory in two different acts of agression, in 1948 and 1967, and that Israel also has engaged in "crimes against humanity," by expelling the Palestinian population from the conquered territory. As such, Professor Quigley asserts that the Oslo Accords must be upheld because the agreements are very favorable to Israel and offer the possibility of peace in a very disruptive region.

Notes and Questions. Is a state obligated, as Professor Beres argues, to continue fighting with a "terrorist" organization, such as the P.L.O., rather than to attempt a peaceful resolution? How many disputes would be resolved if the parties insisted on punishing the other for their crimes of war? Under Beres's argument, is the peace agreement between the Bosnian

Muslims and the Bosnian Serbs legal, or should the Muslims hold out until the Serbs have been punished for their ethnic cleansing? Is Professor Beres' position realistic? Alternatively, if a terrorist organization is not ultimately held responsible for its crimes, what limits are there on the acts it will take to achieve its goals?

3.   THE THIN LINE BETWEEN LIBERATION AND TERRORISM

Beres, The United States and Nuclear Terrorism In a Changing World: A Jurisprudential View

12 Dick. J. Int'l L. 327 (1994).*

Who are the terrorists? Operationally, pertinent departments of the government of the United States currently use the following definitions:

- the unlawful use or threatened use of force or violence by a revolutionary organization against individuals or property with the intention of coercing or intimidating governments or societies, often for political or ideological purposes.

Department of Defense, 1983.

- the unlawful use of force or violence against persons or property to intimidate or coerce a government, the civilian population, or any segment thereof, in furtherance of political or social objectives.

FBI, 1983

- premeditated, politically motivated violence perpetrated against non-combatant targets by subnational groups or clandestine state agents.

Department of State, 1984

- violent criminal conduct apparently intended: (a) to intimidate or coerce a civilian population; (b) to influence the conduct of a government by intimidation or coercion; or (c) to affect the conduct of a government by assassination or kidnapping.

Department of Justice, 1984

- the unlawful use or threat of violence against persons or property to further political or social objectives. It is usually intended to intimidate or coerce a government, individuals or groups or to modify their behavior or policies.

The Vice–President's Task Force on Combatting Terrorism, 1986

None of these definitions is truly suitable * * *.

International law has consistently proscribed particular acts of international terrorism. At the same time, however, it has permitted certain uses of force. These uses derive "from the inalienable right to self-determination and independence of all peoples under colonial and racist regimes and other forms of alien domination and the legitimacy of their struggle, in particular, the struggle of national liberation movements, in accordance with the purposes and principles of the Charter and the relevant resolutions of the

* Reprinted with the permission of the Dickinson School of Law.

organs of the United Nations." This exemption, from the 1973 Generally Assembly Report of the Ad Hoc Committee on International Terrorism, is corroborated, of course, by Article 7 of the UN General Assembly's Definition of Aggression:

> Nothing in this definition, and in particular, Article 3 (inventory of acts that qualify as aggression) could in any way prejudice the right to self-determination, freedom and independence, as derived from the Charter, of peoples forcibly deprived of that right * * *, particularly peoples under colonial and racist regimes or other forms of alien domination; nor the right of these peoples to struggle to that end and to seek and receive support, in accordance with the principles of the Charter and in conformity with the above-mentioned Declaration.

> * * *

This brings us to the first jurisprudential standard for differentiating between lawful insurgency and terrorism, commonly known as "just cause." Where individual states prevent the exercise of human rights, insurgency may express law-enforcing reactions under international law. For this to be the case, however, the means used in that insurgency must be consistent with the second jurisprudential standard, commonly known as "just means."

In deciding whether a particular insurgency is an instance of terrorism or law-enforcement, therefore, states must base their evaluations, in part, on judgments concerning discrimination, proportionality, and military necessity. * * * Once force is applied broadly to any segment of human population, blurring the distinction between combatants and noncombatants, terrorism is taking place. Similarly, once force is applied to the fullest possible extent, restrained only by the limits of available weaponry, terrorism is underway. * * *

SECTION G. LIMITING THE WEAPONS OF WAR

Advisory Opinion on the Legality of the Threat or Use of Nuclear Weapons, Declaration of President Bedjaoui

International Court of Justice, 1996.
35 I.L.M. 1343

> * * *

2. With nuclear weapons, humanity is living on a kind of suspended sentence. For half a century now these terrifying weapons of mass destruction have formed part of the human condition. Nuclear weapons have entered into all calculations, all scenarios, all plans. Since Hiroshima, on the morning of 6 August 1945, fear has gradually become man's first nature. His life on earth has taken on the aspect of what the Koran calls "a long nocturnal journey", like a nightmare whose end he can not yet foresee.

3. However the Atlantic Charter did promise to deliver mankind from fear, and the San Francisco Charter to "save succeeding generations from the scourge of war". Much still remains to be done to exorcise this new terror hanging over man, reminiscent of the terror of his ancestors, who feared being struck by a thunderbolt from the leaden, storm-laden skies. But twentieth-century man's situation differs in many ways from that of his ancestors: he is armed with knowledge; he lays himself open to self-destruction by his own doing; and his fears are better founded. Although endowed with reason, man has never been so unreasonable; his destiny is uncertain; his conscience is confused; his vision is clouded and his ethical co-ordinates are being shed, like dead leaves from the tree of life.

4. However, it must be acknowledged that man has made some attempts to emerge from the blackness of his night. Mankind seems, today at any rate, more at ease than in the 1980s, when it subjected itself to the threat of "star wars". In those years the mortal blast of a space war, a war which would be total, highly sophisticated and would rend our planet asunder, was more likely than ever before to unfurl itself upon humanity. Missiles orbiting close to the Earth could train their infernal nuclear warheads on our globe, while military satellites—for reconnaissance, observation, surveillance or communication—proliferated. The lethal system was about to be established. The "universal government of death", the "thanatrocracy", as the French historian and philosopher of science Michel Serres once called it, said it was ready to set up its batteries in the furthest reaches of the planet. But luckily detente, followed by the ending of the cold war, put a stop to these terrifying preparations.

5. Nevertheless, the proliferation of nuclear weapons has still not been brought under control, despite the existence of the Non–Proliferation Treaty. Fear and folly may still link hands at any moment to perform a final dance of death. Humanity is all the more vulnerable today for being capable of mass producing nuclear missiles.

* * *

———

On July 8, 1996, in response to a General Assembly request for an advisory opinion, the International Court of Justice asserted that it could not declare the threat or use of nuclear weapons to be illegal under all circumstances. The General Assembly had asked, "Is the threat or use of nuclear weapons in any circumstance permitted under international law?" The Court responded by finding as follows:

Advisory Opinion on the Legality of the Threat or Use of Nuclear Weapons

International Court of Justice, 1996.
35 I.L.M. 809.*

105. * * * [The Court finds:]

* Reprinted with the permission of the
American Society of International Law.

A. Unanimously,

There is in neither customary nor conventional international law any specific authorization of the threat or use of nuclear weapons;

B. By eleven votes to three,

There is in neither customary nor conventional international law any comprehensive and universal prohibition of the threat or use of nuclear weapons as such; * * *

C. Unanimously,

A threat or use of force by means of nuclear weapons that is contrary to Article 2, paragraph 4, of the United Nations Charter and that fails to meet all the requirements of Article 51, is unlawful;

D. Unanimously,

A threat or use of nuclear weapons should also be compatible with the requirements of the international law applicable in armed conflict, particularly those of the principles and rules of international humanitarian law, as well as with specific obligations under treaties and other undertakings which expressly deal with nuclear weapons;

E. By seven votes to seven, by the President's casting vote,

It follows from the above-mentioned requirements that the threat or use of nuclear weapons would generally be contrary to the rules of international law applicable in armed conflict, and in particular the principles and rules of humanitarian law;

However, in view of the current state of international law, and of the elements of fact at its disposal, the Court cannot conclude definitively whether the threat or use of nuclear weapons would be lawful or unlawful in an extreme circumstance of self-defence, in which the very survival of a State would be at stake; * * *

F. Unanimously,

There exists an obligation to pursue in good faith and bring to a conclusion negotiations leading to nuclear disarmament in all its aspects under strict and effective international control.

> * * *

Notes and Questions

1. ***In rendering its decision, the court considered provisions*** of the U.N. Charter regarding the use of force, treaties prohibiting the use of weapons of mass destruction, the laws of war, and international humanitarian and environmental laws. The court ultimately avoided reconciliation of the difficult issue—the conflicting requirements of humanitarian law and the right of self defense—by finding that international law was inconclusive regarding the use of nuclear weapons under extreme circumstances. Judge Bedjaoui, who cast the deciding vote on this issue, took pains in his concurring declaration to make clear that the Court was constrained to declare the law, much as it would have liked to create it. He pointed out, however, that having found no customary international law prohibiting

nuclear weapons the Court did not decide that the use would therefore be legal; rather, the Court held that a decision could be rendered only in the context of the facts of a particular situation.

2. ***Today a number of treaties govern the development or use of nuclear weapons.*** These include the Treaty on the Non–Proliferation of Nuclear Weapons, dated July 1, 1968; the Southeast Asia Nuclear Weapon–Free Zone Treaty, dated December 15, 1995; the African Nuclear–Weapon–Free Zone Treaty, dated June 21–23, 1995; the Treaty for the Prohibition of Nuclear Weapons in Latin America, dated February 14, 1967; and the South Pacific Nuclear Free Zone Treaty, dated August 6, 1985. Nearly two hundred states are signatories to the Treaty on Non–Proliferation of Nuclear Weapons; nevertheless, many countries continue to pursue nuclear capabilities. In addition to the known nuclear powers, there are currently forty four states generally deemed capable of developing nuclear power. During the mid–1990s a number of states, including China, France, India, and Pakistan, faced international condemnation as they conducted nuclear tests. This has led to significant international concern and efforts to control proliferation of these weapons, but may, unfortunately, be evidence that the threat of nuclear weapons is not prohibited by customary international law. What do you think the so-called "star-wars" missile shield testing will do to this regime?

States have also acted to ban other types of weapons, in an effort to alleviate the harsh effects of war both on civilians and on the military. One such treaty is the Convention on Prohibitions or Restrictions on the Use of Certain Conventional Weapons Which May be Deemed to be Excessively Injurious or to Have Indiscriminate Effects, dated April 10, 1981. It has three protocols, each of which prohibits use of a specific type of weapon: (1) "any weapon the primary effects of which is to injure by fragments which in the human body escape detection by X-rays"; (2) "time-delay" weapons, such as land mines and other traps; and, (3) incendiary weapons. Another treaty, the Convention on the Prohibition of the Development, Production, Stockpiling and Use of Chemical Weapons and on their Destruction, was adopted on January 13, 1993.

3. ***If the use of nuclear weapons cannot be deemed per se illegal, is there any weapon or form of fighting that is illegal under customary international law?*** Do you agree with the I.C.J. that under certain circumstances the use of a nuclear weapon could be permitted by international law? This decision was rendered by an evenly divided court, with President Bedjaoui casting a second vote. Might this limit the persuasiveness of this advisory opinion?

SECTION H.   USE OF STATE COERCION SHORT OF MILITARY FORCE

Economic Coercion

Notes and Questions. Economic Sanctions: Is non-military coercion subject to the law? Is a state free to impose its will on that of another so long as it refrains from the grosser violations of state personality that are encompassed in physical, military force? Does Article 2(4) of the U.N. Charter proscribe only military force, or also coercions of different types? Is there an emerging law of non-intervention (or a developing body of general international law) that embraces such a proscription? For example, is an economically strong state guilty of illegal conduct if it uses its economic power to seek to force another state to do what it wishes: (a) as to internal non-economic matters, such as establishing honest and democratic governments; (b) as to alignment among power blocs in international relations; (c) as to economic conduct (i) of the same sort as that of the denial practiced by the powerful state (e.g., trade denial as a pressure for change in the trading policy of the pressured state) or (ii) of a different sort (*e.g.*, denial of economic development assistance to induce settlement of a nationalization claim)?

Charter of the Organization of American States

119 U.N.T.S. 3; 2 UST 2394; as amended February 27, 1967, 21 UST 607.

Article 19. "No State may use or encourage the use of coercive measures of an economic or political character in order to force the sovereign will of another State and obtain from it advantages of any kind."

Annex To United Nations General Assembly Resolution 2625 (25) of October 24, 1970

U.N.Gen.Ass.Off.Rec. Annexes, 25th Sess., Supp. No. 28 (A/8028), pp. 122, 123.

Declaration on Principles of International Law Concerning Friendly Relations and Co-operation Among States in Accordance with the Charter of the United Nations

* * *

The principle concerning the duty not to intervene in matters within the domestic jurisdiction of any State, in accordance with the Charter.

No State or group of States has the right to intervene, directly or indirectly, for any reason whatever, in the internal or external affairs of any other State. Consequently, armed intervention and all other forms of interference or attempted threats against the personality of the State or against its political, economic and cultural elements, are in violation of international law.

No State may use or encourage the use of economic, political or any other type of measures to coerce another State in order to obtain from it the subordination of the exercise of its sovereign rights and to secure from it advantage of any kind. * * *

Notes and Questions

1. *With the increasing use of sanctions by the United Nations* and its member states, criticism has developed regarding the efficacy of collec-

tive sanctions and the harms they pose to the citizens of the sanctioned state. Some have argued that collective sanctions violate the norms and principles underlying the U.N. Charter because they actually impose significant suffering on the general population, while the parties in control of the country remain unaffected. *See, e.g.*, Comment, *Does the United Nations' Use of Collective Sanctions to Protect Human Rights Violate its Own Human Rights Standards*, 10 Conn. J.Int'lL. 193 (1994). In addition, because the goals of sanctions are sometimes elusive and their effects unpredictable, sanctions will often adversely affect the state in other ways. *See* Note, *U.N. Sanctions in Haiti: A Contradiction under Articles 51 and 55 of the U.N. Charter*, 20 Fordham Int'l L.J. 1878 (1997). Indeed, it has been argued that the arms embargo imposed by the United Nations on the former Yugoslavia prevented the Bosnian Muslims from getting the weapons they needed to defend themselves from the Serb forces, and therefore violated their inherent right of self defense. *See* Motala & Ritchie, *Self-Defense in International Law, the United Nations, and the Bosnian Conflict*, 57 U.Pitt.L.Rev. 1 (1995). Should the U.N. better define the parameters for collective sanctions? Consider the following proposals.

Note, The Haitian Crisis and the Future of Collective Enforcement of Democratic Governance

27 Law & Pol'y Int'l Bus. 477 (1996).*

The imposition of economic sanctions by the OAS and the United Nations in the Haitian crisis suggests that, although the democratic entitlement ultimately may be protected by such non-forcible measures, special factors govern whether one can expect sanctions to work. As a general matter, the international community has become aware that some programs of economic sanctions may run contrary to the interests of the very people they are supposed to help. Economic sanctions applied to Haiti, for example, were particularly prone to cause misery among the poor and the powerless while the de facto regime remained essentially unaffected and undeterred. Professor Lori Damrosch has developed a series of evaluative standards to be applied to a target of sanctions to determine whether the sanction regime is fundamentally unjust due to its disproportionate impact on the target nation's poor. Damrosch's "differentiation criterion" looks at the effect of sanctions within the target country, attempting to differentiate between innocent civilians and those the sanctions are intended to influence. The "differentiation criterion" proposes two essential claims: first, a program of economic sanctions should not diminish the standard of living of a significant segment of society below the level of subsistence; and second, a program of economic sanctions should target those in whom a change in behavior is sought, and should either diminish their capacity to continue the wrongful behavior or penalize them so that they are induced to desist.

* * *

---

* Reprinted with the permission of the Law and Policy in International Business.

The sanctions' impact on other countries is another factor in the decision to use sanctions for the protection of the democratic entitlement. In the Haitian case, many have argued, not enough attention was paid to the impact that the OAS and the U.N. sanctions had on neighboring countries, most notably the Dominican Republic, which shares the island of Hispaniola with Haiti. Secretary General Boutros–Ghali has recently proposed that "[s]tates suffering collateral damage from the sanctions regime should be entitled not only to consult the Security Council but also to have a realistic possibility of having their difficulties addressed." Finally, sanctions must be applied in a timely manner in order to be effective. One scholar has termed the phenomenon of imposing sanctions too late, "clos[ing] the barn door after the horses have fled." It is, of course, pointless to freeze a bank account after the money has been removed from it; yet in the Haitian case, certain accounts were frozen far too late—one contained less than five dollars.

Professor Christopher Joyner has isolated four specific conditions that will increase the likely effectiveness of a sanctions regime:

> First, sanction measures should be imposed quickly, and should be sweeping in scope. Second, international support for the measures must be strong, despite the costs that will be inflicted on the enjoiners. Third, the enjoiners must maintain their determination to achieve their goal over time. Fourth, it must be determined that the target state is actually vulnerable to sanctions. This means that that state should be involved in international trade.

> * * *

———

Notes and Questions. Are economic sanctions the best means of "enforcement" in international law, short of the actual use of force? What limits should there be on a state's right to control the behavior of other states? Consider this question in light of the Helms–Burton Act, the United States' attempt to further alienate Cuba.

2. *The Helms–Burton Act*

On March 12, 1996, President Clinton signed into law the Cuban Liberty and Democratic Solidarity (Libertad) Act of 1995 (the "Helms–Burton Act" or the "Act"). With this Act the United States is attempting to force other states to join it in the isolation of Cuba, in an effort to remove Fidel Castro from power. The dispute between the United States and Cuba began nearly forty years ago, when Fidel Castro took power in Cuba and expropriated most of the country's privately owned property, including a large amount of property owned by American citizens. Castro then allied Cuba with the Soviet Union, beginning the long period of hostility between the U.S. and Cuba. Despite the fall of the Soviet Union, Cuba has remained communist, and the U.S. has remained determined to remove Castro and install a democratic government. Thus, in 1992, Congress adopted the Cuban Democracy Act, which narrowed the President's discretion relative to Cuba. The Helms–Burton Act was offered early in 1996 and initially condemned by President Clinton. However, in February 1996, Cuba shot down two American civilian aircraft owned by anti-Castro exiles, and in response President Clinton decided to endorse the Act.

Under the Helms–Burton Act, the United States is using the property expropriated nearly forty years ago as a tool for punishing countries that trade with Cuba. Specifically, any company or individual that "trafficks" in confiscated property, *i.e.*, that trades in or derives some benefit from that property, is subject to liability in the United States for the full value of the property, regardless of the benefit derived by the "trafficker." In addition, if the trafficker continues its trafficking, it is subject to treble damages. The benefits of the Helms–Burton Act are not limited to citizens of the U.S. at the time of the expropriation, but also include Cuban citizens who moved to the U.S. following the expropriation. The goals of the Act are extensive, and its enforcement mechanisms will remain in effect until Cuba's government is deemed sufficiently "democratic." Thus, in order to escape the repercussions of the Act, Cuba must not only hold a democratic election and guarantee certain civil rights (including allowing the U.S. to broadcast radio and television signals into its territory), but it must also adopt a market economy and make restitution for all of the expropriated property.

The Act was quickly condemned in the U.S., both because it has extraterritorial effects that are improper under international law and because it uses the federal courts to achieve Congress' foreign policy goals. For the economic side of the Helms–Burton Act, see chapter 13, *supra*. *See, e.g.*, Lowenfeld, *Congress and Cuba: The Helms–Burton Act*, 90 A.J.I.L. 419 (1996); Muse, *A Public International Law Critique of the Extraterritorial Jurisdiction of the Helms–Burton Act (Cuban Liberty and Democratic Solidarity (Libertad) Act of 1996)*, 30 Geo. Wash. J. Int'l L. & Econ. 207 (1996–97); Walker, *The Legality of the Secondary Boycotts Contained in the Helms–Burton Act under International Law*, 3 DePaul Dig. Int'l L. 1 (1997). In addition, some opined that the Helms–Burton Act was actually good both for Cuba and for the Castro regime, because it removed competition from large companies, leaving room for smaller groups to invest in Cuba, and because Cubans may rally behind Castro against their common enemy, America. *See* Comment, *The Helms–Burton Act: Inconsistency with International Law and Irrationality at Their Maximum*, 6 J. Transnat'l L. & Pol'y 289 (1997). The Act received some support, based primarily on the initial illegality of the expropriations, from which other states arguably should not be allowed to benefit. *See* Claggett, *The Controversy over Title III of the Helms–Burton Act: Who Is Breaking International Law—the United States, or the States that Have Made Themselves Co–Conspirators with Cuba in Its Unlawful Confiscations?*, 30 Geo. Wash. J. Int'l L. & Econ. 271 (1996–97).

The international response to the Helms–Burton Act was uniformly negative and often extremely hostile. Canada, the United States' largest trading partner, quickly extended existing legislation to specifically prohibit compliance by its nationals with the Act, and to offer its nationals local remedies for any U.S. claims asserted against them. The European Union Council issued a similar regulation. Within less than six months, on the request of the General Assembly of the Organization of American States, the Inter–American Juridical Committee issued an opinion condemning the U.S. action.

Perhaps in response to the international outcry, President Clinton suspended enforcement of the Act, under the authority given him by Congress. The President is required to review the suspension every six months, and he may continue it so long as he believes that the suspension "[i] is necessary to the national interests of the United States and [ii] will expedite a transition to democracy in Cuba." *See* § 306(b)(1). In announcing the suspension, President Clinton asserted that the international community was united in the goal of bringing democracy to Cuba, and that he intended to continue the suspension for the indefinite future. To formalize his intentions regarding the Act, President Clinton entered into an understanding with the European Union, whereby President Clinton reiterated the "presumption of continued suspension" of the Act, and the European Union agreed to continue their increased efforts of promoting democracy in Cuba. *See* European Union–United States: Memorandum of Understanding Concerning the U.S. Helms–Burton Act and the U.S. Iran and Libya Sanctions Act, 36 I.L.M. 539 (1997).

3. ***Do you believe the U.S. acted properly in enacting the Helms–Burton Act?*** Would the U.S. acquiesce in similar action taken by another state? If the Helms–Burton Act is illegal under international law, what are the limits of economic coercion? At what point does a sanction that affects third parties become improper?

Chapter 16

INTERNATIONAL CRIMINAL LAW

SECTION A. CRIMES AGAINST PEACE, WAR CRIMES AND CRIMES AGAINST HUMANITY

1. INTRODUCTION

"When we neither punish nor reproach evildoers, we are not simply protecting their trivial old age, we are thereby ripping the foundations of justice from beneath new generations." Alexander Solzhenitsyn, THE GULAG ARCHIPELAGO 178 (T. Whitney trans. 1974).

During the twentieth century there has grown a recognition by the international community that individuals may be prosecuted and found liable for international criminal acts, particularly crimes against peace, war crimes and crimes against humanity. These offences, that may be classified as crimes against the peace and security of humankind,[1] are wide-ranging in scope and the aim of this Chapter is to explore them.

---

1. *See* D.H.N. Johnson, *The Draft Code of Offences Against the Peace and Security of*   *Mankind*, 4 *Int. & Comp. L.Q.* 445 (1955); S.A. Williams, *The Draft Code of Offences*

The most poignant examples of a finding of such liability up until the present time were the war crimes trials undertaken by the specially created International Military Tribunals at Nürnberg and Tokyo as well as some national court cases following atrocities committed in the Second World War, a few from the Vietnam War, and more recently the Ad Hoc Tribunals for the former Yugoslavia and Rwanda. The permanent International Criminal Court established in Rome in 1998 is not yet in operation. Other tribunals on the horizon include one for Cambodia and another for Sierra Leone.

The following materials explore these developments from World War I and II trials, through the work of the International Law Commission to the decisions establishing institutions to deal with war crimes in the former Yugoslavia, Rwanda and the International Criminal Court, as well as a sampling of domestic prosecutions.

The last part of this Chapter addresses the way in which states obtain jurisdiction over the person for the purposes of criminal prosecution. This appertains not only to international and transnational crimes but also to any serious criminal offence under domestic law where the alleged or convicted offender is found in another state.

Christopher L. Blakesley, Terrorism Drugs, International Law And The Protection Of Liberty

18–22; 177–179 (1992).*

There have been war crimes and crimes against humanity since antiquity. *See,* the Code of Hammurabi (1728–1686 B.C.), the Laws of Eshnunna (2000 B.C.), and even in the earlier Code of Ur–Nammu (8 2100, B.C.). The Lex Talionis, or law of exact retaliation, is found in the Jewish Torah or Biblical Pentateuch. In virtually all ancient cultures, metaphysics and law were merged; the social cell felt obliged to purge itself of the threat of destruction by the wrath of God or gods. There was a sense that when the group was tainted by crime committed by one of its own or by another against the group, the taint had to be removed to make the group whole again. Punishment of the wrongdoer, combined with religious ceremony, was the cleansing or expiating mechanism. The Code of Manu, [Bk. VII, 18, 23–24; Bk. VIII, 17] provided that rest and happiness for the wrongdoer and society is obtained only by soul-purging punishment of the perpetrator. Blood atonement was required by the Israelites for heinous offenses. [See I Kings 2:28–34]. The Cheyenne banished the one who tainted the food or water supply. The ritual of the "breaking of the arrows," followed to cleanse the group.

Against the Peace and Security of Mankind in I M.C. Bassiouni (ed.) INTERNATIONAL CRIMINAL LAW 109 (1986); Christopher L. Blakesley, *The Modern Blood–Feud, Thoughts on the Philosophy of Crimes Against Humanity,* Chapter in II INTERNATIONAL HUMANITARIAN LAW: ORIGINS, CHALLENGES & PROSPECTS (Edwin Mellen Press, 2001).

* Reprinted with the permission of Transnational Publishers, Inc.

In the very early "modern era," Jean Bodin, Hugo Grotius, and Emerich de Vattel all called for the rule that punishment was necessary for those who commit serious offenses, in their requirement that there be no sanctuary for the criminal. Each nation has an obligation to "prosecute or extradite." The ascendancy of "positivism" in the nineteenth century created the perception that international law was binding only on states and could not impose obligations or impose punishment directly on individuals; that was solely for states to do.

"For centuries military commanders C from Henry V of England, under his famous ordinances of war in 1419, to the American military prosecutions of soldiers involved in the My Lai massacre under the U.S. Code of Military Justice C have enforced such laws against violators. In other cases, states have brought to trial captured prisoners of war for offenses committed against the customary laws of war. Thus, both the accused's own state and the captor state have standing to prosecute. Neither system, however, has functioned with any degree of efficiency."

Telford Taylor, Nuremberg and Vietnam 20 (1970)*

What, then, are the "laws of war"? They are of ancient origin, and followed two main streams of development. The first flowed from medieval notions of knightly chivalry. Over the course of the centuries the stream has thinned to a trickle; it had a brief spurt during the days of single-handed aerial combat, and survives today in rules (often violated) prohibiting various deceptions such as the use of the enemy's uniforms or battle insignia, or the launching of a war without fair warning by formal declaration.

The second and far more important concept is that the ravages of war should be mitigated as far as possible by prohibiting needless cruelties, and other acts that spread death and destruction and are not reasonably related to the conduct of hostilities. The seeds of such a principle must be nearly as old as human society, and ancient literature abounds with condemnation of pillage and massacre. In more recent times, both religious humanitarianism and the opposition of merchants to unnecessary disruptions of commerce have furnished the motivation for restricting customs and understandings. In the 17th century these ideas began to find expression in learned writings, especially those of the Dutch jurist-philosopher Hugo Grotius.

The formalization of military organization in the 18th–century brought the establishment of military courts, empowered to try violations of the laws of war as well as other offenses by soldiers. During the American Revolution, both Captain Nathan Hale and the British Major John André were convicted as spies and ordered to be hanged, the former by a British military court and the latter by a "Board of General Officers" appointed by George Washington. During the Mexican War, General Winfield Scott created "military commissions," with jurisdiction over violations of the laws of war committed either by American troops against Mexican civilians, or vice versa.

* Reprinted with the permission of Quadrangle Books, Inc., New York.

Up to that time the laws of war had remained largely a matter of unwritten tradition, and it was the United States, during the Civil War, that took the lead in reducing them to systematic, written form. In 1863 President Lincoln approved the promulgation by the War Department of "Instructions for the Government of Armies of the United States in the Field," prepared by Francis Lieber, a German veteran of the Napoleonic wars, who emigrated to the United States and became professor of law and political science at Columbia University. These comprised 159 articles, covering such subjects as "military necessity," "punishment of crimes against the inhabitants of hostile countries," "prisoners of war," and "spies." It was by a military commission appointed in accordance with these instructions that Mary Surratt and the others accused of conspiring to assassinate Lincoln were tried.

In the wake of the Crimean War, the Civil War and the Franco–Prussian War of 1870 there arose, in Europe and America, a tide of sentiment for codification of the laws of war and their embodiment in international agreements. The principal fruits of that movement were the series of treaties known today as the Hague and Geneva Conventions. For present purposes, the most important of these are the Fourth Hague Convention of 1907, and the Geneva Prisoner of War, Red Cross, and Protection of Civilians Conventions of 1929 and 1949.

"The right of belligerents to adopt means of injuring the enemy is not unlimited," declared Article 22 of the Fourth Hague Convention, and ensuing articles specify a number of limitations: Enemy soldiers who surrender must not be killed, and are to be taken prisoner; captured cities and towns must not be pillaged, nor "undefended" places bombarded; poisoned weapons and other arms "calculated to cause unnecessary suffering" are forbidden. Other provisions make it clear that war is not a free-for-all between the populations of the countries at war; only members of the armed forces can claim protection of the laws of war, and if a noncombatant civilian takes hostile action against the enemy he is guilty of a war crime. When an army occupies enemy territory, it must endeavor to restore public order, and respect "family honor and rights, the lives of persons, and private property, as well as religious convictions and practices."

Rules requiring humane treatment of prisoners, and for protection of the sick and wounded, are prescribed in the Geneva Conventions. While there is no general treaty on naval warfare, the Ninth Hague Convention prohibited the bombardment of undefended "ports," and the London Naval Treaty of 1930 condemned submarine sinkings of merchant vessels, unless passengers and crews were first placed in "safety."

In all of these treaties, the laws of war are stated as general principles of conduct, and neither the means of enforcement nor the penalties for violations are specified. The substance of their provisions, however, has been taken into the military law of many countries, and is often set forth in general orders, manuals of instruction, or other official documents. In the United States, for example, the Lieber rules of 1863 were replaced in 1914 by an army field manual which, up-dated, is still in force under the title "The Law of Land Warfare." It is set forth therein that the laws of war are part of the law of the United States, and that they may be enforced against both soldiers and civilians, including enemy personnel, by general courts-martial, military commissions, or other military or international tribunals.

Comparable though not identical publications have been issued by the military authorities of Britain, France, Germany and many other countries. These documents, and the treaties on which they are largely based, are regarded as a comprehensive but not necessarily complete exposition of what is really a body of international common law—the laws of war.

Since the mid–19th century, with increasing frequency, the major powers have utilized military courts for the trial of persons accused of war crimes. An early and now famous trial, depicted in a successful Broadway play, was the post-Civil War proceeding against the Confederate Major Henry Wirz on charges of responsibility for the death of thousands of Union prisoners in the Andersonville prison camp, of which he had been commandant. War crimes tribunals were convened by the United States after the Spanish–American War, and by the British after the Boer War.

Following the defeat of Germany in the First World War, the Allies demanded that nearly 900 Germans accused of war crimes, including military and political leaders, be handed over for trial on war crimes charges. The Germans resisted the demand, and in the upshot they were allowed to try their own "war criminals." The trials in 1921 and 1922 were not conducted by military courts, but by the Supreme Court of Germany, sitting in Leipzig. From the Allied standpoint they were a fiasco, as only a handful of accused were tried, and of these nearly all were acquitted or allowed to escape their very short prison sentences. The German court did, however, affirm that violations of the laws of war are punishable offenses, and in the Llandovery Castle case sentenced two German U-boat officers to four-year prison terms (from which both soon escaped) for complicity in the torpedoing of a British hospital ship and the shelling and sinking of her lifeboats. * * *

Notes & Questions

1. **See also**, Telford Taylor, THE ANATOMY OF THE NUREMBERG TRIALS: A PERSONAL MEMOIR (1992). Meron, *The Case for War Crimes Trials in Yugoslavia,* 72 For.Aff. 122, 123 (1993); Blakesley, *Autumn of the Patriarch: The Pinochet Extradition Debacle & Beyond–Human Rights Clauses in Extradition Treaties,* 90 J.Crim.L. & Criminol. 1 (2001); Blakesley, *The Modern Blood Feud: Thoughts on the Philosophy of Crimes Against Humanity,* Ch. in II INTERNATIONAL HUMANITARIAN LAW: ORIGINS, CHALLENGES & PROSPECTS (Edwin Mellen Press 2001); Blakesley, *Obstacles to the Creation of a Permanent War Crimes Tribunal,* 18 Fletch. For. Wld. Affr's 77 (1994). Kelsen, *Collective and Individual Responsibility in International Law with Particular Regard to the Punishment of War Criminals,* 31 Cal.L.Rev. 530, 553–56 (1943) (noting that international law provides for some offenses as criminal, though enforcement is to be undertaken by domestic courts); Orentlicher, *Settling Accounts: The Duty to Prosecute Human Rights Violations of a Prior Regime,* 100 Yale L.J. 2537 (1991); Wright, *The Outlawry of War and the Law of War,* 47 A.J.I.L. 365 (1953).

2. *Nürnberg Principle I*, (1946) provides: "[a]ny person who commits an act which constitutes a crime under international law is responsible therefore and liable to punishment." While you are considering the issues in this chapter, think about Chapter 9, on Human Rights. One question considered herein is whether the growth of individual human rights law has caused a concomitant development of individual duties and accountability under international law? If so, did this individual responsibility pre-exist the Nüremberg Trials or did those trials create the principle that individuals may be recognized as objective actors in international law who may be held accountable for their conduct? If this is a rule, is it part of customary international law or does it require a treaty? If it exists, is it functional without being incorporated into domestic law? What do you think the future holds for the Nüremberg principles? These principles are analyzed in detail below.

3. *The Nürnberg Tribunal concluded* the following: "It was submitted that international law is concerned with the actions of sovereign States, and provides no punishment for individuals; and further, that where the act in question is an act of State, those who carry it out are not personally responsible but are protected by the doctrine of the sovereignty of the State. In the opinion of the Tribunal, both these submissions must be rejected. That international law imposes duties and liabilities upon individuals as upon States has long been recognized * * * *citing Ex parte Quirin*, 317 U.S. 1 (1942) * * * Crimes against international law are committed by men, not by abstract entities, and only by punishing individuals who commit such crimes can the provisions of international law be enforced * * * [T]he very essence of the Charter is that individuals have international duties which transcend the national obligations of obedience imposed by the individual State. He who violates the laws of war cannot obtain immunity while acting in pursuance of the authority of the State, if the State in authorizing action moves outside its competence under international law * * * " International Military Tribunal, Judgment, 6 F.R.D. 69, 110 (1946), *reprinted in* 41 A.J.I.L. 172, 220–21 (1947). "Offenses against the peace and security of mankind * * * are crimes under international law, for which the responsible individuals shall be punished." *See, Draft Code of Crimes Against the Peace and Security of Mankind.* This rule of punishment for "crimes against humanity" or crimes against some "higher law" has existed from antiquity.

4. *The monist-dualist debate* (in Chapter 17, *infra*) is exemplified in international criminal law. Reference is often made to offenses against the "Law of Nations" (*see, e.g.,* U.S. Constitution, article 1, section 8). Does this mean that international law proscribes the conduct and provides for punishment? Or does it mean simply that international law provides nations with jurisdiction to apply their own law for conduct which otherwise would not be within their competence? Through the 18th and into the 19th centuries, writers and jurists believed that rules of international law bound individuals as well as states. *See, e.g., U.S. v. Smith*, 18 U.S. (5 Wheat.) 153, 5 L.Ed. 57 (1820) (piracy violates law of nations; individual liable); *Republica v. De Longchamps*, 1 U.S. (1 Dall.) 111, 1 L.Ed. 59 (1784) (assault on French consul-general violates law of nations; individual liable); 4 Blackstone's COMMENTARIES 66–73 (Welsby ed. 1854) (recounting

various offenses against law of nations, committed by private persons, punishable under English statutory law). Later, in the 19th century, the view emerged that states alone were subjects of international law. They alone were able to assert rights and be held to obligations devolved from the law of nations. Positivists have traditionally believed in non-hierarchical dualism, considering domestic and international law to be in absolutely separate spheres, albeit interdependent and interpenetrated. *See,* Boyle, FOUNDATIONS OF WORLD ORDER; THE LEGALIST APPROACH TO INTERNATIONAL RELATIONS, 1898–1922 (1999); *cf., The Paquete Habana: The Lola,* 175 U.S. 677, 700 (1900) (in Ch. 1, *supra*); Quincy Wright, *Conflicts of International Law with National Laws and Ordinances,* 11 AJIL 1 (1917). *But see,* Starke, *Monism and Dualism in the Theory of International Law,* 17 Brit.Y.B.Int'l L. 66 (1936). *See also,* Dickenson, *The Law of Nations as Part of the National Law of the United States* (pt. 1), 101 U.Pa.L.Rev. 26, 29–30 (1952); (pt. 2) 101 U.Pa.L.Rev. 792, 792–95 (1953); 2 Moore, INTERNATIONAL LAW 951, et seq. (1906); *Harvard Research in International Law, Piracy,* 26 A.J.I.L. 739, 754, 759–60 (1932); Korowitz, *The Problem of the International Personality of Individuals,* 50 A.J.I.L. 533, 534 (1956); Rubin, THE LAW OF PIRACY 305, et seq. (2nd ed. 2000). Meron has argued that human rights law has had a significant impact on international criminal law recently, resulting in a merger of human rights and the law of crimes against humanity. Meron, *On the Inadequate Reach of Humanitarian and Human Rights Law & the Need for a New Instrument,* 77 A.J.I.L. 589 (1983).

5. ***Does international law, itself, condemn certain conduct and call for the punishment of individuals who breach it?*** If so, what legal philosophy backs it up? Consider the following thoughts on Natural Law and Positivism.

David Luban, Alan Strudler, & David Wasserman, Moral Responsibility in the Age of Bureaucracy

90 Mich.L.Rev. 2348, 2350–53 (1993).*

The doctrine of individual responsibility on the part of rulers and ruled alike has played a prominent role in the development of twentieth-century international law. Positivism, including legal realism, was the ascendant view among legal theorists outside the Catholic Church for the country between the 1830's and the 1930's. World War II changed that. If there is a single historical event that accounts for the survival of serious macular interest in natural law, it is surely the Nuremberg trials. The Nuremberg Tribunal held individual Nazi officials responsible for acts that positive law did not forbid at the time they were committed—so-called "crimes against peace" and "crimes against humanity." Anticipating the defendants' protest that they were merely following official orders that carried the force of positive law, Article 8 of the Nuremberg Charter specifically provided that "[t]he fact that the defendant acted pursuant to an order of his government or of a superior shall not free him from responsibility."That Article 8 represents a flat-out rejection of what might be called the positivist excuse

* Reprinted with the permission of the
Michigan Law Review.

for atrocious official acts—the excuse that the acts were licensed by positive law—is intuitively clear. As Stanley Panlson has shown, the defense at Nuremberg relied extensively upon the positivist excuse, which the Tribunal had little difficulty rejecting. The natural law argument that unjust laws lose their obligatory character provides a straightforward philosophical justification for Article 8. Similarly, appeals to natural law * * * form the most obvious justification for criminalizing "murder, extermination, enslavement, deportation, and other inhumane acts * * * whether or not in violation of domestic law * * * where perpetrated." Such crimes against humanity are radically inconsistent with the common good, and any domestic legal system that permits them must violate natural law. In addition, Article 7 of the Charter eliminated the act-of-state defense on the part of those in command positions, thereby recognizing that those who legislate bear moral responsibilities just as surely as do those who follow orders.

Indeed, the view that the Nazi era exposes the moral deficiency of positivism compared with natural law is a commonplace. As early as the mid–1940's, Gustav Radbruch, an eminent pre-War German positivist, repudiated positivism and embraced natural law, arguing in several influential essays that positivism had disarmed German jurists in the face of Nazism. Thus, international revulsion at the official criminality of Hitler's regime, as manifested legally in the Nuremberg trials, represents a triumph for natural law thinking. At the very least, this worldwide condemnation provisionally lays to rest the positivist excuse in international law. But the excuse that "I was only following orders," or "I was only doing my job," was not the only one offered by those implicated in Nazi crimes. In the aftermath of World War II, the world heard with equal frequency the cry, "I didn't know!" This is the epistemological excuse, whose elements present the problem that will occupy our attention in this article. Though it is often insincere, and seldom entirely persuasive, the epistemological excuse seems to come naturally to those who commit wrongs in a bureaucratic setting. We shall argue (1) that bureaucracies function (often by design) to permit their functionaries to truthfully plead the excuse "I didn't know"; (2) that traditional accounts of moral responsibility typically recognize this epistemological excuse, and (3) that it is therefore very difficult to find a workable account of moral responsibility within bureaucratic institutions. The strength and prevalence of the epistemological excuse may render the historic rejection of the positivist excuse an empty or very partial victory.

Perhaps the single most salient characteristic of the Nazi crimes was their bureaucratic nature. They were committed, not by a lawless gang of criminals, but by a regularly functioning state bureaucracy executing official policies. Not only Nazi crimes have this bureaucratic character—it exists as well in the misdeeds of the recently departed regimes of the Soviet empire. Emerging democracies of Eastern Europe—if democracies are what they prove to be—are beginning to come to grips with the bureaucratic crimes committed for generations by officials of their former regimes, many of whom will surely enter the epistemological excuse. Czech novelist Milan Kundera [focuses] directly in The Unbearable Lightness of Being:

> Let us concede that a Czech public prosecutor in the early fifties who called for the death of an innocent man was deceived by the

Russian secret police and the government of his own country. But now that we all know the accusations to have been absurd and the executed to have been innocent, how can that selfsame public prosecutor defend his purity of heart by beating himself on the chest and proclaiming, "My conscience is clear I didn't know."

One might respond with an equally rhetorical question: how can the prosecutor be blamed if he truly did not know? Kundera's rage clearly stems from the ready availability of the epistemological excuse within the secretive Communist bureaucracies, but the fact that an excuse is a bit too handy does not in itself undercut its viability. Thus, the problem of bureaucratic irresponsibility faces post-Communist societies much as it faced post-Nazi Germany. * * *

2.   SOURCES

The London Agreement. This was Agreement by the Government of the United Kingdom of Great Britain and Northern Ireland, the Government of the United States of America, the Provisional Government of the French Republic and the Government of the Union of Soviet Socialist Republics for the Prosecution and Punishment of the Major War Criminals of the European Axis. Signed at London, on 8 August 1945. 82 U.N.T.S. 279.

The Moscow Declaration of 1943, 9 Dept. of State Bull. 311, provided for the punishment by the Allies of Germans who might be found guilty of having committed war crimes. It stated:

> "Those German officers and men and members of the Nazi party who have been responsible for, or have taken a consenting part in the above atrocities, massacres and executions, will be sent back to the countries in which their abominable deeds were done in order that they may be judged and punished according to the laws of these liberated countries and of the free governments which will be created therein ... without prejudice to the case of the major criminals, whose offenses have no particular geographical location and who will be punished by the joint decision of the Governments of the Allies."

On August 8, 1945, an agreement was concluded in London between the Governments of the United Kingdom, the United States, the U.S.S.R. and France, acting in the interests of all the United Nations, which provided for the establishment of an International Military Tribunal for the trial of war criminals whose offences had no particular geographical location. Later, nineteen governments of the United Nations adhered to the agreement. The constitution, jurisdiction and function of the tribunal were defined in the charter annexed to the agreement.

Article 1. There shall be established after consultation with the Control Council for Germany an International Military Tribunal for the trial of war criminals whose offences have no particular geographical location whether they be accused individually or in their capacity as members of organizations or groups or in both capacities.

Article 2. The constitution, jurisdiction and functions of the International Military Tribunal shall be those set out in the Charter annexed to this agreement, which Charter shall form an integral part of this Agreement.

Article 4. Nothing in this Agreement shall prejudice the provisions established by the Moscow Declaration concerning the return of war criminals to the countries where they committed their crimes. . . .

Article 6. Nothing in this agreement shall prejudice the jurisdiction or the powers of any national or occupation court established or to be established in any allied territory or in Germany for the trial of war criminals.

SECTION B. THE INNOVATIONS OF NÜRNBERG: CRIMES AGAINST PEACE AND CRIMES AGAINST HUMANITY

1. CHARTER

The Nürnberg Charter, 1945

Charter of the International Military Tribunal.
59 Stat. 1544, 1546.[a]

Article 2. The Tribunal shall consist of four members, each with an alternate. One member and one alternate shall be appointed by each of the Signatories. * * *

Article 6. The Tribunal established by the Agreement referred to in Article 1 hereof for the trial and punishment of the major war criminals of the European Axis countries shall have the power to try and punish persons who, acting in the interests of the European Axis countries, whether as individuals or as members of organizations, committed any of the following crimes. The following acts, or any of them, are crimes coming within the jurisdiction of the Tribunal for which there shall be individual responsibility:

> (a) CRIMES AGAINST PEACE: namely, planning, preparation, initiation or waging of a war of aggression, or a war in violation of international treaties, agreements or assurances, or participation in a common plan or conspiracy for the accomplishment of any of the foregoing;

> (b) WAR CRIMES: namely, violations of the laws or customs of war. Such violations shall include, but not be limited to, murder, ill-treatment or deportation to slave labor or for any other purpose of civilian population of or in occupied territory, murder or ill-treatment of prisoners of war or persons on the seas, killing of hostages, plunder

a. Editor's note. The Charter was annexed to an Agreement for the Prosecution and Punishment of the Major War Criminals of the European Axis, which came into force on signature, August 8, 1945, by France, the U.S.S.R., U.K., and the U.S. 11 Whiteman Digest 881–82 (1968). In the U.S. it was treated as an executive agreement and was not submitted to the Senate as a treaty for the latter's Advice and Consent. For the distinction between treaties and executive agreements, *see* Chs. 11 and 12.

of public or private property, wanton destruction of cities, towns or villages, or devastation not justified by military necessity;

(c) CRIMES AGAINST HUMANITY: namely, murder, extermination, enslavement, deportation, and other inhumane acts committed against any civilian population, before or during the war;[1] or persecutions on political, racial or religious grounds in execution of or in connection with any crime within the jurisdiction of the Tribunal, whether or not in violation of the domestic law of the country where perpetrated.

Leaders, organizers, instigators and accomplices participating in the formulation or execution of a common plan or conspiracy to commit any of the foregoing crimes are responsible for all acts performed by any persons in execution of such plan.

Article 7.   The official position of defendants, whether as Heads of State or responsible officials in Government Departments, shall not be considered as freeing them from responsibility or mitigating punishment.

Article 8.   The fact that the Defendant acted pursuant to order of his Government or of a superior shall not free him from responsibility, but may be considered in mitigation of punishment if the Tribunal determines that justice so requires.

Article 9.   At the trial of any individual member of any group or organization the Tribunal may declare (in connection with any act of which the individual may be convicted) that the group or organization of which the individual was a member was a criminal organization.

After receipt of the Indictment the Tribunal shall give such notice as it thinks fit that the prosecution intends to ask the Tribunal to make such declaration and any member of the organization will be entitled to apply to the Tribunal for leave to be heard by the Tribunal upon the question of the criminal character of the organization. The Tribunal shall have power to allow or reject the application. If the application is allowed, the Tribunal may direct in what manner the applicants shall be represented and heard.

Article 10.   In cases where a group or organization is declared criminal by the Tribunal, the competent national authority of any Signatory shall have the right to bring individuals to trial for membership therein before national, military or occupation courts. In any such case the criminal nature of the group or organization is considered proved and shall not be questioned.

Article 11.   Any person convicted by the Tribunal may be charged before a national, military or occupation court, referred to in Article 10 of this Charter, with a crime other than of membership in a criminal group or organization and such court may, after convicting him, impose upon him punishment independent of and additional to the punishment imposed by the Tribunal for participation in the criminal activities of such group or organization.

---

1. [The contracting governments signed a protocol at Berlin on Oct. 6, 1945 * * *   which provides that this semi-colon in the English text should be changed to a comma.]

Article 12. The Tribunal shall have the right to take proceedings against a person charged with crimes set out in Article 6 of this Charter in his absence, if he has not been found or if the Tribunal, for any reason, finds it necessary, in the interests of justice, to conduct the hearing in his absence.

Article 26. The judgment of the Tribunal as to the guilt or the innocence of any Defendant shall give the reasons on which it is based, and shall be final and not subject to review.

Article 27. The Tribunal shall have the right to impose upon a Defendant, on conviction, death or such other punishment as shall be determined by it to be just. * * *

Notes and Questions. The Tribunal was composed of four judges and four alternates appointed by each of the four state parties. In the course of its judgment the Tribunal reviewed, *inter alia*, the growth of the Nazi party, the seizure of Austria, Belgium, Czechoslovakia, Denmark, Luxembourg, the Netherlands, Norway and Poland, the aggressive acts against force and the former U.S.S.R., the alleged commission of war crimes and crimes against humanity–all in violation of customary or conventional international law. At the conclusion of the trial, the Tribunal held twelve of the accused guilty and sentenced them to death, three to life imprisonment, and the remainder (except three who were acquitted) to prison for lengthy terms.[b] *See* the chart of Nürnberg dispositions, *infra*. Telford Taylor's ANATOMY OF THE NUREMBERG TRIALS: A PERSONAL MEMOIR (1992), is an excellent book for background on the infighting among the parties involved.

2.   PRINCIPLES

The Nürnberg Principles Report of the International Law Commission

UN GAOR V, Supp. 12 (A/1316) 11–14.

PART III—FORMULATION OF THE NURNBERG PRINCIPLES

95.   Under General Assembly resolution 177(II), paragraph (a), the International Law Commission was directed to "formulate the principles of international law recognized in the Charter of the Nurnberg Tribunal and in the judgment of the Tribunal."

96.   ... In the course of this consideration the question arose as to whether or not the Commission should ascertain to what extent the principles contained in the Charter and judgment constituted principles of international law. The conclusion was that since the Nurnberg principles had been affirmed by the General Assembly, the task entrusted to the

b. Editor's note. *See,* Woetzel, *The Nürnberg Trials in International Law* (1960). *See* the judgment, *infra*.

Commission by paragraph (a) of resolution 177(II) was not to express any appreciation of these principles as principles of international law but merely to formulate them. . . .

Principles of International Law Recognized in the Charter of the Nurnberg Tribunal and in the Judgment of the Tribunal

Principle I. Any person who commits an act which constitutes a crime under international law is responsible therefor and liable to punishment. . . .

99.   The general rule underlying Principle I is that international law may impose duties on individuals directly without any interposition of internal law. . . .

Principle II. The fact that internal law does not impose a penalty for an act which constitutes a crime under international law does not relieve the person who committed the act from responsibility under international law. . . .

102.   The principle that a person who has committed an international crime is responsible therefor and liable to punishment under international law, independently of the provisions of internal law, implies what is commonly called the "supremacy" of international law over national law. . . .

Principle III. The fact that a person who committed an act which constitutes a crime under international law acted as Head of State or responsible government official does not relieve him from responsibility under international law. . . .

104.   The last phrase of Article 7 of the Charter, "or mitigating punishment," has not been retained in the formulation of Principle III. The Commission considers that the question of mitigating punishment is a matter for the competent Court to decide.

Principle IV. The fact that a person acted pursuant to order of his government or of a superior does not relieve him from responsibility under international law, provided a moral choice was in fact possible to him. . . . The idea expressed in Principle IV is that superior orders are not a defence provided a moral choice was possible to the accused.

106.   The last phrase of Article 8 of the Charter "but may be considered in mitigation of punishment, if the Tribunal determines that justice so requires," has not been retained for the reason stated under Principle III, in paragraph 104 above.

Principle V. Any person charged with a crime under international law has the right to a fair trial on the facts and law. . . .

109.   In the view of the Commission, the expression "fair trial" should be understood in the light of the above-quoted provisions of the Charter of the Nürnberg Tribunal.

Principle VI. The crimes hereinafter set out are punishable as crimes under international law:

a. *Crimes against peace:*

(i) Planning, preparation, initiation or waging of a war of aggression or a war in violation of international treaties, agreements or assurances;

(ii) Participation in a common plan or conspiracy for the accomplishment of any of the acts mentioned under (i).

110.   Both categories of crimes are characterized by the fact that they are connected with "war of aggression or war in violation of international treaties, agreements or assurances." . . .

115.   The term "assurances" is understood by the Commission as including any pledge or guarantee of peace given by a State, even unilaterally. . . .

117.   The meaning of the expression "waging of a war of aggression" was discussed in the Commission during the consideration of the definition of "crimes against peace." Some members of the Commission feared that everyone in uniform who fought in a war of aggression might be charged with the "waging" of such a war. The Commission understands the expression to refer only to high-ranking military personnel and high State officials, and believes that this was also the view of the Tribunal. . . .

b. *War crimes:*

Violations of the laws or customs of war which include, but are not limited to, murder, ill-treatment or deportation to slave-labour or for any other purpose of civilian population of or in occupied territory, murder or ill-treatment of prisoners of war, of persons on the seas, killing of hostages, plunder of public or private property, wanton destruction of cities, towns, or villages, or devastation not justified by military necessity. . . .

c. *Crimes against humanity:*

Murder, extermination, enslavement, deportation and other inhuman acts done against any civilian population, or persecutions on political, racial or religious grounds, when such acts are done or such persecutions are carried on in execution of or in connection with any crime against peace or any war crime. . . .

123.   In its definition of crimes against humanity the Commission has omitted the phrase "before or during the war" contained in Article 6(c) of the Charter of the Nürnberg Tribunal because this phrase referred to a particular war, the war of 1939. The omission of the phrase does not mean that the Commission considers that crimes against humanity can be committed only during a war. On the contrary, the Commission is of the opinion that such crimes may take place also before a war in connection with crimes against peace.

124.   In accordance with Article 6(c) of the Charter, the above formulation characterizes as crimes against humanity murder, extermination, enslavement, etc., committed against "any" civilian population. This means that these acts may be crimes against humanity even if they are committed by the perpetrator against his own population.

Principle VII. Complicity in the commission of a crime against peace, a war crime, or a crime against humanity as set forth in Principle VI is a crime under international law.

Notes and Questions. The General Assembly affirmed the principles of international law recognized in the Nürnberg Charter and the judgment of the International Military Tribunal on December 11, 1946. UNGA Res. 95(1), UN GAOR., 1st Sess., Pt. 11 at 188. The International Law Commission at the behest of the General Assembly formulated the Nürnberg Principles. UNGA Res 174(11), UN GAOR., 2nd Sess., UN Doc A/519 at 195–10 (1947). Were they international law when promulgated?

3. TRIALS

Nürnberg War Crimes Trials[a]

(1947), 1 *Trial of The Major War Criminals* 171.

[Twenty-two defendants, the major war criminals whose crimes were not based on having occurred at any particular geographical location, were indicted before the International Military Tribunal established at Nürnberg pursuant to an agreement between France, the United Kingdom, the U.S. and the U.S.S.R. and 19 other adherents. The defendants were charged with crimes against peace, war crimes and crimes against humanity. They were also charged with participating in the formulation or execution of a common plan or conspiring to commit all these crimes. At the conclusion of the trial, the Tribunal held all but three of the accused guilty, twelve of whom it sentenced to death, three to life imprisonment and the remainder to prison for lengthy terms.]

THE TRIBUNAL: . . . The individual defendants are indicted under article 6 of the Charter, which is as follows:

The Tribunal established by the Agreement referred to in Article 1 hereof for the trial and punishment of the major war criminals of the European Axis countries shall have the power to try and punish persons who, acting in the interests of the European axis countries, whether as individuals or as members of organizations, committed any of the following crimes.

The following acts, or any of them, are crimes coming within the jurisdiction of the Tribunal for which there shall be individual responsibility:-

(a) Crimes against peace: namely, planning, preparation, initiation or waging of a war of aggression, or a war in violation of international treaties; agreements or assurances, or participation in a common plan or conspiracy for the accomplishment of any of the foregoing;

(b) War crimes: namely, violations of the laws or customs of war. Such violations shall include, but not be limited to, murder, ill-treatment or deportation to slave labour or for any other purpose of the civilian population of or in occupied territory, murder or ill-treatment of prisoners of war or persons of the seas, killing of hostages, plunder of public or private

a. Editor's note. *See,* Woetzel, The Nürnberg Trials in International Law.

property, wanton destruction of cities, towns or villages, or devastation not justified by military necessity;

(c) Crimes against humanity: namely, murder, extermination, enslavement, deportation, and other inhumane acts committed against any civilian population, before or during the war, or persecutions on political, racial or religious grounds in execution of or in connection with any crime within the jurisdiction of the Tribunal, whether or not in violation of the domestic law of the country where perpetrated.

Leaders, organizers, instigators and accomplices participating in the formulation or execution of a common plan or conspiracy to commit any of the foregoing crimes are responsible for all acts performed by any persons in execution of such plan ...

The making of the Charter was the exercise of the sovereign legislative power by the countries to which the German Reich unconditionally surrendered; and the undoubted right of these countries to legislate for the occupied territories has been recognized by the civilized world. The Charter is not an arbitrary exercise of power on the part of the victorious nations, but in the view of the Tribunal, as will be shown, it is the expression of international law existing at the time of its creation; and to that extent is itself a contribution to international law ...

It was submitted that international law is concerned with the actions of sovereign States, and provides no punishment of individuals; and further, that where the act in question is an act of State, those who carry it out are not personally responsible, but protected by the doctrine of the sovereignty of the State. In the opinion of the Tribunal, both these submissions must be rejected. That international law imposes duties and liabilities upon individuals as well as upon states has long been recognized ... Crimes against international law are committed by men, not by abstract entities, and only by punishing individuals who commit such crimes can the provisions of international law be enforced....

The principle of international law, which under certain circumstances, protects the representatives of a State, cannot be applied to acts which are condemned as criminal by international law. The authors of these acts cannot shelter themselves behind their official position in order to be freed from punishment in appropriate proceedings. Article 7 of the Charter expressly declares: "The official position of the defendants, whether as heads of State, or responsible officials in government departments, shall not be considered as freeing themselves from responsibility, or mitigating punishment."

On the other hand the very essence of the Charter is that individuals have international duties which transcend the national obligations of obedience imposed by the individual State. He who violates the laws of war cannot obtain immunity while acting in pursuance of the authority of the State if the State in authorizing action moves outside its competence under international law.

It was also submitted on behalf of these defendants that in doing what they did they were acting under the orders of Hitler, and therefore cannot be held responsible for the acts committed by them in carrying our these orders. The Charter specifically provides in Article 8: "The fact that the defendant acted pursuant to orders of his Government or of a superior shall not free him from responsibility, but may be considered in mitigation of punishment."

The provisions of this Article are in conformity with the law of all nations. That a soldier was ordered to kill or torture in violation of the international law of war has never been recognized as a defence to such acts of brutality, though, as the Charter here provides, the order may be urged in mitigation of punishment. The true test, which is found in varying degrees in the criminal law of most nations, is not the existence of the order, but whether moral choice was in fact possible.

Judgment of the International Military Tribunal, Nürnberg, Germany, 1946

22 I.M.T., Trial of the Major War Criminals 411, 427 (1948).

* * *

III.   The Common Plan of Conspiracy and Aggressive War

The Tribunal now turns to the consideration of the crimes against peace charged in the indictment. Count one of the indictment charges the defendants with conspiring or having a common plan to commit crimes against peace. Count two of the indictment charges the defendants with committing specific crimes against peace by planning, preparing, initiating, and waging wars of aggression against a number of other States. It will be convenient to consider the question of the existence of a common plan and the question of aggressive war together, and to deal later in this judgment with the question of aggressive war together, and to deal later in this judgment with the question of the individual responsibility of the defendants.

The charges in the indictment that the defendants planned and waged aggressive wars are charges of the utmost gravity. War is essentially an evil thing. Its consequences are not confined to the belligerent states alone, but affect the whole world.

To initiate a war of aggression, therefore, is * * * an international crime [it is] the supreme international crime differing only from other war crimes in that it contains within itself the accumulated evil of the whole. The first acts of aggression referred to in the indictment are the seizure of Austria and Czechoslovakia; and the first war of aggression charged in the indictment is the war against Poland begun on the 1st September 1939.

Before examining that charge it is necessary to look more closely at some of the events which preceded these acts of aggression. The war against Poland did not come suddenly out of an otherwise clear sky; the evidence has made it plain that this war of aggression, as well as the seizure of Austria and Czechoslovakia, was premeditated and carefully prepared, and was not undertaken until the moment was thought opportune for it to be carried through as a definite part of the preordained scheme and plan. For the aggressive designs of the Nazi Government were not accidents arising out of the immediate political situation in Europe and the world; they were a deliberate and essential part of Nazi foreign policy. From the beginning, the National Socialist movement claimed that its object was to unite the German people in the consciousness of their mission and destiny, based on inherent qualities of race, and under the guidance of the Fuehrer.

For its achievement, two things were deemed to be essential: The disruption of the European order as it had existed since the Treaty of Versailles, and the creation of a Greater Germany beyond the frontiers of 1914. This necessarily involved the seizure of foreign territories.

War was seen to be inevitable, or at the very least, highly probable, if these purposes were to be accomplished. The German people, therefore, with all their resources, were to be organized as a great political-military army, schooled to obey without question any policy decreed by the State.

* * *

IV.   Violations of International Treaties

The Charter defines as a crime the planning or waging of war that is a war of aggression or a war in violation of international treaties. The Tribunal has decided that certain of the defendants planned and waged aggressive wars against 10 nations, and were therefore guilty of this series of crimes. This makes it unnecessary to discuss the subject in further detail, or even to consider at any length the extent to which these aggressive wars were also "wars in violation of international treaties, agreements, or assurances."

These treaties are set out in appendix C of the indictment. Those of principal importance are the following:

(A) Hague Conventions

In the 1899 Convention the signatory powers agreed: "before an appeal to arms * * * to have recourse, as far as circumstances allow, to the good offices or mediation of one or more friendly powers." A similar clause was inserted in the Convention for Pacific Settlement of International Disputes of 1907. In the accompanying Convention Relative to Opening of Hostilities, article I contains this far more specific language:

The Contracting Powers recognize that hostilities between them must not commence without a previous and explicit warning, in the form of either a declaration of war, giving reasons, or an ultimatum with a conditional declaration of war.

Germany was a party to these conventions.

(B) Versailles Treaty

Breaches of certain provisions of the Versailles Treaty are also relied on by the prosecution—not to fortify the left bank of the Rhine (art. 42–44); to "respect strictly the independence of Austria" (art. 80); renunciation of any rights in Memel (art. 99) and the Free City of Danzig (art. 100); the recognition of the independence of the Czecho–Slovak State; and the Military, Naval, and Air Clauses against German rearmament found in part

V. There is no doubt that action was taken by the German Government contrary to all these provisions, the details of which are set out in appendix C. With regard to the Treaty of Versailles, the matters relied on are:

1. The violation of articles 42 to 44 in respect of the demilitarized zone of the Rhineland.

2. The annexation of Austria on the 13th March 1938, in violation of article 80.

3. The incorporation of the district of Memel on the 22d March 1939, in violation of article 99.

4. The incorporation of the Free City of Danzig on the 1st September 1939, in violation of article 100.

5. The incorporation of the provinces of Bohemia and Moravia on the 16th March 1939, in violation of article 81.

6. The repudiation of the military, naval and air clauses of the treaty in or about March of 1935.

On the 21st May 1935, Germany announced that, whilst renouncing the disarmament clauses of the treaty, she would still respect the territorial limitations, and would comply with the Locarno Pact. (With regard to the first five breaches alleged, therefore, the Tribunal finds the allegation proved.)

* * *

(E) The Law of the Charter

The jurisdiction of the Tribunal is defined in the Agreement and Charter, and the crimes coming within the jurisdiction of the Tribunal, for which there shall be individual responsibility, are set out in Article 6. The law of the Charter is decisive, and binding upon the Tribunal.

The making of the Charter was the exercise of the sovereign legislative power by the countries to which the German Reich unconditionally surrendered; and the undoubted right to these countries to legislate for the occupied territories has been recognized by the civilized world. The Charter is not an arbitrary exercise of power on the part of the victorious nations, but in the view of the Tribunal, as will be shown, it is the expression of international law existing at the time of its creation; and to that extent is itself a contribution to international law.

* * *

* * * [T]he very essence of the Charter is that individuals have international duties which transcend the national obligations of obedience imposed by the individual State. He who violates the laws of war cannot obtain immunity while acting in pursuance of the authority of the State if the State is authorizing action moves outside its competence under international law.

It was also submitted on behalf of most of these defendants that in doing what they did they were acting under the orders of Hitler, and therefore cannot be held responsible for the acts committed by them in carrying out these orders. The Charter specifically provides in Article 8:

The fact that the defendant acted pursuant to order of his Government or of a superior shall not free him from responsibility, but may be considered in mitigation of punishment.

The provisions of this Article are in conformity with the law of all nations. That a soldier was ordered to kill or torture in violation of the international law of war has never been recognized as a defense to such acts of brutality, though, as the Charter here provides, the order may be urged in mitigation of the punishment. The true test, which is found in varying degrees in the criminal law of most nations, is not the existence of the order, but whether moral choice was in fact possible.

V. The Law as to the Common Plan or Conspiracy

In the previous recital of the facts relating to aggressive war, it is clear that planning and preparation had been carried out in the most systematic way at every stage of the history.

* * *

In the opinion of the Tribunal, the evidence establishes the common planning to prepare and wage war by certain of the defendants. It is immaterial to consider whether a single conspiracy to the extent and over the time set out in the indictment has been conclusively proved. Continued planning, with aggressive war as the objective, has been established beyond doubt. The truth of the situation was well stated by [the] official interpreter of the German Foreign Office:

The general objectives of the Nazi leadership were apparent from the start, namely the domination of the European Continent, to be achieved first by the incorporation of all German-speaking groups in the Reich, and, secondly, by territorial expansion under the slogan "Lebensraum." The execution of these basic objectives, however, seemed to be characterized by improvisation. Each succeeding step was apparently carried out as each new situation arose, but all consistent with the ultimate objectives mentioned above.

The argument that such common planning cannot exist where there is complete dictatorship is unsound. A plan in the execution of which a number of persons participate is still a plan, even though conceived by only one of them; and those who execute the plan do not avoid responsibility by showing that they acted under the direction of the man who conceived it. Hitler could not make aggressive war by himself. He had to have the cooperation of statesmen, military leaders, diplomats, and businessmen. When they, with knowledge of his aims, gave him their cooperation, they made themselves parties to the plan he had initiated. They are not to be deemed innocent because Hitler made use of them, if they knew what they were doing. That they were assigned to their tasks by a dictator does not absolve them from responsibility for their acts. The relation of leader and follower does not preclude responsibility here any more than it does in the comparable tyranny of organized domestic crime.

* * *

VI.   War Crimes and Crimes Against Humanity

The evidence relating to war crimes has been overwhelming, in its volume and its detail. It is impossible for this judgment adequately to review it, or to record the mass of documentary and oral evidence that has been presented. The truth remains that war crimes were committed on a vast scale, never before seen in the history of war. They were perpetrated in all the countries occupied by Germany, and on the high seas, and were attended by every conceivable circumstance of cruelty and horror. There can be no doubt that the majority of them arose from the Nazi conception of "total war," with which the aggressive wars were waged. For in this conception of "total war" the moral ideas underlying the conventions which seek to make war more humane are no longer regarded as having force or validity. Everything is made subordinate to the overmastering dictates of war. Rules, regulations, assurances, and treaties, all alike, are of no moment; and so, freed from the restraining influence of international law, the aggressive war is conducted by the Nazi leaders in the most barbaric way. Accordingly, war crimes were committed when and wherever the Fuehrer and his close associates thought them to be advantageous. They were for the most part the result of cold and criminal calculation.

On some occasions war crimes were deliberately planned long in advance. In the case of the Soviet Union, the plunder of the territories to be occupied, and the ill-treatment of the civilian population, were settled in minute detail before the attack was begun. As early as the autumn of 1940, the invasion of the territories of the Soviet Union was being considered. From that date onwards, the methods to be employed in destroying all possible opposition were continuously under discussion.

Similarly, when planning to exploit the inhabitants of the occupied countries for slave labor on the very greatest scale, the German Government conceived it as an integral part of the war economy, and planned and organized this particular war crime down to the last elaborate detail.

Other war crimes, such as the murder of prisoners of war who had escaped and been recaptured, or the murder of commandos or captured airmen, or the destruction of the Soviet commissars, were the result of direct orders circulated through the highest official channels.

The Tribunal proposes, therefore, to deal quite generally with the question of war crimes, and to refer to them later when examining the responsibility of the individual defendants in relation to them. Prisoners of war were ill-treated and tortured and murdered, not only in defiance of the well-established rules of international law, but in complete disregard of the elementary dictates of humanity. Civilian populations in occupied territories suffered the same fate. Whole populations were deported to Germany for the purposes of slave labor upon defense works, armament production and similar tasks connected with the war effort. Hostages were taken in very large numbers from the civilian populations in all the occupied countries, and were shot as suited the German purposes. Public and private property was systematically plundered and pillaged in order to enlarge the resources of Germany at the expense of the rest of Europe. Cities and towns and villages were wantonly destroyed without military justification or necessity.

(A) Murder and Ill–Treatment of Prisoners of War

Article 6(b) of the Charter defines war crimes in these words:

War Crimes: namely, violations of the laws or customs of war. Such violations shall include, but not be limited to, murder, ill-treatment or deportation to slave labor or for any other purpose of civilian population of or in occupied territory, murder or ill-treatment of prisoners of war or persons on the seas, killing of hostages, plunder of public or private property, wanton destruction of cities, towns, or villages, or devastation not justified by military necessity.

Many Allied soldiers who had surrendered to the Germans were shot immediately, often as a matter of deliberate, calculated policy. * * *

* * *

When Allied airmen were forced to land in Germany they were sometimes killed at once by the civilian population. The police were instructed not to interfere with these killings, and the Ministry of Justice was informed that no one should be prosecuted for taking part in them. The treatment of Soviet prisoners of war was characterized by particular inhumanity. The death of so many of them was not due merely to the action of individual guards, or to the exigencies of life in the camps. It was the result of systematic plans to murder. * * *

* * *

(B) Murder and Ill–Treatment of Civilian Population

Article 6(b) of the Charter provides that "ill-treatment * * * of civilian population of or in occupied territory * * * killing of hostages * * * wanton destruction of cities, towns, or villages" shall be a war crime. In the main, these provisions are merely declaratory of the existing laws of war as expressed by the Hague Convention, Article 46, which stated: "Family honor and rights, the lives of persons and private property, as well as religious convictions and practice, must be respected." The territories occupied by Germany were administered in violation of the laws of war. The evidence is quite overwhelming of a systematic rule of violence, brutality, and terror. On the 7th December 1941, Hitler issued the directive since known as the "Nacht und Nebel Erlass" (night and fog decree), under which persons who committed offenses against the Reich or the German forces in occupied territories, except where the death sentence was certain, were to be taken secretly to Germany and handed over to the SIPO and SD for trial or punishment in Germany. * * *

Even persons who were only suspected of opposing any of the policies of the German occupation authorities were arrested, and on arrest were interrogated by the Gestapo and the SD in the most shameful manner. * * *

* * *

The practice of keeping hostages to prevent and to punish any form of civil disorder was resorted to by the Germans; an order issued by the defendant Keitel on the 16th September 1941, spoke in terms of fifty or a hundred lives from the occupied areas of the Soviet Union for one German life taken. The order stated that "it should be remembered that a human life in unsettled countries frequently counts for nothing, and a deterrent effect can be obtained only by unusual severity." The exact number of persons killed as a result of this policy is not known, but large numbers were killed in France and the other occupied territories; in the east the slaughter was on [a massive] scale. * * *

* * *

(D) Slave Labor Policy

Article 6(b) of the Charter provides that the "ill-treatment or deportation to slave labor or for any other purpose, of civilian population of or in occupied territory" shall be a war crime. The laws relating to forced labor by the inhabitants of occupied territories are found in Article 52 of the Hague Convention, which provides: "Requisition in kind and services shall not be demanded from municipalities or inhabitants except for the needs of the army of occupation. They shall be in proportion to the resources of the country, and of such a nature as not to involve the inhabitants in the obligation of taking part in military operations against their own country." The policy of the German occupation authorities was in flagrant violation of the terms of this convention. Some idea of this policy may be gathered from the statement made by Hitler in a speech on November 9, 1941:

The territory which now works for us contains more than 250,000,000 men, but the territory which works indirectly for us includes now more than 350,000,000. In the measure in which it concerns German territory, the domain which we have taken under our administration, it is not doubtful that we shall succeed in harnessing the very last man to this work.

The actual results achieved were not so complete as this, but the German occupation authorities did succeed in forcing many of the inhabitants of the occupied territories to work for the German war effort, and in deporting at least 5,000,000 persons to Germany to serve German industry and agriculture. * * *

(E) Persecution of the Jews

The persecution of the Jews at the hands of the Nazi Government has been proved in the greatest detail before the Tribunal. It is a record of consistent and systematic inhumanity on the greatest scale. * * *

* * * Adolf Eichmann, who had been put in charge of this program by Hitler, has estimated that the policy pursued resulted in the killing of 6,000,000 Jews, of which 4,000,000 were killed in the extermination institutions.

(F) The Law Relating to War Crimes and Crimes Against Humanity

* * *

The Tribunal is of course bound by the Charter, in the definition which it gives both of war crimes and crimes against humanity. With respect to war crimes, however, as has already been pointed out, the crimes defined by Article 6, section (b), of the Charter were already recognized as war crimes under international law. They were covered by Articles 46, 50, 52, and 56 of the Hague Convention of 1907, and Articles 2, 3, 4, 46, and 51 of the Geneva Convention of 1929. That violation of these provisions constituted crimes for which the guilty individuals were punishable is too well settled to admit of argument.

But it is argued that the Hague Convention does not apply in this case, because of the "general participation" clause in Article 2 of the Hague Convention of 1907. That clause provided: "The provisions contained in the regulations (rules of land warfare) referred to in Article I as well as in the present convention do not apply except between contracting powers, and then only if all the belligerents are parties to the convention." Several of the belligerents in the recent war were not parties to this convention.

In the opinion of the Tribunal it is not necessary to decide this question. The rules of land warfare expressed in the convention undoubtedly represented an advance over existing international law at the time of their adoption. But the convention expressly stated that it was an attempt "to revise the general laws and customs of war," which it thus recognized to be then existing, but by 1939 these rules laid down in the convention were recognized by all civilized nations, and were regarded as being declaratory of the laws and customs of war which are referred to in Article 6(b) of the Charter.

A further submission was made that Germany was no longer bound by the rules of land warfare in many of the territories occupied during the war, because Germany had completely subjugated those countries and incorporated them into the German Reich, a fact which gave Germany authority to deal with the occupied countries as though they were part of Germany. In the view of the Tribunal it is unnecessary in this case to decide whether this doctrine of subjugation, dependent as it is upon military conquest, has any application where the subjugation is the result of the crime of aggressive war. * * *

With regard to crimes against humanity, there is no doubt whatsoever that political opponents were murdered in Germany before the war, and that many of them were kept in concentration camps in circumstances of great horror and cruelty. The policy of terror was certainly carried out on a vast scale, and in many cases was organized and systematic. The policy of persecution, repression, and murder of civilians in Germany before the war of 1939, who were likely to be hostile to the Government, was most ruthlessly carried out. The persecution of Jews during the same period is established beyond all doubt. To constitute crimes against humanity, the acts relied on before the outbreak of war must have been in execution of, or in connection with, any crime within the jurisdiction of the Tribunal. The Tribunal is of the opinion that revolting and horrible as many of these crimes were, it has not been satisfactorily proved that they were done in execution of, or in connection with, any such crime. The Tribunal therefore cannot make a general declaration that the acts before 1939 were crimes against humanity within the meaning of the Charter, but from the beginning of the war in 1939 war crimes were committed on a vast scale, which were also crimes against humanity; and insofar as the inhumane acts charged in the indictment, and committed after the beginning of the war, did not constitute war crimes, they were all committed in execution of, or in connection with, the aggressive war, and therefore constituted crimes against humanity. * * *

Verdicts and Sentences of the International Military Tribunal

Calvocaressi, Nuremberg 141 (1947).

Table of									
	Charges Counts				**Verdicts Counts**				**Sentences**
	1	2	3	4	1	2	3	4	
Goering	X	X	X	X	X	X	X	X	
Ribbentrop	X	X	X	X	X	X	X	X	
Keitel	X	X	X	X	X	X	X	X	
Jodl	X	X	X	X	X	X	X	X	
Rosenberg	X	X	X	X	X	X	X	X	
Frick	X	X	X	X		X	X	X	
Seyss–Inquart	X	X	X	X		X	X	X	Death.
Sauckel	X	X	X	X			X	X	
Bormann	X		X	X			X	X	
Kaltenbrunner	X		X	X			X	X	
Frank	X		X	X			X	X	
Streicher	X							X	
Raeder	X	X	X	X	X	X	X		
Funk	X	X	X	X		X	X	X	Life.
Hess	X	X	X	X	X	X			Life.
Speer	X	X	X				X	X	
Schirach	X							X	20 years.
Neurath	X	X	X	X	X	X	X	X	15 years.
Doenitz	X	X	X			X	X		10 years.
Fritzsche	X		X	X					
von Papen	X	X							Acquitted.
Schacht	X	X							

Notes and Questions: Article 6(c) of the Nürnberg Charter dealing with crimes against humanity, based on the grammatical replacement of a comma for a semicolon referred to *supra*, restricted the jurisdiction of the International Military Tribunal to crimes against humanity committed in the context of the war. Why do think that such a restriction was agreed to? Note that the prosecutions under Allied Control Council Order No. 10 did not have this restriction. See the U.S. Military Tribunal decisions in *In Re Ölhendorf and Others* (Einsatzgrüppen case) 15 I.L.R. 656 (1948) and *U.S.* v. *Alstoetter et al.* (The Justices case), III Trials of War Criminals Before the Nuremberg Military Tribunals Under Control Council Order No. 10, 1946–1949.

4. DEFENSES

In General.

Individual Criminal Responsibility in the Statute for the Ad Hoc Tribunal for the Prosecution of Persons Responsible for Serious Violations of International Humanitarian Law in the Territory of the Former Yugoslavia

Article 7 of the Statute provides for individual criminal responsibility. It reads:

1. A person who planned, instigated, ordered, committed or otherwise aided and abetted in the planning, preparation or execution of a crime referred to in articles 2 to 5 of the present Statute, shall be individually responsible for the crime.

2. The official position of any accused person, whether as Head of State or Government or as a responsible Government official, shall not relieve such person of criminal responsibility nor mitigate punishment.

3. The fact that any of the acts referred to in articles 2 to 5 of the present Statute was committed by a subordinate does not relieve his superior of criminal responsibility if he knew or had reason to know that the subordinate was about to commit such acts or had done so and the superior failed to take the necessary and reasonable measures to prevent such acts or to punish the perpetrators thereof.

4. The fact that an accused person acted pursuant to an order of a Government or of a superior shall not relieve him of criminal responsibility, but may be considered in mitigation of punishment if the International Tribunal determines that justice so requires.

Rome Statute on the Establishment of an International Criminal Court

July 17, 1998, U.N. Doc. A/CONF.183/9.
Articles 25, 27, 28 and 33 in the Documentary Supplement.

Christopher L. Blakesley, Obstacles To The Creation Of A Permanent War Crimes Tribunal

18 The Fletch. Forum of World Affairs 77, 93–96 (1994); reprinted in International Law: Classic & Contemporary Readings (ASIL, Ku & Diehl, eds. 1998).*

Defenses.[a] [Head of State immunity or immunity for acts of government officials or for acts done in an official capacity will not constitute a

---

* Reprinted with the permission of the Fletcher Forum of World Affairs and the American Society of International Law.

a. For more on these defenses, see, D'Amato, *National Prosecution for Interna-*

tional Crimes, in Bassiouni, ed, 3 INTERNATIONAL CRIMINAL LAW, 169, 172–178 (1987).

defense to criminality or even a mitigating factor. Political leaders or other officials, therefore, may be held responsible for giving orders to commit an offense. Liability for criminal negligence is also imposed on a person in a position of superior authority who knew or had reason to know that his or her subordinates were about to commit an offense under the statute and who failed to take whatever action was necessary and reasonable to prevent, deter, or to repress the commission of such crimes by subordinates. On this standard, *see, e.g.*, Paust, *My Lai and Vietnam: Norms, Myths and Leader Responsibility*, 57 Mil.L.Rev. 99, 147–83 (1972), and the numerous cases cited therein. The Report talks of "imputed responsibility or criminal negligence." The same would be true in case of failure to punish those who had committed such an offense. Moreover, Superior Orders is not a defense, but may be considered a mitigating factor, "should the Tribunal determine that justice so requires." The superior orders defense acknowledges that soldiers must obey their superiors. Obviously, if superior officers have the power to inflict punishment, pain or death on a soldier who refuses to obey, duress may be involved, although duress is actually a separate defense. In addition, the ABA Task Force on the Ad Hoc Tribunal for the former Yugoslavia recommended that superior orders should be a legitimate defense if "a defendant acting under military authority in armed conflict did not know the orders to be unlawful and a person of ordinary sense and understanding would not have known the orders to be unlawful." It is hard to conceive, however, of a situation in which the grave breaches covered by the statute of a war crimes tribunal would not be understood to be illegal.]

Duress is traditionally a separate defense from superior orders. It would likely be considered only a mitigating factor when combined with the superior orders defense, where superior orders are conjoined with circumstances of coercion or lack of moral choice. Other standard criminal law defenses, such as minimum age or mental incapacity, for example, would be determined by the Tribunal itself. Certainly, criminal liability would obtain for complicity in such crimes.

In the case of the former Yugoslavia, the ABA Task Force has recommended that mitigation due to duress should be the only type of mitigation allowed under superior orders. This recommendation is sound, but as duress is a distinct defense, it should be separated from the superior orders defense. The mistake-of-law type of superior orders defense should be eliminated and duress retained. It is true that the aspect of the superior orders defense that gives rise to the lack of "moral choice" is a duress-like defense. This relationship was recognized at the Nuremberg Trial, although literally excluded in the London Charter. A second aspect or type of superior orders defense is that based on "ignorance of the illegality." The U.S. Military Field Manual formulates its mistake-based superior orders defense on that basis. Should both types of defense be allowed if a war crimes tribunal were created, or should only duress be allowed as the ABA suggests?

Necessity

In Re Von Leeb and Others (German High Command Trial)

United States Military Tribunal at Nuremberg, Germany, Oct. 28, 1948; 12 War Crimes Reports 1 (1949), 15 I.L.R. 376, at 397 (1948).

THE TRIBUNAL: ... The doctrine of military necessity has been widely urged. In the various treatises of international law there has been much discussion on this question. It has been the viewpoint of many German writers and to a certain extent has been contended in this case that military necessity includes the right to do anything that contributes to the winning of a war....

We content ourselves on this subject with stating that such a view would eliminate all humanity and decency and all law from the conduct of war and it is a contention which this Tribunal repudiates as contrary to the accepted usages of civilized nations. Nor does military necessity justify the compulsory recruitment of labour from an occupied territory either for use in military operations or for transfer to the Reich, nor does it justify the seizure of property or goods beyond that which is necessary for the use of the army of occupation. Looting and spoliation are none the less criminal in that they were conducted, not by individuals, but by the army and the State.

The devastation prohibited by the Hague Rules and the usages of war is that not warranted by military necessity. This rule is clear enough but the factual determination as to what constitutes military necessity is difficult. Defendants in this case were in many instances in retreat under arduous conditions wherein their commands were in serious danger of being cut off. Under such circumstances, a commander must necessarily make quick decisions to meet the particular situation of his command. A great deal of latitude must be accorded to him under such circumstances. What constitutes devastation beyond military necessity in these situations requires detailed proof of an operational and tactical nature. We do not feel that in this case the proof is ample to establish the guilt of any defendant herein on this charge.

Superior Orders and Duress[a]

The importance of the plea of superior orders transcends war crimes trials for it can be resorted to, both in national and in international proceedings, wherever a hierarchical system exists in which subordinates owe obedience to the instructions of their superiors.

See Nürnberg Charter, art. 8. Also Control Council Law, No. 10, Art. II secs 4(a) and 4(b):

---

a. Editor's note. On the superior orders defense, *see*, Dinstein, The Defense of Superior Orders (1965).

4(a) The official position of any person, whether as Head of State or as a responsible official in a Government Department, does not free him from responsibility for a crime or entitle him to mitigation of punishment.

(b) The fact that any person acted pursuant to the order to his Government or of a superior does not free him from responsibility for a crime, but may be considered in mitigation.

In Rome Statute On the Establishment of an International Criminal Court—Art. 33

July 17, 1998, U.N. Doc. A/CONF.183/9.
See Article 33 in the Documentary Supplement.

(1) IN WORLD WAR I

The Dover Castle, Germany, *Reichsgericht,* 4 June 1921, Cmd 1422 (1921), p. 42, Cast No. 231, I.L.R. 429,was a prosecution under articles 228–230 of the Treaty of Versailles, 1919. The accused was charged with having torpedoed, as a commander of a German submarine, on May 26, 1917, the English hospital ship *Dover Castle*, without warning, and with having sunk her with exceptional brutality. When torpedoed she had sick and wounded on board. None of these was drowned when the vessel was sunk, but six members of the crew were killed by the firing of the torpedo. The accused pleaded that in sinking the ship he merely carried out an order of the German Admiralty, which, in the belief that the enemy utilized their hospital ships for military purposes in violation of the Tenth Hague Convention, issued a number of orders instructing the submarines to attack hospital ships as vessels of war. The orders were communicated to the accused before his departure from the base.

The court held that the accused must be acquitted:

It is a military principle that the subordinate is bound to obey the orders of his superiors. This duty of obedience is of considerable importance from the point of view of criminal law. Its consequence is that, when the execution of a service order involves an offence against the criminal law, the superior giving the order is alone responsible.

This was in accordance with the terms of the German Law, s. 47, para. I of the Military Penal Code. The Admiralty Staff was the highest service authority over the accused. He was bound to obey their orders in service matters. So far as he obeyed, he was free from criminal responsibility. The Tribunal then discussed the cases in which, according to Article 47 of the German Military Penal Code, a subordinate is liable although he acted in conformity with his order. These are, first, cases in which a person goes beyond his orders. The accused was not guilty of any such excess. Neither was he guilty of obeying the order although he knew the act in question would involve a crime. He was in the circumstances of the case entitled to hold the opinion that the measures taken by the German authorities against foreign hospital ships were not contrary to international law, but were legitimate reprisals.

In the Llandovery Castle, Germany, Reichsgericht, 16 July 1921, Cmd 1422 (1921), pp. 45–46, (1921), 2 Am. Dig. 436, which involved a similar case the court reached a different conclusion. The two accused were subordinate officers in a German submarine which, after sinking the *Llandovery Castle*, a British hospital ship, fired on her boats with resulting serious loss of life. The commander of the submarine, who gave the firing order, was not within German jurisdiction at the time of the trials, and the prosecution was therefore confined to the two accused who assisted in executing the order of the commander. The latter pledged the accused to secrecy as to the firing, and by making false entries in the log-book and the chart, attempted to wipe out all traces of his action.

The defense of superior orders was not admitted. According to paragraph 2 of Article 47 of the German Military Penal Code the subordinate obeying an order involving a violation of the law is liable to punishment if it is known to him that the order of the superior is contrary to law. The Court found this to be the case with the accused. The killing of the survivors in life-boats was clearly illegal.

----

(2) In World War II

In Re Eck and Others (The Peleus)

Hamburg, British Military Court Oct. 20, 1945; (1945), 13 Am. Dig.

[The accused Eck, who was the commander of a German submarine, and four members of the crew, were charged jointly with the killing of survivors of the crew of the Allied merchant-vessel *Peleus*, which they had torpedoed on the night of March 13–14, 1944. It appeared that most of the members of the crew of the *Peleus* had succeeded in reaching two rafts and floating wreckage. The submarine having surfaced, one of the survivors of the *Peleus* was hailed and interrogated as to the name of the merchant-vessel, its destination, and other particulars. Several members of the crew of the submarine, acting under the orders of the accused Eck, then proceeded to open fire with a machine-gun and throw grenades at those survivors who were still in the water or on the rafts. All but three of the survivors were killed outright or subsequently died of their wounds. The three survivors who escaped death remained on the rafts for more than twenty-five days before they were rescued. The accused Eck pleaded that as commander of the submarine he did not act out of cruelty or revenge but as a matter of operational necessity for the purpose of alienating all traces of the *Peleus*. The four other accused pleaded that they acted in obedience to superior orders. The court held that the five accused were guilty.]

In the course of his summation the Judge Advocate stated:

... It is a fundamental usage of war that the killing of unarmed enemies is forbidden.... To fire so as to kill helpless survivors of a torpedoed ship is a grave breach against the law of nations. The right to punish persons who break such rules of war has equally been recognized for many years....

Let me remind you once more of what ought to be the starting-point of your consideration of this case, the principle of International Law, which is expressed in ... the *Llandovery Castle*.... No one as far as I know has ever challenged the accuracy of the principle which is expressed in the judgment of the Supreme Court of Germany in that case....

The principle is stated in the judgment in the following form: 'The firing on the boars was an offence against the law of nations. In war on land the killing of unarmed enemies is not allowed.... Similarly, in war at sea the killing of shipwrecked people who have taken refuge in lifeboats is forbidden.' My advice to you is that you are entitled to take that statement of the principle as the starting-point of your investigation of this case....

... Each one of the accused ... is entitled in this court to just as fair treatment at your hands and just as much consideration as if he were a citizen of an Alien nation....

... [The Commander of the U-boat] now says, the purpose of [the] firing was primarily the destruction of wreckage in order that every trace of the sinking might be obliterated.... He says he was under an operational necessity to do what he did because he had as his first duty to ensure that the submarine was protected against attack by Allied aircraft. He says that the only way of doing that was to take every possible step ... to destroy every trace of the sinking. If as a result of that survivors were killed it was unfortunate for them, but he was under the paramount necessity of protecting his boat and his crew.

The question whether or not any belligerent is entitled to kill an unarmed person for the purpose of saving his own life has been the subject of much discussion. It may be that circumstances can arise ... in which such a killing might be justified; but I suggest to you that you consider this case on the facts which have emerged from the evidence of Eck [the U-boat's captain]....

... Eck, does not rely upon the defense of superior orders. He stands before you taking the sole responsibility of the command which he issued upon himself.

... It is quite clear that [the weapons] officer Hoffman did fire. He says: "I fired on the rafts. The Kommandant gave me orders; he gave orders directly to me.... Now I am sitting here I do not think it was right to fire as I did." ...

That brings me to the discussion ... of what has been called superior orders, that is to say, orders coming from a higher authority which the accused is by the law and custom of his Service obliged to obey.... The duty to obey is limited to the observance of orders which are lawful. There can be no duty to obey that which is not a lawful order....

... The fact that a rule of warfare has been violated in pursuance of an order of a belligerent government, or of an individual belligerent commander, does not deprive the act in question of its character as a war crime....

Undoubtedly a Court confronted with a plea of superior orders adduced in justification of a war crime is bound to take into consideration the fact that obedience of military orders not obviously unlawful is a duty of every member of the armed forces, and that the latter cannot in conditions of war discipline be expected to weigh scrupulously the legal merits of the order received. The question, however, is governed by the major consideration that members of the armed forces are bound to obey lawful orders only, and that they cannot therefore escape liability if in obedience to a command they commit acts which both violate unchallenged rules of warfare and outrage the general sentiment of humanity.

... It is not fairly obvious to you that if in fact the carrying out of Eck's command involved the killing of these helpless survivors, it was not a lawful command, and that it must have been obvious to the most rudimentary intelligence that it was not a lawful command, and that those who did the shooting are not to be excused for doing it upon the ground of superior orders? ...

Let me now ... deal with the case of [the medical officer] ... [He] says: 'I was ordered to shoot and I did shoot in pursuance of that order.' He admitted in the witness box that he, being a medical officer, was exempted by the regulations of the German Navy from using weapons for the purpose of offence. He enjoys all the privileges which doctors enjoy under International Law in relation to the fighting services of any country. He certainly knew of the exemptions which he enjoyed under the regulations of the particular service to which he belonged. Yet, knowing that, [he] fired with a machine-gun in the circumstances of which you have heard. It is for you to say what you think about it....

... The engineer-officer of this submarine ... was minded to protest at the order which the Kommandant gave, and did in fact protest, telling him that he did not agree with it.

... But having made his protest, having gone below ..., he then comes up on deck.... He saw [the fifth accused, a leading seaman] using the machine-gun. He pushed him away and fired it himself, fired it, as he says, in order that there might be no question of a person to whom he had recently been speaking meaning one of those who had been interrogated, being killed by a bullet fired by the hand of such an undesirable person as he believed [this accused] to be. That, you may think, is a very odd explanation indeed. Whether it is true or not, you may still think that [this officer] might fall within the description of the charge-sheet of a person concerned in the killing of members of the crew of the steamship, because he voluntarily took upon himself at least the possibility of killing somebody on one of those pieces of wreckage, or on a raft.

It is for you to say what you think about it. It is for you to say how much importance is to be attached to the fact that he did make that protest whether it can provide him with a complete answer to this charge....

... You have heard a suggestion made that this Court has no right to adjudicate upon this case because it is said you cannot create an offence by a law which operates retrospectively so as to expose someone to punishment for acts which at the time he did them were not punishable as crimes [*nulla poena sine lege*].... My advice to you is that that maxim and the principle that it expresses has nothing whatever to do with this case. It has reference only to municipal or domestic law of a particular State, and you need not be embarrassed by it in your consideration of the problems that you have to deal with here. . . .

In Re Von Leeb and Others (German High Command Trial)

United States Military Tribunal at Nuremberg, Germany, October 28, 1948.
15 I.L.R. 376 (1948), 12 War Crimes Report 1 (1949).

[Referring to §§ 4(a) and (b) of Control Council Law No. 10, Art. II, quoted *supra*, the tribunal said:] These two paragraphs are clear and definite. They relate to the crimes defined in Control Council Law No. 10, Art. II, Secs. 1(a), 1(b) and 1(c). All of the defendants in this case held official positions in the armed forces of the Third Reich. Hitler from 1938 on was Commander-in-Chief of the Armed Forces and was the Supreme Civil and Military Authority in the Third Reich, whose personal decrees had the force and effect of law. Under such circumstances to recognize as a defense to the crimes set forth in Control Council Law No. 10 that a defendant acted pursuant to the order of his government or of a superior would be in practical effect to say that all the guilt charged in the Indictment was the guilt of Hitler alone because he alone possessed the law-making power of the State and the supreme authority to issue civil and military directives. To recognize such a contention would be to recognize an absurdity.

It is not necessary to support the provision of Control Council Law No. 10 Art. II, Secs. 4(a) and (b), by reason, for we are bound by it as one of the basic authorities under which we function as a Judicial Tribunal. Reason is not lacking.

Inasmuch as one of the reiterated arguments advanced is the injustice of even charging these defendants with being guilty of the crimes set forth in the Indictment, when they were, it is said, merely soldiers and acted under governmental directives and superior orders which they were bound to obey, we shall briefly note what we consider sound reasons for the rejection of such a defense.

The rejection of the defense of superior orders without its being incorporated in Control Council Law No. 10 that such defense shall not exculpate would follow of necessity from our holding that the acts set forth in Control Council Law No. 10 are criminal not because they are therein set forth as crimes but because they then were crimes under International Common Law. International Common Law must be superior to and where it conflicts with, take precedence over National Law or directives issued by any national governmental authority. A directive to violate International Criminal Common Law is therefore void and can afford no protection to one who violates such law in reliance on such a directive.

The purpose and effect of all law, national or international is to restrict or channelize the action of the citizen or subject. International Law has for its purpose and effect the restricting and channelizing of the action of nations. Since nations are corporate entities, a composite of a multitude of human beings and since a nation can plan and act only through its agents and representatives, there can be no effective restriction or channelizing of national action except through control of the agents and representatives of the nation, who form its policies and carry them out in action.

The State being but an inanimate corporate entity or concept, it cannot as such make plans, determine policies, exercise judgments, experience fear or be restrained or deterred from action except through its animate agents and representatives. It would be an utter disregard of reality and but legal shadow-boxing to say that only the State, the inanimate entity, can have guilt, and that no guilt can be attributed to its animate agents who devise and execute its policies. Nor can it be permitted even in a dictatorship that the dictator, absolute though he may be, shall be the scapegoat on whom the sins of all his governmental and military subordinates are wished; and that, when he is driven into a bunker and presumably destroyed, all the sins and guilt of his subordinates shall be considered to have been destroyed with him.

The defendants in this case who received obviously criminal orders were placed in a difficult position, but servile compliance with order clearly criminal for fear of some disadvantage or punishment not immediately threatened cannot be recognized as a defense. To establish the defense of coercion or necessity in the face of danger there must be a showing of circumstances such that a reasonable man would apprehend that he was in such imminent physical peril as to deprive him of freedom to choose the right and refrain from the wrong. No such situation has been shown in this case.

Furthermore, it is not a new concept that superior orders are no defense for criminal action. Article 47 of the German Military Penal Code, adopted in 1872, was as follows:

> If through the execution of an order pertaining to the service, a penal law is violated, then the superior giving the order is alone responsible. However, the obeying subordinate shall be punished as accomplice (Teilnehmer):
>
> > (1) if he went beyond the order given to him,
> >
> > (2) if he knew that the order of the superior concerned an act which aimed at a civil or military crime or offence.

The amendment of this in 1940 omitted the last two words "to him" in Section 1 above in Section 2 changed the words, "civil or military crime or offence", to "general or military crime or offence". If this amendment had any effect, it extended rather than restricted the scope of the preceding act.

It is interesting to note that an article by Goebbels, the Reich Propaganda Minister, which appeared in the *Voelkischer Beobachter*, the official Nazi publication, on 28th May 1944, contained the following correct statement of the law:

> It is not provided in any military law that a soldier in the case of a despicable crime is exempt from punishment because he passes the responsibility to his superior, especially if the orders of the latter are in evident contradiction to all human morality and every international usage of warfare.

In Re Ohlendorf and Others (Einsatzgrüppen Trial)

United States Military Tribunal at Nuremberg, April 10, 1948.
15 I.LR. 656 (1948).

THE TRIBUNAL: ... (7) *Plea of Superior Orders*—Those of the defendants who admit participation in the mass killings which are the subject of this trial, plead that they were under military orders and, therefore, had no will of their own. As intent is a basic prerequisite to responsibility of crime, they argue that they are innocent of criminality since they performed the admitted executions under duress, that is to say, Superior Orders. The defendants formed part of a military organization and were, therefore, subject to the rules which govern soldiers. It is axiomatic that a military man's first duty is to obey. If the defendants were soldiers and as soldiers responded to the command of their superiors to kill certain people, how can they be held guilty of crime? This is the question posed by the defendants. The answer is not a difficult one. The obedience of a soldier is not the obedience of an automaton. A soldier is a reasoning agent. He does not respond, and is not expected to respond, like a piece of machinery. It is a fallacy of widespread consumption that a soldier is required to do everything his superior officer orders him to do. A very simple illustration will show to what absurd extreme such a theory could be carried. If every military person were required, regardless of the nature of the command, to obey unconditionally, a sergeant could order the corporal to shoot the lieutenant, the lieutenant could order the sergeant to shoot the captain, the captain could order the lieutenant to shoot the colonel, and in each instance the executioner would be absolved of blame. The mere statement of such a proposition is its own commentary. The fact that a soldier may not, without incurring unfavourable consequences, refuse to drill, salute, exercise, reconnoitre, and even go into battle, does not mean that he must fulfil every demand put to him. In the first place, an order to require obedience must relate to military duty. An officer may not demand of a soldier for instance, that he steal for him. And what the superior officer may not militarily demand of his subordinate, the subordinate is not required to do. Even if the order refers to a military subject it must be one which the superior is authorized under the circumstances to give. The subordinate is bound only to obey the lawful orders of his superior and if he accepts a criminal order and executes it with a malice of his own, he may not plead Superior Orders in mitigation of his offense. If the nature of the ordered act is manifestly beyond the scope of the superior's authority, the subordinate may not plead ignorance of the criminality of the order. If one claims duress in the execution of an illegal order it must be shown that the harm caused by obeying the illegal order is not disproportionally greater than the harm which would result from not obeying the illegal order. It would not be an adequate excuse, for example, by not obeying it he himself would risk a few days of confinement. Nor if one acts under duress, may he, without culpability, commit the illegal act once the duress ceases.

"The International Military Tribunal, in speaking of the principle to be applied in the interpretation of criminal Superior Orders, declared that: 'The true test, which is found in varying degrees in the criminal law of most nations, is not the existence of the order, but whether moral choice was in fact possible'. The Prussian Military Code, as far back as 1845, recognized this principle of moral choice when it stated that a subordinate would be punished if, in the execution of an order, he went beyond its scope or if he executed an order knowing that it 'related to an act which obviously aimed at a crime'. This provision was copied into the Military Penal Code of the kingdom of Saxonia in 1867, and of Baden in 1870. Continuing even extending the doctrine of conditional obedience, the Bavarian Military Penal Code of 1869 went so far as to establish the responsibility of the subordinate as the rule, and his irresponsibility as the exception. The Military Penal Code of the Austro–Hungarian Monarchy of 1855 provided: 'Art. 158 A subordinate who does not carry out an order is not guilty of a violation of his duty of subordination if: (a) the order is obviously contrary to loyalty due to the Prince of the Land; (b) if the order pertains to an act or omission in which evidently a crime or an offense is to be recognized'. In 1872 Bismarck attempted to delimit subordinate responsibility by legislation, but the Reichstag rejected his proposal and instead adopted the following as Article 47 of the German Military Penal Code: 'Art. 47: If through the execution of an order pertaining to the service, a penal law is violated, then the superior giving the order is alone responsible. However, the obeying subordinate shall be punished as accomplice: (1) if he went beyond the order given to him, or (2) if he knew that the order of the superior concerned an act which aimed at a civil or military crime or offense.' This law was never changed, except to broaden its scope by changing the word 'civil' to 'general', and as late as 1940 one of the leading commentators of the Nazi period, Professor Schwinge, wrote: 'Hence, in military life, just as in other fields, the principle of absolute, i.e. blind obedience, does not exist'. Yet, one of the most generally quoted statements on this subject is that a German soldier must obey orders though the heavens fall. The statement has become legendary. The facts prove that it is a myth.... To plead Superior Orders one must show an excusable ignorance of their illegality. The sailor who voluntarily ships on a pirate craft may not be heard to answer that he was ignorant of the probability he would be called upon to help in the robbing and sinking of other vessels. He who willingly joins an illegal enterprise is charged with the natural development of the unlawful undertaking. What S.S. man could say that he was unaware of the attitude of Hitler towards Jewry? ... But it is stated that in military law even if the subordinate realizes that the act he is called upon to perform is a crime, he may not refuse its execution without incurring serious consequences, and that this, therefore, constitutes duress. Let it be said at once that there is no law which requires that an innocent man must forfeit his life or suffer serious harm in order to avoid committing a crime which he condemns. The threat, however, must be imminent, real and inevitable. No court will punish a man who, with a loaded pistol at his head, is compelled to pull a lethal lever.

"Nor need the peril be that imminent in order to escape punishment. But were any of the defendants coerced into killing Jews under the threat of being killed themselves if they failed in their homicidal mission? The test to be applied is whether the subordinate acted under coercion or whether he himself approved of the principle involved in the order. If the second proposition be true, the plea of Superior Orders fails. The doer may not plead innocence to a criminal act ordered by his superior if he is in accord with the principle and intent of the superior. When the will of the doer merges with the will of the superior in the execution of the illegal act, the doer may not plead duress under Superior Orders. If the mental and moral capacities of the superior and subordinate are pooled in the planning and execution of an illegal act, the subordinate may not subsequently protest that he was forced into the performance of an illegal undertaking. Superior means superior in capacity and power to force a certain act. It does not mean superiority only in rank. It could easily happen in an illegal enterprise that the captain guides the major, in which case the captain could not be heard to plead Superior Orders in defense of his crime. If the cognizance of the doer has been such, prior to the receipt of the illegal order, that the order is obviously but one further logical step in the development of a program which he knew to be illegal in its very inception, he may not excuse himself from responsibility for an illegal act which could have been foreseen by the application of the simple law of cause and effect.... One who embarks on a criminal enterprise of obvious magnitude is expected to anticipate what the enterprise will logically lead to. In order successfully to plead the defense of Superior Orders the opposition of the doer must be constant. It is not enough that he mentally rebel at the time the order is received. If at any time after receiving the order he acquiesces in its illegal character, the defense of Superior Orders is closed to him." The Tribunal also referred to the judgment of the German Supreme Court in the case of the *Llandovery Castle* (see Annual Digest, 1923–24, Case No. 235).

(3) IN VIET NAM

Some background to the My Lai Massacre.

Lippman, War Crimes: The My Lai Massacre and the Vietnam War

1 S.D.Just.J. 295, 299–319 (1993).*

* * *

After C Company was alerted in mid–1967 that they would be sent to Vietnam, they underwent an accelerated training program, much of which was compressed * * * Although the company received routine training in the handling of prisoners, little emphasis was placed on the appropriate treatment of civilians or refugees or on the obligation to report war crimes and atrocities * * * [t]he soldiers had received only "marginal training in several key areas: (1) provisions of the General Conventions, (2) handling and safeguarding of non-combatants, and (3) rules of engagement."

Upon arriving in Vietnam, C Company received a month long indoctrination before being assigned in January 1968 to Task Force Barker, a specially constituted force * * * Task Force Barker was assigned to the northeast portion of Quang Ngai Province which was designated on the military maps as "Pinkville," adjacent to the North Vietnamese border.

* Reprinted with the permission of the San Diego Justice Journal.

The five hundred man task force was faced with a daunting challenge—this was " 'indian country,' "meaning it was firmly under the control of the Viet Cong. Between January 22 and March 15, 1968, Task Force Barker suffered over one hundred friendly casualties, roughly forty percent of which occurred in the month of February. During the same period, the task force killed and wounded an estimated three hundred enemy soldiers, captured fifty combatants and seized roughly twenty weapons. * * *

Calley reported to Officer Candidate School (OCS) in March 1967, a year before the My Lai massacre, and graduated 120th out of a class of 156. He recounted that the overriding lesson taught at OCS was how to kill, with a jungle vine, knife and rifle. It was stressed that the important thing in Vietnam was to get a big kill ratio or body count. Calley learned that in " 'combat you haven't friends—You have enemies—* * * I told myself, I'll act as if I'm never secure. As if everyone in Vietnam would do me in. As if everyone's bad.' " * * *All Vietnamese were the enemy. "Everyone there was VC. The old men, the women, the children—the babies were all VC or would be VC in about three years. And inside of VC women, I guess there were a thousand little VC now." Calley did not recognize complexity—he assumed that all orders were legal * * *

* * * The daily grind of search and destroy missions and life in the jungle took its toll. C Company encountered land mines and snipers and felt frustrated over their failure to directly engage the enemy. The men began to lash out, beating and abusing civilians and prisoners. Various soldiers were assigned by Medina to kill and torture prisoners. In one instance, Calley shot an elderly Vietnamese who had been dropped into a well by his men. Calley reported to Medina that the victim was a Vietnamese sniper who had jumped into the well in order to avoid captivity. Eventually, even those who had initially objected to this brutality began to tolerate the violence. * * *

On February 25, six were killed and twelve were seriously wounded when C Company wandered into a minefield north of Pinkville. Many of the Americans blamed the villagers for having failed to alert them to the mines. The violence escalated—in one case, two platoon members raped a young woman and killed her baby. Calley was on leave at the time of the ambush and coincidentally found himself in a helicopter loaded with gear which had been retrieved from the ambush.

The chopper was filled with gear, rifles, rucksacks * * *. There must have been six boots there with the feet still in them, brains all over the place and everything was just saturated with blood. I believe there was one arm on it and a piece of a man's face, half of man's face on the chopper with the gear. By March 1968, murder, rape and arson had become commonplace. Many units ignored established policy and established "zippo squads," groups whose mission was to follow combat troops through the hamlets and to set them on fire. Few questions were raised over the fact that weapons were seldom recorded as having been seized from dead enemy soldiers. The suspicion was that these were civilian casualties. During a three-day operation in February, Task Force Barker reported having killed eighty Viet Cong and having recovered no weapons. In another February operation, seventy-five Viet Cong were reportedly killed and six weapons were captured. Ronald Grezesik, a member of Calley's platoon, later reflected that the platoon was caught in a vicious cycle which would later culminate in slaughter.

It was like going from one step to another * * * [f]irst, you'd stop the people, question them, and let them go. Second, you'd stop the people, beat up an old man, and let them go. Third, you'd stop the people, beat up an old man, and then shoot him. Fourth, you go in and wipe out a village.

On March 14, two days before the My Lai mission, a small squad from the third platoon, C Company, wandered into a booby trap. George Cox, a popular sergeant, was killed and another GI lost his eyes, an arm and a leg. In retribution, the remaining squad members entered a nearby hamlet, stole a radio and killed a fifteen year old girl and stole her ring. Medina later justified their actions, explaining that the young girl had detonated the booby trap with a remote control device. Gregory Olsen, a devout Mormon, described the incident in a letter to his father: "It was murder, and I'm ashamed of myself for not trying to do anything about it. This isn't the first time * * *. My faith in my fellow men is shot to hell. I just want the time to pass and I just want to come home."

Journalist Richard Hammer writes that the men of C Company had been reduced to killers and thugs:

> In dehumanizing and depersonalizing the Vietnamese, the Americans had themselves become depersonalized and dehumanized, had become vultures on the land, scavengers, * * * leaving in their wake nothing but death and destruction, and the hatred of those they had wronged. * * * like some horrible never-ending chain, they sensed hatred and fear of the Vietnamese toward Americans was translated into even deeper hatred and fear of Americans toward Vietnamese. So the mask of the killer was donned.

Despite this brutality, not a single member of Task Force Barker was court-martialed for an offense against Vietnamese civilians. By mid-March, Task Force Barker had been in the field for almost ten weeks without a respite. Fifteen GI's in the three company task force had been killed and eighty-five wounded. C Company of Task Force Barker soon would be presented with the opportunity [for] revenge.

B.   THE MY LAI MASSACRE

Quang Ngai had been a center of nationalist sentiment. During the struggle against the French, it was a stronghold of Viet Minh strength. * * *

In March 1968, the United States' objective was to engage and to destroy the 48th Battalion of the North Vietnam Army (NVA) which reportedly was headquartered in Son My Village * * * Frustrated at their inability to attract support among the local population, the Americans determined that they would decimate the province. The United States military declared the area to be a "free fire zone," which meant that all targets and suspected targets could be freely attacked without obtaining prior approval. Tens of thousands of tons of bombs, rockets, napalm and artillery ordinance were poured into northeastern Quang Ngai between

1965–1967. Planes with excess ordinance frequently unloaded their bombs on any convenient target, and artillery fire was randomly fired into the area. By 1967, 138,000 civilians had been rendered homeless and about seventy percent of the dwellings in the province had been destroyed.

* * *

Medina also reportedly ordered his men to burn and destroy My Lai (4) and to kill the livestock and to destroy the foodstuffs. No instructions were issued as to the treatment of civilians. According to the Peers inquiry, a significant number of the men reported that Medina had "left little or no doubt" that all persons remaining in the vicinity of My Lai (4) "were enemy, and that C Company's mission was to destroy the enemy." Various witnesses also agreed that Medina made reference to the casualties which had been inflicted by enemy mines, booby traps and sniper fire and that he characterized the forthcoming operation as an opportunity to take revenge against the VC. The Peers inquiry concluded that "[i]n a very real sense … it appears that the operation took the added aspect of a grudge match between C Company and an enemy force in My Lai." Medina also conceded that he had endeavored to work his men into a determined frenzy. He explained that he was attempting to build their morale and to give them the " 'psychological bread to go in and do battle with the 48th VC Battalion.' "Some sense of the mood of C Company is indicated by the question posed to Medina as to whether they should kill women and children. * * *

The platoons split into separate squads. All the participants could hear the continuous stream of weapons firing, and grenade rocket launchers exploding.

* * *

* * * English journalists Michael Bilton and Kevin Sim describe the impressions of Dennis Conti, who operated a mine sweeper:

To Conti the men appeared all psyched up when they landed. The shooting, once it began, created almost a chain reaction * * *. Inside the village his comrades appeared out of control. Families had huddled together for safety in houses, in the yards and in bunkers only to be mown down with automatic weapon fire or blown apart by fragmentation grenades. Women and children were pushed into bunkers and grenades thrown in after them * * *. At one point, wandering off on his own, Conti found a woman aged about 20 with a 4–year–old child. He forced her to perform oral sex on him while he held a gun at the child's head, threatening to kill it. Just at that moment Calley happened along and angrily told him to pull on his pants and get over to where he was supposed to be.

C Company still had not yet received any enemy fire or had encountered any VC. At approximately 0830 hours, Captain Medina reported that the body count now had risen to eighty-four enemy dead. Only a few refused to participate in the brutalities or offered assistance to the Vietnamese. The only American injury in Calley's platoon was an American soldier who shot himself in the foot.

The atrocities escalated. Many GI's became " 'double veterans,' " slang for raping and murdering a Vietnamese woman. Many females reportedly were raped, sodomized, mutilated, and then had their vaginas torn open with knives or bayonets or blasted apart by rifle fire. Victims were stabbed, had their limbs cut off, or were beheaded. Others were scalped, had their tongues cut out or throats slit. Vietnamese were beaten, clubbed, bayoneted and were shot at point blank range. The signature " 'C Company' "or the shape of an Ace of Spades, a Vietnamese sign of bad luck, was carved into the chests of the dead.

The events which made My Lai infamous were now to unfold. Paul Meadlo was standing guard over a group of elderly people, young women and children. [see decision, infra] * * *

Dennis Conti corroborated Meadlo's testimony.

Lieutenant Calley came out and said take care of these people. So we said, okay, so we stood there and watched them. He went away, then he came back and said, "I thought I told you to take care of these people." We said, "We are." He said, "I mean, kill them."

So they—Calley and Meadlo—got on line and fired directly into the people. There were bursts and single shots for two minutes. It was automatic. The people screamed and yelled and fell * * *. The people were pretty well messed up. Lots of heads was shot off, pieces of heads and pieces of flesh flew off the sides and arms. Meadlo fired a little bit and broke down * * *. He gave his weapon into my hands. I said I wouldn't. "If they're going to be killed, I'm not going to do it. Let Lieutenant Calley do it," I told him.

Conti reportedly wandered away and later saw Calley and Sergeant David Mitchell firing into a ditch.

I moved to the left to see what they were shooting at. It was a ditch and there were people there, and Calley and Mitchell were firing down into them. The fire * * * was both automatic and semi-automatic, single shots. A lot of them, the people, were trying to get up and mostly they was just screaming and pretty bad shot up.

The people were lying in the ditch right beneath Calley and Mitchell * * * and both men were holding their weapons at their shoulders and I could see muzzle flashes. I seen a woman tried to get up. I seen Lieutenant Calley fire. He hit the side of her head and blew it off.

Calley was not finished; Radio operator, Charles Sledge, testified. We went up the ditch * * * we came upon a priest almost at the end of the ditch. At least I think he was a priest; he was dressed in white robes. Lieutenant Calley started to ask him some questions and the priest, he would fold his hands and bow his head and say, "No Viet, no Viet." Calley asked him a few more questions and he kept saying, "No Viet." Then Lieutenant Calley hit him with the butt of his rifle.

* * * His mouth was bleeding and then he fell back a little and folded his hands and, sort of like pleading. Lieutenant Calley took his rifle and point-blank pulled the trigger right in his face and blew half his head off. The priest fell. Half his head was blown away.

Sledge then testified that someone shouted that a child was running back toward the village. " * * * Calley ran back and grabbed the baby by one arm. I don't know whether it was a boy or a girl. He picked it up by one arm and threw it into the ditch, and shot it. He flung it into the ditch, the deep end of it. The child was maybe one or two. Calley fired one shot."

Calley, in an interview with journalist John Sack, explained his motivation. "As for me, killing those men in My Lai didn't haunt me. I didn't—I couldn't kill for the pleasure of it. We weren't in My Lai to kill human beings, really. We were there to kill ideology. That is carried by—I don't know. Pawns. Blobs. Pieces of flesh, and I wasn't in My Lai to destroy intelligent men. I was there to destroy an intangible idea [communism]. Those people are monsters, [they] have no qualms, no hang-ups, no holding-backs to the extremes they'll go to. I mean butcherings: that is what communism does, and we were there in My Lai to destroy it. Personally, I didn't kill any Vietnamese that day: I mean personally. I represented the United States of America. My country."

The Peers inquiry concluded that C Company killed between 175 and 200 Vietnamese. The Army Criminal Investigation Division (CID) estimated that the number of dead Vietnamese totalled 347. The company suffered only one self-inflicted injury. Only three or four of the dead Vietnamese were confirmed VC. Three enemy weapons and several sets of web gear and grenades were also captured. The inquiry concluded that there was no evidence that the company had received any enemy fire or had encountered any other form of resistance prior to or after entering My Lai (4).

————

Notes & Questions. **1**. Standard applied in the *Calley case*. Should a soldier be convicted of murder (as opposed to, say, manslaughter) only if he subjectively knew that an order to kill was illegal? Or can he be convicted of murder even if he did not in his own mind know of its illegality but other soldiers knew it was illegal? Was Calley convicted because of what he knew or because of what other people knew? The debate in the opinions in the Calley case centers around what some other person would know: i.e. a person of ordinary sense and understanding, or a person of commonest understanding. Are all the judges saying that Calley can be found guilty, even though he didn't know subjectively, if the person meeting that standard would have known? Or is the standard some rule of evidence, e.g., since an individual of ordinary sense and understanding would know the order was illegal and since Calley is a man of ordinary sense and understanding, therefore Calley "must have known" the order was illegal?

2. In ***Public Prosecutor v. Leopold,*** Austria Supreme Court 1967, 47 Int'l L.Rep. 464 (1974), defendant was convicted of the murder of Poles and Jews, inmates of a labor camp in Poland during the Second World War. Defendant was a German S.S. deputy troop leader, a member of the guard at the labor camp, who claimed to be acting pursuant to orders. The defendant's appeal asserted, inter alia, that he was "unable, owing to his limited intelligence, to realize the criminal nature of the execution of an illegal order." In denying the appeal, the court stated: " * * * [I]t must be said that orders to kill, given without previous proceedings, in respect of individual or groups of inmates of this labour camp could not even as a matter of form have any legal justification. They were therefore straightaway recognizable as illegal. Furthermore, the fact must be considered that orders to kill inmates of the labour camp, irrespective of their form and extent, which were clearly recognizable by anybody as illegal, could never have justified the person executing such orders but could only, in certain circumstances, have excused him from the point of view of absolute coercion (§ 2(g) Penal Code), that is, only if non-execution of such orders would have meant immediate danger to life for the person disregarding them. The reference in the appeal to the power of a commander under martial law to reinforce his orders, in face of the enemy, if necessary immediately by the use of his weapon (which incidentally—as is generally known—was only applied in the last phase of the Second World War), is out of place in this context, since the defendant was not involved in belligerent action by a fighting unit but performed only a guarding function." [Emphasis supplied.]

United States v. Calley

United States Court of Military Appeals, 1973.
48 C.M.R. 19.

■ QUINN, JUDGE:

First Lieutenant Calley stands convicted of the premeditated murder of 22 infants, children, women, and old men, and of assault with intent to murder a child of about 2 years of age. All the killings and the assault took place on March 16, 1968 in the area of the village of My Lai in the Republic of South Vietnam. The Army Court of Military Review affirmed the findings of guilty and the sentence, which, as reduced by the convening authority, includes dismissal and confinement at hard labor for 20 years. The accused petitioned this Court for further review * * *

* * *

[Defendant's second assignment of error is that the evidence is insufficient to meet the reasonable doubt standard. Summary of pertinent evidence follows].

Lieutenant Calley was a platoon leader in C Company, a unit that was part of an organization known as Task Force Barker, whose mission was to subdue and drive out the enemy in an area in the Republic of Vietnam known popularly as Pinkville. Before March 16, 1968, this area, which included the village of My Lai 4, was a Viet Cong stronghold. C Company had operated in the area several times. Each time the unit had entered the area it suffered casualties by sniper fire, machine gun fire, mines, and other forms of attack. Lieutenant Calley had accompanied his platoon on some of the incursions.

On March 15, 1968, a memorial service for members of the company killed in the area during the preceding weeks was held. After the service Captain Ernest L. Medina, the commanding officer of C Company, briefed the company on a mission in the Pinkville area set for the next day. C Company was to serve as the main attack formation for Task Force Barker. In that role it would assault and neutralize My Lai 4, 5, and 6 and then mass for an assault on My Lai 1. Intelligence reports indicated that the unit would be opposed by a veteran enemy battalion, and that all civilians would be absent from the area. The objective was to destroy the enemy. Disagreement exists as to the instructions on the specifics of destruction. Captain Medina testified that he instructed his troops that they were to destroy My Lai 4 by "burning the hootches, to kill the livestock, to close the wells and to destroy the food crops." Asked if women and children were to be killed, Medina said he replied in the negative, adding that, "You must use common sense. If they have a weapon and are trying to engage you, then you can shoot back, but you must use common sense." However, Lieutenant Calley testified that Captain Medina informed the troops they were to kill every living thing—men, women, children, and animals—and under no circumstances were they to leave any Vietnamese behind them as they passed through the villages enroute to their final objective. Other witnesses gave more or less support to both versions of the briefing.

On March 16, 1968, the operation began with interdicting fire. C Company was then brought to the area by helicopters. Lieutenant Calley's platoon was on the first lift. This platoon formed a defense perimeter until the remainder of the force was landed. The unit received no hostile fire from the village.

Calley's platoon passed the approaches to the village with his men firing heavily. Entering the village, the platoon encountered only unarmed, unresisting men, women, and children. The villagers, including infants held in their mothers' arms, were assembled and moved in separate groups to collection points. Calley testified that during this time he was radioed twice by Captain Medina, who demanded to know what was delaying the platoon. On being told that a large number of villagers had been detained, Calley said Medina ordered him to "waste them." Calley further testified that he obeyed the orders because he had been taught the doctrine of obedience throughout his military career. Medina denied that he gave any such order.

One of the collection points for the villagers was in the southern part of the village. There, Private First Class Paul D. Meadlo guarded a group of between 30 to 40 old men, women, and children. Lieutenant Calley approached Meadlo and told him, "You know what to do," and left. He returned shortly and asked Meadlo why the people were not yet dead. Meadlo replied he did not know that Calley had meant that they should be killed. Calley declared that he wanted them dead. He and Meadlo then opened fire on the group, until all but a few children fell. Calley then personally shot these children. He expended 4 or 5 magazines from his M–16 rifle in the incident.

Lieutenant Calley and Meadlo moved from this point to an irrigation ditch on the east side of My Lai 4. There, they encountered another group of civilians being held by several soldiers. Meadlo estimated that this group contained from 75 to 100 persons. Calley stated, "We got another job to do, Meadlo," and he ordered the group into the ditch. When all were in the ditch, Calley and Meadlo opened fire on them. Although ordered by Calley to shoot, Private First Class James J. Dursi refused to join in the killings, and Specialist Four Robert E. Maples refused to give his machine gun to Calley for use in the killings. Lieutenant Calley admitted that he fired into the ditch, with the muzzle of his weapon within 5 feet of people in it. He expended between 10 to 15 magazines of ammunition on this occasion.

With his radio operator, Private Charles Sledge, Calley moved to the north end of the ditch. There, he found an elderly Vietnamese monk, whom he interrogated. Calley struck the man with his rifle butt and then shot him in the head. Other testimony indicates that immediately afterwards a young child was observed running toward the village. Calley seized him by the arm, threw him into the ditch, and fired at him. Calley admitted interrogating and striking the monk, but denied shooting him. He also denied the incident involving the child.

Appellate defense counsel contend that the evidence is insufficient to establish the accused's guilt. They do not dispute Calley's participation in the homicides, but they argue that he did not act with the malice or mens rea essential to a conviction of murder; that the orders he received to kill everyone in the village were not palpably illegal; that he was acting in ignorance of the laws of war; that since he was told that only "the enemy" would be in the village, his honest belief that there were no innocent civilians in the village exonerates him of criminal responsibility for their deaths; and, finally, that his actions were in the heat of passion caused by reasonable provocation.

* * *

The testimony of Meadlo and others provided the court members with ample evidence from which to find that Lieutenant Calley directed and personally participated in the intentional killing of men, women, and children, who were unarmed and in the custody of armed soldiers of C Company. If the prosecution's witnesses are believed, there is also ample evidence to support a finding that the accused deliberately shot the Vietnamese monk whom he interrogated, and that he seized, threw into a ditch, and fired on a child with the intent to kill.

Enemy prisoners are not subject to summary execution * * *. Military law has long held that the killing of an unresisting prisoner is murder. * * * "While it is lawful to kill an enemy 'in the heat and exercise of war,' yet 'to kill such an enemy after he has laid down his arms * * * is murder.' "

Conceding for the purposes of this assignment of error that Calley believed the villagers were part of "the enemy," the uncontradicted evidence is that they were under the control of armed soldiers and were offering no resistance. In his testimony, Calley admitted he was aware of the requirement that prisoners be treated with respect. He also admitted he knew that the normal practice was to interrogate villagers, release those who could satisfactorily account for themselves, and evacuate the suspect among them for further examination. Instead of proceeding in the usual way, Calley executed all, without regard to age, condition, or possibility of suspicion. On the evidence, the court-martial could reasonably find Calley guilty of the offenses before us.

At trial, Calley's principal defense was that he acted in execution of Captain Medina's order to kill everyone in My Lai 4. Appellate defense counsel urge this defense as the most important factor in assessment of the legal sufficiency of the evidence. The argument, however, is inapplicable to whether the evidence is legally sufficient. Captain Medina denied that he issued any such order, either during the previous day's briefing or on the date the killings were carried out. Resolution of the conflict between his testimony and that of the accused was for the triers of the facts. The general finding of guilty, with exceptions as to the number of persons killed, does not indicate whether the court members found that Captain Medina did not issue the alleged order to kill, or whether, if he did, the court members believed that the accused knew the order was illegal. For the purpose of the legal sufficiency of the evidence, the record supports the findings of guilty.

In the third assignment of error, appellate defense counsel assert gross deficiencies in the military judge's instructions to the court members. Only two assertions merit discussion. One contention is that the judge should have, but did not, advise the court members of the necessity to find the existence of "malice aforethought" in connection with the murder charges; the second allegation is that the defense of compliance with superior orders was not properly submitted to the court members.

The existence vel non of malice, say appellate defense counsel, is the factor that distinguishes murder from manslaughter. * * *

* * * In enactment of the Uniform Code of Military Justice, Congress eliminated malice as an element of murder by codifying the common circumstances under which that state of mind was deemed to be present. * * * One of the stated purposes of the Code was the "listing and definition of offenses, redrafted and rephrased in modern legislative language." That purpose was accomplished by defining murder as the unlawful killing of a human being, without justification or excuse. * * *

The trial judge delineated the elements of premeditated murder for the court members in accordance with the statutory language. He instructed them that to convict Lieutenant Calley, they must be convinced beyond a reasonable doubt that the victims were dead; that their respective deaths resulted from specified acts of the accused; that the killings were unlawful; and that Calley acted with a premeditated design to kill. The judge defined accurately the meaning of an unlawful killing and the meaning of a "premeditated design to kill." These instructions comported fully with requirements of existing law for the offense of premeditated murder, and neither statute nor judicial precedent requires that reference also be made to the pre-Code concept of malice. We turn to the contention that the judge erred in his submission of the defense of superior orders to the court. After fairly summarizing the evidence, the judge gave the following instructions pertinent to the issue:

The killing of resisting or fleeing enemy forces is generally recognized as a justifiable act of war, and you may consider any such killings justifiable in this case. The law attempts to protect those persons not actually engaged in warfare, however; and limits the circumstances under which their lives may be taken.

Both combatants captured by and noncombatants detained by the opposing force, regardless of their loyalties, political views, or prior acts, have the right to be treated as prisoners until released, confined, or executed, in accordance with law and established procedures, by competent authority sitting in judgment of such detained or captured individuals. Summary execution of detainees or prisoners is forbidden by law. Further, it's clear under the evidence presented in this case, that hostile acts or support of the enemy North Vietnamese or Viet Cong forces by inhabitants of My Lai (4) at some time prior to 16 March 1968, would not justify the summary execution of all or a part of the occupants of My Lai (4) on 16 March, nor would hostile acts committed that day, if, following the hostility, the belligerents surrendered or were captured by our forces. I therefore instruct you, as a matter of law, that if unresisting human beings were killed at My Lai (4) while within the effective custody and control of our military forces, their deaths cannot be considered justified, and any order to kill such people would be, as a matter of law, an illegal order. Thus, if you find that Lieutenant Calley received an order directing him to kill unresisting Vietnamese within his control or within the control of his troops, that order would be an illegal order.

A determination that an order is illegal does not, of itself, assign criminal responsibility to the person following the order for acts done in compliance with it. Soldiers are taught to follow orders, and special attention is given to obedience of orders on the battlefield. Military effectiveness depends upon obedience to orders. On the other hand, the obedience of a soldier is not the obedience of an automaton. A soldier is a reasoning agent, obliged to respond, not as a machine, but as a person. The law takes these factors into account in assessing criminal responsibility for acts done in compliance with illegal orders.

The acts of a subordinate done in compliance with an unlawful order given him by his superior are excused and impose no criminal liability upon him unless the superior's order is one which a man of ordinary sense and understanding would, under the circumstances, know to be unlawful, or if the order in question is actually known to the accused to be unlawful. * * *

In determining what orders, if any, Lieutenant Calley acted under, if you find him to have acted, you should consider all of the matters which he has testified reached him and which you can infer from other evidence that he saw and heard. Then, unless you find beyond a reasonable doubt that he was not acting under orders directing him in substance and effect to kill unresisting occupants of My Lai (4), you must determine whether Lieutenant Calley actually knew those orders to be unlawful.

* * * In determining whether or not Lieutenant Calley had knowledge of the unlawfulness of any order found by you to have been given, you may consider all relevant facts and circumstances, including Lieutenant Calley's rank; educational background; OCS schooling; other training while in the Army, including basic training, and his training in Hawaii and Vietnam; his experience on prior operations involving contact with hostile and friendly Vietnamese; his age; and any other evidence tending to prove or disprove that on 16 March 1968, Lieutenant Calley knew the order was unlawful. If you find beyond a reasonable doubt, on the basis of all the evidence, that Lieutenant Calley actually knew the order under which he asserts he

operated was unlawful, the fact that the order was given operates as no defense.

Unless you find beyond reasonable doubt that the accused acted with actual knowledge that the order was unlawful, you must proceed to determine whether, under the circumstances, a man of ordinary sense and understanding would have known the order was unlawful. Your deliberations on this question do not focus on Lieutenant Calley and the manner in which he perceived the legality of the order found to have been given him. The standard is that of a man of ordinary sense and understanding under the circumstances.

Think back to the events of 15 and 16 March 1968. * * * Then determine, in light of all the surrounding circumstances, whether the order, which to reach this point you will have found him to be operating in accordance with, is one which a man of ordinary sense and understanding would know to be unlawful. Apply this to each charged act which you have found Lieutenant Calley to have committed. Unless you are satisfied from the evidence, beyond a reasonable doubt, that a man of ordinary sense and understanding would have known the order to be unlawful, you must acquit Lieutenant Calley for committing acts done in accordance with the order. (Emphasis added.)

Appellate defense counsel contend that these instructions are prejudicially erroneous in that they require the court members to determine that Lieutenant Calley knew that an order to kill human beings in the circumstances under which he killed was illegal by the standard of whether "a man of ordinary sense and understanding" would know the order was illegal. They urge us to adopt as the governing test whether the order is so palpably or manifestly illegal that a person of "the commonest understanding" would be aware of its illegality. They maintain the standard stated by the judge is too strict and unjust; that it confronts members of the armed forces who are not persons of ordinary sense and understanding with the dilemma of choosing between the penalty of death for disobedience of an order in time of war on the one hand and the equally serious punishment for obedience on the other. Some thoughtful commentators on military law have presented much the same argument.

The "ordinary sense and understanding" standard is set forth in the present Manual for Courts–Martial, United States, 1969 (Rev.) and was the standard accepted by this Court in United States v. Schultz; and United States v. Keenan. It appeared as early as 1917. Manual for Courts–Martial, U.S. Army, 1917, paragraph 442. Apparently, it originated in a quotation from F. Wharton, Homicide '485 (3d ed. 1907). Wharton's authority is Riggs v. State (Tenn.1866), in which the court approved a charge to the jury as follows: "[I]n its substance being clearly illegal, so that a man of ordinary sense and understanding would know as soon as he heard the order read or given that such order was illegal, would afford a private no protection for a crime committed under such order." * * *

In the stress of combat, a member of the armed forces cannot reasonably be expected to make a refined legal judgment and be held criminally responsible if he guesses wrong on a question as to which there may be considerable disagreement. But there is no disagreement as to the illegality of the order to kill in this case. For 100 years, it has been a settled rule of American law that even in war the summary killing of an enemy, who has submitted to, and is under, effective physical control, is murder. Appellate defense counsel acknowledge that rule of law and its continued viability, but they say that Lieutenant Calley should not be held accountable for the men, women and children he killed because the court-martial could have found that he was a person of "commonest understanding" and such a person might not know what our law provides; that his captain had ordered him to kill these unarmed and submissive people and he only carried out that order as a good disciplined soldier should.

Whether Lieutenant Calley was the most ignorant person in the United States Army in Vietnam, or the most intelligent, he must be presumed to know that he could not kill the people involved here. The U.S. Supreme Court has pointed out that "[t]he rule that 'ignorance of the law will not excuse' [a positive act that constitutes a crime] * * * is deep in our law." Lambert v. California. An order to kill infants and unarmed civilians who were so demonstrably incapable of resistance to the armed might of a military force as were those killed by Lieutenant Calley is, in my opinion, so palpably illegal that whatever conceptional difference there may be between a person of "commonest understanding" and a person of "common understanding," that difference could not have had any "impact on a court of lay members receiving the respective wordings in instructions," as appellate defense counsel contend. In my judgment, there is no possibility of prejudice to Lieutenant Calley in the trial judge's reliance upon the established standard of excuse of criminal conduct, rather than the standard of "commonest understanding" presented by the defense, or by the new variable test postulated in the dissent, which, with the inclusion of such factors for consideration as grade and experience, would appear to exact a higher standard of understanding from Lieutenant Calley than that of the person of ordinary understanding.

In summary, as reflected in the record, the judge was capable and fair, and dedicated to assuring the accused a trial on the merits as provided by law; his instructions on all issues were comprehensive and correct. * * * The decision of the Court of Military Review is affirmed.

■ DUNCAN, JUDGE (concurring in the result):

My difference of opinion from Judge Quinn's view of the defense of obedience to orders is narrow. The issue of obedience to orders was raised in defense by the evidence. Contrary to Judge Quinn, I do not consider that a presumption arose that the appellant knew he could not kill the people involved. The Government, as I see it, is not entitled to a presumption of what the appellant knew of the illegality of an order. It is a matter for the factfinders under proper instructions.

Paragraph 216, Manual for Courts–Martial, United States, 1969 (Rev.), provides for special defenses: excuse because of accident or misadventure; self-defense; entrapment; coercion or duress; physical or financial inability; and obedience to apparently lawful orders. Subparagraph d of ¶ 216 [reads]:

An order requiring the performance of a military duty may be inferred to be legal. An act performed manifestly beyond the scope of authority, or pursuant to an order that a man of ordinary sense and understanding would know to be illegal, or in a wanton manner in the discharge of a lawful duty, is not excusable.

The military judge clearly instructed the members pursuant to this provision of the Manual. The heart of the issue is whether, under the circumstances of this case, he should have abandoned the Manual standard and fashioned another. The defense urges a purely subjective standard; the dissent herein yet another . . .

* * *

Perhaps a new standard, such as the dissent suggests, has merit; however, I would leave that for the legislative authority or for the cause where the record demonstrates harm from the instructions given. I perceive none in this case. The general verdict in this case implies that the jury believed a man of ordinary sense and understanding would have known the order in question to be illegal. Even conceding arguendo that this issue should have been resolved under instructions requiring a finding that almost every member of the armed forces would have immediately recognized that the order was unlawful, as well as a finding that as a consequence of his age, grade, intelligence, experience, and training, Lieutenant Calley should have recognized the order's illegality, I do not believe the result in this case would have been different. * * *

■ DARDEN, CHIEF JUDGE (dissenting):

Although the charge the military judge gave on the defense of superior orders was not inconsistent with the Manual treatment of this subject, I believe the Manual provision is too strict in a combat environment. Among other things, this standard permits serious punishment of persons whose training and attitude incline them either to be enthusiastic about compliance with orders or not to challenge the authority of their superiors. The standard also permits conviction of members who are not persons of ordinary sense and understanding.* * *

The test of palpable illegality to the commonest understanding properly balances punishment for the obedience of an obviously illegal order against protection to an accused for following his elementary duty of obeying his superiors. Such a test reinforces the need for obedience as an essential element of military discipline by broadly protecting the soldier who has been effectively trained to look to his superiors for direction. It also promotes fairness by permitting the military jury to consider the particular accused's intelligence, grade, training, and other elements directly related to the issue of whether he should have known an order was illegal. Finally, that test imputes such knowledge to an accused not as a result of simple negligence but on the much stronger circumstantial concept that almost anyone in the armed forces would have immediately recognized that the order was palpably illegal.

I would adopt this standard as the correct instruction for the jury when the defense of superior orders is in issue. Because the original case language is archaic and somewhat ungrammatical, I would rephrase it to require that the military jury be instructed that, despite his asserted defense of superior orders, an accused may be held criminally accountable for his acts, allegedly committed pursuant to such orders, if the court members are convinced beyond a reasonable doubt (1) that almost every member of the armed forces would have immediately recognized that the order was unlawful, and (2) that the accused should have recognized the order's illegality as a consequence of his age, grade, intelligence, experience, and training.

* * *

In the instant case, Lieutenant Calley's testimony placed the defense of superior orders in issue even though he conceded that he knew prisoners were normally to be treated with respect and that the unit's normal practice was to interrogate Vietnamese villagers, release those who could account for themselves, and evacuate those suspected of being a part of the enemy forces. Although crucial parts of his testimony were sharply contested, according to Lieutenant Calley, (1) he had received a briefing before the assault in which he was instructed that every living thing in the village was to be killed, including women and children; (2) he was informed that speed was important in securing the village and moving forward; (3) he was ordered that under no circumstances were any Vietnamese to be allowed to stay behind the lines of his forces; (4) the residents of the village who were taken into custody were hindering the progress of his platoon in taking up the position it was to occupy; and (5) when he informed Captain Medina of this hindrance, he was ordered to kill the villagers and to move his platoon to a proper position.

In addition to the briefing, Lieutenant Calley's experience in the Pinkville area caused him to know that, in the past, when villagers had been left behind his unit, the unit had immediately received sniper fire from the rear as it pressed forward. Faulty intelligence apparently led him also to believe that those persons in the village were not innocent civilians but were either enemies or enemy sympathizers. For a participant in the My Lai operation, the circumstances that could have obtained there may have caused the illegality of alleged orders to kill civilians to be much less clear than they are in a hindsight review.

Since the defense of superior orders was not submitted to the military jury under what I consider to be the proper standard, I would grant Lieutenant Calley a rehearing.

Notes and Questions

1. *Further proceedings in the Calley case.* In *Calley v. Callaway*, 382 F.Supp. 650 (M.D.Ga.1974), Calley was ordered released on habeas corpus because of pretrial publicity. This was reversed, 519 F.2d 184 (5th Cir. 1975), *cert. denied sub. nom. Calley v. Hoffmann*, 425 U.S. 911 (1976). While these cases were in process, Calley was first paroled by the U.S. Army and then released on bail by the District Court in November 1974, pending appeal. After the Supreme Court denied certiorari, the U.S. Army announced in April 1976 that it would not seek to return Calley to custody for the remaining ten days of his sentence (previously reduced). *See* The

New York Times, Nov. 9, 1974, p. 1; Nov. 10, 1974, p. 1; Sept. 11, 1975, p. 26; Apr. 6, 1976, p. 1.

2. *In Calley's appeal,* he argued that the deaths of the villagers at My Lai were not "legally requitable in that the villagers had no right to continued life cognizable in our law." His argument was founded on the claim that the villagers' support and sympathy for the Viet–Cong was so complete and extensive that they were not entitled to "civilian status." He simultaneously argued that they were not entitled to irregular belligerent status, which would allow them protection of the Geneva POW Convention. *See,* Geneva Convention Relative to the Treatment of Prisoners of War, 12 Aug. 1949, 6 UST 3316 (1956). The Court of Military Appeals rejected Calley's arguments: "[Even if it were true that some of the villagers may have sympathized with and assisted the Viet–Cong, this does not justify killing] 'infants in arms or children of toddler age* * *.' [Moreover, summary executions of 'irregular combatants' may not be condoned], whether an armed conflict be a local uprising or a global war, summary executions as in My Lai (4) are not justifiable * * *." *Discussed in* Lippman, *War Crimes, supra* at 320.

United States v. Staff Sergeant (E–6) Walter Griffen

RA 17542182, U.S. Army, Company D, 1st Battalion (Airborne), 8th Cavalry,
1st Cavalry Division (Airmobile), APO San Francisco 96490 CM 416805.[1]

■ PORCELLA, JUDGE ADVOCATE: In this contested case, the accused was found guilty of acting jointly with others in committing an unpremeditated murder in violation of Article 118 of the Uniform Code of Military Justice. After reducing the period of confinement from ten years, the convening authority approved a sentence of total forfeitures, confinement at hard labour for seven years and reduction to the lowest enlisted grade.

In their assignment of errors, counsel for the appellant contend that the law officer erred prejudicially in failing to instruct the court on the applicable law of the defense of obedience to superior orders. In considering this contention, we will recite those facts which appear pertinent to our disposition of the case.

On 4 April 1967, in Vietnam, a platoon of the 1st Cavalry Division was providing security for an engineer element near Bong Son. About 10 o'clock in the morning, members of the platoon apprehended an indigenous male of military age who, after evacuation and interrogation by a higher echelon, was "confirmed" to be a member of the hostile Viet Cong. Later that day, as the platoon was preparing to cross a large, open rice paddy, a security element on the right flank found an unarmed male native about 40 to 45 years old in a bunker. He was brought to the command post area, and a helicopter was requested for his evacuation. Meanwhile, the accused noticed that activities of his platoon were being observed by a native he suspected might be a member of the Viet Cong. A patrol was dispatched to apprehend him. However, the search was unsuccessful. While the patrol was reconnoitering by fire and discharging grenades in bunkers, one of its

---

1. Petition for review by USCMA *denied,* 39 CMR 293.

members was injured by a secondary explosion. Using radio communications, overheard by several witnesses, Lieutenant Patrick the platoon leader, conversed with Captain Ogg, the company commander. He arranged for the air evacuation of the wounded man but was told this prisoner would not be evacuated by helicopter. The precise conversation concerning the disposition of the prisoner is not clear. However, the understanding of Captain Ogg's order appears to have been that the prisoner should be killed. There is evidence that Lieutenant Patrick gave the accused a direct order to the same effect. Specialist Garcia, the medical technician attached to the platoon, removed the prisoner from the command post area and escorted him, his hands tied behind his back, to an embankment, where the accused and Private First Class Woods each fired several shots at him with M–16 rifles. The prisoner expired as a result. His body contained numerous fragments from M–16 bullets.

The accused testified, in part, to the following effect: He overheard Captain Ogg state in his radio transmission that the prisoner should be killed. Then Lieutenant Patrick said: "Sergeant Griffen, take him down the hill and shoot him. Come back and let me know." The accused admitted firing his rifle at the prisoner and thereafter reporting back to Lieutenant Patrick. He committed the act because he had been ordered to do so and for the safety of his men. He believed the order to be legal because his platoon leader, a lieutenant, had once been relieved when a prisoner who had been securely tied escaped during the night. Also, he felt that the security of the platoon would have been violated if the prisoner were kept, since their operations had already been observed by another suspect. In addition, several months earlier, all the members of his platoon had either been killed or wounded in that same general area after their positions had been observed.

Prior to argument, the defense submitted a proposed instruction on obedience of orders as a defense to the offense charged. The law officer did not give the requested instruction. Rather, he instructed the court as follows on this subject:

"Now, the general rule is that the acts of a subordinate, done in good faith in compliance with his supposed duty or orders, are justifiable. This justification does not exist, however, when those acts are manifestly, beyond the scope of his authority, or the order is such that a man of ordinary sense and understanding would know it to be illegal."

"I tell you as a matter of law that if instructions or orders were received over that radio or were given to the accused in this case to kill the prisoner suspect who was helpless there before them, such an order would have been manifestly an illegal order. You are advised as a matter of law, any such command, if in fact there was such a command, was an illegal order."

"A soldier or airman is not an automation but a reasoning agent who is under a duty to exercise judgment in obeying the orders of a superior officer to the extent, that where such orders are manifestly beyond the scope of the issuing officer's authority and are so palpably illegal on their face that a man of ordinary sense and understanding would know them to be illegal, then the fact of obedience to the order of a superior officer will not protect a soldier for acts committed pursuant to such illegal orders. This is the law in regard to superior orders."

In deciding the issues in this case, we will assume that a superior officer ordered the accused to kill the native male then in the platoon's custody.

The international killing of another person without premeditation is a felony unpremeditated murder (UCMJ, Art 118, 10 USC § 918). However, a homicide committed in the proper performance of a legal duty is justifiable and not a crime. Thus, killing to prevent the escape of a prisoner if no other reasonably apparent means are adequate or killing an enemy in battle are cases of justifiable homicide (MCM, US, 1951, § 197b). Conversely, the killing of a docile prisoner taken during military operations is not justifiable homicide. In this connection, section 85, Department of the Army Field Manual 27–109, Law of Land Warfare, July 1956, promulgates the following doctrine:

> 85. Killing of Prisoners. A commander may not put his prisoners to death because their presence retards his movements or diminishes his power of resistance by necessitating a large guard, or by reason of their consuming supplies, or because it appears certain that they will regain their liberty through the impending success of their forces. It is likewise unlawful for a commander to kill his prisoners on grounds of self-preservation, even in the case of airborne or commando operations, although the circumstances of the operation may make necessary rigorous supervision of and restraint upon the movement of prisoners of war.

The general rule is that the acts of a subordinate, done in good faith in compliance with his supposed duty or orders are, subject to certain qualifications, justifiable. (MCM, US, 1951, § 197b). In his authoritative work, Winthrop stated: "That the act charged as an offense was done in obedience to the order—verbal or written—of a military superior, is, in general, a good defense at military law."

". . . Where the order is apparently regular and lawful on its face, he is not to go behind it to satisfy himself that his superior has proceeded with authority, but is to obey it according to its terms, the only exceptions recognized to the rule of obedience being cases of orders so manifestly beyond the legal power of discretion of the commander as to admit of no rational doubt of their unlawfulness." (Winthrop, Military Law and Precedents, 2d Ed. (1920 Reprint) 296–297.)

The Manual for Courts–Martial, U.S. Conv. 1921 (x. 415, page 355) stated:

> To justify from a military point of view a military inferior in disobeying the order of a superior, the order must be one requiring something to be done which is palpably a breach of law and a crime or an injury to a third person, or is of a serious character (not involving unimportant consequences only) and if done would not be susceptible of being righted. An order requiring the performance of a military duty or act can not be disobeyed with impunity unless it has one of these characteristics.

The Manual for Courts–Martial, United States, 1951 (s. 197B, p. 351, contains the following discussion relating to the defense of duty or orders as justification for a homicide:

> ... the acts of a subordinate, done in good faith in compliance with his supposed duties or orders are justifiable. This justification does not exist, however, then those acts are manifestly beyond the scope of his authority, or the order is such that a man of ordinary sense and understanding would know it to be illegal ... (Emphasis supplied.). (Substantially similar provisions appeared in the MCM, USA, 1928, § 148a and MCM, USA, 1949, § 179a.)

In CM 326604, Gusik, 76 Board of Review 265, 279, the Board of Review said:

> It will be seen, therefore, that, indispensable to the shield of immunity from criminal responsibility afforded one for homicide committed pursuant to lawful orders of his superior, and in the performance of a public duty, are the following:
>
> > (a) That the order or authority was lawful or of such character that he had a right under the circumstances to believe and did believe it to be lawful,
> >
> > (b) That he acted reasonably within the scope of such authority, and
> >
> > (c) Not with malice, cruelty, or by willful oppression flowing from a wicked heart.

A well known treatise contains the following comments (36 Am. Jur. Homicide § 72, p. 208):

> ... But an order which is illegal in itself and not justified by the rules land usages of War, or which is, in its substance, clearly illegal, so that a man of ordinary sense and understanding would know as soon as he heard the order read or given that it was illegal, will afford no protection for a homicide, provided the act with which he may be charged has all the ingredients in it which may be necessary to constitute the same a crime in law.

... United States doctrine expressed in Department of the Army Field Manual 27–10, The Law of Land Warfare, July 1956, is as follows:

> The fact that the law of war has been violated pursuant to an order of a superior authority, whether military or civil, does not deprive the act in question of its character of a war crime, nor does it constitute a defense in the trial of an accused individual, unless he did not know and could not reasonably have been expected to know that the act ordered was unlawful. In all cases where the order is held not to constitute a defense to an allegation of war crime, the fact that the individual was acting pursuant to orders may be considered in mitigation of punishment.

Having considered the foregoing authorities, we accept the foregoing principle for application in this case (§ 197b, MCM, US, 1951, *quoted supra*): The act of a subordinate, done in good faith in compliance with the supposed order of a superior, is not justifiable when the order is such that a man of ordinary sense and understanding would know it to be illegal. (*See* ACM 7321, *Kinder*, 14 CMR 742, 773 (1954)).

We now turn to the question: Did the law officer err in failing to give an appropriate instruction on justification as a defense to a homicide committed in good faith compliance with the order of a superior? As previously noted, the defense counsel made a request for such an instruction, but the law officer instructed contradictorily. He informed the court to the effect that if an order to kill the prisoner had been given, it would have been manifestly illegal.

A law officer is required to give an appropriate instruction when there is some evidence that will allow a reasonable inference that a defense is in issue (*U.S. v. Black*, 12 USCMA 571, 31 CMR 157 (1961)). Evaluating the record, we find the evidence clear and convincing that an unarmed, unresisting prisoner whose hands were bound behind his back was killed at close range by rifle fire discharged by the accused and another soldier. We note no evidence which could provide an inference suggestive of self-defense, or that the killing was to prevent the escape of the prisoner, or for that matter, any other justification or excuse for the killing. Also, there are strong moral, religious, and legal prohibitions in our society against killing others which should arouse the strongest scruples against killings of this kind. In fact, it is difficult to conceive of a military situation in which the order of a superior would be more patently wrong. Accordingly, we view the order as commanding an act so obviously beyond the scope of authority of the superior officer and so palpably illegal on its face as to admit of no doubt of its unlawfulness to a man of ordinary sense and understanding. As there was no evidence which would have allowed a reasonable inference that the accused justifiably killed the prisoner pursuant to the order of a superior officer, it follows, as a matter of law, that this defense was not in issue, the law officer did not err by refusing to give an instruction on it, and that the law officer properly instructed the court that such an order would have been manifestly illegal.

With respect to the law officer's instructions on sentence, appellate defense counsel contend and government appellate counsel concede that the failure of the law officer to instruct the court-martial that it could adjudge reduction in grade as punishment rendered that portion of the sentence excessive. We find the contention meritorious and will act appropriately (*U.S. v. Crawford*, 12 USCMA 203, 30 CMR 203 (1961)).

Further, with respect to the sentence, we observe that the accused was caught up in a rapidly moving sequence of events at the time of the incident. This factor lends mitigating weight to his assertion that he acted without reflection and in honest obedience of a superior's orders. In addition, the accused had approximately eight years of prior service at the time of trial and there were no previous convictions introduced against him. Also, no punitive discharge was adjudged. The staff judge advocate notes in his review, that the accused testified for the prosecution in a subsequent homicide trial of another soldier involving the same incident and that he is "intrinsically remorseful and has a fervent desire to be rehabilitated." He also notes that the two officers involved in this offense were acquitted. Other records of trial before this board of review show that Specialist–Five Raul Garcia was tried by a general court-martial for the same offence and that his approved sentence provides for bad conduct discharge, total forfeitures, confinement at hard labour for three years and reduction. Private First Class David L. Woods was similarly tried. His approved sentence is confinement at hard labour for twelve months, total forfeitures, and reduction to the lowest enlisted grade.

In view of the foregoing, the board of review finds the findings of guilty and sentence as approved by proper authority correct in law and fact and determines on the basis of the entire record that only so much of the sentence as provides for confinement at hard labour for two years and forfeiture of all pay and allowances should be approved. The sentence is modified accordingly. The findings of guilty and the sentence as thus modified are affirmed.

■ PORCELLA, MYERS (concurs) and MILLER (concurs) JUDGE ADVOCATES, 2 July 1968.

Notes and Questions

1. ***The Nürnberg Charter.*** The IMT Charter in article 8 had provided that a superior would not free a subordinate from responsibility but would be considered in mitigation of punishment. In the judgment and the principles extrapolated therefrom by the International Law Commission the tenor was changed in providing that the defence was not possible "providing a moral choice was possible." From the cases extracted above how would you define a moral choice? (See Green, *The Defence of Superior Orders in the Modern Law of Armed Conflict*, 31 Alta. L. Rev. 320 (1993) and Dinstein, The Defence of "Obedience to Superior Orders" in International Law (1965).)

2. ***The Finta case***. The Supreme Court of Canada in *R. v. Finta*, [1994] 28 C.R. (4th) 265 held that "military orders can and must be obeyed unless they are manifestly unlawful." In deciding whether an order is such the Court held that "it must be an order which is obviously and flagrantly wrong. The order cannot be in a grey area or be merely questionable."

3. ***The Rome Statute***. Refer to article 33 in the Documentary Supplement. Orders to commit genocide and crimes against humanity are considered manifestly unlawful.

———

Command Responsibility

See articles 6 and 7 of the Nürnberg Charter, *supra*, and article 28 of the Rome Statute on the Establishment of an International Criminal Court, contained in the Documentary Supplement.

Fenrick, Responsibility of Commanders and Other Superiors, in Triffterer (Ed.) Commentary on the Rome Statute of the International Criminal Court, 515, 516–517 (1999).

The international law doctrine of command responsibility is, to a considerable extent a doctrine concerned with individual criminal responsibility which has developed through customary international law as reflected in war crimes cases decided in the aftermath of the Second World War. The roots of the doctrine can be found in one of the constants of military history, the requirement to place great responsibility in the hands of military commanders * * *. The international law doctrine * * * was a legal vehicle whereby military commanders and certain other persons could be held liable for the criminal activities of their subordinates because they omitted or failed to control [them]. Any individual * * * could be held criminally responsible for an act which he or she planned, instigated, ordered, committed or otherwise aided or abetted.

Additional Protocol I to the 1949 Geneva Conventions

16 *I.L.M.* 1391 (1977)

.   .   .

Article 86—Failure to act

1.   The High Contracting Parties and the Parties to the conflict shall repress grave breaches, and take measures necessary to suppress all other breaches, of the Conventions or of this Protocol which result from a failure to act when under a duty to do so.

2.   The fact that a breach of the Conventions or of this Protocol was committed by a subordinate does not absolve his superiors from penal or disciplinary responsibility, as the case may be, if they knew, or had information which should have enabled them to conclude in the circumstances at the time, that he was committing or was going to commit such a breach and if they did not take all feasible measures within their power to prevent or repress the breach.

Article 87—Duty of commanders

1.   The High Contracting Parties and the Parties to the conflict shall require military commanders, with respect to members of the armed forces under their command and other persons under their control, and prevent and, where necessary, to suppress and report to competent authorities breaches of the Conventions and of this Protocol.

2.   In order to prevent and suppress breaches, High Contracting Parties and Parties to the conflict shall require that, commensurate with their level of responsibility, commanders ensure that members of the armed forces under their command are aware of their obligations under the Conventions and this Protocol.

3.   The High Contracting Parties and Parties to the conflict shall require any commander who is aware that subordinates or other persons under his control are going to commit or have committed a breach of the Conventions or of this Protocol, to initiate such steps as are necessary to prevent such violations of the Conventions or this Protocol, and, where appropriate, to initiate disciplinary or penal action against violators thereof.

Notes & Questions. **1.** ***Protocols I and II to the Geneva Conventions of 1949.*** On June 8, 1977, the Geneva Diplomatic Conference on the Reaffirmation and Development of International Humanitarian Law Applicable in Armed Conflicts adopted two protocols supplementing these conventions: the Protocol Additional to the Geneva Conventions of 12 August 1949, and relating to the Protection of Victims of International Armed Conflicts (Protocol I), with annexes, and the Protocol Additional to the Geneva Conventions of August 12, 1949, and relating to the Protection of Victims of Non–International Armed Conflicts (Protocol II). The protocols entered into force December 7, 1978; they were not in force for the United States as of January 1, 1980. The text of the protocols appears at 72 AJIL 457 (1978) and at 16 ILM 1391 (1977) (Protocol I) and 16 ILM 1442 (1977) (Protocol II).

2. ***In January 1987, President Reagan transmitted Protocol II to the Senate for its Advice and Consent,*** stating that:

[t]he protocol, is essentially an expansion of the fundamental humanitarian provisions contained in the 1949 Geneva Conventions with respect to non-international armed conflicts, including humane treatment and basic due process for detained persons, protection of the wounded, sick and medical units, and protection of noncombatants from attack and deliberate starvation. If these fundamental rules were observed, many of the worst human tragedies of current internal armed conflicts could be avoided. In particular, among other things, the mass murder of civilians is made illegal, even if such killings would not amount to genocide because they lacked racial or religious motives. Several Senators asked me to keep this objective in mind when adopting the Genocide Convention. I remember my commitment to them. This Protocol makes clear that any deliberate killing of a noncombatant in the course of a non-international armed conflict is a violation of the laws of war and a crime against humanity, and is therefore also punishable as murder.

While I recommend that the Senate grant advice and consent to this agreement, I have at the same time concluded that the United States cannot ratify a second agreement on the law of armed conflict negotiated during the same period. I am referring to Protocol I additional to the 1949 Geneva Conventions, which would revise the rules applicable to international armed conflicts. Like all other efforts associated with the International Committee of the Red Cross, this agreement has certain meritorious elements. But Protocol I is fundamentally and irreconcilably flawed. It contains provisions that would undermine humanitarian law and endanger civilians in war. One of its provisions, for example, would automatically treat as an international conflict any so-called 'war of national liberation.' Whether such wars are international or non-international should turn exclusively on objective reality, not on one's view of the moral qualities of each conflict. To rest on such subjective distinctions based on a war's alleged purposes would politicize humanitarian law and eliminate the distinction between international and non-international conflicts. It would give special status to 'wars of national liberation,' an ill-defined concept expressed in vague, subjective, politicized terminology. Another provision would grant combatant status to irregular forces even if they do not satisfy the traditional requirements to distinguish themselves from the civilian population and otherwise comply with the laws of war. This would endanger civilians among whom terrorists and other irregulars attempt to conceal themselves. These problems are so fundamental in character that they cannot be remedied through reservations, and I therefore have decided not to submit the Protocol to the Senate in any form, and I would invite an expression of the sense of the Senate that it shares this view. Finally, the Joint Chiefs of Staff have also concluded that a number of the provisions of the Protocol are militarily unacceptable. 81 AJIL 910 (1987).

————

3. *Do you agree or disagree with President Reagan's reasons* for not becoming party to Protocol I? Even if you agree with them, do they retain their validity after the demise of the Soviet Empire and the end of the Cold War? Protocol I, article 51(2) prohibits "[a]cts or threats of violence the primary purpose of which is to spread terror among the civilian population." Is it appropriate to refuse ratification of this and other salutary rules in Protocol I, because it would provide "national liberation movements" a "rhetorical and political victory"? There may be other reasons for opposing Protocol I. Did it go far enough? Protocol I is not beyond criticism. Michael Reisman suggests that it presents a shift away from the status quo in international affairs. He notes that an existing state that has suffered low intensity incursions or aggression is not allowed by Protocol I to attack another state in which the original low-intensity attackers have found haven, which is an innovation contrary to self-defense in customary international law. This is a valid criticism. One can criticize Protocol I for a basic confusion between humanitarian rules for protecting victims during armed conflict (jus in bello) and rules aimed at determining the status of parties to conflict (jus ad bellum). To the extent that Protocol I makes *jus in bello* dependent on *jus ad bellum* it is unfortunate. Jus in bello originally were undertaken as a matter of self-interest, but had the effect of protecting victims within the embattled state, no matter what "morality" was seen to reside with their "side." Jus in bello in Protocol I is viewed as applying only in certain "acceptable" wars. Protocols I and II made the humanitarian rules applicable to more conflicts, but, unfortunately Protocol I limits their applicability on the basis of an ideological litmus test. Do you agree? What are the arguments favoring Protocol I? *See*, Reisman, *Old Wine in New Bottles: The Reagan & Brezhnov Doctrines*, 13 Yale Int'l J. 171, 193–97 (1988); Rubin, *Int'l Law and the Use of Force by National Liberation Movements*, 13 Fletch.For.Wld.Affairs 410, 414 (1989).

4. *President Reagan's position with respect to Protocol I is vigorously rebutted* by the Legal Adviser to the Directorate of the International Committee of the Red Cross in An Appeal for Ratification by the United States, 81 AJIL 912 (1987).

5. THE LAW OF WAR, HUMANITARIAN LAW AND HUMAN RIGHTS LAW

Conventional and customary legal developments in the law of war during this century have led scholars to refer to this body of law as humanitarian law. See e.g., Detter, The Law of War (2nd ed. 2000); Gutman, Rieff, and Anderson, eds., Crimes of War: What the Public Should Know (1999); Bass Stay the Hand of Vengeance (2000).

Re Yamashita

U.S. Mil.Trib. (1946), 4 Rep. Trials of War Criminals 34–35.

THE PRESIDENT OF THE COURT: "The Prosecution presented evidence to show that the crimes were so extensive and widespread, both as to time and area, that they must either have been wilfully permitted by the accused. Captured orders issued by subordinate officers of the accused were presented as proof that they at least, ordered certain acts leading directly to exterminations of civilians under the guise of eliminating the activities of guerrillas hostile to Japan . . .

. . . As to the crimes themselves, complete ignorance that they had occurred was stoutly maintained by the accused, his principal staff officers and subordinate commanders further that all such acts, if committed, were directly contrary to the announced policies, wishes and orders of the accused. The Japanese Commanders testified that they did not make personal inspections or independent checks . . . to determine for themselves the established procedures by which their subordinates accomplish their missions . . .

This accused is an officer of long years of experience, broad in its scope, who has had extensive command, and staff duty in the Imperial Japanese Army in peace as well as in war . . . Clearly, assignment to command military troops is accompanied by broad authority and heavy responsibility. This has been true of all armies throughout recorded history. It is absurd, however, to consider a commander a murderer or rapist because one of his soldiers commits a murder or a rape. Nevertheless, where murder and rape and vicious, revengeful actions are widespread offences, and there is no effective attempt by a commander to discover and control the criminal acts, such a commander may be held responsible, even criminally liable, for the lawless acts of his troops, depending upon their nature and the circumstances surrounding them. Should a commander issue orders which lead directly to lawless acts, the criminal responsibility is definite and has always been so understood. . . ."

Notes & Questions

1. **The Trials in the Far East.** In addition to the Yamashita Trial, there were other interesting and important trials in the Far East after World War II. For example, in the Collective Ambon (a.k.a. Ceram Island) Trial, held by the Australians and 91 defendants were prosecuted in this single trial. On this, *see*, Ian Kennison, *Recollections of the Australian 'Collective*

Trial' on Ambon, (Japanese Atrocities in Java and in the Moluccas Archipelago [the Spice Islands], essay within sub series, BRITISH WAR CRIMES TRIALS CONCERNED WITH JAPANESE-OCCUPIED TERRITORIES IN THE SOUTH-WEST PACIFIC (vols. 68–78), of THE BRITISH WAR CRIME TRIALS IN THE FAR EAST, 1946–1948) (R. John Pritchard, comp. & ed., forthcoming). There were two large Ambon trials, one Australian and one British. See also, an excellent book by Anthony Cowling, MY LIFE WITH THE SAMURI (Kangaroo Press), especially in Chapter 6, at pp. 84–95, where he provides his vivid and intense account of the events on Haruku in the Moluccas.

2.   ***Orders, knowledge or constructive knowledge.*** What is the appropriate test for liability? Is it strict liability or is it to be based on knowledge or fault?

3.   ***The "Celebici" case***. The ITFY held in *The Prosecutor* v. *Delalic et al*, IT–96–21–T, 16 November 1998 , commonly known as the "Celebici" case after the prison camp where the crimes occurred, that under article 7 of its Statute that a commander had responsibility as discussed above. This was the first time since World War II that the doctrine was applied. It was found to be "firmly placed within the corpus of international humanitarian law". Of particular note was the finding that "persons effectively in command of * * * informal structures, with power to prevent and punish the crimes of persons who are in fact under their control, may be * * * held responsible for their failure to do so." The Tribunal held that the *de facto* position of authority, whether civilian or military was the key component and that formal designation as commander was not a necessary prerequisite. See also before the ICTY *The Prosecutor* v. *Aleksovski*, IT–95–14/1–T, 25 June 1999 and *The Prosecutor* v. *Blaskic*, IT–95–12, 3 March 2000. The ICTR has also addressed the issue in *The Prosecutor* v. *Akayesu*, ICTR–96–T, 2 September, 1998 and *The Prosecutor* v. *Kambanda*, ICTR–97–23–5, 4 September, 1998.

Nullem Crimen Sine Lege

This principle of no crime without law is a fundamental part of international criminal law. An individual can only be prosecuted for acts or omissions that were criminal at international law at the time the conduct occurred.

In Re Ohlendorf and Others (Einsatzgrüppen Trial)

U.S. Military Tribunal at Nürnberg; (1948), 15 Int. L.R. 656.

THE TRIBUNAL: (1) *Jurisdiction of the Tribunal: Control Council Law No. 10 and the Principle of "Nullem Crimen Sine Lege".* The Tribunal said: On December 20, 1945, the Allied Control Council, composed of representatives of the same four above-mentioned nations and constituting the highest legislative authority for Germany, enacted Law No. 10, concerning 'Punishment of Persons Guilty of War Crimes, Crimes Against Peace and Crimes Against Humanity'. This Tribunal came into being under the provisions of the Law, but while the Tribunal derives its existence from the authority indicated, its jurisdiction over the subject matter results from International Law valid long prior to World War II.... Control Council Law No. 10 is but the codification and systemization of already existing legal principles, rules and customs. Under the title of Crimes against Humanity, these rules and customs are the common heritage of civilized peoples, and, in so far as War Crimes are concerned, they have been recognized in various International Conventions, to which Germany was a party, and they have been International Law for decades if not centuries. As far back as 1631, Grotius, in his *De Jure Belli ac Pacis*, wrote: 'But ... far must we be from admitting the conceit of some, that the Obligation of all Right ceases in war; nor when undertaken ought it to be carried on beyond the Bounds of Justice and Fidelity'.... It is indeed fundamental in every system of civilized jurisprudence that no one may be punished for an act which was not prohibited at the time of its commission. But it must be understood that the *lex* referred to is not restricted to statutory law. Law does, in fact, come into being as the result of formal written enactment and thus we have codes, treaties, conventions and the like, but it may also develop effectively through custom and usage and through the application of Common Law. The latter methods are no less binding than the former.... Of course some fields of International Law have been codified to a substantial degree and one such subject is the law of Land Warfare which includes the Law of Belligerent Occupation because belligerent occupation is incidental to warfare. The Hague Regulations, for instance, represent such a codification. Article 46 of these Regulations provides with regard to invading and occupying armies that: 'Family honour and rights, the livers of persons and private property, as well as religious convictions, and practice must be respected'. This provision imposed obligations on Germany not only because Germany signed the Hague Convention on Land Warfare, but because it had become International Law binding on all nations.

But the jurisdiction of this Tribunal over the subject matter before it does not depend alone on this specific pronouncement of International Law. As already indicated, all nations have held themselves bound to the rules or laws of war which came into being through common recognition and acknowledgement. Without exception these rules universally condemn the wanton killing of non-combatants. In the main, the defendants in this case are charged with murder. Certainly no one can claim with the slightest pretense at reasoning that there is any taint of *ex post factoism* in the law or murder. Whether any individual defendant is guilty of unlawful killing is a question which will be determined later, but it cannot be said that prior to Control Council Law No. 10 there existed no law against murder. The killing of a human being has always been a potential crime which called for explanation. The person standing with drawn dagger over a fresh corpse must, by the very nature of justice, exonerate himself. This he may well do, advancing self-defense or legal authorization for the deed, or he may establish that the perpetrator of the homicide was one other than himself. It is not questioned that the defendants were close enough to mass killings to be called upon for an explanation—and to whom are they to render explanation so that their innocence or guilt may be determined? Is the matter of some one million non-military deaths to be denied judicial inquiry because a Tribunal was not standing by, waiting for the apprehension of the suspects?

The specific enactments for the trial of war criminals which have governed the Nuremberg trials, have only provided a machinery for the actual application of international law theretofore existing. In the comparatively recent *Saboteurs Case* (*Ex parte Quirin*, 317 U.S., I, 1942) the Supreme Court of the United States affirmed that individual offenders against the rules and customs of war are amenable to punishment under the common law of nations without any prior designation of tribunal or procedure. In this connection reference may also be made to trials for piracy where, going back centuries, the offenders, regardless of nationality, were always tried in the arresting state without any previous designation of tribunal. Military Tribunals for years have tried and punished violators of the rules of land warfare outlined in the Hague Conventions even though the Convention is silent on the subject of courts.

. . . There is no authority which denies any belligerent nation jurisdiction over individuals in its actual custody charged with violation of international law. And if a single nation may legally take jurisdiction in such instances, with what more reason may a number of nations agree, in the interest of justice, to try alleged violations of the international code of war? In spite of all that has been said in this and other cases, no one would be so bold as to suggest that what occurred between Germany and Russia from June 1941 to May 1945 was anything but war, and, being war, that Russia would not have the right to try the alleged violators of the rules of war on her territory and against her people. And if Russia may do this alone, certainly she may concur with other nations who affirm that right. Thus, Russia's participation in the formulation of Control Council Law No. 10 is in accordance with every recognized principle of international law, and any attack on that participation is without legal support. The Tribunal also finds and concludes that Control Council Law No. 10 is not only in conformity with International Law but is in itself a highly significant contribution to written International Law. . . .

Comment, Punishment for War Crimes: Duty Or Discretion?

69 Michigan Law Review 1312 (1971).*

* * * Immediately prior to the adoption of the 1949 Conventions, it was remarked in reference to one of these earlier conventions that "[i]t is one of the greatest weaknesses of the existing rules on prisoners of war that they do not contain definite and written provisions on sanctions." In view of such criticisms and the ad hoc measures taken to deal with the war crimes of World War II, negotiators in 1949 agreed that specific provisions for punishment of breaches of the new Conventions were essential. Accordingly, each of the Four Conventions adopted in 1949 contained an article requiring each Party to "enact any legislation necessary to provide effective

---

* Reprinted with the permission of the Michigan Law Review.

penal sanctions for persons committing * * * grave breaches" of the Conventions. * * *

Although granted a writ of immunity from military prosecution by the Commanding General of Fort Benning, Georgia, where the trial by court-martial of Lieutenant Calley was conducted, Meadlo consistently refused to testify until the Government issued a federal immunity order protecting him from civilian prosecution. Finally, under threat of arrest for further refusal to testify after having been granted federal immunity, Meadlo took the witness stand on January 11, 1971. Ten days later, Assistant United States Attorney General William H. Rehnquist struck a disquieting note that has been overlooked in the wake of the Calley conviction: [Did the U.S. violate] its treaty obligation under the 1949 Geneva Conventions to prosecute those persons accused of "grave breaches" of the Conventions by granting immunity to a confessed participant in the My Lai slayings?

* * *

Notes & Questions. Did the U.S. not have legislation sufficient to allow effectual penal sanctions? Can compliance with a treaty require elimination of constitutional protection? Could the U.S. enter into a treaty which allows infringement of constitutional rights of U.S. citizens? Could the U.S. enter into the treaty creating the International Criminal Court, wherein defendants (including U.S. nationals) would be tried under circumstances which do not comport with the U.S. Constitution? *See* Blakesley, *Obstacles to the Creation of a Permanent War Crimes Tribunal, supra.*

Bishop, Justice Under Fire 290 (1974)*

* * * All of the Geneva Conventions obligate each signatory power to search for persons alleged to have committed "grave breaches" of those Conventions and to "bring such persons, regardless of their nationality, before its own courts." There is still too little precedent for such enforcement of the law of war. I know of no instance in which * * * any * * * totalitarian government has ever accused a member of its own forces of a violation of the Geneva Conventions or any other war crime. But the most recent available figures show that, as of April, 1971, American courts-martial had tried 117 servicemen and convicted 60 on charges of murdering civilians in Vietnam; an unknown, but probably larger, number had been tried for lesser offenses, such as rape and robbery, against civilians. Murder and other violence against the persons of noncombatants or captured enemies violate the Geneva Conventions, but they are also, of course, violations of the Uniform Code of Military Justice and have been charged as such. The main practical difference is that trial by court-martial for a violation of the Code guarantees the accused procedural protections and appellate review to which he might not be entitled if he were tried by a military commission for a war crime.

---

* Reprinted with the permission of Joseph W. Bishop.

Some of the acquittals were probably unjustified, and in at least one case, that of Captain Ernest Medina, the acquittal may have been based on the military judge's erroneous instruction that Medina had no responsibility for the My Lai massacre unless he had "actual knowledge" of it: as laid down by the Supreme Court in General Yamashita's case, the law is that a commander is responsible for war crimes committed by his subordinates if he knew, or should have known, that they were going on and failed to do what he could to prevent or punish them. It is also safe to assume that many war crimes committed by Americans have never been investigated, tried, or punished. The Pentagon has not shown much enthusiasm for investigating the possible failures of commanders at divisional and higher levels to take adequate measures to prevent and punish war crimes. Moreover, the Department of Justice seems to [have taken] the position that an honorably discharged serviceman cannot be tried for a war crime committed prior to his discharge. The Supreme Court did hold some years ago that such a discharged soldier could not be tried for an ordinary offense, i.e., one that was not a war crime committed prior to his discharge. But it had earlier held, in World War II, that a Nazi saboteur who was an American civilian could constitutionally be tried by a military commission for a war crime, and it did not overrule that decision. I am myself of the opinion (though I seem to be in the minority) that a discharged serviceman can be tried by a military court on a charge of violating the law of war. In any case, Congress could and should give the federal courts jurisdiction to try such cases: under the Geneva Conventions, in fact, the United States is obligated to "enact any legislation necessary to provide effective penal sanctions" for ** " grave breaches."

The record is thus very far from perfect. All that can be said is that it is a better record than that of any other nation in the world and that it lends a degree of credibility to the Pentagon's numerous orders and regulations that aim to prevent and punish war crimes by requiring a report and an investigation of such incidents, and the training and indoctrination of the troops on the subject.

* * *

Notes and Questions

1. **What is the obligation to prosecute?** If the state's obligation is "to prosecute" will it suffice to allow a U.S. prosecutor simply apply his or her discretion to decide whether or not to go forward with a case? Could the U.S. require more? Study the law of land warfare, U.S. Department of the Army Field Manual. [FM 27–10] at 4 (1956) (as amended by Change No. 1, 1976) in the Documentary Supplement.

2. **Atomic weapons.** Paragraph 35 of the Army Field Manual in the Doc.Supp. asserts that the use of explosive atomic weapons cannot as such be regarded as violative of international law in the absence of any customary rule of international law or international convention restricting their employment. Compare this bald statement with the specific prohibitions that are recognized in the manual: against so-called dumdum bullets (paragraph 34), poison (paragraph 37), and chemical and bacteriological

weapons (paragraph 38). Why are atomic weapons not included among these groups? Paragraph 34 states that the prohibition against the use of arms calculated to cause unnecessary suffering does not extend to the use of explosives contained in artillery projectiles, mines, rockets, or hand grenades. Are atomic weapons to be considered as only a new form of explosive device comparable to such devices?

State practice for over fifty years has been not to use atomic weapons in battle. If state practice is some test of a customary rule of international law, it should be noted that the only use of atomic weapons was the two explosions in Japan ending World War II, before the destructive capacity of the atomic bomb and its collateral consequences were fully appreciated. Further, the policy of the atomic superpowers has been based, not upon a claimed lawful first use of atomic weapons, but upon the development of a second strike capacity in response to a first use. The Russians recently indicated that they might consider a first use under certain circumstances.

Richard Falk argues that any use of nuclear weapons is illegal. Is this argument naive, utopian and irrelevant to the real world? Or is it quintessentially practical? Trimble counters that Falk argues that "[t]he effects of nuclear weapons are the 'functional equivalent' of the effects of chemical and biological weapons, therefore nuclear weapons are illegal by virtue of various, prenuclear agreements prohibiting the use of chemical and biological weapons. The use of international law for this argument is neither normative nor persuasive." Is this criticism well taken? Do the development of nuclear weapons and the subsequent international agreements relating to possession and testing indicate that the states-parties sanction the possession and certain uses? What impact do nonproliferation treaties have on this? Does the existence of nonproliferation treaties suggest that the nations holding the weapons consider them to be unacceptable?

Nuclear nations have claimed that earlier treaties on chemical, biological, and other prohibited weapons were not intended to cover all new forms of warfare and weaponry. Nonproliferation treaties have been used to prevent nations from obtaining nuclear weapons. Many nations have not wanted anything to do with nuclear weapons. Some who have the weapons wish to get rid of them. What should be the U.S. position today, now that access to developing or purchasing nuclear weapons is more readily available to other nations or groups? What is the international law? What should it be?

See Chapter 6 on The International Protection of the Environment, section A.3, *supra*, and consider the Advisory Opinion of the International Court of Justice, in the *Legality of the Threat of Nuclear Weapons Case*, 35 ILM 814 (1996).

3. ***Reprisals***. The description of the law of reprisals in ¶ 497 of the Army Field Manual should be considered in the light of the material in Chapters 16 and 17 on the law governing the use of force. For now, note that a reprisal is a retaliatory action taken by one state against another. Reprisals and their "legality" are controversial. They may take the form of military attacks, bombardments, embargos, boycotts of goods, navel or other military demonstrations, The Field Manual's use of the term refers only to the conduct of war rather than to the instigation of war itself, as

suggested by Professor Starke in INTRODUCTION TO INTERNATIONAL LAW 499 (9th ed. 1984). Stark notes that reprisals are only justified, if at all, where the perpetrating state has already committed an international crime, and a request for remedy must be made prior to any reprisal. The reprisal, if allowed at all, must be proportionate to the crime committed. The question for this chapter is whether reprisals may be allowed against individuals who have perpetrated international offenses? Would this make any sense? If a government takes action in reprisal against leaders of other countries, whom the former believe committed international crimes, may the reprisal, if wrongful (disproportionate or mistaken) give rise to international prosecution?

4. ***War Crimes***. Refer to article 8 of the Rome Statute on the ICC in the Documentary Supplement. This article dealing with war crimes lists prohibited weapons. There was major opposition to the inclusion of nuclear weapons. The end result was not only non-inclusion of such but also the omission of biological and chemical weapons, what some delegations called the "poor" states weapons of mass destruction. Note article 8(2)(xx) that provides that further weapons may be added by an amendment after the expiry of seven years after the Statute enters into force.

The Draft Code of Crimes Against the Peace and Security of Mankind,

UN GAOR, 51st Sess., Supp. No. 10; UN Doc. A/51/10 (1996).

See Articles 1–4, 8–9 and 16 in the Documentary Supplement.

Notes & Questions. **1.** The International Law Commission adopted the text of the Draft Code on July 5, 1996. It presented its annual Report to the U.N. General Assembly in the fall of that year. However, the General Assembly has not requested further work on this topic and it is not on the current ILC agenda in 2000–2001. The I.L.C. had been requested by the General Assembly in 1947 to draft the Code and a Statute for an international criminal court. Now that the Rome Statute on the ICC has been adopted in 1998 and the core crimes of genocide, crimes against humanity, war crimes and aggression listed in article 5, contained in the Documentary Supplement, events have probably overtaken the Draft Code in practical terms. Versions of the Draft Code, including the one presented in 1991 to the General Assembly, UN GAOR, 46th Sess., Supp. No. 10; UN Doc. A/46/10 (1991) had contained twelve categories of crimes including colonialism, recruitment, use and financing of mercenaries, international terrorism and illicit traffic in drugs. The 1996 Draft Code was narrowed down with a view to reaching consensus. It lists aggression, genocide, crimes against humanity, crimes against UN and associated personnel and war crimes.

2. ***Individual responsibility***. The articles referred to above in the Draft Code of Crimes deal with, *inter alia*, individual responsibility, punishment and the obligation to extradite or prosecute. Why do you think that international terrorism and drug trafficking, already prescribed by multilateral conventions were omitted. Note that are listed in the Rome Statute on the ICC either. Article 22 of the Rome Statute on the ICC sets out the *nullum crimen sine lege* rule. See also article 23 on *nulla poena sine lege.* Both are contained in the Documentary Supplement.

3. *Does the term "crimes against humanity" include rape* when committed on a mass or systematic scale? *See*, Khusalani, DIGNITY AND HONOUR OF WOMEN AS BASIC AND FUNDAMENTAL RIGHTS (1982), and Nuremberg Charter and Control Council Law No. 10. Certain acts, such as torture and wilfully causing great suffering or serious injury to body or health, are strictly prohibited. In addition to being a "crime against humanity" could rape on such a systematic and massive scale be considered a type of genocide? *See*, Meron, *Rape as a Crime under International Criminal Law,* 87 A.J.I.L. 424, 425 (1993).

4. *There have been suggestions made that Saddam Hussein* be brought to trial in an international tribunal for his conduct during the Persian Gulf War. *See*, Beres, *Prosecuting Iraqi Gulf War Crimes: Allied and Israeli Rights Under International Law,* 16 Hastings Int'l & Comp. L.Rev. 41 (1992); O'Brien, *The Nuremberg Precedent and the Gulf War,* 31 Va.J.I.L. 391 (1991); Moore, *War Crimes and the Rule of Law in the Gulf Crisis,* 31 Va.J.I.L. 403 (1991). If this were done would it comply with the *nullum crimen sine lege* rule? See, *infra*, on the constitutionality of the U.N. Security Council, acting under Chapter VII of the U.N. Charter setting up the ICTY the judgment in *The Prosecutor* v. *Tadic.*

5. *Nürnberg's aftermath–an appraisal.* In JUSTICE UNDER FIRE, *supra*, Professor Bishop asked: "What, then, has the Magna Carta of international law done for the welfare of humanity since its promulgation? The answer is clear and simple: nothing. Since Nuremberg, there have been at least eighty or ninety wars (some calculators exclude armed invasions of neighbors too weak to attempt resistance), some of them on a very large scale. The list includes the Korean war, the Suez invasion of 1956, the Algerian rebellion, the four Arab–Israeli wars, the Vietnam wars (including the accompanying fighting in Laos and Cambodia), and the invasion of Czechoslovakia by the Soviet Union and its myrmidons. In none of these cases, nor in any other, was an aggressor arrested and brought to the bar of international justice, and none is likely to be. For all the good it has done, the doctrine that aggressive war is a crime might as well be relegated to the divinity schools." Is Professor Bishop correct? Could there be an influence not discernable by looking at the numbers of wars?

6. *The Pinochet Case as progeny of Nürnberg*, excerpt from Blakesley, *Autumn of the Patriarch, supra*. It is true that Pinochet's arrest, detention, and the House of Lords decision that he was not immune as a former head of state from prosecution for torture, is very important—a milestone. Nevertheless, there is a "down-side" to the House of Lords decision. The Lords clearly applied a straight forward, traditional dualist position on torture, let alone on all the other horrible crimes with which Pinochet was charged. The House of Lords majority actually insisted on applying classic, rigid, traditional extradition law, applying a pedantic position on the "special use" of dual criminality. I will discuss this in more detail below, but for now, suffice it to say that the House of Lords held: (1) that for extradition to be allowed, not only must the fugitive's conduct be criminal in both states (Spain and England); in addition, (2) a common theory of jurisdiction over the conduct must obtain. This is the special use of double criminality which requires that the jurisdictional theory as well as the conduct proscribed be acceptable in the domestic law of the requested state. The majority's view is, first, that torture was NOT a crime of universal jurisdiction prior to the promulgation of The Convention Against Torture and Other Cruel, Inhuman or Degrading Treatment or Punishment,[1] and that, even if it were, it was not extraditable (or punishable) in England, until promulgation of the Criminal Justice Act of 1988. It insisted that jurisdiction be based on an explicit English "incorporation" of torture as a crime. Thus, although it held that Pinochet was not immune from extradition or prosecution for torture, this was *only* on the basis of the Torture Convention **and** the Criminal Justice Act of 1988, which incorporated it. This position is clearly antagonistic to the idea of torture being a universal crime or a crime that allows universal jurisdiction. Thus, the House of Lords did not embrace customary international law on universality of jurisdiction over heads of state and former heads of state for torture or other crimes against humanity, such as those allegedly committed by Pinochet and his cronies.

Professor David Turns recently argued that the third House of Lords decision in the Pinochet suite provides some hope for British jurisprudence on customary international law, but the Majority, perhaps, could have and should have gone further. Lord Millett's minority opinion maintained that torture was a crime in the United Kingdom well before the incorporation of the Torture Convention, and at least by the time Pinochet came to power in 1973. Lord Millett was a minority of one in the view that torture was a crime under customary international law by that date, and that customary international law was part of English common law. Adoption of his view does not appear likely in the near term.

Notwithstanding its limitations, even the majority opinion does add some momentum to a broader acceptance of the proposition that torture and all crimes against humanity violate both treaty law and customary international law. Eventually, the House of Lords may accept that these offenses are subject to universal jurisdiction, but that surely is for another day.

The English orthodox position on incorporation of customary international law, at least in theory, is that customary international law is automatically part of English law, as long as it is not in conflict with any statute in force or any judicial decision by an English appellate court. In reality, however, English courts virtually never decide cases solely on the basis of customary international law, with a couple of limited exceptions. Exception of prize cases based on ancient Admiralty jurisdiction and in the, now defunct in all but name, Royal Warrant of 1945, which served for the prosecution of German, Italian and Japanese (and, by extension, others such as Koreans, Taiwanese and even one Hungarian who served for Japan) war criminals after WWII. The Royal Warrant was limited to war crimes. It did not cover crimes against humanity, although British military

1. G.A. Res. 46, U.N. GAOR, 39th Sess., Supp. No.51, U.N.Doc. A/39/51.

courts invariably held that crimes against humanity committed in enemy-occupied territory or during the conduct of military operations were subject to military law, hence, were war crimes. These included: single unlawful killings, torture or other forms of maltreatment committed by civilian labor contractors employed by the local Japanese Civil Administration (itself subject to military law and oversight in occupied territories).

Jurisdiction to prosecute international conduct based on customary international law, where individual liberty is at stake, requires an act of Parliament in England and a statute in the United States. This is quite appropriate. To prosecute under circumstances such as when the elements of the offense are too vague, or where there is a question about ne *bis in idem*, would be dangerous. Many treaties were drafted by diplomats and non-criminal law specialists, so some "international crimes" in them or that developed through customary international law are far too vague. Erosion of individual rights before the criminal bar is a realistic thing to worry about, especially when the perpetrator is charged with extremely heinous offenses. This may be particularly true in the current zeal to prosecute those who are charged with having committed crimes against humanity.

The majority of the House of Lords did not even accept the view that torture was a universal crime under customary international law prior to the Torture Convention. Lord Millet said that it was, but cited no settled authority specific to torture for this. He did refer to several human rights instruments, including the Universal Declaration of Human Rights, the International Covenant on Civil and Political Rights, and even the Genocide Convention. He also cited the *Furundzija decision* out of the ICTY.

Torture: Actus Reus and Mens Rea: The position taken by the English and the House of Lords regarding the offense of torture is interesting. Home Secretary Straw agreed with the House of Lords that the Torture Convention, as incorporated into British Law in the Criminal Justice Act of 1988, § 134, requires intent to "[inflict] severe pain or suffering on another in the performance or purported performance of ... official duties...." whether the suffering is caused by act or omission, and whether it is committed directly by the defendant or by aiding, abetting, consent, instigation, by an official person or one acting on his behalf. The House of Lords held that only those acts of torture attributable to Pinochet that occurred after the promulgation of this Act were extraditable or justiciable, if there were to be any prosecution in England. It seems to me that the disappearances and continued pain and suffering caused in the families and loved ones of those who were made to "disappear," constitutes a continuing offense of torture to those families. This should give a basis for any nation to prosecute Pinochet (if he is competent) or his cronies. So, the Spanish request for Pinochet's extradition was refused by the British Government (along with requests from the Belgians, the French, and the Swiss). Amnesty International reported that all four of these nations that had sought Pinochet, are unconvinced that the medical report proves that Pinochet lacks the capacity to stand trial.

6.   THE AD HOC CRIMINAL TRIBUNALS—A PRECEDENT?

Blakesley, Report on the Obstacles to the Creation of a Permanent War Crimes Tribunal

18 The Fletcher Forum of World Affairs 77, 78, 81–86, 97–98 (1994) *reprinted in*, INTERNATION-
AL LAW: CLASSIC & CONTEMPORARY READINGS
(ASIL, Ku & Deihl, eds. 1998)*

Individual criminal responsibility is the cornerstone of any international war crimes tribunal. Nuremberg Principle I provides that "[a]ny person
who commits an act which constitutes a crime under international law is
responsible therefor and liable to punishment."[1] Acts by heads of state or
other government officials, even if committed in an official capacity, may
not provide an immunity defense or mitigate criminality.[2] These officials,
therefore, could also be held responsible for offenses committed pursuant to
their orders. Additionally, liability for criminal negligence may be imposed
on a person in a position of authority who knew, or had reason to know,
that his or her subordinates were about to commit a war crime, and who
failed to take whatever action was necessary and reasonable to prevent, to
deter, or to repress its commission. The same liability obtains for failure to
prosecute those who commit such offenses. When it comes to enforcement
or effecting jurisdiction, will nations unilaterally agree to such liability? Is
agreement required? If not, are they liable pursuant to customary international law or general principles? Who or what institution will be able to
enforce this liability?

Historical and Conceptual Background

Efforts to establish an international criminal tribunal are not new,
although they have intensified recently. One wonders whether this history
of so many attempts and so few successes suggests that the time is ripe for
a permanent tribunal, or that a complete change in the international
system is required before one will succeed. Cherif Bassiouni notes that "the
first prosecution for initiating an unjust war is reported to have been in
Naples, in 1268, when Conradin von Hohenstaufen was executed for that

---

* Reprinted with the permission of the
Fletcher Forum and the American Society of
International Law.

1. The Charter and Judgment of Nuremberg recognize five principles: I.) as indicated in the text; II.) "The fact that domestic
law does not punish an act which is an international crime does not free the perpetrator
of such crimes from responsibility under international law"; III.) "The fact that a person who committed an international crime
acted as Head of State or public official does
not free him from responsibility under international law or mitigate punishment"; IV.)
"The fact that a person acted pursuant to
order of his Government or of a superior does
not free him from responsibility under inter-

national law. It may, however, be considered
in mitigation of punishment, if justice so requires"; V.) "Any person charged with a
crime under international law has the right
to a fair trial on the facts and law." "Nazi
Conspiracy and Aggression Opinion and
Judgment, Nuremberg, 30 September 1945,"
reprinted in 41 A.J.I.L. 186–218 (1946); see
also J. Spiropoulos, "Special Rapporteur, Formulation of Nuremberg Principles," 2 1950
Yrbk. Int'l L.Comm. 181, 191–193.

2. *See, e.g.*, Secretary–General's Report
on the Tribunal for the former Yugoslavia,
Pursuant to ¶ 2 of S.C.Res. 808 (1993) (hereafter "Secretary–General's Report"), at ¶ 55.
* * *

offense." The "modern" idea of establishing an international criminal court could be said to have been launched in 1899 with the Hague Convention for the Pacific Settlement of International Disputes [discussed supra this chapter and in chapters 16 & 17, *infra*].

The 1919 Versailles Treaty was another early step toward establishing a war crimes court. The face of the treaty provided for the prosecution of Kaiser Wilhelm II for a supreme offense against the "international morality and the sanctity of treaties" and for war crimes charged against German officers and soldiers. Also in 1919, the Allies established a special commission to investigate the responsibility "for acts of war" and crimes against "the laws of humanity." The Commission Report contained the following conclusion: "All persons * * * who have been guilty of offenses against the laws and customs of war or the laws of humanity, are liable to criminal prosecution." This provision was developed in response to the killing of an estimated one million Armenians by Turkish authorities and the Turkish people, supported or abetted by the state's public policy. There can be no doubt that those who committed such atrocities knew they were committing * * * "crimes against humanity."[3] U.S. [opposition], however, prevented the Commission's report from including this type of conduct among the offenses that an international criminal court would prosecute. Subsequently, the Treaty of Sèvres, which was the 1920 Treaty of Peace between the Allies and the Ottoman Empire, provided for the surrender by Turkey of such persons as might be accused of crimes against "the laws of humanity," but unfortunately, in 1923, the Treaty of Lausanne gave them amnesty.

Between the two world wars, a wave of terror swept Europe, mostly in connection with nationalist claims in the Balkans. In 1936, Adolf Hitler [exploited] the international community's inability to prosecute or sanction crimes against humanity stating, "And who now remembers the Armenians?" Indeed, it is particularly revealing that he would preface his policy of exterminating Jews, Gypsies, and Slavs by revealing the absence of interest by the world community [to prosecute] such conduct. [That failure and the inability to create efficient] international structures to enforce this proscription, gave Hitler the comfort of knowing that he might succeed in genocide, as others had in the past. In 1937, the League of Nations adopted a Convention Against Terrorism; an annexed Protocol provided for the establishment of a special international criminal court to prosecute such crimes. India was the only country to ratify the Convention. It never entered into force.

After World War II, it became obvious that crimes against peace, war crimes, and what became known, with the London Charter, as "crimes against humanity" had been committed. The London Charter established the International Military Tribunal (IMT) at Nuremberg, which was de-

---

3. See, e.g., Wright, History of the United Nations War Crimes Commission (London: H.M. Stationery Office, 1948), 35 (the governments of Great Britain, France, and Russia had condemned the massacres of Armenians by Turks in 1915 as "crimes against humanity and civilization"); see also, Lansing, "Notes on World Sovereignty," 15 A.J.I.L.: 13, 25 (1921) (former U.S. Secretary of State writing that the slave trade had become a "crime against humanity") * * *.

signed to prosecute major war criminals in the European theater. In 1946, a similar international military tribunal was established in Tokyo to prosecute major Japanese war criminals.

Since World War II, there have been many examples of conduct that violate the Nuremberg principles and which could have been tried in a war crimes tribunal. During the Vietnam War, atrocities were committed by both sides. The depredations of the Khmer Rouge in Cambodia are infamous. The Iraqi Air Force bombed villages in Kurdistan with both mustard gas and nerve gas. The former Soviet Union is alleged to have booby-trapped dolls belonging to Afghan Mujahideen children. Bosnia, Rwanda and Haiti provide more recent examples. The macabre list goes on.

In 1989, the General Assembly urged consideration of the establishment of an international criminal court. This recommendation was predicated on growing international concern for drug trafficking * * * and international terrorism. The International Law Commission (ILC) was requested to prepare a report and, in 1990, proposed the creation of an international criminal court. The G.A. Sixth Committee addressed the issue in 1991, and proposed that it be studied further.

On 8 April 1993 the International Court of Justice (ICJ), in response to the suit filed by Bosnia and Herzegovina, called upon Serbia and Montenegro "immediately * * * [to] take all measures within their power to prevent commission of the crime of genocide * * * whether directed against the Muslim population of Bosnia and Herzegovina or against any other national, ethnical, racial, or religious group."[4] This was an interim decision. The Court noted that facts were still in dispute. It was also unable to render a decision on disputed rights falling outside the ambit of the Genocide Convention. The creation of the Ad Hoc Tribunal for crimes against humanitarian law was the culmination of several earlier Security Council resolutions. * * * In early 1992, Resolution 771 called for preliminary investigations. Resolution 780 of 6 October 1992 created a "War Crimes Commission," which analyzed the information garnered by the earlier investigations, conducted its own investigations, and reported its findings to the Secretary–General. Subsequently, the Secretary–General recommended that the Security Council create the Ad Hoc Tribunal. On 11 February 1993, the Council adopted this recommendation and called for the creation of the Ad Hoc Tribunal in its Resolution 808.

Security Council Resolution 808, paragraph 1, provides: "an international tribunal shall be established for the prosecution of persons responsible for serious violations of international humanitarian law committed in the territory of the former Yugoslavia since 1991."

The Legal Basis and Authority to Establish a Permanent Tribunal

The usual and most appropriate method for establishing an international criminal tribunal would be a convention. All member states, howev-

---

4. *Case Concerning Application of the Convention on the Prevention and Punishment of the Crime of Genocide (Bosnia and Herzegovina v. Yugoslavia* [Serbia and Montenegro]), request for the indication of provisional measures, (1993) I.C.J. Reports 3, 32 I.L.M. 890 (1993) (wherein Bosnia and Herzegovina filed suit against Serbia and Montenegro "for violating the Genocide Convention" and other illegal conduct in violation of customary international law).

er, are likely under a binding obligation to take whatever action is required to enforce the statute under U.N. Charter, Chapter VII. The Secretary–General suggested that the treaty approach would be too long and arduous; drafting an instrument and obtaining the required ratifications for entry into force would not be reconcilable with the urgency expressed by the Security Council in Resolution 808 (Secretary–General's Report, at ¶ ¶ 20–21). Thus, it was recommended that the authority or legal basis for the tribunal be predicated on Chapter VII of the U.N. Charter, which covers Action with respect to Threats to the Peace, Breaches of the Peace, and Acts of Aggression. The creation of the tribunal would be a "measure to maintain or restore international peace and security, following the requisite determination of the existence of a threat to the peace, breach of the peace or act of aggression."

Article 41 of the U.N. Charter provides: "The Security Council may decide what measures not involving the use of armed force are to be employed to give effect to its decisions, and it may call upon the members of the United Nations to apply such measures." Article 42 adds: "Should the Security Council consider that measures provided for in Article 41 would be inadequate or have proved to be inadequate, it may take such action by air, sea, or land forces as may be necessary to maintain or restore international peace and security. Such action may include demonstrations, blockade, and other operations by air, sea, or land forces of Members of the [U.N.]" The argument is that if the use of force is allowed as a "measure" under Article 42, a fortiori, the creation of an ad hoc international criminal court should also be allowed. In "the particular case of the former Yugoslavia, the Secretary–General believes that the establishment of the International Tribunal by means of a Chapter VII decision would be legally justified, both in terms of the object and purpose of the decision [as indicated in the purpose statement in his report] and of past Security Council practice." [Sec.Gen.Report §§ 24, 27].

The Secretary–General's Report relating to the atrocities there noted that the creation of the Tribunal for the prosecution of the alleged breaches of international humanitarian law will apply existing law, including the Geneva Conventions of 1949, and that the Security Council would not be creating law or purporting to legislate. Is this assertion accurate? Where, besides in the Geneva and Hague Conventions, would these crimes be found? Would they be found with sufficient clarity to satisfy due process concerns? Would the Secretary–General's assertions hold for a permanent war crimes tribunal?

Specific Tribunal Characteristics
Propriety

A tribunal will only be acceptable if it proceeds in a manner that is beyond reproach. Basic notions of fairness and human rights in relation to investigation, prosecution, and trial are paramount. Any tribunal unscrupulous in protecting the accused from abuses and deprivation of civil liberties would be a dangerous institution. Justice Jackson summed up the importance of this point in his opening statement during the Nuremberg Trial.

Before I discuss the particulars of evidence, some general considerations which may affect the credit of this trial in the eyes of the world should be candidly faced. There is a dramatic disparity between the circumstances of the accusers and the accused that might discredit our work if we should falter, in even minor matters, in being fair and temperate. Unfortunately, the nature of these crimes is such that both prosecution and judgment must be by victor nations over vanquished foes [a problem not faced by the Ad Hoc Tribunal for the former Yugoslavia].

. . . We must never forget that the record on which we judge these defendants is the record on which history will judge us tomorrow. To pass these defendants a poisoned chalice is to put it to our lips as well. We must summon such detachment and intellectual integrity to our task that this Trial will commend itself to posterity as fulfilling humanity's aspirations to do justice.

International Human Rights Law provides the minimum standards for protection of an accused person. Increasingly, U.S. requests for extradition and hand-overs under Status of Forces agreements have been overridden by international and foreign courts, which have ruled that international human rights provisions take precedence. In two recent cases, concerns over capital punishment have resulted in litigation in which courts outside the United States have held that extradition to states where the death penalty applied would, in certain circumstances, violate provisions of international human rights conventions.

International human rights conventions contain analogues to many of the protections guaranteed by the U.S. Constitution, including the right to fair trial, to "equality of arms" and access to court, to the presumption of innocence, to the right to confrontation, and to the right to counsel of choice. Though some of the international human rights protections meet, and even exceed, U.S. constitutional standards, some do not. Article 20(1) of the Statute for the Ad Hoc Tribunal provides that the "[t]rial chambers shall ensure that a trial is fair and expeditious and that proceedings are rendered in accordance with the rules of procedure and evidence, with full respect for the rights of the accused and due regard for the protection of victims and witnesses." The accused's Geneva Law and human right to consult a lawyer and to have adequate time to prepare a defense must be ensured. To be acceptable, this protection must be applicable to the entire trial process. * * *

Notes and Questions

1. **The atrocities committed** in the territory of the former Yugoslavia and in Rwanda called for immediate action on an *ad hoc* basis.[a] The

---

a. Blakesley, *Obstacles to the Creation of an International Criminal Court, 18* The Fletcher Forum of World Affairs 77, 78, 81–86, 97–98 (1994) (most fns. omitted); *reprinted in*, INTERNATIONAL LAW: CLASSIC & CONTEMPORARY READINGS (ASIL, Ku & Deihl, eds. 1998); Bassiouni, *The Law of the International*

Criminal Tribunal for the Former Yugoslavia (1996); Morris & Scharf, *An Insider's Guide to the International Criminal Tribunal for the Former Yugoslavia* (1995); Forsythe, *Politics and the International Tribunal for the Former Yugoslavia* 5 Crim.L.Forum 401 (1994); H. von Hebel, *An International Tribunal for*

extracts that follow demonstrate how the two tribunals were established by the United Nations Security Council and give a sampling of some of the cases.

2. ***Ad Hoc Tribunal for the Prosecution of Persons Responsible for Serious Violations of International Humanitarian Law in the territory of the former Yugoslavia:*** Nürnberg Principle I is applicable to the depredations which have taken place in the former Yugoslavia. On May 25, 1993, the *Security Council, in Resolution 827,* established a tribunal to try serious violations of international humanitarian law, committed in the territory of the former Yugoslavia, including: murders of men, women and children, mass executions, torture, and forced deportations or expulsion pursuant to "ethnic cleansing." Resolution 827 was based on the Report of the Secretary–General made pursuant to ¶ 2 of Security Council Resolution 808 (1993) (May 3, 1993). [Security Council Doc. S–25704, 3 May 1993].

3. ***The Tribunal has an Appeals Chamber*** consisting of five members and three Trial Chambers with three members each. The President of the Tribunal also presides over the Appeals Chamber. The President, in consultation with the members, will determine who is assigned to each Chamber. Each Trial Chamber elects its own President. At another meeting, the members decided that assignments to the Chambers would be for a period of one year, and thereafter by rotation. * * *

United Nations Charter
Articles 39, 41 and 42

1. *The Ad Hoc Criminal Tribunal for Former Yugoslavia.*

In U.N. Security Council Resolution 808 of February 22, 1993,[a] it was decided that an international tribunal be established for the prosecution of those persons allegedly responsible for serious violations of international humanitarian law in the territory of the former Yugoslavia since 1991.The Secretary General was requested to submit a report on all aspects of the matter, including specific proposals and options for the effective and expeditious implementation of such a tribunal. His extensive report,[b] which took into consideration the suggestions put forward by U.N. member states, meetings of international experts, and non-governmental organizations, recommended that the tribunal be established by a decision of the Security Council on the basis of Chapter VII of the Charter, rather than by multilateral treaty because of the need to act expeditiously. Such Security Council action constituted a measure to maintain or restore international peace and security, following a determination of the existence of a threat to the peace, breach of the peace or act of aggression and had effect immediately, binding member states to take whatever action was required.

the *Former Yugoslavia: An Act of Powerlessness or a New Challenge for the International Community?* 11 *Netherlands Quarterly of Human Rights* 437 (1993); Gross, *The Grave Breaches System and the Armed Conflict in the Former Yugoslavia* 16 *Mich. L.J. Int'l L.*

783 (1995), and Meron, *War Crimes in Yugoslavia and Developments in International Law* 88 *AJIL* 78 (1994).

a. U.N. Doc. S/25704 (1993).

b. U.N. Doc. S/25704 (1993).

On May 25, 1993 the Security Council, in Resolution 827[c] reproduced in part below, decided to set up the tribunal and endorsed the 34–article statute annexed to the Secretary General's Report. The serious violations of international humanitarian law that are within the competence of the Tribunal as listed include (1) grave breaches of the 1949 Geneva Conventions, such as wilful killing, torture, extensive destruction or appropriation of property not justified by military necessity and carried out unlawfully and wantonly, unlawful deportation or confinement of civilians, hostage taking; (2) genocide; and (3) crimes against humanity including murder, extermination, rape, deportation, persecution on political, racial, and religious grounds, and other inhumane acts. The seat of the tribunal is at the Hague and the working languages English and French.[d] The 14 judges, no two of whom may be nationals of the same state, are elected by the General Assembly from a list submitted by the Security Council, drawn from nominations by member states and non-members with permanent observer missions at U.N. Headquarters, for a term of 4 years.[e] The Tribunal consists of 3 Trial Chambers, each with 3 judges and an Appeals Chamber with 5 judges.[f] There is an independent Prosecutor's Office. The Prosecutor is appointed by the Secretary General for a 4–year term. The Prosecutor's staff is appointed by the Security Council on the recommendation of the Prosecutor.[g] The rights of an accused person are provided for in detail, including the right to be presumed innocent until proved guilty, the right to be informed promptly, in detail and in a language that he or she understands of the nature and cause of the charge, the right to counsel of choice, the right to be tried without due delay, the right to examine or have witnesses and the right not be compelled to testify against him or herself or to confess guilt.[h] Penalties are limited to imprisonment. However, in addition, property and proceeds of criminal conduct may be ordered returned to their rightful owners.[i]

Security Council Resolution 827 (1993)

U.N. Doc. S/Res/827 (1993)

The Security Council . . .

Convinced that in the particular circumstances of the former Yugoslavia the establishment as an ad hoc measure by the Council of an international tribunal and the prosecution of persons responsible for serious violations of international humanitarian law would enable this aim to be achieved and would contribute to the restoration and maintenance of peace;

c. U.N. Doc. S/Res/827 (1993).

d. Art. 18(3) of the Statute of the International Tribunal provides that the accused has the right to necessary translation into and from a language that he or she understands.

e. Art. 13. The list shall contain not less than 22 and not more than 39 candidates.

f. Arts. 11 and 12.

g. Art. 16. Justice Richard Goldstone of South Africa was the first Chief Prosecutor, Justice LouiseArbour, of Canada was the second prosecutor of the ICTFY and Ms Carla del Ponte of Switzerland the third.

h. Article 21.

i. Article 24.

Believing that the establishment of an international tribunal and the prosecution of persons responsible for the above-mentioned violations of international humanitarian law will contribute to ensuring that such violations are halted and effectively redressed; . . .

Reaffirming in this regard its decision in resolution 808 (1993) that an international tribunal shall be established for the prosecution of persons responsible for serious violations of international humanitarian law committed in the territory of the former Yugoslavia since 1991;

Considering that, pending the appointment of the Prosecutor of the International Tribunal, the Commission of Experts established pursuant to resolution 780 (1992) should continue on an urgent basis the collection of information relating to evidence of grave breaches of the Geneva conventions and other violations of international humanitarian law as proposed in its interim report (S/25274);

Acting under Chapter VII of the Charter of the United Nations;

1. *Approves* the report of the Secretary General;

2. *Decides* hereby to establish an international tribunal for the sole purpose of prosecuting persons responsible for serious violations of international humanitarian law committed in the territory of the former Yugoslavia between 1 January 1991 and a date to be determined by the Security Council upon the restoration of peace and to this end to adopt the Statute of the International Tribunal annexed to the above-mentioned report;

3. *Requests* the Secretary–General to submit to the judges of the International Tribunal, upon their election, any suggestions received from States for the rules of procedure and evidence called for in Article 15 of the Statute of the International Tribunal;

4. *Decides* that all states shall cooperate fully with the International Tribunal and its organ in accordance with the present resolution and the statute of the International Tribunal and that consequently all States shall take any measures necessary under their domestic law to implement the provisions of the present resolution and the Statute, including the obligation of States to comply with requests for assistance or orders issued by a Trial Chamber under Article 29 of the Statute;

5. *Urges* States and intergovernmental and non-governmental organizations to contribute funds, equipment and services to the International Tribunal, including the offer of expert personnel;

6. *Decides* that the determination of the seat of the International Tribunal is subject to the conclusion of appropriate arrangements between the United Nations and the Netherlands acceptable to the Council, and that the International Tribunal may sit elsewhere when it considers it necessary for the efficient exercise of its functions;

7. *Decides* also that the work of the International Tribunal shall be carried out without prejudice to the right of the victims to seek, through appropriate means, compensation for damages incurred as a result of violations of international humanitarian law;

8. *Requests* the Secretary–General to implement urgently the present resolution and in particular to make practical arrangements for the effective functioning of the International Tribunal at the earliest time and to report periodically to the Council;

9. *Decides* to remain actively seized of the matter.

Notes & Questions. **1**. Do you think that the establishment of such tribunals as ICTFY and ICTR, considered *infra*, have helped to "usher in an era of peace and reconciliation"[a] by placing responsibility on individuals and leaders?

2. Both *Ad Hoc* Tribunals were set up by UNSC Resolutions under Chapter VII of the U.N. Charter, as subsidiary organs of the UNSC. What do you think was the precondition for doing so under article 39 of the U.N. Charter. How was this met in the factual circumstances in both instances? Look at articles 41 and 42 of the U.N. Charter, in the Documentary Supplement. In your opinion do they allow for such tribunals as subsidiary organs of the UNSC? The ITFY was faced at the outset with a challenge on its institutional legitimacy in the *Prosecutor of the Tribunal* v. *Dusko Tadic*. It was held that the Security Council had the authority under Chapter VII of the Charter to establish the ICTFY.

The Prosecutor of the Tribunal v. Dusko Tadic

International Criminal Tribunal for the Former Yugoslavia,
revised and affirmed in part by the Appeals Chamber (2 Oct. 1995)

Decision on the Defense Motion on Jurisdiction (Aug. 10, 1995) (before Judges Cassesse, Li, Deschenes, Abi–Saab and Sidhwa). The following extract demonstrates that the ICTFY was properly established and has subject matter jurisdiction. * * *

2. It is said that, to be duly established by law, the International Tribunal should have been created either by treaty, the consensual act of nations, or by amendment of the Charter of the United Nations, not be resolution of the Security Council. Called in aid of this general proposition are a number of considerations: that before the creation of the International Tribunal in 1993 it was never envisaged that such an ad hoc criminal tribunal might be set up; that the General Assembly, whose participation would at least have guaranteed full representation of the international community, was not involved in its creation; that it was never intended by the Charter that the Security Council should, under Chapter VII, establish a judicial body, let alone a criminal tribunal; that the Security Council had been inconsistent in creating this tribunal while not taking a similar step in the case of other areas of conflict in which violations of international humanitarian law may have occurred; that the establishment of the International Tribunal had neither promoted, nor was capable of promoting, international peace, as the current situation in the former Yugoslavia demonstrates; that the Security Council could not, in any event, create criminal liability on the part of individuals and that this is what the

a. Knight *Legal Issues* in J. Tessitore & Woolfson, *A Global Agenda: Issues Before the*   *52nd General Assembly of the United Nations* 267, 268 (1998).

creation of the International Tribunal did; that there existed and exists now no such international emergency as would justify the action of the Security Council; that no political organ such as the Security Council is capable of establishing an independent and impartial tribunal; that there is an inherent defect in the creation, after the event of ad hoc tribunals to try particular types of offences and, finally, that to give the International Tribunal primacy over national courts is, in any event and in itself, inherently wrong. . . .

8. For the Defense it is said that it is a basic human right of an accused to have a fair and public hearing by a competent, independent and impartial tribunal established by law. The Defense asserts that this right is protected by a panoply of principles of fundamental justice recognized by human rights law. There can be no doubt that the International Tribunal should seek to provide just such a trial; indeed, in enacting its Statute, care has been taken by the Security Council to ensure that this in fact occurs and the Judges of the International Tribunal, in framing its Rules, have also paid scrupulous regard to the requirements of a fair trial. For example, Article 21 of the Statute of the International Tribunal guarantees the accused the right to a fair trial and Article 20 obligates the Trial Chambers to ensure that trials are, in fact, fair. There are several other provisions to the same effect. However, it is one thing for the Security Council to have taken every care to ensure that a structure appropriate to the conduct of fair trials has been created; it is an entirely different thing in any way to infer from that careful structuring that it was intended that the International Tribunal be empowered to question the legality of the law which established it. The competence of the International Tribunal is precise and narrowly defined; as described in Article 1 of its Statute, it is to prosecute persons responsible for serious violations of international humanitarian law, subject to spatial and temporal limits, and to do so in accordance with the Statute. That is the full extent of the competence of the International Tribunal.

* * *

10.   The Defense relies on, or at least refers to, what has been said by the International Court of Justice ("the Court") in three cases: *Certain Expenses of the United Nations*, 1962 I.C.J. 151, 168 (Advisory Opinion of 20 July) (the "Expenses Advisory Opinion"), Legal Consequences for States of the Continued Presence of South Africa in Namibia (South–West Africa) Notwithstanding Security Council Resolution 776, 1971 I.C.I. 16, 45 (*Advisory Opinion of 21 June*) (the "*Namibia Advisory Opinion*") and Caae Concerning Questions of Interpretation and Application of the 1971 Montreal Convention Arising from the Aerial Incident at Lockerbie (*Libya v. U.S.), 1992* I.C.J. 114, 176 (*Provisional Measures Order of 14 April*) (the 'Lockerbie decision"). In the first of these, the Expenses Advisory Opinion, the Court specifically stated that, unlike the legal system of some States there exists no procedure for determining the validity of acts of organs of the United Nations. It referred to proposals at the time of drafting of the Charter that such a power should be given to the Court and to the rejection of those proposals.

11. In the second of these cases, the Namibia Advisory Opinion, the Court dealt very specifically with this matter, stating that: "Undoubtedly, the Court does not possess powers of judicial review or appeal in respect of the decisions taken by the United Nations organs concerned".

12. Finally, in the Lockerbie decision, Judge Weeramantry, in his dissenting opinion, but in this respect not in dissent from other members of the Court, said that "it is not for this Court to sit in review on a given resolution of the Security Council" and, that in relation to the exercise by the Security Council of its powers under Chapter VII: "the determination under Article 39 of the existence of any threat to the peace ... is one entirely within the discretion of the Council.... the Council and no other is the judge of the existence of the state of affairs which brings Chapter VII into operation.... Once [such a determination is] taken the door is opened to the various decisions the Council may make under that Chapter."

13. These opinions of the Court clearly provide no basis for the International Tribunal to review the actions of the Security Council, indeed, they are authorities to the contrary.

14. In support of its submission that this Trial Chamber should review the actions of the Security Council, the Defense contends that the decisions of the Security Council are not "sacrosanct". Certainly, commentators have suggested that there are limits to the authority of the Security Council. It has been posited that such limits may be based on Article 24 (2), which provides that the Security Council: "shall act in accordance with the Purposes and Principles of the United Nations. the specific powers appointed to the Security Council for the discharge of these duties are laid down in Chapters VI, VII, VIII, and XII." One commentator interprets this provision to mean that the Security Council "cannot, in principle, act arbitrarily and unfettered by any restraints." (D.W. Bowett, *The Law of International Institutions* 33, (1982).) Another commentator has taken the position, that although the Security Council has broad discretion in the field of international peace and security, it cannot "act arbitrarily or use the existence of a threat to the peace as a basis for action which ... is for collateral and independent purposes, such as the overthrow of a government or the partition of a State." (Ian Brownlie, *The Decisions of Political Organs of the United Nations and the Rule of Law*, in Essays in Honour of Wang Tieya 95 (1992).)

15. Support for the view that the Security Council cannot act arbitrarily or for an ulterior purpose is found in the nature of the Charter as a treaty delegating certain powers to the U.N. In fact, such a limitation is almost a corollary of the principle that the organs of the U.N. must act in accordance with the powers delegated them. It is a matter of logic that if the Security Council acted arbitrarily or for an ulterior purpose it would be acting outside the purview of the powers delegated to it in the Charter.

16. Although it is not for this Trial Chamber to judge the reasonableness of the acts of the Security Council, it is without doubt that, with respect to the former Yugoslavia, the Security Council did not act arbitrarily. To the contrary, the Security Council's establishment of the International Tribunal represents its informed judgment, after great deliberation,

that violations of international humanitarian law were occurring in the former Yugoslavia and that such violations created a threat to the peace.

* * *

23.   The making of a judgment as to whether there was such an emergency in the former Yugoslavia as would justify the setting up of the International Tribunal under Chapter VII is eminently one for the Security Council and only for it; it is certainly not a justiciable issue but one involving considerations of high policy and of a political nature. As to whether the particular measures of establishing the International tribunal is, inf fact, likely to be conducive to the restoration of peace and security is, again, pre-eminently a matter for the Security Council and for it alone and no judicial body, certainly not this Trial Chamber, can or should review that step.

. . .

27.   That it was not originally envisaged that an ad hoc judicial tribunal might be created under Chapter VII, even if that be factually correct, is nothing to the point. Chapter VII confers very wide powers upon the Security Council and no good reason has been advanced why Article 41 should be read as excluding the step, very appropriate in the circumstances, of creating the International Tribunal to deal with the notorious situation existing in the former Yugoslavia. This is a situation clearly suited to adjudication by a tribunal and punishment of those found guilty of crimes that violate international humanitarian law. This is not, as the Defense puts it, a question of the Security Council doing anything it likes; it is a seemingly entirely appropriate reaction to a situation in which international peace is clearly endangered.

28.   The Defense argues that the establishment of the International Tribunal is not a measure contemplated by Article 41 because the examples included in that Article focus on economic and political measures, not judicial measures. As the Defense concedes, however, the list in that Article is not exhaustive. Once again, the decision of the Security Council in this regard is fraught with fact-based, policy determinations that make this issue non-justiciable.

29.   Further, the Defense contends that the International Tribunal is not an appropriate measure under Article 41 because it has failed to restore peace in the former Yugoslavia. However, the accused is but the first and, as yet, the only accused to be brought before the International Tribunal, and it is wholly premature at this initial stage of its functioning to attempt to assess the effectiveness of the International Tribunal as a measure to restore peace, even were it the function of the International Tribunal to do so.

* * *

32.   Then it is said that international law requires that criminal courts be independent and impartial and that no court created by a political body such as the Security Council can have those characteristics. Of course, criminal courts world-wide are the creations of legislatures, eminently political bodies. The Court, in the Effect of Awards case, specifically held

that a political organ of the United Nations in that case, the General Assembly could and had crated "an independent and truly judicial body". (Effect of Awards of Compensation Made by the U.N. Administrative Tribunal, 1954 I.C.I. 47, 53 (Advisory Opinion of 13 July) (Effect of Awards).) The question whether a court is independent and impartial depends not upon the body that creates it but upon its constitution, its judges and the way in which they function. The International Tribunal has, as its Statute and Rules attest, been constituted so as to ensure a fair trial to an accused and it is to be hoped that the way its Judges administer their jurisdiction will leave no room for complaints about lack of impartiality or want of independence.

33.   The fact that the Security Council has established an ad hoc tribunal is also said to reveal invalidity because it is said to deny to the accused the right conferred by Article 14 of the International Convention on the Protection of Civil and Political Rights ("ICCPR") to be tried by a tribunal "established by law". However, on analysis this introduces no new concept; it is but another way of expressing the general complaint that the creation of the International Tribunal was beyond the power of the Security Council.

34.   It is noteworthy that, in the context of the International Covenant and its entitlement in Article 14 to trial by a "tribunal established by law", this phrase requires only that the tribunal be legally constituted. . . .

51.   The Report of the Secretary–General (U.N. Doc. S/25704 (3 May 1993)) (the "Report") makes it clear, in paragraph 34, that it was intended that the rules of international law that were to be applied should be "beyond any doubt part of customary law", so that problems of non-adherence of particular States to any international Convention should not arise. Hence, no doubt, the specific reference to the law of the Geneva Conventions in Article 2 since, as the Report states in paragraph 35, that law applicable in armed conflict has beyond doubt become part of customary law. But there is no ground for treating Article 2 as in effect importing into the Statute the whole of the terms of the Conventions, including the reference in common Article 2 of the Geneva Convention to international conflicts. As stated, Article 2 of the Statute is on its face, self-contained, save in relation to the definition of protected persons and things. It simply confers subject matter jurisdiction to prosecute what, if one were concerned with the Conventions, would indeed be grave breaches of those Conventions, but which are, in the present context, simple enactments of the Statute.

52.   When what is in issue is what the Geneva Conventions contemplate in the case of grave breaches, namely their prosecution before a national court and not before an international tribunal, it is natural enough that there should be a requirement of internationality; a nation might well view with concern, as an unacceptable infringement of sovereignty, the action of a foreign court in trying an accused for grave breaches committed in a conflict internal to that nation. Such considerations do not apply to the International Tribunal, any more than do the references in the Conventions to High Contracting Parties and much else in the Conventions; all these are simply inapplicable to the International Tribunal. They

do not apply because the International Tribunal is not in fact, applying conventional international law but, rather, customary international law, as the Secretary–General makes clear in his Report, and is doing so by virtue of the mandate conferred upon it by the Security Council. In the case of what are commonly referred to as "grave breaches" this conventional law has become customary law, though some of it may well have been conventional law before being written into the predecessors of the present Geneva Conventions.

53.   It follows that the element of internationality forms no jurisdictional criterion of the offences created by Article 2 of the Statute of the International Tribunal. If it did, there are clear indications in the great volume of material before the Trial Chamber that the acts alleged in the indictment were in fact committed in the course of an international armed conflict. However, little of this material is such that judicial notice can be taken of it and none of it is in the form of, nor has it been tendered as, evidence. In these circumstances the Trial Chamber makes no finding regarding the nature of the armed conflict in question.

––––––––

Notes & Questions. 1. Milosevic, Karadzic, and Mladic: Two of the three most wanted leaders, former President Slobodan Milosevic of FRY, Radovan Karadzic and Ratko Mladic in the Republika Srpska, the Serbian part of Bosnia have been adept at avoiding arrest.

2.   Milosevic's Arrest. Mr. Milosevic may be prosecuted, at least for fraud, corruption, and other financial crimes, but in Serbia, unless new President Kostunica changes his mind and decides to approve Milosevic's surrender to the Hague. On March 30, 2001, Serb police began a tense week-end 26–hour stand-off that finally ended in the early morning of April 1st, 2001, with the arrest of Milosevic in Belgrade on charges of abuse of power, financial crimes, corruption. A few Milosevic supporters had surrounded his home, and as the early morning hours of March 31st arrived, fights broke out and some shots were fired. Some 20 hard-core Milosevic supporters and his body guards vowed not to allow the arrest to happen. Milosevic resisted, vowing that he would rather die than go to jail. It was reported that he brandished a gun and threatened to kill himself and his family. He refused the arrest warrant from the police whom he said were NATO servants and lackeys.

3.   Milosevic could face the Hague, a long prison term, or even the death penalty in the former Yugoslavia. There appears to be some speculation that additional serious charges which may be filed domestically could subject Milosevic to the possibility of the death penalty. If these charges materialize (ordering murder of personal and political enemies), they may actually be an incentive for his transfer to The Hague. The ICTY cannot impose the death penalty. What do you think about this? On the other hand, will it detract from the impact of international criminal law? Recall that this was exactly the position of the Rwandan Government regarding the ICTR. Note that the Rome Statute for the International criminal Court has no death penalty.

Milosevic could face death penalty–wife Mirjana could also face charges , CNN World News, April 3, 2001.*

BELGRADE, Yugoslavia—Former Yugoslav President Slobodan Milosevic could face charges for crimes which carry the death penalty. Serbian interior minister Dusan Mihajlovic revealed on Tuesday that authorities had indications that Milosevic was also involved in "serious crimes" for which the death penalty could apply. He was speaking after Milosevic, who is facing corruption and criminal conspiracy charges, admitted financing conflicts in neighbouring Bosnia and Croatia in an appeal against his detention in a Belgrade jail.

On further possible charges against Milosevic, Mihajlovic, speaking in Vienna, added: "But we are talking about investigations, we need proof. If we get this we will ask the justice authorities to bring charges." He did not specify what the additional charges might be. Authorities in Serbia have not so far accused Milosevic of any offence serious enough to carry the death penalty.

Some of the former president's opponents have however accused him of involvement in politically motivated killings. The death penalty has not been carried out in Serbia for many years. Mihajlovic was speaking as Milosevic's lawyer prepared to appeal against the former president's detention. A court is due to rule on the appeal on Tuesday, a day after the decision to arrest Milosevic paid dividends for Yugoslavia's new leaders as the United States promised to release $50 million in aid for the country.

Milosevic surrendered to the authorities early on Sunday morning following two failed attempts to arrest him, one ending in a gun battle in the grounds of his residence. He is accused of stealing hundreds of millions of dollars from Yugoslavia's treasury. Milosevic submitted a written appeal against his detention from his cell in Belgrade's Central Prison on Monday. He denied using the cash for personal gain but admitted funnelling money to ethnic Serb forces in neighbouring Bosnia and Croatia as they tried unsuccessfully to prevent those republics from breaking away from Yugoslavia. Milosevic's appeal said he financed the purchase "of weapons, ammunition and other needs" for the Bosnian Serb and Croatian Serb armies. "These expenses could not, as a state secret, be accounted for in the state budget," he said.

Milosevic's lawyer said he did not expect the appeal against detention to succeed. "We will have an answer most probably on Tuesday morning. I think it will be a negative one," Toma Fila said. In attempting to clear himself on domestic corruption charges, Milosevic risks building the case against himself at another court—the U.N. war crimes tribunal in The Hague, Netherlands.

Milosevic has already been indicted for crimes against humanity over his brutal crackdown on ethnic Albanians in Kosovo in 1999. The tribunal's chief prosecutor, *Carla Del Ponte*, has revealed she is preparing a second indictment against him over war crimes committed in Bosnia.

* Reprinted with the permission of CNN World News.

Del Ponte expects Milosevic in The Hague

CNN's Belgrade bureau chief Alessio Vinci says Milosevic is unlikely to have given any thought to the tribunal and the potential dangers of his admission. He says the former leader only surrendered to the Belgrade authorities having received assurances that he would not be handed over to The Hague. In any case, Vinci believes, many people in Yugoslavia see Milosevic as having acted in the interest of Serb people. Milosevic's successor, Vojislav Kostunica, has resisted calls to hand him over, saying Belgrade has to pass a law co-operating with the court, which has been viewed within Yugoslavia as anti-Serb. He told the New York Times newspaper on Tuesday: "I must make some compromises, but there is a line I cannot cross."

Western governments have indicated they are ready to give the new Belgrade authorities some time, but they are adamant Milosevic, and all other war crimes suspects, must eventually be transferred to The Hague. The U.S. had threatened to cut off aid if Yugoslavia did not co-operate with the tribunal by the end of March. It has now threatened to block an international donor conference for Yugoslavia unless it continues to make progress in delivering Milosevic to The Hague court. U.S. State Department spokesman Richard Boucher said: "Clearly having Milosevic face international justice for international crimes remains a top priority for the international community." Milosevic is expected to be interrogated again on Tuesday as the criminal investigations against him widen.

Arms cache

He is now also facing charges of inciting his guards to shoot at the authorities sent to capture him. Four police officers were wounded in the attempt, officials said. On Monday police unveiled a cache of weapons allegedly found at Milosevic's residence, including 27 Kalashnikov AK47 rifles, 40 hand grenades, 23 rifle-launched grenades and five crates of ammunition. If tried and convicted on all the charges now pending against him, Milosevic would face five to 15 years in prison. Three of his bodyguards are also in police custody.

However, Serbian Prime Minister *Zoran Djindjic* predicted the former president will also face murder charges. He told The Boston Globe newspaper that Milosevic will be charged within two months of ordering the murders of personal and political enemies. He also said he expected that Milosevic's wife, Mirjana, a key political figure during his tenure in office, would face accusations of murder.

Djindjic told the Globe that Rade Markovic, the chief of the secret police during Milosevic's last three years in office, has begun co-operating with authorities and will link the Milosevics to several murders.

———

Milosevic May Face Death Penalty, Guardian* Unlimited Breaking News, Tuesday April 3, 2001.

* Reprinted with the permission of the Guardian.

BELGRADE, Yugoslavia (AP)—Slobodan Milosevic may face charges at home that carry the death penalty, Yugoslav authorities said Tuesday, and the country's president ruled out extraditing his predecessor to the U.N. war crimes tribunal anytime soon. Milosevic has been jailed at Belgrade's Central Prison while authorities try to build a case for corruption and abuse of power against the 59–year-old deposed leader.

But on Tuesday, Serbian Interior Minister Dusan Mihajlovic said the investigation pointed to more serious offenses allegedly committed during Milosevic's 13–year rule. "There are ... indications that Slobodan Milosevic was involved in severe criminal acts for which the death penalty is provided," Mihajlovic told reporters in Vienna, Austria. Mihajlovic did not elaborate. However, Serbia's prime minister, Zoran Djindjic, told The Boston Globe in an interview that Milosevic will be charged within two months of ordering the murders of personal and political enemies. Djindjic also said that he expected that Milosevic's wife, Mirjana, a key political figure, will also be accused of murder.

Executions in Yugoslavia are carried out by firing squad.

While hailing Milosevic's arrest, the United States and major Western European countries have made clear they expect the architect of the Balkan wars to be handed over to the U.N. war crimes tribunal in The Hague, Netherlands. However, most Yugoslavs consider the tribunal an instrument of American foreign policy established to punish Serbs for what most of them consider their legitimate conduct in the Balkan wars of the last decade, when Yugoslavia disintegrated. At a press conference Tuesday, President Vojislav Kostunica repeated his opposition to extraditing Milosevic anytime soon despite Western pressure. "The Hague court is not on my mind at all," Kostunica said. "We are not thinking about extradition now. We are dealing with Milosevic's responsibility before our own nation and before our own courts."

"Milosevic stands primarily and paramountly responsible before his own nation, his state," Kostunica said. "He is guilty of all the things he did—the country's disintegration and economic collapse—and all the things he failed to do as president."

He said Yugoslavia, which still harbors numerous other indicted war crimes suspects, was willing to cooperate with The Hague but that did not mean subordinating national dignity for "a handful of dollars"—a reference to linking trade and aid to Yugoslavia with extraditing Milosevic. Kostunica also criticized the U.N. tribunal for pursuing "selective justice" by failing to indict leaders of other former Yugoslav republics "and even the leaders of NATO" for the 1999 bombing of his country. Milosevic has steadfastly maintained his innocence. In a statement Monday, he admitted diverting $390 million in Yugoslav dinars and German marks but claimed the money went to bankroll Serb rebels fighting in Croatia and Bosnia–Herzegovina rather than into his personal bank accounts. It was the first time Milosevic had publicly acknowledged financing Serb armies in the Bosnian and Croatian wars.

A Belgrade court Tuesday rejected Milosevic's appeal for immediate release.

Milosevic's Socialist Party threatened Tuesday to launch daily protests if Milosevic is not freed on bail by Friday. A former customs chief, Mihalj Kertes, was questioned for several hours Tuesday, apparently in connection with the corruption charge against Milosevic. He was believed to have been a central figure in the secret financing of rebels in Bosnia and Croatia. Milosevic is accused by The Hague of atrocities committed by his forces against ethnic Albanians during the crackdown in Kosovo two years ago.

The tribunal also says it is preparing more charges in connection with the wars in Croatia and Bosnia when the two former Yugoslav republics gained their independence. Milosevic surrendered early Sunday after a 26–hour standoff with police at his Belgrade villa. He was later charged with inciting his bodyguards to shoot at police. Four policemen were wounded.

The Prosecutor v. Dusko Tadic

ICT for Former Yugoslavia, IT–94–I–AR72 (2 Oct. 1995)

Decision on the Defense Motion for Interlocutory Appeal on Jurisdiction.

[Consider the following extract which looks at the applicability of the "grave breaches" (provisions of the Geneva Conventions 1949.]

■ CASSESSE, J.

* * *

79. Article 2 of the Statute of the International Tribunal provides: "The International Tribunal shall have the power to prosecute persons committing or ordering to be committed grave breaches of the Geneva Conventions of 12 August 1949...."

By its explicit terms, and as confirmed in the Report of the Secretary–General, this Article of the Statute is based on the Geneva Conventions of 1949 and, more specifically, the provisions of those Conventions relating to "grave breaches" of the Conventions. Each of the four Geneva Conventions of 1949 contains a "grave breaches" provision, specifying particular breaches of the Convention for which the High Contracting Parties have a duty to prosecute those responsible. In other words, for these specific acts, the Conventions create universal mandatory criminal jurisdiction among contracting States. Although the language of the Conventions might appear to be ambiguous and the question is open to some debate (see, e.g. (*Amicus Curiae*) Submission of the Government of the United States of America Concerning Certain Arguments Made by Counsel for the Accused in the Case of *The Prosecutor of the Tribunal* v. *Dusko Tadic*, 17 July 1995, (Case NO. IT–94–1–T), at 35–6 (hereinafter, U.S. *Amicus Curiae Brief*)), it is widely contended that the grave breaches provisions establish universal mandatory jurisdiction only with respect to those breaches of the Conventions committed in international armed conflicts. Appellant argues that, as the grave breaches enforcement system only applies to international armed conflicts, reference in Article 2 of the Statute to the grave breaches provisions of the Geneva Conventions limits the International Tribunal's jurisdiction under that Article to acts committed in the context of an international armed conflict.

The Trial Chamber has held that Article 2 [of the Statute of the Tribunal]:

> "[H]as been so drafted as to be self-contained rather than referential, save for the identification of the victims of enumerated acts; that identification and that alone involves going to the Conventions themselves for the definition of persons or property protected. . . .

> [T]he requirement of international conflict does not appear on the face of Article 2. Certainly, nothing in the words of the Article expressly require its existence; once one of the specified acts is allegedly committed upon a protected person the power of the International Tribunal to prosecute arises if the spatial and temporal requirements of Article 1 are met. . . .

> [T]here is no ground for treating Article 2 as in effect importing into the Statute the whole of the terms of the Conventions, including the reference in common Article 2 of the Geneva Convention. [sic] to international conflicts. As stated, Article 2 of the Statute is on its face, self-contained, save in relation to the definition of protected persons and things." (Decision at Trial, at paras. 49–51)

80.   With all due respect, the Trial Chamber's reasoning is based on a misconception of the grave breaches provisions and the extent of their incorporation into the Statute of the International Tribunal. The grave breaches system of the Geneva Conventions establishes a twofold system: there is on the one hand an enumeration of offences that are regarded so serious as to constitute "grave breaches", closely bound up with this enumeration a mandatory enforcement mechanism is set up, based on the concept of a duty and a right of all Contracting States to search for and try or extradite persons allegedly responsible for "grave breaches". The international armed conflict element generally attributed to the grave breaches provisions of the Geneva Conventions is merely a function of the system of universal mandatory jurisdiction that those provisions create. The international armed conflict requirement was a necessary limitation on the grave breaches system in light of the intrusion on State sovereignty that such mandatory universal jurisdiction represents. State parties to the 1949 Geneva Conventions did not want to give other States jurisdiction over serious violations of international humanitarian law committed in their internal armed conflicts—at least not the mandatory universal jurisdiction involved in the grave breaches system.

81.   The Trial Chamber is right in implying that the enforcement mechanism has of course not been imported into the Statute of the International Tribunal, for the obvious reason that the International Tribunal itself constitutes a mechanism for the prosecution and punishment of the perpetrators of "grave breaches". However, the Trial Chamber has misinterpreted the reference to the Geneva Conventions contained in the sentence of Article 2: "persons or property protected under the provisions of the relevant Geneva Conventions". (Statute of the Tribunal, art. 2.) For the reasons set out above, this reference is clearly intended to indicate that

the offences listed under Article 2 can only be prosecuted when perpetrated against persons of property regarded as "protected" by the Geneva Conventions under the strict conditions set out by the Conventions themselves. Clearly, these provisions of the Geneva Conventions apply to persons or objects protected only to the extent that they are caught up in an international armed conflict. By contrast, those provisions do not include persons or property coming within the purview of common Article 3 of the four Geneva Conventions.

82.   The above interpretation is borne out by what could be considered as part of the preparatory works of the Statute of the International Tribunal, namely the Report of the Secretary General. There, in introducing and explaining the meaning and purport of Article 2 and having regard to the "grave breaches" system of the Geneva Conventions, reference is made to "international armed conflicts" (Report of the Secretary–General at para. 37).

83.   We find that our interpretation of Article 2 is the only one warranted by the text of the Statute and the relevant provisions of the Geneva Conventions, as well as by a logical construction of their interplay as dictated by Article 2. However, we are aware that this conclusion may appear not to be consonant with recent trends of both State practice and the whole doctrine of human rights which, as pointed out below (see paras. 97–127), tend to blur in many respects the traditional dichotomy between international wars and civil strife. In this connection the Chamber notes with satisfaction the statement in the *amicus curiae* brief submitted by the Government of the United States, where it is contended that: "the 'grave breaches' provisions of Article 2 of the International Tribunal Statute apply to armed conflicts of a non-international character as well as those of an international character." (U.S. Amicus Curiae Brief, at 35.)

This statement, unsupported by any authority, does not seem to be warranted as to the interpretation of Article 2 of the Statute. Nevertheless, seen from another viewpoint, there is no gainsaying its significance: that statement articulates the legal views of one of the permanent members of the Security Council on a delicate legal issue; on this score it provides the first indication of a possible change in *opinio juris* of States. Were other States and international bodies to come to share this view, a change in customary law concerning the scope of the "grave breaches" system might gradually materialize. Other elements pointing in the same direction can be found in the provision of the German Military Manual mentioned below (para. 131), whereby grave breaches of international humanitarian law include some violations of common Article 3. In addition, attention can be drawn to the Agreement of 1 October 1992 entered into by the conflicting parties in Bosnia–Herzegovina. Articles 3 and 4 of this Agreement implicitly provide for the prosecution and punishment of those responsible for grave breaches of the Geneva Conventions and Additional Protocol I. As the Agreement was clearly concluded within a framework of an internal armed conflict (see above, para. 73), it may be taken as an important indication of the present trend to extend the grave breaches provisions to such category of conflicts. One can also mention a recent judgement by a Danish court. On 25 November 1994 the Third Chamber of the Eastern

Division of the Danish High Court delivered a judgement on a person accused of crimes committed together with a number of Croatian military police on 5 August 1993 in the Croatian prison camp of Dretelj in Bosnia (*The Prosecution v. Refik Saric, unpublished* (Den. H. Ct. 1994)). The Court explicitly acted on the basis of the "grave breaches" provisions of the Geneva Conventions, more specifically Articles 129 and 130 of Convention III and Articles 146 and 147 of Convention IV (*The Prosecution v. Refik Saric, Transcript at* 1 (25 Nov. 1994)), without however raising the preliminary question of whether the alleged offences had occurred within the framework of an international rather than an internal armed conflict (in the event the Court convicted the accused on the basis of those provisions and the relevant penal provisions of the Danish Penal Code. (see *id.* at 7–8)) This judgement indicates that some national courts are also taking the view that the "grave breaches" system may operate regardless of whether the armed conflict is international or internal.

84. Notwithstanding the foregoing, the Appeals Chamber must conclude that, in the present state of development of the law, Article 2 of the Statute only applies to offences committed within the context of international armed conflicts.

85. Before the Trial Chamber, the Prosecutor asserted an alternative argument whereby the provisions on grave breaches of the Geneva Conventions could be applied to internal conflicts on the strength of some agreements entered into by the conflicting parties. For the reasons stated below, in Section IV C (para. 144) [defendant has not been charged with a violation of such an agreement], we find it unnecessary to resolve this issue at this time. . . .

Li, J. (concurring in part)

7. Professor Meron states the customary international law of war crimes very correctly and clearly in the following terms: "Whether the conflicts in Yugoslavia are characterized as internal or international is critically important. The fourth Hague Convention of 1907, which codified the principal laws of war and served as the normative core for the post-World War II war crimes prosecutions, applies to international wars only. The other principal prong of the penal laws of war, the grave breaches provisions of the Geneva Conventions and Protocol I is also directed to international wars. Violations of common Article 3 of the Geneva Conventions, which concerns internal wars, do not constitute grave breaches giving rise to universal criminal jurisdiction. Were any part of the conflict deemed internal rather than international, the perpetrators of even the worst atrocities might try to challenge prosecutions for war crimes or grave breaches, but not for genocide or crimes against humanity". (Meron, *War Crimes in Yugoslavia and the Development of International Law*, 88 AJIL 78, 80 (1994).)

8. The Final Report of 27 May 1994 of the Commission of Experts established pursuant to Security Council resolution 780 (1992) takes the same view as Professor Meron: "If a conflict is classified as international, then the grave breaches of the Geneva Conventions, including Additional Protocol I, apply as well as violations of the laws and customs of war. The treaty and customary law applicable to international armed conflict is well-

established. The treaty law designed for internal armed conflict is in common [A]rticle 3 of the Geneva Conventions, additional Protocol II of 1977, and [A]rticle 19 of the 1954 Hague Convention for the Protection of Cultural property in the Event of Armed Conflict. These legal sources do not use the terms 'grave breaches' or 'war crimes'. Further, the content of customary law applicable to internal armed conflicts is debatable. As a result, in general, unless the parties to an internal armed conflict agree otherwise, the only offences committed in internal armed conflict for which universal jurisdiction exists are 'crimes against humanity' and genocide, which apply irrespective of the conflicts' classification." (S/1994/674, p. 13, para. 42.)

Notes & Questions. With the establishment of the ICTFY and ICTR systematic rape has been recognized as a war crime and crime against humanity. The 1949 Geneva Conventions and two Additional Protocols do not include rape as a grave breach subject to universal jurisdiction.[a] Neither did the IMT's Charter. With the two *Ad Hoc* Tribunals and the new International Criminal Court gender-related crimes have been squarely put as crimes subject to international condemnation and prosecution. Refer to the "Celebici,[b] the FOCA (or the Rape Camp Case), and *Akayesu*[c] cases below.

The Prosecutor v. Delalic, Mucic, Delic & Landzo (Celebici Trial)

(Trial Chamber, ICTFY) Summary of Judgment of November 16, 1998.[a]

[The actual judgment in this case is 500 pages long. The Tribunal, therefore read out a summary of its content which is reproduced below. This case is referred to as *the "Celebici" case* after the prison-camp in Bosnia and Herzegovina where the alleged crimes occurred. The camp housed Bosnian Serbs arrested by the Bosnian forces.]

In Section I, the Judgement contains a description of the charges in the Indictment, which are various counts of violations of Article 2 of the Statute—grave breaches of the Geneva Conventions—and Article 3 of the Statute—violations of the laws of customs of war—alleged to have been committed within the Celebici prison-camp in the Konjic municipality in central Bosnia and Herzegovina over a period of months in 1992.

The fourth accused, Esad Landzo, is thus pursuant to Article 7(1) of the Statute, with wilful killing and murder, torture and cruel treatment and wilfully causing great suffering of serious injury to body or health. The third accused, Hazim Delic, is similarly charged under Article 7(1) with wilful killing and murder, torture—including rape and cruel treatment, inhuman treatment, wilfully causing great suffering or serious injury to

a. Meron, *Rape as a Crime Under International Humanitarian Law* (1993) *A JIL.* 425.

b. *Prosecutor v. Delalic et al.*, Nov. 16, 1998 (ICTFY), summary in 38 ILM 57 (1999)

c. *The Prosecutor* v. *Jean-Paul Akayesu*, Sept. 2, 1998 (ICTR), summarized in) 37 ILM 14 (1998).

a. The full text of the judgment is available at the ICTFY website: w.w.w.un.org/icty.

body or health, the unlawful confinement of civilians, and plunder of private property. Hazim Delic is also charged pursuant to Article 7(3) of the Statute with responsibility as a superior for the crimes which occurred in the Celebici prison-camp at this time.

The second accused, Zdravko Mucic, is also charged pursuant to Article 7(3) with responsibility as a superior for the crimes alleged in the indictment, due to his position as commander of the Celebici prison-camp at the relevant time. Mr. Mucic is further charged as a direct participant in the unlawful confinement of civilians, the plunder of private property and the wilful causing of great suffering or serious injury to body or health and cruel treatment for the inhumane conditions which existed in the Celebici prison-camp. The first accused, Zejni Delalic, is charged pursuant to Article 7(3) with responsibility as a superior for the crimes alleged in the Indictment, due to his overall command over the Celebici prison-camp at the relevant time. Mr. Delalic is also charged as a direct participant in the unlawful confinement of civilians.

* * *

Most importantly, it is found that, in the period relevant to the indictment, a situation of armed conflict existed in Bosnia and Herzegovina, which incorporated the municipality of Konjic. In Konjic, this armed conflict involved the forces of the Bosnian government—the territorial defense forces and the Ministry of Interior forces (MUP), for a time acting jointly with the Croatian defense Council (HVO)—engaging the Bosnian Serb forces—initially the JNA and then the Bosnian Serb army (VRS), joined by local volunteers and militia. It is, furthermore, found that there is a clear nexus between the acts of the accused alleged in the Indictment and this armed conflict.

* * *

The Trial Chamber finds that the conflict in Bosnia and Herzegovina must be regarded as an international armed conflict throughout 1992. There can be no question that forces external to Bosnia and Herzegovina, particularly the forces of the Yugoslav People's Army (JNA), participated in hostilities in that State. In mid-May 1992, there was an attempt by the authorities of the Federal Republic of Yugoslavia (Serbia and Montenegro) to create the appearance that they were no longer involved in Bosnia and Herzegovina, by the division of the JNA into the Bosnian Serb army (VRS) and the Yugoslav army (VJ). The Trial Chamber finds, however, that this was a deliberate attempt to mask the continued involvement of the FRY, whose government remained the controlling force behind the Bosnian Serbs.

The Trial Chamber also finds that, at all relevant times, the persons detained in the Celebici prison-camp, being the victims of the crimes alleged in the Indictment, were persons protected by the Fourth Geneva Convention concerning civilian populations. In particular, it is the firm belief of the Trial Chamber that civilians caught up in an international armed conflict resulting from the dissolution of a State cannot be denied the full protection of the Fourth Geneva Convention solely on the basis of their citizenship status under domestic law.

[The judgment contains a detailed discussion of the concept of command responsibility under customary international law and as incorporated in Article 7(3). This is the first elucidation of the concept of command responsibility by an international judicial body since the cases decided in the wake of the Second World War. Most importantly, it is found that not only military commanders, but also civilians holding positions of authority, are encompassed by the doctrine. Furthermore, for the attribution of criminal responsibility, not only persons in de jure positions of superiority , but also those in such position de facto, may be held criminally responsible if they knew or had reason to know that offences had been or were about to be committed by their subordinates and failed to take the necessary and reasonable measures to prevent or punish such offences.

* * *

[With respect to Mr. Mucic the Tribunal found that as the commander of the prison camp, he was clearly derelict in this duty and allowed those under his authority to commit the most heinous of offences, without taking any disciplinary action. Furthermore, as commander of the Celebici prison-camp, he was the person with the primary responsibility for the conditions in which the prisoners were kept. As discussed in some depth in our written Judgement, the trial Chamber is appalled by the inadequacy of the food and water supplies, and medical and sleeping facilities that were provided for the detainees, as well as the atmosphere of terror which reigned in the Celebici prison-camp.

* * *

[Concerning Mr. Delic the Trial Chamber stated that it was] ... appalled by the details of Mr. Delic's criminal actions, as recounted by many victims and witnesses. He displayed a singular brutality in causing the deaths of two men detained in the Celebici prison-camp and a calculated cruelty in the torture and mistreatment of many others. He raped two defenseless women on several occasions, seeking to exert his power over them and instill absolute fear in them. the Trial Chamber considers the rape of any person to be a despicable act which strikes at the very core of human dignity and physical integrity. As well as showing no mercy to his chosen victims, he has displayed no remorse before this Trial Chamber.

Throughout Mr. Delic's tenure as deputy commander in the Celebici prison-camp he was instrumental in creating an atmosphere of terror by his actions and his threats to and humiliation of the detainees. It appears that he took a sadistic pleasure in causing the detainees pain and suffering, most clearly illustrated by his frequent use of a device to inflict electrical shocks. Mr. Delic abused his position of authority and trust as deputy commander and, although he has been found not to have command responsibility for the offences of others within the prison-camp by his actions he encouraged others among the camp guards to engage in their own forms of mistreatment of the detainees.

Once again, the Trial Chamber would emphasize that the breakdown of society and the mechanisms which ordinarily sanction crimes during times of armed conflict must not be used in avoidance of the responsibility on all individuals to conduct themselves appropriately and exercise moral choice.

Note & Questions. **1.** In the Trial Chamber decision in *The Prosecutor v. Furunzija*,[a] it was held that torture is specifically prohibited by treaty law, particularly article 3 common to the Geneva Convention 1949 and article 4 of Additional Protocol II. Further, in the *Nicaragua* case[b] the International Court of Justice confirmed that article 3 has the status of customary international law. The prohibition against torture imposes upon states an *erga omnes* obligation. Such prohibition is regarded as *jus cogens* with universal jurisdiction conferred on states.

2. In the *Furundzija case* rape as a war crime, crime against humanity or as an act of genocide was considered and the formulation of the crime in the *Akayesu* case, extracted below, was noted.

3. The U.N. Security Council on June 10, 1999 adopted Resolution 1244[c] on the situation relating to Kosovo. It authorized a NATO-led force to establish a safe environment for all people in Kosovo and facilitate the safe return to their homes of all displaced persons and refugees. It also authorized the Secretary–General to establish an international civil presence in Kosovo to provide an interim administration while establishing and overseeing the development of provisional democratic self-governing institutions. In particular, in the context of this Chapter the Security Council recalled the jurisdiction and mandate of the CTFY and demanded full cooperation with it by all concerned including the international security presence.

4. *Note that the ICTY has jurisdiction over any persons violating international humanitarian law in the territory of the FRY.* This would cover the NATO forces as well as the Serbian forces and the KLA. Concerning the NATO bombing campaign refer to the justification of humanitarian intervention in Chapter 17 on The Use of Force by States. The Chief Prosecutor took the position that there was no evidence to justifty the initiation of a prosecution. What principles of customary and conventional international law apply to the level and type of force used in such circumstances? Can "collateral damage" to civilians be justified where the main target was military? If so, when and how? See also the proceedings instituted by Yugoslavia before the International Court of Justice against a number of NATO countries accusing them of bombing Yugoslav territory in violation of international law, of using prohibited weapons and deliberately inflicting conditions of life calculated to cause the destruction of a national group: Case Concerning Legality of the Use of Force, General List 106. The ICJ handed down its decision denying Yugoslavia's request for provisional measures on June 2, 1999. The ICJ remains seized of the case.

a. Case No. IT–95–17/1–T, Dec. 10, 1998.

b. [1986] I.C.J. Rep. 14.

c. U.N. Doc. S/RES/1244 (1999).

The "Rape Camps Case"–The Foca Trial Judgement of Trial Chamber II The Kunarac, Kovac and Vukovic Case

(22 February 2001) JL/P.I.S./566*

[The actual judgment in this case was several hundred pages in length. We have included only the "Summary" of the Judgement of Trial Chamber II, read out by presiding Judge Florence Mumba at today's hearing. This Summary was produced by the Tribunal and it contains the necessary elements of the judgment for purposes of discussion and analysis.]

Dragoljub Kunaric, Sentenced to 28 years; Radomir Kovac, Sentenced to 20 years; Zoran Vukovic Sentenced to 12 Years Imprisonment.

Summary: First convictions by the ICTFY of rape as a crime against humanity Trial Chamber II found that rape was "used by members of the Bosnian Serb armed forces as an instrument of terror"

First convictions of enslavement as a crime against humanity Trial Chamber also states that "lawless opportunists should expect no mercy, no matter how low their position in the chain of command may be"

Today the Trial Chamber delivers its Judgement in the proceedings against the accused.

The full text will be distributed to the parties. I shall read out only a summary and the disposition.

The three accused, who are ethnic Serbs, have been charged by the Prosecution with violations of the laws or customs of war and with crimes against humanity–rape, torture, enslavement and outrages upon personal dignity.

They participated in a Serb campaign in the wider area of the municipality of Foca from early 1992 up to about mid–1993. The campaign was part of an armed conflict between the Serb and Muslim forces in the wider region of Foca, which existed at all times material to the indictments against the accused.

One purpose of the campaign was, among others, to cleanse the Foca area of Muslims; to that end the campaign was successful. Even the town's name was cleansed.

Foca was renamed Srbinje and now lies in the territory of the Republika Srpska. There are hardly any Muslims left in Srbinje today.

One target of that campaign, apart from the Muslim armed forces, were Muslim civilians. In the present case, especially Muslim women.

The method employed was mostly expulsion through terror.

On a general level, the terror expressed itself in the violent destruction of the religious symbols of the Muslims. All mosques in Foca were blown up and the ruins razed to the ground.

* From the ICTY website, The Hague.

Civilian Muslim men and women were rounded up in the villages surrounding Foca, and even as far as the neighbouring municipalities of Kalinovik and Gacko. The men were separated from the women and children.

The men often had to suffer long periods of detention in the Foca KP Dom prison. Detention without justification. Some were severely mistreated when they were captured. Some were killed on the spot, often in the presence or within earshot of their families.

The women and children from the Foca region were taken to collection points, such as Buk Bijela, a settlement south of Foca. From there, they were transferred by bus to Foca High School, where they were detained. Some of them were later taken to other places in and around Foca, such as Partizan Sports Hall, which was about a stone's throw away from the police station, and to private houses in Miljevina and Trnovace. There they would meet women and girls from the other two municipalities.

In the above-mentioned places, the terror took on another, very personal dimension.

Judgment. The trial against the three accused has sometimes been called the "rape camp case", an example of the systematic rape of women of another ethnicity being used as a "weapon of war".

It is to some extent misleading to say that systematic rape was employed as a "weapon of war". This could be understood to mean a kind of concerted approach or an order given to the Bosnian Serb armed forces to rape Muslim women as part of their combat activities in the wider meaning. There is no sufficient evidence for such a finding before the Trial Chamber.

What the evidence shows, is that the rapes were used by members of the Bosnian Serb armed forces as an instrument of terror. An instrument they were given free rein to apply whenever and against whomsoever they wished.

What the evidence shows, is that it was possible for the Serb forces to set up and maintain a detention centre for scores of Muslim women such as Partizan Sports Hall, next to the municipal police building in Foca, from which women and young girls were taken away on a regular basis to other locations to be raped. What the evidence shows, is that the authorities who were meant to protect the victims, such as the local police which had been taken over by the Serbs, turned a blind eye to their suffering. Instead, they helped guard the women, and even joined in their maltreatment when approached by them for help against their oppressors.

What the evidence shows, are Muslim women and girls, mothers and daughters together, robbed of the last vestiges of human dignity, women and girls treated like chattels, pieces of property at the arbitrary disposal of the Serb occupation forces, and more specifically, at the beck and call of the three accused.

What the sum of the evidence manifestly demonstrates, is the effect a criminal personality will have in times of war on helpless members of the civilian population: The actions of the three accused were part of a systematic attack against Muslim civilians. Some of their acts, in peace-time, could doubtlessly be characterized as organized crime. They knew of the military conflict in the Foca region, because they participated in it as soldiers in different units. They knew that one of the main purposes of that campaign was to drive the Muslims out of the region. They knew that one way to achieve this was to terrorize the Muslim civilian population in a manner that would make it impossible for them ever to return.

They also knew of the general pattern of crimes, especially of detaining women and girls in different locations where they would be raped. The actions of all three accused, as will be described below, show beyond any doubt their knowledge of the detention centres, and of the practice of systematically transferring the women and girls to locations where they would be abused by Serb men.

The three accused were not just following orders, if there were such orders, to rape Muslim women. The evidence shows free will on their part. Of the women and girls so detained, one was a child of only 12 years at the time. She has not been heard of since she was sold by one of the accused. The women and girls were either lent or "rented out" to other soldiers for the sole purpose of being ravaged and abused. Some of the women and girls were kept in servitude for months on end.

The three accused are not ordinary soldiers, whose morals were merely loosened by the hardships of war. These are men with no known criminal past. However, they thrived in the dark atmosphere of the dehumanization of those believed to be enemies, when one would not even ask, in the words of Eleanor Roosevelt, "Where, after all, do universal human rights begin? In small places, close to home..."

The three accused are certainly not in the category of the political or military masterminds behind the conflicts and atrocities. However, the Trial Chamber wishes to make it perfectly clear that, although in these cases before this Tribunal it is generally desirable to prosecute and try those in the higher echelons of power, the Trial Chamber will not accept low rank or a subordinate function as an escape from criminal prosecution.

Political leaders and war generals are powerless if the ordinary people refuse to carry out criminal activities in the course of war. Lawless opportunists should expect no mercy, no matter how low their position in the chain of command may be. Indeed, it is opportune to state that, in time of peace as much as in time of war, men of substance do not abuse women. The Trial Chamber will now set out its verdict with regard to each accused.

Would the Accused Dragoljub Kunarac Please Stand:

Dragoljub Kunarac, under Counts 1 to 4 you were charged with rape and torture, both as a violation of the laws or customs of war and as a crime against humanity. The Trial Chamber does not accept your defence of alibi with respect to any of these charges, and that applies equally for all other counts that you were charged with in the indictment. As to the charge that you took Witness FWS–87 to the house at Ulica Osmana Dikica no. 16 at least twice between 13 July and 1 August 1992, where she was allegedly raped by the other soldiers, the Trial Chamber finds that the allegations have not been established beyond reasonable doubt.

As to the charge that on or around 16 July 1992, you took Witnesses FWS–75 and D.B. to Ulica Osmana Dikica no. 16, where they were raped by several soldiers, where you personally raped D.B. and aided and abetted the gang-rape of Witness FWS–75 by several soldiers, the Trial Chamber finds that these charges have been proved beyond reasonable doubt.

As to the charge that on 2 August 1992, you took Witnesses FWS–87, FWS–75, FWS–50 and D.B. to Ulica Osmana Dikica no. 16, and that you, Dragoljub Kunarac, personally raped Witness FWS–87 and aided and abetted the rape of Witnesses FWS–87, FWS–75 and FWS–50 at the hands of other soldiers, the Trial Chamber finds that these charges have been proved beyond reasonable doubt.

As to the charge that at least twice between 13 July and 2 August 1992 you took Witness FWS–95 from Partizan Sports Hall to Ulica Osmana Dikica no. 16, where she was allegedly once raped by you and by three other soldiers, and that the second time she was raped by three soldiers, but not by you, the Trial Chamber finds that it has been proved beyond reasonable doubt that you personally raped Witness FWS–95 on one occasion, but it has not been established that Witness FWS–95 was raped by other soldiers during the two incidents mentioned above.

According to the test set out by the Trial Chamber in its Judgement with respect to cumulative convictions for the same conduct, namely that such convictions are permissible when each offence charged contains at least one distinct element not contained in the other, your conduct can be punished as both rape and torture, both under Article 3 of the Statute as a violation of the laws or customs of war and under Article 5 of the Statute as a crime against humanity. This legal principle applies equally in the indictments against the three accused.

The Trial Chamber therefore finds you GUILTY, under Count 1 of torture as a crime against humanity, under Count 2 of rape as a crime against humanity, under Count 3 of torture as a violation of the laws or customs of war and under Count 4 of rape as a violation of the laws or customs of war.

Under Counts 5 to 8 you were charged with torture and rape, both as a violation of the laws or customs of war and as a crime against humanity. On the evidence before it, the Trial Chamber finds that the charges have not been proved beyond reasonable doubt. The Trial Chamber therefore finds you NOT GUILTY under Counts 5, 6, 7 and 8. Under Counts 9 and 10 you were charged with rape as a violation of the laws or customs of war and as a crime against humanity. As to the charge that sometime in September or October 1992, you went to a place called "Karaman's house" in Miljevina, took Witness FWS–87 to the upper floor and raped her, the Trial Chamber finds that the charges have been proved beyond reasonable doubt. The Trial Chamber therefore finds you GUILTY under Count 9 of rape as a crime against humanity and under Count 10 as a violation of the laws or customs of war. Under Counts 11 and 12 you were charged with torture and rape as a violation of the laws or customs of war.

The Trial Chamber finds that these charges have been fully established. One evening in mid-July 1992, you and two other soldiers took Witness FWS–183 from her home to the banks of the Cehotina River in Foca, where the three of you raped her. You personally raped Witness FWS–183 and aided and abetted her rape by the two other soldiers by encouraging the other men while they were raping her. You further mocked the victim by telling the other soldiers to wait for their turn while you were raping her, by laughing at her while she was raped by the other soldiers, and finally by saying that she would carry Serb babies and that she would not know the father. Accordingly, the Trial Chamber finds you GUILTY under Count 11 of torture as a violation of the laws or customs of war and under Count 12 of rape as a violation of the laws or customs of war. Under Counts 18 to 21 you are charged with enslavement and outrages upon personal dignity as crimes against humanity, and with rape both as a violation of the laws or customs of war and as a crime against humanity. The Trial Chamber finds that on the evidence before it the facts underlying these charges have partly been proved beyond reasonable doubt.

The Trial Chamber finds that you, Dragoljub Kunarac, on 2 August 1992, personally raped Witness FWS–191 in the house in Trnovace and, by taking the girls to the house, aided and abetted the rape of Witness FWS–186 at the hands of the soldier with the pseudonym DP6. However, the Trial Chamber is not satisfied that J.G., whom you had also brought to the house, was raped by the soldier with the nickname "Gaga" on that night.

Furthermore, the Trial Chamber finds that from 2 August 1992 onwards, you, Dragoljub Kunarac, raped Witness FWS–191 whenever you visited the house in Trnovace, while DP6 raped Witness FWS–186 during that period. It has, however, not been established that you aided and abetted the rape of Witness FWS–186 by DP6 during the same period as it has not been shown, apart from the incident when you brought the women to the house, that you were present while DP6 raped Witness FWS–186 or supported him in any other way. It has not been shown that your presence or actions assisted or provided encouragement to DP6 in raping Witness FWS–186. The loose connection between the events at the house and your sporadic presence there would stretch the concept of aiding and abetting with respect to the actual rapes beyond its limits, while it is still close enough for the count of enslavement. The Trial Chamber also finds that Witnesses FWS–186 and FWS–191 were kept for several months in the house in Trnovace, where they where treated as private property by both you and DP6. The Trial Chamber considers the following elements to be of particular relevance for the crime of enslavement: The fact that the girls were detained; (ii) the fact that they had to do everything they were ordered to do, including the cooking and household chores; (iii) the fact that you asserted exclusivity over Witness FWS–191 by reserving her for yourself; (iv) that they were at the constant disposal of you and DP6; (v) other degrading treatment such as offering one soldier the permission to rape her for DM 100 in the presence of Witness FWS–191; and (vi) that they were effectively denied any control about their lives.

The Trial Chamber is of the view that you and DP6 acted in combination and aided and abetted each other regarding the enslavement of these women. The Trial Chamber is, however, of the view that the evidence is not sufficient to support the charge of outrages upon personal dignity in relation to both Witnesses FWS–186 and FWS–191.

The Trial Chamber therefore finds you GUILTY under Count 18 of enslavement as a crime against humanity, under Count 19 of rape as a crime against humanity, under Count 20 of rape as a violation of the laws or customs of war, but NOT GUILTY under Count 21 of outrages upon personal dignity as a violation of the laws or customs of war.

By the totality of these acts you have shown the most glaring disrespect for the women's dignity and their fundamental human right to sexual self-determination, on a scale that far surpasses even what one might call, for want of a better expression, the "average seriousness of rapes during wartime". You abused and ravaged Muslim women because of their ethnicity, and from among their number, you picked whomsoever you fancied on a given occasion. You were a soldier with courage in the field, somebody whom your men undisputedly are said to have held in high esteem. By this natural authority you could easily have put an end to the women's suffering. Your active participation in this nightmarish scheme of sexual exploitation is therefore even more repugnant.

You not only mistreated women and girls yourself, but you also organized their transfer to other places, where, as you were fully aware, they would be raped and abused by other soldiers. This behaviour calls for a severe penalty commensurate with the gravity of your crimes. The Trial Chamber therefore sentences you, Dragoljub Kunarac, to a single sentence of 28 years imprisonment. The sentence shall run from today. The time you have spent in custody shall be credited towards the sentence. You may sit down.

Would the Accused Radomir Kovac Please Stand:

Radomir Kovac, under Counts 22 to 25 you are charged with enslavement and rape as crimes against humanity, and rape and outrages upon personal dignity as violations of the laws or customs of war. On the basis of the evidence received, the Trial Chamber finds that the charges against you have been proved beyond reasonable doubt as follows: On or about 31 October 1992, four girls, Witnesses FWS–87, FWS–75, A.B. and A.S. were transferred to your apartment in the Lepa Brena Building in Foca. Witnesses FWS–75 and A.B. were kept for about a week in the apartment during which time you treated them as your personal property and frequently sexually assaulted them.

They had to do household chores. The hygienic conditions for all the girls were appalling, and they often had to go hungry, because they did not receive sufficient food from you. On one occasion you raped Witnesses FWS–75 and FWS–87 at the same time whilst playing music on your stereo. During their time in your apartment, Witnesses FWS–75 and A.B. were raped by you personally and by other soldiers. In one instance, Witness FWS–75 refused to go with a soldier named Slavo Ivanovic, whom you had brought to the apartment. As a result, you slapped her and sent 12–year-old A.B. in her place. After about a week, you handed the two girls over to other Serb soldiers who continued to rape them. You then visited the house in which they were kept for about two weeks and there pretended to feel sorry for them. They were subsequently handed to yet another group of soldiers who continued to rape them and eventually brought them back to you. The next day, you sold A.B. and handed Witness FWS–75 over to the soldier with the pseudonym DP1. You thus personally raped Witnesses FWS–75 and A.B. and aided and abetted their rape by other soldiers by allowing these soldiers to visit your apartment and to rape the girls, or by encouraging them to do so and by handing over the girls to other men in the knowledge that they would rape them. While they were kept in your apartment, Witnesses FWS–87 and A.S. were constantly raped by you and Jagos Kostic. You personally raped Witness FWS–87, while Jagos Kostic raped Witness A.S., and sometimes also Witness FWS–87, whom you had "reserved" for yourself, without your knowledge. The Trial Chamber therefore notes that it has not been established beyond reasonable doubt that you aided and abetted the rape of Witness FWS–87 by Jagos Kostic, as the evidence indicates that this fact was hidden from you. On an unknown date between about 31 October 1992 and about 7 November 1992, you forced Witnesses FWS–87, A.S. and A.B. to dance naked on a table whilst watching them. However, it has not been established beyond reasonable doubt that Witness FWS–75 was also present on that occasion. Finally, on or about 25 February 1993, you sold both Witnesses FWS–87 and A.S. for 500 DM each to some Montenegrin soldiers. Concerning the count of enslavement with respect to Witnesses FWS–87, FWS–75, A.S. and A.B. the Trial Chamber found the following elements to be of particular relevance: (i) the girls were physically and psychologically detained, because even if they had managed to flee from the apartment, they would have had nowhere to go; (ii) that you sold Witnesses FWS–87, A.S. and A.B.; (iii) that you handed Witnesses FWS–75, A.B. to other soldiers; (iv) the mistreatment, such as beating and slapping; (v) your claim of exclusivity over Witness FWS–87; (vi) the poor living conditions, and the lack of food; (vii) the fact that they had to obey every order and do whatever they were told to do, including the cooking and household chores.

Regarding the count of outrages upon personal dignity against Witnesses FWS–87, FWS–75, A.S. and A.B., the Trial Chamber found the following elements to be of particular relevance:

(i) that you forced the girls to dance naked on a table;

(ii) beating and slapping them;

(iii) the fact that the girls were "loaned" and sold to other men;

(iv) the fact that Witnesses FWS–75 and FWS–87 were once raped by you at the same time while you played music on your stereo.

At all times you were aware that the girls were of Muslim ethnicity, and this was one of the main reasons why you mistreated and abused them.

THE TRIAL CHAMBER ACCORDINGLY FINDS YOU, RADOMIR KOVAC, GUILTY, under Count 22 of enslavement as a crime against humanity, under Count 23 of rape as a crime against humanity, under Count 24 of rape as a violation of the laws or customs of war, and under Count 25 of outrages upon personal dignity as a violation of the laws or customs of war.

Although you have not been convicted of as many counts as the accused Dragoljub Kunarac, the Trial Chamber finds that your guilt is almost as great as his.

Particularly appalling and deplorable is your treatment of 12–year-old A.B., a helpless little child for whom you showed absolutely no compassion whatsoever, but whom you abused sexually in the same way as the other girls. You finally sold her like an object, in the knowledge that this would almost certainly mean further sexual assaults by other men.

You knew that any chance of her being re-united with her mother, whose immense grief the Trial Chamber had to countenance in the hearing, would thus become even more remote than it already was. At the time of trial, some 8 years later, the child had never been seen or heard of again. The treatment of A.B. is the most striking example of your morally depraved and corrupt character.

But what you did to the other girls is no less severe. You kept them as your and Jagos Kostic's slaves, to be used whenever the desire took you, to be given to whomsoever you wished to show a favour. You relished in the absolute power you exerted over their lives, which you made abundantly clear by making them dance naked on a table while you watched. When they had served their purpose, you sold them, too. Your conduct merits serious punishment. The Trial Chamber therefore sentences you, Radomir Kovac, to a single sentence of 20 years imprisonment. The sentence shall run from today. The time you have spent in custody shall be credited towards the sentence. You may sit down.

Would the Accused Zoran Vukovic Please Stand:

Zoran Vukovic, under Counts 21 to 24 you were charged with torture and rape, both as a crime against humanity and as a violation of the laws or customs of war. On the evidence before it, the Trial Chamber finds that none of the allegations underlying these counts have been proved beyond reasonable doubt.

The Trial Chamber therefore finds you NOT GUILTY under Counts 21, 22, 23 and 24.

Under Counts 33 to 36 you were charged with torture and rape, both as a crime against humanity and as a violation of the laws or customs of war. On the evidence before it, the Trial Chamber finds that only one of the incidents underlying those charges has been proved beyond reasonable doubt, namely that on or around 14 July 1992 you personally raped Witness FWS–50. You and another soldier took her out of Partizan after you had threatened her mother that you would kill her if she did not tell you where her daughter was hiding. Her mother then went to find her. You took her to another house where you raped her. She was 15 years old at the time, which you knew, because you told her that had she not been the same age as your daughter–who was about 15 years at the time–you would have done much worse things to her.

The Trial Chamber does not accept the evidence that you were unable to have sexual intercourse because of an injury to the scrotum, which you allegedly suffered.

THE TRIAL CHAMBER THEREFORE FINDS YOU, ZORAN VUKOVIC, **GUILTY** under Count 33 of torture as a crime against humanity, under Count 34 of rape as a crime against humanity, under Count 35 of torture as a violation of the laws or customs of war, and under Count 36 of rape as a violation of the laws or customs of war.

The prosecution evidence in your case has not sustained most counts in the indictment against you, and as a consequence, your sentence must be lighter than for the other two accused.

However, the Trial Chamber regards it as a serious matter that you showed a total lack of remorse and moral stature by talking about your own daughter after having raped Witness FWS–50, who was in addition only 15 years old at the time, and mocked her in her grief by saying that you could have treated her much worse still. Your actions call for serious punishment. The Trial Chamber therefore sentences you, Zoran Vukovic, to a single sentence of 12 years imprisonment. The sentence shall run from today. The time you have spent in custody shall be credited towards the sentence. You may sit down.

————

THE AD HOC TRIBUNAL FOR RWANDA

In April of 1994, the Presidents of Burundi and Rwanda were killed when their aircraft was downed. Immediately, a campaign of widespread killing began with the aim of annihilating the Tutsi population of Rwanda. The Security Council gravely concerned by the reports of genocide and other widespread and systematic violations of international humanitarian law determined that the situation constituted a threat to international peace and security. Acting under Chapter VII of the Charter, on Nov. 8, 1994, it again created an *Ad Hoc* Tribunal, reproduced in part below. It should be noted that at that time the new Government of Rwanda was a non-permanent member of the Security Council and itself requested such action.

————

U.N.S.C. Res. 955, November 8, 1994
The Security Council

* * *

1. Decides hereby, having received the request of the Government of Rwanda (S/1994/1115), to establish an international tribunal for the sole purpose of prosecuting persons responsible for genocide and other serious violations of international humanitarian law committed in the territory of Rwanda and Rwandan citizens responsible for genocide and other such violations committed in the territory of neighbouring States, between 1

January 1994 and 31 December 1994 and to this end to adopt the Statute of the International Criminal tribunal for Rwanda annexed hereto.

2.   Decides that all States shall cooperate fully with the International Tribunal and its organs in accordance with the present resolution and the Statute of the International Tribunal and that consequently all States shall take any measures necessary under their domestic law to implement the provisions of the present resolution and the Statute, including the obligation of States to comply with requests for assistance or orders issued by a Trial Chamber under Article 28 of the Statute, and requests States to keep the Secretary–General informed of such measures.

Notes & Questions. **1.** As with the establishment of the ICTY the Security Council appended to the resolution the Statute of the Tribunal. On account of the fact that the conflict in Rwanda was basically internal the subject-matter jurisdiction, however, differs from the ICTY. It is restricted to genocide, crimes against humanity and violations of article 3 common to the Geneva Conventions 1949 and of article 4 of Additional Protocol II. The temporal jurisdiction of the Tribunal is limited to 1994 and is not open ended as is the ICTFY. Much of the rest of the Statute, however, parallels the ICTY. Both Tribunals share the same Chief Prosecutor and Appeals Chamber. The seat of the ICTR is in Arusha.

2.   *Rwanda, in fact, voted against resolution 955.* The Rwandan Government disagreed with some aspects of the Statute, including the lack of the death penalty which Rwanda retains domestically.

3.   *In 1999, Elizaphan Ntakirutimana was extradited* to the Arusha Tribunal from the United States, despite the lack of an extradition treaty. Until 1996, no extradition from the U.S. was allowed without a treaty. In 1996, however, the extradition law was amended to allow surrender of fugitives to the Ad Hoc Tribunals for the former Yugoslavia and Rwanda.[a] Today, the law reads: "[t]he provisions of this chapter relating to the surrender of persons who have committed crimes in foreign countries shall continue in force only during the existence of any treaty of extradition with such governments."[b] This extradition decision is found in Ch. 3, *supra*. It may be worthwhile reviewing at this point. *See, Ntakirutimana v. Reno*, 184 F.3d 419 (5th Cir.1999) (reversing District Court that had refused extradition of Rwandan *génocidaire*).

----

a. Id. Recently, the U.S. Congress promulgated the Judicial assistance to the International Tribunal for Yugoslavia and to the International Tribunal for Rwanda, Pub.L. 104–106, Div.A., Title XIII, § 1342, Feb. 10, 1996, 110 Stat. 486, provided that: "... [18 U.S.C. § 3181, et seq.], relating to the extradition of persons to a foreign country pursuant to a treaty or convention for extradition ..., shall apply in the same manner and extent to the surrender of persons, including United States citizens, to–(A) [the ICTY]; and (B) [the ICTR]...." *See, Surrender of Ntaki-rutimana*, 988 F.Supp. 1038 (S.D.Tex.1997) (holding this to be unconstitutional); *reversed in*, *Ntakirutimana v. Reno*, 184 F.3d 419 (5th Cir.1999). Also, 18 U.S.C. 3181(b), allows the Attorney General of the U.S. to surrender non-U.S. nationals without a treaty (by way of comity), persons who have committed crimes of violence against U.S. nationals in foreign countries.

b. 18 U.S.C. § 3181, et seq. *See, U.S. v. Herbage*, 850 F.2d 1463, 1465 (11th Cir. 1988); *see discussion, infra*; Blakesley, TERRORISM, DRUGS, *supra* at 224–250.

SUMMARY OF THE JUDGEMENT IN JEAN–PAUL AKAYESU CASE ICTR–96–4–T,
http:/www.un.org/ictr/english/Akayesu/judgment/akay001.htm
Delivered on 2 September 1998

[The actual judgment is nearly 300 pages long. The Trial Chamber, therefore, delivered a summary which is extracted below. The accused was elected *bourgmestre* of Taba commune in 1993 and held that position until June 1994. The *bourgmestre* in Rwanda traditionally has had extensive powers, as the Tribunal noted. He was indicted with 15 counts relating to genocide, crimes against humanity and violations of article 3 common to the Geneva Conventions 1949 and Additional Protocol II of 1977. These Documents are in the Documentary Supplement. Acayesu's specific offenses included murder, torture, rape in addition to the genocide, crimes against humanity, and public incitement to commit genocide.]

. . .

19.   Based on the evidence submitted to the Chamber, it is clear that the massacres which occurred in Rwanda in 1994 had a specific objective, namely the extermination of the Tutsi, who were targeted especially because of their Tutsi origin and not because they were RPF fighters. In any case, the Tutsi children and pregnant women would, naturally, not have been among the fighters. The Chamber concludes that, alongside the conflict between the RAF and RPF, genocide was committed in Rwanda ain 1994 against the Tutsi as a group. The execution of this genocide was probably facilitated by the conflict in the sense that the conflict with the RPF forces served as a pretext for the propaganda inciting genocide against the Tutsi by branding RPF fighters and Tutsi civilians together through the notion widely disseminated, particularly by *Radio Television Libre des Mille Collines (RTLM)*, to the effect that every Tutsi was allegedly an accomplice of the RPF soldiers or "Inkotanyi". However, the fact that the genocide occurred while the RAF were in conflict with the RPF, obviously, cannot serve as a mitigating circumstance for the genocide.

20.   Consequently, the Chamber concludes from all the foregoing that it was, indeed, genocide that was committed in Rwanda in 1994, against the Tutsi as a group. The Chamber is of the opinion that the genocide appears to have been meticulously organized. . . .

21.   The Chamber holds that the genocide was organized and planned not only by members of the RAF, but also by the political forces who were behind the "Hutu-power", that it was executed essentially by civilians including the armed militia and even ordinary citizens, and above all that the majority of the Tutsi victims were non-combatants, including thousands of women and children.

22.   Having said that, the Chamber then recalled that the fact that genocide was, indeed, committed in Rwanda in 1994, and more particularly in Taba, cannot influence it in its findings in the present matter. It is the Chamber's responsibility alone to assess the individual criminal responsibility of the Accused, Jean–Paul Akayesu, for the crimes alleged against him, including genocide, for which the Prosecution has to show proof. Despite the indisputable atrociousness of the crimes and the emotions evoked in the

international community, the judges have examined the facts adduced in a most dispassionate manner, bearing in mind that the accused is presumed innocent.

. . .

26. The Chamber finds that . . . it has been established that throughout the period covered in the Indictment, Akayesu in his capacity as *bourgmestre,* was responsible for maintaining law and public order in the commune of Taba and that he had effective authority over the communal police. Moreover, as "leader" of Taba commune, of which he was one of the most prominent figures, the inhabitants respected him and followed his orders. Akayesu himself admitted before the Chamber that he had the power to assemble the population and that they obeyed his instructions. It has also been proven that a very large number of Tutsi were killed in Taba between 7 April and the end of June 1994 while Akayesu was *bourgmestre* of the Commune. Knowing of such killings, he oppose them and attempted to prevent them only until 18 April 1994, date after which he not only stopped trying to maintain law and order in his commune, but was also present during the acts of violence and killings and sometimes even gave order himself for bodily or mental harm to be caused to certain Tutsi and endorsed and even ordered the killing of several Tutsi.

27. . . . [T]he Prosecutor has shown beyond a reasonable doubt that between 7 April and the end of June 1994, numerous Tutsi who sought refuge at the Taba Bureau communal were frequently beaten by members of the *Interahamwe* on or near the premises of the Bureau communal. Some of them were killed. Numerous Tutsi women were forced to endure acts of sexual violence, mutilations and rape, often repeatedly, often publicly and often by more than one assailant. Tutsi women were systematically raped, as one female victim testified to by saying that "each time that you met assailants, they raped you". Numerous incidents of such rape and sexual violence against Tutsi women occurred inside or near the *Bureau communal*. It has been proven that some communal policemen armed with guns and the accused himself were present while some of these rapes and sexual violence were being committed . . .

29. As regards the facts alleged in paragraphs 14 and 15 of the Indictment, it is established that in the early hours of 19 April 1994, Akayesu joined a gathering in Gishyeshye and took this opportunity to address the public; he led the meeting and conducted the proceedings. He then called on the population to unite in order to eliminate what he referred to as the sole enemy, the accomplices of the Inkotanyi and the population understood that he was thus urging them to kill the Tutsi. . . . The statements thus made by Akayesu at that gathering immediately led to widespread killings of Tutsi in Taba.

30. With respect to the allegations in paragraph 16 of the Indictment, it is also established that on 19 April 1994, Akayesu on two occasions threatened to kill victim U, a Tutsi woman, while she was being interrogated. He detained her for several hours at the Bureau communal before allowing her to leave. In the evening of 20 April 1994, during a search conducted in the home of victim V, a Hutu man, Akayesu directly threat-

ened to kill the latter. Victim V was thereafter beaten . . . in the presence of the accused . . .

. . . [I]t is established that on or about 19 April 1994, Akayesu and a group of men under his control were looking for Ephrem Karangwa and destroyed his house and that of his mother. They then went to search the house of Ephrem Karangwa's brother-in-law in Musambira commune and found his three brothers there. when the three brothers, namely Simon Mutijima, Thaddee Uwanyiligira and Jean–Chrysostome Gakuba, tried to escape, Akayesu ordered that they be captured and ordered that they be killed and participated in their killing.

41. On the crime of genocide, the Chamber recalls that the definition given by Article 2 of the Statute is echoed exactly by the Convention for the Prevention and Repression of the Crime of Genocide. The Chamber notes that Rwanda acceded by legislative decree to the Convention on genocide on 12 February 1975. Thus, punishment of the crime of genocide did exist in Rwanda in 1994 at the time of the acts alleged in the Indictment, and the perpetrator was liable to be brought before the competent courts of Rwanda to answer for this crime.

42. Contrary to popular belief, the crime of genocide does not imply the actual extermination of a group in its entirety, but is understood as such once any one of the acts mentioned in Article 2 of the Statute is committed with the specific intent to destroy "in whole or in part" a national, ethnical, racial or religious group. Genocide is distinct from other crimes inasmuch as it embodies a special intent or *dolus specialis*. Special intent of a crime is the specific intention, required as a constitutive element of the crime, which requires that the perpetrator clearly seek to produce the act charged. The special intent in the crime of genocide lies in "the intent to destroy, in whole or in part, a national, ethnical, racial or religious group, as such".

43. Specifically, for any of the acts charged under Article 2(2) of the Statute to be a constitutive element of genocide, the act must have been committed against one or several individuals because such individual or individuals were members of a specific group and specifically because they belonged to this group. thus, the victim is chosen not because of his individual identity, but rather on account of his being a member of a national, ethnical, racial or religious group. The victim of the act is therefore a member of group, targeted as such; hence, the victim of the crime of genocide is the group itself and not the individual alone.

44. On the issue of determining the offender's specific intent, the Chamber considers that intent is a mental factor which is difficult, even impossible, to determine. this is the reason why, in the absence of a confession from the accused, his intent can be inferred from a certain number of presumptions of fact. The Chamber considers that it is possible to deduce the genocidal intent inherent in a particular act charged form the general context of the perpetration of other culpable acts systematically directed against that same group, whether these acts were committed by the same offender or by others. Other factors such as the scale of atrocities committed their general nature, in a region or a country, or furthermore, the fact of deliberately and systematically targeting victims on account of

their membership of a particular group, while excluding the members of other groups, can enable the Chamber to infer the genocidal intent of a particular act.

45.   Apart from the crime of genocide, Jean–Paul Akayesu is charged with complicity in genocide and direct and public incitement to commit genocide. . . .

. . .

48.   The second crime which comes within the jurisdiction of the Tribunal and of which Jean–Paul Akayesu is charged is that of crimes against humanity. On the law applicable to this crime, the Chamber reviewed the case law on this crime from the judgements rendered by the Nuremberg and Tokyo Tribunals to more recent cases, including the Touvier and Papon cases in France notably and the Eichmann trial in Israel. It indicated the circumstances under which the charge of crimes against humanity would be leveled, as provide for by Article 3 of the Statute, under which the act must be committed as part of a widespread or systematic attack directed against a civilian population on discriminatory grounds.

49.   The third crime on which the Chamber rendered its conclusions is that for which it has competence pursuant to article 4 of the Statute, which provides that the Tribunal is empowered to prosecute persons committing or ordering to be committed serious violations of Article 3 common to the Geneva Conventions of 12 August 1949 for the protection of war Victims and of the Additional Protocol II thereto of June 8 1977. The said Article 3 common to the Geneva Conventions extends a minimum threshold of humanitarian protection as well to all persons affected by a non-international conflict, a protection which was further developed and enhanced in the 1977 Additional Protocol II. The Chamber decided to analyze separately the respective conditions of applicability of Article 3 common to the Geneva Conventions and the Additional Protocol II thereto. It then analyzed the conflict which took place in Rwanda in 1994 in the light of those conditions and conclude that each of the two legal instruments was applicable in this case. Furthermore, the Chamber is of the opinion that all the norms set forth under article 4 of its Statute constitute a part of customary International Law. It finally recalled that the violation of the norms defined in article 4 of the Statute, may, in principle, commit criminal responsibility of civilians and that the Accused belongs to the category of individuals who could be held responsible for serious infringement of international humanitarian law, particularly for serious violations of article 3 common to the Geneva Conventions and the Additional Protocol II thereto.

In light of all the evidence before it, the Chamber is satisfied that the acts of rape and sexual violence described above, were committed solely against Tutsi women, many of whom were subjected to the worst public humiliation, mutilated and raped several times, often in public in the Bureau Communal premises or in other public places, and often by more than one assailant. These rapes resulted in physical and psychological destruction of Tutsi women, their families and their communities. Sexual violence was an integral part of the process of destruction, specifically targeting Tutsi women and specifically contributing to their destruction and to the destruction of the Tutsi group as a whole.

. . .

53. On the basis of the substantial testimonies brought before it, the Chamber finds that in most cases, the rapes of Tutsi women in Taba were accompanied with the intent to kill those women. Many rapes were perpetrated near mass graves where the women were taken to be killed. A victim testified that Tutsi women caught could be taken away by peasants and men with promise that they would be collected later to be executed. Following an act of gang rape, a witness heard Akayesu say "tomorrow they will be killed" and they were actually killed. In this respect, it appears clearly to the Chamber that the acts of rape and sexual violence, as other acts of serious bodily and mental harm committed against the Tutsi reflected the determination to make Tutsi women suffer and to mutilate them even before killing the, the intent being to destroy the Tutsi group while inflicting acute suffering on its members in the process.

54. The Chamber has already established that genocide was committed against the Tutsi group in Rwanda in 1994, throughout the period covering the events alleged in the Indictment. Owing to the very high number o atrocities committed against the Tutsi, their widespread nature not only in the commune of Taba, but also throughout Rwanda, and to the fact that the victims were systematically and deliberately selected because they belonged to the Tutsi group, with persons belonging to other groups being excluded, the Chamber is also able to infer beyond reasonable doubt the genocidal intent of the accused in the commission of the above-mentioned crimes to the extent that the actions and words of Akayesu during the period of the facts alleged in the Indictment the Chamber is convinced beyond reasonable doubt, on the basis of evidence adduced before it during the hearing, that he repeatedly made statements more or less explicitly calling for the commission of genocide. yet, according to the Chamber, he who incites another to commit genocide must have the specific intent to commit genocide that of destroying in whole or in part, a national, ethnical, racial, or religious group, as such.

55. In conclusion, regarding Count One on genocide, the Chamber is satisfied beyond reasonable doubt that these various acts were committed by Akayesu with the specific intent to destroy the Tutsi group, as such.

. . .

Furthermore, the Chamber is satisfied beyond reasonable doubt that in committing the various acts alleged, Akayesu had the specific intent of destroying the Tutsi group as such.

. . .

57. Count 3 of the Indictment on crimes against humanity, extermination, the Chamber concludes that the murder of the eight refugees described in paragraph 19 of the Indictment as well as the killing of Simon Mutijima, Thaddee Uwanyliligra and Jean Chrysostome Gakuba, Samuel,

Tharcisse, Theogene, Phoebe Uwineze and her fiancé facts described during a widespread and systematic attack against a civilian population on ethnic grounds and, as such, constitutes a crime against humanity for which Akayesu is individually criminally responsible.

58. Regarding Count Four, on the basis of the facts described in paragraphs 14 and 15 of the Indictment and which it believes are well founded, the Chamber is satisfied beyond reasonable doubt that by the speeches made in public, Akayesu had the intent to directly crate a particular state of mind in his audience necessary to lead to the destruction of the Tutsi group as such. Accordingly, the Chamber finds that the said acts constitute the crime of direct and public incitement to commit genocide. In addition, the Chamber finds that the direct and public incitement to commit genocide engaged in by Akayesu, was indeed successful and did lead to the destruction of a great number of Tutsi in the commune of Taba.

. . .

64. With respect to Counts 6, 8, 10, 12 and 15, Akayesu is charged with violations of Common Article 3 of the Geneva Conventions of 1949 in counts 6, 8, 10 and 12 and with violations of Common Article 3 of the Geneva Conventions and of Additional Protocol II thereto of 1977 under count 15. The Chamber finds that it has been established beyond reasonable doubt that there was an armed conflict not of an international character between the Government of Rwanda and the RPF at the time of the facts alleged in the Indictment and that the said conflict was well within the provisions of Common Article 3 and of the Additional Protocol II. The Chamber however finds that the Prosecution has failed to show beyond reasonable doubt that Akayesu was a member of the armed forces and that he was duly mandated and expected in his capacity as a public official or agent or person otherwise vested with public authority of a *de facto* representative of the Government to support and carry out the war effort. [The Chamber unanimously found the accused guilty of genocide, incitement to commit genocide and crimes against humanity.]

Notes & Questions. 1. On July 9, 1997 Jean Kambanda who was Prime Minister of the Interim Government of Rwanda from April 8, 1994 until July 17, 1994 was arrested in Kenya. He was transferred to the ICTR. In *Prosecutor* v. *Kambanda,*[a] the accused pleaded guilty to genocide, conspiracy to commit genocide, direct and public incitement to commit genocide and crimes against humanity. The Trial Chamber verified that his guilty plea was voluntary, that he understood the charges and that his guilty plea was unequivocal. Kambanda submitted to the Trial Chamber, as well, a document entitled "Plea Agreement." In it he made full admissions of all relevant facts alleged in the indictment. He acknowledged that as Prime Minister he exercised *de jure* authority and control over members of his government and had the armed forces at his disposal. He also had *de jure* and *de facto* authority over senior civil servants and senior officers in the military. Kambanda was sentenced to life imprisonment.

a. Case No. ICTR 97–23–S, Sept. 4, 1998, *reproduced in* 37 ILM 411 (1998).

2. *Was rape already a war crime before this decision?* Had anyone been convicted of it before this? We have seen in Chapter 10, that the crime of rape has occurred throughout the history of war. Is the offense that was the focus of the *FOCA trial* different from what has occurred in the past or can we say that it is now just finally been recognized by judgment as a crime against humanity? Has it always been considered a crime? In Chapter 9, we see that civil judgments have been rendered in favor of rape victims and rape camp victims.

2. *The Rome Statute of the International Criminal Court,* presented in the Documentary Supplement and discussed immediately below, lists rape, sexual slavery, enforced prostitution, forced pregnancy, enforced sterilization as crimes against humanity in article 7.1(g) and as war crimes in article 8.2 (xxii).

The International Criminal Court the Rome Statute[b]

On July 17, 1998 in Rome the U.N. Diplomatic Conference of Plenipotentiaries on the Establishment of an International Criminal Court adopted the Statute of the International Criminal Court (ICC). The Rome Statute is the culmination of work that began in the International Law Commission,[c] continued in the *Ad Hoc* Committee set up by the General Assembly in 1994,[d] and in the Preparatory Committee (PrepCom.) which met between 1996 and 1998 and prepared the draft text for the Diplomatic Conference.[e]

The five week Rome Conference was the scene of intense negotiations. The draft text had over 1300 square brackets signifying unresolved matters often contentious. Some of the issues that divided states were (1) which crimes would be included; (2) would the ICC have automatic jurisdiction over core crimes once a state had accepted the Court's jurisdiction or would an "opt-in" approach be taken case-by-case; (3) would certain states and if so which have to be parties to the Statute as a precondition to the ICC exercising jurisdiction; (4) would the Prosecutor be able to initiate prosecution;(5) what role would the Security Council play (6) whether the crime of aggression should be included; (7) and if so, what would the definition of aggression be? (See R. S. Lee (ed.) The International Criminal Court: The Making of the Rome Statute (1999), Triffterer (ed.) Commentary on the Rome Statute of the International Criminal Court (1999) and M.C. Bassiouni, *Negotiating the Rome Statute on an International Criminal Court*, 32 Cornell int'l L.J. 443 (1999) and The Statute of the International Criminal Court: A Documentary History (1999). The Conference finally adopted a Statute that is a product of compromise. The portion of the text reproduced in the Documentary Supplement reflects this compromise.

b. Adopted by the U.N. Diplomatic Conference of Plenipotentiaries on the Establishment of an International Criminal Court, on 17 July 1998.U.N. Doc. A/CONF.183/9.

c. See the 1994 Draft Statute in Report of the ILC on its 46th Session, 1994, UN Doc. A

d. U.N. GAOR Res 49/53, Dec. 9, 1994.

e. See M.C. Bassiouni, *International Criminal Court: Compilation of U.N. Documents (1999).*

Sharon A. Williams, The Rome Statute on the International Criminal Court : From 1947–2000 and Beyond

38 Osgoode Hall Law Journal 298–308 (2000).*

* * *

An independent, credible, just and effective international international criminal court with broad state support is an imperative for the twenty-first century.

The International Criminal Court (ICC) was established on 17 July 1998 in Rome by the United Nations Diplomatic Conference * * *. It will have jurisdiction over some of the most serious international crimes. Its value is not only in prosecuting and punishing the alleged perpetrators of the listed crimes, genocide, war crimes, crimes against humanity and potentially aggression, but also in its capacity for deterrence. An impartial international criminal court with an independent prosecutor's office must discourage those who seek to instigate and perpetrate barbarous atrocities in violation of customary international and treaty law. The major challenge for the international community is to make it truly effective and not merely symbolic. * * *

The world community must be prepared to act. Should deterrence fail it must be ready, willing and able to bring to justice those accused, demonstrating that such conduct will not go unchallenged. It is not a question of high-minded revenge, of the victors dictating their terms to the vanquished, but rather a deep-rooted imperative to advance the rule of law and to enhance the quality of human behaviour at the national and international levels. The world community now knows that it is not sufficient to act on an *ad hoc* basis. To do so requires the selective political consent of the United Nations Security Council, acting under Chapter VII of the *Charter* * * * and there is a possibility that one of the five permanent members will veto the action. * * * [A] permanent court not hampered by geographical limits and time is necessary. However, the ICTFY and the ICTR have clearly bolstered world interest in a permanent international criminal court and are preparing the groundwork through their cases for its operation. The ICC is fundamental to international peace and security and the protection of human rights and dignity. * * *

The philosophical and practical underpinnings for the ICC are three-fold * * * deterrence, prosecution of alleged perpetrators, and justice for victims. The critical factor in the establishment of the court is the capacity to enforce. The goal is to replace impunity with accountability. However, there is also another aspect and that is whether the individualization, especially in ethnic conflicts within a single state, will assist in peace and reconciliation between the troubled parties. * * *

On the evening of 17 July 1998 in Rome, the United Nations * * * Conference * * * drew to a climatic end after five solid weeks of intense negotiations, political posturing and, finally accommodations being struck. * * * Amendments of any description at that last stage would have

* Reprinted with the permission of the Osgoode Hall Law Journal.

collapsed the intricately woven package. Still, the tension heightened as first India and then the United States made last ditch efforts to push for acutely controversial amendments. These were defeated in short order by no-action motions. [In the final plenary the United States requested an unrecorded vote. The Statute was adopted by 120 in favor, 7 against and 21 abstentions.] * * * The conference achieved the impossible in many ways. Among the key successes * * * were firstly, the inclusion of automatic jurisdiction over the core crimes of genocide, war crimes, crimes against humanity and aggression, although the latter still has to be defined. Secondly, there is the specific inclusion as crimes against humanity of sexual violence such as rape, sexual slavery, enforced prostitution, forced pregnancy when committed as part of a widespread or systematic attack directed against any civilian population or as war crimes in international and internal conflicts. Thirdly, the statute applies not only to international armed conflicts but also to internal conflicts that meet the threshold test of being more than internal tensions, riots or sporadic acts of violence. Fourthly, there is provision for impartial investigations and an independent prosecutor who may initiate them *proprio motu* with certain inbuilt checks and balances. Thus, the prosecutorial scheme does not depend solely on the initiation of investigations and consequent prosecutions by states parties and the United Nations Security Council. Fifthly, there are rigorous qualifications for judges, no statute of limitations and no reservations are allowed. * * *

It would be naive to suggest that there are not certain weaknesses in the statute. There are. Certain states and most NGOs pressed for the ICC to have universal jurisdiction or a variant thereof, over the listed crimes, but the result at the end of the day was restrictive preconditions in the final text of article 12. In fact, until the proverbial eleventh hour in Rome, article 12 was a make or break provision, and it still today retains its notoriety.

* * * Article 12 is intimately related to article 5 regarding crimes within the jurisdiction of the ICC, article 13 on exercise of jurisdiction, article 17 on complementarity and article 124 on the transitional provision. [These were among the most sensitive and difficult provisions to be negotiated.]

Notes and Questions

1. ***Entry into force***. The Rome Statute needs 60 ratifications to enter into force. As of June 2001 there are 137 signatures and 35 ratifications. States that have ratified include Senegal, Trinidad and Tobago, Italy, Norway, Belgium, France, New Zealand, Venezuela and Canada. The United States signed on December 31, 2000. Following the Rome Conference a Preparatory Commission (to be contrasted with the pre-Rome Preparatory Committee) was established to draft the Rules of Procedure and Evidence for the ICC, guidelines for the Court on the Elements of Crimes, a definition of aggression, a Relationship Agreement between the ICC and the U.N., provisions for immunities and financing of the Court. The Preparatory Commission completed the first two tasks at its session in

June 2000. Many states are in the process of enacting domestic legislation and some constitutional changes to enable ratification. Among the contentious issues are the surrender of nationals to the ICC, the immunity of heads of state and other high ranking government officials and the acceptance of life imprisonment as a penalty. Canada's implementing legislation has been viewed as a prototype. It provides for prosecution of the core crimes as defined in the Rome Statute in Canada based on wide bases of criminal jurisdiction over the offence including universal jurisdiction if the person is found to be present in Canada and for cooperation in surrender to the ICC. See *Crimes Against Humanity Act*, S.C. 2000, c. 24.

2. ***Core crimes***. Although in Rome some delegations wanted the list to be broader and to include international terrorism and drug trafficking, at the end of the day article 5 was restricted largely to cover only those crimes that were covered by customary international law. However, as Meron points out in *Crimes Under the Jurisdiction of the ICC*, in von Hebel, Lammers & Schukking (eds) Reflections on the International Criminal Court (1999), 47, 49, there were departures such as the inclusion of offences against humanitarian and UN personnel and the prohibition on conscription or enlisting children under fifteen.

3. ***Aggression***. Many delegations pressed for the inclusion of aggression. Others wanted to exclude it. The view expressed by some was that this was a crime by states and the ICC is to deal with individual criminal responsibility. Another controversy concerned the role of the United Nations Security Council acting under Chapter VII of the U.N. Charter and how this would interface with prosecutions at the ICC for this crime. The five weeks of the Rome conference did not allow for it to be defined. The compromise was that aggression in accordance with article 5(2) will be within the ICC's jurisdiction once defined by the Preparatory Commission and adopted on amendment by the Assembly of States Parties or by a Review Conference seven years following the entry into force of the Statute. Such an amendment will require a two-thirds majority of the states unless consensus can be reached. Any amendment to the list of crimes, including aggression, shall enter into force only for those states that have accepted the amendment one year after their deposit of instruments of ratification or acceptance. It is further provided that the ICC shall not exercise jurisdiction regarding a crime covered by such an amendment with respect to a state that has not accepted it committed by that state party's nationals or on its territory. Following the Rome Conference, the Preparatory Commission began work on defining aggression and continues as of April 2001.

4. ***No-action motions in Rome***. A no-action motion is where instead of voting on the substance of a proposed amendment, the vote is taken on no action on the amendment. Norway proposed a no action motion on July 17, 1998 on the amendment by India which concerned adding nuclear weapons and other weapons of mass destruction to the list of war crimes, as well as abrogating the role of the Security Council. The no-action motion was adopted by 114 in favor to 16 against with 20 abstentions. Norway then proposed a no-action motion on the United States amendment concerning

article 12 of the Statute, one of the major controversies in Rome. It was adopted by 113 in favor to 17 against with 25 abstentions.

5.   ***The Statute limits the scope of crimes against humanity*** by requiring, in article 7, that "attacks" be "directed against any civilian population ...", and it requires proof that the "[attack be] wide-spread or systematic," and that an element of "knowledge of the attack" be established. Are these limitations wise or too restrictive?

6.   ***Similarly, the term, "attack,"*** is restricted to "multiple commission of [the above-noted] acts ..., [which must be engaged] pursuant to or in furtherance of a State or organizational policy...." [*See*, art. 7(2)]. What does to perpetrate a rape, sexual slavery, enforced prostitution, forced pregnancy, enforced sterilization, pursuant to or in furtherance of organizational or governmental policy mean? Would it be a crime against humanity, if a company commander on his own decided to set-up a rape camp? How would you argue that this would be in furtherance of governmental or organizational policy? What does governmental or organizational mean in this context?

7.   ***The term "War Crime" in article 8***, is also quite limited. It requires that an attack or bombardment, to be considered a war crime be "intentionally direct[ed]." What if a perpetrator, officer or other official is so reckless that similar conduct in any civilian context would be considered (to use the common law term) "depraved heart murder" or reckless homicide, i.e., conduct that is so recklessly in disregard of human life, etc., that it manifests a "malignant heart." What if a leader knew that to bomb a certain place had a 95% chance of wiping-out massive numbers of civilians, and would have a 10% chance of accomplishing a fairly important and legitimate military goal. Would this be a war crime under the ICC Statute?

8.   ***Nuclear Weapons***. Refer to Section B.16 of Chapter 6 on the The International Protection of the Environment concerning this hotly debated issue of whether to include nuclear weapons as prohibited weapons in the Statute. They were not but may be added along with other weapons of mass destruction, namely biological and chemical weapons if the Statute is amended. As to amendments see note 3 above on aggression.

9.   ***Article 12.*** Concerning the preconditions for the exercise by the ICC of jurisdiction, where a case is referred to the ICC by a state party or where the prosecutor had initiated a prosecution, there were several proposals on the table in Rome, ranging from universal jurisdiction, state consent upon ratification by either one of the territorial state where the alleged crime was committed, the custodial state, the state of nationality of the offender or the state of national of the victim, to a state "opt in" proposal, and a case-by-case consent option. For a consideration of these options see Williams, *The Rome Statute on the International Criminal Court: From 1947–2000 and Beyond*, 38 Osgoode Hall Law Journal 298 (2000).The United States position was that the territorial state and the state of nationality, or at a minimum the consent of the state of nationality was fundamental. It was argued that the ICC have no jurisdiction over nationals of non-party states to the Statute as to do so would contravene article 34 of the Vienna Convention on the Law of Treaties, 1969. As Professor Williams notes, *ibid*., at 318, the U.S. "position was that it would not be

acceptable for United States citizens to be accountable in a court not accepted by the United States. The United States made it clear that it could not adhere to a text that allowed for United States forces operating abroad to be brought even conceivably before the ICC * * *.'' This of course still left open referral by the Security Council of a situation acting under Chapter VII of the U.N. Charter as set out in article 13(b) of the Statute. The indispensable requirement of consent by the state of nationality was not acceptable to the overwhelming majority of states. The compromise eventually reached in the final package is as presented in article 12 of the Statute and is discussed in the extract below. See Scheffer, *The United States and the International Criminal Court*, 93 A.J.I.L. 12 (1999) and Wedgwood, *Fiddling in Rome: America and The International criminal Court*, Foreign Aff. 20 (Nov.–Dec. 1998).

Sharon A. Williams, The Rome Statute on the International Criminal Court: From 1947–2000

38 OSGOODE HALL LAW SCHOOL 298, 321 (2000).*

[Article 12] combines state acceptance of jurisdiction for the crimes of genocide, crimes against humanity, war crimes and aggression, when defined, with preconditions for the exercise of jurisdiction by the ICC, in cases where a situation is referred to the prosecutor by a state party or where the prosecutor has initiated a prosecution *proprio motu*. [See article 13(a) and (c).] It allows by states parties the disjunctive acceptance of one or more of the territorial state or the state of nationality of the accused. The transitional provision contained in article 124 was also part of the compromise to gain France's acceptance to the statute. * * *

* * * The compromise was between the "like-minded states", who had for the most part a preference for inherent jurisdiction or for a list of alternative states (territorial state, state of nationality of the accused or the victim and the custodial state) where it was sufficient that one had accepted the jurisdiction of the court by ratifying and the "non like-minded". The latter insisted on either state party acceptance of the state of nationality of the accused or even the stricter requirement that be acceptance conjunctively from a list of states * * *." Article 12 as adopted by the conference is the accommodation that was struck. It reduced the preconditions to the territorial state or the state of nationality of the accused being state parties. These are the two primary bases of jurisdiction over the offence in international criminal law."

Notes and Questions. 1. ***What is your opinion of the U.S. argument based on article 34 of the Vienna Convention on the Law of Treaties,*** 1969 contained in the Documentary Supplement? Is the ICC taking jurisdiction over non-state parties? Do the various conventions dealing with international terrorism assist in answering this question? Consider also that on a domestic criminal law level that when a foreigner commits a crime on the territory of another state, a prosecution in that state is not dependent upon obtaining the consent of the state of nationali-

---

* Reprinted with the permission of the
Osgood Hall Law School.

ty. Is this analogy helpful? Is it a serious gap that the Statute does not allow for the acceptance of the custodial state as a precondition for the ICC to exercise jurisdiction. Even though the U.S. position after Rome was that were fundamental flaws in the Statute it signed. Under the *Vienna Convention on the Law of Treaties*, 1969 what is the impact of signature standing alone?

2. *Non-retroactivity.* According to article 11 the Statute is not retroactive. Consider the earlier section on *nullem crimen sine lege*. If the crimes listed in article 5 are recognized at customary international law why was article 11 included do you think? Neither the war crimes trials post World War II or the ICTY and the ICTR have this limitation. See Williams, *Article 11: Jurisdiction Ratione Temporis*, in Triffterer,(ed.,) Commentary on the Rome Statute of the International Criminal Court, 323 (1999).

3. *Complementarity.* One of the cornerstones of the Statute is article 17 dealing with issues of admissibility The ICC will not have primacy over national criminal courts when the concerned states are investigating or prosecuting in good faith. See Arsanjani, *Reflections on the Jurisdiction and Trigger Mechanisms of the International Criminal Court*, in von Hebel et al., (eds) Reflections on the International Criminal Court 57 (1999), Holmes, *The Principle of Complementarity*, in Lee (ed.) The International Criminal Court: The Making of the Rome Statute 41 (1999) and Sharon A. Williams, *Article 17: Issues of Admissibility* in Otto Triffterer (ed.) Commentary on the Rome Statute of the International Criminal Court 383 (1999).

7.   INDIRECT USE OF NUREMBERG PRINCIPLES: DENATURALIZATION AND DEPORTATION OR DISGUISED EXTRADITION, OR AS A DEFENSE IN DOMESTIC CASES

Courts have applied the Nürnberg principles to Nazi war criminals by expelling, deporting, or other slight-of-hand extraditions.

Ethan Nadelman, The Evolution of U.S. Involvement In the International Rendition of Fugitive Criminals
25 N.Y.U.J.Int'l L. & Pol. 313, 324 (1993).*

The courts have similarly refrained from according any sanctuary to Nazi war criminals who thought they had found a safe refuge in the United States. The one exception occurred in 1959, when a California federal court rejected a request from the government of Yugoslavia for the extradition of Andrija Artukovic, Minister of the Interior of the Independent State of Croatia during World War II. (*Karadzole v. Artukovic*, 170 F.Supp. 383 (S.D.Cal.1959). His alleged crimes, which included control over concentration camps and the murders of thousands of civilians, were viewed by the court as political offenses for which extradition could not be granted. Moreover, until well into the 1970s, the Immigration and Natu-

---

* Reprinted with the permission of the New York University Journal of International Law & Policy.

ralization Service devoted little effort to identifying and deporting Nazi war criminals. During the late 1970s, however, Elizabeth Holtzman, chairperson of the House Judiciary Committee's Subcommittee on Immigration, pushed through legislation requiring the Justice Department to assume responsibility for Nazi war crime cases. Attorney General Griffin Bell responded in 1979 by creating an Office of Special Investigations (OSI), dedicated to finding Nazi war criminals and arranging their extradition or deportation to face charges in foreign courts. The OSI's efforts were aided by the widespread repudiation of the 1959 Artukovic decision by most commentators and all federal courts. By 1991, seventy-five extraditions and deportations had resulted from OSI's investigations, including: the 1986 extradition of Artukovic to Yogoslavia, where he died before his sentenced execution; the 1973 extradition of Hermine Brausteiner–Ryan, a former SS member and Maidanek concentration camp guard, to West Germany, where she was sentenced to life imprisonment for multiple murders; the 1984 deportation of Deodor Fedorenko, a Ukrainian guard in the Treblinka concentration camp, to the Soviet Union, where he was executed for his crimes; the 1987 deportation of Karl Linnas, an Estonian who supervised the killing of Jews in the concentration camps at Tartu, to the Soviet Union, where he died while awaiting action on an appeal for a pardon (*see, U.S. v. Linnas*, 527 F.Supp. 426 (E.D.N.Y.1981); *Linnas v. I.N.S.*, 790 F.2d 1024 (2d Cir.1986)); and the 1986 extradition of John Demjanjuk, a Ukrainian initially identified as a notorious SS guard at the Treblinka and Sobibor death camps known as "Ivan the Terrible," to Israel, where he was tried and sentenced to death.

83–year-old Nazi convicted, **BBC News**, 3 April, 2001

An 83–year-old man who was a Nazi SS commander in World War II has been jailed by a German court for 12 years for murdering Jews in the final months of the war. Julius Viel was convicted of murdering seven Jewish prisoners at a concentration camp in Nazi-occupied Czechoslovakia. Viel, who had denied the charges, sat impassively as the verdict was read out. He is thought to be one of the last Nazis likely to stand trial.

The judge in Ravensburg district court said he had acted "out of lust for murder and base motives", and not on orders. His lawyer said he would appeal, as evidence presented to the court had been contradictory. His legal team had told the court he was stationed in Vienna at the time of the murders. "I'm sorry for my wife's sake," Viel told journalists after the hearing. Viel, who worked as a journalist after the war, was a second lieutenant in the SS at the time of the crimes.

The Jewish people who died were inmates at the Theresienstadt concentration camp, killed in the spring of 1945. They were digging anti-tank trenches at Leitmeritz, near the camp, when they were killed. Viel had been investigated for the murders in the 1960s, but the case was closed after a lack of evidence. A fellow-Nazi broke more than 50 years' silence to testify against Viel. The case was reopened when a former Nazi trainee, Hungarian-born Adalbert Lallier, decided to break half a century of silence to reveal that he had witnessed the killings. Mr Lallier, an economics professor in Canada, told the court in Ravensburg that Viel had shot the victims in cold blood. He was the only person to give evidence, but the German judge said he had believed his account. "Lallier certainly did not imagine what happened," said Judge Hermann Winkler.

He said Viel had escaped a life sentence because of the time which had elapsed since the crime. But he said Viel's exemplary life after the war—which included winning government acclaim for some of his work—did not reduce the enormity of his original crime. "At the beginning of this life's journey, there were seven deaths," said Judge Winkler. "The killing of a human was a crime then as well. The defendant knows it wasn't animals but people he did away with." Around 360 witnesses in Germany, Austria, Britain and Canada were interviewed in a two-year investigation into the case. A number of other investigations into Nazi killings have been continuing, but most defendants are now considered too old or too ill to stand trial.

Can the Nürnberg Principles be used Defensively in Criminal Prosecutions?

Mitchell v. United States

United States Supreme Court, 1967.
386 U.S. 972, 87 S.Ct. 1162, 18 L.Ed.2d 132.* *Certiorari denied.*

■ MR. JUSTICE DOUGLAS, *dissenting*.

Petitioner did not report for induction as ordered, was indicted, convicted, and sentenced to five years' imprisonment and his conviction was affirmed. His defense was that the "war" in Vietnam was being conducted in violation of various treaties to which we were a signatory, especially the Treaty of London of August 8, 1945, * * * which in Article 6(a) declares that "waging of a war of aggression" is a "crime against peace" imposing "individual responsibility." Article 8 provides: "The fact that the Defendant acted pursuant to order of his Government or of a superior shall not free him from responsibility, but may be considered in mitigation of punishment if the Tribunal determines that justice so requires." Petitioner claimed that the "war" in Vietnam was a "war of aggression" within the meaning of the Treaty of London and that Article 8 makes him responsible for participating in it even though he is ordered to do so.[1]

Mr. Justice Jackson, the U.S. prosecutor at Nuremberg, stated: "If certain acts in violation of treaties are crimes, they are crimes whether the United States does them or whether Germany does them, and we are not prepared to lay down a rule of criminal conduct against others which we would not be willing to have invoked against us."

Article VI, cl. 2, of the Constitution states that "Treaties" are a part of the "supreme Law of the Land; and the Judges in every State shall be bound thereby." There is a considerable body of opinion that our actions in Vietnam constitute the waging of an aggressive "war."

* Rehearing denied, 386 U.S. 1042 (1967).

1. The trial court charged the jury that the Treaty of London did not interfere "in any manner in respect to this defendant fulfilling his duty under this order.

This case presents the questions:

(1) whether the Treaty of London is a treaty within the meaning of Art. VI, cl. 2;

(2) whether the question as to the waging of an aggressive "war" is in the context of this criminal prosecution a justiciable question;

(3) whether the Vietnam episode is a "war" in the sense of the Treaty;

(4) whether petitioner has standing to raise the question;

(5) whether, if he has, the Treaty may be tendered as a defense in this criminal case or in amelioration of the punishment.

These are extremely sensitive and delicate questions. But they should, I think, be answered. Even those who think that the Nuremberg judgments were unconstitutional by our guarantee relating to ex post facto laws would have to take a different view of the Treaty of London that purports to lay down a standard of future conduct for all the signatories.

I intimate no opinion on the merits. But I think the petition for certiorari should be granted. We have here a recurring question in present-day Selective Service cases.*

Randall v. Commissioner of Internal Revenue Service

United States Court of Appeals, Eleventh Circuit, 1984.
733 F.2d 1565.

■ PER CURIAM:

This case presents a new twist in two respects to the attempt to claim a credit against income taxes because of the religious beliefs of the taxpayer. First, rather than claiming a credit for just the percentage of his tax that reflects the percentage of the Government's budget utilized for military spending, roughly 61% according to taxpayer, the claim here is for 100% of the taxes he would owe based on the assertion that the payment of any money to the United States Treasury would be the commission of a mortal sin. Second, rather than basing his claim on the First Amendment of the Constitution, taxpayer contends that 26 U.S.C.A. § 7852(d) protects him from payment of taxes. Section 7852(d) states that no provision of the Internal Revenue Code shall apply where it "would be contrary to any treaty obligation of the United States." Taxpayer contends that the requirement that he pay taxes violates treaties of the United States in two ways. First, United States military spending is in violation of international treaty obligations. Second, the United States is obligated by treaty to observe the religious freedom of its citizens, and it is contrary to this treaty obligation to fail to honor taxpayers' free practice of religion by requiring him to pay taxes to the general treasury of the United States, from which military expenditures are made.

* * *

---

* Problems posed by this case are more fully analyzed in Forman, The Nuremberg Trials and Conscientious Objection to War: Justiciability Under United States Municipal Law, in 1969 Proceedings of the American Society of International Law 157 and comments by Telford Taylor and others in 1969 Proceedings 165 ff.

· In sustaining the Commissioner's refusal to allow the tax credit claimed on this basis, the tax court recognized that the sole purpose of section 7852(d) was to insure that the application of the Internal Revenue Code would in no way abrogate any existing tax treaties in the collection of taxes. Plainly, that section is not concerned with the ways in which Government funds, generated by tax revenues, are ultimately spent. * * *

Contrary to taxpayer's argument as to the thrust of the Nuremberg Principles and other principles of international law, the act of paying taxes does not amount to complicity in any war crime committed by the Government. * * * With respect to any violation of international law committed by the Government, the taxpayer as a taxpayer is exempted from complicity by his remoteness and utter lack of direct involvement. * * * It has been consistently held that the Nuremberg Principles furnish no excuse for the non-payment of taxes. * * *

AFFIRMED.

———

Notes and Questions. Nürnberg's apparent adoption of transcendant principles of individual responsibility would seem to provide the individual conscientious objector or disobedient a promising basis for legal defense for refusal to participate. The U.S. judiciary, however, has chosen to interpret the Nürnberg rules strictly, not in favor of the policies they enunciate, but in favor of the state. In Nürnberg itself, were there any other than high ranking officials charged with committing or having a legal duty to prevent war crimes from occurring? If war crimes trials are limited to high ranking officials, does that establish a rule that only high ranking officials have the legal duty? If the average conscript, citizen or member of the armed forces was not charged at Nürnberg, does it mean that those individuals do not have a legal duty and, hence, no defense for refusing to participate? Is this logical or appropriate? If it is the "law" after Nuremberg, has that Judgment been eviscerated? What do the decisions you just read suggest? *See* Lippman, *Civil Resistance: Revitalizing International Law in the Nuclear Age,* 13 Whitt.L.Rev. 17 (1992); Boyle, DEFENDING CIVIL RESISTENCE UNDER INTERNATIONAL LAW (1987); Falk, *Telford Taylor and the Legacy of Nuremberg,* 37 Colum.J.Transnat'l L. 693 (1999).

SECTION C. UNIVERSAL JURISDICTION AND NÜRNBERG PRINCIPLES

1. CASES

Attorney General Of Israel V. Eichmann
Israel, Supreme Court 1962.
36 Int'l L.Rep. 277 (1968).

1. The appellant, Adolf Eichmann, was found guilty by the District Court of Jerusalem of offenses of the most extreme gravity against the Nazi

and Nazi Collaborators (Punishment) Law, 1950 (hereinafter referred to as "the Law") and was sentenced to death. These offences may be divided into four groups:

(a) Crimes against the Jewish people, contrary to Section I(a)(1) of the Law;

(b) Crimes against humanity, contrary to Section I(a)(2);

(c) War crimes, contrary to Section I(a)(3);

(d) Membership of hostile organizations, contrary to Section 3.

2.   The acts constituting these offences, which the Court attributed to the appellant, have been specified in paragraph 244 of the judgment of the District Court * * *. The acts comprised in Group (a) are:

(1) that during the period from August 1941 to May 1945, in Germany, in the Axis States and in the areas which were subject to the authority of Germany and the Axis States, he, together with others, caused the killing of millions of Jews for the purpose of carrying out the plan known as "the Final Solution of the Jewish Problem" with the intent to exterminate the Jewish people;

(2) that during that period and in the same places he, together with others, placed millions of Jews in living conditions which were calculated to bring about their physical destruction, for the purpose of carrying out the plan above mentioned with the intent to exterminate the Jewish people;

(3) that during that period and in the same places he, together with others, caused serious physical and mental harm to millions of Jews with the intent to exterminate the Jewish people;

(4) that during the years 1943 and 1944 he, together with others, "devised measures the purpose of which was to prevent births among Jews by his instructions forbidding child bearing and ordering the interruption of pregnancies of Jewish women in the Theresin Ghetto with the intent to exterminate the Jewish people".

The acts constituting the crimes in Group (b) are as follows:

(5) that during the period from August 1941 to May 1945 he, together with others, caused in the territories and areas mentioned in clause (1) the murder, extermination, enslavement, starvation and deportation of the civilian Jewish population;

(6) that during the period from December 1939 to March 1941 he, together with others, caused the deportation of Jews to Nisco, and the deportation of Jews from the areas in the East annexed to the Reich, and from the Reich area proper, to the German Occupied Territories in the East, and to France;

(7) that in carrying out the above-mentioned activities he persecuted Jews on national, racial, religious and political grounds;

(8) that during the period from March 1938 to May 1945 in the places mentioned above he, together with others, caused the spoliation of the property of millions of Jews by means of mass terror linked with the murder, extermination, starvation and deportation of these Jews;

(9) that during the years 1940–1942 he, together with others, caused the expulsion of hundreds of thousands of Poles from their places of residence;

(10) that during 1941 he, together with others, caused the expulsion of more than 14,000 Slovenes from their places of residence;

(11) that during the Second World War he, together with others, caused the expulsion of scores of thousands of Gypsies from Germany and German-occupied areas and their transportation to the German-occupied areas in the East;

(12) that in 1942 he, together with others, caused the expulsion of 93 children of the Czech village of Lidice.

The acts comprised in Group (c) are:

that he committed the acts of persecution, expulsion and murder mentioned in Counts 1 to 7, in so far as these were done during the Second World War against Jews from among the populations of the States occupied by the Germans and by the other Axis States.

The acts comprised in Group (d) are:

that as from May 1940 he was a member of three Nazi Police organizations which were declared criminal organizations by the International Military Tribunal which tried the Major War Criminals, and as a member of such organizations he took part in acts which were declared criminal in Article 6 of the London Charter of August 8, 1945.

3. The appellant has appealed to this Court against both conviction and sentence.

4. The oral and written submissions of learned counsel who supported the appeal, Dr. Servatius, may, in so far as they are directed against conviction, be classified under two heads:

(1) Purely legal contentions, the principal object of which was to undermine the jurisdiction of a court in Israel to try the appellant for the crimes in question;

(2) Factual contentions the object of which was in essence to upset the finding of the District Court that there was no foundation for the defence of the appellant that he played the part of a "small cog" in the machine of Nazi destruction, that in all the above-mentioned chapters of events he functioned as a minor official without any independent initiative, and that nothing but the compulsion of orders and blind obedience to commands from above guided him in carrying out his work at all stages.

* * *

5. The District Court has in its judgment dealt with both categories of contentions in an exhaustive, profound and most convincing manner. We should say at once that we fully concur, without hesitation or reserve, in all its conclusions and reasons. * * *

[The Jurisdiction of the Court]

6. Most of the legal contentions of counsel for the appellant revolve around the argument that in assuming jurisdiction to try the appellant the District Court acted contrary to the principles of international law. These contentions are as follows:

(1) The Law of 1950, which is the only source of the jurisdiction of the Court in this case, constitutes ex post facto penal legislation which prescribes as offences acts that were committed before the State of Israel came into existence; therefore the validity of this Law is confined to its citizens alone.

(2) The offences for which the appellant was tried are "extra-territorial offences", that is to say, offences that were committed outside the territory of Israel by a citizen of a foreign State, and even though the Law confers jurisdiction in respect of such offences, it conflicts in so doing with the principle of territorial sovereignty, which postulates that only the country within whose territory the offence was committed or to which the offender belongs–in this case, Germany–has the right to punish therefor.

(3) The acts constituting the offence of which the appellant was convicted were at the time of their commission Acts of State.

(4) The appellant was brought to Israeli territory, to be tried for the offences in question, unwillingly and without the consent of the country in which he resided, and this was done through agents of the State of Israel, who acted on the orders of their Government.

(5) The judges of the District Court, being Jews and feeling affinity with the victims of the plan of extermination and Nazi persecution, were psychologically incapable of giving the appellant an objective trial.

* * *

7. We reject all these contentions.

* * *

[Portions of the court's opinion dealing with the second contention–the "extraterritoriality" of the offences–are set forth as follows.]

[Universal Jurisdiction]

12. * * * [I]t is the universal character of the crimes in question which vests in every State the authority to try and punish those who participated in their commission. This proposition is closely linked with the one advanced in the preceding paragraph, from which indeed it follows as a logical outcome. The grounds upon which it rests are as follows:

(a) One of the principles whereby States assume in one degree or another the power to try and punish a person for an offence is the principle of universality. Its meaning is substantially that such power is vested in every State regardless of the fact that the offence was committed outside its territory by a person who did not belong to it, provided he is in its custody when brought to trial. This principle has wide currency and is universally acknowledged with respect to the offence of piracy jure gentium. But while general agreement exists as

to this offence, the question of the scope of its application is in dispute
* * *.

* * *

(b) The brief survey of views set out above shows that, notwithstanding the differences between them, there is full justification for applying here the principle of universal jurisdiction since the international character of "crimes against humanity" (in the wide meaning of the term) dealt with in this case is no longer in doubt, while the unprecedented extent of their injurious and murderous effects is not to be disputed at the present time. In other words, the basic reason for which international law recognizes the right of each State to exercise such jurisdiction in piracy offences–notwithstanding the fact that its own sovereignty does not extend to the scene of the commission of the offence (the high seas) and the offender is a national of another State or is stateless–applies with even greater force to the above-mentioned crimes. That reason is, it will be recalled, that the interest to prevent bodily and material harm to those who sail the seas and to persons engaged in trade between nations, is a vital interest common to all civilized States and of universal scope * * *.

It follows that the State which prosecutes and punishes a person for piracy acts merely as the organ and agent of the international community and metes out punishment to the offender for his breach of the prohibition imposed by the law of nations * * *.

The above explanation of the substantive basis upon which the exercise of the principle of universal jurisdiction in respect of the crime of piracy rests, justifies its exercise in regard also to the crimes which are the subject of the present case.

(c) The truth is–and this further supports our conclusion–that the application of this principle has for some time been moving beyond the international crime of piracy. We have in mind its application to conventional war crimes as well. As we observed in paragraph 11(c) of this judgment, whenever a "belligerent" country tries and punishes a member of the armed forces of the enemy for an act contrary to "the laws and customs of war", it does so because the matter involves an international crime in the prevention of which the countries of the whole world have an interest. * * *

(f) We sum up our views on this subject as follows. Not only do all the crimes attributed to the appellant bear an international character, but their harmful and murderous effects were so embracing and widespread as to shake the international community to its very foundations. The State of Israel therefore was entitled, pursuant to the principle of universal jurisdiction and in the capacity of a guardian of international law and an agent for its enforcement, to try the appellant. That being the case, no importance attaches to the fact that the State of Israel did not exist when the offences were committed. Here therefore is an additional reason–and one based on a positive approach–for rejecting the second, "jurisdictional", submission of counsel for the appellant.* * *

Demjanjuk v. Petrovsky

United States Court of Appeals, Sixth Circuit, 1985.
776 F.2d 571, Cert. denied 475 U.S. 1016 (1986).

■ LIVELY, CHIEF JUDGE.

This international extradition case is before the court on appeal from the denial of a petition for a writ of habeas corpus.

I.   The petitioner, John Demjanjuk, is a native of the Ukraine, one of the republics of the Soviet Union. Demjanjuk was admitted to the United States in 1952 under the Displaced Persons Act of 1948 and became a naturalized United States citizen in 1958. He has resided in the Cleveland, Ohio area since his arrival in this country.

In 1981 the United States District Court for the Northern District of Ohio revoked Demjanjuk's certificate of naturalization and vacated the order admitting him to United States citizenship. * * * Chief Judge Battisti of the district court entered extensive findings of fact from which he concluded that the certificate and order "were illegally procured and were procured by willful misrepresentation of material facts under 8 U.S.C. § 1451(a)."

The district court found that Demjanjuk was conscripted into the Soviet Army in 1940 and was captured by the Germans in 1942. After short stays in several German POW camps and a probable tour at the Trawniki SS training camp in Poland, Demjanjuk became a guard at the Treblinka concentration camp, also in Poland, late in 1942. In his various applications for immigration to the United States the petitioner misstated his place of residence during the period 1937–1948 and did not reveal that he had worked for the SS at Treblinka or served in a German military unit later in the war. In the denaturalization proceedings Demjanjuk admitted that his statements concerning residence were false. * * * He steadfastly denied that he had been at Trawniki or Treblinka, though documentary evidence placed him at Trawniki and five Treblinka survivors and one former German guard at the camp identified Demjanjuk as a Ukrainian guard who was known as "Ivan or Iwan Grozny," that is, "Ivan the Terrible."

Following the denaturalization order the government began deportation proceedings against Demjanjuk. While these proceedings were underway Israel filed with the ... Department of State a request for the extradition of Demjanjuk. The U.S. Attorney, acting on behalf of the State of Israel, filed a complaint in the district court seeking the arrest of Demjanjuk and a hearing on the extradition request. Following a hearing the district court entered an order certifying to the Secretary of State that Demjanjuk was subject to extradition at the request of the State of Israel pursuant to a treaty on extradition between the United States and Israel. * * *

II.

* * *

B.

Before reaching the more technical arguments related to jurisdiction [and] whether the crimes charged were within the treaty provisions, we deal with the sufficiency of the evidence. There was sworn testimony by affidavits from six witnesses who were at Treblinka in 1942 and 1943 who identified Demjanjuk. These witnesses stated that Demjanjuk was a guard who herded prisoners into the gas chambers and then actually operated the mechanism which filled the chambers with gas. In addition, several of the witnesses testified that they saw Demjanjuk beat and maim prisoners, some of whom died. * * *

* * *

III.

A. The pertinent portions of the treaty (Convention on Extradition) between the United States and Israel (hereafter the Treaty) found in the first three articles and the thirteenth article, are set forth:

Article I

Each Contracting Party agrees, under the conditions and circumstances established by the present Convention, reciprocally to deliver up persons found in its territory who have been charged with or convicted of any of the offenses mentioned in Article II of the present Convention committed within the territorial jurisdiction of the other, or outside thereof under the conditions specified in Article III of the present Convention.

Article II

Persons shall be delivered up according to the provisions of the present Convention for prosecution when they have been charged with, or to undergo sentence when they have been convicted of, any of the following offenses:

1. Murder.

2. Manslaughter.

3. Malicious wounding; inflicting grievous bodily harm.

* * *

Article III When the offense has been committed outside the territorial jurisdiction of the requesting Party, extradition need not be granted unless the laws of the requested Party provide for the punishment of such an offense committed in similar circumstances.

The words "territorial jurisdiction" as used in this Article and in Article I of the present Convention mean: territory, including territorial waters, and the airspace thereover belonging to or under the control of one of the Contracting Parties, and vessels and aircraft belonging to one of the Contracting Parties or to a citizen or corporation thereof when such vessel is on the high seas or such aircraft is over the high seas.

* * *

Article XIII A person extradited under the present Convention shall not be detained, tried or punished in the territory of the requesting Party for any offense other than that for which extradition has been granted nor be extradited by that Party to a third State unless:

(Exceptions not applicable).

The Israeli warrant on which the extradition request was based was issued pursuant to a request which charged Demjanjuk with having "murdered tens of thousands of Jews and non-Jews" while operating the gas chambers to exterminate prisoners at Treblinka. It further asserts that the acts charged were committed "with the intention of destroying the Jewish people and to commit crimes against humanity." The complaint in the district court equated this charge with the crimes of "murder and malicious wounding [and] inflicting grievous bodily harm," listed in the Treaty. The warrant was issued pursuant to a 1950 Israeli statute, the Nazis and Nazi Collaborators (Punishment) Law. This statute made certain acts, including "crimes against the Jewish people," "crimes against humanity" and "war crimes committed during the Nazi period" punishable under Israeli law. The statute defines these crimes: "crime against the Jewish people" means any of the following acts, committed with intent to destroy the Jewish people in whole or in part:

1. killing Jews;

2. causing serious bodily or mental harm to Jews;

3. placing Jews in living conditions calculated to bring about their physical destruction;

4. imposing measures intended to prevent births among Jews;

5. forcibly transferring Jewish children to another national or religious group;

6. destroying or desecrating Jewish religious or cultural assets or values;

7. inciting to hatred of Jews; "crime against humanity" means any of the following acts: murder, extermination, enslavement, starvation or deportation and other inhumane acts committed against any civilian population, and persecution on national, racial, religious or political grounds;

"war crime" means any of the following acts: murder, ill-treatment or deportation to forced labour or for any other purpose, of civilian population of or in occupied territory; murder or ill-treatment of prisoners of war or persons on the seas; killing of hostages; plunder of public or private property; wanton destruction of cities, towns or villages; and devastation not justified by military necessity.

B.

Demjanjuk contends that the district court had no jurisdiction to consider the request for extradition. He advances several discrete arguments in support of this position. As he did in the district court, Demjanjuk maintains that the crime he is charged with is not included in the listing of offenses in the treaty. It is his position that "murdering thousands of Jews and non-Jews" is not covered by the treaty designation of "murder." It is a fundamental requirement for international extradition that the crime for which extradition is sought be one provided for by the treaty between the requesting and the requested nation. 18 U.S.C. § 3184; Fernandez v. Phillips, 268 U.S. at 213. We have no difficulty concluding that "murder" includes the mass murder of Jews. This is a logical reading of the treaty language and is the interpretation given the treaty by the Department of State. That interpretation is entitled to considerable deference, as this court noted in Argento v. Horn, 241 F.2d 258, 263 (6th Cir.1957)?

A construction of a treaty by the political department of the government, while not conclusive upon a court called upon to construe such a treaty in a matter involving personal rights, is nevertheless of much weight. [Quoting Charlton v. Kelly.]

Demjanjuk also argues that the district court had no jurisdiction because there is a requirement of "double criminality" in international extradition cases. The Restatement of the Foreign Relations Law of the U.S. (1984) (hereafter "Restatement"), provides in § 487: (1) No person may be extradited pursuant to § 486 [The Basic Rule].

　　　* * *

(c) If the offense with which he is charged or of which he has been convicted is not punishable as a serious crime both in the requesting and in the requested state.

The Supreme Court stated in Collins v. Loisel, "It is true that an offense is extraditable only if the acts charged are criminal by the laws of both countries." See also Brauch v. Raiche ("The requirement that the acts alleged be criminal in both jurisdictions is central to extradition law * * * ").

We believe the double criminality requirement was met in this case. As the Court stated in Collins v. Loisel: "The law does not require that the name by which the crime is described in the two countries shall be the same; nor that the scope of the liability shall be coextensive, or, in other respects, the same in the two countries. It is enough if the particular act charged is criminal in both jurisdictions." If the acts upon which the charges of the requesting country are based are also proscribed by a law of the requested nation, the requirement of double criminality is satisfied. Murder is a crime in every state of the United States. The fact that there is no separate offense of mass murder or murder of tens of thousands of Jews in this country is beside the point. The act of unlawfully killing one or more persons with the requisite malice is punishable as murder. That is the test. The acts charged are criminal both in Israel and throughout the United States, including Ohio. Demjanjuk's argument that to interpret murder to include murder of Jews would amount to judicial amendment of the Treaty is absurd and offensive.

IV.

A.

A separate jurisdictional argument concerns the territorial reach of the statutory law of Israel. Demjanjuk relies on two facts to question the power of the State of Israel to proceed against him. He is not a citizen or resident of Israel and the crimes with which he is charged allegedly were committed in Poland. He also points out that the acts which are the basis of the Israeli arrest warrant allegedly took place in 1942 or 1943, before the State of Israel came into existence. Thus, Demjanjuk maintains that the district court had no jurisdiction because Israel did not charge him with extraditable offenses.

The scope of this nation's international extradition power and the function of the federal courts in the extradition process are set forth in 18 U.S.C. § 3184: * * * Section 3184 clearly provides that the extradition complaint must charge the person sought to be extradited with having committed crimes "within the jurisdiction of any such foreign government," that is, the requesting state. This same condition is reflected in § 486(a) of the Restatement, which requires the requested state to comply with the request to arrest and deliver a person sought "on charges of having committed a serious crime within the jurisdiction of the requesting state." The question is whether the murder of Jews in a Nazi extermination camp in Poland during the 1939–1945 war can be considered, for purposes of extradition, crimes within the jurisdiction of the State of Israel.

B.

We look first at the Treaty. Article III provides that when an offense has been committed outside the territorial jurisdiction of the requesting party, "extradition need not be granted unless the laws of the requested party provide for the punishment of such an offense committed in similar circumstances." Demjanjuk maintains that the "need not" language of Article III prohibits extradition in this case because the laws of the United States do not provide punishment for war crimes or crimes against humanity. * * *

* * *

* * * In our view the treaty language makes two things clear: (1) the parties recognize the right to request extradition for extra-territorial crimes, and (2) the requested party has the discretion to deny extradition if its laws do not provide for punishment of offenses committed under similar circumstances. This provision does not affect the authority of a court to certify extraditability; it merely distinguishes between cases where the requested party is required to honor a request and those where it has discretion to deny a request. That the specific offense charged is not a crime in the United States does not necessarily rule out extradition.

The Israeli statute under which Demjanjuk was charged deals with "crimes against the Jewish people," "crimes against humanity" and "war crimes" committed during the Nazi years. It is clear from the language defining the crimes, and other references to acts directed at persecuted persons and committed in places of confinement, that Israel intended to punish under this law those involved in carrying out Hitler's "final solution." This was made explicit in the prosecution of Adolph Eichmann in 1961. *Attorney General v. Eichmann [supra]*. Such a claim of extraterritorial jurisdiction over criminal offenses is not unique to Israel. For example, statutes of the United States provide for punishment in domestic district courts for murder or manslaughter committed within the maritime jurisdiction (18 U.S.C. § 1111) and murder or manslaughter of internationally protected persons wherever they are killed (18 U.S.C. § 1116(c)). We conclude that the reference in 18 U.S.C. § 3184 to crimes committed within the jurisdiction of the requesting government does not refer solely to territorial jurisdiction. Rather, it refers to the authority of a nation to apply its laws to particular conduct. In international law this is referred to as "jurisdiction to prescribe." Restatement § 401(1).

C.

The law of the United States includes international law. *The Paquete Habana*, 175 U.S. 667, 712 (1900). International law recognizes a "universal jurisdiction" over certain offenses. Section 404 of the Restatement defines universal jurisdiction: § 404: Universal Jurisdiction to Define and Punish Selected Offenses

A state may exercise jurisdiction to define and punish certain offenses recognized by the community of nations as of universal concern, such as piracy, slave trade, attacks on or hijacking of aircraft, genocide, war crimes, and perhaps terrorism, even where none of the bases of jurisdiction indicated in § 402 is present.

This "universality principle" is based on the assumption that some crimes are so universally condemned that the perpetrators are the enemies of all people. Therefore, any nation which has custody of the perpetrators may punish them according to its law applicable to such offenses. This principle is a departure from the general rule that "the character of an act as lawful or unlawful must be determined wholly by the law of the country where the act is done."

The wartime allies created the International Military Tribunal which tried major Nazi officials at Nuremberg and courts within the four occupation zones of post-war Germany which tried lesser Nazis. All were tried for committing war crimes, and it is generally agreed that the establishment of these tribunals and their proceedings were based on universal jurisdiction.
* * *

Demjanjuk argues that the post-war trials were all based on the military defeat of Germany and that with the disestablishment of the special tribunals there are no courts with jurisdiction over alleged war crimes. This argument overlooks the fact that the post-war tribunals were not military courts, though their presence in Germany was made possible by the military defeat of that country. These tribunals did not operate within the limits of traditional military courts. They claimed and exercised a much broader jurisdiction which necessarily derived from the universality principle. Whatever doubts existed prior to 1945 have been erased by the general recognition since that time that there is a jurisdiction over some types of crimes which extends beyond the territorial limits of any nation.

Turning again to the Restatement, § 443 appears to apply to the present case: "§ 443.Jurisdiction to Adjudicate in Aid of Universal and Other Non–Territorial Crimes. A state's courts may exercise jurisdiction to enforce the state's criminal laws which punish universal crimes (§ 404) or other nonterritorial offenses within the state's jurisdiction to prescribe (§§ 402–403)." Israel is seeking to enforce its criminal law for the punishment of Nazis and Nazi collaborators for crimes universally recognized and condemned by the community of nations. The fact that Demjanjuk is charged with committing these acts in Poland does not deprive Israel of authority to bring him to trial.

Further, the fact that the State of Israel was not in existence when Demjanjuk allegedly committed the offenses is no bar to Israel's exercising jurisdiction under the universality principle. When proceeding on that jurisdictional premise, neither the nationality of the accused or the victim(s), nor the location of the crime is significant. The underlying assumption is that the crimes are offenses against the law of nations or against humanity and that the prosecuting nation is acting for all nations. This being so, Israel or any other nation, regardless of its status in 1942 or 1943, may undertake to vindicate the interest of all nations by seeking to punish the perpetrators of such crimes.

D.

We conclude that the jurisdictional challenges to the district court's order must fail. The crime of murder is clearly included in the offenses for which extradition is to be granted under the treaty. Murder is a crime both in Israel and in the United States and is included in the specifications of the Nazis and Nazi Collaborators (Punishment) Law; the requirement of "double criminality" is met; and, the State of Israel has jurisdiction to punish for war crimes and crimes against humanity committed outside of its geographic boundaries.

Though it was not explicitly argued, we have considered whether recognition of the power of Israeli courts to punish for war crimes committed outside of its national territory violates any right of Demjanjuk under the Constitution of the United States. Demjanjuk had notice before he applied for residence or citizenship in the United States that this country, by participating in post-war trials of German and Japanese war criminals, recognized the universality principle. Israel has chosen to proceed under that principle, and we do not supervise the conduct of another judicial system. To do so "would directly conflict with the principle of comity upon which extradition is based." Jhirad v. Ferrandina. In the absence of any showing that Demjanjuk will be subjected to procedures "antipathetic to a federal court's sense of decency," Gallina v. Fraser, this court will not inquire into the procedures which will apply after he is surrendered to Israel. There is absolutely no showing in this record that Israel will follow procedures which would shock this court's "sense of decency." * * * The judgment of the district court is affirmed.

Notes & Questions. 1. Is there any theory upon which Demjanjuk could have been prosecuted in the U.S. for the killings in Poland? Would a state murder statute reach those events? A federal statute? The federal statutes for common crimes listed in Title 18 of the United States Code cover events that take place only within precisely defined jurisdictions (*e.g.*, special maritime and territorial jurisdiction, 18 U.S.C. § 7, *supra*, special aircraft jurisdiction, 49 U.S.C. §§ 1301(38) and

1472(k)). Federal criminal law has expanded only incrementally to reach specific problems that demand extraterritorial prescription, as we have seen with respect to, hostage taking, hijacking and terrorism. Although the court in Demjanjuk identified murder within maritime jurisdiction and murder of internationally protected persons as offenses involving extraterritorial jurisdiction, the killings in that case did not fall within either of those categories.

2. *Lieutenant Calley was convicted of murder under the Uniform Code of Military Justice*, 10 U.S.C. § 801ff., a code applicable to a limited body of persons (e.g., members of the U.S. armed forces and prisoners of war in custody of the armed forces, 10 U.S.C. § 802). There is no statute, state or federal, that in precise terms makes the commission of war crimes punishable. Articles 18 and 21 of the Uniform Code of Military Justice (10 U.S.C. §§ 818 and 821) do so inferentially by conferring jurisdiction on courts-martial, and sanctioning the jurisdiction of military commissions, with respect to the law of war. In *Ex parte Quirin*, 317 U.S. 1 (1942), the Supreme Court stated that Congress, by its recognition of such jurisdiction, "had the choice of crystallizing in permanent form and in minute detail every offense against the law of war, or of adopting the system of common law applied by military tribunals so far as it should be recognized and deemed applicable by the courts. It chose the latter course." But the *Quirin case* involved enemy saboteurs taken in time of war. And the *Yamashita case*, 327 U.S. 1 (1946), involved an enemy general in custody immediately following the cessation of hostilities. But see the argument in Paust, *After My Lai: The Case for War Crime Jurisdiction Over Civilians in Federal District Courts*, 50 Tex.L.Rev. 6 (1971).

3. *Would you favor legislation making war crimes punishable in the United States, beyond the extent to which they may presently be punished under the Uniform Code of Military Justice?* Would you provide for universal prescriptive jurisdiction, i.e., would the statute apply to any war crime, in any war, anywhere in the world, whether or not the United States is a party to the conflict, or whether or not a United States citizen is the actor or the victim? Would such a statute make punishable war crimes in general terms, or would it list specific offenses? What offenses? *See* Komarow, *Individual Responsibility Under International Law: The Nuremberg Principles in Domestic Legal Systems*, 29 Int'l & Comp.L.Q. 21 (1980).

4. *Would you favor legislation making violations of the other Nuremberg principles (crimes against humanity and crimes against peace) punishable in the United States?* Who would be subject to the statute? Foreign citizens, including foreign officials? United States citizens, including United States officials? Again, would the statute apply to any event, anywhere in the world, irrespective of whether United States citizens were the actors or victims, or whether the United States was otherwise involved?

5. *In 1993, the Supreme Court of Israel found that the evidence was insufficient to prove beyond a reasonable doubt that Demjanjuk was "Ivan the Terrible" from Treblinka.* The 6th Circuit Court of Appeals, sua sponte ordered the U.S. Government to respond to allegations

that the prosecution had not disclosed information to the Court in the original extradition hearing that suggested Demjanjuk was not the person named in the extradition request as having been "Ivan the Terrible" of the Treblinka death camp. After Demjanjuk had been returned to the United States, a three-judge federal appeals court panel revoked the 1986 extradition order, which had sent Demjanjuk to Israel. The panel found that Justice Department lawyers committed "fraud on the court," and displayed a "win at any cost" attitude, in failing to disclose key evidence that might have caused the extradition request to be turned down. The Justice Department's Office of Special Investigations (OSI) failed to turn-over statements by two Treblinka guards (made to officials of the former Soviet Union) identifying another man (Ivan Marchenko) as "Ivan the Terrible." The OSI also failed to provide a list of Ukranian guards that it had received from the Polish Government, which included Marchenko and not Demjanjuk. They also did not disclose conflicting statements about whether Demjanjuk was "Ivan the Terrible", obtained from a German guard interviewed by the Justice Department. A "Special Master" had found that the Department of Justice had erred in "good faith", but the three-judge panel disregarded the special master's finding. The Panel noted that the OSI had acted in "bad faith," and in "reckless disregard of the truth." OSI has declared its intent to seek to expel Demjanjuk for being a guard in another Nazi concentration camp (Sobibor) and for lying about his past in his visa application (for which he was stripped of his citizenship in 1981). *See, gen.,* Isikoff, *Appellate Panel Rebukes Justice Dept. on Demjanjuk,* The Wash. Post, Nov. 18, 1993 section A, p. A–01.

6. *Canada amended its Criminal Code in 1987 to provide for the prosecution of past, present and future war criminals in Canada. However, the decision of the Supreme Court of Canada in R. v. Finta [1994]28 C.R. 265 resulted in the need for further new legislation.* The Crimes Against Humanity Act, S.C. 2000, c.24 deals with the prosecution in Canada for genocide, crimes against humanity and war crimes committed inside or outside of Canada. It use wide bases of jurisdiction including universality. The legislation's purpose is also to implement the Rome Statute on the International Criminal Court that Canada ratified in June 2000. Canada has also used extradition and denaturalization and deportation in dealing with war criminals and criminals against humanity.

2.   EXTRADITION & OTHER MEASURES OF OBTAINING JURISDICTION OVER THE PERSON

Introductory Comments and Questions.

1. *The Legal Approach to Rendition of Fugitives—What is Extradition?* International extradition is the legal means whereby sovereign nations render fugitives to the justice of other nations. It is generally a judicial process, but is administrative in some nations. The term, "extradition," was not used until the late 18th century, but it has occurred continuously since antiquity. The earliest known diplomatic document, the Treaty of Peace between Pharaoh Ramses II, and the Hittite King Hattusili III, contains an extradition provision. Treaties authorizing extradition during the Middle Ages began to appear as early as the Treaty of 1174. The first two treaties ever concluded by the U.S. included extradition clauses. U.S. extradition law is a federal, treaty based, judicial process with input and confirmation by the executive branch. Fugitives must be charged with an extraditable offense upon probable cause, not mere suspicion. It is not a means to obtain witnesses or to enforce a civil judgement. The U.S. is currently party to around 100 extradition treaties. Extradition is founded on sovereignty. Sovereign nations by definition must agree to any rendition of a fugitive. Any exercise of legal process on the territory of another, for example abduction in lieu of extradition, violates international law and the sovereignty of the nation from which the fugitive is taken.

The Supreme Court has said that, "... [the] fundamental consideration [is] that *the Constitution creates no executive prerogative to dispose of the liberty of the individual* ... There is no executive discretion to surrender ... [the fugitive] to a foreign government, unless that discretion is granted by law ... Legal authority does not exist, save as it is given by act of Congress or by the terms of a treaty." The executive branch negotiates treaties and executes the transfer. Jefferson and others criticized plenary executive power, claimed by some, as being dangerous to liberty. Traditionally, extraditable crimes were listed in treaties. Today, conduct must be punishable to a minimum level. In 1840, the Supreme Court held that no obligation to extradite existed apart from that imposed by treaty. In 1933 it reiterated: "... international law recognize[s] no right to extradition apart from treaty." In 1933 it clarified: " ... [t]he authority of the President, ... in the absence of statute conferring an independent power, must be found in the terms of the treaty ..., [where a treaty] fails to grant the ... authority, [he] is without power to surrender ..."

2. *Requirement of a Treaty*. Extradition *from* the U.S. generally requires a treaty. *See*, 18 U.S.C. 3181, et seq.; *Valentine v. U.S. ex rel. Neidecker*, 299 U.S. 5 (1936). The first extradition statute in 1848 required a treaty and judicial proceedings in federal court. This was to protect individual liberty by ensuring that all three branches be involved. It interposed the judiciary between the executive and the individual, but still allowed the Departments of State and Justice a powerful influence. From 1848 until 1996, no extradition from the U.S. was allowed without a treaty. In 1996, however, the extradition law was amended to allow surrender to the *Ad Hoc* Tribunals for the former Yugoslavia and Rwanda. *See*, Judicial Assistance Act for these tribunals, 110 Stat. 486 (1998); *see*, Wallach, Extradition to the Rwandan War Crimes Tribunal: Is Another Treaty Required?, 3 UCLA J.I.L. & For.Aff. 59 (1998); *In re Ntakirutimana v. Reno*, 184 F.3d 419 (5th Cir.1999) (reversing District Court that had refused extradition of Rwandan *génocidaire*). Canada introduced a new *Extradition Act*, S.C. 1999, c. 18 which provides for extradition to treaty partners but also to other states or "entities" listed in a schedule to the legislation or with which there is a specific agreement for the purpose of giving effect in a particular case. These "entities" are the *Ad Hoc* Tribunals mentioned above and the International Criminal Court, set up by the 1998 Rome Statute, discussed earlier in this Chapter. See Williams, *Human Rights Safeguards and International Criminal Cooperation in Extradition: Striking the Balance*, 3 Criminal Law Forum 191 (1992). Most other nations have extradition treaties, but will extradite on the basis of comity and their domestic extradition law. The U.S., however, will accept the extradition of a fugitive from a country with which the U.S. has no extant treaty, but we make it clear that reciprocity is not possible. An exception to this rule exists for crimes of violence committed by foreign nationals against U.S. nationals, if the Attorney General certifies that the conduct was terrorism under the *Omnibus Antiterrorism Act*. Extradition from the U.S. requires evidence sufficient for probable cause to believe the fugitive committed the extraditable offense. The 1998 Extradition Treaties Interpretation Act, 112 Stat 3033 made parental abduction an extraditable offense for the first time.

3. *Executive Discretion Not to Extradite.* Legislation allows executive discretion to refuse extradition. Courts cannot bind the Secretary of State to grant extradition in contravention of executive prerogative in foreign relations or its obligation to protect human rights. A fugitive has a due process right to resist extradition through judicial proceedings, but not to a full trial. The hearing must be before a magistrate with participation of counsel. It has the impact of a preliminary hearing, but some courts have held that,"[it] is not a criminal proceeding, and the person whose return is sought is not entitled to the rights available at a criminal trial at common law ...". This has been taken to mean that protections applicable to a preliminary hearing do not obtain. Probable cause is required, but the Federal Rules of Criminal Procedure and the Federal Rules of Evidence have been held not to apply. Documents of questionable authenticity are tolerated. Although the fugitive does have the right to counsel, the exclusionary rule, *ne bis in idem*, and affirmative defenses do not apply, and no right to confrontation and cross-examination applies.

In Canada, the same view is taken: an extradition hearing is not a criminal trial and the constitutional guarantees in the Canadian *Charter of Rights and Freedoms*, such as prevention of double jeopardy and the right to be tried within a reasonable period of time have no application to extradition proceedings. See *United States* v. *Schmidt*, [1987] 1S.C.R. 500 (S.C.C.). The 1971 *Extradition Treaty between Canada and the United States* entered into force in 1976, 1976 Can. T. S. No. 3, 27 U.S.T. 983, T.I.A.S. No. 8237 and was amended by the 1988 *Protocol* in force as of 1991, 1991 Can. T. S. No.37. They are contained in the Documentary Supplement. It is interesting to note that the recent Canadian *Extradition Act*, S.C. 1999, c.18, which repeals the earlier implementing legislation introduces new evidentiary requirements. Under the old legislation Canada required the foreign state to produce a *prima facie* case to substantiate its request, that is sufficient evidence as would justify a trial in Canada if the crime had been committed there. The evidence had to be admissible under Canadian evidentiary rules. The 1999 *Extradition Act* departs from this as many states, particularly civil law jurisdictions, with different evidentiary requirements for committal to trial had difficulty meeting the admissibility rules. Now, it is no longer necessary to submit first party affidavit evidence devoid of hearsay to meet the sufficiency of evidence requirement when it is gathered outside of Canada. The legislation does however require that the "record of the case" summarizing the evidence by the extradition partner for use in the prosecution must be certified by a judicial or prosecuting authority as available for trial, is sufficient to justify prosecution or was gathered according to the law of the extradition partner. Do you think that this differs from the United States approach? Although in Canada, the issue of whether the foreign state had jurisdiction over the offence under its criminal laws was once in the hands of the extradition judge since *United States* v. *Lépine*, [1994] 1 S.C.R. 286, the Supreme Court of Canada has held that the the judge is not vested with this function, but it is the hands of the executive when the request is reviewed and a decision to proceed with the case on behalf of the requesting state is made. In fact the Court has stated repeatedly, including in *Lépine* and *Schmidt* that the role of the extradition judge is the modest one of determining whether there is sufficient evidence to commit for surrender

4. *Multilateral Treaties*. There are treaties that deal with international crimes and provide that states parties may use them as a vehicle for extradition in the absence of a bilateral extradition treaty between them. Review the multilateral conventions dealing with the various aspects of international terrorism contained in the Documentary Supplement.

5. *Double Criminality*. This is one of the fundamental protections for the person sought by the foreign state. The usual approach in older treaties between states was for a schedule or list of extraditable offences to be appended to the treaty. Did this lead to outmoded lists given new international and transnational crimes and the need for states to be cognizant of the need to update by amendments? Was it necessary for both states to classify the criminal conduct in the same way? Note that the U.S. Supreme Court in *Collins v. Loisel*, 259 U.S. 309, 312 (1922) held that "[t]he law does not require that the name by which the crime is described in the two countries shall be the same; nor that the scope of liability shall be coextensive, or, in other respects, the same in the two countries. It is enough, if the particular act charged is criminal in both jurisdictions." See also *U.S. v. Sensi*, 879 F.2d 888 (D.C.Cir.1989). Article 2 of the *Canada-United States Extradition Treaty* provided that for a crime to be extraditable it had to be listed in the Schedule to the Treaty and be punishable by the laws of both contracting parties for a term of imprisonment exceeding one year. Williams in *The Double Criminality Rule Revisted*, 27 Israel L. Rev. 297 (1993) comments that in its decision in *U.S. v. McVey II*, [1992] 3 S.C.R. 475, the Supreme Court of Canada dealt with the list approach and held that " * * * what must be established is that the conduct of the fugitive, if it had occurred in Canada, constitute a crime listed in the Treaty according to a name by which it is known under the law of Canada". It does not matter that the characterization of the criminal conduct under the law of the requesting state is not in the Schedule. See also, Williams, *Extradition Since the Charter of Rights*, in Cameron (ed.) The Charter's Impact on the Criminal Justice System, Ch 22, 383–386. Since 1991 the *Protocol* to the *Canada-United States Treaty* has been in force and Article I now applies the "no-list" approach. All that is necessary for double criminality to be met is for the U.S. and Canada to both consider the conduct as criminal under their respective laws and punishable by imprisonment or other form of detention for a term exceeding one year or any greater punishment.

6. *Jurisdiction Over the Offence by the Requesting State*. The requesting state must establish jurisdiction over the criminal offence under its laws. Many of the early extradition treaties restricted this to the territorial basis of jurisdiction, but this has since been expanded to allow for extraterritorial bases such as the nationality principle. The 1976 *Canada-United Extradition Treaty* in Article 3(3) stated that where the offence was committed outside of the jurisdiction of the requesting state, the requested state "shall have the power to grant extradition if the laws of the requested state provide for jurisdiction over such an offence in similar circumstances', thus providing for a duality of jurisdictional bases. This has been enlarged further by the 1991 *Protocol* in Article III to provide that the requesting state 'shall' extradite in such circumstances and further that even where the requested state law does not provide for the basis been exercised that the 'executive of the requested state may, in its discretion, grant extradition'."

7. *The Maersk Dubai case.* An interesting case that contains several international law issues, including jurisdiction over the offence and the options open to the requested case is *Romania* v. *Cheng*, (1997), 114 C.C.C. (3d) 289. Romania presented an extradition request to Canada. The alleged offences were manslaughter, in that three Romanian stowaways had been thrown overboard on the high seas, the Atlantic Ocean, from the Taiwanese flagged vessel, the *M.V. Maersk Dubai*, by the Captain and several of the other officers. The Captain and the officers were Taiwanese nationals. They were arrested when the vessel reached Halifax, Nova Scotia in Canada, on the information laid by four Filipino crew members. Romania requested extradition based on the 1893 Extradition Treaty between Great Britain (which at that time acted on behalf of Canada in international affairs) and Romania, B.T.S. 1894 No. 14.

In terms of state succession to treaties, Canada upon emerging as an independent state in 1931 assumed all of the treaty obligations entered into on its behalf. The validity of such extradition treaties was explicitly addressed and upheld in *Ex parte O'Dell and Griffen*, [1953] O.R. 170 (Ont. H.C.), concerning the 1842 Webster–Ashburton Treaty between Great Britain and the United States.

Article 1 of the 1893 Treaty provided that for the alleged offence to be extraditable it had to have been committed in the territory of the requesting party. Clearly, Canada could not extradite to Romania. Neither could it extradite Taiwan because Canada does not recognize Taiwan as a sovereign state and has no extradition treaty with it. The third option, prosecution in Canada was also impossible as Canada uses the territorial approach in section 6(2) of the Canadian Criminal Code, subject to express extraterritorial exceptions, such as war crimes, crimes against humanity, genocide, torture and specific international terrorist offences proscribed by multilateral conventions.

Interpretation Of Extradition Treaties.

Sharon A. Williams, Extradition And The Death Penalty Exception In Canada: Resolving The Ng And Kindler Cases

13 Loyola of Los Angeles Int'l and Comp. L.J. 799,801–804.*

* * *

From a purely international perspective, extradition is a treaty matter bearing directly on the rights and duties of states, thus interstate cooperation is emphasized. From a domestic law perspective, extradition is viewed as part of the criminal process [albeit not a trial], and thus may be interpreted in a manner that emphasizes the fugitive's rights.

The fundamental rule of interpretation from the Vienna Convention on the Law of Treaties is to interpret treaties literally according to the ordinary meaning of the words in the text. Treaties must be interpreted in good faith (*pacta sunt servanda*). * * * A treaty must be interpreted in a manner that is calculated to give it effect and content, rather than to deprive it of meaning.

Applying these rules to extradition treaties, the courts in Canada and the United Kingdom have liberally interpreted such agreements in order to give effect to the treaty. * * * In [*U.S.*] v. *Schmidt* [1987] 1 S.C.R 500 (S.C.C.), Justice La Forest ** * stated:

> The present system of extradition works because courts give the treaties a fair and liberal interpretation with a view to fulfilling Canada's obligations, reducing the technicalities of criminal law to a minimum and trusting the courts in the foreign country to give the fugitive a fair trial.

* * *

In *Belgium* v. *Postlewaite*, [1987] 2 All E. R. 985 (H.L.), Lord Bridge addressed this issue stating: "In my judgement those treaties ought to receive a liberal interpretation, which means no more than they should receive their true construction according to their language, object and intent". * * * [He] indicated that courts should look for the underlying intention of the contracting parties when interpreting a treaty provision.

Notes and Questions. 1. Expansion of Extraterritorial Jurisdiction. The "war on drugs" has been used to justify expansion of extraterritorial prescriptive, enforcement and adjudicative jurisdiction. This has included a diminution of limitations to extradition and even approval of extra-legal means, including abduction to obtain fugitives and evidence from abroad. The U.S. Supreme Court has decided that the Constitution, at least the Warrant Clause of the 4th Amendment and possibly other fundamental rights extend only to "the water's edge" or the border. The

---

* Reprinted with the permission of the Comparative Law Journal.
Loyola of Los Angeles International and

infamous torture and execution-style murder of DEA agent Enrique Camarena–Salazar and his pilot, prompted the abduction of *Verdugo–Urquidez* and of *Alvarez-Machain*. In addition, the DEA conducted warrantless searches Verdugo's office and home.

**2. *The"Water's Edge Rule"*—*U.S. v. Verdugo–Urquidez*, 494 U.S. 259 (1990) (discussed below by the Supreme Court in its *Alvarez-Machain* decision) held that the term, *"the people"* in the 4th Amendment (and perhaps that in the 1st, 2nd, 9th, and 10th Amendments) "refer[s] to a class of persons who are part of a national community or who have otherwise developed sufficient connection with this community to be considered part of that community * * *." The actual holding in *Verdugo* was limited to the "Warrant Clause" of the 4th Amendment, which was held not to apply to searches or seizures of a foreign national's foreign home, office, or effects, or to his person. Four justices argued that the 4th amendment did not apply abroad at all, so neither probable cause nor the duty to conduct a search or seizure reasonably obtain. The exclusionary rule did not apply to evidence obtained pursuant to a search that would have been unlawful under the 4th Amendment. Ruth Wedgwood has coined the term, the water's edge rule, "[which], except for citizens and resident aliens, stems from the plurality's sense that U.S. action abroad must be governed by necessity, a sense more familiar to war than to peace * * *." *Verdugo-Urquidez*, 84 AJIL 747, 752 (1990); *see also*, Amann, *A Whipsaw Cuts Both Ways: The Privilege Against Self–Incrimination in an International Context*, 45 UCLA L.Rev. 1201 (1998); Amann, *Application of Fifth Amendment to U.S. Constitution in International Context—Fear of Foreign Prosecution as Ground for Invoking Privilege Against Self–Incrimination*, 92 A.J.I.L. 759 (1998). Is the Court wise to adopt war-founded ideas to limit or exclude the application of constitutional principles? Does "war" beget more or less rationality than peace? What would be the result of the *Verdugo* Court's reasoning on an attempt to exclude a confession or other evidence obtained by extraterritorial torture? Does the *Verdugo* decision suggest that the U.S., otherwise presumably dedicated to the rule of law, is in effect sponsoring—under the Latin motto *male captus, bene detenus*—kidnaping and other illegal practices? *See*, Gurule, *Terrorism, Territorial Sovereignty, and the Forcible apprehension of International Criminals Abroad*, 17 Hastings Int'l & Comp. L. Rev. 457 (1994) (arguing that the Alvarez–Machain decision did not grant federal agents the authority to abduct fugitives). These questions apply to the Alvarez–Machain case, which follows immediately.

United States v. Alvarez–Machain

United States Supreme Court, 1992.
504 U.S. 655, 112 S.Ct. 2188, 119 L.Ed.2d 441.

■ REHNQUIST, C.J. The issue in this case is whether a criminal defendant, abducted to the United States from a nation with which it has an extradition treaty, thereby acquires a defense to the jurisdiction of this country's courts. We hold that he does not, and that he may be tried in federal district court for violations of the criminal law of the United States.

Respondent, Alvarez–Machain, is a citizen and resident of Mexico. He was indicted for participating in the kidnap and murder of United States Drug Enforcement Administration (DEA) special agent Enrique Camarena–Salazar and a Mexican pilot working with Camarena, Alfredo Zavala–Avelar. The DEA believes that respondent, a medical doctor, participated in the murder by prolonging agent Camarena's life so that others could further torture and interrogate him. On April 2, 1990, respondent was forcibly kidnaped from his medical office in Guadalajara, Mexico, to be flown by private plane to El Paso, Texas, where he was arrested by DEA officials. The District Court concluded that DEA agents were responsible for respondent's abduction, although they were not personally involved in it.[a]

Respondent moved to dismiss the indictment, claiming that his abduction constituted outrageous governmental conduct, and that the District Court lacked jurisdiction to try him because he was abducted in violation of the [U.S.—Mexico] Extradition Treaty. The District Court rejected the outrageous governmental conduct claim, but held that it lacked jurisdiction to try respondent because his abduction violated the Extradition Treaty. The district court discharged respondent and ordered that he be repatriated to Mexico . . .

The Court of Appeals affirmed the dismissal of the indictment and the repatriation of respondent, relying on its decision in [U.S. v. Verdugo–Urquidez] . . .[b] Although the Treaty does not expressly prohibit such abductions, the Court of Appeals held that the "purpose" of the Treaty was violated by a forcible abduction, * * * which, along with a formal protest by the offended nation, would give a defendant the right to invoke the Treaty violation to defeat jurisdiction of the district court to try him. The Court of Appeals further held that the proper remedy for such a violation would be dismissal of the indictment and repatriation of the defendant to Mexico.

In the instant case, the Court of Appeals affirmed the district court's finding that the United States had authorized the abduction of respondent, and that letters from the Mexican government to the United States government served as an official protest of the Treaty violation. Therefore, the Court of Appeals ordered that the indictment against respondent be dismissed and that respondent be repatriated to Mexico * * *. We granted certiorari * * * and now reverse.

Although we have never before addressed the precise issue raised, * * *, we have previously considered proceedings in claimed violation of an extradition treaty, and proceedings against a defendant brought before a court by means of a forcible abduction. We addressed the former issue in

---

a. Apparently, DEA officials had attempted to gain respondent's presence in the United States through informal negotiations with Mexican officials, but were unsuccessful. DEA officials then, through a contact in Mexico, offered to pay a reward and expenses in return for the delivery of respondent to the United States. U.S. v. Caro–Quintero.

b. Verdugo–Urquidez was also indicted for the murder of agent Camarena. In an earlier decision, we held that the 4th Amendment did not apply to a search by United States agents of Verdugo–Urquidez' home in Mexico. U.S. v. Verdugo–Urquidez, 494 U.S. 259 (1990).

U.S. v. Rauscher, 119 U.S. 407 (1886); more precisely, the issue of whether the *Webster–Ashburton Treaty of 1842*, which governed extraditions between England and the United States, prohibited the prosecution of defendant Rauscher for a crime other than the crime for which he had been extradited. Whether this prohibition, known as the doctrine of specialty, was an intended part of the Treaty had been disputed between the two nations for some time. Justice Miller delivered the opinion of the Court, which carefully examined the terms and history of the Treaty; the practice of nations in regards to extradition treaties; the case law from the states; and the writings of commentators, and reached the following conclusion: "[A] person who has been brought within the jurisdiction of the court *by virtue of proceedings under an extradition treaty,* can only be tried for one of the offenses described in that treaty, and for the offence with which he is charged in the proceedings for his extradition, until a reasonable time and opportunity have been given him, after his release or trial upon such charge, to return to the country from whose asylum he had been forcibly taken under those proceedings." *Id.*, at 430 (*emphasis added*). In addition, Justice Miller's opinion noted that any doubt as to this interpretation was put to rest by two federal statutes which imposed the doctrine of specialty upon extradition treaties to which the U.S. was a party * * *. Unlike the case before us today, the defendant in Rauscher had been brought to the U.S. by way of an extradition treaty; there was no issue of a forcible abduction.

In *Ker v. Illinois*, 119 U.S. 436 (1886), also written by Justice Miller and decided the same day as Rauscher, we addressed the issue of a defendant brought before the court by way of a forcible abduction. Ker had been tried and convicted in an Illinois court for larceny; his presence before the court was procured by means of forcible abduction from Peru. A messenger was sent to Lima with the proper warrant to demand Ker by virtue of the extradition treaty between Peru and the United States. The messenger, however, disdained reliance on the treaty processes, and instead forcibly kidnaped Ker and brought him to the United States. We distinguished Ker's case from Rauscher, on the basis that Ker was not brought into the United States by virtue of the extradition treaty between the United States and Peru, and rejected Ker's argument that he had a right under the extradition treaty to be returned to this country only in accordance with its terms. We rejected Ker's due process argument more broadly, holding in line with "the highest authorities" that "such forcible abduction is no sufficient reason why the party should not answer when brought within the jurisdiction of the court which has the right to try him for such an offence, and presents no valid objection to his trial in such court." * * *.

In *Frisbie v. Collins*, 342 U.S. 519 * * * (1952), we applied the rule in Ker to a case in which the defendant had been kidnaped in Chicago by Michigan officers and brought to trial in Michigan. We upheld the conviction over objections based on the due process clause and the Federal Kidnaping Act and stated: "... There is nothing in the Constitution that requires a court to permit a guilty person rightfully convicted to escape justice because he was brought to trial against his will."

The only differences between Ker and the present case are that Ker was decided on the premise that there was no governmental involvement in the abduction, * * * and Peru, from which Ker was abducted, did not object to his prosecution. Respondent finds these differences to be dispositive, as did the Court of Appeals in Verdugo, * * *, contending that they show that respondent's prosecution, like the prosecution of Rauscher, violates the implied terms of a valid extradition treaty. The Government * * * argues that Rauscher stands as an "exception" to the rule in Ker only when an extradition treaty is invoked, and the terms of the treaty prove that its breach will limit the jurisdiction of a court * * *. Therefore, our first inquiry must be whether the abduction of respondent from Mexico violated the [U.S.—Mexico] extradition treaty. If we conclude that the Treaty does not prohibit respondent's abduction, the rule in Ker applies, and the court need not inquire as to how respondent came before it.

In construing a treaty, as in construing a statute, we first look to its terms to determine its meaning. * * * The Treaty says nothing about the obligations of the United States and Mexico to refrain from forcible abductions of people from the territory of the other nation, or the consequences under the Treaty if such an abduction occurs. * * *

More critical to respondent's argument is Article 9 of the Treaty:

1. Neither Contracting Party shall be bound to deliver up its own nationals, but the executive authority of the requested Party shall, if not prevented by the laws of that Party, have the power to deliver them up if, in its discretion, it be deemed proper to do so.

2. If extradition is not granted pursuant to paragraph 1 of this Article, the requested Party shall submit the case to its competent authorities for the purpose of prosecution, proved that Party has jurisdiction over the offense.

According to respondent, Article 9 embodies the terms of the bargain which the United States struck: if the United States wishes to prosecute a Mexican national, it may request that individual's extradition. Upon a request from the United States, Mexico may either extradite the individual, or submit the case to the proper authorities for prosecution in Mexico. In this way, respondent reasons, each nation preserved its right to choose whether its nationals would be tried in its own courts or by the courts of the other nation. This preservation of rights would be frustrated if either nation were free to abduct nationals of the other nation for the purposes of prosecution. More broadly, respondent reasons, as did the Court of Appeals, that all the processes and restrictions on the obligation to extradite established by the Treaty would make no sense if either nation were free to resort to forcible kidnaping to gain the presence of an individual for prosecution in a manner not contemplated by the Treaty. * * *

We do not read the Treaty in such a fashion. Article 9 does not purport to specify the only way in which one country may gain custody of a national of the other country for the purposes of prosecution. In the absence of an extradition treaty, nations are under no obligation to surrender those in their country to foreign authorities for prosecution. * * * Extradition treaties exist so as to impose mutual obligations to surrender individuals in

certain defined sets of circumstances, following established procedures
* * *. The Treaty provides a mechanism which would not otherwise exist,
requiring, under certain circumstances, the United States and Mexico to
extradite individuals to the other country, and establishing the procedures
to be followed when the Treaty is invoked.

The history of negotiation and practice under the Treaty also fails to
show that abductions outside of the Treaty constitute a violation of the
Treaty. As the Solicitor General notes, the Mexican government was made
aware, as early as 1906, of the Ker doctrine, and the United States' position
that it applied to forcible abductions made outside of the terms of the U.S.–
Mexico Extradition Treaty.[c] Nonetheless, the current version of the Treaty,
signed in 1978, does not attempt to establish a rule that would in any way
curtail the effect of Ker. Moreover, although language which would grant
individuals exactly the right sought by respondent had been considered and
drafted as early as 1935 by a prominent group of legal scholars sponsored
by the faculty of Harvard Law School, no such clause appears in the
current treaty.[d]

Thus, the language of the Treaty, in the context of its history, does not
support the proposition that the Treaty prohibits abductions outside of its
terms. The remaining question, therefore, is whether the Treaty should be
interpreted so as to include an implied term prohibiting prosecution where
the defendant's presence is obtained by means other than those established
by the Treaty....

Respondent contends that the Treaty must be interpreted against the
backdrop of customary international law, and that international abductions
are "so clearly prohibited in international law" that there was no reason to
include such a clause in the Treaty itself * * *. The international censure
of international abductions is further evinced, according to respondent, by
the [U.N. and O.A.S. Charters]. * * * Respondent does not argue that
these sources of international law prove an independent basis for the right
respondent asserts not to be tried in the United States, but rather that
they should inform the interpretation of the Treaty terms.

The Court of Appeals deemed it essential, * * * for the individual
defendant to assert a right under the Treaty, that the affected foreign

c. In correspondence between the United States and Mexico growing out of the 1905 Martinez incident, in which a Mexican national was abducted from Mexico and brought to the United States for trial, the Mexican charge wrote to the Secretary of State protesting that as Martinez' arrest was made outside of the procedures established in the extradition treaty, "the action pending against the man can not rest [on] any legal foundation." * * * The Secretary of State responded that the exact issue raised by the Martinez incident had been decided by Ker, and that the remedy open to the Mexican government, namely a request to the United States for extradition of Martinez' abductor

had been granted by the United States * * *. Respondent and the Court of Appeals stress a statement made in 1881 by Secretary of State James Blaine to the governor of Texas to the effect that the extradition treaty in its form at that time did not authorize unconsented to abductions from Mexico. * * * This misses the mark, however, for the Government's argument is not that the Treaty authorizes the abduction of respondent; but that the Treaty does not prohibit the abduction.

d. *Editors' note*: The U.S. and Mexico signed, in spring 1994, a treaty supplement, which now explicitly prohibits such abductions.

government had registered a protest * * *. Respondent agrees that the right exercised by the individual is derivative of the nation's right under the Treaty, since nations are authorized, notwithstanding the terms of an extradition treaty, to voluntarily render an individual to the other country on terms completely outside of those proved in the Treaty. The formal protest * * * ensures that the "offended" nation actually objects to the abduction and has not in some way voluntarily rendered the individual for prosecution. Thus the Extradition Treaty only prohibits gaining the defendant's presence by means other than those set forth in the Treaty when the nation from which the defendant was abducted objects.

This argument seems to us inconsistent with the remainder of respondent's argument. The Extradition Treaty has the force of law, and if, as respondent asserts, it is self-executing, it would appear that a court must enforce it on behalf of an individual regardless of the offensiveness of the practice of one nation to the other nation. . . .

More fundamentally, the difficulty with the support respondent garners from international law is that none of it relates to the practice of nations in relation to extradition treaties. In Rauscher, we implied a term in the Webster–Ashburton Treaty because of the practice of nations with regard to extradition treaties. In the instant case, respondent would imply terms in the Extradition Treaty from the practice of nations with regards to international law more generally. Respondent would have us find that the Treaty acts as a prohibition against a violation of the general principle of international law that one government may not "exercise its police power in the territory of another state." * * * There are many actions which could be taken by a nation that would violate this principle, including waging war, but it cannot seriously be contended an invasion of the United States by Mexico would violate the terms of the Extradition Treaty. . . . In sum, to infer from this Treaty and its terms that it prohibits all means of gaining the presence of an individual outside of its terms goes beyond established precedent and practice * * *. The general principles cited by respondent simply fail to persuade us that we should imply in the U.S.–Mexico Extradition Treaty a term prohibiting international abductions.

Respondent and his *amici* may be correct that respondent's abduction was "shocking," * * *, and that it may be in violation of general international law principles. Mexico has protested the abduction of respondent through diplomatic notes * * *, and the decision of whether respondent should be returned to Mexico, as a matter outside of the Treaty, is a matter for the Executive Branch. [*The Mexican Government has requested the extradition of two individuals who allegedly participated in the abduction from Mexico*]. We conclude, however, that respondent's abduction was not in violation of the [U.S.—Mexico Extradition Treaty], and therefore the rule of Ker v. Illinois is fully applicable to this case. The fact of respondent's forcible abduction does not therefore prohibit his trial in a [U.S.] court for violations of the criminal laws of the United States * * *.

■ JUSTICE STEVENS, with whom JUSTICE BLACKMUN and JUSTICE O'CONNOR join, dissenting.

* * * The case is unique for several reasons. It does not involve an ordinary abduction by a private kidnaper, or bounty hunter, as in *Ker* ...; nor does it involve the apprehension of an American fugitive who committed a crime in one State and sought asylum in another, as in *Frisbie* ... Rather, it involves this country's abduction of another country's citizen; it also involves a violation of the territorial integrity of that other country, with which this country has signed an extradition treaty.

A Mexican citizen was kidnaped in Mexico and charged with a crime committed in Mexico; his offense allegedly violated both Mexican and American law. Mexico has formally demanded on at least two separate occasions that he be returned to Mexico and has represented that he will be prosecuted and punished for his alleged offense. It is clear that Mexico's demand must be honored if this official abduction violated the 1978 [U.S.—Mexico] Extradition Treaty ... In my opinion, a fair reading of the treaty in light of our decision in [*U.S. v. Rauscher*] * * *, and applicable principles of international law, leads inexorably to the conclusion that the District Court, [*Caro–Quintero*], and the Court of Appeals for the Ninth Circuit ... correctly construed that instrument.

* * *

I

The Extradition Treaty with Mexico is a comprehensive document * * *. The parties announced their purpose in the preamble: The two Governments desire "to cooperate more closely in the fight against crime and, to this end, to mutually render better assistance in matters of extradition." From the preamble, through the description of the parties' obligations with respect to offenses committed within as well as beyond the territory of a requesting party, the delineation of the procedures and evidentiary requirements for extradition, the special provisions for political offenses and capital punishment, and other details, the Treaty appears to have been designed to cover the entire subject of extradition. Thus, Article 22, entitled "Scope of Application" states that the "Treaty shall apply to offenses specified in Article 2 committed before and after this Treaty enters into force," and Article 2 directs that "[e]xtradition shall take place, subject to this Treaty, for willful acts which fall within any of [the extraditable offenses listed in] the clauses of the Appendix." Moreover, as noted by the Court * * *, Article 9 expressly proves that neither Contracting Party is bound to deliver up its own nationals, although it may do so in its discretion, but if it does not do so, it "shall submit the case to its competent authorities for purposes of prosecution."

Petitioner's claim that the Treaty is not exclusive, but permits forcible governmental kidnaping, would transform these, and other, provisions into little more than verbiage. For example, provisions requiring "sufficient" evidence to grant extradition (Art. 3), withholding extradition for political or military offenses (Art. 5), withholding extradition when the person sought has already been tried (Art. 6), withholding extradition when the statute of limitations for the crime has lapsed (Art. 7), and granting the requested State discretion to refuse to extradite an individual who would face the death penalty in the requesting country (Art. 8), would serve little purpose if the requesting country could simply kidnap the person . . . "[E]ach of these provisions would be utterly frustrated if a kidnaping were held to be a permissible course of governmental conduct [*quoting 9th Cir. decision in U.S. v. Verdugo–Urquidez*]." [A]ll of these provisions only make sense if they are understood as requiring each treaty signatory to comply with those procedures whenever it wishes to obtain jurisdiction over an individual who is located in another treaty nation. [*Id.*]

It is true, as the Court notes, that there is no express promise by either party to refrain from forcible abductions in the territory of the other Nation * * *. Relying on that omission, the Court, in effect, concludes that the Treaty merely creates an optional method of obtaining jurisdiction over alleged offenders, and that the parties silently reserved the right to resort to self help whenever they deem force more expeditious than legal process. If the United States, for example, thought it more expedient to torture or simply to execute a person rather than to attempt extradition, these options would be equally available because they, too, were not explicitly prohibited by the Treaty. That, however, is a highly improbable interpretation of a consensual agreement, which on its face appears to have been intended to set forth comprehensive and exclusive rules concerning the subject of extradition. In my opinion, "the manifest scope and object of the treaty itself," plainly imply a mutual undertaking to respect the territorial integrity of the other contracting party. That opinion is confirmed by a consideration of the "legal context" in which the Treaty was negotiated * * *.

II

* * *

The Court [in *Rauscher*] noted that the [U.S.–U.K.] Treaty included several specific provisions, such as the crimes for which one could be extradited, the process by which the extradition was to be carried out, and even the evidence that was to be produced, and concluded that "the fair purpose of the treaty is, that the person shall be delivered up to be tried for that offence and for no other." * * *. The Court reasoned that it did not make sense for the Treaty to prove such specifics only to have the person "pas[s] into the hands of the country which charges him with the offence, free from all the positive requirements and just implications of the Treaty under which the transfer of his person takes place." * * *. To interpret the Treaty in a contrary way would mean that a country could request extradition of a person for one of the seven crimes covered by the Treaty, and then try the person for another crime, such as a political crime, which was clearly not covered by the Treaty; this result, the Court concluded, was clearly contrary to the intent of the parties and the purpose of the Treaty.

. . .

. . . [T]he, the Extradition Treaty, as understood in the context of cases that have addressed similar issues, suffices to protect the defendant from prosecution despite the absence of any express language in the Treaty itself purporting to limit this Nation's power to prosecute a defendant over whom it had lawfully acquired jurisdiction.

Although the Court's conclusion in Rauscher was supported by a number of judicial precedents, the holdings in these cases were not nearly as uniform as the consensus of international opinion that condemns one Nation's violation of the territorial integrity of a friendly neighbor.[e] It is shocking that a party to an extradition treaty might believe that it has secretly reserved the right to make seizures of citizens in the other party's territory. Justice Story found it shocking enough that the United States would attempt to justify an American seizure of a foreign vessel in a Spanish port: "But, even supposing, for a moment, that our laws had required an entry of the Apollon, in her transit, does it follow, that the power to arrest her was meant to be given, after she had passed into the exclusive territory of a foreign nation? We think not. *It would be monstrous* to suppose that our revenue officers were authorized to enter into foreign ports and territories, for the purpose of seizing vessels which had offended against our laws. It cannot be presumed that Congress would voluntarily justify such a clear violation of the laws of nations." The *Apollon*, 9 Wheat. 362, 370–371 (1824) (*emphasis added*).[f]

The law of Nations, as understood by Justice Story in 1824, has not changed. Thus, a leading treatise explains: "A State must not perform acts of sovereignty in the territory of another State."

" * * *

"It is * * * a breach of International Law for a State to send its agents to the territory of another State to apprehend persons accused of having committed a crime. Apart from other satisfaction, the first duty of the offending State is to hand over the person in question to the State in whose territory he was apprehended." ... Commenting on the precise issue raised by this case, the chief reporter for the American Law Institute's Restate-

---

e. When Abraham Sofaer, Legal Adviser of the State Department, was questioned at a congressional hearing, he resisted the notion that such seizures were acceptable: " 'Can you imagine us going into Paris and seizing some person we regard as a terrorist * * *? [H]ow would we feel if some foreign nation—let us take the United Kingdom—came over here and seized some terrorist suspect in New York City, or Boston, or Philadelphia, * * * because we refused through the normal channels of international, legal communications, to extradite that individual?' "Bill To Authorize Prosecution of Terrorists and Others Who Attack U.S. Government Employees and Citizens Abroad: Hearing before the Subcommittee on Security and Terrorism of the Senate Committee on the Judiciary, 99th Cong., 1st Sess., 63 (1985).

f. Justice Story's opinion continued: "The arrest of the offending vessel must, therefore, be restrained to places where our jurisdiction is complete, to our own waters, or to the ocean, the common highway of all nations. It is said, that there is a revenue jurisdiction, which is distinct from the ordi-

nary maritime jurisdiction over waters within the range of a common shot from our shores. And the provisions in the Collection Act of 1799, which authorize a visitation of vessels within four leagues of our coasts, are referred to in proof of the assertion. But where is that right of visitation to be exercised? In a foreign territory, in the exclusive jurisdiction of another sovereign? Certainly not; for the very terms of the act confine it to the ocean, where all nations have a common right, and exercise a common sovereignty. And over what vessels is this right of visitation to be exercised? By the very words of the act, over our own vessels, and over foreign vessels bound to our ports, and over no others. To have gone beyond this, would have been an usurpation of exclusive sovereignty on the ocean, and an exercise of an universal right of search, a right which has never yet been acknowledged by other nations, and would be resisted by none with more pertinacity than by the American." The Apollon, 9 Wheat., at 371–373.

ment of Foreign Relations used language reminiscent of Justice Story's characterization of an official seizure in a foreign jurisdiction as "monstrous:"

When done without consent of the foreign government, abducting a person from a foreign country is a gross violation of international law and gross disrespect for a norm high in the opinion of mankind. It is a blatant violation of the territorial integrity of another state; it eviscerates the extradition system (established by a comprehensive network of treaties involving virtually all states).

III

A critical flaw pervades the Court's entire opinion. It fails to differentiate between the conduct of private citizens, which does not violate any treaty obligation, and conduct expressly authorized by the Executive Branch . . ., which unquestionably constitutes a flagrant violation of international law, and in my opinion, also constitutes a breach of our treaty obligations. Thus, at the outset, the Court states the issue as "whether a criminal defendant, abducted to the United States from a nation with which it has an extradition treaty, thereby acquires a defense to the jurisdiction of this country's courts." * * * That, of course, is the question decided in *Ker v. Illinois*; it is not, however, the question presented for decision today.

The importance of the distinction between a court's exercise of jurisdiction over either a person or property that has been wrongfully seized by a private citizen, or even by a state-law enforcement agent, on the one hand, and the attempted exercise of jurisdiction predicated on a seizure by federal officers acting beyond their authority conferred by treaty, on the other, [was recognized in 1933, in *Cook v. U.S.* 288 U.S. 102] . . .

[*Discussing common law rules of seizure*] [T]he objection to the seizure is not that it was wrongful merely because made by one upon whom the government had not conferred authority to seize at the place where the seizure was made. The objection is that the Government itself lacked power to seize, since by the Treaty it had imposed a territorial limitation upon its own authority. The Treaty fixes the conditions under which a "vessel may be seized and taken into a [U.S. port], . . . for adjudication in accordance with applicable laws. Thereby, Great Britain agreed that adjudication may follow a rightful seizure. Our Government, lacking power to seize, lacked power, because of the Treaty, to subject the vessel to our laws. To hold that adjudication may follow a wrongful seizure would go far to nullify the purpose and effect of the Treaty. . . ."

The Court's failure to differentiate between private abductions and official invasions of another sovereign's territory also accounts for its misplaced reliance on the 1935 proposal made by the Advisory Committee on Research in International Law . . . [Where] the text . . . plainly states, it would have rejected the rule of [*Ker*]. The failure to adopt that recommendation does not speak to the issue the Court decides today. The Court's admittedly "shocking" disdain for customary and conventional international law principles, . . . is thus entirely unsupported by case law and commentary.

IV

As the Court observes at the outset of its opinion, there is reason to believe that respondent participated in an especially brutal murder of an American law enforcement agent. That fact, if true, may explain the Executive's intense interest in punishing respondent in our courts. Such an explanation, however, proves no justification for disregarding the Rule of Law that this Court has a duty to uphold. That the Executive may wish to reinterpret the Treaty to allow for an action that the Treaty in no way authorizes should not influence this Court's interpretation. Indeed, the desire for revenge exerts "a kind of hydraulic pressure * * * before which even well settled principles of law will bend," *Northern Securities Co. v. U.S.* * * * (1904) (Holmes, J., dissenting), but it is precisely at such moments that we should remember and be guided by our duty "to render judgment evenly and dispassionately according to law, as each is given understanding to ascertain and apply it." ... The way that we perform that duty in a case of this kind sets an example that other tribunals in other countries are sure to emulate.

The significance of this Court's precedents is illustrated by a recent decision of the Court of Appeal of the Republic of South Africa. Based largely on its understanding of the import of this Court's cases—including our decision in *Ker* ...—that court held that the prosecution of a defendant kidnaped by agents of South Africa in another country must be dismissed. *S v. Ebrahim*, S.Afr.L.Rep. (Apr.–June 1991). The Court of Appeal of South Africa—indeed, I suspect most courts throughout the civilized world will be deeply disturbed by the "monstrous" decision the Court announces today. For every Nation that has an interest in preserving the Rule of Law is affected, directly or indirectly, by a decision of this character. As Thomas Paine warned, an "avidity to punish is always dangerous to liberty" because it leads a Nation "to stretch, to misinterpret, and to misapply even the best of laws." To counter that tendency, he reminds us: "He that would make his own liberty secure must guard even his enemy from oppression; for if he violates this duty he establishes a precedent that will reach to himself."

***Notes & Questions.* 1. *For discussion of Alvarez–Machain*,** *see* 86 AJIL 811 (No. 4) (1992) (comment by Jacques Semmelman); Vagts, *Taking Treaties Less Seriously*, 92 A.J.I.L. 458 (1998); Wiehl, *Extradition at the Crossroads: The Trend Toward Extending Greater Constitutional Procedural Protections to Fugitives Fighting Extradition from the U.S.*, 19 Mich. J.Int'l L. 729 (1998); Mitchell, *Domestic Rights & International Responsibilities: Extradition Under the Canadian Charter*, 23 Yale J.I.L. 141 (1998); Glennon, *State–Sponsored Abduction: A Comment on U.S. v. Alvarez–Machain*, 86 AJIL 746 (1992); Halberstam, *In Defense of the Supreme Court Decision in Alvarez–Machain*, 86 AJIL 736 (1992); Gurule, *Terrorism, Territorial Sovereignty, and the Forcible apprehension of International Criminals Abroad*, 17 Hastings Int'l & Comp. L. Rev. 457 (1994) (arguing that the *Alvarez-Machain* decision did not grant federal agents the authority to abduct fugitives).

   2.   *Reservation to abduct*. The majority in *Alvarez* stated that the parties to the extradition treaty silently reserved the right to resort to self-help, if deemed expedient. Do nations have the right or legal authority to resort to such self help? The extradition treaty did not explicitly prohibit abduction. Is the defendant's argument that the treaty implicitly does this a strong one? Is this at odds with the whole rationale behind having extradition treaties that protect state sovereignty and the human rights of the person sought?The U.S. and Mexico have negotiated and entered into a new extradition treaty, which specifies explicitly that extradition is the sole means of obtaining custody of a fugitive for prosecution. See, Cruz, Villereal & Velasco, *Oued listo el tratado de extradition y será signado a más tardar en abril: Tello, EL UNIVERSAL (Mexico City) Feb. 20, 1994,* at p. 31, col. 1.

   3.   *Liberal interpretation*. Is the tradition of interpreting extradition treaties liberally in favor of the requesting state a good one? Is extradition a criminal process? It does put a fugitive in jeopardy of life and liberty much like a preliminary hearing. If this is so, does it deserve the same constitutional protections? On treaty interpretation, read articles 31 and 32 of the *Vienna Convention on Treaties* to which the U.S. is a party [*see* DOC. SUPP.]. These articles provide, not surprisingly, that treaty terms are to be interpreted in light of "their ordinary meaning [read] in their context and in light of [their] object and purpose, [including] any relevant rules of international law." Is this what the Chief Justice did in *Alvarez-Machain*? Does it make sense that parties to an extradition treaty would think it necessary to provide that even if extradition is inexpedient, abduction would not be allowed? The Court did concede that abduction "may be in violation of general international law principles * * * the decision of whether respondent should be returned to Mexico, as a matter outside of the Treaty, is a matter for the Executive branch." Is this point correct under the Constitution? If it is a possible interpretation, is it wise? Is it required? Does or should the judiciary have any role at all in the arena of returning fugitives? Extradition is premised on the principle that nations are sovereign and must agree to any foreign enforcement of law within their territory? Is it not true that this is the very reason for which extradition treaties are necessary? *See* discussion in Chapters 12, 14, and 15 on the Political Question Doctrine and other issues related to the separation and sharing of powers under the Constitution. *See also,* Bederman, *Deference or Deception: Treaty Rights as Political Questions,* 70 U.Colo.L.Rev. 1439 (Symposium, 1999); Goldsmith, *The New Formalism in United States Foreign Relations Law,* 70 U.Colo.L.Rev. 1395 (Symposium, 1999); Blakesley, *Autumn of the Patriarch: The Pinochet Extradition Case & Beyond,* 91 J.Crim.L. & Crim. 1 (2001).

   4.   *"Standing" to object to kidnaping*: In *Ker v. Illinois,* 119 U.S. 436 (1886), the defendant was kidnaped in Peru, but the court held the mode of his arrest was not a constitutional ground for objection to his trial. The defendant was a U.S. national, but the court did not discuss the bearing, if any, of his nationality in holding he had no standing to object to his unlawful arrest. In *Frisbie v. Collins*, 342 U.S. 519 (1952), the Court relied on its decision in *Ker*, holding that a defendant arrested in Illinois by officers from Michigan similarly had no constitutional ground for objecting to his trial.

5. ***Dismissal of the charges against Alvarez–Machain***. On remand, the district court judge dismissed the case against Alvarez for want of evidence, noting that it was noting more than the "wildest speculation." He was allowed to return home. *See*, Mydans, *Judge Clears Mexican in Agent's Killing*, N.Y. Times, A12, Dec. 15, 1992.

6. ***Reflection on U.S. Treaty Commitments***. Vagts wrote:

The mood in the United States about treaty commitments has turned distinctly negative. This has gone so far as to dismay both actual and potential treaty partners of the United States and, in general, all who are concerned about the performance of the country in the realm of international law ... The American reaction is most striking with respect to a willingness to disregard existing treaty obligations ... A series of opinions by the Supreme Court have struck observers abroad and in the United States as extremely restrictive in that sense. Clearly, no international tribunal would be likely to have construed the Extradition Treaty with Mexico as did the Court in United States v. Alvarez–Machain. Such a tribunal would have found, by interpreting the treaty in "good faith," that the United States had an obligation not to bypass the treaty by kidnaping the defendant from Mexican soil, an acknowledged violation of customary international law. The following year, in Sale v. Haitian Centers Council, Inc., [509 U.S. 155 (1993)] the Supreme Court's reading of the United Nations Protocol on the Status of Refugees and the associated portions of our immigration legislation strained the text to free the United States to intercept Haitian refugees on the high seas. The Court found support for that conclusion very largely in negotiating history consisting of statements by the Swiss delegation that, one infers, were trying both to justify Switzerland's exclusion of Jews fleeing the Holocaust in 1942 and to allow future exclusions of "mass migrations." The earlier Aerospatiale case [482 U.S. 522 (1987)] freed U.S. courts to continue to require foreign litigants in U.S. courts to provide discovery under the Federal Rules of Civil Procedure rather than make parties seeking that information resort to international cooperative measures set forth in the Hague Convention. The result in all three cases was to prevent treaty commitments from altering the way we are used to doing things ... Vagts, *Taking Treaties Less Seriously*, 92 A.J.I.L. 458 (1998).

Van Alstine continues the thought.

[U.S.] jurisprudence remains rooted in the ... premise that treaties solely reflect a "contract" between sovereign nations. The consequence has been an inflated view of both the subjective intent of "the parties" and the degree of appropriate deference to the views of the Executive Branch in interpretive inquiries ... [T]he common practical outcome of treaty interpretation by the Court has been of a distinctly conservative nature ... [T]he Court has consistently refused to view a treaty as a body of integrated norms that is capable of generating internal solutions for gaps in its provisions. Instead, when faced with an unsettled question under a treaty, the common approach has been to retreat to otherwise applicable domestic law, "whatever may be the imperfections or difficulties" this may leave in the fulfillment of the international law project.... Van Alstine, *Dynamic Treaty Interpretation*, 146 U. Pa. L. Rev. 687 (1998).

Do you agree with Professors Vagts and Van Alstine? Is this part of what occurred in *Alvarez-Machain*? Is it a different problem with similar roots? For more on treaty interpretation in U.S. law, see Chapter 11.

   7. *Extradition Treaties & Customary International Law.* *Alvarez–Machain's* essential argument was that customary international law prohibits official abduction and requires repatriation. Did the Court gratuitously disparage customary international law as a source of law for decision in the case? Or, can the case be read as one that actually provides subtle support for the customary rule, but not the remedy sought? Extradition is the agreed-upon legal method for rendering fugitives to another's justice. Could Justice Rehnquist's opinion in *Alvarez-Machain* actually be read as holding only that releasing the fugitive would not be the proper remedy? On the subject of the relationship of treaty and custom, in international law and U.S. law, *see* the recent scholarly debate, including: Bradley & Goldsmith, *Customary International Law as Federal Common Law: A Critique of the Modern Position,* 110 Harv.L.Rev. 815 (1997); Koh, *Is International Law Really State Law?,* 111 Harv. L.Rev. 1824 (1998); Bradley & Goldsmith, *The Current Illegitimacy of International Human Rights Litigation,* 66 Fordham L. Rev. 319 (1997); Gerald Neuman, *Sense & Nonsense About Customary International Law: A Response to Professors Bradley & Goldsmith,* 66 Fordham L.Rev. 371 (1997); Stephens, *The Law of Our Land: Customary International Law as Federal Law After Erie,* 66 Fordham L.Rev. 393 (1997); Goodman & Jinks, *Filartiga's Firm Footing: International Rights & Federal Common Law,* 66 Fordham L.Rev. 463 (1997).

   8. *Does the Alvarez decision place U.S. nationals at risk?* Justice Stevens in his dissent quoted Thomas Paine who warned that: "avidity to punish is always dangerous to liberty [because it leads a nation]" stretch, to misinterpret, and to misapply even the best of laws. Does the *Alvarez-Machain* decision create this risk? Certainly, the Executive Branch has "legitimated" abductions to a degree. The U.S. Government publically has repudiated the "abduction" policy, but apparently has continued it in attempted secrecy. Virtually all nations have made it clear that they view such conduct as criminal. President Clinton pledged that the U.S. will not abduct anyone else from Mexico during negotiations modifying the U.S.–Mexico Extradition Treaty. MacChesney & D'Amato, Anthology, at 246. *But see, U.S. Ok's Kidnaping Terrorists: Directive apparently declassified in error,* Chicago Tribune, § 1, p. 10, col. 1 (Feb. 5, 1997) (Clinton Administration continuation) of policy. Do you believe that if U.S. agents were caught in a foreign country attempting to abduct a fugitive that they would risk prosecution? What reaction would be likely, if the U.S. Government caught foreign agents doing similarly? *See, e.g.,* Does this "legitimization" of abductions such as this put the "rule of law" or U.S.

nationals (at home or abroad) at risk? If the *Alvarez* decision is read to provide implicit acceptance of such "enforcement" actions, does this denigrate customary international law on this point or in general? May it tempt other nations to abduct U.S. nationals? While countries will not likely send troops or agents onto U.S. soil to abduct U.S. nationals, they might feel less constrained not to do so abroad or to take other action that injure or render U.S. interests and people vulnerable. How credible will U.S. protests be if abductions ("arrests") of U.S. nationals occur and would seem to violate what has been customary international law? What about parents who "kidnap" their children? On this, see, Blakesley, Comparative Ruminations from the Bayou on Child Custody Jurisdiction–the Hague Convention on Child Abduction, 58 La.L.Rev. 451 (1998); Note, Huynh, *Croll v. Croll: Can Rights of Access Ever Merit a Remedy of Return Under the Hague Abduction Convention?*, N.C. J. of Int'l L. & Comm. Reg. 529 (2001). Article 5 of the Hague Convention defines parental access as "includ[ing] the right to take a child for a limited period of time to a place other than the child's habitual residence." Hague Convention on the Civil Aspects of International Child Abduction, Oct. 25, 1980, T.I.A.S. No. 11,670, 1343 U.N.T.S. 98, reprinted in 51 Fed. Reg. 10,494 (Mar. 26, 1986).

  9. *Protests & Disdain*. Governments around the world, especially in the Western Hemisphere, expressed concern over the implications of the *Alvarez* decision. The U.S. is party to at least 16 bilateral Mutual Legal Assistance Treaties, including treaties with Mexico, Panama, Uruguay, and nations of the Caribbean. The *Alvarez Case*, raised doubt about the vitality of these treaties. Mexico slowed its negotiations on NAFTA. Difficulties arose in matters of extradition and other cooperation in criminal matters. Many countries made formal protests or insisted on modification of treaties or "cooperative" relations. These included Argentina, Brazil, Chile, Paraguay, and Uruguay who issued a joint declaration to the OAS. The State Department reported being inundated with protests from the above-noted countries, along with many others, including Spain, Colombia and Canada. *U.S. Dep't of State Dispatch*, Aug.3, 1992, at 615. Colombia stated that the substance of the U.S. position "threatens the legal stability of [all] public treaties." Canada's Parliament protested and their Minister of External Affairs stated that any U.S. attempt to abduct from Canada would be treated as a criminal offense as well as a violation of the U.S.–Canada Extradition Treaty. Canada had submitted an *amicus brief*, in *Alvarez*, which began by warning: "[t]he issues presented in this case could have a profound effect on Canada–USA extradition relations." The U.S. and Mexico have now completed renegotiation of the extradition treaty making abduction an explicit violation. See *Brief of the Canadian Government as Amicus Curiae in Alvarez–Machain*, 31 ILM 919 (1992).

  10. *Torture or Murder?* What do you think Justice Stevens meant by the point he made in his *Alvarez* dissent that the extradition treaty does not explicitly prohibit the use of torture or the commission of murder by authorities? Is he suggesting that Justice Rehnquist's opinion indicates that torture or murder would not violate the treaty? Or do you think that Justice Rehnquist would agree that, while renunciation of jurisdiction to prosecute would not be a valid remedy, but that prosecution or extradition U.S. officials who perpetrated abduction, torture, or murder would be mandated upon sufficient evidence? Each of those is an extraditable offense. In *U.S. v. Toscanino*, 500 F.2d 267 (2d Cir.1974) the Court distinguished *Ker* and *Frisbie*, by noting that the defendant had been forcibly abducted and allegedly tortured in violation of principles of international law, evidenced by principles of the UN and OAS Charters. *Toscanino* was limited in 1975, when the 2nd Circuit held: "[for] a defendant * * * to interpose the violation of [the U.N. and O.A.S. Charters] as a defense to a criminal prosecution," an official state protest by a state whose sovereignty was violated by the abduction would be required. *U.S. ex rel. Lujan v. Gengler*, 510 F.2d 62 (2d Cir.1975). *Alvarez–Machain*, along with *Matta–Ballesteros v. Henman*, 697 F.Supp. 1040, 1041–42 (S.D.Ill.1988) (7th Cir.1990), show that the current U.S. Supreme Court recognizes that abduction from a foreign country violates international law, the abducted party is left with little, if any, remedy.

11. *Mexico's extradition request*. After the case against Alvarez was dismissed for want of evidence, did the Justice Department contemplate extraditing his abductors? Should it? The Mexican Government sought the extradition of two individuals suspected of abducting Alvarez. Justice Stevens noted in his dissenting opinion that, "[i]t is shocking that a party to an extradition treaty might believe [is now held legitimately to believe] that it has secretly reserved the right to make seizures of citizens in the other party's territory." The dissent noted: "[a]s the Court observes at the outset of its opinion, there is reason to believe that respondent participated in an especially brutal murder of an American law enforcement agent. That fact, if true, may explain the Executive's intense interest in punishing respondent in our courts. Such an explanation, however, provides no justification for disregarding the Rule of Law that this Court has a duty to uphold." Do you agree? The U.S. Government refused to honor Mexico's request for the extradition of those allegedly involved in the Alvarez abduction, although it was kidnaping. Instead, it is reported that the U.S. paid $2.7 million to various prosecution witnesses. Payments to those witnesses are detailed in *Case of Slain Drug Agent*, NY Times, Nov. 8, 1992, at A12.

12. *Civil Suit*. *Alvarez–Machain* sued the U.S. Government and the individuals involved in his abduction and alleged torture. Abduction by U.S. authorities is obviously illegal under international law. Is it illegal under U.S. law? Could or should this lead to civil penalties or criminal prosecution in the offended nation; in the offending nation? Would some form of immunity be a defense?

13. *Other examples of accountability for violation of sovereignty*. In 78 Rev. Gen. de Dr. Int'l. Pub. 1158 (1974) it is reported that a Swiss national, charged with drug trafficking, crossed into France when her fiancee was arrested in Switzerland. The clerk of the Swiss judge in charge of the case went to the woman's residence in France and convinced her to return to Geneva, where she was promptly arrested. In reporting her release, the *Chronique des Faits Internationaux* noted that a French clerk or a French judge would have been severely punished for such conduct. A Spanish police inspector was arrested, prosecuted and sentenced, in 1975, after he entered French territory carrying a hand gun. He stated he had come to do some shopping and had forgotten to leave the gun home. He was sentenced to two months in prison (suspended), 80 *Rev. Gen. Dr. Int'l. Pub.* 248 (1976). Two agents of the Italian Secret Service were at an Swiss airport surveilling an Italian national wanted for espionage. The agents took photographs and recorded automobile registration plates. Notwithstanding the Italian Government's excuses sent through diplomatic channels the agents were prosecuted. 89 *Rev. Gen. de Dr. Int'l. Pub.* 460 (1985). A German national was tried in absentia in Austria and convicted, but his summons had been served by mail. The Supreme Court of Austria held the trial was null and void, because the service was a violation of international law. 38 Int'l L.Rep. 133 (1969).

14. *Rescue raids.* On April 24, 1980, the President Carter ordered a military force to fly into Iran with the objective of rescuing the U.S. nationals held hostage in Teheran. The raid was not successful. Several rescue raids have also occurred for passengers aboard hijacked airliners. Such raids have prompted claims that the territorial sovereignty of the place where the raid occurred had been violated. In relation to sovereignty, are rescue raids different from abductions for prosecution? For a discussion of rescue raids, see Chapter 15, *supra*.

15. *Tu Quo Que?* The U.S. is certainly not the only nation that undertakes abduction. In the mid–1960's, Colonel Argoud, was a French national notorious for his opposition to General de Gaulle's policies leading to independence Algeria's independence. Argoud was sought for prosecution by the French authorities for having invaded France with some of his *Pied-Noir* forces. After the debacle, Argoud found refuge in Germany, but was kidnaped here by "persons unknown" and found tied up in a truck in Paris after an anonymous phone call. The French court ruled that, in the absence of an objection by Germany, no international law issue was presented. In argument before the court, and in the prior proceedings, much was made by the prosecution of applicable precedents in Anglo–Saxon countries; *i.e., Ker–Frisbie*. The French Court did note, however, that the decision would have been different had Germany protested. *In re Argoud*, France, *Cour de Cassation*, 1964, 45 Int'l L.Rep. 90 (1972).

Eichmann. The Israeli Supreme Court held that Adolph Eichmann had no standing to challenge his abduction from Argentina by Israeli agents. Israel's jurisdiction was treated as a matter only between Israel and Argentina and was disposed of by the agreement between the two states to consider the incident closed. *Attorney General of Israel v. Eichmann, supra,* Chapter 1.

16. *Quiet repatriation.* Most violations of a state's sovereignty are caused by overzealous lower echelon law enforcement authorities at or near the border. Instead of becoming *causes célebres*, they are usually resolved quietly and bureaucratically. Ronald Anderson, a U.S. citizen and a conscientious objector during the hostilities in Vietnam, was living in British Columbia. He tried to cross the border to visit his mother in the state of Washington and was seized by U.S. customs officers. A number of witnesses and a journalist's photograph established that the seizure had actually occurred on the Canadian side of the border. The Canadian Department of External Affairs protested and U.S. military authorities quietly returned Anderson to Canada. 79 *Rev. Gen. de Dr. Int'l. Pub.* 462 (1975). For other instances, see the *Canadian Amicus Curiae Brief in Alvarez Machain*, 31 ILM 919 (1992). Consider, however, the following cases.

Buser, THE JAFFE CASE and the Use of International Kidnaping as an Alternative to Extradition, 14 Georgia Journal of International and Comparative Law 357 (1984).*

* * *

The history of bounty hunters in the United States dates from the period of the Old West. In 1872 the Supreme Court * * * recognized that the surety of a person released on bail could appoint someone to pursue a bail jumper and return the bail jumper to the jurisdiction to appear before the court, but only if the bail jumper was located within the territory of the United States. Bounty hunters, however, also had the powers of de facto deputies; they could ride after, capture, and return to the sheriff fugitives from the law. In asserting jurisdiction over fugitives apprehended and returned by bounty hunters, courts use the Ker–Frisbie rule which states that a court may claim jurisdiction over a criminal defendant without regard to the means by which he was brought before the court. The Ker–Frisbie rule follows the ancient Roman maxim male captus, bene detenum, which translates: an illegal apprehension does not preclude jurisdiction.

* * *

Sidney Jaffe was a Florida land developer who ... ran into difficulties ... and was arrested on charges of violating Florida's new Land Sales Act. Bail was posted for Jaffe by a professional bonding company, and he was released from jail. Jaffe fled to Toronto, obtained Canadian citizenship, and failed to appear for his preliminary hearing in Florida. Faced with losing its investment, the company applied to the state Attorney General for the commencement of extradition proceedings.

The extradition proceedings advanced slowly, and the bonding company feared it would have to forfeit its bond. There were also some questions as to whether land sale violation charges were extraditable under the 1971 Treaty. The bonding company, therefore, commissioned one of its agents, Daniel Kear, to abduct Jaffe from his Toronto home. Kear enlisted the aid of Timm Johnsen, a professional bounty hunter.

Kear and Johnsen went to Toronto to retrieve Jaffe. Posing as a policeman, Johnsen approached Jaffe after the latter's morning jog to ask him a few questions. Jaffe was * * * thrown in the back of a rented car and driven to the border, after which he was flown back to Florida [where he] ... was arrested for jumping bail and was incarcerated. He was convicted

---

* Reprinted with the permission of the Georgia Journal of International and Comparative Law.

* * * on twenty-eight counts of illegal land sales and was sentenced to thirty years in prison. * * *

The Canadian government was infuriated by the abduction of Jaffe. As Argentina had done during the Eichmann incident, Canada complained that its national sovereignty had been violated. Federal officials in the United States also sought Jaffe's release, a request refused by Florida authorities. Florida cited an 1872 Supreme Court decision which held that a bondsman or his agent could pursue and return the bail jumper to the jurisdiction to appear before the court. Canadian authorities then requested the extradition of Kear and Johnsen to stand trial on kidnaping charges. The two [were] extradited to Canada . . . for Jaffe's kidnaping.

* * *

Notes. Canada's extradition request was approved the 4th Circuit Court of Appeals. The Court affirmed the District Court's denial of the bounty hunters' writ of habeas corpus, noting: "... Presumably congratulating himself on the outcome [the abduction], Kear no doubt was rudely jolted to learn that Canadian authorities took a very jaundiced view of his behavior. Canada has sought to extradite Kear ... claiming violation of a statute which makes it a crime to kidnap a person with the intent to send or transport the person kidnaped out of Canada against his will ... In sum, circumstances justifying extradition have been established. The denial of a writ of habeas corpus by the district court accordingly was proper. The Canadian court may listen sympathetically to Kear as he seeks to portray himself as someone caught in a complexity of intricate international law beyond his imagination or comprehension. The fact that his cohort Johnson may have posed as a member of the Ontario police force might make things a bit awkward, but in all events the matter is one of defense or mitigation to be raised in the Canadian courts. It is not a grounds [sic] for refusing to honor the Canadian request for extradition." *Kear v. Hilton*, 699 F.2d 181, 182, 185 (4th Cir.1983). Kear and his partner Johnson were convicted in Canada of kidnaping. Jaffe was convicted and sentenced to consecutive jail terms totaling 145 years in prison, but his conviction for fraud was overturned after he had served two years. He was later paroled on the other charge and he returned to Canada. The latter has steadfastly refused to extradite Jaffe on refiled fraud charges.

Brief of the Government of Canada as Amicus Curiae in Support of the Respondent in the Case of United States v. Alvarez Machain

31 International Legal Materials 919 (1992).*

* * *

In the wake of the Jaffee case, the United States undertook in relation to "bounty hunter" abductions only to consult on the return of abducted persons to Canada * * *.

* Reprinted with the permission of the American Society of International Law.

In April 1991, the United States took the formal and unequivocal position *vis à vis* Canada that * * * return of a criminal defendant is not an appropriate remedy under the circumstances of an official abduction. * * *

Notification took place in the case of *Derrick Hills* who, on January 4, 1991, was apprehended by a Windsor City Police officer, some two hundred yards within the United States, in the Windsor–Detroit tunnel. The United States lodged a protest and requested a statement of Canadian intentions. The note asserted, apparently gratuitously, that "under United States law judicial dismissal of the criminal charges, or judicially ordered release * * * is not an appropriate remedy for the violation of territorial sovereignty."

Canada rejected the American position and indicated its understanding that the extant extradition treaty "established the only means under which to obtain the return of fugitive offenders". Canada apologized and hills was returned to American territory to await a proper extradition request. Thereafter, the United States expressed its satisfaction concerning the resolution of the Hills' case but indicated its disagreement with the Canadian position concerning the exclusivity of the Treaty.

Notes and Questions. **1.** *Hills' case.* Does the American protest followed by its statement as to Treaty make sense to you?

2. *Luring.* Does the luring of persons wanted for prosecution in the United States either into the territory of the United States or into an area beyond the territorial jurisdiction of any state, such as the high seas, violate international law? *See United States* v. *Yunis, supra, rev'd on other grounds,* 859 F 2d 953 (D.C. 1988).

Section D.   Extradition & The Political Offense Exception

We have seen that extradition is the process by which nations transfer fugitives from justice for prosecution or punishment. Extradition treaties generally provide that state-parties may refuse to extradite perpetrators of "political offenses." The political offense exception has been among the few defenses to extradition. Traditionally, it was an important means to prevent abuse of the extradition process for political reasons. It has also been one of the most used and most controversial aspects of extradition practice. Political offenses have been characterized as being "purely political" (e.g., treason, sedition, espionage) or as offenses "of a political character," or common crimes committed in a particularly political context. The former are not problematic, but the latter are controversial and difficult. Some recent U.S. treaties have eliminated the exception, except for "pure" political offenses. A more recent use of the political offense exception is where a state will refuse to extradite because the its officials believe that the extradition is actually aimed at prosecuting the fugitive for racial, religious, or political reasons. The political offense exception is explored in the cases and materials which follow.

The State v. Schumann

Ghana, Court of Appeal of Accra, 1966.
39 Int'l L.Rep. 433 (1970).*

[The German government requested the extradition of Dr. Horst
Schumann, who had been charged with murdering more than 30,000
patients in mental establishments within two German concentration camps
from 1942 to 1944 and murdering a large number of Jewish people at
Auschwitz in the course of experiments with mass sterilization from 1939
to 1941. Schumann was employed by the Ghanaian government as a
medical officer at the time the extradition request was made.]

* * * Counsel . . . submitted that the principles relating to an offence
of a political character have been examined and enunciated in the English
cases of Re Meunier [1894] 2 Q.B.D. 415, Re Castioni [1891] 1 Q.B.D. 149;
and R. v. Governor of Brixton Prison, Ex parte Kolczynski [1955] 1 All E.R.
35, and that none of the facts stated in the appellant's evidence fell within
these principles. In the cases of Re Meunier and Re Castioni, the principle
is stated that to constitute an offence of a political nature there must be
some political disturbance or upheaval or there must be some physical
struggle between two opposing political parties for the mastery of the
government of the country, and that the crime in question must have been
committed in furtherance of that disturbance or struggle. The principle was
extended in the Kolczynski case to cover "offences committed in association
with a political object (e.g., anti-Communism) or with a view to avoiding
political persecution or prosecution for political defaults" * * *. It is clear
beyond argument that the appellant's case is not covered by these principles. It is not his case that the poor helpless lunatics at the Munsungen
Asylum or the Jews at Auschwitz had rebelled against the Nazi ideology
and had thereby created some form of political disturbance which needed
quelling, nor indeed does he claim to have committed the offence charged
with a view to avoiding political persecution or prosecution.

[CRABBE, J.A., amplified [*Kolczynski*] somewhat: * * * It seems to
have been established [in *Kolczynski*] that an act committed solely on the
ground of fear of prosecution for a political offence or of political persecution will be sufficient to give the crime a political colouring, if such fear led
immediately or directly to the commission of the crime for which extradition is sought. There must exist a direct connexion of the criminal act with
a political object.

[LASSEY, J., conceded the killings were done "in circumstances which
were not entirely without political significance" and stated]: The crucial
question here is this: In those circumstances is it necessary to widen the
scope or meaning of these magic words, "of a political character", if only
for reasons of humanity? I desire to answer this by saying that to determine the political character of the particular offence so as to make it not
extraditable there must necessarily be present at the time of the commission of the particular crime some element of organized or violent opposition
or resistance to the execution of the planned policy of the ruling political
party and the offence must be committed in the conflict which might result

* Reprinted with the permission of the
Editor of the International Law Reports.

between the opposing parties. In this context any such offence committed either by the agents of the ruling political party seeking to carry out their principal's orders or by the agents of those who dislike or resist the carrying into effect of the particular political policy may be brought under the category of an offence "of a political nature or character" and therefore excusable in extradition proceedings. * * * [N]either the helpless lunatics in the mental institution at "Munsungen" nor the Jews in "Auschwitz" appeared to have offered any organized resistance to the Nazi Party in Germany. . . .

Re Bressano

Argentina, Camara Federal de la Capital, 1965.
40 Int'l L.Rep. 219 (1975).*

The Facts.—Peru requested the extradition of Hugo M. Bressano on charges of bank robbery and assault committed in the Miraflores branch of the Credit Bank of Peru. * * * The Court of first instance refused extradition on the ground that the offences constituted common crimes connected with a political offence and hence were not extraditable * * *. On appeal to the Federal Court of the Capital (Buenos Aires).

Held: that extradition must be granted * * *. Even if we accept the contention that the motive for the principal offence was to provide funds for the support of a programme of training of groups in guerrilla warfare to be directed against the existing political, social and economic order in Peru, and with the ultimate objective of directing this subversive activity against other Latin–American States, we cannot agree that this argument affords a valid reason for treating the offence in question as a political offence, thereby enabling the perpetrators to enjoy protection in any country in which they might seek asylum. [The court *held* that, even if it were not established as positive law that the doctrine of political offenses presupposed the existence of a democratic state. Offenses such as preparation for guerrilla warfare on an international scale did not ever qualify as political.]

Notes and Questions

1. **Lack of Definition**: A political offense has been characterized as referring not to a well-determined criminal transaction which can be specified in terms of a moral and mental element, but as a "descriptive label." No extradition treaty and virtually no legislative act has attempted to define the term, so courts have had to provide guidelines.

2. **Types**: Three basic types of conduct have been found to be political offenses: (1) *"purely political offenses "*such as treason, sedition, or espionage. There is no problem with the application of this form of the exception. (2) *"Offenses of a political character"* are more problematic. These are "common crimes" like burglary or homicide, committed in particular circumstances. Variations on how and when the circumstances are apt varies and presents difficulty. (3) Extradition may be refused, when

---

* Reprinted with the permission of the Editor of the International Law Reports.

it is believed to have been requested for a political purpose or to discriminate against or persecute the fugitive on political, religious, ethnic, or racial
grounds. The French Extradition Law provides that extradition will be
denied "when the crime or the offense has a political character or when it
results from circumstances indicating that the extradition is requested with
a political purpose." [author's translation]. French commentators have
noted that the purpose of the political offense exception is to avoid
extraditing those who are vanquished partisans of a cause. French tribunals refused extradition Spanish Republicans, for example, sought by the
Franco regime after the Spanish Civil War.

3. *Tests*. Despite the difficulty doing so, courts have been required to
define offenses of a political character. They adopted various tests, including: (1) *the political motivation test*; (2) *the political incidence or disturbance test;* (3) *the injured rights theory*; (4) *the model of connexity*; and (5)
several mixed approaches (combining the political incidence, connexity, and
motivation tests).

"The Political Motivation Test" was applied on a few occasions by
courts in several countries, including those in France, Switzerland, and the
U.S., but has been repudiated. French and Swiss courts have modified this
test, calling it the "predominance or proportionality test." This test applies
both subjective and objective criteria to determine whether a given offense
has a sufficient political character. In the *Ockert* decision, a Swiss court
included "acts which have the character of an ordinary crime, ... but
which, because of the attendant circumstances, in particular because of the
motive and the *object*, are of a predominantly political complexion." This
was further refined to require that even when the motive is largely
political, the means employed must be virtually *the only means* available to
accomplish the end pursued and the harm must be proportionate to the
end. In *Ktir*, a Swiss court extradited a French national to France, for
murdering an Algerian F.L.N. brother. The court held that for the political
offense to apply, the motives inspiring the criminal conduct must be of a
predominantly political character: " * * * the act [must be] inspired by
political passion, [and] committed either in the framework of a struggle for
power or for the purpose of escaping a dictatorial authority, and [must be]
directly and closely related to the political purpose. * * * [T]he [harm
caused must] be proportionate to the result sought; * * * the interests at
stake should be sufficiently important to excuse, if not justify, the infringement of private legal rights." Thus, murder will rarely be excepted from
extradition.

The Political Incidence Approach: In 1891, a British judge, in *re
Castioni,* 1 Q.B. 149, 166 (1891), focused not on the motivation, but on the
nature of the conduct itself. He ruled that political offenses are those which
are "incidental to and form a part of political disturbances." In 1894, a
U.S. federal district court held that the political offense exception applied to
government agents seeking to suppress an uprising, as well as to the rebels,
as long as the conduct occurred "... in the course of or furthering of civil
war, insurrection, or political commotion." A crime must be incidental to
and form a part of a political disturbance: a bona fide struggle for political
power. Lately, courts have held that the "disturbance" or "uprising" must

have a reasonable possibility of success. *See, Quinn v. Robinson,* 783 F.2d 776, 797, 798, 202 (9th Cir.1986); Christine van den Wyngaert, THE POLITICAL OFFENSE EXCEPTION TO EXTRADITION 1980).

The model of connexity allows otherwise criminal conduct to be considered a political offense, if it is "closely connected to" a purely political offense:, such as assisting a spy to escape.

The injured rights test requires that the criminal conduct be directed against the state's political organization: " * * * [t]he fact that the reasons of sentiment which prompted the offender to commit the offense belong to the realm of politics does not itself create a political offense. The offense does not derive its political character from the motive of the offender but from the nature of the rights it injures." *Extradition of Gatti, Jdt.Cour d'Appel, France,* 1947 Ann.Dig. 146 (No.70).

"Odious Barbarism"—*Intentional or the Reckless Slaughter of Innocents.* More recently, courts have excepted out conduct that constitutes what may be considered a crime against humanity. This test is based on the idea that there is a level, type, or focus of atrocity that is punishable and extraditable, whether it is political or not. This test is somewhat analogous to war crimes, but in circumstances of non-belligerency. Thus, a perpetrator of a bombing of innocent civilians, or torture of "arrested" or abducted persons should not be exempt from extradition. Some recent decisions have begun to refuse the political offense defense, to those who intentionally or indiscriminately attack innocent civilians, regardless of the motivation or whether it is committed incident to a political upheaval. The French Extradition Law, for example, applies the exception, unless the conduct "constitute[s] ... *odious barbarism* and vandalism prohibited by the laws of war, and only when the civil war has ended." *See, e.g., Eain v. Wilkes,* 641 F.2d 504, 520–21 (7th Cir.1981), *cert. denied,*454 U.S. 894 (1981) ("indiscriminate bombing of a civilian population is not recognized as a protected political act ..."); *In re Doherty,* 599 F.Supp. 270, 275 (S.D.N.Y. 1984) (bombings in public places are not within the political offense exception); *c.f., Quinn v. Robinson,* 783 F.2d 776 (9th Cir.1986). Do you see problems in applying this test?

See also the 1998 *United Nations Convention for the Suppression of Terrorist Bombings,* U.N. Doc. A/RES/52/164, January 9, 1998.Article 11 provides that the offences set forth therein are not to be considered "as a political offence, or as an offence connected with a political offence or as an offence inspired by political motives." All of the previous international terrorism conventions, extracted in the Documentary Supplement did not address this question but rather relied on the obligation *aut dedere, aut judicare,* that is the obligation of a state party to either extradite or submit the case to its own authorities for the purposes of prosecution. Note that *The Terrorist Bombings Convention* does, however, have in article 12 a ground for refusal for extradition or mutual assistance if there are substantial grounds to believe that the request has been made in order to prosecute or punish the person on account of the person's race, religion, nationality, ethnic origin or political opinion. See the discussion of this type of "humanitarian clause" in subsection (g).

Genocide, Crimes Against Humanity and War Crimes. Today it can be fairly stated that under customary international and certain specific treaties such heinous crimes are not considered to be political. *See, The State* v. *Schumann*, extracted above. Note that article 7 of *The Genocide Convention* 1948, 78 U.N.T.S. 277 expressly states that the crimes enumerated in the Convention shall not be considered political for the purposes of extradition. Similarly, *The Apartheid Convention*, 1973, U.N. Doc A/9030 ,1973, article XI so provides. Note also the 1975 *Additional Protocol to the European Convention on Extradition*, E.T.S. No. 86 which excludes genocide, crimes against humanity and war crimes. However, mention should be made of the *Artukovic v. Boyle*, 140 F.Supp. 245 (1956), where in the first decision the District Court for the Southern District of California held that the alleged offences, the ordering of the detention, incarceration in concentration camps and death of approximately 30,000 persons when he was the Minister of the Interior of the German controlled Government of Croatia in World War II were political offences. This decision has been viewed as "the most disturbing misinterpretation of the exemption": Gilbert Transnational Fugitive Offenders in International Law 389 (1998). He was eventually extradited to the former Yugoslavia in 1986, 628 F.Supp. 1370 (1986); 784 F.2d 1354 (1986).)

Note that on the irrelevance of official capacity for prosecution before international tribunals for these crimes article 7 of the ICTY, article 6 of the ICTR and article 27 of the Rome Statute of the ICC, contained in the Documentary Supplement.

Some ad hoc exceptions to the exception have arisen, such as counterfeiting even if connected to a purely political offense. The same is true lately for many forms of terrorism, the *"Clause Belge,"* excepting murder of the head of state or anyone in his family.

4. ***The U.S.–U.K. Treaty & Its Progeny***. In a major shift in U.S. extradition policy occurred in 1986, with the *U.S.—U.K. Supplementary Extradition Treaty*, which narrowed the scope of the political offense exception, providing that certain offenses shall *not* be regarded as being of a political character. Murder, manslaughter, kidnaping, the taking of a hostage, offenses relating to explosives and offenses relating to firearms and ammunition can not be political offenses. The U.S. has similar provisions in its Treaty and Protocol with Canada. These are contained in the Documentary Supplement. This approach has been followed by a series of treaties taking the same approach. It functionally eliminates the exception for crimes of a political character. *Does it deprive the courts of their rightful jurisdiction to decide whether an offense is of a political character?* Is there a "liberty interest" involved in an extradition hearing? The Treaty did provide an exception when the requested state suspects that the true purpose for extradition is to prosecute for racial, religious, or similar reasons. On this topic, *see*, Bassiouni, *The "Political Offense" Exception Revisited: Extradition Between the U.S. and the U.K.–A Choice Between Friendly Cooperation Among Allies and Sound Law and Policy,* 15 Den. J.Int'l L. & Pol. 255 (1987); Blakesley, *An Essay on Executive Branch Attempts to Eviscerate the Separation of Powers,* 1987 Utah L. Rev. 451; Lubet *Taking the Terror Out of Political Terrorism: The Supplementary*

Treaty on Extradition Between the U.S. and the U.K., 19 Conn.L.Rev. 863 (1987); Lubet, *Extradition Unbound: A Reply to Professors Blakesley and Bassiouni*, 24 Tex.Int'l L.J. 47 (1989). In Canada since the mid 1970s the issue of refusing to commit for extradition based on the political offence exception has been taken from the hands of the extradition judge. All the judge can do if evidence is presented on this ground for refusal is to include it in her or his Report to the Minister of Justice that accompanies the order for committal to await surrender. However, once the Minister of Justice makes the final decision to extradite, that decision is subject to judicial review. See the Canadian *Extradition Act*, S.C. 1999, c.18. *The Extradition Act* in sections 46(1)(c) and (2) limits the political offence exception, subject to relevant extradition agreements, in the same way as does the 1991 *Protocol* to the 1976 *Canada-United States Extradition Treaty* contained in the Documentary Supplement.

5. ***The Rule of Non-Inquiry.*** Traditionally, extradition practice has insisted that the requested state not "look behind" the legal system of the requesting state, to consider how just or unjust it might be. This is the "rule of non-inquiry." The rule is not surprising, given the tendency not to want to offend other sovereign nations. On the other hand, this rule risks violation of several important tenets of human rights law. Read U.N. Charter arts. 55(c), 56, and 103, along with the Covenant on Civil and Political Rights, arts. 2, 9, and 26; The Universal Declaration of Human Rights, arts. 2, and 8–10—all in the Documentary Supplement. Do you think that when one nation is deciding whether to send a person to a foreign country for prosecution and punishment, it is important to consider the nature of the system to which the individual is being sent? When the Senate was giving its Advice and Consent to the Supplemental US—UK Treaty, it added a clause that may avoid the rule of non-inquiry. Article 3(a), provides that, ". . . extradition shall not occur if the person sought establishes to the satisfaction of the competent judicial authority by a preponderance of the evidence that the request for extradition has in fact been made with a view to try or punish him on account of his race, religion, nationality, or political opinions, or that he would, if surrendered, be prejudiced at his trial or punished, detained or restricted in his personal liberty by reason of his race, religion, nationality, or political opinions." Article 3(b) adds: "In the United States, the competent judicial authority shall only consider the defense to extradition set forth in [¶ a] for offenses listed in Article 1 of [the Treaty]. A finding under paragraph (a) shall be immediately appealable by either party to [a U.S. district court] or court of appeals, as appropriate [for expedited consideration] . . ." For discussions of this article, see, *U.S. v. Smyth*, 61 F.3d 711 (9th Cir.1995) (art. 3 must be considered with regard to the likely treatment of the particular defendant, not in relation to the general political climate of a place, such as Northern Ireland and the British Diplock Courts); *In re Extradition of Howard*, 996 F.2d 1320 (1st Cir.1993).

6. ***A Humanitarian Exception to Extradition.*** Some have argued that there is (or ought to be) an exception from extradition based not on the "political character" of the offense, but on humanitarian norms. The political offense exception has been important in U.S. jurisprudence, because it has often functioned as a repository for human rights and humani-

tarian protections. Perhaps the difficulties and abuse of the political offense exception would be avoided and the values that it has rightly incorporated could subsist, if a human rights or humanitarian exception to extradition were adopted. *See*, Blakesley, TERRORISM, DRUGS, *supra* at 263–270. Some courts have noted that there is a possibility that an extradited person "would be subject to procedures so antipathetic to a federal court's sense of decency, [that those courts might develop] a humanitarian exception [to the rule of non-inquiry]." *Emami v. U.S.*, 834 F.2d 1444, 1453 (9th Cir.1987); *see*, Cohen, *Implementing the U.N. Torture Convention in U.S. Extradition Cases*, 26 Denv.J.Int'l L. & Pol. 717, 519 (1998). Similarly, article 3 of the U.N. Torture Convention requires a party not to extradite a person if there are substantial grounds to believe that he or she will be subject to torture. The Torture Convention is in the Documentary Supplement, U.N. Doc. A/RES/39/708 (1984), reprinted in 23 ILM 1027 (1984), *modified in* 24 I.L.M. 535 (1985).The Secretary of State has adopted procedures to avoid extradition in violation of the Treaty. Is it likely that U.S. courts may review the Secretary's decision without any implementing legislation? A good argument can be made that this article is self-executing, as the requirement is directly mandated.

The Canadian *Extradition Act*, S.C. 1999, c. 18 § 44(1) provides that the Minister of Justice "shall refuse to make a surrender order if * * * satisfied that (a) the surrender would be unjust or oppressive having regard to all the relevant circumstances; or (b) the request for extradition was made for the purpose of prosecuting or punishing the person by reason of their race, religion, nationality, ethnic origin, language, colour, political opinion, sex, sexual orientation, age, mental or physical disability or status or that the person's position may be prejudiced for any of those reasons." This mandatory ground for refusal applies even where it is not present in the actual extradition treaty being used.

SECTION E.   THE NATIONALITY EXCEPTION

The nationality exception is related to the nationality principle of jurisdiction, so you should refer to Ch. 3, *supra*. Two distinct trends have emerged from state practice. Most Romanist or "civilian" penal systems have been quite uncompromising in not allowing the extradition of their own nationals. The idea is that they are responsible for their nationals both for protection and prosecution for crimes committed. A nation's reputation is put on the line by its nationals. It is considered an unjust burden to allow one's nationals to be prosecuted in a foreign system. This idea developed out of the Medieval German *Realsystem*, which, in turn, stemmed from the practice of the Greek city-states and Rome. Thus, many states are unwilling to extradite their nationals. Having this provenance, they use the concept of nationality in order to take jurisdiction with respect to offences wherever they are committed. For example, France under the Extradition Law of 1927, article 5, expressly prohibits the extradition of nationals. In other states it is expressly forbidden in their constitutions. Today, however, the nationality exemption is breaking down among the nations of Europe, at least as between themselves. It is being replaced there by processes like transfer of prisoners and even transfer of proceedings. In contrast, common law states, such as Canada, the United Kingdom and the United States * * * generally use territoriality as the primary basis of jurisdiction. They are of the view that an offender should be returned to a state that has jurisdiction over the offence regardless of his nationality. * * * This practice appears to be more in harmony with the view that the country with the most substantial connection with the offence should hear the case. Colombia, under pressure of the United States, eliminated its nationality exception. Mexico has done the same.

Notes and Questions. **1. *Common law states***. In the case of common law states where the territorial principle of jurisdiction is the primary basis, if extradition was to be refused on nationality grounds, there would be no way of prosecuting the person unless there was a specific exception for prosecution of citizens. In Canada, for example section 6(2) of the Criminal Code provides that prosecution for criminal offences will only take place for crimes committed in Canada subject to express exceptions in the Criminal Code or other legislation. There are such exceptions using Canadian citizenship as a basis for various acts of international terrorism, war crimes, genocide and crimes against humanity.

2.   *Concurrent jurisdiction*. Situations may occur where criminal conduct transcends international borders and there is concurrent jurisdiction on the territorial basis. For example, X a citizen of Canada operates a telemarketing scheme in Canada. Calls are made from Canada to residents of the United States, where through fraudulent misrepresentations they are induced to purchase shares in companies that turn out to be worthless. Both Canada and the United States would have jurisdiction based on the subjective, objective and effects felt bases of territorial jurisdiction. Similarly, if Z a Canadian citizen masterminds an operation from Canada to smuggle drugs into the United States there would be concurrent jurisdiction. *See Libman* v. *The Queen* (1985), 21 C.C.C. (3d) 206 (S.C.C.) and *Rivard v. U.S.*, 375 F.2d 882 (5th Cir.1967) (5th Cir.); *cert. den.* 389 U.S. 884 (1967). Could X and Z argue that as Canadian citizens they have a constitutional right to be prosecuted in Canada rather than being extradited to the U.S? Section 6(1) of the *Canadian Charter of Rights and Freedoms*, which is part of the *Constitution Act* of 1982 provides that a Canadian citizen has the right to enter, leave and remain in Canada. The same is not true for a U.S. citizen. *In Federal Republic of Germany* v. *Rauca* (1982) 38 O.R. 705 (Ont.H.C.), *aff'd* 145 D.L.R (3d) 638 (Ont.C.A.), where Rauca a naturalized Canadian citizen and former member of the Gestapo was charged in Germany with the murder of approximately 11,500 people in Lithuania in World War II, it was held that even though extradition *prima facie* violated the right to remain in Canada, it was a reasonable limit on that right, as the objective was the protection and preservation of society from criminal activity. At the time of the request, Canada had no war crimes legislation that would have given it a basis on nationality to prosecute in Canada. Today, it would be able to. *See, supra, The Crimes against Humanity Act*, S.C. 2000 c.24.The following extract deals with the concurrent territorial jurisdiction issue where the fugitive sought on the fact that prosecution was an option for Canada to distinguish themselves from *Rauca. See,* Williams, *Extradition From Canada Since the Charter of Rights,* in Cameron (ed.,) THE CHARTER'S IMPACT ON THE CRIMINAL JUSTICE SYSTEM, Ch. 22 (1996); *Nationality, Double Jeopardy, Prescription and the Death Sentence as Bases for Refusing Extradition,* 62 REV. INT'L DE DROIT PÉNAL 259 (1991); Blakesley, *The Law of International Extradition: A Comparative Study,* Ch. 6 in Dugard & Van den Wyngaert eds., INTERNATIONAL CRIMINAL LAW & PROCEDURE 147 (1996).

United States v. Cotroni

[1989] 1 S.C.R 1469 (S.C.C.)

■ LA FOREST J.:

* * * The United States requested the extradition of Mr. Cotroni [a Canadian citizen] on a charge in that country of conspiracy to possess and distribute heroin. All his actions relating to the alleged conspiracy took place while he was in Canada.

In brief, the conspiracy alleged involved the importation and sale of the drug to alleged accomplices of Cotroni in the United States. Delivery of the drug and payment would appear to have taken place in Canada, although most of the prosecution witnesses and the documentary evidence are in the United States. The accused's personal involvement was effectively confined to giving instructions to his accomplices in the United States and one in Canada by telephone in Montreal.

* * *

I do not doubt that Canada has a sufficient interest to warrant [prosecution]. The activities of which [he] is accused constitute serious antisocial acts that would permit prosecution under several criminal provisions. But it is clear * * * that more than one country may have jurisdiction to prosecute an accused for a crime. There are also sufficient links to the United States to warrant that country to prosecute. In fact, the injurious effects of the crime would be felt in that country, for it is there that the illicit drugs would be distributed. Nor is that all. * * * [M]ost, if not all, of the evidence and many of the witnesses are located in the United States.* * *

I see nothing irrational in surrendering criminals to another country, even where they could be prosecuted for the same acts in Canada. * * *

* * * A general exception [based on section 6(1) of the *Charter of Rights*] for a Canadian citizen who could be charged in Canada would, in my view interfere unduly with the objectives of the system of extradition. * * *

* * * [There] is a necessity for permitting a discretion to decide whether a Canadian should be prosecuted in Canada or abroad. Of course, the authorities must give due weight to the constitutional right of a citizen to remain in Canada. They must in good faith direct their minds to whether prosecution would be equally effective in Canada * * *. They have

an obligation * * * to assure themselves that prosecution in Canada is not a realistic option.

SECTION F. THE DEATH PENALTY

> *Behind you swiftly the figure comes softly,*
> *The spot on your skin is a shocking disease.*
> *Clutching a little case,*
> *He walks briskly to infect a city*
> *Whose terrible future may have just arrived ...* W.H. Auden, *Gare du Midi.*

> *"Nobody has the right to take away man's life, because nobody has given it to him." (Dostoevski)*

The focus of this section is on whether extradition should take place when the fugitive will face the death penalty in the requesting state. This issue puts sharply into focus the competing functions of extradition law, namely mutual legal assistance between states in criminal matters and the human rights of the fugitive. In a unanimous judgment of the European Court of Human Rights in *Soering* v. *United Kingdom*, 161 Eur. Ct H. R. (Ser. A) (1989), which involved an extradition request by the United States to the United Kingdom for Jens Soering, on charges of capital murder, the Court held that if the United Kingdom extradited this would violate article 3 of the *European Convention on Human Rights*, 213 U.N.T.S. 221. Article 3 deals with inhuman and degrading treatment. The Court noted that it was not usual to consider potential violations of the Convention, but that it was an exception where extradition would violate article 3 by reason of foreseeable consequences in the requesting state. In *Soering*, the Court "did not address whether the death penalty *per se* violated this right. Rather, the Court viewed the fugitive's subjection to the so-called 'death-row phenomenon' as the applicable question": *See* Williams, *Extradition and the Death Penalty Exception in Canada: Resolving the Ng and Kindler Cases*, 13 Loyola of Los Angeles Int'l & Comp. L. J. 799, 823–824 (1991); Blakesley, Autumn of the Patriarch, *supra* at 90 J.Crim.L. & Criminology, 1, 78–115 (2001); Schakas, The Abolition of the Death Penalty in International Law (2nd ed. 1997).

From a Canadian–United States extradition perspective this issue is of major importance given for geographical reasons the large two way volume of extradition traffic. You should consider Article 6 of the Extradition Treaty of 1976, contained in the Documentary Supplement which provides that:

When the offence for which extradition is requested is punishable by death under the laws of the requesting state and the laws of the requested state do not permit such punishment for that offence, extradition may be refused unless the requesting party State provides such assurances as the requested State considers sufficient that the death penalty shall not be imposed, or, if imposed shall not be executed.

In *Kindler* v. *Canada (Minister of Justice)*, [1991] 2 S.C.R. 779 (S.C.C.), the fugitve, an American citizen, had been convicted of first degree murder, conspiracy and kidnapping in Pennsylvania in 1983. He escaped from custody in 1984 before his sentence was formally imposed. He was arrested in Canada in 1985. In *Reference Re Ng Extradition (Canada)*, [1991] 2 S.C.R. 858 (S.C.C.) Charles Chitat Ng, a British subject born in Hong Kong and a resident of the United States was accused in California of twelve counts of murder, one count of attempted murder, three counts of kidnapping and one count of burglary, when he escaped from custody. He was apprehended in Canada in 1985. Following committal by the extradition judges the Canadian Minister of Justice did not seek assurances from the United States concerning the death penalty before deciding to surrender. In both of these cases the main issue on appeal to the Supreme Court of Canada was whether to extradite where in the one case the death sentence was certain and the other case a potential if found guilty violated the Canadian Constitutional guarantees contained in sections 7 and 12 of the *Charter of Rights*. The Supreme Court of Canada held that section 12 of the Charter which parallels article 3 of the European Convention in *Soering* was in contrast to the holding in that decision not directly applicable, as any cruel and unusual punishment or treatment would not occur in Canada, but that the treatment in the requesting state could effect the interpretation of section 7 of the Canadian Charter of Rights, which provides that everyone, not just Canadian citizens, has the right to life, liberty and security and cannot be deprived thereof except in accordance with the principles of fundamental justice. The Court in these two cases in 1991 was of the view that even though Canada had abolished the death penalty many other states retained it and that the decisions to extradite were taken with the view to deterring fugitives charged abroad with capital offences from seeking a safe haven in Canada. The bottom line in these two cases was that assurances would only be mandated in cases in exceptional cases, that would according to Justice La Forest "shock the conscience of the Canadian people * * * or be in violation of the standards of the international community". In other words the situation for the fugitives must be simply unacceptable, which was not found to be present in the cases at bar.

Ten years down the road the Supreme Court of Canada in a unanimous decision presented another view on this issue as you will appreciate in the extract below.

United States v. Burns And Rafay

2001 Supreme Court of Canada 7.File No: 26129

THE COURT:

* * * The father, mother and sister of the respondent Rafay were found bludgeoned to death in their home in Bellvue, Washington, in July 1994. Both Burns and Rafay, who had been friends at high school in British Columbia, admit that they were at the Rafay home on the night of the murders.They claim to have gone out on the the evening of July 12, 1994 and when they returned, they say, they found the bodies of the three

murdered Rafay family members. The house they say, appeared to have been burgled.

[Burns and Rafay, both aged 18, returned to Canada. The Bellview police sought the cooperation of the RCMP and in an undercover operation the respondents are alleged to have bragged about their respective roles in the murders. The United States requested extradition and a *prima facie* case was found. The Canadian Minister of Justice did not seek or obtain assurances from the United States under article 6 of the Extradition Treaty. The Minister, following submissions by Burns and Rafay stated that]

* * * assurances should be sought only in circumstances where the particular facts of the case warrant a special exercise of discretion and that [they should not be sought routinely]. * * * The age of the respondents, although "youthful", qualified them as adults in the Canadian criminal system. The Minister thought Canadian citizenship was not itself a "special circumstance" to allow the respondents to escape from the full weight of the sentencing process in the United states where the murders were committed.

* * * The Minister felt that Canada should not permit itself to become a safe haven for persons seeking to escape justice, even Canadians. * * * In the end, Canadian nationality was simply one of several factors that the Minister considered but was not determinative.

[Burns and Rafay appealed the decision of the Minister to extradite without assurances to the British Columbia Court of Appeal, (1997), 94 B.C.A.C. 59 which, in a two to one decision held that if they were extradited and put to death in Washington state they would no longer be able to exercise their constitutional right as citizens to return to Canada. The *Kindler* analysis was found to be inapplicable to Canadian citizens.]

* * *

The respondents' position is that the death penalty is so horrific, the chances of error so high, the death row phenomenon is so repugnant, and the impossibility of correction is so draconian, that it is simply unacceptable that Canada should participate, however indirectly, in its imposition. * * * The Minister's decision is a prior and essential step in a process that may lead to death by execution.

The root questions here are whether the Constitution supports the Minister's position that assurances need only be sought in exceptional cases, or whether * * * [they] must *always* be sought barring exceptional circumstances, and if so, whether such exceptional circumstances are present in this case.

* * *

Reviewing the factors for and against unconditional extradition, we conclude that to order extradition of the respondents without obtaining assurances that the death penalty will not be imposed would violate the principles of fundamental justice.

The Minister has not pointed to any public purpose that would be served by extradition *without* assurances that is not substantially served by extradition *with* assurances, carrying as it does in this case the prospect on conviction o life imprisonment without release or parole * * * The evidence shows that on previous occasions when assurances have been requested of foreign states they have been forthcoming without exception. There is no basis in the record to support the hypothesis and counsel for the Minister did not advance it, that the United States would prefer no extradition at all to extradition with assurances.

* * *

The arguments against extradition without assurances have grown stronger since this Court decided *Kindler* and *Ng* in 1991.* * * The international trend against the death penalty has become clearer. The death penalty controversies in the requesting state—the United States—are based on pragmatic, hard-headed concerns about wrongful convictions. None of these factors is conclusive, but taken together they tilt the s. 7 balance against extradition without assurances.

* * *

* * * [W]hether fugitives are returned to a foreign country to face the death penalty or to face eventual death in prison from natural causes, they are equally prevented from using Canada as a safe haven.

* * *

The outcome of this appeal turns on an appreciation of the principles of fundamental justice, which in turn is derived from the basic tenets of our legal system. These basic tenets have not changed since 1991 when *Kindler* and *Ng* were decided, but their application in particular cases (the "balancing process") must take note of factual developments in Canada and in relevant foreign jurisdictions. When principles of fundamental justice as established and understood in Canada are applied to these factual developments, many of which are of far-reaching importance in death penalty cases, a balance which tilted in favour of extradition without assurances in *Kindler* and *Ng* now tilts against the constitutionality of such an outcome. * * *

Notes and Questions. **1. What exceptional circumstances** do you think would following *Burns and Rafay* justify the Canadian Minister of Justice not seeking assurances from a treaty partner that retains the death penalty?

2.   *Nationality*. Unlike the British Columbia Court of Appeal, the Supreme Court of Canada downplayed the importance of the citizenship of Burns and Rafay and the right under the Constitution to enter Canada. With or without assurances, if found guilty they would be unable to return to Canada.

3.   *Jurisdiction*. If Canada did not extradite for the murders charged, the only prosecution that could have taken place in Canada, based on the territorial principle, would have been for a conspiracy hatched in Canada to commit murder abroad.

4.   *International Concerns*. The Supreme Court in *Burns* reviewed in coming to its decision, principles of criminal justice as applied in Canada, the abolition of the death penalty as a Canadian initiative on the international level, international initiatives opposing extradition without assurances, the growing awareness in many states of wrongful convictions and the concerns that have been raised about the death penalty in the United States.

Death Penalty & Violation of the Vienna Consular Convention, from Blakesley, Autumn of the Patriarch: The Pinochet Extradition Debacle & Beyond

91 J. Criminal L. & Criminology 1 (2001).*

In *Breard v. Greene*, 523 U.S. 371 (1998), the State of Virginia convicted Angel Breard, a Paraguayan, and condemned him to death. Upon his arrest, Breard had not been notified of his right to consult a Paraguayan consular officer, as required by the Vienna Convention on Consular Relations.[1] The U.S. Supreme Court held that defendant's failure to assert his Vienna Consular Convention right in the Virginia courts procedurally defaulted any claim he might have had. It also held that the state authorities' violation of the Vienna Convention had no continuing consequences of a nature that would allow Paraguay to sue under the 11th Amendment immunity exception. Paraguay protested and the Department of State requested Virginia's governor to stay Breard's execution. The request for a stay was denied by the governor of Virginia and the U.S. Supreme Court. Paraguay filed an action with the ICJ under article 36(1) of the ICJ Statute and the Optional Protocol Concerning Compulsory Settlement of Disputes, requesting the ICJ to hold that the United States had violated article 36 of the Vienna Convention and sought an order to require the United States to vacate Breard's conviction. These efforts failed and Breard was executed. Not clarifying the issue of the impact of self-executing treaties significantly, the United States Supreme Court, in *Breard v. Greene*, reasoned that, absent a clear and express statement to the contrary, the procedural rules of the forum State govern implementation of the treaty in that State, but noting that the Vienna Convention on Consular Relations arguably confers a right to consular assistance following arrest.[2]

The United States government, certainly invokes the Vienna Convention, to protest other nations' failure to provide United States nationals with proper notice or access to consular officials. Similarly, it has been held

---

* Reprinted with the permission of the Journal of Criminal Law and Criminology.

1. *The Vienna Convention on Consular Relations*, Apr. 24, 1963, art. 36(1), 21 U.S.T. 77, 596 U.N.T.S. 261, at Art. 36, provides in relevant part: "1. With a view to facilitating the exercise of consular functions relating to nationals of the sending state: ... (b) if [the defendant] so requests, the competent authorities of the receiving State shall, without delay, inform the consular post of the sending State if, within its consular district, a national of that State is arrested or committed to prison or to custody pending trial or is detained in any other manner. Any communication addressed to the consular post by the person arrested, in prison, custody or detention shall also be forwarded by the said authorities without delay. The said authorities shall inform the person concerned without delay of his rights under this sub-paragraph." Breard claimed that his rights under the Convention (under Article VI) were violated and the Paraguayan Government also protested.

2. *Breard v. Green*, 523 U.S. 371, 118 S.Ct. 1352, 1354–55 (1998).

that a violation of the *Vienna Convention on Consular Relations* notice requirement *does not require* exclusion of evidence obtained as a result of post-arrest custodial interrogation.[3] The 9th Circuit Court of Appeals noted: "[W]e need not decide whether to accept the government's argument that Article 36 creates no individually enforceable rights, however. We agree with the government's alternative position that assuming that some judicial remedies are available for the violation of Article 36, the exclusion in a criminal prosecution of evidence obtained as the result of post-arrest interrogation is not among them." The Court noted that the 9th Circuit and other circuits have held in recent years that an exclusionary rule is not available for treaty violations. The Vienna Convention, itself, does not indicate expressly whether it provides for a private right of action for its enforcement. On the other hand, it does state in its Preamble that, "the purpose of such privileges and immunities [as set forth in the Vienna Convention] is not to benefit individuals, but to ensure the efficient performance of functions by consular posts on behalf of their respective States." Nevertheless, the courts in the United States are split over whether this pre-ambular language, as well as similar language found in various parts of the Convention itself, forecloses a private right of action for enforcement of rights under the Convention. Nevertheless, even if the Vienna Convention were considered to be self-executing, and to confer private rights, it has been held that it *does not follow* that this includes the right to suppress evidence obtained in an interrogation conducted after failure to notify the accused of his "right" to consular assistance.

On the other hand, a Delaware court held the opposite, noting that, "[t]he text of the Vienna Convention, the intention of the drafters, and the prevailing view among this nation's courts lead this Court to conclude that Defendant's motion to suppress should be granted for the following reasons: (1) the Vienna Convention is the Law of the Land under Article VI, Section 2 of the United States Constitution; (2) the police conduct in this case violated Article 36 of the Convention; (3) Defendant, a Guatemalan citizen, has asserted a Vienna Convention violation in a timely manner [by raising it in a motion at the pre-trial, suppression motion stage]; (4) Defendant has shown adequate prejudice to exist; and; (5) a violation of Article 36 is ground for suppressing incriminating statements made by foreign nationals while in police or government custody."

The fundamental principle, *pacta sunt servanda,* is considered a jus cogens norm, by which, of course, treaties must be enforced.

A minor, claiming Salvadoran nationality, charged with murder, had his case "transferred" from the juvenile court system to the regular, criminal district court for trial on the charges. The juvenile claimed that Vienna Convention, Article 36 (b), entitled him to have his consular officials notified and that he should have been informed that he had the right to speak to a consular official. He also claimed that failure to do this, constituted a jurisdictional error, equivalent to that caused incident to the mandatory notice requirements to make such a transfer under the Texas Family Code. The defendant, then urges that the notice requirements in

---

3. *U.S. v. Lombera–Camorlinga,* 206 F.3d 882 (9th Cir.2000).

Vienna Convention, Article 36, have the same status and effect. The Texas Court of Appeals declined to so hold, noting that it is not settled that an individual has standing to assert a violation of the Vienna Convention on Consular Relations.

Notes and Questions. *See, e.g.* Neuman, *The Nationalization of Civil Liberties, Revisited,* 99 Colum.L.Rev. 1630 (1999); Vadnais, *A Diplomatic Morass: An Argument Against Judicial Involvement in Article 36 of the Vienna Convention on Consular Relations,* 47 UCLA L.Rev. 307 (1999); Halberstam, *The Constitutional Authority of the Federal Government in State Criminal Proceedings that Involve U.S. Treaty Obligations or Affect U.S. Foreign Relations,* 10 Ind.Int'l & Comp.L.Rev. 1 (1999); Alford & Bekker, *International Legal Developments: International Courts & Tribunals,* 33 Int'l Law. 537 (1999); Bradley, *Breard, Our Dualist Constitution,* 51 Stan.L.Rev. 529 (1999); Bederman, *Deference or Deception: Treaty Rights as Political Questions,* 70 U.Colo.L.Rev. 1439 (1999); Ramsey, *The Power of the States in Foreign Affairs: The Original Understanding of Foreign Policy Federalism,* 75 Notre Dame L.Rev. 341 (1999); Kirgis, *Agora: Zschernig v. Miller & the Breard Matter,* 92 A.J.I.L. 704 (1998); Vazquez, *Agora: Breard & the Federal Power to Require Compliance with ICJ Orders of Provisional Measures,* 92 A.J.I.L. 683 (1998).

CHAPTER 17

THEORIES ABOUT INTERNATIONAL LAW

Section A. Some Samples of Theoretical Perspectives.
Section B. Monism & Dualism.
Section C. Principles, Practice and Legitimacy.

1. *Is theory influential on outcomes under international law and on its development?* If you have taken these materials in the order in which we have arranged them, your study of this chapter comes after you have had experience with many of the major aspects of law in the international system. You will have begun to form your own ideas about the similarities and differences between the law you have studied here and the public law you study in other courses. For example: putting to one side the difference between the U.S. Supreme Court and the International Court of Justice as to authorization to decide, do you find these courts acting similarly or in sharply different ways in similar types of cases, i.e. where the Supreme Court is sitting in judgment upon the conflicting interests of two or more states of the Union.

We have put the theory material this far along for three reasons: (a) we wanted you to begin to grope toward theory on your own as you went along; (b) we wanted you to see from case study that so far as professional methodology and involvement go, international law calls upon the same range of skills as other systems of law do; (c) we wanted to avoid raising too many doubts and prospects before you had become more experienced in the subject matter.

Although underdeveloped, the international legal system has engendered extensive theoretical discussion. Why so much doctrine for so few rules and effective institutions to apply them? Is it because the scholars who have committed themselves to this field are creating theories and schools, casting their expectations and preferences as law simply because they have so little in the way of real law stuff to deal with? Do the materials which follow suggest that scholars are theorizing about reality or their dreams? Are they promoting the development of the law?

2. *Critical independence is indispensable.* International public law, more so than other bodies of law, tends to be presented in discrete doctrinal packages. Schools abound. Learned people encourage disciples. Deviation becomes intellectual heresy. Those who do not agree are dolts. Also, international law is often appealed to by advocates highly interested in particular outcomes. This is made possible because much of international law is highly amorphous and hence susceptible to a wide range of assertion or because it becomes an argument of last resort. Or it is found to have a strong rhetorical impact (governments do not wish to be seen as scoff-laws). Sometimes these groups of distorters, the didactic scholars and the argu-

mentative activists, combine forces. In consequence, it is not unusual that spokesmen claim for the international legal system a competence, a completeness and a virtue that it may not in fact possess. In this field the rule of caveat emptor is quite important for shoppers of doctrine.

In methodology, international public law traditionally has been somewhat old-fashioned by the most modern techniques of some domestic systems. It is too often highly exegetic, rigorously logical (even when there are errors in the logic), abstract, antiseptic and remote. Quantification technique as to events, things and attitudes of social groups barely exists. Even the schools that claim for themselves the utmost in realistic modernity are hardly scientific in any sense of association with modern scientific and engineering technology. Major positions are often supported by secondary authorities. In large part, perhaps, the generally backward methodological standard reflects the reality that, after all, the international legal system exists by consensus, and the world does not yet have a full consensus as to what law is and how it should be used.

3. ***Basic jurisprudential problems.*** International law shares with domestic law certain basic problems. These are the relationship of law to justice, the essential nature of law, and the judicial process in relationship to other types of decision-making.

Beyond these, international law throws into issue other fundamental questions:

(a) Is international law "law" in terms of a generally accepted concept of law, whatever that concept is?

(b) If international law is "law" in some sense or other, what is its relationship to other congeries of law, such as natural law, national law, international organizations law, regional systems law?

(c) What are the relations between international law notions and the worlds of social science, policy studies, literary criticism and deconstruction, international relations and doctrines of economics?

(d) Do international and domestic law form two separate legal systems (dualism) or are they each a part of one monolithic system (monism)?

4. ***Philosophy, for what purpose considered?*** What follows is intended to assist you in the development of your philosophic outlook about the legal element in the international system. This includes the development of cognition and analytical skills of both what international law is and what it ought to be or become. You will have been doing these cerebrations, subliminally perhaps, as you have gone through the preceding chapters. Your instructor may have chosen to begin with this part or to go to it immediately after Chapter 1. In any event, problems of international legal theory cannot be avoided. As soon as you think seriously, speak or write about international law, elements of theory will be reflected either as assumptions or affirmations.

5. ***The origins of international law.*** What a majority of modern writers regard as international law began to differentiate from a universalistic public law in the West about 600 years ago. Politically, after the

Roman city-state that became an empire withered away, segments of the old imperium began to see themselves as entities, not as mere extensions of a king's domain. These discrete new entities, despite Louis XIV's famous statement of identity between himself and the state, were incorporeal and distinct from any monarch. Certainly by the time of Ferdinand and Isabella—and probably at least one hundred years earlier—the nation-state as we know it today (territory, population, government) was in being in the West.

These entities soon evolved standards of conduct toward each other beyond the rules of etiquette between monarchs. Some of these were and still are standards of political propriety, such as diplomatic protocol, principles of international relations and comity. Other standards of conduct—always minimum ones—came to be thought of as creating rights and obligations for states, analogous to the rules (or norms) that states themselves imposed on persons within their jurisdiction, not as whim or caprice but as law. Specifically, the part of Roman law that pertained in the heyday of Roman authority to controversies between non-Romans, the jus gentium, became a term used yesterday, and in some measure still, to refer to "customary international law."

The international law of today does not show distinct linkages to ancient Oriental and African practices. Even the modern descendants of very old Oriental cultures accept international law as the product of Western evolution. Ignorance and neglect in the West of the history of law and related institutions in the East constitute the most likely explanation of this omission. Scholars in some of the modern states that have evolved from the Oriental historical matrix sometimes chide the West for this inattention and threaten (usually mildly) to set the matter aright sometime. New states in Africa sometimes are heard in similar vein.

This fact makes the existing international legal system somewhat vulnerable to attacks on its universality by states not present at its creation. More often, however, the states that are not satisfied with the existing order attack specific rules or principles, not the system. Classical, scholarly Marxists, and many who are non-Marxist, deprecate the system of customary international law because it seems to them unavoidably to state, as law, rules and principles fostering the interests of the power elites asserting them. The socialist states of the former Second World, however, came in practice to accept the system and many of its most conventional rules and principles, while selectively seeking to deny status as law to other rules and principles because they are contradictory to national ideological or other preferences.

6. *Naturalists, positivists, the "new wave", and eclectics.* In the West international law was systematized by more or less scholarly writers (publicists), not power-wielding officials. The excerpt from Stone, infra, a modern publicist, refers to some of these. Vitoria (1480–1546) and Suarez (1548–1617) perceived that beyond individual states there was a community of states governed as to their interactions by international rules. These rules were to be found by rational derivation from basic moral principles of divine origin. These Spaniards' concepts developed into a school of natural law, paralleling for international law an earlier jurisprudence about domestic secular law. This is now very important for human rights law and

international criminal law. For those topics see chapters 9 and 16, respectively.

The school of scholastic naturalism was resisted by writers who recognized a legal community but said that its rules came either in whole or in part from state practice, not from God. Gentilis (1552–1608) seems to have been the first to dare say there was more earthliness than theology behind international law. Hugo Grotius (the latinized version of a Dutch name) was born in 1583, and if systematized international law has a single historical beginning it is in his De Jure Belli Ac Pacis, printed in 1625. Grotius served once as Sweden's ambassador, an interesting practice not long continued by states; and as a representative of fishing and sea-trading national interests he gave us, inter alia, the principle of the freedom of the seas as customary international law. Grotius is also type-cast as the first eclectic, because he accepted not only positive law—state practice—as a source of international law, but also natural law. But the natural law of Grotius was more secular than that of the Spanish scholastics, for it was based upon man's rationality—"the dictate of right reason"—rather than upon revelation, exegesis, and deduction of God's will.

A second school of naturalism, secular and rationalist, evolved and had some influence on the early recognition and reception of international law by courts in the United States. Thus, in finding vessels engaged in the slave trade subject to seizure by American privateers, Justice Story, on circuit, wrote:

> " * * * I think it may unequivocally be affirmed, that every doctrine that may be fairly deduced by correct reasoning from the rights and duties of nations, and the nature of moral obligation, may theoretically be said to exist in the law of nations; and unless it be relaxed or waived by the consent of nations, which may be evidenced by their general practice and customs, it may be enforced by a court of justice * * *." U.S. v. The Schooner La Jeune Eugenie, 26 F.Cas. 832, 846 (c.C.D.Mass.1822) (No. 15,551).

But at the Supreme Court commitment to positivism prevailed in a philosophically indistinguishable slave trade situation. Marshall let the slavers keep their "property" [sic]: " * * * This, [slavery], which was the usage of all, could not be pronounced repugnant to the law of nations * * *." The Antelope, 23 U.S. (10 Wheat.) 66 at 120 (1825). Why? The "usage of all [States]" is otherwise and controls. Generally speaking adherence to natural law, especially if of the second or rationalist variety, tends to be a form of idealism about law. Positivism tends to emphasize conduct-phenomenology, e.g. how many states accept that "x" is law, just or unjust?

The role of the writers. Idealism tends to transform into law decision-makers' preferences and down-grade the element of states' volition in accepting a rule or principle as one of law. There has long been in international law a pronounced emphasis on the distinction between the law that is and what ought to be the law. But in some legal philosophies about international law it is harder to discern the line of difference than in others, especially if the publicist is an eclectic, or policy-oriented.

Some modern American writers, for example, devote themselves to telling us how to make better systems, stressing structural and procedural arrangements as if these were the basic need or problem. Others, self-characterized as American philosophic neo-realists, are really so idealistic as to assume that American values are common goal values on the planet and that law is not normative but an argumentative variable in the power process by which authorized decision makers—lawyers, judges, diplomats, politicians—put these goal values into effect with authoritativeness. A few theorists, including those who concentrate in critical legal theory, approach the subject of international law from different perspectives, some challenging the very nature and operation of international law. Perhaps at the central core are those who are essentially mild positivists—in the tradition of American pragmatism—who try to find out what the great weight of acceptance by states shows and to emphasize the norms stated in obligatory form in international agreements.

The writers—and now in the United States, the Restaters—have had, and continue to have, great influence on what judges—and even foreign offices—do in relationship to international law. In civil law countries, where doctrine, i.e. scholarly writing, is the primary influence on jurisprudence, i.e. case law, this is normal. In the common law world it is not normal for domestic law, but it is for international law. For today the judges' perceptions of customary international law are not their own but those of the writer or school they have chosen to follow, rejecting others. And the writers, as we have seen, vary widely in what they perceive. This is the basis of their power and their responsibility. Advocacy in any arena, national or international, as to what the relevant international law rule is requires the advocate to be very familiar with the literature and legal theories, both that which can help his cause and that which might destroy it.

7. *Some questions and issues for you to come back to.* With the above guide, and with questions in mind such as those to follow, evaluate the messages of the excerpts from writings below. Is the writer an idealist or is he reality-oriented? In the historic scheme of differentiation, what label do you give the writer? To your mind does the writer help or hurt the cause of legal order in the world community? Why?

What is international law to you now? Is its existence considered by you to be proved, disproved or not proved? Do you see an identity or a difference between international law and domestic law in the international system? Is international law merely an aspect of a science of international relations? If not, where do you draw lines between principles of international relations and principles of international law? On which side of a line do these fall: self-determination of peoples, nonintervention, equality of states, use of economic force? Can the "rules of international law" be ignored? Would Hitler have had one answer before and another after WWII? What would Saddam Hussein's answer be today? How about the leaders of the various factions in Rwanda, Cambodia, Bosnia and Kosovo? See chapter 9 and 16. How about Mr. Pinochet? What do you think? Are these matters of pure power or is law involved? If so, how? As to the existence or not of international law, should it suffice to note, as then

Professor (later judge of the International Court of Justice) Jessup did in 1940, that foreign ministries have legal staffs, that diplomatic correspondence is full of assertion and counter-assertion as to the international law issues involved in a controversy, that this has been true for at least three centuries, and that, by inference, there are jobs of international lawyering? See Jessup, *The Reality of International Law,* 18 For.Aff. 244 (1940).

———

SECTION A.   SOME SAMPLES OF THEORETICAL PERSPECTIVES

Ratner and Slaughter, Appraising the Methods of International Law: A Prospectus for Readers

In Symposium on Method in International Law, 93 A.J.I.L.291 (1999)*

* * *

To elucidate the theoretical underpinnings of contemporary scholarship through recourse to the methods employed by various theories, we decided upon seven methods for appraisal: legal positivism, the New Haven School, international legal process, critical legal studies, international law and international relations, feminist jurisprudence, and law and economics. In our view, they represent the major methods of international legal scholarship today. Our list does not include methods that may have been utilized by scholars in the past, or that dominated the scholarship of earlier eras—as the absence of Roman law, canon law, and socialist/Soviet law would indicate. It also excludes, owing to space constraints, other approaches that offer important insights, such as natural law, the comparative method and functionalism. Moreover, our identification of seven discrete methods does not preclude other useful ways grouping international legal scholarship. * * *

As the contributors to this symposium will present their respective methods in some detail, here we simply identify their most basic characteristics. We confess that these are purely our own descriptions, informed by our own perspectives, with which the authors may differ.

Positivism. Positivism summarizes a range of theories that focus upon describing the law as it is, backed up by effective sanctions, with reference to formal criteria, independently moral or ethical considerations. For positivists, international law is no more or less than the rules to which states have agreed through treaties, custom, and perhaps other forms of consent. In the absence of such evidence of the will of states, positivists will assume

* Excerpts from additional contributions to this Symposium, on the subjects of critical legal studies, international law and international relations (IR/IL), feminist jurisprudence, and law and economics are included in the selections that follow. These subjects appear after materials on the more traditional subjects of positivism, natural law and sociology of law and functionalism.

Reprinted with the permission of the American Society of International Law.

that states remain at liberty to undertake whatever actions they please. Positivism also tends to view states as the only subjects of international law, thereby discounting the role of nonstate actors. It remains the lingua franca of most international lawyers, especially in continental Europe.

The New Haven School (policy-oriented jurisprudence). Established by Harold Lasswell and Myres McDougal of Yale Law School beginning in the mid–1940s, the New Haven. School eschews positivism's formal method of searching for rules as well as the concept of law as based on rules alone. It describes itself as a policy-oriented perspective, viewing international law as a process of decision making by which various actors in the world community clarify and implement their common interests in accordance with their expectations of appropriate processes and of effectiveness in controlling behavior. Perhaps the New Haven School's greatest contribution has been its emphasis on both what actors say and what they do.

International legal process. International legal process (ILP) refers to the approach first developed by Abram Chayes, Thomas Ehrlich and Andreas Lowenfeld at Harvard Law School in the 1960s. Building on the American legal process school, it has seen the key locus of inquiry of international law as the role of law in constraining decision makers and affecting the course of international affairs. Legal process theory has recently enjoyed a domestic revival, which seeks to underpin precepts about process with a set of normative values. Some ILP scholars are following suit.

Critical legal studies. Critical legal studies (CLS) scholars have sought to move beyond what constitutes law, or the relevance of law to policy, to focus on the contradictions, hypocrisies and failings of international legal discourse. The diverse group of scholars who often identify themselves as part of the "New Stream" have emphasized the importance of culture to legal development and offered a critical view of the progress of the law in its confrontations with state sovereignty. Like the deconstruction movement, which is the intellectual font of many of its ideas, critical legal studies has focused on the importance of language.

International law and international relations. IR/IL is a purposefully interdisciplinary approach that seeks to incorporate into international law the insights of international relations theory regarding the behavior of international actors. The most recent round of IR/IL scholarship seeks to draw on contemporary developments and strands in international relations theory, which is itself a relatively young discipline. The results are diverse, ranging from studies of compliance, to analyses of the stability and effectiveness of international institutions, to the ways that models of state conduct affect the content and subject of international rules.

Feminist jurisprudence. Feminist scholars of international law seek to examine how both legal norms and processes reflect the domination of men, and to reexamine and reform these norms and processes so as to take account of women. Feminist jurisprudence has devoted particular attention to the shortcomings in the international protection of women's rights, but it has also asserted deeper structural challenges to international law, criticizing the way law is made and applied as insufficiently attentive to the role of women. Feminist jurisprudence has also taken an active advocacy role.

Law and economics. In its domestic incarnation, which has proved highly significant and enduring, law and economics has both a descriptive component that seeks to explain existing rules as reflecting the most economically efficient outcome, and a normative component that evaluates proposed changes in the law and urges adoption of those that maximize wealth. Game theory and public choice theory are often considered part of law and economics. In the international area, it has begun to address commercial and environmental issues.

Although, as will be clear from the essays that follow, each of these methods has its own defining characteristics, it is equally apparent that each is a living method, employed by a diverse community of scholars who help ensure its continual evolution. If positivism is simplistically termed the most conservative of the methods, it is safe to say that the positivist method of today might well have been unrecognizable to a lawyer one hundred years ago; if critical legal studies is in some sense the most radical of the methods in the questions it poses about the nature of international law, it too has undergone transformations since its arrival in scholarly circles in the 1980s. The essays can thus present only a snapshot of their method, with perhaps some sense of its path to date and future trajectory. Moreover, although many of the methods have a distinctly American origin, the community of scholars for nearly all of them is now global.

* * *

1 Austin, Jurisprudence 177, 189 (1861)

* * * Speaking with greater precision, international law, or the law obtaining between nations, regards the conduct of sovereigns considered as related to one another.

And hence it inevitably follows, that the law obtaining between nations is not positive law: for every positive law is set by a given sovereign to a person or persons in a state of subjection to its author. As I have already intimated, the law obtaining between nations is law (improperly so called) set by general opinion. The duties which it imposes are enforced by moral sanctions: by fear on the part of nations, or by fear on the part of sovereigns, of provoking general hostility, and incurring its probable evils, in case they shall violate maxims generally received and respected.

* * *

* * * But if perfect or complete independence be of the essence of sovereign power, there is not in fact the human power to which the epithet sovereign will apply with propriety. Every government, let it be never so powerful, renders occasional obedience to commands of other governments. Every government defers frequently to those opinions and sentiments which are styled international law. And every government defers habitually to the opinions and sentiments of its own subjects. If it be not in a habit of obedience to the commands of a determinate party, a government has all the independence which a government can possibly enjoy.

Phillipson, Introduction To Gentili, De Jure Belli Libri Tres (2 Trans., Carnegie Endowment, 1933) 22a*

* * *

5. Conception of the Law of Nations—Society of States—Civil Basis—Membership of the Society. The law of nations, designated by Gentili ius gentium (the customary expression adapted from Roman Law) is that law which all nations or the greater part of them—"maior parsorbis"—agree upon. It is the law of the society or community of states, of the "Societas gentium". This is a concise and simple description, whereby the ambiguous Roman term is made to refer explicitly to international relations. It is not, of course, an exact definition, as it involves, though unavoidably, a tautologism. Indeed, no satisfactory definition had hitherto been formulated. Grotius adopts substantially the conception of Gentili, when he says that the law of nations (ius gentium) is that law which has received obligatory force from the will of all nations or of many; whilst Vattel, like Gentili, verges on tautology in his statement that the law of nations (droit des gens) is the science of the rights and obligations which exist between nations. Some writers emphasize in their definitions the origin of the law of nations, others the nature of the subject-matter, and others again lay stress on those concerned in and bound by it. * * *

* * *

* * * Very frequently we find that Gentili appeals to the ius naturae in order to test the validity of a particular doctrine or the legitimacy of a certain practice; but usually he disregards the current vague metaphysico-legal significance of that term, and interprets it in the sense of humanity, justice, and the best common sense of mankind. And throughout his exposition he insists on the positive juridical sanction quite as much as on the considerations of ethics or on the behests of divine law, and he is careful to discriminate between the work and objects of theologians and the sphere and functions of jurists.

The pioneer work of Gentili was in harmony with the larger movement of the sixteenth century which witnessed a transformation of society, the establishment of a new spirit and wider outlook, the decline of theocracy, and the rise of the modern State. The political conceptions of the Middle Ages, which identified civil and ecclesiastical authority, were derived on the one hand from Greek and Roman doctrines, and on the other from Hebrew and Christian teaching. Towards the end of the thirteenth century the temporal supremacy of the papacy began to be seriously opposed, especially in France, and its decline was further hastened on by the great schism. The conciliar movement of the fifteenth century spread the theory that sovereign power was of the nature of a trust. The Renaissance and the Reformation, two sides of the same great intellectual and moral awakening, revived humanism, scientific curiosity, established a spirit of independence, political as well as spiritual, and a desire to find a more rational basis than the arbitrary theocratic for human society, and substituted civil for clerical

* Reprinted with the permission of the   Peace.
Carnegie   Endowment   for   International

authority, a society of territorial States resting on law and juridical sanction for a theocratic confederation subject to canon law. * * *

* * *

2 Wolff, Classics of International Law
Carnegie Endowment 11, 19 (1934)*

§ 7.—Of the society established by nature among nations. Nature herself has established society among all nations and binds them to preserve society. For nature herself has established society among men and binds them to preserve it. Therefore, since this obligation, as coming from the law of nature, is necessary and immutable, it cannot be changed for the reason that nations have united into a state. Therefore society, which nature has established among individuals, still exists among nations and consequently, after states have been established in accordance with the law of nature and nations have arisen thereby, nature herself also must be said to have established society among all nations and bound them to preserve society.

* * *

§ 25.—Of the positive law of nations. That is called the positive law of nations which takes its origin from the will of nations. Therefore since it is plainly evident that the voluntary, the stipulative, and the customary law of nations take their origin from the will of nations, all that law is the positive law of nations. And since furthermore it is plain that the voluntary law of nations rests on the presumed consent of nations, the stipulative upon the express consent, the customary upon the tacit consent, since moreover in no other way is it conceived that a certain law can spring from the will of nations, the positive law of nations is either voluntary or stipulative or customary.

* * *

Stone, Legal Controls of International Conflict LIII
(1954)**

* * * Is there an international law? In what sense, if any, are its rules binding? To whom are such rules (insofar they exist and bind) directed? Can international law be said to be the law of a society or a community? Nor have the new approaches yielded even substantially new answers to the old questions. John Austin's denial of the *legal* force of international law lacked, no doubt, the temperateness of Professor Corbett or the passionate cynicism of a Lundstedt; but there is little now said that he did not foreshadow a century ago. Today, as centuries ago, those who champion the cause of international law as "law", find its source of validity either in natural law, as did Vitoria and Suàrez, or in positive enactment, as did Gentili and Zouche, or in a mixture of the two as in Grotius. Even Kelsen's reduction of the relations between international law and international

* Reprinted with the permission of the Carnegie Endowment for International Peace.

** © Julius Stone 1954. Reprinted with the permission of Julius Stone and Wm. W. Gaunt & Sons, Inc., Holmes Beach, Fla.

society to the identity of *legal order* and *legal community,* while apparently resolving a traditional perplexity into a mere verbal illusion, has proved to be a new evasion rather than a new solution. Its identification of the international legal order with the international legal community is achieved only by excluding from the notion of "society" the very reference to the world of existence which was the essential source of the exorcised perplexity. * * *

* * *

So, too, it may be striking that modern theories as opposed in temper as to those of Professors Lauterpacht, Lundstedt and Messner converge by different paths on the importance of recognising the role of the individual in international law. But these questions of the "Aye" or "No" of the international status of individuals are in themselves as old as the natural law of a Suàrez or a Grotius: and mere theory is unlikely to advance them further. What theory rather requires is a fuller understanding of the mediating, distorting or obstructing operation of State entities on human relations.

Such fuller new inquiries do not lend themselves to quick answers, nor at all to armchair answers. The need for long and arduous field research within the most inaccessible and dangerously controversial area of human relations is (it is believed) a basic reason for the modern stalemate in juristic thought concerning international law. If such needed inquiries are shunned, then theory is thrown back on such barren questions as whether the actual self-subordination of States to wider international association, functionally limited, warrants the use of the term "community" to describe such an international association. And since the degrees of such self-subordination are potentially infinite in number, ranging from the most transient association on the battlefield by way of a truce for burying the dead, through the intimate organic association (on paper) of a United Nations Organization, to the intimacy in fact of a successful federation such as that of the United States or the Commonwealth of Australia, such inquiries are as interminable as they are barren.

Insofar, therefore, as we are concerned with a "living" or "operative" international law, with "law in action" as distinct from "the books", the continuance of armchair debate whether international law is "law", will not advance understanding. Nor does it really advance matters to interpret "law in action", as do Dr. Schwarzenberger and others, to mean the law enounced or applied by tribunals or competent State organs, as distinct from the writings of publicists. So far as concerns the effects of international law *on men,* and *of men on law,* the law of tribunals and State organs may still be "law in the books" rather than "law in action". Nor has Professor Corbett's search for international "law in action", despite its courage and vigour, really faced the preliminary question, what "international law in action" may mean. It is, in the present view, impossible to study "law in action" without relating the law not merely to the supposed interests and conduct of States, but also (and above all) to those of the men and women of particular times and places. And if this be so, then it becomes apparent that the task of assessing the effect on human interests and human conduct of the interposition of State entities between the great aggregations of mankind, is an inescapable preliminary.

* * *

It is at least probable, that the magic circle of the unsolved classical problems will not be broken until we cease to assume that the categories, conceptions, and methods of municipal law are sufficient, or even necessarily relevant, either for testing the validity of international law or for understanding its actual operation. Certainly our plight seems to cry out for insights which the classical problems, even when clothed in twentieth century philosophical garb, fail to yield. Such an escape from the classical magic circle might also release intellectual energy for tasks more fruitful than those which now engage them.

Kelsen, The Pure Theory of Law[a]

51 Law Quarterly Review 517 (1935).[*]

* * *

28.   The law, or the legal order, is a system of legal norms. The first question we have to answer, therefore, is this: What constitutes the unity in diversity of legal norms? Why does a particular legal norm belong to a particular legal order? A multiplicity of norms constitutes a unity, a system, an order, when validity can be traced back to its final source in a single norm. This basic norm constitutes the unity in diversity of all the norms which make up the system. That a norm belongs to a particular order is only to be determined by tracing back its validity to the basic norm constituting the order. According to the nature of the basic norm, i.e. the sovereign principle of validity, we may distinguish two different kinds of orders, or normative systems. In the first such system the norms are valid by virtue of their content, which has a directly evident quality compelling recognition. * * *

29.   With legal norms the case is different. These are not valid by virtue of their content. Any content whatsoever can be legal; there is no human behaviour which could not function as the content of a legal norm. A norm becomes a legal norm only because it has been constituted in a particular fashion, born of a definite procedure and a definite rule. Law is valid only as positive law, that is, statute (constituted) law. Therefore the basic norm of law can only be the fundamental rule, according to which the legal norms are to be produced; it is the fundamental condition of law-making. The individual norms of the legal system are not to be derived from the basic norm by a process of logical deduction. They must be constituted by an act of will, not deduced by an act of thought. If we trace back a single legal norm to its source in the basic norm, we do so by showing that the procedure by which it was set up conformed to the requirements of the basic norm. Thus, if we ask why a particular act of

a.   The late Professor Albert A. Ehrenzweig, one time a student of Kelsen, always said the correct translation is "the theory of pure law."

* Reprinted with the permission of Stevens & Sons, Ltd., London.

compulsion—the fact, for instance, that one man has deprived another of his freedom by imprisoning him—is an act of law and belongs to a particular legal order, the answer is, that this act was prescribed by a certain individual norm, a judicial decision. If we ask, further, why this individual norm is valid, the answer is, that it was constituted according to the penal statute book. If we inquire as to the validity of the penal statute book, we are confronted by the State's constitution, which has prescribed rules and procedure for the creation of the penal statute book by a competent authority. If, further, we ask as to the validity of the constitution, on which repose all the laws and the acts which they have sanctioned, we come probably to a still older constitution and finally to an historically original one, set up by some single usurper or by some kind of corporate body. It is the fundamental presupposition of our recognition of the legal order founded on this constitution that which the original authors declared to be their will should be regarded as valid norm. Compulsion is to be exercised according to the method and conditions prescribed by the first constitutional authority, or its delegated power. This is the schematic formulation of the basic norm of a legal order.

30.   The Pure Theory of Law operates with this basic norm as with an hypothesis. Presupposed that it is valid, then the legal order which rests on it is valid also. Only under this presupposition can we systematize as law (i.e. arrange as a system of norms) the empirical material which presents itself for legal recognition. On the composition of this material (acts) will depend also on the particular content of the basic norm. This norm is only an expression for the necessary presupposition of all positivistic constructions of legal material. In formulating the basic norm, the Pure Theory of Law in no way considers itself as inaugurating a new scientific method of jurisprudence. It is only trying to make conscious in the minds of jurists what they are doing when, in seeking to understand their subject, they reject a validity founded on natural law, yet affirm the positive law, not as a mere factual assembly of motives, but as a valid order, as norm. With the theory of the basic norm, the Pure Theory of Law is only trying to elucidate, by an analysis of the actual procedure, the transcendental-logical conditions of the historic methods of positive legal knowledge.

31.   Just as the nature of law, and of the community which it constitutes, stands most clearly revealed when its very existence is threatened, so the significance of the basic norm emerges most clearly when the legal order undergoes not legal change, but revolution or substitution. In an hitherto monarchic State a number of men attempt to overthrow by force the legitimate monarchic government and to set up a republican form in its place. If in this they are successful, that is, the old government ceases and the new begins to be effective, in that the behaviour of the men and women, for whom the order claims to be valid, conforms in the main no longer to the old but to the new order, then this latter is operated as a legal order, the acts which it performs are declared legal, the conditions which it proscribes, illegal. A new basic norm is presupposed—no longer that which delegated legislative authority to the monarch, but one which delegates such authority to the revolutionary government. Had the attempt been a failure, had the new order, that is, remained ineffective, in that behaviour

did not conform to it, then the acts of the new government become not constitutional but criminal (high treason), not legislation but delict, and this on the ground of the validity of the old order, which presupposed a basic norm delegating legislative power to the monarch.

If we ask what, then, determines the content of the basic norm, we find, on analyzing judicial decisions back to their first premises, the following answer: The content of the basic norm is determined by the condition of fact out of which the order emerges, given that to the order there corresponds, amongst the human beings to whom it refers, a substantial measure of actual behaviour.

This gives us the content of a positive legal norm. (It is not, of course, a norm of a State's legal order, but a norm of international law, which, as a legal order superior to that of the individual States, legally determines their sphere of jurisdiction.) * * *

      * * *

DeVisscher, Theory and Reality In Public International Law 404 (1968)*

It was doubtless inevitable that a long period of war on a world scale and of unexampled political tensions should have a profound influence on the direction of thought in the field of international law. The descriptive methods of voluntarist positivism in vogue at the beginning of the century, like those derived exclusively from formal logic, are everywhere in retreat. Contemporary legal thought is intensely alive to the need of a new set of values in the foundations of positive international law. From now on it refuses to see in that law merely a technical order without moral inspiration or teleological direction.

The legal thought of today seeks in the direct observation of international life a new field of study. This is not a matter, as there is a tendency to say, of reconstructing international law on a foundation of sociology, but of scrutinizing the *raison d'être* of norms, restoring the contract between the normative apparatus and the underlying realities, and thus sifting through a more broadly informed criticism the rules and practices of international law perceived in the living process of application. In this renewed study the man of law will confront without methodological prejudice realities which at times are ill-adapted to his formal categories. He will not forget, however, that the observation of international life, though it never consists in the mere collection of raw facts, provides only the data for legal elaboration; that legal elaboration has its proper function, which is to select from these data only those which are adapted to social ends and which a complex of characteristics (external prominence, generality, regularity) makes fit material for his particular technique. So understood, enquiries into international relations promise to be fruitful. Properly

* Translated by P.E. Corbett (copyright © 1968 by Princeton University Press). Re-printed with the permission of the translator and the Princeton University Press.

conducted, they will have a vivifying influence; they will re-establish international law in the plenitude of its ends and its efficacity.

Even now this new orientation is apparent on the plane of doctrinal studies. We can find it again in the jurisprudence of the International Court of Justice, in the work of codification going on under the auspices of the United Nations, in the creative effort of international organizations. Everywhere is felt the need to reinvigorate legal technique, to free it from prefabricated categories by associating it more closely with the study of a social milieu in accelerated evolution.

From this realization flow new demands. One is fundamental and moral; in a crisis of human values it insists upon respect for these at the heart of every organized society. There are others, more contingent in character, because tied to the present forms of the distribution of power among nations: such is that demand of effectivity which we have so often encountered and which, in a still primitive order of relations, has a more prominent place than anywhere else.

The study of power, both in its distribution and in its action, has had a large part in our discussion. The reason is that, more than any other, it reveals the tensions and the convergences that characterize the present relations between the political fact and the law. Belonging as it does both to the internal and to the international order, the action of the State is at the center of international relations and is for the moment their most salient feature. It compels the man of law to penetrate beyond the formal manifestations of power into its intimate springs and to do his share towards endowing power with an organization adapted to the common international good.

The problem of the future is that of the transformations of power. There are many signs that the structure of international relations is on the eve of profound changes. Territory, which since the end of the middle ages has provided the firmest base for these relations and ensured their stability, has no longer the same significance. It is all too clear that the existence of atomic weapons, of long-range rockets of increasing accuracy, rob frontiers of their traditional role as bulwarks of power and security. It is not less evident that some of the pacific activities of States cannot go on without more or less serious repercussions in neighboring countries. Consequently some scientific and technological operations (nuclear experiments, diversion and pollution of waters) call for international regulation. Similarly, an economy of international dimensions can no longer conform to political and legal conceptions allied with a configuration of close-walled national units. Association, even integration, are the new forms of power-distribution that force themselves upon States in search of wider markets.

Some of these structural transformations are partially in effect and in course of development.Others are scarcely visible on the horizon. The man of law owes it to himself to watch them; he will go surety for them only in so far as they seem to him factors of progress. No more than any other form of organization do federal structures have value in themselves: like the others they may become the instrument of political or economic antagonisms that divide peoples. The redistribution of power can be efficacious only when based upon solid realities; it can be beneficent only if it guarantees order and peace.

Kaplan and Katzenbach, The Political Foundations of International Law 5 (1961)*

No one can observe the international political system without being aware that order does exist, and that this order is related in important ways to formal and authoritative rules, that is, to a body of law and to a process of law-government. These rules are sustained by the genuine interests which nations have in restraining certain forms of international conduct, even though these constraints must apply to their own conduct as well as to that of other states. To understand the substance and limits of such constraining rules, it is necessary to examine the interests which support them in the international system, the means by which they are made effective, and the functions they perform. * * *

* * *

International Law as "Law:" Sometimes international law is viewed as a rather strange breed of law to which the term "law" is applied only by courtesy if at all. A number of great legal philosophers—Hobbes, Pufendorf, Bentham, and Austin are examples—have all doubted the legal character of international law, and the charges and counter charges which pervade the international community today seem to provide empirical support for their view. Clearly some definitions of law would exclude international law. Disputes, for example, are not routinely decided by an international judiciary, and there exists no coercive agency of formal international status which can effectively enforce the law. Rules do not emanate from any single "sovereign." Indeed, the legal order is not primarily vertical, or hierarchical, as it normally is in domestic government. Rather it is structured horizontally, composed predominantly of formally equal centers of legal authority called "states." We have only the beginnings of supranational authority in the United Nations and in various regional organizations.

* * *

Now, in spite of the differences in terminology and the fact that a critic may get considerable political mileage from invoking the accusation that international law has been flouted, processes in the international and domestic arenas are in some respects comparable. The particular decision disposes of the case and enters into the body of available precedent, whether that decision is persuasive or not. The focus of critical attention is to undercut its status as a norm to be invoked by others in similar circumstances, and it is to this end that some continue to call it a violation of international law. The more arbitrary it can be made to appear, the more radical the innovation, the more it can be related to selfish objectives of a particular state, and the more it offends widely shared and deeply felt values, the less persuasive it will be as precedent for others.

* * *

Doubts about a law-system which lacks judge and sheriff have, we think misleadingly, been frequently expressed as a theory of international law which describes it as a "voluntary" system based on the "consent" of "sovereign" states. It does not require much insight into law-politics to see a parallel between this theory and the consent theory of domestic government. Whatever the moral appeal of the consent theory at both levels (it represents a dislike for coercion), states "consent" to international prescriptions in the same sense that individuals "consent" to existing laws. They recognize the general need for a system of order, they regard the bulk of existing regulation as either desirable or at least tolerable, and they accept what remains because they have to—because they lack the ability to change it. The more intolerable a regulation is, the more pressure there is to seek a change by any means possible.

The point is not, of course, that legal institutions in the international community are adequate to contemporary affairs. Obviously they are not. But these institutions, such as they are, exist and contribute to international order. They will continue until some political combination has the capability to create new institutions more consonant with order and, we can at least hope, with a decent regard for human values. This creative process is presently taking place, on both a universal scale (the U.N. complex) and, perhaps more successfully, in a variety of regional and functional organizations such as NATO and the European Communities.

The authors recognize the merits of criticisms that distinguished observers such as George Kennan have made regarding too great a reliance upon legal processes. American foreign policy has often been formulated without sufficient attention to the role of force and of national interests. We do not wish to encourage naiveté of the sort he describes as "legal idealism," a reliance upon abstract rules that are institutionally unsupported. We concede that nations often do act in partisan ways in support of immediate political objectives. But we contend that much of international conduct is doctrinally consonant with normative standards, even though inconsistent with particular immediate interests, and that long-term self-interest can and does provide political support for internationally lawful conduct. * * *

Question. At this stage of your study are you willing to accept international law as law? Why or why not? In retrospect, does Chapter 1 have a positive, negative, or neutral influence on your attitude? If you do not consider at this point that international law is law, what is the minimum required to make it law?

* * *

Schachter, Philip Jessup's Life and Ideas

80 A.J.I.L. 878, 890 (1986).*

Jessup's Ideas on International Law

In his long, productive life, Jessup expressed himself on virtually all of the major issues of contemporary international law. He did so mainly in articles, lectures and AJIL editorials, many of which were collected and published in books. He never produced a comprehensive treatise or a grand theory. Typically, he addressed specific current issues and that led him often into fundamentals. He felt impelled to rebut the skeptics who questioned the reality of international law and the nationalists who construed the country's interests in a narrow way. Jessup's responses to them were essentially pragmatic. He stressed the essential role of rules in the day-to-day business of world affairs; he pointed to the costs of disorder and conflict in the absence of law; he sought to show how law furthered the shared interests of states. In the same vein, he dealt with the meaning of rules and concepts, pointing out always how the issues bore on the interests of the governments and peoples concerned. His concern with the function of rules is evident particularly in his judicial opinions such as those in Barcelona Traction and the North Sea Continental Shelf Cases and in his writings on state responsibility.

Jessup's practicality led him to make numerous suggestions to improve the process of conflict resolution and the efficacy of international law. He did not disdain small, concrete proposals involving procedural changes or institutional arrangements. Broadly speaking, he was an incrementalist and he tended to be skeptical of grand projects to change the existing order. Experience rather than theory was his guide. * * *

However, his pragmatism was also imbued with a distinct teleological element. Like Elihu Root, his early mentor, Jessup saw the main trends of international society as part of an evolutionary development toward a more organized and effective legal order. The main features of that order could be briefly summarized as follows: recognition of the interest of the international community; protection of the basic rights of individuals; the prohibition of armed force except in self-defense; recourse to judicial procedures or conciliation for dispute settlement; the extension of international regulation and administration in areas of interdependence, global and regional. For Jessup, these ends appeared almost axiomatic. They described the direction in which the world had to move in its enlightened self-interest. The optimism of an earlier age and Jessup's own buoyant spirit are reflected in this outlook.

Jessup's theoretical assumptions were implicit in his analysis of specific issues. They could be characterized as a sophisticated blend of positivism, idealism and pragmatism. He was always careful to distinguish positive law—the *lex lata*—from proposed or predicted future law. At the same time, he was mindful that positive law included principles and concepts that expressed basic values and that these "received ideals" were authoritative guides in construing and extending existing rules. In this manner,

* Reprinted with the permission of the American Society of International Law.

his approach transcended strict positivism. It is well exemplified in The Modern Law of Nations. Concepts as general as the freedom of the seas, pacta sunt servanda, sovereign equality, the obligations of peaceful settlement, self-determination, equitable sharing, are among those persuasively used to infuse values into concrete decisions. Like a good practitioner, Jessup believed a stronger case for a new rule can be made by linking it to an established principle. He was also aware that broadly stated policies in legal instruments must be construed with regard to the consensus of the community on which their authority ultimately depends. The fact that social ends are plural and often conflict impressed him with the necessity for balancing competing considerations in reaching particular decisions.

* * *

Related to Jessup's conception of the international community was his notion of "transnational law," a term he did not invent but which was developed and popularized in his Storrs lectures of 1956. With that notion, Jessup sought to show the growing legal complexity of an interdependent world. The international legal realm could no longer be compartmentalized in its two classic divisions of public international law, applicable only to relations among states, and private international law, governing choice of law and enforcement of national judgments in cases involving nationals of two or more states. The legal rules and process applicable to situations that cut across national lines must now be sought in both public and private international law and, to a significant degree, in new bodies of law that do not fit into either traditional division. As examples of the latter, Jessup cited the growing areas of European Community law, maritime law, international administrative law, war crimes, the law of economic development and the rules applicable to multinational enterprises.

* * *

McDougal, Lasswell, Reisman, Theories About International Law: Prologue to a Configurative Jurisprudence

8 Virginia Journal of International Law 188, 195 (1968).*

* * * The indispensable function of jurisprudence is to delimit a frame of reference appropriate to the study of the interrelations of law and community process and to specify in detail the intellectual tasks by which such study can be made and applied to the solution of the exigent problems it reveals. A jurisprudence of international law which would be relevant to the needs both of specialists in decision and of all who would understand and affect the processes in which they live must, accordingly, comprise a configurative approach, having at least three major characteristics:

1. It must be contextual, i.e., it must perceive all features of the social process of immediate concern in relation to the manifold of events comprising the relevant whole.

2. It must be problem-oriented.

* Reprinted with the permission of the Virginia Journal of International Law.

3.   It must be multi-method.

A jurisprudence aspiring to relevance must be contextual because the comprehensiveness and realism with which an observer conceives his major focus of attention—how he locates law in the community which it affects and is affected by—will determine how he conceives every detailed part of his study, his framing of problems, and his choice of tools for inquiry. It is only by a configurative examination of the larger context that an observer can be assured of extending his inquiry to all relevant variables and of being able to appraise the aggregate consequences of alternatives in decision. A relevant jurisprudence must be problem-oriented if it is to facilitate performance of the various intellectual tasks which confront all who are interested in the study of the interrelations of law and society, to avoid sterile inquiry into meaningless questions, and to contribute as creatively as possible to our institutions of public order in ways that promise to extricate us from the continuing destructive anarchy of our times. A relevant jurisprudence must be multi-method in order to promote mastery over all the necessary intellectual skills, to encourage the employment of strategies in the management of both authority and control, and to insure rationality of choice among alternatives in recommendation and decision.

It may require emphasis that a contextual, problem-oriented, multi-method jurisprudence of international law must provide for the systematic and disciplined performance of a series of distinguishable, but interrelated intellectual tasks. The appropriate specification of a comprehensive set of intellectual tasks, or skills, is important because it is the range of tasks performed, as well as the quality of performance which determines the relevance of inquiry for policy. The most deliberate attempts to clarify general community policy which do not at the same time systematically pursue other tasks, such as the description of past trends in decision and the analysis of factors affecting decision, may achieve only Utopian exercises. The description of past trends in decision, which is not guided by policy priorities and explicitly related to social processes, affords a most meager basis for drawing upon the wisdom of the past. The scientific study of factors affecting decision, which is not oriented by reference to problems in basic community policy, may be of no more than incidental relevance, despite enormous cost. The effort to predict future trends in decision by the mere extrapolation of past trends, without considering whether the factors that affect decision will remain the same, may produce destructive illusion rather than genuine forecast. In confusion about the character of, and appropriate procedures for, the different relevant intellectual tasks, the creativity in the invention and evaluation of policy alternatives, which is indispensable to rational decision, may be lost. The more specific intellectual tasks, for which a policy-relevant jurisprudence must make provision in theory and procedures, must thus include at least:

1.   Clarification of the goals of decision;

2.   Description of the trends toward or away from the realization of these goals;

3.   Analysis of the constellation of conditioning factors that appear to have affected past decision;

4. Projection of probable future developments, assuming no influence by the observer;

5. Formulation of particular alternatives and strategies that contribute, at minimum net cost and risk, to the realization of preferred goals.

Adequate and sufficiently detailed performance of these various tasks in reference to the past, present and future of the various relevant social and decision processes of the world community must obviously require a comprehensive analytic framework which can bring into view the principal features of decision. A "conventional" analysis in terms of government organs and of the technical doctrines employed by officials, an effective technique for certain problems, is on the whole, inappropriate for the study of international decision. Conventional usage must yield to "functional" analysis if comprehensive and realistic orientation is to be achieved. No dependable relationship exists between a structure that is called "governmental" in a particular body politic and the facts of authority and control on the global scale. Analysts of comparative government are well aware of the discrepancy between convention and functional fact for the understanding of the legal and political process at the national or sub-national level, since it is not unusual to discover, for example, that the authority formally provided in a written constitutional charter may be ignored, or totally redefined by unwritten practice. Similarly, when the international arena is examined, the presumed congruence of formal and actual authority of intergovernmental organizations may or may not be sustained by the concurrence of expectations necessary to justify a claim of actual constitutive authority. On a wide range of matters, the principal nation-states may—and do—continue to perceive one another as unilaterally making the critical decisions, for which they accept, and reciprocally enforce, a substantial measure of responsibility.

The comprehensive analytic framework required must, accordingly, include a conceptual technique for delineating the relevant aspects for power and policy of any interpersonal interaction. This technique may be sought by first locating the decision—that is, choosing the phase at which a sequence of interactions appears to culminate in choices enforced by sanctions and deprivation or indulgence. The culminating phase may be organized or unorganized; for example, it may be a formal agreement or a fight, a vote or a combination of unilateral assertion and passive acquiescence. The questions that must be raised in an appropriate phase analysis cover the outcome, pre-outcome and post-outcome dimensions of the whole sequence:

1. Who acted or participated in roles of varying significance in the process which culminated in the decision? (*Participants*)

2. What were the significant perspectives of the participants? With whom were they identified? What value demands were they pursuing, with what expectations? (*Perspectives)*

3. Where and under what conditions were the participants interacting? (*Situations*)

4. What effective means for the achievement of their objectives were at the disposal of the different participants? (*Base Values*)

5. In what manner were these means or base values manipulated? (*Strategies*)

6. What was the immediate result—value allocation—of the process of interaction? (*Outcomes*)

7. What are the effects, of differing duration, of the outcome and process? (*Effects*)

It would, thus, appear that the goal criteria appropriate for the creation of a relevant jurisprudence of international law are entirely comparable to those which experience has demonstrated to be appropriate for national law. For the better appraisal of the potential contributions to a viable jurisprudence of our vast legacy of inherited theories about international law, it may be helpful to make more fully explicit certain goal criteria fashioned after those recommended today as appropriate for a jurisprudence of national law.

———

Notes and Questions about configurative jurisprudence.

1. ***The founders of the Yale School of international law*** have had influence on scholars and teachers, many of them their former students, both in the United States and to some extent abroad. The questions which follow are intended to focus your attention on your personal conception of international law.

2. ***What is the ideal professional training and experience*** for a decision-maker using configurative jurisprudence? Is law training in such jurisprudence enough? Is configurative jurisprudence advocated as a process or as a value-selection system? Or both? Is the lawyer's role expected to be the dominant one in the decision-making process? If so, is this in conformity with reality, considering that the vast majority of decisions about international law are made as a part of the foreign policy process in governments where, unlike in the U.S., lawyers are treated as experts whose role is only to advise?

3. ***Jessup, whose views are discussed above,*** was a professor of international law, an ambassador, an undersecretary of state, and a judge on the International Court of Justice. The protagonists of configurative jurisprudence have not had much experience in non-legal roles in government operations. Do the different experience backgrounds of these lawyers and of Jessup give evidence of having influenced their respective philosophic outlooks about international law?

4. ***In other writings, the above three Yale School authors*** develop some fundamental attitudes that are identifiable in the excerpt under reference here. These include: (i) a rejection of norm-identification-application as the basic function of legal science and an emphasis on policy-choice processes; (ii) the ascription of a relatively low value to the ideal of universality as a goal of international law (such a goal would operate as a

limiter of choice); (iii) strong emphasis in policy science of identifying and reinforcing by decision what are denominated as "common goal values", the most fundamental of which is that of human dignity. Are the above parts congruent, or are there inherent contradictions?

———

Oliver, The Future of Idealism In International Law: Structuralism, Humanism, And Survivalism

The Structure and Process of International Law: Essays in Legal Philosophy Doctrine and Theory 1207, 1208 (Macdonald & Johnston eds. 1983).*

* * *

2.   Idealism and the State of International Law Today

The thesis here is a simple one drawn from many examples in recent political and social history. When a situation or system decays—loses its effectiveness—it either dies or requires unusual social energy to revive it. Such unusual social energy requires mobilization of Purpose and Will. Such mobilization in our species requires an ethical, ennobling component. This component is Idealism, in some form.

It is all too evident that international law is in serious need of resuscitation today, not only in actual effectiveness but in the very expectation of its being able to be effective. Full proof of the degree of decline need not be offered here but the main point must be driven home, largely because it is so often denied or rejected by Idealists who, consciously or in a Freudian subconsciousness, will not face the facts that the *realpolitikers* are always willing to overstate. The truth of the matter is that, as every government international lawyer comes to realize, international legal structures and international legal rules are not in the practice of states treated as superior and ineluctable but as talking, arguing, and negotiating variables. It is always useful for a state to maintain credible "juridical cover" and to avoid—most but not all states think so—becoming an international scoff-law. The point here is not that law is a "variable in the power process" but that the value of fidelity to legal order is not an absolute value in international relations.

* * *

In any closed social system (a society), major value choices are political in their inception and legal order follows along to put these choices into effect. American international lawyers often tend to reverse this sequence, at least in terms of their own sense of mission, importance, and assumed competence (both in the jurisdictional and the capacity meanings). On the whole, U.S. academic international law scholars tend to expect to lead too much as to the value-choice process, rather than being willing to be technicians-after-the-fact of choice. As a result, their legalistic prescriptions for good (improvement, change, better structure, better principles) make less than expected impact on the politicians, national and international, who are ultimately in charge of making the choices (exercises of will and purpose). Thus in today's world we have significant segments of international legal scholarship that are often blind to the deterioration of international law, erroneously confident of competence to fashion the key to growth of what in fact is a semi-moribund science, this to the exclusion of all other cures, and thus widely divergent and combative as to essentials and priorities.

* * *

5. ***Survivalism: Idealistic or Inescapably Realistic?*** Earlier references in this paper have indicated that notions of an irreducible minimum of structural and normative legal order are not widely professed within the academic branch of specialization in international law nor explicitly articulated by official spokespersons for the international legal outlooks of states. It is not difficult to understand these reticences. To too many among the scholars, the facts of degradation in international legal order and the seriousness of the ensuing crisis have simply not penetrated individual universes of perception, busy as each is with cherished projects, determined activism, and the like, from which each derives a degree of optimism that shuts off the unsatisfactory or the unthinkable. Scholars who are also sensitive teachers find it necessary to assure students that what they are studying is real and significant, either or both for the future as well as for now. Some of these also engage in deliberate self-encouragement that understates reality.

Practitioners of international law do not often have time for wide-sweeping reflection, and foreign offices are not given to philosophic disquisitions of an evaluative or programmatic nature. Practitioners tend to live from incident to incident, from crisis to crisis. * * * Another reason that a bed-rock minima approach has not widely appealed is the fear or belief that an imprecise line divides such outlooks from non-expectant, anti-legal *realpolitik*. * * *

A final reason is that a program for an international law of survival brings one immediately to fundamental needs that so far law has failed to regulate: the use of force in fact to achieve national goals; the insufficiency and impotence of legal controls over the first use, in any posture, of nuclear, chemical and bacteriological weapons (and what of laser/maser?); compulsory peaceful settlement of disputes by legal processes and substantive rules; some degree of obligatory sharing of planetary resources on the basis of need, ability to assist, and managerial competence; abolishment of the rule of vested rights to the first exploiter of earth's remaining non-appropriated areas, the moon and other celestial bodies; the provision of more and more assured means for individuals to complain internationally against states, particularly the one to which, willy nilly, they owe "allegiance." In all these instances, there is so far a marked lack of Will–Purpose among states and people who influence states for genuine achievement.Yet without the development first of Will–Purpose in these areas, it is not assured that many of the specific activities in which legal idealists engage will bring effective improvement in planetary conditions. Under these circumstances, the most basic question becomes: how is Will–Purpose to be generated as to a particular line of action through legal structure and normative regulation thereunder? The ultimate pessimist will say, "only after cataclysm." A somewhat more expectant realist will express the hope that, at the very verge of destruction, awareness will come in the nick of time and the whole experience will breed a resolution to ensure a system under which the imminent catastrophe cannot threaten again.

There is some slight evidence that some would risk neither cataclysm nor the brink but wish to revive attention to the fundamentals as a place to begin to build order anew. Expectation and determination (effective Idealism) will become essential to such revival, for there is much frustration and pessimism to be combatted. * * *

In as much as the basic necessity is to develop Will–Purpose, it is desirable to start with the fundamentals, hard to solve though they may be, for it is the vast, planetary mind that must be reached, and there is wider truth in Dr. Johnson's observation as to concentrating the mind than the mere certainty of being hanged in the morning. The notion held by many peoples that they and the states over them are unable to influence outcomes as to the fundamentals—or some of them—needs response, including raising the question whether significant segments of the developing world are acting responsibly in focusing on certain issues of importance to them to the disregard of those of a planetary dimension.

Survivalism is ensuring survival. But it cannot be achieved, as in a lifeboat, by non-idealistic realism. It requires an Idealism about which it will be more difficult to be idealistic than many would like, thus making the task of commitment harder and perhaps less rewarding in terms of personal professional success. The Idealism required ought to be widely communicated in acceptable form for effectiveness outside professional circles. Not all academic international lawyers need be involved, but more than presently are should be. Professional international practitioners ought all to be involved, and the academics and the practitioners ought to improve their collaborations with each other and with other relevant professional groups. Perhaps it is the Idealism of a Sancho Panza not a Quixote that is needed. One recalls that Sancho not only said the windmills were not monsters but that he eventually became an acceptable governor of the island!

The first needs are not the only ones; they only must be met before others can be assured.

Notes and Questions

1. *Questions about "norms".* Are law persons (scholars, judges, practitioners) qualified, strictly on the basis of their professional training, to work well in "non-rule" situations?

The "Yale School", represented by the excerpts from McDougal rejects norm-oriented approaches to legal participation in decision-making. But it articulates principles. What is the difference between a principle and, in Kelsenian terms, a norm?

Kelsen says that legal science is qualified to identify norms, scale them as to authoritativeness, interpret them, and apply them, but that it is not qualified to deal with value choices that lie outside the legal order.Do you agree or disagree? Do lawyers as a class self-limit their qualifications to norm-oriented processes?

In the United States, can it plausibly be argued that the lawyer class is qualified to deal professionally and competently with domestic value choices? With foreign affairs value choices?

2. *General legal philosophy and legal philosophy about international law.* General theories about law have had and are having influences on perspectives about international law. Notions of divine and secular natural law are at home in international law. So would be sociological jurisprudence if chief protagonists of the various schools of sociological jurisprudence (Savigny, Pound, et al.) had been concerned very much about international law. In a very broad and inexact sense, the Yale School adapts old-fashioned sociological jurisprudence to the international arena. The logical positivists too, beginning with that nemesis for international law, John Austin, have given it their attention. Kelsenian philosophy about international law is inherently positivistic in origin and outlook. In fact, a good case can be made that international legal positivism has had a definite influence on general legal philosophy.

The neo-realism movement in American jurisprudence of the twenties and thirties did, especially through Professor Walter Wheeler Cook of Yale, bring private international law into its ambit of attention; but the legal philosophers of this sector did not focus on international public law to any significant degree. Their attention was captured by the judicial process within the U.S. and the need for sharper analyses, in part through sharper nomenclature, in stating and using American law. Their influence on international public law, nonetheless, has come through limited degrees of adoption of their approach by American international legal thinkers. Just as American neo-realism has not died, but has been absorbed into American thinking about internal law, it has come into American methodology about international law, especially as to Hohfeldian nomenclature. (It is very useful in the analysis of international legal situations to know the difference between a right, a privilege, and a power, for instance—or a duty as differentiated from a liability.) Less influential on American international legal philosophy has been the neo-realists' focus on the fact that judges sometimes consciously, more often unconsciously, mask the true reasons for their decisions behind rationalistic use of precedents and analogistic rationales. The reason for this invites fascinating speculations. Perhaps the fact that international law is not wholly American has something to do with it. However, recent criticisms of the judicial stances and methodologies of members of the International Court of Justice in connection with *Nicaragua v. U.S.* may also mark a wider willingness to address the matter.

Recently, a new wave of skeptical examination of law and the realities of power, the Critical Legal Studies movement, has aroused contention, and even furor, by its views about internal American law and international law. The Critical Legal Studies movement although still far from making its way into American law outlooks in the way the older neo-realism has. In many ways, international law is a more vulnerable target for the movement's attacks than internal law, because international law has fewer committed defenders and is structurally more vulnerable. For instance, one element of the less than cohesive Critical Legal Studies movement is "deconstruction", a process borrowed from literary criticism, which focuses on texts and analyzes them to show inherently self-cancelling internal contradictions. International law, alas, for a good deconstructor, would be an easy target! On the other hand, the movement is very suspicious of the masking of naked power behind law.

Critical Legal Studies and International Law

Law, in a broad sense, is indeterminate. Proponents of critical legal studies argue that every legal problem accommodates more than one viable solution and that policy or other non-legal factors determine the choice of the adopted solution. Thus, politics forms the major component of law. Is this insight new or original? Like in the realm of literary criticism, the analytical method of deconstruction is utilized to study law. See whether you think it is inciteful or helpful.

Kramer, Legal Theory, Political Theory, and Deconstruction: Against Rhadamanthus*

238–239; 254–255 (1991).

Deconstructive theory, as a result of anticipating countercritiques and noting its own problems of incoherence, will position itself to seize on problems of incoherence that ravage countercritiques. Its power is made perfect in weakness, its own weakness. Because all critiques become implicated in what they censure, and because careful deconstructionist writing will have stayed keenly alert to both the general dissemination of paradoxes by transference and the specific maelstroms of many of its own paradoxes, our anticipating the countercritiques by helping them with their work may be the most adroit way to gain some leverage in deconstructing countercritiques. Complacent parries will highlight their own weak spots by fastening upon weak spots that have been highlighted in a deconstructionist discourse. At that point, where a deliberate nondefense has become the best defense, battles will be less over (in)coherency and elegiac than over competing ways in which incoherence can articulate itself. * * *
* * *

* * * [a]rguments will be framed in a vocabulary of "struggles", "tactics", "disruption", and "subversion" rather than "truth" * * * Critical and legal force at a particular juncture, not illusive veracity, is the touchstone that guides our choices * * * [a] process of choosing that is based on strategic factors will partake of no fewer problems

* Reprinted with the permission of Indiana University Press.

than a logocentric pursuit of Truth. In a process of either broad type, we shall have to undergo a fatal disquietude * * * Critical power and tactical adroitness must serve as one's leading goals, but the game in which one is strategizing will go on endlessly. One must try—always with a considerable degree of failure to attend carefully to the blindness that will be entailed by each one of one's insights * * *. [What must be] constantly kept in mind is a near-paralyzing tentativeness.

Koskenniemi, Letter To The Editors of The Symposium,

In Symposium on Method in International Law, 93 A.J.I.L. 291, 351 (1999)*

* * *

As I wrote *From Apology to Utopia: The Structure of International Legal Argument* (Helsinki, 1989) at the end of the 1980s, my aim was to examine international law from a standpoint that would be in some ways systematic, perhaps even scientific. My starting point was an observation I had made in the course of having practiced international law with the Finnish Ministry for Foreign Affairs since 1977 that, within the United Nations and elsewhere in international fora as well as legal literature, competent lawyers routinely drew contradictory conclusions from the same norms, or found contradictory norms, embedded in one and the same text or behavior. I never thought that this was because they were simply cynics, manipulating the law to suit the ends of their governments. In some ways what I learned to call the law's indeterminacy was a property internal to the law itself, not introduced to it by "politics" from the outside. As I learned from David Kennedy, the legal argument inexorably, and quite predictably, allowed the defense of whatever position while simultaneously being constrained by a rigorously formal language. Learning to speak that language was the key to legal competence. Such competence was not mere imagination.It was not possible to say just anything that came to one's mouth and pretend that one was making a legal argument. Among other practitioners I had the ability to distinguish between the professionally competent and incompetent uses of legal language—but this ability had little or nothing to do with the identity of the norm or the behavior to be justified or criticized.

I wanted to describe this property of international legal language—its simultaneously strict formalism and its substantive indeterminacy—in terms of a general theory. Hermeneutics was helpful inasmuch as it allowed focusing on law as language. Its interpretive orientation, however, proved disappointing. The search for a "fusion of horizons" seemed altogether too vague and impressionistic to sustain a solid "method." Looking elsewhere, I found that much in the way critical legal scholars in the United States argued sought to grasp precisely this aspect of the law: its formal predictability and substantive indeterminacy.

In search of a method with a critical bite and with some degree of resistance to the most obvious criticisms from recent social and linguistic theory and postanalytical philosophy, I became attached to (classical)

* Reprinted with the permission of the American Society of International Law.

French structuralism, its differentiation between *langue/parole* (or "deep structure" and "surface") and its ability to explain in a hard and positivist—"scientific"—way the construction of language or cultural form from a network of limited possible combinations. Following mainstream structuralism, I described international law as a language that was constructed of binary oppositions that represented possible—but contradictory—responses to any international legal problem. I then reduced international legal argument—what it was possible to produce as professionally respectable discourse in the field—to a limited number of "deep-structural" binary oppositions and transformational rules. To this matrix I added a "deconstructive" technique that enabled me to demonstrate that the apparently dominant term in each binary opposition in fact depended on the secondary term for its meaning or force. In this way, an otherwise static model was transformed into a dynamic explanation as to how the binary structures of international law (rule/exception, general/particular, right/duty, formalism/realism, sovereignty/community, freedom/constraint, etc.) were interminably constructed and deconstructed in the course of any argument, through predictable and highly formal argumentative patterns, allowing any substantive outcome. I felt I had reached a scientific optimum where I had been able to reduce a complex (linguistic) reality into a limited set of argumentative rules.

Ill

Now, however, a new problem emerged. If international law consisted in a small number of argumentative rules through which it was possible to justify anything, what were the consequences to legal dogmatics (the description and systemization of valid law) or indeed to my practice in the legal department of the Foreign Ministry? Or more accurately: I posed no question but continued writing articles about valid law and memoranda to the Minister arriving at definite interpretive statements. The rule R and not -R was valid and was to be interpreted in situation X in the way Y and not -Y. This seemed puzzling to my academic colleagues. Had I not just argued that international legal arguments were indeterminate and that the rule -R was in every conceivable situation as valid as the rule R because, in fact, R and -R entailed each other? How come I now produced texts in which I interpreted treaties and practice just like any other lawyer?—as if my materials were somehow free of the indeterminacy that I claimed elsewhere to be the most striking reality of international law.

This was the problem of the relationship between academic theory/doctrine (I always have difficulty in distinguishing the two from each other) and practice, or of the relations between my (external) description of the structure of legal argument and my (internal) participation in that argument. It soon seemed clear that, however that relationship might be characterized, there was, at least, no direct logical entailment between the one and the other: external description did enhance the facility to make a professionally persuasive argument, but it did not "produce" its outcomes. Such theory/doctrine did not provide readymade solutions for social conflict, or suggest institutional arrangements that could only be "applied" and would then have the consequences they were supposed to have. Which way one's argument as a practitioner went still depended on what one was ready to think of as the "best" (or least bad) or workable, reasonable, humane solution—as well as on what one's client wanted. It was a merit of this theory, however, that it demonstrated that to achieve these strategic goals, the contexts of legal practice offered many different styles of argument. It was sometimes useful to argue as a strict positivist, fixing the law on a treaty interpretation. At other times it was better to conduct an instrumentalist analysis of the consequences of alternative ways of action—while at yet other times moral pathos seemed appropriate. Each of these styles—or "methods" in the language of this symposium—was open-ended in itself, amenable to the defense of whatever position one needed to defend. None of them, however, gave the comfort of allowing the lawyer to set aside her "politics," her subjective fears and passions. On the contrary, to what use they were put depended in some crucial way precisely on those fears and passions.

None of this is to say that lawyers are, or should become, manipulative cynics—apart from the sense that it is a crucial part of professional competence for the lawyer to be able to construct her argument so as to make it credible to her targeted audience. Outside the relationship between the argument and the context, however, there was no external "method," no "theory" that could have proven the correctness of one's reasoning, the standpoint that one was called upon to take as part of one's professional practice.

What works as a professional argument depends on the circumstances. I like to think of the choice lawyers are faced with as being not one of method (in the sense of external, determinate guidelines about legal certainty) but of language or, perhaps better, of style. The various styles—including the styles of "academic theory" and "professional practice"—are neither derived from nor stand in determinate hierarchical relationships to each other. The final arbiter of what works is nothing other than the context (academic or professional) in which one argues.

From this perspective, the tension between academic theory and practice disappears: they, too, are styles that are taken on in a particular context. The "deconstruction" I used in my book provided an effective language and a technique—but only in the academic environment that thinks highly of the linguistic conventions and cultural connotations of deconstruction. More precisely: the academic context is defined by the kinds of cultural conventions—styles—of which that kind of critique forms a part. By contrast, the languages of legal sources, "base values" or economic efficiency are effective in those contexts of legal practice that are identified precisely through those styles. To write a deconstructive memorandum for a permanent mission to the United Nations would be professional and a social mistake—not unlike ordering a beer in a Viennese Heurigen. European rule—positivism might seem hopelessly old-fashioned in front of a postrealist American audience—while informal American arguments about policy goals or economic efficiency associate with European experience in bureaucratic authoritarianism. "Process" language might find a positive echo when debate is about the jurisdiction of international functional organizations, yet feminist styles might better articulate the concerns of activists of nongovernmental organizations, and so on.

It is hard to think of a substantive or political position that cannot be made to fulfill the condition of being justifiable in professionally competent legal ways through recourse to one or another of the legal styles parading through this symposium. The "feel" of professional competence is the outcome of style, more particularly of linguistic style. For international law in all its stylistic variations always involves translation from one language to another. Through it, the languages of power, desire and fear that are the raw materials of social conflict are translated into one or another of the idiolects expounded the contributions to the symposium. Translation does not "resolve" those claims, but makes them commensurate and susceptible to analysis in the professional and bureaucratic contexts in which it is used. But translation is not completely devoid of normative consequences, either.

* * *

Feminist Approaches To International Law

Feminist philosophers and lawyers have been approaching international law from their own various perspectives. See Chapter 9 for feminist approaches to international human rights law. Consider the following views and perspectives.

Fernando R. Tesón, Feminism and International Law: A Reply

33 Va.J.Int'l L. 647 (1993).*

* * *

Until recently international law had not undergone a sustained feminist critique. This gap is now slowly being filled; a notable contribution to that effort is a recent article by Hilary Charlesworth, Christine Chinkin, and Shelley Wright.

This Essay presents a reply to the Charlesworth–Chinkin–Wright critique. Although much of this reply engages more general issues in feminist theory, it would be impossible, within the scope of this work, to address every important political, cultural, biological, epistemological, and metaphysical issue raised by the various feminist critiques of traditional jurisprudence. I therefore confine the analysis to arguments directly relevant to international law, focusing on the analogies and contrasts between the differing feminist approaches to international law and the Kantian theory of international law defended in my previous writings.

The feminist critique of international law contains many disparate strands of theory that must be disentangled. A central difficulty with the article by Charlesworth and her associates is that it conflates divergent arguments from very different (and often irreconcilable) camps within feminist theory. The most important such mismatch is between liberal and radical feminism, which coexist in uneasy tension throughout the article. Much of the analysis in this essay is therefore devoted to separating,

* Reprinted with the permission of Fernando Tesón and the Virginia J. Int'l L.

analyzing, and ultimately evaluating these interwoven but uncongenial threads of feminist thought.

In examining the liberal and radical feminist approaches to international law, as manifested in the Charlesworth article, I distinguish three different levels of criticism. The first level concerns the *processes* of international lawmaking, the second addresses the *content* of international law, and the third attempts to derive a critical theory from the (purported) "nature" or "inherent qualities" of liberal international legal institutions. These critiques are treated differently, in complex ways, by radical and liberal feminism. Yet on all three critical dimensions, my conclusion is the same: although *liberal* feminism has important things to say about international law and relations, radical feminism is inconsistent both with the facts and with a view of international law rooted in human rights and respect for persons.

* * *

Liberal, or Kantian, international legal theory is founded on the idea of the individual as rational and autonomous. Liberal theorists regard individuals as capable of rational choices, possessed of inherent dignity, and worthy of respect. Liberal states in international relations, or members of the liberal alliance, are those nation-states with democratically elected officials, where human rights are generally respected. Liberal internationalism assumes a right to democratic governance, and holds that a state may not discriminate against individuals, including women. This principle is, of course, a centerpiece of the international law of human rights. A corollary of the Kantian thesis is that illegitimate governments may not be embraced as members of the liberal alliance.

Liberal feminists rely on liberal principles of domestic and international law to end abuses against women. Very succinctly, liberal feminism is the view that women are unjustly treated, that their rights are violated, and that political reform is needed to improve their situation, thereby allowing them to exercise autonomous choices and enjoy full equal status as free citizens in a liberal democracy. The governing international principles are the imperatives of human rights, nondiscrimination, and equal opportunity for women, as envisioned in articles 1(3), 8, and 55 of the United Nations Charter. When a state discriminates or deprives women of these human rights, it commits an injustice, a violation of international human rights law for which it is responsible.

Radical feminists agree with liberal feminists that the situation of women must be improved. They believe, however, that liberal institutions are themselves but tools of gender oppression, and that women are exploited by men in even the least suspecting ways. Radical feminists believe that existing states are hierarchically structured according to gender, and that gender hierarchy necessarily infects the process of legal reasoning itself. Radical feminists hold that the "actual choices" of women only *seem* to be autonomous and free; in reality they are *socially* determined. Human beings are not, as liberals would have it, separate, rational entities capable of individual decision-making, but rather beings to some degree defined and determined by their social—and particularly gender—relationships. Under radical feminist theory, no woman is truly free, not even in the "freest" of societies.

III.   Three Feminist Critiques of International Law

In light of the differences in feminist theory it will be convenient to set forth three feminist critiques of international law, and the central claim associated with each: (A) the *processes* of international lawmaking exclude women; (B) the *content* of international law privileges men to the detriment of women; and (C) international law, as a patriarchal institution, *inherently* oppresses women, marginalizes their interests, and submerges their experiences and perspectives.

* * *

Feminists criticize the international lawmaking process for depriving women of the access and opportunity to take part in lawmaking in two important ways. First, feminists argue that women are *underrepresented* in international relations, that is, in high positions in international organizations, in diplomatic services, and as heads of state and government. Second, they contend that because of this underrepresentation, the *creation* of international law is reserved almost exclusively to men. Women are thus effectively prevented from participating in the processes of international lawmaking.

* * *

In addition to criticizing the processes of international lawmaking, many feminists argue that the content of international law privileges men to the detriment of women. The claim that the content of international law favors the interests of men may incorporate either or both of the following arguments: first, international law rules in general are "gendered" to privilege men; and second, international rules such as sovereign equality and nonintervention protect states, and states are instrumental in disadvantaging or oppressing women. * * *

* * * I find little plausibility in the claim of some feminists that the specific content of international law rules systematically privileges men. Positive international law is a vast and heterogeneous system consisting of principles, rules, and standards of varying degrees of generality, many of a technical nature. Rules such as the principle of territoriality in criminal jurisdiction, or the rule that third states should in principle have access to the surplus of the entire allowable catch of fish in a coastal state's exclusive economic zone are not "thoroughly gendered" but, on the contrary, gender-neutral. It cannot be seriously maintained that such norms operate overtly or covertly to the detriment of women. The same can be said of the great bulk of international legal rules.

* * *

Feminists are correct, however, on their second claim that international law overprotects states and governments. International law, as traditionally understood, is formulated in exaggeratedly statist terms. Statism, the doctrine that state sovereignty is the foundational concept of international law, repudiates the central place accorded to the individual in any liberal normative theory; and, by extension, it often results in ignoring the rights and interests of women within states. This criticism is identical to the one made by the Kantian theory of international law.

* * *

[R]adical feminists also attack liberalism. Insofar as this attack is predicated on the perception that liberal philosophy and the liberal state oppress women, it must be met with a philosophical and political defense of the liberal vision. But if the feminist attack on liberalism is predicated on the belief that statism, as an assumption of international law, is necessarily entailed by liberalism, the answer is simply that this is a mistaken inference. Statism is at odds with liberalism. The human rights theory of international law (certainly the most liberal international legal theory) rejects statism because it protects illegitimate governments and is thus an illiberal theory of international law. The whole point of the liberal theory of international law is to challenge absolute sovereignty as an antiquated, authoritarian doctrine inhospitable to the aspirations of human rights and democratic legitimacy.

* * *

[Radical feminists claim] that international law is inherently oppressive of women. Some feminists argue that because current international law derives from European, male, liberal legalism, its very form and structure are inherently patriarchal and oppressive.

* * *

It is significant, in this regard, that Charlesworth and her associates do not emphasize violations of women's rights by particular governments, even though in many countries women are *officially* discriminated against, and sometimes even horribly mutilated with official endorsement or complicity. This omission is related, I believe, to the inherent oppressiveness thesis. Identifying and opposing egregious human rights practices simply holds less *philosophic* interest for the radical feminist than unmasking patriarchal oppression as a pervasive (albeit often "invisible") evil. * * * Their obsession with male dominance leads [these] radical feminists to the grotesque proposition that the oppression of women is as serious in liberal democracies as in those societies that institutionally victimize and exclude women. For feminists to try to improve the condition of women in even the freest societies is a commendable goal, since liberal democracies are not free of sexist practices. This is very different, however, from claiming that liberal democracies and tyrannical states are morally equivalent in the way they treat women. Such an assertion not only perverts the facts; it does a disservice to the women's cause.

* * *

IV.   Conclusion: Defending the Liberal Vision

Legal theory has been much enriched by feminist jurisprudence. Feminists have succeeded in drawing attention to areas where uncritically received legal theories and doctrines have resulted in injustices to women. International law should be no exception, and the contribution of Charlesworth and her associates will rightly force international lawyers to re-examine features of the international legal system that embody, actually or potentially, unjust treatment of women.

* * *

Charlesworth, Feminist Methods In International Law

In Symposium on Method in International Law, 93 A.J.I.L. 291,379 (1999)*

* * *

Feminist methods seek to expose and question the limited bases or international law's claim to objectivity and impartiality and insist on the importance of gender relations as category of analysis. The term "gender" here refers to the social construction of differences between women and men and ideas of "femininity" and "masculine"—the excess cultural baggage associated with biological sex.

The philosopher Elizabeth Grosz has pointed out that feminist theorizing typically requires an unarticulated balance between two goals. Feminist analysis is at once a reaction to the "overwhelming masculinity of privileged and historically dominant knowledges, acting as a kind of counterweight to the imbalances resulting from the male monopoly of the production and reception of knowledges" and a response to the political goals of feminist struggles. The dual commitments of feminist methods are in complex and uneasy coexistence. The first demands "intellectual rigor," investigating the hidden gender of the traditional canon. The second requires dedication to political change. The tension between the two leads to criticism of feminist theorists both from the masculine academy for lack of disinterested scholarship and objective analysis and from feminist activists for co-option by patriarchal forces through participation in male-structured debates.

Feminist methodologies challenge many accepted scholarly traditions. For example, they may clearly reflect a political agenda rather than strive to attain an objective truth on a neutral basis and they may appear personal rather than detached. For this reason, feminist methodologies are regularly seen as unscholarly, disruptive or mad. They are the techniques of outsiders and strangers. Just as nineteenth-century women writers used madness to symbolize escape from limited and enclosed lives, so twentieth-century feminist scholars have developed dissonant methods to shake the complacent and bounded disciplines in which they work. At the same time, most feminists are constrained by their environment. If we want to achieve change, we must learn and use the language and methods of the dominant order.

* * *

* Reprinted with the permission of the American Society of International Law.

Abbott, International Relations Theory, International Law, and The Regime Governing Atrocities In International Conflicts

In the Symposium on Method in International Law, 93 A.J.I.L. 291, 361 (1999).*

Over the last ten years, international relations (IR) theory, a branch of political science, has animated some of the most exciting scholarship in international law. If a true joint discipline has not yet emerged, scholars in both fields have clearly established the value of interdisciplinary cross-fertilization. Yet IR—like international law—comprises several distinct theoretical approaches or "methods." While this complexity makes interactions between the disciplines especially rich, it also makes them difficult to explore concisely.

* * *

IR theory is most helpful in performing three different, though equally significant, intellectual tasks: *description, explanation and institutional design*. First, while lawyers *describe* rules and institutions all the time, we inevitably—and often subconsciously—use some intellectual template (frequently a positivist one) to determine which elements of these complex phenomena to emphasize, which to omit. The carefully constructed models of social interaction underlying IR theory remind us to choose these templates carefully, in light of our purpose. More specifically, IR helps us describe legal institutions richly, incorporating the political factors that shape the law: the interests, power, and governance structures of states and other actors; the information, ideas and understandings on which they operate; the institutions within which they interact.

IR scholars are primarily concerned with *explaining* political behavior—recently, at least, including law—related behavior. Especially within those schools that favor rationalist approaches, scholars seek to identify the actors relevant to an issue, the factors (material or objective) that affect their behavior or otherwise influence events, and the "causal pathways" by which those factors have effect. These elements are typically incorporated in a model that singles out particular factors for study. In designing research, scholars look for ways to test explanatory hypotheses, using case studies or data analysis. Like their counterparts in other social sciences, then, the rationalist schools of IR theory share a common methodological orientation with economics, as described by Jeffrey Dunoff and Joel Trachtman in this symposium.

A scholar applying IR theory might treat legal rules and institutions as phenomena to explained ("dependent variables"). What factors, one might ask, led states in 1949 to adopt the Geneva Conventions, codifying detailed standards of battlefield conduct but drawing sharp distinctions between "international armed conflicts" and other violent situations? (Those "schisms"—senseless from a moral perspective—might prove less arbitrary as a matter of politics.) Alternatively, IR might analyze legal, rules and institutions—including the processes of legal decision making—as explanatory factors ("independent variables"). One might ask, has the existence of

* Reprinted with the permission of the American Society of International Law.

the International Criminal Tribunal for the former Yugoslavia (ICTY), or the way it has handled cases, affected the behavior of governments and other actors in the Balkans? If so, by what means?

Why should a lawyer care about questions like these? Analyses treating law as a dependent variable are valuable in many settings, for they help us understand the functions, origin and meaning of rules and institutions. Analyses treating law as an independent variable are also valuable (though unfortunately less common): they help us assess the workings and effectiveness of legal arrangements in the real world. Both forms of explanation, then, are valuable in their own right. But explanation is at least as important for its forward-looking applications: predicting future developments and *designing institutions* capable of affecting behavior in desirable ways. It is here—conflicting law-based options for the future, as the editors put it—that lawyers can play their greatest role and IR can make its most significant contribution.

* * *

Dunoff and Trachtman, The Law and Economics of Humanitarian Law Violations in Internal Conflict

In the Symposium on Method in International law, 93 A.J.I.L. 291,394 (1999)*

* * *

* * * Law and economics (L & E) is rich in useful theory: it has constructed and refined a body of rationalist theory that can generate refutable hypotheses, and it suggests methodologies by which those hypotheses may be tested. While law and economics is rich in theory, it exalts empiricism (in which it is surprisingly poor). In fact, we are critical of a law and economics that has immodestly been willing to prescribe solely on the basis of theory. In this necessarily brief essay, we do not reach positive conclusions or normative prescriptions because our theoretical and methodological approach does not permit conclusions prior to empirical testing. We are only able to indicate the types of areas that law and economics theory would suggest evaluating, and to describe how law and economics has addressed some related or similar topics. In addition, we show how L & E can assist international lawyers in perhaps their most important creative role—the design and operation of international institutions that permit states to overcome transaction costs and strategic problems and thus to cooperate to realize joint gains.

* * *

Economics is the study of rational choice under conditions of limited resources. Rational choice assumes that individual actors seek to maximize their preferences. The goal of L & E analysis is to identify the legal implications of this maximizing behavior, both in and out of markets, and for markets and other institutions. While the first generation of L & E scholarship often employed cost-benefit analysis to address these issues, our focus is not just on cost-benefit analysis, but also on transaction cost

* Reprinted with the permission of the American Society of International Law.

analysis and game theory, and the application of these methodologies to political contexts through public choice theory.

In many respects these techniques formalize, extend and contextualize insights that are familiar to most international lawyers. But this formalization is important—it allows us to focus on relevant variables, generate hypotheses, and, to some extent, empirically test these hypotheses. Furthermore, it provides a firmer and less subjective basis for argumentation than traditional international law analysis. It is less subjective insofar as it eschews simple natural law or epithet-based argumentation, and provides the capacity to render transparent the distributive consequences of legal rules. Perhaps most important to scholars, it furnishes a basis for a progressive research program built on shared foundations, one that will seek to answer research questions and move on, rather than endlessly address the same tired questions.

* * *

Finally, much of L & E analysis is premised upon the distinction between positive and normative economics. Positive economics is that part of the discipline that, self-consciously modeling itself on the natural sciences, focuses on describing and explaining the world around us. Positive analysis in law, for example, would seek simply to describe the effects of particular legal rules. Thus, the positive analyst may as a professional decline to judge whether international law *should* hold individuals criminally liable for human rights atrocities committed in internal conflict: the positive analyst will not take a position on the *lex-ferenda*. However, given a legal and policy decision that individual criminal responsibility should attach to such behavior, the positive analyst can provide information about the consequences that may be expected to follow from such a rule.

Normative economics, which many economists reject, *evaluates*—rather than simply describes—behavior, and advances reform proposals. Normative economic analysis typically offers reforms designed to maximize "social welfare," usually measured by people's revealed preferences (without suggesting what those preferences should be). It is in this sense that it engages *lex ferenda*.

We recognize that the distinction between "positive" and 'normative' economics is problematic; positive description is often implicitly normative to the extent that it identifies a mismatch between articulated goals and policy or institutional choices. Moreover, even when L & E analysis purports to be positive, it is not neutral. Rather, it is premised upon a normatively determined approach termed "methodological individualism." Under this approach, no particular outcome or norm is a priori deemed desirable; rather, individual choice, sometimes called "consumer sovereignty," is the ultimate source of values. The assumption that individuals are the ultimate source of norms sharply distinguishes L & E analysis from other approaches to international law, such as natural law theories.

When extended to the international realm, the commitment to methodological individualism has substantial normative implications. For example, given the emphasis on individual choice, L & E methods will tend to favor more, rather than less, representative institutions. Moreover, methodological individualism views the state not as a player in its own right with its own normative value, but as a mediating institution with only derivative normative value. Thus, while L & E rejects state-centered positivism, it would rehabilitate the state as an institution, just as it would validate the corporation as an institution: as a vehicle for individuals to work together more productively. Finally, the L & E approach is consistent with the legal positivism that respects the law as written because—and to the extent that—it is the product of legislative processes that reflect individual preferences better than the alternative preference-revealing mechanisms.

* * *

SECTION B. MONISM & DUALISM

1 O'Connell, International Law 38 (2D Ed. 1970)*

The Theory of the Relationship: Monism and Dualism

Almost every case in a municipal court in which a rule of international law is asserted to govern the decision raises the problem of the relationship of international law and municipal law; and in many cases before international tribunals it must also be disposed of when deciding the jurisdictional competence of a State to affect alien interests through its own internal legal order.

There are four possible attitudes towards the question:

(a) That international law has primacy over municipal law in both international and municipal decisions. This is the *monist* theory.

(b) That international law has primacy over municipal law in international decisions, and municipal law has primacy over international law in municipal decisions. This is the *dualist* theory.

(c) That municipal law has primacy over international law in both international and municipal decisions. This is a species of monism in reverse.

(d) That there should be no supposition of conflict between international law and municipal law.

(a) Monism

The monist position is an emanation of Kantian philosophy which favours a unitary conception of law. According to this view, since the capacities of States derive from the idea of law, the jurisdiction to exercise these capacities is granted by the law. It follows that the law to which jurisdictional reference must be made is independent of sovereignty and determinative of its limits. If a State exceeds the limits, its acts are invalid. This argument concedes to international law a broader and more fundamental competence than to municipal law. However, it tends to sidestep the point made by the dualists, namely, that a municipal court may be instructed to apply municipal law and not international law, and hence has

---

* Reprinted with the permission of Stevens & Sons, Ltd., London.

no jurisdiction (using the term as descriptive of the capacity in municipal law to decide a case) to declare the relevant municipal law invalid. Hence, the characterization of the jurisdictional excess as "invalid," or even merely "illegal" (if there is any difference between the terms), is of no meaning internally within the municipal law of the acting State. To this objection, the monist has only one answer, that this conflict of duties, owing to a defect in organization, has been wrongly resolved.

* * *

(b) Dualism

The dualist position is associated with Hegelianism and has governed the judicial attitudes of States where this philosophy has prevailed. The common starting point is the proposition that law is an act of sovereign will, municipal law being differentiated from international law in that it is a manifestation of this will internally directed, as distinct from participation in a collective act of will by which the sovereign undertakes obligations with respect to other sovereigns. This results in a dualism of legal origin, of subjects and of subject matters. International law and municipal law are two quite different spheres of legal action, and theoretically there should be no point of conflict between them. Municipal law addresses itself to the subjects of sovereigns, international law to the sovereigns themselves. If the sovereign by an act of municipal law exceeds his competence in international law it does not follow that municipal law is void; it merely follows that the sovereign has violated international law. Anzilotti has explained the relationship between the dualist thesis and the alleged incapacity of the individual in international law as follows:

> A rule of international law is by its very nature absolutely unable to bind individuals, i.e., to confer upon them rights and duties. It is created by the collective will of States with the view of regulating their mutual relations; obviously it cannot therefore refer to an altogether different sphere of relations. If several States were to attempt the creation of rules regulating private relations, such an attempt, by the very nature of things, would not be a rule of international law, but a rule of uniform municipal law common to several States.

(c) Inverted monism

The theory that municipal law is in its nature superior to international law has never found favour in international tribunals, and is no more than an abstract possibility. It is associated with Bergbohm, whose almost pathological resentment against natural law led to an exaggerated emphasis on the State will. Unlike Austin, who would deny even the term "law" to international law and thereby avoid a potential collision of two systems, Bergbohm allows for international law as a manifestation of the "auto limitation" of the sovereign will. The State is superior to and antecedent to the international community, and remains the only law-making entity. Unlike Triepel, who would distinguish the State will as internally manifested from the State will as externally manifested, Bergbohm allows for only one manifestation, and international law is thus a derivation from municipal law.

(d) The theory of harmonization

According to this view, neither the monist nor the dualist position can be accepted as sound. Each attempts to provide an answer, derived from a single theoretical premise, to two quite different questions. The first question is whether international law is "law" in the same sense as municipal law, i.e., whether both systems are concordant expressions of a unique metaphysical reality. The second question is whether a given tribunal is required by its constitution to apply a rule of international law or municipal law, or vice versa, or authorized to accord primacy to the one over the other. The resemblance between the two questions is only apparent; the lack of jurisdiction in a given tribunal to accord primacy to international law in the event of a conflict between it and municipal law has no relevance to the question whether municipal law does or does not derive its competence from the same basic juridical reality as international law. In some federal systems of law, a State court may be required to apply state legislation which a federal court would declare unconstitutional. The norms of reference are different but the systems are concordant.

The starting point in any legal order is man himself, considered in relation to his fellow man. Law, it has often been said, is life, and life is law. The individual does not live his life exclusively in the legal order of the State any more than he lives it exclusively in the international order. He falls within both jurisdictions because his life is lived in both. Here again, the comparison with a federal system is instructive. It follows that a monistic solution to the problem of the relationship of international law and municipal law fails because it would treat the one system as a derivation of the other, ignoring the physical, metaphysical and social realities which in fact detach them. The world has not yet reached that state of organization where there is only one civitas maxima delegating specific jurisdiction to regional administrations.

But a dualist solution is equally deficient because it ignores the all-prevailing reality of the universum of human experience. States are the formal instruments of will for the crystallization of law, but the impulse to the law derives from human behavior and has a human goal. Positive international law is not pure whim, but an expression of needs and convictions. If it were otherwise, international law and municipal law would be competitive regimes ill-suited to the solution of human problems. The correct position is that international law and municipal law are concordant bodies of doctrine, each autonomous in the sense that it is directed to a specific, and, to some extent, an exclusive area of human conduct, but harmonious in that in their totality the several rules aim at a basic human good.

———

Notes and Questions about monism and dualism. What do you think about this: are these terms descriptive merely of what a particular state does with international law in its own courts and agencies, or do they have direct relevance to the fundamental question whether international law is law? Review Chapters 1 and 12 and take a position as to whether the

United States is properly classifiable as evidencing a monist or a dualist state philosophy. If a federal state has in its constitution a provision that rules of customary international law prevail over state of the union law and constitutions, is that federal state necessarily monist? If any state, federal or unitary, has in its constitution a provision that rules of customary international law prevail over any national law, is that state necessarily monist?

Section C.   Principles, Practice and Legitimacy

A final question on theory. What do you see as the greatest need for the effectiveness of the international legal system today? Acceptance? Structure? Rule, scope and precision? Methodology? Essentiality? Commonality of values? Coercive authority? Other?

Franck, Legitimacy In the International System

82 A.J.I.L. 705 (1988)*

The surprising thing about international law is that nations ever obey its strictures or carry out its mandates. This observation is made not to register optimism that the half-empty glass is also half full, but to draw attention to a pregnant phenomenon: that most states observe systemic rules much of the time in their relations with other states. That they should do so is much more interesting than, say, the fact that most citizens usually obey their nation's laws, because the international system is organized in a voluntarist fashion, supported by so little coercive authority. This unenforced rule system can obligate states to profess, if not always to manifest, a significant level of day-to-day compliance even, at times, when that is not in their short-term self-interest. The element or paradox attracts our attention and challenges us to investigate it, perhaps in the hope of discovering a theory that can illuminate more generally the occurrence of voluntary normative compliance and even yield a prescription for enhancing aspects of world order. * * *

Legitimacy is used here to mean that quality of a rule *which derives from a perception on the part of those to whom it is addressed that it has come into being in accordance with right process.* Right process includes the notion of valid sources but also encompasses literary, socio-anthropological and philosophical insights. The elements of right process that will be discussed below are identified as affecting decisively the degree to which any rule is perceived as legitimate. * * *

A series of events connected with the role of the U.S. Navy in protecting U.S.-flagged vessels in the Persian Gulf serves to illustrate the paradoxical phenomenon of uncoerced compliance in a situation where the rule conflicts with perceived self-interest. Early in 1988, the Department of

---

* Reprinted with the permission of the American Society of International Law. Much of this material also appears in Franck, The Power of Legitimacy Among Nations (New York, 1990).

Defense became aware of a ship approaching the gulf with a load of Chinese-made Silkworm missiles en route to Iran. The Department believed the successful delivery of these potent weapons would increase materially the danger to both protected and protecting U.S. ships in the region. It therefore argued for permission to intercept the delivery. The Department of State countered that such a search and seizure on the high seas, under the universally recognized rules of war and neutrality, would constitute aggressive blockade, an act tantamount to a declaration of war against Iran. In the event, the delivery ship and its cargo of missiles were allowed to pass. Deference to systemic rules had won out over tactical advantage in the internal struggle for control of U.S. policy.

Why should this have been so? In the absence of a world government and a global coercive power to enforce its laws, why did the U.S. Government, with its evident power to do as it wished, choose to "play by the rules" despite the considerable short-term strategic advantage to be gained by seizing the Silkworms before they could be delivered? Why did preeminent American power defer to the rules of the sanctionless system? At least part of the answer to this question, quietly given by the State Department to the Department of Defense, is that the international rules of neutrality have attained a high degree of recognized legitimacy and must not be violated lightly. Specifically, they are well understood, enjoy a long pedigree and are part of a consistent framework of rules—the *jus in bello*—governing and restraining the use of force in conflicts. To violate a set of rules of such widely recognized legitimacy, the State Department argued, would transform the U.S. posture in the gulf from that of a neutral to one of belligerency. That could end Washington's role as an honest broker seeking to promote peace negotiations. It would also undermine the carefully crafted historic "rules of the game" applicable to wars, rules that are widely perceived to be in the interest of all states. * * *

Four elements—the indicators of rule legitimacy in the community of states—are identified and studied in this essay. They are *determinacy, symbolic validation, coherence* and *adherence* (to a normative hierarchy). To the extent rules exhibit these properties, they appear to exert a strong pull on states to comply with their commands. To the extent these elements are not present, rules seem to be easier to avoid by a state tempted to pursue its short-term self-interest. This is not to say that the legitimacy of a rule can be deduced solely by counting how often it is obeyed or disobeyed. While its legitimacy may exert a powerful pull on state conduct, yet other pulls may be stronger in a particular circumstance. The chance to take a quick, decisive advantage may overcome the counterpull of even a highly legitimate rule. In such circumstances, legitimacy is indicated not by obedience, but by the discomfort disobedience induces in the violator. (Student demonstrations sometimes are a sensitive indicator of such discomfort.) The variable to watch is not compliance but the strength of the compliance pull, whether or not the rule achieves actual compliance in any one case.

Each rule has an inherent pull power that is independent of the circumstances in which it is exerted, and that varies from rule to rule. This pull power is its index of legitimacy. For example, the rule that makes it improper for one state to infiltrate spies into another state in the guise of diplomats is formally acknowledged by almost every state, yet it enjoys so low a degree of legitimacy as to exert virtually no pull towards compliance. As Schachter observes, "some 'laws,' though enacted properly, have so low a degree of probable compliance that they are treated as 'dead letters' and * * * some treaties, while properly concluded, are considered 'scraps of paper.' "By way of contrast, we have noted, the rules pertaining to belligerency and neutrality actually exerted a very high level of pull on Washington in connection with the Silkworm missile shipment in the Persian Gulf.

Perhaps the most self-evident of all characteristics making for legitimacy is textual *determinacy*. What is meant by this is the ability of the text to convey a clear message, to appear transparent in the sense that one can see through the language to the meaning. Obviously, rules with a readily ascertainable meaning have a better chance than those that do not to regulate the conduct of those to whom the rule is addressed or exert a compliance pull on their policymaking process. Those addressed will know precisely what is expected of them, which is a necessary first step towards compliance.

To illustrate the point, compare two textual formulations defining the boundary of the underwater continental shelf. The 1958 Convention places the shelf at "a depth of 200 meters or, beyond that limit, to where the depth of the superjacent waters admits of the exploitation of the natural resources of the said areas." The 1982 Convention on the Law of the Sea, on the other hand, is far more detailed and specific. It defines the shelf as "the natural prolongation of * * * land territory to the outer edge of the continental margin, or to a distance of 200 nautical miles from the baselines from which the breadth of the territorial sea is measured," but takes into account such specific factors as "the thickness of sedimentary rocks" and imposes an outermost limit that "shall not exceed 100 nautical miles from the 2,500 meter isobath," which, in turn, is a line connecting the points where the waters are 2,500 meters deep. The 1982 standard, despite its complexity, is far more determinate than the elastic standard in the 1958 Convention, which, in a sense, established no rule at all. Back in 1958, the parties simply covered their differences and uncertainties with a formula, whose content was left in abeyance pending further work by negotiators, courts, and administrators and by the evolution of customary state practice. The vagueness of the rule did permit a flexible response to further advances in technology, a benefit inherent in indeterminacy.

Indeterminacy, however, has costs. Indeterminate normative standards not only make it harder to know what conformity is expected, but also make it easier to justify noncompliance. Put conversely, the more determinate the standard, the more difficult it is to resist the pull of the rule to compliance and to justify noncompliance. Since few persons or states wish to be perceived as acting in obvious violation of a generally recognized rule of conduct, they may try to resolve the conflicts between the demands of a rule and their desire not to be fettered, by "interpreting" the rule permissively. A determinate rule is less elastic and thus less amenable to such evasive strategy than an indeterminate one. * * *

To summarize: the legitimacy of a rule is affected by its degree of determinacy. Its determinacy depends upon the clarity with which it is able to communicate its intent and to shape that intent into a specific situational command. This, in turn, can depend upon the literary structure of the rule, its ability to avoid *reductio ad absurdum* and the availability of a process for resolving ambiguities in its application. * * *

As determinacy is the linguistic or literary-structural component of legitimacy, so *symbolic validation, ritual* and *pedigree* provide its cultural and anthropological dimension. As with determinacy, so here, the legitimacy of the rule—its ability to exert pull to compliance and to command voluntary obedience—is to be examined in the light of its ability to communicate. In this instance, however, what is to be communicated is not so much content as *authority:* the authority of a rule, the authority of the originator of a validating communication and, at times, the authority bestowed on the recipient of the communication. The communication of authority, moreover, is symbolic rather than literal. We shall refer to these symbolically validating communications as cues.

All ritual is a form of symbolic validation, but the converse is not necessarily true. *Pedigree* is a different subset of cues that seek to enhance the compliance pull of rules or rule-making institutions by emphasizing their historical origins, their cultural or anthropological deep-rootedness. * * * Professor Schachter has observed that a body of rules produced by the UN legislative drafting body, the International Law Commission, will be more readily accepted by the nations "after [the Commission] has devoted a long period in careful study and consideration of precedent and practice." Moreover, the authority will be greater if the product is labeled *codification*—that is, the interpolation of rules from deep-rooted evidence of state practice—"than if it were presented as a 'development' (that is, as new law)," even though the Commission (as a subsidiary of the General Assembly) is equally empowered by the UN Charter to promote "the progressive development of international law and its codification." The compliance pull of a rule is enhanced by a demonstrable lineage. A new rule will have greater difficulty finding compliance, and even evidence of its good sense may not fully compensate for its lack of breeding. Nevertheless, a new rule may be taken more seriously if it arrives on the scene under the aegis of a particularly venerable sponsor such as a widely ratified multilateral convention, or a virtually unanimous decision of the International Court of Justice. * * *

* * * Symbols of pedigree and rituals are firmly imbedded in state diplomatic practice. The titles ("ambassador extraordinary and plenipotentiary"), prerogatives and immunities of ambassadors, consuls and others functioning in a representative capacity are among the oldest of symbols and rites associated with the conduct of international relations. The sending state, by the rituals of accreditation, endows its diplomats with pedigree.They become, in time-honored tradition, a symbolic reification of the nation ("full powers" or *plenipotentiary*), a role that is ritually endorsed by the receiving state's ceremony accepting the envoy's credentials. These ceremonies, incidentally, are as old as they are elaborate and are performed with as remarkably faithful uniformity in Communist citadels as in royal

palaces. Once accredited and received, an ambassador *is* the embodiment of the nation. The status of ambassador, once conferred, carries with it inherent rights and duties that do not depend on the qualities of the person, or on the condition of relations between the sending and receiving states, or on the relative might of the sending state. To insult or harm this envoy, no matter how grievous the provocation, is to attack the sending state. Moreover, when an envoy, acting officially, agrees to something, the envoy's state is bound, usually even if the envoy acted without proper authorization. The host state normally is entitled to rely on the word of an ambassador as if his or her state were speaking.

The venerable ritual practices of diplomacy are almost universally observed, and the rules that govern diplomacy are widely recognized as imbued with a high degree of legitimacy, being both descriptive and predictive of nearly invariable state conduct and reflecting a strong sense of historically endowed obligation. When the rules are violated—as they have been by Iran and Libya in recent years—the international community tends to respond by rallying around the rule, as the Security Council and the International Court of Justice demonstrated when the Iranian regime encouraged the occupation of the U.S. Embassy in Tehran. Violations of the elaborate rules pertaining to embassies and immunities usually lead the victim state to terminate its diplomatic relations with the offender. The offended state—as Britain demonstrated after the St. James Square shooting—usually takes care not to retaliate by means that the rules do not permit.

Both determinacy and symbolic validation are connected to a further variable: coherence. The effect of incoherence on symbolic validation can be illustrated by reference to diplomatic practices pertaining to the ritual validation of governments and states. The most important act of pedigreeing in the international system is the deep-rooted, traditional act that endows a new government, or a new state, with symbolic status. When the endowing is done by individual governments, it is known as *recognition*. The symbolic conferral of status is also performed collectively through a global organization like the United Nations when the members vote to admit a new nation to membership, or when the General Assembly votes to accept the credentials of the delegates representing a new government.

These two forms of validation are important because they enhance the status of the validated entity; that is, the new state or government acquires legitimacy, which, in turn, carries entitlements and obligations equal to those of other such entities. Such symbolic validation cannot alter the empirically observable reality of power disparity among states and governments, nor, properly understood, does it give off that cue. It does, however, purport to restrict what powerful states legitimately may do with their advantage over the weak. It is a cue that prompts the Soviets, however reluctantly, to do a lot of explaining when they invade Afghanistan. The pedigreed statehood of Afghanistan, together with the determinacy of the rules against intervention by one state in the internal affairs of another, then combine to render those Soviet explanations essentially unacceptable, global scorn evidencing the inelastic determinacy of the applicable rules.
* * *

To summarize: coherence, and thus legitimacy, must be understood in part as defined by factors derived from a notion of community. Rules become coherent when they are applied so as to preclude capricious checkerboarding. They preclude caprice when they are applied consistently or, if inconsistently applied, when they make distinctions based on underlying general principles that connect with an ascertainable purpose of the rules and with similar distinctions made throughout the rule system. The resultant skein of underlying principles is an aspect of community, which, in turn, confirms the status of the states that constitute the community. Validated membership in the community accords equal capacity for rights and obligations derived from its legitimate rule system.

By focusing on the connections between specific rules and general underlying principles, we have emphasized the horizontal aspect of our central notion of a community of legitimate rules. However, there are vertical aspects of this community that have even more significant impact on the legitimacy of rules. * * *

* * * A rule * * * is more likely to obligate if it is made within the procedural and institutional framework of an organized community than if it is strictly an ad hoc agreement between parties in the state of nature. The same rule is still more likely to obligate if it is made within the hierarchically structured procedural and constitutional framework of a sophisticated community rather than in a primitive community lacking such secondary rules about rules. * * * Of course, there *are* lawmaking institutions in the system. One has but to visit a highly structured multinational negotiation such as the decade-long Law of the Sea Conference of the 1970s to see a kind of incipient legislature at work. The Security Council, the decision-making bodies of the World Bank and, perhaps, the UN General Assembly also somewhat resemble the cabinets and legislatures of national governments, even if they are not so highly disciplined and empowered as the British Parliament, the French National Assembly or even the U.S. Congress. Moreover, there *are* courts in the international system: not only the International Court of Justice, the European Community Court and the regional human rights tribunals, but also a very active network of quasi-judicial committees and commissions, as well as arbitral tribunals established under such auspices as the Algiers agreement ending the Iran hostage crisis. Arbitrators regularly settle investment disputes under the auspices and procedures of the World Bank and the International Chamber of Commerce. Treaties and contracts create jurisdiction for these tribunals and establish rules of evidence and procedure.

The international system thus appears on close examination to be a more developed community than critics sometimes allege. It has an extensive network of horizontally coherent rules, rule-making institutions, and judicial and quasi-judicial bodies to apply the rules impartially. Many of the rules are sufficiently determinate for states to know what is required for compliance and most states obey them most of the time. Those that do not, tend to feel guilty and to lie about their conduct rather than defy the rules openly. The system also has means for changing, adapting and repealing rules.

Most nations, most of the time, are both rule conscious and rule abiding. Why this is so, rather than that it is so, is also relevant to an understanding of the degree to which an international community has developed in practice. This silent majority's sense of obligation derives primarily not from explicit consent to specific treaties or custom, but from *status*. Obligation is perceived to be owed *to a community of states as a necessary reciprocal incident of membership in the community*. Moreover, that community is defined by secondary rules of process as well as by primary rules of obligation: states perceive themselves to be participants in a structured process of continual interaction that is governed by secondary rules of process (sometimes called rules of recognition), of which the UN Charter is but the most obvious example. The Charter is a set of rules, but it is also about how rules are to be made by the various institutions established by the Charter and by the subsidiaries those institutions have created, such as the International Law and Human Rights Commissions. * * * In the world of nations, each of these described conditions of a sophisticated community is observable today, even though imperfectly. This does not mean that its rules will never be disobeyed. It does mean, however, that it is usually possible to distinguish rule compliance from rule violation, and a valid rule or ruling from an invalid one. It also means that it is not necessary to await the millennium of Austinian-type world government to proceed with constructing—perfecting—a system of rules and institutions that will exhibit a powerful pull to compliance and a self-enforcing degree of legitimacy.

*

INDEX

The Text of many of the documents indexed appears in the Coursebook or in the Documentary Supplement of this Coursebook

References are to pages

1479

1-56662-748-6

90000

9 781566 627481